The Dictionary of Art · volume sixteen

The Dictionary of Art

16

Iraq
TO
Janoušek

GROVE

The Dictionary of Art

edited by JANE TURNER, in thirty-four volumes, 1996

This edition is distributed within the United Kingdom and Europe
by Macmillan Publishers Limited, London, and within the United States and Canada by
Grove's Dictionaries Inc., New York.

Text keyboarded by Wearset Limited, Sunderland, England
Database management by Pindar plc, York, England
Imagesetting by William Clowes Limited, Suffolk, England
Printed in the United States of America by RR Donnelley & Sons Company, Willard, Ohio

British Library Cataloguing in Publication Data

The dictionary of art
  1. Art - Dictionaries 2. Art - History -
    Dictionaries
  I. Turner, Jane
  703

ISBN 1-884446-00-0

Library of Congress Cataloging in Publication Data

The dictionary of art / editor, Jane Turner.
  p. cm.
  Includes bibliographical references and index.
  Contents: 1. A to Anckerman
  ISBN 1-884446-00-0 (alk. paper)
  1. Art—Encyclopedias.
  I. Turner, Jane, 1956–
N31.D5   1996   96–13628
703—dc20   CIP

Contents

List of Colour Illustrations   vi

General Abbreviations   vii

A Note on the Use of the Dictionary   xiii

The Dictionary, Volume Sixteen:
Iraq–Janoušek   1

Illustration Acknowledgements   909

List of Colour Illustrations

PLATE I. **Jade**

Jadeite vase, carved with a design of grasshoppers, h. 200 mm, from China, 19th century (Taipei, Taiwan, Ritz Jewellery and Arts Co./Photo: Ritz Jewellery and Arts Co.)

PLATE II. **Jade**

1. Jade burial mask of Pacal (*reg* AD 615–84), from the Temple of the Inscription, Palenque, Mexico, Classic Maya period (ex-National Museum of Anthropology, Mexico City/Photo: Werner Forman Archive, London)

2. Nephrite lanterns, h. 435 mm, from the palace of Emperor Qianlong (*reg* 1736–96), Beijing, China (Taipei, Taiwan, Ritz Jewellery and Arts Co./Photo: Ritz Jewellery and Arts Co.)

PLATE III. **Jade**

1. Nephrite cup with dragon-shaped handle, h. 64 mm, probably from China, 14th century, inscribed in the early 15th century with the name of Ulughbeg (London, British Museum/Photo: Trustees of the British Museum)

2. Nephrite wine vessel, inlaid with enamelled gold plant motifs, h. 104 mm, diam. 116 mm, from India, Mughal, 18th century (London, Victoria and Albert Museum/Photo: Board of Trustees of the Victoria and Albert Museum)

PLATE IV. **Jade**

Jade snuff bottles, Chinese, 18th–19th centuries: (*clockwise from top*) pebble jade, carved in the shape of a fish between the fronds of a lotus plant, h. 80 mm, 1720–80 (the green glass stopper is not the original); flawless nephrite, tourmaline stopper, gilt silver collar, h. 55 mm, 1720–1830; Trojan Embellished Jade, nephrite, carved with bamboo shoot design, coral stopper possibly original, h. 58 mm, perhaps from the Imperial Palace workshops, Beijing, 1750–1830; Meng Haoran Suzhou Jade, nephrite, carved with Meng Haoran riding a donkey, coral stopper, vinyl collar, h. 70 mm, from Suzhou, 1740–1850; Master of the Rocks Noble Occupations Pebble, nephrite, carved with a mountainous landscape, jadeite stopper, h. 63 mm, 1740–1860; (*centre*) Dwyer Lilac Jadeite, jadeite body and stopper, gilt bronze collar, h. 54 mm, 1770–1880 (all Mary and George Bloch private collection/Photo: Robert Hall Photography, London)

General Abbreviations

The abbreviations employed throughout this dictionary, most of which are listed below, do not vary, except for capitalization, regardless of the context in which they are used, including bibliographical citations and for locations of works of art. The principle used to arrive at these abbreviations is that their full form should be easily deducible, and for this reason acronyms have generally been avoided (e.g. Los Angeles Co. Mus. A. instead of LACMA). The same abbreviation is adopted for cognate forms in foreign languages and in most cases for plural and adjectival forms (e.g. A.= Art, Arts, Arte, Arti etc). Not all related forms are listed below. Occasionally, if a name, for instance of an artists' group or exhibiting society, is repeated within the text of one article, it is cited in an abbreviated form after its first mention in full (e.g. The Pre-Raphaelite Brotherhood (PRB) was founded...); the same is true of archaeological periods and eras, which are abbreviated to initial letters in small capitals (e.g. In the Early Minoan (EM) period...). Such abbreviations do not appear in this list. For the reader's convenience, separate full lists of abbreviations for locations, periodical titles and standard reference books and series are included as Appendices A–C in vol. 33.

A.	Art, Arts	Anthropol.	Anthropology	Azerbaij.	Azerbaijani
A.C.	Arts Council	Antiqua.	Antiquarian, Antiquaries	B.	Bartsch [catalogue of Old Master prints]
Acad.	Academy	app.	appendix		
AD	Anno Domini	approx.	approximately	*b*	born
Add.	Additional, Addendum	AR	Arkansas (USA)	BA	Bachelor of Arts
addn	addition	ARA	Associate of the Royal Academy	Balt.	Baltic
Admin.	Administration			*bapt*	baptized
Adv.	Advances, Advanced	Arab.	Arabic	BArch	Bachelor of Architecture
Aesth.	Aesthetic(s)	Archaeol.	Archaeology	Bart	Baronet
Afr.	African	Archit.	Architecture, Architectural	Bask.	Basketry
Afrik.	Afrikaans, Afrikaner	Archv, Archvs	Archive(s)	BBC	British Broadcasting Corporation
A.G.	Art Gallery				
Agrar.	Agrarian	Arg.	Argentine	BC	Before Christ
Agric.	Agriculture	ARHA	Associate of the Royal Hibernian Academy	BC	British Columbia (Canada)
Agron.	Agronomy			BE	Buddhist era
Agy	Agency	ARIBA	Associate of the Royal Institute of British Architects	Beds	Bedfordshire (GB)
AH	Anno Hegirae			Behav.	Behavioural
A. Inst.	Art Institute	Armen.	Armenian	Belarus.	Belarusian
AK	Alaska (USA)	ARSA	Associate of the Royal Scottish Academy	Belg.	Belgian
AL	Alabama (USA)			Berks	Berkshire (GB)
Alb.	Albanian	Asiat.	Asiatic	Berwicks	Berwickshire (GB; old)
Alg.	Algerian	Assist.	Assistance	BFA	Bachelor of Fine Arts
Alta	Alberta (Canada)	Assoc.	Association	Bibl.	Bible, Biblical
Altern.	Alternative	Astron.	Astronomy	Bibliog.	Bibliography, Bibliographical
a.m.	ante meridiem [before noon]	AT&T	American Telephone & Telegraph Company	Biblioph.	Bibliophile
Amat.	Amateur	attrib.	attribution, attributed to	Biog.	Biography, Biographical
Amer.	American	Aug	August	Biol.	Biology, Biological
An.	Annals	Aust.	Austrian	bk, bks	book(s)
Anatol.	Anatolian	Austral.	Australian	Bkbinder	Bookbinder
Anc.	Ancient	Auth.	Author(s)	Bklore	Booklore
Annu.	Annual	Auton.	Autonomous	Bkshop	Bookshop
Anon.	Anonymous(ly)	Aux.	Auxiliary	BL	British Library
Ant.	Antique	Ave.	Avenue	Bld	Build
Anthol.	Anthology	AZ	Arizona (USA)	Bldg	Building

Bldr — Builder

BLitt — Bachelor of Letters/Literature

BM — British Museum

Boh. — Bohemian

Boliv. — Bolivian

Botan. — Botany, Botanical

BP — Before present (1950)

Braz. — Brazilian

BRD — Bundesrepublik Deutschland [Federal Republic of Germany (West Germany)]

Brecons — Breconshire (GB; old)

Brez. — Brezonek [lang. of Brittany]

Brit. — British

Bros — Brothers

BSc — Bachelor of Science

Bucks — Buckinghamshire (GB)

Bulg. — Bulgarian

Bull. — Bulletin

bur — buried

Burm. — Burmese

Byz. — Byzantine

C — Celsius

C. — Century

c. — *circa* [about]

CA — California

Cab. — Cabinet

Caerns — Caernarvonshire (GB; old)

C.A.G. — City Art Gallery

Cal. — Calendar

Callig. — Calligraphy

Cam. — Camera

Cambs — Cambridgeshire (GB)

can — canonized

Can. — Canadian

Cant. — Canton(s), Cantonal

Capt. — Captain

Cards — Cardiganshire (GB; old)

Carib. — Caribbean

Carms — Carmarthenshire (GB; old)

Cartog. — Cartography

Cat. — Catalan

cat. — catalogue

Cath. — Catholic

CBE — Commander of the Order of the British Empire

Celeb. — Celebration

Celt. — Celtic

Cent. — Centre, Central

Centen. — Centennial

Cer. — Ceramic

cf. — confer [compare]

Chap., Chaps — Chapter(s)

Chem. — Chemistry

Ches — Cheshire (GB)

Chil. — Chilean

Chin. — Chinese

Christ. — Christian, Christianity

Chron. — Chronicle

Cie — Compagnie [French]

Cinema. — Cinematography

Circ. — Circle

Civ. — Civil, Civic

Civiliz. — Civilization(s)

Class. — Classic, Classical

Clin. — Clinical

CO — Colorado (USA)

Co. — Company; County

Cod. — Codex, Codices

Col., Cols — Collection(s); Column(s)

Coll. — College

collab. — in collaboration with, collaborated, collaborative

Collct. — Collecting

Colloq. — Colloquies

Colomb. — Colombian

Colon. — Colonies, Colonial

Colr — Collector

Comm. — Commission; Community

Commerc. — Commercial

Communic. — Communications

Comp. — Comparative; compiled by, compiler

Concent. — Concentration

Concr. — Concrete

Confed. — Confederation

Confer. — Conference

Congol. — Congolese

Congr. — Congress

Conserv. — Conservation; Conservatory

Constr. — Construction(al)

cont. — continued

Contemp. — Contemporary

Contrib. — Contributions, Contributor(s)

Convalesc. — Convalescence

Convent. — Convention

Coop. — Cooperation

Coord. — Coordination

Copt. — Coptic

Corp. — Corporation, Corpus

Corr. — Correspondence

Cors. — Corsican

Cost. — Costume

Cret. — Cretan

Crim. — Criminal

Crit. — Critical, Criticism

Croat. — Croatian

CT — Connecticut (USA)

Cttee — Committee

Cub. — Cuban

Cult. — Cultural, Culture

Cumb. — Cumberland (GB; old)

Cur. — Curator, Curatorial, Curatorship

Curr. — Current(s)

CVO — Commander of the [Royal] Victorian Order

Cyclad. — Cycladic

Cyp. — Cypriot

Czech. — Czechoslovak

$ — dollars

d — died

d. — denarius, denarii [penny, pence]

Dalmat. — Dalmatian

Dan. — Danish

DBE — Dame Commander of the Order of the British Empire

DC — District of Columbia (USA)

DDR — Deutsche Demokratische Republik [German Democratic Republic (East Germany)]

DE — Delaware (USA)

Dec — December

Dec. — Decorative

ded. — dedication, dedicated to

Democ. — Democracy, Democratic

Demog. — Demography, Demographic

Denbs — Denbighshire (GB; old)

dep. — deposited at

Dept — Department

Dept. — Departmental, Departments

Derbys — Derbyshire (GB)

Des. — Design

destr. — destroyed

Dev. — Development

Devon — Devonshire (GB)

Dial. — Dialogue

diam. — diameter

Diff. — Diffusion

Dig. — Digest

Dip. Eng. — Diploma in Engineering

Dir. — Direction, Directed

Directrt — Directorate

Disc. — Discussion

diss. — dissertation

Distr. — District

Div. — Division

DLitt — Doctor of Letters/Literature

DM — Deutsche Mark

Doc. — Document(s)

Doss. — Dossier

DPhil — Doctor of Philosophy

Dr — Doctor

Drg, Drgs — Drawing(s)

DSc — Doctor of Science/Historical Sciences

Dut. — Dutch

Dwell. — Dwelling

E. — East(ern)

EC	European (Economic) Community	figs	figures	Heb.	Hebrew
Eccles.	Ecclesiastical	Filip.	Filipina(s), Filipino(s)	Hell.	Hellenic
Econ.	Economic, Economies	Fin.	Finnish	Her.	Heritage
Ecuad.	Ecuadorean	FL	Florida (USA)	Herald.	Heraldry, Heraldic
ed.	editor, edited (by)	*fl*	*floruit* [he/she flourished]	Hereford & Worcs	Hereford & Worcester (GB)
edn	edition	Flem.	Flemish	Herts	Hertfordshire (GB)
eds	editors	Flints	Flintshire (GB; old)	HI	Hawaii (USA)
Educ.	Education	Flk	Folk	Hib.	Hibernia
e.g.	*exempli gratia* [for example]	Flklore	Folklore	Hisp.	Hispanic
Egyp.	Egyptian	fol., fols	folio(s)	Hist.	History, Historical
Elem.	Element(s), Elementary	Found.	Foundation	HMS	His/Her Majesty's Ship
Emp.	Empirical	Fr.	French	Hon.	Honorary, Honourable
Emul.	Emulation	frag.	fragment	Horiz.	Horizon
Enc.	Encyclopedia	Fri.	Friday	Hort.	Horticulture
Encour.	Encouragement	FRIBA	Fellow of the Royal Institute of British Architects	Hosp.	Hospital(s)
Eng.	English	FRS	Fellow of the Royal Society, London	HRH	His/Her Royal Highness
Engin.	Engineer, Engineering			Human.	Humanities, Humanism
Engr., Engrs	Engraving(s)	ft	foot, feet	Hung.	Hungarian
Envmt	Environment	Furn.	Furniture	Hunts	Huntingdonshire (GB; old)
Epig.	Epigraphy	Futur.	Futurist, Futurism	IA	Iowa
Episc.	Episcopal	g	gram(s)	ibid.	*ibidem* [in the same place]
Esp.	Especially	GA	Georgia (USA)	ICA	Institute of Contemporary Arts
Ess.	Essays	Gael.	Gaelic		
est.	established	Gal., Gals	Gallery, Galleries	Ice.	Icelandic
etc	*etcetera* [and so on]	Gaz.	Gazette	Iconog.	Iconography
Ethnog.	Ethnography	GB	Great Britain	Iconol.	Iconology
Ethnol.	Ethnology	Gdn, Gdns	Garden(s)	ID	Idaho (USA)
Etrus.	Etruscan	Gdnr(s)	Gardener(s)	i.e.	*id est* [that is]
Eur.	European	Gen.	General	IL	Illinois (USA)
Evangel.	Evangelical	Geneal.	Genealogy, Genealogist	Illum.	Illumination
Exam.	Examination	Gent.	Gentleman, Gentlemen	illus.	illustrated, illustration
Excav.	Excavation, Excavated	Geog.	Geography	Imp.	Imperial
Exch.	Exchange	Geol.	Geology	IN	Indiana (USA)
Excurs.	Excursion	Geom.	Geometry	in., ins	inch(es)
exh.	exhibition	Georg.	Georgian	Inc.	Incorporated
Exp.	Exposition	Geosci.	Geoscience	inc.	incomplete
Expermntl	Experimental	Ger.	German, Germanic	incl.	includes, including, inclusive
Explor.	Exploration	G.I.	Government/General Issue (USA)	Incorp.	Incorporation
Expn	Expansion			Ind.	Indian
Ext.	External	Glams	Glamorganshire (GB; old)	Indep.	Independent
Extn	Extension	Glos	Gloucestershire (GB)	Indig.	Indigenous
f, ff	following page, following pages	Govt	Government	Indol.	Indology
		Gr.	Greek	Indon.	Indonesian
F.A.	Fine Art(s)	Grad.	Graduate	Indust.	Industrial
Fac.	Faculty	Graph.	Graphic	Inf.	Information
facs.	facsimile	Green.	Greenlandic	Inq.	Inquiry
Fam.	Family	Gr.-Roman	Greco-Roman	Inscr.	Inscribed, Inscription
fasc.	fascicle	Gt	Great	Inst.	Institute(s)
fd	feastday (of a saint)	Gtr	Greater	Inst. A.	Institute of Art
Feb	February	Guat.	Guatemalan	Instr.	Instrument, Instrumental
Fed.	Federation, Federal	Gym.	Gymnasium	Int.	International
Fem.	Feminist	h.	height	Intell.	Intelligence
Fest.	Festival	ha	hectare	Inter.	Interior(s), Internal
fig.	figure (illustration)	Hait.	Haitian	Interdiscip.	Interdisciplinary
Fig.	Figurative	Hants	Hampshire (GB)	intro.	introduced by, introduction
		Hb.	Handbook	inv.	inventory

Inven.	Invention	m	metre(s)	Moldov.	Moldovan
Invest.	Investigation(s)	m.	married	MOMA	Museum of Modern Art
Iran.	Iranian	M.	Monsieur	Mon.	Monday
irreg.	irregular(ly)	MA	Master of Arts; Massachusetts (USA)	Mongol.	Mongolian
Islam.	Islamic			Mons	Monmouthshire (GB; old)
Isr.	Israeli	Mag.	Magazine	Montgoms	Montgomeryshire (GB; old)
It.	Italian	Maint.	Maintenance	Mor.	Moral
J.	Journal	Malay.	Malaysian	Morav.	Moravian
Jam.	Jamaican	Man.	Manitoba (Canada); Manual	Moroc.	Moroccan
Jan	January	Manuf.	Manufactures	Movt	Movement
Jap.	Japanese	Mar.	Marine, Maritime	MP	Member of Parliament
Jav.	Javanese	Mason.	Masonic	MPhil	Master of Philosophy
Jew.	Jewish	Mat.	Material(s)	MS	Mississippi (USA)
Jewel.	Jewellery	Math.	Mathematic	MS., MSS	manuscript(s)
Jord.	Jordanian	MBE	Member of the Order of the British Empire	MSc	Master of Science
jr	junior			MT	Montana (USA)
Juris.	Jurisdiction	MD	Doctor of Medicine; Maryland (USA)	Mt	Mount
KBE	Knight Commander of the Order of the British Empire			Mthly	Monthly
		ME	Maine (USA)	Mun.	Municipal
KCVO	Knight Commander of the Royal Victorian Order	Mech.	Mechanical	Mus.	Museum(s)
		Med.	Medieval; Medium, Media	Mus. A.	Museum of Art
kg	kilogram(s)	Medic.	Medical, Medicine	Mus. F.A.	Museum of Fine Art(s)
kHz	kilohertz	Medit.	Mediterranean	Music.	Musicology
km	kilometre(s)	Mem.	Memorial(s); Memoir(s)	N.	North(ern); National
Knowl.	Knowledge	Merions	Merionethshire (GB; old)	*n*	refractive index of a medium
Kor.	Korean	Meso-Amer.	Meso-American	n.	note
KS	Kansas (USA)			N.A.G.	National Art Gallery
KY	Kentucky (USA)	Mesop.	Mesopotamian	Nat.	Natural, Nature
Kyrgyz.	Kyrgyzstani	Met.	Metropolitan	Naut.	Nautical
£	libra, librae [pound, pounds sterling]	Metal.	Metallurgy	NB	New Brunswick (Canada)
		Mex.	Mexican	NC	North Carolina (USA)
l.	length	MFA	Master of Fine Arts	ND	North Dakota (USA)
LA	Louisiana (USA)	mg	milligram(s)	n.d.	no date
Lab.	Laboratory	Mgmt	Management	NE	Nebraska; Northeast(ern)
Lancs	Lancashire (GB)	Mgr	Monsignor	Neth.	Netherlandish
Lang.	Language(s)	MI	Michigan	Newslett.	Newsletter
Lat.	Latin	Micrones.	Micronesian	Nfld	Newfoundland (Canada)
Latv.	Latvian	Mid. Amer.	Middle American	N.G.	National Gallery
lb, lbs	pound(s) weight	Middx	Middlesex (GB; old)	N.G.A.	National Gallery of Art
Leb.	Lebanese	Mid. E.	Middle Eastern	NH	New Hampshire (USA)
Lect.	Lecture	Mid. Eng.	Middle English	Niger.	Nigerian
Legis.	Legislative	Mid Glam.	Mid Glamorgan (GB)	NJ	New Jersey (USA)
Leics	Leicestershire (GB)	Mil.	Military	NM	New Mexico (USA)
Lex.	Lexicon	Mill.	Millennium	nm	nanometre (10^{-9} metre)
Lg.	Large	Min.	Ministry; Minutes	nn.	notes
Lib., Libs	Library, Libraries	Misc.	Miscellaneous	no., nos	number(s)
Liber.	Liberian	Miss.	Mission(s)	Nord.	Nordic
Libsp	Librarianship	Mlle	Mademoiselle	Norm.	Normal
Lincs	Lincolnshire (GB)	mm	millimetre(s)	Northants	Northamptonshire (GB)
Lit.	Literature	Mme	Madame	Northumb.	Northumberland (GB)
Lith.	Lithuanian	MN	Minnesota	Norw.	Norwegian
Liturg.	Liturgical	Mnmt, Mnmts	Monument(s)	Notts	Nottinghamshire (GB)
LLB	Bachelor of Laws			Nov	November
LLD	Doctor of Laws	Mnmtl	Monumental	n.p.	no place (of publication)
Lt	Lieutenant	MO	Missouri (USA)	N.P.G.	National Portrait Gallery
Lt-Col.	Lieutenant-Colonel	Mod.	Modern, Modernist	nr	near
Ltd	Limited	Moldav.	Moldavian		

Nr E.	Near Eastern	Per.	Period	Ptg(s)	Painting(s)
NS	New Style; Nova Scotia (Canada)	Percep.	Perceptions	Pub.	Public
		Perf.	Performance, Performing, Performed	pubd	published
n. s.	new series			Publ.	Publicity
NSW	New South Wales (Australia)	Period.	Periodical(s)	pubn(s)	publication(s)
NT	National Trust	Pers.	Persian	PVA	polyvinyl acetate
Ntbk	Notebook	Persp.	Perspectives	PVC	polyvinyl chloride
Numi.	Numismatic(s)	Peru.	Peruvian	Q.	quarterly
NV	Nevada (USA)	PhD	Doctor of Philosophy	4to	quarto
NW	Northwest(ern)	Philol.	Philology	Qué.	Québec (Canada)
NWT	Northwest Territories (Canada)	Philos.	Philosophy	*R*	reprint
		Phoen.	Phoenician	*r*	*recto*
NY	New York (USA)	Phot.	Photograph, Photography, Photographic	RA	Royal Academician
NZ	New Zealand			Radnors	Radnorshire (GB; old)
OBE	Officer of the Order of the British Empire	Phys.	Physician(s), Physics, Physique, Physical	RAF	Royal Air Force
				Rec.	Record(s)
Obj.	Object(s), Objective	Physiog.	Physiognomy	red.	reduction, reduced for
Occas.	Occasional	Physiol.	Physiology	Ref.	Reference
Occident.	Occidental	Pict.	Picture(s), Pictorial	Refurb.	Refurbishment
Ocean.	Oceania	pl.	plate; plural	*reg*	*regit* [ruled]
Oct	October	Plan.	Planning	Reg.	Regional
8vo	octavo	Planet.	Planetarium	Relig.	Religion, Religious
OFM	Order of Friars Minor	Plast.	Plastic	remod.	remodelled
OH	Ohio (USA)	pls	plates	Ren.	Renaissance
OK	Oklahoma (USA)	p.m.	post meridiem [after noon]	Rep.	Report(s)
Olymp	Olympic	Polit.	Political	repr.	reprint(ed); reproduced, reproduction
OM	Order of Merit	Poly.	Polytechnic		
Ont.	Ontario (Canada)	Polynes.	Polynesian	Represent.	Representation, Representative
op.	opus	Pop.	Popular	Res.	Research
opp.	opposite; opera [pl. of opus]	Port.	Portuguese	rest.	restored, restoration
OR	Oregon (USA)	Port.	Portfolio	Retro.	Retrospective
Org.	Organization	Posth.	Posthumous(ly)	rev.	revision, revised (by/for)
Orient.	Oriental	Pott.	Pottery	Rev.	Reverend; Review
Orthdx	Orthodox	POW	prisoner of war	RHA	Royal Hibernian Academician
OSB	Order of St Benedict	PRA	President of the Royal Academy	RI	Rhode Island (USA)
Ott.	Ottoman			RIBA	Royal Institute of British Architects
Oxon	Oxfordshire (GB)	Pract.	Practical		
oz.	ounce(s)	Prefect.	Prefecture, Prefectural	RJ	Rio de Janeiro State
p	pence	Preserv.	Preservation	Rlwy	Railway
p., pp.	page(s)	prev.	previous(ly)	RSA	Royal Scottish Academy
PA	Pennsylvania (USA)	priv.	private	RSFSR	Russian Soviet Federated Socialist Republic
p.a.	per annum	PRO	Public Record Office		
Pak.	Pakistani	Prob.	Problem(s)	Rt Hon.	Right Honourable
Palaeontol.	Palaeontology, Palaeontological	Proc.	Proceedings	Rur.	Rural
		Prod.	Production	Rus.	Russian
Palest.	Palestinian	Prog.	Progress	S	San, Santa, Santo, Sant', São [Saint]
Pap.	Paper(s)	Proj.	Project(s)		
para.	paragraph	Promot.	Promotion	S.	South(ern)
Parag.	Paraguayan	Prop.	Property, Properties	s.	solidus, solidi [shilling(s)]
Parl.	Parliament	Prov.	Province(s), Provincial	Sask.	Saskatchewan (Canada)
Paroch.	Parochial	Proven.	Provenance	Sat.	Saturday
Patriarch.	Patriarchate	Prt, Prts	Print(s)	SC	South Carolina (USA)
Patriot.	Patriotic	Prtg	Printing	Scand.	Scandinavian
Patrm.	Patrimony	pseud.	pseudonym	Sch.	School
Pav.	Pavilion	Psych.	Psychiatry, Psychiatric	Sci.	Science(s), Scientific
PEI	Prince Edward Island (Canada)	Psychol.	Psychology, Psychological	Scot.	Scottish
Pembs	Pembrokeshire (GB; old)	pt	part	Sculp.	Sculpture

SD	South Dakota (USA)	suppl., suppls	supplement(s), supplementary	Urb.	Urban
SE	Southeast(ern)	Surv.	Survey	Urug.	Uruguayan
Sect.	Section	SW	Southwest(ern)	US	United States
Sel.	Selected	Swed.	Swedish	USA	United States of America
Semin.	Seminar(s), Seminary	Swi.	Swiss	USSR	Union of Soviet Socialist Republics
Semiot.	Semiotic	Symp.	Symposium		
Semit.	Semitic	Syr.	Syrian	UT	Utah
Sept	September	Tap.	Tapestry	*v*	*verso*
Ser.	Series	Tas.	Tasmanian	VA	Virginia (USA)
Serb.	Serbian	Tech.	Technical, Technique	V&A	Victoria and Albert Museum
Serv.	Service(s)	Technol.	Technology	Var.	Various
Sess.	Session, Sessional	Territ.	Territory	Venez.	Venezuelan
Settmt(s)	Settlement(s)	Theat.	Theatre	Vern.	Vernacular
S. Glam.	South Glamorgan (GB)	Theol.	Theology, Theological	Vict.	Victorian
Siber.	Siberian	Theor.	Theory, Theoretical	Vid.	Video
Sig.	Signature	Thurs.	Thursday	Viet.	Vietnamese
Sil.	Silesian	Tib.	Tibetan	viz.	*videlicet* [namely]
Sin.	Singhala	TN	Tennessee (USA)	vol., vols	volume(s)
sing.	singular	Top.	Topography	vs.	versus
SJ	Societas Jesu [Society of Jesus]	Trad.	Tradition(s), Traditional	VT	Vermont (USA)
Skt	Sanskrit	trans.	translation, translated by; transactions	Vulg.	Vulgarisation
Slav.	Slavic, Slavonic			W.	West(ern)
Slov.	Slovene, Slovenian	Transafr.	Transafrican	w.	width
Soc.	Society	Transatlant.	Transatlantic	WA	Washington (USA)
Social.	Socialism, Socialist	Transcarpath.	Transcarpathian	Warwicks	Warwickshire (GB)
Sociol.	Sociology	transcr.	transcribed by/for	Wed.	Wednesday
Sov.	Soviet	Triq.	Triquarterly	W. Glam.	West Glamorgan (GB)
SP	São Paulo State	Tropic.	Tropical	WI	Wisconsin (USA)
Sp.	Spanish	Tues.	Tuesday	Wilts	Wiltshire (GB)
sq.	square	Turk.	Turkish	Wkly	Weekly
sr	senior	Turkmen.	Turkmenistani	W. Midlands	West Midlands (GB)
Sri L.	Sri Lankan	TV	Television		
SS	Saints, Santi, Santissima, Santissimo, Santissimi; Steam ship	TX	Texas (USA)	Worcs	Worcestershire (GB; old)
		U.	University	Wtrcol.	Watercolour
SSR	Soviet Socialist Republic	UK	United Kingdom of Great Britain and Northern Ireland	WV	West Virginia (USA)
St	Saint, Sankt, Sint, Szent			WY	Wyoming (USA)
Staffs	Staffordshire (GB)	Ukrain.	Ukrainian	Yb., Y.-b.	Yearbook, Year-book
Ste	Sainte	Un.	Union	Yem.	Yemeni
Stud.	Study, Studies	Underwtr	Underwater	Yorks	Yorkshire (GB; old)
Subalp.	Subalpine	UNESCO	United Nations Educational, Scientific and Cultural Organization	Yug.	Yugoslavian
Sum.	Sumerian			Zamb.	Zambian
Sun.	Sunday	Univl	Universal	Zimb.	Zimbabwean
Sup.	Superior	unpubd	unpublished		

A Note on the Use of the Dictionary

This note is intended as a short guide to the basic editorial conventions adopted in this dictionary. For a fuller explanation, please refer to the Introduction, vol. 1, pp. xiii–xx.

Abbreviations in general use in the dictionary are listed on pp. vii–xii; those used in bibliographies and for locations of works of art or exhibition venues are listed in the Appendices in vol. 33.

Alphabetization of headings, which are distinguished in bold typeface, is letter by letter up to the first comma (ignoring spaces, hyphens, accents and any parenthesized or bracketed matter); the same principle applies thereafter. Abbreviations of 'Saint' and its foreign equivalents are alphabetized as if spelt out, and headings with the prefix 'Mc' appear under 'Mac'.

Authors' signatures appear at the end of the article or sequence of articles that the authors have contributed; in multipartite articles, any section that is unsigned is by the author of the next signed section. Where the article was compiled by the editors or in the few cases where an author has wished to remain anonymous, this is indicated by a square box (□) instead of a signature.

Bibliographies are arranged chronologically (within section, where divided) by order of year of first publication and, within years, alphabetically by authors' names. Abbreviations have been used for some standard reference books; these are cited in full in Appendix C in vol. 33, as are abbreviations of periodical titles (Appendix B). Abbreviated references to alphabetically arranged dictionaries and encyclopedias appear at the beginning of the bibliography (or section).

Biographical dates when cited in parentheses in running text at the first mention of a personal name indicate that the individual does not have an entry in the dictionary. The presence of parenthesized regnal dates for rulers and popes, however, does not necessarily indicate the lack of a biography of that person. Where no dates are provided for an artist or patron, the reader may assume that there is a biography of that individual in the dictionary (or, more rarely, that the person is so obscure that dates are not readily available).

Cross-references are distinguished by the use of small capital letters, with a large capital to indicate the initial letter of the entry to which the reader is directed; for example, 'He commissioned LEONARDO DA VINCI . . .' means that the entry is alphabetized under 'L'.

I

[continued]

Iraq, Republic of [Arab. Al-Jumhūriyya al-ʿIrāqiyya]. Country in the Middle East with its capital at Baghdad. Iraq has an area of *c.* 437,500 sq. km, encompassing the valleys of the Tigris and Euphrates rivers, and it is bordered in the west by Syria and Jordan, in the south by Saudi Arabia and Kuwait, in the north by Turkey and in the east by Iran. The economy is largely dependent on the export of oil, although attempts have been made to increase the industrial and agricultural output. The population of *c.* 18,782,000 (1990 estimate) consists of Arabs, Turks, Kurds and other minority groups. Islam is the predominant religion, over 50% of the population being Sunni Muslim and the remainder largely Shiʿa Muslim with a small minority of Christians. Incorporated in the Ottoman empire from the 16th century to the early 20th, after World War I Iraq became a British mandated territory, and in 1921 Amir Faysal (*d* 1933) was proclaimed king. In 1932 the British mandate was terminated, and Iraq was admitted to the League of Nations as an independent state. Iraq was a constitutional monarchy from 1932 to 1958, although during World War II British forces occupied the country. In 1958 a military coup headed by Abdul Karim Kassem overthrew the monarchy, and a republic was declared. Kassem's regime collapsed in 1963, and ʿAbd al-Salam ʿArif (*d* 1966) assumed the presidency. Arab defeat in the Arab–Israeli War (1967) led to unrest in the country, and in 1968 there was an uprising in which the Baʿth Party came to power. Advocating nationalism and Socialism, the Baʿth Party implemented plans for reconstruction and development. Under President Saddam Hussein, Iraq fought a costly war with Iran (1980–88), invaded Kuwait (1990) and was defeated in the Gulf War (1991). This article covers the art produced in the country in the 20th century. For its earlier history *see* ANCIENT NEAR EAST and ISLAMIC ART.

Traditional houses in Baghdad (*see* VERNACULAR AR-CHITECTURE, §II, 7(iv)) are built around open courtyards and may be three to four storeys high including a basement. Large houses often have several courtyards. To counteract high temperatures, houses are densely clustered and may make use of the WIND CATCHER, while light-filtering techniques include screens of coloured glass surrounding the courtyards. The ground-floor walls are usually of baked brick and rubble infill, while the upper storeys have a timber-framed construction with brick infill. Elsewhere in Iraq mud-brick is widely used, while in southern Iraq the marsh Arabs lived in structures made of reeds.

Since the early 20th century much traditional architecture in Baghdad has been destroyed. New roads have been cut through neighbourhoods with courtyard houses in the old town, and in the 1960s and 1970s an area was cleared for a civic centre (completed in 1986). It included the Municipality Building by Hisham Munir (*b* 1930), the Income Tax Building by Mahdi al-Hassani (*b* 1932) and the Water Board Building by Mahmoud al-ʿAli (*b* 1942). New styles of housing have been introduced to Baghdad since the mid-1930s. In the 1950s MOHAMED MAKIYA designed houses and commercial buildings, and in 1959 he founded the department of architecture at the College of Engineering, Baghdad University. Concern about the uncritical adoption of Western styles in Iraq led RIFAT CHADIRJI to seek inspiration in local and regional styles. In 1982 the British architect John Warren (*b* 1938) of the Architecture and Planning Partnership (APP) and the Iraqi firm Mahmoud al-ʿAli and Partners tried to adapt the principles of traditional domestic architecture to modern requirements in conservation schemes of infill housing at Kadhimiyya and Gaylani in Baghdad, where two important shrines are located. Their work stopped in 1984, however, and the schemes were not completed.

Calligraphy flourished in Iraq in the 20th century in the work of HASHEM MUHAMMAD AL-BAGHDADI, whose output ranged from monumental writings on mosques and public buildings to the design of Iraqi banknotes. In 1960 he was appointed lecturer in Arabic calligraphy at the Institute of Fine Arts, Baghdad, and later he became head of the calligraphy department. He awarded only one diploma during his life, to his student Abdul Ghani al-Ani (*b* 1937). The calligrapher HASSAN MASSOUDY, who trained in Baghdad from 1960 to 1969 and then moved to France, where he studied at the Ecole des Beaux-Arts, Paris, has produced novel compositions combining calligraphic skill with painterly elements.

Easel painting in oils commenced in the early 20th century, led by a group of army officers who were taught drawing and painting as part of their military training in Istanbul. The most important figure among this group was Abdul Qadir al-Rassam (1882–1952), who trained at the Military Academy, Istanbul. Al-Rassam gave painting lessons and urged young Iraqi artists to continue their artistic training in Europe. Among his contemporaries were Assim Abdul Hafid (*b* 1886), Hajj Muhammad Salim and Muhammad Salih Zaki (1888–1974). Abdul Hafid and Salim trained at Ottoman military colleges (Abdul Hafid continuing his training in Paris in 1928), while Zaki studied at the Academy of Fine Arts, Istanbul. This group of artists introduced the idea of Western painting to Iraq through their work and teaching. The first Iraqi cartoonist was Hajj Suad Salim (*b* 1918), the son of Hajj Muhammad Salim.

During the 1930s the State encouraged art activities. In 1931 the government, at the instruction of King Faysal, allocated scholarships for art studies abroad, and Akram Shukri (*b* 1910) received a government scholarship to study in England. He was followed by the painter FAIK HASSAN, who in 1933 won a scholarship to study at the Ecole des Beaux-Arts, Paris. Among the other painters who studied abroad was 'Ata Sabri (*b* 1913), who trained in Rome (1937) and after World War II at Goldsmiths College, London, graduating in 1950. In 1936 the Ministry of Education founded the Music Institute in Baghdad, and its success prompted the government to open new departments in drama, painting and sculpture. By 1940 the Institute of Fine Arts was teaching painting and sculpture, and it soon stood at the forefront of the Iraqi modern art movement. In 1941 the Friends of the Arts Society was founded by a group of artists, architects and art-lovers to promote and exhibit Iraqi work. During World War II several young Iraqi painters were inspired by Polish officers who were with the Allied troops in Baghdad, two of whom had studied painting with Pierre Bonnard.

The most important figure to emerge in Iraqi modern art was the painter and sculptor JAWAD SALIM. After studying on government scholarships in Paris (1938–9) and Rome (1939–40), he worked at the Archaeological Museum in Baghdad, where he became acquainted with ancient Iraqi art, and then studied at the Slade School, London (1946–9). After the creation of the Republic in 1958 he was commissioned to make the Monument to *Liberty*, which was placed at the entrance of the National Park in the centre of Baghdad. Jawad Salim was responsible for encouraging many other artists in Baghdad, where he taught sculpture at the Institute of Fine Arts. He also produced designs for book covers, jewellery and other artefacts. Another influential figure was Faik Hassan, who painted such subjects as city-dwellers, peasants and the bedouin. Teaching at the Institute of Fine Arts for over four decades, he experimented with Impressionism, Cubism and abstract art, returning later in his life to Impressionism.

After World War II Iraqi art students studied in increasing numbers on government scholarships in Paris, London and Rome. During the 1950s several societies of artists formed in Baghdad. In 1950 La Société Primitive (later renamed the Pioneers) was founded; Faik Hassan was president, and the members included his pupil Ismail Sheikhley (*b* 1924), Zeid Salih, Mahmoud Sabri and Nouri Rawi. The society focused on painting the countryside, nature and city scenes. A second group of artists, known as the Baghdad Group of Modern Art, was formed in 1951 by Jawad Salim: the members included SHAKER HASSAN AL-SAID, the painter and art critic Jabra I. Jabra,

and the sculptors Muhammad Ghani (*b* 1929) and Khalid al-Rahhal (1926–87). The group was concerned with establishing an identity for modern Iraqi art. In 1953 a third group of artists known as the Impressionists formed around Hafid al-Drubi (*b* 1914), who had trained at Goldsmiths College, London. The members of this group moved away from depicting local subjects in an impressionistic style towards Cubism and abstract art.

In the 1960s output in the fine arts increased. Artists were preoccupied with defining the nature of Iraqi art, especially as many trained abroad, in Europe, the Arab world, the USA, USSR and China. Some Iraqi artists concentrated on folklore or calligraphy (e.g. Jamil Hamoudi) for inspiration; others were inspired by such foreign traditions as 20th-century Mexican art. Iraqi village life was recorded in the paintings of Khalid al-Jader, who trained at the Institute of Fine Arts and on a government scholarship in Paris, becoming dean of the Institute of Fine Arts on his return. Various artists' groups were also formed. In 1965 the Innovationist group was established, which promoted the use of new materials during the four years that it lasted. In 1967 the group Al-Zawiya ('The Religious Fraternity') was formed, led by Faik Hassan and advocating that art should serve national causes. The group held a single exhibition, which included works on political and nationalistic themes. In 1969 a group called New Vision emerged, which included among its members Dia Azzawi (*b* 1939), who later worked in London. In 1971 Shaker Hassan al-Said formed the One-dimension group in Baghdad, which promoted the use of Arabic letters in the composition of a work of art.

Under the Ba'th Party, state patronage of the arts increased. The National Museum of Modern Art in Baghdad multiplied its acquisition of Iraqi art and participated in international exhibitions. Group exhibitions became more frequent, especially those held on occasions marking important political events. In 1969–70 the first annual exhibition commemorating the anniversary of the Ba'th Party was held. An Institute of Applied Arts was founded in Baghdad in 1969, and other institutes were established in such cities as Basra, Mosul and Sulaymaniya. In 1973 the First Congress of Arab Artists was held in Baghdad. Abroad, Iraqi cultural centres in Arab countries, Europe and elsewhere arranged exhibitions. In Iraq large public sculptures were commissioned. Khalid al-Rahhal, for example, who graduated from the Institute of Fine Arts in 1947 and studied on a government scholarship in Rome in 1954, designed the monument to the *Unknown Soldier* (1982) in Baghdad. ISMAIL FATTAH, who had studied with Jawad Salim, conceived the *Martyrs' Monument* in Baghdad (1981–3; see fig.) to commemorate the dead in the Iran–Iraq War; this monument brought him international recognition. The difficult political conditions in Iraq also led to various artists, for example ISSAM EL-SAID, working abroad.

In the early 20th century there was considerable European interest in archaeological sites in Iraq, such as BABYLON, NIMRUD, NINEVEH, HATRA and KTESIPHON. This interest extended to Islamic sites when SAMARRA' was excavated (1911–14). In 1923 a display of archaeological finds in a room of the Serai Building in Baghdad, which had been the residence of the Ottoman governor,

Ismail Fattah: *Martyrs' Monument*, Baghdad, Iraq, 1981–3

occasioned the inception of the Iraq Museum. After independence the Iraqi Directorate of Antiquities became responsible for the preservation of archaeological sites and buildings. The Iraq Museum contains an important collection ranging from prehistoric to Islamic times. Modern art was exhibited at the National Museum of Modern Art in Baghdad (inaugurated in 1962) and the Museum of Pioneer Artists (1979), which exhibited works of the early 20th century. In 1986 the Saddam Arts Centre was opened, with vast halls that could hold large exhibitions. The occasion was marked by the First Baghdad International Festival (entitled *Art for Humanity*), which included works by artists throughout the world. The Centre replaced the National Museum of Modern Art and the Museum of Pioneer Artists, whose permanent collections of Iraqi artists were moved to the new premises. Throughout Iraq there are also provincial museums with archaeological or ethnological collections.

BIBLIOGRAPHY

J. I. Jabra: *Iraqi Art Today* (Baghdad, 1972) [Eng. and Arab. texts]
S. al-Rabi'i: *Al-fann al-tashkīlī al-mu'āṣir fi'l-'Irāq* [Modern painting in Iraq] (Baghdad, 1972)
J. Hamudi: *Dalīl al-fannānīn al-'irāqiyyīn* [A catalogue of Iraqi artists] (Baghdad, 1973)
S. Faris: *Al-manābi' al-tarīkhiyya li'l-fann al-jidārī fi'l-'Irāq al-mu'āṣir* [The historic origins of mural art in contemporary Iraq] (Baghdad, 1974)
J. I. Jabra: *Jawād Salīm wa nasab al-ḥurriyya* [Jawad Salim and the monument to *Liberty*] (Baghdad, 1974)
F. Basmachi: *Treasures of the Iraq Museum* (Baghdad, 1975–6)
N. Salim: *L'Art contemporain en Iraq* (Lausanne, 1977)
Culture and Arts in Iraq, Iraqi Ministry of Culture and Arts (Baghdad, 1978)
I. Fethi: *The Architectural Heritage of Baghdad* (London, 1979)
Iraqi Art of the 50s (exh. cat., London, Iraqi Cult. Cent., 1979)
A.-G. D. el-Basri: *Aspects of Iraqi Cultural Policy* (Paris, 1980)
A. A. Bogdanov: *Sovremennoe izobrazitel'noe iskusstvo Iraka (1900-e–1970-e) godui* [Contemporary art in Iraq] (Leningrad, 1982)
J. Warren and I. Fethi: *Traditional Houses in Baghdad* (Horsham, 1982)
S. H. al-Said: *Fuṣūl min tārīkh al-ḥaraka al-tashkīliyya fi'l-'Irāq* [Chapters from the history of modern art in Iraq] (Baghdad, 1983)
J. I. Jabra: *Judūr al-fann al-'Irāqī* [Monuments of Iraqi art] (Baghdad, 1986)
M. Tournier: *Hassan Massoudy: Calligraphe* (Paris, 1986)
W. Ali, ed.: *Contemporary Art from the Islamic World* (London, 1989), pp. 159–74
S. al-Khalil: *The Monument: Art, Vulgarity and Responsibility in Iraq* (London, 1991)

'Iraq al-Amir ['Araq el-Emir]. Site in Jordan, 18 km west of Amman. A prehistoric mound on the site of the modern village was first occupied in the 5th millennium BC and was encircled by a wall in the 11th century BC. The settlement was abandoned *c.* 1000 BC, until Qasr el-'Abd ('fortress of the slave') was built to the south-west of the mound at the beginning of the 2nd century BC by the Tobiad tax-farmer Hyrcanus (*d* 169 BC) to serve his capital, Tyre. To the west of the mound the so-called 'square building' (37.0×18.5 m), consists of two storeys constructed of large white stones; four towers at the corners each featured a balcony supported by columns. The plan is that of a pronaos, naos and opisthodomos. There are two monumental entrances, which are distyle *in antis*, on the north and south sides. The lower level consists of four storage rooms, accessible through a corridor which received light from seven windows on each façade. The upper storey, designed as living quarters but never completed, had a large central hall with four rooms in the corner towers. The eastern and western sides were decorated with 21 fluted Corinthian columns and the façade bore a frieze representing lions with their cubs. Two basins at the north-east and north-west corners released the overflow of water through fountains. Following Hyrcanus' suicide, the site was again abandoned until *c.* 100 BC, after which the mound continued to be occupied as late as the 14th century AD. H. C. Butler visited the site in 1904 as part of the Princeton Expedition to Syria, producing plans of the ruins and details of elevations and capitals. Excavations were carried out by P. W. Lapp in 1961 and 1962, and from 1976–86 by a programme sponsored by the French Institute of Archaeology.

BIBLIOGRAPHY

Stillwell: "Araq el-Emir'
C. L. Irby and J. Mangles: *Travels in Egypt and Nubia, Syria and Asia Minor* (London, 1823)
C. R. Condor: *The Survey of Eastern Palestine*, i (London, 1889), p. 78
H. C. Butler: *Publications of the Princeton University Archaeological Expedition to Syria in 1904–1905 and 1909* (Leiden, 1919), pp. 1–25
P. W. Lapp: 'The Second and Third Campaigns at 'Araq el –Amir', *Bull. Amer. Sch. Orient. Res.*, clxxi (1963), pp. 8–39
J. A. Goldstein: 'The Tale of the Tobiads', *Stud. Jud. & Late Ant.*, xii/3 (1970), pp. 782–803
J. M. Dentzer, F. Villeneuve and F. Larché: 'The Monumental Gate and the Princely Estate of 'Araq el Amir', *An. Amer. Sch. Orient. Res.*, xlvii (1980), pp. 133–47
N. Lapp and others: 'The Excavation at 'Araq al Amir', *An. Amer. Sch. Orient. Res.*, xlvii (1980)
E. Will, F. Larché and F. Zayadine: *'Iraq al-Amir: Le Chateau du tobiade Hyrcan* , 2 vols (Paris, 1991)

FAWZI ZAYADINE

Irarrázabal, Mario (*b* Santiago, 1940). Chilean sculptor. He studied philosophy and art from 1960 to 1964 at the University of Notre Dame, IN, and theology at the Università Gregoriana Pontificia in Rome from 1965 to 1967. In 1968 he continued his studies under the German sculptor Otto Waldemar. He first exhibited his work in Chile in 1970, consistently using the human figure to express injustice, loneliness, helplessness, sorrow and torture, as in *Judgement* (1978; Valparaíso, Mus. Mun. B.A.). Favouring a directness of expression in his bronzes, for which he used the lost-wax process, he sought to leave visible traces of textures and of the marks made in manipulating the material. He used the nudity of the human body, sometimes lacerated or with exaggerated proportions—the torso is sometimes unduly large in relation to the arms and legs—to emphasize its vulnerability and helplessness, reinforcing this impression by his choice of postures. Whether prone, reclining, seated or standing, the figure is always characterized by the determined way in which the head is held, which completes the expressive effect.

During the 1970s Irarrázabal was unable to work on a monumental scale because of the high cost of casting in bronze. In the 1980s, however, he discovered the possibilities of cement, which he used for commissioned works in Chile and other countries, for example *Monumental Hand* (1982) in Punta del Este, Uruguay, *Monumental Finger* (1987) at the International Sculpture Park in Nairobi, and *Human Group* (1985) at the Galerías Nacionales in Santiago. Irarrázabal's implicit criticism of aspects of human behaviour took on particular poignancy after the installation of a military government of Chile in 1973 when, in order to escape official censorship, he turned to a more conceptual mode.

BIBLIOGRAPHY

M. Ivelić: *La escultura chilena* (Santiago, 1978)
Mario Irarrázabal: Esculturas megalíticas (exh. cat., essay M. Ivelić; Santiago, Inst. Cult. Las Condes, 1985)
M. Ivelić and G. Galaz: *Chile: Arte actual* (Santiago, 1988)

MILAN IVELIĆ

Irbach, Sebastian. *See* IRRWOCH, SEBASTIAN.

Ireland, Republic of [Eire]. Country in north-west Europe, comprising almost 85% of the most westerly of the British Isles. It is bordered to the north-east by Northern Ireland, a part of the United Kingdom, and it is separated from the remainder of the United Kingdom, to the east, by the Irish Sea. The remaining coastline is bordered by the Atlantic Ocean (see fig. 1). Its population in the late 20th century was *c.* 3.5 million, and its capital city is Dublin. Most of the central region is lowland, drained by the River Shannon, but the north and west of the island are characterized by a rugged mountain landscape, and to the south of Dublin are the Wicklow Mountains. Less than 5% of Ireland is forested, and the country's wet climate has led to the accumulation in the midland region of raised peat bogs. The country's economy is based on agriculture, manufacture and services, including tourism.

Ireland was colonized by the Celts during the first millennium BC and subsequently invaded by the Vikings in the 9th and 10th centuries AD. Anglo-Normans colonized part of the island in the late 12th century, and this was followed by increasing settlement from Great Britain, especially in the north-east of the island (Ulster). The whole of the island was ruled directly by the British government from 1801 until 1922, when the Irish Free State was founded, comprising 26 of the island's 32 counties and remaining within the British Commonwealth. The six counties of Northern Ireland, however, continued to be within the United Kingdom. In 1937 a new constitution proclaimed the state of Ireland, still within the Commonwealth, but in 1948 further legislation led to the establishment of a fully independent Irish Republic. This article discusses art throughout Ireland until 1922 and within the Republic of Ireland from 1922. The art of NORTHERN IRELAND from 1922 is discussed in a separate survey.

I. Introduction. II. Architecture. III. Painting and graphic arts. IV. Sculpture. V. Interior decoration. VI. Furniture. VII. Ceramics. VIII. Glass. IX. Gold and silver. X. Objects of vertu. XI. Textiles. XII. Patronage. XIII. Collecting and dealing. XIV. Museums. XV. Art education. XVI. Art libraries and photographic collections. XVII. Historiography.

I. Introduction.

For several centuries after its first colonization, Ireland remained dominated by Celtic culture and society, which was made up of small kingdoms sharing a common Gaelic language. It was never brought within the Roman Empire, but in the 5th century Christianity was introduced by St Patrick, leading to the growth of a distinctive Celtic Christianity, with monastic settlements constituting the main centres of artistic production (*see* CELTIC ART, §II, 5; *see also* INSULAR ART). This skilled artistic output had already begun to falter, however, by the time of the Viking

1. Map of Ireland; those sites with separate entries in this dictionary are distinguished by CROSS-REFERENCE TYPE

invasions, which led to the establishment of a number of coastal towns that became centres of Viking culture and craft (*see* VIKING ART, §II, 4(iii)(b)). The invasion of Ireland by the Anglo-Normans from 1169 led to the introduction of the feudal system in the area around Dublin, known as 'the Pale', and in a broad swathe of territories 'beyond the Pale'. This resulted in the development in these regions of towns, cathedrals, villages and castles, while the western coastal region remained outside English rule. By the late 13th century Ireland was divided into areas of Gaelic culture and English culture, with the new cathedrals being built in the early English Gothic style. During the 14th century the colony was severely damaged by the Black Death, but a Gaelic political and cultural resurgence took place in the 15th century, by which time the Anglo-Normans had largely become absorbed into the Irish polity.

In the early 16th century the cultural and religious unity of Ireland was shattered as the English Tudor monarchs Henry VIII, Mary I and Elizabeth I attempted to impose a centralized English government and law, and Henry and Elizabeth also attempted to introduce Protestant religious reforms. The destruction of the monasteries and continuous warfare naturally prevented the European Renaissance from exerting noticeable influence during this period. There was continued conflict in the early 17th century, when land was confiscated from those who resisted British rule, especially the Gaelic chieftains of the north-eastern region of Ulster, where King James I of England subsequently sponsored British Protestants to settle (the 'Ulster Plantation'). There were further uprisings throughout Ireland in the 1640s, leading to further confiscations after the English Civil War during the Protectorate of Oliver Cromwell. The peace that came with the restoration of the English king Charles II in 1660, and the initiatives of Charles's Irish Viceroy, JAMES BUTLER, 1st Duke of Ormonde, led to a great expansion of Dublin in the late 17th century (*see* DUBLIN, §I, 2). In the 1680s, however, support in the Gaelic community for the Roman Catholic English king James II led to increased repression after James's defeat in 1690 at the Battle of the Boyne by the Protestant king William III. In the early 18th century, with Protestant dominance assured, there was a huge increase in domestic building throughout the country. Magnificent country houses, in the Palladian style, urban terraces, squares, estates and gardens were developed, requiring skilled craftsmanship in stone-carving, stucco and woodwork, together with the provision of furniture, glass and ceramics. English and Italian craftsmen, artists and architects came to practise in Ireland, stimulating native development. Another important influence, particularly for silk- and linen-weavers, was the arrival of Huguenot craftsmen fleeing from persecution in France. This influence became particularly important in Dublin in the 18th century and in the Belfast region in the 19th century.

In 1801 the Irish parliament in Dublin, which, apart from a brief period in the 1790s, had had little independence since Tudor times, was merged with that in London by the Act of Union, passed the previous year. This ended Dublin's life as a capital city and brought a loss of patronage, with the arts becoming increasingly provincial and many artists emigrating. During the 19th century the sectarian division that existed in Ireland between Catholics and Protestants began to take the form of a nationalist division between those who rejected legislative union with Britain and those who accepted it. The nationalism of those who rejected the Union was strengthened by resentment of the Protestant upper class, which owned most land and dominated the professions, and the relative lack of economic support for those parts of Ireland that were mainly inhabited by Catholics. BELFAST in particular flourished during this period as it became caught up in the

Industrial Revolution, but the rest of Ireland was untouched by this new wealth, and Irish nationalism was reinforced by a series of disastrous potato harvests during the 1840s, which resulted in famine and extensive migration, especially to the USA. In the arts this nationalism led to a form of Irish Romanticism known as the CELTIC REVIVAL, while the cultural difference of the north-east from the rest of Ireland was emphasized by its red brick domestic and commercial architecture. Following Catholic emancipation in 1829, the Catholic Revival led to a vast increase in the building of churches and convents, in the Gothic Revival style, in all parts of Ireland.

In the late 19th century and the early 20th there was a political revival as an increasingly dynamic movement grew up demanding a separate Irish parliament within the Union ('Home Rule'), and this was accompanied by a more forward-looking cultural revival. The importance of French art within Europe from the 1880s stimulated many Irish artists to study in Paris and Brittany, leading to the formation of a modern Irish school of landscape painting in the early 20th century. At the same time the British Arts and Crafts Movement was equally influential on Irish stained glass, textiles, metalwork and book production. In 1914 Home Rule was enacted (although northern Protestants vowed to resist it in the 'Ulster Covenant'), only to be immediately suspended because of the outbreak of World War I. Persistent nationalist pressure, however, including an uprising in Dublin in 1916 (the 'Easter Rising') and a war of independence, led to the foundation in 1922 of the Irish Free State. After this, the artistic momentum of the first decades of the 20th century waned, and there was a period of conservative reaction. It was not until after World War II that modernism became the dominant influence in the arts. In the 1960s, particularly, social changes such as increasing industrialization, urbanization and modernization all created a new climate of receptivity for new art and design, with many modern European and American influences transforming the cultural landscape of the state.

BIBLIOGRAPHY

W. Strickland: *A Dictionary of Irish Art*, 2 vols (London, 1913)
F. Henry: *Irish Art in the Early Christian Period* (London, 1965)
——: *Irish Art during the Viking Invasions* (London, 1967)
B. Arnold: *A Concise History of Irish Art* (London, 1969)
F. Henry: *Irish Art in the Romanesque Period* (London, 1970)
R. Stalley: *Architecture and Sculpture in Ireland, 1150–1350* (Dublin, 1971)
J. Hewitt and T. Snoddy: *Art in Ulster: Artists up to 1957* (Belfast, 1977)
P. Harbison, H. Potterton and J. Sheehy: *Irish Art and Architecture* (London, 1978) [with extensive bibliog.]
R. Knowles: *Contemporary Irish Art* (Dublin, 1982)
B. de Breffny, ed.: *Ireland: A Cultural Encyclopedia* (London, 1983)
The Treasures of Ireland (exh. cat. by M. Ryan, Dublin, N. Mus., 1983)
S. B. Kennedy: *Irish Art and Modernism* (Dublin and Belfast, 1991)

JOHN TURPIN

II. Architecture.

1. Before *c.* 1680. 2. *c.* 1680–*c.* 1760: Palladianism. 3. *c.* 1760–*c.* 1860: Neoclassicism and revival styles. 4. After *c.* 1860.

1. BEFORE *c.* 1680. Early Christian monastic and domestic settlements were enclosed by earthen or stone walls, within which wooden or stone buildings were grouped. One such type, mostly found at settlements in Co. Kerry (e.g. at Skellig Michael), is the beehive hut or

clochan. These circular dwellings, stone-built and corbelled, first appeared during the Iron Age, but most date from the Early Christian period. The wooden churches of the Early Christian period were built to a simple box-like design, with roofing of rush or shingle, and they were usually small (*c.* 4.5 m in length). None, however, has survived. Some early stone-built churches, such as Gallurus Oratory, Co. Kerry, appear to be all roof: the silhouette is that of an upturned boat, while the gable end has a simple lintel doorway. St MacDara's Church, Co. Galway, represents another type, based on the early oak-built churches. Large cut stones form four walls supporting a steeply pitched stone roof, with the side walls projecting to create antae at the gable end. In the 10th century, tall and slender round towers began to be built in stone within monastic enclosures. These towers, which are peculiar to Ireland, were usually free-standing structures, although in some cases they formed part of the monastery church itself. Varying in height from 25 m to 30 m, they tapered to a conical stone roof and had an entrance about 2 m to 3 m above ground level, reached by means of a ladder. The tallest (34.28 m) is at Kilmacduagh, Co. Galway. About 70 round towers survive in whole or part across the country. Around 1100, post-and-lintel construction began to give way to round arches, but it was not until the building (1127–34) of Cormac's Chapel, at Cashel, Co. Tipperary, that the Romanesque style reached Ireland (*see* ROMANESQUE, fig. 20). Churches continued to be small, but their sculptural decoration was highly skilled (*see* §IV, 1 below).

In 1142 St Malachy of Armagh invited monks of the CISTERCIAN ORDER to establish foundations in Ireland. With the first of these, Mellifont, Co. Louth, they brought about a radical change in monastic architecture. The piecemeal nature of earlier monastic enclosures was replaced by a more standardized layout, the basic principles of which were utility and simplicity. As in the case of Holycross, Co. Tipperary (see fig. 2), they were usually sited in a remote place, beside running water. The Cistercian layout normally consisted of a cloister, church and conventual buildings. Although an outer court was usually added, to accommodate guest-quarters, schoolhouse, granary, brewery, bakery and gatehouse, only occasional vestiges of these remain. The largest building was the church, cruciform in plan, with an aisled nave, transepts and a square-headed chancel. The transepts had smaller chapels. The Cistercian style was informed by the austere principles of St Bernard of Clairvaux, which were followed by a large proportion of that order's establishments. It was an architecture of smooth surfaces, with little or no decoration, and, since timber roofs were preferred, no vertical shafts were needed for vaulting ribs or transverse arches; thus there was no marked division into bays. A number of establishments in the west of Ireland disregarded the strictures of St Bernard and produced a series of richly sculpted capitals (*see* §IV, 1 below), but after 1220 there was a return to austerity. This lasted until the end of the 14th century, when once again a number of abbeys produced elaborate sculptural programmes, the first of which was for the cloister at Jerpoint Abbey (*c.* 1390–1400), Co. Kilkenny.

2. Cistercian abbey, Holycross, Co. Tipperary, founded 1180, rebuilt 15th century; from a photograph of 1899

The Gothic style was introduced after the Anglo-Norman invasion of 1169. In Cistercian monasteries this meant a greater emphasis on vertical proportions and the use of lancet windows, as at Inch Abbey, Co. Down, founded in 1180. A more elaborate use of Gothic, derived from churches in the west of England, appeared in the independent cathedrals in Dublin, St Patrick's (1220–54) and Christ Church (completed *c.* 1240) (*see* DUBLIN, §IV, 1 and 2). Provincial cathedrals, however, such as Kilkenny (completed in the 1260s) and Limerick (late 12th century), were plainer. The Cistercian style was taken up by Dominicans and Franciscans, although during the 13th century they kept their establishments very simple. During the 14th century the devastation of the Black Death meant that virtually no building work was undertaken. It began again in the 15th century, a period during which the Franciscans were particularly active. They kept to the general layout established earlier by the Cistercians, but a Franciscan friary can be distinguished by its tall narrow church-tower, rising over the crossing of the nave. Many churches built at this time had fine tracery windows as well as elaborate sculpture, found particularly on church furniture such as sedilia and tombs.

Stone castles began to be built in the 1180s, soon after the Anglo-Norman invasion, and continued to be built into the 17th century. English and Welsh prototypes provided the patterns for the first building phase. There were two types, each having one or more wards or bawns enclosed by a curtain-wall with projecting towers. Frequently, as at Carrickfergus (*c.* 1180), Co. Antrim, a massive keep was built in the inner ward, which also accommodated wooden buildings and, often, a low stone hall. Keeps varied considerably, but one type—a rectangular tower with cylindrical corners (e.g. the early 13th-century Carlow Castle, Co. Carlow)—is unique to Ireland.

Castles without keeps, such as Limerick (*c.* 1200) or Roscommon (1278), usually had only one ward enclosed by a defensible curtain-wall. In the 15th century, renewed conflict initiated a new and more prolific building phase. This time both the Irish and the English were involved, using similar styles. Based on earlier keeps, the 15th-century TOWER HOUSE had thinner walls and was smaller in size (e.g. Dunguaire, Co. Galway). Defensive features included bartizans, machicolations, battlements and stone vaulting between the ground and first floors. At the end of the 16th century, tower houses began gradually to give way to larger dwellings, although, of necessity, many defensive features were retained. During the Ulster Plantation in the 17th century, new landlords from Britain imported a variety of styles. Particularly distinctive are the corbelled turrets of many of the Ulster Plantation castles, such as Castle Balfour (1618), Co. Fermanagh, imported by newly established settlers from Scotland. Shortly after 1660 a small number of houses based on fashionable English prototypes were built, such as Beaulieu (1660–67), Co. Louth, a brick house with a hipped roof and dormer windows. Usually they were without defensive features except for a surrounding bawn.

2. *c.* 1680–*c.* 1760: PALLADIANISM. In the late 17th century and the first decades of the 18th century a number of new public buildings were sited in Dublin. The first of these was the Royal Hospital at Kilmainham, built by William Robinson from 1680. In the early 18th century Palladianism became established as the dominant architectural style, with EDWARD LOVETT PEARCE giving the country its finest Palladian building, the Parliament House (now the Bank of Ireland) on College Green, in 1729 (see DUBLIN, fig. 3). This dominance was preserved first through the agency of RICHARD CASTLE and afterwards in the work of native architects, some of whom clung to the style long after it had lost its hold in England. As late as 1773, for example, THOMAS IVORY used Palladian forms and details in his Bluecoat School in Dublin. The same dominance was equally obvious in the field of domestic architecture. The first Palladian house was built *c.* 1709 at Oldtown, Co. Clare, by THOMAS BURGH, but in domestic architecture Pearce (see fig. 15 below) and Castle were again the leading figures. Pearce's first exercise in the style was at Castletown, Co. Kildare, where from *c.* 1730 he added wings with connecting colonnades to the house begun by Alessandro Galilei before 1722. This plan, a main block with connected wings, was much favoured by both Pearce and Castle as well as by many of their contemporaries, although in smaller houses a screen wall was often used instead of colonnades. Pearce's Bellamont Forest (1729; for illustration *see* PEARCE, EDWARD LOVETT), Co. Cavan, where pedimented portico, tripartite division of the façade and Venetian windows were used for the first time in Ireland, is the most perfect Irish Palladian house, but Pearce could also combine the monumentalism of Vanbrugh and Hawksmoor with Palladian elements to produce a more dramatic effect, for example at Summerhill (1731; destr.), Co. Meath. After Pearce's death, Castle came to prominence. Using such features as unsupported pediment, applied temple-front, occuli, niches, tripartite doorways and Venetian windows,

he composed his buildings in a heavy masculine style. Russborough House (1742–55), Co. Wicklow, is considered to be among the best of his works, making use of the full Palladian layout, in which house and farm buildings were organized into one ensemble. At Castle's death, Palladianism was continued, albeit with a leaning towards the Baroque, by the Italian architect DAVIS DUCART and, more simply, by two amateurs: FRANCIS BINDON and Nathaniel Clements (1705–77).

While Palladianism dominated country-house architecture during the early 18th century, wealthy farmers and minor gentry remained content during this period with strong, thatched houses. For smallholders, thatched cabins were the usual type of dwelling throughout the 18th and 19th centuries, while tenants lived in mud-walled cottages. Examples of these smaller dwellings have been collected at the Ulster Folk and Transport Museum at Holywood, Co. Down. Urban domestic buildings for the middle classes varied considerably in size and type, with detached houses being based on country-house types, and terraced houses also retaining a sense of identity while conforming to stipulations established by the lease. The upper classes and prosperous merchants tended meanwhile to favour three- or four-storey houses in the 'Dutch-billy' style, with curvilinear gables fronting on to the street, especially in Dublin and the old part of Limerick.

3. *c.* 1760–*c.* 1860: NEO-CLASSICISM AND REVIVAL STYLES. During the second half of the 18th century there was substantial, if slow, development in many cities outside Dublin. Around 1760, for example, the landlords of Limerick and Belfast began programmes of improvement and expansion on a grid plan, and Cork was also developed, although its hilly terrain did not allow for a regular pattern. Many smaller Irish towns owe their modern appearance to development around this time, with rational planning and wide streets the guiding principles, even if stone and slate buildings were erected only in the main streets or squares, the side streets being lined with simple thatched houses.

During the late 18th century Neo-classicism became the dominant architectural style, especially in domestic and public architecture. Although Gothic and other revival styles became influential in the early 19th century, most notably in the fields of domestic and ecclesiastical architecture, Neo-classicism remained the decisive stylistic influence in the design of public buildings well into the 19th century. The Neo-classical style was first introduced into Ireland by the designs of the English architect WILLIAM CHAMBERS for the Casino (1759) or park temple at Marino, Clontarf, and for Charlemont House (1762), Dublin, both for the Irish peer JAMES CAULFEILD, 1st Earl of Charlemont. After this, encouraged by the various publications on architectural antiquity that were appearing in England at this time, various forms of Neo-classicism became fashionable. Castlecoole (1790–98), Co. Fermanagh, by James Wyatt (*see* WYATT, (2)), is probably the greatest Neo-classical house in Ireland (*see* fig. 16 below), and at the end of the 18th century Wyatt was in great demand both for new country houses and for remodelling interiors of existing ones. At the turn of the century the most prominent architect, however, was FRANCIS JOHN-STON, the first time for many decades that this role had been occupied by a native Irish architect. Although he also drew on examples from Roman antiquity, Johnston was most strongly attracted to the austerity of early GREEK REVIVAL architecture; his effectiveness in this style can best be seen at Townley Hall (1794; see fig. 3), Co. Louth, where an elegant cylindrical hall finds its perfect foil in the massive, undecorated exterior of the house. A simpler, more severe style, dependent on fine proportions for its effect, was meanwhile introduced into urban domestic architecture. The roof was hidden by a solid parapet, and the decoration was restricted to the doorcases, which were enlivened by classical columns in stone or timber and surmounted by a fanlight of delicate iron tracery. The principal building material in the cities was brick, although in the smaller towns stone (which was more widely available) was used, covered in lime plaster.

After the Act of Union in 1800, the exodus of former parliamentarians from Dublin to their country seats led to a country-house building boom. Johnston soon had a rival in the Cork architect Richard Morrison (*see* MORRISON, (1)). Morrison's country-house masterpiece is Ballyfin (1821), Co. Laois, on which he worked with his son William Vitruvius Morrison (*see* MORRISON, (2)). Like Johnston's Townley Hall, Ballyfin has a plain exterior, while its interior is unrivalled in the richness of its decoration, which derives from both Greek and Roman sources.

Another architect who received some country-house commissions was JAMES GANDON, most notably at Emo Park (*c.* 1780), Co. Laois, a work that rivalled Castlecoole. Gandon was more important, however, for his public architecture in Dublin, which radically altered the appearance of the city. Drawing his inspiration from Roman antiquity, Gandon produced such Neo-classical master-pieces as the Custom House (1781), the King's Inns (from 1795) and the Four Courts (1786). He also designed the court-house (1784; destr. 1849) at Waterford. An important impetus was given to public architecture in 1802, when an independent Irish branch of the Board of Works was established. The first principal architect of the Board's civil branch was Robert Woodgate (*d* 1805), who had served as John Soane's clerk during the enlargement in 1791 of Baronscourt, Co. Tyrone. In 1805 Woodgate was succeeded by Francis Johnston, whose main public works were the chapel (1807–14) in Dublin Castle and the Dublin General Post Office (1814–18). With his successor, William Murray (1785–1849), Johnston designed a standard format, in a classical style, for lunatic asylums, to which nine were erected. The court-house was another particularly important building type of this period, with many of the most prominent architects producing examples: John-ston, for example, built the court-house at Armagh in 1805, and William Vitruvius Morrison was responsible for the designs at Carlow and Tralee (both 1828). After a reconstitution of the board in 1831 as the Board of Public Works, Jacob Owen (1778–1870), an Englishman, took over as chief architect. This board was responsible for much of the major public architecture of the 19th century, during which time building activity was much more widely spread. While the austerity of the Greek Revival style

3. Francis Johnston: Townley Hall, Co. Louth, 1794

never became widely popular in domestic architecture, it was often used in the first half of the 19th century for public buildings such as gaols and for Presbyterian and Unitarian churches in Ulster.

Although the GOTHIC REVIVAL style was first introduced into Ireland as early as 1767, at Moore Abbey, Co. Clare, it did not achieve real popularity until after 1800, most notably in domestic and ecclesiastical buildings. Here again the versatile Francis Johnston and William Vitruvius Morrison were among the most important figures. In domestic architecture, the style was most frequently used to dress up an existing house, and at first Gothic detailing was applied only to houses that were fully symmetrical in plan and elevation. For this reason, Johnston's Charleville Forest (begun 1801), Co. Offaly, was entirely novel, being perhaps the first Gothic Revival house in Ireland to feature an irregular outline. The subsequent introduction of the Tudor Gothic style in Ireland is credited to Morrison.

5. Benjamin Woodward: Museum Building, Trinity College, Dublin, stair-hall, 1852–7

Although this was a flourishing period for native Irish architects, English architects continued to be much in demand. JOHN NASH built a number of picturesque castellated houses, including Lough Cutra Castle (1811; altered), Co. Galway, and he sent James Pain (*c.* 1779–1877) with his brother George Richard Pain (*c.* 1793–1838) to Ireland to supervise his works. The Pains stayed and set up their own practice, working in the area around Cork and Limerick. Other English and Scottish architects who sent over designs without visiting Ireland during this period included John Soane, C. R. Cockerell, Thomas Rickman, George Papworth, Edward Blore, William Burn and William Henry Playfair. As architects began to see that the architectural forms and detailing of earlier eras could be highly fruitful in providing fresh ideas, revival architecture grew to embrace styles from many different periods. However, while the Great Famine of 1845–8 did not seriously interrupt public building, its devastating effects brought to an end the era of the great country house.

In ecclesiastical architecture there was a similar period of architectural innovation at the end of the 18th century, when the Board of the First Fruits of the Established Church undertook a vast building programme. Their first new churches, in the Early Gothic Revival style, were unremarkable, except for the highly individual work of JOHN SEMPLE. His church (1830) at Monkstown, Co. Dublin, was based on Portuguese examples illustrated in publications by James Cavanah Murphy, while his St Mary's Chapel of Ease (the 'Black Church'; see fig. 4) in Dublin, built 1828–30, is distinguished by its unusual

4. John Semple: St Mary's Chapel of Ease, Dublin, 1828–30

parabolic-vaulted ceiling. Around the same time, in anticipation of the Catholic Emancipation Act passed by the government in London in 1829, the Roman Catholic Church was busy providing its congregations with large churches redolent of the grandeur of Rome and Greece, such as St Mary's Pro-Cathedral, Dublin, built in 1815. In the 1830s and 1840s the English architect A. W. N. Pugin was an important influence (*see* PUGIN, (2)), introducing designs in 'correct' ecclesiological Gothic for a number of churches in Wexford and for Killarney Cathedral (begun 1842). Interrupted by the Great Famine of the 1840s, the latter building was completed in 1855 by Pugin's son Edward Welby Pugin (*see* PUGIN, (3)) and by the Irish architect J. J. McCARTHY. Together these two architects dominated Catholic church building during the 1850s and 1860s, with the latter producing such works as St Agatha's, Glenfesk, Co. Kerry, begun in 1862. By the middle of the 19th century, however, as with domestic architecture, many other revival styles were being embraced, with Byzantine, Early Christian, Lombardic and Romanesque vying with Gothic as suitable styles for church architecture.

Eventually Gothic Revival and other styles were embraced in public buildings. In 1845 two Irish education acts were passed for the expansion of the Roman Catholic College of St Patrick at Maynooth, west of Dublin, and for the establishment of three Queen's Colleges at Belfast, Cork and Galway. At Maynooth, A. W. N. Pugin added an influential new quadrangle (from 1845), and for the three Queen's Colleges Gothic Revival styles were also chosen: THOMAS DEANE, one of the leading Irish architects to work in a Puginesque manner, produced an asymmetrical Gothic design for Cork, while Charles Lanyon's design for Belfast was symmetrical, and the design by J. B. Keane (*d* 1859) for Galway was in an old-fashioned Early Gothic Revival style. A further series of asylums was commissioned, with consultant architects being employed and Gothic being stipulated as the desired style. Pugin again provided the source for one of the most notable designs, the Killarney Lunatic Asylum (1847–50) by Thomas Deane

and his partner, Benjamin Woodward (*see* DEANE & WOODWARD). Dublin again became the focus of building activity, with Woodward providing a museum building (1852–7; see fig. 5) for Trinity College; other new buildings included the iron-framed extensions to the Royal Irish Academy (1852) and the Natural History Museum (1856), both by Frederick Villiers Clarendon (1820–1904). In 1856 the duties of the Board of Public Works were expanded to include provision of a much wider range of buildings, and subsequently much of the Board's design work was undertaken by its own architects, producing, for example, provincial post offices, schools and police barracks in a variety of eclectic styles. In addition to the numerous Irish architects active in the middle of the 19th century, some English architects continued to work in Ireland. One of the most notable was CHARLES LANYON, who worked mainly in the northern half of the country, on private and public buildings. While his work at the Queen's College (1846–9), Belfast, was characteristic of his absorption of Gothic influences, Lanyon also produced the Custom House (1857) in Belfast, in an Italianate style.

4. AFTER *c*. 1860. In the late 19th century the architectural competition began to play a major role. The Board of Works was responsible for three large buildings in Dublin that were entrusted to consultant architects, two as a result of competitions. All three were built in a Neoclassical style to harmonize with earlier buildings by Gandon: the National Museum and National Library complex (1885) by T. N. Deane (1828–99) and his son Thomas Manly Deane (1851–1932); the Government Building and College of Science (1904) by the English architect Aston Webb; and University College (1914–19), Earlsfort Terrace, by R. M. Butler. Belfast City Hall (1896–1906), designed by another English architect, ALFRED BRUMWELL THOMAS, in a version of Renaissance classicism, was also the result of a competition. Indeed classical-style architecture in one form or another continued to exercise a strong hold throughout Ireland right into the

6. Desmond Fitzgerald: Terminal Building, Dublin Airport, completed 1941 (later altered)

mid-20th century. Thus, modern alternatives were for the most part ignored when, following the 1916 rising, O'Connell Street, Dublin, had to be rebuilt. Perhaps the final major work commissioned by the Board of Works before the advent of Modernism was the capital's Irish National War Memorial, designed by Edwin Lutyens in 1931.

Modernism first appeared in Ireland in the 1930s. At first it was confined mainly to domestic building, although the need for cinemas, hospitals and schools also encouraged the spread of modern design. The concrete structure and geometric lines of Modernism can be seen in the flat-roofed but traditionally planned suburban 'sunshine' houses (*c.* 1932) at Dollymount, Dublin, by Robinson and Keefe. For the new Terminal Building at Dublin Airport (see fig. 6), Desmond Fitzgerald used a type of curvilinear plan to create a convex façade with extensive glass walls and upper-storey terraces, as pioneered by Le Corbusier. In 1953 MICHAEL SCOTT completed the new Irish Transport Board Bus Station and office complex; influenced by Le Corbusier, this was the first fully Modernist building to appear in the heart of Dublin. However, the effects of an economic slump meant that modern architecture did not gain a foothold until the more affluent decade that followed. Scott's partnership, and that of Sam Stephenson (*b* 1933) and Arthur Gibney (*b* 1932), subsequently dominated the architectural scene. Working mainly in a style derived from the work of Mies van der Rohe, Scott's partnership produced the Radio Telefís Eireann Broadcasting Centre (built in phases from 1959) at Donnybrook, Dublin; the Bank of Ireland (1972–8), Baggot St, Dublin; and Carroll's Cigarette Factory (1967–70) at Dundalk, Co. Louth. Arthur Gibney designed the award-winning Irish Management Institute Training Centre (1974), Dublin, while the Bord na Móna Building (1979), Dublin, and the Central Bank (1978), Dublin, are by Sam Stephenson.

Several major competitions during the 1960s resulted in a number of fine modern buildings. Trinity College, Dublin, gained a strong, sculptural library building (1961–7), designed by Paul Koralek (see AHRENDS, BURTON & KORALEK), as a result of a competition in 1960. A 1964 competition to find an overall plan for the new campus at University College, Dublin, was won by Andrzei Wejchert (*b* 1937), who also designed the Arts and Commerce Building, the Aula Maxima (not executed) and, later, the Sports Building, an example of Irish Post-modernist architecture.

BIBLIOGRAPHY

T. W. Sadleir and P. L. Dickinson: *Georgian Mansions in Ireland* (Dublin, 1915)
H. G. Leask: *Irish Castles* (Dundalk, 1941)
——: *Irish Churches and Monastic Buildings*, 3 vols (Dundalk, 1955–60)
B. de Breffny and G. Mott: *The Churches and Abbeys of Ireland* (London, 1970)
P. Harbison: *Guide to the National Monuments in the Republic of Ireland* (Dublin, 1970)
R. Stalley: *Architecture and Sculpture in Ireland, 1150–1350* (Dublin, 1970)
B. de Breffny and R. Ffolliott: *The Houses of Ireland* (London, 1975)
M. J. McDermott: *Ireland's Architectural Heritage: An Outline History* (Dublin, 1975)
S. Rothery: *Everyday Buildings of Ireland* (Dublin, 1975)
P. Shaffrey: *The Irish Town: An Approach to Survival* (Dublin, 1975)
M. Craig: *Classic Irish Houses of the Middle Size* (London, 1976)
M. Bence-Jones: *Ireland*, Burke's Guide to Country Houses, i (London, 1978)
P. Harbison, H. Potterton and J. Sheehy: *Irish Art and Architecture* (London, 1978)
T. O'Beirne: *A Guide to Modern Architecture in Dublin* (Dublin, 1978)
S. Rothery: *The Shops of Ireland* (Dublin, 1978)
G. L. Barrow: *The Round Towers of Ireland* (Dublin, 1979)
A. Rowan: *North West Ulster*, Bldgs Ireland, i (Harmondsworth and New York, 1979)
J. Sheehy: *The Rediscovery of Ireland's Past: The Celtic Revival* (London, 1980)
R. Loeber: *A Biographical Dictionary of Architects in Ireland, 1660–1720* (London, 1981)
F. O'Dwyer: *Lost Dublin* (Dublin, 1981)
M. Craig: *The Architecture of Ireland: From the Earliest Times to 1880* (London, 1982)
P. Shaffrey and M. Shaffrey: *Buildings of Irish Towns* (Dublin, 1983)
——: *Irish Countryside Buildings: Everyday Architecture in the Rural Landscape* (Dublin, 1983)
D. Cruikshank: *A Guide to the Georgian Buildings of Britain and Ireland* (London, 1985)
R. Hurley and W. Cantwell: *Contemporary Irish Church Architecture* (Dublin, 1985)
Public Works: The Architecture of the Office of Public Works, 1831–1987 (Dublin, 1987)
P. Stalley: *The Cistercian Monasteries of Ireland* (London, 1987)
M. Bence-Jones: *A Guide to Irish Country Houses* (London, 1989)
C. Casey and A. Rowan: *North Leinster*, Bldgs Ireland, ii (Harmondsworth and New York, 1993)

NOREEN CASEY

III. Painting and graphic arts.

1. Before 1600. 2. 1600–1799. 3. 1800–1900. 4. After 1900.

1. BEFORE 1600. The earliest examples of painting in Ireland are the illuminated manuscript books produced from the 6th century AD, although only a small number of these survived the Viking raids of the 9th and 10th centuries (see INSULAR ART, §3). The first manuscripts were inspired by continental examples introduced into Ireland by missionary monks returning from Italy and Spain, although their decoration was also influenced by indigenous metalwork and stone-carving (see INSULAR ART, §§2 and 4). The earliest known manuscripts include the Codex Usserianus Primus (early 7th century; Dublin, Trinity Coll. Lib., MS. 55) and the Cathach of St Columba (*c.* 625; Dublin, Royal Irish Acad., s.n.), a copy of the Psalms in which the initial letters are often embellished with Celtic spirals and stylized animal ornament. The late 7th-century Book of Durrow (Dublin, Trinity Coll. Lib., MS. 57), a small manuscript of the Four Gospels in 248 folios, contains the first examples of the 'carpet' page, in which the left-hand page is entirely given over to ornament (see INSULAR ART, fig. 3). It also has the earliest examples of interlaced bands; these are in a variety of colours. This was probably Coptic or east Mediterranean in origin, but it has affinities with contemporary metalwork designs. A product of the chain of monasteries established by St Columba, it is not clear whether the Book of Durrow was made in Ireland, Iona or Northumbria, since these three centres were so closely linked.

Some of the illuminated books produced during the 8th and 9th centuries were small gospel books, intended to be easily portable. Examples include the 8th-century Book of Dimma and the Book of Mulling (both Dublin, Trinity Coll. Lib., MSS 59 and 60), in which symbols or portraits of the Evangelists painted in bright colours accompany texts embellished with geometric and animal decoration. The most celebrated manuscript is the Book of Kells

(Dublin, Trinity Coll. Lib., MS. 58), which may have originated in Iona. This dates from the late 8th century or the early 9th and has coloured ornament on all but two pages. It includes stylized portraits of Christ and the Evangelists and narrative scenes of the *Life of Christ*, in which the emphasis is on symbolism rather than realism (see fig. 7; *see also* KELLS, BOOK OF). The animal ornament is particularly ingenious, and again the illuminator appears to have transformed existing sources as well as inventing motifs. A roughly contemporary work, the Book of Armagh (807; Dublin, Trinity Coll. Lib., MS. 52), the only surviving complete New Testament of the 9th century, shows the quite distinct style followed in the northern region of Armagh. It is decorated with pen drawings of Evangelistic symbols, but colour appears only in a small number of initial capitals. It is of particular historical importance as it contains the writings of St Patrick. Although the influence of the designs and colouring of the Book of Kells continued into the 11th century, illuminated books increasingly tended to feature more simplified designs, and spiral ornament was gradually replaced by stylized figural representations, as in the early 11th-century Southampton Psalter (Cambridge, St John's Coll.). Manuscripts of the 11th and 12th centuries generally lack the carpet pages found in earlier works, and there is evidence of the influence of the invading Vikings' Ringerike style, for example in the 11th-century Liber Hymnorum (Dublin, Trinity Coll.). The final flowering of illuminated manuscript work in Ireland is best represented by Cormac's Psalter (London, BL. Add. MS. 36929), produced in the second half of the 12th century.

Slight traces of figured wall painting discovered at Cormac's Chapel (built 1127–34) at Cashel, Co. Tipperary, and at other sites confirm that the practice of decorating the interiors of Romanesque churches was followed in Ireland. The destruction caused by the Dissolution of the Monasteries during the attempt to introduce Protestant reform in the 16th century, and by the feuds and rebellions that continued into the 17th century, ensured that the loss of ecclesiastical art has been extensive. This includes stained glass. Some of the finest stained glass (probably imported) to be seen in Ireland in the Middle Ages was provided *c.* 1354 by Bishop Richard de Ledrede for the windows of St Canice's Cathedral, Kilkenny; it was all destroyed by Oliver Cromwell's troops in 1650, after they had stormed the city.

2. 1600–1799. During the early 17th century the tower houses of the period were usually decorated with tapestries rather than paintings, although a few aristocrats imported works executed on the Continent. For example, in 1617 Richard Boyle, 1st Earl of Cork (*see* BOYLE, (1)), bought 12 pictures (probably genre scenes) from a Dutch merchant for his dining-room, and four years later his commission for a series of portraits of his immediate family was carried out by a French limner. In general, however, the dearth of patronage discouraged the development of a native school. The artistic climate changed after the Restoration of 1660, when JAMES BUTLER, 1st Duke of Ormonde, was made Lord Lieutenant. He introduced continental tastes and fashions that were quickly taken up by Ireland's upper classes. Patrons began to commission

7. *Temptation of Christ*, miniature from the Book of Kells, 330×250 mm, late 8th century or early 9th (Dublin, Trinity College Library, MS. 58, fol. 202*v*)

portraits as images of status and power, providing employment for numerous visiting artists working in the Netherlandish tradition. The first wave included James Gandy (1619–89) and Thomas Pooley (1646–1723) from England, the Dutch or German artist Gaspar Smitz (*d c.* 1707) and, a little later, the Englishman STEPHEN SLAUGHTER. Together they introduced the conventions of portraiture established in 17th-century London by Anthony van Dyck and Peter Lely. The first native-born portrait painter of ability to emerge was GARRET MORPHEY, probably a Roman Catholic, who painted both the Jacobite gentry (see fig. 8) and their Williamite successors. Other portrait painters included HUGH HOWARD and CHARLES JERVAS, who both studied in Rome; Jervas established himself in London and in 1723 became Principal Painter to George I. One of the finest of these early portrait painters was JAMES LATHAM; he studied in Antwerp, absorbed influences from both French and English art and returned to Dublin *c.* 1730, where he was much sought after. After his death he was succeeded by ROBERT HUNTER, Dublin's dominant portrait painter into the 1780s. Nathaniel Hone the elder (*see* HONE, (1)) was another able artist, whose particular skill in depicting children is evident in such works as *A Piping Boy* (1769; Dublin, N.G.); much of his career was spent in London, however, where he was a founder-member of the Royal Academy. One of the most important factors in the

8. Garret Morphey: *Caryll, 3rd Viscount Molyneux of Maryborough*, oil on canvas, 750×610 mm, *c.* 1690 (Dublin, National Gallery of Ireland)

development of an Irish school of painting in the 18th century was the influence of the Dublin Society (founded 1731) through its schools (*see* §XV below). There, students were provided with some knowledge of the range of continental landscape painting and figurative art, and techniques were taught by practising artists. Chalk and pastel drawing was based on the contemporary French manner, as can be seen in the pastel portraits of ROBERT HEALY and, later, HUGH DOUGLAS HAMILTON (e.g. *Queen Charlotte*, 1769; Berlin, Kupferstichkab.). Premiums were offered annually; these were open to all.

Irish landscape painting, like portrait painting, had its origins in Netherlandish art. Again like portrait painting, its development dates from the 17th century, when surveying and cartography became important in relation to the political control of the land. In the 18th century the Dutchman WILLIAM VAN DER HAGEN, who arrived in Dublin *c.* 1721, was a key influence, both through his topographical views of towns and for his imaginative compositions; his Irish follower Joseph Tudor (*d* 1759) also pursued both types of work. The second major influence on Irish painters was Italian landscape art and, by extension, the Roman Campagna. From the mid-18th century many Irish landscape painters went to Rome. They included Robert Crone (*d* 1779), James Forrester (*fl* 1761–5), Solomon Delane (*d* 1812) and Hugh Primrose Deane (*fl* 1758–84). The most able Irish landscape painter to emerge was Thomas Roberts (*see* ROBERTS, (1)), who studied under George Mullins (*fl* 1756–75). Roberts so

successfully blended the conventions of Dutch and Italian landscape painting with his own personal experience of the Irish landscape that he set the standard for the rest of the century in such works as *Knock Ninney and Part of Lough Erne from Bellisle* (1771; New Haven, CT, Yale Cent. Brit. A.). Subsequent landscape painting in Ireland was dominated until the 1820s by WILLIAM ASHFORD. Arriving from England in 1764, Ashford painted topographical views, notably landowner's demesnes, in a meticulous and elegant manner, but one still couched in classical formulae.

Romantic landscape art first appeared in the work of GEORGE BARRET. The deep influence on Barret of Edmund Burke's *A Philosophical Inquiry into the Origins of our Ideas of the Sublime and the Beautiful* (1757), in which Burke stressed the awe-inspiring moods of nature, is evident in such paintings as the *View of Powerscourt Waterfall* (*c.* 1764; see fig. 9). Such early works differed from the classicism of the 'Irish Italianists', but Barret's later work in London was to be more conventional and dependent on classical models. During the same period, Thomas Sautell Roberts (see ROBERTS, (2)), the younger brother of Thomas Roberts, began to explore a more romantic style, depicting nature's more rugged aspects. The two main scenic areas sought out by late 18th-century painters were Co. Wicklow, around the Powerscourt estate, and Killarney, Co. Kerry, a reflection of changing taste, moving away from tidy images of the well-ordered demesne. Nathaniel Grogan (*c.* 1740–1807), a Cork landscape and genre painter, was unique in his production of pictures depicting Irish peasant life, based on 17th-century Dutch precedents (e.g. *The Wake*, priv. col., see Crookshank and Glin, 1978, fig. 130). Such subject-matter, which marked the first step towards a realistic portrayal of Irish rural life, was to become commonplace in 19th-century travel books of Ireland.

In the mid-18th century theatre design—painted flats and backdrops—became significant in Dublin because of the city's vigorous theatrical tradition. William van der Hagen worked at Smock Alley Playhouse in the 1730s, Tudor in the 1730s and 1740s, followed by John Lewis in the 1750s. Robert Carver (*fl* 1750–91), a landscape painter, also worked there; he later emigrated to London, where he worked at Drury Lane Theatre. There was some decorative and wall painting, usually executed by foreign artists: van der Hagen at Curraghmore House; Peter de Grée (*d* 1789), who worked in grisaille at a number of places; Gaspar de Gabrieli at Lyons House, near Dublin; Vincent Waldré (*d* 1814) at Dublin Castle; and the Pompeian Revival decoration by Thomas Riley in the Long Gallery at Castletown House, also near Dublin.

A lack of state patronage, for example in the decoration of public buildings, discouraged the development of history painting in Ireland and led to many important artists working abroad. For example, during the late 18th century JAMES BARRY established himself as by far the most important Irish Neo-classical artist through a career spent mostly in England. Originally from Cork, Barry first studied there, went to London in 1764 and spent 1765–71 in Rome. Back in London, where he spent the rest of his career, Barry sought to uphold the importance of history painting, decorating the premises of the Royal Society of Arts at his own expense. He became Professor of Painting

9. George Barret: *View of Powerscourt Waterfall*, oil on canvas, 1.0×1.27 m, *c.* 1764 (Dublin, National Gallery of Ireland)

at the Royal Academy but died in poverty. Hugh Douglas Hamilton, a Dublin Society student, also went to Italy (1778–91); he too was influenced by Neo-classical art and painted some fine figure subjects. ROBERT FAGAN, who although born in London considered himself Irish, spent most of his career in Rome, where he evolved an original style of Neo-classical portraiture. Since both he and Barry pursued a career abroad, they had no influence on art in Ireland; even Hamilton practised mainly as a portrait painter after he returned. Foreign portrait painters who worked in Dublin in the late 18th century included a number in flight from their London creditors. FRANCIS WHEATLEY was there from *c.* 1779 (he painted several group portraits depicting members of the Dublin Volunteers); TILLY KETTLE arrived *c.* 1783, and GILBERT STUART stayed between 1787 and 1793. Painting in miniature also flourished in the later 18th century, chiefly through the work of Gustavus Hamilton (*c.* 1739–75), Horace Hone (*see* HONE, (2)), Charles Robertson (1760–1821) and John Comerford (1770–1832).

The development of printmaking in Ireland began in 1645 with an engraved view of Kilkenny by Gaspar Huybrechts (1619–84); at the end of the 17th century Edwin Sandys (*d* 1708) was printing maps and views in

Dublin. Mezzotint, an important 18th-century technique, began with the English engraver Thomas Beard, who worked in Dublin *c.* 1720. The key figure in Irish engraving of this period was John Brooks (*fl* 1730–56), a Dubliner who began by working for a Dutch engraver in London and on his return to Ireland opened a workshop with Andrew Miller (*d* 1763). Their workshop became the training ground for a group of Irish engravers who emigrated to London, where they influenced the development of mezzotints of Old Master and contemporary paintings. THOMAS FRYE, an able portrait painter in oils and pastels, also moved to London, where he made a superb series of portrait and genre subjects in mezzotint. Other engravers, however, remained in Dublin, including William Esdell (*d* 1795), WILLIAM PAULET CAREY and Benjamin Clayton (1754–1814). Many were taught in the Dublin Society Schools by such teachers as Henry Brocas sr (*see under* BROCAS). Seal and gem engravers also benefited from the Schools' teaching, many of them reproducing scenic views made by the leading Irish landscape painters of the day. A developing interest in landscape and antiquarian nostalgia stimulated the market for books such as Thomas Milton's *Collection of Select Views from the Different Seats of the Nobility and Gentry in the*

Kingdom of Ireland (1783–93), Jonathan Fisher's *Views of Killarney* (pubd in the 1770s) or the *Antiquities of Ireland* published by Francis Crose in the mid-1790s. James Malton's *Views of Dublin* (pubd as a volume of aquatints in the 1790s) was the summation of the 18th-century topographical print tradition in Ireland. Apart from engraving for the publishing trade some artists, such as James Barry, used etching as a minor medium.

3. 1800–1900. The Act of Union of 1800 marks an important divide, since from that date Dublin ceased to be a centre of government and aristocratic patronage. The professional and commercial middle classes, and to a lesser extent the country gentry, were to become patrons in the 19th century; their taste was for portraits, smaller landscapes (often in watercolour) and anecdotal genre scenes. This demand was supplied by the Sadler and Brocas families in particular. The genre subjects of NICHOLAS JOSEPH CROWLEY, RICHARD ROTHWELL (e.g. *Novitiate Mendicants*; London, V&A) and Joseph Haverty (1794–1864), and the marine subjects of Edwin Hayes (1820–1904) and Richard Beechy (1808–95), were all typical of the work exhibited at the Royal Hibernian Academy (R.H.A.), the exhibition and market place founded in 1823.

10. Walter Frederick Osborne: *St Patrick's Close, Dublin*, oil on canvas, 690×510 mm, *c.* 1892 (Dublin, National Gallery of Ireland)

The Romantic movement in Irish visual arts was represented chiefly by antiquarianism; this interest in the Early Christian and medieval periods was more archaeological than aesthetic (*see* CELTIC REVIVAL), although one artist who successfully combined both in his watercolours was GEORGE PETRIE. The Ordnance Survey, the employer of Petrie and a number of other artists, stimulated the exploration of remote areas, and this in turn was to foster new landscape subjects discovered in the west of Ireland. Books of topographical views continued to be popular, for example *Picturesque Sketches of Some of the Finest Landscape and Coast Scenery of Ireland* (Dublin, 1835). However, these publications were gradually replaced by travel books, such as Samuel Carter Hall's *Ireland: Its Scenery and Character* (1841), with illustrations by various artists.

It was the demand for a permanent exhibiting organization in Dublin that had led to the formation of the R.H.A. (for further discussion *see* §XV below and DUBLIN, §II). Annual exhibitions were held. Sales of pictures were never high, although the art unions through their sweepstakes helped to dispose of work. The fine art sections of the large international Irish exhibitions of art and industry were influential in fostering a public taste for Old Masters and in the establishment of the National Gallery in 1864. The fine arts were not generally in a thriving state in the mid-19th century, with Ireland suffering from economic depression, famine and emigration. The lack of industrial wealth in turn limited patronage. Belfast, which increasingly had its own distinct cultural characteristics, was an exception, having certain similarities to the north of England and Scotland.

Many of the finest landscape painters moved to England, however, including JAMES ARTHUR O'CONNOR and FRANCIS DANBY in 1813. This was also the case with painters working in other genres. DANIEL MACLISE, originally from Cork, entered the Royal Academy Schools in London in 1828, and he remained in England. His early work concentrated on Irish genre as well as portraiture and book illustration (he contributed to Hall's *Ireland*), but he was to make his reputation as a painter of medieval subjects and developed an increasingly romantic vision of Irish and British history. William Mulready (*see* MULREADY, (1)), born in Co. Clare, specialized in moralizing genre scenes; he spent virtually his entire career in London, as did the portrait painter MARTIN ARCHER SHEE, who became President of the Royal Academy. FREDERIC WILLIAM BURTON, also from Co. Clare, was a fine watercolour painter and had strong antiquarian interests, but he settled in Munich in 1851 and later became Director (1874–94) of the National Gallery in London.

Throughout the 19th century economic depression and lack of patronage continued to encourage Irish artists to emigrate. One exception was the region around Belfast, where ANDREW NICHOLL trained before establishing a significant reputation through his botanical watercolour studies. Although London continued to attract many Irish artists, its lure decreased in the late 19th century, as French art came to dominate the international scene. In 1853 Nathaniel Hone the younger (*see* HONE, (3)), the first of a number of Irish artists to study in France, went to Paris, where he worked under Thomas Couture; in 1857 he settled in Barbizon. His example was followed by FRANK O'MEARA, who studied under Carolus-Duran and painted at Grèz-sur-Loing in the 1870s. Sir JOHN LAVERY, who was born in Belfast but grew up in Glasgow, also went to Grèz in the 1880s to paint landscapes; later he had a highly successful career as a society portrait painter in London. SARAH PURSER went to Paris; on her return to Dublin she brought with her a fresh quality to portraiture, and she became a dynamic catalyst in the Irish art world. In the 1870s Aloysius O'Kelly (c. 1850–1926) painted in Brittany, one of the first Irish artists to do so, and this region of France was to become increasingly popular. During the 1880s large numbers of Irish artists went there, including Helen Mabel Trevor (1831–1900), Henry Jones Thaddeus (1859–1929) and, above all, RODERIC O'CONOR. He became an associate of Gauguin at Pont-Aven and the most avant-garde of all visiting Irish painters, most of whom were more conservative, falling under the influence of the *plein-air* painting of Jules Bastien-Lepage.

During the 19th century the Koninklijke Academie at Antwerp also attracted many Irish artists. Sometimes referred to as the 'Antwerp school', they included NORMAN GARSTIN, J. M. Kavanagh (1856–1918), Richard Moynan (1856–1906) and WALTER FREDERICK OSBORNE, who was influenced early in his career by Jules Bastien-Lepage and later painted street scenes in Dublin (see fig. 10). A number, including Dermod O'Brien (1865–1945), studied both at Antwerp and Paris since, for many students, Antwerp, Paris and Brittany were on the same circuit.

4. AFTER 1900. In the early 20th century a number of Irish artists continued to study in France and Belgium. PAUL HENRY, for example, studied realist and Post-Impressionist art in Paris before returning to become the most celebrated painter of the scenery of western Ireland. The influence of French modernism within Ireland nevertheless remained very limited. There was, however, a gradual diffusion of *plein-air* painting and greater naturalism; and this led to the development of an Irish school that combined elements of realism with a romantic ideology. An increasing number of women artists began to emerge; like their male counterparts, most came from comfortable Anglo-Irish backgrounds, and some belonged more to the British watercolour tradition, such as Rose Barton (1850–1919) and Mildred Anne Butler (1858–1941). The outstanding portrait painter at the turn of the century was John Butler Yeats (see YEATS, (1)), although he spent most of his later career in London and New York. In 1901 an exhibition of work by Yeats and the younger Hone was organized by Sarah Purser. It persuaded HUGH LANE, an Irish art dealer working in London, to campaign for a modern gallery in Dublin (see §XIV below).

Another leading portrait painter in the opening years of the 20th century was WILLIAM ORPEN. He first studied in Dublin and then at the Slade School in London, and between c. 1906 and 1914 he taught at Dublin's Metropolitan School of Art where he influenced a wide circle of Irish artists, including James Sleator (1889–1950), Patrick Tuohy (1894–1930), Leo Whelan (1892–1956), MARGARET CLARKE and the landscape painter Charles Lamb (1893–1964). The strongly academic and traditional nature of Orpen's teaching militated against the influence of

11. Mainie Jellett: *Decoration*, oil on panel, 890×530 mm, 1923 (Dublin, National Gallery of Ireland)

European modernism and tended to limit the horizons of Irish painters working in the 1920s and 1930s. Orpen's teaching could be applied equally well to portraiture and to landscape subjects, and it could therefore be used from 1922 to reflect the traditionalist romantic ideology of the new Irish Free State. JOHN KEATING, one of Orpen's pupils, was the foremost painter of this new cultural identity, one which was also reflected in the west of Ireland landscapes of Maurice MacGonigal (1900–79) and James Humbert Craig (1878–1944). Other painters of the time included Harry Kernoff (1900–74), who painted urban subjects in Dublin, and WILLIAM JOHN LEECH and MARY SWANZY, both of whom pursued their careers outside Ireland.

The leading pioneers of modernism in Ireland were MAINIE JELLETT and Evie Hone (see HONE, (4)). They both studied in Paris under Albert Gleizes and André Lhote, heralding a new wave of Irish students travelling to the French capital. In such paintings as *Decoration* (see fig. 11), and in her lectures in Dublin on Cubism and Abstraction, Jellett tried to overcome the opposition to modern art that she found in what was then a culturally isolated country. During the 1920s and 1930s the R.H.A.

and its exhibitions stood for a traditional, representational, if eclectic, approach to painting, a viewpoint maintained both in its own School and in the city's Metropolitan School of Art, as well as in art schools at Cork, Limerick, Belfast and elsewhere. More adventurous work was exhibited by the Society of Dublin Painters. Paradoxically, World War II provided an opportunity for modern art to emerge in Ireland. Dublin's avant-garde White Stag group of artists and intellectuals included several English artists who had taken refuge there. The group's activities culminated in its 1944 Exhibition of Subjective Art, with a catalogue introduction by Herbert Read. The growing modernist lobby (this included architecture) led to the founding in 1943 of an alternative to the R.H.A.—the Irish Exhibition of Living Art, an annual exhibiting organization. Stylistically, the work exhibited was largely dependent on Parisian art, but with some Expressionist tendencies. A leading exhibitor was Jack B. Yeats (*see* YEATS, (2)), the brother of W. B. Yeats. He had grown up in Sligo but studied in London, where he worked as an illustrator. Yeats was actively promoted by Victor Waddington, who had a gallery in Dublin and later in London. LOUIS LE BROCQUY, another prominent exhibitor, was by the 1960s to become internationally the best-known Irish artist after Yeats. Progressive tendencies in art were to expand under the exclusively modernist patronage of the Irish Arts Council, established in 1951. One current was the semi-abstract landscapes of Nano Reid (1905–81), PATRICK COLLINS, Tony O'Malley (*b* 1913) and Camille Souter (*b* 1929).

During the 1960s, increasing interest in modernism resulted in more art collecting and greater international influence, evident in the work of Hard Edge abstract painters, such as PATRICK SCOTT and CECIL KING. This led to a large number of abstract painters establishing themselves in the 1970s and after, including John Aiken (*b* 1950), Felim Egan (*b* 1952) and Charles Tyrell. The Independents, founded in 1960, favoured a figurative, expressionist style and socially aware subjects, in contrast to the fashionable abstraction of the decade. ROBERT BALLAGH and MICHEAL FARRELL emerged in the orbit of Pop art but developed into broadly urban realist painters. As in many other countries, art in the late 20th century in Ireland was characterized by a wide range of approaches. Such artists as Barrie Cooke (*b* 1931), Eric Van der Grijn (*b* 1941) and Theo McNab (*b* 1940) heralded this period of pluralism. Martin Gale (*b* 1949) and Trevor Geoghegan (*b* 1946) produced detailed realist landscapes; Brian Maguire (*b* 1951), Michael Mulcahy (*b* 1952) and Paddy Graham (*b* 1943) worked in a Neo-Expressionist style; and Cecily Brennan (*b* 1955) produced more lyrical subjects based on nature. The works of BRIAN BOURKE and Michael Kane (*b* 1935) also showed the influence of Expressionism. Members of the R.H.A. continued to provide the mainstay of figurative painting, prominent examples including George Collie (1904–75), Edward McGuire (1932–86), Thomas Ryan (*b* 1927) and Carey Clarke (*b* 1936).

In the graphic arts the setting up by Elizabeth Corbet Yeats of the Dun Emer Press in 1902 and the Cuala Press in 1908 led to a revival of Irish publishing and illustration. Both presses were inspired by the work of William Morris,

and the Cuala published the poems of W. B. Yeats and used illustrations by Jack B. Yeats. The most outstanding illustrator (and stained-glass artist) of the early 20th century was Harry Clarke (*see* CLARKE, (2)), whose illustrations to poems and fairy tales appeared mostly in the 1920s. The work of the publisher Colm O Lochlainn at the Three Candles Press in the 1930s set new standards of book design, typography and art work; in the following decades the publisher Liam Millar continued this tradition at his Dolmen Press. Among the finest illustrated books produced in Ireland in the 20th century was Louis Le Brocquy's limited edition of *The Táin* (1976). At the end of the century this renaissance of publishing in Ireland provided new opportunities for Irish artists and illustrators.

BIBLIOGRAPHY

G. Strickland: *A Dictionary of Irish Artists*, 2 vols (Dublin, 1913)
T. Bodkin: *Four Irish Landscape Painters* (Dublin, 1920/*R* 1987)
F. Henry: *Irish Art in the Early Christian Period to AD 800* (London, 1965)
Irish Houses and Landscapes (exh. cat. by A. Crookshank and others, Dublin, N.G., 1965)
F. Henry: *Irish Art during the Viking Invasions* (London, 1967)
Irish Portraits, 1600–1860 (exh. cat. by A. Crookshank and the Knight of Glin, Dublin, N.G., 1969)
F. Henry: *Irish Art in the Romanesque Period* (London, 1970)
Irish Art in the Nineteenth Century (exh. cat. by C. Barrett, Cork, Crawford Mun. A.G., 1972)
D. Alexander: 'The Dublin Group: Irish Mezzotint Engravers in London', *Bull. Irish Georg. Soc.* (1973), pp. 73–92
Irish Art, 1900–1950 (exh. cat. by H. Pyle, Cork, Crawford Mun. A.G., 1975–6)
Catalogue of Works of Art: Bank of Ireland (exh. cat., intro A. Crookshank, biographical notes by D. Walker; Dublin, 1976)
C. Nordenfalk: *Celtic Manuscript Painting* (Dublin, 1977)
The Treasures of Early Irish Art (exh. cat., New York, Met., 1977)
J. Alexander: *Insular Manuscripts: Sixth to Ninth Centuries* (London, 1978)
A. Crookshank and the Knight of Glin: *The Painters of Ireland, c. 1660–1920* (London, 1978) [with extensive bibliog.]
P. Harbison, H. Porterton and J. Sheehy: *Irish Art and Architecture* (London, 1978)
J. Sheehy: *The Rediscovery of Ireland's Past: The Celtic Revival, 1830–1930* (London, 1980)
R. Knowles: *Contemporary Irish Art* (Dublin, 1982)
The Irish Impressionists: Irish Artists in France and Belgium, 1850–1914 (exh. cat. by J. Campbell, Dublin, N.G., 1984)
A. Crookshank: 'The Visual Arts, 1603–1850', *A New History of Ireland*, ed. T. W. Moody and W. E. Vaughan, iv (Dublin, 1985)
N. Figgis: 'Irish Artists and Society in Eighteenth-century Rome', *Irish A. Rev.*, iii/3 (1986), pp. 28–36
F. Ruane, ed.: *The Allied Irish Bank Collection: Twentieth-century Irish Art* (Dublin, 1986)
N. Figgis: 'Irish Landscapists in Rome, 1750–1780', *Irish A. Rev.*, iv/4 (1987), pp. 60–65
J. Turpin: 'Continental Influence in Eighteenth-century Ireland', *Irish A. Rev.*, iv/4 (1987), pp. 50–57
——: 'Irish History Painting', *Irish A. Rev. Yb.* (1989), pp. 233–47
S. B. Kennedy: *Irish Art and Modernism* (Dublin and Belfast, 1991)
K. McConkey: *A Free Spirit: Irish Art, 1860–1960* (London, 1991)
A. Crookshank and the Knight of Glin: *The Watercolours of Ireland* (London, 1994)
B. Fallon: *Irish Art, 1830–1990* (Dublin, 1994)
B. P. Kennedy and R. Gillespie: *Ireland: Art into History* (Dublin, 1994)

IV. Sculpture.

1. Before 1660. 2. 1660 and after.

1. BEFORE 1660. In the 7th century, after the establishment of Christianity, the most important form of sculpture was the pillar stone inscribed with a cross that became common at monastic settlements. These were followed by the great High Crosses of the 9th to the 12th century. These are also to be found in monastic enclosures,

and they are probably Ireland's most original sculptural contribution (*see* CROSS, fig. 1). Possibly derived from wooden processional crosses covered with metal ornamentation, they were not intended to mark burial places but to assert the site's identification with the Christian faith. Figure sculpture, rare in Irish stone-carving prior to the 9th century, was a major feature of these great scriptural crosses; their subject-matter, based on God's help to man, was typical of Early Christian iconography. Good examples are the Cross of Muireidach at MONASTERBOICE (*see* INSULAR ART, fig. 5) and the Cross of the Scriptures (*c.* 10th century) at Clonmacnois (for illustration *see* CLONMACNOIS MONASTERY); both were carved in sandstone, allowing for fine detail. There is also a distinct group of figured crosses in the Barrow Valley at Moone and Castledermot, Co. Kildare. These crosses were carved in granite, however, resulting in a stiffer, more abstract treatment. On High Crosses of the early 11th century, abstract ornament reappeared, while on very late examples made during the 12th century large figures are depicted, as can be seen on that at Dysert O'Dea, Co. Clare, or at Kilfenora. These indicate that by the 12th century the Romanesque style was beginning to influence Irish sculpture.

The Romanesque church doorways of the 12th century are noteworthy for their elaborate, shallow decorative carving of columns and capitals and for the stylized heads in the voussoirs. As in earlier Irish carving, there is a predilection for abstract ornament, as at Dysert O'Dea, the Nuns' Church at Clonmacnois (1180) and, most notably, at CLONFERT Cathedral, Co. Galway, with its elaborate triangular superstructure displaying tiers of stone-carved heads (*see* ROMANESQUE, fig. 36). The sculptural decoration in such cases was equal in skill and imagination to continental Romanesque work. In their stylized decoration, Romanesque capitals and columns show links with earlier Irish manuscript and metalwork ornament, for example at TUAM, Co. Galway, or the one surviving stone sarcophagus at Cormac's Chapel, Cashel (*see* CASHEL, §2). The influx in the 12th century of Cistercian, Augustinian and other orders was significant, since it led to the introduction in monastic settlements of aisled churches. Despite the austerity of the architectural principles of the Cistercians (*see* §II, 1 above), this allowed opportunities for the sculptural decoration of arcades and capitals not afforded by the earlier simple-cell churches. Finely carved capitals can be seen, for example, at Boyle Abbey, Co. Roscommon, and at Corcomroe Abbey, Co. Clare (*see also* ROMANESQUE, §III, 1(v)(i)). By the early 13th century, Ireland's Anglo-Norman invaders were deeply committed to extensive cathedral building projects, and they introduced foliated capitals and other decorative forms associated with the Early English style. West of England craftsmen, for example, worked on the aisle capitals of Christ Church Cathedral (*see* DUBLIN, §IV, 1). In the Gaelic west of Ireland capitals continued to be carved in a more conservative style, as for example at Cong Abbey (*c.* 1225), Co. Mayo, and in general a flat, decorative aesthetic rather than a three-dimensional naturalism characterized the aims of Irish medieval sculpture in areas remote from English influence.

From the 13th century to the mid-17th, the tomb was the chief object for sculptural decoration. Once the Anglo-Norman colony in eastern Ireland was consolidated, English bishops in Dublin began to have tombs made for themselves after continental models. Even abbots of Gaelic origin copied them, as did the settler knights (e.g. that of the *Cantwell Knight* at Kilfane Church, Co. Kilkenny, of *c.* 1320; see fig. 12). However, the flowering of Anglo-Norman tomb sculpture in Ireland was cut short by the Black Death in the mid-14th century, which

12. Tomb of the *Cantwell Knight*, *c.* 1320 (Kilfane Church, Co. Kilkenny)

profoundly affected the colonized east of Ireland. There was a revival of the form in the 15th century, however, with the Plunkett family in Co. Meath, for example, commissioning carved effigies for the tombs in their churches. Stylistically, the flat effigy was now replaced by the tomb-chest, although in the Gaelic western part of Ireland the wall-tomb was preferred, for example at the Dominican friary at Straide, Co. Mayo. The tomb-chest, however, provided space along its sides for scenes of the *Passion of Christ*, the *Apostles* or other images, a form of display long established in England and on the Continent. A marked contrast is apparent in sculpture of this period between the expert carving of vegetal decorative elements and the stylized rendering of figures, emphasizing the greater interest Irish sculptors had in abstract carving based on plant-forms; the hard Irish limestone, extensively used for tomb carving, lent itself to crisp decorative effects but not to subtle modelling. One of the few families that can be identified by name is the O'TUNNEY family, whose workshop comprised the leading sculptors in Kilkenny. The 'Ormonde school' produced some fine examples, such as the effigies of *Piers Butler, 8th Earl of Ormonde, and his Wife* (*c*. 1539; Kilkenny, St Canice's Cathedral). One outstanding tomb-chest was that of *Bishop Wellsley* (*c*. 1539; removed from Great Connell to Kildare Cathedral), a fine example of Irish Gothic sculpture. The features of the Bishop, shown in effigy, are naturalistically carved, and the chest is surrounded by apostles in relief. The revival of the 15th century also led to a great deal of sculptural work being undertaken at monastic foundations, particularly in the west of the country, for example in the carved tracery of the cloister at Jerpoint Abbey, Co. Kilkenny, with relief figures of nobles and clerics. Late medieval Irish figurative wood-carving was generally undistinguished, however, apart from carvings that were based on animal forms (e.g. the late 15th-century misericords at St Mary's Cathedral, Limerick), and by the 16th century the Irish sculptural tradition was in decline, particularly in Gaelic regions.

A new impetus was given, however, by the wealthy English settler–landlords of the 16th and 17th centuries, such as Richard Boyle, 1st Earl of Cork (*see* BOYLE, (1)), who embellished their houses with carved coats of arms, chimney-pieces and elaborate doorways. Some of the best examples were produced by English sculptors working in Ireland in the prevailing styles of the Elizabethan and Jacobean periods. Renaissance details were taken from foreign engraved sources and used to provide a superficial overlay, as for example on the late 16th-century panels at Moor Abbey, Co. Cork. The tomb meanwhile continued to be the main form of sculpture. Early 17th-century examples include that made to commemorate *Sir Arthur Chichester* (*c*. 1614) in St Nicholas's Church, Carrickfergus, Co. Antrim; the monument to the *1st Earl of Cork* (completed 1620) in St Mary's Church, Youghal, Co. Cork, and a second one (1632) in St Patrick's Cathedral, Dublin; and the monument to *Archbishop Thomas Jones* (1628), also in St Patrick's. The interest in Renaissance detailing also spread to the Gaelic parts of Ireland and can be seen in the O'Connor wall-memorial (1624) in Sligo Abbey. An increasing amount of secular domestic building for wealthy merchants in such cities as Galway and Kilkenny provided

some commissions, since they incorporated carved ornamentation, but this late flowering of a still basically medieval tradition ended with the wars of the mid-17th century.

2. 1660 AND AFTER. Following the Restoration of 1660, foreign sculptors established themselves as Ireland's leading practitioners for a century. The decorative carving of the chapel reredos at the Royal Hospital at Kilmainham, for example, is in the Anglo-Flemish version of the Baroque style and was undertaken by the Huguenot James [Jacques] Tabary (*fl* 1682–8) and his brothers in the 1680s. Their overdoor trophies and other work at Kilmainham set a new standard for architectural carving in 18th-century Dublin churches (e.g. for organ-cases and galleries). The main influence on figure sculpture in the early 18th century was WILLIAM KIDWELL, an English pupil of Edward Pierce. Kidwell's memorial effigies portray the deceased as periwigged and in a reclining pose, following the contemporary English manner, as in his monument to *Sir Donat O'Brien* (see fig. 13). Kidwell also established in

13. William Kidwell: monument to *Sir Donat O'Brien*, *c*. 1717 (Kilnasoolagh Church, Co. Clare)

Ireland the fashion for wall-tablets set in elaborate Baroque frames. Artisans such as John Houghton (*d c.* 1775) and Richard Cranfield meanwhile carved picture-frames, chimney-pieces and exterior ornament in a Rococo manner; their work shows affinities with the ornate and elaborate plasterwork, based on natural forms, of ROBERT WEST.

The arrival in Dublin *c.* 1749 of John van Nost the younger (*see* NOST, VAN, (2)) brought another major development. Van Nost was paid by the Dublin Society to train young Irish sculptors, notably Patrick Cunningham and CHRISTOPHER HEWETSON, and in this role he established the fashion for the portrait bust, which Cunningham continued. Hewetson, on the other hand, settled in Rome; from there he sent home his monument to *Dr Richard Baldwin* in 1784 (Dublin, Trinity Coll.), the first Neo-classical funerary monument seen in Ireland. The architecture of the Neo-classical period also provided greater opportunities for decorative sculptural work than had Palladian architecture before it, and the boom in public and private building in the late 18th century increased the demand for decorative carving, notably for chimney-pieces and doorcases. JAMES CAULFEILD, 1st Earl of Charlemont, brought another influential foreign artist, Simon Vierpyl (1725–1810), from Rome to carve urns for the Casino at Marino, designed by William Chambers (*see* §II, 3 above). Vierpyl, who subsequently also worked for the architect James Gandon, trained EDWARD SMYTH, who worked at Gandon's Custom House, Four Courts and King's Inns, all in Dublin. Smyth excelled in vigorously carved external sculpture, such as the 14 riverine masks on the keystones of the Custom House, and in 1811 he became the first head of the Dublin Society's Modelling School (*see* §XV below). He was later succeeded by his son John Smyth (*c.* 1773–1840), a Neo-classical sculptor of busts and tombs. The School's most notable pupil was JOHN HENRY FOLEY, who left Dublin in 1834 for a brilliant career in London, where he made numerous bronze memorials for Irish patrons.

In the early 19th century a new fashion for public commemorative statues was inaugurated by Thomas Kirk (1781–1845) from Cork, who carved the figure for the top of Nelson's Pillar, built by Francis Johnston (1808; destr. 1966). JOHN HOGAN, who trained in Cork but lived in Rome from 1824 to 1849, also executed many commemorative statues, funerary memorials and busts for Irish patrons. Hogan was deeply influenced by the 19th-century nationalist and Catholic revivals in Ireland, but he continued to work in a Roman Neo-classical style. His finest pieces include *Hibernia with a Bust of Lord Cloncurry* (1844; Dublin, N.G.). In the middle of the century, the leading sculptors were Joseph Kirk (1821–94), who carved the campanile statues for Trinity College, Dublin, as well as a large number of memorials, and THOMAS FARRELL, who made the memorials to *Archbishop Murray* (1855) and *Cardinal Cullen* (1881), both in St Mary's Pro-Cathedral, Dublin. Farrell was trained in his family's stone-carving business, which persevered with a conservative late Neo-classical idiom. The Gothic Revival in architecture also produced a considerable demand for decorative stone-carving, both interior and exterior, as its influence grew during the 19th century. This was met by family stoneyards, such as those owned by C. W. Harrison, the

O'SHEA brothers (whose work included the museum building at Trinity College), James Pearse in Dublin and the Scannell family in Cork. In addition to churches, new clubs, banks and insurance companies all required a considerable quantity of naturalistic ornamental stone-carving.

With revivalist architectural styles dominating sculptural production in the late 19th century, the influence of French Realism and the New Sculpture from England was slow to reach Ireland. Around 1900 the principal young sculptor active and teaching at the Dublin Metropolitan School of Art was JOHN HUGHES, whose main achievement was the *Victoria Memorial* (1901–6; ex-Dublin, Kildare Street; now Sydney, Queen Victoria Bldg). Hughes was succeeded as the School's head of sculpture by OLIVER SHEPPARD. Sheppard specialized in poetic figures, influenced by the Celtic Revival and French Symbolism (e.g. *Cuchulainn*, 1911–12; see fig. 14), but he also created two powerful outdoor bronze nationalist memorials at Wexford and Enniscorthy, dedicated to the rebellion of 1798. His pupil Albert Power (1882–1945) worked in this naturalistic tradition, making portrait busts. Others, such as the Irish-Americans AUGUSTUS SAINT-GAUDENS, Jerome Connor and Andrew O'Connor, worked in a tradition of modelling established by Rodin and provided several of Ireland's public monuments. After 1945 this tradition was continued by Yann Goulet. In the 1930s and 1940s a mode of stylized naturalism became increasingly important, for example in the work of Laurence Campbell

14. Oliver Sheppard: *Cuchulainn*, bronze, 1911–12 (Dublin, General Post Office)

(1911–68), Seamus Murphy (1907–74), Domhnall O'Murchadha, Peter Grant (*b* 1915) and Friedrich Herkner.

The impact of modernism came later in sculpture than in painting. There is a quiet traditionalism, for example, in the sculpture of OISÍN KELLY, visible in such works as *Children of Lir* (1966) in the Garden of Remembrance in Dublin, while many of Kelly's wood-carvings were the result of ecclesiastical commissions. Kelly's work was influential after World War II. Sculpture became more abstract, however, in the 1950s and 1960s in the work of Hilary Heron (1923–77), Ian Stuart (*b* 1926) and Gerda Fromel (1931–75). James McKenna persisted in a modernist figurative style. Edward Delaney reintroduced major public sculpture to Dublin in his monuments to *Wolfe Tone* (Dublin, St Stephen's Green) and *Thomas Davis* (Dublin, College Green), while developments in the 1970s included the Minimalist and conceptual work of Brian King (*b* 1942) and Michael Bulfin (*b* 1939), the installations of JAMES COLEMAN, and the steel sculptures of Alexandra Wejchart (*b* 1920) and Conor Fallon (*b* 1939). The Cork School of Art was an influential centre, where Eilis O'Connell, who emerged in the 1980s, was trained. Others who began to gain recognition included Kathy Prendergast (*b* 1958) and Michael Warren (*b* 1950). An important centre for bronze-casting in the late 20th century was the Dublin Art Foundry, established by John Behan. The Sculptors Society of Ireland played an important role in the 1980s and 1990s in promoting public commissions for sculpture. Conceptual sculpture and installations became a major aspect in the 1980s and 1990s.

BIBLIOGRAPHY

C. Mcleod: 'Medieval Wooden Figure Sculpture in Ireland', *J. Royal Soc. Antiqua. Ireland*, lxxv (1945), lxxvi (1946)

F. Henry: *Irish High Crosses* (Dublin, 1964)

A. Crookshank: 'Irish Sculpture, 1750–1860', *Apollo* (1966)

E. C. Rae: 'Irish Sculptural Monuments of the Later Middle Ages', *J. Royal Soc. Antiqua. Ireland*, c (1970)

A. Crookshank: 'Lord Cork and his Monuments', *Country Life*, cxlix (27 May 1971), pp. 1288–90

R. A. Stalley: *Architecture and Sculpture in Ireland, 1150–1350* (Dublin, 1971)

J. Hunt: *Irish Medieval Figure Sculpture, 1200–1600* (London, 1974)

H. Potterton: *Irish Church Monuments* (Belfast, 1975)

M. de Paor and L. de Paor: *Early Christian Ireland* (London, 1978)

C. Hicks: 'A Clonmacnois Workshop in Stone', *J. Royal Soc. Antiqua. Ireland*, cx (1980)

J. Sheehy: *The Rediscovery of Ireland's Past* (London, 1980)

R. Loeber: 'Sculpted Memorials to the Dead in Early Seventeenth-century Ireland', *Proc. Royal Irish Acad.*, lxxxi (1981)

B. de Breffney, ed.: *Ireland: A Cultural Encyclopedia* (London, 1983)

Treasures of Ireland (exh. cat., ed. M. Ryan; Dublin, N. Mus., 1983)

A. Crookshank: *Irish Sculpture from 1600 to the Present Day* (Dublin, 1984)

D. O'Connell: 'Contemporary Irish Sculpture', *Circa*, xvi (1984)

Cork Art Now (exh. cat. by V. Ryan, Cork, Crawford Mun. A.G., 1985)

R. Loeber: 'Carvings at Moore Abbey, Co. Kildare', *Irish A. Rev.*, iii/4 (1986), pp. 53–5

S. McNab: 'The Romanesque Figure Sculpture at Maghera, Co. Derry, and Raphoe, Co. Donegal', *New Perspectives: Studies in Honour of Anne Crookshank* (Dublin, 1987)

M. Ryan, ed.: *Ireland and Insular Art* (Dublin, 1987)

E. Rynne: *Figures from the Past: Studies in Honour of Helen M. Roe* (Dublin, 1987)

S. McNab: 'Styles Used in Twelfth-century Irish Figure Sculpture', *Peritia*, vii (1988)

J. Turpin: 'The Dublin Society at the Beginnings of Sculptural Education in Ireland, 1750–1850', *Eire-Ireland*, xxiv, no. 1 (Spring 1989), pp. 40–58

JOHN TURPIN

V. Interior decoration.

Academic study of Irish interior decoration is still in its infancy, although research has been carried out on the two notable aspects of the subject, furniture (*see* §VI below) and decorative plasterwork (*see* STUCCO AND PLASTERWORK, §III, 10(i)(c)), and there are many fine 18th- and 19th-century interiors in the country houses that survived the destruction caused by neglect and economic hardship in the early 20th century and the deliberate burnings of the civil war in 1922.

Medieval Ireland was ruled by Gaelic and Anglo-Norman chieftains, some of whom built large castles such as Trim (*c.* 1220), Co. Meath, but these and virtually all medieval ecclesiastical buildings are in ruins. Of the thousands of smaller tower houses built in the 15th and 16th centuries by the lesser gentry, only Dunsoghley in Co. Meath retains its roof. These tower houses were simple and uncomfortable; contemporary accounts complain of the lack of daylight, furniture and bed linen, only partly compensated for by an excess of alcohol and the heat produced by farm animals accommodated on the ground floor. No 'prodigy' houses were built in Ireland to emulate those of Elizabeth I's courtiers in England, although one of her cousins, 'Black Thomas', 10th Earl of Ormonde, built the only surviving Tudor manor house around 1570 at Carrick-on-Suir, Co. Tipperary. Attached to a 15th-century castle for defensive purposes, the house has a long gallery with a fine, elaborately compartmented plaster ceiling. The simple interiors have the same qualities and scale as similar manor houses in Dorset and Somerset. Relatively little building was done in the 16th and 17th centuries, but a few inventories survive, such as that of the 1630s from Dunluce Castle (destr.), Co. Antrim, the seat of the McDonnells, Earls of Antrim; it shows that the castle was full of the best-quality furniture and fittings, acquired by the Earl in London. There were six sets of chairs of state, with lesser chairs and stools to match and canopies, as well as 60 more upholstered chairs and stools, finely inlaid cabinets, celestial and terrestrial globes, travelling four-poster beds and enormous quantities of linen.

Much was destroyed during the Cromwellian wars, and in the 30 years from 1660 the first proper country houses were built, due mainly to the civilizing influence of JAMES BUTLER, 1st Duke of Ormonde and Viceroy to Charles II; he transformed Kilkenny Castle (destr.) during the 1660s and 1670s into a comfortable mansion, with large amounts of silver and elaborately upholstered furniture, much of it French, that put it on a par with Knole, Kent, and Ham House, Surrey. Beaulieu, Co. Louth, built in the 1660s for Sir William Tichborne, is also similar to contemporary English houses with bolection-moulded panelling and ceilings with central ovals surrounded by heavy garlands of plaster flowers and foliage. Eyrecourt Castle (destr.) in Co. Galway, of the same date, had a huge oak staircase with balustrades of carved and pierced panels of scrollwork and panelled newel posts surmounted with carved, flower-filled urns. The Williamite wars of 1688 to 1690 caused further destruction, and little building was carried out for about 20 years. However, the surviving interiors of the Royal Hospital at Kilmainham, Dublin, with spectacular wood-carving by the Huguenot James

Tabary (*fl* 1682–8) and his brothers, ironwork and plaster of the 1680s and 1690s, show the superb workmanship that could be achieved.

The settlement of the Protestant succession in 1689 brought a century of uneasy peace to the country and prosperity to the Anglo-Irish gentry, but the lack of a middle class in any significant numbers meant that few country houses were built; those that were had simple painted and panelled interiors, similar to their English counterparts. Influences came from England either as a result of the owners also living there or via printed sources, but large numbers of French and Dutch craftsmen sought refuge in Dublin from religious persecution in their own countries, bringing new ideas that influenced the decorative details of interiors and furniture. In the early 18th century, exactly contemporary with similar developments in England, the Palladian style made its mark in Ireland (*see* §II, 2 above). Castletown House, Co. Kildare, is the largest and earliest Palladian country house in Ireland, and some of its interiors survive unaltered. Started before 1722 for William Conolly (1662–1729), it was designed initially by Alessandro Galilei and later by EDWARD LOVETT PEARCE. The two-storey entrance hall designed by Pearce shows considerable Italian influence, particularly in the tapering pilasters with flower-basket capitals at the upper level. The first Irish house to have an axial corridor running its full length separating the front and rear ranges of rooms with service staircases at each end, Castletown was considered extremely grand as soon as it was started. The interiors were left incomplete on the death of Conolly in 1729 and were finished during the 1760s and 1770s (see below) to the different taste of his great-nephew's wife, but they impress more by their size and scale than by elaborate or sumptuous decoration. The interiors of Pearce's other surviving buildings, for instance 9 Henrietta Street (see fig. 15), Dublin, have raised and fielded panelling in plaster, whereas his interiors of the House of Lords in Dublin's Parliament House (now the Bank of Ireland), built between 1729 and 1733 and based on studies of Roman basilicas and baths, are panelled in oak. Pearce was probably responsible for three important aspects of Irish interiors: the introduction of a columnar screen in front of the inner wall of an entrance hall to mark the internal cross axis of the house; the placing of a main staircase in a generous separate space to one side of the entrance hall; and the use of a large rectangular top-lit landing entered from the staircase and around which the upper rooms are arranged. These features, rarely seen in England, were almost standard throughout the 18th century in Ireland.

Pearce's architectural successor was Richard Castle, who fused Franco-Dutch, Palladian and Baroque influences with the Irish tradition of exterior reticence and interior elaboration and introduced the fashion for canted and curved storey-height bay windows to further enliven interiors (e.g. Ballyhaise, Co. Cavan, *c.* 1731). His masterpiece is Russborough House, Co. Wicklow, built in 1742–55 for Joseph Leeson, 1st Earl of Milltown. Fairly small in scale and number, the rooms are all simple rectangles without any curves or other special effects. The ceilings and the large coves below them are covered with rich stuccowork, and in all the rooms but one, high mahogany dados, said to be the first use of this wood in Ireland,

15. Plaster chimney-piece and overmantel by Edward Lovett Pearce, 9 Henrietta Street, Dublin, 1731

provide a sober contrast. The walls, except for those of the staircase and the drawing-room, do not have panelling or decoration. These seem to be the principal elements of the 18th-century Irish interior; sadly, no Irish house of the period has its original contents in any quantity, and as contemporary inventories, descriptions and illustrations are rare it is very difficult to be specific or confident about the original appearance of rooms. While the general use of rooms followed that of their more formal English counterparts, with family rooms below the *piano nobile* that contained the principal apartment, life was more relaxed in Ireland; there seems to have been a conscious attempt to impress by informal but lavish displays of hospitality, as recorded by such diarists and correspondents as Mary Delaney (1700–88). Interiors reflected this by the unparalleled luxuriousness of decorative plasterwork, with flowing Baroque and Rococo lines and patterns held within large panels of correct Palladian design. Much of this was designed and executed by the three Swiss-Italian Lafranchini brothers, as at 80 and 85 St Stephen's Green (1731–6 and 1738–40 respectively), Dublin, Carton House (1739–45), Co. Kildare, and Russborough, all by Castle. The Irish love of unrestrained and exuberant plasterwork was realized by many craftsmen, such as BARTHOLOMEW CRAMILLION at the Rotunda Hospital Chapel, Dublin, and Robert West, whose own Dublin house, 20 Lower Dominick Street (1755–8), was a spectacular advertisement of his skills. Based on designs of classical scenes and deities published in French and Italian pattern books from the late 17th century onwards, this plasterwork, daringly undercut, has human, animal and plant forms of extraordinary realism and fantasy. A similarly high level of skill was also achieved in ironwork and other metals; these were combined with particular elaboration in the staircase of the Provost's House (1756) at Trinity College, Dublin.

While the differences between Irish and English practice at this time were clear, there was also a strong desire to emulate the latest London, and hence French, fashions, and this resulted in several English and Scottish architects designing important buildings in Ireland. The Dublin house (now Leinster House) of the Earl of Kildare, for example, was altered and improved c. 1757, although it was less than 20 years old, to the designs of William Chambers. Chambers brought his exquisite Neo-classicism to Ireland in his interiors of the Casino (1759) at Marino, Dublin, for James Caulfeild, 1st Earl of Charlemont, and in his remodelling and completion of Castletown House for the English Lady Louisa Conolly, sister of Emily, Countess of Kildare. A superb stone staircase was inserted into the original staircase hall at Castletown, and the Lafranchini brothers elaborated the otherwise plain coved ceiling and flat walls with plasterwork foliage and portraits of the family. Two drawing-rooms were remodelled with new ceilings, doorcases and chimney-pieces all to Chambers's designs, and c. 1765 one of the 'Palladian' rooms was redecorated as the finest print room in Ireland by pasting engravings and mezzotints directly on to the walls. Ten years later Lady Louisa improved the gallery (24 m long) on the first floor by having the plaster wall panelling 'knocked off smack smooth' and the walls painted with Pompeian grotesques. The gallery was used as a living-room, and its furniture included a pair of commodes by Pierre Langlois and a pair of side-tables by John Linnell (i); three magnificent Venetian chandeliers and four huge sheets of French mirrored glass remain *in situ*.

The first example of Gothic Revival interiors in Ireland was at Castle Ward, Co. Down, built during the early 1760s by an unknown architect for Bernard Ward (later 1st Viscount Bangor) and his wife Lady Anne, where his rooms are planned and decorated in a copybook Palladian manner and hers are Rococo Gothic with spectacular ogee-shaped plaster vaulting. Other interiors of the final 40 years of the 18th century show considerable English classical influence combined with the traditional Irish plan and features. Robert Adam had relatively little influence; the English architects James Gandon, a pupil of Chambers resident in Ireland from 1781, and James Wyatt had far more effect, both through their own work and through the designs of the native Thomas Cooley and the brothers Richard and Francis Johnston. In 1790 Wyatt produced for Armar Lowry-Corry, later 1st Earl of Belmore, the most perfect Irish Neo-classical house, Castlecoole in Co. Fermanagh. The plans have all the standard Irish elements,

and the interiors, of the utmost serenity, simplicity and quality of both materials and craftsmanship, were finished in 1798. They are definitely English in style: the plasterer was Joseph Rose jr (1746–99), who had worked for Robert Adam at Syon House, London, and Harewood House, W. Yorks, and the London sculptor Richard Westmacott (i) provided the chimney-pieces. The hall, drawing-room and dining-room are severe but perfectly proportioned, as are the staircase and central top-lit upper lobby; the oval saloon is more lavish, being encircled with grey scagliola pilasters (see fig. 16). Castlecoole retains its contents, supplied to Armar Lowry-Corry, 2nd Earl of Belmore, by John Preston (*fl* 1793–1825), a leading upholsterer of Dublin, between 1815 and 1824.

Following the Act of Union of 1800 many of the Irish nobility and gentry retreated to their country houses, some of which were then remodelled in the various current fashions. Charleville Forest, Co. Offaly, designed c. 1801 by Francis Johnston for the 1st Earl of Charleville, contains a vast drawing-room with a fan-vaulted ceiling and pendants, and the doors and fireplaces were modelled on genuine medieval designs. Around the same time Johnston had produced elegant and convincing Greek Revival interiors in a manner similar to that of John Soane at Townley Hall, Co. Louth, and Galtrim, Co. Meath, both built in the 1790s with plain, austere exteriors. Richard Morrison and his son and partner William Vitruvius Morrison designed sumptuous Roman-inspired interiors (1822–6) at Ballyfin, Co. Laois, for Sir Charles Coote, Tudor and French Empire ones at Kilruddery (1820–29), Co. Wicklow, for John Brabazon, 10th Earl of Meath, and Greek Revival and French Empire at both Fota (c. 1825),

16. Saloon by James Wyatt, Castlecoole, Co. Fermanagh, c. 1797, with furnishings supplied by John Preston, 1815–24

Co. Cork, for John Smith-Barry, and Baronscourt (1835–43), Co. Tyrone, for James Hamilton, 1st Duke of Abercorn. Ballywalter (begun 1847), Co. Down, built for the rich linen merchant Andrew Mulholland, is the most complete example of a 19th-century Italianate palazzo in Ireland. Designed by Charles Lanyon, the interiors are grouped around a splendid staircase hall lit by a domed skylight. Everything is classical and rather heavy, although superbly detailed and executed. The social and political difficulties experienced after 1845 resulted in few major houses being built in the second half of the century; those that were showed a growing interest in Irish medieval architecture, such as Dromore Castle, Co. Limerick, for William Perry, 3rd Earl of Limerick, by E. W. Godwin and Ashford Castle, Co. Mayo, by James Franklin Fuller (1835–1924) for Arthur Edward Guinness, 1st Lord Ardilaun, both designed in the late 1860s.

BIBLIOGRAPHY
Records of Eighteenth-century Domestic Architecture and Decoration in Ireland, The Georgian Society, 5 vols (Dublin, 1909–13)
T. U. Sadlier and P. L. Dickinson: *Georgian Mansions in Ireland, with Some Account of Georgian Architecture and Decoration* (Dublin, 1915)
H. G. Leask: *Irish Castles and Castellated Houses* (Dundalk, 1946)
C. Curran: *Dublin Decorative Plasterwork in the Seventeenth Century and Eighteenth Century* (London, 1964)
M. J. Craig and others: *Castletown, Co. Kildare* (London, 1969)
D. Guinness and W. Ryan: *Irish Houses and Castles* (London, 1971)
B. de Breffny and R. Ffolliott: *The Houses of Ireland: Domestic Architecture from the Medieval Castle to the Edwardian Villa* (London, 1975)

For further bibliography *see* §VI below.

JOHN REDMILL

VI. Furniture.

Irish furnishings are not easy to study; nearly all the early examples were destroyed, and much of the later work was sold. Exported to England or North America and devoid of provenance, Irish furniture is often indistinguishable from its English prototypes and is sometimes confused with American pieces made by Irish craftsmen who had emigrated. The main centre of production was Dublin, but Limerick, Cork and Waterford also supplied furniture. The trades had been established in Dublin since the 15th century; by the late 17th century guilds were established, and the furniture trade was operating along the same lines as its London counterpart, with upholders often employing the carvers, japanners, gilders, glass-grinders and cabinet-makers essential to their business. Carvers were divided into chair-carvers and frame-carvers; the latter, who were good draughtsmen, specialized in mirror frames, Pier tables and stands. Trade directories and newspapers from the mid-18th century make it possible to list the many craftsmen operating in Dublin, but unfortunately it is difficult to link these names with known furniture. A number of pieces of Irish furniture carry trade labels, but the dispersal of collections has broken the chain of evidence afforded by family records and accounts. The Dublin Society Drawing Schools, established in the 1740s, had an extremely important role in educating craftsmen and contributed to the high standards of design. There was a deliberate policy, encouraged in the 1740s by Jonathan Swift, Samuel Madden (1686–1765) and the Dublin Society, of using Irish materials and craftsmen. This was in retaliation against the punitive trade restrictions that had been imposed on Ireland and the colonies by the English government. In 1782, however, the restrictions were lifted, so English goods became more acceptable. Although the main influences were undoubtedly English, French books and percepts also filtered into Ireland through immigrant Huguenot craftsmen and as a result of the close associations that already existed between the two countries. Robert West, for example, the founder of the Drawing Schools, and his assistant, James Mannin (*fl* 1760–78), had both trained in France.

1. FINE FURNITURE, BEFORE 1800. A few early carved chairs and chests exist in cathedrals and churches, and Limerick Cathedral's 15th-century misericords are the finest examples of medieval carving in Ireland. The 'Armada' table (Bunratty Castle, Co. Clare) is an extremely elaborate piece, its later mahogany top supported on carved lions and allegorical figures, which may have been salvaged from an Armada wreck off the coast of Clare in the 1580s; it was probably made up in Ireland at the end of the 16th century. The finest surviving 17th-century woodwork was made by a Huguenot craftsman, James Tabary (*fl* 1682–8), for the Royal Hospital at Kilmainham, Dublin. The chapel panelling and tabernacle provide a background to the oak altar table of 1687, which is heavily carved in a monumental classical style with a fluted frieze and acanthus-decorated, scrolled legs; this is the first documented piece of Irish furniture known. A John Tabary 'sculptor' and a Louis Tabary 'carver' were both listed as 'French Protestants' in 1685 and were also working at Kilmainham, but nothing further is known about this family or their work.

In the 18th century much of the oak, walnut, japanned and gilt furniture followed English trends but sometimes lagged 10 or 20 years behind, as is demonstrated by a walnut and marquetry chair inscribed *Maher, Kilkenny 1740 Fecit* but made in the Anglo-Dutch style of 20 years earlier (priv. col.; see Coleridge and Fitz-Gerald, fig. 1; another of this set, although not signed, is in the National Museum of Ireland, Dublin). Walnut and mahogany furniture in the Palladian style of William Kent was given an eccentric twist by the Irish love of grotesque animal decoration. This unique style can be seen in seat furniture, card- and side-tables (see fig. 17), bottle stands and blanket chests. Aprons have low-relief, foliated detail set against a punched or geometrically diaper-patterned ground. The carving incorporates eagle heads, birds, festoons, oak leaves and rosettes, and is usually centred on a lion's head, a grotesque mask, a shell or a basket of flowers. Cabriole legs, supported by webbed claw-and-ball feet or by square paws, have acanthus-leaved hocks, masks and scallop shells. The animal features are often bizarre and disturbing: the legs, for example, may be startlingly realistic, with tendons, hair or fishscales. French elements can also be identified: a marble-topped side-table from Co. Limerick of *c.* 1740 (Pickering Forest, Co. Kildare) has a deep pierced apron centred on a vase of flowers similar to those found in *Régence* gilt furniture, and later pieces sometimes combine rocaille scrolls and flowers with masks and other motifs associated with Bacchus, a decoration suitable for the dining-room. The ornament is often profuse and

17. Mahogany side-table with grotesque masks, paw feet and scrolled hocks, *c.* 1750–60 (USA, private collection)

injudiciously applied, the shapes may be clumsy, and old-fashioned forms of construction persisted; stretchers, for example, combine to give furniture a bold but provincial air. Marble table-tops are not common, and instead the furniture displays a lavish use of mahogany in the wide planks used for the tops and the deep carving in the aprons. Very dark mahogany from Santo Domingo and Honduras was a peculiarly Irish taste that may have been formed by the use of black bog oak in the 17th century. Many side-tables are stained black.

A plainer style existed concurrently, its decoration confined to simple fretwork, shell ornaments and elegant curves. Small tea-tables with dished tops, curving aprons and trifid, slipper or club feet with channelled 'panels', and armchairs with serpentine stretchers, curved backs and curved, voluted arms are sometimes similar to Philadelphia and Rhode Island seat furniture. Case furniture was generally restrained in character, dignified on occasion with architectural features: a walnut writing-cabinet with elaborate marquetry inlay (*c.* 1720–30; Chicago, IL, A. Inst.) has pilasters framing the doors of the upper section, as does the mahogany writing-cabinet (*c.* 1760) in the style of Giles Grendey at Castletown House, Co. Kildare. The seaweed marquetry inside the latter is a hangover from the 17th century. A group of walnut bureau-bookcases (London, V&A; Chicago, IL, A. Inst.; and elsewhere) with similarly old-fashioned marquetry, swan-necked pediments and pull-out fronts appears to have been made in Dublin in the 1730s (see fig. 18). A very fine bombé commode (Norwich, Arthur Brett col.), dating between 1745 and 1769, is inlaid with elaborate 17th-century style marquetry bearing the arms of William Stewart, 1st Earl of Blessington. Clocks had been made in Dublin since the

late 17th century. Longcase clocks of the 18th century, which are usually signed, are decorated like the case furniture, with lions' masks, shells, flat foliated acanthus carving, swan-necked pediments, columns and pilasters. Their architectural character may be further emphasized by rustication on the base.

For picture and mirror frames oak and gilded pine and mahogany were used. These were the work of highly skilled carvers, and, since they are occasionally documented and often used trade labels, they can be identified by name. One of the most proficient was John Houghton (*fl* 1730–74), who must have been responsible for the frame of Jan van Beaver's tapestry portrait of *George II* (1738; New York, Met.) with its trophies and rich classical ornaments. It is stylistically very close to his documented elaborate frame of the portrait of *Dean Swift* (Dublin, St Patrick's Deanery). Houghton worked in stone as well as wood, and the pediment of Carton House, Co. Kildare, was executed by him and John Kelly (*fl* 1739–59) in 1739. Kelly's elaborate mahogany four-poster bed with its carved headboard is a rare documented piece of Irish furniture; it was made for Dr Mosse, founder of Dublin's Lying-In Hospital, and cost £19 8s. 6d. in 1759 (Ireland, priv. col., see The Knight of Glin, 1978, pl. 13). Such other craftsmen as Francis and John Booker worked in the manner of Kent. Their father, John Booker sr, started his mirror business in 1725, and the firm continued until 1775. The architectural form of their monumental pedimented mirrors was influenced by the church monuments of William Kidwell, a further example of the close relationship between wood- and monumental carving. Richard Cranfield (1739–1809) was one of the finest carvers in Dublin; he crafted the Italianate gilded chair designed by James

Mannin for the President of the Dublin Society in 1767 (Dublin, Royal Dublin Soc.). He sometimes worked in partnership with another high-quality carver, James Robinson (*fl* 1761–74), and a series of Rococo oval mirrors (1771–4), some bearing his label, are at Newbridge House, Co. Dublin.

From the 1770s Irish furniture lost its distinctive character and followed English Neo-classical styles. Much English furniture was imported, and craftsmen became increasingly reliant on English pattern books for up-to-date ideas. An intriguing instance of this is a mahogany centre-table (London, priv. col; see fig. 19) based on the tomb of Agrippa, which was taken directly from the 1771 English edition of Antoine Desgodetz's *Les Edifices antiques de Rome* (1682); it was inscribed in 1775 by its maker, G. O'Connor, in Dublin. This stylistic shift was also brought about by foreign craftsmen working in Dublin. Pietro Bossi, probably from Florence, who worked in Dublin from 1780 to 1798, was renowned for the

19. Mahogany centre-table by G. O'Connor, Dublin, 1775 (London, private collection)

delicate inlaid Neo-classical designs of his scagliola table-tops and fireplaces. William Moore (*fl* 1785–1814), who had been in the shop of the London firm of Ince & Mayhew, came to Dublin in 1782 and became known for his inlaid satin-wood commodes and demi lune side tables in the Adam style.

2. FINE FURNITURE, AFTER 1800. The Act of Union of 1800 dealt a serious blow to the Irish furniture trade, as Dublin was no longer the seat of Parliament and landowners retired to their country estates or departed for London. There were, however, many important country-house commissions in the early part of the century. Thomas Pakenham, 2nd Earl of Longford, furnished Pakenham Hall (now Tullynally Castle), Co. Westmeath, between 1801 and 1806 with plain furniture that was acclaimed by the novelist Maria Edgeworth for being 'neither Gothick nor Chinese nor gaudy nor frail nor so fashionable that it will be out of fashion in six months' (Tullynally Castle, Pakenham MSS). In the 1810s and 1820s Armar Lowry-Corry, 2nd Earl of Belmore, went to the opposite extreme at Castlecoole, Co. Fermanagh, ordering splendid 'Grecian' furniture (see fig. 16 above) with brass inlay to the value of £17,000 from John Preston of Dublin (*fl* 1793–1825). It is uncertain whether Preston made these furnishings or whether he imported the pieces from England. Otherwise there was a sad decline. Fine carving was replaced by gilded plaster, and the firm of James Del Vecchio (*fl* 1794–1856), who were printsellers, carvers, plasterers, furniture- and mirror makers, specialized in eclectic gilt-wood and plaster Regency side-tables, mirrors, frames etc. Mass production eventually lowered the standards of design and craftsmanship. Despite this, good furniture, some of it reproducing mid-18th-century styles, continued to be made in Dublin throughout the Victorian period. There were two distinctively Irish developments. The first was Killarney work, elaborately inlaid furniture and smaller items for the tourist trade using bog

18. Walnut bureau-bookcase with marquetry, probably made in Dublin, 1730s (Collection of the National Trust of Northern Ireland, Florence Court, Co. Fermanagh, NT)

oak, yew, arbutus and other coloured woods; they included pictorial views of local Killarney buildings and attractions. The second was the Celtic Revival furniture made of bog yew, richly carved with romantic historical themes that were meant to evoke the glories of ancient Ireland. A table (1861; Derrynane Abbey, Co. Kerry) made by Patrick Beakey (*fl* 1853–61) for Daniel O'Connell has a base in the form of a round tower surrounded by harps, oak leaves and three recumbent wolfhounds. The firm of Michael Butler (*fl* 1877–1912) made fine reproduction furniture, such as George II style dining-chairs and elaborately carved sideboards. James Hicks (1894–1936) reproduced the dark mahogany furniture of the Irish Palladian period and the satin-wood commodes and side-tables of William Moore. James Levins sr (*fl* 1900–20) was the carver of many of Hicks's side-tables and Chippendale-style mirrors. Eileen Gray was born in Enniscorthy in Co. Wexford, but her brilliant pioneering modernist designs belong to internationalism. The national yet original manner of Eric Pearce (*b* 1956) can be seen, for example, in his chairs and tables for the dining-hall at Trinity College, Dublin, and in some of the finely crafted woodwork of sycamore inlaid with yew in the restored Government Buildings, Dublin.

3. VERNACULAR FURNITURE. The furniture of the poorer classes was shaped by a shortage of wood and cramped living conditions, constrictions that led to some ingenious multi-functional designs. Dual-purpose settles had hinged box seats that folded out to make a bed, or backs that swung down to rest on the arms and make a table-top. Dressers displaying ceramics were often the only decorative feature in a room. They had a shelved upper storey and cupboards, or a chicken coop, in the base, and some were built-in or acted as a room divider. Their friezes were often decorated with elaborate carving and fretwork. Chairs and stools were simply constructed with a plain, horizontal back rail supported by three or four spindles; the ends of these spindles were tapered and jammed into holes in the seat, as were the legs. The larger items were often made from driftwood, but hedgecuttings and even straw were used for chairs and stools. The wood was disguised by paint, sometimes grained to represent more valuable timbers, otherwise in dark reds and browns or in strongly contrasting colours. Furniture was often made by boatbuilders, coffin-makers, wheelwrights or by the householder himself.

BIBLIOGRAPHY

E. T. Joy: 'Irish Furniture of the Georgian Period', *Country Life Annu.* (1965), pp. 100–01
A. Coleridge and D. Fitz-Gerald [The Knight of Glin]: 'Eighteenth Century Irish Furniture: A Provincial Manifestation', *Apollo*, lxxxiv (1966), pp. 276–89
The Knight of Glin: 'A Family of Looking-glass Merchants', *Country Life*, cxlix (28 Jan 1971), pp. 195–9 [the Booker family]
G. B. Hughes: 'Irish Bog-wood Furniture', *Country Life*, cxlix (27 May 1971), pp. 1318–21
The Knight of Glin: *Irish Furniture*, Irish Her. Ser., xvi (Dublin, 1978)
J. Sheehy: *The Rediscovery of Ireland's Past: The Celtic Revival, 1830–1930* (London, 1980), pp. 78–84
The Knight of Glin: 'The Dublin Del Vecchios', *Antiques*, cxx (1981), pp. 910–14
——: 'Furniture', *Ireland: A Cultural Encyclopedia*, ed. B. de Breffny (London, 1983), pp. 89–93
G. Jackson-Stops: 'A Temple Made Tasteful: A Regency Upholsterer at Castle Coole', *Country Life*, clxxix (10 April 1986), pp. 918–20
The Knight of Glin: 'A Directory of the Dublin Furnishing Trade, 1752–1800', *Decantations in Honour of Maurice Craig* (Dublin, 1992), pp. 47–59
C. Kinmonth: *Irish Country Furniture, 1700–1950* (New Haven, 1993)

THE KNIGHT OF GLIN

VII. Ceramics.

1. BEFORE 1700. Excavations (1986) in Tankardstown, Co. Limerick, unearthed the earliest pottery sherds known in Ireland. Dated to *c.* 5000 BC, the sherds are thin-walled with narrow everted rims and the clay evidently tempered with fine grit. From the Bronze Age until the Middle Ages crude bucket- and barrel-shaped, unglazed storage- and cooking-pots and funerary ware sufficed the general need for ceramic wares. About 1200 the Anglo-Normans introduced a more specialized approach to ceramics, which ensured that pottery was made in specific areas and by specialists. The few excavated kilns from this period show that horizontal kilns with stone-built firing chambers and stoke holes were used. The potter's wheel and lead glazing were also introduced at this time. In the 17th century small potteries were established, which made use of local clays and produced unglazed drainpipes and flowerpots, floor-tiles, glazed crocks for the dairy and decorative kitchen wares.

2. 1700 AND AFTER. From about 1735 to 1739 tin-glazed earthenware was apparently made in Dublin, and between *c.* 1738 and 1743 it was manufactured in Rostrevor, Co. Down. By *c.* 1740 it was also produced in Limerick, Wexford and possibly Youghal, Co. Cork, and by *c.* 1755 apparently in Waterford. In 1752 Captain Henry Delamain (*d* 1757) took over an existing pottery business in Dublin and employed foreign technicians. In 1755 the Dublin Society, which had offered a premium for improving the quality of earthenware, certified the quality of Delamain's tin-glazed wares. After Delamain's death the factory first passed to his wife, Mary Delamain (*d* 1760), and in 1760 to his brother, William Delamain, and Samuel Wilkinson. In 1770 the factory competed for the Dublin Society's prize for earthenware 'in imitation of flint or Paris ware', which was probably a lead-glazed creamware (cream-coloured earthenware), indicating the influence and increasing popularity of Josiah Wedgwood's invention. However, the Delamain factory ceased production *c.* 1770. Between *c.* 1787 and 1799 the Downshire Pottery in Downshire, Co. Wicklow, produced creamware and petitioned the Dublin Society (1792) and the Irish Parliament (1793) for assistance in its production. As with the Delamain establishment, it was necessary to import non-Irish workers, as well as machinery. The factory closed in 1799.

In the late 18th century blanks for decoration and fully decorated wares were imported from England into Ireland. From the late 18th century various local potteries were established in Newry (*c.* 1793–4); Cork (*c.* 1835); Youghal; Lisgoa, Co. Monaghan; Larne (est. first quarter of 19th century–*c.* 1858); Castle Espie (*c.* 1853–*c.* 1879), near Comber; and the Coalisland Pottery (*c.* 1850–*c.* 1890) and the Ulster Fireclay Works (*c.* 1908–14), both in Coalisland, Co. Tyrone. The factories in Newry, Cork, Youghal, Larne and Castle Espie made domestic earthenware; bricks and tiles were made at Castle Espie; and porcelain was made at Coalisland. The porcelain tea-services made by the BELLEEK PORCELAIN FACTORY (est. 1857) in Belleek, Co. Fermanagh, were later imitated by the Coalisland factory. At first the Belleek factory produced useful wares, but later figures and decorative items were introduced (see fig. 20). Items were covered in a nacreous glaze, and some of their more collectable items are openwork baskets and wares decorated with marine forms.

In 1872 Fredrick Vodrey founded the Dublin Pottery, which made items inspired by the Arts and Crafts Movement; the factory closed *c.* 1885. From the 1880s studio ceramics evolved, which mirrored artistic movements in the United Kingdom and Europe. About 1926 the Carrigaline Pottery in Carrigaline, Co. Cork, was founded, which produced both kitchen and art wares and souvenirs for the tourist industry; it closed in 1983. Freedom for the individual potter came with the introduction of the small electric kiln, first used by Kathleen Cox (1904–72) in Dublin in the 1930s. The influence of such art potters as Bernard Leach is evident in the work of Peter Brennan (*b* 1916) and Grattan Freyer.

In 1965 the Kilkenny Design Workshop was opened with government sponsorship in Kilkenny, which indicated the State's increasing concern about design, including that of commercially produced ceramics. A number of workshops were set up during the 1970s in Co. Kilkenny and Co. Cork. In 1986 the Crafts Council of Ireland was reorganized, and in 1987 a new gallery was opened in Dublin. In 1989 it took over the Kilkenny Design Workshop and introduced post-graduate training programmes in craft work including ceramics. Apart from the Belleek Pottery, there have been no long-lasting ceramics factories in Ireland. In the late 20th century ceramics are produced by small-scale, hand-production units, whether in limited editions or as 'one-offs'.

SEAN McCRUM

BIBLIOGRAPHY
M. S. D. Westropp: *Irish Pottery and Porcelain* (Dublin, 1935)
Irish Delftware (exh. cat. by M. Archer and P. Hickey, Co. Kildare, Castletown House, 1971)
P. F. Wallace and M. Kenny: *Pottery in Ireland through the Ages* (Dublin, 1978)
M. Archer: *Irish Pottery and Porcelain*, Irish Her. Ser., xxvii (Dublin, 1979)
M. Reynolds: 'Irish Fine Ceramic Potteries', *Post-med. Archaeol.*, xviii (1984), pp. 251–61
M. Dunlevy: 'James Donovan, the Emperor of China', *Irish A. Rev.*, ii (1985), pp. 28–36
——: *Ceramics in Ireland* (Dublin, 1988)

VIII. Glass.

Glaziers or clear and stained-glassmakers worked in various parts of Ireland from the 13th century. In the late 16th century, licences to make table and window glass were granted to English and continental entrepreneurs. The principal product of those glasshouses situated in or near forests was bottles. The exception may have been that of Abraham Bigo (*fl* 1623–7), which was established *c.* 1623 near Birr and supplied Dublin with window and drinking glass. A government decree of 1641 forbidding the use of wood in furnaces caused a relocation of glasshouses from the forests to ports. Glasshouses had been planned for Dublin from the early 17th century, but it was not until 1675 that a patent was finally granted for

20. Porcelain *Minstrel* comport, h. 304 mm, l. 361 mm, made at the Belleek Porcelain Factory, *c.* 1870 (Dublin, National Museum of Ireland)

the manufacture of 'crystalline glasses resembling rock crystal'. Three lead-glass factories were then established that depended on irregular coal supplies, but produced fine glass. In the 1720s a glass factory was established in Gurteens, near WATERFORD, and production included lead-glass drinking glasses. By 1729 the Round Glass House in Dublin (*see* DUBLIN, §III, 2) was able to advertise such wares as drinking glasses, salvers, baskets with handles and feet for desserts, salts, decanters and lamps.

Throughout the 18th century Irish glassworkers developed their skills in blowing, cutting, engraving and moulding and followed the dictates of the fashionable markets of London and Dublin. Drinking glasses were made in a variety of shapes and were cut or decorated with diamond-point or wheel-engraving; stems were plain baluster shaped or decorated with a 'tear'. From 1746 to 1780 the Irish glass industry was constrained by the order that glass could not be exported from Ireland and that none could be imported into Ireland except through England. In 1771 Benjamin Edwards (*d* 1812) was brought from Bristol by the Tyrone Colleries, and by 1776 he had opened a glass factory in the port of Belfast. From there he advertised enamelled, clear and coloured glass, cut and plain wineglasses, decanters and all kinds of chemical wares. When England crippled its own glass industry with punitive taxes in 1777, other glassworkers, particularly from Bristol and Stourbridge, emigrated to Ireland and established glasshouses for the manufacture of table, ornamental and scientific wares. The glass industry was strengthened by this transfusion of workers from England, and it gained distinction among Irish industries when it was granted permission in 1779–80 to export products to America, the British colonies in the West Indies and Africa, as well as to France, Spain and Portugal. This commercially viable period for Irish glasshouses has been described as the 'age of exuberance' because of the standard and style of the cut-glass decoration. Irish glasshouses were able to specialize in this form of decoration because, unlike England, there was no tax levied on the weight of lead glass, and factories were thus able to produce deeply cut, thick-walled pieces. Cut designs evolved from large flat diamonds, along with horizontal and upright bands, which utilized the soft play of candlelight, to dense patterns of small sharp diamonds and prismatic cutting (see fig. 21), which excelled in gaslight.

Distinctive Irish features and forms also developed, such as the turn-over rim, used on bowls and salt-cellars, and the piggin, a small receptacle for milk or cream that is based on the stave-built wooden pail. The beauty of late 18th-century Irish mirrors lies in the use of a frame embellished with faceted studs and the suspension of a cut-glass half-chandelier in front of the mirror (e.g. c. 1790; Dublin, N. Mus.). Coloured glass was made for epergne liners, salt-cellars, tea-caddies, butter coolers and individual wine-glass coolers. In the late 18th century and the early 19th many Irish factories moulded the fluted bases of such articles as decanters, bowls and goblets, but this cheaper method was used also for such fully moulded tablewares as bottles, decanters, celery glasses, salts and dishes.

By 1825 there were 11 lead-glass factories in full production in Belfast, Dublin, Waterford and Cork (*see* CORK, §1); their size may be gauged by the example of

21. Cut-glass decanter with plain sharp diamonds and flat facets, h. 200 mm, Waterford, c. 1790 (Dublin, National Museum of Ireland)

the Terrace Glass Works in Cork, which employed 24 glassblowers, 16 apprentices and 30 glasscutters, in addition to several clerks, packers and labourers. In the same year the Glass Excise Act was introduced, after which lead glass was taxed in Ireland according to the weight of its metal. Apart from the extra financial burden on the glass factories, the method of tax assessment was so cumbersome that it hampered manufacture. The increasing strength of the English glass industry also had a detrimental effect; the Irish industry began to decline, although it continued in Cork until 1841, Waterford until 1851, Belfast until 1868 and Dublin until 1893. During that period Irish flint glass conformed to the designs fashionable in Britain, yet retained many characteristically Irish cut and moulded motifs and designs. In the late 19th century the Dublin glassworks of T. & R. Pugh produced tableware engraved in Bohemian and Celtic Revival styles. On the establishment of Waterford Glass Ltd in 1947–9, designers studied and produced copies of the 18th-century glass that had made the Waterford name famous. Waterford's international success has encouraged the establishment of many other glass factories in Ireland.

BIBLIOGRAPHY

M. S. D. Westropp: *Irish Glass: An Account of Glass-making in Ireland from the XVIth Century to the Present Day* (London, 1920, rev. Dublin, 1978)
P. Warren: *Irish Glass: The Age of Exuberance* (London, 1970, rev. 1981)
M. Boydell: 'Engravers of Bohemia Working in Ireland and England', *Annals of the 8th Congress of the International Association of Glass History: London and Liverpool, 1981*, pp. 335–43
C. MacLeod: *Glass by Thomas and Richard Pugh in the National Museum of Ireland* (Dublin, 1983)
M. Dunlevy: *Penrose Glass* (Dublin, 1989)

MAIREAD DUNLEVY

IX. Gold and silver.

1. BEFORE 1740. The study of medieval silver in Ireland can be achieved only through tracing the development of the conventional chalice, as no domestic plate survives from this period. The design of the Hubert Walter Chalice (c. 1160), found in Canterbury in 1890, was the model for the design of Irish chalices throughout the 13th century. It comprises a wide, shallow bowl with a rounded plain foot. An early Irish example in the form of a miniature chalice was excavated at Mellifont Abbey, Co. Meath, and assigned to c. 1250 (Dublin, N. Mus.). The bowls of these shallow chalices gradually deepened and grew conical. In the 15th and 16th centuries the bowls became hemispherical. The foot, which had been circular, became hexagonal, in order to avoid the danger of rolling when the chalice was laid on its side to drain into the paten. The stems grew taller and the decorated knop more significant. An example is the De Burgo-O'Malley Chalice (1494; Dublin, N. Mus.), of the English sterling standard; it is inscribed THOMAS DE BURGO ET GRAVINA NI MALLE ME FIERI FECERUNT. Some book shrines and crosses from the 14th and 15th centuries also survive and, together with altar plate, comprise the bulk of the surviving work of medieval Irish silversmiths. There is also a fine example of a mitre and crosier (Limerick, St John's Cathedral) made for Cornelius O'Dea, Bishop of Limerick (*fl* 1400; *d* 1434). It is signed *Thomas O'Carryd Artifex faciens* on the mitre, and the date 1418 appears on both pieces. St Patrick, St

Brigid and St Munchin of Limerick appear on the head of the crosier.

On 22 December 1637 the Company of Goldsmiths of Dublin was formed. It received a royal charter from Charles I that enabled it to regulate the trade throughout Ireland. The charter stipulated that each pound troy of silversmiths' work should contain 11 ounces 2 pennyweight of silver and 18 pennyweight of base metal, usually copper (i.e. 92.5% pure metal). No Irish domestic silver plate made before the mid-17th century survives; in the 1640s the citizens of Dublin were required to submit their plate, gold rings, chains and broken gold for the making and issuing of gold coin to raise funds for Charles I, and the Cromwellian period (1649–60) probably also contributed to the destruction of quantities of gold and silver. It is only from the restoration of the monarchy in 1660 that it is possible to trace the development of the styles and forms of domestic plate.

After c. 1660 the first silver candlesticks appeared. They are usually in the Dutch style with fluted columns and large drip pans or wells at the base of the column, supported on square or hexagonal bases with gadrooned borders. This style was superseded by the baluster shape candlestick at the end of the 17th century. The paten salver—a circular flat dish supported on a central foot—was introduced c. 1660 and was used for serving glasses and probably as a general-purpose tray. These were made until c. 1740 when the central foot began to lose popularity. Salvers were later fitted with three or four legs, and the shape of the tray became more ornamental. Styles in silver during the late 17th century conformed to European and English influences. After the Edict of Nantes in 1685 many Huguenot silver- and goldsmiths arrived, among them Isaac d'Olier, Thomas de Limarest, Timothy Mullineux, Peter Beaulieu and David Romey; they brought with them new forms, including the baluster shape, used particularly for mugs and tankards. A number of pieces made during the reign of William III are extant, for example the mace of the trade guilds of the City of Cork (1696; London, V&A).

After the signing of the Treaty of Limerick on 3 October 1691 a period of peace began that lasted a hundred years. Silversmithing leapt from being a minor craft to a trade that produced splendid domestic silver. Its manufacture continued to increase until it reached its zenith from 1750 to 1800. In 1700 nearly 1 tonne of silverware was manufactured; this increased to 1.7 tonnes by 1725 and gradually rose to over 2.8 tonnes in 1800.

From about 1700 to 1740 domestic silver was made of heavy gauge metal. Plain surfaces and elegant proportions were predominant, the decoration being mostly in the form of crests and coats of arms (e.g. plain caster, 1715–16; London, V&A). Silversmiths produced vast quantities of silver for the dinner- and tea-table, including two-handled cups, often with harp-shaped handles and with slightly tapering sides supported on a squat, moulded foot. Unlike contemporary English examples, Irish two-handled cups were made without covers. As the century progressed the sides of the cups became more tapered, and the base developed a higher step. One of the most popular items in the reign of Queen Anne (reg 1702–14) was the so-called 'strawberry dish', with sides fluted into 16 or 24

panels. These were made in large numbers until the 1730s, but they continued to be made in lesser numbers throughout the 18th century.

Tea had been introduced into Ireland in the mid-17th century, and the first silver teapots appeared c. 1700. They were in use until c. 1730 when they were superseded in popularity by porcelain teapots, and, apart from a few examples manufactured in Cork, they do not seem to have been made between 1730 and 1770. There were originally two basic styles: a bullet shape with a straight spout copied from the globular Chinese porcelain pots popular from c. 1700 to 1730 and a pyriform shape popular from c. 1710 to 1720. In the first half of the 18th century tea was sweetened with sugar held in sugar bowls with removable lids or in plain circular bowls. The lid was often made in the form of a paten salver, which, when inverted, could be used as a stand on which sugar lumps were placed. The first silver cream jugs appeared c. 1732. They are a squat helmet shape and have a central foot (e.g. in Dublin, N. Mus.). This central foot appears to be peculiar to Ireland, and it was not until 1736 that legs appeared on cream jugs.

2. 1740 AND AFTER. By 1740 the elaborate Rococo style, particularly in repoussé decoration, had become fashionable. Coffee was becoming increasingly popular, and the long bodies of coffeepots, together with hot water jugs, were particularly suited to high Rococo decoration. Candlesticks in the Rococo style were produced in large numbers (e.g. made in Dublin by Robert Calderwood, 1746; priv. col.; see fig. 22). From the 1750s human masks began to appear on silver cream jugs with petal-shaped feet. Farmyard scenes became popular from c. 1760. These included cows, sheep and pigs, together with milkmaids, farm buildings, the village church and farmers with their dogs (e.g. sugar bowl with hoof-shaped feet; Dublin, N. Mus.). A typically Irish object produced during this period

22. Silver candlesticks by Robert Calderwood, h. 280 mm, made in Dublin, 1746 (Waterford, private collection)

23. Silver freedom box by Carden Terry and Jane Williams, 22×99×57 mm, made in Cork, 1814 (Washington, DC, National Museum of Women in the Arts)

is the dish ring. As well as being ornamental, these spool-shaped objects were used to protect the polished table from heat. From 1740 they appear with asymmetrical, pierced repoussé work in a great variety of forms with the diameter at the top being narrower than the base (e.g. of 1765; Dublin, N. Mus.).

The Neo-classical style was introduced in Ireland c. 1770, although candlesticks in the form of Corinthian columns were introduced in the late 1750s. The beautiful classical shapes of vessels lent themselves to a new method of decoration known as bright cutting (e.g. sauce tureen made in Dublin, 1787; London, V&A). The variety of engraved designs and motifs includes borders and festoons of husks, palm leaves, lotus flowers and acanthus leaves, together with honeysuckle interspersed with acorns. After 1800 the style began to lose popularity, although it lingered on into the 19th century.

The Act of Union of 1800 had a pernicious effect on the manufacturing industry: Irish silversmiths and allied traders could not compete with cheaper, imported English goods. Patronage was in the hands of a growing middle class of wealthy business and professional people whose tastes were different from those of the aristocracy. In the late 18th century and the early 19th the number of retail shops selling mostly English goods increased, but a few independent silversmiths, for example JAMES LE BAS, continued to operate. Most silver articles were heavy in weight, and there was no particular theme in decoration during the first half of the 19th century. Repoussé chasing with a stippled background was revived.

Freedom boxes were particularly popular in the late 18th century and the early 19th. They are usually in the form of finely engraved snuff- or tobacco boxes and originally contained documents conferring the freedom of a city or town on an important visitor. One made by Aeneas Ryan (1806; London, Apsley House) was presented to Arthur Wellesley, 1st Duke of Wellington. Another example (1814; Washington, DC, N. Mus. Women A.; see fig. 23), made by CARDEN TERRY and

JANE WILLIAMS, is engraved with the coat of arms of the City of Cork and includes a design of Irish harps in the border. The four-piece tea and coffee set, complete with a large tray that could be displayed when not in use on a mahogany sideboard, was also widely used.

The CELTIC REVIVAL style was promoted by international exhibitions in Dublin, including the Great Industrial Exhibition of 1853 and the International Exhibition of Arts and Manufactures of 1865. Many Irish manufacturers, for example G. & S. Waterhouse and James West & Son, produced silverware as well as jewellery in this style. From 1886 Lady Aberdeen (d 1939), the wife of the Lord Lieutenant John Campbell Gordon, 7th Earl of Aberdeen (1847–1934), encouraged cottage industries. In 1894 the Arts & Crafts Society was formed, their first exhibition being held in 1896 at the Royal Dublin Society. Several silversmiths, including Edmond Johnson, West & Son and Hopkins & Hopkins, exhibited sugar bowls, cream jugs and copies of the Ardagh Chalice (8th century; Dublin, N. Mus.).

In the 20th century the Roman Catholic Church, which had begun a spate of building after the Catholic Emancipation Act of 1829, continued to employ craftsmen to manufacture ecclesiastical vessels both for use in Ireland and for Irish Orders in the USA. The Church was one of the main patrons of gold- and silversmiths in the 20th century until Vatican II (1962–5) ordered a reduction in elaborate altar furnishings. To encourage innovative design and to help an ailing gold and silver trade, a commemorative hallmark in the form of *An Claidheamh Solais* ('The Sword of Light') was stamped in 1966 in addition to the existing hallmarks on silver and gold items other than jewellery. A further mark in the form of the 'Glenisheen Collar' was introduced for one year in 1973. There was also a special mark in 1987 to commemorate the 350th anniversary of hallmarking and again in 1989 as part of the celebrations of the Dublin millennium. Important silversmiths working in the late 20th century included Peter Donovan (b 1942), Brian Clarke (b 1947) and Kevin O'Dwyer (b 1953).

See also CORK, §2, DUBLIN, §III, 1 and LIMERICK.

BIBLIOGRAPHY
J. P. Mahaffy and M. S. D. Westropp: *The Plate of Trinity College Dublin* (London, 1918)
J. J. Buckley: *Some Irish Altar Plate* (Dublin, 1943)
K. Ticher, I. Delamer and W. O'Sullivan: *Hallmarks on Dublin Silver* (Dublin, 1968)
Irish Silver, 1630–1820 (exh. cat., intro. G. Dawson; Dublin, Trinity Coll., 1971)
D. Bennett: *Irish Georgian Silver* (London, 1972)
R. W. Jackson: *Irish Silver* (Dublin, 1972)
K. Ticher: *Irish Silver in the Rococo Period* (Dublin, 1972)
Irish Hallmarks on Gold and Silver (Dublin, 1972)
D. Bennett: *Irish Silver*, Irish Her. Ser., vii (Dublin, 1976)
J. Teahan: *Irish Silver*, Dublin, N. Mus. cat. (Dublin, 1979)
Irish Silver: From the Seventeenth to the Nineteenth Century (exh. cat. by J. Teahan, New York, Cooper-Hewitt Mus., 1982)
D. Bennett: *Collecting Irish Silver* (London, 1984)
The Company of Goldsmiths of Dublin, 1637–1987 (exh. cat. by J. Teahan and D. Bennett, Dublin, N. Mus., 1987)
D. Bennett: *The Silver Collection, Trinity College, Dublin*, Trinity Coll. Dublin, Quartercenten. Ser., i (Dublin, 1988)
——: *The Encyclopaedia of Dublin* (Dublin, 1991)

DOUGLAS BENNETT

X. Objects of vertu.

Trade and street directories as well as legal documents show that a wide range of luxury objects were made in Ireland. To supplement local expertise and to ensure a similar standard and style to that produced in London and Paris, specialist craftsmen were attracted from abroad. Although the production of objects of vertu in Ireland is indisputable, it seems that these small objects may have remained so faithful to the style of their foreign counterparts that few have been recognized, unlike furniture and silver, which had distinctive Irish styles. A case in point is seal-engravers: although mentioned regularly in trade lists, their work has been identified only through the motifs or arms used. Yet it was Dr Henry Quin (*fl* 1760s–*c*. 1788), the Regius Professor at the College of Physicians, Dublin, who developed a method of copying antique gems in paste. Quin, a correspondent of Josiah Wedgwood, employed James Tassie as an assistant. Although Tassie left Dublin in 1766, he remained in regular correspondence with Quin throughout his highly successful career. Similarly, ivory turned in Ireland is recognized principally because of its occurrence on Irish musical instruments.

The strength of the Irish decorative art movement is evident in the independent development around 1748 by Samuel Dixon (*fl* 1748; *d* 1768–9) of embossed paper pictures. These were hand-coloured by miniaturists trained at the Dublin Society School (*see* DUBLIN, §II). Dixon followed the illustrations in George Edwards's *Natural History of Uncommon Birds* (London, 1743–51), and the pictures were sold as being not just decorative but also suitable for copying by embroiderers, japanners and shellworkers. His success was such that he had many emulators, or competitors, within a few years.

Jewellery followed foreign fashions so closely that it is difficult to identify Irish examples unless they are clearly marked as such. The standard of craftsmanship was high, however, as shown by the brooch designed by Frederic William Burton and made in gold with white enamel by Edmond Johnson in Dublin (1846–7; Dublin, N. Mus.). A robust piece with Greek masks, coiled snakes and a tragic maiden, it was presented to the actress Helen Faucit for her performance as Antigone.

Jewellery carrying the symbolism of the emerging Irish nation mirrors the growth of that movement. An early example is a gold harp brooch set with rubies, pearls and emeralds in a shamrock shape, reputedly made for and presented by the patriot Robert Emmet to his intended Sarah Curran about 1802 (Cork, Pub. Mus.). From 1848 the growth of interest in the CELTIC REVIVAL was such that designs for copies of brooches of the 8th and 9th centuries AD were registered for mass production as shawl brooches, pins and buckles. Copies and interpretations of Irish Bronze Age jewellery were also made.

BIBLIOGRAPHY
A. K. Longfield: 'Samuel Dixon's Embossed Pictures', *J. Royal Soc. Antiqua. Ireland*, xcvi (1966), pp. 133–40
J. Sheehy: *The Rediscovery of Ireland's Past* (London, 1980)
B. de Breffny, ed.: *Ireland: A Cultural Encyclopaedia* (London, 1983)

XI. Textiles.

The spinning-wheel, horizontal treadle loom and fulling-mill were probably introduced to Ireland about the 13th century. The Guild or Fraternity of Weavers, founded in Dublin in 1446, augured further change through its control of weaving standards, apprenticeship and payment. In the medieval period Ireland was known for its manufacture and export of high-quality weather-proofed woollens. Felt in its smooth and tufted forms (in which jogs of wool were worked into the felt during manufacture) was particularly popular in late medieval Ireland. Irish wool mantles—known then as 'rugg mantles'—were in demand in continental Europe, particularly in the early 16th century when furred mantles (sometimes with the fur on the outside) were in fashion. This cheap alternative was woven in a tabby weave, and the nap then drawn with cards and curled to resemble the wool of sheepskin. During this period it seems that domestic weavers produced a wide variety of woollens, varying from coarse, heavy tabbies to fabrics with sophisticated weaves and decorative patterns. Although the manufacture of finer woollens and draperies was adversely affected by Acts of Parliament of 1698–9, which were intended to protect the English woollen industry, local manufacturers continued to supply the home market with wool carpets and tapestries as well as dress and furnishing fabrics.

Linen was another traditional fabric, since linen tunics had been worn by both sexes from early times. It remained important in the medieval period, when Irish men's shirts required over 30 m of fabric and women's smocks and headdresses were voluminous. Apart from this considerable home market, linen yarn, linen cloth and canvas were also produced for export in the 16th century. The weaving of linen for commercial markets was encouraged in the 17th century, so the industry was well established before Louis Crommelin arrived in 1698 with his Huguenot followers; he introduced the skill of weaving fine linen. A further development was the establishment in 1711 of the Irish Linen Board, which subsidized and regulated the industry and facilitated exports. A wide variety of linens were then in demand, including damasks for table-cloths, lawns or cambric for handkerchiefs and diapers for bed-linens. The Linen Board also gave encouragement to linen printed in the style of chintz, which was used for dress fabrics and furnishings.

By the end of the 18th century the linen industry began to suffer from competition with cotton. For a time, linen and cotton were woven together (see fig. 24) in a union fabric, but when suitable machinery was imported *c*. 1780 cotton was mass-produced and was consequently cheap and popular. Large factories were established in many parts of the country. Linen was able to compete again only when wet-spinning machinery was introduced *c*. 1825, allowing fine yarn to be spun by machine. The introduction of the Jacquard loom about this time simplified the production of figured fabrics. By the 1850s power-looms were able to weave fine linens, and Ulster then supplied the markets of the world. A cottage industry also evolved, particularly in Donegal and other northern areas, for decorating household linens with white embroidery and drawn-thread work.

A fabric that was affected by the development of the linen and cotton industry, and by the subsequent change in fashion, was silk. It is not known when silk was first woven in Ireland, though archaeological evidence shows

24. Furnishing fabric, cotton and linen mixture printed in manganese using copper plates, by Robinson of Ballsbridge, Dublin, pattern repeat 711×762 mm, *c.* 1780 (Dublin, National Museum of Ireland)

that imported silk trimmings were used as early as the 11th century. It is probable that ribbon silk was woven in Ireland before broad-loom silk-weaving was introduced in the early 17th century. Huguenot immigrants, fleeing France after the Revocation of the Edict of Nantes in 1685, seem to have given the industry an important fillip.

The Irish silk industry prospered, despite competition from imported silks and occasional internal upsets, for example that caused by the introduction of labour-saving machinery in 1763. The Irish Parliament encouraged the industry, and in 1765 the Hibernian Silk Warehouse was established in Dublin to promote the fabric. The silk industry survived until the 1820s, but poplin, being more heavily capitalized, survived longer. David Digues de la Touche, a banker, is given credit for the introduction of poplin in the late 17th century. Combining the strength of a wool weft and the visual appeal of a silk warp, Irish poplin became a popular dress fabric. A related poplin, in which the silk warp was woven with a wool, linen or heavy cotton weft, was in demand for furnishings. The introduction of the Jacquard loom in the early 19th century facilitated the weaving of poplin in plaid and brocade designs as well as the usual plain and moiré. By the 1860s Dublin poplin manufacturers could boast that their fabric was used to furnish the courts of Europe. Dress poplin was also in demand, but later the draped gowns of the 1880s required a lighter wool. The use of Australian merino wool satisfied this requirement.

Another luxury textile was lace. Metal lace—gold and silver—was made by lacemen from at least the 16th century. There is documentation that the making of linen lace was taught in Ireland from the early 17th century: bobbin lace

from 1636, lacis by 1644 and needlepoint by 1662. Because bobbin lace was relatively easy to make, its manufacture was encouraged in charity schools; the Dublin Society offered awards from 1740 in an attempt to improve the standard of design. The Society also encouraged the manufacture of needlepoint among the more affluent classes. Its success was short-lived: changing fashion and an Irish penchant for the imported meant that by the late 18th century local production was again confined to charity institutions making bobbin lace and knitted lace trimmings.

The laces with which Ireland is principally identified are those of the 19th century. John Heathcoat's invention in 1808–9 of a machine to make cotton net gave rise to embroidered net laces at Carrickmacross, Co. Monaghan (*c.* 1820), Kells, Co. Meath (1825), and Limerick (1829). Carrickmacross lace is appliqué cambric on net; Limerick is tambour (chain stitch) and run (darn) on net; and both styles were worked at Kells. A wide variety of lace types were produced on country estates under the supervision of philanthropic ladies. Needle lace, based mainly on 17th-century raised Venetian lace, was made at several convent schools, notably the Presentation Convent at Youghal, where it was developed during the 1850s. Its most successful period was during the 1880s and 1890s when, under the direction of James Brenan of the Cork School of Art, new designs were worked in a form of flat needle lace richly decorated with fillings.

Crochet was widely practised during the Great Famine of the 1840s. It had previously been taught in schools using woollen yarn, and the Ursuline Convent at Blackrock, Co. Cork, introduced an interpretation of needlepoint using a crochet hook and linen thread. This technique was also adopted in Co. Kildare and Clones, Co. Monaghan, and in many other convent and Church of Ireland controlled centres. As crochet-work was easily learnt and required little capital investment, it could compete with machine-lace; it was still encouraged as a cottage industry in the early 20th century, particularly in the west of Ireland.

The cottage-industry system was used also for embroideries, in a variety of styles including sprigging (white cotton thread on white linen, often in floral designs), Mountmellick (white knitting cotton on white satin jean in wild-flower designs), Marlfield (coloured wool on wool in Art Nouveau designs) and Kells (wool on wool in Celtic Revival designs). In contrast, the Royal Irish School of Art Needlework in Dublin worked decorative embroideries in the style of their sister school in London. The awakening of a spirit of national identity in the 19th century, coupled with an appreciation of the ideals of the Arts and Crafts Movement in Britain and the designs of the Art Nouveau movement, gave rise to such workshops as that of the Dun Emer Guild, Dublin, which produced quality carpets, tapestries, embroideries etc, frequently in Celtic Revival designs.

Changes in men's outdoor clothing created a demand for homespun weather-proof fabrics in the 1880s. For these, the wool was carded, spun and woven in the traditional way in cottages. To increase the farmer's earning power, the Congested Districts Board introduced *c.* 1893 a loom that was small enough to fit into a cottage home and cheap enough to be purchased by the farmer–weaver. Tweeds continued to be woven on such looms in Donegal in the late 20th century, though changes in living styles from the 1950s encouraged the introduction of lighter-weight tweeds. The Irish linen industry also enjoyed a revival in the late 20th century, when Irish linen was in demand in fashion capitals throughout the world.

BIBLIOGRAPHY

A. K. Longfield: 'History of the Irish Linen and Cotton Printing Industry in the 18th Century', *J. Royal Soc. Antiqua. Ireland*, lxvii (1937), pp. 26–56
——: *Guide to the Collection of Lace*, Dublin, N. Mus. (Dublin, 1942, rev. 1970)
E. Boyle: *The Irish Flowerers* (Belfast, 1971)
M. Reynolds: *Some Irish Fashions and Fabrics, c. 1775–1928* (Dublin, 1984)
W. H. Crawford: *The Irish Linen Industry* (Belfast, 1987)
J. Hoad: *This Is Donegal Tweed* (Inver, 1987)
M. Dunlevy: 'Irish Lace: A Beautiful Craft Revived', *Ireland Welcomes*, xxxviii (1989), pp. 21–7
L. Ballard: *Ulster Needlework: A Continuing Tradition* (Belfast, 1990)
M. Haslam: *Arts & Crafts Carpets* (London, 1991)

MAIREAD DUNLEVY

XII. Patronage.

In early medieval Ireland, the most important patrons of the arts were the monasteries, although these foundations were themselves often wholly under the control of local ruling Gaelic families. Early in the 12th century, for example, Cormac mac Carrthach, King of Desmond and Bishop of Cashel, gave the royal site of the kings of Munster at Cashel to the Church. After the invasions of the late 12th century, the new Anglo-Norman lords provided furnishings, on the English model, for many monastic and cathedral foundations, mostly in eastern Ireland, and during the Gaelic recovery of the 15th century, Gaelic chieftains endowed new friaries, mainly in the west of Ireland. In the Tudor re-conquest of the 16th century, many new powerful English landowners arrived, such as Richard Boyle, 1st Earl of Cork (*see* BOYLE, (1)), who became a major patron of tomb sculpture (*see* §IV, 1 above). Wealthy merchants in cities such as Galway and Kilkenny also patronized architecture and decorative sculpture, but wars and insecurity generally militated against the exercise of patronage in Tudor and early Stuart Ireland.

At the Restoration in 1660, the Viceroy, JAMES BUTLER, 1st Duke of Ormonde, emerged as a major supporter of the arts, both personally and on behalf of the State. He was the moving force, for example, behind the establishment (1680) of the Royal Hospital at Kilmainham, with its superb wood-carvings and portraits. The government welcomed Huguenot immigrants and their craft skills. Building in the 17th century was limited, however, and it was not until the 1730s that there was another period of significant artistic patronage, by which time the Protestant Ascendancy had been consolidated. Grand Tourists such as JAMES CAULFEILD, 1st Earl of Charlemont, JOSEPH LEESON, 1st Earl of Milltown, and FREDERICK AUGUSTUS HERVEY, 4th Earl of Bristol and Bishop of Derry, commissioned architecture and sculpture from Irish and foreign artists, as well as being important collectors. The State also supported a number of building schemes in Dublin in the late 18th century, including the Castle, the Houses of Parliament, the Custom House and Four Courts, with their ornamental carvings and plasterwork,

ceiling paintings and tapestries; outside Dublin, corporations in various towns and the Anglican Church of Ireland commissioned civic buildings and plate. Church memorials and portrait busts, on the other hand, were generally paid for by individual patrons. The luxury crafts of metalworking, glasscutting, silk-weaving and cabinetmaking also responded to the new demands of a wealthy clientele centred on court life in Dublin, with immigrant and local artists and craftsmen supplying this demand.

The removal of power to London with the Act of Union of 1801 severely damaged this patronage, which even the new professional middle classes could not altogether replace. In the years after its foundation in Dublin in 1823, for example, the sales of pictures at the Royal Hibernian Academy were never high. The art unions, which distributed pictures by lottery, maintained a certain level of sales, and some artists earned a steady income from commissions for portraits in oils and sculpted busts, but generally Irish private and civic patronage was very limited. Even the beneficial effects of the Industrial Revolution were confined to the Belfast region, where some industrial patrons emerged. The resurgent Roman Catholic Church was by far the most important patron of the 19th century for buildings and furnishings, although much of the stained glass it commissioned was imported. In the early 20th century, however, the Irish cultural revival led to increased support for the arts and crafts, notably for church interiors. A notable patron in this period was the collector HUGH LANE, who commissioned John Butler Yeats and William Orpen to paint a series of portraits of important social figures. After 1922 the new Irish Free State was innovative in its support for a large series of descriptive paintings of the River Shannon hydroelectric scheme; these were commissioned by the Electricity Supply Board from John Keating during the 1920s. The new State could be an enlightened patron, as exemplified by the Irish Pavilion at the New York World's Fair of 1939. Nevertheless, it was not until 1951, with the establishment of the Irish Arts Council, that the State became fully active in artistic patronage, strongly favouring paintings by modernist artists, notably the work of Louis Le Brocquy. New business collectors commissioned works in the 1960s, and by the 1980s major corporate sponsors of the arts had emerged as patrons. Collections of modern art were formed by the Bank of Ireland and Allied Irish Bank. In the 1960s Carrolls endowed prizes; in the 1980s Guinness Peat Aviation and in the 1990s Glen Dimplex have sponsored awards.

BIBLIOGRAPHY

S. Madden: *Reflections and Resolutions Proper to the Gentlemen of Ireland, as to their Conduct for the Service of their Country* (Dublin, 1738)
W. P. Carey: *Some Memoirs of the Patronage and Progress of the Fine Art in England and Ireland* (London, 1826)
T. Bodkin: *Hugh Lane and his Pictures* (Dublin, 1932)
A. Crookshank: 'Portraits of Irish Houses', *Bull. Irish Georg. Soc.*, v (1962), p. 41
——: 'Lord Cork and his Monuments', *Country Life*, cxlix (27 May 1971), pp. 1288–90
B. de Breffny: *Ireland: A Cultural Encyclopaedia* (London, 1983)
B. Lynch: 'Irish Patrons and Collectors of Indian Art', *G. P. A. Irish A. Rev. Yb.* (1988), pp. 169–84

JOHN TURPIN

XIII. *Collecting and dealing.*

Given the troubled history of the country since the arrival of the Anglo-Normans, it is not surprising that for a long time collecting in Ireland remained sparse. During the 17th century, however, increasing numbers of English and Scottish settlers in Ireland led to a growth in domestic architecture and with it the accumulation of decorative art. Chinese, Dutch and Irish (particularly by Henry Delamain (*see* §VII, 2 above) in Dublin; examples in Dublin, N. Mus.) ceramics were widely collected, particularly in the 18th century. Increasing travel to England, in particular to London, and to continental Europe in the 18th century also presented opportunities for the acquisition of works of art, which were transported back to Ireland. As with the English, Italy was a favourite destination, and Irish aristocrats commissioned portraits by Italian artists in Rome: Robert Clements, 1st Earl of Leitrim, for example, commissioned his own portrait from Pompeo Batoni (1753–4; priv. col.). Other important and active 18th-century collectors in Ireland included JAMES CAULFEILD, 1st Earl of Charlemont, whose portrait was also painted by Batoni (1754; New Haven, CT, Yale Cent. Brit. A.), JOSEPH LEESON, 1st Earl of Milltown, Frederick Augustus Hervey (*see* HERVEY, (1)), 4th Earl of Bristol and Bishop of Derry, and the Dukes of Leinster. One of the most valuable cargoes of statuary returning from the Continent was lost in a storm in Dublin Bay.

The Act of Union reduced the importance of Dublin and made it less attractive to the fashionable. A new native Irish professional and business class was established in the mid-19th century, but while the Anglo-Irish aristocracy remained for at least part of the year in Ireland, a sense of decay and neglect due to the poor economy, as much as anything else, was obvious. The new society surrounded themselves with old objects from a former era and helped stimulate the CELTIC REVIVAL, which expressed a mixture of nationalism and progress. The Gothic, Norman and Elizabethan revivals in England in the 1830s and 1840s were also echoed in Ireland and led to a new interest in archaeology. The discovery of the ancient Tara Brooch and its reproduction and presentation at the Great Exhibition (1851) in London gave impetus to a native art influenced by the Celtic Revival. By the late 19th century, with more widespread education and a greater distribution of wealth, the native Irish were also active in fine art markets, purchasing the objects dispersed at the increasing auction sales of the contents of the established older family homes and collecting the work of such Irish artists as Walter Frederick Osborne, John Lavery, William Orpen, Jack B. Yeats, Paul Henry, John Keating and Frank McKelvey. At about the same time large amounts of 18th-century furniture and other artefacts were increasingly exported from Ireland, especially to the USA, and the country became more and more attractive to foreign dealers and collectors because of the cheapness, quantity and excellent quality of the pieces available. Exports began to exceed imports in a ratio of 10:1, a trend only reversed in the late 20th century. The exporting and importing of works of art have not been legally forbidden, but the imposition of Value Added Tax (VAT), together with loss

of parity with sterling, continued to prove a grave disincentive to importation until 1990, when the rate of VAT on paintings, sculpture and certain articles of antique status (over 100 years) was reduced to 10%. Provisions for preventing national treasures from leaving Ireland have not proved effective, however, although the National Gallery of Ireland is responsible for approving the export of works of art, and even ancient Celtic gold objects have been exported and sold on the London market.

At the end of the 20th century, however, an increasing awareness of the investment value of art works and a growing interest in the preservation of objects of cultural interest were becoming evident. A new class of wealthy international businessman–collector grew up, including Michael Smurfit (*b* 1938), Tony Ryan (*b* 1936) and A. W. F. O'Reilly (*b* 1936), all of whom collected Irish and international art. Corporate support of the arts was also increasing, with the principal banks, such as the Bank of Ireland and the Allied Irish Bank, and many private firms forming collections.

BIBLIOGRAPHY
J. Chapel and C. Gere: *The Art Collections of Britain and Ireland* (New York, 1986)
K. Hudson and A. Nicholls: *The Cambridge Guide to the Museums of Britain and Ireland* (Cambridge, 1987)
B. Arnold: *The Art Atlas of Britain and Ireland* (London, 1991)
BRIAN COYLE

XIV. *Museums.*

The first important museums were established in Dublin in the 19th century. The National Gallery of Ireland, founded by Acts of the British Parliament in 1854, 1855 and 1865, was opened in 1864 and houses a distinguished collection of Old Master paintings and drawings. The National Museum of Ireland (founded in 1877) contains much prehistoric and medieval Irish art, as well as later Irish glass and silver. In 1908, as part of a major effort to introduce the public to French modernism, the Municipal Gallery of Modern Art was opened in Dublin. In 1975 it was renamed after its first benefactor, HUGH LANE, and it occupies an extension to the Georgian Charlemont House in Parnell Square. Trinity College Library, Dublin, although not officially a museum, contains a notable collection of manuscripts, including the Book of Kells (Dublin, Trinity Coll. Lib., MS. 58) and a Matthew Paris manuscript, displays of which are regularly mounted. In 1991 a new Irish Museum of Modern Art was opened at the historic Royal Hospital at Kilmainham, Dublin. Outside Dublin, the Crawford Municipal Art Gallery (founded in 1884), Cork, originally shared a building with the School of Art there, the studios of which were later converted into spacious modern galleries. The City Gallery of Art, Limerick, was opened in 1948, and the Sligo Museum and Art Gallery in 1955; the latter contains a collection of paintings by Jack B. Yeats.

Art museums set up through the generosity of modern benefactors include the Chester Beatty Library and Gallery of Oriental Art (1954), Dublin, which also includes a quantity of medieval and Renaissance European material; the Hunt Museum (1978), Plassey House, Limerick, which houses the John and Gertrude Hunt collection of medieval Irish and other European art and artefacts; and the Glebe

Gallery (1983), Donegal, which displays a collection of modern art presented to the Irish nation by the painter Derek Hill. Lively galleries devoted to temporary exhibitions, mainly of contemporary art, include the Douglas Hyde Gallery, Trinity College, Dublin, and the Guinness Gallery, Dublin.

BIBLIOGRAPHY

W. G. Strickland: 'Art Institutions in Ireland', *A Dictionary of Irish Artists* (Dublin, 1913), ii, p. 579
S. Popplewell, ed.: *The Irish Museums Guide* (Dublin, 1983)
Directory of Irish Museums (Dublin, 1983)
Report on Collecting Activities in Museums of Fine Art in Ireland. Working Papers of the International Committee for Museums of Fine Art: Dublin, 1983
J. Abse: *The Art Galleries of Britain and Ireland* (London, 1985)
J. Chapel and C. Gere: *The National Art-Collections Fund Book of Art Galleries and Museums: The Fine and Decorative Art Collections of Britain and Ireland* (London, 1985)
K. Hudson and A. Nicholls: *The Cambridge Guide to the Museums of Britain and Ireland* (Cambridge, 1987)

MARTYN ANGLESEA

XV. Art education.

The emergence of formally trained Irish-born artists dates from the 18th century, when it was stimulated by improved patronage by the landed class and by the instruction given by the Dublin Society. The Society, founded in 1731, began supporting the drawing school of ROBERT WEST in 1746 and had absorbed it by 1750. A school of ornamental drawing under James Mannin (*d* 1779) was added in 1756; a school of architectural drawing under THOMAS IVORY in 1764; and a school of modelling under EDWARD SMYTH in 1811. The training, inspired by contemporary French practice, gave artists and artisans an understanding of continental styles of art and design, through copying engravings and drawings, and contributed greatly to the quality of 18th-century Irish silversmithing, furniture-carving, plasterwork and the building trades. The teaching of craft skills, however, was by apprenticeship, controlled by the guilds. Painting skills were acquired by working with Irish practitioners or by work or study abroad in England or Italy, while sculptural techniques were learnt in the artisan yard, and architectural education was acquired by apprenticeship in an architect's office.

In the 19th century various design schools were established, based on British models. The Board of Trade in London took over the control and funding of the Dublin Society Schools in 1849 as a school of design, although the Society retained managerial independence until 1877, when it became the Dublin Metropolitan School of Art under the Department of Science and Art in London. In the late 19th century under its headmaster, James Brenan, women were admitted, and lace-making was developed. In 1850 a School of Design was set up in the Royal Cork Institution, replacing the short-lived drawing academy founded by the Cork Society for the Promotion of the Fine Arts in 1818. It was funded municipally from 1856. In 1884 purpose-built studios and an art gallery were opened in Nelson Place (now Emmet Place), Cork, where the school remained until 1979, when it moved to new premises. From 1884 it was also a centre for lace design, having links with nine Munster convent schools, although painting and sculpture remained its chief concerns. In the 1850s the Board of Trade also began supporting a school of practical art at Waterford (from 1852; refounded in 1881 as part of the Municipal School) and a school of ornamental art at Limerick (from 1854; adopted by the corporation in 1896). In 1854 there was also a school of art at the Mechanics Institute of Clonmel. For all these schools, the support of the Science and Art Department was vital in the years before municipal ratepayers took over the burden of financing them.

Fine art education in Ireland in the 19th century was the domain of the Royal Hibernian Academy (R.H.A.). Established in 1823, it maintained a Life and Antique School in Dublin from 1829; by the 1830s this School was the main centre. Leading Irish artists, notably WALTER FREDERICK OSBORNE in the 1890s, were visiting teachers at the R.H.A. Schools, which functioned until 1941. By 1914 the teaching of WILLIAM ORPEN at the rival Dublin Metropolitan School of Art had made the latter the centre of fine art studies in Ireland. In 1936 it was renamed the National College of Art, offering diplomas in painting, sculpture and design. During the 1950s crafts such as pottery, stained glass, metalwork and lithography were added. The leading teachers were JOHN KEATING and Maurice MacGonigal (1900–79) in painting, OLIVER SHEPPARD, Friedrich Herkner (1902–86) and Domhnall O'Murchadha (1914–91) in sculpture, and Harry Clarke (*see* CLARKE, (2)) and Bernardus Romein (1894–1962) in design. In architectural education there was a major development towards the end of the 19th century, when the Dublin Municipal Technical School was set up in 1887, offering a broad range of teaching for its trainees. Qualification was through the examinations of the Royal Institute of Architects of Ireland (founded 1839) or the London-based RIBA. From 1917 architecture was also taught at University College, Dublin.

The teaching of art history at university level began in 1935, with the Purser-Griffith lecture series on European painting at University College, Dublin. This led to the foundation of an art-history department there in 1965. The Trinity College department was founded in 1963. In the 1960s there were major developments in art education. A critical report, *Design in Ireland*, was produced by a group of Scandinavian designers in 1962, and it was echoed by other government reports of the 1960s. Student unrest at the National College of Art between 1967 and 1971, prompted by frustration with the College's conservative teaching methods and excessive bureaucratic control, led to the re-establishment of the College under its own statute in 1971. Elsewhere in Ireland regional technical colleges were set up from 1969. Those at Waterford, Galway, Sligo and Letterkenny included art departments that were primarily orientated towards either the fine arts or crafts, while the long-established art schools at Cork and Limerick, the College of Marketing and Design in Dublin with its first design courses in 1962, and the Dun Laoghaire School of Art, which emerged during the early 1960s from a technical school, all flowered from the 1970s onwards.

BIBLIOGRAPHY

Strickland: 'Art Institutions in Ireland', ii, pp. 579–91
H. F. Berry: *A History of the Royal Dublin Society* (London, 1915)
Design in Ireland (Dublin, 1962)
J. Fowler: 'Art Colleges in Southern Ireland: Against the Odds', *Circa*, xxiv (1985)

J. Turpin: 'The Ghost of South Kensington: The Beginnings of Irish State Qualifications in Art, 1900–1936', *Oideas*, xxx (1987)

P. Murray: 'Cork Art, 1800–1900', *Illustrated Summary Catalogue of the Crawford Municipal Art Gallery* (Cork, 1991)

J. Turpin: 'The Royal Hibernian Academy Schools: The First Eighty Years, 1826–1906', *Irish A. Rev. Yb.* (1991), pp. 198–209

——: 'Irish Art and Design Education', *Irish A. Rev. Yb.* (1994), pp. 209–16

——: *A School of Art in Dublin since the Eighteenth Century: A History of the National College of Art and Design* (Dublin, 1995)

JOHN TURPIN

XVI. Art libraries and photographic collections.

Libraries with important collections of art and architecture are mainly confined to Dublin. Trinity College, Dublin, a British copyright library since 1801, is an essential resource; its acquisition of material from outside the copyright territory has reflected the requirements of the College's art history courses. University College, Dublin, with similar courses, has a particularly important architectural library, and the Bolton Street College of Technology in Dublin also has a good architecture collection, while the collection of the library of the National Gallery of Ireland naturally has an emphasis on Irish art. The purchasing policy of the National Library of Ireland in the late 20th century also concentrated on titles relating to Ireland. The Chester Beatty Library, Dublin, specializes in Oriental material, while the National College of Art and Design, also in Dublin, is strong in its coverage of 20th-century material as well as having an important collection relating to Irish art and design. All of the institutions teaching art and architecture also have slide collections, and the Irish Architectural Archive in Dublin has an important photographic collection relating to Irish architecture, which is being developed on a systematic basis.

EDWARD MURPHY

XVII. Historiography.

The antiquarian movement of the late 18th century stimulated scholarly study of Irish art and architecture. In the 1790s FRANCIS GROSE began *The Antiquities of Ireland* (1791), and Anthony Pasquin (John Williams) published his *Memoirs of the Royal Academicians and an Authentic History of The Artists in Ireland* (1796). W. Carey's *Some Memoirs of the Patronage and Progress of the Fine Arts in England and Ireland* appeared in 1826, and from the mid-19th century romantic cultural nationalism stimulated further writings on Irish art: by GEORGE PETRIE in the *Irish Penny Journal*, by Thomas Davis in the newspaper *The Nation*, and by G. Mulvany in *The Citizen*. Gradually, a case was made for the distinct identity of Irish art and artists, considered hitherto as part of the history of British art. This essentially biographical approach was continued in a series of articles by Sarah Atkinson in the *Quarterly Review*, together with a few monographs by others. In conjunction with primary documents, these secondary sources were used by Walter Strickland for his magnificent and scholarly *Dictionary of Irish Artists* (1913), which became the foundation for all subsequent research. The case for the separate identity of Irish landscape painting was made in 1920 by Thomas Bodkin, who wrote extensively on a wide range of art-historical topics.

The main figure in Irish art-historical scholarship since the 1930s was Françoise Henry, a French scholar who published extensively on illuminated manuscripts and other early medieval subjects. Henry was an influential teacher of Irish art history at University College, Dublin. From the 1960s the leading scholar at Trinity was Anne Crookshank; *The Painters of Ireland* (1978), by Crookshank and Desmond Fitzgerald, the Knight of Glin, was a milestone in the country's art history. Monographic catalogues of exhibitions devoted to Irish art and artists held at the National Gallery of Ireland since the early 1970s made substantial contributions to historiography, as did the three concise catalogues published in the 1980s of the National Gallery's own permanent collection. The development of Irish architectural writing followed from the lead given by the Georgian Society, which published five volumes between 1909 and 1913, and by the numerous publications of Harold Leask and Maurice Craig from the 1940s. The history of design and the decorative arts has also developed since the 1980s. The publication of the *Irish Arts Review*, initially under the editorship of Brian de Breffney, has greatly increased the documentation of the fine and decorative arts.

JOHN TURPIN

Ireland, Northern [Ulster]. Region of the United Kingdom, occupying the north-east section of the island of Ireland. Extending for more than 160 km from east to west and 145 km from north to south, Northern Ireland includes the Sperrin, Mourne and Antrim mountains around an area of lowland, at the centre of which is Lough Neagh, with an area of 400 sq. km. The capital, BELFAST, lies at the head of Belfast Lough (see fig. 1 above). In the late 20th century the population of Northern Ireland was *c*. 1.6 million, made up of three principal groups: those of Celtic or Gaelic descent, who are mainly Roman Catholic; those of lowland Scottish descent, who are mainly Presbyterian; and those of English and Welsh descent, who are mainly Anglican. This article discusses art in Northern Ireland from 1922; for a discussion of art in the region before this date *see* IRELAND.

1. Introduction. 2. Architecture. 3. Painting, graphic arts and sculpture. 4. Decorative arts. 5. Art institutions.

1. INTRODUCTION. Northern Ireland comprises six of the nine counties that made up the ancient Irish kingdom of Ulster. In 1922, when the Irish Free State was established, the majority of the population of these six counties preferred to remain within the United Kingdom. This led to a long-standing conflict ('the Troubles') between these Unionists and Northern Ireland's minority nationalist community, particularly from the late 1960s. There was nevertheless a flowering of talent and a growth of interest in and appreciation of the arts, particularly in the second half of the 20th century. Various influences contributing to this process can be identified: the patronage and careful nurturing of the arts by the Arts Council of Northern Ireland; access to collections and exhibitions at the Ulster Museum in Belfast and at galleries elsewhere; developments in education, which have helped to create among the young a climate more receptive to the arts; and

the stimulus to creative activity and awareness that seems to accompany periods of communal anxiety or stress.

BIBLIOGRAPHY

S. H. Bell, N. A. Robb and J. Hewitt: *The Arts in Ulster* (London, 1951)
M. Longley, ed.: *Causeway: The Arts in Ulster* (Belfast, 1971)
J. Hewitt and M. A. Catto: *Art in Ulster*, 2 vols (Belfast, 1977, rev. 1991)

BRIAN FERRAN

2. ARCHITECTURE. In the two decades following the partition of Ireland in 1922, the newly established government of Northern Ireland conducted a comprehensive building campaign under the direction of its chief architect, Roland Ingleby Smith (1882–1942), who had arrived from England to take up the post. Many police stations and a number of new post offices, telephone exchanges, employment exchanges, educational buildings and servicemen's houses were built across the country, almost all in a rustic Neo-Georgian style and usually in brick or white-painted roughcast. Stranmillis College (1928–30), Belfast, is an outstanding example of the work produced in Smith's Belfast office. The two most important public buildings of the new state were, however, designed by outside architects: the Parliament Buildings (1927–32) at Stormont, Co. Down, near Belfast, by Arnold Thornely (1870–1953) of Liverpool, and the Royal Courts of Justice (1928–33), Belfast, by James G. West of London. Both were built of Portland stone in full-blooded classical style. Some form of Neo-Georgian or restrained classical style prevailed for the secular work of most local architects between the two World Wars, as exemplified by the Sir William Whitla Hall at Queen's University, Belfast, designed by John MacGeagh (1901–85) in 1937. St Malachy's Roman Catholic Church (1937), Coleraine, Co. Londonderry, by Padraig Gregory (1886–1962), is one of the most impressive large churches in a neo-Romanesque style, while St Patrick's Memorial Church (1933) at Saul, Co. Down, by Henry Seaver (1860–1941), is a rare example of Celtic Revivalism, characterized by a belfry in the form of an Early Christian Irish round tower. The schools designed in the 1920s and 1930s for the Belfast Education Committee by Reginald S. Wilshere (1888–1961), who arrived from England in 1926, form an important series. Almost all in rustic brick, they range from the Neo-Georgian Strandtown Primary School (1928–30) to the more Modernist Botanic Primary School (1936–9).

Wartime restrictions and shortages largely curtailed building in the 1940s, except for government-sponsored factories—which were usually built with rustic brick in a pre-war Modernist style, as at the Down Shoe Factory (1949), Banbridge, Co. Down, by W. D. R. Taggart (1872–1940) and R. T. Taggart—and much-needed housing estates erected by the newly formed Northern Ireland

1. James C. Wynnes: Ulster Museum, Belfast, 1924–9; to the left is the extension by Francis Pym, 1963–71

Housing Trust. The estates were usually in roughcast in a conventional domestic idiom, but the best example, the large Cregagh Estate (1945–50), Belfast, designed for the Trust by T. F. O. Rippingham (1896–1964) of the Ministry of Finance, was built in brick with continuous frontages and flat roofs. During the 1950s a large number of secondary schools were built throughout the country, heralding the general acceptance of the Modern Movement in a range of new materials and structural systems. Faughan Valley School (1955–9), near Londonderry, flat-roofed, curtain-glazed and with exposed pilotis to the ground-floor, is the most impressive of an interesting series designed by Noel Campbell (b 1920). Campbell was also responsible for a number of private houses dating from the later 1950s showing American influence. The largest new building in a modern style in the immediate post-war era was Altnagelvin Hospital (1949–60), Londonderry, an arrangement of multi-storey blocks by the English firm Yorke, Rosenberg and Mardall. The most notable later building, the competition-winning Ulster Museum extension (1963–71) in Belfast, was likewise designed by an outsider, Francis Pym of London. It is a robust composition in concrete spliced on to an earlier Neo-classical form in Portland stone that had been erected in the 1920s to the design of James C. Wynnes of Edinburgh (see fig. 1).

In the decades that followed there was interesting work by Shanks, Leighton, Kennedy and FitzGerald, in an avowedly modern idiom, ranging from the expressive board-marked concrete of Portadown Technical College (1973), Co. Armagh, to the studied brickwork of Dungannon Council Offices (1979), Co. Tyrone. Also notable was a series of churches by Gordon McKnight that united modern building techniques with traditional and historic forms, as at the high gabled Chapel of Unity (1968) at Methodist College, Belfast. Ireland's most distinguished

2. Gerard Dillon: *Yellow Bungalow*, oil on canvas, 812×768 mm, *c.* 1954 (Belfast, Ulster Museum)

firm of church architects of the post-war period, Corr and McCormick, was based in Londonderry in Northern Ireland, although their most important works are in the Republic of Ireland. During the 1970s and 1980s the Northern Ireland Housing Executive, against a background of civil unrest, consistently produced good public housing in both urban and rural sites throughout the country. In 1993, however, Ian Campbell, in his large barrel-vaulted Railway Exhibition Centre at the Ulster Folk and Transport Museum in Holywood, Co. Down, recaptured some of the grandeur of 19th-century engineering achievements but also invested it with a crisp precision that recalled the heyday of the Modern Movement.

BIBLIOGRAPHY

Royal Soc. Ulster Architects Yb. (1901–)
R. J. McKinstry: 'Contemporary Architecture', *Causeway: The Arts in Ulster*, ed. M. Longley (Belfast, 1971), pp. 27–42
H. Dixon: *An Introduction to Ulster Architecture* (Belfast, 1975)
D. Evans: *An Introduction to Modern Ulster Architecture* (Belfast, 1977)
P. Larmour: *Festival of Architecture, 1834–1984* (Belfast, 1984)
Ulster Architect (1984–)
——: *Belfast: An Illustrated Architectural Guide* (Belfast, 1987)
M. Patton: *Central Belfast: An Historical Gazetteer* (Belfast, 1993)

PAUL LARMOUR, DAVID EVANS

3. PAINTING, GRAPHIC ARTS AND SCULPTURE. Belfast, while being industrially wealthy, was not a noted artistic centre; before and after partition artists had to look to Dublin or London for any hope of commercial or critical success. Among these was the society portrait painter JOHN LAVERY, who only occasionally worked with Irish sitters and subject-matter. The painter WILLIAM SCOTT and the sculptor F. E. McWILLIAM were among those who embraced modernism and achieved an international reputation, but in both cases most of their work was produced outside Northern Ireland. In later years McWilliam produced a series of sculptures that show his awareness of the darker side of events in Ireland, as with *Woman in Bomb Blast* (Belfast, Ulster Mus.). Among those who continued to work in Northern Ireland, Colin Middleton (1910–83) exemplified the attempt of local artists to make use of the formal and theoretical lessons of such modernist movements as Cubism and Surrealism in order to shape a personal and appropriate regional vision. Of the same generation, there were several painters who went beyond the conventions and stereotypes of romanticized Irish landscape painting to address issues of individual and community identity. They included Gerard Dillon (1916–71), whose work has a fine spatial sense worthy of ancient Celtic decorative art, together with a darkly humorous aspect and a delight in a variety of media and techniques (see fig. 2). Dillon's choice of subjects sums up the concerns that generations of artists in Northern Ireland constantly addressed: issues of belonging to one or other of the political, religious and cultural traditions, issues of personality within or without the community, issues of figuration and symbolism and of the dichotomy between the rural and the urban.

Popular taste elevated the reputation of William Conor (1881–1968) to a local niche analogous to that of L. S. Lowry in the north of England. Unlike Lowry's industrial landscapes, Conor's depictions of Belfast workers and shawled women show no influence of modernism, but the regional popularity of his grainy, smiling images continues, fed no doubt by nostalgia for a vanished and seemingly untroubled urban, industrial, working-class past. The flaw in this approach was addressed by a generation of artists trained in the 1950s at the Belfast College of Art. The work of Basil Blackshaw (*b* 1932) was particularly notable: his images of landscape, of animals and of those people whose lives are bound up with the land were honed down over the years to an essence that was popular with different generations and cultural traditions.

Despite the sporadic conflict between the Unionist majority and the nationalist minority, there was little explicit artistic reference to this until the violence from 1968 onwards, and it was not until *c.* 1975 that there was evidence of a growing number of young artists with a more politicized agenda, who sought to harness any and all forms, media and techniques to confront (or subvert) subjects directly related to 'the Troubles'. Nevertheless, by the 1990s many of the artists working in Northern Ireland were seeking to address a broader range of subjects and issues. Work that is lyrical, or fantastic, or feminist, or expressionist often refers only obliquely to sectarianism and tension, the creators of such work arguing that the local manifestations of such phenomena should be seen as part of a series of global concerns. Other artists looked beyond political borders and used their paintings or sculpture (the latter being particularly successful) to define the identities of place that, while different, were important to both traditions. Apart from some instances of popular political mural painting in Northern Ireland, few works championed party politics or sectarianism. Most artists, e.g. Rita Duffy (*b* 1959) and Dermot Seymour (*b* 1956), held a view of their personal and national identity, of gender/sexuality and of how these related to the religious and cultural differences in all of Ireland, but few sought to present only one viewpoint. In the late 20th century few Northern Ireland artists were represented in major British or international public collections, but the effect of 'the Troubles' was to give a genuine focus and maturity to painters, printmakers, sculptors, photographers and performance and video artists.

BIBLIOGRAPHY

M. Longley, ed.: *Causeway: The Arts in Ulster* (Belfast, 1971), pp. 43–62

A. Bowness: *William Scott: Paintings, Drawings and Gouaches* (London, 1972)

T. P. Flanagan and J. Marle: *F. E. McWilliam* (Belfast, 1981)

J. C. Wilson: *Conor, 1881–1968* (Belfast, 1981)

A. Dunne, J. Fowler and J. Hutchinson: *A New Tradition: Irish Art in the 1980s* (Dublin, 1990)

B. Ferran: *On the Balcony of the Nation* (Belfast, 1990)

J. White: *Gerard Dillon* (Dublin, 1993)

MIKE CATTO

4. DECORATIVE ARTS. The main decorative arts studio in the north of Ireland at the turn of the 20th century was the Irish Decorative Art Association, established in Belfast in 1894, which maintained its position following partition in 1922. The leading figures from the 1920s until the studio's demise in the 1950s were Eva McKee (1890–1955) and Eveline McCloy, who produced graphic designs, painted woodwork and small items of furniture, leatherwork, repoussé copperwork and handmade jewellery in copper and silver, usually decorated in the Celtic or Early Christian Irish style of interlaced zoomorphic ornament.

3. Wilhelmina Geddes: *Rhoda Opening the Door to St Peter*, stained glass, h. *c.* 305 mm, 1934 (Belfast, Ulster Museum)

Other individual figures, all based in Belfast in the 1920s and 1930s, were Edith McDermott, Dorothy Dawson, Alice Britain and Jane Simms, the last two specializing in silver jewellery and natural-dyed hand-weaving respectively. Most craftworkers continued to show works at the important exhibitions in Dublin, but the annual Belfast Arts and Crafts Exhibition, established in 1924, provided a more local focus until 1938, after which it was curtailed by the outbreak of World War II. One of the foremost figures in the Irish Arts and Crafts Movement of the turn of the century was Wilhelmina Geddes (1887–1955), who trained at the Belfast School of Art. She gained an international reputation for her stained-glass work, but she was also a successful graphic artist and the creator of some important embroidered figure panels. Examples of her superb skill in stained glass in the 1920s, designed at first in Belfast but later in London (where she moved in 1925), can be seen at St Cedma's Church in Larne, Co. Antrim. She is also represented by panels of the 1920s and 1930s in the collection of the Ulster Museum in Belfast (see fig. 3). The large rose window of 1938 in Ypres Cathedral in Belgium was one of her greatest achievements outside Ireland.

The staple art industry of the 20th century in Northern Ireland was textiles, and many local professional designers and artists were employed in the 1920s and 1930s providing new patterns for damasks for sale worldwide. The famous 19th-century BELLEEK PORCELAIN FACTORY in Co. Fermanagh continued to reuse its early models (*see* IRELAND, fig. 20) and so did not nurture new designers. After World War II competent stained glass was produced in Belfast by Olive Henry (1902–89) of Clokey & Co. and by Daniel Braniff. In the field of textiles the most notable new figure in this period was the Norwegian designer and hand-weaver Gerd Hay-Eadie, who established her Mourne Textiles business near Rostrevor, Co. Down, and built up an international clientele over the following decades. During the 1960s the Belfast architect Denis O'D. Hanna (1902–73) became interested in a partnership between architects and artists and craftworkers, which came to fruition in some local buildings. At the church of the Pentecost, Cregagh, and St Molua's Church, Stormont, he commissioned various local artists in wood and metal-work, including Elizabeth Campbell, James McKendry and David Pettigrew. Desmond Kinney depicted the figures of early saints and modern workers using gold leaf on glazed panels in both churches. Others followed this lead, but such successful collaborations were only inter-mittent, and no strong tradition of local decorative art in architecture was established.

BIBLIOGRAPHY
P. Larmour: *The Arts and Crafts Movement in Ireland* (Belfast, 1992)
PAUL LARMOUR

5. ART INSTITUTIONS. In 1926 a bequest was made to the Belfast Museum and Art Gallery (opened 1928) by the widow of the linen merchant Robert Lloyd Patterson (1836–1906), consisting mainly of Victorian anecdotal pictures. The bold decision was made to approach the modernist art critic Frank Rutter (1876–1937) for advice, and he recommended the sale of Patterson's collection and the use of the proceeds to buy contemporary paintings of good quality. With the help of the Contemporary Art Society, the Museum soon built up a notable collection, including works by Walter Richard Sickert, Philip Wilson Steer, Spencer Gore, Charles Ginner, William Roberts, Mark Gertler and Stanley Spencer. In 1930 John Lavery presented the gallery with 30 of his own works, to which a special gallery was devoted. Good collections of British and Irish watercolours were assembled during the 1930s and 1950s. In 1961, following the Museum Act (Northern Ireland), the Museum was transferred from the City to the State as the Ulster Museum (see fig. 1 above), and the foundations laid for the policy of buying international contemporary art. Important collecting since the 1970s has been in the fields of international contemporary glass, ceramics, costume and textiles. There is an excellent temporary exhibition gallery that sustains a programme of prestigious loan exhibitions.

The National Trust for Northern Ireland, based at Rowallane, Co. Down, runs nine distinguished country houses, which contain works of art, furniture and textiles. Ireland's oldest regional museum, Armagh County Museum, founded in 1936, has a small art collection, mainly of local topographical views and portraits, as do Fermanagh County Museum in Enniskillen Castle, Down County Museum in Downpatrick, the North Down Heritage Centre in Bangor and the Tower Museum in Londonderry. Work started on the Ulster Folk and Transport Museum at Holywood, Co. Down, in 1958 and it was set up as a National Institution by Act of Parliament in 1961. It has an important collection of craft objects and traditional textiles as well as paintings by the popular Belfast artist William Conor (1881–1968), which formerly belonged to the Linen Hall Library in Belfast. It also comprises

examples of re-erected vernacular buildings. Art collections are also held by the Queen's University of Belfast, Belfast City Hall and the Belfast Harbour Commissioners. Belfast Central Reference Library (built 1890) has a good art section.

The Belfast College of Art, the main training school for decorative artists, painters and sculptors, was moved in the late 1960s from the top floor of the Municipal Technical Institute to newly built premises on York Street. In the 1980s, in accordance with UK policies, it was amalgamated into the University of Ulster as the Faculty of Art and Design. A Department of Architecture was established in the Queen's University, Belfast, in the 1960s. The Arts Council of Northern Ireland runs an exhibition gallery in Belfast and a printmaking studio; it also tours exhibitions and allocates grants. The Royal Ulster Academy of Arts is the youngest of the provincial exhibiting academies. Its roots go back to the Belfast Ramblers' Sketching Club and the Belfast Art Society of the late 19th century. In 1930 it became the Ulster Academy of Arts, with Lavery as its first President, and in 1951 it received its Royal Prefix.

In the first half of the 20th century, the main commercial galleries in Belfast were Rodman's and John Magee's, which are no longer active. The Fenderesky Gallery occupies premises belonging to Queen's University, and the Bell Gallery and the Tom Caldwell Gallery are still active. The Kerlin Gallery was set up in Belfast in the late 1980s, then moved to Dublin. Outside Belfast are the Narrow Water Gallery near Newry and the Peacock Gallery in Portadown. The most original commercial gallery is probably the Orchard Gallery in Londonderry. The art magazine *Circa*, edited in Belfast, was founded in the 1980s and is the leading contemporary art periodical in Ireland. Flourishing art centres of the 1990s are found at the Old Museum and the Crescent Arts Centre in Belfast, and at Newry and Downpatrick.

BIBLIOGRAPHY
N. Nesbitt: *A Museum in Belfast: A History of the Ulster Museum and its Predecessors* (Belfast, 1979)
M. Anglesea: *The Royal Ulster Academy of Arts: A Centennial History* (Belfast, 1981)
S. B. Kennedy: *British Art, 1900–1937: Robert Lloyd Patterson Collection* (Belfast, 1982)
M. Anglesea: *Portraits and Prospects: British and Irish Drawings and Watercolours from the Collection of the Ulster Museum, Belfast* (Belfast and Washington, DC, 1989), intro., pp. xvii–xxii
C. Priestly: *Structures and Arrangements for Funding the Arts in Northern Ireland: A Report to Jeremy Hanley M.P., Minister with Responsibility for the Arts* (Belfast, 1992)
MARTYN ANGLESEA

Irene, Empress. *See* EIRENE.

Irian Jaya [formerly West New Guinea; Western New Guinea; West Irian; Irian Barat]. Indonesian province, comprising the western half of New Guinea and surrounding islands, with a population of *c.* 2.7 million. Formerly a Dutch colony, it was administered by Indonesia under the authority of the United Nations from 1963 until 1969, when it was formally incorporated into the Republic of Indonesia. Culturally Irian Jaya is generally classified as Melanesian rather than Indonesian. Its art has been quite widely studied and illustrated (see bibliography). There are also a number of important museum collections, both in Irian Jaya itself (e.g. Agats, Asmat Mus. Cult. & Prog.) and in the West (e.g. New York, Mus. Primitive A.: Basle, Mus. Vlkerknd.; Amsterdam, Tropenmus.; Leiden, Rijksmus. Vlkenknd.).

1. Introduction. 2. Cendrawasih Bay. 3. Jos Sudarso Bay and the Lake Sentani area. 4. South-west coast.

1. INTRODUCTION. A high mountain range divides Irian Jaya latitudinally into a mountainous northern part and, to the south, a flat, tropical lowland area characterized by vast marshes crossed by sluggish, muddy rivers and infested with mosquitoes and malaria. An inhospitable area, it is as difficult to access from the sea as from the mountainous interior. Perhaps as a result of the country's physical geography, the cultures and languages of Irian Jaya show a bewildering diversity. Nevertheless, certain features distinguish the societies of the north coast from those of the southern plains, and it is possible to make a rough partition of the many languages into two groups: Austronesian and Papuan or Trans New Guinean. The Austronesian languages are related to those spoken in Indonesia and on the Melanesian islands. On New Guinea these are spoken in those areas with regular external contacts, including the northern coastal areas of Irian Jaya. Papuan languages (a general term for those languages that cannot be fitted into the group of Austronesian languages) are mainly spoken in the more isolated parts of New Guinea—the mountainous interior and the southern lowlands. The often difficult, isolated living conditions and the prevailing hostilities between neighbouring groups encouraged the separate development of the New Guinea languages. The resulting diversity of language is enormous: c. 800 languages are spoken, about a quarter of the world's known languages. The language of government and education, however, is Indonesian.

A division between the north coast and the southern plains can also be made on cultural grounds. For example, along the north coast and its numerous islands canoes are heavy, sea-going craft, made of tree-trunks and often heightened by one or more wash strakes. Such canoes are provided with two outriggers and one or two sails. In contrast, the people living in the swampy lowlands of the south depend almost exclusively on slowly meandering rivers for their transportation and communication. Sailing on such a river would be impossible, and an outrigger would make the craft too clumsy to manoeuvre in the narrow, overgrown channels. Consequently they use slender dugout canoes, propelled by up to 20 men, standing one behind the other using long-handled paddles.

Irian Jayan lowland culture was based on a tradition of reverence towards the ancestors. Festivals were elaborated into highly dramatic performances with masked participants representing ancestors and thus required the production of ornate costumes and body paintings. The former practice of headhunting and the regarding of the skull as a sacred object relate to this worship of the dead. Although the highland areas of Papua New Guinea had similar festivals, Irian Jaya's artistic output was confined to the coastal areas, the mountainous interior producing little in the way of art.

2. CENDRAWASIH BAY. This style area extends from the island of Waigeo in the west to the mouth of the Mamberamo River in the east and includes the coastal area and islands of Cendrawasih (formerly Geelvink) Bay. This is the area of the so-called *korwar* style, a word denoting, in the first place, the spirit of the dead and, by extension, the skull and the wooden ancestor figures that served as a medium between the living and the dead (see fig. 1). Although most *korwar* are seated figures, those from the Dore Bay area (see below) are usually standing figures holding in front of them an object resembling a

1. Irian Jayan *korwar* figure sculpture, wood, h. 340 mm, from Sakevem village, Davelung, Cendrawasih Bay, acquired 1893 (Leiden, Rijksmuseum voor Volkenkunde)

shield. The head is always much larger than the body, often in a proportion of 3 to 2. The ancestor skull versions of *korwar* may be placed in a basket, sometimes adorned with a wooden nose and ears. Standing or sitting figures may incorporate a real skull, either placed on a spike, which serves as a neck, or put into a receptacle representing the head of the figure. In the latter case, the front part of the skull may be the face, or the figure may have a carved, wooden face behind which the skull is placed. *Korwar* were placed in houses and their advice sought in such situations as illness or before embarking on a dangerous sailing expedition. The consultation was, in most cases, carried out by the shaman (*mon*) but could also be done by the owner of the *korwar*. As long as a *korwar* was held in honour, it served as a cult focus, because it represented the ancestor to whom offerings were due. However, if *korwar* figures too often gave wrong advice, they lost their usefulness and could be thrown away, sold or even intentionally damaged. Although the making of a *korwar* involved various ritual prescriptions, next to nothing is known about the artists who made them or the aesthetic and technical sides of their production.

Small amulets are made in the same style as *korwar*. Wooden figures representing such animals as dogs, snakes and crocodiles are also found, although very little is known about their specific functions. The large sea-going outrigger canoes are also decorated with various carvings. Among the most impressive are the complicated prows of the large war-canoes (*wai-ron*), consisting of a thin board with openwork scroll ornamentation and the incorporation of one or more heads of *korwar* type, or sometimes a complete figure in the same style. Unlike actual *korwar*, these heads are, as a rule, decorated with cassowary feathers to represent hair. Within the Cendrawasih Bay area there are interesting contrasts of artistic style between the mainly rectilinear construction of the figures and the faces and the elaborate curves of the scrollwork ornamentation seen on canoe prows or in the shield-shaped objects of the Dore Bay *korwar*. Similar scroll ornamentation is found on decorated bamboo tobacco containers and on neck-rests. All of these have an Indonesian style and probably came to Cendrawasih Bay after the typical *korwar* style. Although the *korwar* of the Cendrawasih Bay area share sufficient characteristics to be grouped together, substyles and variations exist within this grouping.

(i) Waigeo Island and the Ajau Islands. The style of this region is characterized by carvings of a seated human form with the arms crossed and laid upon the knees, which are drawn up. The figures are 200 to 250 mm high, the proportion of the head to the body being *c.* 3 to 2. The basic shape of the head is cylindrical with a slightly concave, semi-oval piece removed from the front. The facial area thus formed is delimited along the top by horizontal, projecting eyebrows, from the middle of which the nose forms a perfectly straight vertical ridge ending in a comparatively short, barely modelled horizontal ridge that forms the nostrils. Above the eyebrows, the hairline is indicated by a horizontal brace-shaped groove, which sometimes continues over the cheeks to the jaws. To either side of the nose, just above the nostrils, a slight downward curving line joins the nose to the edge of the

oval face. The lower lip repeats this curve while the upper lip is fairly naturalistic, and teeth are visible. The head is smoothly finished and usually has a raised ridge around the back. Kidney-shaped ears, in relief, are sometimes shown with a carved pendant, shaped like a European pen nib. Sometimes a standing human figure is carved in relief on the sides of the head above each ear.

(ii) Japen Island. In this substyle, the figures are also seated but the elbows rest on the drawn-up knees, and the hands hold an often unidentifiable object. The vertical sides of the head form an obtuse angle with the two planes of the face, the intersection of which forms the ridge of the nose. The nose continues up into the often tapering forehead and down as far as the chin, which ends in a sharp point. The nostrils point upwards at an angle, giving the nose the shape of an anchor. Around the nostrils the face is cut away in the shape of a heart, making the wide slit-mouth jut forward strongly. Its thin lips are carved so that the tongue or teeth show. Eyes are often represented by beads set into the wood. The ears stand out as little ridges. The face is a little deeper than the rest of the head, forming a kind of frame. The proportion of the head to the body is *c.* 2 to 3, and the figures are 250 to 300 mm high. Two or three other styles probably existed on Japen Island. One group of smaller carvings, *c.* 200 mm high, can definitely be identified, with eyes carved as elliptical grooves on a small, raised area. These figures have a heavy, hood-shaped headdress and, in general, are much less angular than other figures of this area.

(iii) The Schouten Islands. In this substyle, seated figures are identical to those of Japen Island except that the head is not composed of flat planes; a horizontal section would be almost egg-shaped. The narrow end is drawn to a point at the front where the two sides of the face meet at an acute angle. The Japen Island figure's heart-shaped part, which is cut away around the nostrils, is either not removed or is only shallowly carved out.

(iv) Wandamen Bay and Umar Bay. With few exceptions, the figures here are seated, again with elbows resting on drawn-up knees. Typically, the head is disproportionately long, about twice as long as it is wide, and projects a long way forward from the short neck at the back. It is sometimes supported under the chin by an ornament held in the hands. At the back of the head there is a large spherical projection, in the shape of a bun of hair. From here the head forms a trumpet shape with the widest part forming a ridge that frames the face. This ridge is often marked on the outside edge with triangular indentations and is reminiscent of a Victorian poke-bonnet. The actual face appears to be attached to this frame; indeed, there is very little sense of an organic relationship between the face and the rest of the head. In its details, the face itself is practically the same as the faces of Japen Island figures. Wandamen and Umar Bay figures are generally 250 to 300 mm tall. Another variation found in this area is the *korwar* figure with an almost perfectly spherical head that is completely smooth and cut off straight on the underside. The face is attached to this head in the same way as in other figures of this area. Many of the well-known skull *korwar* probably belong to this substyle.

(v) Dore Bay and surrounding area. In most cases this substyle is represented by a standing figure that holds a shield, usually with both hands but sometimes with only one, the other arm being stretched out in a threatening way. The shield rests on the ground and consists of scrollwork that appears to be a stylized depiction of two snakes facing each other with open jaws. Occasionally figures hold one or two clearly recognizable snakes that rest their tails on the ground. Sometimes a smaller human figure is worked into the design of the shieldlike form. With this substyle anatomical details are carved in a very naturalistic way. A raised line runs from ear to ear. This substyle is probably the only one to include figures whose arms are fixed to, rather than carved from, the body.

3. JOS SUDARSO BAY AND THE LAKE SENTANI AREA. This stylistic area includes the northern coastal region, the offshore islands stretching from the mouth of the Mamberamo River in the west to the border with Papua New Guinea in the east and the region around Lake Sentani. There are, however, considerable differences in style between the coastal and lakeland regions. Research suggests that contact between the culture of Lake Sentani and that of the Asmat Papuans on the south-west coast was once common (Voorhoeve, 1969). It may be that the two share common roots in the central highlands, possibly near the headwaters of the Sepik River. Again, substyles may be discerned within the area.

The substyle of the Jos Sudarso (formerly Humboldt) Bay area and its islands is characterized by a roundness and a fullness of form that is in sharp contrast to the planes and straight lines of the Cendrawasih Bay style. Although Cendrawasih Bay scrollwork rarely appears, the anchor-shaped *korwar* nose is often found, as is a rounded, up-turned type of nose that has broad, fleshy nostrils and a pierced septum. Most carvings are figureheads, fixed separately to the prows of the outrigger canoes, and they may take one of three forms. The first is a pointed, vertical stick, crossed by one or two horizontal bars, all carved from a single piece of wood. The tips are carved to represent human heads, the heads of birds or sometimes complete birds. The second form is an S-shaped piece of wood, covered with carved human and animal figures. The third is formed by two planes in a V shape, converging in a long tip, slightly turned up towards its end so that the whole resembles the letter Y. On the tip humans or animals or scrolls are carved, the latter probably representing waves. The outsides of the legs of the figure (the inverted Y) are usually decorated with low-relief carvings of groups of stylized birds, probably frigate birds, or fish. Carvings of fish also decorate the hulls of canoes. Animal and human forms are carved as finials on men's houses, but naturalistic representations of human figures are rare.

In the Lake Sentani area there are two stylistic traditions: one may be designated 'chief's art' because of its close association with the chief (*ondoforo*); the other may be labelled 'commoner's art'. To the first category belong the famous decorated house-posts with two pennant-shaped protrusions supporting the ridge-pole of the large chief's houses. Other manifestations are impressive freestanding human figures, many of which were originally the ornamental tops of posts supporting the floor. At least some

aspects of the cultures of Lake Sentani and that of the Asmat on the south-west coast may have common origins. One of the most intriguing aspects of this connection is the striking similarity not only of form but also of function that exists between the house-poles of the *ondoforo* house and those of the ceremonial house (*yeu*) of the Asmat. The ornately carved central posts of the *ondoforo* house were cut from tree trunks and placed with the heavy, plank-like roots uppermost. The roots were carved so that two winglike projections were left on either side of the trunk (see fig. 2). The posts in the Asmat *yeu* are shaped exactly the same way. Functionally, these decorated posts supported the ridge-poles of the buildings that the Asmat regarded as the most prominent in their society. The chief's house on Lake Sentani resembled the Asmat *yeu* in shape much more than it resembled the four- or eight-sided pyramidal Sentani ceremonial house (*mau*), which originated from the Jos Sudarso Bay.

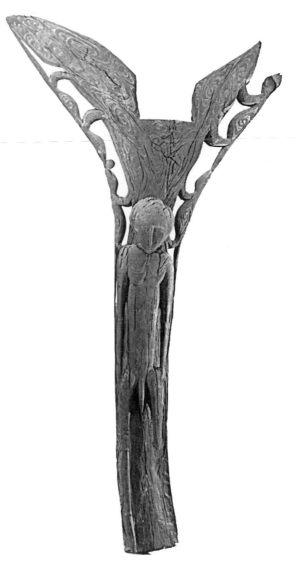

2. Irian Jayan house-post, wood, h. 2.2 m, from Sukarnapura, Lake Sentani (Amsterdam, Tropenmuseum)

The 'commoner's art' is expressed in such objects as hammers, food trays, suspension hooks, lime and tobacco containers, paddles, drums and daggers, all of which may be decorated with characteristic, elegant curvilinear incised motifs and forms based on an S-shaped double spiral. Mention must also be made of barkcloth painted either in the same curvilinear style or with clan motifs, mostly of fish, snakes, lizards, birds and anteaters.

See also PACIFIC ISLANDS, §II, 1.

4. SOUTH-WEST COAST. Within the large area of the south-west coast three stylistic sub-areas can be distinguished, although these do not have rigid boundaries. From west to east they are the Mimika area, which covers the coastal region from the Uta River in the west up to the Otakwa River in the east; the Asmat area, from the Pomac River in the west to the Digul River in the east and the hinterland up to the foothills; and the Marind-anim area, from Yos Sudarso (formerly Kolepom or Frederik Hendrik) Island to the border with Papua New Guinea.

(i) Mimika area. The art here is mainly two-dimensional, characterized by an oval motif, which is filled with a pattern of thin raised edges around which the wood has been cut away. The oval represents a navel (*mopere*), especially a mother's navel. (From *mopere* is derived *mapare*, the innermost, deepest, essential.) The same form is used to represent the eyes and the mouth and is found as a kind of jointmark on the wrists, elbows and particularly the shoulders and knees. The latter have special importance, because after death one's ghost (*ipu*) returns to the kneecap (*iripu*) to claim the spiritual essence (*nata*), without which the ghost could not walk to the mountains that are the dwelling-place of ghosts.

The woodcarver starts by carving the navel and then fills the available space. The patterns are composed of straight lines, dispersed at random across the surface, thus giving the impression of jerky nervousness. The designs are found on the sides of canoes, on paddle blades, on the underside of food bowls, on sago pounders and, most typically, on the surface of long, slender shield-shaped planks (*yamate*). These are exhibited outside the feast houses to be admired by the women. Occasionally the area around the raised edges has been completely cut away, leaving an openwork design. The prows of river-canoes are occasionally decorated with a *yamate*-like carving.

Typical of the Mimika region are the big ceremonial or spirit poles (*mbitoro*). *Mbii* is the spirit of death, a vague form assumed by the personal ghost once it and the spiritual essence have left the body, which remains as an empty container (*kao*) represented by the hollow open-work human figures typical of the spirit poles. These figures stand for specific ancestors, whose names they bear. The poles are made from the same trees that are used for the Sentani house poles and are also placed root-end up. They stand in front of the houses built for the Mirimumake ceremony that accompanies the piercing of the septum of the nose.

The apex of Mimika art is the over life-size pregnant figures that played a central role in the Kiwa ceremony known in the eastern part of Mimika and that were associated with women as the bringers of new life and with female fertility. The figures are carved in the round and covered with typical incised designs including the *mopere* motif that, as the maternal navel, was considered the essence of life. During the ceremony the figures were placed in a specially constructed house, usually four in a row next to the entrance. Only seven examples of these figures are known: six are in the Rijksmuseum voor Volkenkunde, Leiden, and one is in the Rijksmuseum voor Volkenkunde, 'Justinus van Nassau', Breda.

(ii) Asmat area. This area has a wealth of art equalled in New Guinea only by the Sepik region of Papua New Guinea. After a period of decline following the transfer, in 1963, of the former Dutch colony of West New Guinea to Indonesia, Asmat art experienced a revival during the late 1960s that was set in motion by the United Nations Development Programme for West Irian. Though much of the original context of Asmat art has disappeared, late 20th-century research has resulted in a better understanding of the cultural background of Asmat art and of its function (see bibliography).

In Asmat culture mankind is considered as part and middlepoint of a continuously existing universe with no beginning and no end. In Asmat thought there is no place for creation because the world, celestial bodies, mankind, animals and plants always existed and will exist forever. Instead, within this one existence, cyclical changes of status occur. At death, a human changes into a spirit and, in due time, the spirit changes back into a child, who grows up and eventually dies, again becoming a spirit. Transitions from one status to the next are critical, and ritual and religious ceremonies are focused on them. Especially significant is the relationship between the living and the spirits of recently deceased relatives (*ndat*): the ritual life of the Asmat can be seen as an enduring effort to appease the *ndat*. Following death, spirits remain in the world of the living for a time, before entering the realm of the dead (*safan*), and this transitional period is one of great danger. The most effective way of appeasing the spirits is to organize one of the several ritual feasts (*pokmbui*) that involve the collecting of large quantities of food and the making of such wood-carvings as statues that represented, non-naturalistically, specific ancestors (*kavé*), large poles (*mis*) that also represent ancestors with one figure standing on the head of another, and shields (*jemès*), again representing specific ancestors. Each *pokmbui* requires the making of one kind of these wood-carvings.

Another category of Asmat wood-carving symbolizes unspecified ancestors in their particular capacity as head-hunters. These follow a limited number of standardized two-dimensional designs. With one exception these designs are stylized images of fruit-eating, flying animals and are dark-coloured like the Asmat themselves. As the Asmat consider trees to be equal to humans, the fruit of a tree is interchangeable with a human head. Black or dark-coloured animals who feed on fruits and who live above the ground consequently became symbols for head-hunters who lived in the sky (the world of the dead), in other words the ancestors. The animals adopted for this symbolism are the hornbill, the black king cockatoo and the flying fox. The praying mantis also symbolizes the head-hunter, although it does not eat fruit, does not fly and is not dark-coloured. Nevertheless, this insect is human in its movements and, because the parts of the body look like animated sticks, the rendering of the mantis by the Asmat wood-carver resembles a simplified, squatting,

3. Irian Jayan shield, wood, white, red and black pigment, h. 1.34 m, from Sauwa-Erma village, Pomac River, north-west Asmat (Leiden, Rijksmuseum voor Volkenkunde)

human figure. Often two figures are portrayed back-to-back and given the name used to designate an ancestor, *kavé*. Other designs represent the whole being through the use of such parts as the bone or shell nose-piece, an elbow or navel motif or parts of certain animals.

The total number of designs in Asmat art is limited to *c*. 50 or 60, with regional variations of shape and meaning. All such variations in the Asmat picture language or system of ideograms, as one might call their wood-carving, remain well within the general notion of ancestor symbolism. Because ancestors are so important, the ancestor ideo-grams are found on a wide variety of objects, including sago pounders, the blades of paddles, bamboo horns, drums, food and paint bowls, the central section of spears and neck-rests. Their most prominent use, however, is on large shields made from the roots of trees. The designs on the front, which are intended to terrify the enemy by displaying the support of ancestors, vary in style within the Asmat area. The coastal and central Asmat, from Flamingo Bay down to the Casuarina Coast, produce bold designs with smoothly rounded contours. The north-west Asmat use a wealth of small designs surrounding two or three boldly outlined central designs, which usually repre-sent flying foxes (see fig. 3). The eastern Asmat, or Tjitak people, produce similarly bold designs to the coastal Asmat, but the contours are more angular and somewhat clumsily executed, while the people of the Brazza River area also adopt these designs but in an even rougher, more degenerate form.

(iii) The Marind-anim area. This covers the coastal area from Yos Sudarso Island to about halfway between Merauke and the border with Papua New Guinea in the east, stretching inland along the rivers for about a hundred miles. In contrast to the cultures discussed thus far, Marind-anim art is expressed at complicated rituals during which participants carry clumsily made effigies of mythical ancestors and creators (*dema*), often represented by the totem animals of the clan. Such effigies are carved from very light wood, which may be decorated with white, red and black paint and colourful seeds. Artistically unimpres-sive, their full impact would only become clear during the re-enactment of the sacred myths that formed one of the many Marind-anim rituals that were abandoned following the arrival of Western government and religion in the first decade of the 20th century. In a culture where the aesthetic aspect concerns time (dance and drama) rather than space (sculpture), art becomes meaningful only through the understanding of the rituals and the symbolism involved with it.

BIBLIOGRAPHY

J. Pouwer: *Enkele aspecten van de Mimika-Cultuur* (diss., U. Leiden, 1955)
S. Kooijman: 'Art of Southwestern New Guinea: A Preliminary Survey', *Ant. & Survival*, i/5 (1956), pp. 343–72
The Art of Lake Sentani (exh. cat. by S. Kooijman, New York, Mus. Primitive A., 1959)
K. W. Galis: 'De Biak-Noemfoorse Prauw', *Kultuurpatronen*, v/vi (1963), pp. 121–42 [Dut. text with Eng. summary]
J. van Baal: *Dema: Description and Analysis of Marind-anim Culture, South New Guinea*, Koninklijk Instituut voor Taal-, Land- en Volkenkunde, Translation Series 9 (The Hague, 1966)
A. A. Gerbrands, ed.: *The Asmat of New Guinea: The Journal of Michael Clark Rockefeller* (New York, 1967) [incl. cat. of the Michael C. Rockefeller col. of Asmat art at the Museum of Primitive Art, New York]

A. A. Gerbrands: *Wow-Ipits: Eight Asmat Carvers of New Guinea* (The Hague, 1967)

J. Hoogerbrugge: 'Sentani-Meer: Mythe en ornament', *Kultuurpatronen*, ix (1967), pp. 5–91 [Dut. text with Eng. summary]

T. P. van Baaren: *Korwars and Korwar Style: Art and Ancestor Worship in North-west New Guinea* (Paris and The Hague, 1968)

C. L. Voorhoeve: 'Some Notes on the Linguistic Relations between the Sentani and Asmat Languages of New Guinea', *Bijdr. Taal-, Land- & Vlkenknd.*, cxxv/4 (1969), pp. 466–86

The Art of the Pacific Islands (exh. cat. by P. Gathercole, A. L. Kaeppler and D. Newton, Washington, DC, N.G.A., 1979), pp. 277–92

Asmat: Leben mit den Ahnen—Steinzeitliche Holzschnitzer unserer Zeit/Asmat: Life with Ancestors—Stone Age Woodcarvers in our Time (exh. cat. by G. Konrad, U. Konrad and T. Schneebaum, Hofheim am Taunus, Stadtmus., 1981)

L. Hanson and F. E. Hanson: *Art of Oceania: A Bibliography*, Ref. Pubns A. Hist. (Boston, 1984)

S. Kooijman: *Art, Art Objects and Ritual in the Mimika Culture*, Meded. Rijksmus. Vlkerknd., Leiden, xxiii (Leiden, 1984)

T. Schneebaum: *Asmat Images from the Collection of the Asmat Museum of Culture and Progress*, Agats, Asmat Mus. Cult. & Prog. cat. (New York, 1985)

——: *Embodied Spirit: Ritual Carvings of the Asmat* (Salem, MA, 1990)

A. A. GERBRANDS

Iriarte. Spanish family of collectors. Bernardo de Iriarte (*b* Puerto de la Cruz, Tenerife, 18 Feb 1735; *d* Bordeaux, 13 Aug 1814) was the eldest of three brothers from the Canary Islands who made their careers in Madrid. He was a civil servant and at one stage vice-protector of the Real Academia de Bellas Artes de S Fernando in Madrid. Domingo de Iriarte (*b* Puerto de la Cruz, 18 March 1739; *d* Girona, 22 Nov 1795) served primarily in the diplomatic service. The youngest brother, Tomás de Iriarte (*b* Puerto de la Cruz, 18 Sept 1750; *d* Madrid, 17 Sept 1791), was an official translator and archivist as well as poet, playwright and musician. The three came into contact with artistic and literary circles early in their lives through their uncle Juan de Iriarte (1702–71), who was the royal librarian from 1732 to 1771. The brothers built up their collection of prints and paintings as a joint enterprise. When he was at the embassy in Vienna, Domingo bought two portraits from Jusepe de Ribera's series of *Philosophers* (Madrid, Prado) from Prince Eugene of Savoy; Tomás had his portrait painted by Joaquín Inza (Madrid, Prado); and Bernardo sat to Francisco de Goya (1797; Strasbourg, Mus. B.-A.) and acquired an *Interior of a Church with a Priest Celebrating Mass* (possibly *The Communion* of *c*. 1813–18 in Williamstown, MA, Clark A. Inst.) attributed to the same artist. Their gallery was grouped thematically. There were portraits and self-portraits of artists and writers in two rooms, including works by Diego Velázquez, Bartolomé Esteban Murillo and Anton Raphael Mengs (who presented Bernardo with one of his self-portraits); pictures of historic interest in another; portraits by Velázquez and Murillo in a fourth room; and mythological pictures, including a *Venus* ascribed to Leonardo da Vinci in a fifth. Some of the paintings and prints were sold when Bernardo was exiled from Madrid in 1802, and others were sold in Madrid and auctioned in London after his death.

See also CASTILLO, ANTONIO DEL.

BIBLIOGRAPHY
E. Cotarelo y Mori: *Iriarte y su época* (Madrid, 1897)
E. du Gué Trapier: *Goya and his Sitters* (New York, 1964), p. 15
N. Glendinning: 'Goya's Patrons', *Apollo*, cxiv (1981), pp. 236–47 (245)
NIGEL GLENDINNING

Iriarte, Hesiquio (*b* Mexico City, ?1820; *d* Mexico City, ?1897). Mexican illustrator and printmaker. He probably began his career in 1847 in the workshop of the Murguía publishing house. In 1854, in collaboration with Andrés Campillo, he created an outstanding series of illustrations for the book *Los mexicanos pintados por sí mismos*, in which he portrayed character types (e.g. *Great Poet*, lithograph) in the manner of Honoré Daumier. In 1855 he founded the firm Litografía de Iriarte y Compañía. The following year he published portraits of famous personalities in the weekly review *El Panorama*. He was a co-founder in 1861 of the political fortnightly *La Orquesta*, on which he worked for more than ten years as an illustrator and eventually as a caricaturist and as editor. Iriarte continued to contribute to a number of periodicals, including *El Renacimiento*, and his firm also published the weekly *San Baltazar* (1869–70). He collaborated with Santiago Hernández on numerous illustrations for, among others, Vicente Riva Palacio's book *El libro rojo*. Iriarte went into partnership *c*. 1892 with the typographer Francisco Díaz de León to address the demands of new techniques in commercial lithography, and soon after to produce publications illustrated with photogravures.

PRINTS
Los mexicanos pintados por sí mismos (Mexico City, 1854)
V. Riva Palacio: *El libro rojo* (Mexico, 1870)

BIBLIOGRAPHY
M. León Portilla, ed.: 'Hesiquio Iriarte', *Diccionario Porrúa de historia, biografía y geografía de Mexico*, ii (Mexico City, 1964, 5/1986), p. 1536
C. Díaz y de Ovando: 'El grabado comercial en la segunda mitad del siglo XIX', *Hist. A. Mex.*, ed. J. Salvat and J. L. Rosas, xii (Mexico City, 1986), pp. 1708–25
AÍDA SIERRA TORRES

Iriarte [Yriarte], **Ignacio de** (*b* Azcoitia, Guipúzcoa, 16 Jan 1621; *d* Seville, 27 Sept 1670). Spanish painter and printmaker. He was the leading Baroque landscape painter of his generation in Seville. In 1646 he was married in Aracena, Huelva. He soon moved to Seville, where he married again in 1649. Nothing is known of his apprenticeship, and it is doubtful that Francisco de Herrera (i) was his teacher. Iriarte's style was strongly influenced by Flemish landscape, which was then extremely popular in Seville, in particular by the landscapes of Josse de Momper II. The signed and dated *Landscape with Shepherds* (1665; Madrid, Prado) serves as a touchstone for all attributions. Between 1650 and 1700 Iriarte was second only to Bartolomé Murillo as the artist most sought after by collectors in Seville. He also painted religious scenes. An *Annunciation* altarpiece (untraced) was documented in the church of the Brotherhood of Charity in Seville, which also owned a print by Iriarte. A pair of drawings (1669; Paris, Louvre) is signed as if they were to have been made into prints. Palomino reported that Iriarte collaborated with Murillo, whose own landscape style he influenced strongly. A copy after Francisco de Zurbarán with the landscape painted by Iriarte is documented in 1681. Landscapes by Iriarte were usually collected in sets or series. One set is identified as a *Morning* and *Evening* (untraced), and series of architectural perspectives by Iriarte are listed in contemporary inventories.

BIBLIOGRAPHY

Ceán Bermúdez

A. A. Palomino y Castro y Velasco: *El Parnaso español* (Madrid, 1724/R 1947)
C. de Echegaray: 'Fecha de nacimiento del paisajista Ignacio de Iriarte', *Bol. Soc. Esp. Excurs.*, xxii (1915), pp. 316–17
J. Baticle: 'Dibujos españoles para el Louvre', *Archv Esp. A.*, xxxvi (1963), pp. 312–13
D. Kinkead: 'Nuevos datos sobre los pintores don Sebastián de Llanos y Valdés e Ignacio de Iriarte', *Archv Hispal.*, lxii (1979), pp. 191–211
A. Calvo Castellón: *Los fondos arquitectónicos y el paisaje en la pintura barroca andaluza* (Granada, 1982)
J. Brown: 'Drawings by Andalusian Masters', *Apotheca*, iii (1983), pp. 9–20

DUNCAN KINKEAD

Iriarte, Valero (*b* Saragossa, 1680–90; *d* Madrid, after 1743). Spanish painter. In 1711, after painting the portrait (untraced) of the *Prince of Asturias*, the future King Luis, he moved to Madrid, where he remained in the service of Philip V and his consort Elizabeth Farnese, painting numerous portraits of the royal family over the next 30 years. In 1722 Iriarte applied unsuccessfully for the post of court painter, but in 1725 he was appointed, with other Madrid painters, an official valuer of paintings, which elevated him socially and helped him win further commissions. In 1740 he was named court painter. Iriarte's private clients included aristocrats, government officials and members of the bourgeoisie, and some of his works are still preserved in private collections, such as his portrait of *Pedro José de Rojas Contreras* (1740; Madrid, priv. col.). Others are known only through engravings, which demonstrate the extent of his reputation. His portraits in small format and miniature are in an archaizing style reminiscent of the Madrid school towards the end of the 17th century. He also painted religious scenes, such as the *Immaculate Conception* (1713; Saragossa, Mus. Prov. B.A.). In his later works he was influenced by the aesthetic ideas brought to Spain by Michel-Ange Houasse and Jean Ranc. Iriarte's paintings on themes from *Don Quixote* (Madrid, Prado) demonstrate particularly clearly in the choice of subject, the details and the background landscapes the influence of Houasse, whom he would have known at the court of Madrid. He has sometimes been confused with the Valencian painter Cristóbal Valero (*c.* 1707–89).

BIBLIOGRAPHY

A. E. Pérez Sánchez: 'Valero Iriarte', *Bol. Mus. Prado*, ix (1982), pp. 147–56

JUAN J. LUNA

Irimescu, Ion (*b* Preotesti, 1 March 1903). Romanian sculptor, draughtsman and teacher. He studied from 1924 to 1928 at the Fine Arts School, Bucharest, under Dimitrie Paciurea. He made his début at the Official Salon in Bucharest for painting and sculpture, becoming a regular participant there. In 1929 he received a scholarship to the Romanian School at Fontenay aux Roses in France and exhibited at the Salon des Artistes Français in Paris; in the following year he studied at the Académie de la Grande Chaumière under Joseph Bernard. Until 1933 he participated at the Salon d'Automne and Salon du Printemps in Paris, receiving in 1932 the Honorary Mention of the Société des Artistes Français. He returned to Romania in 1934, and from 1937 he took part regularly at the exhibitions of Tinerimea Artistică (The young artists), a society founded in 1901 that included the most prominent Romanian artists; in 1938 he became an associate member of the society. Between 1940 and 1950 he was professor of sculpture at the Fine Arts Academy in Iaşi, and from 1950 he was a professor at the Institute of Fine and Decorative Art 'Ion Andreescu' in Cluj-Napoca. Irimescu became well known not only for his large- and small-scale portrait busts, but also for the neutral stance that he took as an 'official' artist during the years of communist domination. Although he was able to adapt to the requirements of Socialist Realism (e.g. *Steel-smelter*, bronze, 1954; see Oprescu, p. 119), he responded to its abolition by a new creative phase, in which he developed a vegetal morphology inspired by his own calligraphic drawings and the malleability of ceramics. Although Irimescu produced many sculptures in stone, conceived for and erected in public spaces, he concentrated more on modelling and on small-scale sculptures. In 1975 a Ion Irimescu Museum was established in Fălticeni with a substantial donation from the artist.

BIBLIOGRAPHY

G. Oprescu: *Romanian Sculpture* (Bucharest, 1957), pp. 116–22 [in Eng.]

CĂLIN DAN

Irkutsk. Russian city and regional centre in Eastern Siberia. It was founded in 1661 on the right bank of the Angara River on the trade route south to Lake Baikal and Mongolia. By 1686, when it received the status of a town, Irkutsk had two wooden fortresses and a wooden church (1672; destr.). During the 18th and 19th centuries it was one of the most important administrative, trading and cultural centres in Eastern Siberia. The historic centre contains the oldest two-tiered church in Eastern Siberia, the church of the Saviour (1706–10), which was built in the architectural styles of 17th-century Moscow, and the cathedral of the Epiphany (1718–31), decorated with Russian, Baroque and local Siberian ornamentation. From the river the skyline is dominated by the Znamensky Monastery (founded 1689), which contains the multi-storey church of the Sign (1757–62), with intricate Baroque decoration on the façades. The churches of the Arrival in Jerusalem (18th century) and the Exaltation of the Cross (1747–58), which is decorated in Siberian Baroque style (*see* RUSSIA, §III, 2(i)), were built on higher ground. The city's old quarter retains its radial street plan, which developed after 1792. Monuments since the late 18th century include the Neo-classical Governor's Palace (1800–04), the Russian and Asiatic Bank Building (1903) in Modern style and wooden houses (second half of the 19th century–early 20th) with varied sculptural and carved decoration. The art museum (founded 1936) houses a collection of Siberian icons, sculpture and wood-carvings.

BIBLIOGRAPHY

B. Olgy: *Irkutsk: O planirovke i arkhitekture goroda* [Irkutsk: the layout and architecture of the city] (Irkutsk, 1982)
N. Polunina: *Zhivaya starina Priangar'ya* [The varied past of the Angara region] (Moscow, 1990)

M. I. ANDREYEV

Iron and steel. Metals closely related in nature, use and history, steel being a purified form of iron. Iron is the fourth most abundant element and the second most common metal (after aluminium) in the Earth's crust, of which it comprises about 5%. Both iron and steel are notable for their strength, although pure iron is soft and silvery white in colour. It is seldom found in its pure state, however, and it exists most commonly as iron oxide combined with numerous other minerals in iron ore, while meteoric iron contains about 10% of nickel. Iron is extracted from ore by a process of smelting, during which the iron generally absorbs carbon as well as retaining some impurities. Steel is a form of iron with its impurities reduced to a minimum and its carbon content carefully controlled. The earliest examples of meteoric iron fashioned into decorative objects date from the 4th millennium BC, and man-made iron was produced *c.* 2800 BC (*see* §II, 3 below), but the modern tradition of ironworking can be traced back to techniques mastered *c.* 1500 BC by the Hittites in Anatolia. From there these spread eastwards to China and west to Europe, allowing iron to replace bronze as the metal most commonly used for tools and especially arms and armour throughout Europe and Asia and heralding the gradual supersession of the Bronze Age by the Iron Age: the English name 'iron' may derive from the Celtic *isarno*, which in turn is probably related to the Latin word for bronze, *aes*. Steel was also known in antiquity, and the two metals remained important materials in the decorative arts traditions of most European and Asian countries (these traditions are generally discussed within the metalwork sections of regional and country survey articles). Iron also came to be used in Byzantine, Gothic and Islamic architecture, particularly for highly decorative elements, including grilles, railings and door hinges. From the mid-18th century, however, when techniques for its mass production were developed, iron took on a new importance, playing a vital role in the Industrial Revolution through its suitability for use in transport and engineering, including the construction of railways and bridges. In the 19th century wrought and cast iron began to be used for structural members, but in the late 19th century advances in steel technology led to the establishment of that material as the primary structural building material, often used to reinforce concrete (*see* CONCRETE, §II, 1(iii)) and often used in alloys with other metals. It also came to be commonly used for the mass production of countless everyday and household items, including cars, furniture and domestic implements. Wrought iron in particular, however, continued, with steel, to be an important material not only in the applied arts but also in sculpture.

I. Types and properties. II. History and uses.

I. *Types and properties.*

The types and properties of iron and steel relate to the techniques used for their production. The technique of extracting iron from ore by smelting was, until the medieval period, carried out in a hole in the ground, in a stone shaft or (later) in a cupola-shaped shaft made of fired clay (*see* AFRICA, fig. 48). Charcoal and iron ore were heated together and then cooled to form a lump known as a 'bloom', mixed with impurities that could be removed by hand-hammering. The resulting wrought iron was light grey in appearance, with a woody grain. This could be shaped quite freely, hammered (i.e. forged), cut, twisted, stretched, cut and pierced, made malleable by annealing (a process of heating and then slowly cooling the iron). In Europe and the Middle East all iron was produced as wrought iron until the Middle Ages and was available only in fairly small quantities.

Cast iron is produced by melting iron ore in a high-temperature furnace, where it generally absorbs some of the carbon from the fuel used to heat the furnace. The liquid metal is then drawn off and channelled either into finished moulds or into intermediary blocks ('pigs'), which can later be remelted and cast into finished objects. A wide variety of often very intricate forms is therefore possible. Considerable numbers of cast-iron tools and moulds have been excavated from what appears to have been a large foundry in China, dating from the 3rd century BC (*see* CHINA, §XIII, 14(i)(a)). The production of cast iron in Europe, however, dates only from the medieval period and the introduction of such technological developments as the Catalan hearth, an early form of blast furnace that used bellows to heat the charcoal-fuelled furnace to unprecedented temperatures. A shortage of wood and hence charcoal in the 17th century prompted the search for an alternative fuel. Around 1710, at Coalbrookdale, Salop, Abraham Darby II (1711–63) successfully developed coke, a by-product of coal, which could both achieve the required temperatures to liquefy the iron and support larger quantities of ore in the furnace, and this enabled the massive expansion of the cast-iron industries in the 18th and 19th centuries to take place.

In addition to the elemental iron, the chemical components of the common commercial grades of cast iron include carbon (varying from 1.7% to 4%); phosphorus, silicon and sulphur (regarded as impurities and totalling something between 1.1% and 4.2%); and manganese (0.5% to 1%). Cast iron has a high compressive strength, commonly 42,000 kilonewtons, but a relatively low tensile strength, ranging from 13,000 to 18,000 kN. The metal is thus hard but somewhat brittle, making it suitable for structural members in compression (i.e. columns) but unsuitable for those subject to bending and hence tension (i.e. beams); it is also abrasion-resistant and comparatively resistant to corrosion. Modern industrial wrought iron is produced by refining cast iron through reheating it in a furnace in the presence of iron oxide to reduce the amount of carbon. This produces a slag that is then mixed with the iron to produce a workable metal. The iron is not heated to fusion but to a plastic state in which it is rolled or worked to the ultimate form. Wrought iron is hence low in carbon, of which it seldom contains more than 0.02%, and is relatively free also of the usual impurities, which seldom exceed 1.2%. Slag (chiefly iron silicate) runs to 2.5% and is an important factor in giving the worked metal its fibrous structure. Wrought iron has a high tensile strength in the direction of the fibres, ranging from 34,000 to 42,000 kN. This property led to its use in the 19th century for such structural members as beams and girders.

Steel, combining the strength of wrought iron with the malleability of cast, was also produced in antiquity, when it was discovered that cakes of iron partially carburized in charcoal fires produced a material of great hardness and flexibility that could be forged by continued hammering and reheating into swords and other sharp-edged implements. In India and Sri Lanka, a type of crucible steel (*wootz*) was developed, and crucible steel was later produced in Europe. Both methods required great skill, however, and produced only small quantities of steel. Steelmaking therefore remained a specialized and therefore somewhat restricted craft until the late 1850s, when a process for its mass production was introduced by Henry Bessemer (1813–98). This involved forcing air through a bath of molten pig iron, thus bringing oxygen into contact with the iron and reducing its carbon content to the required level. The Bessemer converter also allowed the addition of other elements to improve the qualities of the steel to be strictly controlled, and it facilitated the production of steel for construction and other industrial purposes. Subsequent variations on the Bessemer process were developed in the 1860s (Siemens-Martin or open-hearth method, which allows the use of a large proportion of scrap) and in the 1950s (basic oxygen process, which greatly reduces the time taken in the process). Steel has all the physical properties of cast and wrought iron and only one comparative defect: its vulnerability, except in some special alloys, to oxidation, resulting in the formation of greenish-black ferrous (Iron II) oxide, reddish-brown ferric (Iron III) oxide (rust) or iron ferrous-ferric oxide, containing both Iron II and Iron III. Most steel used for structural and commercial purposes is plain-carbon steel (i.e. it contains no alloys), and any exposed surfaces therefore require frequent painting; galvanized steel, with a protective zinc coating, is commonly used for roof sheeting. The chemical components of plain-carbon steel indicate its relative purity: the essential element, carbon, comprises no more than 0.22% of the total, while the impurities are held to a total of less than 0.3%. In elasticity, stiffness, ductility and malleability, steel is far superior to wrought or cast iron; its tensile strength ranges from 34,000 to 46,000 kN, and its compressive strength matches the 42,000 kN of cast iron. By the end of the 20th century, the majority of iron produced was used as a raw material for the production of steel.

A wide range of alloy steels has been developed to meet the special requirements of hardness, machinability, extreme conditions of stress, and abrasion-, heat- and corrosion-resistance demanded in the modern construction industry and for the manufacture of engines, aircraft and machinery. The two kinds of alloy most commonly used for building purposes are stainless steel and self-weathering steel. The former, which may contain up to 19% chromium (in addition to nickel, manganese and molybdenum), is almost entirely corrosion-resistant and has a tensile strength of up to 77,000 kN. It is primarily used for decorative elements and for the external cladding of buildings or for the external covering of spandrels and columns; its high cost prevents its use for structural members, to which it is otherwise ideally suited. Self-weathering steel (usually identified under manufacturers' trade names, e.g. Cor-Ten steel) does not resist oxidation but renders the oxide that forms on it into a self-renewing protective coating. The alloying elements are generally chromium, copper, manganese and nickel, used in roughly equal proportions. It is the only metal commonly used in building construction to have a distinctive aesthetic quality, because of its dark reddish-brown colour and its soft external texture. Again, because of its high cost it is seldom used for structural purposes and is mainly employed to cover the fire-resistant cladding on structural elements in multi-storey buildings.

Methods of shaping steel include the continuous casting of bars and rods, and the processing of industrial products in a variety of rolling mills; among these are hot-strip and cold-strip mills for sheet steel, and mills for plates, rails, pipes, rods and wire, bars and various structural steel sections. Details of other methods for the shaping and joining of iron and steel (e.g. forging, casting, riveting and welding), as well as decorative techniques (e.g. blueing, carving, damascening and embossing), which are not peculiar to iron and steel, are discussed under METAL, §§III, IV and V.

See also CHROMIUM and ELECTROPLATING.

BIBLIOGRAPHY
C. Hornbostel: *Materials for Architecture* (New York, 1961)
Metals Handbook, i (Metals Park, OH, rev. 9/1978)

CARL W. CONDIT

II. History and uses.

1. Architecture. 2. Sculpture. 3. Applied arts.

1. ARCHITECTURE. From earliest archaeological times until late in the 18th century timber and masonry, in one form or another, dominated almost all building construction. In just over two centuries since, the methods of supporting all but the simplest buildings have been revolutionized, first by the introduction of cast iron, then industrialized wrought iron and finally steel. The heyday of structural cast iron lasted from c. 1790 to the mid-1840s, when wrought iron began to take over, remaining the supreme structural material until in turn it gave way to steel in the last quarter of the 19th century. Cast iron continued to be used quite frequently for columns (always in compression) or for lowly stressed brackets until c. 1900. Today scarcely any truly structural cast iron is used, and no wrought iron is made. Steel is wholly dominant. There are, however, some signs of a limited revival of cast iron, particularly in the new ductile form available since the 1940s. Because of their distinct properties (*see* §I above) and periods of supremacy, it is convenient to consider the achievements with these three ferous materials under three separate but overlapping ages.

(i) c. 1750–c. 1850. (ii) c. 1850–c. 1880. (iii) After c. 1880.

(i) c. 1750–c. 1850. It was not until the mid-18th century, after the introduction of coke for smelting, that cast iron became cheap and plentiful enough and of sufficiently high quality to allow it to play a significant role in architecture—an example of new material being introduced either for its greater economy or to solve specific problems. Fire was one such recurring problem, and it was almost certainly the reason for one very early application of cast iron, in the columns supporting the vast cooker hood and chimney (1752) at Alcobaça Abbey in Portugal. In Britain, cast iron was used in churches from the 1770s, partly for the cheap reproduction of Gothic ornament but also for structural columns, as well as in the construction of a number of bridges. The first of these was an arched bridge

(1777–9) over the River Severn, designed by Thomas Farnolls Pritchard (1723–77) and built by Abraham Darby III (1750–91) at Coalbrookdale, where a 30-m span of cast iron replaced the traditional stone arch (see fig. 1). In Russia, architectural cast iron was used extensively throughout the 18th century, but it is unclear to what extent it was also used to support floors and roofs. Cast iron was a rarity in 18th-century France, but some highly innovative wrought-iron floors and roofs were built, such as Victor Louis's roof at the Théâtre du Palais Royal (1786–90) in Paris, which spanned 21 m.

It is difficult to discern any important trends arising from these early applications of iron to buildings. It was in the multi-storey textile mills of Britain in the 1790s that cast iron was first shown to have an important future in buildings, the disastrous fire at Albion Mill, Blackfriars, London, in 1791 being perhaps the biggest incentive for change. Charles Bage (1752–1822) and William Strutt (1756–1830) were the most important pioneers, developing incombustible interiors with cast-iron columns and brick jack arches spanning between the beams (e.g. Bage's Benyon Marshall & Bage Flax Mill, Shrewsbury, Salop, 1796–7, and Strutt's North Mill, Belper, Derbys, 1803). The earliest interiors had floor spans of only *c*. 2.5–3 m in each direction, as had been the case with timber interiors. Later this iron mill construction spread to warehouses with a gradual opening of spans.

Cast-iron beams were also important in public buildings and large houses, where there was a growing desire for long-span floors that did not sag or bounce. Timber had generally proved inadequate, and between *c*. 1800 and the 1840s there was an increasing interest in cast-iron floor beams, some with floor spans of 12 m or more. At first these castings were used as simple substitutes for the main timbers in essentially timber flooring, but later, brick jack arches—as in the mills of *c*. 1810—or stone slabs were combined with long-span cast-iron beams to give rigidity, sound insulation and fire protection. This development reached its climax in the Palace of Westminster (1837–67), London, by Charles Barry with A. W. N. Pugin, in which the iron roof-plates are the only visible parts of the iron structure. Little is known about the engineers responsible for fixing the shape and size of the beams used by Barry and other architects of this period. Thomas Tredgold's *Practical Essay on the Strength of Cast Iron* (1822) was undoubtedly influential but was dangerously in error in some respects. In most cases it is probable that the widely used test loading of beams provided the main safeguard against misconceptions and poor workmanship.

In the first half of the 19th century cast iron was applied to a wide variety of other uses besides mills and long-span floors, sometimes on its own for complete structures, as for example Hungerford Market (1836) and Bunning's highly decorated Coal Exchange (1847–9), London, and often in combination with timber, as in the New Tobacco Dock (1811–14; destr.), London, or with wrought iron as in the 1837 roof of Euston Station, London. After *c*. 1840 the scale of iron construction and the proportion of wrought iron in composite structures increased substantially. The Palm House at Kew Gardens (1845–8; rest. 1984–91; for illustration *see* KEW, ROYAL BOTANIC GARDENS OF), by Richard Turner and DECIMUS BURTON, was

1. Iron Bridge, Coalbrookdale, by Thomas Farnolls Pritchard and Abraham Darby III, 1777–9

a marked advance on earlier glasshouses and arguably incorporated the world's first rolled I sections. Wrought-iron roofs of increasing spans on cast-iron columns proliferated in the naval dockyards and railway stations, culminating in the roof (1849) designed by engineer Richard Turner (c. 1798–1881) for Lime Street Station, Liverpool, which spanned 47 m.

Outside of Britain cast iron was used more sporadically. Around 1850 American buildings were still largely of timber, while the 'cast-iron age' largely bypassed France, where the wrought-iron techniques of the pre-Revolutionary period lingered, although in the 1830s and 1840s these were applied in combination with cast-iron technology. Nevertheless, some notable iron structures in France date from this period, such as the replacement roof (1837–9) by Mignon for Chartres Cathedral; the iron dome constructed over the Halle au Blé (1813; rebuilt 1889 as the Bourse de Commerce), Paris, by François-Joseph Bélanger and Jacques Ignace Hittorff; the earliest railway stations; and the Bibliothèque Sainte-Geneviève (1843–51), Paris, in which Henri Labrouste achieved a new, monumental expression for an iron structure in an important public building (see LABROUSTE, fig. 1). It also seems certain that the rolled wrought-iron I-beam was first established commercially in France, by Ferdinand Zorés in 1848. In Russia there was a considerable amount of iron construction in the first half of the 19th century, for example at the Alexandrinsky (now Pushkin) Theatre (1828–33; by Karl Rossl and Matthew Clark) and in the cast-iron dome (1837–41; by August Ricard de Montferrand) of St Isaac's Cathedral, both in St Petersburg. A form of riveted plate girder was devised in 1838 for the repair of the Winter Palace after the fire of 1837, ten years before the independent development of riveted wrought-iron beams in Britain.

R. J. M. SUTHERLAND

(ii) c. *1850–c. 1880.* By the middle of the 19th century, partly as a result of the gradual collapse of five storeys of Radcliffe's Mill in Oldham, Lancs, in 1844 and the failure of the Dee Bridge in Scotland in 1847, cast iron was losing much of its reputation for reliability, especially when used for beams. In this context, its place was largely taken by riveted wrought iron, as a result of a brilliant programme of research and testing carried out in 1845–8 by Eaton Hodgkinson (1789–1861) for the Britannia Bridge, Anglesey, designed by Robert Stephenson and Francis Thompson, and patented flooring systems were freely available for public and commercial buildings. In the decades that followed, a mastery of the theoretical structural issues combined with a burgeoning iron industry, not only in Britain but also on the Continent, to enable some of the most spectacular iron-and-glass structures with long-span roofs to be built. Among the best known and most significant was the Crystal Palace, built by Paxton for the Great Exhibition in London in 1851 (for illustration *see* PAXTON, JOSEPH); it had an exhibition space of 98,000 sq. m and was prefabricated away from the site, being erected in only six months (*see also* RATIONALIZED CONSTRUCTION, §2 and fig. 1). It was followed by several notable works in London, including Paddington Station (1852; *see* RAILWAY STATION, fig. 2) by Brunel and Matthew Digby Wyatt, and the 73 m wrought-iron arches of

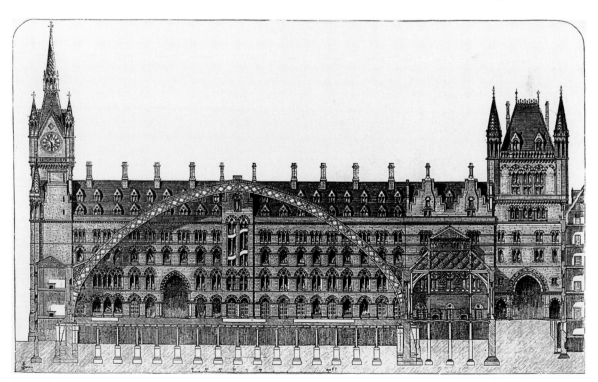

2. Wrought-iron arches at St Pancras Station, London, by W. H. Barlow and R. M. Ordish, 1866–8; section from the north through the train-shed, from *The Engineer*, xxiii (1867), p. 540

St Pancras Station (1866–8; see fig. 2); the ribbed cast-iron dome of the British Library Reading Room (1854–7; *see* LIBRARY, fig. 2) by Sydney Smirke; and the wrought-iron trussed dome of the Royal Albert Hall (1867–71; by Francis Fowke and Henry Young Darracott Scott). These were matched in France by Les Halles (1854–68), Paris, by Victor Baltard (for illustration *see* BALTARD, (2)), which became a prototype for market halls elsewhere in Europe; and in Italy by the Galleria Vittorio Emanuele II, Milan (1861–77; for illustration *see* MENGONI, GIUSEPPE), the culmination of iron-and-glass design for shopping arcades. Most of these buildings, however, had traditional masonry façades: the notable exceptions were the Crystal Palace and Les Halles.

In the USA, too, the superior strength of iron as a primary building material was recognized, for example in the cast-iron dome of the Capitol (1855–63) in Washington, DC, by Thomas Ustick Walter and Montgomery Meigs, and in the wrought-iron structural support of such early skyscrapers as the Cooper Union Building in New York in 1859 by Frederick A. Peterson (*see also* SKYSCRAPER, §1). Decorated cast-iron façades also continued to be used, their structural and decorative possibilities exemplified in the cast-iron and glass commercial buildings in the SoHo district of New York. In 1850 JAMES BOGARDUS patented a prefabricated 'fireproof' iron building, an important forerunner of modern building technology. In his Laing Stores (1848–9), New York, he translated the traditional post-and-lintel system from granite to iron. Cast-iron columns had the effect of providing larger display areas, and the façades were viewed as contemporary, inexpensive and long-lasting. Several companies, such as the Architectural Iron Works founded by DANIEL D. BADGER in New York, took advantage of the new market, creating detailing and ornamentation. Many companies used iron construction from the 1860s to the 1880s (when new fire regulations prohibited the exposure of unprotected iron frames), and the use of prefabrication spread throughout the USA and into Europe, with prefabricated components (e.g. railings) and whole buildings being exported to other continents, such as Africa and Australia.

Iron continued to be popular for ornamental work elsewhere: the Oriel Chambers office building (1864), Liverpool, by Peter Ellis (1804–84) employed iron panels hung between stone piers to create a delicate effect, and cast iron was used for the many new balustrades and railings built in such cities as Paris and New Orleans: the cast-iron fence (1855) of the Cornstalk Hotel, New Orleans, with its ears of corn on their stalks, is a distinctive example. Gates, fences, window lintels, grilles, lighting fixtures and decorative elements from rosettes to graceful openwork are examples of the proliferation of ironwork in the 19th century. Decoratively stamped pressed sheet iron was also used for ceilings. In contrast to some buildings that adopted a simple approach to the design of structural ironwork (see fig. 3), ornamental structures reached their peak with such buildings as the University Museum (1855–61), Oxford, by Deane & Woodward, which has a delicate Gothic Revival iron structure supporting a glass roof; the reading room at the Bibliothèque Nationale (1860–67), Paris, by Henri Labrouste, with

3. Iron and glass roof of the Corn Exchange, Leeds, by Cuthbert Brodrick, 1860–62

multiple domes supported on ornamental iron arches; the department store Au Bon Marché (1867–76), Paris, by Louis-Auguste Boileau and others, with its huge, ornamented stairwells (for illustration *see* DEPARTMENT STORE); and the Menier Chocolate Factory (1871) at Noisiel-sur-Marne, by Jules Saulnier, in which an ornamental effect was achieved with diagonal iron bracing expressed on the exterior of a patterned masonry infill wall. This building was favourably mentioned by Viollet-le-Duc, who promoted the use of iron as a rational structural technique and produced some extraordinary proposals (*see* VIOLLET-LE-DUC, EUGÈNE-EMMANUEL, fig. 4).

(iii) After c. 1880. Although wrought iron had a greater tensile strength than cast iron, it was much more expensive. A cheaper solution to the deficiencies of cast iron was provided in 1856, when Henry Bessemer (1813–98) invented an industrial process for steel production (*see* §I above). Some remarkable iron structures continued to be built, such as the Eiffel Tower in Paris (1887–9; for illustration *see* EIFFEL, GUSTAVE), but by the 1870s and 1880s steel had become the primary structural material, with rolled steel joists being produced in Britain by the mid-1880s. In the USA similar systems of production were developed, and such companies as Carnegie Phipps & Co., who were producing rolled steel beams by 1885, set the stage for that country to become the chief steel-producing nation. Steel soon became the most popular building material in the railway industry as well as in bridges: the Eads Bridge (1867–74; by JAMES BUCHANAN EADS) across the Mississippi River at St Louis, MO, for example, used steel trusses; the Brooklyn Bridge (1869–83; *see* NEW YORK, fig. 4) employed steel cable that had been spun, an

idea developed by its builder John Augustus Roebling (*see* ROEBLING, (1)); and the Firth of Forth Bridge (begun by 1883; by Benjamin Baker and John Fowler), near Edinburgh, proved that steel was the ideal material for long spans (here 520 m). Steel was not only used to build ever taller buildings but also to achieve greater spans. By 1889 the 73 m arches at St Pancras Station had been surpassed by the 115 m span of the Galerie des Machines, Paris (see fig. 4), while in the late 20th century, roofs of much larger spans became quite common: the Louisiana Superdome, for example, built in 1975, is 207 m in diameter, more than 3½ times the span of the Royal Albert Hall.

Most importantly, perhaps, the mass production of steel, together with such technological developments as the introduction of the passenger lift, gave birth to the fully framed tall building (*see* SKYSCRAPER, §1 and fig. 1), which enabled unprecedented building heights to be achieved. The change from internal metal framing with masonry external walls to full skeletal framing was a gradual process, with most of the advances made in the USA. The first virtually fully framed tall building was the 11-storey Home Insurance Building in Chicago (1883–5; destr. 1931; *see* CHICAGO, fig. 1), by WILLIAM LE BARON JENNEY. This used a framework of load-bearing steel and iron that allowed the building to have lighter masonry walls and larger windows, thereby creating more rentable space. Other architects of the CHICAGO SCHOOL turned the city's Loop district into a commercial zone of bold

4. Steel structure of the Galerie des Machines, Paris, by Charles-Louis-Ferdinand Dutert and Contamin, Pierron and Charton, 1889

steel-framed structures, with masonry walls becoming mere curtains connected to a steel skeleton frame by spandrels. Some of the skyscrapers using steel-frame technology were built in New York in a variety of architectural styles, from the Gothicized Woolworth Building (1910–13; for illustration *see* GILBERT, CASS) to the classicized Flat Iron Building (1902) by Daniel H. Burnham. The Ritz Hotel (1904–5; by Mewès & Davis), London, is usually considered to be the first building in the UK with a full metallic frame. In fact the Boat Store (1858–60; by Godfrey Greene) at Sheerness, Kent, has a better claim to this title, but the design of the Ritz clearly owes more to developments in the USA. Elsewhere in Europe, the use of steel provided early demonstrations of the modernist belief that function and structure should be the only expressive media; such buildings include the Beursgebouw (1896–1903), Amsterdam, by H. P. Berlage (for illustration *see* EXCHANGE); Horta's beautiful Art Nouveau structures in Brussels, including the Maison Tassel (1892–3; *see* HORTA, VICTOR, fig. 1); and the AEG Turbinenfabrik (1909), Moabit, Berlin, by PETER BEHRENS (*see* MODERN MOVEMENT, fig. 1).

From as early as the 1850s iron had been used to reinforce concrete (*see* CONCRETE, §II, 1(iii)), and in the 1870s and 1880s steel reinforcement was rapidly developed, its inherent resistance to fire being an important consideration. ERNEST L. RANSOME developed a reinforced concrete frame similar to the steel frames being used in Chicago and elsewhere. In Europe, the PERRET brothers became known for their innovative use of visible reinforced concrete frames (e.g. 25-bis Rue Franklin, 1903; with François Hennebique; *see* PARIS, §II, 6 and fig. 11). From the 1940s glass curtain wall and steel buildings became common among architects associated with the INTERNATIONAL STYLE, many of whom were influenced by the work of Mies van der Rohe; his buildings, for example for the Illinois Institute of Technology, Chicago (e.g. Crown Hall, 1950–56; *see* MIES VAN DER ROHE, LUDWIG, fig. 2), have elegantly detailed, exposed steel columns and steel girders, from which the roof hangs. This form of steel architecture, which allows for uninterrupted interior spaces, harks back to earlier Chicago models of steel-frame construction. In the 1950s and 1960s reinforced concrete was particularly popular for many buildings, although steel began to be used prominently in tensile architecture (*see* TENSION STRUCTURE) and associated buildings, such as the National Gymnasia (1964), Tokyo (for illustration *see* TANGE, KENZŌ). Towards the end of the 20th century there was a strong revival of structural steel, encouraged by the pursuit of 'fast-track' construction and the maintenance requirements of reinforced concrete. This trend was marked by the use of steel space-frames (see fig. 5; *see also* SPACE-FRAME), and a shift towards High Tech styling, seen in the Centre Georges Pompidou (1971–7; by Renzo Piano and Richard Rogers; *see* PARIS, fig. 14); the Lloyds Building (1979–87), London (for illustration *see* ROGERS, RICHARD); the Hongkong & Shanghai Bank (1985), Hong Kong (for illustration *see* FOSTER, NORMAN); and the Renault Distribution Centre (1984), Swindon, Wilts, a cable-stayed structure, also by Foster (for illustration *see* HIGH TECH).

5. Steel space-frame structure of the Crystal Cathedral, Garden Grove, California, by Philip Johnson and John Burgee, 1980

Steel has also been used in combination with other materials. For example, stainless steel, or chromium nickel steel, although in itself very expensive (for which reason it is not usually found as the structural element in large-scale projects), is relatively economical when the cost of maintenance is taken into consideration, making it suitable for decorative purposes. The best example of its decorative use is the Chrysler Building, New York, by William Van Alen (1928–30; see SKYSCRAPER, fig. 2), which has cast stainless steel radiator-cap gargoyles, beautifully fabricated basket-weave entrance portal decorations and lift doors in steel inlaid with wood. With the rise of Art Deco and the taste for streamlining, steel became particularly important as a decorative element: stainless steel doors, lamps and lettering were common in the 1920s and 1930s, as were stainless steel American diners in the 1940s. These usually included coloured enamelled steel panels juxtaposed with stainless steel on the exteriors and stainless steel equipment on the interiors. Steel is also sometimes combined with a small percentage of copper, which creates a patina that resists corrosion. This self-weathering 'Cor-Ten' steel became popular with some sculptors (see §3 below) but was used only occasionally by architects (e.g. Bush Lane House, Cannon Street, London, 1970–76; by Ove Arup); in this building, as in the Centre Pompidou, the externally expressed steel frame was filled with water for fire protection.

BIBLIOGRAPHY

T. Tredgold: *A Practical Essay on the Strength of Cast Iron* (London, 1822)
C. L. G. Eck: *Traité de l'application du fer de la fonte et de la tôle* (Paris, 1841)
J. P. Rondelet: *Traité théorétique et pratique de l'art de bâtir* (Paris, 1847–8)
W. Birkmire: *Architectural Iron and Steel, and its Application in the Construction of Buildings* (London, 1891, rev. 1976)
T. C. Bannister: 'The First Iron-framed Buildings', *Archit. Rev.* [London], cvii (1950), pp. 231–46

S. P. Timoshenko: *History of the Strength of Materials* (New York, 1953)
H. R. Johnson and A. W. Skempton: 'William Strutt's Cotton Mills', *Trans. Newcomen Soc.*, 30 (1955–7), pp. 179–205
H. R. Schubert: *History of the British Iron and Steel Industry, from 450 BC to AD 1775* (London, 1957)
R. Maguire and P. Mathews: 'The Iron Bridge at Coalbrookdale', *Archit. Assoc. J.*, lxxiv (1958), pp. 30–45
A. W. Skempton and H. R. Johnson: 'The Boat Store, Sheerness (1958–60) and its Place in Structural History', *Trans. Newcomen Soc.*, 32 (1959–60)
S. Giedion: *Space, Time and Architecture* (Cambridge, MA, 1962)
A. W. Skempton and H. R. Johnson: 'The First Iron Frames', *Archit. Rev.* [London], cxiv (1962), pp. 175–86
P. Temin: *Iron and Steel in Nineteenth Century America: An Economic Inquiry* (Cambridge, MA, 1964)
C. W. Condit: *American Building* (Chicago, 1968)
F. Hart, W. Henn and H. Sontag: *Multi-storey Buildings in Steel* (New York, 1978)
Metals in America's Historic Buildings, US Department of the Interior (Washington, DC, 1980)
J. G. James: 'The Application of Iron to Bridges and Other Structures in Russia to about 1850', *Trans. Newcomen Soc.*, 54 (1983)
F. H. Steiner: *French Iron Architecture* (Ann Arbor, 1984)
R. J. M. Sutherland: 'The Birth of Stress: A Historical Review', *75th Anniversary International Conference of the Institution of Structural Engineers: London, 1984*
S. Kostoff: *A History of Architecture: Settings and Rituals* (New York, 1985)

PAUL ELI IVEY
(bibliography with R. J. M. SUTHERLAND)

2. SCULPTURE. Steel was first used by artists shortly before World War I, and several factors soon contributed to its popularity as a material for sculpture. Its extensive use in industry attracted those artists who were seeking forms appropriate to the machine age; it also provided an inexhaustible supply of cheap metal in the form of prefabricated parts, offcuts and scrap. Until the 1930s the metal used in sculpture was usually referred to as iron, although much of it must have been steel, which is more

rather than creating them anew, and as the process is usually carried out in iron or steel, artists encouraged the further use of these materials in sculpture. Gargallo meanwhile perfected his characteristic style working in iron on such sculptures as *Harlequin with Flute* (1931; see fig. 7) and *Antinoüs* (1932; for illustration *see* GARGALLO, PABLO).

A consistent use of steel as a sculptural material can be traced to varous developments in the late 1920s. Artists associated with Constructivism, such as ANTOINE PEVS-NER and NAUM GABO, began to use steel in their work, liking its strength and rigidity as well as its associations with engineering. From 1928 to 1931 Picasso made a series of sculptures in collaboration with JULIO GONZÁLEZ in the latter's workshop, using iron wire and flattened metal already available there (*see* PICASSO, PABLO, fig. 8);

6. Steel sculpture in sheet metal and wire by Pablo Picasso: *Guitar*, 775×350×193 mm, 1912 (New York, Museum of Modern Art)

difficult to forge than wrought iron but stronger and more readily available. The malleability and ductility of steel, which enable it to be welded, forged, rolled and extruded, made it possible for artists to express openly the construction of the work and their involvement in it: direct-steel sculpture is assembled with no intervening stage, unlike cast metalwork. Conversely, other artists, especially those associated with Minimalism, deliberately distanced themselves from this manipulation of the material and had their designs fabricated in anonymous industrial conditions. Steel is available in different forms and finishes (*see* §I above), and corroded, chromed, stainless and perforated varieties are among those that have been used by artists; it may also be lacquered or painted.

The impetus for the use of iron and steel for sculpture can be traced to masks made by Pablo Gargallo as early as 1907. Mask-making is usually associated with the decorative arts, and Gargallo's work, in wrought iron and copper, stemmed from the Catalan crafts tradition. When Pablo Picasso saw the masks, he was inspired to create the first steel sculpture, *Guitar* (1912; New York, MOMA; see fig. 6), which is made of flat sheets of steel cut with tin snips. The primary significance of this work, however, was as a sculptural response to Cubist painting, and the importance of the material lay in its flatness rather than its inherent qualities as steel. Picasso also initiated the art form known as ASSEMBLAGE, which later became important to steel sculpture. His first such work, *Glass of Absinthe* (1914; New York, MOMA), a cast bronze incorporating a real spoon, created a precedent for the use of objects with their original identity intact. Welding proved an appropriate method for joining together existing forms

7. Iron sculpture by Pablo Gargallo: *Harlequin with Flute*, 1931 (Paris, Pompidou, Musée National d'Art Moderne)

González taught Picasso to weld. He himself used cut and wrought sheet iron in masks and planar heads inspired by Cubism and by African art (e.g. *Head of Pilar in the Sun*, h. 180 mm; Paris, Pompidou). The open-form constructions that Picasso created introduced a radically new approach to space. He continued with heads and figures composed of found-iron pieces, including kitchen utensils, garden tools and scraps of machinery (e.g. *Head of a Woman*, painted iron, h. 1 m; Paris, Mus. Picasso). The use of a three-dimensional structure to enclose and delineate volume became a constant theme in later steel sculpture. Picasso's liberating influence redirected González's own work: from dabbling in various media, he concentrated on direct, welded iron assemblages and works rooted in Constructivism and drawn from a surreal fantasy of imagined forms.

Also in the late 1920s the American Alexander Calder began to use steel wire for abstract constructions, and in the early 1930s he made his first mobiles of wire and sheet metal, which he exploited for its elegance and relative lightness (for illustration *see* CALDER, (3)); these were followed by vast metal-plate sculptures that he called stabiles, which proved particularly influential on other artists in the 1960s. Another prominent sculptor associated with the use of welded steel was the American David Smith, who became aware of González's work and of his collaborations with Picasso through articles in *Cahiers d'art* published in 1929 and 1935. Smith prized steel for its particular qualities rather than just for its convenience, using prefabricated parts and discarded objects but treating their surfaces in an expressive and individualistic manner by burnishing, polishing and grinding them, as in his *Tanktotem* series of the 1950s (see fig. 8), which incorporated industrial objects (*see also* UNITED STATES OF AMERICA, fig. 23). These and subsequent works, notably the *Voltri* and *Cubi* series of the 1960s, confirmed the validity of steel as a material for sculpture (for illustration *see* SMITH, DAVID). Such works influenced younger sculptors, such as the English artist ANTHONY CARO, who from the early 1960s used steel offcuts and prefabricated parts, often painted in bright colours, as the basis for his elaboration of form. Prominent among other artists in Britain alone who began in the 1960s to produce abstract sculpture in steel (including stainless, painted and corroded steel) were Phillip King, Tim Scott, William Tucker and William Turnbull.

González continued to use iron. The Danish sculptor Robert Jacobsen, arriving in Paris in 1947, chose scrap iron as his medium, cutting and welding the metal in cold state. His early pieces were whimsical anthropomorphs, largely derived from González's example (e.g. *Passenger*, 1955; Copenhagen, Stat. Mus. Kst). González's linear style was also influential on EDUARDO CHILLIDA, who moved towards a muscular, abstract language of his own. In collaboration with the local blacksmiths of his native Basque region, he welded fat iron bars and tubes into twisted, interlocking or gestural forms, free from superfluous detail (e.g. *Dream Anvil XX*, h. *c.* 1.48 m, 1962; Basle, Kstmus.).

In the period after World War II the recycling of discarded objects into art through welding was integral to the work of sculptors associated with JUNK ART, such as

8. Steel sculpture by David Smith: *Tanktotem V*, h. 2.45 m, 1956 (Cannondale, CT, Howard and Jean Lipman private collection)

Richard Stankiewicz, who made elegant constructions out of scrap and industrial parts, and John Chamberlain and César, who used crushed cars as their raw material (for illustration *see* CÉSAR). Kinetic artists also used steel: Jean Tinguely, for example, in assemblages made from motors and found parts; Julio Le Parc in objects using lateral sources of white light against polished metal surfaces (for illustration *see* KINETIC ART); and George Rickey in delicately balancing constructions. Minimalist sculptors such as Sol LeWitt, Tony Smith and Donald Judd exploited the impersonal machined quality of steel, especially in industrially fabricated units, which were ideally suited to an expression of serial repetition (*see* ABSTRACT ART, fig. 3). Whether taken in the form of industrial refuse or in specially produced sheets, steel continued to prove a popular material for sculptors, particularly for those involved with assemblage and other varieties of constructed or welded sculpture.

BIBLIOGRAPHY

H. Read: *A Concise History of Modern Sculpture* (London and New York, 1964)

American Sculpture of the Sixties (exh. cat., ed. M. Tuchman; Los Angeles, CA, Co. Mus. A., 1967)

J. Burnham: *Beyond Modern Sculpture: The Effects of Science and Technology on the Sculpture of This Century* (New York and London, 1968)

H. H. Arnason: *History of Modern Art: Painting, Sculpture, Architecture* (New York and London, 1969; rev. 3/1986)

The Alistair McAlpine Gift (exh. cat., essays by A. Seymour, R. Morphet and M. Compton; London, Tate, 1971) [British sculptors of the 1960s]

W. Tucker: *The Language of Sculpture* (London, 1974)

R. Krauss: *Passages in Modern Sculpture* (London, 1977)

T. Faulkner: *Direct Metal Sculpture* (London, 1978)

E. Lucie-Smith: *Sculpture since 1945* (London, 1987)

STANLEY E. MARCUS

3. APPLIED ARTS. The uses of iron and steel in the applied arts reflect the strength that is the metals' most notable characteristic. Essentially, two traditions have evolved, one relating to the art of working iron and the other to the use of the more malleable but stronger steel; cast iron has a much less extensive history in the applied arts.

(i) Iron. (ii) Steel.

(i) Iron. Beads fashioned from meteoric iron and dating from *c.* 3500 BC have been found at Jirzah in Egypt, but the first man-made iron was probably not produced until *c.* 2800 BC, the date ascribed to fragments of a wrought-iron dagger found at Tell-al-Azmar in Mesopotamia. In northern China wrought-iron artefacts dating from at least the 8th century BC have been found. These may have been brought from the West, but iron artefacts have also been found that were produced within China and dating from the early 5th century BC (*see* CHINA, §XIII, 14(i) and fig. 313). Iron (and steel) implements dating from the early historic period (3rd century BC–4th century AD) have also been found in Sri Lanka, where high-quality iron was later produced using monsoon winds to generate high temperatures in furnaces. Superior weapons-grade iron, and iron arms and armour, were exported from Sri Lanka from the 7th–8th centuries AD, especially to the Islamic world (*see* SRI LANKA, §VI, 1 and 8). Some of the most spectacular iron artefacts from the early Iron Age in Europe include iron swords found at HALLSTATT, Austria, and in Germany (*see* PREHISTORIC EUROPE, §VI, 3(i)). Other early examples of wrought ironwork in the West include a Celtic firedog, dating from the 1st century AD (Cardiff, N. Mus.). Originally one of a pair, its side terminates in a ram's head finial. The treasure from the Sutton Hoo Ship Burial (7th century AD; London, BM) includes an iron cauldron chain consisting of interlocking loops, some shaped as stylized rams' horns.

The early uses of iron were chiefly functional, for example for military equipment (*see* ARMS AND ARMOUR; *see also* ENGLAND, fig. 83). From the medieval period, however, it came to be used more decoratively in the production of such items as wrought-iron gates and grilles, often being worked, for example, into patterns resembling those used in Gothic tracery (*see* GOTHIC, §V). Notable examples are found in the screens (*rejas*) made for Spanish cathedrals (*see* SPAIN, fig. 55) and in grilles for windows (*see* MALTA, fig. 6). Its suitability for such purposes ensured that its use in this context continued for many centuries. In the Baroque period, for example, Jean Tijou, who transformed wrought ironwork in England, executed between 1689 and 1699 the wrought-iron gates and screen to the Fountain Garden (now the Privy Garden) at Hampton Court Palace; Jean Lamour (1698–1771) designed the wrought-iron grilles (*c.* 1755) at Place Stanislas,

9. Wrought-iron 'Armada chest', with engraved steel lock plate, from Nuremberg, *c.* 485×870×430mm, 17th century (London, Victoria and Albert Museum)

Nancy (*see* NANCY, fig. 2); and Henrik Fazola produced the intricate Rococo wrought-iron gates (1758–61) at County Hall, Eger (*see* HUNGARY, fig. 24). During the 19th century wrought iron was frequently used in a similar manner by the artists of the Gothic Revival, while cast-iron techniques were used to produce the miles of decorative railings that characterized the streets and squares of London.

Other items maintained the association with security: iron was frequently used decoratively, for example, in the cladding of doors (*see* DOOR, fig. 4) and in the manufacture of locks, hinges and clasps on wooden chests and caskets. Locksmithing required extraordinary feats of patience and precision in cold-cutting and carving the metal, as well as considerable sophistication in devising elaborate systems of lock construction. The art reached its apogee in France, Switzerland and Germany during the 16th century. French locksmiths executed fine door furniture for the châteaux of Fontainebleau and Anet, for example, and a number of highly elaborate keys survive, including the 'Strozzi key' (London, V&A), reputedly made to admit Diane de Poitiers, the mistress of the French king Henry II, to the latter's private apartments. Probably dating in fact from the early 17th century, the key closely resembles a design in a locksmithing treatise, *La Fidelle Ouverture de l'art du serrurier*, published by Mathurin Jousse in Paris in 1627. Its bow (the loop forming the handle) consists of two grotesque figures back-to-back, a design typical of the period.

In some cases, chests and strong boxes were not only decorated with but also fashioned from iron. Outstanding examples include the 'Armada chest', made in Nuremberg in the 17th century (see fig. 9). A form of early safe, this is made of painted wrought iron, with an engraved steel lock plate that occupies the whole of the underside of the lid. Such chests generally have eight and sometimes as many as twelve bolts, which catch the inturned edges of the sides. Erroneously called 'Armada chests' in the 19th century, most examples were made in southern Germany, and especially in Nuremberg, between the end of the 16th century and the last quarter of the 18th. From there they were exported throughout Europe. Similar late-16th-century chests include Bodley's chest (Oxford, Bodleian Lib.) and the University chest (Cambridge U. Old Schools). Another notable late-16th-century German item is the remarkable chiselled iron throne once owned by the Holy Roman emperor Rudolf II (Longford Castle, Wilts). Signed and dated 1574, it was made by Thomas Rucker of Augsburg (c. 1532–1606), astonishingly apparently as a speculative venture. It was acquired by the City of Augsburg, who presented it to the Emperor. The iconography of its immensely elaborate decoration has never been fully explained but is thought to represent the history of the Roman Empire from the departure of Aeneas from Troy to the time of Rudolf II. Shown in a series of roundels and panels, the imagery amounts to many thousands of figures.

At a humbler level, cast iron was used extensively from the 15th century for a wide variety of domestic utensils and—because of its resistance to heat—firebacks (*see* ENGLAND, fig. 84) and stoves. It was also popular from the early 19th century for furniture and occasionally even jewellery (*see* GERMANY, §IX, 2, and fig. 73; *see also* BERLIN, §III, 2). During the 18th and 19th centuries, the more progressive manufacturers adopted adventurous design policies, working with a number of leading artists, architects and designers. These included the Carron Ironworks, near Falkirk, Scotland, who commissioned Robert Adam (i) to design a number of elegant fire surrounds, stoves and grates (for illustration *see* FIREPLACE FURNISHINGS). In preparation for the Great Exhibition of 1851, the Sheffield ironfounders Henry Hoole & Co. commissioned the British sculptor ALFRED STEVENS to design a series of firegrates, while the Coalbrookdale Company at Ironbridge, Salop, invited Christopher Dresser to design hall and garden furniture for them in the 1870s. Charles Rennie Mackintosh also worked with iron on a domestic scale, for example the fireplace (1904; London, V&A) from the Willow Tea-room, Glasgow.

In France and the USA in the 1920s leading exponents of ironwork included Edgar Brandt (1880–1960) in Paris and Samuel Yellin (1885–1940) in Philadelphia. Brandt's elegant stylization epitomized the stylishness of Art Deco, for example in his treatment of firescreen designs, while Yellin drew on his mastery of wrought iron to work in a more eclectic manner, building up an immensely successful practice that at its height employed 300 smiths. Later in the 20th century there was a considerable international revival of interest in ironwork, stimulated by the high quality of work produced for church and state in Germany by a number of leading smiths, including Fritz Kuhn (1910–67). Other outstanding modern exponents include the Italian sculptor Antonio Benetton (*b* 1910) and the American Al Paley (*b* 1944), who trained and practised initially as a jeweller.

BIBLIOGRAPHY

L. N. Cottingham: *The Smith and Founder's Director* (London, 2/1824)
H. Havard: *Les Arts de l'ameublement: La Serrurerie* (Paris, 1892)
J. Starkie Gardner: *English Ironwork of the 17th and 18th Centuries* (London, 1911)
L. A. Shuffrey: *The English Fireplace and its Accessories* (London, 1912)
C. J. ffoulkes: *Decorative Ironwork from the 11th to the 18th Century* (London, 1913)
Old English Pattern Books of the Metal Trades (London, 1913)
O. Hoever: *An Encyclopedia of Ironwork* (London, 1927); repr. as *A Handbook of Wrought Iron* (London, 1962)
J. Seymour Lindsay: *Iron and Brass Implements of the English House* (London, 1927/R 1964)
J. Starkie Gardner: *Ironwork: From the Earliest Times to the End of the Medieval Period* (London, 1927/R 1978)
M. Ayrton and A. Silcock: *Wrought Iron and its Decorative Uses* (London, 1929)
Wrought Ironwork (London, 1953; rev. 9, Salisbury, 1989)
R. Lister: *Decorative Wrought Ironwork in Great Britain* (London, 1957/R Newton Abbot, 1970)
——: *Decorative Cast Ironwork in Great Britain* (London, 1960)
J. Needham: *Crafts and Craftsmen in China and the West* (Cambridge, 1970), chap. 8
J. F. Hayward: 'Thomas Rucker's Iron Chair', *Waf.- & Kostknd.*, ii (1976), pp. 85–98
J. Andrews: *Edge of the Anvil* (Emmaus, PA, 1977)
E. J. Robertson and J. Robertson: *Cast Iron Decoration: A World Survey* (London, 1977)
J. F. Hayward: 'A Chair from the Kunstkammer of the Emperor Rudolf II', *Burl. Mag.*, cxxii (1980), pp. 428–32
Towards a New Iron Age: The Art of the Blacksmith Today (exh. cat., ed. M. Campbell; London, V&A, 1982)
M. Campbell: *An Introduction to Ironwork* (London, 1985)

DOROTHY BOSOMWORTH

(ii) Steel. While steel implements dating from the 3rd century BC to the 4th century AD have been found in Sri Lanka, the earliest uses of steel in the West probably date from *c.* AD 100, when swords made from twisted steel and iron rods began to be made (*see* METAL, §V and fig. 12; *see also* ROME, ANCIENT, §IX, 3); known as pattern-welded steel, this technique continued in use for many centuries, some examples revealing a distinctive woven effect (e.g. Viking sword blade, *c.* AD 800; Copenhagen, Nmus.). Perhaps a more significant tradition, however, relates to the use, first developed in India, of watered steel (*wootz*), a high-furnaced metal with a surface finish resembling watered silk. This was used for centuries in South and East Asia to make weapons, small boxes, clasps and other articles (e.g. Sword of Aurangzeb, watered steel and gold, Mughal, late 17th century; London, V&A). It was the favoured steel for damascene work, a process traditionally associated with swords and daggers made in India and the Islamic world (*see* INDIAN SUBCONTINENT, fig. 325, and ISLAMIC ART, fig. 231).

The quality of steel was improved by new technical processes introduced in the late 14th century and again from the 16th, when steel was most important for use in armour (e.g. steel gorget, chased with figures in relief, France, *c.* 1610; London, V&A); armour incorporating steel scales knitted to leather was also produced (*see* POLAND, fig. 23). Indian watered steel was highly prized in Europe for more delicate work, but all attempts to reproduce it failed, apart from a crucible steel approximating its properties developed by the Englishman Benjamin Huntsman (*fl* 1742–81). Steelworking remained an art form until the large-scale production of steel for machinery and the construction industries in the 19th century. In areas renowned for metalwork, steel objects, including keys (*see* FRANCE, fig. 81), locks (*see* SPAIN, fig. 56) and scissors (*see* CUTLERY, §2 and fig. 3), were decorated with etched designs and polished, or worked by jewellers and goldsmiths with inlays of gold, silver, copper or bronze (e.g. rapier hilt, blued steel encrusted with gold, France, *c*. 1730; London, V&A). Beautiful examples of this type of work were also produced for mirrors, for example in Islamic art (*see* MIRROR, fig. 6).

In Britain the area of Woodstock, Oxon, was a centre for cut and polished steel objects, and riveted, facet-cut steel nail heads were first used there in the late 17th century to decorate such items as steel boxes, buckles and military medals. Cut-steel jewellery, faceted to resemble the sparkle of diamonds, was introduced by the British around the mid-18th century and later made in France and elsewhere. Birmingham, notably Matthew Boulton's factory, was famous for light steel toys and, from the late 18th century, also produced quantities of cut-steel jewellery (see fig. 10 and METAL, colour pl. II, fig. 3). French designs included steel *pampilles*, or cascades of tiny steel drops.

10. Polished steel châtelaine produced by the Matthew Boulton factory, Birmingham, 1877–82 (London, British Museum)

The town of SHEFFIELD meanwhile became a leading centre for the production of steel cutlery, the major manufacturers including Joseph Rogers & Sons and Thomas Wilkinson & Sons. In Russia the armourers of Tula, near Moscow, were celebrated during the 18th century and early 19th for their luxurious steel furniture and for such objects as chandeliers, candlesticks, sconces, perfume burners, writing sets, toilet boxes, vases and caskets (*see* RUSSIA, figs 49 and 37). Following the European styles of the time, they produced hugely expensive pieces, lavishly decorated with gold, silver (often niello) or gilt-bronze and rose-cut steel facets, sometimes incorporated with the royal cipher or heraldic arms. Cut-steel cross-legged folding chairs and armchairs were popular with the nobility in the 1740s and 1750s, invariably finished with gold, silver or brass detail.

From 1870 such other materials as chromium and nickel were added to molten carbon steel to produce high-alloy or crucible steels used in the manufacture of cutlery, medical instruments and cutting tools. The principles of a streamlined modernist aesthetic sparked a revival in the decorative uses of steel from the 1920s to the 1950s. The first tubular steel cantilevered chair was conceived by Mart Stam in the 1920s (*see* NETHERLANDS, THE, fig. 44) and refined by such artists as LUDWIG MIES VAN DER ROHE (e.g. *MR* side chair, chrome-plated steel, wood and cane, 1928; New York, MOMA), MARCEL BREUER and other artists associated with the Bauhaus (*see* BAUHAUS, §2, and GERMANY, fig. 51). Hailing it as a new material, designers discovered a variety of ways to employ chromium-plated or satin-polished steel, from bar-stools, lamps (e.g. table lamp, chromium-plated and enamelled steel and brass, USA, *c*. 1935; New York, Brooklyn Mus.), cocktail shakers and clocks to the trim on automobiles. Stainless steel proved of enduring value for such household items as kitchen sinks.

For information on the use of steel in engraving *see* ENGRAVING, §I.

BIBLIOGRAPHY
J. Evans: 'Cut-steel Jewellery', *Connoisseur*, xlix (1917), pp. 33–6
L. Aitchison: *A History of Metals* (London, 1960)
H. Hodges: *Artifacts: An Introduction to Early Materials and Technology* (London, 1964)
A. Clifford: *Cut-steel and Berlin Iron Jewellery* (Bath, 1971)
M. D. Malchenko: *Art Objects in Steel by Tula Craftsmen* (Leningrad, 1974)
B. Campbell-Cole and T. Benton: *Tubular Steel Furniture* (London, 1979)
K. C. Barraclough: *Steelmaking, 1850–1900* (London, 1990)

Iroquois. Indigenous people of the Woodlands region of North America (*see under* NATIVE NORTH AMERICAN ART). The League of Iroquois was formed *c*. 16th century AD from the five nations of Mohawk, Oneida, Onondaga, Cayuga and Seneca. The Tuscarora joined in the early 18th century, but the League had collapsed by the 19th century.

Irrwoch [Ihrwach; Irbach; Irwoch]**, Sebastian** (*b* Murau, Styria; *d* Rome, 21 Jan 1813). Austrian medallist, gem-engraver, wax modeller and sculptor. He studied under Franz Anton Zauner at the Akademie der Bildenden Künste in Vienna, and in 1792 he designed and cut a steel medal of a *Vestal Virgin*, for which he received first prize.

That year he also received first prize for his wax model of *Venus Urania*. In 1795 he was awarded a further prize for a terracotta bust of *Achilles* and in 1796 another for a head of *Apollo* after the Giustiniani *Apollo*. In 1797 he won first prize in the sculpture class at the Akademie.

Irrwoch came to be employed by the imperial court and, having been promised a monthly pension of 50 guilders, went to Italy in 1808 as a gem-engraver. The pension was to be made conditional on his establishing good contacts, and although Andreoli, Secretary of the Wiener Kunstakademie in Rome, acknowledged his artistic merits, he apparently lost his financial support and his patronage. The whereabouts of only a few of his medals and wax embossings are known. A jasper cameo of *Archduke Charles of Mecklenburg-Strelitz* (*reg* 1794–1815), signed *Irbach* and showing the ruler in half-length facing left in Roman Imperial style, is listed in the 1821 inventory of the Münz- und Antiken-Cabinet of the Kunsthistorisches Hofmuseum in Vienna. It is also known that Irrwoch designed a similar portrait of the composer *Joseph Haydn* (see Tandler, pl. 11), embossed in wax and dated 1803; it shows the influence of the work of Leonhard Posch. Irrwoch died in hospital in Rome, suffering from depression and hunger.

BIBLIOGRAPHY

BLKO; Forrer; Thieme–Becker
J. Tandler: 'Über den Schädel Haydns', *Mitt. Antropol. Ges.*, xxxix (1909), pp. 260–300

HANNELORE HÄGELE

Irvine, James (*b* Menmuir, Forfarshire, 1833; *d* Hillside, Montrose, 17 March 1889 or 1899). Scottish painter. He studied under the painter Colvin Smith (1795–1875) at Brechin and then at the Edinburgh Academy. It was, however, under the influence of his painter friend George Paul Chalmers (1833–78) that he properly developed as an artist, achieving a mature style that was characterized by strong light effects and low-toned but rich colours. He excelled as a portrait painter and worked in this capacity for some years in Arbroath, briefly in Edinburgh and at Montrose. Recognition finally came in the mid-1870s, after which numerous commissions followed. His work from *c.* 1870–80, for example the three-quarter-length portrait of *William Veitch* (*c.* 1875; Edinburgh, N.P.G.), established him as one of the foremost Scottish portrait painters of the period.

BIBLIOGRAPHY

Wood
J. L. Caw: *Scottish Painting Past and Present, 1620–1908* (Edinburgh and London, 1908), p. 289

☐

Irwin, Harriet Morrison (*b* Davidson, NC, 18 Sept 1828; *d* Charlotte, NC, 27 Jan 1897). American social reformer and writer. She was educated both in the home of her father, the Rev. Robert Hall Morrison, who was the first president of Davidson College, NC, and later at the Salem Female Academy, NC. In 1869 she was the first American woman to patent an architectural design. Prompted by concern for health and economy, she presented plans and an exterior elevation for a hexagonal house in Letters Patent, explaining that 'the objects of my invention are

the economizing of space and building-materials, the obtaining of economical heating mediums, thorough lighting and ventilation and facilities for inexpensive ornamentation'. With husband and brother-in-law, she promoted hexagonal house designs through advertisements, and at least one house was built, at 912 West Fifth Street (*c.* 1869; destr.) in Charlotte, NC, her home town. Others may also have been built.

Irwin's principal interests seem to have been architecture and literature; in her novel *The Hermit of Petraea* she advanced the idea that architecture affects man's physical well-being and that hexagonal dwellings are preferable to other types. Despite her propaganda, the hexagonal house never had the vogue that the earlier octagonal house design of ORSON SQUIRE FOWLER had enjoyed.

WRITINGS

The Hermit of Petraea (Charlotte, NC, 1871)

BIBLIOGRAPHY

O. S. Fowler: *A Home for All* (New York, 1848/*R* New York, 1973)
D. Cole: *From Tipi to Skyscraper: A History of Women in Architecture* (New York, 1973)
M. B. Stern: *We the Women: Career Firsts of Nineteenth Century America* (New York, 1974)
S. Torre: *Women in American Architecture* (New York, 1977)
B. Heisner: 'Harriet Morrison Irwin's Hexagonal House: An Invention to Improve Domestic Dwellings', *NC Hist. Rev.*, lviii (1981), pp. 105–24

BEVERLY HEISNER

Irwin, Robert (*b* Long Beach, CA, 12 Sept 1928). American painter and sculptor. He studied at the Otis Art Institute (1948–50) and at the new and progressive Chouinard Art Institute, Los Angeles (1952–4), where he adopted an Abstract Expressionist painting style. Through his association with the Ferus Gallery, Los Angeles (1959–66), he came into contact with such artists as Ed Moses (*b* 1926) and Billy Al Bengston (*b* 1934). Irwin disdained his early paintings for their lack of 'potency'. In the early 1960s he began a continuous series of experiments. He broke with figuration, searching like Minimalist artists for a way to make the work of art autonomous in content, that is representing nothing but itself, as in the *Disc* series that he began in 1966 (exh. 1968, Pasadena, CA, Norton Simon Mus. A.). Designed to exacting dimensions, colour tones and lighting criteria, the *Discs* appeared suspended, free from the wall and comprising an uncertain mass that dematerialized into its environment.

Irwin wanted the viewer to enter into the work of art, and this led to his installations, the earliest of which date from 1968. He would heighten and alter one's perception of a space using lighting, nylon scrim sheets, which contain and separate the light, and other illusions, for example in *Scrim Veil–Black Rectangle–Natural Light* (1977; New York, Whitney). He coined three terms that defined the relation of his work to its setting: site-adjusted, site-determined and site-dominant. His outdoor works directed the viewers' perceptual experience of the loci, making them confront the conditions and qualities of the site. In *9 Spaces, 9 Trees* (1980; Seattle, WA, Public Safety Building Plaza), a dismal urban space is enhanced through complement and contrast, while *Filigreed Line* (1979; Wellesley Coll., MA, Mus.) brings one repeatedly back to the qualities of the lush natural environment.

WRITINGS
Robert Irwin (exh. cat., New York, Whitney, 1977)
Being and Circumstance: Notes toward a Conditional Art (Larkspur Landing, 1985)

BIBLIOGRAPHY
L. Weschler: *Seeing Is Forgetting the Name of the Thing One Sees* (London, 1982) [biography]

KRISTINA VAN KIRK

Irwoch, Sebastian. *See* IRRWOCH, SEBASTIAN.

Isaachsen, Olaf [Ole Wilhelm] (*b* Mandal, 16 May 1835; *d* Vågsbygd, nr Kristiansand, 22 Sept 1893). Norwegian painter. The years of his childhood and youth, spent in the coastal landscape of southern Norway close to the isolated valley of Setesdal, exerted a formative influence on his activities as an artist. He was a pupil at the Kongelige Tegneskole in Christiania (now Oslo) in 1850, he was apprenticed to Adolph Tidemand in Düsseldorf in 1854, and he studied at the Kunstakademie there between 1854 and 1859. His teachers included Wilhelm Sohn (1830–99) and Theodor Hildebrandt (1804–74). He spent long periods in Paris and was a pupil of Thomas Couture in 1859–60 and Gustave Courbet in 1861–2; both had a profound influence on his technique and pictorial form. In the spring of 1863 he travelled in Italy, where he became particularly interested in Spanish-Neapolitan painting. It is possible that his work was influenced by that of the young French Impressionists, which he encountered during a stay in Paris in 1874. In 1864 Isaachsen returned to Norway and from 1866 lived and worked in Kristiansand, isolated from Norwegian artistic life.

Isaachsen had considerable gifts as a colourist, but the overall quality of his work is very uneven. He was unsuccessful as a painter of historical scenes except in certain highly coloured sketches where he distilled an historical ideal. On the other hand he produced masterful interpretations of the mysterious medieval-style interiors of the timber houses of Setesdal (e.g. *Setesdal House*, 1866 and *Setesdal Loft*, 1878) and visually powerful depictions of peasants in traditional costume (e.g. *Young Man from Setesdal*, 1866; all Oslo, N.G.). Isaachsen also painted landscapes, for a long while in heavy colours inspired by Courbet, but later in a freer form that approached Impressionism, and he produced a number of portraits. His work is mainly represented in museums in Oslo (N.G.), Kristiansand (Christianssands Billedgal.), Bergen (Billedgal.) and Göteborg (Kstmus.).

WRITINGS
'Thomas Couture', *Samtiden*, ix (1898), pp. 168–76
'En selvbiografi (1879)' [An autobiography (1879)], *Kst & Kult.*, xxvii (1941), pp. 165–80

BIBLIOGRAPHY
NKL
S. Willoch: *Olaf Isaachsen* (Oslo, 1926)
A. Boime: *Thomas Couture and the Eclectic Vision* (New Haven and London, 1980), pp. 538–40

SIGURD WILLOCH

Isaacsz. [Isacs; Isaksen], **Pieter (Fransz.)** (*b* Helsingør, 1569; *d* Helsingør, 14 Sept 1625). Dutch painter and draughtsman, active also in Denmark. He was brought up in Denmark, where his parents had fled following the disturbances in the Netherlands. According to van Mander, Isaacsz. began his artistic training in Amsterdam with Cornelis Ketel and later joined Hans von Aachen, whom he accompanied on his journeys through Germany and Italy. From 1590 Isaacsz. was in Amsterdam, where he acquired a reputation as a portrait painter, resulting in commissions to paint large militia group portraits, which reflect the influence of Ketel. The challenge in such pieces lay in depicting a large number of individuals in a natural manner while still maintaining their official character. Isaacsz.'s *Militia Company of Capt. Jacob Hoynck and Lt Wybrand Appelman* (1596; Amsterdam, Rijksmus.) shows the members of the civic guard placed in one line, but in his *Militia Company of Capt Gillis Jansz. Valckenier and Lt Pieter Jacobsz. Bas* (1599; Amsterdam, Rijksmus.) he employed a banqueting table to enliven the composition. He achieved his most successful compositional solution in a preliminary drawing of the 27 members of the *Militia Company of Capt. Adrian Raep* (1603; Amsterdam, Rijksmus.), where a balcony and a balustrade divide the picture into two levels.

Van Mander also recorded Isaacsz.'s success as a history painter, mentioning specifically a small oil on copper of the *Uprising of the Women of Rome* (probably before 1604; Amsterdam, Rijksmus.), which depicts angry Roman women preparing to protest in the Roman senate against Papirius' suggestion that each Roman citizen should have two wives. Isaacsz. is also known to have shared a commission with van Mander to decorate a piano. Before Isaacsz. left Amsterdam to return to Denmark in 1607–8, he trained Hendrick Avercamp.

Once in Denmark, Isaacsz. entered the service of the Danish King Christian IV, for whom he worked intermittently as a court painter until the end of his life. He also acted as agent in artistic matters and oversaw the King's vast programme of purchasing paintings in the Netherlands. The influence of Hans von Aachen and of Venetian art remained strong in Isaacsz.'s paintings carried out in Denmark, as can be seen in *Venus and the Lute-player* (*c.* 1610; Basle, Kstmus.), which is based on a composition by Titian. Isaacsz.'s use of strong Venetian colouring distinguishes him from the more conventional Danish court painters, whose style was based on the more sober treatment of composition and the colouring of Anthonis Mor and the Spanish school. This Venetian influence is especially distinct in his chief work from the year 1615, the three-quarter-length portrait of *Christian IV* (Hillerød, Frederiksborg Slot), the composition of which is directly based on Titian's three-quarter-length portraits. From 1612 Isaacsz. was involved in the decoration of various Danish royal residences. He executed the ceiling paintings in the Winter Room at Rosenborg (destr. 1859) and was leader of the team of artists employed to decorate the castle's Great Hall. His painting of *Herod the Great Tempting the Young Aristobulus to Swim* (originally called *Bathing at an Oriental Harbour*, 1620; Helsingør, Kronborg Slot) was probably part of a series of political allegories Isaacsz. originally executed for the Great Hall at Rosenborg. The subject is based on Flavius Josephus' *De antiquitatibus Judaicis*, which might have been suggested by the artist's brother Johannes Isak Pontanus, a well-known humanist and historiographer. On his father's death in 1617, Isaacsz. took over his government tax post in Helsingør, and it seems that he combined this official post with work as a Swedish secret agent.

BIBLIOGRAPHY

K. van Mander: *Schilder-boeck* ([1603]–1604)

S. Heiberg: 'Art and Politics: Christian IV's Dutch and Flemish Painters', *Leids Ksthist. Jb.* (1983), pp. 7–24

M. Stein: 'Christian IV: A Renaissance Man', *Apollo*, cxx (1984), pp. 368–79

——: *Christian den Fjerdes billedverden* [Christian IV's world of pictures] (Copenhagen, 1987)

Christian IV and Europe (exh. cat., ed. C. Christiansen; 19th A. Exh. of the Council of Denmark, 1988) [exh. held at 10 different Danish locations]

ANTJE SCHMITT

Isabeau of Bavaria, Queen of France. *See* VALOIS, (5).

Isabella, Queen of Castile and León. *See* ARAGON, (6).

Isabella II, Queen of Spain. *See* BOURBON, §II(8).

Isabella Clara Eugenia, Archduchess. *See* HABSBURG, §I(15).

Isabelline style. *See* HISPANO-FLEMISH STYLE.

Isabey. French family of artists. (1) Jean-Baptiste Isabey was one of the leading portrait miniaturists associated with the Napoleonic era. His son (2) Eugène Isabey became one of Louis-Philippe's principal court painters; equally notable for his land- and seascapes, he represents a link between the artists of the Rococo revival and the birth of Romanticism.

(1) Jean-Baptiste Isabey (*b* Nancy, 11 April 1767; *d* Paris, 18 April 1855). Painter, draughtsman and print-maker. He trained in Nancy with Jean Girardet (*d* 1778) and then with Jean-Baptiste-Charles Claudot (1733–1805), master of the miniaturist Jean-Baptiste Augustin. In 1785 he went to Paris, where he began by painting snuff-boxes. In 1786 he received lessons from the painter François Dumont, who had also studied with Girardet in Nancy, before entering the studio of David. Although he had received aristocratic commissions before the Revolution to paint portrait miniatures of the Duc d'Angoulême and Duc de Berry and through them of Marie-Antoinette, he did not suffer in the political upheavals that followed. He executed 228 portraits of deputies for a work on the Assemblée Législative and from 1793 exhibited miniatures and drawings in the Salon. Success came to him in 1794 with two drawings in the 'manière noire', *The Departure* and *The Return*. This type of drawing, using pencil and the stump to simulate engraving, was very fashionable in the last years of the 18th century and reached its peak with Isabey's *The Boat* (exh. Salon 1798; Paris, Louvre), an informal scene including a self-portrait, in which the artist exploited contrasts of light and shade with considerable success.

Isabey took an active part in Parisian artistic and social life and was much sought after by Mme de Staël and Mme Récamier for their salons. He commissioned a portrait of himself and his daughter from François Gérard (for additional information and illustration *see* GÉRARD, FRANÇOIS), and Boilly immortalized Isabey's own brilliant gatherings in the *Studio of Isabey* (1798; Paris, Louvre). At the school of Mme Campan at Saint-Germain-en-Laye, Isabey taught drawing to Hortense de Beauharnais and through her was introduced to the Napoleonic court, where he rapidly established himself. He was one of the first chevaliers of the Légion d'honneur and in 1804 was appointed Dessinateur du Cabinet de l'Empereur, des Cérémonies et des Relations Extérieures. He also organized all the private and public festivities in the Tuileries, at Saint-Cloud and Malmaison. In his capacity as Dessinateur du Cabinet de l'Empereur he produced a watercolour (Paris, Bib. N.) for the frontispiece of a volume of Ossian's poems in Napoleon's library. In 1805 he was made Premier Peintre to the Empress, Josephine, and painted numerous portraits of her, notably the *Empress after the Divorce* (Paris, Louvre) and *Empress Josephine* (after 1803; Angers, Mus. Turpin de Crissé; see fig.). He was on equally good terms with Napoleon's second wife, Marie-Louise, whom he painted in her wedding dress (large miniature, 1810; Vienna, Ksthist. Mus.) and with her son, François-Charles-Joseph, King of Rome (e.g. London, Wallace, 1815; Malmaison, Château N.). His portraits of Napoleon are equally numerous, including *Bonaparte at Malmaison* (exh. Salon 1802; Malmaison, Château N.) and the *Review for Quintidi* (exh. Salon 1804; Paris, Louvre). His miniatures of the Emperor and Empress became so famous that they were used to adorn many snuff-boxes.

In 1807 Napoleon appointed Isabey to succeed I.-E.-M. Degotti (*d* 1824) as principal decorator of the imperial theatres. Isabey also worked for the Sèvres factory, contributing to the decoration of the *Table des maréchaux* (1806; Malmaison, Château N.). During a stay in Vienna he executed 16 portrait miniatures of members of the Austrian imperial family (Vienna, Ksthist. Mus.), which he exhibited in the Salon of 1812. He returned to Vienna

Jean-Baptiste Isabey: *Empress Josephine*, watercolour and wash on paper, 255×198 mm, after 1803 (Angers, Musée Turpin de Crissé)

in 1814 to paint the plenipotentiaries of the Congress of Vienna. Isabey's work did not develop or change, and his popularity began to decline under the Restoration. He was almost forgotten during the July Monarchy, deriving a small pension from a post as assistant curator to the Musées Royaux in 1837. In 1853 Napoleon III remembered that Isabey had been highly regarded by his mother and made him a commander of the Légion d'honneur.

Isabey's fame derived from his portrait miniatures, and within this genre he was considered the leader of a school. In watercolour he created a type of portrait that became extremely fashionable: a woman's face wearing a melancholy, stereotyped smile, framed by roses and wreathed in diaphanous veils fluttering in an imaginary breeze. These portraits, with their fresh, bright colouring, were highly prized by his aristocratic and middle-class clientele. During the Empire and the Restoration, Isabey endlessly repeated this formula, the gracefulness of which sometimes declined into mawkish vapidity. He also produced large drawings such as the *First Consul at the Factory of the Sévène Brothers in Rouen* and *Bonaparte at the Oberkampf Factory* (exh. Salon 1804; Versailles, Château), in which he treated historic events as elegant genre scenes. In the *Staircase of the Louvre* (Paris, Louvre), a large watercolour painted on ivory, he emulated porcelain in the quality of the detail and the sweet, refined colouring. Isabey also made a small number of portraits in oils, including *Napoleon I* (Nancy, Mus. B.-A.) and the *Comtesse de Boigne* (Chambéry, Mus. B. A.).

Isabey's graphic oeuvre is also significant. He was fascinated by drawing in the 'manière noire' when the fashion for this style had only just begun and was one of the first painters to use lithography. In 1818 he published with Godefroy Engelmann a series of small-scale examples of lithography in which he experimented with new ways of rendering effects of light. He also published *Voyage en Italie* (a set of 30 lithographs) and, in a more risqué manner, a collection of 12 *Caricatures de J. J.* (1818). He contributed to Baron Taylor's *Voyages pittoresques et romantiques dans l'ancienne France*, making felicitous use of monochrome printing.

BIBLIOGRAPHY

P. Mantz: 'Jean-Baptiste Isabey', *L'Artiste* (6 May 1855), pp. 1–5
E. Taigny: *J.-B. Isabey: Sa vie et ses oeuvres* (Paris, 1859)
C. Lenormant: 'Jean-Baptiste Isabey', *L'Artiste* (1 March 1861), pp. 97–100
H. Béraldi: *Les Graveurs du XIXe siècle*, viii (Paris, 1889), pp. 151–6
G. Hédiard: *Les Maîtres de la lithographie: J.-B. Isabey* (Châteaudun, 1896)
Mme de Basily-Callimaki: *J.-B. Isabey, sa vie, son temps, 1767–1855: Suivi du catalogue de l'oeuvre gravée par et d'après Isabey* (Paris, 1909)
A. Francastel: 'Quelques miniatures d'Isabey', *Rev. Etud. Napoléoniennes*, ii (1918), pp. 120–28
M. Garçot: 'Jean-Baptiste Isabey, 1767–1855', *Pays Lorrain*, iv (1956), pp. 152–60

MARIE-CLAUDE CHAUDONNERET

(2) (Louis-)Eugène(-Gabriel) Isabey (*b* Paris, 22 July 1803; *d* Lagny, 25 April 1886). Painter and printmaker, son of (1) Jean-Baptiste Isabey. He spent his earliest years in the Louvre among such artists as François Gérard and the Vernet family, and at 7 rue des Trois Frères at the foot of Montmartre. His first works, mostly landscapes in watercolour, painted on the outskirts of Paris, display an independent character that owes little to the influence of his father or the other artists among whom he had lived.

In 1820 he travelled to Normandy with his father, Charles Nodier and Alphonse de Cailleux, the future director of the Louvre. In 1821 he visited Britain with Nodier and discovered British painting; it is uncertain whether Isabey ever met Richard Parkes Bonington (his father certainly knew him), but Bonington's free watercolour technique had a decisive influence on his development. Isabey's admiration for Géricault, the advice of his friends and a passionate temperament also helped to form his style, which was characterized by skilfully worked brushstrokes and a preference for impasto rather than glazing. Between 1821 and 1824 Isabey seems to have returned to Normandy several times, painting on the coast between Le Havre and Dieppe. At the Salon of 1824 he exhibited a series of seascapes and landscapes (untraced), which helped to establish his reputation.

Isabey made a second journey to England in 1825, where he met Delacroix, another important influence on his Romantic vision of landscape. He returned to the Normandy coast in 1826. In 1828 he met Charles Mozin (1806–62) and Paul Huet, who became a close friend, at Trouville, and with them and Théodore Gudin he made famous the genre of Romantic seascape during the 1830s. In 1829 he visited the Auvergne and the Velay, where he made drawings of the region to accompany Charles Nodier's text in the Auvergne volumes of Baron Taylor's *Voyages pittoresques et romantiques dans l'ancienne France*. Isabey's 17 lithographs (1830–32) unify and dramatize the Auvergne sky, landscape and architecture with unusual verve and are among the finest illustrations in this great series (e.g. *Exterior of the Apse of the Church of St Nectaire*).

Isabey was chosen as official artist to accompany the French expedition to Algiers in 1830; he illustrated Denniée's *Précis historique et administratif de la campagne d'Afrique* (Paris, 1830). His enthusiasm quickly changed to disillusion, however, when the drawings and oil studies he brought back failed to sell, and the wide range of subjects he exhibited at the Salon of 1831 reflects the hesitation and confusion he felt at that time. The success there of *The Alchemist* (untraced, see Miquel, no. 1301), then a fashionable subject, the novels of his friend Alexandre Dumas and a certain calculated ambition all encouraged him towards producing anecdotal genre pictures. During the July Monarchy his output alternated between marine subjects, both dramatic (e.g. *Battle of Texel*, 1839; Paris, Mus. Mar.) and placid (*Beach at Low Tide*, 1832, exh. Salon 1833; Paris, Louvre), and historicizing genre subjects—elegant scenes of opening nights in court dress and elaborate re-creations of 16th- and 17th-century ceremonial, often in a maritime setting (e.g. *Arrival of the Duke of Alba at Rotterdam*, 1844; Paris, Louvre). He became one of Louis-Philippe's principal court painters and recorded several important episodes in the life of the July Monarchy (e.g. *Return of the Ashes of Napoleon*; Versailles, Château).

Between 1833 and 1850 Isabey's style fluctuated between the smooth painting loved by the dealers and the thicker impasto found in his large exhibition pieces. At the same time he was producing numerous quickly executed landscape drawings. After 1844, in vast paintings such as the *Disembarkation of Louis-Philippe at Portsmouth on 8 October 1844* (1844; Paris, Louvre, on dep. Versailles,

Eugène Isabey: *Disembarkation of Louis-Philippe at Portsmouth on 8 October 1844*, oil on canvas, 1.48×2.23 m, 1844 (Paris, Musée du Louvre: on deposit at Versailles, Musée National du Château de Versailles et de Trianon)

Château; see fig.), his palette became brighter and his brushwork gained a glimmering quality that was constant from 1850. A journey to Brittany in 1850 marked the start of a free but more compact style in his seascapes, and at the same time he produced a series of *Scenes in the Park*, in which the study of drapery was enriched by a golden Venetian colouring. In the summer of 1856 he moved to Varengeville, near Dieppe, where he produced watercolours of the local cottages and countryside (e.g. Paris, Louvre, Cab. Dessins), which are among his most uninhibited and original works. The increasingly exuberant colour of his paintings of the 1860s and 1870s was applied to scenes of violence, massacres, duels and looting (e.g. *Duel in the Time of Louis XIII*, 1863; Compiègne, Château). He continued to produce marine views, but his boats were now usually painted from models in his studio rather than from life.

From Varengeville, Isabey travelled to Le Havre in 1859 and then to Honfleur with Eugène-Louis Boudin, on whose coastal views he had an important influence. During 1862 he spent some time in Le Havre, Honfleur and Trouville, where he was joined by his pupil, Johan Barthold Jongkind. In his later years he stayed often in Varengeville, working primarily for dealers and exhibiting little at the Salon.

In his costume pieces Isabey did not merely seek to pursue historical truth for its own sake but became both the creator and the victim of the fantasies of the French upper classes, to whom he offered a pleasantly decorative, if artificial, image of their ancestors. He kept alive the elegant frivolity of the world of his father and his father's friends, the Cicéri, and helped to transmit it to the artists of the Rococo revival, such as Adolphe Monticelli. Similarly, in his freshly painted watercolour seascapes he stood between and helped to bridge the worlds of Bonington and Boudin.

BIBLIOGRAPHY
G. Hédiard: *Eugène Isabey: Etude, suivie du catalogue de son oeuvre* (Paris, 1906)
A. Curtis: *Catalogue de l'oeuvre lithographiée d'Eugène Isabey* (Paris, 1939)
Eugène Isabey (exh. cat. by P. H. Schabacker and K. H. Spencer, Cambridge, MA, Fogg, 1967)
P. Miquel: *Eugène Isabey et la marine au XIXe siècle, 1803–1886*, 2 vols (Maurs-la-Jolie, 1980)

PIERRE MIQUEL

Isaia da Pisa (*fl* 1447–64). Italian sculptor. His grandfather, Giovanni di Gante, was a stone-carver, and his father, Pippo di Giovanni de Ghante da Pisa, who worked with Donatello on the Brancacci monument in the Baptistery in Florence in 1426, was documented at the Vatican in 1431 (Müntz). This suggests that Isaia was taken to Rome as a youth. He was probably active as a sculptor before 1447, since Filarete, who was forced to flee Rome at that date, mentioned Isaia in his *Trattato*. Isaia's oeuvre is not easy to define, because the sculptures for which payments exist were all collaborative works. However, a corpus has been assembled, based in part on the style of one of the lunette reliefs from the Tabernacle of St Andrew (Rome, Grotte Vaticane), a project on which he collaborated with PAOLO ROMANO in 1463–4. Porcellio Pandone wrote a poem in his honour (*Ad immortalitatem Isaiae Pisani* *marmorum celatoris*) in which, in the tradition of humanist hyperbole, he compared him to Pheidias, Polykleitos and Praxiteles (Battaglini). Although his work has been called monotonous, the influence of late Roman sculpture on Isaia's style reflects the classicizing taste of his time.

Porcellio described several works by Isaia, including the tomb of *Eugenius IV* (Rome, S Salvatore in Lauro, ex-refectory). Of his work on this tomb, little more than the effigy of the Pope remains, which was also described by the humanist Maffeo Vegio (Kühlenthal), who praised its magnificence. Isaia probably worked on it between the death of Eugenius in 1447 and the sculptor's departure for Naples in 1455. The effigy of *St Monica* (Rome, S Agostino), attributed to Isaia by Porcellio, was probably part of a chapel erected by Vegio in S Agostino and may have been begun by Isaia in 1455 and completed by assistants (Montevecchi). Another early work is the tomb of *Antonio Martínez Chiaves*, the Cardinal of Portugal, originally in S Giovanni in Laterano, Rome. The commission for the tomb was initially given to Filarete; Isaia had apparently not yet completed it in 1449, when Filarete attempted to return to Rome to reclaim the commission. The sculptures from the dismantled tomb are incorporated in two monuments, a Baroque resetting of the *Chiaves* tomb and the tomb of *Cardinal Giulio Acquaviva* (*d* 1574), both in S Giovanni in Laterano. The original tomb can be reconstructed from a drawing (Kühlenthal). The effigy and half-length figures in the centre are flanked by standing allegories in niches; it is probably the first example of a scheme that was to become characteristic of Roman tombs. Isaia's execution of the sculpture does not necessarily imply that he invented the format, but the figures, with their overt references to antique models—*Temperance*, for example, derives from the Venus Genetrix type —is as forward-looking as the design itself. This *all'antica* style helps to explain Isaia's popularity with his humanist patrons; Porcellio Pandone mentioned that he himself owned two works by Isaia of riding figures of Nero and Poppaea, presumably reliefs (both untraced), and Alfonso I and Pius II, the latter a noted humanist, favoured allusions to the Classical past in their commissions.

From 1455 to 1458 Isaia worked on the Arch of Alfonso I of Aragon at the Castelnuovo, Naples (*see* NAPLES, §IV, 4). His precise contribution to the sculptural programme is controversial: Hersey argued that Isaia was the master responsible for the frieze of *Alfonso of Aragon's Triumphal Procession* and its surrounding sculptural detail, but Kruft and Malmanger limited Isaia's and his shop's contribution to the lower fields of the arch. Although both the *Fortitude* and the female genius guiding the King's chariot have been attributed to Paolo Romano, stylistically they are closer to Isaia. Other works that have been plausibly attributed to Isaia include the sacrament tabernacle for S Maria Maggiore (destr.; fragments Rome, S Maria Maggiore, sacristy of the Chapel of Sixtus V; Chicago, IL, A. Inst.; see Middeldorf), a relief of *Apollo* (Warsaw, N. Mus.; see Kaczmarzyk) and the marble high-relief *Virgin and Child*, known as the Orsini *Madonna* (Rome, Grotte Vaticane), which can be identified with a commission of 1451 by Cardinal Pietro Barbo (the future Pope Paul II) in honour of his uncle Eugenius IV (Caglioti). It is evident that Isaia, like many of his

contemporaries, worked with a large number of assistants, and a series of works in locations around Viterbo may be derived from his designs (Negri Arnoldi). One of his last documented activities was working on the construction of the Benediction Loggia for Pius II in 1463–4. After the death of the Pope in 1464, he and Paolo Romano may have worked for private patrons, although it is unlikely that Isaia survived for many years after this date.

BIBLIOGRAPHY
Thieme–Becker

Filarete [A. Averlino]: *Trattato d'architettura* (MS. *c.* 1460–65); Eng. trans. and ed. J. Spencer as *Treatise on Architecture* (New Haven, 1965), pp. 45–77 [facs. of MS.]

G. Vasari: *Vite* (1550, rev. 2/1568); ed. G. Milanesi (1878–85), ii, pp. 472n, 484

A. Battaglini: 'Memoria sopra uno sconosciuto egregio scultore del secolo XV e sopra alcune sue opere', *Atti Pont. Accad. Romana Archeol.*, i (1821), pp. 115–32 [complete text of poem by Porcellio]

E. Müntz: *Martin V–Pie II 1417–1464* (1878), i of *Les Arts à la cour des papes pendant le XVe et le XVIe siècle: Recueil de documents inédits*, ed. E. Thorin (Paris, 1878–82)

A. Venturi: *Storia* (1901–40), vi, pp. 374–87

F. Burger: 'Isaia da Pisa: Plastische Werke in Rom', *Jb. Kön.-Preuss. Kstsamml.*, xxvii (1906), pp. 228–44

L. Ciaccio: 'Scultura romana del rinascimento primo periodo (sino al Pontificato di Pio II)', *L'Arte*, ix (1906), pp. 165–84

A. Riccoboni: *Roma nell'arte: La scultura nell'evo moderno dal quattrocento ad oggi* (Rome, 1942), pp. 8–14

U. Middeldorf: 'The Tabernacle of S. Maria Maggiore', *Bull. A. Inst. Chicago*, xxxviii (1944), pp. 6–10

J. Pope-Hennessy: *Italian Renaissance Sculpture* (London, 1958, rev. 3/Oxford, 1985), pp. 65, 319–20

C. Seymour jr: *Sculpture in Italy, 1400–1500*, Pelican Hist. A. (Harmondsworth, 1966), pp. 118, 134, 137–8, 156, 264–5

V. Golzio and G. Zander: *L'arte in Roma nel secolo XV* (Bologna, 1968)

G. C. Sciolla: 'Fucina aragonese a Castelnuovo, I', *Crit. A.*, n. s. 2, xix/123 (1972), pp. 15–36

G. Hersey: *The Aragonese Arch at Naples, 1443–1475* (New Haven, 1973)

D. Kaczmarzyk: 'Isaia da Pisa, auteur présumé du bas-relief d'Apollon au Musée National de Varsovie', *Bull. Mus. N. Varsovie/Biul. Muz. N. Warszaw.*, xv/1–2 (1974), pp. 28–32

H. W. Kruft and M. Malmanger: 'Der Triumphbogen Alfonsos in Neapel: Das Monument und seine politische Bedeutung', *Acta Archaeol. & A. Hist. Pertinentia*, vi (1975), pp. 213–305

M. Kühlenthal: 'Zwei Grabmäler des frühen Quattrocento in Rom: Kardinal Martinez de Chiaves und Papst Eugen IV', *Röm. Jb. Kstgesch.*, xvi (1976), pp. 17–56

F. Negri Arnoldi: 'Isaia da Pisa e Pellegrino da Viterbo', *Il quattrocento a Viterbo* (Rome, 1983), pp. 324–40

B. Montevecchi: *Sant'Agostino*, Chiese Roma Illus. (Rome, 1985)

F. Caglioti: 'Precisione sulla 'Madonna' di Isaia da Pisa nelle Grotte Vaticane', *Prospettiva* [Florence], 47 (1986), pp. 58–64

□

Isakson, Karl (Oscar) (*b* Stockholm, 16 Jan 1878; *d* Copenhagen, 19 Feb 1922). Swedish painter, active in Denmark. With Carl Kylberg (1878–1952) and Bror Hjorth, he is regarded as a leading painter of biblical themes in 20th-century Swedish art. He studied at the Konstakademi in Stockholm (1897–1901) under Georg von Rosen, Gustaf Cederström and Oscar Björck. In 1902 he went to Italy, where he was especially attracted to the work of Giotto in Santa Croce in Florence. In Cività d'Antino in the Abruzzi he met the Danish painter Kristian Zahrtmann, and in the autumn of that year they went together to Copenhagen, where Isakson continued his studies at Zahrtmann's art school. Isakson settled in Copenhagen but made some trips abroad, chiefly to Paris.

During his time at the Konstakademi Isakson had made a large number of drawings on themes from Old Norse mythology, sometimes reminiscent of the work of Max Klinger or Arnold Böcklin, and he retained this interest during his first years in Copenhagen, as in *Höder and Loki* (1903–4; priv. col.), which depicts the confrontation between the personifications of evil and innocent goodness. The support of patrons, in particular Ernest Thiel in Stockholm, enabled Isakson to stay in Paris from 1905 to 1907. Here he was influenced by the work of Delacroix, the Impressionists and above all Eugène Carrière and Gustave Moreau. *A Self-portrait* (1908; Copenhagen, Stat. Mus. Kst) reveals with its broad brushstrokes and sharply delineated form a move away from the conventional academic style; it is painted in the subdued colours typical of his work in the years 1904 to 1910, which came to be known as his 'grey period', and in 1909 was among works he exhibited at the Free Exhibition in Copenhagen.

Isakson spent several years working on the theme of *Boy Planting* (also known as *Hope*). One version (1909; Stockholm, Nmus.), also shown at the Free Exhibition, has affinities with Ferdinand Hodler's *Consecrated One* (1903–4; Berne, Kstmus.). His work at the exhibition caused a considerable stir, and he was praised as a colourist. He became increasingly interested in formal problems, particularly in the case of still-lifes and nude studies. In spring 1911 he again went to Paris, where he was impressed by Cubism, the art of Matisse and above all that of Cézanne. The confrontation with Cézanne's work led to an important development in Isakson's technique: the application of colours in facets, letting the white ground shine through. In the summer of that year he made his first visit to the picturesque fortress island of Christiansø near the larger island of Bornholm in the southern Baltic Sea. He was to return again and again. His work was reinvigorated during the next few years, as he strove constantly to achieve greater clarity and intensity of light in his colours and ever more simplification of form. This can be seen in the monumental nude study *Model Resting* (1914–15; Göteborg, Kstmus.), where Cézanne's influence is clear. Despite the restrained modelling, the proportions of the female body are convincingly reproduced.

From 1915 to 1918 Isakson produced a large number of still-lifes using complementary colours in luminous planes. In the following years he painted landscapes of Christiansø and Bornholm in the style of Cézanne's work of the mid-1880s, and a series of paintings of a seated woman (version of 1918; Göteborg, Kstmus.), her black clothes reflecting the various colours of the setting. He was by this time working with paler colours thinned with turpentine and made frequent use of diagonal strokes for shading. *Self-portrait* (*c.* 1920; Göteborg, Kstmus.) has luminous shades of yellow, pink, green and blue.

By the early 1920s Isakson had returned to his former interest in symbolic, and particularly religious, subjects. He painted mostly scenes from the life of Christ, such as the *Raising of Jairus' Daughter* (1920–21), *Martha and Mary* (1921), the *Healing of the Blind* (1920–21), the *Woman Taken in Adultery* (1920–21; all Göteborg, Kstmus.); also the *Raising of Lazarus* (two versions, 1920–21; Stockholm, Nmus., and Göteborg, Kstmus.; the iconography of both these works shows a Byzantine influence gained from book illustrations and possibly from the artist's travels in Italy). He painted themes from the Passion such as the *Crowning with Thorns* (1920–22) and the *Soldiers Casting Lots for Christ's Clothing* (1920–21; priv. col.; studies in Copenhagen, Stat. Mus. Kst, and Stockholm, Nmus.). The formal simplicity of these late paintings is combined with an intense expressive power that can recall the work of Emil Nolde.

BIBLIOGRAPHY

SVKL

G. Engwall: *Karl Isakson* (Stockholm, 1944)

N. G. Sandblad: 'Gossen som planterade ett träd' [The boy who planted a tree], *Tidskr. Kstvet.*, xxxii (1957), pp. 195–245

B. Hvas: *Karl Isakson: Ett liv i konst* [Karl Isakson: A life in art] (Lund, 1989)

HANS-OLOF BOSTRÖM

İscehisar. *See* DOKIMEION.

Ischali. *See under* DIYALA REGION.

Ischia. *See* PITHEKOUSSAI.

Iselburg, Peter. *See* ISSELBURG, PETER.

Iseli, Rolf (*b* Berne, 22 Jan 1934). Swiss painter and printmaker. He trained as a lithographer at the School of Decorative Arts in Berne but began his career in the aura of American action painting in the early 1950s, establishing his reputation initially as an exponent of Tachism. In 1963 he acquired land at St Roman, France, where he established a new direction in his art, exemplified by a series of metamorphosed self-portraits inspired by his shadow reflected on a sheet of paper in sunlight. In 1966 he discarded painting on canvas in favour of working with paper, which was collaged, shredded, destroyed and re-placed in free-form assemblages. Also in the mid-1960s he returned to printmaking, exploring etching as his main expressive medium. The powerful intaglio prints bear the stress of vigorously scored marks, creating rich linear textures that obliterate recognizable form. In collaboration with his printer Daniel Divorne, at the Centre Genevois de Gravure Contemporain in Geneva, Iseli gradually evolved his idiosyncratic use of drypoint, characteristically a demanding and aggressive use of the medium. He usually worked without the support of mechanical aids or figurative illusions. He maintained a distance from the successive mainstream Minimalist and conceptual art movements of the 1970s but found a complementary backdrop for his work in European Neo-Expressionism of the 1980s, for example in works by Georg Baselitz, Anselm Kiefer and Rainer Fetting (*b* 1949).

BIBLIOGRAPHY

Rolf Iseli/Georg Baselitz: Monumental Prints (exh. cat., New York, MOMA, 1983)

Rolf Iseli—Das Schwarz und das Weiss: Druckgraphik, 1975–88 (exh. cat. by R. W. Gassen and B. Holeczek, Ludwigshafen, Hack-Mus. & Städt. Kstsamml., 1989)

Rolf Iseli (exh. cat. by E. Billeter and others, Lausanne, Pal. Rumine, 1990)

□

Iselin [Yselin], Heinrich (*fl* 1477–8; *d* Konstanz, 1513). German sculptor. He possibly came from Ravensburg, Upper Swabia, and he was the son-in-law of the cabinet-maker Simon Haider. According to a document of the Konstanz merchants of 1490, Simon and his son Hans, who could not themselves carve, ordered the carvings for a 'werck' for Weingarten Abbey, Upper Swabia, from

Iselin for 100 gulden. This commission was probably for the choir-stalls of the monastery church, which according to 17th-century annals were produced in 1477–8. The 12 busts have survived, representing Moses, King David, an abbot, a master builder, Virgil, an emperor (probably Augustus) and possibly also a sibyl, as well as unidentifiable prophets and seers from pagan antiquity (Berchtesgaden, Schlossmus.). Stylistically the busts are indebted to the work of Nicolaus Gerhaert, and typologically they follow the busts on the choir-stalls in Ulm Cathedral (1469–74). Iselin's attempts to achieve strongly expressive faces using an ornamental system of lines and mimetic wrinkles are striking. Iselin had very probably worked on the choir-stalls of Konstanz Cathedral; the commission, originally intended for Gerhaert, was passed on to Simon Haider after 1467. Here the dorsal reliefs with busts of prophets and apostles, and perhaps also some stall ends, can be ascribed to Iselin. The dorsal reliefs show the animated style of the school of Gerhaert, but their powerful heads are still little differentiated compared with those of the Weingarten busts.

In 1481, after Simon Haider's death, Iselin was given citizenship of Konstanz. He evidently carried on the Haider workshop in conjunction with Hans Haider. In 1506–7 they both worked on a winged altar for Bregenz (destr.). From 1511 to 1513 Iselin was a member of the Inner Council of the city of Konstanz.

BIBLIOGRAPHY
Thieme–Becker
W. Deutsch: 'Die Konstanzer Bildschnitzer der Spätgotik und ihr Verhältnis zu Niklaus Gerhaert', *Schr. Ver. Gesch. Bodensees & Umgebung*, lxxxi (1963), pp. 18–19, 21, 36–48, 58–9, 62–7; lxxxii (1964), pp. 1–60
T. Müller: *Sculpture in the Netherlands, Germany, France and Spain, 1400 to 1500*, Pelican Hist. A. (Harmondsworth, 1966)
Spätgotik am Oberrhein: Meisterwerke der Plastik und des Kunsthandwerks, 1450–1530 (exh. cat., ed. E. Zimmermann and others; Karlsruhe, Bad. Landesmus., 1970), pp. 105–9
M. J. Liebmann: *Die deutsche Plastik, 1350–1550* (Leipzig, 1982)
E. Zimmermann: 'Künstlerische Quellen der Kunst des Veit Stoss am Oberrhein', *Veit Stoss: Die Vorträge des Nürnberger Symposions* (Munich, 1985), pp. 74–6

EVA ZIMMERMANN

Isenbrandt [Isenbrant; Ysebaert; Ysenbrand; Ysenbrandt]**, Adriaen** (*b* ?Antwerp, early 16th century; *d* Bruges, before 21 July 1551). South Netherlandish painter. He became a master in the Bruges Guild of St Luke in 1510, at which time the records specify that he was a 'stranger' and childless. Shortly afterwards he married Maria Grandeel, who bore him one child (*d* 1512). After his wife's death in 1537, Isenbrandt married Clementine de Haerne, with whom he had three daughters. One further daughter was born through an extra-marital relationship with the innkeeper Katelijne van Brandenburch. According to contemporary sources, Isenbrandt was famous and well-to-do. He held important posts in the Bruges Guild of Sculptors and Saddlemakers, serving as deacon nine times between 1518 and 1538 and as governor twice (1526–7 and 1537–8). In 1520 he worked on the decorations for the Triumphal Entry of Emperor Charles V into Bruges, and in the same year the guild archives mention his only official pupil, Cornelis van Callenberghe.

Sanderus claimed that Isenbrandt had been a pupil of Gerard David, but since Isenbrandt was already a master on arrival in Bruges, it is more likely that he may simply have worked in David's studio and been strongly influenced by him. Stylistic similarities and the numerous borrowings from works by David led Weale and Hulin de Loo in 1902 to attribute a large group of paintings to Isenbrandt, a hypothetical proposal that is still generally accepted. This oeuvre had previously been associated by Waagen with the Haarlem painter Jan Mostaert, the painter being known as the Pseudo-Mostaert or Waagen's Mostaert; he was subsequently nicknamed the Master of the Madonna of the Seven Sorrows after the eponymous diptych from the Onze Lieve Vrouwekerk in Bruges.

The works in this group show that Isenbrandt worked in the mature style of Gerard David but also referred to such artists as Jan van Eyck, Rogier van der Weyden, Hans Memling, Albrecht Dürer and Jan Gossart; he was not very inventive or innovative. The quality of his numerous works is very uneven; even within a single painting there are sometimes qualitative differences, a fact probably explained by studio collaboration. His own hand is recognizable in the faces and flesh parts. At least once Isenbrandt repainted works by a painter from another town to suit the local taste. At that time Bruges painters often worked for the art market and for export, and such commercialism was obviously not conducive to complete stylistic unity within a painter's oeuvre. Isenbrandt's best paintings are small and medium-sized idyllic, mostly religious, scenes. The face of his figure of the Virgin is characterized by a narrow chin, small mouth with full lips, a short nose and heavy, lowered eyelids. His donor portraits are mainly rather lifeless and stereotypical, but he showed himself to be a better portraitist in his independent works. Landscape backgrounds are often filled with buildings like those in Gossart's work. David's influence is evident in the dark vegetation and parallel horizontal lines, but the rocks rising vertically from the ground are typical of Isenbrandt. Isenbrandt's decorative shapes are less archaic yet have a tentative feeling. He mixed traditional Gothic details with such fashionable Renaissance elements as antique pillars and volutes, rams' heads and circles. He was a better colourist than David and used warmer tones, particularly red; flesh areas are distinguished by brown pigments. Isenbrandt was often associated with his colleague and fellow townsman Ambrosius Benson, who brought something of the liveliness of the Antwerp school to the calm atmosphere of Bruges art; it is sometimes suggested that Isenbrandt may have come from Antwerp.

There is no documentation or signature for any of the works hypothetically attributed to Isenbrandt. Two pieces are dated and dates can be calculated for two others due to the individuals they depict. The earliest is the *Presentation in the Temple* (*c.* 1510; Bruges Cathedral), in which Philip Wielant and Joanna van Halewijn (*d* 1510) are represented on the wings with their coats of arms. On the back of the central panel there is an Augustinian nun with the quartered coat of arms of Jan de Gros and Guidone Messey. The only connection between the Wielant–Halewijn and Gros–Messey families was the marriage between their children Ferry de Gros and Philippine Wielant (*d* 1521). The triptych was probably commissioned by the donors, who are depicted on it in the traditional way. The date of Joanna van Halewijn's death provides a *terminus ad quem*

Adriaen Isenbrandt: *Virgin of the Seven Sorrows*, oil on panel, 1.38×1.38 m, right-hand panel of a diptych, *c.* 1518 (Bruges, Onze Lieve Vrouwekerk)

for the work. The nun on the *verso* must be Philippine de Gros at the age of about 20, the daughter of Ferry de Gros and Philippine Wielant, who probably had her portrait and coat of arms added when she entered the convent *c.* 1521–2.

Both the dated works by Isenbrandt are from 1518. The first is an inscribed *Bust Portrait of a Man* (Bruges, Groeningemus.), shown facing right, against a neutral background, with his hands joined in prayer. Judging from the subject's physiognomy and name, Paulus Denigro, he is an Italian. The second dated work was a triptych with the *Adoration of the Magi* (Lübeck, Marienkirche; destr. 1942, see Hasse, p. 117), which constituted Isenbrandt's most monumental work. The two oldest wise men were

portraits: the nearest king, kneeling down, was a portrait of Nicholas Brömbse, who became burgomaster in Lübeck in 1520. A third portrait on the left showed Gotthard von Höveln but was painted by another hand *c.* 1560. The figures of the black king and St Joseph, together with the decorative architecture, revealed the influence of the Antwerp Mannerists, while the *Nativity* on the left wing showed that of Gerard David and Jan Gossart. The right wing depicted the *Flight into Egypt*. The outside of the wings showed *Adam and Eve* set against a background of vegetation, definitely indebted to the van Eyck brothers' Ghent Altarpiece (*c.* 1423–32; Ghent, St Bavo).

The last work for which there is an approximate date is regarded as Isenbrandt's masterpiece and for a long time it provided the artist's nickname: the diptych with the *Virgin of the Seven Sorrows* (*c.* 1518; right wing, Bruges, Onze Lieve Vrouwekerk; left wing, Brussels, Mus. A. Anc.). The main, right-hand panel (see fig.) shows the Virgin seated in a niche decorated with such Renaissance motifs as candlestick-shaped pillars and rams' heads with spiral horns. Around her are the seven biblical scenes, two of which indicate a knowledge of woodcuts by Dürer. At some point the left wing was split so that the painting on the outside, a *grisaille* depiction of the Virgin, was separated from the inner left wing, which shows the donors worshipping the Virgin on the main, right-hand inner panel. Joris van de Velde (*d* 1528) is accompanied by St George, his patron saint, and his nine sons; next to him is his wife, Barbara Le Maire (*d* 1535), with her patron saint and her eight daughters. The donors can be identified by the coats of arms painted on the frame. Joris van de Velde was burgomaster of Bruges in 1517 and a year later was installed as provost of the Brotherhood of the Holy Blood. In the painting he wears the Brotherhood's toga, which was designed for his provostship and prescribed for all the brothers in 1518 (it was remodelled a few years later). Van de Velde must have commissioned the painting in 1518, to mark both his appointment as burgomaster and as provost of the Brotherhood of the Holy Blood. Barbara Le Maire probably had funerary crosses added to some of the portraits after her husband's death.

BIBLIOGRAPHY

A. Šanderus: *Flandria illustrata*, ii ('The Hague, 1732), p. 154

J. P. van Male: *Prael toneel der vermaarde mannen van Brugge* [Early theatre of renowned men of Bruges]

G. F. Waagen: *Handbuch der deutschen und niederländischen Malerschulen*, i (Stuttgart, 1862), p. 142 [Mostaert]

W. H. J. Weale: 'Adrien Ysenbrandt', *Le Beffroi*, ii (1864–5), pp. 320–24

Tableaux flamands des XIVe, XVe et XVIe siècles (exh. cat. by W. H. J. Weale, Bruges, Gruuthusemus., 1902), pp. xxiv–xxv, nos 178–85

G. Hulin de Loo: *Bruges 1902: Exposition de tableaux flamands des XIVe, XVe et XVIe siècles, catalogue critique* (Ghent, 1902), pp. lxiii–lxvii, nos 177–85 [a counter-balance to the official catalogue, which gave the lenders' attributions only, prefaced by Weale's essay]

M. J. Friedländer: *Die altniederländische Malerei*, xi (Berlin, 1933), pp. 79–101; Eng. trans. as *Early Netherlandish Painting*, xi (New York, 1974)

R. A. Parmentier: 'Bronnen voor de geschiedenis van het Brugsche schildersmilieu in de XVIe eeuw, IX: Adriaan Isenbrant' [Sources for the history of the artistic life of Bruges in the XVIth century, IX: Adriaen Isenbrandt], *Belg. Tijdschr. Oudhdknd. & Kstgesch.*, ix (1939), pp. 229–92

A. Janssens de Bisthoven: 'Een nieuwe datering voor tween aan Isenbrandt toegeschriven schilderijen' [A new date for two paintings attributed to Isenbrandt], *Miscellanea Jozef Duverger*, i (Ghent, 1968), pp. 175–85

M. Hasse: *Die Marienkirche zu Lübeck* (Munich, 1983)

E. James Mundy: *Paintings in Bruges, 1470–1550: An Annotated Bibliography* (Boston, MA, 1985), pp. 96–8

VERONIQUE VAN PASSEL

Isenmann, Caspar [Gaspard] (*b* Colmar; *fl c.* 1430–84). German painter. His work, with that of Hans Hirtz, Jost Haller and the Master of the Stauffenberg Altar, occupies an essential place in mid-15th-century Alsatian art and testifies to the influence of Netherlandish painting in the upper Rhine. He had an exceptionally long career, being active at the same time as Konrad Witz, Master E.S. and the young Martin Schongauer; although Schongauer must have studied Isenmann's work, there is nothing to prove that he was trained by him. Isenmann worked in his native

city, Colmar, but only a few works survive of an undoubtedly prolific output.

Isenmann's only authenticated surviving work is the group of five panels from an altarpiece (Colmar, Mus. Unterlinden). The date of 1465 on one of the panels and their provenance from St Martin, Colmar, have identified them with the altarpiece commissioned from Isenmann in 1462 by the canons of St Martin, the contract for which survives (Colmar, Archv Mun. SDLS, 5). An important example of late Alsatian Gothic, the altarpiece dominated the choir of the largest church of Haute-Alsace and is one of a series of great painted and sculpted altarpieces that developed in the subsequent 50 years. It was partly destroyed by accident in 1720, but enough evidence survives to enable a reconstruction to be made. With a span of over 8 m, the open altarpiece was dedicated to the Passion: on the left were the *Entry into Jerusalem* and the *Last Supper*, with *Christ on the Mount of Olives* and the *Arrest* above and the *Flagellation* and *Crowning with Thorns*, and probably *Ecce homo* and *Christ Carrying the Cross* (untraced) below. A high and narrow central section must have been occupied by a *Crucifixion*, perhaps sculpted. On the right were the surviving *Lamentation*, *Entombment* and *Resurrection* panels (see fig.), probably followed by a *Noli me tangere*, the *Incredulity of Thomas* and the *Ascension*, *Pentecost* and *Last Judgement* (all untraced). The closed altarpiece, also painted by Isenmann, represented six

Caspar Isenmann: *Resurrection*, oil on panel, 1.10×0.74 m, 1465 (Colmar, Musée d'Unterlinden)

figures of saints; on the left was the surviving dated panel with *SS Catherine, Lawrence and Martin*; on the right only the upper part of *St Barbara* remains, but a drawing (Haarlem, Koenig Col.) suggests that she was perhaps accompanied by SS Erhard and Leo IX. The reverse of the central panels and an early description suggest that the altarpiece may also have had a second opening, essentially sculpted but impossible to reconstruct.

The surviving panels are characterized by the use of a gold ground, sometimes enlivened by tracery in low wood relief in the position of the sky. The scenes are set in true landscapes, however, although some conventional effects are still employed, such as the lines of trees planted on either side of the summit of a hill and winding roads. Isenmann's work is also distinguished by pathos of gesture and a sense of emotion, despite the arrested movement of the figures. The poses are varied, but a certain moderation of expression is retained. The altarpiece has provided a basis for other attributions to Isenmann, the most secure of which is a *Portrait of a Man* (Basle, Kstmus.).

BIBLIOGRAPHY

K. T. Parker: 'Une Feuille d'études de Caspar Isenmann', *Archv Alsac. Hist. A.*, v (1926), pp. 67–72

G. Bergsträsser: *Caspar Isenmann: Ein Beitrag zur oberrheinischen Malerei des 15. Jahrhunderts* (Colmar, 1941)

A. Stange: *Deutsche Malerei der Gotik*, vii (Munich, 1955), pp. 12–15

——: *Die deutschen Tafelbilder vor Dürer*, ii (Munich, 1970), nos 61–4

C. Heck: 'Gaspard Isenmann et le retable de la collégiale Saint-Martin de Colmar', *Bull. Soc. Schongauer* (1973–8), pp. 137–56

CHRISTIAN HECK

Iser, Iosif [Iosef] (*b* Bucharest, 21 May 1881; *d* Bucharest, 25 April 1958). Romanian painter. He studied painting in Munich under Anton Ažbe and Johann Herterich (1843–1905). After a period in Romania (1905–7) he went to Paris, where he studied at the Académie Ranson and mixed with the avant-garde of Montmartre, including Brancusi and Derain. Returning to Bucharest in 1909, he organized the first exhibition of modern art at the Palatul Ateneului. During World War I he fought on the Moldavian front, but he continued to paint, including military personnel (e.g. *Soldiers*, 1917; Bucharest, N. Mus. A.). His work in this period was influenced by that of Cézanne; it was geometric in spirit, but figurative, and it concentrated on representations of the exotic physiognomies and the spectacular landscape of the Tartars of Balcic, a small port on the Black Sea. The best-known of these is the *Tartar Family* (1921; Bucharest, N. Mus. A.), which in its stylized volumes shows the influence of Cubism. Iser's work was also influenced by literature and by the performing arts. He specialized in re-creating the environments of ballerinas and harlequins (e.g. *Harlequin and Dancer*, 1929; Bucharest, N. Mus. A.). He lived again in Paris from 1921 to 1934, and after his return to Romania he remained faithful to his established themes.

BIBLIOGRAPHY

I. Jianu: *Iosif Iser* (Bucharest, 1945/*R* 1957)

P. Comarnescu: *Iosif Iser* (Bucharest, 1965)

Iser, 1881–1958: Expoziție retrospectivă (exh. cat. by G. Pojar, Bucharest, Mus. A., 1983)

ALINA-IOANA ȘERBU

Iserenhod(t), Anton. *See* EISENHOIT, ANTON.

Ise Shrine [Jap. Ise Jingū]. Japanese Shinto shrine in Ise, Mie Prefecture, 90 km east of the city of Nara and near Ise Bay. Of all the shrines in Japan, which number more than 100,000, Ise has the highest standing as it enshrines the ancestral deity of the imperial house. Ise Shrine is divided into two shrine precincts: the Inner Shrine (Naikū) and the Outer Shrine (Gekū). Since the late 7th century, these two shrines have undergone the *shikinen sengū*, the practice of rebuilding the important shrine buildings every 20 years. The main sanctuaries at Ise are called *shōden* (corresponding to the *honden* at other shrines) and are fine examples of an ancient style of main sanctuary (*see* JAPAN, fig. 16).

1. History. 2. Arrangement of the shrine buildings. 3. Style of the *shōden*. 4. *Shikinen sengū*.

1. HISTORY. The Naikū and Gekū are located 4 km apart. The Naikū, formally called the *kōtai jingū* ('large imperial shrine'), enshrines the ancestral goddess of the imperial house, the Sun Goddess, Amaterasu Ōmikami. The Gekū is formally called the *Toyouke daijingū* or *Toyuke daijingū* ('large Toyouke shrine') after the *kami* (deity) of cereals, Toyouke no Ōmikami (or Toyuke no Ōkami), who offers morning and evening meals to Amaterasu. Since ancient times, the Naikū has enjoyed a higher standing than the Gekū.

According to the *Nihon shoki* ('Chronicle of Japan'; AD 720), the goddess of the Naikū, Amaterasu, was initially enshrined in the imperial palace; however, in 92 BC, on account of local unrest, Emperor Sūjin felt unable to continue housing the goddess in the palace. The Princess Toyosuki irihime no mikoto was entrusted with the worship of Amaterasu and erected a *himorogi* ('sacred tree') in the Kasanui village in Yamato Province. Then, in *c.* 5 BC, Emperor Suinin summoned Princess Yamato hime no mikoto and placed her in charge of the worship of Amaterasu. Yamato hime no mikoto travelled throughout the country in an effort to find an appropriate location for a shrine and, on reaching Ise, declared that this was the place where Amaterasu wished her shrine to be built.

The founding of the Gekū is recorded in a document written in AD 804. Emperor Yūryaku is said to have had a divine revelation of Amaterasu in a dream and, in order to feed the goddess morning and evening meals, he moved Toyouke no Ōmikami to Ise in AD 478 from Tanba Province. There are many legends concerning the chronology of the construction of the two shrines, but historical accounts indicate that there were buildings at Ise by the late 7th century. It is recorded that the Naikū underwent the first *shikinen sengū* in 690 and the Gekū in 692. The 61st rebuilding of both shrines took place in 1993, again reproducing the style of the buildings as transmitted from the 7th century or earlier.

In ancient times, the Ise *kami* were worshipped by the court and the people as the protectors of the nation's prosperity and peace. In recorded history, emperors required that the princesses go to Ise to pray to the *kami* on behalf of the court. Even in modern times, shrine visits were not made by the emperors themselves. At one time the general public was forbidden to visit and worship at the shrine, although popular religion had centred around it from the 12th century onwards.

The *shikinen sengū* lapsed during the 15th and 16th centuries in the turmoil caused by domestic wars, and many buildings at Ise were lost, including the all-important *shōden*, which fell into disrepair. The *shinza* (seats for the *kami*) were moved to a *kariden* ('temporary shrine') during this period. In the late 16th century, the shrine received financial support from Oda Nobunaga—the military leader responsible for the reunification of the country—in order to reconstruct its buildings. The rebuilding was completed in 1585. After that time the Tokugawa shogunate (Edo period; 1600–1868) continued the *shikinen sengū*, and Ise Shrine in particular attracted great numbers of worshippers. Mass visits to Ise occur approximately every 60 years: it is said that 2,700,000 people went to Ise in 1771 and nearly 5,000,000 people in 1830. At that time, the study of Japan's past (*see* JAPAN, §XX) was attracting greater interest and in this respect Ise shrine had the highest national standing. After the collapse of the Tokugawa shogunate and with the Meiji Restoration (1868–1912), the emperor once again worshipped at Ise. Since then, the special character of Ise has distinguished it from other shrines.

2. ARRANGEMENT OF THE SHRINE BUILDINGS. In the central area of the shrine is a sacred precinct (known in antiquity as the *Ōmiya'in*). The area of the Naikū precinct is about 3.5 acres and of the Gekū nearly 3.7 acres, each of these also having an eastern and a western side. At any given time, there are buildings on one side only of the eastern and western precincts; the other side remains an empty plot. During the *shikinen sengū*, new buildings are built on the empty plot and then the old buildings on the other side are taken down, so that there is a rotation of the eastern and western spaces every 20 or 21 years. In 1993, it was the eastern plot that was reconstructed. The sacred precincts face south. North of the Naikū *shōden* and south of the Gekū *shōden*, there are two *hōden* ('sacred storehouse' or 'treasure-house'), one removed slightly to the east and the other to the west. The *hōden* are smaller, simplified versions of the *shōden*. Two rows of fences with gates surround the *shōden* and *hōden*. A *yojōden*, a building which the princess would enter for rituals, is located to the south-east, outside the *shōden* and the two inner fences. The *yojōden*, the inner fences, *hōden* and *shōden* are encircled by another two rows of fences.

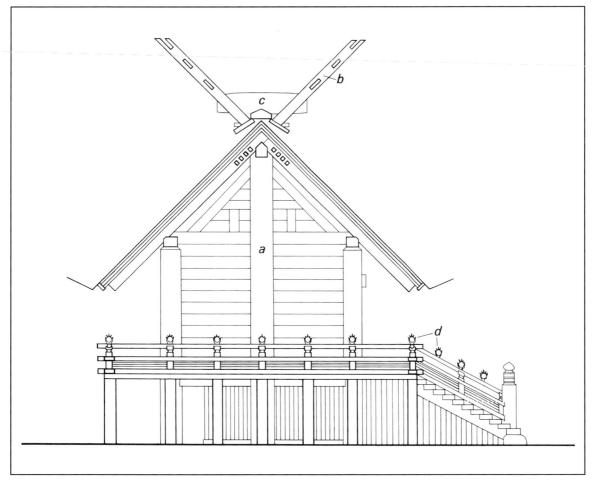

Ise Shrine, *shōden* (main sanctuary) of the Naikū (Inner Shrine), side-view showing *kirizuma zukuri* ('gabled construction') in *shinmei zukuri* ('Shinmei construction') format: (a) *munamochi bashira*; (b) *chigi*; (c) *katsuogi*; (d) *suedana*

The inner *shōden* is consequently surrounded by four rows of fences; each row has a different shape. Outside and north of the Gekū, between the third and the outermost fences, there is another building called the Mikeden. Morning and evening meals are offered daily to the *kami* there. The Mikeden is also important because it retains an ancient construction technique called *ita-azekura* (an ancient form of mortice-and-tenon joinery).

3. STYLE OF THE 'SHŌDEN'. The *shōden* of the Naikū and Gekū are composed of wood and in a similar style. The Naikū *shōden* measures 11.18 m wide×5.45 m deep×6.48 m high; the Gekū *shōden* is marginally smaller (10.18×5.76×6.40 m). Among extant *honden*, those at Ise are relatively large. The two *shōden* are representative of the *shinmei zukuri* ('Shinmei construction'; see fig.), which is one of the oldest styles used in shrine *honden*. There are four round columns across the front of the building and three on the sides, and between the columns the wall is constructed of wooden planks. Centrally positioned on the façade are *tobira* (double hanging doors). There are no windows and the interior contains one room only. The round columns are called *hottate bashira* (column that is placed directly into the ground). This construction technique, preserved by the *shikinen sengū*, dates back to a time before the introduction of Buddhist architecture (*see* JAPAN, §III, 3(i)). In this respect the shrine is unique.

The wooden floor is raised relatively high off the ground, a special trait of Japanese architecture and fundamentally different from Chinese architecture, which also has a tradition of wooden construction. The interior of each *shōden* is approximately the same height. A *mawari'en* (verandah) surrounds the building, and a simple staircase of rectangular timbers leads from the ground to the *shōden* façade. Inside, at each end of the building, detached from the central axis of the wall, there is an additional round column, another feature peculiar to *shinmei zukuri*. It is called *munamochi bashira* (column supporting ridge-tree; see fig. (a)) and is thicker than all other columns in the building. There are no *kumimono* (a complex wooden bracketing system used in temples and shrines that originated in China) on the tops of the *shōden* columns, another vestige of pre-Buddhist architectural style. The roof of the building is gabled (*kirizuma zukuri*), the gable (*hafu*) sloping to the front and back of the building. The thickly thatched roof is straight, unlike many shrine *honden*, which have curvilinear roofs. The barge-boards of the gable extend upwards through the roof ridge to form forked finials (*chigi*; see fig. (b)). The *chigi* at Ise thus illustrate an ancient form, serving as functional elements, while on other shrine *honden* the *chigi* are merely decorative. Also on the roof ridge are a number of short, thick, round crosspieces (*katsuogi*; see fig. (c)). While other shrines generally have two or three *katsuogi*, Ise has a greater number, reaffirming the shrine's high status.

A balustrade is connected to the *mawari'en* and on the top of the balustrade are decorative elements called *suedana* (see fig. (d)). The *suedana* (bulbous bronze ornaments that are encircled by relief flame motifs) are painted in five colours: blue, red, white, black and yellow. The *suedana* form originated in China; the influence of continental culture is thus visible in the style of the oldest shrine

honden. The *honden* of the Kono Jinja (Kono Shrine, Miyazu, Kyoto Prefecture) is the only one, apart from Ise, to have such *suedana*. Another significant feature of the Ise *shōden* is the *shinno mihashira* ('sacred-heart column'). This column is deeply embedded in the ground at the centre of the shrine building beneath the floor. It does not pierce the floorboards and is not connected to any other element of the building. The *shinno mihashira* does not serve a functional purpose but has a religious meaning and is part of the Shinto ceremonies that occur at Ise. On the floor in the centre of the interior of the shrine is a square platform, which serves as the *shinza*.

The Naikū and Gekū *shōden* are broadly similar in style but several features differ. For example, the ends of the *chigi* at the Naikū *shōden* have been cut horizontally, while those of the Gekū *chigi* have been cut vertically. There are ten *katsuogi* on the Naikū *shōden* and nine on the Gekū.

4. SHIKINEN SENGŪ. The term refers to the reconstruction of the buildings on the sacred precinct; it is enormously costly and preparation takes eight years. The 1993 *shikinen sengū* required about 10,000 cu. m of wood. One reason why the practice continues in spite of the expense is that the life of the building—the thatched roof and the wooden *hotatte bashira*, for example—is about 20 years. A magnificent celebration is also held then to give thanks to the *kami* for the annual rice harvest. The *shikinen sengū* therefore not only involves rebuilding but also has spiritual significance: it is a religious deed performed for the worship of the *kami*.

BIBLIOGRAPHY
T. Fukuyama: *Jingū no kenchiku ni kansuru shiteki chōsa* [The historical investigation of the architecture of Ise Shrine] (Ise, 1940)
S. Tanaka: *Jingū no sōshi to hatten* [The foundation and development of Ise Shrine] (Ise, 1960)
K. Tange and N. Kawazoe: *Ise: The Origin of Japanese Architecture* (Tokyo, 1962)
Y. Watanabe: *Ise to Izumo* [Ise Shrine and Izumo Shrine], Nihon no bijutsu [Arts of Japan], iii (Tokyo, 1964); Eng. trans. by R. Ricketts as *Shinto Art: Ise and Izumo Shrines*, Heibonsha Surv. Jap. A., iii (New York and Tokyo, 1974)
E. Inagaki: *Jinja to reibyō* [Shinto shrines and mausolea], xvi of *Genshoku Nihon no bijutsu* [Arts of Japan, illustrated], ed. T. Ouga (Tokyo, 1968)
T. Fukuyama, E. Inagaki and others: *Jingū* [Ise Shrine] (Tokyo, 1975)
                                                    MASAYUKI MIURA

Iseum. *See* BEHBEIT EL-HAGAR.

Isfahan [Iṣfahān, Esfahan; anc. Gabae; Sepahan]. City in central Iran and capital of Isfahan province. Located within the basin of the Zaindeh River, Isfahan was the capital of Iran under the Saljuq (*reg* 1038–1194) and Safavid (*reg* 1501–1732) dynasties and has preserved an almost uninterrupted series of important buildings dating from the Sasanian period to the present day.

1. History and urban development. 2. Art life and organization. 3. Buildings.

1. HISTORY AND URBAN DEVELOPMENT. Known since ancient times as Gabae or Sepahan, the city was connected with the Achaemenid dynasty, but the first remains date from the period of Sasanian rule (*c.* AD 224–651): they include the remains of a palace, erroneously called a fire temple (Pers. *ātishgada*), on the Garladan Hill

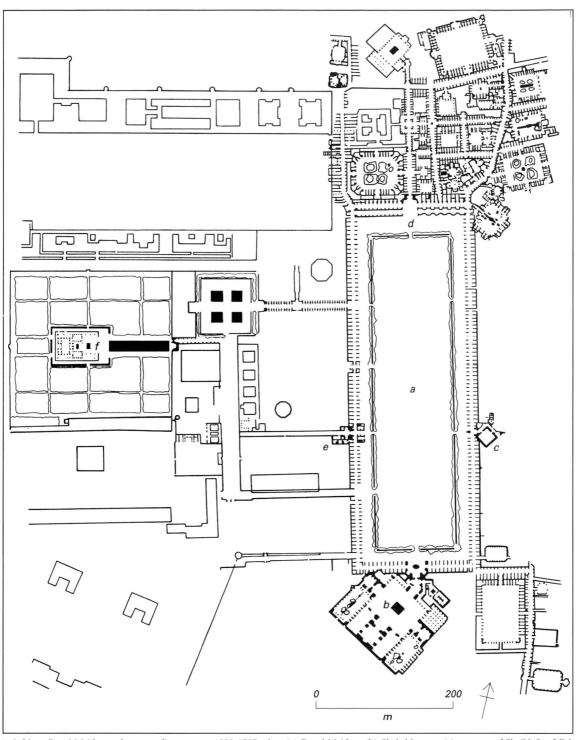

1. Isfahan, Royal Maidan and surrounding areas, *c.* 1590–1707, plan: (a) Royal Maidan; (b) Shah Mosque; (c) mosque of Sheikh Lutfallah; (d) bazaar; (e) ʿAli Qapu Palace; (f) Chihil Sutun Palace

west of the city, and the piers of the Shahristan Bridge to its south-east. When the original administrative centre of Jayy (also called Shahristan, 'the City') declined, Yahudiyya ('the Jewish quarter') became the centre of the city. A Friday Mosque (*see* §3(i) below) was founded there by Arab settlers *c.* 771. Under the Buyid dynasty (*c.* 935–1030) the city was walled and the citadel of Qal'a Tabaraq built to the north-east. The Buyids also built the Jurjir Mosque, known for its elaborately decorated brick portal, and a MUṢALLĀ to the south of the city (*see* ISLAMIC ART, §II, 5(i)(a)). In 1050 Isfahan was conquered by the Saljuq ruler Tughril, and during the long period of Saljuq residence there the city was enriched with many buildings. Most, such as the Nizamiyya Madrasa (*c.* 1070), have been destroyed, but several minarets in the city (e.g. Chihil Dukhtaran, 1107; Saraban, late 12th century) and dozens of mosques and minarets in the environs at Barsiyan (1097–1134), Sin (1134–5), ARDISTAN (rest. 1158–60) and ZAVARA (1135–6; rest. 1156–7) attest to its important role (*see* ISLAMIC ART, §II, 5(i)(b)).

In the early 14th century, when the city became a provincial centre, several small mosques were built in the Zaindeh River basin at Dashti, Gaz and Kaj, and tombs were built in the city and surrounding region. The Pir-i Bakran at Linjan, 30 km south-west of Isfahan, is the tomb of the shaykh Muhammad ibn Bakran (*d* 1303); adjacent to the tomb is a single iwan with extraordinary decoration in carved stucco (*see* ISLAMIC ART, fig. 77). The grave of the shaykh Amu 'Abdallah Suqlha (*d* 1316) at Garladan is marked by an iwan that has transverse vaulting and supports a pair of minarets; their artificially produced vibration gives rise to the popular name of the tomb, 'the Shaking Minarets'. The Imamzada Ja'far (1325), an octagonal tower commemorating a descendant of the Prophet, has fine decoration in glazed tile. Several madrasas and mausolea were built in the later 14th century, when the city was under the control of the Muzaffarid dynasty. Although the main centre of power shifted elsewhere in the 15th century, the few mausolea, *khānaqāh*s (hospices) and restorations carried out in Isfahan and its environs show that the art of ceramic revetment, already widespread in the 14th century, reached its apogee. In almost every period the Friday Mosque was modified and enlarged.

The major transformation of the city (see fig. 1) occurred in 1598, when 'Abbas I (*see* SAFAVID, (2)) made it the capital of his empire (*see* ISLAMIC ART, §II, 7(ii)(a); and GARDEN, §V, 4). He relocated the centre from the old maidan near the Friday Mosque southward to a new 8 ha maidan (1a; *see* §3(ii) below and ISLAMIC ART, fig. 86), which became the seat of religious, royal and commercial power. On the south of the maidan was erected a new congregational mosque, the Shah Mosque (1b; 1611–66; *see* §3(iii) below); on the east was the mosque of Sheikh Lutfallah (1c; 1603–19; *see* §3(iv) below); on the north was the portal (1619–20) to a long covered bazaar (1d; *see* §3(v) below), which connected the new centre with the old; and on the west was the entrance to the royal palace complex (1e; *see* §3(vi)–(viii) below), which contained at least 20 pavilions connected by hanging passageways. Beyond the palace complex, the Chahar Bagh, a wide avenue with trees and water channels, led south to the Si-o-sih pul (Bridge of 33 [Arches]; 1602) and to the Khwaju

Bridge (1650; *see* ISLAMIC ART, fig. 69), which has octagonal pleasure pavilions in the centre and sluices to regulate the flow of the river. On the far side lay the Armenian settlement of New Julfa (*see* §3(ix) below), remarkable for its fine painted houses and churches, and the hunting grounds of Hazar Jarib, an enormous country residence.

One of the richest, most modern and most visited capital cities of its time, Isfahan became the centre of royal patronage for the arts associated with architecture, such as mural painting and tile revetment. The great building fervour that marked the Safavid period in Isfahan lasted until the reign of Husayn (*reg* 1694–1722), under whom a large complex of caravanserai, bazaar and madrasa known as the Madrasa-yi Madar-i Shah (Madrasa of the Shah's Mother) was built. In the 18th century the city suffered repeated invasions and insurrections, and after the Qajars (*reg* 1779–1924) moved the capital to Tehran in 1786, the artistic importance of Isfahan declined.

BIBLIOGRAPHY

Enc. Islam/2

M. B. Smith: 'The "Manārs" of Isfahan', *Āthār-é Īrān*, i (1936), pp. 317–58

A. Godard: 'Isfahan', *Āthār-é Īrān*, ii (1937), pp. 7–176

——: 'The Jurjir Mosque in Isfahan', *Survey of Persian Art*, ed. A. U. Pope and P. Ackerman (London and New York, 1938–9, 2/1964–7), pp. 3100–03

D. N. Wilber: *The Architecture of Islamic Iran: The Ilkhānid Period* (Princeton, 1955/*R* 1969)

L. Hunarfar: *Ganjīna-yi āthār-i tārīkhī-yi Iṣfahān* [Treasury of the historical monuments of Isfahan] (Isfahan, 1965)

W. Blunt: *Isfahan: Pearl of Persia* (New York, 1966)

J. Carswell: *New Julfa: The Armenian Churches and Other Buildings* (Oxford, 1968)

G. Zander, ed.: *Travaux de restauration de monuments historiques en Iran* (Rome, 1968)

E. Galdieri: 'A Hitherto Unreported Architectural Complex at Iṣfahān: The So-called "Lesān al-'arz": Preliminary Report', *E. & W.*, n. s., xxiii (1973), pp. 249–64

R. Holod, ed.: *Studies on Isfahan*, 2 vols, *Iran. Stud.*, vii (1974)

H. Gaube: *Iranian Cities* (New York, 1979), pp. 65–98

Quad. Semin. Iran. U. Venezia, x (1981) [special issue devoted to Isfahan]

R. Hillenbrand: 'Safavid Architecture', *The Timurid and Safavid Periods* (1986), ed. P. Jackson and L. Lockhart, vi of *Cambridge History of Iran* (Cambridge, 1968–91), pp. 759–842

EUGENIO GALDIERI

2. ART LIFE AND ORGANIZATION. Isfahan is best known as the major centre of artistic production in Safavid Iran, and many details of its craft traditions were reported by foreign travellers to the capital. The arts of the book flourished (*see* ISLAMIC ART, §III, 4(vi)(a)). In addition to illustrated manuscripts, artists executed an increasing number of individual paintings and ink drawings, which often depict elegantly dressed men and women of the city. These single-page compositions enjoyed a fairly wide audience, as they were also commissioned by patrons beyond the royal élite. The most celebrated painter was RIZA, whose name has become synonymous with the genre. Royal and commercial workshops in Isfahan also produced fine silk and wool carpets (*see* ISLAMIC ART, §VI, 4(iii)(c)). More importantly, the capital became a major centre for the manufacture of silks, velvets and gold and silver brocades; they were produced for local consumption but also exported to the West in large quantities (*see* ISLAMIC ART, §VI, 2(iii)(c)).

2. Isfahan, Friday Mosque, court façade, 15th century

BIBLIOGRAPHY
Enc. Islam/2
J. B. Tavernier: *Les Six Voyages de Jean Baptiste Tavernier*, 3 vols (Paris, 1679)
J. Chardin: *Voyage en Perse*, 10 vols (Paris, 1811)
I. Stchoukine: *Les Peintures des manuscrits de Shah 'Abbas Ier à la fin des Safavis* (Paris, 1964)
Shah 'Abbas and the Arts of Isfahan (exh. cat. by A. Welch, New York, Asia House Gals, 1973)
R. Holod, ed.: *Studies on Isfahan*, 2 vols, *Iran. Stud.*, vii (1974)
A. Welch: *Artists for the Shah* (London and New Haven, 1976)
B. Gray: 'The Arts in the Safavid Period', *The Timurid and Safavid Periods* (1986), ed. P. Jackson and L. Lockhart, vi of *Cambridge History of Iran* (Cambridge, 1968–91), pp. 877–912
Woven from the Soul, Spun from the Heart (exh. cat., ed. C. Bier; Washington, DC, Textile Mus., 1987)

MASSUMEH FARHAD

3. BUILDINGS.

(i) Friday Mosque. (ii) Royal Maidan. (iii) Shah Mosque. (iv) Mosque of Sheikh Lutfallah. (v) Bazaar. (vi) 'Ali Qapu Palace. (vii) Chihil Sutun Palace. (viii) Hasht Bihisht Palace. (ix) New Julfa.

(i) Friday Mosque [Masjid-i jum'a]. One of the largest and most important buildings of the Islamic period in Iran, the mosque is a palimpsest of religious architecture, as it exemplifies the constructional and stylistic characteristics of all dynasties that reigned over the city. The first mosque on the site (*c.* 771) was a relatively small building (*c.* 52×90 m) made of mud-brick with stucco decoration in a Syro-Mesopotamian style. In 840–41 this building was replaced by a larger one (88×128 m), orientated at an angle of 20° to the original mosque. The new mosque had a large central court surrounded by arcades and baked brick columns supporting a flat roof. A wider aisle led to the mihrab, and the external façade was decorated with blind arches. Towards the end of the 10th century, a row of columns was added around the court façade; the smooth plaster coating used in the earlier work was replaced by brick decoration in relief. The first real transformation of the mosque took place under the Saljuqs (*see* ISLAMIC ART, §II, 5(i)(b) and fig. 29).

A large dome chamber (*c.* 1086–7) was added in front of the mihrab and another domed square was built beyond the north end of the mosque in 1088–9 (*see* ISLAMIC ART, fig. 31). Slightly later, perhaps after the devastation caused by a fire in 1121–2, iwans were inserted on the sides of the court, a rectangular hall was built beyond the south corner, and cross-ribbed vaults were introduced. By the first half of the 12th century, the building had the appearance of the standard Iranian mosque, with four iwans and a dome.

Later changes were more modest. Under the Ilkhanid sultan Uljaytu (*reg* 1304–17) a splendid stucco mihrab (1310) was built abutting the west iwan (*see* STUCCO AND PLASTERWORK, fig. 6), and the courtyard arcade was divided into two levels. Under the Muzaffarids, perhaps under Qutb al-Din Shah Mahmud (*reg* 1358–75), a madrasa was added on the east and a prayer hall on the west, both beyond the old perimeter wall. Most work carried out in the 15th century was limited to rebuilding or repairing structures that were in poor condition. Many complex cross-ribbed vaults can be attributed to this period. A prayer hall, based on a square plan, was added in the south-east corner, and the roof over the hall housing Uljaytu's mihrab was reconstructed. The court façade (*see* fig. 2) was clad with tile revetment; the stunning tile mosaic on the qibla iwan, for example, was ordered by the Aqqoyunlu ruler Uzun Hasan in 1475–6. Almost all Safavid monarchs except 'Abbas I, who was preoccupied with his own large mosque (*see* §(iii) below) on the new maidan, left their mark on the mosque. Several dozen columns were demolished to enlarge prayer halls, a large winter prayer hall was built on the site of the Muzaffarid one, and tilework was added to the iwans and minarets. Further repairs and restorations were carried out under the Afsharids (*reg* 1736–95) and the Qajars.

BIBLIOGRAPHY

A. Gabriel: 'Le Masdjid-i Djum'a d'Isfahan', *A. Islam.*, ii (1935), pp. 11–44

A. Godard: 'Historique du Masdjid-i Djum'a d'Isfahan', *Āthār-é Īrān*, i (1936), pp. 213–82

E. Galdieri: *Isfahān: Masǧid-i Ǧum'a*, 3 vols (Rome, 1972–84)

——: 'The Masǧid-i Ǧum'a Isfahan: An Architectural Façade of the 3rd Century H.', *A. & Archaeol. Res. Pap.*, vi (1974), pp. 24–34

U. Scerrato: 'Notice préliminaire sur les recherches archéologiques dans la Masgid-i Jum'a d'Isfahan', *Farhang-i mi'mārī-yi Īrān*, iv (1976), pp. 15–18

O. Grabar: *The Great Mosque of Isfahan* (New York, 1990)

S. S. Blair: *The Monumental Inscriptions from Early Islamic Iran and Transoxiana* (Leiden, 1992), pp. 160–67

(ii) Royal Maidan [Maydān-i shāh]. An enormous open space fringed by architectural monuments (see fig. 1a above), this royal square was laid out by 'Abbas I between 1590 and 1602. Lying to the south-east of the old city (*see* ISLAMIC ART, fig. 68), it is an elongated rectangle (*c.* 525× 159 m in its final stages) edged by a continuous double order of piers decorated with polychrome glazed tiles. The long modular façades are broken only by the monumental entranceways to four buildings: the Shah Mosque (*see* §(iii) below) on the south, the mosque of Shaykh Lutfallah (*see* §(iv) below) on the east, the portal to the bazaar (*see* §(v) below) on the north and the 'Ali Qapu Palace (*see* §(vi) below) to the west. The creation of the maidan was part of the transformation of the city into the new capital of the Safavid empire and was designed to encourage urban development south towards the Zaindeh River. The square represents an early example of a multi-functional space. A stone channel ran around its perimeter at a short distance from the arcade and separated the space for walking from the central area, which was originally unpaved and covered with gravel. The covered walkway and the outer arcades acted as a bazaar. The great central space generally housed the temporary stalls of merchants, craftsmen, barbers and entertainers but was often cleared for military parades, drill by the shah's personal militia, archery contests and polo matches. For a few years the square also housed a curious horological mechanism with moving figures built for the amusement of the young ruler 'Abbas II (*reg* 1642–66). In addition to its exceptional dimensions and architectonic significance, the square, which was called *naqsh-i jahān* ('Image of the world'), also invoked the political and social philosophy of 'Abbas I, who dreamed of raising his kingdom to the level of the other great monarchies of his day.

BIBLIOGRAPHY

E. Galdieri and R. Orazi: *Progetto di sistemazione del Maydan-i Šāh* (Rome, 1969)

E. Galdieri: 'Two Building Phases of the Time of Šāh 'Abbas I in the Maydān-i Šāh of Isfahan: Preliminary Note', *E. & W.*, n. s., xx (1970), pp. 60–69

H. Luschey: 'Der königliche Marstall in Işfahān und Engelbert Kaempfers Planographia des Palastbezirkes 1712', *Iran*, xvii (1979), pp. 71–9

E. Galdieri: 'Esfahan e la *Domus Spectaculi Automatorum*', *Proceedings of the First European Conference of Iranian Studies, Societas Iranologica Europaea: Turin, 1987*, ii, pp. 377–88

(iii) Shah Mosque [Masjid-i shāh]. This monumental mosque was begun in 1611 by 'Abbas I and finished *c.* 1630 by his successor, Safi (*reg* 1629–42). The entrance vestibule (see fig. 3) is aligned with the southern side of the maidan, but the rest of the building is rotated 45° to align with the qibla and face Mecca (see fig. 1b above). The building consists of a large central court with iwans on the four sides. The iwan on the north-east is a natural extension of the entrance vestibule; those on the south-east and north-west provide access to smaller domed oratories; the one on the south-west leads into the vast domed sanctuary, which is adorned with a monumental mihrab (completed 1666) and alabaster minbar.

The sanctuary communicates with flanking rectangular chambers, each covered by eight domes, and they in turn lead to two rectangular courts in the corners. Paired minarets flank the entrance portal and the sanctuary iwan. Above a continuous marble dado, all vertical surfaces, both interior and exterior, are clad in polychrome glazed tiles, most of which were replaced in the 1930s on the basis of extant remains. The predominant colour is blue except in the rectangular halls, which are revetted in later tiles of yellowy-green shades. The smaller domes have brick exteriors, while the double-shelled sanctuary dome, with an onion-shaped exterior dome covering a hemispherical one, is covered in glazed tiles. Despite its large size (diam. 25 m), the dome with its high drum achieves an effect of great lightness, as it rests on two imposing side arches and an octagonal zone of transition pierced with smaller niches and arches.

3. Isfahan, Shah Mosque, entrance portal, 1611–*c.* 1630

BIBLIOGRAPHY
L. Golombek: 'Anatomy of a Mosque: The Masjid-i Shāh of Iṣfahān', *Iranian Civilization and Culture*, ed. C. J. Adams (Montreal, 1972), pp. 5–11

(iv) Mosque of Sheikh Lutfallah [Masjid-i Sheikh Luṭfallah]. This building lies on the maidan facing the 'Ali Qapu Palace audience chamber (see fig. 1c above). The mosque was ordered in 1603 by 'Abbas I, who entrusted its building and decoration to Muhammad Riza 'Abbasi. Work was finished in 1619, according to the inscription on its beautiful mihrab. The building was originally called the Mosque of the Pontiff (Pers. *Masjid-i ṣadr*) and was entrusted to the theologian Shaykh Lutfallah, who had accompanied the Shah to Isfahan to preach Shi'ite doctrine. Although less famous than the nearby Shah Mosque, the building is distinguished as the only Safavid mosque to diverge from the established norm. It comprises a single domed prayer hall (interior diam. 19 m) with simple service areas and without any external court, side galleries or minarets. Its spare space is comparable to that of the single-domed mosques built under the Ottomans (*see* ISLAMIC ART, §II, 7(i)) or to a private oratory. The prayer hall, which is not aligned with the maidan, is reached through a gloomy corridor that runs along two sides of the prayer room to open opposite the mihrab. The visual and psychological impact achieved by the vast glowing square of the interior, the geometry of which is both emphasized and disrupted by vibrant turquoise tiles, is unforgettable (*see* ISLAMIC ART, fig. 79). The only light is filtered through the double ceramic grilles that cover the 16 windows in the drum under the dome. Below the prayer hall another area, almost of the same dimensions but very low and covered by vaults resting on four octagonal piers, serves as a winter mosque. The exterior of the dome, with its pleasing pointed silhouette, is covered in glazed tile (rest.), with an unusual ochre-coloured design of arabesques. The revetment around the entrance was executed in 1937 on the basis of the few remaining original tiles.

BIBLIOGRAPHY
M. Ferrante: 'La Mosquée de Šaiḥ Luṭfullah à Ispahan: Relevé planimétrique', *Travaux de restauration de monuments historiques en Iran*, ed. G. Zander (Rome, 1968), pp. 421–40

EUGENIO GALDIERI

(v) Bazaar. The main covered bazaar stretches nearly 2 km from the old maidan near the Friday Mosque to the Royal Maidan built by 'Abbas I. The bazaar is a spacious vaulted passage flanked by shops. At short intervals domed intersections (Pers. *chahārsū*) give access to more than 100 service structures, including caravanserais, baths, madrasas, shrines and mosques. The layout probably dates back to medieval times, but the brick fabric and many of the structures have been repeatedly restored and rebuilt. At the south end is the royal bazaar (Pers. *qayṣāriyya*) built by 'Abbas I, laid out with two north–south lanes intersecting three east–west lanes. The entrance from the Royal Maidan (see fig. 1d above) is marked by an elaborate portal with wall paintings and galleries that once housed the royal music pavilion (Pers. *naqqāra khāna*). The two-storey lane behind the portal served in the 17th century as a royal market for fine textiles. The first domed intersection led on the right to the royal mint and on the left to the royal caravanserai. This caravanserai is the largest one in the

city, with 140 rooms for cloth merchants on the ground floor, and jewellers, goldsmiths and engravers on the upper storey. A second domed nodule provides access to another caravanserai, now ruined, behind the first. To the north 'Abbas built a hospital and caravanserai (both destr.), the revenues of which were used to fund the hospital. These buildings mark the extent of 'Abbas's constructions, for buildings further north are orientated slightly differently to conform to the medieval street scheme.

BIBLIOGRAPHY
A. Bakhtiar: 'The Royal Bazaar of Isfahan', *Studies on Isfahan*, ed. R. Holod, 2 vols, *Iran. Stud.*, vii (1974), pp. 320–47
H. Gaube and E. Wirth: *Der Bazar von Isfahan* (Wiesbaden, 1978)

☐

(vi) 'Ali Qapu Palace ['Alī Qāpū]. Situated in the middle of the western side of the Royal Maidan (see fig. 1e above), the 'Ali Qapu (Lofty Gate) was begun by 'Abbas I *c.* 1597 as a simple entrance hall for the royal palace complex but was gradually modified and extended until it reached its present form *c.* 1660 under 'Abbas II. Its function evolved from a guard house to an audience hall and later an official tribune from which to inspect military manoeuvres and games held in the maidan below. The building consists of a main block with a tower and a lower extension crowned by a raised columnar hall (Pers. *tālār*). The towered section (20 m sq., h. 33 m) is subdivided into five levels. Because of the differing elevations of the rooms, the floors had different layouts, and many of the structural elements lack continuity from one floor to the next. The main supporting structures, which are heavy and massive on the lower floors, become lighter towards the top, fading into hollow pilasters on the third floor and ending as a network of thin arches that support and cover the Music Room (*see* ISLAMIC ART, fig. 70). There they are hidden by a skin of plaster *muqarnas* niches painted and pierced for acoustic as well as decorative purposes in shapes typical of Chinese porcelains. The building is richly decorated with wall paintings and small scenes of a mildly erotic nature, which are almost indecipherable. Most of the walls and ceilings are clad in a layer of painted, ornamental plaster, which creates a sculptural effect through a technique similar to champlevé.

BIBLIOGRAPHY
M. Ferrante: 'Dessins et observations préliminaires pour la restauration du palais de 'Alī Qāpū', *Travaux de restauration de monuments historiques en Iran*, ed. G. Zander (Rome, 1968), pp. 137–206
E. Galdieri: *Eṣfahān: 'Alī Qāpū: An Architectural Survey* (Rome, 1979)

(vii) Chihil Sutun Palace [Chihil sutūn]. The only great ceremonial pavilion to have survived from the many built during the Safavid period as part of Isfahan's royal complex, the Chihil Sutun (Forty Columns) comprises a large reception hall (23×11 m) covered by three domes with two symmetrical projections that form a U-shape with the main room. The three sections are preceded on the east by a vast colonnaded porch (Pers. *tālār*) open on three sides and covered with a flat wooden roof (see fig. 4). The pavilion is situated at the centre of an enormous garden (7 ha) with a long pool (110×20 m) on the east–west axis (see fig. 1f above). The building and pool were surrounded by fountains and stone canals with jets of water. The central hall with high ceilings and broad windows is surrounded by smaller rooms arranged on two

4. Isfahan, Chihil Sutun Palace, completed 1706–7, view from the east

levels. Inscriptions suggest that the pavilion was begun by 'Abbas II in 1647, but the original nucleus, perhaps with a different architectural function, may date from an earlier period. The construction of the colonnaded porch in 1706–7 marked the completion of the building. The Chihil Sutun is unusual but not entirely satisfactory in terms of its external architecture and owes its reputation to three factors. First, it gives an idea of what other, now vanished or radically altered official pavilions in the royal Safavid complex were like. Second, it provides an important example of the theatrical nature of Safavid court architecture, achieved by the changing shapes and colours of the 20 wooden columns reflected in the pool and the shimmering decoration of mirror fragments and full-length Venetian-glass mirrors donated by the Doge. Finally, it contains an important series of decorative and figural wall paintings (*see* ISLAMIC ART, fig. 81), including a number of later historical paintings showing official receptions and banquets, battles and visits by European ambassadors.

BIBLIOGRAPHY

M. Ferrante: 'Čihil Sutūn: Etudes, relevés, restauration', *Travaux de restauration de monuments historiques en Iran*, ed. G. Zander (Rome, 1968), pp. 293–322
E. Grube: 'Wall Paintings in the Seventeenth Century Monuments of Isfahan', *Studies on Isfahan*, ed. R. Holod, 2 vols, *Iran. Stud.*, vii (1974), pp. 511–42
S. Babaie: 'Shah 'Abbas II, the Conquest of Qandahar, the Chihil Sutun, and its Wall Paintings', *Muqarnas*, xi (1994), pp. 125–42

(viii) Hasht Bihisht Palace. A small pavilion from the Safavid period, the Hasht Bihisht (Eight Paradises) is situated within the royal palace complex, although it was never intended for official use. An octagon with a cruciform plan, it is arranged on two levels, each with four small rooms at the corners of a central hall. The hall is two-storey and acts like an inner court; it is covered by a dome of almost ovoid shape, richly adorned with painted plaster *muqarnas*. The building has two axes: a north–south one with an arched iwan and an impressive colonnaded porch, and an east–west one with two smaller iwans. The building can be attributed to Sulayman (*reg* 1666–94),

although the Qajar monarch Fath 'Ali Shah (*reg* 1797–1834) made a few superficial alterations, such as four large painted ceramic panels (destr.) depicting the ruler seated on his throne. During the 1920s more drastic alterations effectively destroyed the spatial characteristics of the interior and hid the original plaster decoration beneath ornamental yellow stucco in Rococo taste, but restorations since then have revealed fragments of wall painting, some richly decorative and some delicately descriptive. The complex hydraulic system includes an unusual cascade (Pers. *ābnāma*) of alabaster slabs and ceramic tiles in Turkish style in the south iwan, a large basin and fountain of pierced marble in the north porch and another cascade in stone and alabaster outside the north porch. The surrounding Garden of the Nightingale has also been refurbished. The skilful spatial layout and interplay of different levels visible to passers-by makes the Hasht Bihisht an effective example of theatrical court architecture and dynamic building. It embodies the Iranian way of life in which indoor and outdoor spaces, and natural and man-made environments, are harmoniously integrated.

BIBLIOGRAPHY

D. N. Wilber: *Persian Gardens and Garden Pavilions* (Tokyo, 1962), pp. 107–11
M. Ferrante: 'Le Pavillon de Hašt Bihišt, ou les Huit Paradis, à Ispahan: Relevés et problèmes s'y rattachant', *Travaux de restauration de monuments historiques en Iran*, ed. G. Zander (Rome, 1968), pp. 399–420

EUGENIO GALDIERI

(ix) New Julfa. In 1604 'Abbas I ordered the valley of Ararat on the Ottoman frontier to be evacuated, and several thousand Armenian families from the region were established in a suburb of Isfahan south of the Zaindeh River. Known from 1606 as New Julfa, after the town they had been forced to leave, this quarter of Isfahan flourished as an Armenian Christian community, and between 27 and 30 churches were built there. The 13 surviving examples, dating between 1606 and 1728, combine Safavid style and building techniques with elements imported from the Armenian homeland. Liturgical requirements dictated that the plan developed for churches in Julfa be retained in the new buildings. Traditionally, the exteriors of Armenian churches were relatively plain, and the impact of the buildings derived principally from their form and massing. In New Julfa, the form of the churches, apart from the belfries and crosses crowning the domes, was derived from the Persian architectural tradition, with shallow ovoid domes and pointed arches. The construction of these churches also followed local traditions: baked brick replaced the stone typical in Armenia. The interiors of some churches were richly decorated, and cycles of wall paintings survive in a few of them, notably the Bethlehem Church (1627) and All Saviour's Cathedral (1656), while paintings on panel or canvas survive in many. Like contemporary paintings and book illustrations made for the Safavid court (*see* ISLAMIC ART, §III, 4(vi)(a)), these works show the impact of European modes of representation, through either the presence of European artists or works of art in the Safavid capital. Many of the churches also have underglaze-painted polychrome tile panels or friezes depicting scenes from the New Testament, landscapes and animals. In addition to Armenians, such foreign Christians as Carmelite and Capuchin missionaries lived

in New Julfa. The finest residences, such as those along the Chahar Bagh Avenue, were garden villas modelled on detached royal pavilions. Even modest dwellings were enriched with refined decoration in tile and paint. The house of Petros Valijanian, for example, has murals depicting the *Seven Wonders of the World*.

BIBLIOGRAPHY

T. S. R. Boase: 'A Seventeenth-century Typological Cycle of Paintings in the Armenian Cathedral in Julfa', *J. Warb. & Court. Inst.*, xiii (1950), pp. 323–7

J. Carswell: *New Julfa: The Armenian Churches and Other Buildings* (Oxford, 1968)

V. Gregorian: 'Minorities of Isfahan: The Armenian Community of Isfahan, 1587–1722', *Studies on Isfahan*, ed. R. Holod, 2 vols, *Iran. Stud.*, vii (1974), pp. 652–80

K. Karpetian: *Isfahān, New Julfa: Le case degli Armeni/The Houses of the Armenians* (Rome, 1974)

LAURA GROVES

Isfahani [Iṣfahānī]. Persian family of painters. They were the foremost specialists in painted and varnished ('lacquered') objects (*see* ISLAMIC ART, §VIII, 10) in 19th-century Iran. Their work is marked by meticulous technique, minute detail and delicate finish, and their subjects, such as variations on the theme of the Holy Family, are often inspired by the European pictures and prints that were flooding into Iran at the time. The first known member of the family was Aqa Baba. His elder son, (1) Najaf 'Ali, set the high standards that were passed to other members of the family. His younger brother (2) Muhammad Isma'il was the most brilliant and original member of the family and became a Painter Laureate (Pers. *naqqāsh-bāshī*) of the Qajar dynasty (*reg* 1779–1924). Najaf 'Ali's three sons, Muhammad Kazim (*d c.* 1885), Ja'far and Ahmad, who were active until the 1880s, also painted varnished objects, as did Muhammad Isma'il's son Haydar 'Ali (*fl* 1902–19).

BIBLIOGRAPHY

B. W. Robinson: 'Persian Lacquer in the Bern Historical Museum', *Iran*, viii (1970), pp. 47–50

——: 'Persian Painting in the Qajar Period', *Highlights of Persian Art*, ed. R. Ettinghausen and E. Yarshater (Boulder, 1979), pp. 331–62

M. A. Karīmzāda Tabrīzī: *Ahvāl u āthār-i naqqāshān-i qadīm-i īrān* [The lives and art of old painters of Iran] (London, 1985), nos 80, 230, 324 and 1129

L. S. Diba: 'Lacquerwork', *The Arts of Persia*, ed. R. W. Ferrier (New Haven and London, 1989), pp. 243–54

B. W. Robinson: 'Qajar Lacquer', *Muqarnas*, vi (1989), pp. 131–46

(1) Najaf 'Ali [Najaf 'Alī; Āqā Najaf] (*fl c.* 1815–60). A student of the renowned bird-and-flower painter 'ALI ASHRAF, Najaf 'Ali worked in an archaizing style reminiscent of work produced in the 18th century. Almost all his works are signed *yā shāh-i najaf* ('O King of Najaf'), a punning invocation to 'Ali, the Prophet's son-in-law and first Imam of the Shi'ites, who was buried at Najaf. This signature is found on several penboxes (e.g. Berne, Hist. Mus., MK 987, dated 1854; London, V&A, 849-1889; and Tehran, Mus. Dec. A.). Several unsigned pieces (e.g. Berne, Hist. Mus.) are similar in style and can be attributed to him. In his later work, such as a mirror-case (priv. col., see Robinson, 1989, fig. 12), he often imitated the style of his more famous brother (2) Muhammad Isma'il.

Najaf 'Ali's work is often difficult to identify, and pieces in various other styles are associated with his name, probably because his sons and school not only continued

to paint in his style but also signed his name. A penbox dated 1861–2 (Berne, Hist. Mus., 20-1912) signed by Ja'far, a pair of book covers (*c.* 1870; St Petersburg, Hermitage) signed by Muhammad Kazim, and a penbox dated 1878 (priv. col., see Robinson, 1979, fig. 232) signed by Ahmad all continue the flower-and-bird style of Najaf 'Ali. Muhammad Kazim and Ahmad also worked in painted enamel, and Muhammad Kazim's painted enamels, such as a bowl from a hooka (*c.* 1870; priv. col., see Robinson, 1967, fig. 234), are particularly fine. He was the most important enameller of the late 19th century and produced many fine pieces, such as a hooka base decorated with medallions of the Holy Family set amid flowers (1864; Tehran, Bank Markazi, Crown Jewels Col.).

BIBLIOGRAPHY

B. W. Robinson: 'A Lacquer Mirror-case of 1854', *Iran*, v (1967), pp. 1–6

——: 'Qājār Painted Enamels', *Paintings from Islamic Lands*, ed. R. Pinder-Wilson (Oxford, 1969), pp. 187–204

——: 'Persian Painting in the Qajar Period', *Highlights of Persian Art*, ed. R. Ettinghausen and E. Yarshater (Boulder, 1979), pp. 331–62

M. A. Karīmzāda Tabrīzī: *Ahvāl u āthār-i naqqāshān-i qadīm-i īrān* [The lives and art of old painters of Iran] (London, 1985), no. 1389

B. W. Robinson: 'Qajar Lacquer', *Muqarnas*, vi (1989), pp. 131–46

(2) Muhammad Isma'il [Muḥammad Ismā'īl] (*b c.* 1814; *d* 1882 or 1892). Younger brother of (1) Najaf 'Ali. A prolific artist who painted many penboxes, mirror-cases and caskets, Muhammad Isma'il worked during the early part of his life for the Qajar governor of Isfahan, Manuchihr Khan, known as Muhammad al-Dawla. His court is depicted on a penbox (1848; London, V&A, 763–1876), the earliest signed work by Muhammad Isma'il. The governor is portrayed on other signed works, such as a casket (1850; London, N. D. Khalili priv. col.), and other pieces depicting the governor's court, such as a mirror-case (New York, Brooklyn Mus., 71.49.2), can be attributed to this formative period of Muhammad Isma'il's life. These early works are characterized by large-scale, full-length figures set in highly ordered and conventional compositions.

In the 1850s the artist began to work for the court of the Qajar ruler Nasir al-Din (*reg* 1848–96). A portrait of the king seated on a European settee (1854; London, BL, 1947-2-10-01) is signed *khānazād ismā'īl* ('royal-born Isma'il') and presumably refers to Muhammad Isma'il. A rectangular mirror-case made by the artist in the same year (sold London, Phillips, 15 March 1966, lot 29) was a royal commission. Several figures in the nine historical scenes on the hinged cover can be identified, including the Ottoman sultan Abdülmecid I (*reg* 1839–61) and Tsar Nicholas I of Russia (*reg* 1825–55), who is shown meeting Nasir al-Din Mirza when he was heir-apparent, aged seven. This interest in historical reporting reflects the impact of newspaper printing and lithographed books, which had been introduced in Iran at this time. By 1848 the artist had been designated Painter Laureate (Pers. *naqqāsh-bāshī*), a title used on a pencase with a woman in European dress surrounded by bird-and-flower designs (Karimzada Tabrizi, p. 69).

Muhammad Isma'il's masterpiece is a casket (1865; Berne, Hist. Mus., 71/1913) depicting the campaigns of Muhammad Shah (*reg* 1834–48). The siege of Herat in 1837–8 shown on the lid comprises hundreds of tiny figures and combines Westernizing techniques such as perspective and modelling with the high horizon and bird's-eye view typical of Persian book illustration. A pencase (1866; Baltimore, MD, Walters A.G., 67.3) juxtaposes a scene from the amorous adventures of Bahram Gur in Nizami's *Khamsa* ('Five poems') with a scene of the Virgin and Child. Another penbox from the same year (sold Sotheby's, Sept 1973) contains a self-portrait of the artist on the inner face of the lid. Muhammad Isma'il's last signed work is a mirror-case (1871–2; Berne, Hist. Mus., 73/13). The inner surface of the cover bears a portrait of a nimbed 'Ali holding his forked sword Dhu'l-Fiqar and surrounded by his sons Hasan and Husayn and other figures from Shi'ite theology. This scene, which was inspired by a painting of Abu'l-Hasan Ghaffari, reflects the impact of European altarpieces, such as the one dated 1724 in the church of St Nersus in New Julfa in Isfahan, and shows the increasing popularity of religious subjects in 19th-century Iranian art.

Muhammad Isma'il's nickname was 'the Europeanizer' (Pers. *farangī-sāz*), and his work shows many aspects of European culture that were just beginning to have an impact on Iran: fashions, ways of portraying women, and modes of transport such as carriages, steamboats, trains and suspension bridges. Unlike his older brother Najaf 'Ali, he maintained a distinctive style throughout his long career, and his work is immediately distinguishable by the small puppet-like figures, doll-like faces and heavy scrollwork separating the various events depicted. His style was continued by his son Haydar 'Ali, who painted a fine penbox (1864; priv. col., see 1985 exh. cat., no. 166).

BIBLIOGRAPHY
B. W. Robinson: 'A Lacquer Mirror-case of 1854', *Iran*, v (1967), pp. 1–6
M. A. Karimzada Tabrizi: *Ahvāl u āthār-i naqqāshān-i qadīm-i īrān* [The lives and art of old painters of Iran] (London, 1985), no. 129
Treasures of Islam (exh. cat., ed. T. Falk; Geneva, Mus. A. & Hist., 1985)
M. Ekhtiar: 'Muhammad Isma'il Isfahani: Master Lacquer Painter', *Persian Master: Five Centuries of Painting*, ed. S. R. Canby (Bombay, 1990), pp. 129–43

□

Isham, Samuel (*b* New York, 12 May 1855; *d* Easthampton, NY, 12 June 1914). American writer and painter. After graduating from Yale University in 1875 he travelled to Paris to study art but soon returned to New York to study law at Columbia University. After five years as a practising lawyer (1880–85) he decided definitely to study art and once more went to Paris to work for two years under Louis Boulanger in the Académie Julian. He returned to the USA, where critical acclaim for his landscape and figure paintings eventually attracted the attention of the National Academy of Design, New York, of which he became a full member in 1906. The *Lilac Kimono* (New York, Brooklyn Mus.) displays his broad painterly style. He wrote *The History of American Painting* (1905) with the professed goal of recording the intellectual and cultural growth of the country, although in his widespread coverage 19th-century artists receive most attention. He set each painter within a group, describing individual style and generously giving praise or patiently explaining faults in their work. When the book was reissued in 1927, Royal Cortissoz (1869–1948) updated the original text with a chapter on modern painting. Isham's only other publication was *The Limitations of Verbal Criticism of Works of Art* (1928), which originated as the text of a lecture delivered in 1907 at Columbia University.

WRITINGS
The History of American Painting, iii of *The History of American Art*, ed. J. C. van Dyke (New York, 1905); rev. and suppl. by R. Cortissoz (New York, 1927)
The Limitations of Verbal Criticism of Works of Art (Portland, ME, 1928)
BIBLIOGRAPHY
National Cyclopedia of American Biography, xxxv, p. 343
M. B. Cowdrey: 'A Century of Art History', *A. America*, xlii/3 (1954), p. 225
DARRYL PATRICK

Isham, Sir Thomas (*b* Lamport, Northants, 15 March 1657; *d* London, 27 July 1681). English collector. He succeeded as 3rd Baronet in 1675, while still an undergraduate at Christ Church, Oxford. Shortly afterwards he sat to Peter Lely for his portrait, a more finished version of which was presented to Robert Spencer, Lord Teviot, in 1679 (both Lamport Hall, Northants; *see* LELY, PETER, fig. 4). In October 1676 Isham set out for a tour of the Continent, travelling via Paris and Lyon to Turin, thence to Milan, Padua and Venice. After six weeks in Venice he proceeded via Bologna and Rimini to Rome, which he reached in April 1677 and where he remained for most of his time in Italy. There he acquired, through the mediation of Bruno Talbot, younger son of John Talbot, 10th Earl of Shrewsbury, an impressive group of twenty paintings, nine of which were originals by contemporary Roman masters, including mythological pictures by Giacinto Brandi, Lodovico Gimignani and Filippo Lauri, and two landscapes by Salvator Rosa. The rest were copies of famous works by Raphael, Guido Reni, Pietro da Cortona, Nicolas Poussin and others. Isham also sat for portraits to Carlo Maratti and Ferdinand Voet. This collection (except for two works untraced) remains at Lamport Hall. He returned to England in August 1679 and died unmarried two years later. His two-year sojourn in France, Switzerland and Italy is an early example of the Grand Tour. His choice of paintings, though to some extent determined by Talbot's contacts in the art world, shows a preference for contemporary Roman Baroque works; as for subject-matter, his taste was for pictures depicting the more dramatic episodes of Antiquity.

BIBLIOGRAPHY
G. Burdon: 'Sir Thomas Isham, an English Collector in Rome in 1677–8', *It. Stud.*, xv (1960), pp. 1–25
G. Isham: 'The Correspondence of David Loggan with Sir Thomas Isham', *Connoisseur*, clii (1963), pp. 231–6; cliv (1963), pp. 84–91
Sir Thomas Isham (exh. cat., Northampton, Central Mus. & A.G., 1969)
D. Sutton: 'British Collecting', *Apollo*, cxiv (1981), p. 306
NICHOLAS MARLOWE

Ishān Baḥrīyāt. *See* ISIN.

Ishibutai tomb. Japanese megalithic tomb dating to the 7th century AD in Shimanosho, Asuka village, Takaichi County, Nara Prefecture. Ishibutai ('stone platform') contains the largest stone chamber of the passageway-and-chamber tombs (*see* JAPAN, §III, 2(ii)) and is thought to be the burial place of chief minister Soga no Umako (*d* 626). It was excavated by Kyoto Imperial University (now Kyoto University) in 1933–5 and greatly restored in 1954. The base of the passageway and chamber is a square platform, faced with stones, perhaps once moated. It is not clear whether the passageway and chamber were ever covered by a mound. The internal space is the largest of all Japanese tombs (passageway 11.0×2.5 m; chamber 7.7×3.5 m), and the unusual height of the chamber (4.7 m) is typical of tombs in the Nara–Kyoto area. Drainage ditches run along the walls in the chamber and meet to form a single ditch down the middle of the passageway. The stones of Ishibutai are from a low hillside quarry of hornblende granite near the tomb. Wooden sledges, like the V-shaped sledge (*shura*) found intact at Nakatsuyama Tomb (Fujiidera, Osaka Prefect.), were used with teams of labourers to transport the building materials downhill. Archaeologists have estimated that the tomb was looted around the 9th century, although examples of Sue, a grey stoneware, and Haji, a reddish earthenware (*see* JAPAN, §VIII, 3(i) and 4), have been unearthed from both the passageway and the chamber. Among the Sue pieces were pedestalled vessels (*takatsuki*) with lids, bowls with stands, a pair of small bottles and a large kettle-shaped vessel with raised ridges. Notable among the Haji ware were large bowls (up to 550 mm in diameter) with short 'horn' handles, many of which were broken; bowls on stands or high bases; plates, shallow bowls and pots. These were grave goods, serving as ritualistic containers during interment ceremonies. The finds are impressive in size as in quantity; one Sue pot had a diameter of 900 mm.

BIBLIOGRAPHY

K. Hamada and I. Takahashi: *Yamato Shimanosho Ishibutai no kyoishi kofun* [Megalithic tomb Ishibutai at Shimanosho in (the province of) Yamato], *Kyoto Teikoku Daigaku Bungakubu kōkogaku kenkyū hōkoku* [Report on archaeological research in the Faculty of Literature, Kyoto Imperial University], xiv (Kyoto, 1937)

J. EDWARD KIDDER JR

Ishikawa Jōzan (*b* Izumi, Hekikai district, Mikawa Prov. [now Aichi Prefect.], 1583; *d* Kyoto, 1672). Japanese poet and calligrapher of the early Edo period (1600–1868). He was the son of a samurai named Shinjō. Both his father and grandfather were retainers of the first Tokugawa shogun, Ieyasu (1542–1616), and from his youth Jōzan was an attendant to Ieyasu and joined him in battle. Having, however, violated the command of military leaders during the Summer Battle of Osaka in 1615, he forfeited his fief and went to Kyoto where he took the tonsure. He studied Confucianism with Fujiwara no Seika (1561–1619) and at the same time, on his mother's behalf, entered the service of a daimyo. After his mother's death in 1641, Jōzan constructed a dwelling called Ōtotsuka ('roughness or jaggedness cave') at the temple Ichijōji in Kyoto, where he led the life of a recluse. The building reflected the current Japanese taste for rusticity in architecture but was embellished by its creator with a number of Chinese touches, including a second-storey 'moon-viewing room'. Jōzan commissioned the artist Kanō Tan'yū (*see* KANŌ, (11)) to paint portraits of the *Sanjū rokushisen* ('Thirty-six immortal Chinese poets') of the Han (206 BC–AD 220) to Song (AD 960–1279) periods, whom he selected with his friend Hayashi Razan (1583–1657); the work was in imitation of the *Sanjūrokkasen* ('Thirty-six Japanese immortal poets'). On each of the portraits, Jōzan inscribed one of the poet's own works in clerical script (*reisho*). The works were hung in a room, which was roofed with horizontal timbers and named the Shisendō (Hall of Poetic Immortal Poets).

Jōzan lived at the Shisendō for the last 30 years of his life, writing, reading and singing and mingling with literati masters such as Hayashi Razan and Hori Kyōan. He wrote many poems extolling the beauty of the natural views surrounding his retreat, such as the *Ōtotsuka jukyō* ('Ten borders of the Ōtotsuka') and the *Ōtotsuka jūnikei* ('Twelve views of the Ōtotsuka'). He took charge of the construction of the Kokutei Shōsei'en, a detached pavilion at the temple Higashi Honganji erected during the Kanei era (1624–44). The building was later destroyed by fire several times, but Jōzan's literati tastes are still visible in the stroll garden (*kaiyū*) running along the water's edge at the Ingetsuchi (Pond of the Moon Impression) or at Nakajima (Middle Island), where the connecting corridor bridge is covered by a roof like those used in tea houses.

Many of Jōzan's calligraphies displayed in the Shisendō are in the clerical script (*reisho*) in which he excelled. Indeed, he was one of the few Japanese *reisho* calligraphers. The models available during his lifetime were copies of popular books of the Ming period (1368–1644), not of works written in classical clerical script. Other famous *reisho* calligraphers of the period also wrote in this popular style. It was not until somewhat later in the Edo period that such works were published as the *Shitai senjimon* ('Thousand-character script classic in four script types') and the *Tenrei senjimon* ('Thousand-character classic in seals') in the 18th scroll of the *Sangoku hikkai zensho* ('Complete writings of the Three Kingdoms period'). Jōzan was also highly regarded as a poet of verse in Han period style and published the *Fushōshū*, a collection of poetry and prose in this classical vein. The seal used by Jōzan, like those of other Confucian scholars and poets of the period, was part of the tradition of medieval authorship seals (*see* JAPAN, §XVI, 20). His students compiled the four-volume *Jōzan zenshū* (*Shinpen Fushōshū*) ('Complete collection of Jōzan (New edition of the *Fushōshū*)'). A portrait of Jōzan by Tan'yū is housed in the Shisendō.

BIBLIOGRAPHY

Sho no Nihonshi [History of Japanese calligraphy], vi (Tokyo, 1975)

S. Komatsu, ed.: *Nihon shoseki taikan* [Collection of calligraphy of leading persons in Japan], xiv–xxv (Tokyo, 1978–80)

K. Korezawa, ed.: 'Edo jidai no sho' [Calligraphy of the Edo period], *Nihon no Bijutsu*, 184 (1981) [whole issue]

Masters of Japanese Calligraphy, 8th–19th Century (exh. cat. by Y. Shimizu and J. M. Rosenfield, New York, Japan House Gal. and Asia Soc. Gals, 1984–5)

TADASHI KOBAYASHI

Ishikawa Toyonobu [Nishimura Shigenobu, Magosaburō; Meijōdō, Shūha] (*b* Edo [now Tokyo], 1711; *d* Edo, 1785). Japanese painter, print designer and book illustrator. One of the finest *ukiyoe* ('pictures of the floating world') printmakers active in the mid-18th century, Toyonobu was born into a samurai family. He may have studied under the printmaker Nishimura Shigenaga (?1697–1756), and many scholars identify him with the artist who styled himself Nishimura Magosaburō (before 1730) and Nishimura Shigenobu (1730–47). From 1747 until the end of his career as a print designer, he worked under the name Ishikawa Toyonobu. In the mid-1760s he inherited from his father-in-law an inn in Edo's Kodenmachō district. As innkeeper, he employed the name that was used by successive heads of the family, Nukaya Shichibei. He largely abandoned his artistic activities in the last two decades of his life. Toyonobu's early works reflect the influence of the TORII school. Thus, his *yakushae* ('pictures of actors') and *bijinga* ('pictures of beautiful women') of the 1730s and early 1740s feature robust, columnar figures with heads held erect. His manner later changed considerably, and after 1747 the figures of courtesans and youths became more slender and willowy, with tilted heads and bent knees. Even his depictions of mature actors possess a certain suave elegance. A speciality of Toyonobu was the depiction of beauties in *déshabillé*, with loose robes revealing breasts and legs. *Courtesan Going to Bed* (1750; New York, Met.) is representative of Toyonobu's mature style. Similar qualities appear in the work of Toyonobu's influential, older contemporaries, Okumura Masanobu and Nishikawa Sukenobu.

Ishikawa Toyonobu was a master of the *urushie* ('lacquer pictures') and *benizuri* ('pink-printed pictures'; two-colour prints) printing techniques. Although he was an exquisite colourist, later adding yellow and purple to the limited palette of *benizuri*, he does not appear to have made the transition to full-colour printing (*nishikie*; 'brocade pictures'), which rapidly came to dominate *ukiyoe* after 1765. Toyonobu was an important influence on the *ukiyoe* artists Kitao Shigemasa and Suzuki Harunobu. Ishikawa Toyomasa (*fl* 1770–80) was his student and probably his son. Another son, Ishikawa Masamochi (1753–1830), became famous as a writer under the pseudonym Rokujuen; his work was illustrated by Katsushika Hokusai.

BIBLIOGRAPHY

L. Ledoux: *Japanese Prints of the Primitive Period in the Collection of Louis V. Ledoux* (New York, 1942)
H. Stern: *Master Prints of Japan: Ukiyoe Hanga* (New York, 1969)
H. Munsterberg: *The Japanese Print: A Historical Guide* (New York and Tokyo, 1982)

MARK H. SANDLER

Ishimoto, Yasuhirō (*b* San Francisco, CA, 14 June 1921). Japanese photographer, active also in the USA. He was brought up in Japan and in 1939 returned to the USA, where he studied agriculture and architecture before photography. In 1952 he graduated from the Institute of Design, Illinois Institute of Technology, Chicago, where he had studied under Harry Callahan and Aaron Siskind, and in 1953 returned to Japan. He published works in Japanese photography magazines and a collection of his own photographs, *Aru hi, aru tokoro* ('Someday, somewhere'; Tokyo, 1958). At the same time he photographed the Katsura Detached Palace in Kyoto, one of the great buildings of the 17th century, publishing the results as *Katsura* (Tokyo, 1960). This collection, which showed the influence of Callahan and Siskind, involved a new way of interpreting the traditional beauty of Japan and was somewhat shocking to the Japanese. His uncompromising style had a strong influence on the photographers working in the Vivo (Esperanto: 'life') group, especially Ikko Narahara, Eikoh Hosoe and Kikuji Kawada. Again resident in Chicago from 1958 to 1961, Ishimoto took mainly snapshots; the result, the collection *Chicago, Chicago*

(Tokyo, 1969), won the Mainichi Art Prize. In subsequent years he developed his interest in the Japanese sense of beauty, typified in the Katsura Detached Palace, while also recording the rapidly changing metropolis of Tokyo.

BIBLIOGRAPHY

Contemp. Phot.
New Japanese Photography (exh. cat. by J. Szarkowski and S. Yamagishi, New York, MOMA, 1974), pp. 28–31
The Photographer and the City (exh. cat. by G. Buckland, Chicago, IL, Mus. Contemp. A., 1977)
Japanese Photography Today and its Origin (exh. cat. by A. Colombo and I. Donisello, Bologna, Gal. A. Mod.; Milan, Pal. Reale; Brussels, Pal. B.-A.; London, ICA; 1979), pp. 70–71
The Photography of Yasuhirō Ishimoto (exh. cat. by K. Otsuji and F. Yukoe, Tokyo, Seibu Mus. A., 1989)

KOHTARO IIZAWA

Ishiyama, Osamu (*b* Okayama Prefect., 1 April 1944). Japanese architect and writer. He graduated from Waseda University, Tokyo, in 1966 and completed a graduate course there in 1968, the same year in which he established the office DAM DAN in Tokyo. Through a wide range of activities, of which design was only a part, Ishiyama became a spokesman for the New Wave architects in Japan who turned away from Metabolism and historicism to re-create a sense of place in architecture. An admirer of Buckminster Fuller, Ishiyama also attempted, though not always successfully, to provide general solutions, producing an indeterminate architecture that allowed users maximum freedom within. Inspired by a house in Toyohashi, Aichi Prefecture, constructed in 1962 by Kenji Kawai, an engineer for the early buildings of Kenzō Tange, Ishiyama designed a series of houses of corrugated steel sheets, the best-known of which is the Gen'an (Fantasy Villa) in Aichi Prefecture (1975). These simple houses required only the cheapest of materials and a low standard of construction skills, symbolizing the architect's commitment to making housing easily available to the public. This was a cause he also supported through writing popular books on architecture and initiating a system called 'direct dealing' that recalled, in its intent to bypass the conventional commercial network, the *Whole Earth Catalog*, the book of tools and ideas relevant to independent education published in the 1960s. The Izu no Chohachi Museum (1984) in Matsuzaki, however, was a departure from his previous work. A showcase for the traditional Japanese building craft of plastering, its allusions to Meiji-period (1868–1912) interpretations of Western classical architecture by Japanese carpenters give it a definite Post-modern air. Ishiyama was awarded the prestigious Isoya Yoshida Prize in 1985 for this project.

WRITINGS

'Expedition to Making Houses', *Kenchiku Bunka/Archit. Cult.*, xli (1986), pp. 24–148
Shokunin kyōwakoku dayori [Tidings from the republic of craftsmen] (Tokyo, 1986)

BIBLIOGRAPHY

H. Watanabe: *Amazing Architecture from Japan* (New York, 1991)

HIROSHI WATANABE

Ishmaku, Burhan (*b* Shkodër, 25 May 1926). Albanian woodworker. He was introduced to the furniture-maker's trade at the largest joiner's yard in Shkodër. In 1953 he moved to Tiranë and established a specialist workshop for making such wooden musical instruments as violins, guitars, mandolins, *çifteli* (a type of two-stringed mandolin) and lutes. He joined the Migjeni Artistic Products Enterprise in Tiranë, which was set up in 1966, and became renowned for his designs for mass-produced wooden decorative goods. His designs are characterized by refined and rich floral decoration together with crisp geometric patterns. Most of his work emphasizes the natural colour of the wood. Some of his products, however, are brightly coloured with stylized motifs that imitate traditional Albanian folk designs. A large retrospective exhibition of his work held in the Albanian National Culture Museum in Tiranë in 1984 confirmed him as one of the most distinguished craftsmen of post-war Albania.

UNPUBLISHED SOURCES
Tiranë, A.G. ['Burhan Ishmaku', MSS]

BIBLIOGRAPHY
Albanian Artistic Handicraft Products, 8 Nëntori Enterprise, Chamber of Albanian Trade (Tiranë, n.d.)
'Die Leidenschaft für die Schönheit', *Neues Albanien*, 3 (1984)

GJERGJ FRASHËRI

Isigonos, Epigonos, Stratonikos and Antigonos (*fl c.* 250–200BC). Greek sculptors. They were employed by the Attalid kings of Pergamon to create monuments to Pergamene victories over the Gauls. Isigonos is mentioned only once (Pliny: *Natural History*, XXXIV.xix.84) and may be identical with Epigonos, whom Pliny credits with a *Trumpeter* and a *Weeping Child* 'pitifully caressing its murdered mother' (XXXIV.xix.88), and who also signed eight bases for bronze statues on the Pergamene acropolis, two celebrating victories over the Gauls. No originals by Epigonos survive, but the famous *Dying Gaul* (Rome, Mus. Capitolino; *see* GREECE, ANCIENT, §IV, 2(iv)(b) and fig. 67) may reproduce his *Trumpeter* and be copied from one of the signed monuments of *c.* 223 BC. The warrior wears a Celtic torc and is bleeding from a chest wound, his broken trumpet and sword by his side. The realism of the statue emphasizes its pathos and, by stressing the dignity of the conquered, the statue exalts the achievement of the conquerors. Epigonos signed his work as a native Pergamene, while Stratonikos (who also made 'philosophers') was from Kyzikos; Antigonos came from Karystos in Euboea if, as some scholars think, he is the same person as the antiquarian of that name. This Antigonos combined the formal analysis of art pioneered by XENOKRATES with the study of inscriptions and iconography, thereby anticipating the methods of modern art historians.

See also PERGAMON, §3(i) and (ii).

BIBLIOGRAPHY
U. von Wilamowitz-Moellendorff: *Antigonos von Karystos* (Berlin, 1881)
E. Künzl: *Die Kelten des Epigonos von Pergamon* (Würzburg, 1971)
R. Wenning: *Die Galateranatheme Attalos I* (Berlin, 1978)
A. F. Stewart: *Greek Sculpture: An Exploration* (New Haven and London, 1990), pp. 205–8, 301–3

ANDREW F. STEWART

Isin [now Ishān Baḥrīyāt]. Site in Iraq, 200 km south-east of Baghdad, about 40 km east of Diwaniyyah, consisting of a *tell* (ruin mound) 8 m high. This *tell* has been identified since 1923 as the site of the capital of the Isin I (2017–1794 BC) and Isin II (1157–1026 BC) dynasties (*see* MESOPOTAMIA, §I, 2(ii)(b)), but there is evidence of occupation from at least the Ubaid period (5th millennium BC) to the time of Nebuchadnezzar II (*reg* 604–562 BC).

Isin was first investigated by Stephen Langdon in 1924, and the University of Munich and Bayerische Akademie der Wissenschaften began to excavate there in 1973. Finds are in the Iraq Museum in Baghdad.

The highest point of the site is occupied by the Temple of Gula, goddess of childbirth and healing, the chief goddess of Isin. This temple, which dates to the Old Babylonian period (first half of the 2nd millennium BC), was broader than it was long (68×52 m) and is therefore of the so-called *Breitraum* type, with two cellae dedicated respectively to Gula and to one of her consorts, Ninurta. In 1988 a staircase of at least 19 steps was discovered in front of the building; the temple precinct (*temenos*) was surrounded by a wall. Beneath the temple, walls of plano-convex bricks from the 3rd millennium BC were uncovered. Several cuneiform tablets, mostly dealing with supplies of flour to a palace and several temples, were found in the remains of a building excavated at the same time, and are thought to date from the Isin I dynasty. Some of the most important finds are fragments of life-size terracotta statues of female figures probably belonging to the same period. A large number of smaller terracottas, cylinder seals, pottery and a mace-head of the Akkadian king Maništusu, devoted to Gula, have also been found.

BIBLIOGRAPHY
F. R. Kraus: 'Isin und Nippur nach altbabylonischen Rechtsurkunden', *J. Cuneiform Stud.*, iii (1951), pp. 1–116
B. Hrouda and others: *Isin – Išān Baḥrīyāt*, 3 vols (Munich, 1971–87)

B. HROUDA

Iskandar. *See* TIMURID, §II(4).

Islam [Arab. *islām*: 'surrender (to God)']. Monotheistic religion revealed to the Prophet Muhammad (*d* AD 632) in early 7th-century Arabia. It spread quickly throughout much of Eurasia and Africa to become one of the major world religions. For the arts associated with Islam *see* ISLAMIC ART.

I. Introduction. II. Cult and practice. III. Patronage.

I. *Introduction.*

The Prophet Muhammad received his first revelations *c.* AD 610 while meditating in a cave at HIRA near his home town of MECCA in Arabia. His visions and auditions centred first around the impending resurrection and judgement, then around the One God who is Creator, Sustainer and Judge and whose signs are visible in nature, history and the human soul 'to those who understand'. Muhammad's message, in the Islamic self-conception, is the perfection of previous religions and reinstalment of the pure Abrahamic faith from which Jews and Christians had strayed. With a small group of Muslims ('those who submit [to God]'), Muhammad emigrated from Mecca to MEDINA in 622, and this emigration (hegira, from Arab. *hijra*) marked the beginning of the Islamic era (often designated AH, from *anno hejirae*), which is based on a strictly lunar calendar of about 354 days. As the interpolation of an extra month every three years to keep the lunar calendar in line with the solar year was forbidden, the months of the Islamic calendar have no seasonal associations. The hegira also marked the beginning of Muhammad's political and administrative activities. After reconquering Mecca in

630 and institutionalizing the rites of pilgrimage around the Ka'ba there (*see* §II below), he died at Medina in 632.

In a few decades Islam spread over Arabia, Egypt, Syria, Iraq and Iran (*see* ISLAMIC ART, §I, 5). Muslim troops crossed the Straits of Gibraltar in 711; simultaneously they penetrated Central Asia beyond the Amu (Oxus) River and conquered the lower Indus Valley. The revelations that Muhammad had received were codified by his third successor or caliph 'Uthman (*reg* 644–56), and his redaction of the KORAN, the collected revelations to Muhammad, remained the basis of the faith. It can rightly be called the key to Muslim *Weltanschauung*. To write the Koran beautifully was the duty and joy of calligraphers (*see* ISLAMIC ART, §III, 2).

The Muslim's duties are summed up in five 'pillars'. First, he must attest that 'There is no deity save God; Muhammad is God's messenger.' The first half of this profession of faith (*shahāda*), written with ten vertical strokes, formed a basic calligraphic design and was frequently included during the repetition of religious formulae and divine names (*dhikr*). Second, he must perform a set of prayer formulae and movements (*salāt*, Pers. *namāz*) five times a day in a state of ritual purity (*see* §II, 1 below). He must face Mecca and pray in a clean place. He can pray alone or in congregation, except on Friday at noon; that prayer is congregational and includes a short sermon (Arab. *khuṭba*) delivered from a pulpit (*see* MINBAR). Third, he must pay an alms tax (*zakāt*), which is computed according to income. Free charity is also encouraged in the Koran. Fourth, he must fast during Ramadan, the ninth lunar month. This includes abstention from food, drink, sex and smoking from the beginning of dawn to the end of sunset. At the sight of the new moon, the Feast of the Breaking of the Fast (*'īd al-fiṭr*) is celebrated with communal prayer, often in large open spaces on the outskirts of towns (*see* MUṢALLĀ). Finally, the Muslim must, once in his or her life, carry out the pilgrimage to Mecca (*ḥajj*) during the last month of the lunar year, provided he has the means. The pilgrimage not only requires certain rituals, such as circumambulation of the Ka'ba and the sacrifice of a sheep in remembrance of the willingness of Ibrahim (the biblical Abraham) to sacrifice his son Isma'il (*see* §II, 2 below), but also strengthens the feeling of unity within the Muslim community and has often resulted in reform movements. In addition to these five 'pillars', the Muslim has to believe in the prophets from Adam to Muhammad, the revealed books, the angels, the fact that everything comes from God, and the Last Judgement, when God will decide who deserves Heaven or Hell on the basis of his faith and actions.

The first theological discussions in Islam emerged from the problem of who should lead the community after the Prophet's death. The majority, known as Sunnis or those who follow the Prophet's custom or practice (*sunna*), sided with Abu Bakr (*reg* 632–4), the second caliph. Others saw the rightful leader of the community (*imām*) in prayer and war in Muhammad's cousin and son-in-law, 'Ali ibn Abi Talib (*reg* 656–61). They later became known as the party (*shī'a*) of 'Ali, whence the modern term Shi'ite. During the wars of succession, the Kharijites, the group who advocated that only the most pious be the leader of the community, seceded. The various branches of the Shi'ites clung to the legitimist ideal, but they diverged according to their designation of the final imam. The Zaydis regarded Zayd (*d* 740) as the fifth imam. The Isma'ilis, who included such groups as the Qarmathians and the Fatimids, from whom the Bohoras and the Khojas (followers of the Aga Khan) developed, took Isma'il ibn Ja'far al-Sadiq (*d* 760) as the seventh imam and developed esoteric theories. The majority of Shi'ites, however, continued the line of imams to the twelfth, Muhammad al-Mahdi, who disappeared in 873 and 'will come to fill the earth with justice as it is filled with injustice'. This branch became the official religion of Iran in 1501, although a number of Twelver Shi'ite rulers are known from medieval times. Twelver Shi'ites add to the profession of faith the phrase, "Ali is God's friend'. The imam in Shi'ite understanding is the repository of esoteric wisdom.

Legal schools also developed out of political concerns between 750 and 850. The legal system was based on the Koran and the *sunna* as laid down in the prophetic traditions (*ḥadīth*), for the Prophet was 'the beautiful model' (Koran xxxiii:12). Collecting the traditions and scrutinizing their content and especially the chain of transmitters became a central field of study. The most reliable traditions (*ṣaḥīḥ*) were collected in six works, among which those by Bukhari (*d* 870) and Muslim (*d* 875) are highly esteemed. The need for adjusting the rather slim data from the Koran and traditions to the needs of an ever-growing circle of believers from diverse backgrounds led the ulema, a body of lawyer–divines, to add the principle of analogy (*qiyās*) and the use of intellectual opinion (*ra'y*) to the roots of legislature. The consensus of the ulema was considered to legalize generally accepted decisions and customs; some theologians, however, tried, and still try, to go back to the sources by free investigation (*ijtihād*). The four most important schools of law are the Hanafis, followers of Abu Hanifa (*d* 767), widespread in Turkish areas and in northern India; the Malikis, followers of Malik (*d* 795), a conservative school followed mainly in western North Africa; the Shafi'is, followers of al-Shafi'i (*d* 820), prevalent in most Arab countries; and the Hanbalis, followers of Ibn Hanbal (*d* 855), the most rigorous school, which formed the basis of the form of Islam practised in 20th-century Saudi Arabia.

The confrontation of Islam with such other religions as Christianity and the dualist ZOROASTRIANISM led to theological discussions to keep God absolutely free from anything that might lead man to 'association' (*shirk*), the worst sin for a Muslim. One school, known as the Mu'tazila, therefore denied that the divine attributes were co-eternal with God since this could lead to multiplicity. They refused to believe that the Koran was God's uncreated word, an idea vehemently defended by Ibn Hanbal and others. They emphasized not only God's absolute unity but also his justice: he must recompense good actions and punish bad ones. For a short time in the 9th century, Mu'tazilism was the officially accepted form of Islam, and although ultimately repudiated, its use of philosophical methods encouraged the development of Muslim theology (*kalām*). The theologian al-Ash'ari (*d* 935) developed a compromise theology that became prominent in the central Islamic lands under the Saljuqs.

The Koran was always the basis of Muslim life and thought, as it is God's word 'revealed as a book' and co-eternal with him, according to orthodox belief. At the same time, the personality of the Prophet became more important. Theories about his primordial light were developed *c.* 900, and his role was further highlighted by celebrations of his birthday and by poetry, in both the high and the folk traditions. His heavenly journey (*mi'rāj*) formed the basis for a poetic and pictorial tradition, in which his mount Buraq is represented in diverse media from medieval illustrated manuscripts (*see* ISLAMIC ART, fig. 104) to modern Pakistani trucks. Love for the Prophet is a distinctive feature of Islam, whether he is extolled as intercessor on Doomsday, father figure or beloved, Perfect Man or intermediary between God and his creatures. This development is largely due to mystics or Sufis, who cultivated the inner life of the soul. Their name may have been derived from the typical ascetic's dress of dark blue wool (*sūf*). Growing out of early ascetic trends, they soon discovered the concept of Divine Love, and the history of Sufism includes great philosophers such as Ibn 'Arabi (*d* 1240), poets such as Jalal al-Din Rumi (*d* 1273) and calligraphers such as AHMAD KARAHISARI (*d* 1556). When Sufism became a mass movement in the 12th century due to the growth of fraternities, it offered a more emotional way of piety than did orthodox Islam. Each fraternity had certain characteristics that appealed to various social or ethnic groups. The Sufis played a decisive role in the Islamization of India, China and Africa, and as they often preached their message of love of God and the Prophet not in theological Arabic but in vernacular idioms, they also contributed to the development of regional languages. A number of modern reformers have come from the Sufi tradition, although they may have used the organizational skills they acquired in the fraternity to build up movements that are now called fundamentalist.

BIBLIOGRAPHY

I. Goldziher: *Muhammadanische Studien*, 2 vols (Halle, 1889–90); Eng. trans. by C. N. Barber and S. M. Stern as *Muslim Studies*, ed. S. M. Stern, 2 vols (London, 1967–71)
——: *Vorlesungen über den Islam* (Heidelberg, 1910); Eng. trans. by A. Hamori and R. Hamori as *Introduction to Islamic Theology and Law* (Princeton, 1981)
A. J. Wensinck: *The Muslim Creed* (London, 1932)
G. E. von Grunebaum: *Medieval Islam* (Chicago, 1946)
H. A. R. Gibb: *Mohammedanism* (London, 1949, rev. New York, 1962)
J. Schacht: *The Origins of Muhammadan Jurisprudence* (Oxford, 1950)
G. E. von Grunebaum: *Muhammadan Festivals* (London, 1951)
J. Schacht: *Introduction to Islamic Law* (Oxford, 1964)
G. E. von Grunebaum: *Classical Islam*, trans. K. Watson (Chicago, 1970)
J. S. Trimingham: *The Sufi Orders in Islam* (London, 1971)
A. Schimmel: *Mystical Dimensions of Islam* (Chapel Hill, 1975)
W. Graham: *Divine Work and Prophetic Word in Early Islam* (The Hague, 1977)
A. Schimmel: *And Muhammad is His Messenger: The Veneration of the Prophet in Islamic Piety* (Chapel Hill, 1985)
——: *Islam: An Introduction* (Albany, 1992)
——: *Deciphering the Signs of God: A Phenomenological Approach to Islam* (Albany, 1994)
ANNEMARIE SCHIMMEL

II. Cult and practice.

Islamic rituals focus on activities in the MOSQUE and on pilgrimage. Other life passages, such as circumcision, marriage and death, also involve ceremonies and prayer in the mosque, but the public focus of activity tends to lie in procession. The following discussion relates largely to the pre-modern period.

1. Prayer. 2. Pilgrimage. 3. Circumcision. 4. Marriage. 5. Death.

1. PRAYER. Five daily prayers, at dawn, midday, mid-afternoon, sunset and early evening, are obligatory in Islam. An additional prayer just after dawn is optional. The exact times of prayer are calculated from the beginning of the Islamic day, at sunset, and change daily. They may be performed singly or communally in a mosque or other suitable place. Muslims are summoned to pray by the call to prayer (Arab. *adhān*), which may be given from any suitable high place, although a MINARET became customary at an early date. The call is the same for all five prayers except the dawn prayer, which includes the additional words 'Prayer is better than sleep'. Among Shi'ites, the call includes the terminating words "Ali is God's vice-regent/ friend'. The midday Friday prayer in the congregational mosque is obligatory for all adult males. It is preceded by a sermon (*khuṭba*) from a pulpit (*see* MINBAR) by any male member of the community.

Prayer is preceded by ritual ablution, and fountains and pools are therefore an important feature of mosque design. Clothes must also be clean and the praying place free from impurity. The Muslim faces towards Mecca when praying, and the determination of the qibla—the precise orientation of the Ka'ba, the cubical structure in the centre of the Haram Mosque at MECCA—is extremely important. In general women do not attend the mosque to pray, but where they do so they pray in a reserved area. Worshippers stand in parallel rows, each row separated from the next only by the space required for each man to prostrate himself during prayer. With minor features among the various sects, prayer is the same for all Muslims, involving several sets of prescribed prostrations and recitations, which must be performed in Arabic (see fig. 1).

Prayer at the mosque also takes place on other occasions. During the fasting month of Ramadan, many people break their fast at the sunset prayer in a mosque with water and dates, following the custom of the Prophet Muhammad. Conclusion of the fast and the festival of sacrifice (*'id al-adḥa*) that coincides with the pilgrimage to Mecca are marked by prayer at open-air mosques, usually on the outskirts of towns (*see* MUṢALLĀ). Prayers also take place to commemorate the Prophet's birthday, and in some places droughts and eclipses are also occasions for prayer.

2. PILGRIMAGE. As the direction of Islamic prayer, Mecca is the object of the pilgrimage (*ḥajj*), which every Muslim should attempt to undertake once in his life, during the first days of the twelfth month, Dhu'l-Hijja, although a lesser pilgrimage (*'umra*) may be performed at any time. The pilgrimage focuses on two sites: the Ka'ba at Mecca, and Arafat, a plain 20 km east of Mecca. In earlier times pilgrims to Mecca would make the arduous journey in slow caravans, and the provision of facilities for pilgrims has always been a charitable act. For example, numerous water tanks and way stations were erected along the Darb Zubayda, the route from Baghdad and Kufa in Iraq to Mecca, in the 8th and 9th centuries AD (*see* ISLAMIC ART, §II, 4(i)(b)), and the Ottoman sultans erected forts at watering places along the desert pilgrimage roads in

1. Islamic prayer in a mosque

northern Arabia before building the Hijaz railway (1902–8) as a successor to the ancient pilgrimage road.

The Ka'ba is God's house, and pilgrims are God's guests. According to Islamic belief, the Ka'ba was built by the prophet Ibrahim (the biblical Abraham) and his son Isma'il. Before the advent of Islam, the Ka'ba had been a centre of pagan pilgrimage in the hands of the Meccan tribe of Quraysh, and the hajj represents the Islamization of the pre-Islamic pilgrimage rites, a process instigated by the Prophet Muhammad. The Ka'ba, an empty stone structure with a level roof, is entered by a staircase leading to a single raised door (1982) of solid gold. The Black Stone (al-ḥajar al-aswad) is fixed in the east external corner of the Ka'ba, and pilgrims attempt to kiss it as prescribed or point towards it if prevented by the crowds. The Ka'ba is covered by a great silk drape (kiswa), which is renewed annually at the time of the pilgrimage.

On arrival at the boundaries of Mecca, pilgrims don a two-piece seamless garment (iḥrām) of white cotton. They enter the Haram Mosque to make the ritual circumambulation around the Ka'ba (ṭawāf) in a great swirling mass of humanity (see fig. 2), a movement that ceases only at the obligatory times of prayer. The mosque, where Muslims uniquely pray in concentric circles, has been repeatedly expanded to incorporate the increasing number of pilgrims, which has regularly exceeded one million in the late 20th century. The pilgrims then perform the ritual run (sayy) between the low hills of Marwa and Safa in remembrance of the search for water by Ibrahim's wife Hagar.

The pilgrimage proper begins on the eighth day of Dhu'l-Hijja. Having listened to a sermon at the Haram Mosque on the previous day, the pilgrims head eastward in an immense crowd past Mina towards a rocky outcrop on the plain of Arafat known as the Mount of Mercy. In earlier times residences were maintained near by for Muslims from different regions. The pilgrimage culminates on the ninth day of the month, when pilgrims are required to stand between noon and sunset on the Mount of Mercy and the surrounding plain. The pilgrims then return to Mina, and on the tenth day they sacrifice sheep, goats or camels to commemorate Ibrahim's fulfilment of God's command by sacrificing a beast in place of Isma'il. The pilgrims remain at Mina until the twelfth day, during which time they have their heads shaved and daily cast pebbles at three stones regarded as manifestations of the devil. The rituals end on the twelfth day, and the pilgrims resume their normal garb. Many pilgrims take home prized bottles of water from the holy well of Zamzam in the courtyard of the Haram Mosque; many also include a trip to the Prophet's mosque at MEDINA.

3. CIRCUMCISION. Circumcision (khitān) of male children is universal in Islam and marked by public ceremony. The custom is associated with the prophet Ibrahim and had existed in pre-Islamic Arabia. It spread with the faith to all parts of the Islamic world, although approaches towards it vary with the different schools of law. It should be performed between birth and ten years, with the ages of three and seven preferred. (Female circumcision, common in north-east Africa, is not universally regarded as Islamic and is unmarked by public display.) Details of the ceremony varied, although practice was very similar. In 19th-century Cairo, for example, the

2. Circumambulation of the Ka'ba, Mecca, Saudi Arabia

family of a boy to be circumcised and their friends would gather at one of the major mosques. After prayer, a procession would form and, accompanied by musicians, escort the boy to his house, where a barber would perform the operation. At Mecca, the boy's dress would be lavish, whereas at Cairo he would be dressed as a girl to fend off the evil eye. Among some Muslim communities in Java, a boy would dress as a bridegroom, whereas in others he would wear the pilgrim's *iḥrām*.

Lavish circumcision ceremonies are recorded in textual accounts beginning with the 9th century in Iraq, but circumcision processions are best known from the Ottoman court in Istanbul, when several manuscripts were commissioned to chronicle the elaborate processions accompanying the princes. The *Sūrnāma-i Humāyūn* ('Imperial book of festivals'; *c.* 1583; Istanbul, Topkapı Pal. Lib., H. 1344) shows such processions in the Hippodrome in Istanbul (*see* ISLAMIC ART, fig. 191) celebrating the circumcision of the sons of Murad III (*reg* 1574–95). Vehbi's *Sūrnāma* ('Book of festivals'; Istanbul, Topkapı Pal. Lib., A. 3593; *see* ISLAMIC ART, fig. 195) recounts the festivities accompanying the circumcision of the sons of Ahmed III in 1720 and is illustrated with 137 paintings produced under the supervision of Levni. The Ottoman imperial processions culminated at Topkapı Palace in the Circumcision Room (*Sünnet Odası*), which was built in 1648 by Ibrahim (*reg* 1640–48) and lavishly decorated on the exterior with tiles that had once adorned ceremonial buildings of Süleyman II.

4. MARRIAGE. Marriage ceremonies are initiated with private enquiries and negotiations. Agreement is marked by recitation of Koranic verses and the selection of the marriage day. In Cairo, two or three days before the marriage, the groom's street is decorated with lights and guests dispatch gifts; musicians provide entertainment or there is a religious recitation. Before the wedding, the bride, preceded by musicians, would go in procession under a silken canopy to the public bath, where perfumed water was scattered, incense burned and the hands of the bride and her companions decorated with henna. On the wedding day the bride joined a procession to the groom's house, the scale of display corresponding to the family's status. At marriages of the wealthy, floats reflecting the trades of the town would accompany the procession. The festivities were often accompanied by banquets, as depicted in the copy of Hariri's *Maqāmāt* ('Assemblies'; ?Baghdad, 1225–32; St Petersburg, Acad. Sci., S. 23, p. 205) and Khwaju Kirmani's *Dīvān* (collected poetry; Baghdad, 1396; London, BL, Add. MSS 18113), where the illustration by Junayd on fol. 45*v* depicts *Humay and Humayun on the Day after their Wedding*. Special garments were worn by the bride and groom, and in some cities, such as Fez in Morocco, traditional wedding attire is still produced and worn. Special jewellery, including necklaces and rings, was made for the bride (*see* ISLAMIC ART, fig. 241). Wedding ceremonies were also held in special tents and private gardens.

5. DEATH. According to Islamic law, a dead person should be buried on the day of death. The body is washed and dressed in a simple white seamless garment and then carried in mourning procession on a bier to the mosque, where the corpse may be laid in front of the mihrab and prayers performed. At times it was forbidden to bring the corpse into a mosque, so an annexe might be erected in

3. Islamic funeral procession

which prayers could be said over the body, as at the Qarawiyyin Mosque in Fez. From the mosque the procession (see fig. 3) makes its way to the cemetery outside the town, where the body is laid in a grave orientated towards the qibla. In the simplest and most conservative cases, the place of burial is marked only by stones at the head and foot of the grave. In other cases there may be an inscribed headstone (*see* STELE, §5). In the case of important or revered individuals, a funerary building may be constructed, either before or after death (*see* TOMB, §II). A revered grave may be surrounded by grilles and screens or marked with a CENOTAPH of wood, stone or ceramic, representing a focus for circumambulation where a rite of visitation developed. After the funeral the family of the deceased receives visitors, and prayers and Koran recitations are said at home or under tents erected in the street. These recitations are repeated on the 20th and 40th days after death. The widow continues to mourn for at least four months, during which time she remains at home, wears no jewellery and may not remarry.

The Prophet Muhammad warned Muslims against developing a cult of the dead, and this precept initially inhibited the construction of monumental tombs. The Prophet and his first followers were buried in the mosque of Medina in a manner to ensure the graves did not become objects of worship, but the custom of visiting revered graves spread rapidly, especially among the Shi'ites. The grave of the Prophet's grandson Husayn at Karbala' in Iraq, for example, became a centre of Shi'ite pilgrimage, and by the 10th century burial near the graves of holy figures was considered to confer blessing (*see* SHRINE (i), §II). Muslims also showed interest in the burial places of biblical figures, such as the tomb of Ibrahim at Hebron. These shrines were often rebuilt and restored by successive generations of patrons, and some, such as the shrine of Shaykh Safi at ARDABIL, became repositories of great collections of art.

At the level of popular belief, many religious figures were transformed in death into local saints, and their tombs became objects of local visitation. For example, the cult of a local holy man, Ahmad al-Badawi (*d* 1276), enjoyed enormous success, and by the 19th century his grave at Tanta in Egypt attracted as many pilgrims as did the pilgrimage to Mecca. Other examples of the evolution of the tomb cult of the holy man are represented by the Shadhili cult at al-Mukha in Yemen and that of the Mevlevi whirling dervishes at Konya in Turkey.

BIBLIOGRAPHY
Enc. Islam/2: 'Hadjdj', 'Khitān' [Circumcision]
E. W. Lane: *An Account of the Manners and Customs of the Modern Egyptians* (London, 1836/*R* 1978)
I. Goldziher: *Muhammadanische Studien*, 2 vols (Halle, 1889–90); Eng. trans. by C. N. Barber and S. M. Stern as *Muslim Studies*, ed. S. M. Stern, 2 vols (London, 1967–71)
——: *Vorlesungen über den Islam* (Heidelberg, 1910); Eng. trans by A. Hamori and R. Hamori as *Introduction to Islamic Theology and Law* (Princeton, 1981)
G. E. von Grunebaum: *Muhammadan Festivals* (London, 1951)
F. Rahman: *Islam* (London, 1966)
S. D. Goitein: *Studies in Islamic History and Institutions* (Leiden, 1968)
H. Terrasse: *La Mosquée al-Qaraouiyin à Fès* (Paris, 1968), pp. 21–2
A. S. M. H. Tabataba'i: *Shi'ite Islam* (London, 1975)
G. R. D. King: 'Islam, Iconoclasm, and Declaration of Doctrine', *Bull. SOAS*, xlviii (1985), pp. 267–77
W. Madelung: *Religious Schools and Sects in Medieval Islam* (London, 1985)
G. R. D. KING

III. Patronage.

Religious patronage of architecture and the other arts in the Islamic world was largely regulated by a legal process known as *waqf* (Turk. *vakıf*) or in North and West Africa as *hubūs*. *Waqf* was the alienation in perpetuity of property and the dedication of the revenues arising from the property to the upkeep of a pious foundation. By extension the term *waqf* is also used for the property or funds thus alienated. *Waqf* governed the growth and development of urban centres, the foundation of public works, religious and charitable institutions, and the furnishing and provisioning of these same institutions. Individuals who established charitable foundations might also be private patrons of the arts.

The principle of *waqf* shows some similarities to medieval English mortmain and to the Byzantine *piae causae* as regulated by Justinian I. How far these similarities are the result of a common derivation is difficult to assess. In theory Islam did not recognize *waqf*s created for the benefit of non-Muslim institutions, but exceptions were made for the endowments of churches and monasteries already in existence at the Muslim conquest. In later centuries eastern Christians, particularly Copts and Armenians, recognized principles of endowment based on Islamic practice, while the Mongol rulers of Iran created *waqf*s for Buddhist monasteries before Ghazan (*reg* 1295–1304) converted to Islam in 1296.

The primary requirement concerning a *waqf* is that it be pleasing to God. Foundations included state works such as dams or caravanserais on major trade routes, which the ruler could otherwise have had built at his subjects' expense, and private ventures, typically mosques, madrasas, Sufi institutions (*khānaqāh*s, *tekke*s, *zāwiya*s), Koran schools for children or orphans, fountains for the free distribution of water, and other waterworks, hospitals or lodging places or fortified encampments for pilgrims on the hajj. From the late 12th century onwards, the founder's tomb was often attached to these foundations (*see* ISLAMIC ART, §II, 6(iii)(a)), despite the persistent prejudice in many Muslim societies against conspicuous burial. There are no restrictions on supplementary endowments to fund the restoration of or additions to existing foundations, such as the public fountain the Ottoman sultan Murad III (*reg* 1574–95) added to the Süleymaniye Mosque (1550–57) in Istanbul.

Another requirement is that the endower should be free, legally of age and the unrestricted owner of the property. Since slaves could not own property, some adjustment was needed for endowments in later Islamic states in which armies and administrative personnel were, to a greater or lesser extent, recruited as slaves. In 14th- and 15th-century Egypt such slave recruits were manumitted on the completion of their training; in the Ottoman empire a slave in imperial service who had been conscripted as a youth from the Christian population of the empire might well rise in the administration to be grand vizier and marry a sultan's sister or daughter, although he remained the sultan's slave in law. To establish a foundation on a legal basis, viziers were allowed to alienate property their wives had been granted by the sultan, often however with the specific intention that that should be made *waqf*.

Any property alienated by *waqf* has to be in private ownership. The Iranian view of kingship, which prevailed in many later Muslim cultures, held the ruler to be the sole proprietor of his kingdom. He granted his land by allotment (Arab. *iqtā'*) to military officials, viziers and sometimes the judiciary to hold in fief during their tenure of office or for their lifetime. Any grant of land as private property was therefore at the ruler's expense. In the Ottoman empire, a grant from the sultan was a prerequisite for founding a *waqf*, and the deed generally stated that the grant was made solely for this purpose. This was not always the case where centralized control was weaker. In the early 14th century the founder of the *khānaqāh* of Sayf al-Din Bakharzi (*see* BUKHARA, §2(iv)) met no such official restrictions in acquiring large properties in the surrounding area, where the Mongol invasions a century earlier had left large tracts of land derelict. However, land tenure was often unclear, and many rulers may have justified their periodic confiscations of *waqf* property by citing irregularities in the founders' titles to ownership.

A *waqf* foundation must also be built of permanent materials, although in Iran and western Central Asia, where mud-brick is a basic building material and earthquakes are frequent, many major buildings, such as the mosque of Bibi Khanum (*see* SAMARKAND, §3(ii)), rapidly became ruined and unusable. Hence the importance founders and lawyers attached to specifying the numbers, duties and stipends of the officials who were to keep the foundation in good order, oversee the exploitation of the endowments and maintain the buildings in good repair. Mortgaging or selling the endowments or any part of them was forbidden, and few foundations could have had the financial reserves to cope with major repairs in the event of a disaster or even the regular upkeep of the endowments.

According to the Shafi'i and Hanafi schools of law, the founder of a *waqf* might also be its (paid) administrator (*mutawalli*), whereas the Maliki school held that this

invalidated the *waqf*. In the Maghrib, where the Maliki school prevailed, in general only sovereigns established foundations, since only they could afford to enjoy the prestige and hand the administration to others. The administrator was usually succeeded after his death by his eldest son; should the male line die out, the founder's freed slaves were often named as residuary administrators as a reward for the years spent in their master's service. Female founders of *waqf*s are numerous, but they or their daughters only rarely figure as administrators. The administrators of state foundations or royal *waqf*s were often the holders of a particular office of state; for example, in Mamluk Cairo the Master of the Horse (*amīr ākhūr*) administered the hospital complex of Sultan Qala'un (1284–5; *see* CAIRO, §III, 8). The deeds of foundations endowed by high-ranking eunuchs in the Ottoman empire also often stipulate that the administrators of their foundations should be their successors in office.

After the completion of the building, the conditions of endowment were drawn up in a deed (Arab. *waqfiyya*; Turk. *vakfiye*), which was legally attested and registered in the appropriate state office; when movable property, such as illuminated copies of the Koran or the manuscripts and Chinese porcelains 'Abbas I (*see* SAFAVID, (2)) donated to the shrine at ARDABIL between 1607 and 1611, was made *waqf*, the only record might be an inscription or seal. The strict prohibition against changes to the foundation deed after the founder's death left stipends vulnerable to long-term inflation, with the result that smaller *waqf*s frequently became inoperative. Many of the administrators and higher staff of a charitable institution held several appointments, but they had no incentive to spend anything on the maintenance or development of *waqf* property since their stipends could not be increased.

Relatively early in Islamic history, several of the schools of law accepted that 'movable' property, such as animals, trees, slaves and books, could be made *waqf*. The provision for books was especially important for the development of public libraries in the Islamic lands, particularly in Baghdad under the Saljuq sultans and the last Abbasid caliphs, and in Istanbul under the Ottomans. The deed of *waqf* inscribed in the volumes of a splendidly illuminated 30-part manuscript of the Koran (Cairo, N. Lib., MS. 72) copied at Hamadan in 1314–15 for the Ilkhanid sultan Uljaytu and bequeathed in 1326 to the *khānaqāh* of Bektimur al-Saqi in Cairo provides that the volumes should be accessible to readers and for copying. Many manuscripts bear seals from several *waqf*s: administrators must have considered themselves entitled to dispose of movable property, particularly if old or worn out.

Waqf is of fundamental importance for the history of patronage in Islamic architecture, largely because of an early distinction between foundations that were purely altruistic in their provisions (*waqf khayrī*) and family trusts (*waqf ahlī*) that gave the founder's descendants the right to live off the surplus revenue from pious foundations. One of the earliest recorded family trusts is a deed of the Imam al-Shafi'i (*d* AD 820), the founder of the Shafi'i school of law, making his house at Fustat (Old Cairo) and everything in it *waqf ahlī*. Such *waqf*s were greatly in the majority in a comprehensive review made in 1546 of the *waqf*s of Istanbul, in which the average surplus revenue probably exceeded 50%. Their popularity is often held to be prudential, for they provided a degree of insurance against the arbitrary confiscation of private property. In addition they protected a family fortune or enterprise against the divisive effects of inheritance laws, were partly exempt from taxes and provided for the descendants of officials paid by allotments that reverted to the state at death, retirement or disgrace. The last consideration was particularly important when descendants were debarred by statute from holding high office, as in Mamluk Egypt and Syria. But even if all these considerations were effective, the founder's piety should not be discounted.

The financial advantages of *waqf ahlī* had an important practical consequence. The major shrines of Islam in Mecca, Medina and Jerusalem and the Shi'ite holy places in Iraq and Iran continued to attract large pious benefactions, and even such mosques as al-Azhar in Cairo were the object of disinterested restorations, but as *waqf ahlī* benefited the founder's family as well, creating a new foundation was more attractive than giving to an old one. Hence the great spate of foundations in 14th- and 15th-century Cairo in which both the centre of the city and suburban quarters, such as the southern and the north-eastern cemeteries, rapidly became built up with pious foundations (*see* CAIRO, §I, 2).

As a result whole quarters might become immobilized with endowed property that was often in poor condition. Only two solutions were found to alleviate this congestion: confiscation and exchange. Confiscation, although illegal, was widely practised by the later Mamluk sultans and must often have received some justification, given the frequent irregularities in deeds and conditions of foundation. Exchange was legal, on the strict understanding that it was to the advantage of the *waqf*; it enabled a new founder to buy out an older foundation, demolish property that had become structurally unsound and replace it by a new foundation. Such exchanges often aroused controversy since the price paid generally bore no relation to the current value of the property. Thus the Mamluk sultan Mu'ayyad (*reg* 1412–21) purchased the great brass-plated doors from the complex of Hasan (1356–62; *see* CAIRO, §III, 9, and DOOR, fig. 7) in Cairo to install in his own mosque (1415–20) for a sum so paltry that a contemporary historian stigmatized the transaction as a lapse in decent behaviour. Permission to demolish older *waqf* properties in bad structural condition gave rise to numerous abuses.

Many deeds of endowment have survived while the buildings they refer to no longer exist. These deeds can be surprisingly summary, omitting such information as details of boundaries and water rights and the notional income expected from endowments. Many lack specific details of the buildings and their location. According to its endowment deed, the Rab'-i Rashidi (*see* TABRIZ, §3(i)), a huge foundation built by the vizier RASHID AL-DIN in the early 14th century, included a mosque, madrasas, hospitals, a medical school, various institutions for the study of the Koran, Koran commentary and Prophetic traditions, a mint, a dye-works, a paper mill and a scriptorium for the copying and illustration of his own writings. All of these have disappeared, and the paucity of information in the deed makes it difficult to determine the overall plan of the quarter or the internal plans of the constituent buildings.

Other deeds may designate rooms for a particular purpose without giving any indication of their size or appearance. A characteristic Ottoman example may detail the staff attached to a foundation without giving any idea of the organization of its internal space, as in the deed of Haseki Hürrem Sultan (Roxelana), Süleyman's wife (28 Nov 1540; Istanbul, Mus. Turk. & Islam. A., MS. 2191), endowing a mosque, madrasa, public kitchen and Koran school in the Avratpazarı quarter of Istanbul.

Deeds surviving from 15th-century Mamluk Cairo, however, frequently contain descriptions of individual rooms and their disposition within buildings that can readily be interpreted by comparison with the standing monument or with other buildings of a similar type. Indeed they are an essential adjunct to architectural survey, which rarely gives any indication of the use to which the internal space was put. The most useful of these date from the reign of Qa'itbay (*reg* 1468–96) and relate to the foundations of both the Sultan and his amirs. At this time, the increasing shortage of fine building materials—wood, marble or even limestone—had led to the plundering of material from other standing or ruined buildings, and it may be that founders hoped to avoid a similar fate for their new foundations by precisely describing in the deed all furnishings and decoration. It was never possible to make such building materials *waqf*, but their inclusion seems to have been inspired by the desperate hope that it might be.

BIBLIOGRAPHY

F. Köprülü: 'L'Institution de Vakf et l'importance historique des documents de Vakf', *Vakıflar Derg.*, i (1938), pp. 3–9

L. A. Mayer: *The Buildings of Qāytbāy as Described in his Endowment Deed* (London, 1938) [in Arabic]

F. Köprülü: 'L'Institution de Vakouf: Sa nature juridique et son évolution historique', *Vakıflar Derg.*, ii (1942), pp. 3–44

O. Ergin: *Fatih imareti vakfiyesi* [The endowment deed of the Fatih complex] (Istanbul, 1945)

'A. Ibrahim: 'Al-Wathā'iq fī khidmat al-āthār' [Documents in the service of archaeology], *al-Mu'tamar al-thānī li'l-āthār al-bilād al-'Arabiyya* [Second conference on archaeology in the Arab lands] (Cairo, 1958), pp. 205–87

V. L. Vyatkin: 'Vakufny dokument Ishratkhany' [The *waqf* deed of the Ishratkhana], *Ishratkhana*, ed. M. E. Masson (Tashkent, 1958), pp. 111–36

Y. Eche: *Les Bibliothèques publiques et semi-publiques en Mésopotamie, en Syrie et en Égypte au moyen âge* (Damascus, 1967)

M. Khadr with C. Cahen: 'Deux actes de *waqf* d'un Qaraḫānide d'Asie centrale', *J. Asiat.*, cclv (1967), pp. 305–34

I. Afshar: 'The Autograph Copy of Rashīd al-Dīn's Vaqfnāmeh', *Cent. Asiat. J.*, xiv (1970), pp. 1–38

Ö. L. Barkan and E. H. Ayverdi: *Istanbul vakıflar tahrir defteri 953 (1546) tarihli* [Survey of the *waqf*s of Istanbul dated 953 (1546)] (Istanbul, 1970)

S. Faroqhi: 'Vakıf Administration in Sixteenth-century Konya: The Zaviye of Sadreddin-i Konevî', *J. Econ. & Soc. Hist. Orient*, xii (1974), pp. 145–72

L. A. Ibrahim: 'The Great Ḥānqāh of the Emir Qawṣūn', *Mitt. Dt. Archäol. Inst.: Abt. Kairo*, xxx (1974), pp. 37–64

A. H. Morton: 'The Ardebīl Shrine in the Reign of Shah Ṭahmāsp I', *Iran*, xii (1974), pp. 31–63; xiii (1975), pp. 39–58

J. M. Rogers: 'Waqf and Patronage in Seljuq Anatolia: The Epigraphic Evidence', *Anatol. Stud.*, xxvi (1976), pp. 69–103

——: 'Waqfiyyas and Waqf-registers: New Primary Sources for Islamic Architecture', *Kst Orients*, xi (1976–7), pp. 182–96

——: 'Central Asian *Waqfiyyas* of the Fifteenth and Sixteenth Centuries: The Endowments of Khwāja Ahrār', *International Seminar on Social and Economic Aspects of the Muslim Waqf: Jerusalem, 24–28 June 1979*

L. Fernandes: 'Three Sufi Foundations in a Fifteenth-century Wakfiya', *An. Islam.*, xvii (1981), pp. 141–56

J.-C. David: *Le Waqf d'Ipshir Pāshā à Alep (1063/1653)* (Damascus, 1982)

S. S. Blair: 'Il-Khanid Architecture and Society: An Analysis of the Endowment Deed of the Rab'-i Rashīdī', *Iran*, xxii (1984), pp. 67–90

L. Fernandes: 'The Foundation of Baybars al-Jashankir: Its Waqf, History, and Architecture', *Muqarnas*, iv (1987), pp. 21–42

——: *The Evolution of a Sufi Institution in Mamluk Egypt: The Khanaqah* (Berlin, 1988)

M. M. Amin and L. A. Ibrahim: *Architectural Terms in Mamluk Documents* (Cairo, 1990)

S. Faroqhi: *Herrscher über Mekka* (Munich, 1991)

R. McChesney: *Waqf in Central Asia: Four Hundred Years in the History of a Muslim Shrine, 1480–1889* (Princeton, 1991)

J. M. ROGERS

Islamabad. Capital city of Pakistan. For 10 years after the partition of India and Pakistan in 1947, KARACHI functioned as the temporary national capital, but in 1958 Field Marshal Ayub Khan decided to build a permanent seat of government. In February 1959 an eight-member commission recommended a site on the Pothwar plateau, near the cantonment town of RAWALPINDI, which was to act as a 'mother city' to the new capital during the development process. In September 1959 the Federal Capital Commission was constituted to prepare a master-plan for the project. By January 1960 preliminary reports were completed, and in February the new capital was named Islamabad. In May of the same year, a preliminary master-plan designed by Doxiadis Associates was approved, and in June the Capital Development Authority was established to execute the task. Work began in 1961, and in 1963 the new city received its first residents.

The city of Islamabad occupies an area of 220.15 sq km. It was laid out on a grid plan based on Doxiadis's idea of 'dynapolis'—a city expanding in a fan shape from an initial point. The initial point or Red Area contains national government buildings and cultural institutions. To the south-east is the diplomatic enclave, to the west public buildings. A Blue Area containing the central business district forms a commercial spine flanked by residential sectors along the south-western axis; two industrialized zones are located so as to serve both Islamabad and Rawalpindi.

In the Red Area, Gio Ponti's Secretariat Complex is a successful arrangement of buildings forming a well-integrated unity in which five-storey blocks define a series of quiet enclosures (see fig.) that flow into each other through the building masses. The blocks are connected by horizontal ducts framing dramatic vistas of the surroundings, while the use of water and terraces is reminiscent of Mughal landscaping. In contrast, Government Officers' Hostel by Denis Brigdon attains its architectural integrity

Islamabad, the Secretariat Complex by Gio Ponti, with Antonio Fornaroli and Alberto Rosselli, 1968

from an organic unity of form, function, structure and materials rather than obvious references to historical precedents. Concrete segmental vaults form a ventilated double roof, and the slim bricks lack the traditional thick bed of lime mortar. The Mughal Garden in one of the two courts is only loosely derived from the historical prototype.

The layout of the Presidency Complex, by Edward Durrell Stone, has a formal symmetry, in conformity with the architect's understanding of Mughal concepts. The President's House dominates the main axis of the national square, flanked by the Assembly and the Foreign Office at either end of the minor axis. The President's House rises from the national square as a tiered pyramid. The lowest levels accommodate offices and service areas; over these are the state banqueting and reception halls, while the uppermost tier contains suites for state guests. The entire complex is finished in whitewashed terrazzo. The President's residence itself is located in a separate block set well behind the first block; the two are linked by a formal garden and colonnades. Construction began in 1975 and was completed in 1984. The National Assembly and Foreign Office buildings, by the same architect, have a similar stepped pyramid form but with more austere façades. Vedat Dalokay's mosque, the Shah Faisal Masjid, is raised on a two-storey podium that houses, among other facilities, an entire university. The project is designed to accommodate 100,000 persons in the courtyard and a further 20,000 in the prayer hall and verandah. Construction began in 1976 and was completed in 1984.

BIBLIOGRAPHY

M. H. Raza: *Islamabad and Environs* (Islamabad, n.d.)
K. K. Mumtaz: *Architecture in Pakistan* (Singapore, 1985)

KAMIL KHAN MUMTAZ

Islamic art. The art made by artists or artisans whose religion was ISLAM, for patrons who lived in predominantly Muslim lands, or for purposes that are restricted or peculiar to a Muslim population or a Muslim setting. This article deals with the arts produced from the 7th century to the 19th in the Islamic lands from the Atlantic to western Central Asia (*see also* CENTRAL ASIA, §I) and India (*see also* INDIAN SUBCONTINENT). For 19th- and 20th-century developments in the region, see individual country articles (e.g. EGYPT, IRAN). For Islamic art in other regions, such as Sub-Saharan Africa or South-east Asia, see the appropriate geographical entries (e.g. AFRICA, INDONESIA).

BIBLIOGRAPHY

GENERAL
E. Kühnel: *Islamische Kleinkunst* (Berlin, 1925/*R* 1963); Eng. trans. by K. Watson as *The Minor Arts of Islam* (Ithaca, 1971)
——: *Die Kunst des Islam* (Stuttgart, 1962); Eng. trans. by K. Watson as *Islamic Art and Architecture* (Ithaca, 1966)
K. Otto-Dorn: *Die Kunst des Islam*, A. World (Baden-Baden, 1964); Fr. trans. (Paris, 1967); rev. Eng. trans. (Berkeley and Los Angeles, 1994)
A. U. Pope and P. Ackerman, eds: *Survey of Persian Art* (2/1964–7)
D. Talbot Rice: *Islamic Art*, World A. (London, 1965/*R* 1989)
E. J. Grube: *The World of Islam* (London, 1966)
D. Sourdel and J. Sourdel: *La Civilisation de l'Islam classique* (Paris, 1968)
C. J. du Ry: *Art of Islam* (New York, 1972)
O. Grabar: *The Formation of Islamic Art* (New Haven, 1973/*R* and enlarged 1987)
B. Spuler and J. Sourdel-Thomine: *Die Kunst des Islam*, Propyläen-Kstgesch. (Berlin, 1973)
O. Grabar: 'Islamic Peoples, Art of: IV. Visual Arts', *Encyclopaedia Britannica*, 15th edn (1974)
D. James: *Islamic Art: An Introduction* (London, 1974)
T. Burckhardt: *Art of Islam: Language and Meaning* (London, 1976)
B. Lewis, ed.: *The World of Islam: Faith, People, Culture* (London, 1976)
A. Papadopoulo: *L'Islam et l'art musulman* (Paris, 1976); Eng. trans. (New York, 1976)
M. Rogers: *The Spread of Islam* (Oxford, 1976)
Islamic Art and Architecture, Garland Lib. Hist. A., xiii (New York and London, 1976)
Oxford Studies in Islamic Art (Oxford, 1985–)
R. Ettinghausen and O. Grabar: *The Art and Architecture of Islam, 600–1250*, Pelican Hist. A. (Harmondsworth, 1987)
S. H. Nasr: *Islamic Art and Spirituality* (Albany, 1987)
R. W. Ferrier, ed.: *The Arts of Persia* (New Haven and London, 1989)
N. Atasoy, A. Bahnassi and M. Rogers: *The Art of Islam* (UNESCO, 1990)
B. Brend: *Islamic Art* (London, 1991)
S. S. Blair and J. M. Bloom: *The Art and Architecture of Islam, 1250–1800*, Pelican Hist. A. (London, 1994)

BIBLIOGRAPHICAL WORKS
J. D. Pearson: *Index Islamicus, 1906–1955: A Catalogue of Articles on Islamic Subjects in Periodicals and Other Collective Publications* (Cambridge, 1958); suppl. i, 1956–60 (Cambridge, 1962); ii, 1961–5 (Cambridge, 1967); iii, 1966–70 (London, 1972); iv, 1971–5 (London, 1977); v, 1976–80 (London, 1982)
K. A. C. Creswell: *A Bibliography of the Architecture, Arts and Crafts of Islam to 1st January 1960* (Cairo, 1961/*R* Vaduz, 1978)
——: *A Bibliography of the Architecture, Arts and Crafts of Islam: Supplement Jan. 1960 to Jan. 1972* (Cairo, 1973)
J. D. Pearson, M. Meinecke and G. T. Scanlon: *A Bibliography of the Architecture, Arts and Crafts of Islam: Second Supplement Jan. 1972 to Dec. 1980 (with Omissions from Previous Years)* (Cairo, 1984)

FESTSCHRIFTEN AND COLLECTED WORKS
G. C. Miles, ed.: *Archaeologica Orientalia in Memoriam Ernst Herzfeld* (Locust Valley, 1952)
R. Ettinghausen, ed.: *Aus der Welt der islamischen Kunst: Festschrift für Ernst Kühnel* (Berlin, 1959)
O. Aslanapa, ed.: *Beiträge zur Kunstgeschichte Asiens: In Memoriam Ernst Diez* (Istanbul, 1963)
Studies in Islamic Art and Architecture in Honour of Professor K. A. C. Creswell (Cairo, 1965)
R. Ettinghausen, ed.: *Islamic Art in the Metropolitan Museum of Art* (New York, 1972)
P. Chelkowski, ed.: *Studies in Art and Literature of the Near East in Honor of Richard Ettinghausen* (New York, 1974)
O. Grabar: *Studies in Medieval Islamic Art* (London, 1976)
A. Daneshvari, ed.: *Essays in Islamic Art and Architecture in Honor of Katharina Otto-Dorn* (Malibu, 1981)
C. Adle, ed.: *Art et société dans le monde iranien* (Paris, 1982)
R. Ettinghausen: *Islamic Art and Archaeology (Collected Papers)*, ed. M. Rosen-Ayalon (Berlin, 1984)
R. Pinder-Wilson: *Studies in Islamic Art* (London, 1985)
P. P. Soucek, ed.: *Content and Context of Visual Arts in the Islamic World* (New York, 1988)

PERIODICALS
A. Islam., 16 vols (1934–51)
Āthār-é Īrān, 4 vols (1936–49)
Kst Orients, 11 vols (1950–77)
A. Orient. (1954–)
A. & Archaeol. Res. Pap., 21 vols (1972–84)
Islam. A. (1982–)
Muqarnas (1983–)

I. Introduction. II. Architecture. III. Arts of the book. IV. Metalwork. V. Ceramics. VI. Textiles. VII. Woodwork. VIII. Other arts. IX. Forgeries. X. Historiography. XI. Collectors and collecting. XII. Museums.

DETAILED TABLE OF CONTENTS

I. Introduction   99
   1. Definition   99
     (i) Scope   99
     (ii) Constraints   99
     (iii) Objections   101
   2. Geography and trade   102

(i) Settlement patterns   102
(ii) Commerce and communications   106
3. Ethnography   107
4. Demography   109
5. History   109
    (i) Introduction   109
    (ii) The career of Muhammad (610–32)   110
    (iii) The caliphate and the age of Arab ascendancy
          (632–*c.* 900)   111
    (iv) Early Middle Period (*c.* 900–*c.* 1200)   113
    (v) Later Middle Period (*c.* 1200–*c.* 1500)   115
    (vi) Early Modern Period (*c.* 1500–19th century)   117
6. Patronage and art life   121
    (i) Court   121
    (ii) Urban   123
    (iii) Village and nomad   124
7. Status of the artist   126
8. Subject-matter   127
    (i) Introduction   128
    (ii) Religious themes   128
    (iii) Royal themes   130
    (iv) Secular themes   131
    (v) Vegetal themes   132
    (vi) Geometry   133
    (vii) Writing   134
    (viii) The natural world   135
    (ix) Magic   136
    (x) Heavenly bodies   137

II. Architecture   140
1. Introduction   140
    (i) Materials   140
    (ii) Building types   141
    (iii) Architectural elements and construction
          techniques   142
    (iv) Decoration   142
    (v) Patrons and architects   143
    (vi) Meaning and impact   143
2. Before AD 661   144
3. AD 661–*c.* 750   145
    (i) Introduction   145
    (ii) Religious   146
    (iii) Secular   148
4. *c.* AD 750–*c.* 900   149
    (i) Eastern Islamic lands   150
        (a) Introduction   150
        (b) Iraq   150
            – Cities and settlements   150
            – Building types   152
            – Materials and construction techniques   153
        (c) Iran and western Central Asia   153
            – Mosques   153
            – Residences   154
            – Rural caravanserais   154
    (ii) Central Islamic lands   155
    (iii) Tunisia   156
    (iv) Spain and Morocco   157
5. *c.* AD 900–*c.* 1250   158
    (i) Eastern Islamic lands   158
        (a) Iran and western Central Asia, *c.* 900–*c.* 1050   158
            – Building types   159
            – Materials, techniques, forms and
              decoration   160
        (b) Iran, *c.* 1050–*c.* 1250   161
            – Building types   161
            – Materials, forms and decoration   164

        (c) Afghanistan, Pakistan and western Central
            Asia, *c.* 1050–*c.* 1250   166
            – Building types   166
            – Materials, forms and decoration   168
    (ii) Central Islamic lands   170
        (a) Tunisia and eastern Algeria   170
        (b) Sicily   171
        (c) Egypt   172
            – Urban development   173
            – Palaces   173
            – Mosques   173
            – Minarets   175
            – Funerary architecture   175
            – Madrasas   175
            – Materials, techniques and decoration   176
        (d) Yemen   177
        (e) Syria, the Jazira and Iraq   178
            – Mosques   179
            – Minarets   180
            – Madrasas   180
            – Hospitals   181
            – Mausolea   181
            – Palaces   182
            – Materials, forms and decoration   182
    (iii) Anatolia   183
        (a) Building types   183
            – Mosques   183
            – Madrasas and hospitals   184
            – Funerary architecture   185
            – Secular buildings   186
        (b) Materials, techniques, forms and
            decoration   186
    (iv) Western Islamic lands   187
        (a) Umayyads, 929–1031   187
        (b) Party Kings, 1031–*c.* 1100   189
        (c) Almoravids, 1056–1147   190
        (d) Almohads, 1130–1269   190
6. *c.* 1250–*c.* 1500   192
    (i) Eastern Islamic lands   192
        (a) Iran, *c.* 1250–*c.* 1375   192
            – Building types   193
            – Forms, materials, techniques and
              decoration   194
        (b) Iran, Afghanistan and western Central Asia,
            c. 1375–*c.* 1500   195
            – Eastern Iran   196
            – Western Iran   198
            – Materials, forms, techniques and
              decoration   199
        (c) Indian subcontinent   201
    (ii) Anatolia   201
        (a) Beyliks   202
            – Mosques   202
            – Madrasas, hospitals and hospices   202
            – Funerary architecture   204
            – Secular buildings   204
        (b) Ottomans to 1453   205
    (iii) Central Islamic lands   207
        (a) Egypt and Syria   207
            – Introduction   207
            – Bahri *mamlūk*s, 1250–1390   208
            – Burji *mamlūk*s, 1382–1517   211
        (b) Yemen   213
    (iv) Western Islamic lands   215
        (a) Spain   215
        (b) Morocco and Algeria   217
        (c) Tunisia   219

7. *c.* 1500–*c.* 1900 220
  (i) Ottoman empire 220
    (a) Introduction 220
    (b) Turkey 221
      – 1453–1718 221
      – 1718–1922 225
    (c) Provinces 227
  (ii) Iran 229
    (a) *c.* 1500–*c.* 1700 229
      – History and development 230
      – Artisans, materials, techniques and
        decoration 232
    (b) *c.* 1700–*c.* 1900 233
  (iii) Western Central Asia 235
    (a) Patronage 235
    (b) Building types 235
    (c) Materials, forms, techniques and decoration . 239
  (iv) Indian subcontinent 239
  (v) Morocco 239
8. After *c.* 1900 241
9. Architectural decoration 242
  (i) Sculpture 242
    (a) Non-figural 242
    (b) Figural 245
  (ii) Tiles 248
    (a) Early development 248
    (b) Eastern Islamic lands 248
    (c) Western Islamic lands 250
  (iii) Painting 250
    (a) *c.* AD 700–*c.* 900 250
    (b) *c.* 900–*c.* 1900 252
  (iv) Mosaics 255
  (v) Stained glass 256
  (vi) Epigraphy 257
    (a) Materials, types and languages 258
    (b) Stylistic development 258
10. Urban development 260
  (i) Central and western Islamic lands 260
    (a) Functional organization 260
    (b) Spatial arrangement 262
  (ii) Eastern Islamic lands 264
  (iii) Anatolia and the Balkans 265
11. Housing 267
  (i) Introduction 267
  (ii) Materials 268
  (iii) Forms and regional variation 270
III. Arts of the book 271
1. Introduction 271
2. Calligraphy 273
  (i) Introduction 273
    (a) Forms, materials and equipment 273
    (b) Calligraphers and their education 276
    (c) Treatises 277
  (ii) Before *c.* AD 900 277
    (a) Early evidence 277
    (b) Early Abbasid scripts 278
  (iii) *c.* 900–*c.* 1400 280
    (a) New Abbasid style 280
    (b) *Maghribi* scripts 281
    (c) The Six Pens 282
      – Introduction 282
      – Historical development 282
  (iv) *c.* 1400–*c.* 1800 285
    (a) Old scripts 285
    (b) New scripts 285
      – 15th–17th centuries 285
      – 18th century 287

  (v) After *c.* 1800 287
3. Painted decoration 288
  (i) Manuscripts of the Koran 288
    (a) Introduction and early development 288
    (b) Later regional development 290
  (ii) Other manuscripts 291
    (a) Introduction 291
    (b) Major examples 292
4. Painted illustration 293
  (i) Introduction 293
    (a) Scholarship 294
      – Problems of analysis and attribution 294
      – Publications 295
      – Linguistic classification 296
    (b) Patronage and conventions 296
  (ii) Subject-matter 297
    (a) Scientific and technical works 297
      – 11th century 297
      – 12th–13th centuries 298
      – 14th–15th centuries 299
      – 16th century and later 299
    (b) Belles-lettres 300
    (c) Epic poetry 302
    (d) Historical writing 303
  (iii) Before *c.* AD 1000 304
  (iv) *c.* 1000–*c.* 1250 305
    (a) Egypt 305
    (b) Spain and North Africa 306
    (c) Iraq, Syria and Anatolia 307
      – Northern Mesopotamia 307
      – Southern Mesopotamia 309
  (v) *c.* 1250–*c.* 1500 310
    (a) Egypt and Syria 310
      – *c.* mid-13th century–14th 310
      – 15th century 311
    (b) Iraq and Iran, *c.* 1250–*c.* 1350 313
      – Introduction 313
      – Methods of production 313
      – The Metropolitan style under Ilkhanid court
        patronage, *c.* 1290–*c.* 1310 314
      – The Rashidiyya school, *c.* 1309–18 314
      – Metropolitan painting, 1318–*c.* 1350 315
      – Provincial production in south-west Iran 316
      – Small *Shāhnāmas* 316
    (c) Iraq and Iran, *c.* 1350–*c.* 1400 318
      – Early Jalayirid painting, to *c.* 1375 318
      – Painting during the reign of Ahmad Jalayir
        (*reg* 1382–1410) 319
      – Painting under the Muzaffarids (1364–84) ... 321
    (d) Iran and western Central Asia, *c.* 1400–*c.*
      1500 321
      – Painting during the reign of Timur (*reg*
        1370–1405) 321
      – Painting made for Iskandar Sultan (1384–*c.*
        1415) 322
      – Painting made for Shahrukh (*reg* 1405–47) . 322
      – Painting made for Baysunghur (1397–
        1433) 323
      – Painting made for Ibrahim Sultan (1394–
        1435) 324
      – Other illustrated manuscripts commiss-
        ioned during the reign of Shahrukh 325
      – Painting during the reign of Husayn Bayqara
        (*reg* 1470–1506) 325
    (e) Iraq and Iran, *c.*1450–*c.* 1500 327
    (f) Anatolia 329
    (g) Indian subcontinent 330
  (vi) *c.* 1500–*c.* 1900 331

(a) Iran, *c.* 1500–*c.* 1750   331
– Introduction   331
– The style of Tabriz, 1502–48   331
– The style of Qazvin, 1548–98   334
– The style of Shiraz, *c.* 1500–*c.* 1600   337
– Traditional painting at Isfahan and other
  courts, *c.* 1598–*c.* 1700   338
– Eclectic painting at Isfahan and other
  courts, *c.* 1640–1722   339
(b) Iran, *c.*1750–*c.*1900   341
(c) Western Central Asia   342
(d) Indian subcontinent   344
– Introduction   344
– Painting in the reign of Akbar (*reg* 1556–
  1605)   344
– Painting in the reign of Jahangir (*reg* 1605–
  27)   345
– Painting in the reign of Shah Jahan (*reg*
  1628–58)   345
– Later developments, 1658–*c.* 1900   346
(e) Ottoman empire   346
– 16th century and early 17th   346
– Later 17th century and 18th   350
5. Paper   351
(i) History and development   351
(ii) Production and uses   352
(iii) Special papers   353
6. Papercuts   354
7. Binding   355
(i) Bookbinders, their materials and techniques   355
(ii) Style   356
8. Printing   359
(i) Block-printing   359
(ii) Arabic printing in Europe   360
(iii) Printing in the Islamic lands   360

IV. Metalwork   363
1. Introduction   363
(i) Materials   363
(ii) Metalworking techniques   363
(iii) Decorative techniques   364
(iv) Forms   364
(v) Decorative motifs   366
2. Before *c.* 1100   368
(i) Base metals   368
(a) Spain   368
(b) Egypt and Syria   369
(c) Iraq and western Iran   369
(d) Eastern Iran and western Central Asia   370
(ii) Gold and silver   371
3. *c.* 1100–*c.* 1500   373
(i) Iranian world   373
(a) *c.* 1100–*c.* 1400   373
– Production and patronage   373
– *c.* 1100–*c.* 1250   374
– *c.* 1250–*c.* 1400   376
(b) *c.* 1400–*c.* 1500   377
– Eastern Iran and western Central Asia   377
– Western Iran   378
– Anatolia   378
(ii) Syria and the Jazira, *c.* 1100–*c.* 1250   379
(a) Centres of production   379
(b) Patronage   380
(c) Working practices   380
(d) Forms   381
(e) Decoration   382
(iii) Egypt and Syria, *c.* 1250–*c.* 1500   382
(a) *c.* 1250–*c.* 1400   382

– Centres of production   382
– Patronage   382
– Forms and decoration   383
(b) *c.* 1400–*c.* 1500   384
(iv) Spain and North Africa   386
4. After *c.* 1500   387
(i) Ottoman empire   387
(ii) Egypt and Syria, after *c.* 1800   389
(iii) Iran   390
(a) *c.* 1500–*c.* 1550   390
(b) *c.* 1550–*c.* 1700   391
(c) After *c.* 1700   392

V. Ceramics   393
1. Introduction   393
(i) Materials and techniques   393
(ii) Forms and decoration   394
(iii) Achievement and impact   395
(iv) Collecting   395
2. Before *c.* AD 1000   396
(i) Syria   396
(ii) Iraq   397
(a) Provenance and distribution   397
(b) Fabric, shape and glaze   398
(c) Decorative techniques and motifs   399
(d) Dating and chronology   399
(iii) Iran and western Central Asia   400
(a) Introduction   400
(b) South-west Iran   401
(c) North-east Iran and western Central Asia   401
(iv) Egypt   402
(v) North Africa and Spain   403
3. *c.* 1000–*c.* 1250   404
(i) Egypt   404
(ii) Syria   406
(iii) Iran and western Central Asia   407
(a) *Sgraffito* wares   407
(b) Slip-painted wares   408
(c) Fritwares   408
(d) Lustrewares   409
(e) Enamelled wares   410
(iv) Anatolia   411
(v) Spain and North Africa   411
4. *c.* 1250–*c.* 1500   412
(i) Iran and western Central Asia   412
(a) *c.* 1250–*c.* 1400   412
(b) *c.* 1400–*c.* 1500   413
(ii) Egypt and Syria   415
(a) Unglazed wares   415
(b) *Sgraffito* and slip-painted wares   415
(c) Lustrewares   415
(d) Underglaze-painted wares   416
(iii) Anatolia   418
(iv) Spain and North Africa   418
5. *c.* 1500 and after   419
(i) Eastern Mediterranean lands   419
(a) Introduction   419
(b) Experimentation, *c.* 1500–*c.* 1555   420
(c) Mass production, *c.* 1555–*c.* 1600   421
(d) Decline and diffusion, *c.* 1600 and after   423
(ii) Iran   423
(a) *c.* 1500–*c.* 1700   423
(b) *c.* 1700 and after   425
(iii) North Africa   427

VI. Textiles   428
1. Introduction   428
(i) Fibres and manufacture   428

(ii) Textiles in religious, royal and nomadic life	429
(iii) Textile trade	429
2. Fabrics	431
(i) Before *c.* 1250	431
(a) Egypt	431
(b) Iraq and the eastern Islamic lands	433
(c) Spain and North Africa	436
(d) Yemen	438
(ii) *c.* 1250–*c.* 1500	439
(a) Spain and North Africa	439
(b) Egypt and Syria	441
(c) Eastern Islamic lands	443
(iii) *c.* 1500 and after	444
(a) Eastern Mediterranean lands	444
– Nature of the evidence	444
– Nature of production	445
– Stylistic development	445
(b) North Africa	447
(c) Iran	448
– Materials and techniques	449
– Compund weaves and velvets	449
– Other fabrics	450
(d) Western Central Asia	451
(e) Indian subcontinent	452
3. Dress	452
(i) Introduction	452
(ii) Before *c.* AD 650	454
(iii) *c.* AD 650–*c.* 1200	455
(iv) *c.* 1200–*c.* 1500	457
(v) *c.* 1500 and after	458
(a) North Africa and the central Islamic lands	458
(b) Anatolia and the Balkans	460
– Men's dress	460
– Women's dress	461
– The Balkans	462
(c) Iran	463
– Dress under the Safavids	463
– Dress under the Zands	465
– Dress under the Qajars	465
4. Carpets and flatweaves	466
(i) Introduction	466
(a) Techniques and modes of production	466
(b) Origins and development	467
(c) Scholarship	468
(ii) Before *c.* 1450	469
(iii) *c.* 1450–*c.* 1700	470
(a) Anatolia	470
(b) Mediterranean lands	472
(c) Iran	474
(d) Indian subcontinent	476
(iv) *c.* 1700 and after	476
(a) Anatolia and the Balkans	476
– Economic and social factors	476
– Dating	477
– Geography of production	477
– Impact of trade and the European economy	479
(b) Caucasus	479
– 18th century	479
– 19th–20th centuries	480
(c) Iran	482
– Introduction	482
– Centres of produciton	483
(d) Western Central Asia	484
(e) Indian subcontinent	485
(f) North Africa	485
VII. Woodwork	487
1. Before *c.* 1250	487
(i) Egypt, Syria and Iraq	488
(a) Before *c.* AD 1000	488
(b) *c.* 1000–*c.* 1250	489
(ii) Iran and western Central Asia	491
(iii) Spain and North Africa	492
2. After *c.* 1250	494
(i) Spain and North Africa	494
(ii) Egypt and Syria, *c.* 1250–*c.* 1500	496
(iii) Anatolia, *c.* 1250–*c.* 1500	497
(iv) Ottoman empire, after *c.* 1500	498
(v) Yemen	500
(vi) Iran and western Central Asia	501
VIII. Other arts	503
1. Arms and armour	503
(i) Before *c.* 1500	503
(a) Materials	503
(b) Forms and decoration	503
(ii) After *c.* 1500	505
(a) Ottoman empire	507
(b) Eastern Islamic lands	509
2. Coins	510
(i) 7th–12th centuries	510
(ii) 13th–19th centuries	513
3. Enamel	514
4. Furniture	516
5. Glass	517
(i) 7th–11th centuries	517
(ii) 12th–15th centuries	519
(iii) 16th–19th centuries	522
6. Glass painting	522
7. Ivory	522
(i) Egypt, Syria and Yemen, before *c.* 1500	523
(ii) Spain	524
(iii) Tunisia, Sicily and South Italy	525
(iv) Iran and western Central Asia	526
(v) Ottoman empire, after *c.* 1500	526
8. Jade	527
9. Jewellery	529
(i) Before *c.* 1500	529
(a) Syria, Egypt and North Africa	529
(b) Iraq, Iran and western Central Asia	530
(ii) After *c.* 1500	531
(a) Iran	531
(b) Kurdistan	531
(c) Ottoman empire	531
(d) North Africa	532
(e) Yemen	532
10. Lacquer	533
11. Oil painting	535
(i) Iran	535
(ii) Turkey	536
12. Regalia	537
(i) Crowns	537
(ii) Other regalia	539
13. Rock crystal	540
(i) 7th–11th centuries	540
(ii) 12th–19th centuries	541
14. Seals	542
15. Shadow-puppets	543
IX. Forgeries	545
X. Historiography	546
1. To *c.* 1900	547
2. *c.* 1900–*c.* 1945	548

3. From *c.* 1945   549

XI. Collectors and collecting   551
    1. Islamic lands   551
    2. Europe and North America   553

XII. Museums   555
    1. Europe and North America   555
    2. Islamic lands   557

XIII. Exhibitions   559
    1. 19th century   559
    2. 20th century   559

I. Introduction.

1. Definition. 2. Geography and trade. 3. Ethnography. 4. Demography. 5. History. 6. Patronage and art life. 7. Status of the artist. 8. Subject-matter.

1. DEFINITION. This section discusses the definition of 'Islamic art'; the social, aesthetic and religious constraints on its form and scope; and later 20th-century objections to the traditional notion of a universal Islamic art.

(i) Scope. (ii) Constraints. (iii) Objections.

(i) Scope. Most of what is called Islamic art was made by Muslims for Muslims, but significant exceptions exist. In the 13th century, for example, Christian scenes appear on Syrian and northern Mesopotamian inlaid metalwork in a technique that is 'Islamic' but executed for patrons who may well have been Christians (see fig. 1 and §IV, 3(ii) below), while the decoration of many medieval Hebrew books (e.g. St Petersburg, N. Lib., MS. B192) has appropriately been called Islamic. Furthermore, under the Umayyad dynasty in Syria (*reg* AD 661–750), the Mughal dynasty in the Indian subcontinent (*reg* 1526–1857) or in the contemporary world, non-Muslims have erected buildings, designed cities or decorated objects that were all destined for the use and enjoyment of Muslims. In short, the adjective 'Islamic' when used with the noun 'art' does not refer exclusively to the specific faith known as Islam, but to the complex and varied cultural settings that arose and grew when that faith was accepted by or imposed on a spectacular array of different and frequently very old artistic and cultural traditions. The term 'Islamic' is, therefore, different from such terms as 'Christian' or 'Buddhist'. The latter deal only with a system of beliefs and pious behaviour, while Islam deals with all aspects of life. The term 'Islamic' is also different from such modifiers as 'Gothic' or 'Baroque', as it is not restricted to a period or a style. And 'Islamic' is not, as is 'French' or 'Chinese', tied to a land or space with a continuous chronology of changing artistic forms. Imperfect and even misleading though it may be, the word 'Islamic' is preferable to a host of older terms such as 'Moorish', 'Saracenic' or 'Mohammedan', which have inappropriate or erroneous implications, or to a neologism such as Hodgson's 'Islamicate' (to refer to civilization, where 'Islamic' is limited to the religion), which has not been widely accepted.

Rather than argue about terms, it is more instructive and more useful to identify the reason or reasons why those lands from Morocco to Indonesia and from western Central Asia to Central Africa that became and have remained predominantly Muslim have had an artistic

1. Canteen inlaid with Christian scenes, brass inlaid with silver and black organic material, diam. 369 mm, from Syria, mid-13th century (Washington, DC, Freer Gallery of Art)

history different in kind from the artistic history of western Europe, the Far East and the Americas. In all the latter, regional definitions eventually symbolized by modern countries seem the most appropriate categories around which to group and describe works of art. In dealing with the Muslim world, however, the maintenance of a cultural definition implies that regional, ethnic or national characteristics have been overwhelmed or sublimated into something else. Are there intrinsic, ideological or normative aspects of Islam that radically separate its culture and therefore its art from the art and cultures of other areas? Was it the historiography by non-Muslims of the art of Muslim lands that led to an interpretation of these arts that minimizes regional and national identification? If so, is this interpretation nothing more than the expression of a temporary ideology of understanding that will be replaced by new interpretations as the world changes and new expectations and attitudes arise?

(ii) Constraints. There is no formal Islamic doctrine on the visual or other arts. There are, however, certain attitudes, some directly derived from the Koranic message, others evolved from historical circumstances, that became not so much rules as formal approaches, conscious or hidden intellectual and aesthetic programmes, and eventually social and sensual habits carried on by successive generations of Muslims through whatever means many different Muslim societies had developed for the transmission of commonly held values and constraints. A few examples illustrate the range of these constraints.

The importance of ICONOCLASM, or preferably aniconism, bears deeper consequences for Islamic art than the usual philosophical and theological ones associated with the imitation and representation of living beings. Aniconism led, for instance, to the consistent avoidance of strong visual symbols for states or for dynasties as well as to an apparent paucity of formal and consistent religious symbols. These do exist in folk arts, for example in the hand of Fatima warding off the evil eye or the word *Allāh* as a protective talisman used in all media and circumstances from homes to motorcycles. But in the high art of the State or of urban mosques, there are few such symbolic signs: the MIHRAB, possibly lamps when located on the axis of the mosque, at times the MINARET and in some places inscriptions are the main examples. In a few cases, such as the Aqmar Mosque in Cairo (1125; see fig. 37 below) or the Shah Mosque and the mosque of Shaykh Lutfallah in Isfahan, the decorative sequence of ornament and writing may also send out a religious or pious message of iconographic specificity, but there is nowhere near the visual wealth of a Christian or a Buddhist sanctuary, as most of this visual symbolism is restricted to contemporary audiences and is rarely carried from generation to generation. Even the OTTOMAN empire, which after the conquest of Constantinople in 1453 was closely connected to and often inspired by Italy and ancient Rome, developed an almost fanatical avoidance of mimetic themes or of non representational alternative symbols in both its public art and such industrial arts as ceramics and textiles (see figs 177–9 and 192 below). Contemporary rulers in Iran and the Indian subcontinent, the Safavids and Mughals, were less forceful in this respect, but nevertheless at their courts the visual arts did not appear with the representational brilliance that characterized the patronage of the Medici dynasty in Florence, the dukes of Burgundy or King Louis XIV of France. Whatever explanations exist for the formation of Muslim aniconism, its continuous and ubiquitous presence has, at least until the second half of the 20th century, limited or constricted the possibility of using visual means to transmit messages.

A second constraint seems, at first glance, hardly to be one. The inventiveness of the Muslim world in nearly all techniques of the so-called industrial or decorative arts, such as metalwork, ceramics or textiles, is one of the greater achievements of art there. From the 9th century luxury objects for all of Europe and much of Asia were largely manufactured in the Islamic lands. Christian saints were buried in Islamic silks (e.g. the Shroud of St Josse, see fig. 185 below), and the exterior walls of medieval Italian churches are decorated with *bacini*, complete or fragmentary ceramic objects from Egypt, North Africa and Spain (*see* §V, 1 below). The tsars and patriarchs of Muscovite Russia dressed formally in clothes made in the Muslim world (Moscow, Kremlin), and certain motifs on Chinese ceramics from the Tang period (618–907), and even earlier, derive from the Middle East. These observations lead to two unexpected conclusions. One is the emphasis on the arts that enhance all aspects of life rather than on those such as painting that tend to be ends in themselves. The other is that these arts are almost exclusively secular arts, with the corollary paradox that most of the arts (with the exception of architecture) from a culture defined by its religious identity have been devoted to the beautification of life rather than to the celebration of the divine.

There is no one explanation for this unexpected contrast, but two partly incompatible features of the traditional Muslim ethos may help in understanding it. One is implied by the explanation of Islam provided by the modern philosopher and moralist Muhammed Arkoun, who argued that the repetitive logocentrism of classical Islamic society created a discourse that excluded the experiences of love and death, out of which poetry, mysticism and prophecy could emerge. As these are precisely the major inspirations of art, those activities that were not directly affected by a restricting legal system could expand into almost boundless fantasy and might at certain times and places—as certainly happened in Iran from the 14th century (and perhaps earlier)—acquire a religious Islamic umbrella through the pantheism of mystical thought and behaviour. The second feature, almost the opposite of the first, is that God's total and exclusive power of creation limits human creation to that which is perishable and compels man to develop that which is temporary, showy but not very important. First developed by Louis Massignon in 1922, this interpretation has subsequently been refined without affecting its main argument that man's art must be restricted to the perishable, therefore to the context of life, because the expression of the permanent presence of God is neither permitted nor possible for man to achieve.

The fact that two such largely incompatible interpretations of Islamic art can be argued derives from a third constraint: the absence, or perhaps unavailability, of contemporary written sources on the arts. There are technical manuals, a few of them published, such as the treatise by the 14th-century potter Abu'l-Qasim (*see* ABU TAHIR, §4). There are more abstract manuals of theoretical and applied geometry with implications for the arts, such as al-Kashi's *Miftāḥ al-ḥisāb* ('Key to calculation'; 1427; St Petersburg, Rus. N. Lib., MS. Dorn 131), although few have been studied in sufficient depth. For painting or calligraphy, there is a chronology of names, occasionally with a judgement of an individual's work or an outline of his life, such as that by the 16th-century librarian DUST MUHAMMAD. Nevertheless, the elements for an aesthetic theory or theories, equivalent to the very elaborate aesthetic theories developed in the Islamic lands around poetry and language, are lacking. Although such sources may exist, what has been studied so far—a small fragment from the great theologian al-Ghazali (*d* 1111) or the metaphorical images of Persian poetry—is simply not comparable in depth or potential to such treatises on literature as that by al-Jurjani (*d* 1078), not to speak of post-Renaissance writings in the West. Only further research will tell whether the paucity of usable written sources on Islamic aesthetics is the result of insufficient scholarship or reflects the reality of medieval centuries during which the arts remained in a unique symbiosis of craftsmen who made exciting and wondrous objects and patrons who saw beauty in pleasure and surprise. The Arabic adjective *'ajīb* ('extraordinary', 'fabulous') is the word that most consistently reflects the type of favourable reactions generated by the arts, and the same word was also adopted in Persian and Turkish. But even this remark must be treated with caution, as the investigation of artistic terminology in the languages of Muslim lands has just begun. A better understanding of the traditional discourse of Muslim societies about themselves and their ways of life and of judgement may reveal the true range of an Islamic aesthetic system, if there ever was one.

(iii) Objections. Although it is possible to argue that Islamic culture provided intellectual, aesthetic and social distinctions that affected, eventually transformed and largely unified the artistic traditions found by Muslims wherever Islam appeared, the experience of the 1970s and 1980s introduced questions and issues that may challenge this traditional interpretation of a 'universal' Islamic art.

The first of these issues is the realization that nearly all definitions of Islamic art and most of the studies that led to them were formulated by Western scholars. Some, such as MAX VAN BERCHEM, were Orientalists in the best sense of the word: they knew languages, travelled widely, read chronicles and inscriptions, and reconstructed worlds of form and behaviour that no longer exist. Others, such as Ivan Stchoukine (*see* SHCHUKIN, (2)) or K. A. C. CRESWELL, were curators of a heritage— Persian book illustration in one case, the architecture of Cairo in the other— and were thorough, even if not very well versed in languages and culture. All of them nevertheless sought to create a genuine 'history' based on the national models of 19th-century Europe. They had all emerged at a time when the Muslim world was either under the tutelage of a multiethnic, even if collapsing, Ottoman empire or incorporated into European 'empires', the most important exception being Iran, which remained politically independent. It was useful and natural, if not always necessary, to emphasize the worldwide character of a mode of life and therefore of an art, because it simplified the formation of means to control it. It is not surprising that in the 1920s both the Archaeological Survey of India and the French mandatory powers in Morocco sponsored studies of geometry in the arts as typical of Muslim culture, for such studies substituted a set of abstract and generalized formulae for the complexities of local experience.

Furthermore, the original training of so many specialists as Semiticists led most historians to deal only with the early centuries of Islamic history, when the Abbasid caliphate with its capitals in Iraq extended from the Indus Valley to the Atlantic, or with the later empires, all but one of which (Safavid Iran) were multi-national and alleged some right to the inheritance of the early 'universal' caliphate. Thus, the specifics of Western scholarly concern for the arts, as well as the political and ideological context in which this concern occurred, led to a denial of national identity like that surrounding the development of the study of the arts in continental Europe. The general and universal idea of an all-encompassing Islamic ideology satisfied the needs of colonial rule, and ironically it was picked up by revivalist religious establishments in the late 20th century. Whatever reasons led to this interpretation, it is a reasonable position for whoever deals with the early centuries of Islam (roughly until the mid-13th century), and it alone as a hypothesis can explain why Arabic became so important in western Central Asia and Spain. These centuries can easily be divided into an early Islamic period (to *c.* 900) and a medieval one (*c.* 900–*c.* 1250), both of which have significant correlations to and parallels with the medieval art of Christendom.

But the Islamic world changed in the 13th century, and the notion of universal artistic values across time and space hardly seems to explain the Alhambra (*see* GRANADA, §III, 1) and the Taj Mahal (*see* AGRA, §II, 1), Iznik ceramics (*see* §V, 5(i) below) and Iranian book illustration (*see* §III, 4 below). Scholarship changed as well. Archaeological activities increased knowledge of discrete areas and places. Independent governments and leaders demanded a national or regional aesthetic as a source of local glory and pride. The results of all these novelties still seek their analyst, but a few examples illustrate the range of the reactions. Turkey went through a phase of vertical allegiance to the Hittites rather than to the Ottomans. Egyptian architects at the turn of the 20th century built neo-Mamluk and neo-Pharaonic buildings. Sasanian and Achaemenid models determined the style of official monuments built under the Pahlavi dynasty (*reg* 1924–79) in Tehran. Sogdian art was seen as the precursor of Uzbek and Tajik, rather than Islamic, art in areas of western Central Asia under Soviet rule, although there is some ambivalence about the issue in scholarship. The ruined Buddhist temple at PAHARPUR in Bengal has been identified as the first monument of an art of Bangladesh different from that of Mughal India.

The powerful novelty of Modernism and Post-modernism as well as new economic possibilities led many leading European and American architects, including LOUIS I. KAHN, LE CORBUSIER, Frank Lloyd Wright, GORDON BUNSHAFT, Hans Hollein, ARTHUR ERICKSON, Robert Venturi, Ricardo Bofill and Paul Rudolf, to build or plan to build in the Islamic world. At the same time, international post-Cubist styles of painting appeared in every or nearly every art school from Rabat in Morocco to Dhaka in Bangladesh. All these factors may lead to local historiographies that will become more national or regional than universal.

The tension between cultivated memories of the distant past, an acute and often painful awareness of the immediate past and the new apparent universalism of Western technology and forms has not been resolved. It probably never will be, but it raises the question whether the notion of an Islamic art within a unified Islamic culture will be replaced by a series of national or regional definitions, in which the arts of traditional or classical Islamic times will be only an episode between many ancient traditions and a worldwide contemporaneity, which may or may not allow for individual expressions.

BIBLIOGRAPHY

Ghiyāth al-Din Jamshid al-Kashi: *Miftāḥ al-ḥisāb* [Key to calculation] (1427); ed. A. S. al-Damirdas and M. H. al-Hafani, rev. 'A. H. Lutfi (Cairo, 1967); ed. and Rus. trans. by B. A. Rozenfeld and others as *Kliuch arifmetiki traktat ob okruzhnosti* (Moscow, 1956)

L. Massignon: 'Les Méthodes de réalisation artistique des peuples de l'Islam', *Syria*, ii (1921), pp. 47–53, 149–60

P. Ricard: *Pour comprendre l'art musulman dans l'Afrique du Nord et en Espagne* (Paris, 1924)

E. H. Hankin: *The Drawing of Geometric Patterns in Saracenic Art* (Calcutta, 1925)

R. Ettinghausen: 'Al-Ghazzālī on Beauty', *Art and Thought, Issued in Honour of Dr. Ananda K. Coomaraswamy on the Occasion of his 70th Birthday*, ed. K. Bharatna Iyer (London, 1947), pp. 160–65; also in *Richard Ettinghausen: Islamic Art and Archaeology (Collected Papers)*, ed. M. Rosen-Ayalon (Berlin, 1984), pp. 16–21

M. Arkoun: 'L'Humanisme arabe au IX siècle', *Stud. Islam.*, xv (1961), pp. 63–87

P. P. Soucek: 'Nizami on Painters and Painting', *Islamic Art in the Metropolitan Museum of Art*, ed. R. Ettinghausen (New York, 1972), pp. 9–22

J. W. Allan: 'Abū'l-Qāsim's Treatise on Ceramics', *Iran*, xi (1973), pp. 111–20

O. Grabar: *The Formation of Islamic Art* (New Haven, 1973/R and enlarged 1987)

M. G. S. Hodgson: *The Venture of Islam: Conscience and History in a World Civilization*, i (Chicago, 1974), pp. 56–60

T. Burckhardt: *Art of Islam* (London, 1976)

K. Abu Deeb: *Al-Jurjāni's Theory of Poetic Imagery* (London, 1978)

R. Chadeiji: *Concepts and Influences* (London, 1986)

S. H. Nasr: *Islamic Art and Spirituality* (Albany, 1987)

M.-C. Burgat, ed.: *D'un Orient l'autre*, 2 vols (Paris, 1991)

D. Clevenot: *Une Esthétique du voile* (Paris, 1994)

OLEG GRABAR

2. GEOGRAPHY AND TRADE. The territories where Islam established a permanent political hegemony during its first century and where its most characteristic cultural and social institutions were created and disseminated included Iran from the Hindu Kush and the Amu (Oxus) River in the east to the Zagros and Caucasian highlands in the west, the Fertile Crescent and the Arabian peninsula, the lower Nile Valley and north-west Africa (see figs 2–4). Two adjoining regions were also important: southern Spain (Andalusia), mostly lost to Islam by the mid-13th century, and Anatolia, not fully incorporated into the greater Islamic world until that same era. The distinctive high culture that evolved in these regions was not the creation of any one centre. Rather, it emerged through a centuries-long dialogue, in which Bukhara and Nishapur were in constant communication with Baghdad, Baghdad with Damascus and Cairo, Cairo with Kairouan, Fez and Córdoba. The evolution of Islamic society and culture was strongly influenced by its physical setting, which imposes constraints to which any society must adapt. The topography and climate of the Middle East and North Africa created two crucial problems: severely limited possibilities for dense occupation of the land, and a consequent need for widely scattered settlements, each with a narrow resource base of its own, to exchange goods in order to get beyond bare subsistence.

(i) Settlement patterns. (ii) Commerce and communications.

(i) *Settlement patterns.* This vast region is characterized by an acute scarcity of water—90% is mountain, desert or semi-arid steppe. Water is concentrated in widely scattered areas. Thus Middle Eastern and North African populations are not evenly distributed but found in nodes and narrow bands. This pattern results in a close interaction between urban centres, their immediate agricultural hinterlands and the expanses of steppe and mountain that both separate and connect them.

Few areas get enough rain to support dry farming. Except for Anatolia and scattered valleys in certain favoured mountain ranges (e.g. the Rif of northern Morocco, the Yemen highlands, the Zagros of western Iran and the Caucasus), substantial rainfall is restricted to narrow coastlands that face prevailing winter winds and are backed by substantial mountains: north-west Africa from Casablanca (Morocco) to Cap Bon (Tunisia), the Syro-Lebanese coast, and the southern shore of the Caspian Sea. In north-west Africa the broad coastal plains have produced exportable surpluses of grain and olive oil throughout ancient and medieval times, while the southern Caspian region has been a major rice producer for centuries. The Syro-Lebanese coast is intensively cultivated, but its narrowness has made it much less important in this regard. Finally, mountain valleys can normally provide only a subsistence crop for their hard-pressed cultivators. In short, if agriculture in the traditional Islamic lands were restricted to areas with adequate rainfall, the prospects for human settlement there would be very limited indeed.

Between the Nile and the Amu rivers, however, the densest populations are found in the arid interior. This situation is possible only because these regions can draw excess rainfall from external sources. The most spectacular form of this phenomenon is found in the great river systems, fed by heavy rain and snow in remote highlands: the Nile, the Tigris–Euphrates, the Amu, the Syr and the Zarafshan. Such river systems are the basis for the vast irrigation schemes that have supported the agrarian civilizations of Egypt, Mesopotamia and Transoxiana for millennia. An equally critical role is played by innumerable but widely scattered oases. Small oases are often spring-fed, but the most important ones (e.g. Isfahan, Damascus or the Oued Draa in Morocco) are watered either by small streams that empty into the desert or—particularly in Iran and Afghanistan—by qanats, underground irrigation canals that tap water stored beneath the flanks of nearby mountain chains.

The study of medieval Islamic agriculture is still in its infancy. The most important cereals (the foundation of the Middle Eastern diet) were wheat and, in relatively arid or saline soils, barley. Rice was highy esteemed, but it could be grown only in a few areas and was hence very expensive. In the Mediterranean coastlands olive trees were cultivated, as in antiquity, but vineyards steadily lost their former importance as the population converted to Islam. In the hot interior oases and river valleys, wide tracts were dominated by vast date palm plantations. By the 9th century, at least, the inhabitants had access to a far wider array of fruits and vegetables—some native to the Middle East, but many others imported from India or East Africa—than did Europeans of that era. Sugar cane was cultivated in Egypt, the Levant and the Sous Valley of Morocco; by the 12th century it was an important export item. Finally, a variety of textile- and dye-producing plants—flax in Egypt, cotton in Khurasan and north Syria, indigo in Egypt and Iraq—were cultivated.

The economic, political and cultural significance of these facts is difficult to assess. Cereals yielded a relatively high return of harvest to seed, perhaps as much as 10:1 in irrigated zones. (Compare this to a typical ratio of 3:1 in Carolingian Europe, and 5 or 6:1 by the 13th century.) The effect of such yields was somewhat diluted by the intensive labour required for irrigated agriculture, but the yields could still support a high degree of urbanization as well as complex governmental superstructures. On the other hand, the towns of the region were in no way divorced from the agricultural hinterlands that surrounded them. As market and government centres, they dominated the countryside but were also imbedded within it.

Topographically, the typical configuration of an oasis settlement is that of a central walled city surrounded by smaller 'satellite' settlements, ranging from substantial

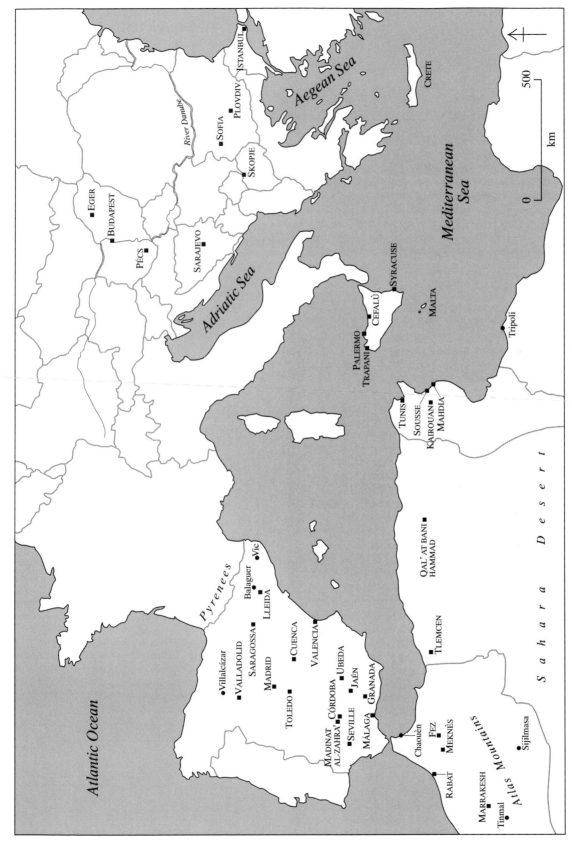

2. Map of the western Islamic lands; those areas with separate entries in this dictionary are distinguished by CROSS-REFERENCE TYPE

3. Map of the central Islamic lands; those areas with separate entries in this dictionary are distinguished by CROSS-REFERENCE TYPE

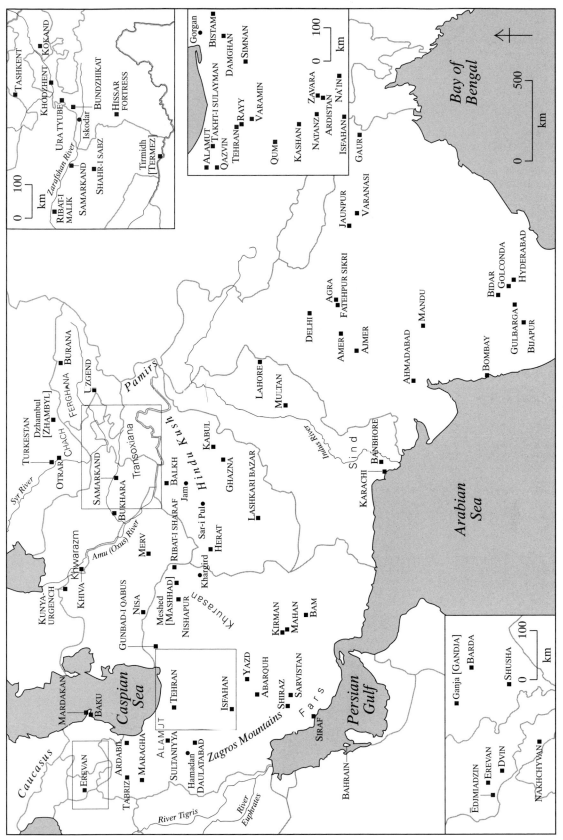

4. Map of the eastern Islamic lands; those areas with separate entries in this dictionary are distinguished by CROSS-REFERENCE TYPE

towns to hamlets (*see* §II, 10 below). Government officials and urban notables controlled most of the land in the adjacent rural districts. While government officials were usually strangers to the districts they ruled, the urban notables typically had close ties (of kinship, clientage or long-standing property rights) to the villages surrounding the cities where they lived. From the other side, villagers flowed into the towns, replenishing their populations and renewing their connections with the countryside. Many townspeople were agriculturalists, cultivating the gardens and orchards that lay adjacent to the city walls. Finally, villagers' sons who hoped to acquire an Islamic education, even to join the ranks of the learned, would gravitate to the nearest substantial town and (literally) sit at the feet of the scholars there.

The mountains, steppes and deserts that flank the oases and river valleys were (then as now) sparsely settled but not empty. They constituted zones of animal husbandry, which took a variety of forms: village sheep-herding, transhumant migration along defined routes between summer and winter pastures, and wide-ranging camel nomadism of the desert. The limited water and pasture in any one district can support a substantial body of people and animals only for a short time; most pastoralist groups thus have to adopt a nomadic way of life to survive. Not surprisingly, they prefer lush pasturage and ample water, and this draws them into lands cultivated by sedentary farmers. Nomad–sedentary interaction (*see* §6(iii) below) is often peaceful and symbiotic: the nomads' flocks pasture on the post-harvest stubble and manure the fields, while flour and simple implements are exchanged for hides and wool. But there is conflict as well. Especially in marginal agricultural districts, thinly settled and too remote for city-based governments to guard, war between 'the desert and the sown' was a recurrent reality.

The philosopher and historian Ibn Khaldun (1332–1406) defined nomadic pastoralism as a form of human social organization that was logically and chronologically prior to all others, and in this he followed the usual opinion of medieval Muslim city-dwellers. But in fact true pastoral nomadism—the herding of domesticated animals as opposed to hunting and gathering—arose along with or even post-dated settled agriculture. The earliest forms of pastoralism used animals (pigs, sheep and goats) that could not wander far from settled areas, and the herders often belonged to the villages and towns. Only the domestication of the horse and (in arid climates) the camel allowed nomadic peoples to achieve full social and political autonomy. But even so, by the rise of Islam in the 7th century nomadic pastoralists constituted an important demographic element in the Middle East and North Africa, especially in the interior steppe of Arabia and Syria. Moreover, they lay outside the direct political control of even the greatest states, though in normal times they could be policed adequately.

(ii) Commerce and communications. The distinctive settlement patterns of the central Islamic lands—scattered patches of dense population separated from one another by vast distances, empty deserts and formidable mountains—demanded commercial exchange. Few districts possessed sufficient resources to ensure anything better than bare subsistence for their populations. For this reason trade—both in staple and luxury goods—has been a major characteristic of Middle Eastern and North African societies since a very remote period. Perhaps no other region in the world has been so deeply shaped by commercial exchange or by the kinds of human and cultural intermingling that trade inevitably brings about.

In spite of appearances, communications within the traditional Islamic lands or with the outside world are not difficult given appropriate technology, and this has been available for a very long time. Ships adequate for long-distance coasting in the inland seas existed by the 3rd millennium BC, and seaborne traffic in the Mediterranean, the Red Sea and the Persian Gulf has been dense at least since the mid-2nd millennium BC. By the early 1st millennium BC, Greeks and Phoenicians had colonized the western Mediterranean and established a regular trade between the Red Sea and Persian Gulf on one side, India and East Africa on the other. Shipbuilding technology was conservative but far from stagnant; ships built for the Mediterranean steadily grew larger, stronger and faster. The seas were never safe: travel was contingent on prevailing winds and seasonal storms, and in spite of all efforts to respect these constraints, the sea bottoms are littered with the wreckage of unfortunate vessels.

Whatever the dangers, however, the sea routes were open and heavily used, ensuring that the Middle East and North Africa would have close contact with many cultures. Cultural borrowing was extremely selective but was always a reality. Commerce ensured a flow of new ethnic groups into the region as well, not only through the voluntary associations of merchants but also through the slave trade—a major channel of access to Sub-Saharan Africa until the late 19th century, and a link between Mediterranean Europe and North Africa until the 18th century.

Overland traffic was established far earlier than shipping; in some form it presumably dates back to the beginnings of human settlement. But for a very long time, regular large-scale exchange could only take place within relatively small zones because there was no way to transport large quantities of goods over the vast distances and arid terrain. Donkeys carried only modest loads and could not traverse the desert. Ox-drawn carts were clumsy and required passable roads. Both modes were therefore useful only for short-distance transport within thickly settled areas. From the 1st century BC, the Romans dealt with this problem through their famed system of roads, but these only smoothed communications within and between areas (Syria, Egypt, Anatolia, Tunisia) that had long been part of a strong commercial network.

By Roman times the problem had already been solved by the domestication of the camel. The Bactrian camel of Central Asia may have been domesticated as a draught animal by 2500 BC, the one-humped dromedary as a herd animal in South Arabia at more or less the same time. However, the dromedary did not become widely used in North Arabia and Syria until *c.* 1000 BC, by which time advances in saddling made it a highly effective beast of burden. Even then, a solid riding saddle for the dromedary, which would enormously increase the mobility and military striking power of the desert peoples of Arabia and Syria, would not be devised until the late Hellenistic–early Roman era (2nd and 1st centuries BC). From *c.* 1000 BC to the 20th century, camels proved to be an unequalled means of transport; they could travel 30 to 40 km per day in favourable circumstances, they could carry well over 250 kg, and they thrived on desert vegetation that other animals could not use. If a camel is a horse designed by committee, it is one of the most successful collective design projects in history. Certainly by Roman times, camel caravans carrying a well-organized long-distance trade were a familiar part of life in south-west Asia. Such caravans not only deepened and broadened trade patterns within the region, but also opened up the possibility of regular contact between north-east Iran and Inner Asia, even China. The famous SILK ROUTE was made possibly by the camel.

In sum, the geography and human ecology of south-west Asia and North Africa provided a generally stable framework for the evolution of political institutions, social patterns and cultural expression under the aegis of Islam. There were important local changes, as irrigation systems were extended or abandoned, as a given district passed from agricultural exploitation to pastureland and back again, as cities waxed and waned, and as important new crops were introduced and took hold. But in a broad sense, the land in 1800 looked much as it had in 650, and the technology of human adaptation and control was not greatly altered.

3. ETHNOGRAPHY. The ethnic groups that make up the population of the central Islamic lands have fluctuated constantly over the centuries. This fluctuation reflects not only the many invasions and migrations that have marked the history of the region, but also the very nature of ethnicity. A group usually perceives its ethnic identity as part of the permanent order of things. In reality, however, ethnicity is subjective and changeable; ethnic identity is no more than one's sense of the broad collectivity to which one belongs by virtue of language, shared customs and values, and distinctiveness *vis-à-vis* other groups. In this light, culture determines ethnicity, not ethnicity culture. Ethnic categories were not the only way in which people classified themselves, and they were seldom the most important. Other forms of social identity (such as religion, occupation and status group) commonly counted for more, ideologically and pragmatically. Nevertheless, ethnicity was deeply felt and played a major role in identifying one's place in society.

The array of ethnic groups and their territorial distribution in south-west Asia and North Africa on the eve of the Islamic conquests was roughly what it had been since the Hellenistic period (323–31 BC) a millennium earlier. Very broadly, the eastern third of this vast region, from the Zagros and Caucasus mountains to Transoxiana, the Pamirs and the Hindu Kush, was dominated by peoples speaking a variety of Iranian languages (many of them mutually unintelligible), who had established themselves on the plateau during the 2nd millennium BC. There were pockets of non-Iranian groups, particularly in the Caucasus and eastern Anatolia. More important, however, was the pressure from Turkic migrations in the north-east steppes beyond the Amu. By the 7th century AD, the steppes were already under Turkic political domination, though the

cities and their oases retained their autonomy and Iranian culture.

The central part of the region, from the Tigris to the Mediterranean and the Taurus Mountains to the Arabian Sea, was largely inhabited by peoples speaking Semitic languages. The majority of the population in the Fertile Crescent consisted of Aramaic-speaking villagers and townsmen, though the socio-political élites belonged to other groups—Iranian in the lower Tigris–Euphrates Valley (the political heartland of the Sasanian dynasty), Greco-Roman in Syria. The interior steppe was dominated by Arabic-speaking oasis-dwellers and nomads. Distinct from the sedentary populations of the Fertile Crescent, the Arabic-speakers intermingled with them, and in certain rural districts many adopted sedentary life. By the time of the Islamic conquests, Syria and the desert fringes of the Euphrates were thoroughly interpenetrated by sedentarized or semi-nomadic Arab tribes.

The Nile Valley showed the same type of mix as the Fertile Crescent—an indigenous population of peasants and townspeople (Copts descended from the ancient Egyptians and still speaking a form of the old Egyptian language), dominated by a Greek-speaking élite of land-owners and Roman officials concentrated in the coastal metropolis of Alexandria. North Africa was inhabited mostly by Berbers, a group of peoples speaking several distinct languages and existing at many cultural levels. A few areas, north-west Tunisia in particular, had a Latin-speaking élite as well. Some were descendants of Roman soldiers and other colonists, others were officials of the Roman Empire or the Church, many were native Berbers who had adopted Latin speech and Roman manners.

The Arab conquests of the 7th century set in motion major changes in this scheme of things, though these changes were not fully worked out for many centuries. The Arabs immediately supplanted the old socio-political élites from Spain to the Hindu Kush. The existing élites either fled (in North Africa, Syria and Egypt) or were compelled to take a second-echelon role (in Iran and Transoxiana). The Arab armies constituted a new élite, demarcated by their language, by their distinctive tribal social structure, and most of all by their new religion of Islam, which they tended to guard jealously. But the Arabs could not retain their élite status for long; by the mid-8th century they were beginning to lose their privileged place within the Islamic polity. Henceforth membership in the élite would require proximity to the throne; the ruling class would be made up of the caliph's servants and clients, whatever their native tongue and ethnic roots.

At this point a more profound impact of the Arab conquests began to be felt—the gradual Arabization of the indigenous populations of the Fertile Crescent, Egypt and North Africa. Bit by bit, beginning in the centres of Arab settlement and spreading outwards, Aramaeans, Copts and Berbers gave up their own languages and adopted Arabic. Likewise they began to adopt the conquerors' religion. Doctrinally, it is only a short step from Christianity to Islam, but culturally it marked a decision to abandon the rituals, habits and values of one's ancestors and to become like the newcomers. It could be argued that the Arabs and their subjects assimilated to one another, but even where the Arabs adopted their subjects' ways, they converted them into elements within an Arab identity. Not everyone adopted Arabic speech or became a Muslim; the process ran rapidly in the major towns and their fertile hinterlands, but far more slowly in the remoter villages and mountains, where Arab troops were not quartered and tribes did not move in.

Iran kept its ancient language for everyday speech, though for some three centuries (c. 650–950) Arabic supplanted it as the sole written language of Iranian converts to Islam. Even after the emergence of New Persian as a literary vehicle in the 10th century, Arabic long continued to be the preferred language of the religious sciences, philosophy and science—in this way playing a role like that of Latin in medieval and Renaissance Europe. Iranians held on to their own cultural heritage and ethnic identity; few ever cared to be regarded as Arabs. Under Islam, indeed, Persian culture came to have a far wider influence than it had ever enjoyed in ancient times. Iranian political ideas were quickly absorbed in the Islamic synthesis, and the kings and heroes of pre-Islamic Iran were eagerly emulated among the Turks. By the 13th century Persian was widely cultivated among Muslims in India (many of them admittedly Iranian immigrants), and India remained a major centre of Persian letters until the 19th century. When Turkish emerged in Anatolia and western Central Asia as a major literary tongue after 1500, it was profoundly shaped by Persian vocabulary, rhetoric and grammar. Islam spread, however, quite as readily in Iran and Transoxiana as elsewhere—by the 10th century a clear majority of Iranians had become Muslims—and the Arabic alphabet rapidly supplanted the older writing system. Even here the Arab conquests had a deep if somewhat attenuated impact: they did not alter the ethnic identity of the indigenous population, but they did change very markedly the content of that identity.

The ethnic impact of the Arab conquests within the traditional Islamic lands was largely absorbed by the 11th century, when a new group, the Turkic peoples of Central Asia, began to penetrate the domains of Islam. The Turks had long been a growing presence in Transoxiana, and many of them had been brought into Islamic territories as slaves, especially from the early 9th century. By the late 10th century many Turkic groups were converting to Islam, due both to its great cultural prestige in Transoxiana and to the work of Sufi missionaries. One outgrowth of this conversion was the establishment of new Muslim kingdoms in Turkish lands, and hence a spread of the Islamic political domain without additional conquests. But soon the Turks began migrating into the Islamic heartlands of north-east Iran, a process that began with the Saljuq incursions of the 1020s and continued, sometimes peacefully, sometimes violently, for another four centuries.

The Turkish impact was different from the Arab, but hardly less significant. The Turks brought no new religion; they came as Muslims, or adopted Islam soon after their arrival. Nor (except in Transoxiana and Anatolia) did they Turkify the existing populations, who quite steadfastly held on to their Iranian, Kurdish, Arab and other identities. But the Turks came in much larger numbers than had the Arabs and competed fiercely for pasture, in both the steppes and highlands. In some regions they became a major element in the ethnic mix (e.g. northern Syria, the

Jazira, Fars); in others they were soon the dominant group (e.g. Azerbaijan and central Anatolia). During this long period Transoxiana was definitively Turkified, leaving only a few islands of Iranian speech and culture in such cities as Bukhara and Samarkand.

Like the Arabs, the Turks constituted the political–military élite of the countries they occupied, but for a far longer period. Arab hegemony had lasted for no more than a century and a half; the Turks created the ruling dynasties of the region and dominated its armies into the 20th century. In spite of their material power, however, they were slow to claim cultural leadership over the lands they ruled. Only in the late 15th century did Turkish become a common literary tongue even in Anatolia or Transoxiana, where Turks were a clear majority of the Muslim population. Until then, most Turkish courts used Arabic or Persian even for their administrative business. In Persian- or Arabic-speaking regions, the Turks deferred to their subjects—no doubt because these languages were those of Islam and Islamic culture, over which the Turks had made themselves protectors.

In spite of the immense changes wrought by the Arab and Turkish invasions in the ethnic structures of the Middle East and North Africa, pockets of the pre-Islamic populations survived. The Fertile Crescent possessed Christian communities that retained not only their religion but their ancient language, as with the Assyrians of northern Mesopotamia. Other groups, such as the Maronites of Mt Lebanon and the Copts in Upper Egypt, adopted Arabic speech but otherwise kept their traditional religion and ethnic identity. In the Atlas Mountains of North Africa the Berbers had uniformly adopted Islam by the 12th century, but they retained their ancient tongues, distinctive social organization and fierce pride in being Berber. In the highlands of eastern Anatolia and north-west Iran, the Armenians held on to their Christian faith as well as their language. The neighbouring Kurds, in contrast, followed the Berber pattern: they soon adopted Islam but remained a people apart. Although educated Kurds wrote in Arabic or Persian or (eventually) Turkish, they continued to speak Kurdish and to insist on their Kurdish identity.

Ethnic change in the traditional Islamic lands has been influenced by religious affiliation and political dominance, but a strong core of identity survives. Ethnic continuity is not a mystical phenomenon. The crucial (though not the sole) variable is probably geographical isolation from the major centres of the dominant culture, and this isolation was best ensured by dwelling in the mountains. Invaders easily dominated the cities, the oases, even the steppe, but the mountains were too difficult to penetrate and too poor to be worth the effort. Here the languages and cultures of the pre-Islamic era could hold on—not unaffected by the vast changes of centuries, but not overwhelmed either.

The ethnic profile of south-west Asia and North Africa thus underwent great changes during the 12 centuries of Islamic domination. Of these the most visible and important were directly connected to the great political convulsions within the region. In AD 600 Arabs and Turks were unimportant frontiersmen within the ancient city-based agrarian societies of south-west Asia and North Africa. In 1800 almost the entire region from the Atlantic coast of

Morocco to the Tigris was Arab in speech and cultural identity. From Tunisia to Central Asia political hegemony was firmly in the grip of various Turkish dynasties and tribal confederations. The Iranians had not expanded their zone of ethnic predominance and now played second fiddle to Turks in the government of their ancient homeland. On the other hand, Iranian cultural influence was felt from Istanbul to Delhi.

4. DEMOGRAPHY. No detailed demographic study of medieval Islamic societies is now possible, nor will it ever be. Even gross population figures are sheer guesswork until the mid-19th century, and there is no usable evidence for such crucial statistics as sex ratios, age-cohort pyramids and birth and death rates. However, a few generalizations can be advanced.

The overall population of the central Islamic lands probably held steady throughout the first seven centuries of Islam (i.e. to 1300). At the time of the Arab conquests, populations in the Mediterranean basin may have been depressed by historic standards, due to the lingering effects of the Justinianic plague, which continued until the mid-8th century. After 750 there may have been some general increase in population over a period of two or three centuries; the clear indications of urban growth and agricultural and commercial expansion during this era make such a statement plausible, albeit far from certain.

Between c. 1000 and 1340 the population probably stagnated and may even have declined slightly. Certain countries, such as Egypt in the 1060s and again from 1200 to 1202, suffered hideous famines. The massacres and destruction of the Mongol invasions in 13th-century Iran far exceeded the usual mortality of medieval warfare. In general, the level of warfare and insecurity was extremely high during this period, a factor that in itself tends to depress birth rates. But catastrophic events were localized and sporadic; overall, there was downward pressure, not sharp decline.

The Black Death, however, was undeniably a demographic disaster, not only in the years 1347–9, when as much as one-third of the population in many districts may have perished, but for centuries after. The Black Death ushered in a new era of endemic plague, characterized by periodic outbreaks throughout the region. These were localized but severe, and it was typical for a city to be 'visited' by a season of plague every 10–20 years. These periodic epidemics, which ended only in the early 19th century, prevented the area from achieving a full demographic recovery until perhaps the beginning of the 20th century. Indeed, it seems likely that, by 1800, overall populations from Morocco to Iran had barely recovered their levels on the eve of the Black Death five centuries earlier.

What numbers are to be associated with these trends? Some crude census statistics for the 1830s and 1840s can serve as a base-line for the early Islamic period. For 1830, Issawi estimated a total population in south-west Asia and North Africa of 34 million; by 1914 (a point at which there is quite reliable data for French North Africa, Egypt and the Ottoman empire, though not for Iran), this figure had doubled. This increase reflects immigration and the simple public health measures of that period, but the bulk

of it must be due simply to the end of major epidemics and improvements in nutrition and living standards. A number between these two extremes (no doubt towards the lower end) probably reflects the population of the period 750–1000.

BIBLIOGRAPHY
G. Le Strange: *Lands of the Eastern Caliphate* (Cambridge, 1905)
W. B. Fisher: *The Middle East: A Physical, Social, and Regional Geography* (London, 1950, rev. 7/1978)
A. K. S. Lambton: *Landlord and Peasant in Persia* (London, 1953, rev. 1969)
S. D. Goitein: *A Mediterranean Society*, 5 vols (Berkeley, 1967–88) [esp. vols i and iv]
A. Miquel: *La Géographie humaine du monde musulman jusqu'au milieu du 11e siècle*, 3 vols (Paris and The Hague, 1967–80) [esp. vol. iii, *Le Milieu naturel*]
W. B. Fisher, ed.: *The Land of Iran* (1968), i of *The Cambridge History of Iran* (Cambridge, 1968–91)
I. M. Lapidus, ed.: *Middle Eastern Cities* (Berkeley, 1969)
R. W. Bulliet: *The Camel and the Wheel* (Cambridge, MA, 1975)
E. Ashtor: *A Social and Economic History of the Near East in the Middle Ages* (London, 1976)
M. W. Dols: *The Black Death in the Middle East* (Princeton, 1976)
Tübinger Atlas des Vorderen Orients (Wiesbaden, 1977–)
R. Weekes, ed.: *Muslim Peoples: A World Ethnographic Survey* (Westport, CT, 1978, rev. 1984)
R. W. Bulliet: *Conversion to Islam in the Medieval Period* (Cambridge, MA, 1979)
W. C. Brice: *An Historical Atlas of Islam* (Leiden, 1981)
C. Issawi: *An Economic History of the Middle East and North Africa* (New York and London, 1982)
A. M. Watson: *Agricultural Innovation in the Early Islamic World* (Cambridge, 1983)

5. HISTORY. Institutional and ideological criteria suggest three broad periods for Islamic history in pre-modern times. The first (c. AD 600–c. 900) is characterized ideologically by a widely shared vision of a single universal community under a single ruler and politically by Arab hegemony. The career of Muhammad was, of course, of prime importance in determining the political history of Islam, which can be viewed from an ideological perspective as the constant struggle of Muslim rulers to demonstrate that they were Muhammad's rightful successors. These three centuries also represent the period when Islam defined itself as a distinctive religion and culture. The long middle period (c. 900–c. 1500), which can be further subdivided at its midway point with the end of Saljuq rule and the devastations of the Mongol invasions, is characterized by political fragmentation and instability on one level, but on another by there emergence of autonomous religious institutions and increasingly diverse cultural expression. The Arab domination of the first period gave way to Turkish (or in North Africa, Berber) political ascendency. In the third period (c. 1500–c. 1800) there was a political reconsolidation in the form of the Ottoman and Safavid empires, as well as that of the Mughals in the Indian subcontinent. These states were not only large and powerful; they were also remarkably durable, and created a framework of institutions and values that lasted into the 20th century.

(i) Introduction. (ii) The career of Muhammad (610–32). (iii) The caliphate and the age of Arab ascendancy (632–c. 900). (iv) Early Middle period (c. 900–c. 1200). (v) Later Middle period (c. 1200–c. 1500). (vi) Early Modern period (c. 1500–19th century).

(i) Introduction. The expression 'Islamic history', almost universally used, is both a misnomer and an anomaly (*see also* §1 above). A misnomer, because it does not refer to

the history of the religion of ISLAM as such, but rather to the whole historical development of a certain group of peoples, of whom many were not even Muslims. An anomaly, because it is rare nowadays to subsume a society under the name of its paramount religion. Yet the very oddness of the term serves a purpose. 'Islamic history' implies that the leading roles in society were taken by those who identified themselves primarily (though never exclusively) as Muslims, who legitimized their privileged status by that identity, and who regarded themselves as members of a great religious commonwealth transcending local loyalties, ethnic divisions and political boundaries.

This section concentrates on the period from the emergence of Islam in the early 7th century to the late 18th century–early 19th, a date marking the beginnings of European political hegemony in much of the Islamic world, when the East India Company attained paramountcy in South Asia under Robert Clive and Warren Hastings, Napoleon occupied Egypt (1798–1801), the Russo-Turkish War (1768–74) led to the Russian occupation of the Tatar Khanates and the weakening Ottoman grip in the Balkans, and the Treaty of Gulistan (1813) was concluded between Russia and Iran. Far more important than European political domination, however, was a profound break in cultural continuity and social organization. A single example will suffice. By the mid-19th century, Islamic law (Arab. *shari'a*), which heretofore had proved both stable and highly adaptable, seemed ill-suited to address many of the legal and economic needs of Muslims. Since the *shari'a* was not merely a code of law, but rather the whole body of religious and social duties incumbent on all believers, its apparent inadequacies struck at the very heart of Muslim identity. What was true for the *shari'a* was true for other realms of life. In literature and the arts, established genres and techniques progressively lost vitality and were replaced by imports of European origin. Soon enough, the old culture and the social order in which it had been rooted were lost beyond recall. There was (and still is) a struggle to reinvigorate certain core elements of tradition and fuse them into an authentically Islamic way of life, but whatever comes out of this struggle will be modern, not a resurrection of the old.

(ii) The career of Muhammad (610–32). Islamic politics, like the religion itself, begin with the Prophet Muhammad (*c.* 570–632). Not only was he the vessel through whom the new revelation was transmitted to the peoples of Arabia, but his career as the founder of a new community was the very model of political action for all later generations. The fundamental principle of Muhammad's legacy was simple but demanding: that the sole legitimate object of politics was to build a society committed to the fulfilment of God's commandments, as given in his revealed word (the KORAN) and in the Prophet's own teaching and example (the Sunna). Anything else was mere worldly ambition.

The kernel of the new religio-social order brought by Muhammad was stated at the very outset of his prophetic career. The earliest revelations he proclaimed in public carry three interwoven doctrines: the absolute oneness and uniqueness of God (Allah), who alone merited worship and obedience, the terrible reality of the Last Judgement, and the virtues of charity and justice that God demanded of every person. The significance of this threefold doctrine was deepened by another message, that God demanded obedience not only from individuals but from communities. In his mercy, God has sent a prophet to every nation. Those that accept the teachings of their prophet will prosper; those that turn away in contempt—the vast majority—face a fearful retribution in this world. A prophet struggles not only to bring salvation in the hereafter to a few individuals, but also to redeem his people from imminent destruction.

According to tradition Muhammad was called to be a prophet *c.* 610 in his native town of MECCA. Mecca had little water and stony soil, but it derived a certain prominence from the regional commerce that it controlled (though it was hardly of global importance, as many have asserted) and from the sanctuary complex centred on the famous shrine of the Ka'ba, the object of an annual pilgrimage among the tribes of west Arabia. The economic and religious life of Mecca had been dominated by the tribe of Quraysh since early in the 6th century AD. Muhammad was himself a man of Quraysh, and for several years he interpreted his mission as the redemption of his fellow tribesmen. To them he brought no new message, but rather the old truths already revealed to the Jews and Christians. During this period Muhammad accepted the basic structures of Meccan society as a given; he strove only to purify that society of vice and false belief. But the leading clans of Quraysh correctly perceived that his message threatened the whole system that they had created and from which they benefited. His efforts were rejected by most of Quraysh and even by many of his near kinsmen. By 619 (marked by the deaths of his wife and closest uncle) his mission was frustrated and his life in danger; if he was to continue, he would have to go elsewhere.

His chance came when leaders of the agricultural oasis of MEDINA, some 325 km north of Mecca, invited him to come and arbitrate a bloody feud between the two tribes dwelling there. The Hegira (*hijra*: 'migration to a place of refuge') in 622 marks the birth date of the Islamic polity. A new political community was created by a treaty between Muhammad, Meccan adherents who had fled with him and the established tribes of Medina. In form this community (*umma*) was a traditional tribal confederation. In substance, however, it was something radically different: the community was to be one of salvation, mandated by God to create a just and righteous society on earth under the leadership of his chosen prophet. In contrast to the existing tribal system, membership in the community was determined not by kinship, but by the voluntary acceptance of Muhammad's teaching.

The new community did not go unchallenged even in Medina. Some of the established tribal leaders resented Muhammad's supremacy and tried to subvert his position. They found natural allies in three Jewish clans long settled in the oasis. These were included in the Medina confederation and were thereby subject to Muhammad's authority, but they rejected the prophetic claims that legitimized his authority. The old tribal chiefs ultimately came around, but the Jews were less fortunate. Religious tensions aside,

Muhammad suspected them of colluding with Quraysh and other opponents. In a chain of disastrous confrontations, two of the clans were exiled, and in 627 the adult males of the third were executed, the women and children enslaved.

Exile from Mecca and the struggle with the Jews of Medina quickly demonstrated to Muhammad and his followers that they were a distinct people with a distinct religious identity. It was now clear that the revelations vouchsafed to Muhammad did not merely renew the ancient stream of prophecy; rather, they completed and superseded the older scriptures. Like the Jews and Christians, Muhammad's people were spiritual heirs of Abraham, but they would restore the original purity of his legacy. In Medina the new religion received its own name, Islam (*islām*: 'devoting oneself to God'); its adherents would be called Muslims.

Muhammad's confederation was founded in Medina, but it could not be confined there. Quraysh had to be brought into Islam if at all possible, the crucial sanctuary of Mecca redeemed from idolatry and restored to worship of the true God. In a series of battles and diplomatic initiatives between 624 and 630, Mecca was challenged, then checked and finally compelled to accept Muhammad's authority. Simultaneously the oasis settlements and desert tribes of western and central Arabia were brought within Medina's network, sometimes by conquest but often through negotiation. In accordance with the confederation's original principles, submission to Muhammad's political authority entailed acceptance of Islam. Jewish and Christian groups were an exception: they could retain their religious beliefs and practices so long as they recognized Muslim political supremacy. By Muhammad's death in 632 the framework of a new religio-political order in Arabia had been erected.

(iii) The caliphate and the age of Arab ascendancy (632–c. 900). Had Muhammad's first successors merely held his confederation together in the face of the severe centrifugal forces that afflicted it, that would have been remarkable enough. The immediate issue—whether the Muslims should continue to be, as in Muhammad's lifetime, not merely a body of believers but also a single polity under a single head—was quickly resolved by the election of Abu Bakr (*reg* 632–4) as his successor (*khalīfa*, hence caliph). Some of the allied tribes tried to secede from the Islamic confederation now that the Prophet was gone, but a bitter two-year war ended this effort. For the next six centuries the majority of articulate Muslims would regard the political unity of the community—real if possible, merely symbolic if necessary—as a central Islamic value.

Abu Bakr's campaigns not only restored Muhammad's confederation, but also led to an enormous territorial expansion. Muslim forces had subjugated all Arabia and penetrated into Palestine and lower Iraq. Under the second caliph, 'Umar (*reg* 634–44), these latter initiatives rapidly became a conquest of the Fertile Crescent, then Egypt and the highlands of western Iran. With these stunning events, which drove the Byzantine empire north of the Taurus Mountains and destroyed the Sasanian empire, the Arabs ceased to be marginal frontiersmen and became rulers of the economic and cultural heartlands of the Ancient Near East. Nor was Islam any longer an odd Arabian cult, but the religion of an imperial élite.

The conquests slowed markedly during the 650s but never came to a halt. By 715, Spain, North Africa, Transoxiana and Sind were under Islamic domination. At this point, however, the Arab–Muslim armies reached their limits; henceforth, until the 11th century, consolidation rather than expansion was the rule. The frontiers of 715 mark the zone within which the fundamental characteristics of medieval Islamic society and culture would be defined. Territorial expansion came with a price. The conquerors retained their ethnic and religious identity in a radically new social and cultural environment, but tensions within the Arab–Muslim élite increased as the early caliphs struggled to transform a loose confederation into a coherent state. Inevitable disparities of status and income led to conflicting visions of the just society mandated by Islam. Those who felt wronged accused their opponents not merely of tyranny but of apostasy. The third caliph, 'Uthman (*reg* 644–56), was murdered in a revolt of disaffected Muslims, an event that forever tainted the legitimacy of the caliphate and opened the gates to a century of intermittent civil war.

Political dissidence quickly turned into religious schism, and schism soon produced a welter of sects with irreconcilable theological doctrines. By the early 700s three broad religio-political orientations had emerged. Many Muslims were devoted to the aspirations embodied in 'Ali ibn Abi Talib—the fourth caliph (*reg* 656–61), the first male convert to Islam and the Prophet's cousin and son-in-law. These were labelled Shi'ites ('partisans [of 'Ali]'). At first they simply pointed to 'Ali's justice, religious knowledge and closeness to the Prophet. Moreover, they argued that the head of the community should be a lineal descendant of Muhammad through 'Ali and the Prophet's daughter Fatima. By the 700s, however, most Shi'ites also held that such a leader would not be merely a ruler but also a divinely guided, infallible religious teacher—not merely *khalīfa* but *imām*. Indeed, the community could only achieve justice and salvation under the guidance of a true imam. Some groups went even further, ascribing supernatural status and powers to the imams, and some of these doctrines entered into the 'classical' formulations of Shi'ite theology in the 10th century.

The Shi'ites appealed to deeply felt values and sentiments and could sometimes command widespread support. But constant divisions within the movement, together with the distaste of many Muslims for the doctrines of its extremists, prevented the Shi'ites from placing an 'Alid imam over the community as a whole. Even in its moments of political triumph, Shi'ism almost always remained a minority movement. In this regard the ABBASID revolution (745–50) is paradigmatic. Its roots lay in a radical Shi'ite sect, and the Abbasids seized power on the basis of a broad (albeit equivocal) Shi'ite programme. Once in power the Abbasids not only turned their backs on their erstwhile partisans, but even subjected many of them to severe persecution.

A second orientation rejected both 'Ali and his rivals; the numerous factions following this line were collectively known as Kharijites ('seceders'). They stressed the equality of all believers and asserted that the head of the community must be replaced if he committed injustice or sinned. For radical Kharijites, sin was tantamount to apostasy, and a 'fallen' leader was thus subject to execution. Such a doctrine did little to promote political cohesion, and the Kharijites were doomed to the margins of Islamic political life. However, certain groups did dominate parts of North Africa for about a century and a half (*c.* 750–*c.* 900). A few isolated Kharijite communities in Oman and the Algerian Sahara have even survived into modern times.

The largest but also the least clearly defined orientation was at first embodied in the caliphal loyalists. These believed that the unity and integrity of the community outweighed all other considerations. So long as the actual caliphs held the community together, provided a modicum of justice and security and adhered to Islam, their government was legitimate. On such grounds, this group denounced the murder of 'Uthman, and after 'Ali's defeat in the first civil war they rallied around his rival and successor, Mu'awiya. When Mu'awiya bequeathed his office to his own kinsmen (the UMAYYAD family), the loyalists continued to recognize them, albeit reluctantly in some cases. Finally, when the Umayyads were overthrown in 750, the caliphal loyalists accepted the claims of their Abbasid successors. No doubt there was an element of passivity or opportunism in all this, but there was also a point of principle: that justice and salvation were impossible in the midst of violence and anarchy. Moreover, the caliphal loyalists believed that the obligation to establish an Islamic doctrine and way of life fell on the believers as a whole, not on a divinely chosen imam. From this perspective, the identity of the community's rulers was in some sense irrelevant so long as they were minimally competent.

By the mid-8th century the caliphal loyalists began to call themselves *ahl al-sunna wa'l-jamā'a* ('the people of tradition and unity')—or more simply, Sunnis—and ultimately they came to represent the mainstream religio-political orientation in Islam. The Sunnis respected the caliph's political prerogatives but rejected his claims to special religious authority. Rather, it was the caliph's duty to submit to and enforce the legal and theological doctrines articulated by the community's learned men ('*ulamā*', hence ulema), scholars whose status was validated not by the State or any formal religious institution, but simply by their mutual reputation among themselves. A determined effort by the Abbasids during the mid-9th century to impose a controversial dogma failed in the face of ulema and popular resistance, and thereafter the autonomy of scholars became a basic principle of Sunni Islam.

Efforts to identify the social roots of these orientations have yielded little. All three originated among Arab Muslims; at bottom they represented ideological, not ethnic cleavages. By the late 8th century the increasing stream of converts to Islam among the conquered peoples was changing the ethnic profile of the new religion. As time went on, conversion certainly altered the social context of these religio-political debates, and inevitably it sharpened their sophistication. However, conversion did nothing to change the basic premises of the three orientations, which had been firmly articulated by 800.

Even as Muslims worked out their key religious doctrines and the political and social principles that should govern the community's life, the caliphate was undergoing a major transformation. Initially *primus inter pares*, the caliph soon had to assert his authority more forcefully in order to control his sprawling empire. 'Uthman came to grief, but Mu'awiya (*reg* 661–80) kept the reins in his own hands by naming a few able governors who had no political base of their own and were firmly committed to his interests. In effect, he exercised power through personal clients. The later Umayyads continued this technique, but also built a bureaucracy and household staff. The bitter civil war (680–92) revealed that caliphal authority now rested ultimately on coercion and increasingly turned the caliphs into autocrats segregated even from their Muslim subjects.

The Abbasid revolution, although it claimed to restore the pristine community of the Prophet, only reinforced these trends. By the 10th century grandiose ceremonial had insulated the caliph from all but his highest officials and intimate courtiers, while the apparatus of government had become extraordinarily complex—the very model of a proper State in the eyes of later Islamic dynasties. The Abbasids strove to eliminate all entities standing between them and their subjects. The Umayyads had recruited their high officials from the notables of favoured Arab tribes, and their armies had been constituted of tribal units as well. The Abbasids made the tribes politically and administratively irrelevant; henceforth every soldier and official would be regarded as a slave or client of the caliph.

This process was perhaps most striking in the military sphere. The Abbasids had been brought to power by an army recruited in the north-east Iranian province of Khurasan. The commanders of this army and the bulk of its manpower were Arabs, but from the outset their tribal affiliations had been suppressed. For 60 years the revolutionary army was the backbone of the regime; as time passed the original troops were replaced by their sons and grandsons. But the old army dissolved in a bitter civil war (810–19) between various scions of the ruling dynasty, and a new army was needed. The solution was found by al-Mu'tasim (*reg* 833–42). While governor of Egypt in the 820s, he had assembled a guard of several thousand Turkish slaves (*mamlūk*s). Slave troops offered important advantages, since they were bound to their master, had no competing loyalties and could be trained to a high standard. On becoming caliph, al-Mu'tasim made his slave corps the élite force in his army. When they clashed with the populace of BAGHDAD, he moved his capital north to the new palace city of SAMARRA', where he segregated them in the palace compound and strictly limited their contact with ordinary citizens. Al-Mu'tasim's mamluks provided him with several able generals and governors but were hard to control; in 861 disgruntled mamluks assassinated the caliph al-Mutawakkil (*reg* 847–61) and seized control of the government for more than a decade. Despite the dangers of the institution, it captured the fancy of Muslim rulers, and from the late 9th century almost every one tried to recruit his own mamluk corps. Indeed, the institution became a trademark of Islamic political life. Moreover, not only did mamluk regiments often dominate the dynasties that they ostensibly served, they were sometimes the seedbed of new regimes.

Al-Mutawakkil's assassination marked a turning-point in the political evolution of Islam. In effect it licensed every adventurer to seek his own fortune. At the geographical extremes of the caliphate, such men had been carving out hereditary spheres of influence for some decades, but now this tendency blossomed in the heartlands of the empire. By 900 the caliphs could assert effective control only over Iraq and south-west Iran; their other dominions were all in the hands of local warlords. From the 10th century down to the end of the Abbasid dynasty in 1258, the caliph's authority as head of the community would be symbolic rather than real. The vision of one body of believers, joined together in a single state under a single head, would remain compelling, but it would seldom be more than a vision.

The local regimes that appeared between 861 and 1000 shared several characteristics. First, most were military dictatorships; their authority was based on the capacity to crush their rivals, inspire fear in their subjects and reward their followers. States of this kind were merely a dense but frail web of vested interests. They possessed no innate legitimacy whatever and were fair game for any challenger who commanded superior resources.

Second, they were perpetually short of cash to pay their troops and could not afford the administrative machinery to collect adequate revenues. They therefore improvised: soldiers (the officers, at least) were to collect their stipends directly from the peasantry. Each payee was assigned a village or group of villages, the tax payments of which were estimated by the central exchequer as equal to his salary and expenses; he would then send his men to collect these payments. In principle these revenue assignments (*iqṭāʿ*) were temporary and revocable, and they conferred no judicial or administrative rights over the villagers. The reality varied with circumstances, but the more powerful states, such as the early Saljuqs and the Mamluks of Syria and Egypt, did supervise their *iqṭāʿ*-holders effectively. At first the *iqṭāʿ* was a makeshift affair, aimed strictly at fiscal goals, but it quickly permeated the whole political–administrative system. By the 12th century *iqṭāʿ*s were often tied to particular offices and ranks: an officer's *iqṭāʿ* often required him to recruit and train a defined number of cavalry, while a provincial governor would meet the expenses of his office out of *iqṭāʿ*s reserved for that purpose. The *iqṭāʿ* was convenient but dangerous, since it gave ambitious soldiers an independent power base; even so, the *iqṭāʿ* and its many variants were the fiscal–administrative foundation of almost every regime from the early 10th century to the mid-19th.

These regimes were typically alien to the lands and peoples they ruled. For example, the progenitor of the Tulunid dynasty in Egypt (*reg* 868–905) had been a Turkish mamluk in Baghdad, while the Buyid rulers of Iraq and western Iran (*reg* 932–1062) were mountaineers from the highlands south of the Caspian. Even genuinely local dynasties, such as the Saffarids of south-east Iran (*reg* 867–1003), were in the hands of rough soldiers. Under these circumstances, ordered government was only possible through an alliance between the military rulers (*amīr*s) and local notables (*aʿyān*). These latter supplied administrative expertise, but equally important, their social prestige and religious learning made the regimes they served acceptable to the people at large. This system would remain a keystone of government in Islam down to modern

times. On another level, the alliance between 'foreign' soldiers and 'indigenous' bureaucrats reflected an important social process that was beginning to transform the Middle East and North Africa. The new political system rested on widespread conversion to Islam, in particular among local social élites. Islamic government in the provinces no longer required the presence of the caliph and his officials.

The notables who staffed the bureaucracy and judiciary were normally men of property. Government service offered enticing career opportunities to them, but it was also a means of defending their family wealth and status against rapacious military chieftains, not to mention bureaucrats from rival clans. To be sure, senior officials seldom stayed at home. Rather, they were usually attached to the entourage of a given prince and followed his peregrinations. Even so, they always retained significant social and economic links with their birthplaces.

The bureaucracy provided the notables with a formal channel of influence on State policy, but their informal roles were equally important. Middle-period Islamic regimes had extremely limited resources; even to impose a modicum of law and order and collect taxes required someone to mediate between rulers and subjects. Notables were simply those 'men of standing' whose family ties, wealth and religious learning allowed them to do this. Some were themselves State officials, others were noted religious scholars, but most often it is impossible to say exactly why one man was a notable while another was not. As with so many of the basic social and political institutions of medieval Islam, the work of notables was informal to an extreme, a matter of consensus and personal ties rather than legally constituted institutions.

(iv) Early Middle period (c. 900–c. 1200). The 10th century began with one last effort to reclaim the vision of a unitary caliphate. A radical Shi'ite movement (the Ismaʿilis) seized control of most of North Africa (909) in the name of a heretofore secret imam claiming direct descent from ʿAli and Fatima. Known as the Fatimid dynasty, they aspired far beyond the Maghrib, aiming to overthrow the Abbasid usurpers and reunite the whole community under their own authority. Since the Fatimids claimed to be imams, moreover, they would be infallible religious teachers as well as temporal rulers; theirs would literally be the government of God. The Fatimid challenge soon faltered. Their religious claims were rejected even by most Shi'ites, and though they conquered Egypt in 969, their dominions never extended much beyond Damascus. By the mid-11th century the Fatimids were just another regional dynasty with delusions of grandeur; in 1171 they were suppressed almost without resistance by Salah al-Din. For the great majority of Muslims the Abbasids still symbolized the fading dream of one community under one head.

Most other middle-period states were military dictatorships (see fig. 5). Some were solo ventures, but more often they were family affairs. Family solidarity in these regimes typically took the form of the family confederation or appanage state, a type of political organization especially characteristic of regimes founded by frontier groups from the steppes or mountains. Examples include the Buyids; the Saljuqs (*reg* 1038–1194; *see* Saljuq, §I), who began as

5. *Court of Badr al-Din Lu'lu'*, regent and later ruler of Mosul (*reg* 1222–59), 170×128 mm; frontispiece from vol. xvii of a copy of Abu'l-Faraj al-Isfahani's *Kitāb al-aghānī* ('Book of songs'), from ?Mosul, *c.* 1218–19 (Istanbul, National Library, Feyzullah Effendi/1566, fol. 1*r*)

wandering Turkomans from the Aral basin; and the AYYUBID dynasty (*reg* 1169–1260), descended from Kurdish soldiers of fortune from south-east Anatolia. Such groups were far removed from the monarchical–bureaucratic traditions of the cities; among them political power was regarded as the rightful possession of an entire lineage. They thought it natural for a man to share power with the kinsmen who had helped him win it. Likewise, on his death he ought to distribute his status and wealth among all his sons and brothers.

A family confederation was thus a polity in which every leading male member of the ruling lineage was assigned a territory to govern in his own right. These princes were not equal in lands and status; they were in principle subordinate to a paramount ruler who was regarded as head of the family. Within his own appanage, however, each prince was autonomous and normally retained the right of hereditary succession. Such confederations could be cohesive when the paramount prince had high prestige within the ruling family, for example as the charismatic founder of an empire or the father of the major appanage princes. Dissension was otherwise inevitable. There were

no clear rules of succession; even the death of an appanage prince, let alone the paramount ruler, was a major crisis. Not surprisingly, most family confederations collapsed within a few generations.

The ideological vacuum of politics in the Early and Later Middle periods was a certain recipe for chaos, and the search to fill it provided many answers, but few good ones. Down to the Mongol catastrophe of 1258, many regimes claimed that they were acting on behalf of the caliph and petitioned Baghdad for diplomas formally investing them with their territories. Since any regional dynast could obtain such a diploma, however, caliphal investiture did little to distinguish the claims of one ruler from another. Other regimes revived the traditions of ancient Iranian kingship, according to which an absolute monarch (Arab. *sulṭān*; Pers. *pādishāh*) was elected by God to be his vicegerent on earth. As God sustained the order of the cosmos, so the king sustained the divinely instituted hierarchy of human society. But kings were made and unmade by God's will—which is to say that any king who fell from power had by definition lost the divine mandate. Although these two theories could not secure real legitimacy for the dynasties that proclaimed them, they did reflect two deep-rooted ideals in medieval Islamic society. Implicit in the fiction of caliphal investiture was the ruler's obligation to uphold God's law (*sharī'a*) and defend the community of believers. Perso-Islamic kingship asserted that social and political harmony were best guaranteed by a ruler who stood above faction, answerable only to God.

An alternative to caliphal investiture and royal autocracy emerged in the Maghrib during the 11th and 12th centuries, when two Berber empires exploded on to the scene and seized control of much of North Africa and Muslim Spain. Both began as frontier revival movements, aimed at intensifying the Islamic commitment of recently converted peoples. The ALMORAVID (Arab. *al-murābiṭūn*: 'men of the frontier fortresses') movement took root among Berber tribes in Senegambia and Mauretania and at first mobilized them against their still-pagan neighbours. Only in the 1060s did the Almoravids move north into the long-established Islamic societies that existed in Morocco and Spain. The ALMOHAD (*al-muwaḥḥidūn*: 'unitarians') movement emerged among the Berbers of the High Atlas, as followers of a militant preacher who saw himself as the rightly guided one who would purify the Maghrib from moral and doctrinal corruption. By 1172 all of North Africa and Muslim Spain lay under the dominion of the Almohads. Revivalist states possessed high legitimacy in Islamic terms, since their whole aim was to re-create the intense faith and pure morality of the Prophet's community. But that mandate proved impossible to realize in practice; such regimes inevitably disintegrated in a few generations as the charisma of their founders faded. Thus they too failed to solve the ideological dilemma of the middle periods. The Almohad empire crumbled under Christian and internal pressures in the early 13th century. The dynasties that replaced it (the NASRID rulers of Granada, the MARINID rulers of Fez and the HAFSID rulers of Tunis, among others) had little if any charisma, though they were generous patrons of religious architecture and learning; as with most Middle period regimes, their authority was frankly of this world.

By the early 11th century political life in south-west Asia was being reshaped by a growing Turkish domination of the army and State. The seeds of this process lay in the Turkish-dominated mamluk regiments. Since these were the élite force in almost every regime in the region, they inevitably commanded tremendous political influence. Indeed, one dynasty of mamluk origin (the GHAZNAVID line) carved out an empire that for a few decades (c. 1000–1040) controlled Khurasan and north-west India. There was no parallel process in the Maghrib, where rulers used black slave-troops from Nubia and the western Sudan, but these rarely gained political paramountcy. West of the Nile, Berber tribesmen remained the paramount military force.

A definitive shift came only with the migration of Turkish nomads into Iran in the early 11th century. The formation of the vast Qarakhanid empire (c. 1000) north of the Amu River by the Karluk Turks signalled the growing influence of Islam in Central Asia. Soon thereafter, bands of recently converted Turkish nomads (the so-called Turkomans) began to infiltrate north-east Iran, led by chiefs from the Saljuq family. The Saljuqs and their followers began as marauders, but quickly turned into immigrants bent on staying in the lands they occupied. In 1040 they annihilated a major Ghaznavid army, and by 1055 they had occupied Baghdad. The Saljuq chief in Iraq, Tughril (d 1063), took the title sultan, thereby claiming plenipotentiary power as the caliph's sole lawful deputy in all matters of this world and the next. Under Malikshah (reg 1072–92), the Saljuqs ruled an empire that nearly replicated the caliphal domains of two centuries before. For a moment, the unity of Islam seemed on the verge of restoration, albeit within a sharply altered political framework.

Saljuq rule brought significant changes to the old Islamic lands but did not transform them. The Turkomans who came with the Saljuqs numbered a few hundred thousand at most; they displaced or absorbed previous ethnic groups only in a few areas, in particular Azerbaijan and central Anatolia. No doubt the Turkomans converted some lands from agricultural to pastoral use in the districts where they were concentrated, but before the 13th century there was no overall shift in Middle Eastern land-use patterns. Nor were the Turkomans the socio-political élite of the new regime, as the Arabs had been in the 7th century. Though the Saljuqs had begun as chiefs of a coalition of Turkoman war-bands, they soon made mamluk troops the core of their standing armies, reducing the Turkomans to a secondary role. Still, the combination of a Turkish dynasty, Turkish-dominated mamluk regiments and Turkoman migration ensured Turkish political domination throughout the region for centuries to come.

The Saljuqs continued the pattern of government established in the 10th century; as foreigners by ethnicity, speech and culture they had no choice. They even carried it a step further by aligning themselves with an already existing movement to establish Sunni Islam as the sole acceptable form of practice and belief. On one level this policy was simply the logical consequence of their claim

to be the caliph's vicegerent. On another, it meant sponsoring an official orthodoxy and a systematic effort to suppress 'deviant' interpretations of Islam.

Heretofore the Sunni ulema had been able to maintain their autonomy from the State, and much the same was true for Shi'ite scholars outside the Fatimid realm, after the occultation, or disappearance, of the twelfth imam. The ulema did this despite a lack of formal institutions to provide unified governance and define doctrine; in Sunni Islam there was a community of believers, but no Church. Religious organization was rudimentary at best, but in the long run it proved amazingly durable. By the mid-9th century the ulema had begun to cluster into distinct 'schools' of law (madhhab). A madhhab was not a formally organized corporation, but rather a group of scholars who shared a common doctrine, traced back to the teachings of an eponymous master, as to the religious and legal obligations incumbent on all Muslims. Thus the Hanafi madhhab consisted of scholars who ascribed their core concepts and doctrines to Abu Hanifa (d 767).

By Saljuq times four of these schools (Hanafis, Malikis, Shafi'is and Hanbalis) dominated the scene; their doctrines differed significantly, and they often quarrelled fiercely, but at bottom each recognized the others as acceptable in God's sight. Within a given city or district the members of a given madhhab were linked by family, patronage and clientship, and student–teacher bonds. On the inter-regional level a madhhab was glued together through the incessant travel of scholars; such travel ensured that important works written in Baghdad would quickly be debated in Nishapur and Damascus. Doctrinal cohesion within these far-flung, loose-knit entities was maintained through the search for consensus (ijmā') on all significant problems. Consensus was not determined by councils and hierarchies; on the contrary, it emerged through decades or centuries of debate and teaching among hundreds of scholars all over the Islamic world. Consensus—an ideal goal as much as a reality—was achieved only when no reputable scholar disagreed on the problem at issue.

The Saljuqs built strong direct ties with the ulema, and by endowing mosques and religious colleges (see MADRASA) on a generous scale they greatly reinforced the institutional infrastructure of Sunni Islam. They rooted their vision of Islam in the State by insisting that all senior bureaucrats have a solid education in the religious sciences; in return they demanded that the ulema lend their support to the regime. On balance, this accommodation between State and men of religion met the interests of both parties, despite moments of friction. It set the model not only for the Saljuqs but for all Sunni regimes down to the 20th century.

(v) Later Middle period (c. 1200–c. 1500). In spite of an official ideology that stressed Perso-Islamic concepts of kingship, the diarchy of caliph and sultan, the unifying power of Sunni Islam and government according to the sharī'a, the Saljuq empire was really an oversized family confederation. This fact became visible immediately on the death of Malikshah in 1092. Some cohesion was maintained in Iran and southern Iraq for another half-century, but thereafter the empire dissolved into a chaos of petty principalities. By the 13th century there was a rough balance of power between several large states (including a revived Abbasid caliphate in southern Iraq), but prospects for a new regional order were quickly shattered by the Mongol cataclysm: in 1218 the vast coalition of Inner Asian peoples created by Genghis Khan (*reg* 1206–27) burst upon the north-east frontiers of Islam. The initial invasion, led by Genghis Khan himself, smashed the most powerful Muslim state of its day, the Khwarazmian empire in eastern Iran and Transoxiana. Expeditions during the following decades annihilated one Muslim dynasty after another, including (to the horror of Muslim observers) the Abbasid caliphate itself in 1258. The only major survivor east of the Nile was a junta that had seized power in Egypt in 1250. The new regime (*see* MAMLUK, §II) fended off a Mongol advance force at 'Ayn Jalut in Palestine (1260)—a tactical victory that unexpectedly proved decisive. For the next two centuries, the region between the Nile and the Amu rivers would be divided between the Mongols and the Mamluks of Egypt and Syria.

The Mongol empire at its peak was an immense apanage state stretching from China to the Ukraine, with each apanage assigned in hereditary title to a lineal descendant of Genghis Khan. For the Muslim peoples, the most important was that established under Hulagu (Hülegü; *reg* 1256–65) and his successors (*see* ILKHANID) in Iran and Iraq from 1256 to 1353. The conversion to Islam by the Golden Horde in Russia (1262) brought immense new territories into the Islamic orbit. The Ilkhanids and their armies were pagans at the time of the conquest and remained so until the conversion of Ghazan (*reg* 1295–1304) to Islam in 1295. Even this did not reduce the immense prestige of Genghis Khan, however. Until the 16th century full sovereignty in the Mongol-dominated lands was exclusively reserved for princes of his line, and all rulers claimed to adhere to the laws and practices established by the conqueror.

The Mongol impact on Iran and Iraq is difficult to assess. The destructiveness of the conquest, together with Ilkhanid hostility to Islam in the early decades of their rule, undoubtedly weakened the institutions of Islamic communal and intellectual life. On the other hand, by the 14th century the Ilkhanids had become active patrons of the arts. Persian literature showed no decline in quality or quantity, as the works of such poets as Sa'di (*d c.* 1290), Hafiz (1325–90) and Jami (1414–92) attest. Moreover, the Mongol conquest opened the gates to an active exchange of artistic techniques and motifs with China, leading to a great enrichment of the resources available to Iranian artists. On the social and economic level, the picture is darker. The Mongol commitment to the nomadic–pastoral traditions of Inner Asia discouraged efforts to restore the infrastructure of urban and agrarian life, damaged so severely during the decades of conquest. Moreover, the Mongols dragged in with them great numbers of Turco-Mongol tribesmen, enough to alter permanently the ethnic make-up of Iran and Anatolia and to shift vast tracts from an agricultural to a nomadic–pastoral economy, despite a return to Islam and Perso-Islamic administrative traditions *c.* 1300. The influx of Inner Asian tribesmen also reduced sharply the political and military significance of mamluk troops in Iran: until the end of the 19th century Iranian

rulers had few troops of their own and were dependent on tribal forces. The rulers' power was thus limited by their relations with the leaders of the powerful nomadic confederations that dominated so much of the country.

The Ilkhanid regime fell apart after around 1350, but a second Mongol empire was soon created by Timur (Tamerlane; *reg* 1370–1405; *see* TIMURID, §II(1)), a Turco-Mongol tribal leader who strove to reunite Genghis Khan's Islamic domains under his own rule. In the customary fashion, he converted his vast conquests into an appanage state, and despite their internecine quarrels his heirs dominated Iran and Transoxiana until 1506. Ideologically, Timur appealed both to the heritage of Genghis Khan and to Islam, a delicate balancing act that succeeded chiefly becuase of his immense personal prestige. Timurid administration followed the Ilkhanid model, favouring the nomadic–pastoral elements of society, but urban life and culture flourished: the Timurid princes were generous and creative patrons of Iranian high culture, and Timur himself was a great builder as well as a destroyer.

Mongol rule did not cross the Euphrates. In Syria and Egypt, power devolved on a self-perpetuating military junta dominated by Turkish-speaking mamluks. The man who emerged as head of the junta at any given time was recognized as sultan. The executive offices of the State were by custom assigned to senior military officers, almost all of whom had begun their careers as military slaves; in theory they were the sultan's ministers, but in fact they were allies and rivals almost as powerful as he. Every succession to the sultanate was a crisis, and the Mamluk empire was continuously ridden by factional violence. Even so, the regime continued without a break and without loss of territory for 250 years until 1517. In contrast to the Mongol regimes, the Mamluk empire was highly centralized; it produced no self-governing appanages, and nomadic pastoralists, whether Arab or Turkoman, remained marginal elements in the political system. This was due in part to the military power of the sultan's mamluk regiments, in part to the deep-rooted bureaucratic traditions of the Nile Valley.

Like its distant Saljuq ancestor, the Mamluk empire insisted on its Islamic identity. The Mamluks made traditionalist Sunnism the only legitimate interpretation of the faith, and they claimed that their chief aim was to defend the *shari'a*. In this light, they honoured the ulema, but allowed them little autonomy or influence in serious matters of state. Even the vigorous Mamluk patronage of mosques and madrasas (*see* §II, 6(iii)(a) below) was an instrument of control, for it ensured that the most lucrative and visible religious positions would be in the gift of the sultan and the military establishment.

By the 13th century the ulema were in any case no longer the sole spokesmen for Islam. For centuries they had claimed that their knowledge of the sacred texts gave them alone the right to say what Islam was. But even as the ulema were first emerging as a distinct group *c.* 800, a few people were stressing a severely ascetic mode of life and a personal, direct experience of the Divine Presence. These came to be known as Sufis (probably derived from the Arabic *suf*, 'wool', hence *sufi* 'wearer of coarse woollen garments'), their doctrine and manner of life as Sufism (*tasawwuf*). Until *c.* 900 their numbers were small, and they kept their distinctive beliefs and practices to themselves. They had no formal organization; leading Sufis certainly knew (or knew of) one another, but each formed his own circle of disciples.

By the 10th century, however, the movement could no longer be kept under wraps. In particular, the ecstatic public teaching of al-Hallaj ibn Mansur (857–922) in Iraq attracted a wide following. Al-Hallaj's doctrines appalled both the stricter ulema and the political authorities, but even his crucifixion did nothing to stifle the rapid spread of Sufism. Indeed, by the 11th century the movement had won over many ulema, perhaps even a majority, and most Muslims now saw *taṣawwuf* and *sharī'a* as complementary rather than contradictory dimensions of Islam. Growth brought no essential change in the intensely personalized structure of Sufism, which still rested on the direct bond between a master (Arab. *shaykh*, Pers. *pīr*) and his disciple (Arab. *murīd*).

In the 12th and 13th centuries Sufism took on a more communal style, although the solitary hermit and the wandering dervish always remained significant figures in Islamic society. Many Sufis began residing in convents (*see* KHĀNAQĀH) founded by such wealthy patrons as rulers or senior military officers. These convents were temporary retreats rather than permanent homes, and they enforced no uniform doctrine and ritual on their inhabitants. Each convent was supervised by a 'respectable' shaykh who was ultimately answerable to the State authorities. In the long term, another form of common life proved more significant. A master's disciples would dwell in his lodge (*zāwiya*), in complete submission to him. Certain of these he ultimately invested with his own spiritual power (*baraka*). At that point some might leave to form their own lodges, but others remained with the master throughout their lives. Nor did his death terminate the existence of the lodge: he was ordinarily buried there, and since his spiritual power did not end with his physical death (it tended rather to increase), the lodge would become a shrine, now headed by his chosen successor—typically a son or intimate disciple. As a shrine it readily became a place of pilgrimage, not to mention a focus of gifts and endowments (*see* SHRINE (i), §II).

Those disciples who left the lodge continued to recognize their master's authority by asserting that the ideas and practices they taught were his. In this way a group of lodges emerged, linked together not only by common rites and teachings, but even more by their connection to a famous shrine. Such a network of Sufi lodges constituted the framework of a *tarīqa* ('order, brotherhood'; literally, 'path'). Each lodge was a coherent organization, held together by the spiritual authority of its shaykh and the wealth that supported it. As a whole, however, an order was simply the body of men who traced their spiritual lineage back to a common ancestor. By the 14th century such orders were found everywhere in Islam; a few had branches throughout the Islamic world. Especially in areas where governments were frail and transitory, such as post-Mongol Iran and the Moroccan Atlas, the shaykhs of the more important lodges often became the real rulers, at least on the local level. Occasionally, as with the Safaviyya of Ardabil (Iran) or the 'Alawiyya of Tafilalt (Morocco),

an order even became the seedbed of a major dynasty (*see* SAFAVID and 'ALAWI).

(vi) Early Modern period (c. 1500–19th century). The 15th century was a time of chaos throughout the Islamic lands. In the far west, the Almohad successor states of North Africa crumbled into ever smaller pieces, until all political cohesion and stability seemed lost. In the east, Timur's vast empire dissolved into a conflict-ridden appanage state, in spite of the unrelenting struggles of Shahrukh to hold it together. His successors could not achieve even that much. Iraq, eastern Anatolia and Azerbaijan were for decades the battleground of two powerful but inherently unstable Turkoman confederations, the QARAQOYUNLU and the AQQOYUNLU. Only the eastern Mediterranean had a degree of security. The Mamluk empire in Egypt and Syria, having survived Timur's assault in 1400, retained both its military prestige and administrative integrity throughout the 15th century, despite an unrelenting economic crisis and savage factional conflicts within the ruling élite. Finally, Anatolia and the Balkans were slowly hammered into a powerful new state under the House of Osman (*see* OTTOMAN). In this context, the 16th century represents an unexpected turnaround, an era in which several remarkably durable empires were formed. Two of them—the SA'DI dynasty in Morocco (and its 'Alawi successor in the mid-17th century) and the Safavid dynasty in Iran—fixed the modern boundaries of those countries. The Ottoman empire, far vaster in extent, was the longest-lived and best-organized state in Islamic history.

The Ottomans emerged from the chaos of post-Mongol Anatolia during the early 14th century. Their eponym Osman (*d c.* 1326), following the path of many other frontier warlords in that period, carved out a tiny principality (Turk. *beylik*) in north-west Anatolia, on the Byzantine borderlands. By 1400 his successors had absorbed most of the other Anatolian principalities, penetrated deep into the Balkans and were on the verge of taking Constantinople itself. Equally important, they had begun to shape their body of household retainers into a centralized state on the Perso-Islamic model. This achievement was almost nullified by Timur in 1402, but the Ottomans still held a few core territories. By the 1420s the empire had been substantially restored, and its power and prestige were permanently secured by the conquest of Constantinople in 1453 by Mehmed II (*reg* 1444–81 with interruption). Territorial expansion continued for the balance of his reign, but his real work was to create a system of government that endured with little change for more than a century and shaped Ottoman political ideals until the mid-19th century.

The reforms of Mehmed II and his successors reflected traditional Perso-Islamic ideals but had a distinctive Ottoman twist. In principle there was a sharp cleavage between subjects (both Muslim and non-Muslim) and the men of the State, but the Ottoman political élite was recruited from all the ethnic and religious groups that made up the population of the empire, and this in itself did something to bridge the gulf between ruler and ruled. One's origins counted for little; what was important was to have adopted Islam, to have learnt Turkish and to have become a loyal servant of the dynasty. The crucial political

6. *Accession of the Ottoman Sultan Süleyman in 1520*, folio size 365×254 mm; double-page illustration to a copy of Arifi's *Sulaymānnāma* ('History of Süleyman'), from Istanbul, 1558 (Istanbul, Topkapı Palace Library, Hazine 1517, fols 17*v*–18*r*)

problem facing the sultans was control over the vast apparatus needed to administer their empire. This they achieved by creating a strong central bureaucracy run literally from the palace, and by staffing key executive offices with men of slave origin. Warfare supplied some of these slaves, but more important was a periodic levy of children (*devşirme*) from the Christians who lived within the Balkan provinces of the empire. This institution (which appeared *c.* 1400) was chiefly intended to fill the élite units of the Ottoman army, in particular the famous janissary infantry; especially promising youths, however, were set apart and educated within the palace. It was from *devşirme* recruits who had risen through the palace service that Mehmed II chose his senior officials; such men continued to dominate high office until the end of the 16th century.

Control over the central government was one thing, control over the far-flung provinces quite another. The makeshift arrangements of the early 15th century were moulded into a system that allowed effective central supervision without undue expense and rigidity. The basic building block was the *tımar*, a land-grant assigned to a cavalryman on life tenure in return for military service. *Tımar*-holders were of disparate background, but typically they were *devşirme* recruits or the sons of previous holders. *Tımar*s were grouped into provinces, the governors of which were also the military commanders of the *tımar*-holders there. In this way, the empire maintained a large,

well-equipped and readily mobilized cavalry throughout its territories. The central government controlled the whole apparatus through close fiscal supervision and the constant rotation of provincial governors.

Even the religious establishment was not exempt from the sultan's control, though its members were always free-born Muslims. By the time of Süleyman (*reg* 1520–66; see fig. 6) all men of religion in the empire were ranked within a state-supervised hierarchy. Gaining an office within the religious hierarchy depended on one's progress through a strictly gradated educational system culminating in the imperial madrasas in Istanbul. Most men of religion sought appointment as a judge (Arab. *qādī*) or madrasa professor, but many entered the civil bureaucracy as scribes and accountants. However, they had no access to military-executive office.

By the mid-16th century the Ottomans had conquered vast tracts beyond their Balkan–Anatolian core: the Mamluks in 1516–17, Hungary, Iraq, Tunisia and Algeria in the following decades. More importantly, these territories were linked together within a remarkably well-integrated commercial–economic network centred on Istanbul. At the same time, problems arose that could not be resolved within the existing system. First, the channels of advancement and promotion were hopelessly clogged, leading to frustration and increasing corruption within the Ottoman élite. Second, the empire was besieged by inflation, which it did not know how to control. Third, changes in the art of war undermined the traditional Ottoman army and provincial administration; in particular, there was now a reduced role for the territorial cavalry, whose *timar*s were increasingly leased to the highest bidder by a cash-starved government. At the same time, the janissaries—once the *corps d'élite*—were becoming too numerous and ill-disciplined. In the 17th century they degenerated into little more than an urban militia. In the end the janissaries were a poor army but a powerful political interest group, and they and their urban allies were able to stifle any serious efforts at military reform during the 18th century. By 1750 the central government no longer had the fiscal or military resources to control most of its provinces; these fell into the hands of local notables and military chiefs who recognized the sultan's supremacy but did not obey his decrees.

By 1800 the Ottoman state faced imminent ruin from internal rebels (Christian in the Balkans, Muslim in Asia and Africa), not to mention Russian and French expansion. The only hope lay in a fundamental transformation of its institutions, a process that required a similar transformation of the Ottoman economy and society. This immense task was shouldered by the 19th-century sultans and their ministers; ultimately it proved beyond their capacities, but that they succeeded even as well as they did merits respect.

While the Ottomans assembled an empire slowly and methodically, their Safavid contemporaries overran the whole of Iran in a decade. Such spectacular beginnings seldom produced lasting results in Islamic history, but the Safavid dynasty endured for more than two centuries and created the geographical and administrative framework of modern Iran. The Safavids traced their origins to a Sufi shaykh of ARDABIL in Azerbaijan, Safi al-Din Ishaq (*d* 1334). For more than a century the Safaviyya order—city-orientated and Sunni—exercised a purely local political influence through its wealth and spiritual charisma, but in the mid-15th century its shaykhs turned it into a militant movement based on the Turkoman tribesmen of Azerbaijan and eastern Anatolia. They adopted a distinctive red headgear, hence their popular name Qizilbash. Safavid preaching stressed *jihād* and popular chiliastic beliefs, and reached a climax under Isma'il I (*reg* 1501–24), who emerged as head of the order in 1499 at the age of 12. Among his followers he was regarded as God incarnate, and this belief inspired them with prodigious daring and energy. By 1510 Isma'il was master of all Iran, and he would have seized Anatolia had not the Ottomans crushed his forces at Chaldiran (1514).

Isma'il's empire was structurally quite primitive. The civilian and religious bureaucracy was recruited from the urban notables, but the State was dominated by the Qizilbash military chiefs, who held both the major provincial governorships (which they exercised almost as rulers of autonomous apanages) and the senior executive posts at the centre. Like most of their predecessors in medieval Iran, the Safavid shahs relied on personal prestige and skill in manipulating tribal factions. Isma'il introduced one crucial innovation by enforcing Twelver Shi'ism as the official religion of his kingdom. This branch of Shi'ism, *sharī'a*-orientated and intellectual, had little in common with the radical beliefs that had brought Isma'il to power,

and his reasons for choosing it are still mysterious. Since Iran possessed few Shi'ite scholars in 1500, the new faith could be established only by recruiting such men from Syria and southern Iraq. Like their Ottoman counterparts, the Safavids closely supervised the religious establishment—at least until the late 17th century, when dynastic decline permitted growing autonomy to the ulema.

Isma'il's regime, which rested on an unsteady foundation of Turkoman troops and religious fervour, was stabilized under his son Tahmasp (*reg* 1524–76), despite fierce pressure from the Ottomans in the west and the Uzbeks in the north-east. By the accession of 'Abbas I (*reg* 1588–1629), however, the Safavid dynasty was on the verge of collapse. In a brilliant reign, the new shah repulsed his foreign enemies, rebuilt his capital, ISFAHAN, opened the country to lucrative foreign trade and reconstructed the State. The essence of this reform was centralization. He reduced the role of the Turkomans and built a powerful quasi-mamluk army with Armenian and Georgian recruits; many provincial governorships were taken from the Qizilbash amirs, converted to crown lands and assigned to his own courtiers (often men of slave origin); the central bureaucracy was enlarged and given greater powers. For the first time, the shah's actual powers approximated those of the Ottoman sultan.

'Abbas's system required a strong ruler, but after the 1660s the Safavid line produced no more. Safavid problems, however, went beyond incompetent shahs; provincial economies were milked dry by officials intent on maximizing short-term revenues, while the army was undermined by rising costs and Qizilbash demoralization. Things fell apart in the early 18th century, as Iran was pillaged by incessant warfare among Turkoman and Afghan tribesmen. In the turmoil, the Safavid dynasty disappeared; for practical purposes, the sack of Isfahan in 1722 marks its end. By the 1790s a new dynasty (from the Turkoman QAJAR tribe) had reassembled the old Safavid dominions. On the structural level, however, the Qajars (*reg* 1779–1924) could not replicate the Safavid achievement. Until the end of the dynasty, the shah's direct control was restricted to his capital of TEHRAN and a few major cities. The greater part of the country was dominated by powerful tribal confederations; in return for gifts and high office, their chiefs swore fealty to the throne and supplied the bulk of its troops. On another front, the Qajars enjoyed little legitimacy among the ulema, whose social prestige and freedom of action were greatly reinforced by their direct control over religious endowments. In this era the seeds were sown for the endemic conflict between the regime and the men of religion in the 20th century. It is no surprise that the Qajars could mount only a belated and superficial response to the challenges of the 19th century; serious efforts to construct a modern state began only with the Constitutional Revolution (1905–9).

The history of Morocco was altogether more modest than that of Iran or the Ottoman empire, but the Sa'di and 'Alawi dynasties did construct a political system that held the country together until the French Protectorate (1912); indeed, the 'Alawis still occupy the throne. Each of the two dynasties had its origins in a Sufi *zāwiya* headed by a lineage of people claiming descent from the Prophet (*sharīf*), and thus each could appeal to the dual charisma of sanctity and kingship to legitimize its rule. In addition, the Sa'dis benefited from their successful *jihād* against Portuguese and Spanish expansion in the late 16th century. Despite the high legitimacy of the two dynasties, however, their power was limited; they dominated the major cities of the Atlantic plain (Fez, Meknès and Marrakesh), but the Berber confederations of the Atlas Mountains and the Saharan oases were attached to the sultan only by periodic tribute and personal alliances. The lack of a centralized regime was no great problem until the mid-19th century, when Morocco began facing unrelenting French military and diplomatic pressures. The sultans simply did not have the money to build a new-style army or the power to create an effective bureaucracy. Skilful policy, combined with limited military and fiscal reforms, could fend off the French for a time, but by the 20th century ingenuity was no longer enough. In the case of Morocco, a modern State was constructed only at the cost of foreign occupation.

In general, the traditional Islamic lands entered the 19th century with their social and cultural traditions intact. As always, these traditions were being redefined in important ways, but they clearly belonged to an unbroken line reaching back to the beginnings of Islam. Political structures, although weakened in relation to the 16th and 17th centuries, still seemed functional to both rulers and subjects. Europe was beginning to pose a real military threat even to major Muslim states, although in 1800 no one could have foreseen how grave that threat would become in the following decades. Economic life was a different matter; the considerable prosperity of the 17th century had given way to stagnation and then crisis in the 18th. But again, the transformation of the following century—the near total domination of capital, production and markets by Europe—was beyond anyone's foresight. A visitor from 1600 would have found North Africa and the Middle East a familiar (albeit sadder) place in 1800. In 1900 that would no longer have been the case.

BIBLIOGRAPHY

GENERAL AND REFERENCE WORKS
Enc. Iran.; *Enc. Islam/1*; *Enc. Islam/2*
E. von Zambaur: *Manuel de généalogie et de chronologie pour l'histoire de l'Islam* (Hannover, 1927)
J. D. Pearson: *Index Islamicus, 1906–1955* (Cambridge, 1958, with suppls at five-year intervals)
C. E. Bosworth: *The Islamic Dynasties: A Chronological Handbook* (Edinburgh, 1967, rev. 1980)
Cambridge History of Islam, 2 vols (Cambridge, 1970)
M. G. S. Hodgson: *The Venture of Islam*, 3 vols (Chicago, 1974)
C. Cahen: *Les Peuples musulmans dans l'histoire* (Damascus, 1977)
——: *Introduction à l'histoire du monde musulman médiéval, VIIe–XVe siècle* (Paris, 1982)
J. M. Abun-Nasr: *A History of the Maghrib in the Islamic Period* (Cambridge, 1987)
G. Endress: *An Introduction to Islam*, trans. C. Hillenbrand (New York, 1988)
R. S. Humphreys: *Islamic History: A Framework for Inquiry* (Minneapolis, 1988, rev. Princeton, 1991)
I. M. Lapidus: *A History of Islamic Societies* (Cambridge, 1988)
A. H. Hourani: *A History of the Arab Peoples* (Cambridge, MA, 1991)

THE RISE OF ISLAM AND THE CALIPHAL ERA
J. Wellhausen: *Prolegomena zur ältesten Geschichte des Islams* (Berlin, 1899)
——: *Das arabische Reich und sein Sturz* (Berlin, 1902); Eng. trans. by M. Weir (Calcutta, 1927/R Beirut, 1963)
L. Caetani: *Annali dell'Islam*, 10 vols (Milan, 1905–26)
W. M. Watt: *Muhammad at Mecca* (Oxford, 1953)
——: *Muhammad at Medina* (Oxford, 1956)

D. Sourdel: *Le Vizirat abbaside de 749 à 936*, 2 vols (Damascus, 1959–60)
M. Rodinson: *Mahomet* (Paris, 1961); Eng. trans. (London, 1971)
H. Laoust: *Les Schismes dans l'Islam* (Paris, 1965)
M. A. Shaban: *The Abbasid Revolution* (Cambridge, 1970)
R. N. Frye, ed.: *From the Arab Invasion to the Saljuqs* (1975), iv of *The Cambridge History of Iran* (Cambridge, 1968–91)
M. M. Ahsan: *Social Life under the Abbasids* (London and New York, 1979)
J. Lassner: *The Shaping of 'Abbāsid Rule* (Princeton, 1980)
F. M. Donner: *The Early Islamic Conquests* (Princeton, 1981)
T. Nagel: *Staat und Glaubensgemeinschaft im Islam* (Zurich and Munich, 1981)
M. Sharon: *Black Banners from the East* (Jerusalem and Leiden, 1983)
M. G. Morony: *Iraq after the Muslim Conquest* (Princeton, 1984)
H. Djait: *Al-Kufa: Naissance de la ville islamique* (Paris, 1986)
H. Kennedy: *The Prophet and the Age of the Caliphates: The Islamic Near East from the Sixth to the Eleventh Centuries* (London, 1986)
P. Crone: *Meccan Trade and the Rise of Islam* (Princeton, 1987)
M. Gil: *A History of Palestine, 634–1099* (Cambridge, 1992)
W. E. Kaegi: *Byzantium and the Early Islamic Conquests* (Cambridge, 1992)
K. Y. Blankenship: *The End of the Jihad State: The Reign of Hisham Ibn 'Abd al-Malik and the Collapse of the Umayyads* (Albany, 1994)
G. R. D. King and A. Cameron, eds: *The Byzantine and Early Islamic Near East: Land Use and Settlement Patterns* (Princeton, 1994)
F. E. Peters: *Muhammad and the Origins of Islam* (Albany, 1994)
D. A. Spellberg: *Politics, Gender and the Islamic Past: The Legacy of 'A'isha bint Abi Bakr* (New York, 1994)

MIDDLE PERIODS
V. V. Barthold: *Turkestan' v' epokhu mongol'skago nachestviya* (Moscow, 1900); Eng. trans. by V. Minorsky as *Turkestan down to the Mongol Invasion* (London, 1928, rev. 1977)
B. Spuler: *Die Mongolen in Iran* (Leipzig, 1939, rev. Leiden, 4/1985)
R. Brunschvig: *La Berbérie orientale sous les Hafsides*, 2 vols (Paris, 1940–47)
B. Spuler: *Iran in früh-islamischer Zeit* (Wiesbaden, 1952)
D. Ayalon: *Gunpowder and Firearms in the Mamluk Kingdom* (London, 1956)
A. Huici Miranda: *Historia politica del imperio almohade*, 2 vols (Tetuan, 1956–7)
J. F. P. Hopkins: *Medieval Muslim Government in Barbary until the Sixth Century of the Hijra* (London, 1958)
A. Darrag: *L'Egypte sous le règne de Barsbay, 825–841–1422–1438* (Damascus, 1961)
C. E. Bosworth: *The Ghaznavids: Their Empire in Afghanistan and Eastern Iran, 944–1040* (Edinburgh, 1963)
N. Elisseeff: *Nur ad-Din: Un Grand Prince musulman de Syrie au temps des croisades*, 3 vols (Damascus, 1967)
I. M. Lapidus: *Muslim Cities in the Later Middle Ages* (Cambridge, MA, 1967)
J. A. Boyle, ed.: *The Saljuq and Mongol Periods* (1968), v of *The Cambridge History of Iran* (Cambridge, 1968–91)
C. Cahen: *Pre-Ottoman Turkey* (London, 1968)
H. Busse: *Chalif und Grosskönig: Die Buyiden im Iraq* (Wiesbaden, 1969)
S. J. Trimingham: *The Sufi Orders in Islam* (Oxford, 1971)
H. Rabie: *The Financial System of Egypt, A.H. 564–741/A.D. 1169–1341* (London, 1972)
C. Cahen: *Turcobyzantina et Oriens Christianus* (London, 1974)
J. E. Woods: *The Aqquyunlu: Tribe, Confederation, Empire* (Minneapolis and Chicago, 1976)
D. Ayalon: *Studies on the Mamluks of Egypt* (London, 1977)
R. S. Humphreys: *From Saladin to the Mongols: The Ayyubids of Damascus, 1193–1260* (Albany, 1977)
D. Ayalon: *The Mamluk Military Society* (London, 1979)
R. P. Mottahedeh: *Loyalty and Leadership in an Early Islamic Society* (Princeton, 1980)
P. M. Holt: *The Age of the Crusades: The Near East from the Eleventh Century to 1517* (London, 1986)
P. Jackson and L. Lockhart, eds: *The Timurid and Safavid Periods* (1986), vi of *The Cambridge History of Iran* (Cambridge, 1968–91)
P. Thorau: *Sultan Baibars I. von Ägypten* (Wiesbaden, 1987); Eng. trans. by P. M. Holt as *The Lion of Egypt: Sultan Baybars I and the Near East in the Thirteenth Century* (London and New York, 1992)
A. K. S. Lambton: *Continuity and Change in Medieval Persia: Aspects of Administrative, Economic, and Social History, 11th–14th Century* (Albany, 1988)

B. F. Manz: *The Rise and Rule of Tamerlane* (Cambridge, 1989)

E. Daftary: *The Isma'ilis: Their History and Doctrines* (Cambridge, 1990)

Y. Lev: *State and Society in Fatimid Egypt* (Leiden, 1991)

J. Berkey: *The Transmission of Knowledge in Medieval Cairo: A Social History of Islamic Education* (Princeton, 1992)

M. Chamberlain: *Knowledge and Social Practice in Medieval Damascus, 1190–1350* (Cambridge, 1994)

C. F. Petry: *Protectors or Praetorians? The Last Mamluk Sultans and Egypt's Waning as a Great Power* (Albany, 1994)

P. Sanders: *Ritual, Politics and the City in Fatimid Cairo* (Albany, 1994)

EARLY MODERN PERIOD

E. Lévi-Provençal: *Les Historiens des Chorfa: Essai sur la littérature historique et biographique au Maroc du XVIe au XXe siècle* (Paris, 1922)

P. Wittek: *The Rise of the Ottoman Empire* (London, 1938)

R. Le Tourneau: *Fès avant le Protectorat* (Casablanca, 1949)

R. Mantran: *Istambul dans le seconde moitié du XVIIe siècle* (Paris, 1962)

H. Inalcik: *The Ottoman Empire: The Classical Age, 1300–1600* (London, 1973)

A. Raymond: *Artisans et commerçants au Caire au XIIIe siècle*, 2 vols (Damascus, 1973–4)

S. J. Shaw and E. K. Shaw: *History of the Ottoman Empire and Modern Turkey*, 2 vols (Cambridge, 1976–7)

J. R. Perry: *Karim Khan Zand* (Chicago, 1979)

R. Savory: *Iran under the Safavids* (Cambridge, 1980)

I. M. Kunt: *The Sultan's Servants: The Transformation of Ottoman Provincial Government, 1550–1650* (New York, 1983)

S. Faroqhi: *Towns and Townsmen of Ottoman Anatolia* (Cambridge, 1984)

A. Raymond: *Grandes villes arabes à l'époque ottomane* (Paris, 1985)

C. Fleischer: *Bureaucrat and Intellectual in the Ottoman Empire: The Historian Mustafa 'Ali, 1541–1600* (Princeton, 1986)

R. D. McChesney: *Waqf in Central Asia: Four Hundred Years in the History of a Muslim Shrine, 1480–1889* (Princeton, 1991)

L. Peirce: *The Imperial Harem: Women and Sovereignty in the Ottoman Empire* (New York, 1993)

C. Kafadar: *Between Two Worlds: The Construction of the Ottoman State* (Berkeley and Los Angeles, 1995)

R. STEPHEN HUMPHREYS

6. PATRONAGE AND ART LIFE. Works of Islamic art created under court patronage have long received primary attention from scholars, museum curators, collectors and the general public. This is because many major works of court patronage have been taken from their place of creation to Western museums, while the use of precious materials in court art or the relatively high degree of documentation have attracted interest. The patronage of the urban middle classes and the beautiful domestic works created in cities, villages and nomadic encampments have, by comparison, only recently come under a similar scrutiny. Despite some reassessment, the record of court patronage is, therefore, to a large extent still regarded as the most characteristic visual artistic tradition in Islam.

(i) Court. (ii) Urban. (iii) Village and nomad.

(i) Court. The existence of a sumptuous tradition of court art would seem to be at odds with the austere rules of personal conduct and the puritanical avoidance of luxury that characterized Muhammad's life and teachings, as described in the *ḥadīth*, the prophetic traditions. In fact, the imperatives of the institution of kingship exerted their independent influence on the civilization developed under his followers, often injecting into Islamic artistic culture pre-Islamic, non-Islamic or—from the strict religious perspective—even anti-Islamic elements. Despite this tension between theology and court art, patronage of the arts by the courts of Islamic states was central to the development of Islamic art and architecture over the centuries.

Court patronage in Islamic history began under the first Islamic dynasty, the Umayyads of Syria in the late 7th century (*see* UMAYYAD, §1). Their surviving architectural commissions show an assimilation of contemporary Helleno-Byzantine and Persian artistic traditions into a new and slowly developing Islamic synthesis under the umbrella of court patronage. Decoration of the Umayyad hunting-lodges in the Syrian desert, such as QUSAYR 'AMRA, often involved large-scale figural painting and sculpture, with depictions of the nude human form quite common, in stark (as it were) opposition to the puritanical and iconoclastic Semitic traditions of the Prophet.

Court artistic patronage over time resulted in the establishment of various institutions. The early emergence of the ṬIRĀZ, a manufactory for the production of luxury textiles operated under close court control, shows the need in Islamic courts for a controlled and reliable supply of the robes of honour that formed such an important aspect of ritual gift-giving in Islam (*see* §VI, 3(i) below). The various sorts of artistic media favoured for court luxury objects in the formative period of Islamic art show a complete adoption of the tastes and in many cases the secular rites and rituals of earlier kingly traditions. Traditional luxury materials such as ivory, rock crystal, silk and precious metals formed the focus of much work by artists under court patronage. As various media came into fashion, they found favour at particular courts. For example, the Umayyad court at Córdoba in the 10th century (*see* UMAYYAD, §2) was famous for ivories (*see* §VIII, 7 below), many carved in the palace suburb of MADINAT AL-ZAHRA'. Under the patronage of the Fatimid dynasty in 11th-century Cairo, the medium of carved rock crystal (*see* §VIII, 13 below and FATIMID) was popular. The OTTOMAN and SAFAVID courts of the 16th century commissioned great carpets (e.g. see fig. 200 below) and countless silk robes of honour as gifts to faithful retainers and foreign ambassadors. At the Mughal courts in the Indian subcontinent, specialists in jade-carving found work for court patrons (*see* INDIAN SUBCONTINENT, §VIII, 11).

The building of large monuments by rulers and their high court officials, especially congregational mosques, shrines and works of urban infrastructure, answered a religious purpose. These monuments carried the additional message of the generosity and power of their royal or noble patrons and conveyed to the public the significance of dynastic patronage for the good not only of the faith but of the *res publica* as well. In early Islamic times the seat of urban power, the *dār al-imāra*, was often situated in the centre of the city next to the congregational mosque, symbolically melding their functions and significance, and from early times the quintessential equality of Islamic believers before God was symbolically marred by the creation of the MAQSŪRA, a decorated walled-off royal precinct within the prayer-hall, indicating the special status of the ruler–patron.

Court patronage served a variety of purposes in Islamic history, and often the aesthetic aspect was secondary. The great institutions for teaching (*see* MADRASA), built from the 11th century in many Islamic lands, exemplify royal patronage. Although their artistic and architectural aspects are important, the foundation of such buildings served the political and religious agenda of establishing Sunni Islam against the various heterodox Shi'ite sects. Throughout Islamic history the royal building and artistic embellishment of religious shrines often served a political end, as when the Umayyads erected the Dome of the Rock (691–2; *see* §II, 3(ii) and fig. 17 below; and JERUSALEM, §II, 1(iii)) as a political, religious and artistic challenge to the dome over the Holy Sepulchre. In the 12th century the Ayyubids built a beautiful shrine for the remains of the great Sunni legalist al-Shafi'i in Cairo in order to have an orthodox shrine in their new capital, which they had just wrested from the Shi'ite Fatimids. The building (*see* CAIRO, §III, 6), with all of its artistry, served as a symbol of Ayyubid political rule and religious piety. In a similar vein, the illustrated manuscripts of dynastic chronicles commissioned by the Ottoman and Mughal courts in later times (e.g. see fig. 132 below) served their very limited audiences as symbolic affirmations of the legitimacy of dynastic rule. The parade art of the Fatimids in Cairo, where processions through the streets, as in many Islamic lands, were the central projections of royal presence and power, seems to have been extremely elaborate, if physically somewhat ephemeral. Sometimes the sheer number and size of the staffs of court artistic establishments projected a political image, in the same way that the unusually large harems of some Islamic rulers served a symbolic rather than a practical purpose.

A view of court patronage in Islam is limited by the vagaries of survival of works of art—for example, the earliest Islamic palaces to have survived even partially intact date only from the 14th century (*see* PALACE, §III)—and by the common practice by larger dynasties of attempting to erase the artistic record of their predecessors. By contrast, a wealth of historical texts and a limited but growing mass of archaeological data from earlier Islamic times give a reasonably clear picture of the practice of royal court patronage, if not of the art itself, even from such sites as BAGHDAD, virtually obliterated by the Mongols in 1258. From Spain and Morocco in the west to the Indian subcontinent and western Central Asia in the east, the patterns of Islamic royal patronage show remarkable similarities over many centuries.

The court patronage of the three late Islamic empires—the Mughals, Safavids and Ottomans—is the best documented and most frequently studied by historians of art. Following models established in Timurid Iran, court artistic patronage (apart from the construction of buildings) focused around a centralized design studio staffed by artists specializing in the arts of the book—designers, calligraphers, painters, illuminators, binders—variously known as the *kitābkhāna/kutubkhāna* (literally, 'house of the book(s)', often translated as 'royal library') or the *naqqāshkhāna* ('house of design', the royal design studio). These royal studios developed various institutions, specialities and working methods. In the Indian subcontinent, for example, it was quite common for several specialist artists to collaborate on a single painting. The Ottoman design studio was divided into two groups: the 'Anatolians' and the 'Persians', each with its own director. In Iran, before Tahmasp (*reg* 1524–76; *see* SAFAVID, §2(1)) turned away from painting, the Shah himself was intimately involved in the day-to-day business of the painting studio in Tabriz (*see* §III, 4(vi)(a) below), in much the same way as the Timurid prince Baysunghur (see fig. 7 and TIMURID, §II(7)) had been in Herat a century earlier (*see* §III, 4(v)(d) below). In the Ottoman empire, court patronage devolved

7. *Baysunghur Seated in a Garden*, opaque watercolour on paper, 287×197 mm; from a copy of *Kalila and Dimna*, from Herat, 1429 (Istanbul, Tokapı Palace Library, R. 1022, fol. 1*v*)

on an elaborate structure of associations, known collectively as the *ehl-i hiref* ('people of talent'), based on individual artistic media from the association of rug-weavers to that of aigrette-makers.

Court artistic patronage in Islam had many different motivations, but among the most interesting is the phenomenon of patronage as related to collecting works of art (*see* §XI below). Islamic rulers collected various kinds of art. The passion of the Ottoman and especially the Safavid rulers for Chinese porcelains has been well documented. The dynastic collections of precious objects and works of art of all kinds amassed by the Safavids and Ottomans formed the basis of world-famous national museums (*see* §XII below), and individual works from royal collections were acquired for European and American collections in the 19th and 20th centuries. The collecting passion among members of the court often sustained artists when large royal commissions were lacking, and the practice of compiling albums of calligraphy, paintings and even design sketches began in Iran in the 15th century (*see* ALBUM, §3) and was practised by such luminaries as the Ottoman sultan Murad III (*see* OTTOMAN, §II(4)), the Mughal emperor Jahangir and the Safavid prince Bahram Mirza (1517–49).

Patronage of the arts was an accepted part of the royal role in Islamic civilization, and most Islamic sovereigns who had the time and the means became patrons of art and architecture whether or not they had any personal inclination towards the arts. Certain court patrons were prominently mentioned in chronicles as having a particular personal interest in the production of art and in the process of artistic creation, and these individuals were in some cases able to bring about almost single-handed great periods of production in the Islamic court art tradition. Concern with artistic patronage to the detriment of other affairs of state is as common a theme in Islamic history as it is in the European traditions, and it is always a temptation to equate the economic consequences of the profligate artistic patronage of the Ottoman sultans Murad III and Ahmed III (*see* OTTOMAN, §II(5)) or the Safavid Tahmasp with the similar afflictions on the French body politic caused by the expense of the building and decoration of Versailles.

BIBLIOGRAPHY

J. A. Pope: *Chinese Porcelains from the Ardebil Shrine* (Washington, DC, 1956)

O. Grabar: *The Formation of Islamic Art* (New Haven and London, 1973, rev. 1987)

R. Ettinghausen: 'The Man-made Setting', *The World of Islam*, ed. B. Lewis (London, 1976), pp. 57–88

M. B. Dickson and S. C. Welch: *The Houghton Shahnameh* (Cambridge, MA, 1981)

R. Krahl: *Chinese Ceramics in the Topkapı Saray Museum, Istanbul*, ed. J. Ayers (London, 1986)

Islamic Art and Patronage: Treasures from Kuwait (exh. cat., ed. E. Atıl; Washington, DC, Trust Mus. Exh., 1990–91)

(ii) Urban. The well-documented tradition of court patronage has often obscured the role of wealthy city-dwellers as patrons in the artistic life of the Islamic lands. Discussions of such patronage tend to be concentrated on media or works of art that most art historians place in the second or third rank of artistic importance, significant for documentary rather than for aesthetic value. In fact, urban patronage of art in the Islamic lands is increasingly recognized for its own aesthetic value; the buildings, books, metal wares, ceramics, textiles and carpets of the urban middle classes, while in some cases following the fashion of the court and partaking of its imagery as well as its styles, in other cases may preserve far older and more elemental traditions out of which court art evolved. The lack of the written documentation, artists' names and institutional continuity often found in Islamic court art is more than compensated for by the sense of freshness, originality and social embeddedness of traditional urban art forms in the Islamic lands.

Islamic domestic architecture and patterns of neighbourhood development have come under close scrutiny only recently; the urban dwellings of Fez and Tunis, Cairo and Damascus, Istanbul and Isfahan present some of the richest and most environmentally adaptive types of Islamic architecture, and the plans, forms, materials and decoration often show a remarkable degree of historical continuity in a given place (*see* VERNACULAR ARCHITECTURE, §II, 7). In the Islamic lands, vernacular and domestic architecture often present the seeds from which the mosques, madrasas, palaces and urban commercial buildings eventually evolved, and the patterns of amenities and embellishments of the urban house, from the lathe-turned latticework

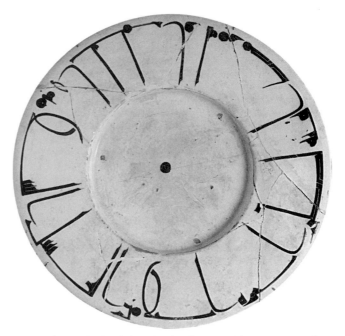

8. Samanid epigraphic bowl, slip-painted earthenware under a transparent glaze, diam. 375 mm, h. 44 mm, from Samarkand, 10th century (Paris, Musée du Louvre, AA96)

window screen (Arab. *mashrabiyya*) of the central Islamic lands to the WIND CATCHER of Iran and Iraq, present combinations of form and function of great beauty and significance in the history of Islamic architecture.

Early evidence of urban patronage survives mainly in the form of ceramics, which, unlike domestic architecture, metalware, textiles, carpets and jewellery, were both non-combustible and non-recyclable. For example, the epigraphic pottery produced in the 10th century under the SAMANID dynasty in eastern Iran and western Central Asia (*see* §V, 2(iii) below), with its elegant calligraphic decoration of moral aphorisms, gives evidence of a pious, discriminating and hard-working bourgeoisie accustomed to surrounding itself with beautiful things (see fig. 8).

Urban patronage at times took the form of a direct command from a patron to an artist, but most commonly its nexus was the bazaar, where works of art were made to be sold to buyers by the artist himself or by an intermediary entrepreneur. The bazaar in turn reflected to a greater or lesser degree the tastes of the court itself, but also reflected interest in art forms that were distinctly middle-class or distinctly nomadic in their social and functional origins (*see* §(iii) below).

Carpets made for middle-class urban Islamic patrons may at times have echoed the one-of-a-kind masterworks made in vast sizes from precious materials for the court, but just as often the carpets sold in the bazaar were of nomadic origins and genre. They served as storage containers, furniture or architectural decoration and displayed simple religious or tribal symbolism, reflecting the nomadic origin of the carpets and the nomadic ancestry of many Islamic city-dwellers. The same situation held for other media as well, from cotton, silk and woollen textiles to the ubiquitous incised and tinned copper tableware.

The functional rituals of everyday life in Islam of necessity dictated that similar genres of art would be required by the urban merchant and his sovereign. The practice of eating food with three fingers of the right hand, for example, meant that washing ewers, basins, napkins and towels of great beauty were made for ruler and subject alike. Dictates of dress, sumptuary conventions and religious traditions about silk ('he who wears silk in this world will forgo it in the next'; see §VI, 3(i) below) and jewellery (fine for women and horses but frowned on for men; see §VIII, 9 below) all moulded the patterns of urban patronage. Calligraphy, the universally approved Islamic art form—which conveyed to practitioner and purchaser alike the aura of prestige and piety—preoccupied middle-class collectors, whether it decorated an album page or a tile, a ceramic plate or a metal ewer.

On occasion, genres of art usually thought to be the sole province of high court notables made a significant impact on urban markets. Such is the case in the mid- to late 16th century with the illustrated and illuminated manuscripts from the workshops of Shiraz in Iran, which were produced for urban patrons outside the orbit of the Safavid court (see §III, 4(vi)(a) below). Dubbed 'provincial schools' by scholars of painting, such centres of workshop production are more appropriately thought of as centres of production for urban patrons. Other examples of such patronage include the illustrated manuscripts of popular narrative poems such as al-Hariri's *Maqāmāt* ('Assemblies') made at Baghdad in the 13th century (see §III, 4(iv)(c) below), and the lavishly illuminated manuscripts of the Koran produced for middle-class patrons in all Islamic societies.

The often arcane and elevated symbolism, sometimes replete with poetic and epigraphic sophistication in inscriptions, found in such genres of Islamic art as the celebrated lustre-painted or enamelled pottery of 13th-century Iran (see §V, 3(iii) below), should not obscure the fact that these pieces exemplify urban bourgeois art and survive in vast numbers when the prototypes made for the court in precious metals, enamels and book illustrations have all but vanished. The brightly coloured Iznik table wares of the 16th-century Ottoman empire represent a technologically sophisticated and vastly appealing group of art objects that were avidly collected by Ottoman urban patrons, while the court was preoccupied to a great extent with collecting blue-and-white Chinese porcelains made for export to the courts of the Middle East (see §V, 5(i) below). Although scholars have sometimes been slow in recognizing the fact, the genres of Islamic art that have always been the most popular among collectors in the West—ceramics, carpets and textiles—and the ones that have found their way in vast numbers into Western collections were for the most part first created for a wealthy, sophisticated and discriminating urban market in the Islamic lands.

BIBLIOGRAPHY

L. Volov [Golombek]: 'Plaited Kufic on Samanid Epigraphic Pottery', *A. Orient.*, vi (1966), pp. 107–33

O. Grabar: 'Imperial and Urban Art in Islam: The Subject Matter of Fāṭimid Art', *Colloque international sur l'histoire du Caire: Cairo, 1969*, pp. 173–89

——: *The Illustrations of the Maqamat* (Chicago and London, 1984)

WALTER B. DENNY

(iii) Village and nomad. The arid plateaux and mountains of the Middle East encouraged a mixed economy of irrigated agriculture and pastoral nomadism, while sea and land routes fostered trade and city life. Urban populations, peasants and nomads differed strongly in lifestyle and tradition while maintaining close economic and political connections.

The nomads of the Middle East had varied origins—they included North African Berbers (see BERBER), Arab bedouins, Iranian Baluch and Turks from the steppe—but their pastoral economy imposed similar lifestyles. Nomads lived off their flocks of sheep and goats, using horses and camels primarily for transport and war. They dwelt in tents (see TENT, §II, 1), moving as their flocks required new pasture, usually in a regular seasonal rotation (see fig. 9). This allowed the nomads to utilize desert and mountain areas unsuitable for agriculture. Although theoretically self-sufficient, pastoral nomads were interested in trade; while separate in consciousness, they usually lived in close contact with settled populations. This could be destructive, as nomads raided villages in times of need, but the different populations often lived in harmony—nomads buying village and city products and providing the important woollen industry with raw materials, while their livestock fertilized the agricultural fields they grazed in winter. Nor were nomad and settled populations entirely distinct. Most nomad groups had a hereditary ruling class, and nomad élites, like settled ones, often lived apart. Wealthy nomads often invested in land to secure their position, becoming part of the local settled élite, and poorer nomads who lost flocks through hunger or disease might take up a settled existence. Both groups could still retain ties to their tribes.

Migration inhibited the development of advanced technology, and nomad artistic production was limited largely to leatherwork and textiles, which formed the major part of their material possessions (see §VI below). Many tents were embellished outside with decorative bands, door and chimney flaps and inside with wall and floor coverings. Both knotted carpets and embroidery were closely associated with nomads, and FELT was worked in appliqué designs. Textile products, used for individual status or produced for the nomad élite, could be of very fine quality. Another possession of artistic importance and status was jewellery (see §VIII, 9 below), for which nomads were in part dependent on city or town craftsmen, who produced works specifically for the nomads' taste. Although it is impossible to say how many products were made for sale before the 18th century, it appears that the development of the commercial carpet industry in Anatolia (see §VI, 4(ii) and (iii)(a) below) began with nomad production.

Nomads also affected the artistic life of the Middle East as mercenaries, conquerors and rulers, since nomad life fostered horsemanship, archery and other military skills. From the 7th century to the 10th the bedouins and Berbers were particularly active. From the 11th century to the 14th the Turks and Mongols of the Eurasian steppe repeatedly invaded the Middle East, and in the 14th and 15th centuries

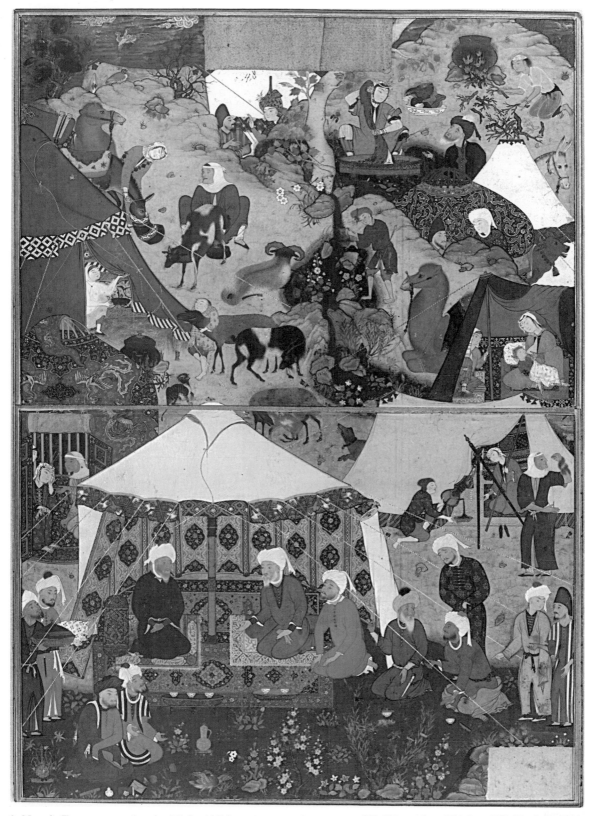

9. *Nomadic Encampment*, attributed to Mir Sayyid ʿAli, opaque watercolour on paper, 278×193 mm, from ?Tabriz, *c.* 1540 (Cambridge, MA, Fogg Art Museum)

two partially nomadic Turkic powers, the OTTOMAN dynasty in the west and the TIMURID dynasty in the east, conquered the Middle East. This ended the nomad conquests, leaving the Turks as the ruling class until the 19th century. Destructive invasions from the steppe were followed by large-scale artistic patronage and the introduction of new ideas. The Saljuq dynasty (*see* SALJUQ, §1) who arrived through eastern Iran in the 11th century brought the artistic styles of that region to the central Islamic world. The ILKHANID and Timurid rulers, interested in world trade, introduced styles and techniques from the Inner Asian steppes and China. Chinese motifs and themes had a strong impact, encouraging, for example, the development of book painting (*see* §III, 4(v)(b) below) in Iran and in other areas.

Since historical sources and surviving artefacts derive largely from either court or urban milieux, the products of the medieval countryside are largely unknown. Historical accounts mention villages primarily as a source of revenue; they were usually taxed collectively and more heavily than urban populations. Middle Eastern landowning and tax-farming systems encouraged absentee landlords, and most large landowners used their incomes to maintain themselves in the cities, leaving local affairs to the village headman. Scholars disagree on the level of connection between the city and the countryside; this clearly varied, probably decreasing in western Islamic lands under Ottoman rule. Most villages differed strongly in lifestyle from the city, and villagers were looked down on by the city populations. Many villagers, however, had close economic ties with the cities, which they provided with food. The organization of cities into quarters also tended to connect villages with the urban centres: people from one region lived in the same quarter and kept in touch with relatives within their village.

Small villages were underdeveloped and involved largely in subsistence agriculture; most profit went to the landlord, who provided seed and capital. Since the usual village building material was mud-brick or pisé, few examples of village architecture or other artefacts remain from the pre-modern period. Simple pottery and cloth production were widespread. Regional markets allowed some villages to specialize in producing specific textiles, pottery or metalwork for surrounding ones. Luxury arts were practised primarily by city craftsmen, but neighbouring villages often played a part in relatively sophisticated crafts. Villages might specialize in a cottage industry, selling through city merchants. Thus both textiles and pottery are often ascribed to a city and its surrounding region. The numerous trade routes through the Middle East allowed remote villages to produce fine crafts for export.

Certain areas far from major cities retained a local culture of tribe and village, sometimes expressed in regional artistic styles. These isolated populations, however, often participated in wider events as allies of a ruling power, mercenaries or bandits, and both artistic styles and techniques were open to new ideas. Western penetration in the 19th century brought greater commercialization of nomad and village production. This was particularly strong in the new cottage industry for the international carpet market (*see* §VI, 4(iv)(c) below). Nevertheless, while economic ties were strengthened, the greater openness to Western ideas in the cities had the effect of widening the gulf between city and countryside in culture and consciousness.

BIBLIOGRAPHY

A. K. S. Lambton: *Landlord and Peasant in Persia* (London, 1953)
I. M. Lapidus: 'Muslim Cities and Islamic Societies', *Middle Eastern Cities*, ed. I. M. Lapidus (Berkeley and Los Angeles, 1969), pp. 47–79
C. Cahen: 'Nomades et sédentaires dans le monde musulman du milieu du moyen âge', *Islamic Civilization, A.D. 950–1150*, ed. D. H. Richards (Oxford, 1973), pp. 93–104
M. Lombard: *Les Textiles dans le monde musulman du VIIe au XIIe siècle* (Paris, 1978)
G. Baer: *Fellah and Townsman in the Middle East: Studies in Social History* (London, 1981)
A. L. Udovitch, ed.: *The Islamic Middle East, 700–1900: Studies in Economic and Social History* (Princeton, 1981)
A. M. Khazanov: *Nomads and the Outside World* (Cambridge, 1983)
M. Brett: 'The Way of the Peasant', *Bull. SOAS*, xlvii (1984), pp. 44–56

BEATRICE FORBES MANZ

7. STATUS OF THE ARTIST. In Islamic societies, as in all societies, the status of the artist depends on the degree of differentiation of the artist's role from that of other craft occupations and consequently on the definition of what constitutes an artist. It depends further on the nature of an artist's reputation and the means by which that reputation is established, measured and enhanced and how the owner of the reputation is recruited, trained, evaluated and remunerated. Finally, there is the status of the art itself; the common Western distinction between the high-status 'fine' arts of painting, sculpture and architecture and the more lowly crafts or 'decorative' arts, comprising almost everything else, is not universally valid. Large-scale painting and sculpture were of little importance in the Islamic tradition, and artists engaged in the production of court art rarely enjoyed public reputations. Indeed, since the process of differentiation of the artistic role that occurred in the European Renaissance has few parallels in the Islamic lands, the documentation of the artist's status in Islam is a complex task. The measures used to indicate status include the appearance of artists' signatures; the mention of artists, their reputations and their work in court chronicles; the surviving data regarding artists' remuneration; the importance of commissions given to certain artists; and, more indirectly, the appearance of pre-modern forged signatures and spurious attributions on works of art (*see* §IX below).

The art of calligraphy (*see* §III, 2 below) is the only artistic genre universally approved by Muslim theologians. Treatises on calligraphy include short professional biographies of artists, list their pupils and works as well as their contributions to the evolution of the art form, and often include anecdotes relating to their status. Such treatises established the reputations of certain artists from the 12th century onwards, and calligraphers have enjoyed a universally high status in the Islamic lands since that time. The situation of painters was different. In Islam, figural images are frowned on as potentially idolatrous (*see* §8 below), and the status of painters depended on patronage, royal and otherwise. Documentary sources on painters—that is, designers and illustrators who worked on the ornamentation of texts and who often created individual works to be sold for the albums (*see* ALBUM, §3) of wealthy collectors—tend to follow the model of sources on calligraphy; the stylistic nature of the works of art themselves is rarely mentioned, but anecdotes indicate the esteem in which a painter's work was held by his peers and patrons (see fig. 10). Diverse sources on calligraphy and painting from later times, such as the fragmentary history of Iranian painting by DUST MUHAMMAD (1544) and the treatises by the Ottoman historian Mustafa 'Ali (1587) and the Iranian Qazi Ahmad (c. 1606), document the status of painters, calligraphers, illuminators, binders and other artists from the early 14th century in Iran to the Safavid, Ottoman and Mughal courts. The status of the painter could also be subject to sudden change as the religious climate altered; the decision c. 1550 by the Safavid shah Tahmasp I, the greatest patron of Iranian painting, to follow a more pious life, left many painters with no income and little alternative but to emigrate to the Ottoman or Mughal courts.

Although court artists worked for a very small, albeit discerning, public, their status as friends and boon companions of rulers enhanced their broad reputation. The

10. Mu'in: *Portrait of Riza*, opaque watercolour on paper, 187×105 mm, from Isfahan, 1673 (Princeton, NJ, Princeton University Library)

late 15th-century Iranian painter BIHZAD attained such status that in later times his name was commonly added to hundreds of paintings of varying and often indifferent provenance, date and quality. In rare cases treatises on art were written by artists themselves: the *Qānūn al-suvar* ('Canons of painting'; c. 1576–1602), for example, by the Safavid painter SADIQI, led to his inclusion in the high-status group of court literati.

The status of other artists and their name recognition varied from medium to medium. Sometimes an artist's signature, perhaps actually used more like a trademark, appears out of nowhere. The name Sa'd that appears on several examples of 12th-century Fatimid lustre-painted pottery is such a case. Weapon-makers, especially sword-smiths, signed their works at different places and times in Islamic art (*see* §VIII, 1 below). The wood-carvers responsible for many of the great wooden pulpits from Anatolia and Syria in the 12th and 13th centuries often signed their works (*see* §VII, 1(i)(b) below). While the names of architects are often known from historical documents, in some periods there are also prominent signatures on buildings—the 13th-century Anatolian works of the enigmatic Keluk ibn 'Abdallah are noteworthy in this respect.

In determining the status of the artist in Islam, it is important not to overemphasize a spurious contrast between the 'honest craftsman' of the Islamic tradition and the genius artist–hero of the post-Vasari era in the West. While the most highly paid and highly regarded artist might append the formula 'the humble, the poor slave' to his signature, scholarship has shown that in many cases artists in the Islamic lands began to develop the same kinds of self-image, status and reputation as their Western counterparts around the same time (15th–16th century). The emergence of these artists from anonymity consequently challenges former suppositions about the status of artists in the Islamic lands and emphasizes the parallels in the artist's status across cultures.

BIBLIOGRAPHY

Dūst Muḥammad: Preface to the Bahram Mirza Album (1544); Eng. trans., ed. W. M. Thackston in *A Century of Princes: Sources on Timurid History and Art* (Cambridge, MA, 1989), pp. 335–50
Ṣādiqī: *Qānūn al-suvar* [Canons of painting] (c. 1576–1602); Azeri Turk. ed. and trans. by A. Yu. Kaziev as *Ganun ös-sövär* (Baku, 1963); Eng. trans. by M. B. Dickson and S. C. Welch in *The Houghton Shahnameh* (Cambridge, MA, 1981), app. I, pp. 259–69
Muṣṭafā 'Ālī: *Manāqib-i hunarvarān* [Virtues of artists] (1587); ed. I. M. Kemal (Istanbul, 1926)
Qāẓī Ahmad ibn Mīr Munshī: *Gulistān-i hunar* [Rose-garden of art] (c. 1606); Eng. trans. by V. Minorsky as *Calligraphers and Painters* (Washington, DC, 1959)
L. A. Mayer: *Islamic Architects and their Works* (Geneva, 1956)
A. Welch: *Artists for the Shah* (New Haven, 1976)
M. B. Dickson and S. C. Welch: *The Houghton Shahnameh* (Cambridge, MA, 1981)
W. B. Denny: 'Contradiction and Consistency in Islamic Art', *The Islamic Impact*, ed. Y. Y. Haddad (Syracuse, 1984), pp. 137–73
M. Jenkins: 'Sa'd: Content and Context', *Content and Context of Visual Arts in the Islamic World*, ed. P. P. Soucek (New York, 1988), pp. 67–90
WALTER B. DENNY

8. SUBJECT-MATTER. For all its rich variety, the subject-matter of Islamic art has always been studied piecemeal, and the lack of a comprehensive survey has vitiated popular understanding of the artistic tradition. Among common misconceptions—usually of Western

origin—are that Islamic art does not evolve significantly, that it is almost exclusively a religious art, and that it avoids depicting living creatures. Even the perception that Islamic art is essentially ornamental is wide of the mark, though no one could deny the strength of the so-called *horror vacui*—the desire to leave no space void—as a basic generative principle in all media, periods and types of decoration (*see* ORNAMENT AND PATTERN, §V). Whether more can be read into it than an affinity for ornamented surfaces is doubtful. Leitmotifs in Islamic art include the continuity of ideas over many centuries and across most of the Islamic lands, the dominating influence of the first century of Islam on what was to follow, and the pervasive impact of the religion on all art. The overarching unity created by such leitmotifs makes the concept of 'Islamic art' meaningful.

(i) Introduction. (ii) Religious themes. (iii) Royal themes. (iv) Secular themes. (v) Vegetal themes. (vi) Geometry. (vii) Writing. (viii) The natural world. (ix) Magic. (x) Heavenly bodies.

(i) Introduction. The distinctive character of Islamic art was due to imaginative changes applied to material borrowed from Late Antiquity, the Ancient Near East, Central Asia, India and the Far East. This astonishing range of sources is largely explained by the geographical position of the Islamic lands, the natural bridge between the Mediterranean world and eastern Asia. Yet the formidable unity of Islamic art transcended not only these borrowings but also regional substyles and chronological evolution. Powerful unifying factors were the annual pilgrimage to Mecca, the land and sea trade routes that criss-crossed these lands, and a shared religion whose language—Arabic—was the lingua franca of the entire culture. Although the major ethnic divisions of Arab, Persian and Turk were strongly marked, each race at times ruled the others, guaranteeing continuous cross-fertilization between artistic traditions. In such contexts designs and motifs migrated frequently from one medium or area to another. Similarly, the various categories proposed for the subject-matter of Islamic art (e.g. geometry, vegetal ornament, writing etc) overlap so much that they merge and challenge the validity of such categories. Yet they are necessary, if only as a convenient means of imposing order on the potentially inchoate mass of material.

The 'gaps'—what is not found in Islamic art—have played a crucial role in its typecasting in the West. Three-dimensional sculpture of substantial scale is rare, perhaps as a result of the religious taboo on devotional images. The virtual absence of easel and oil painting is more difficult to explain on religious grounds. For the Westerner, accustomed to regarding painting as the principal expression of art, it requires an effort of imagination and will to adjust expectations when looking at Islamic art and to encounter it on its own terms. These include a more profound and sophisticated approach to ornament than in Western art and, conversely, little interest in the pursuit of naturalism for its own sake, a pursuit that Western art inherited from the Classical world and that engendered a fascination with the human body, portraiture, genre, still-life and landscape. Islamic art also had little time for myth or figural religious images. Equally, there is little trace of the personality cult that came to surround Western artists, with the concomitant notion that the artist was inspired

and that he could attain privileged social status. Although the names of thousands of Muslim artists, architects and craftsmen are known, their biographies, with few exceptions, are not.

(ii) Religious themes. Much of the subject-matter of Islamic art is religious. For all the theological discussion about the prohibition of images, the prohibition was effective only insofar as devotional images were never produced (*see* §1 above and ICONOCLASM). The iconoclastic controversy in Byzantium may have sharpened Islamic awareness of the issue, but it was not responsible for the particular Islamic stance, and Muslim artists were not dependent on theological approval of their work.

Pride of place goes to architecture, especially the MOSQUE, its furnishings and accessories—the MINARET, MIHRAB, MINBAR and prayer rugs (*see* §VI, 4 below). Other popular building types with religious associations are the MADRASA or theological college and the mausoleum (*see* TOMB, §II), often used as a place for prayer as well as burial. Indeed, some of the principal Islamic shrines have grown up around saints' tombs, expanding to become huge multi-functional complexes (*see* SHRINE (i), §II). The Ka'ba in MECCA became a popular symbol of sanctity, depicted in poetic manuscripts, pilgrimage guides and certificates, and glazed tiles; textile coverings and keys for the Ka'ba served as pious gifts from rulers and high officials.

Special veneration was accorded to manuscripts of the KORAN, and the text was copied by calligraphers on parchment and later on paper in special scripts developed by noted masters (*see* §III, 2 below). Illumination was concentrated on frontispieces and finispieces forming carpet pages of complex geometric interlace (see fig. 11), and chapter headings, marginal palmettes and roundels marking verse counts were frequently illuminated, particularly in gold and ultramarine (*see* §III, 3(i) below). Tooled leather bindings for each volume—often 30 in a single copy—echo in monochrome the carpet pages within. Folding wooden stools allow the book to be displayed open; like the wooden or inlaid metal boxes used to store multi-volume manuscripts of the Koran (see figs 220 and 152 below), they bear Koranic inscriptions. These occur so frequently throughout Islamic art—on buildings, clothing, pottery, metalwork, glass—that they constitute one of its principal subjects, sanctifying even the most everyday objects.

Another religious theme is Paradise. Sometimes it is explicit, as in the depictions of Muhammad's journey to the Seven Heavens (Arab. *mi'rāj*; see figs 104 and 122 below). The trees of Paradise—gigantic and bejewelled—are described at length in the Koran and its commentaries. The trees are represented carefully in the *Mi'rājnāma* ('Book of the [Prophet's] Ascension'; 1436; Paris, Bib. N., MS. suppl. turc 190) and probably in the mosaics of the Dome of the Rock (*see* JERUSALEM, fig. 6) and the Aqsa Mosque, and the Great Mosque of Damascus (see fig. 82 below), as well as the stucco carvings of the Gunbad-i 'Alaviyyan at Hamadan, Iran (?12th century) and the Ardabil Carpet (see fig. 200 below). The houris who await true believers are occasionally depicted, as are the chalices from which the blessed will drink, the buildings in which they will recline and the fruit they will eat. The hybrid birds on the tiled portal of the Shah Mosque (*see* ISFAHAN, fig. 3) may also refer to Paradise, particularly as the inscriptions on the portals of religious buildings and the steel plaques on their gates sometimes play on the concept of such buildings as gates to Paradise. Most references to Paradise, however, are coded or even subliminal. The numerous Koranic verses that describe water as an attribute of Paradise allow the ablution fountains in mosques or the water dispensaries erected for the public good in many Islamic cities (see fig. 66 below and CAIRO, fig. 4) to allude gracefully to this connection, and sometimes the choice of Koranic quotations makes it explicit. The most powerful earthly foretaste of Paradise is the garden (*see* GARDEN, §V). Thus depictions of supernally blossoming gardens in book illustrations (see fig. 120 below), glazed tiles (see fig. 79 below) or carpets (see fig. 209 below and CARPET, colour pl. IV) lend themselves to double meanings. So do actual gardens, from the Generalife (*see* GRANADA, §III, 2) to those of the Taj Mahal (*see* AGRA, §II, 1). Many gardens are walled and thus inaccessible, quartered with water-channels and given a funerary context by their association with a mausoleum.

Hagiography began to affect Islamic art after *c.* 1300, probably when many Muslim taboos were broken following the Mongol invasions. Initially images of the Prophet Muhammad derived from Christian prototypes, but gradually a fuller iconography developed, culminating in the Ottoman period (see fig. 133 below). Illustrated manuscripts of the *Mi'rājnāma* depicted Muhammad in a heavenly setting, and in time this event was treated ecstatically, making Muhammad a more than earthly figure wrapped in flame and escorted by angels. The Prophet, 'Ali and his family were particularly exalted by Shi'ites, with depictions of the lion (*haydar*, a name of 'Ali), 'Ali's martial exploits and Muharram ceremonies (when 'Ali's martyrdom was commemorated) and associated architecture, figural tilework and furnishings. Countless shrines in Iran testify to this devotion. Jewish and Christian sources provided the basis for the *Qiṣāṣ al-anbiyā'* ('Tales of the Prophets'), the popularity of which explains the frequent depiction of Nuh (Noah), Sulayman (Solomon), Da'ud (David), Ibrahim (Abraham), Musa (Moses), Yunus (Jonah) and 'Isa (Jesus) in Islamic painting. The favourite figure was unquestionably Yusuf (Joseph), whose story, as interpreted by poets with Sufi leanings, is widely depicted in manuscripts (see fig. 127 below and BIHZAD), tilework, carpets and murals.

Christian scenes, usually from the lives of Jesus and Mary, appear sporadically on pottery, murals and ceiling paintings, but principally on inlaid metalwork made under the Ayyubids of Syria (see fig. 1 above and §IV, 3(ii) below). The superlative quality of these images shows that Muslim craftsmen were prepared to work on a substantial scale for Christian patrons. Conversely, Muslim objects were used in a Christian context in medieval Europe, as in the rock crystal vessels popularly supposed to hold Christ's blood (for illustration *see* FATIMID), silks and ivory boxes used as reliquaries, episcopal thrones made from heterogeneous fragments of Muslim carvings and Abbasid coins overstruck with the names of Western rulers.

11. Geometric interlace from a double frontispiece, from a copy of the Koran made for the Mamluk sultan al-Jashankir (vol. vii), opaque pigment and gold on paper, 470×320 mm (page), from Cairo, 1304–6 (London, British Library, Add. MS. 22412, fol. 2r)

Mystical themes permeated later Persian book painting (*see* §III, 4(v)(d) and (vi)(a) below). Sometimes, as in Nizami's *Khamsa* ('Five poems') or 'Attar's *Mantiq al-ṭayr* ('Conference of the birds'), the text is crammed with references to mystical experience and teaching, and some protagonists are clearly allegorical. In other cases, however, the artist emphasized or even introduced the Sufi element, as in the illustrations to a copy (Washington, DC, Freer, 32.29–37) of the *Dīvān* (collected poetry) of Ahmad Jalayir. These themes may be tied to a given narrative (e.g. the story of Yusuf and Zulaykha) or may illustrate familiar Sufi practices or symbols (see fig. 127 below). Sufi poets were held in high esteem at court, and important officials manifested Sufi leanings and erected many Sufi foundations (*see* KHĀNAQĀH).

Religious symbols in Islamic art, while not fully understood, include the crescent, often used with a star to denote Islam; the colour green, which can connote sanctity or descent from the Prophet; banners, flags and orbs, often inscribed with some religious motto; the white veil, principally associated with Muhammad; haloes, whether circular on the European model or flaming as in Buddhist art; the various types of turban (e.g. those furnished with a red baton to indicate Safavid allegiance); and a group of images relating to light—pierced domes, hanging lamps, rayed designs etc—that play on the association between God and light (Koran xxiv.35).

Distinctive renderings of supernatural beings established themselves from the 13th century onwards, almost exclusively in book painting. Angels figure in cosmological manuscripts, texts dealing with the life of the Prophet and individual album leaves intended as a test of draughtsmanship. No clear difference can be discerned between the *jinn*s who attend Sulayman in manuscript frontispieces and the *div*s with whom the heroes of Firdawsi's *Shāhnāma* ('Book of kings') fight or the demons who torment the guilty in hell in the *Mi'rājnāma*.

(iii) Royal themes. Much of the finest Islamic art was produced under royal patronage, and royal themes are a central concern (*see* §6(i) above). As with religious art, architecture played a crucial role. Palaces were the most visible embodiment of royal luxury (*see* PALACE, §III), and they transmitted this idea in many forms—entire cities; huge complexes, tightly or loosely organized medieval machines for living; country estates focused on a single royal residence; hunting-lodges; and pavilions. Nor was the element of naked power forgotten. In most major Islamic cities the citadel, often at the city centre, contained the ruler's residence, treasury and a substantial garrison (*see* MILITARY ARCHITECTURE AND FORTIFICATION, fig. 25). Gates and portals drove home the same message by their royal symbols (lions, eagles, dragons) and inscriptions.

The congregational mosque also had a significant political role (*see* §II, 2 below), as the caliph, or his accredited representative, led the people in prayer, and his sermon delivered from the throne-like minbar served as a declaration of political allegiance. The architectural forms employed had a long political history in other cultures: the mihrab can be linked with the niche or apse in which the emperor or bishop sat, the minbar is a type of throne, the MAQSŪRA or royal box recalls the Byzantine *kathisma* (imperial box at the hippodrome), and the dome and axial nave had honorific associations already ancient at the coming of Islam. In time the minaret was also put to use as a symbol of power. Thus the mosque as a whole embodied the theoretical doctrine that religious and secular authority were one. Mausolea too served to glorify secular power, though somewhat less in the western Islamic lands. Sometimes a religious gloss was given by the titulature of the inscriptions, which might vaunt the piety of the tenant; by the location near the tomb of a holy man; or by the addition of a mihrab. But while major mausolea for religious figures are known (*see* CAIRO, fig. 5), the masterpieces of the genre were erected for secular princes (see figs 27, 28, 48, 56, 57 and 58 below). Tents (*see* TENT, §III, 1), despite their impermanence, epitomized courtly luxury by their sheer size and the sumptuousness of their fabrics.

The most original Islamic contribution was the so-called princely cycle, a series of interrelated scenes depicting the pleasures and ceremonies of the royal court: the music of harp, tambourine, flute, trumpet, drum and lute; dancing girls; wrestling, stick fights, jousts and gladiatorial combats with animals; hunting with dogs and falcons, including the retrieval of game; drinking and banqueting; homage and audience scenes; board games; riding on elephants—the range is remarkably wide. Cup-bearers, grooms and servants, chamberlains and various other office-bearers with appropriate attributes are often included. Scenes of country life and agricultural pursuits, such as vintaging or digging, are sometimes incorporated. The cycle is flexible: it is as easily extended as contracted and may have drawn partially on Byzantine and Sasanian sources. It is found as readily in the portable arts, for example in metalwork (see fig. 140 below) or ivory (see fig. 236 below), as in stone sculpture (e.g. the Pila of Játiva; Játiva, Mus. Mun.) or murals (see fig. 80 below). Usually the component images are placed side by side in a single band or roundels to reinforce and intensify each other. Apart from a straightforward description of court life, these images could be intended to evoke graphically the conspicuous consumption expected of royalty. This cycle may also be related to the benedictory inscriptions that so often accompany it. Both say the same thing—one visually, the other in words: this is the Good Life. The epigraphic references to such things as perpetual happiness and lasting security evoke the hereafter, when the Good Life will continue in Paradise for all eternity.

Images of the ruler in majesty were as common in Islamic as in medieval Western or Byzantine art and derived from the same sources. Formal enthronements were most popular, occurring from Umayyad times onwards in three-dimensional sculpture, medals and frescoes, but above all as frontispieces in manuscripts from the 13th century onwards (see figs 110 and 113 below). Frequently the ruler is shown surrounded by his courtiers, amirs and bodyguards. Apart from a few starkly symbolic images, actual portraits are relatively late, beginning *c.* 1420 with frontispieces depicting Baysunghur (*see* TIMURID, §II(7)) and thereafter including depictions of the rulers of the Ottoman, Safavid and Mughal superpowers. The standard method of referring to a ruler was epigraphic. Coins (*see* §VIII, 2 below) provide the perfect laboratory for tracing this evolution, with the ruler's name moving from border to field and gradually taking on titles. Silks and other stuffs made in royal workshops emblazoned the royal name and titles on robes, headgear, armbands and hangings (*see* TIRAZ). Thus inscriptions became a kind of livery, with length and content determined according to a strict hierarchy.

Artists were best able to integrate royal titulature with the shape and design of objects in metal and glass, particularly under Mamluk patronage (*see* MAMLUK, §2). Serried ranks of letters, their uprights forming a bristling phalanx, parade around dishes and bowls proclaiming amiral or royal titles and taking up most of the surface (see figs 154 and 234 below). Emblems punctuate the epigraphy and identify the owner by office rather than by name. In architecture, too, inscription bands and panels, often carefully proportioned and located for maximum legibility, identify the patron, whose name is often accompanied by a list of titles. In tiled inscriptions the ruler's name stands out from the rest of the inscription by the different colour employed—amber (for gold, the royal colour), blue or dark green.

Apart from the ownership of the building, perhaps the most common royal theme expressed by such inscriptions was victory, although the notion of erecting a monument solely to commemorate a victory was foreign to Islamic taste. Thus victory monuments, often identified as such not only by historical circumstances but also by the presence of the Koranic chapter 'Victory' (xlviii) in their inscriptions, may be mosques, minarets or other commemorative buildings. A more coded reference to victory may be made by the use of spolia, usually taken from the religious edifices of other faiths—Christian, ancient Egyptian and Hindu or Jain. Battles were a favourite theme of murals in royal palaces. Few examples survive (*see* §II, 9(iii) below), but they are plentiful in book painting. The victory theme is also expressed in representations of submission or symbolic conquest of an enemy depicted as an (*see* figs 78 and 183 below) or in epigraphic mottoes. Inscriptions of prophylactic character or claiming victory decorate armour (*see* §VIII, 1(ii) below), banners and standards.

The symbols employed in Islamic royal iconography still await the comprehensive study long accorded to their Western counterparts. Many types of crown (*see* §VIII, 12 below), throne (*see* THRONE, §III), parasol, honorific arch and canopy are depicted. Seated rulers are often shown holding a cup, which can be related either to the magical cup of Jamshid in the Persian tradition or to a complicated range of ceremonies (Turk. *and*) among the Turks. Rulers often hold a leafy branch in their other hand, but its significance is still elusive. Some elements of royal costume served symbolic as well as practical ends (*see* §VI, 3(i) below), and some textile designs functioned as dynastic or personal symbols, while others were borrowed from foreign cultures. Colour symbolism in royal costume requires further study. An elaborate system of emblems developed under the Mamluks: emblems set in cartouches comprised simplified symbols (such as napkin, cup, sword, polo-stick) that identified the patron's office. Used on architecture, woodwork, metalware, ceramics, glass, coins and costume, these emblems evoke to perfection the rigid hierarchy of the Mamluk military caste.

Finally, royal life is transfigured and rendered exemplary in the world of myth. In the *Shāhnāma*, the roll-call of monarchs reaches back to the beginning of time and continues until the coming of Islam, so that myth gives way almost imperceptibly to history. But myth and history alike are interpreted through the prism of national sentiment, and Firdawsi's version of Iranian kingship has become part of the heritage of every Iranian. A few Iranian rulers who are historical figures, including Alexander the Great, Ardashir, Bahram V, Khusraw I and Khusraw II, Sultan Mahmud of Ghazna, Sultan Malikshah and Sultan Sanjar, have taken on a mythic identity in Iranian literature. Royal themes from Firdawsi and Nizami, far from being confined to book painting, infiltrated many other media, notably ceramics and tilework, but also carpets, carved stuccos, lacquer and metalwork. Moreover, the popularity of Firdawsi and Nizami spread to Ottoman Turkey and to India. The Indian poet Amir Khusraw Dihlavi (1253–1325) took up the themes of Nizami, and both Arabic versions of the *Shāhnāma* and Ottoman pastiches of it are also known (*see* §III, 4(ii)(b), (c) and (d) below).

(iv) Secular themes. Secular themes play a distinguished role in Islamic art, whether in the field of folk art, science, literature or daily life. Genre images, although underrated, are ubiquitous and include occupations such as building, metalworking, handicrafts, the labours of the months (a popular theme in metalwork) and, above all, agricultural work (a sub-plot in so much of later Persian painting).

The theme of popular entertainment crops up in varied guises. Egyptian lustre pottery under the Fatimids (*see* §V, 3(i) below), for example, depicts scenes of stick-wielding men in combat, wrestling and cock-fighting. Depictions of dances with zoomorphic masks occur sporadically in Islamic art, from murals on Umayyad hunting-lodges to depictions of Ottoman guild processions. These processions, to judge from contemporary book illustrations, encompassed several kinds of public spectacle, such as bands, tumblers and acrobats, stilt-walkers and dwarfs. The Ottoman painter LEVNI specialized in such themes, which were closely connected with the celebration of such major festivals as the Prophet's birthday or the end of Ramadan. These subjects constitute a separate genre in Ottoman painting, while under the Mughals the repertory extended to Hindu festivals and spectacles. Other non-Islamic festivals are depicted because of their strangeness, as in the illustrations to al-Biruni's *Āthār al-bāqiya* ('Chronology of ancient nations'; 1307–8; Edinburgh, U. Lib., Arab. MS. 161), which feature 'outlandish' Zoroastrian, Indian and Babylonian customs.

A far more common theme was genre—the humdrum activities of daily life. Such topics enjoyed a pervasive popularity in Islamic art from the 12th century onwards, whether in Iraq or Spain—where the Pila of Játiva is carved with vignettes of rustic life, or the illustrated romance of *Bayad and Riyad* (see fig. 106 below) is abuzz with swooning lovers, intriguing duennas and literary salons dominated by imperious *précieuses*. A secular bias can be seen in the earliest body of Islamic book painting to survive (*see* §III, 4(iv)(c) below): breech-clouted labourers toil in the fields, assistants mix potions in apothecaries' booths, scholars dispute with each other or lecture their students. Teeming low life abounds in the paintings of numerous manuscripts of al-Hariri's *Maqāmāt* ('Assemblies') produced in 13th-century Iraq and Syria (see fig. 111 below). The smells and squalor, the bustle and noise of contemporary city life are conjured up with uncanny realism in these pages. The hubbub of tavern and slave-market, the ceremonious ritual of mosque and law-court, the fanfares and gala celebrations that announce military processions or the departure of the pilgrim caravan to Mecca—all are captured with the utmost economy, flair and conviction. An entire panorama of 13th-century Arab life unfolds before our eyes. And then, as suddenly as it had appeared, this world vanishes forever for reasons that cannot easily be fathomed.

Henceforth book painting catered principally to aristocratic taste, and the texts of choice were epics and lyrics, except for an enigmatic corpus of paintings associated with SIYAH QALAM depicting the grinding routine of nomadic life—tending animals, shouldering crushing burdens, pitching camp, plodding blindly on. No body of genre scenes in Islamic painting can match these for *gravitas* and emotional depth (see fig. 12). A more muted

12. *Demon in Chains*, attributed to Siyah Qalam, opaque watercolour and gold on paper, 254×337 mm, from ?western Central Asia, 15th century (Cleveland, OH, Cleveland Museum of Art)

realism characterizes the school of BIHZAD, where the emphasis is on the tableau rather than the individual. The formal set-pieces of court life are offset by lively vignettes of woodcutters and melon-sellers, herdsmen, ploughmen and fishermen, and occasionally by an entire *mise-en-scène* drawn from everyday life: a nomadic encampment, a school, a cluttered building site, a busy hammam. This exaltation of ordinary people is quietly revolutionary, but the overriding emphasis on technique seems to prevent anything more than a surface engagement with the appearance of things. Nature methodized seems to have been the watchword of those later Persian painters who toyed with realism, such as MUHAMMADI with his pastel landscapes and al fresco picnics; RIZA, whose sketches from low life and louche pageboys, executed with a dazzling calligraphic line, took Safavid taste by storm; and MU'IN, who produced some notable portraits.

Secular themes in book painting covered subjects as varied as adventures, seafaring, hunting, carousing, battle, banqueting, wrestling and other sports and—above all—romance. In the book of animal fables known as *Kalila and Dimna*, stories of animals sugared a bitter pill of political expediency and worldly wisdom, spiced with moral homilies. Illustrated versions of this text were popular throughout Syria, Iraq, Egypt and Iran in the 13th

and 14th centuries. Artists had free rein in the lively if stereotyped depiction of animals, often shown devoid of habitat and in anthropomorphic contexts (e.g. the king of the birds wears a crown).

In scientific works (*see* §III, 4(ii)(a) below) illustrations were perceived as diagrams explaining the all-important texts, which covered astronomy, military techniques and manoeuvres, automata and especially pharmacology. The plants depicted are schematic, but their ornamental qualities are patent, and thus sheer entertainment steals a march on science. Books on animals also added much Islamic material to a Classical substratum; their interest was as much pharmacological as zoological. Geography and the wonders of creation caught the imaginations of medieval Muslim painters, with depictions of angels and *jinn*, exotic and even fabulous animals and plants, and weird humanoid creatures believed to lie over some distant horizon.

(v) Vegetal themes. Vegetal ornament from various sources was taken to new heights of intensity and sophistication in Islamic art. The Classical world, for example, provided the motifs of the acanthus and the inhabited scroll and familiarized the Islamic world with openwork carving, from which the entire tradition of *mashrabiyya* (spoolwork) may spring, and the Corinthian capital, which served as the point of departure for a series of variations that left

the Classical original unrecognizable. Sasanian Iran and Mesopotamia contributed the palmette and the winged palmette, the rosette and, above all, the notion of repeat designs whereby vegetal forms took on a geometric character. The preference for stucco (*see* STUCCO AND PLASTERWORK, §III, 4), the innate flexibility of which allowed it to accommodate any quirk of design, encouraged this type of even surface patterning. Such trends culminated at Samarra', the Abbasid capital, where moulded and coloured vegetal motifs running the gamut from naturalism to abstraction were employed like wallpaper (*see* SAMARRA', fig. 3).

The principal achievement of Islamic art in the field of vegetal ornament was the invention of the ARABESQUE, whose very name encapsulates its origin. A key characteristic of this geometricized vegetal ornament is its protean variety, which allows it to be adapted to any number of contexts—tightly coiled or loosely undulating, confined to a few leaves or loaded with fruit and blossoms, grand or tiny, background or foreground.

Chinese motifs, which had infiltrated Islamic art at least from the early Abbasid period onwards, came to the fore in the wake of the Mongol invasions in the 13th century. Motifs included the peony, lotus and chrysanthemum, and the combination of these foreign blossoms changed familiar floral designs. Although increasingly schematized, these flowers may have triggered an interest in observing nature more closely, and by the 15th century accurately rendered, botanically distinguishable flowers had entered the repertory of Islamic art: among them the dianthus, hyacinth and above all the tulip. Under OTTOMAN patronage, the SAZ style, an overall surface decoration loosely based on some of these plant forms, developed, and tulipomania reached such a height at the capital in the early 18th century that the period was dubbed *lale devri* ('tulip age').

Vegetal motifs are put to manifold uses. They may be a discreet background for more important decoration, such as epigraphic bands, or they may claim an equal role as foil, as for example the vegetal interlace that constitutes the infill for polygonal patterning on carved woodwork. In both cases, artists exploited the differences between vegetal and other ornament. Vegetal motifs also lend themselves to borders, demarcating one field of ornament from another. The internal logic of a vegetal scroll, helped by colour coding, makes it ideal for palimpsest compositions in which successive designs are superimposed without loss of coherence.

The pervasiveness of vegetal ornament in Islamic art is shown by the transformation of architecture into an organic entity. The process began with window grilles of the Umayyad period, continued in the lambrequin arches of western Islamic architecture (see fig. 44 below) and culminated in panels from the Aljafería Palace (11th century) in Saragossa, where columns, capitals and arches dissolve in a jungle of rank vegetation. Squinches, too, were apt to take on foliate character, as were mihrabs and arches, where the underlying architectural framework is often swamped by the abundance of plant life (see figs 30 and 77 below). The scale, type and location of vegetal ornament may vary from one context to another. It may fill a huge window, dominate the dado or cover a dome;

it is found in manuscript carpet pages and frontispieces. Along with geometry, it provides the basic repertory for carpet design and is equally dominant in carved ivories, pottery and metalwork.

With increasing abstraction, vegetal ornament became fantastic as botanical accuracy was left behind. Geometry is apt to take over, so that vegetal scrolls are disciplined into regular repeating or even concentric circles. Calligraphy assumes organic forms, so that the shafts of letters sprout leaves or even blossoms, as in foliated and then floriated kufic (see fig. 83 below). Similarly, figures of people, animals and birds often take on vegetal character (*see* ORNAMENT AND PATTERN, fig. 14). And only fantasy of the most luxuriant kind can account for the vast supernal trees of Paradise. That same paradisiacal significance can often be sensed in Islamic vegetal decoration, for example in mihrabs or prayer rugs, but it is rarely made explicit. Perhaps artists used vegetal motifs to suggest in general terms the abundance of God's creation. The celebration of fertility would come naturally to people reared in a harsh desert environment; indeed, the image of an oasis is evoked in mosque courtyards with trees and a pool or fountain. A popular motif found in mosaics, silk textiles, architecture (see fig. 43 below) and ivories is a monumental tree flanked by animals. The context of some examples points to a close connection with the immemorially ancient theme of the Tree of Life.

(vi) Geometry. Like vegetal themes, geometry pervades Islamic art at all levels. Its importance in art owes much to the Arab fascination with mathematics seen in scientific instruments and devices—celestial globes, astrolabes, automata—and in treatises on them or on the minutiae of architectural construction and decoration by Abu'l-Wafa' al-Buzajani (AD 940–98) and Abu'l Qasim Jamal al-Din 'Abdallah, also known as al-Kashani (*see* ABU TAHIR, (4)). The many Arabic scientific and mathematical terms that have found their way into English (zenith, nadir, algorithm, algebra), along with 'Arabic' numerals and the very concept of zero, tell the same story. But the translation of such concepts into practice is of prime interest in the visual arts. The construction of Islamic buildings was achieved by squaring the circle, the practical equivalent of calculations involving the square root of two; measurements were achieved by means of ropes and pegs. A system of rotated squares underlies some of the most complex designs in Islamic architecture, for example MUQARNAS vaults. Much practical knowledge was handed on verbally from master to apprentice, but simplified graphic designs served as an aide-mémoire for those with the expertise to decode them. Examples requiring such extrapolation are the rolls that contain only a fraction of the entire plan, the grids that seem to have served as a skeletal framework for the huge religious buildings erected by the Shaybanids in western Central Asia, or the incised plan of a *muqarnas* vault found at Takht-i Sulayman. A grid of equilateral triangles underlies not only window grilles and mosaic floors of the Umayyad period but also mosques and madrasas of the later periods, and the importance of the diagonal as the key generative measurement has been demonstrated in Umayyad palaces and in Persian painting. Proportional relationships help to explain the innate

harmony and symmetry of many Islamic buildings; the use of modular elements such as arches and windows has the same effect. And the Islamic predilection for ornament did not exclude a delight in plain statement by means of solid geometry: cubes, hemispherical domes, cylindrical minarets and conical roofs. Their bare surfaces increased the direct impact of such simple forms.

Geometry makes its principal impact in the patterned surfaces that characterize so much of Islamic art. These patterns can be finite—as in dados, doors, book covers and carpets—or infinite—as in the designs used for borders and curved spaces such as domes and many metalwork shapes. But there are no hard-and-fast distinctions governing the way these two categories operate, or their contexts. Often the framework echoes the nature of the pattern within, so that square panels encase square kufic, or stars enclose stellate designs. Geometrical ornament, like vegetal, lends itself to palimpsest compositions, notably in carpets but also in tile mosaic schemes, for example those with raised polygons. The nomenclature used for geometric patterns, whether in medieval Iraq or in modern Iran and Morocco, reveals that patterns were perceived not in terms of line but as solids. An oval, for example, was called an almond. The craftsman would thus have at his disposal a repertory of named shapes from which to create his pattern.

Geometry finds endlessly varied expression in Islamic art. A given shape, for example, can undergo successive colour changes within a pattern, so that the same lines do double or triple duty simply by reappearing in different colours. Geometry can control the apparently organic exuberance of foliate ornament, as in the case of tightly coiled concentric vegetal scrolls. In the case of calligraphy, a precise set of rules based on the modular diamond shape created by a pen drawn across a surface determined the form of each individual letter. Thus at a fundamental level geometry controls the whole art of writing, although this, like many another use of geometry in Islamic art, is hidden. An instinctive feel for geometry may explain such pervasive features as balance (the preference for mirror symmetry and hierarchies), rotation and repetition. Repetition is most effective within a geometric framework which can control and modulate monotony, infinity, rhythm, mystery and unity—to name only a few associations that it triggers. The repetition of columns and arcades in hypostyle mosques or of domes and vaults can create effects of crescendo and diminuendo, suggest unity in diversity or define a vanishing point.

Medieval Islamic literary sources do not discuss the meanings of geometry in the visual arts, but this has not dampened modern speculation about the meaning of geometry. Muslims occasionally attached symbolic value to numbers, as attested by the various systems of *abjad*, in which each letter of the alphabet was allotted a specific numerical value. And geometry was used to define the concept of the Perfect Man in the writings of the 10th-century group known as the *Ikhwān al-safā'* ('Sincere brethren'). This intriguing evidence, however, cannot begin to account for the dominant role geometry plays in Islamic art. Some expressions could be interpreted as meditations on nature—flowers, stars, crystals, snowflakes, seashells, spiders' webs—and this would be particularly apt

for certain *muqarnas* vaults, carpets or Koran frontispieces. More generally, the ubiquity of geometric themes may suggest that they express the unity (Arab. *tawḥīd*) that is a prime attribute of God. In Christian thought, too, geometry was an archetypal expression of God's thought, but it remains dubious whether the Muslim artist was motivated by such beliefs when he devised a geometric composition.

(vii) Writing. The many references in the Koran to writing contribute to the high regard for calligraphy embedded in Islam from the beginning (*see* §III, 2 below), and the custom of making copies of the Koran clinched the prestige of calligraphy in the Muslim world. Many thousands of manuscripts of the sacred text, most of them now incomplete, show that the text was copied on a much greater scale than was the Bible in the medieval West, although the reasons for this have yet to be explored in appropriate detail. The status of the Koranic scripts was enhanced by the moral dimension of calligraphy, whereby fine writing was regarded as an expression of virtue, and calligraphers copying Korans took care to put themselves in a state of ritual purity before beginning their task.

From almost the beginning of Islam, writing was a major artistic theme. Coins (*see* §VIII, 2 below) bore religious messages—the *basmala* (invocation), the *shahāda* (profession of faith) and quotations from the Koran. Most inscriptions in the Muslim world were written in Arabic, even when that was not the local language: the fact that the Koran was in Arabic gave that language undisputed premier status to Muslims. The longest building inscriptions (*see* §II, 9(vi) below) are Koranic, and thus the building itself serves as the sacred book of Islam. In much the same way, minarets were apt to bear the profession of faith at their summits. Mosque domes were often inscribed on the interior with the 99 Beautiful Names of God, each in a separate cartouche and orbiting like stars in the firmament. In mystical circles, certain letters of the alphabet were assigned special significance, notably *wāw* (which was associated with *tawḥīd*) and the *lām–alif* ligature, which was held to mirror the relationship between the soul and the Beloved. The names of God, Muhammad and 'Ali, reduced to the very limits of legibility in the highly abstracted 'square kufic', were often used as a mantle over an entire building. Kufic inscriptions were used to sanctify everyday objects, often by means of the word *baraka* ('blessing'), but also by the associations that the script had with the Koran and with Koranic inscriptions, associations that lent it a proclamatory air.

In a largely illiterate society, much of the impact of calligraphy and epigraphy was symbolic. Inscriptions are frequently rendered illegible by their complex script or lofty placement. Writing could be used to connote the faith, as in the case of minarets covered with inscriptions (see fig. 32 below) or buildings converted to Islamic use (*see* ISTANBUL, fig. 8). The stereotyped formulae on so much medieval metalwork had an all-embracing symbolic function, at once prophylactic and benedictory, and were probably understood in general terms, even by those who could not decipher them in detail. Other types of epigraphy, such as the closely serried inscriptions so popular in Mamluk art, or the numerous versions of the Ottoman

TUGHRA, had unmistakably royal associations. The special colours used for royal names in monumental inscriptions had symbolic impact. The alphabet took on specific symbolism when *abjad* was used in poetic chronograms or combination locks. Also important are calligraphic pictures, in which letters are coaxed into the shapes of animals, birds, mosques, mihrabs, boats, faces and figures (see fig. 100 below). Sometimes the letters that form the design contain a pun on what is depicted—e.g. the word *haydar* ('lion', a name of 'Ali) written in the form of a lion. Mirror images, necessarily involving writing executed back to front, are also a popular category. The entire genre had a riddling, almost perverse quality about it, inviting the viewer to uncover double meanings and hidden symbolism.

Writing was ornamented in many ways. Perhaps the commonest, so far as kufic was concerned, was for letters to acquire extra decorative devices—foliations, floriations, plaited or bifurcated shafts, rosettes etc. Almost equally popular were various kinds of distortion, whereby the calligrapher would alternate thick and thin strokes or elongate certain letters while cramming others close together. In the 12th and 13th centuries there was a short-lived vogue in inlaid metalwork for animated inscriptions, in which first the terminations of the shafts, then the shafts themselves and finally the entire inscription would be made up of human faces, then human figures and eventually animals too. Presumably the near-illegibility of such inscriptions was part of the fun. Other tricks included *boustrophedon*, in which alternate lines of text would be written directly above the previous line, but upside down; palimpsests, where as many as three inscriptions, each in a different colour or hand, are superimposed on each other; inscriptions written so as to form part of larger geometric patterns or inscriptions; square kufic, in which the letters are forced into interlocking rectilinear shapes; and exercises in virtuosity, some of astounding skill. Entire chapters of the Koran are written on a leaf or even a grain of rice, or a Koran copied on such a tiny scale that it fits into a walnut shell.

A separate category, found most often in metalwork and carpets, comprises pseudo-inscriptions in which real letters formed nonsense words or sequences. Closely linked to this is 'Kufesque', in which the letters not only fail to spell out rational messages but are no longer Arabic letters, even though they have a generic resemblance to them. Kufesque is typically used in a Christian rather than a Muslim context (e.g. the doors of the cathedral of Le Puy in France, the exterior brickwork of HOSIOS LOUKAS in Greece, or on textiles in paintings by GENTILE DA FABRIANO and other late medieval Italian masters). Such 'inscriptions' were prized because of their exotic aura. Many inscription bands, whether on a monumental or small scale, develop their own rhythms by means of massed uprights or descenders, by giving letters serpentine tails and by manipulating spacing.

(viii) The natural world. Nature plays a major role in Islamic art, though more as an inspiration than as a model to be carefully copied. Animals and birds are the principal focus, as shown by early carpets (see fig. 201 below), pottery and stucco decoration. The popularity of the hunt as a theme

13. Bronze griffin, h. 1.07 m, from the western Mediterranean, 11th century (Pisa, Museo dell'Opera del Duomo)

for decoration ensured that the relevant animals—dog, hare, deer, lion etc—were depicted frequently. Animals and birds were suitable for background or secondary ornament, as in the margins of illustrated books, as infill or as borders. Occasionally they are depicted with the most meticulous naturalism, as in the illustrated copies of the *Kalila and Dimna* animal fables (e.g. Istanbul, U. Lib., F. 1422).

Fantasy is more evident than realism. Egyptian woodwork (see fig. 214 below) and pottery from Samarra' (*see* ORNAMENT AND PATTERN, fig. 14) or Nishapur delight in creatures that have botanical, anthropomorphic and epigraphic elements. A deep-rooted fear of idolatry may help to explain the bizarre lengths to which metalworkers went to avoid creating readily identifiable creatures when they fashioned zoomorphic ewers or incense burners; the Pisa griffin (see fig. 13), which partakes of three distinct species as well as having its surface decorated with panels and bands of vegetal, geometric and epigraphic ornament, exemplifies this paradoxical flouting of reality. Scrolls ending in human or animal heads decorate metalwork, *doublures* and carpets. Strangest of all, though, are certain Safavid and Mughal drawings, composite images created out of a plethora of twisted, struggling individual vignettes of living beings enmeshed in the manner of the 16th-century Milanese painter Giuseppe Arcimboldo, and their dating suggests that they were inspired by European models. Another aspect of fantasy is the prevalence of fabulous creatures including double-headed eagles, lions with one face but multiple bodies, the simurgh (see figs 118 and 128 below), winged horses, griffins, sphinxes and harpies. Exotic creatures of Far Eastern derivation—the dragon, *qilin*, unicorn and phoenix—appear in Islamic pottery, textiles and especially book painting following the Mongol invasions. Dragons also guard portals (see fig. 78 below).

Greater importance is accorded to royal creatures, principally the lion, the eagle or falcon, and the elephant. All are the stock-in-trade of costly textiles, on which they are often depicted in heraldic modes in roundels, rampant, passant, regardant, addorsed or affronted (see fig. 185 below) or attacking weaker creatures (see fig. 183 below). Lions act as pedestals for rulers, guard thrones or balustrades and decorate royal mausolea and caravanserais. Rulers such as Bahram Gur are often shown fighting and overcoming them. Eagles decorate ivories, royal buildings and city walls. The words for 'lion' (Arab. *asad*, Pers. *shīr*, Turk. *arslān*) and 'eagle' or 'falcon' (*tughril, toğrul*) figure as royal cognomens or titles. Elephants are depicted carrying monarchs in battle (see fig. 114 below) and as chess pieces. These and other creatures often discharge a symbolic role. Examples include such popular themes as apotheosis, the lion-strangler (see fig. 186 below) and the peacock or 'birds of paradise' that guard the entrances of sacred buildings. Research is gradually revealing the symbolic associations of creatures such as the rabbit, the cat, the camel, the cockerel and others, especially in a literary context in which they represent emotions or states of mind. The fish is a popular theme, often representing the sea, especially in scenes where the ruler is presented as cosmocrator, but also with zodiacal or cosmological associations. In much the same way, the snake represented the earth. The bull—apart from its obvious zodiacal connections, and the lion–bull combat, an ancient Near Eastern theme of royal, apotropaic and calendrical significance—connoted ritual feasting, drinking and sacrifice and was also a symbol of strength in a Turkish milieu. Some animals took on extra importance when the Turco-Mongol animal calendar, which had close links with that of China, came into use alongside the Islamic lunar calendar.

Animals frequently served didactic purposes. The utility of the *Kitāb al-bayṭara*, a treatise on farriery, needed images of horses to accompany the text. The very title of al-Jahiz's *Kitāb al-ḥayawān* ('Book of animals'; Milan, Bib. Ambrosiana, Ar. A. F. D. 140 Inf.) explains why the text is lavishly illustrated with images of animals—stereotyped but recognizable—and often brought vividly to life by a telling detail, such as the ostrich watchfully hatching her eggs. Arabic and Persian books on the usefulness of animals have illustrations depicting animals in their medicinal and pharmacological contexts. Al-Sufi's treatise on the fixed stars includes depictions of animals alongside humans under the appropriate constellation. Animals are a central theme in the principal medieval Islamic encyclopedia of the natural world, al-Qazwini's *'Ajā'ib al-makhlūqāt* ('Wonders of creation'), which exists in many copies, some with hundreds of illustrations.

Landscape was the other major theme from the natural world. It can be found in many media, but its fullest development was reserved for book painting, especially in Iran. It occasionally takes centre stage as a theme, although it mostly provides a background for the ostensible action. Such landscapes were composed by combining a limited number of components, though these are capable of almost infinite variation in colour, tone, size, shape and texture. Rocks are a case in point; in some manuscripts they are treated with Baroque technicolour exuberance, a visual feast in their own right while also serving as a subtle commentary on the action (see fig. 124 below). Many representational conventions, for example those governing fire, smoke, dust and clouds, derived from Chinese prototypes. China also provided, perhaps via woodblock maps, the conventions for water, whether still or in spate, clumps of grass, rocks, mountains, multiple receding planes and trees. Painters often misunderstood the subtleties of these conventions and used them carelessly or with unbecoming brashness. The decorative potential of such landscape symbols became paramount, and their capacity to suggest endless space was destroyed by substituting sharp for blurred outlines and bright colours for the original monochrome. Painters used landscape not as a bearer of meaning, nor as an objective correlative to the themes of the poetry that accompanied it in its original Chinese setting, but as a gorgeous back-cloth to the action. For a time, especially when the influence of Chinese art was at its height, landscape played a decisive part in the creation of mood, thereby deepening and enriching the meaning of the painting (see fig. 115 below). Later 14th-century painters simplified, toned down and tamed such expressionist landscapes (e.g. fig. 119 below). To the extent that the Persian text was hyperbolic, the landscape was its appropriate equivalent, but its role was reduced and less profound than it had been in Chinese painting.

(ix) Magic. Apotropaic images were common. City or citadel gates bear depictions of dragons, serpents, lions and other fearsome beasts; door-knockers feature lions or intertwined serpents, the latter providing doubly effective protection because knots were widely held to have magical efficacy. Doors might bear serpents and, more frequently, knotted designs. Frontispieces and finispieces to books sometimes had images of apotropaic intent; so too did *ex libris* compositions. Knotted devices occur frequently in Islamic pottery (see fig. 163 below), but their meaning is still unexplained, as are those attached to certain types of star (e.g. the hexagram, Solomon's seal). Thresholds were apt places for knotted motifs and for spolia; the message here was one of perpetual victory. In the Umayyad mosque of Damascus, a gold vine (perhaps knotted), the *karma*, marked—and protected—the perimeter of the mosque. When going into battle, Ottoman sultans wore talismanic shirts (see fig. 14) over their armour; these bore lengthy religious inscriptions, mainly from the Koran. Apotropaic powers were attributed to certain automata, for instance the roaring lions that guarded caliphal thrones or the rider placed above the palace at Baghdad; his lance was popularly held to point in the direction from which the city was threatened. Similarly, the winged female figures that flank figures of authority in the frontispieces of medieval

Mesopotamian book painting probably have a protective function—hence the way they look alertly to the left and right of the figure they flank like bodyguards.

Talismanic images are closely related to apotropaic ones and often reflect folk beliefs, for example the *panjah* or *khams*, the 'Hand of Fatima'. People wore amulets with inscriptions that were held to bring good luck, and many vehicles in Afghanistan and Pakistan, for example, still bear inscriptions reading *mashallah* ('What God wills'). Divination bowls have detailed inscriptions invoking blessings and curses in specific circumstances, and mirrors were also used for divination, to judge from the invocatory and magical inscriptions on their reverse sides. The medieval equivalent of registered post was to inscribe an object with the word *budūh*, the *abjad* value of whose letters (2:4:6:8) was held to give a greater degree of security. Muslims attributed talismanic powers to celadon, for it was believed to crack if poison were put into it. Large unglazed water jars bear reliefs perpetuating ancient Mesopotamian iconography, the talismanic power of which had apparently survived the coming of Islam. Illustrated texts such as the *Fālnāma* ('Book of divination') detail magical episodes and practices involving talismans.

Mythical beasts often have something magical about them. Griffins transport Alexander the Great into the empyrean (see fig. 245 below), and Pegasus appears on silks and in manuscripts. A weird array of mythical creatures, deriving partly from Chinese sources but largely from a shamanistic milieu, can be found in the corpus of paintings associated with SIYAH QALAM. Some are creatures of nightmare, having human form but with the heads and appendages of demons, equipped with ravening fangs and claws.

The Islamic world, like the medieval West, tended to place marvels in the East. Thus al-Wasiti, the painter of the Schefer *Maqāmāt* ('Assemblies'; 1237; Paris, Bib. N., MS. arabe 5847), depicted sphinxes and harpies in the wondrous Eastern Isles, where marvels such as the talking or *waqwaq* tree abound. The text and hence the illustrations of al-Qazwini's cosmology teem with outrageous hybrid creatures. Another fruitful source of marvels was poetry, especially in Iran: the bestial tribes of Gog and Magog, Amazons and lion-men, the quest for the Water of Life, the impious ascension of Kay Ka'us into the heavens, such monsters as dragons, lion-apes, unicorns, horned wolves or the Great Worm of Kirman, kings with snakes sprouting from their shoulders, stone warriors, witches and warlocks, demons, fairies and sirens—artists were spoilt for choice. But these texts also struck a more elevated chord as treasure-houses of myth, interpreting the past in heroic terms and providing models for conduct as well as material for entertainment. Hence the emphasis was on the great kings and heroes of Iranian legend—Gayumars, Tahmuras, Jamshid, Kaykhusraw and Faridun, Zal, Suhrab and Rustam—and actual historical figures too, such as Iskandar (Alexander the Great) and the Sasanian monarchs. History and myth mingle, and facts are mythologized (e.g. the Khusraw and Shirin story). Finally, outright thaumaturgy is occasionally depicted. The principal figure here is Solomon; references to him as a wonder-worker, lord of the *jinn*s and master of the speech of animals and birds, are widespread. The popularity of

14. Talismanic shirt of white linen inscribed in black, blue, red and gold with verses from the Koran, l. 1.22 m, from Istanbul, second quarter of the 16th century (Istanbul, Topkapı Palace Museum)

the *Qiṣāṣ al-anbiyā'* helped to spread this iconography and embraced the miracles of the other prophets too, for example Moses, besides influencing the detailed cycle of the life of the Prophet.

(x) Heavenly bodies. For Muslims the lore of the stars embraced astronomy and astrology and was of absorbing interest because the heavenly bodies were widely believed to affect human life. Hence the widespread use of zodiacal imagery in Islamic art (*see* MIRROR, fig. 6). Solar references are particularly numerous and build on foundations laid in the Classical world (e.g. the nimbus) and in the Ancient Near East (e.g. the rosette). The lion is the creature with solar associations *par excellence*, through the zodiacal sign of Leo (often shown overcoming Taurus, the bull), and since the lion was also a popular symbol for the monarch, rulers could also lay claim to solar associations, as in the Fountain of the Lions in the Alhambra (*see* GRANADA, fig. 4). The connection is plainest in the Iranian royal emblem of the lion and sun, the origins of which date to Parthian times, though the motif seems to have attained popularity only in the 13th century. Thereafter it was commonly encountered in coins, pottery, architecture and even—in the 19th century—postage stamps and banknotes. Eagles too could embody solar references. More abstract expressions of the solar theme occur in unmistakably royal contexts, such as the rayed vaulting and mosaics and numerous rosettes at KHIRBAT AL-MAFJAR or the rayed vault mosaics at the Great Mosque of Córdoba. The interiors of domes often display radiating designs, which are replicated on a smaller scale in the *shamsa* motifs in manuscripts. But domes, which by ancient tradition were equated with the vault of heaven—hence the description of so many early Islamic domes as *qubbat al-khaḍrā'* ('dome of the sky')—could have an oculus or star-shaped opening to link with the sky. The poetic quotations on bowls show that they were widely understood to parallel the dome of Heaven. The radiating theme also found

expression in epigraphy, especially in the Mamluk period, when radiating inscriptions, with the shafts mimicking the rays of the sun, were popular (*see* MIRROR, fig. 6). The solar parallel was emphasized by the use of gold inlay. The image of rotation, once again with heavenly associations, was taken up by sphinxes processing in a circle and by the fishpond theme. Textiles employ a wide range of heavenly images, but the sun is paramount in most of them (see fig. 200 below).

The moon had only peripheral importance in Islamic iconography. Lunar eclipses are alluded to in painting and metalwork, and the lunar crescent, which appeared in the Umayyad period, became a major astrological theme on 12th- and 13th-century Mesopotamian coins. Only thereafter did the crescent, often in association with a star, become a symbol of the Islamic faith itself, but the evolution of the process remains obscure. The most obvious example of lunar imagery in Islamic art is the Aqmar Mosque in Cairo (see fig. 37 below); its name ('moonlit') proclaims the connection, and its façade is festooned with radiating epigraphic and Shi'ite images, linking lunar and religious themes.

Solar and lunar references are merely facets of the broader category of *'ilm al-nujūm*, star lore. Knowledge of this branch of science was expected of any educated Muslim, and this may explain the frequency of celestial references in Islamic art. The planets—which in Muslim belief included the sun and moon—and their symbols are the stock-in-trade of hundreds of medieval metal wares and, to a lesser extent, pottery. The so-called planet children, too, are a familiar theme in metalwork and manuscripts right up to Ottoman times. The role of astrology in Islamic art is still unclear, even in familiar stories such as Nizami's *Haft Paykar* ('Seven portraits'), one of the most popular cycles in Iranian painting, which is shot through with astrological references. The zodiac infiltrates the Turco-Mongol animal calendar, religious imagery, city and bazaar gates, bridges, coinage, manuscripts and above all metalwork, where the popularity of zodiacal themes may have had something to do with the choice of metals used in these objects—though why metalwork in particular featured astrological images remains an open question.

Light is a more pervasive theme. Frequent use is made of the celebrated Chapter of Light in the Koran (xxiv), especially verse 35, a favourite inscription for mihrabs since it is often understood to refer to a lamp in a niche; many mihrabs contain depictions of hanging lamps. Minbars are often inscribed with the following verse so that they are thematically linked with the mihrab; indeed they often bear other references to light, for example stellar polygons (for illustration *see* MINBAR), stars or God's name, executed in ivory or bone and therefore standing out as if highlighted from the predominantly dark background of the minbar. Lamps make the same obvious pun by bearing all or part of Sura xxiv.35, as well as rosettes and similar solar motifs. Since they tend to be made of glass or of pierced metal, the letters of the inscriptions stand out like neon signs when the lamp is lit (see fig. 155 below). The transparency of windows is used to the same effect, with pierced grilles, lunettes and spoolwork creating patterns of light, while in the case of stained glass (*see* §II,

9(v) below) polychromy is added. MUQARNAS vaults become metaphors for light in that they mimic the rotating heavens, with expert fenestration creating shafts of light that seem to shoot downwards in several directions. Inscriptions link these ceilings with the Milky Way and the Pleiades, thus proving that the cosmic implications of these light effects were deliberate. The same is true of entire palaces conceived as receptacles of light with alabaster ceilings and glass walls. Some palaces with these features were intended to emulate the legendary palaces of Ghumdan, Sadir and Khwarnaq in pre-Islamic Arabia. The MINARET, which is etymologically linked to notions of fire and/or light, served as a vehicle for actual and spiritual illumination. Minarets were illumined on special occasions (even today they bear neon religious inscriptions) and were used as lighthouses for ships or nocturnal caravans.

Haloes of various kinds—circular, rayed and flame or mandorla—are encountered in Islamic painting. Billowing clouds around inscriptions in manuscripts may be intended to sanctify them and thus act as yet another kind of halo. Various types of metalwork, too, exploited the multiple associations of light, for example by allegorical inscriptions of Sufi intent: candlesticks (see fig. 156 below), incense burners, torchstands (see fig. 158 below), candelabra and polykandela. Finally, many titles used by Muslim potentates employ the concept of light: sun (*shams*), moon (*qamr*, *badr*), light (*nūr*), star (*najm*), celestial sphere (*falak*) and lamp (*sirāj*), in such combinations as 'Light of Religion' (*nūr al-dīn*) or 'Sun of the State' (*shams al-dawla*). Thus the powerful implications of light in a moral and religious context would be made to serve political ends.

BIBLIOGRAPHY

GENERAL

E. Herzfeld: 'Die Genesis der islamischen Kunst und das Mshatta-Prolem', *Der Islam*, i (1910), pp. 27–63

R. Ettinghausen: 'Interaction and Integration in Islamic Art', *Unity and Variety in Muslim Civilization*, ed. G. von Grunebaum (Chicago, 1955), pp. 107–31

F. Rosenthal: *Four Essays on Art and Literature in Islam* (Leiden, 1971)

O. Grabar: *The Formation of Islamic Art* (New Haven, 1973/R and enlarged 1987)

R. Ettinghausen: 'The Man-made Setting: Islamic Art and Architecture', *Islam and the Arab World*, ed. B. Lewis (London, 1976), pp. 57–88

——: 'Originality and Conformity in Islamic Art', *Individualism and Conformity in Classical Islam*, ed. A. Banani and S. Vyronis jr (Wiesbaden, 1977), pp. 83–114

T. Allen: *Five Essays on Islamic Art* (Sebastopol, CA, 1988)

RELIGIOUS AND ROYAL

Enc. Islam/2: 'Hilāl' [Crescent]; 'Rank' [Emblem]

L. A. Mayer: *Saracenic Heraldry* (Oxford, 1933)

R. Ettinghausen: 'Die bildliche Darstellung der Ka'ba im islamischen Kulturkreis', *Z. Dt. Mrgländ. Ges.*, n. s., xii (1934), pp. 111–37

J. Sauvaget: *La Mosquée omeyyade de Médine* (Paris, 1947)

R. Ettinghausen: 'Persian Ascension Miniatures of the Fourteenth Century', *Accademia nazionale dei lincei, atti del XII convegno 'volta' promosso dalla classe di scienze morali, storiche e filologiche, tema: Oriente e occidente nel medioevo: Roma, 1957*, pp. 360–83

W. Hartner and R. Ettinghausen: 'The Conquering Lion: The Life-cycle of a Symbol', *Oriens*, xvii (1964), pp. 161–71

J. Sourdel-Thomine: 'Clefs et serrures de la Ka'ba: Notes d'épigraphie arabe', *Rev. Etud. Islam.*, xxxix (1971), pp. 29–86

R. Ettinghausen: *From Byzantium to Sasanian Iran and the Islamic World* (Leiden, 1972)

D. Shepherd: 'Banquet and Hunt in Medieval Islamic Iconography', *Gathering in Honor of Dorothy E. Miner*, ed. U. E. McCracken (Baltimore, 1974), pp. 79–92

D. E. Klimburg-Salter: 'A Sufi Theme in Persian Painting', *Kst Orients*, xi (1977), pp. 43–84

R. Milstein: 'Sufi Elements in Late Fifteenth Century Herāt Painting', *Studies in Memory of Gaston Wiet*, ed. M. Rosen-Ayalon (Jerusalem, 1977), pp. 357–70

E. Baer: 'The Ruler in Cosmic Setting: A Note on Medieval Islamic Iconography', *Essays in Islamic Art and Architecture of Honor of Katharina Otto-Dorn*, ed. A. Daneshvari (Malibu, 1981), pp. 13–20

C. Williams: 'The Cult of 'Alid Saints in the Fatimid Monuments of Cairo', *Muqarnas*, i (1983), pp. 37–52; iii (1985), pp. 39–60

K. Brisch: 'Observations on the Iconography of the Mosaics in the Great Mosque of Damascus', *Content and Context of Visual Arts in the Islamic World*, ed. P. P. Soucek (University Park, PA, and London, 1988), pp. 13–24

E. Whelan: 'Representations of the *Khāssakīyah* and the Origins of Mamluk Emblems', *Content and Context of Visual Arts in the Islamic World*, ed. P. P. Soucek (University Park, PA, and London, 1988), pp. 219–53

E. Baer: *Ayyubid Metalwork with Christian Images* (Leiden, 1989)

Images of Paradise in Islamic Art (exh. cat., ed. S. S. Blair and J. M. Bloom; Hanover, NH, Dartmouth Coll., Hood Mus. A.; New York, Asia Soc. Gals; Brunswick, ME, Bowdoin Coll. Mus. A.; and elsewhere; 1991–2)

A. Orient., xxiii (1993) [whole issue devoted to Islamic palaces]

R. Hillenbrand: *Islamic Architecture: Form, Function and Meaning* (Edinburgh, 1994)

NATURE, LANDSCAPE AND ANIMALS

A. Riegl: *Stilfragen* (Berlin, 1893); Eng. trans. by E. Kain as *Problems of Style* (Princeton, 1992)

E. Kühnel: *Die Arabeske* (Wiesbaden, 1949); Eng. trans. by R. Ettinghausen as *The Arabesque: Meaning and Transformation of an Ornament* (Graz, 1976)

R. Ettinghausen: *Studies in Muslim Iconography I: The Unicorn* (Washington, DC, 1950)

——: 'Early Realism in Islamic Art', *Studi orientalistici in onore di Giorgio Levi della Vida* (Rome, 1956), i, pp. 250–73

E. Baer: *Sphinxes and Harpies in Medieval Islamic Art* (Jerusalem, 1965)

R. Ettinghausen: 'The Dance with Zoomorphic Masks and Other Forms of Entertainment Seen in Islamic Art', *Arabic and Islamic Studies in Honor of Hamilton A. R. Gibb*, ed. G. Makdisi (Leiden, 1965), pp. 211–24

E. Baer: 'Fish-pond Ornaments on Persian and Mamluk Metal Vessels', *Bull. SOAS*, xxxi (1968), pp. 14–27

G. Azarpay: 'The Eclipse Dragon on an Arabic Frontispiece Miniature', *J. Amer. Orient. Soc.*, xcviii (1977–8), pp. 363–74

B. Brend: 'Rocks in Persian Miniature Painting', *Landscape Style in Asia*, ed. W. Watson, Colloq. A. & Archaeol. Asia, ix (London, 1979), pp. 111–37

P. P. Soucek: 'The Role of Landscape in Iranian Painting to the 15th Century', *Landscape Style in Asia*, ed. W. Watson, Colloq. A. & Archaeol. Asia, ix (London, 1979), pp. 86–110

J. Rawson: *Chinese Ornament: The Lotus and the Dragon* (London, 1984)

A. Daneshvari: *Animal Symbolism in Warqa wa Gulsha* (Oxford, 1986)

J. S. Cowen: *Kalila wa Dimna: An Animal Allegory of the Mongol Court: The Istanbul University Album* (New York, 1989)

R. Hillenbrand: 'Mamlūk and Īlkhānid Bestiaries: Convention and Experiment', *A. Orient.*, xx (1990), pp. 149–87

E. J. Grube: 'Prolegomena for a Corpus Publication of Illustrated *Kalīlah wa Dimnah* Manuscripts', *Islam. A.*, iii (1990–91), pp. 301–481

B. O'Kane: 'Rock Faces and Rock Figures in Persian Painting', *Islam. A.*, iv (1990–91), pp. 219–46

L. Golombek: 'The *Paysage* as Funerary Imagery in the Timurid Period', *Muqarnas*, x (1993), pp. 241–52

GEOMETRY AND SECULAR THEMES

R. Ettinghausen: 'The Bobrinski Kettle: Patron and Style of an Islamic Bronze', *Gaz. B.-A.*, xxiv (1943), pp. 193–208

D. S. Rice: 'The Seasons and the Labors of the Months in Islamic Art', *A. Orient.*, i (1954), pp. 1–39

O. Grabar: 'Imperial and Urban Art in Islam: The Subject Matter of Fāṭimid Art', *Colloque international sur l'histoire du Caire: Caire, 1969*, pp. 173–89

——: 'The Illustrated Maqāmāt of the Thirteenth Century: The Bourgeoisie and the Arts', *The Islamic City*, ed. A. Hourani and S. M. Stern (Oxford, 1970), pp. 207–22

E. Baer: 'The "Pila" of Játiva: A Document of Secular Urban Art in Western Islam', *Kst Orients*, vii (1970–71), pp. 144–66

C. Adle: 'Recherches sur le module et le tracé correcteur dans la miniature orientale', *Monde Iran. & Islam*, iii (1975), pp. 81–105

P. Soucek: 'An Illustrated Manuscript of al-Biruni's *Chronology of Ancient Nations*', *The Scholar and the Saint*, ed. P. Chelkowski (New York, 1975), pp. 103–65

K. Critchlow: *Islamic Patterns* (London, 1976)

U. Harb: *Ilkhanidische Stalaktitengewölbe: Beiträge zu Entwurf und Bautechnik* (Berlin, 1978)

R. Ettinghausen: 'The Taming of the Horror Vacui in Islamic Art', *Proc. Amer. Philos. Soc.*, cxxiii (1979), pp. 15–28

A. Paccard: *Le Maroc et l'artisanat traditionnel islamique dans l'architecture*, 2 vols (Saint-Jorioz, 1979)

L. Golombek: 'The Draped Universe of Islam', *Content and Context of Visual Arts in the Islamic World*, ed. P. P. Soucek (University Park, PA, and London, 1988), pp. 25–50

S. Carboni: 'The London Qazwīnī: An Early 14th-century Copy of the *Ajā'ib al-Makhlūqāt*', *Islam. A.*, iii (1988–9), pp. 15–32

E. Baer: 'Jeweled Ceramics from Medieval Islam: A Note on the Ambiguity of Islamic Ornament', *Muqarnas*, vi (1989), pp. 83–97

G. Necipoğlu: 'Geometric Design in Timurid/Turkmen Architectural Practice: Thoughts on a Recently Discovered Scroll and its Late Gothic Parallels', *Timurid Art and Culture: Iran and Central Asia in the Fifteenth Century*, ed. L. Golombek and M. Subtelny (Leiden, 1992), pp. 48–66

I. el-Said: *Islamic Art and Architecture: The System of Geometric Design*, ed. T. el-Bouri and K. Critchlow (Reading, 1993)

WRITING

D. S. Rice: *The Unique Ibn al-Bawwab Manuscript in the Chester Beatty Library* (Dublin, 1955)

L. Volov [Golombek]: 'Plaited Kufic on Samanid Epigraphic Pottery', *A. Orient.*, vi (1966), pp. 107–33

A. Schimmel: *Islamic Calligraphy* (Leiden, 1970)

R. Ettinghausen: 'Arabic Epigraphy: Communication or Symbolic Affirmation', *Near Eastern Numismatics . . . Studies in Honor of G. C. Miles*, ed. D. Kouymjian (Beirut, 1974), pp. 297–317

——: 'Kufesque in Byzantine Greece, the Latin West and the Muslim World', *A Colloquium in Memory of G. C. Miles, 1904–1975* (New York, 1976), pp. 28–47

E. C. Dodd and S. Khairallah: *The Image of the Word*, 2 vols (Beirut, 1981)

A. Schimmel: *Calligraphy and Islamic Culture* (New York, 1984)

S. Auld: 'Kuficising Inscriptions in the Work of Gentile da Fabriano', *Orient. A.*, n. s., xxxii (1986), pp. 246–65

R. Hillenbrand: 'Qur'anic Epigraphy in Medieval Islamic Architecture', *Rev. Etud. Islam.*, xiv (1986), pp. 173–90

D. James: *Qur'āns of the Mamluks* (London, 1988)

S. S. Blair: *The Monumental Inscriptions of Early Islamic Iran and Transoxiana* (Leiden, 1992)

MAGIC AND HEAVENLY BODIES

W. Hartner: 'The Pseudoplanetary Nodes of the Moon's Orbit in Hindu and Islamic Iconographies', *A. Islam*, v (1938), pp. 113–54

D. S. Rice: *The Wade Cup in the Cleveland Museum of Art* (Paris, 1955)

R. Ettinghausen: 'The "Wade Cup" in the Cleveland Museum of Art: Its Origins and Decorations', *A. Orient.*, ii (1957), pp. 327–66

W. Hartner: 'Zur astrologischen Symbolik des "Wade Cup"', *Aus der Welt der islamischen Kunst: Festschrift für Ernst Kühnel* (Berlin, 1959), pp. 234–43

E. Wellesz: 'An Early Al-Ṣūfī Manuscript in the Bodleian Library in Oxford', *A. Orient.*, iii (1959), pp. 1–26

E. Baer: 'Representations of "Planet-children" in Turkish Manuscripts', *Bull. SOAS*, xxxi (1968), pp. 526–33

W. Hartner: 'The Vaso Vescovali in the British Museum: A Study in Islamic Astrological Iconography', *Kst Orients*, ix (1973–4), pp. 99–130

R. Ettinghausen: 'Abrī Painting', *Studies in Memory of Gaston Wiet*, ed. M. Rosen-Ayalon (Jerusalem, 1977), pp. 345–56

J. W. Allan: *Islamic Metalwork: The Nuhad Es-Said Collection* (London, 1982)

R. Hillenbrand: 'The Symbolism of the Rayed Nimbus in Early Islamic Art', *Cosmos*, ii (1986), pp. 1–52

R. Milstein: 'Light, Fire and the Sun in Islamic Painting', *Studies in Islamic History and Civilization in Honour of Professor David Ayalon*, ed. M. Sharon (Jerusalem, 1986), pp. 533–52

A. S. Melikian-Chirvani: 'The Lights of Sufi Shrines', *Islam. A.*, ii (1987), pp. 117–36

D. Behrens-Abouseif: 'The Façade of the Aqmar Mosque in the Context of Fatimid Ceremonial', *Muqarnas*, ix (1992), pp. 29–38

N. N. N. Khoury: 'The Mihrab Image: Commemorative Themes in Medieval Islamic Architecture', *Muqarnas*, ix (1992), pp. 11–28

J. M. Bloom: 'The Qubbat al-Khadrā' in Early Islamic Palaces', *A. Orient.*, xxiii (1994), pp. 131–7

P. P. Soucek: 'Solomon's Throne/Solomon's Bath: Model or Metaphor?', *A. Orient.*, xxiii (1994), pp. 109–34

ROBERT HILLENBRAND

II. Architecture.

Unlike other forms of Islamic art, such as the illustrated book and inlaid metalwork, architecture is a feature of general occurrence throughout this civilization. It has been used to provide places for communal worship, social service and stately residence. As more money and effort were invested in architecture than in other arts, it is an important indicator of social concerns. Prominent individual patrons deliberately manipulated architecture to express their piety and power. Despite the fragile or less durable materials used and the rigours of the geography and climate (many Islamic lands lie in earthquake zones), large numbers of buildings have survived, even from the early periods, and the architectural record, whether in the buildings themselves or in such ancillary materials as books, accounts and plans, is more complete than that of any other art.

The development of Islamic architecture can be divided into seven periods of unequal length and varying importance. Most of these periods can be subdivided into regions: the eastern Islamic lands, usually comprising Iran, Afghanistan and western Central Asia; the central Islamic lands, usually comprising Arabia, Iraq, greater Syria and Egypt; Anatolia and the Balkans; and the western Islamic lands, usually comprising Spain and North Africa (Tunisia, Algeria and Morocco). The extensive Islamic architecture of the Indian subcontinent is here only summarized, with references to the appropriate discussions elsewhere. These regions are usually treated from east to west, because, apart from the formative period when Mediterranean architectural traditions played a decisive role, most of the architectural innovations that came to characterize Islamic architecture were produced or developed in the eastern Islamic lands. The unusual importance of applied decoration in Islamic architecture merits a separate discussion. Contrary to the stereotyped picture of a desert civilization based in oases, Islamic architecture was the product of a highly urbanized society, and the urban development of its cities, the largest and most important in the medieval world, has long been the subject of study. Housing in the Islamic lands represents a conjunction of regional, local and pan-Islamic trends.

1. Introduction. 2. Before AD 661. 3. AD 661–*c*. 750. 4. *c*. AD 750–*c*. 900. 5. *c*. AD 900–*c*. 1250. 6. *c*. 1250–*c*. 1500. 7. *c*. 1500–*c*. 1900. 8. After *c*. 1900. 9. Architectural decoration. 10. Urban development. 11. Housing.

1. INTRODUCTION. The enormous expanse of the Islamic lands, which stretch in a wide band from the Atlantic to the Indian Ocean, from the steppes of Central Asia to the grasslands of Africa, meant that no single centre was dominant throughout history. Islamic architecture, unlike Roman for example, was multi-centred, and strong regional traditions already evident in pre-Islamic times continued to play an important role within the Islamic world (*see* MESOPOTAMIA, §II and IRAN, ANCIENT, §II).

(i) Materials. (ii) Building types. (iii) Architectural elements and construction techniques. (iv) Decoration. (v) Patrons and architects. (vi) Meaning and impact.

(i) Materials. These were most dependent on geography, largely because building materials were low-value, bulky commodities that were expensive to transport, and particular techniques were developed to use specific materials. The eastern Islamic lands generally favour construction in brick, since little good building stone can be quarried there. As little timber was available for scaffolding, centring or superstructures, ingenious techniques of vaulting in brick were developed. Mud-brick had the advantage of being cheap and remarkably serviceable in areas with little rain; and plaster or stucco revetments were used to protect the fragile surface and, when carved or painted (*see* §9(i)(a) below), to enliven its inherent drabness. Baked brick was more expensive, because it required scarce supplies of fuel for firing; where affordable its durability was preferred in regions with greater precipitation and a more extreme climate. Although it too could be covered with plaster, particularly on interiors, it was left exposed on exteriors, which were enlivened with terracotta and glazed materials. Indeed, stunning exteriors in glazed tile and tile mosaic became a hallmark of architecture in the eastern Islamic lands after *c*. 1250 (see fig. 15 and §9(ii) below).

15. Mausoleum of Timur (Gur-i Mir), Samarkand, Uzbekistan, 1404–5

By contrast, the Mediterranean world inherited the Antique traditions of construction in stone, and fine stone masonry and carving are characteristic of much Islamic architecture in Anatolia, Syria, Egypt, Tunisia and Spain. The great marble quarries of antiquity, however, were not exploited, as Classical and Byzantine spolia, including columns, capitals and bases, were available in virtually unlimited quantities. The ready availability of large quantities of timber from Anatolia, western North Africa and Spain led to the extensive use of wooden coverings, such as trusses and gabled roofs. Especially in the western Mediterranean, which is doused by wet winds off the Atlantic, pitched and tiled roofs were more practical. At various times, however, the power of an international Islamic artistic culture countered regional tendencies, and such materials as stucco and brick were exploited outside their natural habitat. In Egypt, for example, traditionally a land of stone architecture, brick and stucco were favoured for public buildings in the 9th and 10th centuries (see fig. 24 below), due to the prestige of architectural styles at the Abbasid capital in Iraq.

(ii) Building types. The congregational, or Friday, MOSQUE (Arab. *masjid*: 'place of prostration') is by far the most common type of building to survive. In origin a mosque was simply a place set aside for prayer, and this was reflected in its alignment on an axis, known as the qibla, which was directed towards the Ka'ba in Mecca (*see* §2 below). Mosques were built of durable materials and were continuously maintained by the community of believers, who were enjoined to pray collectively in them on Friday at noon. Apart from the liturgical orientation of mosques, the forms they might use and assume were limited only by the ingenuity of the builder and the desires of the patron, although such forms as the MIHRAB (niche in the qibla wall) and the MINARET (tower) became ubiquitous. When centralized power was strongest, as in the first centuries of Islam, a single hypostyle plan, realized in local materials and techniques, was dominant throughout. At other periods, however, local traditions were stronger, and domed mosques, for example, were typical of Ottoman Turkey. From early Islamic times, small oratories were also built as local places of daily prayer. Few early examples have survived, because they were often built of less durable materials and were not permanently endowed. Those few show that a nine-domed type was known in many areas, but regional variations were strong. Mosques provide the armature for understanding the development of Islamic architecture, but the conservatism inherent in religious architecture means that innovations appeared slowly in them. It is far more likely that secular architecture embodied architectural innovation, for it was constructed at the whim of a particular patron to satisfy his own wishes, but far less of it has survived.

In earlier times, the congregational mosque was the centre of the Muslim community, and many educational and charitable functions, such as teaching, lodging and feeding the poor, were carried out there. In later times, the inclusive character of congregational mosques was restricted as they became primarily places of prayer, and other kinds of institutions were thus developed to serve specialized functions. They included theological colleges (Arab. *madrasa, medersa,* Turk. *medrese* etc; *see* MADRASA), hospices for Sufis (Arab. *khānaqāh, zāwiya, ribāṭ; see* KHANAQAH), hospitals (Arab. *māristān,* Pers. *bīmāristān*), alms kitchens (Turk. *imaret*) and drinking-water dispensaries and elementary schools (Arab. *sabīl-kuttāb*). Apart from such specialized spaces as kitchens or fountain-houses, these institutions often shared common forms, with larger rooms for communal activities and small cells for individual residence.

Another common type of building found throughout is the monumental tomb (*see* TOMB, §II). The Prophet Muhammad disapproved of the monumentalization of graves, and orthodox tradition frowned on them, yet there developed a strong tradition of funerary architecture in the Islamic lands; whether this was the result of Shi'ite veneration of the Prophet's family or the continuation of popular pre-Islamic practices is not known. Few tombs have survived from before AD 900, but after that date the tombs of descendants of the Prophet, local saints, mystics and secular figures became increasingly large and magnificent. They came to represent some of the most famous examples of Islamic architecture (e.g. the tomb of Shah Jahan at Agra, known as the Taj Mahal; *see* AGRA, fig. 1). At first these structures were simple canopies, domed cubes or towers, but later they became more elaborate. They were designed to be the formal centrepieces of educational and charitable ensembles in an attempt to counter orthodox disapproval and provide religious justification for the veneration of the dead.

The most common types of secular buildings to survive are those concerned with trade. Rural and urban caravanserais (*see* CARAVANSERAI), warehouses, markets, shopping streets and bridges survive from all over the Islamic lands and testify to the continuous importance of overland trade. At times these were frankly utilitarian, but more often than not they were grandiose constructions advertising the power and prestige of the patron. For example, the splendid caravanserais built by the Saljuq princes throughout Anatolia (*see* §5(iii)(a) below) have unusually elaborate portals of carved stone that go far beyond the necessity of affording protection to the merchants, merchandise and beasts of burden housed within.

Fortresses and citadels (Arab. *burj, qaṣr, ribāṭ* etc) in early Islamic times were built only on the frontiers (they were unnecessary within the empire because of the high degree of internal security). With the breakup of centralized power in the 10th century, however, cities began to be provided with defensive walls and powerful citadels. Citadels and fortifications became particularly important during the Crusades, when there was significant exchange of architectural technology (*see* MILITARY ARCHITECTURE AND FORTIFICATIONS, §IV).

Few palaces have survived, because they were designed more for display than for durability, and those that were in continuous use were repeatedly redecorated (*see* PALACE, §III). Although over time they varied enormously in plan and scale, palaces in the Islamic world tended to be agglomerations of units arranged around interior courts and were formally very different from European châteaux and palaces. Palaces and fine houses were set in gardens or had gardens within them, and these verdant oases provided shade and cooling, fragrant breezes in a generally hot and dry climate (*see* GARDEN, §V). The great palaces in the urban centres of the past are largely built over; those that survive were abandoned and are known only through excavations (e.g. Samarra' in Iraq; *see* SAMARRA', §2), have been preserved as curiosities (e.g. the Alhambra in Granada; *see* GRANADA, §III) or date from relatively recent times (e.g. Topkapı Palace in Istanbul; *see* ISTANBUL, §III, 13). Virtually nothing is known about residential architecture in early times, except for excavated sites such as Fustat (Old Cairo; *see* §4(ii) below) and SIRAF on the Gulf, but domestic architecture after *c.* 1500 is remarkably well documented in many areas (*see* §11 below and VERNACULAR ARCHITECTURE, §II, 7). Public baths (Arab. *ḥammām*) are another common type (*see* BATH (ii), §2). Abandoned baths, such as at KHIRBAT AL-MAFJAR near Jericho and QUSAYR 'AMRA (Qasr al-'Amra) in Jordan (*see* §3(iii) below), show that the Islamic world inherited Late Antique traditions of communal bathing, but the limited availability of water meant that the traditional plunge pool was eliminated. The constantly high heat and humidity of baths weaken the fabric, and few other early examples have survived intact.

(iii) Architectural elements and construction techniques. The common formal elements of Islamic architecture—arches, squinches, vaults, domes and towers—are not unique to the Islamic lands but are often used or combined there in distinctive ways. The need to provide large, relatively undivided spaces for communal gathering and prayer may have led to the development of ingenious techniques of arcuate construction and vaulting, which were then transferred to other types of building. Architects could choose to have many small vaults carried on many relatively slender supports, fewer large vaults carried on massive piers and walls, or some combination. An unusually sophisticated system of vaulting enormous spaces was developed in the Ottoman empire, undoubtedly on the model of earlier Byzantine buildings there. The distinctive profile of these lead-covered domes became one of the most striking features of Ottoman mosques (*see* §7(i) below). Elsewhere mosques and other religious buildings were usually identified from the exterior by tall minarets or by elaborate portals rather than by domes, which became the signifiers of monumental tombs. The simultaneous desire for a pleasing interior space and a dominating exterior profile resulted in unique solutions for domes, perhaps the most unusual being those found in 15th-century buildings of Iran and western Central Asia (*see* §6(i)(b) below). Tall structures were rendered particularly unstable in this land of earthquakes, and the architects often supported a tall and bulbous ribbed dome on a relatively shallow inner shell by means of concealed vertical flanges made of brick. Another solution was to suspend a plaster vault from the exterior one of brick by means of wooden struts and ropes.

The possibilities for supports and coverings were relatively restricted, and Islamic architects focused unusual attention on the zone of transition between the two. Besides such traditional forms as the squinch and the pendentive, new forms, for example a band of prismatic consoles known as Turkish triangles or squinch-net vaulting (see fig. 52 below), were invented to make the transition between base and vault. At times architects preferred to integrate these three zones vertically through the use of ribs and colonnettes, which lead the eye from floor to ceiling. At other times they preferred to distinguish each horizontal band through the repetition of forms. In the zone of transition, for example, the profile of the squinch might be repeated in blind arches over each wall to form a unified eight-sided zone.

One type of transitional device is unique to Islamic architecture: MUQARNAS, which is composed of serried and projecting tiers of small niche-like elements, often likened by Western observers to stalactites or honeycombs (see fig. 49 below). *Muqarnas* is used for cornices separating architectural elements, to fill squinches and to create vaults and semi-vaults. Its origins are still obscure, primarily because of the lack of surviving early examples. It appeared fully fledged in the eastern Islamic lands in the early 11th century and quickly spread throughout the Islamic world. The earliest known examples were made of brick and plaster; later ones were carved from stone or made of glazed ceramic tiles and even mirrored glass. *Muqarnas* vaults, such as those in the Alhambra of Granada, are some of the showiest forms in all Islamic architecture.

The internal courtyard, often with a fountain or pool, was well suited to the hot and dry climate of most Islamic lands and became the organizational focus of many public and private buildings. Open court plans were traditional in the lowlands, but were inappropriate in some regions, such as the Anatolian plateau or the mountains of Iran, where the winters are extremely cold and precipitation is abundant. In Anatolia open courts were reduced in size and covered with vaults; in Iran the court was surrounded on one or more sides by iwans (Arab. *īwān*, Pers. *eyvān*; *see* IWAN), barrel-vaulted spaces that are open at one end and provide shelter and shade or collect sunlight, depending on the season. The fundamental unit of residential construction in the eastern tradition, the iwan was introduced in Mesopotamia as early as the 1st century BC and was widely used in Sasanian and early Islamic architecture in Iraq. Already in pre-Islamic times it was often combined with a dome chamber at its end; this became a favourite architectural unit in Iranian mosques beginning in the late 11th century (*see* §5(i)(b) below). The elaboration of the internal courtyard façade is one of the most characteristic features of Islamic architecture.

By contrast, street façades of buildings in the Islamic lands were often minimal, except for elaborate and monumental portals that extended above the roof-line (Pers. *pīshṭāq; see* PĪSHṬĀQ and fig. 43 below) and were often decorated with such expensive materials as carved stone, glazed brick and tile. It was only in such densely developed cities as Cairo that façades became an important architectural feature, as architects sought to combine the portal, minaret and tomb in a harmonious ensemble visible from the street.

(iv) Decoration. Islamic architecture is distinguished by the extensive use of applied decoration, in such materials as carved, inlaid, painted and gilded stone, wood and plaster,

carved and glazed brick, terracotta or tile, often with designs independent of the underlying structure (*see* §9 below). As in all Islamic art, geometric, vegetal, arabesque and epigraphic motifs predominate. These patterns often had bilateral or fourfold symmetry and could be expanded infinitely to fit any surface. In a region of natural browns and tans, lavishly coloured architectural decoration was a means of making buildings prominent in the landscape and enlivening their surfaces. The glazed azure domes of Iran, for example, mirror the shimmering firmament above and lift the buildings from their humble earthly origins.

(v) Patrons and architects. Contemporary histories of Islamic lands and peoples generally concentrate on the responsible actions of individuals, mentioning specific buildings only when they fit into this schema. The *Khiṭaṭ* ('Districts') of Cairo by the 15th-century historian Ahmad ibn ʿAli al-Maqrizi is a notable exception, which sets the study of Cairene architecture apart from that in virtually all other Islamic cities. Few account-books for buildings have been preserved, except from the Ottoman empire, and more information is generally supplied by the inscriptions on buildings and the endowment deeds for them. These give the names of patrons and rulers, dates, function and the names of builders and architects. Many of the architects or builders (Arab. *bannāʾ*) or engineers (Arab. *muhandis*) were masters of account, in charge of estimating costs and distributing payment. The careers of few architects can be established with certainty, and their oeuvre can rarely be identified by stylistic criteria alone (*see also* §7(ii)(a) below). The major exception is SINAN (ii), chief architect of the Ottoman court, who formulated the principles of Ottoman architecture and is credited with designing nearly 500 buildings. But the identification and development of even the style of this master are still matters of debate.

Architectural knowledge was transmitted largely by gesture and example from master to apprentice in workshop teams. While plans may have been used earlier in the medieval period, the earliest surviving examples date from the 15th century, and they became common only in the Ottoman period. In the Ottoman empire plans were sent to the provinces from the central design studio and realized on the site by local artisans using local materials and techniques (*see* §7(i)(a) below). Few treatises on architecture and design seem to have been written, and those that were seem to have been primarily mathematical or literary exercises rather than practical manuals used by craftsmen. Although the Islamic lands produced the greatest mathematicians of medieval times, there is a lack of evidence to show that the sophisticated traditions of mathematics had any impact on the building trades. The seemingly complicated patterns used in architectural revetment are often the product of simple calculations.

(vi) Meaning and impact. Some authors have found hidden mystical meanings in all the components of Islamic architecture, such as colour, light and shade, and particular geometric shapes. Mysticism was an important element in Islamic society, but its practice was by no means universal, and all buildings do not have mystical meaning. Others

have sought to explain all Islamic architecture with principles of geometric harmonization derived from mathematical treatises and the careful measurement of buildings. Although this may work in individual cases, such as the shrine of Ahmad Yasavi in Turkestan (*see* §6(i)(b) below), these principles cannot be ascribed indiscriminately to all buildings at all times.

Islamic architecture had limited impact on the architecture of the West, as its major formal types were largely inappropriate for reasons of ritual or climate. The bell-towers of post-reconquest Spain that are closely derived from brick minarets of earlier times are a notable exception, as is Brunelleschi's Ospedale degli Innocenti in Florence, which may have been inspired by an Ottoman *māristān* or vice versa. Decorative techniques and motifs had a greater, although still restricted, impact: polychrome masonry and various forms of arches were taken up in Norman Sicily and Romanesque Europe (*see* SICILY, §3; ROMANESQUE, §II, 3–5). More conscious forms of ORIENTALISM have developed at other times, for instance in the 18th and 19th centuries, when the publications of Johann Bernhard Fischer von Erlach and OWEN JONES inspired garden fantasies in the form of mosques, or in the 20th century, when theatres and cinemas were created in the guise of the Alhambra (e.g. H. P. Knowles's Masonic Mecca Temple, New York, 1923–4). Conversely, the architecture of the West had little impact on that of Islam, except in the few instances when Crusader spoils were incorporated into Mamluk buildings as trophies. In the 20th century, however, such Western materials and techniques of construction as reinforced concrete and steel frames were grafted on to traditional forms of Islamic architecture in an uneasy attempt to create an architecture at once modern and Islamic (*see* §8 below).

BIBLIOGRAPHY

Enc. Islam/2: 'Architecture', 'Bina' [building], 'Burdj' [military architecture], 'Madrasa', 'Masdjid' [Mosque]
K. A. C. Creswell: *Early Muslim Architecture*, 2 vols (Oxford, 1932 and 1940/vol. i/R and enlarged 1969; R New York, 1979)
——: *The Muslim Architecture of Egypt*, 2 vols (Oxford, 1952 and 1956/R New York, 1978)
G. Marçais: *Architecture musulmane d'Occident* (Paris, 1954)
L. A. Mayer: *Islamic Architects and their Works* (Geneva, 1956)
K. A. C. Creswell: *A Short Account of Early Muslim Architecture* (London, 1958); rev. by J. W. Allan (Aldershot, 1989)
D. Hill and O. Grabar: *Islamic Architecture and its Decoration, A.D. 800–1500* (London, 1964)
O. Grabar: 'The Earliest Islamic Commemorative Structures', *A. Orient.*, vi (1966), pp. 7–46
U. Monneret de Villard: *Introduzione allo studio dell'archeologia islamica: Le origini e il periodo omayyade* (Rome, 1966)
L. Golvin: *Essai sur l'architecture religieuse musulmane*, 4 vols (Paris, 1970–79)
N. Ardalan and L. Bakhtiyar: *The Sense of Unity* (Chicago, 1973)
O. Grabar: *The Formation of Islamic Art* (New Haven, 1973/R and enlarged 1987)
D. Kuban: *Muslim Religious Architecture*, 2 vols (Leiden, 1974–85)
O. Grabar: 'Islamic Architecture and the West: Influences and Parallels', *Islam and the Medieval West*, ed. S. Ferber (Binghamton, 1975), pp. 60–66
K. Critchlow: *Islamic Patterns* (London, 1976)
D. Hill and L. Golvin: *Islamic Architecture in North Africa* (London, 1976)
J. Hoag: *Islamic Architecture* (New York, 1977)
M. S. Bulatov: *Geometricheskiya garmonizatsiya v arkhitekture Sredney Azii* [Geometric harmonization in the architecture of Central Asia] (Moscow, 1978)
G. Michell, ed.: *Architecture of the Islamic World: Its History and Social Meaning* (New York, 1978)

[Ca'fer Çelebi]: *Risāle-i Mi'māriyye: An Early-seventeenth-century Ottoman Treatise on Architecture*, Eng. trans. by H. Crane (Leiden, 1987)

R. Ettinghausen and O. Grabar: *The Art and Architecture of Islam: 600–1250*, Pelican Hist. A. (Harmondsworth, 1987)

A. Kuran: *Sinan: The Grand Old Master of Ottoman Architecture* (Washington, DC, 1987)

J. Bloom: *Minaret: Symbol of Islam* (Oxford, 1989)

M. K. Ismail, ed.: *The Mosques of Egypt*, 2 vols (London, 1992)

R. Lifchez, ed.: *The Dervish Lodge: Architecture, Art and Sufism in Ottoman Turkey* (Berkeley, 1992)

J. M. Bloom: 'On the Transmission of Designs in Early Islamic Architecture', *Muqarnas*, x (1993), pp. 21–8

A. Orient., xxiii (1993) [entire issue devoted to Islamic palaces]

S. S. Blair and J. M. Bloom: *The Art and Architecture of Islam: 1250–1800*, Pelican Hist. A. (London and New Haven, 1994)

M. Frishman and H.-U.Khan: *The Mosque: History, Architectural Development & Regional Diversity* (London, 1994)

R. Hillenbrand: *Islamic Architecture: Form, Function and Meaning* (Edinburgh, 1994)

——: *Islamic Architecture* (Edinburgh, 1994)

SHEILA S. BLAIR, JONATHAN M. BLOOM

2. BEFORE AD 661. During the lifetime of the Prophet Muhammad (*d* 632) and the rule of his immediate successors (632–61), the caliphs Abu Bakr, 'Umar, 'Uthman and 'Ali, the political centre of the Islamic world remained in western Arabia, in the cities of MECCA and MEDINA. However, because the capital of the new Islamic empire was moved to Syria immediately after the end of this period, the contribution of the building traditions of these two cities, and of pre-Islamic Arabia in general, to the development of Islamic architecture was limited. Only the Ka'ba, the pre-Islamic sanctuary at Mecca that became the focus for Muslim prayer and pilgrimage, and the combined residence and mosque that the Prophet built in Medina seem to have made any impact.

The Ka'ba, which Muslims believe is God's house on earth, was a small, roughly rectangular, roofless enclosure built of dry-laid stone around the sacred well of Zamzam. In 608 the Quraysh, the guardians of the shrine, had it rebuilt with alternating courses of stone and timber and with a timber roof resting on pillars, all features associated with contemporary architecture in Abyssinia (now Ethiopia), a region with which southern Arabia had long been connected. The walls were probably covered with stucco and painted on the interior. The Ka'ba remained unchanged until 683, when it was destroyed by fire during the revolt of the anti-caliph Ibn al-Zubayr. He had it rebuilt in stone and decorated lavishly with mosaics, marble columns and alabaster windows brought from a church in San'a, but these alterations lasted only until 693, when Mecca was reconquered and the building restored to its disposition during the life of the Prophet.

According to Islamic tradition, the form of the MOSQUE was largely determined by the character of the house of the Prophet Muhammad in Medina (see fig. 16). The Prophet built this in 622 as a residence for himself, his family and his followers after their *hijra* ('emigration') from the hostile environment of Mecca to Medina. It was a large and almost empty square enclosed by plain walls 100 cubits (*c*. 56 m) to a side. The three entrances were little more than openings in the wall. Because some of the Prophet's companions complained of the sun during prayer, a shelter (*zulla*) consisting of a roof of palm leaves plastered with mud and resting on palm trunks, was erected along the inside of the qibla wall of the enclosure.

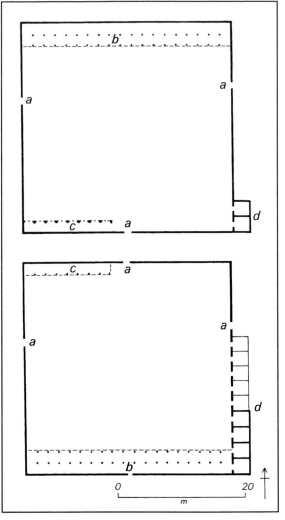

16. House of the Prophet, Medina, Saudi Arabia: (above) plan in AD 622; (below) plan in 623 after change of qibla; (a) entrances; (b) *zulla* (shelter); (c) *suffa* (small covered area); (d) domestic accommodation

A year later, when a divine revelation caused Muhammad to change the qibla from Jerusalem to the Ka'ba in Mecca, the *zulla* was demolished and re-erected along the new qibla wall. Opposite the *zulla* was another small covered area used as a shelter by the most poverty-stricken followers of the Prophet. In seeking the origin of the mosque in domestic architecture, Western scholars have occasionally overemphasized the building's role as Muhammad's house, for it was regularly used for communal prayer and served as the focus of the Muslim community of Medina. Indeed, the large empty courtyard was far bigger than the Prophet's modest household required, and during his lifetime domestic accommodation was limited to nine small rooms along the outer side of the building's east wall. The structure's multiple functions explain both its large size and its architectural design as a public building.

Islam rapidly expanded beyond Arabia, encountering a bewildering variety of cultures and architectural traditions.

The major body of Muslims in each new territory was the army, who needed some serviceable place to gather at noon each Friday for communal prayer. The austere simplicity of their liturgy meant that Muslims could appropriate almost any kind of building for worship, although within the first decade of the Islamic conquests they already showed a preference for purpose-built mosques rather than reused buildings. The mosque did not always take a monumental form, and in many cases only a line of scattered ashes, a reed fence or a shallow ditch marked the enclosure. But more often, particularly in regional centres such as the garrison cities of Iraq and North Africa, mosques assumed a more permanent form. The huge, austere examples built at BASRA (635) and KUFA (638) in Iraq and at Fustat (Old Cairo; 641–2; see CAIRO, §I, 1) in Egypt—and even a bit later at KAIROUAN (670) in Ifriqiya (now Tunisia)—show that the mosque was intended to be inclusive rather than exclusive in character. In essence these mosques were enclosed rectangular spaces oriented towards the qibla. Their most consistent feature was the wall that demarcated the holy ground within from the secular world outside; what was built within the enclosure differed from one mosque to the next, but the irreducible minimum was an open court and a covered area for prayer adjacent to the qibla wall. This prayer-hall comprised either multiple columns supporting a flat roof or arcades supporting a pitched roof. The emphasis on regularly spaced, closely set supports led to the application of the term 'hypostyle' to this type of mosque in modern studies of Islamic architecture, while its popularity throughout the early centuries of Islam, when the Arabs were the predominant ethnic group, has given rise to the alternative name of 'Arab-type' mosque.

The initial austerity of plan and elevation in these mosques ran increasingly counter to contemporary taste, and within a generation all were rebuilt on a much larger scale. Some of the changes, such as the introduction of a continuous portico around all four sides of the court, which unified the space and provided the worshippers with extra protection from the weather, were clearly improvements and were incorporated into the standard vocabulary of the mosque. Paving was introduced in the time of Ziyad ibn Abihi (d c. 675), Governor of Kufa, after the congregation of the great mosque made it their custom to throw handfuls of pebbles at him to express their displeasure at his announcements. He is also credited with introducing brick piers into mosque architecture and crowning them with capitals of 'Persian' type (i.e. with protomes of addorsed bulls or other creatures) and with experimenting with circular mosques in Basra. There was ample room for experiment in this first century, but the guidelines for the future development of the mosque plan were well established within a hundred years of the Prophet's death.

For bibliography see §3 below.

3. AD 661–c. 750. From 661 until the successful Abbasid revolt in 749–50 (see §4 below), the post of caliph, and therefore control of the vast and still-growing Islamic empire (which had conquered the former Byzantine provinces of Syria and Egypt as well as Sasanian Iran), was claimed as a hereditary right by members of the UMAYYAD

family. The new dynasty found itself faced by a number of revolts against its claim to the caliphate, but by the turn of the 8th century these had been suppressed. Secure against external and internal threats, the extensive royal family and numerous notables turned their attention to building splendid religious monuments and luxurious desert residences. This building campaign marked the coming of age of Islamic architecture. It produced a new style, the scale and magnificence of which were a public and visual expression of the caliphs' power, for it was the Umayyads who first recognized the propaganda dimension inherent in splendid buildings and symbolic images (previously viewed with some mistrust). Mu'awiya, the first Umayyad caliph, defended his taste for ostentation on the Byzantine model by saying, 'We are at the frontier and I desire to rival the enemy in martial pomp so that he may be witness to the prestige of Islam'. The Umayyad century defined the regional and dynastic character of Islamic architecture, features that it retained in later centuries. Its architecture, with its blend of structural and decorative elements drawn from the building traditions of the lands it conquered (see EARLY CHRISTIAN AND BYZANTINE ART, §II, 2(i)(d), (ii)(c) and (iii)(c) and IRAN, ANCIENT, §II, 3), also reflects the cosmopolitan nature of the Islamic empire at that time. The buildings of the Umayyad period already possessed several characteristically Islamic features, such as the extensive use of non-figural and epigraphic decoration, especially in religious contexts. Moreover, the building types evolved during this period were so effective that they recurred in various guises in subsequent centuries, though this was due at least partly to the unique glamour that invested this first and most powerful of Islamic dynasties.

(i) Introduction. (ii) Religious. (iii) Secular.

(i) *Introduction.* Umayyad architecture is eclectic, experimental and propagandistic. The eclecticism is easily explained by the fact that the massive building programme was concentrated almost entirely in Syria, whose principal city, Damascus (see DAMASCUS, §1(ii)), became the capital of the caliphate in succession to Medina (except when the court followed the semi-nomadic caliphs as they moved relentlessly from one desert residence to another). The presence of the caliphs in Syria and the flow of booty and taxes into the province were accompanied by a large-scale investment in agricultural installations such as canals, dams and wells; together these factors made it the richest province in the empire and provided the funds for the building boom in the early 8th century. Although Syria remained the centre of the Islamic empire for less than 90 years, its role in the development of Islamic architecture was crucial. The region's own ancient civilization, unified and transformed by hellenization and overlaid with Roman and Christian elements, provided the basis for the new architectural style. The forms and conventions of Classical architecture were better understood in Syria than in the lands further east, and as a result some of the vocabulary of Umayyad architecture—of column and capital, pointed arch and dome, rib and vault—is familiar to a Western observer. These traditions declined in importance, however, as Muslim builders began to adopt the architectural styles of the newly conquered lands to the east—in Mesopotamia, Iran, Central Asia and even India.

Eclecticism in Umayyad architecture was also the consequence of the caliphs' practice of conscripting the labour and materials for their building projects from all over the empire, continuing the system of forced labour employed by their Roman and Byzantine predecessors. They also had the resources to import still more craftsmen and materials from outside the Islamic world, notably from Byzantium. As these large teams of workmen laboured side by side, they both learnt from and competed with one another. The workings of this corvée system is documented by the chance survival of a cache of early 8th-century papyri from Aphrodito in Upper Egypt. Qurra ibn Sharik, the local governor, was responsible for sending a specified number of men to work on the Great Mosque of Damascus (*see* DAMASCUS, §3), and he had to provide money to cover their living expenses too. Literary references and the buildings themselves supplement these documents. According to the historian al-Tabari (*d* 923), both Syrian and Coptic artisans worked on the mosque at Medina. Some Umayyad buildings in Syria feature a Persian type of stucco sculpture, Iraqi techniques of vault construction, mouldings in the style current in south-east Anatolia and a Coptic figural style in the sculpture.

Experiment became widespread in Umayyad architecture in response to the urgings of patrons who delighted in all-over decoration, and the sense of restraint integral to Classical art and its descendants was soon thrown off. The gusto of Umayyad architectural decoration, especially figural stucco and painting, where the effect is heightened by bold, even garish colours, is infectious. Unshackled by convention, open-minded, endlessly inventive, Umayyad artists delighted in turning old ideas to new account, equally ready to trivialize important motifs by dwarfing them and to inflate essentially minor ones so that they acquired an unexpected significance. They were far less inhibited than their contemporaries elsewhere in the Mediterranean world, freely combining features and materials that tradition had hitherto kept apart. At Mshatta, for example, brick vaults of Sasanian type are found a few metres away from a Classically inspired, triple-arched entrance in cut stone. Transpositions are equally common: cornice designs are used for plinths, epigraphy overruns both capital and shaft of column and patterns normally created by quartered marble are imitated in plaster. In this high-spirited and often vulgar art, parody is never far away.

This robustness and often wayward originality are consistently accompanied by a more serious element, for nearly all the significant buildings to survive are the products of royal patronage and have important political and proclamatory dimensions. Sometimes the message is religious, as in the references to Paradise in the lost inscriptions of the mosaics in the Great Mosque of Damascus, or in the frontal attacks on Christianity in the inscriptions of the Dome of the Rock in Jerusalem (*see* JERUSALEM, §II, 1(iii)). More often it is political, asserting—as in the ground-plan of Mshatta—the lonely pre-eminence of the caliph or—as in the floor frescoes of the palace at Qasr al-Hayr West (see fig. 80 below), which combine representations taken from a wide geographical area—the Umayyad dominance over east and west alike.

The apse mosaic in the small audience hall at Khirbat al-Mafjar warns unmistakably of the sudden death that awaits the enemies of Islam. It is peculiarly fitting that Umayyad Syria, rather than Rome or Byzantium, can also claim in the Dome of the Rock the most extensive programme of wall mosaics to survive from ancient or medieval times. The masters of the new Arab *imperium* needed no instruction in the prestige value of such glamorous decoration.

It was inevitable that some of the directions Umayyad art took proved to be dead ends. The Dome of the Rock, for example, despite its central importance in its own time, was fated to have no significant progeny. Similarly, such Classical or Byzantine borrowings as figural sculpture and wall mosaic had little appeal for later Islamic craftsmen. Yet it was the Umayyad period that devised some of the basic types of mosque and palace destined to recur repeatedly in later generations, that established the sovereign importance of applied ornament—geometric, floral and epigraphic—in Islamic art, and finally that created a distinctive new style from the most disparate elements.

(ii) Religious. Much of the credit for the speedy development of the 'hypostyle' or 'Arab-type' mosque (*see* §2 above) belongs to the Umayyad caliph al-Walid I (*reg* 705–15), who was responsible for a trio of strategically sited mosques—the Mosque of the Prophet at Medina, the Aqsa Mosque at Jerusalem and the Great Mosque of Damascus—that consolidated earlier experiments and introduced several features that quickly became canonical. Some of the finest Umayyad mosques have vanished, including the Mosque of the Prophet (707) at Medina, but this can be reconstructed from textual descriptions. The Prophet's house–mosque was quadrupled in size to cover an area 200 cubits (112 m) square, and deep arcades were built around the central court. The qibla wall was fitted with quartered marbles, carved window-grilles and glass mosaics with epigraphic and arboreal ornament. A mihrab, an empty semicircular niche, was inserted in the qibla wall, probably to mark the spot where the Prophet had led prayers, and the bay before it was punctuated by a shield-shaped gilded ceiling. Slender towers were erected at each of the building's four corners. Other Umayyad mosques have been extensively rebuilt. The Aqsa Mosque in Jerusalem, for example, was probably founded by al-Walid I, but its complicated history is not entirely resolved (*see* JERUSALEM, §II, 1(iv)). The Great Mosque of Aleppo was built by the caliph Sulayman (*reg* 715–17), but little of its original aspect can be reconstructed. However, two important Umayyad buildings, the Dome of the Rock in Jerusalem and the Great Mosque of Damascus, survive in something like their intended form. These buildings show that, while early Islamic art was still in the thrall of the Byzantine and Classical heritage, Muslims were already developing their own visual language and were well able to use inherited forms for their own ends. The two buildings belong together as a considered Muslim response to the splendours of Classical and Christian architecture around them.

The Dome of the Rock (see fig. 17) was built in 691–2 by the caliph 'Abd al-Malik after a turbulent decade in which the Umayyads briefly lost control of the holy Arabian cities of Mecca and Medina. It has been suggested

17. Dome of the Rock, Jerusalem, AD 691–2; restored 1552 and 1956–64

that it was intended as a victory monument or as a place of pilgrimage to supplement, if not to supplant, Mecca itself. Yet its site and its form suggest otherwise. It occupied the vast high platform on which Solomon's Temple had stood; this had been shunned by Christians and Jews after its destruction by Titus in AD 70 and had become the principal vacant site in Jerusalem. The dome marks a rocky outcrop traditionally associated by Christians and Jews with the Creation and with Abraham's near sacrifice of Isaac; later Muslims identified it as the spot from which the Prophet ascended during his miraculous Night Journey. Consisting of a domed octagon about 20 m in diameter and 25 m high over the rock and a double ambulatory some 12 m wide, the building is a centralized structure of a type long familiar in Roman mausolea and Christian martyria. The choice of form probably stems from a desire to upstage the nearby domed church of the Holy Sepulchre, also built over a rock. The diameters of the domes are only centimetres apart, but the church is physically confined by the dense urban fabric of Jerusalem, while the Dome of the Rock enjoys an uncluttered and highly visible site. Mosaic was used to decorate the interior and exterior of the Dome of the Rock on a scale unparalleled in any surviving earlier Byzantine church. The inner and outer arcades are decorated with the earliest

epigraphic programme in Islamic architecture, comprising lengthy Koranic quotations exhorting believers and attacking such Christian doctrines as the Trinity and the Incarnation.

The large and splendid Great Mosque of Damascus (706–15; see fig. 18) is comparable in many ways. Another royal foundation, it occupied the most prominent and hallowed site in the city, and its topographical dominance had clear political overtones. The caliph al-Walid I purchased the entire site, comprising the 100×157 m walled enclosure (temenos) of the Temple of Jupiter Damascenus and the church of St John the Baptist within it, and had every structure within its walls demolished. The resulting oblong was divided along its length into an open courtyard and a prayer-hall along its southern side. The prayer-hall is a bold recasting of the standard components of a typical Early Christian basilica to secure a new lateral emphasis in keeping with the needs of Islamic worship. The three aisles remained, but the direction of prayer ran at right angles across them and was marked in elevation by a towering domed gable that clove through the pitched roofs to form a central transept that partitions the prayer-hall and, with the aisle along the qibla wall, forms a T-shape. The façade is a free variation on the standard west front of Syrian churches. Quartered marble formed dados in typical

18. Great Mosque, Damascus, Syria, façade of prayer-hall, AD 706–15

Byzantine fashion. Carved marble window-grilles with elaborate patterns loosely inspired by Late Antique floor mosaics presage the enduring geometric bias of much later Islamic ornament. Above was the glory of the mosque: hundreds of square metres of wall mosaic (*see also* §9(iv) and fig. 82 below), for which the caliph seems to have obtained artists and materials from Byzantium. Human and animal figures are conspicuously absent, indicating, as at the Dome of the Rock, that a distaste for figural ornament in a religious context had already taken root.

Umayyad mosques elsewhere did not share these luxurious features. The mosque (720) at Bosra in Syria (*see* BOSRA, §2) is a small (34×29 m) irregular rectangle with arcades supporting a roof of stone slabs. An exterior stair led to a roof-top aedicule which functioned as a minaret. The earliest phase (*c.* 703–4) of the mosque excavated at Wasit in Iraq was 104 m square with a prayer-hall of five rows of sandstone columns and a single arcade on the remaining three sides of the central court.

(iii) Secular. The many residences founded by the Umayyads in the Syrian desert show the same response to the splendours of Classical and Early Christian architecture as the Dome of the Rock in Jerusalem and the Great Mosque of Damascus, and proclaim the same message of Muslim dominion over the former Christian strongholds of the Near East. Square structures at such sites as Jabal

Says, Khirbat al-Minya and QASR AL-HAYR WEST measure some 70 m to a side. The dimensions, salient gateway, corner towers and battlements show them to have been modelled on Roman frontier forts, but, as they were shorn of virtually all defensive devices and contained luxurious royal apartments and service quarters grouped in two storeys around a central courtyard, their function was closer to that of the Roman villa rustica. This development sprang from the patrons' need to integrate two dissimilar functions, for these residences served at the same time as both the headquarters of working agricultural estates, in which the caliph or prince was lord of the manor, and as symbols of conspicuous consumption and political power. Many of these sites fall into this category, but others, such as Qasr al-Hayr West and QASR AL-HAYR EAST, had caravanserais attesting to their roles as way-stations. Qasr al-Hayr East and Anjar (now in Lebanon) had industrial quarters and were laid out as miniature cities.

QUSAYR 'AMRA and Hammam al-Sarakh, a pair of small bathing establishments east of Amman in the Jordanian desert, represent another free use of a Classical type (*see* BATH (ii), §2). Variously vaulted cold, warm and hot rooms succeed each other in the Roman fashion, but the addition to these humble ensembles of a ceremonial vaulted hall complete with royal apse exalted them to a novel dignity. The sequence of wall and ceiling paintings at Qusayr 'Amra is the most extensive to have survived from the Late Antique and early medieval world (*see also* §9(iii)(a) below). These symbolize the Umayyads' claim to world dominion and show that political concerns infiltrated even the carefree atmosphere of this remote lodge to which the anonymous prince occasionally repaired for a few days of recreation and hunting. (There was no provision for him to live at the site permanently.)

Greatly enlarged multi-functional palaces were built at the very end of the Umayyad period in response to the increasingly extravagant ambitions of the libertine and caliph al-Walid II (*reg* 743–4). Khirbat al-Mafjar, in the fertile Jericho Valley, encloses within its wall a courtyard with an imposing octagonal fountain at its centre, a palace, a mosque, an underground bath with a shower and a huge domed and vaulted bathhall. The plan is a free variation on the loosely designed agglomeration of discrete units found in Roman and Byzantine palaces such as Hadrian's Villa at Tibur (*see* TIVOLI, §2(i)), Piazza Armerina in Sicily (*see* PIAZZA ARMERINA, §1) and the Great Palace in Constantinople (*see* ISTANBUL, §III, 12). The bathhall is the jewel of the site: its floor, spread with 39 adjoining panels, is the largest single floor mosaic to survive from the ancient world and is a fitting match for the elevation, which had vaults of increasing height around a central cupola. Its other amenities included a bathing pool, a wine-filled plunge bath, the diwan (a luxurious royal retiring-room perhaps intended for private audiences, for banqueting or as a tribunal; see fig. 19) and a splendidly appointed latrine designed to accommodate some 33 visitors simultaneously. Fresco paintings and stucco-carvings of unparalleled vigour and inventiveness complemented the spatial subtlety and magnificent mosaics. The sculptures of athletes and serving girls in particular epitomize the sheer *joie de vivre* that the entire establishment exudes (*see also* §9(i)(b) below).

19. Khirbat al-Mafjar, Israel, bathhall diwan, *c.* AD 743–4; restoration drawing by R. W. Hamilton

MSHATTA (probably begun 743), the immense unfinished palace south of Amman, is altogether more sober, even gloomy. Its unprecedented size (144 m per internal side) greatly accentuates its sombre, dominating impact. Enough of the layout remains to reveal that the interior was sequentially subdivided into thirds. The caliph's own quarters, once as lavishly appointed as their counterparts in other Umayyad palaces, occupy only the far third of the central tract, approximately one-ninth of the enclosure. A sumptuously decorated stone façade (Berlin, Pergamonmus.) once extended along the outer face of the central or royal tract (*see* §9(i)(a) below). The huge scale of the ensemble, and especially of the side tracts, which were scarcely begun when work on the whole complex was abruptly stopped, suggests that Mshatta, unlike the other Umayyad residences, was intended to accommodate large numbers of people—perhaps the entire Umayyad court. If Mshatta really was a palace city, it would be the natural precursor to the Round City of Baghdad (*see* §4(i)(b) and fig. 20 below), built no more than a generation later.

Secular architecture outside Syria was less ambitious. Four secular buildings of the Umayyad period have been identified in Iraq. At KUFA, the governor's palace (Arab. *dār al-imāra*) attached to the qibla wall of the mosque has an outer enclosure 169 m square with half-round buttresses. Within this enclosure lies a building 110 m square with four iwans facing on to a courtyard and a surround of subsidiary courtyards. Another late Umayyad building (destr.) was excavated at Tulul al-Shu'aiba outside Basra. It had a four-iwan plan and stucco decorations paralleled at Khirbat al-Mafjar. At Tulul al-Ukhaydir in the desert

west of the Euphrates, a rectangular complex with a mosque and an iwan decorated with stuccowork is probably of slightly earlier date than Tulul al-Shu'aiba. The excavations of another, but undecorated desert palace at Anba' near 'Ana on the Euphrates remain unpublished.

BIBLIOGRAPHY
K. A. C. Creswell: *Early Muslim Architecture*, i (Oxford, 1932, rev. and enlarged 1969)
O. Grabar: 'The Painting of the Six Kings at Qusayr 'Amrah', *A. Orient.*, i (1954), pp. 185–7
K. A. C. Creswell: *A Short Account of Early Muslim Architecture* (London, 1958); rev. by J. W. Allan (Aldershot, 1989)
O. Grabar: 'The Umayyad Dome of the Rock in Jerusalem', *A. Orient.*, iii (1959), pp. 33–62
R. Hamilton: *Khirbat al Mafjar: An Arabian Mansion in the Jordan Valley* (Oxford, 1959)
U. Monneret de Villard: *Introduzione allo studio dell'archeologia islamica: Le origini e il periodo omayyade* (Venice, 1966)
R. Hamilton: 'Who Built Khirbat al-Mafjar?', *Levant*, i (1969), pp. 621–67
B. Finster: 'Die Mosaiken der Umayyadenmoschee', *Kst Orients*, vii (1970), pp. 83–141
O. Grabar: *The Formation of Islamic Art* (New Haven, 1973, rev. 1988)
M. Almagro and others: *Qusayr 'Amra: Residencia y baños omeyas en el desierto de Jordania* (Madrid, 1975)
P. Soucek: 'The Temple of Solomon in Islamic Legend and Art', *The Temple of Solomon: Archaeological Fact and Medieval Tradition in Christian, Islamic and Jewish Art*, ed. J. Gutmann (Missoula, MT, 1976), pp. 73–123
R. Hamilton: 'Khirbat al-Mafjar: The Bath Hall Reconsidered', *Levant*, x (1978), pp. 126–38
R. Hillenbrand: 'Islamic Art at the Crossroads: East versus West at Mshatta', *Essays in Islamic Art and Architecture in Honor of Katharina Otto-Dorn*, ed. A. Daneshvari (Malibu, 1981), pp. 63 86
——: '*La dolce vita* in Early Islamic Syria: The Evidence of Later Umayyad Palaces', *A. Hist.*, v (1982), pp. 1–35
E. Whelan: 'The Origins of the *Miḥrāb Mujawwaf*: A Reinterpretation', *Int. J. Mid. E. Stud.*, xviii (1986), pp. 205–23
R. Hamilton: *Walid and his Friends: An Umayyad Tragedy* (Oxford, 1988)
R. Hillenbrand: *Islamic Architecture* (Edinburgh, 1990)

ROBERT HILLENBRAND

4. *c.* AD 750–*c.* 900. The Abbasid dynasty of caliphs, founded in 749, ruled most of the Islamic lands from capital cities in Iraq during a golden age that lasted at least until the end of the 9th century. New styles of architecture were characterized by forms, techniques and motifs of Iraqi and Iranian origin. Some features of these styles, such as brick vaults and stucco renderings, had already appeared in buildings erected late in the Umayyad period (661–*c.* 750; *see* §3 above), but they became increasingly widespread as a result of the power and prestige of the Abbasid court. In the Islamic lands around the Mediterranean, Late Antique traditions of stone construction roofed with wood continued, although new techniques and styles were eventually introduced from Iraq. The rise of the Abbasids brought economic recession to Syria, however in Egypt, under the Tulunid dynasty (*reg* 868–905), close copies of buildings in the Abbasid capitals were erected in Cairo. Eastern North Africa (now Tunisia) was ruled by the semi-independent Aghlabid dynasty (*reg* 800–909), and the unusually large group of buildings surviving there shows a distinctive regional style. The Iberian peninsula was controlled by a branch of the Umayyad dynasty (*reg* 756–1031), whom the Abbasids had driven out of Syria, and their buildings continue both local Iberian and imported Syrian traditions, although Abbasid styles are increasingly apparent.

(i) Eastern Islamic lands. (ii) Central Islamic lands. (iii) Tunisia. (iv) Spain and Morocco.

(i) Eastern Islamic lands.

(a) Introduction. (b) Iraq. (c) Iran and western Central Asia.

(a) Introduction. The principal tradition of ABBASID architecture developed in Iraq, the capital province of the caliphate. A wide variety of building types, including mosques, palaces, pilgrimage stations, walled race-courses and polo grounds, houses, forts and industrial compounds, succeeded the limited range of distinctive Islamic building types known earlier, because the pre-Islamic building stock, which had still been in use in the Umayyad period, was worn out and had to be replaced. The number of Muslims in the population of the region was growing rapidly, and the needs of this new Islamic society increasingly differed from those of the Late Antique period. Not only were larger mosques required, but new house-plans reflected a perceptible change in the lives of ordinary people, and architectural styles were adapted to meet these developments. Many of the features typical of Abbasid architecture existed before the Abbasids came to power. Barrel vaults over reception rooms, as distinct from the utilitarian barrel vaults used in Roman architecture, were a feature of Mesopotamian and Iranian architecture that had been introduced to Syria in the Umayyad period. The two-centred pointed arch and vault, which were to become standard during the early Abbasid period with an increasing degree of pointing, appeared in the second quarter of the 8th century, although various sorts of pointing had existed before. Decoration with wall painting and carved and moulded stuccos continued traditions of the Umayyad period.

Abbasid architecture in the Iraqi lowlands and on the Iranian plateau shared a common heritage, as both regions had been part of the Sasanian empire, which had had its capital at KTESIPHON in Iraq. In Iraq it was also descended from ancient Mesopotamian architecture, for, despite intervening periods of Iranian, Greek and Roman political control, it is possible to find many direct parallels in techniques and decoration with late Assyrian and Babylonian architecture. The primacy of Mesopotamian ideas in Islamic architecture began to wane in the 10th century, when Iraq entered a period of severe long-term economic decline, and the peoples of the Iranian plateau increasingly dominated politics and architectural innovation (*see* §5(i)(a) below). Geography also differentiated the architecture of the Iraqi lowlands from that of the Iranian plateau, particularly that of eastern Iran, for construction had to be adapted to the different materials available locally. Finally, the nature of the evidence differs: in Iraq the principal sites known are those that were abandoned in favour of other sites, while in Iran the principal sites and monuments have been in continuous use. Thus the archaeological surveys at Iraqi sites have produced synchronic information, while the architectural surveys of Iranian monuments have shown how they changed over time.

(b) Iraq. Architecture in Iraq was strongly influenced by the physical conditions of the country. Stone is available for building in the north around Mosul, in the Iraqi desert west of the Euphrates and on the middle Euphrates between Syria and Iraq, but even individual stones can be rare in the central and southern alluvial plain. The architecture of the region therefore developed primarily in mud-brick, with constantly renewed facings of plaster and frequent rebuildings, sometimes in fired brick. The immense flatness of the land, green only where irrigated by the Tigris and the Euphrates or canals leading from them, also encouraged enormous buildings which were unparalleled in other parts of the Middle East.

Cities and settlements. The most prominent feature of early Abbasid architecture was the construction of large new cities in succession to the garrison cities of the Umayyad period. Architecturally, they were the inheritors of a more ancient Mesopotamian and Iranian tradition of new royal cities, such as Dur-Sharrukin, the city that Sargon II of Assyria (*reg* 721–705 BC) built at Khorsabad in northern Iraq, and Gur, the round city of the Sasanian king Ardashir I (*reg* AD 224–41) at Firuzabad in Iran. Once the Abbasids decided to settle in Iraq, a search was started for a site on which to build a new capital. Two cities called Hashimiyya were begun in the vicinity of Kufa before BAGHDAD, in the outer environs of the Sasanian capital at Ktesiphon, was chosen in 762. The Round City that the caliph al-Mansur (*reg* 754–75) built there, officially called Madinat al-Salam, contained the palace, mosque, administrative offices and residences for the court (see fig. 20). Outside the walls (diam. *c.* 2500 m) were a great cantonment for the army at Harbiyya, markets at the town of al-Karkh and a subsidiary cantonment for the troops of al-Mansur's son al-Mahdi (*reg* 775–85) on the east bank of the Tigris at Rusafa. This combined administrative city and military base was soon transformed into a normal urban entity, particularly after the siege of 812–13 and the replacement of the original Khurasanian army by new units.

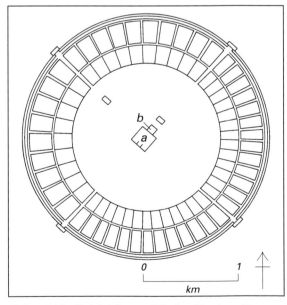

20. Round City, Baghdad, Iraq, AD 762, plan: (a) palace; (b) mosque

Copies of the Round City were built at other sites in Iraq. A horseshoe-shaped city 1500 m across called al-Rafiqa, specifically said to have been a copy of Baghdad, was built in 772 at RAQQA on the Euphrates in Syria to house Khurasanian army units. Air photography has revealed the mosque at its centre and a grid of streets with houses. At Qadisiyya, 20 km south of Samarra', the caliph Harun al-Rashid (*reg* 786–809) began an octagonal city 1500 m across, but it was abandoned in 796. Three avenues led to a square with the site for a mosque in the centre and a palace enclosure on the south. In 836 the caliph al-Mu'tasim (*reg* 833–42) founded Samarra' on the Tigris above Baghdad as an administrative centre and military base for the new Central Asian Turkish and Iranian army units (*see* SAMARRA', §2). Here no defensive wall was built, and the original core of the city spread along the Tigris bank from al-Mu'tasim's palace in the north, known as the Dar al-Khilafa or the Jawsaq al-Khaqani, to the original congregational mosque in the centre of the market area. The traditional placement of the mosque next to the palace, which had continued through the Umayyad period to the founding of Baghdad, was transmuted into a small separation at Qadisiyya and abandoned at Samarra'.

The urban character of early Islamic military settlement is striking. Military cantonments (Arab. *qati'a/qata'i*) are known textually at KUFA, BASRA and Baghdad. The two main cantonments—of the Turks at al-Karkh and of the Central Asian Iranians at al-Matira—were both located 2 *farsakh*s (*c.* 10 km) from Baghdad and Samarra' respectively, although al-Matira was later engulfed by the development of the city, and there were further cantonments in the city itself. They consisted of a main palace, minor palaces, a grand avenue and a grid of streets with houses. The cantonment of the Turks at al-Karkh, measuring 2200 m across, was the largest and might have accommodated 21,000–25,000 soldiers, based on historical information on the density of settlement. Samarra' provides the only architectural evidence for cantonments, but those for the entourages of the caliphs and men of state are indistinguishable from those of the military, except by the proportionate size of palace and housing areas. The defences of the Byzantine frontier from Tarsus to Malatya and ERZURUM were based on a series of fortified cities in which troops were settled. The Roman concept of the frontier fort began to be introduced only at the end of the 8th century in the form of *ribat*s along the Syrian and Tunisian coasts (*see* §§(ii) and (iii) below) and in Central Asia, as Abbasid secular authority collapsed, leaving the *ribat*s to be manned by religious volunteers. Once the frontiers had moved, these developed into religious centres or caravanserais.

The trans-desert pilgrim road from Baghdad and Kufa to Mecca, known as the Darb Zubayda, was built up during the reigns of al-Mahdi and Harun al-Rashid. The Hajj was sometimes led by the caliph, and almost always by a leading man of state. Long stretches of the road were cleared of boulders, and in places the road was walled and drainage ditches dug. The road stations in Saudi Arabia have been surveyed and that at al-Rabadhah excavated. They usually have reservoirs, a large residence with an iwan and lines of rooms, scattered small buildings and a

21. Mosque of al-Mutawakkil (Great Mosque), Samarra', Iraq, AD 848–52

mosque. In the 10th century these arrangements seem to have fallen into decay.

Building types. The five Iraqi mosques from the period employ the courtyard plan. The earliest, known only from texts, was the mosque of al-Mansur in the Round City of Baghdad. Originally it was 200 cubits (*c.* 100 m) square but was later doubled in size. The congregational mosque (Great Mosque) of al-Mutawakkil at Samarra' (848–52; 256×139 m; see fig. 21) had columns supporting a flat wooden roof and was decorated with glass mosaic and marble panels. The other major mosque there, that of Abu Dulaf (859–61), had a prayer-hall of arcades aligned perpendicular to the qibla wall and carried on rectangular brick piers. The 2:3 proportions of the ground-plans of these mosques are found earlier at the unbuilt mosque of the Octagon at Qadisiyya, but the congregational mosques at 'Ana and Sumaka (anc. Uskaf Bani Junayd) have differing overall proportions. Both mosques at Samarra' have helicoidal spiral minarets opposite the mihrab (for that of the Great Mosque *see* MINARET, fig. 1), respectively 52 and 33 m high, a form that is repeated only in the

mosque of Ahmad ibn Tulun in Cairo (*see* fig. 24 below). Four examples of festival mosques (Arab. *muṣalla*), built outside the city and used for prayers on festival days, are known from Samarra'. They are open rectangular enclosures 368×512 m with a smaller enclosure around the mihrab area.

The desert castle at UKHAYDIR, 50 km west of Karbala', is the earliest known Abbasid palace (*c.* 775). A fortified outer wall (175×169 m) is pierced with four gates; three are built into half-round towers, but the main gate on the north is set in a rectangular salient. The palace within has a vaulted entrance hall which leads into a central court with an iwan on the opposite side. The residential accommodation is divided into six courtyard house units with pairs of iwans facing each other.

This plan is descended from late Sasanian architecture, such as the Imarat-i Khusraw at Qasr-i Shirin, and has immediate parallels in late Umayyad palaces at Amman and Mshatta (*see* §3(iii) above). Evidence for late 8th-century house-plans comes from Raqqa in Syria, where a number of grand houses, datable between 796 and 808,

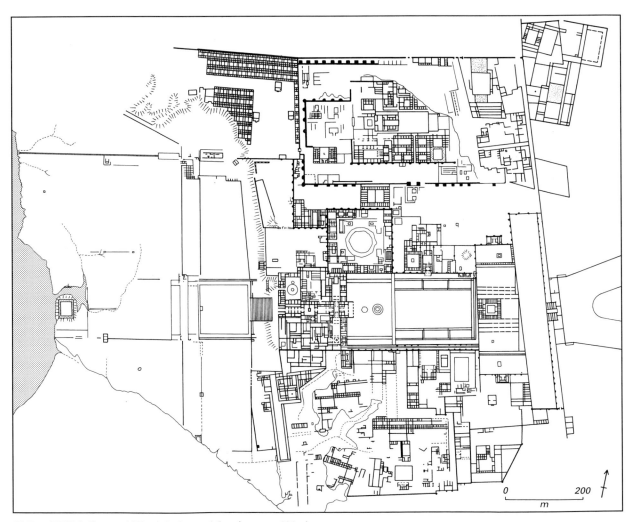

22. Dar al-Khilafa (Jawsaq al-Khaqani), Samarra', Iraq, begun AD 836, plan

the period of Harun al-Rashid's residence there, have been excavated. The buildings have buttressed outer walls and the spread of Mesopotamian buildings, but do not use iwans. The unfinished palace at Hiraqla has a circular outer enclosure with a square central platform, which would, if finished, have had four iwans around a central dome chamber.

A complete range of residential buildings, from caliphal palaces to small single-courtyard houses, is known from Samarra'. The palaces, of which 21 are known, frequently have a square block of reception halls, comprising a central dome chamber with four iwans facing out on to courts or the exterior, and large courtyards, as at the Dar al-Khilafa (see fig. 22) or the Balkuwara. The more private palaces continue earlier practices with rows of courtyard house units.

Forty-five large houses have been excavated. They are often constrained to a rectangular plan by the street grid. The elaborate reception halls of the palaces are replaced by simple closed halls or iwan units, which Herzfeld called 'T-shaped iwans'. These place a transverse rectangular room in front of the iwan and its side rooms, with openings corresponding to the iwan and other doorways, presumably for protection from the weather. The most modest dwellings were in the cantonments, where rows of small houses were arranged in blocks of 10 to 20. Each has seven rooms and a court, but there is considerable variation in the 2252 blocks already identified. Although the houses of Samarra' represent one regional variation, other Abbasid houses excavated at Ktesiphon and 'Ana confirm the pattern. Underground rooms were cut into the conglomerate subsoil for relief from the heat of summer, but evidence for the wind catchers (see WIND CATCHER) common in later Islamic houses has not been found. The Dar al-Khilafa has two sunken areas with pools and flowing water systems: one has a four-iwan plan of rooms cut into the conglomerate, the other has brick built iwans 15 m below ground level. Most of the houses have cold-water bathing facilities and latrines; only two have hot baths with furnaces and hypocausts.   More activities were given monumental form at Samarra' than at previous or subsequent sites. There are 12 polo grounds, walled rectangles measuring 500–530×60–80 m. Two, much like the Safavid Maydan-i Shah at Isfahan (see ISFAHAN, §3(ii)), have viewing pavilions in the middle of one side. There are four race-courses, walled tracks 80–100 m wide. Two have an out-and-back plan measuring 10.5 km, one with a raised viewing mound 21 m high with an 18 m square pavilion. A third is a continuous four-leafed clover with a viewing pavilion in the centre, and the fourth is a linear track nearly 10 km long. Hunting was conducted in a 9×6 km enclosure at Musharrahat; it had a palace and basin on the south side.

Materials and construction techniques. Construction and decoration techniques varied. Outer walls of pisé had half-round buttresses; mud-brick mortared with gypsum and fired brick were also used. Flooring was usually tile, but marble was used exceptionally. Any evidence of upper storeys is unlikely to have been preserved, but the buildings seem nearly all to have been single-storey. The grander buildings have barrel-vaulted reception rooms, but for most buildings the roofing systems are yet to be determined, although flat wooden beams have been proposed. The four-centre pointed arch was introduced at Samarra' in the earliest fully developed examples at the Qasr al-'Ashiq (878–82). Creswell's dating of the introduction of the four-centre pointed arch to the middle of the 8th century was based on the incorrect dating of the Baghdad Gate at Raqqa to 772. The decorative programme of reception rooms at Samarra' included a carved or moulded stucco dado 1–1.2 m high and decorated stucco frames for doors, arches and wall-niches (see §9(i)(a) below). There were three main Samarra' styles (A, B and C). The finest rooms also had glass mosaic, wall paintings, marble panelling and glazed and lustre-painted tiles (see also §9(iii)(a) and (iv) below).

(c) Iran and western Central Asia. Compared to Iraq, a wider variety of materials was used for mosques, residences and caravanserais in this region, including rubble and mortar, fired brick, mud-brick (particularly in north-east Iran and Central Asia) and wood, and construction appears to have been generally smaller in scale.

Mosques. Few of the congregational mosques ascribed to the period can be dated exactly, because most of them have been rebuilt or extensively remodelled in later times. The mosque excavated at Susa measured 56×45 m and had buttressed walls and piers of fired brick. The prayer-hall was four bays deep and ten bays wide; the porticos surrounding the courtyard were two bays deep. The excavators dated the mosque to the first Islamic century (622–718), but traces of stuccos with vine-leaf decoration are probably of early Abbasid date. The Tarik-Khana at DAMGHAN is a smaller (25×27 m) courtyard mosque (see fig. 23). Six arcades perpendicular to the qibla wall form the prayer-hall. Three large piers of fired brick (diam. 1.6 m) in each row support slightly pointed elliptical arches that in turn carry tunnel vaults. Godard (1934) ascribed the building to the 9th century, but as the architectural techniques are transitional from late Sasanian architecture, it has been argued that the building is somewhat earlier. The congregational mosque excavated at SIRAF on the Persian Gulf was erected c. 815–25. It measured 44×51 m and was built entirely of rubble and gypsum mortar. The prayer-hall had three arcades running parallel to the qibla wall, the courtyard was surrounded by a single portico, and there was a square base for a minaret adjacent to the single entrance opposite the mihrab. The mosque was enlarged some 25 years later. The qibla wall was razed and a new one erected further out, and an additional portico around the court further increased the covered area. Perhaps at the same time the prayer-hall was widened three bays to the south-east.

The Masjid-i Jum'a (Friday Mosque) in Isfahan, perhaps the most important of these buildings, was founded c. 771. It was a courtyard mosque measuring approximately 52×90 m and had a rectangular mihrab decorated with carved stuccos, including vine-leaves with four peg-holes in the style used in Iraq up to c. 840. In the reign of al-Mu'tasim the mosque was expanded (88×128 m) and realigned. The exterior walls were decorated with blind arches surmounted by niches. Soundings revealed that the

23. Tarik-Khana Mosque, court façade, Damghan, Iran, 9th century

prayer-hall was six bays deep and that the porticos along the court were two bays deep except on the north, where, unusually, they were four bays deep. Another courtyard mosque in the village of Fahraj near Yazd may date to the second half of the 9th century.

At least ten small mosques were excavated in the residential quarters at Siraf and were dated between the 9th century and the 12th. The buildings, which ranged in size from 5.4×5.5 m to 9.7×10.2 m internally, usually had mihrabs in rectangular salients and prayer-halls divided by one or more transverse arcades and were entered through attached yards. Two had staircase minarets. At BALKH a mosque measuring *c.* 20 m to a side had nine square bays arranged in three rows of three. The arched walls and four central piers originally supported nine vaults, giving the mosque one of its names, the Masjid-i Nuh Gumbad ('Mosque of the Nine Domes'). The extravagant carved stucco decoration of the interior is comparable to Style A and Style B at Samarra' and suggests a mid-9th-century date. Other nine-dome mosques are found in Tunisia, Egypt, Spain, Iraq and western Central Asia.

Residences. Many buildings with iwans, dome chambers and carved stucco decoration known from Iran were routinely thought to be Sasanian palaces, but close examination and careful comparison have demonstrated that some were built in Islamic times. Excavations of houses at Merv (now Mary) in Turkmenia (*see* MERV, §1(ii)) and at Afrasiab (*see* SAMARKAND, §1(i)) have shown that tetrastyle halls and iwans with wooden pillars and roofs characteristic of 7th- and 8th-century Sogdian buildings in the region gave way in the 9th century to vaulted and domed brick architecture, as suggested by walls decorated with Samarra'-style stuccos. The typical country mansion of the feudal aristocracy was a massive mud-brick construction with a series of adjoining semicircular towers; some had a central courtyard surrounded by living-quarters, others a central domed room with vaulted halls on the sides. A two-storey building with four iwans facing on to a narrow central courtyard at Tirmidh (now Termez)

in Uzbekistan has been attributed to the 9th century, and the arrangement continues into the 11th century at Lashkari Bazar in Afghanistan (*see* §5(i)(c) below). The designs on stucco dados in some of the houses excavated at NISHAPUR similarly suggest a late 9th-century date. A group of distinctive rectangular houses with round exterior buttresses and rooms arranged around central yards excavated at Siraf have been dated to the 9th and 10th centuries.

Rural caravanserais. These continued the Sasanian and early Islamic traditions of servicing long-distance trade in the sparsely urbanized regions of Iran and Central Asia. A 9th-century example at Kishman Tepe in southern Turkmenia has an open court surrounded by arcades supporting domed roofs. As the frontiers of Central Asia were made secure, the network of *ribāṭ*s developed to defend them was transformed into caravanserais for the trans-desert routes, and caravanserais built as such in Central Asia were often called *ribāṭ*s. At Darzin in Kirman province, three mud-brick forts, some 25 m square with round buttresses along the exterior walls and tunnel-vaulted chambers on the interior, may date from the 8th century. The buttresses are typical of Umayyad desert castles in Syria and the plans are comparable to those of 9th-century *ribāṭ*s in Tunisia (*see* §(iii) below).

BIBLIOGRAPHY
Abu'l-Hasan Mas'udi: *Murūj al-dhahab* [Meadows of gold] (*c.* 950); Fr. trans. by C. Barbier de Maynard and P. de Courteille as *Les Prairies d'or* (Paris, 1861–77), vii, pp. 192–3
Muhammad ibn Ahmad al-Maqdisi (al-Muqaddasi): *Aḥsan al-taqāsīm fi ma'rifat al-aqālīm* [The finest of selections concerning knowledge of the climes], ed. M. J. de Goeje (Leiden, 1906); Eng. trans. by G. S. A. Ranking and R. F. Azoo as *Selections from Arabic Geographical Literature* (Calcutta, 1897–)
E. Herzfeld: *Erster vorläufiger Bericht über die Ausgrabungen von Samarra* (Berlin, 1912)
——: *Der Wandschmuck der Bauten von Samarra und seine Ornamentik* (Berlin, 1923), i of *Die Ausgrabungen von Samarra* (1923–48)
A. Godard: 'Le Tari Khana de Dâmghân', *Gaz. B.-A.*, n. s. 6, xii (1934), pp. 225–35
K. A. C. Creswell: *Early Muslim Architecture*, ii (Oxford, 1940)
E. Herzfeld: *Geschichte der Stadt Samarra* (Hamburg, 1948), vi of *Die Ausgrabungen von Samarra* (1923–48)

K. A. C. Creswell: *A Short Account of Early Muslim Architecture* (London, 1958); rev. by J. W. Allan (Aldershot, 1989)

R. McC. Adams: *Land behind Baghdad* (Chicago, 1965)

L. Golombek: 'Abbasid Mosque at Balkh', *Orient. A.*, n. s., xv/3 (1969), pp. 173–89

A. S. Melikian-Chirvani: 'La Plus Ancienne Mosquée de Balkh', *A. Asiatiques*, xx (1969), pp. 3–20

J. Lassner: *The Topography of Baghdad in the Early Middle Ages* (Detroit, 1970)

J. M. Rogers: 'Samarra: A Study in Medieval Town Planning', *The Islamic City*, ed. A. H. Hourani and S. M. Stern (Oxford, 1970), pp. 119–55

E. Galdieri: *Isfahân: Masgid-i Gum'a*, 3 vols (Rome, 1972–84)

B. M. Alfieri: 'La moschea Gâmi' [di Fahrag]', *Studi iranici*, ed. A. Bausani and G. Scarcia (Rome, 1977), pp. 65–76

J. Warren: 'The Date of the Baghdad Gate at Raqqa', *A. & Archaeol. Res. Pap.*, xiii (1978), pp. 22–3

J. Lassner: *The Shaping of 'Abbasid Rule* (Princeton, 1980)

M. Shokoohy: 'Monuments of the Early Caliphate at Dārzīn in the Kirmān Region (Iran)', *J. Royal Asiat. Soc. GB & Ireland* (1980), pp. 3–20

D. Whitehouse: *Siraf: The Congregational Mosque* (London, 1980)

R. Hillenbrand: ''Abbasid Mosques in Iran', *Riv. Stud. Orient.*, lix (1985), pp. 175–212

L. Bier: *Sarvistan: A Study in Early Islamic Architecture* (University Park, PA, 1986)

C. K. Wilkinson: *Nishapur: Some Early Islamic Buildings and their Decoration* (New York, 1986)

A. Northedge and R. Falkner: 'The 1986 Survey Season at Sāmarrā', *Iraq*, xlix (1987), pp. 143–73

J. Bloom: *Minaret: Symbol of Islam* (Oxford, 1989)

O. Grabar: *The Great Mosque of Isfahan* (New York, 1990)

(ii) Central Islamic lands. The Abbasid revolution in Iraq in 749 brought economic recession to Syria, once the centre of Umayyad power and architectural patronage, and excavations in Syria and Jordan show that Umayyad building projects came to a sudden halt. Yet a few buildings indicate that Umayyad architectural traditions continued sporadically, especially in Egypt, despite the impact of the eastern tradition in the second half of the 9th century. Syria's brilliant architectural revival late in the 11th century (*see* §5(ii)(e) below) suggests that traditions of ashlar-masonry construction and stone-carving were kept alive throughout the period.

Some Umayyad buildings in Syria were redecorated or renovated in the 8th and 9th centuries. At QASR AL-HAYR EAST, an Umayyad site between Palmyra and the Euphrates, stuccos were added to an official building in the Large Enclosure late in the 8th century. The Aqsa Mosque in Jerusalem was rebuilt soon after the earthquake of 747, although sources complain of a lack of money (*see* JERUSALEM, §II, 1(iv)). The Umayyad model was largely followed, but a new dome was probably added in front of the mihrab. Carved wooden panels with representations of niches and vine-scrolls (*see* §VII, 1(i)(a) and fig. 213 below) have survived from this campaign. In 789, the Bir al-Aneziyya, a vaulted cistern with fine limestone masonry and pointed arches, was built near Ramla by a man identified as a client of the caliph. Sites along the northern frontier with Byzantium and along the Mediterranean coast were fortified. At 'Ain Zarba (now Anavarza, Turkey) new city walls with ashlar masonry, square buttresses and gates with square towers placed in front of a fosse have been dated to the reign of al-Mutawakkil (*reg* 847–61), and the ashlar walls and half-round towers at Eski Malatya (now in Turkey) have also been attributed to the Abbasid period. A square fort with half-round buttresses at Ascalon may have been one of the *ribāt*s on the

Palestinian coast mentioned in the works of the geographer al-Maqdisi (985).

In the 9th century Egypt began to be politically significant for the first time since the fall of the Ptolemys in 30 BC. In 827 the mosque of 'Amr in Fustat (Old Cairo; *see* CAIRO, §III, 1) was enlarged and rebuilt. Within a nearly square enclosure (110×120 m), the prayer-hall had seven arcades of spolia columns parallel to the qibla wall. One wall retains arched windows flanked by colonnettes and engaged piers carrying a wooden architrave decorated with an acanthus frieze in the Late Antique style. The Nilometer on al-Rawda Island, used for measuring the rise of the Nile in flood, is dated to 861–2 and consists of an octagonal measuring column within a 6.2 m square pit. Lined with ashlar masonry, the pit has arched recesses with two-centre pointed arches. Soon afterwards, Ahmad ibn Tulun (*reg* 868–84), the semi-independent governor (*see* TULUNID), built a suburban quarter known as al-Qata'i' (The Allotments), where Iraqi architectural features were first introduced into Egypt. Nothing but lavish descriptions remain of his Maydan palace, but the adjacent mosque (876–9) is well preserved (see fig. 24; *see also* CAIRO, §III, 2). The general form of the Samarra' mosques (*see* SAMARRA', §2), with an outer enclosure and a helicoidal minaret (rest.) opposite the mihrab, was retained, but the 2:3 proportions were abandoned in favour of a squarer shape (122×140 m). The prayer-hall consists of five arcades on rectangular piers parallel to the qibla wall; double arcades enclose the other three sides of the court. The

24. Mosque of Ahmad ibn Tulun, Cairo, Egypt, piers of the east portico, AD 876–9

windows and arches were framed with carved stuccos similar to Samarra'-style work.

BIBLIOGRAPHY
K. A. C. Creswell: *Early Muslim Architecture*, ii (Oxford, 1940)
——: *A Short Account of Early Muslim Architecture* (London, 1958); rev. by J. W. Allan (Aldershot, 1989)
O. Grabar and others: *City in the Desert: Qasr al-Hayr East* (Cambridge, MA, 1978)

ALASTAIR NORTHEDGE

(iii) Tunisia. The establishment of the semi-independent AGHLABID dynasty of governors (*reg* 800–909) in the province of Ifriqiya (corresponding to the Roman Africa Proconsularis and modern Tunisia) ensured a political continuity previously unknown in the region and favoured the realization of architectural projects of a scale and quality previously unattainable. The relatively large number of 9th-century buildings that survive in such a small region is unique for this period and allows the delineation of local styles with unusual precision.

The Aghlabids, who had to contend with raids by the Byzantine fleet until their conquest of Sicily in 827, fortified the principal coastal cities with stone walls, square bastions and small forts at the corners; impressive examples survive at Sousse (859) and Sfax. The tower of Khalaf al-Fata at the highest part of the Sousse ramparts once served as a lighthouse. *Ribāt*s, square structures with semicircular towers at the corners and an open court surrounded by small chambers and larger communal rooms, were erected at regular intervals for coastal defence (*see* MILITARY ARCHITECTURE AND FORTIFICATION, §IV, 1). They combined the functions of fortresses with those of monasteries, for in them pious individuals gathered to prepare for jihad (the struggle to expand the borders of Islam). Examples are preserved at Hergla and Mahares Bourdj Tonga, but the finest are at Sousse and Monastir, which has four.

25. Great Mosque, Kairouan, Tunisia, begun AD 836

Palaces set amid gardens and orchards beautified by vast pools were constructed at Raqqada outside Kairouan. The ruins of one have revealed the plan of a complex building inspired by Umayyad and Abbasid architectural models and decorated with stucco panels reminiscent of those in the Abbasid palaces at Samarra' in Iraq (*see* SAMARRA', §2). An impressive hydraulic system including an aqueduct, an immense pool for storage and a small pool for settling (both perfectly preserved) supplied water to Kairouan, while rainwater was collected at Raqqada in above-ground square reservoirs reinforced with round towers. Bridges, such as those surviving at Hergla and Kairouan, carried roads across rivers and wadis. Texts indicate that baths, caravanserais, hospitals and asylums were also built.

Most of the surviving buildings are mosques, which were built more carefully of more durable materials. On the founding of Kairouan *c.* 670, a congregational mosque had been hastily erected. Although it was repeatedly repaired and enlarged, in 836 Ziyadat Allah ordered the structure to be demolished and entirely rebuilt. The 9th-century Great Mosque of Kairouan largely preserves its Aghlabid aspect (see fig. 25), although it too has been repeatedly restored. The mosque is a rough rectangle with maximum interior dimensions of 122×70 m; the irregularity and extreme elongation from north to south are probably explained by the earlier structures on the site. The court, which is surrounded by double arcades, occupies about two-thirds of the total area. The prayer-hall, which has flat roofs, has seventeen aisles of seven bays perpendicular to, but not reaching, the qibla wall. The interior, a forest of reused antique columns and capitals, has a transverse aisle along the qibla wall and a wider central aisle creating an internal T-plan. The bay where the aisles cross is emphasized with a magnificently conceived ribbed-stone dome resting on an octagonal drum with concave faces, itself supported by a square base. On the interior, the dome rests on a pierced cylindrical drum supported by scalloped squinches, decorated with carved inscriptions and arabesques. A second dome, marking the entrance from the court into the axial aisle, is a late 19th-century reconstruction of a 9th-century original. The mihrab, assembled of openwork marble panels and epigraphic bands and crowned with a semi-dome of wood painted with a scrolling vine bearing leaves and grapes, is surrounded by ceramic tiles lustre-painted in the style of the Abbasid capital at Samarra'. It can be dated to the reign of Abu Ibrahim Ahmad (*reg* 856–63), as can the remarkable wooden minbar (pulpit) to its right (*see* §VII, 1(iii) below). A three-storey minaret with a distinctive battered profile stands astride the mosque's northern wall opposite the mihrab. Once believed to be a vestige of the 8th-century mosque, it is certainly part of the Aghlabid construction and was modelled on the Roman lighthouse at nearby Salakta (anc. Sullecthum).

The Great Mosque of Kairouan provided the model for congregational mosques in Sfax (*c.* 849; extensively remodelled in the 11th century), with nine aisles of three bays, and TUNIS (864), an irregular trapezoid with fifteen aisles of six bays, but without a minaret opposite the mihrab. In the coastal region, however, a distinctive local style developed in which parallel barrel vaults covered each aisle, as at the mosques in the *ribāṭ*s of Sousse and Monastir (both end of the 8th century), the mosque of Bu Fatata (838–41) and the Great Mosque (850–51), both in Sousse. The plan of the mosque of Bu Fatata, with nine bays arranged in a square, was used widely in the eastern Islamic world (*see* §(i)(c) above). The mosque of Muhammad ibn Khairun at Kairouan (866) also has a nine-bay plan, and the three arches of its façade, elaborately decorated with carved stone, have given the building its common name, the Mosque of the Three Doors.

Aghlabid Ifriqiya remained faithful to local traditions inherited from antiquity, which can be seen in the extensive use of stone and the carved openwork panels and the painted semi-dome of the mihrab at the Great Mosque of Kairouan. Nevertheless, the Aghlabids recognized the Abbasid caliph in Iraq as their titular leader, and diplomacy and commerce brought to Kairouan the latest metropolitan styles and techniques. These can be seen in the lustre-painted tiles surrounding the Kairouan mihrab and the minbar next to it, in the stuccos of Raqqada and in the carved stone façade of the mosque of Muhammad ibn Khairun. Carved bands of inscriptions in kufic script were widely but sparingly used for the decoration of buildings.

BIBLIOGRAPHY

G. Marçais: *Tunis et Kairouan* (Paris, 1937)
K. A. C. Creswell: *Early Muslim Architecture*, ii (Oxford, 1940)
G. Marçais: *L'Architecture musulmane d'occident* (Paris, 1954)
A. Lézine: *Le Ribat de Sousse* (Tunis, 1956)
——: *Architecture d'Ifrīqiya* (Paris, 1956)
G. Marçais and L. Golvin: *La Grande Mosquée de Sfax* (Tunis, 1960)
A. Lézine: *Mahdiya* (Paris, 1964)
M. M. al-Shabbi: 'Taqrir mukhtasar hawla 'l-hafariyyat al-jariyya bi-Raqqada' [Short report on current excavations at Raqqada], *Africa: Inst. N. Archéol. & A.*, ii (1968), pp. 5–9 [with Fr. summary, pp. 349–50]
G. Kircher: 'Die Moschee des Muhammad b. Hairun ("Drei-Tore-Moschee") in Qairawân, Tunesien', *Mitt. Dt. Archäol. Inst.: Abt. Kairo*, xxvi (1970), pp. 141–68
D. Hill and L. Golvin: *Islamic Architecture in North Africa* (London, 1976)

LUCIEN GOLVIN

(iv) Spain and Morocco. Architecture during the first centuries of Islamic rule in the Iberian peninsula is principally represented by the buildings of the local branch of the UMAYYAD dynasty, particularly the Great Mosque (Mezquita) of Córdoba (*see* CÓRDOBA (i), §3(i)(a)). Contemporary buildings in Morocco, such as the first stages of the mosques of the Qarawiyyin and of the Andalusians in FEZ, are known exclusively from later literary sources and seem to have been far less ambitious. Fortifications closely followed earlier models (*see* EARLY CHRISTIAN AND BYZANTINE ART, §II, 3(i)(a)), as in the case of the Alcazaba (835) of Mérida. Measuring about 130 m to a side, this fortress has walls 2.7 m thick with towers at the corners and along the sides. The main gate was originally on the north and led into a forecourt and then into a small rectangular enclosure.

The most important extant construction of the Umayyad period is the Great Mosque that 'Abd al-Rahman I (*reg* 756–88), a refugee from Syria and founder of the dynasty, erected on the southern edge of Córdoba in 785 (see fig. 26). Over the 200 years that followed, 'Abd al-Rahman I's successors enlarged and embellished the mosque, its development epitomizing the history of

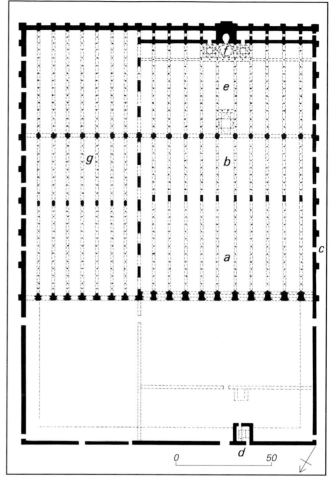

26. Great Mosque, Córdoba, Spain, begun AD 785, plan showing restoration and successive additions: (a) original mosque of 'Abd al-Rahman I; (b) extension of 'Abd al-Rahman II, 836; (c) original portal Bab al-Wuzara', restored 855–6; (d) minaret and expanded court of 'Abd al-Rahman III, 951; (e) extension of al-Hakam II, completed 976; (f) *maqsura*; (g) extension of al-Mansur, 987–8

Umayyad religious architecture. The first mosque measured about 74 m square and consisted of a walled court preceding a covered prayer-hall. A unique system of double-tiered arcades supported the roof. Ten parallel arcades set in the direction of the qibla created eleven aisles of twelve bays each; the outermost aisles were screened off for women. At ground-level reused columns from Roman and Visigothic buildings support horseshoe arches, red shafts having been employed to pick out the broader and higher central nave; at the upper level, thick dressed stone piers support semicircular arches. The voussoirs of the arches at both levels are alternately stone and coursed brick, creating a striped effect that later builders developed further, as they did the decorative possibilities of the horseshoe arch. The Bab al-Wuzara' (now the Puerta de S Esteban) is the only one of the mosque's original portals to survive, although it was already restored in 855–6. Its tripartite composition in cut stone of blind horseshoe arches, crenellations and window-grilles and its deeply carved vegetal ornament bear strong resemblance to Umayyad architecture in Syria (*see* §3 above). Its scheme of a round horseshoe arch with alternately carved and plain voussoirs and an eccentric, raised extrados within a rectangular frame became one of the most characteristic motifs in later western Islamic architecture. Other features, such as the longitudinal aisles of the plan, the striped masonry and the thickness of the upper arcades, may also have been imported from Syria, but the most plausible model for the system of supports is local, specifically the supporting arches of Roman aqueducts (e.g. Los Milagros at Mérida). Even the plan, which has often been compared to that of the Aqsa Mosque in Jerusalem (*see* JERUSALEM, §II, 1(iv)), may owe much to local Christian basilical prototypes. The capitals used in this and the subsequent phase of construction and the spolia columns, the diminutive size of which necessitated the double supports, are the most obvious debt to Spain's Classical heritage.

The prayer-hall of the Great Mosque was enlarged in 836, when 'Abd al-Rahman II (*reg* 822–52) ordered eight additional bays to be added to the south. The elements that had separated the aisles for women were removed, and new women's galleries were laid out in the court. The original qibla wall was then pierced, leaving only a row of thick pillars in the axes of the arcades. The original superposed system of supports was extended into the addition, as it would be in all subsequent phases of the mosque. The new mihrab (destr.) seems to have projected beyond the line of the qibla wall; the twin columns that once flanked it survive and support four capitals that are such close imitations of Roman Corinthian models that they were once regarded as spolia. The bay in front of the mihrab was oblong in plan and therefore provided no space for a dome.

BIBLIOGRAPHY
K. A. C. Creswell: *A Short Account of Early Muslim Architecture* (London, 1958); rev. by J. W. Allan (Aldershot, 1989)
K. Brisch: 'Zum *Bāb al-Wuzara*' (Puerta de San Estebán), der Hauptmoschee von Córdoba', *Studies in Islamic Art and Architecture in Honour of Professor K. A. C. Creswell* (Cairo, 1965), pp. 30–48

CHRISTIAN EWERT

5. *c.* AD 900–*c.* 1250. Although the Abbasid caliphate continued to rule in name, if not in fact, until 1258, when the Mongols captured Baghdad, the cultural hegemony of the preceding period was broken with the emergence of strong regional powers, often non-Arabs who professed heterodox beliefs. Several new building types (e.g. small mosques, madrasas, mausolea and minarets) and stylistic and decorative features (e.g. *muqarnas* and tile revetment) appeared throughout the Islamic lands and testify to the continued movement of men and ideas, but distinct regional styles of architecture developed. The Iranian world and much of the Fertile Crescent came to be dominated by Turkish dynasties, such as the Saljuqs (*reg* 1038–1194) and the Ghaznavids (*reg* 977–1186), staunch Sunnis who strongly supported the spread of orthodox Islam. Much of the central Arab lands from Syria to Tunisia were under the sway of the Fatimid caliphate (*reg* 909–1171), a Shi'ite dynasty that turned Egypt into a new artistic centre in the Mediterranean

region. After its conquest in 1071, Anatolia was opened to Muslim settlement for the first time by a collateral branch of the Saljuqs (*reg* 1077–1307), who introduced Islamic institutions there. In Spain the Umayyads (*reg* 756–1031) assumed the title of caliph in 929 and made Córdoba the most powerful cultural centre in Europe. Following their downfall and a period of political confusion, the entire Muslim west came under the domination of two North African dynasties of zealous reformers, the Almoravids (*reg* 1056–1147) and the Almohads (*reg* 1130–1269), and the region became increasingly isolated from the lands further east.

(i) Eastern Islamic lands. (ii) Central Islamic lands. (iii) Anatolia. (iv) Western Islamic lands.

(i) Eastern Islamic lands. All the distinctive features of Iranian Islamic architecture, such as the introduction of fine-quality baked brick as the primary material of construction and decoration, glazed tile as an important medium of exterior decoration, the four-iwan plan, mausolea, minarets, the tripartite elevation of dome chambers, the subdivision of the squinch into increasingly smaller units and the *muqarnas*, appear for the first time during this period. It is the most creative period in Iranian architecture and justly one of the most renowned periods in the history of Islamic architecture. Most of these features are commonly associated with the Saljuq dynasty (*reg* 1038–1194), whose territories stretched from western Central Asia to Iraq, but many of them were introduced earlier and were not limited to the Saljuq domains.

(a) Iran and western Central Asia, *c.* 900–*c.* 1050. (b) Iran, *c.* 1050–*c.* 1250. (c) Afghanistan, Pakistan and western Central Asia, *c.* 1050–*c.* 1250.

(a) Iran and western Central Asia, c. *900–c. 1050.* The number of buildings surviving from the 150 years before the Saljuq siege of Isfahan (1050) is sufficient to allow regional styles to be delineated for the first time. The most creative region was the eastern Iranian world, which included the provinces of Khurasan and Transoxiana under the SAMANID dynasty (*reg* 819–1005), Khwarazm under the Khwarazmshahs (*reg* 995–1017) and Transoxiana and eastern Turkestan under the Qarakhanids (*reg* 992–1211). This cultural florescence reflected the great agricultural and commercial wealth of the region and its early Islamization. The few standing buildings are complemented by numerous fragmentary remains, but the overall picture has yet to be defined. The mountainous region of northern Iran was ruled by such independent dynasties as the Bawandids (*reg* 665–1349) and the Ziyarids (*reg* 927–*c.* 1090) and is known chiefly for a series of tomb towers with spectacular decoration in patterns of exposed baked brick. Central Iran was tied to Iraq under the BUYID dynasty (*reg* 932–1062), and buildings were decorated with small bricks laid in patterns often covered with stucco. The major developments are the monumentalization of the mausoleum, the proliferation of the minaret, the development of the *muqarnas* and the use of fine baked brick for both construction and decoration, features that became the hallmarks of Iranian architecture under the Saljuqs (*see* §(b) below).

Building types. New congregational mosques were erected to serve the needs of the growing Muslim community. The hypostyle mosque continued to predominate, although the remains are extremely equivocal. The best-preserved example is at NA'IN in central Iran. It measures approximately 42×33 m and has a small (16.1×14.5 m) courtyard surrounded by vaulted spaces of unequal depth. That towards the qibla (south-west) is four bays deep and distinguished by rich stucco decoration in the six bays surrounding the mihrab. The hall opposite is only one bay deep, while those to the north-west and south-east are three and four bays deep respectively, giving a plan that is atypically broader than it is deep. The stucco decoration suggests that the mosque was first constructed in the early 10th century. It has been restored many times, probably first in the late 10th century, when the court façade was remodelled with engaged columns decorated with small bricks set in relief patterns. Similar brick decoration was used on columns of an arcade added around the court of the Friday Mosque at Isfahan (*c.* 975; *see* ISFAHAN, §3(i)), which increased the covered area and gave the mosque a new internal façade. At nearby ARDISTAN, a fragmentary barrel-vaulted arcade and an inscription preserved in the later four-iwan mosque indicate that a hypostyle mosque was erected there *c.* 1000. At KHIVA in the Khwarazm Oasis, wooden columns carved with epigraphic and vegetal decoration suggest that a wooden hypostyle mosque was built there at the same time. The small multi-domed mosques at Hazara and Termez in western Central Asia (*see* TERMEZ, §1(ii)), customarily attributed to the 11th or 12th century, indicate that other mosque types were also used.

Mausolea marked two sorts of graves, those of Shi'ite holy figures and those of secular rulers, but the relationship between the two has yet to be determined. For example, the first tombs over the graves of 'Ali at Najaf and Husayn at Karbala' in Iraq were erected in the late 9th century by an Alid ruler from Tabaristan in northern Iran, but it is unclear whether he was following a local tradition or an imported one. Orthodox Islam had discouraged the veneration of graves, but the strength of heterodox practices during this period countered this reluctance, and the numerous local dynasties may have continued pre-Islamic practices. The veneration of the dead was not limited to Shi'ite rulers alone, for in the second decade of the 10th century the Abbasid caliphs erected a dynastic tomb in BAGHDAD, and their example was followed a decade later by the Samanids, their governors in western Central Asia (*see* TOMB, §II).

Two tomb types can be distinguished: the domed building designed to be entered and the tomb tower designed only to be seen from outside. The earliest extant domed buildings date from the 10th century and continue the structural tradition established in the *chahārṭāq* of Sasanian times, which was a domed cube with arched openings in each of its four walls. Tomb towers, which are novel in form, survive only from the 11th century, but they may well have existed earlier. The classic example of the domed tomb is also the earliest: the Samanid mausoleum at Bukhara (920s; *see* BUKHARA, §2(i)), a 9 m cubic brick structure with battered sides (see fig. 27). Both exterior and interior are enveloped with a variety of brick

27. Mausoleum of the Samanids, Bukhara, Uzbekistan, AD 920s

patterns, the sophistication of which suggests a long but lost tradition preceding it. The Arab-Ata mausoleum at Tim (977) in the Zarafshan Valley is related structurally, but the equal treatment of the exterior walls at Bukhara is replaced by a single monumental façade composed of a rectangular frame around the portal decorated with brick patterns and an inscription. The domed octagonal chamber in the congregational mosque at Natanz was originally free-standing and surrounded by an ambulatory. Dated by inscription to 998–9, it probably served as the tomb of a local Shi'ite saint. The Duvazdah Imam ('Twelve Imams') at YAZD, built in 1037–8 by two Kakuyid amirs, is a more traditional domed cube, but may have served a similar function.

In contrast to domed tombs, tomb towers had plain or simple exteriors enlivened by decorative bands or panels. The earliest surviving example, the GUNBAD-I QABUS (1006–7) near Medieval Gorgan (Arab. Jurjan) in Iran, is also the most spectacular example of the type (see fig. 28). A flanged brick cylinder with a conical roof (diam. 9.67 m; h. 52 m), it marked the grave of Qabus ibn Wushmgir (*reg* 978–1012), the Ziyarid ruler of north-east Iran. The cylindrical examples at Radkan West (1016–21) and Lajim (1022–3) are more modest in scale, and their inscriptions in Arabic and Pahlavi show that pre-Islamic traditions had not died out in the isolated mountainous region south of the Caspian Sea. The only surviving example outside this

28. Gunbad-i Qabus tomb tower, near Gorgan, Iran, 1006–7

region is the octagonal Gunbad-i 'Ali at ABARQUH (1056–7; diam. 12 m), which was built by a Firuzanid amir from Tabaristan in northern Iran for his parents.

The minaret was another form that began to proliferate during this period and continued in later times. Typically it was a tapering brick cylinder about 30 m tall, decorated with horizontal bands of elaborate brick patterns and elegant inscriptions. Gratifyingly visible and not too expensive to build, these structures seem to have been a favourite focus of local patronage. Texts report the existence of minarets in cities such as Isfahan and Bukhara in the 10th century, but the earliest tangible evidence for one is a lead plaque from a now destroyed minaret at Gurganj in western Central Asia (1010–11). The minarets outside the Tarik-Khana Mosque at DAMGHAN and at nearby SIMNAN, built in 1027 and 1031–5 respectively by Abu Harb Bakhtiyar, a governor for the Ziyarids, are the earliest dated minarets to survive in Iran. Another early example survives at Termez (1031–2) on the Oxus River.

The palaces of local rulers, such as those of the Buyid 'Adud al-Dawla (*reg* 949–83) at Baghdad and SHIRAZ, are known through texts as single or grouped pavilions set in gardens supplied with elaborate water systems and decorated with sculpture and painting. Excavations have revealed tantalizing fragments, such as limestone panels from the Hasanwayhid palace at Sarmaj in south-west Iran (*c.* 1000; Tehran, Archaeol. Mus.) and long pillared halls opening on porticos surrounding courts from the palaces at Termez (before 1030). The residential buildings excavated at NISHAPUR in north-east Iran had lavish decoration of painted stucco. Local rulers also patronized civil architecture, such as a series of bridges (984–5, 1008–9 and 1013) on the pilgrimage route near Khurramabad built by Badr ibn Hasanwayh, the Kakuyid gates to Yazd (1040–41) and the city gate at Gandja (1063).

Materials, techniques, forms and decoration. The traditional techniques of brick masonry rendered with carved and/or painted stucco continued. At Natanz the piers were constructed of large rectangular bricks (290×240×50 mm) laid in alternating bands of soldiers with seven courses of common bond. The whole was revetted with plaster and incised with interlaced octagons inscribed in a rectangular border. Carved stucco dados from Nishapur have interlaced geometric designs. The BEVELLED STYLE associated with Samarra' and Balkh in the 9th century (*see* §9(i)(a) below) continued, as in the tympanum over the mihrab of the Duvazdah Imam at Yazd. The major innovation was the use of small rectangular bricks (e.g. 100×150×30 mm) set in relief patterns of diamonds, crosses and other geometric shapes. The technique is best known from Buyid buildings in Isfahan, such as the Jurjir portal and the renovations to the Friday Mosque, and the court façade of the mosque at Na'in, but it was also found at the mound known as Tepe Madrasa at Nishapur. These decorative lays were sometimes rendered with plaster, as at the Jurjir portal, but more typically the bricks were left exposed, as in the minarets and tombs of Damghan and Simnan, setting the style that would predominate in later times. The vertical shafts of minarets were particularly attractive surfaces on which the brick mason might display his mastery of the art. The minaret at Simnan, for example, has six distinct but related patterns enlivening the shaft.

Many of the surfaces were originally painted in vivid colours, but weathering has reduced most to monochrome, and only protected areas have preserved traces of paint. Excavations at Tepe Madrasa at Nishapur, for example, uncovered a brick panel (470×864×76 mm) of interlaced octagons picked out in red and blue, and abstract and figural wall paintings, including some of *trompe l'oeil* brick patterns, were found extensively throughout the site (*see also* §9(iii)(b) below).

A significant formal innovation was the PISHTĀQ, a monumental gateway comprising a free-standing rectangular frame that surrounded an arched opening. First documented in Islamic architecture at the Arab-Ata mausoleum at Tim, it became one of the most distinctive features of later Iranian architecture. The sculptural and deeply moulded portal of the contemporary Jurjir Mosque at Isfahan was an alternative solution to the monumentalization of the entrance, but the screenlike, two-dimensional version eventually proved more popular.

Mihrabs from this period are the earliest surviving in the region and consist of concentric niches within rectangular frames (*see* MIHRAB). The mihrabs at Na'in and Mashhad-i Misriyan (*c.* 1000) in western Central Asia have elaborate decoration in carved stucco; that from Iskodar (*c.* 1000; see fig. 215 below) in western Central Asia is of wood. The arches were usually keel-shaped, but occasionally polylobed, as at Mashhad-i Misriyan.

The interiors of domed buildings were invariably divided into three horizontal zones. The zone of transition between the base and the dome underwent the most formal elaboration as squinches were increasingly subdivided, although the consistent shape of squinch and blind arches unified the zone. The squinches at the Samanid mausoleum in Bukhara consist of two parallel arches buttressed by a perpendicular half-arch in the corner that creates two niche-like elements. Similar elements flank the window above the Jurjir portal at Isfahan. In the squinches at Tim, these same concave elements reappear flanking a smaller arch surmounted by a larger arch; the trilobed profile of the two-tier composition is repeated in the blind arches between. The squinches at the Duvazdah Imam at Yazd take this subdivision even further, replacing the smaller arch in the corner with two blind niches and enclosing the whole trilobed composition within an arched frame.

Niche-like elements were also a major feature of the decorative repertory. Fragments of 11 painted plaster niches were found in a wrecked cellar at Nishapur. The five larger ones (340–60×270–90 mm) have the same projecting shape as the concave squinch elements, while the six smaller ones (290–310×150–220 mm) have a front edge in a single vertical plane. Their smooth white plaster backs give no evidence of how they were attached to the wall, but the use of similar shapes in brick over the portal of the Gunbad-i Qabus suggests that they were arranged in projecting tiers. They are usually considered to be the earliest evidence for the development of the MUQARNAS. *Muqarnas* elements in brick or rubble and mortar were also used for cornices on the exterior of tomb towers (Radkan West, Gunbad-i 'Ali) and minarets (Simnan).

BIBLIOGRAPHY

E. Diez: *Churasanische Baudenkmäler* (Berlin, 1918)

E. Viollet and S. Flury: 'Un Monument des premiers siècles de l'hégire en Perse', *Syria*, i (1921), pp. 226–34, 305–16

G. A. Pugachenkova: *Puti razvitiya arkhitektury yuzhnogo Turkmenistana pory rabovladeniya i feodalizma* [The paths of development of the architecture of southern Turkmenistan in the period of slave-ownership and feudalism] (Moscow, 1958)

——: *Mavzolei Arab-ata* [Arab-Ata mausoleum] (Tashkent, 1963)

C. Adle and A. S. Melekian-Chirvani: 'Les Monuments du XIe siècle du Dâmqân', *Stud. Iran.*, i (1972), pp. 229–97

E. Galdieri: *Isfahân: Masǧid-i Ǧuma'a*, 3 vols (Rome, 1972–84)

C. Adle: 'Le Minaret du masjed-e jâme' de Semnân', *Stud. Iran.*, iv (1975), pp. 177–86

O. Grabar: 'The Visual Arts', *From the Arab Invasion to the Saljuqs* (1975), ed. R. N. Frye, iv of *Cambridge History of Iran* (Cambridge, 1968–), pp. 329–63

M. Bulatov: *Mavzolei Samanidov* [Mausoleum of the Samanids] (Tashkent, 1976)

S. S. Blair: 'The Octagonal Pavilion at Natanz', *Muqarnas*, i (1983), pp. 69–94

R. Hillenbrand: '"Abbasid Mosques in Iran', *Riv. Stud. Orient.*, lix (1985), pp. 175–212

A. Daneshvari: *Medieval Tomb Towers of Iran: An Iconographical Study* (Lexington, KY, 1986)

C. K. Wilkinson: *Nishapur: Some Early Islamic Buildings and their Decoration* (New York, 1986)

J. Bloom: *Minaret: Symbol of Islam* (Oxford, 1989)

S. S. Blair: *The Monumental Inscriptions from Early Islamic Iran and Transoxiana* (Leiden, 1992)

SHEILA S. BLAIR, JONATHAN M. BLOOM

(b) Iran, c. 1050–c. 1250. Between the Saljuq siege of Isfahan in 1050 and the Mongol conquest of Baghdad in 1258, architecture in Iran was dominated by the buildings erected by the rulers of the Saljuq dynasty (*reg* 1038–1194; *see* SALJUQ, §1), especially Sultan Malikshah (*reg* 1072–92) and Sultan Sanjar (*reg* 1118–57). Their first capital was Isfahan in western Iran (*see* ISFAHAN, §1), and a group of monuments dating from the first century of Saljuq rule survives there and in the surrounding area. When Sanjar became supreme sultan, he transferred the capital to Merv (now Mary in Turkmenistan; *see* MERV, §1(ii)), in the hinterland of which other buildings dating from the late 11th century and the early 12th survive. The lands to the north of the Saljuq domains were under the control of rival Turkish dynasties, among them the Khwarazmshahs (*reg c.* 1077–1231) and the Qarakhanids (*reg* 992–1211); those to the east were controlled by the Ghaznavids and the Ghurids (*see* §(c) below). The frontiers shifted constantly, so that buildings in such border sites as Termez (*see* TERMEZ, §1(ii)), Zuzan and Sar-i Pul share characteristics of both regions. As Saljuq power faded, minor dynasties, such as the Ahmadilis and Ildegizids in Azerbaijan and the Salghurids in Fars, were established, and a handful of their buildings from the 12th century and the early 13th remain.

The Saljuq capitals at Isfahan, BAGHDAD and Merv are described as splendid cities with large palaces and elaborate houses for the upper classes, but only at Merv is the general layout of the city known: excavations have revealed the central walled city, the citadel and an extensive suburb. Most of what is known about domestic architecture from other sites is based on a number of stucco plaques. Those from the palace at Termez on the Oxus River are decorated with animal figures, while those from the unpublished excavations at RAYY (New York, Met. and Tehran, Archaeol. Mus.) display a network of geometric and floral motifs in the Bevelled style of Samarra' (*see* §9(i)(b) below).

Building types. The most significant architectural innovation during the period was the development of what would become the standard plan for Iranian mosques. The early Islamic hypostyle mosque was transformed into one in which the arcades around the court were interrupted by four high iwans, one leading to a dome chamber that contained the mihrab. This process of transformation is best seen in the Friday Mosque at Isfahan (see fig. 29; *see also* ISFAHAN, §3(i)), where excavations have shown that the original Abbasid mosque, a large rectangle (88×128 m) with 262 bays and a wider central aisle leading from the court to the mihrab, had already received a new interior court façade in the second half of the 10th century (*see* §(a) above). Under the Saljuqs, the 24 columns corresponding to the 35 bays in front and to either side of the mihrab were replaced by a free-standing domed pavilion supported on giant polylobed piers (see fig. 29a). By interrupting the continuous row of bays, the terminal columns flanking the central pavilion were deprived of

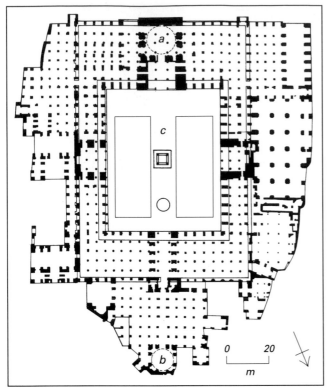

29. Friday Mosque, Isfahan, Iran, begun *c.* AD 771, plan: (a) south dome chamber, 1086–7; (b) north dome chamber, 1088–9; (c) court with four iwans, early 12th century

their counterthrust and rendered dangerously unstable. To remedy this instability, the builders clad these terminal columns with brick crowns that both increased their shear section from 0.92 to 1.25 m and visually prepared the transition from the forest of columns to the huge piers of the new 'sanctuary'.

An inscription running around the base of the dome declares that the chief vizier Nizam al-Mulk ordered the work during the reign of Malikshah; the titles used for the sultan pinpoint the date to 1086–7. During the autumn of 1086 Malikshah and his court had toured Syria, where they would have seen the magnificent new dome recently added to the Great Mosque in Damascus (*see* DAMASCUS, §3), and on returning to his capital Malikshah might well have ordered the new dome in imitation. It is somewhat larger (interior diam. 15 m as against 12.9 m), but must also have served as a MAQṢŪRA (the part of a mosque reserved for the prince).

This symbol of Saljuq sovereignty was soon repeated in other mosques in major cities. The best example survives in the congregational mosque of QAZVIN in north-west Iran. Like the dome chamber at Isfahan, it is a large square 15 m across. The transition to the dome is achieved by an octagonal zone, consisting of four blind arches alternating with four squinches, the squinches being simple arches thrown over the corners, surmounted by a 16-sided zone. Inscriptions and texts indicate that Humartash, Governor of Qazvin, had the new dome chamber added as a *maqṣūra*

between 1106 and 1116. Another dome survives at Gulpayagan, to the north-west of Isfahan. Smaller than the previous examples (interior diam. 10 m), it continues the Isfahan style, but the earlier trilobed squinch has shrunk to a heptafoil filled with three tiers of *muqarnas*. The inscription around the base of the dome dates the construction to the reign of Malikshah's son Muhammad (*reg* 1105–18).

These dome chambers were repeated at smaller towns in the hinterland of Isfahan (ARDISTAN, Barsiyan, Barujird, QUM and Sava) and further north, in Azerbaijan (Marand, Qurva, Sujas and Urmiyya). Their proliferation led André Godard to postulate the existence of the 'kiosk-mosque', a single-domed structure set at the end of a large open space. This he saw as the continuation of the Sasanian domed *chahārṭāq*. Jean Sauvaget vigorously rebutted this theory: in Iran an open courtyard is unsuitable for prayer during much of the year and the small enclosed space would have been inappropriate for Muslim cultic practices. Later excavations at such sites as Barsiyan and Ardistan confirmed some of Sauvaget's points and showed that these dome chambers, built in baked brick, were surrounded by arcades and other structures in mud-brick that have not survived. Whereas the princely connotations of the first dome chambers at Isfahan, Qazvin or even Gulpayagan are clear from their inscriptions, this was not necessarily true for the smaller examples. Repetition dulled the iconographic charge so that these provincial examples were formal, but not necessarily meaningful, copies of the type found in the capital.

The next step in the evolution of the Friday Mosque at Isfahan was the addition of iwans, high vaulted chambers opening on to the court (*see* IWAN). One was built abutting the north façade of the domed pavilion and three others were added along the main axes by knocking down the columns or incorporating them into the new walls. The iwans were fitted to the existing perimeter wall, so that the north iwan was longer and narrower and the side iwans shallower and wider. An inscription on the north-east portal states that it was added during restorations carried out in 1121–2 after the mosque had been damaged by fire; the iwans were probably also added at this time.

This combination of four iwans plus dome chamber was soon repeated in mosques built in nearby towns. At Ardistan, for example, a Saljuq vizier revamped the hypostyle mosque between 1158 and 1160 by adding these elements. The congregational mosque at ZAVARA, built in 1135–6 according to a partially surviving inscription, is a rectangle disposed around a central court with four iwans that vary in shape like those at Isfahan. The wide and shallow qibla iwan leads to a dome chamber 7.45 m square. Arches flank the iwans and lead to barrel-vaulted areas filling the corner spaces; a minaret abuts the portal in the north-west corner. This is the first surviving example of a mosque planned from the start with four iwans and a dome chamber.

Other mosque plans were still used, particularly in north-east Iran. The mosque at Talhatan Baba, 30 km from Merv, is a rectangle measuring 10×18 m with a central dome chamber flanked by two narrow halls. Both its exterior and interior are covered with superb brick patterning, the style of which suggests a date in the late

11th century or the early 12th. Its plan is closest to other rectangular buildings found on the outskirts of such cities as Dihistan, Nisa and Bukhara. These are known locally as *namāzgāh*s, the place where the whole population prayed together at festivals (*see* MUSALLA).

The four-iwan plan soon prevailed, however, in the Isfahan area and became the standard everywhere in later periods. The reason for this is still unclear. The plan is known from pre-Islamic Iran, and Max van Berchem suggested that it was first used in an Islamic religious context for madrasas. These are known to have been built throughout the Saljuq realm, but not a single example has survived intact (*see* MADRASA). Examples from the 14th century allow the possibility that their Saljuq prototypes already had four iwans, but the few remaining traces suggest that the madrasa plan varied according to location. One built at Zuzan at the beginning of the 13th century, for example, had two enormous iwans. Another ruined building at Khargird, probably a madrasa built by Nizam al-Mulk, had a large iwan built in mud-brick flanked by large, two-storey halls. Godard traced the evolution of the four-iwan plan one step further back, suggesting that it had first been the standard house-plan in north-east Iran: houses were often used as teaching establishments before the Saljuqs undertook state sponsorship of madrasas, and so the first madrasas would have been modelled on them. His archaeological evidence for house-plans in this region is tenuous, however, and the houses excavated in the Merv Oasis are small, square, domed buildings constructed of mud-brick, like the country mansions of earlier periods in the same region.

The four-iwan plan was also popular for monumental secular constructions. The governor's palace at Merv was a two-storey mud-brick structure measuring 39×45 m with four iwans opening off a central court 16 m square. Caravanserais too were often built on the four-iwan plan. The best surviving examples, superbly constructed in baked brick, are in western Central Asia. The one at Dayakhatyn in Turkmenistan was on the old road from Amul (now Chardzhou) on the Amu River towards Khwarazm. It is a square building 53 m on each side. A monumental portal on the east leads into a central court (30 m square) surrounded by an arcade interrupted by four iwans. Rectangular rooms lead off the arcade. It can be dated on stylistic grounds to the late 11th century or the early 12th. The caravanserai known as RIBAT-I SHARAF lies near the Iranian border on the old route from Nishapur to Merv. The large rectangular building has a monumental portal leading into a forecourt. Another portal opposite the entrance leads to a second and larger court that is surrounded by four iwans and a dome chamber. Square domed rooms and long vaulted halls, sometimes arranged as apartments, fill the side areas. Only part of the foundation inscription has survived, but the popular name of the building suggests that it should be attributed to the Saljuq vizier Sharaf al-Din Qummi and dated to 1114–15.

Minarets were built in large numbers from the 11th century onwards; a handful still soar above the skyline of Isfahan and some two dozen dot the landscape in Khurasan. This proliferation may indicate a revolution in technique that made these tall towers in baked brick resilient to earthquakes. Surviving examples certainly point

30. Carved stucco from the mihrab of the Imamzada Yahya, Sar-i Pul, Afghanistan, *c.* 1100

to a change in patronage: in addition to those minarets built by sovereigns adjacent to congregational mosques as before, others were erected by viziers, judges and even private individuals as isolated, free-standing constructions. (*See also* MINARET.)

The tombs of the period generally continue earlier forms, the tomb tower and the domed or canopy tomb (*see* §(a) above). The tomb tower at Mihmandust (1096–7), for example, belongs to the same type as two earlier tombs near by in DAMGHAN, but it is considerably larger (interior diam. 7 m; exterior diam. 10 m) and more articulated: the cylindrical body is divided into 12 sides by flanges surmounted by a series of projecting bands. The Imamzada Yahya at Sar-i Pul in Afghanistan (*c.* 1100) is a small domed square (5 m on each side) with a rectangular antechamber. Unprepossessing on the exterior, the interior is encrusted with extraordinary carved stucco (see fig. 30). At times the distinction between the tower and domed types becomes blurred. The Gunbad-i Surkh ('Red Tomb') at MARAGHA (1147–8) is elevated on a plinth so that the inner chamber sits over an interior crypt. The two tombs at Kharraqan (1067–8 and 1093–4) are octagonal with heavy corner buttresses. The grandest is that of Sultan Sanjar at Merv (*see* MERV, §2). In plan it is a simple domed square, remarkable only for its size (27 m on the exterior, 17 m on the interior). Its elevation is more unusual: above the square base, a gallery masks the transition to a soaring 14 m double dome (two shells of slightly varied profile connected by intermittent ties). The tomb obviously impressed medieval viewers, for it remained the example that later sovereigns sought to surpass.

Tomb complexes also developed during the period. Some, such as those at MASHHAD or QUM, surrounded the graves of Shi'ite imams. The building costs were met not only by wealthy Shi'ites but also by government officials seeking to win the support of heterodox elements. Others grew up around the graves of learned figures such as Hakim-i Tirmidhi (*d* 898) or mystics such as Bayazid

Bistami (*d c.* 874). These shrine complexes were often agglomerative, and only detailed archaeological investigation of individual sites will reveal the specific stages of construction.

Materials, forms and decoration. The lack of wood on the Iranian plateau led to the development of brick vaults and domes and new methods to support them. The typical elevation of a dome chamber, already used in the 10th century, was tripartite: four walls arranged in a square supported an octagonal zone of transition in which four squinches alternated with four blind arches, and this in turn supported the dome. In more elaborate examples, an intermediary 16-sided zone or squinch net was inserted between the octagonal zone and the dome. In a single example, the north dome that was added to the Friday Mosque in Isfahan in 1088–9 (see fig. 31), the parts are aligned vertically. From ground-level the eye is drawn up the articulated piers, across the squinches of the octagonal zone and the arches of the 16-sided zone to the inscription band ringing the base of the dome. The elevation logically and architectonically expresses the distribution of force from the base of the dome to the floor. To modern eyes this dome chamber appears to be the pinnacle of Saljuq dome construction, but, as far as is known, it was never repeated.

The form of the squinch varied. In central Iran the typical squinch was trilobed, as in the two dome chambers

31. Friday Mosque, Isfahan, Iran, north dome chamber, 1088–9

at Isfahan. Like the minaret, this form had been known earlier, but it was in this period that it proliferated. The form may well have spread from Isfahan to provincial sites such as Ardistan. In other areas a simpler squinch was used. In the congregational mosque at Qazvin the squinches are large, simple arches, as they are in the mosque at Barujird (*c.* 1140). The variations occur regionally rather than chronologically, and so a building such as the tomb at Sang Bast, once attributed to the early 11th century on the basis of its simple squinches, may really be late 12th century, as a study of its epigraphic ornament has suggested. Elsewhere squinches of different shapes were used in the same building: the caravanserai of Ribat-i Sharaf has five different types, that at Dayakhatyn has three.

Domes too were elaborated and articulated during this period. The tomb towers at Kharraqan show that the double dome already existed in the 11th century and was used to lighten the domical mass both physically and visually. Ribs facilitated construction in a land where wood was unavailable for centring. As the dome was built, the ribs were bonded into the construction and were often exploited for decorative effect: those in the north dome at Isfahan form a complex pentagram; those in Sanjar's tomb at Merv are highlighted in relief. The inventiveness displayed in the manipulation of domed spaces is clear from the Friday Mosque at Isfahan, where over 200 examples cover the individual bays, but their exact chronology has not been established and it is still unclear what percentage can be assigned to this period.

The monumental gateway (Pers. PĪSHTĀQ), a rectangular frame surrounding an arch, continued to develop. The form resembles the façade of an iwan facing an interior courtyard, and at Ribat-i Sharaf the two gateways foreshadow the iwans beyond. It was sometimes grafted on to a smaller mausoleum, hiding the main dome chamber from view, as at UZGEND, where the tomb façades were aligned along a street, or in the tomb at Sarakhs.

Manipulation of brick construction led to the further development of *muqarnas*, which was now cleverly exploited in transitional areas such as squinches, cornices and semi-domes. At Gulpayagan, for example, the squinch consists of a polylobed arch filled with three tiers of *muqarnas*. *Muqarnas* corbels commonly supported the balconies of minarets: three tiers of *muqarnas* remain at the top of the shaft of the minaret at BISTAM, although the upper section has now fallen. *Muqarnas* was clearly designed to provide a visual transition, but its structural role remains to be documented.

Fine baked brick was the pre-eminent material for the construction of important buildings during this period, while mud-brick, pisé and stone were used for subsidiary structures or in specific areas. A standard baked brick measuring *c.* 250×250×50 mm replaced the large, rectangular bricks of early periods and the small brick associated with Buyid buildings in the Isfahan region (*see* §(a) above). They ranged in colour from a cool ochre to a warm reddish brown, depending on the nature of the local clay, and were laid in a variety of flush or basket bonds, from common and double bond to diaper patterns, or in combinations of recessed and projecting bricks. Brick was also the main medium for architectural decoration. Bonding patterns were often exploited for decorative effect: the combination of recessed and projecting bricks was used to create elaborate patterns of light and shadow, for example, and in north-east Iran bricks were sometimes laid in double bond so that the vertical joints created a pattern across the wall. Minaret shafts could be divided into a series of horizontal bands that increased in width to offset visual distortion. The surfaces of other structures were often divided into panels filled with zigzag or octagonal patterns, while vertical bands were used to divide structures such as minaret shafts or dome chambers (see fig. 31) into a number of zones or to outline individual parts of a building, such as squinches, portals and reveals. On the tomb towers at Kharraqan, patterns in the brickwork emphasize structural elements such as buttresses, and brick reveals bearing a variety of patterns decorate each side, creating the effect of a building hung with tapestries. Joints were sometimes filled with plaster endplugs stamped or carved with geometric, floral or epigraphic patterns; or pieces of glazed tile were inserted into the gaps in order to heighten the contrast in colour between brick and interstice. Holes in the brickwork on the earlier tomb tower at Kharraqan (1067–8) were probably filled with these glazed pieces, and small fragments are still preserved in the dome chamber at Gulpayagan.

The potential of this use of colour was soon realized. The minaret at Sin (1132) had a complete inscription in glazed tile. Patterned brickwork and inscription bands in incised brick cover most of the exterior surface of the Gunbad-i Surkh (1147–8) at Maragha. Their matt surfaces contrast with the light-blue glazed strapwork decorating the spandrels and tympanum over the doorway. By the time the nearby Gunbad-i Kabud was built (1196–7), the use of colour had increased to such an extent that the tomb is virtually enveloped by a web of blue glazed tile. *Bannā'ī* ('builder's [technique]') was an easy and effective way of decorating large surfaces (*see* §9(ii)(b) below).

Plaster and terracotta were also used to cover large surfaces, especially in mud-brick buildings. The Imamzada Karrar at Buzun in central Iran (1133–4), a rectangular structure in mud-brick, has magnificent stucco ornament covering the interior. The roundels in the frieze and the side walls and vault of the mihrab were probably precast in a rough form, while the squinches and inscriptions were built up and modelled in place; the whole design was finished with crisp carving. In the Imamzada Yahya at Sari Pul, friezes of floriated script encircle the walls and the zone of transition, and the mihrab is embellished with deeply carved stucco that protrudes in three dimensions (see fig. 30 above). Stucco or terracotta could also be used to emphasize particular parts of a building. In the mosques at Ardistan and Zavara the elaborately carved stucco mihrabs contrast with the baked brick arches and walls. These stucco units were often painted, and traces of red, blue and green are visible under close inspection. Due to its ability to resist weathering, terracotta was preferred for exterior surfaces. The monumental portals on the tombs at Uzgend, for example, have moulded and carved terracotta panels.

The predominance of brick made geometric patterns the most common, but stucco could be carved or moulded

into a wider range of floral and vegetal motifs. Arabesques with undulating stems sprouting leaves and half-palmettes decorate the mihrabs at Ardistan and Zavara, for example. These floral motifs were often confined within geometric panels and sometimes served as beds for bands containing inscriptions. In these, builders or decorators (the distinction between the two is unclear) played off the angular against the cursive by juxtaposing geometric and organic motifs. A few figural motifs are known from secular art. Stucco panels from the palace at Termez show stylized animals that may relate to older Central Asian motifs. Life-size stucco figures depicting princes or courtiers are preserved in a number of museums, but their architectural function, not to mention their provenance, is still unclear.

Decoration was at first used as a means of enhancing structural features and of suggesting, if not actually revealing, the lines of force. But later it gradually began to cover the construction. At Ribat-i Sharaf the brickwork of the original construction was cut in relief or laid in a variety of bonds to create patterns, while the interstices were sometimes decorated with ornamental joints and stars sculpted in plaster. When the building was repaired 40 years later, in 1154–5, the original patterns created by the bonding were covered with plaster, which was then deeply carved and painted in a bewildering array of geometric, floral and epigraphic patterns. In a number of buildings in Khurasan, including Ribat-i Sharaf and the tomb at Sang Bast, interior surfaces were coated with stucco, which was then painted to imitate brick bonding patterns. Elsewhere glazed tile was no longer used as a foil against matt brick, but became a veil enveloping the entire surface. This growing taste for covering up wall surfaces and the increasing use of colour foreshadowed later developments in this direction, but at this time structure and decoration were kept in balance.

BIBLIOGRAPHY

M. Smith: 'Material for a Corpus of Early Iranian Islamic Architecture, i: Masdjid-i Djum'a, Demāwend', *A. Islam.*, ii (1935), pp. 153–73

M. Smith and E. Herzfeld: 'Imām Zāde Karrār at Buzūn: A Dated Seldjūk Ruin', *Archäol. Mitt. Iran*, vii (1935), pp. 65–81

A. Godard: 'Les Anciennes Mosquées de l'Iran', *Athar-é Iran*, i (1936), pp. 187–210

M. Smith: 'The Manārs of Isfahan', *Athar-é Iran*, i (1936), pp. 313–60

——: 'Material for a Corpus of Early Iranian Islamic Architecture, ii: Manār and Masdjid, Barsīān (Isfahān)', *A. Islam.*, iv (1937), pp. 6–41

J. Sauvaget: 'Observations sur quelques mosquées seljoukides', *An. Inst. Etud. Orient. U. Alger*, iv (1938), pp. 81–120

E. Schroeder: 'The Architecture of the Islamic Period: An Historical Outline, F: The Seljūq Period', *Survey of Persian Art*, ed. A. U. Pope and P. Ackerman (London, 1938–9), pp. 981–1045

B. P. Denike: *Arkhitekturnyi ornament srednei Azii* [Architectural ornament of Central Asia] (Moscow, 1939)

A. Godard: 'Khorāsān', *Athar-é Iran*, iv (1949), pp. 7–152

G. A. Pugachenkova: *Puti razvitiya arkhitektury yuzhnogo Turkmenistana pory rabovladeniya i feodalizma* [The paths of development of the architecture of southern Turkmenistan in the period of slave-ownership and feudalism] (Moscow, 1958)

——: *Istoriya iskusstva Uzbekistana* [A history of the art of Uzbekistan] (Moscow, 1966)

D. B. Stronach and T. Cuyler Young jr: 'Three Seljuq Tomb Towers', *Iran*, iv (1966), pp. 1–20

O. Grabar: 'The Visual Arts, 1050–1350', *The Saljuq and Mongol Periods* (1968), v of *Cambridge History of Iran* (Cambridge, 1968–91), pp. 626–58

E. Galdieri: *Isfahān: Masǧid-i Ǧuma'a*, 3 vols (Rome, 1972–84)

R. Hillenbrand: 'Saljuq Monuments in Iran, i', *Orient. A.*, n. s., xviii/1 (1972), pp. 64–77

——: 'Saljuq Monuments in Iran, ii: The "Pir" Mausoleum at Takistan', *Iran*, x (1972), pp. 45–56

D. Wilber: 'Le Masdjid-i Ǧâmi' de Qazwin', *Rev. Etud. Islam.*, xli (1973), pp. 199–229

J. Sourdel-Thomine: 'Inscriptions seljoukides et salles à coupoles de Qazwin en Iran', *Rev. Etud. Islam.*, xlii (1974), pp. 3–43

R. Hillenbrand: 'Saljuq Monuments in Iran, iii: The Domed Masǧid-i Ǧâmi' at Sugâs', *Kst Orients*, x (1975), pp. 49–79

——: 'Saljuq Monuments in Iran: The Mosques of Nûshâbâd', *Orient. A.*, n. s., xxii/3 (1976), pp. 265–77

D. Sourdel and J. Sourdel-Thomine: 'A propos des monuments de Sangbast', *Iran*, xvii (1979), pp. 109–14

M. Kiani, ed.: *Robat-e Sharaf* (Tehran, 1981)

R. Hillenbrand, ed.: *Proceedings of the Saljuq Conference: Edinburgh, August 1982*

O. Grabar: *The Great Mosque of Isfahan* (New York, 1990)

S. S. Blair: *The Monumental Inscriptions from Early Islamic Iran and Transoxiana* (Leiden, 1992)

SHEILA S. BLAIR

(c) Afghanistan, Pakistan and western Central Asia, c. *1050–c. 1250.* A distinctive style of architecture developed in Afghanistan and the surrounding areas under the GHAZNAVID (*reg* 977–1186) and GHURID (*reg c.* 1000–1215) dynasties. It is distinguished by the cumulative effect of several, sometimes minor, characteristics: massive scale, a significant use of stone, unusual arch profiles, new types of glazed tilework, intensive use of terracotta decoration and quantities of panegyric inscriptions written in various experimental angular and cursive scripts, the ornateness of which consistently exceeds anything known in contemporary Iran. Many of these features were innovations of the time, and this school brought terracotta decoration and epigraphic ornament to a pitch of technical mastery never to be exceeded. This brilliant and progressive architecture, parcelled out in remote sites in several modern states (Iran, Afghanistan, Uzbekistan, Tajikistan, Pakistan and India), has been unjustly neglected because the few surviving monuments are poorly preserved and skimpily published.

Building types. The types of buildings correspond to those found in other parts of the contemporary eastern Islamic world but are distributed differently, and some familiar types, such as caravanserais, are absent. Most striking is the relative rarity of mosques and mausolea, the two building types most dominant in the west. Only a half-dozen mosques and four mausolea are known. Among the mosques, the diminutive example at Larwand has such Indian characteristics as dressed-stone construction and decorative techniques; that of Darra-yi Shakh has a plan fortified like a *ribāṭ* (*see* §4(iii) above), while the mosque excavated at LASHKARI BAZAR exhibits a novel combination of a dome chamber with an oblong multi-vaulted prayer-hall and apparently no court. Pride of place must go to the Friday Mosque of HERAT, the Ghurid fabric of which was maintained until the 20th century. The Ghurid mosque had massive piers carrying four-centred arches, often with a slight return at springing level, which are typical of the 12th century, four iwans aligned to the cardinal points and 365 vaults. It is tempting to suggest that the number of vaults was intended to symbolize time with space.

Among mausolea, the 12th-century tomb of Salar Khalil, known as Baba Khatim, in the hamlet of Kim Sane, 60 km west of Mazar-i Sharif, belongs to a Central Asian type: a domed square, the exterior of which is plain on three sides but highlighted on the fourth by a *pīshṭāq* framed by a magnificent kufic inscription. Two mausolea at Chisht (1167 and late 12th century) fall into the same general category, although they are taller, more slender and more refined. A less usual type is the undated mausoleum at Bust, a squat open-plan octagon, or canopy tomb. The interior of the dome has an ornamental revetment of bricks set in alternating rings with flat sides and ends exposed, a technique found also at the minaret of Khwaja Siyah Push. The wedge-shaped piers have two faces set at 45 degrees to each other, and these broaden dramatically to the exterior so that the piers seem spread-eagled. Their lavish articulation by reveals and polygonal engaged columns is similar to the zone of transition in the Ghurid mausoleum in the mosque at Herat. The undated mausoleum of Imam-i Kalan at Sar-i Pul was originally a domed square with rounded buttresses at the corners and axial openings on three sides; the batter of the walls and the arcaded gallery with corner finials are also reminiscent of the Samanid mausoleum at Bukhara (*see* §(a) and fig. 127 above). A well-developed portal probably stood on the south, but it has been lost in the mass of the chamber added in a later building campaign.

One of the few buildings that can clearly be identified as a madrasa is the ruined structure known as Shah-i Mashhad 2 km above the confluence of the Murgab and Kucha rivers in Badgis province. The substantial building (44×41 m) was erected by an unnamed woman in 1175–6. The surviving iwans on the north and south may have been matched by others on the east and west. In the southeast corner are two dome chambers, which may be precursors of the lecture room and assembly hall flanking the main portal in later madrasas, such as the one at Khargird (*see* §6(i)(b) below). The corner of the court is bevelled, a feature also repeated at Khargird. On the exterior east side of the main portal is a niche, presumably a mihrab for travellers, a feature also found at Ribat-i Sharaf (*see* §(b) above). The glory of the building is the splendid decoration in brick, terracotta and carved plaster. The enigmatic building at Danestama, which has public rooms flanking the portal, may also have been a madrasa. Near by are similar buildings in a more ruined state.

Minarets were the most common type of building, to judge by the rate of survival, and they show remarkable formal variety. The most conventional example is the one at Dawlatabad (1108–9): its cylindrical shaft and overall decoration in baked brick and terracotta have numerous parallels in Iran. Other minarets have gadroons or angular flanges. The minaret of Mas'ud III (*reg* 1099–1115) at GHAZNA (original h. *c.* 44 m; partially destr.) had a flanged lower shaft crowned by a cylindrical upper shaft with narrow vertical gadroons separated by guard-bands in high relief. Much of the decoration was epigraphic. The neighbouring minaret built by Sultan Bahramshah (*reg* 1118–52) probably had the same form. The undated minarets of Khwaja Siyah Push in Sistan and Nad 'Ali (medieval Zaranj) have alternately round and angular flanges on the lower shaft. That at Khwaja Siyah Push has decoration in baked brick laid in wide bands of alternately horizontal and vertical bond. The Qutb Minar at Delhi (begun 1198; *see* DELHI, §III, 1 and fig. 2), built in stone, has alternating round and angled flutes on the first storey, gadroons on the second and angular flutes on the third. The masterpiece of the group is the minaret built in 1194 by the Ghurid Ghiyath al-Din Muhammad ibn Sam (*reg* 1163–1203) at Jam in a secluded valley ringed by mountains in central Afghanistan (see fig. 32). It was probably the loftiest (about 60 m) minaret of its time. The shaft is subdivided into three diminishing tiers and was crowned by a domed open-plan aedicule. Within, a double-spiral staircase ensured that those ascending did not meet those descending. The exterior is encased in terracotta ornament, and several latticework panels give the illusion of windows in addition to the actual windows that light the stair. The exuberance of the decorative details is subordinated to the grand design, and its endless ingenuity and sustained panache is rivalled only in the decoration of the Shah-i Mashhad madrasa.

Palaces are known from the ruined suburb of Bust, Lashkari Bazar and from Ghazna. The three main palaces at Lashkari Bazar were set amid gardens with high enclosure walls. The South, or Great, Palace is attributed to Mahmud of Ghazna (*reg* 998–1030) and is outstanding for its scale, rational organization, elaborate bath, and iwan-hall behind the iwan and dome chamber unit on the principal axis of the building which overlooked the Helmand River. The walls of the iwan-hall are decorated with a painted frieze of attendants, Koranic inscriptions including one describing the enthroned Solomon receiving the Queen of Sheba (xxvii.40–41) and geometric ornament in brick and stucco. It was the principal reception hall. The palace has one of the earliest-developed four-iwan plans in Islamic architecture, as well as two- and four-iwan units within the plan. The palace is clearly in the Samarran tradition of a sprawling mud-brick palace-city (*see* §4(i)(b) above), although it is far smaller (170×100 m) than its Mesopotamian forebears. A bazaar some 500 m long led up to the palace on the south. The Centre Palace was entirely different in concept. The extremely compact rectangular structure (56×38 m) was divided into four equal units, each with its own court but differently disposed. Axial passages quartered the building and met in a central court, which was reduced to a well of space as in the country mansions of western Central Asia (*see* §(a) above). These subtleties were hidden by largely blank walls and corner buttresses, except on the east, where a continuous arcade promised easy access. The North Palace, a fortified rectangular enclosure (90×100 m), contains three independent units of four iwans and subsidiary rooms grouped around a court, and three empty enclosures in the remaining space. Secondary palaces, perhaps residences of notables, are scattered over the site of Lashkari Bazar. Some have three storeys and many are rectangular enclosures with rounded corner bastions, semicircular buttresses along the walls and four iwans grouped around a court on the interior. Others have a score or more rooms grouped around a yard and seem more like caravanserais. In the garden to the east of the Centre Palace is a square pavilion 28 m to a side. Its central square hall is surrounded by four iwans opening to the outside and four square chambers in the corners. Its plan is reminiscent of the one Abu Muslim is said to have built at Merv *c.* 745 (*see* MERV,

32. Minaret at Jam, central Afghanistan, 1194

§1(ii)) and prefigures the type of palace exemplified by the Hasht Bihisht at Isfahan (*see* §6(i)(b) below).

The palace of Mas'ud III (*reg* 1099–1115) at Ghazna is less ambitious. It is an irregular quadrilateral (158×127 m) set on a platform. A long iwan served as vestibule to a rectangular court with iwans on the axis of each of its other sides and a square throne-room opposite. An oratory orientated to the qibla opened off the north-west corner of the court, and a smaller four-iwan court is located to the south-west. A bazaar stood some 25 m to the north of the palace, but was parallel to the façade, unlike the one at Lashkari Bazar. It had shops tucked behind a continuous colonnade.

One of the novel building types is the free-standing arch. The Do Baradar near Ribat-i Sharaf is a small version, while the one at Bust, ascribed to Ghurid patronage in the later 12th century, is much larger (see fig. 33). Decorated in cut brick on the front and back, it fronted on a vast empty square at the foot of the citadel and was part of a redesign of the square to channel traffic through the

33. Arch at Bust, Afghanistan, later 12th century

citadel's main gate. It probably had a ceremonial or symbolic function; its imposing span and height would have made comparison with the Sasanian arch at KTESI-PHON mandatory, while its functional aspects seem to be a genuine reworking of the Roman triumphal arch theme. The citadel itself is well preserved, but has been neither planned nor described in detail. The well at Bust comprises a vaulted structure above ground and a complex of vaulted chambers that descends 20 m underground on four levels, with ingenious provision for natural lighting and ventilation. The largest chamber on the second level was distinguished by carved stucco decoration; it might have served as a setting for social gatherings.

Materials, forms and decoration. Most buildings of the period were built of baked brick, but mud-brick was also used for major public buildings on a scale not encountered elsewhere in the Iranian world. This meanest but most accessible of building materials is found at Pishwaran and many other sites in Sistan of the 12th and 13th centuries. At Lashkari Bazar many of the buildings scattered over a field of 14 sq. km are constructed of rammed earth, with mud-brick, baked brick, stone and plaster used more sparingly in key locations. The obvious parallel is to the Abbasid capital at Samarra', also located on a riparian site with royal or seigneurial buildings extending for many kilometres and similar techniques of construction. Wood was occasionally used, both for structural purposes, as in the horizontal frames in the minaret of Mas'ud III at Ghazna, and for decoration, as in the mihrab of the mosque of Charkh-i Lugar, south of Kabul (*see* §VII, 1(ii) below).

Most of the structural forms employed by Ghaznavid and Ghurid builders belonged to the architectural tradition common to the entire Iranian world, but certain features enjoyed a certain vogue. One is the decorated column, which could be multi-ringed ('tomb' of Khalid ibn Walid, near Multan, Pakistan, and several tombstones from Bust) or painted, inscribed or covered with arabesques (South Palace at Lashkari Bazar). The most common form of arch was the horseshoe, distinguished from its counterpart in western Islamic architecture by a pointed apex. It could be used singly (Pishwaran, the field of ruins around the minaret of Khwaja Siyah Push in Sistan), in pairs (arch at Bust) or in arcades (façade of the South Palace at Lashkari Bazar and many areas within it), and the field could be filled with carved stucco. Arches could be cusped, whether with three cusps ('tomb' of Khalid ibn Walid) or more commonly five or seven, a form found extensively on contemporary gravestones and mosques as far away as India (Quwwat al-Islam, Delhi, 1197 (*see* DELHI, §III, 1); and Arha'i Din ka Jhompra, AJMER, 1199). Often the two forms were combined. These arches coexist with types familiar in the rest of the Iranian world, such as the four-centred and shouldered segmental arch (Ghurid mausoleum in the mosque at Herat).

Squinches show remarkable formal variety. At the Imamzada Yahya (known as Imam-i Khurd) at Sar-i Pul, the squinches are composed of a graduated series of 11 semicircular arches bridging the corner. This unusual but logical solution creates a powerful and semi-illusionistic sense of depth, which is emphasized by the plain blind arches between the squinches. A similar squinch composed of a series of graduated rectangles occurs at the South Palace at Lashkari Bazar. Squinches formed of stepped rectangles are also found at the site, which rivals Ribat-i Sharaf for the variety of its squinch forms. Another form of squinch was based on the trilobed arch. At Baba Khatim, the squinches are trilobed arches; the adjoining blind arches repeat the form with a marked stilt in the upper lobe. The whole arrangement is reminiscent of the squinch zone at Tim (*see* §(a) above). A more complex solution of concentric trilobed squinches appears first at Shah-i Mashhad and in a more refined version at the Ghurid mausoleum in the Herat mosque. This arresting image shows how the weight of the dome is rationally divided among its supporting members, and how the multiplicity of large and small curvilinear and flanged forms imparts vitality to the zone. An alternative treatment is found two decades later at the madrasa at Zuzan (1218–19), where the squinch contains a developed *muqarnas*, the standard solution of later centuries.

These buildings display the range of decorative techniques known in Iran. Brick patterning is the major decoration on a few buildings, such as the minarets of Bahramshah and Khwaja Siyah Push and the mausoleum at Bust, and other Iranian techniques are known, such as interlocking hexagonal paving and incising a plastered wall with vertical indentations, but in general an interest in baked brick is replaced by a delight in terracotta. Spindle-shaped plugs form borders. Interlaced medallions animate spandrels, capitals, soffits and columns. Infilled panels parcel up minaret shafts and façades, and illusionistic grilles simulate windows. Inscription bands of blue glazed tile were a relatively new technique, but examples on the portal of the Herat mosque and on the minaret at Jam show a thorough understanding of the decorative potential of the medium (*see also* §9(ii)(b) below). Square floor tiles moulded in relief and glazed yellow, olive, red or brown were found in the palace at Ghazna. Their repertory of animals was repeated in stone sculptures at the same site, and the subject-matter, like the marble frames and grilles there, may have been inspired by booty from the Ghaznavid campaigns in India (*see* §9(i)(b) below). Stucco techniques are in line with contemporary work in Iran and western Central Asia and include the painted imitation of decorative brick bonding, Bevelled style panels and the proliferation of blossoms attached to thin tendrils. The most celebrated frescoes from the period are the images of the royal bodyguard encircling the throne-room of the South Palace at Lashkari Bazar (*see* §9(iii)(b) below). The painted head of a youth on a fragmentary column from the South Palace is close in style to Saljuq lustre pottery (*see* §V, 3(iii) below).

The quantity, content, variety and style of epigraphic decoration distinguishes the architecture of this period (*see also* §9(vi) below). Even in its ruined state, the Ghurid mausoleum at Herat has eight inscriptions; at Shah-i Mashhad fifteen inscriptions, probably a quarter of the original total, survive. The minaret at Jam has seven inscriptions, including all 98 verses of Sura Maryam (xix) of the Koran. Epigraphy dominates the decoration of

several mausolea at Herat, Chisht and Sar-i Pul. The content of the inscriptions has been finely calculated. Koranic quotations are repeatedly taken from *Surat al-Fath* ('Victory') xlviii, and others evoke Solomon, Abraham and a dozen biblical prophets. The profession of faith is displayed prominently over entrances and mihrabs. Lengthy historical inscriptions with the names and titles of the ruler decorate minarets and portals and are often repeated within the building. This unusual emphasis on titulature, confirmed in historical sources, makes Ghurid buildings more propagandistic than those of their contemporaries, and many of the inscriptions strike a strong religious note. Inscriptions present Ghiyath al-Din Muhammad ibn Sam (*reg* 1163–1203), the principal patron of Ghurid architecture, as champion of the faith.

Cursive script is repeatedly used for historical inscriptions at a time when this was a rare practice in the lands to the west. Square kufic script spells out sacred names, as is common in Iran, and also the names and titles of the sultans. Epigraphic roundels are also known. Terracotta is used for large bands of thuluth script, and in the palace at Ghazna gigantic (*c.* 40 mm) terracotta letters were set in high relief against a ground of incised triangles. The extensive use of terracotta permitted a degree of flexibility and curvilinearity not available to craftsmen using brick. At the Ghurid mausoleum at Herat and other buildings, the letter-terminals in cursive inscriptions are punctured with holes and strokes in such a way as to suggest zoomorphic forms. Epigraphy infiltrates every aspect of the decorative ensemble, including brick decoration, minor border designs and the infill of small medallions. Ornament occasionally mimics writing. Decorative devices include the double outlining of letters and the elongation of stems, but the most predominant motif is knotting. The best example is the portal inscription of Shah-i Mashhad, whose never-repeating knots occupy most of the inscription band.

BIBLIOGRAPHY

J. Sourdel-Thomine: 'Deux minarets d'époque seljoukide en Afghanistan', *Syria*, xxx (1953), pp. 108–36
——: 'Stèles arabes de Bust (Afghanistan)', *Arabica*, iii (1956), pp. 295–306
A. Maricq and G. Wiet: *Le Minaret de Djam* (Paris, 1959)
J. Sourdel-Thomine: 'L'Art ghuride d'Afghanistan d'après un livre récent', *Arabica*, vii (1960), pp. 273–80
A. D. H. Bivar: 'Seljuqid *Ziyarats* of Sar-i Pul (Afghanistan)', *Bull. SOAS*, xxix (1966), pp. 57–63
A. Bombaci: *The Kufic Inscription in Persian Verses in the Court of the Royal Palace of Mas'ud III at Ghazna* (Rome, 1966)
A. S. Melikian-Chirvani: 'Eastern Iranian Architecture: A propos of the Ghurid Parts of the Great Mosque of Harat', *Bull. SOAS*, xxxiii (1970), pp. 322–7
M. J. Casimir and B. Glatzer: 'Sah-i Mashad: A Recently Discovered Madrasah of the Ghurid Period in Gargistan (Afghanistan)', *E. & W.*, n. s., xxi (1971), pp. 53–68
J. Sourdel-Thomine: 'Le Mausolée dit de Baba Hatim en Afghanistan', *Rev. Etud. Islam.*, xxxix (1971), pp. 293–320
D. Schlumberger and J. Sourdel-Thomine: *Lashkari Bazar*, 3 vols (Paris, 1978)
H. Crane: 'Helmand-Sistan Project: An Anonymous Tomb in Bust', *E. & W.*, n. s., xxix (1979), pp. 241–6
B. Glatzer: 'Das Mausoleum und die Moschee des Ghoriden Ghiyath ud-Din in Herat', *Afghanistan J.*, vii (1980), pp. 6–22
L. Golombek: 'The Resilience of the Friday Mosque: The Cast of Herat', *Muqarnas*, i (1983), pp. 95–102
B. O'Kane: 'Salguq Minarets: Some New Data', *An. Islam.*, xx (1984), pp. 85–102

S. S. Blair: 'The Madrasa at Zuzan: Islamic Architecture in Eastern Iran on the Eve of the Mongol Invasions', *Muqarnas*, iii (1985), pp. 75–91

K. K. Mumtaz: *Architecture in Pakistan* (Singapore, 1985)

R. Pinder-Wilson: 'The Minaret of Mas'ud III at Ghazni', *Studies in Islamic Art* (London, 1985), pp. 89–102

T. Allen: 'Notes on Bust', *Iran*, xxvi (1988), pp. 56–68

——: 'Notes on Bust (Continued)', *Iran*, xxvii (1989), pp. 57–66

——: 'Notes on Bust (Continued)', *Iran*, xxviii (1990), pp. 23–30

ROBERT HILLENBRAND

(ii) Central Islamic lands. The FATIMID caliphate (*reg* 909–1171) was the most powerful force in the region and the major patron of architecture. The Fatimids supplanted the Aghlabid dynasty of Tunisia and Sicily and in 969 conquered Egypt, to which they moved, leaving their North African territories in the care of Berber governors. Their domains sometimes included Arabia and Syria, which had been in decline since the fall of the Umayyads in 750. Fatimid vassals controlled parts of the Yemen, while other areas were under Zaydi and orthodox control. In the 11th century several Turkish and Kurdish dynasties replaced the Arab tribes that had dominated northern Syria and the Jazira (the lands lying between the upper reaches of the Tigris and Euphrates). Syria, the focus of repeated Crusader attacks, became a vibrant region and was joined to Egypt after 1171. Congregational mosques continued to be the main building type but were increasingly replaced by new types, such as small mosques, madrasas, tombs, minarets and fortifications. Throughout most of the region, stone became the dominant material of construction. The use of *muqarnas* began in the late 11th century and quickly spread throughout the region.

(a) Tunisia and eastern Algeria. (b) Sicily. (c) Egypt. (d) Yemen. (e) Syria, the Jazira and Iraq.

(a) Tunisia and eastern Algeria. The major architectural feature of this region (Ifriqiya) during this period is the creation of the walled cities that contained the palaces of the FATIMID dynasty (*reg* 909–72) and their Berber successors, the ZIRIDS and Hammadids (*reg* 972–1152). In 912 the first Fatimid caliph al-Mahdi began construction of a fortified capital at MAHDIA on a peninsula on Tunisia's east coast. Double land walls and a massive gate, still standing in a much restored state, enhanced the strategic advantages of the site. The congregational mosque there (begun 916; rest. 1960s) has a T-plan, arcades surrounding the court and doubled supports in the central aisle, all features clearly inspired by the 9th-century Great Mosque in Kairouan (see fig. 25 above). The most notable feature of the Kairouan mosque—a massive minaret opposite the mihrab—was replaced by a projecting two-storey portal (see fig. 34) flanked by bastions in the corners, owing to the Fatimid disapproval of giving the call-to-prayer from any place higher than the mosque roof. The formal origins of the portal, built of fine stone masonry, can be traced to Late Antique triumphal arches in the region (e.g. Sufetula, now Sbeitla, Arch of Antoninus Pius). The bastions, once thought to have been bases for minarets, were cisterns for the mosque, since the rocky terrain did not allow digging underground. Features such as the projecting portal, the absence of a minaret, a courtyard surrounded by arcades and the higher and wider transverse aisle that leads to a dome over the mihrab in the prayer-hall continued to

34. Congregational mosque, Mahdia, Tunisia, portal, AD 921

characterize later Fatimid mosques in Egypt (*see* §(c) below).

In 947 the third Fatimid caliph, al-Mansur, founded al-Mansuriyya (or Sabra), another new capital a short distance from Kairouan. It had circular walls, and one enthusiastic contemporary compared it favourably to Baghdad. The palace of the Zirids at Ashir, their hereditary stronghold in central Algeria, is said to have been modelled on a Fatimid palace at Mahdia. Only the plan of the entrance remains at Mahdia, but the palace at Ashir is a large rectangle (72×40 m) with a projecting portal and bent vestibule giving access to a large square courtyard with a portico on the entrance side. Long windowless rooms flank the court, and a large transverse reception hall with a central bay stands opposite the entrance and projects through the exterior wall. Four smaller versions of the same plan flank the central tract.

QAL'AT BANI HAMMAD (Kalaa Bani Hammad), the Hammadid capital in central Algeria, was strategically situated on a mountainous site fortified with ramparts. It contained several large palaces and a mosque, as well as caravanserais and public buildings. It flourished as a refuge from the invasion of bedouins sent by the Fatimid caliphs when the Hammadids rebelled and recognized the authority of the Abbasid caliph in Baghdad. One of the largest palaces (260×160 m) contained a huge pool, and the façades were decorated with blind arcading, similar to that found in the contemporary architecture of Sicily and Egypt (*see* §§(b) and (c) below). Remains of MUQARNAS and *muqarnas*-like decoration mark the earliest appearance in the Muslim west of this quintessentially Islamic motif, but the route by which it arrived from points further east is still to be determined. The minaret, the only significant structure still standing on the site, shows greater affinity to the square minarets of Umayyad Spain and Morocco (*see* §(iv)(a) below) than to earlier Tunisian towers. Its deep recesses were inlaid with polychrome tiles, which were also employed in other areas of the site and would later become one of the most characteristic features of western Islamic architecture. By the late 11th century the site was abandoned in favour of Bijaya (Bougie, now Annaba) on the Mediterranean coast.

BIBLIOGRAPHY
G. Marçais: *L'Architecture musulmane d'occident* (Paris, 1954)
L. Golvin: *Le Magrib central à l'époque des Zirides: Recherches d'archéologie et d'histoire* (Paris, 1957)
——: *Recherches archéologiques à la Qal'a des Banû Hammâd* (Paris, 1965)
A. Lézine: *Mahdiya: Recherches d'archéologie islamique* (Paris, 1965)
L. Golvin: 'Le Palais de Zîrî à Achîr (Dixième siècle J.C.)', *A. Orient.*, vi (1966), pp. 47–76
R. Bourouiba: *L'Art religieux musulman en Algérie* (Algiers, 1973)
J. M. Bloom: 'The Origins of Fatimid Art', *Muqarnas*, iii (1985), pp. 30–38

JONATHAN M. BLOOM

(b) Sicily. The architecture of Sicily from the Islamic conquest in 827 to the mid-13th century shares many features with contemporary architecture in North Africa, but little of it can properly be termed Islamic since most of the surviving monuments date from after 1091, when the Norman conquest was completed. Nevertheless the secular and religious architecture of the Normans in Sicily cannot be understood without reference to its Islamic heritage, and the fragmentary survival of secular architecture from North Africa and Egypt makes the Norman buildings of Sicily particularly important for a clear understanding of contemporary Islamic architecture there. The formal and decorative features of Norman architecture, such as garden palaces amid artificial lakes, blind arcading and *muqarnas* ceilings, are found at the palaces erected by contemporary Muslim princes of North Africa (*see* §(a) above), such as at Ashir, at Qal'at Bani Hammad and at Bejaïa (Bougie).

Sicily shared a common cultural heritage with North Africa because the island was wrested from the Byzantines in 827 by the Aghlabid rulers of Tunisia (*reg* 800–909). They governed it until they were removed by the Fatimids, but the actual rulers, the Kalbid governors (*reg* 948–1091), were effectively independent of North Africa. The arrival of the Normans in 1061 further enriched the artistic culture of the island, giving rise to the anomaly of an Islamic architecture produced for Christian patrons, somewhat equivalent to the Spanish MUDÉJAR. The style of architecture produced by Islamic or Islamicized craftsmen trained in the traditions of North Africa remained substantially unchanged by the addition of Byzantine mosaics or Italian figural sculptures. Only at the end of the period, under Frederick II Hohenstaufen, when the Muslim population was persecuted and destroyed, did Gothic forms, primarily introduced by the Cistercians, begin to exert a major impact. Artistic production came to an almost complete halt with the political unrest in the second half of the 13th century.

Historical sources report that large numbers of cities and villages were founded and many civil and religious buildings erected under Aghlabid, Fatimid and Kalbid rule. Palermo is said to have had 300 mosques, but the only significant remains from the Islamic period are a hypostyle room near Palermo Cathedral (9th century) and a bath covered with ogival barrel vaults at Cefalà Diama (perhaps Kalbid). Ja'far (*reg* 997–1019) constructed an artificial lake in the suburbs of Palermo at the centre of which Roger II Hauteville (*reg* 1130–54) built the Favara (Arab. *fawwara*: 'fountain') Palace. It was laid out around an arcaded courtyard and incorporated a chapel, parts of which still stand.

Under Roger the main Sicilian cities were renovated in an intensive building programme. At Palermo, the seat of the court, the upper part of the city was rebuilt and enclosed within walls to become the site of the Royal Palace and the Cappella Palatina (1131–40; *see* PALERMO, §II, 2). The remarkable ceiling of painted wood over the cappella's nave, which is decorated with tiers of *muqarnas* cells arranged in star patterns (see fig. 35), is undoubtedly derived from now-lost palace ceilings in North Africa, and the high hemispherical dome over its sanctuary, although decorated with Byzantine mosaics, is found in contemporary North African architecture. In 1131 Roger began construction of Cefalù Cathedral (*see* CEFALÙ, §1), which he envisaged as his final resting-place, but only the outer shell and the mosaic decoration of the apse were completed at his death. The ponderous twin towers of the west façade are more like North African minarets than Italian campaniles. In Palermo the churches of S Giovanni degli Eremiti (1132; built over the remains of a mosque), S Maria

35. *Muqarnas* ceiling over the nave, Cappella Palatina, Palermo, Sicily, 1140

dell'Ammiraglio (La Martorana; 1143) and S Cataldo (1160) also display features characteristic of contemporary architecture in North Africa, such as cubic massing relieved only by shallow vertical panelling and horizontal cornices, high hemispherical domes on squinches and cushion voussoirs (*see* PALERMO, §II, 3 and 4).

Building during the reigns of William I (*reg* 1154–66) and William II Hauteville (*reg* 1166–89) is particularly well represented at Palermo and Monreale. In the countryside beyond Palermo, William I built the Ziza (Arab. *'azīza*: 'splendid') Palace during the last two years of his life. Set in a paradisiacal garden, this stone building (36.30×19.75×25.70 m) has towerlike projections at either end. The three-storey elevation is emphasized by shallow blind arcades and was originally crowned with an inscribed cornice. The building contains two superposed cruciform rooms flanked by smaller chambers on three levels. The lower room has a typical Islamic fountain opposite the entrance; water springs from the wall and flows down a stepped and rippled cascade (Arab. *salsabīl*) into a series of pools and channels on the floor. *Muqarnas* hoods crown many of the recesses of the interior. Under William II, the cathedrals of Monreale (1172–6) and Palermo (1184–5) were erected speedily, due to great advances in building techniques (*see* MONREALE CATHEDRAL and PALERMO, §II, 1). The decorative polychromy of the exteriors, the floors decorated with mosaic and the painted wooden ceilings all relate to contemporary architecture in North Africa.

The Cuba (1180; Arab. *qubba*: 'dome'), located in the suburbs of Palermo, is, like the Ziza, a garden pavilion set in the middle of a pool. Mentioned in Boccaccio's *Decameron* (Day V, vi), it is a tall rectangular block (*c.* 30×18 m) with limestone walls and rectangular projections in the middle of each side. Blind arcades along the exterior divide the façades into vertical registers that run from the water level to the cornice. Inside, a square central courtyard was bounded by tall arcades. To one side is a cruciform room like the fountain room at the Ziza, to the other is one with three entrances. Near by in the gardens stands a small kiosk known as the Cubola. It consists of a cubic base (6.33 m to a side) with arched openings outlined with mouldings and cushion voussoirs in each face. Squinches support a hemispherical dome. The Aula Verde (Green Hall) in the Royal Palace at Palermo, where the king held public audience, was a porticoed atrium probably like the cloister in the Benedictine monastery of Monreale. The long covered passageway linking the Royal Palace to Palermo Cathedral and similar royal passages in the Cappella Palatina and in Monreale Cathedral recall the passages linking the palaces of Muslim rulers to congregational mosques (*see* §(iv)(a) below).

Muslim culture in Sicily declined with the arrival of Henry VI in 1194 and HOHENSTAUFEN domination. The most conspicuous building project of the period was a strategic defence system of Frederick II (*reg* 1220–50) that extended throughout the Hohenstaufen dominions in Sicily and southern Italy. The fortifications made use of building techniques that dated back to antiquity, but were reinforced by a long familiarity with Muslim fortified buildings. Of the many castles founded by Frederick II, those at Catania (1239; *see* CATANIA, §2) and Augusta

(1231–42) have plans similar in design to those of *ribāṭ*s in the Maghrib, while the Castello Maniace at Syracuse (1232–9; *see* SYRACUSE, §2), which was also a luxurious residence, has a large hypostyle hall with magnificent groin vaults along with a Cistercian-inspired great doorway.

BIBLIOGRAPHY

G. de Prangey: *Essai sur l'architecture des arabes et des maures en Espagne, en Sicile et en Barbarie* (Paris, 1841)
A. Goldschmidt: 'Die Favara des Königs Rogers von Sizilien', *Jb. Kön.-Preuss. Kstsamml.*, xvi (1895), pp. 199–215
——: 'Die normanischen Königspaläste in Palermo', *Z. Bauvsn*, xlviii (1898), cols 541–90
S. Bottari: 'La genesi dall'architettura siciliana del periodo normanno', *Archv Stor. Sicilia Orient.*, xxviii (1932), pp. 320–27
G. Agnello: *L'architettura sveva in Sicilia* (Rome, 1935)
H. Schwarz: 'Die Baukunst Kalabriens und Siziliens im Zeitalter der Normannen', *Röm. Jb. Kstgesch.*, vi (1942–4), pp. 1–112
U. Monneret de Villard: *Le pitture musulmane al soffitto della Cappella Palatina in Palermo* (Rome, 1950)
G. Marçais: *L'Architecture musulmane d'occident* (Paris, 1954), pp. 118–25
G. Bellafiore: 'Edifici d'età islamica e normanna presso la cattedrale di Palermo', *Boll. A.: Min. Pub. Istruzione*, 5th ser., lii (1967), pp. 178–9
F. Basile: *L'architettura della Sicilia normanna* (Rome, 1975)
G. Bellafiore: *Dall'Islam alla Maniera* (Palermo, 1975)
——: *La Zisa di Palermo* (Palermo, 1978)
F. Gabrieli and U. Scerrato: *Gli arabi in Italia* (Milan, 1979)
G. Bellafiore: 'Architettura e cultura delle città fatimite in Sicilia', *Stor. Città*, xvii (1980), pp. 3–10
——: 'I giardini paradiso a Palermo nella età islamica e normanna', *Argomenti Stor. A.*, i (1983), pp. 5–22
——: *Architettura delle età islamica e normanna in Sicilia* (Palermo, 1990)

GIUSEPPE BELLAFIORE

(c) Egypt. Architecture from the 10th century to the mid-13th is dominated by the patronage of the FATIMID (*reg* 909–1171) and AYYUBID (*reg* 1169–1252) dynasties in Cairo, founded by the Fatimids in 969. The revival of stone masonry for public buildings, the use of monumental inscriptions on their exteriors and the new responses to an increasingly dense urban environment are the most notable developments, and their ramifications in Egyptian Islamic architecture continued for centuries. Some 40 religious buildings, ranging from enormous congregational mosques to small mausolea, survive in Cairo, and five minarets and dozens of rather crude mausolea have been found in the towns of Upper Egypt, notably ASWAN. Several medieval Arabic literary works, particularly the *Khiṭaṭ* ('Districts') by Ahmad ibn 'Ali al-Maqrizi (1364–1442), the Mamluk historian and littérateur, describe many other buildings, particularly the secular architecture that has vanished, as well as their decoration and furnishings. Taken together, the buildings and the texts give an unusually rich picture of medieval Islamic architecture. Architecture of the period falls into three phases. The first, characterized by large-scale caliphal patronage of palaces and congregational mosques adapted to the needs and tastes of the new Shi'ite rulers of Egypt, began with the founding of Cairo and the transfer there of the Fatimid capital in 972 (*see* CAIRO, §I) and ended with the terrible economic and social crises of the 1060s caused by the repeated failure of the Nile to flood. The second, characterized by the refortification of Cairo against the double threat of the Saljuq Turks and the Crusaders and the transfer of political power to members of the court who constructed small mosques, mausolea and shrines, began with the restoration of Fatimid authority under Badr al-Jamali, who served as vizier to the caliph al-Mustansir

from 1073 to 1094, and ended with the fall of the dynasty in 1171. The third is marked by the continued fortification of Cairo and the adaptation of older models of religious architecture to the demands of the new Sunni Ayyubid dynasty.

Urban development. The most important urban foundation of the Fatimid dynasty was their third capital, originally established in 969 as a camp to the north-east of Fustat, the old Muslim capital of Egypt. Eventually named al-Qahira ('the Victorious'), from which the name Cairo is derived, this settlement became the political and administrative centre of their realm. It was enclosed in mud-brick walls approximately 1 km on each side, which were protected by a canal and a moat and pierced by massive gates. Several palaces, gardens, barracks, commercial establishments and residences within the walls are mentioned in medieval texts, but only the congregational mosque survives. Excavations at nearby Fustat, which continued to be a major residential and commercial quarter, have provided a unique glimpse of a medieval Islamic city: a dense agglomeration of multi-storey houses, shops, public baths and industrial establishments linked by networks of streets, water channels and sewers.

The most visible remains of Fatimid Cairo are the parts of the fortifications rebuilt by Badr al-Jamali between 1087 and 1092. He replaced some of the original mud-brick walls with finely coursed masonry quarried from an ancient site across the river, possibly Memphis, and rebuilt three of the city gates. Badr is said to have imported architects

from Edessa (now Urfa in south-eastern Turkey), and the construction and decoration of the gateways and walls are close to those found in the stone architecture of that region. The first Ayyubids further repaired and extended the walls and connected them to the citadel they built on a hill dominating Cairo from the south-east, to which they transferred the seat of power from the old Fatimid palaces within the city. Impressive curtain walls set with half-round towers ring the roughly rectangular enceinte that enclosed the royal residences.

Palaces. Both of the splendid Fatimid palaces of Cairo have disappeared, but they were described as vast yet irregular walled precincts containing pavilions, courtyards and splendid gardens on either side of the main north–south artery of the city, consequently known as Bayn al-Qasrayn ('Between the Two Palaces'; now Shari' Mu'izz li-Din Allah). The Eastern Palace was built in the 970s and the Western Palace in the mid-11th century. Several wooden boards splendidly carved with figures of musicians, dancers and animals (Cairo, Mus. Islam. A.; *see* §VII, 1(i)(b) below) are thought to have been made for the Western Palace and reused in the hospital of Qala'un (destr.), which was built on the site in 1284–5.

Mosques. Two of the congregational mosques constructed by the early Fatimids survive in Cairo, and texts mention or describe several others. The Azhar Mosque (*see* CAIRO, §III,3) was begun in 970, the year following the foundation of Cairo, as the mosque of the Fatimid

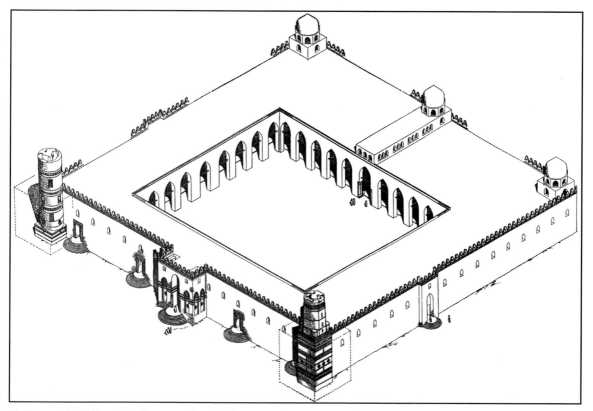

36. Mosque of al-Hakim, Cairo, Egypt, completed 1013; axonometric reconstruction by Farid Shafi'i

encampment. The transfer of the capital to Egypt in 972 made it the principal mosque of the entire urban agglomeration. It measured about 85×70 m, but its original aspect has been lost since its interior and exterior façades have been entirely encased in later construction. The courtyard surrounded by arcades, hypostyle prayer-hall, wider central aisle and dome in the bay in front of the mihrab are so similar to those in the earlier Fatimid mosque at MAHDIA (*see* §(a) above) that the architect or plans for the new mosque may have been sent from North Africa. The materials and techniques of construction are clearly local: the arcades are supported on marble columns taken from an earlier building, as in the 9th-century renovation of the mosque of 'Amr in Fustat (*see* CAIRO, §III, 1); carved (and perhaps painted) stucco decorated the interior of the brick walls with vegetal and epigraphic ornament. Carved stucco decoration over brick and Koranic inscription bands had already been used in the mosque of Ibn Tulun, the other great pre-Fatimid mosque in Egypt (*see* CAIRO, §III, 2).

The mosque of al-Hakim (see fig. 36), immediately outside the north wall of Cairo, was begun by the caliph al-'Aziz in 989 or 990 and completed by his son al-Hakim in 1013 (*see also* CAIRO, §III, 4). Measuring 120×113 m, it is nearly two and a half times larger than the Azhar Mosque. Although the plan shares many features of the earlier mosque, including the domes in the rear corners of

the prayer-hall, the materials and techniques of construction differ markedly, perhaps because marble columns were no longer available. Its exterior walls are of rough-hewn stone, except for the beautifully carved masonry of the portals and corner towers. In the interior, which was heavily and inappropriately restored in the 1980s, massive brick arcades supported a flat timber roof. Apart from the furnishings, which cost some 5000 dinars, the only interior decoration was a frieze at the top of the plainly plastered walls inscribed in floriated kufic script with quotations from the Koran. In 1011 massive stone salients were built which enclosed the finely carved stone towers at the ends of the main façade. Although their archaeological history is clearly understood, they are the most unusual feature of this mosque and their meaning remains controversial. Undoubtedly they are tied to the erratic religious policy of al-Hakim, but they had no effect on later building.

Whereas the large congregational mosques built during the first period of Fatimid architecture in Cairo were free-standing structures that ignored their settings, two smaller mosques from the second period show a new interest in integrating architecture into the increasingly crowded city around them. The elegant Aqmar Mosque was ordered by the vizier Ma'mun al-Bata'ihi in 1125 for an irregular site on the east side of the main artery just north of the palace. As the courtyard measures only 10 m square, the small scale forced all the elements typical of Fatimid mosques to be reduced to essentials. The mosque's most interesting

37. Aqmar Mosque, Cairo, Egypt, façade, 1125

feature is its splendidly carved stone façade (see fig. 37), which for the first time in Islamic architecture was aligned to the pre-existing street that runs roughly north–south, while the interior of the building was orientated towards Mecca, here the south-east. The triangular block created by the divergence of the façade from the internal orientation was filled with service rooms, a feature that would become standard in later Cairene architecture. The design of the façade condenses typical earlier forms: originally it consisted of a central portal which projected slightly from two lateral flanks (right flank destr.). The stone-carving brilliantly displays the entire repertory of Fatimid ornament: the decoration is concentrated between two long inscription bands that wrap the façade and proclaim the name and titles of the patron. The portal block, a large central arch flanked by two storeys of blind niches, recalls the first Fatimid mosque at Mahdia in Tunisia (*see* §(a) above), but differs in the variety of niche-hoods, which are scalloped, fluted or crowned with *muqarnas*. The mosque built by the vizier al-Salih Tala'i' in 1160 on a site just beyond the Bab Zuwayla gate has a typical Fatimid design, except that it was elevated on a basement storey containing tunnel-vaulted shops, the rental of which provided for the upkeep of the mosque. This is the first-known instance of a religious building incorporating commercial functions, a feature frequently repeated in later Cairene architecture.

Minarets. The Ayyubids, adherents of the Shafi'ite school of law, believed that one congregational mosque was sufficient in any urban agglomeration and were content to use the congregational mosques they found in Cairo. They nonetheless provided mosques with minarets, features that had by now become standard in Sunni mosques, although the Fatimids had eschewed them (*see* MINARET). Indeed, as early as the mid-11th century, minarets were erected in towns and villages of Upper Egypt, showing the weakening of Fatimid control over the region. These minarets, of which five survive, stand on square stone or brick bases, and their cylindrical brick shafts are crowned with domed lanterns, which resemble contemporary mausolea at Aswan. The peculiar forms of these minarets and of the mausolea at Aswan suggest that their architectural origins are to be found in the contemporary architecture of western Arabia, to which Upper Egypt was linked by the pilgrimage route across the Red Sea.

Funerary architecture. The monumentalization of tombs and the concomitant architectural development of large cemeteries outside the city walls are highly significant, since early Muslims frowned on ostentatious memorials to the dead. Textual and epigraphic evidence indicates that large tombs were built as early as the mid-9th century, but they became increasingly popular from the 10th century onwards. Although monumental tombs appeared simultaneously in other Muslim lands, their emergence in Egypt was linked to the veneration of the graves of descendants of the Prophet (Arab. *sharif* or *sayyid*, feminine *sayyida*) considered saints and martyrs by Shi'ites. This cult was encouraged by the Fatimid caliphs (who were themselves buried in a dynastic tomb within the palace grounds) and their viziers, but even before the Fatimid conquest of

Egypt the great cemetery to the south of Cairo had been an important focus of Shi'ite popular piety, especially among women. Under the Fatimids, women's religious activities were centred on a mosque built in the cemetery by a wife of the caliph al-'Aziz. The Ayyubids desecrated the Fatimid dynastic mausoleum, but they preserved the shrine of Husayn (the Prophet's grandson) in it, which remains one of Cairo's most venerated sites. They attempted to redirect popular piety from Shi'ite to Sunni saints, most notably the celebrated jurisconsult al-Shafi'i (*d* 820), who had been buried in the great southern cemetery.

The earliest Cairene mausoleum to survive—at least in plan—is the martyrium (Arab. *mashhad*) of the Sharif Tabataba (943), a nine-domed open pavilion about 18 m square. The most common type, however, was a smaller domed cube containing a cenotaph for the deceased, who was buried in the ground below. Dozens survive in Aswan from the 11th and 12th centuries and give some idea of how other cemeteries of the period must have appeared. The domed brick cubes at Aswan are extremely simple, with decoration only in the zone of transition, which is enlivened on the exterior by concave sides and fantastic acroteria and on the interior with something modelled on a *muqarnas* squinch. Some of the surviving mausolea in Cairo are flanked or preceded by modest chambers, anterooms and vestibules. The most elaborate is the *mashhad* of Sayyida Ruqayya (1133), which has handsome stucco decoration in and around the main and subsidiary mihrabs that stand on either side of the entrance and in the rooms flanking the main chamber. The ribbed dome is supported by an octagonal zone of transition; its squinches are subdivided into two tiers of small vaulted compartments, the design of which is repeated between the squinches in trefoil windows divided by a central Y-shaped framework.

Somewhat more complex in form is the structure built on the order of the vizier Badr al-Jamali in 1085 on the scarp of the Muqattam Hills overlooking Cairo from the south-east, an extremely inaccessible, if prominent, location. Known today as the mosque of al-Juyushi, from Badr's title, Commander of the Armies (Arab. *amīr al-juyūsh*), the building is called a *mashhad* in its foundation inscription. Its plain exterior clearly reveals its constituent parts: an entrance complex under a tall tower, a small courtyard flanked by vaulted chambers and a vestibule preceding a domed prayer-hall. Although the building now contains a tomb in a dome chamber added on the left, its original function is unclear. The elegantly carved stucco inscriptions decorating the splendid mihrab (see fig. 38; *see also* §9(i)(a) below) and dome suggest that the building was erected to commemorate Badr's triumph over his opponents.

Madrasas. The madrasa, the spread of which was the major architectural development elsewhere in the Islamic world during the period, did not reach Egypt until after 1171, since one of its purposes was to counter Shi'ite propaganda. The Sunni Ayyubids introduced the first madrasas to Egypt, but only the magnificent wooden cenotaph remains of the madrasa that Salah al-Din ordered near the grave of the Imam al-Shafi'i in 1176–7. The

38. *Mashhad* al-Juyushi, Cairo, Egypt, mihrab, 1085

Materials, techniques and decoration. After 969 stone was revived for public architecture, but structures remained conservative. Although external walls were increasingly built of finely coursed masonry, interiors continued to be hypostyle spaces with stuccoed brick supports and flat wooden roofs. Domes were rare, except for the small brick cupolas covering places of special significance, such as the bay in front of the mihrab in a congregational mosque or over a tomb. The only exceptions seem to have been the Fatimid dynastic tomb in the palace and the huge dome erected over the tomb of Imam al-Shafi'i.

Indifferently built brick walls continued to be covered with carved stucco revetments. Scarce supplies of wood were used with careful emphasis for beams and doors. Literary evidence suggests that some interiors that are now whitewashed were originally painted in bright colours. This must have created a truly sumptuous effect when accompanied by ornately carved and inlaid wooden panels, glimmering lamps and richly patterned textiles. Apart from fragments of figural reliefs that once decorated the palace, the subject-matter of architectural decoration was primarily epigraphic, consisting of magnificent kufic inscription bands that outline and define architectural elements (see figs 37 and 38; *see also* §9(vi)(b) below). The interiors and exteriors of Fatimid buildings were decorated with monumental inscriptions to an unparalleled degree, and the presence of the elegant but extremely legible foliated script immediately identifies Fatimid work. Large fields of stucco arabesque derived from 9th-century prototypes were reduced to subservient roles after the 10th century. Exterior decoration in carved stone used the same repertory of epigraphic and ornamental bands, although the exterior of the Aqmar Mosque preserves some unique panels representing a mosque lamp and a flowering plant. Vertical panelling with blind niches, which became the ubiquitous exterior treatment for later Cairene urban architecture, is first seen on the street façade of the Aqmar Mosque, itself perhaps inspired by the now lost palace façade.

The typical arch profile employed before *c.* 1100 was pointed, but after that date the standard was a keel arch, a four-centred arch in which the part struck with the greater radius tends to become straight. The particularly fine examples carved on the façade of the Aqmar Mosque (see fig. 37) have ribs radiating from a pierced boss decorated with arabesques and inscriptions. This arrangement became common in stucco mihrabs, where the increasingly intricate scalloped edges became bands of *muqarnas*-like ornament.

Throughout the Islamic world the major decorative development at this time was the widespread use of MUQARNAS to form a cornice, to effect the transition between a dome and its support and to create entire domes and semi-domes. *Muqarnas* cornices and hoods were known in Egypt from the late 11th century, when they were probably imported from Syria. The *muqarnas* squinch arrived in Cairo independently, apparently via Upper Egypt, which had a lively vernacular style dependent on western Arabia. *Muqarnas* squinches first appeared in 11th-century mausolea in Aswan and later in the Cairo cemetery (e.g. the *mashhad* of Sayyida Ruqayya). A contemporary domed bay added to the Azhar Mosque, however, has squinches without *muqarnas* filling; the

domed mausoleum over the cenotaph, built some 35 years later, measures *c.* 15 m square internally, and its massive walls could easily support a stone or brick dome, although the present dome is wooden (*see* CAIRO, §III, 6). The only madrasa from this period to survive in part is that built in 1242 by the Ayyubid sultan al-Salih Najm al-Din Ayyub (*reg* 1239–49, with interruption) on the site of the Fatimid Eastern Palace. Its two blocks (most of the south block destr.) are separated by a vaulted alley, and the whole complex is, like the Aqmar Mosque, aligned to the street on the exterior and the qibla on the interior. Each block consists of two iwans on opposite ends of a vast rectangular courtyard, and they are united by an ashlar façade 72 m long, decorated with keel-arched recessed panels. The panels echo those on Fatimid buildings along the same street, but the joggled voussoirs and striped masonry are distinctly Syrian features introduced by the Ayyubids. The portal in the centre of the façade that leads to the alley is a reinterpretation of the portal of the Aqmar Mosque crowned with a multi-storey minaret. The large domed tomb for the founder (diam. 10 m, h. 21 m) at the northern end of the complex inaugurated a series of funerary madrasas built within the city by the Mamluk sultans over the next 250 years (*see* §6(iii)(a) below).

difference may be that the *muqarnas* squinch still reflected a more popular level of taste that would have been inappropriate for the city's most prestigious mosque and centre of learning.

BIBLIOGRAPHY

Aḥmad ibn ʿAlī al-Maqrīzī: *Al-mawāʿiz wa'l-i'tibār bi dhikr al-khiṭaṭ wa'l-athār* [Exhortations and consideration for the mention of districts and monuments], 2 vols (Cairo, 1853)
U. Monneret de Villard: *La necropoli musulmana di Aswan* (Cairo, 1930)
K. A. C. Creswell: *The Muslim Architecture of Egypt*, 2 vols (Oxford, 1952–9)
J. Amer. Res. Cent. Egypt, iv– (1965–) [preliminary rep. on the excavations at Fustat by G. T. Scanlon]
S. D. Goitein: *A Mediterranean Society*, 5 vols (Berkeley, 1967–88)
Y. Ragib: 'Sur deux monuments funéraires du cimetière d'al-Qarafa al-Kubra au Caire', *An. Islam.*, xii (1974), pp. 67–83
——: 'Deux Monuments fatimides au pied du Muqattam', *Rev. Etud. Islam.*, xxvi (1978), pp. 91–117
——: 'Les Mausolées fatimides du quartier d'al-Mašahid', *An. Islam.*, xvii (1981), pp. 1–30
J. M. Bloom: 'The Mosque of al-Hakim in Cairo', *Muqarnas*, i (1983), pp. 15–36
C. Williams: 'The Cult of ʿAlid Saints in the Fatimid Monuments of Cairo, i: The Mosque of al-Aqmar', *Muqarnas*, i (1983), pp. 37–52
J. M. Bloom: 'Five Fatimid Minarets in Upper Egypt', *J. Soc. Archit. Historians*, xliii (1984), pp. 162–7
C. Williams: 'The Cult of ʿAlid Saints in the Fatimid Monuments of Cairo, ii: The Mausolea', *Muqarnas*, iii (1985), pp. 39–60
J. M. Bloom: 'The Mosque of the Qarafa in Cairo', *Muqarnas*, iv (1987), pp. 7–20
——: 'The Introduction of the Muqarnas into Egypt', *Muqarnas*, v (1988), pp. 21–8
——: *Minaret: Symbol of Islam* (Oxford, 1989)
D. Behrens-Abousief: 'The Façade of the Aqmar Mosque in the Context of Fatimid Ceremonial', *Muqarnas*, ix (1992), pp. 29–38

JONATHAN M. BLOOM

(d) Yemen. Architecture in the Yemen was conservative, and pride in the cultural achievements of the pre-Islamic past survived for centuries. Few of the earliest Islamic buildings known through texts survive in unaltered condition, and it is only from the 10th century that formal types and styles can be distinguished. The tumultuous religious and political history of the region complicates the story of its architecture. Its remoteness from the centre of Abbasid power in Iraq made the Yemen a centre for Shi'ite heterodoxy. The ZAYDI dynasty (*reg* 898–1962), followers of the fifth imam, settled at Saʿda in the northern highlands and often extended their power as far south as SAN'A in the centre of the country. The SULAYHID dynasty (*reg* 1047–1138), followers of the seventh Shi'ite imam and consequently nominal vassals of the Fatimids of Egypt (*see* §(c) above), controlled San'a and Jibla in the southern highlands. The coastal lowlands and the south, including Hadramawt, were generally Sunni in affiliation, and the Sunni AYYUBID dynasty of Egypt and Syria extended its control over the Yemeni highlands from 1174 to 1229.

Several types of mosque remain from this period. The simplest type is a closed, unlit cubic chamber with a single entrance. The interior is divided by rows of monolithic supports with simple capitals. The entrance lies on the axis of the mihrab. The most impressive examples are the mosque of al-ʿAbbas at Asnaf in the Khawlan (1126) and the mosque of Sarha (13th century), which are remarkable for the magnificent decoration of their ceilings. The richly carved, painted and gilded designs, which consist mainly of interlacing and star patterns, divide and orientate the otherwise undifferentiated space. The type can be traced

back to the mosque at Tamur (7th or 8th century), the Ka'ba at Mecca (*see* §2 above) and ultimately pre-Islamic temples such as that at Ghaybun. A larger variant, also with pre-Islamic antecedents, has a transverse rectangular plan, several entrances and multiple supports, which are often pre-Islamic columns set on top of each other to achieve the required height. These mosques were occasionally preceded by a court, but it was not integrated into the ensemble. Examples of this type include the mosque of Sulayman ibn Dawud (1089) at MARIB and the congregational mosque of Damar (12th–13th century).

The hypostyle courtyard mosque, common elsewhere in the Islamic world, was in the beginning comparatively rare in the Yemen, although the type had been introduced by the UMAYYAD caliphs for the Great Mosque of San'a (705–15). In the 10th century this was still the only courtyard mosque in the city. The mosque at Shibam near Kawkaban (9th–10th century) is another early example of this type. It is a rectangle (38×26 m) enclosing a courtyard surrounded by hypostyle halls. The prayer-hall on the north is four bays deep and, like the Great Mosque of San'a, has a coffered and richly painted wooden ceiling. The hall on the south is three bays deep, while those on the east and west are two bays deep. The columns supporting the roof-beams are all nearly 8 m high. Their cylindrical shafts and palm or square capitals imitate pre-Islamic forms. Despite the archaic form of the supports, the orientation and spatial organization of the mosque are reminiscent of Abbasid mosques of the 9th century (*see* §4(i) above). The courtyard façade is composed of a continuous arcade surmounted by a blind gallery. At some later date, the arcades were filled with screen walls.

The mosque of Arwa bint Ahmad (1088–9; see fig. 39) in Jibla, north of Ta'izz, was, according to historians, originally the palace of the Sulayhid dynasty but was converted into a courtyard mosque. Like other courtyard mosques in the Yemen, it has a courtyard surrounded by arcades and a prayer-hall with columns supporting a flat wooden roof. Unusually, the prayer-hall with four aisles parallel to the qibla wall is intersected by a wider central aisle leading from a domed bay in the centre of the courtyard arcade to the mihrab. These features, found in mosques built by the Fatimid dynasty in Egypt, were probably introduced because the Sulayhids shared the Fatimids' Isma'ili Shi'ite beliefs and were their nominal vassals. The wider central aisle was adopted for mosques later built by the Zaydi rulers of the Yemen, such as the mosque of Zafar Dhibin (*c.* 1200). Here the mihrab bay is domed, although the wooden domes of the central aisle, painted like the rest of the coffered ceiling, are not visible from the exterior.

Arwa bint Ahmad was buried in the north-west corner of her mosque in a tomb richly decorated with epigraphic and floral bands. The Zaydi imams also had richly decorated tombs. Those at Zafar Dhibin (13th century) are the earliest monumental examples. The domed squares have plain exteriors with open arcades on three sides, but on the interior the zones of transition are decorated with elaborate inscription bands and carved stucco. Other types of buildings, such as the domed mosque and the madrasa, are known to have been introduced to the Yemen by the

39. Mosque of Arwa bint Ahmad, Jibla, Yemen, courtyard, 1088–9

orthodox Ayyubid dynasty, but none of their buildings has survived.

The earliest surviving mihrab with elaborate decoration is in the mosque of Jibla, although the mihrab niche of the Umayyad mosque at San'a is said to have been so richly decorated that the Abbasid governor had it painted over in white. The Jibla mihrab consists of a rectangular epigraphic frame enclosing a tall blind arch and a smaller vaulted niche. Niche and blind arch are covered with a dense pattern of arabesques, while the outer spandrels have bulging prismatic bosses. Later mihrabs, including those in the Zaydi zone, copied this arrangement, but under the Ayyubids simple niches with only one frame were preferred; their vaults were richly decorated with stucco, such as the mihrab in the mosque of Ğanad (1215).

The earliest surviving minarets are at the Great Mosque of Zabid (*c.* 1200), the Great Mosque of San'a and the Great Mosque of Zafar Dhibin (14th century). The octagonal shaft of that at Zabid, articulated by blind arcades, sits on a relatively tall square base and is surmounted by a lantern resembling a *muqarnas* dome. This minaret served as a model for the 13th-century tower at the mosque of Mahjam and for various towers in the city of Zabid. The shaft of the unusual brick minaret of the mosque of Zafar Dhibin has zigzags in the form of confronted snakes with open jaws.

The monumental portal is first seen in a doorway in the qibla wall of the Great Mosque at San'a (1158). The arch is raised on engaged columns with block capitals on which falcons are depicted and is covered by a ribbed semi-dome. Reliefs to the right and left depict striding lions, a figural theme common in the art of northern Mesopotamia.

Architecture was generally trabeate, with stone columns and capitals, or piers constructed with bricks, supporting richly decorated coffered wooden ceilings. Arcades, occasionally found in the pre-Islamic Christian architecture of San'a and used in the Great Mosque of San'a in the 8th century, became increasingly common in the period. External walls were usually built of stone and bricks, but façades were occasionally faced with stucco, as at the mosque of Zafar Dhibin. Tilework appears only in isolated instances in the Zaydi zone, as in the façade of the mosque of Zafar Dhibin, where small, bright greenish-blue discs were inserted in stucco decoration.

BIBLIOGRAPHY

R. Lewcock and G. R. Smith: 'Two Early Mosques in the Yemen: A Preliminary Report', *A. & Archaeol. Res. Pap.*, iv (1973), pp. 117–30
P. Costa: 'La Moschea Grande di San'a', *Annali: AION*, xxxiv (n. s., xxiv) (1974), pp. 487–506
B. Finster: 'Die Freitagsmoschee von San'a. Vorläufiger Bericht. I. Teil', *Baghdad. Mitt.*, ix (1978), pp. 92–133
——: 'Die Freitagsmoschee von Sibam-Kaukaban', *Baghdad. Mitt.*, x (1979), pp. 193–228
B. Finster and J. Schmidt: 'Die Freitagsmoschee von San'a. Vorläufiger Bericht. II. Teil', *Baghdad. Mitt.*, x (1979), pp. 179–92
B. Finster: articles in *Archaeol. Ber. Yemen*, i (1982), pp. 213ff, 223ff; iii (1986), pp. 109ff, 161ff, 185ff
E. J. Keall: 'Zabid and its Hinterland', *Proc. Semin. Arab. Stud.*, xiii (1983), pp. 53–70
R. B. Serjeant and R. Lewcock: *San'a': An Arabian Islamic City* (London, 1983)
E. J. Keall: 'A Preliminary Report on the Architecture of Zabid', *Proc. Semin. Arab. Stud.*, xiv (1984), pp. 51–65
R. Lewcock: 'Jemenitische Architektur im Mittelalter', *Jemen*, ed. W. Daum (Innsbruck and Frankfurt am Main, 1987), pp. 181ff   □

(e) Syria, the Jazira and Iraq. Architecture in Syria and the Jazira revived only in the late 11th century from the

decline that had set in after the Abbasids moved the capital to Iraq in 750 (*see* §4(ii) above). The Fatimids of Egypt had managed to rule southern Syria in the late 10th century and the early 11th, and a number of Arab tribal dynasties reigned over parts of northern Syria and the Jazira, but few buildings erected before 1080 survive. In Iraq, which remained the capital province despite the domination of the Buyids (*see* §(i)(a) above), no buildings have been preserved from the first half of the period. After the invasions of Saljuq Turks and Crusaders in the late 11th century, most of the area was controlled by such Turkish and Kurdish dynasties as the Saljuqs (*reg* 1038–1194; *see* SALJUQ, §1), and the ARTUQID (*reg* 1102–1408), ZANGID (*reg* 1127–80) and AYYUBID (*reg* 1180–1260) dynasties, although the Abbasid caliphs briefly reasserted their authority in Iraq before the Mongols conquered Baghdad in 1258. Many building types survive from the second half of this complex period, including an unusually large number of palaces. Forms and decoration were drawn from a wide variety of sources; the most striking are survivals of Classical elements in the architecture of northern Syria and the Jazira.

Mosques. These usually followed the model established in the Umayyad period (*see* §3 above) at the congregational mosques of Damascus (*see* DAMASCUS, §1(ii)) and ALEPPO: an oblong prayer-hall with two, three or four aisles and an open courtyard surrounded by porticos. In Aleppo and its environs, the prayer-hall was often covered with groin vaults, although crude domes may be seen at such slightly later sites as Sarmin (1305–6) and al-Bab (1305). In Damascus, timber gable roofs continued to be used to the end of the period, for example in the Jami' al-Hanabila (early 13th century). In the Jazira, mosques generally had tall masonry barrel vaults (which gives them a basilical appearance) and large domes covering the bay in front of the mihrab (Arab. *maqsūra*), a feature common to Saljuq mosques in central Iran (*see* §(i)(b) above). The penchant for elaborate stone-carving throughout much of the region and the free-standing nature of mosques in the Jazira led to the creation of some of the most complex and original façades in medieval Islamic architecture.

The congregational mosque of DIYARBAKIR is strikingly similar to the Umayyad mosque of Damascus, although it lacks a dome. Columns and mouldings from a Roman theatre were reused and adapted for its courtyard façades. The western (1117) and eastern (1164; see fig. 40) façades consist of superposed Classical orders framing pointed arcades and windows and combine such ancient forms and motifs as architrave, brackets and cornice with such purely Islamic ones as floriated kufic inscriptions and arabesque patterns. The eastern façade, excepting its ancient columns, is an Islamic interpretation of a Roman one. At Silvan (Arab. Mayyafariqin; *c.* 1152–7) a dome with a diameter of 13.5 m dominates the prayer-hall of four alternately wide and narrow aisles. The dome may have been conceived as an independent unit in the heart of the mosque, as it was once surrounded by roofless aisles on three sides, an unusual design parallel to that of the dome chamber added to Isfahan's Friday Mosque in 1086–7. The upper level of the north façade was once decorated with a continuous band of little foliate arches

40. Congregational mosque, Diyarbakır, Jazira, east façade, 1164

resting on squat colonnettes within cornices of antique derivation, of which only two fragments remain. The lobed arches and the angled voussoirs enhance the illusion of instability. The masterpiece of Artuqid architecture is the congregational mosque at Kızıltepe (Arab. Dunaysir; 1204), for the dome (diam. *c.* 10 m) is perfectly integrated within the three arcades of the prayer-hall, giving the mihrab area focus and unity without dominating the mosque. The mihrab itself, a *tour de force* of stone-carving, is covered with intricate geometric and vegetal patterns, the curvilinear and slightly three-dimensional qualities of which are similar to contemporary work from MOSUL. The court façade has a central foliate arch in *ablaq* (bichrome) masonry flanked by a mihrab and three smaller arched openings on each side; all nine arches are framed by continuous mouldings, the meanders of which simulate a foliate arch.

The mosque of Nur al-Din at Mosul (1170–72) was typologically related to the domed mosques of the Artuqids but has been totally rebuilt. The original hemispherical dome was replaced by a conical dome similar to those used in local shrines. The bent-brick minaret, some columns and the mihrab (1148), which came from another mosque, are the only medieval parts remaining. The extremely thick octagonal columns of veined dark-blue alabaster are composed of several thin slabs to compensate for the weakness of the material, widely used in Mosul. The mihrab (as well as several others in the Mosul Museum) are related to Iranian mihrabs in composition, and the intricate carved motifs were adapted from Iranian stucco and Iraqi brick-carving traditions. The Jami' al-Tawba in Damascus, built by the Ayyubid sultan al-Ashraf Musa in 1235, also relates to the Artuqid domed mosque. It has a wide transept leading from a central door across a two-aisled timber-roofed prayer-hall to the mihrab. The bay in front of the mihrab is covered by a typical Damascene cupola: four squinches create an octagonal zone; eight more squinches create a 16-sided drum alternately pierced by little windows, on which rests a smooth dome. The single entrance on the east is covered by a *muqarnas* vault and supports an octagonal minaret in *ablaq* masonry, an unusual arrangement necessitated by the mosque's minimal street frontage.

Congregational mosques at RAQQA and HARRAN depend on earlier Iraqi models for their squarish plans and dimensions (*c.* 100 m to a side). The Raqqa mosque, built of brick and having multiple entrances to the courtyard, is closer to the prototype than the Harran mosque, of which the cut-stone walls and three axial entrances are derived from the Syrian tradition. Other Syrian features in both mosques are the relatively shallow prayer-halls and the gabled timber roofs. The only remains of the mosque at Raqqa are the fortified outer enclosure (possibly 8th century), a circular brick minaret in the courtyard and an 11-bay arcade of pointed arches resting on rectangular brick piers with engaged colonnettes forming the courtyard façade. It is securely dated (1165–6) by an inscription plaque above the central arch. The mosque at Harran, the chronology of which is complicated by the ancient spolia used and occasional references to the forms of antique architecture, contains two late 12th-century inscriptions. The decoration effectively blends such Late Antique forms as capitals, friezes, mouldings and entablatures with such typically Islamic ones as arabesques, cursive inscriptions, trefoil arches and *muqarnas*. The depth, precision and richness of the carving produce a sumptuous effect recalling alabaster carving from Mosul.

Minarets. Minarets in the Jazira were typically brick cylinders based on Iranian prototypes, while most early Ayyubid ones in Syria are square, often of stone and probably derived from square Syrian church towers. Octagonal minarets, modelled on Mesopotamian prototypes (e.g. 'Ana), appear in brick first at Balis (Meskene), about 100 km east of Aleppo, where one was built in the reign of al-Malik al-'Adil Abu Bakr (1193–1218). In the second quarter of the 13th century, stone replaced brick to create a minaret type that remained popular well into later centuries.

Madrasas. The madrasa was introduced to Damascus soon after Syria passed to the Saljuqs in the last quarter of the 11th century, and within 75 years the city boasted no less than 11 examples. The earliest surviving is the madrasa of Kumushtakin (Gümüshtekin) in Bosra (1136; *see* BOSRA, §2). It measures 20×17 m and consists of a vestibule, two iwans and a longitudinal prayer-hall disposed around a small domed courtyard. Stairs in the vestibule once led to a second storey containing rooms for students. The domed courtyard is unique among early Syrian madrasas, but the iwans, prayer-hall and second storey became standard features. One of the earliest surviving madrasas in Damascus is the Nuriyya (1172), built by Nur al-Din.

It has a modified four-iwan plan with a central courtyard containing a large pool filled by channels from a fountain in the western iwan; its southern side contained a timber-roofed prayer-hall. The entrance is crowned with a pendent *muqarnas* vault. Beside it stands the founder's mausoleum, a new feature that subsequently became extremely popular in Syria and then Egypt. It is a square room covered with a conical *muqarnas* vault of an Iraqi type used earlier in Nur al-Din's hospital. The plan of the madrasa and the pendent portal vault are repeated on a more monumental scale in the 'Adiliyya Madrasa (1224), but the prayer-hall is groin-vaulted and only the mausoleum's pendentives are embellished with *muqarnas*.

Madrasas built in Aleppo during the second half of the 13th century epitomize Ayyubid architecture. The Zahiriyya Madrasa, a free-standing stone building, was begun by al-Malik al-Zahir Ghazi (*reg* 1186–1216) in a sparsely inhabited region south of Aleppo. The architect made no attempt to monumentalize or ornament its exterior and only pierced it unobtrusively with a few grilled windows. The severity of the exterior walls is mitigated only by the opulent *muqarnas* vault of the portal and by the undulating profile of its six domes. The interior consists of a mosque, mausoleum, study halls and residential units arranged around an oblong courtyard. The Firdaws (Paradise) Madrasa, built by Princess Dayfa Khatun in 1235–7, has, in sharp contrast, a large exterior iwan in the middle of its northern sector. Residential units to either side indicate that it may have been the patron's audience hall; a garden beyond the iwan watered by channels would have completed the verdant image implied by the building's name. On the interior (see fig. 41), exquisite *muqarnas* capitals adorn the columns surrounding the courtyard on three sides; on the fourth a spacious iwan, decorated with a wide inscription frieze of a type that became extremely popular in Mamluk architecture, contains large niches intended for book storage. The utter simplicity of the interior is unbroken except in the mosque, where the dome above the mihrab springs from a five-tier *muqarnas* zone and the mihrab itself is adorned with polychrome interlaced masonry, a feature that had originated in Aleppo late in the 12th century and spread to Konya, Damascus, Jerusalem and Cairo by the 13th.

In comparison the Jazira had few madrasas, reflecting its recent conversion to Islam and relative marginality in Islamic scholarship. Two in Diyarbakir, the Zinciriye (1198) and the Mesudiye (1198–1223), have courtyards surrounded by arcades resting on piers and interrupted by iwans. The dour effect of the local black stone is softened by *ablaq* masonry, *muqarnas* portals, foliate and pendent arches and cursive inscription bands on an arabesque ground, all decorative devices brought by one of the Aleppan architects. The largest (106×48 m) and most impressive madrasa of the period was the one built by the caliph al-Mustansir in BAGHDAD (1228–33). The large central court (62×27 m) is surrounded by two-storey arcades leading to student cells interrupted by three iwans and the triple-arched opening of a prayer-hall. Other rectangular rooms fill the subsidiary spaces. Designed for instruction in the four major rites of Islamic jurisprudence, the Mustansiriyya reflects the Caliph's interest in sponsoring ecumenical Sunnism.

41. Firdaws Madrasa, Aleppo, Syria, courtyard, 1235–7

Hospitals. All Syrian cities had at least one hospital (Arab. *bīmāristān*) by the middle of the 13th century. The most important is that built by Nur al-Din (1154) immediately after his conquest of Damascus. It is a four-iwan building with a central courtyard and groin-vaulted corner rooms used for treatment or incarceration; two doors originally led to another courtyard that may have been for the treatment of women. The portal has a bronze-sheathed wooden door with overall geometric ornament surmounted by an antique pediment over which rises a flat plaster *muqarnas* vault. A conical *muqarnas* vault, also made of plaster, surmounts the vestibule and bears traces of its original colour. The hospital overlooking Damascus (1250–56) built by the Kurdish prince Sayf al-Din Qaymari was clearly modelled on that of Nur al-Din, but the Qaymari Hospital shows how Syrian architecture had been systematized in the intervening century. The lateral iwans are reduced in size to accommodate two extra rooms, domes have been replaced with barrel or groin vaults, and the awkward portal of Nur al-Din's hospital has been replaced by a stone *muqarnas* vault framed by striped and joggled voussoirs. Except for the main iwan, which is decorated with painted plaster, the building is unadorned.

Mausolea. The typical mausoleum in Iraq was a small square building crowned with an elaborate *muqarnas* vault. The earliest surviving is the shrine of Imam al-Dawr

(Imam Dur; 1085–90; *see also* MUQARNAS) north of Samarra'. It was built by an Uqaylid prince to honour a descendant of the fifth Shi'ite imam. From the exterior, the battered brick walls, 10 m to a side and 12 m high, support a high octagonal drum and three tiers of convex and angular elements crowned with a small cupola. The interior is a riot of carved plaster ornament culminating in five diminishing tiers of *muqarnas*. The type continued to be popular in Iraq, to judge from the 20 or so examples remaining. The handful of shrines to minor Shi'ite saints in Mosul, such as those to Imam Yahya ibn al-Qasim (1239) and Imam 'Awn al-Din (1248), are the only significant ones in the Jazira. They measure some 8 m square, are orientated with their corners to the cardinal points and are covered with *muqarnas* vaults closely related to Iraqi prototypes. Only the tile mosaic linings and protective pyramidal roofs are local features. The interiors, a few steps below ground-level, contain the cenotaph and a mihrab in the south corner. Most Syrian mausolea are small, independent structures of limited architectural interest. Those located in the various cemeteries of Damascus and especially in the northern suburb of Salihiyya consist of a square stone chamber surmounted by a lobed brick dome and contain a single entrance, a mihrab and one or more cenotaphs. The zone of transition consists of two rows of squinches and the walls are often decorated with pious inscriptions and painted stucco ornament.

Palaces. These present striking parallels to contemporary madrasas in such features as *muqarnas* or pendent-vault entrances, courtyards with iwans, tripartite court façades and the use of water, but their vestibules are more elaborate and their decoration more ostentatious. The gate of the palace at Qal'at Sahyun (*c.* 1200) is a *tour de force* of stereotomy, being the only portal in Syria to have three vaults with two pendent keystones. The portal leads to a domed cruciform vestibule, a bent corridor and a courtyard with water-channels excavated in the bedrock instead of the usual pool. Three of the four iwans facing the courtyard are flanked by smaller arches. The Matbakh al-'Ajami ('Kitchen of the al-'Ajami family') in Aleppo, probably once their residence, is surmounted by a dome on *muqarnas* pendentives, the largest preserved Ayyubid dome. The arch of the main iwan contains a double tier of massive arrow-shaped pendants, and its roof consists of two stone *muqarnas* vaults with a pendent keystone. The entrance to the palace of the Ayyubid sultan al-'Aziz Muhammad (*reg* 1216–37) in the citadel of Aleppo is surmounted by a superb *muqarnas* vault typical of the restrained luxury of late Ayyubid patronage. The fountain in the central courtyard is identical in arrangement to those in the Nuriyya Madrasa in Damascus and the Ziza Palace in Palermo (*see* §(b) above). The Artuqid palace at Diyarbakır (1201–22) had four iwans facing a square courtyard containing a large octagonal pool filled by water-channels and decorated with tiles and glass and stone mosaic. The cruciform design and water system recall the fortress of Sahyun and the Ayyubid palace at Aleppo. The one remaining pavilion from the Artuqid palace in Mardin (1239–60) consists of a large central iwan flanked by a pair of small superposed iwans overlooking a large cistern filled by water channels from the iwans. Typologically related to earlier palaces in North Africa and Sicily, it also resembles the palace of Badr al-Din Lu'lu' in Mosul, which had three iwans overlooking the Tigris. The much restored palace of the caliph al-Nasir (*reg* 1180–1225) in Baghdad has a courtyard (20×15 m) with two-storey porticos interrupted by two iwans. It is distinguished by the extensive use of *muqarnas* vaulting and carved terracotta ornament.

Materials, forms and decoration. Stone was the primary building material in Syria and most of the Jazira, gradually changing to brick near the Euphrates valley, where brick was used exclusively from the region of Raqqa to Iraq. Rubble masonry revetted with stone and vaulted with brick was characteristic of the Mosul region, and brick was used throughout the Jazira for vaulting and minarets. In northern Syria, buildings were roofed with cut-stone vaults, while in central and southern Syria, including Jerusalem, buildings were covered with rubble or brick vaults or timber roofs. In the Hawran, a basaltic region in southern Syria, stone was used for all parts of the building, including vaults and even flat slab roofs.

The variety of forms used in the Jazira is unequalled elsewhere in the medieval Islamic world as it combines Late Antique survivals, borrowings from local Christian structures and imports from eastern Islamic architecture. The excellent stone masonry and the use of columns, entablatures and mouldings, particularly the continuous moulding characteristic of northern Syria, reveal the Classical legacy. While spolia were salvaged from ancient monuments, other elements were made after Antique models. Brick or stucco forms such as minarets and *muqarnas* vaults were sometimes adopted unchanged from Iranian and Iraqi architecture; at other times they were reworked in stone, but the material's hardness and heaviness forced non-load-bearing forms, such as *muqarnas* vaults and foliate arches, into structural roles. In Mosul Zangid buildings are often decorated with a wide inscription band made of deep-blue marble inlaid with white alabaster.

Most buildings in Syria, including free-standing ones, presented plain exteriors, except for some discreetly placed mouldings, grilled windows or a recessed portal covered by a *muqarnas* or pendent vault, although striped *ablaq* masonry appears in the latest Ayyubid buildings in Damascus. The pointed arch, sometimes slightly horseshoe in shape, was most frequent, although a flat arch with joggled stone voussoirs in contrasting colours marked important portals, often below a *muqarnas* vault. Vaults included the barrel vault, groin vault and groin vault supporting a cupola and domes. A few early *muqarnas* vaults were of the Iraqi type, but most were slightly pointed hemispherical domes resting on *muqarnas* pendentives or a double zone of squinches. Domes were used over single structures and as parts of larger ensembles. The differing materials and building traditions of northern and southern Syria gradually submitted to the equalizing effects of travelling craftsmen and the new political and sectarian unity of the region. The period was dominated by the style of Aleppo, the excellent masons of which found ready employ in Damascus, Jerusalem and ultimately Cairo. The *muqarnas* vaults of brick and plaster typical of Iraq were transformed into masonry domes on *muqarnas* pendentives and an original style notable for its rigour and sobriety was created. The exuberance of Iraqi stucco decoration was transformed in Syria into finely proportioned stone-carving, and strict axial or coaxial symmetry was sacrificed to more functional plans.

BIBLIOGRAPHY

M. van Berchem and J. Strzygowski: *Amida-Diyarbakr* (Heidelberg, 1910)
F. Sarre and E. Herzfeld: *Archäologische Reise im Euphrat- und Tigris-Gebiet*, 4 vols (Berlin, 1911–20)
J. Sauvaget: 'Inventaire des monuments musulmans de la ville d'Alep', *Rev. Etud. Islam.*, v (1931), pp. 59–114
M. Ecochard: 'Notes d'archéologie musulmane, i: Stéréotomie de deux portails du XII siècle', *Bull. Etud. Orient*, vii–viii (1937–8), pp. 83–108
J. Sauvaget and M. Ecochard: *Les Monuments Ayyoubides de Damas* (Paris, 1938–40)
A. Gabriel: *Voyages archéologiques dans la Turquie orientale*, 2 vols (Paris, 1940)
E. Herzfeld: 'Damascus: Studies in Architecture, I–IV', *A. Islam*, ix (1942), pp. 1–53; x (1943), pp. 13–70; xi–xii (1946), pp. 1–71; xiii–xiv (1948), pp. 118–38
——: *Matériaux pour un corpus inscriptionum arabicarum, deuxième partie: Syrie du Nord, inscriptions et monuments d'Alep*, 2 vols (Cairo, 1954–6)
K. A. C. Creswell: *The Muslim Architecture of Egypt*, ii (Oxford, 1959)
O. Aslanapa: 'Erster Bericht über die Ausgrabungen des Palastes von Diyarbakır', *Istanbul. Mitt.*, xii (1962), pp. 115–28
——: *Turkish Art and Architecture* (New York, 1971)
H. Schmidt: *Die Madrasa des Kalifen al-Mustansir in Baghdad* (Mainz, 1980)
R. Hillenbrand: 'Eastern Islamic Influences in Syria: Raqqa and Qal'at Ja'bar in the Later 12th Century', *The Art of Syria and the Jazira, 1100–1250*, ed. J. Raby (Oxford, 1985), pp. 21–48

T. Sinclair: 'Early Artuqid Mosque Architecture', *The Art of Syria and the Jazira, 1100–1250*, ed. J. Raby (Oxford, 1985), pp. 49–68

Y. Tabbaa: 'The Muqarnas Dome: Its Origin and Meaning', *Muqarnas*, iii (1985), pp. 61–74

T. Allen: *A Classical Revival in Islamic Architecture* (Wiesbaden, 1986)

Y. Tabbaa: 'The Medieval Islamic Garden: Typology and Hydraulics', *Garden History, Issues, Approaches, Methods*, ed. J. D. Hunt (Washington, DC, 1992)

——: 'Circles of Power: Palace, Citadel, and City in Ayyubid Aleppo', *A. Orient.*, xxiii (1993), pp. 181–200

——: 'Survivals and Archaisms in the Architecture of Northern Syria, ca. 1080–ca 1150', *Muqarnas*, x (1993), pp. 29–41

——: *Constructions of Power and Piety in Medieval Aleppo, 1178–1260* (University Park, in preparation)

YASSER TABBAA

(iii) Anatolia. Architecture from the conquest of Anatolia in 1071 to the late 13th century is often identified with the Saljuqs of Rum (*reg* 1077–1307; *see* SALJUQ, §2), the major power during the period, but it was actually the product of several Turkoman principalities in the region. In the late 11th century Turkoman tribes under the leadership of a collateral branch of the Iranian Great Saljuq royal house overwhelmed the Byzantine army and administration and established ephemeral control over most of the Anatolian plateau. Byzantine and Crusader counter-attacks at the end of the century drove the Turkomans from the coasts to the interior and led to the emergence of the Danishmend principality at KAYSERI and SIVAS, the Saltuqid principality at ERZURUM, Bayburt and Erzincan (*see* ALTINTEPE), the Mangujak principality at DIVRIĞI and the Saljuq principality at KONYA (Iconium). In the second half of the 12th century the Saljuqs gradually incorporated the other principalities, to which in the early 13th century they added the south and north coasts of Anatolia and the region from upper Mesopotamia east to Lake Van. During this period indigenous Byzantine and Armenian architectural forms and techniques were synthesized with those of Iran, Syria, Iraq and Central Asia to create a distinctive and powerful building style, primarily in stone. By the mid-12th century modest and eclectic buildings were erected in such towns as Tokat, Niksar, AMASYA, Konya and Erzurum. With the unification of central and eastern Anatolia, commercial prosperity grew and construction increased in pace and scale. The military–bureaucratic élite were the major patrons, while princes exerted most of their architectural effort on military foundations and caravanserais on the major trade routes. Although Anatolian architecture retained its eclecticism in the 13th century, it became more stylistically and conceptually consistent. With the defeat of the Saljuqs in 1243 and the extension of a Mongol protectorate over their lands, royal sponsorship came to an abrupt and complete halt, although powerful amirs continued to build lavishly (*see* §6(ii)(a) below).

(a) Building types. (b) Materials, techniques, forms and decoration.

(a) Building types.

Mosques. Examples of the 12th and 13th centuries are generally plain and conservative constructions of three broad types: hypostyle, basilical and single-domed square. Despite the prestige enjoyed by Iranian culture in Saljuq Anatolia, Iranian Saljuq mosques were rarely copied. The Great Mosque of Malatya (1224), the brick iwan court of which clearly derives from Iranian antecedents (*see* §(i)(b) above), is a notable exception. The hypostyle mosque, exemplified by the Great Mosque of Sivas (1197), is the earliest type. Its prayer-hall, a shallow rectangle of cut stone, is divided into eleven aisles by ten arcades carried on heavy stone piers supporting a flat timber and earthen roof. The north façade of the prayer-hall is preceded by a modern wooden portico, but the rectangular courtyard is contemporary with the mosque. The brick minaret attached to the south-east corner of the prayer-hall probably dates to the early 13th century, when the mosque was repaired. The impression is one of low, massive horizontality, the mosque's plain exterior walls enhancing its inward orientation. Quite different is the eastern wing of the Alaeddin Mosque in Konya (late 12th century), the reused Hellenistic and Byzantine columns of which give the interior a sense of openness and spaciousness. Variations on the hypostyle type have an enlarged aisle on the mihrab axis, a dome over the bay in front of the mihrab and a small open fountain court in the central bay of the axis. The Great Mosque of Divriği (1228–9), the most renowned example, is part of a complex that includes a hospital and tomb built by the Mangujak prince Ahmad Shah and his wife Turan Malik. A high octahedral cap on an octagonal drum conceals a hemispheric dome over the bay in front of the mihrab, and an oculus in the dome over the central bay of the middle aisle admits light and air. The mosque is also remarkable for the varied and elaborate vaults of its five aisles and the exuberant high-relief stone decoration of its portals and mihrab (*see* §9(i)(a) below).

The basilical type of mosque has antecedents in 12th-century buildings such as the Kale Mosque of Divriği (1180–81), where the vaulted central nave is distinguished from the domed side aisles. The most developed examples date from the 13th century and include the Alaeddin Mosque of Niğde (1223) with three domes ranked along the qibla wall and open central nave bay and the Burmalı Minare Mosque of Amasya (1237–46) with three domes along the nave to emphasize the mihrab axis. The Gök Medrese Mosque in Amasya (third quarter of the 13th century) is divided into fifteen bays by the eight piers of its nave arcades; they are covered by a system of domical vaults that foreshadows the multi-domed congregational mosques built by the Ottomans in the 14th and 15th centuries (*see* §6(ii)(b) below).

The third type of mosque consists in its simplest form of a square, single-domed prayer-hall opening directly on to the street. Walls are generally of brick or rubble, occasionally faced with cut stone. Domes are brick and rest on either squinches or a belt of prismatic consoles known as Turkish triangles. The type, which did not contain a minbar (pulpit) and therefore was not used for Friday prayer, is associated particularly with Konya (e.g. mosques of Şekerfuruş, 1220, and Abdalaziz, 1253), but is encountered in Akşehir (e.g. mosque of Ferruh Shah, 1224) and other towns. A more elaborate variant found several times in Konya (e.g. the mosques of Haci Ferruh, 1215–16, Beşarebey, 1219, and Erdemşah, 1220) is preceded by a closed vestibule or colonnaded portico. Large brick minarets, sometimes decorated with tile, are attached to the north-east or north-west corners, as on the mosque of Hoca Hasan and the Ince Minareli Mosque in Konya (*c.* 1264).

Madrasas and hospitals. Examples of the 12th and 13th centuries have either closed courts, a type unique to Anatolia, or open courts, a more common type that derives conceptually from Iran and Mesopotamia (*see also* MADRASA). The closed-court type appeared first: the oldest in Anatolia are the Danishmend Yaghıbasan Madrasa of Niksar (1157–8) and the Çukur Madrasa of Tokat (mid-12th century). Built of rubble faced with cut ashlar, they have square courtyards covered by domes on squinches with two iwans at right angles to each other and student cells ranged around the other two sides. Attempts to derive this arrangement from the Kumushtakin Gümüshtekin Madrasa in Bosra (1136) in Syria remain unpersuasive. Early Saljuq examples include the single-iwan Ertokuş Madrasa in Atabey (1224) and the four-iwan hospital of Turan Malik in Divriği (?1228). The Karatay (1251–2) and Ince Minareli (*c.* 1265) madrasas in Konya and the Taş Madrasa (1278–9) in Çay all have single iwans at the back, student cells along either side and great hemispheric brick domes on fan pendentives over the central courtyard. The Karatay Madrasa has splendid tile revetments on the interior; the Ince Minareli has a dramatic relief-carved stone portal, some of the most spectacular architectural decoration of the period (see fig. 42).

Open-court madrasas appeared at the beginning of the 13th century and have either two or four iwans. The contiguous two-iwan madrasa and hospital known as the Çifte ('Double') Medrese (1205) in Kayseri is the earliest securely dated Saljuq madrasa extant. Others, such as the madrasa of Huand Hatun in Kayseri (1237–8), the Sırçalı Madrasa in Konya (1242) and that of Süleyman Pervane in Sinop (1262), have pairs of iwans (an entry hall and a classroom) on the long axis and student cells along the sides of the courtyard. Four-iwan examples, such as the hospital (Turk. *şifaiye*) built by Sultan 'Izz al-Din Kayka'us in Sivas (1217–18), the Sahibiye Madrasa in Kayseri (1267–8) and the Buruciye and Gök madrasas (1271–2) in Sivas, have iwans on all four sides of the central courtyard. Normally the buildings are only one storey high, although some of the larger and grander examples, such as the Gök Medrese in Tokat (*c.* 1275) and the Çifte Minareli Madrasa in Erzurum (*c.* 1250; see fig. 43), have an upper storey. The founder's tomb is commonly included within the building, as is a small mosque, although on rare occasions it is contiguous.

A few dervish cloisters (Turk. *zaviye, hanikah; see* KHANAQAH) survive from the period. The oldest is the

42. Ince Minareli Madrasa, Konya, Turkey, *c.* 1265

43. Çifte Minareli Madrasa, Erzurum, Turkey, *c.* 1250

Ribat-i Eshab-i Kchf at Afsin near Elbistan (13th century). The Boyalikoy Hanikahi near Afyon (first half of the 13th century), a typical example, has a domed central hall with four iwans opening off it, a plan perhaps modelled on Central Asian domestic architecture.

Funerary architecture. Commemorative architecture derived typologically and morphologically from Iranian canopy tombs and tomb towers. Anatolian tombs are typically two-storey structures of brick or stone. They often have partially buried crypts, entered through separate doors below ground-level, and raised prayer-chambers reached via double staircases and elevated portals. The crypt sometimes housed one or more mummified corpses; the prayer-chamber contained the elaborate cenotaph(s) of the deceased. Tombs are usually independent structures, although they are occasionally integrated into other buildings. The most common types have square, semi-subterranean crypts; circular, square or polygonal shafts; and conical, tetrahedral or polyhedral caps. Relief carving with motifs derived from the Saljuq repertory frequently enriches façades, especially in eastern Anatolia (*see* §9(i)(b) below). The earliest examples, found in northern and eastern Anatolia, date from the second half of the 12th century. In the first half of the 13th century tombs became more common, appearing in Konya, Kayseri and other central Anatolian towns, and after the Mongol invasion tomb-building became particularly important throughout Anatolia.

The polygonal tomb tower is the most common type, accounting for a third of the extant examples. All are octagonal except for the unique decagonal tomb of Sultan Kiliç Arslan II (*reg* 1156–92) in the Alaeddin Mosque, Konya (*c.* 1190). Some are sparsely decorated (e.g. the tomb of Tac ül-Vezir at Konya, 1239), while others, such as the Çifte Künbed in Kayseri (1247–8), are richly ornamented with an elaborately worked portal and elegant epigraphic border. Variants, such as the tomb of Melik Gazi at Kırşehir (last quarter of the 13th century), have an octagonal drum and conical cap. The tomb of Emir Saltuq at Erzurum (late 12th century) has an octagonal base topped by a tall cylindrical drum and conical cap; its striped masonry and surface decoration resemble Armenian work. The extraordinary tomb of Mama Hatun in Tercan (first quarter of the 13th century) is an octagonal tower, each face of which is composed of a cylindrical segment, covered with a fluted conical cap. The interior is articulated by eight lobes mirroring the exterior. The tomb stands within a high stone enclosure lined with 11 burial niches; a portal carved in relief gives access to the complex. Square tombs are also common in the 13th century, especially in central Anatolia. The tombs of Şeyh Ahmed (1221–2) and Şeyh Aliman (1288), both in Konya, have simple square prayer-chambers covered by brick domes on squinches or Turkish triangles. Larger and more elaborate examples, such as the much restored tomb of Ebu'l-Kasim in Tokat (1233–4) and the tomb attached to the Gök Madrasa in Amasya (*c.* 1275), have high octagonal drums on squinches; the exterior is covered with prismatic elements and octahedral caps. Others, such as the brick tomb of Melik Gazi at Pazarören, Kayseri province (?13th century), recall the Gunbad-i Surkh at Maragha in Iran (*see* §(i)(b) above).

The small group of so-called iwan tombs found most commonly in central Anatolia are typologically different. Rectangular in plan, both crypt and prayer-chamber are covered with barrel vaults. The prayer-chamber is left open at one of the short ends, which is treated as the principal façade to form an iwan. Both indigenous, pre-Islamic Anatolian and Iranian sources have been posited, unpersuasively, for the iwan-type tomb. The Danishmend period tomb of Hacı Cikirik at Niksar (1183), which seems to have been part of a larger structure (destr.), is the earliest example extant. Particularly fine examples are the tombs of Seyit Gazi in the province of Eskişehir (1207–8), of Emir Yavtaş in the village of Reis, Akşehir province (*c.* 1250), and of Gühertaş (*c.* 1275) and Gömeç Hatun (last quarter of the 13th century) in Konya.

Secular buildings. A series of more than 100 stone caravanserais (Turk. *han*) built between 1200 and 1270 along the key commercial routes radiating from Konya are the most impressive monuments of the period. Located at intervals of one day's stage (about 30 km), they are characterized by their often grand scale and the fine quality of their stone construction and decoration. At least eight were erected by Saljuq sultans and several others were founded by members of the royal family, but the great majority were built by members of the ruling military–bureaucratic élite. They seem to have been erected to open Anatolia to international commerce and thereby enhance the prosperity of the Saljuq state. Anatolian caravanserais derive in plan and to a lesser extent decoration from Syrian, Iranian and Central Asian prototypes. Three basic designs can be distinguished. The simplest is a rectangular hall without courtyard; typically the interior is divided by piers into three aisles covered by barrel vaults. Walls are thick and solid with only a few small windows. Such buildings are apparently of local design and are found mostly in central Anatolia, such as Eğret Han on the Afyon–Kütahya road (first quarter of the 13th century) or Çiftlik Han on the Sivas–Amasya road (mid-13th century). Courtyard caravanserais, of which only five are attested, are closely related to Syrian prototypes and date from the early 13th century. They are large rectangular structures with monumental stone portals and large central courts surrounded by deep arcades. Outstanding examples are the Evdir Han, built by Sultan 'Izz al-Din Kayka'us I in 1215–19, and the Kırkgöz Han, perhaps built by Sultan Ghiyath al-Din Kaykhusraw II (*reg* 1237–46), both on the road from Antalya to Burdur. The third type of caravanserai combines the basilical hall of the first type with the arcaded court of the second. The most notable examples are two buildings known as Sultan Han, which were built by Sultan 'Ala' al-Din Kayqubadh on the Konya–Aksaray road (1229) and at Tuzhisar on the Kayseri–Sivas road (1236–7). Both have high, fortress-like walls with half-round towers at regular intervals, magnificently ornate portals, and courtyards containing an elevated mosque and

surrounded by open stables, guest-rooms, storerooms and baths. A second monumental portal leads to the basilical hall at the back, which has a raised lantern and conical cap over its central bay.

Other surviving secular buildings include fortifications, baths and portions of palaces. The best-preserved ensemble of military architecture is at Alanya; it includes extensive walls, a seaside bastion and a naval arsenal. Lesser fragments are found in Kayseri, Bayburt, Divriği, Antalya and Ankara. The only part remaining from the Saljuq royal palace in Konya is a fragmentary pavilion built on one of the citadel towers by Kiliç Arslan II (*reg* 1156–92). The pavilion once consisted of a square room surrounded by a balcony on consoles and revetted with glazed tiles. 'Ala' al-Din Kayqubadh's summer palace near Kayseri, known as Kaykubadiye, consisted of three small buildings on an artificial lake, a boathouse, mosque and two-room hall decorated with glazed tiles. Kubababad, his larger summer palace on Lake Beyşehir, had a fortified wall enclosing 16 modest structures, including two tiled residential buildings.

(b) Materials, techniques, forms and decoration. Stone, brick and timber, the traditional building materials of the region, continued to be used in 12th- and 13th-century Anatolia, but stone - in ashlar, ashlar-faced rubble and rubble masonry - was used most widely and effectively. Techniques for shaping and decorating it were well developed long before the coming of Islam. Brick, used much more rarely, is particularly associated with the region of Konya and is curiously absent from east Anatolia, where Anatolian masonry traditions were tenaciously adhered to, despite proximity to Iran and the active borrowing of Iranian architectural forms and decorative elements. Where used, brick rarely rivals the rich decorative patterning found in Iranian architecture. It was frequently combined with stone in vaults and domes. Timber was used for vertical supports and beams.

With the exception of the tomb tower, architecture of the period is characterized by horizontal massing and inward orientation. Outer walls function as screens containing the inner architecture and do not articulate interior space. Only the occasional dome or conical cap breaks the overall horizontality of form. Walls are massive and fenestration is minimal. Structures are generally covered by vaults, which display a remarkable variety of form. Domes are carried on squinches and pendentives or by belts of prismatic consoles. Architectural functions are frequently grouped together in building complexes (Turk. *külliye*).

Surfaces are sparsely decorated. Ornament is concentrated around portals and windows on the exterior and around the mihrab on the interior. Techniques include relief-carved stone, striped masonry, decorative brickwork, glazed tile and, rarely, stucco and painting. Motifs derive from Iranian and Syrian as well as Turkish and indigenous Anatolian (Armenian and Byzantine) sources and include geometric and vegetal bands and fields, occasional zoomorphic motifs and epigraphy. In many instances, Iranian stucco motifs have been translated into stone (*see* §9(i) below).

BIBLIOGRAPHY

F. Sarre: *Konia, seldschukische Baudenkmäler* (Berlin, 1921)
A. Gabriel: *Les Monuments turcs d'Anatolie*, 2 vols (Paris, 1931–4)
M. Ferit and M. Mesut: *Selçuk veziri Sahip Ata ile oğullarının hayat ve eserleri* [The life and works of the Saljuq vizier Sahip Ata and his sons] (Istanbul, 1934)
F. Sarre: *Der Kiosk von Konia* (Berlin, 1936)
A. Gabriel: *Voyages archéologiques dans la Turquie orientale*, 2 vols (Paris, 1940)
M. F. Uğur and M. M. Ferit: *Selçuklu büyüklerinden Celalettin Karatay ve kardeslerinin hayat ve eserleri* [The life and works of the Saljuq notable Jalal al-Din Karatay and his brothers] (Konya, 1940)
M. Z. Oral: 'Kayseri'de Kubadiye sarayları' [The palaces of Kaykubadiye in Kayseri], *Türk Tarih Kurumu: Belleten*, xvii (1953), pp. 501–17
S. Lloyd and D. S. Rice: *Alanya ('Ala'iyya)* (London, 1958)
K. Otto-Dorn: 'Seldschukische Holzsaulenmoscheen in Kleinasien', *Aus der Welt der islamischen Kunst: Festschrift für Ernst Kühnel* (Berlin, 1959), pp. 58–88
K. Erdmann: *Das anatolische Karavansaray des 13. Jahrhunderts*, 3 vols (Berlin, 1961–76)
O. Aslanapa: 'Kayseri'de Keykubadiye köşkleri kazısı' [Excavations of the palaces of Kaykubadiye in Kayseri], *Türk Arkeol. Derg.*, xiii (1964), pp. 19–40
K. Otto-Dorn and M. Önder: 'Bericht über die Grabung in Kobadabad', *Archäol. Anz.*, ii (1965), pp. 170–83
J. M. Rogers: 'The Çifte Minare Medrese at Erzurum and the Gök Medrese at Sivas', *Anatol. Stud.*, xv (1965), pp. 63–85
S. Ögel: *Anadolu Selçukları'nın taş tezyinatı* [Anatolian Saljuq stone ornamentation] (Ankara, 1966)
M. O. Arık: 'Erken devir Anadolu–Türk mimarısında türbe biçimleri' [Tomb types in Anatolian–Turkish architecture of the early period], *Anatolia*, xi (1967), pp. 57–100
R. H. Ünal: *Les Monuments islamiques anciens de la ville d'Erzurum et de sa région* (Paris, 1968)
A. Kuran: *Anadolu Medreseleri* [Anatolian madrasas] (Ankara, 1969)
J. M. Rogers: 'Recent Work on Seljuk Anatolia', *Kst Orients*, vi (1969), pp. 134–69
S. Dilaver: 'Anadolu'daki tek kübbeli Selçuklu mescitlerinin mimarık tarihi yönünden önemi' [The importance of single-dome Saljuq mosques in Anatolia in the history of architecture], *Sanat Tarihi Yıllığı*, iv (1971), pp. 17–28
M. Sözen: *Anadolu medreseleri: Selçuklu ve beylikler devri* [Anatolian madrasas, the Saljuq and Beylik periods], 2 vols (Istanbul, 1972)
J. M. Rogers: 'Royal Caravanserais and Royal Inscriptions in Seljuk Anatolia', *Edebiyat Fak. Araştırma Derg.*, viii (1978), pp. 397–431
Ü. Ü. Bates: 'The Impact of the Mongol Invasion on Turkish Architecture', *Int. J. Mid. E. Stud.*, ix (1978), pp. 23–32
A. Kuran: 'Anatolian–Seljuk Architecture', *The Art and Architecture of Turkey*, ed. Ekrem Akurgal (New York, 1980), pp. 80–110
H. Crane: 'Notes on Saldjuq Architectural Patronage in Thirteenth Century Anatolia', *J. Econ. & Soc. Hist. Orient*, xxxvi (1993), pp. 1–57

HOWARD CRANE

(iv) Western Islamic lands. A distinctive style of architecture arose in Spain, Morocco and central Algeria as a result of the increasing isolation of the entire region from the eastern Islamic lands and easy communication across the Straits of Gibraltar. It is characterized by such forms as horseshoe, cusped and intersecting arches with alternately coloured or patterned voussoirs, ribbed domes and square minarets. Architectural activity falls into four distinct phases, which correspond to four political periods. The first coincided with the patronage of the UMAYYAD caliphate (*reg* 929–1031) of Córdoba, when a new palace was erected at Madinat al-Zahra' outside the city and the congregational mosque was enlarged. Architecture during the confusing period in the 11th century when numerous petty kingdoms under the rule of the Party Kings (Arab. *mulūk al-tawā'if*; Sp. *Reyes de Taifas*) ruled the Iberian peninsula is exemplified by palaces, such as the Aljafería in Saragossa. Towards the end of the 11th century, the

ALMORAVID dynasty (1056–1147) of Morocco conquered Spain and unified the region. Their mosques in Algeria show the direct impact of Andalusian forms and motifs. They were succeeded in turn by another North African reforming power, the ALMOHAD dynasty (1130–1269), whose congregational mosques in Morocco refined and standardized earlier forms and decoration.

(a) Umayyads, 929–1031. (b) Party Kings, 1031–*c.* 1100. (c) Almoravids, 1056–1147. (d) Almohads, 1130–1269.

(a) Umayyads, 929–1031. After 'Abd al-Rahman III (*reg* 912–61) had had himself declared caliph in 929, he introduced a monumental building programme without precedent in the Islamic west. The old palace in Córdoba, which stood adjacent to the mosque on the site of the former episcopal palace, was no longer adequate for the official and social requirements of a caliph, so in 936 a new palace city was begun some 8 km west of the city centre at MADINAT AL-ZAHRA' (see fig. 44). The site chosen lay at the foot of the Sierra de Córdoba where the southern slopes ran gently out into the verdant plain. The rectangular outline of its double-faced walls (1518×745 m) was modified to the curve of the slope on the side facing the mountain. Only the centre of the northern part of the enclosure has been excavated, to reveal parts of an extensive palace complex against the north wall. The palace complex lacks any ordering principle, such as the

44. Madinat al-Zahra', Spain, begun 936

45. Great Mosque, Córdoba, Spain, *maqsūra* and mihrab, AD 976

rigid symmetry characteristic of Umayyad religious architecture (and earlier palatine architecture elsewhere in Islam); its axes organize only the immediate surroundings of the principal buildings. Aisled halls are flanked by anterooms and preceded by transverse porticos opening on to square courtyards surrounded by porticos and rooms. The three-aisled disposition of the Salón Rico, the most lavishly decorated hall, is repeated in a free-standing pavilion from which it is separated by a courtyard with water basins. The long axis is broken by ramps, which bend and branch out to connect one area of the palace to another across the irregularities of the terrain. Texts describe a functional division into three terraced zones for the palace, dwellings and gardens; the palace undoubtedly constituted the crown of the city.

Ornamental panels from Madinat al-Zahra' show the impact of Mesopotamian Abbasid forms and techniques (*see* §4(i) above) on Umayyad decoration, but the characteristic stucco of the Abbasids was replaced by the soft local limestone, a material so unresisting and malleable that it was ideally suited to experiments with form. Some marble panels, however, are more conservative in effect and preserve Syrian Umayyad (*see* §3 above) or even Sasanian motifs (*see* IRAN, ANCIENT, §II, 3). The dado panels of the Salón Rico bear the richest vegetal compositions of thick-stemmed scrollwork growing out of a densely woven undergrowth laden with composite, often hypertrophied palmette and fruit-like forms which interlace almost without a background.

The other facet of 'Abd al-Rahman's building programme was the extension of the Great Mosque in the capital (see fig. 26 above; *see also* CÓRDOBA (i), fig. 2). In 951–2 he enlarged and refurbished the mosque's court, razing the 8th-century minaret in the process and placing a new tower on the north side of the expanded courtyard.

Rising over 47 m, it measured some 8.5 m square and contained twin staircases. Its proportions (1:5) and exterior decoration later served as prototypes for the monumental Almohad minarets of the 12th century and for the bell-towers of MUDÉJAR churches. 'Abd al-Rahman also had plainer minarets added to the two congregational mosques of FEZ in Morocco, which he had recently captured.

Al-Hakam II (*reg* 961–76), 'Abd al-Rahman's son, had already supervised work at Madinat al-Zahra' as heir apparent, and he continued his father's work on the mosque of Córdoba until 976, achieving unprecedented splendour. Directly after his accession in October 961, he had the prayer-hall extended by an additional 12 bays, the size of the original mosque, and transferred the columns of 'Abd al-Rahman II's mihrab to the new one. The earlier plan and elevation were maintained in the extension, but several new features were introduced: columns and capitals were arranged hierarchically, a domed space marked the first few bays of the central aisle, a transept-like space was introduced along the new qibla wall, and a *maqsūra*, or space reserved for the ruler, was created in the five bays in front of and beside the new mihrab (see fig. 45).

The principal concept in al-Hakam II's extension was the heightening and intensification of devices found in the earlier mosque—horseshoe arches, for example—to define and enhance important areas. The transverse arcade separating the qibla aisle from the rest of the mosque is strongly marked in elevation by enormous round horseshoe arches, and the five bays of the *maqsūra* are further differentiated by increasingly complex arch profiles: voluted soffits on the outermost pair, twin bays of two-tier systems enriched by five-lobed arches on the intermediate pair and a two-tiered system of intersecting arches over the central bay, which is itself subdivided into three. The intersecting arches are transformed into three dimensions in the ribbed domes of the central three bays of the *maqsūra*. The ruler entered the mosque from the palace across the street via a bridge and a passage within the qibla wall itself. The mihrab is the most splendid in western Islam, displaying the entire repertory of decorative forms (e.g. horseshoe and cusped arches, alternating voussoirs and inscriptions) and techniques (e.g. carved plaster, marble and stone, mosaic and quartered marble). Mosaic decorated the dome over the mihrab (*see* CÓRDOBA (i), fig. 2), the walls surrounding the mihrab and the flanking portals. The niche itself is a small heptagonal room covered with a monolithic shell vault rather than the semicircular recess characteristic of mihrabs in central and eastern Islamic lands. Its particular shape may be related to the horseshoe-shaped apses of contemporary Mozarabic churches (e.g. SAN MIGUEL DE ESCALADA), and it became a model for mihrabs throughout the region. Several of the mosque's features are direct or indirect references to earlier buildings. The spatial articulation of the qibla area in a series of square bays seems to preserve the Syrian tradition of the Aqsa Mosque in Jerusalem (*see* JERUSALEM, §II, 1(iv)) rather than the continuous transept found in the congregational mosque in Kairouan. Al-Hakam II is reported to have commanded the Byzantine emperor to send him a master mosaicist and materials to decorate the mosque, just as the Syrian Umayyad caliph al-Walid I (*reg* 705–15), his ancestor, had asked for Byzantine mosaicists to work on the mosque of Damascus (*see* §3(ii) above). Indeed, the 10th-century expansion of the mosque can be understood as a conscious revival of Syrian Umayyad architecture as one part in the revival of the Umayyad caliphate in Spain.

The final and largest extension to the mosque was ordered by al-Mansur, the all-powerful vizier of Hisham II, in 987–8 after an influx of Berber recruits for the campaigns against the Christians had swelled the population of the capital. As the Guadalquivir River was too close to allow the prayer-hall to be extended further south, the mosque was extended along the entire east side. Unlike the earlier extensions, which had moved the mihrab, al-Mansur's addition left the focus of al-Hakam II's prayer-hall unchanged. It not only maintained the aisled plan with two-tiered arcades of the earliest mosque, but structurally unnecessary transverse rows of piers in the new hall continued those that had once indicated the limits of the earlier phases. Unlike the careful arrangement of columns and capitals in al-Hakam II's extension, those of the addition were arranged somewhat haphazardly.

The only surviving private religious foundation from the Umayyad period is the mosque near the Bab al-Mardum in Toledo (999–1000; now El Cristo de la Luz; *see* TOLEDO, §I, 1); its Cordoban motifs, including two-tiered arches and the hierarchical intensification of space, suggest that stylistic developments in the capital were eagerly imitated elsewhere in the realm. The mosque is a brick structure measuring 8 m square and consists of nine vaulted bays arranged in a square. The east and west sides had arched openings into each bay; the south side contained the mihrab, and the north side had horseshoe and lobed arches disposed in two storeys. The vaults of the interior rest on a grid of horseshoe arches springing from four central columns and corresponding piers projecting from the outer walls. At the lowest level the compartments are directionally neutral, but they become directional and hierarchical to emphasize the mihrab through increased complexity in the intermediary storeys and the vaults themselves.

(b) Party Kings, 1031–c. 1100. The Aljafería (Arab. *al-Ja'fariyya* but originally *Dār al-surūr*: 'House of happiness') Palace in SARAGOSSA is the only Islamic princely seat of 11th-century Spain to survive more or less intact, although there are fragments of contemporary work at the Alcazaba of Almería, the Alcazaba of MÁLAGA, the Alcazaba of Balaguer (Lleida province) and perhaps even the Alhambra in Granada (*see* GRANADA, §III, 1). It is also one of the few palaces of the period identifiable in contemporary Arabic literature. The second lord of the Hudids, Abu Ja'far Ahmad ibn Sulayman al-Muqtadir bi-llah (*reg* 1049–82), brought the kingdom of Saragossa to its political and cultural zenith and built a formidable castle close to the western walls of his capital around the remains of a great 9th-century tower. Its walls have projecting round towers, like the Roman walls of the city. The interior space is trisected into longitudinal tracts, of which the central one, the official and social area, is further trisected into suites of rooms flanking a courtyard. The outer sectors were never completed, although they were perhaps intended

46. Fragment of stucco decoration, Alcazaba, Balaguer, Spain, 11th century

for dwelling quarters. An octagonal oratory directly adjoins the north block. Its mihrab holds strictly to the Cordoban scheme of twin columns supporting a round horseshoe arch with an eccentric, raised extrados and alternately carved and plain voussoirs. The north hall was the heart of the palace and perhaps contained the throne. Its inner face copies the general scheme of the arcade systems around the *maqsūra* in the mosque of Córdoba. The principle of horizontal impost lines has been abandoned in the bent intersecting arches of the court façades, but the periodic appearance of dwarf columns on the imposts of the intersecting arches recalls the multi-storey articulation of the arcades at Córdoba. The capitals of the arches are clearly intended to be understood as structural elements, since they rest on colonnettes. The upper register of the entrance to the presumed south hall, however, differs markedly from the Cordoban repertory, for complicated arches of composite profile replace the horseshoe arches of the north hall. The tectonic supports separating the registers of intercrossing arches have disappeared, and the arches have become an atectonic net, initiating a motif that became widely popular in succeeding centuries. The repeated tripartite division of the plan had already been used in the Syrian Umayyad palace at Mshatta (Qasr al-Mushatta) (*see* §3(iii) above), but the hierarchical articulation of the palace area develops themes seen in the mosque of Córdoba.

The remains of stucco and painting found at Balaguer are so closely related to those of the Aljafería that both complexes can be regarded as part of the same repertory. The finest stucco elements in Balaguer (see fig. 46) are identical to the last detail to the paintings of the Aljafería, suggesting that the same artists were masters of both crafts. Painted composite palmettes in the upper arcade of the Aljafería Mosque are direct transpositions of the stuccos, for they share the same longitudinal grooved elements alternating with contrasting fronded leaves that are so striking in Balaguer. The standard repertory was so developed that highly schematized forms could be combined almost arbitrarily.

(c) *Almoravids, 1056–1147*. The Almoravids (Arab. *al-murābiṭūn*: 'the people of the *ribāṭ*s'), a fundamentalist group of Berbers, founded MARRAKESH c. 1062. From this capital they conquered large portions of North-west Africa, crushed the petty kingdoms in Spain and incorporated them into their already considerable domains. Marrakesh became a centre of Andalusian art as Spanish artists, perhaps whole workshops, came to southern Morocco, bringing their considerable artistic heritage. The square Andalusian minaret, which had already been introduced to Fez in the 10th century, was unknown in Almoravid mosque architecture. Brick piers had probably been the preferred means of support in the pre-11th-century mosques of North-west Africa, since the ready supply of spolia columns available to Umayyad and Aghlabid builders did not exist. Piers continued to be the major means of support in Almoravid mosques, although columns were occasionally used in limited roles, particularly on either side of the mihrab. Three well-preserved Almoravid mosques in Algeria show how deeply Andalusian elements penetrated the architecture of North-west Africa.

The congregational mosque in Algiers (c. 1097) stands squarely between earlier Umayyad and later Almohad mosques. Measuring 38.2×46.3 m, its courtyard is included within a 9×11 grid of square bays crossed by four transverse arcades. The central aisle, a series of single bays culminating in a square bay in front of the mihrab, is emphasized by its greater width. Pointed horseshoe arches are used in the longitudinal arcades and around the courtyard; lobed arches are used in the interior transverse arcades and are further enriched in the area of the three central aisles. In comparison to the interpenetrating T-plan of al-Hakam II's extension at Córdoba, the articulation of the qibla area, where the arcades and the roofs run right to the qibla wall, is indecisive. The diminutive courtyard, the T-plan, the profiles of the piers, the arches of the arcades and their hierarchic distribution all reappear in later Almohad mosques.

Two other Almoravid mosques in TLEMCEN (rebuilt 1136) and in nearby Nedroma (before 1145) have only some of these features, although Nedroma's eccentric location, small size (28.3×20.0 m) and simplicity may partly explain this difference. Although transverse arcades divide the prayer-hall, neither mosque has a transept along the qibla wall, and only the bay in front of the mihrab is marked by a dome. The mosque at Tlemcen is larger (49.3×45.6 m) and far more elaborate. The central aisle has several lobed arches with lambrequin relief decoration in stucco, and the stucco dome in front of the mihrab, consisting of 12 ribs supporting a small cupola, is a *tour de force*. The interstices between the ribs are decorated with splendid pierced arabesque patterns which allow light to filter into the mosque. Although the deep mihrab recess, the lobed horseshoe arch with an eccentric extrados and

alternating voussoirs, the ribbed dome and the elaborate stucco carving are directly in the Cordoban manner, *muqarnas* in the corner squinches and cupola are a new element in Almoravid decoration.

Only one small cupola, the Qubbat al-Ba'diyyin (or Barudiyyin; 1106–42), remains from the principal Almoravid mosque in Marrakesh. Once the centre of the ablution complex, this diminutive structure (7.3×5.4 m) documents the impact of Andalusian decorative motifs (e.g. ribbed domes and intersecting horseshoe arches) on Almoravid architecture and illustrates the process by which *muqarnas* vaulting replaced ribbing as the characteristic decoration of domes in the architecture of the region.

The elegant stucco decoration at Marrakesh, at Tlemcen and in the Almoravid restorations to the Qarawiyyin Mosque in Fez show the role plant ornament played in Almoravid architectural decoration. Excavations at Chichaoua, 70 km west of Marrakesh, revealed stuccos probably made by a metropolitan workshop that first developed features seen during the rule of the Party Kings in the 11th century in Spain. The fronded leaf is more dominant, as is the drop-shaped palmette base. Contrasting effects were achieved in composite motifs, especially with fronded leaf elements juxtaposed at an angle. The almost arbitrary combinations of base and upper parts of decoration under the Party Kings are now systematically extended to asymmetrical composite leaf forms. The principle of the widest possible variation within the narrowest possible repertory of elements is taken to an extreme.

(d) *Almohads, 1130–1269*. The Almohad caliphs inherited the artistic and political traditions of the Almoravids. They fused North-west Africa and Andalusia into a unified artistic sphere, of which the capitals at Marrakesh and Seville (*see* SEVILLE, §I, 1) were the two main centres of artistic life. The types of buildings were clarified and architectural elements standardized; the exuberance of the Andalusian or Andalusian-trained decorators who had worked on Almoravid buildings was restrained to suit the more austere Almohad taste. Their art, especially mosque architecture, is marked by their role as religious reformers.

The Kutubiyya ('Booksellers') Mosque in Marrakesh was erected in two stages: the first took place directly after the Almohad occupation of the city in 1147; the second, an almost exact replica of the first set against it at a slight angle, was probably finished by 1158. Only foundations (87×58 m) remain from the first mosque, but the beautiful stone minaret (12.5 m square; h. 67.5 m; *see* MINARET, fig. 2), erected between the two stages, became a model for virtually all other minarets in North-west Africa. The Almoravid type of mosque with piers and longitudinal aisles was clarified and enriched, particularly in the qibla area. A wider central nave and qibla transept give rise to the familiar T-plan, but the nave as well as the outermost of each group of side aisles generate *muqarnas* domed bays at the intersection with the qibla transept. In elevation the hierarchy of arches for which Almoravid architects had provided the prototype was perfected: pointed horseshoe arches were standard, except where they were embellished with lobes, trefoils, lambrequins and *muqarnas* in the transverse arcades and especially around the domed bays along the qibla wall. Comparable domed bays had been used at either end of the qibla wall in Fatimid mosques in Egypt (*see* §(ii)(c) above), but their purpose is unknown; visually they recall the bays of Córdoba's *maqsūra* shifted laterally.

Tinmal, high in the Atlas mountains, was the village where Ibn Tumart, the founder of the Almohad movement, had lived and worked. Its mosque (1153–4; see fig. 47), erected between the two stages of the Kutubiyya in Marrakesh, is much smaller than the first Kutubiyya (9 as opposed to 17 aisles wide) but was evidently entrusted to artisans from the ruler's workshop in the capital, to judge from the superb quality of the craftsmanship. Instead of the massive Kutubiyya minaret that stood to the side of the mosque, the architect ingeniously integrated the mihrab, minbar (pulpit) recess and imam's door into a relatively low but massive masonry block, the internal staircase of which indicates that it served as the minaret. Oddly enough, Almohad architects never repeated the arrangement.

Other Almohad congregational mosques exhibit variations on the standard scheme. That of Seville (1172–98) must have been much like the double Kutubiyya in plan, although only its minaret, the Giralda, remains after a cathedral was built on the site. The minaret (11.6 m square; original h. *c.* 60 m) was saved to become the cathedral's bell-tower. It stands in the same relative position as the Kutubiyya Minaret in Marrakesh. The Mosque of the Kasba in Marrakesh, built by Ya'qub al-Mansur (*reg* 1184–99), is unusually planned around five courts; the central one reverses the relation of open and covered spaces typical of Almohad mosques and recalls the four-iwan plans of contemporary eastern Islamic architecture (*see* §(i)(b) above), since each of its internal façades has a wider and slightly higher central arch. The Hasan Mosque in RABAT (1195–6) was designed to be the largest (180×140 m) mosque in the western Islamic world. Twenty-one aisles wide, it has a three-aisled transept along the qibla wall, a disproportionately small oblong courtyard

in the north and two subsidiary oblong courtyards perpendicular to the qibla which light the interior. Because of the mosque's inordinate size, several hundred dressed-stone columns replaced the usual brick piers. The minaret, set opposite the mihrab, dominates the exterior and was meant to be nearly 60 m high, but the dreams of the founder, Ya'qub al-Mansur, the last Almohad caliph of importance, were shattered and the mosque was never completed.

The rationalized standardization of Almoravid decoration suited the fundamentalist mentality of the Almohads. Ornamental elements were reduced in size but extended in number, and detail was monumentalized. Large network panels composed of foliate arches were used to decorate minarets. The interior drawing of plant elements was eliminated or reduced to a few grooves or notches; the frond gave way to an almost flat half-palmette, which was used only on capitals as a means of contrast. The capital lost the vestiges of its Classical origins and became the favourite surface for plant decoration, particularly in the austere prayer-halls of Almohad mosques. The second Kutubiyya, for instance, preserves more than 250 examples. These plant capitals, usually on over-slender half columns placed against brick piers or the wall, are the only powerful plastic members and delimit the zones of the supports from those of the arches. Not only was the single decorative element rethought, but the distribution of decoration in Almohad architecture was conceived anew. The unarticulated or sparsely detailed surfaces of individual leaves are paralleled by the largely unadorned surfaces on the whole structure. This formulation of the values of decoration was new, but its formal and structural principles were deeply rooted in the traditions of pre-Almohad Spanish–Islamic art.

BIBLIOGRAPHY

H. Terrasse: 'La Grande Mosquée almohade de Séville', *Mémorial Henri Basset*, ii (Paris, 1928), pp. 249–66
H. Basset and H. Terrasse: *Sanctuaires et forteresses almohades* (Paris, 1932)
H. Terrasse: *L'Art hispano-mauresque des origines au XIIIe siècle* (Paris, 1932)

47. Congregational mosque, Tinmal, Morocco, 1153–4

M. Ocaña Jiménez: 'La inscripción fundacional de la Mezquita de Bîb al-Mardûm en Toledo', *Al-Andalus*, xiv (1949), pp. 175–83

E. Lévi-Provençal: *Histoire de l'Espagne musulmane*, 3 vols (Paris, 1950)

M. Gómez-Moreno: *El arte árabe español hasta los almohades: Arte mozárabe* (1951), iii of *Ars Hispaniae* (Madrid, 1947–51)

J. Caillé: *La Mosquée de Hassan à Rabat* (Paris, 1954)

G. Marçais: *L'Architecture musulmane d'Occident* (Paris, 1954)

J. Meunié, H. Terrasse and G. Deverdun: *Nouvelles recherches archéologiques à Marrakech* (Paris, 1957)

L. Torres Balbás: 'Art hispanomusulmán: Hasta la caída del califato de Córdoba', *Historia de España*, ed. R. Menéndez Pidal, v (Madrid, 1957)

K. Brisch: 'Madîna az-Zahrâ' in der archäologischen Literatur Spaniens', *Kst Orients*, iv (1963), pp. 5–41

G. Marçais: 'Sur les mosaïques de la Grande Mosquée de Cordoue', *Studies in Islamic Art and Architecture in Honour of Professor K. A. C. Creswell* (Cairo, 1965), pp. 147–56

L. Seco de Lucena: 'Los palacios del taifa almeriense al-Mu'tasim', *Cuad. Alhambra*, iii (1967), pp. 15–26

P. Berthier: 'Campagnes de fouilles à Chichaoua d'avril–mai 1965 à octobre–novembre 1967', *Bull. Soc. Hist. Maroc*, i (1968), pp. 23–8

C. Ewert: 'Spanisch–islamische Systeme sich kreuzender Bögen, i: Die senkrechten ebenen Systeme sich kreuzender Bögen als Stützkonstruktionen der vier ehemaligen Hauptmoschee von Córdoba', *Madrid. Forsch.*, ii (1968) [whole issue]; ii: 'Die Arkaturen eines offenen Pavillons auf der Alcazaba von Málaga', *Madrid. Mitt.*, vii (1966), pp. 232–53; iii: 'Die Aljafería in Zaragoza', *Madrid. Forsch.*, xii (1978–80) [whole issue]

H. Terrasse: *La Mosquée al-Qaraouiyin à Fès* (Paris, 1968)

P. Berthier: 'Campagnes de fouilles à Chichaoua d'avril–mai 1965 à avril–mai 1968—2e partie', *Bull. Soc. Hist. Maroc*, ii (1969), pp. 7–26

C. Ewert: 'Islamische Funde in Balaguer und die Aljafería in Zaragoza', *Madrid. Forsch.*, vii (1971) [whole issue]

——: 'Der Miḥrâb der Hauptmoschee von Almería', *Madrid. Mitt.*, xiii (1972), pp. 286–336

——: 'Die Moschee am Bâb al-Mardûm in Toledo: Eine "Kopie" der Moschee von Córdoba', *Madrid. Mitt.*, xviii (1972), pp. 287–354

R. Bourouiba: *L'Art religieux musulman en Algérie* (Algiers, 1973)

F. Hernández Giménez: *El alminar de 'Abd al-Raḥmân III en la mezquita major de Córdoba* (Granada, 1975)

H. Stern: 'Les Mosaïques de la Grande Mosquée de Cordoue', *Madrid. Forsch.*, xi (1976) [whole issue]

L. Golvin: *L'Art hispano-musulman* (1979), iv of *Essai sur l'architecture religieuse musulmane* (Paris, 1970–79)

C. Ewert: 'Baudekor-Werkstätten im Kalifat von Córdoba und ihre Dispersion in nachkalifaler Zeit', *Künstler und Werkstatt in den orientalischen Gesellschaften*, ed. J. Gail (Graz, 1982)

J. Hassar-Benslimane and others: 'Tinmal 1981', *Madrid. Mitt.*, xxiii (1982), pp. 440–66

S. López-Cuervo: *Medina az-Zahra: Ingeniería y formas* (Madrid, 1983)

F. Hernández Giménez: *Madînat al-Zahrâ': Arquitectura y decoración* (Granada, 1985)

C. Ewert: *Die Kapitelle der Kutubîya-Moschee in Marrakesch und der Moschee von Tinmal* (1991), iv of *Forschungen zur almohadischen Moschee*, by C. Ewert and J. P. Wisshak (Mainz, 1981–91)

M. Barrucand and A. Bednorz: *Moorish Architecture in Andalusia* (Cologne, 1992)

CHRISTIAN EWERT

6. *c.* 1250–*c.* 1500. The Mongol invasions at the beginning of the 13th century destroyed any semblance of unity in the Islamic world, and the distinct regions that emerged remained independent centres of power until the 16th century. In this period of political, social and economic instability, when institutions of religious legitimacy and political authority were absent, secular figures sought a place in posterity by endowing charitable foundations. Often centred on the tomb of the founder or a famous mystic, these architectural ensembles combined building types developed earlier, such as mosques, madrasas, minarets, hospices, hospitals and mausolea. Similarly, the use of such decorative techniques as *muqarnas* and glazed tile, which had been limited in earlier centuries, was expanded to create an immensely appealing architecture of showy

exteriors and brilliant colouristic effects. Exquisite revetments in carved and painted plaster, glazed tile, carved wood and stone masked simple construction; structural innovations were largely confined to vaulting, particularly in the Iranian world, as larger and new types of vaults were developed to cover a wide variety of spaces.

(i) Eastern Islamic lands. (ii) Anatolia. (iii) Central Islamic lands. (iv) Western Islamic lands.

(i) Eastern Islamic lands. Throughout the period the Iranian world was dominated by two Mongol dynasties from Central Asia, first the Ilkhanids (*reg* 1256–1353), initially subordinates of the Great Khan in China, who had their capitals in western Iran, and then the Timurids (*reg* 1370–1506), also descendants of Genghis Khan, who had their capitals in Transoxiana and Khurasan. Designed to underscore their world-conquering ambitions, the buildings they erected are some of the most impressive in all of Iranian architecture. Structures were larger, higher and more monumental than before, and traditional building types, such as mosques, madrasas, tombs and hospices, were often combined in multifunctional complexes. Brick remained the principal material of construction, but it was increasingly concealed on the exterior by glittering tile revetments and on the interior by elaborately carved and painted plaster.

In India, although Muslims had founded trading settlements in Sind as early as the 8th century, a distinctive tradition of Islamic architecture emerged only at the end of the 12th century, when the Ghurid sultan of Khurasan, Muhammad ibn Sam, conquered northern India, and his commander Qutb al-Din Aybak established Delhi as the capital. Delhi remained the seat of several dynasties, collectively known as the Delhi sultanates, which ruled successively until the definitive Mughal conquest in 1555, while other independent Muslim states emerged throughout India. Indigenous building techniques were adapted for the new types of buildings required by Muslims, particularly mosques and tombs. In regions where stone was the primary material of construction, spolia, particularly columns from temples, were used extensively. The indigenous tradition of trabeate architecture was modified by the arcuate system typical of Islamic architecture in Afghanistan, Iran and western Central Asia.

(a) Iran, *c.* 1250–*c.* 1375. (b) Iran, Afghanistan and western Central Asia, *c.* 1375–*c.* 1500. (c) Indian subcontinent.

(a) Iran, c. *1250–c. 1375.* For the century and a half between the Mongol conquests in the 1250s and the campaigns of Timur in the 1380s and 1390s, architecture in Iran was affected by the changing religious and political outlook of the Mongol ILKHANID dynasty (*reg* 1256–1353) and of its clients and successors, notably the MUZAFFARID dynasty (*reg* 1314–93) in southern Iran and the JALAYIRID dynasty (*reg* 1336–1432) in Iraq and western Iran. At first the Ilkhanid dynasty, founded by Hulagu (*reg* 1256–65), a grandson of Genghis Khan, remained true to Mongol tradition: its members adapted the nomadic practices of the steppe to their new environment, wintering in the warmer lands of Iraq, summering on the grassy plains of Azerbaijan and continuing to live in tents. Until 1295 the Ilkhanid rulers were mostly shamanists or Buddhists and

recognized the supremacy of the Great Khan in Mongolia or China. However, after his accession, Ghazan Khan (*reg* 1295–1304) was converted to Islam and threw off allegiance to the Great Khan, thereby assuring the ascendancy of the culture of the sedentary Iranians over that of the nomadic Mongols. Ghazan and his chief minister RASHID AL-DIN inaugurated a vast programme of reforms that revitalized the economy and provided the funds for new construction, particularly of religious buildings. The effects of Ghazan's reforms continued to be felt under his two successors, Uljaytu (*reg* 1304–16) and Abu Sa'id (*reg* 1316–35). After the death of Abu Sa'id, political power became fragmented among the great amirs and the rival claimants to the throne they supported, and the major building projects of the previous 50 years were replaced by work on individual monuments sponsored by members of local dynasties.

Earthquakes, invasions and subsequent building works have destroyed all but a few monuments in the Ilkhanid capitals at MARAGHA, Tabriz (see TABRIZ, §1), BAGHDAD and SULTANIYYA; it is thus only in provincial cities of central and western Iran that a substantial number of buildings from the period survive. Inscriptions on the buildings give some information about dates of construction, patronage and builders. Rashid al-Din mentioned the building activities of his contemporaries in his *Jāmi' al-tawārīkh* ('Compendium of histories'), and he provided information on the buildings attached to his charitable foundation (*waqf*) near Tabriz (destr.; see TABRIZ, §3(i)) in the endowment deed he composed for it. Other court historians were hired to record the architectural commissions of their patrons, while such foreign visitors as the Moroccan globe-trotter Ibn Battuta (1304–c. 1370) and the Italian friar Odoric of Pordenone (c. 1286–1331) noted the buildings they saw. Architectural remains show that there was general continuity with the preceding period in the types of buildings constructed, whether palaces, caravanserais, mosques, madrasas, *khānaqāh*s (Sufi hospices) or tombs, and in the plans, design features and materials used. New features include increased emphasis on verticality and a more extensive use of colour.

Building types. The earliest surviving building, and one of the most unusual, is the observatory that Hulagu had built in 1258 for the celebrated astronomer Nasir al-Din Tusi (1201–74) on a hill north of his capital at Maragha. Traces of the central tower for the quadrant (diam. 45 m) and several round and straight-sided subsidiary buildings have been uncovered, all built of brick on rubble foundations and revetted with tiles decorated with lustre or with enamel over a blue glaze (*lājvardīna*; *see also* §9(ii)(b) below).

Palaces were mostly built of wood or were relatively fragile constructions of cloth, carpeting and felt, and none has survived. They were extraordinarily elaborate: Ghazan's summer palace was a tent of golden tissue which took two years to make. It consisted of an audience hall with several appendages and required a month to erect. At the winter site of Ujan, in what is now Azerbaijan, courtiers had individual tents of horsehair cloth or felt; temporary mosques and bazaars were set up along broad avenues, and when summer came, all lesser tents were

burned. The only palace of which anything survives is the summer residence begun c. 1275 by the Ilkhan Abaqa (*reg* 1265–82) at Saturiq (now TAKHT-I SULAYMAN) and built directly on the foundations of the Sasanian sanctuary of Shiz (*see* IRAN, ANCIENT, fig. 5). A large courtyard (125×150 m), orientated on a north–south axis, encompassed an artificial pond and was surrounded by porticos and four iwans. Behind the north iwan was a domed room which was built on the site of the Sasanian fire temple and probably served as the Ilkhanid audience hall. Behind the west iwan was a transverse hall flanked by two octagonal kiosks; it had served as the Sasanian throne-room and became the living quarters of the Ilkhanid sovereign. The quality and abundance of the architectural décor, particularly the marble carvings and the lustre and *lājvardīna* tiles, show that Abaqa spared no expense. Both the site, which the Ilkhanids thought was where the Sasanian emperors had been crowned, and the elements of the decoration, i.e. the lustre tiles with quotations and scenes illustrating themes from the 11th-century Persian epic, the *Shāhnāma* ('Book of kings') of Firdawsi, may have been chosen for their association with pre-Islamic Iranian kingship.

As part of Ghazan's economic reforms, caravanserais were erected at staging posts along the principal routes to provide safe lodging for merchants. Only traces of these have survived at such sites as Sin, Sarcham and Marand. They are rectangular in plan, with monumental portals and projecting bastions. Caravanserais were also built within cities. The Khan al-Mirjan (or Khan al-Urtma) in Baghdad (1359) is one of the few urban commercial buildings to survive. Mirjan, the Governor of Baghdad for the Jalayirids, built it as a source of revenue for the adjacent religious foundation that included his tomb. The rectangular brick building consists of two-storey structures surrounding a long central hall. The hall, 14 m high, is spanned by eight transverse arches supporting stepped vaults which are crowned by domes resting on squinches. The sophisticated roofing system, which allows light into the interior, shows that the Governor considered the caravanserai to be as important as the other parts of his complex. Ghazan also issued an edict requiring the construction of a bath and mosque in every community, with the receipts from the bath supporting the mosque, but no Ilkhanid baths have survived.

The four-iwan-plus-dome plan developed in earlier centuries (*see* §5(i)(b) above) continued to be used for congregational mosques. The best-preserved example was built between 1322 and 1326 at VARAMIN, south of Tehran, by the local family of governors under Abu Sa'id. The mosque (*see* MOSQUE, fig. 2) is a large rectangle (66×43 m) containing a rectangular central court; four iwans, connected by two-storey arcades, sit at the centre of each of its sides. The four iwans are not equal in size; rather, a strong longitudinal axis orientated on the qibla is created by the monumental portal, the wider qibla iwan and the majestic dome beyond. The congregational mosque at KIRMAN, built by the Muzaffarids in 1349 and later, is another example, although it lacks the typical dome on the qibla axis. Other mosques, such as those at Hafshuya, Ashtarjan and Faryumad, had two iwans, while one of the largest congregational mosques of the period, that built by the vizier 'Alishah in Tabriz, consisted of a

48. Mausoleum of Uljaytu, Sultaniyya, Iran, 1305–15

single monumental iwan (25 m to the springing of the vault), which was intended to surpass the celebrated Sasanian iwan at Ktesiphon.

In north-west Iran severe winters rendered the open court unsuitable, and various types of hypostyle mosque with no courtyard were built. That at Ardabil (early 14th century) consists of a rectangular chamber with a flat roof supported on two rows of tree trunks; that at Asnaq is square with four monolithic stone columns supporting the flat wooden roof. Smaller mosques in central Iran often consisted of a single dome chamber, as in the group built along the Zaindeh River downstream from Isfahan at Kaj, Dashti and Aziran.

Other types of religious buildings designed for communal use, such as madrasas and *khānaqāh*s, also followed the four-iwan plan. The Madrasa Imami (1354) in Isfahan is a near-perfect example, with four iwans grouped around a central courtyard and connected by two-storey arcades with living chambers.

In the funerary architecture of the 14th century both the tomb tower and the domed square chamber continued to be erected. Mausolea built for lesser figures, such as descendants of the imams or minor princes, were relatively small, free-standing buildings. The Imamzada Ja'far at Isfahan (1325), for example, is an octagonal tomb tower some 7 m in diameter. Wealthier patrons, mainly sultans and their chief ministers, built larger tombs as part of elaborate funerary complexes. The best surviving example is the mausoleum of Sultan Uljaytu (*reg* 1304–17) at Sultaniyya. The tomb is a huge octagon, 38 m in diameter, with a rectangular prayer-hall (15×20 m) appended to the south. The central octagonal space, 25 m in diameter, is surmounted by a dome 50 m high and ringed by eight minarets. While it now stands in splendid isolation (see fig. 48), Uljaytu's tomb was once the centre of a large pious foundation, including places for prayer, instruction and Koran reading, living quarters and a hospital. Hardly anything of these other buildings has survived, but the scale of these imperial foundations is suggested by the

endowment deed for the Rab'-i Rashidi, Rashid al-Din's foundation outside Tabriz (*see* TABRIZ, §3(i)). A gateway complex gave access to the founder's tomb, a hospice, a *khānaqāh* and a hospital. Over 300 people were permanently attached to the foundation: more than 100 salaried employees and day-labourers and 220 slaves. The endowment amounted to almost 50,000 dinars; that of Sultan Uljaytu for his funerary complex at Sultaniyya was reported to have been almost double that amount.

Other funerary complexes were built around the tombs of Sufi saints, both contemporary figures and those long dead. Golombek has called them 'the little cities of God' and singled out five as the most brilliant and best preserved: the shrine of 'Abd al-Samad at NATANZ; that of Shaykh Safi, eponym of the Safavid dynasty, at ARDABIL; the Pir-i Bakran near Isfahan; the shrine of Bayazid at BISTAM; and the complex of Shaykh Ahmad at Turbat-i Shaykh Jam. The one at Natanz, for example, was built by an Ilkhanid vizier in the first decade of the 14th century around the tomb of 'Abd al-Samad, a spiritual master of the Suhrawardi order of Sufis. In addition to the tomb, the complex contained a *khānaqāh* for the master's disciples, a congregational mosque and a minaret, all executed in the most up-to-the-minute techniques and materials.

Forms, materials, techniques and decoration. One of the highlights of Iranian architecture of the previous centuries had been the inventive variety of its brick vaulting. An interest in structure had led to new uses of ribs covering bays and new methods of breaking up the squinch to create more elaborate transitions from walls to dome. Now architects shifted their attention to methods of covering space, especially rectangular areas. The solid walls of earlier buildings were pierced with openings and bays, and types of transverse vaulting were developed to admit light and air. Proportions were also altered: rooms became taller, arches more pointed and minarets more attenuated. Typical of the new verticality and refinement of form are the monumental portals with soaring double minarets preserved in Isfahan, YAZD and ABARQUH.

Along with this interest in space came the use of the MUQARNAS for vaulting. Previously *muqarnas*, in the form of serried tiers of squinch-like niches, had been part of the structural fabric and confined to squinch zones and cornices. Now it became more decorative and was used to create entire vaults. In the complex at Natanz, for example, an elaborate stucco vault covers the tomb, where ten tiers of *muqarnas* rise from the piers to converge on a 12-pointed star (see fig. 49), and brick *muqarnas* fills the vault of the *khānaqāh* portal. These *muqarnas* units are not integral parts of the structure, but shells hung from the pyramidal roof of the tomb or the back wall of the portal.

Baked brick continued to be the main material of construction in this period, but more and more attention was paid to ways of adding colour to it. Small glazed elements had already been introduced in the interstices between bricks, where their shining light- and dark-blue glazes played off against the matt surface of the reddish bricks. Fragments from Ghazan's and Rashid al-Din's funerary complexes at Tabriz show that by *c.* 1300 surfaces

19. Tomb of 'Abd al-Samad, shrine complex, Natanz, Iran, *muqarnas* vault, 1307–8

were being covered in continuous expanses of tile mosaic, in which pieces of various shapes were cut from monochrome tiles and arranged to form a pattern. New colours were added to the two shades of blue: black and white, then purple, green and ochre. Geometric patterns gave way to increasingly naturalistic floral ones. For the portal of the Imamzada Baba Qasim at Isfahan (1340–41), five colours were used in floral and arabesque patterns. For the portal of the congregational mosque at Kirman (1349), a full seven-colour palette was used. Alternatively, whole wall surfaces could be enlivened by using glazed bricks of different colours to spell out pious names and phrases in square kufic script in the technique called *banna'ī* (*see* §9(ii)(b) below). Colour and pattern could be used, as at the shrine of 'Abd al-Samad at Natanz, to create a unified exterior façade.

Colour was also extended to interior surfaces. The patterns formed by brick bonding had earlier served as interior decoration, but now interior walls were often covered with stucco and painted (*see also* §9(i)(a) below). Sometimes the patterns imitated brick bonding; at other times they consisted of large floral or ogival motifs, as in the tomb of Rukn al-Din in Yazd (1325). Epigraphic panels and friezes were also popular. Many of the patterns and motifs have close parallels in contemporary book decoration, suggesting that designers and calligraphers worked in various media during this period.

BIBLIOGRAPHY

D. M. Wilber: *The Architecture of Islamic Iran: The Il Khanid Period* (Princeton, 1955)

L. C. Bretanitsky: *Zodchestvo Azerbaydzhana XII–XIV vv. i yego mesto v arkhitekture Perednego Vostoka* [The architecture of Azerbaijan in the 12th–14th centuries and its place in the architecture of the Near East] (Moscow, 1966)

L. Golombek: 'The Cult of Saints and Shrine Architecture in the Fourteenth Century', *Near Eastern Numismatics, Iconography, Epigraphy, and History: Studies in Honor of George C. Miles*, ed. D. K. Kouymjian (Beirut, 1974), pp. 419–30

P. Vardjavand: 'Rapport préliminaire sur les fouilles de l'observatoire de Maraqé', *Monde Iran. & Islam*, iii (1975), pp. 199–224

R. Naumann: *Die Ruinen von Tacht-e Suleiman und Zendan-e Suleiman* (Berlin, 1977)

U. Harb: *Ilkhanidische Stalaktitengewölbe* (Berlin, 1978)

B. O'Kane: 'The Friday Mosques of Asnak and Saravar', *Archäol. Mitt. Iran*, xii (1979), pp. 341–51

S. S. Blair: 'Ilkhanid Architecture and Society: An Analysis of the Endowment Deed of the Rab'-i Rashidi', *Iran*, xxii (1984), pp. 67–90

A. S. Melikian-Chirvani: 'Le *Shahname*, la gnose soufie et le pouvoir mongol', *J. Asiat.*, ccxxii (1984), pp. 249–338

S. S. Blair: *The Ilkhanid Shrine Complex at Natanz, Iran* (Cambridge, MA, 1986)

——: 'The Mongol Capital of Sultaniyya, "The Imperial"', *Iran*, xxiv (1986), pp. 139–51

——: 'The Epigraphic Program of the Tomb of Uljaytu at Sultaniyya: Meaning in Mongol Architecture', *Islam. A.*, ii (1987), pp. 43–96

——: 'The Ilkhanid Palace', *A. Orient.*, xxiii (1993), pp. 239–48

SHEILA S. BLAIR

(b) *Iran, Afghanistan and western Central Asia, c. 1375–c. 1500.* During this period architecture in eastern Iran was closely identified with the patronage of the TIMURID dynasty (*reg* 1370–1506), which ruled an area now divided between Iran, Afghanistan, Uzbekistan and Kazakhstan. Western Iran was controlled by two Turkoman confederations, the QARAQOYUNLU (*reg* 1380–1468) and the

AQQOYUNLU (*reg* 1378–1508). All these rulers saw architectural patronage as a means of reinforcing their legitimacy and erected impressive brick monuments revetted in richly coloured tilework. Important developments in technique occurred during the period.

Eastern Iran. The most significant Timurid monuments survive in and around the cities of MASHHAD, HERAT, SAMARKAND and BUKHARA and in such isolated locations as TURKESTAN (now in Kazakhstan) and Khargird in north-east Iran. Fine work was also produced in provincial centres, notably Isfahan (*see* ISFAHAN, §1) and YAZD, in the first half of the 15th century. Although none of the buildings surviving in Yazd attains the standard of the best metropolitan examples, the cumulative effect of its many fine neighbourhood mosques makes it an important showcase of Timurid patronage. In addition to extant buildings, a wide range of other sources makes this period one of the best documented in the history of Iranian architecture. Timurid courts supported a large number of official biographers and historians, such as Hafiz-i Abru (*d* 1430), Nizam al-Din Shami (*fl* 1404), 'Abd al-Razzaq Samarqandi (*d* 1482), Khwandamir (*d* after 1535–6), Mir Khwand (*d* 1498) and Sharaf al-Din Yazdi (*d* 1454), who chronicled the exploits and achievements of their patrons, including their building works. The glowing reports of Timurid court chroniclers should be set against the anti-Timurid polemic of the Damascene historian Ibn 'Arab-shah (*d* 1450), who as a boy had been deported to Samarkand by Timur, and the more sober, but credulous, travelogue of the Spanish ambassador Ruy Gonzalez de Clavijo (*d* 1412). Other sources include two 15th-century histories of Yazd, which give an account of contemporary building activities more detailed than that for any other city, even Herat. The architecture of the period is also frequently represented in minute detail in contemporary book illustration, but the images are often schematic and stereotyped and are of limited value for the history of architecture. British and Russian military and scientific expeditions during the 19th century recorded some buildings that were subsequently destroyed.

These sources provide information of a kind not available for earlier periods. For example, Yazdi's brief account of the foundation of the shrine of Ahmad Yasavi at Turkestan even notes the dimensions of several rooms in *gaz*, enabling its metric equivalent (606 m) to be calculated. It is likely that the building was originally planned on a squared grid based on the *gaz*, although the earliest surviving examples of architectural plans using a squared grid (Tashkent, Alisher Navoi Lib.) date from at least a century later. The texts also mention the name of one architect, QAVAM AL-DIN SHIRAZI, whose works can also be identified from inscriptions. The names of other builders with the epithet 'Shirazi'—indicating that they or their ancestors came from Shiraz—appear in inscriptions of the period, and this has led some scholars to posit the existence of a 'school of Shiraz', but this term may be misleading. Despite this rich documentation, the difficulties of access to this now divided region have often precluded comprehensive treatment.

The buildings constructed by Timur (*reg* 1370–1405), the founder of the dynasty, are notable for their gigantic

size, best seen in the towering hulks of his congregational mosque at Samarkand (132×99 m, interior court 76×64 m; later known as the Mosque of Bibi Khanum; *see* SAMARKAND, §3(ii)) and the ruined portal of the Aq Saray, his palace at SHAHR-I SABZ (*see* CENTRAL ASIA, fig. 12). In carrying off artisans from the cities he captured to Samarkand, his avowed aim was to make it the most beautiful capital in the world; he built on such a grand scale not for the aesthetic pleasure that such buildings afforded but in order to inspire his subjects with awe. None of Timur's successors had the same ambitions, and their architectural projects were on a correspondingly reduced scale. The greatest patron of architecture in the first half of the 15th century was not the ruling sultan, Timur's son Shahrukh (*reg* 1405–47), but Shahrukh's wife Gawharshad. Her constructions in Mashhad and Herat were the finest of the age, outstanding by virtue of their size and the quality of their decoration. Other patrons might compete in number of commissions, but not in quality. Complex designs, inventive vaulting systems and dazzling tilework characterize her buildings. They mirror her formidable political power, which was so great that Sultan Abu Sa'id was impelled to have her executed in 1457, when she was well over 70 years old. She was the only female member of the dynasty deemed worthy of this fate.

Architectural trends in the second half of the 15th century are more difficult to assess, since the major buildings of the period have vanished. Contemporary sources record a great deal of building activity, especially during the reign of Sultan Husayn Bayqara (*reg* 1470–1506), when the leading patron was the amir 'ALISHIR NAVA'I. 'Alishir is credited with commissioning 50 caravanserais, 19 cisterns, 15 bridges, 9 baths, 18 mosques and 17 other religious buildings. In contrast to the first half of the century, other amirs and viziers do not appear as architectural patrons: 'Alishir must have used his position as Sultan Husayn Bayqara's confidant to monopolize the funds available. His major endowment was the Ikhlasiyya complex, located near that of Gawharshad in Herat. Nothing of it remains, but its large scale put it in the tradition of the Rab'-i Rashidi, the huge foundation established near Tabriz by the Ilkhanid vizier Rashid al-Din (*see* TABRIZ, §3(i)). In contrast to the situation in the Ilkhanid period (*see* §(a) above), when viziers were the greatest patrons after the rulers themselves, under the Timurids it was the amirs who filled this role. This change may be the result of the greater homogeneity of the state: unlike their Mongol predecessors, Timurid military chiefs had come to power in a Muslim milieu and shared many of the cultural values of those they ruled. While Timurid princes, female members of the royal family and viziers vied with each other to build and endow magnificent complexes of buildings serving a variety of private, public and religious functions, religious dignitaries, merchants and bureaucrats commissioned buildings that, due to their limited resources, were on a more modest scale.

Congregational mosques of the period continue to use the four-iwan-plus-dome plan that had been standard in Iran since the 11th century (*see* §5(i)(b) above). That ordered by Timur for Samarkand (1398–1405) is distinguished by its great size: it covers an area 132×99 m; its main dome is 18.5 m in diameter and 37 m high. Timurid historians reported that Timur was dissatisfied with the appearance of his buildings on a number of occasions and ordered them to be rebuilt on a grander scale. This may account for the unfinished state of its main portal. There was no room for such a portal at the congregational mosque (completed 1418) that Gawharshad added to the shrine of Imam Riza in Mashhad. The mosque is unusual for a Timurid building in having no well-defined or decorated exterior; instead, it focuses inwards. This introspection is emphasized by the mosque's most radical feature, the upper galleries flanking the side iwans: from the courtyard these resemble the entrances to the students' cells in a two-storey madrasa. The court façade is truly magnificent. Its dazzling multicoloured tilework, in which tile mosaic and underglaze- and overglaze-painted tiles were used, is anchored to the strong lines of the architecture. Its centrepiece, the qibla iwan, is decorated with a superb inscription written by Gawharshad's son Baysunghur. Gawharshad also had a four-iwan congregational mosque built as part of her complex in Herat (1417–38), while 'Alishir Nava'i restored the main congregational mosque of the city in 1498–1500. This restoration included structural consolidation, the rebuilding of the Ghurid portal and extensive redecoration, but the quality of the tilework, particularly that painted in overglaze, had declined, and earlier interest in the play of light and shadow over articulated surfaces had given way to a taste for a smooth finish.

Madrasas of the period are even more homogeneous, with courts surrounded by two storeys of students' cells and four iwans. The most famous of these is the Ghiyathiyya Madrasa at Khargird in Iran, built in 1444–5 for the vizier Pir Ahmad Khwafi, a native of the region. Its nearly symmetrical plan was accomplished by moving the mosque, which usually occupied the larger qibla iwan, to the right of the entrance, where it is balanced by a domed lecture hall on the left. This shift enabled the architect to create four iwans of equal size. The desire for symmetry led to the bevelling of the corners of the court, although this added no spatial advantage. The earlier emphasis on height is here replaced by strong horizontal façades, the clean lines of which provide the base for tile revetment in blazing colours. The madrasas of Shahrukh's son Ulughbeg in Bukhara (1417–20) and on the Registan in Samarkand (c. 1420; see SAMARKAND, §3(iv)) are variations on the same theme.

While some madrasas, especially in Khurasan, contained the tombs of their founders, whether rulers or court notables, the free-standing tomb was also common. The greatest number can be found in the necropolis of the Shah-i Zinda (see SAMARKAND, §3(i)). Many of the small mausolea that line the street leading to the principal shrine were built for female members of Timur's family. Most are small square or octagonal structures covered with domes. At the beginning of the period they were decorated with deeply incised moulded tiles glazed in up to four colours (white, light and dark blue and manganese black), but this was later replaced by a combination of underglaze- and overglaze-painted tiles or tile mosaic (see also §9(ii)(b) below); the drums beneath the domes increased in height and the gap between inner and outer domes widened

correspondingly, culminating in the exaggerated profile of the mausoleum of Tuman Agha (1405–6).

Timur's own tomb in Samarkand, the Gur-i Mir (1404–5; see fig. 15 above; see also SAMARKAND, §3(iii)), exhibits the same exaggerated profile and elaborate tile decoration. It originally formed part of a madrasa and khānaqāh complex for his grandson Muhammad Sultan, but when Muhammad Sultan died prematurely the site became a dynastic mausoleum. The four-iwan madrasa that Gawharshad had built near her mosque in Herat included a dome chamber in which she and many of her descendants were buried. Only this chamber and a single minaret survive to bear witness to the extraordinary skill of the architect, Qavam al-Din Shirazi.

Monumental tombs of various kinds were also built for holy men. Some, such as the shrine of Chashma-yi Ayyub in Bukhara (1380 or 1385–6), were built over the supposed burial place of prophets of the pre-Islamic past (in this case, Job). More common were those erected in honour of famous Sufi shaykhs, such as the shrines of Ahmad Yasavi (d 1166) at Turkestan (1399) and of 'Abdallah Ansari (d 1089) at Gazur Gah outside Herat (begun 1425). A considerable body of scholarly opinion condemned building mausolea, and in some cases, as at Gazurgah, Turbat-i Shaykh Jam and Taybad, the cenotaph stood in the open air before an iwan, an arrangement that has been called a ḥaẓīra.

In other cases a tomb chamber was incorporated in a larger complex. In the plan of Timur's shrine for Ahmad Yasavi at Turkestan (see fig. 50), rooms with different functions were organized within a rectangle measuring 65×46 m. In addition to the domed mausoleum, the shrine boasts a huge central dome chamber (diam. 18 m; h. 37 m), as well as various other rooms. These served the resident community of Sufis and would have included an assembly-room, living quarters, a library, a mosque and rooms for meditation. In shrine complexes built earlier in the century, these functions had been dispersed among groups of buildings arranged in a more haphazard fashion. The Turkestan shrine remained an anomaly, however, for later complexes built under the Timurids follow the older tradition. Another new feature of the shrine at Turkestan is its regular, decorated exterior, clearly intended to be seen from all sides.

The ruins of the Aq Saray, the palace Timur built at Shahr-i Sabz (1379–96), show these same concerns for size and imposing exteriors. Only the base of its immense portal, the vault of which must have soared over 50 m, survives. Tent palaces, often set in gardens, were more common. The string of vast gardens with which Timur adorned the outskirts of Samarkand contained sumptuous pavilions, 'each with its complement of chambers magnificently ornamented in blue and gold, the walls being panelled with tiles of these and other colours' (Clavijo). In other cases embroidered silk tents provided an informal counterpoint to the rigidly organized parterres of the gardens. Timur may have wanted to re-create the upland meadows to which the court moved each summer. Streams and bowers provided the necessary cool breezes and shade, enabling him to move at will from one to another with urban civilization still close at hand.

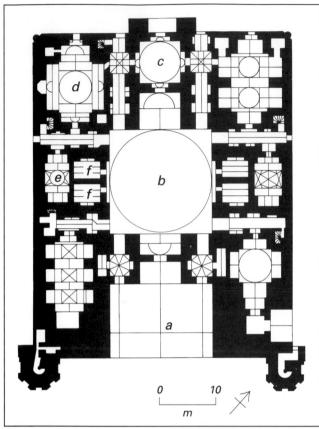

50. Shrine of Ahmad Yasavi, Turkestan, Kazakhstan, 1399, plan: (a) entrance portal; (b) kazanlik; (c) mausoleum; (d) mosque; (e) library; (f) cells

The Timurids in Herat were equally alive to the delights of the garden. By the end of the 15th century the area north of the city was filled with gardens irrigated by canals. In some cases streams were diverted to bisect religious buildings such as Sultan Husayn Bayqara's madrasa and 'Alishir's Ikhlasiyya complex. A setting for picnics, musical and literary parties, wedding and circumcision feasts, gardens also served as the locus for the quotidian affairs of state. The most splendid garden in Herat was Sultan Husayn Bayqara's Bagh-i Jahanara, where, as the chronicler Khwandamir related, the 'soul-refreshing air which breathed through every avenue, like the zephyr breeze of the loveliest month of spring, possessed the influence to assuage the sorrows of the most afflicted'.

Many examples of civil and military engineering remain: fortresses, such as the citadel of Herat (rebuilt 1415–17); the dams of Kirat, Akhlamabad and Gulistan (10 km north of Mashhad); canals; bathhouses, such as the one beside the congregational mosque in Yazd (1421–2); and caravanserais (three on the route from Astarabad to Isfara'in, one in Sang Bast and one at Kushrabat, all in Iran). The most important of the civil structures is the observatory founded by Ulughbeg in Samarkand in 1420 (*see* SAMARKAND, §3(v)). The three-storey circular building (diam. 48 m) contains a giant sextant, a solar quadrant, galleries and annexes containing lodgings for the astronomers.

Western Iran. Both of the Turkoman confederations that vied for power in western Iran had originated in eastern Anatolia. The Qaraqoyunlu supplanted their former Jalayirid suzerains in Azerbaijan and Iraq in 1410–11 and expanded into western and then southern Iran under Jahanshah (*reg* 1438–67). They were overcome by the Aqqoyunlu ruler Uzun Hasan (*reg* 1453–78) in 1467–8. The Aqqoyunlu were in turn overthrown by Shah Isma'il, the founder of the Safavid dynasty, between 1501 and 1508 (*see* §7(ii) below). Only a few buildings erected under Turkoman patronage survive in their capital Tabriz and in the cities of Isfahan and Yazd, which they held in the second half of the 15th century. Their lost splendour is reflected in contemporary Ottoman buildings in northwest Turkey.

The most spectacular of the surviving buildings, despite its ruined state, is the Blue Mosque in Tabriz (*see* TABRIZ, §3, (ii)). The mosque was originally part of the Muzaffariyya complex, built for the wife of Jahanshah Qaraqoyunlu, but the other elements, the *khānaqāh*, cistern, library and tomb, have disappeared. An inscription above the portal gives the name of the architect, Ni'matallah ibn Muhammad al-Bawwab, and the date of construction AH 870 (1465). The core of the building, a rectangle measuring 52×34 m, contains a domed central courtyard surrounded on three sides by a series of domed or transverse-vaulted spaces. The 'sanctuary', a cruciform chamber covered with a dome (diam. 16 m), is aligned with the main entrance and projects from the fourth, or qibla, side. This plan (a double-domed prayer-hall surrounded by smaller rooms) has been compared to mosques built by the Ottomans in Bursa (*see* §(ii)(b) below), but it differs in the larger scale of the main dome and the chain of smaller rooms. Enough of the decoration survives to show that its materials and design were of the highest quality. Arabesques and inscriptions worked in luminously intense and exquisitely delicate tile mosaic cover the walls (see fig. 51). Even lustre tiles, rarely used by this date, are found at the base of the main portal. The most sumptuous decoration was reserved for the 'sanctuary'. The walls above the marble dado, the vaulting and the dome were covered in dark-blue hexagonal tiles, overlaid with patterns stencilled in gold leaf, foreshadowing the overall tile revetment of the 17th-century mosque of Shaykh Lutfallah in Isfahan (*see* ISFAHAN, §3(iv)).

Immediately after taking possession of the Qaraqoyunlu territories, Uzun Hasan moved his capital to Tabriz, where he built the Nasriyya complex (destr.). Enlarged by his son Ya'qub (*reg* 1478–90), this eclipsed the Muzaffariyya in the eyes of contemporaries. In addition to the madrasa in which Uzun Hasan was buried, it comprised a mosque, a kitchen where meals were served to the poor, and a bazaar. In turn, the Nasriyya was eclipsed by Uzun Hasan's palace at Isfahan, the Hasht Bihisht ('The Eight Paradises'; also destr.). Surrounded by a garden and adjacent to a parade ground, mosque and hospital, it was described by an anonymous Venetian merchant as having four corner rooms, four antechambers (?iwans) and a dome. These parts correspond to a standard palace type known later in Iran, Turkey and India.

Three Turkoman buildings still stand in Isfahan: the Darb-i Imam Mausoleum (1453–4), the tomb of Shaykh

51. Interior tile decoration, Blue Mosque, Tabriz, Iran, 1465

Abu Mas'ud (1489–90) and the Darb-i Kushk (1496–7), a *zāwiya* or 'hermitage' for Sufis. The repairs that Uzun Hasan ordered for the Friday Mosque in 1475–6 also survive (*see* ISFAHAN, §3(i)). In Yazd the congregational mosque was repaired in 1457, while construction of and repairs to smaller buildings, usually mosques, were carried out in many of the surrounding villages and towns, such as Ashkizar, Bundarabad and Taft. The large number of these indicates the great prosperity of the region under the Turkoman confederations. Most share a similar plan deriving from that of the congregational mosque in Yazd. A small courtyard is surrounded by low arcades on three sides and a large iwan on the qibla side. The iwan leads to a domed chamber flanked by low vaulted closed prayer-halls (Pers. *shabistān*). The mosque at Bundarabad (1473–4) is remarkable for its fine tile mosaic minbar.

Two monuments built by the Ottomans, the Green Mosque in BURSA (1412–24) and the Çinili Kiosk in Istanbul (1472), are closely connected to now-lost buildings of the same period in western Iran. The Green Mosque preserves fine examples of tile mosaic and *cuerda seca* tiles, the latter signed by craftsmen from Tabriz. These techniques had never previously appeared on Ottoman buildings: Turkoman craftsmen seem to have adopted the latest ceramic techniques developed in Central Asia, as seen, for example, on the mausolea in the Shah-i Zinda cemetery in Samarkand, and to have transmitted them to Anatolia. Similarly, the almost symmetrical centralized

plan, tilework and squinch-net vaulting of the Çinili Kiosk have often been attributed to Central Asian sources, but the plan probably reached Anatolia via the intermediary of Turkoman buildings, such as the Hasht Bihisht Palace in Tabriz.

Materials, forms, techniques and decoration. Iranian architecture of the 15th century was built of brick—mud-brick for walls and fortresses, and baked brick for more prestigious structures. Foundations were normally built of rubble. Stone was used in rare instances, such as the portals and columns of the congregational mosque at Samarkand, which were made from stone imported from India. Wood was scarce and was used sparingly for lintels, doors and tie-beams, especially those connecting the inner and outer shells of double domes.

Most interior spaces were covered by brick vaults clad with tiles on the outside and stucco on the inside. The period was one of extraordinary development in vaulting techniques. The three dome chambers in the shrine of Ahmad Yasavi at Turkestan are cruciform in plan—even the main dome chamber, where there was room only for the shallowest of side recesses. Each recess is vaulted with *muqarnas*, which leads the eye up to the inner dome, itself a plaster *muqarnas* shell. Compared with earlier *muqarnas* shells, such as that at Natanz (see fig. 49 above), those at Turkestan are of unparalleled complexity. The individual units are reduced in size and multiplied in number, but confusion is averted by ordering this mass with regular deep furrows and clusters of smaller units. No further development of these *muqarnas* vaults took place; instead the transverse vaulting, used experimentally in the smaller side rooms at Turkestan, was combined with the cruciform plan of the dome chambers to produce important innovations.

In the tomb of Gawharshad at Herat, broad ribs spring from the edges of the four recesses in the dome chamber and interlace to produce a square smaller than the room below. Small squinches lead up to rows of *muqarnas* and a 16-sided dome. This arrangement required less buttressing than one with a dome equal in diameter to the span of the room below: the supporting walls could be pierced by large openings or recesses, and the compartments formed by the intersecting ribs could be filled with whatever the architect desired, be it *muqarnas*, rhomboidal faceting or yet smaller ribs to produce further subdivision. The result is a more fluid transition from floor to ceiling than had been achieved earlier. The rigid vertical division of dome chamber into cube, squinch and cupola gave way to a variety of possibilities limited only by the architect's imagination. This new-found freedom, combined with the reduction in the load-bearing elements and consequent opening of wall spaces, led to the refashioning of concepts of interior space, which was the most important development in 15th-century Iranian architecture.

Structural elements were invariably covered with decorative revetments. The most common and economical method of covering large exterior wall surfaces was the *bannā'ī* technique (*see* §9(ii)(b) below), which is seen, for example, on the Gur-i Mir and the madrasa at Khargird. Tile mosaic, far more expensive and labour-intensive, became more refined in colour and design, but few new patterns were created. Whereas *bannā'ī* technique, with its rectangular tiles, was ideal for geometric ornament and kufic inscriptions, tile mosaic was suitable for curved designs—floral and arboreal motifs, arabesques and cursive inscriptions. Individual tiles decorated with underglaze painting in the *cuerda seca* technique or with monochrome glaze were combined in large compositions. The moulded turquoise and white and the underglaze-painted tiles seen in the earliest tombs in the Shah-i Zinda necropolis at Samarkand soon fell out of fashion, although very limited quantities of the latter reappear in Khurasan during the first half of the 15th century. Several types of decorative revetments are combined on major monuments: tile mosaic, underglaze-painted tiles and *cuerda seca* tiles were used together at Gawharshad's mosque at Mashhad and her complex in Herat. The Turkoman buildings in Isfahan show exceptionally fine tile mosaic: in the Darb-i Imam there effective use was made of the amber gold that was to figure so prominently in the later Blue Mosque in Tabriz.

Interior surfaces, less exposed to the elements, were often plastered and painted. While some buildings were decorated with plaster carved in high relief, as they had been in the 14th century, a more popular method was to cover the entire surface with a decorative plaster shell which mimicked structural forms. Buildings in Herat and its environs (e.g. Gazur Gah, Taybad and Khargird; see fig. 52) display a sophisticated use of plaster squinches and *muqarnas*. Nothing remains of the rich wall paintings that once adorned the palaces of Timur and Abu Sa'id.

The best-preserved examples of wall painting are in the small building known as the Zarnigarkhana within the shrine at Gazur Gah: these share the delicacy of contemporary manuscript painting and may be related to carpet design. (*See also* §9(iii)(b) below.)

BIBLIOGRAPHY

D. Price: *Chronological Retrospect, or Memoirs of the Principal Events of Mohammedan History*, III/ii (London, 1821)

'The Travels of a Merchant in Persia'; Eng. trans. by C. Grey, *Travels in Tana and Persia*, ed. Lord Stanley of Alderly, Hakluyt Society Publications (London, 1873), pp. 141–207

R. Gonzalez de Clavijo: *Vida y hazañas del gran Tamorlan con la descripción de las tierras de su imperia y señoria* (St Petersburg, 1881/*R* 1971); Eng. trans. by G. le Strange as *Embassy to Tamerlane, 1403–1406* (London, 1928)

E. Cohn-Wiener: *Turan* (Berlin, 1930)

F. Saljuqi: *Gāzurgāh* (Kabul, 1962)

G. A. Pugachenkova: "Ishrat-Khaneh and Ak-Saray: Two Timurid Mausoleums in Samarkand', *A. Orient.*, v (1963), pp. 177–89

A. Mawlavi: 'Masjid-i Shāh yā maqbara-yi Amīr Ghiyāṣ al-Dīn Malikshāh' [The Masjid-i Shah of the tomb of Amir Ghiyath al-Din Malikshah], *Hunar va Mardum*, cxxiv–cxxv (Iran. Solar 1343/1965), pp. 37–45

F. Saljuqi: *Risāle-yi mazārāt-i Harāt* [Treatise on the shrines of Herat] (Kabul, 1967)

J. T. Tabataba'i: *Naqshhā va nigāshtahā-yi Masjid-i Kabūd-i Tabrīz* [Pictures and images of the Blue Mosque of Tabriz] (Tabriz, Iran. Solar 1347/1968)

L. Golombek: *The Timurid Shrine at Gazur Gah* (Toronto, 1969)

I. Afshar: *Yādgārhā-yi Yazd* [Monuments of Yazd], 3 vols (Tehran, Iran. Solar 1348–54/1970–76)

L. Hunarfarr: *Ganjīna-yi āsār-i tārīkhī-yi Isfahān* [A treasury of the historical monuments of Isfahan] (Isfahan, Iran. Solar 1350/1972)

A. Mawlavi: *Āsār-i bāstānī-yi Khurāsān* [Ancient monuments of Khurasan], i (Tehran, Iran. Solar 1354/1976)

B. O'Kane: 'The Madrasa al-Ghiyāṣiyya at Khargird', *Iran*, xiv (1976), pp. 79–92

52. Stucco vaulting, lecture hall, Ghiyathiyya Madrasa, Khargird, Iran, 1444–5

The Citadel and Minarets of Herat, Afghanistan, UNESCO (n.p., 1976)

L. Hunarfarr: *Isfahān dar dawra-yi jānishīnhā-yi Timūr* [Isfahan at the time of the successors of Timur] (Tehran, Iran. Imp. 2535/1977)

N. B. Nemtseva: 'Istoki kompozitsii i etapy formirovaniya ansamblaya Shakhi-Zinda' [The origins and architectural development of the Shah-Zinda]; Eng. trans. with additions by J. M. Rogers and A. Yasin, *Iran*, xv (1977), pp. 51–74

M. E. Masson and G. A. Pugachenkova: 'Shakhri Syabz pri Timure i Ulug Beke' [Shahr-i Sabz from Timur to Ulughbeg]; Eng. trans., ed. J. M. Rogers, *Iran*, xvi (1978), pp. 103–26; xviii (1980), pp. 121–44

B. O'Kane: 'Tāybād, Turbat-i Jām and Timurid Vaulting', *Iran*, xvii (1979), pp. 87–104

N. B. Nourmoukhammedov: *The Mausoleum of Hodja Ahmed Yasavi* (Alma-Ata, 1980)

T. Allen: *A Catalogue of the Toponyms and Monuments of Timurid Herat* (Cambridge, MA, 1981)

C. Melville: 'Historical Monuments and Earthquakes in Tabriz', *Iran*, xix (1981), pp. 159–77

G. A. Pugachenkova: *Chefs d'oeuvre d'architecture de l'Asie Centrale, XIVe–XVe siècles* (Paris, 1981)

T. Allen: *Timurid Herat* (Wiesbaden, 1983)

B. O'Kane: 'Timurid Stucco Decoration', *An. Islam.*, xx (1984), pp. 61–84

L. Man'kovskaia: 'Towards the Study of Forms in Central Asian Architecture at the End of the Fourteenth Century', *Iran*, xxiii (1985), pp. 109–29

B. O'Kane: 'The Tiled Minbars of Iran', *An. Islam.*, xxii (1986), pp. 133–53

——: *Timurid Architecture in Khurasan* (Costa Mesa, 1987)

L. Golombek and D. Wilber: *The Timurid Architecture of Iran and Turan*, 2 vols (Princeton, 1988)

B. O'Kane: 'From Tents to Pavilions: Royal Mobility and Persian Palace Design', *A. Orient.*, xxiii (1993), pp. 248–68

BERNARD O'KANE

(c) Indian subcontinent. Architectural developments under the Delhi sultanates are epitomized by the Quwwat al-Islam Mosque in the capital (begun 1197; *see* DELHI, §III, 1). Arches and domes were initially simulated with corbelling, as in the Aybak screen (1199), but by the time of the KHALJI dynasty (*reg* 1290–1320) true arches with voussoirs became the rule and true domes on squinches were often used, as at the 'Ala'i Darvaza (1305). The Qutb Minar (1199 and 1368; h. 72.5 m), like minarets erected earlier by the Ghaznavids in Afghanistan (*see* §5(i)(c) above), has superimposed flanged and cylindrical shafts separated by *muqarnas* cornices and decorated with inscriptions; unlike them it is built of sandstone. The domed tomb of Ghiyath al-Din Tughluq (1320–25; *see* DELHI, §III, 2) has battered walls in the style of MULTAN built of rubble faced with red sandstone and white marble. The battered walls, prominent dome capped by a finial and four-centred arch become prominent features in Indo-Islamic architecture.

Distinctive regional styles developed in the other Muslim states. That of JAUNPUR in north India, for example, is characterized by tall gateways, such as the one in front of the Atala Mosque (1377–1404). A particularly distinctive regional style developed in Gujarat and Rajasthan in western India and is exemplified by the congregational mosque at Ahmadabad (1423; *see* AHMADABAD, §3). Its trabeate hypostyle hall is covered with 15 corbelled domes and screened by an exquisitely carved arched façade. Multan and Sind had strong links to Afghanistan and eastern Iran, and its distinctive architectural style used bricks, glazed tile and wood for roofs and tie-beams. The tomb of Rukn al-Din 'Alam at Multan (1320–24), erected by Ghiyath al-Din Tughluq, has an octagonal plan, battered walls, corner turrets and finials. Architecture in Bengal

continues the indigenous tradition of brick construction. Many of the mosques there are characterized by multiple mihrabs, such as that of Zafar Khan Ghazi in Tribeni (1298), which has five. They are distinguished from pre-Islamic construction by curved cornices, fine terracotta decoration and engaged corner towers. Under the sultans of Malwa (*reg* 1401–1531) major buildings were erected on high plinths, and colour was used extensively in tile revetments and polychrome inlay of marble and stone. Mosques, tombs and palaces in Dhar and MANDU show the strong impact of the earlier Delhi tradition. In the Deccan the BAHMANI sultanate largely ignored indigenous architectural traditions. Buildings in its first capital at GULBARGA (1347–1425) followed the style of contemporary architecture in the Delhi sultanate in such features as battered walls, while at Bidar, capital from 1425 to 1518, the architectural style of contemporary Iran and Central Asia under the Timurids became increasingly apparent in such features as domes raised on tall drums, glazed tilework and the four-iwan plan (*see* INDIAN SUBCONTINENT, §III, 6(ii)).

□

(ii) Anatolia. Architectural patronage in Anatolia from the mid-13th century to the late 15th was in the hands of numerous Turkoman principalities (Turk. *beylik*). Two of them, the Aqqoyunlu and the Qaraqoyunlu, who ruled the eastern region, became major powers in western Iran (*see* §(i)(b) above). Another principality, the Ottoman, which ruled in the north-west, eventually subsumed the others and expanded into Europe. After the Ottomans had conquered the Byzantine empire of Constantinople (now Istanbul) in 1453 and moved their capital there, they became a major world power, and their architecture began to express their imperial role in new ways (*see* §7(i) below). The regional diversity of the principalities is reflected in their varied architectural styles, which were eventually subsumed by the homogeneous imperial style of the Ottomans.

Architecture in central and eastern Anatolia shows a strong sense of continuity with the preceding period (*see* §5(iii) above). In principalities such as Karaman and Eretna, stone, brick and wood continued to be used in the traditional manner. Low, massive walls with small windows support vaults and domes on squinches, pendentives or Turkish triangles. Plans are conservative, although new elements, such as the mosque portico and tomb vestibule, are occasionally introduced. Architectural decoration in tile and relief-carved stone also strongly follows earlier prototypes, although such details as the width of portals change.

The western principalities, such as Menteşe, Aydin, Saruhan and Germiyan (and the Ottomans), located in regions rich in Greek, Roman and Byzantine monuments and closely linked to the Mediterranean world, experimented not only with traditional Anatolian Turkish formal and structural elements but with Byzantine and Mediterranean ones as well. Alternating courses of brick and stone follow the Byzantine mode, marble revetments cover façades, new mosque plans appear and porticos are often appended to façades. The domical vaults of mosques are enlarged to unify interior space, and courtyards are appended to them. In contrast to the earlier period when the madrasa and the caravanserai were the most significant building types, the mosque became the outstanding expression of the builder's craft. Western Anatolia during the 14th century and the early 15th gave rise to elements of a new style of Turkish architecture that found its highest development under the Ottomans.

(a) Beyliks. (b) Ottomans to 1453.

(a) Beyliks. The Saljuqs of Rum were defeated by the Mongols at Kösedagh in 1243 (*see* §5(iii) above), but they continued to rule in name for the remainder of the century. Under indirect ILKHANID rule in the nominally Saljuq lands of the east, local patrons erected modest buildings in such towns as SIVAS, Tokat, Niksar and ERZURUM in the late 13th century and the early 14th. The Turkoman princes of the southern and western frontier regions built little at first, but by the mid-14th century they began to express their ambition and piety through patronage, and Karaman, Ermenak, Muğla, Peçin, Manisa, Kütahya, Iznik (*see* IZNIK, §2) and BURSA emerged as new centres of architecture. This proliferation of architectural centres ruptured the stylistic unity of the preceding period. Central and eastern Anatolia, with old and deeply rooted Islamic traditions, continued the style of earlier centuries, but the western principalities experimented by synthesizing older elements with ideas encountered in the newly acquired lands on the western frontier.

Mosques. Five types of mosques were built: single-domed square, hypostyle, wooden, basilical and the T-plan (also known as the Bursa- or zawiya-type [Turk. *zaviyeli*] and multi-purpose) mosque. The single-domed square, built throughout Anatolia in the 14th and 15th centuries, is the most common type; its antecedents lie in the early 13th century. The simplest ones, for example the Saray Mosque in Sinop (1374) or the Pekmez Pazarı Mosque in Kütahya (1381), have a square prayer-hall covered with a domical vault. More elaborate examples, such as the Kurşunlu Mosque in Kütahya (1377) and the Ak Mescid in Afyon (1397), have porches of two, three or five domed or vaulted bays across the façade. The transition from square base to dome was made either by squinches, as in the Kazırzade Mosque in Tire (late 14th century) and the Ilyas Bey Mosque in Balat (1404), or, more frequently, by a belt of prismatic consoles, usually called Turkish triangles, as in the Kubbeli Mosque in Afyon (1330) and the Yelli Mosque in Peçin (late 14th century). Minarets were built at the ends of façades, although many smaller mosques lack minarets and a few have them appended to the qibla wall. The minaret is detached at the Kazırzade Mosque in Tire and the Şeyh Matar Mosque in DIYARBAKIR (1500).

Hypostyle mosques show considerable diversity. The archaic type associated with the beylik of Karaman has interior arcades or colonnades parallel to the qibla wall. The Ulu Cami of Ermenak (1302), for example, is a plainly constructed building with a rectangular prayer-hall covered by a flat timber and earthen roof; a small entry vestibule stands to the west. A closely related type, chiefly associated with the Ottomans, has piers or columns dividing the

interior space into equal bays covered by domical vaults. The earliest securely dated example is the Hamidid Yivli Minare Mosque in Antalya (1373). Built on the foundations of a Byzantine church, the mosque has twelve reused columns dividing the interior into six bays covered with red-tiled domical vaults on Turkish triangles and a long, narrow barrel vault in the west. In eastern Anatolia, the Qaraqoyunlu and Aqqoyunlu Turkomans used this type in the Kızıl Mosque in Bitlis (14th century) and the Ibrahim Bey Mosque in Diyarbakır (late 15th century). A third variant, with clear 13th-century prototypes, has arcades perpendicular to the qibla wall and often a wider and higher central aisle and dome over the bay in front of the mihrab. The Saruhanid congregational mosque of Manisa (1371; see fig. 53) has a dome (diam. 10.8 m) that rests on an octagonal drum and eight piers and dominates the hypostyle prayer-hall. The prayer-hall is preceded by a fountain court which has arcades on three sides and is similar to the mosque in size and plan. A similar fountain court is found at the Isa Bey Mosque of Selçuk, near Ephesos (1374; see fig. 54), built for the amir of Aydin by 'Ali ibn al-Dimishqi (of Damascus). Its plan, based on the 8th-century Great Mosque of Damascus (*see* §3(i) above), features an arcade that is parallel to the qibla wall and divides the broad rectangular prayer-hall into two aisles; it is intersected by a transept of two domes on pendentives. Minarets flank the façade to the courtyard, which is surrounded by colonnaded porticos and monumental gateways.

Wooden mosques, with wooden interior supports and flat wooden roofs, are variants on the hypostyle type. Notable early examples, dating to the latter part of the preceding Saljuq period, include the Sahib Ata/Larende Mosque in KONYA (1258), the Great Mosques of Afyon (1372) and Sivrihisar (1275) and the Arslanhane Mosque in ANKARA (1289–90). The Eşrefoğlu Mosque in Beyşehir (1297) has an asymmetrical five-sided stone wall enclosing a hypostyle prayer-hall with six rows of great timber supports at right angles to the qibla wall. The aisle on the mihrab axis is emphasized by greater width and height, by a dome in front of the mihrab and by a tiny fountain court in the middle bay. Later examples, such as the Şah Mosque in Niğde (1343) and the Meram Mosque outside Konya (1402–24), are found in central Anatolia, although several of the finest wooden mosques have survived in the region of Kastamonu on the Black Sea coast (e.g. the Mahmud Bey Mosque in Kasaba Köyü; 1366).

Basilical mosques, such as that of Sungur Bey in Niğde (1335; reconstr. 18th century), continued to be built in the traditional style. It was a conservative three-aisled basilical structure with four domes along the central aisle and curious Gothic elements over its east portal. Other examples are the Great Mosque in Milas (1378) built by Ahmet Gazi and the Ulu Cami in Bergama (1398). The T-plan mosque was used almost exclusively by the Ottomans (*see* §(b) below), but one was built in 1394 at Milas by Firuz Bey, the Menteşeid governor for the Ottomans.

Madrasas, hospitals and hospices. Madrasas and hospitals, like those of the preceding period, are essentially similar in form and are of two types. The more common open-court type is found throughout Anatolia and is hardly

53. Congregational mosque, Manisa, Turkey, 1371

54. Isa Bey Mosque, Selçuk, Turkey, 1374

distinguished in plan or decoration from 13th-century examples. The two-iwan Hatuniye Madrasa in Karaman (1382), for example, is a rectangular structure with classroom and entry iwans on the axes of the short sides of the courtyard and student cells behind the arcaded portico along the long sides. A monumental stone portal in the 13th-century manner further enhances its archaism. The finely wrought Ak Medrese in Niğde (1404) is remarkable for its two-storey construction and balcony with ogee arcades across the upper part of the main façade flanking a traditional monumental portal. The large and traditional Zincirli Madrasa in Aksaray (1336) is notable for its four-iwan plan. Closed-court madrasas also derive from earlier models. The Yakutiye and Ahmediye madrasas in Erzurum (1310 and 1314, respectively) are the earliest Beylik examples. Both have groin- and barrel-vaulted central courts similar to 13th-century examples, and the fine relief-carved portal, two-minaret façade and domed mausoleum of the Yakutiye clearly imitate the nearby Çifte Minareli Madrasa (*c.* 1250; *see* MUQARNAS, fig. 1). The Emir Musa Madrasa (1352; destr.) and the Ibrahim Bey Imaret (1433), both in Karaman, and the Germiyanid Vacidiye Madrasa in Kütahya (1314) are closer to the Konya tradition of closed-court madrasas, having a single large hemispherical dome over a square central court. The Ibrahim Bey Imaret is especially fine: the two-storey complex included a soup-kitchen (Turk. *imaret*), mosque, madrasa and Koran school. The zone of transition below its dome is particularly conservative, being one of the latest examples of the use of fan pendentives.

Dervish cloisters (Turk. *hankah, tekke, zaviye; see* KHANAQAH) are generally modest in scale. Several late 13th-century examples are found in the region of Tokat, such as those of Sumbul Baba (1291–2) and Halifet Gazi (1291–2) in the city itself. The cloister of Sitti Zeynip outside Alanya (15th century) has three irregular vaulted chambers of rubble masonry adjacent to the saint's tomb. Far grander is the Köşk Medrese outside KAYSERI, built by the Amir of Eretna in 1339. High crenellated walls of cut stone, a small portal and tall slit windows give the rectangular structure a fortified appearance. Within, a pair of vaulted rooms flank the entry iwan, which opens on to a small courtyard enclosed with arcaded porticos. At the centre stands the octagonal tomb of Suli, the patron's wife.

Funerary architecture. Commemorative architecture proliferated rapidly in the Anatolian Beyliks, and was considerably more diverse and experimental than in the earlier Saljuq period. The 13th-century arrangement of partially buried crypt and superimposed prayer-chamber was retained in the Turkoman principalities, and polygonal, circular and square tower tombs with conical, tetrahedral or polyhedral caps continued to be standard, although a great variety of new devices was developed to monumentalize portals, facilitate the transition from base to shaft and enrich façades. Most mausolea of the period are variants on the tomb-tower type, but a small number continue the iwan type of the 13th century. The octagonal tomb tower is most common, ranging from the plain tomb of Şeyh Süleyman (1301) adjoining the Eşrefoğlu Mosque in Beyşehir to the elaborate tomb of Hüdavend Hatun in Niğde (1312), the exterior surfaces of which are richly worked in geometric, vegetal and zoomorphic relief patterns. Occasionally tombs of this sort, such as that of Ali Cafer in Kayseri (*c.* 1350), have a small porch-vestibule or domed portico added to the entry façade. Other polygonal tombs are hexagonal, such as those of the Mansur Baba and Şeyh Şeraffedin of Harput (both 14th century); pentagonal, such as the Yörük Dede Tomb in Ankara (late 14th century); and dodecagonal, a type particularly associated with the Qaraqoyunlu in the region of Lake Van, such as the tomb of Halime Hatun in Gevaş (1358).

Cylindrical tombs with conical caps are less common and are found mainly in central and eastern Anatolia. The Eretnid Sırçalı tomb in Kayseri (mid-14th century) is simple and dignified, while the tomb of the Aqqoyunlu amir Bayindir at Ahlat (1481) stands on a high square crypt with bevelled corners. Its cylindrical shaft is open for more than half its circumference with an arcade on squat columns. The Aqqoyunlu tomb of Zeynel Mirza at Hasankeyf (second half of the 15th century) has a cylindrical shaft of brick decorated with tile mosaic in the manner of contemporary Timurid buildings in western Central Asia (*see* §(i)(b) above). Square tomb towers form a more complex group. The typical example, such as the tomb of Fakih Dede in Konya (1454), has a square base supporting an octagonal drum with prismatic elements in the zone of transition that resemble exposed squinches. The Güdük Minare Türbesi (1348) in Sivas, which is the tomb of Hasan Beg, the amir of Eretna, has a system of exposed Turkish triangles separating the cylindrical shaft and conical roof. The tombs of Seyyid Mahmud Hayrani in Akşehir and Celal al-Din Rumi in Konya, which have great fluted cylindrical drums above their square bases, were 13th-century foundations rebuilt by Karamanid amirs in the early 15th century. The most extraordinary variant is the marble tomb of Aşık Pasha in Kirşehir (1322–33). A monumental gateway enriched with a knotted border and scallop-headed niche opens on to a long, narrow corridor leading to a square prayer-chamber surmounted by a low octagonal drum and dome.

Secular buildings. Several palaces and pavilions have been identified from the period, although most civil and commercial structures have been extensively reworked in later times. The most important is the early 14th-century palace of Taşkin Pasha at Damsa Köyü near Ürgüp. Larger and more spacious than surviving 13th-century palaces, it has a monumental portal in the Saljuq style leading to the interior, where a series of small rooms open off a large central hall. It is constructed of rubble except for a small mosque built of marble ashlar with a finely worked mihrab. The flat roof was of thick timber beams overlaid with earth. More modest palaces and pavilions have been identified near Alanya, at Aksaray and at Peçin.

Baths such as the Eşrefoğlu Hammam in Beyşehir (1297) survive from the early years of the period. Their organization ultimately derives from Roman *thermae*, but the domed *caldarium* often has a four-iwan plan with private chambers in the corners. Baths from the 14th and 15th centuries are found in many regions of Anatolia, including Konya, Peçin and Balat. The Hasbey Hammam in Meram outside Konya (1424) is a large double bath symmetrically planned with separate facilities for men and women. Fourteenth-century covered bazaars (Turk. *bedestan*) survive in Beyşehir and Tire, although they were substantially altered in later centuries. Caravanserais were modest in scale and execution, since individual principalities could not support great programmes to develop trade routes of the kind that had taken place under the Saljuqs. Such buildings as the Menteşeid Üçgöz (Karapaşa) Caravanserai at Peçin and the Karamanid caravanserai at Alanya perpetuate earlier types. The great Yeni Han on the Tokat–Sivas road is substantially an Ottoman building despite its inscription dating it to 1330.

BIBLIOGRAPHY
A. Gabriel: *Les Monuments turcs d'Anatolie*, 2 vols (Paris, 1931–4)
R. Riefstahl: *Turkish Architecture in Southwestern Anatolia* (Cambridge, MA, 1931)
K. Wulzinger, P. Wittek and F. Sarre: *Das islamische Milet* (Leipzig, 1935)
I. H. Uzunçarşılı: 'İbrahim Bey'in Karaman imareti vakfiyesi' [The vakfiye of the *imaret* of Ibrahim Bey in Karaman], *Türk Tarih Kurumu: Belleten*, i (1937), pp. 65–164
A. Gabriel: *Voyages archéologiques dans la Turquie orientale*, 2 vols (Paris, 1940)
A. S. Ülgen: 'Kırşehir'de Türk eserleri' [Turkish monuments in Kırşehir], *Vakıflar Derg.*, ii (1942), pp. 253–61
A. Sayılı: 'Vacidiye medresesi' [The Vacidiye madrasa], *Türk Tarih Kurumu: Belleten*, xii (1948), pp. 663–7
E. Diez, O. Aslanapa and M. M. Koman: *Karaman devri sanatı* [The art of the Karaman period] (Istanbul, 1950)
K. Otto-Dorn: 'Die Isa Bey Moschee in Ephesus', *Istanbul. Forsch.*, xvii (1950), pp. 115–31
O. Aslanapa: 'Doğu Anadolu'da Karakoyunlu türberleri' [Qarakoyunlu tombs in eastern Anatolia], *Ankara Ü. İlahiyat Fak. Yıllık Araştırmalar Derg.*, i (1956), pp. 105–13
A. Kızıltan: *Anadolu beyliklerinde cami ve mescitler* [Congregational and quarter mosques of the Anatolian principalities] (Istanbul, 1958)
K. Erdmann: 'Saraybauten des dreizehnten und vierzehnten Jahrhunderts in Anatolien', *A. Orient.*, iii (1959), pp. 77–94
M. Arel: 'Muttakı Karamanoğulları devri eserleri' [Monuments in Mut of the Karamanid period], *Vakıflar Derg.*, v (1962), pp. 241–50
T. Özgüç: 'Monuments of the Period of Taşkın Paşa's Principality', *Atti del secondo congresso internazionale di arte turca: Napoli, 1965*, pp. 197–201
I. Akçay: 'Yakutiye medresesi' [The Yakutiye madrasa], *Vakıflar Derg.*, vi (1966), pp. 146–52
M. O. Arık: 'Erken devir Anadolu-Türk mimarısında türbe biçimleri' [Tomb types in Anatolian–Turkish architecture of the early period], *Anatolia*, xi (1967), pp. 57–100
A. Arel: 'Menteşe beyliği devrinde Peçin şehri' [The city of Peçin in the period of the principality of Menteşe], *Anadolu Sanatı Araştırmaları*, i (1968), pp. 69–98
R. H. Ünal: *Les Monuments islamiques anciens de la ville d'Erzurum et de sa région* (Paris, 1968)
Ü. Ü. Bates: *The Anatolian Mausoleum of the Twelfth, Thirteenth and Fourteenth Centuries* (diss., U. Michigan, 1970)
A. Akarca: 'Beçin' [Peçin], *Türk Tarih Kurumu: Belleten*, xxxv (1971), pp. 1–37
O. Aslanapa: 'Kazısı tamamlandıktan sonra Van Ulu Camii' [The congregational mosque of Van after completion of its excavation], *Sanat Tarihi Yıllığı*, v (1972–3), pp. 1–25
M. Sözen: *Anadolu medreseleri: Selçuklu ve beylikler devri* [Anatolian madrasas: the Saljuq and Beylik periods], 2 vols (Istanbul, 1972)
N. Emre: 'Aydınoğulları ve esereler' [The Aydinids and their monuments], *Arkitekt*, x–xi (1973), pp. 307–20
I. Aslanoğlu: *Tire'de camiler ve üç mescid* [Congregational mosques and three smaller mosques in Tire] (Ankara, 1978)
M. O. Arık: 'Turkish Architecture in Asia Minor in the Period of the Turkish Emirates', *The Art and Architecture of Turkey*, ed. E. Akurgal (New York, 1980), pp. 111–36

HOWARD CRANE

(b) Ottomans to 1453. The architecture of the Ottoman principality in north-west Anatolia and Thrace from its emergence *c.* 1300 to the conquest of Constantinople in 1453 (*see* OTTOMAN, §I) was similar to that of the other Beyliks in the region (*see* §(a) above) in combining elements of traditional Anatolian Islamic architecture with local building materials and techniques. Early Ottoman architecture differed, however, in its simplicity, rationality and reliance on domes.

The early Ottomans built three types of mosque: a single-domed square, a multi-unit mosque and a T-plan mosque. The single-domed mosque became common in western Anatolia in the 14th century when the Ottomans, like other princelings, built scores of them. Preceded by a three-bay portico, the typical mosque has a square base, a band of Turkish triangles and a hemispheric dome (diam. 8–11 m). For example, the Alaeddin Bey Mosque in BURSA (1335–6) has walls built of alternating courses of stone and brick; the three arches of its portico are supported by four Byzantine columns. Only a few examples depart from the model. The Orhan Gazi Mosque in Bilecik (first half of the 14th century) has no portico, and its dome is supported by four large arches that spring from the corners of the room and allow the interior space to be expanded in four large recesses. The Green Mosque (Turk. Yeşil Cami) in Iznik (1378–91; *see* IZNIK, §2), built by Hacı bin Musa for the grand vizier Hayreddin Pasha, was expanded with an interior vestibule of three bays. The mosque of Yıldırım Bayezid in Mudurnu (1382) has an unusually large dome (diam. 19.65 m), which stretched the limits of the single-unit type in early Ottoman architecture.

Larger spaces were traditionally obtained with a hypostyle structure repeating smaller units. Several early Ottoman mosques belong to this type. The most important is the Great Mosque (Turk. Ulu Cami) of Bursa (1396–1400), a rectangular stone building measuring 56 by 68 m. The walls and 12 massive piers support a grid of 20 lofty domes (diam. 9 m) resting on pendentives. The domes along the central north–south axis are slightly higher; an oculus in the second bay creates an interior court, which has a fountain for ablutions. Other mosques of this type were built in Bolu, Çankırı, Kütahya and Söğüt, but only the Eski Cami in EDIRNE (1402–13) survives. The Üç Şerefeli Mosque in Edirne (1437–47; *see* MOSQUE, fig. 3), built by Murad II and perhaps the most important mosque erected before the conquest of Constantinople, is entirely different: its massive central dome, arcaded courtyard and multiple minarets foreshadow later imperial Ottoman mosques (*see* §7(i) below).

T-plan mosques, the most original type in early Ottoman architecture, combined mosques with dervish hostels. Sultans often built them for the religious brotherhoods they supported. The mosques were arranged somewhat like closed-court madrasas of the 13th century. The earliest example was the mosque of Orhan Gazi at Iznik (1334; destr.), which had a porch leading to a domed central hall and a barrel-vaulted iwan; on either side were long, narrow rooms for itinerant dervishes. The mosque of Murad I at Çekirge near Bursa (1385; see fig. 55), often known as the Hüdavendigâr Mosque, is a more complex version in which each wing of the lower storey contains an auxiliary iwan and three rooms for dervishes; the upper storey has a 16-unit madrasa surrounding the central hall. In the reign of Bayezid I (1389–1402) Ottoman architects began to replace barrel vaults with domes, first in the iwans and then in the hostel rooms. As the superstructure became

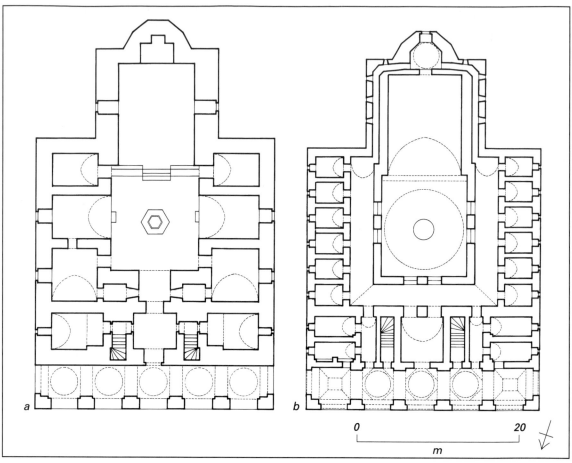

55. Mosque of Murad I (Hüdavendigâr Mosque), Çekirge, near Bursa, Turkey, 1385, plans: (a) lower storey; (b) upper storey

domed, the plan became increasingly geometric. Domes surmount the main iwan and hostel rooms in the mosque of Bayezid Pasha in Amasya (1419) and all the spatial units in the mosque of Gedik Ahmed Pasha in Afyon (1472–3). Some multi-purpose mosques were parts of larger building complexes. The Yeşil complex of Mehmed I in Bursa (1412–24), for example, combines a madrasa, soup-kitchen, bath and tomb with a mosque, but the individual elements are placed in response to the terrain and vistas, and the resulting arrangement is somewhat haphazard.

Hexagonal and octagonal tombs were common. Among the most remarkable are the hexagonal tomb of Şehzade Mustafa in the Muradiye Cemetery in Bursa (*c.* 1479) and the octagonal tomb of Mehmed I in the same city (*c.* 1421). The latter's turquoise, blue and yellow tiles covering the portal, interior walls, mihrab and cenotaph represent the finest ceramics from the pre-Iznik period and give the building its common sobriquet, Yeşil Türbe (Green Tomb).

Unlike the Saljuqs, who developed commerce by build-ing caravanserais (Turk. *han*) along the Anatolian trade routes, the early Ottomans concentrated on building urban commercial centres consisting of caravanserais and *arastas* (streets lined with shops selling the same type of com-modity), for wholesale and retail trade respectively, and a bazaar (*bedestan*), where the most valuable merchandise was sold. The early Ottoman urban caravanserais, such as the Emir Han of Orhan Gazi (*reg c.* 1324–60) and the Ipek (Silk) Han of Mehmed I (*reg* 1403–21), both in Bursa, were two-storey structures arranged around spacious courtyards. Storerooms and business offices occupied the ground floor, with guest rooms upstairs. During the reign of Bayezid I the bazaar became the most important building, after the congregational mosque, in the core of an Ottoman town. Typically a sturdy rectangular structure with a gateway in the middle of each of its four sides, it was a double-aisled building with domes arranged in pairs. Depending on the size of the town and the volume of trade, the number of domes could range from four at Amasya to fourteen at Bursa and Edirne. The Issız ('Desolate') Han near Ulubat (*c.* 1394), an early Ottoman rural caravanserai, has two rooms flanking the entrance iwan and a long triple-aisled hall.

Anadolu Hisar (1394–5) and Rumeli Hisar (1452), the forts on the Anatolian and European shores of the Bosporus at its narrowest point, are good examples of early Ottoman military architecture. They were built by Bayezid I and Mehmed II respectively to control naviga-tion between the Black Sea and the Sea of Marmara (*see* MILITARY ARCHITECTURE AND FORTIFICATION, §IV, 3).

The most remarkable of the numerous early Ottoman bridges is the Uzun Köprü (Long Bridge; 1443–4) near Edirne, which is 1254 m long and has 164 (originally 174) arches spanning the marshy Ergene Valley. It attests to the level of engineering skill acquired by the Ottomans prior to the conquest of Constantinople.

The basic element of construction was the thin square brick. Arches, vaults and domes were built exclusively of brick and covered with terracotta roof-tiles, now usually replaced by lead sheets. Walls were often constructed of two or three courses of brick alternating with one of stone, a typical Byzantine technique. Important buildings often had ashlar walls and brick domes sheathed with lead. Reused Roman or Byzantine capitals and Byzantine motifs often enlivened exteriors. Behind them, however, traditional Turkish elements, such as squinches and bands of prismatic consoles (Turkish triangles), supported domes, and glazed ceramic tiles and marble fretwork decorated important areas of interiors, such as the sultan's loge and the wall surfaces around the mihrab.

BIBLIOGRAPHY
K. Otto-Dorn: *Das islamische Iznik* (Berlin, 1941)
A. Gabriel: 'Bursa'da Murad I. camii ve Osmanli mimarisinin menşei meselesi/La Mosquée de Murat 1er à Brousse et le problème des origines de l'architecture ottomane', *Vakıflar Derg.*, ii (1942), pp. 37–43, 49–57
——: *Une Capitale turque: Brousse*, 2 vols (Paris, 1958)
S. Eyice: 'İlk osmanli devrinin dini-içtimai bir müessesesi: Zaviyeler ve zaviyeli camiler' [A socio-religious institution of the early Ottoman period: zawiyas and zawiya-mosques], *Istanbul U. Iktisat Fak. Mecmuası*, xxxiii (1962–3), pp. 1–80 [with Fr. summary]
O. Aslanapa: 'Iznik'te Sultan Orhan Imaret camii kazisi/Die Ausgrabungen der Sultan Orhan Imaret Moschee von Iznik', *Sanat Tarihi Yıllığı*, i (1964–5), pp. 16–38
E. H. Ayverdi: 'Bursa Orhangazi camii ve Osmanli mimarisinin mesei meselesi' [The mosque of Orhan Gazi in Bursa and the problem of the origin of Ottoman architecture], *Vakıflar Derg.*, vi (1965), pp. 69–83
A. Kuran: *The Mosque in Early Ottoman Architecture* (Chicago and London, 1968)
O. Aslanapa: *Turkish Art and Architecture* (London, 1971)
G. Goodwin: *A History of Ottoman Architecture* (Baltimore and London, 1971)

APTULLAH KURAN

(iii) Central Islamic lands. The Mongol devastation of Iraq made Syria and particularly Egypt the centre of a distinct Arab Islamic culture as Iraq was incorporated into the Iranian world and northern Mesopotamia into Syria and Anatolia. Egypt, Syria and western Arabia were controlled by the Mamluk sultans (*reg* 1250–1517), whose capital, Cairo, became the largest and most populous city of the Mediterranean world. Pious foundations built of fine masonry were wedged into the increasingly dense urban fabric of Cairo, Damascus, Aleppo and Jerusalem. In the Yemen, which maintained its close political ties with Egypt, a distinct but related style of architecture developed under the RASULID (*reg* 1229–1454) and Tahirid (*reg* 1482–1526) dynasties.

(a) Egypt and Syria. (b) Yemen.

(a) Egypt and Syria. Dominated by the patronage of the Mamluk amirs, a self-perpetuating corporation of military slaves (*see* MAMLUK, §II, 1), the architecture of this period is characterized by prolific and splendid monumental construction in Cairo, the most populous city in medieval Islamic lands (*see* CAIRO, §I, 2), and in such other leading cities of the empire as Damascus (*see* DAMASCUS, §1(ii)) and ALEPPO. Architectural style was characterized by an exchange between Syria and Egypt, which was still dominated by the distinctive tradition of urban architecture in Cairo (*see* §5(ii)(c) above). There were also occasional contacts with contemporary architecture in North Africa, Anatolia, Iran, possibly western Central Asia, as well as crusader buildings in Sicily and along the Syrian littoral. Financed by flourishing east–west trade, Mamluk buildings symbolized the power of their patrons, first Bahri Turkish *mamlūk*s (*reg* 1250–1390), and then Burji Circassian *mamlūk*s (*reg* 1382–1517).

Introduction. The most characteristic monument was the funerary complex, which combined the mausoleum of the founder with a mosque, madrasa, *khānaqāh*, drinking-water dispensary, Koran school and occasionally a hospital. Tomb complexes were subsidized by pious endowments (Arab. *waqf*; *see* ISLAM, §III) that set aside in trust such income-producing properties as rentals, baths, mills, shops and agricultural lands. The religious functions and associations of these pious foundations made their preservation more likely than that of such other Mamluk constructions as palaces, public baths and fortifications, which have perished through destruction, use or neglect. The Koran school and drinking-water dispensary provided the 'two mercies' most commended by the Prophet: teaching the Koran and giving water to the thirsty. These charitable institutions furnished justification for a monumental tomb, a type of building on which the pious often frowned.

There was also a strong economic incentive in this period for such endowments. Mamluk amirs were recruited exclusively from slaves (usually Turks or Circassians), and since no amir's son could become a slave (because he was a Muslim) he was excluded from entering the élite corps or inheriting his father's position. All that an amir possessed could be considered crown property, so his descendants might inherit little from him directly. But property set aside to support a pious foundation was not liable to seizure by the sultan, and the patron could provide for his descendants by making them supervisors or beneficiaries of the trust. The sultan, with much greater resources at his disposal than most amirs, had the same incentive to build monuments that might provide livelihoods for his descendants. He himself was usually one of the amirs, although occasionally a sultan's son was allowed to succeed him, often as the creature of strong amirs. Sultans and amirs therefore built to seek immortality in living memory and to foster intercessionary prayer for the life to come. According to the scholar Ibn Khaldun, who lived in Cairo for the quarter-century before his death in 1382, incomes and profits from endowments became huge, and the numbers of students and teachers multiplied because of the generous stipends available.

Cairo, the capital of the empire, seat of the sultan and the city where the amirs vied most dramatically for dominance and repute, received the largest, most spectacular and greatest number of foundations: 910 documented projects of which 210 remain. Other centres of patronage were the vice-regal cities of Damascus (253 projects of which 50 remain) and Aleppo (232 projects of which 49 remain). The holy city of MECCA had 101 documented projects and MEDINA had 50. Other important religious centres were Jerusalem (*see* JERUSALEM, §I, 3), with 147 projects of which 62 remain, and Hebron, with 24 projects of which 6 remain. TRIPOLI of Syria, seat of a Mamluk governorate, had 46 building projects (35 remain), Hama had 25 (6 remain; *see* HAMA, §2), Safad had 15 (4 remain). Elsewhere in Syria, Qal'at al-Hisn had 14 (7 remain), and Baalbek, Ramla, Homs and Nablus are each said to have had over a dozen foundations. In Egypt, Alexandria had 32 (*see* ALEXANDRIA, §4), and buildings were erected in such smaller cities as Siryaqus, Qus and Faiyum. During Timur's invasion of Syria in 1400–01, both Aleppo and Damascus were burnt, and many fine buildings were destroyed, especially in Damascus, so few examples of early Mamluk architecture survive in Syria.

As symbols and sources of power, Mamluk buildings had to be sited prominently. In Cairo the choicest sites were along the *qaṣaba*, the processional way that ran between the gates known as the Bab al-Futuh and the Bab Zuwayla within the Fatimid walled city. Sites there were available only to the sultan, and the amirs usually built on the winding side streets or in the suburbs, especially along the Darb al-Ahmar, which stretched from the Bab Zuwayla to the Citadel. No other city could compete with Cairo in prestige, but amirs who resided in other cities and derived power from local support had considerable incentive to build in them.

Within each site builders had to meet three requirements. Any parts of a building intended to be used for prayer had to be orientated towards Mecca, which in the case of Cairo lies to the south-east. The façade of the building had to be aligned with streets already laid out without concern for the qibla. Finally, the tomb, which often provided the justification for the building, had to be placed prominently on the façade, as did the portal and the minaret, so as to dominate visually the public space of the street. Urban building sites, usually acquired by purchasing and razing old residences which had grown up arbitrarily, were often irregular, and architects in Cairo learnt to build on almost any shape of site. No other Muslim city exhibits so many ingenious adaptations of monument to site, and Cairo seems occasionally to have provided an example for other Mamluk cities.

The building traditions of Cairo, Damascus and Aleppo dominate architecture of the period. In Cairo the highly conservative tradition of architecture meant that materials, forms and techniques adopted earlier under the patronage of the Fatimid and Ayyubid dynasties, such as fluted brick domes, keel arches, panelled façades and cushion and joggled voussoirs, continued to be used. No device, once adopted, was likely to be discarded later. In Damascus the Umayyad mosque, one of the great monuments of early Islamic architecture (*see* DAMASCUS, §3), provided inspiration for construction under the Mamluks. Such features as arcaded courtyards, a wider central aisle leading to the mihrab, square minarets, fine ashlar masonry, sometimes in striped bands (Arab. *ablaq*), roofs on wooden rafters and interior decoration of polychrome marble panels and mosaic of mother-of-pearl and glass tesserae all derive from great monuments of the Umayyad period. In Aleppo buildings were also constructed with fine ashlar masonry but were often vaulted with barrel and groin vaults and

domes on pendentives, sometimes decorated with *muqarnas*. Polychrome stone intarsia of interlaced designs accentuated mihrabs, portals and other distinctive areas; *muqarnas* hoods often crowned portals.

Bahri mamlūks, 1250–1390. Baybars I (*reg* 1260–77), the first great Mamluk sultan and real creator of the empire, built his own madrasa (1262–3) in Cairo. The site was once part of the eastern Fatimid palace and lay along the *qaṣaba* to the north-east of the madrasa–mausoleum complex built by his former master, the Ayyubid sultan al-Salih, and had Baybars not died in Damascus he would probably have been buried in Cairo. Only a fragment of the madrasa remains, but its façade had striped masonry, a portal with a *muqarnas* hood, the first in Egypt, and a minaret over the portal. The interior court had four iwans for the teaching of four subjects. The major surviving building from Baybars's reign is a congregational mosque (1269; *see* CAIRO, §III, 7) for al-Husayniyya, his new suburb to the north-east of the Fatimid city. This vast construction (106×103 m) has outer walls of ashlar with projecting monumental entrances on three sides; they open on to halls of varying depth with columns and piers supporting brick arcades and flat roofs around a large open court. The portals are decorated with blind niches and *muqarnas*, much like the Aqmar Mosque (1125) in Cairo, although the interlacing strapwork designs on either side of the passage within the north-western portal are more characteristic of Aleppo. The plan is clearly modelled on that of the mosque of al-Hakim, built some 250 years earlier (*see* CAIRO, §III, 4), except for the great square space in front of the mihrab, which originally supported a vast wooden dome similar in scale and construction to that over the mausoleum of Imam al-Shafi'i (*see* CAIRO, §III, 6). The interior, mostly gutted, had marble columns, fine stucco ornament and a marble mihrab.

Qala'un (*reg* 1280–90), another former *mamlūk* of Sultan al-Salih Ayyub, built his own tomb complex, which included a madrasa and hospital, directly opposite Baybars's madrasa on an irregular L-shaped site, measuring about 100 m in each direction (*see* CAIRO, §III, 8). The site formerly contained the western Fatimid palace, once the residence of the heirs to the throne, and the symbolism was obvious. A monumental portal in the centre of the façade leads to a long corridor; to its left are the remains of the madrasa, which has one great iwan and a mosque at opposite ends of a court and many rooms for students; to its right are the tomb and minaret. At the end of the corridor, along the base of the L, was the hospital (destr.), a complex arrangement of iwans and T-shaped rooms around a court measuring 21×33 m. The building is richly syncretistic: antique columns support pointed arches on the pseudo-Gothic façade; a portal with Aleppo-style intarsia also has horseshoe arches in the western Islamic style, and the mihrab in the madrasa is decorated in the Syrian style with glass and mother-of-pearl mosaic above polychrome marble panels. The tomb-chamber, originally with a wooden dome resting on Ptolemaic granite columns (see fig. 56), is modelled on the Dome of the Rock in Jerusalem and has walls covered with polychrome marble inlay in the style of Damascus. The coffered wooden ceilings above the ambulatory around the tomb are similar

56. Complex of Qala'un, Cairo, interior of mausoleum, 1284–5

to those in the tomb of Imam al-Shafi'i and in the madrasa of al-Salih Ayyub, probably first inspired by the stone ceiling of the old temple of Bel in Syrian Palmyra. The windows were of stained glass set in stucco. The original finial of the minaret, destroyed by the great earthquake of July 1303, was probably a fluted and keel-shaped dome.

Qala'un's *mamlūk* Kitbugha (*reg* 1295–7) usurped the throne of Qala'un's son al-Nasir Muhammad (*see* MAM-LUK, §II, 2(3)) and built his own madrasa and mausoleum to the north of Qala'un's complex in a clear desire to advertise himself as the true heir to his former master. A much smaller and more limited version of Qala'un's building next door, it has an entrance in the centre of the façade and a corridor separating the tomb from the madrasa. The Gothic portal in white marble was removed from a crusader church in Acre by Sultan Khalil (*reg* 1290–94) and reused here. The Egyptian historian al-Maqrizi (1364–1442) considered it one of the most marvellous things made by man. The madrasa was the first cruciform example in Cairo, with iwans on all four sides of the court for teaching the four schools of Sunni law. When al-Nasir returned to the throne in 1299 after a *coup d'état*, he took over the incomplete building, changed the inscriptions (the building is known after him) and buried his mother and son there. Al-Nasir intended to be buried in his *khānaqāh* at Siryaqus, north of Cairo, but was actually buried in his father's mausoleum.

Such a prominent site on the *qaṣaba* was not available to the amirs Salar (*d* 1310) and Sanjar al-Jawli (*d* 1344–5), who built their funerary complex (1303–4) on a stone outcrop known as Qal'at al-Kabsh ('Ramscastle') near the

mosque of Ibn Tulun. The difficult terrain of the site has been ingeniously overcome by building on several levels. A flight of steps leads to an elevated portal and a cruciform vestibule; to its right an internal staircase leads to a small domed vestibule. From it one enters either a short groin-vaulted passage on the left that leads to the madrasa and a *khānaqāh*, or a long groin-vaulted corridor that leads to three mausolea. The two larger ones of Salar and Sanjar (diams 9.98 and 9.16 m), which overlook the street, are crowned with fine fluted domes of brick covered with stucco; a third mausoleum at the end of the corridor, believed to be that of their Sufi mentor, is covered with a small (diam. 6.38 m) hemispheric stone dome. The mina-ret, placed between the portal and the amirs' tombs, has three storeys separated by *muqarnas* tiers. The lower storey is a tall square shaft of ashlar; it is decorated on the south and west with mock balconies supported on *muqarnas* corbels and surmounted by horseshoe arches with cushion voussoirs. The two upper storeys are of brick, the lower octagonal with eight keel-shaped arches with fluted hoods, and the upper cylindrical and crowned with a fluted dome of brick covered with stucco. This elongated and com-manding minaret is one of the most elegant built before 1340, when a new type without the square shaft was introduced.

The third reign of al-Nasir (1309–41), when he returned to the throne firmly in control of the quarrelsome amirs, was the greatest period of growth and monumental construction in Cairo. All that remains of the vast building programme the Sultan undertook on the Citadel is a congregational mosque (1318–35). Built of dressed ashlar, it has a rectangular courtyard surrounded by hypostyle halls supported by columns taken from Ptolemaic, Roman and Christian buildings. The court façade has a two-storey arcade of polychrome masonry and is crowned with merlons. The nine bays in front of the mihrab are covered by a great wooden dome resting on eight red granite Pharaonic columns. The interior was richly decorated with dados of fine polychrome marble, since looted, and a wooden ceiling of octagonal coffers like those in Qala'un's tomb, painted blue and silver. At the north-east corner and over the north-west portal are two minarets; their fluted-dome finials are decorated in blue and white ceramic tiles, an Iranian feature unusual in Cairo, where colouristic effects are usually sought in stone.

Al-Nasir also encouraged his amirs to transform the cemetery between the Fatimid city and the Citadel into a new suburb. No less than seven new congregational mosques were added there in his lifetime, four of them by his sons-in-law, who were also prominent amirs. This form of patronage was also encouraged by the relaxation of the restriction limiting the number of congregational mosques in which the Friday sermon (Arab. *khuṭba*) could be delivered. Of these new foundations, the best preserved and most imposing is that of Altinbugha al-Maridani (*c.* 1340) on the Darb al-Ahmar. It shares many features with al-Nasir's mosque on the Citadel, for it was planned by the same court architect, Master (Arab. *mu'allim*) Ibn al-Suyufi. It is a square building (*c.* 43 m to a side) with reused and new poly-faceted columns supporting hypo-style halls around a central court. Above the court arcades are blind ribbed keel arches, lozenges and medallions like

57. Congregational mosque, complex of Hasan, Cairo, court, 1356–9; from D. Roberts: *Egypt and Nubia*, iii (London, 1849)

those on the Aqmar Mosque; the arcades on the qibla side are separated from the court by a splendid screen of turned wooden spoolwork (Arab. *mashrabiyya*). As in al-Nasir's mosque, eight red Pharaonic granite columns around the bays before the mihrab support a wooden dome. The mihrab itself is decorated with a mosaic of coloured stone and mother-of-pearl; turquoise-glazed ceramic colonnettes support miniature blind arcades. The east corner of the building is inset to adjust to the angle of the street, and the resulting zigzag wall is decorated with shallow panels with *muqarnas* hoods, each containing two windows. The minaret is of the new form that became dominant for the rest of the period: the square base is little more than a transition between the mosque and the two receding octagonal storeys, the upper one surmounted by a circle of slender colonnettes supporting a bulbous stone finial.

In this fertile period of Cairo's greatest prosperity and security, the populace may have been over half a million, a prodigious number for a 14th-century urban infrastructure to support. A number of imposing *khānaqāh*s and madrasas were built (for illustration *see* KHANAQAH), as well as a new kind of neighbourhood religious centre incorporating a congregational mosque, madrasa and *khānaqāh*. The older type of hypostyle mosque with an open courtyard was sometimes replaced by a new type somewhat like a four-iwan madrasa with the court roofed over. In the first example, the mosque of Aslam al-Silahdar (1344–5), the south-east (qibla) and north-west iwans were replaced with small hypostyle halls. The technique of constructing domes entirely of stone was introduced to

Cairo by artisans from Aleppo during the period of al-Nasir. The first extant example is the small plain one built by Salar and Sanjar al-Jawli (1304), which follows Syrian prototypes. Cairene examples soon became fluted like brick domes there, as in the mausoleum of Muzaffar 'Alam al-Din Sanjar (1322).

The period following al-Nasir's death in 1341, when his many sons and grandsons came and went on a throne controlled by the leading amirs, was scarcely less productive of fine buildings. The Black Death (1347–9) carried off at least a quarter of the population, but ironically seems to have stimulated building, for the wealth of those who died without heirs increased the sums available to the sultan, since according to Islamic law it devolved to him. To this period belongs the mosque of Aqsunqur (1347), another king-maker and son-in-law of al-Nasir. It is a fine large hypostyle and courtyard mosque with octagonal ashlar piers bearing groin vaults in the qibla arcades, and two mausolea, one for the founder and one for several of the infant sons of al-Nasir, whom he and his fellow amirs placed briefly on the throne. In 1652 Ibrahim Ağa Müstahfizan, an Ottoman janissary officer, built himself a mausoleum next to the mosque's entrance; he redecorated the mosque with marble dados in the Mamluk style and blue and green tiles made in Damascus in imitation of Ottoman tiles from Iznik (*see* §V, 5(i) below and IZNIK, §2), which have given rise to the building's popular name, the Blue Mosque.

The greatest of all Mamluk buildings is the immense (7900 sq. m) complex built for Sultan Hasan (*reg* 1347–61 with interruption), a son of al-Nasir, at the foot of the

Citadel (*see* CAIRO, §III, 9; see also fig. 57). It contained a cruciform congregational mosque with four madrasas and a mausoleum of imperial scale (diam. 21 m; originally crowned with a bulbous dome of wood, since replaced), as well as an orphanage, a covered bazaar with shops, a hospital, water-tower, baths and kitchens (all destr.). The enormous sums needed seem to have been obtained in part by confiscating lands of the Coptic Church. The complex is notable for its height. The four madrasas in the corners of the central court are each four or five storeys, and the entrance portal (h. 26 m) would have been flanked by two lofty minarets had not an earthquake dissuaded the builders. The decoration is equally splendid, from the carved stone *muqarnas* of the portal hood and vestibule vault to the chinoiserie stucco on the interior. Both the plan and the decoration seem to have been inspired by earlier Anatolian and Iranian buildings (*see* §§(i)(a) and (ii) above).

Bulbous domes appeared in Cairene architecture at this time. Resting on a high drum decorated with projecting tiers of *muqarnas*, they have a dominating external profile and occasionally an interior vault proportionate to the chamber below. Some, such as the one over the tomb of Amir Sarghatmish (1356), have smooth profiles, while others, such as those on al-Sultaniyya (*c.* 1350), the curious building in the Qarafa Cemetery with domes on either side of an iwan, have ribbed profiles in which each flute of the dome rises from a separate *muqarnas* corbel. The tendency towards elongation is taken to an extreme in the small mausoleum of Yunus al-Dawadar (1382). The obvious similarity of these domes to those on buildings erected by the Timurid dynasty in Iran and Central Asia (*see* §(i)(b) above) has led to speculation about the origins of the type, but the tradition of double domes had been well established in Iran since the 11th century, and structural considerations suggest that the Cairene examples are translations of brick building techniques into stone.

Burji mamlūks, 1382–1517. Intense strife in the Mamluk corps brought to power a new élite, recruited not from Turkish slaves but from Circassians from the Caucasus. The leader who emerged, Barquq, built a mosque, madrasa, *khānaqāh* and mausoleum on the *qaṣaba* just north of al-Nasir's madrasa. The site provided some 45 m of street frontage, and the building was made all the more prominent by having it project 3 m into the street. The plan shows some similarities to that of Qala'un's madrasa near by, but the building incorporates features developed in Sultan Hasan's complex such as the monumental entrance and vestibule, cruciform plan and court façade. The decoration of marble panelling, bronze-plated doors and carved stone and the elaborately worked minaret set the style for Cairene architecture in the first half of the 15th century.

From 1400 to 1422 the Mamluk state suffered its greatest period of external threat and internal conflict. After Timur's devastation of Syria, famine and plague broke out, and civil strife ensued. Aleppo's fortunes soon revived, due to its role as the entrepôt between Venetian trade in the eastern Mediterranean and Iranian silk trade from the Caspian. Great stone warehouses, such as the Khan al-Qadi (1441), were erected. The populous new

suburbs along caravan routes were endowed with fine, often polychrome ashlar buildings such as mosques, usually with prominent minarets (e.g. Jami' al-Utrush; 1399–1409) and *khānaqāh*s. Damascus recovered some of its population, but the architecture of the 15th century is for the most part showy and meretricious. Patrons wanted a good display, so colourful façades and tall polygonal minarets conceal buildings that are otherwise undistinguished, such as the Jaqmaqiyya Madrasa (1421) and the Sabuniyya Mosque (1464).

Cairo also suffered enormously, as half the city and its environs were ruined and bustling markets abandoned. Despite the devastation, monuments continued to be built, due to the determination and priorities of the rulers. Although Barquq had been buried in his mausoleum on the *qaṣaba* for reasons of state, in his will he requested that his final resting-place be in the northern cemetery, near the graves of his father (whom he had brought from Circassia) and revered Sufi shaykhs. Accordingly, Barquq's son Faraj (*reg* 1399–1412 with interruption) built a *khānaqāh*, madrasa, congregational mosque and double mausoleum there (1399–1410). Because it was built on open land, the complex had an unusual plan: it is a vast freestanding square (*c.* 75 m to a side) with four façades and elements arranged symmetrically around a large open court. The two huge mausolea flanking the hypostyle prayer-hall, in which Barquq, Faraj and his family are buried, are covered with monumental stone domes (diam. 14 m) decorated with chevrons. In the midst of an epidemic of plague so severe that the workmen dropped dead at their labours, Sultan Mu'ayyad Shaykh (*reg* 1412–21) ordered a great complex, with a congregational mosque, madrasa, *khānaqāh*, mausoleum, bath, residence, library and kitchen, at the southern end of the *qaṣaba*, just inside the Zuwayla Gate, on which its two minarets were placed. Resources were always found for building, and anything lacking was taken from earlier foundations. The magnificent doors and chandelier, for example, were highhandedly removed from the complex of Sultan Hasan against payment of a sum to its endowment.

Barsbay (*reg* 1422–38) built a mausoleum with a *khānaqāh* and madrasa on the *qaṣaba* (1424), but an outbreak of plague in 1429 led him to construct another complex in the northern cemetery (1432), not far from that of Faraj. It comprised a tomb, *khānaqāh*, madrasa, mosque, two domed halls for Sufi prayer sessions, kitchens and residences for Sufis and for his own descendants. The mosque (15×20 m) has a central aisle flanked by raised ones, an arrangement previously more typical of palaces but found in many later religious buildings. The stone domes of the complex are carved with increasingly complex star interlace patterns, which replaced the chevrons typical earlier. The interior decoration of the complex is among the finest in the northern cemetery, particularly the marble mosaic pavements.

Under Qa'itbay (*reg* 1468–96; *see* MAMLUK, §II, 2(10)), the greatest of the later Mamluk sultans, Alexandria and Aleppo were refortified; Cairo, Alexandria, Jerusalem and provincial centres were endowed with bridges, commercial houses, canals and religious foundations; and the shrines in Mecca and Medina were extensively restored. It was a period of fine architecture, although the Mamluk realm

58. Complex of Qa'itbay, Cairo, 1472–4

was threatened by the growing power of the Ottomans and was frequently at war in Anatolia. Financial arrangements were precarious, and extortion and confiscation provided much of the necessary monies for building. The hallmarks of architecture during Qaʾitbay's reign are charm and elegance rather than monumentality. Qaʾitbay's funerary complex in the northern cemetery (1472–4; see fig. 58; *see also* CAIRO, §III, 10) is the best-known and most admired structure of the period. It comprised a madrasa, *khānaqāh*, mausoleum, hospice for commercial travellers, cistern, water-dispensary, Koran school, apartments for his descendants and reception area. The carved masonry dome over his mausoleum is the finest in Cairo, combining strapwork tracery with an undulating vegetal arabesque (*see* MUQARNAS, fig. 2). Among the Sultan's many other buildings in Cairo are madrasas at Qalʿat al-Kabsh (1475–6) and on Rawda Island (1481–90), two caravanserais (1477 and 1480), and a water-dispensary and Koran school (Arab. *sabīl-kuttāb*; 1479), which also had apartments for his descendants. He also restored the Azhar Mosque and the mausoleum of Imam al-Shafiʿi. Like al-Nasir, Qaʾitbay encouraged his amirs to build. The madrasa–mausoleum complexes of Qajmas al-Ishaqi (1480–81) and Azbak al-Yusufi (1494–5) are scarcely less splendid than the Sultan's. Azbak also constructed a palace and madrasa beside an artificial lake he had dug in Cairo; the district, al-Azbakiyya, became well known for light living. The amir and Grand Secretary Yashbak min Mahdi constructed two large domed buildings (Arab. *qubba*) on the outskirts of Cairo (1477 and 1479). Unlike funerary domes, they are plain on the exterior but heavily decorated on the interior and were probably pleasure-domes where aristocrats could attend Sufi performances at leisure.

Two years after Qaʾitbay's death the Portuguese gained control of the Indian Ocean and denied the Mamluks the spice trade, their richest source of revenue. Building continued unabated in Cairo, however, until the Ottoman conquest of 1517, and the legacy of the Qaʾitbay style remained strong, particularly in the work of the sultan Qansuh al-Ghawri (*reg* 1501–17). His funerary complex on both sides of the *qaṣaba* (1503–4) has the mosque-madrasa and minaret on the west and the mausoleum, *khānaqāh*, Koran school and water-dispensary on the east. Near by is a caravanserai and commercial hotel (Arab. *wakāla*), the revenues from which helped support the complex. The worsening financial situation meant that construction was shoddy and the quality of workmanship declined: the marble revetments were illegally confiscated from other foundations, and the minaret and dome had to be reconstructed within the Sultan's reign.

BIBLIOGRAPHY

Enc. Islam/2: 'Dimashq', 'Halab', 'al-Kahira'
Aḥmad ibn ʿAlī al-Maqrīzī: *Al-mawāʿiẓ waʾl-iʾtibār bi dhikr al-khiṭaṭ waʾl-athār* [Exhortations and consideration for the mention of districts and monuments], ii (Cairo, 1853), p. 382
E. Herzfeld: *Inscriptions et monuments d'Alep* (Cairo, 1954–5)
Ibn Khaldun: *The Muqqadimah: An Introduction to History*, ii, trans. F. Rosenthal (Princeton, 1958), p. 435
K. A. C. Creswell: *The Muslim Architecture of Egypt*, ii (Oxford, 1959)
D. Brandenburg: *Islamische Baukunst in Ägypten* (Berlin, 1966)
S. L. Mostafa: *Kloster und Mausoleum des Farag ibn Barquq in Kairo* (Glückstadt, 1968)
C. Kessler: 'Funerary Architecture within the City', *Colloque international sur l'histoire du Caire: Caire, 1969*, pp. 257–68

S. L. Mostafa: *Moschee des Farag ibn Barquq in Kairo* (Glückstadt, 1972)
L. A. Ibrahim: 'The Great Hanqah of the Emir Qawsun in Cairo', *Mitt. Dt. Archäol. Inst.: Abt. Kairo*, xxx (1974), pp. 37–64
J. Revault and B. Maury: *Palais et maisons du Caire du XIVe au XVIIIe siècle*, 3 vols (Cairo, 1975–9)
C. Kessler: *The Carved Masonry Domes of Medieval Cairo* (London, 1976)
M. Meinecke: *Die Madrasa des Amirs Mitqal in Kairo* (Mainz, 1976)
——: 'Die mamlukischen Faience Dekorationen: Eine Weststätte aus Tabriz in Kairo (1330–1350)', *Kst Orients*, xi (1976–7), pp. 85–144
J. M. Rogers: 'The Stones of Barquq', *Apollo*, ciii (1976), pp. 307–13
M. Meinecke:: *Die Moschee des Amirs Mitqal* (Mainz, 1980)
D. Behrens-Abouseif: 'The North-eastern Extension of Cairo under the Mamluks', *An. Islam.*, xvii (1981), pp. 172–8
L. E. Fernandes: 'Three Sufi Foundations in a Fifteenth-century Wakfiya', *An. Islam.*, xvii (1981), pp. 141–56
J. M. Bloom: 'The Mosque of Baybars al-Bunduqdari in Cairo', *An. Islam.*, xviii (1982), pp. 45–78
D. Behrens-Abouseif: 'The *Qubba*: An Aristocratic Type of *Zāwiya*', *An. Islam.*, xix (1983), pp. 1–8
H. Salam-Leibich: *The Architecture of the Mamluk City of Tripoli* (Cambridge, MA, 1983)
L. A. Ibrahim: 'Residential Architecture in Mamluk Cairo', *Muqarnas*, ii (1984), pp. 47–60
A. Raymond: 'Cairo's Area and Population in the Early 15th Century', *Muqarnas*, ii (1984), pp. 21–32
J. A. Williams: 'Urbanization and Monument Construction in Mamluk Cairo', *Muqarnas*, ii (1984), pp. 33–46
D. Behrens-Abouseif: 'Change in Function and Form of Mamluk Religious Institutions', *An. Islam.*, xxi (1985), pp. 73–94
M. Meinecke: 'Mamluk Architecture. Regional Architectural Traditions: Evolution and Interrelations', *Damas. Mitt.*, ii (1985), pp. 163–76
R. B. Parker, R. Sabin and C. Williams: *Islamic Monuments in Cairo: A Practical Guide* (Cairo, 1985)
M. H. Burgoyne: *Mamluk Jerusalem* (London, 1987)
D. Behrens-Abouseif: 'The Citadel of Cairo: Stage for Mamluk Ceremonial', *An. Islam.*, xxiv (1988), pp. 25–80
C. Karim: 'The Mosque of Aslam al-Bahaʾi al-Silahdar (764/1345)', *An. Islam.*, xxiv (1988), pp. 233–52
D. Behrens-Abouseif: *Islamic Architecture in Cairo: An Introduction* (Leiden, 1989)

JOHN A. WILLIAMS

(b) Yemen. Under such staunchly Sunni dynasties as the RASULID (*reg* 1229–1454) and Tahirid (*reg* 1454–1536), cultural and political links with Egypt remained strong, and there was intense and unprecedented architectural activity in their domains. Sultans and their families, officials and scholars commissioned mosques, madrasas and hospices. Of these only three or four monuments survive in Taʿizz, the primary residence of the Rasulid court, while smaller and less spectacular buildings remain in ZABID, Hays, Mahjam, Jibla, Ibb and Ridaʿ. The birka (water feature) of the famous garden of Sultan Mugahid, near Taʿizz, is all that remains of the splendid palaces. The Rasulids controlled SANʿA, in the centre of the country, for 150 years, but the Zaydi imams maintained their influence in the northern highlands, where they preserved a conservative and distinct style of building (*see* §5(ii)(d) above).

The earliest preserved examples of domed mosques date from the Rasulid period, although they may have been modelled on mosques erected by the Ayyubids (*reg* 1174–1229) that have not survived. The prayer-hall typically comprises a large central domed bay flanked by pairs of smaller ones, as in the Asadiyya Madrasa (before 1258) at Ibb. The mosque is preceded by a court surrounded by arcades, with domes covering the corner bays. In the Muzaffariyya Mosque at Taʿizz (1249–95; see fig. 59), which was built with an adjoining madrasa, the large central domed bay is flanked by several pairs of

59. Muzaffariyya Mosque, Ta'izz, Yemen, 1249–95

domed bays, which are flanked in turn by larger domed bays, creating an extremely wide (53 m) but shallow prayer-hall. The qibla wall, which faces the town, is unusually treated as the main façade and is decorated with blind niches and a wide band of interlacing. The mihrab projection on the exterior is surmounted by a short tower crowned with a small dome. Rows of windows allow light to flood the interior, which had traditionally been left dark. Many of these innovations were retained under the Tahirids and differentiated orthodox places of worship from those of the Zaydis, who adhered to the older tradition. Smaller mosques, which had previously had flat roofs, also acquired domes, for example the mosque of Malhuki (1499), in north-eastern Ibb, which has nine domed bays arranged in a three-by-three grid.

Madrasas were introduced to the Yemen by the Ayyubids to serve the struggle of the orthodox ruling dynasty against the Zaydis and other Shi'ites. Although Ayyubid madrasas purportedly used a four-iwan plan, surviving Rasulid madrasas, such as the Asadiyya, the Mu'tabiyya (1392) and the Ashrafiyya (1397–1401) in Ta'izz, are entirely different. The Mu'tabiyya is a rectangle (23.4×28.8 m) divided in two parts: to the north is a prayer-hall of six equal domed bays embraced on three sides by a U-shaped corridor; to the south is a court flanked by subsidiary vaulted and domed rooms which were used for teaching. The Ashrafiyya's plan is similar but larger and more complex. The prayer-hall, like the typical Rasulid mosque, consists of a large domed bay flanked by two pairs of smaller ones. It is preceded by a courtyard (10×11 m) flanked by rectangular vaulted halls, which served as libraries. Three cenotaphs of the royal family have been erected in the court itself. To the south lies a domed *khānaqāh* with adjoining iwans. This square unit, measuring 27 m to a side, is in turn enclosed on the west and east by an open-roofed loggia from which project

two portals. A third portal on the south leads to a passage. On the fourth (qibla) side, the exterior is enlivened with superimposed blind arcades and cresting which lend rich texture to the façade. These buildings are sumptuously decorated on the interior with carved stucco and painted ornament. Many of their architectural and decorative features, such as projecting portals of multicoloured sandstone, triple arches, framing fillets and gadrooned domes, have parallels in the architecture of the Jazira and southeast Anatolia (*see* §5(ii)(e) above) and seem to have been imported by Ayyubid and Rasulid patrons. The typical features of Rasulid madrasas, such as monumental portals and multi-storey minarets, were repeated in Tahirid ones. In the great madrasa built in Rada' by 'Amir II (*reg* 1488–1517), the U-shaped passage was extended to surround the mosque on the north (qibla) side, forming a loggia with fountains. Other Tahirid madrasas, such as the Mansuriyya in Juban (1482), introduce features derived from the architecture of India (*see* §(i)(c) above), with which the Yemen was traditionally linked. Innumerable small madrasas dotted provincial towns and followed local traditions in plan and decoration. The madrasas of Ibb, for example, which are mostly of the Rasulid period, have small, cube-shaped mosques facing halls or porticos. The madrasas of Zabid are equally simple, although domes and barrel vaults are more frequent.

*Khānaqāh*s were less common. The one founded in Hays by the Rasulid al-Muzaffar (*reg* 1250–95) is the only one to survive. It has an unusual plan of a two-aisled, barrel-vaulted prayer-hall, a square courtyard also flanked by barrel vaults and a large iwan. A portal surmounted by a small turret leads to a transverse room with cisterns and then via a bent axis into the courtyard.

Richly decorated tombs were generally reserved for the Zaydi imams. The domed tombs of the imams in the south of the mosque of Hadi at Sa'da, which are open on three sides, merge into one another in an unplanned complex (14th–15th century). Other members of the imams' family were buried under open, domed kiosks partially decorated with stucco inscriptions and geometric designs, although those preserved at Sa'da mostly date from the 15th century. The tomb of the imam Salah al-Din (*d* 1391) in San'a is unusual, for the domed square is extended on the north by an iwan, on the south by an apse and on the west by a rectangular space. Other tombs, such as the simple ones at Hijrat al-Felle near Sa'da, are closed and can be entered only from one side. Gadrooned domes were used intermittently at Sa'da, while simple hemispheric ones were used at Zafar Dhibin, Dhibin and elsewhere. The tombs of the Rasulids were normally integrated into madrasas, but the cenotaphs in the courtyard of the Ashrafiyya Madrasa at Ta'izz are baldachin structures with painted and gilded decoration as elaborate as that of the tombs of the Zaydi imams.

Minarets incorporated in later Rasulid madrasas in Ta'izz derive ultimately from Egyptian models built under the Mamluks (*see* §(a) above). The shaft, set on a square base, is subdivided into several storeys, usually octagonal in plan, and decorated with blind arcades resting on engaged columns. Towers in the Zaydi zone were simpler, at least in the early period. A round shaft set on a square basc had a smooth profile, broken only by an octagonal band in the lower section. Blind niches with stucco ornament were sometimes inserted there, as at the Masjid al-Abhar in San'a (late 14th century).

Muqarnas elements were used occasionally, for example in the zone of transition in the dome of the tomb of the imam Salah al-Din in San'a and on the façade of the mosque of the madrasa in Haqla, eastern Ibb (14th century). Carved stucco and painted ornament were used extensively to decorate Rasulid and Tahirid buildings, but tilework appears only in isolated instances and evidently only in the Zaydi zone, where small, greenish/light-blue discs were inserted in stucco decoration, as on the minaret of the Masjid al-Abhar in San'a and the Nizamiyya at Sa'da (*c*. 1400). An exception is the tile panel at the Great Mosque of Zabid.

BIBLIOGRAPHY
R. B. Lewcock and G. R. Smith: 'Three Medieval Mosques in the Yemen', *Orient. A.*, xx (1974), pp. 75–86, 192–203
R. B. Serjeant and R. Lewcock: *San'a': An Arabian Islamic City* (London, 1983)
E. J. Keall: 'A Preliminary Report on the Architecture of Zabid', *Proc. Semin. Arab. Stud.*, xiv (1984), pp. 51–65
U. Scerrato and others: articles in *E. & W.*, xxxiv (1984), pp. 440ff; xxxvi–xxxvii (1986), pp. 422ff
B. Finster: 'Die Architektur der Rasuliden', *Jemen*, ed. W. Daum (Innsbruck and Frankfurt am Main, 1987), pp. 237ff
N. Sadek: 'Rasulid Women: Power and Patronage', *Proc. Semin. Arab. Stud.*, xix (1989), pp. 121–6

(iv) Western Islamic lands. The collapse of the Almohad empire in the mid-13th century led to the emergence of the Nasrid dynasty of Granada (*reg* 1230–1492) and three rival Berber dynasties in western, central and eastern North Africa, respectively the Marinids of Fez (*reg* 1196–1549), the Abdalwadids of Tlemcen (*reg* 1236–1550) and the Hafsids of Tunis (*reg* 1228–1574). Mainly palaces survive in Spain, but North Africa preserves a wider range of civic and religious buildings, including madrasas, which were first introduced during this period. Often known as Hispano-Moresque (or Hispano-Maghribi), this western school of architecture typically combines revetments of richly carved plaster and wood with colourful tile mosaic dados and floors, as interest in structure gave way to a preoccupation with decoration.

□

(a) Spain. (b) Morocco and Algeria. (c) Tunisia.

(a) Spain. After the defeat of the Almohads at Las Navas in 1212 (*see* §5(iv) above), the NASRID court (*reg* 1230–1492) at Granada became a brilliant centre of Islamic civilization, particularly in the second half of the 14th century (*see* GRANADA, §I, 1). The principal architectural remains include some of the most famous buildings in all Islamic architecture, such as the Alhambra and Generalife palaces in Granada (*see* GRANADA, §III, 1). In contrast to other regions and periods where most of the remaining buildings served religious functions, almost all surviving buildings are palaces or civic structures. At its finest, Nasrid architecture is immensely sensual: intimate spaces are intricately decorated with coloured tile and carved stucco open to the sky and the landscape; gardens provide colour and aroma, pools mirror buildings and reflect light, and fountains and water-channels add sound and motion.

Four stylistic periods can be distinguished. In the first, covering the sultanates of Muhammad I (*reg* 1232–72), Muhammad II (*reg* 1272–1302), Muhammad III (*reg* 1302–8) and Nasr (*reg* 1308–13) citadels at Granada (the Alhambra), MÁLAGA and Almería were built on the remains of 11th-century fortresses. The first two have double or triple concentric sets of walls with towers that enclose military and residential quarters. City gates have flat façades (e.g. Granada, Alhambra, the Hierro gate and west façade of the Vino gate). Initially towers were conceived as simple dwellings, for their walls lack decoration and arc pierced only by square or slit windows (e.g. Granada, Alhambra, Homenaje Tower), but under Muhammad II and Muhammad III they were decorated luxuriously and became the principal palace halls.

A typical house or palace was arranged around a rectangular courtyard. A gallery at either end precedes a rectangular room or (in a tower) a square room, which had windows on three sides or lateral chambers and small alcoves set into the thickness of the wall facing the entrance. The finest example is the Cuarto Real de S Domingo (Dar al-Manjara al-Kubra) in Granada. The throne-room, the only surviving part, shows consummate mastery of design in carved stucco, lustre ceramics and tile mosaic worked in a variety of geometric, vegetal and epigraphic motifs. As in earlier buildings, arches and galleries rest on piers or columns (e.g. Granada, courtyard of the Salvador Church), and foliate designs and both decorative and structural vaults of inter-crossing arches follow Almohad models (e.g. Granada, hermitage of S Sebastian). Ornamental panels have compositions inspired by textiles such as the great banner of Las Navas de Tolosa (Burgos, Monastery of Las Huelgas, Church). The epigraphy is adapted from Almohad art, with squat, cursive lettering and elegant geometric kufic in two types and sizes, the smaller script occupying the top of the cartouche (e.g. Granada, Cuarto Real de S Domingo and Alhambra, Portal). The geometric designs fix the canon for all Nasrid art, and radial eight-pointed stars are more common than the traditional quadrangular and diagonal networks (e.g. Granada, minaret of S Juan de los Reyes). Other geometric designs combine six-, ten- and twelve-pointed stars. Floor-tiles have geometric designs in blue on a white ground. Two types of tile mosaic (Sp. *alicatado*) were used for dados: coloured interlaced bands on a white ground and white interlaced bands over blue, green and black. Lustre tiles were used on the jambs of the entrance arch to the Cuarto Real de S Domingo.

The second period spans the sultanates of Isma'il I (*reg* 1313–25), Muhammad IV (*reg* 1325–33) and Yusuf I (*reg* 1333–54). Part of Granada's walls (including the Bab Ilbira (now Puerta de Elvira) and Bab al-Tawwabin), the gate of Málaga's shipyards and modifications to Málaga's fortress belong to the end of the period. City gates were richly ornamented, their external façades under Yusuf I flanked by two projecting tower-like bodies (Granada, the Bab al-Ramla, now Puerto de las Orejas, rebuilt 1935; Granada, Alhambra, the Bab al-Ghudur and Bab al-Shari'a). The interiors of military towers were remodelled as luxurious dwellings (Granada, Alhambra, Torre de la Cautiva). Plans evolved to a 'classical' state: a transverse room with alcoves at either end was inserted between the gallery and the square hall, which has small cupboard-alcoves cut into the thickness of the walls. Porticos usually rest on columns (e.g. Granada, Casa Zafra), although pillars were still used. Square lanterns were introduced over the rooms in baths, madrasas and palaces (e.g. Granada, Alhambra, Torre del Peinador and Palacio de Comares) to break up spaces. The great entrance porch of the Corral del Carbón (14th century), the only remaining *funduq* (caravanserai) in Granada, is a local interpretation of an iwan, a common feature in eastern Islamic architecture. *Muqarbas* (also called *muqarnas* or *mocárabes*) was introduced in arches, projecting eaves and squinches to transform a square base into an octagon (e.g. Granada, Yusufiyya Madrasa, rest.; now Casa del Cabildo Antiguo). Ceramic mosaic in galleries and on dados and floors attained its maximum splendour. Complex geometric designs were worked in warm colours and purple tones (e.g. Granada, Alhambra, Torre de la Cautiva, Salón de Comares). Ceramic was also used in spandrels and decorative panels (e.g. Granada, Alhambra, the Shari'a Gate). The kufic lettering shows further geometric evolution and now decorated the upper and middle sections of the epigraphic cartouche. The use of wood reached its culmination, notably in ceilings. At first designs were carved and painted, but later designs are only painted (e.g. Granada, Alcazar Genil). Flat and brightly coloured figural paintings (e.g. Granada, Alhambra, Casita del Partal) depict medieval hunting and military life. The finest ensemble is the Palacio de Comares in the Alhambra. A portico of seven arches overlooks the pool and fountains of the court and precedes a *mocárabes* arch leading into the Sala de la Barca, a long transverse room celebrated for its wooden ceiling (reconstr. 1964–5) supported by stucco *mocárabes*. Two sets of paired arches lead into the throne-room of the Palacio de Comares (Hall of the Ambassadors); its colouring, Koranic text and wooden ceiling geometrically

decorated with seven concentric levels of stars may symbolize the seven heavens of the Islamic paradise.

The third period coincides with the sultanate of Muhammad V (*reg* 1354–9; 1362–9). Public buildings, such as the Maristán (1367; destr.) in Granada, remained architecturally conservative, but palatine architecture achieved a splendid distribution of volumes and spaces. The palace dwelling, epitomized by the Palacio de los Leones at the Alhambra, centred around great halls, such as the Qubba Mayor of the palace, called Dos Hermanas, and the Qubba of the Abencerrajes, which were occasionally used for public functions. In these ample halls varied spaces are creatively grouped as square ground-plans ascend to pierced octagonal or star-shaped *mocárabes* vaults. The alternation of illuminated square spaces with shaded rectangular ones, as in the Sala de los Reyes (or de la Justicia), creates an impression of extraordinary depth. This great spatial achievement derived from earlier Almohad religious architecture, for example the bays along the qibla wall in the Kutubiyya Mosque in Marrakesh (*see* §5(iv)(d) above). Marble columns became slimmer and were placed alone or in groups, as at the Patio de los Leones (*see* GRANADA, fig. 3 (xii)). The disposition of arches around overlapping axes and the central belvederes in the north and south porticos there can be traced back to the portico of the Dar al-Jund at MADINAT AL-ZAHRA', the 10th-century Umayyad palace near Córdoba. Dados have new geometric designs with multicoloured bands interlacing on a white ground. Other large geometric patterns contained smaller and finer designs. Curvilinear patterns reached their highest evolution, although designs with straight lines continued to be used and some walls were decorated with plain incised lines. New forms of flora included bunches, sometimes held in a clasped hand. Kufic scripts attained their greatest splendour in Hispano-Muslim epigraphy as complex triangular compositions were woven with axial symmetry. Paintings of hunting, fighting and courtly life decorated the walls and ceilings of the Sala de los Reyes (or de la Justicia) and other buildings at the Alhambra (*see* §9(iii)(b) below), and sculptures of stylized lions adorned palaces and public buildings such as the Alhambra's Palacio de los Leones and the Maristán in Granada (Granada, Alhambra).

The political and economic decline of the sultanate led to a decline in architecture during the fourth and final period of Nasrid art (1391–1492), as ideas were reiterated and quality deteriorated. At the Alhambra the plan of the Qubba Mayor (Dos Hermanas) was adapted to the interior of the Qalahurra of Muhammed VII (Infantas Tower) by drastic alterations: the belvedere was reduced to the thickness of the tower wall, the alcoves were placed in the back room, and the sides of the lantern hall were turned into galleries. The Dar al-Hurra Palace (probably 15th century; now convent of S Isabel la Real) in Granada used an antiquated architectural scheme. Decoration featured large plain surfaces of stucco framed by borders with completely decadent geometric patterns and elongated and narrow foliate designs. Although panels of kufic calligraphy were still axially symmetric, the letters are coarser. Medallions and geometric figures appeared in the middle of spandrels, and these medallions eventually became the only ornament on the arches.

In Nasrid architecture, the construction of utilitarian buildings—fortresses, bridges and underground cisterns—was distinguished from that of palaces and civic buildings by the use of vaulted structures of brick or concrete. Those used included barrel, groin, basket-shaped, hemispheric and *mocárabes* vaults. They were supported by free-standing or embedded piers, sometimes with an attached column, segmental, semicircular or pointed horseshoe arches and walls of brick, ashlar and marble masonry or concrete reinforced with masonry. City walls, towers and vaults were covered with stucco. Vaults were occasionally painted to simulate red brick, or white ashlar with red joints in the 10th-century style, as at the Bab al-Ghudur and Bab al-Shari'a at the Alhambra, which was also decorated with painted marble. Pavements were normally tightly laid pebblework with a central drainage spine, or plain or herringbone brickwork.

Palaces and civic buildings, in contrast, were of trabeate construction: lintelled doors, windows, porticos and galleries were sometimes decorated with simulated arches of coloured plaster to give the illusion of dynamism and ethereality. Gravity is apparently absent from Nasrid architecture, but in reality structures are static and primitive in composition, for thick walls counterbalance the thrusts of the light wooden roofs, below which hang decorative ceilings of wood or occasionally plaster. Vaults were used to roof large palace towers, as at the Qalahurra of Yusuf I (Cautiva Tower) and Comares Tower at the Alhambra, and also in the baths (*ḥammām*s), where civic-palatine and military styles were combined, the former being used for the cool rooms and the latter for the hot ones.

60. Cuarto Dorado (façade of the Palacio de Comares), Alhambra, Granada, Spain, mid-14th century

Nasrid architecture is richly ornamented with a variety of vividly coloured elements, such as carved stucco and ceramic tile, which give the impression of silks and fine fabrics. Areas of white stucco highlight the intense painted decoration, give depth to spaces and indirectly light the walls, as at the Partal and in the courtyard galleries and façade of the Palacio de Comares (see fig. 60). Abstract vegetal and geometric designs are accompanied by epigraphic panels and bands of poems and laudatory phrases in kufic and cursive scripts.

BIBLIOGRAPHY
Enc. Islam/2: 'Muḳarbas', 'Naṣrids'
L. Torres Balbás: *Arte almohade; arte nazarí; arte mudéjar*, A. Hisp., iv (Madrid, 1949)
M. Gómez-Moreno: 'Granada en el siglo XIII', *Cuad. Alhambra*, ii (1966)
A. Fernández-Puertas: *The Alhambra*, 2 vols (London, 1996)

ANTONIO FERNÁNDEZ-PUERTAS

(b) Morocco and Algeria. Under the patronage of the MARINIDs, Wattasids (*reg* 1196–1549) and Zayyanids (*reg* 1235–1550), their capitals at FEZ and TLEMCEN (now in Algeria) achieved their distinctive identities. Undistinguished materials and methods of construction were usually hidden behind non-structural architectural units and elaborate and eclectic surface decoration derived from earlier buildings in Morocco and Spain. This Hispano-Moresque style survived with little innovation and decreasing vigour until the 20th century (*see* §7(v) below).

In response to the political and economic insecurity of the times, Marinid society turned to the cult of local holy men and saints, the mysticism of Sufi institutions and the conservative orthodoxy of the ulema (learned men of Islam). Marinid building programmes are characterized by large numbers of small religious endowments, such as mosques around saints' tombs, hospices for Sufi fraternities (Arab. *zāwiya*; *see* KHANAQAH) and madrasas to educate the orthodox bureaucracy. This phenomenon was parallel to that in contemporary Egypt (*see* §(iii)(a) above). These public expressions of piety were accompanied by private displays of wealth and luxurious living, for domestic disorder and the disastrous defeats in Spain and Ifriqiya (now Tunisia) in the early 14th century did not curtail prolific royal patronage. The reigns of Abu Sa'id 'Uthman (*reg* 1310–31), Abu'l-Hasan 'Ali (*reg* 1331–48) and Abu 'Inan Faris (*reg* 1348–59) produced more than 20 major constructions and renovations.

The congregational mosque erected in 1276 when New Fez was built to the west of Fez is a typical Marinid foundation. Relatively small (54×34 m), with seven aisles perpendicular to the qibla wall, it has a T-plan (a wide central aisle leading to a wide aisle parallel to the qibla wall) and dome over the first bay of the prayer-hall. The minaret in the north-west corner of the courtyard is colourfully decorated with a raised brick interlace pattern on a background of glazed tile mosaic (Arab. *zallīj*) and an upper register of stellar tile patterns. Similar plans were used in Fez for the Hamra and Abu'l-Hasan mosques (mid-14th century), and in Tlemcen for the Zayyanid mosque of Sidi Brahim (1308–18) and the mosques around the tombs of Abu Madyan (Sidi Bou-Médine; mosque of al 'Ubbad; 1338) and Sidi al-Halwi (1354). The main portal is usually on the mihrab axis and, in a Marinid innovation, is embellished with tile mosaic, carved stucco and heavy wooden corbels. The mosque in al-Mansura, the Marinid siege town outside the walls of Tlemcen, is unusually large (85×60 m) and copies the Almohad mosque of Hasan in Rabat in size, plan and materials and technique of construction (pisé with some use of stone). Begun by Abu Ya'qub (*reg* 1286–1307), it seems never to have been completed. Thirteen aisles run perpendicular to the three aisles parallel to and adjoining the qibla wall. The stone minaret (h. 38 m) stands opposite the mihrab; its base houses the main portal, of which the shallow decoration in relief combines cusped and interlaced arches, framing inscriptions and arabesque spandrels in a successful reinterpretation of earlier portals designed under the Almohads (*see* §5(iv)(d) above). Aisles parallel to the qibla wall characterize the small mosque at the necropolis of Chella, near Rabat, and the mosques in the Shrabliyin, Lala al-Zhar and Bu 'Inaniyya madrasas in Fez. Derived from the plan of the Qarawiyyin Mosque in Fez, which the early Marinids restored along with the tomb of Mulay Idris there, it became the standard plan for later mosques. The Marinids also enlarged the congregational mosque of Taza and gave it a remarkable pierced ribbed dome modelled on the dome in the bay in front of the mihrab in the congregational mosque of Tlemcen (1136), as well as a bronze mosque lamp cast from a bell brought as booty from Christian Spain (*see* §IV, 3(iv) below).

Many madrasas were built in Fez, Salé and MEKNÈS between 1271 and 1355. The seven remaining in Fez range in size and design from the small and plain Saba'iyyin (1323–5), which has only 11 students' rooms and no oratory, to the monumental Bu 'Inaniyya (1350–55), which housed 100 students and had its own congregational mosque, minaret, water-clock and Koran school (*see* MADRASA, fig. 2). All had courts, the surfaces of which were covered with geometric, floral and epigraphic designs in carved stucco, cedarwood and marble, and tile mosaic (see fig. 61; *see also* §9(ii)(c) below). Students' cells with small windows overlooked a fountain or pool in the centre of the court, a prayer-hall stood opposite a single entrance bent for privacy, and a second court housed latrines. Small arcades filled with openwork wooden screens added visual interest to the court spaces. The jewel-like decoration, often extensively restored in the 20th century, is similar to that found in the contemporary Nasrid palaces of Granada (*see* §(a) above), although an increasingly distinct Fez style, distinguished by fewer marble columns, more wood and a different overall treatment of the parts, emerged after the early 14th century. Abu'l-Hasan's madrasa in Salé (1340) retains its delightful arcaded courtyard and carved stone portal in the local Almohad tradition, but it is reduced in scale and effectiveness. A door in a similar style is all that remains of Abu 'Inan's Zawiyat al-Nussak outside Salé, where excavations revealed an unusually spacious plan. It follows Abu'l-Hasan's ruined *zāwiya* in the funerary complex at Chella, which had a single-storey courtyard containing a large pool with fountains. Another ruined building discovered at Aïn Qarwash was first thought to be a house, but was then identified as either a madrasa or a *zāwiya*, a confusion that reveals the parallel traditions of decoration and plan used in religious and secular architecture.

Although city walls, gates, caravanserais, public baths, aqueducts, public fountains and storehouses remain from

61. 'Attarin Madrasa, Fez, Morocco, courtyard, 1323–5

the period, royal palaces survive only near Tlemcen. At al-Mansura the court of Abu'l-Hasan's unfinished palace contained a pool similar in proportions to the Patio de los Arrayanes of the Alhambra (*see* GRANADA, §III, 1). The two other palatial remains outside Tlemcen have yet other types of courts. The trend towards building lavish houses and palaces in Fez and the introduction of such techniques as tile mosaic began in the reign of Abu Rabi' Sulayman (*reg* 1308–10), according to the historian Ibn Khaldun (1332–82). Several Marinid houses in Fez have exquisite decoration similar to that of the madrasas. Small and irregular plots forced builders to develop regular but ingenious plans, which resulted in extreme height (e.g. a courtyard under 4 m to a side is over 12 m high). Wide and shallow rooms, the depth of which was limited by the length of beams available, are articulated by alcoves at either end and gain access to the courtyard, light and air through a single large door surmounted by decorated windows. A Marinid residential tower remains at Belyunes near Ceuta, and small courtyard houses have been excavated there and further west at Ksar el-Srhir. The tower is similar to Nasrid examples, and its groin-vaulted rooms demonstrate, along with the baths of Fez, Rabat and Oujda and the storehouses of Fez, that Marinid secular construction—mainly of brick, mortar and rubble, with wooden supports and occasionally of pisé or stone masonry—was not strictly trabeate, nor was it always a skeleton on which surface decoration was hung.

BIBLIOGRAPHY

G. Marçais and W. Marçais: *Les Monuments arabes de Tlemcen* (Paris, 1903)
A. Bel: 'Les Inscriptions arabes de Fès', *J. Asiat.*, 11th ser. (1917–19), ix, pp. 303–29; x, pp. 81–170, 215–67; xii, pp. 189–276; xiii, pp. 5–96; xv, pp. 467–79
——: *Les Inscriptions arabes de Fès* (Paris, 1919)
H. Basset and E. Lévi-Provençal: 'Chella: Une Nécropole mérinide', *Hespéris*, ii (1922), pp. 1–92, 255–316, 385–425
——: *Chella: Une Nécropole mérinide* (Paris, 1923)
C. Terrasse: *Médersas du Maroc* (Paris, 1927)
B. Maslow: *Les Mosquées de Fès et du nord du Maroc* (Paris, 1937)
H. Terrasse: 'Trois bains mérinides du Maroc', *Mélanges William Marçais* (Paris, 1950), pp. 311–20
G. Marçais: *L'Architecture musulmane d'Occident* (Paris, 1954)
J. Meunié: 'La Zaouiat en-Noussak: Une Fondation mérinite aux abords de Salé', *Mélanges d'histoire et d'archéologie de l'Occident musulmane, hommage à Georges Marçais* (Algiers, 1957), pp. 129–45
R. Le Tourneau: *Fez in the Age of the Marinides* (Norman, OK, 1961)
H. Terrasse: 'Quelques Remarques sur les édifices de Belyunes', *Al-Andalus*, xxviii (1963), pp. 213–30
R. Bourouiba: *L'Art religieux musulman en Algérie* (Algiers, 1973)

NADIA ERZINI

(c) Tunisia. Of the dynasties ruling North Africa, only the HAFSID dynasty (*reg* 1228–1574) presented itself as the successor of the Almohads (*see* §5(iv)(d) above), and their administration strongly followed Almohad custom. The Hafsids reinvigorated urban life in such coastal cities as TUNIS, Sousse and Sfax, which had preserved their Zirid inheritance, despite the Hilalian invasions of the 11th century and the bedouinization of much of the region. KAIROUAN, once the political and commercial capital of North Africa, became a backwater, preserving only its religious pre-eminence. The Hafsids constructed mosques, madrasas and hospices for Sufi fraternities (*zāwiya*), they fortified Kairouan and Tunis, repaired the walls of Sousse and Sfax and built palaces in and near Tunis. The architecture of the region, which traditionally had been inspired by that of the eastern Islamic world, began to adopt Moroccan and Andalusian ideas brought by refugees from the Christian reconquest of Spain.

The Mosque of the Qasba in Tunis (1231–5) was begun slightly before the Hafsid governor Abu Zakariya declared his independence from the Almohads. The impact of Moroccan architecture is evident in the *muqarnas* and imposts in the dome over the bay in front of the mihrab, capitals profusely decorated with palmettes and fleurons in the Almohad style and a square stone minaret decorated with lozenge-net panels and topped by a lantern crowned with a pyramid of green tiles. The building remains faithful to local principles in its massing, use of stone, prayer-hall roofed with groin vaults resting on columns and vertical grooves decorating the mihrab niche. The Hawa Mosque, founded in the suburbs of Tunis by Abu Zakariya's widow, the princess 'Atf, has an oblong prayer-hall divided into seven aisles of six bays perpendicular to the qibla. The 42 square bays are covered with brick groin vaults supported on columns. The bay in front of the mihrab has four scalloped squinches, a feature seen in Aghlabid buildings of the 9th century (*see* §4(iii) above), supporting a cylindrical drum and a bulbous dome. The buttresses that bristle on the exterior give the building a military aspect. Neither mosque has a courtyard. The Hafsids refurbished Kairouan's congregational mosque in an attempt to restore some of its lost prestige. They constructed the galleries surrounding the courtyard and remodelled the portals, of which the Bab Lalla Rihana (1294; see fig. 62) on the east is a projecting rectangular pavilion covered with a fluted dome. The blind arcade on the exterior, crowning merlons and carved plaster arabesques on the soffits are inspired by Andalusian models, but realized in traditional Tunisian terms.

Madrasas flourished under Hafsid patronage, and they clustered around the Zaytuna, the congregational mosque of Tunis that the Hafsids restored and provided with a remarkable ablution facility. Abu Zakariya founded the Shamma'iyya Madrasa (1249), the first in the Islamic west, which was a simple urban house reworked to accommodate students and offer them a place of instruction and prayer, and his widow built another. The Muntasiriyya, begun by the caliph al-Muntasir (*reg* 1434–5), has a square central courtyard with a rectangular recess 3 m wide covered with a flat wooden roof opening on the middle of each side. The recess on the north leads to the entrance, that opposite to a nine-bay mosque and that on the east to a classroom. The recess on the west has been destroyed. The plan was undoubtedly modelled on the four-iwan madrasa plan common in the Islamic east; it was probably imported from Mamluk Egypt, with which the Hafsids maintained close relations.

62. Great Mosque, Kairouan, Tunisia, Bab Lalla Rihana portal, 1294

Hospices for Sufis (Arab. *zāwiya, khānaqāh*) began to appear in Tunisia in the 14th century, probably imported from the Islamic west. Focused on the tomb of a saint, and located in both urban and rural areas, they provided teaching and accommodation for devotees, as well as centres of pilgrimage, gathering and retreat for the community at large. The oldest are believed to be in Kairouan, for example those of Sidi Sahib, built around the grave of Abu Zama'a al-Balawi, a companion of the Prophet (reconstr. 17th century), and Sidi 'Abid al-Gharyani, begun by a Hafsid prince before 1324 but finished only in 1402 when the present tomb was associated with it. The most celebrated in and near Tunis are those of Sidi Ben 'Arus (1490) and Sidi Qasim al-Jalizi (for al-Zalliji; *c.* 1496). The latter centres around an arcaded courtyard paved with white marble inlaid with black marble and coloured tile. One side contains the square tomb of the saint, the others are occupied by a mosque and rooms for pilgrims and the poor. The tomb is decorated with such local features as blind arcades, rectangular recesses and corner colonnettes, but it is roofed with a pyramid of green tiles, a distinctly Moroccan substitution for the usual dome. The decoration of columns, capitals, carved plaster and ceramic on the interior similarly combines local and western Islamic features. The abundance of tile decoration reflects the occupation of Sidi Qasim (*d* 1496), a maker of tiles (*zallīj*) who emigrated from Andalusia to Tunis, where his spiritual merits brought him to the attention of the Hafsid princes. The *zāwiya* was decorated, if not by him, then by disciples who learnt from him the Andalusian craft of tile-cutting.

The beautiful residences, flowered parks and large gardens built by the Hafsid caliph al-Mustansir (*reg* 1249–77) are known only through literary descriptions. The Ras al-Tabiya Palace and park in the suburbs of Tunis had a vaulted passage permitting the women of the harem to go to the park without being seen. In the late 15th century a Flemish traveller wrote that it had four buildings arranged in a cross around a court paved with polychrome tiles. Four pools were fed from a central fountain. Al-Mustansir also built the Qubba Asarak (1253) and the Abu Fihr Palace on the outskirts of Tunis, which had pavilions at either end of an enormous basin. All of these are reminiscent of extant Moroccan and Andalusian palaces. The Hafsids remodelled and enlarged the covered market streets of Tunis in the 13th and 14th centuries; the most famous, the Suq al-'Attarin (Perfumers' Market), adjoins the Zaytuna Mosque and consists of three streets of shops covered with brick barrel vaults. Charitable foundations of the Hafsids included many public baths, hospitals and lazarettos.

BIBLIOGRAPHY

G. Marçais: *Tunis et Kairouan* (Paris, 1937)
R. Brunschvig: *La Berbérie orientale sous les Hafsides des origines à la fin du XVe siècle*, 2 vols (Paris, 1940–47)
G. Marçais: *L'Architecture musulmane d'Occident* (Paris, 1954)
J. Revault: *Palais et demeures de Tunis, I (XVIe et XVIIe siècles)* (Paris, 1967)
——: 'Une Résidence Hafside: L''Abdalliya à la Marsa', *Cah. Tunisie*, xix (1971), pp. 53–65
A. Daoulatli: *Tunis sous les Hafsides* (Tunis, 1976)
D. Hill and L. Golvin: *Islamic Architecture in North Africa* (London, 1976)

LUCIEN GOLVIN

7. *c.* 1500–*c.* 1900. The buildings of this period include some of the finest, best-preserved and most famous examples of Islamic architecture. The regional styles that had evolved over the preceding centuries were shaped into three imperial styles under the patronage of the Ottomans (*reg* 1281–1924) in the eastern Mediterranean region, the Safavids (*reg* 1501–1732) and other dynasties in Iran and the Mughals in India (*reg* 1526–1858). In other regions, such as western Central Asia and north-west Africa, distinct architectural styles were maintained under the SHAYBANID dynasty (*reg* 1500–98) and their collateral branches who ruled until 1785, and the Sharifan dynasties of Morocco (*reg* 1511–). Despite stylistic variations, all of these regions (except north-west Africa) shared a common architectural vocabulary of arches, domes and slender towers, but these forms were used for different purposes within the well-established repertory of types of Islamic architecture such as mosques, tombs and palaces. Traditional forms and techniques were increasingly affected by European architecture and architects, especially in the 19th century.

(i) Ottoman empire. (ii) Iran. (iii) Western Central Asia. (iv) Indian subcontinent. (v) Morocco.

(i) Ottoman empire. After the conquest of Constantinople (now Istanbul) in 1453 and particularly after the conquest of Syria and Egypt in 1517, architecture throughout the eastern half of the Mediterranean was dominated by the patronage of the Ottoman dynasty (1281–1924; *see* OTTOMAN, §I). Domed mosques flanked by pencil-shaped stone minarets formed the centrepieces of large building complexes erected by rulers and government officials throughout the empire. The consistent style was assured by central control of architectural design, although local techniques of construction often resulted in distinct provincial variants.

(a) Introduction. (b) Turkey. (c) Provinces.

(a) Introduction. Architectural practice under the Ottomans was dominated by the imperial Corps of Court Architects, of whom the greatest figure was the architect SINAN (ii). Founded in the 1520s when central control of all major building activity in the empire became desirable, the Corps prepared designs, procured materials and kept construction books for all religious and secular buildings initiated by the sultan, his family, the grand vizier and other high-ranking state officials. The Corps also approved and supervised all major architectural projects throughout the empire. The Chief Court Architect either discharged this responsibility himself, used the branch offices in major provincial centres or sent someone from the central office in Istanbul to the site. When a court architect executed a provincial project, a local architect helped with the construction. The Corps also trained apprentices, who assisted court architects in their tasks before being allowed to build a small tomb, fountain or wooden-roofed mosque independently.

The Corps was an efficient organization with an effective mechanism of centralized control, but it failed to produce aesthetic uniformity. Buildings designed and constructed by court architects in Istanbul were visibly different from those in the distant provinces. The purity of the Ottoman classical style could be sustained in provincial areas only when supervision was adequate. Thus, the Genabi Ahmed Pasha Mosque in ANKARA (1565–6), designed in Istanbul by Sinan, has an unnecessarily large base for the minaret, uneven window sequences on the sides and an asymmetrical portico. In keeping with Syrian building traditions, the mosque of Behram Pasha in DIYARBAKIR (1572), the Adiliye Mosque in ALEPPO (1565) and the Sulaymaniyya Mosque in Damascus (1554–5; see DAMASCUS, §1(ii)) are constructed of alternating courses of white and dark-grey stone. Similarly, the mosques of Süleyman Pasha (1528) and Malika Safiya (1610) in Cairo wear decorative Mamluk cloaks over their Istanbul designs (see CAIRO, §I, 3).

Ottoman architecture in the 16th century, despite the centralized planning, was still a personal art form in which design and execution were part of the same process. Key decisions concerning the design, such as the diameter of the dome, transition system, thickness of the outer walls and type of portico or arcade, were made in the central office, but almost everything else had to be devised on the site by the executive architect. He played the principal role in the formation of the building: the more capable he was, the more successful was the finished product. This explains why the buildings Sinan designed and constructed in and around Istanbul usually turned out better than those designed by him but constructed by his less gifted subordinates.

Sixteenth-century Ottoman architects, unlike their contemporaries in Italy, did not write treatises on architecture, so knowledge of architectural practice is limited. The earliest work on the subject, Ca'fer Efendi's *Risāle-i Mi'māriyye* ('Treatise on architecture'), dates from the first quarter of the 17th century and is a mine of information about the life and works of MEHMED AĞA, Chief Court Architect from 1606 to c. 1622. Ottoman architects in the classical period worked with simple floor-plans drawn on paper prepared with a grid of squares. Costs were estimated in some detail, but specifications (in the contemporary sense) were not articulated; the executive architect had to make many of the decisions on his own as the walls went up.

In the 19th century Corps-trained architects lost their jobs to architects recruited from Europe or to those with European training, such as Krikor Balyan (see BALYAN, (1)). The Imperial College of Military Engineering was established in 1801, but not until 1883 was a full architectural curriculum, modelled on that of the Ecole des Beaux-Arts in Paris, taught at the Istanbul Academy of Fine Arts. Many of the instructors of the School of Civil Engineering (established 1884) were recruited from Germany and Austria. (*See also* ISTANBUL, §I, 5.)

Axiality, centrality and exteriority are the three principal characteristics of Ottoman architecture. The typical building is the domed congregational mosque, while the domed tomb, favoured earlier, became relatively unimportant. The hemispheric dome was the predominant form in religious architecture because it expressed the concept of a central space. The integration of the interior space under the central dome can be seen as a metaphor for the oneness of God, just as the pyriform superstructure of the imperial mosque, in which semi-domes and smaller domes surround the great central vault, may be likened to the hierarchical Ottoman social order. The integration of space under a large dome led architects to accentuate the vertical. Verticality produced increased outer wall surfaces, which prompted articulation and externalized the building mass. Ottoman architects gave their buildings true exterior façades and dramatic profiles, yet at the same time they reintegrated the courtyard into the mosque plan. The impact of Byzantine and European architecture played a major role in reversing the traditional Islamic disregard for a building's exterior. Domes of brick and stone also covered the arcades surrounding the courts in mosques and caravanserais, and grids of domes covered the marketplaces of Ottoman cities.

Cut stone faced the most important public buildings, but brick was also used, particularly in alternation with stone, as in the kitchens of Topkapı Palace in Istanbul. Marble, quarried at Prokonnessos on the island of Marmara, was used for specific purposes, such as mihrabs, minbars (pulpits) and paving. Ruins in Istanbul, Baalbek in Syria and Alexandria in Egypt (see ALEXANDRIA, §4) provided antique marble and granite columns and slabs, which could be reused and recut for the arcades and dados of such buildings in the capital as the Süleymaniye Mosque and the Baghdad Pavilion at Topkapı Palace.

Elaborate tile-panels with floral, vegetal and epigraphic motifs covered lower interior surfaces, particularly the area in mosques surrounding the mihrab or the entire qibla wall. The finest quality tiles were produced at Iznik (see IZNIK, §2) for specific buildings, such as the mosque of Rüstem Pasha in Istanbul (see also §9(ii)(b) below); later, however, cheaper tiles and tile-panels were mass-produced and applied somewhat haphazardly to fit the space available. Coloured glass, imported from Venice and set in plaster, filled windows and diffused light in mosque interiors, but little has survived in its original condition. Upper surfaces, particularly vaults and domes, were decorated with paint on plaster. Standard motifs included epigraphic roundels in the pendentives and sunburst medallions in the centres of domes. Many of these were freely restored in the 19th century by the FOSSATI brothers, Gaspare Trajano and Giuseppe.

(b) Turkey. The spatial experiments of early Ottoman architecture (see §6(ii)(b) above) were codified in the 16th and 17th centuries in a classical style exemplified in a series of noble imperial mosque complexes in Istanbul. Built of superb stone masonry and decorated with precious marbles and exquisite tiles, they are some of the finest and most attractive monuments of Islamic architecture ever built, and they attest to the enormous power and sophistication of the Ottoman empire during its golden age. Beginning with the Tulip period (early 18th century), European elements were increasingly introduced in generally smaller buildings.

1453–1718. Mosques were usually the centrepieces of pious foundations (Turk. *külliye*) that might encompass shops, markets, baths and caravanserais to support the mosque, schools, hospices and soup-kitchens. Complexes of religious buildings built after the conquest of Constantinople were more rationally planned than those built before in Bursa and Edirne. Two of the most characteristic features of Ottoman mosques, an integral courtyard and the multiple minarets that distinguish imperial mosques, had first appeared at the Üç Şerefeli Mosque in Edirne (1437–47).

Ottoman mosques can be divided into two groups according to their superstructures. Mosques with wooden roofs were once more numerous than those with masonry domes, but wood's inherent vulnerability to fire means that few have survived. The Ramazan Efendi Mosque in Istanbul (1585) has a lead-covered tetrahedral roof covering both prayer-hall and portico and superb Iznik tiles inside. The Takkeci Ibrahim Ağa Mosque (1590) outside the walls of Istanbul near the Topkapı Gate has a U-shaped portico supported by wooden posts and a wooden dome concealed by a pitched roof.

Masonry-domed mosques, which range in size from tiny single-domed structures to monumental imperial mosques surmounted by scores of domes, are covered in a rich variety of ways. The Firuz Ağa Mosque in Istanbul (1490) established the classical prototype of the single-unit mosque with a dome on pendentives, cut-stone walls, two-tiered windows, a three-bay portico on four marble columns and a pencil-like stone minaret. During the 16th and 17th centuries scores of them were built throughout the empire. Most are located in Istanbul (e.g. the mosques of Hürrem Sultan (1538) and Hadım Ibrahim Pasha (1551)), but others are found at Gebze, Izmit, Karapınar, KAYSERI, Edirne and URFA, Aleppo in Syria, Cairo in Egypt, Trikkala in Greece, SOFIA in Bulgaria, Pécs in Hungary (*see* PÉCS, §1) and Mostar (partly destr.) in Bosnia and Herzegovina. Variations on the single-unit mosque involved the portico. The mosques of Bali Pasha in Istanbul (1504), Ali Pasha in Tokat (before 1572) and Grand Vizier SOKOLLU MEHMED PASHA in Luleburgaz (1569) have five, seven and nine bays respectively, while the mosques of Lari Çelebi in Edirne (1514–15) and Ivaz Efendi in Istanbul (*c.* 1585) have U-shaped porticos embracing the prayer-hall on the front and sides. Bases for the columns that once supported an outer shed roof show that double porticos first appeared in the Süleymaniye Mosque in Çorlu (1512). Extant examples, such as the mosques of Mihrimah Sultan at Üsküdar in Istanbul (1548), Damad Ferhad Pasha in Çatalca (1575–80), Behram Pasha in Diyarbakır (1572) and the ʿAdiliyya in Aleppo (built by the viceroy of Egypt, Dukaginzade Gazi Mehmed Pasha, in 1565), show the widespread popularity of this feature. Imperial mosques outside Istanbul were often of the single-unit type, and most of the provincial imperial mosques from the period were simple, modest structures.

Architects in Istanbul and Edirne experimented with a variety of ingenious and attractive mosque schemes including central domes on square, hexagonal and octagonal bases surrounded by semi-domes and smaller domes. The mosque of Mehmed Fatih in Istanbul (1470; destr. 1766; rebuilt; *see* ISTANBUL, §III, 9(ii)) was the first to introduce a single semi-dome on the qibla side of the central dome and three small domes on each side. It was preceded by a courtyard surrounded by domed arcades. The patron, Sultan Mehmed II Fatih (the Conqueror; *reg* 1451–81), was an enlightened ruler who sought to balance his

country's Islamic and Byzantine past with such contemporary developments of the Mediterranean world as the Italian Renaissance. The site on Istanbul's fourth hill had once supported Justinian's church of the Holy Apostles. The huge dome and central position of the mosque dominated the complex (1463–70), which had a hospital, double bath, kitchen, hospice, eight madrasas and two tombs arrayed along three parallel axes around a vast plaza 210 m on each side. The plan of the mosque, but with a seven-bay porch, was reproduced in the Selimiye in KONYA (*c.* 1566) and the Zal Mahmud Pasha Mosque in Eyüp (*c.* 1580), where deep galleries covered by flat-topped vaults enclose the central space on three sides.

Mehmed's son, Bayezid II (*reg* 1481–1512), built complexes in Edirne, AMASYA and Istanbul, of which the one in Istanbul (completed 1505–6) by the architect Yaʿqub Shah ibn Sultan Shah is the greatest. Its mosque, flanked by hospices and minarets, has semi-domes to the north and south of the central dome, an arrangement undoubtedly suggested by the great Byzantine church of Hagia Sophia (*see* ISTANBUL, §III, 1(ii)(a)) and a logical progression from the Fatih Mosque. The Şehzade Mehmed Mosque (1543–8; by Sinan) has a cruciform scheme of four semi-domes, one on each side of the central dome. It is preceded by a courtyard equal to the mosque in size. The hierarchical massing of the superstructure gives the mosque a plastic quality, and its colonnaded lateral façades brought a new concept of exteriority to Ottoman architecture, which had been largely introverted. The surrounding complex is asymmetrically organized: the mosque and tomb stand on the west side of a rectangular plaza, the madrasa and caravanserai on the east, and the kitchen and school at an angle across the street on the south.

The Süleymaniye (1552–9; see fig. 63 and ISTANBUL, §III, 10) is the most magnificent of all mosques in Istanbul and one of Sinan's finest works. Set on a dramatic site overlooking the Golden Horn, it is a largely symmetrical complex of pious foundations and service buildings terraced into the hillside (for plan *see* KÜLLIYE). Two sets of handsome minarets mark the four corners of its forecourt. The central dome (diam. 26.2 m) rises to a height of 53 m, and the interior space is extended along the qibla axis by two semi-domes and on either side by a row of five domed units in two different sizes. Like the mosque of Bayezid II, the plan follows the basic scheme of Hagia Sophia, but the space is more open.

The seven madrasas surrounding Süleyman's mosque made it the most prestigious centre of higher learning in the Ottoman world. The First and Second (1552) and Third and Fourth Madrasas (1558) were organized around courtyards, while the other three were organized longitudinally. The *imaret* (lodging and/or dining facilities; see below) comprises three buildings in a row on the north side of the mosque plaza: a hospice (Turk. *tabhane*), a guest house (Turk. *darüzziyafe*) containing kitchens on the ground floor and a caravanserai in the basement, and a hospital (Turk. *darüssifa*).

The hexagonal scheme of the Üç Şerefeli Mosque in Edirne was repeated first in the Kara Ahmad Pasha Mosque at Topkapı in Istanbul (*c.* 1560), where the dome rests on six columns and is bolstered by a pair of semi-domes on either side, and again in Sinan's mosque for

63. Süleymaniye Mosque, designed by Sinan, Istanbul, Turkey, 1552–9

Sokollu Mehmed Pasha at Kadırga in Istanbul (1571–2), where the central dome rests on two pairs of semi-domes supported by the rectangular outline of the walls. Another type of mosque inspired by the Üç Şerefeli Mosque had a large domed unit flanked by pairs of domed units half as large and two wings. It became popular in the latter part of the 15th century and was used widely during the reign of Süleyman. The mosque of Hafsa Sultan in Manisa (1522) is a typical example, while at the mosque of Mihrimah Sultan at Edirnekapı in Istanbul (c. 1565) the central dome is raised on four great arches to form a monumental baldachin allowing daylight to flood the lofty interior through screen walls with many windows.

Sinan's Selimiye Mosque in Edirne (1569–75; see fig. 64) achieves the optimum open interior space in Ottoman architecture by having its huge dome (diam. 31.28 m) rest on an octagonal baldachin expanded with semi-domes on the angles. The four minarets at the corners of the mosque, the tallest (70.89 m) in Ottoman architecture, frame the logical progression of domes, semi-domes and buttresses. The mosque, preceded by a rectangular courtyard, is set within a symmetrical complex that does not detract from the mosque's centrality. Octagonal support systems were used on a smaller scale at the Rüstem Pasha (1561), Azapkapı (1577) and Nişancı Mehmed Pasha (1588) mosques in Istanbul, but the Selimiye effectively marks an end to spatial development in the Ottoman imperial mosque.

In the 17th century the cruciform scheme of the Şehzade Mosque became the ideal for imperial mosques, emulated by both the Yeni Cami (New Mosque, begun by Davud Ağa in 1594, continued by Ahmed Dalgiç 1599–1603, and finally completed in 1663 by Mustafa Ağa) of the two queen mothers Safiye Sultan and Turhan Sultan and the mosque of Sultan Ahmed I (Blue Mosque, 1609–16, by Mehmed Ağa; see ISTANBUL, §III, 11). The plaza of the Yeni complex, placed on one side of the mosque probably because of the marshy site, is framed by an L-shaped covered bazaar and a tomb. The Sultan Ahmed Mosque is unique in having six minarets at the corners of the mosque and courtyard. Its interior, lit with windows of coloured Venetian glass, is clad with panels of tiles at ground and gallery level and with blue-stencilled plaster above. The subsidiary buildings of the complex are clustered in groups on the three sides of the mosque: the tomb and madrasa on the east, kitchen and hospital on the west, and shopping street (Turk. arasta) on the south. The asymmetrical formation and arbitrary setting of the three clusters, however, obscures the unity of the whole.

Most Ottoman madrasas were part of larger charitable complexes and either stood next to the mosque, as in that of Mihrimah Sultan at Üsküdar (1547), or shared the mosque's forecourt by surrounding its arcade on three sides, as in that of Mihrimah Sultan at Edirnekapı (c. 1565). Wrapping the madrasa around the courtyard allowed non-royal patrons, such as Sokollu Mehmed Pasha, to usurp

64. Selimiye Mosque, designed by Sinan, Edirne, Turkey, 1569–75

the imperial prerogative of having a courtyard before their mosques. Madrasas were also built independent of mosques. Süleyman the Magnificent built a madrasa in Halıcılar Köşkü (1548) to commemorate his father Selim I, and Rüstem Pasha built an exceptionally attractive one in Istanbul (1550) with an unusual octagonal courtyard inscribed within square walls. It contained a mosque-classroom and cells for students.

The word *imaret*, which had denoted a group of buildings, came to mean the lodging and/or dining facilities of a complex. Those in small complexes, such as those of Hürrem Sultan in Istanbul (1550) and of Murad III in Manisa (1586), had kitchens, storage rooms, a bakery and a refectory arranged around a single courtyard, while large complexes such as the Süleymaniye had separate buildings for each function (see above). At the Atik Valide complex in Üsküdar (c. 1574–83; by Sinan) one vast building with several courtyards encompasses a hospital, hospice, kitchen and two-winged caravanserai.

The caravanserai with wings on either side of a domed hall was often built on major trade routes during the period, for example those of Çoban Mustafa in Gebze (c. 1523) and Ekmekçioğlu Ahmed Pasha in Edirne (1609–10). When the complex was located in or near a market town, a shopping street might be integrated with the caravanserai, as in the complexes of Sokollu in Luleburgaz (1568), Lala Mustafa Pasha in Ilgın (1584) or Kara Mustafa Pasha in Incesu (1670). The Rüstem Pasha Han in Edirne (1560; for illustration *see* CARAVANSERAI) combines an urban caravanserai for local merchants and another for travelling traders.

Baths, like caravanserais, provided revenues to maintain the other buildings within a complex; they were located either on the periphery of the complex or in busy commercial centres to attract more clients. Single baths survive in the Süleymaniye and Kılıç Ali Pasha (completed 1583) complexes in Istanbul. The Barbaros Hayreddin Pasha Bath in Zeyrek, popularly known as the Çinili ('Tiled') Hammam (c. 1545), is a double bath with men's and women's sections placed side by side in a compact cluster. Both sections contain a domed hall, a vaulted *tepidarium* and a cruciform *caldarium*. The bath of Haseki Sultan (1556), called the Ayasofya Hamamı because of its location opposite Hagia Sophia in Istanbul, is also a double bath. Here, however, the identical men's and women's sections are back to back and consist of large halls, a three-unit *tepidarium* and a *caldarium* around a domed octagonal space with four alcoves on the sides and four rooms at the angles. Other double baths survive in Samatya, Edirne and Üsküdar. Ottoman bathing establishments had heated plunge pools only where hot springs provided the water, as at Rüstem Pasha's Yeni Kaplıca (New Spa; 1552) in Bursa or at the bath of Sokollu Mehmed Pasha in Budapest (c. 1578; *see* BUDAPEST, §I, 1).

Aqueducts and bridges as well as foundations and domes exemplified the skill of Ottoman structural engineers and the importance of their work. Roman aqueducts, improved by the Byzantines and repaired by Mehmed the Conqueror, were adequate for Istanbul's needs in the 15th

65. Baghdad Pavilion, Topkapı Palace, Istanbul, Turkey, 1639

century, but the population increase of the 16th century caused a severe water shortage. Between 1555 and 1563 the waters of the Kâğithane River in the Belgrade Forest were tapped, and 50 km of conduit, one main reservoir and four aqueducts were built, of which the two-tiered Mağlova (l. 257 m) is notable for its sturdy triangular flanges. Other Ottoman aqueducts brought water to Edirne, MECCA and MEDINA as well as a host of small towns. The Büyük Çekmece Bridge at Silivri near Istanbul (by Sinan, 1563–7) crosses 600 m of water with four hump-back sections connecting three artificial islands to either bank. The beautiful 185-m bridge over the Drina at Visegrád (Bosnia and Herzegovina), ordered by Sokollu Mehmed Pasha in 1577, has 11 arches and two resting platforms in the middle.

Few residential buildings from the period remain, since earthquakes and fires periodically razed the modest wooden homes of Istanbul and other Ottoman cities. Apart from the Atmeydani (Hippodrome) Palace in Istanbul (now the Museum of Turkish and Islamic Art), only Topkapı Palace (*see* ISTANBUL, §III, 13), the chief palace of the Ottoman sultans, preserves some semblance of a classical Ottoman setting, although the sultans repeatedly reconstructed, restored and renewed its parts. The oldest surviving pavilion is the Çinili ('Tiled') Kiosk, built in 1473 following a plan adapted from Iranian models (*see* ISTANBUL, fig. 7).

Three pavilions—the early 17th-century Circumcision Room, the Revan Pavilion that Murad IV built in 1636 to commemorate his capture of Yerevan, and the Baghdad Pavilion, built in 1639 to commemorate the conquest of Baghdad—exemplify the architectural character of the period. The Baghdad Pavilion (see fig. 65) is a large domed room with four alcoves and an outer gallery covered by broad eaves. Marble and tiles cover the exterior and interior walls, stained-glass windows subdue the light to the interior, wooden shutters and doors are inlaid with ivory and mother-of-pearl, and a brass-hooded fireplace at one corner warmed the low sofas in the alcoves.

1718–1922. European elements foreign to the classical Ottoman architectural vocabulary were introduced during the Tulip period under Ahmed III (*reg* 1703–30; *see* OTTOMAN, §II(5)) and gained popularity under Mahmud I (*reg* 1730–54). Fountains assumed monumental dimensions, and the Baroque style was adopted for palaces and the houses of the rich. Under Osman III (*reg* 1754–7) and Mustafa III (*reg* 1757–74) Baroque elements appeared on imperial mosques, leading to the emergence of the Ottoman Baroque, in which flamboyant Baroque ornament was liberally applied to a classical Ottoman armature. Baroque ornament did not destroy the classical essence because Ottoman life in the 18th century did not yet require foreign building types. In the 19th century, however, new types, such as monumental military barracks (e.g. those erected in Haydarpasa in Istanbul) replaced traditional forms, and the classical architectural framework collapsed, radically transforming the Ottoman cityscape.

66. Fountain of Ahmed III, Topkapı Palace, Istanbul, Turkey, 1729

Enthusiastic dispatches describing life in France by Mehmed Yirmisekiz Çelebi (*d* 1732), ambassador plenipotentiary, revolutionized the Ottoman court by introducing the European Baroque. The Sultan built himself a palace in the French style at Kâğıthane, and the notables followed suit. These plaster-and-lath fantasies have not survived, but the pavilion of Osman III at Topkapı Palace also emulates the French Rococo. Its apartment of several rooms decorated and furnished in the European manner clearly illustrates the break with the traditions of the Baghdad Pavilion.

The grand vizier Damad Ibrahim Pasha built the most important mosque of the Tulip period in 1726 in Mushqara (now Nevşehir), his home town. Set inside a rectangular plaza, a traditional domed-cube prayer-hall is preceded by a minaret and five-bay portico, but the classical style is weakened as parts seem unrelated to the whole. Domed turrets are too thin to be of any structural use, and weight towers at the corners are like finials. The attenuated walls, windows, dome, drums, columns and twin minarets of the Laleli Mosque in Istanbul (1763) further illustrate this slenderizing process. The Nuruosmaniye Mosque in Istanbul, begun by Mahmud I and completed in 1755 by Osman III, whose name it bears, has a horseshoe-shaped courtyard in the spirit of the European Baroque. The prayer-hall, in contrast, retains the classical formation of the 16th century: the dome rests on four pendentives between great arches buttressed by weight towers at the corners. The transparent screen walls are reminiscent of the Mihrimah Sultan

Mosque at Edirnekapı, built two centuries earlier. Europeanizing decorative details break with the past and reveal new and foreign sources. A simplified form of Ionic capital replaced the lozenge and *muqarnas* capitals of the classical period, arches became round and multifoil, portals became unusually tall and were crowned by tiers of diminishing semicircles instead of the conventional *muqarnas*, and circular rings replaced the *muqarnas* consoles on the balconies of the minarets. The mosque, however, does not invoke the spirit of the European Baroque, for Baroque elements were applied superficially and do not penetrate the building's skin.

Turkish Baroque architecture has surface plasticity but lacks the intricate conception of space and the strong sense of movement of its European counterpart. The most successful buildings of the 18th century are consequently small works, such as fountains and tombs, in which interior space plays little or no part. The fountain of Ahmed III (1729; see fig. 66) in front of the principal gate to Topkapı Palace is a square structure covered by a leaded roof with deep projecting eaves. The core contains a reservoir with spouts in the middle of each façade and triple-grilled cylindrical fountains at the corners. Although the intricate floral and foliate designs decorating the fountain are not new to Ottoman architecture, their exuberance and quantity differ from the restraint of classical decoration. The white marble tomb attached to the complex of Mihrişah Sultan at Eyüp in Istanbul (1792) has a dodecahedral body, the convex facets of which are separated by slender engaged columns, verd-antique below and pink granite above. Small voluted buttresses surround the recessed drum.

Ottoman architecture became more sensitive to European fashion in the 19th century, when Europe had pushed its way closer. The Neo-classical Empire style of Napoleon's France found an enthusiastic reception during the reigns of Mahmud II (reg 1808–39; see OTTOMAN, §II(6)) and his son Abdülmecid (reg 1839–61). Two works in the Ottoman Empire style are the Nusretiye Mosque at Tophane in Istanbul (1826), designed by the architect Krikor Balyan for Mahmud II to commemorate his victory over the janissaries, and the Sultan's tomb on the Divanyolu in Istanbul (1840), built by Abdülmecid to venerate his father's name. More outwardly Baroque are the mosques of Bezmialem Valide Sultan in Dolmabahçe (1853) and Abdülmecid in Ortaköy (1854). Each consists of a domed prayer-hall behind a medium-sized Renaissance-style palace flanked by two slender minarets in the form of Corinthian columns. Imperial palaces, such as the Dolmabahçe (1853) and the Beylerbeyi (1864), which Abdülaziz (reg 1861–76; see OTTOMAN, §II(7)) built on the shores of the Bosporus, are neo-Baroque, although their interiors, separated into men's and women's quarters and organized around traditional four-iwan halls, are traditionally Turkish.

Towards the end of the 19th century, a variety of Orientalism began to overshadow Western revivalism. The mosques of Pertevniyal Valide Sultan in Aksaray (1871) and of Abdülhamid II in Yıldız (Hamidiye; 1885) point to a critical change in the Ottoman socio-political outlook and represent something more than a new fashion. Just as the total absorption of Renaissance and Baroque features in the Mosque of Abdülmecid at Ortaköy symbolized the court's aspirations towards Westernization, the Eastern and Islamic motifs that imbue the Hamidiye in Yıldız symbolized an Ottoman resurgence. Jachmund, a German professor at the new School of Civil Engineering, designed the Sirkeci railway terminal (1890), of which the neo-Mamluk horseshoe arches, striped masonry and rose windows perfectly exemplify the eclectic Orientalism of the day.

The third and last phase of Ottoman revivalism rehabilitated Turkish classicism of the 16th century, in keeping with Turkish aspirations towards cultural identity. Intricate details from the era of Sinan featured in the new style, which enjoyed a wide popularity between the proclamation of the Second Constitution in 1908 and the end of the empire in 1922. Among the best examples of the Turkish neo-classical style in Istanbul are the Land Registry Building in Sultanahmed (1908) and the Central Post Office Building in Sirkeci (1909), both by VEDAT, Mehmed V's tomb and elementary school in Eyüp (1911), and the Bebek mosque (1913) and the Fourth Vakif Han in Bahçekapi (1912–26), both by KEMALETTIN. The Vakif Han is an immense seven-storey office block of which the cut-stone façade conceals a steel skeleton. Such classical elements as tiled panels, geometric carvings, profiled mouldings, pointed domes and well-arranged windows have been applied to create a neo-Renaissance elevation in Ottoman guise.

BIBLIOGRAPHY

E. H. Ayverdi: *Fatih devri mimarisi* [Architecture in the reign of Mehmed the Conqueror] (Istanbul, 1953)
D. Kuban: *Türk barok mimarisi hakkinda bir deneme* [Essay on Turkish Baroque architecture] (Istanbul, 1954)
——: *Osmanli dini mimarisinde iç mekan tesekkülü* [Formation of space in Ottoman religious architecture] (Istanbul, 1958)
T. Öz: *Istanbul camileri* [Mosques of Istanbul], 2 vols (Ankara, 1962–5)
S. Turan: 'Osmanli teskilâtinda hassa mimarlari' [Royal architects in Ottoman administration], *Ankara Ü. Dil Ve Tarih Araştırmaları Derg.*, i (1963), pp. 157–202
D. Kuban: 'An Ottoman Building Complex of the Sixteenth Century: The Sokollu Mosque and its Dependencies in Istanbul', *A. Orient.*, vii (1968), pp. 19–39
A. Kuran: *The Mosque in Early Ottoman Architecture* (Chicago and London, 1968)
S. H. Eldem: *Köşkler ve kasirlar/Kiosks and Pavilions* (Istanbul, 1969)
Yirmisekiz Mehmet Çelebi: *Fransa seyahatnamesi* [Journey to France] (Istanbul, 1970)
O. Aslanapa: *Turkish Art and Architecture* (London, 1971)
G. Goodwin: *A History of Ottoman Architecture* (Baltimore and London, 1971)
E. H. Ayverdi: *Osmanli mimarisinde Çelebi ve II. sultan Murad devri, 806–855 (1403–1451)* [The era of Mehmed Çelebi and Murat II in Ottoman architecture, 806–55 (1403–51)] (Istanbul, 1972)
Ö. L. Barkan: *Süleymaniye Camii ve İmareti İnşaatı, 1550–1557* [The construction of the Süleymaniye Mosque and its adjoining buildings, 1550–57)], 2 vols (Ankara, 1972–9)
E. H. Ayverdi: *Osmanli mimarisinde Fatih devri, 855–886 (1451–1481)* [The period of Mehmed II in Ottoman architecture, 855–86 (1451–81)], 2 vols (Istanbul, 1973–4)
Z. Nayir: *Osmanlı mimarlığında sultan Ahmed külliyesi ve sonrası, 1609–1690* [The complex of Sultan Ahmed and its influence in Ottoman architecture, 1609–90] (Istanbul, 1975)
A. Kuran: 'Eighteenth-century Ottoman Architecture', *Studies in Eighteenth-century Islamic History*, ed. T. Naff and R. Owen (London and Amsterdam, 1977)
D. Kuban: 'Architecture of the Ottoman Period', *The Art and Architecture of Turkey*, ed. E. Akurgal (Oxford and New York, 1980)
J. M. Rogers: 'The State and the Arts in Ottoman Turkey: The Stones of Süleymaniye', *Int. J. Mid. E. Stud.*, xiv (1982), pp. 71–96
M. Cezar: *Typical Commercial Buildings of the Ottoman Classical Period and the Ottoman Construction System* (Istanbul, 1983)
Y. Yavuz and S. Özkan: 'The Final Years of the Ottoman Empire', *Modern Turkish Architecture*, ed. R. Holod and A. Evin (Philadelphia, 1984)
G. Necipoğlu-Kafadar: 'The Süleymaniye Complex in Istanbul: An Interpretation', *Muqarnas*, iii (1985), pp. 92–117
——: 'Plans and Models in 15th- and 16th-century Ottoman Architectural Practice', *J. Soc. Archit. Historians*, xlv (1986), pp. 224–43
Ca'fer Çelebi: *Risala-i Mi'mariyya: An Early Seventeenth-century Ottoman Treatise on Architecture*, Eng. trans. by H. Crane (Leiden, 1987)
D. Kuban: 'The Style of Sinan's Domed Structures', *Muqarnas*, iv (1987), pp. 72–97
A. Kuran: *Sinan: The Grand Old Master of Ottoman Architecture* (Washington, DC, and Istanbul, 1987)
M. Cerasi: 'Late Ottoman Architects and Master Builders', *Muqarnas*, v (1988), pp. 87–102
J. Erzen: 'Sinan as Anti-Classicist', *Muqarnas*, v (1988), pp. 70–86

APTULLAH KURAN

(c) *Provinces.* In the classical period, the Ottoman court style of architecture was diffused through government institutions established in the main provincial cities of the empire (see OTTOMAN, §I). Plans in the court style were sent from Istanbul (see §(a) above), but local materials and labour force meant that vaulting, elevation and façade might differ from the classical ideal. This system changed in the 18th century, when the power of the central administration waned: tax revenues owed to the state were seized by regional governors and notables, who adopted a new bourgeois way of life. This was also the time when European styles began to be adopted.

67. Sulaymaniyya complex, Damascus, Syria, 1554–5

The eastern half of the Balkans, which had been devastated by war among the Byzantines, Bulgarians and Ottomans, was colonized by the Ottomans from the 14th century, and thousands of buildings were erected quickly to serve the needs of the new Muslim population and Ottoman government. Traditional stone and brick cloisonné techniques continued to be used until the mid-15th century, when ashlar construction began to predominate. At the same time, experiments in the construction of large domes, such as that in the great mosque of Yambol in Bulgaria (1420s; diam. c. 25 m), provided a model for the enormous interior spaces of classical-style mosques in the capitals. The western Balkans, including Albania, Bosnia and central Macedonia, were not immediately converted to Islam, and their architectural traditions, such as decorative brickwork (e.g. the Hacı Mahmud Mosque in Bitola, in the Republic of Macedonia, 1527) and tiled roofs, were maintained for longer. Fortresses were undoubtedly the most essential and monumental constructions; the building of several in Hungary was depicted in contemporary Ottoman manuscript painting. Caravanserais and bridges, such as the beautiful example at Mostar (Bosnia and Herzegovina; 1566; destr.), were constructed along military or commercial routes. Many fine examples of late Ottoman domestic architecture are preserved, particularly the verandah houses of Berat and the fortified stone houses of Gjirokastër, both in Albania.

After the Ottomans defeated the Safavids of Iran at the Battle of Chaldiran (1514; see SAFAVID, §1), the provinces of MOSUL, BAGHDAD and BASRA in Iraq were incorporated into the Ottoman empire. Under Ottoman rule, shrines were restored and new mosques erected. In Baghdad, pre-Ottoman architectural features, such as brick

construction, high arched portals with muqarnas semi-domes and exterior surfaces revetted with glazed tile, continued to be used, as on the Ahmadiyya Mosque (1795). In Mosul, which was more closely tied to Anatolia, such buildings as the Shaykh 'Abbas Mosque (1669) show a far greater impact of the metropolitan style of Ottoman architecture.

Syria, Arabia and Egypt were conquered in 1516–17 and remained under Ottoman control for centuries. Aleppo, Damascus and Cairo continued to be the principal cities in the region (see ALEPPO; DAMASCUS, §1(ii); CAIRO, §I, 3), but the new importance of the pilgrimage route from Turkey to the holy cities of Arabia meant that smaller cities were also endowed with accommodations for pilgrims. Multi-purpose complexes, combining mosques, madrasas, kitchens and caravanserais, were common (e.g. the Khusraw Pasha complex in Aleppo, 1546, and the Sulaymaniyya complex in Damascus, 1554–5; see fig. 67). Commercial structures, particularly urban caravanserais (Arab. khān), with associated markets, bazaars and shops, were especially important in Aleppo, which became the centre for commercial transactions linking Europe and the Mediterranean with Anatolia, the Jazira, Iran and India. Ottoman religious architecture in Syria is distinguished by the continued use of bichrome (Arab. ablaq) masonry, except at the Dome of the Rock in Jerusalem, where the ruined mosaics on the exterior were replaced with multi-coloured tiles specially commissioned for the purpose (see JERUSALEM, §II, 1(iii)). Domestic buildings, of which splendid examples remain in Damascus ('Azam Palace, begun 1749; now Museum of Popular Arts and Traditions) and Aleppo, are characterized by irregular spreading plans arranged around several interior courts for men and women, often with large iwans. Interiors were splendidly revetted in painted, carved, gilded and inlaid wood, marble and tile. In the 19th century many Syrian cities were remodelled as streets were widened, public squares laid out and new European types of buildings erected.

Under Ottoman guardianship, shrines in the holy cities of MECCA and MEDINA in Arabia quickly took on such Ottoman features as domes, slender minarets and glazed tiles. The Masjid al-Haram, the mosque around the Ka'ba in Mecca, was enlarged to the Ottoman taste in the 16th century; the Mosque of the Prophet in Medina was rebuilt in 1849. Many other Ottoman constructions were subsequently razed by the conservative Sa'ud dynasty (*reg* 1746–) because they considered domes and minarets to be heretical innovations. In the Yemen, which the Ottomans ruled until 1635, the earlier type of domed mosque remained in use (*see* §6(iii)(b) above), but in plan and elevation it followed the type developed in Turkey. The octagonal domed plan, masonry techniques, articulation of the walls, and decoration of the Husayniyya in Ta'izz (16th or 17th century) are characteristic of metropolitan Ottoman architecture. The traditional mihrab frame was elongated to the Ottoman taste, and new ornamental motifs, such as bands of carnations and peonies, introduced. Elements of traditional painted and stucco decoration continued to be used, however, as in the Bakiriyya Mosque in SAN'A (1597).

In Egypt, the annual remittance owed the government in Istanbul meant that less money was available for local construction than had been the case under the Mamluks (*see* §6(iii)(a) above), although hundreds of small buildings survive from the period in Cairo. The local Mamluk style continued to be used without interruption, but a few buildings, such as the mosque of Malika Safiya (1610), were built in the metropolitan Ottoman style. The *sabīl-kuttāb*, a combination drinking-water dispensary and elementary school which had been known in the Mamluk period, became the most characteristic building type, undoubtedly for reasons of economy. Nearly 100 survive, and such elegant examples as those of 'Abd al-Rahman Katkhuda (1744) and Ruqayya Dudu (1761) attest to continued architectural vitality. Interior revetments of marble were still popular, although tiles were sometimes introduced, as in the mosque of Aqsunqur (Blue Mosque), which was redecorated (1652) with low-quality tiles. Perhaps the most famous example of Ottoman architecture outside Turkey is the mosque of Muhammad 'Ali (Cairo, 1828–57; *see* CAIRO, §III, 11), designed on a plan similar to that of the mosque of Sultan Ahmed in Istanbul (1609–16; *see* ISTANBUL, §III, 11).

Algeria and Tunisia were incorporated into the empire by corsairs in the 16th century; they later came under the control of semi-autonomous rulers who imitated court life in Istanbul. The hypostyle mosque, traditional in North Africa, was replaced by central-plan domed mosques roughly inspired by metropolitan Ottoman examples, such as the mosque of Sidi Mahrez in TUNIS (1726) and that of the Fishermen (Jami' al-Jadid; the New Mosque) in Algiers (1660–61). Painted and glazed tile-panels and carved and painted stucco were used to decorate the interiors of mosques, fine houses and palaces (e.g. Algiers, Beylerbey Palace, 16th century and later; Tunis, Dar 'Uthman, 18th

century), although exteriors retained their traditional aspect.

BIBLIOGRAPHY

J. A. Williams: 'The Monuments of Ottoman Cairo', *Colloque international sur l'histoire du Caire: Caire, 1969*, pp. 453–65

R. Dokali: *Les Mosquées de la période turque à Alger* (Algiers, 1974)

G. Goodwin: 'Ottoman Architecture in the Balkans', *A. & Archaeol. Res. Pap.*, ix (1976), pp. 55–9

M. Kiel: 'The Ottoman Hamam and the Balkans', *A. & Archaeol. Res. Pap.*, ix (1976), pp. 87–96

R. I. Lawless: 'Albania: The Legacy of Turkish Islam', *A. & Archaeol. Res. Pap.*, ix (1976), pp. 60–67

S. Stamov: 'Les Monuments islamiques sur les terres bulgares', *A. & Archaeol. Res. Pap.*, ix (1976), pp. 68–74

E. H. Ayverdi and others: *Avrupa'da osmanli mimari eserleri* [Ottoman buildings in Europe], 4 vols (Istanbul, 1977–82)

M. Kiel: 'Some Reflections on the Origins of Provincial Tendencies in the Ottoman Architecture of the Balkans', *Islam in the Balkans: Persian Art and Culture of the 18th and 19th Centuries*, ed. J. M. Scarce (Edinburgh, 1979), pp. 19–28

R. I. Lawless: 'Berat and Gjirocastër: Two Museum Towns of Albania', *Islam in the Balkans: Persian Art and Culture of the 18th and 19th Centuries*, ed. J. M. Scarce (Edinburgh, 1979), pp. 9–17

N. Hanna: *An Urban History of Bulaq in the Mamluk and Ottoman Periods* (Cairo, 1983)

Ü. Ü. Bates: 'Two Ottoman Documents on Architects in Egypt', *Muqarnas*, iii (1985), pp. 121–7

F. Yenisehirlioglu: *Türkiye dısındaki osmanli mimari yapıtları* [Ottoman architectural works outside Turkey] (Ankara, 1989)

□

(ii) Iran. The architectural traditions established by the Timurids in Khurasan and Transoxiana were continued under the patronage of the Safavid (*reg* 1501–1732), Zand (*reg* 1750–94) and Qajar (*reg* 1779–1924) dynasties, but the centres of patronage moved to their capitals in Isfahan, Shiraz and Tehran. Religious architecture was still built of brick and revetted with glazed tile inside and out, while palaces, which often included wooden hypostyle porches, were decorated on the interior with carved plaster and sometimes painted with figural scenes adapted from the repertory of contemporary book illustration. Increasing contact with the West led to the introduction of European ideas and motifs.

(a) *c.* 1500–*c.* 1700. (b) *c.* 1700–*c.* 1900.

(a) c. *1500*–c. *1700*. Architectural patronage in Iran was dominated by the SAFAVID dynasty (*reg* 1501–1732), whose domain stretched from eastern Turkey to western India and from the southern Caucasus and Bukhara to the Persian Gulf and Indian Ocean. Despite the temporal and geographic extent of their empire, the period is best known for buildings erected in a single city, Isfahan, in the 60 years after Shah 'Abbas I (*reg* 1588–1629) transferred the capital there in 1598 (*see* ISFAHAN, §1). The buildings of the period simultaneously exhibit two tendencies. The first is towards a well-planned (although often hastily and crudely executed), three-dimensional, open architecture based on careful study and refinement of earlier traditions. The result is a sensitive style that can be fully enjoyed and easily appreciated. The other tendency is towards a more static and artificial architecture based on grandiose but set schemes and fixed perspectives. The result is a theatrical, courtly style that tends to the sensational and is more difficult to encompass freely. Only rarely are the two tendencies balanced and merged into a harmonious synthesis. Rather, most architectural works are ambiguous,

perpetually poised between a static and ceremonial vision and a need for rationality and functionalism in organizing a single structure, group of buildings or urban system. The modest architectural lexicon inherited from the Timurids in north-east Iran (*see* §6(i)(b) above) was barely sufficient for the demands of a new imperial Persian architecture. This obstacle was overcome, particularly in Isfahan, by architects who produced more sophisticated and ambitious versions of traditional buildings, and the resulting style was exported to the furthest corners of the empire. Although architectural compositions remained tied to local motifs, regional forms were sometimes integrated into a coherent imperial style which was disseminated by the wide circulation of labour, artists and ideas.

History and development. Shah Isma'il I (*reg* 1501–24), who established Twelver Shi'ism as the state religion, built throughout the empire, but his major works, such as a large official building at Khoy between Tabriz and the Turkish frontier, have been destroyed and only minor ones remain. At SHIRAZ two modest, centrally planned tombs stand over the graves of Khatun Qiyamat and Bibi Dukhtaran, and at Kalkhuran near ARDABIL a larger tomb with an unusual apsidal plan covers the grave of Shaykh Jibra'il, father of the eponymous founder of the Safavid dynasty. At Isfahan the Harun-i Vilayat (1513) is a traditional domed square tomb with a fine tile façade, and the nearby Masjid-i 'Ali (1522) has a traditional four-iwan mosque plan with a domed sanctuary and an elaborate tiled façade. At Sava the Friday Mosque and the Maydan Mosque were restored.

More than 40 buildings date from the long reign of Shah Tahmasp I (*reg* 1524–76), but the monarch himself was responsible for only a few architectural projects, as he was more interested in book painting (*see* §III, 4(vi)(a) below). Most of his architectural work was in QAZVIN, the new capital, which was subsequently devastated by earthquake. He ordered a royal mosque and palace with large gardens, guest rooms and separate pavilions; all that remains is the monumental entrance iwan, the 'Ali Qapu ('Lofty gate'), and the much restored pavilion known as the Chihil Sutun ('Forty columns') or the Kula-yi Farangi ('European hat'). Shrines were repaired or enlarged. The grand Jannat Saray, an octagonal domed hall for Sufi gatherings and prayer (*c.* 1540), was added to the dynastic shrine at Ardabil and a caravanserai added to the tomb of the Eighth Shi'ite imam at MASHHAD (*see* SHRINE, colour pl. IV, fig. 1). At Isfahan the qibla iwan of the Friday Mosque was refurbished with tile (*see* ISFAHAN, §3(i)). New works in the city included a pavilion for royal receptions, an aqueduct and the Qutbiyya Mosque; the only surviving fragment is the tile-ornamented doorway of the mosque (1543), reinstalled in the park of the 17th-century Chihil Sutun Palace (*see* ISFAHAN, §3(vii)). An extensive palace at NA'IN with elaborately painted plaster decoration has been attributed to *c.* 1560 on stylistic grounds.

The most ambitious patron of the period was Shah 'Abbas I, who earned the regal, though somewhat rhetorical, epithet 'Constructor of the World'. He transferred the capital further south to Isfahan, and, under the watchful eyes of merchants, jewellers, adventurers, ambassadors, missionaries and technicians, the city was transformed into a large metropolis and international entrepôt that for many outshone all other contemporary cities in the world, including those of Europe. 'Abbas I relocated the city's commercial and political centre to open land near the Zaindeh River. Trade was diverted from the old centre near the Friday Mosque to a 2 km-long bazaar (*see* ISFAHAN, §3(v)) lined with caravanserais and culminating in a dramatic portal. The portal (1619–20) opens on to an enormous maidan (*c.* 525×159 m; see fig. 68), surrounded by a continuous two-storey arcade linking the portal on the north with the small oratory known as the mosque of Shaykh Lutfallah (1603–19; see fig. 79 below) on the east, the large congregational Shah Mosque (1611–*c.* 1630) on the south and the entrance to the palace grounds on the west (*see* ISFAHAN, §3(ii)–(iv)). To the west of the palace, a long avenue called Chahar Bagh ('Four gardens') leads to the Si-o-sih pul ('Bridge of thirty-three [arches]'). It was erected in 1602 by Allahvardi Khan, favourite and generalissimo of 'Abbas I, and has a main passage for caravans flanked by lanes for pedestrians with several semicircular towers at intervals. It connected the city to the great hunting reserves, Hazar Jarib ('Thousand acres'), across the river. (*See also* §10(ii) below.)

This complicated urban development was designed to create an ideal city in which the members of different social, ethnic and religious classes could coexist peacefully. Some 23 churches were built in New Julfa. They combined local materials of construction, such as brick, and techniques of decoration, such as tile and painted stucco, with traditional forms from Armenian stone architecture, such as belfrys. Residences for Carmelite and Capuchin missionaries, like those of rich Persians, were garden villas, modelled on detached royal pavilions, such as the Bagh-i Fin at KASHAN and the Hasht Bihisht at Isfahan (*see* ISFAHAN, §3(viii)). Even modest dwellings were enriched with new architectural features and refined decoration. The dominant feature in many of these private dwellings was the skilful and inventive use of water in fountains and pools.

'Abbas I and his courtiers also ordered works outside the capital. At the dynastic shrine at Ardabil, the Chinikhana, housing the royal porcelain collection donated in 1612, was redecorated and the Dar al-Huffaz, a large hall for Koran reading, refurbished (1627–8). At the shrine at Mashhad an upper esplanade was built across the old courtyard and Allahvardi Khan constructed the octagonal dome chamber (1612). At the shrine for the Sufi shaykh Ni'matallah Vali (*d* 1431) at MAHAN near Kirman, a covered gallery and courtyard were added to the dome chamber (1601). Innumerable mausolea dedicated to the cult of saints and martyrs were built throughout the country, such as the tomb of Khwaja Rabi' (1620) outside Mashhad, which is a fine octagonal structure with a high double dome revetted in tile. Between 1596 and 1606 Ganj 'Ali Khan rebuilt the centre of KIRMAN after he had been appointed its governor. A series of public buildings including a bath, caravanserai, mint, water-tower and mosque are harmoniously positioned and connected by a continuous portico around a large rectangular maidan (100×50 m). The innovative planning, unified character

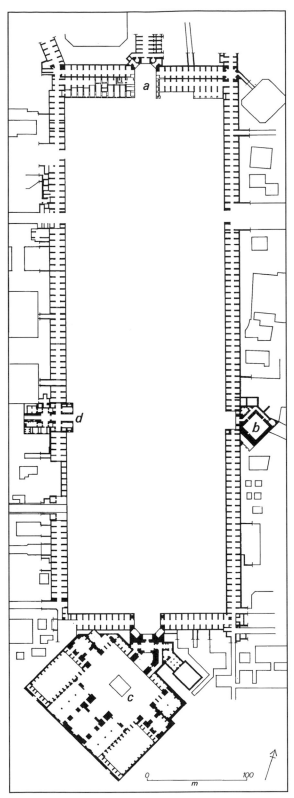

68. Royal Maidan, Isfahan, Iran, c. 1590–c. 1630, plan: (a) bazaar portal, 1619–20; (b) mosque of Shaykh Lutfallah, 1603–19; (c) Shah Mosque, 1611–c. 1630; (d) 'Ali Qapu Palace, begun c. 1597

and social import of the complex make it one of the major architectural achievements of the period, although it is unclear whether it was the prototype for or a minor replica of the more famous one at Isfahan.

The quantity, scale and quality of architectural patronage slackened after the reign of 'Abbas I. His successors did not fully understand the Shah's ecumenical policies, which were devoted to realizing a vast urban building programme, although they continued to construct public and religious buildings, especially in Isfahan and in the holy cities of QUM and Mashhad. 'Abbas II (reg 1642–66) constructed two masterpieces in the capital: the Chihil Sutun ('Forty columns') Palace, a large rectangular hall preceded by an iwan and a hypostyle porch (Pers. talar), and the Khwaju Bridge (1650). Probably erected for the Shah by the general Hasan Beg, the bridge has two levels, separate lanes for pedestrians and caravan traffic and a central viewing pavilion (see fig. 69). Its Baroque spatial organization represents the culmination of bridge construction under the Safavids. Under Sulayman (reg 1666–94) the shrine at Mashhad was restored following the earthquake of 1673, and two palaces built at Isfahan. The Hasht Bihisht ('Eight paradises'; 1669) has a central domed hall with open porches on the four sides and closed rooms in the four corners. The Talar-i Ashraf (c. 1690) is simpler in plan: it has a central hall roofed with a groin vault and flanked by smaller rooms. The most striking, if theatrical, construction of Husayn I (reg 1694–1722) is a mosque-madrasa, caravanserai (later transformed into a hotel) and bazaar off the Chahar Bagh in Isfahan. Known as the Madrasa-yi Madar-i Shah ('Madrasa of the Shah's mother'), the complex marks a return to the grand scale of architecture under 'Abbas I, although the plan is stereotyped and the decoration, particularly the tilework, is coarse.

Public works assumed great importance throughout the country, particularly under 'Abbas I. Numerous aqueducts, dams and other projects for water control and fluvial diversion were initiated, but not all of them were carried out. To satisfy the demand of Isfahan's 600,000 residents, 'Abbas I wanted to join a river beyond the first range of the Zagros Mountains to the Zaindeh. Only the insurmountable technical difficulties of drilling through the mountain dissuaded him. Bridges developed from purely functional structures into pleasure spots and opportunities for architectural display. At Isfahan, for example, within 50 years defensive and regulatory buildings were added to the north head of the Shahristan Bridge, the Si-o-sih pul and Khwaju bridges erected, the Marnan Bridge refurbished and the Jubi Bridge built to transport water from Suffa Mountain south of the city. The building or restoration of five bridges along 4 km of the Zaindeh River in such a brief period demonstrates the robust start given to urbanization and the rapid physical development of the capital that paralleled its political growth. As these bridges were fitted with wooden gates for regulating the flow of water, they also served as dams for irrigation.

Aqueducts assumed great importance because of the increase in new settlements, and an extensive system of qanāts, subterranean aqueducts directly linked to the water-bearing stratum, was dug. The forms and types of buildings for collecting and storing water were expanded. The typical

69. Khwaju Bridge, Isfahan, Iran, 1650

water-storage tanks (Pers. *āb-anbār*) are enormous semi-underground cisterns covered with domes and ventilated by means of pipes (Pers. *bādgīr*); their façades often resemble richly decorated iwans. Ingenious structures for the production and storage of ice (Pers. *yakhchāl*) were developed, with protective walls, often of mud-brick, gaily decorated with inventive brickwork. Pigeon towers (Pers. *burj-i kabūtar*) were another architectural genre that ʿAbbas I encouraged for economic and agricultural reasons. Thousands were built on the fertile plain of Isfahan from monies provided by the Shah, who then heavily taxed the guano harvest. The first simple circular types (perhaps based on designs provided directly by government technicians) soon evolved into more complicated forms designed to increase the number of holes for nesting. The extensive network of clearing stations and resting posts for caravans was renewed and extended with public monies, private funds and the proceeds of religious foundations. The typical rural caravanserai is a rectangle set in open countryside with rounded towers at the corners, three plain walls and a fourth marked by a boldly projecting portal. A vaulted vestibule leads to the interior, a court surrounded by one or two storeys of vaulted rooms linking iwans in the middle of each of its four sides. Some of the larger examples, such as the one at Mahyar (1502–24; rest. 1666–94) located some 40 km from Isfahan towards Shiraz, have two storeys and interior façades resembling those of contemporary mosques or madrasas. The urban Madrasa-yi Madar-i Shah Caravanserai in Isfahan similarly displays a high degree of functional and architectural refinement.

Artisans, materials, techniques and decoration. Town planning and building on such a wide scale necessitated the employment of dozens of architects and master builders. They were assisted by calligraphers who decorated buildings with monumental epigraphs, often containing a chronogram; tile-makers and cutters who designed and executed ceramic revetments; plasterers who prepared mihrabs, panels, grilles and *muqarnas*; woodworkers who

carved doors and window-grilles and inlaid ceilings; and painters who decorated interiors with wall paintings, usually conceived as manuscript paintings enlarged to a monumental scale. The work-force, especially at the top, was highly mobile and dominated by the Isfahan school. Many craftsmen who worked in Isfahan had epithets suggesting that they were recruited from elsewhere. For example, Shams al-Din of Tabriz signed the inscription in tile mosaic dated AH 929 (1522–3) for the portal of the Masjid-i ʿAli, and the calligrapher Kamal al-Din Husayn of Herat designed the one dated AH 938 (1531–2) in the south iwan of the Friday Mosque. Other craftsmen attached the epithet Isfahani ('of Isfahan') to their name (e.g. Yusuf ibn Taj al-Din, the builder of Isfahan who collaborated with Kamal al-Din Husayn of Herat on the repairs to the south iwan of the Friday Mosque). Isfahani craftsmen were sent to work on major projects throughout the realm. Hajji Shujaʿ of Isfahan, for example, repaired the *muṣalla* (open-air prayer-ground) in Mashhad for Sulayman.

Only a few architects are named in contemporary chronicles and only a few signed more than one building, but how they worked can be seen from the career of one of the most famous monumental calligraphers, Muhammad Riza al-Imami, who signed some 60 inscriptions between 1628 and 1677 in Isfahan, Natanz, Qazvin, Qum and Mashhad. His patrons ranged from four successive shahs to a humble fruit-seller; his commissions ranged from such major projects as the Shah Mosque in Isfahan and the shrine of Imam Riza in Mashhad to such small works as the tomb of Baba Qasim in Isfahan. He came from a family of monumental calligraphers, for others with the name Imami had signed buildings in Isfahan 75 years earlier. His son Muhammad Muhsin and his grandson ʿAli Naqi continued the family tradition.

The vast scale of architecture during this period led architects to produce buildings with uniform exteriors and to experiment with structure. The system of ribbed vaults developed during the 15th century was perfected through empirical study of the yield strength of materials. Rooms are spanned by ribbed arches which, when the spans are large, have forked bases so as to distribute the weight more equally on to piers, which are often concealed within the interior and exterior walls. The courtly style, however, discouraged such structural experiments from being displayed, and they have been revealed only during the course of restoration. Such techniques are best seen in the upper two floors of the 'Ali Qapu Palace at Isfahan (see ISFAHAN, §3(vi)). In the Music Room (see fig. 70), which crowns the palace, load-bearing structures, although boldly conceived, are hidden by a rich and obsessive decorative cover, which is split and fragmented into painted stucco *muqarnas* and niches in the form of Chinese porcelains. Elsewhere, flat walls are covered with paintings, the subject-matter of which varied from such Persian classics as the romance of Khusraw and Shirin to such current events as a series of European embassies and the Battle of Chaldiran depicted on the walls of the Chihil Sutun Palace at Isfahan (see §9(iii)(b) and fig. 81 below). A few, such as the wall paintings in the Imamzada Zayd in Isfahan, depict religious scenes, and some others, such as the seven wonders of the world in the house of Petros Valijanian at New Julfa, depict scenes foreign to Persian culture.

BIBLIOGRAPHY

A. U. Pope, ed.: *Survey of Persian Art from Prehistoric Times to the Present* (Oxford and London, 1930), pp. 1165–225
M. Siroux: *Caravansérails d'Iran et petites constructions routières* (Cairo, 1949)
D. Wilber: *Persian Gardens and Garden Pavilions* (Washington, DC, 1962)
J. Carswell: *New Julfa: The Armenian Churches and Other Buildings* (Oxford, 1968)
G. Zander, ed.: *Travaux de restauration de monuments historiques en Iran* (Rome, 1968)
E. Galdieri and R. Orazi: *Progetto di sistemazione del Maydan-i Shah* (Rome, 1969)
I. Luschey-Schmeisser: 'Der Wand- und Deckenschmuck eines safavidischen Palastes in Nayin', *Archäol. Mitt. Iran*, ii (1969), pp. 183–92
E. Galdieri: 'Two Building Phases of the Time of Shāh 'Abbās I in the Maydān-i Shāh of Iṣfahān', *E. & W.*, n. s., xx (1970), pp. 60–69
M. Siroux: *Anciennes voies et monuments routiers de la région d'Ispahan* (Cairo, 1971)
Iran. Stud., vii (1974) [2-part issue entitled *Studies on Isfahan*, ed. R. Holod]
A. H. Morton: 'The Ardabil Shrine in the Reign of Tahmasp I', *Iran*, xii (1974), pp. 31–64; xiii (1975), pp. 39–58
W. Kleiss: 'Der safavidische Pavillon in Qazvin', *Archäol. Mitt. Iran*, ix (1976), pp. 290–98
R. Orazi: *The Wooden Gratings in Safavid Architecture* (Rome, 1976)
E. Beazley: 'Some Vernacular Buildings of the Iranian Plateau', *Iran*, xv (1977), pp. 89–102
E. Galdieri: *Esfahān: 'Ālī Qāpū. An Architectural Survey* (Rome, 1979)
——: '*De ambiguitate*: Apparenze e realtà nell'architettura d'età safavide', *Quad. Semin. Iran. U. Venezia*, x (1981), pp. 145–69
D. Pickett: 'Inscriptions by Muhammad Riḍā al-Imāmī', *Iran*, xxii (1984), pp. 91–102
R. Hillenbrand: 'Safavid Architecture', *The Timurid and Safavid Periods* (1986), ed. P. Jackson and L. Lockhart, vi of *Cambridge History of Iran* (Cambridge, 1968–), pp. 759–842
W. Kleiss: 'Safavid Palaces', *A. Orient.*, xxiii (1993), pp. 269–80

EUGENIO GALDIERI

(b) c. *1700–c. 1900*. Iranian buildings from this period are associated mainly with the patronage of the ZAND dynasty in SHIRAZ (*reg* 1750–94) and the QAJAR dynasty in northern Iran (*reg* 1779–1924). Sixteen buildings remain of the twenty-seven attributed to Muhammad Karim Khan Zand, who served at Shiraz as regent for the Safavids from 1750 to 1779. The most important were grouped around a great maidan, following the arrangement introduced by the Safavids at Isfahan and Kirman (see §(a) above). Although modernized and traversed by a boulevard, the original disposition can be reconstructed. On the south is the deeply recessed entrance to the Masjid-i Vakil (Regent's Mosque; begun 1766; rest. 1827–8), a congregational mosque with a square court (60 m to a side) surrounded by single-storey arcades with iwans on the north and south. The north iwan connects to the entrance, while the south iwan leads to the main prayer-hall, a deep rectangle (36×75 m) with five rows of vaulted bays supported on 48 fluted stone columns. The court façade is revetted with a stone dado and overglaze-painted tiles with floral motifs, heavily restored in the 19th century (see fig. 71). A bath behind the mosque and a vaulted bazaar to its east complete the Vakil complex. On the north of the maidan is the Arg, a square citadel with massive brick walls and circular towers at the corners decorated with bricks set in high relief to form bands of geometric patterns. Inside are apartments on two storeys around a court. To the east of the citadel is the Divankhana, an audience hall, the high *talar* (columnar porch) of which was encased in the Central Post Office in the 20th century. The porch is decorated with marble low reliefs of scenes from Persian epics. Of the palace grounds to the south-east of the citadel, only a small octagonal pavilion remains. It comprises a central room with an octagonal pool, deeply pointed iwans on the four axes and small closed rooms on several levels in the corners. The exterior is decorated with overglaze-painted

70. 'Ali Qapu Palace, Isfahan, Iran, vault of the Music Room, begun c. 1597

71. Masjid-i Vakil (Regent's Mosque), Shiraz, Iran, court, begun 1766; restored 1827–8

tiles depicting flowers, animals and people in pink, blue, green and yellow on a white ground.

Under the Qajars, the classic plan of the open court with four iwans continued to be used in religious architecture, but variations were introduced as interior façades were articulated with kiosks, wind catchers or clock-towers. Royal mosques at QAZVIN (1806), Zanjan (1827–8) and SIMNAN (1827–8) all have prominent entrance portals with *muqarnas* vaults linked to the north iwans by dome chambers, but the articulation of the court arcades varies. The arcades at Qazvin and Zanjan are one storey high, while at Simnan an upper storey is recessed behind the lower one to form an open terraced walk. At Qazvin and Zanjan the four iwans are of equal height, while at Simnan the north and south ones are higher. The south iwans, which are usually richly decorated in tile mosaic and overglaze-painted tiles with floral and tendril designs, lead to domed sanctuaries. At Qazvin and Simnan angled squinches ease the transition from a square chamber to the circular base of the dome. The mosque of Nasir al-Mulk at Shiraz (1876–88), one of the many mosques built under Nasir al-Din Shah (*reg* 1848–96), has a rectangular court surrounded by a single storey of arcades and a columnar prayer-hall on the west. A shallow iwan in the south is flanked by two blind niches surmounted by kiosks on the roof and leads into a high chamber containing the mihrab; the same elements appear on the north. The overglaze-painted tilework displays luxuriant bouquets of roses in pink, blue, yellow, violet and green on a white ground. The great Sipahsalar Mosque at Tehran (1881–90), which also functioned as a madrasa, has a low and wide entrance on the west, the curving sides of which are flanked by two imposing minarets. Around the spacious court two-storey arcades open on to small rooms. In the

centre of each side is a massive iwan; framed by two pairs of minarets, that on the south leads to a large domed sanctuary flanked by subsidiary chambers. Decoration in tile mosaic and overglaze-painted tile uses geometric and calligraphic motifs and exuberant flowers and fruits on a scale appropriate to the large size of the building.

Major shrines, notably those of Imam Riza at MASHHAD and of Fatima at QUM, were restored and extended by the Qajar monarchs, and the *takya*, an arena set up for the performance of the play lamenting the martyrdom of the imams Hasan and Husayn, is first known from this period. The *takya* of Mu'avin al-Mulk at Kirmanshah (completed 1929) has two courts linked by a central dome chamber and is decorated with polychrome tilework illustrating the events commemorated in the play.

Secular architecture is best exemplified by palaces in Tehran. The Gulistan Palace, which served as winter residence and administrative centre, is a rambling series of buildings and gardens within a walled enclosure. Such traditional forms as the *talar*, here a marble-columned recess used as an audience hall, were built by Fath 'Ali Shah, but Nasir al-Din's alterations made between 1867 and 1892 dominate the plan and introduce European-inspired forms. The façade of his audience hall has tall windows and engaged pilasters; the two storeys on the interior are linked by a formal stair decorated with mirror-work. Nasir al-Din's private palace, the Shams al-'Imarat, is a multi-storey building with two turrets. Both palaces are decorated with tile mosaic and underglaze-painted tiles in which traditional themes are mingled with floral, figural and landscape scenes in the Victorian style. Luxurious summer palaces in the hills north of Tehran show that the Qajars maintained the custom of seasonal migration. Fath 'Ali Shah's impressive palace, Qasr-i Qajar (destr.), can be reconstructed as a series of terraces ascending to the royal apartments, which consisted of a modest two-storey pavilion enclosing a garden court. Two of Nasir al-Din's summer palaces constructed in the 1880s abandoned this elegant symmetry. The palace at 'Ishratabad has a four-storey brick tower like the Shams al-'Imarat and women's quarters of 17 chalets around a lake. At Sultanatabad a large garden surrounded separate buildings, including a five-storey polygonal tower that served as private apartments and a three-storey rectangular building with a deep *talar* that was the audience hall. The painted ceiling and underglaze-painted tile dado in the reception room mix traditional Persian subjects with whimsical copies of European ones. Many of these forms were repeated in domestic architecture. The 19th-century house in the settlement of Sidih outside Isfahan, for example, is a self-contained compound of baths, stables, a bakery and gardens. An octagonal entrance hall with niches opens on to a long corridor dividing men's and women's quarters. Although the men's quarters are much more lavishly decorated with mirrors and carved and painted plaster, both have the same plan: a colonnaded courtyard (22×15 m) surrounded by reception and living rooms, with *talar*s replacing the traditional iwans.

BIBLIOGRAPHY

'A. N. Bihruzi: *Julga-yi Shiraz* [The plain of Shiraz] (Shiraz, Iran. Solar 1347/1969), pp. 125–267

Y. Zoka: *Tarikhcha-yi sakhtamanha-yi arg-i saltanati-yi tihran: Rahnamayi kakh-i gulistan* [A short history of the construction of the Tehran citadel: guide to the Gulistan Palace] (Tehran, Iran. Solar 1349/1971)

J. Scarce: 'Function and Decoration in Qajar Tilework', *Islamic in the Balkans: Persian Art and Culture of the 18th and 19th Centuries* (Edinburgh, 1979), pp. 75–86

A. A. Bakhtiar and R. Hillenbrand: 'Domestic Architecture in Nineteenth-century Iran: The Manzil-i Sartip near Isfahan', *Qajar Iran: Political, Social and Cultural Change, 1800–1925*, ed. E. Bosworth and C. Hillenbrand (Edinburgh, 1983), pp. 383–401

R. Hillenbrand: 'The Role of Tradition in Qajar Religious Architecture', *Qajar Iran: Political, Social and Cultural Change, 1800–1925*, ed. E. Bosworth and C. Hillenbrand (Edinburgh, 1983), pp. 352–82

J. Scarce: 'The Royal Palaces of the Qajar Dynasty: A Survey', *Qajar Iran: Political, Social and Cultural Change, 1800–1925*, ed. E. Bosworth and C. Hillenbrand (Edinburgh, 1983), pp. 329–51

——: 'The Arts of the Eighteenth to Twentieth Centuries: Architecture, Ceramics, Metalwork, Textiles', *From Nadir Shah to the Islamic Republic* (1991), ed. P. Avery, G. Hambly and C. Melville, vii of *Cambridge History of Iran* (Cambridge, 1968–)

JENNIFER M. SCARCE

(iii) Western Central Asia. Architecture from the 16th to the 19th century is noteworthy for complexes of religious structures developed around earlier buildings; the individual buildings were complementary in design and function but increasingly stereotyped in plan and execution. The construction of elaborate mausolea, which had been characteristic of the region earlier, fell from favour as prominent figures were usually buried near the tombs of saints or in other buildings such as madrasas. Buildings of the 16th and 17th centuries continue many of the traditions of Timurid architecture (*see* §6(i)(b) above); many of the same building types, such as four-iwan congregational mosques, were built in similar techniques of brick revetted with glazed tile. Written sources refer to more than 350 public buildings erected between 1500 and 1700. This growth in public building seems to have been caused by increased private wealth. Much of that wealth, especially

in the form of commercial and agricultural enterprises, was used to fund endowments for new buildings. The building boom tapered off towards the end of the 17th century, perhaps because the stock of land available for endowments had already been encumbered. KHIVA, situated on the increasingly important trade route between the expanding Russian empire and Iran and India, was an exception to the stagnation in architectural activity after 1700.

(a) Patronage. (b) Building types. (c) Materials, forms, techniques and decoration.

(a) Patronage. Patrons came from three distinct groups: the political leadership drawn from families descended from Genghis Khan (e.g. the SHAYBANID dynasty), the military leadership of the Uzbek Turkic tribal organizations, and the spiritual leaders of the various Sufi orders, principally the Naqshbandiyya. The first group is typified by 'Abdallah Khan II (*reg* 1583–98), whose enduring reputation as a builder was such that later observers tended to attribute any monumental building to him. The second group is exemplified by Qul Baba Kukaltash, confidant of 'Abdallah Khan, who built a large madrasa in Bukhara (*see* BUKHARA, §1) as well as a variety of other projects including madrasas, small mosques, caravanserais and reservoirs, and Yalangtush Bi Alchin, who in the mid-17th century sponsored two large madrasas at the Registan in Samarkand and also spent considerable sums on buildings in Dahpid, a village north of Samarkand where his Sufi order was centred. The third group is represented by the Juybari family in Bukhara, which acquired its wealth first as administrators of religious endowments and then as landlords and investors in commerce and manufacturing. Khwaja Sa'd Juybari (*d* 1589) is recorded as having financed more than 60 major renovations or new constructions.

(b) Building types. New buildings, particularly religious structures, were integrated with older ones in complexes, and efforts were made to harmonize exteriors. New buildings never replicated older designs exactly, but balanced the old and highlighted earlier artistic achievements with new techniques of brickwork or revetment. Complexes of public buildings were arranged around an open plaza (the Registan at Samarkand) or a large tank or reflecting pool (the Lab-i Hawz in Bukhara) or faced each other across a thoroughfare (the double madrasa complexes at Bukhara). The most famous of these complexes is the Registan in Samarkand (see fig. 72 and SAMARKAND, §3(iv)), which was a focus of the city's commercial and public life and already contained several large buildings. In 1501 Shaybani (or Shibani) Khan began a large double madrasa (destr.) on the east of the square, which was completed after his death in 1510. The building became the burial place of its founder and 33 of his descendants and relatives, whose cenotaphs were placed on a massive stone platform, some 2 m high and 4 m square. At the same time, Abu Sa'id ibn Kuchkunji (*d* 1533), a leading political figure in Samarkand, added a madrasa (destr.) on the south side of the Registan, where he and his brother were buried. In the mid-17th century during the governorship of Yalangtush Bi Alchin, the Registan was again

72. Registan square, Samarkand, western Central Asia, 15th century and later

the focus of architectural activity. A *khānaqāh* was ordered by a shaykh of the Yasawi order on the west, and a madrasa was built by a member of the Ata'i sub-order on the east (both destr.). Two large madrasas were sponsored by the Governor himself: the Shir Dar ('lion-possessing', so called because of the rampant lions in the spandrels of the entry arch; 1616–36) on the east and the Tilla Kar ('gold-work'; *c.* 1646–60), which included a congregational mosque.

Other sites were developed and redeveloped in a manner similar to the Registan. A few kilometres west of Bukhara is the old Sunni Muslim shrine known as Char Bakr (the Four Bakrs), honouring four early religious scholars from Bukhara named Abu Bakr. In the 1560s the shrine was under the care of the Juybari family, and 'Abdallah Khan II financed construction of a mosque, madrasa and *khānaqāh* as well as an elaborate two-storey gateway to the shrine precinct. The buildings were heavily endowed and received a significant annual income into the 20th century. The Lab-i Hawz ('Edge of the reservoir'), also in Bukhara, developed around the enormous (69×86 m) madrasa founded by Qul Baba Kukaltash in 1568–9. Forty years later Nadr Bi Arlat, another important military figure, developed the site between the madrasa and a branch of the Zarafshan River with a rectangular stone reservoir (36.0×45.5 m), flanked on the west by a combined mosque and hospice and on the east by a madrasa. Work on the complex was completed by 1620 and may have inspired the final plan of the Registan at Samarkand. The Abu Nasr Parsa complex in BALKH was built around the tomb of a 15th-century shaykh. The tomb was incorporated into a madrasa some time before the middle of the 16th century, when that structure was renovated by one of the shaykh's descendants. At the end of the century the building was revetted with blue tile and

its entrance (re)built by 'Abd al-Mu'min, the son of 'Abdallah Khan II, and framed with distinctive twisted mouldings. By the mid-17th century the shrine covered 3 ha and included other madrasas, a large one by 'Abdallah Khan II and another large one (begun 1612; destr.) opposite it by Nadhr Muhammad, who reigned at Balkh. The latter had a tall entrance iwan, four lecture halls, a mosque, numerous cells for students and a library of 2000 volumes. The porticos were decorated with lapis lazuli and faced with tiles. The builder was Mir Qasim, and the masters Hajji and Mir Muhammad assisted him. At the same time, a fourth madrasa and mosque were added beside that of 'Abdallah Khan II by Allah Yar, a military leader, and in 1660 a fifth madrasa was added by Subhan Quli, the son of Nadhr Muhammad, facing the first one with the tomb. These five madrasas may have been aligned along a thoroughfare or set in a quadrangle like the complexes of the Registan and the Lab-i Hawz.

The major types of individual religious buildings were mosques with minarets, madrasas and *khānaqāh*s. Congregational mosques are usually large rectangular structures with interior courts; iwans in the middle of each of the four sides are linked by single-storey roofed spaces. The Masjid-i Kalan (Grand Mosque) in Bukhara (*see* BUKHARA, §2(iii)), for example, had been founded in 1121, but the structure (78×127 m) was extensively renovated by the early 16th century with arched entrances, stone columns and 288 vaulted bays. The traditional form of hypostyle mosque also continued to be used. The Friday Mosque at Khiva, for example, was rebuilt (1788–9) reusing wooden columns from several earlier mosques on the site. The typical small, or quarter, mosque is a one- or two-storey rectangular building with an L-shaped porch on two adjacent sides; the roof of the porch is supported on tall wooden columns. The form responded to the region's climate, allowing prayer to be performed out of doors in warm weather protected from rain or sun. Two outstanding examples are the Masjid-i Boland and the Masjid-i Zayn al-Din, both in Bukhara and datable to c. 1550. Foundations cut from massive blocks of stone elevate their floors a metre above ground level.

Minarets were often modelled on the Kalan Minaret in Bukhara (1127). Built of brick, they are often free-standing and have a distinctive tapering cylindrical shaft decorated with horizontal bands of geometric ornament executed in glazed tile and crowned by a *muqarnas* cornice. Smaller-scale copies of the 46 m original proliferated in Bukhara and the surrounding countryside. In contrast, the minarets framing the two madrasas sponsored by Yalangtush Bi in Samarkand are integrated into the structure and are covered with a network of tile mosaic patterns like those of the Ulughbeg Madrasa near by (*see* SAMARKAND, §1(ii)). In Khiva, the Friday Mosque is flanked by a towering minaret of the Bukharan type, which continued to be built throughout the 19th century. A 70 m minaret was planned for the madrasa of Muhammad Amin Khan, but it was left unfinished at the patron's death in 1855.

Madrasas followed the open-interior plan standard for congregational mosques. Their façades consist of a central iwan flanked by arcades, often two-storey, while the other three sides of the exterior are usually blank. They have assembly halls in the corners and cells around the court-yard, sometimes arranged on two storeys. Some are quite large: the Qul Baba Madrasa in Bukhara (1568–9), the largest surviving example in Central Asia, measures 69×86 m and could accommodate over 300 students. Many, such as the Mir-i ʿArab Madrasa in Bukhara (1530–36), contain the tomb of the founder, here in the north-west corner. Madrasas following the traditional plan continued to be built into the 19th century, for example that built by Allah Quli at Khiva (1835), one of the largest

(62×47 m) in the city. Hospices were usually smaller versions of madrasas, with only one assembly hall.

Existing tombs and shrines were enlarged with madrasas, hospices and mosques. In the eastern suburbs of Bukhara, the tomb of Baha' al-Din Naqshband received a formal enclosure (Pers. *haẓīra*) and a hospice in 1545; another hospice, perhaps the one with the distinctive squat, ribbed central dome, was erected in 1599. In Samarkand the grave of Khwaja Ahrar (*d* 1490), the pre-eminent Sufi of his time, was embellished (c. 1630) with an enclosure, madrasa and *khānaqāh*. At Balkh, the grave of ʿAli ibn Abi Talib, the Prophet's son-in-law and a major Shiʿite saint, which had been discovered c. 1480 in the village of Khwaja Khayran, east of Balkh (now Mazar-i Sharif, Afghanistan), was repeatedly restored and enlarged in the 16th and 17th centuries. The Gunbad-i Kabudi ('Azure dome'), a domed tomb for Gistan Kara ibn Jani Beg, the sovereign at Balkh, was erected beside the shrine c. 1539 by his widow Tursun Begi. Towards the end of the 16th century, it was renovated by ʿAbd al-Muʾmin, who also expanded and retiled the mausoleum of ʿAli. Around 1602 the new ruler at Balkh, Wali Muhammad ibn Din Muhammad, increased the structure in height to 30 *dharʿ* (c. 24 m) and developed the land around it into formal gardens, adding a stone reservoir on one side. In 1704, the *khānaqāh* that Sultan Husayn Bayqara had built in 1480 was levelled by an earthquake and rebuilt. At Khiva, the tomb of Pahlavan Mahmud, a popular poet of the 14th century, was repeatedly restored and enlarged. In 1701 a monumental entrance was added, in 1810 the domed mausoleum was reconstructed with a side gallery, which served as a tomb of the Khans of Khiva, and in 1825 another side gallery and lavish tile decoration were added.

Commercial architecture is exemplified by the caravanserai, warehouse (Pers. *tīm*) and retail market buildings

73. Taki-Zargaran (Dome of the Goldsmiths), Bukhara, western Central Asia, 1570s

(Pers. *ṭāq* or *chahārsū*). Caravanserais were large rectangular buildings with or without an interior court. The two-storey caravanserai of Allah Quli Khan at Khiva (1822–3) has shops on the exterior and stalls and rooms for merchants surrounding an interior court. A warehouse adjacent to the Goldsmiths' Market in Bukhara (late 16th century) is one storey high and measures 50 m on each side. On the west the main entry iwan, flanked by two smaller iwans, leads to a domed interior space surrounded by smaller domed units. Retail markets were domed buildings erected over main intersections. During the 1570s three of the most important in Bukhara were (re)built by 'Abdallah Khan II. Known as the domes of the Goldsmiths (see fig. 73), Hatters and Moneychangers, they are spaced along a 650 m stretch of the main north-south route through the city. Each has a large dome surrounded by lower domes radiating from the centre to cover adjacent shops, storerooms and alleys.

Royal architecture of the 16th and 17th centuries is known only from literary descriptions. The sprawling palace complex built by Nadhr Muhammad Khan at Balkh was organized around 12 closed courts. One of them was planted with gardens around a large pavilion and was intended for relaxation; others were reserved for women and bathing. Separate buildings within this complex included a mosque with arcade and porticos large enough for 5000 worshippers, a huge kitchen, furniture and bedding storerooms, and a large audience hall (24×9×25 m) that faced a 9×18 m salon surmounted by a dovecote. The buildings were revetted with tile and inscriptions, and one source mentions rooms panelled with marble and a 'Chinese picture gallery'.

The grounds of this huge complex contained 200 workshops, a falconry, a banquet hall and separate assembly areas of amirs and other notables. The same sovereign also built a number of hunting-lodges in the mountains south of Balkh. They contained workshops, women's quarters, sleeping areas and salons. Several 19th-century palaces are preserved in Khiva. The Tash Hawli ('Stone court'), inside Ichan Fortress, was erected in stages between 1830 and 1838. An irregular trapezoid, it has 163 rooms arranged around several courtyards (see fig. 74). Its most characteristic feature is the *talar*, a high porch supported on tall and elegantly carved wooden columns, which opens on to a court. Many of the walls are revetted with *cuerda seca* tiles (*see* §9(ii)(b) below) decorated with colourful arabesque ornament. The principal architects were Nur Muhammad Tajikhan and Qalandar Khivaki; 'Abdallah Jan did the tiles.

The residences of the wealthy were walled compounds (Pers. *ḥawili*) comprising separate buildings and a small courtyard. A property sold in Bukhara in 1559, as one example, covered an area of 300 sq. m and had seven suites, two salons (one for receiving guests) and a kitchen. A much larger one (1500 sq. m) had two stables, a granary and second-storey apartments. The most common facility for relaxation was the Persian garden (Pers. *chahārbāgh; see also* GARDEN, §V, 4). These parks varied according to individual taste but were usually walled enclosures including open pavilions, stone water-channels with cascades

74. Tash Hawli Palace, Khiva, western Central Asia, courtyard, 1830–38

and pools, and terraced gardens. There was no standard size, but Bukharan examples from the 16th century ranged from 10 to 25 ha.

(c) Materials, forms, techniques and decoration. Architects and engineers took into account the natural environment in ways perhaps not seen earlier, including measures to cope more effectively with the region's relatively high level of seismic activity. For example, there were no attempts made to build massive structures on the scale of the mosque of Bibi Khanum in Samarkand, the fabric of which began to disintegrate even before it was completed. Preventive measures in the form of anti-seismic foundations were designed into large buildings. Brick continued to be the major material of construction, and glazed tile and brick the major technique of decoration. Structures were less daring and inventive than before, and glittering tile revetments may have been used to conceal structural banality in new buildings and dress up older ones. Patterns of decoration became bolder and more stereotyped and execution coarser, although the overall effect is often charming. Tile mosaic was replaced by *cuerda seca* panels and large bands of glazed brick laid in geometric patterns. White, light blue and dark blue remain the predominant colours, but yellow, green and black were used in the first half of the period. Flamboyant figural ornament was introduced into the repertory. The madrasa of Nadr Bi Arlat (1618–20) at the Lab-i Hawz in Bukhara, for example, sports two large birds of paradise facing each other on the spandrels over the main entry. The Shir Dar Madrasa in Samarkand has sunbursts with human faces rising behind lions attacking gazelles. An unusually large number of wooden architectural elements, such as doors, windows, columns, brackets, lintels and ceilings, have survived in the dry climate. They were often finely carved in low relief in a variety of geometric, vegetal and epigraphic patterns.

See also CENTRAL ASIA, §I, 2(i)(f).

BIBLIOGRAPHY
Enc. Iran.: 'Bukhara, v: Archaeology and monuments'
V. L. Viatkin: *Pamyatniki drevnostei samarkanda* [Samarkand's monuments of antiquity] (Samarkand, 1927)
B. N. Zasypkin: *Arkhitektura srednei Azii* [Architecture of Central Asia] (Moscow, 1948)
N. M. Baginskii: *Antiseismika v arkhitekturnykh pamyatnikakh srednei Azii* [Anti-seismics in the architectural monuments of Central Asia] (Moscow, 1949)
V. M. Dmitrev: 'Kompozitsionnye osobennosti bukharskoi arkhitektury vtoroi poloviny XVI veka' [Compositional characteristics of Bukharan architecture of the second half of the 16th century], *Materialy po istorii i teorii arkhitektury uzbekhistana* [Materials for the history and theory of the architecture of Uzbekistan], i, Soyuz Sovetskikh Arkhitektorov UZSSR: Nauchnaya Seriya (Moscow, 1950), pp. 31–44
G. A. Pugachenkova and L. I. Rempel': *Vydayushchiesya pamyatniki arkhitektury uzbekistana* [Outstanding architectural monuments of Uzbekistan] (Tashkent, 1958)
V. Voronina, ed.: *Arkhitekturnye pamyatniki srednei Azii: Bukhara, Samarkand* [Architectural monuments of Central Asia: Bukhara, Samarkand] (Leningrad, 1969)
D. Brandenburg: *Samarkand* (Berlin, 1972)
V. A. Nil'sen and V. N. Manakova: *Arkhitekturny dekor pamyatnikov uzbekistana* [Architectural decoration of the monuments of Uzbekistan] (Leningrad, 1974)
B. Brentjes: *Mittelasien: Kunst des Islams* (Leipzig, 1979)
L. Mankovskaya: *Khiva* (Tashkent, 1982)
G. A. Pugachenkova: *Pamyatniki iskusstva Sovetskogo Soyuza: Srednyaya Aziya: Spravochnik-putovoditel* [Artistic monuments of the Soviet Union: Central Asia: a guide] (Leipzig, 1983)
R. D. McChesney: 'Economic and Social Aspects of the Public Architecture of Bukhara in the 1560s and 1570s', *Islam. A.*, ii (1987), pp. 217–42

ROBERT D. MCCHESNEY

(iv) Indian subcontinent. Islamic architecture in northern India in this period was dominated by the patronage of the MUGHAL dynasty (*reg* 1526–1858), which traced its descent from the Timurids of Khurasan and Transoxiana. Such emperors as Akbar (*reg* 1556–1605), Jahangir (*reg* 1605–27) and Shah Jahan (*reg* 1628–58) erected splendid and elegant mosques, tombs and palaces; in the 17th century, too, the nobility became more important as patrons of architecture. These buildings, some of the best-known examples of Islamic architecture, combine the indigenous traditions of Indo-Islamic architecture with those of Iran and Central Asia in a distinctive and elegant style. A precise linearity and division of flat surfaces into panels replaced the solid three-dimensional massing characteristic of earlier Islamic architecture in India. Stone, particularly white marble and red sandstone, became more widely used, replacing the brick and tile of earlier times, and the use of colour was restrained in favour of high polish and meticulous finish. Characteristic forms include the ogee arch and the bulbous dome, although trabeate techniques continued to be used in secular construction.

The most famous buildings of the period, such as the Taj Mahal in Agra (1631–47; *see* AGRA, §II, 1), are monumental tombs set on platforms amid formal gardens and pools. Both the garden setting and typical octagonal plans of the tombs derive from Persian prototypes, particularly in secular architecture, where octagonal plans and walled gardens with watercourses had paradisaical connotations. Pleasure gardens, such as the Shalimar Gardens at LAHORE (1633–42), were large walled and terraced enclosures; they too derived from the prototype of the Timurid *chahār-bāgh* ('four-[plot] plan'). Congregational mosques, such as the one at Delhi (1644–58; *see* DELHI, §III, 6) built by Shah Jahan, have immense open courts surrounded by shallow arcades, except on the qibla side, where a large iwan, flanked by covered prayer-halls and minarets, leads to a dome chamber containing the main mihrab. Magnificent forts and fortified palaces were constructed throughout the Mughal empire, particularly in the capitals at Lahore, Delhi (*see* DELHI, §III, 5) and Agra (*see* AGRA, §II, 3). The most famous is the palace-city at FATEHPUR SIKRI (c. 1560–85), which is divided into religious and residential–administrative areas arranged on a modular grid (*see also* INDIAN SUBCONTINENT, §III, 7(i)(a)).   □

(v) Morocco. Architecture under the patronage of the SA'DI (*reg* 1511–1659) and the 'ALAWI (*reg* 1631–) dynasties, often collectively known as the Sharifs of Morocco, was based on traditional forms and techniques. Innumerable mosques, shrines, palaces, citadels and bridges were built, but the lack of a systematic survey makes it difficult to distinguish general, dynastic and local styles, although the Sa'dis are identified with religious architecture and the 'Alawis with secular monuments. Architectural conservatism makes dating on stylistic grounds extremely hazardous. In addition to the vast numbers of buildings that have survived in varying states of repair, information can be

75. Mihrab, three-aisled mosque to the south of the Saʿdian necropolis, Marrakesh, Morocco, 16th century

gleaned from the history of Abu'l-Qasim al-Zayyani (*d* 1833), from hyperbolic evocations in panegyric court poetry and from sensational accounts by European captives, missionaries and ambassadors.

While the Saʿdis and the ʿAlawis controlled large, if varying, areas of Morocco, they concentrated their architectural patronage in their capital cities. MARRAKESH, founded by the Almoravids and dominated by the imposing monuments of the Almohads (*see* §5(iv)(d) above), remained the centre of the Saʿdi dynasty; all significant Saʿdian architecture is found there, except two pavilions added to the courtyard of the Qarawiyyin Mosque in FEZ. Most ʿAlawi buildings are in MEKNÈS, which became the capital under Ismaʿil (*reg* 1672–1727), although Rashid (*reg* 1664–72) built the Sharratin Madrasa in Fez and Muhammad III ibn ʿAbdallah (*reg* 1757–90) erected buildings in RABAT (al-Sunna, or Great Mosque) and Marrakesh (Berrima Mosque).

Architectural originality of this period lies in small complexes that combined mosques with other institutions, such as a fountain–school (Arab. *sabīl-kuttāb*), madrasa, bath or ablution facility. The most beautiful is the Ben Yusuf Madrasa in Marrakesh (1564–5), which has a harmonious central courtyard flanked by galleries. Corridors lead to more than 100 cells for students on several storeys. Shrines, such as those of Sidi Ben Sulayman al-Jazuli (*c.* 1554) and Sidi Bel ʿAbbas al-Sabti (*c.* 1605) in Marrakesh, included the saint's tomb and lodgings for permanent residents and guests. Saʿdian mosques, such as the Bab Dukkala (1557) and the Muwassin (1562–72) mosques in Marrakesh, continue the T-plan (in which longitudinal arcades with a wider central aisle abut a broad qibla arcade), which had been typical of prayer-halls in the

western Islamic world for centuries. They combine such Marinid features as a square courtyard (*see* §6(iv)(b) above) with such Almohad ones as three domes along the qibla arcade. The use of horseshoe arches and piers instead of columns is typically Moroccan. In ʿAlawi religious architecture, such as the mosque of Lalla ʿAwda in Meknès (1672–1727) and that built in Fez by ʿAbdallah (1729–35), the aisles are usually parallel to the qibla wall and occasionally cut by a perpendicular central aisle. They retain the same annexes as in the Saʿdian period, but their decoration is simplified and sometimes rather monotonous, revealing the speed with which the mosque was executed.

The Saʿdis set their dynastic necropolis against the south wall of the Almohad mosque of the Kasba in Marrakesh, perhaps to take advantage of the site's holiness. The tombs are enclosed in a walled garden. The first tomb was originally a typical square funerary structure, but it was enlarged in 1590 when Ahmad al-Mansur buried his mother there. His own tomb is more ambitious: the Room of Twelve Columns containing the cenotaphs is flanked by a three-aisled mosque on the south (see fig. 75) and a lecture room on the north, an arrangement probably inspired by the now lost Nasrid mausoleum in Granada. Its rich decoration in stucco, marble, tile mosaic and wood epitomizes the finest Saʿdian craftsmanship.

The Saʿdis built their kasba or royal city within the Almohad walls of Marrakesh, but its internal organization seems to have been their own creation. Its original plan, reconstructed from a Portuguese drawing of 1585 and contemporary Arabic and European descriptions, shows distinct public and private areas and a garden zone. Only the ruins of the audience palace, the Badiʿ, constructed by Ahmad between 1578 and 1593, have survived. The palace followed Andalusian models in integrating pools, fountains, gardens and open pavilions within massive walls. Of the once splendid decoration, only bare walls of beaten earth and baked brick remain. The ʿAlawis erected princely establishments throughout their realm. The most famous is the immense palace of Ismaʿil at Meknès. It combines conventional Hispano-Moresque features with a sense of efficiency and, paradoxically, a preference for large volumes. Ismaʿil also erected 76 fortresses to control the countryside; Boulaouane and Kasba Tadla exemplify this unrefined but spectacular military architecture. ʿAbdallah built his principal palace in Fez, and his son Muhammad built his in Marrakesh. Their successors restored and enlarged them or built new government cities such as the Mashwar (or Mechouar) in Rabat. In the late 19th century courtiers still constructed sumptuous private palaces in traditional style.

In both materials and forms the architecture of this period continues Moroccan traditions. Walls were built of beaten earth and baked brick. These humble materials were sometimes covered by marble panels, but more often were revetted in sculpted plaster, tile mosaic or carved wood, following the style typical of earlier buildings in Morocco and Spain. Decoration includes vegetal, geometric and epigraphic motifs and is always strictly aniconic. Although some new floral elements followed Ottoman models, the style is more stereotyped than in earlier times and is not particularly creative. In secular architecture, however, there was a new sense of volume and rational organization, inspired perhaps by European ideas.

BIBLIOGRAPHY
G. Rousseau and F. Arin: *Le Mausolée des princes saadiens à Marrakech*, 2 vols (Paris, 1925)
B. Maslow: *Les Mosquées de Fès et du nord du Maroc* (Paris, 1937)
G. Marçais: *L'Architecture musulmane d'Occident: Tunisie, Algérie, Maroc, Espagne et Sicile* (Paris, 1954)
G. Deverdun: *Marracech: Des origines à 1912*, 2 vols (Rabat, 1959–66)
M. Barrucand: *L'Architecture de la Qasba de Moulay Ismaïl à Meknès*, 2 vols (Rabat, 1976)

MARIANNE BARRUCAND

8. AFTER *c.* 1900. The interaction of architecture in the Islamic world with that of the West, which had begun in the 19th century (*see* §7(i) above), intensified in the 20th century, and the traditional architectural vocabularies that had distinguished one region from another were subsumed. Such cities as Tunis, Cairo, Istanbul, Baghdad, Aleppo and Tehran were transformed by the introduction of wide, straight thoroughfares, which cut through the existing maze-like fabric of narrow, winding lanes and culs-de-sac and defined the patterns of future urban growth. The street, which had been an artery of communication, became a more distinct component of the urban composition and demanded more attention from surrounding structures. Traditional elements and planning concepts were gradually abandoned in favour of Western ones. Such features as complicated entry sequences separating the interior of a structure from the street and wooden latticework (Arab. *mashrabiyya*) disappeared, while new ones, such as concepts of overall symmetry and frontal axiality and the use of Classical orders, became customary. Western building types gradually replaced traditional ones. The primary and secondary school, the polytechnic and the university, for example, were substituted for the madrasa, and the villa or apartment unit replaced the courtyard house. At the same time new construction methods and building materials were introduced; steel and, more importantly, reinforced concrete became ubiquitous. Western-trained architects and engineers gained ascendancy. Some were Westerners, but others were natives trained either in the West or in local schools newly established on Western models. Professional organizations and, to a lesser extent, labour unions replaced guilds.

This break with the architectural traditions of the Islamic world had already been under way in the 19th century, but interest in documenting and understanding these traditions developed only in the 20th. The systematic investigation of architectural history, initiated in the West and concerned with the Classical world, was slowly extended to the architecture of the Islamic world, and the notion of Islamic architecture as a distinct entity came into existence.

As architecture in the Islamic world became increasingly integrated into international styles, only one type of building, the mosque, maintained a clear and autonomous Islamic identity. The mosque of al-Rifa'i in Cairo, one of the largest and most important Islamic religious buildings of the period, was conceived in 1869 when Princess Khushyar, Consort of Ibrahim Pasha and mother of Khedive Isma'il (*reg* 1863–79), commissioned the architect Husayn Pasha Fahmy to replace the *zāwiya* of al-Rifa'i with a funerary mosque, but the death of both architect

and patroness led to suspension of the work, and the mosque was largely constructed between 1905 and 1911. It is a clear example of architectural revivalism, but in contrast to earlier eclectic structures such as the Ortaköy Mosque in Istanbul (1846), which incorporated neo-classical features, or the mosque of Sayyidna Husayn in Cairo (1874) and the Hamidiye in Istanbul (1886), which used Gothic-Revival ones, the mosque of al-Rifa'i returned to a more exclusively Islamic vocabulary. The Islamic revival, which was a Western design methodology, had appeared in the 1860s and dictated a return to the heritage of the Islamic world for prototypes. The mosque of al-Rifa'i imitated features typical of architecture built under the Mamluks (*see* §6(iii)(a) above), but it also adhered to principles of overall symmetry and frontal axiality in both its plan and its façades. The structure's Islamic aspects are limited to surface components rather than planning concepts. The decoration, for which the architect left no plans, was executed by Max Herz Bey after examples taken from earlier mosques in Cairo.

Revivalism played a dominant role in mosque architecture of the first half of the 20th century, but the commitment expressed in the mosque of al-Rifa'i to the architecture of the region in which the building is located was not a prevalent attitude. The Mamluk revival, for example, was popular for mosques throughout the Arab Middle East, such as that of al-Husayni in AMMAN (1922), the state mosque of the newly founded emirate of Transjordan. More often, Islamic revivalism was used eclectically, as in the Islamic Center in Washington, DC (1949), which has minarets borrowed from the traditional architecture of Egypt under the Ayyubids (*reg* 1169–1252), along with arch forms used in Andalusia since the 10th century and tilework modelled on that produced under Ottoman patronage in the 16th century.

Some of the earliest attempts to break away from architectural historicism are found in the works of the architect Hassan Fathy. In his design for the village of New Gourna near Luxor (1945; *see* THEBES (i), §III), Fathy sought inspiration in the architecture of the Egyptian countryside, using vernacular forms for the various structures, including the mosque, and local materials and techniques of construction. The buildings, erected by the villagers themselves, have bearing walls and vaults of mud-brick, not reinforced concrete (for illustration *see* FATHY, HASSAN). Fathy's work passed largely unnoticed in the short term, but by the 1970s it had affected not only architects in the Islamic world but those in the developing world as well.

By the 1950s such architects as Sayyid Kurayyim (*b* 1911) of Egypt, SEDAD HAKKI ELDEM of Turkey and RIFAT CHADIRJI of Iraq began to reject direct revivalism and advocate a sparser use of surface ornament for most types of buildings. The mosque, however, proved to be somewhat problematic, because providing a sense of visual continuity with the past was difficult to reconcile with the opposing need to incorporate the essentially ahistorical architectural developments of recent times. One solution was to adhere to historicism and ignore modern developments, as in the 'Uthman Mosque in Damascus (designed by Muhammad Farra in 1961, completed 1974). Another

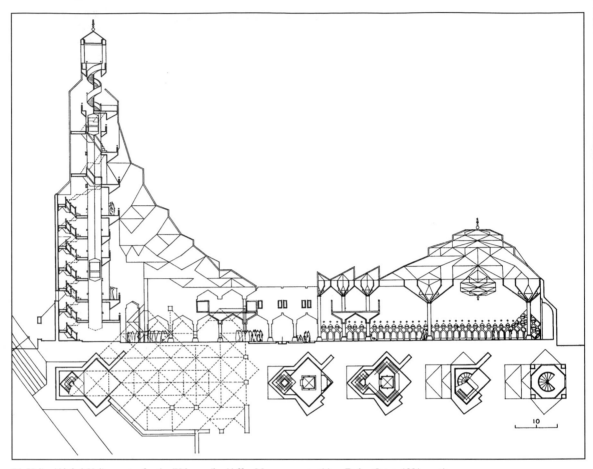

76. Halim 'Abd al-Halim: entry for the 'Uthman ibn 'Affan Mosque competition, Doha, Qatar, 1981; section

solution attempted to synthesize the two needs by preserving traditional elements, usually the minaret and the dome, but abstracting them into a more contemporary arrangement that maintained a visual link with the past. Early examples of this synthesis include Eriche Baharuddin's Negara Mosque in Kuala Lumpur (1956, completed 1967) and Walter Gropius's project for the mosque at Baghdad University (1958; see BAGHDAD), which included a large bulbous dome touching the ground at three points and placed within a circular reflecting pool. A third solution rejected revivalism. Mosques belonging to this approach, such as the mosque for the Etimesgüt Armed Units in ANKARA (designed in 1965 by Cengiz Bektas), the Sherefudin White Mosque in Visoko, Bosnia and Herzegovina (designed in 1967 by Zlatko Ugljen, completed 1980), and the 'A'isha Bakkar Mosque in Beirut (designed in 1970 by Ja'far Tuqan (b 1938)), reflect the influence of such 20th-century masters as Le Corbusier and Alvar Aalto. In all three, visual connections with the past are almost non-existent. The dome is abolished, while minarets are transformed into highly abstracted vertical elements. Despite their architectural merit, these ahistorical mosques have not achieved much popularity and remain few in number.

In the 1970s mosque construction expanded because of the rise in religious sentiment and the expanded revenues following the increase in oil prices in 1973. This quantitative change was accompanied by more varied approaches towards design. Earlier efforts to combine the traditional with the contemporary continued. More conservative combinations are found in the works of such architects as MOHAMED MAKIYA. In his mosques, most notably the Kuwait State Mosque in KUWAIT City (1976–84), traditional elements are emphasized, while contemporary ones remain subdued. The courtyard of the mosque is surrounded by porticos, which are made of exposed concrete and have flat lintels instead of arches. Mosques showing a higher level of experimentation, such as the King Faisal Mosque in ISLAMABAD, Pakistan (designed in 1970 by Vedat Dalokay, completed 1984), which abstracts the model for the imperial Ottoman mosque, have been quite popular. As with Gropius's design for the mosque at Baghdad University, these structures are highly expressionist, if not flamboyant. A number of architects have modified ideas advocated by Hassan Fathy. In a series of mosques designed for the Saudi Arabian cities of Jiddah and Medina, primarily during the 1980s, the architect ABDEL WAHED EL-WAKIL maintained some of Fathy's vernacularly inspired forms and his use of traditional materials and construction techniques, but these characteristics were combined with direct revivalism, usually of

Egypt's Mamluk and Ottoman architectural heritage. The architect RASIM BADRAN emphasized the regional sensitivity Fathy had expressed in his design for New Gourna. In the Great Mosque in RIYADH (1985), for example, he attempted to relate to the vernacular architecture of the Najd, the region in which the mosque is located, but used contemporary technology. Other innovative approaches can be seen in two unbuilt projects. In Robert Venturi's entry for the State Mosque competition in Baghdad (1983; see VENTURI, RAUCH AND SCOTT BROWN), he consciously reinterpreted and rearranged accepted architectural norms by placing a massive *muqarnas* dome over the courtyard instead of the prayer-hall, its customary location. In Halim 'Abd al-Halim's entry for the 'Uthman ibn 'Affan Mosque competition in Doha, QATAR (1981; see fig. 76), the architect abandoned traditional architectural forms and prototypes and referred to the geometric principles used in Islamic art and architecture, transforming two-dimensional geometric patterns into a three-dimensional composition.

BIBLIOGRAPHY

J. Abu-Lughod: *Cairo: 1001 Years of the City Victorious* (Princeton, 1971)
H. Fathy: *Architecture for the Poor* (Chicago, 1973)
Guide to Kuala Lumpur's Notable Buildings (Kuala Lumpur, 1976)
Albenaa (1979–)
Mimar (1981–)
W. J. R. Curtis: *Modern Architecture since 1900* (Oxford, 1982)
B. Lewis: *The Muslim Discovery of Europe* (New York, 1982)
A. Evin and R. Holod, eds: *Contemporary Turkish Architecture* (Philadelphia, 1983)
R. Holod and D. Rastofer, eds: *Architecture and Community: Building in the Islamic World Today* (New York, 1983)
S. Cantacuzino, ed.: *Architecture in Continuity: Building in the Islamic World Today* (New York, 1985)
K. K. Mumtaz: *Architecture in Pakistan* (Singapore, 1985)
D. Rastofer, J. M. Richards and I. Serageldin: *Hassan Fathy* (Singapore, 1985)
Z. Celik: *Remaking of Istanbul* (Seattle, 1986)
M. Al-Asad: 'The Mosque of al-Rifa'i in Cairo', *Muqarnas*, x (1993), pp. 108–24

MOHAMMAD AL-ASAD

9. ARCHITECTURAL DECORATION. Applied decoration is one of the most characteristic features of Islamic architecture, and the exteriors and interiors of buildings throughout the Islamic world were enlivened with colourful revetments of carved and moulded stucco, carved stone, glazed brick and ceramic tile, paint, stone and glass mosaic. The primacy of the written word in Islam meant that inscriptions played a pre-eminent role in architectural decoration, and the antipathy towards figural representation (see §I, 8 above) meant that figural themes were less popular than geometric, vegetal and epigraphic ones; indeed the geometricized vegetal motif, or ARABESQUE, is one of the hallmarks of Islamic decoration. (*See also* ORNAMENT AND PATTERN, §V.)

(i) Sculpture. (ii) Tiles. (iii) Painting. (iv) Mosaics. (v) Stained glass. (vi) Epigraphy.

(i) Sculpture. Most of the three-dimensional decoration of Islamic architecture consists of geometric, vegetal and arabesque patterns worked in low relief. Figural decoration was popular in only two periods: the first half of the 8th century in Syria and the 12th and 13th centuries in Anatolia, the Jazira, Syria and Iraq. Such materials as stone, stucco, brick and terracotta were carved or moulded and often painted, but only traces of colour remain. The early taste

for three-dimensional decoration was subsumed by a growing interest in colour (*see* §(ii) below). (For wooden features *see* §VII below.)

(a) Non-figural. (b) Figural.

(a) Non-figural. In the early Islamic period, indigenous traditions of Late Antique, Early Byzantine and Near Eastern architectural decoration in carved stone and stucco were continued, as motifs and techniques from a wide range of sources were combined in a distinctive new style. Spolia from pre-Islamic buildings, particularly columns, capitals and bases, were often employed in major public buildings, especially mosques. Early congregational mosques, such as those at Córdoba (*see* CÓRDOBA (i), §3(i)(a)) and KAIROUAN (Tunisia), preserve hundreds of Late Antique and Byzantine capitals and columns. As the supply of spolia was exhausted, distinctively Islamic capitals were made in increasingly fanciful interpretations of Corinthian models. Other three-dimensional ornament in mosques was usually restrained and maintained the Late Antique tradition of emphasizing structure.

Three-dimensional ornament was much more profuse and innovative in palace architecture. The importation of the technique of stucco revetment from Iraq and Iran in the early 8th century allowed structures to be transformed into surfaces for exuberant decoration. For example, the façade of the Umayyad palace at QASR AL-HAYR WEST in Syria (early 8th century; *see also* §3(iii) above) has an essentially Classical composition of a portal flanked by two half-round towers, but the panels of vegetal and geometric ornament that cover it tend to modify and minimize the underlying architectural forms. Intensely naturalistic ornament was consciously juxtaposed with highly stylized forms. The extraordinary eclecticism of motifs and themes used was due to the vast empire from which the Umayyads drew their inspiration and labour force. The superbly carved stone façade from the Umayyad palace at MSHATTA (Berlin, Pergamonmus.; see fig. 252 below) is the most elaborate of all Umayyad sculptural programmes. The portal was flanked by a horizontal band of 40 triangles, separated by a zigzag band of acanthus leaves. Each triangle contains a rosette set on a ground of finely worked vine scrolls. The lively movement of stems, leaves and bunches within the triangles contrasts with the conventional borders and the static circles in which the vegetation is inscribed. The unfinished state of the carving shows that much of the work was done *in situ*. While some examples, such as the façades of Mshatta and KHIRBAT AL-MAFJAR near Jericho, are executed in high relief, the trend was towards an overall flattening of design.

This trend towards flattening is continued in the stucco decoration of the Abbasid palaces at Samarra' in Iraq (mid-9th century), where three increasingly abstract styles of carved and moulded ornament have been identified. The first (Style A) is characterized by a recognizable vine leaf, which is pierced with four 'eyes' and is distinguished from the deeply recessed void of the background. In the second style (Style B), the contrast between subject and ground is less apparent, the vegetal forms are increasingly abstracted and the surface of each leaf is covered with small dots. While styles A and B are logical developments of earlier traditions of technique and design, the third style

(Style C, or the BEVELLED STYLE) points in new directions. The moulded design consists of endless rhythmic and symmetrical repetitions of curved lines with spiral terminals. The bevelled cut (Ger. *Schrägeschnitt*) introduced a new feeling of plasticity and movement. In the Balkuwara Palace (849–59), for example, walls covered with a continuous dado in the Bevelled style are surmounted by small arched recesses framed with pearl borders (*see* SAMARRA', fig. 3).

Stucco moulded or carved in the Samarra' styles became extraordinarily popular for both secular and religious architecture throughout the Abbasid realm. At the nine-domed mosque at BALKH in Afghanistan (9th century; *see also* §4(i)(c) above), stucco relief ornament covers most of the superstructure; at the congregational mosque of Ibn Tulun in Cairo (876–9; see fig. 24 above and CAIRO, §III, 2), restrained bands of patterned stucco outline the arcades and soffits. At the Regent's Palace at Termez (12th century) in Uzbekistan, geometric and arabesque ornament in a debased Samarra' style decorates the dados. The Bevelled style persisted; it is found, for example, in a large stucco panel beside the mihrab at the 14th-century shrine of Pir-i Bakran at Linjan in central Iran.

With the break-up of Abbasid hegemony, distinctly regional styles of three-dimensional ornament began to emerge. In the western Islamic world, the Late Antique and early Islamic traditions of using decoration to emphasize structure were maintained longer, and Abbasid styles of carving seem to have had little direct impact. The carved stucco dados from the palace at Sédrata in the Algerian Sahara (10th–11th century) are rigorously geometric and flat, and they are thought to derive from local traditions. The superbly carved marble panels from the 10th-century additions to the Great Mosque of Córdoba display naturalistic vegetal themes and a lively sense of movement, but they are equally flat. In the 11th and 12th centuries attempts were made to heighten the relief (see fig. 46 above). A portal from the Aljafería Palace in SARAGOSSA (11th century; Madrid, Mus. Arqueol. N.) is decorated in high relief with exuberant variations on the interlaced cusped arches used at the mosque of Córdoba. The underside of the Almoravid cupola in MARRAKESH, Morocco (early 12th century), is also richly sculptural, but this type of deeply carved stucco (*see also* §5(iv)(c) above) was not continued in later centuries, when extensive ensembles of stucco and wood carved in shallow relief decorated the upper surfaces of walls and the undersides of vaults. The primary motif is the arabesque, although epigraphic themes, *muqarnas* and lambrequin arches are also common. In the finest examples, such as the 'Attarin Madrasa in Fez (1323–5; see fig. 61 above), the carving displays a subtle plasticity within the confines of shallow relief, but in such later examples as the 16th-century *zāwiya* of Sidi Bel 'Abbas in Marrakesh, the wealth of intricate ornament becomes increasingly monotonous.

In Egypt, the Samarra' styles of carving wood and stucco introduced in the 9th century were replaced by increasingly naturalistic and crisply carved themes. The development can be traced in the architecture of Cairo (*see also* §5(ii)(c) above). Even the letters of inscriptions sprout leaves and flowers, as in the decoration of the Azhar (972) and Hakim (1013) mosques (see fig. 83 below

and CAIRO, §III, 3 and 4). The stucco surround of the mihrab in the mosque of al-Juyushi (1085; see fig. 38 above) is perhaps the finest example of this restrained and elegant style, where inscriptions, arabesques and floral motifs executed in shallow relief are superbly balanced within a composition fitted to the lines of the structure. In later centuries, three-dimensional stucco decoration continued to play a minor, but occasionally spectacular, role as in the stuccos surrounding the mihrab of the madrasa of al-Nasir Muhammad (1304). More striking is the Mamluk tradition of carved masonry domes. Ribbed domes of the early 14th century, modelled on earlier brick and stucco examples, were succeeded by domes in which carved zigzag decoration was coordinated with the structure, as in the dome over the tomb of Mahmud al-Kurdi (1394–5). In the early 15th century interlaced star patterns were adapted to the curved surfaces of the domes, and in the late 15th century star patterns were combined with arabesques, as in the dome over the tomb of Sultan Qa'itbay (1474; see fig. 58 above and CAIRO, §III, 10), the masterpiece of the series.

Another distinct regional style developed in the greater Iranian world, where brick buildings were enhanced with three-dimensional decoration on both exterior and interior. On the exterior, the interstices between bricks were manipulated to create patterns of light and shade, and carved endplugs of stucco and terracotta were also inserted between bricks to vary the surface patterns. The bricks themselves were also laid at varying depths to increase

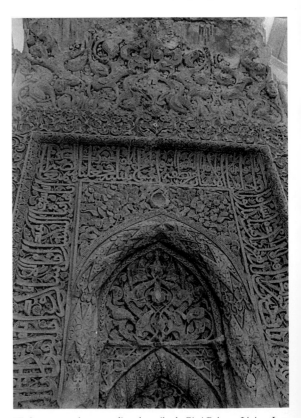

77. Stucco panel surrounding the mihrab, Pir-i Bakran, Linjan, Iran, early 14th century

further the play of light and shadow over the surface (*see also* §5(i)(b) above). The exterior decoration of the Kalan Minaret at Bukhara (1127; *see* BUKHARA, §2(iii)), for example, is divided into horizontal bands, each with a different motif, and the relief changes according to the height. Terracotta, which allowed great fineness of detail, was especially favoured in western Central Asia (*see* §5(i)(c) above), as on the portals of the mausolea at UZGEND (12th century). On the interior, stucco was the favoured material for three-dimensional ornament (see fig. 30 above). While the Samarra' styles and techniques of shallow relief were continued, a tradition of increasingly high relief can be traced in the decoration in and around mihrabs. In the finest examples, such as the mihrabs at the congregational mosques at ARDISTAN (1135) and Isfahan (*see* STUCCO AND PLASTERWORK, fig. 6) and the shrine at Pir-i Bakran (see fig. 77), arabesques of stems and leaves on intersecting levels create a sense of movement and depth.

In Anatolia, where Late Antique and Byzantine traditions of stone-carving were maintained for centuries, the themes developed in Iranian stucco were translated into stone (see fig. 41 above). At DIVRIĞI (1228–9), for example, the portals of the hospital and the congregational mosque are embellished with a bewildering array of fantastic vegetal and arabesque motifs that project from the wall in high and even undercut relief. This unusual style may owe something to Armenian and Georgian stone-working traditions, as did the accompanying interest in figural ornament (*see* §(b) below).

For bibliography *see* §(b) below.

SHEILA S. BLAIR, JONATHAN M. BLOOM

(b) Figural. The Islamic world was remarkably united in an instinctive and rooted distaste for figural sculpture as architectural decoration. Even when figural sculpture was most popular, as in Syria in the first half of the 8th century or in Anatolia and the Jazira in the 12th and 13th, an appreciation of figural sculpture was an acquired and unusual taste. The theological prohibition of figural art in all contexts began to be formulated in a precise and exhaustive manner in the 8th century, but the unequivocal presence of figural sculpture on the palaces of the Umayyad caliphs (*see* §3 above), who were the temporal and spiritual heads of the Muslim community, shows either that the prohibition was not yet in effect or that there was a clear dividing line between the religious and secular spheres. Later, an aversion to figural art operated primarily in the religious sphere, and the ban on sculpture was contravened only in specific contexts. In the public domain these included talismans and expressions of victory on bridges and city or castle gates; in a more private context such images were confined to bath and palace interiors. The taste for sculpture usually evinced a latitudinarianism, a broad-minded indifference to the finer points of theological detail, rather than a marked enthusiasm for such decoration.

Pre-Islamic or non-Islamic figural sculpture was sometimes used in Islamic architecture for triumphal purposes. For example, pharaonic reliefs were reused as thresholds in the Islamic monuments of Cairo, such as the funerary madrasa of Barquq *intra muros* (1386), and Indian sculptures from Somnath were sent by Mahmud of Ghazna (*reg* 998–1030) for the threshold of the *haram* at MECCA. Less obviously religious in tenor were Classical statues placed at intervals along the city walls of KONYA. In Iran the mosque at QAZVIN was known as the Mosque of the Bull, presumably because Achaemenid bull-headed *protomes* were reused to support the roof. In the Yemen pre-Islamic figural carving was reused in the congregational mosques at SAN'A and Dhamar.

The unusual interest in figural sculpture during the later Umayyad period in Syria was triggered by the Romano-Byzantine art of the eastern Mediterranean region. In all probability such work was also produced further afield in Egypt and Iraq. This figural sculpture was employed exclusively in palatial residences and vividly expressed the sybaritic lifestyle followed there. Virtually all the surviving sculpture comes from three excavated sites, QASR AL-HAYR WEST, KHIRBAT AL-MAFJAR and MSHATTA. All three were caliphal residences and had figural sculpture on their exterior façades in plain public view. Khirbat al-Mafjar and Mshatta are attributable to the patronage of al-Walid II (*reg* 743–4), who even as heir-apparent delighted in flying in the face of public opinion, but Qasr al-Hayr is attributable to Hisham (*reg* 724–43), a ruler who observed religious forms punctiliously.

These sculptures show a wide range of subjects in unprecedented combinations. A cycle of images associated with the princely lifestyle had been developed by the end of the Umayyad period. This princely cycle is expressed most fully in the stucco sculptures from Qasr al-Hayr, which include enthroned rulers, in both the Byzantine and Sasanian manner, female attendants offering flowers and beverages, male servants carrying animals and dishes, bodyguards, reclining figures (perhaps intended to represent banqueters), strutting birds and pacing lions. They occupy the interstices of a continuous balustrade encircling the upper storey of the palace court, a location that enabled them to function as visual referents to the courtly activities pursued in the rooms behind. At Khirbat al-Mafjar the porch of the bath-hall is dominated by the image of a caliph with drawn sword supported by a pair of snarling lions. Traces of colour indicate that polychromy and gilding were essential parts of the decorative scheme. Figures of mountain sheep on the ledge below were presumably intended as royal symbols in the Persian manner. Within the porch at gallery level, a bevy of bare-breasted maidens offer drinks and flowers to the visitor. Among them was an incongruous figure garbed like a Roman centurion. Athletes in loincloths, whose poses parody atlantids, occupied the pendentives. The dome over the diwan, the private audience chamber within the bath-hall, was decorated with birds, winged horses and a striking arrangement of six heads emerging from a flower (*see* STUCCO AND PLASTERWORK, fig. 5), all suggestive of apotheosis. The significance of other themes, such as the heads emerging from knotted medallions in the vault of the entrance vestibule, remains enigmatic. On the façade at Mshatta, almost all the triangular panels to the left of the entrance are inhabited by real and imaginary animals, whereas those to the right, behind the palace mosque, have no living beings.

The western Islamic world, including Spain, was generally hostile to figural decoration. Few examples of architectural sculpture survive, and the scattered references in literary sources indicate that figural decoration was primarily used in palaces. According to al-Maqqari (*d* 1632), the Umayyad caliph 'Abd al-Rahman III al-Nasir (*reg* 912–61) placed a statue of his favourite wife al-Zahra' over the gate of MADINAT AL-ZAHRA', the palace-city near Córdoba named after her, and excavations there have yielded a fragmentary sculpture of a draped figure executed in the Roman tradition. Lions formerly adorned the city gate at MAHDIA, the Fatimid capital in Tunisia inaugurated in 921, and a marble relief of a cross-legged ruler listening to a flautist was unearthed there; the remains of lead in the crevices suggest that the surface was enlivened by pieces of stone in variegated colours. Stucco sculptures representing various creatures, including a parrot with fruit in its beak and lions, were found in the ruins of Sabra al-Mansuriyya, the next Fatimid capital in Tunisia. According to the poet Ibn Hamdis (*d* 1132–3), lion sculptures adorned the gate of the Zirid palace at Bougie (Algeria) and acted as waterspouts in fountains there. A grey marble lion found at QAL'AT BANI HAMMAD in Algeria apparently adjoined the springing of the arch of a palace gate, and the same place on the Gate of the Udayas at RABAT (*c.* 1195–9) was decorated with a sculpted fish. A column in the *zāwiya* of Sidi 'Abid al-Gharyani at KAIROUAN in Tunisia shows two confronted and highly stylized birds drinking from a chalice. The principal example of later architectural sculpture from Spain is a stucco slab depicting interlaced arches weirdly interspersed with human heads (Berlin, Mus. Islam. Kst). It was probably made for the Nasrids (*reg* 1230–1492; *see* §6(iv)(a) above), and the hairstyles suggest the impact of western European models. Block-like lions whose stylized ferocity excludes naturalism decorate fountains in the Patio de los Leones and the Palacio del Partal at the Alhambra in Granada (*see* GRANADA, §III, 1).

The most significant body of figural sculpture to survive from the western Islamic world is a series of carved basins and tanks or troughs, perhaps intended for ritual ablution. The earliest dated piece is the tank made in 987–8 at Madinat al-Zahra' for the chief minister Ibn Abi-'Amir, known as al-Mansur (Madrid, Mus. Arqueol. N.). Its propagandistic purpose is clear from its decoration, which juxtaposes the patron's name and titles with lions crouching on the wings of eagles grasping deer. A similar but larger (700×1550×820 mm) tank now in the Ben Yusuf Madrasa in MARRAKESH was made for al-Mansur's son 'Abd al-Malik, probably at Madinat al-Zahra' between 1002 and 1007. The best-known piece is the Pila of Játiva (Játiva, Mus. Mun.), which was probably made for a rich commoner in the 11th century. Its repertory of images from the princely cycle is the fullest yet encountered on a single work of art from Muslim Spain.

Figural sculpture in relief or in the round enjoyed a certain vogue in palace decoration in the Iranian world between the 11th and 13th century. A large number of almost life-size stucco reliefs and sculptures of princes, attendants and scenes of court life are said to have come from RAYY in Iran, but their authenticity has been questioned. The largest quantity of figural sculpture in stucco scientifically excavated in the Iranian world was found in the ruined palace at Termez on the Oxus River. Figural panels were set above a dado of geometric, floral and epigraphic motifs. Arched panels containing animals were flanked by others with strapwork patterns or with curvilinear motifs in a debased BEVELLED STYLE (*see also* §(a) above). Two of the four panels depict fearsome pairs of lions emerging from a single head: the head above the rampant pair has an extended tongue and Medusa-like mane. Two other damaged panels depict a pair of addorsed crouching felines and a lion bringing down a bull, and fragments were found of two griffins sculpted in the round. The subject-matter and decoration with rosettes and solar discs suggest a zodiacal or apotropaic meaning. Similar motifs characterize the contemporary marble sculpture found at GHAZNA in Afghanistan, capital of the Ghaznavid dynasty (*reg* 977–1186), where an octagonal water basin is bordered with a variety of real and imaginary animals. A series of waterspouts in the form of lions with gaping jaws seems to have been part of the irrigation system in the palace garden. A panel depicting a leaping monkey and a man carrying a basket is undoubtedly derived from Indian models, as are the lotus shape of the basin and creatures sharing a single head. The extensive campaigns waged by the Ghaznavids in north India and the fabulous booty they amassed there easily explain this transfer of motifs.

An unusually rich tradition of figural sculpture emerged during the 12th and 13th centuries in parts of Turkey, Syria, Iraq and Iran, which were then under the control of several Turkish dynasties, including the Saljuks of Anatolia and the Artuqids. This tradition waned rapidly in the 14th century when the area came under the domination of the Ilkhanid dynasty. Most surviving examples were carved in stone, but excavations of the Saljuq palaces at Kubadabad near Beyşehir and at KONYA have revealed significant quantities of figural decoration in stucco. Figural sculptures decorated a variety of building types, including castles, palaces, caravanserais, bridges, mausolea, madrasas and even mosques. Nevertheless, this taste was clearly exceptional, for figural decoration is found on only eight of the hundred surviving caravanserais and only three mausolea, but its presence on six mosques and three madrasas shows that it was not an aberration. The repertory includes real and imaginary animals, birds and people. Lions were most commonly represented, followed by single- and double-headed eagles; leopards, bulls, panthers, dogs, horses, hares, deer, peacocks, serpents, dragons, sphinxes and harpies were also shown. These creatures were depicted singly or in confronted or addorsed pairs. Representations of the human figure include rulers, court officials, servants, angels and sirens. One of the most famous depictions was on the Talisman Gate at BAGHDAD (1221; destr. 1917; *see* fig. 78), where a seated monarch, presumably the Abbasid caliph al-Nasir, held two dragons by their tongues. Animals and figures were occasionally shown in association with fruiting trees, as at the Çifte Minareli Madrasa at ERZURUM (1243) and the Döner Kümbed at KAYSERI (late 13th century), or with signs of the zodiac, as in the combination of the lion and sun at the bridge at Cizre (1164). The most complete zodiacal cycle survives at the octagonal mausoleum at Khachen Dorbatly in Azerbaijan

78. Figural terracotta decoration on the Talisman Gate, Baghdad, Iraq, 1221 (destr. 1917)

(1314), but the dodecagonal tomb of the Ilkhanid sultan Ghazan Khan at Tabriz (1304; destr.; *see* TABRIZ, §I) probably displayed the full zodiacal cycle in a more appropriate setting. These figural representations were usually distributed somewhat haphazardly over the exterior of buildings, but they were also used as gargoyles or applied to such significant locations as window and door surrounds and the spandrels of arches or gateways.

The meaning of these images has been hotly disputed. Some were heraldic emblems, such as the panther found at Lydda (Israel), which is associated with Baybars I (*reg* 1260–77), the Mamluk sultan of Egypt. The eagles on the walls of DIYARBAKIR are Artuqid emblems. Many were references to royalty. Lions and eagles, quintessential images of sovereignty, often decorate buildings erected under royal patronage, and others, such as the lions at the castle of Mayyafariqin (1156) or the double-headed lion at Alay Han (*c.* 1215), are more generalized symbols of royalty. Some are personal crests, while others referred to ownership, as in the simplified images of animals included in the *tamgha*s, or brands, used by Turkish nomads. Other images express shamanistic, totemic or magic beliefs. Many

representations were probably apotropaic in function, but the role of others, such as the menageries at Ak Han (1253–4) and Karatay Han (completed 1240–41) or the series of animal heads at the Sunqur Bey Mosque at Niğde (1335; destr.) and the Gök Madrasa at SIVAS (1271), is unclear. Images of the sun and moon at the hospital of Kayka'us at Sivas (1217–18), the minaret of Abu'l Muzaffar at Mayyafariqin (1212) and the mosque of Alaeddin at Niğde (1223) may have been references to spiritual illumination or a survival of the age-old veneration of heavenly bodies by the Turkic tribes of Central Asia, Mongolia and Siberia. The combination of the lion and the sun on the Incir Han and the bridge at Cizre was presumably intended in a zodiacal sense, as the planet Sun under the influence of Leo. Some images may also have been intended to refer to the afterlife, for 'He became a falcon' is a common Turkish expression to describe death, and the tree of life surmounted by an eagle is often used as a symbol of paradise.

It is hard to reconcile a single directed iconography with the often haphazard nature and placement of these images. Many of these representations may have been inspired by the Armenian tradition of stone sculpture (*see* ARMENIA, §IV, 1), for they share high relief, haphazard distribution over the exterior and emblematic significance. The unique architectural example of zoomorphic script, found around the main keep of the fortress at BAKU on the Caspian Sea (1234–5), may also have been derived from Armenian manuscripts, although it was commonly used on Islamic metalwork (*see* §IV, 1(v) below).

BIBLIOGRAPHY
S. M. Flury: *Die Ornamente der Hakim- und Ashar-Moschee* (Heidelberg, 1912)
R. M. Riefstahl: 'Persian Islamic Stucco Sculpture', *A. Bull.*, xiii (1931), pp. 439–63
K. A. C. Creswell: *Early Muslim Architecture*, i (Oxford, 1932/*R* and enlarged 1969)
M. Dimand: 'Studies in Islamic Ornament, i: Some Aspects of Omaiyad and Early Abbasid Ornaments', *A. Islam.*, iv (1937), pp. 293–337
B. P. Denike: *Arkhitekturnii ornament srednei Azii* [The architectural ornament of Central Asia] (Moscow, 1939)
M. Dimand: 'Studies in Islamic Ornament, ii', *Archaeologica Orientalia in Memoriam Ernst Herzfeld* (Locust Valley, NY, 1952), pp. 62–8
R. Ettinghausen: 'The "Beveled Style" in the Post-Samarra Period', *Archaeologica Orientalia in Memoriam Ernst Herzfeld* (Locust Valley, NY, 1952), pp. 72–83
L. I. Rempel': *Arkhitekurni ornament uzbekistana* [The architectural ornament of Uzbekistan] (Tashkent, 1961)
D. Hill and O. Grabar: *Islamic Architecture and its Decoration, A.D. 800–1500* (Chicago, 1964)
A. U. Pope and P. Ackerman, eds: *Survey of Persian Art* (London and New York, 1938–9, 2/1964–7), iii, pp. 1258–364
E. Baer: 'The "Pila" of Játiva: A Document of Secular Urban Art in Western Islam', *Kst Orients*, vii (1970–71), pp. 144–66
D. Hill and L. Golvin: *Islamic Architecture in North Africa* (London, 1976)
C. Kessler: *The Carved Masonry Domes of Mediaeval Cairo* (London, 1976)
M. S. Bulatov: *Geometricheskaya garmonizatsiya v arkhitekture srednei Azii, IX–XV vv.* [Geometric harmonization in the architecture of Central Asia, 9th–15th centuries] (Moscow, 1978)
G. Öney: 'Architectural Decoration and the Minor Arts', *The Art and Architecture of Turkey*, ed. E. Akugral (New York, 1980), pp. 170–74
C. Ewert and J.-P. Wisshak: *Forschungen zur almohadischen Moschee*, i (Mainz, 1981)
E. Whelan: 'Representations of the *Khāssakīyah* and the Origins of Mamluk Emblems', *Content and Context of Visual Arts in the Islamic World*, ed. P. P. Soucek (New York, 1988), pp. 219–53

ROBERT HILLENBRAND

(ii) Tiles. Ceramic decoration of Islamic architecture is notable for the range of techniques used, the superb quality of the tiles, especially those produced at KASHAN in central Iran and Iznik in western Turkey (*see* IZNIK, §2), and, most importantly from an architectural standpoint, for its ability (admittedly not always achieved) to clothe a whole building in colour and, by judiciously varying the type, pattern and location, to preserve the integrity of the underlying architecture. Wall tiles were used on both interior and exterior surfaces and display a range of subjects, including geometric motifs, writing, flowers, animals, birds, human figures and scenes from epic narratives. The choice of subject depended on the building's function, with mosques and religious buildings usually having non-figural decoration. The tradition of ceramic decoration apparently developed slowly in the early centuries of Islam before exploding in the 11th century in parallel but distinct ways in the eastern and western Islamic worlds. In the post-classical period older styles were repeated at a lower level of quality.

(a) Early development. (b) Eastern Islamic lands. (c) Western Islamic lands.

(a) Early development. Large figurative panels of glazed bricks were used extensively in Assyrian, Babylonian and Achaemenian architecture, but wall tiles appeared in Islamic architecture only in the 9th century. Several examples of polychrome lustre tiles, showing a cock within a wreath, were uncovered in excavations of the Dar al-Khilafa (Jawsaq al-Khaqani) palace (*c.* 836) at Samarra' in Iraq (*see* SAMARRA', §2), and an extensive series with vegetal motifs decorates the mihrab of the Great Mosque at KAIROUAN (862) in Tunisia. Despite the great strides in ceramic production over the next two centuries (*see* §V, 2 below), the few surviving examples of wall tiles, either those in champlevé technique from north-west Iran or those in lustre from Egypt, suggest that ceramic decoration played a minor role in any architectural ensemble.

(b) Eastern Islamic lands. By the late 11th century architects in the eastern Islamic world had reached the ultimate exploitation of carved and patterned brick decoration and were ready to experiment with glazed revetment. The clay-coloured bricks of buildings such as the two tomb towers at Kharraqan (1067–8 and 1093–4; *see* §5(i)(b) above) in north-west Iran are the same hue as the surrounding countryside, and the addition of a contrasting colour was a natural step in the evolution of decoration. Rectangular tiles could be simply arranged in friezes, but patterns with arabesques, strapwork or epigraphy required fitting small pieces together like a jigsaw in the technique known as tile mosaic or mosaic faience (Pers. *kāshī*). The technique is extremely labour-intensive, and therefore expensive, but the freedom of design it permitted and the growing intensity of the colours obtained justified the cost. The most common glaze was light or turquoise blue, readily available from cobalt deposits in Iran. It was used frequently and effectively for external inscriptions (e.g. the minarets at Sin (1132) in central Iran and at Jam (1194) in central Afghanistan) and for increasingly complicated strapwork patterns (two tomb towers at MARAGHA (1147–8 and 1196–7) in north-western Iran). Two additional colours, white and dark blue, are found in one monument erected shortly before the Mongol invasions, the madrasa at Zuzan (1219) in north-eastern Iran.

The Mongol invasions cut short the evolution of Iranian tilework, and potters may have sought refuge in Anatolia, where the next developments are found. KONYA, a city never sacked by the Mongols, has a series of 13th-century buildings with extensive ceramic decoration. The most magnificent is the Karatay Madrasa (1251–2). Much of the interior of the central dome chamber is covered in tile (the harsher climate of Anatolia was injurious to exterior tilework). Manganese black is added to the three colours used at Zuzan, although the white of the Karatay Madrasa is plaster and not glaze. A similar effect of contrasting white was often achieved by sgraffito, scratching away the glaze to reveal the biscuit colour of the tile beneath, for example in the mihrab (*c.* 1235) of the Alaeddin Mosque in Konya, while a further contrast was attained by incorporating stucco within the design, as in the Arslanhane Mosque in ANKARA (*c.* 1290).

Subsequent development of tile mosaic occurred mainly in Iran and Transoxiana (*see also* §6(i)(a) above). During the 14th century ochre and green were added to the palette and patterns evolved from geometric to naturalistic and floral, as in the portal to the congregational mosque at KIRMAN (1349) in central Iran. The technique reached its apogee in Timur's palace of Aq Saray at Shahr-i Sabz (Uzbekistan; 1395–6; *see* CENTRAL ASIA, fig. 12), although works done in Iran in the 15th century under Qaraqoyunlu patronage (e.g. the Darb-i Imam at Isfahan, 1453–4, and the Blue Mosque at Tabriz, *c.* 1465; *see* TABRIZ, §3(ii) are comparable (*see also* §6(i)(b) and fig. 51 above). In general, tilework produced under the Safavid dynasty (*reg* 1501–1732) failed to advance on previous work, with the exception of the dome chamber in the mosque of Shaykh Lutfallah at Isfahan (1603–19; *see* ISFAHAN, §3(iv)), the interior lines of which are so simple that they can readily support the variety and intensity of the tilework applied to the walls (see fig. 79).

While tile mosaic was the dominant technique of ceramic decoration in the eastern Islamic world during the 13th and 14th centuries, a wide range of other techniques were used alongside or in place of it. Carved and glazed tilework was virtually confined to Transoxiana. In the 12th century it was primarily used for cursive inscriptions, the finest example being the turquoise upper inscription encircling the minaret at Vapkent (Uzbekistan; 1198–9). By the time of Bulyan Quli Khan's tomb in Bukhara (*c.* 1358) white and dark-blue glazes were added and virtually all the interior and exterior surfaces were covered, although many pieces have been removed to Western museums (Hamburg, Mus. Kst & Gew., and London, V&A). Surprisingly, the technique died out by the end of the 14th century.

Underglaze painting, used extensively on ceramic vessels from the end of the 12th century (*see* §V, 3 below), was adapted for wall tiles and became widespread in the 13th and 14th centuries. Most examples, such as the Saljuq palace at Kubadabad (*c.* 1236) on Lake Beyşehir in central Anatolia, were laid in friezes which formed a small part of the overall decoration. Underglaze-painted decoration predominates on only one extant building, the Tomb of

79. Tilework, dome chamber, mosque of Shaykh Lutfallah, Isfahan, completed 1619

Shad-i Mulk in the Shah-i Zinda at Samarkand (1371; *see* CENTRAL ASIA, §1, 2(ii)(b)); the portal spandrels display the boldest panels, and the cenotaphs have enlarged chinoiserie motifs enhanced by light relief. Two mihrabs attributable on stylistic grounds to lustre workshops in Kashan (New York, Met., and Cairo, Mus. Islam. A., dated AH 719/1319–20) also have large areas of underglaze painting, while two early 14th-century cenotaphs in western Central Asia, one for Najm al-Din Kubra at KUNYA-URGENCH and one for Sayyid 'Ala' al-Din in Khiva (*see* CENTRAL ASIA, fig. 15), are very different in style, with Chinese lotuses and peonies and much turquoise staining. Three groups of underglaze-painted tiles from the 15th century are hexagonal and show a strong influence of Chinese blue-and-white wares. One group is found in the complex of al-Tawrizi (1428–9; *see* DAMASCUS, §1(ii)) at Damascus in Syria, the finest are in the mosque of Murad II (1435–6) at EDIRNE in Turkey, and a third group datable to the late 15th century is preserved in the Islamic Museum in Cairo.

The earliest tiles attributed to the site of Iznik in southwestern Turkey, four large (1.27×0.48 m) blue-and-white panels in the Sunnet Odasi of Topkapı Palace in Istanbul (*c.* 1555–65; *see* ISTANBUL, §III, 13(ii); *see also* TILE, colour pl. XIII, fig. 1), are very different in quality. Birds and dragons sporting amid chinoiserie leaves and blossoms are painted in two shades of blue on a luminous white ground. The painting is of a richness and delicacy not found in other tilework and is a tribute to the artists of

the Sultan's atelier who drew the original cartoons and to the potters who executed them. Later tiles produced at Iznik were fired with the same brilliance and intensity but use the full range of colours found on contemporary vessels—green, purple and the famous tomato-red. When applied on a modest scale, as in the mosque of Sokollu Mehmed Pasha in Istanbul (*c.* 1572), the effect is unsurpassed. All-over revetment, as in the mosque of Rüstem Pasha in Istanbul (*c.* 1561), is less successful, as the brilliance of the tiles detracts from the architectonic solidity of the building.

Lustreware, produced continuously from 1200 to 1340 at Kashan, was the most expensive type of ceramic produced in medieval Iran and was restricted to interior surfaces. The bulk of surviving examples are star tiles for dados and square or rectangular inscription friezes, but the finest efforts were reserved for mihrabs or panels covering cenotaphs. Over 30 of these assemblages survive, in whole or in part. The largest ones measure more than 2 m and contain more than 40 individual tiles, and those from the pre-Mongol period are higher in quality than later pieces. The mihrab dated AH 612 (1215) in the shrine of Imam Riza at MASHHAD, for example, has a bold design of three niches set within large rectangular friezes decorated with angular and cursive writing. The design is enhanced by the pronounced moulding of the inscriptions and the arabesques on the tympanum and spandrels of the main arch, and the background painting is as finely detailed as that on any contemporary vessel.

Cuerda seca tiles, in which different glazes were separated by a greasy substance mixed with manganese, leaving a matt black line between the colours after firing (*see also* TILE, §I, 2(i)), was first used extensively in late 14th-century Transoxiana. Such buildings as the mausoleum of Qutluq Aqa (1361) in the Shah-i Zinda at Samarkand display a wide range of colours and motifs and are larger and more ambitious than later examples from Iran. The technique may have continued in destroyed buildings from 15th-century Tabriz, since artisans from that city made high-quality examples for the Yeşil complex in BURSA (*c.* 1421). The mihrab of the mausoleum, in particular its central panel with a lamp suspended on a luxuriant ground of chinoiserie flowers, is the cynosure of the genre. The Tabriz atelier continued to work in Turkey for a short time (e.g. the mosque of Murad II at Edirne), but the technique was eventually abandoned in favour of underglaze-painted tiles. It was taken up enthusiastically in 17th-century Iran, however, when it provided a cheap substitute for tile mosaic in Shah 'Abbas's grandiose plans for Isfahan. Figural panels from the Safavid period are related to contemporary album painting, but are more naive in style. The technique was also used widely in architecture built under the Qajars (*reg* 1779–1924; *see* §7(ii)(b) above), although frequently with a strident, predominant pink.

Mīnā'ī or polychrome overglaze-painting, a popular technique for vessels, was rarely used for tilework. Only a few tiles survive in museum collections (Cairo, Mus. Islam. A.), and the only building recorded as having used them on a large scale is the kiosk of Kiliç Arslan II in Konya (second half of the 12th century). The related technique of *lājvardīna*, in which enamels are painted over a dark-blue or turquoise glaze, is used for tiles with Chinese lotuses, dragons and phoenixes from the palace at TAKHT-I SULAYMAN (*c.* 1275) in north-western Iran. *Lājvardīna* tiles rarely appear on later architecture produced under the Ilkhanids (*reg* 1256–1353), but had a brief florescence in several monuments in the Shah-i Zinda at Samarkand before dying out at the end of the 14th century. The masterpiece in this technique is the cenotaph for Qutham ibn 'Abbas (1334–5), the focal point of the Shah-i Zinda. Gilded lotuses on tear-drop bosses contrast with the white ground that imitates *mīnā'ī* technique, and the scale and liberal application of gilding give the cenotaph a richness unparalleled by any pottery vessel. In *bannā'ī* (builder's technique) glazed bricks were alternated with ordinary baked bricks to create geometric patterns over the surface of a wall or to spell out sacred names or pious phrases, as in the 12th-century mosque at Nushabad. This was an easy and effective way of decorating large surfaces and became exceedingly popular in later periods, when the colour range was increased from the two tones of blue and the patterns became more elaborate.

(c) Western Islamic lands. By the 11th century the technique of tile mosaic (Arab. *zallīj*, Sp. *alicatado*) had reached a sophisticated level in the western Islamic world, as seen in the elaborate pavements found at QAL'AT BANI HAMMAD in southern Algeria. The technique may well have developed earlier, as fragments from Sabra/al-Mansuriyya near Kairouan in Tunisia could date from the original Fatimid foundation in the mid-10th century or from the later Zirid occupation in the mid-11th. The technique continued in the 12th century, when intricate imbrication in tile mosaic was used to decorate the minarets of the Kutubiyya and Kasba mosques in MARRAKESH. The flowering of tile mosaic in the western Islamic world, however, occurred in 14th-century monuments built by the Marinids (*reg* 1196–1549) in Morocco (*see* §6(iv)(b) above). Unlike the eastern Islamic world, where blue predominated, in the west the main colours were green and light brown, usually on a white ground. Stucco decoration on the upper walls was set off by tiled dados, which were usually capped by epigraphic friezes in which the black letters were formed by sgraffito. Floors, unlike those in the east, often had glazed highlights or were completely covered in tiles (see fig. 61 above; *see also* TILE, colour pl. XIII, fig. 3). Even the piers and columns in courtyards were revetted in tile, as in the 'Attarin Madrasa in FEZ (1323–5) and the Bu 'Inaniyya madrasas in Salé (1341–2) and Fez (1350–55). While the overall effect is glistening, the resulting dissolution of surface provided an insufficient visual foundation for the intricate carved stucco and woodwork above. Tile mosaic was also used on minarets and portals. Most patterns, especially on minarets, were geometric, but occasional exceptions, such as the vegetal arabesques on the spandrels of the portal to the Abu Madyan Mosque at TLEMCEN (1338–9), rival the delicacy of the finest stuccowork. *Cuerda seca* tiles produced a similar effect, as the spandrels on the Puerta del Vino in the Alhambra at Granada (second half of the 14th century; *see* GRANADA, §III, 1) show.

Tile panels in the Italian maiolica technique were produced in Tunisia and became popular throughout North Africa from the 18th century onwards. Although they sometimes had ambitious designs of flowering trees in vases, the muddied colour of the glazes and the occasional smearing of the colours represent a distinct decline in quality.

BIBLIOGRAPHY

T. Öz: *Turkish Ceramics* (Ankara, n.d.)
M. P. Blanchet and H. Saladin: 'Description des monuments de la Kaala des Beni Hammad, commune mixte des Maadid, province de Constantine (Algérie)', *Nouv. Archvs Miss. Sci.*, xvii (1908), pp. 1–21
G. Audisio: *La Marqueterie de terre émaillée (mosaïque de faïence) dans l'art musulman d'Occident* (Algiers, 1926)
D. Wilber: 'The Development of Mosaic Faience in Islamic Architecture in Iran', *A. Islam.*, vi (1939), pp. 16–47
A. Lane: *Victoria and Albert Museum: A Guide to the Collection of Tiles* (London, 1960)
O. Aslanapa: *Türkische Fliesen und Keramik in Anatolien* (Istanbul, 1965)
N. S. Grazhdankina, M. K. Rakhimov and I. E. Pletnev: *Arkhitekturnaya keramika uzbekistana* (Tashkent, 1968)
J. Carswell: 'Six Tiles', *Islamic Art in the Metropolitan Museum of Art*, ed. R. Ettinghausen (New York, 1972), pp. 99–124
B. P. Maldonado: *El arte hispanomusulmán en su decoración geometrica* (Madrid, 1975)
M. Meinecke: *Fayencedekorationen seldschukischer Sakralbauten in Kleinasien* (Tübingen, 1976)
W. Denny: *The Ceramics of the Mosque of Rustem Pasha and the Environment of Change* (New York, 1977)
O. Watson: *Persian Lustre Ware* (London, 1985)

BERNARD O'KANE

(iii) Painting. Painting was used in many ways in Islamic architecture: by itself on plaster walls and floors or to emphasize relief carvings on stucco and wood (*see* §§(i) above and VII below). The fragile nature of the medium means that most paintings, particularly from the early periods, have been destroyed. Surviving fragments come mainly from buildings that were abandoned, such as palaces, since buildings that were in constant use, such as mosques and shrines, were repeatedly replastered and redecorated. Even palaces were often flimsily built and demolished or abandoned at a ruler's whim or radically redecorated by his successors. Throughout the Islamic world the preponderant type of wall painting has been non-figural, but little has survived and even less has been published. In Iran architectural inscriptions were painted in blue on interiors (e.g. the knotted kufic inscription around the Pir-i 'Alamdar at DAMGHAN, 1027–8), and roundels and ogival medallions in many colours are found, for example at the Rukniyya at YAZD (1324–5). In Cairo contemporary paintings are preserved in the mosque and hospice of Shaykhu (1355). Those in the madrasa of Khushqadam al-Ahmadi (1366 or 1376) and the madrasa al-Ghannamiyya (1372–3) are particularly luxurious, perhaps because they had been reception rooms of private houses of the earlier 14th century. Figural wall paintings were far less common in the Islamic world, but interest in their subject-matter has led to their study and publication.

(a) *c.* AD 700–*c.* 900. (b) *c.* 900–*c.* 1900.

(a) c. AD *700–c. 900.* Evidence of figural wall painting in the centuries preceding the Muslim conquests is poor, and the mosaics of Antioch in Syria (*see* ANTIOCH (i), §2(iii)), rock-reliefs at the Sasanian site of TAQ-I BUSTAN in Iran, textiles from Alexandria and even Pompeian wall paintings have all had to bear excessive weight in reconstructing the historical context of the two ensembles of figural wall painting to survive from the early 8th century

in Syria. The earlier are found on the interior walls of the bath at QUSAYR 'AMRA in Jordan. The bathing scenes with female nudes and children, one of them clearly based on a *Birth of Venus*, and elaborate hunting scenes, mostly of onagers, show surprisingly strong classicizing reminiscences, despite their variety and their damaged and now lacunary state. They seem to illustrate two main functions of great baths in Late Antiquity, as places of public assembly and as places of entertainment. One painting, at the left end of the west wall of the right bay of the great hall, shows six kings. Four of them are identified by inscriptions in poor Greek: the Byzantine Emperor or one of his generals; Roderick, the last Visigothic King of Spain, who was killed at the Battle of Guadalete on 19 July 712; Chosroes, the last Sasanian monarch; and the ruler of Abyssinia. Except for the last, they could all represent rulers defeated by the early Muslims, and the other two kings have accordingly been identified as the Emperor of China and either the Turkish ruler of the western Khaqanate, who was defeated at Samarkand in 712, or Dahir, a Hindu king defeated in the same year. The identifications indicate a *terminus post quem* of 712, which would date the bath to the reign of al-Walid I (*reg* 705–15) or one of his successors. Although this painting has been the subject of considerable scholarly attention, it was never the focus of the pictorial programme.

Other paintings in the vaults of Qusayr 'Amra show musicians in a lozenge diaper and craftsmen in panels. They are closely related to mosaic designs known from Antioch and Palestine in the 5th and 6th centuries. Other classicizing figures include cupids, victories and the muses, also titled in inept Greek. The style of the larger figures with heavy limbs and even heavier modelling has not so far been paralleled in any local school of Late Antiquity. The dome over a side chamber is decorated with a zodiac with the constellations arranged in descending rows from the North Pole at the centre: since the celestial equator lies well above the base of the dome, some of the constellations of the southern hemisphere are also included. The constellations are shown as they would appear on the surface of a celestial globe, not as they would appear in the heavens. Because of the arrangement in tiers they have been squeezed into the space available, and it has not been possible to date precisely the globe on which the zodiac was based. Iconographically, the star-pictures are much closer to the Ptolemaic–Greek tradition than to the *sphaera barbarica* — the repertory of constellation-pictures showing the influence not only of Hellenistic but also of Babylonian models — that was used by later Abbasid astronomers.

The only other architectural paintings to survive from the Umayyad period are two floor paintings from QASR AL-HAYR WEST, the desert palace in the Palmyrene steppe built by the caliph Hisham (727; Damascus, N. Mus.). The one in room XIV is a copy, or a pastiche, of a mosaic showing a central medallion with a bust of Ge (Earth) bearing fruit, and Tritons or Lapiths in two of the spandrels. The other, in room XIX, is divided into three

80. Floor painting of a mounted archer, from room XIX, Qasr al-Hayr West, Syria, AD 727 (Damascus, National Museum)

registers: two musicians in an arcade, a mounted archer or hunter (see fig. 80), and huntsmen returning to the *ḥayr* (walled enclosure) with their captured animals. Their dress, posture and accoutrements owe much to the decoration of Sasanian silver and rock reliefs, although Sasanian seals were probably the immediate source. The two ensembles show that Umayyads inherited a hellenized tradition of architectural decoration yet were affected by such Parthian–Sasanian traditions as a taste for frontality in figural representation, an orientalizing vocabulary of royal symbols and a preference for low relief over sculpture in the round.

With the fall of the Umayyads in 750, the political and geographical centre of the caliphate shifted to Iraq and Iran, and the hellenizing tradition weakened. Wall painting under the Abbasids continued pre-Islamic traditions of painting in Mesopotamia, Iran and western Central Asia. The historian al-Mas'udi (*d* 956) alluded to paintings at the Sasanian capital at KTESIPHON and in the tombs of the Sasanian kings, but excavations at Ktesiphon yielded only fragmentary paintings of uncertain date in baths and elsewhere. The rich tradition of painting on the eve of the Muslim conquest, however, is now well documented thanks to extensive discoveries in western Central Asia (*see* CENTRAL ASIA, §I, 4(iv)). Paintings (Tashkent, Aybek Mus. Hist. Uzbekistan; copies in Samarkand, Afrasiab Mus.) found in the ruins of a palace at Afrasiab, ancient Samarkand (*see* SAMARKAND, §1(i)), show fragmentary scenes identified by inscriptions in Bactrian and Sogdian of embassies to Varkhuman (Vargoman), the ruler of Sogdiana (*c.* 650–75), from the rulers of Chach (the Tashkent area), Chaghanian, China and even, to judge by their costumes, Korea. The figures from Chaghanian and Sogdiana have overgarments with wide lapels over trousers and boots exactly like those on the figures in the Grotto of the Sixteen Swordbearers at Qizil in Chinese Turkestan, including such details as patterned roundels of boars' heads, deer and guinea-fowl with Sasanian scarves in pearled surrounds. The paintings were sketched in red on dry plaster and then strengthened in black. Many of their details are unfinished, but they show no evidence of damage from the Muslim conquest of 712. Some of the wall paintings (mostly in St Petersburg, Hermitage) discovered in the ruins of Pendzhikent in the Zarafshan Valley probably date from the period after the Muslims occupied Sogdiana, although the interpretation of their subject-matter is still a matter of debate. In addition to important cycles of paintings illustrating the exploits of Rustam, datable to *c.* 740, a cycle of pictures of the same date has been identified as illustrating tales from the *Pañcatantra*. These Indian tales were translated into Pahlavi and then into Arabic as *Kalila and Dimna*, and illustrations in the earliest surviving manuscripts of the Arabic version (e.g. Paris, Bib. N., 3465), probably made in Syria in the first decades of the 13th century, show significant resemblances to the Pendzhikent murals. Both wall paintings and manuscript paintings doubtless derived from a common source, perhaps a scroll, and argue for the persistence of a continuous tradition of painting from pre-Islamic to Abbasid times (*see* §III, 4(ii) below).

Figural paintings excavated by ERNST HERZFELD at the 9th-century Abbasid capital at Samarra' (*see* SAMARRA', §2) show the impact of iranicizing textiles from Central Asia, as worn by the 'Sogdian' God of Silk from DANDANOILIK (6th–8th century; London, BM). Many fragments of small compositions (Berlin, Pergamonmus.; London, BM; Istanbul, Mus. Turk. & Islam. A.; and elsewhere), some barely more than miniatures, were brought to light. Although a few were found in the larger houses, most were excavated at the Dar al-Khilafa (Jawsaq al-Khaqani), the palace built by the caliph al-Mu'tasim, and were accordingly dated to *c.* 836–9. These fragments are problematic in several ways. Many of the fragments in London have several layers of plaster showing radically different compositions, and they could well have been painted over several decades. Considerably more was excavated than was published in 1927, but many of the finds had been mislaid during World War I and the site disturbed. The lack of any technique for rapid recording of the finds meant that, as the painted fragments emerged from the ground, Herzfeld, a fine draughtsman, was obliged to touch in the designs with watercolour before they dried out. The published colour illustrations, which have become a standard part of the repertory, are likewise all in his own hand.

Figural decoration was found in three areas of the Jawsaq al-Khaqani. The Sardab, an underground refuge from the heat of summer, had friezes in low relief of Bactrian camels on a blue ground. The bath in what Herzfeld identified as the harem contained the largest reconstructible composition, evidently from a dome: a heavy cornucopia scroll reminiscent of the mosaics in the Dome of the Rock in Jerusalem (*see* §(iv) below) but inhabited by eagles, hares, other fauna and scantily clad human figures. Both scroll and fauna are strongly hellenizing, although many of the animals wear scarves in the Sasanian manner. The bath and the throne-room, the third area with painting, had small panels with female or epicene dancers, cup-bearers and hunters. One showing a barelegged hunter in a starry gown slaying a bull is reminiscent of Mithraic imagery and may be astrological in purport. Numerous other fragments, some sketched in black on plaster or on marble, belong to unidentified compositions. The rich repertory of birds—herons, geese, eagles, partridges, guinea-fowl, parrots and cockerels—derives from Sasanian seals. Also found in the throne-room were earthenware wine-jars painted with figures and inscriptions.

(b) c. 900–c. 1900. To judge from sporadic remains the early tradition of figural wall painting persisted throughout the Islamic world. A bath excavated at Fustat (Old Cairo) had arched niches painted with confronted doves, a dancer and a cup-bearer (Cairo, Mus. Islam. A.); the paintings have been attributed to the 10th century, under either late Tulunid or early Fatimid patronage. Contemporary sources suggest that figural painting was widespread in baths, and that some paintings were of an indecent character. The 15th-century Cairene historian al-Maqrizi, quoting an anonymous treatise, the *Ḍaw' al-nibrās wa-uns al-jullās fī akhbār al-muzawwiqīn* ('The light of the lamp and the essence of good company in anecdotes of painters'), alluded to a contest before the Fatimid vizier al-Yazuri (in office 1050–58) in which two painters, Ibn

'Aziz and al-Qasir, represented dancing girls. By means of colour contrasts, some seemed to emerge from the walls and others to retreat into them. And a mosque in the Qarafa Cemetery near Cairo (976–7; *see* CAIRO, §I, 1) was decorated with a painting of a fountain which appeared three-dimensional from one angle. Al-Maqrizi's description of such feats as 'the height of the painter's art' suggests a marked taste for such illusionistic painting. The best-preserved specimen of wall painting in the Fatimid style is the wooden *muqarnas* ceiling of the Cappella Palatina in Palermo, Sicily (probably begun 1132; inaugurated 28 March 1140; *see* §5(ii)(b) above; PALERMO, §II, 2(ii)). It has astonishingly varied vignettes from the repertories of both courtly and everyday life and subjects drawn from narrative and legend. With contemporary lighting, however, the paintings must have been nearly invisible. While there are evident parallels with the figural repertory used on Fatimid lustre ceramics of the 11th and 12th centuries, the differences in style and subject-matter suggest that they were executed by local painters employed in the workshops of Roger II (*reg* 1130–54). They, like his other court craftsmen, were probably Muslim and were highly influenced by the arts of Islamic Egypt and North Africa.

The earliest evidence for figural wall painting in the western Islamic world is minute fragments excavated at MADINAT AL-ZAHRA', the palace-city outside Córdoba built by the Umayyad caliph 'Abd al-Rahman III al-Nasir (*reg* 912–61). Wall paintings from the Torre de las Damas in the Alhambra of Granada (Granada, Alhambra) were doubtless executed for the Nasrid ruler Muhammad V (*reg* 1354–9, 1362–91), who ordered extensive work there (*see* GRANADA, §III, 1). Small in format and set in superimposed rows, they include an encampment scene and scenes of court life somewhat reminiscent of 14th-century illustrated manuscripts of al-Hariri's *Maqamat* ('Assemblies'; *see* §III, 4(v)(a) below). Their hybrid appearance must be partly the result of subsequent restoration.

In the eastern Islamic world the remains are richer, and fragments of wall paintings from the 10th and 11th centuries are preserved at several sites. Wall paintings with tiers of smallish figures were found at Hulbuk, the capital of the Khuttalan region on the upper Oxus River, and at the adjacent site of Sayod. One striking find is a depiction of the Lupercalian wolf suckling Romulus and Remus (see 1980 exh. cat.). The style derives from that of paintings (St Petersburg, Hermitage) of the Sogdian pantheon excavated at Kalay-i Kakhkakha, the ruler's palace at BUNDZHIKAT (Tajikistan; 7th–9th century), chief city of the Ustrushana region (*see* CENTRAL ASIA, §I, 4(iv)). Excavations carried out in the 1930s at NISHAPUR in eastern Iran brought to light several fragmentary layers of figural wall paintings at various sites (*see also* §5(i)(a) above). A hunting scene with male and female heads was found in a bathhouse at Qanat Tepe; dados with calyx ornament framed by fat scrolls with human hands were found at Tepe Madrasa; and painted *muqarnas* with foliate vases, some with eyes, were found at Sabz Pushan. A heavily armed mounted hunter, his face obliterated, with traces of a standing figure to his left (Tehran, Archaeol. Mus.), was found at Vineyard Tepe in a room where the decoration may never have been completed. The figure is

comparable to those on local ceramics of the 10th and 11th centuries (*see* §V, 2(iii) and 3(iii) below) but is much more detailed. Elements of clothing and drapery recall those found at Hulbuk and Sayod. The paintings must date before the site was seriously damaged by an earthquake in 1145 and sacked by the Ghuzz Turks eight years later. The South Palace at LASHKARI BAZAR in southern Afghanistan was excavated in the 1950s (*see also* §5(i)(c) above). The audience hall had large paintings of standing, moon-faced male figures wearing knee-length tunics with fine medallion patterns and belts with pendent straps. The figures are shown frontally, but their boots are in profile. Their stance, accoutrements and features are strikingly reminiscent of the male figures at Samarra', and they must represent the Turkish slave-guards of the Ghaznavid ruler Mahmud (*reg* 998–1030), builder of the palace. Contemporary sources state that Mahmud himself was also depicted in battle or revelry, but nothing resembling a portrait or portrait type has come to light at any Ghaznavid site.

Figural wall painting is unknown from the 12th, 13th and 14th centuries in Iran and Anatolia, apart from the few fragments acquired on the art market that allegedly came from RAYY in central Iran. They show small figures in tiers and are similar in style to the figural decoration of *mīnā'ī* (enamelled) ceramics of the period (*see* §V, 3(iii)(e)) below). The absence of figural wall painting may be explained by the popularity of tilework and stucco, which were often decorated with figural subjects. In the 15th century interiors painted in blue and white were popular, to judge from illustrations in manuscripts, and wall paintings are mentioned in several contemporary sources. The Bagh-i Dilkusha (*c.* 1402), Timur's garden pavilion in Samarkand is said to have been decorated with scenes of his Indian triumphs, and the observatory of Ulughbeg there (1420) had representations of the heavenly bodies, the seven climes and doubtless zodiacal and other astrological figures, which were probably more decorative than heuristic. The palace of the Aqqoyunlu ruler Ya'qub (*reg* 1478–90) at Tabriz had wall paintings of battle scenes and triumphs, according to an anonymous Italian merchant who saw it.

Under the Safavid dynasty (*reg* 1501–1732) wall painting became increasingly popular, and the subject-matter broadened to include scenes from literature and popular religious themes. Figural wall paintings have been discovered in a pavilion built by Tahmasp I (*reg* 1524–76) at QAZVIN in north-western Iran and are similar in style to contemporary manuscript painting. In his panegyric *Gulistān-i hunar* ('The rose garden of art'), Qazi Ahmad mentioned that Tahmasp himself executed several scenes in the Chihil Sutun Palace there. One, depicting *Joseph and Potiphar's Wife*, was probably on cloth, for it is said to have been pasted on the lower part of the western pavilion together with a topical couplet. Elaborately painted plaster decoration found in a palace at NA'IN has been dated to *c.* 1560 on stylistic grounds. Persian wall paintings came into their own in the 17th century, when they were used extensively to decorate the public buildings in Isfahan erected by 'Abbas I (*reg* 1588–1629), such as the Allahverdi Bridge (1602–3), the portal from the maidan to the bazaar and various palaces (*see* ISFAHAN, §3(ii), (v), (vii)). Those on the Allahverdi Bridge, which were destroyed in the

19th century, were condemned by European travellers as obscene, but the paintings' lasciviousness may have been exaggerated. The ones in the Chihil Sutun Palace, restored by 'Abbas II in 1647–8, are the best preserved. They are in the manner of the painter RIZA and his pupils and show drinkers, both male and female, in gardens and larger historical scenes (see fig. 81). These large compositions show great moments in Safavid history, such as the victory of Isma'il I over the Uzbek chief Muhammad Shaybani Khan, Tahmasp I receiving the Mughal ruler Humayun, 'Abbas I receiving the Governor of Turkestan, Nadir Muhammad Khan and 'Abbas II receiving an embassy from the Uzbeks. Traces of wall paintings have also been found on Safavid palaces at Ashraf, Lahijan and other resorts on the Caspian. The Safavid tradition of wall painting also spread to India under the Mughal dynasty (*see* INDIAN SUBCONTINENT, §V, 4(i)). Iranian shrines and mosques were first decorated with figural paintings in this period, although they were executed in a less courtly and more popular style. Examples in the Friday Mosque at Sidih, a mosque in Lahijan and the Imamzada Zayd at Isfahan (1685–6, although the paintings are later) show episodes from the lives of the Shi'ite martyrs 'Ali, Hasan and Husayn. Wall paintings with popular themes, such as the coffee-house paintings in a popular style depicting early Shi'ite leaders, were produced in the 19th century,

although they were often replaced by large figural tile panels and paintings on canvas.

In the Ottoman empire, the earliest representational wall paintings to survive were done in the 18th century under strong European influence and depict fantastic architecture in garden landscapes. As in Iran, however, scattered references suggest that the tradition is much older. Gentile Bellini, for example, is said to have painted erotic scenes (*cose de lussuria*) in Istanbul between 1479 and 1481, but the report could well have been hearsay, and the paintings could anyway have been on panels or canvas. According to Ogier Ghiselin de Busbecq, who was in Istanbul between 1554 and 1562, folding doors on a pavilion built by Süleyman the Magnificent along the Bosporus depicted the defeat of the Safavids at Chaldiran in 1514.

BIBLIOGRAPHY

Ahmad ibn 'Alī al-Maqrīzī: *Al-mawā'iz wa'l-i'tibār bi dhikr al-khiṭaṭ wa'l-athār* [on the districts and monuments of Cairo], ii (Cairo, 1853), p. 318

A Narrative of Italian Travels in Persia, trans. by C. Grey (London, 1873), p. 175

The Letters of Ogier Ghiselin de Busbecq, trans. by E. S. Forster (Oxford, 1922, rev. 1968), p. 39

E. Herzfeld: *Die Malereien von Samarra* (Berlin, 1927)

F. Saxl: 'The Zodiac of Qusayr 'Amra', *Early Muslim Architecture*, ed. K. A. C. Creswell, i (Oxford, 1932/*R* and enlarged 1969), pp. 424–31

E. Kühnel: 'Baudekor und Kleinfunde', *Die Ausgrabungen der zweiten Ktesiphon Expedition (Winter 1931/32)*, ed. E. Kühnel and F. Wachtsmuth (Berlin, 1933), pp. 25–6

81. Wall painting of a man seated by a tree, Chihil Sutun Palace, Isfahan, Iran, 1647–8

Y. Godard: 'L'Imamzade Zaid d'Isfahan: Un Edifice décoré de peintures religieuses musulmanes', *Āthār-é Īrān*, ii (1937), pp. 341–8

R. Ettinghausen: 'Painting in the Fatimid Period: A Reconstruction', *A. Islam.*, ix (1942), pp. 112–24

U. Monneret de Villard: *Le pitture musulmane al soffitto della Cappella Palatina in Palermo* (Rome, 1950)

O. Grabar: 'The Painting of the Six Kings at Qusayr 'Amrah', *A. Orient.*, i (1954), pp. 185–7

R. Ettinghausen: 'Early Realism in Islamic Art', *Studi orientalistici in onore di Giorgio Levi della Vida* (Rome, 1956), i, pp. 250–73

D. S. Rice: 'Deacon or Drink: Some Paintings from Samarra Examined', *Arabica*, v (1958), pp. 15–33

Qāḍī Aḥmad: *Gulistān-i hunar* [The rose-garden of art], trans. by V. Minorsky as *Calligraphers and Painters* (Washington, DC, 1959), p. 182

R. Ettinghausen: *Arab Painting* (Geneva, 1962)

L. Torres Balbás: 'Arte califal', *España musulmana hasta la caída del Califato de Córdova, 711–1031 de J.-C.*, ed. E. Lévi-Provençal (1965), v of *Historia de España* (Madrid, 1935–)

P. Mura: 'La Restauration des peintures murales du Chihil Sutūn', *Travaux de restauration de monuments historiques en Iran*, ed. G. Zander (Rome, 1968), pp. 323–83

Islamic Art in Egypt, 969–1517 (exh. cat. by A. Hamdy and others, Cairo, Semiramis Hotel, 1969)

E. Grube: 'Wall Paintings in the Seventeenth Century Monuments of Isfahan', *Iran. Stud.*, vii (1974), pp. 511–42

A. A. Abdurazakov and M. K. Kambarov: *Restavratsiya nastennykh rospisei Afrasiyaba* [Restoration of the wall paintings of Afrasiyab] (Tashkent, 1975)

L. I. Al'baum: *Zhivopis' Afrasiyaba* [The painting of Afrasiyab] (Tashkent, 1975)

M. Almagro and others: *Qusayr 'Amra: Residencia y baños omeyas en el desierto de Jordania* (Madrid, 1975)

W. Kleiss: 'Der safavidische Pavillon in Qazvin', *Archäol. Mitt. Iran*, n. s., ix (1976), pp. 253–61

G. Renda: *Batılaşma döneminde Türk resim sanatı, 1700–1850* [Turkish painting in the period of westernization, 1700–1850] (Ankara, 1977)

D. Schlumberger and J. Sourdel-Thomine: *Lashkari Bazar*, 3 vols (Paris, 1978)

J. D. Dodds: 'The Paintings in the Sala de Justicia of the Alhambra: Iconography and Iconology', *A. Bull.*, lxi (1979), pp. 186–97

Oxus: 2000 Jahre Kunst am Oxus-Fluss im Mittelasien (exh. cat., Zurich, Mus. Rietberg, 1980), no. 91

G. Azarpay: *Soghdian Painting* (Berkeley, 1981)

C. K. Wilkinson: *Nishapur: Some Early Islamic Buildings and their Decoration* (New York, 1986)

H.-C. Graf von Bothmer: 'Architekturbilder im Koran: Eine Prachthandschrift der Umayyadenzeit aus dem Yemen', *Pantheon*, xlv (1987), pp. 4–20

J. Raby: 'Between Sogdia and the Mamlūks: A Note on the Earliest Illustrations to Kalīla wa Dimna', *Orient. A.*, n. s., xxxiii (1987–8), pp. 381–98

Oxus: 2000 Jahre Kunst am Oxus-Fluss im Mittelasien. Neue Funde aus der Sowjetrepublik Tadschikistan (exh. cat., Zurich, Mus. Rietberg, 1989)

J. M. ROGERS

(iv) Mosaics. The highpoint of mosaic production in Islamic architecture occurred under the Umayyad dynasty of Syria (*reg* 661–750; *see* §3 above), when mosaics were commonly used to decorate the walls of religious structures and the floors of palaces. The Umayyads generally employed craftsmen trained in the mosaic tradition of Syria and Palestine, and in special circumstances they imported masters from Byzantium. The techniques and forms used in the Christian world were continued, but their aniconic and epigraphic content gave them a distinctively Islamic character. In general glass tesserae were used on walls and stone tesserae on floors.

The first Islamic religious building known to have had mosaic decoration is the Ka'ba in MECCA. In 684–5 its walls above the marble dado were covered with mosaics, perhaps obtained from the 6th-century church of Abraha at SAN'A in the Yemen; they were destroyed when the

82. Barada Panel, mosaic from west side of court, Great Mosque, Damascus, AD 705–15

Ka'ba was rebuilt in 693. Mosaics and other opulent decoration characterized the great religious monuments commissioned by the Umayyad caliphs 'Abd al-Malik and his son al-Walid, such as the Dome of the Rock in Jerusalem (691–2; *see* JERUSALEM, §II, 1(iii)) and the early 8th-century mosques at MEDINA, Mecca, Jerusalem, probably Fustat (all destr.) and Damascus (*see* DAMASCUS, §3). During the reign of the Umayyad caliph Sulayman (*reg* 715–17) the mosque in ALEPPO was also decorated with mosaics (destr.). The surviving mosaics in Jerusalem and Damascus show that the decorative programmes were aniconic and epigraphic. The mosaics on the exterior of the Dome of the Rock were replaced with glazed tiles in the 16th century, but acanthus leaves, calix tendrils, palm trees, jewels and inscriptions predominate on the interior. In the mosque of Damascus wall surfaces above the quartered marble dado were covered with landscape panels depicting trees alternating with architectural conceits arranged along the banks of a watercourse; only one fragment, the Barada Panel on the west side of the court, survives (see fig. 82). In part the architectural compositions are determined by convention; in part they depict real constructions. Arcades and soffits were decorated with trees, tendrils and candelabra. Many of these motifs had been attributes of the saints in paradise in Christian art, but these secondary elements became the principal subjects in the decoration of the Damascus mosque. The programme at Damascus has been interpreted (among other theories) as a depiction of paradise, particularly in view of texts that record the presence of Koranic verses on this theme, and the programme on the Dome of the Rock may be construed similarly.

The tradition of mosaic decoration on religious architecture continued under the Abbasids (*reg* 749–1258). The caliph Mansur (*reg* 754–75) widened the colonnades around the Ka'ba and decorated them with mosaics in imitation of the works of al-Walid. He also commissioned mosaics for the tholos (circular building) over the well of Zamzam near by. Mosaic decoration was used on several 9th-century mosques. At the mosque of al-Mutawakkil at Samarra' (848–52; *see* SAMARRA', §2), mosaics covered the tholos over the well and the prayer-hall. At the Great Mosque at Damascus, the Treasury, a small aedicule in the court, was decorated with mosaics using traditional motifs. The Umayyad ruler of Spain, al-Hakam II, continued the tradition by importing masters from Byzantium in 965 to decorate the mihrab and *maqṣūra* of the Great Mosque of Córdoba (*see* CÓRDOBA (i), §3(i)(a)). The last major programme of mosaic decoration was the restoration of the Aqsa Mosque in Jerusalem by the Fatimid caliph al-Zahir (*reg* 1021–36; *see* JERUSALEM, §II, 1(iv)). Under the Ayyubids (*reg* 1169–1252) and Mamluks (*reg* 1250–1517) mosaics were used occasionally to decorate mihrabs, the most notable example being the one in the tomb of Shajarat al-Durr in Cairo (1250), but in general later examples are less successful. Mosaic decoration in the tomb of the Mamluk sultan al-Zahir Baybars in Damascus (1277–81; *see* DAMASCUS, §1(ii)) and his restorations to the north end of the Barada Panel in the Great Mosque repeat Umayyad motifs in a simplified form.

Wall mosaics in secular settings seem to have been rare. The only two surviving examples are at Minya on Lake Tiberias (early 8th century) and at MADINAT AL-ZAHRA' outside Córdoba (936). Colourless glass forms were found at the early Abbasid palace at RAQQA in Syria, but they might have been intended for the floor. Floor mosaics of coloured stone were commonly used in 8th-century buildings in Syria, such as the palaces at Minya, KHIRBAT AL-MAFJAR, Qasr al-Hallabat, Qastal and Amman and baths at QUSAYR 'AMRA and 'ANJAR. The 39 adjoining panels on the floor of the bath-hall at Khirbat al-Mafjar (30×30 m) constitute the largest single floor mosaic to survive from the ancient world. Syrian floor mosaics continued pre-Islamic motifs and in some cases intimate carpets. The basic designs are composed of ornaments derived from the square and the root-of-two system of proportion, and also the hexagon and the root-of-three system. Geometrical ornaments, which had been important for Christian floor mosaics, became the principal decoration. Patterns became denser and more ambiguous as secondary forms were added. A unique figural mosaic survives in the audience room at Khirbat al-Mafjar; it depicts a central tree flanked by two grazing gazelles and a lion attacking another gazelle, the meaning of which seems to continue old symbolical traditions. Floor mosaics were also used in the palaces of the Aghlabids (*reg* 800–909) and Fatimids (909–72) in Tunisia. The patterns of Late Antiquity were reworked, but the palette was restricted to black and white. In the 13th century the floor mosaics in the baths at Sinjar in northern Iraq were famed for their beauty.

The mosaics used in Umayyad buildings are unsurpassed in quality. Glass cubes generally measure 10 mm each side,

but the stone cubes from Minya measure 7 mm. In the mosque of Damascus, tesserae were set into a plaster layer 10–15 mm thick made of chalk and straw. Brightly coloured areas were marked out with red lines and darker areas with black lines; the cubes were then set directly into the wall. To reflect light, gold cubes were fixed at angles of up to 30° depending on the height of the wall. The palette of glass tesserae found at Damascus and Jerusalem comprises eight shades of green, six of blue, indigo, violet, brown, grey, pink and yellow. Cubes of various colours were also backed with gold and silver leaf. Mother-of-pearl served as a supplementary material. The palette of stone tesserae for floors comprised black and white for outlines and yellow, yellow–green, grass green, dark green, olive green, blue–green, grey, light blue, dark blue, violet and brick red. (For tile mosaic *see* §(ii) above.)

BIBLIOGRAPHY

M. van Berchem: 'The Mosaics of the Dome of the Rock in Jerusalem and of the Great Mosque in Damascus', *Early Muslim Architecture*, ed. K. A. C. Creswell, i (Oxford, 1932/*R* and enlarged 1969), pp. 213–372

O. Grabar: 'The Umayyad Dome of the Rock in Jerusalem', *A. Orient.*, iii (1959), pp. 33–62

R. Hamilton: *Khirbat al-Mafjar: An Arabian Mansion in the Jordan Valley* (Oxford, 1959)

H. Stern: 'Recherches sur la Mosquée al-Aqsa et sur ses mosaïques', *A. Orient.*, v (1963), pp. 27–47

C. Kessler: 'Die beiden Mosaikböden in Qusayr 'Amra', *Studies . . . in Honour of K. A. C. Creswell* (Cairo, 1965), pp. 105–31

B. Finster: 'Die Mosaiken der Umayyaden-Moschee von Damaskus', *Kst Orients*, vii (1970–71), pp. 83–141

M. Meinecke: 'Das Mausoleum des Qala'un in Kairo: Untersuchungen zur Genese der mamlukischen Architekturdekoration', *Mitt. Dt. Archäol. Inst.: Abt. Kairo*, xxvii (1971), pp. 47–80

H. Stern: *Les Mosaïques de la Grande Mosquée de Cordoue*, with contributions by M. Ocaña Jiménez and D. Duda (Berlin, 1976)

G. Bisheh: 'Pavimentazioni musive ommiadi da Qasr al-Hallabat in Giordania', *I mosaici di Giordania*, ed. M. Piccirillo (Rome, 1986), pp. 129ff

——: 'Qasr al-Hallabat', *Archv Orientforsch.*, xxxiii (1986), pp. 185ff

P. Cartier and F. Marin: 'Qastal', *Archv Orientforsch.*, xxxiii (1986), pp. 187ff

G. Hellenkemper Salies: 'Die Mosaiken der Grossen Moschee von Damascus', *Corsi Cult. A. Ravenn. & Biz.*, v (1988), pp. 95–6

BARBARA FINSTER

(v) Stained glass. Coloured glass was used throughout the Islamic world in many periods for windows in religious and secular buildings. The tradition is as old as Islam, which undoubtedly adopted it from Byzantine art. The mid-8th-century sites of KHIRBAT AL-MAFJAR near Jericho and QASR AL-HAYR WEST in Syria had stained-glass windows, as did the palace built for the Abbasid caliph al-Mu'tasim (*reg* 833–42) at Samarra' in Iraq (*see* SAMARRA', §2). Fragments of coloured glass were also excavated in such North African sites as Sabra/al-Mansuriyya (10th century) near Kairouan and QAL'AT BANI HAMMAD (11th century) in Algeria. It became particularly common in later periods, when distinct regional traditions emerged. Early geometric designs gradually gave way to floral and arabesque motifs.

The development of the art is inseparable from the use of window-grilles. Made of marble, stone, wood or plaster, they are used throughout the Islamic lands, a region of strong sun and great heat, to soften light, admit refreshing breezes and permit one to see without being seen. Grilles combine solids and voids, light and shadow; stained glass adds coloured light, which enlivens and modulates the interior space and decoration. Six marble grilles, the oldest examples of geometric design in Islamic art, are preserved at the Great Mosque of Damascus (706–15; *see* DAMASCUS, §3), and they, or others like them, may have provided a model for those in the Great Mosque of Córdoba (785–6; *see* CÓRDOBA (i), §3(i)(a)). In Cairo, the mosques of Ibn Tulun (876–9) and al-Azhar (970–72) have arches and windows decorated with geometric and vegetal motifs in pierced plaster (*see also* CAIRO, §III, 2 and 3). The tradition continued into later Islamic times, for virtuoso examples of pierced marble grilles are known from India under Mughal rule (1526–1858), as at the tomb of Shaykh Salim Chisti (1581–2; rest. 1605) at FATEHPUR SIKRI. The art of stained glass is also inseparable from the art of carved stucco. The stucco screen carries the decoration of the wall surface across voids, by using the same techniques of carving and the same motifs and decorative ideas. It was only a small step for the artisan to fix fragments of coloured glass into pierced plaster panels. In exceptional cases, glass was set with lead kames, as in European stained-glass windows.

Windows with double grilles first appeared in Cairo in the 11th century. As the stained-glass window was conceived to be seen from the interior, only the interior grille was glazed; the exterior one was left open. The unglazed exterior grille protected the interior grille from projectiles. It also decorated the exterior, by masking the embrasure of the bay and hiding the outer, less elegant side of the glazed window. The window with double grilles further softens the bright light passing through the window that could harm the studied aesthetic effects in the interior. This system of double windows was often taken up in the richly decorated mosques built by the Ottomans in the 16th and 17th centuries, and in the 19th and 20th centuries in the grand private houses of SAN'A in the Yemen, where the traditional geometric and vegetal themes are enlivened in a popular style.

Architecture in Cairo under the Mamluks (*reg* 1260–1517) offers numerous examples of grilles and glazed windows of both coloured and uncoloured glass set in an armature of plaster. These were found in mosques, such as those built for sultans Barquq *intra muros* (1384), Mu'ayyad (1314) and Qa'itbay *extra muros* (1474; *see* CAIRO, §III, 10), mausolea (e.g. that of Qala'un, 1285; *see* CAIRO, §III, 8), as well as in the large reception rooms (Arab. *qā'a*) of Mamluk palaces, where they decorated bays surmounted by an oculus or the bays of the small lanterns surmounting the central court (Arab. *dūrqā'a*). This was the case in the palaces of Alin Aq (1293), Beshtak (1334–9), Yashbak (*d* 1482) and Qa'itbay (1485). After the Ottomans took Egypt in 1517, it became the mode in domestic architecture to decorate the upper parts of projecting grilles of turned wood (Arab. *mashrabiyya*) with rectangular stained-glass windows, as in the Bayt al-Suhaymi (1648 and 1796), the Bayt al-Razzaz (rest. 1778) or the Musafirkhana Palace (1779–88).

Ottoman architecture in Turkey offers remarkable examples of stucco grilles and stained glass, from the Yeşil Cami (Green Mosque) in BURSA (1424) and the Selimiye in EDIRNE (1574) to the Süleymaniye (1552–9; *see* ISTANBUL, §III, 10) and the mosque of Kiliç Ali Pasha (1580–81) in Istanbul. The coloured glass was often imported from Venice, as at the Yeni Valide (1597–1663) and Sultan

Ahmed I (1616; *see* ISTANBUL, §III, 11) mosques in Istanbul. Stained-glass windows were also used in Ottoman palatial architecture, as at the Baghdad Pavilion (1639) at Topkapı Palace in Istanbul. The apartments of the sultan adjacent to the mosque of Yeni Valide (mid-17th century) preserve some very fine examples, in which floral motifs dominate. Many windows have not resisted the ravages of time, and the original glass has been replaced (e.g. Istanbul, Mihrimah Mosque). The colours are less nuanced, and the Baroque motifs clash with the interior decoration. Elsewhere in the Ottoman empire, the stained-glass windows that decorate the Dome of the Rock (691–2) in Jerusalem date from the restoration by Süleyman the Magnificent in 1528 (*see* JERUSALEM, §II, 1(iii)).

In Iran, the mosque of Shaykh Lutfallah (1603–19) at Isfahan has 16 double-grilled windows, glazed predominantly in blue, illuminating the exquisite tile decoration of the interior (see fig. 79 above and ISFAHAN, §3(iv)). In the same city the Chihil Sutun royal pavilion (rest. 1706–7; *see* ISFAHAN, §3(vii)) preserves plaster grilles filled with stained glass that were taken from the Darb-i Imam Shrine (1453). In Iran coloured glass was sometimes replaced by mirror-glass, a technique known as *ā'ina-kārī*. This began in the 17th century (e.g. the entrance to the Chihil Sutun), but became particularly characteristic of architecture under the Qajars (*reg* 1779–1924), where it was used for portals and iwans (e.g. QUM, shrine of Fatima).

Stained glass was also popular in the western Islamic lands. At the Alhambra in Granada (*see* GRANADA, §III, 1), the Mirador de Lindaraja (or deo Daraxa) is roofed with a pierced stucco vault glazed with red, blue, green and yellow glass in geometric patterns. In the mosques built by the Marinid (*reg* 1196–1549) and Sa'dian (*reg* 1511–1659) dynasties in FEZ and MARRAKESH, carved stuccowork extends over the wall openings. These pierced bays are known as *shammasiyya*, a word derived from the Arabic word for 'sun'; in contrast, the same grilles are known in Cairo and the Yemen as *qamariyya*, from the Arabic word for 'moon'. Throughout North Africa, the examples in religious architecture were followed in domestic architecture, whether in the great Marinid or Sa'dian houses of Fez or the Hafsid ones of Tunisia. The tradition of stucco grilles and stained glass continues in Morocco, most notably in royal architecture.

BIBLIOGRAPHY

Enc. Iran.: 'Ā'ina-kārī'

K. A. C. Creswell: *Early Muslim Architecture*, 2 vols (Oxford, 1932–40/vol. i *R* and enlarged 1969)

G. Marçais: *L'Architecture musulmane d'Occident* (Paris, 1954)

K. A. C. Creswell: *The Muslim Architecture of Egypt*, ii (Oxford, 1959), pp. 91–2

H. E. Wulff: *The Traditional Crafts of Persia* (Cambridge, MA, 1966), p. 135

J. Revault: *Palais et demeures de Tunis*, 4 vols (Paris, 1967–78)

G. Goodwin: *A History of Ottoman Architecture* (Baltimore and London, 1971)

A. Paccard: *Le Maroc et l'artisanat traditionnel islamique dans l'architecture*, 2 vols (Saint-Jorioz, 1979)

G. Bonnenfant and P. Bonnenfant: *Les Vitraux de Sanaa* (Paris, 1981)

J.-C. Garcin and others: *Palais et maisons du Caire*, 2 vols (Paris, 1982–3)

J. Revault, L. Golvin and A. Amahan: *Palais et demeures de Fès* (Paris, 1985)

PAUL BONNENFANT

(vi) Epigraphy. The first monument of Islamic architecture, the Dome of the Rock in Jerusalem (692; *see* §3 above;

JERUSALEM, §II, 1(iii)), was decorated with religious and historical texts inscribed in bands that emphasized architectural forms. Throughout the course of Islamic civilization such religious and historical inscriptions proliferated, becoming more elaborate in content and style. The extensive use of inscriptions, on both the exterior and interior of buildings, is one of the distinguishing features of Islamic architecture, and inscriptions continue to be a major decorative feature of such modern buildings as the mosque (1984) in the King Khalid International Airport at RIYADH, Saudi Arabia.

(a) Materials, types and languages. The materials used depend on local techniques of construction and decoration. In those regions of the Mediterranean basin where stone is used for construction, inscriptions are incised and carved in relief in the stone itself or added in mosaic, wood or stucco. In the eastern Islamic lands where the preferred medium of construction is brick, inscriptions are executed in brick or added in such other earthenwares as stucco, terracotta or glazed tile. Throughout, inscriptions on bands and plaques outline and define such common architectural forms as arcades, iwans, domes and tympana, and inscriptions incorporated into brick bonding cover entire wall surfaces.

Religious inscriptions are by far the most common type. They include passages from the Koran, traditions ascribed to the Prophet Muhammad (Arab. ḥadīth), pious phrases and ejaculations, prayers and poems. Often dismissed as mere banalities, these inscriptions can shed light on the meaning and function of a building, since even the most stereotyped formulae, such as blessings on the Prophet's family, often reflect sectarian beliefs or theological positions, and longer Koranic passages were often chosen or spurious hadith coined with reference to contemporary events. Scholars have paid more attention to historical inscriptions, which can be divided into four categories. Foundation inscriptions often supply the names of the patron and reigning sovereign, the type of building, the date, and the names of builders or artisans. Commemorative inscriptions or epitaphs give the names of the deceased for whom the building was erected. Administrative decrees reveal the workings of contemporary bureaucracy and government. Endowment deeds (Arab. waqfiyya) supply lists of property endowed and topographical details. Historical inscriptions can often be used to correct or supplement textual sources, which are more liable to redaction and corruption. While a single inscription can supply specific historical information, corpora of inscriptions allow the unusual to be discerned amid the standard.

Until the 11th century almost all monumental inscriptions were in Arabic, the official language of the caliphate. Persian played an important role in the literary renaissance that took place in the eastern Islamic lands under the Ghaznavids (reg 977–1186) and was soon introduced into monumental epigraphy. The first surviving foundation inscription in Persian occurs on a tomb erected for a Qarakhanid prince c. 1055 at Safid Buland in the Farghana Valley of western Central Asia. Persian inscriptions occur on other buildings erected by the Qarakhanids, for a Persian poem is inscribed over the portal on the RIBAT-I MALIK, a caravanserai between Samarkand and Bukhara

rebuilt by the Qarakhanid Shams al-Mulk Nasr in 1078–9. These Persian inscriptions are difficult to read: an epic poem in floriated kufic that encircles the court of the palace at GHAZNA (1111–12) defied decipherment until the excavators realized it was written not in Arabic but in Persian, and the inscription at Ribat-i Malik is still undeciphered. When cursive scripts, which commonly used points to distinguish letters of similar shape and marks to indicate short vowels, became standard for inscriptions, texts in Persian became readable and common. Turkish remained a lingua franca for a longer period: the first example of an inscription in Turkish survives in the madrasa of Ya'qub Çelebi in Kütahya (1411), but only under the Ottomans in the 16th century did it become common in commemorative inscriptions. Inscriptions in other languages, sometimes written in Arabic script, are also recorded in Africa, India and South-east Asia during the later centuries of Islam.

(b) Stylistic development. Monumental inscriptions, executed in a clear sober script and designed for both rhetorical and decorative purposes, had long been used in the Classical world, and the first Islamic dynasty, the Umayyads of Syria (reg 661–750; see §3 above), continued the epigraphic traditions of the region by ordering inscriptions in stone and mosaic and using the same formulae and style while substituting Arabic for Latin. This angular monumental script, often known as kufic as it was once thought to have originated in the Iraqi city of KUFA, is characterized by simple geometric shapes, harmonious proportions and wide spacing. The juxtaposition of horizontal and vertical strokes lends the inscription band a strong internal rhythm which is subtly enhanced by the elongation of such horizontal letters as dāl and kāf.

In early kufic script most of the letters are concentrated in the lower part of the inscription band, and new devices were developed to fill the upper zone. Few inscriptions have survived from Iraq, the capital province of the Abbasid caliphate (reg 749–1258), but the development of kufic over the next few centuries can be traced in a long series of limestone and marble tombstones from Egypt. They provide fixed dates for the introduction of such decorative devices as the bevelled stem, arc, barb, palmette and rising tail and show that, as ornament filled the upper zone, the script became more cramped. In the 9th century artists in Egypt, the Hijaz (western Arabia) and the western Islamic lands continued to embellish the apexes of the letters so that foliated script evolved into a floriated one in which flowers, tendrils and scrolls seem to grow from the terminal or medial forms of the letters. Floriated kufic was favoured by the wealthy and sophisticated Fatimids of Egypt (reg 909–1171; see §5(ii)(c) above), for example in the mosque of al-Hakim (989/90–1013; see CAIRO, §III, 4 and fig. 83), the mosque of al-Juyushi (1085; see fig. 38 above) and the Aqmar Mosque (1125; see fig. 37 above), all in Cairo. In the eastern Islamic lands another decorative device, interlacing, was used to meet the same need to fill the upper zone. In the western Islamic lands elaboration of the stems of the letters had led from bevelling to foliation and then to floriation; in the east the tendency towards elongation and distortion of horizontal letters led to internal modifications and superimposed ornament.

83. Floriated kufic inscription on the western minaret, mosque of al-Hakim, Cairo, Egypt, 1003

The tomb tower (1016–21) for the Bawandid ruler Abu Ja'far Muhammad at Radkan West in the mountains of northern Iran shows a complex use of knots and plaiting in and around the letter shapes. Such plaiting was particularly suitable for inscriptions in brick. By the 11th century these decorative devices threatened to obscure the legibility of kufic inscriptions. Symbolic affirmation may have superseded communication, and inscriptions were probably recognized visually rather than read literally. At the same time, small semi-independent dynasties proliferated, and the titulature of rulers expanded rapidly, so that even petty princes had long strings of flowery epithets attached to their names.

To resolve these conflicting demands—the basic illegibility of many highly decorated but unpointed kufic scripts and the increasing number of titles in any historical inscription—designers turned to cursive scripts. Cursive scripts had been used alongside monumental kufic for chancellery documents since the Umayyad period, and such famous calligraphers as IBN MUQLA (d 940) and IBN AL-BAWWAB (d 1022) had refined and elevated them to a rank suitable for copying the Koran. Cursive first appeared in monumental epigraphy in the 11th century (see also §5(i)(c) above). It was used initially for religious inscriptions, such as the Koranic verses across the façade of the south dome added to the Friday Mosque in Isfahan in 1086–7 (see §5(i)(b) above and ISFAHAN, §3(i)). With its greater legibility, cursive script was quickly adopted for historical texts. In the eastern Islamic lands this was a gradual process; the first surviving examples are stucco panels in the tomb of al-Hakim al-Tirmidhi at Termez (see TERMEZ, §1(ii)) in the name of the Qarakhanid Ahmad (d 1089) and stone fragments from Ghazna in the name of the Ghaznavid sultan Ibrahim (d 1100). In the central

Islamic lands the change was more abrupt, as the Zangid ruler Nur al-Din (reg 1146–74; see §5(i)(e) above) ordered the adoption of cursive scripts in monumental inscriptions. Kufic lost its pre-eminence in monumental epigraphy and became stereotyped and repetitive. In the Islamic west kufic remained typical for large Koranic bands used as foils to historical inscriptions in cursive (e.g. the stucco cartouches in the Alhambra Palace at Granada; 14th century). In the eastern Islamic lands kufic survived longer, for angular scripts were well suited to brick construction. Wall surfaces could be quickly covered by large panels executed in banna'i technique (see §(ii)(b) above), for example the façade of the Madrasa al-Ghiyathiyya (1444–5) at Khargird.

In the central Arab lands designers reserved their greatest artistic efforts for elaborating cursive scripts. To balance the inscription and fill the upper zone, designers dropped the rigid base line characteristic of kufic and divided words into short groups of letters suspended on the diagonal, as in the construction text by the Ayyubid al-Malik al-Mu'azzam 'Isa on the citadel of Jerusalem (1213). The phrases became more crowded as texts grew longer and incorporated administrative decrees written in several lines within rectangular frames (e.g. the decree in the name of the Mamluk sultan Jaqmaq added to the mosque of Princess Asal-bay in the Faiyum in 1441–2). In Iran stucco-carvers and tile-workers elongated the stems of the letters and filled the upper zone with a wealth of floral ornament (e.g. the minaret at Dawlatabad, Afghanistan; 1109), arabesques (tomb at Sangbast in eastern Iran; 12th century) and even a second inscription inserted among the stems of the main text (e.g. Pir-i Bakran, Linjan, early 14th century, see fig. 77 above; also the tomb of Uljaytu at SULTANIYYA, 1315). The introduction of tile mosaic made colour an important feature in inscriptions (*see* §(ii) above), and designers juxtaposed white letters against a dark-blue ground with vocalization in accent colours (mosque of Shaykh Lutfullah; see fig. 79 above) and set off the name of the ruler in gold, as in the restoration text in the name of the Aqqoyunlu ruler Uzun Hasan added to the qibla iwan of the Friday Mosque at Isfahan in 1475–6. Ottoman tile-workers adapted and refined many of these techniques, as in the tiled tympana in the Üç Şerefeli Mosque at EDIRNE (1437–47); and in Iran, Turkey and India cartouches replaced rectangular frames as poetic inscriptions in local languages became more frequent.

BIBLIOGRAPHY

Enc. Iran.: 'Arabic inscriptions'; *Enc. Islam/2*: 'Kitābāt'
M. van Berchem: *Matériaux pour un corpus inscriptionum arabicarum, i: Egypte 1*, Mém.: Miss. Archéol. Fr. Caire (Cairo, 1894–1903)
M. Sobernheim: *Matériaux pour un corpus inscriptionum arabicarum, ii: Syrie du Nord*, Mém.: Inst. Fr. Archéol. Orient. Caire (Cairo, 1909)
M. van Berchem and H. Edhem: *Matériaux pour un corpus inscriptionum arabicarum, iii: Asie Mineure 1*, Mém.: Inst. Fr. Archéol. Orient. Caire (Cairo, 1910–17)
M. van Berchem: *Matériaux pour un corpus inscriptionum arabicarum, ii: Syria du Sud*, Mém.: Inst. Fr. Archéol. Orient. Caire (Cairo, 1920–22)
G. Wiet: *Matériaux pour un corpus inscriptionum arabicarum, i: Egypte 2*, Mém.: Inst. Fr. Archéol. Orient. Caire (Cairo, 1929–30)
E. Combe, J. Sauvaget and G. Wiet, eds: *Répertoire chronologique d'épigraphie arabe* (Cairo, 1931–)
H. Hawary and H. Rached: *Les Stèles funéraires*, i and iii, Cairo, Mus. Islam. A. cat. (Cairo, 1932 and 1938)
G. Wiet: *Les Stèles funéraires*, ii and iv–x, Cairo, Mus. Islam. A. cat. (Cairo, 1936–42)
E. Herzfeld: *Matériaux pour un corpus inscriptionum arabicarum, ii: Syrie du Nord 2*, Mém.: Inst. Fr. Archéol. Orient. Caire (Cairo, 1954–6)
R. Ettinghausen: 'Arabic Epigraphy: Communication or Symbolic Affirmation', *Near Eastern Numismatics . . . Studies in Honor of G. C. Miles*, ed. D. Kouymjian (Beirut, 1974), pp. 297–317
F. T. Dijkema: *The Ottoman Historical Monumental Inscriptions in Edirne* (Leiden, 1977)
E. C. Dodd and S. Khairallah: *The Image of the Word* (Beirut, 1981)
H. M. el-Hawary and G. Wiet: *Matériaux pour un corpus inscriptionum arabicarum, iv: Arabie*, Mém.: Inst. Fr. Archéol. Orient. Caire (Cairo, 1985)
S. S. Blair: *The Monumental Inscriptions from Early Islamic Iran and Transoxiana* (Leiden, 1991)

SHEILA S. BLAIR

10. URBAN DEVELOPMENT. No single type of city characterizes the traditional Islamic world; rather, several different types developed as a result of natural, religious, cultural and historical circumstances. The courtyard house, often considered a salient characteristic of the Islamic city, can be explained as a standard response to the generally hot and dry climate that prevails from the Atlantic to the Hindu Kush, and many examples can be found well before the rise of Islam (*see* §11 below). Irregular urban plans, another feature said to be typical of the Islamic city and juxtaposed with the highly organized and strictly geometric plans typical of Hellenistic or Roman cities, are characteristic of some ancient Oriental towns. The increasing irregularity of plan, disorganized layout of public zones, and development of specialized markets, or souks, where wheeled traffic was normally absent—usually considered to be characteristics of the Islamic city—were already present in the Byzantine period. Nevertheless, distinct urban types developed in three of the major cultural zones of the Islamic world: the Islamic lands of the Mediterranean and Near East, Iran and western Central Asia, and Anatolia and the Balkans. Since few Islamic cities have been excavated, their structure is best established for the period after 1500.

(i) Central and western Islamic lands. (ii) Eastern Islamic lands. (iii) Anatolia and the Balkans.

(i) Central and western Islamic lands. The fundamental feature of the Arab Islamic city is the separation between public centres for economic, religious and cultural activities, and private zones, mainly reserved for residence. These economic and residential zones developed in concentric rings around the centre. While literary, legal and archaeological evidence provides limited information about early cities in the Arab world, a wealth of information for the period from the 16th century to the mid-19th clearly shows the character of the classical Arab city. Its evolution was interrupted in the mid-19th century by external influences and constraints. New economic and technical conditions imposed such sudden and brutal changes that adaptation was impossible, and the traditional city was transformed into an 'Old Town', often known as medina (Arab. *madina*: 'city'), which is decaying or has already disappeared.

(a) Functional organization. (b) Spatial arrangement.

(a) Functional organization. In the absence of precise data about pre-Islamic Arab cities, it is difficult to find the origins of the separation between a public centre and a private zone, but these features are conspicuous in the plan of traditional Arab cities, where a central zone crossed by a fairly regular network of open and relatively large streets contrasts sharply with peripheral zones having an irregular network of roads. In pre-colonial Algiers, for example, culs-de-sac made up only one-quarter of the total street length in the lower city, which contained the commercial centre, administration and residences of the ruling élite, whereas they comprised more than half the street length in the upper city, where the native population lived.

Most of a city's economic activities were concentrated near the congregational mosque in the centre around the covered market (Arab. *qaysariyya*, Turk. *bedesten*), often closed by doors, for cloth and valuable goods. Some covered markets were quite large; the one in FEZ, for example, covers 3000 sq. m. The goldsmiths' market (Arab. *ṣāgha*) was also located in the market centre because of its role in commercial transactions, particularly money-changing. Clustered around it were the souks (Arab. *sūq*), or specialized markets, and the caravanserais (Arab. *khān*, *wakāla* and *funduq*), for wholesale and international trade (*see* CARAVANSERAI). This central area is easily delimited on a map by its fairly regular street network. In TUNIS, for example, the congregational mosque is surrounded by a square zone with an orthogonal street pattern. The area of this central zone varied according to the economic importance of the city and its role in international trade: it covered 1.1 ha in Algiers, 6 ha in Tunis, 8.7 ha in Damascus (*see* DAMASCUS, §1(ii)), 10.6 ha in ALEPPO (see fig. 84), 11.8 ha in BAGHDAD, and an astonishing 58 ha in Cairo (see fig. 85; *see also* CAIRO, §I, 2–4), the second city of the Ottoman empire. In Aleppo the central zone was distinctive enough to have a particular name, Madina, and

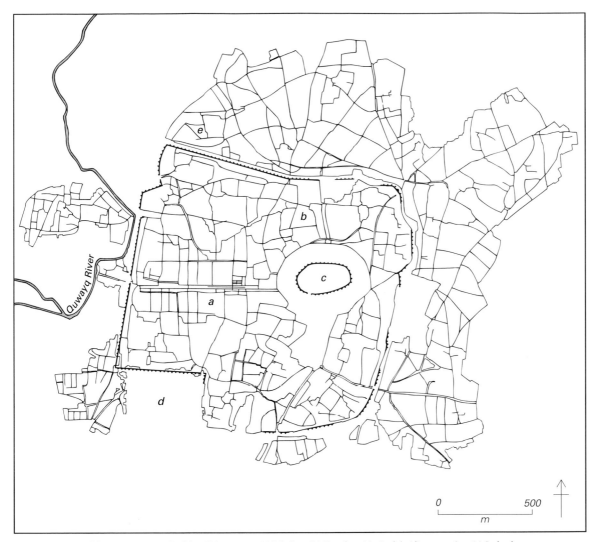

84. Aleppo, plan of the city centre, end of the 18th century: (a) Madina; (b) Farafira; (c) citadel; (d) cemeteries; (e) Judayda

the 19 caravanserais there (of the 53 known at Aleppo) occupied nearly half of its area. In Cairo the central zone corresponded to al-Qahira, the Fatimid city founded in 969 (*see* §5(ii)(c) above), and it boasted 229 caravanserais (of 348 known). The *qaṣaba*, the central thoroughfare of the city, occupied only 1.2% of its area but monopolized 57% of its economic activity.

These urban centres normally remained in the same place, perhaps because of their close relationship to the congregational mosques at their core. Only in MOSUL during the Ottoman era (16th–18th century) were the markets moved from the centre near the congregational mosque to the outskirts along the Tigris. Despite the stable position of urban centres, they evolved with the environment; in the Ottoman era the trading zones of such great Arab cities as Tunis, Cairo and Aleppo increased by half as these cities expanded vigorously. Their central commercial zones were characterized by relatively large and straight streets, since too much irregularity would have hindered economic activity. These regular central

streets included the *qaṣaba* of Cairo (6 m wide) and the thoroughfares of the great souks of Aleppo, which developed on two or three parallel lines. In some cases, such as Damascus, Aleppo and probably Tunis, these streets were inherited from antiquity, but in others they were Arab foundations. The *qaṣaba* in Cairo, for example, followed the course of the Fatimid avenue between their two palaces. Central zones were often linked to the suburbs by straight roads; in Tunis for example, which had an orthogonal grid in the centre, pairs of roads led from the gates of the city to suburbs in the north, south and west.

The urban space beyond this central economic zone was occupied by residential quarters. These quarters, known as *ḥawma* in Algiers and Tunis, *ḥāra* in Cairo and Damascus and *maḥalla* in Aleppo, Mosul and Baghdad, typically had a main street (*darb*), often closed by a gate (*bāb*), and were subdivided into secondary streets and then into culs-de-sac. The characteristic network of narrow irregular streets and culs-de-sac, often described as the typical feature of the Arab city (although it is only one of

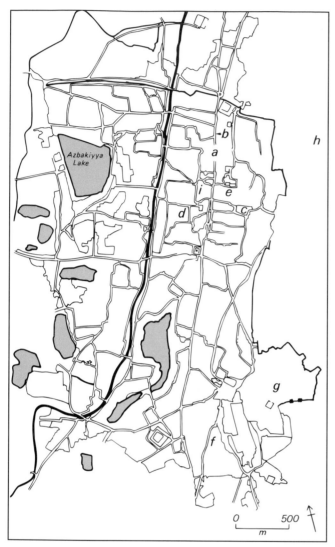

85. Cairo, plan of the city centre, end of the 18th century: (a) al-Qahira; (b) *qaṣaba*; (c) al-Azhar Mosque; (d) Khan al-Hamzawi; (e) Khan al-Khalili; (f) Suq al-Ghanam; (g) citadel; (h) cemeteries; (i) Jewish quarter

activities in residential quarters were limited to non-specialized markets, the small souks (Arab. *sūwayqa*) comprising such shops as bakers and grocers that catered to the daily needs of the inhabitants. Those in Aleppo and Damascus have been remarkably described by JEAN SAUVAGET. Other amenities might include an oratory for daily prayer, a mosque, public baths or a small market. Family life in these quarters extended into community life, from such private celebrations as circumcisions and weddings, to religious ceremonies around the shrine of a local saint or community festivals, such as the *ʿaraḍa* in Damascus. This collective life could also degenerate into traditional conflicts with neighbouring quarters.

This twofold urban structure was recognized in Islamic jurisprudence. Hanafi jurists, for example, distinguished between the 'public' zone of the city and the 'private' zone. In the centre political authorities were responsible for unsolved crimes, whereas the inhabitants of the residential quarters had to compensate collectively for the consequences of such deeds.

(b) Spatial arrangement. Both commercial and residential functions were arranged in concentric rings around the city centre. Commercial and craft activities were arranged according to a hierarchy that relegated trades of lesser importance to more remote areas. In the central zone near the congregational mosque was the booksellers' souk, which served the shaykhs and students. Markets for the most expensive goods, such as precious metals, spices, coffee and luxury cloth, were grouped together near the covered market and the goldsmiths' souk, as were caravanserais for international trade, multi-storey buildings with warehouses for goods on the ground floor and accommodation for traders upstairs. In 18th-century Cairo, for example, the 62 caravanserais for the spice and coffee trade were all located in the central area defined by the Azhar Mosque, the Khan al-Hamzawi and the Khan al-Khalili. In Tunis, the shops of the spice merchants and drapers were located in the prestigious streets abutting the congregational mosque.

Markets linked to the countryside were found on the outskirts of the city in large open squares (Arab. *raḥba*). They dealt in products of little worth compared to their weight; these were difficult to stock and too bulky to transport to the centre. They included grain, fruit and vegetables, and cattle, which required vast spaces and whose noise and dust would have been quite intolerable in town centres. Crafts that required considerable space, such as mat-weaving and rope-making, or that entailed grave nuisances for the neighbourhood, such as slaughter-houses, tanneries, ovens and furnaces, were located towards the outskirts of the city or even rejected beyond its limits. This configuration was so constant that changes of location often signal important urban changes. By the 18th century the open market square once on the outskirts of Algiers had become surrounded by the lower city; this became the 'old market' (*raḥba qadīma*) when a new open square was located on the outskirts near Bab ʿAzzun. In the Ottoman period a street near Bab Zuwayla in the centre of Cairo was still called Suq al-Ghanam ('sheep market'), although the actual sheep market had been moved to the south of the city. The displacement of

its aspects), developed in the residential zone: culs-de-sac represented 52% of the street network in Fez, 48% in Algiers, 47% in Cairo, 43% in Damascus and 41% in Aleppo. The number of quarters depended on the size of the city: Tunis had 41, Algiers about 50, Baghdad 61, Aleppo 72 and Cairo probably 100. Their surface area was also variable; the average quarter in Cairo covered about 2 ha and housed some 200 families, an average density of 300–400 inhabitants per ha. These communities were small enough to allow for quasi-family ties among their members and for easy control by the shaykhs who administered them. The quarter formed an isolated unit which was closed at night and in case of trouble, but it was not really cut off from the urban centre as the inhabitants went there to work, to shop for goods not available locally and to pray in the congregational mosque on Fridays. Economic tanneries in Aleppo (*c.* 1570), Cairo (*c.* 1600) and Tunis (1770) was the result of active expansion in these cities.

This same concentric arrangement also applied to residential zones, although it is less obvious and was more difficult for historians of Arab cities to accept. Archaeological investigations in and archival documents from Tunis, Cairo and Aleppo show that the quality of housing was hierarchically distributed from the bourgeois houses in the centre to the poorer houses in the outskirts. Wealthy quarters characterized by rich and vast houses, such as those in Tunis described by Revault, developed in the vicinity of the central souks. In Aleppo, the bourgeoisie and shaykhs lived in the Farafira quarter and around the Citadel and Madina, where the most beautiful houses were located. These houses, which closely resembled the palaces of the rulers, were large (200–400 sq. m in Tunis, 400–900 sq. m in Aleppo) and had numerous rooms for specific purposes and refined decoration. It is logical that the central sector should have been reserved for the residences of the wealthy, for the merchants and shaykhs wanted to live close to their places of business. The heart of the city was monopolized by economic activities and left little space for residential construction: the scarcity and cost of land and the necessity of resorting to vertical and more expensive architecture made these areas accessible only to the wealthy.

The houses of the middle class were located at a greater distance from the centre. In Cairo these houses did not have courtyards, but in many other Arab cities they were scaled-down versions of the classical courtyard house. Their reduced size (100–150 sq. m in Tunis, 80–190 sq. m in Aleppo) did not allow domestic functions to be differentiated as they were in the houses of the wealthy. The poor lived near the outskirts in houses that were poorly built of cheap and flimsy materials. They had to be rebuilt often, leaving little or no archaeological evidence, and they pass unmentioned in historical accounts. Their rural character was due to the origins of a large part of the population of these peripheral zones. The thatched cob-walled huts (Arab. *nuwayl*) in the outer quarters of Fez and Tunis must have resembled modern shanty towns. In other cities, such as Cairo, Damascus, Aleppo and MEDINA, low houses were grouped around a common courtyard. This arrangement (Arab. *hawsh*) ensured a highly collective life that prevented the strict observation of family isolation and feminine seclusion. It is another example of popular housing that diverges sharply from the stereotypical 'Islamic house', with its familial unit turned inward towards a courtyard. These popular quarters were also characterized by a dynamic religious life centred on Sufi brotherhoods, probably because of the close ties these suburbs kept with the surrounding rural zones where these brotherhoods were active.

This hypothetical model was always transformed in reality by geographical, historical, religious, economic and social factors. Tunis, for example, is wedged between two lakes, so the city developed in two large suburbs on the north (Bab Suwayqa) and south (Bab Jazira). A small river, the Quwayq, prevented Aleppo from developing to the west. The Muqattam hills, which dominate Cairo on the east, hindered expansion in that direction until the late 20th century. The citadel the Ayyubids built to the south-east of Cairo at the end of the 12th century encouraged expansion of the city in that direction, while large cemeteries to the north-east of Cairo and the south of Aleppo discouraged development there. The increased importance of Damascus as a pilgrimage station in the Ottoman period explains the development of the Midan suburb, which extends nearly 2 km south of the city. The tendency to separate the Christian and Jewish communities led to the creation of minority quarters which did not conform to the general rules of urban spatial organization (see below). Members of the ruling class often chose to settle in the outskirts, where they could find sufficient space for large palaces and such amenities as abundant water and vegetation for vast gardens. In 18th-century Cairo, for example, the Mamluk and military aristocracy settled around the Azbakiyya Lake, a peripheral area normally occupied by non-specialized, polluting industries and by the houses of the poor and Christian minority.

Arab cities were strongly segregated, although the supposed egalitarianism of Islamic society is often thought to have led to an integrated population within a city, with the houses of the poor adjoining those of the rich, all behind undifferentiated, modest façades. The most striking feature of the urban population, however, is the great inequality between rich and poor. For Cairo, inheritance documents from the 17th and 18th centuries reveal that the largest legacy, that of a coffee merchant who died in 1735 (8,845,550 paras), was 60,000 times greater than the smallest legacy, that of a vegetable seller who died in 1703 (145 paras). Such tremendous inequality was reflected in the quality of housing and in the clear separation between the wealthy quarters of the ruling class and rich bourgeoisie of merchants and shaykhs and middle-class or poor quarters. The relative toleration enjoyed by Jews and Christians, the 'protected' minorities, is also said to have justified close contact among people of different faiths, but Arab cities typically had distinct quarters for minorities. The Jews of Tunis lived within the Hara, a quarter the limits of which in the 19th century are shown by a 1959 map of streets, where more than 75% of the population was Jewish. At the end of the 19th century, the Christians of Aleppo still occupied, more or less exclusively, the western half of the northern suburbs and comprised all of the population of Judayda and neighbouring areas. Judayda was a wealthy residential area in an outer zone of the city, which would normally have been occupied by poorer housing. The Jewish quarter of Cairo, by contrast, was a poor area located in the centre near the souks of the goldsmiths and money-changers, who were often Jews. Political factors may also have played a role, for this site offered greater scope for control and protection by the administration. National communities were also segregated, in direct proportion to their distance from the dominant Sunni Muslim population. The most extreme case is Antioch in northern Syria, which was still an aggregate of cities in 1930. Each of the three communities that made up the town (Turks, Christians and Alawites) lived in their own closed quarters. The geographical arrangement of these quarters is significant: the Turks, who were until 1918 the politically and socially dominant group, occupied the centre, whereas the Alawites, who were subjected to double discrimination because of their poverty and their adherence to a minority sect of Islam, had been pushed to the northern and southern ends of the town.

The topographical realization of diverse and contrasted social and economic communities in the traditional Arab city meant that the city ran the risk of disintegrating into its constituent units, as in Aleppo and Antioch. The organization of the urban space, however, with its strong city centre, combining economic, religious and cultural activities, and its logical distribution of activities and housing from the centre to the periphery, endowed the Arab city with a strong internal unity that prevented it from falling into anarchy. On the contrary, such cities as Aleppo and Cairo show a real prosperity and splendour from the 16th to the 18th century. The consolidation of the city structure and the organization of its expansion owed much to such Islamic institutions as the judicial system and charitable endowments. The traditional Arab city did not just conserve worn and outdated forms, but was a coherent and dynamic whole linked to its society and economy.

BIBLIOGRAPHY

M. Clerget: *Le Caire: Etude de géographie urbaine et d'histoire économique*, 2 vols (Cairo, 1934)
J. Sauvaget: 'Esquisse d'une histoire de la ville de Damas', *Rev. Etud. Islam.*, viii (1934), pp. 421–80
J. Weulersse: 'Antioche: Essai de géographie urbaine', *Bull. Etud. Orient.*, iv (1934), pp. 27–79
J. Sauvaget: *Alep*, 2 vols (Paris, 1941)
R. Brunschvig: 'Urbanisme médiéval et droit musulman', *Rev. Etud. Islam.*, xv (1947), pp. 127–55
J. Caillé: *La Ville de Rabat*, 3 vols (Paris, 1949)
R. Le Tourneau: *Fès avant le Protectorat* (Casablanca and Paris, 1949)
E. Pauty: 'Villes spontanées et villes créés en Islam', *An. Inst. Etud. Orient. U. Alger*, ix (1951), pp. 52–75
G. von Grunebaum: 'The Structure of the Muslim Town', *Islam: Essays on the Nature and Growth of a Cultural Tradition* (London, 1955, rev. 1961), pp. 141–58
R. Le Tourneau: *Les Villes musulmanes de l'Afrique du Nord* (Algiers, 1957)
P. Sebag: *La Hara de Tunis* (Paris, 1959)
I. Lapidus: *Muslim Cities in the Later Middle Ages* (Cambridge, MA, 1967)
J. Revault: *Palais et demeures de Tunis*, 4 vols (Paris, 1967–78)
I. Lapidus, ed.: *Middle Eastern Cities* (Berkeley, 1969)
G. Cladel and P. Revault: *Medina: Approche typologique* (Tunis, 1970)
A. Hourani and S. M. Stern, eds: *The Islamic City* (Oxford, 1970)
J. Abu-Lughod: *Cairo: 1001 Years of the City Victorious* (Princeton, 1971)
L. Torrès-Balbás: *Ciudades hispano-musulmanas*, 2 vols (Madrid, 1972)
L. C. Brown, ed.: *From Madina to Metropolis* (Princeton, 1973)
J.-C. David: 'Alep: Dégradation et tentatives actuelles de réadaptation des structures urbaines traditionelles', *Bull. Etud. Orient.*, xxviii (1975), pp. 19–49
R. Serjeant, ed.: *The Islamic City* (Paris, 1980)
B. Johansen: 'The All-embracing Town and its Mosques', *Rev. Occidente Musulman & Médit.*, xxxii (1981)
M. Meriwether: *The Notable Families of Aleppo, 1770–1830* (diss., Philadelphia, U. PA, 1981)
A. Bouhdiba and D. Chevallier, eds: *La Ville arabe dans l'Islam* (Tunis, 1982)
A. Raymond: *Artisans et commerçants du Caire au XVIIIème siècle* (Paris, 1982)
J.-C. Garcin and others: *Palais et maisons du Caire*, 2 vols (Paris, 1982–3)
H. Gaube and E. Wirth: *Aleppo* (Wiesbaden, 1984)
A. Raymond: *Grandes villes arabes à l'époque ottomane* (Paris, 1985)
P. Cuneo: *Storia dell'urbanistica: Il mondo islamico* (Rome, 1986)
N. Hanna: *Les Maisons moyennes du Caire et leurs habitants au 17ème et 18ème siècles* (diss., U. Aix–Marseille I, Aix-en-Provence, 1989)
A. Marcus: *Aleppo in the Eighteenth Century* (New York, 1989)
P. Sebag: *Tunis au XVIIème siècle* (Paris, 1989)

(ii) Eastern Islamic lands. Iranian cities of the Islamic period are less well known than those of Arab Islamic lands. Because the favoured material of construction was mud-brick, cities often developed horizontally, as one centre was abandoned in favour of another. Few sites have been excavated, except in the marginal areas of Iraq and western Central Asia. Textual problems are also significant, as it is often difficult to distinguish between a district and its major town of the same name.

The aridity of the Iranian plateau means that the major cities are oases and settlements along the foothills of the high mountain chains where the supply of water is assured by rivers or subterranean aqueducts (Pers. *qanāt*). Settlements were usually established along trade routes or at strategic sites and are surrounded by broad agricultural lands, market-gardens and pasture.

The typical urban arrangement in pre-modern times was an inner city (*shahristān*) centred on a citadel (*kuhandiz*) and flanked by suburbs (*bīrūn*). The inner city was usually a modification of a pre-Islamic one. Those that were circular or quadrilateral usually had four gates on the cardinal sides, and in Islamic times a fifth gate was often added. Following the upheavals of the 10th and 11th centuries, cities were usually fortified. Major arteries led from the gates to the city centre, and the quarters between them were divided into residential blocks. Within the blocks twisted culs-de-sac gave pedestrian access to individual buildings.

This typical arrangement is found from the southern fringes of the Dasht-i Lut to western Central Asia (e.g. MERV, BUKHARA, KHIVA and SHAHR-I SABZ). One of the best examples is HERAT in Afghanistan. The inner city (1500×1600 m) is cardinally orientated. There are five gates: three in the centres of the west, south and east sides, and two on the north, one behind the citadel in the north-west quadrant and the other behind the congregational mosque in the north-east. Streets 4–5 m wide and lined with shops and workshops lead from the gates and intersect in a central domed bazaar (*chahārsū*). The four main streets are divided into small blocks (10,000–15,000 sq. m), which are largely residential as all religious buildings other than the congregational mosque are located on the fringes. The inner city is surrounded by suburbs, which expanded dramatically in the 15th century when the members of the TIMURID dynasty (*reg* 1370–1506; *see* §6(i)(b) above) built palaces, mosques and madrasas in lush garden settings along the canals to the north of the city.

The arrangement of residential blocks defined by streets and comprised of footpaths and houses has been clarified by detailed studies of Isfahan in central Iran (*see* ISFAHAN, §1). The typical house is arranged around a central court, the façades of which have symmetrical tripartite plans. The main façade, on the south, incorporates the most public room (*urusī* or *shāhnishīn*). Most houses have two courtyards, called *bīrūn* ('inner') and *andarūn* ('outer'), but many houses have several courtyards joined by common access vestibules (*hashtī*). These blocks are in a constant state of flux, as changes of ownership lead to houses expanding or contracting in courtyard-defined units, and the internal arrangement of the blocks is totally transformed within two to three generations. The houses, generally built of mud-brick and wood, are ephemeral, and none of those recorded in the 1970s was more than 150 years old (*see* VERNACULAR ARCHITECTURE, §II, 7(viii)).

Neighbourhood service nodes were typically located at the intersection of the streets surrounding the residential blocks or near the mouth of a *qanāt*. These architectural complexes were often centred on a mosque, tomb or *khānaqāh* and might also include such public buildings as baths, shops and fountains. These service nodes were continually repaired and replaced, but one built (1713–15) by 'Ali Quli Agha in the Bidabad quarter of Isfahan gives a good idea of the type. It contains a combined mosque–madrasa, in which Friday prayers are performed by the inhabitants of the quarter, a double bath, several fountains and a bazaar centred on a monumental *chahārsū* and containing workshops for weaving and furniture and 36 shops, catering primarily to the needs of the area.

The city of Isfahan also shows how the traditional city type could be transformed by imperial fiat. The city had been the capital under the Buyids (*reg* 932–1062) and Saljuqs (*reg* 1038–1194) and remained a regional centre and emporium under the Ilkhanids (*reg* 1256–1353) and Timurids, but the Safavid monarch 'Abbas I transformed it in 1598 when he made it the capital of his empire (*see* §7(ii)(a) above). The centre of the new district was a new maidan located close to the Zaindeh River to the south of the old city. It was intended to supplant the old open market that adjoined the Friday Mosque, and to that end the monarch erected the Qaysariyya, the royal bazaar, on the north side. Consisting of two parallel north–south

roads and three east–west ones, it housed many shops, the mint, the royal bath and the royal caravanserai, the largest in the city, with 140 rooms for cloth merchants on the ground floor and jewellers, goldsmiths and engravers above. On the maidan opposite the entrance to the bazaar, 'Abbas I ordered a new congregational mosque, the Shah Mosque (*see* ISFAHAN, §3(iii)). To the west of the maidan was the royal palace compound, comprising a gatehouse, kitchens, storage-sheds, chicken-houses, private living quarters for the royal family and pavilions in large parks (see fig. 86). This compound extended west to the Chahar Bagh ('four-[plot] plan'), the wide boulevard bordered by the palaces of the nobility that stretched south across the river to the quarter of New Julfa, where 'Abbas I had settled 3000 Armenian families.

See also CENTRAL ASIA, §I, 2(iii)(b).

BIBLIOGRAPHY
G. A. Pugachenkova: *Puti razvetiya arkhitektury yuzhnogo Turkmenistana* [Paths of development in the architecture of southern Turkmenistan] (Moscow, 1958)
J. Aubin: 'Eléments pour l'étude des agglomérations urbaines dans l'Iran médiéval', *The Islamic City*, ed. A. H. Hourani and S. M. Stern (Oxford, 1970), pp. 65–77
Iran. Stud., vii (1974) [2-part issue entitled *Studies on Isfahan*, ed. R. Holod]
K. Karpetian: *Isfahan, New Julfa: Le case degli Armeni/The Houses of the Armenians* (Rome, 1974)
M. Bonine: *Yazd and its Hinterland: A Central Place System of Dominance in the Central Iranian Plateau* (Austin, 1975)
L. Golombek and R. Holod: 'Preliminary Report on the Isfahan City Project', *Akten des VII. International Kongresses für iranische Kunst und Archäologie: München, 7–10 Sept. 1976*, pp. 578–90
H. Gaube: *Iranian Cities* (New York, 1979)
T. Allen: *Timurid Herat* (Wiesbaden, 1983)
S. S. Blair: 'The Mongol Capital of Sultaniyya, "The Imperial"', *Iran*, xxiv (1986), pp. 139–51

SHEILA S. BLAIR

(iii) Anatolia and the Balkans. Most of the information on Islamic cities in Anatolia and the Balkans concerns the period from the 16th to the 18th century when the area was controlled by the Ottoman dynasty (*reg* 1281–1924). It is debated whether towns in the Balkans survived the wars and epidemics of the later Middle Ages and were still flourishing when the Ottomans conquered the region in the 14th and 15th centuries. The degree to which Balkan towns of the 16th century were new creations of the Ottomans is also a matter of discussion. In Anatolia, the Ottoman state had to accommodate earlier patterns of urbanization that were Turkish and Muslim but associated with rival Turkoman states such as the Karamanids (*reg c.* 1256–1483) and the Dhu'l-Qadr (*reg* 1337–1522). In most cases major mosques and other foundations established by pre-Ottoman rulers were permitted to continue in operation, and summaries of their charters (Turk. *vakifname*) were inserted into Ottoman tax registers.

The most significant institution for the structure of the Ottoman city was the pious foundation. Mosques, madrasas, *khānaqāh*s, guest-houses, soup-kitchens, drinking fountains and primary schools were grouped in complexes which formed the core of a town quarter (*mahalle*). These institutions were assigned rural or urban income-producing properties in perpetuity, and their services, offered free of charge to users, were financed by taxes paid by villagers, as well as by the revenues of caravanserais and

86. Palace compound, Isfahan, Iran, 1684–5; engraving by Engelbert Kaempfer from *Amoenitates politico-physico-medicarum*, v (Lemgo, 1712) (London, British Library)

covered markets. These institutions thus served as a means to transfer rural wealth into towns. The pious foundations established in Istanbul by Sultan Mehmed I (1472–3) and Sultan Süleyman II (1557) have been particularly well studied (*see* ISTANBUL, §II, 2), but similar complexes on a smaller scale functioned in such provincial towns as BURSA, EDIRNE, Trikkala and Trabzon.

The most important monuments in the city centre are the major mosques, citadel, covered market (*bedestan, bedesten, bezazistan*) and caravanserais (*han*). Even modest towns had more than one congregational mosque. Citadels were common, though by no means universal, and city walls surrounding a town were exceptional: the walls around Istanbul were built by the Byzantines, and the wall built around Ankara *c.* 1600 was financed by the townsmen as protection from the Celali rebellions that were devastating the countryside. In the 16th century the covered market, which comprised a few dozen shops and offered storage facilities for such valuable goods as textiles, distinguished towns involved in inter-regional trade from more modest, rural marketing centres. Caravanserais, which were two-storey buildings arranged around a courtyard, provided storage for trade goods and accommodation for merchants in transit. They were generally clustered about the covered market so as to minimize disruption to residential neighbourhoods. The caravanserai district, such as the one known in ANKARA around 1600, often had a street for wheeled traffic, since peasant carts were used for short-haul traffic in Anatolia, while the camel caravan was the favoured means of transportation for long-distance traffic. In many parts of the Balkans, where carts and wagons dominated long-distance traffic as well, a special commercial area (*araba pazarı*) was sometimes set aside for them on the edge of town. Shops were often built in clusters near pious foundations and rented out against payment of an entry fee and a low perpetual rent. Artisans and merchants also converted their shops into pious foundations that could be passed on to specified descendants without subdivision on condition that the heirs fulfilled certain religious obligations.

By the 16th century the most important Ottoman towns had developed a business district that contained almost no habitations, as a single building rarely served both commercial/artisanal and residential functions except in 18th-century Istanbul. Residential districts had only shops providing daily necessities and domestic workshops, such as those in Ankara where the renowned mohair cloth was woven. Town quarters usually grouped several households that shared the same ethnic and/or religious background. Rich and poor typically lived in the same neighbourhood, although in certain cases wealthier neighbourhoods can be distinguished from poor ones, which were usually located on the outskirts. Ghettos did not exist; both in Istanbul and in Anatolia Muslim residents mingled with non-Muslims, despite official and unofficial attempts to maintain the homogeneity of town quarters.

The palaces of sultans and high-level administrative officials in Istanbul and, from the 17th century onwards, the residences of provincial notables in Anatolian and Balkan towns were elaborate constructions, but apart from Topkapı Palace in Istanbul (*see* ISTANBUL, §III, 13(iii)) they were built of perishable materials and with very few

exceptions, only those dating from the second half of the 18th century and later have survived. Wealthy residences in the provinces imitated the style of the capital Istanbul, and from the mid-18th century onwards the vogue for landscape painting and Baroque decoration can be seen in such outlying Anatolian towns as Birgi and Yozgat. House types (see fig. 87) varied from region to region. By the 18th century in Istanbul, residential construction was generally of wood, and three-storey houses were common, even in the suburbs along the Bosporus. In certain parts of central Anatolia, houses were built of mud-brick supported by wooden frames; 17th-century examples had one or two storeys. In the area around KAYSERI and Ürgüp where good building stone is abundant, single-storey houses with roof terraces remained the norm well into the 19th century. Ecological constraints were by no means the only factors that determined house type: the influence of Istanbul styles of construction was pervasive, even in unfavourable environments.

The desire for family privacy was important and was manifested in a variety of ways. Culs-de-sac were much less widespread than previously thought, and ingenious solutions were found to provide a view of natural scenery and the street and to allow residents to see without being seen. One solution was to concentrate inhabited rooms on the second and third floors, which often had belvederes. Another solution to the problem of privacy was to construct second homes outside the city, in the case of inland towns among gardens and vineyards or in the case of Istanbul along the waterfront. There, social interaction was more informal than in the city itself, and this relaxation

87. Tokat, Turkey, view of a street

of constraints was part of the attraction provided by summer residences.

BIBLIOGRAPHY

O. L. Barkan: 'Süleymaniye Camii ve Imareti tesislerine ait yillik bir muhasebe bilancosu, 993–994 (1585–1586)' [Yearly accounts of the Süleymaniye Mosque and Hospices, 993–4 (1585–6)], *Vakıflar Derg.*, ix (1947), pp. 109–62

——: 'Essai sur les données statistiques des registres de recensement dans l'empire ottoman aux XVe et XVIe siècles', *J. Econ. & Soc. Hist. Orient*, i (1958), pp. 11–36

——: 'Osmanli Imparatorluğunda imaret sitelerinin kuruluş ve işleyiş tarzına âit araştırmalar' [Research on the establishment and functioning of hospice complexes in the Ottoman empire], *Istanbul Ü. Iktisat Fak. Mecmuası*, xxiii (1962–3), pp. 239–96

N. Todorov: 'Quelques aspects de la ville balkanique aux XVe et XVIe siècles: Nombre et populations', *Histoire*, ii of *Actes du II. Congrès international des études du sud-est européen: Athènes, 1970*, pp. 209–19

K. Kreiser: 'Bedesten-Bauten im osmanischen Reich: Ein vorläufiger Überblick auf Grund der Schriftquellen', *Istanbul. Mitt.*, xxix (1979), pp. 367–400

H. Inalcik: 'The Hub of the City: The Bedestan of Istanbul', *Int. J. Turk. Stud.*, i (1979–80), pp. 1–17

Ö. Ergenc: 'XVII yüzyilin baslarinda Ankara'nin yerlesim durumu üzerine bazi bilgiler' [Some information on settlement patterns in early 17th-century Ankara], *Osmanli Araştırmaları*, i (1980), pp. 85–108

N. Todorov: *La Ville balkanique aux XVe–XIXe siècles: Développement socio-économique et démographique* (Bucharest, 1980)

G. Necipoğlu-Kafadar: 'The Süleymaniye Complex in Istanbul: An Interpretation', *Muqarnas*, iii (1985), pp. 92–117

S. Faroqhi: *Men of Modest Substance: House Owners and House Property in Seventeenth-century Ankara and Kayseri* (Cambridge, 1987)

A. Kuran: *Sinan: The Grand Old Master of Ottoman Architecture* (Istanbul, 1987)

T. Artan: *Architecture as a Theater of Life: Profile of the 18th-century Bosphorus* (diss., Cambridge, MA, MIT, 1989)

SURAIYA FAROQHI

11. HOUSING. From time immemorial in the great river valleys of the Middle East, tribes and communities have survived by living in cohesion, finding it easiest to make compact settlements using earth or mud-brick for mass with timber for horizontal support and lighter top structures. Termites devoured the timber, and consequently the next generation would rebuild on the previous foundations. Each generation brought materials within the walls and discarded them where they had decayed; so the towns rose, each making its little flat-topped plateau encapsulating layer upon layer over a period many times longer than written history. This testimony has enabled archaeologists to show that the fundamental evolution of the Mediterranean or courtyard house took place in what is known as the Middle East, flowing from the combination of intuitive design, practical response and precedent that defines vernacular architecture.

(i) Introduction. (ii) Materials. (iii) Forms and regional variation.

(i) Introduction. Since the 7th century AD the region has been dominated by Islam, but throughout its long documented history the building of towns and villages has reflected the philosophies and cultures of the many peoples who inhabited and passed through it. All have contributed to the multiple vernacular of this complex region, and many strands have been woven into a complex pattern for which there is no simple description. The task of unravelling the strands is made easier by the persistence of ethnic and tribal traditions even in alien environments and distant places. For example, the Greek vernacular was carried to the Indus, and Yemeni migrants in northern Nigeria have continued to build their square tower houses

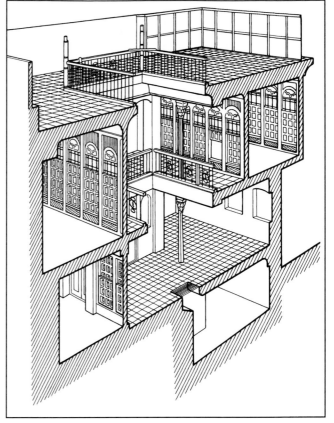

88. Traditional courtyard house, Baghdad, Iraq; sectional perspective showing the projecting oriel (*shanashil*) window over the street to the right

in a land of round thatched huts. So it is that the courtyard houses of UR, built some 4000 years ago, are echoed in the typical houses still found in southern Iraq.

In the wide alluvial plain created from the silt carried by the Tigris and Euphrates rivers from the northern mountains, traditions have been so persistent that even the foods described in ancient texts can be recognized in the traditional menus of the countryside. Similarly, the houses and vernacular community buildings, though young in themselves, represent something as old as civilization itself. The basic building type, the courtyard house (see fig. 88), was evolved in response to a climate where shelter is needed against extremes of heat and occasionally cold, but where rain is neither persistent nor unwelcome. In consequence circulation between usable spaces takes place in the open.

The courtyard house is essentially a family entity, usually in the sense of the extended family, with several generations living together and in more wealthy instances with servants and dependants living in secondary courtyards (see fig. 89). It formed the fundamental and universal cell of the urban structure, but within the house there might be individual cells of specific privacy relating to a couple, an individual wife or another dependant. Powerful family traditions make the protection of women a pillar of the social structure, and the community would go to considerable lengths to ensure that no individual woman lived in

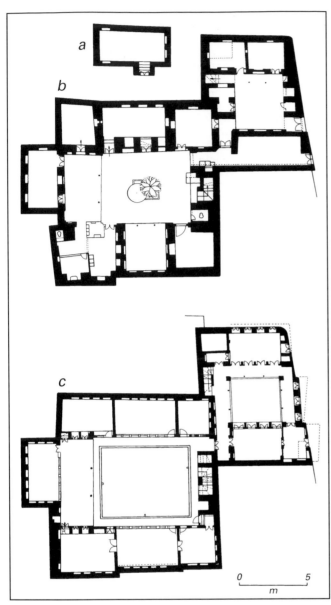

89. Courtyard house, Kadhimiya district, Baghdad, plan: (a) basement; (b) ground floor; (c) first floor

secondary grouping, rather looser than the first, would arise. These groupings of ten or a dozen households in turn join into a small urban entity, often known as a *mahalla* (sometimes *hawna*, *hāra* etc), which varied widely in size, but typically comprised some hundred households. A principal street leading into or through such a small district would focus within this urban village on some place of trade and the local centre of the community with its well, school, bath, church, mosque or synagogue. While there is nothing unique in such an arrangement, being part of the natural way of human life, it reached a level of consistency and continuity in the cities of the Middle East that made a fundamental statement of human values before the divergent tendencies of the modern era. The social groupings extend in upward gradation through the city; above the neighbourhood group, however, conscious architecture supersedes vernacular in importance.

(ii) Materials. Vernacular building is more dependent on the use of local materials than more sophisticated forms of architecture. In volumetric terms, unburnt earth must have constituted the greater part of the material used in vernacular building: in many areas it was virtually universal, if reinforced occasionally with burnt brick or stone. Earth was used widely as render or as mortar with gypsum or lime as an additive and a variety of organic materials to aid consolidation. Dung, milk, egg and blood have been used to provide albumin, allowing higher consolidation by lubricating the clay particles during placing. Resinous plant juices have also been used, similarly allowing the earth to be consolidated, burnished or even polished at the wet stage.

Being more permanent, fired brick has been widely used, particularly in the lower and more vulnerable parts of buildings. It has a long history in the region. Ancient piers in which every brick bears the name of Nebuchadnezzar still project from the bed of the Tigris, having survived millennia of flood and erosion. The inventive systems of vaulting, doming, arching and decorative walling that gave form and character to the houses of Iraq and the Nile valley relied on brick. As a material it could be carved and worked, and even in vernacular buildings was frequently used to provide spiral colonettes, decorative spandrels, lunettes or panels. These panels identify and give status to the street door. The patterns in which brick was deployed are fundamental, for Middle Eastern brick is generally uniform in colour. In more sophisticated architecture it was frequently glazed, but this was rare in vernacular building. Burnt brick was important throughout the region as a paving material, and, in the north, fired clay tiles perpetuated Roman traditions of pitched roofing.

The region is well endowed with gypsum (calcium sulphate), which forms a quick-setting mortar (plaster of Paris) when heated moderately. Various combinations of this native material were used to solidify and stabilize earths, and it provided a basis for the stucco used from early times to decorate such buildings. Mortars of this type also provided the quick-setting cements that allowed the building of uncentred vaulting and domes, encouraging the inventive forms of roof construction typical of Afghanistan, Uzbekistan, Iran and northern Iraq. Mazar-i

isolation. Concern for privacy reached high and sometimes obsessive levels in Middle Eastern society. One consequence was the subdivision of the family cell into two sections: the area where guests were welcome, generally known as *selamlık* (Turk.), and the private area, the unenterable preserve of the household, in particular of the women, known as *haremlik* or *harem*. The cellular house is linked to the rest of the world through very limited access points—ideally one door to the street. The lower walls are pierced by minimal openings to the ouside world.

Within the town several such cells were grouped together on small streets, leading to organic fingering street patterns with culs-de-sac off which a relatively small number of houses could open (*see* §10 above). Thus a

Sharif, Bukhara, Merv, Mashhad, Bam, Yazd, Isfahan, Tabriz and Mosul have been centres of this tradition.

Much of the stone used is rubble bonded with stabilized earth mortar, but dressed stone has also been important, employed not only to emulate the higher quality buildings of the upper strata of society but also as reused materials. Stone and stone dressings for openings were used in the coastal regions of the Mediterranean Sea and the Red Sea. Coral rock was used on the Red Sea coast, as at the abandoned trading city of SUAKIN. In the basaltic region of the Hawran in southern Syria, a totally lithic architecture was developed with floors and roofs of stone planks, and in antiquity even the doors and window shutters were of stone. In central Anatolia, buildings have been carved into pillars of soft volcanic tufa. Traditions of stoneworking and the consequent box-like architectural forms have persisted in vernacular building to the 20th century. Close clustering has produced the angular conglomerates that have typified the cities of Palestine and Syria, such as Hama, Sidon, Damascus and Jerusalem, as well as the many picturesque villages of the region.

Timber, being relatively scarce throughout the Middle East, has generally been reserved for joinery and structural functions. One of the most typical features of vernacular construction is the flat roof formed of pole joists overlaid by smaller timbers or fibrous materials such as palm leaf or cane and roofed with compacted mud. A parapet carried up on masonry walls completes the basic form, and the spans of the available timbers determine the dimensions of the building. Available timber varies distinctly region by region. In many areas poplar has consistently been the most readily available, but in Iraq, Egypt and the Saudi Peninsula the palm has been important, usually halved as joists and as posts, although its fibrous boards can scarcely be called timber. In the Gulf, mangrove poles have been extensively imported. Burmese teak, much valued as a joinery timber because of its resistance to termite attack, has long been imported into the region. Vernacular architecture also responds to seismic problems, and the introduction of horizontal courses of timber in some areas of the Yemen and the Abha region of Saudi Arabia has given rise to a distinctive architectural style resistant to earth tremors. There is also a strong tradition of timber-frame building across the northern belt, perhaps also for earthquake resistance. Small scantlings, often of poplar but, in some areas, of pine, are typical. Since termites render timbers other than teak an impermanent material, such a reliance on timber framing may seem short-sighted; but the quality of the architecture, nevertheless, has relied heavily on the carpenter.

Timber framing was used as a light structure added to the upper levels of the building. Lower walls of masonry, perhaps laced with timber, would give way at the upper levels to carpentry. This led, in turn, to the widespread use of jettying, the joists being carried out across the masonry wall as a short cantilever. The effect was to stiffen the floor by reversing the stresses in the joists, allowing the more economical use of timber with the secondary advantage of gaining additional space. More could be achieved with less, and the sense of airiness and lightness gained was a further advantage. From Thrace to Uzbekistan and beyond in both directions light pole framing with brick or earth-block nogging is widespread. Floors were often cantilevered or jettied, and roofs were hidden behind parapets to be used for a multiplicity of household functions, particularly for sleeping. Flooring and the decks of roofs might be waterproofed with no more than a mud plaster, perhaps enriched with gypsum or even bitumen, which occurs naturally and has long been traded throughout the region. Alternatively, fired brick or tile would be used to create a waterproof surface. Techniques of waterproofing were evolved in which a fibre-rich clay would be rolled into the surface after rain. As persistent rain is not usual in much of the region, these rudimentary techniques were effective. In parts of the northern belt, however, such as the Caucasus, on the Black Sea and in northern Anatolia, tile pitched roofs have long provided a better answer to the more persistent rains of the area and have dominated the vernacular tradition.

Timber was widely employed for screened projecting balconies enclosed externally to form part of the room. This device took on local names: *mashrabiyya* in Egypt and the Hijaz, *shanashil* in Iraq (see fig. 88 above) and the Gulf, while further north and elsewhere it was given derivative names such as *baghdadi*. Its use extends far beyond the region, from Morocco to India, for it allowed areas that were 'harem' to project out into the street or to oversail the more public rooms of the house so that women could watch what was going on. Internally the device was known as *kabishkan*. Socially and visually it took on an importance far beyond its proportionate extent, as it became the key visual characteristic of much vernacular building. Variations typified local, regional or national qualities and did much to identify the place of origin of the architectural form. An Ottoman-style *shanashil* appearing in Egypt or a Basra-style one in Muscat could identify the origins and movements of peoples. Often the balconies were constructed very lightly, of lattices and filigree in slender frames. They were part of a more wide-reaching tradition that transcended the boundaries of the vernacular, reaching out to the intricate geometries of the finest interlocking timber screen and panel-making that played so great a part in the more polite architecture of the Islamic lands (*see* §VII, 2(ii)-(iii) below).

Timber has advantages of lightness and insulation as well as strength, so it was used for complete façades and multi-storey buildings. The now-destroyed streets of Basra repeated from Mosul to Muscat were echoed in the timber-faced merchants' houses of Jiddah and the waterside timber façades on the Bosporus. Timber played an important and apparently unlikely role elsewhere. Belts of reed mat, cane or timber have been built into the lowest courses of walling, apparently as a precaution against earthquakes and rising salts. Timber framing lies behind many smooth earth-rendered façades; timber ties and lacing members restrain the tower houses of the Yemen and hold together the wind towers of the Gulf and the Persian highlands. As a material, timber has the advantage of tensile strength, giving cohesion to the building. It is also economical, for building in brick would consume substantially more wood as fuel and would also require the burning of limestone or gypsum.

Other dwelling types in the region include latticed tunnels of reed used by the marsh Arabs of southern Iraq (*see* VERNACULAR ARCHITECTURE, fig. 29). Where the Tigris and Euphrates join near Basra, extensive reed-beds grow in the sluggish waters providing the only building material other than mud. Long halls are built using the lamella lattice principle, in which a diagonal weave provides strength. A tradition of brick vaulting is strong in Upper Egypt, where barrel vaults are generally preferred to domes, which are typical in the Iranian plateau. In northern Syria south and east of Aleppo, a strong local vernacular was evolved where every chamber is roofed with a high parabolic dome. Because of their high form, these were structurally stable using thin shells of unbaked earth studded with projecting foot supports to provide access for maintenance. In the Iranian uplands interlacing arches carry domes above square chambers. When sequenced around courtyards these domes produce the bubbled rooftops characteristic of such towns as YAZD. Requiring substantial compressive strength, the domes are generally made of baked brick, although structures of mud-brick are also common, and ingenious secondary vaulting lightens the haunches to support a flat floor or deck above.

(iii) Forms and regional variation. Although Islam has given social coherence to vernacular building throughout the region, it is often difficult to distinguish vernacular constructions by religion or race. The predominant form of the Middle Eastern vernacular is the courtyard plan, which offers physical and social advantages. The protection offered by the compound wall is psychologically and practically important, being adopted in the countryside as well as in the town. In town the compound walls are party walls between dwellings, and the courtyard offers privacy at the expense of outward views other than to the street itself. This system allows a high density of site usage, an important consideration when city walls had to be defended and water carried. The courtyard is also very effective in moderating climatic conditions. With minimal ground exposure, a complex of courtyard housing has the advantage of providing a high level of protection against solar gain (see fig. 90). Consequently the lower levels of habitation are well protected, as are the narrow streets overhung by jettied windows. The functional and climatic advantages of such an arrangement were the cause of its retention, development and persistence. An important corollary, furthermore, is the control of height. Where dwellings were built so close together and rooftops were sleeping areas, it became unacceptable that one structure should be higher than another. Overlooking became an invasion of privacy, and in consequence there arose a web of common law effectively controlling the height of buildings and limiting them all to the same level. The consequent characteristic urban form was found through much of the region, particularly in the great cities of the plains—Baghdad, Basra and Karbala'—the traditional cities of the Gulf, and Aleppo and Diyarbakır.

Climatic subtleties within the region cause the types to vary. Height and orientation are determined by matters such as the prevailing wind. Projecting structures—towers and scoops—reach up to catch these regular breezes (*see* WIND CATCHER). At Dubai in the Gulf and in Iran, Afghanistan and Pakistan these structures stand four-square as towers, quartered to catch any wind. In Karbala',

90. Part of Rusafa district, Baghdad; aerial view

Mosul and Baghdad, windscoops project above the walls to catch the summer winds from the north-west, deflecting the dry air into the cool damp basements. Each different type gives a distinct local character.

Local traditions arose in such cities as Cairo, where open balconies were built in corners to provide ventilation and view. In Kuwait and other trading cities, the courtyard meeting houses for the men of the family (Arab. *dīwāniyya*) were set along the shoreline with open breezy rooms. In response to social and practical needs, builders in the Islamic lands created a structural matrix in which the individual building dissolves in the greater conglomerate and becomes unimportant to the point of sometimes being invisible. Many a substantial house in Cairo, Aleppo or Baghdad has no greater opening to the world than a single door to the street. Such a building has no external elevation or prospect whatever. A fundamental cause of this cohesion is the philosophical background of Islam, which tends to be at one with Christianity and Judaism in emphasis on social kinship. Urban society is drawn into closely knit groups of which the most important focuses on the mosque attended daily by the local male population. The geographically determined orientation of the mosque itself (Arab. *qibla*) may set the alignment of the housing at large. This orientation is often reinforced by rituals within the home and the conception that certain directions are more propitious than others. Thus the remarkable cohesion of the Muslim city is a product of long tradition, available materials, climatic control, the social ethic and the influence of religion.

Other distinct traditions are found in Arabia. In the Hijaz, the part of Saudi Arabia bordering on the northern end of the Red Sea, the upland cities of Mecca and Medina have stone buildings. Although the earlier vernacular has virtually been obliterated by the regeneration that accompanies wealth, there was an impressive multi-storey tradition of building, with street façades up to four storeys fronting a complexity of courtyard structures. The Red Sea port of Jiddah, lesser towns such as Ta'if in the highlands and Wajh on the coast share the tradition of relatively bland façades dressed by occasional screened overhanging windows to project wealth and influence. Further south a distinctive additional flavour is apparent in Abha, a highland region benefiting from greater rainfall where there is a strong tradition of banded rubble walling laced with timber. Battered walls and small openings combine to produce a semi-fortified aspect even more apparent in the higher and greener lands of the Yemen. Here the courtyard traditions are abandoned. The clustered multi-storey houses of Jiddah become towered streets, patterned and pulsating with visual energy. In the San'a' region overt display covers many walls with whitened brick in patterns as intricate as carpets. Heights vary and the buildings cluster, as at stone-built Hajjara in the mountains and al-Mukalla on the Arabian Sea coast. Inland, the cities of the Hadramawt rise eight or nine floors, the 'skyscrapers' of vernacular tradition, earth-rendered, many-windowed, built in mud and stone. Shibam is the most famous of these once-remote towns of tightly planned houses towering above the date palms of their fertile wadis, the upper rooms airy and private, increasingly windowed as the buildings rise.

Equally liveable houses of similar floor plan rise five and six storeys above the sparkling waters of the Bosporus. Waterside timber façades have lined these shores of Asia and Europe from Istanbul to the village of Emirgan. Leaning gently as decay has bitten into their lower levels, they too are the result of the similar patterns and philosophies of life that run across the region. Beneath them, in favoured positions on the shore, stand the single-storey and balconied pleasure houses (Turk. *yalı*), the centralized plans of which are effectively that of the courtyard house, the key to the domestic architecture of the region.

For more information and additional bibliography, *see* VERNACULAR ARCHITECTURE, §II, 7.

BIBLIOGRAPHY
O. Reuther: *Das Wohnhaus in Baghdad und anderen Städten des Irak* (Berlin, 1910)
L. Gardet: *La Cité musulmane: Vie sociale et politique* (Paris, 1969)
J. L. Abu-Lughod: *Cairo: 1001 Years of the City Victorious* (Princeton, 1971)
L. C. Brown: *From Madina to Metropolis: Heritage and Change in the Near Eastern City* (Princeton, 1973)
J. Revault and B. Maury: *Palais et maisons du Caire du XIVe au XVIIIe siècle*, 3 vols (Cairo, 1975–9)
J. P. Greenlaw: *The Coral Buildings of Suakin* (London, 1976)
G. Michell, ed.: *Architecture of the Islamic World: Its History and Social Meaning* (London, 1978)
S. Bianca: *Städtebau in islamischen Ländern* (Zurich, 1980)
A. Abdel Nour: *Introduction à l'histoire urbaine de la Syrie ottomane* (Beirut, 1982)
I. Serageldin and S. El-Sadek: *The Arab City: Its Character and Islamic Cultural Heritage* (Riyadh, 1982)
F. Varanda: *The Art of Building in Yemen* (Cambridge, MA, 1982)
J. Warren and I. Fethi: *Traditional Houses in Baghdad* (Horsham, 1982)
S. H. Eldem: *Turkish Houses: Ottoman Period*, 2 vols (Istanbul, 1984–6)
F. Fusaro: *La città islamica* (Rome, 1984)
Ö. Küçükerman: *Turk evi, Turkish House* (Istanbul, 1984)
K. Talib: *Shelter in Saudi Arabia* (London, 1984)
A. Raymond: *Les Grandes Villes arabes à l'époque ottomane* (Paris, 1985)
H. Djait: *Al-Kufa: Naissance de la ville islamique* (Paris, 1986)
S. B. Hakim: *Arab-Islamic Cities: Building and Planning Principles* (London, 1986)
A. D. C. Hyland and A. Al-Shahi: *The Arab House* (Newcastle upon Tyne, 1986)
M. Musselmani: *Damascene Homes* (Damascus, 1988)
S. Bianca: *Hofhaus und Paradiesgarten* (Munich, 1991)
K. Mechta: *Maghrib: Architecture, urbanisme* (Paris, 1991)

JOHN WARREN

III. Arts of the book.

The arts of the book were of extraordinary importance throughout the Islamic lands because of the primacy Islam accorded the written word. The Islamic world inherited earlier traditions of book format, such as the codex and roll, but developed a distinctive form of the codex with a horizontal format for early manuscripts of the Koran and used the roll in a vertical format exclusively for legal documents (*see* TUGHRA). Books were elaborately calligraphed in a variety of scripts and decorated with non-representational and figural ornament and illustration, although figural decoration is restricted primarily to non-religious texts. The art of papermaking was developed to a high degree in the Islamic world, which was responsible for the transfer of this technique from China to the West, and such related techniques as marbling and papercuts were also turned into arts. Manuscripts and albums of calligraphy and painting were enclosed in fine bindings of leather and pasteboard, which were often stamped, cut, painted and gilded. Although block-printing was used sporadically, the manuscript tradition remained vital; printing with movable type was introduced only at a relatively late date.

1. Introduction. 2. Calligraphy. 3. Painted decoration. 4. Painted illustration. 5. Paper. 6. Papercuts. 7. Binding. 8. Printing.

1. INTRODUCTION. As the languages written in the Arabic script (e.g. Arabic, Persian, Ottoman Turkish and Urdu) read from right to left, books in the Islamic lands have a format opposite to that of books written in Western languages: they are hinged on the right side, and the fore-edge and envelope flaps of the bindings are on the left. The text reads from what would be to Western eyes the back of the book. The flyleaf (fol. 1*r*, and in all Islamic books a left-hand page) is often left blank or inscribed with the ex-libris. This may contain a simple inscription, seal or elaborate rosette with such information as the name of the person for whom the manuscript was copied or its owner. The text itself usually begins on fol. 1*v* (in all Islamic books a right-hand page), and the title of the work is often written above the text in a larger and more decorative hand. Some books have pairs of decorative pages inserted between the flyleaf and the beginning of the text. In manuscripts of the Koran these frontispieces might be geometric and arabesque designs, while in other types of manuscripts they might display scenes showing the author or patron (see fig. 110 below). In almost all cases these pages have elaborate marginal decoration with triangular projections into the right- and left-hand margins (see fig. 103 below). The colophon, found at the end of the text (or occasionally at the end of a section of the

text), gives information about the scribe and date and place of copying (see COLOPHON, §4). Since Islamic bindings were easily detached from the body of the book, the front and back pages were most subject to wear and are often missing. Basic information about books has thereby been lost.

Illustrated books, which were always a tiny minority of those produced in the Islamic world, have received attention from art historians, who have usually considered them quite separate from unillustrated books, which have normally been the domain of librarians and historians of literature. The calligraphy can range from the pedestrian to the superb, the decoration from the simple to the sublime. Patrons of the arts of the Islamic book enjoyed plain, decorated and illustrated copies equally, but the study of the luxury book within the larger context of book production is relatively new.

The patronage of books ranged from royal commissions, such as the mammoth and heavily illustrated copy (dispersed, ex-Houghton priv. col.; e.g. New York, Met.) of Firdawsi's *Shāhnāma* ('Book of kings'; see §4(vi)(a) below) made for the Safavid shah Tahmasp I (reg 1524–76), to books made for the market. The latter included repetitive and hackneyed copies in the Turkoman Commercial style (see §4(v)(e) below) of such standard works as the *Shāhnāma* as well as fine manuscripts by famous hands. The only surviving manuscript of the Koran by the noted Baghdadi calligrapher IBN AL-BAWWAB, for example, is a small copy (Dublin, Chester Beatty Lib., MS. 1431; see fig. 97 below) made in 1000–01 for sale, to judge from the absence of a patron's name on the flyleaf or in the colophon. Manuscripts made on commission for noted patrons may reveal specific concerns of the patron, while those made for sale can illustrate more general tastes of the time.

Books were prized possessions throughout the Islamic world and were available for consultation in public and private libraries (Arab. *maktaba*; Pers. *kitābkhāna*; Turk. *kütüphane*). Rulers often had large libraries. One of the most famous was that founded by the ABBASID caliph al-Ma'mun (reg AD 813–33) at Baghdad in conjunction with an academy designed to procure translations of ancient texts. The library of al-Hakam II (reg 961–76), the Umayyad caliph of Spain, is said to have contained 400,000 volumes listed by title in a catalogue of 44 volumes, each of 20 folios. When the library of the Fatimid caliphs of Egypt was plundered in 1068, one witness saw 25 camels laden with books brought to the residence of a single vizier, and another reported that the piles of burning books made the streets run with molten silver and gold. Libraries were often housed in separate buildings: that of the BUYID ruler 'Adud al-Dawla (reg 949–83) at Shiraz, for example, was a complex of structures surrounded by gardens with lakes and waterways; it had 360 domed rooms on two storeys. Nevertheless, collections of books did not always remain in place: the Mughal emperor Humayun (reg 1530–56 with interruption) reportedly took his library of rare books on campaign in boxes strapped on the backs of camels, and the number of books captured by the Ottomans from the Safavids at the Battle of Chaldiran in 1514 (see §4(vi)(a) below) suggests that this practice was not limited to the Mughals alone. Books were

also prized booty: Timur (reg 1370–1405; see §4(v)(d) below) sent captured books and craftsmen back to his capital at Samarkand, and the Ottoman sultan Mehmed II (reg 1444–81 with interruption) stipulated that books should be part of the ransom for the Aqqoyunlu prince Yusufça Mirza, captured in 1472.

Libraries were staffed with a director, librarian(s), attendants and copyists, for copying was the major method used to acquire texts in the era before printing. The Ilkhanid vizier RASHID AL-DIN, for example, specified in the endowment deed for his tomb complex that manuscripts of his works and other texts were to be copied annually and distributed throughout the realm. In later periods, under the Timurid, Safavid, Ottoman and Mughal rulers, royal scriptoria produced particularly elaborate volumes which were often illustrated. Some patrons were noted littérateurs themselves, such as Ahmad Jalayir (reg 1382–1410; see JALAYIRID, (1)) and Husayn Bayqara (reg 1470–1506; see TIMURID, §II(8)) of Herat; the Zirid ruler al-Mu'izz ibn Badis (reg 1016–62; see also §2(i)(c) below) was a noted authority on the arts of the book, including papermaking, binding and gilding. The most famous patron of the arts of the book is the Timurid prince Baysunghur (1397–1433; see §2(iv)(a) below and TIMURID, §II(7)); his studio in Herat is known to have produced over 20 de luxe, illustrated manuscripts which remained a standard to which others aspired for generations. One of the greatest patrons, the Mughal emperor Akbar (reg 1556–1605; see §4(vi)(d) below), is said to have been illiterate, although he appreciated having books read to him and the many dramatic illustrations accompanying his books would have enhanced their appeal.

In earlier periods the several steps in the preparation of a book may have been accomplished by the same person. Yahya ibn Mahmud al-Wasiti, for example, is known to have transcribed and illustrated a copy of al-Hariri's *Maqāmāt* ('Assemblies') in 1236 (Paris, Bib. N., MS. arab. 5847; see §4(iv)(c) below). By the 15th century the production of luxury manuscripts was such an elaborate process that specialists, or even teams of specialists, were required for calligraphy, decoration, gilding, illustration and binding. A manuscript of Jami's *Haft awrang* ('Seven thrones'; Washington, DC, Freer, 46.12), for example, was copied by no fewer than five master calligraphers working over nine years (1556–65) in three different cities. The complicated paintings in such luxury manuscripts were undoubtedly executed by several artists and apprentices; by the late 16th century in the Indian subcontinent their specific roles are described as design, painting or colouring, and portraits or faces.

The arts of the book reached an apogee in the 16th century, particularly in the Ottoman empire, Iran, western Central Asia and the Indian subcontinent. A wide range of literary, historical and scientific manuscripts was illustrated for a variety of patrons, and single pages of calligraphy and painting were collected in albums (see ALBUM, §3), together with European prints and drawings acquired through increased commercial and diplomatic contacts with Europe. Despite the increased popularity of single images and panel paintings, the manuscript tradition remained vital until the 19th century, when printing

Arabic-script languages with movable type or lithography became accepted.

BIBLIOGRAPHY

Enc. Islam/2: 'Kitāb' [book]
A. Grohmann and T. W. Arnold: *Denkmäler islamischer Buchkunst* (Leipzig, 1929); Eng. trans. as *The Islamic Book* (New York, 1929)
J. Pedersen: *Den arabiske bog* [The Arabic book] (Copenhagen, 1946); Eng. trans. by G. French, ed. R. Hillenbrand (Princeton, 1984)
B. W. Robinson, ed.: *Islamic Painting and the Arts of the Book*, The Keir Collection (London, 1976)
F. Çağman and Z. Tanındı: *Topkapı Saray Museum: Islamic Miniature Painting* (Istanbul, 1979); rev. as *The Topkapı Saray Museum: The Albums and Illustrated Manuscripts*, ed. J. M. Rogers (Boston, 1986)
Arts of the Islamic Book: The Collection of Prince Sadruddin Aga Khan (exh. cat. by A. Welch and S. C. Welch, New York, Asia Soc. Gals; Fort Worth, TX, Kimbell A. Mus.; Kansas City, MO, Nelson–Atkins Mus. A.; 1982–3)
G. D. Lowry with S. Nemazee: *A Jeweler's Eye: Islamic Arts of the Book from the Vever Collection* (Washington, DC, 1988)
F. Déroche: *The Abbasid Tradition*, The Nasser D. Khalili Collection of Islamic Art, i (London, 1992)
D. James: *The Master Scribes*, The Nasser D. Khalili Collection of Islamic Art, ii (London, 1992)
——: *After Timur*, The Nasser D. Khalili Collection of Islamic Art, iii (London, 1992)

SHEILA S. BLAIR, JONATHAN M. BLOOM

2. CALLIGRAPHY. The calligrapher and his art were central to Islamic culture. The KORAN, the word of God revealed in Arabic to the Prophet Muhammad, gives the art of writing a special place in Muslim thought and life. The letters in which the Koran was recorded spread to all areas where Muslims were found and became the badge of identity for the Muslim community. The Arabic script was adopted for writing Persian and Turkish; to change the script, as Kemal Atatürk did in Turkey in 1928, signalled a break from this religious and cultural tradition. The earliest Arabic books were written on parchment in angular scripts, often known as kufic (*see* §(ii)(b) below). By AD 900 parchment began to be replaced by paper and the angular scripts by cursive hands. These had long been used for everyday writing, but they were codified and made suitable for the copying of books. After 1400, calligraphers in the Iranian lands developed new scripts particularly suited to Persian poetry. Despite the impact of printing and lithography after 1800, calligraphy remains the pre-eminent art form in the Islamic world and has moved into such new media as painting on canvas and sculpture. Writing also appears prominently on virtually every other medium of Islamic art (e.g. *see* §II, 9(vi) above; and §§IV, 1(v) and V, 1 below) in different styles according to the nature of the material. These epigraphic scripts often degenerated because many craftsmen were illiterate and merely copied designs prepared by master calligraphers. Pseudo-inscriptions often appear on metalwork, ceramics and woven fabrics, especially carpets, testifying to the symbolic importance of writing in Islamic art.

(i) Introduction. (ii) Before *c.* AD 900. (iii) *c.* AD 900–*c.* 1400. (iv) *c.* 1400–*c.* 1800. (v) After *c.* 1800.

(i) Introduction. The central role of writing in Islamic culture is stated unequivocally in the Koran. It speaks of the 'well-preserved tablet' and the 'celestial pen' and states that God 'taught man by the pen' (*Sūrat al-balad* ('The city') xc.3). *'Nūn* ('By the pen'), the first verse of the chapter entitled *Sūrat al-qalam* ('The pen'; lxviii), is often understood as an allusion to the exalted status of writing.

Angels sit on everyone's shoulders to record their actions in the book of works that will be presented on the Day of Judgement (*Sūrat al-infiṭār* ('The cleavage') lxxxii.10–12). When the Koran was first revealed the text was scribbled on various materials such as bovine shoulder blades, leather and parchment in an ungainly script that represented only the consonants and long vowels in angular characters. It was soon considered important to write the word of God in clear, beautiful letters, which helped the reciters (Arab. *qāri'*) and at the same time had an iconic quality. Cursive scripts for daily use always existed alongside the more formal scripts, and the burgeoning bureaucracy necessitated specialists for various types of chancellery scripts. These scribes (Arab. *kātib*) co-existed with copyists (*warrāq*; often also booksellers) and calligraphers (*khaṭṭāṭ*). Calligraphers underwent arduous training and often achieved high rank. From early Islamic times connoisseurs eagerly collected specimens of master calligraphers, preserving many early works and encouraging copying; forgeries are also known from an early date. Biographical dictionaries, which mention anyone noted for fine handwriting in a certain style, and numerous treatises on calligraphy, are other sources of information.

(a) Forms, materials and equipment. (b) Calligraphers and their education. (c) Treatises.

(a) Forms, materials and equipment. Like Hebrew and Syriac, Arabic is written and read from right to left. The Arabic alphabet (see fig. 91) contains 28 letters, of which three can represent consonants or long vowels. Short vowels are not usually written; sometimes they are represented by small marks above or below the consonant. There are only 17 letter forms to represent the 28 letters, and small dots called diacritical points are placed above or below the consonant to distinguish different consonants of the same form. Most letters can be connected to those around them by means of ligatures, or connecting strokes; six can be connected only to preceding letters. The letter forms change according to their position in a word; the free-standing form is usually distinct from the initial, medial and final forms. Most letters sit on an imaginary base-line; some, such as *alif* and *lām*, which together form the common definite article *al-*, are vertical strokes, while others, such as the tails of *sīn*, *nūn* and *yā'*, descend below the line. A combination of the letters *lām* and *alif* is often recognized as the 29th letter of the alphabet. Persian, Ottoman, Urdu, Sindhi, Pashto, Malay and other languages add extra diacritical points or marks to represent additional consonants.

The art of calligraphy comprised many parts. A system of proportion was developed by Ibn Muqla in the early 10th century to regularize the shapes of individual letters as well as the relations between letters. The rhombic dot produced by a short stroke of the traditional reed pen was used as the proportional module: letters were measured in numbers of dots (*see* §(iii)(c) below). Different letters connect in different places: *mīm*, for example, connects to the preceding letter on the top right and to the following letter on the bottom left. The letters of a word with several *mīm*s, such as Muhammad, could be stacked along a line oblique to the page. The calligrapher had to anticipate the requirements of the script, and often used the ligatures to

The Arabic Alphabet					
Name	Transcription	Final	Medial	Initial	Independent
alif	ā	ﻞ	ﻟ	ا	ا
bā'	b	ﺐ	ﺒ	ﺑ	ب
tā'	t	ﺖ	ﺘ	ﺗ	ت
thā'	th	ﺚ	ﺜ	ﺛ	ث
jīm	j	ﺞ	ﺠ	ﺟ	ج
ḥā'	ḥ	ﺢ	ﺤ	ﺣ	ح
khā'	kh	ﺦ	ﺨ	ﺧ	خ
dāl	d	ﺪ	ﺪ	ﺩ	د
dhāl	dh	ﺬ	ﺬ	ﺫ	ذ
rā'	r	ﺮ	ﺮ	ﺭ	ر
zā'	z	ﺰ	ﺰ	ﺯ	ز
sīn	s	ﺲ	ﺴ	ﺳ	س
shīn	sh	ﺶ	ﺸ	ﺷ	ش
ṣād	ṣ	ﺺ	ﺼ	ﺻ	ص
ḍād	ḍ	ﺾ	ﻀ	ﺿ	ض
ṭā'	ṭ	ﻂ	ﻄ	ﻃ	ط
ẓā'	ẓ	ﻆ	ﻈ	ﻇ	ظ
'ayn	'	ﻊ	ﻌ	ﻋ	ع
ghayn	gh	ﻎ	ﻐ	ﻏ	غ
fā'	f	ﻒ	ﻔ	ﻓ	ف
qāf	q	ﻖ	ﻘ	ﻗ	ق
lām	l	ﻞ	ﻠ	ﻟ	ل
mīm	m	ﻢ	ﻤ	ﻣ	م
nūn	n	ﻦ	ﻨ	ﻧ	ن
hā'	h	ﻪ	ﻬ	ﻫ	ه
wāw	w/ū	ﻮ	ﻮ	ﻭ	و
yā'	y/ī	ﻲ	ﻴ	ﺑ	ي
lām-alif	lā	ﻼ	ﻼ	ﻻ	ﻻ

91. Chart of the Arabic alphabet

display his skill and inventiveness. The extension of the rhombic dot produced by the reed pen into the vertical stroke representing *alif*, the first letter of the alphabet, and the importance of *alif* for the proportion of all other letters, offered Sufis a symbol for the creation of the world out of the One: *alif*, the first letter of Allah (God), stands for his unity and unicity.

Parchment was the favoured material for manuscripts during the first centuries of Islam, and it was produced in various qualities. Copies of the Koran (Arab. *muṣḥaf*) on parchment were gathered in boxes or bound volumes, not kept in scrolls as was typical of books in Classical antiquity. Some copies were very large, with a broad format and only three to five lines per page; others were miniature, the smallest known measuring 40×70 mm (e.g. Cambridge, MA, Sackler Mus.). After the conquest of Egypt in 641 papyrus became a common material used primarily for secular writings, such as official correspondence, legal documents, registers, tax receipts and the like (*see also* PAPYRUS, §2). The great revolution in material came after the Muslims became acquainted with paper (*see* §5 below), which is traditionally ascribed to the capture of Chinese prisoners in 751 near Samarkand. Although Chinese paper continued to be used for special purposes, paper-mills were soon established in various parts of the Islamic world. The introduction of paper, which was cheaper than parchment and much easier to handle than papyrus, seems to have had a considerable effect on the shape of books and the evolution of styles of writing (see fig. 92). The earliest surviving book written on paper (866–7) is a fragmentary copy of Abu 'Ubayd's work on unusual terms in the Hadith (Leiden, Bib. Rijksuniv.); the earliest surviving Koran manuscript on paper (971–2; Istanbul, U. Lib., A. 6778) has a rectangular format instead of the broad, horizontal one of earlier vellum copies. As a result of the change in format, vertical letters became more elongated and the crouching lower letters more distinct from the slim taller ones. As paper was smoother than papyrus, the single letters could be drawn with greater fluidity. Coloured papers, like coloured parchment, were used for important texts. Paper was usually treated with a kind of starch (Arab. *ahar*) and burnished with a round stone, preferably an agate. A blind-tooled ruler (Arab. *mastar, mistar*) was sometimes used to mark the lines lightly before writing. It

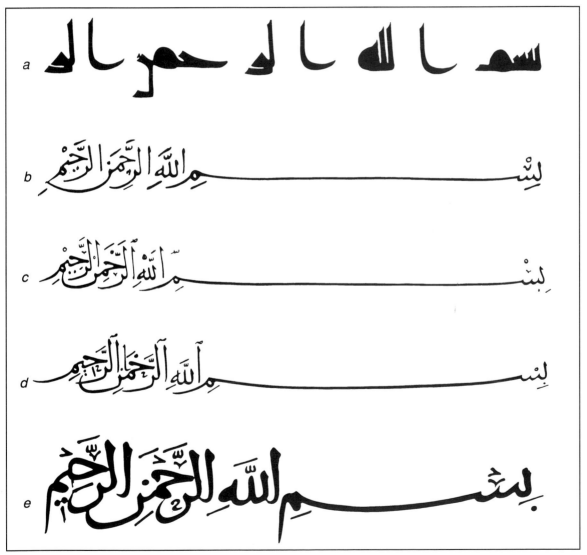

92. Different forms of the basmala, the invocation of the name of God that starts most chapters in the Koran: 'In the name of God, the merciful, the compassionate' (Arab. *bismillāh al-raḥmān al-raḥīm*): (a) Kufic from a manuscript of the Koran transcribed probably in the 10th century; (b) *naskh* from a manuscript of the Koran transcribed by Ibn al-Bawwab at Baghdad, 1000–01; (c) *rayḥān* from a manuscript of the Koran transcribed by Arghun al-Kamili, *c.* 1335; (d) *muḥaqqaq* from a manuscript of the Koran transcribed at Cairo, *c.* 1370–75; (e) *thuluth* from a manuscript of the Koran transcribed at Cairo, 1304–6

consisted of a frame with cotton or silk threads drawn between its borders and was inserted between two sheets of paper and rubbed so that it left a fine imprint. Until the 15th century the margins of the page were usually left unmarked; in later manuscripts the text block was surrounded by fine lines, and in luxury manuscripts marginal decorations were often as elegant as the calligraphy itself.

The standard writing instrument was the reed pen (Arab. *qalam*; cf. Gr. *kalamos*). The best reeds came from Iraq, Egypt and Shiraz in Iran. Trimming the pen correctly was as important as knowing the rules of writing, for each style of script required a nib trimmed to a different shape. The prepared reed was placed on a small (*c.* 100 mm) tablet made of a hard material such as bone, ivory or tortoise-shell, often beautifully decorated. The nib was cut to the desired shape with a sharp penknife, and a small incision in the nib guaranteed an even flow of ink. To secure blessing, pious calligraphers preserved the cut-off pieces of pens with which they had copied the Koran or Hadith to heat the water for their funeral baths. The pens of great masters were collected by connoisseurs. Quills were rarely used; in later times a few calligraphers used steel pens. Chinese Muslims and some early Indian calligraphers used brushes.

The preparation of ink (Arab. *hibr*, *midād*) was often a trade secret. Frequently, ink was made of soot and could be washed off easily (hence the common allusion by poets to their tears of repentance that might wash off the record of their black sins). Ottoman calligraphers sometimes collected the soot produced by the oil lamps in the Süleymaniye Mosque for their ink, again to ensure heavenly blessing. The inks used on early parchment manuscripts often appear brownish. Coloured ink was used in documents and Korans where gold letters highlighted important words such as the name of God. The ink was kept in an inkwell (Arab. *dawāt*), which often formed part of a pencase. These were made of various materials ranging from brass to porcelain and were richly decorated. To control the amount of ink picked up by the pen, loose threads of raw silk or cotton (Arab. *līqa*) were placed inside the inkwell.

Special techniques of writing included *découpage* (*see* §6 below) and 'fingernail script' (Pers. *khatt-i nākhun*), in which the letters were scratched with a fingernail into the reverse side of the paper so that they appeared in relief and were often coloured or gilded.

(b) Calligraphers and their education. The Turkish saying 'Calligraphers are destined for Paradise for copying the Koran, while painters will most probably go to Hell' shows the central role of calligraphers in Islamic art. 'I could not grasp the forelock of calligraphy easily', said MIR 'ALI TABRIZI, the 15th-century calligrapher, and indeed learning this art was, and is, a long and complicated process. Guidance by a master is essential. The calligrapher resembles the Sufi, entrusting himself to a master who not only teaches him the outward skills, such as the correct position for writing with the right hand, ink preparation, pen trimming, paper burnishing and repeating the individual letters thousands of times with the paper resting on his left knee, but also introduces him to the etiquette demanded of calligraphers, who should be modest and soft,

who should maintain a state of ritual purity (as required for reciting or writing the Koran) and who must never cease practising small letters during the day and large letters in the evening. The master often instructed disciples in the secrets of letters according to the mystical tradition: each letter of the alphabet had not only an outward form and a numerical value but also an inner meaning, and Sufi thought often used metaphors drawn from the calligrapher and his art.

Students should be apprenticed at a young age because an elderly person rarely became a true master. The methods were sometimes harsh: pupils studied 'under the rod of the master'. To disobey him was a terrible breach of etiquette, and stories abound of unfortunate disciples who were cursed by the offended master and developed wounds in their fingers that never healed, or even turned blind. The master charged a fee in cash or kind, although some calligraphers gave free lessons to talented but needy children. Family members were often instructed by their elders, and thus a number of women such as Shuhda (*d* 1178) were instructed in the art. In later centuries many Muslim rulers, especially from Iran, the Indian subcontinent and Ottoman Turkey, but also from the western Islamic world, excelled in calligraphy (see fig. 93). Some made a living from copying and selling the Koran so as not to use moneys from the public treasury.

After many years of instruction and practice copying classical works, the calligrapher received his *ijāza*, permission to sign his pages using the formula 'so-and-so has

93. Calligraphic exercise by the Timurid prince Baysunghur and his companions, ink on paper, 680×600 mm, from Herat, *c.* 1420–30 (Istanbul, Topkapı Palace Library, H. 2152, fol. 31b)

written it' (*katabahu . . .*). The practice sheets of good calligraphers became collectors' items because of the elegant shapes, even of meaningless combinations of letters. A calligrapher's speed varied between 50 and 500 lines of Persian poetry per day. Some boasted of writing one-thirtieth of the Koran daily; others needed a year to complete a fine copy. If a calligrapher was appreciated by his patron he received a good salary and grants of property; in Iran and India he was sometimes honoured by such lofty titles as 'golden pen' (Pers. *ẕarrīn qalam*) or 'one with jewel-like letters' (Pers. *jawāhir raqam*) and attained a high rank.

(*c*) *Treatises.* The interest in calligraphy led to the composition of numerous treatises on the subject, including rhymed instructions in both Arabic and Persian. One of the first known special treatises is the *'Umdat al-kuttāb* ('Staff of the scribes') by the Zirid ruler al-Mu'izz ibn Badis (*reg* 1016–62). This book describes the preparation of pens, inks, dyed papers and bookbindings. Other treatises were written for the Mamluk sultans of Egypt (*reg* 1250–1517). They themselves were hardly masters of the craft, since many were illiterate, but they commissioned magnificent copies of the Koran for their charitable foundations. There are also numerous handbooks for secretaries containing remarks on literary style, protocol and calligraphic techniques, such as *Adab al-kuttāb* ('Etiquette for secretaries') by al-Suli (*d* 946). The most comprehensive is *Ṣubḥ al-a'shā fī ṣinā'at al-inshā* ('The morning of the nightblind person in the technique of official writing') by al-Qalqashandi (*d* 1418), which includes a good introduction to the calligraphic styles (in vol. 3). Some artists told their life stories and the secrets of their art in lengthy Persian poems, as for example Majnun of Herat (*d* after 1503) and SULTAN 'ALI MASHHADI, whose poem is included in the compendium on calligraphy compiled in early 17th-century Iran by Qazi Ahmad ibn Mir Munshi ('the secretary'). Similar studies were written in Ottoman Turkey, where Mustafa Ali composed his *Manāqib-i hunarvarān* ('Wonderful deeds of the artists') for Sultan Murad III (*reg* 1574–95), a noted connoisseur and calligrapher himself. An important 18th-century work, Mustaqimzade's *Tuhfat-i khaṭṭāṭīn* ('Gift of the calligraphers'), enumerates hundreds of masters in various styles and, like the works mentioned above, includes personal remarks about the author's colleagues. At the end of the 19th century the first printed edition of a treatise of this kind appeared, the small but frequently used compilation by Habib, *Khaṭṭ u khaṭṭāṭān* ('Calligraphy and calligraphers').

BIBLIOGRAPHY
Enc. Islam/2: 'Dawāt' [inkwell], 'Kāghad' [paper], 'Kalam' [reed pen], 'Khaṭṭ' [writing]

Abu Bakr Muhammad ibn Yahya al-Suli: *Adab al-kuttāb* [Etiquette of secretaries] (*c.* AD 946); ed. M. Bahjat (Baghdad, AH 1341/1922)

Al-Mu'izz ibn Badis: *'Umdat al-kuttāb* [Staff of the scribes] (*c.* 1060); Eng. trans. by M. Levey as 'Mediaeval Arabic Bookmaking and its Relation to Early Chemistry and Pharmacology', *Trans. Amer. Philos. Soc.*, n. s., lii/4 (1962) [whole issue]

Shihab al-Din Ahmad al-Qalqashandi: *Ṣubḥ al-a'shā fī ṣinā'at al-inshā* [The morning of the nightblind person in the technique of official writing] (*c.* 1418); ed. M. A. Ibrahim, 14 vols (Cairo, 1931–2)

Mustafa Ali: *Manāqib-i hunarvarān* [Wonderful deeds of the artists] (1587); ed. İ. M. Kemal (Istanbul, 1926)

Qazi Ahmad ibn Mir Munshi: *Gulistān-i hunar* [Rose-garden of art] (1606); Eng. trans. by V. Minorsky as *Calligraphers and Painters* (Washington, DC, 1959)

Mustaqimzade Süleyman Sadeddin: *Tuhfet al-hattatin* [Gift of the calligraphers] (*c.* 1780); ed. İ. M. Kemal (Istanbul, 1928)

Habib: *Hatt u hattatan* [Calligraphy and calligraphers] (Istanbul, AH 1306/1888–9)

B. Moritz: *Arabic Palaeography* (Cairo and Leipzig, 1906)

C. Huart: *Les Calligraphes et les miniaturistes de l'Orient musulman* (Paris, 1908/*R* Osnabrück, 1972)

E. Kühnel: *Islamische Schriftkunst* (Berlin and Leipzig, 1942/*R* Graz, 1972)

J. Pedersen: *Den arabiske bog* [The Arabic book] (Copenhagen, 1946); Eng. trans., ed. R. Hillenbrand (Princeton, 1984)

F. Rosenthal: 'Abū Ḥaiyān al-Tawḥīdī on Penmanship', *A. Islam.*, xiii–xiv (1948), pp. 1–30

A. J. Arberry: *Specimens of Arabic and Persian Palaeography* (London, 1949)

G. Vajda: *Album de paléographie arabe* (Paris, 1958)

F. Rosenthal: 'Significant Uses of Arabic Writing', *A. Orient.*, iv (1961), pp. 15–23

J. Sourdel-Thomine: 'L'Ecriture arabe et son évolution ornementale', *L'Ecriture et la psychologie des peuples* (Paris, 1963), pp. 249–61

A. Grohmann: *Arabische Paläographie*, 2 vols (Vienna, 1967–71)

N. Zayn al-Din: *Muṣawwar al-khaṭṭ al-'arabī* [Atlas of Arabic calligraphy] (Baghdad, AH 1388/1968/*R* AH 1394/1974)

A. Schimmel: *Islamic Calligraphy* (Leiden, 1970)

M. Lings: *The Quranic Art of Calligraphy and Illumination* (London, 1976)

The Qur'ān (exh. cat. by M. Lings and Y. H. Safadi, London, BM, 1976)

Y. H. Safadi: *Islamic Calligraphy* (London, 1978)

Calligraphy in the Arts of the Muslim World (exh. cat. by A. Welch, New York, Asia Soc. Gals; Cincinnati, OH, A. Mus.; Seattle, WA, A. Mus.; St Louis, MO, A. Mus.; 1979)

G. Endress: 'Die arabische Schrift' and 'Handschriftenkunde', *Grundriss der arabischen Philologie*, ed. W. Fischer, i (Wiesbaden, 1982), pp. 165–97, 271–96

A. Schimmel: *Calligraphy and Islamic Culture* (New York, 1984)

M. Bayani: *Ahvāl va āṣār-i khwushnavīsān* [Biographies and works of calligraphers], 2nd edn in 4 vols (Tehran, Iran. Solar 1363/1984–5)

From Concept to Context: Approaches to Asian and Islamic Calligraphy (exh. cat. by S. Fu, G. D. Lowry and A. Yonemura, Washington, DC, 1986)

Islamic Calligraphy/Calligraphie islamique (exh. cat., Geneva, Mus. A. & Hist., 1988)

ANNEMARIE SCHIMMEL

(*ii*) *Before* c. AD *900.* This was the period in which the plain writing of Arabic was transformed into a calligraphic script, one of the most sublime products of Islamic civilization. The genesis of the Arabic alphabet probably began in the second half of the 4th century and was complete by the beginning of the 6th, when the fundamental and distinctive marks of Arabic writing seem to have been fixed. The development of Arabic writing in the first century of Islam (early 7th century to early 8th) can only be gleaned from various papyri and inscriptions. But the development of the arts of the Arabic book, and particularly its calligraphy, can be traced confidently from the period when the ABBASID caliphs ruled at Baghdad (749–1258).

(*a*) *Early evidence.* Reconstructing the early history of Arabic script requires prudence. According to certain Arabic texts, which depend on late 8th- and early 9th-century sources, the Arabic alphabet originated in Mesopotamia, to the west and south of Baghdad, in the ancient cities of al-Anbar and then al-Hira (both on the Euphrates), and from there it spread to the Hejaz (western Arabia) at the end of the 6th century. Epigraphic evidence, however, points to the frontier between Arabia and Syria. The oldest examples of Arabic writing, dating between 512 and 568, are three inscriptions from the south and south-east of Damascus and the trilingual inscription (Brussels, Musées Royaux A. & Hist.) found to the south-east of Aleppo at Zabad (Zebed). The most commonly proposed hypothesis connects the ductus, or general shape of the letters, used in these inscriptions with Nabataean script, particularly that found in late inscriptions of the 3rd and 4th centuries. The most important of these is from al-Namara in south-west Syria (328), and is an Arabic text written in Nabataean characters. Another hypothesis, which fits fairly well with textual accounts, sees Syriac, as written at al-Hira, as the prototype from which the Arabic alphabet developed. But there is no physical evidence to support this view.

The Arabic system of writing (see fig. 91 above) belongs to a north-west Semitic alphabet, the history of which began in the second half of the 2nd millennium BC. The Arabic alphabet basically records consonants like its predecessors, but it differs from them in several important ways. Arabic did not maintain a monumental form, in which the letters are separated from each other, alongside a cursive form, in which the letters are connected; instead Arabic writing is characterized by ligatures between letters. Therefore 'cursive' can only be used in describing Arabic writing to distinguish styles derived from the natural movements of the hand from other styles, the execution of which is more studied. Arabic also had more consonants than other north-west Semitic languages, and introduced diacritical points to expand the limited repertory of 17 different characters to record its 28 phonemes. (*See also* §(i)(a) above.)

When Muhammad began to preach Islam, in the early 7th century AD, writing was already practised in the Hejaz and the rest of Arabia: pre-Islamic poetry makes numerous references, both direct and indirect, to writing. In the Koran the message transmitted by Muhammad is called a writing or a book (Arab. *kitāb*), and the text abounds with technical terms such as reed pen and tablet. Finally, the diverse accounts relating to Muhammad, including the Hadith, biographies of him and lists of his secretaries, show that knowing how to write was in no way exceptional. The Koran speaks of *al-nabī al-ummī* (*Sūrat al-a'rāf* ('The ramparts') vii.158), which is read by traditionalists as the 'unlettered Prophet' and is taken as evidence that Muhammad did not know how to read or write. Western Orientalists, however, often interpret this phrase as the 'Prophet of the common folk'. Whatever the case may be, the revelations of the Prophet began to be written down during his lifetime, well before the third caliph 'Uthman (*reg* 644–56) had a definitive recension of the Koranic text made and copies distributed to the important centres of the Muslim lands. Unfortunately none of these manuscripts has been preserved. Sources have, however, preserved the names of calligraphers and even vague biographical information about them, but their styles of writing are described too summarily to allow a reconstruction of the history of calligraphy on this basis. For example, Khalid ibn Abu'l-Hayyaj is recorded in the *Fihrist* ('Index') of al-Nadim (late 10th century) as a calligrapher and epigrapher for the UMAYYAD caliph al-Walid (*reg* 705–15): he was the first to calligraph the Koran, and he also designed the Koranic inscription that once decorated the

mihrab in the mosque of Medina, but the nature of his work remains a mystery.

The only evidence of Arabic writing in the 7th century is provided by early (and rare) papyri and some inscriptions, which date between 642 and 677. The papyri, although ungainly, show a utilitarian cursive close to standard Arabic script. This cursive, often called *naskh* (from the verb 'to copy'), is clearly connected to pre-Islamic prototypes, as are the inscriptions, although these are stylized, regularized and geometricized. The caliph 'Abd al-Malik (*reg* 685–705) imposed Arabic as the official language of the chancellery, and the rough scripts used earlier were transformed into codified systems of calligraphy. The inscription on the Dome of the Rock in Jerusalem (691–2; *see* JERUSALEM, §II, 1(iii)) is stunning proof of the new style of writing. Historical and literary texts suggest similarly that styles of writing began to multiply, rules of usage to be defined and the position of the calligrapher to be elevated.

Calligraphy was naturally applied to the copying of the Koranic text. At first the script used in Koran manuscripts remained relatively close to the standard hand; this style, succinctly described in the *Fihrist* as that of Mecca and Medina, was identified by Amari in the middle of the 19th century and renamed *hijāzī* by Abbott in the 20th. The salient characteristic of this script, which is basically cursive, is that the stroke of the *alif* leans towards the right and has a lower return; it is found in manuscripts executed in a variety of styles. Each *hijāzī* manuscript is internally consistent, reflecting the independence of the copyists from any imposed uniformity. *Hijāzī* is found on many fragments datable to the 7th century (e.g. Paris, Bib. N., MS. arab. 328a) and was common in the 8th, showing that the use of this style, which was identified with the most sacred moments in Islamic history, was maintained despite the introduction of other more elaborate styles. This style of writing is not found in any of the Koran manuscripts traditionally attributed to the caliph 'Uthman (e.g. Istanbul, Mus. Turk. & Islam. A., MS. 457) or the fourth caliph 'Ali (*reg* 656–61; e.g. Istanbul, Topkapı Pal. Lib., E.H. 2), which are actually later manuscripts of the 8th or 9th century. Distinct variants of *hijāzī* also existed, one of which is known as *mā'il* ('sloping'). It is distinguished by a staff-like *alif* without a lower return (e.g. London, BM, Or. MS. 2165). These variants may reflect the influence of later non-cursive styles; on the other hand, these later non-cursive styles may have been adapted to the canons of *hijāzī* in deference to it.

(b) Early Abbasid scripts. The following phase in the history of Arabic calligraphy is traditionally discussed under the rubric 'kufic', referring to Kufa, a city in southern Iraq and intellectual centre in the first centuries of Islam. Historical sources do not describe the characteristics of the term kufic but use it imprecisely to designate all ancient scripts. Orientalists began to use the term at the end of the 18th century, but by the beginning of the 19th they realized that it was inadequate to describe the astonishing variety of scripts used. It is preferable, at least as far as manuscripts are concerned, to use the term 'early Abbasid scripts' for those used from the second half of the 8th century to the first half of the 10th. This period coincides

with the height of Abbasid sovereignty, although the origins of some scripts are to be found earlier. Cursive hands were still used in daily affairs, but the art of calligraphy sought its inspiration elsewhere.

Calligraphy flourished during this period, to judge from surviving manuscripts. These are primarily Korans, but several non-Koranic specimens (e.g. Paris, Bib. N., MS. arab. 2047) suggest a more generalized use of these scripts. Production was essentially anonymous: signed and dated works are exceptional. Lacking such precise indicators, the chronology, localization and even classification of manuscripts and styles are problematic. These manuscripts can, however, be tentatively classified on palaeographic grounds. Early Abbasid scripts developed in connection with a new format: while most of the *ḥijāzī* Korans have a vertical format, those of the 8th to 10th centuries were generally copied on horizontal pages. The reasons for this break with tradition, whether aesthetic or ideological, are obscure. Texts indicate that styles of script were defined by their size, and the study of manuscripts reveals the close connection between a style of script and a fixed module. Two styles of the 9th century, which Déroche (1983–5) labelled BII and DI, demonstrate that the shapes of letters combine with features relative to their size. In manuscripts copied in BII style (e.g. Paris, Bib. N., MS. arab. 340f), each line occupies c. 4–6 mm, whereas in DI (e.g. Dublin, Chester Beatty Lib., MS. 1407; see fig. 94), each line occupies between 11 and 22 mm.

After the formative period, in which verticality was the most striking characteristic, calligraphers favoured relatively 'thick' scripts in which horizontality dominated. The horizontality is emphasized by the ligatures and the letters that follow the line (e.g. *ṣād* or *dāl*); it is reinforced by the teeth of such letters as *bā'* and *sīn* and by the circular forms of the letters *fā'* and *mīm*. In early Abbasid scripts the ductus is balanced between the vertical and horizontal axes. Apart from such forms as the isolated *alif*, or the final *jīm* or *'ayn*, developed curves are relatively rare, but it cannot properly be called angular. The horizontal elongation of the body of the letter (Arab. *mashq*) is quite common, whether for convenience or because of the artist's desire for a particular effect. The calligrapher was still relatively free to do as he pleased: he could cut off words at the end of a line, something unthinkable later, superpose letters, create geometric motifs over the whole page, juxtapose inks of different colours, or even make the text stand out by using a tinted ground. For example, the dispersed Blue Koran (9th or 10th century; e.g. Tunis, Mus. N. Bardo) has gold letters and silver markers on vellum dyed deep blue with indigo. The calligrapher had total latitude to create hybrid styles and could mix the letter forms of different styles or use a style in a smaller or larger module than usual.

In the late 9th century and early 10th there was a return to manuscripts in the vertical format. This change may have been connected to the substitution of paper for parchment as the primary writing surface. The aesthetic that had dominated most of the 9th century was gradually abandoned, and a vertical tension is discernible in the styles designated by Déroche as D Vb (e.g. Paris, Bib. N., MS. arab. 373a) and D Vc (e.g. London, N. D. Khalili priv. col., MS. KFQ91; see Déroche, 1992, no. 58), in

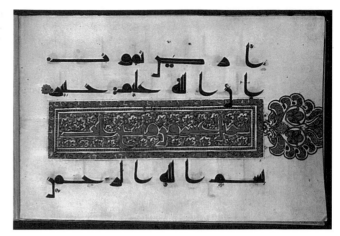

94. Early Abbasid script from a Koran, 218×323 mm, 9th century AD (Dublin, Chester Beatty Library and Gallery of Oriental Art, MS. 1407, fol. 2*v*)

which the vertical letters are much more elongated. At the same time certain less elaborate styles (Déroche group E) seem to approach cursive. Early Abbasid scripts differed considerably from the scripts used in daily life and were difficult for the untrained to read, so old forms began to be replaced by cursive ones.

BIBLIOGRAPHY

al-Nadim: *Fihrist* [Index] (987–8); Eng. trans., ed. B. Dodge as *The Fihrist of al-Nadim: A Tenth-century Survey of Muslim Culture*, 2 vols (New York, 1970)

M. Amari: 'Bibliographie primitive du Coran', annotated by H. Dérembourg, *Centenario della nascita di M. Amari*, i (Palermo, 1910), pp. 5–22

G. Bergsträsser: 'Zur ältesten Geschichte der kufischen Schrift', *Z. Dt. Ver. Bwsn & Schr.*, v–vi (1919), pp. 54–66

G. Bergsträsser and O. Pretzl: *Geschichte des Qorans*, iii (Leipzig, 1936)

N. Abbott: *The Rise of the North Arabic Script and its Kur'anic Development* (Chicago, 1939)

A. Grohmann: *Einführung und Chrestomathie zur arabischen Papyruskunde*, i (Prague, 1955)

——: 'The Problem of Dating Early Qur'ans', *Der Islam*, xxxiii (1958), pp. 213–31

S. Y. al-Jabburi: *Al-khaṭṭ al-'arabī wa-taṭawwuruhu fī'l-'uṣūr al-'abbāsiyya fī'l-'Irāq* [Arabic script and its development in the Abbasid period in Iraq] (Baghdad, 1962)

J. Sourdel-Thomine: 'Les Origines de l'écriture arabe: A propos d'une hypothèse récente', *Rev. Etud. Islam.*, xxxiv (1966), pp. 151–7

S. al-Munajjid: *Dirāsāt fī ta'rīkh al-khaṭṭ al-'arabī mundhu bidāyatihi ilā nihāyat al-'aṣr al-umawī* [Studies on the history of Arabic calligraphy from its origin until the end of the Umayyad period] (Beirut, 1972)

F. Déroche: 'Les Ecritures coraniques anciennes: Bilan et perspectives', *Rev. Etud. Islam.*, xlviii (1980), pp. 207–24

R. G. Khoury: 'Papyruskunde', *Grundriss der arabischen Philologie*, ed. W. Fischer, i (Wiesbaden, 1982), pp. 251–70

F. Déroche: *Les Manuscrits du Coran: Aux origines de la calligraphie coranique* (1983), I/i of *Manuscrits musulmans*, pt 2 of *Catalogue des manuscrits arabes*, Paris, Bib. N. cat. (Paris, 1983–5)

Maṣāḥif Ṣan'ā' [The Koran manuscripts of San'a] (exh. cat., Kuwait City, Mus. Islam. A., 1985)

J. M. Bloom: 'The Blue Koran: An Early Fatimid Kufic Manuscript from the Maghrib', *Les Manuscrits du Moyen-Orient: Essais de codicologie et de paléographie*, ed. F. Déroche (Istanbul and Paris, 1989), pp. 95–100

F. Déroche: 'A propos d'une série de manuscrits coraniques anciens', *Les Manuscrits du Moyen-Orient: Essais de codicologie et de paléographie*, ed. F. Déroche (Istanbul and Paris, 1989), pp. 101–11

E. Whelan: 'Writing the Word of God: Some Early Qur'ān Manuscripts and their Milieux, Part I', *A. Orient.*, xx (1990), pp. 113–48

F. Déroche: *The Abbasid Tradition: Qur'ans of the 8th to the 10th Centuries AD*, The Nasser D. Khalili Collection of Islamic Art, i (London, 1992)

(iii) c. 900–c. 1400. The most important development in this period was the replacement of so-called angular scripts by round hands. The latter, which had long been used for daily affairs, were codified and regularized and became suitable for copying the Koran and other manuscripts. Even before 900 early Abbasid scripts had begun to show more cursive features: the New Abbasid style that developed was transformed in the western Islamic lands (Arab. *maghrib*) into a group of distinctive regional scripts, known collectively as *maghribī*, while in the central and eastern Islamic lands six prominent round hands were canonized as the classic scripts, known collectively as the Six Pens.

(a) New Abbasid style. (b) *Maghribī* scripts. (c) The Six Pens.

(a) New Abbasid style. In the 9th century, the different types of writing—from everyday cursive hands to more studied calligraphic styles—began to come together in what Déroche (1983–5) has called the New Abbasid style (NS). This movement may have been the work of a particular individual or the result of many disparate efforts. Sources preserve the names and contributions of many calligraphers in the chancelleries, but their works have not survived. At most, textual information only supports what can be observed in the manuscripts: the relations between one script and another, the role of the module (*see* §(i)(a) above) and the size of the support. Various terms have been used to refer to this new style: eastern kufic, broken kufic, western kufic and kufic-*naskh*. This last succinctly

characterizes the new style: a cursive hand, the most elaborate versions of which preserve vestiges of early Abbasid styles. Early Abbasid scripts long co-existed with the new style, and influences were reciprocal. The new scripts were widely used to copy a great variety of manuscripts: they were popular because they were elaborate calligraphic variants of common cursive hands.

The new style, a vertical and elongated script with an accentuated angular character and deliberate contrast between thick and thin, was used from the second half of the 9th century (e.g. Dublin, Chester Beatty Lib., MS.1417) to the beginning of the 13th (e.g. Meshed, Imam Riza Shrine Lib., MS. 84). It was used over a wide area: the same style is found in the 10th century at Isfahan (e.g. Istanbul, Mus. Turk. & Islam. A., MSS 453–6) and Palermo (London, N. D. Khalili priv. col., MSS QUR261 and QUR368, dated 982–3; see Déroche, 1992, no. 81). It was also used for a variety of purposes, from personal writings and humble manuscripts (e.g. Milan, Bib. Ambrosiana, MS. 56/X) to luxury books, such as the so-called Qarmathian Koran (dispersed, e.g. Dublin, Chester Beatty Lib., MS. 1436; see fig. 95; Istanbul, Topkapı Pal. Lib., E.H. 12) and the *Kitāb al-diryāq* ('Book of antidotes', 1199; Paris, Bib. N., MS. arab. 2964; *see* §3(ii) below). The basic repertory of calligraphic letter forms is found in the script that Déroche has termed New Style I (NS I), which could be transformed by the pen of a master into a display of talent. Far from hiding the line traced by the pen, as had

95. New Abbasid style script from a dispersed manuscript of the Koran, 335×238 mm, 11th century (Dublin, Chester Beatty Library and Gallery of Oriental Art, MS. 1436, fols 9*v*–10*r*)

been the case with early Abbasid scripts, the new style made the ductus visible. The use of angular elements and the striking contrast between thick and thin give NS I a stately formality. The role of the calligrapher is clearly evident.

The apogee of NS I was the 11th century, although a mannerist tendency already appears, filling the letters with flourishes or flowers (e.g. Istanbul, Topkapı Pal. Lib., E.H. 42). This tendency may show the influence of epigraphy on calligraphy, for floriated scripts had long been common for monumental inscriptions (*see* §II, 9(vi) and fig. 83 above). At the end of the period legibility seems again to have become more important, to judge from the small-scale examples that have survived. The marked contrast between thick and thin is relegated to second place in NS III (e.g. Paris, Bib. N., MS. arab. 382a), a less polished and more rounded script. By the 13th century, New Style scripts had been totally supplanted by round hands (*see* §(c) below) and relegated to book titles and chapter headings in Koran manuscripts. The letters were transformed into deliberately complex forms, closer in character to those used in monumental epigraphy. Finally, New Style scripts degenerated into the 'kufic' of 20th-century typographers.

BIBLIOGRAPHY
S. Y. al-Jabburi: *Al-khaṭṭ al-ʿarabī wa-taṭawwuruhu fiʾl-ʿuṣūr al-ʿabbāsiyya fiʾl-ʿIrāq* [Arabic script and its development in the Abbasid period in Iraq] (Baghdad, 1962)
F. Déroche: *Les Manuscrits du Coran: Aux origines de la calligraphie coranique* (1983), I/i of *Manuscrits musulmans*, pt 2 of *Catalogue des manuscrits arabes*, Paris, Bib. N. cat. (Paris, 1983–5)
B. St Laurent: 'The Identification of a Magnificent Koran Manuscript', *Les Manuscrits du Moyen-Orient: Essais de codicologie et de paléographie*, ed. F. Déroche (Istanbul and Paris, 1989), pp. 115–24
F. Déroche: *The Abbasid Tradition: Qurʾans of the 8th to the 10th Centuries AD*, The Nasser D. Khalili Collection of Islamic Art, i (London, 1992)

(b) Maghribī scripts. Scripts used in the western Islamic lands between the 10th and the 15th century were long thought to have derived from kufic scripts (*see* §(ii)(b) above), but their origin can be traced to the New Abbasid style (*see* §(a) above); the appearance of *maghribī* should be seen as one facet of the trend that brought cursive to the fore. Certain peculiarities of the New Abbasid style were maintained throughout the long history of *maghribī*: the incurving and the upper swelling of the shafts in medium and large scripts, a hook or spur at the bottom of the final *alif*, the sloping shafts of *ṭā'* and *kāf* and ligatures with indentations. At the same time the angularities of the New Abbasid style were replaced in *maghribī* by curved and circular forms, such as the sweeping curve and deep bowl of the final *nūn* and other letters, the final form of which can be extended in this way (e.g. *lām, mīm, rā'*). The letters *fā'* and *qāf*, which in eastern Islamic lands have respectively one and two dots above the letters, have in *maghribī* script a single dot below and above the letter.

Although the major features of *maghribī* script were already in place by the late 10th century, calligraphers still seem to have used the New Abbasid style for their finest efforts, to judge from the Nurse's Koran, a manuscript copied and illuminated in 1020 by ʿAli ibn Ahmad al-Warraq ('the paperseller') for the nurse of the Zirid ruler

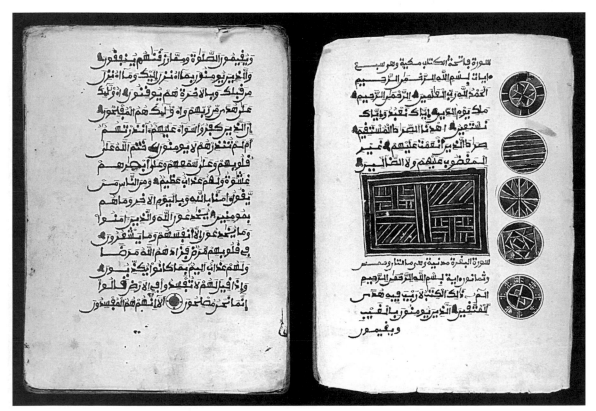

96. *Maghribī* script from a Koran, sub-Saharan Africa; 19th century (Dublin, Chester Beatty Library and Gallery of Oriental Art, MS. 1599)

al-Muʿizz ibn Badis (dispersed, e.g. Kairouan, Mus. A. Islam.; Tunis, Mus. N. Bardo). Later manuscripts show certain peculiarities that have been tentatively named after the three great centres of civilization in the western Islamic lands. Manuscripts in a small script with fine and clear letters are called *andalusī* (Andalusian). This style was maintained at least from the 12th to the 15th century (e.g. Istanbul, U. Lib., A. 6754; 1304, Paris, Bib. N., MS. arab. 385). The characteristics of the idiosyncratic *qayrawānī* (from Kairouan in Tunisia) and the larger and less compact *fāsī* (from Fez in Morocco) are not as precisely defined. This situation resulted either from the lack of systematization similar to that which took place in the East under such masters as Ibn Muqla (*see* §(c) below) or from a different system of apprenticeship. The term *maghribī* has therefore been used in a general fashion for scripts of medium and large size with the same features as the small script. Within the general rubric *maghribī*, a certain evolution can be traced in such contorted forms as the hook-like terminals of *rā'* or *ṣād* (e.g. Paris, Bib. N., MSS arab. 438–40) that were added to the simple script inherited from the prototypes. Despite a certain conservatism, marked for example by a prolonged attachment to parchment and to the old system of noting vowels with coloured marks, the calligraphic versions of *maghribī* integrated new features that reflected the vitality of a style of writing deeply rooted in daily practice. The particular aesthetic of the western Islamic lands also transformed the eastern styles, such as *thuluth*, that were adopted in the region. *Maghribī* script was further developed only in sub-Saharan Africa, where the *sūdānī* style of writing is distinguished by coarse, rough forms and frequent irregularities (e.g. Dublin, Chester Beatty Lib., MS. 1599; see fig. 96), which might reflect older practices in North Africa (e.g. *see* HAUSA, §5).

BIBLIOGRAPHY

O. Houdas: 'Essai sur l'écriture maghrébine', *Nouveaux Mél. Orient.*, 2nd ser., xix (1886), pp. 85–112

A. D. H. Bivar: 'The Arabic Calligraphy of West Africa', *Afr. Lang. Rev.*, vii (1968), pp. 3–15

A. Brockett: 'Aspects of the Physical Transmission of the Qur'an in 19th-century Sudan: Script, Decoration, Binding and Paper', *MSS Mid. E.*, ii (1987), pp. 45–67

N. van den Boogert: 'Some Notes on Maghribi Script', *MSS Mid. E.*, iv (1989), pp. 30–43

F. DÉROCHE

(c) The Six Pens.

Introduction. By far the most important development during this period in the eastern Islamic lands was the canonization of six prominent calligraphic styles as the classic scripts, known collectively as the Six Pens (Arab. *al-aqlām al-sitta*; Pers. *shash qalam*). The six consist of three sets of majuscule–minuscule pairs: *thuluth–naskh*, *muḥaqqaq–rayḥān* and *tawqīʿ–riqāʿ*. All six are round hands, and for normal uses they totally supplanted the angular scripts (*see* §§(ii)(b) and (iii)(a) above), which were then relegated to ornamental uses in frontispieces and chapter headings. The distinctions among these scripts are minor; there are almost no radical differences in letter shapes or forms among the various classic styles, although the *tawqīʿ–riqāʿ* pair allows for connections between letters that must be separated in other styles.

Scripts of the *thuluth–naskh* group are the most curvilinear. The descending tails of the letters *nūn*, *sīn* and *ṣād* are continuous curves, which can be more or less open, and the *alif* is a straight stroke tapering towards the base. *Muḥaqqaq* script is characterized by a narrow zone below the base-line, so the bowls of such descending letters as *lām* and *nūn* are quite shallow. Such letters as *rā'* and *wāw* generally end in straight, sharp tips without upturn. The top of such letters as initial *alif* and *lām* has a characteristic barb or hook (Arab. *irsāl*). *Tawqīʿ* script is characterized by distended final *nūn*s, often indistinguishable from *rā'*. The *alif* in the *alif–lām* pair dissolves into a small horizontal stroke leading into the *lām*, the initial *hā'* is distorted into a wavy line and numerous unorthodox connections are made, such as *alif* to *dāl* and *rā'* to *jīm*.

Naskh became the calligraphic norm for the copying of ordinary books and small-scale Koran manuscripts. *Thuluth* was often used for chapter headings in Koran manuscripts. It replaced the angular script for the calligraphic ornamentation of architecture, particularly in tile, a medium in which the curvilinear *thuluth* script could be easily executed (see fig. 79 above). *Naskh* and *thuluth* were taken as the exemplars for modern typography and are the most familiar and legible to ordinary readers. *Muḥaqqaq* became the almost exclusive vehicle for large-scale manuscripts of the Koran, such as the enormous 30-part copy bequeathed by the Ilkhanid sultan Uljaytu (*reg* 1304–17) to his mausoleum at Sultaniyya in Iran (1306–13; dispersed, e.g. Istanbul, Topkapı Pal. Lib., E.H. 234, 243, 245; Leipzig, Bib. U., xxxvii, K1). The more fluid *tawqīʿ* and *riqāʿ* scripts, developed for use in chancellery documents, were generally employed for colophons in manuscripts and for calligraphy in carved plaster.

Historical development. According to tradition, *muḥaqqaq* was the first round style to emerge, and it was *muḥaqqaq* that the Abbasid vizier IBN MUQLA, in the early 10th century, defined by the use of circles and rhomboids. Although his definitions were not as precise as the geometric definitions of the Roman alphabet, they served to establish the various proportions in terms of the rhombic 'dot' created by one stroke of the nib. For example, the height of the *alif* measures eight dots in *muḥaqqaq*, seven in *thuluth* and six in *tawqīʿ*; the maximum length of a horizontal bowl measures seven in *muḥaqqaq* and six in *thuluth*. These proportions give *muḥaqqaq* a more slender and elongated line than *thuluth*. Tradition also credits Ibn Muqla with the definition of *thuluth* and *naskh*. No examples of his calligraphy are known to exist.

The system established by Ibn Muqla was refined by IBN AL-BAWWAB. Attempts have been made to re-create his 'well-proportioned script' (Arab. *al-khaṭṭ al-mansūb*), but interpretations vary widely since the term itself means only 'fine script'. The only example of Ibn al-Bawwab's handwriting to survive is a small manuscript of the Koran copied in Baghdad (1000–01; Dublin, Chester Beatty Lib., MS. 1431; see fig. 97). It is the earliest surviving Koran manuscript in cursive script on paper, but there were undoubtedly earlier efforts. Written in a regular, bold *naskh* hand, the letters, words and lines are set closely

97. *Naskh* script by Ibn al-Bawwab; double page from a Koran, each folio 177×137 mm, copied at Baghdad, 1000–01 (Dublin, Chester Beatty Library and Gallery of Oriental Art, MS. 1431, fols 151*v*–152*r*)

together without sacrificing clarity. The lines of the script are meticulously straight and parallel and show no evidence of the use of a blind-tooled ruler. The decoration of the manuscript, with chapter headings, verse markers and geometric and floral arabesques in the margins and on the frontis- and finispieces, is executed in gold and a restrained palette of black, blue and white and is as remarkable as the calligraphy itself.

This system was perfected in the late 13th century by the master calligrapher YAQUT AL-MUSTA'SIMI. He replaced the straight-cut nib of the pen with an obliquely cut one, thereby creating a more elegant ductus. For this he earned the epithets 'sultan', 'cynosure' and 'qibla' of calligraphers. He is reported to have copied two Koran manuscripts each month, but few genuine examples have survived (e.g. 1289, Paris, Bib. N., MS. arab. 6716; 1294, Istanbul, Topkapı Pal. Lib., E.H. 74). His work was prized by later calligraphers and collectors, and some of his manuscripts were later refurbished with splendid illumination under the Ottomans and Safavids (e.g. 1283–4, Istanbul, Topkapı Pal. Lib., E.H. 227; 1286–7, with 16th-century illumination on the opening pages, Tehran, Archaeol. Mus., MS. 4277). Despite their small size, these Koran manuscripts are notable for the spaciousness of the layout. This is achieved in part by the fineness of the *rayḥān* calligraphy, characterized by the shallow but broad bowls of the descending letters and by the extension of the ligatures between letters.

These figures were the most notable exceptions to a tradition of anonymity, for in the early centuries of Islam calligraphers were seldom known by name and rarely signed their works. In the 14th century, however, master calligraphers emerged from the obscurity of nameless artisanship as they increasingly signed their works, and their names are preserved in literary and historical sources. Calligraphy in the 14th century was dominated by the students of Yaqut, known collectively as the Six Masters. The group comprised Nasrullah al-Tabib (Nasr al-Din

Mutatabbib; *fl* 1328–35), Ahmad al-Suhrawardi, often called Shaykhzada (*fl* 1301/2–28), Arghun ibn 'Abdallah al-Kamili (*fl* 1300–52), Mubarakshah ibn Qutb Tabrizi (*fl c.* 1323), Haydar and Yusuf Mashhadi. The Six Masters are known for the splendid Koran manuscripts they penned.

AHMAD AL-SUHRAWARDI is best known for a large 30-part Koran manuscript produced at Baghdad (1302–8; dispersed, Dublin, Chester Beatty Lib.; Istanbul, Topkapı Pal. Lib.; New York, Met.; Tehran, Archaeol. Mus.). This stunning manuscript, probably produced under royal auspices, has pages with five lines of majestic *muḥaqqaq* script without the least speck of colour. Each line has its own visual harmony, yet is conceived as part of the page as a whole. The distinctive quality of the script suggests that Ahmad was responsible for the most splendid but unsigned manuscript of the Koran produced for the Ilkhanids, that endowed to Uljaytu's mausoleum at Sultaniyya. A more modest example of his work is a one-volume manuscript copied in a careful *naskh* hand (Nov 1318; Istanbul, Mus. Turk. & Islam. A.). Mubarakshah ibn Qutb is known for a small single-volume manuscript of the Koran in *naskh* (1323; Baltimore, MD, Walters A.G.). Arghun al-Kamili, one of the finest exponents of *rayḥān*, signed two medium-sized copies of the Koran (Oct 1320, Istanbul, Mus. Turk. & Islam. A.; 1329–30, Istanbul, Topkapı Pal. Lib.). These calligraphers also prepared inscriptions for execution in other media. HAYDAR, for example, who was often known as Kanda-navis ('writer in large/cut characters'), is named in superb carved stucco inscriptions at Natanz (1309) and Isfahan (1310) in Iran. Specimens of calligraphy by the Six Masters were avidly collected, particularly by the Timurid prince and bibliophile Baysunghur (1397–1433; *see* TIMURID, §II(7)), who had examples of their work put together in the oldest known album of calligraphy (Istanbul, Topkapı Pal. Lib., H. 2152).

The Six Masters in turn passed their traditions to their pupils in Iran. YAHYA AL-SUFI is known for Koran manuscripts in *naskh* (1338–9, Istanbul, Mus. Turk. & Islam. A.; 1339–40, Dublin, Chester Beatty Lib.), as well as a larger one in *rayḥān* script (1344–6; Shiraz, Pars Mus.). 'ABDALLAH SAYRAFI was a pupil of Haydar and, like his master, designed architectural inscriptions in glazed tile. He was known as the Yaqut of his age and penned a short treatise on calligraphy (Berlin, Staatsbib. Preuss. Kultbes., Orientabt., MS. or. oct. 48). 'Umar Aqta' (literally 'one-armed') was a rare left-handed calligrapher. He is said to have presented Timur (*reg* 1370–1405) with a tiny copy of the Koran in minuscule *ghubār* ('dust') script. Timur refused to accept it as he found it too small, whereupon 'Umar penned another copy, in which each line was at least a cubit in length. Having finished, decorated and bound the manuscript, the scribe tied it on a barrow and took it to Timur's palace, where the Sultan received him in state.

In Syria and Egypt, which became the centre of Arab Islam after the Mongol conquests of the mid-13th century, the styles of writing established by Yaqut and his pupils flourished under the patronage of the Mamluk sultans, who ordered large multi-volume manuscripts of the Koran copied in *muḥaqqaq* script for their charitable foundations. In comparison with the Iranian world, the names of few calligraphers are known, although the quality of the work is extremely high. Sharaf al-Din Muhammad ibn Sharaf ibn Yusuf, known as Ibn al-Wahid (*d* 1311), is one of the few exceptions: born in Damascus, he studied under Yaqut in Baghdad, where he mastered all scripts. He then went to Cairo, where he worked for Baybars al-Jashankir (*reg* 1309), producing an unusual seven-volume Koran in

gold *thuluth* script outlined in black. The tradition of Yaqut was continued by Mubarakshah ibn Ahmad al-Dimishqi al-Suyufi, known for his superb *rayḥān* hand (e.g. a one-volume manuscript of the Koran, 1344; Istanbul, Topkapı Pal. Lib., Y. 365). Perhaps the finest manuscripts of the Koran produced under the Mamluks are associated with the patronage of Sha'ban II (*reg* 1363–76) and his mother. Six enormous manuscripts, mostly in single-volume format, are written in superb *muḥaqqaq* script. Considering the exceptionally high quality of the script and illumination, it is surprising that most of the calligraphers chose to remain anonymous.

BIBLIOGRAPHY

Qazi Ahmad ibn Mir Munshi: *Gulistān-i hunar* [Rose-garden of art] (1606); Eng. trans. by V. Minorsky as *Calligraphers and Painters* (Washington, DC, 1959)

D. Sourdel: 'Le Livre des secrétaires de 'Abdallah al-Baġdādī', *Bull. Etud. Orient.*, xiv (1952–4), pp. 115–63

D. S. Rice: *The Unique Ibn al-Bawwab Manuscript in the Chester Beatty Library* (Dublin, 1955/R Paris, 1972) [with facs.]

S. al-Munajjid: *Al-kitāb al-'arabī'l-makhṭūṭ ilā'l-qarn al-'āshir al-hijrī* [Arabic manuscript books until the 10th century of the Hegira] (Cairo, 1960)

H. Fadayili: *Aṭlas-i khaṭṭ: Taḥqīq dār khuṭūṭ-i islāmī* [Atlas of scripts: examples of Islamic scripts] (Isfahan, Iran. Solar 1350/1971)

N. Zayn al-Din: *Badā'i' al-khaṭṭ al-'arabī* [Splendours of Arabic calligraphy] (Baghdad, 1972)

A. Khatibi and M. Sijelmassi: *The Splendour of Islamic Calligraphy* (London, 1976)

The Qur'ān (exh. cat. by M. Lings and Y. H. Safadi, London, BM, 1976)

Y. H. Safadi: *Islamic Calligraphy* (London, 1978)

P. P. Soucek: 'The Arts of Calligraphy', *The Arts of the Book in Central Asia, 14th–16th Centuries*, ed. B. Gray (Boulder, CO, London and Paris, 1979), pp. 7–34

D. James: *Qur'āns of the Mamlūks* (London and New York, 1988)

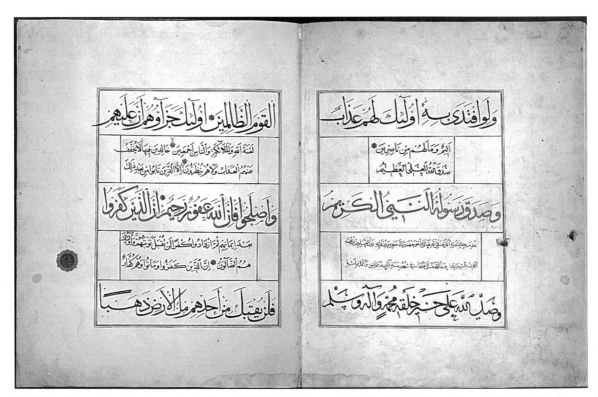

98. Calligraphic exercise with various scripts by Zayn al-'Abidin ibn Muhammad al-Katib al-Shirazi; from a Koran, 1483–4 (Dublin, Chester Beatty Library and Gallery of Oriental Art, MS. 1502, fols 24a–b)

(iv) c. 1400–c. 1800. The distinctive *maghribī* scripts continued to flourish in North Africa, and large manuscripts of the Koran continued to be produced in the central Arab lands, but the centre of creativity in all the arts of the book shifted to the Iranian world as Persian became the language of literature and art, even in the Ottoman and Mughal empires. Although written in a script developed for the Arabic language, the distinctive requirements of Persian allowed the development of new calligraphic styles, particularly more fluid scripts. These scripts were known by many names, and confusion and duplication of terminology abound. Connoisseurs began to collect specimens of fine handwriting and assemble them in albums; calligraphers began to produce calligraphic exercises in which they displayed their skill by juxtaposing several scripts (see fig. 98) or by arranging the letters and words in unusual ways. The names of many more calligraphers are known because they signed many more works and were included in biographical literature.

(a) Old scripts. (b) New scripts.

(a) Old scripts. The arts of the book had been taken to new heights of refinement and lavishness in the second half of the 14th century under the sponsorship of the successors to the Ilkhanids in the great centres of book production and illumination at Baghdad and Tabriz, but the most splendid manuscripts were those produced for the Timurid princes at Herat in western Afghanistan during the 15th century. The tradition of the Six Pens perfected by the Six Masters in the early 14th century (*see* §(iii)(c) above) continued in the early 15th. Ahmad ibn Mas'ud, known as al-Rumi (from Anatolia), for example, was a master of the Six Pens who worked in Herat under the patronage of the Timurid prince Baysunghur (1397–1433; *see* TIMURID, §II(7)), a great patron of the arts of the book and an accomplished calligrapher himself. Ahmad Rumi used *naskh* to copy the first manuscript associated with Baysunghur's patronage, al-Juzjani's history of the Mu'izzi Mamluks of Delhi, *Ṭabaqāt-i Nāṣirī* (1411–12; Berlin, Staatsbib. Preuss. Kultbes., MS. Peterman I, 386). He may well have instructed the prince, for a calligraphic exercise in which Baysunghur and his companions copied a phrase that Ahmad had executed in *riqā'* is included in the prince's album of calligraphy (Istanbul, Topkapı Pal. Lib., H. 2152, fol. 31*v*). Other masters of the Six Pens who worked at Herat during the reign of Baysunghur's father, Shahrukh (1405–47), included 'Abdallah Tabbakh, Shaykh Mahmud Haravi, Abdallah 'Murvarid' Bayani and Shams al-Din Baysunghuri.

Thuluth (Turk. *sülüs*) and *naskh* (Turk. *nesih*) became the primary scripts in the Ottoman empire. Indeed, for clarity and artistic discipline the productions of Ottoman calligraphers have never been surpassed. The most famous early Ottoman calligrapher was ŞEYH HAMDULLAH, who worked for Bayezid II (*reg* 1481–1512). He is particularly known for his calligraphic exercises that juxtapose a line of large script with several lines of smaller script, together with panels of painting and marbled paper, the whole enclosed within a ruled frame (e.g. a page in *muḥaqqaq* and *rayḥān*, Istanbul, Topkapı Pal. Lib., E.H. 2078). He and his followers in the 16th century were known as the

Seven Masters of Anatolia. They included his son and pupil, Mustafa Dede Shaykhzada (*d* 1539–40), Abdullah of Amasya, the brothers Jalal and Jamal of Amasya, Ibrahim Sharbatchizade of Bursa and Ahmad Karahisarî, who was the most famous calligrapher during the reign of Süleyman.

In addition to the Six Pens, Ahmed is known for his practice of the *musalsal* ('chained') method, where an entire phrase was written without lifting the pen from the page, such as the well-known frontispiece with the basmala (invocation of the name of God) written in *musalsal* between two panels of square writing (Istanbul, Mus. Turk. & Islam. A., MS. 1443, fols 1*r*–2*v*). This tradition was refined by HAFIZ OSMAN, the finest Ottoman calligrapher of the 17th century. He evolved an apparently simple style of *naskh* based on the principles of Yaqut (*see* §(iii)(c) above) and Hamdullah that epitomizes the clarity and elegance of Ottoman scripts (e.g. a Koran manuscript, 1663–4, Istanbul, U. Lib., A. 6549; and a calligraphic specimen, Istanbul, Topkapı Pal. Mus., 3655).

(b) New scripts.

15th–17th centuries. In 15th-century Iran the increase in lavishness in the production of fine Persian manuscripts was accompanied by the development of a new script called *nasta'līq*, a contraction of *naskh* and *ta'līq*. It combined the principles of *naskh*, the round hand used for common copying, and *ta'līq* (see below), a stylized chancellery script with more curved and elongated forms than in *tawqī'-riqā'*. Words are written with a distinct diagonal slant to the lower left, which creates a sense of forward movement on the page. The *alif* is shorter than in *naskh*, and other letters, especially *sīn* and *tā'*, are elongated to conform to the flowing lines of the script and intensify the visual effect. The invention of *nasta'līq* (see fig. 99) is universally attributed to MIR 'ALI TABRIZI.

The first generation of practitioners of *nasta'līq* about whom any detailed knowledge exists and whose works survive in numbers are described in the sources as the students of Mir 'Ali. Most of them were active in Herat during the first third of the 15th century and were associated with Baysunghur's patronage (*see* §(a) above). JA'FAR BAYSUNGHURI and his student Azhar (*fl* 1421–72), both accomplished calligraphers of the Six Pens, introduced the *nasta'līq* style to Herat. Ja'far supervised 40 calligraphers in Baysunghur's scriptorium, and examples of his writing in the classic styles of *thuluth*, *naskh* and *muḥaqqaq* are preserved in an album (Istanbul, Topkapı Pal. Lib., H. 2153, fols 27*r*, 58*r* and 160*v*). His *nasta'līq* hand, as in the manuscript of the *Shāhnāma* ('Book of kings'; 1430; Tehran, Gulistan Pal. Lib., MS. 61), which he penned for Baysunghur, already shows the characteristic placement of individual graphic units at a 30-degree angle to the horizontal base-line and is extraordinary for the discipline of rhythm and spacing. The *nasta'līq* hand of his pupil Azhar is even more elegant, as seen, for example, in a manuscript of Nizami's *Haft paykar* ('Seven portraits'; New York, Met., 13.228.13). Azhar is reported to have been the calligrapher who began one of the most superb illustrated manuscripts of the 15th century, a copy of Nizami's *Khamsa* ('Five poems') commissioned by the

99. *Nastaʿlīq* script by ʿAli ibn Hasan al-Sultani, copied from Nizami: *Khusraw and Shirin*, Tabriz, c. 1405–10 (Washington, DC, Freer Gallery of Art, MS. 31.37*v*)

Timurid ruler Abuʾl-Qasim Babur (*reg* 1449–57), which then passed to several Qaraqoyunlu, Aqqoyunlu and Safavid princes (Istanbul, Topkapı Pal. Lib., H. 762).

In the next generation the eastern variety of *nastaʿlīq* was given its classical 'Khurasanian' form by SULTAN ʿALI MASHHADI, who spent most of his career in Herat working for the major bibliophiles Husayn Bayqara (*see* TIMURID, §II(8)) and ʿALISHIR NAVAʾI. His script, more fluid and spacious than that of Jaʿfar, is found in some of the most luxurious illustrated manuscripts of the period, such as a copy of ʿAttar's *Manṭiq al-ṭayr* ('Conference of the birds'; 1483; New York, Met., 63.210) and a copy of Saʿdi's *Būstān* ('Orchard'; 1488; Cairo, N. Lib., Adab Farsi 908), which is the only manuscript with illustrations undisputedly by Bihzad, the master of Persian painting. In 1514, when he had retired to Mashhad, he wrote a verse treatise on calligraphy that was later incorporated in Qazi Ahmad's biography of calligraphers and painters (*see* §(i)(c) above). It contains both practical and autobiographical information and demonstrates the close association between religious discipline and the practice of calligraphy.

MIR ʿALI HUSAYNI HARAVI worked in Mashhad and Herat for the Timurids and Safavids until 1529, when he was taken to Bukhara by the Uzbeks. His *nastaʿlīq* lacked some of the discipline and formality of that by Sultan ʿAli. His Persian poetry is written on the diagonal with a thick ductus (stroke); some of the diacritical dots are omitted,

and he never added the stroke to distinguish *gāf* from *kāf*. Professional calligraphers considered him an autodidact lacking the discipline of rigorous training, and in his own day his art was not universally appreciated. Later connoisseurs, however, avidly collected his manuscripts and calligraphic specimens, which they incorporated in albums with elaborate marginal decoration. Virtually all the calligraphy in the Kevorkian Album (New York, Met.; Washington, DC, Freer) and the Berlin Album (*see* §4(vi)(d) below), prepared for the Mughal emperors of India, bears the signature of Mir ʿAli. The *nastaʿlīq* tradition was continued under the Safavids (*reg* 1501–1732) by such masters as Shah Mahmud Nishapuri (1487–1564/5; *see also* §3(ii) below) and MIR ʿIMAD. *Nastaʿlīq* was rarely used for copying the Koran, but a notable exception was prepared by Shah Mahmud in 1538 (Istanbul, Topkapı Pal. Lib., H.S. 25). Like Mir ʿAli, Mir ʿImad favoured the single folio with Persian poetry written on the diagonal (e.g. his signed folio, St Petersburg, Acad. Sci., Inst. Orient. Stud., E/14).

Nastaʿlīq, practically from the time of its inception, became the preferred script of Persian. In Azerbaijan and western Iran, the land of its birth, a slightly different style of *nastaʿlīq* was cultivated by ʿAbd al-Rahman Khwarazmi (*fl* 1430s–60s) and his two sons, ʿAbd al-Rahim and ʿAbd al-Karim (*fl* 1460s–90s). Variations in the width of the ductus were produced by a different cut of the nib, and, compared to the standard of Jaʿfar, the style is somewhat impulsive, with some letters crowded together while others are exaggerated. This can be seen in the *Khamsa* of Nizami copied by ʿAbd al-Rahman in Shiraz (1435–6; London, BL, Or. MS. 12856). The unusual canon of proportion is continued in the work of ʿAbd al-Karim (e.g. a page of poetry, Istanbul, Topkapı Pal. Lib., H. 2153, fol. 32r). Often called Iraqi *nastaʿlīq*, because western Iran was known as Persian Iraq, this style was taken in the 16th century to Ottoman Turkey, where it flourished as a minor style under the misnomer *taʿlīq*, and to the Indian subcontinent, where it became the model for Indian *nastaʿlīq*, which developed an ever thicker horizontal stroke and became the standard script for Urdu. This thick horizontal stroke is also found in a style called *bihārī*, which has wedge-shaped letters, thick round bowls for endings and wide spaces between words. It was developed in India specifically for manuscripts of the Koran; the script is first documented in a small copy of the Koran (1399; Geneva, Prince Sadruddin Aga Khan priv. col., MS. 32; see 1979 exh. cat., no. 75) and continued to be used for copying the Koran long after the classical styles had been adopted for other works. Manuscripts in *bihārī* script are reminiscent of those in *maghribī* script in the unbalanced ratio of one letter to another and in their colourfully decorated margins and frontispieces.

Another script popular in Iran during the period was *taʿlīq*, the 'hanging' script, a highly ornamental form of *tawqīʿ-riqāʿ* which revels in the use of extraneous loops and unorthodox connections and is extremely difficult for the uninitiated to decipher. Tradition credits various individuals with its invention, including Taj al-Din Salmani (*d* 1491), but the classic definition of eastern *taʿlīq* was given by Khwaja ʿAbd al-Hayy (*d* 1501), chief secretary to the Timurid sultan Abu Saʿid Mirza. *Taʿlīq* was practically limited to the production of diplomatic correspondence and letters of patent and congratulation. A western variety was developed for the Aqqoyunlu chancellery in Azerbaijan and Iraq. Under the Ottomans *ta'līq* was transformed into *dīvānī*, a highly elaborate and decorative script in which firmans (edicts) were written until the end of the empire (e.g. firman of Sultan Ahmed II, 1694; Washington, DC, Freer). It was also brought to the Mughals in India.

18th century. Shikasta nasta'līq developed in 18th-century Iran, and is to *nasta'līq* what *ta'līq* is to *tawqī-riqā'*, that is, it adds numerous ligatures and contractions to the letter forms of the base-script. Words and phrases may be written at all angles to each other and are often surrounded by reserve panels to set them off from the surrounding page. Of all forms of classical calligraphy, examples of *shikasta nasta'līq* are the least constrained by convention, and many of the superb specimens produced by Iranian calligraphers in the 18th and 19th centuries resemble abstract designs in which the eye revels in the overall composition without having to decipher individual words, which in many cases is all but impossible. One of the greatest masters of *shikasta nasta'līq* was 'Abd al-Majid Taliqani (*d* 1771). In rare cases the script was used for administrative documents, such as the plea for tax relief written by Mirza Kuchik Khan (1795–6; Cambridge, MA, Sackler Mus.). The individual lines, eight of which are upside down and record the successful outcome of the plea, are unified by the parallel sweeping curves of the script.

Zoomorphic calligraphy of the 18th century and later shaped words and phrases into the forms of birds, animals and human faces. It differed from the zoomorphic script that had been used in Iranian metalwork of the 12th century, where the individual letters had been decorated with or transformed into humans and animals (*see* §IV, 1(v) below). The texts generally chosen for incorporation into zoomorphic calligraphy were the basmala and the names Allah, Muhammad, 'Ali, Hasan and Husayn. For example, Ibn Hajji Muhammad 'Ali of Isfahan penned the basmala in the form of a bird and presented it to the Safavid prince Mahmud Mirza (Springfield, MA, Mus. F.A.). Lions, the symbol of 'Ali, the 'Lion of God', are often used in Shi'ite invocations. Zoomorphic calligraphy flourished particularly among the Bektashi dervishes of the Ottoman empire (e.g. a verse by 'Attar in the form of a lion killing a serpent, 1795; Munich, Staatl. Mus. Vlkerknd.) and in India (e.g. the Throne Verse, Koran ii.255, in the shape of a horse, late 16th century; see 1979 exh. cat., no. 77). Another calligraphic *tour de force* is the black exercise (Pers. *siyāh mashq*), which consists of a given letter, group of letters or word in *nasta'līq* script written repeatedly, each time slightly to the left, so that the entire page may be almost completely blackened with ink, hence the name of the style. Initially a calligraphic exercise, the *siyāh mashq* of master calligraphers became in time an end in itself, and specimens were avidly collected by connoisseurs.

UNPUBLISHED SOURCES

Istanbul, Topkapı Pal. Lib., y.y. 599 [Majnun al-Rafiqi: *Rasm al-khaṭṭ* ('Illustration of scripts')]

BIBLIOGRAPHY

Mustafa Ali: *Manāqib-i hunarvarān* [Virtues of artists] (1587); ed. İ. M. Kemal (Istanbul, 1926)

Qazi Ahmad ibn Mir Munshi: *Gulistān-i hunar* [Rose-garden of art] (1606); Eng. trans. by V. Minorsky as *Calligraphers and Painters* (Washington, DC, 1959)

Muhammad ibn Hindushah Nakhchivani: *Dastūr al-kātib fī ta'yīn al-marātib* [Instruction of scribes in the establishment of degrees]; ed. A. A. Alizade, 2 vols (Moscow, 1964–76)

M. İzzet: *Khuṭūṭ-i 'uthmāniyya* [Ottoman scripts] (Istanbul, AH 1309/1891–2)

İ. H. Baltacıoğlu: *Türklerde yazı sanatı* [Calligraphy among the Turks] (Ankara, 1958)

A. A. Ivanov, T. B. Grek and O. F. Akimushkin: *Album indiskikh i persidskikh miniatur XVI–XVIII vv* [Album of Indian and Persian miniatures, 16th–18th centuries] (Moscow, 1962)

A. Alparslan: 'Ecoles calligraphiques turques', *Islam Tedkikleri Enst. Derg.*, v (1973), pp. 265–78

L. Fekete: *Einführung in die persische Paläographie: 101 persische Dokumente*, ed. G. Hazai (Budapest, 1977)

P. P. Soucek: 'The Arts of Calligraphy', *The Arts of the Book in Central Asia, 14th–16th Centuries*, ed. B. Gray (Boulder, CO, London and Paris, 1979), pp. 7–34

Calligraphy in the Arts of the Muslim World (exh. cat. by A. Welch, New York, Asia Soc. Gals; Cincinnati, OH, A. Mus.; Seattle, WA, A. Mus.; St Louis, MO, A. Mus.; 1979)

H. Lowry: 'Calligraphy: Hüsn-i hat', *Tulips, Arabesques & Turbans: Decorative Arts from the Ottoman Empire*, ed. Y. Petsopoulos (New York, 1982), pp. 169–92

M. Bayani: *Aḥvāl va āṣār-i khwushnavīsān* [Biographies and works of calligraphers], 2nd edn in 4 vols (Tehran, Iran. Solar 1363/1984–5)

Hakkak-zade Mustafa Hilmi: *Mizânül-hatt* [Scale of scripts], ed. Abdül-kadır Dedeoğlu (Istanbul, 1986)

S. C. Welch and others: *The Emperors' Album* (New York, 1987)

WHEELER M. THACKSTON

(v) After c. 1800. The practice of traditional calligraphy continued into the 19th century: every aspiring calligrapher had to copy classical models before his training was complete. In Ottoman Turkey, for example, the style of Şeyh Hamdullah and Hafiz Osman was continued by such masters as MUSTAFA RAQIM). He is renowned for his calligraphic pictures, such as the basmala written in the shape of a bird, and the intertwined letters of the expression: 'There is no power and no strength save in God' (Arab. *lā ḥawl wa-lā quwwat illā bi'llāh*). This type of calligraphic picture continues to be popular (see fig. 100). Descriptions of the Prophet's inner and outer qualities (Arab. *ḥilya*) were written in the style developed by Hafiz Osman. The style of *nasta'līq* script perfected by Mir 'Imad and developed by ESAD YESARI was made into a distinctive Turkish hand by the latter's son, Mustafa Izzet Yesarizade (*d* 1849). Modernization created new opportunities for calligraphers, who were called on to produce inscriptions for coins, postage stamps and banknotes. After 1928, however, when the new Turkish republic replaced the Arabic script with the roman alphabet, calligraphy became an art form separated from everyday life since fewer people were able to read the script. 'Aziz Rifa'i (1872–1934), the leading exponent of the Hafiz Osman tradition, left Turkey for Egypt, where he produced luxury copies of the Koran and trained a new generation of calligraphers. Despite attempts to maintain a high standard, their work was rendered largely superfluous by the printing press (*see* §8 below), since even the finest calligraphy could be reproduced mechanically, particularly by lithography.

Calligraphers therefore looked for new ways to use their skills. Some (for example, the Turkish calligrapher İsmayil Hakki Baltacıoğlu) ventured into new forms such as the

100. Calligraphic picture of the basmala by Nik Zainal Abidin, 460×450 mm, *c.* 1983

Flame script, in which the letters resemble flames, or the Crown script used in some Arab countries. After World War II a new feeling of Islamic identity caused many artists who had formerly imitated European painting to turn to calligraphic pictures because the substitution of letters for living figures seemed more in tune with Islamic ideals. Some artists reinvigorated the tradition of square writing formerly used for tiles, walls and other architectural settings. The Pakistani artist Anwar Jalal Shemza, for example, achieved Mondrian-like effects using a single, geometrized Arabic letter as his main motif. Other artists arranged texts in circular form. These circular calligraphies were sometimes inspired by the decoration on ceramics produced under the Samanid dynasty (*reg* 819–1005) in the eastern Islamic world (*see* §V, 2(iii) below). They were also turned into mandala-like forms in which circles, sometimes combined with octagons or plaiting, are filled with hundreds of minute repetitions of a single phrase such as 'There is no god but he' (Arab. *lā ilāha illā huwa*). Other calligraphers devised word pictures. The Iranian artist Adharbod (*b c.* 1917), for example, created paintings in which the letters of the word 'war' (Pers. *jang*) were composed of images of bones and skulls. Colour, produced with such non-traditional techniques as batik, colour etching and screenprinting, is particularly important for modern calligraphers and is used to highlight the message of their paintings. In contrast, traditional calligraphers generally restricted colour to border decoration, opening pages and the like. Only rarely did colour become a means in itself for the calligrapher, for example in the work of the North African master al-Qandusi (*d* 1861), who elaborated on the more outspoken coloration of manuscripts in *maghribī* script.

This new form of calligraphic painting is practised throughout the Islamic world. Calligraphic pictures from Malaysia and India daringly transform letters into almost organic forms, while the highly refined calligrams of HASSAN MASSOUDY and his group in Paris capture the best spiritual dynamics of this art. In Pakistan experimentation has been especially strong, although traditional writing styles are still used and some young artists have tried to develop new variants. The artist Sadeqain (1930–87) was a painter rather than a traditionally trained calligrapher, who even illustrated verses of the Koran. The letters grow, not always convincingly, into palm trees, cityscapes and sailing boats, but his most inventive composition is the depiction of the Koranic phrase 'Be! And it becomes' (Arab. *kun fayakūn*, e.g. *Sūrat al-baqara* ('The cow') ii.117) with two extended round endings to the letter *nūn* in the shape of a spiral nebula out of which emerge suns, stars and galaxies. His younger colleague Aslam Kamal (*b* 1935) keeps to strictly geometric forms in a stylized angular script, combining religious sentences with Mughal architectural silhouettes. The work of another artist, Rashid Ahmed Arshad (*b* 1937), has been described as 'scribbling on the canvas like a doctor's prescription in *shikasta*', and one wonders to what extent these younger artists were influenced by such European painters as Paul Klee, some of whose paintings were themselves inspired by Arabic lettering. The calligraphies of the London-based Egyptian Ahmad Moustafa display an inexhaustible imagination and a skilful use of modern technology. Sculptors have also turned to calligraphy. Sculptures repeating the word 'God' (Arab. *Allāh*) are comparatively easy to form because of the three vertical shafts of the letters, and the Iranian sculptor PARVIZ TANAVOLI has created delightful works from the word 'nothing' (Pers. *hīch*).

BIBLIOGRAPHY

İ. M. K. İnal: *Son hattatlar* [The last calligraphers] (Istanbul, 1954/*R* 1970)
İ. H. Baltacıoğlu: *Türklerde yazı sanatı* [Calligraphy among the Turks] (Ankara, 1958)
H. von Halem, ed.: *Calligraphy in Modern Art* (Karachi, 1975)
H. Massoudy: *Calligraphie arabe vivante* (Paris, 1981)
A. Moustafa: *The Attributes of Divine Perfection* (Jiddah, 1991)
J.-P. Sicre: *Hassan Massoudi* (Paris, 1991)

ANNEMARIE SCHIMMEL

3. PAINTED DECORATION. From the first century of Islam, vegetal, geometric and epigraphic motifs were added to the text block and margins of manuscripts of the Koran to divide and embellish the text. This decoration, in gold and an increasingly broad range of colours, is often called illumination, to distinguish it from illustration (*see* §4 below). According to Muslim belief the Koran cannot be illustrated, so manuscripts of it often have elaborate non-representational decoration. Following the model of Koran manuscripts, decoration was then applied to other kinds of manuscripts, particularly Persian poetic texts, the production of which flourished from the 14th century in Iran, western Central Asia, Turkey and the Indian subcontinent. The traditional repertory was eventually expanded in literary texts to include such representational motifs as animals, birds, flowers and human figures.   □

(i) Manuscripts of the Koran. (ii) Other manuscripts.

(i) Manuscripts of the Koran.

(a) Introduction: Early development. (b) Later regional development.

(a) Introduction and early development. Painted decoration was used primarily to indicate divisions in the Koranic

text. It is found within the text block, in the margins and over the whole page (most often over facing pages). Within the text, markers divide verses or groups of verses, and bands separate chapters. Marginal decoration complements the decoration within the text. It is also used to indicate the prostrations (Arab. *sajda*) prescribed in the Koran, as well as the divisions of the text into sixtieths (Arab. *hizb*), thirtieths (Arab. *juz'*), thirds and halves which facilitate daily, weekly or monthly reading. These divisions also gave rise to a more complex pattern of decoration, which spread over two pages, normally at the beginning or end of the volume—be it a single- or multi-volume manuscript. The function of this third type of decoration is less clear, and these full pages may have been conceived as adjuncts to the binding (*see* §7 below), which often has similar designs. Only a few motifs are used within the text. A circle commonly marks the end of a verse, while groups of five verses are often indicated by the letter *hā'*, the alphabetic equivalent (Arab. *abjad*) of the numeral five. It was written in kufic script, and its shape became increasingly stylized. In some manuscripts similar but more elaborate motifs are placed in the margin to emphasize the divisions within the text block. Within the illumination the verse number, spelt out in letters, or in early manuscripts written in *abjad*, facilitates reference to the text. Marginal dividers are either circular designs (like verse dividers) or geometric motifs.

The most important decorative elements in early manuscripts of the Koran are the bands separating chapters (with or without an accompanying marginal vignette), frames for the text and full-page designs (see fig. 101). In the earliest *hijāzī* manuscripts of the Koran, a diverse group attributed to western Arabia in the early centuries of Islam, the bands are simple geometric designs traced in ink and rarely coloured (e.g. Dublin, Chester Beatty Lib., MS. 1615, fol. 20*r*). Within a short time architectural, vegetal and geometric themes began to be used. The most spectacular example of an architectural design is found in a large-format manuscript in San'a (Dar al-Makhtutat, MS. 20–33.1) attributed to the 8th century, which has a frontispiece depicting a mosque and consecutive text pages framed by decorative bands. Another large-format manuscript (Cairo, N. Lib., MS. 139; Paris, Bib. N., MS. arab. 324a) has arcaded bands separating some chapters. Vegetal and geometric designs were, however, more lastingly popular and were often combined to produce an effect of great vitality. The vegetal elements are often stylized, but chapter divisions in a more naturalistic style are also found (e.g. Istanbul, Mus. Turk. & Islam. A., S.E. 80).

The decoration of early Koran manuscripts was governed by geometric principles, which may have been derived from mosaic decoration. They are already evident in horizontal-format manuscripts from the late 8th century and the 9th (e.g. Dublin, Chester Beatty Lib., MS. 1406). When the decoration spreads over two pages, one side mirrors the other. In several manuscripts from this period the full-page illuminations have the same dimensions as the written surface, suggesting that the calligrapher and illuminator were the same person, as was the case in later times. The famous 11th-century calligrapher IBN AL-BAWWAB, for example, was also an illuminator of some repute and was probably responsible for both text and decoration of a manuscript copied in Baghdad in 1000–01 (see fig. 97 above). The decoration of these early manuscripts always incorporates vegetal elements (often traced in sepia), but they are somewhat abstract and generally subordinate to the overall geometric scheme.

Frame bands were used to surround a central field. When the field is an elongated rectangle, the frame band is wide. The field contains plaited motifs, arabesques and vegetal designs, while the band itself is a complex mesh of interwoven gold bands (e.g. Dublin, Chester Beatty Lib., MS. 1407, fols 3*v*–4*r*). When the central section is composed of one or two squares the frame is narrower but contains the same decorative repertory (e.g. Paris, Bib. N., MS. arab. 351, fol. 105*v*). Compositions based on circular

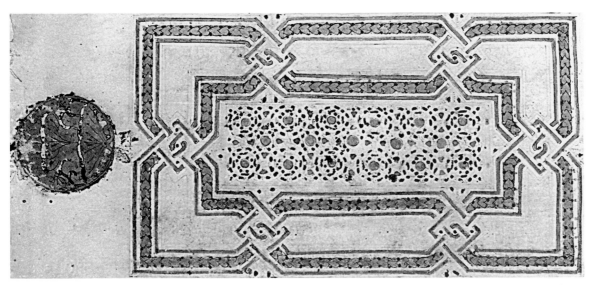

101. Full-page design from a Koran, h. 223 mm, endowed to the Great Mosque at Damascus, 910–11 (Istanbul, Topkapı Palace Library, E.H. 16, fol. 39*r*)

elements are comparatively rare; calligraphy is sometimes integrated into the decoration, and gold became increasingly popular. Chapter headings were decorated in similar ways. The earliest manuscripts rarely have chapter titles; the space left empty at the end of a chapter is filled with decoration. With time, the decoration became standardized. The chapter title was written against an illuminated ground, and the more systematic use of bands is accompanied by a greater regularity of forms and motifs. Marginal vignettes, however, remain extremely varied.

At the end of the 10th century, when the vertical format regained its popularity, a central circular composition, sometimes accompanied by a St Andrew's cross, became the predominant design (e.g. Dublin, Chester Beatty Lib., MS. 1411, fol. 1v). These designs can be elaborate, but the basic decorative elements remain the same. On other illuminations a single motif, usually vegetal, is repeated either on the whole surface or enclosed within a rectangle, as in the frontispiece to a manuscript signed by 'Ali ibn Shadhan al-Razi (972; Dublin, Chester Beatty Lib., MS. 1434, fols 1v–2r). This type of design had already been used on earlier horizontal-format manuscripts and remained popular into the 13th century, as in the manuscript copied by al-Hasan ibn Juban ibn 'Abdallah al-Qunawi in Konya (Sept 1278; Dublin, Chester Beatty Lib., MS. 1466, fols 330v–331r).

Geometric designs, already evident in the 9th century, continued to develop in the later period. Full-page designs were conceived as a pattern of stars, polygons or circles radiating from a central point, as in a Koran manuscript made in Bust, southern Afghanistan, in 1111–12 (see

102. Full-page design from a Koran, 140×115 mm, from Bust, Afghanistan, 1111–12 (Paris, Bibliothèque Nationale, MS. arab. 6041, fol. 2r)

fig. 102). The unity of the double page of decoration was emphasized by a band enclosing the three external sides of the designs, as in the decoration on a double page with the last two chapters of the Koran, done in Egypt (c. 1400; Dublin, Chester Beatty Lib., MS. 1628). Geometric decoration reached its apogee under the Ilkhanids (reg 1256–1353) in Iran and the Mamluks (reg 1250–1517) in Syria and Egypt. The highest standard of production can be seen in books produced by such workshops as the one headed by Abu Bakr Sandal in Cairo in the first decade of the 14th century (e.g. Dublin, Chester Beatty Lib., MS. 1479). The rectangular format is often compartmentalized into a square central section between two smaller rectangles, usually epigraphic, above and below. Marginal vignettes, whether accompanying a chapter heading or a full-page design, display a new range of forms and are often decorated with slender arabesques. Arabesques, peony flowers and lotus blossoms appear in other parts of the decoration, but the plaited motifs used in earlier manuscripts still prevail in the borders. Gold continued to dominate the palette, but the introduction of other colours such as red, black and green gives a more balanced effect. The bands with chapter headings contain subtly shaped cartouches which emphasize the titles. Large rosettes resembling sunbursts (Arab. *shamsa*) were placed at the beginning of the manuscript.

(b) Later regional development. Under the Timurids (reg 1370–1506) of Iran and Transoxiana, the decoration on the page diminished in importance in favour of the frame surrounding the beginning of the text. Geometric compositions were still used, but to a lesser extent, and an undulating stem with golden foliage occurs frequently. The marginal vignette was incorporated into the frame band, which is usually fringed with blue palmettes, as in the opening pages to the splendid manuscript penned by Timur's grandson Ibrahim Sultan (1424; Mashhad, Imam Riza Shrine Mus., MS. 414, fols 1v–2r). A deep blue is characteristic of these illuminations, but bright green, orange and pink were also used. These principles and compositions continued to be used in manuscripts produced during the Safavid period (reg 1501–1732). Floral sprays appear with increasing frequency, and a darker blue became popular. The focal points of the manuscript are the frames marking the beginning and end of the text. Sometimes there was a frontispiece decorated with a large rosette or sunburst containing a Koranic phrase, as in the Koran written and decorated by Ruzbihan Muhammad al-Tab'i al-Shirazi (c. 1520; Dublin, Chester Beatty Lib., MS. 1558, fols 1v–2r). In single-volume manuscripts the double-page frame is reserved for the first chapter, while a more modest design is used for the second chapter. The middle and end of the text—eventually each of the 30 *juz'*—are often indicated by an illuminated frame. The bands bordering the text are enlivened by arabesque stems carrying delicately coloured flowers. The marginal vignette was permanently incorporated within the decorative frame, and only a triangular tip protrudes into the margin. Greens, purples and black were added to the traditional blues and gold.

Migrating craftsmen took the Safavid style to the Indian subcontinent (e.g. London, BL, Or. MS. 11544, fols 3v–

4*r*) and, sometimes reluctantly, to the Ottoman empire, such as the manuscript endowed in 1594 to the mosque in Yaniq (Györ, Hungary) by the Ottoman Grand Vizier and conqueror of Hungary, Sinan Pasha (Paris, Bib. N., MS. arab. 418, fols 2*v*–3*r*). A large number of Koran manuscripts were made for the Ottomans, but they lack creativity: well-established models were constantly repeated. Increasingly the roles of calligrapher and decorator were separated. Frames were still used at the beginning of the manuscript, but textual divisions were indicated by numerous marginal designs. At the end of the 18th century the Rococo style was introduced into Koran decoration as artists emulated European styles, as seen in the floral borders of a manuscript made for Sultan Selim III (1806; Dublin, Chester Beatty Lib., MS. 1581, fols 1*v*–2*r*).

In the western Islamic world a square format for Koran manuscripts on parchment prevailed until the 14th century; designs based on circular motifs, as in the frontispiece to a manuscript (Paris, Bib. N., MS. arab. 423) done for the Marinid sultan Abu 'Inan Faris (*reg* 1348–58), were used alongside those with a vertical trellis, as in the opening and closing pages to a manuscript done probably in Granada (1303; Paris, Bib. N., MS. arab. 385, fols 1*v*–2*r*, 129*v*–130*r*). The same style continued even when a vertical format was adopted, as in the manuscript written for a prince of the 'Alawi dynasty of Morocco (1729–30; Cairo, N. Lib., MS. 25, fols 261*v*–262*r*). As in earlier manuscripts, mesh bands are used to outline the design. This is particularly the case for roundels, themselves composed of epigraphic motifs, as in the opening and closing pages to a manuscript written in Valencia (1182–3; Istanbul, U. Lib., A. 6754, fols 1*v*–2*r*, 131*v*). The marginal vignettes accompanying the chapter headings or indicating the sections are particularly fine, especially on parchment manuscripts, such as one attributed to 12th-century Spain (Istanbul, Mus. Turk. & Islam. A., MS. 360). Chapter headings were placed within a band only rarely and at the beginning of the volume, but the ornamental effect of the gold letters in the title is striking.

BIBLIOGRAPHY

R. Ettinghausen: *Arab Painting* (Geneva, 1962)
——: 'Manuscript Illumination', *Survey of Persian Art*, ed. A. U. Pope and P. Ackerman, iv (London, 2/1964), pp. 1937–74
A. J. Arberry: *The Koran Illuminated: A Handlist of Korans in the Chester Beatty Library* (Dublin, 1967)
M. Lings: *The Quranic Art of Calligraphy and Illumination* (London, 1976)
M. Lings and Y. H. Safadi: *The Qur'ān* (London, 1976)
Qur'āns and Bindings from the Chester Beatty Library (exh. cat. by D. James, London, Islam. Cult. Cent., 1980)
F. Déroche: *Les Manuscrits du Coran: Aux origines de la calligraphie coranique* (1983), I/i of *Manuscrits musulmans*, pt 2 of *Catalogue des manuscrits arabes*, Paris, Bib. N. cat. (Paris, 1983–5)
D. James: 'Some Observations on the Calligraphers and Illuminators of the Koran of Rukn al-Dīn Baybars al-Jāshnagīr', *Muqarnas*, ii (1984), pp. 147–57
H.-C. von Bothmer: 'Frühislamische Koran-Illuminationen: Meisterwerke aus dem Handschriftenfund der Grossen Moschee in Sanaa/Yemen', *Kst & Ant.* (1986), pp. 22–33
——: 'Architekturbilder im Koran', *Pantheon*, xlv (1987), pp. 4–20
——: 'Masterworks of Islamic Book Art: Koranic Calligraphy and Illumination in the Manuscripts found in the Great Mosque in Sanaa', *Yemen: 3000 Years of Art and Civilisation in Arabia Felix*, ed. W. Daum (Innsbruck, 1987), pp. 178–81
D. James: *Qur'āns of the Mamlūks* (London and New York, 1988)
——: *The Master Scribes: Qur'ans of the 10th to the 14th Centuries AD*, The Nasser D. Khalili Collection of Islamic Art, ii (London, 1992) [text in Eng. and Arab.]
——: *After Timur: Qur'ans of the 15th and the 16th Centuries*, The Nasser D. Khalili Collection of Islamic Art, iii (London, 1992) [text in Eng. and Arab.]

F. DÉROCHE

(ii) Other manuscripts.

(a) Introduction. (b) Major examples.

(a) Introduction. Like their Koranic counterparts, Islamic secular manuscripts frequently contain complex programmes of illumination (Arab. *tadhhīb*; Pers. *tazhīb*) comprising many non-representational (and sometimes figural) motifs designed to enhance the pleasure of reading the text and perusing the folios, as well as to increase the overall artistic value. Illumination is usually quite limited in Arabic secular manuscripts, but it developed extensively in Persian ones, where it was often coordinated with elaborate programmes of illustration. From Iran this style of decoration was taken to Turkey and the Indian subcontinent, where it also flourished. Primary sources often give the names of artists known for their skill as illuminators (Arab. *mudhahhib*), but the decoration of Islamic manuscripts other than Korans is often overlooked, primarily because of art historians' preoccupation with painted illustration. There is, consequently, little agreement on nomenclature or descriptive terminology, and no corpora of illuminated manuscripts or decorative forms have been published.

The decorative programme of illuminated secular manuscripts typically begins with several folios of front matter, starting on the first page with a circular or oval rosette often inscribed with the title of the text or name of the patron. This is generally called a *shamsa*, from the Arabic word for sun, or sometimes *dībācha*, from the Persian word for brocade. This can be followed by a frontispiece (Pers. *sarlawh*) of at least two equally common types. The first is a double page of decoration, usually forming a mirror-image composition within a vertical field. The second type is an illuminated frame around the opening lines of text, with the writing encased in colourful contour lines (Pers. *tahrīr*) or cloud panels (Pers. *ābrī, tarsi'*). Many manuscripts contain both types of frontispieces. In others, the opening text page may be set off with an illuminated titlepiece or headpiece, variously referred to as *'unwān* (Arab.) or *sarlawh* (Pers.), at the top of the written surface. It is quite typical for manuscripts comprising more than one text, such as the collected works of one author, the *Khamsa* ('Five poems') of Nizami for example, to contain a decorated superscription at the beginning of each section of text.

Coloured rulings (Pers. *jadval*), usually red or frequently multicoloured, were used to set off the text area from the margins in virtually all non-Koranic manuscripts made in Iran, at least from the 13th century. In prose manuscripts the text is written as a single block, while in poetry the text is written in two, four or six columns of rhyming distichs to be read across the line. The distichs are separated by vertical rulings, generally two pairs of gold lines flanked by thin black lines. Illuminated rubrics (Pers. *lawh*) were often placed at regular intervals in de luxe manuscripts to separate parts of the text, such as narrative actions or divisions between prose and poetry. In poetic texts with four or more columns these rubrics span the central two columns and the text reads continuously from right to left, jumping over the rubric. Poetic texts may be further embellished with intercolumnar designs and with square and triangular panels when verses are written diagonally, conventionally thought to stretch out the text in preparation for an illustration on a following page, as seen, for example, in a manuscript of 'Attar's *Mantiq al-tayr* ('Conference of the birds'; 1483; New York, Met., MS. 63.210), copied by Sultan 'Ali Mashhadi in Herat. The margins (Pers. *havashī*) outside the text block and the rulings provide yet another surface for illumination, which can range from simple flecking with gold (Pers. *zar-afshān*) or dusting (Pers. *ghubār*) to painted or stencilled designs (Pers. *'akssāzi mistar*), including triangular thumbpieces in the centre of the side margins.

As in other medieval manuscript traditions, gold was the predominant colour for illumination, with blue a common contrast. By at least the 14th century the palette incorporated a full range of colours, plus black, white and occasional pastels. The principal design elements include scrolls or arabesques of seemingly limitless size and shape, flowers in both bud and full bloom, and geometric motifs ranging from simple squares and circles to complex patterns of interlacing and radial designs. The design patterns are extremely varied and often combine and superimpose forms and motifs within a frame. The overall design is determined in part by the location of the decoration within the manuscript and its function, whether a titlepiece or rubric, and in part by regional and aesthetic factors, but the overall tendency was towards the multiplication of fields and the miniaturization of forms. Headpieces in Persian manuscripts from the early 14th century generally consist of rectangular panels enclosing large, recognizable blossoms, such as lotuses and peonies, with broad stems and leaves, for example the headpiece from the second volume of the Great Mongol *Shāhnāma* ('Book of kings') probably made in Tabriz (*c.* 1335; ex-Demotte; Paris, Bib. N., MS. supp. pers. 2137, fol. 1*v*). By the end of the 15th century the rectangle had been expanded with large triangular projections (Pers. *tāj*: 'crown') and radiating finials (Pers. *shuraf*: 'crenellations'), as can be seen in a copy of the poet 'Arifi's *Hālnāma* ('Book of ecstasy') decorated in Herat by Yari, the royal illuminator (1495–6; St Petersburg, Rus. N. Lib., Dorn 440, fol. 1*v*). Both upper and lower fields abound with small trefoils and quatrefoils, dense and delicate palmette scrolls, and intersecting bands of checks and crosses.

(b) Major examples. Few early manuscripts have survived, and illuminated pages at the front and back of books were particularly vulnerable to wear. One of the earliest is a copy (Leiden, Bib. Rijksuniv., MS. 437) of Abu Bakr Muhammad ibn 'Abdallah's *Kitāb khalq al-nabī wa-khulqih* ('Book of the moral and physical characteristics of the Prophet'), written and illuminated by Abu Bakr Muhammad ibn Rafi', the copyist in Ghazna, for the Ghaznavid amir 'Abd al-Rashid (*reg* 1050–53). The ex-libris on fol. 1*r* is written in gold on a vertical field (180×110 mm) decorated with gold scrolls outlined in red. A double-page frontispiece (fols 1*v*–2*r*) in gold, red, blue and green has a broad band at the top of each page with the title; below, the text blocks contain the invocation and the author's name in gold, and the beginning of the text

in black. Marginal vignettes project into the outer margins from the title and the bottom of the text block. Elsewhere in the manuscripts, chapter headings, written in gold outlined in black, have palmettes projecting into the margins. The decoration shows the impact of contemporary Koran manuscripts.

A more elaborate programme of decoration is found in a manuscript of Pseudo-Galen's *Kitāb al-diryāq* ('Book of antidotes'; 1199; Paris, Bib. N., MS. arab. 2964) made in northern Iraq. Fols 2*r*–7*v* contain a series of frontispieces, with and without writing. They have two formats: a square central field containing a medallion or illustration with rectangular panels above and below, or a rectangular field surrounded by broad epigraphic borders on all four sides. The ground is usually decorated with elaborate gold scrolls outlined in black. Triangular thumbpieces project into the outer margins. (*See also* §4(ii)(a) and (iv)(c) below.)

Many of these early features continued to be used in Persian manuscripts of the 13th and 14th centuries. The double-page frontispiece (Dublin, Chester Beatty Lib., Pers. MS. 104.29) to the second volume of the First Small *Shāhnāma* has broad bands across the top and bottom of the page inscribed with verses against a scrolling ground. They extol the beauty of calligraphy and painting. The 1341 *Shāhnāma* made for the Injuid vizier Qivam al-Din Hasan has a double-page frontispiece containing rosettes within square fields enclosed within narrow borders. The ex-libris is inscribed in the rosette on the right, the title and date in the one on the left (Washington, DC, Sackler Gal., S86.0110–11).

Book production reached its apogee in the Iranian world during the 15th and 16th centuries, and elaborate illumination was standard in all luxury manuscripts. One of the most celebrated is a copy (London, BL, Or. MS. 2265) of Nizami's *Khamsa* made for Tahmasp I (*reg* 1524–76), second ruler of the Safavid dynasty of Iran, at his court in Tabriz. Copied by the famous scribe Shah Mahmud Nishapuri between 1539 and 1543, the volume originally contained almost 400 folios (now 360×250 mm), of which all had some form of illumination and at least 17 had full-page illustrations (*see* §4(ii)(b) and (vi)(a) below). The illumination is not signed, but Mirak the Illuminator and his son Qivam al-Din, who are known to have worked for Tahmasp, may have worked on the manuscript. This splendid manuscript epitomizes the art of illumination at its peak in 16th-century Iran, although the manuscript is actually a composite of early and late Safavid taste, for it was refurbished towards the end of the 17th century, a relatively common process for de luxe Islamic manuscripts, when a number of the illuminated borders were replaced and several paintings added.

The opening pages (fols 1*v*–2*r*) have a pair of matching rosettes, each in the form of a 12-pointed star with a scalloped gold circle in the centre, set against a blue ground decorated with green palmette scrolls and multicoloured blossoms. On fol. 2*r* the braided gold band that encircles this motif is pricked in a minute pattern, creating the impression of relief; this technique appears frequently in Islamic illumination and enhances the reflective quality of the gold. The outer field has trilobed medallions alternating with pairs of superimposed pendants in green and light blue on a blue ground with gold palmette scrolls and blossoms. The rosettes are edged in white and have blue finials at their tips. The central gold fields might have been intended to contain the ex-libris (e.g. fol. 16*r* of the Tahmasp *Shāhnāma*; see 1980 exh. cat., p. 44).

The text begins (fols 2*v*–3*r*; see fig. 103) with an extremely elaborate double frontispiece. Each half contains a double column of seven lines of text, each outlined by pricked gold lines forming contour panels with blue sprigs and leaves against a gold ground. This central element is flanked by vertical rectangles illuminated with a bold design of interlacing palmette bands on a densely pricked gold ground. Above and below are horizontal panels enframed by a gold arabesque band. The fields contain a central gold cartouche inscribed in white and outlined by a thin white band with tiny black crosses that extend outwards to form a lattice-like pattern. The lattice creates 26 lobed units distributed in reciprocal pairs around the central cartouche. The lobed units are filled with red or gold pendants decorated with floral or palmette scrolls. This entire composition is enclosed on three sides by a narrow black band densely decorated with a scroll with split palmettes and blossoms and edged with thin coloured lines similar to rulings and a broad outer border, with large gold medallions alternating with gold pendants set against a dark blue ground. A large gold-cusped triangle projects from the outer side of each half. These borders visually join the two halves of the frontispiece at the gutter to create a unified composition. Thin blue finials overlap the marginal illumination, painted in two colours of gold and depicting real and fantastic animals and birds amid foliage. Almost every folio of the manuscript has similar scenes of flora and fauna in the margins, although they seem to have been executed in two styles. Some of this variation may be due to the refurbishment of the manuscript when later artists sought to emulate or improve on the original illumination. The principle of symmetry, used in all the other illuminations, did not apply in the margins, for the iconography and composition differ on facing folios.

BIBLIOGRAPHY

Dict. Middle Ages: 'Manuscript Illumination: Islamic'

Qazi Ahmad ibn Mir Munshi: *Gulistān-i hunar* [Rose-garden of art] (1606); Eng. trans. by V. Minorsky as *Calligraphers and Painters* (Washington, DC, 1959)

L. Binyon: *The Poems of Nizami* (London, 1928)

R. Ettinghausen: 'Manuscript Illumination', *Survey of Persian Art*, ed. A. U. Pope and P. Ackerman, iv (London, 1939, 2/1964), pp. 1937–74

B. Farès: *Le Livre de la thériaque: Manuscrit arabe à peintures de la fin du XIIe siècle conservé à la Bibliothèque nationale de Paris* (Cairo, 1953)

S. M. Stern: 'A Manuscript from the Library of the Ghaznawid Amir 'Abd al-Rashid', *Paintings from Islamic Lands*, ed. R. Pinder-Wilson (Oxford, 1969), pp. 7–31

R. Ettinghausen: 'Abri Painting', *Studies in Memory of Gaston Wiet*, ed. M. Rosen-Ayalon (Jerusalem, 1977), pp. 345–56

O. F. Akimushkin and A. A. Ivanov: 'The Art of Illumination', *The Arts of the Book in Central Asia, 14th–16th Centuries*, ed. B. Gray (Boulder, CO, London and Paris, 1979), pp. 35–57

Wonders of the Age: Masterpieces of Early Safavid Painting, 1501–1576 (exh. cat. by S. C. Welch, Cambridge, MA, Fogg, 1980)

MARIANNA S. SIMPSON

4. PAINTED ILLUSTRATION. Book illustration is one of the most familiar aspects of Islamic art in the West, and it has been appreciated there for longer than most other forms of Islamic art. This interest is undoubtedly due to the attractive story-book images, exquisite detail and jewel-like colours characteristic of the classical style of manuscript painting that developed primarily in Iran in the 15th century. Images removed from manuscripts were appreciated by connoisseurs, who added them to their collections of European paintings and drawings and had them mounted and framed for exhibition on walls, and complete illustrated manuscripts were appreciated by bibliophiles, who added them to their collections of European manuscripts and printed books. Despite the splendours of binding, paper, decoration and calligraphy in many Islamic manuscripts, it was the narrative and often lyric imagery of the paintings that appealed most directly to Western taste.

(i) Introduction. (ii) Subject-matter. (iii) Before *c.* AD 1000. (iv) *c.* 1000–*c.* 1250. (v) *c.* 1250–*c.* 1500. (vi) *c.* 1500–*c.* 1900.

(i) Introduction. The apparent contradiction between what was understood to be a Koranic prohibition of figural imagery and the existence of relatively large numbers of books illustrated with figural scenes attracted the attention of Western scholars from the first. Such early scholars as Arnold (1928) noted that figural paintings and sculptures survive from the early period of Islamic architecture in Syria (*see* §II, 3 above) and that the earliest illustrated books to survive were made in the same area. Nevertheless they understood the illustrated Islamic book to be largely a feature of Iranian art and tried to explain its florescence in the period from the 14th to the 17th century as a revival

103. Illuminated frontispiece, 360×250 mm; from Nizami: *Khamsa* ('Five poems'), made for Tahmasp I, Tabriz, 1539–43 (London, British Library, Or. MS. 2265, fol. 2*v*)

of the figural tradition of pre-Islamic Iran, notably in Manichaeism. Scholars contrasted this Iranian tradition with a supposedly Semitic tradition of iconophobia. More recent scholarship, however, has shown that the Islamic world had a continuous tradition of figural imagery in private and secular contexts and that the art of the illustrated book developed in the 9th century as part of the revival of Classical learning sponsored by the Abbasid caliphate (*reg* 749–1258) as well as a continuation of the tradition of imagery practised in western Central Asia (*see* CENTRAL ASIA, §I, 4(iv) and (v)). The florescence of the illustrated book in 14th-century Iran has also been connected to the Mongol domination of much of the Islamic world and increased contacts with China, where illustrated texts were a major art form.

(a) Scholarship. (b) Patronage and conventions.

(a) Scholarship.

Problems of analysis and attribution. The study of painted illustrations from Islamic manuscripts has largely been a product of Western scholars who followed models established for the study of Western art and focused primarily on such questions as the identification of regional schools and the hands of individual painters. This approach has been fruitful for such famous painters as BIHZAD, but it has been less successful with others, as few artists before the 16th century signed their work. There is little, if any, contemporary evidence for the identification of individual artists before the 16th century, and only in the 17th century can their careers be established on the basis of signed works. It was also at this point that artists and patrons became interested in the earlier history of manuscript painting in Iran and began to collect examples of it in albums, add attributions to earlier works and write its history. Many so-called 'signatures' are later attributions of dubious value.

The identification of schools and hands is further complicated by the lack of information about the working methods of artists in the medieval Islamic world. It is not known, for example, whether a master painter was usually responsible for drawing the outlines and his students responsible for colouring, or whether there were specialists for the application of gold or the drawing of faces or animals. Traditional workshop practices encouraged the repetition of compositions through the use of pounces, pattern books and standardized scenes. The depiction of such a well-known scene from Persian literature as *Khusraw Espying Shirin Bathing* (from Nizami's *Khamsa* ('Five poems'); *see* §(ii)(b) below) remained virtually unaltered for generations, and images from such important manuscripts as the *Dīvān* (collected poetry) of Khwaju Kirmani, made for the Jalayirid sultan Ahmad (Baghdad, 1396; London, BL, Add. MS. 18113; *see* §(v)(c) and fig. 119 below), served as models for artists throughout the 15th century. It also seems probable that artists could work in several styles, for it is known that calligraphers had to master several styles of script and copied the work of their masters so adeptly that the difference could not be detected.

All these factors mean that the study of Islamic manuscript painting has often been divorced from the context in which it was produced and appreciated in the Islamic world, that is, the illustrated book. Until the 16th century the calligrapher was more important than the painter, and the names and careers of many more calligraphers than painters are known. From that time, however, the balance began to shift, and the artist emerged as a distinct personality. Already in the 16th century, paintings attributed to famous artists were removed from manuscripts and collected with independent images and specimens of calligraphy in albums prepared for the most discerning connoisseurs.

Only in the second half of the 20th century did scholars begin to investigate the relations between all the parts of the book, such as text, calligraphy, image, decoration and binding. The space allotted for the illustration was determined by the calligrapher. In earlier manuscripts the calligrapher left a space in the text which he, or another, would later illustrate. But as the importance and size of the image increased, several changes occurred. To ensure that the space for an image would be properly placed on the page, the calligrapher often manipulated the layout of the text preceding the image, particularly by writing on the diagonal, which took up more space than writing horizontally. The triangular interstices were often filled with decorative motifs, which served to cue the reader that an illustrated page would soon follow. In later manuscripts, the illustration took such pre-eminence over the text that an illustrated page might have only one or two couplets of text integrated into the image. These verses were often penned after the image was completed, for many completed images lack text. In some cases a laminate was made: a full-page image was painted on one sheet of paper, which was then pasted to the blank side of another sheet that had the text copied on the other side.

Many of the technical aspects of book illustration in the Islamic world have only begun to attract the attention of scholars. Scholars such as Adle studied the relations between the module or scale of the image and the layout and size of the calligraphy. Lowry and others (1988) had the pigments analysed, with the goal of establishing groups of painted images on technical grounds. It is well known, for example, that *peori*, or Indian yellow, a pigment made from the urine of cows fed on mango leaves, was not used in Persian painting and can be used therefore as a criterion to distinguish manuscripts in a provincial Iranian style from those produced in India. Visual analysis shows that the green pigment used in manuscripts attributed to Shiraz is of lesser quality (and more corrosive) than that used in Herat. The investigation of pigments is complicated by the retouching and 'improvement' to which manuscript paintings were often subjected as fashions and ideals of beauty changed. Several images in the Great Mongol *Shāhnāma* ('Book of kings'; Tabriz, *c.* 1335; dispersed, ex-Demotte), for example, were retouched in the 19th century. Not only were faces changed and eyes darkened, but flaking pigments were painted over, often with such modern pigments as Prussian blue.

Single-page paintings and manuscript illustrations have been particularly subject to faking and forgery, undoubtedly because of the value of single images and the relative ease and availability of the necessary materials. In the 16th century the reputation of the painter Bihzad was so great that his work was copied and his name inscribed on works patently not by him, such as the *Seated Scribe* (Boston, MA, Isabella Stewart Gardner Mus.). Similarly, many drawings attributed to Riza, the great 17th-century master (*see* §(vi)(a) below), are not by his hand. In some cases these images can be understood as a form of tribute to the master, as exact copying was the most sincere form of admiration and the craft tradition encouraged the exact repetition of compositions, figures and style. Indeed, the style of Riza was copied and emulated for a century after his death. In many cases the attributions added to an image or in the margin are the later work of well-intentioned connoisseurs. The Mughal emperor Jahangir (*reg* 1605–27), for example, often added attributions and identifications to the Persian manuscripts in the royal library.

Throughout the history of illustrated manuscripts from the Islamic world, incomplete or damaged texts have been repaired and restored, and illustrations completed and repainted. For example, a magnificent copy of Nizami's *Khamsa* (Istanbul, Topkapı Pal. Lib., H. 762; see fig. 124 below and COLOUR, colour pl. V) was begun in the mid-15th century for the Timurid ruler Abu'l-Qasim Babur (*reg* 1449–57), continued for several Turkoman princes and, still unfinished, passed into the hands of one of the Safavid amirs, for whom the last illustrations were added in the early 16th century (*see* §(vi)(a) below). Another superb copy of the same text (see figs 104 and 107 below)

104. *Ascent of the Prophet to Heaven*, 287×186 mm; illustration from Nizami: *Khamsa* ('Five poems'), Tabriz, 1539–43 (London, British Library, Or. MS. 2265, fol. 195*r*)

was prepared for the Safavid ruler Tahmasp I between 1539 and 1543; it was refurbished and given additional illustrations in the late 17th century by the leading artist of the day. In more recent times manuscripts and their images have been altered to increase their sale value. Most collectors would only accept images on a text page, and some preferred a double-page spread that recalled the open book. Images on damaged pages have been trimmed and pasted on to irrelevant text pages. Illustrated leaves have been joined to unillustrated ones to create double-page spreads. Pages with illustrations on recto and verso have been split and new unillustrated backs commissioned. All these alterations were possible because of the elaborate way books were produced and because collectors rarely read the text accompanying the image and were not troubled by words that might have nothing to do with the image. Only in the rarest cases has an entire illustrated manuscript been forged. The *Andarznāma* ('Book of Andarz') appeared on the art market in the 1950s and purported to be the earliest illustrated Persian manuscript. It was quickly shown to be a crude forgery on the grounds of an inconsistent text, modern pigments (i.e. Prussian blue) and spurious iconography (depiction of stirrups).

Publications. Many of the advances in the study of manuscript illustration in the Islamic world have resulted from international exhibitions (*see* §XIII below), which have been accompanied by catalogues and other volumes that have played a key role in the dissemination of information. A standard reference work such as Binyon, Wilkinson and Gray's *Persian Miniature Painting* was written to commemorate the Burlington House exhibition of Persian art in 1931; subsequent international exhibitions and catalogues have dealt with particular aspects of the history of the Islamic illustrated manuscript, such as those of the early Safavid or Timurid dynasties. Equally important in the refinement of knowledge about Islamic manuscript illustration has been the publication of the major museum collections with illustrated catalogues. Without a doubt, the largest and finest collection, much of which was once the property of the Ottoman sultans, is housed at the Topkapı Palace Library in Istanbul, but only some of its manuscripts and paintings have been published. Smaller but no less important public collections in Paris, Dublin, London and Washington have been published, as have a few private collections, such as those of Edmund de Unger (Ham, Surrey, Keir priv. col.) and Prince Sadruddin Aga Khan.

Other publications have focused on the manuscripts produced under a particular dynasty, such as the systematic studies of Ilkhanid, Timurid, Safavid and Ottoman illustrated books by Ivan Stchoukine (*see* SHCHUKIN, (2)), or on a particular manuscript, such as Grabar and Blair's monograph on the Great Mongol *Shāhnāma*, or Dickson and Welch's monograph on another copy (dispersed, ex-Houghton priv. col.; e.g. New York, Met.) of the same text prepared for Tahmasp I two centuries later. Quite another genre has been the study of a particular text, such as Firdawsi's *Shāhnāma* or Nizami's *Khamsa*. This topic has been approached either through indexes of scenes illustrated, such as Dodkhudoeva's catalogue of *Khamsa* illustrations, or through analyses of a text repeatedly illustrated at a particular time, such as Simpson's work on the Small *Shāhnāmas*. A further approach has been the study of manuscripts produced in a particular city or workshop, such as Guest's study of the manuscripts illustrated at Shiraz in the 16th century.

Linguistic classification. The study of Islamic illustrated books has traditionally been divided along ethnic lines into Arab, Persian and Turkish groups. The problems with these convenient but misleading divisions can be seen in the case of Baghdad: the paintings produced there in the 13th century are considered Arab, those of the 14th and 15th centuries Persian, while those of the late 16th century are Turkish. Similarly, a division along linguistic lines can be misleading, for the royal workshops in 15th-century Herat produced manuscripts in Chaghatay Turkish (written in Uyghur script) and Persian (in Arabic script) and illustrated them in the same classical Persian style. Manuscripts written in Persian were also prepared for the Ottoman and Mughal rulers of Turkey and India.

(b) Patronage and conventions. Given the importance of the written word in Islam, it is likely that a larger segment of society was familiar with books than in other contemporary cultures. Nevertheless, illustrated books were always a rare commodity and restricted in circulation to the court and highest levels of the urban bourgeoisie. Only a few patrons or owners of illustrated books are known from the medieval Arab world; some books were made on commission for princes while others were made for the market, but no direct correlation between quality and patronage can be established. In the Persian book tradition, and in the related Ottoman and Mughal ones, the finest illustrated books were made for royal libraries: the patronage of fine illustrated manuscripts was an important attribute of princes. These books, which often had deliberate programmes of images to make didactic points, can be distinguished from those more numerous examples of commercial production that had no deliberate programme beyond the presentation of familiar images and heroes.

The earliest surviving illustrations in books from the Islamic world are simple and diagrammatic, with only the merest suggestions of setting, space, action and detail. These pictures developed out of a tradition of scientific and technical illustration and were designed only to express visually the information conveyed verbally in the text. Soon, however, the possibilities of the image were expanded and a complex language of illustration was developed. This development is incipient in several copies of al-Hariri's *Maqāmāt* ('Assemblies'; *see* §(iv)(c) below) produced at Baghdad in the first half of the 13th century, where more complex images both illustrate the text and comment on it, but it is principally a feature of the book tradition in the Iranian world in the 14th century and later. At first both the pictorial conventions and expressive possibilities of the image were expanded in manuscripts produced under the patronage of the ILKHANID dynasty (*reg* 1256–1353) in Iran. The representation of pictorial space became more important, and devices taken from foreign traditions of representation, such as Chinese scroll

painting and Byzantine illustrated manuscripts, were assimilated into the visual vocabulary. These devices included cutting off figures at the edge of the picture-plane, repoussoir figures in the foreground, horizon lines, receding lines of hills and pure landscape images. The expressive potential of images was also exploited, and several paintings, particularly from the Great Mongol *Shāhnāma* (*see* §(v)(b) below), dramatically depict such strong emotions as grief.

This period of experimentation in the pictorial and expressive potential of images soon ended; by 1370 a canon of representation had been established that was to be followed until the 19th century in the book tradition of much of the Islamic lands. In general, emotional involvement was replaced with lyrical detachment, so that the goriest of battles is frozen in a choreographed ballet. The only uncontrolled feature is the exuberance with which the image spills over the outer edge of the frame into the margin, but even this feature became regularized and conventionalized. Time and the elements have been stopped in an unchanging moment of perpetual springtime, where birds sing and flowers bloom forever. Skies are indifferently blue or gold, and the few night-time scenes known are indicated only by a crescent moon and the golden flames of candles and torches. There is no light and shade in this immutable world, and colours are unmodulated. Colour is not used to characterize a particular substance but is applied arbitrarily to unify compositions and to lead the eye from one vibrant spot to another. Pattern is applied uniformly to bricks, tiles and textiles, only minimally revealing the volume of the surface beneath. Figures are normally depicted in three-quarter view, with the exception of such stock figures as an old crone.

Scenes set in the distant past are peopled with figures in contemporary dress; in the finest manuscripts produced for royal patrons the protagonists may be portraits of major figures and the scenes may depict the court of the ruler. The double-page frontispiece to a copy of Sa‘di's *Būstān* ('Orchard', Herat, 1488; Cairo, N. Lib., Adab Farsi 908), illustrated by Bihzad, clearly depicts the court of the patron, Husayn Bayqara (*see* TIMURID, §II(8)). The sultan himself, seated under a canopy inscribed with his titles, is distinguished by physiognomy and dress. This is an early example of portraiture, which became more frequent in later periods, although common only in India.

Spatial perspective is often said to be absent from these pictures, but it does exist: it merely uses a series of conventions different from those used in the West. The horizon line is arbitrarily set about two-thirds of the way up the picture, and most of the action takes place below it. The ground is seen from a bird's-eye perspective, but the figures on it are seen from the ground. Thus carpets on the floor are shown as flat rectangles with their edges parallel to the margins of the picture: their patterns are clearly visible. Vanishing-point perspective, introduced in the 17th century as a result of increased familiarity with European prints, was only superficially assimilated into traditional modes of spatial representation, as were other conventions of European representation such as atmospheric perspective and shading.

From the 14th to the 17th century the production of luxury illustrated manuscripts was one of the major art forms in the greater Iranian world, and the importance of illustrated books spread beyond the limits of the medium. The production of luxury books was normally entrusted to a royal studio or scriptorium; the designs produced there were used for other arts, such as carpets, textiles, metalwork and ceramics. Thus the illustrated book was not only important in its own right but also played a central role in the creation of other arts.

BIBLIOGRAPHY

GENERAL

P. W. Schultz: *Die persisch-islamische Miniaturmalerei* (Leipzig, 1914)

T. W. Arnold: *Painting in Islam* (Oxford, 1928)

T. W. Arnold and A. Grohmann: *The Islamic Book: A Contribution to its Art and History from the VII–XVIII Century* (Leipzig and Paris, 1929)

E. Blochet: *Musulman Painting, XIIth–XVIIth Century* (London, 1929/R New York, 1975)

A. Sakisian: *La Miniature persane du XIIe au XVIIe siècle* (Paris and Brussels, 1929)

L. Binyon, J. V. S. Wilkinson and B. Gray: *Persian Miniature Painting* (Oxford, 1933/R New York, 1971)

G. D. Guest: *Shiraz Painting in the Sixteenth Century* (Washington, DC, 1949)

B. Gray: *Persian Painting* (Geneva, 1961)

R. Ettinghausen: *Arab Painting* (Geneva, 1962)

E. J. Grube: *Muslim Miniature Paintings from the 13th to 19th Century, from Collections in the United States and Canada* (Venice, 1962)

O. F. Akimushkin and A. A. Ivanov: *Persidskiye miniatyury XIV–XVII vv.* [Persian miniatures of the 14th–17th centuries] (Moscow, 1968)

R. Pinder-Wilson, ed.: *Paintings from Islamic Lands* (Oxford, 1969)

L. Golombek: 'Toward a Classification of Islamic Painting', *Islamic Art in the Metropolitan Museum of Art*, ed. R. Ettinghausen (New York, 1972), pp. 22–31

C. Adle: 'Recherche sur le module et le tracé correcteur dans la miniature orientale', *Monde Iran. & Islam*, iii (1975), pp. 81–105

M. S. Simpson: *The Illustration of an Epic: The Earliest Shahnama Manuscripts* (New York, 1979)

O. Grabar and S. Blair: *Epic Images and Contemporary History: The Illustrations of the Great Mongol Shahnama* (Chicago and London, 1980)

Wonders of the Age: Masterpieces of Early Safavid Painting, 1501–1576 (exh. cat. by S. C. Welch, Cambridge, MA, Fogg, 1980)

M. B. Dickson and S. C. Welch: *The Houghton Shāhnāmeh* (Cambridge, MA, 1981)

N. Rohani: *A Bibliography of Persian Miniature Painting* (Cambridge, MA, 1982)

M. S. Simpson: 'The Production and Patronage of the *Haft Aurang* by Jami in the Freer Gallery of Art', *A. Orient.*, xiii (1982), pp. 93–119

L. N. Dodkhudoeva: *Poemy Nizami v srednekovoy miniaturnoy zhivopisi* [The poems of Nizami in medieval miniature painting] (Moscow, 1985) [with Eng. summary]

T. W. Lentz and G. D. Lowry: *Timur and the Princely Vision* (Washington, DC, 1989)

S. Canby, ed.: *Persian Masters: Five Centuries of Painting* (Bombay, 1990)

COLLECTIONS

F. R. Martin: *The Miniature Painting and Painters of Persia, India and Turkey, from the 8th to the 18th Century*, 2 vols (London, 1912)

G. Marteau and H. Vever: *Miniatures persanes tirées des collections de Georges Marteau et Henri Vever et exposées au Musée des arts décoratifs, juin–octobre 1912*, 2 vols (Paris, 1913)

E. Schroeder: *Persian Miniatures in the Fogg Museum of Art* (Cambridge, MA, 1942)

B. W. Robinson: *A Descriptive Catalogue of the Persian Paintings in the Bodleian Library* (Oxford, 1958)

A. J. Arberry and others: *The Chester Beatty Library: A Catalogue of the Persian Manuscripts and Miniatures*, 3 vols (Dublin, 1959–62)

A. Welch: *Collection of Islamic Art: Prince Sadruddin Aga Khan*, 4 vols (Geneva, 1972–8)

B. W. Robinson, ed.: *Islamic Painting and the Arts of the Book*, The Keir Collection (London, 1976)

N. M. Titley: *Miniatures from Persian Manuscripts: A Catalogue and Subject Index of Paintings from Persia, India and Turkey in the British Library and the British Museum* (London, 1977)

——: *Persian Miniature Painting and its Influence on the Art of Turkey and India: The British Library Collections* (London, 1983)

G. D. Lowry and others: *An Annotated and Illustrated Checklist of the Vever Collection* (Washington, DC, 1988)

B. Schmitz: *Islamic Manuscripts in the New York Public Library* (New York, 1992)

A. Soudavar: *Art of the Persian Courts: Selections from the Art and History Trust Collection* (New York, 1992)

S. P. Camby: *Persian Painting* (London, 1993)

SHEILA S. BLAIR, JONATHAN M. BLOOM

(ii) Subject-matter. A wide variety of texts was illustrated in the Islamic world but, paradoxically, the Islamic authors and books most popular in the West, such as the poetry of Omar Khayyam and *The Arabian Nights*, were rarely if ever illustrated in the Islamic world. Most of the earliest illustrated manuscripts to survive are scientific and technical works, but a range of literary and poetic writings, subsumed under the rubric '*belles-lettres*', was also popular in the Arab world, and illustrated copies survive from the years after 1000. Many kinds of literature were also illustrated in the Persian- and Turkish-speaking lands, including a few religious texts, although the Koran, the major religious text in the Islamic world and its most common book, was never illustrated. In the Persian-speaking lands, epic poetry, particularly Firdawsi's *Shāhnāma* ('Book of kings'), was the most commonly illustrated type of literature. Illustrated histories, which first survive from 14th-century Iran, became more important in later times and spread to Turkey and India.

□

(a) Scientific and technical works. (b) *Belles-lettres*. (c) Epic poetry. (d) Historical writing.

(a) Scientific and technical works. Scientific and technical texts are among the earliest illustrated manuscripts surviving from the Islamic world and comprise a distinct category within the tradition of illustrated manuscripts. This development may be explained by the extraordinary interdependence of text and illustration that they exhibit. The illustrations served primarily to elucidate the text and in some cases were necessary to understand it. Consequently illustrations developed as integral parts of the works and appeared consistently and relatively unchanged in successive copies. The production of scientific and technical manuscripts was due to the burst of intellectual and scientific activity in the Islamic world that began in the 9th century with the translation into Arabic of a full range of Greek scientific and learned texts. It continued with the creation of original works by Islamic scholars deeply indebted to the Classical tradition, a development encouraged by contact with Middle Byzantine texts. It was only natural, therefore, that both textual and visual components of these works were firmly rooted in the Classical tradition and would remain relatively faithful to it throughout the long history of their production, which extended at least to the 16th century in various regions of the Islamic world.

11th century. Many of the hallmarks associated with scientific manuscript illustration are already established in two of the earliest surviving fully illustrated manuscripts: a copy of 'Abd al-Rahman ibn 'Umar al-Sufi's celebrated astronomical catalogue of the stars and constellations, *Kitāb ṣuwar al-kawākib al-thābita* ('Book of the fixed stars'; 1009–10; Oxford, Bodleian Lib., Marsh 144), and a copy of an Arabic translation of Dioskurides' herbal with

105. *Machine for Washing the Hands*, 314×219 mm; illustration from al-Jazari: *Automata*, 1315–16 (Washington, DC, Freer Gallery of Art, MS. 30.75r)

descriptions of plants and their medicinal uses, *De materia medica* (1083; Leiden, Bib. Rijksuniv., MS. Or. 289, Warn.). Despite the visual dissimilarities between these works, they exemplify and share the distinct characteristics of illustrated scientific manuscripts: both are seminal works in Islamic science that were repeatedly illustrated, both emphasize the overriding explanatory function of the illustrations, and both preserve a close affinity to the Classical tradition. Al-Sufi's work, an original scholarly endeavour, is a synthesis of known Classical scholarship and contemporary Arabic treatises. *De materia medica* was first translated from Greek into Arabic in the 9th century and formed the basis of all Islamic pharmacology.

12th–13th centuries. During the late 12th century and the 13th, the production of illustrated scientific manuscripts expanded dramatically. Earlier works were continually executed with fresh illustrations. Many more illustrated copies of the works of al-Sufi and Dioskurides survive from this period, even from such remote areas of manuscript production as Spain and North Africa (e.g. a copy of the *Kitāb ṣuwar* made in Ceuta in 1224; *see* §(iv)(b) below). There also appeared a wealth of other illustrated texts on such scientific and empirical subjects as astronomy, botany, cosmology, engineering, medicine and zoology, all of which maintained their underlying ties to their

Classical sources. Some of these manuscripts, especially those of a specialized, technical nature, contain precise diagrams that were copied unchanged into the 16th and 17th centuries. For example, diagrams of the anatomy of the human eye can be found in a 13th-century manuscript of the treatise on optics *Kitāb al-'ashr maqālāt fī'l-'ayn* ('Book of the ten discourses on the eye'; Cairo, N. Lib., Tibb Taimur 100) by the great scholar and translator Hunayn ibn Ishaq al-'Ibadi (809–73). The *Kitāb fī ma'rifat al-ḥiyal al-handasiyya* ('Book of knowledge of ingenious mechanical devices') or *Automata*, written by al-Jazari for the Artuqid ruler Nasir al-Din (*reg* 1201–22), survives through a spectacular series of closely related illustrated copies, beginning with a manuscript (Istanbul, Topkapı Pal. Lib., A. 3472) copied in 1206, shortly after the autograph work, and ending with a 19th-century Persian translation (Paris, Bib. N., MS. supp. pers. 1145 and 1145a). Both text and illustrations are based on Classical sources as known through Greek compendia on mechanics and mathematics by such writers as Heron of Alexandria and Philon of Byzantium. The treatise owes its popularity not only to its scientific interest but also to its capacity to entertain. Closely following the models of their Classical predecessors, the illustrations contain many diagrams in order to explain the technical complexities of the mechanical contrivances (see fig. 105 and CLOCKS AND WATCHES, fig. 1). Even where accessory figures are inserted, adding some animation to the images, the figures maintain their underlying Classical ties despite stylistic changes over time. In a manuscript of Ahmad ibn al-Hasan ibn al-Ahnaf's *Kitāb al-bayṭara* ('Book of farriery'; Baghdad, 1208–9; Cairo, N. Lib., Khalil Agha 8f), which was based on a Greek veterinary text, the artist generally stayed within the explanatory needs of the text in representing the animal and human accessory figures, but in one instance he introduced a narrative spontaneity and naturalized the figures into their new Islamic milieu.

Such a venture into narrative expansion beyond the literal needs of the text characterizes the most outstanding manuscript illustration of this period, the celebrated copy (1224; dispersed, e.g. Istanbul, Topkapı Pal. Lib., Ayasofya 3703) of Dioskurides' *De materia medica*. The illustrations of the preparation of drugs by the physician and his assistants and the elaborate representation of fully equipped pharmacies go well beyond the demands of the text. In two illustrated copies of the *Kitāb al-diryāq* ('Book of antidotes') by Pseudo-Galen (1199, Paris, Bib. N., MS. arab. 2964; mid-13th century, Vienna, Österreich. Nbib., Cod. A.F. 10; *see* §(iv)(c) and fig. 110 below), contemporary agricultural activities and genre scenes are captured in colourful detail.

The enrichment of imagery and the unprecedented variety in human representation in scientific manuscripts of the 12th and 13th centuries reflect the broader explosion of imagery that occurred in all the portable arts during this period. An expanded medieval Islamic definition of scientific works, to include a wider range of empirical, philosophical and learned disciplines based on both Classical and popular traditions, seems to have encouraged a more fluid exchange of imagery between the scientific and literary branches of Islamic manuscript illustration. A series of copies were made of the moralistic animal fables

Kalila and Dimna, written by Ibn al-Muqaffaʿ (*d c.* 757–9) and based on the Indian *Fables of Bidpai*. The earliest surviving copy (?from Syria; Paris, Bib. N., MS. arab. 3465) dates between 1200 and 1220. The depiction of the two jackals, who are the main characters, and the other animals is closely related to the Classical tradition of zoological illustration as well as to a long tradition of pictorial representation in western Central Asia. The *Mukhtār al-ḥikam wa-maḥāsin al-kalim* ('Choicest maxims and best sayings'), written by the Fatimid prince al-Mubashshir ibn Fatik in the 11th century, contains biographies and sayings of such great Greek physicians, philosophers and scientists as Galen, Hippokrates, Aristotle, Socrates and Solon. The texts were not only derived from Greek anthologies but were sometimes direct quotations from Greek sources, already available in Arabic translation. The illustrations in a 13th-century copy (Istanbul, Topkapı Pal. Lib., A. 3206) follow Classical figural types, compositions and iconographic groupings. Another illustrated manuscript, the *Rasāʾil ikhwān al-ṣafāʾ* ('Epistles of the sincere brethren'; Baghdad, 1287–8; Istanbul, Süleymaniye Lib., Esad Ef. 3638), is a 10th-century encyclopedic work deeply affected by Classical thought and philosophy while expounding a new Muslim truth.

The integration of assorted scientific and non-scientific subjects within a single work is epitomized by the cosmology entitled *ʿAjāʾib al-makhlūqāt wa-gharāʾib al-mawjūdāt* ('The wonders of creation and their singularities'), written by al-Qazwini in 1276. The earliest surviving illustrated copy (Munich, Bayer. Staatsbib., C. arab. 464) was made in Wasit (south-east Iraq) only four years later, within the lifetime of the author, by Muhammad ibn Muhammad ibn ʿAli, who probably copied the original illustrations along with the text. A catalogue and study of all natural phenomena known at the time, both heavenly and earthly, scientific and fantastic, real and mythological, al-Qazwini's cosmology fully benefited from the pool of images available in literary and scientific illustrations. The text enjoyed enormous popularity; three Arabic copies survive from the end of the 14th century, and translations into Persian and Turkish were later illustrated. This series of illustrated manuscripts provides a substantial body of Islamic astronomical and astrological images. As is characteristic of scientific illustration, the images closely follow earlier iconography, although modifications in style and fashion appear in the later Persian and Turkish versions.

14th–15th centuries. The basic repertory of illustrated scientific manuscripts had been established by the time of the Mongol invasions in the mid-13th century. With a few exceptions, illustrated manuscripts produced after this time were copies of older works, some of which do not survive in earlier editions, or new anthologies. An outstanding work, again combining scientific and fantastic elements, is a manuscript of Ibn Bakhtishu's *Manāfiʿ al-ḥayawān* ('Usefulness of animals'; 1297–9; New York, Pierpont Morgan Lib., MS. M.500) copied at Maragha in north-west Iran. Despite the obvious infusion of Persian and East Asian elements in the superb illustrations of animals, the systematic survey of the subject is still faithful to the Classical tradition. Astrological compendia continued to be popular under the JALAYIRID dynasty (*reg* 1336–

1432), as can be seen in a profusely illustrated copy (1399; Oxford, Bodleian Lib., Or. MS. 133) of tracts on astrology, divination and prognostication known as the *Kitāb al-bulhān*, a manuscript of the *Majmūʿa al-mubārak* ('Blessed compendium'; Ham, Surrey, Keir priv. col., MS.III.29–68; U. Sarajevo, Inst. Orient. Res.) and a copy of Nasir al-Din al-Tusi's *ʿAjāʾib al-makhlūqāt* (1388; Paris, Bib. N., MS. pers. 332). The Timurid prince Iskandar Sultan (1384–c. 1415; *see* TIMURID, §II(4)) was a noted patron of lavishly illustrated manuscripts on scientific subjects, such as an anthology with astrological and zodiacal images (London, BL, Add. MS. 27261). Much of this astronomical and astrological imagery was repeated with little innovation in later works, such as an 18th-century manuscript of al-Qazwini's *ʿAjāʾib al-makhlūqāt* (Munich, Bayer. Staatsbib., C. arab. 463).

Zoological works, especially *Kalila and Dimna*, were popular under the Mamluk dynasty (*reg* 1250–1517) of Egypt and Syria, and several careful copies were made in the 14th century (e.g. 1354; Oxford, Bodleian Lib., Pococke 400; Paris, Bib. N., MS. arab. 3467). Related works in the first half of the 14th century include Ibn Zafar al-Siqilli's *Sulwān al-muṭāʿ* ('Prescription for pleasure'; Kuwait, Homeizi priv. col.; Geneva, Prince Sadruddin Aga Khan priv. col.; Washington, DC, Freer, 54.1–2), al-Jahiz's *Kitāb al-ḥayawān* ('Book of animals'; Milan, Bib. Ambrosiana, Ar. A.F.D. 140 Inf.) and Ibn Ghanim al-Maqdisi's *Kashf al-asrār* ('Disclosure of secrets'; Istanbul, Süleymaniye Lib., Lala Ismail 565; *see* §(v)(a) below). By the second half of the 14th century distinctive Mamluk works on horsemanship and military exercises (Arab. *furūsiyya*) appeared. The technical and instructive nature of their diagrams is exemplified by a copy of Isa ibn Ismaʿil al-Aqsaraʾi's *Nihāyat al-suʾl waʾl-umniyya*, a treatise on horsemanship (1366; Dublin, Chester Beatty Lib., Add. MS. 1). A noteworthy example (Istanbul, U. Lib., A. 4689) from the 15th century is the *Kitāb al-zardaqa* ('Book of farriery') written for Yalbay, Keeper of the Horse for the Commander-in-Chief of Damascus during the reign of Barsbay (1422–38).

16th century and later. Scientific illustration continued well into the 16th and 17th centuries, and later in some areas. The output mainly consisted of copies of older works; the influential works of al-Sufi, Dioskurides, al-Jazari, al-Qazwini and manuscripts of *Kalila and Dimna* were the most popular. These manuscripts remained true to the nature of scientific illustration and preserved their links with the original Islamic works and their Classical predecessors.

BIBLIOGRAPHY

Ibn al-Razzaz al-Jazari: *Kitāb fī maʿrifat al-ḥiyal al-handasiyya* [Book of knowledge of ingenious mechanical devices] (*c.* 1206); Eng. trans., ed. D. R. Hill (Dordrecht and Boston, 1974)

K. Weitzmann: 'The Greek Sources of Islamic Scientific Illustrations', *Archaeologica Orientalia in Memoriam Ernst Herzfeld*, ed. G. C. Miles (Locust Valley, NY, 1952), pp. 244–66; also in *Studies in Classical and Byzantine Manuscript Illumination*, ed. H. L. Kessler (Chicago and London, 1971), pp. 20–44

E. J. Grube: 'Materialien zum Dioskurides Arabicus', *Aus der Welt der islamischen Kunst: Festschrift für Ernst Kühnel*, ed. R. Ettinghausen (Berlin, 1959), pp. 163–94

S. Walzer: 'The Mamlūk Illuminated Manuscripts of Kalīla wa-Dimna', *Aus der Welt der islamischen Kunst: Festschrift für Ernst Kühnel*, ed. R. Ettinghausen (Berlin, 1959), pp. 195–206

E. Wellesz: 'An Early al-Ṣūfī Manuscript in the Bodleian Library in Oxford: A Study in Islamic Constellation Images', *A. Orient.*, iii (1959), pp. 1–26

R. Ettinghausen: *Arab Painting* (Geneva, 1962)

S. H. Nasr: *Islamic Science: An Illustrated Study* (London, 1976)

D. Haldane: *Mamluk Painting* (Warminster, 1978)

E. Atıl: *Kalila wa Dimna: Fables from a Fourteenth-century Arabic Manuscript* (Washington, DC, 1981)

——: *Renaissance of Islam: Art of the Mamluks* (Washington, DC, 1981)

D. Brandenburg: *Islamic Miniature Painting in Medical Manuscripts* (Basle, 1982)

E. R. Hoffman: *The Emergence of Illustration in Arabic Manuscripts: Classical Legacy and Islamic Transformation* (diss., Cambridge, MA, Harvard U., 1982)

R. Ward: 'Evidence for a School of Painting at the Artuqid Court', *The Art of Syria and the Jazira, 1100–1250*, ed. J. Raby (Oxford, 1985), pp. 69–84

S. Carboni: 'Two Fragments of a Jalayirid Astrological Treatise in the Keir Collection and in the Oriental Institute in Sarajevo', *Islam. A.*, ii (1987), pp. 149–86

EVA R. HOFFMAN

(b) *Belles-lettres.* Various literary works in Arabic and then Persian and Turkish were prepared in illustrated copies. As was the case with scientific manuscripts, the earliest examples derived from the Classical and Byzantine tradition of book illustration. A 20-volume copy of Abu'l-Faraj al-Isfahani's *Kitāb al-aghānī* ('Book of songs') made between 1217 and 1220 for BADR AL-DIN LU'LU', regent to the last Zangids in Mosul, had illustrated frontispieces; of the six volumes that survive, five preserve frontispieces depicting courtly life (*see* §(iv)(c) below). The earliest illustrated manuscripts of prose fiction in Arabic are copies of the *Kalila and Dimna* animal fables (e.g. ?Syria, 1200–20; Paris, Bib. N., MS. arab. 3465; *see* §(a) above).

The illustration of literary works flourished in the Arab world after 1200. Four additional illustrated copies of *Kalila and Dimna* and eleven illustrated copies of the *Maqāmāt* ('Assemblies') of al-Hariri (1054–1122) are known before 1350. The *Maqāmāt*, which recounts the adventures of the rogue Abu Zayd of Saruj as told by the merchant al-Harith, enjoyed enormous popularity, primarily for its linguistic ingenuity and punning style. The illustrations emphasize another aspect of the text, the protagonists' adventures throughout the Islamic world, thereby providing a rare glimpse of medieval daily life, for example the village scene in the Schefer Hariri (1236–7; Paris, Bib. N., MS. arab. 5847, fol. 138r; see fig. 111 below). Romances were rarely illustrated in the Arab world. One exception is a fragmentary manuscript of the tale of the lovers *Bayad and Riyad* (see fig. 106) copied in Spain or Morocco (*see also* §(iv)(b) below). The surviving illustrations depict an aristocratic milieu distinct from the popular settings of the *Maqāmāt*; the additive quality of the images and the local architectural details show that the artist was working outside traditional modes.

In the Persian-speaking world entirely different types of literature were illustrated. In addition to epic poetry and historical writing (*see* §§(c) and (d) below), lyric and mystical poetry was commonly illustrated. The earliest surviving manuscript is a unique copy of 'Ayyuqi's verse romance *Varqa and Gulshah* (*c.* 1250; Istanbul, Topkapı Pal. Lib., H. 841), probably illustrated at Konya in Anatolia (*see* §(v)(f) and fig. 125 below). Other literary works were added to the repertory in the 14th century. The most popular was the *Khamsa* ('Five poems') of Nizami, one of

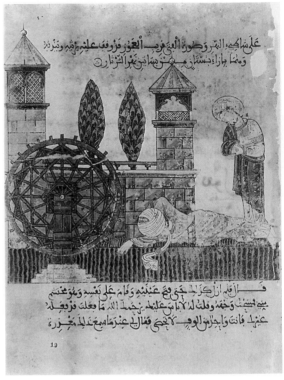

106. *Bayad Lying Unconscious at the River*, 210×198 mm; illustration from *Bayad and Riyad*, Spain or Morocco, *c.* 1200 (Rome, Vatican, Biblioteca Apostolica, MS. arab. 368, fol. 19r)

the greatest poets in the Persian language. The text comprises five romances: *Makhzan al-asrār* ('Treasury of secrets'), an ethico-political poem containing parables, reflections and allegories; *Khusraw and Shirin*, the story of the love of the Sasanian king Chosroes II for Shirin and the fate of his unfortunate rival Farhad; *Layla and Majnun*, the story of two children from the Arabian desert whose parents' foolishness brings about their unhappy fate; *Haft paykar* ('Seven portraits'), the story of the Sasanian king Bahram Gur, who represents the ideal king, and his marriages to seven princesses, who represent the different climes (see fig. 124 below); and *Iskandarnāma* ('Book of Alexander'), depicting Alexander as warrior, philosopher and prophet. At least 250 illustrated manuscripts of the text are known. The earliest is a manuscript (1318; Tehran, U., Cent. Lib., MS. 5179) in which space was left for 16 illustrations, although the actual paintings were only added in a provincial style typical of the mid-14th century. With the increased popularity of this work towards the end of the 14th century a standard repertory of images was developed, much like that of the *Shāhnāma* ('Book of kings'; *see* §(c) below). Most of the poems have well-known characters as protagonists whose exploits were easily illustrated. In the *Makhzan al-asrār*, however, there are no consistent protagonists and the most common subjects for illustration were the parables, such as *Sanjar and the Old Woman* and *Nushirvan and his Vizier in the Ruined Palace* (see fig. 107).

107. *Nushirvan and his Vizier in the Ruined Palace*, 305×194 mm; illustration from Nizami: *Khamsa* ('Five poems'), 1539–43 (London, British Library, Or. MS. 2265, fol. 15*v*)

The popularity of Nizami's *Khamsa* led to several imitations. The *Khamsa* of Amir Khusraw Dihlavi (1253–1325) closely follows that of Nizami but is somewhat shorter. It was particularly popular in India, the author's native land. Another *Khamsa*, comprising two romances and three ethical poems imbued with Sufi mysticism, was written by Khwaju Kirmani (1290–1352). The most famous copy (London, BL, Add. MS. 18113; see fig. 119 below), which incorporates three of the five works, was illustrated by JUNAYD at Baghdad in 1396 with some of the most lyrical images in all Islamic art.

The works of other famous poets were also illustrated. Sa'di's *Gulistān* ('Rose-garden'), a collection of anecdotes illustrating ethical truths, was written in short prose passages with verse endings. It was illustrated more often than his *Būstān* ('Orchard'), a treatise on didactic and ethical questions (*see* §(i) above and fig. 131 below). A particularly splendid copy of the *Gulistān*, with fine calligraphy, illumination and eight illustrations (Herat, 1426–7; Dublin, Chester Beatty Lib., Pers. MS. 119), was made for the Timurid prince and bibliophile Baysunghur (*see* TIMURID, §II(7)).

One of the most popular works of Persian poetic literature, the *Dīvān* (collected poems) of Hafiz (1325–90), was less frequently illustrated, probably because most of the poems are *ghazal*s, relatively short lyrics that did not lend themselves easily to illustration. The most notable example is a luxury copy prepared for the Safavid prince Sam Mirza (*c.* 1526; dispersed, ex-Cartier priv. col.; e.g. Cambridge, MA, Sackler Mus.; New York, Met.; see fig. 126 below). Its five illustrations develop themes mentioned in the couplets, such as the celebration of the sighting of the new moon after Ramadan or lovers drinking wine in a garden, into full-page images drawn from contemporary life.

The poets Nizami, Sa'di and Hafiz were long dead before their poems were illustrated; by contrast, the works of another famous Persian poet, Jami (1414–92), were illustrated within the author's lifetime. His works comprise three *dīvān*s of lyric poetry and seven *masnavī*s (poems written in rhyming couplets) collectively called the *Haft awrang* ('Seven thrones'), which exists in well over one hundred illustrated copies. The most famous of the *masnavī*s, *Yusuf and Zulaykha*, is a mystical account of the biblical and Koranic story of Joseph and Potiphar's wife. The most famous illustrated manuscript of the *Haft awrang* (Washington, DC, Freer, 46.12; *see* §(vi)(a) and fig. 127 below) was copied between 1556 and 1565 for the Safavid prince Ibrahim Mirza. Its 28 splendid full-page illustrations embellish the essential narrative elements of the text with an appreciation of the author's mystical message. The *dīvān*s of such lesser poets as the Jalayirid sultan Ahmad Jalayir (*see* JALAYIRID, (1)) and the Timurid courtier ʿALISHIR NAVAʾI were also illustrated, as were poems by such figures as Shams al-Din Muhammad ʿAssar (*d* 1382) and anthologies. The latter were particularly favoured by the Timurid ruler Iskandar Sultan (*see* TIMURID, §II(4)).

Religious literature in Persian and Turkish was another genre produced in illustrated copies. Illustrated histories, epics and lyric poetry sometimes contained single scenes of religious subjects, but cycles of images illustrated works devoted to events in the life of the Prophet Muhammad. His mystical ascension to Heaven (Arab. *mi'rāj*) was a favourite subject; a lavishly illustrated copy (Paris, Bib. N., MS. supp. turc 190) of the *Mi'rājnāma* ('Book of the ascension') in Chaghatay Turkish was prepared at Herat *c.* 1436. Its 61 illustrations are striking for the lavish use of gold and fantastic images of Heaven and Hell (*see also* §(v)(d) below). A six-volume copy of the *Siyār-i Nabī* ('Life of the Prophet') prepared for the Ottoman sultan Murad III has more than 800 illustrations (*c.* 1594–5; dispersed, e.g. Dublin, Chester Beatty Lib., Turk. MS. 419; Istanbul, Topkapı Pal. Lib., H. 1221–3; New York, Pub. Lib., Spencer MS. 157). It is the largest single cycle of religious illustration in Islamic art and the most complete visual portrayal of Muhammad's life (*see also* §(vi)(e) and fig. 133 below). Another popular religious text was the *Fālnāma* ('Book of divination'), ascribed to various authors including the sixth Shi'ite imam, Ja'far al-Sadiq (*d* 765). Several illustrated copies were prepared; all have an unusually large format (600×450 mm), with illustrations on one side and text on the other, although the cycle of illustrations and iconography differ.

BIBLIOGRAPHY

R. Ettinghausen: *Arab Painting* (Geneva, 1962)
Sixteenth-century Miniatures Illustrating Manuscript Copies of the Work of Jami from the USSR Collections (Moscow, 1966)
A. S. Melikian-Chirvani: 'Le Roman de Varqé et Golšâh', *A. Asiat.*, xxii (1970) [whole issue]

P. J. Chelkowski: *Mirror of the Invisible World: Tales from the Khamseh of Nizami* (New York, 1975)

M.-R. Séguy: *The Miraculous Journey of Mahomet: Mirâj nâmeh* (London, New York and Paris, 1977)

I. Stchoukine: *Les Peintures des manuscrits de la 'Khamseh' de Nizâmî au Topkapi Sarayî Müzesi d'Istanbul* (Paris, 1977)

M. S. Simpson: 'The Production and Patronage of the *Haft Aurang* by Jami in the Freer Gallery of Art', *A. Orient.*, xiii (1982), pp. 93–119

N. M. Titley: *Persian Miniature Painting* (London, 1983)

C. G. Fisher: 'A Reconstruction of the Pictorial Cycle of the *Siyar-i Nabī* of Murad III', *A. Orient.*, xiv (1984), pp. 75–94

O. Grabar: *The Illustrations of the Maqamat* (Chicago, 1984)

L. N. Dodkhudoeva: *Poemy Nizami v srednevekovoy miniaturnoy zhivopisi* [Poems of Nizami in medieval miniature painting] (Moscow, 1985) [with Eng. summary]

J. Raby: 'Between Soghdia and the Mamluks: A Note on the Earliest Illustrations to *Kalīla wa Dimna*', *Orient. A.*, n. s., xxxiii (1987–8), pp. 381–98

SHEILA S. BLAIR, JONATHAN M. BLOOM

(c) Epic poetry. Epic poetry was particularly popular in the Persian-speaking lands, and the most commonly illustrated book in Islamic art is the *Shāhnāma* ('Book of kings'), which recounts the history of Iran from the creation of the world to the end of the Sasanian dynasty (651). Most *Shāhnāma* illustrations depict enthronements of rulers and combats between individuals or armies.

108. *Court of Gayumars*; illustration from Firdawsi: *Shāhnāma* ('Book of kings'), made for Tahmasp I, *c.* 1525–35 (Geneva, Prince Sadruddin Aga Khan private collection)

Abu'l-Qasim Firdawsi (*d c.* 1020) began work on the *Shāhnāma c.* 980 and completed it *c.* 994; a revised copy was prepared *c.* 1010 for presentation to the Ghaznavid sultan Mahmud, who purportedly did not appreciate either the text or its author and was niggardly in his recompense. Nevertheless the poem of some 50,000 rhyming couplets in *mutaqārib* metre soon became popular, and excerpts were included in an 11th-century anthology by Mas'ud ibn Sa'd. The text is based in part on an unfinished poem by Daqiqi (*d* 980) and prose works derived from pre-Islamic texts. Firdawsi's text was used as a source by many Islamic historians, and the incidents and characters described in it are alluded to by many poets.

The *Shāhnāma* has four major sections corresponding to the principal dynasties: the Pishdadians, the Kayanians, the Ashkanians or Parthians (*reg* mid-3rd century BC–AD 220s) and the Sasanians (*reg* 224–651). The text is subdivided into the reigns of 50 kings, into which is woven a cycle of heroic tales. The first section is mythical, the second essentially legendary; only the last two are based on historical fact. The first section includes the creation of the world, the invention of civilization and the origins of the long feud between the lands of Iran and Turan. The Kayanian section includes the deeds of Rustam, Isfandiyar and Bizhan, heroes linked to different regions or literary traditions. The life of Rustam links together episodes concerning the rulers on whose behalf he combats the natural and supernatural enemies of Iran. The most important human opponents were the rulers of Turan, particularly Afrasiyab, and many battles between Iranians and Turanians are described. Supernatural enemies include demons, dragons and witches, who often appear in disguise. The Ashkanian section is briefer and less colourful than the concluding section about the Sasanians, where important events are described in considerable detail.

Historical accounts record that manuscripts of the *Shāhnāma* began to be copied in Firdawsi's lifetime, but the earliest surviving manuscript (Florence, Bib. N. Cent., MS. Cl III.24 (G.F. 3)) is dated 1217. It has illumination but no illustration; the first known illustrated copies were produced during the rule of the Ilkhanids (*reg* 1256–1353). It soon became the most popular text for illustration, but copies differ markedly in the number, character and subject of their images. Certain stories were popular in most periods, especially those that depict colourful or dramatic moments in the lives of rulers or heroes. Gayumars, the first king, is often portrayed with his courtiers clothed in garments of animal skins (see fig. 108). Other scenes from the Pishdadian section include the evil Zahhak with serpents growing from his shoulders and the noble Faridun mounted on an ox and carrying a mace. The exploits of Rustam were particularly popular subjects for illustration, as were the lives of his parents, the white-haired Zal and Rudaba, the daughter of a Turanian ruler. Rustam's tragic battle with his son Suhrab provides an emotional climax that was often illustrated. The last two sections have far fewer illustrations. Alexander the Great, although he conquered Iran, was treated as an Iranian hero, and his exploits, such as his combat with the Iranians and the death of his opponent Dara, were particularly popular, but only the deeds of the most famous Sasanian rulers, such as Nushirvan, Bahram Gur, Chosroes I and Chosroes II, were usually depicted.

It is difficult to distinguish between the general popularity of the themes and characters in the *Shāhnāma* and specific knowledge of Firdawsi's text. Images of Bahram Gur and the slave-girl who mocked his skill as a hunter and of the contest between Faridun and Zahhak are depicted without text on ceramics (e.g. a 12th- or 13th-century overglaze-painted bowl; New York, Met., 57.36.2) and metalwork (e.g. a late 13th- or early 14th-century candlestick; Paris, Mus. A. Déc., 4421). Conversely the text itself could be inscribed on architecture and be used as a source of royal symbolism, as on the Saljuq palace at Konya in Turkey.

The *Shāhnāma* was regarded as a historical text, and some of the most impressive manuscripts, with fine calligraphy, illustration, illumination and binding, were commissioned by princely patrons to underscore their connection to the great heroes of the past. These manuscripts can differ from those made for the market in having illustrations chosen for their relevance to the life and character of the sponsor. A splendid copy known as the Great Mongol or Demotte *Shāhnāma* (*c.* 1335; dispersed; see §(v)(b) and fig. 115 below) has unusual scenes of death and mourning and emphasizes legitimacy and the right of foreigners to rule Iran, subjects that would have been appropriate for its probable sponsor, a vizier at the court of the Ilkhanid Abu Saʿid (*reg* 1317–35). A copy (1430; Tehran, Gulistan Pal. Lib., MS. 61) made for the Timurid prince and bibliophile Baysunghur (see TIMURID, §II(7)) has scenes of princely education. The best known of these royal *Shāhnāma* manuscripts is the one made for the Safavid shah Tahmasp I (*c.* 1525–35; dispersed, ex-Houghton priv. col.; see fig. 108). Many of its 258 illustrations were done by the leading artists of the day and depict the glorious setting of kingship (see also §(vi)(a) below).

The popularity of Firdawsi's *Shāhnāma* led to translations and imitations. An Arabic prose translation was prepared by the historian al-Bundari in 1227, although it appears never to have been illustrated. The *Shāhnāma* was translated into Turkish several times. The most popular Turkish translation was completed in 1511 by Sharif Amidi in Cairo; the holograph copy with 62 illustrations is preserved in Istanbul (see §(v)(a) below). The text was also illustrated at the Ottoman court, as were other translations of uncertain authorship (e.g. *c.* 1530; Istanbul, Topkapı Pal. Lib., H. 1116). Firdawsi's text provided a model for several versified and illustrated chronicles about mythic, legendary and historical figures. The earliest, written by Asadi in 1066, is the *Garshāspnāma* ('Book of Garshasp'), which concerns the exploits of Rustam's great-great-grandfather. One copy (1354; Istanbul, Topkapı Pal. Lib., H. 674) has five illustrations depicting the hero and his exploits, and space for other illustrations that were never executed. The *Iskandarnāma* ('Book of Alexander'), a Turkish epic chronicling the exploits of Alexander the Great, was composed by Ahmadi in 1390. The earliest of several illustrated copies was produced at Amasya (1416; Paris, Bib. N., MS. supp. turc 309). Most of its illustrations were cut from 14th-century Persian manuscripts, but three rough depictions of riders were prepared especially for it. The *Khāvarānnāma*, celebrating the virtues and exploits of

ʿAli, the son-in-law of the Prophet Muhammad and fourth caliph, was composed by Ibn Husam in 1426. A copy (*c.* 1477; dispersed, e.g. Tehran, Riza ʿAbbasi Mus.) made at Shiraz has illustrations distinguished by flaming gold haloes around the head of the Prophet. The *Shāhnāma* also served as a model for several versified histories, of which those of the Ottoman dynasty were particularly lavish (see §(d) below).

BIBLIOGRAPHY

N. Atasoy: 'Un Manuscrit mamlūk illustré du Šāhnāma', *Rev. Etud. Islam.*, xxxvii/1 (1969), pp. 151–8

J. Norgren and E. Davis: *Preliminary Index of Shah-nameh Illustrations* (Ann Arbor, MI, 1969)

M. S. Simpson: *The Illustration of an Epic: The Earliest Shahnama Manuscripts* (New York, 1979)

O. Grabar and S. Blair: *Epic Images and Contemporary History: The Illustrations of the Great Mongol Shahnama* (Chicago and London, 1980)

A. M. Piemontese: 'Nuova luce su Firdawsi: Uno Šāhnāma datato 614 H./1217 a Firenze', *AION*, n. s., xxx (1980), pp. 1–38, 189–242

M. B. Dickson and S. C. Welch: *The Houghton Shahnameh* (Cambridge, MA, 1981)

M. S. Simpson: 'Narrative Allusion and Metaphor in the Decoration of Medieval Islamic Objects', *Pictorial Narrative*, ed. H. L. Kessler and M. S. Simpson (Washington, DC, 1985), pp. 131–49

PRISCILLA P. SOUCEK

(d) Historical writing. The Arab historian al-Masʿudi wrote that *c.* 915 he saw an illustrated *History of the Kings of Persia* belonging to a noble family in southern Iran (see §(iii) below). The earliest surviving illustrated manuscripts of historical texts, however, were only produced during the period of ILKHANID rule in Iran (1256–1353). This was one of the most prolific periods for historical writing in Iran and the time when illustrated copies of the *Shāhnāma*, the Persian national epic (see §(c) above), began to proliferate. These historical manuscripts were illustrated in varying styles: the early Metropolitan style, as in a copy of al-Biruni's *Āthār al-bāqiya* ('Chronology of ancient nations'; 1307–8; Edinburgh, U. Lib., Arab. MS. 161; see §(v)(b) below) and the Provincial style associated with Shiraz, as in a copy of Balʿami's Persian adaptation of al-Tabari's *Annals* (Washington, DC, Freer, 30.21, 47.19, 56.16), but the most distinctive was the style of the Rabʿ-i Rashidi, the quarter of Tabriz (see TABRIZ, §3(i)) founded by the vizier RASHID AL-DIN. Manuscripts of his *Jāmiʿ al-tawārīkh* ('Compendium of histories'; e.g. ?1314, Edinburgh, U. Lib., Arab. MS. 20; London, N. D. Khalili priv. col.) have large folios with horizontal line drawings enhanced with coloured washes (see fig. 114 below), a format and style heavily indebted to Chinese handscrolls. Other, detached illustrations (Berlin, Staatsbib. Preuss. Kultbes., Orientabt. Diez A 70–73) have a squarer format but exhibit the same style.

The Rabʿ-i Rashidi style was revived *c.* 1425 in Herat under the Timurid ruler Shahrukh for manuscripts of Rashid al-Din's *Jāmiʿ al-tawārīkh* and Hafiz-i Abru's continuation of it, the *Majmaʿ al-tawārīkh* ('Assembly of histories'). Some manuscripts, such as Hafiz-i Abru's holograph copy (1425; Istanbul, Topkapı Pal. Lib., H. 1653), continue the horizontal format for illustrations; others, such as a *Jāmiʿ al-tawārīkh* (Paris, Bib. N., MS. supp. pers. 1113), have larger, rectangular paintings, but both are done in what has been called the historical style of Shahrukh, in which the simple compositions of the 14th-century models are repeated, but the polychrome pigments, developed landscape with high horizons, and sartorial details reveal their 15th-century origins (*see also* §(v)(d) below).

Dynastic histories continued to be popular under the Timurids (*reg* 1370–1506) and their successors in Central Asia, the Indian subcontinent, Iran and Turkey. One of the most famous was Sharaf al-Din 'Ali Yazdi's life of Timur, the *Zafarnāma* ('Book of victory'). Most illustrated copies are in the style of the period in which they were done, but occasionally a manuscript seems to have been commissioned for commemorative purposes. For example, a copy made for the Timurid prince Husayn Bayqara (1467–8; Baltimore, MD, Johns Hopkins U., Garrett Lib.) has six double-page illustrations that have been interpreted as celebrations of the Prince's conquest of Khurasan (*see also* TIMURID, §II(8)). Later patrons commissioned their own dynastic histories, which were often illustrated. The *Shaybānīnāma* (1510; Vienna, Österreich. Nbib., Cod. Mixt. 188), for example, is a verse epic about Muhammad Shaybani, the founder of the SHAYBANID dynasty of Transoxiana (*reg* 1500–98). Dynastic chronicles prepared for the MUGHAL dynasty (*reg* 1526–1858) include the *Bāburnāma*, the memoirs of the dynasty's founder, Babur, and the *Akbarnāma*, a chronicle of the first 46 years of the reign of Akbar (*reg* 1556–1605). Members of the SAFAVID dynasty of Iran (*reg* 1501–1732) commissioned both prose and verse histories (London, BL, Or. MS. 3248, Add. MS. 7784) of the dynasty's founder, Isma'il I, and a more general dynastic history, the *Tārīkh-i jahānārā* ('History of the world-adorning'; 1683; Dublin, Chester Beatty Lib., Pers. MS. 278). Histories were also commissioned for specific events, such as Imamquli Khan's taking of Hurmuz (on the island of Jarun) from the Portuguese in 1622, which Qadri recorded in his poem, the *Jarūnnāma* (1623; London, BL, Add. MS. 7801).

Under the Ottoman dynasty of Turkey (*reg* 1281–1924) the tradition of illustrated histories flourished in the early 16th century and remained a distinct mode until the 19th. Among the most unusual illustrated manuscripts are those by the writer and painter NASUH MATRAKÇI, such as the *Bayān-i manāzil-i safar-i Irāqayn* ('Description of the stages of the journey to the two Iraqs'), also known as the *Majmu'-i manāzil* ('Compendium of stages'; 1537–8; Istanbul, U. Lib., T. 5964). Its illustrations realistically depict the cities and ports conquered by Süleyman (*reg* 1520–66; *see* §(vi)(e) below). Manuscripts by members of the Ottoman administration were the foundation of the classical style of Ottoman painting that evolved in the imperial studio in the 1550s. One of the most important works was Arifi's history of the Ottoman dynasty written in Persian verse and modelled on the *Shāhnāma*. A sumptuous five-volume set was transcribed in 1558, and the last volume, the *Sulaymānnāma* (Istanbul, Topkapı Pal. Lib., H. 1517; see fig. 132 below), recounting the history of Sultan Süleyman, has 69 large illustrations documenting the magnificence of his reign and magnifying his achievements (*see also* OTTOMAN, §II(3)). Vehbi's *Sūrnāma* ('Book of festivals'; Istanbul, Topkapı Pal. Lib., A. 3593) recounts the festivities accompanying the circumcision of the sons of Ahmed III in 1720. Its 137 illustrations, painted by LEVNI between 1720 and 1732, depict the enormous range of entertainments presented during the 15-day festival and shed light on 18th-century Turkish life.

BIBLIOGRAPHY

R. Ettinghausen: 'An Illuminated Manuscript of Ḥāfiẓ-i Abrū in Istanbul, Part 1', *Kst Orients*, ii (1955), pp. 30–44

E. Atıl: *An Eighteenth-century Ottoman Book of Festivals* (diss., U. MI, 1969)

D. T. Rice and B. Gray: *The Illustrations to the 'World History' of Rashid al-Din* (Edinburgh, 1976)

H. G. Yurdaydın: *Naṣūḥü's-Silāḥī (Matrākçī), Beyān-i menāzil-i sefer-i 'Irākeyn-i Sulṭān Süleymān Hān/Maṭrākçī Naṣūḥ and his 'The Description of the Stages of Sulṭān Süleymān Hān's Campaign in the Two 'Irāks'* (Ankara, 1976) [facs., modern Turk. transcription and Eng. trans. of text with commentary]

B. Gray: *The World History of Rashid al-Din: A Study of the Royal Asiatic Society Manuscript* (London, 1978)

N. M. Titley: *Persian Miniature Painting* (Austin, TX, 1984)

E. Atıl: *Süleymanname: The Illustrated History of Süleyman the Magnificent* (Washington, DC, and New York, 1986)

E. Sims: 'Ibrāhīm-Sulṭān's Illustrated *Zafar-nāmeh* of 839/1436', *Islam. A.*, iv (1991), pp. 175–218

——: 'Ibrahim-Sultan's Illustrated *Zafarnama* of 1436 and its Impact in the Muslim East', *Timurid Art and Culture*, ed. L. Golombek and M. Subtelny (Leiden, 1992), pp. 132–43

——: 'The Illustrated Manuscripts of Firdausī's *Shāhnāma* Commissioned by Princes of the House of Tīmūr', *A. Orient.*, xxii (1992), pp. 43–68

SHEILA S. BLAIR

(iii) Before c. AD *1000.* Literary accounts attest that books with painted illustrations were produced in the Islamic world before the year 1000, but not a single dated example survives. The introduction to *Kalila and Dimna*, the moralistic animal fables by Ibn al-Muqaffa' (*d c.* 757–9; *see* §(ii)(a) above), specifies the inclusion of illustrations, and the historian al-Tabari (*d* 923) noted in his *Annals* the existence of illustrated books, including *Kalila and Dimna*. Around 915 the historian al-Mas'udi wrote that he saw an Arabic translation of a Persian chronicle about the Sasanian dynasty. It had been compiled in 731 and contained portraits of twenty-five Sasanian kings and two queens. This or a similar work was also described by the historian Hamza al-Isfahani (*d c.* 967). Colophons of two illustrated manuscripts from the 11th century specify that they were copied from 10th-century versions, which presumably had illustrations: a manuscript of al-Sufi's astronomical work, *Kitāb ṣuwār al-kawākib al-thābita* ('Book of the fixed stars'; 1009–10; Oxford, Bodleian Lib., Marsh 144), and a copy of an Arabic translation of Dioskurides' botanical work, *De materia medica* (1083; Leiden, Bib. Rijksuniv., MS. Or. 289, Warn.).

An extraordinarily large body of undated, fragmentary works on paper was preserved in Egypt, notably in Old Cairo (Fustat). Among this motley material of varied date and function, scholars have cautiously identified certain fragments as leaves from early illustrated manuscripts. Most of them have been attributed to the years when the Fatimids (*reg* 969–1171) ruled in Egypt, a period of unprecedented artistic creativity, particularly in the realm of figurative representation (*see* §(iv)(a) below). One fragment (Vienna, Österreich. Nbib., Rainer Col. Ar. 25612) with an illustration of a tree between two stepped grave covers has been dated on palaeographic grounds to the late 9th century or early 10th and identified as the closing illustration of a story about two lovers. While the fragments exhibit a great range of quality, style and subject-matter, the pre-eminent sources for their form and function are the Late Antique and Byzantine traditions of book illustration.

When examined collectively many of these illustrations can be grouped into a distinct class of scientific, empirical and learned illustrations stemming from the Classical tradition of illustrated manuscripts. Several leaves contain representations of animals, of which the most striking example is one depicting a hare on the recto and a lion on the verso; it is inscribed with the title 'Book on the speech of wild animals' and the name of the early 7th-century author Ka'b al-Ahbar (New York, Met., 54.108.3). The leaf may have been part of a zoological text rooted in the tradition of the zoological handbook of Classical times, which contained animal illustrations, later widely adopted in Islamic manuscripts. Another leaf (New York, Met., 54.108.1) depicts a rooster and may have served as a zoological illustration. The execution, with a full and free brush to suggest depth and texture, clearly stems from Hellenistic practice in the metropolitan centres of Late Antiquity. Other fragments, such as a leaf showing the centaur Sagittarius shooting a bow and arrow (Cairo, Mus. Islam. A., 15610), may have illustrated books on astronomy or astrology. A drawing of a mounted horseman (Vienna, Österreich. Nbib., Rainer Col. 954) may have been part of a military or hippological handbook, of a type known from Classical times and preserved in the Greek *hippiatrika* of Byzantine times. Inscribed on the recto *al-faras bi'l-ṣadīm* ('the horse in vigorous onslaught'), the fragment has been dated on palaeographic grounds to the 10th century. One fragmentary piece, composed of five scraps of paper, is from an erotic manuscript (Vienna, Österreich. Nbib., Rainer Col. Ar. 25613). The illustration shows a couple engaged in sexual intercourse and is placed between lines of text describing and amplifying the scene. That the illustration was added after the text was completed is indicated by the crowding of the representation. The two figures have flat, linear bodies and large heads and features. Both illustration and text follow a format found in a specific Hellenistic–Roman erotic catalogue known as the Serial Type, where pairs of figures appear at intervals in the text; the illustrations exemplify popular Hellenistic forms that had evolved in Egypt. Some other fragments may be sketches rather than finished works. The use of sketches preserved the tradition of the Classical model-book, which had been maintained in Egypt at least as late as the 5th or 6th century. Model-books from the Fatimid period may have played a role in perpetuating this tradition, for it has been suggested that model-books were used in designing the decoration of later Islamic metalwork in the 13th century.

BIBLIOGRAPHY

Abu Ja'far Muhammad ibn Jarir al-Tabari: *Ta'rikh al-rusul wa'l-mulūk* [Annals of prophets and kings] (early 10th century); (Cairo, 1967–76), ix, p. 108

T. W. Arnold and A. Grohmann: *The Islamic Book: A Contribution to its Art and History from the VII–XVIII Century* (Leipzig and Paris, 1929)

D. S. Rice: 'The Oldest Illustrated Arabic Manuscript', *Bull. SOAS*, xxii (1959), pp. 207–20

E. J. Grube: 'Fostat Fragments', *Islamic Painting and the Arts of the Book*, ed. B. W. Robinson, The Keir Collection, ii (London, 1976), pp. 126–32

EVA R. HOFFMAN

(iv) c. 1000–c. 1250. More evidence for the production of illustrated books survives than from the previous period,

for textual references are complemented by manuscripts and fragments of scientific and literary works. Virtually all the surviving manuscripts were produced in the Arabic-speaking lands of the Mediterranean and Near East. Production in Egypt coincided with the heyday of the Fatimid dynasty (*reg* 969–1171), but the meagre remains are only a faint shadow of contemporary production, since textual references and reflections in other media indicate that the arts of the book flourished. The situation is similar in contemporary Spain and North Africa. The majority of manuscripts surviving from the period were produced in the cities of Iraq, Syria and south-eastern Anatolia in the 12th and 13th centuries.

(a) Egypt. (b) Spain and North Africa. (c) Iraq, Syria and Anatolia.

(a) Egypt. The arts of the book, as well as the other pictorial arts, underwent unprecedented development during the period of Fatimid rule in Egypt (*reg* 969–1171). Textual accounts refer to the production of luxury manuscripts, which were housed in royal and private libraries, but most of these codices were destroyed with the looting of the palace library in the middle of the 11th century, and the range of illustrated manuscripts in the period has to be reconstructed on the basis of scattered and fragmentary evidence. The library in the Fatimid palace in Cairo is said to have contained more than 100,000 bound volumes on a wide range of topics. The 18,000 scientific and technical works ranged from astronomy to zoology, all types of texts that had been illustrated in Classical times. Other references state that the vizier Yazuri (*d* 1058) liked to peruse illustrated manuscripts, and it is generally assumed that at least some of the manuscripts in the library were illustrated.

The largest group of tangible remains consists of paper fragments with sketches, drawings and paintings found in the rubbish-heaps of Fustat, which are attributable to the Fatimid period on stylistic grounds. Over 150 fragments have been recorded (Grube: *Studies in Islamic Painting*, 1994, pp. 70–125). Only a small number are clearly from illustrated manuscripts, having text that relates to the image. One of the most important is a leaf from a poetic anthology (11th century; Ham, Surrey, Keir priv. col., I.7): the recto has a few lines of writing that have been identified as by the great Umayyad poet Kuthayyir (*d* 723) addressed to his beloved 'Azza; below this is the name Abu Ayyub Sulayman ibn Muhammad ibn Abu Ayyub al-Harrani, possibly the editor of the collection. The verso (see fig. 109) has a rectangular frame enclosing a painting of a figure seated on a throne. It may well have been one half of a double frontispiece, for the arrangement conforms to a tradition transmitted to Islamic painting from Late Antique and Byzantine models. Other fragments from illustrated manuscripts attributed to the Fatimid period include a leaf formerly in Moscow (see Denike, 1938, pl.6), two leaves in New York and others in Vienna (*see* §(iii) above).

The paintings and drawings that decorate these few surviving pages are in such different styles, ranging from coloured line drawings with only the slightest touches of colour, to fully fledged, full-brush paintings with no graphic detail, that it is still impossible to delineate a

109. *Seated Figure*, 207×124 mm; illustrated leaf from a poetic anthology, from Cairo, 11th century (Ham, Surrey, Keir private collection, I.7*v*)

coherent stylistic development of manuscript painting in Fatimid Egypt. The enormous range of representations from this period in other media, however, has allowed scholars to establish with greater precision the styles of painting in the Fatimid period. Many of the illustrated paper fragments show no evidence of ever having been part of a manuscript: most are simple sketches, often not more than scribbles, possibly annotations a painter or illustrator may have made for future use in his work, but a few are more finished works. The most famous is the extraordinary drawing of a nude and tattooed dancing-girl wearing a necklace, bracelets, anklets and a ribbon around her head and holding a lute and wine-goblet (Jerusalem, Israel Mus., M 165–4–65). A work of considerable size (280×180 mm), quality and astonishing realism, the painting is done in red ink overlaid in black with traces of white and crimson.

The many styles of Fatimid painting in Egypt are documented principally on lustre-decorated pottery, of which many pieces of superb quality have survived (*see* §V, 3(i) below). These paintings are both non-representational and figural, and include elaborate scenes that appear to reflect contemporary manuscript and wall painting. They combine the Abbasid style, introduced into

Egypt in the 9th century, with a more lively and impressionistic style of drawing associated with the survival of Hellenistic traditions in Egypt. Many wall paintings are mentioned in the sources (*see* §II, 9(iii) above), but the few fragments that have survived probably pre-date the arrival of the Fatimids in Egypt. Fatimid painters may also have migrated from Egypt to Sicily, where they may have been responsible for the splendid wooden ceilings of the Cappella Palatina in Palermo (*c.* 1140) and Cefalù Cathedral. Ettinghausen's idea (1956) that Fatimid painting developed a new sense of realism on the basis of observation of everyday life has been questioned by Grube (1984), who suggested that the subjects represented follow the time-honoured traditions of princely and courtly iconography, recording and glorifying the ruling class.

BIBLIOGRAPHY

B. Denike: *La Peinture iranienne* (Moscow, 1938)
R. Ettinghausen: 'Painting in the Fatimid Period: A Reconstruction', *A. Islam.*, ix (1942), pp. 112–24
——: 'Early Realism in Islamic Art', *Studi Orientalistici in onore di Giorgio Levi della Vida*, i (Rome, 1956), pp. 250–73
G. Wiet: 'Recherches sur les bibliothèques égyptiennes au Xe et XIe siècles', *Cah. Civilis. Méd.*, vi (1963), pp. 1–11
E. J. Grube: 'Fostat Fragments', *Islamic Painting and the Arts of the Book*, ed. B. W. Robinson, The Keir Collection, ii (London, 1976), pp. 126–32
R. Milstein: *Islamic Painting in the Israel Museum* (Jerusalem, 1984)
E. J. Grube: 'La pittura islamica nella Sicilia normanna del XII secolo', *Alto medioevo*, ed. C. Bertelli, Pitt. Italia (Milan, 1994), pp. 416–31
——: *Studies in Islamic Painting* (London, 1994)

ERNST J. GRUBE

(b) Spain and North Africa. As in Egypt, the destruction and dispersion of major libraries makes delineating the style of book painting in Spain and North Africa difficult, although literary evidence attests to a flourishing tradition of book production. The library of the Umayyad caliphs of Spain (*reg* 756–1031) was expanded during the reign of al-Hakam II (*reg* 961–76), who, according to the historian al-Maqqari (*d* 1632), converted Muslim Spain into a great market where the literary productions of every region were immediately brought for sale, and collected round him the most skilful men of his time in the art of transcribing, binding or illuminating books. The scientific and philosophical manuscripts were burnt during the reign of al-Hakam's son Hisham II (*reg* 976–1013 with interruption) in order to appease a powerful orthodox contingent, and the remainder of the library was plundered, destroyed or sold with the collapse of the caliphate in the 11th century.

The only manuscript with figural illustration to survive is a copy of the romance *Bayad and Riyad*, a tortured and complex love odyssey (*see* §(ii)(b) and fig. 106 above). The manuscript was probably produced *c.* 1200 in north-west Africa or, more likely, Spain, on the basis of the architectural forms of the settings, such as balconies and miradors giving on to sumptuous gardens, and complex lobed arch forms. The illustrator relied on many Eastern motifs and compositional formulae, which can be seen, for example, in the 1228–9 manuscript of the Arabic translation of Dioskurides' *De materia medica* (*see* §(c) below). The muted and refined tone that distinguishes the *Bayad and Riyad* manuscript seems to grow from a courtly Spanish tradition. Indeed, the figures and settings, which are painted directly on the page without a background, are rounded forms whose contained, graceful movements are echoed in the circular designs of the soft drapery folds. In this way the figures offer a strong contrast to the dramatic, jabbing gestures in the illustrations to a copy of the *Maqāmāt* ('Assemblies') of al-Hariri produced in Syria (1222; Paris, Bib. N., MS. arab. 6094).

An illustrated copy of al-Sufi's *Kitāb ṣuwar al-kawākib al-thābita* ('Book of the fixed stars'; Rome, Vatican, Bib. Apostolica, MS. Ross. 1033) was made in 1224 at Ceuta. As in most copies of the work, the illustrations are linear pictures of constellations that emphasize the scientific nature of the pictures over the mythological identification of the constellations. For example, on fol. 19*v* the constellation Hercules is depicted as a dancer with a beard and a lively, striped tunic, his body contorted in a pose choreographed to express the relationship between his constellation's stars.

The divergent nature of the surviving types of manuscripts, a romance and an astronomical treatise, prohibit further generalization, but they offer tantalizing hints of a refined tradition of book production with connections to the East and its own canons of taste. Koran manuscripts of the 12th century executed in the distinctive *maghribī* script characteristic of the region (*see* §2(iii)(b) above) contain elaborate frontispieces that juxtapose geometric and floral ornament (e.g. Valencia, 1182; Istanbul, U. Lib., A. 6754). Further hints of the lost tradition are found in Christian and Jewish manuscripts produced in the Iberian peninsula. The illustrations to the Biblia Hispalense (988; Madrid, Bib. N., Cod. Vit. 13–1), completed in or near Seville, bear witness to an Islamic tradition of figural illustration. Decorative palmettes link it to surviving manuscripts of the Koran, while prophets wearing turbans rendered in a linear, calligraphic hand suggest the possibility of a lost, abstracted figural style. Similarly, later Hebrew Bibles and Haggadahs executed in the Iberian peninsula (e.g. the First Kennicott Bible, 1476, Oxford, Bodleian Lib., Ken. MS. 1; a Hispano-Moresque Haggadah, Castile, 1300, London, BL, Or. MS. 2737) retain geometric and vegetal decoration that relate them to earlier Islamic examples, and suggest that they may be repositories of lost details of Spanish Islamic illustration.

BIBLIOGRAPHY
Al-Maqqari: *Nafḥ al-ṭib* (1629); Eng. trans., ed. D. Pascual de Gayangos as *The History of the Mohammedan Dynasties in Spain: Extracted from the 'Nafhu-t-tib'*, ii (London, 1843), pp. 168–9
U. Monneret de Villard: 'Un codice arabo-spagnolo con miniature', *La Bibliofilia*, xliii (1941), pp. 209–23
A. R. Nykl: *Historia de los amores de Bayad y Riyad: Una chantable oriental en estilo persa* (New York, 1941)
R. Ettinghausen: *Arab Painting* (Geneva, 1962)
J. Williams: *Early Spanish Manuscript Illumination* (New York, 1977)

JERRILYNN D. DODDS

(c) Iraq, Syria and Anatolia. The production of illustrated Arabic manuscripts flourished in Iraq, southeastern Anatolia and northern Syria during the 12th and 13th centuries. As most of this region coincides with ancient Mesopotamia, manuscripts produced there are commonly called 'Mesopotamian'. Colophons and inscriptions in the manuscripts and stylistic features in the illustrations allow a provisional distinction to be made between works produced in northern Mesopotamia, especially at Mosul, and in southern and central Mesopotamia, where the main centre was Baghdad. Production was

generally carried out in workshops presumably attached to the courts of local rulers. Since production depended on the temperament and tastes of the ruler, the durability of his political power and the fluctuating importance of Islamic orthodoxy, artists were frequently forced to move and try their luck at another court. The cultural framework for this system of patronage was made up of a highly educated urban class that had an interest in literature and from which calligraphers and painters were recruited.

The major political and religious power in the region was the ABBASID dynasty (*reg* 749–1258), whose capital at Baghdad remained the pre-eminent intellectual centre of the Islamic world until it was sacked by the Mongols in 1258. Since 1055 the Abbasid caliphs had been subject to the domination of the Saljuq dynasty of Iran (*reg* 1038–1194), but they regained some political authority in the late 12th century. To the north, one branch of the Zangid dynasty ruled at Mosul from 1127 to 1222, when they were succeeded by their vizier Badr al-Din Lu'lu'. Other parts of northern Iraq, northern Syria and south-eastern Anatolia were contested in the 12th and 13th centuries between another branch of Zangids and various branches of the Artuqid and Ayyubid dynasties.

Northern Mesopotamia. The Classical tradition of technical and naturalistic illustration was continued in northern Mesopotamia. Al-Jazari wrote the *Automata* (*see* §(ii)(a) above) for the Artuqid ruler of Diyarbakır, Nasir al-Din (*reg* 1201–22), and numerous illustrated copies were produced beginning in the author's lifetime. The earliest surviving manuscript (Istanbul, Topkapı Pal. Lib., A. 3472) was copied by Muhammad ibn Yusuf ibn 'Uthman al-Hisnkayfi in 1206. The technical diagrams follow Classical precedent, but their colour and stylization are typical of the period. The Classical tradition was also continued in Mosul under the Zangids, as can be seen in manuscripts of al-Sufi's *Kitāb ṣuwar al-kawākib al-thābita* ('Book of the fixed stars'; northern Mesopotamia, 1131; Istanbul, Topkapı Pal. Lib., A. 3493; Mosul, 1170–71; Oxford, Bodleian Lib., Hunt 212). The Classical tradition of naturalistic and illusionistic plant illustration, represented by the manuscript of Dioskurides' *De materia medica* made *c.* 512 for the Byzantine princess Juliana Anicia (Vienna, Österreich. Nbib., Cod. med. gr. 1), was partly continued in Arabic translations of the works of Dioskurides and Pseudo-Galen, but the strictly scientific attitude was abandoned in favour of narrative images with less precise botanical representations and the inclusion of such figures as physicians preparing and administering medicines. Portraits of authors and scholars acquired an almost magical and mythical quality since they were considered miracleworkers. The lack of a direct relationship to nature led to increased stylization, and anecdotal and mythological aspects were introduced, particularly in the illustrations to luxury manuscripts. A copy of the Arabic translation of *De materia medica* done in northern Mesopotamia (1228–9; Istanbul, Topkapı Pal. Lib., A. 2127), signed by the painter ?'Abd al-Jabbar ibn 'Ali, illustrates the merging of the scientific and narrative styles. The title-page shows Dioskurides as a teacher and mingles iconographic and stylistic elements of antique, Byzantine and medieval origin. Some of the plant illustrations are illusionistic, others are abstract.

Eastern Islamic sources also contributed to the evolution of this style. The style of representation seen in metalwork and ceramics produced in Iran under Saljuq rule (*see* §§IV, 3(i)(a) and V, 3(iii) and below) became particularly well-established in northern Mesopotamia, quite possibly as a result of artists fleeing from the Mongol invasions to the peaceful states of the region. The Saljuq style is evident in a manuscript of Pseudo-Galen's *Kitāb al-diryāq* ('Book of antidotes'; Jan 1199; Paris, Bib. N., MS. arab. 2964) copied by Muhammad ibn Saʿid Abi'l-Fath ʿAbd al-Wahid for his nephew. The detailed colophon states that the scribe, who came from a distinguished Shiʿite (probably Iraqi) family, also illustrated the manuscript. The illustrations show the discovery and preparation of antidotes. Their style and iconography indicate that the manuscript was made in northern Mesopotamia. Although the Classical tradition is still visible in the representation of some plants, the decorative accessories are typical of the medieval narrative style. Iconographic features typical of Saljuq art include the crenellated architecture, the cross-legged manner of sitting, the delicate proportions of the figures and their bright clothes covered with garlands of flowers and palmettes. The Hellenistic arrangement of folds in the depiction of drapery has been converted into an inorganic moiré pattern. The physicians' heads are surrounded by nimbi, used in other Arabic manuscripts for high- and low-ranking individuals and even birds. The doll-like figures epitomize the Saljuq ideal of beauty, and the genre scenes provide insight into medieval Islamic life. The unusual iconography of the double frontispiece has provoked much speculation. Each page has two interlaced snake-like dragons framing a circular medallion in which an enthroned female attended by two female dancers holds a crescent moon in each hand; winged female genii hover in the four spandrels. The frontispiece has been interpreted in terms of astral symbolism, as heraldic motifs or as the depiction of the solar eclipse that occurred in the month mentioned in the colophon.

Another copy of the *Kitāb al-diryāq* (Vienna, Österreich. Nbib., Cod. A.F. 10), probably made at Mosul *c.* 1220–40, is almost identical in content and style to the Paris manuscript, but plants, animals and human figures are even more stylized. Line is vigorous, colour and proportion are harmonious and human figures and ornament are in the Saljuq style, although antique models are dimly reflected in the medallion portraits of famous physicians on fol. 1*v* and the illustrations of snakes. The scenes portraying the discovery and preparation of theriac are more narrative than scientific. The red-ground frontispiece (fol. 1*r*; see fig. 110) depicts the sovereign—and presumed patron of the manuscript—seated on a golden throne; this central image is surrounded by scenes of hunting, feasting, music, games and travel that reflect the pastimes of a Turkish ruler. The style of representation in the Vienna manuscript is similar to that of the unique illustrated copy of ʿAyyuqi's *Varqa and Gulshah* (?Konya, *c.* 1250; Istanbul, Topkapı Pal. Lib., H. 841; see fig. 125 below) and to polychrome overglaze-painted ceramics produced in Saljuq Iran. Although Aleppo and Diyarbakır have been suggested as possible places of origin, it is generally

110. *Enthroned Sovereign*, 325×250 mm; illustrated frontispiece from Pseudo-Galen: *Kitāb al-diryāq* ('Book of antidotes'), probably from Mosul, *c.* 1220–40 (Vienna, Österreichische Nationalbibliothek, Cod. A.F. 10, fol. 1*r*)

accepted that the Vienna manuscript was produced in Mosul during the reign of the atabeg Badr al-Din Lu'lu', who is portrayed on the frontispiece.

The same sovereign's portrait is identified by inscriptions on the armbands in five frontispieces to the *Kitāb al-aghānī* ('Book of songs') compiled by the 10th-century poet Abu'l-Faraj al-Isfahani. Six of the original twenty volumes survive: vols ii, iv and xi in Cairo (N. Lib., Adab 579), xvii and xix in Istanbul (Millet Lib., Feyzullah Ef. 1565–6) and xx in Copenhagen (Kon. Bib., Cod. arab. 168). Vol. xi is dated AH 614 (1217–18) and vol. xx is dated AH 616 (1219–20); both are signed by the calligrapher Muhammad ibn Abi Talib al-Badri (an epithet deriving from his master's honorary title), who stated that he also penned the previous volumes. The five dedicatory pictures show Badr al-Din Lu'lu' engaged in typical royal activities: seated on a throne, giving audience, riding in ceremony, hunting with falcons and celebrating with concubines and musicians. The gilding, rich colouring, winged genii and other symbols serve to glorify the sovereign and link this life with the next.

One of the most popular literary works in the medieval Islamic world was the sequence of animal fables known as *Kalila and Dimna*. In the oldest surviving illustrated copy (?Syria, 1200–20; Paris, Bib. N., MS. arab. 3465) many of the representations of animals, which were presumably based on zoological works, are as symmetrical as heraldic beasts and are heavily stylized. This heraldic quality and the lavish gilding reveal the courtly character of the manuscript. Persian traditions are noticeable in the stylized plants, although Late Antique realism still survives in the shapes of the animals and their powerfully lifelike movements. This style continued in Syria and Egypt under Mamluk rule (*see* §(v)(a) below).

Southern Mesopotamia. Manuscripts produced in southern Mesopotamia exhibit many of the features found in northern Mesopotamian painting, such as elements of Hellenistic illusionism and Late Antique realism and a pictorial language derived from Early Christian and Byzantine painting. In southern Mesopotamia, however, Western and Eastern traditions confronted each other more intensely, and the manuscripts attained an unprecedented level of artistic achievement, visible in their sophisticated and integrated compositions and the tendency towards expressionism, trenchant characterization and even uglification. This mature style appeared shortly after 1220 in Baghdad, seat of the Abbasid caliphate and intellectual centre of the Islamic world, and flowered there in the succeeding decades.

The few surviving examples of illustrated Syriac manuscripts produced in Christian monasteries and of early Islamic monumental painting (*see* §II, 9(iii) above) only hint at the rich cultural background against which the most famous illustrated manuscripts associated with Baghdad arose, those of the *Maqāmāt* ('Assemblies') of al-Hariri (*see* §(ii)(b) above). Of the five illustrated copies thought to date between 1220 and 1260, two (Paris, Bib. N., MSS arab. 6094 and 3929) belong to the northern Mesopotamian group. The other three appear to have been produced in Baghdad. One of the most famous and impressive, and possibly the oldest (St Petersburg, Acad. Sci., Lib., S. 23), is attributed to Baghdad *c.* 1225–35 because of stylistic comparison with other dated manuscripts and the realistic depiction of such details as brick architecture. The many realistic and expressive illustrations are set against highly animated landscapes with buildings, groups of tents and dense crowds of people. These create a new sense of three-dimensional space due to the use of bird's-eye perspective, the skilful distribution of vegetation and the semicircular or oval compositions of overlapping figures and objects. The few but expertly handled graphic and pictorial devices capture people and animals in characteristic poses and movements. Genre-like subsidiary elements transform the images into an almost autonomous pictorial narrative. A closely related copy, the Schefer Hariri (Paris, Bib. N., MS. arab. 5847), was written and illustrated by Yahya ibn Mahmud al-Wasiti in 1236–7. His name shows that he came from the town of Wasit south of Baghdad, and an inscription on fol. 164*v* names the caliph al-Mustansir (*reg* 1226–42). Both points suggest a Baghdadi provenance. The manuscript has 99 brightly coloured illustrations, some double-page, which are more balanced and elegant in style than those in the St Petersburg copy. They provide humorous insight into the varied life of a medieval Arab village (see fig. 111). The third copy of the *Maqāmāt* (Istanbul, Süleymaniye Lib., Esad Ef. 2961) is badly preserved but equalled the other two in style, richness and quality. An inscription on fol. 204*r*

111. *Village Scene* by Yahya ibn Mahmud al-Wasiti, 348×260 mm; illustration from al-Hariri: *Maqāmāt* ('Assemblies'), probably from Baghdad, 1236–7 (Paris, Bibliothèque Nationale, MS. arab. 5847, fol. 138*r*); known as the Schefer Hariri

names the last Abbasid caliph, al-Musta'sim (*reg* 1242–58), and is the basis for its attribution to Baghdad.

Illustrated copies of scientific manuscripts were also produced in Baghdad. Several manuscripts about horses and other animals, produced in northern and southern Mesopotamia, have survived. Two copies of the *Kitāb al-bayṭara* ('Book of farriery') by Ibn al-Ahnaf were copied by the calligrapher 'Ali ibn al-Hasan ibn Hibatallah in Baghdad, the first (Cairo, N. Lib., Khalil Agha 8f; *see also* §(ii)(a) above) in 1208–9 and the second (Istanbul, Topkapı Pal. Lib., A. 2115) a year later. The numerous illustrations with their sparing but confident lines capture the build and temperament of the horses and also show the veterinary surgeons and assistants treating them. Two illustrated copies of the Arabic translation of Dioskurides' *De materia medica* show that the long-standing interest in translations of Classical texts continued in Baghdad. The colophon in the first (Istanbul, Topkapı Pal. Lib., Ayasofya 3703) gives the name of the scribe (and illustrator?) 'Abdallah ibn al-Fadl and the date AH 621 (1224–5). The illustrations, 30 of which were removed and are dispersed in European and American collections, depict plants and scenes with human figures, including physicians and patients. The colophon of the second (Oxford, Bodleian Lib., Cod. Or. Arab. d. 138) states that it was copied at Baghdad in AH 637 (1239–40). Despite the reliance on antique models for the author-portrait and depiction of plants, the vegetation is abstract and stylized. The simplicity and clarity make the highly realistic figural scenes immediately comprehensible.

The powerful southern Mesopotamian style survived the Mongol conquest of Baghdad in 1258. A copy of al-Qazwini's *'Ajā'ib al-makhlūqāt wa-gharā'ib al-mawjūdāt* ('Wonders of creation and their singularities'; 1279–80; Munich, Bayer. Staatsbib., C. arab. 464) was produced in Wasit during the author's lifetime. A copy of the *Rasā'il ikhwān al-ṣafā'* ('Epistles of the sincere brethren'; Istanbul, Süleymaniye Lib., Esad Ef. 3638) was made in Baghdad in 1287–8. These two manuscripts continued the developed Baghdadi style while introducing more decorative tendencies characteristic of manuscript illustration under the Ilkhanids, the Mongol rulers of Iran (*see* §(v)(b) below).

BIBLIOGRAPHY

Ibn al-Razzaz al-Jazari: *Kitāb fī ma'rifat al-ḥiyal al-handasiyya* [Book of knowledge of ingenious mechanical devices] (*c.* 1206); Eng. trans., ed. D. R. Hill (Dordrecht and Boston, 1974)
K. Holter: 'Die Galen-Handschrift und die Makamen des Harîrî der Wiener Nationalbibliothek', *Jb. Ksthist. Samml. Wien*, n. s., xi (1937), pp. 1–48
——: 'Die islamischen Miniaturhandschriften vor 1350', *Zentbl. Bibwsn*, liv (1937), pp. 1–34
H. Buchthal: 'The Painting of the Syrian Jacobites and its Relation to Byzantine and Islamic Art', *Syria*, xx (1939), pp. 136–50
——: ' "Hellenistic" Miniatures in Early Islamic Manuscripts', *A. Islam.*, vii (1940), pp. 125–33; also in H. Buchthal: *Art of the Mediterranean World, A.D. 100 to 1400* (Washington, DC, 1983); pp. 1–10
H. Buchthal, O. Kurz and R. Ettinghausen: 'Supplementary Notes to K. Holter's Check List of Islamic Illuminated Manuscripts before A.D. 1350', *A. Islam.*, vii (1940), pp. 147–64
H. Buchthal: 'Early Islamic Miniatures from Baghdad', *J. Walters A.G.*, v (1942), pp. 18–39; also in H. Buchthal: *Art of the Mediterranean World, A.D. 100 to 1400* (Washington, DC, 1983); pp. 18–31
K. Weitzmann: 'The Greek Sources of Islamic Scientific Illustrations', *Archaeologica Orientalia in Memoriam Ernst Herzfeld*, ed. G. C. Miles (Locust Valley, NY, 1952), pp. 244–66; also in *Studies in Classical and Byzantine Manuscript Illumination*, ed. H. L. Kessler (Chicago and London, 1971), pp. 20–44
B. Farès: *Le Livre de la thériaque: Manuscrit arabe à peintures de la fin du XIIe siècle conservé à la Bibliothèque nationale de Paris* (Cairo, 1953)
D. S. Rice: 'The Aghānī Miniatures and Religious Painting in Islam', *Burl. Mag.*, xcv (1953), pp. 128–36
E. J. Grube: 'Materialien zum Dioskurides Arabicus', *Aus der Welt der islamischen Kunst: Festschrift für Ernst Kühnel*, ed. R. Ettinghausen (Berlin, 1959), pp. 163–94
R. Ettinghausen: *Arab Painting* (Geneva, 1962)
G. Azarpay: 'The Eclipse Dragon on an Arabic Frontispiece Miniature', *J. Amer. Orient. Soc.*, xcviii (1977–8), pp. 363–74
O. Grabar: *The Illustrations of the Maqamat* (Chicago, 1984)
R. Ward: 'Evidence for a School of Painting at the Artuqid Court', *The Art of Syria and the Jazira, 1100–1250*, ed. J. Raby (Oxford, 1985), pp. 69–84
J. M. Rogers, F. Çağman and Z. Tanındı: *The Topkapı Saray Museum: The Albums and Illustrated Manuscripts* (London, 1986), pp. 29–57
D. Duda: *Die Handschriften in arabischer Sprache* (1992), v of *Die illuminierten Handschriften und Inkunabeln der Österreichischen Nationalbibliothek* (Vienna, 1983–)
E. R. Hoffman: 'The Author Portrait in Thirteenth-century Arabic Manuscripts: A New Islamic Context for a Late-Antique Tradition', *Muqarnas*, x (1993), pp. 6–20

DOROTHEA DUDA

(v) c. *1250*–c. *1500*. This was the heyday of the illustrated manuscript in much of the Islamic world. In Egypt and Syria the traditions established earlier in the regions (*see* §(iv)(a) and (c) above) were continued, while in the eastern Islamic lands, which came directly under the control of the Ilkhanid dynasty of Iran (*reg* 1256–1353), the illustrated book was transformed into a major art form.

This tradition was continued under their successors in the second half of the 14th century, and under the patronage of the Timurid dynasty (*reg* 1370–1506) in Iran and western Central Asia the art of the book achieved its classical moment, when exquisite illustration was integrated into a harmonious ensemble of paper, calligraphy, illumination and binding. Under the Qaraqoyunlu and Aqqoyunlu Turkomans, the Timurids' rivals in Iraq and southern and western Iran, illustrated books were produced for the court and the open market. The pre-eminence of Persian as a language of literary discourse meant that Iranian models were followed in other lands, particularly Anatolia and the Indian subcontinent.

□

(a) Egypt and Syria. (b) Iraq and Iran, *c.* 1250–*c.* 1350. (c) Iraq and Iran, *c.* 1350–*c.* 1400. (d) Iran and western Central Asia, *c.* 1400–*c.* 1500. (e) Iraq and Iran, *c.* 1450–*c.* 1500. (f) Anatolia. (g) Indian subcontinent.

(a) Egypt and Syria. The book illustration of this period is traditionally called 'Mamluk' after the sequence of sultans who ruled in Egypt and Syria from 1250 to 1517. However, only one Mamluk sultan, Qansuh al-Ghawri (*reg* 1501–16), is known to have commissioned illustrated manuscripts, and only three manuscripts contain dedications to high-ranking Mamluk officers. Other illustrated books may have been owned by Mamluks, among them the many manuals on horsemanship (Arab. *furūsiyya*) illustrated from the 1360s onwards (the earliest copy, Dublin, Chester Beatty Lib., Add. MS. 1, is dated AH 767/1365–6). They depict the equestrian exercises that formed a regular part of the Mamluks' training, and contain only simple illustrations in which clarity is dominant. No artistic innovations were made in producing them.

Before the end of the 14th century most patrons and collectors of illustrated literary manuscripts were not the Turkish-speaking Mamluks but educated members of the Arabic-speaking middle class, which included the sons of Mamluks. Several illustrated manuscripts contain the names of sons of Mamluks, and, although Arab patrons were not in the habit of adding their names to manuscripts, the name of a tax inspector from Damascus appears on a copy (1323; London, BL, Add. MS. 7293) of the *Maqāmāt* ('Assemblies') of al-Hariri, which he bought in 1375–6. Many of the texts popular with these patrons—the tales of the roguish adventurer Abu Zayd that al-Hariri brought together in his *Maqāmāt*, the sequence of animal fables known as *Kalila and Dimna*, the Arabic translation of Dioskurides' *De materia medica* and al-Jazari's *Automata*—had been illustrated before, under Ayyubid rule.

Mamluk book painting developed from that practised in Syria and northern Iraq in the 13th century. In the second quarter of the 14th century a more elaborate style with lavish gold compositions and Chinese-inspired motifs was introduced. In the 15th century the Turkoman style from Iran became increasingly influential, and patronage shifted from the middle class to the court.

c. *mid-13th century–14th*. Paintings in early Mamluk manuscripts have a diagrammatic quality well suited to their role as narrative illustrations. They are unframed, except when architecture serves as a framing device. The compositions are two-dimensional: dishes of fruit float unsupported in the air in order to fill empty spaces, and figures are restricted to the lower edge of the picture, which is often just a ruled base-line. The compositions are reduced to their essential ingredients: a canopy symbolizes the sky, a curtain suggests an interior. Figures are stock types without individual characterization, and their costumes are decorated with flat patterns or 'scroll folds' which make no attempt to imitate the natural fall of cloth.

This early Mamluk style is exemplified by a *Maqāmāt* manuscript (London, BL, Or. MS. 9718), one of whose illustrations includes the name of Ghazi ibn 'Abd al-Rahman al-Dimashqi. He was a well-known calligrapher (*d* 1310) who trained many pupils; his studio in Damascus may have been the centre for this style. However, the style was already established by the time of the earliest surviving manuscript produced under the Mamluks, a copy of Ibn Butlan's *Da'wat al-aṭibbā'* ('Banquet of the physicians'; 1272–3; Milan, Bib. Ambrosiana, MS. A. 125 Inf), and it continued well into the middle of the 14th century, as shown by a manuscript of *Kalila and Dimna* (1354–5; Oxford, Bodleian Lib., Pococke 400).

A second, equally distinctive style emerged during the second quarter of the 14th century. The earliest example is found in a copy of the *Maqāmāt* (1333–4; Vienna, Österreich. Nbib., MS. A.F. 9). The style of illustration has many similarities with contemporary Koran illumination (*see* §3(i) above) and the chinoiserie style found in Iranian manuscripts of the same period (*see* §§(b) and (c) below). All the manuscripts in this tight group are lavishly decorated. The paintings are executed on a gold ground and have a thick gold frame surrounded by a ruled blue line with finials at each corner. The text is ornamented with whirling gold rosettes and illuminated chapter-headings in the manner of contemporary Korans. Despite the gold ground, the illustrations experiment with landscape and composition; they use the frame to create spatial tension and allow figures or animals to break out of it for increased dramatic effect. These spatial experiments and the exotic flora and fauna depicted—lotuses, peonies, gnarled trees, phoenixes and dragons—show the impact of Chinese pictorial conventions, which were probably received via Persian illustrated manuscripts as well as from the Chinese textiles and porcelains so popular at the Mamluk court. A new figural type with heavy Mongol features and thick black hair is probably intended to resemble members of the Mamluk élite. An important manuscript within this group is a copy of Ibn al-Durayhim's bestiary, the *Manāfi' al-ḥayawān* ('Usefulness of animals'; see fig. 112). Ibn al-Durayhim, who is identified in the colophon as the author, copyist and illustrator of the manuscript, was a prominent member of the religious establishment at Damascus. In the 1350s he taught at the Great Mosque of Damascus, and his position may explain why the textual illumination in the manuscript resembles contemporary Koran manuscripts. This manuscript suggests that the second style should also be associated with Damascus rather than Cairo, the Mamluk capital.

Numerous Mamluk manuscripts fall outside mainstream developments, perhaps because of the lack of a central source of patronage. One of the most interesting is a huge copy of the *Maqāmāt* (1323; London, BL, Add. MS. 7293). If finished, this would have been the most

112. *Two Herons in a Chinoiserie Landscape*; illustration from Ibn al Durayhim: *Manāfi' al-ḥayawān* ('Usefulness of animals'), from Damascus, 1354–5 (Madrid, Escorial, Biblioteca del Monasterio de San Lorenzo, Cod. 898, fol. 80*r*)

extensively illustrated copy of the text to survive. Its paintings reproduce the complex architectural structures, animated figures and even costume details seen in paintings produced in the 13th century by members of the southern Mesopotamian school at Baghdad, and must have been copied from an illustrated manuscript of the *Maqāmāt* of that period. Executed a century or so after its presumed prototype, it is the only Mamluk manuscript to show the impact of the innovative and productive Baghdad school.

The fragile market for illustrated books seems to have collapsed at the end of the 14th century, probably because the predominantly middle-class patrons were badly affected by the social and economic crisis that beset Mamluk society at that time. Illustrated copies of al-Hariri's *Maqāmāt* were no longer produced, and other illustrated manuscripts of a literary character are rare and of poor quality. A manuscript of *Kalila and Dimna* (1389; Cambridge, Corpus Christi Coll. Lib., MS. 578) contains crude compositions and sketchy figural drawing. The simple clarity of the first style and the lavish gold grounds and stylistic innovations of the second have completely disappeared.

15th century. The few illustrated manuscripts attributed to Egypt or Syria during the first half of the 15th century already show signs of the Turkoman style of book painting (*see* §(e) below) that would dominate Mamluk painting in the second half of the century. A copy of a *Kitāb al-zardaqa* ('Book of farriery'; *c*. 1425; Istanbul, U. Lib., A. 4689) was produced in Damascus for a Mamluk called Yalbay, who was Keeper of the Horse for the governor of Damascus during the reign of Barsbay (1422–38). It contains 11 paintings or diagrams of horses, some of which are displayed on a ground filled with scattered grasses and flowers in a style unknown in earlier Mamluk painting. Such an innovative style was presumably not restricted to this practical manual with its second-rate illustrations: it is much more likely that by the 1420s there was an active school of painting, probably based in Damascus, that looked to contemporary Iranian work for inspiration. A copy of Ibn Ghanim al-Maqdisi's *Kashf al-asrār* ('Disclosure of secrets'; Istanbul, Süleymaniye Lib., Lala Ismail 565) may also belong to this school. It contains numerous depictions of animals and figures in landscape settings within thick gold frames. Various models were used, but such elements as the scattered flowers and grasses on the ground, windswept trees with close-leaved foliage, Chinese cloud bands and sartorial details were taken from illustrated manuscripts produced under the Turkomans in Iran.

During the second half of the 15th century the Turkoman style predominates, as in a copy of the *Iskandarnāma* ('Book of Alexander'; *c*. 1467; Istanbul, U. Lib., T. 6044), Ahmadi's Turkish version of the Alexander legend. This manuscript was produced for Khushqadam ibn 'Abdallah, the treasurer of Sayfi 'Ali Bay, secretary to Sultan Timurbugha (*reg* 1467–8). Its 12 paintings (see fig. 113) can be directly compared to those in manuscripts produced for Pir Budaq, the Turkoman governor of Baghdad and Shiraz. The complex and detailed compositions, the elegant figures and the depiction of architecture and landscape are totally Iranian in execution and lack any trace of earlier Mamluk styles. Atıl (1984) has therefore suggested that the manuscript was illustrated by artists who had fled to Cairo after Pir Budaq's death in 1466. The same artists may also have worked on two very similar *furūsiyya* manuscripts, one in Istanbul (1466–7; Topkapı Pal. Lib., R. 1933), the other divided between Ham, Surrey (Keir priv. col., II.7–37), and Cairo (Mus. Islam. A., 18019 and 18235–6). These two manuscripts imitate Turkoman figural styles and costumes and ignore the well-established Mamluk tradition of illustrating such texts.

Court patronage of Turkish literature, first seen in Khushqadam's copy of the *Iskandarnāma*, was continued by Sultan Qansuh al-Ghawri. He commissioned a Turkish translation of the Persian national epic, the *Shāhnāma* ('Book of kings'; *see* §4(ii)(c) above), from the poet Sharif Amidi, and had a copy prepared in Cairo with 62 illustrations (1511; Istanbul, Topkapı Pal. Lib., H. 1519). According to the introduction, the Sultan, as a bibliophile who could read Persian himself and had many copies of the *Shāhnāma* in his library, commissioned the translation so that others could read and understand the work. The illustrations in his Persian *Shāhnāma*s served as models for those in his Turkish translation: a copy produced under the Aqqoyunlu (1486; Istanbul, Topkapı Pal. Lib., H. 1506) must have been in the Sultan's library, as its paintings are clearly the source for many of those in the Turkish version. The illustrations also include local Egyptian details

113. *Enthroned Sovereign*; illustrated frontispiece from Ahmadi: *Iskandarnāma* ('Book of Alexander'), made for Khushqadam ibn 'Abdallah, Cairo, *c*. 1467 (Istanbul, University Library, T. 6044, fol. 1*v*)

of architecture, furniture and costume, which give a fascinating insight into court life and represent a new development in Mamluk painting. Qansuh al-Ghawri also commissioned an anthology of Turkish poetry, which includes some of his own verses. The manuscript (Berlin, Staatsbib. Preuss. Kultbes., Orientabt., MS. or. oct. 3744) is undated, but the frontispiece, showing an enthroned ruler flanked by two attendants in an elaborate architectural setting, was probably painted by one of the artists who worked on the *Shāhnāma*.

This belated development of Mamluk court patronage came to an abrupt end when the Ottomans conquered Cairo in 1517. Although many artists and manuscripts were carried off to Istanbul, illustrated manuscripts continued to be produced in Egypt and Syria (*see also* §(vi)(e) below). The first illustrated copy of the *Humayūnnāma*, Ali Çelebi's Turkish translation of *Kalila and Dimna* (1566–7; Istanbul, Topkapı Pal. Lib., H. 359), which was produced in Cairo, shows that book painting could still be of the best quality.

BIBLIOGRAPHY
Ibn Zafar al-Siqilli: *Sulwān al-mutā'* [Prescription for pleasure] (*c*. 1170); Eng. trans., ed. A. S. Melikian-Chirvani, 3 vols (Kuwait, 1985) [contains facs. of MS. in priv. col.]

Ibn al-Razzaz al-Jazari: *Kitāb fī ma'rifat al-ḥiyal al-handasiyya* [Book of knowledge of ingenious mechanical devices] (*c.* 1206); Eng. trans., ed. D. R. Hill (Dordrecht and Boston, 1974)

E. de Lorey: 'Le Bestiaire de L'Escurial', *Gaz. B.-A.*, xiv/6 (1935), pp. 228–38

K. Holter: 'Die frühmamlükische Miniaturenmalerei', *Graph. Kst.*, ii (1937), pp. 1–14

——: 'Die Galen-Handschrift und die Makamen des Harīrī der Wiener Nationalbibliothek', *Jb. Ksthist. Samml. Wien*, n. s., xi (1937), pp. 1–48

H. Buchthal: 'Three Illustrated Hariri Manuscripts in the British Museum', *Burl. Mag.*, lxxvii (1940), pp. 44–52

O. Lofgren and C. J. Lamm: *Ambrosian Fragments of an Illuminated Manuscript Containing the Zoology of al-Ğāḥiẓ* (Uppsala, 1946)

D. S. Rice: 'A Miniature in an Autograph of S̲h̲ihāb al-dīn Ibn Faḍlallāh al-'Umarī', *Bull. SOAS*, xiii (1951), pp. 856–67

S. Walzer: 'The Mamlūk Illuminated Manuscripts of Kalīla wa-Dimna', *Aus der Welt der islamischen Kunst: Festschrift für Ernst Kühnel*, ed. R. Ettinghausen (Berlin, 1959), pp. 195–206

N. Atasoy: 'Un Manuscrit mamlūk illustré du S̲āhnāma', *Rev. Etud. Islam.*, xxxvii/1 (1969), pp. 151–8

M. Mostafa: 'Miniature Paintings in some Mamluk Manuscripts', *Bull. Inst. Egyp.*, lii (1970–71), pp. 5–15

D. James: 'Mamluke Painting at the Time of the Lusignan Crusade, 1365–70', *Human. Islam.*, ii (1974), pp. 73–87

G. İnal: 'Kahire'de yapılmış bir Hümâyûnnâme'nin minyatürleri' [Miniatures from a *Hümâyûnnâme* made in Cairo], *Belleten*, xl (1976), pp. 439–65

D. James: 'Arab Painting', *Marg*, xxix/3 (1976), pp. 1–50

B. Flemming: 'Literary Activities in the Mamluk Halls and Barracks', *Studies in Memory of Gaston Wiet*, ed. M. Rosen-Ayalon (Jerusalem, 1977), pp. 249–60

D. Haldane: *Mamluk Painting* (Warminster, 1978)

E. Atıl: *Renaissance of Islam: Art of the Mamluks* (Washington, DC, 1981)
: 'Mamluk Painting in the Later Fifteenth Century', *Muqarnas*, ii (1984), pp. 159–71

A. Contadini: 'The *Kitāb Manāfi' al-Hayawān* in the Escorial Library', *Islam. A.*, iii (1988–9), pp. 33-58

RACHEL WARD

(b) Iraq and Iran, c. 1250–c. 1350.

Introduction. A tradition of illustrated manuscripts can be documented in the Persian-speaking lands of Iraq and western Iran during the rule of the ILKHANID dynasty (*reg* 1256–1353), when several distinct styles of book painting emerged. Narrative representation had been used earlier in the greater Iranian world, but it survives only in such media as architecture and ceramics. For example, the walls of the audience hall in the southern palace at LASHKARI BAZAR in Afghanistan (*c.* 1000) depict the Turkish guard who surrounded the Ghaznavid sultan Mahmud (*reg* 998–1030), and lustre-painted and polychrome enamelled wares of the 12th and 13th centuries (*see* §V, 3(iii) below) show individual scenes of such epic heroes as Zahhak, Faridun and Bahram Gur. Manuscript illustration had long flourished in the Arab world, including Iraq; and an illustrated copy of 'Ayyuqi's romance in Persian verse, *Varqa and Gulshah*, can probably be attributed to Konya in central Anatolia *c.* 1250 (*see* §(f) and fig. 125 below). Numerous examples of illustrated manuscripts survive, however, only after the establishment of the Mongol dynasty of the Ilkhanids. The reasons for this apparent spurt in production are not totally clear, but it was undeniably related to the general cultural revival sponsored by the Ilkhanids and more particularly to the interest in historical writing shown by the Mongol rulers and their Iranian ministers. Familiarity with Chinese illustrated scrolls may also have played a role in this development.

Surviving manuscripts can be arranged in five groups. They do not form a simple, evolutionary series but show conscious experimentation in style. Older traditions were continued, and a wide range of foreign and local sources were exploited for new motifs and ideas. Some of these, such as the portrayal of emotion, were soon abandoned; others, such as the programmatic use of colour or the high horizon, were incorporated into the standard range of conventions. The function of the illustrated manuscript was also extended in this period. While some manuscripts had simple pictures inserted regularly into the text, manuscripts commissioned by important court patrons had carefully scrutinized texts and specific cycles of illustration. These manuscripts were meant to make an ideological point, to project the concerns or policies of the court. In later Persian painting this range of functions continued, from more popular manuscripts meant mainly to delight the eye and mind of the beholder to more elaborate ones designed for rhetorical purposes.

Methods of production. The Ilkhanids continued the nomadic practices of the steppe: even when not on campaign, the court regularly migrated from summer pastures in north-west Iran to warmer winter quarters in Iraq. Artisans joined this mobile court and may even have produced luxury manuscripts *en route*. Identifying sites of production is therefore difficult, and the strictly geographical names used by some scholars, such as the 'school of Tabriz', 'of Baghdad' and 'of Shiraz', are unsuitable, as are dynastic ones, such as the 'Inju school'. The identification of hands is also problematic, for production practices are almost unknown. Extant manuscripts show that the scribe first copied the text, leaving blanks for the illustrations. Sometimes the scribe himself painted the pictures, as in a copy of al-Qazwini's *'Ajā'ib al-makhlūqāt* ('Wonders of creation'; 1279–80; Munich, Bayer. Staatsbib., C. arab. 464); sometimes another artist did, as in a copy of the *Dīvān* (collected poetry; London, BL, Add. MS. 18113; see fig. 119 below) of Khwaju Kirmani, penned by Mir 'Ali ibn Ilyas Tabrizi and illustrated by JUNAYD in 1396. It is unclear how specialized artists were: whether they performed a variety of tasks or whether they were restricted to certain techniques, such as line drawing or illumination, or to certain materials, such as gold or opaque watercolours. The best example of a 14th-century scriptorium is the one founded by the vizier RASHID AL-DIN in the Rab'-i Rashidi, his quarter in Tabriz (*see* TABRIZ, §3(i)). Its endowment deed provided for the annual copying of the Koran and other religious manuscripts, and an addendum provided for the annual copying of the vizier's collected works in Arabic and Persian. Some of the 220 slaves attached to the complex were assigned to the tasks of calligraphy, painting and gilding, and all manuscripts were to be done on good Baghdadi paper in a neat hand, collated with the originals in the library and bound in fine leather. Not all copies of Rashid al-Din's *Jāmi' al-tawārīkh* ('Compendium of histories') were illustrated there, for the Baghdadi biographer Ibn al-Fuwati (1244–1323) mentioned meeting a famous master who was illustrating one of Rashid al-Din's works while in the sultan's camp at Arran in Azerbaijan.

The earliest account of manuscript painting in this period was written in the mid-16th century by the Safavid court librarian DUST MUHAMMAD as the preface to an album (Istanbul, Topkapı Pal. Lib., H. 2154) he compiled illustrating the evolution of calligraphy and painting. In an often-quoted statement, he said that during the reign of Abu Sa'id (1317–35) the master Ahmad Musa withdrew the veil from Persian painting and invented the kind of painting still current in Dust Muhammad's day. Ahmad Musa's mantle then passed to his pupil Shams al-Din and from him to 'ABD AL-HAYY and finally to Junayd of Baghdad, all of whom worked for successive Jalayirid sultans. Junayd signed one painting in the 1396 copy of Khwaju Kirmani's collected poems, but this is the only signed painting from the 14th century, and the lack of other dated and signed material makes it impossible to trace Dust Muhammad's account back in time.

The Metropolitan style under Ilkhanid court patronage, c. *1290*–c. *1310.* A mature tradition of manuscript illustration had been established in the Abbasid capital at Baghdad in the early 13th century (*see* §(iv)(c) above); this Mesopotamian style survived the Mongol conquest of the city in 1258, as can be seen in such manuscripts as the Munich al-Qazwini, which was produced at Wasit in Iraq in 1279–80, and a copy of the *Rasā'il ikhwān al-ṣafā'* ('Epistles of the sincere brethren') completed at Baghdad in 1287–8. While the patrons of these two manuscripts are unknown, two manuscripts from the 1290s are linked to the Ilkhanid court and show the origins of the Metropolitan style. The earlier is a copy of 'Ata Malik Juvayni's *Tārīkh-i jahāngūshā* ('History of the world conqueror'; Paris, Bib. N., MS. supp. pers. 205) finished in 1290. The double-page frontispiece shows on the right a squatting groom leading a caparisoned horse and on the left a scribe seated beneath a tree taking dictation from a standing figure in a flowered coat, presumably the author, who was chief vizier to the Ilkhanid court. The second manuscript from the 1290s (New York, Pierpont Morgan Lib., MS. M.500) is the Persian translation of Ibn Bakhtishu's Arabic bestiary, *Manāfi' al-ḥayawān* ('Usefulness of animals'), which was commissioned by Ghazan (*reg* 1295–1304). The manuscript was copied in one of the Ilkhanid capitals, Maragha in Azerbaijan, in 1297 or 1299, and is illustrated with 94 paintings, some no bigger than 50 mm in each direction. Those on the first folios follow a conservative Mesopotamian style: the paper is left plain as a background and there is no attempt to depict space illusionistically. In other paintings towards the end of the manuscript an awareness of Chinese painting and a new sense of atmosphere and space are apparent. Figures are smaller in scale and more integrated into their setting. Landscape is more developed, with such new motifs as gnarled trees and convoluted clouds. In contrast to the symmetrical compositions of the earlier paintings, figures are sometimes cropped at the edge of the picture, suggesting a world beyond its narrow plane.

Two other dated illustrated manuscripts are closely related to this court-sponsored school. One is the earliest surviving copy of Sa'd al-Din al-Varavini's *Marzbānnāma* ('Book of Marzban'; Istanbul, Archaeol. Mus., MS. 216), completed at Baghdad in May 1299. The text belongs to the literary genre of mirrors for princes, consisting of didactic fables intended to guide a future ruler along the correct ethical and moral path. Contrary to normal practice, the three illustrations at the beginning of the manuscript were painted before the text; they depict the Prophet Muhammad, the author and the patron. The paintings are set off by thick gold borders and show traditional compositions and figure types, but new sartorial and tonsorial details, such as overlapping kaftans, looped coiffures and varied hats, are introduced. A manuscript of al-Biruni's *Āthār al-bāqiya* ('Chronology of ancient nations'; Edinburgh, U. Lib., Arab. MS. 161) is slightly later in date (1307–8). The text discusses the calendars used by pre-Islamic peoples, and the 24 small illustrations show some of the historical events relating to these. Gold rulings and patterned borders frame the illustrations; the simple, symmetrical compositions, haloed figures with turbans and robes, and patterned drapery are typical of the earlier Baghdad style, but the convoluted clouds and coloured grounds are new. The image of the *Investiture of 'Ali at Ghadir Khumm* (fol. 162*r*) depicts the Prophet Muhammad designating his son-in-law 'Ali as his successor, a crucial event in Shi'ite theology. It shows the interest of 14th-century patrons in varied religious movements, including Shi'ism, and uses new features, such as direct communication between the figures and swirling red and gold clouds set against a dark sky, to enhance the drama of the moment.

All these early Metropolitan manuscripts combine Near Eastern and Chinese styles, injecting traditional compositions with such new motifs as lotus blossoms, swirling clouds, pomegranates, patterned kaftans and looped coiffures. Although the paintings within the text are relatively small, they exhibit a new interest in space: frame bands separate illustrations from the text, and receding groundlines, grassy tufts and circular arrangements of figures expand the setting.

The Rashidiyya school, c. *1309–18.* The trend of incorporating Chinese elements and opening up the image continued in the manuscripts produced under the auspices of Rashid al-Din. The Mongol ruler Ghazan had commissioned his vizier to extend Juvayni's *Tārīkh-i jahāngūshā,* and Rashid al-Din turned the work into a four-volume world history, the *Jāmi' al-tawārīkh.* He provided for copies of both the Arabic and Persian versions of his history to be made each year at his scriptorium; the bound manuscripts were to be displayed in the mosque of the Rab'-i Rashidi, registered at the judiciary and then sent to different cities throughout the realm. Despite these precautions, no manuscript has survived intact, and only fragments of three contemporary copies of vol. ii, which contains the history of non-Mongol Eurasian peoples, have survived. Fragments of the Persian text are preserved in two manuscripts in Istanbul (Topkapı Pal. Lib.). The first (H. 1653) is a copy of the *Majma' al-tawārīkh* ('Assembly of histories'), Hafiz-i Abru's 15th-century continuation of Rashid al-Din's work; its middle section belongs to a manuscript of Rashid al-Din's history made in 1314. The second (H. 1654) is an almost complete text finished in 1317 (*see* §(c) below). These two copies can be used to determine the size, rate and subjects of illustration,

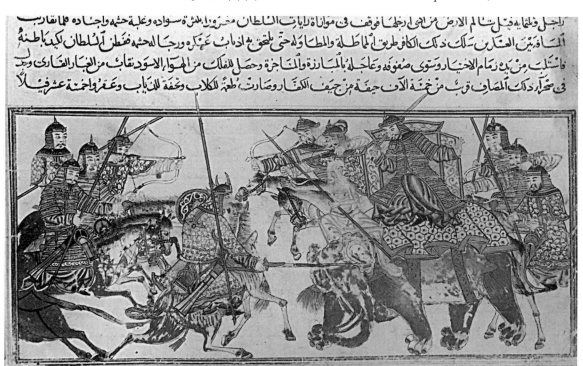

114. *Mahmud Invades the Punjab, c.* 116×250 mm; illustration from Rashid al-Din: *Jāmiʿ al-tawārīkh* ('Compendium of histories'), from Tabriz, *c.* 1314 (Edinburgh, University Library, Arab. MS. 20, illus. 53)

but most of their images were not painted until the late 14th century or early 15th. The only manuscript of Rashid al-Din's universal history with contemporary illustrations is the fragmentary Arabic version divided between Edinburgh (U. Lib., Arab. MS. 20) and London (ex-Royal Asiat. Soc., London; N. D. Khalili priv. col.). It seems likely that these two belonged to the same manuscript, as they have the same dimensions and contain different but contiguous sections of the text. They were certainly once bound together, for they are paginated in the same hand with succeeding numbers. Neither fragment includes a colophon, but the date 1314 added to the fragment in London seems plausible.

All the 14th-century copies of Rashid al-Din's universal history are large-format: each page has a written area *c.* 350×250 mm containing more than 30 lines of text. The narrow illustrations extend across the page and occupy about one-third of its height. The text is not illustrated regularly; instead, certain subjects (e.g. the battles of Badr and Uhud) are repeated and certain cycles (e.g. the history of the Ghaznavid dynasty) preferred. This selectivity suggests that the images were not intended to be merely illustrative but to make a political point. The illustrations (see fig. 114) are done in a common house style using coloured washes, a technique derived from Chinese brush painting. The horizontal format of the images and the abrupt cutting-off of the figures at the margins echo Chinese handscrolls, and conventional depictions of water, rocks and peaks behind peaks imbue the landscape with a Chinese spirit. These images do not copy contemporary Yuan painting but are filtered through another medium,

such as textiles or ceramics. The manuscripts illustrate the cosmopolitan atmosphere in Tabriz, entrepôt between East and West, for when Rashidiyya artists lacked Eastern models they turned to Western ones, basing the composition of a scene such as the *Birth of Muhammad* (Edinburgh, U. Lib., Arab. MS. 20, fol. 44*r*) on a Christian *Nativity.*

The Rashidiyya house style is so specific that other works can be attributed to the same milieu. A manuscript (London, BL, Orient. & India Office Lib., Ethé MSS 903, 911, 913) containing the collected works of several poets was certainly done at the Rashidiyya, for it is dated 1313–15 and the strip-like images are similar in format to those in the *Jāmiʿ al-tawārīkh.* Detached paintings preserved in four albums (Berlin, Staatsbib. Preuss. Kultbes., Orientabt., Diez A 70–73) formerly belonging to Heinrich Friedrich von Diez, the Prussian ambassador to the Sublime Porte from 1784 to 1791, probably illustrated vol. i of the *Jāmiʿ al-tawārīkh*, which contained the history of the Mongols. The same coloured washes and stylistic conventions are used as in the fragments of vol. ii, and the paintings are similar in width, although many are considerably taller and would have filled almost the entire page. In this respect they prefigure another fragmentary copy of vol. i (Calcutta, Asiat. Soc., MS. D31), but its *nastaʿlīq* script, stylized plants and high horizon suggest an attribution to the 15th century.

Metropolitan painting, 1318–c. 1350. Rashid al-Din's scriptorium was plundered after his execution in 1318, but its impact survived owing to the widespread distribution of its products. The largest, and perhaps the most spectacular, manuscript of the entire century is the Great Mongol *Shāhnāma* ('Book of kings'), known also as the Demotte *Shāhnāma* after the infamous dealer who broke it up for sale at the beginning of the 20th century (*see* DEMOTTE, GEORGES). It originally contained about 300 large-format folios (written space 410×290 mm) with some 200 illustrations, of which only 58 are known today. The paintings show an extraordinary range of styles and techniques. A few, such as *Alexander Visiting the Brahmans* (Washington, DC, Sackler Gal.), reflect the direct impact of the Rashidiyya style and iconography, but most are much bolder in concept; they use a varied palette and a broad range of expressive devices to expand the compositions and turn illustrations into complete images. The large-scale figures dominate the landscape and display a quality of emotion rarely found in Persian painting. In *Ardawan Captured by Ardashir* (see fig. 115) the circular composition focuses attention on the mounted victor, impassive before the bowed and humbled Ardawan. Contorted trees and hooded soldiers add exoticism and drama to the event. No colophon from the manuscript has survived, and traditional stylistic analysis is inadequate to deal with the bewildering array of hands and styles, but on historical and ideological grounds the manuscript should be attributed to 1330–36, when Rashid al-Din's son Ghiyath al-Din revived his father's scriptorium.

115. *Ardawan Captured by Ardashir*, 405×292 mm; illustration from the Great Mongol *Shāhnāma*, from Tabriz, *c.* 1335 (Washington, DC, Arthur M. Sackler Gallery, MS. 586.0103); also known as the Demotte *Shāhnāma*

Manuscript production in the Metropolitan style continued during the political chaos of the last two decades of Ilkhanid rule. A manuscript of Asadi's *Garshāspnāma* ('Book of Garshasp'; 1354; Istanbul, Topkapı Pal. Lib., H. 674) contains five completed paintings and has space for many more. The illustrations have affinities in figural style and composition with the Great Mongol *Shāhnāma*, but the high horizon, projection of images into the margin and stilted and more formal figures indicate its later date and provincial place of production. Detached paintings preserved in albums in Istanbul and Berlin are more directly in the mainstream Metropolitan tradition, using the same format, bold compositions and lively colours as the Great Mongol *Shāhnāma*, but they are traditionally ascribed to the reign of the Jalayirid sultan Uways I (1356–74), who was a major patron of the arts of the book (*see* §(c) below).

Provincial production in south-west Iran. South-west Iran also maintained an active tradition of manuscript production, as can be seen in four *Shāhnāma* manuscripts dated between 1330 and 1352 (Istanbul, Topkapı Pal. Lib., H. 1479; St Petersburg, Rus. N. Lib., Dorn 329; see fig. 116; and two dispersed copies, the second known as the Stephens *Shāhnāma*). The dedication of the dispersed copy dated 1341 to a vizier of the Injuid family, who governed south-west Iran from *c.* 1303 to 1357 (*see* §3(ii) above), allowed Stchoukine to formulate a 'Shiraz school under the Injuids', but the court often moved between Isfahan and Shiraz. Several other manuscripts, such as a dispersed *Kalila and Dimna* dated 1333, the *Kitāb-i samak-i 'ayyār* ('Book of Samak the Paladin'; Oxford, Bodleian Lib., Ouseley MSS 379–81) and the Persian adaptation of the *Annals* of al-Tabari (Washington, DC, Freer, 30.21, 47.19, 56.16), can be attributed to the same school on stylistic grounds. These manuscripts are all medium-sized (the written page is *c.* 300 mm high) and have vibrant, energetic, even slapdash illustrations. The paint is often unevenly applied so that the underdrawing shows. While the palette is extensive, certain colours are repeated, especially red or ochre backgrounds. Landscape is imaginatively depicted but is strictly planar and uses a limited range of conventions, the most distinctive being conical hills.

This productive school blossomed under the economic revival sponsored by the Injuids, but its origin is difficult to trace due to lack of dated manuscripts. One key piece is a manuscript of *Kalila and Dimna* copied in 1307–8 (London, BL, Or. MS. 13506). Although tiny (the written page measures 140×50 mm), it contains a double-page frontispiece and 66 small paintings. The meander borders, inverted cloud conventions and bamboo tree trunks hark back to the Mesopotamian style of the 13th century, but the red backgrounds, flowered robes and lotus-petal borders are all typical of the group produced in southwest Iran in the 1330s and 1340s, and the small dome-shaped hills seem to be forerunners of the more pointed conical ones used in Injuid manuscripts.

Small Shāhnāmas. As well as the large-format Metropolitan works and the medium-sized works from southwest Iran, there is a group of four dispersed *Shāhnāma* manuscripts, which lack dedications, colophons or dates,

116. *Bahram Chupin Killing a Lion*; illustration from a *Shāhnāma*, from Shiraz, 1332–3 (St Petersburg, Russian National Library, Dorn 329, fol. 343*r*)

but which can be grouped together on stylistic grounds. All are extremely small in format (e.g. the pages in Washington, DC, Freer, have written surfaces that measure 250×170 mm) and have some 300 folios with more than 100 paintings that were carefully executed using a palette

117. *Gurdiyah Presenting an Equestrian Cat to Khusraw Parviz*; illustration from a Small *Shāhnāma*, probably from north-west Iran, early 14th century (Geneva, Musée d'Art et d'Histoire, MS. Add. Pozzi 382)

of bright, thickly applied colours and lavish amounts of gold for background and secondary motifs (see fig. 117). Patterned designs crowd the compositions, and the small, vivacious figures seem to burst from the frame. The small figures and lack of a high horizon show that these manuscripts belong to the late 13th century or early 14th, but their exact provenance is still open to question. They were once attributed to Shiraz under the Injuids on the basis of a comparison with a dispersed copy of the scientific anthology *Mu'nis al-aḥrār*, compiled by Muhammad ibn Badr Jajarmi at Isfahan in 1341; while the localization and date of the latter are undisputed, its value for localizing the Small *Shāhnāma*s is limited. Some of the compositions in the Small *Shāhnāma*s occur in the Great Mongol *Shāhnāma*, but they are totally different in scale and much more restricted in conception. The Small *Shāhnāma*s have also been attributed to the Indian subcontinent, while Simpson (1979) has placed them in Baghdad *c.* 1300 on the basis of a comparison with the *Marzbānnāma* of 1299, but none of these hypotheses has prevailed. The quality and number of these manuscripts bespeak a consistent level of taste, which may represent a different level of patronage rather than a distinct geographical or chronological locale.

BIBLIOGRAPHY

Dust Muhammad: Preface to the Bahram Mirza Album (1544); Eng. trans. by W. M. Thackston in *A Century of Princes: Sources on Timurid History and Art* (Cambridge, MA, 1989), pp. 335–50

I. Stchoukine: *La Peinture iranienne sous les dernières Abbasides et les Il-khans* (Bruges, 1936)

K. Holter: 'Die islamischen Miniaturhandschriften vor 1350', *Zentbl. Bibwsn*, liv (1937), pp. 1–34

E. Schroeder: 'Ahmad Musa and Shams al-Din: A Review of Fourteenth-century Painting', *A. Islam.*, vi (1939), pp. 113–42

H. Buchthal, O. Kurz and R. Ettinghausen: 'Supplementary Notes to K. Holter's Check List of Islamic Illuminated Manuscripts before A.D. 1350', *A. Islam.*, vii (1940), pp. 147–64

D. Barrett: *Persian Painting of the Fourteenth Century* (London, 1952)

R. Ettinghausen: 'On some Mongol Miniatures', *Kst Orients*, iii (1959), pp. 44–65

B. Gray: *Persian Painting* (Geneva, 1961)

R. Ettinghausen: *Arab Painting* (Geneva, 1962)

G. İnal: 'Some Miniatures of the *Jāmiʿ al-tavārīkh* in Istanbul, Topkapı Museum, Hazine Library no. 1654', *A. Orient.*, v (1963), pp. 163–75

A. S. Melikian-Chirvani: 'Le Roman de Varqé et Golšâh', *A. Asiat.*, xxii (1970) [whole issue]

J. M. Rogers: 'The Burial Rites of the Turks and the Mongols', *Cent. Asiat. J.*, xiv (1970), pp. 195–227

P. Soucek: 'An Illustrated Manuscript of al-Biruni's *Chronology of Ancient Nations*', *The Scholar and the Saint*, ed. P. Chelkowski (New York, 1975), pp. 103–65

N. Titley: 'An Illustrated Persian Text of Kalila and Dimna Dated 707/1307–8', *BL J.*, i (1975), pp. 42–61

D. T. Rice: *The Illustrations to the 'World History' of Rashid al-Din* (Edinburgh, 1976)

B. Gray: *The World History of Rashid al-Din: A Study of the Royal Asiatic Society Manuscript* (London, 1978)

E. J. Grube: 'Persian Painting in the Fourteenth Century: A Research Report', *AION*, xxxviii/17 (1978) [suppl.]

B. Gray, ed.: *The Arts of the Book in Central Asia, 14th–16th Centuries* (Boulder, CO, London and Paris, 1979)

M. S. Simpson: *The Illustration of an Epic: The Earliest Shahnama Manuscripts* (New York, 1979)

O. Grabar and S. Blair: *Epic Images and Contemporary History: The Illustrations of the Great Mongol Shahnama* (Chicago and London, 1980)

M. S. Simpson: 'The Role of Baghdad in the Formation of Persian Painting', *Art et société dans le monde iranien*, ed. C. Adle (Paris, 1982), pp. 91–116

A. T. Adamova and L. T. Gyuzal'yan: *Miniatyury rukopisi poemy 'Shakhname' 1333 goda* [Miniatures from the manuscript of the *Shāhnāma* poem dated 1333] (Leningrad, 1985)

S. Carboni: 'The London Qazwīnī: An Early 14th-century Copy of the *ʿAjāʾib al-makhlūqāt*', *Islam. A.*, iii (1988–9), pp. 15–32

P. P. Soucek: 'The Life of the Prophet: Illustrated Versions', *Content and Context of Visual Arts in the Islamic World*, ed. P. P. Soucek (University Park and London, 1988), pp. 193–218

S. S. Blair: 'On the Track of the "Demotte" *Shahnama* Manuscript', *Les Manuscrits du Moyen-Orient: Essais de codicologie et de paléographie*, ed. F. Déroche (Istanbul and Paris, 1989), pp. 125–32

K. Rührdanz: 'Illustrationen zu Rašīd al-Dīn's Taʾrīḫ-i Mubārak-i Ġāzānī in den Berliner Diez-Alben', *L'Iran face à la domination mongol, Pont-à-Mousson: 26–28 octobre 1992*

S. S. Blair: 'The Development of the Illustrated Book in Iran', *Muqarnas*, x (1993), pp. 266–74

Illustrated Poetry and Epic Images: Persian Painting of the 1330s and 1340s (exh. cat. by M. L. Swietochowski and S. Carboni, New York, Met., 1994)

S. S. Blair: *Compendium of Chronicles: Rashid al-Din's Illustrated History of the World* (London, 1995)

M. S. Simpson: 'A Reconstruction and Preliminary Account of the 1341 *Shāhnāma*', *Festschrift for B. W. Robinson* (London, in preparation)

S. S. Blair and J. M. Bloom: 'Epic Images and Contemporary History: The Legacy of the Great Mongol Shahnama', *Islam. A.*, v (in preparation)

SHEILA S. BLAIR

(c) Iraq and Iran, c. 1350–c. 1400. In the years following the break-up of Ilkhanid power a new style of Persian manuscript painting appeared, one that would lay the groundwork for the classical styles of the 15th and 16th centuries (*see* §§(d) and (vi)(a) below). The painters of this transitional period not only fused Chinese and Near Eastern pictorial elements into a coherent whole but also developed a new formula for the depiction of space. Manuscript illustrations of the late 14th century also show a change in subject-matter and mood: the repertory of manuscripts illustrated was expanded greatly, and the emotionalism of the early 14th century was replaced by a lyrical detachment that became a hallmark of later Persian manuscript painting.

Following the disintegration of the Ilkhanid empire from 1336, the JALAYIRID dynasty (*reg* 1336–1432), a Mongol family that had provided provincial governors for the Ilkhanids, seized power in Iraq and north-west Iran.

Their capitals at Tabriz and Baghdad became major centres of book production in the Ilkhanid tradition. Two Jalayirid rulers, Uways I (*reg* 1356–74) and Ahmad (*reg* 1382–1410), stand out as important patrons of the arts of the book. The Muzaffarids (*reg* 1314–93), another family that had provided governors for the Ilkhanids, established control over southern Iran; their capital at Shiraz continued the traditions of book production established there under the Injuids (*reg c.* 1303–57). The major historical source for painting during the period is the Safavid court librarian Dust Muhammad (*see also* §(b) above), who traced the origins of Persian manuscript painting from Ahmad Musa to his pupil Shams al-Din, who learnt his art in the reign of Uways I. Dust Muhammad attributed the illustrations of a *Shāhnāma* ('Book of kings') to Shams al-Din, who in turn was teacher to three important artists: 'Abd al-Hayy, the master Junayd and Pir Ahmad Baghshimali, 'the zenith of his time'.

Early Jalayirid painting, to c. 1375. The works in the middle decades of the 14th century are disparate, ranging from those that have an affinity with earlier styles to others with expanded spatial compositions closer to the manuscripts dated to the reign of Sultan Ahmad. There appears to be a transition from the emotional pathos of the Ilkhanid works to the refined reserve that would mark later styles of Persian manuscript painting. Given the eclectic quality of the works and lack of securely dated examples, it is almost impossible to establish a coherent evolution of forms.

One of the great disappointments of this crucial period is the low quality of the few dated manuscripts surviving from the mid-14th century. The mediocre quality of three manuscripts produced between the decline of the Ilkhanids from 1336 and the beginning of the reign of Uways in 1356 seems to bear out Dust Muhammad's silence concerning any major patrons during this period. An anthology of alchemy and magic (1339; Istanbul, Topkapı Pal. Lib., A. 2075) has a double frontispiece and anticipates illustrated copies of scientific manuscripts produced under the later Jalayirids. A manuscript of *Kalila and Dimna* (1343–4; Cairo, N. Lib., Adab Farsi 61) has uninspired illustrations that were probably added or repainted later in the century. A copy of Asadi's *Garshāspnāma* ('Book of Garshasp'; 1354; Istanbul, Topkapı Pal. Lib., H. 674) has paintings that, while retaining a certain robustness, lack the emotional drama of the Great Mongol *Shāhnāma* of *c.* 1335.

By contrast, the undated manuscripts ascribed to this period are of superb quality, but in the 15th and 16th centuries several key paintings were cut from their original manuscripts and pasted into albums with other works from different periods. Many of these pages have traditionally been attributed to the reign of Uways, who is known to have been an active patron of the arts, but it is difficult to assign them to an exact date, artist, place of production or patron. Dust Muhammad made the point that an unbroken chain from master to student linked the Ilkhanid and Jalayirid workshops, so it is not surprising that certain elements that had appeared in such Ilkhanid masterpieces as the Great Mongol *Shāhnāma* were expanded and refined in the second half of the century. The high quality of these undated works can be seen in the illustrations to a manuscript of *Kalila and Dimna* pasted in an album (Istanbul, U. Lib., F. 1422) prepared for the Safavid shah Tahmasp I (*reg* 1524–76). The *Kalila and Dimna* manuscript was surely a royal commission and may have been initiated by an Ilkhanid patron, as Cowan suggested, but some of the most impressive illustrations, such as the *Clever Merchant and the Gullible Thief* (fol. 24*r*), burst beyond the frame into the margins and are more sophisticated than earlier works in depicting space, suggesting that they, at least, should be given a date in the 1350s or 1360s.

Paintings probably cut from several *Shāhnāma* manuscripts in another album (Istanbul, Topkapı Pal. Lib., H. 2153) may also date from the early years of the reign of Uways, for much of the drama so prevalent in the Great Mongol *Shāhnāma* has been retained in such images as *Isfandiyar and the Dragon* (fol. 157*r*). There are also affinities between this page and certain illustrations in the cut-up *Kalila and Dimna*, most particularly the tendency to suggest animal faces in the rocky landscape. The hand of a revolutionary artist has also been at work in the page (fol. 23*r*; see fig. 118) illustrating the legendary bird, the

118. *Simurgh Carrying the Infant Zal to its Nest*, 317×168 mm; illustration cut from a *Shāhnāma* and mounted into an album, from ?Tabriz, *c.* ?1370 (Istanbul, Topkapı Palace Library, H. 2153, fol. 23*r*)

simurgh, soaring aloft to its mountain retreat. The fabulous bird cradles the abandoned child Zal as it slows for its approach hovering over a group of writhing and convoluted rocks. Above, a towering mountain peak is crowned by trees set against windswept clouds. The painting is permeated by the drama of untamed nature animated by mysterious energies. The concept of nature as a backdrop for human drama had been introduced in the Great Mongol *Shāhnāma* but is developed to an even greater degree here; within a generation, however, this passion would be transformed into more conventionalized forms. The vertical format of the illustration breaks completely with the horizontal format traditionally used in Near Eastern painting. No longer is the painting a mere footnote to the text; it is a visual entity in itself. This new format may reflect the impact of the Chinese hanging scroll. After it became thoroughly Persianized in the late 14th century, the vertical composition remained a favourite for the next three centuries of painting in the greater Iranian world.

The album (Istanbul, Topkapı Pal. Lib., H. 2154) prepared in 1544 by Dust Muhammad for the Safavid prince Bahram Mirza contains a series of ten extraordinary paintings from a copy of the account of the Prophet Muhammad's journey to the Seven Heavens, the *Mi'rājnāma* ('Book of the ascension'). The large scale and heroic energy of such illustrations as the *Angel Gabriel Carrying Muhammad over a Celestial Landscape of Mountains and Fire* (fol. 42*v*) announce this as the work of an important artist. Four of the paintings have been attributed by a 16th-century hand to Ahmad Musa. According to Dust Muhammad, Ahmad Musa was active in the reign of the Ilkhanid sultan Abu Sa'id (1317–35), but his career may have continued into the reign of Uways. Further fine works that date from this period are found in four albums (Berlin, Staatsbib. Preuss. Kultbes., Orient. Abt., MSS Diez A 70–73) acquired by Heinrich Friedrich von Diez, Prussian ambassador to the Ottomans from 1784 to 1791. Some illustrations also show the legacy of the artists of the Great Mongol *Shāhnāma*, and such compositions as a footwashing scene (Diez A 70 fol. 16) show advancements in the depiction of space parallel to those seen in the Istanbul albums.

*Painting during the reign of Ahmad Jalayir (*reg *1382–1410).* Ahmad Jalayir (*see also* JALAYIRID, (1)) was a gifted poet, calligrapher and painter who was responsible for the patronage of some of the finest works produced in this period. He had capitals in both Tabriz and Baghdad, but in 1386 Timur occupied Tabriz, centre of the Ilkhanid and Jalayirid scriptoria, forcing Ahmad and his most skilled artists to retreat to Baghdad. In 1393 Timur entered Baghdad and Ahmad had to retreat to Damascus and then Cairo. By the next year, however, he was able to return to Baghdad, where his workshop continued to produce until June 1401, despite a brief interruption by Timur in 1399. Ahmad then fled again to Egypt. After Timur's death in 1405 Ahmad returned to Baghdad. He briefly reoccupied Tabriz, only to be driven out. He died in his attempt to retake it in 1410. The earliest dated manuscripts associated with the reign of Ahmad are not as fine as the ones associated with his father, Uways I. A copy of Nizami's *Khamsa* ('Five poems'; 1386–8; London, BL, Or.

MS. 13297) is important for its new subject-matter rather than for the beauty of its illustrations. The shift from the illustration of history, legends and epics to lyrical and romantic poetry is one of the innovations of painting under Ahmad.

This new mood is perfectly expressed in the finest of all Jalayirid manuscripts, a copy of the *Dīvān* (collected poetry) of Khwaju Kirmani (1396; London, BL, Add. MS. 18113). It contains nine paintings in a similar style of the highest quality. One of them, depicting *Humay and Humayun on the Day after their Wedding* (fol. 45*v*), is signed by JUNAYD, who must be the Junayd described by Dust Muhammad as a pupil of Shams al-Din. This is the only signed masterpiece that can be linked indisputably to Dust Muhammad's account. Junayd's paintings are worthy of their lofty heritage, for they are revolutionary in several ways. Their strong vertical compositions are the logical result of the spatial experiments seen in paintings from the Istanbul albums. The Khwaju Kirmani illustrations retain the earlier fascination with the forces of nature, yet blend it with a sweet atmosphere of delicacy and refinement. In comparison to these illustrations, the raw emotional themes of earlier Ilkhanid illustrations seem almost brutal. The dramatic page (fol. 31*r*; see fig. 119) in which the parted lovers Humay and Humayun recognize each other after their combat in a clearing in the wood has a marvellous counterplay of stillness and motion and of

space and pattern. The excitement inherent in this emotional encounter is suggested by the rearing horse, the whip-like movements of the curvilinear trees and the soaring birds that flutter up from the forest in reaction to the human drama below. It is not surprising that such a work was the direct inspiration for some of the finest works of the 15th century. Another painting was detached from this manuscript and bound into the album prepared by Dust Muhammad (Istanbul, Topkapı Pal. Lib., H. 2154, fol. 20*v*). It has the same dreamy beauty, doll-like figures and resolution of the tension between exterior and interior space that is seen in the works by Junayd, but it bears a 16th-century attribution to 'ABD AL-HAYY, who Dust Muhammad said was another pupil of Shams al-Din. 'Abd al-Hayy was carried off by Timur to his capital at Samarkand and played a role in the development of Timurid book illustration.

Other works from the first half of Ahmad's reign are of lesser quality. These include a copy of *Kalila and Dimna* (1392; Paris, Bib. N., MS. supp. pers. 913) and the illustration added to a copy of Rashid al-Din's *Jāmiʿ al-tawārīkh* ('Compendium of histories'; Istanbul, Topkapı Pal. Lib., H. 1654) penned in 1317, both of which are rather pedestrian. Illustrations to a copy of a Persian adaptation of al-Qazwini's cosmology, *ʿAjāʾib al-makhlūqāt* ('Wonders of creation'; 1388; Paris, Bib. N., MS. supp. pers. 332), and to a copy of the astrological text, the *Kitāb al-bulhān* (1399; ?Oxford, Bodleian Lib., Or. MS. 133), show some new landscape and decorative elements despite the conservative compositions characteristic of scientific manuscripts. The illustrations are connected to the Western tradition of depicting the seasons and labours of the months. An astrological manual (Ham, Surrey, Keir priv. col.; U. Sarajevo, Inst. Orient. Res.) with illustrations stylistically similar to those in the *Kitāb al-bulhān* is thought to have been produced in Baghdad under the Jalayirids.

Two remarkable manuscripts are usually assigned to the second, troubled half of Ahmad's reign. The first is a beautiful copy of Nizami's romance *Khusraw and Shirin* (Washington, DC, Freer, 31.32–31.37). The manuscript was copied by 'Ali ibn Hasan al-Sultani (*see* MIR 'ALI TABRIZI and §2(iv)(b) above) 'in the capital Tabriz'; its fine quality and similarities to the *Dīvān* of Khwaju Kirmani indicate that Timur had not been able to carry off all the best Jalayirid artists to Samarkand. This manuscript lacks the absolute refinement of Junayd's work, but the innovations of his style have been retained. A copy of the *Dīvān* of Ahmad himself (Washington, DC, Freer, 32.29–37) is also attributed to this period. The poetry gives a glimpse into Ahmad's character and helps to explain the refined elegance of royal manuscripts prepared during his reign. The text blocks of exquisite calligraphy on 8 of the 337 folios have marginal drawings in black ink with slight touches of blue and gold depicting the life of the nomad and scenes of daily life in the country. The illustrations are charming in their fine draughtsmanship and narrative quality and, with their reflections of Far Eastern ink painting, are the best examples of chinoiserie in the Jalayirid period. The spread of Sufism may also have contributed to the sense of an animated landscape bursting with life and energy that pervades these illustrations.

119. Junayd: *Humay and Humayun in Combat*, 324×241 mm; illustration from Khwaju Kirmani: *Dīvān* (collected poetry), from Baghdad, 1396 (London, British Library, Add. MS. 18113, fol. 31*r*)

Painting under the Muzaffarids (1364–84). The province of Fars in southern Iran had always been a centre of traditional Persian culture; here the Muzaffarid ruler Shah Shuja (*reg* 1364–84) was the patron of Hafiz, the great Persian lyric poet of Shiraz. The few manuscripts remaining from this period show a radical shift from the provincial red-ground style practised under the Injuids to one that reflects contemporary Jalayirid innovations. A manuscript of the *Shāhnāma* (1371; Istanbul, Topkapı Pal. Lib., H. 1511) includes elements that would become typical of the Shiraz school, such as a high horizon line with distinctive cleft rocks, a repetitive semé ground with tufts of grass, and large expanses of pure colour, especially in the sky. The tendency to turn everything into a pattern and to conceptualize nature is already present. These localized features are repeated in another copy of the *Shāhnāma* (Cairo, N. Lib., Adab Farsi 6) dated 1393, the year in which Timur conquered Shiraz.

The production of luxury manuscripts expanded in Shiraz after the arrival of the Timurids, to judge from a sumptuous two-volume copy of a collection of five epic poems (1397–8; Dublin, Chester Beatty Lib., Pers. MS. 114; London, BL, Or. MS. 2780). It contains several pictorial conventions of the Shiraz style, such as gold skies, tufa-like rocks and figures emerging half-hidden behind the high horizon, that allow its attribution to that city. The superior quality of materials and execution may indicate the hands of Jalayirid artists who had fled the unstable situations in Tabriz and Baghdad, or captured artists in Timur's entourage. The tenacity of older traditions in Fars is exhibited in a poetic anthology copied by Mansur Bihbihani (1398; Istanbul, Mus. Turk. & Islam. A., 1950). Eleven of the twelve paintings accompany the poems of Nizami and are pure landscapes devoid of figures; Aga-Oglu suggested that they represent a survival of Mazdean beliefs. The subject-matter of these paintings sets the manuscript apart from metropolitan works and attests to the surprising variety of book painting in late 14th-century Iran.

BIBLIOGRAPHY

M. Aga-Oglu: 'The Landscape Miniatures of an Anthology Manuscript of the Year 1398 A.D.', *A. Islam.*, iii (1936), pp. 77–98

E. Kühnel: 'A Bidpai Manuscript of 1343–4 in Cairo', *Bull. Amer. Inst. Iran. A. & Archaeol.*, v/2 (1937), pp. 137–4

R. Ettinghausen: 'Persian Ascension Miniatures of the Fourteenth Century', *Accademia nazionale dei Lincei, atti del XII convegno 'volta' promosso dalla classe di scienze morali, storiche e filologiche. Tema: Oriente e occidente nel medioevo: Roma, 1957*, pp. 360–83

——: 'On Some Mongol Miniatures', *Kst Orients*, iii (1959), pp. 44–65

M. S. Ipsiroglu: *Saray-Alben: Diez'sche Klebebande aus der Berliner Sammlungen* (Wiesbaden, 1964)

R. Pinder-Wilson: 'Paintings of the Jala'irid Period: A Reconsideration', *Memorial Volume of the Vth International Congress of Iranian Art and Archaeology: Tehran, 1968*, pp. 161–6

N. Atasoy: 'Four Istanbul Albums and Some Fragments from Fourteenth Century Shahnamas', *A. Orient.*, viii (1970), pp. 19–48

D. Duda: 'Die Buchmalerei der Ǧalā'iriden, 1', *Der Islam*, xlviii (1971), pp. 28–76

N. Titley: 'A Fourteenth-century Khamseh of Nizami', *BM Q.*, xxxvi (1971), pp. 8–11

D. Duda: 'Die Buchmalerei der Ǧalā'iriden, 2: Die Malerei in Tabriz unter Sultān Uwais und Husain', *Der Islam*, xlix (1972), pp. 153–240

D. E. Kimburg-Salter: 'A Sufi Theme in Persian Painting: The Diwan of Sultan Ahmad Gala'ir in the Freer Gallery of Art, Washington, DC', *Kst Orients*, xi (1977), pp. 43–84

V. A. Prentice: 'A Detached Miniature from the *Masnavī*s of Khwaju Kirmani', *Orient. A.*, xxvii (1981), pp. 60–66

S. Carboni: 'Two Fragments of a Jalayirid Astrological Treatise in the Keir Collection and in the Oriental Institute in Sarajevo', *Islam. A.*, ii (1987), pp. 149–86

T. Fotouhi: 'Les Illustrations d'un manscrit persan de la Bibliothèque nationale: Le livre des merveilles de la Création', *Rev. Hist. A.*, 4 (Dec 1988), pp. 41-52

J. S. Cowan: *Kalila wa Dimna: An Animal Allegory of the Mongol Court: The Istanbul University Album* (New York, 1989)

For further bibliography *see* §(b) above.

JULIE BADIEE

(d) Iran and western Central Asia, c. *1400–*c. *1500.* Painted illustration in finely copied and illuminated manuscripts assumed its classical format and reached the apogee of quality during the rule of the TIMURID dynasty (*reg* 1370–1506) in Iran and western Central Asia. For the first time in Iranian Islamic cultural history, the dynastic name and stylistic adjective 'Timurid' function virtually as one, and the history of book production in the Timurid capitals at Samarkand, Herat and Shiraz can best be understood as the result of individual royal patronage.

*Painting during the reign of Timur (*reg *1370–1405).* No painted images made for Timur or indisputably associated with his patronage survive, although wall paintings are described by contemporary authors such as the historian Ibn 'Arabshah (1392–1450) and the panegyrist Sharaf al-Din 'Ali Yazdi (*d* 1454). The paintings depicted the ruler, his court, his exploits and his family and were executed by artists from the conquered lands of Iran, Iraq and possibly even Syria. The earliest surviving paintings of the Timurid period are found in two illustrated volumes (Dublin, Chester Beatty Lib., Pers. MS. 114; London, BL, Or. MS. 2780), perhaps originally a single larger volume, of Persian epic poems. Although they have no dedication, they are dated 1397–8 and are written and illuminated in a Shiraz-style hand on unmistakably Shiraz paper; they have 16 illustrations in a style that combines Jalayirid features with others typical of painting in western Central Asia. These paintings differ from Jalayirid court painting in several ways: the figures are ample and natural and fill the pictorial space; the compositions are simple with virtually no architecture and a rather high horizon; the rulings around the paintings are wide gold lines instead of bundles of lapis-blue, black and gold lines. The landscapes often comprise only a series of steeply angled planes differentiated by colour and the surface texture of rock or desert. Subsidiary figures are only partially visible, placed at a dip in the horizon or cut by the margin. This mannerism, in addition to the Central Asian appearance of the demons (Pers. *dīv*) that figure in some of the illustrations, reflects the impact of the pictorial tradition of western Central Asia for the content of some illustrations and of Chinese scroll paintings for the compositions. Chinese elements had already appeared in painting under the Ilkhanids (*see* §(b) above) and can be seen in several paintings of uncertain date and origin mounted in three celebrated albums in Istanbul (Topkapı Pal. Lib., H. 2152, H. 2153 and H. 2160). These are clearly not manuscript illustrations, and Timur's court at Samarkand is one of the hypotheses proposed for their date and place of production.

Painting made for Iskandar Sultan (1384–c. 1415). Many of these features were retained in the manuscripts made for Timur's grandson Iskandar Sultan (*see* TIMURID, §II(4)) in the southern city of Shiraz, where he was appointed governor in 1409. The illustrated manuscripts known to have been made for him date between 1410 and 1413: an *Anthology* (1410; Lisbon, Mus. Gulbenkian, LA 161; the paintings were completely ruined by a flood in 1968 and have been entirely repainted); a smaller *Miscellany* (1410–11; see fig. 120); a horoscope (1411; London, Wellcome Inst. Hist. Medic. Lib., Persian MS. 474); an astrological compendium (1411; Istanbul, U. Lib., F. 1418); and some large folios from an anthology copied in Isfahan (1413; Istanbul, Topkapı Pal. Lib., B. 411). To this list may be added others lacking documentation: an *Anthology* of poetry copied in Yazd (1407; Istanbul, Topkapı Pal. Lib., H. 796), several undated manuscripts and single paintings, some of them tiny, and some free and vivacious pen drawings that often have a Chinese flavour. All are unmistakably similar in style and execution to the paintings in manuscripts commissioned by Iskandar Sultan as well as to the Persian epic poems of 1397–8. Compositions are as elaborate, exteriors are integrated within the shape of the image, interiors are well designed and the figures are numerous and surely disposed throughout the picture. Some episodes illustrated in the *Miscellany*, especially from

120. *Shirin Sees the Portrait of Khusraw*, 107×74 mm; illustration from a *Miscellany*, from Shiraz, 1410–11 (London, British Library, Add. MS. 27261, fol. 38*r*)

the *Shāhnāma* ('Book of kings') of Firdawsi and the *Khamsa* ('Five poems') of Nizami, so perfectly convey the spirit of the text they illustrate that they assumed canonical status early in the 15th century. Such images as *Khusraw Sees Shirin Bathing, Iskandar Sees the Sirens* or *Rustam Rescues Bizhan from the Pit* remained canonical well into the 16th century. In stories with less fantastic or magical content and more resemblance to 15th-century life, such as princely audiences and military clashes, the paintings match Ibn 'Arabshah's description of wall paintings in the time of Timur. Figures remain ample in all the paintings connected with Iskandar; faces are notably oval in shape and often tilted to one side in a mannerism that survived for many decades.

These manuscripts also differ in content from most later Timurid illustrated manuscripts: they are compendia of religious texts and prayers, scientific works, histories and belles-lettres. To accommodate multiple works in one volume, as had been done in Muzaffarid Shiraz, one text would be written diagonally in the margins of a folio bearing another text or illustration; the diagonal lines meet at the middle of the vertical margin in a triangular space that was then illuminated. At least ten unillustrated manuscripts connected with Iskandar Sultan by reasons of scribe, locus of production or style of calligraphy and illumination can be added to these illustrated manuscripts and detached paintings. They form a coherent school, one created by a particular Timurid prince with an interest in specific subjects and a marked taste for certain styles of calligraphy, illumination and painting. This pattern of patronage was repeated throughout the century by other members of the Timurid family.

Painting made for Shahrukh (reg 1405–47). The illustrated manuscripts associated with Timur's son Shahrukh and his circle have, with perhaps two exceptions, a specifically historical cast: when considered with a number of unillustrated historical texts, they document a preoccupation of the new Timurid ruler with establishing his dynasty's legitimate claim to rule Iran. As works of art, the earliest of the illustrated histories is the best (Istanbul, Topkapı Pal. Lib., B. 282). It is a large, handsomely illuminated and illustrated *Kulliyyāt-i tārīkhī* ('Historical compendium'), which includes Bal'ami's Persian adaptation of al-Tabari's *Annals*, part of the *Jāmi' al-tawārīkh* ('Compendium of histories') of the great Ilkhanid vizier Rashid al-Din and the earliest version of the *Zafarnāma* ('Book of victory'), the panegyric history of Timur by Sharaf al-Din 'Ali Yazdi, with additions and supplements by Shahrukh's court historian, Hafiz-i Abru (*d* 1430). Completed in 1415–16, the manuscript has 20 illustrations accompanying Bal'ami's text and depicting the lives of the prophets from Abraham to Muhammad and the pre-Islamic kings of Iran. They are large, squarish compositions executed in four distinct styles; most include large figures in open landscapes whose antecedents can be found in Shiraz manuscripts produced under the Muzaffarids and Iskandar Sultan. They anticipate many later illustrations in an autograph copy of the *Majma' al-tawārīkh* ('Assembly of histories') by Hafiz-i Abru (Istanbul, Topkapı Pal. Lib., H. 1653), as well as in manuscripts done for Shahrukh's bibliophile son Baysunghur. Compositions (or parts of them), the drawing of figures and the oval, tilted faces, as well as the wide gold bands framing the images recall the manuscripts commissioned by Iskandar Sultan. Some compositions make daring use of empty space, a novel feature not found in the best Timurid illustrations, and the most memorable have a forceful, dramatic energy. Despite the variation in quality, the paintings use similar shades of gold and colours. The entire manuscript has a breadth of scale and magnificent illuminations that distinguish it from the other historical manuscripts of the century.

Illustrations in the autograph copy of Hafiz-i Abru's *Majma' al-tawārīkh*, dated 1425 but containing fols 149–435 from a 14th-century copy of Rashid al-Din's *Jāmi' al-tawārīkh*, and another, slightly later copy of Hafiz-i Abru's text (dispersed, ex-Tabbagh and Watson priv. cols) show a consistent pictorial conception and style of illustration which Ettinghausen called the 'historical style of Shahrukh'. Almost all the episodes are depicted in a hilly landscape devised with stencil-like monotony. The narrative may be vividly conveyed but with few figures clumsily disposed in pictures of old-fashioned format, squat bands placed horizontally across the written surface of the folio. In varying degrees these paintings, as well as those in two fragments of copies of the *Jāmi' al-tawārīkh* (Paris, Bib. N., MS. supp. pers. 1113, relating events from the reign of Genghis Khan to Ghazan; and Calcutta, Asiat. Soc., D31, concerning Mongol history from *c.* 1220 to 1298–9), demonstrate a dependence on the pictorial prototypes and formulae that had evolved for the illustration of these texts in the Ilkhanid period, combined with a simplified rendition of figural types, clothing and accoutrements as found in finer manuscripts made for the Timurids. They all share roundish and flaccid faces and a palette of simple, strong primary colours.

Perhaps the finest example of the facial type and bright colours characteristic of the historical style is found in the 61 large illustrations to a manuscript of the *Mi'rājnāma* ('Book of the ascension'; Paris, Bib. N., MS. supp. turc 190). It recounts the miraculous night-journey of the Prophet Muhammad accompanied by the archangel Gabriel through the Seven Heavens and Hell. It is unusual for the supernatural world it depicts, for the lack of a dedication or colophon, and for the material differences between it and most other surviving fine Timurid volumes. Unlike them it is calligraphed in both Uyghur Turkish and Arabic scripts; it is written on thick white paper, and the images illustrating the Prophet's journey are distinctly Buddhist in content and Central Asian in style. The gold and pigments used for the illumination and illustrations are of extremely high quality. Similarities of the paper to that in an astrological manuscript (Paris, Bib. N., MS. arab. 5036), which was calligraphed for Shahrukh's son Ulughbeg in Samarkand in the 1430s, and its Uyghur calligraphy suggest that this unique manuscript should be dated 1435–40. It is a product of the part of the Timurid world that continued to draw on its Central Asian past for inspiration.

Painting made for Baysunghur (1397–1433). Timurid manuscript painting attained its classical status under the patronage of Shahrukh's third son, Baysunghur (*see* TIMURID, §II(7)). For most of his short adult life he seems to have been his father's trusted regent. In 1420 he was sent to take Tabriz from the Aqqoyunlu Turkomans, where he presumably encountered the Jalayirid calligraphers and artists whom he took back to Herat. There he appears to have established a workshop, referred to in a rare and important progress report (*c.* 1429; Istanbul, Topkapı Pal. Lib., H. 2153, fol. 98*r*; see Thackston) as a *kutubkhāna* (literally, 'books-house', but meaning scriptorium, workshop or library), in which his scribes, gilders, binders and artists assembled to carry out his commissions. Herat's position as the Timurid capital city was thus reinforced as the Timurid artistic capital for the rest of the century. By the second quarter of the 15th century, Baysunghur's painters had digested the exuberance and expressiveness of manuscript illustration produced under the Ilkhanids a century earlier. They had also taken up and assimilated compositional formulae, canons of figural elegance and architectural embellishment, and traditions of manuscript illumination used under the Jalayirids, as well as borrowing other compositions for favourite subjects from Iskandar Sultan's Shiraz-trained artists. Baysunghur's artists compressed these disparate elements and codified them into a flexible style capable of illustrating a variety of texts and of conveying a specific message in a pictorial language of compositions, forms and colours and in the choice and treatment of the subjects chosen. It is a style characterized by fluid perfection, extravagant line and colour, and even monotony.

Among the more than twenty manuscripts, ten pictorial and text fragments and numerous drawings that can be associated with Baysunghur, eight manuscripts dedicated to him contain superb paintings that exemplify the essence of Timurid painting. They are dated between 1426 and 1432 and include some of the best-known texts of classical Persian poetry and prose: a manuscript of Sa'di's *Gulistān* ('Rose-garden'; 1426–7; Dublin, Chester Beatty Lib., Pers. MS. 119); an anthology of poetry and treatises on music and chess (1426–7; Florence, I Tatti); a manuscript of Khwaju Kirmani's *Humay and Humayun* (Vienna, Österreich. Nbib., N.F. 382); two copies of *Kalila and Dimna*, dated respectively 1429 and 1431 (Istanbul, Topkapı Pal. Lib., R. 1022 and H. 362), although the paintings in the later manuscript may be late Jalayirid or modelled on Jalayirid court painting; a magnificent copy of the *Shāhnāma* (see fig. 121); a copy of Nizami 'Arudi's *Chahār maqāla* ('Four discourses'; 1431; Istanbul, Mus. Turk. & Islam. A., MS. 1954); and one poem from a *Khamsa* of Nizami, 'Layla and Majnun', from which two paintings (Ham, Surrey, Keir priv. col., III. 74–5, see Robinson, 1976, pp. 149–50, colour pls 8–9) have been detached. Each of these manuscripts has a distinct character that depends on the subject illustrated, the drawing and palette of the paintings and the date of execution. In the entire group of over 90 paintings several different hands may be distinguished. Despite the differences in style of illustration, the volumes embody their patron's notion of what a fine manuscript should be. Baysunghur's exacting standards extended beyond the subjects, compositions and quality of illustrations, for the majority of the superb volumes he commissioned were not illustrated. All his

121. *Luhrasp Told of the Disappearance of Kay Khusraw*; illustration from a *Shāhnāma*, from Herat, 1430 (Tehran, Gulistan Palace Library, MS. 61, p. 362)

volumes were written by renowned scribes (appropriate for a prince who was himself a fine calligrapher), on paper thicker than Shiraz paper and of a warm brownish-cream colour. The books are exquisitely illuminated using compositions derived from Jalayirid rather than Muzaffarid models. The bindings of leather and of cut and gilded paper are equally exquisite (*see* §7 below). All the quantifiable aspects of the volumes—paper, rulings, paintings, even the height of the calligraphy—are proportionately related, a fact that contributes profoundly, if subtly, to the overall harmony. These features, together with the accepted practice of repeating compositions, shaped a classical style that retained its currency for the next three centuries throughout the Islamic world from Egypt and Turkey to the Indian subcontinent.

A comparison of Baysunghur's copy of the *Shāhnāma* with another copy of the same text (London, Royal Asiat. Soc., Morley MS. 239), prepared in Herat a decade later for his younger brother Muhammad Juki, demonstrates the potential of Baysunghur's classical style. The earlier manuscript is 40 mm larger in height and width but has only 21 paintings compared to the 31 remaining in the Muhammad Juki manuscript. The palette of the earlier manuscript is deep, with a predominant dark purple cast,

while the palette of the later one is brighter and lighter, with white pigment added to many colours. The clearest difference between the manuscripts is seen in the choice of subjects and compositions: many of the paintings in the earlier manuscript invoke such concepts of high seriousness as princely legitimacy and the responsibility of good government, while the paintings in the later manuscript emphasize the deeds of the great hero Rustam. In the earlier manuscript the settings are either Timurid gardens of the kind created in Herat or closed architectural compositions of a unique and complex character, while the feats of prowess in the later manuscript are set in a fairy-tale world of unearthly towering mountains and desert landscapes.

Painting made for Ibrahim Sultan (1394–1435). Shahrukh's second son, Ibrahim Sultan (*see* TIMURID, §II(6)), was responsible for another stylistically distinct group of manuscripts made in Shiraz, where he was appointed governor in 1414. The manuscripts connected with him continue the scribal, decorative and pictorial traditions of earlier Shiraz manuscripts, some being written by such Shiraz scribes as Mahmud ibn Murtaza al-Husayni. He had copied the Gulbenkian *Anthology* for Iskandar Sultan and had remained in Shiraz, where in 1420 he copied another *Anthology* of Persian poetry (Berlin, Mus. Islam. Kst, J. 4628). This was presumably offered by Ibrahim Sultan to Baysunghur, for the ex-libris states that it was made for the latter's library. The lavish illumination is in the earlier minute and unoutlined Shiraz style; its 29 illustrations, which must have been painted by a number of hands, also recall the distinctive style of paintings made for Iskandar Sultan. Two illustrations in the *Anthology* are in a new style which became the hallmark of manuscripts made at Shiraz for Ibrahim Sultan over the next 15 years: relatively few figures, which are tall and slender and which move with simple but forceful gestures in desert landscapes or architectural settings with strong lines but minimal details. The narrative details have been reduced to essentials, leaving images with an overall stark, farouche and curiously modern quality. An undated manuscript of the *Shāhnāma* (Oxford, Bodleian Lib., Ouseley Add. MS. 176) dedicated to Ibrahim Sultan has forty-seven paintings and five tinted drawings in this remarkable style. It is also seen in the first illustrated copy of Sharaf al-Din 'Ali Yazdi's *Zafarnāma*, which was completed in 1436 after the death of Ibrahim Sultan. The subjects of the 24 illustrations (dispersed; see fig. 122) recall Ibn 'Arabshah's description of wall paintings in Timur's garden pavilions. This distinctive style continued to be used for another decade in Shiraz, to judge from a copy of Nizami's *Khamsa* (1436; London, BL, Or. MS. 12856), a copy of Juvayni's *Tārīkh-i jahāngūshā* ('History of the world conqueror'; 1438; Paris, Bib. N., MS. supp. pers. 206, and at least five dispersed paintings) and a copy of the *Shāhnāma* (1444; Paris, Bib. N., MS. supp. pers. 494; frontispiece in Cleveland, OH, Mus. A., 45.169, 56.10), to name only a few. It is rarely found in Iran after the mid-15th century, by which time workshops in Shiraz had begun to produce commercial quantities of illustrated volumes that reflected the style of manuscripts produced at the Turkoman courts of Tabriz

122. *Yildirim Bayezid Arms for Battle against Timur in 1402*, opaque pigment and gold on paper, 227×155 mm; from Sharaf al-Din 'Ali Yazdi: *Zafarnāma* ('Book of victory'), 1436 (Jerusalem, L.A. Mayer Memorial Institute for Islamic Art, 23–68, fol. 260*r*)

and Baghdad (*see* §(e) below), although it appears in some early Ottoman manuscripts.

Other illustrated manuscripts commissioned during the reign of Shahrukh. Several copies of Nizami's *Khamsa* produced in the second quarter of the 15th century illustrate the stylistic variations that could be played on Baysunghuri themes for illustrating a classical text in a classical manner. One manuscript (St Petersburg, Hermitage, VR-1000) was completed for Shahrukh at Herat in 1431. Its 38 paintings are conceptually and stylistically related to those in manuscripts made for Baysunghur, but they are not so fine in the quality of their finish. The manuscript is written in three columns, the outer written on the diagonal in one direction only, a vestige of the Shiraz format of framing a text block with a second text written on the diagonal. This archaizing feature is curious in a manuscript the illustrative programme of which is so advanced, especially when compared with another *Khamsa* (ex-Cartier priv. col.) that is said to have borne Shahrukh's ex-libris. This *Khamsa* is datable between 1415 and 1420; the compositions, facial types and the wide gold rulings show that its paintings were done by artists who had worked for Iskandar Sultan, but its text is laid out in the four-column format standard in most Herat manuscripts.

The composition of the paintings of the St Petersburg *Khamsa* are the most varied of all surviving manuscripts produced at Herat for princely patrons. They also provide the best surviving example of the (Timurid) pictoral aesthetic in which copies of traditional compositions, reworked versions and entirely new compositions all ranked of equal importance within the context of a princely manuscript. They show many different hands whose work spanned several decades in Timurid Iran. *Shirin Sees the Portrait of Khusraw* (fol. 55*r*) reproduces a composition that had already been used in Iskandar Sultan's *Miscellany* of 1410–11 (fol. 38*r*; see fig. 120 above) and that was repeated in another, tiny manuscript of the *Khamsa* (London, BL, Add. MS. 25900, fol. 41*r*) copied in 1442 but mostly illustrated later in the century. Several attendants on the right side of the St Petersburg *Khusraw Holding Court in a Garden* (fol. 125*v*) have round faces and snub noses, characteristics also found in other fine Herat manuscripts copied in the 1430s and 1440s, such as a splendid, detached folio (Paris, Mus. A. Déc., 3727) presumably from a copy of Khwaju Kirmani's *Humay and Humayun*. The artist who painted these works is the principal painter of yet another fine copy of the *Khamsa* (1445–6; Istanbul, Topkapı Pal. Lib., H. 781) made for Ismat al-Dunja, the wife of Muhammad Juki. The colophon names the illustrator and illuminator as KHWAJA 'ALI of Tabriz, possibly to be identified with the 'portraitist' of that name Baysunghur brought from Tabriz, according to Dust Muhammad. This is a rare occurrence of a colophon naming a painter; painters' signatures do not appear until the last two decades of the century. Moreover, biographical dictionaries (Pers. *tazkira*) of the 15th and 16th centuries mention few Timurid painters; when they do they use terms that hardly permit one to be distinguished from another, at least by modern standards. One exception is Khalil, who figures in Dust Muhammad's treatise and is also named in the progress report submitted to Baysunghur by Ja'far, in which Khalil is said to be working on two paintings in the *Gulistān* prepared for Baysunghur.

Both the 1442 and 1445–6 copies of the *Khamsa* are incomplete. The former has only one painting contemporary with the text; fourteen fine ones were added towards the end of the 15th century (see below) and another four added *c.* 1530. The latter has eleven contemporary paintings, one blank space, and two paintings (fols 160*r* and 279*v*) added in a curious hybrid style that combines European elements with later Turkish ones. The unfinished state of these manuscripts doubtlessly reflects the uncertainty of Timurid life in the mid-15th century. With Shahrukh's death in 1447, Timurid control over Iran and western Central Asia weakened. For the next two decades princes of the dynasty fought among themselves, leaving little time or inclination for the patronage of the arts. The commissioning of fine manuscripts passed to members of the Turkoman tribal confederation, whose princes gradually took control of Iran, Khurasan and even, briefly, Herat.

Painting during the reign of Husayn Bayqara (reg 1470–1506). As early as 1467 Husayn Bayqara (*see* TIMURID, §II(8)) had anticipated his reconquest of Herat from the Turkomans by commissioning a copy of the *Zafarnāma*, although he did not actually take the city until 1470. From that date until his death, Herat returned to the position it had enjoyed during the reign of Shahrukh, as a city whose ruler was said to have encouraged all the arts and crafts of the world to such a degree that in each profession he produced an unsurpassed master. In addition to the sultan and members of his immediate family, other notables, including his formidable vizier 'ALISHIR NAVA'I, commissioned fine manuscripts. The very finest, with superb calligraphy, illumination and illustration, number fewer than ten, a small proportion of the number of manuscripts produced there in the last quarter of the century. Many good illustrated manuscripts are not of the highest quality; many were never intended to be illustrated; some of the finest transcribed in Herat were illustrated only in the following century in Bukhara, Tabriz or Delhi; in some cases paintings were removed (and thus survived) from manuscripts that no longer exist. The volumes from which some paintings were removed are known (e.g. the *Abduction of a Maiden*, ?1498; Washington, DC, Freer, 37.27, from a *Khamsa* of Amir Khusraw Dihlavi), but most detached paintings (e.g. a large, impressive battle scene, Cambridge, MA, Sackler Mus., 1960.199; or *Sultan Husayn in a Garden*, right half, Tehran, Gulistan Pal. Lib., MS. 1663–4; left half untraced) have not yet been connected to their parent texts and it is unlikely that they ever can be.

Such texts as the *Shāhnāma* seem to have been less popular in late 15th-century Herat than the poems of Sa'di or Amir Khusraw Dihlavi, or mystical poems such as 'Attar's *Mantiq al-tayr* ('Conference of the birds') or the *Khamsa* of 'Alishir himself. Fine manuscripts had fewer illustrations than those from the first half of the century, but often paintings are signed in ways that leave no doubts about the authenticity of the signatures, and the names of painters are also found in a variety of contemporary and later sources. The best-known painter of this period is BIHZAD, but QASIM 'ALI, MIRAK *naqqāsh* ('painter'), Hajji Muhammad *naqqāsh*, Maqsud and Ustad Baba Hajji are also named in contemporary written sources.

The earliest manuscript produced under Husayn Bayqara is his copy of the *Zafarnāma* (Baltimore, MD, Johns Hopkins U., Garrett Lib.); although the text was completed in 1467–8, its unusual illustrative complement of six paired paintings is surely to be dated a decade later, if not more. A five-volume copy of 'Alishir's *Khamsa* in Chaghatay Turkish was made for Husayn Bayqara's son Badi' al-Zaman (1485; Manchester, John Rylands U. Lib., Turk. MS. 3; Oxford, Bodleian Lib., Elliott MSS 287, 317, 339, 408) and has at least 18 paintings. A copy of Sa'di's *Gulistān* (1486; Houston, TX, Art and History Trust col.) prepared for Husayn Bayqara has three fine paintings, and a copy of Sa'di's *Būstān* ('Orchard'; 1488; Cairo, N. Lib., Adab Farsi 908) with five paintings was also made for him (*see* §(i) above). A beautiful example of 'Attar's *Mantiq al-tayr* was copied in 1483 for the Sultan (New York, Met., 63.210); one of its four contemporary paintings is dated 1487 (see fig. 123). Fourteen paintings were added *c.* 1493 to the tiny manuscript of Nizami's *Khamsa* copied in 1442, as attested by the date on fol. 77*v*. Another manuscript of the *Khamsa* copied for one of Husayn Bayqara's amirs in 1494–5 (London, BL, Or. MS. 6810; *see* MANUSCRIPT, colour pl. VI) has 21 paintings, the most of any manuscript in the group. A large and beautiful manuscript of Amir

123. Mirak: *The Beggar who Professed his Love for the Prince*, 222×114 mm; illustration from 'Attar: *Mantiq al-tayr* ('Conference of the birds'), from Herat, 1487 (New York, Metropolitan Museum of Art, 63.210.28, fol. 28*r*)

Khusraw Dihlavi's *Khamsa* copied for another amir in 1496–7 (Istanbul, Topkapı Pal. Lib., H. 676) has only a magnificent double-page frontispiece.

Of the four manuscripts associated with Husayn Bayqara, Bihzad is associated with three: the *Zafarnāma*, which has attributions written on the flyleaf by the Mughal emperors Akbar (*reg* 1556–1605) and Jahangir (*reg* 1605–27), a noted connoisseur of painting; the *Gulistān*, in which two paintings have attributions to Bihzad; and the celebrated *Būstān*, which has four signed paintings. In addition, three paintings added to the tiny *Khamsa* of 1442 bear his signature, as do seven in the *Khamsa* of 1494–5, but many of these 'signatures' should be treated with caution. The same can be said for Mirak's 'signature' on two paintings in the *Khamsa* of 1494–5, although he was probably responsible for the four contemporary paintings in the *Mantiq al-tayr*, and he probably planned the compositions for the other four that were not finished until the early 17th century (*see* §(vi)(a) below).

All these paintings, whether or not they bear a true signature or an attribution, share a naturalism, a sense of human ease, variety of movement and a preoccupation with daily life in late 15th-century Iran: battles and hunts, the construction of mosques and palaces, wrestling matches and bath-house scenes, feasts in gardens or pavilions, meetings in mosques and religious gatherings, and episodes in the countryside (although these are quite specific to the mystical texts they illustrate). For all their naturalism, however, such pictures are composed of stock figures and compositional patterns developed throughout the century. It is questionable whether the individual work of any late Timurid painter may be distinguished from that of his fellows; it seems more likely that even in the late 15th century classical Persian manuscript painting was still an art with a canonical ideal of perfection. What pleased was not originality or idiosyncratic interpretation but the extent to which an artist's work adhered to the classical canons, within which only the most subtle adjustments of draughtsmanship, composition, form and colour-balance constituted the difference between the titans who were lauded as challenging Mani, the legendary inventor of painting, and those fine workmen who never invited comment from contemporaries.

With the capitulation of Herat in the early 16th century to the Shaybanid dynasty of Transoxiana, the equilibrium of this visual language used to illustrate classical texts was destroyed, to emerge in various guises in the following century. In Bukhara, towards the middle of the 16th century, painting in the classical late Timurid manner was often added to manuscripts copied at Herat in the reign of Husayn Bayqara (see §(vi)(c) below). In Tabriz, Qazvin and Isfahan, successively the capitals of the Safavid dynasty (reg 1501–1732), adherence to the classical and virtually anonymous canon perfected by Baysunghur's artists between 1420 and 1435 was less and less a desirable end. Indeed, the history of the court-sponsored schools of Persian manuscript painting in the 16th and 17th centuries is that of painters with distinct artistic personalities interpreting classical texts in new, and sometimes distinctly unclassical, versions of the classical style of Timurid painting.

BIBLIOGRAPHY

F. R. Martin and T. Arnold: *The Nizami MS Illuminated by Bihzad, Mirak and Qasim Ali, written 1495 for Sultan Ali Mirza Barlās, ruler of Samarqand, in the British Museum (Or. 6810)* (Vienna, 1926)

T. Arnold: *Bihzād and his Paintings in the Zafar-Nāmah MS.* (London, 1930)

J. V. S. Wilkinson: *The Shāh-Nāmeh of Firdausī: The Book of the Persian Kings* (Oxford, 1931)

B. W. Robinson: 'Unpublished Paintings from a XVth-century Book of Kings', *Apollo Miscellany*, ed. W. M. Jennings (London, 1951), pp. 17–23

B. Gray: 'An Unknown Fragment of the "Jāmi' al-tawārīkh" in the Asiatic Society of Bengal', *A. Orient.*, i (1954), pp. 65–76

I. Stchoukine: *La Peinture des manuscrits timurides* (Paris, 1954)

R. Ettinghausen: 'An Illuminated Manuscript of Ḥāfiz-i Abrū in Istanbul, Part 1', *Kst Orients*, ii (1955), pp. 30–44

M. Mostafa: *Persian Miniatures of Behzad and his School in Cairo Collections* (London, 1960)

I. Stchoukine: 'La Peinture à Yazd au début du XVIe siècle', *Syria*, xliii (1966), pp. 99–104

——: 'Les Peintures turcomanes et ṣafavies d'une Khamseh de Nizāmī, achevée à Tabriz en 886/1481', *A. Asiat.*, xiv (1966), pp. 3–16

M. L. Swietochowski: 'The Language of the Birds: The Fifteenth Century Miniatures', *Bull. Met.*, xxv (1967), pp. 317–38

I. Stchoukine: 'Une Khamseh de Nizāmī de la fin du règne de Shāh Rokh', *A. Asiat.*, xvii (1968), pp. 45–58

The Classical Style in Islamic Painting: The Early School of Herat and its Impact on Islamic Painting of the Later 15th, the 16th and 17th Centuries (exh. cat. by E. J. Grube, New York, Pierpont Morgan Lib., 1968)

E. G. Sims: 'Sultan Husayn Bayqara's Zafar-Namah and its Miniatures', *The Memorial Volume of the VIth International Congress of Iranian Art and Archaeology: Oxford, 1972*, pp. 299–311

I. Stchoukine: 'La Khamseh de Nizāmī, H. 753, du Topkapi Sarayī Müzesī d'Istanbul', *Syria*, xlix (1972), pp. 239–46

E. G. Sims: 'Prince Baysunghur's Chahar Maqaleh', *Sanat Tarihi Yıllığı*, vi (1974–5), pp. 375–409

B. W. Robinson, ed.: *Islamic Painting and the Arts of the Book*, The Keir Collection, ii (London, 1976)

M.-R. Séguy: *The Miraculous Journey of Mahomet: Mirâj nâmeh* (London, New York and Paris, 1977)

I. Stchoukine: *Les Peintures des manuscrits de la 'Khamseh' de Nizāmī au Topkapi sarayî müzesi d'Istanbul* (Paris, 1977)

B. Gray, ed.: *The Arts of the Book in Central Asia, 14th–16th Centuries* (London and Paris, 1979)

B. W. Robinson: 'The Shāhnāma of Muḥammad Jūkī, RAS. MS 239', *The Royal Asiatic Society: Its History and Treasures*, ed. S. Simmonds and S. Digby (Leiden, 1979), pp. 83–102

E. J. Grube: 'Two Kalīla wa Dimnah Codices Made for Baysunghur Mīrzā: The Concept of the "Classical Style" Reconsidered', *Atti del III convegno internazionale sull'arte e sulla civiltà islamica: Problemi dell'età timuride, Quad. Semin. Iran. U. Venezia*, viii (1980), pp. i–xi, 114–22

Islam. A., i (1981) [issue devoted to Istanbul albums]

T. W. Lentz: *Painting at Herat under Baysunghur ibn Shahrukh* (diss., Cambridge, MA, Harvard U., 1985)

A. S. Melikian-Chirvani: 'Khwāje Mīrak Naqqāsh', *J. Asiat.*, cclxxvi (1988), pp. 97–146

T. W. Lentz and G. D. Lowry: *Timur and the Princely Vision* (Washington, DC, 1989)

E. Sims: 'Painting in Timurid Iran', *Asian A.*, ii/2 (1989), pp. 62–79

W. M. Thackston, ed.: *A Century of Princes: Sources on Timurid History and Art* (Cambridge, MA, 1989)

E. G. Sims: 'Ibrahim-Sultan's Illustrated Zafar-Namah of 839–1436', *Islam. A.*, iv (1990–91), pp. 177–276

A. T. Adamova: 'Repetition of Compositions in Manuscripts: The Khamsa of Nizami in Leningrad', *Timurid Art and Culture: Iran and Central Asia in the Fifteenth Century*, ed. L. Golombek and M. Subtelny, Studies in Islamic Art and Architecture, Supplements to *Muqarnas*, vi (Leiden, 1992), pp. 67–75

A. Soudavar: *Art of the Persian Courts: Selections from the Art and History Trust Collection* (New York, 1992)

E. G. Sims: 'The Illustrated Manuscripts of Firdausi's Shahnama Commissioned by Princes of the House of Timur', *A. Orient.*, xxii (1993), pp. 43–68

A. T. Adamova: article in *Islam. A.*, v (in preparation) [on the St Petersburg *Khamsa* of 835/1431]

ELEANOR SIMS

(e) Iraq and Iran, c. 1450–c. 1500. After the death of the Timurid sultan Shahrukh in 1447, Iraq and most of Iran were occupied by two Turkoman confederations, the Qaraqoyunlu ('Black Sheep'; reg 1380–1468) and the Aqqoyunlu ('White Sheep'; reg 1378–1508). Their main capital was Tabriz in north-west Iran; it became the Aqqoyunlu capital when they defeated the Qaraqoyunlu in 1468, but Shiraz remained an important centre of book production. With one possible exception—the manuscript of al-Qazwini's *'Ajā'ib al-makhlūqāt* ('Wonders of creation'; New York, Pub. Lib., Spencer MS. 45; Washington, DC, Freer, 54.33–114, 57.13) bought in Algiers by Friedrich Sarre, which has been attributed to Aqqoyunlu Diyarbakır in the early 15th century (Badiee, 1984)—the Turkomans had no tradition of court painting. They employed captured artists of varying origins and traditions, and Turkoman manuscripts from the mid-15th century contain paintings in three distinct styles often side by side in the same volume (e.g. a copy of Nizami's *Khamsa* ('Five poems'); London, Royal Asiat. Soc., MS. Pers. 246). The first style continued the traditions associated with manuscripts produced in Shiraz under the Timurids, the second was founded on the classical canon associated with Timurid Herat, and the third is a comparatively simple style which apparently originated in north-west Iran.

By the late 1450s or early 1460s the Herat-inspired style had triumphed for court painting at the expense both of the Shiraz style, which had disappeared, and the northwest style, which was relegated to the illustration of commercially produced manuscripts. The Herat style was used for all the manuscripts executed *c.* 1455–65 under the patronage of the Qaraqoyunlu prince Pir Budaq, who was governor of Shiraz and then Baghdad for his father Jahanshah (*reg* 1438–67). A copy of the *Khamsa* of Khusraw Dihlavi (Istanbul, Topkapı Pal. Lib., R. 1021), for example, was done in 1463 at Baghdad and illustrated with eight paintings in the Turkoman variant of the Herat style. Robinson (1979) has argued that the finest achievement of this school is the manuscript of *Kalila and Dimna* (Tehran, Gulistan Pal. Lib.), which he attributed to Baghdad *c.* 1460–65.

The Herat tradition established under Pir Budaq was developed under the Aqqoyunlu between 1468 and 1478 in a group of small but exquisite manuscripts in which the figures have round and rather childish faces, tiny feet and turbans set high on the head. Although unusually large, a copy of the *Annals* of al-Tabari (Dublin, Chester Beatty Lib., MS. 144) belongs to the group, as does a double-page frontispiece later inserted into a copy of Jami's *Silsilat al-ẓahab* ('Chain of gold'; 1549; St Petersburg, Rus. N. Lib., Dorn 434, fols 81*v* and 82*r*). Their size and quality suggest that they may have been executed for the Aqqoyunlu ruler Uzun Hasan (*reg* 1453–78). The finest flowering of the Turkoman court style took place under Uzun Hasan's younger son Ya'qub (*reg* 1478–90). His two leading artists were SHAYKHI and DARVISH MUHAMMAD. Their best work can be seen in a copy of Nizami's *Khamsa* (Istanbul, Topkapı Pal. Lib., H. 762; *see* COLOUR, colour pl. V). This volume, begun in the mid-15th century, was taken over by Pir Budaq and then Uzun Hasan's elder son Khalil; it then passed to Ya'qub, under whose patronage the text was completed in 1481 and 11 paintings supplied. The style of the paintings has become less academic and has fantastic features of colour and drawing (see fig. 124 and COLOUR, colour pl. V; *see also* §(vi)(a) below). Other examples of the court style of this period can be found in two albums (Istanbul, Topkapı Pal. Lib., H. 2153 and H. 2160) known as the albums of Ya'qub. They contain many works attributed to Shaykhi but only three to Darvish Muhammad. They also contain a considerable body of paintings and drawings attributed to the master (Pers. *ustād*) Muhammad SIYAH QALAM ('Black pen'), many of which depict demons, monsters and scenes of nomad life. The works of Siyah Qalam have sometimes been attributed to a much earlier date in western Central Asia, but stylistic similarities between them and the works of Darvish Muhammad are a good reason to assign the whole group to the patronage of Ya'qub. Indeed, Muhammad Siyah Qalam and Darvish Muhammad may have been one and the same man.

Two fine Turkoman manuscripts are of royal quality but fall outside the main tradition. A copy of Nizami's *Khamsa* (Dublin, Chester Beatty Lib., Pers. MS. 137) is said to have been done at Isfahan in 1463–4, according to a now-lost colophon. The paintings have bright colours, fine draughtsmanship and bushy vegetation, while the figures are sometimes grotesque, with thin long necks and heavy bulbous bodies. A two-volume copy of the *Shāhnāma* (1494; vol. i, Istanbul, Mus. Turk. & Islam. A., MS. 1978 and dispersed; vol. ii, Istanbul, U. Lib., Y. 7954/310) was produced for Sultan 'Ali Mirza, identifiable

124. *Bahram Gur in the Green Pavilion* (detail); illustration from Nizami: *Khamsa* ('Five poems'), from Tabriz, 1481 (Istanbul, Topkapı Palace Library, H. 762, fol. 189*v*)

with the ruler of Gilan in northern Iran. Many of its 300 illustrations have large figures with big heads, an idiosyncrasy that has led to its nickname, the Big-head *Shāhnāma*.

Since the 14th century, Shiraz had probably been the main centre for the production of manuscripts for commerce and export; under Turkoman rule in the last quarter of the 15th century this role was expanded. The paintings in well over 100 illustrated manuscripts are in the Turkoman Commercial style, a simple but effective and utilitarian idiom that retains the stocky child-like figures and simplified landscapes of the north-west style of mid-century. The style seems to have crystallized in the hands of Farhad, the painter who signed several paintings dated 1477 in a manuscript of the *Khāvarānnāma* (Tehran, Riza 'Abbasi Mus. and dispersed), celebrating the virtues and exploits of 'Ali, the son-in-law of the Prophet Muhammad. Manuscripts illustrated in the Turkoman Commercial style outnumber by more than two to one all other 15th-century illustrated manuscripts combined, and whenever the place of production is named, it is invariably Shiraz.

Another style also found in the commercial manuscripts of the 1470s and 1480s is known as the Brownish (Turk. *kumral*) style, owing to the predominant use of brown instead of black for hair and other facial features. It is lighter and more delicate than the Turkoman Commercial style; figures are smaller and slimmer and landscapes more delicately drawn. The grass tufts, in particular, are placed closer together. Its origins can be traced to the *Khamsa* of 1463–4. Whenever the colophon includes such information, Shiraz is always the place of production, as in a copy of 'Assar's *Mihr and Mushtari* (1478; Washington, DC, Freer, 49.3), made by the scribe Shaykh Murshid at Shiraz and illustrated with two paintings in the Brownish style.

BIBLIOGRAPHY

B. W. Robinson: 'Origin and Date of Three Famous *Shāh-Nāmeh* Illustrations', *A. Orient.*, i (1954), pp. 95–110

——: 'The Turkman School to 1503', *The Arts of the Book in Central Asia, 14th–16th Centuries*, ed. B. Gray (London and Paris, 1979), pp. 215–47

——: 'Siyah Qalam', *Islam. A.*, i (1981), pp. 62–5

J. Badiee: 'The Sarre Qazwini: An Early Aq Qoyunlu Manuscript?', *A. Orient.*, xiv (1984), pp. 97–113

B. W. Robinson: *Fifteenth Century Persian Painting: Problems and Issues* (New York, 1991), chap. 2, pp. 21–43

B. W. ROBINSON

(f) Anatolia. References to painting in Anatolia in the *Maṣnavī* (a mystical poem in rhyming couplets) by Jalal al-Din Rumi (1207–73) may simply be literary topoi, for only two illustrated manuscripts appear to have survived from the period of Saljuq rule there (*reg* 1077–1307; *see* SALJUQ, §2). One is a copy of 'Ayyuqi's romance of *Varqa and Gulshah* (c. 1250; Istanbul, Topkapı Pal. Lib., H. 841), which is also the oldest extant illustrated manuscript in Persian (see fig. 125). The 71 illustrations of small, haloed

figures set against a coloured ground are in the narrow horizontal format typical of wall painting; the figural style is also found on contemporary overglaze-painted ceramics from Iran. There is no general agreement on its attribution, but the painter's name, 'Abd al-Mu'min ibn Muhammad al-Khuvayyi (from Khvoy in north-west Iran), which appears on fol. 58r of the manuscript, also appears among the witnesses to the endowment deed of the madrasa of Jalal al-Din Karatay at Konya endowed in 1253. The other is a magical miscellany (Paris, Bib. N., MS. pers. 174) by Muhammad ibn Ibrahim, who was known as Nasir al-Rammali ('the geomancer') al-Sivasi (from Sivas in Anatolia). It includes two works, one completed at Aksaray in 1268, the other completed at Kayseri in 1272. The original illustrations are line drawings of magical scripts and talismanic figures, although few were ever completed and the blanks were filled, possibly as late as the Ottoman period, with highly coloured figures of demons, the planets and marvels from the Alexander Romance (the stories of a mythical Alexander) or popular stories based on the lives of the Koranic prophets (Arab. *qiṣaṣ*). Many of these have little to do with traditional stereotypes and seem to derive rather from Byzantine art.

The earliest illustrated manuscript produced under the Ottoman dynasty (*reg* 1281–1924) is a copy of Ahmadi's *Iskandarnāma* ('Book of Alexander'; Amasya, 1416; Paris, Bib. N., MS. supp. turc 309), although only three of the twenty illustrations are original, and the remainder have been pasted in from at least two different manuscripts.

125. *Combat of Rabi and Varqa*, 70×175 mm; illustration from 'Ayyuqi: *Varqa and Gulshah*, possibly from Konya, c. 1250 (Istanbul, Topkapı Palace Library, H. 841, fol. 13v)

No other illustrated manuscripts survive until the reign of Mehmed II (*reg* 1444–81 with interruption), an active collector of albums and illustrated books. He stipulated, for example, that they should form part of the ransom of the Aqqoyunlu prince Yusufça Mirza, who had been captured in 1472. The rich booty taken when Mehmed defeated the Aqqoyunlu ruler Uzun Hasan in 1473 could have included the well-known albums of painting and calligraphy from Tabriz and Herat (Istanbul, Topkapı Pal. Lib., H. 2152, H. 2153 and H. 2160), unless they were acquired later as booty from the Battle of Chaldiran in 1514. These are, however, of only marginal relevance to the history of Ottoman painting, since Ahmed I (*reg* 1603–17) is the only sultan known to have looked at them. Undoubtedly motivated by political interest in the culture of the later Timurids, Mehmed II had a copy of the *Dīvān* (collected poetry) of the great Chaghatay poet 'ALISHIR NAVA'I in his personal library; illustrated manuscripts of Nava'i's works from the early 16th century, which reached Istanbul as booty or gifts, long remained an important factor in Ottoman painting. Under Mehmed II and Bayezid II (*reg* 1481–1512) a number of small-format verse works also seem to have been produced for the royal libraries. These include a copy of Amir Khusraw Dihlavi's *Khamsa* ('Five poems'; 1493; Istanbul, Topkapı Pal. Lib., H. 799), which has artless illustrations in an eclectic style. The *Cerrahiye-i haniye* by Sharaf al-Din, copied at Amasya in 1456–6 (Paris, Bib. N., suppl. turc 693), a translation of a Persian version of the treatise on fractures and sprains by Apollonius of Kitium, was presented to Mehmed II.

Both text and illustrations of an unfinished copy of Firdevsi Burusevi's *Sulaymānnāma* ('Solomon romance'; Dublin, Chester Beatty Lib., Turk. MS. 406) dedicated to Bayezid II are also eclectic. The double frontispiece depicts Solomon and Bilqis each enthroned above tiers of ministers, angels, demons and monsters. The subject-matter derives largely from the text of the Greek *Testamentum Salomonis*, an illustrated, although unrelated, copy of which was in the library of Mehmed II, while the arrangement and style derive from one or more southern Spanish prototypes which probably reached Ottoman Turkey with the great Jewish diaspora following the fall of Granada in 1492. The unfinished state of the manuscript is probably explained by the author's fall from grace at the Ottoman court before Bayezid's death in 1512.

BIBLIOGRAPHY

A. S. Melikian-Chirvani: 'Le Roman de Varqé et Golšâh', *A. Asiat.*, xxii (1970) [whole issue]

M. K. Özergin: 'Selçuklu sanatçısı nakkaş 'Abdü'l-Mü'min el-Hoyî hakkında' [The Saljuq artist 'Abd al-Mu'min al-Khuvayyi, the painter], *Belleten*, xxxiv (1970), pp. 219–29

E. Atıl: 'Ottoman Miniature Painting under Sultan Mehmed II', *A. Orient.*, ix (1973), pp. 103–20

F. Çağman: 'Sultan Mehmet II. dönemine ait bir minyatürlü yazma: Külliyat-i Kâtibi' [A manuscript with miniatures from the age of Mehmed II: Katibi's *Külliyat*], *Sanat Tarihi Yıllığı*, vi (1974–5), pp. 333–46

N. M. Titley: 'Istanbul or Tabriz? The Question of the Provenance of Three Sixteenth-century Nevai Manuscripts', *Orient. A.*, n. s., xxiv/3 (1978), pp. 292–6

E. J. Grube: 'Notes on Ottoman Painting in the 15th Century', *Essays in Islamic Art and Architecture in Honor of Katharina Otto-Dorn*, ed. A. Daneshvari (Malibu, 1981), pp. 51–63

E. J. Grube and E. Sims, eds: *Islam. A.*, i (1981) [whole issue devoted to four albums in Istanbul]

E. J. Grube: 'The Date of the Venice Iskandar-nama', *Islam. A.*, ii (1987), pp. 187–95

M. Barrucand: 'The Miniatures of the *Daqā'iq al-Haqā'iq* (Bibliothèque Nationale, Pers. 174): A Testimony to the Cultural Diversity of Medieval Anatolia', *Islam. A.*, iv (1991), pp. 113–42

J. M. Rogers: 'The Chester Beatty *Süleymanname* Again', *Essays in Honour of B. W. Robinson*, ed. R. Hillenbrand (Edinburgh, in preparation)

J. M. ROGERS

(g) Indian subcontinent. The book was the only art, other than architecture, in which a distinctive tradition evolved under the succession of sultanates that ruled in the Indian subcontinent from the early 13th century to the mid-16th. Indigenous traditions of book production were unsuitable to meet the new demands for copies of the Koran and other books required by pious Muslims. Few manuscripts survive from the first two centuries of Muslim rule there, probably because many were destroyed with Timur's sack of Delhi in 1398, and the first steps in the development of a distinctive tradition of book production can only be traced under the independent sultanates in the 15th century. Manuscripts of the Koran were copied in an idiosyncratic script (*see* §2(iv)(b) above), and illustrations were added to other manuscripts in a distinctive idiom in which Indian motifs and themes were combined with traditional Iranian models.

This pictorial style was first identified in a group of eight illustrated manuscripts dated between 1417 and 1440, as well as in other undated manuscripts and detached leaves. The images show features of Timurid provincial work done at Shiraz (*see* §(d) above) such as the high horizon line, ground decorated with a semé pattern of leaves and flowers, and coral-like hills. The drawing is drier and simpler, and there are such archaisms as horizontal formats depicting shallow space, stepping along the upper frame and crosshatching to indicate the groundplane. Typical Indian features include large groups of figures in serried rows and identical poses, and bright, unusual colours. The paintings often have narrow, decorated bands, a feature also found in manuscripts in the Western India style; the texts are often copied in a peculiar calligraphic hand in which the bowls of the letters are nested inside each other. Most of these features can be seen in a manuscript of the *Shāhnāma* ('Book of kings'; 1438; London, BL, Or. MS. 1403). Its Indian provenance is confirmed by the use of *peori*, a yellow pigment made from the urine of cows fed on mango leaves and unknown in Iran, and by an extraneous textual reference to the king of Delhi. Other manuscripts and detached paintings in the same style lack these two essential pieces of evidence, and it is still a matter of debate whether some of them were produced in the Indian subcontinent or in another provincial Timurid centre.

Another group of four manuscripts produced in Mandu *c.* 1500 shows the direct impact of contemporary Persian painting. The most famous is a copy of the *Ni'mātnāma* ('Book of delicacies'; London, BL, Orient. & India Office Lib., Pers. MS. 149), an illustrated cookbook prepared for the Khalji sultans of Malwa between 1495 and 1505. The paintings are done in the Turkoman style of Shiraz (*see* §(e) above) but show details of daily life in the Indian subcontinent such as cooking pots and patterned textiles. That the artists at Mandu could work in various imported styles is shown by a manuscript of Sa'di's *Būstān* ('Orchard'; 1500–03; New Delhi, N. Mus., MS. 48.6/4), copied by Shahsavur al-Katib and illustrated by Hajji Mahmud; it has 43 paintings in a provincial version of the classical Timurid style of Herat.

See INDIAN SUBCONTINENT, §VI, 3(ii)(d) for a fuller discussion and bibliography.

(vi) c. 1500–c. 1900. The classical tradition of book illustration established under the Timurid dynasty in western Central Asia (*see* §(v)(d) above) reached its culmination in Iran during the first half of the 16th century under the patronage of the Safavid dynasty (*reg* 1501–1732) in their capitals at Tabriz and Qazvin. In the later part of the century, however, the importance of the illustrated book as a work of art gave way to the single-page drawing or painting, often destined for mounting in albums, although illustrated manuscripts of modest pretensions were still produced for the market in such provincial centres as Shiraz. Increased contact with Europe in the 17th century brought about the introduction of Western subjects and pictorial conventions, such as vanishing-point perspective, shading and atmospheric colour. The illustrated book never regained its importance in the 18th and 19th centuries, although under the Qajar dynasty (*reg* 1779–1924) a distinctive and attractive style of miniature painting emerged. In western Central Asia the Timurid and Safavid traditions of book illustration were faithfully maintained under the Shaybanid dynasty (*reg* 1500–98) and their successors in the first half of the 17th century, but, as in Iran, the art of the illustrated book then lost its importance. The most important developments in the art of the illustrated book during this period occurred in the Indian subcontinent under the Mughals (*reg* 1526–1858), where a distinct style evolved that combined traditions of earlier Indian painting, both Islamic and non-Islamic, with features imported from contemporary Iran and Europe. An equally distinctive style emerged in the Ottoman empire, where Persian models were adapted to depict contemporary events in manuscripts prepared for royal patrons. ☐

(a) Iran, *c.* 1500–*c.* 1750. (b) Iran, *c.* 1750–*c.* 1900. (c) Western Central Asia. (d) Indian subcontinent. (e) Ottoman empire.

(a) Iran, c. 1500–c. 1750.

Introduction. Painting under the Safavid dynasty (*reg* 1501–1732; *see* SAFAVID, §1) is distinguished from that of the previous period in that far more of it survives and in many different scales and media. Unlike the 15th century, when the finest manuscript painting can be understood with direct reference to the Timurid princes who ruled on the Iranian plateau and in western Central Asia, fine painting executed under the Safavids is better described by the name of the city or province in which a manner of painting was developed. Thus Safavid painting may be described as being in the style or manner of Tabriz, Qazvin and Isfahan, the series of capitals in which the Safavid shahs held court; Mashad and Herat, where governors or regents ruled; or Shiraz and Khurasan, provincial cities and regions where traditional modes of

painting were only partly affected by metropolitan developments in the pictorial arts. These names signify distinctive styles and sometimes types of painting rather than specific geographical provenances.

Book painting under the Safavids includes the most spectacular ensembles of Persian manuscript illustration as well as the most pedestrian; between these two poles are many manuscripts that are good, interesting, captivating or distinguished in one way or another but that may never merit special discussion. Yet Safavid painting should be understood not only as traditional book illustration but as other pictorial modes as well. Most numerous are evocative single-figure compositions, both drawings and paintings, which are often bound into albums alternating with handsome examples of calligraphy. Equally important, although less known, are the large mural ensembles decorating the walls of private and public buildings (*see* §II, 9(iii) above), many erected not only for Muslims but also for the sizeable Armenian Christian community in New Julfa across the Zaindeh River from Isfahan, and a smaller number of large, independent oil paintings on canvas (*see* §VIII, 11(i) below). Some of the same figural compositions occurring in illustrated manuscripts, finished coloured drawings and large-scale paintings were adapted for the decoration of textiles and ceramics, which were important and widely exported Safavid trade goods. Trade was a central element of Safavid life and art. Contacts with the Indian subcontinent and Europe brought people and objects to Iran that had a lasting influence on the styles and techniques of contemporary and later painting.

During the Safavid period the revolution espousing 'equal rights for pen and brush', which had begun at the end of the Timurid century, culminated. This fundamental change forever altered the traditional relations between wealthy patrons and anonymous artists. By the end of the 16th century, Safavid painters and illuminators routinely signed and/or dated their works, whereas in previous centuries a reliable signature, especially in conjunction with a date, was rare and notable. In addition to the number of artists known from authentically signed paintings and drawings, the number of artists discussed in contemporary written sources amounts to a small explosion of information. Stchoukine (1959) could name 75 artists documented by at least one source or picture; many more have been recorded since. Moreover, the emergence of the artist as a personality no less worthy of recognition than the calligrapher seems to be coeval with the breakdown of the traditional Persian pictorial aesthetic that eschewed originality and rewarded adherence to classical canons in the making of fine pictures. It is no coincidence that more distinctive and personal styles of painting and drawing may be noted during the two centuries of Safavid rule than at any other time in the history of Persian art.

The style of Tabriz, 1502–48. Painting in Iran during the first half of the 16th century is inextricably tied to the turbulent events accompanying the rise of the Safavid dynasty. In 1502 the Safavids defeated the Aqqoyunlu Turkomans and took over their capital at Tabriz in northwest Iran, including the Turkoman court library and its book-making workshops. In 1507 Badi' al-Zaman (*reg* 1506), the last ruler of the Timurid line, fled west to the protection of the Safavid court, bringing with him the portion of the Timurid royal library that had not already been taken to Bukhara. By 1514 the Safavids were already on the defensive at their western frontier, facing the first of four invasions by Ottoman armies. This continued Ottoman threat eventually forced the Safavids to move their capital southwards to Qazvin in 1548.

The movement from Herat of artists, patrons and the works of art that accompanied them accounts for many aspects of the later history of Persian painting. The most notable of these are the development of painting in the Safavid court at Tabriz and in the Shaybanid court at Bukhara (*see* §(c) below) and the final deposit of the greater part of the Timurid and Turkoman libraries in the Ottoman capital at Istanbul after the Ottomans defeated the Safavids at the Battle of Chaldiran in 1514. According to a document purportedly dated 1522, Isma'il I (*reg* 1501–24) invited Bihzad, the most celebrated Timurid painter, to come to Tabriz as director of the royal library.

Whether Isma'il actually cared for the arts of the book or had only, but astutely, recognized the Timurid practice of using fine illustrated manuscripts as an instrument of dynastic propaganda is not clear; the general quality of the painting in manuscripts made during his reign is not especially high. There are, however, some notable exceptions. One is the group of 11 paintings added to the copy of Nizami's *Khamsa* ('Five poems'; Istanbul, Topkapı Pal. Lib., H. 762) that had been commissioned by Abu'l-Qasim Babur (*reg* 1449–57), a son of the Timurid prince Baysunghur, and, after attempts by the Qaraqoyunlu prince Pir Budaq and the Aqqoyunlu rulers Khalil and Ya'qub to finish it, was finally completed in the reign of Isma'il (*see* §(v)(e) and fig. 124 above). Nine Safavid paintings are still in the manuscript in company with ten of the Turkoman paintings already finished at Ya'qub's death in 1490. The other two Safavid paintings (one dated 1504–5) and one Turkoman painting were detached from the manuscript (Ham, Surrey, Keir priv. col., III.207–9). The 15th-century paintings in the manuscript are considered the finest of all Turkoman court painting. Given that Isma'il was both nephew and son-in-law of Ya'qub, this manuscript was probably one of the principal conduits for the transmission to the Tabriz workshops of a fundamental element of Turkoman court painting, the energetically charged, almost frantic compositions in which usually inanimate landscape is as active as humans and animals.

The dimensions (*c.* 300×195 mm) of the Istanbul *Khamsa* are almost identical to an illustrated manuscript of Muhammad 'Asafi's *Dastān-i Jamāl va Jalāl* ('Story of Jamal and Jalal'; 1502–3; Uppsala, U. Lib., O Nova 2), which was copied in Herat but the 34 remaining illustrations of which were almost certainly painted in Tabriz. They similarly divide into later Turkoman court and earliest Safavid stylistic groups. In both manuscripts the Safavid paintings show the distinctive Safavid headgear (Pers. *kulāh*), with its protruding red baton, still thick and stumpy, around which the turban was wrapped. While the *Jamal and Jalal* paintings remain a curious pictorial dead-end, the paintings in the *Khamsa* prefigure Safavid painting as it was to develop under the sponsorship of Tahmasp I (*reg* 1524–76), Isma'il's son and successor; they are highly

sophisticated creations, complex in composition and refined in style, execution and colouring. The best of the *Khamsa* pictures have been attributed to SULTAN-MUHAMMAD, who later worked on the *Shāhnāma* ('Book of kings') connected with Tahmasp I. The hand of Sultan Muhammad has also been discerned in another painting (London, BM, 1948-12-11-023), the exotic and supercharged *Rustam Sleeps while Rakhsh Fights the Lion* from a lost manuscript of the *Shāhnāma*.

A third superb manuscript made during the reign of Isma'il is an undated copy of the Shah's own *Dīvān* (collected poetry; Washington, DC, Sackler Gal., S 86.0060), which he composed in Turki under the penname Khata'i. Incomplete and damaged, the manuscript now contains three paintings, the subjects of which appear to be generalized scenes of courtly life; analysis of the pictures in the context of the poetry surrounding them shows how explicitly each painting renders in images the words of the poem in which each is embedded. Smaller, finer and more conventional in composition than *Rustam Sleeps* and the Safavid pictures of the *Khamsa*, these are the only paintings that may be indisputably connected with Isma'il's patronage.

The undoubted glory of Safavid painting, and perhaps of all Persian painting, are the manuscripts produced in the long reign of Tahmasp I (*see* SAFAVID, §2(1)). His patronage falls into two distinct phases. From 1524 until at least the mid-1540s his taste, position and means encouraged a bibliophile's paradise in which manuscripts were created that are truly wonders of the age. There followed a decade during which he apparently renounced the visual arts, but his recovery from an illness *c.* 1566 brought a return to the passion for painting he had had in his earlier life and caused him to recall from exile Ibrahim Mirza, a favourite nephew who shared his interest. In 1514, when he was barely a few months old, Tahmasp had been sent to Herat as nominal governor, and his love of fine manuscripts, his skill as a calligrapher and his connoisseurship of the arts of the book are surely connected to his exposure to the aesthetic modes and mores of Herat conferred by his early life in that city and by the presence in Tabriz of Bihzad, the great master of the Herat style of painting.

Presumably Tahmasp established his own scriptorium-library (Pers. *kitābkhāna*) on his return to Tabriz, for several fine illustrated manuscripts were produced in the next few years. By 1524, when he succeeded to the throne, his hand was already trained enough to copy the text of 'Arifi's verse romance *Gūy va chawgān* ('Ball and bandy') for a pocket-sized manuscript ornamented with fine illumination and 16 unsigned paintings (St Petersburg, Rus. N. Lib., Dorn 441). Another fine manuscript, a copy of Nizami's *Khamsa*, was penned by the celebrated calligrapher of Herat, Sultan Muhammad Nur (1524–5; New York, Met., 13.228.7). Most of its 15 paintings and a detached picture in Dublin (Chester Beatty Lib., Pers. MS. 228.vi) have been attributed to SHAYKHZADA. Also attributed to Shaykhzada are five of six paintings in a contemporary copy of the *Dīvān* of 'Alishir Nava'i copied at Herat (1526–7; Paris, Bib. N., MS. supp. turc 316–17). The masterpiece of early Safavid painting is a superb manuscript of the *Dīvān* of Hafiz (ex-Cartier priv. col.;

divided Cambridge, MA, Sackler Mus.; New York, Met.; Houston, TX, A. & Hist. Trust col.). It is undated, its calligrapher is unidentified, and even the place where it was executed is uncertain, although it was probably made at Tabriz. Each of its four (originally five) paintings is unusual. *Princely Entertainment* is remarkable for the dark intensity of its green garden setting. *Feast of 'Id*, which bears a dedication to the Safavid prince Sam Mirza and is signed by Sultan-Muhammad, makes sly visual comments on the behaviour of the court on the eve of an important festival. *Allegory of Drunkenness* (see fig. 126), also signed by Sultan-Muhammad, is an audacious and wickedly humorous portrayal of a Sufi gathering, with realistic portraits of an entire community in the throes of spiritual (and literal) intoxication. *Episode in a Mosque*, which bears an attribution to Shaykhzada, is unusually large. It shows an elaborate interior which juxtaposes an agitated crowd of men against highly decorated rectilinear shapes, comprising architectural components and textiles placed on them. Although this image recalls Bihzad's compositions, it is extremely similar in such features as figures, faces and compositional units to the painting attributed to Shaykhzada of *Khusraw Enthroned* (fol. 64*r*) in the *Khamsa* of 1524–5.

The largest and most ambitious project of the Tabriz workshop is the *Shāhnāma* made for Tahmasp (dispersed, ex-Houghton priv. col.; e.g. New York, Met.). Dust Muhammad wrote that it was so beautifully illustrated that the pen was inadequate to describe it and that it contained one painting before which 'the hearts of the boldest of painters were grieved and they hung their heads in shame' (*Court of Gayumars*; see fig. 108 above). Virtually intact until *c.* 1960, it was a large (470×318 mm) volume of 760 gold-sprinkled folios with 258 illustrations. The scribe is unknown, it bears only a single date (AH 934/1527–8 on fol. 516*v*, depicting *Ardashir and Gulnar*) and only two paintings bear attributions (*Manuchihr Enthroned* on fol. 60*v* to MIR MUSAVVIR and *Haftvad and the Worm* on fol. 521*v* to DUST MUHAMMAD). Tahmasp, during his period of renunciation, gave the manuscript to the Ottoman sultan Selim II (*reg* 1566–74) soon after his accession; it remained in Istanbul until early in the 20th century.

The creation of the manuscript must have occupied a small army of craftsmen and artists over a considerable period. It may have been begun shortly after Tahmasp's accession in 1524 and completed shortly before 1540, when artists turned to Tahmasp's next major commission. It is extremely uneven in quality, for some of the paintings are superlative and merit every word of praise, contemporary or modern, ever lavished on them; others are fine but undistinguished illustrations; some are banal and boring. Towards the middle of the volume the need to produce large numbers of pictures at some speed dictated a formula: pictures occupy only part of the written surface with essential figures or other elements placed in the simplest of settings, often with a void in the centre. Such pictorial expediency seems hard to reconcile with a princely manuscript of such quality in all the other aspects of its production, including paper, calligraphy, ornamentation, binding and, above all, the quality of such images as Sultan-Muhammad's *Court of Gayumars*. The illustrations of Tahmasp's *Shāhnāma* represent all the stylistic currents of

126. Sultan-Muhammad: *Allegory of Drunkenness*, 215×150 mm; illustration from Hafiz: *Dīvān* (collected poetry), probably from Tabriz, *c.* 1526 (Cambridge, MA, Harvard University Art Museums, and New York, Metropolitan Museum of Art, fol. 135*v*)

Persian painting in various stages of development. Virtually every important painter in Tabriz is presumed to have worked on the manuscript, although the paucity of signatures is curious in view of the later Safavid habit of signing pictures.

The next major project of the Tabriz workshop was a copy of Nizami's *Khamsa* (London, BL, Or. MS. 2265; see fig. 103 above). It was copied in Tabriz by the famous scribe Shah Mahmud Nishapuri and bears dates between 1539 and 1543. It has splendid ornamentation, and its wide margins are further enhanced by drawings executed in gold touched with silver of animals cavorting in windblown landscapes. Smaller (360×250 mm) than the *Shāhnāma*, it has fewer illustrations: fourteen are contemporary with the manuscript, at least three others have been detached (Cambridge, MA, Sackler Mus., 1958.75 and 1958.76; Edinburgh, Royal Mus. Scotland, 1896–70) and three more were added by Muhammad Zaman in 1675–6. Nevertheless it is aesthetically more coherent and its illustrations are more uniform in conception, execution and finish than is the *Shāhnāma*. Inscriptions written on the pictures attribute them to Tabriz painters of the highest stature: Sultan-Muhammad, his son MIRZA 'ALI, AQA MIRAK, MUZAFFAR 'ALI and MIR SAYYID 'ALI. A couplet inscribed on *Nushirvan and his Vizier in the Ruined Palace* (see fig. 107 above) is followed by the name of Mir Musavvir and the date AH 946 (1539–40). The paintings were executed separately and pasted into spaces left for them in the text. The manuscript remained unfinished in the 16th century: not all the spaces for illustration were filled.

The large paintings in this last of Tahmasp's great manuscripts exemplify the Tabriz style. These paintings are more temperate and less cramped than earlier Safavid pictures and often variations on a pictorial aesthetic, with a surprisingly wide range of differing styles in each. In them are merged the components of earlier Safavid painting: the frenetic type of landscape with unusual colouring, and visionaries or other-worldly beings, associated with painting in late 15th-century and very early 16th-century Tabriz; the limpid, cool and balanced compositions associated with Herat; the increasingly naturalistic depiction of humans engaged in daily activities, and the taste for the multiplication of patterns, in textiles, tile panels, tents, architecture, pools, fountains and the smaller accoutrements of Safavid life. Beneath such pictorial elaboration lie traditional compositions, which illustrate many of the best-known of Nizami's stories. Each is set out of doors or includes a garden background. Palatial terrace or nomad camp, enchanted wilderness pool or barren hunting-ground, each picture is a broad, balanced composition conveying a sense of limitless space, whether it has many figures (*Khusraw Enthroned*, fol. 60*v*) or relatively few (*Bahram Gur Displays his Prowess*, fol. 211*r*). The court scenes suggest Tahmasp's own court, and he may have been flatteringly portrayed as Bahram Gur on fol. 211*r*.

The *Ascent of the Prophet to Heaven* (see fig. 104 above) is the most striking, beautiful and moving image in this *Khamsa*, on a par with Sultan-Muhammad's *Court of Gayumars* from the *Shāhnāma*. Against a star-spangled blue sky with white clouds in curling Chinese shapes that half-hide the golden moon with a white halo around it, soars the Prophet Muhammad. He is mounted on Buraq, the human-headed horse that bears him through the Seven Heavens into the Divine Presence. Dressed in green, his face veiled with white, he blazes with a huge halo of flame. The archangel Gabriel, with a smaller flaming nimbus, escorts him. Angels wearing crowns or foliage headdresses and bearing offerings surround him. The composition is classical, but none of the earlier examples approaches the grandeur of this picture or conveys its other-worldly atmosphere nor achieves its nobility of form and colour. Whoever imagined, and painted, this vision of faith and glory (for it carries no attribution), it is a fitting final image in any discussion of Tabriz painting under the sponsorship of Shah Tahmasp.

The style of Qazvin, 1548–98. The repeated Ottoman invasions of Iran during the reign of Tahmasp seem to have persuaded the Shah, probably in 1548, to move his capital away from the Ottoman threat south-east to Qazvin. Also in the mid-1540s Tahmasp is said to have wearied of calligraphy and painting and occupied himself with important affairs of state, the well-being of the country and the tranquillity of his subjects (Qazi Ahmad,

p. 135). By 1556 he had issued a ban against the secular arts throughout his kingdom, but it is unclear how complete Tahmasp's weariness of the pictorial arts was. Qazi Ahmad records that the Shah himself painted several group or genre pictures (Pers. *majlis*), including one of *Yusuf Appearing before Zulaykha and her Ladies*, for the Chihil Sutun Palace in Qazvin. The earliest surviving copy of the *Fālnāma* ('Book of divination'; dispersed) has also been associated with Tahmasp's patronage at this time on the grounds that its subject, the picturing of omens and their interpretations, might have appealed to the increasingly religious ruler. At least 28 paintings are known and more are unpublished. They are large (*c.* 590×445 mm), vivid, highly coloured compositions of religious or literary subjects; some are narrative and some hieratic. They vary in style, but the overall quality is high, even when the solution to composing pictures on such a scale is to fall back on strict symmetry, large areas of abstract pattern, or the division of landscape into well-differentiated bands of colour against which the protagonists, whether of this world or another, are displayed. One of the most striking images (Geneva, Mus. A. & Hist., 1971–107/35) is set in a mosque: men pray and prostrate themselves before an enormous and wondrously illuminated representation of the sandals of the Prophet. None of the pictures is signed, although some have been attributed to Aqa Mirak and possibly 'Abd al-'Aziz. The Shah's waning interest in the illustrated book may not have extended to all the arts of the book: calligraphers were needed to design monumental inscriptions on buildings in the new capital and to copy religious texts, such as a manuscript of the Koran (London, Nasser D. Khalili Col., Qur 729, see D. James, *After Timur*, London, 1992, pp. 172–81) completed in July–August 1552. Its superb quality has led to the supposition that it was made in Qazvin and possibly for Tahmasp himself.

Painters had to look elsewhere for their livelihood. Some went west to the Ottoman court in Istanbul and others went east, either to the Mughal court in exile at Kabul or to the independent states in the Deccan. Other painters found congenial employment at the court of Tahmasp's nephew Ibrahim Mirza (1543–77) in Mashhad. Named governor of this city in 1555, Ibrahim Mirza apparently established a celebrated scriptorium-library, which followed him for a decade around Khurasan after his dismissal as governor in 1564. Its first product might have been an album reported to have been a wedding-gift to Gawhar Sultan, Tahmasp's daughter and Ibrahim Mirza's wife, later that year. Ibrahim Mirza is said to have possessed a library of some 3000 volumes, but only two of the illustrated books made for him are known to have survived: a copy of the *Naqsh-i badī'* ('Beautiful script') of Muhammad Ghazzali Mashhadi, copied at Sabzevar (1574–5; Istanbul, Topkapı Pal. Lib., R. 1038), and a copy of Jami's *Haft awrang* ('Seven thrones'; Washington, DC, Freer, 46.12), the most important illustrated manuscript to survive from the second half of the 16th century.

The *Haft awrang* remains Ibrahim's aesthetic testament by virtue of the quality of its calligraphy, its 28 illustrations and its superb decoration. The manuscript has survived virtually intact and in surprisingly good condition; the eight colophons and details of its physical assembly provide a previously unimaginable amount of information about the workings of the scriptorium-library. The manuscript (375×254 mm) is similar to the *Khamsa* made for Tahmasp and also has wide, illuminated margins of paper differing from that on which the text was written. It was copied by five scribes over nine years (1556–65) in three different cities: Mashhad, Herat and Qazvin. The scribes were highly distinguished: Shah Mahmud Nishapuri had copied Tahmasp's *Khamsa*; Rustam 'Ali was Bihzad's nephew and had worked for Ibrahim Mirza's father, Bahram Mirza; Muhibb 'Ali was the son of Rustam 'Ali, and Malik Daylami was the calligrapher recalled to Qazvin to design building inscriptions for Tahmasp. Simpson's codicological analysis of the manuscript suggests that the non-sequential order and varied locales in which the seven poems were copied is proof of the ad hoc, nomadic nature of Ibrahim Mirza's scriptorium. The nine-year period may also be misleading since the dates refer to the copying of the text. Only after the text (and presumably the paintings as well) was complete and the volume assembled could the extraordinary illuminations and decorated borders have been executed. Ibrahim Mirza himself may have been the primary illuminator, as the manuscript has lavish quantities of illumination but preserves the name of only one gilder, 'Abdallah al-Shirazi, and Qazi Ahmad described Ibrahim Mirza as having golden hands in painting and decoration and being a master in various techniques of illumination.

The paintings of the *Haft awrang* are unsigned but have been attributed to six artists, of whom five—Aqa Mirak, Mirza 'Ali, Muzaffar 'Ali, Qadimi and Shaykh Muhammad—had worked on important manuscripts for Tahmasp. The subjects of the paintings are relatively uncommon, and many were devised from stock compositional elements that were put to striking and original uses. Some (e.g. *Jami Kissing the Feet of Khizr*, fol. 207v) are based on 15th-century compositions; one (*The Arabian's Hospitality*, fol. 169v) recalls early 16th-century painting but is set with more elegantly coiffed and bearded figures in the style of Tabriz. Others are constructed on the example of the most mature Tabriz compositions with ample rhythms and in settings that are gorgeous (*A Father's Discourse on Love*, fol. 52r) or intensely lyrical (*A City Dweller Desecrates a Garden*, fol. 179v). Some are unforgettable images in which taut lines of buildings or tents provide a structure for complex assemblages of people whose expressions and interactions convey nuances beyond the meaning of the episode illustrated. Among them are figural types anticipating the distortion of proportion and pose that is one of the hallmarks of Qazvin-style painting and drawing. Another characteristic is the confusion and refined chaos of the setting: the languid and contorted figures are virtually lost among fantastic rock landscapes (*Yusuf's Escape from the Well*, fol. 105r) or amid the skewed geometry of palace pavilions (*Yusuf Entertained at Court before his Marriage to Zulaykha*; see fig. 127) or tents and canopies in the wilderness (*Majnun Eavesdrops on Layla's Camp*, fol. 253r).

The image of *Yusuf Entertained at Court* (attributed to Shaykh Muhammad), like so much Qazvin-style painting, can be taken not only as an illustration of the text but also as a glimpse of a Safavid court entertainment. The all-male party displays varied physiognomies and builds, racial

types and ages; the setting is a brick palace decorated with tile panels and wooden grilles, spread with rugs and overhung with patterned canopies. In drawing, colour and detail the image conforms with surviving Safavid palaces and rugs. But this picture is surely to be read on several more levels: as a Sufi meditation on divinity, embodied in the beautiful figure of Yusuf in his flaming nimbus, and also as a salute to the patron, for the handsome Yusuf is an idealized portrait of Ibrahim himself. It is no coincidence that the patron's names and titles are inscribed in gold letters above the arch directly over Yusuf's head. By contrast, the image of *Salman and Absal on the Heavenly Isle* (fol. 191v, attributed to Mirza 'Ali) is the quintessential and perfectly executed image of an ideal world, epitomizing to Western eyes a sense of Oriental fantasy. A pair of graceful lovers has alighted on to a verdant shore from a swan-prowed vessel floating on a silver sea. Turtles and fish swim in the water, parrots, monkeys and rabbits cavort on the land and birds on the branches of trees. The sun sets amid curling clouds streaked with gold and trailing pink and red. Salman is keen-eyed and ready to display his prowess with bow and arrow; Absal, perched precariously on a rock, is sloe-eyed and double-chinned, bejewelled and beguiling.

The same figural types and faces occur in the more conventional setting of a double-page composition (Boston, MA, Mus. F.A., 14.624; New York, Met., 12.233.1), also attributed to Mirza 'Ali, showing a rocky glade in which a courtly hawking party rests. Despite the absence of any signature, date or association with a text, it has been proposed that the composition was intended as the frontispiece to a manuscript undertaken jointly by Tahmasp and Ibrahim Mirza on Ibrahim's return to the court at Qazvin about 1574. The entire composition is aesthetically similar to images in Ibrahim Mirza's *Haft awrang* in the way the painted landscapes give way to gold-drawn landscapes in the wide margins and then to gold-sprinkled marbled frames. The gold borders are more elaborate than the floral borders of the *Haft awrang*; they extend the hunting theme into the imagination, for in them simurghs and dragons, as well as leopards, wolves and bears, prey on gazelles, rabbits and birds. The older men in this splendid picture have faces with well-differentiated features and expressions, as is the case in many pictures in the *Haft awrang*. The younger figures, however, are depicted in the full-blown, highly mannered figural style associated with Qazvin: the bodies are slim and often sway-backed, the eyes large and smudgy or long-lashed, widely set in faces fuller than they are high, with marked double chins, the heads apparently too heavy for the necks from which they bend at improbable angles. Such figural types occur occasionally in the illustrations to a manuscript of Nizami's *Khamsa* (New York, Pub. Lib., MS. M. 836) begun in 1572 and completed in 1581 at Qazvin, and more frequently in those in a copy of Hilali's *Sifat al-'ashiqin* ('Dispositions of lovers'; 1582; priv. col., see 1985 exh. cat., no. 76).

The figural style associated with Qazvin is best seen in a large number of single-figure paintings and drawings from the late 16th century. Far more than many contemporary drawings of multiple figures set in landscapes, these

127. *Yusuf Entertained at Court before his Marriage to Zulaykha*, attributed to Shaykh Muhammad, 342×232mm; illustration from Jami: *Haft awrang* ('Seven thrones'), made for Ibrahim Mirza, 1556–65 (Washington, DC, Freer Gallery of Art, 46.12, fol. 132*r*)

drawings portray the details of Safavid life, its accoutrements and its practices with special immediacy. Many exist in multiples, as nearly identical copies of finished drawings. Two late 16th-century versions of a *Kneeling Youth* (Geneva, Prince Sadruddin Aga Khan priv. col., Ir.M. 73; New York, Met., 1973.92) show the same figure with hands pressed firmly on to one raised knee and head bent, as if in obeisance, under the weight of a brocaded or embroidered cap lined with the finest fluff of fur. They reveal the subtle differences of line and ornament, finish and quality, that may occur in two renditions of the same subject. Shaykh Muhammad, one of the artists connected with the *Haft awrang*, repeated his image of a *Kneeling Youth* with subtle differences of pose, line and detail: in one version (Paris, Louvre, AO, SI 3427) the youth reads from a book in his right hand and holds a narcissus in his left; in another version (Washington, DC, Freer, 37.23) he plays with a parrot perched on his right hand. *Wayward Youths*, another drawing attributed to Shaykh Muhammad (Paris, Louvre, AO, SI 7121), pushes the aesthetic of the Qazvin figural type to the point at which it is hard to separate the image on the paper from what has been written about the dissipated society at the end of Tahmasp's reign. Two adolescents hold hands and gaze intensely into each other's eyes, one playing with the chin of the other; hair escapes from underneath the twists of their turbans, one of which is askew. Their long waists could hardly be thinner, their legs seem to have no bones and the smudging of the right-hand figure creates an ambiguity in the lower part of the picture no less unsettling than that of their faces.

Although these and similar images anticipate the style and manner that characterize much painting and drawing in the 17th century, conservative notions of illustrating texts, which had shaped the tradition of Persian painting for over two centuries, still controlled many artists, and despite Tahmasp's withdrawal of patronage the traditional format continued to find both patrons and painters during the third quarter of the 16th century. In addition to illustrated manuscripts, there are single sheets of paintings, drawings and calligraphy that would have been bound into albums; they vary in style and quality, as might be expected when patrons were less wealthy than the royal connoisseur and his family. Among them were minor princes of the Safavid family; Tajik and Qizilbash noblemen who were governors, guardians and generals; and provincial patrons in the Caspian coastal provinces and the lands under Uzbek control (*see* §(c) below). The best of these manuscripts might well have been made in Mashhad or Qazvin and include paintings that approach the finest court work. They include a copy of Jami's *Silsilat al-zahab* ('Chain of gold'; St Petersburg, Rus. N. Lib., Dorn 434) completed by the noted calligrapher Shah Mahmud Nishapuri on 1 Sha'ban AH 956 (25 Aug 1549). It has a magnificent double-page frontispiece depicting a hunting scene; its composition was reused for the frontispiece to the dispersed copy of the *Shāhnāma* made in 1576–7 for Isma'il II.

Among the finest of the manuscripts made in the last quarter of the century is the *Shāhnāma* made for Isma'il II (*reg* 1576–7), who apparently followed the princely practice of commissioning an illustrated copy of the text on his accession. This large manuscript (460×315 mm), dispersed in the early 20th century, was apparently left unfinished at the patron's death, since the 52 known paintings illustrate stories from the first two-thirds of the text. They are executed in the general manner of Qazvin but without its extreme mannerisms and bear contemporary attributions to eight painters, including 'Ali Asghar, Zayn al-'Abidin, Murad Daylami, the irascible but highly literate and well-connected SADIQI, and SIYAVUSH, known as the 'Georgian'. Siyavush is credited with nineteen paintings and Sadiqi with seven; both had been pupils of Tahmasp's painter Muzaffar 'Ali, who may have been the first director of the project. Isma'il's ineffectual successor, Muhammad Khudabanda (*reg* 1578–87), was pictorially inactive, and painters had to seek work from other patrons, most notably the Shamlu khans who governed Herat as regents for the Safavid princes in the last quarter of the 16th century. Manuscripts made for this important tribe have illustrations mixing classical Herat compositions, Qazvin- and Mashhad-style landscapes and 16th-century-style figures whose garments and features anticipate the new style and spirit of 17th-century Isfahan.

The style of Shiraz, c. *1500–c. 1600.* Throughout the 16th century Shiraz was an important centre for the commercial production of manuscripts of good, although not superb, quality. A large number of manuscripts bear colophons stating that they were made in Shiraz, and many scribes and/or illustrators bear the epithet Shirazi ('from Shiraz'). Shiraz manuscripts have similar dimensions and illustrations of distinct shape and proportion. The distinctive Shiraz style seems to have developed out of the Turkoman Commercial style practised there in the 15th century (*see* §(v)(e) above). At least half a dozen manuscripts copied between *c.* 1510 and 1522 were made in a workshop associated with the tomb complex (Pers. *astāna*) of Mawlana Husam al-Din Ibrahim, and there must have been a number of similar establishments where manuscripts were produced commercially. The quantities of texts produced throughout the century were illustrated in the prevailing court styles of Tabriz and Qazvin or, by *c.* 1545, in a distinctive Shiraz aesthetic controlling both written surface and pictorial layout. The typical image is sandwiched between two areas of text and projects into the outer margin by half the width of the text block, creating a vertical division into thirds. The projection extends for the full height of the text block, creating a characteristic T-shaped field. Within the image, the ratio 3:5 is repeatedly used; for example, the horizon line rests at three-fifths the height of the image. These features were first noticed in a dispersed copy of Sharaf al-Din 'Ali Yazdi's *Zafarnāma* ('Book of victory'), copied by the noted Shiraz scribe Murshid in 1546; the mathematically controlled plotting of the page design was found to be characteristic of manuscripts from the middle of the century. The distinctive Shiraz canon continued to be used throughout the century: it is found in a copy of Siyaqi-Nizam's *Futūhāt-i humāyūn* ('Conquests of the emperor'; Paris, Bib. N., MS. supp. pers. 226), concerning the reconquest of the province of Khurasan by 'Abbas I (*reg* 1587–1629), produced at Shiraz in the opening years of the 17th century.

The uncertain political situation in the last quarter of the 16th century led artists trained in the Shiraz style to seek work elsewhere in Iran. A copy of the *Shāhnāma* has been assigned to Qazvin (*c.* 1580–85; Windsor Castle, Royal Lib., Holmes 150 (A/5)). Its 88 paintings are the work of four hands: one artist from Qazvin and three adhering in various degrees to the Shiraz style. Another copy of the *Shāhnāma* (London, India Office Lib., MS. 3450) was probably done a decade later in Shiraz. Its 56 paintings are the work of two hands: the more conventional one is entirely in the style of Shiraz, the other has been linked to one of the three painters who worked on the Windsor Castle copy and tentatively identified as Zayn al-ʿAbidin, who was associated with the *Shāhnāma* made for Ismaʿil II.

Traditional painting at Isfahan and other courts, c. 1598– c. 1700. The state of painting at the time of the accession of ʿAbbas I in 1587 is reflected in the paintings from the fragmentary *Shāhnāma* (Dublin, Chester Beatty Lib., Pers. MS. 277) thought to have been commissioned by him about that time. The 21 surviving folios of this large manuscript (407×261 mm) are embellished with lavish marginal drawings in gold. Since Muhammad Zaman painted two of the sixteen extant paintings and touched up several others in 1675–6, the manuscript must have been intact at that time, but it has since lost its colophon, which might have supplied information about the date and place of production. The fourteen paintings are attributed on stylistic grounds to three artists, two of whom are well known in literary sources and whose works epitomize the salient features of contemporary painting: Sadiqi and RIZA. Sadiqi, who had already worked on several manuscripts including the copy of *The Shāhnāma* made for Ismaʿil II, was appointed the new shah's librarian. His finest painting in the *Shāhnāma* made for ʿAbbas I is the *Simurgh Carrying the Infant Zal to its Nest* (see fig. 128), a quintessential Persian text illustration that transcends the details of its creation. This well-known story (see also fig. 118 above) has here been given its most beautiful and fantastic setting. Exquisitely designed and placed on the page, this painting differs greatly from the two others attributed to Sadiqi: *King Sarv, his Daughters and the Three Sons of Faridun* and *Zal before Rudaba's Castle*, which are distinguished by figural style and scale. Only the landscape backgrounds, with their fantastic curving shapes, share a similar spirit.

Sadiqi is also associated with a copy of Kashifi's *Anvār-i Suhaylī* ('Lights of Canopus'; Geneva, Prince Sadruddin Aga Khan priv. col.), illustrated with an astonishing 107 paintings. Its colophon bears the date AH 1002 (1593), surrounded by an inscription in gold containing the ambiguous statement that 'it is written as it is ordered by the rare man of the time...Sadiqi the painter [Pers. *muṣavvir*]'. The paintings have been attributed to Sadiqi and are remarkably homogeneous in style, palette and draughtsmanship, as well as in their overall conception and consistent liveliness, but the date of the colophon raises questions about Sadiqi's role in the royal library.

The sublimity of Sadiqi's paintings in the *Shāhnāma* manuscript for ʿAbbas I and elsewhere has been ascribed to the presence in the royal library of the young Riza,

128. *Simurgh Carrying the Infant Zal to its Nest*, attributed to Sadiqi, gold and coloured inks on paper, 407×261mm; illustration from Firdawsi: *Shāhnāma* ('Book of kings'), *c.* 1597 (Dublin, Chester Beatty Library and Gallery of Oriental Art, Pers. MS. 277, fol. 12)

whose period of activity coincides with a change in the aesthetic of the ideal human figure that is the virtual hallmark of the Isfahan style in the 17th century. Many of the features of this new aesthetic can already be found in the painting *Faridun Spurning the Ambassador from Salm and Tur* (Dublin, Chester Beatty Lib., Pers. MS. 277), generally ascribed to Riza. Although the setting could hardly be more formulaic and unimaginative, the painting is peopled with a fascinating mix of sharply observed individuals and idealized Isfahan youth. The two modes co-exist in the same picture: Faridun, the vizier and the ambassador on the steps at the lower right could almost be portraits of specific people, while the attendants display such standard features as large oval faces, big eyes with black pupils hanging below the lid, cupid's-bow mouths and double chins. Their hair is black and wavy, often creeping down the cheek and escaping from headdresses or the enormously broad, flattened and loosely wound turban that is a sartorial feature of the period. Heads are shown in three-quarter view, hands and feet are small and figures increasingly corpulent. Most distinctive are the impossibly wind-blown garments and poses of standing figures. Many of these features can be found in other works of Riza, such as single-page studies of languid youths (e.g. *Young Man in a Blue Cloak*; Cambridge, MA, Sackler Mus., 1936.27), which also show the most characteristic feature of Persian painting and drawing in this period: the renewed emphasis on a calligraphic line of varied breadth for the depiction of humans. This is less perceptible in finished book illustrations but quite evident in single-page paintings, especially in such places as waists, wrists, hems and turbans where fabric is bunched or moves, and in the faint gold-drawn landscapes that serve as rudimentary settings. This feature is most evident in pen drawings, of which Riza signed many (e.g. *Man Scratching his Head*, 1598–9; Washington, DC, Freer, 53.12).

In 1598 'Abbas I formally established his capital at Isfahan. While many buildings erected there were enhanced with painted decoration, only one manuscript can be connected with the ruler: a restoration of the exceptionally fine but unfinished copy of 'Attar's *Mantiq al-tayr* ('Conference of the birds'; New York, Met., 63.210), in which the text is dated 1483 (*see* §(v)(d) above). Some time before 1609 when 'Abbas I endowed the manuscript to the shrine of Shaykh Safi at Ardabil, a pair of illuminated frontispieces was executed by Zayn al-'Abidin, paintings were made for four blank spaces and the manuscript was re-margined and re-bound. Three unsigned pictures (fols 4, 18 and 22) set Isfahan-style figures, and buildings in mixed style, in landscapes largely composed of elements characteristic of the Timurid style. The fourth painting, *The Conference of the Birds* (fol. 11), is Timurid in virtually every aspect save the face of the hunter at the right margin, whose musket extends over the wide rulings and on to the gold-flecked blue–green margin. The painting is signed by Habiballah, an artist mentioned by Qazi Ahmad and documented as early as the reign of Isma'il II. His work is distinguishable from that of the prolific Riza only by his signature. Other painters who perpetuated the figural style associated with Riza include MUHAMMAD YUSUF, MUHAMMAD QASIM, Riza's son Shafi' and his pupil MU'IN. They and many others made innumerable drawings and paintings which were mounted in albums, often with apposite specimens of calligraphy. Such composite folios constituted one of the principal markets for the arts of the book in a period when public and private buildings in the capital were being decorated with paintings on walls or tiles in larger versions of Riza-style compositions. The only difference between these two modes of Safavid painting is scale; such figural designs were also adapted to the repertory of ceramics and both woven and knotted textiles.

Many other manuscripts, some of good quality, were made for royal and non-royal patrons in the first half of the 17th century. One of the earliest is a copy of 'Alishir Nava'i's *Dīvān* (c. 1615; ex-Rothschild priv. col.; sold London, Colnaghi's; see 1976 sale cat., no. 43) with nine paintings signed by Riza. A copy of Nizami's *Khusraw and Shirin* (London, V&A, 364–1885 and L. 1613–1964) with 19 paintings (one detached) is dated AH 1091, clearly an error for AH 1041 (1631–2) because one of the paintings is dated AH 1042. One of the most impressive manuscripts is a large copy of 'Abd al-Rahman al-Sufi's *Kitāb suwar al-kawākib al-thābita* ('Book of the fixed stars'; 1630–33; New York, Pub. Lib., Spencer Col., MS. 6). It has 71 illustrations, many of them double page. Three copies of

the *Shāhnāma* include an undated manuscript (London, India Office Lib., MS. 1256) with superb illumination and 28 unsigned paintings, some probably by Mu'in. A two-volume copy (1644–5; Dublin, Chester Beatty Lib., Per. MS. 270; Geneva, Prince Sadruddin Aga Khan priv. col., MS. 22) made for 'Abbas II (*reg* 1642–66) has 50 illustrations, most signed by Mu'in. A splendid copy (1648; Windsor Castle, Royal Lib., Holmes 151 (A6)) made for Qarajaghay Khan, a guardian of the shrine at Mashhad, has 148 paintings, one signed by Muhammad Yusif; others are attributed to Muhammad Qasim. An unsigned and undated copy of Muhammad Riza Naw'i's *Sūz va gudāz* ('Burning and melting'; Dublin, Chester Beatty Lib., Pers. MS. 268) has ten superb paintings attributed to Muhammad Qasim around the middle of the 17th century.

Eclectic painting at Isfahan and other courts, c. 1640–1722. A stream of European diplomats, priests, merchants and adventurers made their way to Isfahan in the 17th and 18th centuries. An official embassy from the Mughal emperor Jahangir in 1618 was recorded by Persian and Mughal artists (e.g. a finished picture by Riza in the Hermitage Album; 1633; St Petersburg, Hermitage). The exotic presence of such foreigners and their retinues, the exchange of diplomatic gifts and the sale of foreign merchandise had a cumulative effect on the pictorial techniques and styles of Persian painting in the 17th century, an effect that lasted until the 19th century. In addition to large oil paintings on canvas and mediocre devotional paintings, smaller pictures, portrait miniatures, illustrated books and prints introduced other techniques of European painting into 17th-century Iran. European craftsmen, including jewellers, watchmakers and gunsmiths, came with many of the missions, but references to specific and identifiable European painters are frustratingly vague. The European presence was visually documented by Persian artists in several ways. A number of figural compositions by conventional Persian painters show European figures (e.g. Riza's *Seated Portuguese Youth with a Dog*, 1633–4; Detroit, MI, Inst. A., 58.334). Court painters adopted such European conventions as linear perspective and cast shadows, modelling with colour, and the use of colour and scale to give the illusion of distance. These conventions must have been learnt in Iran, as there is no reliable record of any Persian painter travelling to Europe in this period. Painters also adopted such features of contemporary Mughal painting as a more realistic depiction of flora and fauna, artificially lit settings and an interest in portraiture, but it is unclear whether these features, which characterize much Persian painting in the second half of the 17th century, were learnt in the Indian subcontinent or at home, as several Persian artists, particularly such masters of eclecticism as SHAYKH 'ABBASI and 'ALIQULI JABBADAR, may have travelled to Kashmir.

There are no written documents about later 17th-century painting, and its course must be deduced from the works of art themselves and the inscriptions they bear. Two features deserve comment: the uncalligraphic quality of most work and the distinctive and recognizable styles of individual artists. It is difficult to mistake a fine picture by one artist for that by another. Shaykh 'Abbasi's style is distinguished by perfectly observed details of dress and grooming; thin and washy colour combined with sooty black for textural details of hair, beards, fur and feathers; shading along contours of people, architecture and landscape. The style of MUHAMMAD ZAMAN is equally personal and equally different. His finest work (see fig. 129) dates from the reign of Sulayman (*reg* 1666–94), when he added pictures to 16th-century royal manuscripts, such as the *Khamsa* made for Tahmasp and the *Shāhnāma* made for 'Abbas I. He often added foreign mannerisms and exotic accessories of dress and setting to traditional Persian subjects and compositions. Suavity of draughtsmanship, stippled application of colour and meticulous finish characterize all his works, whether manuscript paintings or painted and varnished penboxes and caskets. In his paintings in the Hermitage Album, 'Aliquli Jabbadar conveyed the frozen atmosphere of royal audiences and documented the dress and arms worn by sharply observed princes and courtiers. By the end of the century this type of realistic setting with exotic accoutrements was often adopted for the illustration of traditional poetic texts, such as a copy of the *Shāhnāma* (New York, Met., 13.228.17) written between 1663 and 1669 but illustrated between 1693 and 1698. By the early 18th century the exotic accoutrements that a small number of eclectic painters had introduced in the 17th century had become standard elements in the traditional compositions used to present traditional tales.

129. Muhammad Zaman: *Fitna Astonishing Bahram Gur*, 195×138mm; illustration added to Nizami: *Khamsa* ('Five poems'), 1675–6 (London, British Library, Or. MS. 2265, fol. 213*r*)

BIBLIOGRAPHY

EARLY SOURCES

Qazi Ahmad ibn Mir Munshi: *Gulistān-i hunar* [Rose-garden of art] (1606); Eng. trans. by V. Minorsky as *Calligraphers and Painters* (Washington, DC, 1959)

W. M. Thackston, ed.: *A Century of Princes: Sources on Timurid History and Art* (Cambridge, MA, 1989)

GENERAL

T. W. Arnold: *Painting in Islam* (Oxford, 1928)

L. Binyon, J. V. S. Wilkinson and B. Gray: *Persian Miniature Painting* (Oxford, 1933/*R* New York, 1971)

E. Schroeder: *Persian Miniatures in the Fogg Museum of Art* (Cambridge, MA, 1942)

G. D. Guest: *Shiraz Painting in the Sixteenth Century* (Washington, DC, 1949)

A. J. Arberry and others: *The Chester Beatty Library: A Catalogue of the Persian Manuscripts and Miniatures*, 3 vols (Dublin, 1959–62)

I. Stchoukine: *Les Peintures des manuscrits safavis de 1502 à 1587* (Paris, 1959)

I. Stchoukine: *Les Peintures des manuscrits de Shah Abbas I à la fin des Safavis* (Paris, 1964)

Persian Miniature Painting from Collections in the British Isles (exh. cat. by B. W. Robinson, London, V&A, 1967)

O. F. Akimushkin and A. A. Ivanov: *Persidskiye miniatyury XIV–XVII vv.* [Persian miniatures of the 14th–17th centuries] (Moscow, 1968)

The Classical Style in Islamic Painting: The Early School of Herat and its Impact on Islamic Painting of the Later 15th, the 16th and 17th Centuries (exh. cat. by E. J. Grube, New York, Pierpont Morgan Lib., 1968)

Shah 'Abbas and the Arts of Isfahan (exh. cat. by A. Welch, New York, Asia Soc. Gals; Cambridge, MA, Fogg; 1973–4)

B. W. Robinson: *Persian Paintings in the India Office Library: A Descriptive Catalogue* (London, 1976)

A. Welch: *Artists for the Shah* (New Haven and London, 1976)

S. C. Welch: *Persian Painting: Five Royal Safavid Manuscripts of the 16th Century* (New York, 1976)

Rothschild and Binney Collections: Persian and Mughal Art (exh. cat., ed. B. W. Robinson; London, Colnaghi's, 1976)

E. Atıl: *The Brush of the Masters: Drawings from Iran and India* (Washington, DC, 1978)

Wonders of the Age: Masterpieces of Early Safavid Painting, 1501–1576 (exh. cat. by S. C. Welch, London, BL; Washington, DC, N.G.A.; Cambridge, MA, Fogg; 1979–80)

B. W. Robinson: *Persian Paintings in the John Rylands Library: A Descriptive Catalogue* (London, 1980)

B. Schmitz: *Miniature Painting in Harāt, 1570–1640* (diss., New York U., Inst. F.A., 1981)

Treasures of Islam (exh. cat., ed. T. Falk; Geneva, Mus. A. & Hist., 1985)

M. L. Swietochowski and S. Babaie: *Persian Drawings in the Metropolitan Museum of Art* (New York, 1989)

S. R. Canby, ed.: *Persian Masters: Five Centuries of Painting* (Bombay, 1990)

SPECIALIST STUDIES

M. M. Qazwini and L. Bouvat: 'Deux Documents inédits relatifs à Behzad', *Rev. Monde Musulman*, xxvi (1914), pp. 146–61

L. Binyon: *The Poems of Nizami* (London, 1928)

I. Stchoukine: 'Les Peintures turcomanes et ṣafavies d'une Khamseh de Niẓâmî, achevée à Tabrîz en 886/1481', *A. Asiat.*, xiv (1966), pp. 3–16

B. W. Robinson: 'Two Manuscripts of the "Shahnama" in the Royal Library, Windsor Castle—I: Holmes 150 (A/5), and II: Holmes 151 (A/6)', *Burl. Mag.*, cx (1968), pp. 73–89; 133–40

——: 'The Shāhnāmeh Manuscript Cochran 4 in the Metropolitan Museum of Art', *Islamic Art in the Metropolitan Museum of Art*, ed. R. Ettinghausen (New York, 1972), pp. 73–86

——: 'Two Persian Manuscripts in the Library of the Marquess of Bute (Part II)', *Orient. A.*, xviii (1972), pp. 50–56

S. C. Welch: *A King's Book of Kings* (New York, 1972)

C. Ade: 'Recherche sur le module et le tracé correcteur dans la miniature orientale', *Monde Iran. & Islam*, iii (1975), pp. 81–105

P. J. Chelkowski: *Mirror of the Invisible World: Tales from the 'Khamseh' of Nizami* (New York, 1975)

B. W. Robinson: 'Ismā'īl II's Copy of the *Shāhnāma*', *Iran*, xiv (1976), pp. 1–8

E. Sims: 'The European Print Sources of Paintings by the Seventeenth-century Persian Painter, Muhammad-Zamān ibn Hājī Yūsūf of Qum',

Atti del XXIV congresso internazionale di storia dell'arte: Bologna, 1979, pp. 73–83

M. B. Dickson and S. C. Welch: *The Houghton Shah Nameh* (Cambridge, MA, 1981)

M. S. Simpson: 'The Production and Patronage of the *Haft Aurang* by Jami in the Freer Gallery of Art', *A. Orient.,* xiii (1982), pp. 93–119

E. Sims: '16th-Century Persian and Turkish Manuscripts of Animal Fables in Persia, Transoxiana, and Ottoman Turkey', *A Mirror for Princes from India: Illustrated Versions of the Kalilah wa Dimnah, Anvar-Suhaylī, Iyar-Danish, and Humayun Nameh,* ed. E. J. Grube (Bombay, 1991), pp. 98–123

ELEANOR SIMS

(b) Iran, c. *1750–*c. *1900.* The continuous military activity, political confusion and civil war in 18th-century Iran was not conducive to the production of illustrated manuscripts, and virtually none has survived. In the only peaceful reign, that of Karim Khan Zand at Shiraz (*reg* 1750–79), manuscript illustration was neglected in favour of varnished paintings on papier-mâché (*see* §VIII, 10 below) and large oil paintings (*see* §VIII, 11(i) below). The leading painter, Muhammad Sadiq, produced a few separate miniature paintings, but no book illustrations by him are known.

The art of book illustration revived during the reign of the Qajar monarch Fath 'Ali Shah (*reg* 1797–1834). Perhaps the finest manuscript of the period is a copy of the *Dīvān* (collected poetry; Windsor Castle, Royal Lib., Holmes 152) by the ruler himself, who wrote poetry under the name Khaqan. It was sent as a gift to the Prince Regent (later George IV, King of England) in 1812. MIRZA BABA, a leading painter in oils, was responsible for the two excellent portraits in the volume, one of the royal poet (see fig. 130) and another of his uncle and predecessor, the eunuch Agha Muhammad (*reg* 1796–7), as well as the gold marginal paintings, lavish illuminations and the beautiful painted and varnished covers. The portraits are dated 1802, by which time the artist had been named Painter Laureate (Pers. *naqqāsh-bāshī*), a title not previously known but subsequently awarded to several artists of the later 19th century. The illustrations in a fine copy of the *Anvār-i Suhaylī* ('Lights of Canopus'; Mahboubian priv. col., see 1970 exh. cat., no. 928) may also be attributed to him. There are several large and fully illustrated copies (Oxford, Bodleian Lib., Elliott MS. 327; London, BL, Orient & India Office Lib., Ethé MS. 901; Vienna, Österreich. Nbib., Flügel MS. 639 and Tehran, Majlis Lib., MS. 15234) of a voluminous epic by Fath 'Ali Shah's Poet Laureate. Entitled the *Shāhanshāhnāma* ('Book of the king of kings'), it celebrated, with poetic licence, the monarch's early career. The illustrated copies were mostly designed as gifts to foreign potentates; the unsigned illustrations, although generally competent, are somewhat repetitive and monotonous. There are also numerous manuscripts of the classical poets illustrated in the same style, but seldom with distinction and sometimes quite crudely executed. The rich enamel-like pigments of previous centuries have given way to comparatively thin watercolours.

If Fath 'Ali Shah's *Dīvān* is the finest Qajar manuscript, the most lavish and spectacular is a Persian translation (Tehran, Gulistan Pal. Lib., MSS 12367–72) of *The Thousand and One Nights* commissioned in 1853 by Nasir al-Din (*reg* 1848–96). The six folio volumes contain 1134

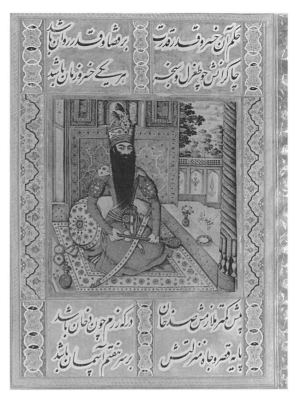

130. Mirza Baba: *Fath 'Ali Shah*; illustration from Fath 'Ali Shah: *Dīvān* (collected poetry), from Tehran, 1802 (Windsor, Windsor Castle, Royal Library, MS. A/4)

illustrated pages, each containing two to three separate images. This enormous work was directed by the court painter Abu'l-Hasan Ghaffari, later known as Sani' al-Mulk ('Painter of the Kingdom'; *see* GHAFFARI, (2)), who designed most of the compositions and executed a considerable proportion of them; he was assisted by a team of 34 painters. The style is unified, westernized, sometimes almost photographic, and the execution is meticulous throughout. This work set the style for most small-scale painting in Iran during the remainder of the 19th century. One exception is a copy of the *Shāhnāma* made for the family of the Shiraz poet Visal (?Tehran, Nigaristan Mus.); the paintings, dated between 1857 and 1863, were mainly executed by the Shiraz painter Lutf 'Ali Khan in an original manner, with a few added by the poet's sons.

Single-page paintings and drawings have survived in considerable numbers. Many of the finest are flower paintings, a field dominated by the Shiraz artists Muhammad Hadi and Lutf 'Ali Khan. Most of the leading oil painters of the 19th century also worked in miniature, executing fine portraits of princes and courtiers dressed in voluminous patterned and fur-trimmed robes. A portrait (*c.* 1850–65; ex-Rothschild priv. col., see Robinson, 1985) attributed to Sani' al-Mulk is a penetrating, although unfinished, study of a bearded minister in a tall astrakhan cap; another (1846; see Robinson, 1985) by Mirza Baba al-Husayni depicts the corrupt vizier Hajji Mirza Aghasi in a white cloak set against an almost hallucinatory cloudy sky. One distinctive genre of single-page painting is the 'tourist picture'. Sir William Ouseley, the British Orientalist, was offered a large variety at Isfahan in 1811, and many were brought back by 19th-century travellers. They consist of well-executed representations of single figures wearing Persian costumes or depictions of trades set against a plain ground. They are similar in subject and presentation to contemporary Company paintings from India and rice-paper paintings from Canton and were produced for the same European clientele.

Lithography, which had been invented in Germany at the end of the 18th century, reached Iran some 40 years later; its capabilities of combining calligraphy, line drawings and decorative designs were exploited in numerous lithographed editions of the classics, popular fiction and translations from Western languages which were printed in Tehran and Tabriz from the 1840s onwards. The most prolific and competent illustrator was 'Aliquli Khuvayyi, whose illustrations for the works of Nizami (1848), al-Qazwini (1848) and Firdawsi (1850) are naive but often effective and sometimes display, intentionally or not, an impish sense of humour. The lithographic work of Sani' al-Mulk, however, is infinitely superior to that of his contemporaries. He produced a fine lithographed portrait of *Peter the Great* for a Persian translation (1846) of Voltaire's *Histoire de l'empire de Russie sous Pierre le Grand.* In 1861, at the behest of the Shah, Sani' al-Mulk began the publication of a government weekly newspaper, *Rūznāma-yi dawlati 'aliyya-i Īrān*, which continued publication for some years after his death in 1866. This was copiously illustrated by him with incisive and sometimes merciless portraits of princes, statesmen and generals and scenes of current happenings, all superbly drawn but sometimes poorly printed. Lithographed books continued to be published well into the 20th century, but none of their increasingly westernized illustrations approached the standard he set.

BIBLIOGRAPHY

J. de Rochechouart: *Souvenirs d'un voyage en Perse* (Paris, 1867), chap. xxiii
H. Massé: 'L'Imagerie populaire de l'Iran', *A. Asiat.*, vii (1960), pp. 163–78
Treasures of Persian Art after Islam: The Mahboubian Collection (exh. cat., Austin, U. TX, A. Mus., 1970)
B. W. Robinson: 'The Tehran Niẓāmī of 1848 and Other Qājar Lithographed Books', *Islam in the Balkans: Persian Art and Culture of the 18th and 19th Centuries*, ed. J. M. Scarce (Edinburgh, 1979), pp. 61–74
——: 'Lacquer, Oil-paintings and Later Arts of the Book', *Treasures of Islam* (exh. cat., ed. T. Falk; Geneva, Mus. A. & Hist., 1985), pp. 176–205

B. W. ROBINSON

(c) Western Central Asia. Under the patronage of the SHAYBANID dynasty (*reg* 1500–98) and in the first decades of the rule of their Tughay-Timurid successors (*reg* 1598–1753), artists in western Central Asia illustrated epics, histories and poetic manuscripts in a succession of styles derivative of Timurid and Safavid painting (*see* §§(v)(d) and (vi)(a) above). These books were produced in moderate quantity for local patrons, including members of the ruling élite, and, during the middle third of the 16th century, for export to the Indian subcontinent as well. In the last 60 years of the 17th century, artists increasingly followed Indian, probably Kashmiri, styles rather than Persian ones. In the 18th and 19th centuries local folk

styles were displaced by imported Kashmiri books, reflecting conquests in the Indian subcontinent by the Durrani kings of Afghanistan (*reg* 1747–1819).

The study of book production in western Central Asia during this period is complicated by an apparent shortage of artists and models. The shortage of artists meant that manuscripts were often illustrated many years after they were copied and dated. Many illustrations were added at Bukhara in the first half of the 16th century to manuscripts copied at Herat between 1490 and 1525; paintings were added by Muhammad Murad Samarqandi in the first quarter of the 17th century to a manuscript of the *Shāhnāma* ('Book of kings') copied for 'Ish Muhammad, the ruler of Khiva (1556–7; Tashkent, Orient. Inst. Lib.), and crude paintings following Persian styles of the late 16th century were added *c.* 1600 to a copy of Muhammad Salih's *Shaybānīnāma* ('Book of the Shaybanids'; 1510; Vienna, Österreich. Nbib., Cod. Mixt. 188). The shortage of models can be seen in the numerous copies of Sa'di's *Būstān* ('Orchard') and Jami's *Yusuf and Zulaykha* and *Subhat al-abrār* ('Rosary of the pious'), in which illustrations of the same episodes show little variation in composition from volume to volume. The retardataire nature of these works makes it difficult to construct a meaningful stylistic chronology.

Like the Safavid dynasty in Iran, the Shaybanids were heirs to the Timurid cultural tradition, and the paintings in the first important manuscript produced under their patronage—a copy of Muhammad Shadi's *Fathnāma* ('Book of conquests'; Tashkent, Orient. Inst. Lib., MS. 5369)—could easily be confused with the large-figure illustrations made in the mid-15th century at the Timurid capital of Samarkand, except that the book chronicles the exploits of the Uzbek Muhammad Shaybani Khan (*reg* 1500–10). Manuscripts illustrated in this old-fashioned style, such as a copy of Hatifi's *Khusraw and Shirin* (Oxford, Bodleian Lib., Ouseley MS. 19), have been documented to Samarkand and Tashkent. The style is thought to have been abandoned soon after the death of its main patron, Keldi Muhammad Sultan, ruler of Tashkent, in 1532–3.

A finer style of painting developed in Bukhara, where 'Ubaydallah Khan, ruler there from 1512 to 1539, took calligraphers, artists and manuscripts captured in raids on Herat between 1512 and 1536. Bukhara paintings of the first half of the 16th century reflect Herat models in two different ways. One group copied the styles and compositions used in Herat in the last decade of the 15th century. Several dated manuscripts of the 1520s, such as a copy of 'Assar's *Mihr and Mushtarī* (1523; Washington, DC, Freer, 32.5/8) attributed to Bukhara, have figures wearing costumes indistinguishable from those in Herat manuscripts painted 30 years earlier. The latest manuscript of this retardataire group is a copy of Sa'di's *Gulistān* ('Rosegarden'; Cologny, Bodmer Found.) transcribed by SULTAN 'ALI MASHHADI at Herat in 1500 but only illustrated for 'Ubaydallah Khan's son 'Abd al-'Aziz Sultan at Bukhara in 1547. The compositions and large figures in its paintings closely follow those in another copy of the *Gulistān* (A. Soudavar priv. col.) painted some 60 years earlier.

A second style of painting derived from Herat models can be associated specifically with the patronage of 'Abd al-'Aziz Sultan, who ruled in Bukhara from 1540 to 1549.

It is believed that this style was introduced by SHAYKH-ZADA, a disgruntled Safavid court artist who was perhaps the most outstanding student of the famous Herat artist Bihzad (Soudavar, 1992, pp. 189–97). Comparison of Shaykhzada's work in several manuscripts made for Sam Mirza, Safavid governor of Herat from 1522 to 1529, with the style used by 'Abd al-'Aziz's artists in Bukhara in the 1530s and 1540s reveals many similarities in the representation of unusually flat architectural motifs, ornate tile decoration, and female figures. Shaykhzada's presence at Bukhara in 1537–8 is documented by dedications alongside paintings in a copy of Hatifi's *Haft manzar* ('Seven countenances'; Washington, DC, Freer, 56.14). The artist may have arrived in Bukhara c. 1529 in the company of the calligrapher MIR 'ALI HUSAYNI HARAVI (*see also* §2(iv)(b) above), whose removal to Bukhara by 'Ubaydallah Khan is documented by the early 17th-century chronicler Qazi Ahmad. During the 1530s Shaykhzada must have trained Mahmud Muzahhib, 'Abdallah and Shaykhan [Shahm] ibn Mulla Yusuf al-Haravi, whose signed works are known from several manuscripts made for 'Abd al-'Aziz in the 1540s. These court artists produced scenes derivative of Herat models of the 1520s as well as studies of single figures and couples, a genre that they may have invented.

The Shaykhzada style practised in the workshop of 'Abd al-'Aziz Sultan in the 1540s was followed, with diminishing artistic results, until the end of the 16th century. A copy of the *Shāhnāma* (1564; Istanbul, Topkapı Pal. Lib.) made for 'Abdallah Khan, the *de facto* ruler of western Central Asia during the second half of the 16th century, has simple paintings with rolling hills dividing the picture horizontally and motifs abstracted from earlier Bukhara paintings which have been enlarged and centred in the compositions (İnal, 1974–5). Certain texts, such as Jami's *Tuhfat al-ahrār* ('Gift of the noble'), were popular in these years (e.g. 1548; Dublin, Chester Beatty Lib., Pers. MS. 215), with artists closely repeating compositions and stylistic features from one manuscript to another. In another type of manuscript, exemplified by a copy of Kashifi's book on ethics, *Akhlāq-i muhsinī* (London, BL, Orient. & India Office Lib.), large numbers of simple figures are depicted with little or no background and rarely have any relation with the text. After the death of 'Abd al-'Aziz Sultan royal patronage was curtailed in Bukhara, and some artists migrated to Golconda in the Deccan; manuscripts produced there, such as a copy of Hatifi's *Khusraw and Shirin* (1568; Bankipur, Patna, Khuda Bakhsh Lib.), maintain the figural types and costumes of contemporary Bukhara painting but use a different palette and are less finely painted.

In the early years of the 17th century Bukhara painting received a new infusion of Persian motifs as a direct result of the Shaybanid conquest of Khurasan and control of Herat and Mashhad from 1586 to 1598. Paintings produced in both cities served as models: a copy of the *Majālis al-'ushshāq* ('Conferences of lovers'; 1606; Tashkent, Orient. Inst. Lib.), made in Bukhara, repeats the tall figural style associated with Shahqasim, a calligrapher and painter in Herat, while a copy of Sharaf al-Din 'Ali Yazdi's *Zafarnāma* ('Book of victory'; 1628–9; Tashkent, Orient. Inst. Lib., MS. 4472) has the elaborate rock formations—

131. Muhammad Sharif: *Court Scene*; illustration from Sa'di: *Būstān* ('Orchard'), 1616 (Dublin, Chester Beatty Library and Gallery of Oriental Art, Pers. MS. 297, fol. 183*v*)

often outlined by smaller, whitish rocks—and prominent use of blue pigment typical of compositions painted in Mashhad some 40 years earlier. The gifted but eccentric artist Muhammad Murad Samarqandi (*fl* 1600–25) injected a satirical realism into his work of this period, as did his talented contemporary MUHAMMAD SHARIF (see fig. 131). The names and works of several court painters and calligraphers in Bukhara during the second half of the 17th century are cited in Muhammad Amin Bukhari's world history, *Muhīt al-tawārīkh*, and works by them are included in two copies of Nizami's *Khamsa* (1648, St Petersburg, Rus. N. Lib., MS. P.N.S. 66; 1668–71, Dublin, Chester Beatty Lib., Pers. MS. 276). They show a new awareness of Indian or Kashmiri painting in the depiction of landscape, but the costumes and facial characteristics still derive from Bukhara traditions. Book illustration apparently ended in Bukhara c. 1700, although a few illustrations in a crude folk style have been attributed to the 18th century. A large number of illustrated books were imported from Kashmir in the 19th century.

See also CENTRAL ASIA, §I, 4(vi)–(vii).

BIBLIOGRAPHY

Enc. Iran.: ''Abd Allāh'; 'Bukhara VI: The Bukharan School of Miniature Painting'

B. W. Robinson: 'An Unpublished Manuscript of the Gulistan of Sa'di', *Beiträge zur Kunstgeschichte Asiens: In Memoriam Ernst Diez*, ed. O. Aslanapa (Istanbul, 1963), pp. 223–36

G. İnal: 'Topkapı Sarayı Koleksiyonundaki Suntani bir Özbek Şehnamesi/A Royal Uzbeck Shahnameh in the Topkapı Palace Museum and its Significance for Uzbeck Painting', *Sanat Tarihi Yıllığı*, vi (1974–5), pp. 303–32 [Eng. summary]

B. W. Robinson: *Persian Painting in the India Office Library* (London, 1976)

M. M. Ashrafi-Aini: 'The School of Bukhara to *c.* 1550', *The Arts of the Book in Central Asia, 14th–16th Centuries*, ed. B. Gray (London and Paris, 1979), pp. 248–72

O. Galerkina: *Mawarannahr Book Painting* (Leningrad, 1980)

O. F. Akimushkin and A. A. Ivanov: 'Une Ecole artistique méconnue: Boxara au XVIIe siècle', *Art et société dans le monde iranien*, ed. C. Adle (Paris, 1982), pp. 127–39

M. S. Randhawa: 'Rare Bukhara Manuscript, "Raudat-ul-Muhibbin"', *A. & Islam. World*, i/4 (1983–4), pp. 7–10

R. Skelton: 'The Relationship between Mughal and Central Asian Painting in the Seventeenth Century', *Proceedings of the Second European Seminar on Central Asian Studies: London, 1987*

B. Schmitz: *Islamic Manuscripts in the New York Public Library* (New York, 1992), pp. 57–60

A. Soudavar: *Art of the Persian Court* (New York, 1992), pp. 101–9

BARBARA SCHMITZ

(d) Indian subcontinent.

Introduction. Under the patronage of the Mughal emperors (*reg* 1526–1858) a distinctive new idiom of book illustration emerged in the Indian subcontinent, in which the style of 15th-century Timurid illustration (*see* §(v)(d) above) was combined with indigenous traditions of representation and European ones known through the medium of prints. The Mughal style of painting was characterized by a new interest in naturalism and portraiture, which was used to great advantage in the illustration of albums and contemporary histories prepared for imperial patrons from the late 16th century to the late 17th. The Mughals, who claimed descent from the Timurid dynasty of Iran and western Central Asia, continued their ancestors' patronage of the arts of the book at the highest level, not only for the visual delight these books provided but also as an expression of dynastic power.

Mughal rulers amassed large libraries in which the great works from the libraries of their Iranian ancestors were found. For example, the copy of Firdawsi's *Shāhnāma* ('Book of kings'; *c.* 1440; London, Royal Asiat. Soc., Morley MS. 239), made for the Timurid prince Muhammad Juki, and the superb copy of Sharaf al-Din 'Ali Yazdi's history of Timur, the *Zafarnāma* ('Book of victory'; 1467–8; Baltimore, MD, Johns Hopkins U., Garrett Lib.), made for the Timurid prince Husayn Bayqara, bear the stamps of the Mughal emperors on the flyleaves. These libraries also functioned as workshops, and, in contrast to Persian manuscript painting, much information about individual artists has been preserved through signatures, marginal attributions and contemporary descriptions of workshop practice.

The few surviving paintings from the reign of Humayun (*reg* 1530–56 with interruption) show a deep indebtedness to Persian models (*see also* INDIAN SUBCONTINENT, §VI, 4(i)(a)). In 1540 the Emperor was forced into exile at the court of the Safavid ruler Tahmasp I, who was beginning to lose interest in the patronage of painting just at this time. In 1555, when Humayun regained his throne, such Iranian painters as 'ABD AL-SAMAD and MIR SAYYID 'ALI formed the core of the new imperial workshop at Delhi and brought with them the latest developments in book painting as practised at Tabriz, Qazvin and Bukhara. The impact of the Persian tradition can be seen in the fine calligraphy, rich decoration, margins with figural paintings in gold, painted and varnished bindings and the assemblage of albums.

Painting in the reign of Akbar (reg 1556–1605). A distinct Mughal style of painting developed during the reign of Akbar (*see also* INDIAN SUBCONTINENT, §VI, 4(i)(b)), who assembled a huge workshop that followed him as he moved among his capitals at Delhi, Fatehpur Sikri (1569–85) and Lahore (1585–98). One of the workshop's first projects was to refurbish an earlier copy of the *Tūtīnāma* ('Tales of a parrot'; Cleveland, OH, Mus. A., 62.279) in the 1560s. The 218 splendid illustrations combine features seen in several of the local styles of the pre-Mughal period and reflect not only the complicated history of the manuscript but also the regions from which the artists of the imperial workshop had been assembled. The other major project begun early in Akbar's reign was a 14-volume copy of the *Ḥamzanāma* ('Tales of Hamza'; *c.* 1562–77; *see* INDIAN SUBCONTINENT, fig. 259). This 15-year project was begun under the direction of Mir Sayyid 'Ali and completed under 'Abd al-Samad. The manuscript originally comprised 1400 large paintings on cotton; they depict the legendary exploits of Hamza, an uncle of the Prophet Muhammad. The surviving paintings, although widely varied in quality, show the early Mughal style. It is still strongly derived from Persian models, but the decorative patterning of Persian illustration has given way to naturalism, realistic depiction of space, clear presentation of narrative and interest in portraiture. This last may have been introduced to Indian painting via European prints and representations, but the large forms and bold palette are distinctively Indian. This coherent Mughal style is clearly seen in the illustrations to the first de luxe manuscript to survive intact from Akbar's workshop: a copy of Kashifi's Persian version of the *Kalila and Dimna* animal fables, *Anvār-i Suhaylī* ('Lights of Canopus'; 1570; U. London, SOAS, Lib., MS. 10102).

In the 1580s, after the completion of the *Ḥamzanāma*, artists began to illustrate different types of manuscripts. Some were translations of Sanskrit texts into Persian, the court language. A copy of the *Razmnāma* ('Book of wars'; Jaipur, Maharaja Sawai Man Singh II Mus., MS. AG. 1683–1850), made between 1582 and 1586, is a translation of the *Mahābhārata*. Other illustrated manuscripts chronicled the life of Akbar and his ancestors. These historical works include a copy of the *Tīmūrnāma* ('History of Timur'; *c.* 1584; Bankipur, Patna, Khuda Bakhsh Lib.), several copies of the *Bāburnāma*, the memoirs of Akbar's grandfather (e.g. London, BL, Or. MS. 3714, and Baltimore, MD, Walters A.G., W. 596), and two copies of the *Akbarnāma*, the emperor's biography completed in two volumes by the court historian Abu'l-Fazl in 1596 and 1598 (*c.* 1590, London, V&A, IS. 2–1896; *c.* 1596–7, Dublin, Chester Beatty Lib., Ind. MS. 3, London, BL, Or. MS. 12988 and dispersed; *see* INDIAN SUBCONTINENT, figs 262 and 263). These manuscripts are characterized by their full-page illustrations, with images exploding from the traditional boundaries of the text block to encompass the entire page. To create such a large number of images in such a short time, production was organized in teams, with different artists responsible for outlines, colour, finishing touches, faces etc. In some cases, particularly the first *Akbarnāma*, paintings prepared for earlier manuscripts were removed and pasted into new ones. In these paintings, which are among the most advanced projects of the imperial workshop in the 1590s, established masters and novices worked together to achieve compositional clarity and spaciousness. Akbar's workshop also produced luxury copies of the Persian classics, exemplified by a copy of the *Dīvān* (collected poetry) of the 12th-century Persian poet Anvari (1588; Cambridge, MA, Sackler Mus., 1960.117.15). This pocket-sized volume on the finest thin paper has 15 illustrations, each apparently executed by a single artist. The illustrations show superb technical control of volume, spatial recession and colouring, and contain penetrating portraits of individuals and groups.

Works were also produced for the nobility and members of the merchant class in either the imperial or independent workshops. A copy of the *Kitāb-i sā'at* ('Book of hours'), for example, was written for Mirza 'Aziz Koka, Akbar's foster-brother, at Hajipur near Patna in 1583. Its paintings so closely resemble those in a second copy of the *Ṭūṭīnāma* (Dublin, Chester Beatty Lib., Ind. MS. 21), which was made c. 1580 for Akbar, that imperial artists must have been responsible. Other illustrated works for this patron are entirely different in style and must be the work of other artists. At least one patron, 'Abd al-Rahim Khan-i Khanan (1561–1626/7), who was commander-in-chief of the Mughal armies under Akbar and Jahangir, was a major patron of books and supported his own private workshop. He had a splendid copy of the Sanskrit epic *Rāmāyaṇa* (Washington, DC, Freer, 07.271) prepared between 1597 and 1605 in imitation of the one Akbar had ordered. Such works, often called Sub-imperial, generally follow the subject-matter and style of imperial painting but use the simpler compositional patterns and brighter colours of traditional Indian painting (see INDIAN SUBCONTINENT, §VI, 4(ii)). A more Persianate style was used for the illustration of the Persian classics, such as a copy of the *Khamsa* ('Five poems') of Khusraw Dihlavi (Berlin, Staatsbib. Preuss. Kultbes., Orientabt. 1278), refurbished in 'Abd al-Rahim's workshop between 1603 and 1617. Styles of painting apparently depended on the subjects illustrated. Commercial production during the period is exemplified by numerous copies of the *Shāhnāma* (e.g. 1601; New York, Met., 13.228.22). They have small illustrations, with crude, oversized figures set on simple grounds.

A parallel but independent style of painting developed in the Deccan (see INDIAN SUBCONTINENT, §VI, 4(vi)), where independent Muslim states had close ties with Iran and lands to the west. Many of the works identified as Deccani are single paintings and portraits destined for albums. One of the earliest dated manuscripts is a copy of the *Nujūm al-'ulūm* ('Stars of the sciences'; 1570–71; Dublin, Chester Beatty Lib., Ind. MS. 2) made in Bijapur and illustrated with 876 paintings in a charming but naive style when compared with contemporary Mughal works. A more Persianate style was used at Golconda, to judge from a late 16th-century copy of the *Kulliyyāt* ('Collected

works') of Sultan Muhammad Quli Qutb Shah (Hyderabad, Salar Jung Mus.). These Deccani styles developed and flourished during the following century.

Painting in the reign of Jahangir (reg 1605–27). Akbar's son Salim, who reigned as Jahangir, developed a deep and lively interest in the arts of the book before his accession and was an acute connoisseur of the hands of individual artists. His preference for small books with fewer but finer illustrations is seen in a copy of the *Dīvān* of Najm al-Din Hasan Dihlavi (1602; Baltimore, MD, Walters A.G., W. 650). Under Jahangir the imperial workshop was reduced in size, thereby freeing lesser painters to seek work elsewhere. Painters became more specialized: such artists as MANOHAR, DAULAT and BISHAN DAS did portraits, ABU'L HASAN large court scenes and MANSUR natural history subjects. These individual works were often bound into albums, which are one of the most characteristic products of the imperial workshop at this time. Two large albums survive: the Gulshan Album (Tehran, Gulistan Pal. Lib., MS. 1663/64) contains work dated from 1599 to 1609, and the Berlin Album (Berlin, Staatsbib. Preuss. Kultbes., Orientabt., MS. A.117) contains work dated from 1608 to 1618. The albums were assembled with double spreads of calligraphy and painting contained within elaborate painted and gilded borders. The calligraphic examples, largely from the 15th and 16th centuries by SULTAN 'ALI MASHHADI and MIR 'ALI HUSAYNI HARAVI, have borders with a variety of European and Indian figures and scenes. The paintings comprise Persian works, earlier Mughal paintings, contemporary portraits of court figures, a few Deccani paintings and European prints and paintings with Mughal versions and copies of them. The portraits show a warmth and perspicacity that make them among the finest paintings of the period.

Painting in the reign of Shah Jahan (reg 1628–58). During the reign of Shah Jahan (*see also* INDIAN SUBCONTINENT, §VI, 4(i)(d)), Jahangir's son and successor, the imperial workshop became even smaller, as the patron was not particularly interested in illustrated works of literature, although a few illustrated copies of Sa'di's Persian classics were refurbished or prepared. The greatest paintings of the period are associated with the *Pādshāhnāma* ('History of the emperor'; *see* INDIAN SUBCONTINENT, fig. 268). The single extant volume (1657–8; Windsor Castle, Royal Lib., MS. HB.149), copied by Muhammad 'Amin Mashhadi, retains 44 full-page images, most of them illustrating the first decade of Shah Jahan's reign. The emphasis in the paintings, as in the text, is on such major events as darbars (royal receptions), battles and state occasions, which are filled with meticulous profile portraits of Shah Jahan and his courtiers, probably produced from studies kept on file. Approximately a dozen dispersed paintings are so close in size and style to those of the Windsor volume that they must have been intended for it or other volumes of the text. Many of the Windsor paintings, which are attributable to such major painters as BALCHAND, BICHITR, 'ABID and PAYAG, seem to have been made close to the time of the events depicted for an earlier version of the text that was never completed. Technically among the most brilliant of Mughal paintings, with a complete assimilation of European perspective and landscape devices, these static and stylized images lack the warmth of portraits produced earlier under Jahangir. Fine paintings were also made for albums, such as the Minto Album (Dublin, Chester Beatty Lib., Ind. MS. 7; London, V&A, IM. 8–1925 to 28–1925). Portraits in early albums were usually mounted within illuminated borders decorated with a pattern of animals and flowers outlined in gold, while those in the Late Shah Jahan Album (dispersed) have borders with figures echoing those in the main composition.

Later developments, 1658–c.1900. The great age of imperial patronage was brought to an end with Aurangzeb (*reg* 1658–1707; *see also* INDIAN SUBCONTINENT, §VI, 4(i)(e)). As artists retreated from realism, reverted to more traditional concepts of composition and produced simplified, rather lifeless portraits, book illustration reached a technical and stylistic plateau. In 1680 painting and music were banned from the court. After the ruler's death, fine paintings and manuscripts were again produced for the court but on a limited scale (*see also* INDIAN SUBCONTINENT, §VI, 4(i)(f)). One example is the dedication copy of the *Kārnāma-i 'ishq* ('Book of affairs of love'; London, BL, Orient. & India Office Lib., Johnson Album), a romantic tale composed in Persian in 1731 by Rai Anand Ram, known as 'Mukhlis', which was dedicated to Muhammad Shah (*reg* 1719–48). The 37 paintings, done by Govardhan between 1733 and 1738, combine the sureness of 17th-century technique with a new hardness of line and coolness of colour. This brief revival was cut short in 1739 when Nadir Shah (*reg* 1736–47) sacked Delhi and carried off the imperial treasures, including such fine manuscripts as the Gulshan Album. Many of the remaining artists moved to independent states in the Deccan, Bengal and Avadh, where few if any books were illustrated in the traditional style. During the twilight of the Mughal empire in the early 19th century several illustrated copies of the histories of Shah Jahan were made, apparently as presents for Europeans who were fascinated by the pomp and state of the Mughals and their buildings. Copies of the *Pādshāhnāma* (London, BL, Add. MS. 20734, and Bankipur, Patna, Khuda Bakhsh Lib.) have about 30 paintings depicting great architectural monuments commissioned by Shah Jahan, such as the Taj Mahal and the Red Fort. Later manuscripts of this type, for example a copy of the *'Amal-i ṣāliḥ* (*c.* 1830; London, BL, Or. MS. 2157), a history of Shah Jahan by Muhammad Salih Kanbu, even depict Europeans admiring the Mughal monuments.

A distinctive style of illustrated books is identified with the region of Kashmir in the north (*see* INDIAN SUBCONTINENT, §VI, 4(viii)). These small paintings are enclosed by the text and have simple compositions, often depicting a group of people in front of a pavilion set in a landscape. A copy of the *Shāhnāma* (1719; London, BL, Add. MS. 18804) has been identified as an early example of the style that flourished in the 18th and 19th centuries. Such manuscripts as a *Dīvān* of Hafiz (*c.* 1796; London, BL, Add. MS. 7763) are characterized by extremely fine paper, burnished and sprinkled with gold, lavish floral borders in gold, blue and pink, and busy but naive compositions. This style had a direct impact on the arts of the book in

western Central Asia, as Kashmiri illustrated books were increasingly exported there during the 18th and 19th centuries (*see* §(vi)(c) above).

See INDIAN SUBCONTINENT, §VI, 4 for a fuller discussion and bibliographies.   □

(e) Ottoman empire. The interest of the early Ottoman sultans in the arts of the illustrated manuscript (*see* §(v)(f) above) developed greatly after their conquest of Constantinople (now Istanbul) in 1453. A palace scriptorium was established there in the late 15th century or early 16th, and production flourished into the 17th century. Initially derived from Iranian illustrated and decorated models, the Ottoman tradition developed a distinct character with the incorporation of European traditions such as topographical illustration. In contrast to Iran, where virtually all illustrated manuscripts were epic and literary works, those produced for the Ottoman sultans were largely accounts of contemporary and dynastic history couched in traditional poetic forms. As in Iran, exquisite albums with leaves of portraits, flower paintings and fine calligraphy were also produced.

16th century and early 17th. The value of the materials required for the production of fine manuscripts—paper, fine leathers, precious pigments and gold—and the urgency of imperial demand led, as in contemporary Iran and the Indian subcontinent, to a concentration of calligraphers, marginators, illustrators, illuminators and binders in a palace scriptorium. In Ottoman Turkey this institution is generally known as the *nakkaşhane* (from Pers. *naqqāsh*: 'artist, painter, illuminator, decorator'), although in its early years the term was rarely used. The origins of the institution can be traced to the reign of Bayezid II (*reg* 1481–1512), when artists from the Aqqoyunlu workshops at Tabriz in Iran were recruited for work in Istanbul. Some of these craftsmen advanced to high rank, and the expertise they brought must have influenced not only the organization of the studio but also the style and repertory of the images made there. The corporate nature of their work makes it hazardous to attribute images to specific individuals; painters' signatures in fine manuscripts made for the Ottoman court before the later 16th century are far rarer than those of calligraphers. Shah Mansur Tabrizi, a chief artist (Ott. *ser-nakkaşan*) in a list of painters conscripted from Tabriz following the victory of Selim I over the Safavids at Chaldiran in September 1514 (Istanbul, Topkapı Pal. Lib., D.10734), is not known by any signed work at the Ottoman court, but SHAHQULI (Şahkulu), who appears in the same list, was head of the 'Rumi' painters and chief artist by the time of his death (*c.* 1556). His long residence at the Ottoman court, however, has left only one or two signed works (e.g. a line drawing of a dragon; Istanbul, Topkapı Pal. Lib., H. 2154, fol. 2*r*).

Many of the images produced for Ottoman manuscripts are of types long established in the Persian manuscript tradition, such as enthronements, hunts and battles, but the Ottoman interest in the illustration of contemporary history led to the development of several distinct new genres of illustration. The most striking and novel genre in 16th-century Ottoman painting is the campaign journal.

Credit for its invention is due to a talented amateur, MATRAKÇI NASUH, whose first and most remarkable exercise in the genre is the *Beyān-i menāzil-i sefer-i 'Irākeyn-i Sultān Süleymān Khān* ('Description of the stages of the campaign of Sultan Süleyman Khan in the two Iraqs'; ?1537–8; Istanbul, U. Lib., T. 5964), an account of Süleyman's campaign against the Safavids in 1534–5. Executed by divers hands and mostly by painters unschooled in the court style, the illustrations show the towns through which the Sultan passed and the shrines he visited. They draw upon such varied sources as Venetian bird's-eye views, engineers' siege-plans, shrines depicted in guides for pilgrims to the holy places of Islam and direct observation. Later works by Nasuh—such as the *Tārīkh-i Sultān Bāyazīd* ('History of Sultan Bayezid'; c. 1540; Istanbul, Topkapı Pal. Lib., R. 1272), about the campaigns of Bayezid II in the eastern Mediterranean in 1499, and the *Tārīkh-i fath-i Şikloş ve Ustūrgūn ve Ustunibelgirād* (c. 1545; Istanbul, Topkapı Pal. Lib., H. 1608), about the Ottoman campaigns of 1543–4 at sea and on land—drew on images of Mediterranean ports from the sea by European prisoners or renegade siege engineers, as well as Hungarian topographical material. Estimates of Nasuh's own contribution to the illustration of his works have varied, but topography remained an important Ottoman preoccupation and can be seen in the liberal use of Venetian cartographic prints, which circulated widely in the Ottoman empire. A conspicuous example is the double-page view of the fortress of Szigetvár in Hungary in Ahmed Feridun's *Nuzhat asrār al-akhbār dar safar-i sigitvār* (chronicle of the Szigetvár campaign; 1568–9; Istanbul, Topkapı Pal. Lib., H. 1339, fols 32v–33r), which is based directly on a print by the Venetian cartographer and draughtsman Domenico Zenoi or Zenoni.

Ottoman topographical illustration was also advanced by the work of another amateur, the corsair Piri Reis (d 1552). The surviving third of his famous map of 1513 (Istanbul, Topkapı Pal. Lib., R. 1633 *mük*) is partly based on maps used by Columbus and shows the Americas; it bears illustrative vignettes most reminiscent of the 'Catalan' atlases of the late 14th century and 15th. The principal work of Piri Reis was the *Kitāb-i bahrīye* ('Book of the mariner'), an atlas of the Mediterranean with town views based largely on Italian *isolarii* ('island books'). The presentation copy (Istanbul, Topkapı Pal. Lib., R. 642) is dated 1525–6. The book became widely popular in the 16th and 17th centuries, not only as a practical guide for mariners but also in larger formats, often with additional views of cities and ports to which the text makes no reference. This tradition of topographical illustration had little direct impact on the illustrated Ottoman chronicles of the later 16th century: the increasing role of the official court historian (Ott. *şāhnāmagū*, Turk. *şahnameci*) as panegyrist led to the decay of the illustrated campaign journal.

The historian Çelebi 'Arif (d 1561–2), known as 'Arifi, was of Iranian origin and seems to have arrived at the Ottoman court c. 1545. He was appointed court historian and set about writing a five-volume history of the Ottoman dynasty in Persian, the *Shāhnāma-yi āl-yi 'Uthmān* ('Book of kings of the Ottoman house'), in the metre of Firdawsi's classic *Shāhnāma* ('Book of kings'). The presentation copy of the fifth volume, the *Sulaymānnāma* ('Book of Süleyman'; 1558; Istanbul, Topkapı Pal. Lib., H. 1517), is the first important panegyric history of Süleyman's reign. It is a lavishly illustrated chronicle, with 617 folios of fine gold-speckled and polished paper, excellent *nasta'līq* calligraphy (*see* §2(iv)(b) above) by 'Ali ibn Amir Beg Shirvani, exquisite illumination and 69 large illustrations (including four double spreads; see fig. 132). Most of the pictorial and spatial formulae of contemporary Persian book illustration are retained, but these images are distinguishable by the distinctive Ottoman headgear worn by many of the figures and the introduction of European perspective in views of such cities as Belgrade (fol. 108v) or Temesvár (now Timişoara) (fol. 533r). The *Sulaymānnāma* project was plainly important for the reorganization of the court scriptorium, which had been preoccupied with the production of the fine manuscripts of the Koran endowed to the Süleymaniye Mosque (inaugurated in 1557), and it must have been necessary to bring in illustrators from outside. The office of court historian and the newly reorganized scriptorium must therefore be seen as consecutive, rather than parallel, developments. Without a strong central organization it is unlikely that so many grand illustrated manuscripts could ever have been produced, and it is striking how many of the panegyric histories concern the reign of Süleyman I, either as contemporary chronicles or as immediate reminiscences.

The scriptorium reached its peak of productivity in the reign of Murad III (reg 1574–95), when the historian Lokman cooperated with the chief artist (Ott. *nakkāşbāşı*) OSMAN in the writing and illustrating of histories and genealogical works. Lokman consistently alternated panegyrics of his patron with rehearsals of the exploits of Süleyman in several works, including another history of Süleyman, the *Sulaymānnāma* (1579; Dublin, Chester Beatty Lib., MS. 413), the first volume of the *Shāhanshāhnāma* ('Book of the king of kings'; 1581–2; Istanbul, U. Lib., F. 1404) with 58 paintings, and the two volumes of the *Hunarnāma* ('Book of achievements'; Istanbul, Topkapı Pal. Lib., H. 1523 and H. 1524) completed respectively in 1584–5 and 1588 with 112 paintings. Osman's participation is recorded in the preface to the first volume of the *Hunarnāma*, although he may have been appointed under Selim II (reg 1566–74). Other historical works associated with Lokman and Osman include the *Shāhnāma-yi Salīm Khān* ('Book of kings of Selim II'; Jan 1581; Istanbul, Topkapı Pal. Lib., A. 3595) with 44 paintings and the presentation copy of Mustafa 'Ali's *Nuṣratnāma* ('Book of victories'; 1584–5; Istanbul, Topkapı Pal. Lib., H. 1365) recording the campaigns of Lala Mustafa Pasha in Iran and Transcaucasia in the late 1570s.

The pictorial repertory in these works is largely conventional—enthronements, feasts, receptions of ambassadors, processions, hunts, campaigns on land or at sea—but other subjects, such as the sultan's public works, are introduced. A series of double-page illustrations in the first volume of the *Hunarnāma* shows, for example, the successive courtyards of the Topkapı Palace, the innermost court (fols 23v–32r) also showing the harem but with its façades discreetly blank. The general aim of these illustrations was legibility rather than graphic accuracy. The elaborate processions in the Hippodrome in Istanbul depicted in the *Sūrnāma-i*

132. *Battle of Mohács*, each folio 365×254 mm; double-page illustration from 'Arifi: *Sulaymānnāma* ('Book of Süleyman'), 1558 (Istanbul, Topkapı Palace Library, H. 1517, fols 219*v*–220*r*)

humāyūn ('Imperial book of festivals'; *c.* 1583; Istanbul, Topkapı Pal. Lib., H. 1344; see fig. 191 below) are given an almost diagrammatic clarity, markedly different from the complex, much more naturalistic scenes of the same events as depicted in the second volume of the *Shāhanshāhnāma* (Istanbul, Topkapı Pal. Lib., B. 200). It bears the date November 1592, showing that Osman must have had a good deal to do with it, although it was completed only in 1597–8, after his dismissal.

A collection of portraits of the Ottoman sultans, the *Qiyāfat al-Insānīya* or *Shamā'ilnāma*, which was composed by Lokman in 1579 and illustrated under the supervision of Osman, shows that portraiture was a persistent interest of Ottoman painting. Its origins can be traced back a century to the well-documented interest of Mehmed II in European portraiture. A portrait bust showing him in old age (Istanbul, Topkapı Pal. Lib., H. 2153, fol. 145*v*) is closely related to the portrait medal of him, the second state of which is dated 1481, by COSTANZO DA FERRARA, based on sketches he must have made in Istanbul in the early 1470s. A large-format line-and-wash portrait in the same album (fol. 10*r*), showing him as a much younger man, has speculatively been attributed to Sinan Beg, a painter claimed by Mustafa 'Ali to have been of Venetian birth, though there is no evidence for this. The brushwork, modelling and use of wash have no parallels in Islamic art, but neither in style nor in technique can the portrait be described as northern Italian. By the mid-16th century,

HAYDAR RA'IS's portraits of Ottoman sultans and court officials are distinguished by their vivid colours and dramatic use of dark grounds. Lokman acknowledged help in producing faithful likenesses (little interest is shown in conveying character) from portraits by south German painters, which must also have included prints of the sultans' portraits collected by Paolo Giovo and supplied to the Grand Vizier SOKOLLU MEHMED PASHA. The earliest copy of the *Shamā'ilnāma* (Istanbul, U. Lib., T.'7), presented to Murad III with Osman's illustrations, is dated 1579–80, but there are various slightly later copies, possibly made as gifts for foreign ambassadors. The *Shamā'ilnāma* illustrations were also the prototypes for the royal portraits in later 16th-century illustrated genealogical works, such as one made for the Grand Vizier Siyavuş Pasha (1585–6; Istanbul, Topkapı Pal. Lib., H. 1321).

The final project of the reign of Murad III was a six-volume copy of the *Siyar-i Nabī* ('Life of the Prophet'), Mustafa Darir's biography of the Prophet Muhammad composed in the late 14th century. Of the original six volumes, four survive more or less intact (Dublin, Chester Beatty Lib., Turk. MS. 419; Istanbul, Topkapı Pal. Lib., H. 1221–3; New York, Pub. Lib., Spencer MS. 157), one is fragmentary and the other survives only as scattered pages. The 814 illustrations seem to have been supervised by NAKKAS HASAN, later the chief artist of Mehmed III. Hasan evidently worked on volume i and on some of volume vi (dated 1594–5); his portrait appears above the colophon of the *Shāhnāma* of Mehmed III (Istanbul, Topkapı Pal. Lib., H. 1209). The artists were apparently unfamiliar with earlier illustrations relating to the life of Muhammad. Although many of the illustrations are repetitive, even slapdash, the limited expressiveness of Ottoman historical illustration is here replaced by striking colourism and expressionistic stylization (see fig. 133). In many respects the *Siyar-i Nabī* shows Ottoman painting at its most original. Unfortunately this great work had no sequel, perhaps because the project dragged on and on. When Mehmed III acceded to the throne in 1595, Lokman and Osman and his staff were all dismissed, allegedly for their lack of productivity, but that could simply have reflected the absence of surplus capacity in the scriptorium.

The production of non-figural illumination at the scriptorium was no less important than that of figural painting, but its study is complicated by the widespread and persistent use of stencils and the extreme rarity of illuminators' signatures. The evolution of Ottoman illumination owes much to later versions of the international Timurid style as practised at Tabriz. Only two illuminators' names are known from the earlier 16th century: Bayram ibn Derviş Şir in a manuscript of the Koran (1523–4; Istanbul, Topkapı Pal. Lib., E.H. 58) and Mehmed ibn Ilyas in

another copy of the Koran (1547–8; Istanbul, Topkapı Pal. Lib., Koğuşlar 23). The most important innovator, however, was KARA MEMI, some of whose earliest work dated 1554–5 appears in a refurbished manuscript of the Koran (Istanbul, Topkapı Pal. Lib., E.H. 49) attributed to 'Abdallah Sayrafi (*fl* 1310–44; *see* §2(iii)(c) above). Kara Memi's masterpiece is a copy of the *Dīvān* (collected poetry) of Süleyman I (*reg* 1520–66), who wrote under the pen-name Muhibbi (1566; Istanbul, U. Lib., T. 5647). It has exquisite naturalistic floral motifs within the text block and in the margins.

Another important duty of the palace scriptorium was to prepare pages of calligraphy, paintings and drawings for mixed albums offered to the sultans on the great feasts of the Muslim year. With the exception of an album of Ahmed I (*reg* 1603–17; Istanbul, Topkapı Pal. Lib., B. 408), these were generally small in format and, at least by the 17th century, often incorporated earlier material. In addition to such genre scenes as grooms with horses, camel fights or elegantly dressed male or female figures, Ottoman painters of the 16th century excelled in line-and-wash pictures of angel figures or dragons in foliage. Conscious adaptations of Aqqoyunlu and Safavid types, these paintings are distinguished by their greater simplicity of composition and heavier modelling. Wholly original, however, are studies of foliage and composite blossoms in which animal motifs are relatively inconspicuous. The basic element is a long, feathery leaf (*saz*: 'reed', but other senses have been suggested), although chinoiserie elements may be present. The *saz* style reached its apogee under Murad III, for example in an album compiled for the future Sultan in 1572–3 (Vienna, Österreich. Nbib., Cod. Mixt. 313), in which *saz* leaves have even been treated as repeating borders. These compositions were adapted to tilework and textiles, but it is difficult to see any of them as actual cartoons for other media.

The most prominent of the later 16th-century painters associated with these album leaves is VELI CAN; he worked for Murad III, and many album pages (e.g. Istanbul, Topkapı Pal. Lib., H. 2162, fol. 8*v*) are, more or less speculatively, attributed to him. To judge from these, he was primarily interested in figural subjects. Pages executed for 17th-century Ottoman palace albums increasingly show that artists were aware of contemporary Safavid drawing at Isfahan, particularly by the successors of Riza (*see* §(vi)(a) above), but often with a seriously weakened effect.

By the early 17th century the albums prepared for presentation to the sultan had attracted attention outside the palace, especially from foreigners in Istanbul, and bazaar artists made numerous low-quality collections of images depicting costumes and picturesque scenes, such as strangely dressed dervishes, Turkish baths, executions, tortures, low women and the Bagnio where the galley-slaves were chained. Few if any of these appear to be signed, but the earliest dated album of this type, the *Dürr-i Şāhvār* ('Royal pearl'; Geneva, priv. col., see 1985 exh. cat., no. 108), a verse anthology illustrated with costumed figures, was made in 1589, perhaps for Murad III.

Other types of manuscripts include astrological works, such as a copy of the *Maṭāli' al-sa'āda* ('Rising of auspicious constellations'; 1582–3; Paris, Bib. N., MS. supp. turc 242)

133. *First Revelation to Muhammad on Mt Hira*, 220×175 mm; illustration from Mustafa Darir: *Siyar-i Nabī* ('Life of the Prophet'), *c.* 1594–5 (Istanbul, Topkapı Palace Library, H. 1222, fol. 155*r*)

made for Fatma Sultan, a daughter of Murad III. The prototypes from which they were copied determined their style. With these can be associated two manuscripts of a work on numerology, the *Tarjuma-i Miftāḥ-i jafr-i jāmi'* ('Translation of the Key to general divination'; Istanbul, Topkapı Pal. Lib., B. 373; Istanbul, U. Lib., T. 6624), ordered by Mehmed III (*reg* 1595–1603) but executed under his successor, Ahmed I (*reg* 1603–17). A sumptuous large-format copy of the *Fālnāma* ('Book of divination'; Istanbul, Topkapı Pal. Lib., R. 1703), in rather similar style, was ordered by Kalendar Pasha, Master of the Works to Ahmed I. Genealogical works are often difficult to distinguish precisely from historical ones since such earlier historical works as 'Arifi's *Sulaymānnāma*, dealing with contemporary subjects, were evidently conceived as parts of larger works going back to the origins of the Ottoman dynasty, if not to the Creation itself. The illustrations to a copy of the *Zubdat al-tavārīkh* ('Cream of histories'; 1583–4; Istanbul, Mus. Turk. & Islam. A., 1973) are markedly different in style from those of the illustrated histories of the same decade. Although more innovative in theme, the representations of biblical patriarchs and Koranic prophets are closer to the magical than to the historical manuscripts in style.

In the late 16th century and 17th there was a vogue for long verse or prose romances, based partly on the *Shāhnāma* but also on other oral or written sources, with rather stiff and simplified illustrations. The works include a copy of the *Qissa-yi Farrūkhrūz* ('Story of Ferruhruz'; London, BL, Or. MS. 3298), with a dedication to Murad III on fol. 36*v*; a copy of the *Dastān-i Farrūkh u Hūmā* ('Tale of Ferruh and Huma'; 1601–2; Istanbul, U. Lib., T. 1975); and a copy of Faramarz ibn Khudadad Arrajani's *Qissa-yi Shahr u Shatrān* ('Story of Şahr and Şatran'; 1648; Istanbul, U. Lib., T. 9303). A copy of a Turkish translation of Firdawsi's *Shāhnāma* was illustrated *c.* 1620 by AHMED NAKŞÎ (New York, Pub. Lib., Spencer MS. 1). There are also numerous Ottoman copies of al-Qazwini's *'Ajā'ib al-makhlūqāt* ('Wonders of creation'), often with mediocre illustrations and attributable to provincial centres. The text is usually the Persian version, but Sururi's abridged Turkish version may well be the one used in the copy (Istanbul, Topkapı Pal. Lib., A. 3632) made for Şehzade Mustafa, the son of Süleyman I, which was left unfinished at his execution in 1553.

Although Istanbul was the primary centre of manuscript production in the 16th and 17th centuries, a few manuscripts were illustrated elsewhere in the Ottoman empire. Illustrated manuscripts do not appear to have been produced in the Balkans except at Edirne, which may have been an important centre, but whatever evidence existed was lost when the palace and library there were destroyed in the 19th century. In Syria, Mustafa 'Ali succeeded in having the first copy of his *Nuṣratnāma* illustrated at Aleppo (1582; London, BL, Add. MS. 22011); the presentation copy made for Murad III in Istanbul was based on it (see above). To judge from the blanks, Mustafa 'Ali also intended to have another historical work illustrated, *Jāmi' al-hubūr der majālis-i sūr* (an account of the circumcision ceremonies; 1582–6; Istanbul, Topkapı Pal. Lib., B. 203), evidently in Baghdad, where he was subsequently transferred. That project was abandoned, but Baghdad,

particularly between 1598 and 1602 when Hasan, who had been the chief artist of Mehmed III, was governor there, is associated with a series of illustrated Shi'ite pietistic works, such as Fuzuli's martyrology, the *Hadīqat al-su'adā* ('The garden of the blessed') and Lami'i Çelebi's *Maqtal-i āl-i Rasūl* ('The killing of the family of the Prophet'). They are, however, markedly like Shiraz manuscripts in style and have little in common with the *Siyar-i Nabī* in which Hasan himself played such an important role. A copy of 'Ali Çelebi's *Humayūnnāma* ('a version of the Kalila and Dimna fables'; 1566–7; Istanbul, Topkapı Pal. Lib., H. 359) was made in Cairo, doubtless a commission from an Ottoman governor; a second copy (London, BL, Add. MS. 15153) may also have been made there in 1588–9. Illustrated hagiographical works from the early 17th century on the life of Jalal al-Din Rumi also suggest that Mevlevi dervish lodges at Konya and elsewhere may have patronized the arts of the book, with or without the stimulus of the sultans.

Later 17th century and 18th. Very little is known about Ottoman painting between the death of Osman II in 1622 and the early 18th century. Virtual facsimile copies of earlier illustrated manuscripts were produced, such as a *Salīmnāma* (1687–8; London, BL, Or. MS. 7043), which is closely related to Lokman's *Shāhnāma-yi Salīm Khan* of 1581, and a volume of the *Siyar-i Nabī* (*c.* 1700; Istanbul, Mus. Turk. & Islam. A., MS. 1974). There was a notable, although short-lived, revival of figural painting in the early 18th century under Ahmed III (*reg* 1703–30; *see* OTTOMAN, §II, (5)), not merely in the exquisite fashion-plates and portraits by LEVNI, his chief artist, but also in the animated compositions of his unfinished presentation copy of the *Sūrnāma-i Vehbī*, Vehbi's account of the circumcision festivities of 1720. Levni's portraits of Ahmed III (e.g. in a *Silsilanāma*; *c.* 1720; Istanbul, Topkapı Pal. Lib., A. 3109) are in traditional style, but those by 'Abdullah Buhari and the Armenian Rufail, who worked in larger format, are increasingly westernized. This feature is seen in the illustrations to another ambitious enterprise, a translation (1747–8; Istanbul, Topkapı Pal. Lib., B. 274) of al-'Ayni's *'Iqd al-jumān* ('Necklace of pearls').

Only a small and rather miscellaneous group of illustrated works survives from the period following Levni's death in 1732. The *Ma'rifatnāma* ('Book of esoteric knowledge'), a mystical work with eschatological illustrations and diagrams composed in 1756–7 by Ibrahim Hakkı, achieved some popularity, as did the *Khūbānnāma* ('Book of handsome men') and the *Zanānnāma* ('Book of women') of Fazil Enderuni (e.g. a copy of 1791–2; Istanbul, U. Lib., T. 5502). There are fine flower paintings, surprisingly late in view of the well-documented Ottoman interest in floriculture two centuries or more before, signed by Ali Usküdari in an album dated 1727–8 (Istanbul, U. Lib., T. 5650), and the so-called *Sunbulnāma* ('Book of hyacinths'; 1736–7; Istanbul, Topkapı Pal. Lib., H. 413), which illustrates hyacinths ordered from the Dutch Republic by the Ottoman court in 1722. The sudden decline of manuscript painting is difficult to explain. It can scarcely be a direct consequence of the printing press established in 1726 by Ibrahim Müteferrika at Istanbul (*see* §8(iii) below), for its influence remained extremely restricted for decades after its foundation. It does, however, coincide with a widespread fashion for landscape painting and architectural views in both religious and secular buildings.

BIBLIOGRAPHY

A. S. Ünver: *Nigârî: Hayatı ve eserleri* [Nigari: his life and works] (Istanbul, 1946)

——: *Levnî* (Istanbul, 1951)

Z. Akalay (Tanındı): 'Tarihi konuda ilk osmanlı minyatürleri' [The first Ottoman miniatures on historical subjects], *Sanat Tarihi Yıllığı*, ii (1966–7), pp. 102–15

F. Çağman: 'Şāhnāme-i Selīm Han ve minyatürleri' [The *Shāhnāma* of Selim II and its miniatures], *Sanat Tarihi Yıllığı*, v (1972–3), pp. 411–42

G. Renda: 'Topkapı Sarayı Müzesindeki H. 1321 no.lu Silsilename'nin minyatürleri/The Miniatures of Silsilename, No. 1321 in the Topkapı Saray Museum Library', *Sanat Tarihi Yıllığı*, v (1972–3), pp. 443–80 [Eng. version, pp. 481–95]

H. Yağmurlu: 'Tezhip sanatı hakkında genel açıklamalar ve Topkapı Sarayı Müzesi kütüphanesinde imzalı eserleri bulunan tezhip ustaları' [General observations on the art of book illumination and illuminators whose signed works are in the library of the Museum of the Topkapı Palace], *Türk Etnog. Derg.*, xiii (1973), pp. 79–131

N. Atasoy and F. Çağman: *Turkish Miniature Painting* (Istanbul, 1974)

G. İnal: 'Kahire'de yapılmış bir Hümâyûnnâme'nin minyatürleri' [The miniatures of a *Hümâyûnnâme* made in Cairo], *Belleten*, xl (1976), pp. 439–65

H. G. Yurdaydın: *Naṣūḥü's-Silāḥī (Matrākçī), Beyān-i menāzil-i sefer-i 'Irākeyn-i Sultān Süleymān Khān/Matrākçī Naṣūḥ and his 'Description of the Stages of the Campaign of Sultan Süleyman Khan in the Two Iraks'* (Ankara, 1976)

Y. Demiriz: '16 yüzyıla ait tezhipli bir Kuran' [An illuminated 16th-century Koran], *Sanat Tarihi Yıllığı*, vii (1976–7), pp. 41–58

E. Atıl: 'Ahmed Nakşi: An Eclectic Painter of the Early Seventeenth Century', *Proceedings of the Fifth International Congress of Turkish Art: Budapest, 1978*, pp. 103–21

E. G. Sims: 'The Turks and Illustrated Historical Texts', *Proceedings of the Fifth International Congress of Turkish Art: Budapest, 1978*, pp. 247–72

Z. Akalay (Tanındı): 'XVI yüzyıl nakkaşlarından Hasan Paşa ve eserleri' [The 16th-century painter Hasan Pasha and his works], *I. milletlerarası türkoloji kongresi, iii. Türk sanat tarihi: İstanbul, 1979*, pp. 607–25

E. Atıl: 'The Art of the Book', *Turkish Art*, ed. A. Atıl (Washington, DC, and New York, 1980), pp. 137–238

Z. Tanındı: *Siyer-i Nebî: İslâm tasvir sanatında Hz. Muhammed'in hayatı* [The *Siyer-i Nebî*: the life of the Prophet Muhammad in Islamic pictorial art] (Istanbul, 1984)

Treasures of Islam (exh. cat., ed. T. Falk; Geneva, Mus. A. & Hist., 1985)

E. Atıl: *Süleymanname: The Illustrated History of Süleyman the Magnificent* (Washington, DC, and New York, 1986)

Y. Demiriz: *Osmanlı kitap sanatında natüralist üslûpta çiçekler* [Naturalistic floral motifs in Ottoman book art] (Istanbul, 1986)

B. Mahir: 'Saray nakkaşhanesinin ünlü ressamı Şah Kulu ve eserleri' [The famous artist Şahkulu of the palace scriptorium and his works], *Topkapı Sarayı Müz.: Yıllık*, i (1986), pp. 113–30

I. H. Uzunçarşılı: 'Osmanlı sarayında ehl-i hiref "sanatkârlar" defterleri' [Account-books of the palace craftsmen in the Ottoman palace], *Belgeler*, xv (1986), pp. 23–76

J. M. Rogers: 'East and West in Mehmed the Conqueror's Library', *Bull. Biblioph.*, iii (1987), pp. 297–321

——: 'Pride and Prejudice: Mehmed the Conqueror and the Italian Portrait Medal', *Stud. Hist. A.*, xxi (1987), pp. 171–94

T. Reyhanlı: 'The Portraits of Murad III', *Erdem*, iii/8 (1987), pp. 453–78

The Age of Sultan Süleyman the Magnificent (exh. cat. by E. Atıl, Washington, DC, N.G.A.; Chicago, IL, A. Inst.; New York, Met.; 1987)

Süleyman the Magnificent (exh. cat. by J. M. Rogers and R. M. Ward, London, BM, 1988)

L. Klinger and J. Raby: 'Barbarossa and Sinan: A Portrait of Two Ottoman Corsairs from the Collection of Paolo Giovio', *Arte veneziana e arte islamica*, ed. E. J. Grube (Venice, 1989), pp. 47–67

S. Pinar, A. Mill and I. Altıntaş, eds: *A History of Turkish Painting* (Seattle and London, 1989)

R. Milstein: *Miniature Painting in Ottoman Baghdad* (Costa Mesa, CA, 1990)

A. T. Karamustafa: 'Military, Administrative and Scholarly Maps and Plans', *The History of Cartography*, ed. J. B. Harley and D. Woodward, ii (Chicago and London, 1992), pp. 209–27

J. M. Rogers: 'The Illuminator Karamemi and the Role of *ser-nakkaşan*', *Soliman le Magnifique et son temps*, ed. G. Veinstein (Paris, 1992), pp. 227–38

——: 'Itineraries and Town Views in Ottoman Histories', *The History of Cartography*, ed. J. B. Harley and D. Woodward, ii (Chicago and London, 1992), pp. 228–55

S. Soucek: 'Islamic Charting in the Mediterranean', *The History of Cartography*, ed. J. B. Harley and D. Woodward, ii (Chicago and London, 1992), pp. 263–92

J. M. ROGERS

5. PAPER. The earliest books in the Islamic world were written on parchment and papyrus, the writing surfaces known in antiquity, but paper, which was introduced from China, quickly replaced them both. The Islamic world was famous for its fine paper in the medieval period and was responsible for the introduction of papermaking technology to Europe. By the 14th century, European papers began to replace those of the Islamic world. (*See also* PAPER, §§I and III.)

(i) History and development. (ii) Production and uses. (iii) Special papers.

(i) History and development. The introduction of paper to the Islamic world is traditionally dated to the Battle of Talas in western Central Asia, when in AD 751 the Muslims defeated the Chinese. Among those taken prisoner were supposedly some who knew the art of papermaking and who introduced it to Samarkand. One Arabic word for paper (*kāghad* or *kāghid*) is possibly borrowed via the Persian from the Chinese *chuzhi*, paper from the bark of the paper-mulberry tree. This new support for writing rapidly spread westward and progressively replaced papyrus and parchment. At the end of the 8th century the Abbasid caliph Harun al-Rashid (*reg* 786–809) is said to have encouraged the use of paper in the chancellery. The earliest extant book written on paper (866–7) is a fragmentary copy of Abu 'Ubayd's work on unusual terms in the Hadith (Leiden, Bib. Rijksuniv.). There must have been certain resistance to the use of the new material, for parchment was retained for copying the Koran for some time, and the earliest known surviving Koran manuscript on paper (Istanbul, U. Lib., A. 6778) is dated 971–2 (*see* §2(i) above). Parchment, either on its own or combined with paper, continued to be used in the western Islamic lands when it had already been abandoned elsewhere. By contrast, paper was used from the 8th and 9th centuries by Christian copyists in areas of the Byzantine empire captured by the Muslim armies.

The earliest centres of manufacture were located in the eastern part of the Muslim world at Samarkand and in the province of Khurasan in north-east Iran. They retained their pre-eminent position for a considerable time and also maintained their reputation for a product of exceptional quality, much in demand by copyists. Production spread to all parts of the Islamic world, including such regions as Egypt where papyrus was traditionally used. The technology of papermaking spread throughout the area between the Indian subcontinent and Spain (the importance of the Spanish town of Játiva for the diffusion of paper is well known). In the 10th century paper-mills are known to have existed in Iraq, Syria and Palestine, although the date of their introduction to Baghdad and Cairo is still debated.

In the 11th century papermakers in the Islamic world enjoyed a favourable position, not only supplying domestic needs but also exporting their product to the Byzantine empire and western Christian countries. Muslim paper-makers were also responsible for the transmission of the technique to Europe. In the Islamic world the introduction of paper was accompanied by the appearance of specific trades: the artisans who collaborated in the actual production of paper, and the *warrāq*, who became principally known as a papermerchant but whose role spread to encompass aspects of manuscript production such as bookbinding. The *Fihrist* ('Index') written in 987–8 by al-Nadim, a *warrāq* of Baghdad, is one of the most valuable sources for the early history of Islamic calligraphy (*see* §2(ii)(a) above).

With the development of paper-mills in Europe and improvements in the manufacturing process, the favourable position of Islamic papermakers declined. The Islamic world became a net importer of paper, and, from the 14th century, an increasing number of manuscripts were copied on European paper, easily recognizable by the presence of watermarks. North Africa was the first to be affected by this change, but the rest of the Islamic world followed rapidly. European paper-mills, notably the Italian ones, were able to adapt to the taste of their clientele by choosing watermark motifs that were acceptable to Muslims (in particular the famous *trelune*: three crescent moons aligned). In the face of this competition local production declined, and when new paper-mills were established in the Ottoman empire in the 18th century, European experts were sometimes employed in order to create a product similar to that from the West. In this way watermarks first appeared in Islamic papers. This attempt to face competition was not seriously pursued in the 19th century, when technological advances, such as the introduction of wood-pulp, widened the gap between East and West. The lack of raw materials, notably timber and water, in the region increased the dependence on Western supplies of paper.

(ii) Production and uses. Information about production methods is almost entirely based on literary sources: so far no physicochemical analysis of old paper has been carried out to check seriously the authenticity of these texts. The Chinese origin of papermaking makes it plausible that Islamic papermakers used linen (rags) and hemp (rope) as raw materials in the preparation of the pulp. It is uncertain whether cotton was used: the traces that have been detected can be explained by an insufficiently careful selection of rags. Two other elements were also used to prepare the pulp: the North African ruler and author al-Muʿizz ibn Badis (*reg* 1016–62; *see* §7(i) below) appears to have been aware of the use of unrefined flax, and examination of papers suggests that old paper was sometimes recycled. After having been cut up, the fibres were carefully softened, cleaned and then pounded, manually according to the traditional practice described by Ibn Badis, or mechanically in more recent times. These operations continued until the pulp achieved a satisfactory degree of purity and texture.

The rectangular mould used in the production of sheets comprised a frame, inside which thin parallel strands were attached. These strands, which were of vegetable fibre (explaining the irregularities observed on the paper), left a number of parallel marks, known as laid-lines, on the sheet when extracted by the papermaker from the tank of pulp. These are often the only wiremarks that can be observed on Islamic papers. It is also reasonable to suppose that the configuration of these marks would vary according to local practice, relating to preference for one fibre over another and ways of arranging the strands within the mould. Western papers have two different types of wiremarks in addition to the watermark: laid-lines in one direction and, perpendicular to these, chain-lines, which correspond to the strands that hold the laid-lines in place. In most Islamic papers only the laid-lines are visible; the chain-lines are not clearly visible except in a few papers with irregularly spaced groups of two or three chain-lines. The production of this kind of paper appears to have been concentrated in a zone stretching from Egypt to southeast Turkey and lasted for several hundred years until the 15th century or the beginning of the 16th. A third type of Islamic paper bears no wiremarks at all due to the interposition of a fine textile between the mould and the pulp.

Two types of mould seem to have been in use: an earlier floating one, and a supple one. The floating mould was filled with paper pulp, and the sheet was left to dry in the mould. The supple mould was dipped with a regular movement into the receptacle containing the paper-pulp. After having withdrawn it from the tank, the papermaker extracted a sheet from the mould, which he then put out to dry. Having eliminated excess moisture, he either hung it on a line or applied the sheet to a flat surface. This method resulted in a difference in texture between the two sides of the sheet, which had later to be corrected to make both sides equally suitable for writing. With both methods the paper was sometimes extremely thin and, for this reason, it was often preferable, particularly in early times, to glue two or more sheets together, so as to increase the strength of the paper. Early manuscripts of the Koran copied on to this type of paper sometimes comprise sheets that resemble very thin cardboard. In some cases the text was written on only one side of two sheets, which were later glued together to form a composite page. The tradition of such collage was never lost in later manuscripts, but the purpose changed, as did the techniques. For example, a copy of the *Haft awrang* ('Seven thrones') of Jami (1556–65; Washington, DC, Freer, 46.12) is made up of sheets formed by laminating several different types of paper to create margins of different effect and colour from the text block. Scrolls, used for decrees and documents, were formed by gluing a succession of sheets or partial sheets end to end.

Before it was ready for use as a writing support, the dried sheet of paper had to be subjected to sizing, an operation that rendered the surface smooth and non-porous. A starch-based product, in the form of a liquid, paste or powder, or albumin was spread over the paper to prevent it from absorbing ink. Each sheet was then laid on a completely smooth work surface and rubbed with a rounded tool, either egg-shaped of a very hard substance or a wooden pestle, the handle of which allowed great pressure to be exerted. When the paper reached a satisfactory degree of glazing, it only remained for the copyist to draw the lines required to guide his writing. For this purpose the copyist used a piece of card on which threads were strung at regular intervals. By pressing the sheet of paper with his nail against these lines, he obtained the necessary guide for his work.

The format of Islamic papers is still a subject of debate. Literary sources give an extensive list of various types of paper. Most of the names are geographic, such as *Baghdādī* (from Baghdad), *Shāmī* (from Syria) and *Dawlatābādī* (from Daulatabad in India). Occasionally the names refer to the appearance of the paper, for example *ḥarīrī*, a paper resembling silk rather than using silk as raw material. Some of these names undoubtedly indicated a format, even if terminology was loose, to judge from what is known from other media. The dimensions of these papers are never given in the sources, and the only line of investigation is empirical. Reconstructing the size of folios is further complicated by the copyists' distinctive way of making gatherings. Instead of using gatherings of four or eight pages, which derive from a simple folding of the full sheet of paper, they used, until the 19th century, gatherings of ten pages, which do not correspond to any simple folding process. Some clue to dimensions may be provided by Byzantine manuscripts copied on Islamic paper: Irigoin (1991) has established formats of 660/720×490/560 mm, 490/560×320/380 mm and 320/370×235/280 mm. A careful examination of the texts might provide additional information: for example, a beautiful copy of pamphlets on religion and philosophy by Rashid al-Din (1310; Paris, Bib. N., MS. arab. 2324) was copied, if one is to believe the preface, on sheets that each had a length of six sheets of the Baghdad format.

(iii) Special papers. Manuscripts were frequently copied on tinted papers, a practice that derives from an older tradition. Several examples are known of manuscripts on dyed parchment, notably the 10th-century Blue Koran (dispersed, e.g. Tunis, Mus. N. Bardo). A wide variety of colours was used, of which saffron yellow was the most common; according to textual sources the use of colours had a clear code of meaning. An early 15th-century manuscript of the Koran (Paris, Bib. N., MS. arab. 389–92) has pages tinted predominantly purple, although the paper shows marked differences in hue from one page to another. According to Ibn Badis, paper could be tinted in two ways: either the sheet was dipped in a coloured bath, or a colorant (e.g. saffron) was added to the size during the process of smoothing the surface. Paper sprinkled with gold flecks (Pers. *zarafshānī*) was used as a support for calligraphy and for margins in such luxury manuscripts as the copy of the *Shāhnāma* ('Book of kings') prepared for the Safavid shah Tahmasp I (*c.* 1525–35; dispersed, ex-Houghton priv. col.; e.g. New York, Met.).

Marbled paper (Pers. *kāghaẓ-i abrī*; Turk. *ebru*) may have reached the Indian subcontinent from the East at the end of the 15th century or, according to an Iranian source, around the middle of the 16th (*see also* PAPER, DECORATIVE). From there the technique spread to Iran and Turkey. Drops of colorant were deposited with a brush or pipette on the surface of a bath, usually containing a mixture of gum tragacanth and water. Gallate was also used to aid the dispersion of the colours on the surface. The drops of colour were then worked with pointed instruments and combs to create shot patterns. When the desired pattern had been obtained, the marbler delicately

placed a sheet of unprepared paper on the surface of the bath, and, in a few seconds, this took up the design created. For each sheet it was necessary to recommence the operation, using the same bath.

Marbled paper became increasingly fashionable as a support for calligraphy (in which case pale colours were preferred), as a margin for pages of precious manuscripts (e.g. fig. 134), as endpapers (e.g. a *Dīvān* (collected poetry) of Anvari; 1515; London, V&A, 169–1923) or even for book covers. Marbled paper began to replace leather in Ottoman bindings of the 17th century, due to the economic crisis, and it continued to be used for centuries. The arts of calligraphy and marbling were closely associated; for example, MEHMED RASIM, known as Hatib, and

134. Marbled paper, each folio 245×150 mm; from a collection of hadith, *c.* 1540, transcribed by ʿAbd al-Hayy ʿAli for Şehzade Mehmed (Istanbul, Topkapı Palace Library, E.H. 2851, fol. 2*r*)

Necmeddin Okyay (1883–1976) were skilled in both. Several types of marbled paper can be identified. The simplest (Turk. *battal ebrusu*) forms the basis for the more elaborate varieties, created either with a thin wire or a needle passed over the design in alternating directions (*tarama*) or turned around on itself (*bülbülyuvası*, literally 'nightingale-nest'), or with a comb with narrow- or widely spaced teeth (*taraklı ebru*). Floral patterns were also made, a process perfected by Necmeddin Okyay, in varying degrees of stylization: pansies (the oldest), carnations, hyacinths, tulips and daisies.

BIBLIOGRAPHY

Al-Mu'izz ibn Badis: *'Umdat al-kuttāb* [Staff of the scribes] (*c.* 1060); Eng. trans. by M. Levey as 'Mediaeval Arabic Bookmaking and its Relation to Early Chemistry and Pharmacology', *Trans. Amer. Philos. Soc.*, n.s., lii/4 (1962), pp. 3–79

Qazi Ahmad ibn Mir Munshi: *Gulistān-i hunar* [Rose-garden of art] (1606); Eng. trans. by V. Minorsky as *Calligraphers and Painters* (Washington, DC, 1959), pp. 189–94

J. von Karabacek: *Das arabische Papier* (Vienna, 1887); Eng. trans by D. Baker and S. Dittmar (London, 1991)

C. Huart: *Les Calligraphes et les miniaturistes de l'Orient musulman* (Paris, 1908/*R* Osnabrück, 1972)

F. Babinger: *Zur Geschichte der Papiererzeugung im osmanischen Reiche* (Berlin, 1931)

D. Hunter: *Papermaking: The History and Technique of an Ancient Craft* (New York, 1943)

J. Irigoin: 'Les Premiers Manuscrits grecs écrits sur papier et le problème du bombycin', *Scriptorium*, iv/1 (1950), pp. 194–204

C.-M. Briquet: 'Le Papier arabe au Moyen Age et sa fabrication', *Mnmt Chart. Pap. Hist. Illus.*, iv (1955), pp. 162–70

——: 'Recherches sur les premiers papiers employés en Occident et en Orient du Xe au XIVe siècle', *Mnmt Chart. Pap. Hist. Illus.*, iv (1955), pp. 129–61

J. Irigoin: 'Les Types de formes utilisés dans l'Orient méditerranéen (Syrie, Egypte) du XIe au XIVe siècle', *Papiergeschichte*, xiii (1963), pp. 16–21

O. Ersoy: *XVIII ve XIX yüzyıllarda türkiye'de kâğıt* [Turkish paper of the 18th and 19th centuries] (Ankara, 1965)

A. Grohmann: *Arabische Paläographie*, i (Vienna, 1967), pp. 98–105

R. B. Loring: *Decorated Book Papers* (Cambridge, MA, 1973)

M. Beit-Arié: *Hebrew Codicology: Tentative Typology of Technical Practices Employed in Hebrew Dated Medieval Manuscripts* (Paris, 1976)

M. A. Kağıtçi: *Historique de l'industrie papetière en Turquie/Historical Study of Paper Industry in Turkey* (Istanbul, 1976) [bilingual text]

U. Derman: *Türk sanatında ebru* [Marbling in Turkish art] (Istanbul, 1977)

Islamic Bindings and Bookmaking (exh. cat. by G. Bosch, J. Carswell and G. Petherbridge, U. Chicago, IL, Orient. Inst. Mus., 1981)

M. A. Doizy and S. Ipert: *Le Papier marbré* ([Paris], 1985)

F. Richard: 'Un Manuscrit méconnu: L'Anthologie poétique de la B.N. illustrée et signée par Behzâd', *Stud. Iran.*, xx/2 (1991), pp. 263–74

Y. Porter: *Peinture et arts du livre: Essai sur la littérature technique indo-persane* (Paris and Tehran, 1992)

J. Irigoin: 'Les Papiers non filigranés: Etat présent des recherches et perspectives d'avenir', *Ancient and Medieval Book Materials and Techniques*, ed. M. Maniaci and P. F. Munafò, i (Vatican City, 1993)

F. DÉROCHE

6. PAPERCUTS. The two techniques of collage and *découpage* (Pers. *qit'a*; Turk. *kaatı*) as a serious and refined art have their origins in Syria and Egypt under the Mamluks (*reg* 1250–1517), where openwork designs in leather were first used for the doublures (linings) of bookbindings (*see* §7 below). The technique was extended to paper in Iraq and Iran during the rule of the Timurid dynasty (*reg* 1370–1506). Papercutting was first applied to ornamental calligraphy in *nasta'līq* script in 15th-century Herat, when so many of the crafts associated with fine Persian book production were perfected (*see* §4(v)(d) above). Specimens of collage (cut-out letters pasted on to a background of contrasting colour, usually light on dark) and, more rarely,

découpage (a sheet of contrasting colour mounted behind a sheet from which letters are cut out) survive from the 15th and 16th centuries. Perhaps the most famous example of collage is a copy of the *Dīvān* (collected poetry; dispersed, e.g. Istanbul, Mus. Turk. & Islam. A., MS. 1926) in Chaghatay Turkish by Husayn Bayqara, the last ruling Timurid prince of Herat (*reg* 1470–1506). The lines of *nasta'līq* script have been cut from sheets of light-blue, tan and beige paper and pasted on a dark-blue ground; the pages are enhanced with exquisite illumination and set within gold-flecked borders (see fig. 135). The names of only a few practitioners of the art of cut-out calligraphy have been preserved. The best known is Shaykh 'Abdallah of Herat, the son of Mir 'Ali Haravi; he is said to have been responsible for the *Dīvān* of Husayn Bayqara. The master papercutter (Pers. *qāṭi'*) Sangi 'Ali Badakhshi produced a *découpage* of some autograph verses of Mir 'Ali, and other examples of his work (e.g. New York, Met., 67.266.76) show that *découpage* continued to flourish in the Iranian world after 1500.

The arts of collage and *découpage* passed to Turkey under the Ottomans in the early 16th century with the many Iranian craftsmen and artists who emigrated there.

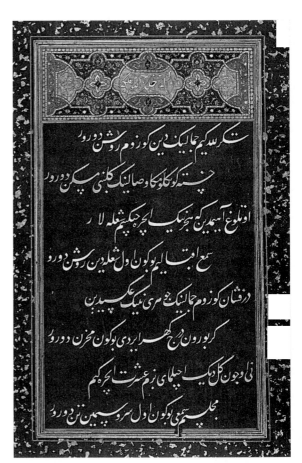

135. Papercut calligraphy, opaque watercolour, gold and paper on paper, 225×142 mm; from Husayn Bayqara: *Dīvān* (collected poetry), from Herat, *c.* 1490 (Los Angeles, CA, County Museum of Art, MS. M73.55.99)

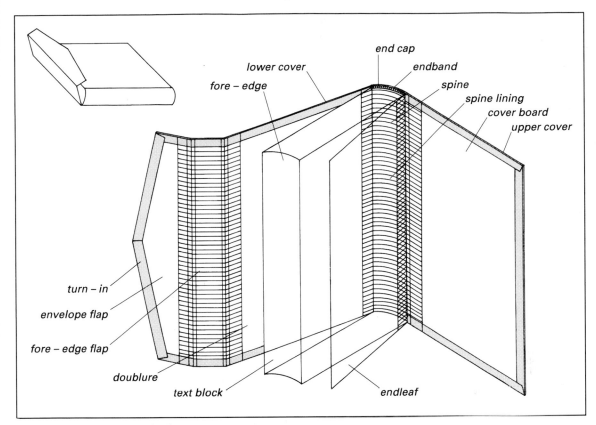

end cap

lower cover

fore – edge

endband

spine

spine lining

cover board

upper cover

turn – in

envelope flap

fore – edge flap

doublure

text block

endleaf

136. Diagram of a typical Islamic binding

Not only calligraphy (e.g. an illuminated frontispiece to a manuscript of hadith prepared for the prince Mehmed; *c.* 1540; Istanbul, Topkapı Pal. Lib., E.H. 2851, fols 1*v*–2*r*) but also miniature gardens replete with flowers, shrubs and trees were produced by Ottoman *découpeurs*, in collage. The many surviving specimens by Fakhri of Bursa (*d* 1617) such as a two-tiered garden scene in his style (Vienna, Österreich. Nbib., Cod. Mixt. 313, fol. 12*r*), attest his consummate skill with the paper-knife. Among the works of the artist Naqshi is a calligraphic specimen (Washington, DC, Sackler Gal., S86.0335) in which collage calligraphy in white is surrounded by an imitation of gold flecking (Pers. *zarafshānī*) composed of tiny gilt diamonds cut out and pasted on to the background in a floral design. Interest in papercuts continued in the 17th and 18th centuries (e.g. four pages glued in the back of an *Anthology*; London, BL, Or. MS. 13763 *a–d*) and may well have been the source for European papercuts.

BIBLIOGRAPHY

Mustafa Ali: *Manāqib-i hunarvarān* [Virtues of artists] (1587); ed. İ. M. Kemal (Istanbul, 1926), p. 63

Qazi Ahmad ibn Mir Munshi: *Gulistān-i hunar* [Rose-garden of art] (1606); Eng. trans. by V. Minorsky as *Calligraphers and Painters* (Washington, DC, 1959), p. 193

J. M. Rogers: *Islamic Art and Design, 1500–1700* (London, 1981), pp. 18–23

A. Schimmel: *Calligraphy and Islamic Culture* (New York, 1984), p. 55

M. Bayani: *Aḥvāl va āṣār-i khwushnavīsān* [Biographies and works of calligraphers], 2nd edn in 4 vols (Tehran, Iran. Solar 1363/1984–5), pp. 452–3

T. W. Lentz and G. D. Lowry: *Timur and the Princely Vision* (Washington, DC, 1989), pp. 268–70

WHEELER M. THACKSTON

7. BINDING. Bookbinding was one of the most esteemed arts in the Muslim world because of its close association with the written word. Islamic bindings are distinguished from Western ones by a right-hand hinge, a fore-edge flap on the left and boards that do not project beyond the body (see fig. 136). After paper replaced parchment in the 10th and 11th centuries as the usual body material, bindings were made in a standard two-step process: preparation of the body and preparation of the cover. The two were only loosely joined in the areas most subject to flexing, and the cover often became detached from its intended body. The two could be rejoined or a new cover could be made, but usually elaborate covers were preserved separately or reused with other bodies, explaining why the earliest Islamic bindings known are detached from their bodies. Most of the early Islamic bindings known come from Tunisia or Egypt, so that regional styles are impossible to distinguish before the 14th century. Bindings after that date are usually divided into regional groups: Egypt and Syria, north-west Africa and Spain, South Arabia, Iran, Turkey and the Indian subcontinent.

(i) Bookbinders, their materials and techniques. (ii) Style.

(i) Bookbinders, their materials and techniques. The elevated status of the bookbinder means that many names are

known. In the *Fihrist* ('Index'), a 10th-century compilation of books and their authors, al-Nadim named eight; Mustafa Ali, the 16th-century Turkish author, included many more in his treatise *Manāqib-i hunarvārān* ('Virtues of artists'). Other bookbinders, such as al Amin, signed their works. Two texts provide a great deal of additional information about the materials and techniques of Islamic bookbinding: '*Umdat al-kuttāb* ('Staff of the scribes'), probably composed by the Zirid ruler al-Mu'izz ibn Badis (*reg* 1016–62), and *Ṣinā'a tasfīr al-kutub wa ḥall al-dhahab* ('Craft of bookmaking and the dissolving of gold'), composed in 1619 by Abu'l-'Abbas Ahmad ibn Muhammad al-Sufyani, a master binder from Fez. Bookbinders at work are depicted on marginal illustrations in an album (Berlin, Staatsbib. Preuss. Kultbes., Orientabt., S. 83, and Washington, DC, Freer, 54.116) prepared for the Mughal ruler Jahangir (*reg* 1605–27).

The materials and techniques of Islamic bookbinding remained remarkably constant throughout the Islamic world over time. The earliest manuscripts were written on parchment and papyrus, but these materials were quickly superseded once Muslims gained knowledge of papermaking (*see* §5(i) above). The folios were collated and assembled in gatherings, which were normally sewn into a single body using a link-stitch (sometimes termed Coptic- or chain-stitch). The typical Islamic manuscript has two sewing stations connected by a simple link-stitch that picks up the preceding gathering, but the coloured linen or silk thread used was often too thin for its function and broke. After sewing, the spine was lined, usually with linen, to allow flexing, distribute stresses and provide an even surface on which to paste the leather covering. The lining projected beyond the spine 20–25 mm on either side to form hinges by which the body was attached to the cover boards. After the body edges were trimmed, endbands were sewn to the head and tail of the spine to consolidate the structure and decorate the body. By the 14th century the standard headband had silk threads of two different colours to produce a pattern of small chevrons.

The typical Islamic book cover, of leather made rigid with pasteboard, had fore-edge and envelope flaps. Sometimes flexible covers of skin, paper or cloth were used; early Islamic parchment codices had wooden boards, the weight, stiffness and thickness of which, together with the restraining action of straps, ties or clasps, shielded the skins from the cockling caused by atmospheric changes. By the 12th or 13th century the head and tail flaps, which had been used in the earliest bindings preserved at Kairouan in Tunisia, were replaced by fore-edge and envelope flaps. This arrangement, in turn, disappeared in the 18th century under the impact of European bookbinding. The earliest example of the classic type of binding is a fragment of a lower cover and flap that can be dated to the 11th century (Vienna, Österreich. Nbib., Rainer Col.). Thinly pared leather, dyed red, yellow, green or black, was dampened, pasted and smoothed into place over the boards, flaps and spine. The corners were not systematically fixed: sometimes the mitres were lapped; occasionally they were butted. The boards were then left to dry, and the turn-ins were trimmed near their edges. The leather covers could be left plain, tooled, stamped or painted and gilded (*see* GILDING, colour pl. II, fig. 1). Varnished covers

(usually known as 'lacquer' covers; *see* §VIII, 10 below) were produced in Iran, Turkey and India; at first the varnish was applied to leather, but, as the covers had a tendency to crack, varnished pasteboard became more common.

Islamic bindings often had doublures (linings) of paper, leather or fabric pasted on to the inner face of the upper and lower boards and overlapping the adjacent flyleaf. Essentially structural, they also became one of the prime decorative features of the Islamic book. The typical doublure was made of leather, although the earliest surviving Islamic bindings from Kairouan have parchment doublures, often made from reused manuscript leaves. Although some leather doublures were tooled like covers, those made in Egypt, Syria and Arabia from the 14th to the 16th century were block-pressed with intricate vegetal and geometric interlacing. The blocks were cut in intaglio, in contrast to the relief-cut blocks used in textile printing. Brown was the preferred colour. From the 15th century Iranian doublures were of leather or paper painted blue to highlight elaborate, applied filigree decoration. Turkish doublures were often coloured red. Plain paper, sometimes dyed yellow, was used to line the inside of less elaborate covers. Even modest volumes produced from the 17th to the 19th century had doublures, endpapers and pastedowns made of marbled or gold-sprinkled papers.

Asphodel paste, wheat starch and gum arabic were used to paste book boards and attach paper, leather and textiles, while animal glues made from cattle hocks, snails and fish were used as vehicles for gold, silver and pigments. Bookbinding tools remained unchanged over the centuries: many of the implements Ibn Badis mentioned are depicted in 17th-century images, such as those in the album made for Jahangir, and still form the basic kit of traditional bookbinders in Istanbul. A slab, usually made of marble, formed the work surface since Islamic bookbinders did not work at tables. Rope-tightened and wooden screw-presses were used. On Arab bindings a compass and ruler were used to lay out the design for blind-tooling. Although Ibn Badis suggested using a warm tool, most tooling was done cold. Before the 15th century, binders used individual tooling irons for designs such as the almond, 'breast of the falcon' and dot and roundel, which they combined in various larger patterns. Panel stamps were first used for the borders of Arab bindings, but in later centuries, particularly in Iran, binders used larger stamps that could emboss up to half the cover at once. The most popular central motif was the *turunja* or 'citrus' shape.

(*ii*) *Style*. Most of the earliest Islamic bindings preserved come from North Africa. The most important are the 179 fragments that were found in the library of the Great Mosque of Kairouan in Tunisia and date from the 9th to the 13th century. These, along with other fragments preserved in Cairo (N. Lib.), show that binders continued many of the techniques and motifs used in Coptic bindings, such as blind-tooling, coloured inpainting, incising, cutting and geometric diaper patterns. As the typical vertical format for manuscripts was replaced by the horizontal format preferred for early parchment Korans, the typical layout of the cover evolved from a square central panel

137. Binding, goatskin with blind- and gold-tooling, upper cover 259×175 mm, from Egypt or Syria, 14th century (Dublin, Chester Beatty Library and Gallery of Oriental Art, Moritz Collection 64)

with narrow friezes above and below to a single oblong panel filled with twisted band ornament and surrounded by a wider border. The earliest designs were small in scale, with motifs used in a frieze or repeat to form frames and borders or to fill a larger decorative form. Complex decorative areas were built up with fillets, bars, arcs and dots. Different designs were also used for the front and back covers. For example, the upper and lower covers of a 9th-century binding from Kairouan (130×83 mm; see Marçais and Poinssot, no. 1) are decorated with a blind-tooled torsade circumscribing a rectangular field containing a kufic inscription. The three-word inscription begins on the front cover and ends on the back, a common arrangement. In other cases, the two covers show variations on the same design. The front cover of a square binding from Egypt (10th–11th century; Baltimore, MD, Walters A.G.) is decorated with openwork tracery of spiral *rinceaux* ending in palmettes or leaves over a gilded ground; the back cover is a simplified version of the front.

The widespread production of paper manuscripts was accompanied by a return to the vertical format. The group of bindings in Kairouan attributed to the 12th and 13th centuries typically has a central geometric figure in a plain field with tooled borders of fillets and twists and triangular corner elements. These bindings are similar to a group preserved in the Ben Yusuf Madrasa in Marrakesh, Morocco, attributed to the period of Almohad rule (*reg* 1130–1269). The binding on a magnificent copy of the Koran (1256; London, BL, Or. MS. 13192), written in Marrakesh by the penultimate Almohad sultan Abu Hafs ʿUmar al-Murtada (*reg* 1248–66), is an early example of gold-tooling and strapwork in reserve against a tooled ground, although two centuries earlier Ibn Badis mentioned a more primitive form of stamping with gold. Gold-tooling did not appear on European bindings for another two centuries.

Regional variations can be detected in bindings produced after the 14th century. 'Arab' bindings, comprising those ascribed to Egypt and Syria, Spain and North Africa, and the Yemen, are generally simpler, with less elaborate tooling than those ascribed to Iran, Turkey or the Indian subcontinent. Two types of geometric layouts predominate in Arab bindings: central medallions and strapwork patterns emanating from a central star. Colour is used sparingly, and the main effect is achieved by contrasting gold against untooled strapwork bands. Typical doublures are made of light-brown or cream leather that is block-pressed with arabesque and floral designs. Bindings from North Africa and Spain are done in dark, coarse-grained leather and have somewhat simple patterns; a cover in London (180×130 mm; V&A, 366/22–1888) attributed to North Africa in the 14th or 15th century has a central roundel filled with strapwork and plain, triangular corner-pieces. Examples from Egypt and Syria are often particularly fine, with tooling and cut-outs adding a sense of vitality, and gold, silver and blue paint enhancing the pattern. The bindings on a 30-volume copy of the Koran (371×275 mm; Baltimore, MD, Walters A.G.; Dublin, Chester Beatty Lib.; London, BL, and V&A; Washington, DC, Freer, and Lib. Congr.) made for Aytmish al-Bajasi (*d* 1400), an amir of the Mamluk sultan Barquq, all have central medallions composed of geometric interlaces radiating from an eight-pointed star worked in blind- and gold-tooling and stamping. The medallions are set in plain fields, the corners of which are filled with quarter medallions. A binding in Dublin (see fig. 137) made of brown goatskin over pasteboard is decorated with blind- and gold-tooling in strapwork patterns. The upper and lower covers have the same frames, but the fields have different patterns. Bindings produced for the Zaydi rulers of Yemen in the 15th century form another coherent group. Most are of light-brown leather, quarto size with polished surfaces decorated with flat blind-tooling and calligraphic stamps with religious mottoes or binders' signatures (e.g.

138. Binding, leather filigree, lower cover 258×175 mm, made for Husayn Bayqara, Herat, 1482–3 (Istanbul, Museum of Turkish and Islamic Art, MS. 1905)

U. Chicago, IL, Orient. Inst. Mus., A12125, signed by al-Rabiʿ).

Iranian bindings are laid out with central medallions and corner-pieces or overall patterns in the field. Borders are often filled with elaborate cartouches. In contrast to the angular geometry of Arab bindings, Iranian bindings are more curvilinear. Colour is more prominent and motifs are more elaborate and naturalistic. The same techniques of stamping and tooling were used to more elaborate effect. A binding in Dublin (1435; Chester Beatty Lib., MS. 5282) has 550,000 blind stamps and 43,000 gold stamps; it must have taken about two years to complete. Gilding was often applied with a fine brush. Poetic texts often had quatrains stamped on the fore-edge flap or spine so that the contents could be identified when the books were stacked. One of the earliest surviving Iranian book-bindings encloses a copy of Ibn Bakhtishuʿs bestiary, *Manāfiʿ al-ḥayawān* ('Usefulness of animals'; 1297 or 1299; New York, Pierpont Morgan Lib., MS M.500), copied at Maragha in north-west Iran. Measuring 339×254 mm, the covers are made of dark reddish-brown leather decorated with blind-tooling applied with a small number of punches. There are no traces of gilding. The front and back covers have almond-shaped medallions with three different radiating elements. All the patterns are symmetrical, except two graceful arabesques on the flap. The total effect is of austere dignity.

In the early 15th century the arts of the book in Iran were transformed under the patronage of the Timurid prince Baysunghur (1397–1433) at Herat. The typical layout of a central medallion with quarter medallions in the corners was elaborated by relief and lobing. New techniques—such as leather filigree, often on a blue ground, and varnish—were introduced, colour was increased through the use of silk inlays and paint, and naturalistic vegetal and figural motifs were added. These innovations suggest that manuscript painters were closely involved in the design and execution of bindings. The decoration of inner covers was often as elaborate as that on the outer covers, and the protected location often ensured better preservation. The binding on a copy of *Kalila and Dimna* made for Baysunghur (1429; Istanbul, Topkapı Pal. Lib., R. 1022) has a landscape in relief filled with birds, animals and flowers. Two confronted dragons fill the triangular flap. Even more spectacular is the binding for a copy of the *Sitta* ('Six poems') of ʿAttar made for Baysunghurʾs father, Shahrukh, in 1438 (Istanbul, Topkapı Pal. Lib., A. 3059). The upper cover, depicting a fantastic landscape inhabited by deer, monkeys, dragons and ducks, was stamped with a single large block; the flap depicts Chinese-style lions amid dragons, ribbons and foliage in the same technique. The fore-edge bears a stamped dedication to Shahrukh. The inner covers, worked in filigree against a deep-blue ground, are equally splendid. The upper cover has a central medallion containing a tree flanked by dragons; the quarter medallions, borders and flap are inhabited by ducks, rabbits, monkeys, deer and lions in a foliate ground. Leather covers could also be decorated with gold and varnish, as on the binding of a copy of Jalal al-Din Rumiʾs mystical poem, the *Maṣnavī*, made for Sultan Husayn Bayqara at Herat (see fig. 138). The outer covers have been stamped with central medallions and lobed quarter-panels, varnished in black and painted with peonies and other flowers in gold. The similarly executed fore-edge flap bears a quatrain admonishing the reader to read the book. The inner covers bear a spectacular example of leather filigree set against a blue ground, depicting wild animals cavorting in a landscape.

In the 16th century a layout of the central panel surrounded by block-stamped border panels and cartouches became increasingly popular for Iranian bindings. They were often gilded to create an impression of great sumptuousness; decoration included arabesques, cloud-scrolls, medallions, inscriptions and landscapes. To save money, paper filigree often replaced leather, and large metal blocks allowed half the cover to be stamped at once. An early 16th-century binding enclosing an album of calligraphy attributed to the royal scribe Mir ʿAli (232×137 mm; London, V&A, 685–1876) depicts a landscape showing three birds perched in a tree. Cranes and ducks fly between clouds, and rabbits cavort on the ground. The inner covers, with the traditional layout of a central medallion and quarter panels, are inlaid with gold paper filigree set against a red, blue, green and black paper ground. Painted and varnished covers often depict princely pastimes, such as hunting and feasting and scenes from literature. The outer covers of a varnished set in London (304×185 mm; V&A, 353–1885) have single fields with figural scenes. The upper cover depicts a prince in a garden surrounded by servants roasting food and playing musical instruments; the lower shows the prince hunting. The inner covers, done in the same technique but with a medallion format, show *Majnun among the Animals* from the *Khamsa* ('Five poems') of Nizami and a tiger attacking a deer. The iconography suggests that the covers may have belonged to a manuscript of the *Khamsa* made for a royal patron.

From the 17th to the 19th century book covers continued to use the same formats and techniques but were simpler in execution. A complete leather cover in London (378×265 mm; V&A, 1948–1981), for example, is done with gold block-stamping and traces of gold paint. The field has an almond-shaped medallion with two pendants at either end and scalloped corner panels; the narrow border is stamped with cartouches and quatrefoils. The single-field format became increasingly popular; leather was replaced by pasteboard when varnished covers became standard, and the flap tended to disappear. The single field often contains arabesques, floral or figural scenes; the art of the bookbinder was subsumed by the art of the painter.

Bindings produced in Turkey under the Ottomans (reg 1281–1924) generally followed the Iranian layout of a central medallion and quarter medallions in the corners, but they used a greater combination of coloured leathers and distinctive Ottoman motifs, such as the sawtoothed leaf (Turk. saz), carnation, arabesque (Turk. rumi) and Chinese cloud band. The quarter medallions were often joined to form ogee arches, and medallion contours are often scalloped (e.g. Washington, DC, Sackler Gal., S86.0478). Medallions on the inside covers show a wide range of colours (blue, orange, turquoise, black and red) and material (paper, silk and cotton), as on a complete cover in London (V&A, 123–1897). Production was centralized in Istanbul, where 700 binders are said to have worked in the 17th century. The impact of European books in the 18th and 19th centuries led binders to drop the characteristic Islamic flap in favour of slipcases and to adopt Europeanizing decorative motifs. The European-format covers to a book of prayers (182×106 mm; March 1825; London, V&A, 801–1942) are made of papier-mâché painted and varnished with an overall design of trees, leaves and acorns on a green ground within a narrow cable border.

Islamic bindings from the Indian subcontinent continue the styles and techniques of their Iranian models, as for example in the stamped leather covers to a Būstān ('Orchard') of Sa'di made for Nasir al-Din Khalji (reg 1500–10; New Delhi, N. Mus., 48.6/4). In the 19th century a distinct local school of book production flourished in Kashmir. Typical bindings are of varnished pasteboard painted with floral scenes: a Koran in London (382×232 mm; V&A, 1392–1922) has an elaborate all-over floral pattern of pink and yellow blossoms against a black ground.

BIBLIOGRAPHY
Al-Mu'izz ibn Badis: 'Umdat al-kuttāb [Staff of the scribes] (c. 1060); Eng. trans. by M. Levey as 'Mediaeval Arabic Bookmaking and its Relation to Early Chemistry and Pharmacology', Trans. Amer. Philos. Soc., n.s., lii/4/(1962), pp. 3–79
Mustafa Ali: Manāqib-i hunarvarān [Virtues of artists] (1587); ed. İ. M. Kemal (Istanbul, 1926)
Ahmad ibn Muhammad al-Sufyani: Sinā'a tasfir al-kutub wa hall al-dhahab [Craft of bookmaking and the dissolving of gold] (1619), ed. P. Ricard (Fez, 1919)
F. Sarre: Islamic Bookbinding (Berlin, 1923)
E. Gratzl: Islamische Bucheinbände des 14. bis 19. Jahrhunderts (Leipzig, 1924)
P. Ricard: 'Reliures marocaines du XIIIe siècle', Hespéris, xvii (1933), pp. 109–27
——: 'Sur un type de reliure des temps almohades', A. Islam., i (1934), pp. 74–9
M. Aga-Oglu: Persian Bookbindings of the 15th Century (Ann Arbor, 1935)
J. Pedersen: Den arabiske bog [The Arabic book] (Copenhagen, 1946); Eng. trans., ed. R. Hillenbrand (Princeton, 1984)
G. Marçais and L. Poinssot: Objets kairouanais: IXe au XIIIe siècle (Tunis and Paris, 1948)
R. Ettinghausen: 'The Covers of the Morgan Manāfi' Manuscript and Other Early Persian Bookbindings', Studies in Art and Literature for Belle da Costa Greene (Princeton, 1954), pp. 459–73
T. C. Petersen: 'Early Islamic Bookbindings and their Coptic Relations', A. Orient., i (1954), pp. 41–64
The History of Bookbinding, 525–1950 AD (exh. cat. by D. E. Miner, Baltimore, MD, Walters A.G. and Mus. A., 1957–8)
B. van Regemorter: Some Early Bindings from Egypt in the Chester Beatty Library (Dublin, 1958)
M. Weisweiler: Der islamische Bucheinband des Mittelalters, nach Handschriften aus deutschen, holländischen und türkischen Bibliotheken (Wiesbaden, 1962)
E. Gratzl: 'Book Covers', Survey of Persian Art, ed. A. U. Pope and P. Ackerman, iv (2/1964), pp. 1975–94
O. Aslanapa: 'The Art of Bookbinding', The Arts of the Book in Central Asia, 14th–16th Centuries, ed. B. Gray (Boulder, CO, and London, 1979), pp. 59–92
Qur'āns and Bindings from the Chester Beatty Library (exh. cat. by D. James, London, Islam. Cult. Cent., 1980)
Islamic Bindings and Bookmaking (exh. cat. by G. Bosch, J. Carswell and G. Petherbridge, U. Chicago, IL, Orient. Inst. Mus., 1981)
D. Haldane: Islamic Bookbindings in the Victoria and Albert Museum (London, 1983)
T. W. Lentz and G. D. Lowry: Timur and the Princely Vision (Washington, DC, 1989), nos 40, 99

GULNAR K. BOSCH, GUY PETHERBRIDGE

8. PRINTING. As Arabic script has joins between most letters, it presents problems quite unlike those of the Roman, Greek and Hebrew alphabets that preoccupied the first few generations of European typographers. Not only is a higher degree of punch-cutting skill required, especially if calligraphic norms are to be imitated, but matrices must be justified even more minutely if the breaks between adjacent sorts are to be disguised. The compositor likewise must constantly avoid using the wrong letter form. Moreover, as well as different initial, medial, final and free-standing sorts for most letters, an abundance of ligatures is also needed for pairs or groups of letters (see §2(i) and fig. 91 above). If short-vowel marks (Arab. ḥarakāt) are required for Koranic and certain other texts, then even more sorts are needed, as well as huge quantities of quadrats and leads to be interspersed between the vowel marks. A full Arabic fount can therefore contain over 600 sorts. Although some simplification was introduced in later periods, the Arabic script has never really acquired separate typographic norms, either aesthetic or practical, that could permit a decisive break with its scribal past. Since typography in its true sense has now been superseded, and modern methods of electronic 'typesetting' permit a return to almost any variety of genuinely cursive script, this is unlikely to occur in the future.

(i) Block-printing. (ii) Arabic printing in Europe. (iii) Printing in the Islamic lands.

(i) Block-printing. Printing was practised in the Islamic world probably as early as the 10th century. Block-prints on paper, found in Egypt, survive in several collections, notably Vienna (Nbib.), Cambridge (U. Lib.) and New York (Columbia U. Lib.), and further pieces have been excavated at Fustat (Old Cairo). At least one printed papyrus (Dublin, Chester Beatty Lib.) and two parchment pieces (see Arnold and Grohmann, 1929, pl. 15) are also preserved. The only literary and historical testimony to block-printing in the Arab world is two obscure references in Arabic poems in the 10th and 14th centuries to the

production of amulets with *ṭarsh*, a non-classical Arabic term. It may refer to tin-plates with engraved or repoussé lettering used to produce multiple copies of Koranic and incantatory texts for sale to the illiterate poor: the style of the surviving pieces indicates that they were not intended to gratify any refined literary or artistic taste, since the script is far from calligraphic and there are even errors in the Koranic texts. Some examples have headpieces with designs incorporating bolder lettering and ornamental motifs, sometimes white on black, which may have been printed with separate woodblocks. In 1294 the Ilkhanid sultan Gaykhatu (*reg* 1291–5) introduced paper money printed in Tabriz by Chinese artisans living there, but it was rejected by the Iranian people. Some block-printed patterns have also been found on the endpapers of manuscript codices (see Arnold and Grohmann, 1929, pl. 29A). The origin of the process used is unknown: while China or Central Asia has been suggested, the marked difference in techniques and the contrast with the luxury character of other Chinese imports and their imitations make this improbable, but a link with the printing of patterns on textiles, also practised in medieval Egypt, cannot be ruled out. Islamic block-printing seems to have died out in the 14th or 15th century, and there is no evidence that it was ever used to produce books or substantial literary texts in any form. These remained the monopoly of scribes in the Islamic world until the 18th century, and the origins of Arabic typography and printed book production must be sought not in the Middle East but in Europe.

(ii) Arabic printing in Europe. Arabic printing with movable type originated in Italy in the early 16th century. The first book was the *Kitāb ṣalāt al-sawāʾī* ('book of hours') printed by the Venetian printer GREGORIO DE' GREGORIIS at Fano in 1514 and sponsored by Pope Julius II for the use of Arab Melchite Christians in Lebanon and Syria. The type design is inelegant, and it was set in a clumsy, disjointed manner. Rather better was the typography of Paganino de' Paganini (1470–1541), who printed the whole text of the Koran at Venice in 1537–8, probably as a commercial export venture; but it was still so remote from calligraphic norms as to make it quite unacceptable to the Muslims for whom it was intended, especially as it also contained errors in the Koranic text. Italy remained the home of Arabic printing for the rest of the 16th century, and it was in Rome in the 1580s that Robert Granjon (*fl* c.1523–c. 1593) produced his elegant Arabic types, which for the first time achieved calligraphic quality, with their liberal use of ligatures and letter-forms derived from the best scribal models. They were used principally in the lavish editions of the Tipografia Medicea Orientale between 1590 and 1610, and they set the standard for nearly all subsequent work, especially that of the Dutch scholar–printer Franciscus Raphelengius (1539–97) and his successor Thomas Erpenius (1584–1624), who produced many Arabic texts with his more practical and workmanlike founts in the early 17th century, and whose type-styles were much used or copied in Germany, England and elsewhere. Another elegant and beautiful fount was commissioned by the French scholar–diplomat François Savary de Brèves (1560–1628) and evidently based on Arab or Turkish specimens of calligraphy acquired while he was French ambassador in Istanbul between 1592 and 1604; it was executed in Rome before 1613 and later used both there and at the Imprimerie Royale in Paris in the mid-17th century, and again in the Napoleonic period. It subsequently provided a model for others, notably that of the Propaganda Fide, which had a monopoly of Arabic printing in Rome from 1662 onwards, and that of the monastic presses of 18th-century Romania.

There was a steady flow of Arabic printed books from most of the European centres of learning in the 17th, 18th and 19th centuries. After Granjon, other leading typographers, such as William Caslon (1692–1766) and GIAMBATTISTA BODONI, were also involved in the design of Arabic founts. As well as Orientalist editions, the European presses produced Biblical and other Christian texts for use in the Middle East, and also some 'secular' texts as a commercial export commodity aimed at Muslims, although these met with little success.

(iii) Printing in the Islamic lands. Arabic typography was not used in the Muslim world until the 18th century; all printed books in use had previously been imported from Europe. The reasons for this delay must be sought both in the nature of Islamic societies and in the supreme religious and aesthetic role accorded to the written word in the Islamic world. The segmentation and mechanization of the Arabic script by typesetting seemed tantamount to sacrilege; at the same time mass production of books challenged the entrenched monopoly of intellectual authority enjoyed by the learned class (Arab. *ʿulamāʾ*) and threatened to upset the balance between that authority and the power of the State. This was one important reason why printing was eventually sponsored by modernizing rulers in the 18th and 19th centuries.

As in Europe, the earliest Arabic books printed in the Middle East were Christian texts. The earliest book printed in Arabic type is a Psalter, the *Kitāb al-zabūr al-sharīf*, printed at Aleppo in 1706 by the priest ʿAbdallah Zakhir and published by the Melkite patriarch. Arabic printing in the Arab world remained in the hands of Syrian and Lebanese Christians for over a century. They used types cut and cast locally, modelled partly on local Christian book-hands and partly on the European tradition of Arabic type design, especially that of Orthodox Romania and of the Propaganda press in Rome.

Printing by Muslims was revived in Istanbul in the second decade of the 18th century, when Ibrahim Müteferrika began printing engraved maps using copperplates and probably techniques imported from Vienna; the earliest extant example is dated 1719–20. This was part of a programme of westernizing innovations in the Ottoman capital that also led, less than ten years later, to the establishment of Müteferrika's famous book-printing establishment, complete with Arabic types cut and cast locally and modelled on the normal clear Ottoman *nesih* (Arab. *naskh*) script of the period (*see* §2(iv)(a) above). The first book, an Arabic–Turkish dictionary, was printed in 1728 and was followed by 16 others in Ottoman Turkish before the press was closed in 1742. Since the printing of the Koran and other religious texts was still forbidden, these books were all secular works, on history, geography, language, government (by Müteferrika himself), navigation and chronology. Several were illustrated with maps and engravings. Apart from a reprint in 1756, the press was not restarted until 1784, after which Ottoman Turkish printing had a continuous history until the adoption of the Latin alphabet in 1928.

Arabic printing in Egypt dates from 1822, apart from the relatively insignificant output of the presses of the French occupation in 1798–1801. The first book was printed at the state press of Muhammad 'Ali (*reg* 1805–48) at Bulaq near Cairo. This press was started by an Italian-trained typographer, Niqula Masabiki, and the first types were imported from Milan and are perceptibly European in style. They were soon replaced by a succession of locally cut and cast founts based on indigenous *naskh* hands, which are somewhat cramped and utilitarian rather than calligraphic; they set the norm for Arabic typography in Egypt and at many other Muslim Arabic presses elsewhere for the rest of the 19th century. Types based on the more flowing *nasta'līq* script (*see* §2(iv)(b) above) were also employed, both for Persian texts and for headings in Arabic works, and a fount in the distinctive *maghribī* script (*see* §2(iii)(b) above) was also created but little used.

In the first half of the 19th century many Arabic books were imported into the Middle East by Christian missionaries. Most of these books were printed at a British-run press in Malta between 1825 and 1842; they included secular educational works as well as religious tracts. At first the types were brought from England, but in the 1830s a new fount was cut and cast locally from calligraphic models, almost certainly prepared by the famous Lebanese writer Faris al-Shidyaq (1804–87), who had been a scribe in his youth and worked at the Malta press in this period. These books set new standards among the Arab (mainly Christian) pupils who used them, and the tradition was later continued by the American mission press in Beirut, which introduced a new typeface in the late 1840s, again based on calligraphic models. Known as American Arabic, it has a characteristic attenuated and forward-sloping appearance and was also used by several other presses in the Arab world. A more orthodox face, which was clear and workmanlike and based on Turkish models, was adopted by the press of the Jesuit mission in Beirut *c.* 1870 and became popular throughout the Levant.

Other Catholic mission presses inaugurated Arabic printing in Jerusalem in 1847 and in Mosul in 1856; in both cases their first founts were brought from Europe (Vienna and Paris respectively). The first press in Iraq, however, had operated in Baghdad in 1830, using a fount similar to those in Iran (presses had been established at Tabriz *c.* 1817 and Tehran *c.* 1823): an elegant Persian-style *naskh* with such curious idiosyncrasies as the shortened top stroke of the letter *kāf*. *Nasta'līq* typography was never favoured in Iran, despite the prevalence of this style in the scribal tradition (including lithography). It was, however, used in the Indian subcontinent as early as 1778 and remained in use there, for both Persian and Urdu, until the mid-19th century; it was later revived in Hyderabad. Arabic typography burgeoned from the mid-19th century onwards, with presses starting in Damascus in 1855, Tunis in 1860, San'a in 1877, Khartoum in 1881, Mecca in 1883 (see fig. 139) and Medina in 1885. Most of

139. Printed Arabic script; from 'Abd al-Malik al-Tha'alibi: *Kitāb al-nihāya fi'l-ta'rīḍ wa'l-kināya* ('Book of the outcome of intimation and allusion'), the first book printed in Mecca, 1883 (Cambridge, University Library)

these used local types in the Istanbul and Bulaq traditions, and many of them produced newspapers as well as books.

Since the late 1820s, however, many books, and some newspapers, had been printed not from type but by lithography (*see* §4(vi)(b) above). This process was favoured in many quarters, especially in Morocco, Iran, western Central Asia and the Indian subcontinent, where it almost completely displaced typography for more than half a century. Its perceived advantages were that scribal calligraphy—including *nasta'līq*, which is difficult to reproduce typographically—could be directly reproduced and that it enabled many small publishers to avoid expensive investment in founts. At best, lithographed texts can rival in beauty and clarity well-executed manuscripts of the period; at worst, they can degenerate into barely legible grey scrawls.

Arabic typography was revived in the Middle East in the late 19th century and early 20th, with considerable improvements in typefaces, especially in Egypt, where the new founts of the Matba'at al-Ma'arif, and the Bulaq Press from 1902 onwards, set higher standards of clarity and elegance. In 1914 another new fount at the Bulaq Press halved the number of sorts by eliminating many ligatures while retaining some of the calligraphic features of the older Bulaq types. The introduction of Linotype hot-metal machines further simplified the setting of Arabic-script texts, while inevitably moving further away from traditional calligraphy and book-hands. With the decline of metal types and the introduction of photo- and computer-generated typesetting, however, the way was opened for a return to calligraphic norms.

Apart from type styles, other aesthetic features of the Islamic printed book must be noted. As with early European *incunabula*, the tendency at first was to imitate manuscript styles and layouts. Words and lines were set closely, paragraphs and punctuation were lacking, the main type area was often surrounded by rules, and glosses or even complete commentaries appeared in the margins. Red ink was sometimes used for headings or keywords, following the scribal practice of rubrication. Traditional tapered colophons were common. Title-pages were often lacking, but the verso of the first leaf was commonly begun by a decorative headpiece (Arab. *'unwān*), often containing the title and/or the basmala, the invocation of the name of God. The earliest headpieces were engraved on wood; later, elaborate designs were constructed from fleurons and other single-type ornaments following a European printing practice, the aesthetic origins of which lay in the infinitely repeatable geometric and foliate patterns of Islamic art. In the late 19th century some elaborate pseudo-Islamic designs were used for headpieces and borders, especially in Ottoman Turkey, perhaps reflecting a European rather than an indigenous taste. Later, other European artistic styles such as *Jugendstil* can be detected in decoration and page design. By this time European norms of title-pages, paragraphing, punctuation, running heads and the like had begun to dominate book production in the Islamic world.

Illustrations in Islamic printed books, until the introduction of modern half-tone techniques at the end of the 19th century, can be divided into two categories. The first is woodcuts and engraved or lithographed plates used in typographic books, mainly for maps, diagrams and didactic or technical illustrations. They often incorporate linear perspective, an innovation in many areas of the Islamic world. The second is pictures introduced into the texts of lithographed books; they are often copied from, or in the style of, paintings in manuscripts. They usually accompany literary texts from an earlier period, but sometimes modern elements intrude, as in the depiction of a gramophone in the illustration to an Uzbek lithographed text of 1913 (see Chabrov, 1984). By reproducing pictorial elements in a standard, repeatable form for a much wider readership than that of illustrated manuscripts, both kinds of illustration helped to transform artistic awareness among educated Muslims of the 19th and 20th centuries.

BIBLIOGRAPHY

Enc. Islam/2: 'Maṭba'a'
C. F. Schnurrer: *Bibliotheca arabica* (Halle, 1811, *R*/Amsterdam, 1970)
E. G. Browne: *The Press and Poetry of Modern Persia* (Cambridge, 1914)
F. Babinger: *Stambuler Buchwesen im 18. Jahrhundert* (Leipzig, 1919)
T. F. Carter: *The Invention of Printing in China and its Spread Westward* (New York, 1925, rev. 2/1955)
T. W. Arnold and A. Grohmann: *The Islamic Book: A Contribution to its Art and History from the VII–XVIII Century* (Leipzig and Paris, 1929)
C. A. Storey: 'The Beginning of Persian Printing in India', *Oriental Studies in Honour of Cursetji Erachji Pavry* (London, 1933), pp. 457–61
S. N. Gerçek: *Müteferrika matbaası* [The Müteferrika press], i of *Türk matbaacılığı* [Turkish printing] (Istanbul, 1939)
J. Nasrallah: *L'Imprimerie au Liban* (Beirut, 1948)

A. Demeerseman: 'La Lithographie arabe et tunisienne', *Rev. Inst. B.-Lett. Arab.*, xvi (1953), pp. 347–89; as booklet (Tunis, 1954)
Abu'l-Futuh Ridwan: *Ta'rīkh maṭba'at Būlāq* [History of the Bulaq press] (Cairo, 1953)
A. Demeerseman: 'L'Imprimerie en Orient et au Maghreb: Une Etape décisive de la culture et de la psychologie islamiques', *Rev. Inst. B.-Lett. Arab.*, xvii (1954), pp. 1–48; as booklet (Tunis, 1954)
A. J. Arberry: *Arabic Printing Types: A Report Made to the Monotype Corporation Limited* (n. p., *c.* 1955)
Khalil Sabat: *Ta'rīkh al-ṭibā'a fi'l-sharq al-'arabī* [History of printing in the Arab East] (Cairo, 1963, rev. 2/1966)
K. Jahn: 'Paper Currency in Iran', *J. Asian Hist.*, iv (1970), pp. 101–35
M. Krek: *Typographia Arabica: The Development of Arabic Printing as Illustrated by Arabic Type Specimens* (Waltham, MA, 1971)
R. Meynet: 'Les Difficultés de l'imprimerie', *L'Ecriture arabe en question: Les Projets de l'Académie de langue arabe du Caire de 1938 à 1968* (Beirut, 1971), pp. 30–35
G. Duverdier: 'Les Caractères de Savary de Brèves, les débuts de la typographie orientale et la présence française au Levant au 17e siècle', *L'Art du livre à l'Imprimerie Nationale* (Paris, 1973)
R. Hamm: *Pour une typographie arabe: Contribution technique à la démocratisation de la culture arabe* (Paris, 1975)
M. Krek: *A Bibliography of Arabic Typography* (Weston, MA, 1976)
W. Henkel: *Die Druckerei der Propaganda Fide: Eine Dokumentation* (Munich, 1977)
M. Krek: *A Gazetteer of Arabic Printing* (Weston, MA, 1977)
Y. Safadi: 'Arabic Printing and Book Production', *Arab Islamic Bibliography: The Middle East Library Committee Guide* (Hassocks, Sussex, 1977), pp. 221–34
H. A. Avakian: 'Islam and the Art of Printing', *Uit bibliotheektuin en informatieveld* (Utrecht, 1978), pp. 256–69
M. Krek: 'The Enigma of the First Arabic Book Printed from Movable Type', *J. Nr E. Stud.*, xxxviii (1979), pp. 203–12
M. W. Albin: 'Iraq's First Printed Book', *Libri*, xxxi (1981), pp. 167–74
E. Krüger: 'Vom Ende einer Kunst: Die Gestaltung des osmanischen Buchdruckes', *Gutenberg-Jb.*, lvi (1981), pp. 218–22
H. D. L. Vervliet: *Cyrillic and Oriental Typography in Rome at the End of the Sixteenth Century: An Inquiry into the Later Work of Robert Granjon (1578–90)* (Berkeley, 1981)
V. Cândea: 'Dès 1701: Dialogue roumano-libanais par le livre et l'imprimerie', *Le Livre et le Liban jusqu'à 1900* (Paris, 1982), pp. 281–93
G. Duverdier: 'Les Impressions orientales en Europe et le Liban', *Le Livre et le Liban jusqu'à 1900* (Paris, 1982), pp. 157–280
G. Endress: 'Die Anfänge der arabischen Typographie und die Ablösung der Handschrift durch den Buchdruck', *Grundriss der arabischen Philologie*, ed. W. Fischer, i (Wiesbaden, 1982), pp. 291–6, 312–14
G. Roper: 'Arabic Printing: Its History and Significance', *Ur* (1982), 1, pp. 23–30
J. Balagna: *L'Imprimerie arabe en Occident: XVIe, XVIIe et XVIIIe siècles* (Paris, 1984)
G. N. Chabrov: 'Illyustratsiya v turkestanskoy litografirovannoy knige, 1908–1916 gg.' [Illustrations in the lithographed books of Turkestan, 1908–16], *Kniga*, xlix (1984), pp. 95–106
W. Gdoura: *Le Début de l'imprimerie arabe à Istanbul et en Syrie: Evolution de l'environnement culturel, 1706–1787* (Tunis, 1985)
M. Krek: 'Arabic Block Printing as the Precursor of Printing in Europe: Preliminary Report', *Amer. Res. Cent. Egypt Newslett.*, cxxix (1985), pp. 12–16
G. Roper: 'Arabic Printing and Publishing in England before 1820', *Brit. Soc. Middle E. Stud. Bull.*, xii (1985), pp. 12–32
J. Nasrallah: 'Les Imprimeries melchites au XVIIIe siècle', *Proche Orient Chrét.*, xxxvi (1986), pp. 230–59
R. W. Bulliet: 'Medieval Arabic ṭarsh: A Forgotten Chapter in the History of Printing', *J. Amer. Orient. Soc.*, cvii (1987), pp. 427–38
G. Duverdier: 'Savary de Brèves et Ibrahim Müteferrika: Deux drogmans culturels à l'origine de l'imprimerie turque', *Bull. Biblioph.* (1987), 3, pp. 322–59
A. Nuovo: 'Il Corano arabo ritrovato (Venezia, P. e A. Paganini, tra l'agosto 1537 e l'agosto 1538)', *La Bibliofilia*, lxxxix (1987), pp. 237–71
A. Tinto: *La tipografia medicea orientale* (Lucca, 1987)
M. W. Albin: 'An Essay on Early Printing in the Islamic Lands with Special Relation to Egypt', *Institut Dominicain d'Etudes Orientales du Caire: Mélanges (MIDEO)*, xviii (1988), pp. 335–44
M. Borrmans: 'Observations à propos de la première édition imprimée du Coran à Venise', *Quad. Stud. Arab.*, viii (1990), pp. 3–12
A. Nuovo: *Alessandro Paganino (1509–1538)* (Padua, 1990)

——: 'A Lost Arabic Koran Rediscovered', *The Library*, 6th ser., xii (1990), pp. 273–92

K. K. Walther: 'Die lithographische Vervielfältigung von Texten in den Ländern des Vorderen und Mittleren Orients', *Gutenberg-Jb.*, lxv (1990), pp. 223–36

M. Borrmans: 'Présentation de la première édition imprimée du Coran à Venise', *Quad. Stud. Arab.*, ix (1991), pp. 93–126

R. Smitskamp: *Philologia Orientalis: A Description of Books Illustrating the Study and Printing of Oriental Languages in 16th and 17th-century Europe* (Leiden, 1992)

G. ROPER

IV. Metalwork.

The transformation of utilitarian objects into sophisticated works of art made metalwork one of the most important art forms in the Islamic world. At first Classical and Sasanian metalworking traditions were continued (*see* ROME, ANCIENT, §§IX and X, 5; EARLY CHRISTIAN AND BYZANTINE ART, §VII, 6–7; and IRAN, ANCIENT, §V), but by the 12th century a new style evolved in which wares made of copper alloys were given rich surface decoration in copper, gold and silver inlay. By *c.* 1500 this characteristic type of inlaid ware had been largely superseded, and Islamic metalwork had lost much of its originality. In the 19th century older forms and decorative themes were revived, particularly in Egypt and Iran.

1. Introduction. 2. Before *c.* 1100. 3. *c.* 1100–*c.* 1500. 4. After *c.* 1500.

1. INTRODUCTION. The metalworkers of the Islamic world created objects of great beauty using the same materials (principally gold and silver and alloys of copper, tin, zinc and lead; *see* METAL, §I), the same production processes and metalworking techniques (casting, spinning, and raising and sinking; *see* METAL, §§II–III) and the same decorative techniques (repoussé, chasing, punching, engraving, piercing and inlay; *see* METAL, §V) as their predecessors. These resources were employed to produce domestic and religious objects, architectural fittings and scientific and medical instruments, as well as arms and armour, coins and jewellery (*see* §VIII, 1, 2 and 9 below). Objects for domestic and religious use form the largest category of surviving pieces. Pre-Islamic shapes continued in use at first, but by the late 8th century or the 9th a new taste developed for heavier forms, faceted bodies and combinations of disparate elements. In the 12th and 13th centuries shapes were refined and zoomorphic features added, and in later centuries profiles became more sinuous and attenuated. These utilitarian objects were often distinguished by rich surface decoration. Geometric, vegetal and animal motifs and panels and bands containing inscriptions were common in all periods. Scenes including human figures were depicted primarily on metalwork made between the 10th and 14th centuries and were re-introduced on wares made in Iran from the 16th century onwards. □

(i) Materials. (ii) Metalworking techniques. (iii) Decorative techniques. (iv) Forms. (v) Decorative motifs.

(i) Materials. Despite the importance of gold and silver wares in the pre-Islamic period, religious scruples seem to have reduced the demand for such objects from the early 8th century, although silver objects continued to be made in Iran in some quantities (*see* §2(ii) and figs 143 and 144 below). The disapproval of precious metal tablewares by pious Muslims appears to have affected production intermittently over the following centuries, but other factors, such as metal shortages and the melting down of gold and silver objects for bullion, may have been of equal importance in explaining the lack of surviving examples.

Most surviving metal objects are made of copper and its alloys. Few Islamic pieces have been analysed, so that terms such as 'bronze' and 'brass' have been applied indiscriminately. The terminology in medieval Arabic and Persian texts is often ambiguous: the term *ṣufr* was often used for both copper and bronze, and al-Jazari (*fl* 1206), supposedly a metalworker by profession, referred to the lattice decoration on a palace door in Amida (now Diyarbakır, Turkey) as 'brass' (Arab. *shabah*), although surviving portions of this and other doors are of cast bronze. Similarly, the word *raṣāṣ* was used indiscriminately for both lead and tin. One copper alloy—'white' or high-tin bronze—has a silver colour, and, according to the Persian author al-Biruni (*d c.* 1050), it served as a substitute for silver after al-Hajjaj (*c.* 661–714), the pious governor of Iraq, had banned the use of precious metals. This statement is supported by the number of surviving 8th-century wares made of white bronze—drinking vessels, basins of different sizes and water jugs. White bronze is particularly suitable for such vessels, as it does not produce verdigris. It was also known for its ringing sound, a quality it shares with bell metal (speculum), and al-Jazari recommended its use in the construction of clocks for this reason. It continued to be used alongside silver until the late 12th century.

In the early period iron may have been used to replace bronze for the plating of doors and city gates and became important in the production of steel for weapons and tools. By the 19th century steel was being used in Iran for household and religious objects as well as arms (*see* §4(iii)(c) below). Other metals were used occasionally, as in the case of the encrusted zinc wares now in Istanbul that are thought to have been made there and in Iran from *c.* 1500.

(ii) Metalworking techniques. Casting was used in several ways. Work in the round was usually cast in open moulds, but objects of more complex shape were cast in piece moulds and then soldered together. Closed shapes were produced by the lost-wax process, of which al-Jazari, writing in northern Mesopotamia in 1206, gave an accurate, if sketchy, account. This method was probably used to produce an aquamanile with a lion-shaped handle and a body in the form of a zebu suckling a calf (?eastern Iran, 1206); it may possibly have been used for a penbox made even earlier (?eastern Iran, 1148; both St Petersburg, Hermitage). Casting with green sand was also described by al-Jazari, this time in connection with the production of lattice work. Although not mentioned in any written source, the process of spinning on a lathe was evidently used to make hollow, primarily circular, vessels from discs of sheet-metal, such as brass or white bronze. Raising and sinking, in which thin metal sheets were hammered into a variety of shapes, from flat trays to drum-shaped candlesticks, was widely employed for hollow vessels such as jugs, bottles, cups, bowls and ewers; it reached its greatest degree of sophistication in the ewers and candlesticks

produced in and around Herat in eastern Iran (now in western Afghanistan) in the late 12th century and the early 13th (*see* §3(i)(a) below).

(iii) Decorative techniques. Repoussé work (raising the design from inside) was often combined with chasing (working from the outside): repoussé was used for the rough features of a design and chasing for refining the surface texture of the ornament and sharpening its contours. Both techniques are linked to the work of the gold- and silversmith. A number of gold and silver objects decorated in repoussé and chasing survive from pre-13th-century Iran, but reports by such later Muslim travellers as Ibn Battuta (*d* 1367–8) suggest that they were manufactured over a wider area and in greater quantities. On bronze objects repoussé is generally restricted to small surfaces such as the animal and bird figures and friezes on trays, ewers and candlesticks hammered in sheet-metal. Bronzes with their entire surface decorated with repoussé work are rare, although such a practice had been known in the Near East since remote antiquity. The earliest surviving Islamic example is a gilt repoussé mosque lamp made by 'Ali ibn Muhammad al-Nisibini at Konya in Anatolia in 1280–81 (Ankara, Mus. Ethnog.).

Chasing could be carried out with variously shaped punches, chisels and tracers. The punches were stamps in the form of small bars with square, round, oval or ring-shaped ends. Punching, or ringmatting as it is called when an annular punch is used, is particularly appropriate in creating a repetitive design. Rows of punch marks were also used to attach strips or wide areas of gold, silver and copper inlay to objects made of copper alloys. Punched circles were the principal decoration on earlier metalware and vessels made of white bronze, but the technique was used most frequently to make inscriptions and other motifs stand out from the background. Although ringmatting was never completely abandoned, it seems to have gone out of fashion for bronzes in the early 13th century: the latest dated medieval example occurs on an inlaid penbox made for a vizier of the Khwarazmshahs in 1210–11 (Washington, DC, Freer).

Chasing with chisels and tracers, also called tracing or incising, was used to produce grooved surfaces and linear decoration (see fig. 156 below), as was engraving, in which grooves were made by cutting out the metal with a graver, burin or scraper. The effects produced by tracing and engraving are so similar that it is often difficult to distinguish the two. Both were used on all types of metal, either on their own or in combination with other techniques, and both were employed to trace patterns on everything from unpretentious household utensils to finer pieces decorated with intricate arabesques, to enrich repoussé and to prepare the surfaces of metal wares for inlay. Both are still commonly used in bazaar workshops.

Piercing (making holes in a metal by drilling, sawing, punching or filing) was employed for objects that required a porous or openwork surface such as lamps, incense burners and handwarmers, as well as for decorative purposes (see figs 145 and 155 below). The technique was also popular in Iran and Turkey after *c*. 1500 for plaques, handles and fine instruments.

A particularly refined form of decoration was achieved by overlaying parts of an object's surface with patterns formed from metal wires (in the case of linear inlay) or small pieces of sheet-metal (in the case of spatial inlay), the colour of the inlay differing from that of the ground. Thin pieces of red copper were sometimes hammered into small cavities to mark the eyes or feathers of a bird or to accentuate fruits or flowers, as on bronzes attributed to Mesopotamia in the 8th or 9th century. Silver wire was rarely used in these early examples. From the middle of the 12th century inlay in silver, copper, gold and other substances began to be used much more widely and to much greater effect (see figs 140 and 146–54 below). Al-Jazari described an elaborate inlay technique used for doors at Amida: a lattice work was made by cutting the pattern for the inlay from a sheet of metal, casting the grooved ground by the lost-wax technique and fitting both parts together. The use of this method cannot be confirmed from preserved examples.

Linear inlay of copper and silver was often set into deeply chased punch marks, which were usually aligned in two or three rows on either side of an incised guideline. In some instances punches with rectangular, triangular or oval edges were used to create lines with stepped, zigzag or undulating profiles. Silver was also laid into a chiselled depression, the slightly undercut or dovetailed edges of which held the inlay in place. Copper was also applied in slight depressions, but these were formed by engraving three parallel grooves the ridges of which secured the copper once it had been hammered into place. During the finishing process the inlay was made flush with the surrounding surfaces. For spatial inlays, relatively deep recesses were formed by punching the outlines and chiselling away the central area. Sheets of silver or copper were then beaten into the undercut spaces and subsequently engraved. In another method, used for gold from the mid-13th century onwards, the design was chased in shallow grooves into which the thin gold leaf was hammered. For larger areas the ground was roughened with punches or finely chased hatchings. Such roughened areas are still visible on surfaces that have lost their original gold inlay. Various black materials were used for outlines and background scrolls. For gold and silver objects, the material was niello, a mixture variously composed of silver, copper, gold and lead sulphides, which was usually set into grooves cut into the surface of the metal, heated to fuse it to its bed and then finished with abrasives. For bronze and brass objects, a black, bituminous substance was used, but its exact composition has not been established.

(iv) Forms. Metal lampstands, oil lamps, candlesticks and other lighting implements were used in great numbers in the Islamic world. The Dome of the Rock and the Aqsa Mosque in Jerusalem, for example, were said to have been lit by 5000 suspended lamps, which were supplemented by 2000 wax candles on Friday nights and special occasions. The traditional Byzantine lampstand was gradually transformed by breaking the plain surfaces of the tripod base into angular facets. Oil lamps had the same globular bodies and projecting spouts as their Roman prototypes, but their parts were more distinct, and bird and animal elements were added. Candlesticks usually had a tubular

neck between the candle socket and a large base of varying shape (e.g. drum-shaped, concave, nine-sided; see figs 147 and 156 below), although pillar lampstands were popular in 16th- and 17th-century Iran (see fig. 158 below). The few metal mosque lamps surviving from the early period are made of pierced and perforated sheet-metal and have globular bodies and flaring necks. From the late 13th century they were gradually replaced by glass lamps. In Egypt and the western Islamic world the Byzantine type of polycandelon was gradually transformed into a multi-tiered chandelier (see fig. 155 below). Many large examples made under the Mamluk sultans (reg 1250–1517; e.g. Cairo, Mus. Islam. A.) are prismatic, pyramidal and even architectural in shape.

Early Islamic incense burners have a low cylindrical body on three feet, a domed cover and a long handle. Incense burners with square bodies are rare; the unusually large example in Washington, DC (h. 315 mm; Freer), is surmounted by five domes and was probably modelled on architectural forms. A cylindrical type with a hood was popular in eastern Iran from the 11th to the 13th century, while the Byzantine type with a domed cover was preferred in the western Islamic world from the early 13th century to the mid-14th. Incense burners were given animal forms in north-eastern Iran in the 12th century (see fig. 145 below), and spherical censers were used in Egypt and Syria in the 14th and 15th centuries; they were suspended or rolled along the floor.

Small metal flasks, zoomorphic phials and bottles with elongated or pear-shaped bodies and tall, tubular necks were used for perfume. Other toilet accessories include mirrors with handles, a form that follows a long Mediterranean tradition. A larger group of small mirrors (diam. 100–200 mm) have a central perforated boss for a cord; they are based on Chinese prototypes and may have had magical or talismanic functions.

Metal inkwells, penboxes and other writing accessories were often sumptuously produced (see fig. 148 below and METAL, colour pl. I, fig. 1), although those made of precious metals and decorated with human and animal forms were regularly condemned by religious authorities, not least because these implements could be used while copying out the Koran. Inkwells, probably modelled on glass prototypes, were usually squat cylinders. A cast bronze fragment found at Nishapur suggests that the type was already in use in eastern Iran in the 10th century. Examples from the 12th and 13th centuries have lids with domed centres and small loops or handles for fastening the pots to the scribes' hands. Iranian examples from the 16th to the 18th century are taller and have bulbous lids. Penboxes usually have separate compartments for reed pens, ink, the threads placed in the inkwell to control the amount of ink taken up by the pen, sand for blotting and starch-paste for preparing the paper. The earliest dated example (1148; St Petersburg, Hermitage) is a bronze parallelepiped with openings at either end for the ink and pens. More common is the open, wedge-shaped type made in two parts so that the inner, compartmented box can be slid out. This type could be worn pushed through the belt. Rectangular open penboxes with separate, hinged covers were apparently based on wooden models. The earliest known metal examples date from the mid-12th century

and have rounded ends. This type continued to be popular in Iran (see fig. 148 below), but in Egypt and Anatolia a square-ended penbox was more common. It was the emblem of Mamluk secretaries, and in the 16th century Turkish and Chinese potters imitated the form in ceramic. Another type of penbox worn through the belt in Ottoman Turkey was a flattened tubular pen container with a small inkpot attached.

Metal caskets and boxes assumed a considerable variety of shapes and sizes, ranging from miniature receptacles 20 to 30 mm across to large containers 200 to 300 mm a side. Larger chests were made of wood and bound or plated with metal. The two basic types are rectangular caskets and cylindrical boxes. Silver caskets from 10th- to 12th-century Spain were modelled on ivory prototypes; brass or bronze caskets from 12th- to 14th-century Iran imitated the forms and decoration of those in silver. The earliest cylindrical boxes, attributed to Iran in the 12th century, are large; later brass examples from Mesopotamia or Syria are smaller and more slender and always have flat covers with bevelled edges. Cylindrical boxes with low bodies and domed covers were probably made in Syria from the late 13th century to the early 14th. Besides these two basic types, there are other pieces with unusual shapes and dimensions, such as a kidney-shaped box in London (BM). Unusual shapes and inscriptions sometimes elucidate a container's function. Mamluk lunch boxes, for example, have three separate units stacked one on top of the other; they are bronze that has been tinned to prevent food poisoning, and their rounded shape facilitated cleaning. Koran boxes were large squares, usually made of plated wood (see fig. 152 below).

Large metal ewers were often made in sets with matching basins for ablutions. Early Islamic ewers were made in such a wide variety of shapes—oval bodies and handles with thumb rests (see fig. 142 below) and round bodies with zoomorphic spouts, for example—that their grouping is still controversial. Iranian workshops in the 11th and 12th centuries experimented further with shapes, creating embossed, fluted and faceted forms (see fig. 146 below) and composite ewers with vase-shaped bodies and spouts like oil lamps. In Mesopotamia shapes with broad surfaces that could be enriched with figural decoration were preferred; ewers made there in the late 12th century and the early 13th have wide shoulders and are heavier and less elegant (see fig. 151 below). Later Iranian and Turkish ewers are increasingly attenuated and curvaceous. Metal water-flasks were often modelled on those in other materials. The Freer Canteen, a large round flask with flat sides attributed to 13th-century Syria (Washington, DC, Freer), is based on Late Antique pilgrim flasks, and pot-bellied water flasks in gold and gilt copper produced under the Ottomans had leather prototypes.

Drinking cups and bowls of precious metal are described as princely accoutrements, but few have survived from the early Islamic period. Hemispherical bowls were made of silver or white bronze in the early period. Stemmed cups and bowls, probably derived from pre-Islamic Iranian prototypes, were popular in Iran from the 10th to the 12th century. Inlaid hemispherical bowls from the 13th century include such masterpieces as the 'Vaso Vescovali' (London, BM), the Wade Cup (Cleveland, OH,

140. Bobrinsky Bucket by Muhammad ibn 'Abd al-Wahid and Hajib Mas'ud ibn Ahmad al-Naqqash, bronze inlaid with copper and silver, h. 180 mm, from Herat, 1163 (St Petersburg, Hermitage Museum)

Flat metal dishes and trays were often made in sets, such as the five trays bearing the name of Yusuf, the second Rasulid sultan of Yemen (*reg* 1250–95). Circular trays were usually decorated with concentric bands (see fig. 150 below), while rectangular trays, which were particularly popular in the eastern Islamic world in the 12th century, had recessed wells. A variety of flat dishes, occasionally fitted with three legs, were also used in the eastern Islamic world.

Metal cooking vessels ranged enormously in size. Tiny pots with long spouts were used for preparing indigo. A series of medium-sized cauldrons from the eastern Islamic world (diam. 500 mm) have narrow everted rims and four flanges and are often inscribed with the maker's name. A large basin for drinking water (diam. 1.75 m) was donated to the mosque at Herat in 1375, and Timur ordered a gargantuan basin (diam. 2.45 m) for the shrine of Ahmad Yasavi at Turkestan (now in Kazakhstan) in 1399. Bronze mortars were widely used for pharmaceutical purposes and had cylindrical bodies, often decorated with facets, flanges and bosses.

Architectural furnishings were also made of metal. Iron door plates are known from two gates erected in Yazd in 1040; they are decorated with inscriptions, archers and elephants with armed riders. Several examples of plated doors are known from northern Mesopotamia (*see* §3(ii)(d) below). Most extant examples are plated with iron or bronze alloys: the examples made of silver described in texts have probably been melted down. Knockers were often made of cast bronze in the shape of open-work arabesques and confronted dragons. Screens and grilles made of iron bars connected by balls were often of high quality. A particularly fine iron example in the Is'irdiyya madrasa in Jerusalem (1359) is signed by Muhammad ibn al-Zayn, the same name that occurs on the 'Baptistère de St Louis', while three brass balls inlaid with silver and gold are inscribed with the name of the Ilkhanid sultan Uljaytu (*reg* 1304–17) and probably came from his tomb at Sultaniyya. Iranian padlocks were made in an extraordinary variety of zoomorphic shapes despite their small size (50×35 mm on average). The locks and keys made for the Ka'ba in Mecca are important historical documents as they are usually inscribed with the names and titles of the donors. Scientific and medical instruments—astrolabes, globes, knives and scissors—form a final category of utilitarian metalwares. They were often of fine quality and beautifully decorated.

(v) Decorative motifs. Geometric patterns on Islamic metalwork are confined within closed borders or medallions and rarely form continuous surface patterns or the main decorative feature, as they do in other Islamic arts. Instead they provide a network of squares, lozenges, circles or hexagons into which other motifs are set, or, like swastikas and basket weaving, they function as background patterns or space fillers. Circles are often interlaced, and a circle circumscribing six or eight interlaced circles was a common design in the 13th and 14th centuries. From the early 12th century, particularly in Iran, the most frequently used patterns were those based on hexagons. Geometry also provided the foundation for vegetal and floral arabesques.

Mus. A.) and the Peytel Cup (priv. col.). From the 15th century the bowl-shaped cup was supplemented in Iran and Turkey by a covered tankard with a bulbous body, cylindrical neck and single handle. In the second half of the 16th century a straight-sided tankard modelled on wood and metal prototypes became popular in the Ottoman empire. Larger metal bowls served other functions. After the 13th century the well-balanced proportions of earlier examples were gradually replaced by more angular types, whose sharply convex sides give them a heavy and clumsy appearance. Many examples are known from Iran, Syria and Egypt (see fig. 154 below). Bowls used by itinerant dervishes for begging (Pers. *kashkūl*) have a characteristic boat shape. Basins have flat bases, straight, curved or faceted sides and flaring or fluted rims. Extremely fine examples such as the 'Baptistère de St Louis' (Paris, Louvre; see fig. 153 below) and the d'Arenburg Basin (Washington, DC, Freer) show an extraordinary range of decoration. Buckets with bail handles were necessary bathhouse utensils, but they too include such superb examples as the Bobrinsky Bucket (St Petersburg, Hermitage; see fig. 140), made for a merchant in Herat in 1163 and decorated with friezes of merrymakers, animals and animated inscriptions in inlaid copper and silver.

The basic elements of vegetal ornament on Islamic metalwares—the pomegranate, vine, acanthus and lotus—derive from Ancient Near Eastern and Hellenistic sources, but these elements were combined in new ways, were articulated differently and were assigned new functions. Vegetation not only formed the principal decoration, but also provided a neutral ground for other elements. Denaturalized plants, similar to those found on stone and stucco decoration made under the Umayyad caliphs (*reg* AD 661–750), occur on early bronze and silver vessels and serve both as ornament and as formal devices to subdivide the surface. Less ambitious objects have undulating stalks with shoots that branch off the main stem and carry vine and palmette leaves. Scrolls inhabited with birds, hares and other animals appear on late 8th-century bird figures and on the Marwan Ewer (Cairo, Mus. Islam. A.; *see* §2(i)(b) below). Fully developed arabesques appear by the 10th century in various forms. That on a silver cup in New York (Met., 64.132.2) has pairs of axially opposed split palmettes, while others, particularly on brasses signed by artists associated with Mosul, have pairs of knotted, bifurcated palmettes blossoming from crescent-shaped loops. Arabesques could also swirl over the entire surface of an object, as on the ewer made for the Ayyubid ruler of Aleppo in 1232 (Washington, DC, Freer).

A single plant, isolated sprout or flower was occasionally set against a plain ground to give the illusion of a garden or outdoor environment. This occurred on early Islamic silver or bronze objects in the Sasanian style, as on a silver vase in Jerusalem (Mayer Mem. Inst. Islam. A., M107–69), or in a more conventionalized manner on 13th-century Mesopotamian brasses and their derivatives. A tray in Cleveland, OH (Mus. A., 45.386), for example, has single sprouts set against a neutral background of regularly winding spiral scrolls. More naturalistic plants begin to appear in the 13th century, and flowers from the repertory of Chinese design such as the lotus, peony and morning glory become dominant motifs.

Animals commonly appear on Islamic metalwork produced for non-religious purposes before the 13th century. Birds, fish and animals related to the hunt were supplemented by such imaginary creatures as simurghs, griffins, sphinxes, harpies and unicorns. Occasionally whole vessels, such as fountainheads and incense burners, were fashioned in the shape of animals (see fig. 141 below), and animals served as handles, feet and spouts. Animals were depicted in many different compositions: singly in medallions, paired, in combat, revolving around a central axis, in friezes and in scrolls. These creatures expressed good wishes as well as serving as ornamental devices.

The most common figural theme depicted was that of pleasures and pastimes. On early pieces banquet and hunt scenes occur in the centre of plates and dishes, but by the mid-12th century scenes of merrymaking were applied to a variety of shapes in different compositions, including continuous bands, individual frames and concentric bands. Besides banqueting scenes, often with musicians and dancers, and episodes from the hunt, there were depictions of boating, riding in a howdah and polo matches. These princely themes continued the Ancient Near Eastern tradition of royal diversions and were popular in all times and periods. Other subjects, such as scenes from outdoor life, labour and recreation, and fighting warriors, were limited to specific regions.

The cosmic and terrestrial cycles found on many vessels made after the 12th century reflect a growing concern with magic and astrology. The symbols of the planets follow the Hellenistic tradition in their essentials and are analogous to planetary figures in Islamic illustrated manuscripts. The signs of the zodiac are usually shown in combination with their astrological lords, the planets. On a penbox made by Mahmud ibn Sunqur (London, BM; see fig. 148 below and METAL, colour pl. I, fig. 1), for example, the planet Mars, represented by a warrior with a sword and severed head, rides a ram, representing Aries. New and unconventional symbols are inserted into the astrological cycle, such as human-headed birds in the sign of Gemini or variations on the traditional representation of Venus as a female lute-player. A princely figure surrounded by six planets and the twelve signs of the zodiac appears on a series of objects made between the late 12th century and the late 13th. The Labours of the Months, a popular theme in Byzantine and European medieval art, are found on a group of candlesticks attributed to north-western Iran or eastern Anatolia in the late 13th century and the early 14th.

Scenes from epics and legends also occur on Islamic metalwares. Some, such as Bahram Gur hunting, continue Sasanian conventions of the royal hunter. Others, such as Faridun bringing Zahhak to Mt Damavand, appear later in illustrated manuscripts of the *Shāhnāma* ('Book of Kings'), the Persian national epic. Still others, such as the inhabited fish pond, go back to the Alexander Romance and other popular legends.

Christian scenes and figures occur on 18 inlaid wares that can be attributed to 13th-century Syria on technical and stylistic grounds. They range in quality from the splendid d'Arenburg Basin (Washington, DC, Freer), dedicated to the Ayyubid sultan al-Salih Ayyub (*reg* 1240–50), to a rather crude incense burner in Cleveland, OH (Mus. A.). The scenes do not form any coherent Christian cycle and have anomalous details. On the d'Arenburg Basin, for example, the *Raising of Lazarus* incorrectly follows *Christ's Entry into Jerusalem*, and Lazarus is represented in a way otherwise unknown in eastern Christian art.

Inscriptions containing signatures, dates or short blessings appeared on metalwares of the early Islamic period but were not integrated into the decoration. By the late 10th century or early 11th, they had been adapted to the shape of the object and integrated into the overall decorative schema. On later Iranian wares, inscriptions were often placed in cartouches set within floral and geometric patterns, while on later pieces from Egypt and Syria they constituted the major part of the decoration and appeared in continuous and intersecting bands and radial arrangements. In general, the same kinds of monumental scripts were used on metalwork as are found in other media. The earliest inscriptions were written in the simple angular script known as kufic, while plaited, foliated and floriated forms of kufic appeared on bronzes attributed to Khurasan (eastern Iran) in the 11th and 12th centuries. The plaiting and knotting of kufic letters spread westward from Khurasan, and by the 13th century they were appearing on wares made in Syria and Mesopotamia. In the 12th century cursive script was introduced; the first dated example, in which cursive and kufic scripts are juxtaposed, is a penbox made in 1148 (St Petersburg, Hermitage). Cursive scripts gradually replaced kufic, and inscriptions on later wares are done in increasingly attenuated styles, such as the *thuluth* used on Syrian and Egyptian wares and the *nasta'liq* used in Iran.

One type of script, however, is unique to metalwork: in it part or all of the letters assume human or animal form. A script in which the letters were transformed into birds or in which the tails of the letters end in birds' heads was already in use on slip-covered ceramics made in the eastern Iranian world in the 10th century and was then transferred to bronzes produced there. Human-headed, zoomorphic and anthropomorphic scripts are all documented on the Bobrinsky Bucket (see fig. 140 above). In the upper inscription in cursive, for example, the top half of the letters are transformed into figures of revellers, dancers and musicians, while the lower sections assume bird and animal shapes or end in bird and animal heads. Gradually, more animal heads and new species of lively and humorously drawn creatures were added, as on the masterful zoomorphic script on the Wade Cup (Cleveland, OH, Mus. A.). In the 13th century all three types were transferred to northern Mesopotamia and Syria, where they became increasingly elaborate so that scenes of merrymaking obscured their legibility and they became merely ornamental.

BIBLIOGRAPHY

D. Barrett: *Islamic Metalwork in the British Museum* (London, 1949)
L. A. Mayer: *Islamic Metalworkers and their Works* (Geneva, 1959)
U. Scerrato: *Metalli islamici* (Milan, 1966)
J. Sourdel-Thomine: 'Clefs et serrures de la Ka'ba', *Rev. Etud. Islam.*, xxxix (1971), pp. 29–86
G. Fehérvári: *Islamic Metalwork of the Eighth to the Fifteenth Century in the Keir Collection* (London, 1976)
P. Tanavoli and J. T. Wertime: *Locks from Iran* (Washington, DC, 1976)
J. W. Allan: *Persian Metal Technology, 700–1300 A.D.* (London, 1979)
——: *Islamic Metalwork: The Nuhad Es-Said Collection* (London, 1982)
A. S. Melikian-Chirvani: *Islamic Metalwork from the Iranian World, 8–18th Centuries* (London, 1982)
E. Baer: *Metalwork in Medieval Islamic Art* (Albany, NY, 1983)
E. Atıl, W. T. Chase and P. Jett: *Islamic Metalwork in the Freer Gallery of Art* (Washington, DC, 1985)
Pots and Pans: A Colloquium on Precious Metals and Ceramics, Oxford, 1985
J. W. Allan: *Metalwork of the Islamic World: The Aron Collection* (London, 1986)
F. Bodur: *Türk maden sanatı/The Art of Turkish Metalworking* (Istanbul, 1987)

EVA BAER

2. BEFORE *c.* 1100. Base metal wares were produced in large numbers throughout the Islamic world between the 7th and 11th centuries, and many pieces survive. Far fewer gold and silver objects are known, and almost all can be attributed to Iran.

(i) Base metals. (ii) Gold and silver.

(i) Base metals. While earlier metalworking and decorative techniques were continued, metalware produced in the Islamic world before 1100 introduced three new features: zoomorphic shapes for whole vessels or for appendages such as spouts and handles; ornamental inscriptions; and inlay in metals of contrasting colour. Base metal wares such as oil lamps and ewers exemplify these developments.

These objects can be grouped typologically and geographically, but attributions to particular regions must be treated with caution, as the shapes and techniques of much early Islamic metalwork were spread over a vast area by trade: a common lamp form has been found in Egypt, at Kairouan, on Mallorca and at several medieval Spanish and Portuguese sites, for example. Nevertheless, four major regions may be delineated.

□

(a) Spain. Self-sufficient in both base and precious metals, Islamic Spain inherited a flourishing metalworking industry from the Visigothic period, and its continued existence was noted by later authors such as Ibn Sa'id (*d* 1286), who reported that brass and iron objects were regularly exported to North Africa. Córdoba and Madinat al-Zahra', as the capitals of the Spanish branch of the Umayyad dynasty (*reg* 756–1031), must have attracted the finest craftsmen of the day. Several pieces were found there, and texts mention extravagant objects such as a fountain basin with 12 water-spouts, each in the shape of a different animal, made of gold inlaid with pearls; other examples were made of silver and copper. Other centres known from textual references include Almería, famous for its copper and iron utensils under the Almoravids (*reg* 1056–1147); Málaga, which produced iron knives and

141. Fountain-head in the shape of a deer, cast bronze, h. 400 mm, found at Madinat al-Zahra', near Córdoba, Spanish, 10th century (Córdoba, Museo Arqueológico)

scissors according to the 14th-century geographer al-'Umari; and Toledo and Seville, which were recorded as important metalworking centres by al-Maqqari in the 16th century.

The most important surviving objects from the Umayyad period are two fountain-heads in the shape of deer: one (Córdoba, Mus. Arqueol.; see fig. 141) has a cast body covered with a denatured net of circles formed by vine scrolls and was found in the ruins of Madinat al-Zahra'; the other (Madrid, Mus. Arqueol. N.) was found in Córdoba. A peacock-shaped aquamanile (Paris, Louvre) bears an inscription in both Arabic and Latin and has been attributed to both Spain and Sicily. Zoomorphic pieces continued to be produced in the region in later periods (*see* §3(iv) below). Astrolabes were made in great quantity, especially in the 11th century. Many are dated: there are examples from Toledo dated 1028, 1067 and 1068; from Valencia dated 1071 and 1086; from Saragossa dated 1079–80; and from Guadalajara dated 1081–2. Other early bronzes from Islamic Spain are more important as evidence for a flourishing Mediterranean trade than for their artistic qualities.

(b) Egypt and Syria. Shapes scarcely changed between the 6th century, when the Middle East was under Byzantine rule, and the 8th. The form of basin found at the 7th-century Anglo-Saxon ship burial at Sutton Hoo in England, for example, also occurs at Pella (i), an early 8th-century site in Jordan, and a brazier with ivory inlay typical of 6th-century Egyptian work was excavated at Mafraq, a site of the Umayyad period (AD 661–750), also in Jordan. Except for specifically Christian objects, recognizable by their liturgical function or motifs such as the Cross, it is impossible to distinguish those made for Muslim patrons from those made for Christians; the label 'Coptic' is therefore inappropriate and should be avoided when referring to metalwork of the Islamic period. Alexandria in Egypt was an important centre of production in the classical world, and it probably continued to be so in early Islamic times, although there is no specific evidence. Harran in northern Syria (now in Turkey) is the only centre in the Levant to be specifically associated with a particular product: according to the *Fihrist* ('Index') of al-Nadim (*d* AD 995), it was a centre of astrolabe production.

The most famous piece associated with Egypt is the Marwan Ewer (Cairo, Mus. Islam. A.), so called because it was found near the spot where the last Umayyad caliph, Marwan II, was killed and buried in AD 750. Variously attributed to 8th- or 9th-century Egypt, Syria, Iraq and Iran, it can be dated to the late 8th century by comparison with two bird-shaped aquamaniles of cast bronze. One (St Petersburg, Hermitage) has traces of silver inlay and is dated 796; the other (undated; Berlin, Mus. Islam. Kst) is decorated with incised designs—rosettes, rabbits and birds in roundels among scrolling vine-stems—that are very similar to those on the Marwan Ewer. An Egyptian source for the ewer is suggested by two stylistic features: the dolphins supporting the handle base follow the classical taste for such creatures; and the rabbits incised on its body are also found in Coptic (i.e. pre-Islamic Egyptian) art and became a popular subject on Fatimid ceramics. The ewer

was found with two typically Egyptian objects, a three-footed bucket and another, concave-sided ewer. Other Egyptian vessels of this period have three feet, while concavity is typical of early Islamic bronzes from Egypt and can be found in bowls, ewers, basins, bottles and albarellos.

The Marwan Ewer sheds light on the hierarchy of media in early Islamic times. Its shape and the steps at the top and bottom of the globular body show that it owes its form to cameo glass, and the elaborate spout and perforated funnel top suggest that the glass prototype has bejewelled precious metal mounts. The circular cavities around the body would originally have held small, ruby-like copper discs in imitation of a bejewelled original. Another form of bronze ewer that may also be Egyptian has a pear-shaped or globular body, a thin neck and an unusual form of handle with a rhomboid knop, sometimes pierced, halfway up. One example (Richmond, Surrey, Kier priv. col., see Fehérvári, no. 2) was purchased in Egypt, while others have been found in Sicily, Lebanon, Syria and Spain.

(c) Iraq and western Iran. Written sources name several centres in Iraq and western Iran that produced metalware in the early Islamic period (the 10th-century geographer al-Muqaddasi, for example, mentioned Hamadan as a centre for high-tin bronze), but only two sites, Isfahan and Basra, can be specifically related to objects. The name al-Isfahani, associating the bearer with Isfahan, occurs first on 10th-century astrolabes and then fairly frequently over the next two centuries, suggesting that the city continued to be a metalworking centre during this period. The other centre, Basra in Iraq, is named on the Tiflis Ewer (Tbilisi, Mus. A. Georgia; see fig. 142), which has a high, flaring foot, a fluted body and neck and a handle with a large palmette-shaped thumb-rest. The inscription on its round, open mouth says that it was made in Basra by Ibn Yazid in AH 67 or 69 (AD 686 or 688), but the hundreds digit may have been omitted for lack of space, in which case the object should be dated to either the 8th or 9th century on stylistic grounds. This would put the ewer in the Abbasid period (750–1258), when cultural trends moved eastward from Iraq, and would account for similar ewers with round mouths attributed to 10th-century Iran (e.g. ex-Lewisohn priv. col.; untraced) and 12th- and 13th-century eastern Iran and Central Asia (e.g. the Samarkand Ewer, St Petersburg, Hermitage). Other forms of metalwork reinforce the idea that Abbasid Iraq set the taste for Iran. Ewers with inverted, pear-shaped bodies and cylindrical necks, for example, are known from Abbasid Iraq (e.g. Baghdad, Iraq Mus.), 10th-century Iran (e.g. New York, Met., 32.86) and 12th- and 13th-century eastern Iran (e.g. the Nishapur Ewer; New York, Met.), as are tubular-spouted ewers and cosmetic articles.

An outstanding group of ewers with copper inlay was also produced in 9th- or 10th-century Iraq. The two finest examples (St Petersburg, Hermitage, KZ 5750; Baltimore, MD, Walters A.G., 54.457) have heavy palmette and other vegetal designs in relief, while another (London, V&A) is virtually undecorated. These weighty cast ewers are unrivalled in monumentality and show the sophistication of the base metal industry of Abbasid times.

142. Tiflis Ewer by Ibn Yazid, bronze, h. 648 mm, from Basra, Iraq, AD 686 or 688 (Tbilisi, Museum of Art of Georgia)

(d) Eastern Iran and western Central Asia. The period before 1100 was the age of fine bronze casting in eastern Iran; once the technique of decorating metal objects with large areas of copper and silver inlay developed in the 12th century, the art of bronze casting declined. Before 1100, for example, there are many forms of cast lamp, but in the 12th century there is only one standard inlaid form.

A group of 'white', or high-tin, bronze objects has been attributed to the province of Khurasan in eastern Iran in the early Islamic period (e.g. a bowl from Nishapur; Tehran, Archaeol. Mus., 9797). They are decorated with geometric patterns composed of dot-and-circle motifs, dots, lines and discs. A number of large hemispherical basins, probably also made of high-tin bronze, are slightly later in date. They can be linked by the bifurcated hats worn by the courtly figures depicted on them to the Ghaznavid dynasty, which ruled Khurasan and lands further east from 977 to 1186. The pieces are notable for the inscriptions they bear, which continue the tradition of maxims used on 10th- and 11th-century ceramics from Khurasan and Transoxiana (*see* §V, 2(iii) below). These

objects confirm the statement by al-Biruni (*d c.* 1050) that in his day the people of the province of Sistan in eastern Iran were particularly skilled in the manufacture of high-tin bronze.

There are many more examples of cast objects made from a quaternary alloy of copper, lead, zinc and tin. They form three groups. The first consists of objects bearing inscriptions of the type current before *c.* 1100 or designs related to those on glazed ceramics produced in Khurasan and Transoxiana before the rise of the Saljuq dynasty in the 11th century. It includes animal- and bird-shaped incense burners and ewers with zoomorphic spouts, as well as aquamaniles, lampstands and dishes. The second group, which includes bottles, ewers and incense burners, has almond-shaped bosses as virtually the only form of decoration. They can be tentatively dated to the 11th and 12th centuries. The third group consists of undecorated lamps and ewers and can be dated to the period before *c.* 1100 by association with ceramics excavated at Nishapur, at Paykand near Bukhara and at Samarkand.

Bronzes, often of a rather idiosyncratic type, were produced in Transoxiana. Noteworthy among the surviving pieces are bowls and ewers of a curious angular shape, some of which were signed by a metalworker called Ahmad. The geographer al-Muqaddasi (*d* AD 985) mentioned Bukhara, Samarkand and the smaller settlement of Shargh near by as centres for the production of copper or copper alloys and specified Rabingan between Samarkand and Bukhara as a centre for high-tin bronze. The quantity of animal- and bird-shaped objects from eastern Iran may be linked with the Buddhist bronze-casting industry in Kashmir and nearby regions, which produced many images in the pre-Islamic and early Islamic periods. The continued existence of this industry in early Islamic times would account, for example, for the small amounts of inlay used on the incense burners. Small pieces of copper and turquoise set into the surface of these replaced the silver inlay commonly used on the Buddhist pieces. It is uncertain whether this was the inspiration for all the inlay used in the eastern Islamic world at this time. Linear inlay for inscriptions is found on a number of pieces, including a late 9th- or 10th-century ewer (Herat Mus.).

Metalware from the eastern Iranian world also shows ties to older western Central Asian traditions. A number of horse bronzes excavated at Nishapur (Tehran, Archaeol. Mus.; New York, Met.) have designs based on the felt- and woodworking traditions of western Central Asia and the Altai Mountains. A belt piece from the site is decorated with a stylized flower with four leaves and two symmetrical stems similar to the design on a belt plate of the Migration Period found in Russia. Other designs imitate those of precious metal. Base metal jewellery from Nishapur and Rayy, for example, imitated that in gold and silver and was probably made for less affluent members of the population.

BIBLIOGRAPHY

M. Gómez-Moreno: *El arte español hasta los almohades: Arte mozárabe* (1951), iii of *Ars Hispaniae* (Madrid, 1947–77), pp. 324–41

A. A. Ivanov: 'O proizvodstve bronzovykh izdeliy v Maverannakhre v domongol'skoye vremya' [On the production of bronze wares in Transoxiana in the pre-Mongol period], *Kratkiye Soobshcheniya Inst. Arkheol. AN SSR*, cxxii (1970), pp. 101–5

J. W. Allan: *Nishapur: Metalwork of the Early Islamic Period* (New York, 1972)

B. I. Marshak: 'Bronzovyy kuvshin iz Samarkanda' [A bronze jug from Samarkand], *Srednyaya Aziya i Iran* [Central Asia and Iran], ed. A. A. Ivanov and S. S. Sorokin (Leningrad, 1972), pp. 61–90

L. Torres Balbás: 'Arte califal', *España musulmana hasta la caída del Califato de Córdoba* (1973), v of *Historia de España*, ed. R. Menéndez Pidal (Madrid, 1935–), pp. 745–69

A. S. Melikian-Chirvani: 'The White Bronzes of Early Islamic Iran', *Met. Mus. J.*, ix (1974), pp. 286–91

G. Fehérvári: *Islamic Metalwork of the Eighth to the Fifteenth Centuries in the Keir Collection* (London, 1976)

J. W. Allan: 'Silver: The Key to Bronze in Early Islamic Iran', *Kst Orients*, xi (1976–7), pp. 5–21

A. S. Melikian-Chirvani: 'Les Thèmes ésotériques et les thèmes mystiques dans l'art de bronze iranien', *Mélanges H. Corbin* (Tehran, 1977), pp. 367–406

Al-Andalus: The Art of Islamic Spain (exh. cat., ed. J. D. Dodds; Granada, Alhambra; New York, Met.; 1992)

J. W. ALLAN

(ii) Gold and silver. Gold and silver plate, particularly the latter, had been widely used in the Mediterranean world of Late Antiquity, in the Sasanian empire (AD 224–651) and in pre-Islamic western Central Asia. Such luxury objects were known in Arabia when Islam emerged in the early 7th century AD, and the early Muslims must have acquired many more as booty during their conquests, particularly when they captured the Sasanian capital at Ktesiphon in AD 637. The Koran frequently mentions the denizens of paradise using gold and silver cups, but only once does it refer to their use by humans, when it forbids the hoarding of precious metals (Koran, ix.34). By the early 8th century official opinion had hardened against the use of gold and silver for vessels and jewellery. The emphasis placed on these sumptuary prohibitions suggests that Muslims of the period were wearing gold jewellery and using gold and silver vessels like those employed in the Sasanian wine-drinking ceremony (Pers. *bazm*).

Little early Islamic plate has survived, but this may be due as much to its destruction in financial emergencies as to religious scruples. Gold and silver plate was always considered a currency reserve that could be melted down for minting (an early 13th-century parcel-gilt silver cup in the Keir priv. col., Richmond, Surrey, has been deliberately broken into large fragments, probably for this purpose). Surviving plate shows that pre-Islamic decorative themes such as banquet scenes, the hunt, and musical entertainments continued to be used, although the designs were simplified and made more geometric and abstract. Surfaces were increasingly compartmentalized, and backgrounds, which had previously been undecorated, were patterned with ringmatting. As in all the Islamic decorative arts, inscriptions became increasingly common. Gold and, even more so, silver were used extensively for architectural fittings in the medieval Islamic world, but nothing has survived subsequent financial emergencies. The Ka'ba at Mecca had silver doors, silver door-rings and locks, silver mihrabs, silver panels and gold inscription bands, while gold and silver lamps once illuminated the Dome of the Rock in Jerusalem and other major shrines. Extraordinary precious metal objects were looted from the treasuries of the Fatimid caliphs in 1067 by hungry troops. Among them were bejewelled golden birds and animals and a miniature garden of silver planted with gilt trees and flowers set with gems.

Sasanian-style silver plate decorated in high relief with scenes of the king hunting and feasting continued to be produced in those mountainous areas of Iran along the Caspian Sea that had remained unconquered by the Muslims. In these 'post-Sasanian' or 'Tabaristan' wares the relief tended to be flattened, the scale of individual figures was reduced, the figures became stylized to the point of caricature, and the barrier between figure and ornament broke down. Examples include three silver bowls and two forks found in the province of Mazandaran (all Tehran, Archaeol. Mus.). The bowls are inscribed with the name of Windad Ohrmazd, a local ruler in the late 8th century. On the exterior rows of niello hearts create four radial compartments containing single female figures derived from the Sasanian motif of bacchantes accompanied by auspicious attributes; they have been transformed into musicians, and Sasanian naturalism has given way to a flatter, more abstract style. Similarly, the Sogdian tradition of silver plate continued after the Islamic conquest of western Central Asia, but the stylization of older forms is even more pronounced.

143. Silver ewer made for Abu'l-'Abbas Valgin ibn Harun, diam. 266 mm, found at Hamadan, western Iran, *c.* 1000 (Tehran, Archaeological Museum)

144. Octagonal gilt silver tray, diam. 358 mm, from Iran, 10th century (Berlin, Museum für Islamische Kunst)

Fewer than 100 other silver and gold objects survive from medieval Islamic times, and they also come from the Iranian world, suggesting that traditional Iranian values may have outweighed Islamic prohibitions. Two hoards of silver objects were found in Iran, and individual pieces have been unearthed in the former Soviet Union. Most of the remainder do not have a clear provenance, and their authenticity, like that of many other objects attributed to 10th-century Iran, has often been questioned. The first hoard of silver was found at Hamadan in western Iran (Tehran, Archaeol. Mus.) and consisted of three conical bowls, two saucers, a tray, a ewer, two small jugs, a bottle and a cup; these have been identified as the wine-service of Abu'l-'Abbas Valgin ibn Harun, whose name appears on seven of the pieces in inscriptions that invoke blessings and good wishes on him. He is identified as 'client of the Commander of the Faithful', a title that suggests that these objects date from c. 1000. Angular inscription bands inlaid in niello encircle each piece, which is otherwise plain (see fig. 143). The second hoard of silver, reportedly found in northern Iran (Jerusalem, Mayer Mem. Inst. Islam. A.; ex-Harari priv. col.), included seven perfume sprinklers, six incense burners, three jugs, two caskets, a cup, a spoon and several sets of horse-trappings. The pieces, decorated with gilt or niello, fall into two stylistic groups that have been attributed to 10th-century Khurasan (north-eastern Iran) and 11th-century Iran. The shapes of many of these objects are repeated in later bronze and brass wares and in other precious metal objects attributed to the same period.

A type of small jug (h. c. 150 mm) with a round body and a tall flaring neck, sometimes provided with a curved handle, is found in both silver and gold. An example in silver decorated with peacocks in roundels is inscribed with the name of an amir who held the same high rank as Valgin ibn Harun; another with a handle and three feet and more attenuated proportions offers blessings to Husayn ibn 'Ali (both St Petersburg, Hermitage). A gold jug without handle (Tehran, Riza 'Abbasi Mus.) is decorated in shallow relief with inscription bands and birds in roundels. Two other jugs with handles (Washington, DC, Freer and Cleveland, OH, Mus. A.) are inscribed with the names of Buyid amirs. The example in Washington, naming Abu Mansur Bakhtiyar (d AD 978), has a curvaceous profile with little distinction between body and neck, while that in Cleveland, with a poem dedicated to Samsam al-Dawla in AD 983–5, has the more traditional rounded body and flaring neck. Shallow bowls, or cups, were similarly made with and without handles. Some were simple hemispherical vessels; others, with more vertical sides, foot-rings and handles with finger holes and thumb-rests, are distinguished by decoration on the exterior, which ranges from chased inhabited vine-scrolls (e.g. priv. col., see Baer, 1983, fig. 78) to epigraphic and animal friezes (Jerusalem, Mayer Mem. Inst. Islam. A., M40–68).

Flat dishes or trays were usually round and derived from Byzantine prototypes, although octagonal and rectangular examples are known (see fig. 144). They are decorated on the upper surface, often with concentric bands. An engraved and partly gilt example was found in 1903 at Izgirli in Bulgaria (diam. 315 mm; Paris, Bib. N., Cab. Médailles) along with Byzantine coins indicating that the hoard was buried c. 1200. It has an interlaced hexagram in the centre, circumscribed by a frieze of running animals in an undulating vine scroll. The most famous example is a large flat dish or salver in Boston, MA (diam. 430 mm; Mus. F.A.). Its inscriptions state that a queen ordered it from Hasan of Kashan for the Saljuq sultan Alp Arslan (reg 1063–72) in 1066, but the unusually lengthy inscription, jumbled titulature and peculiar style cast doubt on its authenticity. A rectangular tray in St Petersburg (Hermitage) is exquisitely inscribed with the name and titles of Abu Ibrahim, who ruled Khwarazm in western Central Asia in the 11th century. Its simple decoration and the understated elegance of its epigraphy contrast sharply with the crowded design of the Alp Arslan Salver. Small flat dishes with slightly inverted sides and three feet have been identified as incense burners. One (ex-Kelekian priv. col.) is of silver decorated with niello and gilding. It has a central medallion depicting a sphinx surrounded by six tear-shaped pendants. An inscription band, punctuated with circular medallions, runs along the exterior walls. Two other examples in Jerusalem belong to the Harari hoard, which also included four incense burners with long handles, a type also known in base metal.

Precious metals were also used for commemorative medallions. The historian Ibn al-Athir (d 1233) stated that on 1 Muharram AH 378 (21 April AD 988; New Year's Day) the vizier Ibn 'Abbad presented Fakhr al-Dawla, the Buyid ruler of Rayy, with a gold dinar weighing 4.25 kg. On one side it had seven lines of Arabic poetry extolling the piece as a sun and the ruler as king of kings; on the other it was inscribed (like a coin) with chapter cxii of the Koran and the names of the caliph, of the Buyid ruler and of the place where it was struck (Gurgan). No such enormous piece survives, but smaller ones are known: a silver medallion with a coin-like obverse and a neo-Sasanian reverse (Momignies, Belgium, Gournet priv. col.) struck in the name of the Buyid prince Rukn al-Dawla in AD 962; a gold medallion with two neo-Sasanian portraits struck by his son 'Adud al-Dawla at Fars in AD 969–70 (Tehran, priv. col.); and three gold presentation pieces issued at Baghdad in the name of another Buyid prince, 'Izz al-Dawla, between AD 973 and 976. One of the 'Izz al-Dawla pieces (ex-Gans priv. col.) represents a lion attacking a stag or an ibex; another, known only through a cast, shows an eagle seizing a duck or a gazelle; and the third (Istanbul, Archaeol. Mus.) depicts a seated king and a lute-player. An uninscribed medallion in gold (Washington, DC, Freer) depicts an enthroned prince drinking and a mounted falconer, and one in silver (St Petersburg, Hermitage) depicts a mounted hunter shooting gazelles.

BIBLIOGRAPHY

Y. I. Smirnoff: *Argenterie orientale / Vostochnoye serebro* (St Petersburg, 1909)

R. Harari: 'Metalwork After the Early Islamic Period', *Survey of Persian Art*, ed. A. U. Pope and P. Ackerman (London, 1937–8, 2/1964–7), pp. 2466–529

M. Bahrami: 'A Gold Medal in the Freer Gallery of Art', *Archaeologica orientalia in memoriam Ernst Herzfeld* (Locust Valley, NY, 1952), pp. 5–20

R. Ghirshman: 'Argenterie d'un seigneur sassanide', *A. Orient.*, ii (1957), pp. 77–82

G. C. Miles: 'A Portrait of the Buyid Prince Rukn al-Dawlah', *Amer. Numi. Soc. Mus. Notes*, xi (1964), pp. 283–93

A. S. Melikian-Chirvani: 'La Coupe d'Abu Sahl-e Farhad-Jerdi', *Gaz. B.-A.*, lxxi (1968), pp. 129–46

B. I. Marshak: *Sogdiyskoye serebro* [Sogdian silver] (Moscow, 1971)

G. C. Miles: 'Numismatics', *The Period from the Arab Invasions to the Saljuqs*, ed. R. N. Frye (1975), iv of *The Cambridge History of Iran* (Cambridge and London, 1968–), pp. 364–77

V. P. Darkevich: *Khudozhestvennyy metall Vostoka* [Art metal of the Orient] (Moscow, 1976)

J. W. Allan: 'Silver: The Key to Bronze in Early Islamic Iran', *Kst Orients*, xi (1976–7), pp. 5–21

A. S. Melikian-Chirvani: 'Essais sur la sociologie de l'art islamique; i: Argenterie et féodalité dans l'Iran médiéval', *Art et société dans le monde iranien*, ed. C. Adle (Paris, 1982), pp. 143–75

E. Baer: *Metalwork in Medieval Islamic Art* (Albany, 1983)

J. W. Allan: 'The Survival of Precious and Base Metal Objects from the Medieval Islamic World', *Pots and Pans: A Colloquium on Precious Metals and Ceramics, Oxford, 1985*, pp. 57–70

G. H. A. Juynboll: 'The Attitude towards Gold and Silver in Early Islam', *Pots and Pans: A Colloquium on Precious Metals and Ceramics, Oxford, 1985*, pp. 107–15

A. S. Melikian-Chirvani: 'Silver in Islamic Iran: The Evidence from Literature and Epigraphy', *Pots and Pans: A Colloquium on Precious Metals and Ceramics, Oxford, 1985*, pp. 89–106

B. Marschak: *Silberschätze des Orients* (Leipzig, 1986)

R. Ward: *Islamic Metalwork* (London, 1993)

SHEILA S. BLAIR, JONATHAN M. BLOOM

3. *c.* 1100–*c.* 1500. This was the heyday of Islamic metalwork, when inlaid bronzes and brasses replaced the cast bronzes and precious metal wares of the preceding period. From the mid-12th century the centre of creativity was in Khurasan (eastern Iran). The innovative techniques, unusual shapes and elaborate motifs developed there later appeared in wares produced in the Jazira (northern Mesopotamia), Syria and Egypt. In the 15th century the quality of inlaid wares produced in Egypt and Syria generally declined, whereas eastern Iran re-emerged as a centre of luxury metalwork. Throughout the period Spain and North Africa remained relatively isolated from these developments, and comparatively few pieces from there have been identified.

(i) Iranian world. (ii) Syria and the Jazira, *c.* 1100–*c.* 1250. (iii) Egypt and Syria, *c.* 1250–*c.* 1500. (iv) Spain and North Africa.

(i) Iranian world. Almost all the surviving metalwork produced in Iran and adjacent regions between the mid-12th century and the end of the 15th century is made of bronze or brass. Many of these base metal wares are lent a rich appearance by elaborate surface decoration using such techniques as engraving, incising, inlay in copper, silver and gold, and tinning (see fig. 140 above and figs 146, 147 and 149 below); a smaller group has spectacular repoussé decoration (see fig. 146 below). The exuberant forms of 12th-century wares gradually gave way to a narrower range of conventional shapes, while the wide variety of figural scenes, geometric and vegetal designs and inscriptions characteristic of earlier pieces was replaced in the 15th century by a more limited repertory of floral and vegetal motifs and inscriptions.

☐

(a) *c.* 1100–*c.* 1400. (b) *c.* 1400–*c.* 1500.

(a) c. 1100–c. 1400. Brass and bronze wares produced in the Iranian world from the 1140s onwards survive in far greater numbers than those made in the preceding period, and this can be taken as evidence for increased production. The manufacture of these objects appears to have been concentrated first in the metalworking centres of Khurasan, a region now divided between Iran, Afghanistan and Turkmenistan, and then in Azerbaijan and Anatolia after the Mongol conquests of the mid-13th century.

Production and patronage. Information on centres of production comes from literary sources and from the few pieces inscribed with their place of manufacture; more bear the artist's name, which often includes a reference to his or his family's place of origin, but this does not necessarily give the location of his workshop. From these sources it appears that from the 12th century to the mid-13th production took place in the cities of Herat (now in Afghanistan), Nishapur (now in Iran), Ghazna (now in Afghanistan) and possibly Merv (now in Turkmenistan). Herat was a major centre for inlaid bronze vessels, and its style can be delineated as it is named on both the Bobrinsky Bucket (1163; St Petersburg, Hermitage; see fig. 140 above) and a ewer made in 1181–2 (Tblisi, Mus. A. Georgia). At the end of the 13th century new centres of production in Azerbaijan and Anatolia appear in the written sources. Tabriz in Azerbaijan produced so many metal objects that they were used in commercial transactions according to Qazvini (*d* 1283), and Erzincan in north-east Anatolia was renowned for its candlesticks according to Ibn Battuta (*d* 1355). The province of Fars in south-west Iran has been identified as the home of a local school of metalworking in the 14th century on the basis of the titles used in the inscriptions. The development of these western centres did not mean that those in Khurasan ceased to function, for a large basin in the congregational mosque in Herat was made there for the Kart ruler Ghiyath al-Din in 1374–5.

The quantity, high quality and aesthetic refinement of metalwares produced in the region imply the existence of an organized production process and of patrons willing and able to pay for the expense involved. The exceptional quality of the Bobrinsky Bucket may well have required the skills of several artisans: according to the Persian inscription on its rim, it was cast (*żarb*) by Muhammad ibn 'Abd al-Wahid; it was worked ('*amal*) by Hajib Mas'ud ibn Ahmad, 'the decorator' of Herat; it was ordered by 'Abd al-Rahim ibn 'Abdallah al-Rashidi; and its owner was a merchant called Khwaja Rukn a-Din Rashid al-Din 'Azizi ibn Abu'l-Husayn al-Zanjani. Other masterpieces of the same period, including an aquamanile in the form of a zebu suckling her calf while a lion attacks her back (Khurasan, 1206; St Petersburg, Hermitage), was manufactured by two different metalworkers, one responsible for the casting or fashioning, the other for the engraving or inlay. However, the role of these craftsmen and the nature of the production process have not been completely elucidated.

The system of patronage that lay behind the production of these objects is also a matter of debate. Some ideas, such as attributing all inlaid brasses to princely patrons, have been discarded, for it is clear that some 12th- and 13th-century merchants were rich enough to buy high-quality metalwares, as in the case of the Bobrinsky Bucket. An eastern Iranian penbox dated 1148 (St Petersburg, Hermitage) was made by a metalworker who described himself as *al-bayyā* ('the tradesman'), and Giuzalian has argued that the owner, who may have been a close relation of the maker, also belonged to the merchant class. Yet a general middle-class patronage cannot be established. The owners mentioned in most inscriptions were sultans, male, and occasionally female, members of the royal household, local rulers and civil and religious dignitaries. Some 14th-century objects, such as a candlestick (Boston, MA, Mus. F.A.) donated to the shrine of the mystic Abu Yazid (Bayazid) at BISTAM during its restoration in 1308, were pious donations to religious institutions.

Illustrations in 12th- and 13th-century manuscripts also provide evidence for the increasing demand for metal artefacts by members of princely and upper-class households. In a copy of the Arabic version of Dioskurides' *De materia medica* (Mesopotamia, 1228–9; Washington, DC, Freer) one illustration (fol. 32.20*v*) depicts a doctor instructing his attendant in the preparation of cataplasm; the attendant is stirring the poultice in a large metal mortar, while a lampstand carrying a bird-shaped bronze lamp is placed between them. Pencases and inkwells are also frequently illustrated. The Irano-Mesopotamian type of pencase, open or closed with rounded ends, is depicted in association with the Nine Sages of Antiquity in a copy of the Arabic version of Pseudo-Galen, the *Kitāb al-diryāq* ('Book of antidotes'; ?northern Mesopotamia, Jan 1199; Paris, Bib. N., MS. arab. 2964, fols 5*v*–*r*). In a copy of the *Maqāmāt* ('Assemblies') of al-Hariri (?Baghdad, before 1235; St Petersburg, Acad. Sci., MS. S. 23) one illustration (p. 250) shows the judge of Sa'da seated behind a table on which stands a typical inkwell of the early 13th century: gilt, cylindrical and with a domed cover. Common metal shapes such as jugs with zoomorphic or S-shaped handles, composite ewers of the type whose upper apertures are

like oil lamps, hemispherical bowls with or without covers (like the famous Wade Cup; Cleveland, OH, Mus. A.) and drum-shaped candlesticks are also depicted. On another page (p. 205) of the St Petersburg *Maqāmāt* the illustrator showed banqueters at a wedding feast eating and drinking from gilded stem cups whose fluted bodies and low feet resemble similar contemporary cups worked in bronze and repoussé, as well as the rare surviving parcel-gilt silver cup made for Badr al-Din Ulugh Qaymaz (Richmond, Surrey, Keir priv. col.; see Fehérvári, no. 127); the latter shows signs of having been deliberately broken up into large pieces, presumably in order to be melted down. Such a practice, doubtless carried out in times of financial crisis, might explain the paucity of precious metal objects from this early period, for, although the visual evidence of illustrations is corroborated by travellers' accounts mentioning gold and silver wares, little else survives except for a few examples of gold and silver jewellery, belt plaques and jugs.

c. 1100–c. 1250. The surviving metalwork of the period before the Mongol conquests of the mid-13th century is notable for the variety of its shapes. Some forms—for instance hooded incense burners, inkwells with covers in the shape of melon-shaped domes, and ewers with longitudinally fluted bodies—were already associated with Khurasan, while others, such as wedge-shaped penboxes, rectangular pencases with round edges, cylindrical boxes of different sizes and candlesticks with drum-like bodies, were new. Vessels were often given zoomorphic forms

145. Incense burner, incised and pierced bronze, h. 175 mm, probably from eastern Iran, 12th century (New York, Metropolitan Museum of Art)

(see fig. 145), and different types of objects were combined to create composite shapes. One group of ewers, for example, has upper apertures like oil lamps and spouts that point upwards, recalling animal or bird heads. This form of ewer seems to have originated in the provinces east or north of Samarkand in the late 10th century or early 11th, and a type derived from it became popular in Khurasan in the late 12th century and early 13th (see fig. 146). The earliest example is a ewer made for 'Uthman al-Nakhchavani in 1190–91 (Paris, Louvre).

Some of the most elaborate objects produced during this period were made by raising and sinking and decorated with repoussé work. Ewers fashioned by this method have a cylindrical, faceted or fluted body; a flat, slightly upward sloping shoulder; a raised spout projecting from a cylindrical neck; a low foot; and a handle. Apart from the handle, each part was made of a separate sheet, and then carefully and nearly invisibly soldered to the others. Tremendous skill was required to manufacture these ewers, especially for the repoussé decoration in the form of real or imaginary birds or animals hammered from the inside

on the neck and body. A 12th-century ewer in New York (Met., 44.15), for example, has a frieze of birds hiding the seam between the body and shoulder. The same technique was used to make a group of seven candlesticks. The most sophisticated and technically advanced (Washington, DC, Freer, 51.17) has two rows of lions sitting on their haunches worked in repoussé on the upper and lower registers of the high base; staggered octagons, also hammered in relief, in the middle register of the base; and pyramids in relief on the socket. Its body, neck and socket were formed from a single sheet that has been stretched to its limit. All these ewers and candlesticks can be attributed to Khurasan in the late 12th century and the early 13th by comparison with the ewer made by Mahmud ibn Muhammad of Herat in 1181–2.

Copper and silver inlay, used to an extent hardly known before the 12th century, may well have originated in Khurasan, for the inlay on the penbox in the Hermitage dated 1148 seems to be a metalworker's experiment with a technique that had been out of fashion for centuries. Less than 20 years later such inlay was being handled with complete assurance. The wider range of motifs used from the 12th century onwards includes scenes of pleasure and pastime drawn in an animated style. These appear in continuous bands that have to be read in sequence to be understood: crowded friezes of isocephalic figures standing, walking, squatting or riding and pairs of musicians, dancers or banqueters are shown as though part of a narrative, although no individual group or figure is emphasized. Their round faces, long plaited hair, exaggerated upper bodies, poses and gestures resemble representations on contemporary ceramics (*see* §V, 3(iii) below). The most celebrated example is the Bobrinsky Bucket, but these features already occur on the penbox dated 1148. On many other pieces a rich variety of vividly drawn animals, both real and imaginary, fill the central panel within a design or form border patterns; the animals chase one another, fight in pairs or are linked by their wings or other members. This fascination with fabulous, often human-headed, creatures coincided with a growing interest in astrology. First documented on a magic mirror (1153; Cairo, Mus. Islam. A.), zodiacal and planetary figures occur in many different combinations and in a variety of configurations on pieces made in Iran in the 12th and 13th centuries and in Syria and Egypt at a later period (*see* §(iii) below).

While astrological figures are also found to a lesser extent on other Islamic art forms such as ceramics and manuscripts, figural script, in which the letter is transformed into a bird, a person or an animal, is almost exclusive to metalwork (the avian type was used on ceramics *c.* 1000) and may have been invented by artists working in bronze and brass. The Bobrinsky Bucket is the first dated example in bronze: the uppermost of its three inscription bands is in a cursive script in which the upper halves of the vertical strokes are transformed into revellers, dancers, musicians and the like, while the lower sections of the letters are zoomorphic. The central inscription band has plaited, rather than animated, kufic characters, but in the bottom band, again in cursive script, the vertical strokes are human-headed. These types of figural script were used for less than 50 years in eastern Iran, but the

146. Ewer, bronze inlaid with silver and gold, h. 394 mm, from Herat, *c.* 1200 (New York, Metropolitan Museum of Art)

147. Base of a candlestick, brass, h. 205 mm, probably from Shiraz, Iran, first half of the 14th century (Edinburgh, Royal Museum of Scotland); original silver and gold inlay is now lost

tradition was taken up in the first half of the 13th century in Mesopotamia and Syria (*see* §(ii) below), although the pieces produced there lack the spontaneity of their Iranian precursors.

In the case of some inlaid wares, it is possible to establish the relationship between an object, its function and its owner on the basis of its decoration and inscriptions. A mid-12th-century inkwell in Toronto (Royal Ont. Mus.), for example, has three arched medallions enclosing the figure of a scribe with his writing utensils (a pointed pen and paper, an unidentifiable rectangular object and an inkwell of the same type as the vessel). An inscription on the lid gives the owner's name and profession (inspector of the treasury). Other inscriptions, phrased as if the object itself were speaking, express the hope that the owner will enjoy good health while using it and praise the object's qualities. Occasionally the craftsmen praise their own accomplishments, as did Mahmud ibn Muhammad of

Herat, the maker of the ewer with repoussé decoration dated 1181–2 that is now in Tbilisi. Such expressions first appeared on metalwork and in other arts during this period, but they continued in use long after it.

This brief florescence of Iranian metalwork was part of a burst of creativity in all the portable arts. Some of the technical and stylistic innovations seen at this time were the result of new ideas from western Central Asia, but the enormous increase in productivity and the sudden popularity of princely, astrological and figural themes are still to be explained.

c. *1250*–c. *1400*. In the second half of the 13th century composite and zoomorphic forms gave way to conventional shapes. Wedge-shaped pencases went completely out of fashion, while the rectangular type with rounded ends was retained. Drum-shaped candlesticks assumed more refined, variegated forms (see fig. 147). New shapes appeared, such as 12-sided caskets with relatively low containers and high domed covers, and small, bell-shaped candlesticks with flat shoulders. Some traditional decorative themes were retained. A penbox made by Mahmud ibn Sunqur (1281; London, BM; see fig. 148 and METAL, colour pl. I, fig.1), for example, is still decorated with signs of the zodiac, and other 14th-century brasses show princely pastimes with friezes of hunters and polo players or medallions with an enthroned dignitary, revellers or attendants. But the designs became drier, more rigid and less imaginative. On some vessels gold inlay replaced the copper used in previous centuries. Contacts with China brought about by the Mongol conquests of the 13th century are reflected in the application of Chinese ornament to traditionally Islamic shapes and in the introduction of Far Eastern floral and animal motifs. Peony and lotus blossoms are drawn in a lively, naturalistic style, as are creatures from Chinese mythology, the phoenix and the *qilin*, a stag with a dragon's head and a bushy tail.

Themes used in the decoration of 14th-century pieces include epics and legends from Persian literature. Episodes from the *Shāhnāma* ('Book of Kings') of Firdawsi, including Bahram Gur's master shot in front of his harpist Azada, Faridun capturing Zahhak, and Zal's deportation

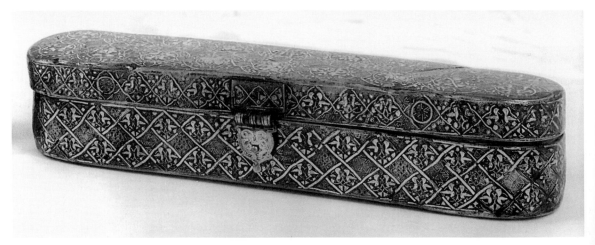

148. Penbox by Mahmud ibn Sunqur, brass inlaid with silver and gold, l. 197 mm, from Iran, 1281 (London, British Museum)

to Manuchihr on the back of an elephant, form part of a frieze on a brass bowl made by Turanshah in 1351 (London, V&A). Other subjects, such as a solar symbol surrounded by real and fabulous sea beasts, may go back to popular legends such as the Alexander Romance. The design first occurs on a bowl dated 1305–6 in Modena (Gal. & Mus. Estense), and it was repeated with slight variations at the bottom of many 14th-century bowls. The Labours of the Months are represented on a group of candlesticks attributed to north-west Iran or south-east Anatolia in the late 13th century or early 14th. Introduced into the Islamic world from Byzantium or Georgia, the meaning of these scenes seems never to have been fully understood and, except for a few Egyptian ivory carvings (*see* §VIII, 7 below), remained a local phenomenon.

Metal objects from the late 13th century and the 14th also provide evidence of a growing interest in the written word. Medallions with figural motifs alternate with large cartouches, each of which contains a portion of a text, which is often a poem connected allegorically to the type of object on which it figures. A stem cup in Paris (Bib. N., Cab. Médailles, Chabouillet 3193) has verses around its rim that praise wine while evoking Alexander's Water of Life and thereby implying that whoever drinks from the vessel will live eternally. References to the moth that seeks the candle flame as an allegory for the human soul seeking God are contained in a quatrain on a candlestick in Berlin (north-west Iran or south-east Anatolia, 14th century; Mus. Islam. Kst), and verses suggesting an allegorical relationship between the pen and the inkwell appear on penboxes. More often the epigraphic bands placed prominently on the body of the object contain good wishes for the beholder. This fashion, typical of contemporary pieces from Syria and Egypt, is found on a group of bowls attributed to the province of Fars that have inscription bands interrupted by roundels enclosing court scenes set against a floral ground. Generally inlaid with silver and gold, they have elongated figures that resemble the princely images depicted in manuscripts made for the Jalayirids *c.* 1400 (*see* §III, 4(v)(c) above).

BIBLIOGRAPHY
R. Ettinghausen: 'The Bobrinski Kettle: Patron and Style of an Islamic Bronze', *Gaz. B.-A.*, xxiv (1943), pp. 193–208
E. Baer: 'Fish-pond Ornaments on Persian and Mamluk Metal Vessels', *Bull. SOAS*, xxxi (1968), pp. 14–27
L. T. Giuzalian: 'The Bronze Qalamdan (Pen Case) 542/1148 from the Hermitage Collection', *A. Orient.*, vii (1968), pp. 95–119
A. S. Melikian-Chirvani: 'Bassins iraniens du XIVe siècle au Musée des beaux arts', *Bull. Mus. & Mnmts Lyon.*, iv (1969), pp. 189–206
R. Ettinghausen: 'The Flowering of Seljuk Art', *Met. Mus. J.*, iii (1970), pp. 113–31
E. Atıl: 'Two Il-Khanid Candlesticks at the University of Michigan', *Kst Orients*, vii (1972), pp. 1–36
E. Baer: 'An Islamic Inkwell in the Metropolitan Museum of Art', *Islamic Art in the Metropolitan Museum of Art*, ed. R. Ettinghausen (New York, 1972), pp. 199–212
D. Shepherd: 'Banquet and Hunt in Medieval Islamic Iconography', *Gathering in Honor of Dorothy E. Miner*, ed. U. E. McCracken (Baltimore, 1974), pp. 79–92
A. S. Melikian-Chirvani: 'Les Bronzes du Khorasan, i–vi', *Stud. Iran.*, iii–vii (1974–8)
G. Fehérvári: *Islamic Metalwork of the Eighth to the Fifteenth Century in the Keir Collection* (London, 1976)
A. S. Melikian-Chirvani: 'Silver in Islamic Iran: The Evidence from Literature and Epigraphy', *Pots and Pans: A Colloquium on Precious Metals and Ceramics, Oxford, 1985*, pp. 89–106
E. Baer: 'Wider Aspects of Some Ghaznavid Bronzes', *Riv. Stud. Orient.*, lix (1987), pp. 1–15

EVA BAER

(b) c. *1400–c. 1500.* Timur's campaigns of conquest in central and western Asia in the late 14th century and the early 15th provided the catalyst for the development of a distinctive style of metalwork that may be termed 'Timurid'. This style is known from almost 100 objects of brass that were either inlaid or engraved and then tinned; most were made in the province of Khurasan in north-east Iran, and during this period its capital, Herat, re-emerged as a centre for the production of luxury metalwork. Pieces in the Timurid style were also manufactured on a much smaller scale in western Iran and Anatolia.

Eastern Iran and western Central Asia. The earliest pieces of metalwork produced in western Central Asia under Timurid patronage are a bronze basin and six brass oil lamps commissioned by Timur himself. The basin (St Petersburg, Hermitage, SA 15930), most notable for its enormous size (h. 1.58 m, diam. 2.43 m), was made in 1399 for the shrine of Ahmad Yasavi in Yasi (now Turkestan, Kazakhstan). The oil lamps (average h. 900 mm) can be dated between 1401 and 1405; they are associated with the same shrine, which still houses three of them. They are decorated with epigraphic, vegetal and geometric ornament, some of which preserves fine gold and silver inlay. Their forms, function, inlay, decoration and epigraphy amalgamate different artistic traditions from Iran and elsewhere; these must have been brought to western Central Asia, along with the metalworkers themselves, as a direct consequence of Timur's victorious campaigns.

The distinctive Timurid style of metalwork had emerged by the second quarter of the 15th century and continued into the 16th. It is documented by 25 objects that are dated and/or signed. A further 75 pieces can be attributed to Khurasan in the 15th and 16th centuries on the basis of analogy with these dated and signed wares. These objects, primarily of cast brass, can be divided into two broad classes: one consists of inlaid wares, the other of engraved and tinned wares. They can be distinguished from earlier Iranian wares by their shapes, the techniques used and their epigraphic and other decoration. Their shapes were unknown in earlier times or have been modified considerably. A pot-bellied jug with an S-curved dragon handle (average h. 135 mm) was especially common (see fig. 149). Other shapes include shallow dishes, deep basins and covered bowls, and candlesticks that occasionally preserve a socket in the form of a pair of open-mouthed, entwined dragons. Many of these types are depicted in contemporary manuscript illustrations. The inlay technique used was much finer than that of the 14th century: linear inlays using slender strips of sheet-metal or wire replaced the earlier spatial inlay that had used small pieces of sheet-metal. Engraved and tinned wares were made by the same techniques as were used in the 14th century, but their higher quality and greater quantity show that they were produced as luxury wares in the Timurid period. Tinning was used to give a silvery surface to a variety of wares, and colour was added to both inlaid and engraved objects by filling the cross-hatchings in the

149. Pot-bellied jug with S-curved dragon handle by Habiballah ibn 'Ali Baharjani, brass inlaid with silver, h. 130 mm, probably from Herat, 1461–2 (London, Victoria and Albert Museum)

background with a black material that is still unidentified. Floral and vegetal motifs and epigraphy replaced the figural representation typical of pieces made between the 12th and 14th centuries. Geometric and abstract ornament played a limited role. Previously decoration had been organized horizontally within clearly defined compartments, but the new or differently proportioned shapes called for new ways of organizing decoration. Dishes, for example, are often decorated with radial designs well-suited to their circular interior.

A series of inlaid wares dated between 1456 and 1505 shows the development of an increasingly unified programme of design: the characteristic repetitive floral and leaf motifs, leaf arabesques and inscriptions gradually became finer, more closely packed and less varied, until, at the turn of the 16th century, they formed a dense surface patterning made up of small-scale decorative and epigraphic elements. In contrast, the engraved and tinned wares of the 15th century are decorated with large-scale floral motifs such as peonies and lotus blossoms, often boldly drawn. These may have been inspired by the Chinese blue-and-white porcelains that were exported to Iran in large numbers to supply members of the Timurid ruling élite.

Inscriptions on Timurid metalwares consist of Persian poetic texts written in a great variety of cursive scripts. These were generally well-written and free of mistakes and, on occasion, reflect contemporary developments in calligraphy, such as the use of the new *nasta'liq* script. The texts usually allude to the objects on which these are inscribed and include verses by poets of the 10th to 14th centuries such as Hafiz, as well as contemporaries who

were active in Khurasan such as Qasim al-Anwar, Jami and Salihi. The appearance of their verses on metalwork produced during their lifetimes confirms the attribution of these pieces to Khurasan. Some bear makers' signatures that give the artists' or their families' place of origin; all but one refer to places in Khurasan near Herat, which must have been the main centre of production. A jug dated 1498 (London, BM) is inscribed with the name of the Timurid ruler of Herat, Sultan Husayn Bayqara.

Western Iran. The few wares that can be attributed to western Iran in the late 14th century or the early 15th show that, despite the presumed disruption of artistic activity caused by Timur's invasions, the metalworking centres in the provinces of Fars and Azerbaijan continued to work in the manner established in the 14th century. A pencase in Lyon (Mus. B.-A., D 617) and a bowl in London (V&A, 554–1876) can be attributed to Azerbaijan during this transitional period. Their floral and abstract design, which bears traces of fine inlay, exhibits the new stylistic and technical features that were also transmitted to the Timurid east. The only object from the later 15th century that can be ascribed with any certainty to western Iran is a tall oil lamp decorated with engraved and silver inlaid inscriptions and vegetal designs (h. 1.21 m; priv. col.; see Melikian-Chirvani, 1987, pls vii–viii). The inscriptions name the Aqqoyunlu ruler Uzun Hasan (*reg* 1453–78), whose capital was at Tabriz in Azerbaijan, and suggest that the lamp was made for a Sufi shrine. (*See also* VENETO-SARACENIC for further possible attributions to western Iran during this period.)

Only a handful of objects fashioned from precious metal are preserved from 15th-century Iran, in contrast to the abundant gold and silver tableware described in contemporary texts and the numerous gold- and silver-coloured vessels and implements depicted in manuscript illustrations. Extant examples include a gilt silver bottle and jug from the early 15th century (both St Petersburg, Hermitage, SK 585 and 586) and a silver bowl inlaid with gold and niello from the turn of the 16th century (Washington, DC, Freer, 54.115).

Anatolia. Copper and brass wares produced in 15th-century Anatolia were gilded or tinned to give them the appearance of precious metal. Inlaid pieces are exceedingly rare; one important example is a silver inlaid bowl inscribed with the name of the Ottoman sultan Murad II (*reg* 1421–51), which is strongly influenced by, if not actually of, Mamluk workmanship (St Petersburg, Hermitage). Other, later objects made for a royal patron are two large gilt brass candlesticks (h. 980 mm; Istanbul, Mus. Turk. & Islam. A., 139-B) made for Sultan Bayazid II, possibly for his mosque complex in Edirne (begun 1484). Several smaller brass candlesticks datable to his reign (1481–1512) resemble some late 15th-century Timurid candlesticks in form and vegetal decoration, but similarities to other decorative arts show that they are certainly of Ottoman manufacture.

BIBLIOGRAPHY

A. A. Ivanov: 'Gruppa khorasansikh mednykh i bronzovykh izdeliy vtoroy poloviny XV v.' [A group of Khurasanian brass and bronze wares from the second half of the 15th century], *Trudy Gosudarstvennogo Ermitazha*, x (1969), pp. 157–67

E. Grube: 'Notes on the Decorative Arts of the Timurid Period', *Gururajamañjarika: Studi in onore di Giuseppe Tucci* (Naples, 1974), pp. 233–69

A. S. Melikian-Chirvani: 'Recherches sur l'école du bronze ottoman au XVIe siècle', *Turcica*, vi (1975), pp. 146–67

Timur and the Princely Vision: Persian Art and Culture in the 15th Century (exh. cat. by T. W. Lentz and G. D. Lowry; Los Angeles, CA, Co. Mus. A.; Washington, DC, Sackler Gal.; 1979)

L. Komaroff: 'Timurid to Safavid Iran: Continuity and Change', *Marsyas*, xx (1979–80), pp. 11–16

A. A. Ivanov: 'O bronzovykh izdeliyakh kontsa XIV v. iz mavzoleya Khodzha Akhmeda Yasevi' [On the bronze wares from the end of the 14th century from the mausoleum of Khwaja Ahmad Yasavi], *Srednyaya Aziya i yeyo sosedi* [Central Asia and its neighbours], ed. B. A. Litvinsky (Moscow, 1981), pp. 68–84

J. W. Allan: 'Copper, Brass and Steel', *Tulips, Arabesques and Turbans*, ed. Y. Petsopoulos (London, 1982), pp. 33–42

N. T. Ölçer: 'Türkische Metallkunst', *Türkische Kunst und Kultur aus osmanischer Zeit* (Recklinghausen, 1985), pp. 274–81

A. S. Melikian-Chirvani: 'The Lights of Sufi Shrines', *Islam. A.*, ii (1987), pp. 117–36

L. Komaroff: 'Pen-case and Candlestick: Two Sources for the Development of Persian Inlaid Metalwork', *Met. Mus. J.*, xxiii (1988), pp. 89–102

J. W. Allan: 'Metalwork of the Turcoman Dynasties of Eastern Anatolia and Iran', *Iran*, xxix (1991), pp. 153–60

L. Komaroff: *The Golden Disk of Heaven: Metalwork of Timurid Iran* (Costa Mesa, CA, 1992)

——: 'Persian Verses of Gold and Silver: The Inscription on Timurid Metalwork', *Timurid Art and Culture: Iran and Central Asia in the Fifteenth Century*, ed. L. Golombek and M. Subtelny (Leiden, 1992), pp. 144–57

LINDA KOMAROFF

(ii) Syria and the Jazira, c. 1100–c. 1250. Surviving examples of metalwork produced in Syria and the Jazira (northern Mesopotamia) during this period consist almost exclusively of inlaid brasses. They are simpler in shape than contemporary objects from the eastern Iranian world (*see* §(i) above), but, like the latter, have richly decorated surfaces. The motifs used in this decoration include a wide variety of figural subjects, with genre scenes as well as astrological figures and representations of royal pastimes similar to those on eastern Iranian objects. The bold inscriptions on these pieces name the local rulers who commissioned them and the craftsmen who made them, indicating the high status that the latter enjoyed. Many of the craftsmen bore the name al-Mawsili, associating them with the city of Mosul.

(a) Centres of production. (b) Patronage. (c) Working practices. (d) Forms. (e) Decoration.

(a) Centres of production. Mosul was the main centre of the inlaid brass industry in the Jazira. The first object that can be associated with this area is a key made for the Ka'ba in Mecca and dated 1180 (Istanbul, Topkapı Pal. Mus.). Its decoration is related to objects made in Mosul in the first half of the 13th century, and its date suggests that the city was already established as a centre of production by the second half of the 12th century. A steady succession of objects bear dates in the second quarter of the 13th century, beginning with a box made by Isma'il ibn Ward al-Mawsili in 1220 (Athens, Benaki Mus.). An undated ewer (Paris, Louvre) was probably produced there even earlier, since its maker was Isma'il's teacher, Ibrahim ibn Mawaliya.

Written sources confirm Mosul's role in the production of inlaid brass. The geographer Ibn Sa'id, who travelled in the area in 1250, wrote that many crafts were practised in Mosul, especially the manufacture of inlaid brass vessels. Together with silk garments woven in the city, these were exported in the course of trade or as gifts to other courts. Sibt ibn al-Jawzi (*d* 1258) reported that when the ruler of Mosul, Badr al-Din Lu'lu' (*reg* 1222–59), was defeated by the army of the Khwarazmshah in 1237, the Khwarazmians looted Badr al-Din's chattels and treasures and all the possessions of his army, and 'a pencase inlaid with silver worth 20 *dirhams* fetched only 5 and a basin and ewer brought 20'. Five objects owned by Badr al-Din Lu'lu', and presumably made in his capital, have survived: a large and elaborately decorated tray (Munich, Staatl. Mus. Vlkerknd.; see fig. 150), a basin (Kiev, Acad. Sci.), a candlestick (St Petersburg, Hermitage), a small tray (London, V&A) and the Henderson Box (London, BM). The box made by Isma'il ibn Ward in 1220 and the ewer made by his master can also be connected with Mosul on the basis of textual evidence, for Isma'il ibn Ward, who describes himself as an 'engraver (Arab. *naqqāsh*) from Mosul', finished copying a manuscript on the *Traditions of the Prophet* (Dublin, Chester Beatty Lib., MS. 3130) in February 1249; a reading note states that the manuscript was in the city of Mosul three months later. Additional evidence for the importance of Mosul in the production of inlaid brass is the frequent occurrence of the name al-Mawsili ('of Mosul') among the craftsmen who made such wares during the rest of the 13th and 14th centuries. This shows that association with Mosul was a source of prestige for a metalworker, even if it does not necessarily mean that he worked in the city.

Is'ird (now Siirt in Turkey) was another centre of production. The 14th-century geographer Mustawfi noted that good vessels of copper or copper alloy were produced there and that the town was famous for its splendid drinking cups. The name al-Is'irdi was borne by several 13th-century craftsmen. Abu'l-Qasim ibn Sa'd ibn Muhammad al-Is'irdi signed an undated cup, a pencase dated 1236–7, and a pencase and candlestick dated 1245–6; Sa'd al-Din al-Is'irdi designed coins in Cairo under the Mamluk sultan Aybak (*reg* 1250–57); and 'Umar al-Is'irdi signed an undated pencase. In addition to a group of drinking cups appropriate to Mustawfi's description, a number of candlesticks and other objects of high-tin bronze have been attributed to the town, but they could also have come from other centres in the Jazira or Anatolia.

The earliest dated object from Damascus, another possible centre of the industry, is a ewer made by Husayn ibn Muhammad al-Mawsili in 1259 (Paris, Louvre); how much earlier the industry might have begun there is unknown. The lack of signatures containing the name al-Dimashqi ('the Damascene') on later metalwares suggests that, despite its political importance, Damascus never achieved the prominence of Mosul or even Is'ird. Smaller towns may well have had their own inlaying industries and local petty rulers their own craftsmen. The scholar–craftsman al-Jazari, for example, spent a number of years in the late 13th century in service to Nasir al-Din Mahmud, the Artuqid ruler of Amida (now Diyarbakır), for whom he designed and made mechanical devices, door revetments and the like. Such craftsmen were probably itinerant,

150. Tray made for Badr al-Din Lu'lu', brass inlaid with silver, diam. 620 mm, probably from Mosul, second quarter of the 13th century (Munich, Staatliches Museum für Völkerkunde)

selling their services wherever wealthy patrons could offer them employment.

(b) Patronage. Local rulers such as Badr al-Din Lu'lu' of Mosul played an important role in the development of the metalworking industry in the towns of the Jazira. Other patrons are known from inscriptions: Artuq Arslan, the Artuqid ruler of Mardin (*reg* 1200–39), commissioned a candlestick whose base is in Jerusalem (al-Haram al-Sharif Mus.); and Abu'l-Qasim Mahmud ibn Sanjar Shah, who ruled at Cizre in the first half of the 13th century, ordered a ewer (Nuhad Es-Said priv. col., on loan to Oxford, Ashmolean; see Allan, 1982, no. 6) and a basin (ex-Sarre priv. col., see F. Sarre: *Sammlung F. Sarre*, i: *Metall* (Berlin, 1906), pl. vi). A similar situation occurred in Syria, for at least 16 pieces of inlaid metalwork bear the names of Ayyubid sultans.

Objects made in the name of high-ranking courtiers are suprisingly rare. A ewer dated 1232 (Washington, DC, Freer) was made for Shihab al-Din Tughril, *atabek* (preceptor) of al-'Aziz, the Ayyubid ruler of Aleppo; and a

bowl in Bologna (Mus. Civ. Med.) bears the name of Najm al-Din 'Umar, an officer of Badr al-Din, presumably Badr al-Din Lu'lu'. Equally rare are objects commissioned by members of other social groups, such as the divination table dated 1241 (London, BM) made for a market inspector, Muhammad al-Muhtasib al-Najjari. The large number of fine-quality anonymous objects that survive suggests that there were enough wealthy customers for inlaying workshops to produce ready-made metalwares for sale in the local market. Further evidence for this is the fact that many objects bearing owners' names were apparently made with a blank space to which the name was added later, rather than having a design based around the name and titles of a specific patron.

(c) Working practices. The signatures used by the 23 craftsmen with the name al-Mawsili show something of the organization of this industry. They describe themselves as the 'pupils' (Arab. *tilmidh*) or 'hired men' (Arab. *ajir*; also *ghulām*, lit. 'slave') of their masters, but how they were hired or became attached to their teachers is not known.

Family businesses certainly existed in the second half of the 13th century, but as yet none is known for the period before 1250. In one case, a candlestick in Cairo (Mus. Islam. A.), two craftsmen signed the work: it was made by Hajj Isma'il and decorated by the inlayer Muhammad ibn Fatuh, who was the hired man of another metalworker, Shuja' ibn Man'a. Some artisans, especially astrolabists, worked in several crafts. Such versatility is illustrated by Muhammad ibn Khutlukh of Damascus: his divination table (London, BM) suggests by its nature and the form of the piece used to suspend the instrument (the *kursī*) that he was also an astrolabist, while his incense burner (Aron priv. col., see Allan, 1986, no. 1) shows that he also made utilitarian, if individualistic, metal objects.

(d) Forms. Typical shapes in Syria and the Jazira include bowls, basins and other vessels with concave sides; flat trays; and ewers with an inverted pear-shaped body and a straight spout rising from the shoulder. According to Allan (1985), these shapes are almost exclusively based on earlier Egyptian forms that are ultimately Late Antique in origin. Three important sets of door revetments survive from the period: those in bronze made for the hospital of Nur al-Din in Damascus (1154), impressive examples in iron in the citadel of Aleppo (1211), and the bronze door coverings of the mausoleum of Imam 'Awn al-Din at Mosul signed by the craftsman 'Umar ibn al-Khidr (1248; all *in situ*). They are comparable to contemporary work in Cairo, such as the door revetments from the mausoleum of the Imam al-Shafi'i (Cairo, Mus. Islam. A.) and the mosque of al-Salih Tala'i' (*in situ*). The Mosul doors closely resemble the revetments described by al-Jazari in his *Kitāb fī ma'rifat al-hilal al-handasiyya* ('Book of knowledge of ingenious mechanical devices'), written in Damascus in 1206, as do the door handles from the Great Mosque at Jazarit ibn 'Umar (now Cizre, Turkey), divided between Copenhagen (Davids Saml.) and Istanbul (Mus. Turk. & Islam. A.). A magnificent pair of door-knockers (Kuwait, priv. col., see *Louisiana Revy*, xxvii/3, 1987, no. 96) have designs that also suggest Mosul as their place of origin.

(e) Decoration. The rich decoration of the inlaid metalwork of this period was based on a variety of patterns and motifs. Backgrounds consisted of patterns derived from textile designs such as T-frets and swastikas, as on the Blacas Ewer (see fig. 151), or arabesques, as on a candlestick in Paris (Mus. A. Déc., 4414); they could also be plain, as on the small tray commissioned by Badr al-Din Lu'lu' (London, V&A). Cusped roundels containing figures or arabesques were usually set against these grounds, but various forms of arcading also occur. The 'belted' layout, in which the object appears to be wearing a belt with a large clasp in the form of a sun-disc (a design more popular in works produced in Syria and Egypt in the 14th century), is found occasionally, as on the incense burner dated 1243–4 (London, BM). Narrow bands of angular and cursive inscriptions are common; they contain good wishes for the owner or, in the case of royal objects, the name and titles of the patron. Many of the decorative motifs, such as arabesque scrolls and angular kufic inscriptions, resemble those used on metalware from the eastern Iranian world. Such similarities have traditionally been

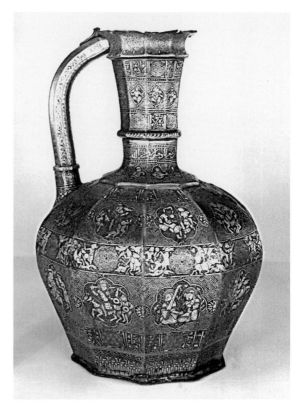

151. Blacas Ewer by Shuja' ibn Man'a al-Mawsili, brass inlaid with silver and copper, h. 304 mm, 1232 (London, British Museum)

explained as the result of the westward migration of craftsmen fleeing the Mongol invaders, but Allan (in Raby, ed., 1985) has argued that they result from a common inheritance from illuminated and illustrated manuscripts that circulated throughout the lands controlled by the Saljuqs in the 12th century.

At least 18 of the pieces decorated with figural motifs bear scenes with Christian subject-matter, the most famous being a canteen in Washington, DC (Freer). Some objects, such as a box decorated with a frieze of priests bearing crosses and censers (London, V&A), were clearly made for use by the local Christian communities; others were designed for Muslim patrons. The d'Arenburg Basin (Washington, DC, Freer), for example, was made for the Ayyubid sultan al-Salih Ayyub (*reg* 1240–49) and has an arcade with Christian figures and small cusped roundels with scenes from Christ's life. None of the extant pieces shows scenes from Christ's crucifixion or resurrection, two episodes rejected by Islam as spurious attempts to attribute divinity to the Prophet Jesus. This suggests that the clients were mainly Muslims, who tolerated Christianity insofar as it did not clash with their own beliefs, and that within the Muslim community there was a fashion for Christian motifs on metalware in the 1240s.

The imagery on other objects with figural decoration is secular. It includes enthronement scenes and other episodes from court life, as on the Gambier-Parry Wallet (U. London, Courtauld Inst. Gals); friezes of mounted horsemen, as on the Freer Canteen; and genre scenes of men digging, ploughing with oxen or hunting birds with blow-pipes, such as those seen on a ewer dated 1223 (Cleveland, OH, Mus. A.). Astrological scenes are less common than on contemporary pieces from eastern Iran, but they occur occasionally, as on the large tray commissioned by Badr al-Din Lu'lu' (see fig. 150 above). Both Christian and secular figures are clearly linked to illustrations in contemporary manuscripts.

The decoration sometimes had a symbolic meaning. An early 13th-century box lid (London, V&A, 320–1866) has a rosette in the centre; this is surrounded by six discs joined by interlacing strapwork; a pre-Islamic Arabic poem on the shoulder links the pattern on the lid to celestial imagery in a way that would please a royal client: 'Do you not see that God has granted you a degree of power that makes all kings [grovel at your feet], for you are the sun; the kings, the stars. When the sun rises, no star will be seen.' Similar imagery is found on a penbox in Bologna (Mus. Civ. Med., 2119): figures representing the planets and signs of the zodiac form concentric rings around an enthroned ruler who wears a rayed crown. This clear evidence has been used to interpret less explicit motifs on later Near Eastern metalwork and to suggest that such cosmic symbolism continued as a decorative theme in the later 13th century and the 14th.

BIBLIOGRAPHY

D. S. Rice: 'The Brasses of Badr al-Din Lu'lu', *Bull. SOAS*, xiii (1950), pp. 627–34
——: 'Studies in Islamic Metalwork—ii and iii', *Bull. SOAS*, xv (1953), pp. 61–79, 229–38
——: 'Inlaid Brasses from the Workshop of Ahmad al-Dhaki al-Mawsili', *A. Orient.*, ii (1957), pp. 283–326
J. Sourdel-Thomine: 'Clefs et serrures de la Ka'ba: Notes d'épigraphie arabe', *Rev. Etud. Islam.*, xxxix (1971), pp. 29–86
L. T. Schneider: 'The Freer Canteen', *A. Orient.*, ix (1973), pp. 137–56
D. James: 'An Early Mosul Metalworker: Some New Information', *Orient. A.*, xxvi (1980), pp. 318–21
E. Baer: 'The Ruler in Cosmic Setting: A Note on Medieval Islamic Iconography', *Essays in Islamic Art and Architecture in Honor of Katharina Otto-Dorn* (Malibu, 1981), pp. 13–20
J. W. Allan: *Islamic Metalwork: The Nuhad Es-Said Collection* (London, 1982)
——: 'Concave or Convex? The Sources of Jaziran and Syrian Metalwork in the 13th Century', *The Art of Syria and the Jazira, 1100–1250*, ed. J. Raby (Oxford, 1985), pp. 127–40
——: 'The Survival of Precious and Base Metal Objects from the Medieval Islamic World', *Pots and Pans: A Colloquium on Precious Metals and Ceramics, Oxford, 1985*, pp. 57–70
——: *Metalwork of the Islamic World: The Aron Collection* (London, 1986)
E. Baer: *Ayyubid Metalwork with Christian Images* (Leiden, 1989)

(iii) Egypt and Syria, c. 1250–c. 1500. The metal wares produced under the Mamluk sultans of the Bahri line (*reg* 1250–1390) include some of the finest inlaid brass objects produced in the Islamic world. In the late 14th century and the early 15th, however, the metalworking industry suffered a severe crisis due to plague, inflation, civil war and a shortage of silver and copper, especially in Cairo. Inlaid brass, for which Egyptian and Syrian craftsmen had been famous throughout the Mediterranean for two centuries, virtually disappeared, and far fewer bronze objects survive than from earlier periods. The production of luxury metalwork revived in the last quarter of the 15th century under the patronage of Sultan Qa'itbay (*reg* 1468–96).

(a) *c.* 1250–*c.* 1400. (b) *c.* 1400–*c.* 1500.

(a) c. 1250–c. 1400.

Centres of production. Evidence concerning centres of production in Egypt and Syria during this period comes mainly from inscriptions. Cairo is named on a candlestick made by Muhammad ibn Hasan al-Mawsili (1269; Cairo, Mus. Islam. A.), a ewer (1275; Paris, Mus. A. Déc.), a candlestick (1283; Cairo, Mus. Islam. A.) and a basin made by 'Ali ibn Husayn ibn Muhammad, but the design, shape and technical characteristics of these four objects vary, and it is impossible to define a recognizable Cairene style. The evidence regarding Damascus is more specific and suggests a calligraphic style and a taste for royal and official titles. In 1293 Sultan Khalil instructed his vizier to write to Damascus for 200 candlesticks, 100 of copper, bearing the Sultan's titles, and 50 each of gold and silver. The 'copper' candlesticks were presumably inlaid brass. Two surviving candlesticks, one of beaten brass made by Husayn ibn Muhammad al-Mawsili in 1257 (Paris, Louvre) and another made by 'Ali ibn Kasirat al-Mawsili in 1277 for the mihrab of the mosque of Ibn Tulun (Cairo, Mus. Islam. A.), bear inscriptions that state they were made in Damascus. Both are decorated with calligraphic designs and serve as the basis for attributing a long series of candlesticks to the same workshop in Damascus. Several name 13th- and 14th-century Mamluk sultans such as Kitbugha, al-Nasir Muhammad and Hasan, and the series continues into the 15th century.

Metalworkers of this period were clearly indebted to the school of Mosul of the early 13th century since most of the 17 known craftsmen bear the name al-Mawsili ('of Mosul'). One exception is Muhammad ibn al-Zayn, the maker of the famous 'Baptistère de St Louis' (*c.* 1300–10; Paris, Louvre; see fig. 153 below) as well as an iron grille for the Is'irdiyya madrasa in Jerusalem (*in situ*). Another is Muhammad ibn Sunqur al-Baghdadi (i.e. of Baghdad), who made the Koran box in Berlin and a hexagonal table for Sultan al-Nasir Muhammad (1327–8; Cairo, Mus. Islam. A.). He may have been the brother of the Mahmud ibn Sunqur who made a penbox in a style more characteristic of the eastern Islamic world (London, BM; see fig. 148 above and METAL, colour pl. I, fig. 1), suggesting that he was of Iraqi origin.

Most metalwork was produced in the bazaar, and the historian al-Maqrizi (1364–1442) described how the metalworkers of Cairo, like other craftsmen, had their own quarter there, but in 1374 the governor of Damascus set up a workshop in his palace to make textiles and other luxury goods. The workshop was equipped with furnaces, and goldsmiths were employed there to produce objects made of or decorated with gold and silver, such as stirrups and camel saddles. Presumably these craftsmen had to work in the palace so that the governor could monitor the amount of precious metal used.

Patronage. The patrons named on inlaid metal objects made in this period were all members of the Mamluk military aristocracy, either sultans or their amirs. The court of Sultan al-Nasir Muhammad, to which 28 pieces can be assigned, was particularly prolific. During the latter half of the 14th century objects were produced that bore the title but not the name of a specific individual, and this suggests that the ruling class had less control over the industry, allowing pieces to be sold to a wider clientele. Many pieces were made for export, and some were done for non-Muslim patrons such as Hugh IV of Lusignan, King of Cyprus and Jerusalem (*reg* 1324–59), named on a basin in Paris (Louvre). Many other examples from the end of the 14th century and the 15th bear European coats of arms or have shields left blank to receive such arms on arrival at their destination. Others were made for foreign Muslim patrons, such as a large group of objects, including two made in Cairo, that bear the names of the four members of the Rasulid dynasty, who ruled Yemen from 1250 to 1377, or of their officers of state. Basins from the 14th century also appear in pagan shrines in Ghana; they probably reached Ghana via the trans-Saharan gold trade, but it is not clear whether they were there as objects of trade or simply as the personal possessions of Arab merchants.

Forms and decoration. The most striking style of this period, that based on the decorative use of calligraphy, is exemplified by the magnificent Koran box made by Muhammad ibn Sunqur al-Baghdadi and inlaid by al-Hajj Yusuf ibn al-Ghawabi (first half of the 14th century; Berlin, Mus. Islam. Kst; see fig. 152), which is decorated with Koranic inscriptions in various scripts: a wide band of *thuluth* around the body of the square box is set against narrow bands in other cursive and angular scripts. The first dated example of this style is a candlestick made by Husayn ibn Muhammad al-Mawsili in 1257 (Paris, Louvre), and its evolution can be traced through a series of candlesticks to its full development *c.* 1300. Numerous

examples survive from the reign of Sultan al-Nasir Muhammad (*reg* 1294–1340 with interruptions). The style may be linked to contemporary manuscript production, but the precise relationship remains to be investigated. An important development in the 14th century was the incorporation of inscriptions within circular motifs. Initially the prerogative of the sultan, these designs were gradually taken over by the Mamluk amirs. At first the sultan's titles were left in the central disc, while the amir's own titles were placed in the surrounding sunburst. At a later stage the centre was filled with the amir's armorial devices. These changes reflect the increasing power of the officers of state following the death of al-Nasir Muhammad in 1340. The arrangement is related to the 'belted' style, in which the objects appear to be wearing a belt with a large clasp in the form of a sun-disc with rays, as in the incense burner made in the name of al-Nasir Muhammad (Nuhad Es-Said priv. col., on loan to Oxford, Ashmolean; see Allan, 1982, no. 15).

Another important group of objects bears figural representations. Court scenes depicting rulers and their amirs, already seen in the Syrian and Jaziran wares made before 1250, continued in the work of Muhammad ibn al-Zayn. His bowl (Paris, Louvre) shows the enthroned sultan flanked by various functionaries bearing symbols of office. More important is the figural design on his other work, the 'Baptistère de St Louis' (see fig. 153). On the exterior four panels with standing figures alternate with four roundels containing mounted huntsmen. The interior follows the same arrangement, but the four panels have mounted warriors, while two of the roundels have enthroned sultans and the other two originally bore the

152. Koran box by Muhammad ibn Sunqur al-Baghdadi, wood covered with brass and inlaid with gold and silver, h. 270 mm, first half of the 14th century (Berlin, Museum für Islamische Kunst)

153. 'Baptistère de St Louis' by Muhammad ibn al-Zayn, brass chased and inlaid with gold and silver, h. 232 mm, from Egypt or Syria, c. 1290–1310 (Paris, Musée du Louvre)

owner's armorial device. The standing figures on the exterior include members of the Mamluk ruling class (Mongoloid; armed; wearing turbans, surcoats, slipper shoes and spats) and indigenous servants (non-Mongoloid; some bearing eating or drinking vessels, others birds or animals related to the hunt; wearing hats of different kinds, kerchiefs, cloaks and boots). The basin is unique in portraying the members of both the military and the lower classes and gives a rare example of an individual portrait, that of the probable owner, the amir Salar.

Metalwork decorated with figures was rare after the beginning of the 14th century, and the themes taken up by Muhammad ibn al-Zayn were never developed. Some figures are astrological, as on a bowl in Paris (Louvre, 6032) and a magnificent inlaid steel mirror in Istanbul (Topkapı Pal. Mus.). By the 1370s figures also appear on wares produced in Damascus: a visitor to the city in 1384–5, Simone Sigoli, mentioned basins and ewers decorated with figures and leaves, and the box made for Aydamur al-Ashrafi, governor of Aleppo, in 1371 (Paris, Louvre) shows animals and birds placed in a paradisal setting.

A great deal of architectural metalwork survives from this period, including large numbers of 13th- and 14th-century bronze or brass doors in Cairo. A comparison of doors of this period (e.g. those of the madrasa of Sultan Qala'un; 1284–5) with earlier examples (e.g. those of the mosque of al-Salih Tala'i', 1160) shows that there was continuity in their production. The type of splendid cast bronze door facings seen in the funerary complex of Sultan Hasan (1356–62; see DOOR, fig. 7) occur only once thereafter, in the main doors of the mosque of Sultan Barquq (1384–6; all four examples in situ), and are then replaced by thin, pierced facings that were cheaper in terms of material and labour costs. Numerous window grilles also remain, including fine examples in inlaid brass bearing the names of Sultan Hajji (reg 1346–7) and Sultan Hasan (reg 1356–61; both Cairo, Mus. Islam. A.) and undecorated iron grilles still in situ.

BIBLIOGRAPHY

G. Wiet: Catalogue général du Musée Arabe: Objets en cuivre (Cairo, 1932)
L. A. Mayer: Saracenic Heraldry (Oxford, 1933)
D. S. Rice: The Baptistère de St Louis (Paris, 1951)
——: 'Arabic Inscriptions on a Brass Basin Made for Hugh IV de Lusignan', Studi orientalistici in onore di Giorgio Levi della Vida, ii (Rome, 1956), pp. 390–402
H. Batanouni: 'Catalogue of Mamluk Doors with Metal Revetments' (MA thesis, Amer. U. Cairo, 1975)
Renaissance of Islam: Art of the Mamluks (exh. cat. by E. Atıl, Washington, DC, N.G.A., 1981)
J. W. Allan: Islamic Metalwork: The Nuhad Es-Said Collection (London, 1982)
R. A. Silverman: 'Akan Kuduo: Form and Function', in Akan Transformations: Problems in Ghanaian Art History, ed. D. H. Ross and T. F. Garrard (Los Angeles, 1983), pp. 10–29
J. W. Allan: 'Sha'ban, Barquq and the Decline of the Mamluk Metalworking Industry', Muqarnas, ii (1984), pp. 85–94
J. M. Bloom: 'A Mamluk Basin in the L. A. Mayer Memorial Institute', Islam. A., ii (1987), pp. 15–26

J. W. ALLAN

(b) c. 1400–c. 1500. The production of fine metal objects in Egypt and Syria had declined in quantity and quality towards the end of the 14th century, and by the beginning of the 15th century smaller objects were being made in a narrower range of shapes and techniques. Basins and ewers, common in the 14th century, became exceedingly rare, while shallow dishes became one of the most typical forms. Decoration became coarser and more repetitive. Inscriptions became less important and rarely identify either patron or maker. The emblems used by the sultan and Mamluk amirs proliferate, but few are identifiable. Floral designs continue but are simplified and merely scratched into the surfaces of objects. Stamped motifs, frequently geometric and interlocking, appear with increasing regularity, particularly on bronze and tinned copper objects.

Bronze seems to have been unavailable in Cairo by the later 14th century, for Sultan Sha'ban (*reg* 1363–76) commanded the governor of Damascus to collect bronze objects and send them to Cairo for use in his mausoleum. This suggests that the Egyptian industry failed due to the scarcity of raw materials; the financial crisis under Sultan Faraj (*reg* 1399–1412) probably exacerbated the situation. The Syrian industry, renowned for its fine wares in the 14th century, came to an end in 1401 when Timur sacked Damascus, its principal centre, and took its artisans captive. The decline in metalworking may also have resulted from the growing taste for Chinese ceramics noted by the Egyptian historian al-Maqrizi *c.* 1440.

Fine metalwork was still needed for the great public monuments of Cairo, which continued to be built on a large scale. Few objects were made expressly for these new buildings, and many of their furnishings, such as candlesticks and chandeliers, were plundered from older foundations. Sultan Mu'ayyad, for example, furnished his mosque in Cairo (*c.* 1420) with extremely fine pieces produced 60 years earlier for the funerary complex of Sultan Hasan. A lantern fragment bearing the name of Sultan Khushqadam (*reg* 1461–7; Cairo, Mus. Islam. A.) demonstrates the mediocre quality of the few objects that were made. Bronze door facings continued to be produced for major architectural projects, although a comparison between those for the madrasas of Sultan Barquq (*c.* 1386) and those for Sultan Barsbay (*c.* 1424) in Cairo illustrates the sharp change in style. The facings made for the madrasa of Sultan Barquq consist of intricate interlocking units in high relief that have been engraved and inlaid with arabesque and chinoiserie designs; they form a repeating geometric design that covers the entire wooden door. In Barsbay's madrasa double framing bands surround a tripartite composition of two narrow epigraphic compartments enclosing a large central compartment, which contains a central ogee medallion and elaborate corner devices. The flat design, strongly reminiscent of contemporary bookbindings and manuscript frontispieces, is attached to the door with nails, the heads of which are in high relief. This type of door, using much less metal and showing much more of the underlying wood, remained standard through the century.

Metalworking revived in the last quarter of the century under the patronage of Sultan Qa'itbay (*reg* 1468–96), who was a prolific builder and restorer of monuments in Mecca, Medina and Jerusalem as well as in Cairo. The demand for furnishings generated by these public projects probably spurred the revival, but an accompanying increase in private demand is also evident. Sophisticated metalworking techniques such as inlay and repoussé were again used to make fine brass basins, dishes, bowls and ewers with articulated bottoms, bevelled or faceted sides and scalloped

154. Brass bowl made for Sultan Qa'itbay (*reg* 1468–96), inlaid with gold and silver, from Cairo (Istanbul, Museum of Turkish and Islamic Art)

rims inspired by the greatly prized Chinese ceramics. The finest example of the revived inlay technique is a small brass bowl inlaid with gold and silver (Istanbul, Mus. Turk. & Islam. A.; see fig. 154). Engraving continued but designs were enhanced by the application of a bituminous paste to the background. Four types of ornament—floral, arabesque interlace, elaborate knots and geometric patterning—were used, usually simultaneously, but the inscription, normally enclosed in a cartouche of strapwork, was the primary element of design. A new form of *thuluth* script in which the thick vertical strokes rise up in pairs and cross to form pincers was used only on royal metalwork, such as an engraved beaten-brass bowl in New York (Met., 91.1.565), probably made for secular use.

Copper, tinned copper and tinned bronze objects, typically shallow dishes, lunch boxes and trays, appear in large numbers in the later 15th century. They are decorated with rather crudely engraved designs, frequently strapwork, Y-fret patterns, simple scrolls and cross-hatching. Some of these pieces bear composite emblems (circular shields divided horizontally into three fields filled with assorted cups, napkins, penboxes and powder horns) as well as inscriptions indicating that they were made for Mamluk amirs. Other pieces bear anonymous benedictory inscriptions that are largely illegible (e.g. Oxford, Ashmolean, 1959.24, 1959.30; London, V&A, 1242–1888). Although metalwork was again fashionable, the poor quality of these objects suggests that the materials and craftsmanship at Qa'itbay's command were not available to either his non-royal contemporaries or his successors. Among the most interesting of the post-Qa'itbay pieces are bronze chandeliers and polycandela that are curiously architectonic in form. A chandelier made for the complex of Sultan Qansuh al-Ghawri (*reg* 1501–17; Cairo, Mus. Islam. A.) has a finial-topped dome, the surface of which is engraved with designs strongly reminiscent of the carved stone domes of contemporary buildings.

After Syria and Egypt became provinces of the Ottoman empire in 1516–17, tinned coppers and bronzes of the pre-conquest type continued to be produced, but the cartouches, strapwork, fretwork and dense floral scrolls of the Mamluk period were increasingly replaced by metropolitan Ottoman motifs such as the cypress tree and the spray of flowers issuing from a vase. Few of these provincial pieces are notable for the quality of their design or for technical excellence.

BIBLIOGRAPHY

G. Wiet: *Catalogue général du Musée Arabe du Caire: Objets en cuivre* (Cairo, 1932)

D. S. Rice: 'Studies in Islamic Metalwork—i', *Bull. SOAS*, xiv (1952), pp. 564–78

——: 'Studies in Islamic Metalwork—iv', *Bull. SOAS*, xv (1953), pp. 489–503

J. W. Allan: 'Later Mamluk Metalwork: A Series of Dishes', *Orient. A.*, n.s., xv/1 (1969), pp. 38–43

A. S. Melikian-Chirvani: 'Cuivres inédits de l'époque de Qa'itbay', *Kst Orients*, vi (1969), pp. 99–133

J. W. Allan: 'Later Mamluk Metalwork: A Series of Lunchboxes', *Orient. A.*, n.s., xvii/2 (1971), pp. 156–64

A. Raymond and G. Wiet: *Les Marchés du Caire, traduction annotée du texte de Maqrīzī* (Cairo, 1979)

Renaissance of Islam: Art of the Mamluks (exh. cat. by E. Atıl, Washington, DC, N.G.A., 1981)

AMY W. NEWHALL

(iv) *Spain and North Africa.* Seville seems to have been the most important metalworking centre in Islamic Spain in the period between *c.* 1100 and its conquest by Ferdinand III of Castile in 1248. It is noted as such by the 16th-century author al-Maqqari and is named on a series of five astrolabes dated between 1212 and 1237 and made by a craftsman called Muhammad ibn Fattuh (Rome, Osservatorio Astron.; Paris, Bib. N.; Oxford U., Mus. Hist. Sci.; Cairo, Mus. Islam. A.; Chicago, IL, Adler Planetarium). Subsequent generations of astrolabists worked in other cities under the rule of the NASRID dynasty of Granada (*reg* 1230–1492): Muhammad ibn Fattuh's son Muhammad signed an astrolabe he made at Murcia in 1252–3 (Barcelona, Observatori Fabra); Ahmad ibn Husayn ibn Baso was responsible for three made in Granada itself between 1265 and 1310 (Madrid, Real Acad. Hist.; Genoa, Soc. Ligure Stor. Patria; Paris, M. G. Pin priv. col.); and Ibrahim ibn Muhammad ibn al-Raqqam made one at Guadix in 1320–21 (Madrid, Real Acad. Hist.).

A few bronzes surviving from 12th-century Spain, such as a mortar from Palencia (h. 200 mm; Villanueva y Geltrú, Mus. Balaguer), show that the forms and style of decoration that had evolved under the Umayyad dynasty continued in use after the dynasty's fall in 1031. Under the Nasrids gilt bronze was popular. Surviving examples include a magnificent bucket (h. 170 mm; Madrid, Mus. Arqueol. N.), three small cylindrical boxes or inkwells (Arezzo, Mus. Dioc.; Kuwait, Homaizi priv. col., for illustration see Allan; Madrid, Pidal priv. col., for illustration see S. M. Imamuddin: *Muslim Spain, 711–1492 A.D.* (Leiden, 1981), pl. iv, no. 1) and a pear-shaped box or reliquary (Rome, Basilica S Marco). The most important surviving bronze is the great chandelier with pierced inscriptions and arabesque decoration made for the Nasrid sultan Muhammad III in 1305, presumably at Granada (Madrid, Mus. Arqueol. N.; see fig. 155). It conforms to the type of chandelier current in the Mediterranean world in earlier times, which had a tall, pierced, conical or pyramidal body, with the glass containers suspended from the polycandelon-like base. It shares these features with late Mamluk brass and early Ottoman silver pieces.

Another group of objects is associated with the last Nasrid ruler, Abu 'Abdallah Muhammad XI ('Boabdil'; *reg* 1482–3, 1487–92). Many of his single- and double-edged swords are in Madrid (Mus. Ejército). They have magnificent mounts of gilt bronze with gold filigree and enamel work and show that metal wares of superb quality were still being produced despite the Nasrids' declining power. Some of the surviving pieces of Nasrid gold jewellery are also enamelled and display geometric designs. In general, metalwork from Muslim Spain uses relatively few figural motifs, apart from a tradition of making fountain-heads in the shape of animals. (A lion (Paris, Louvre), found in the province of Palencia and dated to the 12th or 13th century, was probably a fountain-head.) Instead, geometric and arabesque patterns were more popular, and under the Nasrids the decorative possibilities of the cursive Arabic script known as *naskh* were explored.

Surviving metalwork from Morocco is equally rare. The finest works are chandeliers. The 'Great Chandelier' in the Great Mosque in Taza, made in 1294, weighs 32 *qinṭār* (*c.* 15 kilos), has 514 oil holders and cost 8000 *dīnār*s. A

155. Bronze chandelier with pierced inscriptions and arabesques, made for the Nasrid sultan Muhammad III, h. 540 mm, probably from Granada, 1305 (Madrid, Museo Arqueológico Nacional)

work of extraordinary skill and sophistication, its internal ribbed dome imitates the design of the dome over the bay in front of the mihrab in the mosque. Two other late 13th-century chandeliers in the Great Mosque of Taza are less exotic, but also stand out for their pierced arabesque work: the 'Small Chandelier' and one made from a church bell probably captured in a Marinid raid into southern Andalusia. This tradition continued into the 14th century and is exemplified by the fine lamp in the name of the Marinid Abu Sa'id 'Uthman made in 1323 for his Attarin Madrasa in Fez, the chandelier made in 1337 for the Qarawiyyin Mosque in Fez from a bell captured in Gibraltar four years earlier and at least six other contemporary chandeliers in the same mosque. The earliest surviving chandelier from North Africa is in the Andalusiyyin Mosque in Fez; it probably dates from the reign of the Almohad caliph al-Nasir (1199–1214). Two others in the same mosque date from the late 14th century and the 15th. Other objects made in North Africa during this period include alms bowls of cast bronze decorated solely with inscriptions detailing their function. Bronze and iron door fittings also survive, as do sets of three bronze balls of the type that

have topped mosques and minarets in Morocco for centuries, but the significance of which is not clear.

BIBLIOGRAPHY

C. Terrasse: *Médersas du Maroc* (Paris, 1927)
H. Terrasse: *La Mosquée des Andalous à Fès* (Paris, n.d.)
——: *La Grande Mosquée de Taza* (Paris, 1943)
M. Vicaire: 'Note sur quatre mesures d'aumône inédits', *Hespéris*, xxxi (1944), pp. 1–14
L. Torres Balbás: *Arte almohade; arte nazarí; arte mudéjar* (1949), vi of *Ars Hispaniae* (Madrid, 1947–77), pp. 224–34
H. Terrasse: *La Mosquée al-Qaraouiyin à Fès* (Paris, 1968)
The Arts of Islam (exh. cat., London, Hayward Gal., 1976), nos 174–6
J. W. Allan: 'Inkwell', *Louisiana Rev.*, xxvii/3 (March 1987), cat. no. 174
Al-Andalus: The Art of Islamic Spain (exh. cat., ed. J. D. Dodds; Granada, Alhambra; New York Met.; 1992)

J. W. ALLAN

4. AFTER *c.* 1500. For Islamic metalwork during this period in Central Asia and India *see* CENTRAL ASIA, §I, 5(i)(d) and (ii)(g) and INDIAN SUBCONTINENT, §VIII, 15.

(i) Ottoman empire. (ii) Egypt and Syria, after *c.* 1800. (iii) Iran.

(i) Ottoman empire. The eastern Mediterranean was dominated by the Ottoman Turks for 300 years after the conquest of Syria and Egypt by Sultan Selim I in 1516–17; Egypt broke away from the empire in the 19th century, but Syria remained under Ottoman control until World War I. During this period the Ottoman capital, Istanbul, was the dominant centre of production, and designs created in the court studios there were employed throughout the empire on all types of wares. Two categories can be distinguished in the vast amount of material that has survived (Topkapı Palace Museum alone holds 6000 pieces): costly items commissioned by the court circle; and wares made in imitation for the rest of the population using cheaper materials and less laborious techniques. The palace treasury held pieces made for the personal use of the sultan or for ceremonial occasions as well as supernumerary items that were periodically given as gifts or recycled. Their history can be traced from treasury inventories and from seals or dedications engraved on them. Other high-quality wares were presented by members of the imperial family or officers of state to religious or charitable foundations such as mosques, madrasas, tombs and libraries (most now in museums).

Production for the court was carried out by craftsmen (*ehl-i hiref*) who were retained on the palace payrolls. At the end of the 16th century, 100 Istanbul gold- and silversmiths were retained in this way, and the lists also include craftsmen specializing in gold inlay, gold wire making, moulds for seals, stamps and coins, gold and silver-thread making, iron work, metal casting and arms and armour. Smaller groups of approved craftsmen were established in provincial cities, particularly those where Ottoman princes served as governors. All the major cities of the empire also had a large number of metalworkers organized in guilds and serving both domestic and foreign markets, while the various sections of the Ottoman army and navy had their own workshops for weapons and other military equipment.

Items produced for the court were fashioned in gold, silver, and, from the mid-16th century to the mid-17th, zinc. They were frequently inlaid with gold, enamels, niello and table-cut gemstones. Copper, its alloys (brass and bronze), iron and steel were generally reserved for utilitarian pieces and architectural decoration; copper wares were often enhanced by tinning and gilding. Casting, spinning and hammering from sheet-metal were used to shape metal wares, while decoration was applied by chasing, incising, repoussé, punching, overlay and inlay. Designs were primarily floral, both naturalistic and stylized, with scrolls and sprays covering surfaces. Figural representations, which had been prevalent in earlier Islamic traditions, are noticeably absent from the repertory of Ottoman metalwork. Apart from jewellery most pieces are essentially functional, whether designated for the sultan's treasury or for the humble household. They include a variety of items for serving food and beverages, writing equipment, arms and armour, and architectural components and furnishings.

Decorative themes produced in the court studios became more prominent on metalwork produced after the first quarter of the 16th century. A court payroll dated 1526 lists a number of metalworkers employed in the court who had trained in the eastern and western provinces of the empire, notably in Azerbaijan and Bosnia. The collaborative efforts of artists from diverse backgrounds are evident in a group of silver or gilt-silver jugs with dragon-shaped handles (e.g. London, V&A, 158–1894; h. 140 mm). Their pot-bellied shape derives from pieces made in eastern Iran during the 15th century (*see* §3 (i)(b) above); their technique (chasing, repoussé or both against a ring-matted ground) reflects that used in eastern Europe; but their decorative themes (scrolls combined with split-leaves and stylized lotus blossoms) are purely Ottoman. Similar materials, techniques and themes were applied to bowls, boxes, plates and trays, some of which were decorated with niello.

These relatively understated pieces with refined and harmonious designs were produced at the same time as gold, silver and zinc pieces inlaid with gold scrolls bearing gem-encrusted blossoms. The same technique was used to decorate carved jade, rock crystal and Chinese porcelains and was typical of objects produced for the court between the 1550s and 1650s. Some spectacular gold pieces, such as a ceremonial canteen (Istanbul, Topkapı Pal. Mus., 2/3825) have jade plaques similarly decorated with gold inlays and gems; other pieces, including a penbox and a jug (Istanbul, Topkapı Pal. Mus., 2/22, 2/8) have rock crystal components lined with illuminated paper. These imperial wares display superb craftsmanship and show the combined talents of artists from several court workshops.

Work from this period is characteristically decorated in the *saz* style, in which floral scrolls with fantastic blossoms and leaves, sometimes intermingled with cloud bands, spiral across the surface and create a three-dimensional effect with two or more superimposed layers. The master goldsmith who excelled in this style was the Mehmed who appears as Mehmed the Bosnian in palace documents dating from between 1596 and 1605. He created delicate designs in chasing and repoussé, filigree work, niello inlays and gem incrustation. Three of his signed and dated pieces are preserved in Istanbul: a binding for the poems of Murad III (1588), a box for the Prophet's mantle (1592–3) and a lock and key for the Ka'ba (1593–4; all Topkapı Pal. Mus.). Other pieces in a similar style, such as the gold

canteen mentioned above, a crown presented by Sultan Ahmed I to Stephen Bocskay, the ruler of Transylvania, in 1605 (Vienna, Ksthist. Mus.), decorative components for ceremonial and sacred swords and other bindings, can also be attributed to him.

Unadorned or simply chased pieces, such as candlesticks (see fig. 156), ewers, basins and bowls with bold and striking shapes contrast with the jewelled gold objects. Made of silver, copper or brass, the latter two sometimes tinned or gilded, they represent a different aesthetic approach to metalwork. Among the more impressive pieces are a pair of large silver candlesticks datable to the second quarter of the 17th century (h. 1.175 m; Istanbul, Mus. Turk. & Islam. A., 93A–B). These materials and techniques continued to be used for metalwork made between the mid-17th century and the early 20th, but the decorative repertory changed. Pieces from the 18th century are done in a Rococo style with floral bouquets, garlands and fluttering ribbons. Gilt-copper, known as *tombak*, was one of the most popular materials. In the 19th century copper and gilt-copper were fashioned into a variety of functional pieces frequently decorated with naturalistic flowers and fruit. Silver was used for such household items as mirrors and matching sets of basins and ewers and for

156. Candlestick with chased and incised decoration, brass, cast in sections and soldered, h. 260 mm, from Turkey, *c.* 1500 (Washington, DC, Freer Gallery of Art)

accessories including belts, pendants and bracelets, some inlaid with niello, others embellished with wire filigree.

BIBLIOGRAPHY

A. S. Melikian-Chirvani: 'Recherches sur l'école du bronze ottoman au XVIe siècle', *Turcica*, vi (1975), pp. 146–67

J. Allan and J. Raby: 'Metalwork', *Tulips, Arabesques and Turbans*, ed. Y. Petsopoulos (London, 1982), pp. 97–109

F. Çağman: 'Serzergeran Mehmet Usta ve Eserleri' [Chief jeweller Mehmet and his works], *Kemal Çığ'a Armağan* [*Festschrift* for Kemal Çığ] (Istanbul, 1984), pp. 51–88

N. Tapan Ölçer: 'Türkische Metallkunst', *Türkische Kunst und Kultur aus osmanischer Zeit* (exh .cat., Frankfurt am Main, Mus. Ksthandwic 1985), ii, pp. 274–81

E. Atıl: *The Age of Sultan Süleyman the Magnificent* (Washington, D.C., and New York, 1986), pp. 113–75

F. Bodur: *Türk Maden Sanatı / The Art of Turkish Metalworking* (Istanbul, 1987)

ESIN ATIL

(ii) Egypt and Syria, after c. *1800.* By the beginning of the 19th century Egyptian and Syrian metalworkers were producing 'nothing but mediocre pieces' (*Description de l'Egypte*, p. 509), for they had suffered from a scarcity of materials since the 14th century and from the competition of Turkish imports since the 16th. Locally produced objects were typically tinned copper trays lightly engraved with designs adopted from Ottoman metropolitan work such as cypress trees and sprays of flowers issuing from vases. When Muhammad 'Ali established Egypt's independence from the Ottoman empire in 1841, he opened the country to European imports, and English and German metalwork flooded the market. At the same time European taste for orientalia was growing (*see* ORIENTALISM), and, to meet the new demand, the production of fine inlaid and engraved metalwork was revived in Cairo, Damascus and Jerusalem at the end of the century. The main source of inspiration was the objects made for Mamluk sultans (*reg* 1250–1517) and their amirs (*see* §3(iii) above), but new shapes along the lines of European expectations, such as the undulating urns and fantastic chandeliers seen in many photographs of Victorian interiors, were also created. This revival lasted until World War I, when taste changed; later production was for the tourist market and lacks both historical resonance and creative verve.

In 1880 the Khedive 'Abbas II founded the Arab Museum in Cairo (now Mus. Islam. A.), where local artisans were able to study the inscriptions and decoration on antique pieces and the old techniques of inlay and engraving in order to produce the exact replicas their clients required. One example is a copy of an inlaid bronze lamp made for Sultan Baybars II (1309) commissioned by Lord Curzon for the Taj Mahal (untraced). Some copies were so successful that they were taken for genuine antiques. A pair of inlaid bronze doors long thought to belong to the madrasa of Sultan Barquq (1384–6; New York, Hisp. Soc. America Mus.) were actually made for the Street of Cairo in the Midway Plaisance at the Columbian Exposition in Chicago in 1893. One of the most widely copied objects, and one widely illustrated in contemporary books on art and history, was a hexagonal stand of pierced brass with silver and gold inlay made for the Mamluk sultan al-Nasir Muhammad (1327–8; Cairo, Mus. Islam. A.). This unique piece (the only similar object is made of wood) bears the signature of the artisan who made it, Muhammad ibn Sunqur al-Baghdadi, and this

may have added to its appeal in the West, where the individual artist is venerated (copies in Istanbul, Topkapı Pal. Mus.; Cambridge, MA, Harvard U., Semit. Mus.; Philadelphia, U. PA, Mus.; and several priv. cols; see fig. 157). One of the most notable entrepreneurs in this trade at Cairo was Giuseppe Parvis, who ran his own workshop as well as being a dealer.

In Damascus the art of inlaying metal with silver revived after a hiatus of 500 years. Beautiful and opulent calligraphy (usually simple aphorisms or good wishes) inlaid in silver is normally considered the hallmark of Damascus work. Damascene craftsmen are thought to have adhered less closely to Mamluk models and to have been more inventive than their counterparts in Cairo, but most attributions are made without the benefit of identifying inscriptions. In his survey of occupations in Damascus in the 1890s, Sa'id al-Qasimi noted that Jews were the greatest practitioners of

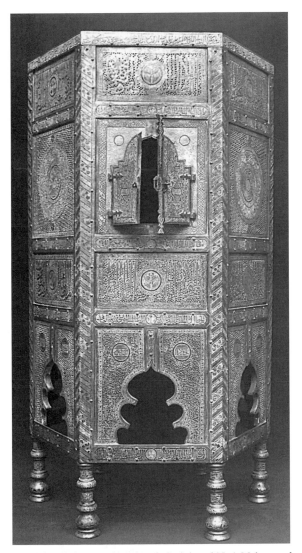

157. Copy of a hexagonal stand made for Sultan al-Nasir Muhammad by Muhammad ibn Sunqur al-Baghdadi in 1327–8, pierced brass with silver and gold inlay, h. 860 mm, diam. 422 mm, Cairo, late 19th century (Cambridge, MA, Harvard University, Semitic Museum)

metal inlay; he stated that European taste stimulated the metalwork revival and that the wares were exported to Egypt and Europe as well as being sold on the local market. In 1909 Avraham Bar-Adon, head of the copper department of the new Bezalel Craft School in Jerusalem, went to the Damascus atelier of B. Asfar to learn the craft of inlay, and his letters contain valuable information on technique and workshop practice in Damascus at that time. The workshop he founded in Jerusalem became known for inlaid objects, often with representational and religious decoration.

BIBLIOGRAPHY

E. Jomard and others, eds: *Description de l'Egypte: Etat moderne*, ii/2 (Paris, 1822)

M. du Camp: *Le Nil, Egypte et Nubie* (Paris, 1854), p. 47

M. S. al-Qasimi: *Qāmūs al-ṣanāʿat al-shāmiyya/Dictionnaire des métiers damascains*, 2 vols (Paris, 1960)

The Mamluk Revival: Metalwork for Religious and Domestic Use (exh. cat. by E. Whelan, New York, Jew. Mus., 1981)

AMY W. NEWHALL

(iii) Iran. Metalwork from the early 16th century continued the forms, techniques and styles that had evolved in the preceding century in eastern Iran (*see* §3(i)(b) above). In the second half of the century a new aesthetic emerged: sleek, tapered forms were introduced; inlay in precious metal was abandoned; figural decoration reappeared, but remained less important than vegetal and abstract ornament; and inscriptions in *nastaʿlīq* script proliferated. Metal wares produced under the Zand and Qajar dynasties (*reg* 1750–94 and 1779–1924 respectively) survive in their tens of thousands but are of modest artistic merit.

(a) *c.* 1500–*c.* 1550. (b) *c.* 1550–*c.* 1700. (c) After *c.* 1700.

(a) c. 1500–c. 1550. Iranian metal wares from the early 16th century can be distinguished from earlier examples produced under the Timurid dynasty (*reg* 1370–1506) only on the basis of the dates or the content of their inscriptions. The most common type of dated object is a pot-bellied jug with an S-curve dragon handle and gold and silver inlay (examples dated 1508–9, 1512, 1513 and 1517 respectively in Tehran, Archaeol. Mus.; Copenhagen, Davids Saml.; London, BM; Istanbul, Mus. Turk. & Islam. A.; see fig. 149 above for an earlier example). Another common form is a small, cylindrical inkwell with a dome-shaped cover (an example dated 1513 in London, V&A), a type that had often been shown accompanied by a double-barrelled pencase in late 15th-century manuscript illustrations such as one in a copy of the *Khamsa* ('Five poems') of Nizami dated 1494–5 (London, BL, Or. MS. 6810, fol. 214*r*). Whereas many 15th-century wares were inscribed with verses in Persian, these pieces often bear prayers in Arabic. The inkwell dated 1513 has two prayers, one invoking the names of the Prophet Muhammad and the Twelve Imams, the other addressed to ʿAli. The Shiʿite character of these inscriptions—ʿAli and the Twelve Imams were held in particular respect by Shiʿites—does not specifically place this object within the milieu of the Shiʿite Safavid dynasty (*reg* 1501–1732), but the prayer to ʿAli, for example, first appeared on coins struck in the name of the first Safavid shah Ismaʿil I (*reg* 1501–24) and was frequently inscribed on later 16th-century and 17th-century wares. Its inclusion on inlaid wares is an important means of

distinguishing early 16th-century pieces from 15th-century ones in the same style. The decoration of these jugs and inkwells continued the tendency towards a compressed, dense network of inlaid design composed of delicate, interlaced leaf arabesques in which the system of quatrefoils and epigraphic cartouches is often barely distinguishable from the all-over patterning. A bowl dated 1510–11 (London, V&A) is decorated with undulating cloud scrolls and entwined leaf scrolls like those on non-inlaid wares from the 15th century. The background is filled by hatched and cross-hatched lines; cross-hatching, a hallmark of 15th-century metalwork, is rarely found on later 16th-century engraved wares.

These inlaid wares were probably made in Herat (now in Afghanistan), which was the capital of the Timurid rulers of eastern Iran until 1507, and must have continued to be an important centre for metalware production during the first two decades of the 16th century. The bowl dated 1510–11 is inscribed in *nastaʿlīq* script with verses by Hilali (*d* 1535–6), a poet who worked in Herat, and is signed by Sultan-Muhammad, a calligrapher attached to the court of the last Timurid ruler of Herat, Badiʿ al-Zaman (*reg* 1506–7). Production at the Safavid capital of Tabriz in northwest Iran in the 1510s or 1520s is attested by three cylindrical dome-covered inkwells, all inlaid, signed by Mirak Husayn Yazdi (two in London, V&A; one in Athens, Benaki Mus.). This shape is also documented in contemporary manuscript illustrations from Tabriz such as one in a copy of the *Khamsa* of Nizami (1539–43; London, BL, Or. MS. 2265, fol. 77*v*). The epithet Yazdi does not necessarily mean that Mirak Husayn himself came from the town of Yazd in central Iran, but it certainly differentiates him from metalworkers trained in the 15th-century style who invariably had epithets derived from places in eastern Iran (the latest example is a jug signed by ʿAli ibn Muhammad ʿAli Shahab al-Ghuri—that is, of Ghur, now in Afghanistan—in 1512; Copenhagen, Davids Saml.). The inkwells are decorated with medallions filled with radial designs of stylized cloud scrolls and split palmettes marked by hooked spirals and curved lines, and the overall scheme is more spacious and rhythmic and less hieratic than the precise, crowded designs typical of 15th-century wares.

In the second quarter of the 16th century decoration became stiffer and more schematized, and new motifs such as a scrolling leaf background to the inscriptions appeared. This transitional style is found primarily on engraved and tinned bowls. On a bowl dated 1535–6 (New York, Met.) the traditional decorative vocabulary—vegetal and abstract ornament divided among interlocking and overlapping compartments—is maintained, but the motifs are abstracted and the calligraphy is more prominent. This type of metalware continued to be produced in a provincial style in eastern Iran and western Central Asia well into the second half of the 16th century. Other pieces can be attributed to a transitional period in western Iran. A jug (London, V&A, 241–1896) maintains the traditional shape and decoration of polylobed medallions, epigraphic cartouches and five-petalled flowers and clover leaves, but the design is more sharply defined, livelier although more stylized, and less linear and compact. Similarly a large bowl (London, V&A, 535–1876) is decorated with fine *nastaʿlīq* inscriptions and a fretwork of polylobes filled with slender cloud scrolls and stylized flowers.

(b) c. *1550–*c. *1700.* Several dated objects show that a new style of metalwork emerged in western Iran in the later 16th century, most probably in the third quarter. A number of previously unknown or substantially modified shapes were introduced. The most important is a column-shaped lampstand, a tapered cylinder with a chamfered or faceted middle section and a flared base. The earliest dated example is one that was donated to a shrine in Iraq in 1561–2 (Baghdad, Iraq Mus.), but the shape may have been introduced from northern India during the second quarter of the century. Closely related examples include one dated 1578–9 (New York, Met.; see fig. 158), another dated 1579–80 which preserves its lamp in the form of a footed cup (St Petersburg, Hermitage) and a third dated 1587–8 (Paris, Mus. A. Déc.). They are engraved with all-over patterns of spiralling split-leaves or zigzag bands and with lozenge-shaped cartouches filled with vegetation, and the decoration emphasizes the contours of the form. Several other lampstands, as well as globular-bodied, slender-necked ewers with thin, curved spouts and buckets with slender bases and upward curving sides, can be dated to the same period because of their similar decoration and characteristic *nasta'līq* inscriptions with Persian verses. Dates and owners' names are often inscribed in cartouches, but the number of empty cartouches suggests that such inscriptions were added after the object was purchased.

Under Shah 'Abbas I (*reg* 1588–1629) the same shapes and decorative vocabulary were continued. A common form was a wine bowl with shallow foot and flaring lip. Bowls, lampstands and other vessels were typically decorated with repetitive vegetal and abstract patterns similar to those found in contemporary carpets or manuscript illumination. Figural ornament was reintroduced to Iranian metalwork as a major decorative device after a hiatus of nearly 200 years. Animal and human figures, similar to those in contemporary drawings and illustrated manuscripts, are set against a background of vegetal scrolls within cartouches or lobed frames. The same style of figural decoration was used on one of the rare pieces of later 16th-century inlaid metalware, a cylindrical inkwell with domical cover (New York, Met., 41.120 a, b). Engraved pieces, such as bowls in London (V&A, M.718–1910) and Paris (Louvre, 7880–117), occasionally bear Armenian inscriptions alongside the more common Persian verses and probably belonged to members of the Armenian community established by Shah 'Abbas in New Julfa, south of his capital, Isfahan. The style associated with Shah 'Abbas continued throughout the 17th century, as is demonstrated by several dated objects, such as a covered bowl decorated with a figural band of combatant animals set against a scrolling floral ground (1678–9; London, V&A). These wares are usually ascribed to western Iran, sometimes more specifically to Isfahan, because of their similarity to other arts produced there or because of the Armenian inscriptions engraved on them. Other engraved and tinned brass wares datable to the late 16th century or the early 17th have been attributed to Khurasan (eastern Iran), as the owners' names inscribed on them contain references to places in the region. They are decorated with the same type of abstract and figural ornament found on pieces from western Iran, but the decoration is organized in a more spacious manner and includes cross-hatching. The dates and attributions for much later 16th- and 17th-century metalware are often open to question, for the inscriptions, in contrast to those on 15th- and early 16th-century pieces, often give the name of the owner but rarely contain artists' signatures or other clues to provenance.

A group of cut steel objects overlaid with gold can be attributed to western Iran in the 16th and 17th centuries. Beginning in the 16th century cut steel was used to make vessels as well as pierced plaques and medallions. Exceptional objects are signed, including two begging bowls for itinerant mystics signed by Hajji 'Abbas, one dated 1606–7 (ex-Nuhad al-Said priv. col.). The decoration of such objects is related more to contemporary cut and gilded armour (*see* §VIII, 1(ii) below) than to contemporary engraved brass and tinned wares.

158. Lampstand, cast and engraved brass, h. 337 mm, from western Iran, 1578–9 (New York, Metropolitan Museum of Art)

BIBLIOGRAPHY

A. A. Ivanov: 'O pervonachal'nom naznachenii tak nazyvayemykh iran-skikh "podsvechnikov" XVI–XVII vv.' [On the original function of the so-called Iranian 'candlesticks' of the 16th–17th centuries], *Issledov-aniya po istorii kul'tury narodov Vostoka* [Studies in the history of the culture of the peoples of the East] (Leningrad, 1960), pp. 337–45

A. S. Melikian-Chirvani: *Le Bronze iranien* (Paris, 1973), pp. 96–125

A. Welch: *Shah 'Abbas and the Arts of Isfahan* (New York, 1973)

A. S. Melikian-Chirvani: 'Safavid Metalwork: A Study in Continuity', *Iran. Stud.*, vii (1974), pp. 543–85

L. Komaroff: 'Timurid to Safavid Iran: Continuity and Change', *Marsyas*, xx (1979–80), pp. 11–16

J. W. Allan: *Islamic Metalwork: The Nuhad Es-Said Collection* (London, 1982), pp. 114–17

A. S. Melikian-Chirvani: *Islamic Metalwork from the Iranian World, 8th–18th Centuries*, London, V&A cat. (London, 1982), pp. 260–355

J. M. Rogers: *Islamic Art and Design, 1500–1700* (London, 1983), pp. 141–8

LINDA KOMAROFF

(c) After c. *1700.* Brass wares continued to be the commonest type of metalwork produced in Iran during the 18th and 19th centuries, and they bear engraved, repoussé or pierced decoration that is sometimes set off against a ground overlaid with niello or a black bituminous substance. The Safavid capital of Isfahan continued to be a leading centre of production, especially for yellow brass wares, despite the shift of the capital to Shiraz under the Zand dynasty (*reg* 1750–94) and to Tehran under the Qajars (*reg* 1779–1924). Production also flourished at Shiraz and Kirman, the latter specializing in tinned copper, which also continued to be produced in the province of Khurasan in eastern Iran.

A few new forms were added to the range that had been elaborated by the late 16th century (*see* §(iii)(b) above): hookahs, for example, and pendants in the shape of hands. Older forms continued to be made with great technical skill but lost much of their former elegance. Their fate is illustrated by the bloated look of a squat household vessel (London, V&A, 558–1878) with a broad neck and bulging sides (h. 147 mm; diam. 292 mm).

Decoration covers the entire visible surface of most objects. Inscriptions and traditional arabesque motifs continued to appear on tinned copper wares from eastern Iran, as on a hemispherical bowl in Kabul (*c.* 1820; Mus.). Elsewhere a wide range of small figural motifs (humans, animals and imaginary creatures) were used to a much greater extent than in the Safavid period (1501–1732). The figures are displayed paratactically, either singly or in pairs. They are set within cartouches against a background of simple arabesques usually consisting of a bare-stem spiral terminating in a peony-like blossom. The classical arabesque of spiralling stems bearing half-palmettes was retained for the subtle framework that outlines the structure of the object and divides its surface. Cartouches are round, rectangular with rounded corners, polylobed, pointed or lozenge- or star-shaped and are defined by a frame or outlined by the stems of the arabesques. The figures are shown feasting or hunting, themes that were part of a traditional repertory of princely pastimes. Some figures carry goblets to their lips and brandish pitchers of wine in a garden set with bottles and fruits; some sleep with their heads resting on their knees, illustrating the topos from Persian literature of 'plunging the head on to the knee of contemplation'; others are shown seated on large, high-backed chairs in the European manner (e.g.

London, V&A, 1366–1874). A whole panoply of entertainers—musicians, dancers, actors, tight-rope walkers and wrestlers—appears on some pieces, such as a bowl in London (1827–8; V&A) and a late 19th-century lantern in Chicago, IL (A. Inst.). Amorous couples are depicted, but the overt eroticism of such scenes in other media of Qajar art is absent. Huntsmen on horseback and a range of wild animals—hares, gazelles, lions, dogs, birds and boars—are shown on objects such as a soap carrier in London (BM; see fig. 159). Animal combats are also portrayed, and combat with a snake, previously a rare motif, was particularly popular during the Qajar period. The depiction of wild animals may also be a punning reference to the theme of the feast, for the Persian word for the wilderness inhabited by the animals (*bādiya*) also means 'wine-cup'. In earlier periods this association between decoration and function had been established by inscriptions. A similar metaphorical interpretation may also have been intended for the animal- and demon-headed figures that often alternate with banqueters or appear separately on a large group of 19th-century wares from Isfahan, such as a lampstand in London (V&A, 500–1874).

A smaller group of brass wares are decorated with continuous scenes with monumental figures in a neo-Safavid style that was part of an attempt to re-create the

159. Soap carrier, brass with pierced lid and cast handle, h. 340 mm, diam. 197 mm, from Iran (probably Isfahan) 19th century (London, British Museum)

Iranian court culture of the 16th and 17th centuries. Another strand in this revivalism was the appearance of motifs derived from Achaemenian and Sasanian models of the 6th–1st centuries BC and 3rd–7th centuries AD, which had become familiar through 19th-century archaeological discoveries.

The technique of gold and silver inlay on iron and steel, which had been kept alive by armourers (*see* §VIII, 1(ii) below), was employed for the axes, clubs and begging bowls used by wandering dervishes, for small figurines of animals, particularly elephants and peacocks (e.g. London, V&A, 1305–1874), and for ornaments in the shape of fruits such as pears, apples and pomegranates, which were hung up to symbolize the tree of life and to bring good luck and were given as wedding and New Year presents. All of these objects were decorated with traditional vegetal motifs, and begging bowls in particular had inscriptions enclosed within cartouches. One example (Aron priv. col., see Allan, no. 6) is inscribed with a Persian poem that refers to its function and is signed as the work of Hajji 'Abbas and dated AH 1015 (1606–7), but its coco-de-mer shape, its decoration and the technique used all suggest that it was made in the 19th century.

Most late Iranian wares were made for the market, but a group of ceremonial objects was commissioned by the court. This group shows the impact of European styles and iconography, which were often absorbed via Russia, as well as archaeological references to ancient Iran. These features can be seen on the enamelled gold basins, ewers, vases and rosewater-sprinklers made for Fath 'Ali Shah (*reg* 1797–1834; *see also* §VIII, 3 below).

BIBLIOGRAPHY

EWA: 'Qajar school'

R. M. Smith: *Persian Art*, London, S. Kensington Mus. (now V&A) cat. (London, 2/1876), pp. 58–75

T. H. Hendley: *Memorials of the Jeypore Exhibition, 1883*, ii (London, 1884), pls liii–lvi

A. A. Ivanov: 'Dannyye epigrafiki i voprosy datirovki iranskikh mednykh i bronzovykh izdeliy XIX v.' [Epigraphic data and problems of dating Iranian copper and bronze wares of the 19th century], *Epig. Vostoka*, xvii (1966), pp. 65–71

U. Scerrato: 'Coppia di candelabri di Isfahan di epoca Qāğār', *Arte orientale in Italia*, ii (Naples, 1971), pp. 27–48

A. S. Melikian-Chirvani: 'Qajar Metalwork: A Study in Cultural Trends', *Qajar Iran: Political, Social and Cultural Change, 1800–1925*, ed. E. Bosworth and C. Hillenbrand (Edinburgh, 1983), pp. 311–29

J. Allan: *Metalwork of the Islamic World: The Aron Collection* (London, 1986)

UMBERTO SCERRATO

V. Ceramics.

The history of Islamic ceramics can be divided into four periods. In the first, the traditional techniques inherited from Byzantine and Sasanian ceramics were revolutionized during the 9th and 10th centuries under the impact of Chinese imports, when Islamic potters sought to imitate the white porcelains of the Tang period. Overglaze painting in lustre, an invention of artisans in the Islamic world, was first applied to ceramics associated with the 9th-century Abbasid capitals in Iraq. In the following centuries, the technique of lustre, known to only a few workshops, was carried to other regions, most notably Egypt and Iran, and the development of an artificial paste body, capable of supporting an extremely wide range of decorative techniques including underglaze painting, led to an almost unparalleled explosion of ceramic art. The Mongol conquests of the mid-13th century brought new types of Chinese porcelains, particularly blue-and-white wares, to the Islamic lands, where they initiated a widespread vogue for chinoiserie. In the final period this infatuation with Chinese wares continued. The finest collections of Chinese ceramics to survive were assembled at the Ottoman palace in Istanbul and the Safavid dynastic shrine at Ardabil, and most potters continued to work under the thrall of Chinese blue-and-white, although potters in the western Islamic lands seem to have had little interest in Chinese precedents. In the Ottoman empire potters broke away from Chinese models and created distinctive wares underglaze-painted on a frit body.

1. Introduction. 2. Before *c.* AD 1000. 3. *c.* 1000–*c.* 1250. 4. *c.* 1250–*c.* 1500. 5. *c.* 1500 and after.

1. INTRODUCTION. Most of the lands that came to be ruled by Muslims after the 7th century AD had long traditions of producing pottery and related wares, and the history and geography of the region serve to explain many of the characteristic features of Islamic ceramics. The production of earthenwares in Iran, for example, can be traced back to the Neolithic period (*see* IRAN, ANCIENT, §VI, 1(i)), and moulded earthenwares had been produced on the southern and eastern shores of the Mediterranean in Roman times (*see* ROME, ANCIENT, §X, 8(ii)(a)). Indeed, the earliest Islamic ceramic vessels are direct continuations of these pre-Islamic wares. Faience artefacts and architectural decorations had been used centuries earlier in Iraq (*see* ANCIENT NEAR EAST, §II, 5) and Egypt (*see* EGYPT, ANCIENT, §XVII, 5).

(i) Materials and techniques. (ii) Forms and decoration. (iii) Achievement and impact. (iv) Collecting.

(i) Materials and techniques. The great riparian centres of Near Eastern civilization had a virtually unlimited supply of the raw materials from which earthenware ceramics are made: clay, sand and water. The most important ceramic centres, such as Kashan in central Iran, an important pottery centre for six millennia, and Iznik in Anatolia, which flourished in the 16th century, were located near the source of the heavy materials from which their products were made, although some particularly fine clays were transported several hundred kilometres. *Sang-i chīnī* (Pers.: 'China stone'), a kaolinized quartz porphyry, for example, is found in the Karkas Mountains near Natanz, south of Kashan. The clay was slaked and sieved, sometimes through a silk screen. In Iran the clay was tempered by the addition of silica in the form of flint or ground quartz pebbles from dry riverbeds, but potters in Syria added sand.

Other raw materials were mined throughout the region and formed a major item of commerce. Lead, which as red lead (Arab. *isrinj*, Pb_3O_4) fluxed or lowered the firing temperature of a silica-based glaze, was mined near Balkh, in Anatolia, in upper Mesopotamia, in eastern Algeria and in Spain. Tin, which as an oxide opacifies a lead-silicate glaze and also keeps underglaze paint from running, was found in the Algarve of southern Spain, but it was also imported from Britain and the Malaysian peninsula (Kala), whence the Arabic name *qal'ī* for the metal. Alkaline

160. Fritware plate by Sayyid Shams al-Din al-Hasani with 29 scallops overglaze-painted in lustre, diam. 352 mm, from Kashan, 1210 (Washington, DC, Freer Gallery of Art)

glazes, which are extremely transparent but tend to degrade and iridesce, were made from quartz, soda, potash and occasionally salt. They adhere only to some clays and change the colours produced.

Copper, mined in various regions of Iran and Transoxiana, western Algeria and Spain, in the form of copper oxide gives a green colour to a lead glaze and a turquoise-blue colour to an alkaline glaze. Cobalt was mined near Kashan and Qum and was exported to China as early as the 7th century. As smalt it was still exported from Iran in the 14th century, although by the 15th century the Chinese had begun to mine their own cobalt ore. It gives a sapphire-blue colour (Pers. *lājvardī*) to an alkaline glaze. Ferric oxide (Fe_2O_3) gives a yellow or orange colour to a lead glaze; under reducing conditions it becomes ferrous oxide (Fe_2O), which gives a pale-green colour. Other colouring agents included manganese, which produces a violet or blackish-brown, antimony and arsenic. Some potters made their own glazes; others bought them prepared as frits from specialist craftsmen.

The design of kilns followed local precedents, the dimensions and construction depending on the size and nature of the wares produced. Vertical kilns, in which the fire burns at the bottom and the gases pass the stacked pottery on their way to exhaust at the top, have been used in Mesopotamia since the 4th millennium BC. In the down-draught kiln, used in Iran, hot gases descend through the stacked pottery to exhaust at the bottom through a chimney. A medieval ceramic workshop, with moulds, wasters and kilns, was excavated in the ruins of Nishapur in north-east Iran. Special reducing kilns, which produce a smoky atmosphere, were used for the production of lustrewares, in which oxides of copper and silver are applied to a fired alkaline glaze. The second firing deposits a thin film of metal on the surface of the glaze; burnishing

enhances the reflective qualities. Fuel, often scarce in this arid region, was provided by burning such materials as dung, olive-pits, brush and grasses, although some regions, notably Spain and Anatolia, had access to ample supplies of firewood. Many of the traditional ceramic techniques, described in a treatise (1303) by the Persian potter Abu'l-Qasim (*see* ABU TAHIR, (4)), were used in the 19th century by 'ALI MUHAMMAD ISFAHANI and continue to be used in the 20th.

Techniques of fabricating the finest wares included throwing on a wheel and moulding, although some rural potters used simpler techniques of coiling and slab building. One mould could be used repeatedly: for example, a mould for a plate 352 mm in diameter with 29 scallops in the cavetto is known to have been used to make several pieces, including four painted overglaze with lustre (see fig. 160) and one painted in black under a turquoise glaze (see Ettinghausen, fig. 24). Ceramic workshops undoubtedly produced works of different techniques and qualities for patrons of differing means and tastes.

(ii) Forms and decoration. By far the largest number of ceramic vessels made in the Islamic lands were unglazed earthenwares used by the entire population for the transportation and storage of liquids and the cooling of water through evaporation. Shapes include jugs, jars, ewers, amphorae and flasks. Most of these quotidian wares were left plain, but some were decorated with barbotine ornament in soft clay, while others, particularly from Egypt, had elaborately pierced and carved filters. Many of the shapes, particularly in finer qualities, were also glazed, making them suitable as tablewares. People usually ate communally from large flat dishes or chargers, with smaller plates and bowls for condiments and soups and goblets for beverages. Bowls, which might be hemispheric, conical or bell-shaped, usually had a low foot. Although many ceramics with the finest decoration have the shape of common tablewares, their elaborate and directional decoration suggests that they were intended more for display than for eating. Glazed jars (e.g. see fig. 173 below) were used in different sizes for storing and transporting foodstuffs and drugs, including wine, water, butter, honey and olives. The most common ceramic furnishing was the small oil lamp that held a single wick; candelabra with several reservoirs were also made. Mosque lamps, made in 16th-century Anatolia in imitation of those in glass, were symbolic, since their opaque body would have rendered them unusable as lamps. Other ceramic furnishings include tabourets, flower vases, incense burners, decorative figurines and toys. One of the most common but enigmatic types of object is a small sphero-conical vessel with a short neck and small opening. Hypotheses for its function have ranged from a container for mercury, a hand-grenade, an aeolipile to heat up the kiln, an alchemical vessel and a perfume flask to a gourd for beer and a hooka base.

Just as potters in the Islamic lands employed a wide range of techniques to decorate their wares, they also used a wide range of motifs (*see also* §I, 8 above). Logically, such closed shapes as jugs and bottles have their decoration on the exterior, while such open shapes as bowls and dishes have their major decoration on the interior. The traditional division of the surface of a dish into well, cavetto and rim (see fig. 160) was dissolved in only a few examples, such as some wares produced at Iznik in the 16th century (see fig. 178 below). From earliest times, the most popular motifs were geometric and vegetal, including interlacing, arabesques, palmettes, scrolls and blossoms (see figs 163–4 below). Geometricized vegetal ornament remained a constant theme, despite changes in techniques and the impact of Chinese ornament (see figs 172–5, 177–82 below). Animals, birds and more rarely humans were also popular, particularly during the period before c. 1250 (see figs 165–9 below). These depictions have been interpreted in many ways, ranging from generalized pronouncements of good luck and happiness in the hereafter to specific representations of astrological themes and princely power. Some of the most ambitious pieces show distinctly narrative imagery (see fig. 160), which has often been thought to illustrate Sufi or literary themes. An early 13th-century enamelled beaker from Iran (Washington, DC, Freer), for example, is decorated with scenes in three registers showing the story of Bizhan and Manizha from Firdawsi's *Shāhnāma* ('Book of kings'). It is clear that these narrative scenes are connected to the development of the illustrated manuscript in Iran (*see* §III, 4(v)(b) above), but the exact relationship between painting on ceramics and in manuscripts remains a matter of lively debate.

Epigraphy, as in other areas of Islamic art, was the most distinctive subject used to decorate Islamic ceramics. From the earliest times ceramics were decorated with Arabic inscriptions in angular script (see fig. 162 below). Simple and anonymous expressions of good wishes continued to be used on Islamic ceramics for centuries and became increasingly elaborate in both form and content (see figs 166 and 176 below). Iranian ceramics were often decorated with several inscription bands in both Arabic and Persian. These might include such information as the name of the maker, the date, the patron and surprisingly banal verses that seem to bear little or no relation to the scenes depicted in the field or the ostensible function of the object (see fig. 160 and figs 168–9 below). Interpreting these inscriptions is often difficult, for an inscription such as *sa'd* may be read either as 'happiness' or as the proper name of a potter or workshop. The reading may depend on the location of the inscription and the historical context, and sometimes such ambiguity may have been intentional.

(iii) Achievement and impact. Potters in the medieval Islamic world transformed the earthenwares of the pre-Islamic period into a major art form, primarily by the application of an extraordinary range of surface decoration, including—but not limited to—slip decoration, lead, tin and alkaline glazes, overglaze, inglaze and underglaze painting, carving and incising. Many of these techniques were also applied to ceramic tiles, a distinctive feature of Islamic architectural decoration (*see* §II, 9(ii) above). The interest in elaborating surfaces is the most characteristic and persistent feature of Islamic pottery. Potters in the Islamic world were also constantly inspired by the hard body, elegant shapes and fine glazes of Chinese wares, and although they were unable to duplicate Chinese porcelains, by the 12th century they had created a relatively fine, hard and white fritted body by resurrecting the technique of

faience, in which ground quartz was mixed with small amounts of white clay and glaze. From an early date Islamic wares also inspired Chinese potters, and blue-and-white ware, one of the most distinctive Chinese types, seems to have been inspired by Islamic models (*see* BLUE-AND-WHITE CERAMIC). A singular contribution of potters in the Islamic world was the development of overglaze painting in lustre, which gives pieces a distinctive metallic sheen. The most important contribution of Islamic ceramics, however, was the development of underglaze painting on the fritted body, for this gave the ceramic artist an excellent surface on which to paint freely; the underglaze-painted ceramics produced at Iznik in western Anatolia in the 16th century can be seen as culminating nearly a millennium of creative ceramic production in the Islamic lands. Islamic lustrewares and underglaze-painted wares were admired in medieval Europe, and the production of luxury ceramics there owes much to Islamic precedents. In the 19th century the rediscovery of the decorative qualities of Islamic ceramics inspired such European artists as William De Morgan and Christopher Dresser.

(iv) Collecting. Although European potters learnt the techniques for producing such luxury wares as maiolica, Delft and faience from the Islamic world, Islamic ceramics were comparatively less familiar in Europe than were Chinese wares, which were imported in great quantities from the 17th century. The exterior walls of medieval Italian churches had often been inset with dishes (It. *bacini*) imported from Egypt, North Africa and Spain, and such precious commodities as drugs and unguents were exported from the Middle East to Europe in glazed and occasionally lustre-painted vessels (see fig. 173 below) and apothecary jars (*albarelli*). A series of Iznik jugs were set in precious metal mounts in late 16th-century England (e.g. London, BM, AF23), and European patrons also commissioned Iznik ceramics painted with their coats of arms. Iznik ceramics were imitated by Italian potters under Medici patronage (e.g. a Medici porcelain bowl with everted rim; c. 1575–87; London, V&A, 5760–1859) and in the so-called Candiana wares made at Padua in the 17th century (e.g. a maiolica dish, c. 1630–40; Vienna, Hochsch. Angewandte Kst, Ke. 989).

The serious collecting of Islamic ceramics began only in the 19th century. ROBERT MURDOCH SMITH, director of the Persian Telegraph Department, acquired ceramics for the new South Kensington Museum, and Iznik ceramics were amassed by such connoisseurs as FREDERICK DUCANE GODMAN, whose collection was acquired by the British Museum in 1983. ALAN BARLOW's collection, formed largely between 1905 and 1926, initially focused on Iznik ceramics as well. Most Iznik ceramics were found outside Turkey: more than 532 pieces, for example, were acquired between 1865 and 1869 by the French consul Auguste Salzmann on the island of Rhodes, hence the misnomer Rhodian ware. The industrialist Charles Lang Freer began collecting 'Raqqa' pottery in the early 20th century; he particularly admired the iridescent degradation of the glaze on pieces that had been buried and only slowly came to appreciate the technical and design qualities intended by their makers. Other collectors followed suit, often led by such dealers as Dikran Kelekian and Hagop Kevorkian.

The demand of collectors for Islamic ceramics encouraged clandestine excavations, and many famous pieces of Islamic pottery have unknown provenance. Dealers assigned names of sites (e.g. Raqqa, Sultanabad, Rayy, Gurgan or Kubachi) to describe types of ceramics, but few of these sites have shown evidence for production, such as kilns and wasters, of the ceramic types with those names. Excavations at Samarra' in Iraq, for example, have failed to reveal any evidence for the production of lustrewares traditionally associated with this site. Ettinghausen was able to delineate the specific style of lustreware associated with Kashan (see fig. 160 above) on the basis of signatures and extant pieces, rather than of kilns and wasters. At Iznik, by contrast, excavation of kilns has produced important evidence for the development of the ceramic industry there over several centuries.

The high prices paid for many Islamic ceramics have also encouraged forgery. Some pieces have been ingeniously re-created from a few authentic fragments, while others are entirely new. New methods of technical examination, such as thermoluminescence and petrographic analysis, serve not only to differentiate the real from the fake but also to help identify the products of distinct potteries.

BIBLIOGRAPHY

Enc. Iran.: 'Ceramics'; Enc. Islam/2: 'Khazaf' [Ceramics]
Abu'l-Qasim Jamal al-Din 'Abdallah: 'Arā'is al-Jawāhir wa Nafā'is al-Aṭā'ib [Brides of gems and delicacies of amenities] (1303), ed. I. Afshar (Tehran, 1967); partial ed. and Ger. trans. by H. Ritter, J. Ruska and R. Winderlich as 'Orientalische Steinbücher und persische Fayencetechnik', Istanbul. Mitt., iii (1935) [whole issue]; Eng. trans. by J. W. Allen as 'Abū'l-Qāsim's Treatise on Ceramics', Iran, xi (1973), pp. 111–20
'Ali Muhammad Isfahani: On the Manufacture of Modern Kashi Earthenware Tiles and Vases, Eng. trans. by J. Fargues (Edinburgh, 1888); also in W. J. Furnival, Leadless Decorative Tiles, Faience and Mosaic (Stone, 1904)
R. L. Hobson: A Guide to the Islamic Pottery of the Near East (London, 1932)
R. Ettinghausen: 'Evidence for the Identification of Kashan Pottery', A. Islam., iii (1936), pp. 44–70
A. U. Pope and P. Ackerman, eds: Survey of Persian Art (London, 1938–9; 2/1964–7), pp. 1446–706
A. Lane: Early Islamic Pottery (London, 1954)
——: Later Islamic Pottery (London, 1957, rev. 1971)
C. K. Wilkinson: 'The Kilns of Nishapur', Bull. Met. (May 1959), pp. 235–40
J. Sauvaget: 'Introduction à l'étude de la céramique musulmane', Rev. Etud. Islam., xxxiii (1965), pp. 1–64
H. E. Wulff: The Traditional Crafts of Persia (Cambridge, MA, 1966), pp. 102–71
E. Atil: Ceramics from the World of Islam (Washington, DC, 1973)
G. Fehévári: Islamic Pottery: A Comprehensive Study Based on the Barlow Collection (London, 1973)
E. J. Grube: Islamic Pottery of the Eighth to the Fifteenth Century in the Keir Collection (London, 1976)
H. Philon: Early Islamic Ceramics: Ninth to Late Twelfth Centuries (London, 1980)
M. Jenkins: 'Islamic Pottery: A Brief History', Bull. Met., xl/4 (Spring 1983) [whole issue]
Arte islamica in Italia: I bacini delle chiese pisane (exh. cat., ed. G. Berti and P. Torre; Rome, Pal. Brancaccio, 1983)
A. Caiger-Smith: Lustre Pottery: Technique, Tradition and Innovation in Islam and the Western World (London, 1985)
O. Watson: 'Ceramics', Treasures of Islam, ed. T. Falk (Geneva, 1985), pp. 206–9
——: Persian Lustre Ware (London, 1985)
Blue and White Chinese Porcelain and its Impact on the Western World (exh. cat. by J. Carswell, U. Chicago, IL, Smart Gal., 1985)
A. Y. al-Hassan and D. R. Hill: Islamic Technology: An Illustrated History (Cambridge and Paris, 1986), pp. 160–69
N. Atasoy and J. Raby: Iznik: The Pottery of Ottoman Turkey (London, 1988)
E. Baer: 'Jewelled Ceramics from Medieval Islam: A Note on the Ambiguity of Islamic Ornament', Muqarnas, vi (1989), pp. 83–97
[J.] M. Rogers: 'Ceramics', The Arts of Persia, ed. R. W. Ferrier (New Haven and London, 1989), pp. 255–70
A. Ghouchani and C. Adle: 'A Sphero-Conical Vessel as Fuqqā'a, or a Gourd for "Beer"', Muqarnas, ix (1992), pp. 72–92
E. J. Keall: 'One Man's Mede is Another Man's Persian; One Man's Coconut is Another Man's Grenade', Muqarnas, x (1993), pp. 275–85

SHEILA S. BLAIR, JONATHAN M. BLOOM

2. BEFORE c. AD 1000. The earliest ceramics in the Islamic lands continue those of the conquered territories, but during the 9th and 10th centuries there was an extraordinary explosion in ceramic technology. A range of fine ceramics was developed in Iraq, heartland of the Abbasid empire (reg 749–1258), and was probably inspired by fine wares imported from Byzantium and especially China. Luxury ceramics were exported to other areas of the Islamic world, where local traditions of lead- and tin-glazing and slip-painted wares developed.

(i) Syria. (ii) Iraq. (iii) Iran and western Central Asia. (iv) Egypt. (v) North Africa and Spain.

(i) Syria. The earliest distinctive traditions of ceramic production in the Islamic world seem to have appeared in the province of Syria, seat of the Umayyad dynasty (reg 661–750). The identification of Umayyad ceramics has been problematic, but archaeological fieldwork in the 1970s and 1980s has produced better information, although it is still difficult to determine which layers of continuously occupied settlements post-date the Islamic conquest. Moreover, the lack of Abbasid copper coins and continued use of Umayyad copper coins in the period of Abbasid rule (reg 749–1258) have misled archaeologists into ascribing an Umayyad date to later ceramics.

The Umayyad ceramic sequence known in greatest detail is that of north-central Jordan, where excavations have been published from Pella, Jerash (anc. Gerasa), Amman and several desert castles of the Umayyad period. In the Late Byzantine period, fine wares were supplied partly by imports from the Mediterranean of Late Roman C (Phocian red slip) and African red slip wares and partly by local production in Jerash of unglazed ware painted in red and white (see EARLY CHRISTIAN AND BYZANTINE ART, §VII, 1). Coarse wares often have ribbed decoration on the bodies fired red or black. After the Islamic conquest, with the disappearance of Mediterranean imports, the ribbed decoration on coarse wares began to disappear too, and a buff surface finish was initially common.

Early in the 8th century red-painted designs appeared on both fine and coarse unglazed wares. The finest style, known as Umayyad Palace ware, has a red-firing earthenware body 3–5 mm thick with a buff slip and fine red-painted designs (see fig. 161). Flat-bottomed bowls with vertical sides, deep bowls with incurving rims and closed jars are known. Designs include Arabic inscriptions and interlaced patterns known from floor mosaics of the Umayyad period. In the semi-fine wares a different technique is used of broad brush-painted designs of sprigs, whorls and wavy lines on a surface fired buff rather than slipped. These vessels are in the form of cups, water jars,

161. Umayyad Palace ware, early 8th century

cooking pots with lids, and two-handled kraters. There is also a parallel tradition of white-painted designs on a dark surface. The red-painted tradition continued into the Abbasid period, probably disappearing c. 800, and at least three phases have been identified.

Ribbed coarse wares of the Byzantine type also continued to evolve, and an Islamic ceramic type, the flat-bottomed basin, was introduced in grey- or buff-slipped ware with incised decoration. Byzantine-style moulded lamps with dated inscriptions in Arabic are known from Jerash. From c. 800 to c. 1000 the coarse wares retained similar forms but became smaller in size, as the sand found as a temper in the pottery of the Umayyad period ceased to be used. In Palestine during the 9th century local lead-glazed bowls with designs painted in brown and green were introduced, and the interiors of red-ware cooking pots also began to be glazed. The typical Islamic splash-glaze bowls having a clear lead glaze with brown and green over a white slip and occasionally sgraffito decoration were not introduced to Palestine and Jordan until the 10th century.

Little clear information emerged from the excavations in central and northern Syria at the Umayyad sites of Qasr al-Hayr West and Qasr al-Hayr East. The red coarse wares of the Byzantine period continued, with buff coarse wares in the Euphrates area. Brittle ware, a fine north Syrian cooking-pot ware widely traded down the Euphrates and across northern Mesopotamia from the late 2nd century to the late 9th, developed c. 750 into an open form with lug handles and rouletted decoration. With the establishment of Raqqa on the upper Euphrates in 772, a new industry of Iraqi-style ceramics began in northern Syria (see §(ii) below). Fine 'eggshell' buff jars with a turban on the single handle, a type that continued until the 13th century, had already appeared in Iraq, and variants were

produced at Raqqa, particularly vessels in the form of cups, ewers and large jars with moulded decoration and kufic inscriptions. Some of these vessels have the blue–green glaze typical of Sasanian ceramics in Iraq (see IRAN, ANCIENT, §VI, 3). Coincident with the import of wares identified with the Abbasid capital at Samarra', probably in the early 9th century, there developed a local tradition of polychrome glazing with designs painted in green and yellow.

BIBLIOGRAPHY

A. Lane: 'Medieval Finds at Al Mina in North Syria', Archaeologia [Soc. Antiqua. London], lxxxvii (1937), pp. 19–78
R. de Vaux and A.-M. Stève: Fouilles à Qaryet el Énab Abu Gôsh (Paris, 1950)
G. L. Harding: 'Excavations on the Citadel of Amman', Annu. Dept Ant. Jordan, i (1951), pp. 7–16
Y. Crowe: 'Early Islamic Pottery and China', Trans. Orient. Cer. Soc., xli (1975–7), pp. 263–78
O. Grabar and others: City in the Desert, 2 vols (Cambridge, MA, 1978)
R. B. Harper: 'Athis-Neocaesaria-Qasrin-DibsiFaraj', Le Moyen Euphrate, ed. J. C. Margueron (Leiden, 1980)
P. Sodini and others: 'Dehès (Syrie du Nord): Recherches sur l'habitat rural', Syria, lvii (1980), pp. 1–301
A. McNicoll and others: Pella in Jordan, i (Canberra, 1982)
J. A. Sauer: 'The Pottery of Jordan in the Early Islamic Periods', Studies in the History of Archaeology of Jordan, i, ed. A. Hadidi (Amman, 1982), pp. 329–38
F. Zayadine, ed.: Jerash, i (Amman, 1986)
D. Whitcomb: 'Khirbat al-Mafjar Reconsidered: The Ceramic Evidence', Bull. Amer. Sch. Orient. Res., cclxxi (1988), pp. 51–67

ALASTAIR NORTHEDGE

(ii) Iraq. Pottery-making in Iraq underwent an extraordinary surge in production, quality and variety in the 9th and 10th centuries, a development that coincided with the resplendent taste and demands of the Abbasid caliphs (reg 749–1258) at their capitals, Baghdad and Samarra'. The opening up of new lands to agriculture and strong political and commercial ties, particularly with Iran and the Far East, brought material and cultural gains. Foreign imports included a vast range of ceramics, prompting Mesopotamian potters, already endowed with a local heritage based on Greco-Roman tradition, to adapt their aesthetic and technical skills and produce new types marked by an Islamic–Arab character. The main types of ceramics produced in Iraq during this period were yellow and green splashed ware, mottled ware, lustreware, blue-on-white ware, moulded-relief ware, sgraffito and local imitations of imported Chinese vessels. All these types were dispersed throughout the medieval Islamic world. Splashed wares had the widest distribution, being recorded at most major Islamic sites. Large numbers of mottled wares were unearthed at Samarra' and Kish in Iraq, at Susa and Nishapur in Iran and at Al-Mina in Syria. Iraqi lustreware was even more widely dispersed, reaching as far west as Madinat al-Zahra in Andalusia. Blue-on-white wares were found at Hira, Kish and Samarra' in Iraq, at Siraf, Susa, Istakhr, Nishapur, Sirjan and Rayy in Iran, and at Antioch in Syria.

(a) Provenance and distribution. (b) Fabric, shape and glaze. (c) Decorative techniques and motifs. (d) Dating and chronology.

(a) Provenance and distribution. Most of the well-known and complete pieces from this period are preserved in collections throughout America, Europe and the Middle East, but their original provenance and distribution are unclear. Production in the 9th and 10th centuries is often known as 'Mesopotamian' without precise reference to specific manufacturing centres or find spots. The earliest excavators of Mesopotamian sites were primarily interested in pre-Islamic material and dug through Islamic levels haphazardly. Sarre's publication of the ceramics from Samarra' (1925) was the first serious record of Islamic finds. Excavation reports from such sites as Susa and Siraf have added coherence and scientific information, but archaeological evidence is still inconclusive.

The variety and abundance of the Samarra' finds might suggest that the ceramics were produced locally, but only one kiln site—without associated wasters—has been found near by. At Susa the only kiln found was dated to the 9th century on the basis of associated wasters and lustre fragments. The quantity and quality of the pieces found, however, suggest that it was an important production centre despite its provincial location. Excavations at Siraf on the Persian Gulf uncovered remains of 30 kilns from the 10th century, attesting to strong pottery activity, but many of the ceramic finds, especially the 9th- and 10th-century Samarra' types, were probably imported from Iraq.

According to literary and historical accounts, the cities of Basra, Kufa and Baghdad were also centres of pottery production during this period, but this has not yet been confirmed by archaeology. The fine quality of the white clay found near Basra is described by two Abbasid writers. Abu'l-Mutahhar al-Azdi mentions that the clay is 'extracted of a white layer from Sawad [an area near Basra]', and al-Jahiz refers to the 'whiteness of the vessels and the delicious taste of the water contained in their jars'. Pieces of pottery (and glass) have been found bearing signatures containing the epithet *al-basri* ('from Basra'). Baghdad was linked with the making of the mihrab lustre tiles in the Uqba ibn Nafi' (Congregational) Mosque, Kairouan, and medieval authors referred to the beautiful and colourful pots of Baghdad, but noted that when the capital was moved to Samarra, potters were transferred from Basra and Kufa (al-Ya'qubi). The sources remain mute, however, about wares produced at Samarra'.

(b) Fabric, shape and glaze. Earlier scholars such as Arthur Lane (see also Sarre and Koechlin) emphasized the role of Chinese products, particularly porcelain, in the development of fabric, shape and glaze. The excavations at Samarra' unearthed the first physical evidence of Chinese material, including white stoneware, porcelain, green-and-grey glazed stoneware and a type of white ware coloured with green and yellow splashes that is usually associated with polychrome vessels once thought to date to the 8th-century Tang dynasty. The large number of Chinese sherds found in major towns and seaports such as Samarra', Susa and Siraf suggests the extent of the Far Eastern trade. The Iranian polymath al-Biruni (*d* 1048) recounted the coveted qualities and shapes of Chinese pieces reaching the Near East in the 10th century: 'The best Chinese pots are those apricot in colour, fine-walled and clear. When tapped, they produce a sharp continuous ring.' He also enumerated at least nine different types of Chinese glazed wares collected by a merchant from Isfahan. The Iranian historian Abu'l-Fadl Bayhaqi (*d* 1077) described a gift of 20 pieces of imperial Chinese porcelain

(*chīnī faghfūrī*), in addition to 2000 ordinary porcelain pieces that the governor of Khurasan, 'Ali ibn Isa, offered to the Abbasid caliph Harun al-Rashid (*reg* 786–809).

The whiteness, strength and elegance of Chinese imports must have impressed local potters. Lacking materials to produce the vitreous and porcellanous bodies of Chinese wares, Iraqi craftsmen refined local clays, producing a well-levigated, compact, cream-coloured earthenware body that modern scholars identify as the Samarra' clay body. It was used for most types, including cobalt-decorated white ware, finely potted lustre pieces and polychrome splashed vessels. Variations in body tonality and quality may indicate different production centres, even some outside Mesopotamia. In excavations at Fustat (Old Cairo) in Egypt, for example, a few finely potted fragments coated with white slip and decorated with green and mustard spots and streaks under a clear glaze were found beside others of inferior fabric and lesser quality. The finer fragments must have been imported from Mesopotamia, the others made locally.

Some shapes demonstrate clear affinities with Chinese forms. Curvilinear bowls with everted rims and foot-rings, a typical form found at Samarra' and Susa, were probably based on Chinese stoneware bowls that had arrived in Mesopotamia in the 9th century. Potters also copied the Yuëh-type ribbed bowl with a lobed rim and a slightly splayed foot-ring. While generally left plain like their models, these forms were sometimes decorated with cobalt-blue designs (see fig. 162) or splashed with polychrome colours. The elaborate decoration of some lustre-ware bowls conceals the ribbed walls and notches on the rims. The limited repertory of shapes also includes a flat plate (see fig. 163), either with an angular outline and a clear division between the base-wall and rim or with softly flaring walls, possibly imitating metal prototypes. Some flat plates have three button legs (e.g. Tehran, Archaeol. Mus.) and occasional spouts attached to the lower end of

162. Earthenware bowl decorated in cobalt blue on opaque white glaze, diam. 253 mm, from Iraq, 9th century AD (Munich, Staatliches Museum für Völkerkunde)

the wall near the base-line. The origin and function of this form is unclear, but it might have derived from Zoroastrian cult vessels. Closed forms are rare. Jugs have wide flaring necks and squat bodies. A large white jar painted in blue (London, BM) is similar to one painted in lustre (Chicago, IL, A. Inst.), with a flat base, short neck and exaggerated loop handles on the shoulders. Shapes were not exclusive to one decorative technique but occur in lustre, polychrome and blue-on-white wares, all of which might have been produced in the same workshops.

It was once thought that the Mesopotamian potter applied an opaque white glaze over a thin white slip covering the clay body, but microscopic study of sherds from Samarra' at the University of Michigan in 1941 showed that only yellow and green Tang-style glazed objects had a thin slip. Otherwise, the white glaze was applied directly over the compact yellow paste of the body. The composition of the white glaze is controversial. Earlier scholars believed its main component to be lead and, since lead has tin as an opacifying agent, they called these pieces 'tin glaze'. Adams and Whitehouse, the excavators of Tell Abu Sarifa and Siraf, challenged this theory and attributed the opacity to incomplete vitrification of alkaline glazes, an evolution of a Sasanian glazing technique. The examination of some opaque white-and-grey wares from Susa by beta-ray back-scatter, a lead-detection test, confirmed this theory (Crowe, 1974). Moreover, analysis of 13 sherds from Siraf found no lead, proving the alkaline nature of the glazes. On refiring some of the Susa samples, the glazes melted at temperatures below 750° C, suggesting that the original firing was done at such low temperatures that some quartz particles were left in suspension and produced the white colour. It is possible that two glazing procedures existed simultaneously, for analysis of two fragments of blue-on-white ware from Hira (Oxford, Ashmolean) showed a lead/tin glaze on the interior and an alkaline one on the exterior. Lead glazing, a Roman–Byzantine tradition connected with Syrian and Mesopotamian glass and enamel production, continued to be a popular method in the Islamic period for relief wares and monochrome glazed objects. Thus, in order to obtain the milky-white effect of Chinese porcelain, the Mesopotamian potter could have used either of two techniques: opacifying lead glazes with tin or incomplete firing of alkaline glazes.

(c) Decorative techniques and motifs. Pottery produced in this period shows new decorative schemes, ranging from the quasi-abstract, masterful cobalt-blue brushwork on opaque white glazes to the denser lustre designs and the carefree green and yellow splashes applied without regard to the carefully incised patterns beneath. Iraqi and Iranian sites have also yielded unornamented sherds, probably made locally to imitate plain porcelain vessels imported from China. The most radical innovation in embellishing the surface was the invention of lustre decoration, a technique of applying metallic oxides to opacified white glazes and firing them a second time in a reducing atmosphere to produce shimmering designs. The decorative repertory depended largely on Classical and Iranian motifs, and traditional palmettes, rosettes and flowers were combined and reshaped. Interlaced bands formed intricate

163. Flat earthenware plate with moulded relief decoration, lustre glaze and overglaze green splashes, diam. 280 mm, from Iraq, 9th century (Washington, DC, Freer Gallery of Art)

geometric patterns. Figural imagery is rare, but frontal human figures and stylized animals were occasionally painted in lustre (e.g. Washington, DC, Freer, 25.6 and 53.90).

Prominence was given to a new decorative form, the inscription (see fig. 162 above). Apart from a generalized assertion of the faith, inscriptions also became a mark of distinction used to label luxury objects in an artistically written, angular kufic script. The name of the craftsman or a benediction was incorporated into the design, as in the moulded relief and lustre objects, or was used as an exclusive motif, particularly in blue-on-white wares. The most popular phrases were *Baraka li-sahibih* ('Blessings to its owner') and *al-mulk [li-llah]* ('Dominion [belongs to God]'), but sometimes longer aphorisms were included, such as 'May you eat [from this dish] with satisfaction and beauty.' The signatures of potters or decorators, especially of blue-on-white ware, were prominently displayed on open surfaces. Muhammad al-Salih signed three blue-on-white bowls, and at least seven other artisans signed examples of this type. Several glazed relief fragments are signed Abu Nasr (e.g. Athens, Benaki Mus., 453), and a condiment dish (London, BM) is inscribed 'the work of Abu Nasr al-Basri [or al-Nasri]'. Ernst Grube suggested that the signatures were made for patrons who collected pieces made in famous workshops.

(d) Dating and chronology. The dating and chronology of pottery from this period has undergone reassessment since 1925, when Sarre assumed that Mesopotamian pottery could be encapsulated between the foundation of Samarra' in 836 and the transfer of the capital back to Baghdad in 892. As Samarra' continued to function long

after the court had departed, the traditional fixed dates have been expanded to allow for evolution in technique, shape and decoration. Some scholars, however, continue to attribute the majority of production at Samarra' to the 9th century and to use that date for the attribution of similar wares from other sites. Only sound stratigraphic excavation of all sites will establish a clear evolution and explain the extraordinary challenges and creative responses of Mesopotamian potters before 1000.

For many years, the splashed ware of this period was considered an imitation of Chinese Tang ware, on the assumption that both used the same colours over a lead-glazed slip, but the Chinese origin of the Islamic type is now discredited. The shapes differ, and Islamic splashed wares use manganese, a colour unrecorded in Chinese examples. Such wares were produced in China only in the first half of the 8th century and were manufactured exclusively for imperial tombs, making them unlikely exports. Rather, the three-coloured splashed wares that appeared in Iraq during the 9th century must have been an independent creation of local potters.

The evidence from Susa is also important in dating early Islamic wares since it, unlike the capital Samarra', was a site of uninterrupted habitation. Excavations between 1851 and 1972 allowed a relative sequence of types to be posited, and the discovery of two coin hoards, one dated 860–79 and the other 914–56, fixed the sequence chronologically. Furthermore, the second hoard was contained in a splashed yellow and green jar, suggesting that that type could be attributed to the first half of the 10th century.

Whitehouse's excavations at Siraf (1966–73) further discredited the narrow Samarra' horizon, both as a dating criterion and as evidence of the evolution of pottery types in the period. According to him, the evidence of coins found in the congregational mosque at Siraf showed that a gradual evolution of most pottery types took place during the 10th century: white glazed wares, either plain or painted with cobalt blue, were followed by splashed wares without incision and by white wares painted with green or brown; these preceded both white glazed ware painted with lustre and incised splashed wares. Allen, however, argued that the coins do not necessarily indicate a *terminus post quem* or completion date of the mosque but rather a *terminus ante quem* or starting-point, and recommended pushing Whitehouse's dates back to the 9th century.

The abundance of lustrewares found at Samarra' and elsewhere in Iraq and Iran lends an additional complexity to delineating the ceramic chronology of the period. The connections between lustrewares and blue-on-white pottery in their shared milky-white opaque surface and shapes suggest that, although decoratively different, both types were produced simultaneously in the same workshops. Both monochrome and polychrome lustre tiles adorned the Jawsaq al-Khaqani, the palace of the caliph al-Muʿtasim (*reg* 833–42) at Samarra'; a proximate date (862–3) has been proposed for the lustre tiles decorating the mihrab of the congregational mosque at Kairouan in Tunisia, said to have been imported from Iraq. The dates for the Kairouan tiles, however, are unreliable as they are based on a 15th-century source. Whitehouse (1979, p. 47) presents J. Hansman's view of a later dating on the basis of material collected in Khuzistan in southern Iran. Hansman

advocates a later dating for the introduction of white glazed pottery, pushing the dates of lustreware, including the tiles from Samarra' and Kairouan, a century later.

BIBLIOGRAPHY

Ahmad ibn Abi Yaʿqub ibn Wadah al-Yaʿqubi: *Kitab al-buldan* (Leiden, 1891)
Abuʾl-Mutahhar al-Azdi: *Hikāyat Abiʾl-Qāsim*, ed. A. Mez (Heidelberg, 1902)
F. Sarre: *Die Keramik von Samarra* (1925), ii of *Die Ausgrabungen von Samarra* (Berlin, 1923–48)
R. Koechlin: *Les Céramiques musulmanes de Suse au Musée du Louvre* (1928), xix of *Mémoires de la mission archéologique en Perse* (Paris, 1899–)
G. Marçais: *Les Faïences à reflets métalliques de la grande mosquée de Kairouan* (Paris, 1928)
D. T. Rice: 'The Oxford Excavations at Hira', *A. Islam.*, i (1934), pp. 51–73
G. Reitlinger: 'Islamic Pottery from Kish', *A. Islam.*, ii (1935), pp. 198–213
al-Biruni: *Kitāb tahdīd nihāyāt al-amākin* [Book of the regions]; Eng. trans. by A. Zeki Validi Togan as *Biruni's Picture of the World*, Mem. Archaeol. Surv. India, liii (New Delhi, 1941)
R. McC. Adams: 'Tell Abu Sarifa: A Sassanian Islamic Ceramic Sequence from South Central Iran', *A. Orient.*, viii (1970), pp. 87–119
G. Scanlon: 'The Fustat Mounds: A Shard Count 1968', *Archaeology*, xxiv (1971), pp. 220–33
Y. Crowe: 'Certains types et techniques de la céramique de Suse', *Atti del VII convegno della ceramica: Albisola, 1974*, pp. 75–83
M. Rosen-Ayalon: *La Poterie islamique: Ville royale de Suse IV* (1974), l of *Mémoires de la délégation archéologique en Iran* (Paris, 1899–)
al-Jahiz: *Epistles*, iii, ed. Ubaid-allah ibn Hasan (Cairo, 1979)
D. Whitehouse: 'Islamic Glazed Pottery in Iraq and the Persian Gulf: The Ninth and Tenth Centuries', *AION*, n. s., xxix (1979), pp. 44–61
——: *Siraf III: The Congregational Mosque and Other Mosques from the Ninth till the Twelfth Centuries* (London, 1980); review by T. Allen in *A. Orient.*, xiii (1982), pp. 188–9

VERA TAMARI

(iii) Iran and western Central Asia. The Muslim conquest of Iran between 642 and 715 did not immediately precipitate a revolution in the production of ceramics. Rather, the wares associated with the end of the Sasanian dynasty (*reg* 224–651), coarse vessels either unglazed or with clear or turquoise alkaline glazes (*see* IRAN, ANCIENT, §VI, 3), continued to be made well into the 8th century. This survey, therefore, concentrates on the wares produced after the establishment of the Abbasid caliphate in Iraq (*reg* 749–1258), where the innovative styles and techniques of early Islamic ceramics had developed fully by the early 9th century (*see* §(ii) above).

(a) Introduction. Despite, or perhaps because of, Western commercial interest in Iranian ceramics, the scientific study of techniques, schools and kiln sites has hardly reached maturity. A few excavation reports from such sites as Susa, Siraf, Nishapur, Sirjan and Qasr Abu Nasr in Iran and Merv and Afrasiab (old Samarkand) in western Central Asia shed light on the types of wares available in some areas, but until other potentially rich sites in northwest and central Iran are excavated and the results published, the story will remain incomplete. Production sites were determined by the availability of clay, a fact unaffected by political changes, whereas trade in ceramics and especially the introduction of fine Chinese wares at the court of the Abbasid caliph Harun al-Rashid (*reg* 786–809) played a decisive role in the stylistic development of ceramics in 9th-century Iran and western Central Asia.

Abbasid potters tried to imitate the shapes and the whiteness of Tang stoneware and porcelains, and Iraqi potters and their Iranian emulators experimented with new glazes, abandoning the alkaline glazes used earlier in favour of the lead glazes used by the Chinese as well as the Byzantine makers of *terra sigillata*. Tang potters of white wares and *san cai* wares, on which Abbasid potters modelled their white wares and splashed wares, apparently tailored the products destined for export to the Middle East to the taste of their customers. Pieces dating from the 9th century with moulded, applied and/or stamped relief decoration and green or yellow lead glazes reminiscent of pre-Islamic pottery of the eastern Mediterranean have also been found at sites in Iran and Afghanistan. Infused with the dual inspiration of Chinese and Mediterranean ceramics, Islamic potters created their own styles. Ceramics produced in south-west Iran in the 9th and 10th centuries closely follow those of the Abbasid capital at Samarra' in Iraq, whereas those produced in north-east Iran and western Central Asia show a range of local idioms, some influenced by Abbasid wares, others unique to the area.

(b) South-west Iran. Excavations at Susa have unearthed Umayyad as well as Abbasid ceramics closely related or identical to those found at Samarra'. Unglazed pottery without decoration or with incised, applied or stamped ornament was found on all three levels of Islamic habitation. In addition to large storage jars, there were many types of pitchers, for which the porous surface ensured cool liquid contents. Sometimes the unglazed surface was painted with simple decoration of undulating bands, stripes or floral motifs. Intricately moulded pots were found on the first (mid-7th century to mid-8th) and second (mid-8th century to 9th) levels. The glazed ceramics from Susa range from bowls with monochrome green, turquoise, blue, yellow and brownish-purple glazes to various polychrome wares closely related to Mesopotamian wares. A large group, mainly bowls, from the second level consists of splashed wares, in which drips or spots of black, green, yellow, blue, turquoise and brown oxides cover a yellowish-white slip. They were probably imported from Mesopotamia or inspired by Mesopotamian rather than Chinese prototypes, for all the splashed wares have a yellowish body and no Chinese *san cai* sherds were found at the site. Round-sided bowls covered with opaque white glaze and decorated with cobalt blue, alone or with copper oxides ranging from green to turquoise, may have been imported from Mesopotamia. In addition to central rosettes, linear decoration and mottling on the rim, these bowls have epigraphic decoration, either signatures or maxims. It has been a subject of debate whether the whiteness of the glaze was obtained through tin opacifiers or through low firing of alkaline glaze.

The largest group of Islamic wares excavated at Susa were lustrewares, primarily bichrome and monochrome lustre-painted bowls. The mention of kiln wasters by earlier writers led to the belief that monochrome lustrewares were produced at the site, but as no kiln sites have been mentioned in more recent literature, the argument for local manufacture rests on determining whether the wasters were actually rejects or simply pieces of lesser quality imported from Mesopotamia. The decoration of

these pieces parallels that of Iraqi lustrewares, with complex vegetal and geometric compositions on the interior of bichrome lustre bowls and simpler vegetal, geometric, animal and human forms silhouetted on an opaque white ground in the monochrome wares. The bichrome pieces date to the 9th century, the monochrome ones to the 9th and 10th.

The finds from Siraf complement those from Susa. A major Gulf port on the east–west maritime route during the Sasanian and early Islamic periods, Siraf has yielded more than a million potsherds. This enormous sample mitigates the possible muddling of the stratigraphy by the rubble used as landfill beneath major buildings. As at Susa, numerous blue–green alkaline-glazed ceramics imported from Iraq were unearthed in levels dating from the 7th and 8th centuries. Unlike Susa, many Chinese ceramics were found at Siraf, reflecting its status as entrepôt. The most numerous Chinese ceramics were various types of stoneware (grey-bodied and green-glazed, painted and glazed, and white), white porcelains and green wares. The first Islamic wares modelled on Chinese wares, dating *c.* 825, were white-glazed, plain or with cobalt-blue decoration. These were followed after 900 by splashed wares without incised decoration and then by white wares with lustre glaze and splashed wares with incised ornament. According to the excavator Whitehouse, new types of imports were introduced gradually over the 9th and 10th centuries, and local production of slip-painted ware began only in the 11th century.

Sirjan, the capital of Kirman province in early Islamic times, was another important pottery-producing site. Williamson's brief excavation of the waster heaps from pottery kilns there turned up wasters of slip-painted wares, *sgraffito* and splashed types as well as a few stray sherds of the distinctive white-ware shapes. Slip-painted wares imitating those of Nishapur were produced in great quantity: they have the same designs of birds and inscriptions, but the palette is limited to shades of yellows and browns. Slip-painted wares made at other sites in central Iran such as Jiruft, 500 km east of Sirjan, and Zarang, the capital of Sistan province, also imitated Khurasani wares with a limited range of colours.

(c) North-east Iran and western Central Asia. Nishapur, a city in the province of Khurasan in north-east Iran, is known for a range of locally produced pottery types that bear little relation to the wares of Abbasid Iraq. Extensive finds of 9th- and 10th-century ceramics illustrate the growing importance of the city as a centre of trade under the Samanid dynasty (*reg* 819–1005). Wilkinson, one of the excavators of the site, divided the ceramic finds according to decoration and glaze into 12 groups, 10 of which were produced locally in the 9th and 10th centuries. The first group, buff ware, is unique to the site, but closely related to buff ware from Merv. The buff body is decorated with black, yellow and green and covered with a transparent lead glaze. The earlier 9th-century pieces are decorated with animate subjects, including humans, and are frequently crowded with birds, pseudo-inscriptions, flowering branches and quadrupeds; the 10th-century pieces have inanimate motifs such as leaves, dots, hatching and strips, often arranged in quadrants. While these buff wares

164. Earthenware splashed ware bowl with *sgraffito* decoration, h. 72 mm, diam. 260 mm, from Nishapur, 10th century (New York, Metropolitan Museum of Art)

may have been made for any one of the various religious or ethnic groups in the city, the significance of this *mélange* of motifs is elusive.

Two other types, monochrome and unglazed wares, also show little dependence on Abbasid prototypes. Monochrome glazed pieces, mainly bowls, vases, pitchers and lamps, have red earthenware bodies usually covered in white or coloured slip under a coloured glaze. Monochrome glazing was introduced in Khurasan only in the 9th century, much later than in south-west Iran. Green glaze predominated, except on certain types of bowls, although it is found on bowls with *sgraffito* decoration. As at Susa, the majority of the unglazed wares were used for storing and serving water. The surface colour ranges from greenish to buff, and the limited decoration includes incised, straight or wavy lines and chattering, achieved by letting a loosely held tool bounce off the leather-hard surface of a vessel as it turned on the wheel. The shapes of various types of unglazed wares changed from the 9th to the 10th century, but essentially this remained a ware made and used locally.

Other types of ceramics from Nishapur relate to those of Abbasid Iraq. Opaque white wares have tin-opacified glazes of poor quality, decoration in manganese instead of cobalt blue and a body of reddish earthenware instead of yellow. Lustrewares were apparently imported from Iraq, and local imitations were made by painting designs either on a poor opaque white glaze or, more commonly, on a white engobe which was then covered with a transparent lead glaze. Opaque yellow wares with decoration in green were found in a variety of coarse shapes. Splashed wares, both plain and *sgraffito*, abounded at Nishapur and attest to the broad popularity of the type (see fig. 164). One of the most numerous and striking groups of Nishapur wares

was black-on-white ware, which has inscriptions and decoration in manganese slip on a white engobe. The type may be modelled on Abbasid white wares or possibly on inscribed textiles (*see* TIRAZ), which have a similar aesthetic effect. Polychrome on white ware, slip-painted ware with coloured engobe, and ware with yellow-staining black have elaborations of motifs found on black-on-white ware, suggesting that these three types were produced towards the end of the period (mid- to late 10th century).

For further information on the pottery produced in western Central Asia, *see* CENTRAL ASIA, §I, 7(iv)–(vi).

BIBLIOGRAPHY

R. Koechlin: *Les Céramiques musulmanes de Suse au Musée du Louvre* (1928), xix of *Mémoires de la mission archéologique en Perse* (Paris, 1899–)
S. B. Lunina: 'Goncharnoye proizvosto v Merve X nachala XIII vv' [Ceramic production in Merv from the 10th century to the early 13th], *Trudy Yuzhno-Turkmen. Arkheol. Kompleksnoi Eksped.*, xi (1962), pp. 217–418
E. Z. Zaurova: 'Keramischeskiye pechi VII–VIII vekov na gorodischche Gyaur-Kale starogo Merva' [Ceramic kilns of the 7th–8th centuries on the citadel of Gaur Kale, Old Merv], *Trudy Yuzhno-Turkmen. Arkheol. Kompleksnoi Eksped.*, xi (1962), pp. 174–216
Iran, vi–xii (1968–74) [excavation reports from Siraf by D. Whitehouse]
N. B. Nemtseva: 'Stratigrafiya yuzhnoy okrainy gorodishcha Afrasiab' [Stratigraphy of the southern outskirts of the city of Afrasiyab], *Afrasiab*, i (1969), pp. 153–205
C. K. Wilkinson: *Nishapur: Pottery of the Early Islamic Period* (New York, [1973])
M. Rosen-Ayalon: *La Poterie islamique: Ville royale de Suse IV* (1974), l of *Mémoires de la délégation archéologique en Iran* (Paris, 1899–)
Y. Crowe: 'Early Islamic Pottery and China', *Trans. Orient. Cer. Soc.*, xli (1975–7), pp. 263–78
J.-C. Gardin: 'The Study of Central Asian Pottery: Some Reflections on Publication', *Amer. J. Archaeol.*, lxxxi (1977), pp. 80–81
M. Kervran: 'Les Niveaux islamiques du secteur oriental du tepe de l'Apadana: Le matériel céramique', *Cah. Dél. Archéol. Fr. Iran*, vii (1977), pp. 75–160
R. Naumann: *Die Ruinen von Tacht-e Suleiman und Zendan-e Suleiman und Umgebung* (Berlin, 1977)
Afghan Stud., i (1978) [excavation reports from Kandahar by A. McNicoll and D. Whitehouse]
D. Whitehouse: 'Islamic Glazed Pottery in Iraq and the Persian Gulf: The Ninth and Tenth Centuries', *Annali: AION*, n. s., xxix (1979), pp. 44–61
——: *Siraf III: The Congregational Mosque and Other Mosques from the Ninth till the Twelfth Centuries* (London, 1980); review by T. Allen in *A. Orient.*, xiii (1982), pp. 188–9
D. S. Whitcomb: *Before the Roses and Nightingales: Excavations at Qasr-i Abu Nasr, Old Shiraz* (New York, 1985)
P. Morgan and J. Leatherby: 'Excavated Ceramics from Sīrjān', *Syria and Iran: Three Studies in Medieval Ceramics*, ed. J. Allen and C. Roberts, Oxford Studies in Islamic Art, iv (Oxford, 1987), pp. 23–174
A. Williamson: 'Regional Distribution of Mediaeval Persian Pottery in the Light of Recent Investigations', *Syria and Iran: Three Studies in Medieval Ceramics*, ed. J. Allen and C. Roberts, Oxford Studies in Islamic Art, iv (Oxford, 1987), pp. 11–22
J. M. Rogers: 'Ceramics', *The Arts of Persia*, ed. R. W. Ferrier (New Haven and London, 1989), pp. 255–69
E. J. Keall and R. B. Mason: 'The 'Abbasid Glazed Wares of Sīrāf and the Basra Connection: Petrographic Analysis', *Iran*, xxix (1991), pp. 51-66

SHEILA R. CANBY

(iv) Egypt. The technique of glazing arrived *c.* 700 in Egypt from the old Parthian lands of Iran via Syria, where it had been used since the Roman period (*see* ROME, ANCIENT, §X, 8(ii)(a)). Although glazing on a frit base had originated in Egypt (*see* EGYPT, ANCIENT, §XIII), in the era before the Islamic conquest decoration in various slips, generally on a bisqued underslip, had been preferred (*see* COPTIC ART, §V, 2). At first vessels were simply coated with

transparent glazes, either green or a variety of tints ranging from yellow to gold, a process seen most noticeably on lamps. Later, slips were employed to provide decorative schemes, which included geometric, slap-dash, vegetal, anthropomorphic and eventually crude epigraphic motifs. Sometimes these slipped designs were applied to a surface without an overall underglaze, so that sections were left gritty to the touch after the glaze was applied and fired. In the 8th century better-quality vessels had the decoration painted on an overall underslip, which was then covered with the desired glaze. The designs were applied to rather simple shapes, a studied continuation of Classical and Coptic models.

A more sophisticated mode of decoration involving stamped and moulded motifs was brought from the eastern Islamic lands some time before the mid-8th century. The first pieces simply imitated imported wares, but later pieces were adapted to local taste, with amusingly realistic zoomorphic designs and two or three coloured glazes on the same surface. A fragment from the flat base of a dish (see fig. 165) has a horned, winged animal moulded in relief; the animal's body is covered in a green glaze, its horns, wings, belly and hoofs in a brown glaze, and the surface of the vessel in a mustard-coloured glaze. Although the earlier type of lead-glaze ware continued to be made well into the 10th century, the more sophisticated moulded and stamped wares are rarely found after the end of the 9th.

165. Fragment of an earthenware dish with moulded decoration and three colours of glaze, diam. 60 mm, from Egypt, *c.* AD 900 (Athens, Benaki Museum)

Chinese ceramics appeared in Egypt *c.* 850 and did not disappear from local markets until the 18th century, although the quantity and quality varied. The early porcelains were especially admired and their shape assiduously imitated, with the result that the Egyptian potter was emancipated from his millennial heritage. At the same time splashed wares were imported from Iraq, prompting a wide range of glaze-on-glaze decorated vessels that have been misnamed Fayyumi wares. These so seized local fancy that they continued to be produced until the 13th century with a seemingly infinite variety of motifs and combination, but with declining aesthetic quality. Another import from eastern Islamic lands that was adapted to the local aesthetic was the technique of incising a design in the overall slip beneath a free-flowing transparent glaze of various tints. In the 11th century the technique was applied to *sgraffito* designs more clearly modelled on Northern Sung celadons.

BIBLIOGRAPHY

La Céramique égyptienne de l'époque musulmane (Cairo and Basle, 1922)
A. Bahgat and F. Massoul: *La Céramique musulmane de l'Egypte* (Cairo, 1930)
W. B. Kubiak: 'Medieval Ceramic Oil Lamps from Fusṭāṭ', *A. Orient.*, viii (1970), pp. 1–18
G. T. Scanlon: 'Egypt and China: Trade and Imitation', *Islam and the Trade of Asia*, ed. D. S. Richards (Oxford and Philadelphia, 1970), pp. 81–95
——: 'Fustat Expedition: Preliminary Report 1968, Part II', *J. Amer. Res. Cent. Egypt*, xiii (1976), pp. 69–89
——: 'Fustat Expedition: Preliminary Report 1973, Back to Fustat-A 1973', *An. Islam.*, xvii (1981), pp. 407–36
W. B. Kubiak and G. T. Scanlon: *Fusṭāṭ-C* (1989), ii of *Fusṭāṭ Expedition: Final Report* (Lake Winona, IN, 1986–)

GEORGE SCANLON

(v) *North Africa and Spain.* An active ceramic tradition developed in the western Islamic world in the 9th and 10th centuries. Large quantities of non-lustred painted wares with designs of birds, animals and humans have been found at several sites in North Africa associated with the Aghlabid (*reg* 800–909), Fatimid (*reg* 909–1171) and Zirid (*reg* 972–1152) dynasties. The site of Raqqada, founded in 876 as Aghlabid capital near Kairouan in Tunisia, yielded local and folk imitations of well-known Abbasid types. The most common pieces are flat-sided bowls with mustard slip and manganese and green decoration and bowls with straight flaring sides decorated with the same colours on a white ground. A few similar pieces were found at Mahdia, which served briefly as Fatimid capital from 912–13 until 947–8, when the caliph al-Mansur (*reg* 946–53) moved the capital to a new site near Kairouan. Known as Sabra/al-Mansuriyya, the satellite city remained the capital until the mid-11th century. A kiln there produced flat-sided bowls decorated with green, yellow and manganese on a white ground. Figural decoration included animals with cross-hatched or diagonally lined bodies and hunters, falconers and horsemen as well as a narrative frieze showing the siege of a palace (Tunis, Mus. N. Bardo).

Similar wares were produced in Spain during the period of Umayyad rule (756–1031). Excavations at the site of Madinat al-Zahra', the palace-city founded outside Córdoba in 936 and sacked in 1010, yielded two types of pottery. The finer buff-bodied wares have a creamy-white lead glaze, opacified with tin on both interior and exterior, and are decorated on the interior in manganese and green. The most common shape is a bowl with well-formed foot-ring and gently sloping sides. The fineness of the potting and glazing and the shape are reminiscent of Abbasid wares. The second, more numerous type of pottery found at Madinat al-Zahra' is a red-bodied ware with a mustard-yellow lead glaze on the exterior and a lead glaze opacified with tin on the interior, which serves as a white ground for decoration painted in manganese and green. The most common shape is a bowl with flat bottom and slightly flaring sides; it is decorated with animals, figures or kufic inscriptions (e.g. Madrid, Mus. Arqueol. N., 63.043). A similar bottle found at Córdoba (h. 245 mm; Madrid, Mus. Arqueol. N., 11.282) has a long narrow neck and round belly decorated with a frieze of musicians and other figures. This type was produced throughout Andalusia with local variations: for example, a bowl found at Granada (diam. 350 mm; Granada, Mus. Arqueol. Prov., 855) has a naturalistic horse. Similar wares were found during excavations at the Qal'at Bani Hammad, the site in central Algeria that served as capital of the Hammadid branch of the Zirid dynasty (*reg* 1015–1152). They too are decorated with cross-hatched animals and lack yellow in the palette for decoration.

There is no clear evidence that lustrewares were produced in Aghlabid Tunisia, and no lustreware kilns have been found. The mihrab (862) in the congregational mosque at Kairouan is surrounded by some 150 monochrome and polychrome tiles lustre-painted in the style of the Abbasid capital at Samarra'. Although a much later source reported that some tiles were imported and others made on the spot by an Iraqi craftsman, all the tiles around the mihrab are stylistically and technically uniform and were probably imports from Iraq. A lustre bowl decorated with a field of foliage interrupted by four splashes of colour (diam. 270 mm; Kairouan, Mus. A. Islam) also found at Kairouan has the same motifs and style of decoration as the tiles and was probably also imported from Iraq as it is similar in shape to Abbasid bowls produced there.

BIBLIOGRAPHY

G. Marçais: *Poteries et faïences de la Qal'a des Beni Ḥammād* (Constantine, 1913)

——: *Les Faïences à reflets métalliques de la Grande Mosquée de Kairouan* (Paris, 1928)

M. Jenkins: 'Western Islamic Influences on Fāṭimid Egyptian Iconography', *Kst Orients*, x (1975), pp. 91–107

M. Retuerce and J. Zozaya: 'Variantes geográficas de la cerámica omeya andalusí: Los temas decorativos', *La ceramica medievale nel mediterraneo occidentale: Atti del III congreso internazionale: Siena-Faenza, 1984*, pp. 69–128

G. Rosselló Bordoy: *El nombre de las cosas en al-Andalus: Una propuesta de terminología cerámica* (Palma de Mallorca, 1991)

——: 'The Ceramics of al-Andalus', *Al-Andalus: The Art of Islamic Spain* (exh. cat., ed. J. D. Dodds; Granada, Alhambra; New York, Met.; 1992), pp. 97–105

□

3. *c.* 1000–*c.* 1250. During this period ceramics became a major art form throughout the Islamic world. The lustre technique spread to Egypt, Syria, Iran and Spain, and other luxury wares that required a double firing were also introduced. The development of a new frit body enabled potters to produce myriad shapes, which were covered in an extraordinarily wide range of glazes and techniques, including *sgraffito*, champlevé and slip, underglaze and overglaze painting.

(i) Egypt. (ii) Syria. (iii) Iran and western Central Asia. (iv) Anatolia. (v) Spain and North Africa.

(i) Egypt. With the establishment of the Fatimid dynasty in Egypt (*reg* 969–1171), a ceramic renaissance took place there. Pride of place must go to lustrewares, a technique derived from Samarra' wares (*see* §2(ii) above) in which a design painted in a fluxed silver or copper nitrate on a matt tin-opacified glaze turned lustrous following a session in the reducing kiln. When the lustre technique was first achieved in Egypt in the 7th century, it was applied to glass (*see* §VIII, 5(i) below). Following the conquest of Egypt by the Abbasids in the mid-8th century, the technology was taken to Iraq; there it was applied to ceramics, which were exported to Egypt in quantity well into the 10th century.

Egyptian potters soon shed their commitment to the Abbasid decorative repertory, preferring a revived classicism and the exuberance of the court cycles seen in other forms of artistic expression, notably carved wood (*see* §VII, 1(i)(b) below). A complicated form of floriated kufic script, echoing the splendid inscription bands in stone and stucco seen on the mosques, walls and gates of Cairo (see fig. 83 above), was adapted to the various curves and planes of pottery. In addition to traditional geometric and floral motifs, Fatimid lustrewares are decorated with a wide range of figural subjects, including rabbits, birds, horsemen and dancers, often set within a scalloped border around the rim (see fig. 166). Ettinghausen attributed the new sense of realism to a closer observation of everyday life, and Grabar suggested that popular taste had been affected by the flood of imperial objects following the looting of the Fatimid treasuries in the mid-11th century. In addition to the courtly iconography, more homely motifs can be traced to pre-Islamic Egyptian culture (Grube, 1962), while Jenkins (1975) has found their source in the 10th-century pottery of Tunisia and Algeria.

Few lustrewares are dated; a rare exception is a fragmentary large plate (Cairo, Mus. Islam. A.) dedicated to Ghaban, who served as commander-in-chief for the Fatimid caliph al-Hakim from 1011 to 1013. During this period Egyptian artists began to sign their work, and the characteristics of workshops, notably those of MUSLIM, make it possible to comprehend the development and diffusion of one distinguished genre. A *terminus ante quem* can be established for other dishes that were set into the walls of Italian churches at construction (It. *bacino*). For example, a Fatimid lustre bowl with four fish can be dated to the mid-11th century as it decorates the church of S Stephano in Pisa, and another showing a seated figure holding a wine-cup can be dated to the last quarter of the century as it decorates the church of S Sisto there (see 1983 exh. cat., pls VIII and VII).

Lustring on different-coloured underglazes was made possible by the discovery of a siliceous glaze that would hold the lustre. This discovery can be dated by an albarello with a procession of peacocks (Ann Arbor, U. MI, Kelsey Mus.) excavated at Fustat in an undisturbed find-spot datable *c.* 1075. Since the mid-10th century Egyptian potters had imitated the shapes and colouring of the best

Chinese porcelains and celadons (*see* §2(iv) above), and with the introduction of siliceous glazes the nature of the imitation changed in two ways: a porcellanous effect was achieved by using colours other than gleaming white or clear green, notably turquoise, honey brown and manganese, and lightly incised designs inspired by the feather-brush decoration beneath the finer Northern Sung imports were cut through the slip under the various siliceous glazes. These incised wares have been called Fustat Fatimid Sgraffito ware (FFS) because of the large number of wasters found at the site. In time these tight inscaped designs were allied to others more generally associated with lustrewares, particularly epigraphic, zoomorphic and anthropomorphic designs, so that one can trace the parallel chronological and aesthetic developments of the two wares. Some of the FFS wares carry parts of the design in low relief and/or two or three colours of overglaze.

As Fatimid lustrewares herald a shift from the opacified to the siliceous overglaze, so the FFS wares demonstrate an evolution in the clay body. The omnipresent buff-brown body of most of the finer vessels began to carry an increasing admixture of quartz. The resulting whitening of the base clay, although not evident to the naked eye, is nonetheless important in that it points the way to the frit bodies encountered at the end of the 12th century in Syria (*see* §(ii) below). Certain Fatimid lustrewares made from this frit-like composite clay might have reached Iran and sparked the search for the superbly ductile and strong fritware emanating from the kilns at Kashan (*see* §(iii) below).

Although the early so-called Faiyum wares continued to cater to more popular taste during this period, they too were subjected to the shift from opaque to siliceous underglaze and a contraction of the palette to a ripple effect of flowing manganese on a transparent underglaze that shows the white slip. Green and honey-brown glazes disappeared, as did the epigraphic and zoomorphic motifs so popular in the comparable ware of the 9th and 10th centuries.

Decoration with underglaze slips reappears in the 11th century as an attempt to imitate Fatimid lustre, perhaps for a less prosperous market. Discrete themes from the lustre canon are slip-painted in manganese or black slip and then covered by either a colourless or a transparent turquoise glaze to achieve a silhouette effect. Some very rare finds at Fustat proved that rather early in the 11th century the Egyptian potter was experimenting with polychrome underglaze slip painting as though in anticipation of later Raqqa painted wares. Finally, a technically novel ware based on the unmistakable buff-brown clays used by Egyptian potters appeared twice in 11th-century loci at Fustat. The decoration consists of an opaque coloured underglaze, either red, blue or a light streaky lilac tint, over which is pulled a trail of an opaque glaze of a different colour, generally white. This technique puts the design in relief and creates the effect of an enamel or a coloured glass overthreading. It might be either a clumsy ceramic parallel to marvered glass or a prefiguring of the enamelled glass that appeared in Syria in the early 13th century.

With the establishment of the Ayyubids in Egypt (*reg* 1169–1252), the Fatimid aesthetic was quickly eclipsed, as seen in the marked contrast between the glazed pottery

166. Earthenware plate with flat rim painted in golden lustre over an opaque white glaze, h. 70 mm, diam. 383 mm, from Egypt, 12th century (Washington, DC, Freer Gallery of Art)

available in 1100 and that dominating the market in 1200. Two types of fritware produced in Iran, silhouette ware and underglaze-painted ware, were copied in Syria, and these imitations were exported to Egypt, where the elements were promptly adapted to local taste. It is often difficult to distinguish a piece of Syrian Raqqa ware from an Egyptian product, as both were based on a coarse whitish frit. The use of transparent green and manganese glazes in silhouette wares and the gradual addition of red and green in the underglaze-painted wares are Egyptian glosses on received models. These fritwares continued to be produced up to the 13th century, bridging the change of power wrought by the Mamluks (*reg* 1250–1517).

Unglazed ceramics had no real importance after the advent of glazing in Egypt, but the filter or gargoulette was always a subject of artistic expression, and the finish and variety of those made in this period, some glazed and/or lustred, point to an undiminished commerce. In the 12th century these delicately cut designs gave way to the large and more robust filters associated with the period of Ayyubid rule. In addition, the old-fashioned polished redware, sometimes called Pseudo-Samian, was still manufactured in appreciable quantities into the middle of the 11th century. As this type had been made in Egypt since the Late Kingdom (*see* EGYPT, ANCIENT, §XIV), it is the longest-lived speciality ceramic in the Mediterranean world.

BIBLIOGRAPHY
R. Ettinghausen: 'Painting in the Fatimid Period: A Reconstruction', *A. Islam.*, ix (1942), pp. 112–24
——: 'Early Realism in Islamic Art', *Studi orientalistici in onore di Giorgio Levi della Vida*, i (Rome, 1956), pp. 250–73
H. al-Basha: 'Tabaq min al-khazaf bi-ism Ghaban Mawlā al-Hākim bi'amrillāh' [A pottery plate with the name Ghaban Mawla al-Hakim

bi-amrillah written on it], *Bull. Fac. A., Cairo U.*, xviii (1958), pp. 71–85

E. J. Grube: 'Studies in the Survival and Continuity of Pre-Muslim Traditions in Egyptian Islamic Art', *J. Amer. Res. Cent. Egypt*, i (1962), pp. 75–97

M. Jenkins: 'Muslim: An Early Fatimid Ceramicist', *Bull. Met.*, xxvi (1968), pp. 359–69

O. Grabar: 'Imperial and Urban Art in Islam: The Subject Matter of Fāṭimid Art', *Colloque international sur l'histoire du Caire: Caire, 1969*, pp. 173–89

M. Jenkins: 'Western Islamic Influences on Fatimid Egyptian Iconography', *Kst Orients*, x (1975), pp. 91–107

Arte islamica in Italia: I bacini delle chiese pisane (exh. cat., ed. G. Berti and P. Torre; Rome, Pal. Brancaccio, 1983)

E. J. Grube: 'Realism or Formalism: Notes on Some Fatimid Lustre-Painted Ceramic Vessels', *Studi in onore di Francesco Gabrieli* (Rome, 1984), pp. 423–32

G. T. Scanlon: *Filters* (1986), i of *Fusṭāṭ Expedition: Final Report* (Lake Winona, IN, 1986–)

——: 'Fatimid Underglaze Painted Wares: A Chronological Readjustment', *A Way Prepared: Essays on Islamic Culture in Honour of Richard Bayly Winder*, ed. F. Kazemi and R. McChesney (New York, 1987)

GEORGE SCANLON

(ii) Syria. Pottery made in Syria in the 11th century and early 12th continued earlier types (*see* §2(i) above). Moulded earthenware pouring vessels elaborately decorated with friezes of running animals or calligraphic bands continue the tradition of moulded vessels of the Abbasid period. Other earthenwares not exclusive to Syria are stoneware pear-shaped vessels with a bulbous top and narrow opening often with stamped or moulded ornament and sometimes inscribed with the names of makers or owners. Their use is uncertain, and suggestions include bombs containing naphtha, containers for ointments, unguents or mercury, and aeolipiles to heat up the kiln. A group of champlevé wares decorated with arabesques and palmettes have been attributed to Caesarea on the basis of ten bowls excavated from a ship that was wrecked *c.* 1025

at Serçe Limanı off the southern coast of Turkey. They may have been local imitations of the lustrewares produced in the Fatimid capital at Cairo (*see* §(i) above).

Between the mid-12th century and the mid-13th, two technically and stylistically distinct phases of fritwares were produced. Both phases were probably made at sites on the Euphrates, although the precise location of the potteries is still uncertain. The pottery from the first phase (*c.* 1150–*c.* 1180) is sometimes called Tell Minis ware after the village near Ma'arrat al-Nu'man where a large cache was found. Associated finds in the area and the large quantity of material excavated at the citadel at Hama reinforced the view that this early phase was produced in central Syria, but subsequent research uncovered examples of the first phase at sites in northern Syria that are usually associated with the later phase, such as Raqqa and Balis on the Euphrates. Indeed, the pottery of the second phase (*c.* 1180–*c.* 1250) is usually called Raqqa ware, although Euphrates ware might be a better term. These potteries had a vast output, ranging from unglazed earthenwares to fine glazed fritwares. A mass of sherds has been found at major Islamic sites in Syria and as far as Anatolia, and there are numerous complete pieces in museums and private collections in Syria and abroad (e.g. New York, Met., and Washington, DC, Freer).

Wares from the first phase have a hard, compact, white and very fine frit body comparable to that used at Kashan in Iran (*see* §(iii) below) and clear or opacified alkaline glazes. The most characteristic shape is a small shallow bowl with straight flaring sides and sharply turned foot. These vessels are decorated in lustre or with patterns carved beneath monochrome glazes. The lustre, the colour of which ranges in tone from strong orange to pale greenish-yellow, is usually painted on to the opacified glaze. Details are often scratched through the lustre before firing in the reducing kiln, and the overall style of painting is unrestrained and sketchy. Designs have a consistency of style suggesting production in a single workshop, and the similarity to Fatimid lustrewares indicates the direct participation of Egyptian craftsmen. Designs include geometric or vegetal motifs arranged symmetrically, calligraphic compositions repeating a single word such as happiness (Arab. *sa'd*) or good health (*'afiya*), and figural motifs of animals, harpies and seated humans (see fig. 167). Common to all designs are scrolls with sketchy curling leaves, which act as filler pattern or become the main motif with the addition of a trilobed leaf. The same range of shapes is found in monochrome wares, which are carved or incised with arabesque or geometric motifs. They have manganese, turquoise or clear glazes, usually not opacified and often applied over a quartzy slip.

Another group from the first phase known as Laqabi ('nicknamed') wares have underglaze colours separated by incised lines. The lines outline a bold design, often harpies or eagles, and also prevent the colours from running during firing. Shapes include jars, large dishes with flat rims, and a figurine in the shape of a horseman (Damascus, Mus. N.). Although some Laqabi wares may have been made at Kashan, finds at Syrian sites and the strong similarity in fabric and style between many Laqabi vessels and carved wares suggest Syrian manufacture for some pieces.

167. Fritware bowl painted in lustre over an opaque white glaze, h. 70 mm, diam. 205 mm, from Syria, *c.* 1150 (Copenhagen, Davids Samling)

Wares from the second phase have a thick, sandy and pink frit body quite distinct from the hard white frit of the earlier wares and alkaline glazes that are rarely opacified and tend to iridize. The most frequent shapes are conical bowls and hemispherical bowls with flat rims; among other shapes are figurines and stands with colonettes and arches. These wares include monochrome wares, two types of underglaze-painted wares and lustre. Underglaze painting, a technique perfected by Syrian potters, was done either in black under a brilliant turquoise glaze or in blue and/or black under a clear glaze. Designs include animals or birds painted with broad sweeping brushstrokes reminiscent of Fatimid lustrewares and a range of swirling patterns of dots, spirals and arabesque motifs. Red and green were also used on pieces with figures or tightly knit geometric patterns. These designs were inspired by contemporary enamelled (Pers. *mīnā'ī*) wares made in Iran, but curiously Syrian potters made no attempt to reproduce the enamelled technique, although enamelled glass was made there. This group is often called Rusafa ware since many pieces were found at Rusafa, but there is no evidence of a separate production centre there.

The lustre pottery of Raqqa, produced from *c.* 1200, is also inspired by Iranian wares from Kashan, but the designs are almost entirely non-figural and have dense patterns of tightly knit scrolls and leaf or calligraphic patterns painted in reserve against the chocolate-coloured lustre ground. Sherds from the site of Qasr al-Banat in northern Syria show that the lustre was also painted on cobalt, turquoise and manganese glazes. The impact of Raqqa was most strongly felt in Egypt, where, as in Syria, the tradition of underglaze painting began during the period of Ayyubid rule (1169–1252) and continued under the Mamluks (*reg* 1250–1517).

BIBLIOGRAPHY

F. Sarre: 'Die Keramik im Euphrat- und Tigris-Gebiet', *Archäologische Reise im Euphrat- und Tigris-Gebiet*, iv (Berlin, 1920), pp. 1–25

P. J. Riis and V. Poulsen: *Les Verreries et poteries médiévales* (1957), iv/2 of *Hama: Fouilles et recherches de la Fondation Carlsberg, 1931–1938* (Copenhagen)

E. J. Grube: 'Raqqa-Keramik in der Sammlung des Metropolitan Museum in New York', *Kst Orients*, iv (1963), pp. 48–78

R. Ettinghausen: 'The Uses of Sphero-conical Vessels in the Muslim East', *J. Nr E. Stud.*, xxiv (1965), pp. 218–29

J. M. Rogers: 'Aeolipiles Again', *Forschungen zur Kunst Asiens in Memoriam Kurt Erdmann* (Istanbul, 1969), pp. 147–58

G. Öney: 'Kubadabad Ceramics', *The Art of Iran and Anatolia* (1974), iv of *Percival David Foundation Colloquies on Art and Archaeology in Asia* (London, 1970–), pp. 68–84

V. Porter: *Medieval Syrian Pottery* (Oxford, 1981)

H. Philon: 'Stems, Leaves, and Water-weeds: Underglaze-painted Pottery in Syria and Egypt', *The Art of Syria and the Jazira*, ed. J. Raby, Oxford Studies in Islamic Art, i (Oxford, 1985), pp. 113–26

K. Tweir: 'Der Qasr al-Banat in ar-Raqqa: Ausgrabung, Rekonstruktion und Wiederaufbau 1977–1982', *Damas. Mitt.*, ii (1985), pp. 258–65

V. Porter and O. Watson: ' "Tell Minis" Wares', *Syria and Iran: Three Studies in Medieval Ceramics*, ed. J. Allen and C. Roberts, Oxford Studies in Islamic Art, iv (Oxford, 1987), pp. 175–248

C. Tonghini and E. J. Grube: 'Towards a History of Syrian Islamic Ceramics before 1500', *Islam. A.*, iii (1988–9), pp. 59–94

M. Jenkins: 'Early Medieval Islamic Pottery: The Eleventh Century Reconsidered', *Muqarnas*, ix (1992), pp. 56–66

VENETIA PORTER

(iii) Iran and western Central Asia. Ceramic styles and technologies that had developed in Khurasan and western Central Asia in the 9th and 10th centuries (*see* §2(iii)

above) filtered westward and were adopted at sites in northern and central Iran in the 11th and 12th centuries. Similarly, techniques and decorative motifs current in Egypt were transferred through Syria to Iran (*see* §§(i) and (ii) above). The period is characterized by a plethora of ceramic styles and techniques, but efforts to assign these stylistic groups to production centres are frustrated by the lack of archaeological evidence and by the stubborn adherence of site names assigned in the art trade. Moreover, it is unclear to what extent fine ceramics were traded overland and how much and how often they were copied locally. Many of the types originated and flourished during the period when the Saljuq dynasty ruled Iran (1038–1194), but the actual impact of the Saljuq rulers on these wares is debatable. Although rulers might have facilitated trade between ceramic centres, they did not necessarily stimulate the development of new styles. Several major Iranian sites such as Rayy and Istakhr were excavated in the 1930s, but the results were published only partially. Excavations from other sites such as Takht-i Sulayman have been published, but they were provincial centres of ceramic production. The same situation pertains in western Central Asia. Thus, many of the finest Iranian pieces from the 12th and 13th centuries do not have known find-spots and must be dated and localized on the basis of their inscriptions and by comparison, when possible, with glazed wall tiles still *in situ*.

(a) *Sgraffito* wares. (b) Slip-painted wares. (c) Fritwares. (d) Lustrewares. (e) Enamelled wares.

(a) Sgraffito wares. The technique of incising through white slip under a transparent colourless glaze in order to reveal the reddish body of the pot had already been developed in Nishapur in the 9th and 10th centuries, and it continued in the 11th and 12th centuries and spread to Rayy, Takht-i Sulayman and other sites in northern Iran. On bowls found at Lashkari Bazar in Afghanistan, the incised areas occur not in the centre but on the walls, where they form triangles or circles associated with spots of green oxide. The *sgraffito* bowls from the late 12th- and early 13th-century Rayy, like those from Lashkari Bazar, are sketchily decorated, often with single birds in the centre and wave motifs near the rim. More attractive *sgraffito* wares known as Amol wares feature densely incised designs of animals, birds and geometric figures on crosshatched grounds. These too are covered with transparent colourless glaze and varying quantities of green oxides. Some of these designs may have derived from metal prototypes.

Two other forms of *sgraffito* are noteworthy. Aghkand wares of the 12th and 13th centuries (e.g. Washington, DC, Freer, 67.4, and Paris, Louvre), named because many were reportedly found at the site 250 km south-east of Tabriz, have imposing birds or animals and vine scrolls defined by lines incised through white slip and coloured with the green, yellow and purple pigments of splashed wares. This type was adopted in Syria and the Christian Levant by the early 11th century (*see* EARLY CHRISTIAN AND BYZANTINE ART, §VII, 1). Champlevé, another technique related to *sgraffito*, was used in Azerbaijan province in north-west Iran at such sites as Takht-i Sulayman and Garrus. Instead of incising the design, the potter carved away the background, leaving the slip-painted decoration intact. Sometimes he left the carved area bare, sometimes he painted it with manganese oxide before covering the whole vessel with transparent colourless or green glaze. The result was a bold design on a dark ground and a striking, if folkish, style of pottery.

(b) Slip-painted wares. Potters in north-east Iran and western Central Asia in the 9th and 10th centuries had already found a solution to the problem of producing a white surface on which to decorate ceramic vessels by covering the reddish or buff earthenware bodies of their vessels with white slip, made of diluted fine white clay. On this they painted various metallic oxides mixed with diluted clay to form such colours as green, red, black, yellow and brown, which in turn were covered with transparent colourless lead glaze. This technique enabled the potters to produce myriad classes of pottery, all based on one technique but ranging in decoration from stark epigraphic wares to imitation Abbasid lustrewares and animate wares. Debased adaptations of the black-on-white wares were found at Lashkari Bazar, as were wares in white on a black ground and in black, white and yellow on a red ground. The ornament of these slipwares at Lashkari Bazar remained closely related to that of wares made at Nishapur, but a related group of slipwares associated with the site of Sari near the Caspian Sea in northern Iran features large, hastily rendered birds and stylized vegetal scrolls in green or red, yellow and brown pigments on a white slip ground. As this technique flourished as far south as the Kirman region and the style varied from place to place, the type should not be connected only with Sari.

(c) Fritwares. In the second half of the 12th century ceramic production in Iran was revolutionized by the introduction of the frit body, a mixture of ground quartz and white clay that results in a strong hard fabric to which alkaline glazes adhere well. Not only did the frit body obviate the need for white slip, but its strength and cohesiveness also enabled potters to make vessels with extremely thin walls and even to pierce them. Although fritware was probably first used in Egypt, the technique was adopted in Syria and then in Iran, where its decorative properties were fully developed at two major ceramic centres, Rayy and Kashan, and smaller sites in the centre and north of the country.

As with the tin-opacified white wares associated with the Abbasids (*see* §2(ii) and fig. 162 above) and the slip-painted wares associated with the Samanids (*see* §2(iii) above), fritwares were inspired by Chinese white wares. Extremely thin white bowls and beakers with carved or pierced decoration and transparent colourless glazes emulate the pure forms and translucence of Chinese porcelains. Iranian potters, however, were never slaves to their prototypes, and transparent blue, turquoise and purple glazes soon took precedence over colourless glaze. Moulded and carved decoration is derived from the Iranian repertory of astrological, animal, vegetal and epigraphic motifs. The versatile frit body allowed potters to vary shapes and fashion almost every type of vessel without fear of sides collapsing or glazes running. On Laqabi ('nicknamed') wares, for example, glazes of different

colours were combined by carving designs with grooved or raised outlines that segregated the glazes, a technique similar to that of cloisonné enamelling. As a last nod to the slip-painting tradition, potters of the second half of the 12th century painted designs in black slip on the white frit body, sharpened their outlines with a knife and covered them with a transparent turquoise or colourless glaze. The result is a small but distinctive series of bowls (e.g. London, V&A) and jugs (e.g. Washington, DC, Freer, 67.3), often called silhouette, shadow or black-slip ware.

By the first half of the 13th century the possibilities suggested by silhouette ware were realized in the development of true underglaze painting. Blue from cobalt and black from a mixture of oxides were found to be reliable pigments unlikely to run when applied to a frit body. Although the most famous examples of underglaze-painted wares from the early 13th century come from Kashan, similar wares may well have been produced at several centres. At their best, they display the sculptural, painterly and colouristic qualities that set medieval Iranian ceramics apart from the ceramics of other eras and regions of the Islamic world. Luxury items such as a reticulated ewer with a rooster-headed spout, a handle shaped like a tail-feather and decoration of Persian verses (see fig. 168) were adapted and copied widely in lesser-quality wares,

168. Fritware doubled-shelled ewer in the shape of a rooster, black and blue paint under a transparent turquoise glaze, h. 291 mm, from Iran, early 13th century (Washington, DC, Freer Gallery of Art)

suggesting that the fine ceramics and their replicas were highly fashionable in the early 13th century and accessible to large segments of the population.

(d) Lustrewares. By the third quarter of the 12th century some ceramic vessels produced in Iran were decorated in lustre overglaze, a technique previously used in Iraq, Egypt and Syria. Although lustrewares had been available in Iran in the 9th and 10th centuries, the Iraqi potters who knew the technique apparently emigrated to Egypt, and no lustreware was made in Iran until around the time of the fall of the Fatimid dynasty in 1171. Presumably, Egyptian craftsmen introduced the technique to Iran, for Egyptian and Iranian bowls of the 12th century share many compositions and decorative motifs. Because of its complexity, cost and luxurious appearance, the lustre technique remained a closely guarded secret until the late 12th century.

Abu'l-Qasim, the early 14th-century member of the famous Abu Tahir family of Kashani potters (*see* ABU TAHIR, (4)), described the process of making fritware and enumerated the steps needed to add lustre glaze to a frit bowl. After a first firing of 12 hours in the heat and six and a half more days' cooling in the kiln, the pots were removed from the kiln and were ready to be painted with overglaze. The lustre glaze consisted of a mixture of red and yellow arsenic, gold and silver marcasite, yellow vitriol, copper, and silver ground with sulphur dissolved in grape juice or vinegar. Once the design was painted on the pot, the vessel was placed in a special kiln and fired in 'light smoke for 72 hours' until the painted surface had turned golden. In the smoky muffle kiln the reduction of oxygen caused the metallic oxides to fuse with the slightly softened alkaline glaze. Despite numerous possibilities for error in production, lustrewares soon became one of the predominant forms of luxury ceramics in the late 12th century and early 13th.

The earlier identification of three main styles of lustreware, the Monumental, the Miniature and the Kashan styles, with two main sites, Rayy and Kashan, has been seriously questioned. Watson demonstrated that the only concentration of lustreware wasters was found at Kashan and cited epigraphic evidence of signatures by Kashani potters at such other sites as Sava and Gurgan. The most telling inscription is that on a bowl (London, V&A, C162-1977) found at Gurgan and signed 'Muhammad ibn Muhammad of Nishapur living in Kashan' (Arab. *al-muqīm bi qāshān*). Watson concluded that, following a possible initial phase of production in Rayy, by the 1180s Kashan had become the major centre of lustreware manufacture and that Kashan lustrewares were traded throughout Iran and exported as far east as Sind and as far west as Spain.

Of the three stylistic groups, the Monumental relies most on prototypes from Fatimid Egypt and possibly Syria. On many Monumental-style wares the major design elements (human figures, animals and arabesques) are reserved on a lustre ground. The rims of some bowls are decorated with lustre scallops derived from those found on many Fatimid bowls (*see* §(i) and fig. 166 above). Unlike the figures on Egyptian wares, those on the Iranian ones have moon-shaped faces and slanted eyes, perhaps derived from Buddhist images or figures on Chinese ceramics.

Subjects of decoration include horsemen, seated drinkers and musicians, animals and a few multi-figure scenes suggesting narrative content. Half-palmette scrolls, epigraphic bands and sketchy vines and leaves often fill defined areas on these bowls. Most pieces in this style are large flat dishes or bowls with slightly flaring rims and cylindrical foot-rings, shapes not used for pots in the other two styles. In addition to bowls and dishes, the Monumental style adorned bottles, jugs, sweetmeat dishes, jars and a variety of faceted or lobed moulded bowls. Although potters may have derived some of these shapes from metalwork, they apparently did not look to earlier Iranian ceramics for models. Lacking any dated examples, the Monumental style has been dated to the last quarter of the 12th century by comparison with silhouette wares, which have the same shape of bowl with slightly everted lip and the same aesthetic of contrasting light and dark passages. According to Watson, both the Monumental style of lustreware and silhouette ware disappeared *c.* 1200 when the straight-sided flaring bowl typical of the Kashan style and underglaze painting were adopted.

The Miniature style, so named after its relation to manuscript illustration (*see* §III, 4(iv)(c) above), differs from the Monumental style not only in decorative technique but also in vessel shape. Rather than reserving large-scale motifs on a lustre ground, potters working in the Miniature style painted small-scale designs in bands or panels on a variety of vessel shapes or occasionally single larger-scale motifs mainly on bowls. Motifs include humans, animals, arabesques and inscription bands, often the buffer between one zone and another. Many decorative elements of this style parallel those found on enamelled wares (*see* §(e) below), another type of ceramic that is fired twice. Both types, for example, feature trees with chequered foliage, textiles with intricate repeating designs and plants with long stalks and small dot-like leaves. Four pieces in the Miniature style are dated between 1179 and 1199, and one of them dated 1191 (ex-Bahrami priv. col., see Watson, pl. 53) is signed by ABU ZAYD, a potter also known from earlier enamelled bowls and lustrewares in the Kashan style. Given the stylistic range of signed pieces, Abu Zayd can be credited with the development of the Kashan style, which flourished from *c.* 1200 to the 1220s.

The Kashan style derives neither from foreign prototypes nor from other media. Rather, it uses passages of intricate yet lively detail formed by scratching a multitude of spirals and half-palmettes through the lustre ground surrounding the primary elements of the composition. These consist of groups of large-scale human and animal figures and non-figural motifs such as arabesques, inscriptions and geometric designs. Most bowls contain compositions with a pair of seated figures, rows of figures with a prince or tree in the centre, horsemen, or single large animals. In addition to the characteristic shape of bowl with flaring straight sides, high foot-ring and angular transition from wall to foot, vessels in the Kashan style range from long-necked bulbous-bodied bottles to flat dishes with straight, moulded and scalloped edges. The latter shape derives from metalwork, and examples are known from one or more moulds with the same dimensions (29 scallops, diam. 352 mm; see fig. 160 above). Just

169. Fritware enamelled bowl, attributed to Abu Zayd, h. 98 mm, diam. 210 mm, from Iran, 1187 (London, British Museum)

as the shapes and motifs found on Kashan-style lustrewares were duplicated in underglaze-painted pieces, so a series of human and animal figurines were decorated in all three styles of lustreware as well as in the underglaze technique and in opaque monochrome glazes. Some of these figurines functioned as aquamaniles or vases, but others with no openings may have been purely decorative.

Only nine pieces in the Kashan style are signed, and the only name to appear more than once is Abu Zayd. Dated works are more common: 56 are known from the period 1202–26. The Mongol invasions in the 1220s must have seriously curtailed the production of lustreware, because no known vessels are dated between 1226 and 1260. Although some signed pieces are of top quality, many lesser works are also dated, leading Watson to suggest that dates and signatures were added when space was available but were not the potters' first priority. Otherwise the inscriptions on vessels, as opposed to those on tiles, consist of Persian and occasionally Arabic verses that rarely relate to the activities or figures depicted on them. A large plate made by Shams al-Din Hasani in 1210 for an unidentified amir (Washington, DC, Freer), for example, shows a horse attended by a sleeping groom and five other figures; the exergue below is filled with an aquatic scene of a naked woman among fish. The unusually detailed iconography suggests a specific scene, but the verses inscribed on the rim give no clue and the meaning of the image has yet to be explained.

(e) Enamelled wares. At the same time as the three styles of lustreware were produced at Kashan, another luxury overglaze ware, unique to Iran, was introduced, presumably also at Kashan. Called enamelled (Pers. *mīnā'ī*) ware, this fritware comprises bowls, jugs, beakers, ewers, vases

and bottles covered first with a transparent colourless or opaque turquoise glaze and then fired. Colours such as turquoise and cobalt blue were applied prior to the first firing, whereas black, red, white and gold were painted on to the cold glaze and fixed in a second firing. The result was a group of polychrome pots decorated in a style closely allied to that of book illustration. Indeed, several pieces contain scenes from the *Shāhnāma* ('Book of kings'), and one large bowl (Washington, DC, Freer) shows an actual battle that took place in the 1220s.

Enamelled wares with figural decoration pose more questions concerning iconography than do the lustrewares. In addition to identifiable narrative scenes on bowls, tiles and a beaker (Washington, DC, Freer), five bowls are inscribed with the month Muharram and the years AH 582 or 583 (AD 1186 or 1187; see fig. 169). One bowl (ex-Tabbagh priv. col.) is signed by Abu Zayd, so the group has been assigned to him. At least two of the dated bowls and a related piece contain the scene of a ruler or single individual sitting apart from a group of figures and separated from them by a tree. In the foreground is a pool with fish swimming in it; birds fly to and fro in the sky. Another bowl (ex-Parrish-Watson priv. col., see Ettinghausen, 1938–9, pl. 686), dated 1 Muharram 583 (corresponding to 13 March 1187), shows a figure riding a donkey while attendants walk near by and an angel hovers above. Since Muharram is the first month of the Muslim year, it is possible that these bowls were presented as gifts for the New Year (Pers. *nawrūz*), a tradition already established in Iran. Whether or not the bowls were made for specific patrons, their decoration, such as loving couples or rulers with their wives and attendants, often implies well-being, as do inscriptions offering blessings to the owner.

Dated enamelled wares range from 1186 to 1224. In that period potters of enamelled wares did not limit themselves to their original palette, but experimented with combinations of lustre and enamel glazing. At their best they produced extremely sumptuous wares, at their worst a surfeit of opulence. Ultimately in the mid- and later 13th century enamelled wares developed away from the Miniature style, as bowls and other vessels increasingly had moulded arabesque decoration that was glazed turquoise and highlighted with lustre and white overglaze painting. The Miniature style may have been so closely identified with Abu Zayd that it did not survive him. Certainly the Mongol invasions of the 1220s and 1250s precipitated changes in the style of decorating ceramics in Iran and ushered in a new wave of Chinese influence in the visual arts. Yet, as a native Iranian style of ceramics, enamelled wares stand alone, and their uniqueness has been recognized by modern fakers, who quickly understood the appeal of the charming worlds found within enamelled bowls.

BIBLIOGRAPHY

R. Ettinghausen: 'Evidence for the Identification of Kashan Pottery', *A. Islam.*, iii (1936), pp. 44–70

——: 'The Ceramic Arts in Islamic Times, B: Dated Faience', *Survey of Persian Art*, ed. A. U. Pope and P. Ackerman (London, 1938–9; 2/1964–7), pp. 1667–95

M. Bahrami: *Gurgan Faiences* (Cairo, 1949/R Costa Mesa, CA, 1988)

G. D. Guest and R. Ettinghausen: 'The Iconography of a Kashan Lustre Plate', *A. Orient.*, iv (1961), pp. 25–64

J.-C. Gardin: *Lashkari Bazar II: Les Trouvailles: Céramiques et monnaies de Lashkari Bazar et de Bust*, Mém.: Dél. Archéol. Fr. Afghanistan, xviii (Paris, 1963)

R. Ettinghausen: 'The Flowering of Saljuq Art', *Met. Mus. J.*, iii (1970), pp. 113–31

J. W. Allan: 'Abū'l-Qāsim's Treatise on Ceramics', *Iran*, xi (1973), pp. 111–20

M. S. Simpson: 'The Narrative Structure of a Medieval Iranian Beaker', *A. Orient.*, xii (1981), pp. 15–24

——: 'Narrative Allusion and Metaphor in the Decoration of Medieval Islamic Objects', *Pictorial Narrative in Antiquity and the Middle Ages*, ed. H. L. Kessler and M. S. Simpson, Studies in the History of Art, xvi (Washington, DC, 1985)

O. Watson: *Persian Lustre Ware* (London and Boston, 1985)

A. Williamson: 'Regional Distribution of Mediaeval Persian Pottery in Light of Recent Investigations', *Syria and Iran: Three Studies in Medieval Ceramics*, Oxford Studies in Islamic Art, iv (Oxford, 1987)

SHEILA R. CANBY

(iv) Anatolia. Despite the renown of ceramic tiles from Anatolia under the Saljuq dynasty of Rum (*reg* 1077–1307; *see* §II, 9(ii) above), few ceramic vessels were known from this period until such sites as Kubadabad, Kalehisar near Alaca Höyük, Ahlat, Eskikahta, Adiyaman (Samsat) and Kurucutepe near Elaziğ were excavated, as were several other sites flooded by the Keban and Atatürk dams in south-east Anatolia. A large number of unglazed vases, ewers, bowls, plates and similar artefacts were discovered. Made of soft red, grey or yellow clay, they were either painted with dark grey or red stripes or decorated in relief with grooves and scrolls, moulded or carved figures and animals, masks, rosettes and arabesques. Although most excavated wares were not glazed, there were considerable numbers of simple dishes, pots, bowls and oil lamps made of a coarse reddish or dirty-white clay with a thick monochrome glaze in turquoise, green, violet or yellow-brown.

The most common ceramics are earthenwares. *Sgraffito*, a popular technique when the area was under Byzantine control (*see* EARLY CHRISTIAN AND BYZANTINE ART, §VII, 1), continued to be made. Designs include abstract foliate and geometric motifs and bird, animal and human figures. The brick-red, grey or beige body is covered with a monochrome cream, yellow-brown, green or polychrome transparent glaze. The rarer champlevé wares were usually painted in dark brown or black under a colourless, green, brown or polychrome transparent glaze. The slender and elongated faces on pieces with figural decoration distinguish them from those of other areas, which display round faces and almond-shaped eyes. A few slipwares have also been found.

More expensive fritwares were also produced. Lustrewares, found mainly in south-east and eastern Anatolia, have colourless, greenish, violet or rarely dark-blue glazes decorated in different shades of brown. Colourless glazes are occasionally enlivened with cobalt-blue decoration in the glaze. The designs of stylized plants, rings and pseudo-kufic inscriptions are coarsely drawn. Vessels with black designs under a transparent turquoise glaze, a type produced in Syria (*see* §(ii) above), were also made in Anatolia; they can be distinguished by their coarse, granular and dirty-white body. Others have black, blue and brown decoration under a colourless glaze. The great variety of forms are decorated with abstract leaves and flowers within geometric frames. Stylized borders with pseudo-kufic inscriptions are also common.

BIBLIOGRAPHY
K. Otto-Dorn: *Türkische Keramik* (Ankara, 1957)

O. Aslanapa: *Türkische Fliesen und Keramik in Anatolien* (Istanbul, 1965)

G. Öney: 'Human Figures on Anatolian Seljuk Sgraffito and Champlevé Ceramics', *Essays in Islamic Art and Architecture in Honor of Katharina Otto-Dorn*, ed. A. Daneshvari (Malibu, 1983), pp. 113–26

The Anatolian Civilisations III: Seljuk/Ottoman (exh. cat., 18th Council of Europe exh.; Istanbul, 1983), D.61–D.91

GÖNÜL ÖNEY

(v) Spain and North Africa. In the western Islamic world, as elsewhere, production centres, varieties of vessel shapes and techniques of decoration proliferated during this period. In Spain, for example, local potteries have been identified at Toledo, Saragossa, Valencia, Málaga, Mallorca, Badajoz and Murcia. Most surviving vessels are bowls or plates, but cooking manuals attest to a wider variety of forms. The green-and-manganese wares with colourless glaze common in the earlier period (*see* §2(v) above) became increasingly elaborate, and bowls decorated with lateen-rigged three-masted sailing ships (e.g. Pisa, Mus. N. S Matteo) were used to decorate Italian churches (It. *bacini*) in the early 11th century. Once attributed to Tunisia, these bowls have been assigned to Mallorca on the basis of the clay used. Similar wares produced in Sicily or Tunisia are decorated with animals, birds and geometric and floral elements and include yellow in the palette. The pigments, particularly on the bowls decorated with birds and animals, often run during glazing, producing a blurred design. *Cuerda seca* wares were also introduced. An early 11th-century bowl from Alcalá de Henares (Madrid, Mus.

170. Earthenware drinking vessel with handles having all-over *sgraffito* decoration, h. 134 mm, from Murcia, mid-13th century (Murcia, Centro de Estudios Arabes y Arqueológicos 'Ibn Arabi')

Arqueol. N., 74/48/30) is decorated with a white and yellow peacock on a black ground, while a late 11th-century bowl from Morocco, used to decorate the church of S Sisto in Pisa (see 1983 exh. cat., pl. IX), has lozenges and palmettes in green and yellow on a white ground. By the late 11th century the *cuerda seca* technique deteriorated and parts of the surface were left unglazed.

Other techniques include stamped wares covered with monochrome glazes. Several flat bowls made in Morocco were used in the late 11th century and early 12th to decorate the churches of S Sisto and S Andrea in Pisa (see 1983 exh. cat., pl. X and fig. 24). Stamped relief wares also became popular in Spain under the Almohads (*reg* 1130–1269), as did *sgraffito*, which eventually replaced *cuerda seca*. The most sophisticated vessels produced at Murcia in the mid-13th century (see fig. 170) have arabesque designs incised over the entire surface in imitation of metal prototypes with niello. Lustrewares, first imported from Fatimid Egypt, were then produced locally. A rare bowl with confronted horses painted on a tin glaze in yellow lustre, which was discovered at Tudela, Navarra (Tudela, Archv Mun.), may be a local imitation of Fatimid wares. Other Spanish lustre bowls incorporated into Italian churches in the 12th century have birds and flowers painted in metallic-coloured lustre with hints of olive green over a thin white tin glaze, which does not conceal the red colour of the clay beneath.

BIBLIOGRAPHY

La Céramique médiévale en Méditerranée occidentale Xe–XVe siècles: Colloque international du Centre national de la recherche scientifique: Valbonne, 1978

Arte islamica in Italia: I bacini delle chiese pisane (exh. cat., ed. G. Berti and P. Torre; Rome, Pal. Brancaccio, 1983)

La cerámica islámica en Murcia (exh. cat. by J. Navarro Palazón, Murcia, ?1986)

G. Rosselló Bordoy: 'The Ceramics of al-Andalus', *Al-Andalus: The Art of Islamic Spain* (exh. cat., ed. J. D. Dodds; Granada, Alhambra; New York, Met.; 1992), pp. 97–105

☐

4. *c.* 1250–*c.* 1500. The Mongol invasions in the 13th century opened the channels by which Chinese celadons and blue-and-white porcelains were imported to the Islamic lands. Chinese wares became the standard of excellence to which Near Eastern potters aspired, and local techniques of producing underglaze-painted fritwares were adapted to this new chinoiserie taste. The one exception was the Maghrib, where a distinct tradition of lustreware developed under the splendid patronage of the Nasrid court in Granada.

(i) Iran and western Central Asia. (ii) Egypt and Syria. (iii) Anatolia. (iv) Spain and North Africa.

(i) Iran and western Central Asia. In the period following the Mongol conquest of the eastern Islamic lands, ceramics played a lesser role than in earlier times, perhaps because the arts of the book became increasingly important (*see* §III, 4(v)(b) above). Porcelains imported from China provided much of the inspiration for local ceramic production under the rule of the Ilkhanid dynasty (*reg* 1256–1353) in western Iran and of the Timurid dynasty (*reg* 1370–1506) in Khurasan and Transoxiana and their Turkoman contemporaries in western Iran.

(a) *c.* 1250–*c.* 1400. (b) *c.* 1400–*c.* 1500.

(a) c. *1250*–c. *1400.* Iranian ceramics from the period are far less varied in technique than earlier examples. Most are made of a soft white frit, which precluded the subtle shapes of earlier times. The cheaper technique of underglaze painting, which did not require repeated and complex firings, generally replaced overglaze decoration. Lustreware was still produced, but the painting became simplified and stylized, designs less detailed and drawing cruder, although new chinoiserie motifs such as simurghs and lotus blossoms were added to the repertory. Lustre tiles for architectural revetment were produced until 1340, but the dozen lustre vessels dated between 1261 and 1284 (e.g. a dish dated 1277; Washington, DC, Freer, 09.317) have sombre and heavy decoration. The city of Kashan in central Iran remained the major centre of lustreware, where the same families controlled production. The fourth generation of the Abu Tahir family included the potter Yusuf and his brother Abu'l-Qasim, who composed a treatise on gems and minerals (1303), the major source for the art of making ceramics in medieval Iran.

A second group of luxury ceramics produced in Ilkhanid Iran is known as *lājvardīna* ware, from the Persian word *lājvard* ('lapis lazuli'), because of the deep-blue glaze on many examples (*see* CERAMICS, colour pl. IV), although some are glazed in turquoise blue (e.g. a sweetmeat dish, Washington, DC, Freer, 09.318). The pieces were leaf gilded and overglaze painted in red, black and white. These wares, mainly bowls and tiles, but occasionally *albarelli* (e.g. New York, Met., 1957.61.12) and other shapes, apparently replaced the enamelled wares of the pre-Mongol period and must have been expensive because they were made of costly materials and required a second firing in a special kiln. Despite their expense, vessels have coarse greyish bodies and clumsy potting. Bowls are often decorated with radial patterns filled with scrolls, circles and dots. *Lājvardīna* wares were produced throughout the 14th century: Abu'l-Qasim had described the technique in his treatise, and one of the earliest dated pieces is a fragmentary star tile (1315; ex-R. Ettinghausen priv. col.). A bowl dated 1374–5 (Berlin, Mus. Islam. Kst, I. 24/66) must have been made near the end of the series.

The major type of underglaze-painted ware is known after the city of Sultanabad, located on the road from Hamadan to Isfahan. Many pieces were found there, but as the city was established only in 1808 and no kiln sites have been discovered there, the name is a convenient if misleading label. Similar wares were also excavated at Saray, the city founded by Berke Khan (*reg* 1257–67), which became the capital of the Golden Horde under Uzbek Khan (*reg* 1312–41) and was destroyed by Timur in 1395, but they have different shapes and stiffer drawing (e.g. St Petersburg, Hermitage). A few of the more finely potted Sultanabad wares transfer designs characteristic of lustrewares to the underglaze technique; they have been attributed to Kashan. Most of the pieces have coarse and clumsy potting with a thick glassy glaze that forms greenish pools and drops. The typical shape (see fig. 171) is a deep conical bowl with a wide rim overhanging interior and exterior. The rim is decorated with a pearl border, while the interior shows an animal or a bird with a spotted body on a ground of thick-leaved foliage. The greenish or greyish-brown slip makes the surface uneven. Other shapes include large jars and *albarelli*.

A fourth group, comprising moulded monochrome wares, displays a similar interest in surface texture. Shapes include large jars, bowls with vertical sides, jugs, figurines and models. Examples are glazed in either blue or green and moulded in relief with vegetal, epigraphic and figural motifs. A large dark-blue jar (h. 502 mm; 1284–5; Washington, DC, Freer, 08.198) has moulded decoration of gazelle-like animals on the body and an inscription on the shoulder; a similar piece in New York (Met.) is dated 1282–3. Other pieces in this group imitate Chinese Longquan celadons (*see* CHINA, §VII, 3(iv)(b)): a green-glazed dish (London, V&A, C.10–1947) is decorated with four fish and radiating ribs on the cavetto.

BIBLIOGRAPHY
R. Ettinghausen: 'New Affiliations for a Classical Persian Pottery Type', *Parnassus*, viii (March 1936), pp. 10–12, 20–21
G. Reitlinger: 'The Interim Period in Persian Pottery: An Essay in Chronological Revision', *A. Islam.*, v (1938), pp. 155–78
——: 'Sultanabad: Classification and Chronology', *Trans. Orient. Cer. Soc.* (1944–5), pp. 25–34
A. Lane: *Early Islamic Pottery* (London, 1947)
——: *Later Islamic Pottery* (London, 1957)
J. W. Allan: 'Abu'l Qasim's Treatise on Ceramics', *Iran*, xi (1973), pp. 111–20
E. Atıl: *Ceramics from the World of Islam* (Washington, DC, 1973)
O. Watson: *Persian Lustre Ware* (London, 1985), pp. 178–9

(b) c. 1400–c. 1500. During this period in all the arts there developed an insatiable appetite for chinoiserie, and this was especially true for ceramics. Pottery produced under the Timurids (*reg* 1370–1506) is either turquoise-and-black or blue-and-white, imitating Chinese porcelains, which were brought as gifts by embassies from China to the Timurid courts in Khurasan and Transoxiana. According to the Spanish envoy Clavijo, the tables of Timur (*reg* 1370–1405) were laden with Chinese porcelains, gold and silver, and from the end of the 14th century blue-and-white vessels of Chinese type are depicted in Persian manuscript paintings. Ulughbeg, Governor of Samarkand for his father Shahrukh (*reg* 1405–47), built a special pavilion to house his porcelain collection (Pers. *chīnī-khāna*). Excavation at this site revealed several blue-and-white porcelain tiles which, according to the Timurid descendant and Mughal emperor Babur (*reg* 1526–30), Ulughbeg had ordered directly from China.

China alone could not have satisfied the Timurids' need for tablewares, and the Timurid craftsmen, who made superb tiles, must also have turned their hand to ceramic vessels. While some potters simply worked to supply the insatiable demand at every level for goods of Chinese type, others strove to perfect the quality of the blue and the clarity of the white. In addition to the ubiquitous earthenwares, they produced fine wares, which, like the Kashan wares of the earlier period (*see* §3(iii)(c) above), were made from a quartz paste obtained by crushing cobbles collected from stream beds. Local geology and tradition gave each production centre a unique ceramic body, and several centres have been identified through microscopic studies of their petrofabric combined with stylistic analysis.

Despite the new taste for Chinese porcelains, some workshops maintained traditional techniques and styles

171. Fritware Sultanabad bowl, diam. 286 mm, from Iran, first half of the 14th century (New York, Metropolitan Museum of Art)

well into the 15th century. A lustre-painted bowl (1418; sold Paris, Nouveau Drouot, 14 April 1981, lot 70) and several lustre-painted tiles (e.g. a pair dated 1455; New York, Met., 30.95.26, and Berlin, Mus. Islam. Kst., I. 3940) indicate that this popular technique continued, despite a decline in quality. Some *lājvardīna* wares attributed to the 14th century may actually date from the early 15th, since this technique of blue glaze with overglaze enamel and gold was still used during the reign of Timur to make tiles in Samarkand.

A large quantity of pottery was excavated at the Timurid citadel in Samarkand, and other finds come from unspecified locations in the area. Some fragments bear traditional decoration, but many blue-and-white sherds were also found of a type (e.g. a dish depicting a landscape; *c.* 1405; London, V&A, C206–1984) that copied not Yuan originals, but Syrian imitations of Yuan porcelains. Most popular were those with the characteristic Syrian spiky blossom and water-lotus bouquet. An extremely fine group with a tin-opacified glaze displays superbly drawn phoenixes (e.g. a fragment of a candlestick, *c.* 1405; Samarkand, Inst. Archaeol.). The use of sand rather than cobbles to make the paste, a Syrian technique, bears out Clavijo's statement that Timur brought potters from Damascus in 1402. In addition to deep bowls copying Chinese shapes, other forms include ewers and bell-shaped candlesticks with twin shafts in the form of dragons. The Samarkand workshops declined after 1411 when Ulughbeg issued an edict allowing those forcibly brought to Samarkand to return home. Some potters apparently went to Syria and Anatolia and produced the blue-and-white tiles decorating buildings in Damascus and Edirne (*see* §§(ii) and (iii) below). An unidentified centre (possibly Diyarbakır in eastern Turkey) exported low-grade wares as far as Siraf

172. Nishapur blue-and-white dish decorated with peonies, diam. 430 mm, Iran, 1450–70 (Ham, Surrey, Keir private collection)

on the Persian Gulf; from there they were shipped to East Africa, where they were embedded—along with genuine Chinese porcelains—in the walls of early 15th-century houses at Kilwa. Other potters went to Khurasan and joined the workshops of Nishapur.

The Nishapur workshop, responsible for turquoise-and-black and superb blue-and-white wares, has been identified by associating pieces found at a kiln site discovered by Charles Wilkinson with the petrofabric of other well-known and dated pieces. Wares painted in black under a transparent turquoise glaze (e.g. a dish with cloud-point design; 1468–9; Rome, Pal. Brancaccio, 178) seem to have been inspired by Cizhou scrollwork, as well as Yuan geometric compositions. Four examples are dated between 1468 and 1495, and production continued into the 16th century. These wares were widely imitated, in both stone-paste and earthenware, from Anatolia (e.g. Miletus ware) to Sistan and Transoxiana, and in some instances potters from Nishapur may have migrated. In the mid-15th century the Nishapur workshop began to produce two lines of blue-and-white wares. One line comprises beautiful peony plates based on Xuande designs (see fig. 172). Like their Chinese models, the dishes are divided into three zones on the interior. A derivation of the wave border-decoration of the Yuan period (1279–1368; *see* CHINA, §VII, 3(v)) was favoured for rims. The centre displays either a continuous undulating peony band or an isolated spray of camellia blossoms, both drawn from models of the early Ming period (1368–1644; *see* CHINA, §VII, 3(vi)). The back, however, shows a reductive version of the peony scroll that becomes further simplified as the double scroll, a hallmark of the Nishapur workshop. The painterly quality of the best peony dishes is superb.

The application of the cobalt blue resembles the heaped-and-piled technique so admired in China: different shades of blue were achieved by applying varying amounts of pigment. Designs include bird-and-flower compositions and animals. The second line of Nishapur blue-and-white wares displays interlaced geometric designs incorporating Chinese cloud-collar points (e.g. a dish, 1460–90; New York, Met., 36.20.4). Towards the end of the century quality declined (e.g. a dish with large blossom; *c.* 1500; Toronto, Royal Ont. Mus., 992.117.1).

The most successful workshop inspired by Nishapur was at Mashhad, where distinct variations of all the Nishapur types were produced. Two dishes with the same petrofabric are inscribed with the date and place of manufacture: one painted in chromium green on white (1444–5; Edinburgh, Royal Mus. Scotland, 1888.570) and another with three blossoms (1473–4; St Petersburg, Hermitage, VG.2650). Inscribing the place of manufacture is unusual in the history of Iranian ceramics and can best be explained here by the importance of the shrine of Imam Riza at Mashhad under the Timurids. The circulation of souvenirs would also explain why products from Mashhad were so widely copied, for example in earthenwares produced in Khwarazm. Another ware associated with the province of Khurasan, but not identified with any known workshop, consists mainly of small bowls decorated on the exterior with one or two dragons (e.g. Berlin, Mus. Islam. Kst., I. 5380).

As the power of the Timurids declined in the east, the Turkoman confederations of the Aqqoyunlu (*reg* 1378–1508) and the Qaraqoyunlu (*reg* 1380–1468) lured craftsmen to their courts, most notably at Tabriz. Here another major workshop was established, which first produced very fine copies of Chinese porcelain as well as copies of the better Khurasan wares. Ottoman sources state that the group of potters that eventually went from Tabriz to Istanbul came originally from Khurasan. A small group of Tabriz wares is characterized by precise drawing that regularizes or geometricizes the Chinese prototypes. Some pieces (e.g. a dish with central blossoms, last quarter of the 15th century; Oxford, Ashmolean, 1978.1484) resemble early blue-and-white wares from Iznik in Anatolia and may have been produced at either site. The two predominant shapes, dishes with wide or narrow foot-rings, may be contemporary, but the narrow foot-ring type (with water-weed design on the back) seems to have continued into the middle of the 16th century. These wares make up the bulk of the Kubachi wares, which were found in large quantity in the village of that name in Dagestan, where a few Nishapur and Mashhad wares were also found.

BIBLIOGRAPHY
Zahir al-Din Muhammad Babur (*d* 1530): *Baburnāma* [Book of Babur]; Eng. trans. by A. Beveridge, 2 vols (London, 1922)
Ruy Gonzalez de Clavijo (*d* 1412): *Embajada a Tamorlan*; Eng. trans. by G. Le Strange as *Embassy to Tamerlane (1403–1406)* (London, 1928)
A. Lane: 'The So-called "Kubachi" Wares of Persia', *Burl. Mag.*, lxxv (1939), pp. 156–62
N. Chittick: *Kilwa* (Nairobi, 1974)
E. J. Grube: 'Notes on the Decorative Arts of the Timurid Period', *Gururajamanjarika: Studi in onore di Giuseppe Tucci*, ed. A. Forte and others (Naples, 1974), pp. 233–79
A. A. Ivanov: 'Faiansovoe bliudo XV veka iz Mashhada' [A faience dish of the 15th century from Meshed], *Soobshcheniya Gosudarstvennogo Ermitaza*, xlv (1980), pp. 64–6

O. Watson: *Persian Lustre Ware* (London, 1985)
E. J. Grube: 'Notes on the Decorative Arts of the Timurid Period II', *Islam. A.*, iii (1988–9), pp. 175–208
Timur and the Princely Vision (exh. cat. by T. W. Lentz and G. D. Lowry, Washington, DC, Sackler Gal.; Los Angeles, CA, Co. Mus. A., 1989)
R. B. Mason and L. Golombek: 'Differentiating Early Chinese-influenced Blue and White Ceramics of Egypt, Syria and Iran', *Archaeometry '90: Proceedings of the 27th International Archaeometry Symposium: Basel, 1990*, pp. 265–74
G. Necipoğlu: 'From International Timurid to Ottoman: A Change of Taste in Sixteenth Century Ceramic Tiles', *Muqarnas*, vii (1990), pp. 136–70
L. Golombek: 'The *Paysage* as Funerary Imagery in the Timurid Period', *Muqarnas*, x (1993), pp. 241–52
L. Golombek, R. B. Mason and G. Bailey: *Tamerlane's Tableware: A New Approach to the Chinoiserie Ceramics of Fifteenth- and Sixteenth-Century Iran* (in preparation)

LISA GOLOMBEK

(ii) Egypt and Syria. Seven types of ceramics developed during the period when the Mamluk sultans (*reg* 1250–1517) dominated the eastern Mediterranean. The most mundane are unglazed ceramics and *sgraffito* and slip-painted wares under mustard, yellow or green glazes. The sumptuous wares painted in lustre over transparent blue or colourless glazes continue traditions established under the Fatimids (*reg* 969–1171; *see* §3(i) above). Three types of underglaze-painted wares imitate Longquan celadons and blue-and-white porcelains from China (*see* CHINA, §VII, 3(v)) and Sultanabad wares from Iran (*see* §(i)(a) above). These seven types, which fall into four broad groups, display marked differences of shape, quality of execution, colour and decoration, dissimilarities that reflect not only the impact of various traditions, both local and foreign, but also varied functions.

(a) Unglazed wares. (b) *Sgraffito* and slip-painted wares. (c) Lustrewares. (d) Underglaze-painted wares.

(a) Unglazed wares. Unglazed moulded wares in a dense buff or yellow–buff paste and related wares of lesser quality with incised motifs or scratched lines belong to the vernacular tradition. Common shapes include utilitarian objects such as pitchers, pilgrim flasks (e.g. Damascus, Mus. N., A1557) and spherical ampoules. Examples have been found and were probably made in Egypt, Syria, Palestine and northern Iraq. The incised wares are difficult to date, but they can be compared to vessels of similar shape in the moulded group. On these the blazons, floral designs, animals, arabesques and calligraphic themes parallel those found on *sgraffito* or slip-painted wares datable from the late 13th century to the 15th.

(b) Sgraffito and slip-painted wares. *Sgraffito* and slip-painted wares account for more than half of the glazed ceramics produced in Egypt, and they have also been found in Syria, along the Red Sea, in the coastal cities of the Byzantine empire and in the Khanate of the Golden Horde. Thrown in a red clay that ranges from loose to compact depending on the surface treatment, these wares share similar shapes and glazes but differ in their decorative techniques and themes. *Sgraffito* wares are decorated with designs incised and/or carved through a thin layer of white slip, with coloured slips to highlight the motifs, under transparent lead glazes in different shades of yellow, brown and occasionally green. Similar glazes are attested on slip-painted wares, except that the patterns are painted

in white, yellow or yellowish-brown slips. Shapes range from bowls with straight or flared foot-rings (a form with local and eastern Mediterranean antecedents) to footless bowls, small jars, and dishes with rounded cavettos and upward-flaring flat rims (a type imitating 13th-century Syrian wares; *see* §3(ii) above). Bowls where the cavetto or body breaks or is redirected upwards or outwards as it rises from the foot are a new shape and appear to have been inspired by imported Cypriot wares of the 12th and 13th centuries. A vessel distinguished by a tall foot-ring supporting a rounded or carinated cavetto was probably made in imitation of 14th-century Mamluk metal shapes (*see* §IV, 3(iii)(a) above).

On *sgraffito* wares the imitation of metal objects is further shown by the division of the surface into concentric bands. These bands are enlivened by calligraphic, floral, geometric and occasionally human and animal designs. The heraldic emblems of the Mamluk military aristocracy also appear, but no examples of composite blazons have so far been recorded, implying that the *sgraffito* wares went out of fashion by c. 1400. The poorly rendered calligraphic designs often state that the object was 'one of the things made for …' followed by the honorific titles of unidentified officials, suggesting that these objects were probably mass-produced to be sold to the households of various amirs. Many vessels bear potters' signatures, especially that of Sharaf al-Abawani (e.g. Washington, DC, Egyp. Embassy, see 1981 exh. cat., no. 95), a practice also found on the underglaze-painted wares.

The formal rendering of the designs on *sgraffito* wares contrasts with the sketchy inscriptions, blazons and foliate and animal motifs on slip-painted vessels. Fleshy, wavering leaves painted with a full brush (e.g. Cairo, Mus. Islam. A., 23438) and animals with a foreshortened front leg recall the styles decorating the ceramics of the Ayyubid period, especially those painted in black under a clear turquoise–green glaze. The motifs and styles on other pieces show similarities to *sgraffito* and underglaze-painted wares of the 14th and 15th centuries, suggesting that the slip-painted wares lasted longer than *sgraffito* wares.

(c) Lustrewares. In contrast to unglazed, *sgraffito* and slip-painted wares, which have clay bodies, lustrewares and underglaze-painted wares have a whitish gritty composite paste. The rarest but also the most costly type has designs painted in lustre over a blue or colourless glaze. Examples have been found in Egypt, along the Red Sea, in the coastal cities of the eastern Mediterranean, in Italy, along the Euphrates and in the Khanate of the Golden Horde. A blue ovoidal jar with olive-green lustre decoration (Kuwait City, Mus. Islam. A., LNS 188C), inscribed 'made for Asad al-Iskandarani, the work of Yusuf in Damascus', identifies the most probable centre of production. From Syria, *albarelli* and ovoidal jars filled with spices were exported throughout the western Mediterranean, and several intact examples have been found in Sicily (see fig. 173), whence these vessels have been known as Siculo-Arabic. They are also mentioned in 14th-century European apothecary lists, and their popularity prompted Valencian potters to copy them, according to a contract dated 1420.

Albarelli, ovoidal jars and dishes continue forms attested in Syria and Egypt since the 12th century. A dish with

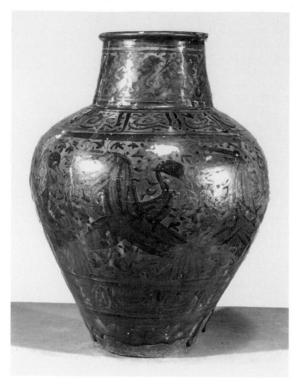

173. Large fritware jar, underglaze-painted in blue, overglaze-painted in golden lustre, h. 381 mm, found at Trapani, Sicily, from ?Damascus, 14th century (London, Victoria and Albert Museum)

steep rounded cavetto rising from a tall base is a familiar shape, first attested on Longquan celadons of the late 13th century and 14th. These vessels are enlivened by calligraphic and animal motifs on a ground of wiry stems and leaves, exemplifying the persistence of earlier styles. Others painted with Chinese-inspired motifs in black-and-blue or blue-and-white suggest that the blue-glazed lustre-painted wares and ones with similar decorative schemes painted in lustre on a clear glaze date from the 13th to the 15th century.

(d) Underglaze-painted wares. Wares underglaze painted in a bichromatic palette, either black-and-blue or blue-and-white, have been found at most Islamic sites between the eastern Mediterranean coast and the Iranian frontier. Wasters found in Fustat and Damascus, Hama and other Syrian cities suggest that these types were produced in several centres and exported as far afield as the Red Sea, the Euphrates, the Byzantine empire and the emerging Turkish beyliks of Anatolia. In the two capitals of the Golden Horde on the Volga, underglaze-painted wares of Mamluk origin as well as those from Ilkhanid Iran have been found beside locally produced vessels, as shown by wasters of both black-and-blue and blue-and-white types. Both Mamluk and Iranian potters copied Chinese originals. Dishes with flat everted rims and a raised ridge at the tip of the lip, deep rounded bowls and other bowls with cavettos rising steeply from a tall narrow foot-ring and often ending in an inverted rim are first attested on Longquan celadons and blue-and-white porcelains of the

Yuan dynasty (reg 1279–1368). Other shapes from Egypt and Syria, however, continued local traditions. The sombre bichromatic black-and-blue palette is occasionally enriched by the use of a deep-red colour, descended from the three-colour 'Rusafa' wares of the earlier period, or by a green pigment under a greenish transparent glaze. The same designs are sometimes interpreted in a black palette under a green glaze or in manganese under a clear one, the latter reminiscent of North African colour schemes. On most examples the surface is divided into panels of various shapes that can be aligned differently, although on several complete and fragmentary objects the outside of the vessel is treated as a unified space. The two-dimensional aspect of the composition is strengthened by the linear rendering of the motifs.

Among the earliest examples are those pieces decorated with a lozenge formed out of four dots next to angular scrolls, cursive inscriptions and animal figures usually on a plain ground. A chronological framework is provided by an albarello (Naples, Capodimonte) dated 717/1317 and a fragment (Cairo, Mus. Islam. A.) inscribed 'the year [seven hundred and] forty-five' (AD 1344–5), suggesting that this type began to be produced c. 1300. Contemporary with this group is another decorated with radiating panels and designs on a hatched ground (e.g. Damascus, Mus. N., A5356), a design found also on early 14th-century manuscripts of the Koran. This group is the first to show motifs of Chinese derivation, such as the phoenix, peony and lotus, as well as the typical shape of blue-and-white porcelains, a dish with inverted rim. This type was introduced c. 1300, and production continued throughout the century.

A third group is characterized by the unified spatial treatment of the surface. Stemmed cups, trees, fish, horses, lotus flowers, inscriptions and even Christian themes are depicted on a ground of arrow-shaped leaves and outlined in black on either a white or a grey slip, often rendered in relief. Several fragments are dated [7]44 or [7]45 (AD 1343–5), arrow-shaped leaves also appear on metalwares dated to the third reign (1309–40) of the Mamluk sultan al-Nasir Muhammad, and the shapes have parallels with Chinese blue-and-white imports. This type originated in the second quarter of the 14th century and extended into the second half of the century. On vessels with a turquoise or sage-green pigment, the designs are more sketchy, and this rather coarse type can be dated to the late 14th century or the 15th, as the same green hue is found on several vessels inspired by early 15th-century Chinese blue-and-white porcelains. The blue-and-black palette apparently continued to be used even after the more luminous blue-and-white colour scheme was introduced.

The blue-and-white colour scheme was inspired by Chinese porcelains that began to reach the Near and Middle East in the second half of the 14th century. The widespread popularity of chinoiserie makes it difficult to identify the centres of production, but differences in body, glaze and painterly modes and the presence of signatures (attested only on Syro-Egyptian pieces) allow the material to be grouped regionally. Wasters from Fustat and Damascus testify to the manufacture of blue-and-white imitations in both regions. Although Syrian products have a whiter, finer and more compact body, wares from the two areas share colour schemes, motifs and styles. They were exported to the Volga, southern Italy, the coast of Asia Minor, Iraq, the Red Sea coast and the Yemen.

Although the shapes of these Far Eastern imports are varied and their motifs plentiful, few imports were copied until *c.* 1400. Apart from dishes with foliate or inverted bevelled rims, other forms are local, and the widespread use of wall tiles (*see* §II, 9(ii)(b) above) is also without Chinese precedent. The earliest Mamluk imitations of Chinese wares are those that copy Yuan linear styles in the outline-and-wash technique (e.g. vases dated 1351, Copenhagen, Davids Saml.) and use such Chinese motifs as the lotus pond, the spiked lobed leaf, waves, classic scrolls, diaper patterns, cloud-collar motifs and dragons without the admixture of Islamic elements (see fig. 174). On several vessels Yuan designs with rocky landscapes, flower sprays or doubled fruits are combined with composite scrolls of Ming origin and rendered in styles paralleled only on the tiles from the mosque of Ghars al-Din al-Tawrizi in Damascus (1423) and those from the mosque of Murad II in Edirne (1435–6). From this point Islamic patterns such as ewers or winding sprays embracing trees are depicted in conjunction with Chinese motifs in either a blue-and-white or a blue-and-black palette in a linear style of Yuan origin or in quick brushstrokes without tonal variations. Workshops of potters re-emerged, and they can be identified by signatures inside the foot-ring. The finely potted vessels decorated in an eclectic manner can be ascribed to the studios of GHAYBI, 'Ajami and Ustad al-Misri. From the mid-15th century, potter–painters slowly began to free themselves from the Chinese hold, choosing motifs and styles from a variety of Chinese and Islamic sources. Chinese motifs might be painted in a multicoloured palette of blue, black, green and red, while Islamic motifs could be rendered in blue. Many vessels decorated in this multicoloured palette are not as finely potted as those signed by the masters and are bigger, coarser and decorated in quick brushstrokes reminiscent of Italian maiolica or contemporary Spanish wares.

174. Blue-and-white fritware dish, diam. 335 mm, from Syria, 15th century (New York, Madina private collection)

BIBLIOGRAPHY

G. C. Pier: 'Saracenic Heraldry in Ceramic Decoration', *Bull. Met.*, iii (1903), pp. 8–11
A. Abel: *Gaibi et les grands faïenciers égyptiens d'époque mamelouke* (Cairo, 1930)
A. Bahgat and F. Massoul: *La Céramique musulmane de l'Egypte* (Cairo, 1930)
J. Sauvaget: *Poteries syro-mésopotamiennes du 14e siècle* (Paris, 1932)
R. L. Hobson: 'A Fourteenth-century Egyptian Albarello', *BM Q.*, ix (1934), pp. 51–2
L. A. Mayer: 'Huit objets inédits à blasons mamluks en Grèce et en Turquie', *Mél. Maspéro*, iii, Mém.: Inst. Fr. Archéol. Orient. Caire (1940), pp. 97–104
J. Sauvaget: 'Tessons de Rakka', *A. Islam.*, xiii–xiv (1948), pp. 31–45
J. Lacam: 'La Céramique au Musée des Arts Décoratifs', *Faenza*, xxxvii (1951), pp. 98–104
M. A. Marzouk: 'Three Signed Specimens of Mamluk Pottery from Alexandria', *A. Orient.*, ii (1957), pp. 497–501
V. Poulsen and E. Hammershaimb: *Les Fouilles de Hama, 1931–38: Les verreries et poteries médiévales* (Copenhagen, 1957)
M. A. Marzouk: 'Egyptian Sgraffito Ware Excavated at Kom-ed-Dikka in Alexandria', *Bull. Fac. A.* [Alexandria], xiii (1959), pp. 3–23
M. A. al-'Ush: 'Namathij min al-khazaf al-'arabiyya al-islāmiyya fī'l-mathaf al-watanī bi Dimishq' [Examples of Arab Islamic ceramics in the National Museum, Damascus], *Al Ma'rifa* (1963), pp. 103–11
J. Carswell: 'A Fourteenth-century Chinese Porcelain Dish from Damascus', *American University of Beirut Festival Book*, ed. F. Sarruf and S. Tamim (Beirut, 1966), pp. 39–52
A. 'Abd al-Raziq: 'Documents sur la poterie d'époque mamelouke: Sharaf Al Abawani', *An. Islam.*, vii (1967), pp. 21–32
W. B. Kubiak: 'Overseas Pottery Trade of Medieval Alexandria as Shown by Recent Archaeological Discoveries: A Preliminary Communication', *Fol. Orient.*, x (1969), pp. 5–30
——: 'Medieval Ceramic Oil Lamps from Fustat', *A. Orient.*, viii (1970), pp. 1–18
T. Rayhanli: 'Türk ve Islam Eserleri Müzesinde Bulunan Memluk Keramikleri' [Mamluk ceramics in the Museum of Turkish and Islamic Art], *Sanat Tarihi Yıllığı*, iv (1970–71), pp. 215–35
A. H. S. Megaw: 'Excavations at "Saranda Kolones", Paphos', *Rep. Dept Ant., Cyprus* (1971), pp. 117–46
G. T. Scanlon: 'Fustat Mounds: A Shard Count, 1968', *Archaeology*, xxiv (1971), pp. 220–33
J. Carswell: 'Six Tiles', *Islamic Art in the Metropolitan Museum of Art*, ed. R. Ettinghausen (New York, 1972), pp. 99–125
M. Meinecke: 'Zur mamlukischen Heraldik', *Mitt. Dt. Archäol. Inst.: Abt. Kairo*, ii (1972), pp. 213–65
K. Toueir: 'Céramiques mameloukes à Damas', *Bull. Etud. Orient.*, xxvi (1973), pp. 209–17
B. Gray: 'The Export of Chinese Porcelain to the Islamic World: Some Reflections on its Significance for Islamic Art before 1400', *Trans. Orient. Cer. Soc.*, lxi (1975–7), pp. 231–61
M. Meinecke: 'Die mamlukischen Fayencemosaikdekorationen: Eine Werkstätte aus Tabriz in Kairo (1330–1350)', *Kst Orients*, xi (1976–7), pp. 85–144
G. T. Scanlon: 'Some Mamluk Ceramic Shapes from Fustat: "Sgraff" and "Slip"', *Islam Archaeol. Stud.*, ii (1980), pp. 59–147
Renaissance of Islam: Art of the Mamluks (exh. cat by E. Atil, Washington, DC, N. Mus. Nat. Hist.; Minneapolis, MN, Inst. A.; New York, Met.; and elsewhere, 1981), pp. 146–92
H. Philon: 'A Mamluk Deposition from the Cross', *Graeco-Arabica*, ii (1983), pp. 265–74
M. Jenkins: 'Mamluk Underglaze-painted Pottery: Foundations for Future Study', *Muqarnas*, ii (1984), pp. 95–114
G. T. Scanlon: 'Mamluk Pottery: More Evidence from Fustat', *Muqarnas*, ii (1984), pp. 115–26
H. Philon: 'Thessaloniki, Andalusia and the Golden Horde', *Balkan Stud.* (1985)
Blue and White Chinese Porcelain and its Impact on the Western World (exh. cat. by J. Carswell, U. Chicago, IL, Smart Gal., 1985)

HELEN PHILON

175. Blue-and-white fritware charger, diam. 445 mm, from Iznik, *c.* 1480 (The Hague, Haags Gemeentemuseum)

(iii) Anatolia. The production of ceramic vessels continued to be a minor art during the rule of the Turkoman principalities (*see* BEYLIK) from the 13th to the 15th century, when architectural revetments in glazed tile (*see* §II, 9(ii)(b) above) were more important. The typical ceramic vessel is an unpretentious earthenware. The most widespread type is Miletus ware, so called because quantities of it were excavated at Balat, ancient Miletos, but subsequent excavations showed that Iznik was the major site of production, although Kütahya and Akcaalan near Ezine were other centres. Produced throughout the 15th century, these wares were potted in a coarse red clay covered with a white slip and painted usually in blue or green under a clear lead glaze. The typical convex bowl or deep dish (e.g. Bursa, Mus. Turk. & Islam. A., 2659) has a centralized design of fish decorated with spirals.

Towards the end of the 15th century Anatolian potters began to produce ceramics (see fig. 175) with a hard and dense frit body covered with a brilliant white slip and painted in cobalt blue under a transparent lead-fluxed glaze, which shows no tendency to crackle and little tendency to pool. These blue-and-white ceramics are of a technical standard unmatched in the Islamic world since the fritwares produced at Kashan in Iran in the early 13th century (*see* §3 (iii)(c) above) and are often quite large, some chargers measuring over 400 mm in diameter. Numerous kiln sites have been discovered in Iznik and its environs. The earliest of these ceramics (*c.* 1480), decorated with elaborate arabesques and floral scrolls in cobalt blue reserved on white, are known by such misleading modern names as Abraham of Kütahya ware after an atypical ewer (1510; London, BM, G.1983.1) and Baba Nakkaş ware after the painter in the court studio of the Ottoman sultan Mehmed II (*reg* 1441–81 with interruption). Although these wares were inspired by Chinese blue-and-white porcelains, the designs on the interiors are an Ottoman variation of the International Timurid style (see fig. 172 above) in which the languid rhythms of the prototype have been transformed into a forceful design with a greater sense of three-dimensionality and a more intense and contained quality. Despite the decorative origins of these exquisite wares, they are technically distinct not only from contemporary Iranian ceramics but also from contemporary tile revetments, such as those on the Fatih Mosque or the Çinili Kiosk at Istanbul (*see* ISTANBUL, §III, 9 and 13(ii)). The technology to make these vessels was probably an invention of Anatolian potters, who were encouraged by the expanded patronage of the Ottoman court at Istanbul to produce the finest wares of the 16th century (*see* §5(i) below).

BIBLIOGRAPHY

F. Sarre: 'Die Keramik der islamischen Zeit', *Das islamische Milet*, ed. K. Wulzinger and P. Wittek (Berlin, 1935)
K. Otto-Dorn: *Das islamische Iznik* (Berlin, 1941)
O. Aslanapa: *Türkische Fliesen und Keramik in Anatolien* (Istanbul, 1965)
——: 'Pottery and Kilns from the Iznik Excavations', *Forschungen zur Kunst Asiens in Memoriam Kurt Erdmann* (Istanbul, 1969), pp. 140–46
The Anatolian Civilisations III: Seljuk/Ottoman (exh. cat., 18th Council of Europe exh.; Istanbul, 1983), D.92–D.94
O. Aslanapa: 'Iznik çini firinlari 1985 çalismalari' [Ceramic kilns excavated at Iznik in 1985], *VIII. kazi sonuçlari toplantisi*, ii (Ankara, 1986), pp. 315–34
N. Atasoy and J. Raby: *Iznik: The Pottery of Ottoman Turkey* (London, 1989)

(iv) Spain and North Africa. The major development in this period was the florescence of the ceramic industry at MÁLAGA. Ceramics had been produced there from the 10th century and lustre-painted earthenwares from the early 13th, but under the patronage of the Nasrid sultans of Granada (*reg* 1230–1492), Málaga became the major centre of ceramic production, and its products were exported throughout Europe. Production there ceased abruptly some time before the mid-15th century, but continued elsewhere under Christian patronage, especially in Valencia (*see* CERAMICS, colour pl. IV, fig. 3 and SPAIN, §VII, 1). Nevertheless, the memory of Málaga persisted in the common European term maiolica, the original Italian name for lustreware. In North Africa, despite the importance of glazed-tile revetments (*see* §II, 9(ii)(c) above), glazed ceramic vessels seem to have been relatively uninspired. For example, a small spherical jar (13th–14th century; Paris, Mus. N. A. Afr. & Océan., 1967.3.1) found at Sidi Kacem in Morocco has pseudo-epigraphic decoration in green and brown applied without slip or glaze.

Nasrid lustrewares are characterized by a yellowish-amber lustre with a pronounced iridescence and a limited repertory of designs. The Malagan technique of using fluxed pigments has a tendency to overfiring, in which the clay medium adheres to the glaze and dulls the metallic film. Compared to the finest Kashan lustrewares, the painting is coarse and loose, although the best pieces are more elegant and their great size shows enormous skill in firing. For example, the Fortuny Tablet (Madrid, Inst. Valencia Don Juan), named after the painter Mariano Fortuny y Madrazo who purchased it in the Albaicín quarter of Granada in the mid-19th century, is a single slab (1.08×0.63 m) with a carpet-like design of a central field with arabesques and swan, peacock and dragon heads surrounded by a rectangular border with cartouches inscribed with the name of Yusuf III (*reg* 1407–17). Typical bowls (e.g. London, V&A, 486-1864; diam. 508 mm) have a conical profile and raised rim; they are decorated in a coppery-brown lustre, often with scenes of ships.

The best-known ceramics of the period are the Alhambra vases, so called because several were found in the Alhambra at Granada in the 18th century. The largest lustreware pots ever produced (average h. 1.25 m), they are all shaped like amphorae with a narrow base, swelling body, sloping shoulder, ribbed neck and broad flat handles shaped like wings. The ten surviving examples can be assigned to two groups. The first, characterized by a bulbous shape, short neck, bold angular inscriptions in a wide central register and monochrome lustre, can be dated to the late 13th century or early 14th (e.g. Palermo, Gal. Reg. Sicilia, 5229). The second, more elongated and elegant in shape, with a narrow band of cursive script and additional decoration in cobalt blue or gilding, can be dated to the late 14th century or early 15th. Several of the earlier examples (e.g. St Petersburg, Hermitage, F.317) have depictions of a stylized hand on the handles, an apotropaic device. Two of the later examples (Granada, Mus. N. A. Hispanomusulmán; see fig. 176; Washington, DC, Freer) include the depiction of confronted gazelles on the body. In shape these jars represent the culmination of a tradition of large unglazed earthenware jars to store and serve water, but the practical function of these elephantine luxury objects is unclear.

BIBLIOGRAPHY
A. W. Frothingham: *Lusterware of Spain* (New York, 1951)
R. Ettinghausen: 'Notes on the Lusterware of Spain', *A. Orient.*, i (1954), pp. 133–56
M. Olagnier-Riottot: 'Etude d'un vase des XIIIe/XIVe siècles trouvé dans la région de Sidi Kacem', *Hespéris*, ix (1968), pp. 229–32
B. Martínez Caviró: *La loza dorada* (Madrid, 1983)
A. Caiger-Smith: *Lustre Pottery: Technique, Tradition and Innovation in Islam and the Western World* (London, 1985)
S. S. Kenesson: 'Nasrid Luster Pottery: The Alhambra Vases', *Muqarnas*, ix (1992), pp. 93–115
G. Rosselló Bordoy: 'The Ceramics of al-Andalus', *Al-Andalus: The Art of Islamic Spain* (exh. cat., ed. J. D. Dodds; Granada, Alhambra; New York, Met., 1992), pp. 97–105 and 354–61

176. Earthenware Alhambra vase, overglaze-painted in lustre, h. 1.35 m, from Málaga, late 14th century or early 15th (Granada, Museo Nacional de Arte Hispanomusulmán)

5. *c*. 1500 AND AFTER. In this period underglaze-painted ceramics supplanted the overglaze-painted wares popular in the earlier periods. The 16th century was the heyday of ceramic production in the Ottoman empire, when Iznik became the major centre and a distinctive Ottoman type of ceramics was developed there. In Iran, Chinese wares continued to be popular and to inspire local production. North Africa revived as a centre of ceramic production with the influx of refugee potters from Spain.

(i) Eastern Mediterranean lands. (ii) Iran. (iii) North Africa.

(i) Eastern Mediterranean lands. In the lands under the control of the Ottoman dynasty (*reg* 1281–1924) after *c*. 1500, ceramics continued to be used for tableware and architectural decoration, but tiles became increasingly important and underglaze-painted fritwares supplanted earthenwares for all ceramics of artistic pretension. The great bulk of ceramic production continued to be simple wares made for local use, but the major centres of production prospered after *c*. 1500 as improvements in long-distance trade and unprecedented market demand made trade in these expensive and attractive products more practicable, despite their fragility. Ottoman ceramics therefore form part of an artistic environment that includes the Mediterranean to the west and the Islamic world to the east and south. Ceramics were a means by which artistic ideas were transmitted from one medium and region to another. They were an important basis for middle-class patronage of the arts and a barometer of artistic preferences and taste, especially with regard to the continuing fascination in the Islamic world with the ceramic arts of China.

(a) Introduction. (b) Experimentation, *c*. 1500–*c*. 1555. (c) Mass production, *c*. 1555–*c*. 1600. (d) Decline and diffusion, *c*. 1600 and after.

(a) Introduction. The use of an artificial ceramic body, the development of underglaze-painting and tin glazes,

and the fascination with Chinese porcelain all affected the production of fine tablewares in the Ottoman empire from the 15th to the 17th century. These changes had profound effects on both style and the organization of production: not only did they make it possible for ceramic decoration to imitate styles of book painting and illumination (*see* §III, 4(vi)(e) above), but they also allowed for a division of labour among those who created the shapes, applied the slip, drew the designs and coloured the outlines. The production of fine ceramics in later Islamic times is often associated with court design workshops and almost always shows the impact of other media, especially painting. It therefore exhibits the same blurring of the borders of the genre that had been a characteristic of ceramic art since Classical Greek times.

By 1500, experiments in the Turkoman realms of northwest Iran and in the city of Iznik in north-west Anatolia had led to the production of blue-and-white ceramics (*see* §4(iii), fig. 175 above and CERAMICS, colour pl. IV, fig. 1) imitating the porcelains exported to Middle Eastern markets in large quantities from China under the Ming dynasty (*reg* 1368–1644; *see* CHINA, §VII, 3(vi)). The addition of ground flint or quartz and frit to white potters' clay, a process already used successfully in Iran in the 12th century (*see* §3(iii)(c) above), produced an artificial white body akin to the strong, white and translucent porcelain. Potters often enhanced the whiteness of this material by coating the body of a vessel with an even whiter slip to which tin oxide had been added. On this white surface, which had analogies to paper as well as porcelain, ceramic artists painted designs in the familiar cobalt blue as well as a range of colours, including ochre, purple, olive, green, turquoise, red, yellow and black. The development of a transparent, almost colourless glaze, incorporating a lead flux to enhance its melting properties, allowed the design to be covered with a thin, glassy coating that protected the decoration while enhancing its visual properties.

The traditional barrier between tablewares and tile revetment had already begun to crumble in the 13th century with the development of lustre painting in Iran, but after *c.* 1500 the new underglaze technique resulted in the use of shiny white-ground tiles in architectural revetment, often as accents in a field of monochrome turquoise or dark-blue tiles. Since underglaze painting is close technically and conceptually to book painting, calligraphy and illumination, the technological developments in ceramic centres forged a closer bond between the arts of design and those of architectural decoration in the Ottoman empire. Indeed, the dissolution of the boundaries between ceramics and book painting is one of the outstanding technical and artistic accomplishments of Ottoman ceramic art.

Iznik seems to have been the major centre of ceramic production from the 15th to the 17th century; nevertheless, the tortuous history of scholarship concerning Ottoman ceramics has resulted in a peculiar and often misleading terminology. For example, sherds of the early and simple wares of 15th-century Iznik were excavated on the site of ancient Miletos and were consequently known as Miletus ware. Early blue-and-white wares were once ascribed to kilns run by the Armenian community at nearby Kütahya, because two examples bear Armenian inscriptions mentioning that city. One, a ewer (1510; London, BM, G. 1983.1), names the donor, a certain Abraham of Kütahya; the other, a fragmentary waterbottle (1529; London, BM, G. 1983.118), states that it was ordered there as a gift for a monastery in Ankara. Golden Horn wares, another group of blue-and-white wares from Iznik bearing designs of tight vine spirals, were once ascribed to the potteries of the Golden Horn, the inner Istanbul harbour. Damascus wares, fine tablewares decorated with an exceptional palette of grey–green, turquoise and pale purple produced briefly in the second quarter of the 16th century, were once ascribed to Damascus, where some poorer wares in the same palette were produced in the late 16th century. Finally, the splendid polychrome wares mass-produced in Iznik were long ascribed to Rhodes. Provincial variations of Iznik wares were indeed made at Rhodes as well as Kütahya, Damascus, Diyarbakır, Jerusalem and in the Balkans, but these misleading placenames have generally been abandoned in favour of chronological typologies. An overview of the vast numbers of surviving wares shows not only the historical evolution of various groups of pottery, reflecting both technical developments and the history of taste, but also the stylistic identities of particular workshops within Iznik.

The succession of stylistic groups shows that the production of Ottoman ceramics was dynamic and open to technical experimentation and stylistic change. The assumption of a historical sequence among technical groups, however, is not entirely valid; the market demand for blue-and-white objects continued long after the development of brilliant polychromy in Iznik (e.g. a blue-and-white dish with foliate rim, *c.* 1575; Ecouen, Mus. Ren., Cl. 8326), and the diversity of both the production centre and the market-place meant that different stylistic groups were produced side by side throughout the 16th century.

The popularity of Iznik pottery is attested not only by the thousands of surviving examples and their continued weighty presence in the art market, but also by evidence of export throughout the period of production. Excavations from Fustat (Old Cairo) in Egypt to York Minster in Britain have yielded sherds of Ottoman pottery. As objects of the sincerest form of flattery, Iznik wares left their impact on the contemporary ceramic production of Kirman and Tabriz, Damascus and Cairo, Valencia and Padua.

(b) Experimentation, c. 1500–c. 1555. By 1500 the fledgling Ottoman ceramic workshops at Iznik had begun to produce fine ceramic wares that eventually reached a level of astonishing variety, quality and volume. Iznik had been a centre for production of simple pottery since Byzantine times: deposits of potters' clay were available locally, and the abundant wood of the Bithynian forests fuelled the kilns. Proximity to the established trade routes across north-west Anatolia and to the new Ottoman capital at Istanbul brought kilns, artists and prosperity to Iznik in the 16th century. Ceramic artisans of Iznik began experimenting with the challenge of imitating Chinese porcelain before 1500. The body of their early work was strikingly dense and heavy, and was close in weight and colour (if not in hardness and translucency) to the much admired Chinese prototypes. The shapes used by the early Iznik

experimenters include small ewers with dragon-like handles (e.g. the Abraham of Kütahya ewer), covered pots and dishes with cusped rims. These shapes were derived from porcelain and metalwork prototypes, and the decorative motifs employed were derived either directly from Chinese art or indirectly through the international Timurid style of the 15th century, with its reliance on intertwining and interpenetrating vines, split-leaf motifs (Turk. *rumi*) and leaves that fold over each other. Outstanding examples show the application of Islamic designs to vessels with shapes of Chinese porcelain (e.g. a charger, *c.* 1510; Paris, Louvre, 7449) and 15th-century Islamic metalwork.

Ottoman potters invented an original form of decoration consisting of tight spiralling dark-blue whorls with tiny flowers and leaves, which also recalls the illumination of monograms that introduced imperial Ottoman decrees (*see* TUGHRA). Such pieces, the so-called Golden Horn ware, show a delicacy of decoration in sharp contrast to the traditional shapes and robust potting. Some of the best examples include a charger (*c.* 1525–35; Kuwait City, Mus. Islam. A., LNS 231C) and a bowl (*c.* 1530–40; London, V&A, 790-1905). This style persisted after a black outlining pigment was introduced *c.* 1525, and some of the largest and finest masterpieces of this later variation include huge footed bowls (see fig. 177 and CERAMICS, colour pl. IV, fig. 1) and large, long-necked bottles (h. 430 mm; London, BM, 78.12-30.519).

The potential of this new medium of underglaze-painted fritware was recognized immediately. As early as the first quarter of the 16th century, tentative steps were made to break into the market for architectural decoration, and Iznik potters created a new palette of warm turquoise and then black (used for outlining), grey-green and pale-purple underglaze pigments, although the green and purple were rarely used in tilework. They also expanded their stylistic repertory to include developments in the arts of the book at the court design workshop in Istanbul. Two trends in the court style had a great impact: a sinuous leaf and arabesque (Turk. *saz*) and a vocabulary of flowers cultivated in the Ottoman empire, including carnations, tulips, hyacinths, honeysuckles and rosebuds. For example, a fragmentary deep dish with foliate rim showing a bird among sinuous foliage (*c.* 1530; Vienna, Österreich. Mus. Angewandte Kst, OR 788) is extraordinarily close to a set of huge tiles painted in cobalt blue and turquoise, now affixed to the Circumcision Room of Topkapı Palace in Istanbul. The exquisitely detailed execution suggests that the artist who applied the coloured pigments was probably the same individual who created the cartoon.

Surviving documents indicate that from the outset the fine pottery of Iznik was very expensive, with a single tile selling for more than five times the daily wage of a skilled craftsman and tablewares bringing even higher prices. Although nominally destined for table use, Iznik wares were apparently regarded primarily as objects for visual display and enjoyment, and not as cheaper or theologically more acceptable substitutes for tablewares of precious metal. Iznik potters quickly began to expand their markets, not only into architectural decoration but into the traditional domains of glass and metalwares as well. By 1520 potters were creating a variety of shapes. Large vessels in the shape of traditional glass mosque lamps were used for

177. Large footed fritware bowl with spiral decoration, underglaze-painted, h. 280 mm, diam. 425 mm, from Iznik, *c.* 1545 (London, Victoria and Albert Museum)

symbolic purposes in mosques, tombs and shrines (e.g. a set of four lamps from the tomb of Bayezid II (*d* 1512); Istanbul, Topkapı Pal. Mus., Çinili Köşk, 41/3–6). Unusual forms include a penbox (*c.* 1510; London, BM, G. 1983.7), traditionally made of painted wood or inlaid metal.

At the same time that the palette was extended, Iznik artisans began to fall under the spell of the style of illumination taking form at the court workshops in Istanbul. Many of the acknowledged masterpieces of Ottoman ceramics were created during this period, when designers often disregarded the natural zones dictated by the shape of the vessel and covered traditional shapes with designs that flow from the centre of the plate over the cavetto and rim (see fig. 178). This tondo painting imposed on a tableware form serves as a paradigm of the new style. Designs invariably have a top and bottom; the large size and great expense of these wares also suggest that they were intended primarily for display and decoration and not for eating. Some particularly magnificent objects, such as a plate painted in black, two blues, green and pale purple (USA, priv. col.; see Atasoy and Raby, fig. 352), show the collaboration of court artists in the production of tablewares; other objects show a division of labour among artisans.

(c) Mass production, c. 1555–c. 1600. The creation by the early 1560s of a brilliant green and the famous Iznik red, a pigment composed of red clay that stood up in relief under the clear transparent glaze, ushered in the most brilliant period in the history of Iznik ceramics, when the workshops mass-produced thousands of tiles for imperial Ottoman buildings, private foundations, residences (*see* TILE, colour pl. IV, fig. 1) and provincial architectural projects, as well as vast numbers of technically masterful and colourful tablewares in a variety of shapes and decorative schemes. The precise dates known for tile revetments allow a relative chronology to be established

178. Deep fritware dish with foliate rim, underglaze-painted, diam. 370 mm, from Iznik, c. 1545 (London, Victoria and Albert Museum)

179. Polychrome fritware plate with cypress and flowers and wave-and-foam border, underglaze-painted, diam. 291 mm, from Iznik, c. 1575 (Washington, DC, Freer Gallery of Art)

for technically and stylistically similar tablewares. The introduction of the red pigment can be dated with some precision, for it first appeared on the tile revetment of the qibla wall of the Süleymaniye Mosque (1550–57; see

ISTANBUL, §III, 10). A lamp reputed to have been made for the mosque (c. 1557; London, V&A, 131-1885) is a rare early example using red and black as ground colours.

The uneven application of red seen on the lamp was soon corrected, and examples from c. 1560 to c. 1575 show complete technical mastery, although the cobalt blue and green occasionally ran into the glaze. This mature style is exemplified by a group of polychrome plates, bottles, pitchers, tankards, jars and covered bowls decorated with bouquets of charming stylized flowers and occasionally birds, often with a heavily stylized wave-and-foam border of tight black spirals separated at intervals by a host of arbitrary shapes in blue outline (see fig. 179). Traditional designs were also realized for a short time in novel palettes: several pieces datable c. 1560–75 are painted in black, white and other colours on a coloured slip that ranges from soft lavender (e.g. a plate, Kuwait City, Mus. Islam. A., LNS 323 C) through pale blue (e.g. a plate, Ecouen, Mus. Ren., Cl. 8549) to salmon red (e.g. a dish, London, BM, 78.12-30.493).

Documentary evidence shows that the Iznik workshops preferred producing ceramic wares for sale on the open market to executing royal tile commissions pegged to an artificially low price. A royal decree sent to Iznik in 1585 demanded that the ceramic workshops cease producing tablewares for the market and turn their energies instead to making tiles for the palace in Istanbul. The thriving trade between the Ottoman empire and the West meant that the new wares quickly found foreign as well as domestic markets. High prices led to imitation Iznik wares and tiles being made in Italy and Hungary as well as in such Ottoman provincial centres as Diyarbakır and Damascus. Syria became a centre for the tile industry, and its wares are distinguishable by a distinctive green, the absence of red, a thick glaze with a tendency to crackle and three cockspur marks on the centre of dishes (e.g. a deep bowl, diam. 330 mm; London, BM, ex-Godman priv. col.). Nevertheless, Iznik remained the most important centre of production and seems to have been responsible exclusively for royal commissions; much of the raw material used was brought from Karahisar and other mining centres, some quite far from Iznik.

The concept of a matched set of tableware hardly existed in Ottoman pottery. Each work, despite general stylistic similarities to other works that may indicate a common origin or artist or general dependence on a model or even a cartoon, is in its execution an individual freehand object. Exceptions occur in matched sets of mosque lamps made for particular buildings (e.g. those from the tomb of Bayezid II), and in works made to order for foreign patrons. For example, a dispersed set of at least two large and eight small shallow dishes (e.g. Lisbon, Fund. Gulbenkian; Iznik, Archaeol. Mus.; London, BM; Sèvres, Mus. N. Cér.) bears the coat of arms of an anonymous Italian or Italo-Dalmatian client. This contrast with the strict uniformity demanded by tile production emphasizes the diversity and adaptability of the Iznik manufactories and the ability of many individual artists to work jointly under the direction of a master for large royal commissions and independently for the market in tablewares.

(d) Decline and diffusion, c. 1600 and after. The quality and quantity of Iznik production began to decline gradually during the 17th century. Due to strict government control of the price of tiles, which were executed under royal order, the Iznik kilns were evidently forced to produce large royal commissions at a financial loss; fires in the Iznik potters' quarter and the cumulative effects of silicosis and lead poisoning probably also contributed to the decline of production. Ceramic production, especially the manufacture of architectural tiles, seems to have served almost as a symbolic barometer of government power through its public or semi-public patronage, a fact that probably explains the broad revival of the classical Ottoman style sponsored by the court in the early 18th century. This included a short-lived attempt to resurrect the royal ceramic workshops by moving them to a site near the ruined Byzantine palace of Tekfur Saray on the Istanbul city walls.

Also in the 18th century the kilns of Kütahya, long a secondary centre of ceramic production, began to produce pretty polychrome underglaze-painted wares in considerable quantity. A polylobed censer with polychrome decoration (Cincinnati, OH, A. Mus., 1952.272) bears an Armenian inscription stating that it was made in 1176 (AD 1726–7), presumably at Kütahya. In the 20th century Kütahya wares have not been held in very high artistic esteem, but they do mark a continuation of the Ottoman ceramic tradition of underglaze-painted pottery. The sizeable Armenian population of Kütahya introduced into the Ottoman decorative vocabulary a range of Christian figural subjects (e.g. a wine-bowl signed by Toros with Christ flanked by the 12 Apostles; diam. 200 mm; Athens, Benaki Mus., 7649), and widespread social changes led to the emergence of a new type of ware, the bowl-like coffee-cup and saucer (e.g. New York, Met., 06.388a-b), to serve the needs of the many coffee-houses that became a common Ottoman institution. By the 19th century Kütahya commercial production also began to decline, but royal Ottoman patronage of ceramics returned with the establishment of a porcelain manufactory at Yıldız near Istanbul in 1894. Despite the use of some Islamic motifs and patterns, Yıldız porcelain remained a provincial version of European royal porcelain manufactured in the same period (e.g. a porcelain coffee-service with polychrome and gold decoration; *c.* 1895; Istanbul, Topkapı Pal. Mus., 16/437-68).

Local pottery traditions such as that of Çanakkale on the Dardanelles enjoyed a brief vogue during the 19th century, and an equally brief Neo-classical surge in Ottoman architecture in the last quarter of the 19th century brought about a limited revival at Kütahya and other centres of tiles in eclectic versions of early styles. Provincial Ottoman cousins and descendants of the Iznik tradition continued to be produced in the Balkans, the Aegean, Syria, Palestine and Egypt well into the 20th century, despite the inroads made by cheap European tablewares. In addition to this remarkable persistence of artistic memory within the Ottoman empire, Iznik techniques and styles were adopted by major studio potters of 19th-century western Europe (e.g. Joseph Théodore Deck, William De Morgan and E. Lachenal) and by ceramic and glass-making factories (e.g. Zsolnay Ceramics Factory in Hungary, Minton Ceramic Factory in England, J. & L. Lobmeyr in Austria, Longwy in Belgium and Cantagalli in Italy). Iznik pottery has been imitated in the 20th century from Morocco to Japan, and its motifs continue to inspire designers for almost all decorative media from textiles to wallpaper.

BIBLIOGRAPHY

R. Anhegger: 'Quellen zur osmanischen Keramik', in K. Otto-Dorn, *Das islamische Iznik* (Berlin, 1941), pp. 165–95

A. Lane: 'The Ottoman Pottery of Isnik', *A. Orient.*, ii (1956), pp. 247–81

K. Otto-Dorn: *Türkische Keramik* (Ankara, 1957)

K. Erdmann: 'Neue Arbeiten zur türkischen Keramik', *A. Orient.*, v (1963), pp. 191–219

T. Öz: *Turkish Ceramics* (Ankara, 1964)

O. Aslanapa: *Türkische Fliesen und Keramik in Anatolien* (Istanbul, 1965)

J. Carswell and C. J. F. Dowsett: *Kütahya Tiles and Pottery from the Armenian Cathedral of St James, Jerusalem*, 2 vols (Oxford, 1972)

S. Yetkin: *Anadolu'da Türk çini sanatının gelişmesi* [Development of Turkish tile art in Anatolia] (Istanbul, 1972, rev. 1986)

W. Denny: 'Islamic Blue and White Pottery on Chinese Themes', *Bull. Mus. F.A., Boston*, lxxi (1974), pp. 76–99

——: *The Ceramics of the Mosque of Rüstem Pasha* (New York and London, 1977)

J. Raby: 'Diyarbekir: A Rival to Iznik', *Istanbul. Mitt.*, xxvii (1977–8), pp. 429–59

W. Denny: 'Ceramics', *Turkish Art*, ed. E. Atıl (Washington, DC, and New York, 1980), pp. 239–98

——: 'Turkish Ceramics and Turkish Painting: The Role of the Paper Cartoon in Turkish Ceramic Production', *Essays in Islamic Art and Architecture in Honor of Katharina Otto-Dorn*, ed. A. Daneshvari (Malibu, 1981), pp. 29–36

J. Raby and Ü. Yücel: 'Blue-and-white, Celadon, and White Ware: Iznik's Debt to China', *Orient. A.*, xxix (1983), pp. 38–48

Blue and White Chinese Porcelain and its Impact on the Western World (exh. cat. by J. Carswell, U. Chicago, IL, Smart Gal., 1985)

N. Atasoy and J. Raby: *Iznik: The Pottery of Ottoman Turkey* (London, 1988)

O. Aslanapa, Ş. Yetkin and A. Altun: *The Iznik Tile Kiln Excavations (The Second Round: 1981–1988)* (Istanbul, 1989)

G. Necipoğlu: 'From International Timurid to Ottoman: A Change of Taste in Sixteenth Century Ceramic Tiles', *Muqarnas*, vii (1990), pp. 136–70

WALTER B. DENNY

(ii) Iran. A variety of ceramics continued to be produced in Iran, although they rarely, if ever, achieved the technical and aesthetic qualities of contemporary wares produced in the Ottoman empire. Underglaze- and overglaze-painted wares—especially lustre—often imitated Chinese originals. From the 18th century, imports of Chinese and European ceramics increasingly supplanted local production of fine wares.

(a) *c.* 1500–*c.* 1700. (b) *c.* 1700 and after.

(a) c. 1500–c. 1700. Several important types of ceramics were produced in Iran during the two centuries of Safavid rule (1501–1732). Despite incursions by the Ottomans from the west and by the Uzbeks from the northeast, the traditional areas of ceramic production—the provinces of Azerbaijan, Jibal, Khurasan and Kirman—remained within its frontiers. Although such traditional centres as Mashhad, Tabriz and Kirman have been proposed, locating specific potteries is a problem. One group of ceramics, heavily potted in a soft and porous white body covered with a thin, glassy glaze, is often known as Kubachi ware after a remote town in Dagestan in the Caucasus where many examples were found in the late 19th century. The town was better known for its foundries

180. Blue-and-white flask, soft-paste body, h. 246 mm, from Iran, 1523–4 (London, Victoria and Albert Museum)

than its ceramics, and presumably the dishes had been made and purchased further south in exchange for firearms before being set as decoration into the fabric of local houses. Both blue-and-white and polychrome wares were normally made of a soft-paste body, combining fine white clay and glaze components. The quality of the glaze varied from mediocre with a crackled surface on Kubachi wares to excellent on certain blue-and-white dishes, in which the underglaze painting is applied to a buffer layer closer to glaze than slip set over the body proper to secure the painting and close fitting of the glaze.

The relatively few ceramics to survive from the early Safavid period show a taste for chinoiserie, particularly blue-and-white. The earliest dated Safavid ceramic (1523–4; see fig. 180) is a damaged blue-and-white pilgrim flask with a somewhat blasphemous verse surrounding a balanced composition of blossoms with a central bird on both circular flanks. A plaque, overglaze-painted in lustre and signed by Master Muhammad of Kashan, records in very poor calligraphy the endowment of a minbar in 1528 to the Friday Mosque at Kuhpayeh in central Iran. It, along with a tombstone in the same technique (1560; Hamburg, Mus. Kst & Gew.), shows that lustre painting continued at Kashan, although at a modest level. Tomb plaques were also produced in blue-and-white: one (401×355 mm; 1532; New York, H. Anavian priv. col.) is decorated with trees.

By the second half of the 16th century ceramic painting had become less bold and more refined in composition. A new type of Kubachi ware, with polychrome slip painting and an occasional pink slipped ground (e.g. Sèvres, Mus. N. Cér., 22693), was introduced. Typical decorative motifs include animals, flowers, stylized figures

and busts and geometric patterns, with little reference to Chinese-inspired designs. A dish depicting the zodiac painted by 'Abd al-Vahid in two tones of blackish blue on white (1563–4; Berlin, Mus. Islam. Kst, I.1292) shows a geometric composition of 12 zodiac circles with chinoiserie small clouds and scale-fillers in the interstices.

Under 'Abbas I (*reg* 1588–1629) the arts were promoted and international trade flourished, particularly after 1597 when he moved the capital to Isfahan in central Iran. The perennial popularity of Chinese blue-and-white ceramics is shown by the 1162 pieces of Chinese porcelain that 'Abbas donated to the dynastic shrine at Ardabil between 1607 and 1611. Whereas Ottoman potters had by this time long forsaken Chinese models, their Safavid counterparts found renewed inspiration in the export pieces of the Wanli period (1573–1620; see CHINA, §VII, 3(vi)) brought to Iran by merchants of the Dutch East India company. Known as Kraak ware, after the Dutch approximation of 'carrack', the type of Portuguese ship that first brought these dishes to Europe, these ceramics echo the lively Chinese decoration of ducks, birds, insects, lotus ponds, deer and Buddhist symbols. Over half-a-dozen pieces of imitation Kraak ware are dated between 1616 (a teapot, London, BM) and 1641 (a *kendi*, a type of water-container of South-east Asia). Undated dishes of various sizes (e.g. London, V&A, 419-1874) adopt a design of deep panel borders around a central filler. Such designs continued to be used until the end of the 17th century in a variety of styles, often in a black-and-white colour scheme. Marks inside the base appear from the 17th century and show square seals, 'tassel marks' and various signatures. Kubachi wares also continued to be produced until the first quarter of the 17th century in both polychrome (e.g. a tomb slab dated 1628; London, V&A) and blue-and-white schemes of central figures, flowers, animals or geometric patterns on dishes and tiles.

By the end of the 1650s ceramic shapes underwent a radical change away from Chinese prototypes, such as the *kendi*, which became a kalian, a hooka bottle. One (1658; London, V&A, 616-1889) displays a sparse pattern in white slip with touches of yellow applied to a blue ground. On large dishes the white slip was applied to a coffee-coloured glaze or to a celadon-type finish recalling Swatow wares (e.g. a dish with a spray of dianthus; London, V&A). The effect was also obtained by carving away a delicate pattern through the coloured glaze, often blue (e.g. a large dish with a six-pointed arabesque design, diam. 505 mm; London, V&A). Trumpet-neck vases, a number with four secondary necks on the shoulder, are often decorated with broad aquatic and genre scenes in blue and white. The long neck of ewers and water-sprinklers responded to a change in taste, perhaps due to the patronage of the last firm ruler of the dynasty, 'Abbas II (*reg* 1642–66).

The same change in taste is visible in a magnificent series of large dishes in which the decoration combines geometric mouldings with central and radial compositions outlined in blue. Fillers recall embroidery repeats of dianthus and dense leafy scrolls; faded touches of ochre or yellow enliven the blue-and-white compositions. The new colour scheme was also applied to bottles, ewers, kalians and small dishes of oblong or octagonal shape. On occasion a circular inscription in white against a broad black band (see fig. 181) encircles the cavetto within the rim. One example (1666; London, V&A) has a commemorative verse for the newly enthroned Sulayman/Safi II (*reg* 1666–94) encircling a large incised flower-spray. *Blanc de Chine*, a popular type of export ware in the second half of the 17th century, inspired the Persian potter to create small incised dishes (e.g. London, V&A) as well as ewers in the best kind of manmade soft-paste body. A similar fine body could be covered with an opaque turquoise glaze or even vivid yellow, lavender or midnight blue. A high quality of glazing can also be found on moulded bottles or bases for opium-smokers, decorated with hunting scenes, *scènes galantes*, camels or simple geometric and floral scrolls in green and amber. Special dinner-sets with Armenian monograms either on plain white pieces with incised patterns or on dishes with the aster pattern of Chinese blue-and-whites were ordered by richer members of the Armenian trading community.

A brief revival of ceramics overglaze-painted in lustre occurred in the second half of the 17th century. The shades of lustre range from deep copper to ruby red. A denser style, with highly stylized depictions of willow trees, flowery stems, deer and streams, or compact geometric repeats on either a white or blue glaze, points to late 17th-century manuscript borders. The only dated example is a long-necked bottle with trees on a blue glaze (?1673; ex-Wallis priv. col.; see Watson, 1985, fig. 136). Although only one tile (London, V&A, C5-1913) is known, large numbers of vessels have survived. The shapes, rather smaller than usual and fired on spurs, include dishes, coffee-cups, long-necked bottles and vases. The name of the potter Khatim is recorded on several pieces; a dish (Berlin, Mus. Islam. Kst) bears the phrase *'amal-i khatim* ('the work of Khatim') written boldly against floral sprays. The name Muhammad Riza on the bottom of a bowl (London, BM, ex-Godman priv. col.) may be that of either a potter or a patron. The evolution of late Safavid ceramics is still unclear. Dishes and small bowls excavated at Kandahar (Afghanistan) and Merv (Turkmenistan) have hasty brushwork. In wares from southern Iran, roughly incised lines can emphasize the mushy pattern in cobalt blue; sage-green, grey or black are also quite common.

BIBLIOGRAPHY

Enc. Iran.: 'Ceramics, xv'
Trudy Yuzhno-Turkmen. Arkheol. Kompleksnoi Eksped., ii (1951), pp. 7–72, 147–68
A. Lane: *Later Islamic Pottery* (London, 1957)
O. Watson: 'Persian Lustre Ware from the 14th to the 19th Centuries', *Monde Iran. & Islam*, iii (1975), pp. 63–80
Y. Crowe: 'A Preliminary Enquiry into Underglaze Decoration of Safavid Wares', *Decorative Techniques and Styles in Asian Ceramics* (1978), viii of *Percival David Foundation Colloquies on Art and Archaeology in Asia* (London, 1970–), pp. 104–25
A. W. McNicoll: 'Excavations at Qandahar 1975: Second Interim Report', *Afghan Stud.*, i (1978), pp. 41–66
M. D. Whitman: *Persian Blue and White Ceramics: Cycles of Chinoiserie* (diss., New York U., 1978)
O. Watson: *Persian Lustre Ware* (London and Boston, MA, 1985), pp. 157–75
B. Gray: 'The Arts in the Safavid Period', *The Timurid and Safavid Periods*, ed. P. Jackson and L. Lockhart (1986), vi of *The Cambridge History of Iran* (Cambridge, 1986), pp. 910–12
Y. Crowe: 'The Glazed Ceramics', in *Excavations at Old Kandahar, 1974 and 1975: Conducted by the British Institute of Afghan Studies*, Soc. S

181. Dish, soft-paste body, diam. 272 mm, from Iran (Edinburgh, Royal Museum of Scotland)

Asian Stud., monograph no. 1, by A. McNicoll and W. Ball (Oxford, in preparation)

YOLANDE CROWE

(b) c. 1700 and after. The vigorous ceramic production that had existed during the period of Safavid rule declined in the 18th century. A report by the East India Company on manufacturing and trade in Iran in the 1780s did not even mention ceramics, and imports, ranging from quotidian Russian pottery to fine European and Chinese porcelains, comprised most of the ceramics used in Iran. Under the patronage of the Zand dynasty at Shiraz (*reg* 1750–94), however, quality polychrome wares, usually with a distinctive pink, were produced as tiles to decorate mosques and tablewares in imitation of Chinese *famille rose* wares.

The taste for exports was particularly strong in northern Iran under the rule of the Qajar dynasty (*reg* 1779–1924). Fath 'Ali Shah (*reg* 1797–1834), for example, ordered dinner-services inscribed with his name and the date 1234 (AD 1820) for the Gulistan Palace in Tehran from the factories of Crown Derby and Wedgwood. Examples of Chinese *famille rose* export porcelains range from a plate decorated with a border of flower-sprays enclosing Persian inscriptions and the date 1201 (AD 1787; see Christie's, 14 March 1977, lot 144) to a more flamboyant group of bowls painted with figures, birds and flowers framing a central inscription with a name. A change in taste also depressed the market for ceramics, as the standard ceramic shapes of vessels, vases, water-pipes and containers were often fashioned of metal or glass. Indeed, the Qajar monarchs often preferred enamelled and jewelled gold and imported glass.

The most common everyday wares were unglazed earthenwares, and good-quality pieces were made at Qum and Kashan. The drinking vessels from Qum are either

182. Tin-glazed earthenware bowl painted with polychrome enamels by 'Ali Akbar of Shiraz, diam. 415 mm, from Iran, 1846 (London, Victoria and Albert Museum)

plain or decorated with figural and foliate designs in trailed slip, and containers from Kashan are pale greenish yellow. The largest group are monochrome glazed wares, which are related to unglazed wares in shape and function. They are usually fine-textured orange or buff earthenwares in such simple shapes as open bowls, dishes and globular and pear-shaped vases. The most common glaze was turquoise, easily obtained by combining copper oxides in an alkaline-based glaze. Other common colours include copper green and yellow, and violet was reportedly used at Meybod, a village 40 km north-west of Yazd still renowned for its ceramics. Fine-quality wares were made at Kashan, where at least 100 potters were employed according to Comte Julien de Rochechouart, who travelled in Iran in 1867.

A composite paste of finely ground white clay, quartz and a glassy frit was used for finer wares and produced a fabric varying from granular pinkish buff to fine hard white. Underglaze-painted wares were produced in a variety of styles at different centres. Qum produced lamps and plates painted in black under a transparent blue glaze. According to Rochechouart and L. J. Olmer, Professor of Physics and Chemistry at the Imperial Polytechnic in Tehran in the late 19th century and early 20th, the city of Na'in in central Iran was known for a more distinguished group of wares painted in dark blue (e.g. a bowl; London, V&A, 59.1889). They have a pinkish-buff body painted with bright cobalt blue that tended to run during firing. Designs include Chinese pagodas, sprigs of flowers perhaps inspired by imports of contemporary Staffordshire, and birds and fishes. They include a series of signed and

dated pieces (1864–1901), but production continued until 1935 when it was replaced by the more profitable carpet industry. Other polychrome pieces with similar fabric, shape and glaze are sketchily painted in cobalt blue, manganese purple, brownish pink and black.

A finer group of polychrome underglaze wares (e.g. a vase; London, V&A, 517.1889) can be attributed to Tehran in the late 19th century as they were acquired there in 1887 by Robert Murdoch Smith. Made of white paste superior to that used in Na'in, they are covered with a lustrous transparent alkaline glaze that has a tendency to crackle. The painting is done in a varied palette of cobalt blue, turquoise, olive green, purple, yellow and pink, with black used for outlines, hatching and shading. The sophisticated shapes include chalices, flat-sided flasks and pear-shaped vessels with flaring trumpet or long narrow necks. Designs are arranged in panels or medallions containing roses and carnations reserved against contrasting ground, scrolls and geometric borders. Several pieces are signed by Husayn, and, according to Murdoch Smith, others were made by 'ALI MUHAMMAD ISFAHANI, who also made a group of similar tiles purchased by Murdoch Smith at the same time.

Overglaze-painted wares cannot be linked to specific centres of production. The fine-textured orange-buff earthenware is covered with an opaque white tin-glaze and painted in bright enamels in cobalt blue, purple, rose pink, yellow, green, red and black with touches of gold. Their eclectic designs combine Persian, Chinese and European motifs. For example, a large bowl (see fig. 182) signed by 'Ali Akbar of Shiraz is decorated on the interior with the

Qajar emblem of the lion and sun surrounded by a border of Chinese figures, butterflies, rocks and peonies and on the exterior with scenes of hunting and reception divided by borders of peonies and chrysanthemums. These overglaze-painted wares may have been cheaper imitations of 'lacquered' (i.e. painted-and-varnished) and enamelled gold objects. The traditional technique of lustreware was also revived in the late 19th century, probably as a result of European interest in the technique and in collecting early examples. Potted in a granular pinkish-buff frit and painted in golden-brown lustre over a white tin-glaze, these lustre vessels (e.g. a vase; London, V&A, 1332.1904) are painted with crowded designs in a technique similar to contemporary book illustration.

BIBLIOGRAPHY

J. Polak: *Persien: Das Land und seine Bewohner* (Leipzig, 1865)
Comte Julien de Rochechouart: *Souvenirs d'un voyage en Perse* (Paris, 1867)
L. J. Olmer: 'Rapport sur une mission scientifique en Perse', *Nouvelles archives des missions scientifiques*, xvi/1 (Paris, 1908), pp. 49–61
M. Centlivres-Demont: *Une Communauté de potiers en Iran: Le Centre de Maybod (Yazd)* (Wiesbaden, 1971)
C. Issawi: *An Economic History of Iran, 1800–1914* (Chicago, 1971)
O. Watson: 'Persian Lustre Ware from the 14th to the 19th Centuries', *Monde Iran. & Islam*, iii (1975), pp. 63–80
J. Scarce: 'Ali Mohammad Isfahani: Tile Maker of Tehran', *Orient. A.*, n. s., xxii/3 (1976), pp. 278–88
——: 'The Arts of the Eighteenth to Twentieth Centuries', *From Nadir Shah to the Islamic Republic*, ed. P. Avery, G. Hambly and C. Melville (1991), vii of *The Cambridge History of Iran* (Cambridge, 1968–91), pp. 930–39

□

(iii) North Africa. The fine ceramic tradition associated with Málaga (*see* §4(iv) above) continued after the Christian conquest in Spain (*see* SPAIN, §VII, 2) and in the Muslim kingdoms of North Africa, to which some potters emigrated, although the technique of lustre decoration seems not to have been carried there. In contrast to the eastern Islamic lands, fritwares were not produced and Chinese ceramics had little, if any, impact. Rather, the majority of vessels are lead-glazed earthenwares with polychrome decoration, although a blue-and-white palette remained popular in Morocco. Tiles for floors and wall revetments (*see* §II, 9(ii)(c) above) were also made throughout the region. The city of Fez in northern Morocco became a major centre of ceramic production: by the end of the 16th century it had some 180 workshops. Meknès was known for its monochrome green-glazed wares, and Safi, some 200 km north of Agadir on the Atlantic coast, produced simple salt-glazed earthenwares until the second half of the 19th century, when distinctive polychrome wares began to be made there.

Glazed earthenwares painted on a white slip and decorated in cobalt blue and polychrome were produced at Fez from the 17th century. Typical forms include large plates, footed bowls, pitchers and small oil flasks with large mouths, but the most distinctive types are short bulbous vessels with a knob handle on the cover (Arab. *jabbāna*) and tall covered storage jars with a swelling profile (*ḥabya*). The earliest blue-and-white ceramics are sparsely decorated with geometric and floral motifs. For example, an 18th-century earthenware platter (diam. 400 mm; Paris, Mus. de l'Homme) displays an eight-pointed star surrounded by foliate scrolls on a white ground. Decoration gradually seems to have become denser, as shown by a mid-19th-century covered dish (h. 340 mm; Tangiers, Mus. Kasbah), the entire surface of which is covered with designs in a pale, thin blue. Early polychrome wares have decoration in pale blue, pale green and yellow-orange, with geometric designs sometimes outlined in a pale brown (e.g. bowl, diam. 320 mm; Stuttgart, Linden-Mus.). Pieces combining blue-and-white with polychrome decoration (e.g. a dish, diam. 460 mm; Rabat, Mus. A. Maroc.) show that both types were produced simultaneously in the same workshops. Colours became stronger in the 18th and 19th centuries: a mid-19th-century covered jar (h. 805 mm; Tangiers, Mus. Kasbah) is decorated with cobalt blue, emerald green and lemon yellow within brownish-black lines. As with the blue-and-white wares, decoration became denser, and vegetal motifs inspired by Andalusian models were gradually modified as the repertory was expanded under the impact of imports from Europe, Ottoman Turkey, Iran and even India. Among the most distinctive and attractive pieces is a group of flat dishes depicting stylized sailing-boats (e.g. Paris, Mus. A. Afr. & Océan., 1962.361).

Emigrés from Andalusia also reinvigorated the ceramic industry in Tunisia. The Sufi saint Sidi Qasim al-Jalizi (or al-Zalliji; *d* 1496), a maker of tiles (*zallīj*), emigrated from Andalusia to Tunis, and the shrine complex around his tomb there is elaborately decorated with tiles. In the 16th century potters also emigrated from the island of Jerba to Nabeul, on the Gulf of Hammamet south-east of Tunis. Specialists in plain wares, they quickly adapted their products to the Tunisian taste. The transfer of techniques was further accelerated when Philip II expelled the Moors from Spain in 1610. The workshops of the Qallalin quarter in Tunis produced not only tiles, but also earthenware basins, bowls, vases, lamps, jars, amphorae and pitchers (*qulāl*) painted in emerald green, yellow and manganese brown under a transparent glaze. A 17th-century basin painted in polychrome under a transparent glaze (diam. 460 mm; Paris, Mus. A. Afr. & Océan., M.67.1.4) is decorated on the interior with a ship accompanied by fish, a traditional theme since ancient times and often found on Italian *bacini* (*see* §3(v) above). At the end of the 18th century, Italianate motifs such as rosettes and garlands with grotesques, as well as Turkish ones such as domed mosques with minarets, were added to the traditional vocabulary, particularly on tiles. Objects for domestic use, such as lamps, vases and cruets, were made of earthenware and dipped into monochrome yellow, green, blue or brown lead glaze; some bicoloured pieces were dipped twice. A 19th-century moulded penbox with a brown glaze (150×95×90 mm; Sèvres, Mus. N. Cér., 3551), for example, has wells for pens and ink on the top and architectural decoration on the sides.

The ceramic production of Algeria remains largely unstudied, except for the rural pottery made by women in the mountains of the Grande Kabylie to the east of Algiers. These low-fired earthenwares were modelled by hand from slabs and coils into such domestic utensils as amphorae, pots, bowls, cruets with multiple compartments, oil lamps and chandeliers. After firing they were painted with geometric designs in black and sometimes red ochre on a resinous varnish or white slip. These attractive wares have been compared with prehistoric or

Neolithic pottery, the designs of which would have been passed from generation to generation. A 19th-century vessel with a ring-handle on the top, wide spout on one shoulder and slender spout on the other (Paris, Mus. A. Afr. & Océan., M.65.3.68), for example, has intricate geometric decoration painted on a white slip; it has been identified as a nursing bottle.

BIBLIOGRAPHY

A. Van Gennep: 'Etudes d'ethnographie algériennes, III: Les poteries kabyles', *Rev. Ethnog. & Soc.*, ii (1911), pp. 277–331
A. Bel: *Les Industries de la céramique à Fès* (Algiers, 1918)
M. A. Bel: *Les Arts indigènes féminins en Algérie* (Algiers, 1939)
H. Balfet: 'Les Poteries modelées d'Algérie dans les collections du Musée du Bardo', *Lybica*, iv (1956), pp. 289–346
A. Boukobza: *La Poterie marocaine* (Casablanca, 1974)
L'Islam dans les collections nationales (exh. cat., Paris, Grand Pal., 1977)
J. Soustiel: *La Céramique islamique: Le guide du connaisseur* (Fribourg, 1985)
Marokkanische Keramik (exh. cat. by B. Hakenjos, Düsseldorf, Hetjens-Mus., 1988)

SHEILA S. BLAIR, JONATHAN M. BLOOM

VI. Textiles.

Textiles have been an especially important art form in the Islamic lands. In addition to their use in dress, textiles were also the major form of furnishing, particularly as carpets, at all levels of traditional Islamic culture, from the nomadic encampment to the royal court. Textiles were the primary indicators of social status and, at times, of ethnic and occupational status, and they formed the major item of commerce, fuelling long-distance trade, the financial systems to support it and consequently wars of conquest. Furthermore, textiles were often the means by which artistic styles and motifs spread, particularly before the widespread adoption of paper and cartoons.

For further information *see* TEXTILE, §I.

1. Introduction. 2. Fabrics. 3. Dress. 4. Carpets and flatweaves.

1. INTRODUCTION. In Islamic civilization, as in other traditional societies, most textiles were simple, inexpensive and plain, made from humble materials by uncomplicated processes and intended to serve the basic needs of clothing, shelter and everyday utility. Nevertheless, many different types of fine textiles were produced in the Islamic lands, and these were among the most prized in the medieval world. In addition to their utilitarian functions, fine textiles were used as flags and banners, carpets and canopies, places of prayer or devotion, robes or gifts of state, adornment for rites of power or passage, and even as necessary parts of ceremonies associated with death. Most traditional Islamic societies were, and still are, weaving cultures; custom and the temperate dry environment militated against the use of furs, leather and felts as clothing, while climate, religion and social custom supported the covering of the body with woven fabrics. Long-distance trade in textiles formed a basis of the pre-Islamic economy into which the Prophet Muhammad was born in the late 6th century AD, and early Islamic civilization inherited a long and rich tradition of fine weaving from the Sasanian and Byzantine empires (*see* ANCIENT NEAR EAST, §II, 6(ii)(b) and EARLY CHRISTIAN AND BYZANTINE ART, §VII, 3).

(i) Fibres and manufacture. (ii) Textiles in religious, royal and nomadic life. (iii) Textile trade.

(i) Fibres and manufacture. Of all fibres used in Islamic textiles, wool has the most complex lineage and importance to the social order as it is the major economic product of nomadic herding societies. Wool has been used on all levels of textile production, from the coarsest felts (*see* FELT) and woven stuffs used for tents (*see* TENT, §I) to the finest carpets and court textiles. The raising of sheep was prevalent in the semi-arid region extending from the Iberian Peninsula across north-west Africa to Central Asia long before the birth of the Prophet. Sheep herding was closely linked with nomadism in the semi-mountainous areas where there was less competition between the depredations of grazing flocks and the restriction on grazing necessary for agriculture to survive. With the coming of Islam, the trade in both raw wool and woollens increased across this region, and numerous documents attest to a thriving production in virtually all Islamic lands capable of sustaining grazing. In certain cases, such as the invasion of Anatolia by Turkish tribes after 1071, the arrival of Central Asian nomads and their flocks appears to have increased wool production dramatically.

Flax is another fibre with a long tradition of use in the Islamic world. The main centres of production were in Egypt, Syria and lower Mesopotamia, where rivers provided large quantities of fresh water for processing the raw material into linen threads. Although some significant early Islamic textiles (e.g. the Veil of Ste Anne, 1096–7; for illustration *see* TIRAZ) are linen, the importance of this fibre for luxury fabrics waned in the face of increased production of cotton and silk. Cotton, which requires a subtropical climate and irrigated fields, was gradually introduced into the Middle East and North Africa from India in the 1st millennium AD, and became well established from early Islamic times in Transoxiana, Khurasan, Mesopotamia and Syria, areas that have continued to be important centres of production. Despite the prominence of Egyptian cotton in modern times, cotton does not seem to have been a major product there in medieval times.

SILK, introduced to the Middle East from China and a major medium of artistic expression from the early days of Islam, rapidly became the pre-eminent fibre for luxury textiles. Sericulture, which requires a temperate climate and adequate rainfall for the cultivation of mulberry trees on which the silkworms feed, had been introduced into Central Asia from China along the Silk Route (*see* SILK ROUTE, §2) in the 4th century AD. By early Islamic times, major centres of cocoon production included Transoxiana, the Caspian littoral and Syria. Iran, in particular, inherited from the Sasanian era a complex drawloom technology, and Islamic silks of immense complexity were produced in the medieval period (*see* §2(i)(b) below). Silk weaving spread as far as Spain in the west where equally magnificent fabrics, often copying eastern prototypes, were made (*see* §2(i)(c) below). In later Islamic times silk was produced throughout the Islamic lands, with monarchs establishing royal manufactories to produce silks for the court. Typically the taste for silk began with the importation of Chinese fabrics and then led to the importation of cocoons or threads for local looms and finally to the cultivation of mulberry trees. The city of BURSA in western Anatolia, for example, reached prominence first as a market for the transhipment of cocoons across the Mediterranean and then as a major centre for the cultivation of mulberry trees, which covered the surrounding plain by the mid-17th century (*see* §2(iii)(a) below). Northern Syria was another major area of production, and by the 15th century commerce in silk was a mainstay of the economy of the Ottoman empire (1281–1924) and as a result of trading contacts with European purchasers fuelled the development of European banking.

The making of textiles has long been a basic element of socialization in many Islamic lands. Young urban women were taught the domestic art of embroidery, which not only served to indicate their neatness and industriousness but also contributed to the value of their dowries. In villages and encampments very young girls were taught the craft of spinning, while weaving, especially of carpets, was often the exclusive province of women. Men generally controlled large-scale and commercial operations, such as dyeing and marketing. Further, in nomadic and village societies the designs of fabrics and carpets often serve as visual symbols of tribal and family groups.

Certain genres of textiles are closely allied to daily life in the Islamic lands. In Central Asia, for example, elaborate animal trappings were used to decorate the bridal procession. In Morocco, intricately woven silk wedding-sashes constituted a major element of artistic weaving and perpetuated a wide repertory of traditional patterns. In many parts of the Middle East a wide range of textiles was developed for common social rituals: the protocol of the formal meal required tablecloths, napkins (Arab. *mandīl*) and other textiles; towels and coverings were used in the bathhouse; embroidered kerchiefs featured as prizes in athletic contests; and elaborate embroidered textiles depicting flowers carried an entire glossary of iconographic messages.

(ii) Textiles in religious, royal and nomadic life. Costly and ostentatious personal adornment with elaborate textiles is generally frowned on in Islam, especially for men; but at the same time the Koran (e.g. lv. 35–78) promises silken garments, cushions and carpets in Paradise as a reward to believers who submit to God's will on earth. The Hadith include numerous references to clothing and textiles; one of the most famous is the saying attributed to the Prophet that he who wears silk in this world will forgo it in the next. This prophetic tradition meant that religious figures rarely, if ever, wore silk, although as the primary luxury fabric in Islamic civilization it was frequently worn by court officials and others of high status and great wealth. Traditions and stories of the Prophet's life mention his cloak and banner, both conserved as relics in Istanbul (probably wool; Topkapı Pal. Mus.). Coloured textiles, such as the black banners of the Abbasid dynasty (*reg* 749–1258), were major political symbols in early Islamic religious struggles, and in later Islamic times the green banner became a symbol of religious revolt.

Textiles figure strongly in various religious rituals. A seamless white cloth is required for a burial shroud (*see* ISLAM, §II), while for many people the turban in its various forms is the primary outward indication of the wearer's adherence to Islam. Textile coverings for women, from the chadar worn in Iran to the *ehram* in Anatolia, developed as a response to the religious demand that women's bodies be covered in public. Many Islamic sumptuary conventions, such as the wearing of green turbans by some religious figures, are based directly on religious custom or legislation. The use of textiles is so pervasive in the Islamic world that Golombek has described it as a 'draped universe'. Its central shrine, the Ka'ba in MECCA, is adorned annually with a new woven veil (Arab. *kiswa*), and numerous works of art and architecture are covered with patterns reminiscent of textile designs.

Throughout most of Islamic history there has been an implicit conflict between the concepts of religious duty and kingship, and this conflict is particularly clear in the area of fine textiles. They had served prominently in the ritual giving of royal gifts that characterized many Near Eastern monarchies long before the rise of Islam. In early Islamic times, a state-controlled system of manufactories producing textiles for such gifts and other royal purposes came into being (*see* TIRAZ). Likewise, the preference for silk for royal garments meant that from early times Islamic courts participated directly in developing the commerce and weaving of silk.

The prototypes for the textiles produced for early Islamic rulers may be found in the complex brocaded silks produced for the Byzantine and Sasanian courts. Hieratic designs of roundels with confronted animals, both real and imaginary, and images of royal symbols and pastimes passed into the Islamic repertory with ease, continuing to be found on Islamic textiles from Central Asia to Spain at least until the 13th century (see fig. 183 below). The production of elaborate silks, especially with figural designs, seems to be associated with periods of relative religious tolerance. The inscriptions on a Nasrid silk from Granada proclaim 'I am made for pleasure, for pleasure am I' (Washington, DC, Textile Mus.), while the production of figural silks in Iran under the Safavid ruler Tahmasp I (*reg* 1524–76) apparently went into decline when the Shah turned to religion in his old age (*see* SAFAVID, (1)).

Textiles, especially those made from wool, were the major artistic form among nomads, from the Arab Bedouins and Berbers in the West to the Turks and Mongols in the East. Since these peoples often came to assume political leadership in the Islamic world, the art of the knotted carpet and other textiles associated with nomadic society, economy and culture gained a more general importance and continued to be practised long after nomads had adopted sedentary lifestyles based on agriculture, trade and artisanry in the cities. Examples of the widespread persistence of textiles of nomadic origin include the large tents and canopies used for royal ceremonies, which sometimes attained enormous scale and size; the cushions that line the walls of traditional Islamic houses; the quilt that covers the charcoal brazier; and the various bags and wrappers that serve for storage and display.

(iii) Textile trade. Trade in textiles and fibres created and supported many commercial arteries in the Islamic lands. Throughout the Middle Ages silk reached the West through the Islamic lands, and by the 15th century the transhipment of cocoons and silk thread accounted for a

major part of the economies of such prominent Islamic dynasties as the Mamluks (*reg* 1250–1517) in Egypt and Syria, the Timurids (*reg* 1370–1506) in Iran and western Central Asia, and the Ottomans in the eastern Mediterranean. Fabrics made of linen, cotton, wool and animal hair were also important at various times, along with the more glamorous silks. The impact of this trade on European cultures is demonstrated by such words entering European languages as cashmere (the fine underhair of Kashmir goats), pashm (a fine wool or goat hair, from Pers. *pashm*: 'wool'), camlet (camels' hair), mohair (the fine hair of the Angora goat, from Arab. *mukhayyar*: 'by choice, deliberately', referring to watered mohair), damask (from Damascus), muslin (from Mosul) and organdy (from Urgench). From the 9th century silks woven in Iran with historical inscriptions were taken by trade or conquest to Europe, where they acquired legends linking them with Christian events and personalities and became relics, such as the 'Shroud of St Josse' (see fig. 185 below). Islamic silks of this kind were virtually synonymous with power and authority, both secular and ecclesiastical, in western and northern Europe. From the 10th century the records of the Cairo Geniza, a trove of medieval Jewish documents, attest to a brisk Mediterranean trade in textiles. The stupendous coronation robe of the Holy Roman emperors (Vienna, Schatzkam.; see fig. 183) was made in Palermo for the Norman king of Sicily Roger II Hauteville (*reg* 1130–54; *see* HAUTEVILLE, (1)) in 1133–4 (*see* §2(i)(c) below). In later times Turkish silks were used extensively for ecclesiastical vestments in Russia and Poland, and Bursa amassed incredible wealth not only as an entrepôt for textiles, but also as a major manufacturing centre for velvets.

The role of textiles as vectors for designs can be seen in one of the celebrated 14th-century Konya carpets (*see* §4(ii) below), which features a design of lotus blossoms adapted from a Chinese silk made under the Yuan dynasty

(*reg* 1279–1368). Turkish carpets with Chinese silk designs then entered the Mediterranean commerce and were copied by Spanish weavers. A *Mudéjar* carpet with a unique pattern of hooked motifs in staggered rows (Washington, DC, Textile Mus.) clearly shows that designs of Chinese origin were carried as far as the western limits of the Islamic world.

Many bazaars in the Islamic world were built around the cloth market (Turk. *bezzāzistān*), a building that bears a striking analogy to the cloth-hall of medieval Europe. The role of the market supervisor (Arab. *muhtasib*; Turk. *mühtesib*) included keeping track of the quality of fibres, weaving and dyestuffs used in textile production, as well as assuring a fair market price for such textiles. Regulation and taxation of textile production were central to the economies of many Muslim states, and expansion of markets coupled with access to raw materials influenced state policy in many Islamic realms.

BIBLIOGRAPHY

Enc. Islam/2: 'Harīr' [silk]

P. Ackerman: 'Islamic Textiles: History', *Survey of Persian Art*, ed. A. U. Pope and P. Ackerman (London, 1938–9; 2/1964–7), pp. 1995–2162

R. B. Serjeant: 'Islamic Textiles: Material for a History up to the Mongol Conquest', *A. Islam*, ix (1942), pp. 54–92; x (1943), pp. 71–104; xi–xii (1946), pp. 98–145; xiii–xiv (1948), pp. 75–117; xv–xvi (1951), pp. 29–85; as book (Beirut, 1972)

E. Kühnel and L. Bellinger: *Catalogue of Dated Tiraz Fabrics* (Washington, DC, 1952)

F. May: *Silk Textiles of Spain* (New York, 1957)

F. Dalsar: *Bursa'da ipekçilik* [The Bursa silk industry] (Istanbul, 1960)

H. Inalcik: 'Bursa and the Commerce of the Levant', *J. Econ. & Soc. Hist. Orient*, iii (1960), pp. 131–47

E. H. Schafer: *The Golden Peaches of Samarkand* (Berkeley and Los Angeles, 1962)

S. D. Goitein: *Economic Foundations* (1967), i of *A Mediterranean Society* (Berkeley and Los Angeles, 1967–88)

F. Rosenthal: 'A Note on the *Mandīl*', *Four Essays on Art and Literature in Islam* (Leiden, 1971), pp. 63–99

M. Lombard: *Les Textiles dans le monde musulman* (Paris, 1978)

183. Red silk robe embroidered with gold and pearls, diam. 3.42 m, made in Palermo for the coronation of Roger II, King of Sicily, 1133–4 (Vienna, Schatzkammer)

L. Golombek: 'The Draped Universe of Islam', *Content and Context of Visual Arts in the Islamic World*, ed. P. P. Soucek (University Park, PA, and London, 1988), pp. 25–50

Images of Paradise in Islamic Art (exh. cat., ed. S. S. Blair and J. M. Bloom; Hannover, NH, Dartmouth Coll., Hood Mus. A.; New York, Asia Soc. Gals; Brunswick, ME, Bowdoin Coll. Mus. A.; and elsewhere; 1991–2)

WALTER B. DENNY

2. FABRICS. Fine fabrics of wool, linen, silk and cotton were produced in the Islamic lands, continuing the textile traditions of earlier times. Before *c*. 1250 embroidered and tapestry woven linens and cottons made in state factories were particularly important. Patterned silks, which had been made in some regions during the early period, became significant throughout the Islamic lands after *c*. 1250. Court production of luxury fabrics, such as figured silk velvets and brocades, was encouraged by many of the great powers that arose in the Islamic lands after *c*. 1500.

(i) Before *c*. 1250. (ii) *c*. 1250–*c*. 1500. (iii) *c*. 1500 and after.

(i) Before c. *1250.* The textile traditions of the Byzantine and Sasanian empires continued and developed under the rule of the Umayyad (*reg* 661–750) and Abbasid (*reg* 749–1258) dynasties. Manufactories were established throughout the Islamic lands for weaving cotton and linen fabrics and decorating them with wool and silk for official presentation and use. Extraordinarily elaborate drawloom silks were also produced, particularly in Iran and in Spain, whereas a distinct group of ikats was made in the Yemen.

(a) Egypt. (b) Iraq and the eastern Islamic lands. (c) Spain and North Africa. (d) Yemen.

(a) Egypt. The Egyptian textile industry that flourished in antiquity (*see* EGYPT, ANCIENT, §XVI, 17) continued after the Arab conquest in AD 640–41, when Egypt became one of the main centres for the production of fine textiles in the Islamic world. Flax remained the major fibre and was spun with a characteristic S-twist and Z-plied before being woven into fine linens, which were often embellished with tapestry bands or embroidery. This decoration, which often included figural representations as well as inscriptions, was worked in wool or silk, both imported fibres, although woollen and silk textiles were also produced locally. Because of Egypt's unusually dry climate, many textiles have been preserved, particularly in graves. Some fabrics were undoubtedly imported, but those made in Egypt can often be distinguished by fibre, spinning and decoration. The large number of examples inscribed with dates and names of individuals and places of manufacture allows them to be sequenced to a degree impossible for fabrics from other areas of the Islamic world. Even so, the surviving fragments hardly reflect the wealth of textiles mentioned in medieval sources.

The prevalence of linen in Egypt allowed the production of a tightly woven fabric, in contrast to the loosely woven fabrics—cotton, silk and *mulham* ('half-silk'; *see* §(b) below)—of the eastern Islamic lands. The tight weave allowed fabrics to be embroidered with stitches that created uneven tension on the face and reverse, giving a puckered effect, and a great variety of stitches including stem stitch, flat stitch and couching was used. Furthermore, in contrast to cotton, linen did not need to be glazed, though the absence of glaze made it difficult if not impossible to draw a preliminary design on the fabric before embroidering the

decoration. As a result, other methods of planning the design, such as couching and counting threads, were generally employed in Egypt, and these serve to distinguish Egyptian work from other early Islamic textiles.

Textile production in Egypt was concentrated in three areas: Upper Egypt, the Faiyum and Lower Egypt. Production sites in Upper Egypt known from inscriptions and texts include ASYUT, Taha, al-Qais and Bahnasa. Those in Lower Egypt include Misr (Fustat or Old Cairo) at the head of the Nile Delta, Damietta and Tinnis at the eastern edge of the Delta, and Alexandria at the western edge of the Delta. Upper Egypt was known for its wool tapestry work, while wool, silk and linen were woven in the Faiyum. Lower Egypt, dominated by the Delta with its abundance of fresh water for retting flax, was naturally the centre of linen manufacture.

The tapestry technique and pictorial representation that had been characteristic of Egyptian textiles produced before the Arab conquest (*see* COPTIC ART, §V, 3) continued in Islamic times, although there was a change in the organization and execution of the design on the loom. Coptic robes were usually unshaped linen garments decorated in wool or linen with narrow vertical bands on the front and back and tapestry medallions on the shoulders, front, back and sleeves. The warp ran vertically on the finished garment. The typical Arab dress was similarly a loose linen robe, but the warp ran horizontally in the finished garment, so that the tapestry stripes on either side of the neck and across the top of the sleeves follow the weft. These garments were often woven in the form of a cross and finished without cutting. This fashion continued until the 11th century, when it was superseded by a cut and tailored garment of the Persian type.

Coptic textiles (Arab. *qubāṭī*) are reported to have been used by the caliphs 'Umar (*reg* 634–44) and 'Uthman (*reg* 644–56) for the covering (*kiswa*) annually draped over the Ka'ba in Mecca. *Qubāṭī* continued to be used for this purpose for several centuries, although it is likely that the term eventually took on the more general meaning of a white linen cloth. Such fabrics are generally associated with the Tinnis–Damietta group of factories, which is also known to have produced fine napkins, cloaks and shirts. Egypt was a centre for the production and trade in alum, natron and indigo, used in the dyeing and preparation of cloth, and the inclusion of Egypt in the Islamic empire provided new sources for dyestuffs and materials: madder and kermes, for example, were increasingly supplanted by lac from India, which produced a stronger and clearer red dye, and silk from Syria began to replace wool.

A considerable number of two-coloured silk textiles, woven as trimmings for tunics, have been found in Egyptian graves, especially at AKHMIM. Woven in a pictorial style derived from late Hellenistic art, they have been attributed to Egypt or Syria in the 8th and 9th centuries. Some bear Greek or Coptic names, indicating that they were made for the Christian market; others in an identical style bear inscriptions in Arabic, which are often indecipherable (e.g. London, V&A, 2150-1900, a compound twill of undyed silk warp and two colours of silk weft showing stylized figures under a tree).

The major innovation of the coming of Islam was the introduction of state manufactories for textiles. The fabrics they produced, known in Arabic as TIRAZ from their inscriptions containing good wishes and the name and titles of the ruling caliph, were made up into robes of honour worn by the caliph or bestowed by him as official gifts. Inscriptions and texts mention both public ('āmma) and private (khāṣṣa) factories, but the distinction between the two types is unclear. Although the institution was probably introduced to Egypt under the Umayyad dynasty (*reg* 661–750), the production of ṭirāz can be clearly documented there only from the 9th to the 13th century: one tapestry fragment (Cairo, Mus. Islam. A., 3084) was woven in the public factory at Misr under the Abbasid caliph al-Amin (*reg* 809–13), and the earliest embroidered ṭirāz (Cairo, Mus. Islam. A., 9439) was made in a private factory for his successor al-Ma'mun (*reg* 813–33) in 831–2. Over time, both the titles and the style used in the inscriptions became more elaborate. Egyptian ṭirāz are distinguished by such features of calligraphy as horizontal bars across tall letters and the use of peculiar locutions.

Although tapestry weaving had a very long history in Egypt, embroidery was apparently introduced from Iraq in the Islamic period. Tapestry weaving continued to be used for non-caliphal pieces, but throughout the 9th century and into the first decades of the 10th, ṭirāz fabrics ordered by caliphs in Egypt almost always had embroidered texts. With the establishment of the Tulunid dynasty (*reg* 868–905), whose leader was initially sent from Iraq as governor for the Abbasids, Z-spinning was introduced to Egypt, probably by craftsmen brought from Iraq. Z-spinning continued to be used along with traditional S-spinning until *c.* 940, when, presumably, the last of the foreign workers died. A characteristic group of tapestry weaves, often with large-scale animal and figural compositions (e.g. Washington, DC, Textile Mus.), is attributed to the Faiyum and Upper Egypt and dated to the late 9th century because of similarities with other arts assigned to the Tulunid period.

Because weaving linen was a very old craft in Egypt, it is difficult to distinguish the product of one factory from another, but by the 10th century technical and stylistic features of the embroidery make it possible to distinguish the work of individual factories, such as those at Alexandria, Tinnis, Misr and Tuna. Although the vast majority of pieces in the name of the caliph al-Muqtadir (*reg* 908–32) were embroidered, a few individual examples of ṭirāz were tapestry woven (e.g. 920–21; Ann Arbor, U. MI, Kelsey Mus., 22509). The new technique seems to have determined the style of the inscription, for the short letters, many without descending tails, indicate a lack of refinement in comparison to earlier embroidered texts. By the middle of the 10th century, tapestry weaving seems to have become the norm, for under al-Muti' (*reg* 946–74) embroidery was rare.

The arrival of the Fatimid caliphs (*reg* 909–1171) in Egypt in 972 brought about an increased demand for luxury textiles, since Cairo became the capital of a caliphate with an elaborate court ceremonial. The Fatimids had already shown a taste for luxury textiles before their conquest of Egypt in 969, for several Egyptian ṭirāz fabrics made before that date are inscribed with their names and titles. New robes of honour with inscriptions naming the caliph were distributed to courtiers in summer and winter,

and medieval sources describe the extraordinary contents of the Dār al-kiswāt, a treasury of textiles in the caliphs' palace. The Persian traveller and spy Nasir-i Khusraw, who visited Egypt from 1047 to 1050, gives an impressive list of shot silks and fine muslins or linens produced in various Egyptian towns. Silk brocade (dībāj) is known to have been woven at the Dār al-dībāj in Cairo.

Fatimid ṭirāz production can be divided into four periods on the basis of its decoration. In the first period (969–1021), foliate designs and animals or birds appear affronted or addorsed within hexagonal or oval medallions between kufic borders (e.g. Cairo, Mus. Islam. A., 9444). The decorative bands are few and narrow at first but eventually increase in number and breadth. Under al-Hakim (*reg* 996–1021) a more subtle type of decoration became fashionable. The miniature designs, with small and elegant birds and palmettes, are well drawn and clearly defined with simple inscriptions. In the second period (1021–94) the technique became finer and a greater variety of decorative motifs was used, although the general disposition of medallion bands between kufic borders was maintained. Textiles from the mid-11th century are marked by graceful calligraphy with symmetrical and clear small letters, a tall curve in the final letters and elaborate interlacing with vines and palmettes (e.g. Boston, MA, Mus. F.A., 30.675).

In the third period (1094–1130), the finest in Fatimid Egypt for the production of ṭirāz, the decorative style was developed with broad bands of plaited ribbons containing animal or arabesque motifs in the interstices. Some epigraphic borders show an early use of cursive script. The most famous example, the Veil of St Anne (Apt Cathedral; for illustration *see* TIRAZ), made of bleached linen tabby, has three parallel bands of tapestry-woven ornament in coloured silk and some gold filé (thread). The central band has interlacing circles joining three medallions containing pairs of addorsed sphinxes. Kufic inscriptions around the medallions name the Fatimid caliph al-Musta'li (*reg* 1094–1101) and his vizier al-Afdal, the supervisor of the work. Lateral bands decorated with birds and animals contain another inscription stating that the textile was woven in the royal factory at Damietta in 1096–7. The piece was probably intended as an over-garment or mantle, the central band containing the medallions falling down the back; it was probably acquired either by the bishop or lord of Apt, both of whom participated in the first crusade in 1099.

In the fourth period (1130–64), the plaited decoration became increasingly elaborate, and the bands are so wide that they cover the entire fabric (see fig. 184). The ground colour is generally bright yellow, probably in imitation of even finer luxury fabrics that were embroidered with gold thread. Other types of luxury textiles appear in this period, including fabrics printed with gold and outlined in red or black (e.g. Cairo, Mus. Islam. A., 10836). Inscriptions, in a debased cursive script, became increasingly stylized. A silk fabric assigned to the period of Ayyubid rule in Egypt (1169–1252) has continuous undulating bands forming lozenge-shaped medallions containing paired birds and griffins flanking a tree (dispersed, e.g. New York, Met.).

184. Egyptian linen and silk tapestry, 380×155 mm, made during the reign of the Fatimid caliph al-Hafiz (*reg* 1130–49) (Boston, MA, Museum of Fine Arts)

BIBLIOGRAPHY

Nāṣir-i Khusraw (*d c.* 1075): *Safarnāma* [Book of travels], Eng. trans. by W. M. Thackston jr as *Nāser-e Khosrāw's Book of Travels* (Albany, 1986)

Aḥmad ibn ʿAlī al-Maqrīzī (1364–1442): *al-Mawāʾiz waʾl-iʾtibār bi-dhikr al-khiṭaṭ waʾl-āthār* [On the districts and monuments of Cairo], 2 vols (Cairo, 1853), ii, pp. 409–13

O. von Falke: *Kunstgeschichte der Seidenweberei* (Berlin, 1913); Eng. trans. as *Decorative Silks* (New York, 1922, London, 3/1936)

A. F. Kendrick: *Catalogue of Textiles from Burying Grounds in Egypt* (London, 1921)

E. Kühnel: *Islamische Stoffe aus ägyptischen Gräbern* (Berlin, 1927)

E. Combe and others: *Répertoire chronologique d'épigraphie arabe*, 19 vols (Cairo, 1931–)

G. Marçais and G. Wiet: 'Le "Voile de Sainte Anne" d'Apt', *Mnmts Piot*, xxxiv (1934), pp. 177–94

H. A. Elsburg and R. Guest: 'The Veil of Saint Anne', *Burl. Mag.*, lxviii (1936), pp. 140–45

R. Pfister: 'Matériaux pour servir au classement des textiles égyptiens postérieurs à la conquête arabe', *Rev. A. Asiat.*, x (1936), pp. 1–16 and 73–85

N. P. Britton: *A Study of Some Early Islamic Textiles in the Museum of Fine Arts Boston* (Boston, 1938)

E. Kühnel: 'La Tradition copte dans les tissus musulmans', *Bull. Soc. Archéol. Copte*, iv (1938), pp. 79–89

R. Pfister: 'Toiles à inscriptions abbasides et fatimides', *Bull. Etud. Orient.*, xi (1945–6), pp. 47–90

E. Kühnel and L. Bellinger: *Catalogue of Dated Ṭirāz Fabrics: Umayyad, Abbasid, Fatimid, The Textile Museum, Washington, D.C.* (Washington, DC, 1952)

R. B. Serjeant: *Islamic Textiles: Material for a History up to the Mongol Conquest* (Beirut, 1972), pp. 135–64

Y. Stillman: 'New Data on Islamic Textiles from the Geniza', *Textile Hist.*, x (1979), pp. 184–95

C. Rogers, ed.: *Early Islamic Textiles* (Brighton, 1983)

H. Glidden and D. Thompson: 'Ṭirāz Fabrics in the Byzantine Collection, Dumbarton Oaks, Part One: Ṭirāz from Egypt', *Bull. Asia Inst.*, ii (1988), pp. 119–39

SHEILA S. BLAIR, JONATHAN M. BLOOM

(b) Iraq and the eastern Islamic lands. Of the enormous quantities of textiles known from contemporary sources to have been produced in the lands of the eastern caliphate, only a relatively small number of embroideries, printed and/or painted textiles and fabrics with woven decoration have survived.

The earliest embroideries belong to a well-defined technical group: all are chain-stitched in polychrome wools and usually white cotton yarns on a cotton ground that was originally embroidered with red wool. The most important of these, showing the fragmentary figure of a mounted Sasanian king with soldiers (Athens, Benaki Mus.), probably dates from the end of the period of Sasanian rule (AD 226–637). Others continue the Sasanian tradition but can be attributed to the period of Umayyad rule (661–750) after the Islamic conquest of the region. One example in Cairo (Mus. Islam. A.) shows an Iranian soldier killing a horseman within a field bordered by double rows of pearls, while other fragments in Swedish collections (see Lamm) are worked with floral motifs, rosettes or a frieze of birds between single rows of pearls.

The largest number of surviving embroideries are TIRAZ textiles, which feature a band of inscription embroidered on a ground of *mulḥam* ('half-silk': silk warps and cotton wefts) or cotton. The fabric was often glazed—probably with wheat starch—to stiffen and polish it, and pressed. The most common embroidery stitches are chain, double-chain and split stitches, although blanket, coiled double-running, couching and back stitches are also found. Dated or datable pieces fall between the caliphate of al-Muʿtazz (*reg* 866–9) and the fall of Baghdad to the Saljuqs in 1055. The only weaving centres named in the inscriptions are Merv, Bishapur and Baghdad; a very rare *mulḥam* fragment (Cairo, Mus. Islam. A.) has an embroidered inscription naming Merv as the place of manufacture, and a tapestry-woven border.

A small group of sumptuous embroideries are worked with polychrome silks and gold thread on a *mulḥam* ground; they have been assigned to the 11th and 12th centuries for stylistic and epigraphic reasons. The silk floss was embroidered primarily in split stitch, although running, self-couching and outline stitches were also used; the gold threads were couched, in some cases over a layer of ivory silk floss. The largest piece (Boston, MA, Mus. F.A. and Cleveland, OH, Mus. A.) is a fragmentary hanging with a design of large linked roundels enclosing single birds or animals, bordered by animal friezes and with small roundels in the interstices. At the bottom is a kufic inscription surmounted by a border of tangent roundels formed by a vine, the only complete one of which encloses a large bird. Small fragments with lions aligned in rows (Washington, DC, Textile Mus.) may also be from a hanging. Many other embroidered pieces consist of borders, in one instance with inscription bands beside friezes of winged horses (Washington, DC, Textile Mus.), and in another with an alternating design of paired peacocks within a roundel and a star that encloses a bird (Cleveland, OH, Mus. A.). Further types of border, although in more fragmentary condition, show a bird amid scrolling vines below a frieze of geometric ornament (Cleveland, OH, Mus. A.), or cartouches enclosing inscriptions or harpies within framing bands of scrolling vines (Athens, Benaki Mus.; Boston, MA, Mus. F.A.), while one rare embroidery (New York, Met.) is ornamented with a frieze of Christian saints under an arcade. Yet other fragments (e.g. Cleveland, OH, Mus. A.; Washington, DC, Textile Mus.) have designs based on *ṭirāz* bands, or merely display inscriptions in foliated kufic.

A number of examples of printed and painted textiles survive (Cairo, Mus. Islam. A.; Athens, Benaki Mus.; Lyon, Mus. Hist. Tissus; New York, Met.; New York, Cooper-Hewitt Mus.; Washington, DC, Textile Mus.; Cleveland, OH, Mus. A.; Boston, MA, Mus. F.A.; Toronto, Royal Ont. Mus.; former Lamm priv. col., now divided between Göteborg, Röhsska Kstslöjdmus.; Lund, Kulthist. Mus.; Stockholm, Medelhavsmus.; Stockholm, Nmus.). On a cotton or *mulḥam* ground, designs were printed with wooden blocks and gold and polychrome pigments, or drawn with dark brown or red ink, with other colours, particularly gold, often applied as well. Both techniques were occasionally used together. One painted cotton attributed to the 9th century (see Lamm, pl. XVIIA) is decorated in bands: a bird enclosed in a pearl roundel, a pearl border and a fragmentary section with a female head and a Sasanian flag. Fragments attributed to the 11th and 12th centuries show animals and/or birds enclosed in roundels or arranged in rows, squares and bands, together with tripartite bands similar to *ṭirāz* textiles, or simple inscriptions. Many designs resemble those of embroidered and woven pieces, suggesting that they may have been less expensive alternatives.

Textiles with woven decoration from the 8th and 9th centuries include tapestry fragments with warps of wool and wefts of wool and cotton; their designs are strongly based on Sasanian models. Some (Krefeld, Dt. Textilmus.; Cairo, Mus. Islam. A.) have bands of rosettes within tangent diamonds, birds enclosed by medallions of pearls and cabochons, or geometric designs. Some dozen fragments (Cairo, Mus. Islam. A.; New York, Met.; Athens, Benaki Mus.; Cleveland, OH, Mus. A.; former Lamm priv. col.) show rams, framed singly or standing in a frieze, as well as small palmette trees flanked by birds and borders of debased rosettes. Additional isolated fragments include one with rosettes within a geometric floral design and another (Cleveland, OH, Mus. A.) with a female head. A final group woven entirely of wool (Cairo, Mus. Islam. A.; Washington, DC, Textile Mus.) were found in Egypt but have been attributed to Iran or Iraq. Usually displaying birds or animals within roundels that are arbitrarily cut by ornamental borders, they typically have red grounds and designs in pastel colours. Five have a rare twill tapestry weave, and several have Arabic inscriptions datable on epigraphic grounds to the 8th century, including one (Washington, DC, Textile Mus.) bearing the name of Marwan, presumably the Umayyad caliph Marwan II (*reg* 744–50).

Compound weaves from this early period include fragments woven of wool and cotton showing Sasanian-inspired motifs such as birds in pearl roundels, or geometric patterns (Cleveland, OH, Mus. A.; Washington, DC, Textile Mus.; Paris, Mus. Cluny). A few silks show Sasanian-inspired birds or simurghs in roundels or polygonal compartments (e.g. Wolfenbüttel, Herzog August Bib.; Aachen, Domschatzkam.; St Petersburg, Hermitage; London, V&A; Reims, Mus. St-Remi). Another group attributed to 9th-century Baghdad (Washington, DC, Textile Mus.; Athens, Benaki Mus.) is brocaded in silk and gold and silver. The pieces are woven with lozenges, often enclosing cocks within octagons or stars, or with a dense mesh of geometric figures, within which are many motifs from the earlier Sasanian tradition. One (Berlin, Mus. Islam. Kst) is inscribed with the title of the Abbasid caliph al-Muntasir (*reg* 861–2).

A number of silks can be dated from the 10th to the 12th century. One, a compound silk (Berlin, Mus. Islam. Kst), is woven with an inscription band with a title typical of the Buyid rulers of Iran and Iraq (*reg* 934–1062). A second (Bamberg, Diözmus.), brocaded with gold, has an inscription band followed by aligned roundels enclosing pairs of birds. Four others, of which three are lampas or variations of lampas weaves (Berlin, Tiergarten, Kstgewmus.; Maastricht, St Servaasbasiliek; ex-Uwaroff priv. col., Moscow; Boston, MA, Mus. F.A.), have designs of paired animals or birds flanking a floral element and often enclosed by a roundel bordered by animals, birds or inscription bands. Another small group of silks (Bamberg, Diözmus.) with a tabby foundation weave and twill binding of supplementary wefts is ornamented with diverse designs incorporating animals and birds; these appear to date from the late 12th century or early 13th. Several silk-and-gold textiles can be attributed to the end of the period: one from a reliquary at Siegburg (Berlin, Tiergarten, Kstgewmus.) is woven with double-headed eagles within shields; another, a lampas textile (Augsburg, Maximilianmus.) woven with dodecagons depicting the well-known tale of Bahram Gur and Azada riding on camelback, was retrieved from the tomb of Bishop Hartmann (*d* 1286) in Augsburg Cathedral. A third, from a grave in Bamberg Cathedral, is a lampas weave with a design of animals in linked roundels and an inscription at the top.

Eleven pieces, scattered around the world, are documented in the archives of the Victoria and Albert Museum, London, as having been found at the necropolis at RAYY, south of Tehran, between 1925 and 1930. They include two with inscription bands naming Buyid rulers: a linen *ṭirāz* brocaded in silk with the name of Fakhr al-Dawla (*reg* 977–97; Washington, DC, Dumbarton Oaks); and a compound twill silk tomb-cover with the name of Baha’ al-Dawla (*reg* 998–1012; Washington, DC, Textile Mus.). Another large compound twill silk (dispersed; see *Survey of Persian Art*, pl. 992A and figs 644a and b) has a pattern of birds flanking a tree, while fragments of a compound tabby silk (London, V&A) show paired lions in roundels with octagonal figures in the interstices. Four of the Rayy pieces are silk doublecloths: one (Riggisberg, Abegg-Stift.) is adorned with linked octagons enclosing paired falconers on horseback, and the interstices are filled with ovals enclosing paired birds on a diapered ground; two more (London, V&A; Washington, DC, Dumbarton Oaks) show aligned roundels, bordered with animals and birds, enclosing paired animals and birds, while smaller roundels or octagons fill the interstices; the fourth (London, V&A; Washington, DC, Textile Mus.; Paris, Mus. Cluny) features paired sphinxes flanking a palmette tree within an inscribed octagon, and the interstices are filled with a geometric grid. Two more of the Rayy discoveries are tabby weaves with supplementary pattern wefts: one, the Ganymede Silk (divided), has crowned figures supported by double-headed eagles within a rectangular grid of kufic inscriptions; the other (Paris, Mus. Cluny; Paris, Mus. A. Déc.; New Haven, CT, Yale U. A.G.) has alternating bands of kufic inscriptions and scrolling vines. Another piece is a lampas weave with a design of polygons enclosing four pairs of sphinxes and foliate ornament.

Many other silks attributed to this period are said to have come from Rayy, but have no documentation (principal collections: Cleveland, OH, Mus. A.; Washington, DC, Textile Mus.; Riggisberg, Abegg-Stift.; New Haven, CT, Yale U. A.G.). They are woven with a wide range of patterns, often similar to those on the documented pieces, and in addition to the structures known from the documented pieces they include triplecloths and lampas weaves that are brocaded or have twill grounds. Their authenticity has been the subject of intense debate. A study using epigraphic and radiocarbon analysis of 17 textiles has revealed inconsistencies between the inscribed texts of many of the textiles and their purported dates; the results indicated that textiles in this group may range in date from the medieval period to post-1950, when new isotopes of carbon were introduced into the atmosphere.

Silks also survive from the eastern boundaries of Iran and Transoxiana. An early group, all compound weaves, has been assigned to Sogdiana, the region between Bukhara and Samarkand (principal collections: St Petersburg, Hermitage; Sens Cathedral; Liège, Mus. A. Relig. A. Mosan; Berlin, Mus. Islam. Kst; London, BM; London, V&A). On the reverse side of one (Huy, Collegiate Chruch of Notre Dame) is an ink inscription penned in Sogdian identifying the textile as *zandanījī*, that is derived from the town of Zandane near Bukhara. Although the Sogdian

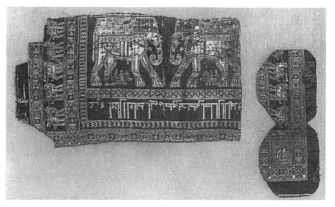

185. Eastern Iranian silk textile known as the ‘Shroud of St Josse’, fragments 520×940 mm and 620×245 mm, from Khurasan, 10th century (Paris, Musée du Louvre)

school of weaving is recorded in documents as early as the 6th century, from archaeological, documentary and epigraphic evidence the existing silks appear to have been produced from the late 7th century to the 9th. They can be divided into three broad categories on technical grounds, two of which—Zandaniji II and III—have been assigned to the Islamic period in the 8th and 9th centuries. Designs typically consist of rows of geometric compartments enclosing paired animals or birds, rosettes, geometric figures or scenes repeated in mirror reverse. Many motifs are derived from Byzantine sources, Sasanian and post-Sasanian Iran and the Far East, yet they have been transformed into a distinctly Sogdian style within which various degrees of stylization and geometricization can be observed. The Lion Silk (10th–11th century) at Maastricht (Schatkamer St-Servaasbasiliek) is related technically and stylistically to this group, but is later in date. Another silk attributed to the province of Khurasan in eastern Iran is the ‘Shroud of St Josse’ (see fig. 185). The fragments show a highly stylized design of confronted elephants above a kufic inscription inside a wide border with a procession of Bactrian camels, a cock in the corner and framing bands of geometric ornament. According to its inscription, this compound twill silk was made for the Turkish commander of Khurasan, Abu Mansur Bakhtakin (*d* 961).

BIBLIOGRAPHY

O. van Falke: *Kunstgeschichte des Seidenweberei* (Berlin, 1913); Eng. trans. as *Decorative Silks* (New York, 1922, London, 3/1936)

F. E. Day: ‘Dated Tirāz in the Collection of the University of Michigan’, *A. Islam.*, iv (1937), pp. 420–47

C. J. Lamm: *Cotton in Medieval Textiles of the Near East* (Paris, 1937)

R. Pfister: ‘L’Introduction de coton en Egypte musulmane’, *Rev. A. Asiat.*, xi/3 (Sept 1937), pp. 167–72

G. Wiet: ‘Tissus brodés mésopotamiens’, *A. Islam.*, iv (1937), pp. 54–62

N. P. Britton: *A Study of Some Early Islamic Textiles in the Museum of Fine Arts, Boston* (Boston, 1938), pp. 23–35, 70, 76–7

P. Ackerman: ‘Islamic Textiles: History’, *Survey of Persian Art*, ed. A. U. Pope and P. Ackerman (London, 1938–9, 2/1964–7), pp. 1995–2162

G. Wiet: *Soieries persanes* (Cairo, 1948)

E. Kühnel and L. Bellinger: *Catalogue of Dated Tiraz Fabrics in the Textile Museum* (Washington, DC, 1952)

E. Kühnel: ‘Abbasid Silks of the Ninth Century’, *A. Orient.*, ii (1957), pp. 367–71

D. G. Shepherd and W. Henning: ‘Zandaniji Identified?’, *Aus der Welt der islamischen Kunst: Festschrift für Ernst Kühnel* (Berlin, 1959), pp. 15–40

A. Mordini: 'Une Soierie abbasside du IXe siècle', *Bull. Liaison Cent. Int. Etud. Textiles Anc.*, xxxi (1970), pp. 50–64

M. Bernus, H. Marchal and G. Vial: 'Le Suaire de Saint Josse', *Bull. Liaison Cent. Int. Etud. Textiles Anc.*, xxxiii (1971), pp. 22–5

A. A. Jerusalimskaya: 'K slozheniiu shkoly khudozhestvennogo sholkot-kachestva v Sogde' [On the formation of the Sogdian school of silk weaving], *Srednaya Aziya i Iran* [Central Asia and Iran], ed. A. A. Ivanov and S. S. Sorokin (Leningrad, 1972), pp. 5–46

R. B. Serjeant: *Islamic Textiles: Material for a History up to the Mongol Conquest* (Beirut, 1972) [repr. of *A. Islam.*, ix–xvi (1942–51)]*Bull. Liaison Cent. Int. Etud. Textiles Anc.*, xxxvii (1973) and xxxviii (1973) [two issues devoted to the 'Buyid' silks in the Abegg-Stiftung, Riggisberg]

D. G. Shepherd: 'Medieval Persian Silks in Fact and Fancy (A Refutation of the Riggisberg Report)', *Bull. Liaison Cent. Int. Etud. Textiles Anc.*, xxxix/xl (1974) [whole issue]

L. von Wilckens: 'Sieben Seidengewebe und ein Stickereifragment', *Anz. Ger. Nmus.* (1975), pp. 140–46

K. Riboud: 'A Newly Excavated Caftan from the Northern Caucasus', *Textile Mus. J.*, iv (1976), pp. 21–42

L. Golombek and V. Gervers: 'Tiraz Fabrics in the Royal Ontario Museum', *Studies in Textile History, in Memory of Harold B. Burnham*, ed. V. Gervers (Toronto, 1977), pp. 82–125

S. Müller-Christensen: 'En persisk brokade fra Domkirken i Augsburg', *By og Bygd* [Town and country], *Festskrift til Marta Hoffmann, Norsk Flkmus. Ab.*, xxx (1983–4), pp. 185–94

Internationales Kolloquium: Textile Grabfunde aus der Sepultur des Bamberger Domkapitals: Schloss Seehof, 1985

D. King: 'The Textiles Found near Rayy about 1925', *Bull. Liaison Cent. Int. Etud. Textiles Anc.*, lxv (1987), pp. 34–58

S. S. Blair, J. M. Bloom and A. E. Wardwell: 'Reevaluating the Date of the "Buyid" Silks', *A. Orient.*, xxii (1993), pp. 1–41

(c) Spain and North Africa. Textiles produced in the western Islamic world before the 13th century show a wide variety of styles and techniques and a high level of artistic achievement. The cultivation of the silkworm, the weaving of silk textiles and the institution of the TIRAZ, or official factories, were all introduced to the Iberian peninsula under the Umayyads of Spain (*reg* 756–1031). Documents mention official factories at Córdoba, Almería, Fiñana, Seville and Málaga; weaving was also an important industry at Valencia, Lleida and Toledo. Because most of the surviving textiles were preserved in churches, the vast majority were adapted to serve Christian liturgical functions and therefore no longer preserve their original form. No examples have been preserved in North Africa, although a fragmentary silk twill with an inscription embroidered in yellow thread (divided: London, V&A, 1314–1888, T.13-1960; New York, Brooklyn Mus.; and Brussels, Musées Royaux A. & Hist.) was probably made for the Umayyad caliph of Syria Marwan II (*reg* 744–50) in the official workshop of Ifriqiyya, presumably located at Kairouan. Other official factories were located at Sousse in Tunisia, the Qal'at Bani Hamad in Algeria and Fez in Morocco; in Tunisia weaving was an important industry at Mahdia, while from Gabès, famous for its sericulture, silk production was introduced to Sicily by the Aghlabid dynasty (*reg* 800–909), which took control of the island.

The earliest dated Spanish textile is the celebrated *ṭirāz* of the Spanish Umayyad ruler Hisham II (*reg* 976–1013 with interruption), which was preserved in the church of S María del Rivero, San Esteban de Gormaz Soria Province (Madrid, Real Acad. Hist.). Both its design and technique—silk and gold tapestry inwoven in a silk tabby ground—can be traced to Egypt. The gold wefts are typical of those found in Spanish Islamic textiles: silvered and gilded strips of membrane Z-wrapped around a silk core. Another

11th-century textile in the form of a *ṭirāz* and woven in the same inwoven-tapestry technique is preserved in Huesca (Mus. Episc. & Capitular Arqueol. Sagrada). Several related but smaller inwoven tapestries datable to the 9th to 11th centuries include borders from San Pedro de Montes and San Pedro de Arlanza (Madrid, Inst. Valencia Don Juan; Covarrubias, Mus. Parroq.); parts of the shrouds of St Froilan and St Columba (León and Sens cathedrals); a fragment from a reliquary in Oviedo Cathedral (untraced); and a band from the mitre of St Valerius (Roda de Isábena Cathedral). A further example, a 10th-century band (Madrid, Inst. Valencia Don Juan), is woven in the same technique, but its pattern of linked roundels, the most complete of which encloses a peacock, reflects Near Eastern designs. Fragments from a reliquary in the cathedral of El Burgo de Osma, and from the alb of Abbot Biure (Barcelona, Mus. Dioc.), are additional examples of Spanish textiles attributable to the 11th century.

The earliest drawloom textiles include three 11th-century compound-twill silks in the church of S Isidoro, León. Two, with designs of aligned roundels enclosing either floral motifs or paired animals, and stars or four-directional palmettes in the interstices, are based on Near Eastern models; that with animals has inscriptions around the roundels stating that it was made in Baghdad, but the epigraphy betrays its Spanish origin. The third silk has wide and narrow bands ornamented with inscriptions, opposing rows of paired animals and birds, and inhabited vines. Two important compound-twill silks, the Witches Pallium (Vic, Mus. Episc.) and the lining of the reliquary of St Millán (Logroño, Monasterio de Yuso-PP Agustinos Recoletos), are woven in red, with friezes of paired animals or birds and Trees of Life in dark green and yellow. A slightly later (11th–12th century) compound-twill silk from the tomb of St Bernard Calvó at Vic (dispersed, e.g. Cleveland, OH, Mus. A.) has rows of double-headed eagles grasping lions, a motif borrowed from the Near East. Contemporary with this textile is a group of compound-twill silks modelled after Byzantine textiles. Their Spanish origin is indicated by the Arabic inscription on one (Vic, Mus. Episc.) woven with ogival inscription bands framing paired griffins. This fragment is related stylistically both to a silk in Amsterdam (Rijksmus.) and to another reportedly from the monastery of Santa Maria de l'Estavy (New York, Cooper-Hewitt Mus.).

Another group of drawloom silks unified by design and technique can be attributed to the 12th century (Boston, MA, Mus. F.A.; Cleveland, OH, Mus. A.; New York, Cooper-Hewitt Mus.; New York, Met.; Quedlinburg, Schlossmus.; Burgos, S Juan de Ortega; Riggisberg, Abegg-Stift.; Salamanca, Mus. Dioc.; Vic, Mus. Episc.). They are sometimes known as the Baghdad Group because the inscription on one of them, from the church of El Burgo de Osma (Boston, MA, Mus. F.A.), states that it was made in Baghdad. However, both the epigraphy and the technique are Spanish. Another, the chasuble of San Juan de Ortega at Quintanaortuña (Burgos), has an inscription naming the Almoravid ruler 'Ali ibn Yusuf (*reg* 1106–42). The design of this group of textiles consists of aligned, slightly elliptical roundels framed by friezes of animals or birds and enclosing paired animals or birds. The exception is the Lion Strangler Silk (dispersed, e.g. Cleveland, OH,

Mus. A.; New York, Cooper-Hewitt Mus.; see fig. 186), found in the tomb of St Bernard Calvó at Vic, which presents a bearded and turbaned central figure strangling confronted lions. The whole group has four-directional palmettes that fill the interstices, and horizontal inscription bands sometimes interrupt the roundels. The ground is typically ivory-coloured, and the pattern predominantly red and green with details in yellow or brocaded with gold. The weave is lampas, except for the horizontal inscription bands, which are a compound weave; the warps are typically arranged in groups of two and four, and the gold wefts are bound in a honeycomb pattern.

Another group of 12th-century lampas silks brocaded with gold is characterized by double-headed eagles, grasping gazelles or birds, which flank concentric bulb palmettes. Examples from the tombs of Alfonso VII of Castile (d 1157) and the infante Don García (d 1145 or 1146) are now in Toledo Cathedral and the parochial church at Oña (Burgos); others are in the cathedrals of Bremen and Bamberg. Closely related in design but from the 13th century is a fragment (Bamberg Cathedral) with gazelles and bulb palmettes. Additional silk-and-gold lampas textiles depicting animals and birds in roundels (e.g. Provins Cathedral; Berlin, Staat. Mus.; Madrid, Inst. Valencia Don Juan, 2059) are distinguishable from the

Baghdad Group by technical details. A large (2.25×1.75 m) and nearly complete compound twill panel (Burgos, Real Monasterio de las Huelgas, Mus. Telas & Preseas) woven c. 1200, with inscribed roundels enclosing paired lions, borders and an inscription across the top, served as a pall for Maria de Almenar (d 1234). One of the most accomplished compound-twill silks is the Cope of King Robert, a chasuble used in 1258 to wrap the relics of St Exupère at St Sernin, Toulouse. Pairs of large peacocks and small animals flanking Trees of Life are arranged in horizontal rows; beneath each is a kufic inscription repeating the word *baraka* ('blessing'). Palmette trees separate the units.

Sicily under Islamic rule was renowned for its silk textiles, and the industry continued there under the Normans (reg 1061–1194). Textiles formerly thought to originate from Sicily are now attributed to Spain; the only group of textiles clearly attributable to Sicily is part of the set of coronation robes of the Holy Roman Emperor and Empress (Vienna, Schatzkam.). The most famous is the stupendous mantle (see fig. 183 above) of Roger II Hauteville (see HAUTEVILLE, (1)), which bears an Arabic inscription along the hem stating that it was made in the royal workshop at Palermo in 1133–4. A hemicircle (diam. 3.42 m) of red silk, it is embroidered in gold thread and pearls and features a central tree separating addorsed lions attacking camels. It is partially lined with a sumptuous silk and gold tapestry-woven fabric with figural scenes. The Holy Roman set also includes an alb made for William II Hauteville (see HAUTEVILLE, (2)) on which a bilingual Latin and Arabic inscription embroidered in pearls and gold states that it was made in 1181 at Palermo (see also ROMANESQUE, §X, EMBROIDERY, §1 and ITALY, §XI, 1).

BIBLIOGRAPHY

R. B. Serjeant: *Islamic Textiles: Material for a History up to the Mongol Conquest* (Beirut, 1972) [repr. of *A. Islam.*, ix–xvi (1942–51)]

D. G. Shepherd: 'The Hispano-Islamic Textiles in the Cooper Union Collection', *Chron. Mus. A. Dec. Cooper Un.*, i (1943), pp. 357–401

M. Gómez-Moreno: *El Panteón real de las Huelgas de Burgos* (Madrid, 1946)

——: 'Tapicería, bordados y tejidos', *El Arte árabe español hasta los Almohades*, A. Hisp., iii (Madrid, 1951), pp. 344–51

D. G. Shepherd: 'The Textiles from Las Huelgas de Burgos', *Bull. Needle & Bobbin Club*, xxxv (1951), pp. 3–26

F. Day: 'The Tirāz Silk of Marwān', *Archaeologica Orientalia in Memoriam Ernst Herzfeld*, ed. G. C. Miles (Locust Valley, NY, 1952), pp. 39–61

D. G. Shepherd: 'The Third Silk from the Tomb of Saint Bernard Calvo', *Bull. Cleveland Mus. A.*, xxix (1952), pp. 13–14

C. Bernis: 'Tapicería hispano-musulmana (siglos IX–XI)', *Archv Esp. A.*, xxvii (1954), pp. 189–212

F. E. Day: 'The Inscription of the Boston "Baghdad" Silk', *A. Orient.*, i (1954), pp. 191–4

E. Grohne: 'Mittelalterliche Seidengewebe aus Erzbischofsgräbern im Bremer Dom', *Alte Kostbarkeiten aus dem bremischen Kulturbereich* (Bremen, 1956), pp. 107–67

E. Kühnel: 'Die Kunst Persiens unter den Buyiden', *Z. Dt. Mrgländ. Ges.*, cvi/1 (1956), pp. 78–92 (90 and fig. 26)

F. L. May: *Silk Textiles of Spain: Eighth to Fifteenth Century* (New York, 1957)

D. G. Shepherd: 'A Dated Hispano-Islamic Silk', *A. Orient.*, ii (1957), pp. 373–82

——: 'Two Medieval Silks from Spain', *Bull. Cleveland Mus. A.*, xlv (1958), pp. 3–7

D. G. Shepherd and G. Vial: 'La Chasuble de St-Sernin', *Bull. Liaison Cent. Int. Etud. Textiles Anc.*, xxi (1965), pp. 20–31

R. A. Lazaro Lopez: 'Découverte de deux riches étoffes dans l'église paroissiale d'Oña', *Bull. Liaison Cent. Int. Etud. Textiles Anc.*, xxxi (1970), pp. 21–5

D. G. Shepherd: 'A Treasure from a Thirteenth-century Spanish Tomb', *Bull. Cleveland Mus. A.*, lxv (1978), pp. 111–34

186. Spanish silk textile known as the Lion Strangler Silk (detail), 680×165 mm, from the tomb of St Bernard Calvó, Vic, 12th century (New York, Cooper-Hewitt Museum, Smithsonian Institution, National Museum of Design)

C. Partearroyo: *Historia de las artes aplicadas e industriales en España* (Madrid, 1982)

Internationales Kolloquium: Textile Grabfunde aus der Sepultur des Bamberger Domkapitals: Schloss Seehof, 1985

R. M. Martín i Ros: 'Tomba de Sant Bernat Calbó: Teixit dit de Gilgamés', *Osona II* (1986), iii of *Catalunya romànica* (Barcelona, 1975–), pp. 728–31

——: 'San Joan de las Abadesses: Teixit anomenat *Palli de les Bruixes*', *El Ripollès* (1987), x of *Catalunya romànica* (Barcelona, 1975–), pp. 399–402

C. Partearroyo Lacaba: *La seda en España: Leyenda, poder y realidad* (Tarrasa, 1991)

J. D. Dodds, ed.: *Al-Andalus: The Art of Islamic Spain* (New York, 1992)

ANNE E. WARDWELL

(d) Yemen. The manufacture and trade in textiles were already important to the highly developed civilization of South Arabia in pre-Islamic times. Textiles may have been exported to Egypt soon after 3000 BC, textile merchants of Sheba are mentioned in a biblical reference from the 6th century BC, and Yemeni textiles were esteemed outside the Arabian peninsula from the 4th century AD. They were used to confer status and to pay taxes and tribute in the Hijaz and Sasanian Iran. Finely striped Yemeni cloth was used to cover the Ka'ba in Mecca, a tradition maintained by the Prophet Muhammad (whose body was also wrapped in Yemeni shrouds) and continued until the mid-7th century when Coptic cloth was substituted.

Yemeni textiles maintained their fine reputation in the Islamic period and were exported for use by the caliphs and the élite. The Umayyad (*reg* 661–750) and early Abbasid (*reg* 749–1258) caliphs favoured Yemeni tie-dyed and brocaded cotton cloth with bands of inscriptions (*see* TIRAZ), specially woven in San'a. Yemeni textiles, in particular cloaks with borders and striped cloth manufactured in San'a and Aden, were in great demand in the Levant, Egypt, Baghdad and China, although after AD 1000 there was increased competition from other sources. From the 11th to the 13th century, as Yemeni exports declined, Jewish and Muslim merchants based in Aden dominated the east–west textile trade.

Cotton (probably indigenous) was cultivated in antiquity, and silk was introduced by the 4th century AD. In Islamic times, Yemen was also known for its dyes: its specialities were madder, indigo and *wars* (*Flemingia grahamiana*, an unusual yellow/orange dye, derived from a plant), cultivated for both local use and export. The most important centres of textile production were Aden, renowned for its fine linen stuffs, and San'a, with its cotton, silk and woollen decorated stuffs, most notably the famous

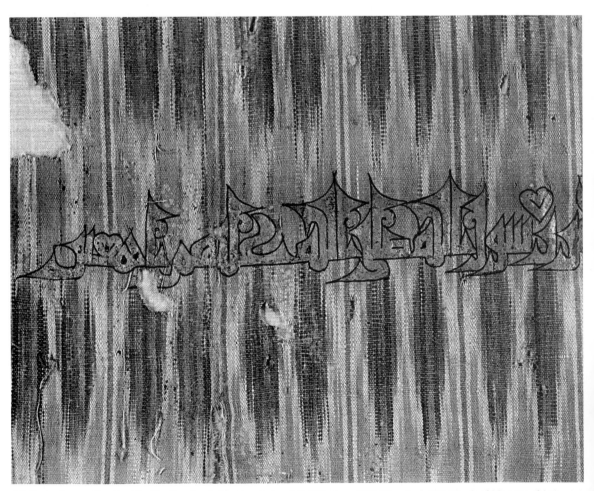

187. Yemeni cotton ikat (detail) with painted and gilded inscription, 625×581 mm, *c.* 1000 (Cleveland, OH, Cleveland Museum of Art)

ikat cloths (see TEXTILE, §III, 1(ii)(a)). Indeed, the Malaysian word *ikat* may derive from the Arabic *'aqada*, to tie or knot, and some experts regard South Arabia as the original home of ikat. These cotton ikats, called *'aṣb* (referring to the technique of binding the warp threads for resist dyeing), *washī* (decorated), *burd* or *ridā'* (referring to the cloaks and gowns made of ikat), were of exceptionally fine quality and were imitated by weavers in Egypt, Spain and Iran, who had probably learnt the techniques from Yemeni craftsmen. The tie-dyed warps were usually dyed in shades of blue and yellow prior to weaving, and this patterned yarn was woven in wide stripes alternating with narrower ones in plain colours. As these textiles were woven in tabby weave, often warp-faced, the fabric had pronounced stripes, although sometimes a tartan effect was achieved when the wefts were dyed as well. The most common decoration was an inscription embroidered in undyed cotton or painted, gilded and outlined in black ink (e.g. Cleveland, OH, Mus. A., 50.353, cotton tabby with painted inscription naming the Yemeni imam Yusuf ibn Yahya (*reg* 955–1003); see fig. 187). Ornaments in silk or cotton tapestry weave or brocaded cotton were less frequent.

BIBLIOGRAPHY
C. J. Lamm: *Cotton in Medieval Textiles of the Near East* (Paris, 1937)
A. Bühler: *Ikat Batik Plangi* (Basle, 1972)
R. B. Serjeant: *Islamic Textiles: Material for a History up to the Mongol Conquest* (Beirut, 1972)
L. Golombek and V. Gervers: 'Tiraz Fabrics in the Royal Ontario Museum', *Studies in Textile History in Memory of H. B. Burnham*, ed. V. Gervers (Toronto, 1977), pp. 82–125
J. Baldry: *Textiles in Yemen* (London, 1982)
S. S. Blair: 'Legibility Versus Decoration in Islamic Epigraphy: The Case of Interlacing', *World Art: Themes of Unity in Diversity: Acts of the XXVIth International Congress of the History of Art: Washington, DC, 1986*, ii, pp. 229–31

JENNY BALFOUR-PAUL

(ii) c. 1250–c. 1500. The end of the Abbasid caliphate brought about the decline of official manufactories for textiles in the Islamic lands, but exquisite silks continued to be woven on drawlooms. Three regional groups can be identified.

(a) Spain and North Africa. (b) Egypt and Syria. (c) Eastern Islamic lands.

(a) Spain and North Africa. The major innovation in 13th-century textiles was the gradual replacement of animal patterns characteristic of the earlier period by a style often identified as Hispano-Moresque. These small-scale designs formed by interlacing strapwork are largely geometric and floral but sometimes include paired animals, and larger pieces have inscription bands. The trend towards the increased use of geometric forms, visible in other arts produced under the Almohad dynasty (*reg* 1130–1269) in north-west Africa and Spain, is already apparent in works of the late 12th century; the earliest example is a silk-and-gold tapestry made into a cap for the infante Ferdinand of Castile in the late 12th century or early 13th (Burgos, Real Monasterio de las Huelgas, Mus. Telas & Preseas). The most famous textiles of this type include those found in the tombs of Don Felipe (*d* 1274; see fig. 188) and Doña Leonor at Villalcázar de Sirga (dispersed: e.g. Madrid, Inst. Valencia Don Juan.; New York, Cooper-Hewitt Mus.; New York, Hisp. Soc. America; Cleveland, OH, Mus. A.), two of the three silk-and-gold

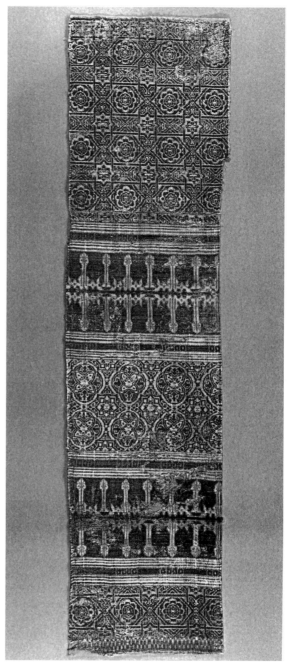

188. Spanish silk textile, fragment of tunic, 680×165 mm, from the tomb of Don Felipe (*d* 1274), S María la Blanca, Villalcázar de Sirga (Riggisberg, Abegg-Stiftung)

textiles from the San Valero vestments (*c.* 1279; Madrid, Inst. Valencia Don Juan) and the shroud of Sancho IV (*d* 1295) at Toledo Cathedral. These are compound weaves, some with areas of double cloth; other textiles with small-scale geometric patterns were woven differently. Two silks at the Real Monasterio de las Huelgas in Burgos (Gómez-Moreno, nos 4 and 5) are lampas weaves with areas of compound weave; their gold pattern wefts are bound in a honeycomb pattern. Additional textiles from Burgos (Gómez-Moreno, nos 15–20), together with a blue-and-gold striped silk from the tomb of Don Felipe (dispersed: e.g. Cleveland, OH, Mus. A.), have bands of linear lozenge designs woven in fancy weave alternating with bands of inscriptions or other geometric ornament formed by additional gold and silk pattern wefts. Fancy weave inwoven with silk-and-gold tapestry is used in the ornamented panels on the cope and dalmatics of San Valero (Barcelona, Mus. Tèxtil & Indument.), a cushion cover from the tomb of Leonor of Castile (*d* 1244) at Burgos (Real Monasterio de las Huelgas, Mus. Telas & Preseas) and a garment for the infante Alfonso (*d* 1291) at Valladolid (Mus. Dioc. & Catedralicio).

Three surviving textiles intended for furnishings exhibit the technique of silk-and-gold tapestry inwoven in a tabby ground. One of these, a fragmentary example showing pairs of drinking ladies in roundels surrounded by strapwork in the typical Hispano-Moresque style (New York, Cooper-Hewitt Mus.), is ascribed to the early part of the 13th century. Another, the cushion cover of Queen Berengaria of Castile (*d* 1246; Burgos, Real Monasterio de las Huelgas, Mus. Telas & Preseas), has top and bottom borders in gold with Arabic inscriptions which define a crimson field with four octagrams and a central roundel enclosing a pair of women flanking a Tree of Life. The third example, fragments from a large hanging retrieved from the tomb of Don Arnaldo de Gurb (*d* 1284), Bishop of Barcelona (dispersed: e.g. Cleveland, OH, Mus. A.; New York, Cooper-Hewitt Mus.; Madrid, Mus. Arqueol. N.; Granada, Mus. N. A. Hispmus.), preserves parts of the roundels that were originally arranged in aligned rows and portions of the end borders. Similar to these three furnishing fabrics is the splendid Las Navas de Tolosa Banner (3.3×2.2 m; Burgos, Real Monasterio de las Huelgas, Mus. Telas & Preseas), worked in gold, crimson, white, blue, black and green silk, with a central octagram enclosed by pearl borders and Koranic inscriptions. The banner is thought to have been a trophy won by Ferdinand III (*d* 1252) and donated to the monastery when it was reconstructed in the first half of the 13th century.

Similar textiles were also woven for Christian patrons in the 13th century, to judge from three groups of MUDÉJAR textiles made according to different techniques. A mantle from the tomb of Ferdinand III (Madrid, Real Armeria) and the chasuble of the Sancho of Aragon (*d* 1275; Toledo Cathedral) are entirely tapestry-woven with heraldic designs. By contrast, several textiles from the monastery of Las Huelgas (Gómez-Moreno, nos 35, 32–43), plus a number of vestments and fragments from other European churches, are the most important of the many 'half-silks': these compound weaves have linen main warps, silk binding warps and wefts, and gold thread usually consisting of strips of silvered and gilded membrane S-wrapped around a linen core. Their designs are clearly related to stucco ornament at Las Huelgas, Burgos: compartments enclosing animals, birds, stars, and occasionally heraldry, often interrupted by bands of pseudo-Arabic inscriptions. The third group, silks known as Cloths of Aresta, are preserved in many European churches as well as at Las Huelgas, Burgos (Gómez-Moreno, nos 21–33). Woven in weft-faced lozenge or diagonal twill weaves,

their designs consist of small fleurs-de-lis, lions, castles, birds, plants or occasionally armorials against a diapered ground.

A small group of brocaded lampas silks from the early 14th century have designs of gazelles, basilisks and concentric bulb palmettes reminiscent of the gazelle/eagle/palmette designs of the 12th century (e.g. Cleveland, OH, Mus. A.; Paris, Mus. Cluny; Sens Cathedral). The most common 14th-century textiles, however, are drawloom silks with Hispano-Moresque designs of stars and other geometric figures formed by interlacing strapwork. The fields are interrupted by bands with merlons, interlacing, inscriptions or (rarely) figures or animals, as in a large textile (New York, Hisp. Soc. America). These designs were often woven with gold and polychrome silks until the end of the 14th century, when gold became too expensive to use in this way. Typical textiles from the late 14th century have designs of strapwork combined with kufic and cursive inscriptions closely modelled after tile and stucco decoration at the Alhambra Palace and sometimes known as Alhambra arabesques. The undulating design on one silk-and-gold lampas textile with vines, palmettes, heraldic shields and rampant lions (Cleveland, OH, Mus. A.) shows the impact of Chinese textiles. The only textiles known to have been woven in North Africa are two banners, silk-and-gold tapestry inwoven in a tabby ground (Toledo Cathedral). Both were made at Fez and captured at the battle of the Rio Salado in 1340. The first (2.8×2.2 m) was made in 1312 for the Marinid ruler Abu Sa'id 'Uthman (*reg* 1310–31); the second (3.74×2.67 m) was made in 1339 for Abu'l-Hasan 'Ali I (*reg* 1331–48). Both were probably woven by Andalusians or weavers trained in Spain and should therefore be regarded as products of the great Hispano-Islamic textile tradition rather than indigenous North African forms.

During the 15th century variations on the star and tile patterns continued to be woven in silk. Whether they were made in Spain or in North Africa by Muslims fleeing the Christian reconquest is debated. A complete silk curtain (Cleveland, OH, Mus. A.; *see* TEXTILE, colour pl. VII, fig. 1) has two identical lateral panels with rectangular fields of arabesques framing tile patterns, elaborate borders with knotted kufic and Alhambra arabesques, and a central panel with Alhambra arabesques flanked by narrow bands of inscription, interlacing and merlons; the Nasrid motto (*lā ghālib ilā'llah*: 'There is no victor save God') on all the panels confirms their Spanish origin. Other textiles from the 14th and 15th centuries include those with variously striped patterns with repeating bands of inscriptions, interlacing and floral motifs, and *Mudéjar* silks with heraldic designs or combinations of strapwork and European-style floral motifs, animals and birds. Both Islamic and *Mudéjar* silks from this period are predominantly lampas weaves, sometimes combined with areas of compound weave.

BIBLIOGRAPHY

D. G. Shepherd: 'The Hispano-Islamic Textiles in the Cooper Union Collection', *Chron. Mus. A. Dec. Cooper Un.*, i (1943), pp. 357–401

M. Gómez-Moreno: *El Panteón real de las Huelgas de Burgos* (Madrid, 1946)

L. Torres Balbas: *Arte almohade, arte nazarí, arte mudéjar*, A. Hisp., iv (Madrid, 1949), pp. 57–61, 198–203, 384–9

C. Bernis: 'Tapicería hispano-musulmana (siglos XIII y XIV)', *Archv Esp. A.*, xxix (1956), pp. 95–115

F. L. May: *Silk Textiles of Spain: Eighth to Fifteenth Century* (New York, 1957)

D. G. Shepherd: 'La Dalmatique d'Ambazac', *Cieta Bull.*, xi (1960), pp. 11–29

M. J. Ainaud de Lasarte: 'La Devise des rois de Grenade sur un tissu hispano-mauresque', *Bull. Liaison Cent. Int. Etud. Textiles Anc.*, xxxii (1970), pp. 14–21

D. G. Shepherd: 'A Treasure from a Thirteenth-century Spanish Tomb', *Bull. Cleveland Mus. A.*, lxv (1978), pp. 111–34

C. Partearroyo: *Historia de las artes applicadas e industriales en España* (Madrid, 1982)

A. E. Wardwell: 'A Fifteenth-century Silk Curtain from Muslim Spain', *Bull. Cleveland Mus. A.*, lxx (1983), pp. 58–72

S. Desrosiers, G. Vial and D. de Jonghe: 'Cloth of Aresta: A Preliminary Study of its Definition, Classification, and Method of Weaving', *Textile Hist.*, xx (1989), pp. 199–223

C. Partearroyo Lacaba: *La seda en España: Leyenda, poder y realidad* (Tarrasa, 1991)

J. D. Dodds, ed.: *Al-Andalus: The Art of Islamic Spain* (New York, 1992)

(b) Egypt and Syria. The textile industry in Egypt and Syria under the Mamluks (*reg* 1250–1517) was very important. Social position and court and military rank were reflected in the fabric, colour and cut of dress; the *kiswa*, the cloth covering the Ka'ba in Mecca, was made in Egypt; and robes of honour (Arab. *khil'a*) were produced as state gifts. Although weaving is mentioned by many travellers, chroniclers and European pilgrims, and the resultant fabrics feature in European church inventories, the only significant textual information is the description of drawloom weaving in Alexandria by the encyclopaedist and historian al-Nuwayri (*d* 1332). In Egypt there were official factories (Arab. *ṭirāz*) at Alexandria and Cairo; cotton was woven at Alexandria and silk and linen in both cities, while Bahnasa in the Faiyum was noted for its linen and woollen fabrics. In Syria, luxury silks were produced at Damascus—also the site of an official factory—and at Antioch. Other important centres were Baalbek and Aleppo, while Ramla and Sarmin were known for cotton weaving. Dyestuffs from Egypt are mentioned by the chroniclers Qalqashandi (1355–1418) and al-Maqrizi (1364–1442). Weaving flourished in the politically and economically stable conditions under the Bahri, or Turkish, Mamluks (*reg* 1250–1390) but declined as a result of the civil wars and economic depression that beset the state from 1388 to 1422. Although Damascus and Alexandria remained important weaving centres under the Burji, or Circassian, Mamluks (*reg* 1382–1517), a census taken of weavers in Alexandria in 1434 revealed that only 800 looms were operating out of the 14,000 that had been in use in 1388.

Textiles have been preserved in burials—principally in Upper Egypt and Old Cairo (Fustat)—and in European church treasuries. Representing only a tiny fraction of the quantities produced, surviving fragments nevertheless reveal a wide variety of techniques, styles and fabrics from sumptuous silks to everyday fabrics. A core group can be attributed to this period on the basis of technique, style and occasionally epigraphy, although it is sometimes difficult to distinguish Egyptian or Syrian textiles from those woven in Italy and Asia. Silks woven on drawlooms may be lampas or compound weaves, doublecloth or a variation with multiple sets of warps and wefts (often called triple or incomplete triple weave), and damask. These are occasionally combined with bands of extended tabby, which have a ribbed effect. Metal thread consists of a silk core around which were spun metal strips or gilded or silvered animal substrate. In addition to drawloom silks, other survivals include tapestry fragments (e.g. New York, Met.; Cairo, Mus. Islam. A.), several tabby or twill textiles with striped designs, doublecloth cottons, and fragments of resist-printed cottons and linens.

Only one drawloom textile has been scientifically excavated: a yellow silk garment (Cairo, Mus. Islam. A., 23903) found in 1966 in a church crypt at Jabal Adda in Upper Egypt and attributed to the late 13th century. A close variation of its star-and-cross pattern combined with animals and latticework exists in a silk damask (Riggisberg, Abegg-Stift.) which may indicate a similar date. Study of the inscriptions on fabrics has allowed dating of several examples. Some drawloom textiles can be dated by the names of the rulers inscribed on them. The earliest is a silk (Cairo, Mus. Islam. A.) with inscription bands forming ogival compartments which enclose heart-shaped palmettes; the inscriptions repeat a dedication to Qala'un (*reg* 1280–90). Dating from the reign of his successor Khalil (*reg* 1290–94) is an inscribed tapestry fragment (Cairo, Mus. Islam. A.) in which the tripartite division of medallions and diamonds flanked by inscription bands derives from official textiles made under the Fatimids (*see* §(i)(a) above). Two drawloom silks bear the titles of al-Nasir Muhammad (*reg* 1294–1340 with interruptions): a yellow damask with inscribed medallions and vines terminating in long curving leaves (Berlin, Mus. Islam. Kst) and a fragmentary cap preserving medallions with inscribed borders and lattice centres (Göteborg, Röhsska Kstslöjdmus.). Three damasks with designs of inscribed bulb palmettes on parallel curving vines (Berlin, Mus. Islam. Kst and Tiergarten, Kstgewmus.; London, V&A) bear the Persian form of al-Nasir Muhammad's name, suggesting that these textiles may have been made in Iran for export to the Mamluk court.

Several other drawloom textiles can be attributed to specific Mamluk rulers on the basis of the titles in their inscriptions. Five give the title *al-malik al-nāsir*: a cap (Cleveland, OH, Mus. A.) and two fragments with bands of crescent moons and/or inscriptions and animals (London, V&A; Cairo, Mus. Islam. A.); a silk with tangent dodecagons, inscribed borders and paired lions (Berlin, Mus. Islam. Kst); and a fragment (Göteborg, Röhsska Kstslöjdmus.) preserving a band of inscribed medallions, fish, crescent moons and lozenges between bands of extended tabby. Although this title was used by four sultans in the 14th century, the silks are generally attributed to the reign of al-Nasir Muhammad. A striped silk with an inscription 'Glory to our lord, the sultan *al-malik al-mu'ayyad*', double-headed eagles, paired animals, lotus flowers and latticework (divided: Göteborg, Röhsska Kstslöjdmus.; New York, Met., see fig. 189) is stylistically earlier than the reigns of the two Mamluk sultans who bore that title in the 15th century. The textile was probably intended for the Rasulid sultan of Yemen, Mu'ayyad Da'ud (*reg* 1296–1322), for whom metalwares were also made in Egypt. A fragmentary silk garment for a child (Berlin, Mus. Islam. Kst) with ogives framing paired griffins within medallions bears the title *al-sulṭān al-malik al-muzaffar*. Although five Mamluk sultans assumed that title between

189. Egyptian or Syrian silk double weave, 922×527 mm (mounted), early 14th century (New York, Metropolitan Museum of Art)

1259 and 1421, the style and design suggest a date not later than the reign of Baybars II (*reg* 1309). Three drawloom silks are inscribed 'Glory to our master the sultan *al-malik al-ashraf*', a title assumed by six Mamluk sultans between the 13th and the 15th century. The first, a blue damask (London, V&A), probably dates to the reign of Kujuk (*reg* 1341–2) or earlier, since a variation of its pattern was painted in 1354 by Puccio di Simone and Allegretto Nuzi. The second, a striped silk-and-gold textile (Cairo, Mus. Islam. A.), was probably woven during the reign of Kujuk or of Sha'ban II (*reg* 1363–76), judging from its 14th-century design of animals, flowers, cartouches and inscriptions. The third, a lampas silk-and-gold orphrey (London, V&A), may date as late as the reign of Barsbay (*reg* 1422–37), because its ogival design of vines, lotuses, cartouches and bulb palmettes was depicted *c.* 1430 by the Master of the Bambino Vispo. Two variations of this design occur in a silk-and-gold lampas cape (Cleveland, OH, Mus. A.) and a silk damask (London, V&A) of approximately the same date.

Several drawloom silks with inscriptions but no titles can be attributed to the 14th century for stylistic reasons. Two, a hat (Cleveland, OH, Mus. A.) and a fragment (Berlin, Mus. Islam. Kst), are woven with bands of inscriptions 'Glory to our master the sultan', running animals and pin stripes, while in another fragment (Washington, DC, Textile Mus.) bands of floral ogives alternate with bands of inscription, 'the sultan, the king'. A tunic (Cairo, Mus. Islam. A.) has a design of ogival medallions alternating with crescent moons, both inscribed *al-sultān*; they are arranged in staggered rows with fish and rosettes in the interstices. Similar medallions within an ogival net of crescent moons, rosettes and small medallions occur in

two silks belonging to a dalmatic and cope (Lübeck, Marienkirche). The word *al-sultān* also appears in the crescent moons ornamenting a child's sandal (Richmond, Surrey, Keir priv. col.). Other drawloom silks without inscriptions (Cleveland, OH, Mus. A.; Washington, DC, Textile Mus.; Cairo, Mus. Islam. A.; Berlin, Tiergarten, Kstgewmus.; Toronto, Royal Ont. Mus.; New York, Met. and Lyon, Mus. Hist. Tissus) display a variety of patterns— bands, squares, scrolling vines and ogives—which include such typically Mamluk motifs as crescent moons, fish, lotus flowers, latticework, rosettes and pin stripes.

A green, white and gold textile making up a chasuble (London, V&A) can be attributed to the 15th century, since its design of ogives enclosing medallions is similar to one painted *c.* 1500 by the MASTER OF ST GILES (*see* MASTERS, ANONYMOUS, AND MONOGRAMMISTS, §I). Several lampas silks (Berlin, Tiergarten, Kstgewmus.) may also date from the 15th century; some have ogival patterns similar to the chasuble, others have designs of diamonds, squares or stars. The rosette, latticework and fleurs-de-lis in these repetitive geometric patterns recall the repertory of earlier designs, but animals and birds are no longer found.

In addition to drawloom textiles, several textiles have striped designs which were usually achieved by supplementary warps and/or wefts. Small-scale geometric motifs and diaper patterns frequently ornament the narrow bands of these textiles, though two silk-and-gold winding sheets excavated at Jabal Adda (Cairo, Mus. Islam. A.) and a fragment (New York, Met.) incorporate inscriptions and animals or rosettes. Some (Cleveland, OH, Mus. A.; Cairo, Mus. Islam. A.; Berlin, Mus. Islam. Kst) are woven of silk-and-gold thread; others (Berlin, Mus. Islam. Kst; New York, Met.) use silk or combinations of silk and cotton, linen or wool. This striped group is loosely attributed to the 13th to 15th centuries, except for the pieces excavated at Jabal Adda which can be dated more precisely.

Block-printed cottons and linens, reflecting Egypt's trade with India, often emulate drawloom patterns or metalwork designs. They have been attributed to dates from the 13th to the 15th century, but without reliable documentation. Two linen fragments (Cairo, Mus. Islam. A.), one with a design nearly identical to that of the yellow silk excavated at Jabal Adda and the other with an inscription inhabited by figures among the letters, certainly date to the late 13th century or early 14th. Certain fragments (Cleveland, OH, Mus. A.; Athens, Benaki Mus.) with crescent moons and/or fish can be assigned to the 14th century for iconographic reasons, while other pieces (Cairo, Mus. Islam. A.) with medallions, stars or cartouches and bands of inscription, together with a fragment (Washington, DC, Textile Mus.) with bands of inscription, have been attributed on stylistic grounds to the 15th century.

BIBLIOGRAPHY

A. F. Kendrick: *Catalogue of Muhammadan Textiles of the Medieval Period, Victoria and Albert Museum* (London, 1924), pp. 38–42

E. Kühnel: *Islamische Stoffe aus ägyptischen Gräbern* (Berlin, 1927)

H. J. Schmidt: 'Damaste der Mamlukenzeit', *A. Islam.*, i (1934), pp. 99–109

C. J. Lamm: 'Dated or Datable Tirāz in Sweden', *Monde Orient.*, xxxii (1938), pp. 103–25

R. Pfister: *Les Toiles imprimées de Fostat et l'Hindoustan* (Paris, 1938)

M. A. Marzouk: *History of Textile Industry in Alexandria, 331 B.C.–1517 A.D.* (Alexandria, 1955), pp. 66–79

H. J. Schmidt: *Alte Seidenstoffe* (Brunswick, 1958), pp. 151–72

N. B. Millet: 'Gebel Adda Preliminary Report, 1965–66', *J. Amer. Res. Cent. Egypt*, vi (1967), pp. 53–63

J. Brookner: 'Textiles', *Quseir al-Qadim: Preliminary Report*, ed. D. S. Whitcomb and J. H. Johnson (Cairo, 1979), pp. 183–95

Renaissance of Islam: Art of the Mamluks (exh. cat. by E. Atıl, Washington, DC, Smithsonian Inst.; Minneapolis, MN, Inst. A.; New York, Met.; Cincinnati, OH, A. Mus.; 1981), pp. 223–48

L. W. Mackie: 'Toward an Understanding of Mamluk Silks: National and International Considerations', *Muqarnas*, ii (1984), pp. 127–46

D. Thompson: 'Cotton Double Cloths and Embroidered and Brocaded Linen Fabrics from 10th to 14th Century Egypt: Their Relation to Traditional Coptic and Contemporary Islamic Style', *Bull. Liaison Cent. Int. Etud. Textiles Anc.*, lxi–lxii (1985), pp. 35–49

ANNE E. WARDWELL

(c) Eastern Islamic lands. The Mongol conquest of Asia in the mid-13th century led to the opening of trade routes from China to Italy along which, from the mid-13th century to the mid-14th, luxury fabrics were traded, resulting in a brief period of international design. Woven silks, cottons, linens, woollens, carpets, felts, furs, embroideries and quilting were all produced in quantities. About 100 silk textiles of the 13th century to the mid-14th survive from Iran, Iraq and western Central Asia, but only a few from Anatolia; all are preserved in museums and churches in Europe and North America. Archaeological evidence is confined to a few samples excavated in Xinjiang Province in China.

Records of Asian chroniclers and travellers indicate the importance of textile weaving in western Central Asia and Iran during the 13th and 14th centuries, and silk cultivation increased in Iran during the period. The Persian vizier Rashid al-Din, the Italian merchant Marco Polo (1254–1324), the Moroccan traveller Ibn Battuta (1304–77) and Ruy Gonzalez de Clavijo (*d* 1412), Spanish envoy at Timur's court, specified centres of production including Mosul, Tabriz, Urgench and Samarkand and some broad categories of textiles, but the accounts are inconsistent. European documents of the late 13th century and the 14th list luxury fabrics from western Central Asia and Iran as *panni tartarici* ('Tartar cloths'), indicating their place of origin as the Mongol empire, but are rarely more specific. Techniques and styles are not usually described in inventories, but patterns are. Examples include cocks and horseman in the Canterbury Inventory (1315), human figures and animals in the Vatican Inventory (1361) and curtains with griffins in the Prague Inventory (1355). Other motifs described include roses, lilies, lotus-bulbs, monkeys, bands and strips. Contemporary literary descriptions, such as those in Dante's *Inferno* and Langland's *Piers Plowman*, also indicate the desirability of these fabrics.

Luxury textiles were made from silk and metal thread, the latter a strip of silvered and/or gilded animal substrate either woven flat or wound on a core, usually cotton or occasionally silk. Structural differences distinguish textiles woven in Iran, western Central Asia and the Middle East from those produced in Italy and Spain. Central Asian textiles have selvages reinforced with silk warps, but never linen cords as is usual with Italian and Spanish silks. Central Asian textiles are often woven with silk warps and ground wefts of cotton, whereas only one small group produced in the Mediterranean area has mixed fibres. In Central Asian textiles having metal thread combined with animal membrane, the thread is either woven flat or wound on a cotton core, whereas Italian and Spanish textiles with metal thread and membrane used silk and linen cores. The predominant weave is lampas, but compound weave, doublecloth and velvet are also found.

Only one group of textiles with technical similarities, including selvage construction, paired main warps and gold filé pattern wefts with a silk core, reflects a continuous weaving tradition predating the Mongol conquest. This group can be assigned to the Ilkhanid territories by virtue of one textile, a *ṭirāz* inscribed with the name of the Ilkhanid sovereign Abu Saʿid (*reg* 1317–35; Vienna, Dom- & Diözmus.), produced in a royal workshop, probably at Tabriz. It is a lampas and compound weave with bands containing peacocks and animals. The earliest example of this group, a fragmentary textile with a design of Bahram Gur and kings found in the grave of Bishop Hartmann (*d* 1286; Augsburg, Maximilianmus.), is datable by its style and iconography to the mid-13th century.

Several textiles can be attributed to western Central Asia in the late 13th century or the 14th for three principal reasons: the selvage structure; the composition of their metal threads; and the use of pre-Mongol iconographic elements. Some have cotton ground wefts, including a few assigned to Transoxiana. Designs often include a combination of Islamic, Central Asian and Chinese motifs, indicating the commercial role and cultural diversity of western Central Asia at that time. Most are lampas silks with flat strips of gilded animal membrane. Five silks of this type were found in the tomb of Cangrande della Scala (*d* 1329) in Verona (Verona, Castelvecchio, A, D, E, G and H). Two further examples (Regensburg, Alte Kapelle) are a chasuble showing grape leaves and vines, a design inspired by Italian silks of the 1340s–1400; and a stylistically related tunic, which must be of the same date.

A large number of silks having pattern wefts with gilded or silvered leather strips on a cotton core and with more concentrated warps than in Central Asian textiles were formerly attributed to Italy, Egypt or Iran, but are now attributed to Khurasan, the easternmost province of Iran. Most of them combine pre-Mongol Islamic and Chinese motifs. A silk and silver lampas (Cleveland, OH, Mus. A., 45.14) is one of three extant textiles of this type with a pattern of paired birds flanking palmettes, a design found in 12th-century Iranian ceramics. A silk with Chinese-style dragons (*chi-lin*; Berlin, Tiergarten, Kstgewmus., 78.744) and another with a design of ogival medallions with paired animals, floral motifs and dragons (formerly Berlin, Tiergarten, Kstgewmus., 68.2742) also show the impact of Chinese motifs.

Another group of textiles has selvages with single main warps in a different colour from the rest of the fabric; these warps appear on the face while the pattern wefts appear on the back. The metal threads usually have a linen core. The patterns on this group vary, showing Chinese, Central Asian and Italian motifs. One, a lampas (Lyon, Mus. Hist. Tissus, 28.340), has a design of grapevines copied directly from a 14th-century Italian silk. Two others, a chasuble and a dalmatic (London, V&A, 594-1884 and 8361-1863; see fig. 190), have a pattern of fish-eating birds, which may relate to the 1341 inventory entry

190. Silk textile made into a dalmatic, lampas woven in blue silk and metal thread, 2.32×1.22 m, from ?western Iran, 14th century (London, Victoria and Albert Museum)

of the church of S Francesco, Assisi, describing a *panno tartaresco* with a design of pelicans. The predominant use of linen in the metal thread core and the presence of Italian motifs in a few of these textiles suggest western Iran or Iraq as a likely provenance. Italian commerce was concentrated in Tabriz, Sultaniyya and Urgench, and as the region of Urgench is not known for using linen as a core material, the first two cities seem a more likely provenance. The production of luxury textiles clearly continued after the mid-14th century, but no representative corpus of weaving dating from before the 16th century has survived, and textiles are rarely documented.

Anatolia had a weaving industry of some significance in the 13th century, to judge from two compound twills with gilt threads: one (Lyon, Mus. Hist. Tissus, 23.475) is decorated with lions and inscribed with the name of Kayqubad I (*reg* 1219–37), the Saljuq sultan of Anatolia; the other (Berlin, Tiergarten, Kstgewmus.) is decorated with a double-headed eagle. The earliest textile attributable to Anatolia under the rule of the Ottoman dynasty (*reg* 1281–1924) is a late 14th-century silk in the monastery of Studenica, Serbia, with a decorative composition and arrangement similar to contemporary Ilkhanid and Mamluk silks. Ottoman textiles may have inspired weavers over a wide geographical area, as several fragments from 15th-century Egypt have pattern motifs usually identified with the Ottomans, such as three crescent balls in pyramidal form. The Anatolian silk and velvet weaving industries developed rapidly in the late 14th century. By 1421 at least 100 different fabrics were produced in Ottoman Anatolia, and by 1500 over 90 types of high-quality silks, including velvets, were manufactured in Bursa alone (*see* §(iii)(a) below).

BIBLIOGRAPHY

P. Toynbee: 'Tartar Cloths', *Romania*, xxix (1900)
G. Wiet: *L'Exposition persane de 1931* (Cairo, 1933)
N. A. Reath and E. B. Sachs: *Persian Textiles* (Oxford, 1937)
Le stoffe di Cangrande (exh. cat., ed. L. Majagnato; Verona, Castelvecchio, 1983)
A. E. Wardwell: 'Flight of the Phoenix: Crosscurrents in Late Thirteenth- to Fourteenth-century Silk Patterns and Motifs', *Bull. Cleveland Mus. A.*, lxxiv (1987), pp. 1–35
——: 'Panni Tartarici: Eastern Islamic Silks Woven with Gold and Silver (13th and 14th Centuries)', *Islam. A.*, iii (1988–9), pp. 95–173

LINDA WOOLLEY

(iii) c. *1500 and after.* The large number of textiles that survive from the Islamic lands in the period show an extraordinarily wide variety of techniques, especially for luxury fabrics, such as figured silk velvets and brocades. Increasing competition from European fabrics, particularly in the 19th century, led to a decline in the production of luxury fabrics in major urban workshops, although village and nomadic production remained important.

(a) Eastern Mediterranean lands. (b) North Africa. (c) Iran. (d) Western Central Asia. (e) Indian subcontinent.

(a) Eastern Mediterranean lands. Because of the political control, albeit often nominal in the final years, exercised by the Ottoman sultans (*reg* 1281–1924) over the eastern and southern Mediterranean lands, the inspiration for textile design and the demand for production in the region stemmed from the Ottoman court established at Istanbul in 1453. Silk fabrics including patterned silk weaves, velvets and monochrome light-weight satins and embroideries played an important role throughout the Ottoman empire, where they were a major commodity, used for such furnishings as coverings, curtains and pillows and clothing including kaftans, sashes, kerchiefs and headbands. Although archives, pictorial sources and garments preserved in royal collections and church treasuries provide some information, so few textiles are dated and so few technical analyses have been published that textiles can only be grouped into broad stylistic categories based on the designs and motifs used. Production of luxury silk fabrics developed during the 15th century and reached its apogee in the late 16th century and the 17th; during the 18th century embroidery techniques were featured more than woven ones, and designs became more stylized.

Nature of the evidence. Archival sources for Ottoman textiles range from royal inventories to records of tax farm revenues, but few have been published in critical editions. Most research has focused on the economic rather than the art-historical development of textile manufacture in the region, using in particular the archives of Topkapı Palace in Istanbul and those held by municipal authorities in such cities as BURSA in Anatolia. Diplomatic and personal reports from European travellers, merchants and official envoys contain more general information as well as subjective views of the visual and tactile qualities of contemporary fabrics.

For the early period pictorial evidence from Ottoman book illustration is ambiguous. Illustrations in a copy (1498; Istanbul, Topkapı Pal. Lib., H. 799) of Khusraw Dihlavi's *Khamsa* ('Five poems'), for example, offer little evidence for the textural quality of textiles and do not confirm the passion for figured and inscribed fabrics recorded in texts. The artist probably selected his colours to create harmony within the composition, not to depict dress dyes accurately. The emphasis on recording historical events and personalities that developed in the 16th century resulted in a more careful representation of fabric patterns by court artists. Illustrations in copies (e.g. Istanbul, Topkapı Pal. Lib., H. 1344, A. 3593 and A. 3594) of the *Sūrnāma* ('Book of festivals') depict details of equipment and processes used in the creation of textiles, such as swifts and chain warping. European artists and printmakers had little personal knowledge of the region, and their work shows misunderstanding if not flights of imagination. In the 19th century photography allowed more accurate depictions, but rarely recorded technical details.

The largest collection of Ottoman silks is in the Topkapı Palace Museum, where about 1000 kaftans and other garments worn by sultans and members of the court were preserved in bundles after their deaths. The names on the bundles were once thought to provide reliable dates for the textiles, but the labels are not necessarily contemporary and their accuracy cannot be assumed. Some Ottoman textiles were presented as gifts to foreign dignitaries and have been preserved in royal Swedish and Russian collections; others, used as ecclesiastical vestments, survive in churches and monasteries in northern and central Europe. Other textiles were seized as booty when the Ottomans were defeated at Vienna (1683) and Buda (1686). The presence of any of these textiles in European inventory records therefore provides historians with a *terminus ante quem*.

Few studies of Ottoman fabrics have been published giving precise technical and structural details. As a result, for example, it is not possible to distinguish the compound-weave fabric woven with silver and gold metallic threads (Ott. *seraser*) produced in Istanbul from that of Bursa, and indeed there is disagreement on the exact definition and technical characteristics of such famous Ottoman stuffs as *zarbaft* ('woven with gold'), *hatai* ('Chinese'), *serenk* (compound-weave fabric using two or three colours of silk), *kemha* (compound-weave fabric of polychrome silk and metallic threads), *çatma* (voided silk velvet woven with gold, gilded silver and silver metallic threads) and *seraser* itself. It has therefore been general practice to date the textiles according to the character of the pattern motif and its arrangement within the decorative composition. It is presumed that complex detailed patterns devolved over the decades into more fluid, less intense compositions, which in time became even more simplified linear forms with consequent loss or alteration in the nature of tension and energy created by the design. Intricacy and complexity of pattern and motif are thus considered hallmarks of high aesthetic standards. This emphasis on decorative motif, however, has little relevance for plain or overall decoratively woven fabrics, but these textiles have received scant attention from textile and art historians.

Nature of production. The main centre of silk production was Bursa, and by 1500 over 90 types of high-quality silk, including velvets, were manufactured there. It was the major depot for the export of Iranian silk to Europe, but in the 16th century, when imports were curtailed because of wars with Iran, the Ottoman sultans encouraged

domestic silk production. By the mid-17th century the plains around Bursa were covered with mulberry trees, the leaves of which fed the silkworms, and by the 18th century the Ottoman state rivalled Iran in exporting unwoven silk to Europe. Other centres of silk production included Edirne, Hereke, Bilecik and Amasya in Anatolia and Aleppo and Damascus in Syria. Light and heavy cottons, the latter suitable for military use and theoretically restricted to internal purchase, were produced on the Aegean and south Mediterranean coasts. Cyprus also became a major cotton producer after it was annexed to the Ottoman empire in the late 16th century. Until cloth began to be imported from western Europe on a large scale, woollen textiles were produced mainly in the European provinces of the Ottoman empire, although the area around Izmir in Turkey was known for its serge (Turk. *çuha*) cloth. Ankara was famous for the manufacture of mohair, and the watermarking of mohair cloth there is recounted by 17th-century travellers.

By the 16th century a network of cloth trade guilds had been established; each guild had its own patron saint, such as Adam and Enoch for tailors and Job for silk workers. The guilds usually had a hierarchy of masters, journeymen and apprentices under the administration of a chief, steward, chief fellow and council of elders. Bursa guilds of the early 17th century, however, did not follow this organization, perhaps because of the comparatively late introduction of sericulture or the use of slave labour. The central government used the guilds to implement its economic policies, whether directed against tax evasion or smuggling proscribed yarns and textiles to foreign merchants. For example, in the 1520s textile merchants were forbidden to deal in Persian silks because of an official economic blockade, and in the 1570s the Bursa guilds agreed not to use gold thread in face of the shortage of gold bullion. With the rising costs of raw materials, official concern centred on declining standards of workmanship, in particular the use of cheaper dyes, inferior yarn quality, short measures and debased metallic thread. Despite this development, textile production was still considered a profitable concern, and workshops were bought by court and army officials or included in tax farms. Government edicts then increasingly dealt with price fixing, although questions about quality were still raised. In return, the guilds expected the central government to protect their interests by safeguarding supplies of raw materials, hindering competition by expelling foreign workers, reducing equipment and forbidding the sale of certain items.

Stylistic development. Despite technical advances in the 15th century, home demand quickly outstripped supply, and court documents from the reign of Mehmed II (*reg* 1444–81 with interruption) record that at one stage over 14% of total court expenditure went to purchasing European, particularly Italian, silks. Although contemporary documents refer to a fashion for dress fabrics with figures and inscriptions, pictorial evidence suggests a preference for monochrome garments occasionally relieved with gold, perhaps embroidered, decoration. Several items of clothing (Istanbul, Topkapı Pal. Mus.) are associated with Mehmed II on the basis of labels attached to them, although the authenticity of these labels has been

191. *Guild of Kemha Weavers on Parade*, 303×200 mm; illustration from Lokman: *Sūrnāma-i Humāyūn* ('Imperial book of festivals'), *c.* 1582–3 (Istanbul, Topkapı Palace Library, H. 1344, fol. 331*v*)

importation of Italian patterned textiles, but it is difficult to distinguish Italian fabrics made for the Ottoman market from indigenous Ottoman fabrics and thus to establish a chronology for Ottoman textile designs in this period. These problems are particularly apparent in the case of luxurious silk and velvet textiles containing floral and arabesque motifs within undulating ogival lattice forms. Reath's supposition that all velvets employing cut and uncut pile (e.g. New York, Met., 12.49.5) were made in Italy cannot be accepted as a clear-cut rule.

Patterns usually rendered in bright colours dominate a light or dark ground. Ogier Ghiseli de Busbecq (Busbequius), the envoy of the Holy Roman emperor to the Ottoman court from 1554, noted that as a rule the dark colours, as prescribed for non-Muslims in the Ottoman empire, were not favoured in high social circles. When the field colour has a rich and vibrant tone, the pattern is highlighted by the use of metallic thread, either flat or 'purled'. When gold or silver thread is used in secondary wefts as the ground colour, its two-dimensional quality is often complemented by more formal stylized design motifs, picked out in pastel shades, the tension being created by the juxtaposition of motif and ground. The *seraser* trousers (Istanbul, Topkapı Pal. Mus., inv. no. 13/131–2/4414) attributed to Süleyman (*reg* 1520–66) are a fine example. Conversely, on vibrant fields the decorative elements appear to be arranged in layers, giving an illusion of depth. This can be seen in the spectacular silk fabric in a ceremonial kaftan associated with Prince Bayezid (*d* 1561; Istanbul, Topkapı Pal. Mus., 13/37; see fig. 192)

questioned. These demonstrate a wide range of sophisticated weave techniques incorporating both simple and complex pattern motifs in various compositional arrangements, but no figural depictions. There is evident concern for surface texture as well as colour, ranging from pale pastel shades to sombre rich hues.

The apogee of Ottoman textile production ran from the second half of the 16th century to the late 17th. This was the period of sumptuous silks and velvets carrying gold and silver threads in secondary wefts, types of textiles depicted in contemporary book illustrations as clothing worn by courtiers and paraded or tossed before the royal family (see fig. 191). It is assumed that the complex patterned motifs employed in these textiles had developed from earlier compositions, often rendered in twill weave, in which the pattern elements, striking in their simplicity of outline, are set against the field in staggered repeats or in stripes (e.g. early 16th-century garment fragments, London, V&A). The more elaborate and complicated floral motifs, in which small stylized flower heads or sprays such as hyacinths and tulips decorate the petals or leaves of large blossoms (e.g. New York, Met., 49.32.79), are thought to be examples of later production, perhaps reflecting the growing complexity and refinement of the Ottoman court. It could also be argued, however, that the increased intricacy of the designs was linked to the

192. Ottoman kaftan made from a compound-weave silk in six colours and gold on a dark ground, mid-16th century (Istanbul, Topkapı Palace Museum)

woven in gold and six colours on a dark ground. Arabesque scrolls unroll with controlled energy over the field; serrated or flame-edged leaves or rush plumes create secondary circular movements, unhalted by sprays with full or bud flower heads falling across their stems in rhythmic order; both leaves and flowers contain secondary floral patterns. Many of these motifs appear in contemporary manuscripts, metalwork and ceramics made for the Ottoman court, suggesting that court studios had a strong impact on textile designers and weavers.

In the 18th and 19th centuries the fondness for floral motifs continued, and during the Tulip Period (1718–30) the tulip dominated the composition of both furnishing and dress fabrics, in form becoming more elongated and stylized. Small, separate floral elements were often repeated in parallel horizontal rows and later vertically in the manner of contemporary French silks and Indian chintzes (e.g. an embroidered gown belonging to Fatma Sultan, daughter of Mustafa III (reg 1757–74); Istanbul, Topkapı Pal. Mus., 13/815). The passion for flowers and also for a garden setting can be seen most vividly in the magnificent Ottoman tent interiors (e.g. 17th century; Kraków, N.A. Cols, 896), as well as in the more humble linen towels and sashes with deftly embroidered ends (e.g. a towel end embroidered with houses, a tent and trees beside a river, Chicago, IL, A. Inst.). Patterns became increasingly static, and the motifs appear to have been laid on the surface of the fabric. Metallic threads within the weave were replaced by gold, silver and coloured silk embroidery on a monochrome ground, perhaps reflecting bullion shortages, changes in taste and a shortage of skilled weavers. Pastel or rich sombre shades were considered marks of good taste, while vibrant, dramatic tones were relegated to less refined, bourgeois sensibilities.

In the early 19th century demand for traditional Ottoman fabrics declined. The adoption of European styles was considered a mark of culture and intelligence, an association strengthened by various official reform programmes, including dress laws, aimed at modernization (see §3(v)(b) below). Complicated pattern-weaving techniques ceased, and decoration was usually applied after weaving by embroidery, needle-lace and printing, although ikat was still produced. Colour remained important, but textural qualities became harsher and more emphatic in character. There was a marked increase in heavily worked embroidery, often in satin or couching stitch over pads, using metallic thread, wire and strips with spangles and sequins and incorporating motifs from the contemporary decorative repertory of western Europe.

The Ottoman textile industry suffered further setbacks in 1838 with the signing of the Anglo-Turkish Commercial Convention. Foreign imports were liable only to a 5% tax on entry, whereas domestic products were subject to provincial dues, transit tax and additional levies amounting to 12 to 50% on value. The impact was immediate and severe. Although 2000 cotton looms had operated at Tirnova (now Malko Tŭrnovo, Bulgaria) and Scutari (Üsküdar in Turkey) in 1812, only 200 remained in 1841. Between 1815 and the middle of the century Bursa production dropped a similar 90%, despite the importation of silk-reeling mills to cut production and labour costs. The government then intervened with measures aimed at revitalizing domestic production. Import levies were raised, trade fairs set up and industrial training programmes introduced. So much foreign machinery and labour were imported that a foreign technician redefined Turkish cloth as 'cloth made in Turkey by European machinery, out of European material and by good European hands' (Macfarlane, p. 453). The revival succeeded, despite such internal problems as the spread of pébrine, the silkworm disease, and such external factors as the opening up of China and Japan to European trade and the cheaper transportation costs through the Suez Canal, and textile production in Turkey boomed in the years before World War I.

BIBLIOGRAPHY

Enc. Islam/2: 'Ḥarīr' [Silk], 'Kuṭn' [Cotton]
C. Macfarlane: Turkey and its Destiny, ii (London, 1850)
N. A. Reath: 'Velvets of the Renaissance from Europe and Asia Minor', Burl. Mag., l (1927), pp. 298–304
T. Öz: Türk kumaş ve kadifeleri [Turkish textiles and velvets], 2 vols (Istanbul, 1946–51); Eng. trans. of vol. i as Turkish Textiles and Velvets, XIV–XVI Centuries (Ankara, 1950)
R. Ettinghausen: 'An Early Ottoman Textile', Communications of the First International Congress of Turkish Art: Ankara, 1959, pp. 134–40
W. Denny: 'Ottoman Turkish Textiles', Textile Mus. J., iii (1972), pp. 55–66
M. Gönül: Türk elişleri sanati: XVI–XIX yüzyil (Ankara, 1973); Eng. trans. as Turkish Embroideries, XVI–XIX Centuries (Istanbul, 1976)
H. Gerber: 'Guilds in 17th-century Anatolian Bursa', Asian & Afr. Stud., ii (1975), pp. 59–86
M. Çizakça: 'A Short History of the Bursa Silk Industry', J. Econ. & Soc. Hist. Orient, xxiii (1980), pp. 142–52
D. King and M. Goedhuis: Imperial Ottoman Textiles (London, 1980)
L. W. Mackie: 'Rugs and Textiles', Turkish Art, ed. E. Atıl (Washington, DC, and New York, 1980), pp. 299–374
H. Tezcan and S. Delibaş: Topkapı Sarayi Müzesi (Tokyo, 1980); trans. and ed. J. M. Rogers as The Topkapı Saray Museum: Costumes, Embroideries and Other Textiles (Boston, 1986)
Ö. Barişta: Osmanli imperatorluk dönemi türk işlemelerinden örnekler [Examples of Turkish embroideries from the Ottoman imperial period] (Ankara, 1981)
W. Denny: 'Textiles', Tulips, Arabesques and Turbans: Decorative Arts from the Ottoman Empire, ed. Y. Petsopoulos (London, 1982), pp. 121–68
S. Faroqhi: Towns and Townsmen of Anatolia (Cambridge, 1984), pp. 125–55
P. Johnstone: Turkish Embroideries in the Victoria and Albert Museum (London, 1986)
E. Atıl: The Age of Sultan Süleyman the Magnificent (Washington, DC, 1987), pp. 177–224

PATRICIA L. BAKER

(b) North Africa. The great tradition of silk-weaving known in Spain and North Africa was continued after c. 1500 in Spain under Christian patronage and to a lesser extent in North Africa. A pilgrim banner of brocaded maroon silk with metallic thread (3.61×1.88 m, 1683; Cambridge, MA, Sackler Mus., 1958.20) is attributed to Morocco on the basis of its distinctive maghribī letter forms. Large silk tomb-covers were also woven with gold threads; one with large thuluth script in the Ottoman style (Paris, Mus. A. Afr. & Océan., 1862.827) is attributed to Tunis in the 16th or 17th century; another with varied styles of calligraphy in cartouches (Paris, Mus. A. Afr. & Océan., 1961.5.1) was woven at Fez in the 18th century for the hospice (Arab. zāwiya) of the Sherqawi order of mystics at Boujad in the Middle Atlas. The tradition of weaving fine silks on drawlooms has continued at Fez into the 20th century, where elements of wedding costumes,

193. Moroccan embroidered panel, silk on linen, 650×650 mm, from Chaouèn, 19th century (London, Victoria and Albert Museum)

including elaborately patterned sashes for men, are produced according to traditional techniques.

Ottoman and European imports began to supplant local textiles in the 18th century, and surviving costumes from the 19th century show that imported fabrics from France and the Middle East were combined with local textiles that copied them. For example, Tunisian silks and cottons from the late 19th century imitate contemporary French and Turkish fabrics. Conversely, at the end of the 19th century Europeans began to collect the beautiful and varied embroideries of Algeria and Morocco. These collections are the major source of information about textile production in North Africa between the 17th and the 19th century, but their uneven, eclectic and personal nature makes generalization about the development of North African textiles in this period extremely difficult.

Despite their geographical proximity and the shared use of a particular shade of purple found in no other Mediterranean embroideries, the designs and techniques of embroideries from Algeria and Morocco differ markedly. In Algeria, curtains, headdresses and kerchiefs with which to wrap the head after bathing were embroidered. They were made of linen (until the 19th century when cotton was introduced) and embroidered with floss silk using double-darning, double-running, brick and satin stitches, among others, together with eyelet holes. As many as nine separate colours, and occasionally silver and gold thread, were used. The characteristic motif is a large floral medallion that resembles both the artichoke motif of Turkish embroideries and the *glastra* (a motif of folk embroidery) of the Dodecanese Islands in the Aegean. The three types of piece are distinguished by differing layouts of design. Curtains have three loom-widths of fabric joined with an uneven number of imported, possibly French, silk ribbons.

Narrow embroidered borders run along the top and sides of each piece, and a whitework band forms the bottom border. A line of five or more large floral medallions runs vertically down the centre of each loom-width. Headdresses and kerchiefs were made from long, narrow lengths of fabric. For the headdress, it was folded end-to-end and sewn to form a hood with lappets, with the embroidery concentrated on the hood and the ends of the lappets. The kerchief was left unsewn, with wide embroidered borders along its entire length. In the earliest examples, dating to the late 17th century or early 18th, red and blue silks featuring brick stitch predominate; by the beginning of the 19th century, shades of purple had become popular, as had double-running and satin stitches with eyelet holes.

In Morocco curtains, bed furnishings, cushion covers and costume accessories were embroidered. They were made of the same materials as Algerian pieces (linen until the 19th century and embroidered with floss silk), but the repertory of popular stitches was limited to double-running, satin and long-armed cross. No stylistic development has been determined, and most pieces are attributed to the late 18th century or later. In contrast to Algerian work, however, regional styles can be distinguished. The embroideries of Fez, Rabat and Salé are geometric and based on tree forms. Those from Fez are worked in double-running stitch and are monochrome red or blue; those from Rabat, in satin stitch, are usually monochrome red or purple, though sometimes the two colours are combined; those from Salé, in double-running stitch, can be either monochrome blue or polychrome. Embroideries from Tetouan have more naturalistic floral motifs worked in double-running stitch using brightly coloured silks on a silk or linen ground (e.g. an 18th-century mirror-veil; Cambridge, Fitzwilliam). Those from the nearby town of Chaouèn (Xauen; Chéchaouen) are also in double-running stitch and polychrome floss, but are worked on linen and have geometric motifs reminiscent of Hispano-Moresque tilework (see fig. 193). Those from Azemmour on the Atlantic Coast are worked in long-armed cross stitch in monochrome red, blue or green, and the background is embroidered so that the unworked linen forms the designs, which include birds and animals. They differ from other Moroccan embroideries and are often indistinguishable from earlier Italian pieces.

BIBLIOGRAPHY
A. D. Howell Smith: *Catalogue of Algerian Embroideries*, London, V&A (London, 1915); rev. A. J. B. Wace (London, 1935)
P. Ricard: *Arts marocains: Broderie* (Algiers, 1918)
G. Marçais: 'Les Broderies turques d'Algers', *A. Islam.*, iv (1938), pp. 145–53
E. Newberry: 'The Embroideries of Morocco', *Embroidery*, vii/2 (1939), pp. 29–35
W. Denny: 'A Group of Silk Islamic Banners', *Textile Mus. J.*, iv (1974), pp. 67–81
L'Islam dans les collections nationales (exh. cat., Paris, Grand Pal., 1977), nos 241–2
C. Stone: *The Embroideries of North Africa* (London, 1985)
Broderies marocaines, Paris, Mus. A. Afr. & Océan. (Paris, 1991)

JENNIFER WEARDEN

(c) Iran. Fine textiles had long been produced in the Iranian world, but many more textiles and fragments have survived from the period after 1500. Those from the years of Safavid rule (*reg* 1501–1732) in Iran demonstrate an

extraordinary mastery of techniques and designs, particularly figural silks of complex weave structure. Both textile production in Iran and international trade in finished textiles declined in the second half of the 18th century, following the destruction of Isfahan by the Afghans in 1722. Attempts at revitalization in the 19th century were not entirely successful, as Iranian textile industries suffered from the import of cheaper manufactured goods from abroad and from the disease (pébrine) that spread among silkworms in the 1860s. Textiles were presented as royal and diplomatic gifts to foreigners and have been preserved in European and Indian armouries, treasuries and museums. Depictions of textiles appear in 16th- and 17th-century book illustrations, album pages, wall paintings and ceramics. Textiles from the 18th and 19th centuries, when Iran was under the domination of the Afsharid (*reg* 1736–95), Zand (*reg* 1750–94) and Qajar (*reg* 1779–1924) dynasties, are also documented in small painted or enamelled objects and oil paintings on canvas. Textual sources for textiles range from local and regional histories and chronicles to the archives of foreign trading companies active in Iran. Those of the Dutch East India Company in The Hague, the India Office Library in London and the British East India Company in Bombay, for example, yield extraordinary documentation for the trade in textiles, the import and export of dyestuffs and glazing compounds, and local customs of dress.

Materials and techniques. The complicated fabric structures and patterns of such fabrics as lampas and velvet were woven on drawlooms, used in Iran for centuries. The wide range of colours used in Persian textile arts reflects deep understanding of the technology and properties of dyes. Domestic madder and indigo imported from India were used to produce reds and blues. Imported cochineal and lac, both red dyes, were more expensive and were used primarily to dye silk; safflower produced a bright orange characteristic of many Safavid silks, which has often faded over time. Additional dyestuffs were derived from other insects and such plant materials as pomegranate rind, walnut husks and weld.

Silk, traditionally cultivated along the mountain slopes bordering the Caspian Sea in northern Iran, was a major export from the 16th century onward. 'Abbas I (*reg* 1588–1629) encouraged the Armenian communities to become involved in production and gave them protected status. Cotton, the tensile strength of which led to its use as warp and weft in some Safavid carpets, was extensively cultivated as a cash crop in the mid-19th century and exported to supply the industrialized looms of England and Russia. Wool and goat hair were the main fibres of nomadic weavings and were traded extensively on the international market as early as the 17th century. The hair from the underbelly of Kirman goats was favoured in Kashmir and England, since its softness and strength made it an ideal fibre for weaving shawls. Coarser grades of wool were used for weaving shawls in Kirman and Mashhad.

Compound weaves and velvets. Safavid textiles can often be distinguished from contemporary Ottoman fabrics by the prevalence of figural motifs, including scenes of animals in combat, paired birds and fish, intertwined fruit and flowering trees, hunting and falconry, all popular subjects in contemporary poetry and painting. Images from favourite stories from Firdawsi's *Shāhnāma* ('Book of kings') and Nizami's *Khamsa* ('Five poems') were adapted to the rectilinear requirements of loom-weaving. A satin lampas signed by Ghiyath (*c*. 1600; divided: e.g. Washington, DC, Textile Mus., 3.312), for example, depicts Layla riding in a howdah on a camel while her lover Majnun pines among animals in the desert, and a contemporary velvet (divided: Cleveland, OH, Mus. A., 44.499–500; New York, Met., 1978.60; Washington, DC, Textile Mus., 3.220) shows the celebrated scene in which Khusraw sees Shirin bathing.

KASHAN and YAZD are frequently mentioned as centres for the production of fine silks and velvets, but it is not yet possible to assign definitive attributions. ISFAHAN served as the major emporium from 1598, when 'Abbas I made it the capital, although TABRIZ remained a major centre, particularly for trade with Turkey. International trade via the Persian Gulf was served by the ports of Hormuz in the 16th century, Bandar Abbas (Gambroon) in the 17th and 18th centuries and Bushire in the 19th century.

Satin lampas and velvets reached unprecedented levels of aesthetic and technical achievement in the 16th century. All lampas textiles produced during the Safavid period have a satin foundation with a supplementary twill weave, while the unit of repeat is disguised by the design and alternation of colour. A good example is a lampas depicting a slender courtier holding a ewer and cup in a landscape with animals, birds, cypresses and flowering trees (divided: Washington, DC, Textile Mus., 3.306 (see fig. 194); Cleveland, OH, Mus. A., 24.743; London, V&A, 282–1906; New York, Met., 08.109.3); colours of the courtier's garment, the bird's plumage and the rocks alternate from red to yellow. Safavid velvets are often richly patterned with designs related in style to contemporary manuscript painting and other courtly arts. An early 17th-century cut and voided silk velvet (divided: Berlin, Mus. Islam. Kst; New York, Met., 46.156.5; Washington, DC, Textile Mus., 3.320), for example, shows a falconer with fluttering turban and sash in the style associated with the great painter Riza.

Other textile structures were less complicated. A red and white silk doublecloth (?16th century; divided: New Haven, CT, Yale U. A.G.; New York, Met., 46.156.7; Washington, DC, Textile Mus., 3.280) is divided into rectangular compartments; some of these contain polylobed cartouches inscribed with poetry, others frame figural and architectural scenes. Brocaded taffetas and satins utilized discontinuous supplementary wefts, which allowed the weaver to create multicoloured repeat patterns that reproduce complicated floral designs ranging from naturalistic depictions to highly abstract forms. Several examples from the 17th century introduce representations of such imported flora as the calla lily or such exotic fauna as the Javanese sparrow. More popular, to judge from the number that survive, were fanciful depictions of flowering plants, repeated across the field (e.g. a 17th-century brocaded taffeta with composite flowers resembling thistles, pansies and carnations; Washington, DC, Textile Mus., 3.138). The bright colours and silken sheen give these textiles a sense of flashy opulence. In the 18th and 19th centuries such designs were reduced in scale, and

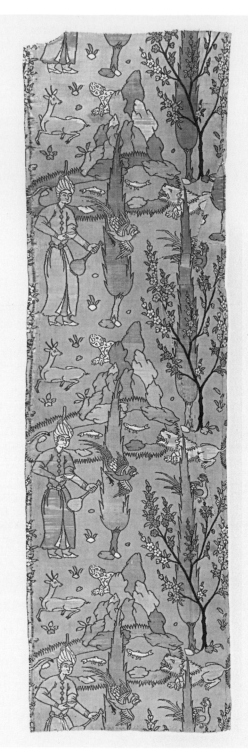

194. Iranian silk, satin lampas depicting a wine-bearer in a landscape, 1.17×0.34 m, 16th century (Washington, DC, Textile Museum)

The presence of metallic yarns in many Iranian textiles from this period makes them shimmer in the light. These textiles are often termed 'metal-ground textiles', but as these fabrics show a variety of compound weave structures, the term defines a stylistic, rather than a technical group. Sparkling and glittering gold and silver effects were achieved by several techniques. Foil strips, produced either by cutting a hammered sheet into narrow widths or by flattening a drawn metal wire, were used alone as weft yarns or more commonly wrapped around yellow or white silk cores to produce yarns that give the impression of gold and silver. The finished textile was sometimes beaten or heat-pressed to smooth the surface, protect the metal and preserve its sheen. Common designs include single or paired flowers or birds repeated across the field. The motifs are often carefully and accurately depicted, as on a twill weave with irises and daisies (divided: Berlin, Mus. Islam. Kst; New York, Met., 09.50.1110; Washington, DC, Textile Mus., 3.118). In later pieces, the designs decrease in size and the overall repeat patterns appear to be more crowded. For example, a compound silk with complementary wefts and inner warps (divided: Lyon, Mus. Hist. Tissus; Washington, DC, Textile Mus., 3.193) shows a crowded scene of courtiers on horseback hunting with falcons; it can be attributed to the 18th century on the basis of the tall pronged hats worn by the courtiers.

Other fabrics. The vast majority of textiles were plain weaves, which could be ornamented after weaving by such techniques as painting and printing, embroidery, appliqué, quilting or pieced patchwork. By the late 17th century or early 18th, Iran was producing printed cottons (Pers. *qalamkār*), using hand-carved wooden blocks. Isfahan and later Tehran became important centres for the production of printed fabrics. Elaborate and complicated designs were achieved through the use of several blocks, one for each colour. Red and blue are predominant, with black often used for outlines. Inscriptions with historical information, quotations from poems, or a dedication were added by hand-painting with a brush. Bolt fabric for garments or linings frequently shows small overall repeat patterns in red and blue, as in a 19th-century woman's jacket (Washington, DC, Textile Mus., 1983.68.5). Small complete loom widths and lengths were decorated to serve as covers and hangings, often with a niche format and symmetrical layout of lions, tigers, birds and flowers around a central tree, such as a hanging (1.67×1.04 m; Washington, DC, Textile Mus., 1980.8.5) made at Isfahan *c.* 1861.

Embroidery in silk or cotton seems to have been a home-based activity and reflected local styles until the end of the 19th century, when materials, techniques and designs begin to follow European models. Designs might be pictorial, floral or geometric, repeated to form elaborate overall patterns sometimes with a central medallion format. A fragment of an unusually elaborate embroidered plain weave attributed to the 16th or 17th century (divided: Paris, Mus. A. Déc.; Washington, DC, Textile Mus., 3.43) contains a repeating design depicting the lovers Yusuf and Zulaykha, a pattern that shows the same design principles as contemporary compound weaves. In the 19th century Rasht, Yazd and Tabriz were famous centres for embroidery. Wool embroideries and appliqués from Rasht were

they are often difficult to distinguish from contemporary Indian work. The repeated pear or teardrop shape (Pers. *buta, boteh*: 'shrub', 'flowering bush') also became popular.

produced in a variety of ornamental designs with symmetrical compositions. A type of embroidery practised in and around Tabriz incorporated drawn and deflected threads and is also seen throughout eastern Turkey, Armenia and Azerbaijan. In Kirman, traditional wool embroidery on curtains, coverlets and cushions often made use of floral patterns as well as those with birds and animals.

BIBLIOGRAPHY

N. A. Reath and E. B. Sachs: *Persian Textiles* (New Haven, 1937)
A. U. Pope and P. Ackerman, eds: *Survey of Persian Art* (London and New York, 1938–9, 2/1964–7), pp. 1995–2226
J. Gluck and S. Gluck, eds: *A Survey of Persian Handicraft* (Tehran, London and New York, 1977)
H. Landolt-Tüller and A. Landolt-Tüller: *Qalamkār-Druck in Isfahan: Beiträge zur Kenntnis traditioneller Textilfarbetechniken in Persien* (Basle, 1978)
M. McWilliams: 'Prisoner Imagery in Safavid Textiles', *Textile Mus. J.*, xxvi (1987), pp. 4–23
Woven from the Soul, Spun from the Heart: Textile Arts from Safavid and Qajar Iran, 16th–19th Centuries (exh. cat., ed. C. Bier; Washington, DC, Textile Mus., 1987)
R. Neumann and G. Murza: *Persische Seiden* (Leipzig, 1988)
B. Tietzel: *Persische Seiden des 16.–18. Jahrhunderts aus dem Besitz des deutschen Textilmuseums Krefeld* (Krefeld, 1988)
J. Scarce: 'The Persian Shawl Industry', *Textile Mus. J.*, xxvii–xxviii (1988–9), pp. 22–39
J. Allgrove McDowell: 'Textiles', *The Arts of Persia*, ed. R. W. Ferrier (New Haven, 1989), pp. 151–70
M. McWilliams: 'Allegories Unveiled: European Sources for a Safavid Velvet', *Textiles in Trade: Proceedings of the Textile Society of America Biennial Symposium: Washington, DC, 1990*, pp. 136–48
J. Scarce: 'Textiles', *From Nadir Shah to the Islamic Republic*, ed. P. Avery, G. Hambly and C. Melville (1991), vii of *The Cambridge History of Iran* (Cambridge, 1968–91), pp. 945–58

CAROL BIER

(d) Western Central Asia. The textile arts of the region encompassing parts of Afghanistan, Uzbekistan and eastern Turkestan (Xinjiang province of China) were highly developed, particularly the silk and silk-and-cotton fabrics produced there since late antiquity. This textile art was centred in such cities as Samarkand, Bukhara, Kokand and Andizhan, towns populated mainly by Uzbeks, Persian-speaking Sarts and a considerable number of Jews. The Uyghurs had a similar but less sophisticated textile culture. The other Turkic peoples of the area, such as the Turkomans, Kazakhs, Kirgiz and Karakirgiz, and the Persian-speaking Tajiks maintained distinctive tribal traditions. Weaves include a ribbed fabric of warp-faced plain weave (*adras*), broken twill (*atlas*), satin (*khanatlas*) and, rarely, velvet (*bakhmal*). After weaving, fabrics were beaten on a wooden block with a heavy mallet to impart lustre. Fabrics can be classified into three major groups on the basis of their dyeing and decoration: two of these, ikats and block-printed fabrics, were made for the market by highly skilled craftsmen, often Jews who specialized in dyeing; the third type, embroidered pieces, was worked at home by women and girls for trousseaus.

Except for some archaeological finds, such as those of the 7th–8th century AD from TURFAN in Xinjiang, surviving fabrics appear to date from the 19th century. Both older and newer fabrics were woven and decorated in narrow strips (some 500 mm wide), then sewn together to produce larger pieces for wall hangings, blankets or coverlets (Uzb. *parda*: 'curtain'; *qulkarpa*: 'curtain for covering wall niches'; *ruijoi*: 'nuptial bedsheets'), bedspreads and prayer-rugs. Surviving tailored garments include a woman's robe (*kaltacha*) and a man's and woman's overcoat (*khalat, chapān*), shirt and trousers. Smaller embroideries, some on a woollen foundation, include caps, saddle-covers, trappings and many kinds of bags; diminutive embroidered tray covers and other pieces of stitchwork (*lakai*) of the Lakai Uzbeks are particularly noteworthy. The patterns and colours of ikatted overcoats were so gaudy that Western travellers in the 19th century ridiculed the men wearing these garments; furthermore, the rooms of the wealthy were decorated with wall hangings, coverlets, pillow-cases and covers in similar brightly coloured fabrics, so that the residents blended with the environment. Tents and temporary walls were adorned with hangings during festivals. In addition, textiles played a major role in the ceremonial surrounding marriage: rooms and tents used for the wedding feast; the animals carrying the bride and her company to the bridegroom's house; the betrothed couple; and many other elements, including the nuptial bed, were all covered for the occasion with richly decorated textiles.

Ikat fabrics (known in Uzbekistan as *abr* ('cloud') because of the vague contours of the decorative patterns, or *khalat* because of its favoured use for coats) have only tie-dyed warps. Ferghana, roughly equivalent to the Khanate of Kokand, was the ikat centre of the region. The often intricate and strikingly colourful patterns are geometrical and kaleidoscopic, consisting mainly of large and small red circles and bands of elongated figures. Most ikat designs are now industrially printed, although small workshops in Xinjiang still produce silken ikats of modest quality.

The most spectacular fabrics of Central Asia are the embroideries known as *sūzanī* ('needlework'), a term applied particularly to large pieces used as wall hangings. The more popular versions are dominated by large round floral motifs and hence resemble tie-dyed fabrics. More intricate patterns feature small motifs including geometricized birds (typical of rural areas) and branches, bushes or trees with slim leaves and large red flowers or fruits, particularly pomegranates (typical of urban areas). Such fabrics usually have a central panel filled with several flowering bushes and surrounded by a border with larger flowers in garlands. The best-known examples, densely covered with leaves and flowers, appear to have been made in the 19th century in Uzbekistan, although simpler versions were made throughout east and west Turkestan.

See also CENTRAL ASIA, §I, 6.

BIBLIOGRAPHY

G. L. Chepelevezkaya: *Suzani uzbekistana* [The embroidery of Uzbekistan] (Tashkent, 1961)
S. Makhkamova: *Uzbekskiye avroviye tkani* [Uzbek 'Abrovy' textiles] (Tashkent, 1963)
A. Bühler: *Ikat, Batik, Plangi*, 3 vols (Basle, 1972)
A. Leix: *Turkestan and its Textile Crafts* (Basingstoke, 1974)
Folk Art of Uzbekistan (Tashkent, 1978)
Suzani: Stickereien aus Mittelasien (exh. cat., Mannheim, 1981)
J. Kalter: *Aus Steppe und Oase* (Stuttgart, 1983)
M. Klimburg and S. Pinto: *Tessuti ikat dell'Asia centrale* (Turin, 1986)
J. Taube: *Suzani: Raumschmückende Stickereien aus Mittelasien und ihr kulturhistorisches Umfeld* (Halle, 1987)
——: 'Suzani: Stickereien aus Mittelasien', *Kleine Beitr. Staatl. Mus. Vlkerknd. Dresden*, xii (1991)

MAX KLIMBURG

(e) Indian subcontinent. Under the patronage of the Mughal emperors (*reg* 1526–1857) and especially from the late 17th century to the early 19th, the Indian subcontinent was the textile workshop of the world. The cotton, silk and woollen textiles produced there were brightly decorated in an amazing variety of techniques, including dyeing, printing, painting and embroidery, and were exported throughout Asia and Europe. From an early date Indian textiles had been imported into the central Islamic lands, where these fabrics provided models for such local products as the block-printed cottons of 18th-century Iran.

For more information and bibliographies *see* INDIAN SUBCONTINENT, §VI, 1.

SHEILA S. BLAIR, JONATHAN M. BLOOM

3. DRESS. Throughout the history of man, dress has reflected the economic, political and religious divisions of society, and the Islamic world was no exception. Although dress in the Islamic world changed continuously, it was constantly a mark of status and position. Before *c.* 1500, the evidence for the history of dress rests largely on literary and historical evidence, supplemented by a few depictions in illustrated manuscripts and murals, and a handful of garments. After *c.* 1500, the evidence is broader and includes many garments, particularly those of the ruling class, large numbers of paintings, drawings and, in the 19th century, photographs, and descriptions by both natives and foreigners.

For dress in India *see* INDIAN SUBCONTINENT, §VIII, 7.

(i) Introduction. (ii) Before *c.* AD 650. (iii) *c.* AD 650–*c.* 1200. (iv) *c.* 1200–*c.* 1500. (v) *c.* 1500 and after.

(i) Introduction. Dress in the Islamic world is often viewed as traditional and static, but both major and minor elements changed continually, and at different rates in different areas. Some of the most important changes in dress were associated with the ascendancy of a particular ethnic or social group, such as the Turks under the Abbasid caliphs (*reg* 749–1258) or the Georgians under the later Safavid rulers of Iran (*reg* 1501–1732). The distinct styles of dress worn by these groups consequently gained wide currency, only to fade as the power of the specific group waned. Most of the evidence for the history of dress in the Islamic world relates to the court and upper social stratum. Literary and visual sources, normally produced for the rich and powerful, are the primary evidence for the early period (i.e. before *c.* 1500), while actual items of dress, again usually made for the upper classes, survive in greater numbers from the later period. Until the advent of photography in the 19th century, there was little precise information about the dress of the urban and rural masses. The exact relationship between court dress and that of the urban, rural and tribal communities in pre-modern times is difficult to define, although texts suggest that throughout the centuries the fashions of the court strongly influenced fabric and clothing markets.

Increasingly, after the establishment of an Islamic empire in the mid-7th century, the public display of courtiers and officials in costly and ostentatious attire was acknowledged to demonstrate the wealth, power and magnificence of the ruling regime. The devout Muslim sought guidance in matters of dress from the Hadith, the

traditions of the Prophet Muhammad, as expounded by the particular sect or school of law that the individual followed. The wearing of silks and brightly coloured and heavily patterned textiles, for example, was theologically deemed reprehensible, particularly among Sunnis, and simple unpatterned garments of linen, wool and cotton were considered the mark of a humble believer. Muslim rulers known for their piety, such as the Umayyad caliph 'Umar (*reg* 717–20), the Ayyubid sultan Salah al-Din (*reg* 1169–93) and the Ottoman sultan Süleyman (*reg* 1520–66), were described in contemporary literature as preferring austere dress, whereas extravagant and amoral leaders were supposed to have favoured trailing, perfumed and luxurious apparel. This contradiction between pious austerity and courtly display was never resolved.

The Islamic concept that the social order has been created by God meant that an individual's dress ought to reflect his social rank, occupation or profession, and political and religious affiliation. Wearing apparel associated with a lower rank displayed proper humility, while donning the fabric, style and colour of garments associated with a higher rank showed the wearer's dissatisfaction with the established order and his/her challenge to spiritual and temporal authority. An individual might demonstrate loyalty to society in general and a secular or religious leader in particular by wearing a certain item or colour of dress. The wearing of black, for example, was associated with the Abbasid dynasty, and in later times the wearing of green was reserved for descendants of the Prophet. A particular kind of turban with a white sash wrapped around a red cap with a high, spiked protrusion became the hallmark of the Safavid dynasty in Iran, and yellow footwear was favoured at the court of the Ottoman dynasty (*reg* 1281–1924). Either the neglect or the disinclination to wear such an item could be interpreted as a calculated insult. If the wearer was found guilty of betraying the government or a fraternity, the special item of dress was publicly removed to signify the wearer's exclusion from the group. A military man usually assumed bureaucratic dress on accepting an administrative post. For example, the sultans of the Ayyubid (*reg* 1169–1252) and Mamluk (*reg* 1250–1517) dynasties in Egypt discarded their short close-fitting military dress for their investiture and donned the long ample robes associated with the ulema (jurists/theologians) in order to acknowledge the spiritual responsibilities of office. Distinctions of rank were reflected in the system of presenting courtiers with robes of honour (Arab. *khil'a*) and other garments.

Women's dress seems to have followed a similar system. In upper social circles the system was in operation from the mid-13th century, if not before, and became increasingly elaborate. At the most basic level, unmarried women were distinguished from married ones. At the Ottoman court, for example, the type of fur trimmings and waist girdle indicated social and maternal status, while at the Safavid court the type of headdress was the distinguishing feature. The costumes worn by dancers and musicians are known from early depictions: a wall painting from the palace at Samarra' in Iraq known as the Jawsaq al-Khaqani (836–9), for example, shows two female dancers dressed in long flowing gowns, draped with scarves and bedecked with pearl fillets and gold earrings. Similar outfits distinguish musicians and dancers in later representations, such as a lustre bowl from 12th-century Egypt (Washington, DC, Freer, 46.30). Under the Mamluks, prostitutes were required to wear red trousers and wrap.

Outdoors, women's garb usually covered and concealed the dress worn at home. At no time was veiling compulsory throughout the Islamic lands, and there was no universal rule about the area to be concealed by the veil or the status (e.g. married or unwed, free-born or slave) it indicated and age at which it had to be worn in public. In the 20th century veiling has been associated with families moving from rural areas into cities, and conversely discarding the veil has been linked with greater educational opportunities and higher social status. Since the mid-20th century, however, the issue of veiling has been revived with the growth of fundamentalism and the rejection of Western social and moral values.

Non-Muslims, both male and female, were subject to sumptuary regulations of dress (Arab. *ghiyār*), but the evidence about their effectiveness is conflicting. Christians and Jews were initially required only to dress differently from Muslims, and no distinction was made between them. Under the Abbasids and the Fatimids (*reg* 969–1171) of Egypt, the colour and fabric of dress and the type of shoe were stipulated, and later these were further distinguished for specific communities, with religious groups outside the Judeo-Christian traditions, such as Zoroastrians, generally receiving the harshest regulation. There was a steady, if episodic, stream of sumptuary legislation from government and the courts. Such actions were usually justified with reference to declining moral values and growing social disharmony, but legislation was also issued to protect home production of textiles and clothing. The government and the ulema looked to the local inspector of markets to ensure that sumptuary regulations were upheld in the streets and bazaars. In addition to controlling quality and quantity at the retail end so that no purchaser received a short length or sub-standard work, he was responsible for ensuring that in public non-Muslims wore only their permitted colours and fabrics and that women had the correct sleeve-length or headdress. Broadly speaking, these restrictions about colour and the quality of fabric continued with regional variations until the mid-19th century in the Ottoman empire and until the early 20th century in Iran.

The ruling family and its household were considered the arbiters and guardians of good taste. The conventions of culture (Arab. *adab*) were never precisely defined, but at times they extended to texture, weave and colour of dress fabric. Rulers who did not defend these principles were criticized, while those who attempted to encourage adherence, such as the Mamluk sultan Qala'un (*reg* 1280–90) and his son Khalil (*reg* 1290–94), were lauded in contemporary chronicles. The ulema constantly reminded the community of the public behaviour expected from those in authority. There was an underlying belief among political and religious leaders that a decline in the standards of dress reflected the decline in social and moral standards and consequently that social unrest could be minimized if people wore dress traditionally associated with their status,

profession and religious affiliation. Conversely, the stipulations in the dress reform laws of Turkey and Iran in the 19th and 20th centuries supported governmental reform and modernization programmes.

Some beliefs about dress were common to rich and poor alike. Personal wealth was often measured in terms of textiles and clothing, as seen in the frequent references in trousseau lists, bequests and investments. At least from Abbasid times, aesthetic sensitivity to textiles has been taken as a sign of connoisseurship and wealth. Those with sufficient means had winter and summer wardrobes, and it was the duty of the court astronomer to announce the time for the seasonal change. Public rituals frequently include the donning of special clothing; the most important is the pilgrimage to Mecca, when male pilgrims have to wear seamless white garments (Arab. *izār* and *ridā'*). Other rituals include the celebration of the month of Muharram, when mourning clothes are put on in commemoration of the martyrdom of the Prophet's grandson Husayn on the 10th of the month; and the great festival on the 10th day of the month of Dhu'l-Hijja (Arab. *'īd al-adhā*, Turk. *büyük bayram*), when new clothes are donned.

There was a common belief that garments could possess magical power, both for good and bad, which could then be passed on to the owner. Such magic was durable, inasmuch as a piece of clothing from a saintly person or even the water used for washing it, as in the case of the Prophet's mantle (Arab. *burda*, Pers. *khirqa-yi sharīf*), would continue to hold blessing. Indeed, the story of the Prophet's mantle became the focus of a literary genre, exemplified by the poem written by the 13th-century Egyptian al-Busiri; known as *Burda*, the ode was supposed to convey the mantle's blessing to all who heard it. Garments cut and sewn on days deemed auspicious automatically held good magic. Bad luck, however, could be brought upon the owner by evil-wishers secreting spells or charms within the fabric or touching the clothing. To minimize this risk, the wearer would seek God's blessing when dressing in newly acquired or laundered stuffs. Similarly, talismanic legends on garments, such as a linen shirt (Istanbul, Topkapı Pal. Mus., 13/1150) inscribed with Koranic verses and prayers, were intended to safeguard the wearer from adversity. Authority, like magic, could be transferred from master to disciple through garments. Thus the story of the Prophet giving his turban to his son-in-law 'Ali is understood by Shi'ites to mean that spiritual and temporal power was passed to him. Under the Abbasids, the caliph repeatedly emphasized the legality and authority of his office by wearing the Prophet's mantle. This idea is echoed in the initiation ceremonies of certain dervish orders, where the master's cloak is placed over the novice's shoulders to signify his entry into the order.

The structure of most garments was based on the loom width of the fabric. The untailored wraps favoured by the first caliphs were soon replaced by cut and sewn garments, as tailoring came to be seen in the medieval Islamic period as the mark of a civilized society. Nevertheless, the cut of dress was essentially simple in form, with one or two panels folded to form front and back and then sewn. Sleeves were set in at right angles to the sides with, where necessary, underarm gussets or slits and side panel slits for ease of movement. In the later period, outer tunics assumed a more tailored structure, with a series of triangular inserts attached to the main front and back panels as seen in Mamluk shirts, Ottoman robes and 18th-century Safavid garments. This structure may have originated from narrow fabric widths produced by back-strap looms. It is uncertain whether this simple structure was retained to complement the use of richly patterned and coloured luxury fabrics, but the tailoring of garments became more complex as the use of monochrome self-patterned textiles increased. With the adoption of Europeanized dress in metropolitan centres during the 19th century, elements of European tailoring appeared, such as sloping and padded shoulders, darts and pleats, and shaped armholes. Although robes retained their function as markers of office and status, certain structural elements changed over the centuries. Some of these relate to changes in the wearer's function or role. In the 18th century, for example, the uniform of the Ottoman Janissary corps became more ceremonial in style and less suited to the demands of active service. In other cases alterations could be linked with changes in attitude regarding the human form, as for example in 17th-century Iran when emphatically hipped and narrow-waisted robes became fashionable in court circles.

The type, size, form and colour of the headdress became visually and emblematically dominant over the whole ensemble of dress from Abbasid times on. The colour often related to the wearer's political and/or religious affiliation; for example, the Abbasids and the Qajar dynasty of Iran (*reg* 1779–1924) preferred black, the Ayyubids yellow. The headdress identified profession or occupation, and the bureaucrat, for instance, was careful not to sport the style identified with the military. The actual form and decoration of the headdress often had a religious significance. The 12 padded flutes of the Safavid turban and the headgear worn by Teslim dervishes demonstrated the wearer's belief in the doctrine of Twelver Shi'ism, while the topknob of the Husayni dervish turban symbolized divine unity. In the 20th century the wearing of Western (i.e. Christian) clothing and hats has been seen by some orthodox Muslims as official and personal renunciation of Islam. Rank was also expressed by headgear. Ottoman court paintings from the 18th century show that the highest-ranking court officials wore the tallest or most conspicuous headdresses (see fig. 195). Men of the Qashqa'i tribal confederation in Iran donned peaked or unpeaked caps according to rank and age. In both examples the form and style are associated more with the level of responsibility and status than with the nature of the duties.

BIBLIOGRAPHY
Enc. Islam/2: 'Ghiyār' [Distinction]; 'Khil'a' [Robe of honour]; 'Khirḳa-yi sherīf' [Mantle of the Prophet]; 'Libās' [Clothing]
R. Dozy: *Dictionnaire détaillé des noms des vêtements chez les Arabes* (Amsterdam, 1845/*R* Beirut, 1969)
G. E. von Grunebaum: *Muhammadan Festivals* (London, 1951)
M. M. Ahsan: *Social Life under the Abbasids* (London, 1979)
P. L. Baker: 'The Fez in Turkey: A Symbol of Modernization?' *Costume*, xx (1986), pp. 72–86
A. S. Rugh: *Reveal and Conceal: Dress in Contemporary Egypt* (Cairo, 1986)
J. M. Scarce: *Women's Costume of the Near and Middle East* (London, 1987)
P. L. Baker: *A History of Islamic Court Dress* (diss., U. London, 1988)

195. *Shaykh al-Islam Followed by Three Viziers, with Various Troops in the Lower Registers*; illustration from Vehbi: *Sūrnāma* ('Book of ceremonies'), *c.* 1720 (Istanbul, Topkapı Palace Library, A. 3593, fol. 12*v*)

Y. K. Stillman and N. Micklewright: 'Costume in the Middle East', *Mid. E. Stud. Assoc. Bull.*, xxvi (1992), pp. 13–38

PATRICIA L. BAKER

(ii) Before c. AD *650.* The earliest dress worn by Muslims was the same as that worn by others in 7th-century Arabia, with certain modifications reflecting the new moral sensibilities of the Muslim community. Since antiquity, Arab attire for both sexes had been characterized by simple, untailored garments consisting primarily of loose wraps. Several basic articles of clothing had been in vogue for centuries before the advent of Islam. Herodotus (*Histories* VII.lxvi), for example, reported that the Arabs of his day wore a long flowing garment (*zeira*) which was cinched with a belt. This was undoubtedly the *izār*, a large sheet-like wrap worn by men and women both as a sarong-like waist cloth and as a mantle, which is still worn by Muslim pilgrims to Mecca. The report of Herodotus was corroborated by Strabo (*Geography* XVI.iv.26), who related that the Arab Nabataeans 'go without tunics, with girdles about their loins and with slippers on their feet'. The Bedouin predilection for dark garments also predates the rise of Islam; to define a blue-black colour, the Babylonian Talmudic tractate *Nidda* ('The menstruant', 20a) cites the dark clothes of an Arab.

The Arabs who lived within the cultural spheres of the great empires of Late Antiquity followed the fashions of these higher civilizations. The Arabs who ruled Hatra in northern Mesopotamia during the Parthian period, for example, are depicted in surviving sculptures wearing Persian attire: some wear sleeved mantles and chitons, others trousers and Parthian military festoons. In marked contrast, the Arab inhabitants of the oasis towns of the Syrian desert dressed in the fashion of the eastern Hellenistic world. Bas-reliefs from the caravan city of Palmyra depict deities and humans wearing tunics and mantles draped in the Greco-Roman style. By the advent of Islam in the early 7th century, these three styles had already begun to fuse. The Hadith (canonical traditions concerning the Prophet Muhammad) contain numerous references to indigenous Arabian garments and items of foreign provenance, including such humble articles as underdrawers (Arab. *sirwāl*) for women and such luxurious ones as a brocade *qabā'*, a sleeved robe, slit in front and fastened with frogs. Both of these were Persian styles, whereas the basic body shirt (*qamīs*, from Lat. *camisia*) and tunic (Arab. *jubba* and *thawb*) were worn throughout the Byzantine Near East.

The basic outlines of the Islamic vestimentary system can already be discerned in the earliest years of Islam in Arabia, although almost all information about dress is based on textual sources written a century or more later. The system remained remarkably constant through the Middle Ages, despite changes in fashion and regional variation. The norm was several layers of clothing. A person might wear one garment or many, depending on such factors as weather, occasion and economic means. By the time of the Prophet (*d* 632), the Ancient Near Eastern practice of covering the head out of modesty and respect was already the norm for both men and women. The turban (*'imāma*), which had been worn by Arabs since pre-Islamic times, became 'the badge of Islam' in the late Middle Ages, and Muslim men are depicted with turbans not only in Islamic art but also in Christian illustrated manuscripts, such as the early 14th-century copy (Madrid, Bib. N., MS. Vitr.26, 2) of the *Synopsis of Histories* by the Byzantine historian John Skylitzes and a late 13th- or early 14th-century copy of the *Cantigas de Santa María* of Alfonso X (Madrid, Escorial, Bib. Monasterio S Lorenzo, MS.J.b.2).

(iii) c. AD *650–c. 1200.* In keeping with his ascetic creed, Muhammad frowned on Muslim men wearing garments of costly fabrics with rich ornamentation (although he did not object to women wearing such clothes), but such scruples were abandoned within a generation or two of his death with the establishment of an Islamic empire and the rise of a leisured class, which enjoyed wearing fine clothing. The haute bourgeoisie found religious sanction for their luxurious taste in fabricated traditions that Muhammad had permitted men to wear silks and brocades. As regards monarchs, Arab historians relate that the Umayyad caliph 'Abd al-Malik (*reg* 685–705) wore embroidered garments, and that his son and second successor Sulaiman (*reg* 715–17) and his retinue wore only garments of variegated silk (*washī*), including tunics, cloaks or mantles (*ridā'*), drawers, turbans and brimless caps (*qalansuwa*).

In common with the rulers of Byzantium and Sasanian Iran, the Umayyads (*reg* 661–750) wore special embroidered fabrics (*see* TIRAZ) produced in royal factories. *Tirāz* garments such as robes of honour (*khil'a*) were bestowed by the caliphs and their governors as tokens of favour. The oldest surviving piece of a *tirāz* garment is a 600 mm length of a linen turban with a red silk inscription bearing the date AH 88 (AD 707; Cairo, Mus. Islam. A.). *Tirāz* garments became extremely popular in the Middle Ages and were worn not only by members of the caliphal entourage and the bureaucracy, but also by the bourgeoisie. Both Islamic and Byzantine illustrated manuscripts frequently depict Muslim men wearing robes with *tirāz* bands on the upper sleeves (see fig. 196).

Islamic society became highly fashion-conscious during the caliphate of the Abbasids (*reg* 749–1258). Under their rule the empire became increasingly cosmopolitan. In 9th- and 10th-century Iraq the Persian secretarial class propagated the polite education and cultural ideal of *adab*, the Islamic equivalent of the ancient Greek *paideia* and the medieval European *courtoisie*. Elegance in writing, speech and dress were as essential for the haute bourgeoisie as they were for the ruling class. Simple woollen garments were considered fitting only for the poor and for Sufis, ascetics whose name in Arabic is derived from the word for wool (*sūf*); people of culture preferred finer fabrics. The sophisticate Muhammad al-Washsha' (*d* 936) devoted several chapters of his treatise on *adab*, *Kitāb al-muwashshā aw al-zarf wa'l-zurafā'* ('The ornamented book, or elegance and elegant people'), to the subject of proper dress.

196. *The Fortieth Assembly*; illustration from al-Hariri: *Maqāmāt* ('Assemblies'), second quarter of the 13th century (Paris, Bibliothèque Nationale, MS. arab. 3929, fol. 134*r*)

According to him, a fashionable gentleman was outfitted with a fine undershirt and a lined tunic, both of high-quality linen. Over these, he wore a lined robe or another tunic of linen, silk or *mulḥam* ('half-silk'). His head was covered at all times. When going out of doors he would drape over his clothes a cloak, sometimes with decoration at either end, while a headscarf or cowl (*ṭaylasān*) was placed over his turban. Making a good appearance meant avoiding unpleasant or clashing colours, dirty clothes or clothes perfumed like those of slave girls. Shoes and sandals could be of various leathers, colours and designs, and shoes in such colour combinations as black and red or yellow and black were permitted. The Persian custom of wearing stockings (*jawrab*) inside one's shoes was already in vogue.

Al-Washsha' provided less detail in his chapter on female attire, which is subtitled 'Concerning those clothes that differ from those of fashionable men'. The author began again with intimate garments. The gentlewoman's lingerie consisted of a smoky-grey shift (*ghilāla*) and drawers. The type of dress was not specified, but it had to have wide sleeves and a collar with a drawstring, in contrast to most depictions of female figures on ceramics and wall paintings, which show females wearing narrow sleeves. By the time of al-Washsha', a woman was expected to be totally swathed when going out of doors. She wore several layers of wraps and veils, beginning with a mantle and continuing with the all-enveloping body-wrap. In addition, she covered her face with a veil (*miqna'a*), the finest of which came from the city of Nishapur in eastern Iran, and wore a black turban on her head. Black was considered particularly stylish, while white garments, with the exception of underdrawers, were to be avoided as unfeminine.

Many new garments of Persian origin came into fashion during the Abbasid period. One was the *qalansuwa ṭawīla*, a tall, conical brimless hat consisting of a frame of reed or wood covered with fabric; it was nicknamed *danniyya* because of its resemblance to an inverted amphora-like wine jar (*dann*). According to a famous anecdote, Harun ar-Rashid (*reg* 786–809), the Abbasid caliph of *Arabian Nights* fame, wore one of these hats emblazoned with 'pilgrim' on one side and 'holy warrior' on the other, symbolizing the duties he undertook in alternate years of leading pilgrims to Mecca and leading men on the Holy War. The hat is commonly depicted in illustrated manuscripts of al-Hariri's *Maqāmāt* ('Assemblies') where the hero Abu Zayd often wears it in its long and regular versions. Another Persian garment that became extremely popular throughout the Arab world was the kaftan (Pers. *khaftān*, Turk. *qafṭān*). Originally a cuirass, by Abbasid times the kaftan had become a luxurious sleeved robe which buttoned down the front. The caliph al-Muqtadir (*reg* 908–32) wore a silver brocade silk kaftan from Tustar in Iran, and his son wore one of Byzantine silk ornamented with figures. Illustrations in manuscripts, representations on ceramics, and wood and ivory carvings show men wearing ornamented kaftan-like garments, but in most cases it is difficult to identify the precise type.

Goods from all over the world, including garments, flowed into the Abbasid capitals of Baghdad and Samarra'. One was the *fūṭa*, a long piece of *sārī*-like cloth which served as loincloth, apron and shawl. Chinese oilcloth

raincloaks (Arab. *mimṭara*) were mentioned by al-Tha'alabi (*d* 1037) in his entertaining little encyclopedia *Laṭā'if al-ma'arif* ('Refined bits of information'). They must have been costly, since the poet al-Buhtari (*d* 897) begged his patron to give him one. Fur came to be widely used for luxury garments. The ancient Arabs had known only sheepskins with the fleece left on, but in cosmopolitan Abbasid society furs were imported from Europe, Central Asia and China for use as decorative trim, linings and entire robes. The most popular were squirrel, fox, beaver, weasel, rabbit, sable, ermine, lynx and mink. Although fur garments are frequently mentioned in medieval Arabic and Persian texts, the only ones commonly depicted in Islamic art before the 16th century are the fur caps worn by Turkish soldiers. Two rare exceptions are royal robes: a fur-trimmed coat of gold brocade in the frontispiece to a 13th-century copy (Vienna, Österreich. Nbib., MS.A.F.10, fol. 1*r*) of Pseudo-Galen's *Kitāb al-diryāq* ('Book of antidotes'; see fig. 110 above) and a robe with fur shoulders, lapels and hem.

The Fatimid rulers (*reg* 909–1171) of North Africa and Egypt were the most clothes-conscious of the medieval Islamic world. They exhibited a dramatic flair for pomp and ceremony that exceeded anything the Abbasids had done, and clothing played a major part in creating the aura of majesty and splendour. Every functionary from the caliph to the clerk had a ceremonial costume (*badla mawkibiyya*) supplied by an official government bureau, which not only distributed these outfits, but also oversaw their production and storage in the caliphal supply house (*dār/khizānat al-kiswa*). The Egyptian historian al-Maqrizi (*d* 1442), who quoted extensively from Fatimid authors and provided almost all the surviving information about Fatimid ceremonial dress, reported that the outfit given to each individual had as many as 12 items and comprised a complete ensemble from turban to underdrawers. Clothing of different weight was provided according to the season. Fatimid ceremonial dress was made of the finest textiles, such as high-grade silk (*ḥarīr*), fine linens (*sūsī*, *dabīqī*, *sharab* and *dimyaṭī*), royal brocade (*khusrawānī*) and siglaton (*siqlaṭīn*, a rich silk). These costumes were usually white and embroidered with gold and silver threads in accordance with the official Fatimid imagery of luminous splendour and divine light, as opposed to the official black robes of the rival Abbasid caliphate. The selection of the caliph's costume was a ritualized event before every holiday.

Every rank and office in the Fatimid caliphate was distinguished by its costume. The caliph had an enormous turban consisting of a cap (*shāshiyya*) around which was wound a cloth (*mandīl*) in the shape of a myrobalan, a plum-shaped fruit; the special way of winding this turban was called the 'winding of majesty'. It probably resembled the enormous, oddly shaped turban worn by an equestrian figure on a fragment of a lustre bowl attributed to the period of Fatimid rule in North Africa (Tunis, Mus. N. Bardo). According to al-Maqrizi, the caliph's turban was ornamented with jewels, and a high solitaire was mounted on a silk band centred on the brow. The entire headgear was dubbed 'the noble crown'. When the Fatimids moved their capital from Mahdia in Tunisia to Cairo in 972, they brought with them a new style of turban, the *ḥanak* or *taḥnīk al-'imāma*, which was distinguished by running the winding cloth from one temple to the other under the chin and jaw. It was officially worn by military commanders, viziers, chief eunuchs and often by the caliph himself, and became so fashionable that its motif of the winding cloth under the chin and jaw was carried over into women's jewellery where it reappeared as a chin- or jaw-band. An Egyptian trousseau list from the 12th century mentions one such band or chain studded with pearls, and another with pearls or gold discs. A specifically North African fashion, the *ḥanak* is still worn in parts of the Maghrib, especially among such Berber groups as the Touareg in southern Algeria and Morocco.

A prime source in documenting medieval Islamic dress is the Cairo Geniza, an enormous cache of discarded papers (dispersed) that was preserved in a storeroom of a synagogue in Fustat (Old Cairo) and in the nearby cemetery of Basatin. The Geniza manuscripts include 750 trousseau lists of Jewish brides in Egypt during the rule of the Fatimid, Ayyubid (*reg* 1169–1252) and, to a lesser extent, Mamluk (*reg* 1250–1517) dynasties. Commercial documents and private letters also provide important data on men's clothing. The information supplied by the Geniza documents pertains to the history of dress throughout the Islamic world, since the discriminatory dress code of differentiation for non-Muslims (*ghiyār*) was ignored under the Fatimids, and non-Muslims could wear clothes of the same cut, colour and fabric as Muslims. The Geniza documents also present a picture of bourgeois dress at a time of ecumenical prosperity when the commercial revolution in the Islamic world was at its peak and when there was a significant middle class with both the means and desire to be fashionable.

The bourgeoisie during the Fatimid and Ayyubid periods consciously or unconsciously tried to imitate the modes and mores of the ruling class. Well-to-do merchants, for example, bestowed robes of honour and other *ṭirāz* garments upon family members and friends. Medieval Arab geographers and historians noted that there were separate factories producing *ṭirāz* for the ruling élite and for commoners. The Geniza documents clearly show that people of means wore all the precious fabrics known from literary descriptions of Fatimid ceremonies: more than 60 textiles are mentioned in the Geniza documents, including 12 different kinds of silk; 17 of them were unknown hitherto.

The archaeological, artistic and literary sources agree that during this period people enjoyed clothing in a wide variety of colours and patterns. This richness and diversity was perhaps as much a psychological reaction to the dull, buff tones of the Middle Eastern landscape as it was a sign of wealth and prosperity. Textile dyes took their names from all sorts of natural phenomena, such as spices, fruits, nuts, animals, plants and stones. Fabrics were dyed the colour of quince, bitter orange, basil, apricot, chickpea, clover, mandrake, wine, peacock, sand grouse, pearl and ruby. Even the common colours were distinguished according to shade: blue could be sky-blue, cloudy-blue or azure, to cite but a few; white could be white-grey, cloudy-white or wax. Although cloudy-green, clover, pistachio, emerald and viridescent are mentioned, shades of green seem to have been much less common than any of the other colours. The rarity of green may have been due to the technical difficulties of achieving good dyes that would hold well over time. In later times, green was reserved for descendants of the Prophet, but such an explanation is anachronistic for the Fatimid and Ayyubid periods. Black garments also seem to have been comparatively rare during Fatimid times, perhaps for political reasons, due to associations with the Abbasids. Some of the few variations mentioned are bluish-black (*kuḥlī*: 'the colour of kohl'), brownish-black (dubbed with the rather sensual and suggestive name of 'slave girl's thigh'), blackish, peppery and leaden. The patterns that embellished clothing were as varied as the colours. In addition to the usual decorated hems, sleeves and clavi (vertical bands), garments could have all-over patterns, including a wide variety of checks and stripes with such names as 'chessboard' and 'the flowing of the pen'. Avian, animal and anthropomorphic designs were popular on embroidered bands and as all-over patterns.

(iv) c. *1200*–c. *1500*. Until the latter part of the Fatimid period a cosmopolitan Islamic style, with some regional variations, was shared by the Arabic-speaking urban bourgeoisie throughout the Muslim world, but this situation changed dramatically in the 12th and 13th centuries. In the Muslim East, Turkish military dynasties introduced many Central Asian styles, particularly in military and ceremonial dress. At first, the Arab populations of Egypt and the Levant were little affected by the styles of their Turkish overlords. The two classes are clearly distinguished in 12th- and 13th-century manuscript paintings by their ethnic features and clothing. The typical outer garment of the ruling Turkish élite was a coat (Arab. *qabā'*) that crisscrossed over the chest. The Saljuqs (*reg* 1038–1194) and the Ayyubids preferred the 'Turkish' coat, which closed with the right side overlapping the left, whereas the Mamluks favoured the 'Tartar' coat, which closed the opposite way. Over the coat was a belt of metal plaquettes (*ḥiyāṣa*) or a sash (*band*). There were a variety of caps: the principal ones were the triangular *sharbūsh*, which was sometimes trimmed with fur or wrapped with a small kerchief to form a sort of turban; and the rounded *kalawta*, which was usually yellow in the Ayyubid period and red in the Mamluk.

In the West indigenous Berber and Hispanic elements became stronger with the rise of the Berber empires that united the Maghrib with what remained of Muslim Spain. The Saharan costumes of the Almoravid dynasty (*reg* 1056–1147) were distinctive because of the veil (*lithām*) that covered the lower half of the face. The Almoravids also wore the North African hooded cape, the burnous (*burnūs*). Although the face veil was forbidden to outsiders, other garments were adopted by some Iberian subjects who wanted to ingratiate themselves with their new masters, despite ridicule from their fellow Andalusians. After a generation or so, however, the trend was reversed as the Almoravids came under the spell of the sophisticated Andalusian culture and themselves adopted fashions that filtered back to North Africa.

The Almohad caliphate (1130–1269) had a greater and more lasting impact on the history of clothing in the Maghrib, since the puritanism of the movement's founder and spiritual guide, Muhammad ibn Tumart (*d* 1130), extended to dress. As a result, veiling for women was more strictly observed through North Africa and Islamic Spain, and non-Muslims were compelled to wear distinctive clothing. Although Almohad courtiers, like the Almoravids before them, eventually succumbed to the luxuries of Andalusia, the Almohad simplicity of dress remained the norm for most North Africans throughout the Middle Ages and into modern times. By contrast, in the Nasrid kingdom of Granada (1230–1492) there was a revival of brightly coloured clothing and fine silks, and the Berber-style turban was abandoned. The fashions of Christian Spain were increasingly influential, although Moriscos continued to wear their own distinctive dress after the fall of Granada in 1492.

BIBLIOGRAPHY

Enc. Islam/2: 'Libās' [Clothing]

Muḥammad al-Washshā' (*d* 936): *Kitāb al-muwashshā aw al-ẓarf wa'l-ẓurafā'* [The ornamented book, or elegance and elegant people], ed. R. E. Brünnow (Leiden, 1886/*R* Cairo, 1953)

al-Tha'alabi (*d* 1037): *Laṭā'if al-ma'arif* [Refined bits of information]; Eng. trans. by C. E. Bosworth as *The Book of Curious and Entertaining Information* (Edinburgh, 1968)

Aḥmad ibn 'Alī al-Maqrīzī (*d* 1442): *al-Mawā'iẓ wa'l-i'tibār bi-dhikr al-khiṭaṭ wa'l-athār* [Exhortations and instructions on the districts (of Egypt) and its antiquities] (Cairo, 1853–4)

R. Dozy: *Dictionnaire détaillé des noms des vêtements chez les Arabes* (Amsterdam, 1845/*R* Beirut, 1969)

J. Jouin: 'Documents sur le costume des musulmans d'Espagne', *Rev. Afr.*, lxxv (1934), pp. 43–6

R. Levy: 'Notes on Costumes from Arabic Sources', *J. Royal Asiat. Soc. GB & Ireland* (1935), pp. 319–38

R. B. Sergeant: 'Islamic Textiles: Material for a History up to the Mongol Conquest', *A. Islam*, ix (1942), pp. 54–92; x (1943), pp. 71–104; xi–xii (1946), pp. 98–145; xiii–xiv (1948), pp. 75–117; xv–xvi (1951), pp. 29–85; as book (Beirut, 1972)

L. A. Mayer: *Mamluk Costume: A Survey* (Geneva, 1952)

R. Dussaud: *La Pénétration des Arabes en Syrie avant l'Islam* (Paris, 1955)

G. Bernis: *Indumtaria española en tiempos de Carlos V* (Madrid, 1962)

R. Arié: 'Quelques remarques sur le costume musulman au temps des Naṣrides', *Arabica*, xii (1965), pp. 244–61

M. Fendri: 'Un Vêtement islamique ancien au Musée du Bardo', *Africa: Inst. N. Archéol. & A.*, ii (1967–8), pp. 241–71

M. V. Gorelik: 'Blizhnevostochnaya miniatura xii–xiii vv. kak etnograficheskiy istochnik' [Near Eastern miniatures of the 12th and 13th centuries as an ethnographic source], *Sov. Etnog.*, clxxii/2 (1972), pp. 37–50

Y. K. Stillman: *Female Attire of Medieval Egypt, According to the Trousseau Lists and Cognate Material from the Cairo Geniza* (diss., Pennsylvania State U., 1972)

——: 'The Importance of the Cairo Geniza for the History of Medieval Female Attire', *Int. J. Mid. E. Stud.*, vii (1976), pp. 579–89

——: 'New Data on Islamic Textiles from the Geniza', *Textile Hist.*, x (1979), pp. 184–95

S. D. Goitein: *Daily Life* (1983), iv of *A Mediterranean Society* (Berkeley, Los Angeles and London, 1967–88), pp. 150–200

YEDIDA K. STILLMAN

(v) c. 1500 and after. From the 16th to the 19th century, dress in the Islamic world followed regional patterns, roughly but not exactly corresponding to the political situation. North Africa and the central Islamic lands were largely under the control of the Ottoman dynasty (*reg* 1281–1924), and Turkish dress was worn by officials and the military, while the rest of the population continued to wear traditional Arabo-Islamic styles. In Anatolia and the Balkans, dress followed the precedents set by the Ottoman court at Istanbul, with distinctive styles for military and religious groups. In Iran styles of dress followed the precedents set by the Safavid (*reg* 1501–

1732), Zand (*reg* 1750–94) and Qajar (*reg* 1779–1924) dynasties at their courts in Isfahan, Shiraz and Tehran. Throughout the Islamic world, European fabrics and styles of dress began to be adopted in the 19th century by the urban élites.

□

(a) North Africa and the central Islamic lands. (b) Anatolia and the Balkans. (c) Iran.

(a) North Africa and the central Islamic lands. Until the introduction of European fashions in the late 19th century, dress in the Arab world continued according to traditions established before *c.* 1500. In North Africa the styles current under the late Almohads and their successors remained stable. In the central Islamic lands of Egypt and the Levant, the basic dichotomy of Turkish dress for official attire and for the military apparel of the ruling élite, and Arabo-Islamic dress in urban, rural or bedouin form for the rest of the population, remained the norm even after the region came under Ottoman rule in 1516. The dichotomy was not absolute, and some Ottoman fashions, such as the Turkish-style kaftan for men and women, the close-fitting coat (Turk. *yelek*) and pantaloons (*çakṣir*), were adopted by members of the urban bourgeoisie. A similar phenomenon occurred in Tunisia and Algeria, which succumbed piecemeal to Ottoman control in the 16th century. In all provinces of the Ottoman empire, Turkish synonyms for certain items of clothing were used alongside native Arabic equivalents (e.g. Turk. *yashmaq* for Arab. *burqu'*, a woman's face veil).

European travel literature supplants indigenous artistic and literary sources for the history of dress, as this was a period of cultural eclipse in the Arabic-speaking world. Such works, frequently accompanied by drawings and engravings, provide important descriptions of local clothing. In addition, illustrations in Ottoman and Persian manuscripts, especially works of a religio-historical nature, occasionally depict Arab subjects in native attire, e.g. the illustrations to a 6-volume 16th-century copy (dispersed) of Mustafa Darir's biography of the Prophet, *Siyar-i Nabī* (see fig. 133 above).

Outside the main urban centres of administration, regional styles predominated. The clothing of one region was distinguished from that of another not by differences in the forms of the basic garments themselves, but by minor variations in the sleeves, collar, ampleness and length. There were also significant variations, particularly for female attire, in such decorative details as the pattern of the fabric, colour of the embroidery, trimming and fastenings. Male attire was more uniform in style (except in Morocco), since men enjoyed greater physical and social mobility than women, whose *de facto* confinement in small local communities intensified individual style from region to region. Accordingly, when a plate from E. W. Lane's *An Account of the Manners and Customs of the Modern Egyptians* (London, 1836) was reused for a book on Syria, its caption 'A Syrian Gentleman . . . *ca* 1860' was only slightly inaccurate.

From Egypt to Iraq, the basic male wardrobe consisted of underdrawers (Arab. *sirwāl*, *shakshīr*, often simply called *libās*, the common word for clothing), a tunic (called *gallābiyya* in Egypt, *thōb* in Palestine, *badan* in Arabia and *dishdāsha* in Iraq) or long shirt (called *qamīṣ(a)* almost universally), an outer robe and a mantle. The outer robe (called a *jubba* almost everywhere, a *qumbāz* in Syria, Palestine and Iraq, a *banīsh* in Iraq and Arabia) and mantle (called *'abā'(a)* everywhere, with special names given to particular varieties such as the white wool *masūmī* of Baghdad) varied according to socio-economic status and time of year. Until the late 19th century (and indeed much later in many places), the prescribed headgear for men of the urban élite was the tripartite turban, consisting of a skullcap (*'araqiyya, ma'raqa* or *ṭāqiyya*), a felt cap (tarboosh or fez) and a white muslin winding cloth (*shāsh*, but also *laffa* and *ṭarḥa*). The bedouin, villagers and even many townspeople in the Near East wore a flowing headscarf over the skullcap. This headscarf, called by the general name of *kāfiyya* or *kūfiyya*, was also known by particular regional names, such as *ghabāna* in the Hejaz, *ghuṭra* in Najd, and *ḥaṭṭa* in Palestine. It was usually white, but could also be completely covered with a pattern of coloured checks or lozenges. Normally, the headscarf would be made of cotton, but a fine one could be of silk with embroidered decoration. It was held in place by a circlet of cord, rope or leather (*'aqāl*, or *brīm* in Syria and Palestine) made of one to four coils, the latter being standard for Arabian royalty.

In North Africa males wore outer garments in addition to the usual layers of tunics and gowns. The two most distinctive outer wraps were the burnous (also *silhām* in Morocco) and the *ḥayk*. The burnous was a large hooded cape of black or white wool, which was felted in the finer examples. One particularly striking variety of the burnous, the *akhnīf*, was worn by the Berbers of the Anti Atlas and High Atlas mountains during the winter months. Made of black goat hair and embroidered on the lower back with a red-orange, eye-shaped design, it frequently captured the attention of European artists and ethnographers. The *ḥayk* was a large outer wrap, usually white, which could envelop the body in a variety of ways, some extremely complex. Together with its cousins, the *ksā'* and the *barrakān*, which differed according to fabric, colour and weight, it was an indigenous garment, which predated the Arab conquest in the 7th century. These wraps caught the attention of medieval Arab writers and later European travellers and artists, notably Delacroix, who visited the region in the 19th century. Another outer garment worn in Morocco and western Algeria was the *jellaba* (also *jellābiyya* and *jellāb*), a hooded robe with long sleeves. It could be of the heaviest wool or the lightest cotton, and was normally plain white, brown or black, but could also be striped. Most men in North Africa wore a small simple turban (*shedd(a)*), consisting of a winding cloth with or without a skullcap, although large tripartite turbans were worn by members of the Turkish élite in the cities of Algeria, Tunisia and Tripolitania. Also common was a soft brimless cap (*shāshiyya*) of felted wool in a variety of styles and colours. In Morocco and Algeria, peasant men (and women) frequently wore wide-brimmed straw hats (Arab. *taraza, tarazala* or *tarazal*) when working out of doors.

Unlike male dress in the two main zones of the Arabic-speaking world, female attire exhibited tremendous regional variation. Within a single country, there were marked differences according to regional, ethnic and class criteria, especially where veils, headdresses and the decorative details of dresses and robes were concerned. For example, the *shaṭwa*, a conical hat shaped like an inverted flowerpot and covered with horizontal rows of coins, was the distinctive headcovering of women from Bethlehem, whereas the *ṣmāda*, a thick padded cap attached to a stiff padded rim of tightly wound fabric shaped like a horseshoe and decorated with a row of coins, was the typical headcovering of women from Ramallah, Samaria and Lower Galilee. Women in the coastal plain of Palestine wore a bonnet (*ṣaffa* or *wuqā*). In the Hebron Hills women had a special hat for weddings called the *wuqāyat al-darāhim* ('hat of coins'); it was round with a flat top and encrusted with overlapping layers of small coins sewn to resemble fish scales.

In 19th-century Egypt upper-class urban women wore a composite turban (*rabṭa*) consisting of one or more printed cloths wound around a skullcap or tarboosh; a jewelled crown piece (*qurṣ*) was frequently placed on top of it. Women of the lower classes, on the other hand, wore a simple kerchief (*'aṣba*). In the hill country of Lebanon and Syria, women of all three major ethno-religious groups (Muslim, Christian and Druze) wore a high, pointed, mitre-like headdress (*ṭanṭūr(a)* or *tartūr*) of wood, horn or metal; it was sometimes ornately carved and was held in place by a kerchief or band. In northern Palestine and parts of Syria, this coif was restricted to Druze women; a similar headdress, but with half a cone, was worn by Muslim and Jewish women in urban Tunisia and Algeria.

Female headcovering varied greatly throughout North Africa. This was especially true among the large Jewish minority, and Jewish women in Morocco still wear many types of headdresses. In Tunisia, the bonnets (*kūfiyya, shkūfiyya* and *dūka*) worn by married Muslim women for festive occasions varied in shape from conical to round and sometimes had fabric coming down the back and sides. They could be ornately embroidered, studded with pearls or covered with coins, depending on regional style. Even headscarves varied greatly in colour, size, shape and decoration. In Morocco, Algeria and Tunisia, the scarf (*sibniyya*) worn in a variety of turban-like fashions by Jewesses and Muslim women of Andalusian descent was fringed, whereas the scarves (such as the *wiqāya* and the *qṭīb*) worn there by other women usually did not have a fringe.

Female attire, even everyday wear, was richly embellished, unlike that of males, which usually had little decoration beyond embroidered trim or multicolour striping (festive garments in the Levant are exceptional). Dresses, coats, jackets and wraps were often richly embroidered (*muqaṣṣab*) in Syria, Palestine and among the tribes of the Arabian Peninsula. Many regions, towns and tribal groups had their own distinctive decorations. Bethlehem, for example, was famous for its combination of gold-thread couching and multicoloured satin-stitch embroidery in silk on its finest dresses, such as the *thōb malakī* ('royal dress') and *thōb ikhḍārī* ('green dress'); the combination produced a pyrotechnic display of colours and golden arabesques. Ramallah was noted for its finely executed embroidery in red cross stitch on white or blue linen dresses (see fig. 197) and on white head veils. The black dresses worn by women in the Najd were traditionally

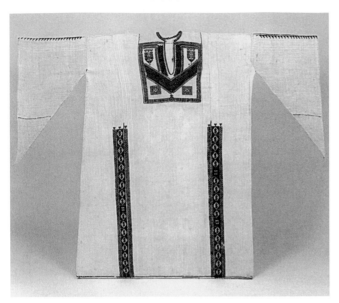

197. Woman's dress (*thōb*), linen, from Ramallah, late 19th century (Santa Fe, NM, Museum of International Folk Art)

BIBLIOGRAPHY

W. al-Jādir: *al-Malābis al-sha'biyya fī'l-'Irāq* [Folk costume in Iraq] (Baghdad, n.d.)
G. Cyr: *Lebanese and Syrian Costume* (Beirut, n.d.)
G. Marçais: *Le Costume d'Alger* (Paris, 1930)
G. Rousseau: *Le Costume au Maroc* (Paris, 1938)
R. Tresse: 'L'Evolution du costume des citadins syrolibanais depuis un siècle', *La Géographie*, lxx (1938), pp. 1–16, 76–82
——: 'L'Evolution du costume des citadins en Syrie depuis le XIXe siècle', *La Géographie*, lxxi–lxxii (1939), pp. 29–40, 257–71
J. Besancenot: *Costumes du Maroc* (Paris, 1942/*R* Aix-en-Provence, 1988)
M. Chehab: 'Le Costume au Liban', *Bull. Mus. Beyrouth*, vi/6 (1942–3), pp. 47–79
E. Racknow: 'Das Beduinenkostüm in Tripolitanien: Dargestellt am Beispiel des Nuâil-Stammes', *Baessler-Archv*, xxv (1943), pp. 24–50
——: *El traje musulman femenino en Africa del Norte* (Madrid, 1953)
M. C. Keatinge: *Costumes of the Levant* (Beirut, 1955)
S. Galloy-Jorelle: 'Les Tissages ras de Djebala', *Cah. A. & Tech. Afrique N.*, vi (1960–61), pp. 10–15
R. Arié: 'Notes sur le costume en Egypte dans la première moitié du XIXe siècle', *Rev. Etud. Islam.*, xi (1968), pp. 201–13
C. Sugier: 'Les Coiffes féminines de Tunisie', *Cah. A. & Trad. Pop.*, i/2 (1968), pp. 61–78
Ḥayyē ha-Yehūdim be-Marōqō [Costumes of the Jews of Morocco] (exh. cat., Jerusalem, Israel Mus., 1973)
Maroc: Costumes, broderies, brocarts (Paris, 1974)
Y. K. Stillman: *Palestinian Costume and Jewelry* (Albuquerque, NM, 1979)
P. L. Fiske, W. R. Pickering and R. S. Yohe, eds: *From the Far West: Carpets and Textiles of Morocco* (Washington, DC, 1980)
Y. K. Stillman: 'The Costume of the Jewish Woman in Morocco', *Studies in Jewish Folklore*, ed. F. Talmage (Cambridge, MA, 1980)
H. C. Ross: *The Art of Arabian Costume: A Saudi Arabian Profile* (Fribourg, 1981)
A. B. Rugh: *Reveal and Conceal: Dress in Contemporary Egypt* (Syracuse, NY, 1986)
Palms and Pomegranates: Traditional Dress of Saudi Arabia (exh. cat., ed. Y. Stillman; Cambridge, MA, Harvard U., Semit. Mus., 1987–9)

YEDIDA K. STILLMAN

enlivened with coloured silk appliqués, sequins and embroidery in metallic and silk threads. Women from Shafa in the Hejaz wore distinctive dresses (*durrā'a*) pieced together in horizontal bands and covered with geometric embroidery in metallic and silk threads. In North Africa embroidery was common on dresses and robes, especially on kaftans, which were couched with gold thread in a technique known there as *siqillī* ('Sicilian work'). Silk threads of various shades were occasionally used for colourful floral designs, but metallic embroidery normally predominated. Embroidery on waist sashes and shawls was also common.

During the second half of the 19th century and the first half of the 20th, Europe's increasing economic, political and cultural penetration of the Middle East and North Africa had a marked impact on the dress of the region. Cheap, factory-produced fabrics replaced hand-loomed ones. New embroidery motifs and decorations were copied from imported textiles or learnt from Christian missionaries in craft schools. Aniline dyes manufactured in Europe were used instead of local vegetal dyes and frequently gave clothing gaudier hues. In the 20th century silk was commonly superseded by synthetic fabrics, called *ḥarīr nabaṭī* ('Nabataean silk') in the Levant and *ḥarīr rūmī* ('European silk') in North Africa. A more radical transformation was the abandoning of traditional, loose, flowing garments in favour of Western tailored clothing. This change in the basic vestimentary system did not happen at a uniform rate. It occurred first among westernizing Muslim élites and members of Jewish and Christian minorities in the major urban centres, especially along the Mediterranean coast where European impact was strongest. Elsewhere the pace varied, with most of the people in North Africa and the Arabian Peninsula resisting Western dress much longer than their counterparts in Egypt and the Levant.

(b) Anatolia and the Balkans. The social diversity within the Ottoman empire was reflected in its dress. Muslims dressed differently from the ethnic minorities of Christians, Jews, Greeks and Armenians; city and town dwellers dressed differently from villagers; and subjects from the European regions of the empire dressed differently from those from Anatolia. Most information from contemporary sources, such as manuscript illustration, travel literature, paintings, photographs and the few surviving costumes, documents the dress of the wealthy, urban, culturally dominant class in Istanbul. Consequently the main types of dress that can be distinguished are the male and female attire of the capital, although there is also considerable information on the attire worn in the Balkans.

Men's dress. Male attire in Anatolia reflected occupational and social identity in a specific and public way. Details, such as the colour of shoes and the configuration of headgear, were closely regulated by sumptuary laws, as was the use of certain luxury fabrics and furs. Men's dress falls into civilian, military and religious groups, reflecting the major social divisions. Civilian dress includes court dress, which is well documented due to the Ottoman habit of saving a sultan's clothing after his death and to the precise depictions of court attire found in illustrated manuscripts (see fig. 195 above). Court dress consisted of a loose shirt (Turk. *iç gömlek*) of wool, cotton or a cotton-silk blend; straight, loose-fitting trousers extending to the ankle (*şalvar*); an inner robe (*entari*); and an outer kaftan. The inner robe opened at the front and was either wrapped with a sash or belt, or closed or fastened with a series of corded buttons and loops. The sleeves were long or cut at the elbow, and in some cases separate sleeves (*kolluk*) could be buttoned on at the elbow. The kaftan, which was worn open, was similar in construction to the inner robe, but was often of a heavier and more luxurious fabric, and could be quilted or lined with fur for warmth. A type of kaftan with narrow, floor-length sleeves and slits at the shoulders through which the arms passed (*merasim*) was worn on ceremonial occasions and given as a royal gift. Shorter kaftans could be worn for outdoor activities, particularly riding, sometimes with close-fitting trousers (*çakşır*) to which socks were attached. Less important officials and court bureaucrats often wore the inner robe without the kaftan. Court rank was further indicated by other vestimentary features such as the type of fabric, headdress and accessories. The elaborately patterned silks and velvets preserved in the Topkapı Palace Museum in Istanbul (*see* §2(iii)(a) above) were reserved for sultans and the highest officials; others wore plain-coloured fabrics of cotton or wool. Every man who worked at court, including members of the military, had a specific type of headgear which identified his job and rank. The men responsible for guarding gates and doors within the palace, for example, wore white headdresses which were held in place by a wide embroidered gold band around the forehead and fell halfway down the back. Military and court officials were also distinguished by their accessories, such as swords, ceremonial axes, flywhisks, handkerchiefs or pencases tucked into belts.

Military uniforms were strictly regulated, but generally resembled the dress of other groups, while allowing for more freedom of movement. The traditional dress of the Janissary corps included boots, trousers and the inner robe closed with a wide belt. Rank was indicated by such elements of the costume as colour, headgear and weaponry, as well as by the way in which the inner robe was draped. A more formal costume was worn for ceremonial occasions. Members of the religious community wore garments similar to those worn at court, but of restrained colour and fabric. Their headdresses often included green, the colour reserved for descendants of the Prophet and conventionally identified with Islam. Each of the religious orders or dervish groups had a distinctive dress. The ceremonial dress of the Mevlevi order, for example, consisted of a long, full shift (*tennure*), a long-sleeved waist-length jacket (*destegül*), cummerbund (*elifenemed*) and hat (*sikke*). Dervish costume often included symbolic accessories: members of the Bektashi order, for example, wore a belt (*kemer*), around which was wound another belt tied with a stone at the end (*kamberiye*), in memory of Kamber, the groom of the Prophet's son-in-law 'Ali. Attached to the belt was a bag (*cilbent*), inscribed twice with the name of 'Ali and a double image of Zulfikar (Arab. *dhū'l-fiqār*), his twin-bladed sword.

Clothing styles in the Ottoman empire changed markedly in the late 18th century and 19th, when it underwent a period of rapid social transformation. During the reign of Selim III (*reg* 1789–1807) military dress became a symbol of the sultan's efforts to modernize the army. The introduction of a new uniform, more European in style than the traditional Janissary garb, led to a mutiny and the sultan's deposition. Thirty years later in 1826, military

uniforms again became the focus of attention when Mahmud II (*reg* 1808–39; *see* OTTOMAN, §II(6)) decreed that members of the newly formed army that was to replace the Janissaries would wear serge trousers, a broadcloth vest and jacket, and a red head covering, which quickly evolved into the fez. Mahmud continued his attempts to modernize Ottoman society through dress with his decree of 1829 that all male subjects were expected to wear trousers, frock coat, shirt, European-style shoes and fez. Only the ulema (professional theologians) were exempted from this ruling and permitted to wear traditional dress, and they continued to do so until 1934, when they were made to adopt European dress. From the 1830s the clothing of most men, apart from villagers, came to resemble that of their European counterparts.

Women's dress. Like male attire, female attire in Anatolia combined layers of garments and rich mixtures of colours and textures for indoor and outdoor wear and was subject to sumptuary regulation. Unlike male attire, women's indoor dress was rarely subject to public scrutiny. The basic outfit consisted of undergarments covered by a tunic and a dress tied with a sash or belt, a headdress and slippers. These basic garments remained in use over the centuries, although stylistic details changed.

Women's dress in the 16th century, as described by contemporary travellers and illustrated in a few manuscripts, began with two undergarments: straight, loose-fitting trousers (Turk. *şalvar*) extending to the ankle, made of plain white fabric, and an underdress (*gömlek*) with a long skirt, long full sleeves, a round neck and a front opening, made of thin white fabric decorated at the selvages with gold or another colour. Over these, women wore a variety of brightly coloured tunics (*yelek*) or dresses (*entari*). The tunic and dress were related structurally; the tunic had no sleeves or collar and fastened at the front with a series of small buttons, sometimes decorated with rows of gold braid around the buttons. It was usually hip-length, sometimes longer, and was worn over the underdress. The dress was a long robe buttoning down the front to the hips with full, three-quarter-length sleeves and a round collarless neck. It was usually worn unbuttoned to the breasts, with the skirt open to reveal the trousers, underdress and tunic. Like the tunic, the front of the dress was often decorated with rows of braid. A number of garments illustrated in contemporary manuscripts are neither tunic nor dress. Women invariably wore sashes (*kuşak* or *kemer*) wound around the waist or slightly lower; made of a fabric that contrasts in colour to the dress, they were draped and knotted in a variety of ways. The 16th-century headdress consisted of a small pillbox hat (*takke*) of velvet or felt, decorated with jewels, plumes or flowers and kept in place by an embroidered scarf (*yemeni*) wound around it. Shoes for indoors were either slippers of leather or velvet decorated with embroidery or jewels, or high wooden clogs (*nalān*) sometimes covered with silver or precious stones, which were worn primarily in the bathhouse. Outdoors, women wore yellow leather boots, a long full coat (*ferace*) and a white headdress (*yaşmak*) in two pieces.

Most of these garments were also used in the 17th century, but sometimes a fur-lined tunic was added on top of the dress, and the belt and headdress changed. Belts, still worn around the hips over the dress, were often of metal or of stiff cloth, heavily decorated with metal studs or plates. Cloth sashes were also worn, either tied in elaborate knots or fastened with a large metal buckle. The small pillbox hat and scarf were replaced by a tall conical hat (*tantura*), often of silver brocade, with a scarf of a different colour wound around the base and hanging either to the side of the face or down the back. For the street, the white headdress was draped over the conical hat.

In the 18th century, the basic elements remained the same but the shape and fabric changed. Trousers, made of printed or striped fabric in a variety of light colours, became voluminous, falling over the feet; the underdress was sometimes tucked into the trousers rather than worn over them; and the tunic was replaced by a second robe worn over the dress which could be long- or short-sleeved and was sometimes trimmed with fur. Both the dress and the outer robe were more graceful, perhaps due to lighter or softer material. By the end of the 18th century, the sash was often an entire shawl of silk or wool, draped elaborately around the hips (see fig. 198), although the earlier style of belt also continued to be worn. The conical hat was replaced by a small cap, sometimes decorated with jewels and with one or more scarves wound around it. Streetwear still consisted of a coat and the two-piece white headdress, but the coat had a large square collar which extended down the back, almost like a cape, varying in length from a few inches to the entire length of the coat.

In the late 18th and the 19th centuries women's dress, like that of men, showed the increasing influence of European fashion. With the growing popularity of imported fabrics, the traditional garments became softer and more exaggerated in form. Trousers were wider and the fabric of the underdress was finer and more transparent. The dress was longer, often trailing on the floor, and it was necessary to tuck it under the shawl (which was wound around the hips) in order to walk. The sleeves of the dress extended below the fingertips and were always worn open from the elbow. A second dress, sometimes trimmed with fur, or a short waist-length jacket (*cepken*) with long, close-fitting sleeves was worn on top of the underdress. The fabrics used for these garments were delicate, light-coloured silks and cottons of stripes or floral prints, decorated with ribbons, sequins, gold braid and trim crocheted of silk. The same changes in form occurred in the coat and white headdress. Over the course of the 19th century dress became more conspicuously European in style. Greek and Armenian women took the lead in adopting elements of European dress, perhaps because they had the strongest contacts with the foreign community, and by the mid-19th century their dress was often entirely European. Change proceeded more slowly among Turkish women, who adopted European fashions piecemeal, as for example in the substitution of a French-style jacket for the traditional one in a 19th-century costume in Istanbul (Topkapı Pal. Mus., 13/2082) and in the increasing use of gloves and stockings. Details of cut or decoration were initially modified to look more European, and then garments of the new style replaced older ones.

The 1860s marked the turning-point for women's fashion in the Ottoman world. By the middle of the

198. *Ottoman Woman*; from the *Zenanname* ('Book of women'), *c.* 1793 (London, British Library, Or. MS. 7094, fol. 28*v*)

decade, European dress was sometimes worn by the women of the imperial harem and by wealthy Istanbul ladies who emulated court style. Royal visits by Empress Eugenie and the Prince and Princess of Wales in 1866 removed any remaining barriers to the enthusiastic adoption of European fashions by the upper-class women of Istanbul. During the last three decades of the 19th century, the gradual transition from traditional dress to European styles was greatly accelerated, as changes in dress mirrored the larger political and social changes taking place in Turkey.

The Balkans. Dress in the Balkans was enormously rich and varied and reflected the range of social and political identities. This geographically, ethnically and religiously diverse region came under Ottoman rule in the 15th and 16th centuries, and for the most part it remained within the Ottoman sphere of influence until the 19th century, when nationalist movements and the weakening of Ottoman control led to independence. Anatolian and eastern textiles were highly valued in the Balkans, and there was an extensive trade in cotton, wool and silk fabrics, velvets, silk and cotton yarn for embroidery and braids, furs, silver- and gold-wrapped threads, and embroidered goods. In the 17th century Ottoman court dress, worn by officials sent as local administrators and their wives, was copied by the Hungarian Christian aristocracy. The most direct examples of the adoption of Turkish styles occurred in urban areas; the costume of wealthy Hungarian women in the 16th and 17th centuries, for example, included face coverings and veils. Local dress in areas where large segments of the population converted to Islam also included several Turkish elements. In late 19th-century Sarajevo, for example, men wore shirt and trousers, a short jacket, sash around the waist and fez; women wore the Turkish-style underdress and trousers covered by a tunic or dress, and their garments resembled those of women in other provinces of the empire.

Village dress in the Balkans displayed wide regional diversity, but in many areas it is possible to trace Turkish influence on some aspects of traditional costume, particularly in such accessories as knitted socks, men's sashes or belts, and women's embroidered woollen aprons. Embroidered sleeveless vests (*jelek*, from Turk. *yelek*) worn in many areas by men and women are similar in construction and decoration to Turkish provincial tunics.

BIBLIOGRAPHY

O. Hamdy and M. de Launay: *Les Costumes populaires de la Turquie en 1873* (Constantinople, 1873)
L. E. Smart: *The Durham Collection of Garments and Embroideries from Albania and Yugoslavia* (Halifax, 1939)
M. Vlahović: *National Costumes of Serbia* (Belgrade, 1954)
A. S. Ünver: *Geçmiş yüzyıllarda kıyafet resimlerimiz* [Pictures of costumes from past centuries] (Ankara, 1958)
A. Rubens: *A History of Jewish Costume* (New York, 1967)
J. Bjeladinović: *Folk Costumes of Yugoslavia* (Belgrade, 1976)
J. Scarce: 'Turkish Fashion in Transition', *Costume*, xiv (1980), pp. 144–67
H. Tezcan and S. Delibaş: *Topkapı Sarayı Müzesi* (Tokyo, 1980); trans. and ed. J. M. Rogers as *The Topkapı Saray Museum: Costumes, Embroideries and Other Textiles* (Boston, MA, 1986)
J. Scarce: *Middle Eastern Costume from the Tribes and Cities of Iran and Turkey* (Edinburgh, 1981)
V. Gervers: *The Influence of Ottoman Turkish Textiles and Costume in Eastern Europe with Particular Reference to Hungary* (Toronto, 1982)
P. Petrescu: *Romanian Folk Costume* (Bucharest, 1985)
P. Baker: 'The Fez in Turkey: A Symbol of Modernization?', *Costume*, xx (1986), pp. 72–86
F. Davis: *The Ottoman Lady: A Social History from 1718 to 1918* (New York, 1986), pp. 187–207
E. Atıl: *The Age of Sultan Süleyman the Magnificent* (Washington, DC, 1987), pp. 176–81
N. Micklewright: 'Tracing the Transformation in Women's Dress in Nineteenth-century Istanbul', *Dress*, xiii (1987), pp. 33–40

NANCY MICKLEWRIGHT

(c) *Iran*. Iranian dress between 1500 and 1900 spanned three distinct historical and political phases. Two, the reigns of the Safavid (*reg* 1501–1732) and Qajar (*reg* 1779–1924) dynasties, are comparable in length and degree of stability; the third, a turbulent interregnum, was distinguished only by the few relatively tranquil years of Zand rule (*reg* 1750–94). Fluctuating political and economic conditions, changing tastes and external influences affected both the production of textiles and other materials

associated with dress and its accessories, and also the nature and content of the primary and secondary sources.

Dress under the Safavids. One of the most important economic features of Iran under Safavid rule, notably after 'Abbas I (*reg* 1588–1629) transferred the capital to Isfahan in 1597, was the encouragement of a thriving textile industry, which concentrated on a wide range of sophisticated weaves suitable for clothing and household needs. Only a few isolated examples of dress have survived, including fragments of expensive plain and figured silks and velvets dating from the late 16th century to the early 18th, some sash and turban lengths decorated with striped and flowered motifs, a rare sumptuous example of a man's coat dating to the late 16th century (Moscow, Kremlin, Armoury) and a random selection of jackets and coats dating from the late 17th century to the early 18th. This arbitrary and sparse material can be supplemented by contemporary representations and European descriptions of clothes and manners. Manuscript illustration, in which scenes are conventionally depicted in a clear, even light, and figures and their environment are shown with meticulous clarity, is invaluable for giving a good impression of the overall look, shape, colour and decoration of dress and of the surface pattern of fabrics. This source does not, however, enable specific types of fabric, weave, decorative technique or methods of construction to be identified. Moreover, it provides only a limited social perspective, since the characters of epic and romantic literature are invariably depicted as richly dressed aristocrats. The accounts of the more observant European travellers, such as the French Huguenot John Chardin (1643–1713), can offer a corrective balance.

Collectively the sources reveal general principles of dress which remain constant. Both men and women wore layers of garments of elegant cut and shape, which were combined in striking combinations of colour and pattern according to the wearer's status and personal taste. In the 16th century the basic garment of men's dress was a close-fitting knee-length jacket (Pers. *qabā*) with long tapering sleeves and an overlapped and fastened front; these were characterized by strong colours such as blue, orange, yellow and green. The jacket could function equally as an undershirt, worn with loose white pants, or as a shirt, either tucked into or belted over long full trousers (*shalvār*). By the 17th century shirts patterned with narrow white and crimson stripes were fashionable and could be worn with a white sleeveless waistcoat. Robes and coats were worn over the jacket and trousers. The principal garment was an ankle-length belted robe with long sleeves and wrapover front. It was usually made of plain fabric in a wide range of colours, including orange, red, green, yellow, blue, brown and white; patterned fabrics with white or yellow ground and floral scrolls or ribbon cloud motifs in gold, which simulated the effect of brocaded silk, were also occasionally worn. The use of contrasting colours for lining and facing fabrics added a decorative touch to what was essentially a functional item. For use with this robe, two kinds of belt were fashionable: a finely pleated and knotted girdle made of fabric, and a band of linked gold medallions and clasps; both were hung with such personal accessories as handkerchiefs, pencases and daggers. The

199. Muhammad Zaman: *Prince on Horseback, with a Courtier and Servants*, 143×206 mm, from Isfahan, *c.* 1670–85 (London, British Museum)

outfit was completed by a long coat (*bālāpūsh*) in a choice of styles worn over the robe. One style, usually worn belted, was of loose straight shape with wide elbow-length sleeves; it was normally made in a plain fabric intended either to contrast or to harmonize with the robe beneath it. This type of coat was often lavishly decorated with looped gold braid and button fastenings from neck to waist and with borders of gold foliage motifs at the neck and shoulders. Sometimes, however, a richly patterned fabric ornamented in gold with scrolling foliage or medallion designs was used. A second style, worn unbelted, had exaggeratedly long sleeves, slit horizontally at mid-arm level. The wearer could either insert his arms through these slits, so that the sleeves trailed behind him, or could drape the coat over his shoulders as a cloak. Heavy brocaded silks or velvets were suitable fabrics for this style.

By the late 16th century, fabric designs changed while these basic shapes and combinations of garments continued to be worn. Large flower rosettes and animal, bird and even human figural motifs, all worked in strong bright colours on bright grounds, replaced the earlier scrolling foliage designs. In the 17th century the shape of the garments themselves became more flamboyant. The main robe, usually of a quilted plain fabric, had a tight bodice, a bell-shaped mid-calf-length skirt and either a wrapover or centre-front fastening. A broad sash wrapped around the waist replaced the narrow belt. A loose hip-length jacket or long coat of flower-patterned fabric with seasonal fur

collar and lining was worn. The most conspicuous change in fashion, however, affected the turban (*dūl band*). Turbans in the 16th century were usually of fine white cloth with gold edgings, coiled into a graceful tulip shape around a tall pointed red felt cap (*tāj ṣafavī*). Because of their distinctive headgear, the Safavids were often disparagingly called 'red caps' (*kulāh-i surkh*; Turk. *qizil bāsh*). By the 17th century this type of turban had expanded into a broad shape swathed around a flat cap. Jewellery was relatively modest, consisting of gold belt and weapon mounts, plain gold finger-rings and earrings and chains of pearls around turbans. Personal grooming complemented the restraint of dress; young men were clean-shaven and turbans concealed their hair (although by the 17th century young men were permitted to frame their faces with tendrils of hair); older men sported moustaches and beards of varying length. Footwear was simple and colourful; cloth stockings of red, blue, green and violet, tied at the knee with string garters, were in vogue, while for formal occasions, such as court ceremonies, a lightweight backless slipper or mule was worn. Cuban-heeled clogs in black, red, yellow or green leather over flat-soled slippers were used for outdoor wear, and boots were worn for riding (see fig. 199).

Women's dress was equally colourful and elegant, and depended for effect on a tasteful combination of layers of garments. Underwear consisted of an ankle-length shirt (*pīrāhan*) with long full sleeves, a round neck and deep central opening at the front. It could be tucked into straight trousers of plain or patterned fabric. Over this layer, the 16th-century woman wore one or two narrow-cut long robes, which fell loose and unbelted, and which had tight wrist-length sleeves. These were usually yellow, red, blue or green. Fabrics were also patterned with delicate scrolling motifs in gold. A third layer, consisting of richly patterned coats with either elbow-length or long trailing sleeves, could be worn over the robes, and a third type of coat with long tight sleeves could be worn with a contrasting scarf knotted around the hips. By the 17th century women's clothing, like that of men, underwent a change in shape. Robes became close-fitting, with tight bodices and bell-shaped skirts of mid-calf length. The most popular fashion was to wear two robes in striking combinations of colour and design, such as rich orange over purple with gold sprigs. By the late 17th century light silks of white or pink patterned with lotus and peony motifs among interlaced leafy stems were popular. Plain or flowered silk sashes were draped and looped around the hips. Occasionally a fur-lined short jacket was placed around the shoulders to function as a cape. Legs were covered with flowered stockings, and footware consisted of embroidered, brocaded silk and knitted slipper socks for indoor use and leather shoes with Cuban heels for outdoor wear.

Women distinguished between indoor and outdoor wear. They covered their heads with white scarves folded tightly around the face and tied under the chin, and added a selection of bandeaux and shawls (*chārqad*) according to personal taste. Jewellery was elaborate, ranging from pearl necklaces to heavy gold chains with pendants, diadems, aigrettes, finger-rings and earrings. Hair and face received much attention: wavy tendrils framed the face, and long hair was braided into many plaits interwoven with strands of jewellery. Eyes and lips were boldly emphasized with kohl and rouge, while nails and hands were decorated with patterns in deep orange-red henna. Outdoors a woman's finery was concealed by an all-enveloping white cloak (*chadār*), worn with a white face veil or a black visor-like mask.

Dress under the Zands. The disintegration of the Safavid state in the first decades of the 18th century disrupted such crafts as textile weaving, and the evidence for dress is limited to changes recorded at the Zand capital of Shiraz in south-west Iran. The large flamboyant motifs of Safavid fabrics gave way to small floral patterns. Men continued to wear long, well-cut robes, but the large turban was replaced by either a turban wrapped tightly around a tall narrow cap, or a puckered felt hat. Women's dress evolved from long or mid-calf-length robes to tight short jackets with flaring skirts worn over straight trousers patterned with oblique floral stripes. Surviving lengths of trouser fabric are made either of silk in a complex weave or of white cotton calico entirely embroidered in fine stitches.

Dress under the Qajars. The establishment in 1779 of stable rule by the Qajars encouraged a revival in dress from their capital at Tehran, and contemporary sources are both plentiful and informative. Details of cut and construction can be studied in a wide range of garments in such fabrics as brocaded silks, twill-weave wool, block-printed cotton and imported European broadcloth. Life-size paintings in oils on canvas and on the walls of palaces

and homes of the wealthy depicted the splendidly dressed Qajar shahs, their families and their courtiers and eclipsed the art of manuscript illustration. Diplomatic and commercial contacts with Europe increased the flow of official reports, travel accounts and diaries, in which descriptions of textiles and clothing were often accompanied by engravings and drawings. From the late 19th century photographs taken by both Iranians and Europeans provide an additional visual source.

Men's dress evolved rapidly, both because of natural change and the impact of European styles and fabrics. In the early 19th century dress continued to develop along traditional lines. A loose hip-length white undershirt with long sleeves was still worn. Ankle-length flaring trousers, usually of red or black fabric and worn with finely knitted silk slipper socks, replaced the loose underpants and knee-length cloth stockings of Safavid and Zand fashions. Cuban-heeled shoes, usually of dark green leather, continued to be worn. Robes were stylishly cut with close-fitting bodices, long tight sleeves and ankle-length flaring skirts. They were made either in plain or finely patterned fabrics: narrow vertical stripes of floral bands and repeated floral cone motifs were popular choices. Such textiles were products of the Kirman wool industry. Following traditional custom, robes were worn either singly or in pairs with harmonizing fabric designs. The outer coat, usually of plain colour (black, blue, red or white), was enlivened with facing and hem bindings in striped bias-cut fabric. Sashes of plain fabric with deep floral cone borders or with narrow sprigged stripes were swathed around the waist and knotted in front. Headdresses ranged from tall, firmly wound turbans worn by some court and religious dignitaries to black, tightly curled lambskin hats of pointed or cylindrical shape. Hair was styled in curls and sidelocks, while facial hair varied from full and bushy moustaches to heavy beards. This mode was customary among upper- and middle-class Qajar society. Fath 'Ali Shah (*reg* 1797–1834) and his family, however, wore luxurious versions made of rich brocaded silks, usually lavishly embellished with cuffs and collars of pearls, rubies and emeralds. They also wore elaborate jewelled crowns, which were modified versions of ancient Sasanian styles.

The introduction of European-style army uniforms and formal dress during the 1840s substantially changed men's fashion, as traditional and Europeanized garments mingled in varying degrees. Rural and urban working-class men, for example, continued to wear loose ankle-length trousers, while courtiers and officials wore smartly cut black or white European trousers which were often decorated with stripes of gold braid along the outer leg. Close-fitting quilted jackets were complemented by sleeveless waistcoats, while double-breasted frock coats and greatcoats, made in either plain dark or patterned fabrics, replaced the traditional robes. Accessories also changed to suit the new fashions: narrow belts replaced swathed sashes, and smart dark leather shoes or knee-high boots were adopted. Headdresses varied according to occupation: Muslim clergy continued to wear white or green turbans, while government officials adopted a neat pillbox-shaped black lambskin hat, which was worn over short hair. The use of jewellery was restrained, as there was no place for extravagantly gem-studded collars and cuffs on frock coats.

Nasir al-Din (*reg* 1848–96) confined himself to diamond aigrettes pinned to his hat and jewelled epaulettes and buttons on his coat.

The change in women's dress during the 19th century was more gradual and occurred within a traditional context, although with some surprises. The long loose undershirt continued to be worn, often with jewelled borders added to neck and front openings; occasionally a minuscule sequined brassière was worn beneath it. Long bell-shaped skirts or voluminous flaring trousers were made in plain coloured fabrics (red, blue and green) or in heavy and stiff brocaded silk with stylized flower motifs against a gold ground. Long robes and coats went completely out of fashion and were replaced by short tight jackets with long sleeves and flaring peplums, often in a fabric that matched the skirt or trousers. This graceful dress changed dramatically in the late 19th century: layers of short skirts, ranging from mid-thigh to knee length and worn over tight trousers or white stockings, replaced the long full skirts and trousers. Headdresses varied from jewelled caps positioned over elaborately curled long hair to scarves pulled tightly around the face and secured under the chin. Faces were boldly emphasized with cosmetics: kohl was used to shape eyebrows and enlarge and elongate the outline of the eyes; a delicate flower *boteh* or rosette was drawn on the forehead, and beauty spots were applied to the cheeks, chin and occasionally to the neck; rouge was applied to cheeks and lips; and henna was used to colour nails, hands and feet. Outdoors, women were still concealed in a voluminous cloak, usually of black or dark blue, and their faces covered with long, white, rectangular veils with a lattice at eye-level worked in cut-and-drawn thread embroidery. Loose stocking-boots tied at the knee evolved by the end of the 19th century into a pair of ample leggings; both were worn with low-heeled leather clogs.

BIBLIOGRAPHY

C. Colliver Rice: *Persian Women and their Ways* (London, 1923)
J. Chardin: *Travels in Persia, 1673–1677* (London, 1927/*R* New York, 1988)
J. Housego: 'Honour Is According to Habit: Persian Dress in the Sixteenth and Seventeenth Centuries', *Apollo*, xciii (1971), pp. 204–9
S. J. Falk: *Qajar Paintings: Persian Oil Paintings of the 18th and 19th Centuries* (London, 1972)
A. Welch: *Shah Abbas and the Arts of Isfahan* (New York, 1973)
J. M. Scarce: 'The Development of Women's Veils in Persia and Afghanistan', *Costume*, ix (1975), pp. 4–14
——: 'A Persian Brassière', *A. & Archaeol. Res. Pap.*, vii (1975), pp. 15–21
——: *Middle Eastern Costume from the Tribes and Cities of Iran and Turkey* (Edinburgh, 1981)
——: *Women's Costume of the Near and Middle East* (London, 1987)
——: 'Vesture and Dress: Fashion, Function and Impact', *Woven from the Soul, Spun from the Heart: Textile Arts of Safavid and Qajar Iran, 16th–19th Centuries*, ed. C. Bier (Washington, DC, 1987), pp. 33–56

JENNIFER M. SCARCE

4. CARPETS AND FLATWEAVES. In the Islamic lands, carpets occupy a place of prominence not found in other artistic traditions, as these textiles provided comfortable and attractive surfaces for seating and sleeping in a region where hard furniture was largely unknown. They have been woven in a wide geographical area known as the 'Rug Belt', distinguished by a temperate climate, terrain suitable for sheep grazing, and historical and cultural links to a nomadic or tribal past. The major areas of traditional carpet production in the central Islamic lands are Anatolia (including northern Syria and the south-eastern Balkans), Iran, the Caucasus and western Central Asia (including western China, parts of Afghanistan, Uzbekistan, Tajikistan and Turkmenistan). There is also a historic tradition of carpet production in Spain and North Africa, in northern India and for a brief period in Egypt, the only carpet-producing land that fulfils none of the normal environmental conditions for carpet production. The concept of the 'Oriental' carpet has become so all-pervasive that carpets with Oriental designs are produced by machine in France, Belgium, the United States, Britain and even the Middle East, and carpets with traditional hand-knotting in Romania, China, India and other areas that have cheap labour and a need for hard currency.

(i) Introduction. (ii) Before *c.* 1450. (iii) *c.* 1450–*c.* 1700. (iv) *c.* 1700 and after.

(i) Introduction. Broadly defined, a carpet is a heavy textile, usually but not invariably rectangular in shape and almost always meant to be used in the form in which it was made, without cutting or sewing, on flat surfaces such as walls, floors or tables. 'Rug' is often used synonymously, but in this article its use will be restricted to small pile-woven carpets.

(a) Techniques and modes of production. (b) Origins and development. (c) Scholarship.

(a) Techniques and modes of production. The vast majority of traditional carpets in the Islamic world are made exclusively or primarily of sheep's wool and similar animal fibres by a variety of processes. The simplest carpets are felted, largely from undyed, carded and unspun wool. This is usually white, but can often be light or dark brown; it is fulled with hot water and an alkaline solution (*see* FELT). Felt carpets may be plain or patterned, with designs added either in the felting process or afterwards using appliqué or mosaic techniques. Woven carpets fall into two main categories: pile carpets, where knots of yarn are tied on the warp foundation, with varying numbers of wefts between the rows of knots, to produce a fur-like surface; and flat-woven carpets, produced by a variety of techniques. Among the best-known types of flat-woven carpets are tapestry-woven pieces, which usually have slits where two colours meet along a warp line; and brocaded carpets, which have extra decorative wefts creating patterns on a warp and weft ground (*see* KILIM). Embroidery is rarely encountered in carpets of the Islamic lands.

Pile-woven carpets are categorized according to the material used and the technique of construction. Most examples use wool for the pile, but the warp and weft may be wool, goat or camel hair, cotton or silk, among other fibres. Although the thickness, disposition and relative numbers of warps and wefts in the foundation may vary extensively, from relatively coarsely knotted pieces in wool with 1000 knots per sq. decimetre to the finest silk carpets with over 12,000 knots per sq. decimetre, the technical categories of pile carpets are usually defined by the type of knot used: the symmetrical (Turkish or Gördes) knot, the asymmetrical (Persian or Sehna) knot and the single-warp (Spanish) knot. These techniques of construction are to some extent geographically or ethnically specific;

with the exception of the extreme western part of the Islamic world, where the single-warp knot predominates, and the Caucasus, where the symmetrical knot predominates, both symmetrical and asymmetrical knots are found in carpets produced in Iran, Anatolia and western Central Asia.

Most carpets are rectangular and have a field framed by borders and guard bands. The field is often filled with a symmetrical pattern which is cut off at the edges but could continue into infinity. Many carpets have a central medallion; in Iranian examples this is often framed by quarter medallions in the corners of the field (see fig. 200). Some carpets have a design that is intended to be viewed from only one direction, as in the case of prayer-rugs and ṣaff (row) carpets used to indicate the direction of prayer (see fig. 205 below). Given the techniques of production, the simplest motifs to weave are geometric; but with increased

200. Ardabil Carpet, wool knotted pile, 10.5×5.3 m, from Iran, 1539–40 (London, Victoria and Albert Museum)

fineness, curvilinear designs are also possible. These include not only scrolling arabesques and floral motifs, but also animals and figures. Garden carpets have a grid design showing a bird's-eye view of a garden, in which the rectangular field is divided into compartments filled with trees and flowers by water channels which are themselves filled with fish and which intersect to form pools. Borders are filled with repeating geometric motifs such as cartouches, palmettes or pseudo-kufic or kufesque inscriptions, often joined by an arabesque scroll. A small number of carpets have other woven inscriptions giving the name of the weaver, place of production or date.

(b) Origins and development. The reasons why the art of carpet-weaving flourished in the Islamic world are the subject of controversy. Some scholars associate the knotted pile carpet with the Turkic-speaking nomadic peoples, and point to the Turkish origins and a predominance of Turkish designs in the earliest surviving carpets. Others emphasize the traditional use of carpets to cover the floors of mosques as a factor in their widespread acceptance by Islamic cultures. Certainly, two of the most common types are the individual prayer-rug (Arab. *sajjāda*; Turk. *seccade*; see CARPET, colour pl. III), which usually incorporated an arch-like design suggestive of a mihrab in a mosque and at times the gateway to heaven; and the *ṣaff* carpet, the design of which represents the arcades of a hypostyle mosque, which was used to arrange worshippers in rows facing Mecca. These two types, however, account for only a fraction of the wide variety of carpet genres and designs in the Islamic world, so further scholars have suggested that the making and using of carpets in the Middle East may also be associated with pre-Islamic and non-Islamic cultures.

In the 1940s an almost perfectly preserved carpet, woven with symmetrical knots, was excavated in a south Siberian burial site. Dated at least to the 4th century BC, the PAZYRYK carpet (St Petersburg, Hermitage) created a 1600-year gap in the history of the knotted carpet. The explanation of this gap has proved problematic, and disputes have erupted over the origin of various techniques and designs. These disputes often devolve to the problem of race (the association of early surviving carpets and traditional carpet designs with nomadic societies and migrations of Turkic-speakers) versus place (the association of early carpets from Anatolia with societies and peoples who inhabited that area long before the Turks migrated there, beginning in the 11th century). As with the earlier controversy of *Orient oder Rom* that permeated and even blighted the study of Roman and Near Eastern art in the early 20th century, the eventual resolution of the carpet debate will probably and unsurprisingly acknowledge that traditional carpet designs and techniques evolved from a variety of sources.

By the 14th century, the date of the earliest group of extant carpets, commercial production had certainly developed. By the late 15th century a carpet revolution had occurred, as artists trained in or familiar with such arts of the book as calligraphy, illumination, illustration and binding, and with such techniques of architectural decoration as wall painting, tiles and stone-carving, turned their attention towards the design of carpets. By the 16th century in Iran and Turkey (and at the end of the century in India) workshops under court control produced carpets on commission for the imperial courts. These court carpets, which have close parallels to other artefacts designed in the royal workshops, were some of the most significant artistic products of the 16th and 17th centuries, and their impact on commercial carpet production is still felt.

The most unusual aspect of the carpet-weaving tradition in the Islamic world is its permeation of the social and economic strata of traditional society. Carpets were woven by nomadic tribeswomen and by village women in many lands, primarily for personal use and secondarily as a 'cash crop' that could be bartered or sold to obtain goods not available in the local pastoral or agricultural economy. From early times carpets formed a major component of trade, not only within the Islamic world but also externally with southern, central and western Europe. The popular and costly Turkish commercial carpets in particular inspired from an early date an imitative carpet production in western Europe, most notably in Spain, where a carpet tradition had long existed under Islamic rule. The commercial production of carpets in Egypt that began under the Mamluks in the 15th century appears to have been another enterprise begun with European as well as local markets in mind.

(c) Scholarship. Carpets have traditionally been classified according to their general geographic origin: Anatolia, Iran, western Central Asia and the Caucasus. In many cases these traditional geographic classifications are meaningless and confusing, since within these areas there are separate traditions of nomadic, village and commercial weaving, each with its own multitude of technical subgroups and localized designs. KURT ERDMANN (1977) first proposed a method of looking at carpets based on the social context and intent of production. He divided carpets into four types: those produced exclusively for local use, those with a secondary commercial purpose, those with a primary commercial purpose and those made on royal commission. This approach has spawned much productive scholarship, which focuses on the relationships among different kinds of production and gives new stature to nomadic and village carpets. These recent and undocumented artefacts, often artistically impressive, have long been favoured by collectors and constitute the commodity of a very high-priced and fad-prone market.

Iconography and symbolism have long been important subjects in the study of carpets. The designs on elaborate carpets produced in Islamic courts from the 15th to the 17th century have been investigated in relation to the arts of the book, while the carpet art of nomadic peoples has been studied in the context of the iconography of tribal traditions. Since the meaning of forms is intimately connected to the larger questions of the origins and development of the carpet, the debate over meaning and symbolism is linked to other central issues of carpet scholarship. Cammann, for example, looked to the east, especially China, for the origin of many forms found in Islamic carpets and, in the light of this, argued for a reinterpretation of many carpet motifs.

Another aspect of carpet studies involves the use of analytic techniques to study materials, dyestuffs and structure, in order to determine age and provenance. The early structural analyses of A. U. Pope and S. Troll were continued by ERNST KÜHNEL and L. Bellinger, and both structural and dye analysis have become routine facets of carpet study. When used in combination with other tools of art-historical analysis, such techniques can help scholars to determine geographic and ethnic origins, authenticity and age (*see* TECHNICAL EXAMINATION, §VIII, 9). Cochineal, for example, was brought by Spaniards from the New World in the early 16th century and replaced other, more expensive insect dyes such as kermes and lac; its presence can therefore help determine the age of a fabric. The twist of the yarn, whether Z- or S-spun, can also help determine provenance: yarns are traditionally S-spun in Egypt, whereas they are Z-spun elsewhere in the Islamic lands. The field of fibre study, in which basic materials, especially wool, are analysed to cast light on a carpet's age and origins, is relatively new, but holds considerable promise.

In the 1970s and 1980s many new examples of early carpets were discovered. Fragments have been excavated in Iraq, Egypt and Central Asia, while unusual and impressive examples of early carpets in relatively good states of preservation have surfaced in mosques in the Middle East, in store-rooms and attics of European stately homes and museums, and even in such unlikely venues as a north Italian synagogue, where an early carpet with mixed Egyptian, Turkish, Italian and Hebrew antecedents came to light.

Carpet studies suffer from two major handicaps. First, carpet scholarship has been enmeshed with the thriving market and with dealers and collectors of these very costly and very rare artefacts, a connection that has had both beneficial and deleterious effects on published research. Second, and partly as a result of this, few specialists of Islamic art have shown a serious interest in carpet studies, so leaving the subject to individuals who frequently lack the requisite methodological and linguistic competence; this has led, in turn, to a highly problematic scholarly literature. The scarcity of young professional scholars in the field casts a shadow over the future of carpet studies.

Art historians have concentrated attention on the early court and commercial carpets, but an overview of the carpet tradition in the Islamic world reveals the aesthetic as well as the cultural importance of the arts of village and nomadic peoples, which both affect and reflect the arts of the court and related manufactories. Certainly the finest carpets of the 15th, 16th and 17th centuries are among the most significant artistic creations of their respective traditions, and in terms of scale and expense and as emblems of kingship they rank with architecture as major monuments of royal patronage. The importance of carpets in the hierarchy of royal gifts, plus the creation in court-controlled workshops of important types of carpet, which appear to have been used as royal gifts, shows the association of carpets with the ideas of kingship and conspicuous consumption. The additional historical associations of carpets with nomadism and tribal traditions, together with the ceremonial tents that formed such an important part of secular ritual at the courts of the Safavids, Ottomans and Mughals, provide a link between the art of the court and the art of the common people that is without parallel in other cultures (*see* TENT, §I). Moreover, the village tradition is still deemed one of the chief glories of the Islamic world. The productive interplay of Islamic carpets across boundaries of social environment, economic class, ethnic origin, geography and time is, then, one of the major reasons for both the popularity of the form and the fact that Islamic carpets constitute virtually the only traditional form of Islamic art to have survived with all its complexity and diversity into modern times.

BIBLIOGRAPHY
Enc. Iran.; *Enc. Islam/2*: 'Bisāṭ' [Carpets]
A. U. Pope and S. Troll: 'Carpet Making: The Technique of Persian Carpet Weaving', *Survey of Persian Art*, ed. A. U. Pope and P. Ackerman (London, 1938–9, 2/1964–7), pp. 2437–55
K. Erdmann: *Der orientalische Knüpfteppich* (Tübingen, 1955; Eng. trans., London, 1962/*R* Fishguard, 1976)
E. Kühnel and L. Bellinger: *Cairene Rugs and Others Technically Related* (Washington, DC, 1957)
K. Erdmann: *Siebenhundert Jahre Orientteppich* (Herford, 1966; Eng. trans., Berkeley and Los Angeles, 1970)
M. H. Beattie: *The Thyssen-Bornemisza Collection of Oriental Carpets* (Castagnola, 1972)
M. Dimand and J. Mailey: *Oriental Rugs in the Metropolitan Museum* (New York, 1973)
S. Cammann: 'Symbolic Meanings in Oriental Rug Patterns', *Textile Mus. J.*, iii/3 (1974), pp. 5–34
Prayer Rugs (exh. cat. by R. Ettinghausen and L. Mackie, Washington, DC, Textile Mus., 1974)
K. Erdmann: *History of the Early Turkish Carpet* (London, 1977)
F. Spuhler: *Islamic Carpets and Textiles in the Keir Collection* (London, 1978)
W. B. Denny: *Oriental Rugs* (Washington, DC, 1979)
Ş. Yetkin: *Historical Turkish Carpets* (Istanbul, 1981)
W. B. Denny: 'Turkoman Rugs and the Origins of Rug Weaving in the Western Islamic World', *Hali*, iv/4 (Spring 1982), pp. 329–37
The Eastern Carpet in the Western World (exh. cat. by D. King and D. Sylvester, London, Hayward Gal., 1983)
A. Boralevi: 'Un tappeto ebraico-egiziano', *Crit. A.*, xlix/2 (1984), pp. 34–47
D. Black, ed.: *The Macmillan Atlas of Rugs and Carpets* (New York, 1985)
F. Spuhler: *Die Orientteppiche im Museum für Islamische Kunst Berlin* (Berlin, 1987)
C. G. Ellis: *Oriental Carpets in the Philadelphia Museum of Art* (Philadelphia, 1988)
J. Thompson: *Oriental Carpets from the Tents, Cottages and Workshops of Asia* (New York, 1988)
W. B. Denny: 'Saff and Sejjadeh', *Orient. Carpet & Textile Stud.*, iii/2 (1990), pp. 92–104

WALTER B. DENNY

(ii) Before c. 1450. The evidence for the production of floor coverings made of woven, knotted and felted wool in western Central Asia and the Near East in the period before *c.* 1450 is very patchy. A nearly intact knotted carpet (1.8×2.0 m; St Petersburg, Hermitage) discovered in a tomb at PAZYRYK in southern Siberia has been dated to the end of the 4th century BC. The rectangular field shows 24 framed squares containing stylized flowers; the broad borders show either friezes of fallow deer and horses, or medallions with stylized lions. Fragments found in Sasanian levels (6th century AD) at Shahr-i Qumis in northern Iran (New York, Met.) include a looped pile carpet and a flat-woven floor covering of wool and cotton. These two modest examples are considered the earliest of their type to have been excavated in Iran, but literary sources provide evidence for the rich tradition of floor coverings in the Sasanian period. When the Arabs conquered the Sasanian capital at Ktesiphon in AD 637, they found a huge carpet (destr.), some 60 cubits (27 m) square, which may have

covered the floor of the royal audience hall. Known as the Spring of Khusraw, it depicted paths and streams between garden plots planted with trees and flowers and was enriched with silk, gold, silver and gemstones.

Evidence for the production of carpets from the advent of Islam in the 7th century to the Mongol conquests in the mid-13th combines a rich literary tradition with scant and fragmentary remains. A wide variety of textiles, flat-woven and pile carpets and fibre mats are known to have been produced in Iran and western Central Asia as floor coverings, and the techniques apparently spread to other regions of the Islamic world. The Aghlabid (*reg* 800–909) rulers of North Africa, for example, sent carpets as tribute to the Abbasid caliphs in Baghdad, so these carpets must have been perceived as precious objects of artistic value. Three fragments of pile carpets, believed to date from the 11th century, were excavated in 1980 at Fustat (Old Cairo) in Egypt. All are made of Z-spun wool, which is found everywhere in the Islamic world but Egypt, suggesting that these carpets were imported. One has a single-warp knot typical of later Spanish carpets, while two have symmetrical knots with multiple weft shoots and may well have come from carpet-weaving centres in northern Iran and Armenia. In 1986 the Asian Art Museum in San Francisco acquired a small (1.68×0.89 m), symmetrically knotted carpet with a large stylized lion in the field. This carpet is also said to have been found at Fustat. Radiocarbon analysis produced results consistent with an 8th- or 9th-century date, and the carpet is commonly attributed to the Iranian world.

The techniques for the production of knotted carpets were apparently introduced to Anatolia with the arrival of Islam in the region in the 12th century. The group known as the Konya Carpets comprises 18 large pieces discovered in central Anatolia at the congregational mosques of KONYA in 1903 and Beyşehir in 1925, and smaller fragments subsequently discovered in Cairo. The carpets are rather coarsely knotted, with less than 1000 symmetrical knots per sq. decimetre, and show a limited range of strong colours (medium and dark red, medium and dark blue, yellow, brown, and ivory). The typical layout consists of a central field with small, angular motifs arranged in staggered rows and a contrasting border with large pseudo-kufic designs or stars. They were initially attributed to the patronage of the Saljuq sultans (*reg* 1077–1307) at Konya, but a date in the first half of the 14th century is more likely, for at least one features an asymmetrical motif derived from the cloud pattern on silks woven under the Yuan dynasty (*reg* 1279–1368) in China. The size of the Konya Carpets (the largest measures 2.58×5.50 m) suggests that they were produced on a commercial rather than village or nomad scale. These carpets seem to have been made for local consumption, as only a few fragments of them have been found outside Anatolia and they are not depicted in contemporary Italian paintings.

Commercial carpet production in the Islamic world is attested from the 13th century by Western as well as Muslim travellers. Both Marco Polo, who passed through Anatolia in 1271–2, and the Moroccan globe-trotter Ibn Battuta (1304–77) mentioned carpets in their accounts. Carpets, long an object of trade within the Islamic lands, were exported to Europe from the 13th century, and trade

201. Animal carpet, wool knotted pile, 1.53×1.26 m, from Anatolia, 14th century (New York, Metropolitan Museum of Art)

increased in the 14th century. A Florentine manuscript of *c.* 1320 records four carpet entrepôts: Saffi and Zamurro (Safi and Azemmour in Morocco) and Setalia and Altoluogo (Antalya and Selçuk (anc. Ephesos) in Turkey). The archives of Francesco di Marco Datini of Prato indicate that Alexandria, Beirut, Constantinople (Istanbul) and Trebizond were also centres of carpet production *c.* 1380–*c.* 1410.

Depictions of carpets began to appear in paintings of the 14th century, both Iranian and Italian. The earliest Iranian depictions of carpets are found in a dispersed manuscript of the *Shāhnāma* ('Book of kings'), made in Tabriz *c.* 1335. In the image of *Zahhak Enthroned* (Washington, DC, Freer) the King is seated on a throne below which is spread a carpet showing octagons enclosing stylized quadrupeds. In *King Faridun Mourning his Son Iraj* (Washington, DC, Sackler Gal.) the King is seated on a carpet showing a dragon within a rectangular field. Similar depictions of carpets showing animals, either birds or quadrupeds, within hexagons or octagons appear in Italian, particularly Sienese, paintings. The three known animal carpets, knotted in wool with symmetrical knots of fairly low density in a limited colour range, including various tones of red, yellow and blue, are dated by comparison with representations in paintings. A carpet acquired by the Metropolitan Museum of Art in New York in 1990 shows a rectangular field with four stylized quadrupeds, themselves decorated with stylized quadrupeds; it has about 1240 symmetrical knots per sq. decimetre (see fig. 201).

Although radiocarbon analysis produced results consistent with a date as early as 1040–1290, a 14th-century date has conventionally been accepted, since a similar carpet appears in an anonymous Sienese painting from the early 15th century of the *Marriage of the Virgin* (London, N.G., 1317). The other two animal carpets are attributed to the first half of the 15th century. The one in Berlin (1.72×0.90 m; Pergamonmus.), acquired by Wilhelm von Bode in Rome in 1886, reportedly from a church in central Italy, shows stylized dragons and phoenixes within octagons. It, or one very like it, appears in Domenico di Bartolo's fresco of the *Wedding of the Foundlings* (Siena, Osp. S Maria della Scala), painted between 1440 and 1444. The Marby Carpet (1.45×1.09 m; Stockholm, Stat. Hist. Mus.), found in the Swedish village of Marby in 1925, displays confronted birds separated by a Tree of Life within squares. A similar carpet with stylized birds in squares is depicted in the *Betrothal of the Virgin* (Rome, Pin. Vaticana) by the 15th-century painter Sano di Pietro.

BIBLIOGRAPHY
Enc. Iran.: 'Bahār-e Kesrā' [Spring of Khusraw]; 'Carpets'
C. J. Lamm: 'The Marby Rug and Some Fragments of Carpets Found in Egypt', *Svensk. Orientsällskapets Åb.* (1937), pp. 51–130
R. Ettinghausen: 'New Light on Early Animal Carpets', *Aus der Welt der islamischen Kunst: Festschrift für Ernst Kühnel*, ed. R. Ettinghausen (Berlin, 1959), pp. 93–116
A. Geijer: 'Some Thoughts on the Problems of Early Oriental Carpets', *A. Orient.*, v (1963), pp. 79–87
K. Erdmann: *Siebenhundert Jahre Orientteppich* (Herford, 1966; Eng. trans., Berkeley and Los Angeles, 1970)
L. W. Mackie: 'Covered with Flowers: Medieval Floorcoverings Excavated at Fustat in 1980', *Orient. Carpet & Textile Stud.*, i (1985), pp. 23–5
——: 'An Early Animal Rug at the Metropolitan Museum', *Hali*, 53 (1990), pp. 154–5
T. Kawami: 'Ancient Textiles from Shahr-i Qumis', *Hali*, 59 (1991), pp. 95–9

(iii) c. 1450–c. 1700. Increased numbers of carpets survive from the period after the mid-15th century, primarily because more carpets were made and many were exported as luxury goods to be treasured and preserved. Many types of carpets, particularly Turkish ones, were also depicted in contemporary European paintings. This relative wealth of information allows distinctions to be made on the basis of place of manufacture and patronage. Although small carpets continued to be produced, some larger examples were made, either as commissions by local and Western patrons or for general sale on the market.   □

(a) Anatolia. (b) Mediterranean lands. (c) Iran. (d) Indian subcontinent.

(a) Anatolia. The types of carpets attributed to commercial production in Anatolia between the mid-15th century and the 17th are numerous and interrelated, and large numbers of them were exported to Europe where they were depicted by contemporary artists and preserved as valuable items. Many are classified by similarities in technique and design; but the names commonly used for groups of related carpets are taken either from the painters in whose works they are shown, among them Carlo Crivelli (*see* CRIVELLI, (1)), Gentile Bellini (*see* BELLINI, (2)), Hans Holbein (ii) (*see* HOLBEIN, (3)), HANS MEMLING and Lorenzo Lotto, or from the towns in which it is thought the carpets were made, the most notable being Ushak

(now Uşak) in western Anatolia. These classifications are highly subjective and not exclusive, and one scholar may classify a particular carpet by its technique or design while another may use the supposed place of origin. All these carpets, however, are knotted entirely in wool, with a symmetrical knot of fairly low density. In the 15th and 16th centuries the colour range was limited to varying tones of red, yellow and blue; in the 17th century the range was expanded, although tones of red still predominated. Designs are almost entirely geometric; even animal and floral motifs are reduced to angular forms.

The Crivelli type, depicted in paintings that Carlo Crivelli executed in the 1480s, is related to earlier so-called animal carpets, but the composition is more elaborate, consisting of large stars in various colours that enclose confronted animal motifs; a fragmentary example is preserved in Budapest (Mus. Applied A.). A carpet of the Bellini type first appears in Gentile Bellini's *Virgin and Child Enthroned* (London, N.G.), attributed to the last two decades of the 15th century. This type has a meandering inner border that forms a geometric niche terminating in a cusp at the top; at the bottom the border projects into the field in a keyhole shape, whence the alternative names Keyhole or Re-entrant carpet. Bellini carpets may also contain a pendant (lamp) at the top or a medallion in the middle of the niche and pseudo-kufic inscriptions in the outer border (e.g. 1.70×1.24 m, 1368; Berlin, Mus. Islam. Kst, inv. no. 87). Sub-groups of this type continued to be produced into the early 17th century.

There are two types of Holbein carpet. Those with large patterns, sometimes called Wheel carpets (e.g. 4.3×2.0 m; Berlin, Mus. Islam. Kst, inv. no. I.5526), usually have two or three broad octagons separated by connecting bands that link them to the borders (*see* HOLBEIN, (3), fig. 4). Both the number of octagons (sometimes depicted as a single medallion surrounded by four smaller ones) and the colour arrangement can vary. Small-pattern Holbeins (e.g. Istanbul, Mus. Turk. & Islam. A., 303) have two types of geometric motif—octagons and cross-shaped lozenges—arranged in a diaper pattern. The design is executed with great freedom of colour and is arranged without a fixed scheme. The borders are often decorated with elegant pseudo-kufic inscriptions with intertwined stems. Both Large- and Small-pattern Holbein carpets date from the 15th and 16th centuries, and both seem to have been knotted in Spain (e.g. Boston, MA, Mus. F.A.; *see* CARPET, §II, 2(i)) as well as in Anatolia. The relatively rare Memling carpets have an all-over pattern of octagonal medallions, arranged in parallel or staggered rows (e.g. a fragment in Budapest, Mus. Applied A.). The medallions contain stepped lozenges with small hooks at the corners.

The large group of Lotto carpets is characterized by an elaborate all-over design of an arabesque invariably executed in yellow on a red ground with small fields of blue, green or black (see fig. 202). The design is inspired by the stylized floral repertory and represents a variation of the octagon and cross-shaped lozenge design of Small-pattern Holbeins. Borders vary considerably, from alternating medallions and cartouches to pseudo-kufic inscriptions and floral motifs of different complexity and geometric design. One example (New York, Met., 62.231) was presumably commissioned by a Western patron for a

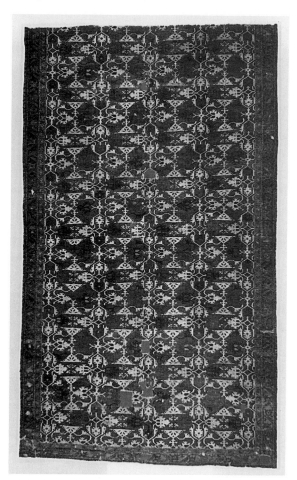

202. Lotto carpet, wool knotted pile, 3.69×2.11 m, from Anatolia, 16th century (Berlin, Museum für Islamische Kunst, inv. 82, 707)

wedding, as it bears the coat of arms of the Doria and Centurione family. These carpets vary considerably in quality and in size, ranging from large examples measuring 5.0×2.5 m (Florence, Bargello) to small pieces in Transylvanian churches, which measure 1.7×1.0 m; this range indicates a long period of production.

Several types of carpet are attributed to the manufacturing centre of Ushak: these include the medallion Ushak, the star Ushak, and the white-ground Ushak. Medallion Ushaks are large carpets knotted in traditional Anatolian colours—light and dark blue, yellow, red, dark brown, white and occasionally green—and have a large central medallion of slightly ovoid shape flanked by pendants and half polylobed medallions (e.g. 5.44×2.61 m; Lugano, Col. Thyssen-Bornemisza). The field is densely patterned with floral motifs of leaves and flower buds. Medallion Ushaks have been attributed to the second half of the 15th century on iconographic grounds, but they were manufactured mainly in the 16th and 17th centuries. Star Ushaks are mostly knotted on a red field and have a repeated design of dark blue eight-pointed medallions or 'snowflakes' alternating with dark blue lozenges or other smaller motifs decorated with yellow arabesques (*see* CARPET, colour pl. II). The geometric ground is filled with leafy and flowery buds in white, yellow, blue, red and green (e.g. 4.27×2.27 m; New York, Met., 58.63). They can be dated to the 16th century. The third type of Ushak carpet has a white or beige ground with decoration in brown, green, light yellow and, rarely, red. One sub-group has a repeat design of stylized birds, leaves and rosettes connected by a floral grid (e.g. 3.38×1.79 m; New York, Met., 22.100.127); another sub-group has a design of three small balls over two wavy lines (Turk. *çintimani*; e.g. 3.15×2.02 m; Washington, DC, Textile Mus.).

Commercial production in Anatolia continued in local centres during the 17th century. Commercial commissions were influential in spreading certain types, such as the Lottos and white-ground Ushaks, to Europe. Both Lotto carpets and star Ushaks were copied in England during the late 16th century and the 17th and perhaps in southeastern Europe as well (*see* CARPET, §II, 2(ii)). Some carpets of Anatolian manufacture take the name Transylvanian from the region in Romania where large numbers, taken there by merchants, were found in the 19th century; small and distinctive, they have a centralized design with flowers within four corner spandrels (e.g. Ham, Surrey, Keir priv. col.). It seems likely that other western Anatolian centres known for the manufacture of carpets in later times, such as Lâdik (or Konya-Lâdik), Gördes, Kula, Milâs and Mucur, produced carpets as early as the 17th century, although surviving examples are not securely dated. Many of these carpets are small (1.6–1.8×1.1–1.3 m) carpets of the so-called prayer-rug type (Turk. *seccade*), the design of which includes a niche-like element recalling the mihrab in a mosque. A tradition of flatweaving must have co-existed alongside the knotting of pile carpets, but the earliest surviving flatweaves date from the 18th century.

BIBLIOGRAPHY

J. Zick: 'Eine Gruppe von Gebetsteppichen und ihre Datierung', *Berlin. Mus.: Ber. Ehem. Preuss. Kstsamml.*, xi/1 (1961), pp. 6–14

C. G. Ellis: 'The Ottoman Prayer Rugs', *Textile Mus. J.*, ii/4 (1969), pp. 5–23

The Splendor of Turkish Weaving (exh. cat. by L. W. Mackie, Washington, DC, Textile Mus., 1973)

C. G. Ellis: 'The "Lotto" Pattern as a Fashion in Carpets', *Festschrift für Peter Wilhelm Meister* (Monaco, 1975), pp. 19–31

K. Erdmann: *The History of the Early Turkish Carpet* (London, 1977)

J. Mills: 'Lotto Carpets in Western Paintings', *Hali*, iii/4 (1981), pp. 278–89

The Eastern Carpet in the Western World (exh. cat. by D. King and D. Sylvester, London, Hayward Gal., 1983)

R. Pinner and W. B. Denny, eds: 'Carpets of the Mediterranean Countries, 1400–1600', *Orient. Carpet & Textile Stud.*, ii (1986) [whole issue]

J. Mills: 'Carpets in Paintings: The "Bellini", "Keyhole" or "Re-entrant" Rugs', *Hali*, 58 (1991), pp. 86–103

(b) Mediterranean lands. In contrast to contemporary production in Anatolia, where the symmetrical knot was used, another group of carpets was knotted with an asymmetrical knot open to the left. These have been attributed to several centres on the eastern and southern shores of the Mediterranean in the period from the 15th to the 17th century, and most have been identified conventionally with the Mamluk sultans (*reg* 1250–1517) in Egypt and Syria and the Ottoman dynasty (*reg* 1281–1924) in Anatolia and the eastern Mediterranean. On technical and stylistic grounds, four sub-groups (Mamluk, Para-Mamluk, Ottoman Court and Compartment carpets)

have been distinguished, but their traditional names should not be seen as accepted indications of places of production or patronage. Indeed, the provenance of these carpets remains a matter of lively debate.

Mamluk carpets are one of the most readily recognizable types, characterized by intricate centralized designs, executed in red, green, blue and yellow, revolving around one or more large octagonal medallions. There may be a single octagon, as in the many small (*c.* 1.3×1.8 m) examples (e.g. New York, Met., 41.190.266; see fig. 203); three medallions, as in the large (over 4×10 m) carpets belonging to the Scuola di S Rocco in Venice (1541) and the Medici family in Florence (1557–71; Florence, Pitti); or five medallions, as in the splendid Simonetti carpet (8.97× 2.39 m; New York, Met.). Generally, the entire field is densely decorated with geometrical motifs composed of more-or-less regular octagons, hexagons and triangles that produce an almost kaleidoscopic effect. Warp, weft and pile are S-spun, a technique normally associated with Egypt, and Z-twined. Mamluk carpets are made of wool except for one three-medallion silk example (Vienna, Östcrrcich. Mus. Angcwandtc Kst).

The provenance of these carpets, which were particularly popular in Italy, has long been debated. On the basis of frequent references in European documents from the late 15th century and early 16th, the period during which most were imported to Europe, Mamluk carpets were

203. Turkish Mamluk carpet, wool knotted pile, 1.8×1.3 m, 16th century (New York, Metropolitan Museum of Art)

once attributed to Damascus, but beyond these sometimes contradictory references no objective evidence of Damascene manufacture has been found. Rather, four factors suggest that Cairo was the principal centre of production, beginning in the second half of the 15th century and continuing to the mid-16th, despite the Ottoman conquest of the region in 1516–17. First, the terms *cairino*, *caiarino* and *cagiarino* (all derivatives of the name Cairo) were used in inventories. Second, one carpet (Washington, DC, Textile Mus.) bears a Mamluk emblem datable between 1468 and 1516. Third, the Venetian traveller Giuseppe Barbaro stated that the Persian carpets he saw at Tabriz in 1474 were superior to those manufactured in Bursa and Cairo. Finally, in 1585 the Ottoman sultan Murad III (*reg* 1574–95) ordered 11 artisans and their materials to be transferred from Cairo to Istanbul, implying that there was a tradition of great technical achievement in Egypt.

The iconography of Mamluk carpets has also attracted scholarly attention, particularly because the limited palette makes it extremely difficult to discern the individual motifs within the design. A small floral element composed of three flowers, in which the corolla opens in the shape of an umbrella, has been identified as papyrus stalks, implying artistic continuity with pre-Islamic Egypt. Ellis (1974) has somewhat provocatively compared the design of Mamluk carpets to Tibetan mandalas, and others have compared the carpets to the inlaid floors and fountains that once adorned the interior courtyards of Cairene houses. On the basis of archival references, comparison with iconographic motifs in other media, and sociological and political considerations, several sub-groups of Mamluk carpets have been identified, one of which has been tentatively assigned to Morocco.

Three types of carpets manufactured in the eastern Mediterranean lands during the 16th century are technically and iconographically analogous to the Mamluk type, but they are knotted with Z-twist wool and use madder instead of lac to dye the wool red. One grouping, the Para-Mamluk carpets (e.g. Philadelphia, PA, Mus. A., 55.65.2; 1.80×1.38 m), has distinct octagonal designs in which a central large octagon is flanked by smaller ones at either end. Cypress trees are characteristic filler motifs, and borders have bands of elegant pseudo-kufic designs. Para-Mamluk carpets are thus related to both Mamluk carpets and Large-pattern Holbeins (*see* §(a) above). The provenance of Para-Mamluk carpets is controversial. They were certainly produced in an urban setting, probably on commission. Despite some claims for Anatolia, they should be attributed to Cairo or North Africa.

Octagonal designs recur in Compartment carpets, also known as Chequerboard or Chessboard carpets, of which some 30 examples are known (e.g. 3.77×2.43 m; Washington, DC, Textile Mus.). The field of the typical carpet is subdivided into squares, within which are hexagons, octagonal stars and other small connecting motifs including cypress trees. The palette, although limited, is more varied than in Mamluk carpets. As with Para-Mamluk carpets, the provenance of Compartment carpets is controversial: they have been attributed to Damascus, Cairo, Adana in Anatolia, and even the island of Rhodes. Although Rhodes was an important entrepôt, it was never a centre of production; Damascus is plausible, but in the absence of

positive evidence the most likely attribution is Cairo or North Africa.

Ottoman Court carpets share with Para-Mamluk and Compartment carpets the use of an asymmetrical knot, but in this case warp and weft are often silk, and the pile is knotted in cotton as well as wool. Their floral patterns differ markedly from the geometric ones of the other two groups. The repertory includes such motifs as large buds, tulips and long leaves with jagged edges, all of which are identical to those used to decorate ceramic tiles, textiles and the margins of manuscripts associated with the OTTOMAN court in the mid-16th century. The shared vocabulary implies a common design source in the court workshop (Ott. *nakkaşhane*), which produced cartoons used in a variety of media; hence the name Ottoman Court to distinguish them from those contemporary carpets thought to have been manufactured in Anatolia without imperial patronage. The characteristic floral ground of Ottoman Court carpets supports central round and oval medallions, lateral half medallions and angular quarter segments, which are all probably derived from Persian designs. Although Persian designs had already been influential in the Ottoman design studios, a more markedly Persian character appears following the Ottoman victory over the Safavids at Chaldiran in 1514 and the sack of the Safavid capital at Tabriz, after which artists and art objects were brought to the Ottoman capital.

Ottoman Court carpets vary considerably in size, from fairly small specimens (*c.* 1.2×1.7 m) to large ones (e.g. 10.0×3.3 m; Florence, Pitti). Unusual cruciform examples (e.g. San Gimignano, Mus. Civ. and London, V&A) were special orders from Europe intended as table covers. One sub-group of Ottoman Court carpets depicts either a niche filled with ornate floral motifs (e.g. Vienna, Österreich. Mus. Angewandte Kst) or two columns supporting an arch with floral elements on a monochrome field (e.g. the Ballard Rug; New York, Met.). The borders of these carpets were done with particular care. Three possible centres of manufacture have been proposed: Cairo, Istanbul and Bursa. Production probably took place in all three at different but overlapping times. Floral carpets began to be produced in Cairo after 1570, when the production of Mamluk carpets was declining. Murad III's removal of artisans from Cairo to Istanbul in 1585 may mark an improvement in quality or a shift in the production site to Istanbul or to nearby Bursa, already a renowned textile centre. Nevertheless, important works were still produced in Cairo at the end of the 16th century and the beginning of the 17th. An Ottoman Court carpet in Florence, for example, was described in contemporary inventories of the Medici wardrobe as *cairino*; it was presented to Grand Duke Ferdinando II by Admiral da Verrazzano in 1623.

BIBLIOGRAPHY

K. Erdmann: 'Kairene Teppiche, ii: Mamluken- und Osmanenteppiche', *A. Islam.*, vii (1940), pp. 55–81

E. Kühnel and L. Bellinger: *Cairene Rugs and Others Technically Related* (Washington, DC, 1957)

K. Erdmann: 'Neuere Untersuchungen zur Frage der Kairener Teppiche', *A. Orient.*, iv (1961), pp. 65–105

C. G. Ellis: 'Mysteries of the Misplaced Mamluks', *Textile Mus. J.*, ii/2 (1967), pp. 2–20

——: 'Is the Mamluk Carpet a Mandala? A Speculation', *Textile Mus. J.*, iv/1 (1974), pp. 30–51

J. Thompson: *The Sarre Mamluk and 12 Other Classical Rugs* (London, 1980)

Hali, iv/1 (1981) [special issue devoted to Mamluk carpets]

R. Pinner and W. B. Denny, eds: 'Carpets of the Mediterranean Countries, 1400–1600', *Orient. Carpet & Textile Stud.*, ii (1986) [whole issue]

GIOVANNI CURATOLA

(c) Iran. The tradition of carpet-making in Iran can be documented with examples beginning only in the late 15th century or early 16th, but the high technical quality of the early pieces indicates that carpets had been made there for some considerable time. This is confirmed by the few fragments from the earlier period that may be attributed to Iran, representations of carpets in manuscripts and references to them in texts. Those illustrated in Persian manuscripts of the 14th century and early 15th have geometric patterns (see fig. 121 above), some of which are related to the Small-pattern Holbein carpets of Anatolia (*see* §(a) above). Carpets with floral patterns began to be depicted in the mid-15th century (see fig. 127 above). Although they do not show an abrupt departure from earlier types in terms of the underlying principles of composition, they introduce a new decorative vocabulary typical of the arts produced under the patronage of the TIMURID dynasty (*reg* 1370–1506).

Only one small fragment of a 15th-century carpet in the geometric style is known to have survived (Athens, Benaki Mus., 16147), but there exist a few floral carpets, similar in spirit to those depicted in manuscript paintings of the Timurid period, that may date from the second half of the 15th century. A spectacular example (5.30×2.22 m; Lisbon, Mus. Gulbenkian) has a central lobed medallion framed by four medallion segments in the corners of the field, a composition typical of contemporary bookbinding and manuscript illumination. The carpet has cotton warps and wefts and asymmetrical wool knots in a wide range of colours, including red, light and dark blue, green, white, yellow and salmon pink. The turbulent field of double split-leaf motifs, stylized lotus blossoms, flowers and palmettes is held in check by a trellis of stems. Flowers and birds (animals and even human figures occur in other examples) appear to be placed in a random way, but on closer examination the composition is carefully orchestrated.

The refined and sophisticated aesthetic of Timurid court workshops continued under the patronage of the SAFAVID dynasty (*reg* 1501–1732). Approximately 1500 carpets and fragments survive from this period. In the first half of the 16th century designs became more elaborate, perhaps because of an increased role that book illustrators may have played in their inspiration. Compositions with a central medallion and quarter medallions repeated in the corners continued to be favoured. Field patterns became increasingly complex: some are entirely floral, while others show birds and animals in idealized natural settings. Carpet weavers were able to achieve such detail thanks to the introduction of silk for warps, wefts and even pile.

Early 16th-century carpets are thought to have been made in Safavid capitals at Tabriz and subsequently Qazvin. Later Safavid rulers established royal factories in such other cities as Kashan, Kirman and Isfahan, but records do not link specific carpets or types of carpet to particular centres. Only three signed and dated carpets survive from this period. One (5.70×3.65 m; Milan, Mus. Poldi Pezzoli) has silk warps and three shoots of cotton weft after each row of asymmetrical knots, with approximately 4100 knots per sq. decimetre. The lobed central medallion, depicting 40 flying cranes, is surrounded by a lively hunting scene. The huntsmen—some mounted, others on foot—fight ferocious lions, cavorting deer and other animals. The figures wear the distinctive Safavid turban, a white cloth wrapped around an upright red baton, which can be seen in contemporary book illustration. The medallion is red, the field is dark blue and the pattern is worked in a wide range of colours. The inscription gives the name Ghiyath al-Din Jami, perhaps to be identified with the weaver, and a date that can be read as either AH 929 (1522–3) or, more probably, AH 949 (1542–3).

The other signed and dated carpets are a matched pair known as the Ardabil carpets, after the shrine in northwest Iran where they were once thought to have originated. The outer borders and lower field of one of them, in Los Angeles (7.3×4.1 m; Co. Mus. A.), were cut down, probably in the late 19th century, and used to repair the other, in London (10.5×5.3 m; V&A; see fig. 200 above). Both are knotted in wool on undyed silk warps and wefts; the warp is Z-spun and S-ply, and three shoots of weft follow each row of knots. The carpets differ, however, in knot count, texture and pile length. The example in London has approximately 4600 knots per sq. decimetre; that in Los Angeles has 6200. On both carpets, 16 small ovoid medallions splay out from a larger lobed medallion; two representations of mosque lamps hang from small medallions on the longitudinal axis. A quarter of the central motif is repeated in each corner of the field. These elements seem to float above a galaxy of floral motifs on a deep blue ground, but the apparently random array is actually united by stems forming an intricate arabesque. Cartouches on both carpets are inscribed with the first couplet from an ode by the Persian poet Hafiz (*d* 1390) and the signature, 'The work of a servant of the court, Maqsud of Kashan, in the year 946' (AD 1539–40).

KASHAN, the town where Maqsud or one of his forebears was born, was a well-known weaving centre. Although it is not certain that the Ardabil carpets were woven there, a small group of carpets is generally attributed to its workshops in the mid-16th century. Characterized by brilliant colour and technical perfection (sometimes over 12,000 knots per sq. decimetre), they are woven entirely in silk and usually measure less than 3×2 m. In colour, design and texture, they recall velvets attributed to Kashan. Ten of these carpets have centralized compositions of medallions in a field of floral ornament and double split-leaves; four others contain directional scenes with animals. One example in 14 colours (New York, Met., 14.40.721; see fig. 204) depicts a woodland scene in which a range of animals play and fight while others, including two ferocious winged lions of decidedly Chinese character, look on. Pairs of pheasants flanking lotus blossoms create an elegant border.

In the second half of the 16th century, Tahmasp I (*reg* 1524–76) apparently lost interest in the patronage of the arts, and the best carpets seem to have been produced

204. Silk carpet, 2.38×1.80 m, from Kashan, Iran, mid-16th century (New York, Metropolitan Museum of Art)

in provincial centres. A large group of carpets with varied designs, but all woven with the same structure, is usually attributed to Kirman in southern Iran and dated to the late 16th century and early 17th. They have depressed warps and three weft shoots, the first and third of which are wool and the second silk or cotton, a structure characteristic of 19th- and 20th-century carpets from Kirman. Some 15 carpets and fragments are known as Sanguszko carpets after the finest example (Paris, Prince Roman Sanguszko priv. col.), said to have been captured from the Ottomans at the battle of Khotim in Ukraine in 1621. Sanguszko carpets maintain the classical composition of a centralized medallion on a field of animals and birds, but both the rendering of motifs and the use of muted colours differ from those in earlier Safavid carpets. The medallions in the borders are similar to tiles on buildings commissioned by Ganj 'Ali Khan, governor of Kirman from 1596 to 1621. Another sub-group known as Vase carpets have directional rather than centralized compositions (e.g. Berlin, Mus. Islam. Kst; Vienna, Österreich. Mus. Angewandte Kst; London, V&A and New York, Met.). The field appears as a random assortment of flowers (peonies, lotuses and lilies) as well as palmettes, floral sprays, pomegranates and rosettes, among which vases sometimes appear, but the composition is highly regular, often laterally symmetrical, and usually structured on an intricate lattice composed of three planes of stems from which blossoms issue at regular intervals. The blossoms, once the background motif, have expanded to dominate the composition. Several examples of Garden

carpets (e.g. Glasgow, Burrell Col.; the Wagner Garden Carpet, see CARPET, colour pl. IV and GARDEN, fig. 13) are related in technique and style to the group with depressed warps. The field schematically shows a bird's-eye view of a Persian garden, the parterres of which are bisected by watercourses emanating from a central pond. Each parterre is filled with a variety of flowers, shrubs, trees and birds; the streams may contain fish. In such an arid land as Iran, garden iconography remained popular; Garden carpets of a more stylized character were made in the 17th and 18th centuries and are often ascribed to Kurdistan.

Another group of carpets, characterized by a deep pink field and a blue-green border, is assumed to have been made in HERAT. The best-known examples are the Emperor's Carpets (New York, Met. (7.5×3.3 m)); Vienna, Österreich. Mus. Angewandte Kst), which Peter the Great of Russia gave to Leopold I of Austria in 1698. Knotted in wool on silk warps with some 5500 asymmetrical knots per sq. decimetre, the carpets are worked in 18 colours. Fantastic large blossoms facing in all directions run a stately dance over the field, while animals and birds sport amid a tracery of twirling stems, rosettes and cloud bands. Cartouches in the inner guard band contain Persian poetry celebrating nature and lauding the shah, presumably Tahmasp. In other Herat carpets, parts of the ground were brocaded in gold and silver thread.

Carpets with gold and silver thread were also among the gifts that 'Abbas I (reg 1588–1629) bestowed on those he wished to please or impress. He presented the English entrepreneur Sir Anthony Shirley with six mules, each carrying four carpets, of which four were of silk and gold and twenty of 'crewel'. Those in silk and gold were probably examples of a type later known as Polish or Polonaise carpets. Much sought after in the great houses of 17th-century Europe, some 300 of them survive. Some must have been special commissions, for they bear European coats of arms, including one example (Kraków, N. Mus.) with arms once thought to be those of the Czartoryski family. They acquired the misnomer Polonaise when several were exhibited at the International Exhibition at Paris in 1878, but they are known to have been woven in Safavid court factories established by 'Abbas and his successors. Knotted in silk on silk or cotton warps and wefts, these carpets are now faded but were once bright green, blue, yellow and pink, enriched with silver and gold. Their designs vary considerably but are composed of fleshy overblown blossoms or palmettes and swirling leaves arranged in compartments or around a central medallion. Similar designs of a central medallion framed by quarter medallions appear on flatweaves (see KILIM), including several (Munich, Residenzmus.) bearing the arms of Sigismund III, King of Poland (see VASA, (2)). He had sent an Armenian merchant to Kashan to purchase carpets, and a document dated 12 September 1602 may well relate to these pieces. In contrast to the pile carpets, the flatweaves often include representations of animals, birds and human figures. With their meticulously rendered designs and restrained colours, these carpets are strikingly different from those of the early 16th century and mark the heyday of the Iranian carpet. In later years, classical motifs and designs became increasingly stiff and stylized.

BIBLIOGRAPHY

Enc. Iran.: 'Ardabīl Carpet'; 'Carpets IX. Safavid Period'
T. Mańkowski: 'The Art of Carpet Making, B: Some Documents from Polish Sources Relating to Carpet Making in the Time of Shāh 'Abbās I', *Survey of Persian Art*, ed. A. U. Pope and P. Ackerman (London and New York, 1938–9, 2/1964–7), pp. 2431–6
R. Stead: *The Ardabil Carpets* (Malibu, 1974)
K. Erdmann: *Oriental Carpets* (Fishguard, 1976)
Carpets of Central Persia (exh. cat., ed. M. H. Beattie; Sheffield, Mappin A.G.; Birmingham, Mus. & A.G.; 1976)
The Eastern Carpet in the Western World (exh. cat., ed. D. King and D. Sylvester; London, Hayward Gal., 1983)
F. Spuhler: 'Carpets and Textiles', *The Timurid and Safavid Periods* (1986), vi of *The Cambridge History of Iran* (Cambridge, 1968–91), pp. 698–727
L. W. Mackie: 'A Piece of the Puzzle: A 14th–15th Century Persian Carpet Fragment Revealed', *Hali*, xi/5 (1989), pp. 16–23

JENNY HOUSEGO

(d) Indian subcontinent. Knotted woollen floor coverings may have been made in India for centuries, but the earliest surviving examples (e.g. Boston, MA, Mus. F.A., 93.1480) are dated to the end of the 16th century on the basis of their similarities to manuscripts produced at the end of the reign of the Mughal emperor Akbar (*reg* 1556–1605), although the carpets may have been woven later. The evident similarities to the carpets of Safavid Iran suggest that designs or weavers were brought from Iran, much as painters and manuscripts were. Characteristic Indian features include lively asymmetrical designs in the field which depict foliage and figures, and wisteria-like clusters of flowers. The finest carpets were produced during the reign of Shah Jahan (*reg* 1628–57), when some examples had silk warps and wefts and a pile of fine goat hair with 39,500 knots per sq. decimetre (e.g. the Altman fragment, New York, Met., 14.40.722). Typical Indo-Persian carpets, in which Indian single-flower motifs were combined with Iranian-style palmettes, were modified for the European market by the addition of heraldic motifs (e.g. *c.* 1631; London, Girdlers' Co.). Indian carpets of the period are epitomized by red-ground pieces with rows of flowering plants (e.g. New York, Frick). In the middle of the 17th century the typical palmette borders were replaced by strapwork and guilloche bands (e.g. Lisbon, Mus. Gulbenkian, T. 72), and in the second half of the century the typical tree and flower motifs became more rigid (e.g. Jaipur, Maharaja Sawai Man Singh II Mus.) or enclosed within lattices. Compositions became increasingly elaborate, eventually culminating in the *millefleurs* carpets (e.g. Oxford, Ashmolean) produced at the end of the Mughal period.

For more information and bibliography *see* INDIAN SUBCONTINENT, §VIII, 4.   □

(iv) c. 1700 and after. By the 18th century the three traditional modes of carpet production—commercial, village and nomadic—are well documented. In the 19th century production responded strongly to Western demands, taste and entrepreneurial activities, particularly when Oriental carpets became important in European and American interior decoration. Although traditional modes of production continued, large commercial ventures were established, primarily in Iran and the Caucasus, and most of the carpets known today in the West as Oriental rugs were produced for export.

(a) Anatolia and the Balkans. (b) Caucasus. (c) Iran. (d) Western Central Asia. (e) Indian subcontinent. (f) North Africa.

(a) Anatolia and the Balkans. The three traditions of carpet-weaving embedded in Turkish Anatolian culture—commercial, village and nomadic—continued to flourish *c.* 1700, long after the court-controlled weaving establishments that provided a major part of their historical and artistic heritage had ceased to operate (*see* §(iii)(a) above). Commercial carpet-producing establishments were located in such centres as Uşak (Ushak) and Gördes (Ghiordes) in west Anatolia and Konya in western central Anatolia, where access to the Mediterranean markets had made carpets important for export as well as the domestic economy. The declining interest of Europeans in Oriental carpets after 1700 coincided with Louis XIV's *grand goût* in France and the heyday of such manufactories as Gobelins (*see* GOBELINS, §2) and SAVONNERIE, where carpets were produced in a style consistent with other contemporary French decorative arts, although some copies of Turkish models were produced (*see also* CARPET, §II, 2(iii)). When carpet-weaving re-emerged as an important commercial undertaking in the Middle East in the later 19th century, it was often under the aegis of European economic and political control, which influenced not only the means of production but also style. Carpet-weaving in Anatolia and the Balkans in the 18th and 19th centuries therefore combines local and foreign artistic sources, old and new economic systems, social conservatism and change, and Western and Turkish tastes.

Economic and social factors. Anatolian village weaving, highly localized as regards designs, techniques and types of market, served a mixture of social and economic purposes. To some extent village women wove carpets for local use, as practical furnishings for their houses and mosques; to a greater extent, nomadic weavers created a multitude of bags, covers, animal trappings and decorations to serve the practical and ceremonial needs of nomadic life. The commercial potential of village and nomadic carpets gave them an important economic function from early times as one of the few creations of the village or encampment economy (apart from agricultural and animal products) that could be turned into cash.

Both the carpets themselves and the process of weaving them form an important part of village culture: carpets often perpetuate local techniques and designs that belong to the artistic tradition of a village, and the weaving of such carpets was and still is a traditional form of socialization and economic activity for young women. By the 19th century the skill of the village carpet-weavers was increasingly harnessed by cottage-industry entrepreneurs, and the resulting products varied widely in artistic quality. Although some cottage weavers continued to weave traditional designs for new commercial purposes, some entrepreneurs dictated new patterns and introduced new colours deemed to reflect European and American tastes. The growth of cottage and piecework industries affected the designs, colours and markets of village carpets, while the introduction into Turkey from Europe of power-driven Jacquard and other looms using steam and water and the importing of cheap textiles from Europe sometimes led in the villages themselves to the replacement of traditional hand-woven carpets with industrially produced substitutes.

The nomadic weaving tradition is probably the oldest and certainly the most conservative in Anatolia, although the reason for this is still disputed by anthropologists and carpet scholars. The high degree of self-sufficiency in the nomadic economy and the tight strictures of tribal society probably provided a certain degree of insulation against economic and artistic change. Nomadic weaving traditions in Anatolia continued to preserve early designs while many village weavers abandoned them. This is especially true in the case of flat-woven carpets (see KILIM), which commanded little interest from either domestic or foreign markets and were woven in non-carpet formats to serve such specific functions as tent furnishings, provision sacks and animal trappings.

The persistence of designs among certain tribal groups as they migrated or in specific locations even as the indigenous populations changed is a complex issue given the lack of firmly datable examples of early village and nomadic weaving. Some scholars posit that the designs of Anatolian flatweaves date to prehistoric times, seeing in some abstract geometric motifs reflections of the prehistoric art of Anatolia and the imagery of ancient mother-goddess cults. Others interpret the same designs as Turkic symbols that have been carried westward from Central Asia since the 11th century, while still others find such arguments to be unprovable (and hence pointless) or regard the alleged historical similarities as a product of the limited range of designs dictated by the techniques of carpet-weaving, especially flat-weaving.

Dating. Whereas earlier Turkish carpets can be dated reliably from their depiction in European paintings, the more numerous recent Turkish carpets are far more difficult to date. The tendency of the market to date objects early, which enhances their value in the eyes of some collectors, has led to a countervailing tendency among the few scholars who concern themselves with the subject to date everything to the 19th century or later, thereby making the 18th century a prominent hole in carpet history. Most physical and chemical tests are of limited value for carpets woven within the last 250 years. The presence of aniline dyes in a carpet is a helpful indicator of a late date, as long as the dyed fibres do not belong to later repairs or restorations. It has, however, become a common practice to remove small tell-tale areas of aniline orange and grey-purple from traditionally dyed carpets to improve their appearance and increase their apparent age and thus their market value. The condition of a carpet is no measure of its age, since sophisticated means of distressing a carpet, which range from such simple measures as shearing dark brown pile to simulate the corrosive effects of time on that particular colour, to physical abrasion and chemical alteration of colour, are quite common.

Dating of more recent Anatolian carpets therefore depends primarily on the traditional methods of art history. One means of dating is provided by carpets themselves when they have reliable inscriptions including dates; another is through written documents, old photographs and (rarely) European paintings. The chief means of constructing the history of later Turkish weaving, however, is by extrapolating absolute dates from a sequence of relative ones. First a technical and stylistic archetype—a carpet or carpets that, for persuasive reasons, can be said to represent the earliest available stage in the gradual evolution of design and technique—is identified, and then the degree of deviation from the prototype within the weaving of a precisely defined geographical area is measured. This method allows scholars to define a regular chronological process of stylization, for the dictates of the weaving process and the individuality of weavers gradually assert themselves as carpets are copied from other carpets. Thus the more a carpet deviates from the prototype, the later it is assumed to be. By using such a relative sequence and such other factors as works datable because of inscriptions and the evidence of inventories, and the presence of aniline dyes, reliably accurate dating of many kinds of Turkish carpets is possible. The most famous example of relative sequencing of designs involves a prototype that was invented in the mid- to late 16th century, an Ottoman court prayer-rug with an architectural design showing a triple arch and paired columns (e.g. the Ballard Rug; New York, Met.). Later examples (e.g. Washington, DC, Textile Mus., R 34.22.1; early 18th century) show an increasing stylization of design. Anatolian kilims, with their bold geometric designs, are harder to date. Although dealers and collectors have made extravagant claims for a very early date for certain kilims, most serious students of carpet history view these claims with extreme caution.

Geography of production. By the end of the 19th century the distinctive products of several Anatolian weaving centres had become important items of commerce in the Ottoman empire, and dealers and subsequently some scholars assigned various names to carpets in an attempt to identify their geographic origins. Among large format carpets, the traditional Turkey carpet, coarsely woven with a preponderance of red and blue, was produced in Uşak, Isparta and surrounding areas. Nevertheless, most Anatolian carpets entering the market were small, for the small prayer-rug (Turk. *seccade*) with the design of an arch at one end had predominated in traditional village weaving, and small rugs filled a new Western taste for decorating with scatter rugs. A wide variety of small carpets using traditional Anatolian techniques and dyestuffs combined with designs recalling local village and nomadic traditions as well as the great age of Ottoman court art was produced at Lâdik, Mucur (Mudjur, Mujur) and Kırşehir (Kirshehir) in central Anatolia. The designs of many of these pieces can be traced to prayer-rugs and small medallion carpets of the Transylvanian type. The production of more finely woven carpets using non-traditional techniques, materials and designs was developed by entrepreneurs in Kayseri during the 19th century for urban markets at home and abroad.

In western Anatolia the market-town of Bergama (ancient Pergamon) gave its name to the long-piled and coarsely woven products of nomadic and village weavers in north-west Anatolia, often bearing designs of great antiquity. For example, a 19th-century fragment (1.42× 0.88 m; Berlin, Mus. Islam. Kst, 04/77) bears a design

205. Gördes prayer-rug with an arched design, wool knotted pile, 1.93×1.35 m, from Turkey, late 18th century (Springfield, MA, George Walter Vincent Smith Art Museum)

arch in the field and the border motifs all derive from 16th-century prototypes, but are strongly geometricized. Together with the carpets traditionally attributed to Mucur and Milâs, Lâdik carpets represent a weaving tradition that long resisted Western designs and coloration and only succumbed to cheap aniline dyes with the economic and social upheavals of the late 19th century and early 20th. By contrast, the traditional type of Kırşehir carpet was produced well into the 20th century alongside examples using a totally Europeanized design vocabulary.

Traditional modes of carpet-weaving and design persisted in many places in Anatolia even after the growth of commercially oriented cottage industries serving domestic and foreign markets. Because the market virtually ignored slit tapestry-woven kilims until the last third of the 20th century, they continued to be woven in traditional formats and designs throughout Anatolia and the Balkans long after aniline dyes had blighted their glorious tradition of colours. Traditional techniques persisted in east and southeast Anatolia, in the Taurus Mountains along the south coast, in certain Anatolian towns and above all in the north-west, where many kinds of tribal weaving persisted into the later 20th century. That of the Yüncü nomads, for example, had a distinctive palette dominated by red

derived from that of a Large-pattern Holbein carpet. The towns of Gördes, Milâs and Kula also gave their names to distinctive carpet types. The products of Gördes became the best known and commanded the highest prices, being highly prized in the West. Gördes carpets, which sometimes use cotton rather than wool in both foundation and pile, often employ muted colours (see fig. 205). The non-traditional and intricate designs reflect both domestic embroideries and European styles. Cottage industries throughout Turkey—from Thrace and Bandirma in the north-west to Kayseri in the east—used traditional Gördes designs, eventually prompting large numbers of copies from the Iranian looms of Tabriz as well. Gördes carpets, in common with those of Kayseri, Istanbul and Kula, were often altered for the market by the addition of elaborate false fringes and the application of bleach to mute the colours. Thus the commercial magic of the Gördes name led to its attachment to carpets of entirely different provenance, design and technique.

Carpets attributed to Lâdik in Konya province stand at the opposite pole from the traditional Gördes type: woven in brilliant colours using traditional materials, Lâdik carpets reflect a distinctively Anatolian blend of nomadic designs and the classical Ottoman style (see fig. 206). The triple

206. Lâdik rug with triple arched design, wool knotted pile, 1.88×1.17 m, from Anatolia, 19th century (St Louis, MO, Art Museum)

and blue and a preponderance of powerful interlocking geometric shapes, while nomadic weaving of the northwest traces its designs directly back to early Holbein and Lotto carpets and often shows striking parallels with the weaving of nomadic Turkic peoples of Transcaucasia, Turkmenistan and Kazakhstan (see §(d) below).

Other areas of Anatolia also preserved traditional techniques and styles of carpet-weaving together with a thriving production through much of the 19th century. These include the districts of Karapinar in Konya province and the 'Yörük Triangle' to the east, which extends from the Taurus mountains in the south to the market town of Şarkişla in the north. Certain groups of carpets can be localized on the basis of evidence gathered by anthropologists and historians and from the collection of carpets preserved as religious endowments (Turk. *vakf*) in local mosques.

Impact of trade and the European economy. As Ottoman political and military fortunes declined after 1700, a shifting of economic power and the establishment of independent Western commercial ventures on a large scale within the Ottoman empire meant that the production of Turkish carpets began to be affected by European markets. Although Western entrepreneurship and markets had some impact on Gördes and Kayseri carpets, Western tastes became even more dominant in the realm of large carpets. As the fashion for the brightly coloured red Turkey carpet waned in the second half of the 19th century, manufactories at Uşak and other centres turned to making large carpets of coarse weave in pale colours, often depending on aniline dyestuffs and on the process of 'washing' carpets with chemicals after weaving to make their palette more acceptable in Western markets. These carpets appear to have been produced for an aesthetic and a market entirely different from that of the more complex and finely knotted contemporary carpets of Iran (see §(c) below). Eventually, Turkish manufactories responded to the popularity of Iranian styles by producing cheaper Iranian-style carpets in Kayseri and more expensive ones in Sivas and in the state-controlled manufactories established at Hereke near Istanbul in 1844.

In the 20th century Turkish production was further affected by the development of carpet collecting in the West. Imitations of Gördes carpets were made in a variety of centres; finely knotted reproductions of classical Persian and Ottoman carpets were produced at Hereke and in ateliers in the Armenian quarter of Kukapı in Istanbul. In the late 20th century a renaissance in the use of traditional dyestuffs in Anatolia, together with the spectacular performance of older Turkish village and nomadic carpets on the art market, led to the weaving of reproduction carpets that were new and faithful versions of older village and nomadic types. Some of these have been subjected to clipping and bleaching to make them more acceptable to buyers with a preference for old carpets, while others, notably those produced by the DOBAG cooperatives (see Thompson, 1988), reach the market as they left the loom, honest modern re-creations of traditional carpet types.

BIBLIOGRAPHY

M. Beattie: 'Coupled-column Prayer Rugs', *Orient. A.*, xiv (1968), pp. 243–58

W. Denny: 'Anatolian Rugs: An Essay on Method', *Textile Mus. J.*, iii (1973), pp. 7–25

M. L. Eiland: *Oriental Rugs: A Comprehensive Guide* (Greenwich, CT, 1973, rev. Boston, MA, 1976), pp. 104–37

M. Beattie: 'Some Rugs of the Konya Region', *Orient. A.*, xxii (1976), pp. 60–76

C. G. Ellis: 'The Rugs from the Great Mosque at Divriği', *Hali*, i/3 (1978), pp. 269–74

A. N. Landreau, ed.: *Yörük: The Nomadic Weaving Tradition of the Middle East* (Pittsburg, 1978)

W. Denny: 'Classical Roots of Anatolian Kilim Designs', *Hali*, ii/3 (1979), pp. 105–9

Y. Petsopoulos: *Kilims* (New York, 1979)

B. Balpinar and U. Hirsch: *Flatweaves of the Vakiflar Museum İstanbul* (Wesel, 1982)

W. Brüggemann and H. Böhmer: *Rugs of the Peasants and Nomads of Anatolia* (Munich, 1983)

B. Balpinar and U. Hirsch: *Vakiflar Museum İstanbul: Carpets* (Wesel, 1988)

W. Denny: 'Turkish Rugs', *The Markarian Album*, ed. W. Denny and others (Cincinnati, 1988), pp. 75–150

J. Thompson: *Oriental Carpets*, rev. edn (New York, 1988), pp. 124–5

WALTER B. DENNY

(b) Caucasus.

18th century. Carpets and flatweaves were probably produced in the Caucasus, the rugged isthmus bordered by the Black and Caspian seas and crossed by the Greater and Lesser Caucasus mountains, long before the 17th century, when the region was nominally under the control of the Safavid dynasty (*reg* 1501–1732) of Persia. 'Abbas I (*reg* 1588–1629) is reported to have established carpet manufactories in Shirvan and Karabagh provinces, but no example of their products has yet been identified, and the earliest examples are datable *c.* 1700. Since early Caucasian carpets are larger than most tribal or nomadic pieces, yet stouter, coarser and less sophisticated in pattern than carpets made in Iran for the Safavid court (*see* §(iii)(c) above), they were probably produced commercially for export.

Early Caucasian carpets are typically long (often over 5 m) and relatively narrow with narrow borders. They feature symmetrically knotted wool pile on undyed warps, and their wool wefts are almost always dyed red. The knot count is usually well under 15.5 per sq. cm. These carpets once bore the trade name Quba carpets after the town in eastern Dagestan, but they were probably not manufactured there, as the town only developed late in the 18th century. It is more likely that they were manufactured to the south and west in the urban centres of Shusha in Karabagh province and Shemakhy in Shirvan, since 19th-century carpets produced in Karabagh have the same heavy coarse texture and bold motifs.

Dragon carpets are the oldest, largest and most discussed group of early-Caucasian carpets. The field of a typical Dragon carpet—red, or less often blue or brown—is covered with a large-scale trellis of jagged leaves, overlapped at their intersections by large palmettes. Within irregular compartments formed by the trellis appear the dragons after which the carpets are named: upright and S-shaped with vestigal crests and flaming shoulders and haunches. Older examples (see fig. 207) include such other fauna as lions battling dragon-headed stags (*chi'lin*) in the compartments not occupied by the dragons, and ducks and pheasants in the leafy latticework. Even in the oldest carpets of the group, the animals are so stylized as to be

207. Dragon carpet, wool knotted pile, 4.69×2.23 m, from the Caucasus, *c.* 1700 (Ham, Surrey, Keir private collection)

barely recognizable. Despite the Chinese ancestry of the animal motifs, Dragon carpets probably derived from Safavid carpets. Many Dragon carpets and other early Caucasian pieces share with the Vase carpets of 17th-century Kirman a directional trellis pattern and the structural peculiarity of the periodic addition of a heavy single weft.

Despite the important role played by Armenian weavers and clients in the carpet production of the Caucasus, theories proposing an Armenian origin for Dragon carpets must be discounted. FREDRIK MARTIN first argued for a 13th- or 14th-century origin there, but his dating must be rejected in light of their derivation from Safavid designs. No Dragon carpet is inscribed in Armenian; the only signed piece (Washington, DC, Textile Mus., R 36.1.4;

4.45×1.83 m) bears the name of Husayn Beg written in Arabic script and a date readable as either 1001 or 1101 (AD 1592 or 1689). As this carpet is anomalous in so many ways, however, including the unusual colours and drawing and the central medallion imposed on the latticework, it is thought to be a freely adapted 19th-century Kurdish recreation of a Dragon carpet. Only later do designs taken from Dragon carpets appear on many carpets inscribed in Armenian. The Gohar carpet (USA, priv. col. *see* ARMENIA, §V), for example, is inscribed 'I, the sinful Gohar, made this with my newly learned hands, may the reader pray for me', and has a date in the form of a chronogram, which can be read as 1679–80, 1699 or 1732. In the field, vestiges of dragons in addorsed pairs surround palmettes that have become pendants to a large central medallion. The design is clearly transitional between the directional, overall latticework of Dragon carpets and the centralized format of some 19th-century carpets from the Karabagh region.

Other pieces with technical similarities to Dragon carpets display different designs. The leafy trellis of Dragon carpets may be maintained, although the dragons and other fauna are omitted in favour of long-stemmed flowering plants (e.g. Philadelphia, PA, Mus. A., 43.40.62; 3.66×1.46 m). Cypress trees may alternate with medallions that sprout curving, serrated leaves in X-shaped groups of four (e.g. Washington, DC, Textile Mus., R 36.2.4; 4.88×2.08 m). Sunburst carpets are named for the arresting, white-rayed floral motif that appears singly or in multiples among large palmettes and leaves (e.g. Washington, DC, Textile Mus., R 36.2.12; 5.31×2.31 m). Towards the end of the 18th century patterns that were dramatically reduced in scale and probably borrowed from brocaded silks became fashionable. The semé design (Pers. *afshān*: 'scattering'), featuring an endless repeat of vines, palmettes, roundels and forked lilies (e.g. a fragment, Washington, DC, Textile Mus., 1970.14.1; 3.71×2.49 m), proved so successful that it continued to be reproduced virtually unchanged in 19th-century carpets from several districts of the Caucasus.

BIBLIOGRAPHY

F. R. Martin: *A History of Oriental Carpets before 1800* (Vienna, 1908)

A. U. Pope: 'The Myth of the Armenian Dragon Carpets', *Jb. Asiat. Kst*, ii (1925), pp. 147–58

A. Sakisian: 'Les Tapis à dragons et leur origine arménienne', *Syria*, ix (1928), pp. 238–56

U. Schürmann: *Teppiche aus dem Kaukasus* (Brunswick, 1964; Eng. trans., London, 1965/*R* Accokeek and Basingstoke, 1974)

S. Yetkin: *Early Caucasian Carpets in Turkey*, 2 vols, trans. A. and A. Mellaarts (London and Atlantic Highlands, 1978)

Early Caucasian Rugs (exh. cat., ed. C. G. Ellis; Washington, DC, Textile Mus., 1978)

I. Bennett: *Caucasian* (1981); i of *Oriental Rugs* (n.p. and Woodbridge, 1981–9)

L. Kerimov and others: *Rugs and Carpets of the Caucasus: The Russian Collections* (Harmondsworth and Leningrad, 1984)

Weavers, Merchants and Kings: The Inscribed Rugs of Armenia (exh. cat., ed. L. der Manuelian and M. Eiland; Fort Worth, TX, Kimbell A. Mus., 1984)

JULIA BAILEY

19th–20th centuries. In the last quarter of the 19th century the Caucasus region was linked to Europe by modern transportation and communication systems, and the making of carpets was transformed from a local craft supplying the home and bazaar into a major industry producing exports for Europe and America. Although weaving remained a cottage industry, synthetic dyes were introduced in the 1880s and were rapidly adopted for their ease of use. Marketing considerations led to the choice of some Western designs, the most common being the European rose. The export boom peaked after 1900, but World War I, pestilence and civil strife destroyed the weaving economy, although the industry revived early in the Soviet period (*c.* 1926) when motifs from traditional patterns of Caucasian carpets were reused separately. The result was a distinctive type of scatter rug (less than 3×2 m) with a central field of one colour surrounded by borders of another; both contrast with the colours used in the superimposed pattern. This creates a geometric art with strong centres and repeated and alternating motifs. Although animals are present, floral motifs predominate and the main border pattern is a stylized vine with blossoms and tendrils.

Current nomenclature includes 35 to 40 terms referring to sites, areas or ethnic groups; nonetheless, two main types of pile carpets can be distinguished. One group comes from the western Transcaucasus and is called Kazakh/Borchaly (Bordjalou) after the small districts in north-west Azerbaijan and south-east Georgia settled centuries earlier by Kazakhs from western Siberia. This type has thick yarn and a high pile. Several wefts pass between rows of knots and are visible on the back, and cotton wrapping is occasionally used for side finishes. The designs are spacious because of the wide separation between motifs (which are relatively abstract), the abrupt jumps in motif size, and the use of contrasting colours, mainly bright reds and violets made from cochineal (see fig. 208). By 1910 the quality of the Kazakh group had declined considerably.

The second group comes from the eastern lowlands along the Caspian Sea and is called Quba or Shemakhy after the towns in the heartland of Baku province, although the type was produced northward into coastal Dagestan (Kiurin district) up to Derbent and southward to the Djevat and Lenkoran districts. The typical carpet has fine-spun yarn and short pile. The two wefts between each row of knots are barely visible on the back of the carpet. Many, often complementary, colours are used; blue is the most common. Motifs are quasi-representational and of graduated sizes, and patterns are intricate. The highest quality and the most numerous pieces came from Quba itself: in 1913 its 40,000 weavers comprised 80% of the district's craft-industry labour force. Quba carpets also show the greatest fidelity to traditional designs and dyes. Products from Shemakhy are similar, but less fine; those of Lenkoran are poorly dyed. A sub-set of the Quba/Shemakhy type is comprised of pictorial carpets, bearing representations of stories, scenes and people. They were rarely exported.

Other carpets show some characteristic features of the two main types. One intermediate group originated in Elizabetpol province and can be called Gandja/Karabagh after its northern and southern cities. This group is technically similar to the Kazakh/Borchaly type, but resembles the Quba/Shemakhy type in design. Other intermediate carpets resemble the Quba/Shemakhy type, but with coarser materials, motifs and patterns. They

208. Kazakh carpet, wool knotted pile, 2.39×1.63 m, from the Caucasus, early 19th century (Berlin, Museum für Islamische Kunst, inv. 4/69)

probably came from several still unidentified sites. Shusha was the capital of Karabagh (Kariega) where the surge of commercial weaving began in the 1880s. Some of the ten principal Shusha patterns are curvilinear and resemble Persian ones rather than the indigenous Gandja/Karabagh type.

The Transcaucasus was also the source of many handsome flatweaves (*see* KILIM). A large group from the Quba district are woven with a floating weft, which gives them a thick, matted back, a technique known as sumak after the town of Shemakhy. Many bear the same patterns as pile carpets, with a main field enclosed by borders composed of a continuous meander-and-bar pattern or a repeated single motif. Other flatweaves from the western Transcaucasus, known as verneh, are made of narrow strips sewn together and brocaded with depictions of stylized camels, dragons or snakes. Reversible types of flatweaves include covers woven in narrow bands of different colours, covers with a unitary or repeat pattern, and all-purpose fabrics made from a composite of narrow strips, which bore supplemental designs.

BIBLIOGRAPHY

Enc. Iran.: 'Carpets XV'

R. E. Wright: *Rugs and Flatweaves of the Transcaucasus* (Pittsburgh, 1980)

For further bibliography *see* §(b) above.

RICHARD E. WRIGHT

209. *Millefleurs* carpet, wool knotted pile, 2.02×1.36 m, from Shiraz, Iran, second half of the 18th century (London, Victoria and Albert Museum)

(c) Iran. With the exception of Shiraz, stable under the prosperous rule of the Zand regent Muhammad Karim Khan (*reg* 1750–79), 18th-century Iran experienced political disruptions that were not conducive to carpet production. The installation of the Qajar dynasty (*reg* 1779–1924) in Tehran brought about a revival of court patronage, although the magnificent silk and brocade carpets of the Safavid period were no longer manufactured, at least in significant numbers. Stability led to an increase in urban, village and nomad production, the three traditional modes of carpet manufacture, and these expanded dramatically towards the end of the 19th century when manufactories were established to meet the demand of export markets, particularly in Europe and the USA.

Introduction. Production in the 18th century is exemplified by a carpet woven (and signed) by Muhammad Sharif Kirmani (1758; Tehran, Archaeol. Mus.) bearing a traditional design of a lattice with flowering plants in its compartments. Knotted with the same technique of depressed warps used in Vase carpets (*see* §(iii)(c) above) and associated with the city of Kirman, from which the weaver (or his ancestors) evidently came, it serves as the

basis for identifying a group of related carpets and fragments. Other examples with non-traditional motifs, including fields strewn with small flowers (often called *millefleurs* or *millefiori*; e.g. London, V&A, T. 99-1973; see fig. 209) and the repeated pear or teardrop shapes familiar from paisley patterns (Pers. *buta, boteh*; see Housego (1989), fig. 30), are attributed to Shiraz because carpets bearing these designs are depicted in contemporary paintings of Zand notables. Persian carpets were not favoured in Europe in the first half of the 18th century, but by the 1780s and 1790s merchants of the English East India Company reopened carpet trade with Iran through Bushehr (Bushire), the port of Shiraz on the Gulf.

By the second quarter of the 19th century sizeable numbers of carpets were being produced in both traditional and new centres, including Herat, Kirman, Yazd, Borujerd, the Turkoman areas of Khurasan, Isfahan and Azerbaijan. A popular design of the period combined different types of floral motifs, such as the graceful symmetrical schemes of floral palmettes on a background of close-textured leaves (e.g. a carpet made in Faraghan in 1817; London, V&A, 200.1925). Popularized through international expositions, museum exhibitions, the Arts and Crafts Movement in Britain and changes in styles of interior decorating, Iranian carpets were produced and exported in increasing numbers from the 1870s. At first commercial and custom production was financed locally by loom owners, merchants and notables. The growing international market, however, demanded new capital, which was provided by wholesalers, traders, merchant bankers and Western importers. Ziegler & Co., the Manchester firm that made and imported carpets, was the first to organize production with foreign capital. Initially the firm exported new and used carpets, including the famous Ardabil carpets (London, V&A; see fig. 200 above; Los Angeles, CA, Co. Mus. A.) made in the 16th century. Between 1877 and 1882 it established an enterprise in Sultanabad (now Arak), a town in western Iran on the trade route between Tehran and Baghdad. Ziegler & Co. provided weavers with raw materials, including wool and patterns, and cash advances. Carpets were made in standard dimensions to suit Western houses (e.g. 4×6, 8×10 ft and runners) and designs. The success of the venture allowed the company to expand operations; 111 villages around Sultanabad were involved by 1894. Other entrepreneurs followed suit, and in addition to organizing cottage and workshop production through local agents, all these firms established their own manufactories in Iran.

Most Iranian carpets in the West, therefore, were produced in the second half of the 19th century or later in standard sizes, designs and quality. In contrast to Anatolia, where villagers continued to produce small carpets with traditional patterns which were exported to Western markets, in Iran villages weavers quickly adapted to Western demands for carpets to fit rooms, areas, hallways and stairs. Furthermore, long-wearing knotted carpets were produced for export, in anticipation of use in Western interiors where street shoes are worn indoors, bringing dirt on to the carpet and grinding it into the pile. As a result, the design and production of Persian village looms were controlled by Western retail merchants to an unprecedented extent; however attractive, these carpets hardly represent a folk art rooted in native traditions.

The enormous area of Iran and the varying conditions under which carpets were produced make generalization difficult. Nonetheless, four main groups can be distinguished: luxury products woven in special manufactories for the court, carpets woven in cities and towns, village carpets and carpets woven by nomadic tribes. In contrast to Anatolia and the Caucasus, where geometric designs predominated, designs in Iran were usually based on floral and medallion motifs. Colours were adapted to consumers' taste; typical schemes balance deep red, dark blue and orange with lighter tones of green, turquoise and beige. Synthetic dyes were introduced by the 1870s, but the harsh colours were unsuited to Western taste, so to subdue them the carpets were washed in chemical baths. Cotton warps are common, and both symmetrical and asymmetrical knots were used.

Nomenclature is confusing, for a single term (e.g. 'Herati') can refer to the place where a particular carpet was made (Herat), the type of design (arabesque) or the quality of work (fine, with up to 4500 knots per sq. decimetre). Despite the bewildering range of names, designs and colours, however, most Persian carpets of the 19th century show a preference for elaborating motifs, and by the late 19th century flamboyant floral designs similar to those on architecture and tilework were popular. Large-scale pictorial carpets were introduced in the mid-19th century. Often inscribed with graceful calligraphy in the border, they present scenes from such literary works as Firdawsi's *Shāhnāma* ('Book of kings') and Nizami's *Khamsa* ('Five poems'). From the 1870s pictorial carpets also bore images from Western sources, including scenes from Classical mythology and portraits of European figures. The images were derived from newspapers, books, postcards, paintings and photographs, and the carpets were very fine in technique, particularly when imitating stippling and hatching in the original image.

Centres of production. Carpets have been made in Azerbaijan, the Turkish-speaking region in north-west Iran, since Safavid times, and are known by various names. The oldest known carpets of the Heriz type date from the 19th century and are woven on an all-wool foundation. Often called Serabi/Serapi, Heriz carpets combine the dignity of large Persian formats (5×7 m is not uncommon) with the appeal of geometric designs typical of carpets produced in nearby Anatolia and the Caucasus. In the late 19th century extremely fine silk carpets (up to 2500 knots per sq. decimetre) were woven at Tabriz; their designs were based on Anatolian and European prototypes (e.g. Springfield, MA, Smith A. Mus.; 1.83×1.27 m).

In Kurdistan to the south of Azerbaijan such types as Hamadan, Senna (Sanandaj) and Bijar (Bidjar) were made. These carpets are distinguished by their technical variety, ranging from the sturdy, hard-wearing quality of many Hamadan carpets (e.g. London, V&A, 363–1897; 3.71× 1.81 m) to the astonishing fineness and suppleness associated with the relatively small, asymmetrically knotted carpets of Senna (e.g. Berlin, Mus. Islam. Kst, 35,179; 3.11×1.51 m, with 2030 knots per sq. decimetre). The single weft between each row of knots gives the back of

Senna carpets a distinctive granular texture. Senna also produced flat-woven carpets of extraordinary fineness (e.g. London, V&A, 321-1896; 1.87×1.36 m), and production there was apparently less affected by the Western market than elsewhere. The extremely thick and stiff carpets associated with Bijar were woven on a wool foundation with closely set warps and tightly beaten knots (e.g. Amherst Coll., MA, Mead A. Mus.; 8.23×4.57 m).

The district to the south-east of Hamadan around Arak became a major centre of commercial production in the 19th century, particularly after Ziegler & Co. established its enterprise there. It was largely a home-based industry, employing weavers in towns and surrounding villages; only gradually were factories established in the cities. The 19th-century carpets of Sarouk are finely woven small carpets with traditional floral medallion designs in a limited range of muted colours, including pink. Other names applied to carpets of the district include Sultanabad and Ziegler (carpets primarily made for Europeans), and

210. Faraghan carpet, wool knotted pile, 2.84×1.71 m, from Iran, second half of the 19th century (Berlin, Museum für Islamische Kunst)

Faraghan (Ferahan) and Lilihan, villages in the surrounding district. Faraghan carpets (e.g. Berlin, Mus. Islam. Kst, with 1400 knots per sq. decimetre; see fig. 210) are finely woven with designs based on the traditional *herati* pattern, derived from the International Timurid style of the 15th and 16th centuries.

The city of Kashan in central Iran had been a centre of carpet production in Safavid times, and in the late 19th century workshops in the surrounding villages began to produce velvety wool and occasionally silk carpets based on traditional designs for both local and Western markets (e.g. Berlin, Mus. Islam. Kst, I.6/78; 1.90×1.46 m; with 5000 knots per sq. decimetre). Kirman had also been a centre of carpet production since the 16th century, but in the 19th century large carpets were produced there for the Western market. They are distinguished by subdued colours, fine weave (up to 5500 knots per sq. decimetre) and hard-wearing qualities. Designs (e.g. Washington, DC, Textile Mus., 1969.52.1; 2.52×2.11 m, with 7500 knots per sq. decimetre) were often transferred from the famous goat-hair shawls of Kirman, although other patterns were based on floral medallions, flowering trees, interpretations of classical Iranian and European carpets, and pictorial themes.

The supple and thin carpets of the province of Khurasan in north-east Iran are often known after Mashhad, its principal city. They have a common structure of asymmetrical knots around two pairs (Pers. *juftī*) of cotton warps, three shoots of cotton weft between each row of knots, and side finishes of a single bundle of warps, usually overcast in red. The distinctive and intense palette of pinky red, pale blue and ivory is often set against a dark blue ground, with a typical *herati* design (e.g. London, V&A, 256-1892; 5.12×2.66 m). Other typical designs include zigzag floral scrolls (e.g. a carpet made in Mashhad in 1876; London, V&A, 839.1877).

Carpets produced by nomads throughout Iran are generally smaller and more geometric in design than their urban counterparts. The carpets are generally loosely woven and knotted in brilliantly coloured soft wool, showing an astonishing variety of designs and techniques. Such nomad groups as the Qashqa'i and the Bakhtiari in south-west Iran continued to weave traditional pieces into the 20th century. Qashqa'i carpets, generally identified with Shiraz, the main marketing centre, often bear geometricized figural motifs; the ends are often extra weft-brocaded with herringbone or chequered stripes. Bakhtiari carpets are distinguished by bright colours and compartmentalized patterns; the loosely strung warps and tightly pulled single wefts give them a granular texture similar to but much coarser than that of Hamadan carpets. Nomadic carpets were relatively unaffected by the commercialization of production in the 19th century and were not discovered by collectors until the 20th century. In south-east Iran the Afshar produced large carpets with European-style floral designs in the 19th century; Baluch carpets show a limited palette of varying shades of red and blue, and sometimes beige. Nomads also produced many flatweaves in a variety of techniques, from interlocking tapestry to sumak brocading (*see* KILIM).

BIBLIOGRAPHY

Enc. Iran.: 'Carpets X–XI'

J. Housego: 'The 19th Century Persian Carpet Boom', *Orient. A.*, n. s., xix/2 (1973), pp. 169–71

——: *Tribal Rugs* (London, 1978)

P. Fontaine: 'The Carpet Weaving Industry in the Arak Region: Permanence and Change in the Technical Organization of Production', *Orient. Carpet & Textile Stud.*, iii (1987), pp. 52–64

L. M. Helfgott: 'Production and Trade: The Persian Carpet Industry', *Woven from the Soul, Spun from the Heart: Textile Arts of Safavid and Qajar Iran: 16th–19th Centuries*, ed. C. Bier (Washington, DC, 1987), pp. 107–20

J. Housego: '18th-century Persian Carpets: Continuity and Change', *Orient. Carpet & Textile Stud.*, iii (1987), pp. 40–51

——: 'Carpets', *The Arts of Persia*, ed. R. W. Ferrier (New Haven and London, 1989), pp. 118–56

SHEILA S. BLAIR, JONATHAN M. BLOOM

(d) Western Central Asia. Fine knotted carpets and related textiles were produced after 1700 by the tribes who migrated seasonally in search of pasture for their flocks and herds. Unlike their counterparts elsewhere in the Islamic lands, these carpets are almost exclusively the products of tribal weavers, although many are erroneously named after Bukhara (Bokara), the main market centre. More generally known as Turkoman (Turkmen) carpets after the predominant ethnic group, these carpets can be distinguished from Anatolian, Caucasian and Iranian examples by the presence of the characteristic *gul* (*göl*), an octagonal medallion of variable shape, often decorated with geometric patterns or stylized animals and birds (see fig. 211). The medallions are arranged in regular rows of dominant and subordinate elements, and the resulting

211. Salor Turkoman carpet, wool knotted pile, 3.22×2.50 m, from western Central Asia, first half of the 19th century (New York, Metropolitan Museum of Art)

infinite-repeat patterns invite comparison with Small-pattern Holbein carpets attributed to 15th- and 16th-century Anatolia (see §(iii)(a) above), although the history of Turkoman carpet weaving before the late 18th century remains a matter of lively conjecture.

Following their conquest of the area in the mid-19th century the Russians gave scholarly attention to traditional Turkoman tribal weaving and published several studies in the second half of the century. The Russian governor of Transcaspia, General A. A. Bogolyubov, for example, amassed and published his collection from all the major tribal groups, which formed the basis for the collection in the State Museum of Ethnography in St Petersburg. Turkoman weavings are usually classified according to tribe and type. Up to the Russian conquest, the most important tribe to weave carpets was the Salor (Salur); the other main tribes were the Tekke (the dominant tribe), the Saryk, the Chodor (Chaudor), the Arabatchi and the Yomut. European and American scholarship on the subject developed considerably in the late 20th century, but there is still no consensus of opinion about the classification of patterns, symbolism of design and origin of motifs. As motifs were often exchanged among tribes and modified over time, technical characteristics are a surer guide to distinguishing the products of particular tribal groups.

In all types of Turkoman carpets, warp, weft (usually two) and pile yarns are Z-spun and S-plied. Red predominates as the ground colour, because of the ubiquitous use of madder root and insect dyes. Different dyeing techniques, however, and the use of mordants, most commonly alum, produced many shades of red, ranging from dark walnut brown through mahogany to purple-crimson and brilliant scarlet. The red ground is complemented by blue, green, yellow, ivory (undyed), brown and orange. Natural dyes were used until the late 19th century, when the introduction of aniline dyes resulted in harsher tones. Pile and foundation are usually sheep's wool, although goat or other animal hair is sometimes used. Silk and occasionally cotton, purchased from merchants, are sometimes employed for small accents in the pile. Various knots are used among the different tribal groups: Salor pieces have asymmetrical knots open to the left and sometimes right, and closely packed warps on two levels; Tekke carpets have symmetrical or asymmetrical knots open to the right, often with a single weft; Saryk carpets have symmetrical knots; Yomut and Ersari carpets may have any of the three types of knots; while Arabatchi and Chodor carpets have both types of symmetrical knots.

Turkoman tribal weavings include knotted pile and tapestry weavings for use as tent furnishings and animal trappings. The extreme popularity of these pieces among 20th-century collectors and the wide range of uses to which they were put have led to a bewildering variety of terms in the literature. In general, large pile carpets (khali, chaly) and flatweaves were laid on the floor. Felts were used on the floor and as tent walls (see FELT). Tents were decorated with door-hangings (ensi, engsi), door surrounds (kapunuk, deslik) and horizontal bands. Storage bags (torba) ranged in size from the larger chuval (juval, tschowal) to the smaller mafrash. Pentagonal animal trappings (asmalyk), sometimes embroidered, and rectangular

ones (kejebe, kedshebe) were woven for special occasions, as were trappings for the bridal litter (khalyk).

For more information and additional bibliography see CENTRAL ASIA, §I, 6(iii).

BIBLIOGRAPHY
Enc. Iran.: 'Carpets XVI'
A. A. Bogolyubov: Kovry Sredney Azii [Carpets of Central Asia] (St Petersburg, 1908; Eng. trans., ed. J. M. A. Thompson, Ramsdell, 1973)
V. G. Moshkova: Kovry narodov Sredney Azii kontsa XIX–nachala XX vv. Materialy ekspeditsii 1929–1945 godov [Carpets of Central Asia of the late 19th and early 20th centuries. Materials found by the expedition of 1929–45] (Tashkent, 1970)
S. Azadi: Turkoman Carpets and the Ethnographic Significance of their Ornaments, trans. R. Pinner (Fishguard, 1975)
R. Pinner and M. Frances, eds: Turkoman Studies (London, 1980)
Turkmen Tribal Carpets and Traditions (exh. cat., ed. L. Mackie and J. Thompson; Washington, DC, Textile Mus., 1980)
W. Denny: 'Turkoman Rugs and the Origins of Rug Weaving in the Western Islamic World', Hali, iv/4 (1982), pp. 329–37
L. Tsareva: Rugs and Carpets from Central Asia (Leningrad, 1984)
W. Kupke and others: Like Flowers in the Desert: The Culture of Turkmen Nomadic Tribes of Central Asia (Hamburg, 1993)

CAROLYN KANE

(e) Indian subcontinent. With the decline of the Mughal empire, production shifted to such provinces as Rajasthan, the Punjab, Kashmir, Avadh, Bengal and the Deccan, where copies of earlier carpet types were made. Particularly popular were millefleurs designs (e.g. a Kashmiri carpet, New York, Met., 1970.302.7), which have often been confused with contemporary work in southern Iran (see §(c) above). By the mid-19th century few knotted carpets were made in north India, although fine millefleurs carpets continued to be made in the Deccan and vast quantities of cotton flatweaves (dari, dhurrie) were produced. Increased European and American interest in carpets spurred a revival of the craft in the second half of the 19th century, and factories were established at Srinagar, Amritsar, Mirzapur and Agra. The most successful were the prison workshops, which were not required to be profitable.

For more information and bibliography see INDIAN SUBCONTINENT, §VIII, 4.

(f) North Africa. The early history of carpets in North Africa is obscure. According to a 14th-century source, the Aghlabid ruler of Kairouan sent 120 large carpets (Arab. busut) as tribute to the Abbasid caliph al-Ma'mun (reg 813–33), and these must have been precious objects. The geographer Yaqut (1171–1229) described busut from the region of Tebessa in eastern Algeria as sumptuous, well-made and long-lasting. The carpets of Tlemcen in western Algeria are mentioned in several later sources, both Islamic and European. None of the texts, however, gives any indication of the type of carpet, design or colour. Carpet-weavers may have been among the emigrés from southern Spain to north-west Africa after the fall of the Kingdom of Granada in 1492, bringing with them the distinctive techniques of Spanish carpet-weaving (see CARPET, §II, 2(i) and SPAIN, §XI, 1), and the Ottoman domination of most of the region from the mid-16th century introduced Anatolian carpets (see §(iii)(a) above) to North Africa. Nevertheless, the earliest surviving carpets from the region can only be attributed to the 19th century, although one scholar has used structure, format and design to assign a group of Mamluk carpets (*see* §(iii)(b) above) to north-west Africa in the 14th, 15th and 16th centuries.

The long tradition of carpet production in North Africa is confirmed by the weavings of the BERBER tribes, generally very conservative, who produced pile carpets using diverse and sometimes original procedures. The white woollen *tanchra*, a thick, loop-knotted carpet, which could be used as a mattress, of the Mzab region in central Algeria, has long, barely twisted tufts coiled into loops which stand out from the warp and are held in place by the weft. Measuring some 1.85×2.1 m, these carpets have no decoration and are thought to imitate sheepskins. The knotted carpets used in tents known as *qtif* or *qatifa*, made by nomads throughout the region, are more refined in technique and design, but are based on the same principles. Specialized male weavers (*reggam*) tie the knots, while women behind the loom cut the loops, shear the surface, and beat the weft tight with a special heavy comb. These very long carpets (*c.* 2×6 m) have red grounds and geometric patterns in many colours. They are made in Tunisia by the Hamama and Mahadba tribes and in Algeria by the Nemencha and Harakta tribes in the region south of Constantine. Those made in the Djebel Amour to the south of Oran have geometric decoration in blue or black pectinate lines and woven bands of various colours at both ends; they remained true to local tradition into the 20th century.

The Berber pile carpets of the High and Middle Atlas mountains in Morocco are similar to the *qtif* and show an extraordinary variety. The carpets produced in the Haouz, the plains surrounding Marrakesh, are also known as Chichaoua carpets after the town some 70 km south-west of the city. These large (2.2×5.5 m maximum) carpets with overlapping rows of coarse symmetrical knots have red grounds with sombre decoration of triangles, squares or even figures in green, browns or orange. The fine carpets of the Aït Ouaouzguit, made by the Glaoua tribes of the High Atlas Mountains to the south of Marrakesh, have more elaborate compositions: narrow borders enclose a field filled with a single lozenge or a lattice forming lozenges in various colours on a red or brown ground. The carpets range in size from small rectangular or square pieces meant to be used as prayer- and saddle-rugs to large (1.5×4.5 m) examples used as floor coverings and mattresses. The knotted carpets of the tribes inhabiting the Middle Atlas Mountains have a high pile (80 mm maximum). Various kinds of knots are used, including distinctive Berber or overlapping knots, tied around four warps. The designs also vary widely. Zemmour carpets have a red ground and very regular patterns, while others have designs of diamond patterns with pectinate lines. Zaïane carpets have multicoloured diamond patterns on a red ground, those of the Beni M'tir have parallel vertical bands, those of the Beni Mguild have a red ground with decoration often reduced to sparse elements on a white ground, and those of the Marmoucha have decoration of pectinate lines.

The best known of the urban pile carpets (Arab. *zerbiya, sajjada*) are those of Kairouan in Tunisia, which began to be produced in the 18th or 19th century. Their designs, with borders of stylized kufic script enclosing a central elongated hexagon, are modelled on those of Anatolian carpets, but Kairouan carpets are not as finely woven (4 knots per sq. cm). The introduction of aniline dyes in the late 19th century led to a decline in quality; in the 20th century fine undyed carpets (*alloucha*) began to be woven in shades of white, beige, brown and grey wool. Algerian Guergour carpets are similarly dependent on Anatolian prototypes, particularly Gördes carpets (see fig. 205 above). These large carpets (1.5–2×4–5 m) have red grounds with motifs woven in shades of green, blue, yellow, pink and white. The *qtif* of the Bedouin also became dependent on Anatolian models, featuring large central lozenges with corner-pieces decorated with such floral motifs as carnations and tulips. Carpets were also produced at Rabat and Mediouna (near Casablanca) in Morocco, beginning in the late 18th century. The finest may have 19 knots per sq. cm and, like most North African carpets, are long and narrow (e.g. Rabat, Mus. A. Maroc., 1968–9–1; 5.14×1.89 m; 19th century). They generally have red grounds and show a wide variety of colours, including yellow, orange, green, blue and brown. Their designs recall those of Gördes carpets, but compositions are stiffer. Mediouna carpets have a longer pile and brighter colours; the field design of three large medallions overwhelms the borders. The carpets from Qal'at Bani Rashid to the south-east of Oran have designs of multiple compartments and a finely nuanced colour range. They are presumably related to the carpets of Andalusia, as Andalusians emigrated to this region in the 16th century, but they also share similarities with the carpets of the Djebel Amour. Carpets have been made in factories at Tlemcen since the beginning of the 20th century and are a great commercial success, although they retain no element of traditional production. The commercial production of pile carpets has been established throughout North Africa in the 20th century.

Flat-woven carpets (*klim, mergoum*) have remained faithful to the tradition of purely geometrical decoration and are some of the most distinctive weavings from North Africa. The heavy *mergoum*s of Kairouan often have a pale green ground and a design of parallel zigzag bands or a more complicated pattern of chevrons and diamonds in the field. They also use the pectinate lines so typical of Berber art. Similar weavings are also produced in the Tunisian Sahel (e.g. the *ksaya* or wall-covering and *mouchtiya* or shawl of El Djem) and in the south where they share similarities with the flatweavings of Tripolitania (*klim trabelsi*). At Gafsa in central Tunisia, the distinctive bright weavings have bold geometric designs, often including lines of camels and even people. In the region south of Constantine, very long, magnificently decorated hangings (*draga*) served to separate men from women in the tent. Similar pieces were known in the Djebel Amour as *tag*. The variety and splendour of Moroccan flat-woven carpets (see fig. 212) exceed those produced elsewhere in the Maghrib. Woven in both the High and Middle Atlas mountains, they are the glory of museums in Marrakesh, Fez, Meknès and Rabat, and are vibrant proof of the high quality of Berber art. Other flat-woven textiles of the Bedouin include the *flij*, a long (0.5–0.8 ×7–12 m) band of wool mixed with goat or camel hair. Undecorated or striped examples were sewn together to form the roof of the tent; more elaborately decorated pieces were sewn

212. Flat-woven *hanbel* (blanket or floorcovering; detail), 4.63× 1.90m, Berber, from the Middle Atlas Mountains, Morocco, *c.* 1930 (Meknès, Musée Dar Jamai et Palais)

together as floor coverings. Among the most beautiful are the hangings of Oulad Naïl (in the region of Laghouat, Algeria), which have red grounds and geometric patterns in orange, green and yellow.

BIBLIOGRAPHY

P. Ricard: *Corpus des tapis marocains*, 4 vols (Paris, 1923–34)
R. P. Giacobetti: *Les Tapis et tissages du Djebel-Amour* (Paris, 1932)
L. Poinssot and J. Revault: *Tapis tunisiens*, 4 vols (Paris, 1937–57)
L. Golvin: *Les Arts populaires en Algérie*, 6 vols (Algiers, 1950–56)
From the Far West: Carpets and Textiles of Morocco (exh. cat., ed. P. L. Fiske, W. R. Pickering and R. S. Yohe; Washington, DC, Textile Mus., 1980)
I. Reswick: *Traditional Textiles of Tunisia and Related North African Weavings* (Los Angeles, 1985)
J. Housego: 'Literary References to Carpets in North Africa', *Orient, Carpet & Textile Stud.*, ii (1986), pp. 103–8
——: ' "Mamluk" Carpets and North Africa', *Orient. Carpet & Textile Stud.*, ii (1986), pp. 221–42

LUCIEN GOLVIN

VII. Woodwork.

Despite the scarcity of the raw material and the virtual absence of domestic furniture, woodwork occupied an unusually important place among the arts of the Islamic world. The mountain forests of Syria, North Africa and Spain were famous for their stands of cypress, cedar and pine, but Iraq and Egypt, equally important as woodworking centres, had to import wood from Syria, the Sudan or India. Only in Central Asia, northern Iran, Anatolia, the Balkans, Morocco and Spain was wood available in sufficient quantity to allow its free use for timber-frame construction. It was widely but sparingly used throughout the region for ceilings, lintels, doors and screens, and the high cost of the material encouraged techniques such as marquetry and grillework that minimized waste through the use of small pieces of wood. In a society that preferred cushions and rugs to chairs and benches, domestic wooden furniture was limited to small low tables and chests, but mosques were often provided with fine wooden minbars (pulpits; *see* MINBAR), *maqsūra*s (screened enclosures for the ruler; *see* MAQSURA), bookcases and reading stands and storage-boxes for manuscripts of the Koran. These mosque furnishings provide the best source for the study of technical and stylistic evolution. A considerable amount of Islamic woodwork has survived, as the inherent perishability of wood was countered by the aridity of the climate in many parts of the Islamic world; the religious function of the objects has also helped to preserve them owing to the longevity of the institutions to which they belonged and the respect with which they were treated.

1. Before *c.* 1250. 2. After *c.* 1250.

1. BEFORE *c.* 1250. At the beginning of the Islamic period (7th–8th centuries AD) Africa, Anatolia and northern Iran were still heavily forested, and wood was an essential material for shipbuilding, carpentry and joinery throughout the Islamic world: even the Damascus oasis produced enough poplar for reinforcement timbers to be commonly used in local construction in Syria. Deforestation, however, began to affect the availability of wood in the eastern Mediterranean and led to the afforestation programme instituted by the Fatimid dynasty (*reg* 969–1171) and its Ayyubid successors (*reg* 1169–1252) in Egypt. By the end of the period wood was so scarce and expensive that it had to be imported. The export of timber from Catholic Europe to Islamic lands was periodically banned by the Pope to prevent its use for building warships, but on at least one occasion the Venetians circumvented this embargo by exporting wood in sizes that were useless for shipbuilding. The increasing scarcity of wood, particularly in Syria and Egypt, may explain the change in taste from the use of large planks carved with arabesques to tongue-and-groove strapwork panels and turned screens composed of small pieces arranged in geometric patterns (Arab. *mashrabiyya*). Such strapwork appears on pieces made in the 11th century in Syria, Egypt, Spain and North Africa.

Five different decorative techniques were employed: joining (methods included mortice and tenon, tongue and groove, dowelling or pinning, scarfing, and dovetailing); carving, which was usually done with a vertical cut until a new style with a bevelled cut developed at Samarra' in Iraq *c.* AD 850 (*see* BEVELLED STYLE); turning, few examples of which survive from before *c.* 1250; inlay and mosaic work done with ivory, bone and precious woods set in geometric patterns and fixed with glue or wooden dowels; and painting, known from the traces that survive on many objects.

Native woods used included sycamore, jujube, tamarisk and *Acacia nilotica*, along with such acclimatized species as padauk, East Indian rosewood (*Dalbergia latifolia*), pudding pipe tree (*Cassia fistula*), cypress and lime. The date palm, whose fibrous strands mean that it is hardly wood at all, was regularly used for rafters in Egypt, but was boxed in with thin planks, which were then painted or carved. Aleppo and parasol pines, oak, birch, box, walnut and poplar were imported from Asia Minor and Europe, teak from East Asia and shea (karite) from the Sudan. Ebony came from India or the Sudan. These woods tended to be used where they were most readily available: African ebony was used more often in Egypt, teak more commonly in Iraq. In 11th-century Egypt, the principal materials were holm-oak and cypress, and such precious woods as East Indian rosewood, padauk, African ebony and *Cassia fistula* were used for inlay. Although several varieties of wood were readily available in Anatolia, only a few isolated pieces of Anatolian woodwork survive from the period before 1250; these are discussed with the more numerous later examples in §2(iii) below.

BIBLIOGRAPHY

W. Heyd: *Histoire du commerce du Levant au Moyen Age*, 2 vols (Leipzig, 1885–6)

M. Lombard: 'Arsenaux et bois de marine dans la Méditerranée musulmane (VIIe–IXe siècles)', *Le Navire et l'économie maritime du Moyen Age au XVIIIe siècle* (Paris, 1958)

□

(i) Egypt, Syria and Iraq. (ii) Iran and western Central Asia. (iii) Spain and North Africa.

(i) Egypt, Syria and Iraq.

(a) Before *c.* AD 1000. (b) *c.* 1000–*c.* 1250.

(a) Before c. AD *1000.* Large rectangular wooden panels and planks prepared using techniques and decorative motifs taken over from Late Antiquity have survived from the period between the rise of Islam (early 7th century AD) and *c.* 850. The outstanding pieces are the several dozen carved panels from the Aqsa Mosque in Jerusalem (900–1100×350–600 mm; now divided, Jerusalem, Islam. Mus. and Rockefeller Mus.). At one time they served as false consoles at the ends of the 20 beams supporting the roof over the central nave, but their original position in the mosque is unknown. Four decorative elements reminiscent of Late Antique ornament are found: architectural forms, particularly a pair of columns supporting an arch; vases and baskets; plant elements such as fruits and leaves; and geometric designs, including lozenges and circles. Their stylized vegetal motifs juxtapose contrary elements (e.g. grapes with acanthus leaves) and superimpose fruits and leaves on other leaves. The fields between the carved panels are painted with blue and white motifs outlined in black. Related fragments have been found at sites in Syria, Jordan and Egypt.

A smaller group of panels bears elements derived from Sasanian art, particularly winged motifs and pine-cones; the motifs are smaller, flatter and more densely packed into their frames. On stylistic grounds these pieces have been attributed to the second half of the 8th century AD, when the political centre of the Islamic world shifted from Syria to Iraq. This transitional style is best exemplified by a rectangular panel, probably teak, found at the 'Ayn al-Sira cemetery near Cairo (320×1920 mm; Cairo, Mus. Islam. A., 2462). Narrow bands carved with a Koranic inscription in Kufic script border a central field of seven compartments separated by lancet leaves or rosettes. Alternating compartments are filled with wing motifs

issuing from paired horns against a ground of vine scrolls with small leaves. The end compartments have a trellis pattern, and the other two compartments have arched niches filled with vegetal motifs. The carving is uniformly flat. A rectangular teak panel found at Takrit in Iraq (New York, Met.) is extraordinarily similar in style and technique.

A third style, characterized by greater relief in carving, is seen on pieces found throughout the central Islamic lands. Those found in Iraq include fragments from a door or portable minbar (h. 1.79 m; New York, Met., 31-63-1), a pair of doors (each leaf 2.25×1.23 m; Athens, Benaki Mus., 9121) and part of a door frame (Baghdad, Iraq Mus.), but the major examples are still *in situ*: a double door in the monastery of St Macarius (Deir Abu Maqar) in the Wadi Natrun of Egypt and the teak minbar in the Great Mosque of Kairouan in Tunisia. The Kairouan minbar, the oldest in existence (AD 862–3; 3.31×3.93 m), has a triangular framework held together by mortice-and-tenon joinery. Each side consists of 17 upright beams supporting 52 rectangular panels arranged in a triangle and is surmounted by a balustrade with 17 additional panels. The openwork panels are mostly decorated with geometrical or arabesque grilles, carved with the utmost delicacy in several planes. While most of the individual design elements, such as the five-lobed leaf, pine-cone, acanthus whorl and winged motif, are known from earlier examples, here they are combined and integrated in designs of unparalleled richness. A later report that Abu Ibrahim Ahmad, the Aghlabid governor of Kairouan from 856 to 863, had teak brought from Baghdad and made into a minbar probably refers to these panels.

The first distinctly Islamic style of wood-carving emerged in the mid-9th century at the Abbasid capital at Samarra' in Iraq, where wooden doors and panels were carved in the Bevelled style. This form of endlessly repeating arabesques carved with a distinctive slanted cut is based on abstracted vegetal forms, but the distinction between background and foreground has disappeared. The style is exemplified by a pair of teak doors (New York, Met., 31.119.3–4; see fig. 213), each with four rectangular panels set in a plain wooden frame. Each panel is carved with a pear-shaped form from which spring kidney-shaped leaves, a trilobed leaf and a split palmette; the 'pears' rest on volutes ending in trilobed palmettes. This court style was imitated throughout the Abbasid realm. In Egypt it is identified with the patronage of the TULUNID dynasty (*reg* 868–905), but the Egyptian version of the Bevelled style incorporated several new features. Broad surfaces were subdivided, a narrow bead was introduced to emphasize smaller elements, and the abstracted vegetal motifs of the Iraqi style were often transformed into recognizable birds and occasionally into animals. Arched panels, for example one in Cairo (h. 580 mm; Mus. Islam. A., 13173), usually depict confronted or addorsed birds. The well-known panel in Paris (h. 0.73 m; Louvre) depicting a duck-like bird whose bill and body transmute into palmettes and calyxes may once have had a mate. Friezes were decorated with bands of paired birds (e.g. Cairo, Mus. Islam. A., 6280–2, with traces of paint) or bevelled palmette scrolls and inscriptions (e.g. Cairo, Mus. Islam. A., 3498). A great quantity of woodwork survives at the mosque of Ibn Tulun (876–9; *see* CAIRO,

213. Pair of teak doors, each 2.64×0.47 m, from Samarra', 9th century (New York, Metropolitan Museum of Art)

§III, 2). A frieze inscribed with verses from the Koran in Kufic script (letter h. 150–90 mm) ran above the interior arcades, just below the roof; its original length was an

astounding 1988 m. Other panels carved with geometric and non-figural ornament in the Bevelled style decorate the door frames and ceiling. The Bevelled style continued to be used in Egypt during the 10th century, but few major buildings were erected, and few dated pieces have survived.

BIBLIOGRAPHY

J. David-Weill: *Les Bois à épigraphes jusqu'à l'époque mamlouke* (Cairo, 1931)

E. Pauty: *Les Bois sculptés jusqu'à l'époque ayyoubide* (Cairo, 1931)

M. Dimand: 'Arabic Woodcarvings of the Ninth Century', *Bull. Met.*, xxvii (1932), pp. 135–7

——: 'Studies in Islamic Ornament', *A. Islam.*, iv (1937), pp. 293–337

K. A. C. Creswell: *Early Muslim Architecture*, ii (Oxford, 1940), pp. 317–19, pls 89–90

G. Marçais: 'The Panels of Carved Wood in the Aqsa Mosque at Jerusalem', in K. A. C. Creswell: *Early Muslim Architecture*, ii (Oxford, 1940), pp. 127–37

F. Shafi 'i: 'Al-akhshāb al-muzakhrafa fi'l-ṭirāz al-umawī' [Decorated woodwork in the Umayyad style], *Bull. Fac. A., Fouad I U.*, xiv/2 (1952), pp. 65–112

H. Stern: 'Quelques Oeuvres sculptées en bois, os et ivoire de style omeyyade', *A. Orient.*, i (1954), pp. 119–30

M. F. Abu Khalaf: *The Early Islamic Woodwork in Egypt and the Fertile Crescent* (DPhil. thesis, Oxford U., 1985)

R. Hillenbrand: 'Umayyad woodwork in the Aqsa Mosque', *Bayt al-Maqdis: 'Abd al-Malik's Jerusalem*, ed. J. Raby and J. Johns (in preparation), ix/2 of *Oxford Studies in Islamic Art* (Oxford, 1985–)

MARWAN F. ABU KHALAF

(b) c. *1000–*c. *1250.* The relatively large quantity of Egyptian and Syrian woodwork surviving from this period makes it possible to delineate its stylistic evolution with far greater precision than for the contemporary period in Iraq. Under the Fatimid dynasty (*reg* 969–1171) woodcarvers continued to use the Bevelled style which had been imported into Egypt in the Tulunid period (*see* §(a) above), as on a pair of doors ordered for the Azhar Mosque in Cairo by the caliph al-Hakim in 1010 (Cairo, Mus. Islam. A.). Each leaf is composed of seven carved rectangular panels set within a simple mortised frame, and all but the two panels bearing the inscription are decorated with retardataire vegetal arabesques. The style was soon superseded: a wooden screen from the church of St Barbara (Sitt Barbara) in Cairo, attributed to approximately the same date (Cairo, Coptic Mus.), shows new elements, such as figural representations, which became typical somewhat later. The vine and vase motifs on the screen, undoubtedly inspired by the same motifs on a 6th-century Coptic door in the church (*see* COPTIC ART, fig. 8), are considered to be a distinguishing feature of Egyptian woodwork.

The same type of layout can be seen in examples from the mid-11th century, such as the sanctuary screen in the chapel of the convent of St George (Deir Mari Girgis) in Old Cairo. This has 73 carved panels set in a plain rectangular matrix and displayed on the valves of the doors and the doorcase; the four panels joined diagonally at the top left and right are cut down, showing that all the panels are reused. Two teak panels from unidentified doors (330×215 mm; Cairo, Mus. Islam. A.; see fig. 214; and New York, Met.) have arabesques terminating in paired horses' heads. The bridles and medallions are outlined with beaded bands; the carving is deeply undercut. Panels of deeply carved symmetrical arabesques continued to be popular in Cairo until the end of the Fatimid period, as on a set of cupboard doors for the Aqmar Mosque

214. Carved teak door panel, 330×215 mm, from Egypt, 11th century (Cairo, Museum of Islamic Art)

(1125) and doors to the Fakahani Mosque (1148–9). Eleventh-century woodwork is best known, however, for a figural style whose subject-matter included scenes of princely pleasures, Christian saints and everyday life. It was used in both secular and Christian contexts, and the most important examples are the numerous carved boards thought to have encased ceiling beams in the 'Lesser' or 'Western' Palace of the Fatimid caliphs in Cairo. The boards may have been ordered by the caliph al-Mustansir when he restored the palace between 1058 and 1065. The palace was razed some two centuries later to make way for the complexes of Sultan Qala'un and his son al-Nasir Muhammad, in both of which the boards were later reused; their reuse emphasizes the great value of large pieces of wood. One leaf of a door and over 31 m of carved boards (300 mm wide) are preserved (most in Cairo, Mus. Islam. A.). The boards, bordered by intermittent scrolls, contain a frieze of alternating hexagonal and rhomboidal cartouches formed by intertwining fillets. The cartouches have a foliate ground set with representations of peacocks, hares, gazelles, birds of prey, ducks, griffins, harpies and sphinxes, as well as those of princes, warriors, falconers, banqueters, musicians and merchants. Detailing was achieved by paint on a gesso ground, as is shown in some traces. Almost identical carved boards (two in Cairo, Coptic Mus.; one in New York, Met.) once decorated the convent of St George (Deir Mari Girgis) in Old Cairo.

Marquetry, a very different technique, was used in contemporary Syrian woodwork. Large panels were typically formed of angular interlacing strapwork radiating from central stars. The earliest extant example (1091–2) is the minbar ordered by the Fatimid vizier Badr al-Jamali for the shrine of Husayn at Ascalon (later transferred to Hebron, mosque of Abraham). The triangular fields on either side of the minbar are decorated with a geometric interlace of hexagons and hexagrams delineated by scrolled bands, and the interstices are filled with richly carved delicate arabesques. Turned-work panels form the railings on either side of the stairs.

Marquetry soon became popular in Egypt, where two masterpieces were produced—the portable wooden mihrab made for the shrine of Sayyida Nafisa in Cairo (1138–47; Mus. Islam. A.) and the minbar ordered by the vizier al-Salih Tala'i' for the 'Amri Mosque at Qus in 1155–6. The slender niche of the mihrab is carved with strapwork and lacy arabesques and is set within a rectangular field delineated by inscriptions in floriated Kufic. Within the rectangular field grooved laths intersect to form a geometric pattern of stars, elongated hexagons and T-shapes; the interstices are filled with arabesque motifs which are similar to those in the niche and contrast sharply with the moulded strapwork patterns. On the minbar at Qus patterns based on a similar hexagonal system of strapwork and stars cover the whole of each side. The grooved mouldings intersect but do not overlap, and the angular strapwork contrasts sharply with the curved arabesque filler motifs.

The finest marquetry, however, was apparently produced in Syria at Aleppo, where several masters and their sons signed works. The mihrab (1167–8) of the Maqam Ibrahim in the citadel of Aleppo is the work of Ma'ali ibn Salam, who used three different patterns for the frame, semi-dome and lower niche, each striking in its boldness. Most of the rest of the woodwork in the building has perished: the lintels over the windows had similar patterns, but the most intricate was on a panel above a side door, which had strapwork revolving around 11-pointed rather than the usual 8-, 10- or 12-pointed stars. Such complexity was never repeated again. Ma'ali's son Salman was one of four artisans from the same Aleppan workshop who signed the minbar (destr.) made in 1168–9 for the Aqsa Mosque in Jerusalem. Commissioned by Nur al-Din, the Zangid ruler of Aleppo, in anticipation of taking Jerusalem from the Crusaders, the minbar was moved there by his nephew Salah al-Din (Saladin) after he captured the city in 1187. The extensive use of inlaid ivory, both for the outlines of the polygonal figures and for some of the smaller interstitial stars, predates by a century the similar use of ivory on Mamluk minbars (*see* §2(ii) below).

The wealth of woodwork in the mausoleum of Imam al-Shafi'i in the southern cemetery of Cairo (1211; *see* CAIRO, §III, 6) exemplifies the ways in which wood was used and decorated under the Ayyubids. The cenotaphs, screens, doors, coffers, friezes, beams, brackets, pendentives and dome are all made of wood; the finest piece is the cenotaph of al-Shafi'i himself (*see* CENOTAPH, §2), which Salah al-Din commissioned in 1178. It is signed by 'Ubayd ibn Ma'ali, who probably came from the Aleppan family responsible for the mihrab in the Maqam Ibrahim and the minbar in the Aqsa Mosque. The overall design, the inscriptions and especially the floriate polygons are of the highest quality, and it outshines Salah al-Din's own cenotaph in Damascus (1195). Shafi'i's mausoleum was commissioned by Salah al-Din's nephew al-Kamil in honour of his mother, who was also buried there; her cenotaph, together with several pieces of a surrounding screen (Cairo, Mus. Islam. A.), is still extant. Apart from a magnificent openwork Kufic inscription which ran around the upper part (largely destr.), al-Kamil's mother's cenotaph is a pale reflection of that of al-Shafi'i made three decades earlier. Three pairs of doors from the mausoleum of al-Shafi'i also survive: one, on the inner face of the present entrance, has a radiating strapwork pattern; another (Cairo, Mus. Islam. A.) consists of large rectangular panels, exquisitely carved with arabesques, but juxtaposed in the manner of earlier Fatimid woodwork. The doors of the original entrance, now a window, could easily be mistaken for those of a century earlier, but the octagonal wooden coffers above them are the first in a series that continued through later Mamluk architecture. A wooden frieze ran around the dome chamber above the dado, connecting the projecting beams from which oil lamps were suspended; both the beams and the frieze are carved with an exuberant floriated Kufic script on a spiral background.

What little Iraqi woodwork survives from this period shows that woodworkers continued the traditions of carving seen in the 9th century (*see* §(a) above). A pair of 12th-century doors from the mosque of Nabi Jirjis in Mosul (2.3×0.62 m; Baghdad, Iraq Mus.) is richly decorated with foliated Kufic inscriptions and fine arabesques reminiscent of the earlier style associated with Takrit. A tamarisk-wood minbar ordered in 1153 for the al-'Amadiyya Mosque in a village near Mosul (2.5×0.96 m; Baghdad, Iraq Mus.) is decorated with rather coarse marquetry and arabesque panels carved in a retardataire Bevelled style. The raised polygonal plaques on the rear are separated by wide flat bands that follow the geometric contours of the plaques; this is the first appearance of a feature found in many later tile mosaic panels. An inscription on a panel parallel to the handrails states that it was the work of three Georgians: 'Ali ibn al-Nahi, Ibrahim ibn Jami' and 'Ali ibn Salama. A mulberry-wood cenotaph was ordered by the Abbasid caliph al-Mustansir in 1227 for the tomb of Musa al-Kazim (*d* 799), the seventh imam of the Twelver Shi'ites (0.95×2.62×1.95 m; Baghdad, Iraq Mus.). Rectangular panels on the sides are deeply carved with elegant foliated and knotted Kufic inscriptions within finely carved arabesque borders.

BIBLIOGRAPHY

M. van Berchem: 'La Chaire de la Mosquée d'Hébron et le martyrion de la tête de Husain à Ascalon', *Festschrift Eduard Sachau* (Berlin, 1915), pp. 298–310

—: *Jérusalem*, Mém.: Inst. Fr. Archéol. Caire, xliv/2 (1927), ii/2 of *Syrie du Sud*, Mat. Corp. Inscrip. Arab., pt ii (Cairo, 1920–27), pp. 393–402

J. David-Weill: *Les Bois à épigraphes jusqu'à l'époque mamlouke* (Cairo, 1931)

E. Pauty: *Les Bois sculptés jusqu'à l'époque ayyoubide* (Cairo, 1931)

G. Wiet: 'Les Inscriptions du mausolée de Shāfi'ī', *Bull. Inst. Egyp.*, xv (1933), pp. 167–85

C. J. Lamm: 'Fatimid Woodwork, its Style and Chronology', *Bull. Inst. Egyp.*, xviii (1935), pp. 59–91

B. Fransis and N. Naqshbandi: 'Al-āthār al-khashab fī Dār al-āthār al-'arabiyya' [Woodwork in the Arab Museum], *Sumer*, v (1949), pp. 55–64

E. Herzfeld: *Inscriptions et monuments d'Alep*, Mém.: Inst. Fr. Archéol. Caire, lxxvi/1–2 (1955–6), ii of *Syrie du Nord*, Mat. Corp. Inscrip. Arab., pt ii (Cairo, 1909–56), pp. 121–8

L. A. Mayer: *Islamic Woodcarvers and their Works* (Geneva, 1958)

S. Dīhwahjī: 'Jāmi' al-Nabī Jirjis fī'l-Mawṣil' [The Mosque of Nabi Jirjis in Mosul], *Sumer*, xvii (1960), pp. 100–12

M. Jenkins: 'An Eleventh-century Woodcarving from a Cairo Nunnery', *Islamic Art in the Metropolitan Museum of Art*, ed. R. Ettinghausen (New York, 1972), pp. 227–40

S. Z. al-Kawākibī: 'Minbar al-Masjid al-aqṣā' [The minbar of the Aqsa Mosque], *Majallat 'Adiyat Ḥalab*, iv–v (1978–9), pp. 31–66

M. F. Abu Khalaf: *The Early Islamic Woodwork in Egypt and the Fertile Crescent* (DPhil. thesis, Oxford U., 1985)

C. Williams: 'The Qur'anic inscriptions on the *Tabut* of al-Husayn in Cairo', *Islam. A.*, ii (1987), pp. 3–14

E. Anglade: *Musée du Louvre: Catalogue des boiseries de la section islamique* (Paris, 1988)

JONATHAN M. BLOOM, BERNARD O'KANE

(ii) Iran and western Central Asia. The history of woodwork in the eastern Islamic lands before the Mongol invasions of the mid-13th century can be pieced together from textual references and a few surviving pieces. Woods such as walnut, plane, juniper, birch, box and erica (Arab. *khalanj*) were available in the mountain forests south of the Caspian Sea and in Central Asia. Cities such as Amul, Rayy, Qum and Isfahan were known for the production of ladles, combs, plough-handles, scales, bowls, platters and deep plates. Few of these everyday objects have survived, but a small turned bowl (diam. 60 mm) datable to the 11th or 12th century was excavated at RIBAT-I SHARAF in north-east Iran. It is decorated with polychrome lacquer depicting seven seated figures (*see* §VIII, 10 below). Wood was also used in the construction of buildings and for architectural furnishings, and the motifs and style of carving are analogous to decorative schemes found in architectural surface ornament, metalwork and textiles of the same period. A 10th-century history of the city of Qum stated that the tomb of a descendant of Imam Ja'far was built of wood, and it is possible that the decorative brickwork of such structures as the 10th-century mausoleum of the Samanids in Bukhara (*see* BUKHARA, §2(i) and fig. 27 above) reflects earlier wooden construction. The earliest datable pieces are architectural fragments that have been incorporated in later buildings, but they come from such a broad geographical region and so few are dated that it is impossible to arrange them stylistically. Many are decorated in the Bevelled style, which remained in vogue well into the 14th century.

Surviving pieces include columns, capitals, beams, mihrabs, minbars, doors, grilles and panels. Several columns, capitals and fragments have been found in village mosques in the Zarafshan Valley in the mountains of Tajikistan. The columns are decorated with carving in the Bevelled style in horizontal bands just below the capitals. The capital from Oburdon (Tashkent, Aybek Hist. Mus.) supported four consoles carved with vegetal elements. Columns from the congregational mosque at Khiva show a wide variety of styles. Four columns decorated with geometric strapwork patterns are inscribed with the name of the patron Abu Fadl Muhallabi, and the style of the simple Kufic script suggests a date *c.* AD 1000. Other columns with finely carved basket- or bell-shaped capitals

215. Wooden mihrab from the mosque at Iskodar, Tajikistan, ?11th century (Dushanbe, Republican Historical, Regional and Fine Arts Museum)

probably date from the late 11th century or the 12th. Three mihrabs have survived. One (1103) in the winter prayer hall of the Maydan Mosque at Abyana in central Iran has a mortised frame containing an arched recess and rectangular panels carved in a variety of styles, particularly the Bevelled style. The two undated mihrabs have panels of varying shapes set side by side. That from Iskodar in the Zarafshan Valley (see fig. 215) is probably 11th century because of its simple Kufic script; that from the mosque of Shah Muhyi'l-Din in Charkh-i Logar in Afghanistan is somewhat later. Both illustrate the amalgamation of decorative motifs from such diverse media as brick, stucco, textiles and metalwork. The mosque at Abyana also preserves a minbar dated 1073 and two wooden capitals attributed to the same date, all finely carved in the Bevelled style. The undated minbar at Muhammadiyya near Nayin probably belongs to the same period.

Tomb furnishings were often of wood. If genuine, the earliest are five wooden panels ordered by the Buyid amir 'Adud al-Dawla in AD 974. Widely varying in size, shape and decoration, they are all inscribed in a similar plain Kufic script. The three largest (Cairo, Mus. Islam. A., and ex-Rabinou priv. col.), which bear the date and patron's name, are carved in a rather flat style and have gabled fields bordered by undulating stems filled with a foliate motif similar to Sasanian palmettes, a pattern derived from

early Islamic vine scrolls. The two smaller ones (Cairo, Mus. Islam. A., and ex-Acheroff priv. col.), inscribed with similar litanies, have keel-shaped arches surrounding deeply cut vegetal arabesques, reminiscent of contemporary Syrian work. A few other funerary pieces are attributed to Buyid patronage (e.g. a cenotaph in Jerusalem, Israel Mus.), but the authenticity of some (e.g. a pair of doors, Washington, DC, Freer) has also been questioned. The finest surviving ensemble from the period is a set of two folding doors from the tomb of Mahmud of Ghazna (*d* 1030) in Afghanistan, which were transferred to the Agra Fort in 1842. The interior face of each of the four panels consists of a plain mortised frame set with seven squares. Each square, carved in a late version of the Bevelled style, is framed with a narrow band of bevelled ornament, which is a condensed and abstracted version of that found on the larger 'Adud al-Dawla panels. The carving on the rectangular panels on the exterior, like the smaller ones ordered by 'Adud al-Dawla, adds new elements: the sinuous lines are carved in deep relief, the palmettes are rhythmical and symmetrical, and the whole design is marked by an unprecedented sense of plasticity. Despite their certain provenance from Mahmud's tomb, it is unclear whether the doors were installed at the time of his death or in the 12th century during a revival of interest in his cult.

For additional information and bibliography *see* CENTRAL ASIA, §I, 8(viii).

BIBLIOGRAPHY

S. Flury: 'Das Schriftband an der Türe des Mahmud von Ghazna (998–1030)', *Der Islam*, viii (1918), pp. 214–27

G. Wiet: *L'Exposition persane de 1931* (Cairo, 1933), no. 6

Hasan ibn Muhammad Qumi: *Tārīkh-i Qum* [History of Qum], ed. S. J. Tihrani (Tehran, AH 1313/1934), p. 225

B. Deniké: 'Quelques monuments de bois sculptés au Turkestan occidental', *A. Islam.*, ii (1935), pp. 69–83

M. B. Smith: 'Minbar: Masdjid-i Djami', Muhmmmadiyè', *Athar-é Iran*, i (1936), pp. 175–80

V. L. Voronina: 'Reznoye derevo Zarafshanskoy doliny' [Wood-carving of the Zarafshan Valley], *Materialy & Issledovaniya Arkheol. SSSR*, xv (1950), pp. 210–20

R. Ettinghausen: 'The "Beveled Style" in the Post-Samarra Period', *Archaeologica Orientalia im Memoriam Ernst Herzfeld*, ed. G. C. Miles (Locust Valley, NY, 1952), pp. 72–83

B. Brentjes: 'Zu einigen samanidischen und nachsamanidischen Holzbildwerken des Seravschantales im Westen Tadshikistans', *Cent. Asiat. J.*, xv (1971), pp. 295–7

A. S. Melikian-Chirvani: 'Un Chef-d'oeuvre inconnu dans une vallée afghane', *Conn. A.*, cccviii (1977), pp. 76–9

M. Kiani, ed.: *Robat-e Sharaf* (Tehran, 1981), pp. 45–53, figs 1–3, pls 1–7 [Eng. summary, pp. 6–7]

S. S. Blair: *The Monumental Inscriptions from Early Islamic Iran and Transoxiana* (Leiden, 1992)

ABBAS DANESHVARI

(iii) Spain and North Africa. The forests of the Iberian peninsula and north-west Africa provided abundant timber, particularly pine, walnut, cypress and some other types, for example alerce (sandarac tree); these woods were used for architectural fittings and furniture. The remains of mosque ceilings, doors and minbars provide the best evidence for technical and stylistic developments in woodwork in this area, but wooden structures can occasionally be deduced from their equivalents in stone or plaster. The principal centres of woodwork production were Córdoba and Seville (in Spain) and Fez (in Morocco).

The Rustamid rulers of central North Africa (*reg* AD 761–909) erected a wooden hypostyle mosque (771; destr.) in their capital at Tahart (now in Algeria), and Idris I (*reg* 789–93) ordered an inscribed wooden minbar for his mosque (790) at Tlemcen (also in Algeria) to which his son Idris II (*reg* 793–828) added another inscription. However, the oldest extant woodwork in the region is the minbar (862–3) in the Great Mosque at Kairouan. This minbar and a later example from Córdoba were the models for most later minbars in the western Islamic world. Several of the ceiling beams from the Kairouan mosque are tree trunks boxed in with planed cypress planks. Some of these planks, reused in the 11th century, preserve 9th-century decoration of brightly painted, regularly repeating composite vegetal and floral motifs.

The oldest surviving pieces of woodwork from Islamic Spain are two ceiling beams (Granada, Mus. N. A. Hispmus.) from Córdoba, decorated with carved floral and geometric patterns and dating from the caliphate of 'Abd al-Rahman III (*reg* 912–61). When his son al-Hakam II (*reg* 961–76) enlarged the mosque at Córdoba in 965, a flat ceiling was formed by boards attached to horizontal beams, the ends of which were covered by wooden boxes. The ornamental ceiling (*armadura*) was protected by a gabled roof. The boards were carved and painted, over which were superimposed separate carved and painted pieces; like many contemporary crafts, these show design elements imported from Iraq. Wooden vaults may also have been the prototypes for the unusual rib-vaulted stone cupolas added to the mosque in 965. Decorative stone corbels over the door known as the Bab al-Wuzara' (now Puerta de San Esteban; 785–7) and in what is now commonly known as the Salón Rico at Madinat al-Zahra', the caliphal residence outside Córdoba, further indicate a developed tradition of wooden roof construction. Archaeological remains from Madinat al-Zahra' show that wood was used for gabled roofs, single, double and folding doors, windows and cupboards, which were often decorated with brass sheets and nail heads. According to chronicles, a new minbar and *maqsūra* were made for the mosque of Córdoba in *c.* 965, but the only 10th-century minbar preserved is a Fatimid example in the mosque of the Andalusians in Fez, for which in 979–80 the Umayyad minister al-Mansur ordered a new back (probably made in Córdoba). The original minbar had been severely damaged, and al-Mansur also had it repaired with a panel imitating the original work, composed of closely set turned balusters and a new backrest. It was restored again in the 14th century in Marinid times.

No 11th-century wooden ceilings have survived in Spain, but their existence can be judged from a plaster version in the Aljafería Palace in Saragossa, which has a fascia board and a double row of corbels with floral decoration. It resembles contemporary work in Toledo. The 11th-century ceiling of the congregational mosque of Kairouan had carved and painted panels, as well as deeply carved and richly painted consoles. The most important example of 11th-century woodwork is the magnificent wooden *maqsūra* (restored 1625) that the Zirid ruler al-Mu'izz ibn Badis (*reg* 1016–62) ordered for the mosque. Enclosing a 6×8 m area to the right of the minbar, it consists of a rectangular framework, heavily carved with

arabesques and supporting grilles of turned spindles and spools; these are crowned with a magnificent foliated kufic inscription and pierced merlons. Some of the panels have bevelled carved ornament (a style that had developed at Samarra' in Iraq in the 9th century AD), while the letters and vegetation enclosed by a continuous raised bead are distinctively Zirid.

Under the Almoravids (*reg* 1056–1147) the ornamental ceiling of planks suspended below the gabled roof was eliminated from mosque architecture. The congregational mosque of Tlemcen (1136) preserves the oldest surviving example of decorated rafters, tie-beams and brackets. At the mosque of the Qarawiyyin (1134–43) at Fez the brackets are decorated with serpentine forms. The doors of the mosque are covered with plain metal bands or geometric designs in a manner already used in 10th-century Spain. Painted friezes with floral and epigraphic decoration and fragments of corbels, one of them with pierced carving (Granada, Alhambra), were discovered on the Mauror Hill in Granada, Spain. A door at the monastery of Las Huelgas in Burgos shows very fine interlocked geometric decoration with individual pieces decorated with delicate foliage, a technique found on several important Almoravid minbars surviving in North Africa. The minbar from Nedroma in Algeria (late 11th century; Algiers, Mus. N. Ant.) is decorated with adjoining squares. That in the congregational mosque in Algiers (1097) has square panels of relief-carved arabesque set in a framework like that of the minbar of the mosque of the Andalusians

216. Wooden minbar (detail), from the Kutubiyya Mosque, Marrakesh, Morocco, made in Córdoba, *c.* 1120 (Marrakesh, Bahia Palace)

in Fez. The finest is the minbar made in Córdoba *c.* 1120 for the mosque of 'Ali ibn Yusuf in Marrakesh in Morocco, which the Almohads (*reg* 1130–1296) then transferred to the Kutubiyya Mosque (Marrakesh, Bahia Palace; see fig. 216). The sides have an all-over strapwork frame of ivory and wood intarsia; the elaborate geometric design is based on interlocking squares, which at the corners form eight-pointed stars which are themselves surrounded by four further eight-pointed stars. The risers of the stairs are decorated with an exquisite strapwork of pearl bands defining horseshoe arcades. The minbar made for the mosque of the Qarawiyyin in Fez in 1143 uses the same techniques on the sides but the risers are somewhat simpler.

Similar strapwork patterns appear for the first time on some of the wooden ornamental ceilings of the Almohad Kutubiyya Mosque in Marrakesh (1162). The galleries of the Almohad Mosque of Seville, however, had gabled ceilings with crossbeams, great eaves on the gateway into the courtyard (restored in 1975), and its door lined with metal strapwork and moulded hexagonal pieces and four-pointed stars with kufic inscriptions and foliate designs. Its bronze knockers, with palm leaves and cursive inscriptions, are exceptional pieces. The Mudéjar door of the principal portal to the mosque at Córdoba was a copy of this one, also covered with metal plaques in a geometric design, the individual pieces decorated with foliate designs and epigraphy.

BIBLIOGRAPHY

S. Flury: *Islamische Schriftbänder Amida-Diyarbekr XI. Jahrhundert. Anhang: Kairuan, Mayyafariqin, Tirmidh* (Basle, 1920), pp. 35–44

G. Marçais: *Coupole et plafonds de la grande mosquée de Kairouan* (Tunis, 1925)

——: 'Note sur la chaire à prêcher de la Grande Mosquée d'Alger', *Hespéris*, vi (1926), pp. 419–22

F. Hernández Jiménez: 'Arte musulmán: La techumbre de la Gran Mezquita de Córdoba, *Archv Esp. A. & Arqueol.*, iv (1928), pp. 191–225

H. Basset and H. Terrasse: *Sanctuaires et forteresses almohades* (Paris, 1932), pp. 234ff

K. A. C. Creswell: *Early Muslim Architecture*, ii (Oxford, 1940)

L. Torres Balbás: *Arte almohade; arte nazarí; arte mudéjar*, A. Hisp., iv (Madrid, 1949)

M. Gómez-Moreno: *El arte árabe español hasta los Almohades; arte mozárabe*, A. Hisp., iii (Madrid, 1951)

H. Terrasse: *La Mosquée des Andalous à Fès* (Paris, [*c.*] 1952])

L. Torres Balbás: *Artes almorávide y almohade*, Arte y Artistas (Madrid, 1955)

F. Hernández Jiménez: 'El almimbar móvil del siglo X de la mezquita de Córdoba', *Al-Andalus*, xxiv (1959), pp. 381–99

L. Torres Balbás: 'Arte hispanomusulmán hasta la caída del califato de Córdoba', *Historia de España*, ed. R. Menéndez-Pidal, v (Madrid, 1965)

H. Terrasse: *La Mosquée al-Qaraouyin à Fès* (Paris, 1968)

Ibn Sahib al-Sala: *Al-männ bil imäma* (Valencia, 1969)

H. Terrasse: 'Un Bois sculpté du XIIe siècle trouvé à Marrakech', *Al-Andalus*, xl (1969), pp. 419–20

A. Fernández-Puertas: 'Tabla epigrafiada de época almorávide o comienzos de la almohade', *Misc. Estud. Arab. & Heb.*, xx (1971), pp. 109–12

——: 'Tabla epigrafiada almohade', *Misc. Estud. Arab. & Heb.*, xxi (1972), pp. 77–86

——: 'Tablas epigrafiadas de época almorávide y almohade', *Misc. Estud. Arab. & Heb.*, xxiii (1974), pp. 113–19

——: 'Las puertas chapadas hispanomusulmánas', *Misc. Estud. Arab. & Heb.*, xxix–xxx (1980–81), pp. 163–76

——: 'Dos vigas califales del Museo Nacional de Arte Hispanomusulmán', *Homenaje al Prof. Dario Cabanelas Rodriguez, of. m., con motivo de su LXX aniversario* (Granada, 1987), pp. 203–40

ANTONIO FERNÁNDEZ-PUERTAS

2. AFTER *c.* 1250. Wood continued to be scarce and expensive, in the Islamic lands around the Mediterranean, and virtually all the woodwork produced in the area after *c.* 1250, from furniture to ceilings, is based on the assemblage of small pieces. In the eastern Islamic lands large timbers continued to be available for use in structures, fittings and furnishings, but the taste for geometric compositions based on small wooden units also spread to these regions: although it was not functionally requisite, large panels were often carved to resemble assemblages of small pieces. Lattice-like screens of turned wood (Arab. *mashrabiyya* or *al-shimāsa*; Sp. *ajimeces*) became widespread. Painting often replaced carving as the primary decorative technique, and other techniques, such as inlay and 'lacquer' (*see* §VIII, 10 below) were used to enhance surfaces.

□

(i) Spain and North Africa. (ii) Egypt and Syria, *c.* 1250–*c.* 1500. (iii) Anatolia, *c.* 1250–*c.* 1500. (iv) Ottoman empire, after *c.* 1500. (v) Yemen. (vi) Iran and western Central Asia.

(i) Spain and North Africa. The art of woodwork continued to flourish after 1250 in Spain, under the Nasrids (1230–1492), who took Granada in 1238, and in North Africa, particularly under the Marinid dynasty (*reg* 1196–1549) of Fez and the Abdalwadids of Tlemcen (in Algeria; *reg* 1236–1550). As in earlier periods, stylistic and technical developments are best seen in the joined ceilings of palaces and mosques and in liturgical furniture. During this period the interlaced patterns introduced earlier became so complex that they often completely hide the underlying structure.

Structural or ornamental wooden ceilings (Sp. *armaduras*), which had first been developed under the Almoravids (*reg* 1056–1147), reached their apogee between the 13th and the 15th century. The mosque of Sayyidi ibn al-Hasan (Sidi Bel Hasan; 1296) at Tlemcen retains only a portion of its original ornamental ceilings of pieces of cedar, but the late 13th-century ceiling of the Cuarto Real de S Domingo (Dar al-Manyarah al-Kubra) in Granada has magnificently coloured interlaced designs between its rafters. In the Alhambra in the same city the portico of the early 14th-century Palacio del Partal has a flat ornamental wooden ceiling (*armadura ataujerada*) with small *mocárabes* vaults (*muqarnas* in eastern Arab lands) and a central carved polygonal ceiling. At the Generalife to the north-east of the Alhambra a flat wooden ceiling has decorated background panelling and interlaced patterns. Inspired by the work of several centuries earlier in Córdoba are the ceilings of the rooms in the Generalife and in the Alcázar Genil (1319) to the south of Granada, with their respective interlaced and superimposed designs, which appear to float above a projecting cornice of plaster *mocárabes*, ultimately the evolution of the boxes that cover the ends of the beams, at the mosque at Córdoba. The masterpiece of Islamic geometric design in wood is the ceiling of the throne-room in the Palacio de Comares (first half of the 14th century) in the Alhambra (see fig. 217). It is supported on a richly painted *mocárabes* cornice, and each of its four sides consists of three inclined planes. These 12 planes culminate in a horizontal panel supporting a small *mocárabes* vault. Over 8000 individual elements are joined in a design of seven concentric bands of alternating large and small stars, which probably represents the seven heavens of paradise described in the Koran (lxvii). The

217. Wooden ceiling of the throne-room, Palacio de Comares, Alhambra, Granada, *c.* 1333–54

bulbous wooden ceilings in the projecting pavilions of the Patio de los Leones (1380s) may also have had cosmic or zodiacal meanings. Hemispherical ceilings on a larger scale, such as the Hall of the Ambassadors in the Alcázar of Seville (1427), were also built by *mudéjar* artisans, who until the 17th century produced thousands of wooden *armadura* ceilings.

Carved wood was used extensively for corbels, lintels, eaves, spandrels and entablatures, and joined panels were employed for doors, shutters and lattice-like screens (*ajimeces*). Nasrid eaves have upturned rafters and corbels, whereas many Marinid and some *mudéjar* eaves have horizontal rafters and corbels (e.g. the Montería in the Alcázar of Seville). The eaves of the façade of the Palacio de Comares in the Alhambra are perfectly proportioned to their setting and are unsurpassed in their size, magnificent carving and colouring. Nasrid, Marinid and *mudéjar* doors were lined with metal bands or metallic pieces; they were of plain wood with decorative nails; or they had interlaced geometric designs with coloured pieces that were either plain or carved or had superimposed carving (e.g. the Puerta de la Justicia, the façade of the Palacio de Comares and the Patio de los Leones in the Alhambra respectively). Particularly fine Marinid ensembles are the interior façades of the 'Attarin (1323–5) and Bu 'Inaniyya madrasas (1350–55) in Fez in Morocco and the Bu 'Inaniyya madrasa in Meknes (*c.* 1345), also in Morocco.

Other wooden elements were lattice grilles and balustrades with turned or interlaced decoration. The mosque of the Qarawiyyin in Fez retains the wooden *'anaza*, an auxiliary mihrab in a grille in the court façade of the prayer hall, placed there in 1289. Although its exterior surface is heavily weathered, the interior preserves its inlaid interlace decoration and kufic inscriptions. The library added to the mosque in 1350 is decorated with a fine set of wooden fixtures and a decorated ceiling. Several important examples of liturgical furniture are preserved in the mosque of the Andalusians in Fez. The earliest is a wooden mihrab (1307) inserted in the *'anaza* (restored). It is finely carved in shallow relief with scalloped arches and imbrecated designs characteristic of architectural decoration. The door to the imam's room (15th century) combines panels of shallow relief with grilles of turned spindles, and the contemporary balustrades of the staircases to the Mosque of the Dead display a vigorous hexagonal interlace.

Marinid minbars, such as the minbar of the mosque at Taza in Morocco, continue the proportions and techniques of strapwork decoration established in earlier centuries and suggest the form of vanished Nasrid minbars. Although earlier minbars had contrasting carved and inlaid decoration, both the strapwork and the polygons on the minbar at Taza are decorated with ebony and ivory inlays. The same woodworking technique used for the Marinid minbars—carved and inlaid with ivory, bone, silver, ebony or other fine woods—was used for objects made for Nasrid royal palaces. Among those that have survived are the richly decorated door cupboards (Granada, Mus. N. A. Hispmus.) from the Cetti Merien Palace (destr.), which are inlaid with bone, silver and precious woods in superimposed networks of hexagons and six-, eight- and twelve-pointed stars. Many wooden boxes and jewel caskets with flat or hipped lids are similarly covered in geometric patterns of bone and wood inlay (*see* MARQUETRY, colour pl. VIII, fig. 3). A folding chair, with a leather seat and back, also made for a royal patron (Granada, Mus. N. A. Hispmus.), has a wooden X-frame richly covered by intarsia of repeated polygons with inserted stars made of silver, bone and precious-coloured woods. Another wooden royal item, a sultan's sceptre (now at Alcalá de Hernares), consists of decorated wooden and bone spools held on a metal rod core.

BIBLIOGRAPHY

M. Gómez-Moreno: *La ornamentación mudéjar toledana/Mudejar Ornamental Work in Toledo* (Madrid, 1924)
L. Torres Balbás: 'Hojas de puerta de una alacena en el Museo de la Alhambra de Granada', *Al-Andalus*, iii (1935), pp. 438–42
J. Fernandis Torres: 'Muebles hispanoárabes de Taracea', *Al-Andalus*, v (1940), pp. 459–65
M. Gómez-Moreno: 'El bastón del Cardenal Cisneros', *Al-Andalus*, v (1940), pp. 192–5
L. Torres Balbás: 'El más antiguo alfarje conservado en España', *Al-Andalus*, ix (1944), pp. 441–8
——: 'Ajimeces', *Al-Andalus*, xii (1947), pp. 415–27
——: *Arte almohade; arte nazarí; arte mudéjar*, A. Hisp., iv (Madrid, 1949)
H. Terrasse: *La Mosquée des Andalous à Fès* (Paris, [*c.* 1952])
G. Marçais: *L'Architecture musulmane d'occident* (Paris, 1954)
H. Terrasse: *La Mosquée al-Qaraouiyin à Fès* (Paris, 1968)
A. Fernández-Puertas: *El lazo de ocho occidental o andaluz: Su trazado, canon proporcional, series y patrones* (Granada and Madrid, 1975)
A. Prieto y Vives: *El arte de la lacería* (Madrid, 1977)
D. Cabanelas: *El techo del Salón de Comares en la Alhambra* (Granada, 1988)
A. Fernández-Puertas: *The Alhambra*, 2 vols (London, 1996)

For further bibliography *see also* §1(iii) above.

ANTONIO FERNÁNDEZ-PUERTAS

(ii) Egypt and Syria, c. 1250–c. 1500. Despite its perennial scarcity in Egypt and Syria, wood continued to play an essential role in religious and secular architecture after the establishment of the Mamluk sultanate (1250–1517; *see* MAMLUK, §II, 1). Imported from as far away as the Sudan and India, it was used for structural elements such as ceilings and domes and fixed and portable furnishings such as window grilles and shutters, minbars and Koran stands. Decorative techniques of earlier periods, such as painting, carving, turning and joining, continued to be used, although techniques based on assemblages of small pieces of wood were increasingly important, and painting replaced carving as the major means of decorating ceiling planks. Turned and carved grilles and marquetry strapwork (Arab. *qanāt*) designs, known as early as the 11th century, increased in popularity after *c.* 1250, perhaps due to the scarcity of wood for panelling, although the fitting together of small pieces also helped to combat shrinkage and warping in the hot, dry climate of Egypt. The new taste for interlacing strapwork designs composed of small polygonal panels can be explained in the same way: they could be fitted together without a noticeable break in the pattern more easily than could the carved arabesques. Inlaid ivory, bone, ebony and other woods often provided additional colour.

Following the precedent of the dome over the mausoleum of Imam al-Shafi'i (1211; restored 1480; *see* §1(i)(b) above), wood remained the choice material for the largest domes in Cairo: those of the mosque of Baybars (1269) and the mausoleum of Sultan Hasan (1362; *see* CAIRO, §§7 and 9) and the mausoleum of Sultan Barquq (1386; incorrectly restored in brick). Wood, usually painted, was also used for ceilings, for *muqarnas* cornices and pendentives and for inscription bands. Turned and joined wooden screens and grilles provided privacy or shade in both secular and religious architecture, and *mashrabiyya* grilles enclosed cenotaphs and partitioned off prayer halls and tomb chambers in religious architecture. The earliest and finest wooden ensemble is preserved in the mausoleum and madrasa of Sultan Qala'un (1284–5; *see* CAIRO §III, 8). The great corridor has a ceiling of light transverse beams supporting longitudinal planks, the whole resting on a cornice. The beams are carved with a delicate arabesque design which is hardly visible at a distance, despite its painted highlights. A *mashrabiyya* screen nearly 4 m wide and pierced with two doors composed of alternating diagonal grid and baluster sections guards the entrance to the mausoleum, in which splendid *mashrabiyya* screens, added by Qala'un's son, al-Nasir Muhammad, enclose the cenotaph (see fig. 218) and divide the interior. Coffered wooden ceilings (restored) cover eight sections of the ambulatory around the cenotaph. The large amount of wood needed to accomplish this work led to the reuse of 11th-century wood-carvings from the 'Western' Palace that previously occupied the same site. A room behind the mihrab in the 9th-century mosque of Ibn Tulun in Cairo (restored after 1296) has distinctly un-Egyptian wooden corbels that may be the work of Muslim craftsmen who had fled the Christian reconquest of Spain.

The best guide to the stylistic evolution of woodwork during this period is the series of dated minbars produced in Syria and Egypt under Mamluk patronage. The high

218. Wooden *mashrabiyya* screen added by al-Nasir Muhammad to the mausoleum of Sultan Qala'un, Cairo, *c.* 1303

proportion of signed examples indicates the esteem in which the craft was held, although the names do not usually indicate the relationship between craftsmen, as occasionally happened in earlier times. The first Mamluk sultan, Baybars I (*reg* 1260–77), commissioned a minbar (destr.) from Abu Bakr ibn Yusuf for the mosque of the Prophet in Medina. The earliest, and one of the finest, minbars extant was ordered by Sultan Lajin for the mosque of Ibn Tulun (1296). Made of sycamore, teak and ebony, it has been extensively restored, but many of the original plaques (many in London, V&A) show that the arabesque carving of the polygons varied from piece to piece, inviting contemplation of the design from near as well as from afar. This feature derives almost certainly from the minbar (destr.) commissioned in 1168–9 by Nur al-Din for the Aqsa Mosque in Jerusalem. The Cairo minbar is also the first extant example to display the bulbous dome over the seat that was to become a characteristic feature of Mamluk minbars. The almost contemporary minbar ordered by Qarasunqur for the Great Mosque of Aleppo (*c.* 1300) and made by Muhammad ibn 'Ali, a craftsman from Mosul, shows a much greater use of ivory inlay, a feature that appeared slowly in Cairene minbars but became common in numerous examples produced under Qa'itbay (*reg* 1468–96). For all the technical virtuosity, however, the exact repetition of the arabesque pattern in each polygon has a certain mechanical feel, although the perfect integration of the interlace pattern into the triangular field shows great sensitivity to design. Minbars were major collaborative efforts: that ordered by Kitbugha for the congregational mosque of Hama in Syria was signed by 'Ali ibn

Makki and 'Abdallah Ahmad in 1302; it was inlaid by Abu Bakr ibn Muhammad and decorated by 'Ali ibn 'Uthman. Ahmad ibn 'Isa, who signed the minbar made for the mosque of al-Ghamri in Cairo (*c.* 1446; later transferred to the complex of Sultan Barsbay), attempted to enliven the ubiquitous interlacing angular strapwork by consistently curving the lines radiating from the 12-pointed stars. He also signed a minbar made in 1480–81 for the madrasa of Abu Bakr ibn Muzhir in Cairo and is thought to have been responsible for the minbars sent to Mecca by the sultans Khushqadam in 1462 and Qa'itbay in 1475. When angular and curving strapwork is combined, as in the minbar of the mosque of Abu'l-'Ila in Cairo (*c.* 1485), the effect is awkward.

Other items of mosque furniture displaying intricate ivory and coloured wood inlay include Koran boxes and *kursīs*, a name used both for large lecterns on which Koran readers sat and for small tables. The hexagonal table and Koran box from the madrasa of Khwand Baraka, the mother of Sultan Sha'ban, in Cairo (1368–9; Cairo, Mus. Islam. A.) are particularly fine. The table is covered with large inlaid panels of interlace designs, while the box is inlaid with marquetry designs in ivory, ebony and tin. A Koran box and small folding Koran stand (*rahla*) bearing the name of Sultan al-Ghawri (*reg* 1501–16; Cairo, Mus. Islam. A.) show a change in taste at the end of the era. The box is painted with a central medallion and four quarter medallions in the corners. The medallions are decorated with gold lotus leaves and arabesques on a black ground, clearly showing the impact of Persian bookbinding. The stand, on which the only decoration is a three-line inscription boldly inlaid with ivory, shows a return to simplicity which is found in some contemporary Ottoman woodwork (*see* §(iv) below).

BIBLIOGRAPHY

S. Lane-Poole: *The Art of the Saracens in Egypt* (London, 1886/*R* n.d.), pp. 111–50

J. David-Weill: *Les Bois à épigraphes depuis l'époque mamlouke* (Cairo, 1936)

E. Kühnel: 'Der mamlukische Kassettenstil', *Kst Orients*, i (1950), pp. 55–68

H. 'Abd al-Wahhāb: 'Tawqī'āt al'ṣunnā' 'alā āthār Miṣr al-islāmiyya' [Craftsmen's signatures on Islamic Egyptian works of art], *Bull. Inst. Egypte*, xxxvi (1953–4), pp. 533–58

E. Herzfeld: *Inscriptions et monuments d'Alep*, Mém.: Inst. Fr. Archéol. Caire, lxxvi/1–2 (1955–6), ii of *Matériaux pour un Corpus inscriptionum arabicarum; deuxième partie: Syrie du Nord* (Cairo, 1909–56), pp. 168–71

Exhibition of Islamic Art in Egypt (exh. cat., ed. A. Hamdy and others; Cairo, Semiramis Hotel, 1969), pp. 217–48

G. S. Ohan: *Cairene Bahri Mamluk Minbars, with a Provisional Typology and a Catalogue* (MA thesis, Amer. U. Cairo, 1977)

Renaissance of Islam: Art of the Mamluks (exh. cat. by E. Atıl, Washington, DC, Smithsonian Inst., 1981), pp. 195–210

BERNARD O'KANE

(*iii*) *Anatolia, c. 1250–c. 1500.* The ready availability of fine timber in Anatolia allowed painted and carved woodwork to be used freely for structural elements in mosques, houses and pavilions. The few examples that survive from the period before 1250 are included below, as it is only in the period between *c.* 1250 and *c.* 1500 that enough examples are preserved to begin to delineate the development of woodworking in the area.

Elaborate joinery was used for furnishings, especially minbars in mosques. Unusually wide boards were employed for shutters, doors and the sides of minbars; sometimes they were carved with centralized compositions, but often they were carved with strapwork patterns in imitation of joinery. Inlay was introduced towards the end of the period and soon replaced the earlier techniques.

Many mosques had wooden structural elements such as columns, capitals, beams and consoles and furnishings such as window-shutters and doors. They were painted with stylized foliate and floral motifs and geometric patterns in red, dark blue, yellow and white. Typical examples are the congregational mosques (Turk.: *Ulu Cami*) at Afyon (1272), Sivrihisar (1274) and Ayas (13th century) and the Arslanhane Mosque at Ankara (1289–90). In rare cases painted wood was also used for mosque furniture. An unusual lacquered wooden lectern (1278; Konya, Mevlana Mus.) is decorated with a double-headed eagle and lion over a field of arabesques on the inner sides of which the Koran was placed.

The side panels for minbars were usually made with interlocking pieces. Tongue-edged lozenges, octagons and stars carved with arabesques are joined by grooved frames without glue or pins, a technique known in Turkish as *kündekâri.* The pieces were set with the grain perpendicular to the grain of the frame to prevent warping, and the joined panels were further supported on a wooden substructure. Earlier examples such as the minbars from the mosque of Alaeddin in Konya (1155–6) and the congregational mosques of Siirt and Malatya (both 13th century; Ankara, Mus. Ethnog.) have angular pieces. Those from the 14th century, such as the minbars from the congregational mosques at Birgi (1322), Manisa (1376) and Bursa (1499), have finer, more intricate and shallower carving and are decorated with large rosettes and bosses. This joinery technique demanded meticulous workmanship to make the tongues and grooves fit tightly, so it was often imitated by carving a single board in relief with lozenges, octagons and stars. The boards were mounted side by side on the frame of the minbar, but warping and shrinkage eventually caused the joints to open and interrupt the strapwork patterns. Minbars in such 'false joinery' are found in the mosque of Alaeddin at Ankara (1197–8), the congregational mosques at Kayseri (1237) and Divriği (1228–9) and the Arslanhane Mosque at Ankara (1289–90; see fig. 219). A few later examples from the 14th and 15th centuries, such as the minbar from the Ahi Elvan mosque in Ankara (1382), are much simpler in technique, for both the frame bands and the strapwork panels have been glued or pinned to boards.

Woodwork from this period is deeply carved. The Bevelled style that had been popular in Egypt, Syria and Iraq (*see* §2(i)(a) above) is rare, although there are exceptional examples (e.g. the 13th-century minbar from the congregational mosque at Malatya; Ankara, Mus. Ethnog.). Geometric, floral and arabesque motifs were carved in flat relief, while inscription bands had rounded contours and seem to float on the arabesque ground. The inscriptions often mention the artisan. Hacı Mengimberti, for example, carved the minbar in the mosque of Alaeddin in Konya (1155–6), and 'Abdallah ibn Mahmud al-Naqqash made the doors for the mosques at Kasabaköy (1366) and

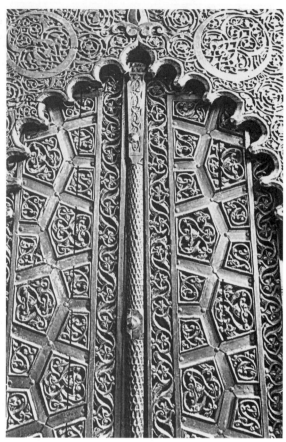

219. Wooden minbar of boards carved to resemble joinery ('false joinery'), from the Arslanhane Mosque, Ankara, 1289–90

Ibni Neccar (1367) outside Kastamonu. Latticework was commonly used for the balustrades of minbars and the pedestals of lecterns.

Inlay was first used for small panels in the second half of the 14th century and quickly became popular. The 15th-century doors from the mosque of Hacı Bayram in Ankara (Ankara, Mus. Ethnog.) are inlaid with ivory and wood, and the walnut doors from the mosque at Balıkesir built by Zağanos Pasha, vizier to the Ottoman sultan Mehmed II (*c.* 1460; Istanbul, Topkapı Pal. Mus.), are inlaid with ivory, boxwood and metal wire.

BIBLIOGRAPHY

B. Ögel: 'Selçuklu devri ağaç işçiliği hakkında notlar' [Notes on Anatolian woodwork of the Seljuk period], *Yıllık Araştırmalar Derg.*, i (1956), pp. 199–220

K. Otto-Dorn: 'Seldschukische Holzsäulenmoscheen in Kleinasien', *Aus der Welt der islamischen Kunst: Festschrift für Ernst Kühnel* (Berlin, 1959), pp. 59–88

M. Z. Oral: 'Anadolu'da sanat değerleri olan ahşap minberler, kitabeleri ve tarihçeleri' [Wooden minbars of artistic value in Anatolia, their inscriptions and histories], *Vakıflar Derg.*, v (1962), pp. 23–77

Ç. Çulpan: *Türk-Islam tahta oymacılık sanatında rahleler* [Koran stands in Turkish Islamic wood-carving] (Istanbul, 1968)

G. Öney: 'Die Techniken der Holzschnitzerei zur Zeit der Seldschuken und während der Herrschaft der Emirate in Anatolien', *Sanat Tarihi Yıllığı*, iii (1969–70), pp. 299–305

Y. Demiriz: 'XIV. yüzyılda ağaç işleri' [Woodwork in the 14th century], *Yüzyıllar boyunca Türk sanatı* [Turkish art through the centuries], ed. O. Aslanapa (Istanbul, 1977), pp. 61–71

G. Öney: 'Architectural Decoration and the Minor Arts', *The Art and Architecture of Turkey*, ed. E. Akurgal (Fribourg, 1980), pp. 201–3

Anadolu medeniyetleri/The Anatolian Civilisations, iii: *Seljuk/Ottoman* (exh. cat., ed. Ş. Aykoç and others; Istanbul, Topkapı Pal. Mus., 1983), pp. 86–94

GÖNÜL ÖNEY

(iv) Ottoman empire, after *c.* 1500. By the early 16th century, wood itself was not considered a sufficiently spectacular material for furniture in the imperial mosques of the Ottoman empire. Joined wood was replaced by other materials with painted and carved decoration recalling the treatment of woodwork. The minbar of the Süleymaniye Mosque in Istanbul (1557), for example, was made of Proconnesian marble. Instead, luxury wooden objects—thrones, chests and musket stocks inlaid with ivory, precious metals, mother-of-pearl and tortoiseshell and encrusted with hardstones—were produced in small numbers for the Ottoman court.

Furniture of superlative quality and considerable individuality was already being made for the court by the early 16th century. The most famous piece is a hexagonal walnut chest for a 30-part Koran made by Ahmed ibn Hasan Kalibî Fânî (*ḳālibî*: 'maker of musket stocks') in 1505–6 for the mosque of Sultan Bayezid II (Istanbul, Mus. Turk. & Islam. A., 3; see fig. 220). The exterior is veneered with ebony, encrusted with ivory panels and inset with fine marquetry. It is the earliest dated piece of furniture in the Ottoman court style, but a walnut quiver (Istanbul, Topkapı Pal. Mus., 1/10463) is similarly veneered and richly inlaid. A variety of sources can be suggested for this early 16th-century monumental furniture. Elaborately inlaid musical instruments were produced in Iran in the late 15th century and the early 16th, to judge from miniature paintings and registers. Many were probably taken to Turkey as booty, as were small artefacts such as a carved sandalwood casket made for the Timurid ruler Ulugh Beg (*d* 1449), which was probably reworked in Istanbul (Istanbul, Topkapı Pal. Mus., 2/1846; see 1989 exh. cat., no. 49). Northern Italian marquetry was highly developed by 1500, and its smooth, high finish and angular meander borders, whether single, double or plaited, would have appealed to Ottoman taste. A combined reading stand and chest-of-drawers, possibly a calligrapher's table, from the mausoleum of Sultan Ahmed I (*reg* 1603–17; Istanbul, Mus. Turk. & Islam. A., 33), for example, combines elongated cross motifs similar to the openwork on a north Italian comb (London, V&A, 4229.1857) with a medallion and corner pieces taken from a pattern used in bindings. Another source was Mamluk Egypt: such Ottoman pieces as the preacher's chair in the Süleymaniye Mosque and the cenotaph and canopy dated 1543–4 in the tomb of Şehzade Mehmed in Istanbul have elaborate meander borders like those on Koran chests and stands made in Egypt in the 14th and 15th centuries. The materials used in Mamluk work, however, were of far lower quality.

Later 16th-century woodwork evolved independently and rather strangely. A square Koran box installed by Sultan Mahmud I (*reg* 1730–54) in the library of Hagia Sophia was probably made in the reign of Süleyman the Magnificent (1520–66; Istanbul, Mus. Turk. & Islam. A., 5). Veneered in ebony, ivory and mother-of-pearl, its sides have rectangular panels with central medallions and corner pieces. Cusped skirting between the legs repeats the profile of the panel decoration in contrasting materials. The cover, originally surmounted by a large knob-finial, is boldly inlaid with a chevron design with a frieze of palmettes and hexagons at the top.

Mother-of-pearl, used earlier for inlay, was also inlaid itself. A polygonal Koran box with a large dome made of hardwood veneered with ivory, dark woods and mother-of-pearl was found in the mausoleum of Sultan Mehmed III at Hagia Sophia (*d* 1603; Istanbul, Mus. Turk. & Islam. A., 13). The mother-of-pearl rosettes on the lid were themselves inlaid with foliate tracery in black mastic and bear the remains of gold settings for jewels. Even more elaborate are the bejewelled mother-of-pearl stars at the centre of star-polygon compositions on the sides of a tall domed Koran chest from the mausoleum of Sultan Selim II (*d* 1574; Istanbul, Mus. Turk. & Islam. A., 2). It is made of hardwood veneered with ebony, ivory, mother-of-pearl and marquetry panels of these and reddish boxwood, yellow metal and silver wire.

Tortoiseshell was also incorporated into veneered decoration. A pair of doors in the pavilion in the Harem at Topkapı Palace in Istanbul built by Sinan for Sultan Murad

220. Hexagonal walnut chest for a 30-part copy of the Koran, made by Ahmed ibn Hasan Kalibî Fânî, from Istanbul, 1505–6 (Istanbul, Museum of Turkish and Islamic Art)

III in 1578–9 have ingeniously varied panels of minute marquetry (allegedly in mahogany, lead and tin as well as ebony and ivory) and veneer in ivory, ebony, mother-of-pearl and tortoiseshell, this last set over gold foil to give it added glitter. Technically similar is a tall hexagonal Koran chest inlaid with tortoiseshell and mother-of-pearl found in the mausoleum of Sultan Mehmed III (Istanbul, Mus. Turk. & Islam. A., 19). It is signed by the court architect Ahmed Dalgıç, who also signed a pair of wooden doors for the mausoleum, which are magnificently inlaid with mother-of-pearl. His dual role of architect and wood-worker is explained by the fact that one of the court architect's duties was to provide models of projected buildings.

Fewer signed or attributable masterpieces were produced after the 16th century. The canopied throne executed under Ahmed Dalgıç's successor, Mehmed Ağa, for Sultan Ahmed I (Istanbul, Topkapı Pal. Mus., 1/1652) is made of walnut inlaid with mother-of-pearl floral sprays on a tortoiseshell ground. To increase the brilliance, the inlay is nailed to the wood over silver foil and encrusted with peridots, rubies and turquoises. It is more sumptuous but not more novel than the shutters and door panels for the two pavilions, the 'Baghdad Kiosk' (1635) and the 'Revan Kiosk' (1639–40), built by Sultan Murad IV in the Topkapı Palace, or the canopied throne of St James the Lesser in the Armenian Patriarchate of St James in Jerusalem (1656). In the 17th century the quality of both technique and materials declined, although wooden stocks of firearms continued to be made (*see* §VIII, 1(ii) below). Those captured in the field are not of very high quality and must have been mass produced. They are inlaid with ivory (often stained), mother-of-pearl and ring-and-dot ornament in brass wire, studded with brass or, occasionally, encrusted with hardstones. Arms now in Wawel Castle in Kraków, for example, show that the decorative repertory was close to that of monumental furniture. The minute marquetry typical of 20th-century bazaar craftsmanship in Turkey, Syria and Egypt may date from a revival of this craft in 18th-century Syria.

Wood was also used for the interior decoration of domestic buildings. Although huge numbers have been destroyed by fire, many examples from the 18th and 19th centuries survive in former Ottoman towns such as Plovdiv in Bulgaria. Rooms in traditional homes such as the house of Nur al-Din in Damascus (1707; New York, Met.) had wooden panelling and ceilings painted and gilded, usually on a gesso ground, with raised designs of abstract and floral patterns, poems and architectural vignettes.

BIBLIOGRAPHY

C. Kerametli: 'Osmanlı devri ağaç işleri: Tahta oyma, sedef, bağ ve fildişi kakmaları' [Woodwork of the Ottoman period: wood-carving and incrustation with mother-of-pearl, ivory and tortoiseshell], *Türk Etnog. Derg.*, iv (1961), pp. 5–13

E. Yücel: 'Osmanlı ağaç işçiliği' [Ottoman woodwork], *Kült. ve Sanat*, v (1977), pp. 58–71, 190–91

J. M. Rogers: 'The State and the Arts in Ottoman Turkey: Part ii: The Furniture and Decoration of Süleymaniye', *Int. J. Mid. E. Stud.*, xiv (1982), pp. 283–313

Anadolu medeniyetleri/The Anatolian Civilisations, iii: *Seljuk/Ottoman* (exh. cat., ed. Ş. Aykoç and others; Istanbul, Topkapı Pal. Mus., 1983), pp. 154–7, 196–8

J. M. Rogers: 'Osmanische Holzarbeiten', *Türkische Kunst und Kultur aus osmanischer Zeit* (exh. cat., Frankfurt am Main, Mus. Ksthandwerk, 1985), pp. 320–32

C. Köseoğlu and J. M. Rogers: *The Topkapı Saray Museum: The Treasury* (Boston, 1987), pp. 187–8

The Age of Sultan Süleyman the Magnificent (exh. cat. by E. Atıl, Washington, DC, N.G.A.; Chicago, IL, A. Inst.; New York, Met.; 1987–8), pp. 166–72

Süleyman the Magnificent (exh. cat. by J. M. Rogers and R. M. Ward, London, BM, 1988), pp. 156–63

Timur and the Princely Vision: Persian Art and Culture in the Fifteenth Century (exh. cat. by T. W. Lentz and G. D. Lowry, Washington, DC, Sackler Gal.; Los Angeles, CA, Co. Mus. A.; 1989)

J. M. ROGERS

(v) *Yemen.* Wood was used for fine architectural fittings and furnishings throughout the region, but the fragility of the material makes it difficult to trace the history of traditional woodworking techniques, which disappeared in the middle of the 20th century. Wood was used in domestic architecture for doors, window-frames, shutters and grilles. In religious architecture it was used for ceilings and such furnishings as cenotaphs and minbars. The antiquity of this tradition is indicated by wooden ceilings in the great mosque at San'a, where the four bays at the west end of the northern prayer-hall (?10th century) are elaborately coffered and painted. Abyssinian cordia was preferred for exterior doors, as it is resistant to insects and water, but acacia and jujube were also used. Tamarisk was used for tool handles, locks, spoons, mortars and pestles, and fruit woods—for example apricot, pomegranate, pear and nut—were used for such turnings as waterpipes. Mustard-seed oil or paints based on it were applied as preservatives. Various techniques of joinery created large planks which were painted or carved in relief, with either a vertical or a bevelled cut. Screens were made of pierced planks, crossed laths or turned work. Wood was also inlaid with mother-of-pearl, ivory and coloured woods, and the effect of the finest pieces approaches marquetry.

Doors, which mark the boundary between public and increasingly private spaces, are set with the more important decoration visible to the visitor to denote the prestige of the owner. Outer doors are often massive affairs of planks joined side by side and decorated with metal knockers and nails, the heads of which are shaped like stars, cones and hemispheres. Inner doors often have rectangular frames around three rectangular panels, two horizontal ones above and a vertical one below. Sometimes each valve may have more than a dozen panels. The rectangular panels are decorated with oval medallions and cartouches, carved in a range of vegetal, geometric and epigraphic motifs, and occasionally animals and birds.

Window openings are covered with shutters, screens and flaps and sometimes have projecting grilles of wood. The use of grillework may go back to pre-Islamic times, to judge from a medieval Islamic description of the palace of Ghumdan in pre-Islamic San'a, although the two earliest examples of grillework to survive are the wooden lunette grille in the great mosque at San'a (1110–1230) and the wooden screen in Ashrafiyya Madrasa in Ta'izz (1397–1401). Lattice-like screens of turned wood (Arab. *mashrabiyya*) were only introduced to the Yemen in the 20th century from Egypt and the trading cities of the Red Sea coast; they replaced projecting oriel windows of brick and stone.

The earliest wooden cenotaphs, such as that of Sayyida in the mosque at Dhu'l-Jibla (1088–9), are simple rectangular solids decorated with inscriptions, but later examples are more elaborate constructions with a rectangular socle more than 1 m high surmounted by a smaller rectangular middle section and a cross-shaped upper storey with a pitched roof and polygonal domed aedicule at the crossing. The cenotaph in the Abhar Mosque at San'a for the imam al-Mansur al-Husayn (*reg* 1727–48) has a framework decorated with vegetal *rinceaux* enclosing nearly 100 carved and pierced panels showing geometric, arabesque and epigraphic ornament (see fig. 221). The tomb of al-Mutawakkil (*reg* 1716–27) in the corner of the mosque he erected in San'a is enclosed within an L-shaped wooden screen of seven units. Six of the units have four registers of openwork panels; the central panel in the second register is a window to allow the cenotaph to be seen. The seventh unit is a double door. The cenotaph itself follows the model of that erected for al-Mansur al-Husayn, except that the pitched roof is bowed. The tomb is dated by inscription to 1741 and was built by al-Mansur to honour his father. Al-Mansur's son Mahdi 'Abbas (*reg* 1748–75) also erected a magnificent cenotaph. It follows the standard type, but is distinguished by ogive arches on the gable ends, a dome over the aedicule and sumptuous painted decoration which highlights the splendid pierced carving of the panels. In the mosque at Sa'da the cenotaph (18th or 19th century) for Yahya al-Hadi (854–911), the first ZAYDI imam of the Yemen, has eliminated the middle

221. Wooden cenotaph for the imam al-Mansur al-Husayn, Abhar Mosque, San'a, Yemen, 1748

storey and replaced the openwork panels of the socle with horizontal cartouches carved with inscriptions in the Ottoman style.

BIBLIOGRAPHY

R. B. Serjeant and R. Lewcock: *San'a': An Arabian Islamic City* (London, 1983)

M. Schneider: 'Les Inscriptions arabes de l'ensemble architectural de Zafar-Di Bin (Yemen de Nord)', *J. Asiat.*, cclxxiii (1985), pp. 61–137, 293–369

G. Bonnenfant and P. Bonnenfant: *L'Art du bois à Sanaa: Architecture domestique* (Aix-en-Provence, 1987)

☐

(vi) Iran and western Central Asia. After *c.* 1250 wood continued to be used in the eastern Arab lands for functional items such as combs and bowls, for construction purposes and for fixed and movable furnishings. Many more examples survive from this period, so that regional styles and chronological developments can be discerned. While carving continued to be the primary means of decoration, much painted woodwork has also survived. The palmettes and rosettes used in vegetal ornament were replaced by the acanthus, lotus and vine as arabesques became increasingly geometricized and polygonal figures, particularly eight-pointed stars, became more important.

The two most important pieces surviving from the early 14th century are minbars in the congregational mosques of Na'in and Isfahan. The example in Na'in (1311) was ordered by a merchant and was signed by the 'designer' (Arab. *naqqāsh*) Mahmud Shah ibn Muhammad from Kirman. Of typical form and size (h. 5.22 m, w. 1.05 m., d. 3.19 m.), it is made of jujube wood. The triangular sides are composed of rectangular panels within a mortised frame. The panels and frame are carved with shallow Bevelled style arabesques, the balustrade is a lattice of interlaced octagons, and larger raised panels with stellate designs are used for emphasis on the canopy and the lintel. The minbar in Isfahan has complex octagonal tracery designs and fine intaglio-carving. It can be attributed to approximately the same date, as it is similar in size and form to the minbar in Na'in, although it lacks a canopy. The carving on the geometric panels resembles that from Na'in, but the decoration includes two new elements which are also found in contemporary architectural decoration in carved stucco: inscriptions in a stylized square Kufic script and naturalistic leaves in high relief. Many of these features can be found on other contemporary pieces, such as the doors to the mosque in the shrine of Bayazid Bistami at Bistam (1307–9), a group of cenotaphs from the area around Sultaniyya, the Mongol capital in north-west Iran (early 14th century), and a folding Koran stand dated 1359 (see fig. 222). They all show great technical ability and a rich decorative repertory; the Koran stand, in particular, has deeply undercut naturalistic flowers, inscriptions and arabesques worked on several levels. Perhaps the most unusual piece is the cenotaph of Esther from the mausoleum of Esther and Mordechai at Hamadan. All the decorative motifs and forms are typical of early 14th-century Persian woodwork except for the Hebrew inscription.

Superb craftsmanship was also known in western Central Asia. A cenotaph for Yahya ibn Ahmad (*d* 1336; Bukhara, Reg. Mus.), a grandson of the noted mystic Sayf

222. Carved wooden Koran stand, h. 1.30 m, from Turkestan, Kazakhstan, 1359 (New York, Metropolitan Museum of Art)

al-Din Bakharzi, is remarkable for its fine execution and the variety of its decoration. Its rectangular panels are carved in varying relief with hexagonal and octagonal star patterns, vegetal arabesques and a polylobed arch resting on columns. Work of this quality continued under the Timurid dynasty (*reg* 1370–1506). Carved wooden doors are preserved from many of the major buildings the Timurids erected, including the shrine of Ahmad Yasavi at Turkestan (1397–9; *see* TURKESTAN) and several buildings in Samarkand: the shrine of Qutham ibn 'Abbas (1403–4) and the tomb of Tuman Aqa (1404–5) in the Shah-i Zinda cemetery and the Gur-i Mir (1405; St Petersburg, Hermitage). The typical valve has three rectangular fields: a larger vertical panel in the centre with a smaller horizontal panel, often inscribed, above and below. Traces of paint indicate that the doors were once brightly coloured. The doors to the tomb of Tuman Aqa are the work of Sayyid Yusuf from Shiraz, and the unusual ivory and wood marquetry on doors from the Gur-i Mir is a technique previously associated with Syria and Egypt. Following Timur's campaigns in western Iran, Iraq and Syria, he forcibly moved craftsmen to western Central Asia to work on his new buildings. Multi-level floral and

223. Columns made from the trunks of oriental plane-trees, 'Ali Qapu Palace, Isfahan, 17th century

arabesque carving continued throughout the 15th century and transferred to other media, such as stone. A door in New York (Met.; 2.05×0.76 m) is carved with large blossoms on arabesque scrolls in a manner reminiscent of late 15th-century tombstones.

In 15th-century Iran woodwork continued to be produced at a more modest level of patronage, and many contemporary innovations from Central Asia went unnoticed. Two pairs of doors (1427–8) survive at the mosque at Afushta near Natanz in central Iran. One was donated by a local notable and the other is signed by the master Husayn ibn 'Ali, a woodworker and inlayer from Ubbad, a neighbouring village. Each valve has the traditional tripartite division, but the carving is less lively and broad flat borders contrast sharply with the carved arabesque ground. The richly forested, but remote province of Mazandaran was a major woodworking centre, and many of its mosques and shrines were fitted with carved wooden doors, shutters and cenotaphs. A cenotaph ordered in 1473 by a local ruler for the shrine of Abu'l-Qasim (1.13×1.18×1.86 m; Providence, RI Sch. Des., Mus. A.; *see* CENOTAPH, fig. 1) is signed by the masters Ahmad the carpenter and Hasan ibn Husayn. The shallow relief, geometric patterns and absence of vegetal arabesques recall work of previous centuries.

Much woodwork survives from the Safavid period, particularly from Isfahan, the city Shah 'Abbas I made his capital in 1596–7. Palaces and pavilions, such as the 'Ali Qapu, Hasht Bihisht and Chihil Sutun (all 17th century; *see* ISFAHAN, §3(vi) to (viii)) have wooden porticos (Pers. *tālār*) with columns made from the trunks of oriental

planes (see fig. 223). The columns are hexagonal or octagonal and are crowned with wooden *muqarnas* capitals. Columns and capitals were richly painted in tempera (Chihil Sutun, southern portico) or decorated with mirror mosaic (Chihil Sutun, eastern portico). Wooden ceilings were also richly ornamented. That of the Hasht Bihisht has geometric tracery composed of hexagons and eight-pointed stars, richly painted wooden panels (east and west porticos) and star-shaped mirrors, all meant to suggest the heavenly vault. Similarly, the ceiling of the great eastern portico of the Chihil Sutun was painted in blue with five-, eight- and ten-pointed stars. Wooden doors were frequently painted and varnished in the technique erroneously called 'lacquer' (*see* §VIII, 10 below), which was used on both leather and papier mâché. A pair of doors from the Chihil Sutun (h. 1.95 m; London, V&A) maintains the traditional tripartite composition but introduces figural scenes on the panels and floral arabesques for the frame.

Wooden grilles were used as balustrades and window screens. The two most frequent types are the rectangular grille surmounted by a pointed arch and the large grille composed of three or more movable panels. Both types use triangular, square or rectangular grids to create varied polygonal and stellate shapes. Their initial simplicity and wide mesh differentiates them from the *mashrabiyya* work of Egypt and Syria (*see* §(ii) above). The grilles of the great eastern portico of the Chihil Sutun have been restored on the basis of fragments found *in situ*. In later examples, the mesh is smaller, and the fillets are thinner, creating denser and more complex compositions in which stars and polygons proliferate. The central motif is often surrounded by narrow bands decorated with mirrors and covered in a fretwork of small pieces of wood. In the 18th century the decorative vocabulary of earlier times was repeated monotonously in fretwork and mosaic, but under the Qajar dynasty (*reg* 1779–1924) the decorative motifs changed completely. The mesh widened, designs were simplified, and linear geometric patterns were relegated to subsidiary positions. Curvilinear designs predominated, creating floral patterns, as in the Anguristan House at Isfahan. These grilles were often decorated with mirrors and uncoloured and coloured glass.

Wood continued to be used for columns, grilles, doors and shutters in the religious and domestic architecture of western Central Asia until the 19th century. The principal centres were Samarkand, Bukhara, Tashkent, Kokand and especially Khiva, where several mosques and palaces preserve extensive ensembles of carved wood. Most notable are the hypostyle halls and columnar porticos. The columns, which often rest on stone bases, are generally carved with horizontal bands of floral and spiral arabesques in low relief except at the base, which is carved in high relief with six ogival pendants surmounting a pear-like shape. Some have *muqarnas* capitals. The columns support corbelled brackets, carved beams and flat wooden roofs. Painted wooden ceilings are typical of important spaces. The tripartite compositions of earlier times are often found on carved doors, but other decorative schemes based on single large panels and many small panels were also used.

For additional information and bibliography, *see* CENTRAL ASIA, §I, 8(viii).

BIBLIOGRAPHY

L. H. Rabino: *Mazanderan and Astarabad* (London, 1928)
B. Deniké: 'Quelques Monuments de bois sculptés au Turkestan occidental', *A. Islam.*, ii (1935), pp. 69–83
A. Godard: 'Natanz', *Athar-é Iran*, i (1936), pp. 104–6
M. B. Smith and P. Wittek: 'The Wood Mimbar in the Masdjid-i Djami', Nain', *A. Islam.*, v (1938), pp. 21–35
L. Bronstein: 'Decorative Woodwork of the Islamic Period', *A Survey of Persian Art*, ed. A. U. Pope and P. Ackerman (2/London, 1969), pp. 2607–27
R. Orazi: *Wooden Gratings in Safavid Architecture* (Rome, 1976)
A. D. H. Bivar and E. Yarshater, eds: *Mazandaran Province, portfolio 1: Eastern Mazandaran—I* (1978), vi of *Persian Inscriptions down to the Early Safavid Period*, Corp. Insc. Iran., iv (London, 1977–)
L. Man'kovskaya: *Khiva* (Tashkent, 1982)
F. Noci: 'Un antico minbar in legno della Masjid-i Jam'a di Isfahan', *Quad. Ist. Stud. Islàm.*, ii (1982), pp. 1–12
G. Curatola: 'Some Ilkhanid Woodwork from the Area of Sultaniyya', *Islam. A.*, ii (1987), pp. 97–116
Timur and the Princely Vision: Persian Art and Culture in the Fifteenth Century (exh. cat. by T. W. Lentz and G. D. Lowry, Washington, DC, Sackler Gal.; Los Angeles, CA, Co. Mus. A.; 1989), pp. 45–6, 206–8

R. ORAZI

VIII. Other arts.

1. Arms and armour. 2. Coins. 3. Enamel. 4. Furniture. 5. Glass. 6. Glass painting. 7. Ivory. 8. Jade. 9. Jewellery. 10. Lacquer. 11. Oil painting. 12. Regalia. 13. Rock crystal. 14. Seals. 15. Shadow-puppets.

1. ARMS AND ARMOUR. Islamic arms and armour are often distinguished by rich surface decoration, including inlay with gold and silver, damascening and engraving. The introduction of firearms in the 15th century radically changed the nature of arms and armour in the Islamic lands, and far more examples survive from the later period. □

(i) Before *c.* 1500. (ii) After *c.* 1500.

(i) Before c. *1500.* The arms and armour of the early Islamic period continued pre-Islamic traditions of the Late Antique, Sasanian and Visigothic lands. Forms and decorative motifs characteristic of the arms used by the Turkic nomads of the Central Asian steppe were gradually introduced in the eastern Islamic lands, while in the western Islamic lands a separate tradition evolved in which Turkish forms and practices were far less apparent. These developments can be pieced together from the few surviving objects, the relatively obscure written sources and the more abundant, albeit highly stylized, pictorial sources.

(a) Materials. Iron was the most common material in the construction of Islamic arms. The mixing of metals was typical: a mail shirt or a cuirass might mix iron and bronze links or lamellae; a bronze hilt could be paired with an iron blade. The continued use of bronze set Islamic arms and armour apart from those in much of early medieval Europe. The use of bronze could have resulted from a lack of iron, a wealth of the metals used to form bronze and brass alloys, or the strength of a bronzeworking tradition in non-military metalwork.

Surface decoration was at first rare, as it was in other types of Islamic metalwork. Engraved inscriptions and arabesques then appeared (e.g. a 15th-century iron mask; London, Khalili priv. col., MTW 1390), followed by inlay with silver, copper and eventually a small amount of gold

(e.g. a Mamluk helmet with inlaid and engraved decoration; see fig. 224b) and from the 12th century with enamel (224g). Carved ivory or bone was used for hilts, and the use of soft stone for dagger grips is recorded in written sources. Leather was employed decoratively to cover sword grips (see fig. 225l and m) and scabbards. Hardened leather (cuir-bouilli) was used throughout the region for the segments of helmets, probably in conjunction with metallic frames, for lamellar armour and for shields, although the only surviving examples come from western Central Asia. Written sources indicate that such hardened leather could be tooled, gilded or painted, and thus leather for armour was decorated in the same manner as in such other arts as bookbinding. Buff leather seems to have been used as soft armour in Muslim Spain, parts of North Africa and the eastern Islamic lands, at least after the Mongol invasions of the 13th century. Wood was used for shields and seems to have been painted or covered with leather, although texts also mention polished wood. Textiles were also common, and a decorative layer of fabric covered at least one form of Islamic armour, the mail-lined *kazaghand*, a form of padded and fabric-covered body armour probably of Transoxianan or east Iranian origin, which came into widespread use before the 12th century. Jade was used for hilts and quillons in a group of swords and sabres (e.g. New York, Met. and Istanbul, Topkapı Pal. Mus.) generally attributed to the first half of the 15th century, when the Timurid prince Ulughbeg ruled Samarkand and when many Chinese features were adopted in the eastern Islamic lands.

(b) Forms and decoration. The huge area from Syria to Spain that the Arabs conquered was essentially Romano-Byzantine in its military traditions, and the short Roman stabbing sword (Lat. *gladius*) continued to be used for many centuries, as attested by written sources and surviving sword-hilts (see fig. 225e, h, j and k). In regions neighbouring Iran, Sasanian traditions were continued. A sword found in Oman, for example (untraced), has a longer blade in the Sasanian tradition. Indian weaponry may also have played a role, for early Arabic texts often mention Indian swords (Arab. *suyūf al-hind*), and a Hindu mythological bird was used as a decorative motif in a sword-hilt (225h), the metallurgical analysis of which points to Azerbaijan or Anatolia as the place of origin. In the Iberian peninsula, Visigothic models were probably continued. Although no examples survive from early Islamic Andalusia, a sword of essentially western form but with Islamic constructional features (Saint-Raphaël, Mus. Archéol.) has been found in a North African ship that sank in the 11th–12th century; it was discovered off the French coast outside Agay, east of Saint-Raphaël.

Until the 12th century most Islamic swords were straight and double-edged. Hilts were correspondingly symmetrical, though their designs varied. Some lacked cross-guards (225c, e, h, j and k); some had curved quillons (225l); others had cross-like quillons that resembled European types (225f, g, i and m).

The curved sabre was known in early Islamic Iran (225f) and probably further west, but it became popular only in the 13th century and commonly appears on metalwork from the 14th century (e.g. an inlaid cauldron;

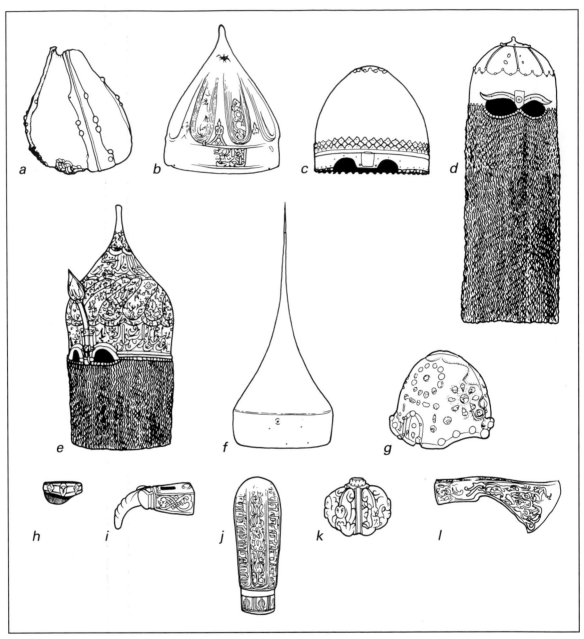

224. Islamic arms and armour, 7th–15th centuries: (a) segmented iron helmet covered with bronze or copper, found at Nineveh, northern Iraq, 7th–8th centuries AD (London, British Museum); (b) one-piece iron helmet with inlaid and engraved decoration, from ?Egypt or Syria, late 13th century–14th (Brussels, Musée de la Porte de Hal); (c) iron helmet with riveted brow-band, 14th century (Kraków, National Art Collections); (d) segmented iron helmet with riveted brow-band and brass or gilt decoration, late 13th century–14th (Istanbul, Military Museum); (e) one-piece gilt iron helmet inlaid with silver, from western Iran or Anatolia, *c.* 1450–*c.* 1500 (untraced); (f) one-piece iron helmet with Ottoman Topkapı Palace Armoury mark, from Anatolia, 15th century (London, Tower of London); (g) iron helmet gilded and inlaid with enamel medallions, from Granada or Morocco, *c.* 1480 (New York, Metropolitan Museum of Art); (h) silver archer's thumb-ring, from Egypt, *c.* AD 750–*c.* 850 (Cairo, Museum of Islamic Art); (i) bronze war-hammer head, from Iran, 11th–13th centuries (Ham, Surrey, Keir private collection); (j) engraved bronze macehead, found at Nishapur, 11th–12th century (Tehran, Archaeological Museum); (k) cast-iron macehead, from Iran, 11th–13th centuries (London, British Museum); (l) inlaid iron axehead, from Volga Bulgar, late 12th century–early 13th (untraced)

Konya, Mevlana Mus.). Early Islamic daggers excavated in Jordan are simple workaday objects, but highly decorated examples are also known. Part of a dagger grip, probably from 10th-century Iran (untraced), is made of silver embossed with a hunting motif, while an ear dagger, a type of dagger with twin discs at the pommel of the hilt, from 15th-century Spain (225d) is made of ivory laid over wood and bronze.

The mace was a popular weapon. Maceheads in cast bronze had been used in Iran at least from the 8th century BC, while bronze war-axes are among the weapons excavated at DURA EUROPOS in Syria (3rd century AD). Such weapons probably spread from Iran both before and during the early Islamic centuries. The mace was a symbol of authority as well as an offensive weapon, as demonstrated by miniature maceheads which had no real military function (225a). Maceheads also assumed many different forms. These included an elongated and often inlaid type, such as an 11th- or 12th-century example from Nishapur in north-east Iran (224j), a bulbous fluted type which could also be highly decorated (224k) and an animal- or monster-headed style, such as a 12th- or 13th-century example from the eastern Islamic world (225b). The war-hammer, sometimes with a hook or spike at the rear, was another specialized form of mace (see fig. 224i). Few war-axes survive from this early period (224l), although they became widespread in later centuries.

Helmets were generally made of iron and decorated with costlier materials. One of the earliest to survive (224a) is attributed to the 7th or 8th century. Although much corroded, it probably had a splendid covering in copper or bronze. It follows the Central Asian tradition of segmented construction that was used until the late 13th century or early 14th (224d) but was gradually supplanted by single-piece construction (224b, c, e, f and g). A one-piece iron helmet has also been discovered in an early 8th-century context at Varakhsha, in Uzbekistan.

A fragmented 7th- or 8th-century cuirass from southern Iran (New York, Met.) mixes iron and bronze/copper lamellae. Such a mixture may be the reality behind the rows of blue and gold lamellae depicted on 12th- and 13th-century ceramics and in illustrated manuscripts, such as a copy of ʿAyyuqi's *Varqa and Gulshah* (Istanbul, Topkapı Pal. Lib., H. 841; see fig. 125 above), and gives credence to the almost invariable medieval European description of Saracen helmets as golden. Bronze links had been used in mail armour in the pre-Islamic Middle East and are shown in late 11th-century Spanish manuscript illustrations, such as those in Beatus' commentary on the Apocalypse (London, BL, Add. MS. 11695).

Most archery equipment was made of perishable material and has not survived, but a silver archer's thumbring found at Fustat (Old Cairo; 224h) shows that expensive materials were also used. Numerous pictorial sources from at least the 12th century onwards, including manuscripts, ceramics and decorated metalwares, suggest that Turkish horse archers used abundantly decorated bows, quivers and bowcases comparable to those found in various graves throughout most of the Eurasian steppes, such as a Turkish bowcase from Khir-Yurt (7th–8th century; St Petersburg, Hermitage), an Alan bow and bowcase from Moshchevaya Balka in the northern Caucasus (8th–9th century; St Petersburg, Mus. Ethnog.), numerous quivers from western Central Asia and an almost perfectly preserved bowcase from western Siberia (14th–15th century; St Petersburg, Hermitage). Shields may also have followed nomadic prototypes; a silver gilt plate probably made in 9th-century Sogdiana (St Petersburg, Hermitage) shows typical Central Asian quivers, early forms of bowcase and small round shields.

Arms and armour typical of the Turkic nomads of the Central Asian steppe were gradually incorporated into the Islamic repertory, the most common examples being small lamellar cuirasses, which are depicted on many 10th-century ceramics from Nishapur, and the curved sabre. Even decorative motifs, such as the dragons' heads found on a 12th-century sword from Iraq (225l), were copied from Turkic prototypes. In the 15th century more naturalistic plant motifs were introduced (224e).

A separate evolution took place in the 14th and 15th centuries in the western Islamic lands, particularly in Andalusia and North Africa. Geometric designs, arabesques and calligraphy dominated the decorative repertory (225d), and distinct types of weapons developed. The earlier Roman stabbing sword evolved into the highly decorated 'Grenadine' swords of the 15th century, and the few curved swords were distinguished from Central Asian types by their different forms of hilt. A kidney-shaped shield (Arab. *daraqa*, Span. *adarga*; e.g. Vienna, Ksthist. Mus., C195) was produced in Morocco and Granada and probably evolved from larger ones made of hide that had been typical in earlier periods.

Arms were also imported from western Europe. The most famous, though controversial, example is the Helmet of Boabdil (224g). Essentially a 15th-century Italian or Spanish sallet, it is a type of light helmet with a neck guard, which was probably decorated in Muslim territory. The abundant enamelled medallions set into its surface might explain the carbuncles and other jewels mentioned in 12th- and 13th-century French chansons de geste as decorating helmets of Muslim warriors.

A few features were also imported from the eastern Islamic world. Two highly corroded swords from Gibraltar (London, BM, on loan to London, Tower) have quillons made by sandwiching two pieces of metal on either side of the blade and tang, a method originally used in Iran or Central Asia. The swords can be dated to the 12th–14th century, and this form of hilt construction and the spherical pommels, as well as the scale-decorated tin covering the grip on one of them, suggest an Islamic provenance.

BIBLIOGRAPHY

H. Stocklein: 'Die Waffenshätze im Topkapu Sarayi Müzesi', *A. Islam.*, i (1934), pp. 200–18

A. R. Zaki: *Al-siyah fi'l-islām* [Arms in Islam] (Cairo, 1951)

A. B. de Hoffmeyer: *Arms and Armour in Spain, a Short Survey*, 2 vols (Madrid, 1972–82)

D. C. Nicolle: *Early Medieval Islamic Arms and Armour* (Madrid, 1976)

R. Elgood, ed.: *Islamic Arms and Armour* (London, 1979)

A. S. Melikian-Chirvani: 'Notes sur la terminologie de la métallurgie et des armes dans l'Iran musulmane', *J. Econ. & Soc. Hist. Orient*, xxiv (1981), pp. 310–16

——: 'The Westward Journey of the Kazhagand', *J. Arms & Armour Soc.*, xi (1983), pp. 8–35

A. North: *An Introduction to Islamic Arms* (London, 1985)

D. C. Nicolle: *Arms and Armour of the Crusading Era, 1050–1350* (New York, 1988)

D. Alexander: *The Arts of War: Arms and Armour of the 7th to 19th Centuries* (1992), xxi of *The Nasser D. Khalili Collection of Islamic Art*, ed. J. Raby (London and New York, 1992–)

Al-Andalus: The Art of Islamic Spain (exh. cat., ed. J. D. Dodds; Granada, Alhambra, and New York, Met., 1992), nos 60–69

DAVID NICOLLE

(ii) After c. 1500. With the conquest of Egypt and Syria in 1516–17, the Turkish Ottoman dynasty (*reg* 1281–1924) established rule over much of the Mediterranean and Near

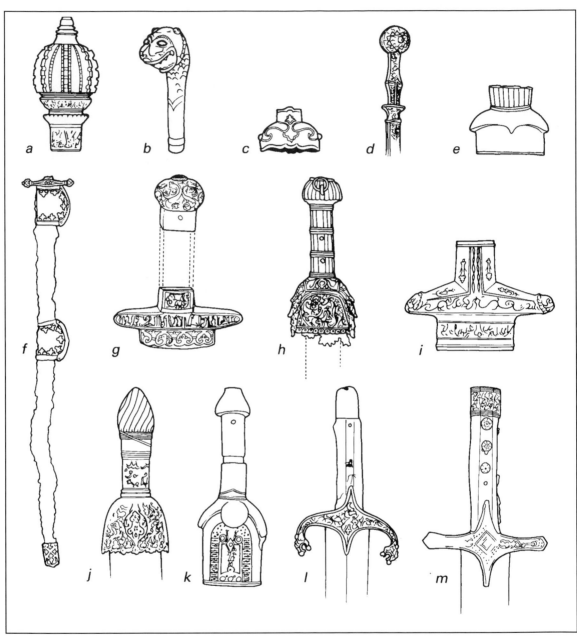

225. Islamic arms and armour, 8th–15th centuries: (a) miniature silvered macehead inscribed with the name of Abu'l-Fath Muhammad ibn Sultan, from Transoxiana or north-east Iran, 1199–1220 (exh. Spink and Son Ltd, London, 1977; untraced); (b) brass zoomorphic macehead, ?from Iran, 12th–13th centuries (Los Angeles, CA, County Museum of Art); (c) bronze matrix for shaping sword guards, ?from Iran, 12th–14th centuries (New York, Metropolitan Museum of Art); (d) 'ear' dagger, ivory, wood and bronze, from Andalusia, late 15th century (Madrid, Real Armeria); (e) iron sword-guard, found at al-Rabadhah, Saudi Arabia, 8th–9th century AD (Riyadh, King Saud University); (f) slightly curved iron sabre with gilt-bronze quillons, scabbard mounts and chape, found at Nishapur, 9th–11th century (New York, Metropolitan Museum of Art); (g) bronze sword pommel and quillons engraved with Koran cxii, from Egypt (London, Storm Rice private collection); (h) bronze sword-hilt in the form of a lotus plant, from Azerbaijan or eastern Anatolia, late 10th century AD (Bodrum, Bodrum Museum); (i) engraved gold quillon, from Iran, 13th–14th centuries (St Louis, MO, Art Museum); (j) bronze sword-hilt, from Andalusia, late 13th century–15th (Istanbul, Military Museum); (k) bronze sword-hilt, ?from Egypt or Syria, 13th–15th centuries (Istanbul, Military Museum); (l) sword of an unnamed caliph, Iraq, late 12th century–13th (Istanbul, Topkapı Palace Museum); (m) second sword of Caliph al-Mustaʿsim, from Iraq, mid-13th century, with pommel added in Istanbul, 1451–81 (Istanbul, Topkapı Palace Museum)

East. As in the case of non-military metalwork, the weapons produced in the Ottoman capital at Istanbul set the style for the rest of the empire, and these can be distinguished from arms and armour made in the Islamic east.

(a) Ottoman empire. (b) Eastern Islamic lands.

(a) Ottoman empire. Many examples of Ottoman arms and armour have been preserved in the former imperial armouries in Istanbul, which also received large amounts of booty from Ottoman successes in Iran, the Near East and western Europe. Most of the finer pieces are in the Topkapı Palace Museum, Istanbul, while others are preserved in Turkish military museums (e.g. Istanbul, Mil. Mus.). Collections outside Turkey (e.g. Kraków, N. A. Cols) contain booty seized when the Ottomans were defeated at the second siege of Vienna in 1683.

The main form of Turkish armour at the beginning of the 16th century was a mail corslet reaching down to the thighs with short sleeves. A series of rectangular plates were arranged horizontally over the mail at the front and back to form a panel of overlapping lames. A second type consisted of a large, circular convex plate at front and back with a series of smaller plates linked by mail providing a defence for the upper chest and shoulders; shaped vambraces of plate covered the forearm and hand, and narrow greaves with oval plate defences for the knee-joints were sometimes added, linked by rings to the main areas of mail. This was the armour worn by the janissaries, and much of it is of undistinguished quality and was clearly munition armour for the ordinary soldiers. Some examples were richly decorated with damascening in gold and silver and fine engraving; these were presumably made for their officers.

Helmets of the 16th century were usually made of steel and followed the conical forms introduced in the preceding century, but the profile had a much sharper taper towards the top, and the base was formed by a broad band. Protection for the face and brow was provided by a small peak at the front, combined with a vertically sliding bar. One type of helmet, which may have been made in one workshop for one detachment of the army, has almost parallel sides so that it is wide enough to fit over a turban; the sharply tapering top is skilfully hammered into broad spiral flutes and terminates in a polygonal knob, while the surface has been blued and then damascened in silver and gold. Some still preserve their mail aventails. In addition to fluting and damascening, decoration could consist of patterns of scrolling foliage, arabesques and palmettes in the Ottoman taste, incised into the surface or worked as copper or brass inlay. Inscriptions were also added, usually in the form of grand titles or pious invocations, although they occasionally included the owner's name. An example probably made for the sultan (see fig. 226) is inlaid with gold arabesques and encrusted with gold medallions studded with rubies, turquoises and amethysts. During the 16th and 17th centuries, conical helmets were also made of gilt-copper (*tombak*) for use as parade armour and bore engraved decoration of ring-matting. Some 17th-century helmets of this type are formed of vertical straps pierced in openwork and lined with velvet.

226. Parade helmet, iron, damascened with gold and enhanced with niello, set with gold plaques and relief tracery and encrusted with rubies, turquoises and amethysts, h. 270 mm, from Istanbul, mid-16th century (Istanbul, Topkapı Palace Museum)

Two other types of helmet were also used. One, a cap-like adaptation of the conical helmet known as the chichak, was worn by the Ottoman cavalry by 1500. The main component was a rounded bowl with earflaps to which a peak and an extension at the back to protect the neck were usually attached by riveting; the face was protected by a vertically sliding bar that passed through a hole in the peak; and the earflaps were sometimes extended with plates to protect the cheeks. Most were made of steel, and their quality varied enormously. The chichak was still in use in the 17th century, when it was transmitted to Europe, forming the prototype for the Civil War 'pot' in England. A simplified form of the janissary headgear—a distinctive white felt cap with a long flap hanging over the shoulders—was also produced during the 16th century. It consisted of a steel, silver or gilt-copper cone-shaped helmet with a convex top and a plume-holder shaped rather like a vambrace riveted to the front.

Horse armour from the 16th and 17th centuries consists mainly of a large number of rectangular plates arranged horizontally and linked by mail to circular or square plates designed to defend the more exposed areas. Chanfrons were formed of either a single plate or a series of plates linked by mail; single-plate chanfrons were made in gilt-copper as well as the more usual steel.

Ottoman wicker shields have a distinctive round shape with a convex profile. Lightweight and sturdy, they measure from 600 to 670 mm in diameter and are formed of cane wrapped in coloured silk that has been wound around a central steel or iron boss that is often inlaid with gold. The silk wrapping is sometimes worked into precisely rendered patterns on a crimson ground, and the underside is often padded and lined with velvet. A steel version was also produced. The cavalry was usually equipped with long lances with leaf-shaped heads. Short wooden javelins with small triangular heads and long flights to steady them have also survived. Standards were distinctive, consisting of either a flat, leaf-shaped box of brass or gilt-copper or a crescent mounted on a pole with horsehair and textiles suspended from it. War maces of the 16th and 17th centuries have large onion-shaped heads of steel, sometimes divided into separate lobes, or have a series of flanges arranged around a central column. The latter type, made in silver or gilt-copper, was used in the 17th century as a symbol of office, and some ceremonial maces made of precious metals and hardstones such as rock crystal and jade are of imperial quality. One example (Istanbul, Topkapı Pal. Mus., 2/715) has an iron or steel core sheathed in gold and is studded with small rubies and turquoises in the same manner as the helmet in the same collection. Flails and war-axes were also carried in battle and on parade. Under Ottoman domination the Mamluks of Egypt carried a crescent-shaped broad-bladed axe set with a hammer head on the opposite side. The blades were often fretted out with inscriptions. The handles are usually of steel or wood, the more elaborate parade axes being inlaid with ivory and mother-of-pearl or decorated with lacquer.

The usual sword carried for war was a curved single-edged sabre with small pommel and grip formed of horn or wood plaques pinned through the tang, although steel examples are known (see fig. 227a). A sabre made for Sultan Süleyman (*reg* 1520–66; Istanbul, Topkapı Pal. Mus., 1/463) has a leather-covered hilt held in place by three gilt studs and a blackened steel pommel and guard inlaid with gold; the steel blade has gold damascened inscriptions on each side; the wooden, leather-covered scabbard has blackened steel mounts inlaid with gold to match the pommel and guard. A short sword (yataghan) was also widely carried. It has a forward-curving single-edged blade and a grip with two ears at the top and was carried in the waistband (see fig. 227c).

In medieval times the Turks had developed a very powerful short bow for use by horsemen. Archery in Turkey reached its peak in the mid-16th century. These short bows were composed of laminations of horn sinew and wood which combined elasticity with power. The bow was in general more effective than the musket.

Firearms were introduced to Turkey at the end of the 15th century, and the earliest illustrations in manuscripts such as a copy of the *Süleymannāme* ('History of Süleyman'; 1558; Istanbul, Topkapı Pal. Lib., H. 1517) depict matchlocks with square-sectioned stocks and round barrels. A type of musket used by the janissaries until the 18th century had a short polygonal stock decorated with metal inlays and a heavy barrel of watered steel. The snap-lock mechanism known as the miquelet was adopted in the 17th century, but by 1700 was replaced by an imported lock operating on the flintlock principle. Turkish gun barrels of watered steel were widely exported, and others with round or polygonal walls so thick that designs could

227. Swords and scabbards (from left to right): (a) scabbard and sword, watered steel blade inlaid in gold and hilt of blued steel damascened in gold, l. 965 mm, from Turkey, *c.* 1850, the blade probably earlier; (b) sword, watered steel blade inlaid with the name Kalb 'Ali, hilt chiselled and overlaid with gold, l. 955 mm, from Iran, late 17th century; (c) scabbard and yataghan, steel mounts overlaid in gold, ivory grip, blade inscribed with pious invocations and heroic verses, the name of the maker 'Umar and the name of the owner, Muhammad Rashid Paşa, l. 730 mm, from Istanbul, 1840 (London, Victoria and Albert Museum)

be chiselled into the surface without affecting their strength were highly prized in the West. One is fitted to a musket in Louis XIII's 'cabinet d'armes' (London, V&A, 12-1949). By the 17th century the typical stock was polygonal in section and straight-sided with a step behind the breech. Butts are made of separate blocks of ivory joined by dowels, and stocks are elaborately decorated, either by overlaying with pierced and engraved silver, inlaying with coral, mother-of-pearl and metals, or by covering with velvet pinned with decorative studs. Guns are signed in various ways: lockplates are stamped with the name of the maker; barrels are inlaid with dates and names, including that of the owner; silver mounts are stamped with tughras. Some 18th-century guns are engraved with pseudo-European lettering imitating the signatures on European flintlocks.

Large wall guns were a speciality of Turkish gunmakers; a series in the Topkapı Palace have long thick barrels and muzzles chiselled in the form of monsters' heads or with repeating foliate patterns. Blunderbusses with bell-shaped muzzles and short stocks inlaid with scrolling wire were made in the late 18th century and early 19th for use on horseback. Most surviving pistols also date from the 18th and 19th centuries. A few exemplify an indigenous Ottoman style characterized by a curious rat-tail stock, silver sheet embossed over the entire surface, and an extended tubular capucine at the muzzle. More common are those with down-curving stocks and prominent butts that imitate Western styles.

With Selim I's conquest of Egypt in the early 16th century, Ottoman styles of arms and armour were transmitted to North Africa. In the Sudan a short-sleeved mail shirt formed of interlinked riveted rings was worn split up the middle for riding. Better-quality helmets were round and had a fixed nasal defence and a large aventail. In the 19th century the khedive of Egypt ordered helmets from Birmingham and mail shirts made from split key-rings. The straight double-edged sword with cruciform hilt typical of the medieval period was retained in the Sudan and elsewhere in North Africa until the end of the 19th century. Blades were often imported from such western European sources as Solingen and mounted in silver. The standard North African gun was long and had as many as 25 simple round bands to attach the barrel to the stock, which was mounted in brass or steel set with crudely engraved bone or ivory plaques and overlaid with silver bands. Most pistols were made of imported elements which were decorated locally. A group with coral decoration, for example, was made in Algiers in the 19th century.

The classic weapons in Arabia from the 16th century were the sword and the dagger. Swords were distinguished by grips with angular extensions. Hilts were nielloed to contrast with the silver or gold punched ground, and gold filigree, sometimes set with rows of precious stones, was used for the mounts. Daggers had strongly curved scabbards, and the same elaborate filigree was used to decorate hilts, scabbards and the accompanying belts.

(b) Eastern Islamic lands. Armour made in the eastern Islamic lands after 1500 combined plate with mail or leather and textile garments. Rectangular or circular plates (Pers. *chahār a'ina*) protected the body; tubular vambraces (*bāzūband*) covered the arms from wrist to elbow and were secured by straps. The typical helmet is a rounded cone and has a nasal defence, tall crest and mail aventail with pointed ends. Examples from the 16th and 17th centuries have almost parallel sides and are generally made of heavier metal than later examples. The typical decoration consists of gold damascening and stylized floral ornaments chiselled into the surface. After 1830 designs taken from book illustrations were engraved and then inlaid with silver and gold. Pieces were often inscribed with well-known Koranic quotations such as the Throne Verse (ii.255) or the Sura of Victory (xlviii), the names of God, common exhortations such as 'Open, O Opener of Gates' and couplets by such famous poets as Firdawsi or Hafiz. Armour was often made 'en suite'. One of the earliest and most elaborate examples is a set of body-plates, vambraces, helmet and shield made for Sulayman I (*reg* 1666–94; Kraków, N. Mus.) in which plain steel surfaces are played off against cartouches and bands with

scrolling arabesques and dedicatory inscriptions in gold and silver; the most unusual decoration is the bosses in the shape of suns with faces. Another set (Berne, Hist. Mus.) includes a long-sleeved garment, shirt and cape of riveted mail, body-plates and a round conical helmet with a mail aventail and a distinctive peak at the front. While the defence for the body follows the classical Persian forms, the helmet is based on Chinese or Mongol prototypes, and the set was probably made in western Central Asia.

Staff weapons such as lances and spears show considerable ingenuity. Examples from the 17th and 18th centuries include tridents, twin-bladed forks with wavy blades, and pikes with triangular blades of hollow-ground section. The cavalry also used short javelins, which were usually made in sets of three and housed in a wooden case, often mounted in silver. Those made for war have wooden shafts with long triangular-sectioned heads and flights. Javelins made of tubular steel sections and damascened in gold were used in the 19th century.

The saddle-axe with a small, hatchet-shaped blade was also popular in Iran. Several signed by Lutf'Ali Ghulam are remarkable for their fine craftsmanship and artistry. One dated 1735–6 (Milan, Mus. Poldi Pezzoli) is decorated with calligraphy, while another made four years later (London, Wallace) depicts a hawk attacking a heron. Larger, crescent-shaped double-axes were used as symbols of office and had lavish decoration; the watered steel head was chiselled and overlaid with gold. Similar materials were used for a distinctive form of mace which had a head shaped like a bull or a demon. Used in medieval times, it was revived in the 18th and 19th centuries for parades. Flanged maces were larger and more elegant than contemporary Turkish examples, and both shaft and head were sometimes damascened in gold. Many are signed by Hajji 'Abbas, an Iranian craftsman who specialized in chiselled steel and supposedly worked in the 17th century, although most works bearing his signature date from the 19th.

The typical sword had a broad single-edged curved blade, usually of watered steel, and short, rounded quillons. Blades were chiselled with shallow grooves or were broad and flat. Pieces made before the 18th century are gently curved and comparatively heavy and have hilts of ivory or bone plaques riveted to the tang. Later pieces are more severely curved and lighter and have pommels set at right angles to the tang. In the late 18th century the straight double-edged sword was revived and was often fitted with a steel hilt engraved with Koranic inscriptions. Many pieces are signed by such famous 17th-century craftsmen as Asadallah of Isfahan or Kalb 'Ali (227b), but the signatures occur on pieces of varying date and may have been used as a mark of quality. Daggers often had finely carved hilts, made of ivory or bone and set with stones. They were decorated with floral designs, figures and poetic verses about daggers (see fig. 231 below).

Iranian gunsmiths specialized in long guns of relatively light construction. Their general shape seems to have been inspired by Ottoman models, but their narrow proportions and considerable length make them appear more elegant. Barrels were made of watered steel. Examples from the 18th century have scrolling palmettes damascened in gold along the top of the barrel, while later ones are entirely chiselled with designs based on contemporary textiles.

BIBLIOGRAPHY

P. Holstein: *Armes orientales* (Paris, 1931)
R. Zeller and E. F. Rohrer: *Orientalische Sammlung Henri Moser Charlottenfels* (Berne, 1955)
K. A. C. Creswell: *A Bibliography of Arms and Armour in Islam* (London, 1956)
H. R. Robinson: *Oriental Armour* (London, 1967)
R. Elgood, ed.: *Islamic Arms and Armour* (London, 1979)
C. Blair, ed.: *Pollard's History of Firearms* (London, 1983)
A. Jacob: *Les Armes blanches du monde islamique* (Paris, 1985)
A. North: *An Introduction to Islamic Arms* (London, 1985)
D. Alexander: *The Arts of War: Arms and Armour of the 7th to 19th Centuries* (1992), xxi of *The Nasser D. Khalili Collection of Islamic Art*, ed. J. Raby (London and New York, 1992–)
R. Elgood: *Arms and Armour of Arabia in the 18th, 19th, and 20th Centuries* (Aldershot, 1994)
D. G. Alexander, L. Kalus and T. Tezcan: *Épées et armes apparantes* (in preparation), i of *Catalogue des armes de mains de la collection du palais du Topkapı à Istanbul* (Istanbul)
D. G. Alexander: *Catalogue of the Islamic Arms and Armour in the Metropolitan Museum* (New York, in preparation)

A. R. E. NORTH

2. COINS. The inscriptions on Islamic coins were engraved in reverse on the polished end of cylindrical iron dies using a pointed tool. There is evidence on the coins that letter groups or entire lines of script were sometimes formed as a punch that was stamped into the die, and also that letters were inscribed with some sort of rotating burin, but both these techniques were exceptional, the first at the beginning of the 8th century AD only and the second at the end of the 8th century and beginning of the 9th. Sometimes, as in Egypt under the Fatimids and Ayyubids (*reg* 1169–1252), the surface of the dies was polished to provide a mirror-smooth background for the inscriptions on the coins. Two dies were needed to make a coin: the lower die was fixed solidly in place, a disc of metal placed on it, and the upper die mounted on that, held more or less vertical by a worker. A hammer blow, or several blows, on the end of the upper die impressed the engraving of both dies on the two faces of the coin. The general technique was the same as that in Europe, inasmuch as the different civilizations inherited the same monetary technology from antiquity. The inscriptions on nearly all Islamic coins include the city and year of issue, making each coin a miniature historical document, bearing information intentionally placed on it by its issuers and unintentionally conveyed by its style, manufacture, weight and alloy.

(i) 7th–12th centuries. (ii) 13th–19th centuries.

(i) 7th–12th centuries. During the lifetime of the Prophet Muhammad (*c.* 570–632), the Arabs of Mecca and Medina minted no coins of their own but used the gold and silver coins of the Byzantine and Persian empires. The earliest coins with Arabic inscriptions were issued in Iran from 651 and are almost exactly like the silver coins of the Sasanian empire, which had just been conquered: they have the same standard portrait of the Sasanian emperor, the same Zoroastrian fire altar on the reverse and the same inscriptions in Pahlavi (middle Persian) (*see* ANCIENT NEAR EAST, §II, 8(iii)). The coinage issued in Iran by the Arabs differed at first only in having short religious phrases in Arabic written in the margins (see fig. 228a). Later in

the 7th century the names of Arab officials, still written in Pahlavi script, were substituted for the name of the Sasanian emperor, and at the very end of the century, one governor had his name written in Arabic instead of Pahlavi. The epigraphic style of the Arabic inscriptions can be defined as 'Pahlavesque', for the letters are the same as in modern Arabic but the strokes that form them are the strokes used in Pahlavi. There is nothing remarkable in the continuity of this coinage from Sasanian times, since the workmen who made the coins were the same men (or their descendants) who had made coins under the Sasanians. Coins such as these Arab–Sasanian issues are sometimes known as imitations, but the term is unjust since the workmen can hardly be accused of imitating their own work.

In Egypt also, perhaps after a hiatus following the Arab conquest in 641, minting was resumed at Alexandria with coins so similar to those of the Byzantine period that they have often confused the most erudite catalToguers, since Arabic inscriptions were not used on the earliest Islamic coins in Egypt. In Syria, where there were no Byzantine mints, there was no official Arab minting until the Umayyad caliph 'Abd al-Malik (*reg* 685–705) reorganized the caliphate in 692, but there also the first coins were adaptations of Byzantine types in gold (228b) and copper (228c) and the Sasanian type in silver (228d). These earliest Damascus coins, with adaptations of Roman and Sasanian imagery, lasted only two years (692–4) before being replaced by coins with a new image, the caliph standing, girt with his sword (228e). But this imagery was apparently also controversial, perhaps because the caliph was not supposed to be an analogue of previous emperors, so in 697 a new and original completely Islamic design was invented for the coinage, with only religious inscriptions in Arabic, plus the date and, on silver, the name of the mint (228f). This design, with several horizontal lines of inscription surrounded by a circular inscription on obverse and reverse, became the standard Islamic type for centuries. It is characteristic of Islamic coins that they have no images, only inscriptions; although occasionally Muslims have issued coins of Western type with images, especially following the acquisition of new territories. Conversely, Islamic designs were sometimes issued by Christian powers, such as the Crusaders, the Normans of Sicily and the kings of Spain; these coins either copied the inscriptions of some Muslim coinage or had Christian inscriptions in Arabic.

With the foundation *c.* 705 of Wasit in Iraq as eastern capital of the Umayyad dynasty, there began a new style of epigraphy, which was characteristic of Islamic coinage for the next few centuries (see fig. 229a). This style is known to numismatists as kufic, and in some European countries it has given its name to the entire coinage of early Islam. The script is similar to that used in manuscripts and on buildings in that the letters are rigid and angular, composed of straight lines and circle segments. Within this general characterization, however, a variety of scripts is included. At the beginning, on Umayyad gold dinars and silver dirhams, the script is exceedingly rectilinear, but the inscriptions on the coins are well proportioned and laid out with plenty of space. In the course of the 8th century, when power passed to the Abbasid caliphs, the

228. Islamic coins of the 7th century, obverse and reverse: (a) silver drahm with the name of Khusraw, diam. 28 mm, minted at Darapgird, Iran, year 30 of the Yazdegird era, AD 661–2; (b) gold solidus, diam. 20 mm, minted at Damascus, Syria, AD 692–4; (c) bronze fals, diam. 21 mm, minted at Emesa (Homs), Syria, AD 693–4; (d) silver drahm, diam. 31 mm, minted at Damascus, Syria, AD 693–4; (e) gold dinar, diam. 20 mm, minted at ?Damascus, Syria, AD 694–5; (f) gold dinar, diam. 19 mm, minted at ?Damascus, Syria, AD 696–7 (New York, American Numismatic Society)

letters became increasingly stretched, extending horizontally while decreasing in height. This attenuation can be seen most vividly in letters with upper and lower horizontal lines, such as *dāl* and *kāf*. At the peak of this trend (*c.* 780) the letters extend across the entire face of the coin, cramping the other letters of the same line into a small area (229b). This extremely mannered script was used from North Africa to western Central Asia. In the second half of the 8th century, the name of the caliph and other officials also began to be put on coins. As the names and titles grew longer and more and more officials were mentioned on a single coin, the inscriptions became cramped, ugly and hard to read.

The political disintegration of the Abbasid caliphate in the 9th and 10th centuries gave rise to greater regional diversity in coin epigraphy, all still within the general definition of kufic script and generally with the same religious inscriptions and arrangement (on each face, three or four horizontal lines of script surrounded by one or more circular inscriptions). At Baghdad, the capital, under the caliph al-Ma'mun (*reg* 813–33 with interruption), a new style was introduced *c.* 820, successfully resolving the problem of engraving some 200 words on the two circular

faces of a coin some 25 mm in diameter: the letters are small but well proportioned vertically and horizontally and easy to read; the obverse has a new circular inscription in the margin (229c). Under al-Ma'mun the new-style coins were once again anonymous, but his successor, al-Mu'tasim (*reg* 833–42), restored his name to the coinage, and henceforth all coins issued under the caliph's direct authority had no names other than that of the caliph and his designated heir, if any. For this reason, when rulers belonging to such dynasties as the Tulunids (*reg* 868–905), the Samanids (*reg* 819–1005) and the Saffarids (*reg* 867–*c.* 1495) had their names added to that of the caliph on coins, it was taken as an expression of their independence. Subsequently the right of *sikka*, to have one's name on the coinage, even along with that of the caliph and other overlords, became a mark of independent sovereignty in the Islamic world.

This new style, including its inscriptions and their arrangement, was the basis for regional variations in the eastern Islamic lands from the 9th to the 13th century. Within its well-defined parameters, die engravers could employ their often considerable talents only in minor variations. While the overall kufic style was maintained,

229. Islamic coins of the 8th–11th centuries, obverse and reverse: (a) silver dirham, diam. 27 mm, minted at Wasit, Iraq, AD 704–5; (b) silver dirham with the name of the Abbāsid caliph al-Mahdi, diam. 22 mm, minted at Madinat al-Salam (Baghdad), Iraq, AD 778–9; (c) silver dirham, diam. 27 mm, minted at Madinat al-Salam (Baghdad), Iraq, AD 821–2; (d) gold dinar with the name of the Ghaznavid ruler Mahmud, diam. 26 mm, minted at Nishapur, Iran, 1003–4; (e) silver dinar with the name of the Fatimid caliph al-Mu'izz, diam. 23 mm, minted at al-Mansuriyya, Tunisia, AD 953–4; (f) gold dinar with the name of the Fatimid caliph al-Musta li, diam. 22 mm, minted at Misr (Cairo), Egypt, 1097–8 (New York, American Numismatic Society)

inscriptions might be more or less rectilinear, and it became common to ornament the letters with arabesques. Sometimes part of the inscriptions on a coin might be engraved in a script so miniscule that it cannot be read without magnification. Such inscriptions were probably engraved by older short-sighted engravers, and a tendency towards short-sightedness may have been hereditary among die engravers. At other times certain words or phrases might be engraved in a large and muscular kufic. Long double horizontals might be plaited, that is engraved so that two horizontal strokes appear to intertwine. The first line of the central inscription on the obverse, *lā ilah illā* ('there is no god but . . .'), begins and ends with the ligature *lāmalif*, and these two prominent characters were elaborated in all sorts of ways. Although the position of the main inscriptions was fixed, ancillary words and phrases could be varied in location. At some mints for extended periods, a pattern once used was never repeated; every die was different. As an art—and it generally was an art for many engravers, evidenced not only by the creativity of their work but also in a few instances by their signatures on the dies—coin epigraphy reached its peak in this period in eastern Iran, in Merv, Balkh and especially Nishapur (229d). Unfortunately the superbly engraved dies were not often matched by similar care in the production of the coins themselves, so that areas of the design are often weakly impressed on the metal flan or blurred.

One dynasty that took a radically different approach to coin design was the Fatimids of North Africa, Egypt and Syria (*reg* 909–1171). In 953 the caliph al-Mu'izz (*reg* 953–75) introduced an entirely new coinage with nearly all the inscriptions arranged in concentric circles (229e). The Fatimid rejection of the Abbasid Sunni consensus was evidenced, even to the illiterate, in their coinage. The skill of the die engravers of Cairo under the Fatimids in the 10th and 11th centuries was equal to that of their counterparts in eastern Iran, but—perhaps because of the more centralized bureaucracy—the Egyptians lacked the originality of the Iranians. The Fatimids used several different designs, but each one was employed at all mints uniformly throughout the period of its use. Although Fatimid coinage was imitated by European Christians and other Muslims, the imitations, no matter how faithful to their prototype, never duplicate the precision and finish of Cairene engraving (229f). Moreover, in Egypt the coins were better made than in the east, so the calligraphy appears to better effect. Yet compared to the contemporary coins of eastern Iran, the aesthetic effect of Egyptian coins is like the lettering of a finely made scientific instrument compared to the calligraphy of an art poster.

(ii) 13th–19th centuries. The 13th century was a watershed in the stylistic evolution of Islamic coinage. In the west and in the east there were radical innovations that completely changed the appearance of Islamic coins. One of these was the introduction of a new style of cursive script, known as *naskhī* to numismatists but actually a form of *thuluth*. Kufic had been standard on coins long after it had become archaic in manuscripts and monumental calligraphy; before the 12th century, cursive was used very rarely on coins, to emphasize one or two words such as a ruler's name. The general adoption of cursive script originated, like so many other innovations in coinage, in a political upheaval: the conquest of North Africa and Spain by the Almohad dynasty (*reg* 1130–1269), leaders of a radical fundamentalist movement. Like the Fatimids before them,

they marked their rise to power by a distinctive coin design, enclosing the central inscriptions in a square surrounded by a circle; all the inscriptions, for the first time, were in ordinary cursive script instead of angular kufic. The design and new style of script remained standard in the western Islamic lands until the 16th century (see fig. 230a). At the beginning of the 13th century, cursive was introduced in Egypt, although still with the traditional arrangement of inscriptions. By the end of the century, it had spread throughout Iran and into India. Henceforth kufic was only one of several variant scripts in the die engraver's repertory.

Although the Fatimids and Almohads introduced new designs to signal their religious dissent, the Mongol Il-khanid rulers of Iran (*reg* 1256–1353) changed the design of their coinage merely to distinguish changes in the weight standard or alloy of their issues. Nevertheless, the frequency of these changes from the end of the 13th century onwards, and the breakdown of central authority in 14th-century Iran, gave die engravers and their administrative masters almost total freedom in the design and arrangement of coin types. The two sides of the coin are usually quite different, and the inscriptions may be enclosed in

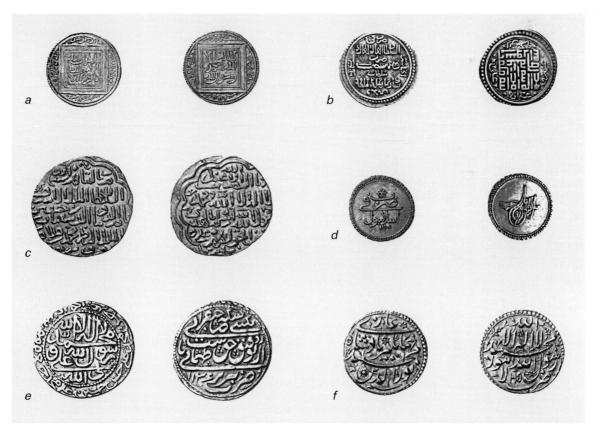

230. Islamic coins of the 12th–18th centuries, obverse and reverse: (a) gold half dinar with the name of the Almohad ʿAbd al-Muʾmin, diam. 20 mm, minted at Isbiliyya (Seville), Spain, *c.* 1130–63; (b) silver dirham with the name of the Ilkhanid sultan Abu Saʿid, diam. 20 mm, minted at Sultaniyya, Iran, in the Ilkhanid year 33, 1333–4; (c) gold dinar with the name of the Mamluk sultan al-Ashraf Shaʿban, diam. 27 mm, minted at al-Qahira (Cairo), Egypt, 1372–3; (d) gold *zer-i mahbub* with the name of the Ottoman sultan Ahmed III, diam. 18 mm, minted at Islambul (Istanbul), Turkey, 1703–4; (e) silver *ʿabbasi* with the name of the Safavid shah Tahmasp II, diam. 28 mm, minted at Tabriz, Iran, 1723–4; (f) gold *mohur* with the name of the Mughal emperor Jahangir, diam. 23 mm, minted at Lahore, Pakistan, 1606–7 (New York, American Numismatic Society)

simple squares or circles or in complex ornamented polygons. Within these various cartouches, the inscriptions may be monumental bold cursive or tiny square kufic, with a mixture of several styles preferred over uniformity (230b). A single design might be imposed in a single year in mints from Anatolia to Transoxiana, only to be replaced four or five years later by something quite different.

While coinage in Iran continued to be original and creative, coin design and epigraphic style in Egypt and Syria under the Mamluks (*reg* 1250–1517) evolved more slowly and uniformly, and the end result was rather different from the classical Abbasid format from which it had begun (230c). In Egypt, the outer boundaries of the coin design disappear: there are no longer any outer circular inscriptions nor any framing cartouches in the east. The script is inscribed in stolid horizontal lines across the coin from one edge to the other, or even, one might say, beyond the edges, since the area of the engraving on the dies expanded beyond the diameter of the coins themselves, so that only the centre of the design is actually impressed on the metal flan. Nevertheless, what can be seen is always straightforwardly legible, unlike contemporary designs from Iran where words sometimes seem to have been placed randomly on the coin, more for aesthetic effect than for sense.

From the 16th century onwards the Islamic world can be divided numismatically into two spheres which perpetuated the distinctions that can be perceived between Egypt and Iran as far back as the 10th century. Coins issued under the Turkish Ottoman dynasty (*reg* 1281–1924) are handsome, majestic, often elegant, especially those issued during the Tulip Period in the early 18th century (230d). In the 18th and 19th centuries the sparse inscriptions (always in *thuluth*), surrounded by large open spaces and minimal decoration, have a serenity that is most impressive. A unique feature of Ottoman coin design from the beginning of the 18th century is the use of the sultan's signature in the form of a TUGHRA, a complex curvilinear monogram that incorporates his name and titles with those of his father.

The Perso-Indian sphere, represented by coins issued by the Safavid dynasty of Iran (*reg* 1501–1732) and the Mughal dynasty of India (*reg* 1526–1857), continues the coinage tradition of the Ilkhanids and Timurids (*reg* 1370–1506) in Iran. By the beginning of the 16th century, coinage in the Iranian cultural sphere had become rather monotonous; there are still variant cartouches, but the coins are so crowded with inscriptions in a tall, thin *thuluth* script that no overall design emerges to the eye. This style was brought to India by the first Mughals, Babur (*reg* 1526–30) and Humayun (*reg* 1530–56 with interruption). The situation did not improve until the end of the 16th century under the Safavid shah 'Abbas I and the Mughal emperors Akbar and Jahangir. Under these rulers, a simpler, bolder *thuluth* began to appear, especially under Akbar, most of whose coinage is quite handsome. More importantly for the future, a new style of script began to appear at the end of the 16th century and beginning of the 17th in both countries (chronological priority is difficult to establish). This is *nasta'liq*, a script characterized by sweeping horizontal strokes that seem to drop down to the left, quite similar to the normal script in which Persian and Urdu are

written in the 20th century. In Iran *nasta'liq* is almost always used along with *thuluth*, often each on a different side of the same coin (230e), while in India it became the only normal script for coinage (230f). In both countries, for the first time since Islamic coinage had begun, a language other than Arabic became common on coins: rhyming verses in Persian contain the ruler's name and punning references to his monetary authority.

The introduction of European mint machinery in the 19th and 20th centuries raised the question whether to adopt with it European notions of coin design. In general, only monarchies under Western domination, such as Egypt and Iraq, placed the ruler's portrait on coins. Most Muslim states in the 20th century avoid human portraits on coins, but use inanimate images such as historical monuments, a traditional sailing vessel or date palms. At the extremes, the coinage of Turkey is no different from that of any European state, while coins in Saudi Arabia have only inscriptions with the national symbol of a palm above crossed swords.

BIBLIOGRAPHY

Enc. Iran.: 'Coins'
L. A. Mayer: *Bibliography of Moslem Numismatics, India Excepted* (London, 1954)
L. Volov [Golombek]: 'Plaited Kufic on Samanid Epigraphic Pottery', *A. Orient.*, vi (1966), pp. 107–33
R. Plant: *Arabic Coins and How to Read Them* (London, 1973)
M. L. Bates: 'Islamic Numismatics', *Mid. E. Stud. Assoc. Bull.*, xii/2 (May 1978), pp. 1–16; xii/3 (Dec 1978), pp. 2–18; xiii/1 (July 1979), pp. 3–21; xiii/2 (Dec 1979), pp. 1–9
A. Welch: *Calligraphy in the Arts of the Muslim World* (Austin, 1979), pp. 204–11
M. L. Bates: *Islamic Coins* (New York, 1982)
The Coinage of Islam: Collection of William Kazan (Beirut, 1983)
M. L. Bates and R. E. Darley-Doran: 'The Art of Islamic Coinage', *Treasures of Islam*, ed. T. Falk (London, 1985), pp. 350–95
M. Broome: *A Handbook of Islamic Coins* (London, 1985)
L. Komaroff: 'The Epigraphy of Timurid Coinage: Some Preliminary Remarks', *Amer. Numi. Soc. Mus. Notes*, xxxi (1986), pp. 207–32
G. Rispling: 'Names of Die Engravers on 10th Century Islamic Coins', *Numi. Meddel.*, xxxvii (1989), pp. 329–35
S. Album: *A Checklist of Popular Islamic Coins* (Santa Rosa, CA, 1993)
T. El-Hibri: 'Coinage Reform under the 'Abbasid Caliph al-Ma'mun', *J. Econ. & Soc. Hist. Orient*, xxxvi (1993), pp. 58–83

MICHAEL L. BATES

3. ENAMEL. The technique of enamel (Arab. and Pers. *mina*), in which gold, silver and copper objects are decorated with heat-fused glass pastes coloured by metal oxides (*see* ENAMEL, §1), was used sporadically in the Islamic world from the 10th to the 15th centuries. Textual descriptions imply that the cloisonné technique (*see* ENAMEL, §2(i)) was introduced from the Byzantine empire (*see* EARLY CHRISTIAN AND BYZANTINE ART, §VII, 7(ii)), probably as a cheaper substitute for precious stones, especially emeralds. A few pieces of gold filigree jewellery decorated with small areas of opaque cloisonné enamel (*see* §9(i) below) can be attributed on stylistic grounds to Egypt or Spain in the 10th–12th century. The historian al-Maqrizi (1364–1442) listed enamelled wares among the treasures looted from the Fatimid palace in Cairo in the 1060s, including enamelled trays from Byzantium.

The only large object with enamel decoration that survives from the early period is a gilded bronze dish (diam. 226 mm; Innsbruck, Tirol. Landesmus.) of highly skilled workmanship and complex design. It includes a central roundel showing the ascension of Alexander the

Great surrounded by six smaller roundels that enclose stylized animals and birds. According to an inscription around the inside rim, the dish was made for Da'ud (*reg* 1114–44), the Artuqid ruler of northern Mesopotamia, but the mixed iconography, jumbled inscription and unusual form suggest a Byzantine or Armenian provenance. Cloisonné enamelling continued to be used for jewellery made in Egypt and Spain from the 13th to the 15th century, and several swords made for the Nasrid dynasty of Granada in the 15th century (Madrid, Mus. Ejército, and Kassel, Hess. Landesmus.) have gilt-bronze mounts decorated with gold filigree and enamel. The most characteristic form of Islamic enamelling during this period was that used for Iranian ceramics in the 12th century (*see* §V, 3(iii) above) and Syrian and Egyptian glassware from *c.* 1200 (*see* §5(ii) below).

In the 17th century a variety of new enamelling techniques—champlevé, *basse taille*, painted and repoussé, for example (*see* ENAMEL, §2(ii), (iii) and (vii))—appeared in Iran and Turkey, as well as in India (*see* INDIAN SUBCONTINENT, §VIII, 15(iv)). They were either introduced by the European craftsmen who worked at the Islamic courts of the period, or they originated in local attempts to reproduce the European enamels sent as diplomatic gifts and trade goods. Indian enamels of the 17th century, probably produced at the imperial ateliers at Agra, Delhi and perhaps Jaipur, are remarkable for their clear, rich colours and fine designs and were used to decorate objects ranging in size from thumb-rings to thrones, although only the base of one Mughal enamelled throne survives (Istanbul, Topkapı Pal. Mus., 735). Enamels continued to be produced in India in the 18th and 19th centuries, principally at Jaipur.

Mughal and European enamels were known in Iran by the late 17th century, and the trade of enameller was established in the local and Armenian communities; indeed, by the end of the century the Safavid court at Isfahan had a post of chief enameller. Early production is documented by the enamelled daggers and other fine-quality objects that entered the Russian imperial collections before the 1730s (St Petersburg, Hermitage; see fig. 231). They show the same qualities that enabled 19th-century Iranian enamellers to surpass their European counterparts: brilliant colours (primarily pinks, royal blue, turquoise and translucent green) used effectively against gold or opaque white grounds, rich detail, and delicate figural and flower designs. Objects from the 18th and 19th centuries that were decorated in this manner include tableware, hookas, caskets, jewellery, such as pendants and turban ornaments, regalia and weapons. Many pieces are signed and dated, and more than 25 artists are known from the 1770s to the early 20th century.

The art of enamelling flourished in Iran under the patronage of the Qajar monarch Fath 'Ali Shah (*reg* 1797–1834), and many of the objects made for him form part of the Iranian Crown Jewels collection (Tehran, Bank Markazi). Probably the finest painted enamel in the collection is a seated portrait of the Shah signed by the painter 'ALI and mounted on the back of an oval mirror with a carved jade handle. A teapot enamelled with busts of Fath 'Ali Shah and floral swags and a dedication to the monarch was painted by BAQIR, who was renowned for

231. Enamelled dagger and sheath, damascened steel and gold, l. 410 mm, from Iran, late 17th century or early 18th (St Petersburg, Hermitage Museum)

his delicate execution and brilliant colours. Several large gold dishes decorated with a lion and sun in the centre panel surrounded by alternating birds and floral swags were made as presents from the Shah. A solid gold example weighing *c.* 3 kg, presented to the Court of Directors of the British East India Company on 18 June 1819 (London, V&A, I.S. 09406), was painted by MUHAMMAD JA'FAR, the most prolific painter in enamels at the court. The most important enameller of the late 19th century, Muhammad Kazim, was a member of the ISFAHANI family of painters; he painted many fine pieces, such as a hooka base decorated with medallions of the Holy Family set amid flowers (1864; Tehran, Bank Markazi, Crown Jewels Col.). The range of objects decorated with overall enamel painting was very wide and comparable to Indian production, with the addition of royal insignia.

Enamelled wares were also produced in the Ottoman empire, but because of the proximity to European centres of production and the cosmopolitan character of Istanbul craftsmen, it is often difficult to distinguish fine local products in a highly Europeanized style from imports. In the mid-17th century enamelling was used for clock dials (e.g. Istanbul, Topkapı Pal. Mus., 53.85), and it became increasingly popular for jewellery such as gold turban ornaments (e.g. Istanbul, Mus. Turk. & Islam. A., 447).

BIBLIOGRAPHY

M. Aga-Oglu: 'The Origin of the Term Mīnā and its Meanings', *J. Nr E. Stud.*, v (1946), pp. 241–57
V. B. Meen and A. D. Tushingham: *Crown Jewels of Iran* (Toronto, 1968)
B. W. Robinson: 'Qājār Painted Enamels', *Paintings from Islamic Lands*, ed. R. Pinder-Wilson (Oxford, 1969), pp. 187–204
C. Köseoğlu: *Topkapı Sarayı Müzesi* (Tokyo, 1980), Eng. trans. and ed. by J. M. Rogers as *Topkapı Saray Museum: The Treasury* (London and Boston, 1987)
M. Jenkins and M. Keene: *Islamic Jewelry in the Metropolitan Museum of Art* (New York, 1982)
A. A. Ivanov, V. G. Lukonin and L. S. Smesova: *Oriental Jewelry from the Collection of the Special Treasury, the State Hermitage Oriental Department* (Moscow, 1984)
M. A. Karimzada Tabrizi: *Aḥvāl u āthār-i naqqāshān-i qadīm-i īrān* [The lives and art of old painters of Iran] (London, 1985)
S. Redford: 'How Islamic Is it? The Innsbruck Plate and its Setting', *Muqarnas*, vii (1990), pp. 119–35
Al-Andalus: The Art of Islamic Spain (exh. cat., ed. J. D. Dodds; Granada, Alhambra; New York, Met.; 1992), nos. 19, 61–3, 65, 67–8, 72–3

LAYLA S. DIBA

4. FURNITURE. The paucity of domestic furniture in the Near East, where life is traditionally lived on or near ground level, has been a characteristic feature of the region at least since the early Islamic period. Beds, chairs, stools, tables and the like were hardly needed when the custom was to sit cross-legged and sleep on a rug, cushion or low sofa (Arab. *ṣuffa*), the back supported by cushions and bolsters, perhaps with a small low table near by. Many of the functions associated with furniture in other cultures were filled in the Islamic lands by knotted carpets and flat-woven textiles. Nevertheless, some portable furniture, such as the MINBAR or pulpit and stands and boxes to hold copies of the Koran (see fig. 157 above), was used in mosques and other religious settings, and thrones of various types were used by rulers (*see also* §12 below).

Most of the meagre information about furniture in the medieval Islamic world comes from written sources. Pieces of furniture are mentioned in the Hadith (traditions of the Prophet), histories, geographies and works of belles-lettres. An unusually rich source is provided by the Genizah documents, an enormous cache of discarded papers preserved in a storeroom of a synagogue in Fustat (Old Cairo). The 300,000 documents, dating mainly from the mid-10th century to the mid-13th, include marriage contracts, wills, trousseau lists, commercial documents and personal letters relating to the Jewish community, and this information can be extrapolated to describe the habits of the medieval Islamic world. The range of names and functions provided by textual sources are supplemented by occasional depictions on ceramics and metalwork and in manuscript illustrations, although the conventionalized nature of the imagery can limit the value of these sources.

Rigid seats were used to differentiate those in authority from the general population, who sat on the floor. The minbar, which derived from the judge's seat in pre-Islamic Arabia, enabled the preacher to be seated at a level above that of the standing congregation; similarly the throne differentiated the ruler from the ruled (*see also* THRONE, §III). The Umayyad dynasty of Syria (*reg* 661–750) apparently adopted the Antique tradition of chair-like thrones, for a figure (perhaps the caliph) is shown seated in a stucco relief (Damascus, N. Mus.) from QASR AL-HAYR WEST. A similar chair is depicted at the Umayyad site of QUSAYR 'AMRA in Jordan, where a mural at the end of the apse shows the ruler enthroned. The Abbasid dynasty (*reg* 749–1258), which drew its initial support from the eastern Islamic lands, favoured the traditional Persian type of throne on which the ruler sat cross-legged but raised above the crowd. A silver medallion (diam. 28 mm; Berlin, Bodemus.), for example, shows the caliph al-Muqtadir (*reg* 908–32) seated on a low throne, his back resting against a cylindrical bolster. This type of low throne, with or without a back, was widely dispersed in the medieval Islamic lands, thanks to the esteem that the practices of the Abbasid caliphs held.

A third type of seat derived from the folding stool of Classical times. A scribe is depicted sitting on one on the painted ceiling of the Cappella Palatina in Palermo (mid-12th century), and one frontispiece to a 21-volume manuscript of the *Kitāb al-aghānī* ('Book of songs'), made at Mosul in 1218 (Istanbul, U. Lib., Hb 300), shows Badr al-Din Lu'Lu', the vizier and future atabeg (regent) of Mosul, seated on a folding stool, perhaps because the throne was reserved for the sultan or caliph as the symbol of authority. Early 14th-century manuscript illustrations, such as those to a copy of Rashid al-Din's *Jāmi' al-tawārīkh* ('Compendium of histories'; Edinburgh, U. Lib., MS 20), often show the scribe or vizier seated on a folding stool next to the enthroned ruler. Several new types of royal furniture based on Chinese models were introduced to the eastern Islamic lands as a result of the Mongol conquest in the 13th century, although it is not clear whether actual examples of Chinese furniture or depictions of it were imported. For example, a throne with a flat seat enclosed on three sides by decorative panels, sometimes with dragon or phoenix finials, is often depicted with a low footstool in front of it in manuscript illustrations from the 14th century onwards (see fig. 121 above). According to textual and iconographical sources, there were several kinds of thrones and seats with arms and backs (sometimes consisting of cushions tied to metal or wooden poles).

Large worktables were used by some craftsmen, as shown by *The Monkey and the Carpenter*, image on two detached pages from a 14th-century copy of *Kalīla and Dimna* (Paris, Bib. N., Ar. 3465, fol. 47*r*; Istanbul, U. Lib., F. 1422, fol. 22*r*). Most craftsmen, however, worked on the ground. MUʿIN's well-known portrait of the artist RIZA (Princeton U., NJ, Lib., Garrett Coll. 96G), for example, shows him seated on the ground and holding a drawing on his lap. People traditionally ate seated in a circle around the communal food, from which the food was taken and eaten over the lap. Sometimes the food was placed at ground level on a mat, at other times it was raised on some sort of low stand or table. A stand might support either a bowl or a tray on which the bowls of food were placed, and it could be made of wood (e.g. an Ottoman octagonal pine table, veneered with walnut and carob and inlaid with mother-of-pearl and horn, h. 355 mm; Paris, Louvre, 934), ceramic (e.g. a moulded hexagonal stand with a transparent turquoise-blue glaze, h. 320 mm, Syria, 13th century; Copenhagen, Davids Saml.) or metal (e.g. an Egyptian stand of inlaid brass, 14th century; New York, Met.). In addition, many objects with leg-like bases, stems or tall feet that have been identified as dishes, bowls, beakers or compot dishes were in fact dining-tables or stands for trays.

Chests ranged in size from small caskets of metal or ivory to hold precious items (see fig. 237 below) to large boxes of wood, decorated with paint or inlaid with mother-of-pearl (e.g. Copenhagen, Davids Saml., 22/1983; *see also* MARQUETRY, colour pl. VIII, fig. 3). Walls sometimes had shaped cavities for storage, as in the Abbasid palaces at Samarra' (*see* SAMARRA', fig. 3) and the music room of the ʿAli Qapu Palace at Isfahan (see fig. 70 above). Some libraries had wooden bookcases with hinged doors which could be locked, and an illustration in a copy (Paris, Bib. N., MS. arabe 5847, fol. 5*v*) of al-Hariri's *Maqāmāt* ('Assemblies'), painted by Yahya al-Wasiti in 1237, shows books stacked flat on shelves within arched niches. Many examples of exquisitely decorated wooden doors, some undoubtedly used to close closets, have been preserved (*see* §VII above).

BIBLIOGRAPHY
Enc. Islam/2: 'Athāth' [Furniture], 'Kursī' [Seat], 'Minbar'
A. Mazahéri: *La Vie quotidienne des musulmans au moyen âge* (Paris, 1951), pp. 75–82
J. Sadan: *Le Mobilier au Proche-Orient médiéval* (Leiden, 1976)
M. M. Ahsan: *Social Life under the Abbasids* (London and New York, 1979), pp. 190–95
S. D. Goitein: *Daily Life and the Individual* (1983), iv of *A Mediterranean Society* (Berkeley and Los Angeles, 1967–88), pp. 105–38
J. Rawson: *Chinese Ornament: The Lotus and the Dragon* (London, 1984), pp. 150–62
J. Sadan: 'Furniture, Islamic', *Dictionary of the Middle Ages*, v (New York, 1985), pp. 313–16
                      based on information supplied by J. SADAN

5. GLASS. The history of glass production in the Islamic lands may be divided into three periods. The first period, in which many Late Antique and Sasanian techniques continued to be employed, included the reigns of the Umayyad (*reg* 661–750) and Abbasid (*reg* 749–1258) dynasties. During the second period a brilliant series of gilded and enamelled glasswares, particularly beakers and mosque lamps, was produced in Syria and Egypt, which were under the control of the Ayyubid (*reg* 1169–1260) and Mamluk (*reg* 1250–1517) dynasties. The third period is characterized by the introduction and imitation of European products. Islamic glass sometimes imitated precious stones, and many of the finishing techniques that glassmakers employed were the same as those used by lapidaries; indeed, the same craftsmen may have worked with both materials (*see* §13 below).

BIBLIOGRAPHY
C. J. Lamm: *Mittelalterliche Gläser und Steinschnittarbeiten aus dem nahen Osten* (Berlin, 1929–30)
The Arts of Islam (exh. cat., London, Hayward Gal., 1976), pp. 131–46
J. Kröger: *Glas* (1984), i of *Islamische Kunst: Loseblattkatalog unpublizierter Werke aus deutschen Museen: Berlin, Staatliche Museen preussischer Kulturbesitz: Museum für islamische Kunst* (Mainz, 1984–)
M. Jenkins: 'Islamic Glass: A Brief History', *Bull. Met.*, xliv/2 (1986) [whole issue]   □

(i) 7th–11th centuries. (ii) 12th–15th centuries. (iii) 16th–19th centuries.

(i) 7th–11th centuries. Knowledge of the earliest Islamic glass is derived from objects found by chance, by clandestine 'excavators' or in controlled archaeological excavations. The best-known archaeological site is Samarra' in Iraq, the capital of the Abbasid caliphs from 836 to 892. Early excavations at Samarra', however, were conducted without regard for stratigraphy, and few finds can be dated with certainty to the caliphal occupation. Controlled excavations have taken place at such sites as Hama in Syria, Fustat (Old Cairo) in Egypt (*see* CAIRO, §I, 1) and Siraf in Iran. The most closely dated collection of early Islamic glass, however, was found under water at Serçe Limanı near Bodrum in Turkey, where archaeologists recovered complete vessels and a cargo of broken glass from a ship that sank *c.* 1026.

In the first two centuries after the Islamic conquest, glassmakers in the central Islamic lands followed existing traditions. In Syria and Palestine they adapted the Roman cosmetic tube by reducing its size and placing it on the back of a 'camel' made by manipulating hot glass and adorning it with trails. These 'dromedary flasks' (e.g. h. 120 mm; New York, Met., 69.153) were extremely popular, and examples have been found in Egypt, Syria, Iraq and Iran. Other forms with applied decoration include bottles and flasks decorated with blobs of glass which were manipulated while hot to resemble extended animal skins. In Egypt glassmakers experimented with pincered and stamped decoration. The former was made by pinching the hot glass with tongs, the jaws of which were decorated with patterns that include inscriptions and zoomorphic motifs. The most common variety of stamped glass consists of 'coin weights', which were produced in Egypt in large numbers between the 8th and the 15th centuries. The earliest known example bears the date AH 90 (AD 708–9). Stamped appliqués bearing the names of governors or officials and the capacity that they guaranteed were attached to vessels used for measuring. In western Asia glassmakers produced vessels with stamped medallions adorned with human heads, birds and winged horses of Sasanian type (e.g. a vase, h. 152 mm; New York, Met., 37.56).

Glass was used even more extensively in the 9th century, and products ranged from utilitarian vessels, some of which have applied or mould-blown ornament, to exquisite

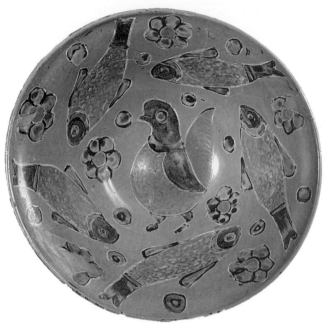

232. Lustre-painted glass bowl, diam. 158 mm, from Egypt, 11th century (private collection, on loan to Corning, NY, Museum of Glass)

luxury items. Vessels with moulded decoration (e.g. a jug; New York, Met., 47.85.2) were made by blowing the glass into decorated moulds, a technique that allowed the glassblower to make decorated objects almost as quickly as plain ones. Early Islamic glassmakers produced a wide variety of mould-blown decoration, from geometric patterns, common in the finds from Serçe Limanı, to birds, animals and inscriptions.

Luxury objects of the 9th to the 11th centuries include glass with scratched decoration, mosaic-glass, gold-glass, glass decorated with lustre and cut glass. The scratched glass consists of vessels incised with vegetal or geometric motifs, sometimes accompanied by inscriptions (e.g. Damascus, Mus. N., A 11403, discovered at Raqqa). Many such vessels are of translucent deep blue glass. Several examples were found in the crypt of the Buddhist temple at Famen, west of Xi'an in Shaanxi Province, China; the crypt was sealed in 874. The glass from Samarra' includes fragments of mosaic-glass tiles (e.g. seven fragments in Berlin, Mus. Islam. Kst). Early Islamic mosaic-glass is rare, but surviving objects include plates, cups and perfume bottles, many of which are formed from 'bull's-eye' canes (e.g. a bowl, diam. 135 mm; Copenhagen, Davids Saml., 33/1978). Only a handful of gold-glass objects are known. Apart from fragments excavated at Antioch, none of these objects was found in a controlled archaeological context, and hence their dating depends on stylistic criteria. Two of the most distinctive objects (a fragmentary bowl, h. 85 mm; Copenhagen, Davids Saml., 4/1987 and London, BM) have gold inscriptions enlivened with spots of blue enamel. The inscriptions are similar to a script used on manuscripts of the 9th and 10th centuries, and it is likely that the gold-glass objects were made at this time. As one example is said to have been found in Iran and

another resembles wheel-cut glass from Iran, the objects were probably made in western Asia.

A more common variety of luxury glass was decorated with lustre. This shiny effect, which appears to have been an invention of the Islamic world and became extremely popular on ceramics (see §V, 3(i) above), was obtained by painting the glass surface with a suspension of finely powdered oxides of copper or silver and then firing the object in oxygen-free conditions at a temperature of c. 600°C. The temperature was high enough to fuse the metal to the surface but insufficient to soften the glass and cause the object to collapse. The lustre may be brown, yellow, green or red, and the colours were applied either singly or in combination. A fragment of a lustre-painted goblet discovered in Fustat (Cairo, Mus. Islam. A.) bears the name of a governor who ruled for a month in 773, and another fragment (Cairo, Mus. Islam. A., 12739/6) is dated AH 163 (AD 779–80). A third object (Corning, NY, Mus. Glass) bears an inscription stating that it was made at Damascus. It is not known whether Damascus was the only place of manufacture or how long lustre painting on glass was practised before and after the dates on these objects, but pieces have been attributed on stylistic grounds to 11th-century Egypt (see fig. 232).

Lapidary techniques, such as wheel-cutting, which had been practised extensively by the Romans and Sasanians, were revived in the 9th century, and they were used between the 9th and the 11th centuries to produce some of the masterpieces of Islamic glass. Early examples include vessels decorated in the BEVELLED STYLE, in which outlines are cut on a slant and there is no distinct plane forming the background (e.g. a beaker, h. 125 mm; Berlin, Mus. Islam. Kst, I.4/59). A second style consists of relief-cutting, in which the entire background was removed, leaving the ornament in relief (e.g. a bottle, h. 215 mm; Berlin, Mus. Islam. Kst, I.92/63). Many relief-cut glasses have been found in north-east Iran, and the style is often associated with the city of NISHAPUR, although other centres almost certainly existed elsewhere in western Asia and in Egypt. The same styles of cutting were applied to rock crystal (see §13(i) below). Most early Islamic relief-cutting was carried out on monochrome blanks of glass. These were usually colourless, but a group of brilliant green glasses (e.g. Corning, NY, Mus. Glass, 55.1.136) and one opaque turquoise bowl (h. 60 mm, diam. 186 mm; Venice, S Marco; see GLASS, colour pl. V, fig. 2) are known.

Glasscutters also decorated blanks made in the cameo technique, in which a layer of glass of one colour was applied to an object of a different colour. Subsequently, most of the outer layer was removed mechanically, leaving the ornament in relief on a background of a different colour. Islamic cameo glass usually has coloured decoration on a colourless ground. Although cameo glass had been made by the Romans, there is no reason to suppose that production persisted into the Islamic period; presumably the technique was reinvented in western Asia or Egypt. Islamic cameo glass falls into two groups. In the first, patches of coloured glass were applied to the vessel. This 'marquetry' technique allowed the glassmaker to produce objects with small isolated designs (e.g. a flask with confronted lion and dove, h. 230 mm; Copenhagen, Davids Saml., 2/1972). It was unsuitable, however, for decoration covering the entire surface. For this, the vessel had to be covered almost completely with an overlay, either by dipping the parison into a pot of molten glass or by inflating it in a preformed 'cup' made from glass of the second colour. Perhaps the earliest example of this second type to survive is a bottle decorated with confronted birds flanking a palmette (h. 150 mm; Copenhagen, Davids Saml., 3/1971). Other complete or restored examples include the Corning Ewer (see fig. 233), decorated with animals and birds of prey. The ewer was reportedly found in Iran, and its form has numerous parallels among glass, pottery and metal objects from that country. It also resembles rock crystal ewers attributed to Cairo under the Fatimid dynasty (*reg* 969–1171), and hence its place of manufacture is uncertain.

BIBLIOGRAPHY
C. J. Lamm: *Das Glas von Samarra* (1928), iv of *Die Ausgrabungen von Samarra* (Berlin and Hamburg, 1923–48)
——: *Mittelalterliche Gläser und Steinschnittarbeiten aus dem nahen Osten* (Berlin, 1929–30)
P. Oliver: 'Islamic Relief Cut Glass: A Suggested Chronology', *J. Glass Stud.*, iii (1961), pp. 9–29
S. Fukai: *Persian Glass* (New York, Tokyo and Kyoto, 1977)
S. M. Goldstein, L. S. Rakow and J. K. Rakow: *Cameo Glass: Masterpieces from 2000 Years of Glassmaking* (Corning, 1982)

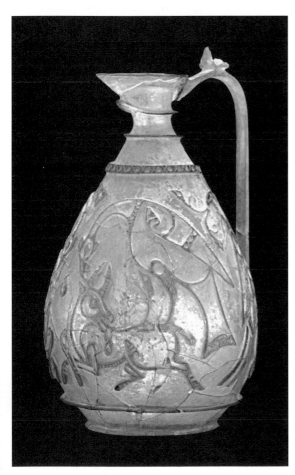

233. Cameo glass ewer, colourless, with a transparent green glass overlay, h. 160 mm, from Egypt or Iran, 11th century (Corning, NY, Museum of Glass)

G. F. Bass: 'The Nature of the Serçe Limanı Glass', *J. Glass Stud.*, xxvi (1984), pp. 64–9
A. H. Morton: *A Catalogue of Early Islamic Stamps in the British Museum* (London, 1985)
R. Charleston: 'Glass', *The Arts of Persia*, ed. R. W. Ferrier (New Haven and London, 1989), pp. 295–305
R. Pinder-Wilson: 'The Islamic Lands and China', *Five Thousand Years of Glass*, ed. H. Tait (1991), pp. 112–39

DAVID WHITEHOUSE

(ii) 12th–15th centuries. Much of the glass that remains from this period, when Syria and Egypt were under the control of the Ayyubid (*reg* 1169–1260) and Mamluk (*reg* 1250–1517) dynasties, is preserved in museums and church treasuries throughout the world. Several pieces were obtained at an early date for the collections of European potentates who admired these luxury wares, and several items, particularly mosque lamps, remained in the religious establishments for which they had been made. Incomplete vessels and fragments have been excavated from rubbish dumps in Egypt at Fustat (Old Cairo), Qus, Antinoë and Qasr Ibrim in the Nile Valley, and at Quseir on the Red Sea; in Sudan at Sennar and 'Aydhab; in Syria at Raqqa and Hama; and at Jerusalem. Further finds have been made in Malaysia at the medieval entrepôt of Pengkalan Bujang near Penang Island, western Europe and the south of England.

Many techniques and forms were continued from the previous period. Items produced include bottles, flasks, vials, perfume sprinklers, lamps, stands and tableware. Drinking vessels were frequently made of glass, but glass bowls were unusual and plates were rare. Glass was also used for small items such as gaming pieces, disc-shaped coin weights and figurines of fish and birds, sometimes made as sprinklers. The repertory was perhaps wider in the Mamluk period than in the Ayyubid and included drinking vessels in the form of cups and stemmed goblets as well as beakers. A notable Mamluk type was the large mosque lamp, made in the form of a sphere resting on a conical base and surmounted by a funnel, with applied glass loops from which it was suspended (see fig. 234 and GLASS, colour pl. IV, fig. 1).

The Egyptian glass industry was centred on Alexandria and Fustat, where almost all types have been excavated, and a parallel glass industry flourished in Palestine and Syria. Aleppo and Damascus are known as centres for the production of enamelled glass in the 13th and 14th centuries, and enamelled glass excavated at Raqqa in Syria may have been manufactured there. Non-figural enamelled glass has been found at Hama, along with prunted beakers decorated with applied glass knobs. Coloured glass with white impressed trails has been found at Jerusalem and at Belus Na'aman in Israel, suggesting that Islamic-type glass continued to be produced in areas under Crusader control.

Coin weights suggest that opaque turquoise glass continued to be popular in the Ayyubid period, although it became progressively darker and went out of style *c.* 1250. Translucent yellow-green glass was used until the 13th century. Opaque white and black glass was used throughout the 12th century but was replaced *c.* 1229 by translucent red-purple, itself replaced *c.* 1315 by clear crystal-like glass. This was standard from 1371 to 1494 when weights ceased to be produced. Decoration of contrasting colour continued to be swirled in the molten batch or marvered

234. Glass mosque lamp, enamelled and gilded, h. 267 mm, diam. 203 mm, from Syria or Egypt, *c.* 1286 (New York, Metropolitan Museum of Art)

The origins of enamelled glassware are unknown, but the technique in Syria and Egypt was contemporary with the production of enamelled ceramics in Iran. Early pieces of gilded and enamelled glass have predominantly figural decoration, but include one or more inscription bands almost always in cursive script.

Two methods of applying gold to glass were characteristic of the Ayyubid period. One used flat gold silhouettes with scratched detailing (e.g. an opaque black fragment with the wing of an eagle in gold; Oxford, Ashmolean, P2719). This style can be seen on a flask (London, BM, 1906 7–19 1) bearing an inscription naming the ruler of Mosul, 'Imad al-Din Zangi (*reg* 1127–46). A variant of this technique has red enamel drawing over the gold silhouette work. A bottle (h. 320 mm; Cairo, Mus. Islam. A., 4261) mentioning the last Ayyubid ruler of Aleppo, Salah al-Din Yusuf (*reg* 1237–60), includes free-floating gold arabesques, roundels with touches of blue and bands of small cursive script. The second method of applying gold used a thick enamel ground for lettering and motifs to give a sumptuous relief effect. A fragment from Egypt (London, BM, 1900 6–21 39) depicts an animal against some foliage and shows some similarities to contemporary enamelled ceramics from Iran. A beaker with relief gilded borders (Kassel, Hess. Landesmus., destr.) was decorated with a group of mounted falconers, whose dress and trappings paralleled those on a frontispiece (Copenhagen, Kon. Bib., Cod. arab. 168) thought to depict the ruler of Mosul, BADR AL-DIN LU'LU' (*reg* 1222–59). This style of gilded glass seems to have gone out of production in the mid-13th century.

Several examples of gold silhouette with red drawing can be dated to the mid-13th century. The motifs are generally scattered over the surface and often combined with inscription bands, several of which can be joined together to form a continuous text. Popular motifs include shark-like fish; on a beaker found in Lübeck they are combined with seated revellers and an inscription, and on a mosque lamp (London, V&A, 330–1900) they are combined with arabesques, birds and small polychrome horsemen. These fish also appear with other polychrome decoration on another beaker (London, V&A, 335–1900) bearing the lion emblem and titles of the Mamluk sultan Baybars I (*reg* 1260–77). Narrow gilded strips outlined in red border the inscription, the letters of which are outlined in red on a sky-blue enamel ground. A similar style of inscription is found on a fragmentary beaker excavated near Oxford (Abingdon Mus.). A few pieces with horseman-style friezes have a second inscription band in which the letter is painted in gold on the exterior while the field is painted red or blue on the interior, such as a beaker (see fig. 235) found in the late 19th century under an altar in the church of S Margarita in Orvieto.

In the mid-13th century the arrangement of figures in friezes was abandoned in favour of smaller figures in roundels or cartouches. A two-handled pilgrim flask of olive-green glass (London, BM, 691–20 3), gilded and enamelled in blue, three shades of red, green, yellow, white and black, has the traditional motif of mounted hunters on the shoulders, but roundels on the sides contain a turbaned reveller and a harpist, and large cartouches on the front and back are filled with arabesque designs. The

into the main body. Marbled glass, which had been popular in the 11th century, was again popular in the late 13th century and early 14th.

A group of cut-glass beakers (h. *c.* 140 mm; e.g. London, BM, 1959 4–14 1), known as Hedwig beakers because one or more are associated with the Silesian princess St Hedwig (1174–1245), is traditionally attributed on stylistic grounds to 12th-century Egypt. All these objects are made of colourless glass with a smoky or topaz tinge and have deep wheel-cut decoration of lions, griffins and eagles with details indicated by hatching. Most of the 14 intact examples were preserved in church treasuries or aristocratic collections in Europe; fragments of four others were excavated in Italy and Germany and at Novogrudok in Belarus'. As neither the place of manufacture nor the date of Hedwig glasses has been established, they have also been attributed to the Byzantine world, Russia or southern Italy.

The best-known luxury vessels from this period are decorated with gold and polychrome enamel. These vessels, which were sometimes blown into moulds to obtain a ribbed or rippled effect, were painted with gold designs, either outline or solid, which were then filled in or enhanced by enamel colours and gently fired. The enamel consisted of powdered glass or frit, which was applied in the form of paste. The heat required to fuse the enamel (normally 650–750°C) was lower than the temperature at which the vessel would have begun to soften (*c.* 850°C).

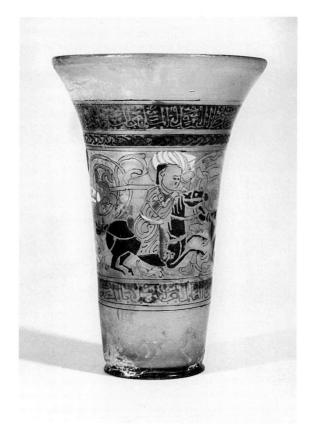

235. Glass beaker, enamelled and gilded, h. 150 mm, diam. 105 mm, possibly from Aleppo, c. 1260 (Paris, Musée du Louvre)

compositional style imitates that of inlaid metalwork produced in the second half of the 13th century at Damascus and Cairo, and this derivative style of enamelling glass was probably produced in the same centres. Chinoiserie motifs, which found favour in other arts of the Mamluk period, were also incorporated into enamelled glass at this time. For example, a vase (h. 339 mm; Lisbon, Mus. Gulbenkian, 2378) was enamelled in blue, red, green, yellow and white with birds and phoenixes, common chinoiserie motifs, and a band of foaming water in place of the traditional inscription.

In the 14th century chinoiserie motifs continued to be popular on enamelled glass, as did designs based on inlaid metal prototypes. As in metalware, the popularity of figural motifs declined as inscription bands became wider and were set on a floral ground interrupted by roundels with emblems, areas of contrasting pattern or suspension handles on mosque lamps. The inscriptions on mosque lamps generally mention the donor and include the well-known Light Verse from the Koran (xxiv.35), which likens God, the light of the heavens and the earth, to a glass lamp. Over a dozen mosque lamps from the three reigns of al-Nasir Muhammad (reg 1294–1340 with interruptions) represent the summit of 14th-century enamelled glass. A band of tall script at the neck with blue lettering on a gilded ground decorated with polychrome scrolls, leaves and buds contrasts with another band on the body

inscribed with gold letters on a blue ground with scattered gold blossoms. At least 50 lamps inscribed with the Light Verse and the name of Hasan (reg 1347–61 with interruption) are known. By the end of the century this traditional style had evolved, as seen in many of the 40 surviving mosque lamps made for Barquq (reg 1382–99 with interruption), on which epigraphy plays a lesser role and the drawing is hasty. One example (London, V&A, 326–1900) seems to revive earlier features with an inscription, a row of red and green medallions, outlines on the exterior of the vessel and colour-fill on the interior.

Production of enamelled glass seems to have declined sharply in the 15th century. Timur's sack of Damascus in 1401 may explain the collapse of the industry there, and archaeological evidence suggests that Mamluk taste changed and enamelled drinking-ware fell out of use in Egypt. A few enamelled lamps were ordered for charitable establishments by notable 15th-century Mamluks, but most of the glass excavated in 15th-century levels is archaic in technique. Instead of translucent or tinted wares, clear glass was decorated with blue trails or nearly opaque purple glass with green and white marvered trails. It was once thought that Venetians supplied the Mamluks with enamelled glass at the end of the 15th century, but enamelled glass was probably produced in Venice well before that time. Venetian glass of the 15th century resembles Mamluk glass of some two centuries earlier, although unpainted Venetian glass is similar to the clear, blue-trailed Mamluk glass. Mamluk-style gilded and enamelled glass was widely imitated in 19th-century Europe by such masters as EMILE GALLÉ and Joseph Brocard and the glass company J. & L. LOBMEYR.

BIBLIOGRAPHY

G. Wiet: *Lampes et bouteilles en verre émaillé*, Cairo, Mus. Islam. A. cat. (Cairo, 1929/R 1982)
C. J. Lamm: *Oriental Glass of Medieval Date Found in Sweden and the Early History of Lustre-painting* (Stockholm, 1941)
P. J. Riis: 'Saracenic Blazons on Glass from Ḥamā', *Studia Orientalia Ioanni Pedersen* (Copenhagen, 1953), pp. 295–302
P. J. Riis and V. Poulsen: *Les Verreries et poteries médiévales*, iv of *Hama: Fouilles et recherches de la Fondation Carlsberg, 1931–38* (Copenhagen, 1957)
A. Lamm: 'A Note on Glass Fragments from Pengkalan Bulang, Malaya', *J. Glass Stud.*, vii (1965), pp. 35–40
Masterpieces of Glass (exh. cat., ed. D. B. Harden and others; London, BM, 1968), pp. 114–21
B. Gray: 'Thoughts on the Origin of "Hedwig" Glasses', *Colloque international sur l'histoire du Caire: Caire, 1969*, pp. 191–4
R. H. Pinder-Wilson and G. T. Scanlon: 'Glass Finds from Fustat', *J. Glass Stud.*, xv (1973), pp. 12–30
R. J. Charleston: 'A 13th-century Glass Beaker Excavated at Lübeck', *Lübeck 1226: Reichsfreiheit und frühe Stadt* (Lübeck, 1976), pp. 321–37
The Arts of Islam (exh. cat., London, Hayward Gal., 1976), pp. 131–46
R. J. Charleston, M. Archer and M. Marcheix: *The James A. de Rothschild Collection at Waddeston Manor: Glass and Stained Glass, Limoges and Other Painted Enamels* (London and Fribourg, 1977), pp. 78–81
Renaissance of Islam: Art of the Mamluks (exh. cat. by E. Atil, Washington, DC, Smithsonian Inst. Traveling Exh. Serv., 1981–2), pp. 118–44
A. Engle: 'A Forgotten Glassmaking Centre of the Islamic Period', *Readings Glass Hist.*, xiii–xiv (1982), pp. 9–33
R. Hasson: 'Islamic Glass from Excavations in Jerusalem', *J. Glass Stud.*, xxv (1983), pp. 109–13
J. G. Kolbas: 'A Color Chronology of Islamic Glass', *J. Glass Stud.*, xxv (1983), pp. 95–9
D. S. Whitcomb: 'Islamic Glass from Quseir al-Qadim, Egypt', *J. Glass Stud.*, xxv (1983), pp. 101–8
M. Wenzel: 'Thirteenth-century Enamelled Glass Found in Medieval Abingdon', *Oxford J. Archaeol.*, iii/3 (1984), pp. 1–21

A. H. Morton: *A Catalogue of Early Islamic Stamps in the British Museum* (London, 1985)

M. Wenzel: 'Towards an Assessment of Ayyubid Glass Style', *The Art of Syria and the Jazira, 1100–1250*, ed. J. Raby (Oxford, 1985), pp. 99–112

MARIAN WENZEL

(iii) 16th–19th centuries. Glass production in this period is marked by the introduction of European glass, and its domination of markets in the Middle East and Asia. Venice and Spain, followed by England and Holland, were the main European exporters. Gilded, enamelled or filigree hollowware (beakers, goblets, ewers and decanters), mosque lamps, spectacles, mirrors and sheet glass all found a ready market. Special designs and shapes in the Turkish style were created, and a principal export was the glass water-pipe bowl (Pers. *nārgīl, ḥuqqa*), known as a hooka or hubble-bubble. From the 18th century the cut and engraved glass of Bohemia became popular, as well as French opalines and Russian glassware. Chandeliers and table lamps were also in great demand. Glass continued to be used in architectural decoration in the form of stained glass for windows and mirrorwork (*ā'ina-kārī*) for interior wall surfaces (*see* §II, 9(v) above) as well as for painting on glass (*see* §6 below).

Documentary evidence exists for the local production of high-quality glass in Turkey in the 16th and 17th centuries. For example, the *Sūrnāma-yi humāyūn* ('Imperial book of festivals'; *c.* 1583; Istanbul, Topkapı Pal. Lib., H. 1344, fols 32*v* and 33*r*) depicts the guild of glassblowers on parade in the Hippodrome in Istanbul; they blow glass in a furnace carried on a float and carry examples of their work. The earliest surviving examples of Ottoman glass, however, date from the late 18th century and the 19th when glass factories were established near Istanbul. The best known, Beykoz, was established during the reign of Selim III (*reg* 1789–1807) by a Turkish artisan who trained at Murano. Beykoz has become the generic term for all later glass produced under the Ottoman dynasty (*reg* 1281–1924). Another workshop was opened at Incirköy in 1846–7: it produced filigree ware (Turk. *çeşm-i bülbül*), decorated with stripes of opaque white and translucent coloured glass that imitated the Venetian and Bohemian *vetro a fili*. Colourless vessels decorated with opaque red marbling (e.g. a rosewater sprinkler, h. 229 mm; New York, Met., 83.7.230) are characteristic. Other production consisted of imitation Venetian cut and gilded glass, opalines and Bohemian-style cut glass, good enough to compete with European imports for the Middle Eastern market. Many fine examples are preserved in Istanbul (Topkapı Pal. Mus.).

Documentary evidence from Iran shows that glass was produced at Shiraz and Isfahan from the first half of the 17th century. Extant pieces, however, are extremely difficult to date, and many may be 19th-century examples of types still produced at Isfahan, Shiraz and Tehran. Vessels in rich blue, green and amber as well as transparent glass were blown or moulded in whimsical and graceful shapes and decorated with threading and punching. Rosewater sprinklers, long-necked ewers and decanters were especially common, and fine examples are preserved in Tehran (Abgina Mus.) and New York (Met.).

Local histories, travellers' accounts and book paintings document the possibility of local glass production in India under the patronage of the Mughal dynasty (*reg* 1526–1858), but extant examples can be securely dated only from the 18th century. Gilded and enamelled glasswares as well as moulded and relief-cut wares were produced in a highly decorative and ornate style immediately identifiable through contemporary book painting, textile designs and architectural ornament. The matrix itself was often lead glass imported from England.

See also INDIAN SUBCONTINENT, §VII, 9.

BIBLIOGRAPHY

R. Charleston: 'On the Import of Western Glass into Turkey: 16th–18th Centuries', *Connoisseur* (May 1966), pp. 18–26

M. G. Dikshit: *History of Indian Glass* (Bombay, 1969)

F. Baymaroğlu: *Turkish Art and Beikoz Glassware* (Ankara, 1976)

L. S. Diba: 'Glass and Glassmaking in the Eastern Islamic Lands: Seventeenth to Nineteenth Centuries', *J. Glass Stud.*, xxv (1983), pp. 187–93

J. M. Rogers: 'Glass in Ottoman Turkey', *Istanbul. Mitt.*, xxxiii (1983), pp. 239–67

M. Jenkins: 'Islamic Glass: A Brief History', *Bull. Met.*, xliv/2 (1986) [whole issue]

R. Charleston: 'Glass', *The Arts of Persia*, ed. R. W. Ferrier (New Haven and London, 1989), pp. 295–305

LAYLA S. DIBA

6. GLASS PAINTING. The art of painting behind glass (Fr. *eglomisé*; *see* GLASS PAINTING) flourished principally in Iran in the 19th century. In this technique the unpainted side of the glass is displayed to the viewer and the picture is built up in precisely the reverse order to that of a painting on canvas or paper, beginning with surface details and highlights and finishing with the background. The technique was exported from Europe in the 18th century to China and India where Company painters executed the same technique on mica (*see* INDIAN SUBCONTINENT, §VI, 4(ix)). The earliest Iranian examples date from the reign of the Qajar monarch Fath 'Ali Shah (*reg* 1797–1834).

Painting on glass was one of the many branches of painting in which Qajar court artists were expected to excel, but the rate of breakage must have been high as the glass employed was thin and some of the paintings are large. Among surviving examples are fine portraits of the Shah and his sons signed by such noted court artists as MIRZA BABA and MIHR 'ALI (Tehran, Ethnog. Mus.). Many other glass paintings of inferior quality were produced by journeymen; they show sloe-eyed beauties indulging in wine and were used as mural decoration. According to the traveller John Johnson, in the audience chamber of the palace at Tehran 'the niches were filled with glasses of different figures, having a half-length portrait in each, of either man or woman, in the manner of Chinese paintings on glass, which perhaps they actually were'. Paintings on glass continued to be produced during the reign of Nasir al-Din (*reg* 1848–96), and in later times floral borders were sometimes painted on mirrors, but in a rather perfunctory style.

BIBLIOGRAPHY

J. Johnson: *A Journey from India to England, through Persia, Georgia, Russia, Poland and Prussia in the Year 1817* (London, 1818), pp. 166–7

B. W. ROBINSON

7. IVORY. Luxury objects made of or decorated with IVORY were produced in those parts of the Islamic world

where the material was available: as India could satisfy only her own needs, the ivory used came mostly from eastern and central Africa, and consequently the Mediterranean Islamic lands—particularly Syria, Egypt, Spain and Sicily—were the primary centres of ivory-working. Bone was occasionally used as a substitute, particularly in Egypt. The range of ivory objects was limited by the shape and size of the elephant's tusk: small objects such as combs, boxes and chessmen were carved whole from the block, while larger boxes were made of separate pieces that were usually assembled using ivory pegs. Ivory was carved in relief, incised, painted and gilded. Wooden surfaces were also decorated with ivory in intarsia, in which ivory shapes were countersunk, and incrustation, in which the shapes were fixed to the surface (*see also* §VII above).

(i) Egypt, Syria and Yemen, before *c.* 1500. (ii) Spain. (iii) Tunisia, Sicily and South Italy. (iv) Iran and western Central Asia. (v) Ottoman empire, after *c.* 1500.

(i) Egypt, Syria and Yemen, before c. *1500.* Late Antique traditions of ivory-working continued in Syria and Egypt after the Islamic conquest in the 7th century. Two small ivory pyxides (cylindrical boxes; diam. 75 and 85 mm; London, V&A, and Kuwait City, Mus. Islam. A.) and one of bone (Berlin, Mus. Islam. Kst) and a fine panel in Athens (150×70 mm; Benaki Mus.) are carved in relief with vine scrolls issuing from a vase, one of the many Greco-Roman motifs that survived into the early Islamic period. Similarly carved ivory and bone plaques were excavated at Fustat (Old Cairo) and have been dated to the 7th and 8th centuries. A group of 'abstract' chessmen incised with dots and circles filled with brown pigment (New York, Met.; Boston, MA, Mus. F.A.; Paris, Louvre; Berlin, Mus. Islam. Kst) is usually attributed to Syria or Egypt. A pyxis with a conical lid is similarly decorated with incised dots and circles filled with black and red pigments (h. 175 mm; Cologne, St Gereon) but was made in Aden for 'Abdallah ibn al-Rabi', governor of the Yemen from 778 to 784. There is no other evidence of ivory-working in the Yemen at this time, and the Cologne pyxis may be the work of a Syrian or Egyptian craftsman. Among the exceedingly rare 'naturalistic' chessmen attributed to this period are an elephant (Florence, Bargello), an elephant and rider (probably a king; Berlin, Mus. Islam. Kst) and a horseman (i.e. a knight; St Petersburg, Hermitage). The most famous single chessman is a king mounted on an elephant accompanied by warriors and horsemen (h. 160 mm; Paris, Bib. N., Cab. Médailles). An inscription on the base states that it was the work of Yusuf al-Bahili. Al-Bahili is an Arab tribal name well attested in the early Islamic period, but the carving is in the sculptural style of 9th-century India.

A group of inlaid rectangular wooden panels found in a cemetery near Fustat shows that craftsmen in Egypt continued Late Antique techniques of intarsia and incrustation. The pieces vary in size and are thought to have been either from coffins or (less probably) from bookcovers. They have been dated on stylistic grounds to the 9th and 10th centuries. Some large panels are inlaid with representations of arcades or columns or intricate geometric compositions of squares and roundels (e.g. Paris, Louvre, A. O. AA20).

Egyptian carved ivories of the 10th and 11th centuries were produced for Islamic and Christian clients. Many ivory or bone panels of varying shapes and sizes have been found in the ruins of Fustat. Most display a limited repertory of animals, birds and, more rarely, human figures against a scrolling ornament on a smooth ground. Generally of mediocre quality, they were intended for the decoration of caskets or furniture and are closely related to contemporary wood-carving (*see* §VII, 1(i)(b) above). A small group of rectangular panels ascribed to the 11th or 12th century are of outstanding workmanship, carved with consummate skill and assurance in two openwork planes. Four panels (see fig. 236 for two of them) that are carved with scenes of courtly pursuits, the chase, feasting and music-making form a rectangular frame that may once have adorned the back of a throne. The tiny figures, acutely observed with particular attention to clothing and textile patterns, frolic on a ground of regular vine scrolls which give added depth to the composition. Two other panels with similar subjects (Paris, Louvre) are closely related. One horizontal and five vertical panels (125–170×62–80 mm) depict scenes of the hunt and the grape harvest. Two of them are remarkably like sculptures of the Labours of the Month on the portal of S Marco in Venice and may

236. Ivory panels, two of four that form a frame 419×365 mm, from Egypt, 11th–12th centuries (Berlin, Museum für Islamische Kunst)

represent a rare instance of this iconography in Islamic art. Parallels in composition and posture can be found between the whole group and wooden panels from the Western Palace of the Fatimid caliphs in Cairo (Cairo, Mus. Islam. A.). A wooden casket with rounded ends and a domical lid in Palermo (Cappella Palatina) is encrusted with ivory and a black substance and decorated with birds, animals, sphinxes and other paired figures set in volute scrolls as well as Arabic verses extolling the casket. It can be dated to the late 12th century or the early 13th.

Figural ornament, so popular in the early period, is virtually unknown after 1300. Intarsia replaced incrustation as the primary technique of decorating wooden objects with ivory, perhaps inspired by the magnificent inlaid wooden minbars that Mamluk patrons were ordering for their mosques. Typically, intersecting strapwork panels enclose ivory polygons carved in relief with arabesques and inscriptions, as on a high table made for Khwand Baraka, mother of Sultan Sha'ban, in 1369 (Cairo, Mus. Islam. A.). Five pierced pyxides are among the rare ivory objects in the round produced in this period. One of them (ex-Rothschild priv. col.; see Migeon, pl. 8) is inscribed around the lid with the name and titles of Sultan Salih (*reg* 1351–4), and four others (London, BM, 74.3–2.5 and 91.6–23.8; V&A, 4139–1856 and A68–1923) share the same delicate pierced decoration and encircling inscription bands executed in low relief on a ground filled with a black substance.   .

(ii) Spain. There was no indigenous tradition of ivory-working in the Iberian peninsula before the third quarter of the 10th century, when splendid ivories suddenly began to be produced in the court workshops of the Umayyad caliphs. Their technical mastery and assured style are difficult to explain unless the craftsmen came from Syria or Egypt or were trained by artisans sent from Byzantium, but neither hypothesis is wholly satisfactory. The 29 objects in this group are mostly rectangular caskets with lids that are either flat or in the form of a truncated pyramid and pyxides with domical lids; a folding spice box (Burgos, Mus. Arqueol. Prov.) is exceptional. Many are thought to have been jewellery boxes, but the verses inscribed on one pyxis (New York, Hisp. Soc. America) indicate that it was a container for perfumes. To this group should be added the arms of a processional cross (Paris, Louvre, and Madrid, Mus. Arqueol. N.) and a wooden portable altar inlaid with carved ivory strips (Madrid, Mus. Arqueol. N.). All are characterized by high relief carving in a single plane on a ground that has been left smooth. All but the smallest and largest caskets are made of ivory plaques joined by ivory pegs; the small casket with cover in Madrid (Inst. Valencia Don Juan) is carved from two solid blocks, while the large casket in the cathedral of Palencia has plaques attached to a wooden frame. Pairs of hinged braces fasten the lids of caskets; a single brace suffices for pyxides. Where original, they are made of nielloed silver with lanceolate terminals and are attached to the lower edge of the back and to the upper surface of the lid. A lock and hasp are attached to the front.

Many pieces have Arabic inscriptions carved in relief in a plain or foliated kufic script on the lower edge of the lid. They may record names of the owner and the craftsman and the date and place of manufacture. Ivories were made for the caliph al-Hakam II (*reg* 961–76), members of the royal house and other dignitaries. Several objects are dedicated to female members of the court, including a daughter of 'Abd al-Rahman III (London, V&A) and Subh, a concubine of al-Hakam II and mother of the caliph Hisham II (Madrid, Mus. Arqueol. N.). Inscriptions on caskets in the parish church at Fitero in Navarra and in Madrid (Inst. Valencia Don Juan) state that they were made in 966 at Madinat al-Zahra' (*see* CÓRDOBA (i), §2), the palace suburb of Córdoba, and ten other ivories have been attributed there on stylistic grounds. All share a dense vegetal decoration, comprising full and half palmettes, quatrefoils and berries on a continuous stem disposed symmetrically about a vertical axis. A distinctive feature is the precise carving of the serrations and the veining of the leaves. Confronted or addorsed birds and animals appear on pyxides in Madrid (Mus. Arqueol. N.), Lucerne (E. Kofler-Truniger priv. col.; see Kühnel, 1971, no. 39) and New York (Met.). The pyxides at Fitero and the Hispanic Society of America in New York are signed by a craftsman named Khalaf. The spice box in Burgos must have been made before 962 as it bears a dedication to a daughter of 'Abd al-Rahman III while he was still living and is therefore the earliest piece in the group.

A distinct group of nine other ivories is attributed to Córdoba between 968 and 1005, although their inscriptions do not specify the place of production. Their decoration is organized in cartouches, usually with eight lobes, interlaced with each other and with the framing bands. The cartouches depict scenes of feasting, music-making, hunting, jousting and animals or birds fighting, while the interspaces are filled with plant ornament. A pyxis in Paris (Louvre) was made in 968 for al-Mughira, son of 'Abd al-Rahman III. Four eight-lobed cartouches on the lid and walls depict different scenes in mirror symmetry: a standing musician flanked by two seated figures on a dais supported on the backs of paired lions, paired horsemen flanking a palm tree from which they gather dates, two men grasping a nest containing an eagle, and paired lions attacking a buffalo. The plant ornament of the interspaces contains paired falconers, wrestlers, griffins, peacocks, birds, butting goats and animals of the chase. A large rectangular casket in Pamplona (see fig. 237), made in 1005 for the son of al-Mansur, chief minister to Hisham II (*reg* 976–1009), is equally fine. On the lid ten eight-lobed cartouches show paired animals, fabulous beasts and horsemen at the chase; ten similar cartouches on the sides show scenes of jousting, feasting or music-making on a dais supported by paired lions, and a man defending himself with a sword and shield against attacking lions. The inside of the lid is inscribed 'the work of Faraj and his pupils', of whom at least four signed various parts of the decoration.

As the Umayyad caliphate collapsed, the court ivory-carvers found a refuge at Cuenca in Castile, which was under the rule of the Dhu'l-Nunids of Toledo from 1020 onwards. Inscriptions on three carvings state that the pieces were made in Cuenca, and five others are attributed to this centre on stylistic grounds. Their ornament is organized in narrow horizontal or vertical registers and is composed of the plant ornament found on the objects produced at Madinat al-Zahra' and the creatures and human figures of those from Córdoba, but the workmanship is inferior and the designs lack the inventiveness of earlier periods. The earliest is a casket in Burgos (Mus. Arqueol. Prov.) made in 1026 by Muhammad ibn Zayyan; an encrusted wooden casket in Madrid (Mus. Arqueol. N.) was made in 1050 for the ruler's son Abu Muhammad Isma'il by 'Abd al-Rahman ibn Zayyan, Muhammad's brother or son.

Ivory was also used for the incrustation of wooden objects. Texts describe an encrusted minbar made in Córdoba in 966, but the earliest minbar of Córdoban workmanship to survive was made for the Kutubiyya Mosque in Marrakesh between 1125 and 1130. Wood and ivory cubes, some stained, were encrusted in chequerboard patterns to form framing bands, and ivory panels were carved with cursive inscriptions and inlaid. A group of three encrusted rectangular caskets with truncated pyramidal lids has been attributed to the 13th century. Two of them are decorated with large roundels enclosing animals and human figures arranged in strict mirror symmetry, like the Córdoban carved ivories. A magnificent pair of encrusted cupboard doors from a private house in Granada (Granada, Mus. N. A. Hispanomusulmán) and a large rectangular casket decorated with interlaced star patterns in stained ivory and various woods (Madrid, Mus. Arqueol. N.) show that the craft was still practised in 14th-century Granada.

(iii) Tunisia, Sicily and South Italy. Painted caskets and carved oliphants (hunting horns), often known as 'Siculo-Arabic' or 'Saracenic' ivories, are ascribed to Tunisia, Sicily and South Italy between the 10th and the 13th centuries. They share techniques used elsewhere in the Islamic world, and elements from the Islamic decorative repertory and Arabic inscriptions appear on many of them, but only a few can be ascribed with certainty to Muslim patrons. An important, if anomalous, rectangular casket with bulbous legs and finials (420×240×200 mm; Madrid, Mus. Arqueol. N.) has scrollwork border panels painted in green and red. An Arabic inscription painted on the lid records that the casket was made for the Fatimid caliph al-Mu'izz (*reg* 953–75) in al-Mansuriyya, the town founded by his father near Kairouan in Tunisia that was his capital until 972. This rare early Fatimid luxury object bears a signature that has been read as Ahmad al-Khurasani.

Some 220 ivories, including caskets, pyxides, combs and crosiers ornamented with polychrome decoration and often gilded, comprise a more homogeneous group attributed to Sicily in the 11th and 12th centuries. In contrast to the Spanish ivories, which were made in limited quantities for aristocratic patrons, the large number of painted ivories that survive suggests that they were intended for a wider clientele. Rectangular caskets (l. 100–485 mm) have flat or truncated pyramidal lids, oval caskets have domical lids and pyxides have flat lids. The water-based pigments used were red, green and more rarely blue; outlines and inner details are in black. Very little of the original gold leaf they once bore has survived. Gilt metal braces with lanceolate terminals and locks join the lids to the main bodies. Roundels, presented singly, paired or in multiples, but never interwoven, are the predominant

237. Ivory casket by Faraj and his pupils, h. 350 mm, from Córdoba, 1005 (Pamplona, Museo de Navarra)

format for their decoration. Invariably inscribed with a compass, they are filled with elements from the Islamic repertory of the 12th and 13th centuries, such as geometric figures, arabesques, birds (often peacocks), animals and human figures, as well as depictions of Christ and of saints. These same elements may also appear without the enclosing roundel, and a few rare cases present miniature scenes (e.g. Palermo, Cappella Palatina). Many of the caskets and pyxides are embellished on the lower edge of the lid with benedictory verses or amatory phrases in angular or cursive Arabic script. The absence of historical dedications supports the suggestion that they were made for sale on the market rather than the result of individual commissions; most were probably intended as bridal caskets, although over 100 were preserved in Western church treasuries.

The formal, technical and stylistic homogeneity of these ivories would be explained by a single regional provenance, but the variations in the handling of common motifs, inscriptional formulae and roundel ornament indicate that they were produced by several workshops at different stages of development. Some 20 caskets, pyxides and crosier heads have rather sparingly dispersed ornament of crosses, stars and birds formed of tiny circles incised in the ivory surface and filled with green or red pigment, a technique known already in the 8th century (*see* §(i) above). An oval casket in York Minster that cannot be later than 1148 suggests that the incised group be assigned to the first half of the 12th century. The only other oval casket (Trent, Mus. Dioc.) combines incised circles stained red or black with gilded decoration of Greek crosses, birds and arabesques and links the incised and the painted groups. The painted ivories are generally dated to the second half of the 12th century and the first half of the 13th. The earliest recorded example is the Reliquary of St Petroc from Bodmin, Cornwall (London, BM), first mentioned in 1177, and others are recorded between 1215 and 1309.

The painted ivories show similarities to contemporary Spanish and Egyptian work, but their decorative treatment and organization do not conform entirely to the canons of the main artistic centres of the Islamic world, and this suggests that they were produced outside the mainstream of Islamic art. Diez argued unconvincingly for Syria, and Monneret de Villard (1950) believed they were made in Mesopotamia. Citing resemblances to the paintings, mosaics, textiles, carved wood and painted pottery of Norman Sicily, Kühnel (1914) plausibly attributed them to Sicily under Norman and Hohenstaufen rule, although it is also possible that they were produced in South Italy, perhaps at Amalfi. Ivory workshops staffed by the isolated Muslims of Sicily would explain both the Christian elements and the divergences from mainstream Islamic art. After the rebellion of 1221 the Muslim population of Sicily was mostly dispersed to North Africa, and it is unlikely that the industry survived long into the 13th century.

Thirty ivory oliphants and six caskets preserved in Western church treasuries are commonly called 'Saracenic', but were probably produced in South Italy, possibly Amalfi, in the 10th and 11th centuries. Although they owe much of their form, technique and decoration to the arts of Islam, none has been found in an Islamic context, and oliphants were neither used as hunting horns nor as drinking vessels in the Islamic world. The earliest of the three types is distinguished by its undecorated main field. The upper and lower ends are relief carved in a single plane on a smooth ground with borders containing acanthus scrolls and animals in the Islamic style. Of the seven examples known, only that in the treasury of Aachen Cathedral may be of Islamic workmanship. The second group is distinguished by a main field carved with interlaced roundels each enclosing a real or fabulous bird or animal (e.g. Berlin, Mus. Islam. Kst), the third by a field divided into longitudinal bands (e.g. Florence, Bargello). Although some of the images belong to the Islamic repertory, others come from the Romanesque bestiary, so it is doubtful whether any is Islamic work. Of the six caskets decorated in a similar style and technique, two (Berlin, Mus. Islam. Kst, and St Petersburg, Hermitage) may be of Islamic workmanship. The St Petersburg casket has carved openwork decoration similar to contemporary Egyptian work, for example. An ivory penbox (New York, Met.) is crudely inscribed TAUROFI[LIUS]MANSO ('Taurus son of Manso'), apparently by a craftsman unfamiliar with Latin. The Mansoni family played a prominent role in Amalfitan affairs in the 10th and 11th centuries, and Amalfi, which had important commercial relations with Egypt and the Levant, is known to have been a centre of ivory-working (e.g. the Paliotto in Salerno Cathedral). An act of the Angevin king in 1301 referred to the Muslim craftsmen ('Saracenos artistas') of South Italy in such terms as to suggest that they were as numerous as their crafts were various.

(iv) Iran and western Central Asia. Only a handful of ivory carvings have been attributed to medieval Iran. A rectangular penbox (230×70 mm; Brussels, Stoclet priv. col.; see von Falke, pls opposite pp. 280 and 282) is carved in relief with arcades on the sides and with three interlaced roundels on the lid. The central roundel depicts Bahram Gur mounted on a camel and hunting a hare, while those to either side of it depict simurghs. The iconography is clearly

of Sasanian inspiration, but the style suggests an early Islamic date. A mirror-back carved in relief with addorsed birds with crossing tails (diam. 104 mm; Athens, Benaki Mus.) has been attributed on stylistic grounds to 11th-century Iran. There are references to the carving of ivory and ebony in the region of Isfahan in the 13th century, but the earliest physical evidence for the existence of this craft is a pair of early 15th-century inlaid wooden doors from the Gur-i Mir in Samarkand (St Petersburg, Hermitage). Five ivory panels (*c.* 203×44 mm; Tehran, Archaeol. Mus.) from the tomb of the Safavid ruler Isma'il I (*reg* 1501–24) at Ardabil are carved in openwork with Koranic inscriptions against a scrolling floral ground.

See also CENTRAL ASIA, §I, 8(iv).

(v) Ottoman empire, after c. 1500. Ivory was used in the Ottoman court workshops to make small objects such as mirrors, belts, buckles, handles and hilts, or to decorate larger wooden objects in the techniques of incrustation and intarsia (*see* §VII, 2(iv) above). A deeply carved oval mirror-back was made by Ghani in 1543–4 and dedicated to Süleyman (see fig. 238). The central area of scrolling chinoiserie flowers has an inner border of scrolling flowers and cloud bands and an outer border of Turkish couplets in complex *thuluth* script wishing beauty and brightness to the user's face. The pieces of the mirror were assembled using gold nails. A circular mirror (mid-16th century; Istanbul, Topkapı Pal. Mus.) has lotus flowers and split palmettes radiating from a central turquoise rosette set in gold. The ivory hilt of a sword made for Süleyman (1526–7; Istanbul, Topkapı Pal. Mus.) is lightly incised with delicate floral scrolls filled with a black substance and overlaid with a gold openwork net of lotus scrolls. Belt plaques decorated in the same technique of black inlay overlaid with gold scrollwork can also be dated to the first half of the 16th century. A belt plaque carved in openwork with radial scrollwork panels (diam. 83 mm; Istanbul, Topkapı Pal. Mus., 538) has been attributed to both Turkey and India in the 17th or 18th century. Ivory was also used for pen-holders, the handles of knives used for trimming pens, penrests, penboxes and spoon handles. Walrus ivory was preferred for the hilts of swords and daggers.

BIBLIOGRAPHY

G. Migeon: *Exposition des arts musulmans au Musée des Arts Décoratifs* (Paris, 1903)

E. Diez: 'Bemalte Elfenbeinkästchen und Pyxiden der islamischen Kultur', *Jb. Kön.-Preuss. Kstsamml.*, xxxi (1910), pp. 231–44; xxxii (1911), pp. 117–42

E. Kühnel: 'Sizilien und die islamische Elfenbeinmalerei', *Z. Bild. Kst*, xlix (1914), pp. 162–70

A. Bahgat and A. Gabriel: *Fouilles d'al-Foustat* (Paris, 1921)

H. Terrasse and J. Hainaut: *Les Arts décoratifs au Maroc* (Paris, 1923)

A. Basset and H. Terrasse: 'Sanctuaires et forteresses almohades', *Hésperis*, vi (1926), pp. 107–270

O. von Falke: 'Ein sassanidischer Elfenbeinkasten', *Pantheon*, i (1928), pp. 144–6

J. Ferrandis: *Marfiles árabes de Occidente*, 2 vols (Madrid, 1935–40)

U. Monneret de Villard: *La Cassetta incrostata della Cappella Palatina di Palermo* (Rome, 1938)

P. B. Cott: *Siculo-Arabic Ivories* (Princeton, 1939)

E. Kühnel: 'Die mamlukische Kassettenstil', *Kst Orients*, i (1950), pp. 55–68

U. Monneret de Villard: *Le pitture musulmane al soffitto della Cappella Palatina in Palermo* (Rome, 1950), pp. 29–30

J. Beckwith: *Caskets from Cordoba* (London, 1960)

Al-Andalus: The Art of Islamic Spain (exh. cat., ed. J. D. Dodds; Granada, Alhambra; New York, Met., 1992)

RALPH PINDER-WILSON

8. JADE. Nephrite jade (Pers. *yashm*) has been known in the Islamic lands at least since the 10th century AD. It is mentioned in the anonymous Persian geography *Ḥudūd al-'alam* (982), and an account of its sources in Khotan, its properties and its uses appears in the treatise on mineralogy *Kitāb al-jamāhir fī ma'rifat al-jawāhir*, written by the polymath al-Biruni (973–*c.* 1050) for the Ghaznavid sultan Shihab al-Dawla Mawdud (*reg* 1041–50). Dishes of jade encrusted with gold are said to have been brought to the Yemen from China by a Syrian merchant in 1303 and jade vessels sent from Yemen to the Mamluk sultan of Egypt in the following year. Although the material was thus known in the Islamic lands before the 15th century, there is no evidence of it being worked by lapidaries under Islamic patronage until Timur's grandson Ulughbeg (1394–1449; *see* TIMURID, §II(5)) acquired two large blocks of greenish-black nephrite in 1425 (*see also* CENTRAL ASIA, §I, 8(v)). These were taken to Samarkand to be carved and inscribed for use as Timur's tombstone in the Gur-i Mir (*see* SAMARKAND, §3(iii)).

The earliest jade object known to have been in Timurid possession is the cup inscribed with Ulughbeg's name (l. 194 mm; London, BM, OA 1959.11-20.1(36); *see* JADE, colour pl. III, fig. 1). This Chinese scholar's vessel for grinding ink (Chin. *cheng*), with a handle in the form of a hornless dragon, is not considered to be of imperial Ming workmanship but was doubtless sent with one of several Chinese embassies and is a possible exemplar for a series of wine cups made under Timurid patronage. Unlike Ming jades, these follow metal or ceramic forms. The shape of a small green jade cup with a duck's head (Varanasi, Banaras Hindu U., Bharat Kala Bhavan, 3/8860) is evidently inspired by a type of Mongol loop-handled silver cup used for drinking kummis. This cup is also inscribed with Ulughbeg's name and that of its later owner, the Mughal emperor Jahangir (*reg* 1605–27). Other uninscribed cups (e.g. London, BM, 1961.2-13,1, and Tehran, Archaeol. Mus.), circular, lobed or elliptical in plan, have dragon handles with either the snout or the lower jaw of the dragon resting on the rim. Dragon heads, like those seen in Timurid metal candlesticks (*see* §IV, 3(i)(b) above), also terminate the jade quillon blocks of swords (e.g. 51×102 mm; New York, Met., 02.18.765). Such objects, often coarsely polished, have a severe appearance which is emphasized by the aggressive power of the dragon terminals and the black or dark green colour of the nephrite.

An alternative type of vessel, of which at least four examples have survived, is copied from a well-known series of inlaid brass jugs in which a high cylindrical neck rises from a torus moulding above a globular body (see fig. 149 above). They usually have serpentine handles with dragon heads, either integral or joined to the body, and originally had domed lids. The finest is a magnificent white nephrite vessel (see fig. 239) which marks the culmination of Ulughbeg's patronage since it bears the full regnal titles that he held from 1447 to 1449. In this object the grinding and polishing of the jade reaches the highest level of

238. Ivory mirror-back by Ghani, 140×122 mm, from Istanbul, 1543–4 (Istanbul, Topkapı Palace Museum)

E. Kühnel: *Die islamischen Elfenbeinskulpturen, VII–XIII Jahrhundert* (Berlin, 1971)

R. H. Pinder-Wilson with C. N. L. Brooke: 'The Reliquary of St Petroc and the Ivories of Norman Sicily', *Archaeologia*, civ (1973), pp. 261–305

The Arts of Islam (exh. cat., London, Hayward Gal., 1976), pp. 147–56

C. Köseoglu: *Topkapı Sarayı Müzesi* (Tokyo, 1980), Eng. trans. and ed. by J. M. Rogers as *Topkapı Saray Museum: The Treasury* (Boston, 1987)

The Anatolian Civilisations III: Seljuk/Ottoman (exh. cat., 18th Council of Europe exh., Istanbul, 1983)

J. M. Rogers: 'Osmanische Elfenbeinkunst', *Türkische Kunst und Kultur aus osmanischer Zeit* (exh. cat., Frankfurt am Main, Mus. Ksthandwerk, 1985), i, pp. 339–42

Süleyman the Magnificent (exh. cat. by J. M. Rogers and R. M. Ward, London, BM, 1988)

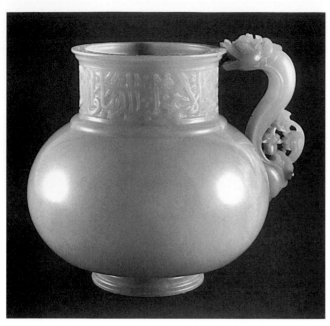

239. Nephrite jade jug, h. 145 mm, 1447–9 (Lisbon, Museu Calouste Gulbenkian)

sophisticated mastery, in which the pearl-like texture of the white material is fully exploited. Two other white jade objects known from the Timurid period are a small two-handled vessel in the Danish royal collections and an even smaller pot (h. 35 mm, diam. 30 mm; San Francisco, CA, Asian A. Mus.) inscribed with the titles of Ulughbeg's nephew 'Ala' al-Dawla (1417–60).

Several jade objects can be assigned to the reign of the Timurid sultan Husayn Bayqara (*reg* 1470–1506) on the basis of the only precisely dated Timurid hardstone object, an agate bowl (1470–71; Houston, TX, Art and History Trust priv. col.). Based in shape on a type of Ming blue-and-white porcelain vessel that was imported into Iran, it has a band of verse celebrating wine engraved below the rim as well as decorative cartouches on its walls. A dark green jade bowl (Paris, Louvre, MR199), even closer to a porcelain prototype, having a slightly flared rim, has the same verses below and a wider central band containing an elegant peony scroll engraved in intaglio around the sides. A phoenix-handled cup (London, V&A), with a quatrain praising Jahangir added in 1613, probably also dates to Husayn Bayqara's reign. The late phase of Timurid jade workmanship is seen in two dishes with arabesque scrolls in circular medallions. The marginally finer plate (Paris, Louvre, MR 198 (E175)) is uninscribed, but a similar one (sold at Christies, 27 April 1993) was owned by the Mughal emperor Babur in 1509–10 and may represent what was then current production when he visited the Timurid capital.

Unlike the Timurids, their Safavid successors in Iran (*reg* 1501–1732) appear to have had no interest in jade, though a black jade jug (h. 110 mm; Istanbul, Topkapı Pal. Mus.) of Timurid form with a metal handle was inlaid with gold arabesques for Isma'il I (*reg* 1501–24) before it was carried off to Istanbul in 1514. A rather plain bowl (London, V&A), after a porcelain model and rather poorly inscribed with verses, was presented to the shrine at ARDABIL by 'Abbas I in 1611. A seal-handle (Berlin, Mus. Islam. Kst) of 'Abbas II (*reg* 1642–66) has confidently executed intaglio arabesques, indicating that Iranians possessed the competence to work jade had it appealed to them.

The Ottomans showed the same predilection for jade as the Timurids in Transoxiana and the Mughals in the Indian subcontinent. Sixteenth-century Ottoman examples generally follow Timurid models, but the execution is often coarse and clumsy. A dominant feature is the application of gold scrolls with tiny leaves and gems mounted above the surface of the stone in flower-like settings. An alternative mode, particularly in the 17th century, is a rather severe arabesque of scrolling stems with bifurcated leaves inlaid flush with the jade surface. Unlike the Timurids and Mughals, the Ottomans frequently added small inlaid jade plaques to weapons, quivers and other military and ceremonial equipment (e.g. a gold canteen, h. 270 mm; Istanbul, Topkapı Pal. Mus., 3825) because they believed that jade brought victory in battle, would ward off lightning and possessed curative properties. From the 17th century Ottoman jade sword hilts frequently copied the 'pistol-grip' form of Mughal swords and daggers, and a similar emulation of Mughal taste affected the design of jade vessels. As in the subcontinent (*see* INDIAN SUBCONTINENT, §VIII, 11), a taste developed for light green and white nephrite. Forms became less heavy and more sensuous in outline, though never as closely influenced by organic models as Mughal pieces. By contrast with similar Mughal examples, later Ottoman pieces often have flat-sawn horizontal or vertical handles and are closer to Chinese taste in the use of stems trailing from bud handles to end in coils under the base.

Luxury objects produced for the Qajar court of Iran (*reg* 1779–1924) combined jade with other precious materials. A jewelled nephrite dish (Vienna, Ksthist. Mus., Plastik-Sammlung no. 3223) presented by the Persian ambassador Abu'l-Hasan Khan to the Austrian emperor Francis II (*reg* 1804–35) has a central gold plaque enamelled by the painter 'ALI, who also painted an oval mirror with a carved jade handle (Tehran, Bank Markazi, Crown Jewels Col.).

BIBLIOGRAPHY

Ḥudūd al-'alam [The regions of the world] (982); Eng. trans by V. Minorsky (London, 1937/*R* 1970), p. 86

al-Bīrūnī (*d c.* 1050): *Kitāb al-jamāhir fī ma'rifat al-jawāhir* [The sum of knowledge about precious stones], ed. F. Krenkow (Hyderabad, AH 1355/1936–7)

R. Skelton: 'The Relations Between the Chinese and Indian Jade Carving Traditions', *The Westward Influence of the Chinese Arts from the 14th to the 18th Century*, ed. W. Watson (London, 1972), pp. 101–3

E. J. Grube: 'Notes on the Decorative Arts of the Timurid Period', *Gururājamañjarikā: Studi in onore di Giuseppe Tucci*, ed. A. Forte and others (Naples, 1974), pp. 252–6

R. Skelton: 'Characteristics of Later Turkish Jade Carving', *Fifth International Congress of Turkish Art: Budapest, 1975*, pp. 795–807

C. Köseoglu: *Topkapı Sarayı Müzesi* (Tokyo, 1980); Eng. trans. ed. by J. M. Rogers as *Topkapı Saray Museum: The Treasury* (Boston, 1987), pp. 52–3, 196

Islamic Art and Design, 1500–1700 (exh. cat. by J. M. Rogers, London, BM, 1983), pp. 149–51

E. J. Grube: 'Notes on the Decorative Arts of the Timurid Period II', *Islam. A.*, iii (1988–9), pp. 176–80

T. W. Lentz and G. D. Lowry: *Timur and the Princely Vision: Persian Art and Culture in the Fifteenth Century* (Los Angeles, 1989), pp. 142–3, 221–5, 311, 317, 321, 354

R. Skelton: 'Islamic and Mughal Jades', *Jade*, ed. R. Keverne (London, 1991), pp. 274–95

R. Pinder-Wilson: 'Jades from the Islamic World', *Marg*, xliv/2 (1992), pp. 35–48

A. Soudavar: *Art of the Persian Courts: Selections from the Art and History Trust Collection* (New York, 1992), pp. 92–3

ROBERT SKELTON

9. JEWELLERY. The disapproval by Islamic religious authorities of luxury materials had little effect in restraining the wealthy from adorning themselves with gold, silver and precious stones, but only a small percentage of the jewellery produced in Islamic lands has survived. Grave goods, one of the main sources for jewellery historians of other cultures, are forbidden in Islam, and the jewellery that remained above ground was subject to the demands of fashion and economy: gold and silver were melted down and stones reused. Very few of the pieces that do survive have a known date or provenance. The few published excavations, occasional chance finds of treasure and rare objects bearing a clue to their date and place of manufacture, as well as pictorial representations and textual descriptions, provide the only reliable evidence. Most attributions depend on stylistic and technical comparison with the few objects of known provenance and have to be treated with caution, for the styles and techniques of this conservative craft often endured for centuries and, when innovations were introduced, they were swiftly spread by itinerant jewellers (mainly Jews, as gold was considered impure), making it difficult to differentiate between centres of production until the later period.

BIBLIOGRAPHY

Enc. Islam/2: 'Djawhar' [Jewellery]

M. Jenkins and M. Keene: *Islamic Jewelry in the Metropolitan Museum of Art* (New York, 1982)

Islamic Jewelry (exh. cat. by N. Brosh, Jerusalem, Israel Mus., 1987)

M. Wenzel: *Ornament and Amulet: Rings of the Islamic Lands* (1993), xvi of *The Nasser D. Khalili Collection of Islamic Art*, ed. J. Raby (London, 1992–)

(i) Before *c.* 1500. (ii) After *c.* 1500.

(i) Before c. *1500.* The most popular forms of jewellery worn by women were pairs of bracelets, armlets and anklets, necklaces, amulets, earrings, finger-rings, nose-rings and diadems. Men wore belts, amulets, finger-rings (including seal rings) and earrings. Precious stones were the most prestigious material used; they were left *en cabuchon*, were bored and strung, or were simply set. Gold was also highly prized, and silver and brass were often gilded in imitation. Shells, stones, glazed ceramic, coloured glass etc were used for their aesthetic rather than intrinsic value. Most of the techniques and decorative motifs continued pre-Islamic traditions. The Islamic contribution was the gradual increase of epigraphic decoration, on decorative pieces as well as amulets, and a corresponding decrease in the use of the figural decoration so popular in antiquity.

(a) Syria, Egypt and North Africa. Painted and stucco depictions of the Umayyad caliphs (*reg* 661–750) and their court from the palaces in Syria show that their jewellery, like their costume and other arts, followed Late Antique traditions. Excavated pieces dating from the first centuries of Islam are usually indistinguishable from their predecessors. A distinctly Islamic style first appeared in the period of Fatimid rule (*reg* 969–1171) in Egypt. Finds from the ruins of Fustat (Old Cairo) have revealed that the finest jewellery was made of gold and skilfully decorated with filigree and granulation, a traditional technique that reached a peak of excellence during this period and was used on earrings, pendants (*see* JEWELLERY, colour pl. III, fig. 1), bracelets and even finger-rings. Small cloisonné enamel plaques, usually intended for pendent centrepieces to gold necklaces, were also found at Fustat. Byzantine techniques and motifs, such as paired birds beneath a tree, were used in their manufacture. Ibn al-Zubayr, writing in the mid-11th century, listed enamels among the gifts sent from the Byzantine emperor to the Fatimid caliph in 1045 to 1052, but some must have been produced locally, as several pieces have fluent Arabic inscriptions in both angular kufic and cursive *naskh* scripts. An enamelled gold brooch (Cairo, Mus. Islam. A., 4337), for example, bears a quotation from the Koran (xxi.64) in kufic script.

Cairo, as the seat of the Fatimid court, must have been the main centre of production, and high-quality pieces found in other parts of the Fatimid empire may have been imported from there, but it is equally likely that there were several centres of production, as well as itinerant jewellers moving about the empire. A hoard of gold jewellery with filigree decoration, found in the Tarabia region south-west of El Kef in Tunisia in association with coins minted at Mahdia or Mansuriyya between 1003 and 1045, was probably produced locally. The forms (bracelets, earrings and necklace elements), the gold filigree work and certain decorative motifs relate the pieces to those found at Fustat and show how widespread styles and techniques were at this time.

Two hoards of jewellery were unearthed in the 1963 excavations at Caesarea in Israel. The first, thought to have been buried before the Crusader invasion of the city in 1101, included biconical and oval gold beads as finely decorated in filigree and granulation as anything from Fustat, as well as engraved silver amulet boxes and strung stone and glass beads. The second contained a pair of anklets, armlets and bracelets. These were made of silver and decorated in repoussé with animals and other motifs familiar from Fatimid woodwork. Similar bangles made of silver, gold or brass sheet were found in Syria.

The same style probably continued after the fall of the Fatimid dynasty in 1171, and many of the pieces attributed to the Fatimids were probably made later under the Ayyubids (*reg* 1169–1252) or even the Mamluks (*reg* 1250–1517). Some types of objects known from the Fatimid period, such as enamel plaques and repoussé sheet bangles, have inscriptions in a style of script that suggests a later date. A gold pendant (Cairo, Mus. Islam. A., 9455), for example, has an enamel plaque inscribed in *naskh*, a style of script not used for such purposes under the Fatimids. Reattributing some of the Fatimid pieces would explain why so little material has survived from the later periods. A few pieces bear the emblems of Mamluk officers or are decorated with chinoiserie motifs such as dragons, lotus or peony flowers and lobed borders that did not become popular until the 14th and 15th centuries. Because these East Asian motifs were received mainly via Iran, it is not always possible to distinguish between Egyptian and Iranian pieces.

Leather belts with metal fittings became important as status symbols at the Ayyubid and Mamluk courts, although painted ceramics and the frescoes of the Cappella Palatina in Palermo, which are attributed to painters familiar with the art of the Fatimid court, indicate that men had worn little or no jewellery under the Fatimids. The finest belts were made of gold set with precious stones and were presented by the sultan to his highest-ranking officers. The most lavish examples described in contemporary chronicles have not survived, but there is a group of belts with massive buckles and rectangular plaques, often made from gilded silver with fine openwork of scrolling vegetation and animal motifs. One (Jerusalem, Mayer Mem. Inst. Islam. A., J.23) is inscribed with the names and titles of al-Sultan al-Malik al-Salih Abu'l-Fida Isma'il, which makes it possible to establish an unusually specific provenance and date for this piece, as Abu'l-Fida, an Ayyubid prince who ruled at Hama in Syria, was granted the title sultan by his Mamluk suzerain only a year before his death in 1321. Similar belts have been found in Turkey and southern Russia, and the type may have originated in the Eurasian steppes, whence many Mamluk sultans and their courtiers were recruited (*see* MAMLUK, §II, 1).

(b) Iraq, Iran and western Central Asia. Sasanian traditions remained strong in this area after the Muslim conquest. Virtually no jewellery has survived from Iraq from the period when it was the centre of the Abbasid caliphate (749–1258), but two 9th-century frescoes from an Abbasid palace at SAMARRA' depict men wearing a type of belt with pendent straps decorated with close-fitting arrowhead-shaped plaques that is also seen in the Sasanian rock reliefs at TAQ-I BUSTAN.

The most accessible and complete body of material dating from the early medieval period (8th–10th century) was excavated at NISHAPUR in north-east Iran (New York, Met.). It includes stone and glass beads; gold hoop and bead earrings; bronze crescent- and pear-shaped pendants; gold, silver and bronze finger-rings with stone settings; gilded-bronze rectangular belt fittings similar to those

depicted on courtiers in frescoes at Nishapur and LASH-KARI BAZAR; and a gold snake-headed bracelet. These pieces show that pre-Islamic forms and decoration continued well into the Islamic period, but Arabic inscriptions were added to the traditional repertory of animal and vegetal motifs on the finest objects, such as a silver and nielloed cylindrical amulet box and several of the belt fittings.

Two identical gold bracelets (New York, Met., 57.88 and Washington, DC, Freer; see fig. 240) are attributed to Nishapur, even though they are of a much higher quality than anything excavated at the site. They have shanks made of hollow tubes tapering towards the clasp, and the repoussé decoration and fine wire wound round them give a twisted effect. The clasps are boldly decorated with turquoises and four large and several smaller hemispheres covered in fine granulation. Four discs on the underside of the clasps have been stamped over coins minted in Nishapur in the name of the Abbasid caliph al-Qadir (*reg* 991–1031) during the reign of the Ghaznavid sultan Mahmud (*reg* 998–1030). The bracelets provide important evidence that Khurasan produced high-quality gold jewellery decorated with filigree and granulation like that known from Egypt.

A hoard of damaged silver jewellery, probably gathered to be melted down, is more closely dated than the finds from Nishapur, as it was buried near Chimkent in Kazakhstan with coins minted between 949 and 1040. It contained a similar mix of objects: beads, earrings, pendants, finger-rings, bracelets, belt fittings and amulet cases. Decorative techniques include niello, gilding and filigree. Most of the decorative motifs are vegetal, but some are animal, and the amulet cases have Arabic inscriptions.

Another hoard, attributed on stylistic grounds to the 11th or 12th century, was found at Nahavand in western Iran (London, BM). It contained an engraved gold wine bowl and silver gilded and nielloed weapon fittings, belt or harness trappings, beads and an amulet case. They were the valued possessions of one man, Abu Shuja' Inju Takin, whose name was inscribed on a suspension ring and who must have been a member of the ruling Turkish military élite. The quantity of silver probably reflects his limited financial resources rather than a preference for silver over gold.

Between the 12th and the 15th centuries the quantity of pictorial evidence compensates for the lack of archaeological material. Women depicted on pottery and in manuscripts of the 12th and 13th centuries wear diadems, crescent earrings outlined with seed pearls and pairs of anklets, armlets and bracelets. Figural and animal motifs are common on all media during this period, and jewellery is frequently decorated with chasing animals, paired birds and even human figures. With the Mongol invasions in the mid-13th century, East Asian motifs permeated all the arts of Iran, including jewellery. Manuscript illustrations from the 14th and 15th centuries depict cusped and lobed crowns and pendants, dragon-headed bangles and ring bezels, with lotus and peony flowers as favourite motifs of decoration. In the 15th century, rosette-shaped belt fittings executed in delicate gold filigree replaced the earlier rectangular ones, and strings of pearls were suspended around women's faces.

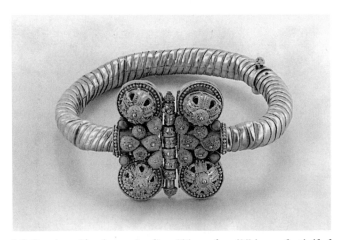

240. Bracelet, gold and turquoise, diam. 106 mm, from ?Nishapur, first half of the 11th century (Washington, DC, Freer Gallery of Art)

Many pieces of jewellery in this style have been found in graves and hoards in the territory of the Golden Horde along the north coast of the Black Sea and the lower reaches of the River Volga. These can be attributed to the 14th and 15th centuries by associated coins. One example, the Simferopol Treasure (Moscow, State Hist. Mus.), included rectangular and rosette-shaped belt fittings, headdress ornaments, earrings, amulet cases and bracelets, and was buried with coins and an official pass from the first half of the 14th century. Techniques used to decorate the jewellery included fine filigree work and some rather crude enamel. The amount of jewellery found in this area and its consistent style indicate that it was produced locally, but its close resemblance to jewellery in Persian manuscript illustrations suggests that similar material was produced in Iran, although little has survived.

BIBLIOGRAPHY

al-Qāḍī al-Rashīd ibn al-Zubayr (mid-11th century): *Kitāb al-dhakhā'ir wa'l-tuhaf* [Book of treasures and gifts], ed. M. Hamidullah (Kuwait, 1959)

A. Spitsin: 'Iz kollektsiy imperatorskago Ermitazha' [From the collections of the Imperial Hermitage], *Zapiski Russ. Arkheol. Obshchestva*, viii (1906), pp. 249–74

A. Bahgat and A. Gabriel: *Fouilles d'al-Foustāt* (Cairo, 1921)

B. Gray: 'A Seljuk Hoard from Persia', *BM Q.*, xiii (1938–9), pp. 73–9

G. Marçais and L. Poinssot: *Objets kairouanais, IXe au XIIIe siècle*, 2 vols (Tunis, 1948–52)

V. P. Darkevich: *Khudozhestvenny metall Vostoka, VII–XIII vv.* [Fine metalwork of the East: 8th–13th century] (Moscow, 1976)

J. W. Allan: *Nishapur: Metalwork of the Early Islamic Period* (New York, 1982)

D. J. Content: *Islamic Rings and Gems: The Benjamin Zucker Collection* (London, 1982)

M. G. Kramarovsky: 'Serebro Levanta i khudozhestvenny metall severnogo Prichernomorya, XII–XV vekov' [Silver of the Levant and fine metalwork of the area north of the Black Sea in the 13th–15th century], *Khudozhestvennyye pamyatniki i problemy kul'tury Vostoka* [Art objects and problems of the culture of the East], ed. V. Lukonin (Leningrad, 1985), pp. 152–80

R. Hasson: *Early Islamic Jewellery*, Jerusalem, Mayer Mem. Inst. Islam. A. cat. (Jerusalem, 1987)

The Simferopol Treasure, Moscow, State Hist. Mus. cat. (Moscow, n.d.)

M. Wenzel: *Ornament and Amulet: Rings of the Islamic Lands* (1993), xvi of *The Nasser D. Khalili Collection of Islamic Art*, ed. J. Raby (London, 1992–)

RACHEL WARD

(ii) After c. *1500.* Most surviving examples of jewellery date from the late 18th century and the 19th, when distinctive styles had evolved in different regions.

(a) Iran. (b) Kurdistan. (c) Ottoman empire. (d) North Africa. (e) Yemen.

(a) Iran. Iranian jewellery from the 16th and 17th centuries can be studied from contemporary book illustrations. Women wore long necklaces composed of rosette-shaped gold medallions, often set with precious stones of green and red, sometimes with a central shield-shaped medallion. Belts, for both men and women, resemble the necklaces by design: they were dark straps on which rosette-shaped medallions were pinned at fixed intervals. Buttons on men's robes were the same shape. Another female ornament fashionable in the 16th century was a string of pearls hung under the chin, connecting both sides of the headscarf. Men's turbans were decorated with a few short chains of gold beads or with gold pins ornamented with feathers. Both men and women wore long earrings with suspended pear-shaped rubies, while Sufis and servants wore simple earrings of gold hoops. By the 17th century, necklaces of rose-shaped medallions had gone out of fashion, and turbans were bigger but lacked the chains of gold beads. In the second half of the century, women wore gold chokers set with precious gems, usually red. Belts were made of square plaques, also set with stones, and men wore studded rings on their little fingers.

Under the Qajars (*reg* 1779–1924), jewellery styles and designs changed drastically, and the upper class wore far more. Distinctive gold jewels were set with coloured gems on one side and enamelled on the other. Pieces include long dome- or crescent-shaped earrings decorated with motifs of flowers, birds and leaves; pear- or teardrop-shaped (*boteh*) hair and turban pins; chokers; cylindrical or hexagonal amulet cases; and pendants with portraits of young ladies including the Virgin and Child. The richness and quantity of jewellery set with rubies, emeralds, sapphires, diamonds and pearls are documented in contemporary oil paintings (see fig. 243 below). Collars, cuffs, hems and shoes were decorated with enormous quantities of shining white pearls.

For further information about jewellery in western Central Asia *see* CENTRAL ASIA, §I, 8(vi)(b).

(b) Kurdistan. A distinctive style of jewellery developed in the late 19th century and early 20th in Kurdistan, the region between Iran and the Ottoman empire in northern Mesopotamia. Traditional goldsmithing techniques and patterns were used, and fine filigree was a speciality of the Kurdish goldsmith. Precious stones were rare, but turquoise, a stone that adds magical significance to the decoration, was common. Scrolls, leaves, flowers, fish and birds were used along with geometric patterns. Necklaces were comprised of gold beads, at times combined with oblong plaques set with turquoises and European or Ottoman coins. The typical Kurdish necklace for festive occasions was made of oblong plaques with fish-shaped suspended elements. There were also chains of gold coins with a large one in the centre. Bracelets with English coins or appliquéd crescents and stars were common. Most earrings were made in filigree and shaped like crescents or baskets with suspended small pearls or gold balls. Silver belt buckles were done in repoussé with floral patterns in contemporary Ottoman style.

(c) Ottoman empire. Under the patronage of the Ottoman dynasty (*reg* 1281–1924), Istanbul became a centre of goldsmithing. Many silver and gold mines and quarries for precious stones were incorporated in the empire, which expanded rapidly in the 15th and 16th centuries, and many goldsmiths came—either voluntarily or involuntarily—to the capital. In the 16th century a distinctive Ottoman style, incorporating elements from Iran, India and the Balkans, was established. Turkish paintings from the late 15th century onwards show sultans and princes with large turbans decorated with magnificent gold pins set with precious gems. They wore belts with gold buckles and gold rings set with diamonds, rubies, emeralds and sapphires on their little fingers. From the 16th century they wore archers' thumb-rings made of jade decorated with gold scrolls. Several luxury belts (Istanbul, Topkapı Pal. Mus.) were made of mother-of-pearl or ivory plaques inlaid with a black organic material and gold and set with

gems. The jewellers' techniques were also applied to many objects of jade and rock crystal in the sultan's treasury (*see* §§8 above and 13(ii) below), which were decorated with precious stones set into gold collar mounts, a distinctively Ottoman technique. Beginning in the 18th century the Ottoman arts, including goldsmithing, became strongly dependent on European styles, and in the 19th and 20th centuries traditional jewels were refashioned following European tastes.

Jewellery with gold chains includes bracelets, necklaces, headbands and chokers. The typical bracelet was hinged and made of several parallel rows of chains welded on to flat plaques that serve as the hinge and pin clasps. Chokers were similar, except that the huge clasp was fastened in front. Headbands made of several chains fastened to the headdress were used until the late 19th century. In the second half of the 17th century, rose diamonds became increasingly popular for hatpins, earrings and rings. Hatpins were designed after ladies' turban-pins in the shape of roses, bouquets, flower stems, stars, crescents and various types of birds. Rings have an almond-shaped bezel, similar to the European marquise ring. Pearl necklaces were popular, to judge from paintings and photographs, but the original necklaces have been unstrung and the pearls reused. Necklaces of gold coins, genuine or imitation and often bearing the typical Ottoman seal (*tughra*), were used in many areas of the empire. In the late 19th century European coins were preferred for their value. Silver belts and buckles, sometimes gilded, were an essential accessory of traditional Ottoman dress (*see* §VI, 3(v)(b) above). They vary in shape, style and technique: some are set with turquoises and corals; others are decorated in repoussé, filigree and enamel with scrolls and geometric motifs.

(d) North Africa. Most of the extant jewellery from Morocco, Algeria and Tunisia dates from the 19th century, although a few pieces, such as a pair of pendent gold earrings set with rubies and emeralds (New York, Met., 1981.5.6,17), are ascribed to the 17th century. Although silver was common in rural areas, gold jewellery was worn in the cities and by tribal people of the Sahara, who were in close contact with sub-Saharan Africa. The need to protect oneself against the evil eye is a prominent feature of North African jewellery. The spread hand, known as the *khamsa* ('five') or Hand of Fatima, after the Prophet's daughter, is the most common talisman in the region. Magical powers are also attributed to the cross and other geometric forms such as the triangle and the hexagram or Seal of Solomon. The decorative repertory includes fish, snakes, scorpions, doves and salamanders, each with certain apotropaic powers.

Morocco is known for the great variety of *khamsa*s, which range from the simple ones used in rural areas, cast or cut of silver sheets with engraved floral decoration, to the magnificent urban examples, set with diamonds and emeralds. Fibulae, the pins inherited from the Roman tradition and used by Berber women to fasten their upper garments, were embellished with triangular silver plaques, engraved and set with coral or glass, and often linked by a chain decorated with circular or oval elements. The most common element of gold jewellery was the *tizara* worn by rich urban women, a necklace of medallions in openwork arabesques set with precious stones and pearls. Other necklaces are studded with solid elements on one side and decorated in champlevé enamel on the other. Pendent earrings common in the cities are done in openwork with settings and are suspended around the ears. Both necklaces and earrings copied Ottoman jewellery and Baroque jewellery from southern Spain. Bracelets from Fez and Tangier known as the 'Sun and Moon' are comprised of diagonal stripes alternating silver with gold. Other bracelets were cast and decorated in floral or geometric patterns, and spike bracelets were designed to protect the wearer during raids. Enamelled jewellery from Tiznit is done mainly in yellow and green; niello is a speciality of Taguemont, a small town in the Anti Atlas; and amber, valued for its medicinal power, is extensively used in southern Morocco and Mauritania.

Algerian jewellery, mainly fibulae and diadems, necklaces and bracelets, is made of silver and decorated with cloisonné enamel in green, blue and yellow and in fine filigree. Jewellery is often set with coral to take advantage of its remedial and magical powers. Traditional Tunisian jewellery is also silver, sometimes gilded. The major ornaments are amulet cases, either triangular, cylindrical or rectangular, and hoop and suspended earrings. Crescent-shaped fibulae are engraved with doves (the symbol of blessing and good tidings), fish (the symbol of fertility and life), flowers and hexagrams, the same motifs found on bracelets. Other jewellery is done in filigree, and cloisonné in red and blue on a ground of gilded silver is common. The major centres of production are Tunis, Djerba and Sfax. The Tuareg tribes of the Sahara also made silver jewellery, especially cast bracelets and crosses, in which the arms of the cross and its embossed centre replace the traditional hand as the symbol of the number five. Tuareg silver jewellery was often decorated with balls and pyramidal protuberances or engraved and nielloed. Bracelets were also made of horn or wood. In the Sahara coral, as well as cowrie shell, is used for pendants and hair ornaments.

(e) Yemen. The earliest Yemeni jewellery to survive dates from the late 18th century and was made mainly in San'a. The origins of the tradition are unclear, and suggestions have ranged from pre-Islamic South Arabia to India. Yemeni Jews had a virtual monopoly on the production of jewellery, and the art was passed from father to son. Yemeni jewellery therefore shows a uniform conservative style in which motifs and shapes are repeated in varied combinations. Traditional jewellery is of silver, sometimes gilded, and uses such techniques as repoussé, filigree, granulation and appliqué. The different elements are composed of numerous small elements welded together. Decorative elements often carry a symbolic meaning; for example, fish and ears of wheat indicate fertility and rattlers are intended to ward off demons.

The typical decorative elements are small flowers made of silver granules, rhomboidal plaques coupled in appliqué, mulberry-shaped beads of welded granulation, and small beads shaped like pomegranates or nuts. Triangles decorated in filigree serve as the ends of necklaces. Snake-like chains are made of flattened links, and other chains are crocheted in foxtail plaits. Bracelets—with or without clasps—are always made in pairs. The Kubur bracelet, which has protuberances shaped like tombs (Arab. *qubūr*), is worn by the bride as a reminder, even on her wedding day, of death. Several rings were worn simultaneously. The typical example has a raised bezel, wedding rings are made of delicate filigree, and other rings are set with amber, pearl or red or green glass. Amulet cases, cylindrical or rectangular, are either an integral part of the jewellery or worn independently as a talisman.

The Lazem necklace (see fig. 241) is comprised of several rectangular plaques linked by parallel rows of small beads from which cylindrical amulet cases are suspended. It is usually given to a girl on reaching marriageable age. The Labbeh necklace is composed of chains made up of many small plaques; it is tied under the chin while pendants, chains and rosettes suspend from it. It is given to the bride by her father. The Ma'anakeh necklace is comprised of chains of beads, usually polyhedral or berry-shaped, hanging between triangles at the ends. It is worn in a twisted fashion by married women. Necklaces include coins, mainly the Austrian thaler, known as the riyal. Earrings are long, suspended and connected to the *gargush*, a headdress that completely covers the ears.

BIBLIOGRAPHY

Enc. Islam/2: 'Khamsa' [five]
P. Eudel: *L'Orfèvrerie algérienne et tunisienne* (Algiers, 1902)
R. Berliner and P. Borchardt: *Silber Schmiedearbeiten aus Kurdistan* (Berlin, 1922)
M. Narkiss: *The Artcraft of the Yemenite Jews* (Jerusalem, 1941)
J. Besancenot: *Bijoux arabes et berbères du Maroc* (Casablanca, 1953)
G. Marçais: *Les Bijoux musulmans de l'Afrique du nord* (Algiers, 1958)
Haye ha-Yehudim be-Maroko [Jewish life in Morocco] (exh. cat., ed. A. Muller-Lancet; Jerusalem, Israel Mus., 1973; Fr. trans., 1986)
Jewelry from Persia: The Collection of Patti Birch (exh. cat., Pforzheim, Schmuckmus., 1974)
C. Köseoglu: *Topkapı Sarayı Müzesi* (Tokyo, 1980), Eng. trans. and ed. by J. M. Rogers as *Topkapı Saray Museum: The Treasury* (Boston, 1987)
The Art of the Goldsmith and Silversmith in Jewish Communities in the East: Jerusalem, 1981 [papers published in *Peamim*, xi (1982)]
The Jews of Kurdistan (exh. cat., ed. O. Schwartz-Beeri; Jerusalem, Israel Mus., 1981) [in Heb.]
A. Fischer: *Africa Adorned* (London, 1984)
R. Hasson: *Later Islamic Jewelry* (Jerusalem, 1987)
Jewellery and Goldsmithing in the Islamic World: International Symposium: Jerusalem, 1987
M. Russo-Katz: 'Jewelry', *Sephardi Jews in the Ottoman Empire* (exh. cat., ed. E. Juhasz; Jerusalem, Israel Mus., 1989), pp. 173–95
M. Wenzel: *Ornament and Amulet: Rings of the Islamic Lands* (1993), xvi of *The Nasser D. Khalili Collection of Islamic Art*, ed. J. Raby (London, 1992–)

RACHEL HASSON

10. LACQUER. Two techniques were used to produce what is commonly known as 'Islamic lacquer'. In the first, lac, the resin-like substance produced as a protective covering by lac insects, was applied to objects made of wood or metal. It was used until the 14th century for a small number of objects such as the 11th- or 12th-century wooden bowl (diam. 60 mm) decorated with seated musicians that was excavated at Ribat-i Sharaf in north-east Iran (see Kiani, fig. 1 and pls 3–6). At the same time, the second, and more common, technique, that of protecting painted decoration with a layer of resin varnish, was being applied to utilitarian objects, such as a varnished wooden dish decorated with a jackal (London, V&A), whose style suggests an attribution to 13th- or 14th-century Egypt. In Iran this resin-varnish technique subsequently developed

241. Silver necklace fabricated from sheet, wire and shot, decorated with granulation, filigree and tiny plates of silver, set with green glass, 254×190 mm, from Yemen, 19th century (New York, Metropolitan Museum of Art)

into a high-quality art form applied to papier-mâché objects that had been covered with a thin coat of plaster or gesso.

The handful of varnished bookbindings that survive from the 15th century (Istanbul, Topkapı Pal. Lib.) bear the same non-figural designs as are found on contemporary leather bindings (*see* §III, 7 above). In the 16th century figural subjects drawn from contemporary book illustration (*see* §III, 4(vi)(a) above), such as picnics, hunts and other scenes of court life, began to appear. They are characterized by plants and trees outlined in gold. The first signed examples were made by Rizal 'Abbasi at the beginning of the 17th century. These, and bookbindings made 50 years later by his pupil Mu'in Musavvir, show that lacquer painting was regarded as a respectable activity in which the foremost painters might engage. Other leading artists at the Safavid court in Isfahan, such as Muhammad Zaman and 'Aliquli Jabbadar, painted lacquered objects in the Europeanizing style that came into fashion in the second half of the 17th century.

From the mid-17th century resin varnish began to be applied to a wider range of objects, such as penboxes, caskets and mirror-cases, which consist of a frame (usually rectangular, but sometimes octagonal or oval) and a cover for the mirror that was either hinged or slotted into the frame. In the 18th century production of these items increased. Figural scenes continued to be depicted, and designs of roses and nightingales became popular and remained so during the subsequent history of Iranian lacquer. The Europeanizing style continued to be used at the court of Karim Khan Zand (*reg* 1750–79; see ZAND) in Shiraz. Muhammad Sadiq, for example, produced oil paintings, miniatures and lacquer wares (see fig. 242), while 'Ali Ashraf worked only in lacquer, specializing in fine flower and bird designs on a black ground.

The 19th century was the heyday of Iranian lacquer. In 1811 Sir William Ouseley saw piles of penboxes several feet high in the Isfahan bazaar, as well as numerous mirror cases and caskets. Most pieces bore designs with figural subjects executed by anonymous artists, but some were signed by the foremost court artists—Mirza Baba, Mihr 'Ali and Sayyid Mirza, for example. Towards the end of the reign of the Qajar monarch Fath 'Ali Shah (*reg* 1797–1834) Najaf 'Ali of Isfahan began to make his name, and he and his family became the leading lacquer painters of the mid-century. Besides his three sons, Muhammad Kazim, Ja'far and Ahmad, this group included his younger brother, Muhammad Isma'il, who was perhaps the best of them all and who delighted in European subjects with innumerable small figures. A casket done by him in 1865 (Berne, Hist. Mus.) is the most remarkable surviving piece of its kind. Every surface is covered with the finest painting, particularly on the exterior, where hundreds of tiny figures are depicted taking part in scenes from the campaigns against the Afghans and the Turkmen.

Shiraz and Tehran were also important centres in the second half of the 19th century. At Shiraz the leading exponent in the 1850s was Aqa Buzurg, an able portrait painter, while at the end of the century the work of the painter Fathallah combined meticulously painted figural medallions with gold scrollwork and sprays of roses. Good work of all kinds was done at Tehran. Figural subjects show the influence of Sani' al-Mulk, although he himself produced only one or two pieces of painted lacquer. In the 1880s the intricate arabesque designs used in manuscript illumination were executed in lacquer by Razi and his followers. Around the turn of the century, highly Europeanized figural subjects, sometimes of a mildly erotic character, were done by 'Abd al-Husayn and 'Abd al-Latif, two painters who shared the title Sani'-i Humayun. At this time many lacquered objects, particularly doors and caskets, were painted with imitations of Safavid miniatures and were often provided with misleading inscriptions and dates. Inconsistencies and anachronisms in details of costume and other accessories reveal their true date. The revival of miniature painting from the 1920s onwards encouraged the production of a few lacquered objects

242. Lacquer mirror-case (rear of mirror left, front of hinged cover right), painted by Muhammad Sadiq, 260×184 mm, from Shiraz, Iran, 1775 (London, Victoria and Albert Museum)

decorated in a pseudo-Safavid style; although finely executed, they are not particularly original.

From Iran the technique of applying resin varnish on papier mâché spread to Turkey and India. For the most part, painted lacquer produced there followed Iranian models in technique and design. In Turkey the main centre was Edirne, and the designs were almost exclusively floral; no examples earlier than the 18th century survive. In India a few bookbindings from the 17th and 18th centuries have arabesque designs, but the majority of Indian painted lacquer was executed in Kashmir from the 18th century onwards. The designs are either massed flowers, usually outlined in gold, or figures from Iranian legend, drawn in the rather clumsy style characteristic of Kashmiri book painting.

BIBLIOGRAPHY

B. W. Robinson: 'A Lacquer Mirror-case of 1854', *Iran*, v (1967), pp. 1–6
——: 'Persian Lacquer in the Bern Historical Museum', *Iran*, viii (1970), pp. 47–50
M. Y. Kiani, ed.: *Robat-e Sharaf* (Tehran, 1981), pp. 45–54; Eng. summary, pp. 6–7
Lacquerwork in Asia and Beyond: Percival David Foundation Colloquium on Art & Archaeology in Asia, no. 11: London, 22–24 June 1981
B. W. Robinson: 'Persian Lacquer and the Bern Historical Museum Casket', *Orientations* (Oct 1985), pp. 24–9
——: 'Lacquer, Oil Paintings and Later Arts of the Book', *Treasures of Islam* (exh. cat., ed. T. Falk; Geneva, Mus. Rath, 1985), pp. 176–205
Eastern Lacquer: An Exhibition of 50 Pieces of Persian, Indian and Turkish Lacquer (exh. cat. by B. W. Robinson, London, Bernheimer F.A., 1986)

11. OIL PAINTING. The traditional formats for painting in the Islamic world were book illustration and wall painting; oil paintings on canvas were a relatively late development. In Iran they began to be produced after the intensification of contacts with Europe in the 17th century, but the link with book production remained strong, so that the best examples give the impression of being enlarged miniatures. In Turkey an indigenous tradition of oil painting was established only in the 19th century.

(i) Iran. The earliest examples of painting in oils to survive in Iran—the murals of the Chihil Sutun Palace (*see* ISFAHAN, §3(vii))—were done for Shah 'Abbas II (*reg* 1642–66) and were executed in pigment that was mixed with oil and painted directly on the plaster walls; the earliest examples of oil painting on canvas date from the second half of the 17th century. They show large, full-length figures, whose treatment resembles that of contemporary miniatures in the westernizing style of SHAYKH 'ABBASI, MUHAMMAD ZAMAN and 'ALIQULI JABBADAR (*see also* §III, 4(vi)(a) above). The oil paintings were probably inspired by portraits of princes and ladies brought to the Safavid court by European envoys, but may also owe something to the Armenian community of the New Julfa quarter (*see* ISFAHAN, §3(ix)). Among the few oil paintings to survive from the early 18th century are two portraits of the Afsharid ruler Nadir Shah (*reg* 1736–47), one showing him half-length (London, Commonwealth Relations Trust), the other full-figure, seated (London, V&A, I.M. 20–1919). Both are in a thoroughly Europeanized style, perhaps modelled on English paintings seen during Nadir Shah's invasion of India. A contemporary but less sophisticated painting (untraced) shows a bridal pair, the bridegroom apparently one of Nadir Shah's sons.

A recognizably Persian style of painting developed in the work of MUHAMMAD SADIQ under the patronage of Muhammad Karim Khan (*reg* 1750–79), the Zand ruler at Shiraz. Muhammad Sadiq added still-lifes and groups to the range of subjects. His figures are stiff, with modelled features very much in the European manner. Perspective is arbitrary, carpet-patterns are shown in ground-plan, and landscapes rarely appear. A typical example of his work is *Girl Playing a Mandolin* (1769–70; Faroughi priv. col.). The other important artist of the time was Ja'far, who produced a large oil painting of *Muhammad Karim Khan and his Court* (Shiraz, Pars Mus.). In this work the contrast between the stiff and formal courtiers and the easily lounging figure of the sovereign, pulling at his water-pipe and winking knowingly at the spectator, is well shown.

Sadiq's style was developed under the patronage of the Qajar dynasty (*reg* 1779–1924). The inscription on a painting of *Shirin Visiting Farhad as he Carves Mt Bisitun* (1793–4; 1.45×0.88 m, priv. col.; see Robinson, 1985, no. 184) shows that the artist MIRZA BABA was already working for the Qajars at Astarabad before they established their capital at Tehran. The painting shows an often-illustrated scene from Nizami's *Khamsa* ('Five poems'), but the most characteristic works of the early 19th century are life-size portraits of Fath 'Ali Shah (*reg* 1797–1834). Mirza Baba's best portrait of the Shah (1798–9; London, Commonwealth Relations Trust) was presented by the Shah to the East India Company in 1822. Mirza Baba's rival MIHR 'ALI also produced portraits of the Shah, of which the finest—perhaps the finest of all Persian oil paintings (see fig. 243)—shows the ruler full-length, wearing a robe of gold brocade embroidered with roses, the towering Qajar crown on his head, and the staff of Solomon, surmounted by a jewelled hoopoe, in his hand. The emphasis on the ruler's fine eyes, wasp-like waist and majestic beard alludes to his handsome appearance and personal vanity.

Other popular subjects were courtiers and princes. MUHAMMAD HASAN KHAN, for example, painted several fine portraits, such as *Prince Holding a Flintlock* (1.95×0.91 m; Tehran, Nigaristan Mus.), which emphasize the sitter's clothing and textiles. An enormous mural by 'ABDALLAH KHAN for the Nigaristan Palace in Tehran (1812–13; destr.) depicted Fath 'Ali Shah enthroned with 12 of his sons and flanked by serried rows of court officials and foreign ambassadors. The painting, known from several small-scale copies (e.g. London, India Office Lib., Add. Or. MS. 1239–42), contained in all 118 rather stiff life-size figures. In the second half of Fath 'Ali Shah's reign, a younger generation of court painters came to the fore: SAYYID MIRZA, a painter of royal portraits who worked in a more impressionistic style; AHMAD, who probably trained under Mihr 'Ali and first imitated his style, but whose manner became more westernized; and MUHAMMAD, who painted distinctive portraits of moon-faced beauties with huge eyes and tiny mouths.

In the mid-19th century all branches of painting were dominated by Abu'l-Hasan GHAFFARI, known by the title Sani' al-Mulk ('Painter of the Kingdom'). His most celebrated work is a huge mural painted for the prime minister's palace (1856; now divided into seven panels, Tehran, Archaeol. Mus.). It depicts Nasir al-Din (*reg* 1848–

243. Mihr 'Ali: *Fath 'Ali Shah*, oil on canvas, 2.46×1.25 m, 1812–13 (Tehran, Nigaristan Museum)

96) enthroned between his sons and ministers and attended by courtiers and foreign envoys, in much the same way as 'Abdallah Khan had depicted the court of Fath 'Ali Shah. Sani' al-Mulk's forte was portraiture, uncompromising and sometimes merciless. His tradition was carried on by his nephew Muhammad Ghaffari, known as Kamal al-Mulk ('Perfection of the Kingdom'). He studied in Europe, and his mature work, including portraits, landscapes and genre scenes, is completely Europeanized in style. Two other oil painters enjoyed the patronage of Nasir al-Din. ISMA'IL JALAYIR, an early student in the Polytechnical School (Dar al-Funun) founded in Tehran in 1851, worked in the 1860s in an individual, though westernized, style, sometimes entirely in grisaille. His paintings are infused with an atmosphere of gentle melancholy. The paintings of Mahmud Khan (1813–93), who was also Poet Laureate, consist mainly of landscapes and views of the royal palaces, executed with almost photographic realism, but he also

produced several striking figural studies (e.g. *Two Men Reading by Candlelight*; exh. RA 1931; untraced).

BIBLIOGRAPHY
B. W. Robinson: 'The Court Painters of Fath 'Ali Shah', *Eretz-Israel*, vii (1964), pp. 94–105
S. J. Falk: *Qajar Paintings: Persian Oil Paintings of the 18th and 19th Centuries* (London, 1972)
E. G. Sims: 'Five Seventeenth-century Persian Oil Paintings', *Persian and Mughal Art* (exh. cat., London, Colnaghi's, 1976), pp. 223–51
J. Taboroff and L. S. Diba: 'A Nineteenth-century Isfahan Painting', *Akten des VII. internationalen Kongresses für iranische Kunst und Archäologie: München, 1976*, pp. 628–34
B. W. Robinson: 'Persian Painting in the Qajar Period', *Highlights of Persian Art*, ed. R. Ettinghausen and E. Yarshater (Boulder, 1979), pp. 331–62
——: 'Persian Royal Portraiture and the Qajars', *Qajar Iran*, ed. E. Bosworth and C. Hillenbrand (Edinburgh, 1983), pp. 291–310
M. A. Karimzada Tabrizi: *Ahval u āthār-i naqqāshān-i qadīm-i īrān* [The lives and art of old painters of Iran] (London, 1985)
B. W. Robinson: 'Lacquer, Oil-paintings and Later Arts of the Book', *Treasures of Islam* (exh. cat., ed. T. Falk; Geneva, Mus. A. & Hist., 1985), pp. 176–206
——: 'Painting in the Post-Safavid Period', *The Arts of Persia*, ed. R. W. Ferrier (New Haven and London, 1989), pp. 225–31
——: 'Persian Painting under the Zand and Qājār Dynasties', *From Nadir Shah to the Islamic Republic* (1991), vii of *The Cambridge History of Iran* (Cambridge, 1968–91), pp. 870–89

B. W. ROBINSON

(ii) Turkey. Oil painting on canvas has been known since the Ottoman sultan Mehmed II (*reg* 1444–81 with interruption) invited Gentile Bellini (*see* BELLINI, (2)) to Istanbul in 1479, and oil portraits of the sultans were collected in the Topkapı Palace at various times. Until the 19th century, oil paintings were largely produced by travelling and émigré European artists for European patrons. Jean-Baptiste van Mour (1671–1737) and JEAN-ETIENNE LIOTARD made their reputations with Orientalist works of Turkish subjects, and in the 19th century the European painters resident or travelling in the Ottoman empire included such figures as ALEXANDRE-GABRIEL DECAMPS and EDWARD LEAR. European artists of lesser stature, such as the Italian count Amadeo Preziosi (1816–82), also settled in Turkey and appear to have sold their paintings to travellers and resident Europeans.

Although the European painting tradition had an impact on the traditional Turkish media of book illustration (*see* §III, 4(vi)(e) above) and mural painting (*see* §II, 9(iii)(b) above), at least from Bellini's time, an indigenous Turkish tradition of oil painting began only in the early 19th century. At that time the military academies of Istanbul started to teach linear perspective as an adjunct to producing images for military operations, and oil painting seems to have accompanied perspective, almost as an afterthought. A government-sponsored programme of educating Ottoman artists in France ensued, and by the time of the Second Empire many Turkish painters were resident in Paris, studying at the studios of various painters. AHMET ALI and SÜLEYMAN SEYYIT, both painting instructors in military academies, were sent to Paris in the 1860s. After a preparatory course of language studies at the Ottoman School, they entered the Ecole des Beaux-Arts and worked with such academic painters as GUSTAVE BOULANGER and JEAN-LÉON GÉRÔME. OSMAN HAMDI, who was not a product of the military schools, also studied in Paris, before founding the Fine Arts Academy (Sanayi-i Nefise Mektebi) in Istanbul (*see* ISTANBUL, §II, 3).

The early Turkish painters in oils followed the European genres of their masters. Still-life, landscape and topographical painting were especially popular, as these genres did not conflict with traditional religious views against depicting humans (*see* §I, 8 above). Nevertheless, some of the most talented of the early generation of Turkish painters also painted portraits. Osman Hamdi, who became an influential figure, seems to have openly flouted traditional Islamic values, producing a prodigious number of canvases incorporating details from Istanbul monuments and works of art to lend authenticity to his work. Although Hamdi Bey, as he was known in the West, never seems to have produced nude studies or to have depicted the nude in his finished paintings, his work *Mihrab* (see fig. 244) shows a woman in a décolleté *entari* (traditional dress) sitting in a *rahle* (Koran-stand) in front of a tiled mihrab with copies of the Koran in disarray under her feet. This work seems almost calculated to offend religious sensibilities and contrasts remarkably with the gentle still-lifes of Ahmet

244. Osman Hamdi: *Mihrab*, oil on canvas, 2.10×1.08 m, 1901 (private collection)

Ali and Süleyman Seyyit and the somewhat naive architectural landscapes of the military-trained Ahmet Ragıp (*fl* 1890s), Hüseyin Zekaî Pasha (1860–1919) and Ahmet Ziya Akbulut (1869–1938).

By the end of the 19th century, Ottoman painters in oils were working in a wide variety of genres, producing not only Orientalist genre paintings but seascapes, portraits and Istanbul street scenes. The artists tended to be in the thrall of the academic painters, being for the most part untouched by the realism of Courbet and Manet. Drawing on a variety of European sources, their work ranged from the meticulous architectural studies of Ahmet Ziya Akbulut to the elegant society portraits of Mihri Musfik (1886–1954), one of Turkey's first significant women painters in oils, and to the popular Barbizon-inspired landscapes of Ali Riza (1858–1930), affectionately dubbed Hoca ('teacher') by his many students and friends. One of the most capable of the second generation of painters was the Ottoman prince Abdülmecid (1868–1944), who, after the deposition of the last sultan Mehmed VI Vahdettin, in 1922, became caliph until that office was abolished by Atatürk in 1924. Given the traditional Islamic injunctions against figural painting, it is ironic that this rather retiring figure excelled in portraiture and genre scenes; his best-known work, *Beethoven in the Saray* (Istanbul, Mus. F.A.), depicts a musical afternoon in the Sultan's palace, with a piano trio performing for onlookers in front of a plaster bust of Beethoven, with the artist himself depicted listening at the right.

BIBLIOGRAPHY

M. Cezar: *Sanatta batı'ya açılış ve Osman Hamdi* [Osman Hamdi and Western trends in art] (Istanbul, 1971)
T. Erol: 'Painting in Turkey in XIX and Early XXth Century', *A History of Turkish Painting* (Seattle and London, 1988), pp. 87–234
S. Başkan: *Contemporary Turkish Painters* (Ankara, 1991)

WALTER B. DENNY

12. REGALIA. As successors to the Prophet Muhammad, the caliphs often used objects associated with him, such as his mantle (Arab. *burda*), sword and staff (*qadīb*), as insignia of office, but contact with Byzantium and the revival of the royal traditions of Sasanian Iran led to the introduction and adoption of more elaborate regalia, including crowns and thrones (*see* THRONE, §III), particularly in the eastern Islamic lands where Sasanian traditions were the strongest.

(i) Crowns. (ii) Other regalia.

(i) Crowns. The traditional headgear in the Islamic lands is the turban (Arab. *'imāma*; Pers. *dūl band*; Turk. *tülbend*); and indeed it is commonly said that the turban is the crown of the Arabs. Following the example of the Prophet Muhammad, Muslim rulers traditionally wore the turban or its variants. Crowns of the defeated Sasanian and Byzantine enemies of Islam are pictured on several buildings erected by the Umayyad dynasty (*reg* 661–750) in Syria and Palestine. Several crowns are depicted on the interior mosaics at the Dome of the Rock (692; *see* JERUSALEM, §II, 1(iii)). The most elaborate has prominent wings and a central crescent moon on the top; it is similar to the headgear on the Sasanian king depicted in a mural at QUSAYR 'AMRA. Diadems depicted in the Dome of the Rock are composed of jewelled plaques with pendent pearl chains or have pointed triangular pieces or pinnacles above

245. Crowned figure of ?Alexander on an enamelled bronze dish, made for Da'ud of northern Mesopotamia, 1114–44 (Innsbruck, Tiroler Landesmuseum Ferdinandeum)

the plaques and longer chains. These can be identified as crowns of the Byzantine emperor and empress, as similar ones are worn by Justinian and Theodora in the mosaics of S Vitale (547). By the 10th century the Byzantine imperial diadem was worn over a silk skullcap, and this feature was also copied in Islamic representations.

As examples of crowns survive only from the late periods, the early history of crowns must be studied from their depiction in other arts. Crowns were worn by three types of figures in Islamic art. The first group of crowned figures include portraits of early Islamic rulers in stucco sculptures and coins and medallions. Fragments of a large figure wearing a winged crown were excavated at QASR AL-HAYR WEST (c. 730). The prominent location on the main gate and large size of the statue suggest that it represents an Islamic prince, perhaps the Umayyad caliph Hisham (reg 724–43), to whom the structure is attributed. A comparable statue was excavated from a similar location at KHIRBAT AL-MAFJAR, but the top of the head is missing. Several coins and medallions made for the Abbasid caliphs (reg 749–1258) show crowned figures. A gold presentation piece (971; Paris, Bib. N., Cab. Médailles) depicts a crowned figure holding a wine-cup on one side and a falcon on the other, and an inscription identifies the figure as the Abbasid caliph al-Muti' (reg 946–74). This identification suggests that the crown worn by figures on a series of presentation coins minted between the 9th and the 12th centuries may be the crown of the caliphate (Arab. tāj al-khalīfa), one of the insignia of sovereignty (ālāt al-mulūkiyya) worn by the caliph for ceremonial occasions and festivals. A less sumptuous series of pictorial coins issued by several dynasties in northern Mesopotamia shows enthroned crowned figures at royal ease.

A second group of crowned figures in Islamic art pertains to celestial imagery and includes zodiacal figures,

angels, harpies, sphinxes and other fabulous animals. The largest cycle is found on the ceiling of the Cappella Palatina in Palermo (1132–53) and was executed by painters familiar with traditions of pictorial representation in the Islamic lands. Zodiacal figures represented in copies of al-Sufi's popular treatise, Kitāb ṣuwar al-kawākib al-thābita ('Book of the fixed stars'; e.g. 1009–10; Oxford, Bodleian Lib., MS. Marsh 144), are sometimes crowned. A crowned figure, thought to be Alexander and seated on a platform borne to heaven by large birds, appears on an enamelled bronze dish made for the Artuqid ruler of northern Mesopotamia, Da'ud (reg 1114–44; Innsbruck, Tirol. Landesmus.; see fig. 245). Crowned harpies and sphinxes are depicted on pottery and manuscripts made in the medieval Islamic period. Most of the crowns have two or three peaks decorated with palmettes. Buraq, the Prophet's steed on the mi'rāj, his miraculous night journey to heaven, is always shown crowned (see fig. 104 above), and angels are often shown crowned, as in a drawing by the Ottoman court painter SHAHQULI (Washington, DC, Freer, 37.7).

The third group of crowned figures consists of representations of historical kings. Although the Arab historian al-Mas'udi wrote in the 10th century that he had seen a copy of a book with pictures of the Sasanian monarchs depicted in their regalia, the earliest surviving representations of this type date from the 12th century to the early 14th, when manuscripts and overglaze-painted ceramics show figures wearing crowns loosely based on the Sasanian winged type, with crescent omitted and the wings patterned with large palmettes. These crowns become common in illustrations to Firdawsi's Shāhnāma ('Book of kings') and other Persian epics and romances. A new type of crown, featuring crenellated headband, high dome with top finial surrounded by a cloud collar, and jewels studding the band, points and topknot, appeared in the mid-14th century, as seen, for example, in illustrations to the Great Mongol ('Demotte') Shāhnāma (see fig. 115 above). This new crown, probably derived from those of the Middle Byzantine period, remained standard for crowns depicted in Persian manuscripts over the next four centuries (e.g. see fig. 121 above).

A distinctive new type of headgear was introduced to Iran in the early 16th century under the Safavid rulers (reg 1501–1732). Comprising a crimson cap with 12 gores wrapped in a white turban, it is said to commemorate the 12 Shi'ite imams. It was supposedly devised by the Aqqoyunlu ruler Haydar in 1487 after receiving instruction in a dream from imam 'Ali himself, but it may derive from the headgear worn by the Bektashi dervishes of Anatolia as early as the 13th century. The first depictions of this headgear appear in a manuscript of Muhammad 'Asafi's Dastān-i Jamāl-ū Jalāl ('Story of Jamal and Jalal'; 1503–5; Uppsala, U. Lib., MS. O Nova 2). During the reign of Tahmasp I (reg 1524–76), the red cap became so elongated that it resembled a baton, and the hat was worn by everyone from prince to stable-boy, to judge from manuscript illustrations. Under 'Abbas I (reg 1588–1629) the symbolic crown of the Safavids was revived in a new shape: a short knobbed baton was wrapped in a horizontal, wheel-like fashion. Although not usually worn by the shah himself, this hat was worn by men with immediate allegiance to him, such as governors, generals, envoys and personal guards. The symbolic Safavid headgear was apparently transformed into an actual crown of state, possibly in the late 17th century. According to the Huguenot jeweller John Chardin, Sulayman I (*reg* 1666–94) wore a crown at his coronation, and engravings illustrating Chardin's travels show a crown similar to the one worn by courtiers to 'Abbas II (*reg* 1642–66), although the jewelled plumes are more elaborate.

A new form of Persian crown was introduced by the Afsharid ruler Nadir Shah (*reg* 1736–47), who reportedly wore a gold crown shaped like the tall bulbous headdress of an Armenian bishop and adorned with gems and pearls. Portraits of the Shah show him wearing a four-pointed, red felt hat adorned with jewelled plumes and gems, and it is likely that the crown was a gilded version of a contemporary felt hat. The Qajar ruler Agha Muhammad (*reg* 1779–97) is credited with introducing a new type of crown of high ovoid form, the lower two-thirds studded with pearls and the plain upper part terminating in a large jewelled finial. It is depicted in several portraits by MIRZA BABA (Windsor Castle, Royal Lib., MS. A/4; e.g. see fig. 130 above), and a copper crown of this type with poor quality enamel inlays (Tehran, Gulistan Pal.) may have been made as a replica. Fath 'Ali Shah (*reg* 1797–1834) commissioned a new imperial crown, a *c.* 300 mm-high confection of diamonds, pearls, emeralds and rubies, with a giant red spinel topping the red velvet skullcap (Tehran, Bank Markazi, Crown Jewels Col.). Known as the Kayani crown, it was used by all successive Qajar monarchs (see fig. 243 above) and refashioned under Nasir al-Din (*reg* 1848–96), who also commissioned a tiara in Paris. The Pahlavi ruler Riza Shah (*reg* 1926–41) commissioned several Iranian jewellers to make a new imperial crown inspired by Sasanian models, and Muhammad Riza Shah (*reg* 1941–79) commissioned the Parisian jeweller Pierre Arpels to make a crown of emeralds, pearls, rubies and spinels for the coronation of Empress Farah in 1967.

Under the Ottomans (*reg* 1281–1924), the turban—often decorated with a jewelled aigrette—remained the standard royal headgear until the 19th century, except under Süleyman (*reg* 1520–66), who ordered a spectacular gold helmet from Venetian goldsmiths in 1532. The helmet comprised four crowns with enormous pearls, a headband with diamonds, and a neck guard with straps, as well as a plumed aigrette. The ensemble, valued at 144,400 ducats, featured 50 diamonds, 47 rubies, 27 emeralds, 49 pearls and a large turquoise. It apparently symbolized Süleyman's political aspirations in western Europe by alluding to the papal tiara and the Habsburg crown, but its meaning was soon lost and it was melted down.

(ii) Other regalia. The early caliphs used only a few objects as regalia, but by the Abbasid period a tall cap (*qalansuwa*) wrapped with a turban was an additional mark of sovereignty (*see* §VI, 3(iii) above). The Fatimid caliphs of Egypt (*reg* 969–1171) had the most elaborate ceremonial in the medieval Islamic world, perhaps imitating Byzantine court ceremonial. Fatimid ceremonial included the use of the parasol (*mizalla*), and many relics of the early Shi'ite martyrs, such as 'Ali's twin-bladed sword known as Dhu'l-fiqar, were miraculously discovered and used as regalia. Lesser but powerful princes adopted elaborate regalia and

ceremonial. The Hamdanid amir of Aleppo, Sayf al-Dawla (*reg* 945–67), for example, was invested with a diadem set with precious stones, neck chain and two gold arm buckles also set with precious stones. The Saljuq Turks (*reg* 1038–1194) regarded the bow and arrow as regal attributes but also adopted various Islamic insignia. The *ghāshiyya*, a saddle-cover probably studded with precious stones, was carried in processions before the Saljuq ruler as a mark of sovereignty. Many of these items were adopted by the Mamluk sultans of Egypt and Syria (*reg* 1250–1517), who regularized and codified the systematic usage of weapons and implements, such as the mace, bow, sword and penbox, to symbolize the power of the state. Indeed, much of the information about medieval Islamic regalia is derived from Mamluk historians, particularly Ibn Khaldun (1332–82) and al-Qalqashandi (1355–1418).

Although some regalia is depicted in medieval Islamic imagery, few examples survive from before *c.* 1500. The few medieval pieces include carved rock crystals (e.g. a spherical knop of a silver chalice carved in low relief with a lion and griffin; Leuven, St Jacob) thought to have been ceremonial mace- or sceptre-heads. After the Ottomans conquered the Mamluks in 1517, many relics of the Prophet Muhammad, including his mantle, bow and standard, and of the early caliphs were brought to Istanbul (Topkapı Pal. Mus., Holy Mantle Pavilion), where they became regalia of the Ottoman sultans in their role as caliphs. Other Ottoman *objets d'art* such as a golden water canteen encrusted with jewels (Istanbul, Topkapı Pal. Mus.) also seem to have served as royal insignia. The Ottoman investiture ceremony included the girding on of the sword of 'Uthman [Osman], founder of the dynasty, in the mosque of Eyüp, although this symbolic rite was largely invented in the 19th century.

The regalia of the Safavid rulers of Iran included a throne, sword and dagger. In addition to a jewel-encrusted shield and sabre (Tehran, Bank Markazi, Crown Jewels Col.), the peripatetic ruler Nadir Shah had four sets of horse furniture set with pearls, rubies, emeralds and diamonds that may have served as thrones. Muhammad Karim Khan (*reg* 1750–79), the Zand ruler of Shiraz, is depicted in an oil painting (Shiraz, Pars Mus.) with a large water-pipe, possibly of Venetian glass, in an elaborate jewelled mount; a jewelled water-pipe became a usual part of the regalia of the later Iranian monarchs, such as Agha Muhammad. The jewelled epaulets, swordbelt and decorations adopted by the Qajar monarch Muhammad (*reg* 1834–48) imitated the attire of contemporary European monarchs, and his successor, Nasir al-Din, ordered other imperial regalia inspired by what he had seen in Europe, including a golden globe (Tehran, Bank Markazi, Crown Jewels Col.) weighing some 34 kg and set with 51,000 gems, the land masses indicated in rubies and the seas in emeralds.

BIBLIOGRAPHY

Enc. Iran.: 'Crown', 'Crown Jewels'; *Enc. Islam/1*: 'Tadj' [Crown]; *Enc. Islam/2*: 'Marāsim' [Official court ceremonies], 'Mawākib' [Processions], 'Mizalla' [Parasol]

J. Chardin: *Travels of Sir John Chardin into Persia and the East Indies*, ii (London, 1686), pp. 38–45

M. Canard: 'Le Cérémonial fatimide et le cérémonial byzantin: Essai de comparaison', *Byzantion*, xxi (1951), pp. 355–420

M. Bahrami: 'A Gold Medal in the Freer Gallery of Art', *Archaeologica Orientalia in Memoriam Ernst Herzfeld*, ed. G. C. Miles (Locust Valley, NY, 1952), pp. 5–20

G. C. Miles: 'Miḥrāb and 'Anazah: A Study in Early Islamic Iconography', *Archaeologica Orientalia in Memoriam Ernst Herzfeld*, ed. G. C. Miles (Locust Valley, NY, 1952), pp. 156–71

V. B. Meen and A. D. Tushingham: *Crown Jewels of Iran* (Toronto, 1968)

O. Kurz: 'A Gold Helmet Made in Venice for Sultan Sulayman the Magnificent', *Gaz. B.-A.*, lxxiv (1969), pp. 249–58

C. Köseoğlu: *Topkapı Sarayı Müzesi* (Tokyo, 1980), Eng. trans. and ed. by J. M. Rogers as *Topkapı Saray Museum: The Treasury* (London and Boston, 1987)

B. Schmitz: 'On a Special Hat Introduced during the Reign of Shāh 'Abbās the Great', *Iran*, xxii (1984), pp. 103–12

L. Ilich: 'Münzgeschenks und Geschenkmünzen in der mittelalterlichen islamischen Welt', *Münster. Numi. Ztg*, xv (1985), p. 11, no. 39

E. Whelan: 'Representations of the *Khāssakīyah* and the Origins of Mamluk Emblems', *Content and Context of Visual Arts in the Islamic World*, ed. P. P. Soucek (New York, 1988), pp. 219–53

G. Necipoğlu: 'Süleyman the Magnificent and the Representation of Power in the Context of Ottoman–Hapsburg–Papal Rivalry', *A. Bull.*, lxxi (1989), pp. 401–27

BARBARA SCHMITZ

13. ROCK CRYSTAL. Clear colourless quartz in hexagonal crystals was imported from East Africa, the Laccadive and Maldive Islands in the Indian Ocean, and North Africa; it was carved in the central Islamic lands (Iran, Iraq, Syria and Egypt) from the 8th to the 11th century. The most common forms are containers, such as phials, flasks, ewers, cups and dishes, but maceheads, sword-pommels, chessmen, small pendants, beads, seals and amulets are also known. Carving was the primary means of decoration. Most of the 180 objects known are preserved in European royal and church treasuries, but a few pieces have been excavated, notably at Fustat (Old Cairo) and Susa in Iran. Five centuries later the technique was revived in Turkey under the Ottoman dynasty (1281–1924), in Iran under the Safavids (*reg* 1501–1732) and in India under the Mughals (*reg* 1526–1857), when crystals were often combined with gold and set with gems.

(i) 7th–11th centuries. Rock crystal had been carved in the Late Antique Mediterranean lands and in Sasanian Iran, but by the Islamic conquests in the 7th century, the industry is believed to have died out in Egypt and Syria, leaving Mediterranean production concentrated at Constantinople and other centres in Europe. The industry flourished continuously in the Sasanian lands, as exemplified by the Cup of Solomon (late 5th century or 6th; Paris, Bib. N., Cab. Médailles), a dish formed of a lattice of gold with inset roundels of garnet, green glass and rock crystal. A large central medallion of rock crystal depicts the Sasanian emperor seated on a throne supported by winged horses. The continuation of this tradition can be seen in one of the earliest Islamic pieces known, a small shallow dish mounted in gold and once set with precious stones that was excavated at Susa (l. 95 mm; Paris, Louvre). Carved in relief with fan palmettes issuing from a central area, the dish can be attributed to the early 9th century.

Other pieces can also be attributed broadly to the eastern Islamic world in the 9th and 10th centuries. Each of a group of small crescent-shaped pendants, all found in Iran, represents a small leather bag with grooved lines indicating straps and imitates a well-known type of amulet-case. A goblet found at Qazvin (h. 97 mm; London, BM) has a flanged rim and collar at the base of the bowl, features that characterize contemporary Persian relief-cut glass. Nishapur in north-eastern Iran has been suggested as the place of production because it is thought to have produced superb relief-cut glass goblets of this form, and the split-leaf palmettes on the Qazvin goblet are similar to those found on fragments of frescoes excavated there. An oil lamp in St Petersburg (Hermitage) has been attributed to Mesopotamia on the basis of its acanthus leaves and pearl borders. According to the great polymath al-Biruni (*d* 1048), Mesopotamia was the centre of the Islamic rock crystal industry, for unworked crystal was imported to Basra where it was carved.

Many pieces were carved in the BEVELLED STYLE, current at SAMARRA' in Iraq, the capital of the Abbasid caliphs from 836 to 892. This style of carving was also introduced into Egypt under the Tulunid dynasty (*reg* 868–905) and into the eastern Islamic world. Thus the style is a broad indication of date but is less useful in establishing provenance. The finest examples, carved with great assurance and a clearly defined decorative composition, are now mounted in a pair of 16th-century Venetian candlesticks (see fig. 246). The Bevelled style is also found on a group of small cylindrical flasks with a band of carved ornament around the mid-section. One example (Baghdad, Iraq Mus.) was excavated at Wasit in Iraq; others have been found in Egypt.

A dozen small flasks or ampullae carved in the form of fish have been attributed to Egypt on iconographic grounds, since the fish was a common motif there. One was found at Samarkand, another was acquired in Iran, and at least two were found in Egypt. Some (e.g. Cologne, cathedral of St Severin) reproduce only the forked tail and fins of fish, while others (e.g. London, BM) are decorated with foliage in the Bevelled style. A group of small flasks in the shape of molars are attributed to Egypt in the Tulunid period. They are octagonal in section and rest on four pointed feet. Each of the four alternate sides is decorated with a lentiloid shield. One was excavated at Fustat; an identical example was preserved in the church at Burscheid, Germany. They are attributed to Egypt because the glass houses there had sufficiently mastered the glasscutting technique necessary to shape these small flasks. A group of objects in which the sole decoration is an inscription carved in relief can also be attributed to Egypt in the mid-10th century because of the style of the simple or foliate kufic inscriptions, which invoke blessings and good wishes on the owner. One of these, a phial (h. 91 mm, diam. 35 mm; Cairo, Mus. Islam. A.), has a flaring neck and cylindrical body, but the splayed foot has been broken.

The Bevelled and relief styles were often used side by side for small pieces beginning in the 10th century in Egypt, perhaps because relief carving was more difficult. A set of 15 chessmen (Kuwait City, Mus. Islam. A.) includes a king and queen decorated with palmettes in the Bevelled style and a knight, bishop and rook carved with trefoil leaves in relief on a garlanded stem. A group of 14 relief-carved flasks in the shape of a crouching lion (e.g. London, BM) should also be attributed to this period. Most have a cylindrical boring (diam. 13 mm) from the animal's chest to near the hindquarters, and the haunches and shoulders are decorated with lentiloid leaves and

246. Rock crystal carved in the Bevelled style, 210×85 mm, possibly from Egypt, 9th–10th centuries AD; mounted in a silver gilt candlestick, h. 460 mm, from Venice, 16th century (Venice, Museo di San Marco)

the caliph al-'Aziz (reg 975–96); the inscription on another ewer (ex-Medici col.; Florence, Pitti) indicates that it was made personally for the Commander of Commanders, a title borne by Husayn ibn Jawhar between 1000 and 1008; and a rock crystal crescent (Nuremberg, Ger. Nmus.) is inscribed with the name of the caliph al-Zahir (reg 1021–36). The two inscribed ewers belong to a group of six of similar shape and size (ex-Saint-Denis Abbey; Paris, Louvre; Fermo Cathedral; Venice, S Marco; London, V&A). Made of flawless crystal, they have pear-shaped bodies, thin walls, mouths with prominent lips, necks with two or three sharp mouldings, another moulding (except on the London piece) below a flared footring, and a handle cut from the same piece of crystal as the body, pierced and surmounted by an animal. The bodies have a central stylized foliate motif, flanked by animals decorated with intaglio discs. The animals vary: paired birds (Paris, Florence and Fermo), confronted seated lions (the 'Aziz ewer), running moufflon (the second Venice ewer) and falcons attacking gazelles (London). The Paris and Fermo ewers are inscribed with an anonymous supplication. The six ewers can be placed in chronological order on the basis of style: the 'Aziz ewer, Florence, Paris, Fermo, the second Venice ewer and London. The last two represent the pinnacle in the development of Egyptian rock crystal carving: they are characterized by a smoothly polished ground, low relief and an even secondary plane, and their decoration is denser than on the other pieces. Their vegetal arabesques have notched stems and are more three-dimensional than the others.

Other large pieces can be attributed to the same period in Egypt. Notable examples include a handled cup and saucer given by Henry II in 1014 to the cathedral at Aachen, where it is mounted in the golden ambo, and a similar cup in the Residenz, Munich, said to have been given by Henry II to the chapel at Regensburg. All three objects are decorated in relief with looping stems from which full and half-palmettes emerge. The decoration is restrained and controlled; the surface is smoothly polished. Related examples include a heart-shaped flask (h. 170 mm; Kuwait City, Mus. Islam. A.) decorated with half-palmettes disposed symmetrically on a vertical stem.

The production of rock crystal objects continued at least to the mid-11th century, because the Persian traveller Nasir-i Khusraw, who visited Egypt between 1046 and 1050, mentioned that fine rock crystal vessels were produced and sold in the Lamp Market of the Cairo bazaar. He also said that fine-quality unworked crystal from Qulzum on the Red Sea began to replace the poorer-quality material from north-west Africa. Other accounts state that the treasury of the Fatimid caliphs contained 18,000 (or 36,000) items of rock crystal, including large basins, carafes and jars, which could hold up to 16 litres. None of these enormous pieces is known to have survived the looting of the Fatimid treasuries in the 1060s, when it is thought that the craft died out in Egypt.

(ii) 12th–19th centuries. A group of vertically faceted crystal cups or jugs has traditionally been attributed to the Near East or Egypt between the 12th and the 14th centuries, but they bear datable European metal mounts and are more likely to be of European, possibly Burgundian,

paired interlocking half-palmettes. Several spherical crystals are thought to have been ceremonial mace or sceptre heads. The finest (Leuven, St Jacob), reused as the knop of a silver chalice, is decorated with a lion and griffin carved in low relief and set within raised circular frame bands.

After the Fatimid dynasty (reg 909–1171) conquered Egypt in 969, larger objects in rock crystal began to be produced, including three bearing names of prominent individuals. One ewer (h. 180 mm, diam. 125 mm; Venice, S Marco; for illustration see FATIMID) bears the name of workmanship. In the early 15th century, the Egyptian historian al-Maqrizi, who knew the accounts of the dispersal of the Fatimid treasury, lamented that crystal was no longer available in Egypt.

Crystal was fashioned elsewhere in the Islamic lands. The 17th-century French visitors to the Safavid court, J.-B. Tavernier and the Huguenot Sir J. Chardin, mentioned hardstone-cutting among the crafts practised in the Isfahan bazaar, and the technique may well have included the fashioning of rock crystal. A dagger (Istanbul, Topkapı Pal. Mus.) made for the Ottoman sultan Selim I (reg 1512–20) has a rock crystal handle and a gold-encrusted blade with a chronogram equivalent to 1514–15; the piece probably commemorates his victory over the Safavids at Chaldiran, and the handle may well be a trophy taken from the Safavid palace at Tabriz.

Rock crystal soon became popular at the Ottoman court. A pot-bellied jug with a cylindrical neck (second quarter of the 16th century; Istanbul, Topkapı Pal. Mus.) is decorated only with vertical oblong panels with trefoil heads that allow the beauty of the material to shine

247. Rock crystal canteen, with gold, rubies and emeralds, octagonal, h. 322 mm, from Turkey, 16th–17th centuries (Istanbul, Topkapı Palace Museum)

through. All other examples of rock crystal in the Topkapı Palace Treasury are elaborately embellished. They include imported European vessels with chip-carving or wheel-cut foliate sprays to disguise natural flaws, as well as vessels sheathed in gold or encrusted with precious stones, both cabuchon and cut, in gold collar-mounts with scroll traceries. Masterpieces include an octagonal canteen carved from a single piece of rock crystal with a gold head and foot and encrusted with rubies and emeralds (see fig. 247), and a round-ended penbox made of panels of rock crystal framed with gold bands, set with emeralds and rubies, and lined with white paper illuminated with fine blue and gilt foliate sprays. These pieces represent the high point of Ottoman rock crystal and incrustation workmanship; the technique of encrustation became increasingly repetitive in the 17th century. In contrast, pieces from Mughal India (e.g. a dish; London, BM, 1964 4-19 1) are closer to the European taste that lets the material stand alone, although European motifs such as acanthus scrolls are transmuted into Eastern ones such as lotuses and chrysanthemums.

BIBLIOGRAPHY

Enc. Islam/2: 'Billawr' [Rock crystal]
C. J. Lamm: Mittelalterliche Gläser und Steinschnittarbeiten aus dem nahen Osten (Berlin, 1929–30)
R. Pinder-Wilson: 'Some Rock Crystals of the Islamic Period', BM Q., xix (1954), pp. 84–7; also in Studies in Islamic Art (London, 1985), pp. 145–50
D. S. Rice: 'A Datable Islamic Rock Crystal', Or. A., n. s., ii/3 (Autumn 1956), pp. 85–93
H. R. Hahnloser and others: Il tesoro di San Marco (Florence, 1971)
The Arts of Islam (exh. cat., London, Hayward Gal., 1976), pp. 119–28
Islamic Art and Design, 1500–1700 (exh. cat. by J. M. Rogers, London, BM, 1983), pp. 150–51
E. Atıl: The Age of Sultan Süleyman the Magnificent (Washington, DC, and New York, 1987), pp. 127–31
R. Pinder-Wilson: 'Islamic Rock Crystals', Dar al-Athar al-Islamiyyah Newslett., xx (1989), pp. 16–21

RALPH PINDER-WILSON

14. SEALS. Islamic seals follow pre-Islamic, particularly Sasanian traditions, especially in the choice of materials. Engraved gemstones were used throughout the Islamic period as seals, and also possibly as talismans or ornaments. Seal gemstones are carved in intaglio, in contrast to talismanic and ornamental gemstones, which are usually carved in relief. Gemstones were an ideal material for seals, but occasionally they were replaced by precious or base metals or even glass. Their decoration is almost exclusively epigraphic, especially from the 7th to the 14th or 15th century, and most surviving examples come from the eastern Islamic world.

Seals from the 7th to the 12th century have inscriptions in the angular script often known as kufic. The inscriptions are brief, sober and pious and contain three kinds of text. Some are religious in content, bearing Koranic quotations, prayers to God (see fig. 248a), Muhammad or 'Ali (248f) or moral aphorisms (248b and e). Texts of the second type contain the name of the owner accompanied by a set religious expression indicating his relationship to God and his humility and resignation (248c). Texts of the third type (248d and h) contain only the owner's proper name, usually in the traditional Islamic pattern of 'A son of B'. In many cases it is impossible to identify the individual concerned.

248. Islamic seals: (upper row, left to right) (a) haematite, inscribed 'My God, the living', 9×10×3 mm; (b) cornelian, inscribed 'Rely [on God], that will suffice thee; ask [him], thou shalt receive', 11×14.5×3 mm; (c) black jasper, inscribed 'God is the trust of Muḥammad', 11×12.5×3 mm; (d) onyx, inscribed 'Aḥmad ibn al-Ḥusayn', 10.5×14×4.5 mm; (e) haematite, inscribed 'My hope from God is [his] pardon', 12×14.5×2.5 mm; (f) ?haematite, inscribed 'Muḥammad and 'Alī, the two of them are my hope', 11×13×1 mm; (g) ?cornelian, inscribed 'Trust in the Most-great King, O Nāṣir ibn Ja'far', 13.5×15×4 mm; (lower row, left to right): (h) haematite, inscribed 'Muḥammad ibn Aḥmad', 8×11×3.5 mm; (i) lapis lazuli, inscribed 'God is sufficient for us' (Koran iii.173) and 'The transcendent Patron, the transcendent Helper' (Koran viii.40), 16.5×16.5×3 mm; (j) brass, inscribed 'He who trusts in the sublime Sovereign the servant Barī ibn Kamāl', diam. 26.5 mm; (k) cornelian, inscribed 'There is no god but God, the sovereign, the manifest truth. His servant 'Abbāsqulī, 1234', 19×22×4 mm, 1818–19; (l) cornelian, inscribed '. . . ibn Ḥ'asan, 1302', 14×21×3 mm, 1884–5 (New York, Benjamin Zucker private collection)

The oldest seals use a simple kufic script characterized by a straight horizontal base line (248a). This simple kufic script is typical of seals made from the 7th to the 9th century, but was also used in later periods, when owners wished to imitate the earlier style in order to add magical power to the usual, signatory function of the seals. During the 10th century some letters became more rounded (248e and f). This evolution can be seen most easily in inscriptions containing the name of the owner and his father, because the loop of the letter *nūn* in the word *ibn* ('son') developed decoratively. At first it became deeper and rounded, but later, probably during the 10th or 11th century, it was transformed into a long oblique stroke that descends below the base line. At roughly the same time, certain tails and loops climb towards the top of the engraved space (248g), a distinctive feature for dating these objects. Summary decorative elements, such as schematized small leaves, were added occasionally to the lower end of the letter *nūn* or rarely to other characters extending below the base line or to the tips of the long upstrokes that reach the top of the engraved space (248e and g). As other letters gradually lost their rigidity, a cursive script developed, either in the 12th century or possibly earlier in the eastern Islamic world, as suggested by coins from the late 10th century.

From the 13th century and especially after the 15th, new tendencies developed in seal carving. Inscriptions became considerably longer (248i, j and k). Their decoration, hitherto limited to a few schematized motifs such as a six-pointed star formed by three short crossed strokes (248c, d and h), became more naturalistic and filled the area more completely, including the space between the characters. The variety of gemstones became more limited, by far the most popular being cornelian. In addition to texts in Arabic, there are inscriptions in Persian, usually short poems, and later in Turkish. From the 16th century many inscriptions include the year in which the seal was made (248k and l). These dates are sometimes difficult to read, as the figures are executed summarily and can be confused with the overall decoration. The word for thousand is often omitted as obvious and has to be supplied where appropriate. These later seals are quite common and can be obtained in the bazaars in the region.

BIBLIOGRAPHY

J. T. Reinaud: *Monumens arabes, persans et turcs, du cabinet de M. le Duc de Blacas et d'autres cabinets*, 2 vols (Paris, 1828)

J. Hammer-Purgstall: *Abhandlung über die Siegel der Araber, Perser und Türken* (Vienna, 1849)

H. L. Rabino: *Coins, Medals and Seals of the Shāhs of Iran (1500–1941)* (Cambridge, 1945)

——: 'La Sigillographie iranienne moderne', *J. Asiat.*, ccxxxix (1951), pp. 193–207

I. H. Uzunçarşılı: *Topkapı Sarayı Müzesi mühürler seksiyonu rehberi* [Topkapı Palace Museum: guide to the seals section] (Istanbul, 1959)

'U. N. al-Naqshabandi and H. 'A. 'A. al-Hurri: *Al-akhtām al-islāmiyya fi'l-mathaf al-'irāqī* [Islamic seals in the Iraq Museum] (Baghdad, 1975)

A. G. Mu'ini: 'Muhr-u naqsh-i muhr' [Seals and their inscriptions], *Hunar va Mardum*, xvi (Iranian solar 1357/1978), pp. 42–63

L. Kalus: *Catalogue des cachets, bulles et talismans islamiques*, Paris, Bib. N., Cab. Médailles cat. (Paris, 1981)

P. Gignoux and L. Kalus: 'Les Formules des sceaux sasanides et islamiques: Continuité ou mutation?' *Stud. Iran.*, xi (1982), pp. 123–53

L. Kalus: *Catalogue of Islamic Seals and Talismans*, Oxford, Ashmolean cat. (Oxford, 1986)

D. J. Content, ed.: *Islamic Rings and Gems: The Benjamin Zucker Collection* (London, 1987)

LUDVIK KALUS

15. SHADOW-PUPPETS. The shadow theatre was much appreciated in the Islamic lands by all social levels, from the court to the poor, until the beginning of the 20th

century. The term *khayāl al-zill* ('shadow fantasy') is of Arabic origin, but shadow-puppets are known primarily from the lands of the former Ottoman empire, where the shadow theatre developed from the 16th century and reached its apogee in the 17th. Earlier traditions elsewhere are known only through literary sources. Karagöz, the name of the principal hero of the Turkish shadow theatre, has often come to designate the entire genre, even in non-Turkish speaking countries, such as Tunisia, Algeria or Greece. Nearly all surviving shadow-puppets, except for a few Egyptian examples, correspond to the Turkish type. Shadow-puppets were not considered worthy of collecting until the beginning of the 20th century, and no preserved puppet seems more than one or two centuries old. Although there may have been professional puppet-makers, the puppeteer usually made his own puppets, copying older puppets that had to be replaced. Some costume details help to date certain models, while more recent puppets may be distinguished by their realistic style and less elaborate workmanship; puppets with filigree work, in contrast, seem to date from the 19th century. Despite its widespread popularity, shadow theatre could not survive against cinema and television, and it has been preserved only by organized endeavours to revive popular art forms.

In the shadow theatre a substantial curtain separates the operator from the public. A rectangle (formerly 2×2.5 m; more recently *c.* 1×0.6 m) cut in the curtain some 1.5 m above ground level is covered by a thinner white fabric: the puppeteer sits behind this screen and holds the puppets (which stand *c.* 200–400 mm high) against it. Two lamps, placed between him and the screen, illuminate the puppets from behind; the light shining through their translucent bodies makes them glow like stained glass. The puppeteer moves the puppets by means of sticks and speaks the dialogue, adapting his voice to each character, as he recites or improvises the text. It is essentially a one-man show, although he is often accompanied by a singer and tambourine player.

The puppets, cut from thin but stiff pieces of translucent leather, are flat and coloured. Their joints are fixed simply by strings. They have a round hole with a socket, where the manipulating stick (*c.* 500 mm) is fixed. Some puppets, including Karagöz, have two sticks. Nearly all puppets are caricatures of standard characters. The two main characters are Karagöz (Turk.: 'black' + 'eye'), a rough, poor, lazy and clownish gypsy (see fig. 249), and his neighbour Hacivat, who is more bourgeois, polite, cunning and opportunistic. The numerous female roles are always gossips and intriguers. There are also many heavily caricatured stock figures based on professionals, provincials and foreigners, as well as dwarfs, opium-addicts, idiots etc. Certain characters, such as Farhad and Shirin, were made for specific plays. Some types, such as Nile boatmen, are peculiar to Egyptian plays. Animals, real or fantastic, appear quite often. Props are scarcely used, but a wide range of decorative showpieces are employed to fill the empty stage before the beginning of the play.

All plays follow the same four-part programme. The play opens with the 'Poem of the curtain' explaining the mystical and didactic character of shadow plays. This is followed by blessings, then Hacivat calls for Karagöz, who

249. Shadow-puppet of Karagöz disguised as a woman, translucent leather, Turkish, 19th or 20th century (Jerusalem, L. A. Mayer Memorial Institute for Islamic Art)

appears and fights him. The second part, the 'Dialogue', is a humorous improvisation between Hacivat and Karagöz, which ends with another fight between the protagonists. The third part, the 'Performance', is the play proper. It is not necessarily related to the 'Dialogue', and its contents can be inspired by classic literary romances (e.g. Farhad and Shirin), by popular narratives or by sketches from daily life. This last form was used by political satirists from the end of the 19th century. The concluding element, the 'Epilogue', resembles the 'Dialogue' and announces the next performance. All plays, even those of the literary type, have farcical elements. The traditional plays have been written down only in the later 20th century; 47 have been recorded, but some were taken from the same prototype. As a new play was usually presented every night but one during the month of Ramadan, one could expect a repertory of some 28 or 29 plays.

The origins of the Islamic shadow theatre are controversial. Popular tradition suggests an origin in the Anatolian city of Bursa in early Ottoman times, as Şeyh Kuşteri, the legendary inventor of the shadow theatre, and the two protagonists are supposed to have lived in Bursa during the days of the Sultan Orkhan (*reg c.* 1324–60). Although this theory was accepted by the 17th-century Ottoman historian Evliya Çelebi, it is not very reliable. Two other theories suggest that the shadow theatre originated in

China or India respectively, then spread to Central Asia, whence it was brought by the Turks to Anatolia. However, these two hypotheses, based on the mediation of Central Asian tribes, confuse puppets and shadow-puppets, as it seems that there were only three-dimensional puppets in Central Asia. A fourth theory, which proposes an Indian origin and subsequent transmission to the Near East by gypsies, relies on the fact that Karagöz himself is a gypsy. A fifth hypothesis posits an Egyptian origin and introduction to Anatolia by the Ottoman sultan Selim I (reg 1512–20) after the conquest of Egypt in 1517. This theory goes back to the 16th-century Egyptian chronicler Ibn Iyas, a usually reliable source.

The Islamic shadow theatre seems closer to the Chinese than to the Indian or Indonesian types, and may have come to the Near East from China and reached Egypt before Anatolia. In any event, shadow theatre is known to have existed in China and Egypt from the 13th century. Three shadow plays by the 13th-century Egyptian ophthalmologist Ibn Daniyal anticipate later Karagöz plays. Shadow theatre is known only through literary references in Iran, Syria and Spain, but they are too allusive to allow the reconstruction of the ways shadow-puppets were used, the kinds of plays or the form of the puppets. Major collections of shadow-puppets are held in Hamburg, Museum für Kunst und Gewerbe, and Jerusalem, L. A. Meyer Memorial Institute for Islamic Art.

BIBLIOGRAPHY
Enc. Islam/2: 'Karagöz'; 'Khayāl al-zill' [Shadow fantasy]
G. Jakob: *Geschichte des Schattentheaters* (Hannover, 1925)
J. M. Landau: *Shadow Plays in the Near East* (Jerusalem, 1948)
M. And: *A History of Theatre and Popular Entertainment in Turkey* (Ankara, 1963–4)
A. Tietze: *The Turkish Shadow Theatre and the Puppet Collection of the L. A. Mayer Memorial Foundation* (Berlin, 1975)
A. Gökalp: 'Les Indigènes de la capitale et le kaleïdoscope culturel ottoman: Les "figures ethniques" sur la scène du Karagöz turc', *Théâtre d'Ombres: Tradition et modernité* (Paris, 1986)
S. Moreh: 'The Shadow Play (Khayâl al-Zill) in the Light of Arabic Literature', *Journal of Arabic Literature*, xviii (1987)

MARIANNE BARRUCAND

IX. Forgeries.

There is little evidence for the forging of works of art in the early centuries after the coming of Islam in the 7th century AD; there was no mystique of a pre-Islamic classical tradition, and there were no famous named artists to stimulate the production of forgeries. Following the development of a systematic artistic approach to calligraphy by the 9th century, there appeared a tendency to emulate the works by great practitioners of this pre-eminent form of Islamic art. The renowned calligrapher Ibn al-Bawwab (d 1022), for example, was commissioned to write a missing section (Arab. *juz'*) of a Koran manuscript penned by his teacher Ibn Muqla. Ibn al-Bawwab found old paper resembling that used for the original manuscript and carefully copied the script and illumination, giving the gold an antique appearance. His work was so successful that the new section could not be distinguished from the old ones. This emulation of famous hands may have resulted in the adding of spurious signatures or at least optimistic attributions to various works of calligraphy. A superb copy (Istanbul, Topkapı

Pal. Lib., B. 125) of the *dīvān* (collected poetry) of the pre-Islamic poet Salama ibn Jandal, for example, has a colophon saying that it was copied by Ibn al-Bawwab in 1017, but the colophon must be spurious, for the calligrapher died a decade before the patron of the manuscript, the Saljuq vizier Abu Sahl (d 1064), was born. Under the Timurid dynasty (reg 1370–1506) in Iran, the reputations of individual calligraphers and painters developed in court circles. Collecting works of art on paper in albums became fashionable, and signatures and attributions on such works became more frequent, particularly under the Safavid dynasty (reg 1501–1732) in Iran, the Ottoman dynasty (reg 1281–1924) in the eastern Mediterranean basin, and the Mughal dynasty (reg 1526–1858) in north India.

Only in the 19th century, however, did the production of forgeries of Islamic art begin in earnest. In some cases it was due to the reverence that developed for the 'classical ages' of the past; in other cases it was a response to the high prices paid by Western collectors. In Iran, signatures of such famous artists as Bihzad were frequently added to paintings of various stylistic parentage and age. In Syria and Egypt, high-quality inlaid and engraved metal wares were made in the style later known as Mamluk Revival, in which the main sources of inspiration were objects made for the Mamluk sultans (reg 1250–1517) and their amirs (see §IV, 4(ii) above). These metal wares were produced to meet the increasing European demand for orientalia, but in the hands of unscrupulous dealers or naive art historians they later acquired the aura of authenticity. In a workshop at Valencia, an eccentric individual, D. Francisco Pallás y Puig (1859–1926), produced copies of the Hispano-Arab ivory caskets that had been made at Córdoba in the late 10th century and early 11th under the Umayyad caliphate (reg 756–1031). The copies were first sold at ordinary commercial prices as frank imitations, but with time they passed for originals, although they would not be thought so today.

Other more serious fabrications occurred as a response to Western collecting. Paintings from the well-known manuscript (New York, Pierpont Morgan Lib., MS. M. 500) of Ibn Bakhtishu's Persian translation of the Arabic bestiary *Manāfi' al-hayawān* ('The advantages of animals'), copied at Maragha in Azerbaijan in the 1290s, for example, were tampered with to suggest that Chinese paintings had been used as models. It has also been suggested that all the illustrations in some manuscripts are forgeries. The paintings in a copy (New York, Pub. Lib., Spencer col.) of Firdawsi's *Shāhnāma* ('Book of kings') prepared for the Safavid ruler 'Abbas I in 1614 were once thought to be 17th-century paraphrases of illustrations in the copy of the epic prepared for the Timurid prince Baysunghur in 1430 (Tehran, Gulistan Pal. Lib.; see fig. 121 above). The paintings in the Spencer *Shāhnāma* have been discovered to be the work of Iranian forgers in the late 19th century who added them to a genuine manuscript, the illustrations for which were never realized, with the intent to deceive local patrons. In certain cases, such as a manuscript (divided, Cincinnati, OH, A. Mus., and New York, Kevorkian priv. col.) of the *Andarznāma* ('Book of Andarz'; July 1090), it has been suggested that leading scholars may have played a role in the creation and publicizing of what is now recognized to be a bizarre forgery. In few cases, however, has the suspected or discredited work of art been the subject of frank discussion in the scholarly literature. Instead, a certain coyness predominates, presumably to avoid institutional or personal embarrassment to museums and colleagues and possibly with an eye to potential litigation as well.

Despite the tendency to avoid publication on the subject, scholars have long discussed suspected cases of forgery. The authenticity of a silver salver (Boston, MA, Mus. F.A.) bearing the incised name of the Saljuq sultan Alp Arslan (reg 1063–72) and dated 1066–7 has been hotly disputed, despite the subsequent appearance of other objects in the same style and a respectable report on its metal content (see §IV, 2(ii) above). A large group of complex woven silks allegedly excavated at Rayy and attributed to the patronage of the Buyid dynasty (reg 932–1062) in Iran has excited even more controversy, in which the arguments of art historians have been questioned or buttressed by the often ambiguous results of physical tests for age and chemical tests for dyestuffs. Of all the suspected forgeries in Islamic art, the Buyid silks have been written about at greatest length, sometimes in a polemical fashion.

Carpets have been an especially rich field for forgers, and the workshops of Teodor Tuduk in Bucharest in the late 19th century and early 20th have attained almost legendary status in the field as the purported source of many suspect pieces. The unmasking of carpet forgeries has been quite simple in some cases, such as those carpets with aniline dyes or those worn down with pumice, but recent evidence, still unpublished, has indicated that the scale used to calibrate carbon-14 dates for carpets is seriously skewed. In one case, carbon-14 testing on a piece with a 19th-century signature and date produced results consistent with a date several hundred years earlier, and in another, a rare example of an animal carpet (New York, Met.), carbon-14 testing provided a range of 1040–1290, but the piece has been attributed on art-historical grounds to the second half of the 14th century. As village and nomadic carpets have commanded astronomical prices on the market since 1970, they have been the subject of very clever forgeries, some of them reusing materials obtained by unravelling old flat-woven carpets. (See also §VI, 4(i) and (iv)(a) above.)

The vast majority of allegations of forgery made about Islamic works of art never appear in print, and as a consequence there is little open discussion of the phenomenon. The authenticity of such major works as the Anhalt carpet (New York, Met.) has been doubted privately, but there has been no concerted effort either by the carpet's critics or by its defenders to find a systematic approach to the whispered controversy. The large yield of genuine archaeological objects uncovered in uncontrolled excavations results in a parallel market in artificially patinated bronze and ceramic objects in Middle Eastern bazaars, but in general there has been little systematic effort to address problems of such faked objects by scholars and even less by dealers and auction houses. In most cases, the results of physical and chemical tests to determine age and authenticity have been inconclusive, and the traditional methods of connoisseurship, epigraphy and palaeography have been central to the unmasking of fakes and forgeries.

BIBLIOGRAPHY

M. Gomez Moreño: 'Los marfiles cordobeses y sus derivaciones', Archv Esp. A. & Arqueol., iii (1927), pp. 233–43
A. Coomaraswamy: 'An Eleventh-century Silver Salver from Persia', Bull. Mus. F.A., Boston, xxxii (1934), pp. 56–8
D. S. Rice: The Unique Ibn al-Bawwab Manuscript in the Chester Beatty Library (Dublin, 1955)
R. Ettinghausen and others: Andarz Nama, Proceedings of the IVth International Congress of Iranian Art and Archeology: New York, Philadelphia, Baltimore & Washington DC, 1960
E. Kühnel and D. G. Shepherd: 'Buyid Silks', Proceedings of the IVth International Congress of Iranian Art and Archeology: New York, Philadelphia, Baltimore & Washington DC, 1960
Bull. Liaison Cent. Int. Etud. Textiles Anc., xxxvii/1 (1972) [issue devoted to the Buyid silks in Abegg Stiftung in Berne]
D. G. Shepherd: 'Medieval Persian Silks in Fact and Fancy (A Refutation of the Riggisberg Report)', Bull. Liaison Cent. Int. Etud. Textiles Anc., xxxix–xl (1974) [whole issue]
S. S. Blair, J. M. Bloom and A. E. Wardwell: 'Re-evaluating the Date of the "Buyid Silks" by Epigraphic and Radiocarbon Analysis', A. Orient., xxii (1993), pp. 1–42

WALTER B. DENNY

X. Historiography.

The study of Islamic art and architecture is a comparatively new field, which until the latter part of the 20th century was of interest only to scholars from Europe, Russia and North America. Since then, increased numbers of people from the Islamic lands have developed an interest and expertise in the history of their art during the last 1400 years, although many of the major centres of scholarship remain in the Western world. The speed with which the field has grown means that many central questions remain to be answered. Few individuals can command all the necessary tools, particularly the languages, required for serious research, and access to sites and collections in this often volatile region is difficult. Scholarship has frequently been less than rigorous, and many smooth pages of generalities conceal yawning gaps of knowledge.

There is no evidence that any artist or patron in the centuries covered by this survey ever thought of his art as 'Islamic', and the notion of a distinctly Islamic tradition of art and architecture, eventually encompassing the lands between the Atlantic and the Indian oceans, is a phenomenon of late 19th- and 20th-century Western scholarship, as is the terminology used to describe it. Until that time European scholars had used such restrictive geographic or ethnic terms as 'Indian' ('Hindoo'), 'Persian', 'Turkish', 'Arab', 'Moorish' and 'Saracenic' to describe distinct regional styles, but such all-embracing terms as 'Mahommedan/Mohammedan', 'Moslem/Muslim' and 'Islamic' came into favour only when scholars began to look back to a golden age of Islamic culture in the 8th and 9th centuries and project it simplistically on to the kaleidoscopic modern world. This initial focus on the early period has led to the relative neglect of the period after 1500. Nationalist and universalist currents have long existed in the study of the arts of the region. Many scholars maintain nationalist views, studying Islamic art only in Turkey, Iran or western Central Asia and chauvinistically ignoring contemporary developments in neighbouring lands. The universalist view of some early scholarship is no longer fashionable; in any event, few have the interest or intellectual equipment to study the continuities between pre-Islamic and Islamic art, particularly as modern scholarship tends to compartmentalize knowledge unduly and stress the breaks over the continuities in the arts.

1. To *c*. 1900. 2. *c*. 1900–*c*. 1945. 3. From *c*. 1945.

1. TO *c*. 1900. Apart from a few exceptional cases—such as al-Maqrizi, the 15th-century local antiquarian and historian of Egypt, or Qazi Ahmad, the early 17th-century chronicler of Persian calligraphers and painters—scholarly interest in the architecture, art and archaeology of the Islamic lands developed in the West, where it followed diplomatic, commercial and colonial involvement in the Islamic lands of North Africa, the Middle East, western Central Asia and the Indian subcontinent. Islamic objects were acquired by legitimate or illegitimate means for collections in Europe, although paradoxically the first objects to arouse scholarly interest were 8th- to early 11th-century coins that had been traded in Scandinavia, northern Germany and Russia in the early Middle Ages. The first scholarly book on Islamic numismatics was G. J. Kehr's *Monarchiae Asiaticae–Saracenicae status qualis VIII et IX. . .seculo fuit, ex nummis argenteis prisca Arabum scriptura kufica. . .cusis, et nuper. . .effossis, illustratus* (Leipzig, 1724), in which the author correctly read the kufic inscriptions and provided commentary. By the late 18th century other collections of Islamic coins had been catalogued, culminating in the systematic classification by C. M. Frähn (1782–1851), *Das muhammedanische Münzkabinett des asiatischen Museum der kaiserliche Akademie der Wissenschaften zu St Petersburg* (1821). Coins remain a well-studied aspect of Islamic art.

This interest in epigraphy led in the 18th century to the study of other inscribed works of Islamic art. The traveller and scholar CARSTEN NIEBUHR was one of the first to record Islamic inscriptions, and in his description of Arabia he illustrated a page in kufic script from an early manuscript of the Koran. Inscriptions played a large part in the first catalogue of an entire collection of Islamic decorative arts, the *Monumens arabes, persans et turcs, du cabinet de M. le Duc de Blacas et d'autres cabinets* (Paris, 1828) by the French Orientalist J. T. Reinaud (1795–1867). Other noted epigraphers of the period included the Ottoman historian J. von Hammer-Purgstall (1774–1856), who published several inscriptions, and the Italian abbot Michelangelo Lanci (1779–1867), whose three-volume *Trattato delle simboliche rappresentanze arabiche e della varia generazione de' musulmani caratteri sopra differenti materie operati* (Paris, 1845–6) includes engravings of inscriptions on talismans, amulets, arms and armour, metal wares and textiles.

Superficial familiarity with Islamic architecture was spurred by the publication of *Entwurff einer historischen Architektur* (Vienna, 1721), the general history of architecture by Johann Bernhard Fischer von Erlach (*see* FISCHER VON ERLACH, (1)). It included representations of Arab, Turkish and Persian architecture taken from coins and the accounts of travellers and archaeologists. Fischer von Erlach's images inspired the design of several kiosks, pavilions and palaces in a quasi-Oriental manner, such as the mosque-shaped pavilion (1778) and other buildings in

the gardens at SCHWETZINGEN near Mannheim by NICOLAS DE PIGAGE. The exotic—but gratifyingly accessible—Islamic buildings in Spain began to be known towards the end of the 18th century. The architects Juan de Villanueva (*see* VILLANUEVA, (2)) and Pedro Arnal (1735–1805) were sent by the Real Academia de San Fernando to make drawings of Granada and Córdoba under the direction of José de Hermosilla. Published in 1780 as *Antiguedades árabes de España*, the drawings were the basis for J. C. Murphy's *Arabian Antiquities of Spain* (London, 1813), which brought the buildings to an even wider audience. A veritable avalanche of visual accounts ensued: JOSEPH-PHILIBERT GIRAULT DE PRANGEY published *Souvenirs de Grenade et de l'Alhambra* (Paris, 1836–7), *Monuments arabes et moresques de Cordoue, Séville et Grenade* (Paris, 1836–9) and *Essai sur l'architecture des Arabes et des Mores, en Espagne, en Sicile, et en Barbarie* (Paris, 1841), which also introduced monuments in North Africa, recently colonized by the French. The two atlas folios by Jules Goury (1803–34) and OWEN JONES, *Plans, Elevations, Sections, and Details of the Alhambra* (London, 1842–5), conceived as a pattern book for architects, further familiarized European audiences with Islamic architecture and launched a craze for Oriental fantasies in the West. Sicily was the other European region with a strong Islamic presence, and its Islamic monuments were the focus of the Italian Orientalist Michele Amari (1806–89). Born in Palermo, he became a pioneer in Arabic studies in Italy and an authority on the Islamic monuments of Sicily.

Egyptian Islamic architecture became known to Europeans from the *Description de l'Egypte* (Paris, 1809–28), the scientific record of Napoleon's expedition to Egypt (1798–1801) and one of the greatest achievements of the encyclopedic tradition of the French Enlightenment. Published in nine volumes of text, ten elephant folios of plates and an atlas, and covering everything from Egyptian antiquities to popular music, the work included accurate views of Islamic buildings and reproductions of inscriptions, many now destroyed. Like views of the Alhambra, these images were adapted by European artists for their own purposes: Baron ANTOINE-JEAN GROS, for example, transformed the depiction of the mosque of Ibn Tulun in Cairo into the setting of his painting *Bonaparte Visiting the Victims of the Plague at Jaffa* (1804; Paris, Louvre). The traditional artistic life of Egypt in the early 19th century was described by E. W. Lane in his early Victorian bestseller, *An Account of the Manners and Customs of the Modern Egyptians* (London, 1836).

The tradition of describing exotic architecture found in the *Description de l'Egypte* was continued by others, such as the Marseillais architect PASCAL COSTE, who worked for the Egyptian ruler Muhammad 'Ali (*reg* 1805–48) and published *Architecture arabe* (Paris, 1839). Jules Bourgoin (1838–1907) published a minute study of geometric designs, principally in Mamluk architecture, and detailed if imaginative plates in *Les Arts arabes* (Paris, 1873); much the same can be said of the work by A. C. T. E. Prisse d'Avennes (1807–79), *L'Art arabe d'après les monuments du Kaire* (Paris, 1877). Islamic architecture in other countries was also depicted. Coste, for example, accompanied the French embassy to Iran in 1840–41 and, with the painter Eugène Flandin (1809–76), produced *Voyage en*

Perse in eight volumes (Paris, 1843–54), as well as *Monuments modernes de la Perse* (Paris, 1867). Coste and his contemporaries preferred the later showier architecture with its emphasis on glittering coloured revetments to earlier, more sober styles, and he was unaware of the spectacular north dome chamber of the Friday Mosque at Isfahan (see fig. 31 above), now considered the masterpiece of 11th-century Persian architecture. The French government also sponsored the travels of CHARLES TEXIER in the 1830s to Asia Minor, Armenia and Iran, as well as the travels of Xavier Hommaire de Hell (1812–48) in 1846–8; the plates reproduced in his *Voyage en Turquie et en Perse* (Paris, 1853–60) followed the tradition of pretty *vedute*, charmingly enlivened by groups of picturesque natives.

2. *c*. 1900–*c*. 1945. A new scholarly interest in Islamic architecture and art developed around the turn of the 20th century, when several European scholars went beyond 19th-century Orientalism and attempted to understand Islamic art in terms of the culture that produced it. This new approach can be seen in the work of the Swiss scholar MAX VAN BERCHEM, who, following a trip to the Near East in 1889, developed the idea of Islamic archaeology, in which monuments and works of art would be studied in their historical contexts. Van Berchem persuaded the Académie Française to sponsor the series *Matériaux pour un corpus inscriptionum Arabicarum*, and he prepared volumes dealing with the Arabic inscriptions of Cairo, Jerusalem and part of Anatolia. His activities were paralleled by those of the Austrian Joseph von Karabacek (1845–1918), a numismatist, epigrapher and founder of the study of Arabic papyrology and Islamic heraldry. Like van Berchem, von Karabacek was a pioneer in placing Islamic art in a wider historical perspective, for he realized the importance of epigraphy and textual sources for interpreting an object. His unfettered imagination, however, often led him to erroneous conclusions, but these spurred others to refute his hypotheses. As the knighted director of the Hofbibliothek in Vienna and secretary to the Vienna Academy, von Karabacek made the study of Islamic art acceptable both professionally and socially.

Berlin became a centre for the new scholarly approach. German interest in the Ottoman empire, which controlled large areas of the Levant, and the close relationship between the emperor William II (*reg* 1888–1918) and the Ottoman sultan Abdülhamid II (*reg* 1876–1909) led to the acquisition of the façade from the palace at Mshatta in Jordan, along with the Pergamon altarpiece and the stoa gate from Miletos, for the Kaiser-Friedrich-Museum (now the Pergamonmuseum). The Mshatta façade, which was acquired as a Late Antique work but soon reattributed to the early Islamic period, became an important exhibit in the Islamic section (founded in 1904). Such Berlin-based scholars as ERNST HERZFELD, who travelled with FRIEDRICH SARRE through Iraq, combined a first-hand knowledge of the architectural and artistic monuments of the region with expertise in languages, history and culture to produce seminal works on the development of Islamic art that remain essential reading.

Following World War I, European scholars developed regional specialities, often following the colonial or diplomatic interests of the scholar's country of origin. German scholars, such as Sarre, continued to work on the former Ottoman lands. They were joined by the Frenchman ALBERT GABRIEL, who after working in Egypt and Syria became the director of the French Institute in Istanbul and wrote extensively on the Islamic architecture of Anatolia, particularly in the pre-Ottoman period. The French also worked in North Africa and Syria: HENRI TERRASSE studied western Islamic art and architecture, as did GEORGES MARÇAIS, who focused on the Classical substratum there. The brilliant scholar JEAN SAUVAGET followed van Berchem's notion of Islamic archaeology and focused on similar issues in Syria. British interest in Egypt and Syria is epitomized by the work of K. A. C. CRESWELL, who wrote a monumental history of Islamic architecture in the Arab lands, with particular reference to Egypt, where he lived throughout most of his long life. Creswell's positivist approach, seen in his seminal tomes, *Early Muslim Architecture* (Oxford, 1932–40) and *The Muslim Architecture of Egypt* (Oxford, 1952–9), led him to string monuments together in series to explain architectural developments and to compile massive bibliographies on the architecture, arts and crafts of Islam. Italian involvement in North Africa is reflected in the work of UGO MONNERET DE VILLARD, who worked on Christian and Islamic monuments of Upper Egypt and Nubia, as well as Islamic art in Italy. His synthesizing approach led him to explain Islamic art as a logical development from previous traditions.

Iran was opened to Western scholars (and development) following the establishment of the Pahlavi line in 1924. The Frenchman ANDRÉ GODARD became the director of the Department of Antiquities, recording monuments throughout the country; similarly the Americans ARTHUR UPHAM POPE, Myron Bement Smith and Donald Wilber made several research trips throughout Iran. Foreign interest in Iranian art culminated in the monumental *Survey of Persian Art from Prehistoric Times to the Present* (London, 1938–9), edited by Pope and his wife, Phyllis Ackerman. Published in six hefty tomes, it contains articles by a wide range of experts arranged by the different media and periods. Although much of the information has been superseded, the *Survey* remains the starting-point for most work on Persian art and is still unique in the field. As in other works from the 1920s and 1930s, architecture was treated separately from the other arts, and this approach was continued by Wilber in his monographs on Ilkhanid and (with Lisa Golombek) Timurid architecture.

In the early 20th century the study of the decorative arts, of unusual importance in the Islamic lands, emerged as a distinct scholarly speciality, often associated with wealthy collectors and museum curators. Following Stanley Lane-Poole (E. W. Lane's nephew), who had published *The Art of the Saracens in Egypt* (London, 1886) as well as studies of Islamic coins, Henri Saladin and Gaston Migeon published their two-volume *Manuel d'art musulman* (Paris, 1907). The great 1910 exhibition of Islamic art in Munich was commemorated in a monumental scholarly catalogue by Sarre and FREDRIK MARTIN that made the finest of the 3500 objects assembled from all over Europe accessible to a wide audience. These publications spurred the writing of several handbooks on the Islamic decorative arts by such scholars as Heinrich Glück and ERNST DIEZ (1925), ERNST KÜHNEL (1925), ZAKI MUHAMMAD HASAN and MAURICE S. DIMAND. Some scholars developed specialities in particular media: for example, DAVID STORM RICE in metalware, ARTHUR LANE in ceramics and C. J. Lamm in textiles and glass. Carpets, which had been imported into the West since the 15th century and had already attracted the interest of WILHELM BODE, became the particular interest of Dimand, KURT ERDMANN and others. In all these areas, scholars focused on the finest examples of each type, often leaving the mass of poorer or incomplete pieces unstudied. This interest in the decorative arts also led such scholars as ALOIS RIEGL, Herzfeld and Kühnel to study ornament, particularly the development of arabesque.

Painting, central to the history of European art, has played a comparatively smaller role in Islamic culture, but nevertheless it became one of the major subspecialities of 20th-century scholarship. Alois Musil's discovery in 1898 of extensive figural murals in the early Islamic bath complex at Qusayr 'Amra provoked a generation of scholars, including THOMAS ARNOLD and BISHR FARÈS, to revise traditional views on the lawfulness of painting in Islam. Interest in manuscript painting was spurred by such scholar-collectors as Martin, Georges Marteau and HENRI VEVER. The study of Persian manuscript painting continued under the next generation of scholars, including BASIL GRAY, keeper at the British Museum, and the Russian émigré Ivan Sergeyevich Stchoukine (*see* SHCHUKIN, (2)), based in Paris and Beirut, who used stylistic criteria to delineate individual hands and schools and write surveys of particular periods. This interest in connoisseurship remains unusually important in the study of Islamic painting.

Epigraphy, the first aspect of Islamic art to be studied, remained an important subspeciality. GASTON WIET continued van Berchem's work on the *Corpus* and—along with Etienne Combe and Sauvaget—began publication of the *Répertoire chronologique d'épigraphie arabe* (Cairo, 1931–), a multi-volume list of Arabic inscriptions on buildings and objects. As in other media, scholars developed regional expertise: the historian Evariste Lévi-Provençal, for example, studied the Arabic inscriptions of Spain, while Ghulam Yazdani studied those of the Indian subcontinent in *Epigraphia Indo-Moslemica*, begun by Josef Horovitz (1909–12). The inscriptions of western Central Asia, inaccessible to most Western scholars, were the subject of a special journal, *Epigrafika Vostoka*, which includes important contributions by such scholars as V. A. Kratchkovskaya and A. A. Semenov. Palaeography, however, has not been studied to the same degree. The method Samuel Flury (1874–1935) developed in the early 20th century for studying letter shapes was followed by later scholars, particularly Janine Sourdel-Thomine, who continued the work of Sauvaget, integrating the study of epigraphy and texts into the history of architecture and art. The pioneering palaeographic studies of Adolf Grohmann were never finished, although they have inspired a new generation of scholars, including François Déroche, to reinvestigate the development of Arabic script.

3. FROM *c.* 1945. The disruptions caused by World War II reconfigured the study of Islamic art, as such traditional centres as Berlin were displaced and many European scholars emigrated to the USA, which became an important centre of research. Dimand and Mehmet Aga-Oglu had already emigrated to the USA in the 1920s, and they were joined in the 1930s by Herzfeld and RICHARD ETTINGHAUSEN. In addition to museums in New York and Washington, DC, centres of higher learning such as the Institute for Advanced Study at Princeton, the University of Michigan at Ann Arbor, New York University and Harvard University established positions in Islamic art, where scholars participated in the general development of the history of art as an academic discipline in the postwar period. The number of students increased exponentially, as the PhD became a necessary union card for entrance into the profession. The study of Islamic art continues to reflect contemporary political developments: the explosion of oil wealth, for example, encouraged many to enter the field in the 1970s, and the Soviet occupation of Afghanistan and the Iranian Revolution caused some specialists to switch their purview to the Islamic arts of India or the Ottoman empire. Indeed, scholarly fashion has led to the bunching of investigation in certain areas at certain times; other areas, particularly North Africa, have been woefully neglected, and research tools, such as meticulous Creswellesque surveys of Islamic architecture in other regions, have never been undertaken.

Traditional approaches to scholarship have been continued and refined. Ettinghausen, for example, built on the traditions of German scholarship to produce masterful investigations of iconography and style, with particular reference to the Islamic arts of Iran. B. W. Robinson, keeper at the Victoria and Albert Museum, used stylistic criteria to delineate individual hands and schools of Persian painting, producing a corpus of scholarly catalogues and expanding the field to include the arts of the Qajar dynasty in Iran. A. S. Melikian-Chirvani transformed the study of Islamic, particularly Iranian, metalwork by exploring the relationships between art, mysticism and myth. Michael Meinecke (*d* 1995) meticulously expanded the encyclopedic study of Mamluk architecture begun by Creswell.

Other scholars of Islamic art have broadened the scope of enquiry, building on the work of pioneers to investigate new topics and reinvestigate old ones. For example, Barbara Finster and Jürgen Schmidt re-examined such early Islamic sites as Ukhaydir to put them in broader archaeological and historical contexts. In the study of Islamic manuscripts, work has addressed such questions as the relationship of text and image, the role of subject-matter, or the manuscript as an entire work of art. Another important development has been the reintegration of architecture and the decorative arts, notably by Oleg Grabar in *The Formation of Islamic Art* (New Haven, 1973), dealing with the Umayyad and Abbasid dynasties. His work was followed during the 1970s and 1980s by several of his colleagues and students in exhibitions and catalogues on the arts of later dynasties, most notably by Esin Atıl in Washington. The study of architectural history has been broadened to include the study of architectural types, such as the minaret, and the iconography of forms.

The increased interest in the history of Islamic art has expanded the range of the techniques used from traditional art-historical analysis of style and iconography to broader social and economic analyses. A general interest in the use of written documents for explaining artefacts has led scholars to investigate archival sources, such as endowment deeds, registers, account books and the like, which survive in Cairo, Istanbul and elsewhere. Some scholars, such as L. A. Ibrahim, have used endowment deeds to establish vocabularies, while others, such as H. E. Wulff in Iran, André Paccard in Morocco and Henry Glassie in Turkey, building on the work of Oskar Reuther, Herzfeld and Felix Langenegger in Iraq, have interviewed artisans to understand techniques and terminology. Following the monographs by L. A. Mayer (1895–1959) on Islamic artists and their works, interest in the personalities—both artists and patrons—has revived, countering the widespread conception of anonymous masters in Islamic art.

A distinct field of Islamic archaeology developed in the post-war period. As archaeology had been developed as a method to compensate for the absence of written sources in the study of cultures and civilizations, it was less appropriate for Islamic civilization where written sources are comparatively available, particularly in the later periods. Early excavations at the Qal'at Bani Hammad in Algeria by General de Beylié in 1908, at Madinat al-Zahra' in Spain by R. Velásquez Bosco *c.* 1910, and at Samarra' in Iraq by Herzfeld and Sarre in 1911–13 had sought to uncover luxury residences and artefacts to be transferred to European museums. At other sites, Islamic levels had been quickly dug through by archaeologists interested in earlier periods, although sympathetic excavators at such sites as Miletos, Tarsus and Susa recorded Islamic finds, especially coins. Archaeology tends to be more appropriate for the study of the early Islamic period, and many Umayyad sites have been the focus of archaeological investigations. The first excavations, such as those in the 1930s by Daniel Schlumberger at Qasr al-Hayr West, focused on material remains, but post-war investigations of such sites as Qasr al-Hayr East in Syria, Quseir and Fustat (Old Cairo) in Egypt, Siraf in Iran, and Lashkari Bazar and Ghazna in Afghanistan have tried to situate the sites in broader geo-historical contexts.

Archaeology has also been used to uncover the structural history of complex buildings, as in R. W. Hamilton's work on the Aqsa Mosque in Jerusalem and Eugenio Galdieri's work on the Friday Mosque at Isfahan. The technique of surface survey was used by R. McC. Adams to document settlement patterns in the Diyala Basin of Iraq over several millennia, and aerial surveys, first used by Erich F. Schmidt to document cities and sites in Iran, have yielded important information about the development of the Samarra' region in the Abbasid period. Scholars have also used archaeological material to place the arts of the Islamic lands in broader contexts. For example, John Carswell, Nurhan Atasoy, Julian Raby and others have studied the impact of Chinese blue-and-white ceramics on those of the Islamic lands.

New scientific techniques have been used in the post-war period to examine works of Islamic art, understand how they were made and determine their authenticity. The technical laboratory at the Freer and Sackler Galleries in Washington, DC, has been a pioneer in this respect. Thermoluminescence has been used to determine when ceramics were fired, and petrography to study the bodies and glazes of individual pieces. Non-destructive techniques such as X-ray fluorescence analysis have been used to group and compare metal objects other than those made of iron. Radiocarbon analysis was initially of only limited use for analysing Islamic art, for large samples of organic materials, such as fabrics, paper or wood, were destroyed in neutron-activation analysis. The development of accelerator-mass spectrometry has permitted minute samples of problematic pieces, such as many of the 'Buyid' silks, purportedly from 10th- and 11th-century Iran, to show that they were manufactured in the 20th century. PIXE (Proton-induced X-ray examination), a non-destructive technique for analysing pigments and paper, promises to be of great value in the study of the Islamic arts of the book.

The study of Islamic art is carried out in many venues. In addition to museums and universities in Europe, North America, Russia and the Islamic lands—there are 68 paid posts in Turkey alone—there are many local, European and American research institutes in the Islamic lands, particularly in such cities as Cairo, Damascus, Istanbul, Tehran and Kabul. Local departments of antiquities supervise the conservation and documentation of Islamic works of art and architecture. The first was the Comité de Conservation des Monuments de l'Art Arabe, founded in Cairo in 1881.

Information about Islamic art is published in a variety of ways. Major journals include the organs of departments of antiquities (such as *al-Atlāl* in Saudi Arabia and *Sumer* in Iraq). *Ars Islamica* (1934–51), the first journal devoted specifically to Islamic art, was superseded by *Ars Orientalis* (1954–). Eleven volumes of *Kunst des Orients* appeared between 1950 and 1976. More recent journals devoted to the field include *Muqarnas*, published since 1983 for the Aga Khan Program in Islamic Architecture at Harvard University and the Massachusetts Institute of Technology, and *Islamic Art*, published by the Islamic Art Foundation since 1984. Articles on Islamic art also appear in an extraordinarily wide range of journals, *Festschriften* and collected works in many languages and alphabets; these titles are largely accessible through *Index Islamicus*, a continuing bibliography of periodical literature begun by J. D. Pearson in 1958, and the massive bibliography on the architecture, arts and crafts of Islam begun by Creswell. This bibliography also provides access to the enormous range of checklists and catalogues of museum and private collections, public exhibitions and sales.

BIBLIOGRAPHY

GENERAL

M. van Berchem: 'Notes d'archéologie arabe', *J. Asiat.*, 8th ser., xvii (1891), pp. 411–95; xviii (1891), pp. 46–86; xix (1892), pp. 377–407; 10th ser., iii (1904), pp. 5–96

E. Kühnel: 'Ergebnisse und Aufgaben der islamischen Archäologie', *Der Orient in deutscher Forschung* (Leipzig, 1944), pp. 255–9

J. Sauvaget: 'Comment étudier l'histoire du monde arabe', *Rev. Afr.*, xc (1946), pp. 5–23; also in *Mémorial Jean Sauvaget* (Damascus, 1954–61), i, pp. 165–86

——: 'L'Archéologie musulmane en France de 1939 à 1945', *A. Islam.*, xiii–xiv (1948), pp. 150–61

R. Ettinghausen: 'Islamic Art and Archaeology', *Near Eastern Culture and Society*, ed. T. Cuyler Young (Princeton, 1951), pp. 17–47; also in *Richard*

Ettinghausen: *Islamic Art and Archaeology (Collected Papers)*, ed. M. Rosen-Ayalon (Berlin, 1984), pp. 1229–69

J. M. Rogers: 'From Antiquarianism to Islamic Archaeology', *Quad. Ist. It. Cult. R. A. E.*, n. s. 2 (1974) [whole issue]

O. Grabar: 'Islamic Art and Archaeology', *The Study of the Middle East: Research and Scholarship in the Humanities and the Social Sciences*, ed. L. Binder (New York, 1976), pp. 229–63

C. Cahen: *Introduction à l'histoire du monde musulman médiéval, VIIe–XVe siècle: Méthodologie et éléments de bibliographie* (Paris, 1982), pp. 41–9

O. Grabar: 'Reflections on the Study of Islamic Art', *Muqarnas*, i (1983), pp. 1–14

R. S. Humphreys: *Islamic History: A Framework for Inquiry* (Princeton, 1988/R 1991)

J. Sweetman: *The Oriental Obsession: Islamic Inspiration in British and American Art and Architecture, 1500–1920* (Cambridge, 1988)

Europa und der Orient, 800–1900 (exh. cat., ed. G. Sievernich and H. Budde; Berlin, Berlin Gal., 1989)

Muqarnas, viii (1991) [whole issue entitled *K. A. C. Creswell and his Legacy*]

D. M. Reid: 'Cultural Imperialism and Nationalism: The Struggle to Define and Control the Heritage of Arab Art in Egypt', *Int. J. Mid. E. Stud.*, xxiv (1992), pp. 57–76

WORKS MENTIONED IN TEXT

Aḥmad ibn ʿAlī al-Maqrīzī (1364–1442): *Al-Mawāʿiz waʾl-iʿtibār bi-dhikr al-khitat waʾl-āthār* [Exhortations and consideration for the mention of districts and monuments], 2 vols (Cairo, 1853)

Qāzī Aḥmad ibn Mīr Munshī: *Gulistān-i hunar* [Rose-garden of art] (*c.* 1606); Eng. trans. by V. Minorsky as *Calligraphers and Painters* (Washington, DC, 1959)

J. T. Reinaud: *Monumens arabes, persans et turcs, du cabinet de M. le Duc de Blacas et d'autres cabinets*, 2 vols (Paris, 1828)

J. von Karabacek: *Das arabische Papier* (Vienna, 1887)

H. Saladin and G. Migeon: *Manuel d'art musulman*, 2 vols (Paris, 1907, 2/1927)

F. Sarre and F. R. Martin: *Die Ausstellung von Meisterwerken muhammedanischer Kunst*, 4 vols (Munich, 1911–12)

G. Marteau and H. Vever: *Miniatures persanes exposées au Musée des arts décoratifs juin–octobre 1912*, 2 vols (Paris, 1913)

E. Diez: *Die Kunst der islamischen Völker (Handbuch der Kunstwissenschaft)* (Berlin, 1915)

H. Glück and E. Diez: *Die Kunst des Islam*, Propyläen-Kstgesch., v (Berlin, 1925)

E. Kühnel: *Islamische Kleinkunst* (Berlin, 1925)

M. S. Dimand: *A Handbook of Mohammedan Decorative Arts* (New York, 1930; rev. 2 as *A Handbook of Muhammadan Art*, 1944)

E. Combe, J. Sauvaget and G. Wiet, eds: *Répertoire chronologique d'épigraphie arabe* (Cairo, 1931–)

A. U. Pope and P. Ackerman, eds: *A Survey of Persian Art*, 6 vols (London, 1938–9), rev. 16 vols (London, 1964–7/R Tokyo, 1977)

D. Schlumberger: 'Les Fouilles de Qasr el Heir el Gharbi', *Syria*, xx (1939), pp. 195–238, 324–73

E. F. Schmidt: *Flights over Ancient Cities of Iran* (Chicago, 1940)

Z. M. Hasan: *Funūn al-islām* [The arts of Islam] (Cairo, 1948)

R. W. Hamilton: *The Structural History of the Aqṣā Mosque* (Oxford, 1949)

J. Sourdel-Thomine: 'Deux minarets d'époque seljoukide en Afghanistan', *Syria*, xxx (1953), pp. 108–21

G. Marçais: *L'Architecture musulmane d'Occident: Tunisie, Algérie, Maroc, Espagne et Sicile* (Paris, 1954)

D. M. Wilber: *The Architecture of Islamic Iran: The Il Khānid Period* (Princeton, 1955)

L. A. Mayer: *Islamic Architects and their Works* (Geneva, 1956)

B. W. Robinson: *A Descriptive Catalogue of the Persian Paintings in the Bodleian Library* (Oxford, 1958)

R. McC. Adams: *Land Behind Baghdad* (Chicago, 1965)

U. Monneret de Villard: *Introduzione allo studio dell'archeologia islamica: Le origini e il periodo omayyade* (Rome and Venice, 1966/R 1968)

H. E. Wulff: *The Traditional Crafts of Persia* (Cambridge, MA, 1966)

E. Galdieri: *Isfahān: Masǧid-i Ǧumʿa*, 3 vols (Rome, 1972–84)

E. Atıl: *Ceramics from the World of Islam* (Washington, DC, 1973)

O. Grabar: *The Formation of Islamic Art* (New Haven, 1973, rev. 1987)

B. Finster and J. Schmidt: 'Sasanidische und frühislamische Ruinen in Iraq', *Baghdad. Mitt.*, vii (1976) [whole issue]

O. Grabar and others: *City in the Desert: Qasr al-Hayr East* (Cambridge, MA, 1978)

F. Gabrieli and U. Scerrato: *Gli Arabi in Italia* (Milan, 1979)

A. Paccard: *Le Maroc et l'artisanat traditionnel islamique dans l'architecture*, 2 vols (Saint-Jorioz, 1979)

A. S. Melikian-Chirvani: *Islamic Metalwork from the Iranian World, 8th–18th Centuries*, London, V&A cat. (London, 1982)

E. Atıl, W. T. Chase and P. Jett: *Islamic Metalwork in the Freer Gallery of Art* (Washington, DC, 1985)

Blue and White Chinese Porcelain and its Impact on the Western World (exh. cat. by J. Carswell, U. Chicago, IL, Smart Gal., 1985)

L. Golombek and D. Wilber: *The Timurid Architecture of Iran and Turan*, 2 vols (Princeton, 1988)

G. D. Lowry and others: *An Annotated and Illustrated Checklist of the Vever Collection* (Washington, DC, 1988)

N. Atasoy and J. Raby: *Iznik: The Pottery of Ottoman Turkey* (London, 1989)

J. Bloom: *Minaret: Symbol of Islam* (Oxford, 1989)

M. Meinecke: *Die mamlukische Architektur in Ägypten und Syrien*, 2 vols (Glückstadt, 1992)

S. S. Blair, J. M. Bloom and A. E. Wardwell: 'Re-evaluating the Date of the "Buyid" Silks by Epigraphic and Radiocarbon Analysis', *A. Orient.*, xxii (1993), pp. 1–42

H. Glassie: *Turkish Traditional Art Today* (Bloomington and Indianapolis, 1993)   □

XI. Collectors and collecting.

1. Islamic lands. 2. Europe and North America.

1. ISLAMIC LANDS. The collecting of calligraphy preceded all other forms of collecting in the Islamic lands. The works of prominent calligraphers, such as Ibn Muqla, were already collected as art by *c.* AD 1000, for the extensive library of the Buyid ruler Baha' al-Dawla (*reg* 998–1012) at Shiraz contained an incomplete 30-part Koran by the noted calligrapher. Other rulers elsewhere amassed collections of calligraphy and art: by the mid-11th century the treasuries of the Fatimid caliphs at Cairo, for example, contained many copies of the Koran written by such calligraphers as Ibn Muqla and his successor Ibn al-Bawwab, as well as many fine textiles, *objets d'art* and curiosities.

The collecting of illustrated manuscripts became particularly important in Iran, India and the Ottoman empire in the 15th and 16th centuries, where collecting paintings and manuscripts seems to have been deemed a standard princely attribute. The Timurid ruler Shahrukh, for example, marked with his seal one of the folios of an incomplete 14th-century copy (London, Nour priv. col.) of Rashid al-Din's *Jāmiʿ al-tawārīkh* ('Compendium of histories') and commissioned the contemporary historian Hafiz-i Abru to complete the manuscript. Shahrukh's son, the prince and bibliophile Baysunghur, is known to have acquired and commissioned many books with splendid calligraphy and illustrations for his library, as well as albums (e.g. *c.* 1430; Istanbul, Topkapı Pal. Lib., H. 2310) with specimens of calligraphy by well-known masters of the 14th century. A particularly fine copy of Nizami's *Khamsa* ('Five poems'; Istanbul, Topkapı Pal. Lib., H. 762), begun in the mid-15th century for the Timurid prince Babur, passed to several Turkoman princes, before passing, still unfinished, into the hands of a Safavid amir, for whom the last illustrations were added in the early 16th century.

Under the Safavids, interest in the history of calligraphy was complemented by a new interest in the history of book illustration in Iran, and albums containing fine specimens were assembled from the collections of important individuals and prefaced with essays by experts in the field (*see* ALBUM, §3). In 1564–5 the calligrapher MIR

SAYYID AHMAD, for example, prepared an album of calligraphy for the Safavid military commander Ghayb Beg by reviewing and inspecting tomes and calligraphic specimens. The Safavid amir Husayn Beg commissioned an album in which calligraphy was paired with painting on two-page spreads (1560; Istanbul, Topkapı Pal. Lib., H. 2151). Perhaps the most important of these albums was that prepared for Prince Bahram Mirza in 1544 by Dust Muhammad, the historian of painting and calligraphy (Istanbul, Topkapı Pal. Lib., H. 2154). Bahram Mirza's collection of Persian manuscript painting was apparently encyclopedic, for Dust Muhammad was able to select for inclusion in the album splendid examples of work by virtually every master from the 14th century to his own day. The Safavid royal collection apparently included the great Mongol copy of the *Shāhnāma* ('Book of kings'; dispersed, ex-Demotte priv. col.), for its format and some of its illustrations served as models for early Safavid books and paintings. Some manuscripts from the royal collections were given as gifts, such as the superbly illustrated and illuminated two-volume copy of the *Shāhnāma* made for Tahmasp (*reg* 1524–76), which was presented to the Ottoman sultan Selim II (*reg* 1566–74). Others were endowed to shrines, such as a superb copy of Farid al-Din 'Attar's *Manṭiq al-ṭayr* ('Conference of the birds'; see fig. 250), which 'Abbas I (*reg* 1588–1629) endowed to the Safavid dynastic shrine at ARDABIL, along with a collection of 1162 Chinese porcelains. The collecting of engraved metal

250. Library seal of 'Abbas (upper right) and statement of endowment (Arab. *waqf*; upper left) on *Men Gathering Wood and a Man Drowning*, 185×130 mm; illustration from Farid al-Din 'Attar: *Manṭiq al-ṭayr* ('Conference of the birds'), from Herat, 1483 (New York, Metropolitan Museum of Art, 63.210.44, fol. 44*r*)

wares also seems to have been important in Iran, as examples of 14th-century Iranian metalwork bear the names of as many as five later owners.

The Mughal emperors of India were avid collectors. Many of the works in the Timurid library, such as the copy of Firdawsi's *Shāhnāma* (London, Royal Asiat. Soc., MS. 239) made for the Timurid prince Muhammad Juki and the copy (Baltimore, MD, Johns Hopkins U., Garrett Lib.) of the *Ẓafarnāma* ('Book of victory') made for Sultan Husayn Bayqara, eventually passed to the Mughals, who traced their descent from the Timurids and often inscribed their names on the flyleaves of important luxury books immediately after their accession. The Mughal imperial collections also contained fine luxury wares, such as antique and contemporary Chinese porcelains and Timurid *objets d'art*. The most famous example is a white jade jug (Lisbon, Mus. Gulbenkian; see fig. 239 above) made for Ulughbeg (*reg* 1447–9), which was proudly inscribed with the names of the Mughal emperors Jahangir in 1613–14 and Shah Jahan in 1646–7.

The Ottoman sultans were also keen collectors. Mehmed II actively collected illustrated books and albums, some of which were apparently taken from the Aqqoyunlu library at Tabriz. Mehmed also stipulated that books should form part of the ransom for the Aqqoyunlu prince Yusufça Mirza, captured in 1472. The rich booty captured when Mehmed defeated the Aqqoyunlu ruler Uzun Hasan (*reg* 1453–78) in 1473 may have included the specimens of painting and calligraphy now mounted in several albums (Istanbul, Topkapı Pal. Lib., H. 2152, H. 2153 and H. 2160). Mehmed's taste also ran to Florentine engravings and Italian portrait medals, but the taste of his son Bayezid II was more traditional, and he sold most of his father's collection for the benefit of the great mosque he established in Istanbul in 1505. Bayezid collected manuscripts and catalogued the royal library. A copy of Ibn Bakhtishu's *Manāfi' al-ḥayawān* ('Benefits of animals'; 1297 or 1299; New York, Pierpont Morgan Lib., MS. M 500) bears Bayezid's seal. After the Battle of Chaldiran in 1514, works of art were seized as booty from the Safavids, including manuscripts and several jade objects, and they entered the palace collection.

There is little evidence, however, that later Ottomans perused these works of art: Ahmed I (*reg* 1603–17), for example, is the only sultan known to have looked at the albums associated with Mehmed, and Mehmed Arif, keeper of guns in the imperial armoury, is the only person known to have read the *Shāhnāma* made for Tahmasp and presented to Selim, for he wrote synopses of the stories on the sheets protecting the paintings in 1801. As the Ottoman empire persisted into the 20th century, the imperial collections have largely survived intact at Topkapı Palace in Istanbul, although some items were removed and eventually sold on the market. The Tahmasp *Shāhnāma*, for example, was acquired in 1903 by Edmond de Rothschild, whose heirs eventually sold it to the American collector Arthur A. Houghton jr, who had the manuscript dismembered and its folios sold separately.

In the 19th century, although the centre for the collecting of Islamic art moved to Europe, individuals in several areas of the Islamic lands continued to collect Islamic works of art. The Qajar rulers of Iran maintained the royal library in Tehran, although individual manuscripts, such as the great Mongol *Shāhnāma*, were removed from the collection *c.* 1900. In the Ottoman capital at Istanbul, Isma'il Ghalib (1848–95), son of the grand vizier Ibrahim Edhem Pasha and brother of Osman Hamdi, director of the Imperial Museum, assembled an important collection of coins, which the imperial mint bought after his death. In Egypt, Mustafa Fadil, the brother of Khedive Isma'il (*reg* 1863–79), collected Persian manuscripts. These eventually became part of the national collection, which includes such works as a splendid copy of Sa'di's *Būstān* ('Orchard'; 1488; Cairo, N. Lib., Adab Farsi 22) with calligraphy by Sultan 'Ali Mashhadi and illustrations by Bihzad. The physician 'Ali Ibrahim collected rugs and ceramics, which form the core of the Museum of Islamic Art, Cairo.

Collectors from the Islamic lands have entered the international market with increasing prominence in the second half of the 20th century. With the rising revenues from oil and development in many areas of the Middle East, the collecting of Islamic art has flourished, and many private collections have been established in Iran, Kuwait, Saudi Arabia and elsewhere. The most encyclopedic is that begun in the mid-1970s by Nasser Sabah al-Ahmad al-Sabah and his wife Hussa, much of which has been housed in the Museum of Islamic Art, Kuwait City. An extensive collection, particularly of Turkish metalwork, has been amassed by the Koç family (Istanbul, Sadberk Hanım Mus.).

BIBLIOGRAPHY

J. Alsop: *The Rare Art Traditions: The History of Art Collecting and its Linked Phenomena* (Princeton and New York, 1982)
A. S. Melikian-Chirvani: *Islamic Metalwork from the Iranian World, 8th–18th Centuries*, London, V&A cat. (London, 1982)
J. Raby: 'East and West in Mehmed the Conqueror's Library', *Bull. Biblioph.*, iii (1987), pp. 297–321
——: 'Pride and Prejudice: Mehmed the Conqueror and the Italian Portrait Medal', *Stud. Hist. A.*, xxi (1987), pp. 171–94
W. M. Thackston: *A Century of Princes* (Cambridge, MA, 1989), pp. 335–56
S. Markel: 'Fit for an Emperor: Inscribed Works of Decorative Art Acquired by the Great Mughals', *Orientations*, xxi/8 (1990), pp. 22–36
Islamic Art and Patronage: Treasures from Kuwait (exh. cat., ed. E. Atıl; Baltimore, MD, Walters A.G.; Fort Worth, TX, Kimbell A. Mus.; St Louis, MO, A. Mus. and elsewhere, 1990–92)
S. S. Blair and J. M. Bloom: 'Epic Images and Contemporary History: The Legacy of the Great Mongol *Shahnama*', *Islam. A.*, v (in preparation)

JONATHAN M. BLOOM

2. EUROPE AND NORTH AMERICA. The thoroughness with which Islamic artefacts have been collected by Europeans is understandable in light of the collaboration that has emerged between individual endeavour and state institutions since the 17th century. Before this, church treasuries and princely collections contained only a small number of items, acquired as spoils or gifts. The Treasury of S Marco in Venice, for example, contains several Islamic rock crystals and glass objects (*see* GLASS, colour pl. V, fig. 2) acquired during the Crusades, and Eleanor of Castile (*d* 1290) received 56 pieces of Málaga lustreware in 1289. With the formation of the British, Dutch and French trading companies in the 17th century and the emergence of national museums in the 18th, this situation altered. During the 19th century, in an atmosphere of colonial expansion, the Islamic arts were gradually re-evaluated

in Europe; by the early 20th century, amid much commercial speculation, their aesthetic qualities were widely recognized.

Manuscripts were sought in the 17th century primarily with the aim of recovering lost Classical texts or for scientific information. Arabic, Persian and Turkish texts were acquired at Istanbul and Aleppo, especially by the English Orientalist Edward Pococke (1604–91), the Dutch Orientalist Jacob Golius (1596–1667) and by Levinus Warner (1619–65), who was appointed Dutch Resident in Istanbul in 1654. Archbishop WILLIAM LAUD ensured that the ships of the British Levant and East India companies returned with manuscripts, and the Dutch East India Company fulfilled the same purpose in Holland. In France, Jean-Baptiste Colbert (*see* COLBERT, (1)) organized missions of acquisition and appealed to merchants and negotiators. Some collectors, such as the Habsburg emperor Rudolf II (*see* HABSBURG, §I(10)), recognized the quality of the Islamic arts of the book. Rembrandt owned Mughal paintings, perhaps for costume studies; these entered the collection of Nicolaas Witsen, burgomaster of Amsterdam, and were acquired in the 18th century by the Habsburg empress Maria-Theresa for Schönbrunn Palace, Vienna.

Textiles and pottery, including Safavid wares imitating Chinese blue-and-white, were also brought to Europe in the vessels of the trading companies. Sigismund III (*see* VASA, (2)), King of Poland, sent the Armenian Sefer Muratowicz to Kashan in 1601 to purchase carpets and tents. Objects of trade and utility, such as textiles and pottery, however, were not necessarily regarded as items for collectors' cabinets, where the typical objects were weapons, armour, bezoars, shells, hardstones and other curiosities.

The activities of the British East India Company in Bengal in the 18th century gave rise to a group of collectors, especially of manuscripts, in the circle associated with the governor-general Warren Hastings (1732–1818). Foremost among them was RICHARD JOHNSON, whose large collection of manuscripts and albums (London, BL, Orient. & India Office Lib.) was formed in such centres as Lucknow and Hyderabad. Many other individuals, such as Elijah Impey (*d* 1809), the Chief Justice of Bengal (1774–83), and Jonathan Scott, Hastings' Persian secretary, also collected. In the province of Avadh (Oudh), where Europeans of various nationalities came in contact with the Shi'ite nawabs, fortunes were made and collections easily formed; in addition to Johnson, for example, Jean Baptiste Gentil (1726–99), Claude Martin (1735–1800) and Antoine Polier (1741–95) made their acquisitions here. Most collectors were, however, Company employees, and as they returned home, their manuscripts appeared increasingly on the London market.

The political involvement of European nations in Egypt and Asia was accompanied by a growth of intellectual enquiry. In Calcutta in 1784, William Jones (1746–94) founded the Asiatic Society of Bengal, the first learned Orientalist society. Thereafter learned societies and institutions developed throughout Europe, and specialist libraries and museums were founded. Like the national collections of Europe, many of these were to become enlarged by the widespread removal of objects that accompanied 19th-century colonial expansion. The French invaded Egypt in 1798 and returned with numerous items. British forces at Seringapatam, India, acquired Tipu Sultan's library in 1799 and in later years removed manuscripts from Bijapur and Delhi. Precious manuscripts in the shrine at Ardabil in north-west Iran were removed by Russian forces in 1827. Only in the late 19th century, under the necessity of ensuring the survival of indigenous arts, was a more concerted effort made by colonial administrators to protect the cultural traditions under their control.

Individual travellers and diplomats contributed to this process of acquisition, particularly long-term residents. Heinrich Friedrich von Diez (1751–1817), plenipotentiary minister of Frederick the Great to Istanbul (1784–91), amassed many manuscripts including four albums containing 430 paintings, drawings and sketches. Ignored by 19th-century cataloguers because they contained no text, these albums only began to be fully appreciated in 1955. Gore Ouseley (1770–1844) and his brother William (1767–1842) acquired some of their manuscripts and paintings during a diplomatic mission (1811–14) to Iran. The collection of manuscripts, coins and antiquities formed when Claudius Rich (1787–1821) was ambassador at Baghdad was purchased for the British Museum with a Parliamentary grant in 1825.

The Romantic taste for the exotic resulted in a new breed of collectors more tolerant of non-European styles, such as WILLIAM BECKFORD, but it was in the context of design that Islamic art was at first re-evaluated, especially by OWEN JONES and his circle. This outlook was encouraged in the mid-19th century by the founding of the South Kensington (later Victoria and Albert) Museum, which

acquired a wide range of Islamic items. ROBERT MURDOCH SMITH, the director of the Persian Telegraph Department based in Tehran, offered his services in 1873 to supply the museum with Iranian artefacts. He made substantial purchases at low cost and acquired the collection of Jules Richard (1816–91), who had lived in Iran since the 1840s. First in Murdoch Smith's office, and later in the diplomatic service, Sidney Churchill (1862–1921) collected book covers and manuscripts and joined forces with Richard to search for artefacts. FREDERICK DUCANE GODMAN, who from c. 1865 specialized in ceramics, also acquired some of Richard's items. Meanwhile calligraphy, which was less easy for many Western collectors to appreciate, was acquired by Frederick Ayrton, who resided for 25 years in Cairo.

Algeria was accessible to collectors after the French invasion in 1830, and Tunisia after 1881, but the European presence in Morocco was slight until the French and Spanish occupation in the early 20th century. The intellectual interest in items from the Maghrib was primarily ethnographic. Some collectors, such as Prosper Ricard (1874–1952), held relevant positions in the colonial administration: as a French government official, he directed the preservation and documentation of indigenous arts.

Paris became the principal centre for collectors in the late 19th century. There was a steady growth of commercial dealing, and when Japanese items became harder to find, Islamic art seemed a viable option to which to turn. Exhibitions of Islamic art became more frequent after the Exposition Universelle of 1878, and important collections, such as those of Albert Goupil (1840–84; son of ADOLPHE GOUPIL), Charles Schéfer (1820–98), Hakky Bey and Octave Homberg, were sold on the market. The linear style of Safavid drawing, seen for example in the works of Riza, bore comparison with the stylistic tendencies of Art Nouveau artists, and jewellers such as HENRI VEVER became interested in the Islamic arts of the book. Edward Moore, President of Tiffany & Co. (see TIFFANY, §1), gave the first major collection of Islamic art to the Metropolitan Museum in New York in 1891. Influential dealers, many of whom were Armenian, advised collectors. Dikran Khan Kelekian, for example, introduced Henry Havemeyer (1847–1907) to Iranian ceramics and guided the taste of Henry Walters (see WALTERS, (2)). JACQUES DOUCET was attracted to Islamic art when he met the influential dealer Charles Vignier (1863–1934) in 1906. Scholar–collectors also emerged, notably FREDRIK MARTIN, FRIEDRICH SARRE and P. W. Schulz.

Persian and Indian carpets began to be collected in the 19th century and were perhaps the most popular aspect of Islamic art in America, attracting a broad spectrum of financiers, industrialists and other wealthy collectors, such as J. PIERPONT MORGAN and John D. Rockefeller jr (see ROCKEFELLER, (1)). The collection of fine Indian and Persian rugs and fragments belonging to BENJAMIN ALTMAN went to the Metropolitan Museum. James F. Ballard (1851–1931) of St Louis, MO, assembled one of the largest carpet collections in the USA; between 1922 and 1924 he gave 129 rugs to the Metropolitan Museum and many more to the St Louis Art Museum. The remainder of his collection was inherited and augmented by his daughters, Nellie Ballard White, most of whose collection also went

251. Ceramic fluted bowl with underglaze-painted decoration, diam. c. 220 mm, from Iran, 14th century (Ham, Surrey, Keir private collection)

to the St Louis Art Museum, and Bernice C. Ballard, whose collection was sold at Parke-Bernet in 1950. The extensive collection of antique Oriental carpets and fragments assembled by GEORGE HEWITT MYERS formed the basis of the Textile Museum in Washington, DC.

A wide range of collectors became interested in other aspects of Islamic art, from barons Edmond and Maurice de Rothschild and the financier CALOUSTE SARKIS GULBENKIAN to such connoisseurs as Henri d'Allemagne and Claude Anet. The British politician Leopold Amery acquired Qajar paintings before they became fashionable; his collection was later acquired by the Nigaristan Museum, Tehran. ALFRED CHESTER BEATTY, who began his career as a mining engineer, wintered in Egypt and formed a collection from c. 1920 to 1965 to represent the arts of the book. ALAN BARLOW, by contrast, concentrated on ceramics: his Islamic collection, formed largely between 1905 and 1926, initially emphasized wares from Iznik. GERALD REITLINGER formed his ceramic collection after journeys to KISH and Hira in 1930–32. The tradition of the scholar-collector has continued through the 20th century with Edwin Binney III (d 1986), much of whose collection passed to the San Diego Museum of Art and the Sackler Museum at Harvard University, and Abolala Soudavar, who has assembled the Art and History Trust Collection. Prince Sadruddin Aga Khan began his collection of Islamic art in the early 1950s. Edmund de Unger's Keir Collection (Ham, Surrey) embraces all aspects of Islamic art (see fig. 251), as does Nasser David Khalili's Nour Collection (London).

BIBLIOGRAPHY

J. T. Reinaud: *Monumens arabes, persans et turcs du cabinet de M. le duc de Blacas et d'autres cabinets* (Paris, 1828)
P. W. Schulz: *Die persisch-islamische Miniaturmalerei*, 2 vols (Leipzig, 1914)
G. Reitlinger: *The Economics of Taste*, 3 vols (London, 1961–70)
R. Lightbown: 'Oriental Art and the Orient in Late Renaissance and Baroque Italy', *J. Warb. & Court. Inst.*, xxxii (1969), pp. 228–79
M. H. Beattie: *The Thyssen-Bornemisza Collection of Oriental Carpets* (Castagnola, 1972)
T. J. Falk: *Qajar Paintings: Persian Oil Paintings of the 18th and 19th Centuries* (London, 1972) [the Amery Collection]
A. Welch: *Collection of Islamic Art, Prince Sadruddin Aga Khan*, 4 vols (Geneva, 1972–8)
E. Binney: *Turkish Miniature Paintings and Manuscripts from the Collection of Edwin Binney, 3rd* (New York, 1973)
R. Ettinghausen: 'The Impact of Muslim Decorative Arts and Painting on the Arts of Europe', *The Legacy of Islam*, ed. J. Schacht with C. E. Bosworth (Oxford, 1974), pp. 292–320
G. Fehérvári: *Islamic Metalwork of the Eighth to the Fifteenth Century in the Keir Collection* (London, 1976)
E. J. Grube: *Islamic Pottery of the Eighth to the Fifteenth Century in the Keir Collection* (London, 1976)
B. W. Robinson, ed.: *Islamic Painting and the Arts of the Book: The Keir Collection* (London, 1976)
Rothschild and Binney Collections: Persian and Mughal Art (exh. cat., ed. B. W. Robinson; London, Colnaghi's, 1976)
F. Spuhler: *Islamic Carpets and Textiles in the Keir Collection* (London, 1978)
S. C. Welch: 'Private Collectors and Islamic Arts of the Book', *Treasures of Islam* (exh. cat., ed. T. Falk; Geneva, Mus. A. & Hist., 1985), pp. 25–31
C. G. Ellis: *Oriental Carpets in the Philadelphia Museum of Art* (Philadelphia, 1988), pp. ix–xii
G. D. Lowry with S. Nemazee: *A Jeweler's Eye: Islamic Arts of the Book from the Vever Collection* (Washington, DC, 1988)
B. W. Robinson, ed.: *Islamic Art in the Keir Collection* (London and Boston, 1988)
J. Raby, ed.: *The Nasser D. Khalili Collection of Islamic Art* (London and Oxford, 1992–)

Art of the Persian Courts: Selections from the Art and History Trust Collection (exh. cat. by A. Soudavar, Los Angeles, CA, Co. Mus. A.; U. Chicago, IL, Smart Gal.; and Houston, TX, Menil Col., 1992–3)

XII. Museums.

Since the late 17th century, when the museum first emerged in Europe as a public institution, various types have been created and some have developed collections of Islamic art. As a result Islamic objects, particularly in the West, have been placed in several contexts depending on the purpose of the institution and the nature of the artefact. For example, libraries house many Islamic books and works on paper. Museums devoted entirely to the presentation of Islamic art, however, are still comparatively rare. By contrast, the idea of the 'national' museum, embracing a wide variety of items from many eras, has been more influential both in the West and in the Islamic lands.

1. Europe and North America. 2. Islamic lands.

1. EUROPE AND NORTH AMERICA. A few Islamic items were already present when the British Museum opened to the public in 1759 as the first major 'national' museum in Europe, and from the outset the museum contained a library, which accepted Oriental manuscripts. During the 19th century Islamic manuscripts began to enter the British Museum in greater numbers, and a Department of Oriental Manuscripts was formed in 1867. By 1913 a sub-Department of Oriental Prints and Drawings had also been established. Islamic artefacts entered the museum in increasing numbers from the late 19th century, especially after the Department of Oriental Antiquities was established in 1861, and the collection is one of the most comprehensive, with particular emphasis on the arts of the book, metalwork and ceramics. From 1973 the Department of Oriental Manuscripts and Printed Books became part of the British Library. In France, a 'national' museum was established in Paris in 1793 to contain treasures confiscated in the Revolution, but the collection of Islamic artefacts at the Louvre developed in particular under the direction of EMILE MOLINIER in the 1890s, and by 1906 a Department of Islamic Art had been created. The important collection, was, however, rarely displayed to the public until the new Islamic gallery was opened in 1993. The Bibliothèque Nationale in Paris also houses an important collection of manuscripts, coins and other Islamic objects.

Other types of repositories relevant for Islamic artefacts were established in Europe during the course of the 19th century. These ranged from the museums of learned Orientalist societies to those connected with trade and colonial activities. In 1801, for example, the library and museum of the East India Company opened in London, and manuscripts, albums, paintings, penboxes and other Islamic items were purchased or bequeathed to this collection. Plunder also arrived, most notably from the campaign against Tipu Sultan (reg 1782–99) at Seringapatam in 1799, which included his throne, weapons and a musical tiger. In 1880 the India Museum was incorporated in the South Kensington (now the Victoria and Albert)

Museum, and the library later became the India Office Library.

Museums of ethnography and particularly of 'applied' or 'industrial' art are two other types of museums established in Europe in the mid-19th century that developed collections of Islamic items. Following the Great Exhibition (1851) the South Kensington Museum (1857) promoted education in 'applied' art and design, and the museum is noted for its collections of Islamic textiles, ceramics, metalwork and other objects. Similar collections soon appeared throughout Europe: at Vienna (1863), and then at Berlin, Brno, Budapest, Dresden, Frankfurt, Hamburg, Kassel, Kiel and Leipzig. In Paris in the 1880s, the collection of the Musée des Arts Décoratifs developed after a lottery yielded to the Central Union of Decorative Arts about six million francs. With this money artefacts were purchased and a temporary home for them was established at the Palais de l'Industrie. The first Islamic items for the museum were acquired in 1886 at the Paris sale of the collection of Albert Goupil (1840–84).

The Islamic department of the Staatliche Museen in Berlin was, until World War II, at the forefront of enquiry into Islamic art. The cordial relationship between the German emperor William II and the Ottoman sultan Abdülhamid II (*reg* 1876–1909) led to the installation of the façade of the palace of Mshatta (see fig. 252) in the Kaiser-Friedrich-Museum, and, in 1904, the Islamische Kunstabteilung was founded on the initiative of WILHELM BODE. FRIEDRICH SARRE, who gave 400 items from his private collection in 1921, was director of the department until 1931. In 1932 the considerably enlarged collection was transferred to the newly constructed Pergamonmuseum. ERNST KÜHNEL remained in charge during World War II, when many of the portable objects in the collection were dispersed for safekeeping in Germany. The Mshatta façade and many of the fine carpets, however, were severely damaged by bombs. In 1954 those objects that had been stored in West Germany were exhibited in the new museum complex at Dahlem (West Berlin), while those temporarily removed from East Germany to the Soviet Union were again displayed in the Pergamonmuseum. Under KURT ERDMANN, who became director of the museum in Dahlem in 1958, Islamic items were purchased for the first time since the war. After German reunification the two halves of the collection were reunited administratively in 1992, although they are displayed separately pending the construction of a new exhibition space on Museum Island. The collection is extremely broad and is notable for its fine architectural fragments, many from German excavations in Iraq and Palestine, ceramics, woodwork, carpets, metal wares and ivories.

Other European museums with fine collections of Islamic art include the Hermitage in St Petersburg, notable for many Iranian and Turkish objects from the Russian imperial collections. Islamic objects in the Habsburg collection passed to the Kunsthistorisches Museum in Vienna. The Benaki Museum in Athens is distinguished for its collection of decorative arts, particularly from the Mediterranean Islamic lands. The Gulbenkian Museum in Lisbon has a particularly fine collection of Islamic ceramics as well as many splendid textiles, carpets, manuscripts and bindings. The Museo Nacional de Arte Hispanomusulmán was established by the scholar L. Torres Balbás in Granada. The Davids Samling in Copenhagen, housed in the residence of its founder, C. L. David, continues to expand its encyclopedic collection of Islamic decorative arts. The Institut du Monde Arabe in Paris, founded in 1980 to encourage the knowledge of Arab civilization and culture

252. Façade from the palace of Mshatta, 8th century AD (Berlin, Pergamonmuseum); restored

in France, has a museum in which objects from its own collection and other French public collections are exhibited. The Ashmolean Museum at Oxford has an important collection of Islamic ceramics and metal wares; the Bodleian Library has notable Islamic manuscripts, as does the John Rylands Library in Manchester.

In the United States, the Freer Gallery of Art in Washington, DC, has had a collection of Islamic ceramics since its foundation in 1923, but particularly under the curatorship (1944–67) of RICHARD ETTINGHAUSEN the collections were expanded to include many fine examples of metalwork and manuscripts. The superb collection was further enriched by the founding of the adjacent Sackler Gallery, which acquired in 1986 some 500 Islamic manuscripts, paintings, albums, bindings and calligraphic specimens from the collection of HENRI VEVER. These collections at the Freer and Sackler galleries are complemented by those of the Textile Museum, which houses the incomparable collection of Oriental carpets assembled by GEORGE HEWITT MYERS. In New York City the Metropolitan Museum of Art, founded in 1870 on the inspiration of the South Kensington Museum, added a Near Eastern Department in 1932 with MAURICE S. DIMAND as curator. Under Ettinghausen's curatorship (1969–79), splendid new exhibition galleries were opened and the most comprehensive collection of Islamic art in the United States put on permanent display. The New York Public Library has a fine collection of Islamic manuscripts, and the Brooklyn Museum has a good collection of artefacts, particularly ceramics. Other significant collections in the United States include those in Boston (Mus. F.A.), Cambridge, MA (Fogg and Sackler museums), Cleveland (Mus. A.), Philadelphia (U. PA, Mus.; Mus. A.), Los Angeles (Co. Mus. A.) and San Diego (Mus. A.).

2. ISLAMIC LANDS. The oldest museum in Asia is reputedly that of the Asiatic Society of Bengal, established in Calcutta in 1814. Now the Indian Museum, its scope was defined in 1814 as 'the illustration of Oriental manner and history, and to elucidate the peculiarities of art and nature in the East'. During the 19th century many other museums were created in India by British administrators, and many contain Islamic artefacts.

In the Islamic lands museums began to be established from the late 19th century. In Egypt, Khedive Isma'il (*reg* 1863–79) tried to counter the removal of architectural and artistic items to Europe by planning an Arab museum in 1869. The scheme was realized by his successor Tawfiq (*reg* 1879–92) in 1880, who created a museum to preserve valuable items from mosques and private collections, and the enterprise formed the nucleus of the present Museum of Islamic Art in Cairo. Julius Franz (1831–1915) of the Ministry of Awqaf (pious foundations) was entrusted with the organization, and the rescued items were first deposited in the eastern arcades of the mosque of al-Hakim. Ya'qub Artin (*d* 1916) and Edward Rogers (1831–84) helped to classify the objects. To oversee the affairs of the museum and related projects, a khedival decree instituted in 1881 created the Comité de Conservation des Monuments de l'Art Arabe. The collection grew quickly and was moved to a building constructed in 1883 in the courtyard of the

mosque of al-Hakim. In 1892 Max Herz (*b* 1856) was appointed director, and he wrote a catalogue and saw the collections open in new premises in 1903. From 1923 to 1951 GASTON WIET served as director. This museum did not have a monopoly on all items: Islamic manuscripts continued to be housed in the khedival library in Cairo, directed by the German Orientalist Bernhard Moritz (1859–1939) from 1896 to 1911.

In Turkey, Sultan Abdülhamid II established in 1877 the Imperial Ottoman Museum at the Çinili Kiosk at the Topkapı Palace. Under the directorship of OSMAN HAMDI from 1881 to 1910, an order against the traffic in antiquities was put into effect and excavations were organized. In 1891 the archaeological collection was opened to the public in a new building, and in later years annexes were built. After Abdülhamid was deposed in 1909, his collection at Yıldız Palace was moved back to the Topkapı Palace at the insistence of Hamdi's brother HALIL EDHEM, who became director of the Imperial Ottoman Museum on Hamdi's death. Following the declaration of the Turkish Republic in 1923, museums developed apace. In 1924 a decision was made to repair buildings at the Topkapı Palace and admit the public. An extraordinary range of Islamic art collected by the sultans is displayed there, including manuscripts, textiles, metal wares and *objets d'art*. Çinili Kiosk has become a museum devoted to Islamic ceramics. The Islamic museum at the Süleymaniye complex, which opened in 1914, was reopened in 1927 as the Museum of Turkish and Islamic Art (Türk ve Islam Eserleri Müzesi), now housed in the palace of IBRAHIM PAHA on the Atmeydanı. Museums were also established in many other centres, particularly after 1925, when a law closing dervish tekkes came into effect and valuable items they contained were moved to local museums. The Mevlana Museum in Konya, for example, opened in 1926. In 1928 the Museum of Ethnography, noted for its woodwork, was opened in Ankara. The ministry of pious endowments (Vakıflar) has also opened the Carpet Museum (1979) and the Kilim and Flat-Woven Rug Museum (1982) in Istanbul.

In Iran, museums were founded from the 1930s, the decade when exhibitions of Iranian art proliferated in Europe and the United States. The Ethnographical Museum was founded in Tehran in 1938, and the Archaeological (Iran Bastan) Museum in 1946. The latter contains a vast collection of pre-Islamic as well as Islamic items. In the 1970s several other museums opened in the city, including the Nigaristan Museum, specializing in the art of the Qajar period, the Riza 'Abbasi Museum for decorative arts, the Carpet Museum and the Museum of Glass and Ceramics. Other notable museums include the Imam Riza Shrine Museum in Mashhad, which contains a wealth of material donated to the shrine over the centuries.

In most other Islamic countries the creation of the nation state and the founding of museums have gone together. The National Museum in Damascus, founded in 1919 when the Ottoman sultan relinquished control over Syria, has a department of Arab–Islamic antiquities exhibiting finds from many sites, including the reconstructed façade from the palace at Qasr al-Hayr West. An archaeological museum was established in Baghdad, the capital of Iraq, in 1923, the same year that Turkey gave up its claim to rule there. Plans for an Iraqi national museum developed from 1932, the year in which the British mandate was terminated and Iraq became a sovereign state. The Iraq Museum in Baghdad, completed in 1963, contains material dating from the prehistoric period to the 19th century, and the Arab Museum houses a collection of Islamic antiquities from such sites as Samarra' and Wasit. In North Africa the Musée National du Bardo in Tunis, the Musée National des Antiquités in Algiers and the Musée des Antiquités in Rabat are the major depots for Islamic artefacts, although important items are to be found in museums of ethnography and smaller collections in provincial cities. The Museum of Islamic Art in Kuwait City (Dar al-Athar al-Islamiyya), containing the al-Sabah collection, opened in 1983, although the building was heavily damaged in the Gulf War (1991) and much of the collection was temporarily removed to Iraq.

In Jerusalem archaeological finds from excavations at such sites as Khirbat al-Mafjar are housed in the Rockefeller Museum, founded as the Palestine Archaeological Museum. The Islamic Museum of the Aqsa Mosque houses an incomparable collection of artefacts and documents relating to the Haram al-Sharif (Temple Mount in the Islamic period). The Mayer Memorial Institute for Islamic Art was founded by Mrs V. B. Salomons (d 1969) to honour the scholar L. A. Mayer (1895–1959), who had been professor of Islamic art and archaeology and rector of the Hebrew University. The collection, which was formed under Ettinghausen's direction, contains a broad range of Islamic art from many lands. Other Islamic objects, particularly paintings and manuscripts, are in the Israel Museum.

BIBLIOGRAPHY

EUROPE

M. Demaison: 'Le Musée des Arts Décoratifs', *Les Arts* [Paris], xlviii (1905), pp. 1–45

A. F. Kendrick: *Catalogue of Muhammadan Textiles of the Medieval Period, Victoria and Albert Museum* (London, 1924)

L. Binyon: *L'Art asiatique au British Museum: Sculpture et peinture*, A. Asiat., vi (Paris and Brussels, 1925)

E. Blochet: *Les Enluminures des manuscrits orientaux—turcs, arabes, persans—de la Bibliothèque Nationale* (Paris, 1926)

E. Kühnel: 'The Islamic Department of the Berlin Museum', *A. Islam.*, xv–xvi (1951), pp. 143–5

B. W. Robinson: *A Descriptive Catalogue of the Persian Paintings in the Bodleian Library* (Oxford, 1958)

A. J. Arberry and others: *The Chester Beatty Library: A Catalogue of the Persian Manuscripts and Miniatures*, 3 vols (Dublin, 1959–62)

Museum für Islamische Kunst, Berlin: Katalog, 1971 (Berlin, 1971)

Persian Art: Calouste Gulbenkian Collection (Lisbon, 1972)

Museu Calouste Gulbenkian (Lisbon, 1975) [checklist]

B. W. Robinson: *Persian Paintings in the India Office Library: A Descriptive Catalogue* (London, 1976)

N. M. Titley: *Miniatures from Persian Manuscripts: A Catalogue and Subject Index of Paintings from Persia, India and Turkey in the British Library and the British Museum* (London, 1977)

L'Islam dans les collections nationales (exh. cat., Paris, Grand Pal., 1977)

B. W. Robinson: *Persian Paintings in the John Rylands Library: A Descriptive Catalogue* (London, 1980)

N. M. Titley: *Miniatures from Turkish Manuscripts: A Catalogue and Subject Index of Paintings in the British Library and the British Museum* (London, 1981)

R. Desmond: *The India Museum, 1801–1879* (London, 1982)

A. S. Melikian-Chirvani: *Islamic Metalwork from the Iranian World, 8th–18th Centuries*, London, V&A cat. (London, 1982)

F. Déroche: *Les Manuscrits du Coran*, 2 of i/1 of *Bibliothèque Nationale, Département des Manuscrits: Catalogue des manuscrits arabes*, 2 vols (Paris, 1983–5)

D. Duda: *Die illuminierten Handschriften und Inkunabeln der österreichischen Nationalbibliothek: Islamische Handschriften I. Persiche Handschriften*, 2 vols (Vienna, 1983)

D. Haldane: *Islamic Bookbindings in the Victoria and Albert Museum* (London, 1983)

K. Brisch, ed.: *Islamische Kunst: Löseblattkatalog unpublizierter Werke aus deutschen Museen* (Mainz, 1984–)

F. Spuhler: *Die Orientteppiche im Museum für Islamische Kunst Berlin* (Berlin, 1987)

E. Anglade: *Musée du Louvre: Catalogue des boiseries de la section islamique* (Paris, 1988)

K. von Folsach: *Islamic Art: The David Collection* (Copenhagen, 1990)

N. Erzini: '"Moorish" Pottery in the Victoria and Albert Museum: The Contribution of George Maw of Maw and Co. to the Knowledge of Moroccan Ceramics in Britain', *Morocco*, iii (1993), pp. 57–72

NORTH AMERICA

N. P. Britton: *A Study of Some Early Islamic Textiles in the Museum of Fine Arts, Boston* (Boston, 1938)

E. Schroeder: *Persian Miniatures in the Fogg Museum of Art* (Cambridge, MA, 1942)

E. Kühnel and L. Bellinger: *The Textile Museum: Catalogue of Dated Tiraz Fabrics: Umayyad, Abbasid, Fatimid* (Washington, DC, 1952)

R. Ettinghausen: 'Almost One Hundred Years Ago', *Islamic Art in the Metropolitan Museum of Art*, ed. R. Ettinghausen (New York, 1972), pp. 1–8

M. S. Dimand and J. Mailey: *Oriental Rugs in the Metropolitan Museum of Art* (New York, 1973)

Ceramics from the World of Islam (exh. cat. by E. Atıl, Washington, DC, Freer, 1973)

P. Pal, ed.: *Islamic Art: The Nasli M. Heeramaneck Collection* (Los Angeles, 1974)

The Brush of the Masters: Drawings from Iran and India (exh. cat. by E. Atıl, Washington, DC, Freer, 1978)

M. S. Simpson: *Arab and Persian Painting in the Fogg Museum of Art* (Cambridge, MA, 1980)

E. Atıl, W. T. Chase and P. Jett: *Islamic Metalwork in the Freer Gallery of Art* (Washington, DC, 1985)

C. G. Ellis: *Oriental Carpets in the Philadelphia Museum of Art* (Philadelphia, 1988)

G. D. Lowry with S. Nemazee: *A Jeweler's Eye: Islamic Arts of the Book from the Vever Collection* (Washington, DC, 1988)

M. L. Swietochowski and S. Babaie: *Persian Drawings in the Metropolitan Museum of Art* (New York, 1989)

B. Schmitz: *Islamic Manuscripts in the New York Public Library* (New York and Oxford, 1992)

ISLAMIC LANDS

G. Wiet: *Catalogue général du Musée Arabe du Caire: Lampes et bouteilles en verre émaillé* (Cairo, 1929)

——: *Album du Musée Arabe du Caire* (Cairo, 1930)

J. David-Weill: *Catalogue général du Musée Arabe du Caire: Les Bois à épigraphes jusqu'à l'époque mamlouke* (Cairo, 1931)

E. Pauty: *Catalogue général du Musée Arabe du Caire: Les Bois sculptés jusqu'à l'époque ayyoubide* (Cairo, 1931)

G. Wiet: *Catalogue général du Musée Arabe du Caire: Objets en cuivre* (Cairo, 1932)

J. David-Weill: *Catalogue général du Musée Arabe du Caire: Les Bois à épigraphes depuis l'époque mamlouke* (Cairo, 1936)

M. Bahrami: *Iranian Art: Treasures from the Imperial Collections and Museums of Iran* (New York, 1949)

Moslem Art in the Fouad I University Museum (Cairo, 1950)

R. O. Arık: *L'Histoire et l'organisation des musées turcs* (Istanbul, 1953)

M. A. al-'Ush: *Musée National de Damas: Département des antiquités arabes islamiques* (Damascus, 1976)

S. R. Dar: *Repositories of Our Cultural Heritage: A Handbook of Museums in Pakistan, 1851–1979* (Lahore, 1979)

B. Balpınar and U. Hirsch: *Flatweaves of the Vakıflar Museum Istanbul* (Wesel, 1982)

M. Jenkins, ed.: *Islamic Art in the Kuwait National Museum* (London, 1983)

R. Milstein: *Islamic Painting in the Israel Museum* (Jerusalem, 1984)

F. Çağman and Z. Tanındı: *The Topkapı Saray Museum: The Albums and Illustrated Manuscripts*, trans. and ed. by J. M. Rogers (London and Boston, 1986)

H. Tezcan and S. Delibaş: *The Topkapı Saray Museum: Costumes, Embroideries and Other Textiles*, trans. and ed. by J. M. Rogers (London and Boston, 1986)

C. Köseoğlu: *The Topkapı Saray Museum: The Treasury*, trans. and ed. by J. M. Rogers (London, 1987)

K. Çiğ, S. Batur and C. Köseoğlu: *The Topkapı Saray Museum: Architecture: The Harem and Other Buildings*, trans. and ed. by J. M. Rogers (London and Boston, 1988).

D. M. Reid: 'Cultural Imperialism and Nationalism: The Struggle to Define and Control the Heritage of Arab Art in Egypt', *Int. J. Mid. E. Stud.*, xxiv (1992), pp. 57–76

XIII. Exhibitions.

The international exhibitions held in Europe from the mid-19th century onwards, beginning with the Great Exhibition of 1851 in London, encouraged an awareness of the aesthetic quality and commercial value of Islamic objects and were the forerunners of the public exhibitions of Islamic art that have flourished in the 20th century.

1. 19TH CENTURY. At first the interest in Islamic objects at the international exhibitions was primarily as manufactures, with the emphasis on technical skill and design quality, but this initial interest gradually developed into a greater appreciation of antiquarian and aesthetic values. All areas of the Islamic world, with or without a colonial status, were encouraged to contribute to these exhibitions by sending products. At the Exposition Universelle in Paris in 1867, the notable Turkish contribution was made all the more significant by the presence of Sultan Abdülaziz (*reg* 1861–76), the first Ottoman sultan to visit western Europe. In 1873 the Weltausstellung at Vienna was attended by the Qajar monarch Nasir al-Din (*reg* 1848–96); this was the first visit of an Iranian monarch to Europe.

Iranian objects were increasingly esteemed. In 1876 the South Kensington (later the Victoria and Albert) Museum in London arranged an Exhibition of Persian Art, which displayed items recently acquired for its collection through the activities of ROBERT MURDOCH SMITH, the director of the Persian Telegraph Department, based in Tehran. Although this exhibition still emphasized Islamic objects as manufactures in accordance with the philosophy of art prevailing at the museum, it was nevertheless significant for highlighting the artistic achievement of a specific Islamic nation. By the time of the Exposition Universelle in Paris in 1878, the usual national pavilions and displays were supplemented by a range of Islamic objects belonging to such European collectors as PHILIPPE BURTY, Albert Goupil (1840–84), JULES JACQUEMART, EUGÈNE PIOT and Charles Schéfer (1820–98). The exhibition was therefore important for encouraging the connoisseurship of Islamic art in Europe and indicates the extent to which it had already begun to develop.

Persian and Arab Art, an exhibition of more than 600 items held at the Burlington Fine Arts Club, London, in 1885, gathered for the first time objects belonging to a large number of private collectors in Britain. It emphasized ceramics, and enthusiasm was again directed towards the arts of Iran. As HENRY WALLIS stated in the catalogue, the aim was 'to illustrate the more important phases of the art of Persia, and its effluent arts of Damascus and Rhodes', a reference to the supposed origins of Ottoman ceramics. The first exhibition in Paris devoted solely to Islamic art was the Exposition d'Art Musulman, held in 1893 at the Palais de l'Industrie. Organized by Georges Marye, keeper

of the Musée d'Alger, the exhibition was the largest presentation of Islamic objects to date, with 2500 items on display. It was accompanied by a display of work from the Peintres Orientalistes Français and was visited by the young Henri Matisse. In Vienna an exhibition of Oriental pile carpets was held as early as 1880, and this interest continued: in 1891 the city hosted an exhibition of carpets at the Handelsmuseum, and in 1901 there was an important exhibition of book paintings at the Hofbibliothek. Elsewhere in Europe, scholars of Islamic art began to exhibit items from their own collections: FREDRIK MARTIN at Stockholm in 1897, FRIEDRICH SARRE at the Königliches Kunstgewerbemuseum, Berlin, in 1899 and P. W. Schulz at the Kunstgewerbemuseum, Leipzig, in 1900.

2. 20TH CENTURY. The turning-point for the connoisseurship of Islamic art came in Paris in 1903 with the Exposition des Arts Musulmans, organized by Gaston Migeon (1861–1930) and Raymond Koechlin (1860–1931) at the Union Centrale des Arts Décoratifs. The exhibition comprised a wide range of items of extremely high quality lent by a large number of collectors. A high level of erudition was attained, as MAX VAN BERCHEM read the Arabic inscriptions and Clément Huart (1854–1926), Professor at the Ecole des Langues Orientales, the Persian ones. Four years later a smaller exhibition of paintings and textiles was held at the Musée des Arts Décoratifs.

The great Munich exhibition (May–October 1910), which brought together Islamic objects from collections in Germany, France, Britain, Spain, Turkey, Egypt and Russia, demonstrated the extensive interest in Islamic art among German scholars. The ulterior motive for the exhibition was the passion play produced once every decade in Oberammergau. As an exhibition of Islamic art, the Munich exhibition was larger than any yet held, with 3555 works of art and sections on trade and music. Organized by Sarre and Martin, it was commemorated by a large catalogue, *Die Ausstellung von Meisterwerken muhammedanischer Kunst*, although only a small format handlist accompanied the exhibition. In Britain, interest in Islamic art was more muted than on the Continent, and ceramics continued to preoccupy collectors, as indicated by the exhibition at the Burlington Fine Arts Club in 1907. By comparison, interest in the Islamic arts of the book was greatest in France, where an exhibition held at the Musée des Arts Décoratifs from June to October 1912 was devoted to this field alone. An appeal was made to Parisian collectors, and more than 500 items were assembled, including paintings, manuscripts and bookbindings dating from the 12th to the 17th century. With the outbreak of World War I the enthusiasm among European scholars and connoisseurs of Islamic art was temporarily checked.

In the United States, where collectors had considerable purchasing power, interest in Islamic art had begun to develop even before war broke out. For example, an exhibition of Persian and Indian manuscripts and paintings was held in 1914 at the Boston Museum of Fine Arts. Exhibitions of Oriental carpets were arranged at the Metropolitan Museum of Art in New York in 1910 and 1921. The collector James F. Ballard (1851–1931) of St Louis lent 69 of his carpets to the 1921 exhibition, and the following year he presented the Metropolitan Museum with 126 carpets, which constituted the finest part of his collection.

The 1920s were years of economic and political recovery in Europe, and few exhibitions of Islamic art were held. In 1921 European and Oriental manuscripts belonging to the American collector ALFRED CHESTER BEATTY were exhibited at Baroda House, his London home. In 1925 Martin's collection was exhibited at the Victoria and Albert Museum, while the Exposition d'Art Oriental, Chine—Japon—Perse in Paris presented objects from private collections. By the 1930s exhibitions of Islamic art had gathered momentum again, and during this decade a great number were held throughout the world, with the arts of Iran still emphasized. The large Exhibition of Persian Art at Burlington House, London, in 1931 set the standard for those that followed: the Exposition d'Art Persan in Cairo in 1934–5, the Leningrad exhibition of 1935, the Paris exhibition of Iranian art in 1938, and Six Thousand Years of Persian Art organized by ARTHUR UPHAM POPE for the Iranian Institute, New York, in 1940. There were also many smaller exhibitions: in 1930 at Detroit; in 1935 at Toledo, OH, Brooklyn, NY, and Warsaw; in 1936 at Zurich and in 1937 at San Francisco, the first exhibition of Islamic art on the west coast of the United States. Turkish art began to be exhibited more frequently, perhaps justified by the emergence of the new Turkish state out of the old Ottoman empire. Turkish art was exhibited at Vienna in 1932, at the New York World's Fair in 1939, and at Splendeur de l'Art Turk at the Musée des Arts Décoratifs, Paris, in 1953.

The devastation of World War II made another period of recovery necessary before momentum could gather again. Items from the Berlin Museum that had been deposited in the salt mine of Grasleben to escape destruction were exhibited at Celle in the Province of Hannover in April 1947. The break-up of the old colonial empires also inspired exhibitions: the granting of independence to India, for example, was marked in Britain by The Art of India and Pakistan at the Royal Academy, London, 1947–8, which included Islamic objects from collections in India, Pakistan, Britain, France and the United States. Political considerations also lay behind other exhibitions, such as the exhibition of Syrian art at the Hermitage, Leningrad (now St Petersburg), in 1957.

Exhibitions had already served to present the national heritages of Iran and Turkey, and this trend continued with 5000 Years of Egyptian Art, held at the Royal Academy, London, in 1962, and 7000 Years of Iranian Art, held in eight American cities in 1964–5. These exhibitions and other similar ones consciously stressed the national histories of specific areas of the Islamic world and embraced pre-Islamic as well as Islamic objects. This approach has continued: In the Image of Man, held at the Hayward Gallery, London, in 1982, for example, presented 'the Indian perception of the Universe through 2000 years of painting and sculpture'.

In more recent decades, however, the nationalist approach has sometimes been countered by a greater appreciation of the unity of the Islamic heritage across national boundaries. The Arts of Islam, held at the Hayward Gallery, London, in 1976, was a comprehensive presentation of Islamic art equal in scope to the Munich exhibition

of 1910. Treasures of Islam, held in Geneva in 1985, also encouraged a broad view of Islamic culture, albeit with an emphasis on Iranian book painting. There has also been increased interest in contemporary Islamic art and calligraphy.

In the later years of the 20th century exhibitions of Islamic art have focused on particular rulers, dynasties and periods, and many have benefited from the involvement of Islamic nations as lenders. Shah 'Abbas & the Arts of Isfahan documented the art and architecture of 17th-century Iran. Wonders of the Age (1979) focused on manuscript painting between 1501 and 1576 under the early Safavid rulers of Iran; its exhibition schedule, however, was curtailed by the Iranian Revolution. Renaissance of Islam: Art of the Mamluks, which travelled through the United States, focusing on the various arts of Egypt and Syria between the 13th and 16th centuries, was enriched by loans from Egypt and Europe. The Age of Sultan Süleyman the Magnificent, which travelled in the United States and Europe during 1987–8, drew on the extensive collections of the Topkapı Palace in Istanbul to illustrate the sumptuous arts produced during the reign of this 16th-century monarch. Shortly after, Timur and the Princely Vision brought together from around the world fine objects from 15th-century Iran.

International politics have played an increasingly important role. For example, 120 objects from the extensive collection of Islamic art in the Hermitage were exhibited at the Museum of Islamic Art, Kuwait City, in 1990, and a similar group of objects from the al-Sabah collection on loan to the Kuwait National Museum were exhibited in Leningrad (now St Petersburg). As the al-Sabah pieces were abroad, they escaped damage during the Iraqi occupation of Kuwait (1990–91) and were available for the exhibition Islamic Art & Patronage: Treasures from Kuwait, which travelled extensively in the United States and in France.

BIBLIOGRAPHY

Illustrated Catalogue of Persian and Arab Art, Exhibited in 1885 (exh. cat., ed. H. Wallis; London, Burlington F.A. Club, 1885)
F. Sarre and F. R. Martin: Die Ausstellung von Meisterwerken muhammedanischer Kunst, 4 vols (Munich, 1911–12)
G. Marteau and H. Vever: Miniatures persanes exposées au Musée des arts décoratifs, 2 vols (Paris, 1913)
Catalogue of the International Exhibition of Persian Art (exh. cat., London, RA, 1931)
Persian Art: An Illustrated Souvenir of the Exhibition of Persian Art at Burlington House (exh. cat., London, RA, 1931)
L. Binyon, J. V. S. Wilkinson and B. Gray: Persian Miniature Painting (London, 1933/R New York, 1971)
Guide to the Exhibition of Persian Art (exh. cat., ed. P. Ackerman; New York, Iran. Inst., 1940)
L. Ashton, ed.: The Art of India and Pakistan: A Commemorative Catalogue of the Exhibition Held at the Royal Academy of Arts, London, 1947–8 (London, 1949)
Shah 'Abbas & the Arts of Isfahan (exh. cat. by A. Welch, New York, Asia Soc. Gals, and Cambridge, MA, Fogg, 1973–4)
The Arts of Islam (exh. cat., London, Hayward Gal., 1976)
Carpets of Central Persia (exh. cat., ed. M. H. Beattie; Sheffield, Mappin A.G.; Birmingham, Mus. & A.G., 1976)
The Qur'ān (exh. cat. by M. Lings and Y. H. Safadi, London, BM, 1976)
Wonders of the Age: Masterpieces of Early Safavid Painting, 1501–1576 (exh. cat. by S. C. Welch, London, BL; Washington, DC, N.G.A.; Cambridge, MA, Fogg, 1979–80)
Renaissance of Islam: Art of the Mamluks (exh. cat. by E. Atıl, Washington, DC, N. Mus. Nat. Hist.; Minneapolis, MN, Inst. A.; New York, Met., and elsewhere, 1981)

The Anatolian Civilisations III: Seljuk/Ottoman (exh. cat., 18th Council of Europe exh.; Istanbul, 1983)

Islamic Art & Design, 1500–1700 (exh. cat. by J. M. Rogers, London, BM, 1983)

Treasures of Islam (exh. cat., ed. T. Falk; Geneva, Mus. A. & Hist., 1985)

The Age of Sultan Süleyman the Magnificent (exh. cat. by E. Atil, Washington, DC, N.G.A.; Chicago, IL, A. Inst., and New York, Met., 1987–8)

Süleyman the Magnificent (exh. cat. by J. M. Rogers and R. M. Ward, London, BM, 1988)

Timur and the Princely Vision: Persian Art and Culture in the Fifteenth Century (exh. cat. by T. W. Lentz and G. D. Lowry, Washington, DC, Sackler Gal., and Los Angeles, CA, Co. Mus. A., 1989)

Islamic Art & Patronage: Treasures from Kuwait (exh. cat., ed. E. Atil; Washington, DC, Trust Mus. Exh., 1990–91)

Masterpieces of Islamic Art in the Hermitage Museum (exh. cat., Kuwait City, Mus. Islam. A., 1990)

Images of Paradise in Islamic Art (exh. cat., ed. S. S. Blair and J. M. Bloom; Hanover, NH, Dartmouth Coll., Hood Mus. A.; New York, Asia Soc. Gals; Brunswick, ME, Bowdoin Coll. Mus. A., and elsewhere, 1991–2)

Z. Çelik: *Displaying the Orient: Architecture of Islam at Nineteenth-century World's Fairs* (Berkeley, Los Angeles and Oxford, 1992)

Eredità dell'Islam (exh. cat., ed. G. Curatola; Venice, Doge's Pal., 1993)

S. J. VERNOIT

Isma'il Jalayir [Ismāʿīl Jalāyīr] (*fl c.* 1860–70). Iranian painter. The son of Hajji Muhammad Zaman Khan Jalayir of Khurasan, Isma'il Jalayir trained in the 1860s at the Dar al-Funun, the college founded in Tehran by the Qajar monarch Nasir al-Din (*reg* 1848–96). The artist worked in a variety of media including oil, miniature, grisaille and varnished paint ('lacquer'; *see* ISLAMIC ART, §VIII, 10). In addition to portraits, his subjects ranged from Christian scenes, such as the *Sacrifice of Isaac* (ex-Schulz priv. col., see Schulz, i, pl. F), to depictions of historical events. In 1861 he added a battle scene of the Qajar ruler Muhammad (*reg* 1834–48) to a varnished penbox (sold London, Sotheby's, 1978) decorated some two decades earlier by MUHAMMAD HASAN AFSHAR with scenes of the Last Judgement. Isma'il Jalayir was a favourite of Nasir al-Din and painted a fine portrait of him (1862–3; Tehran, Mus. Dec. A.). The artist's work is Europeanized on the surface, as in a painting of a group of ladies drinking tea from a samovar in a garden pavilion (London, V&A, P.56–1941), but maintains the traditions of Persian painting and is often tinged with gentle melancholy. Isma'il Jalayir committed suicide at a young age.

BIBLIOGRAPHY
P. W. Schulz: *Die persisch-islamische Miniaturmalerei* (Leipzig, 1914)

B. W. Robinson: 'Persian Painting in the Qajar Period', *Highlights of Persian Art*, ed. R. Ettinghausen and E. Yarshater (Boulder, 1979), pp. 331–62

M. A. Karimzada Tabrizi: *Ahvāl āthār-i naqqāshān-i qadīm-i īrān* [The lives and art of old painters of Iran] (London, 1985), no. 131

B. W. Robinson: 'Qajar Lacquer', *Muqarnas*, vi (1989), pp. 131–46

——: 'Persian Painting under the Zand and Qājār Dynasties', *From Nadir Shah to the Islamic Republic*, vii of *The Cambridge History of Iran* (Cambridge, 1991), pp. 870–90

Isoda Koryūsai [Haruhiro] (*fl* 1765–80s). Japanese painter and woodblock-print designer. He was active during the Edo period (1600–1868) and is said to have been born into the samurai class. His use of the art name (*gō*) Haruhiro around 1766–7 has led some scholars to conjecture that he was a pupil of Suzuki Harunobu, but there is no decisive evidence for this. Koryūsai principally created *ukiyoe* ('pictures of the floating world'; *see* JAPAN, §VI, 4(iii)(b)), which frequently depicted scenes from the

pleasure quarters of the large cities. He was important in Edo (now Tokyo) for his contribution to the development, started by Harunobu, of *nishikie* ('brocade prints'; polychrome prints resembling cloth woven in colours). He is known for depictions of beautiful women (*bijinga*), for example the *First Designs of the Young Leaves, in Pattern Form* series (*Hinagata wakana no hatsu moyō*; woodblock prints; *c.* late 1770s; e.g. New York, Met.; see fig.), in which young courtesans (the 'young leaves' of the title) are shown wearing the latest fashions (*see also* JAPAN, §IX, 2(iii)(b) and fig. 168). His images bear some resemblance to those of Harunobu, but his frequent use of the reddish colour known as *tan* is a distinctive feature, and his figures are perhaps more worldly. In the *First Designs* series, the beauties are depicted on a larger scale and are more decoratively attired than the women designed by Harunobu.

Koryūsai also designed many bird-and-flower compositions (*kachōga*), such as *Crow and Heron in the Snow* (*c.* 1770s; Tokyo, Riccar A. Mus.), and produced at least 250 of the long, narrow prints known as *hashirae* ('pillar prints'), for example *Beauty and Monkey* (*Bijin to saru*; see Kikuchi, 1968, pl. 16), in which a mischievous monkey is shown playfully pulling at a girl's kimono. The girl's body is partially cropped, almost as if she is leaving the scene, and the rest of her twists back to look down at the monkey.

Isoda Koryūsai: *Nanakoshi of the Ogiya*, woodblock print, 387×266 mm; from his series *First Designs of the Young Leaves, in Pattern Form*, *c.* late 1770s (New York, Metropolitan Museum of Art)

Other *hashirae* employ this element of cropping or cutting off, which emphasizes the format and heightens the sense of a moment frozen in time. In his later years, Koryūsai devoted himself to brush paintings, in which the stylistic influence of the Kanō school is noticeable. In 1781 he received the honorary religious rank of *hokkyō* (Bridge of the Law), an unusual official reward for a *ukiyoe* artist.

BIBLIOGRAPHY
S. Kikuchi: *Ukiyoe* [Pictures of the floating world], Genshoku Nihon no bijutsu [Arts of Japan, illustrated], xvii (Tokyo, 1968, 2/1977)
L. P. Roberts: *A Dictionary of Japanese Artists: Painting, Sculpture, Ceramics, Prints, Lacquer* (Tokyo and New York, 1976/R 1980)
R. Neurer, H. Libertson and S. Yoshida: *Ukiyo-e: 250 Years of Japanese Art* (New York, 1979)

BRENDA G. JORDAN

Isola Bella [formerly Isola di San Vittore]. Island in Lake Maggiore, northern Italy, the principal of three islands near Stresa known as the Isole Borromeo, where the 17th-century Palazzo Borromeo was built; this is a significant example of the harmonious integration of architecture, sculpture and garden design in the Baroque style. Before the 17th century the island was a barren rock with a few cottages and a church, inhabited only by poor fishermen. Count Carlo III Borromeo (1586–1652) initiated a grand project of building and landscaping in 1632 and renamed the island Isabella (later corrupted to Isola Bella) in honour of his wife Isabella d'Adda. Carlo's scheme was finished under his sons Vitaliano Borromeo and Cardinal Giberto Borromeo (1615–72), Vitaliano taking over most of the supervision of the project. Several artists collaborated on the scheme; Angelo Crivelli (*d* 1630), who conceived the original plan for the gardens and palace, Francesco Maria Ricchini, Francesco Castelli (1655–*c*. 1692), Gian Andrea Biffi and Carlo Fontana, who was brought from Rome in 1688. Additions were made to the building in the 18th and 19th centuries, and the north façade was completed only in 1959.

The design incorporates terraces rising to the palazzo (see fig.), which is four storeys high in the central block and three in the lateral wings. In the courtyard of the palace stands the chapel, designed in 1790 by Giuseppe Zanoia (1747–1817) and built in 1840; it contains fine tombs by Giovanni Antonio Amadeo and Agostino Busti, including parts of Busti's tomb of *Gian Marco and Zenone Birago* (1522), which were brought in 1796 from the church of S Francesco Grande in Milan. In the basement of the palace are artificial grottoes. The interior of the palace is furnished with fine pieces of furniture and hung with numerous paintings. The ballroom (1794–5), designed by Zanoia, is decorated with frescoes by Giambattista Tiepolo. Elsewhere are works by Annibale Carracci, Francesco Bianchi (*fl* 1506–10), Luca Giordano, Giovanni Battista Crespi and Bernardino Campi. There are also numerous views by Pieter Mulier (1637–1701), portraits by Cesare Tallone and views by Francesco Zuccarelli and

Isola Bella, Palazzo Borromeo, begun 1632

Giovanni Paolo Panini. The palazzo also contains a fine collection of 16th-century English tapestries, and there are 17th-century Flemish tapestries in the Salone degli Arazzi.

The garden was created at the same time as the house and is one of the finest examples of Italian Baroque gardens. It rises in ten terraces—the lowest built over piles thrown out into the lake—which are decorated with statues, vases, arches and fountains, all in an ornate style, together with a wide variety of rare and exotic plants. The sculptors Carlo Simonetta (*d* 1693) and Resnati were commissioned to embellish the gardens with statues. The famous Teatro Massimo was built on the final terrace, with a backdrop in stone embellished with the coats of arms of the Borromeo family. The palace now incorporates the Museo Borromeo.

BIBLIOGRAPHY
M. Ferrero Viale: 'Quelques nouvelles données sur les tapisseries de l'Isola Bella', *Bull. Mus. Royaux A. & Hist.*, xlv (1973), pp. 77–142
A. Ferrari-Bravo, ed.: *Lombardia (esclusa Milano)*, Guida Italia TCI (Milan, 1987), pp. 233–4

□

Isoya Yoshida. *See* YOSHIDA, ISOYA.

Isozaki, Arata (*b* Oita, 23 July 1931). Japanese architect, teacher and theorist. One of the leading architects of his generation, he became an influential proponent of the avant-garde conceptual approach to architecture that characterized the New Wave in Japan in the 1970s and after (*see* JAPAN, §III, 5(iii)(b)). He studied at the University of Tokyo under Kenzō Tange and after graduating (1954) he worked for Kenzō Tange & Urtec until 1963. From 1960 Isozaki began to develop his own practice, first as an architectural designer, completing the Ōita Medical Center (1960) and Ōita Prefectural Library (1966), and then as a theorist, loosely associated with Japanese Metabolism and creating such ironic projects as his 'Ruin Future City' and 'Clusters in the Air' (both 1962). His first large public commission was the Ōita branch of the Fukuoka Mutual Bank, completed in 1967. Other important public works followed in relatively rapid succession, and he quickly established his reputation with such buildings as the Gunma Prefectural Museum of Modern Art (1971–4), Takasaki; the Kitakyushu City Museum of Art (1972–4); the Kitakyushu Municipal Central Library (1972–5); and the West Japan General Exhibition Center (1977), Kitakyushu.

Isozaki took a critical position towards the Functionalist line in the Modern Movement, irrespective of whether this was expressed in the *wakonyosai* reinforced-concrete architecture of Tange or the visionary projects of the Metabolists. He favoured instead a conceptual approach that would bestow upon architecture an independent cultural significance. In pursuit of this goal, Isozaki attempted to evolve his own *maniera*, which was predicated as much on a subtle reinterpretation of Japanese culture as on the legacy of Japanese Modernism. His approach was initially inspired by the ironic observations of the Japanese novelist Jun'ichiro Tanizaki (1886–1965), who wrote a witty and perceptive elegy on the passing of the Japanese tradition in his famous text *In'ei raisan* ('In praise of shadows'; 1933–4). In *Yami no kukan* ('Spaces of darkness'; 1964), a paradoxical updating of this essay,

Isozaki not only responded to Tanizaki's nostalgia but also formulated an alternative technological aesthetic that he dubbed 'twilight gloom'. He went on to combine this highly illusory, gridded, atectonic treatment of mass and space—first evident as a discernible mode in the small bank buildings he designed for the Fukuoka Mutual Bank between 1968 and 1971 (e.g. in Fukuoka, Tokyo and Saga)—with equally mannered devices drawn from the West, such as the Renaissance technique of anamorphic projection or disjunctive tropes drawn from the work of Adolf Loos and Marcel Duchamp.

Of his 'twilight gloom' aesthetic Isozaki wrote in 1972:

> The building has almost no form; it is merely a grey expanse. The multi-level grid guides one's lines of sight but does not focus them on anything in particular. At first encounter, the vague grey expanse seems impossible to decipher and utterly odd. The multi-level lattice disperses vision throughout the space much as various images might be thrown around an area from a central projector. It absorbs all individual spaces that establish strict order. It conceals them, and when that concealment process is over, only the grey expanse remains. The process itself has an order of sanctity, like a brilliant crime committed in the midst of dusty daily life.

This metal-clad, atectonic aesthetic was perfected in his Gunma Prefectural Museum of Modern Art and appeared last in its fully amplified form, in which everything is subjected to the same overriding grid, in his Shukosha Building (1975), Fukuoka City. In 1974 Isozaki characterized his Gunma Museum as so many Sol Lewitt 'cubes on a lawn', in which the membrane-like metal gridded coverings are only extended as far as needed for appropriate scenographic effect.

Between 1972 and 1975 Isozaki started to move away from his dematerialized atectonic manner to explore an architecture based on the tectonic form of the vault, as seen in the semicircular precast concrete vaults of his Kitakyushu Municipal Central Library (*see* JAPAN, fig. 41) and also in the shell concrete roof of his Fujimi Country Club (1974), Fujimi, planned in the form of a question mark that can only be seen as such from the air. Isozaki's so-called 'rhetoric of the cylinder' culminated in the 1970s and early 1980s in a series of barrel-vaulted concrete houses, derived as much from primitive Japanese *haniwa* tombs as from the Western megaron. In 1980, however, fragmentary Post-modern historicist quotes began to appear in his work, disrupting the purity of its gridded form with stylistically disjunctive passages, as in his Tsukuba Civic Center (1983; see fig.). This building is 'cannibalistic' in its use of Modernist references, for these are invaded by neo-classical tropes that are hard to identify (e.g. the rustication that is vaguely reminiscent of the work of Claude-Nicolas Ledoux), which are deliberately mixed up with episodes drawn from Isozaki's gridded 'twilight gloom' manner. Isozaki followed this auto-destruction of his own late manner with a series of free sculptural compositions, including the administrative headquarters (1992) for the Disney Corporation in Orlando, FL. Perhaps the finest building of his late career, however, is one that formed part of his so-called 'red desert' sequence: the Museum of Contemporary Art (1987), Bunker Hill, Los Angeles.

Arata Isozaki: Tsukuba Civic Center, Tsukuba, 1983

In many respects Isozaki's architecture can be seen as an aesthetic but savagely ironic comment on a spectacular but technologically ruined late modern reality. There is thus always an undercurrent of morbid scepticism lying beneath the exuberance of his aesthetic form—a darkness of spirit that became overt from time to time. In his Electric Labyrinth (1968), designed for the Triennale in Milan, for example, the exhibition was haunted by an image of the devastated Hiroshima, combined with traditional Japanese ghosts and demons representing the revengeful spirits of the nuclear disaster. Throughout his career Isozaki was a visiting professor of architecture at several universities, notably in the USA; his work was widely exhibited and won many awards.

WRITINGS

Kukan-e [Collected writings, 1960–69] (Tokyo, 1971)
'About my Method', *Japan Architect*, xlvii/8 (1972), pp. 22–8
'The Metaphor for the Cube', *Japan Architect*, li/3 (1976), pp. 27–46
Shuho-ga [Collected writings, 1969–78] (Tokyo, 1979)
'A Rethinking of Space of Darkness', *Japan Architect*, 287 (1981), pp. 9–26
'The Ledoux Connection', *Archit. Des.*, lii/1–2 (1982), pp. 28–9

BIBLIOGRAPHY

A New Wave of Japanese Architecture (exh. cat., ed. K. Frampton; New York, Inst. Archit. & Urb. Stud., 1978)
P. Drew: *The Architecture of Arata Isozaki* (New York and London, 1982)
B. Barattucci and B. Di Russo: *Arata Isozaki: Architettura, 1959–1982* (Rome, 1983)
B. Bognar: *Contemporary Japanese Architecture: Its Development and Challenge* (New York, 1985)
——: *The New Japanese Architecture* (New York, 1990)
N. Florenz: *Arata Isozaki: Architecture, 1960–1990* (New York, 1991)

KENNETH FRAMPTON

Israel. Country on the east Mediterranean coast. It was established as an independent nation on land that was part of the British Mandate of Palestine. Israel occupies an area of *c.* 27,000 sq. km, bordering to the north with Lebanon and Syria, to the east with Jordan and to the south-west with Egypt (see fig. 1). It also occupies the territories of the Golan Heights, the West Bank and the Gaza Strip (still disputed 1996), and in 1980 it proclaimed the formerly disputed city of Jerusalem as its capital (*see also* JERUSALEM, §I, 4). Its terrain and climate include the temperate and fertile Mediterranean coastal plain, the hill regions of northern Galilee and central Israel, where rainfall is heaviest, the dry Great Rift Valley and the southern, arid Negev Desert. Israel's main water resource, the River Jordan, flows into the Dead Sea, which, at 400 m below sea level, is the lowest point on earth.

I. Introduction. II. Architecture. III. Painting, graphic arts and sculpture. IV. Ceramics. V. Metalwork. VI. Textiles. VII. Patronage. VIII. Collecting and dealing. IX. Museums. X. Art education. XI. Art libraries and photographic collections.

I. Introduction.

Located at the junction of Asia, Africa and Europe, Israel has always been on a strategic trade route as well as being a battlefield for armies contending for the Holy Land. Prior to the 19th century a small Jewish population was concentrated in Galilee, while the predominant Muslim and Christian inhabitants, with the exception of the nomadic Bedouin in the Negev, lived in hill townships of traditional stone dwellings. New forms of Jewish settlement along the coastal plain in the 1870s and later in the northern and central hilly regions altered the region's traditional physical character. After the rebirth of Zionism in the 19th century, Britain supported the establishment of a Jewish homeland in the Balfour Declaration (1917). The fall of the Turkish Ottoman Empire led to the British Mandate over Palestine (1922), which was opposed by Arab extremists. Established as a parliamentary democracy, Israel became an independent state in 1948. Subsequent Jewish immigration from all over the world brought a cultural diversity, firing the imagination of local architects and artists. To absorb the waves of immigration the government created development towns in previously unpopulated areas (*see* §II below). By the late 20th century the population had more than quadrupled to *c.* 5 million, 85% of whom Jews, 11% Muslims and 4% Christians, with 85% of the population living in urban areas (principally Jerusalem, TEL AVIV, Jaffa and Haifa). The continuing Arab–Israeli conflict lessened after international peace efforts initiated in 1979 with the Camp David peace accord between Israel and Egypt. In 1993 new peace negotiations began.

BIBLIOGRAPHY

G. Canaan: *Rebuilding the Land of Israel* (New York, 1954)
R. Shechori: *Art in Israel* (Tel Aviv, 1974)
A. Barzel: *Art in Israel* (Milan, 1987)
Archit. Israel, 1 (Jan 1988), pp. 5–84 [issue ded. to Isr. archit.]

II. Architecture.

Three distinct periods of an emerging Israeli architecture can be identified from the mid-19th century. During the Ottoman period the expansion of the ancient walled cities of Jerusalem and Jaffa took place (*see* OTTOMAN, §II; *see also* JERUSALEM, §I, 3). The new buildings drew on a range of influences brought by Eastern and Western immigrants, with Western influences predominating at the turn of the century; the Arts and Crafts Movement in particular had a notable effect on neo-classical and neo-eastern (or pseudo-Hebraic) trends. During the period of the British Mandate architecture was influenced by the strong presence of new European ideas. The eclectic Oriental style continued until the beginning of the 1930s, by which time two diverging trends could be discerned: the British School, based in Jerusalem and represented by British architects employed by the Mandate (*see also* JERUSALEM, §I, 4); and European modernism, practised by European immigrants.

By 1948 new solutions were already being sought for the problems inherent in the settlement of an increasing flow of immigrants. Mature European-trained architects such as ADOLF RADING, RICHARD KAUFFMANN, LEOPOLD KRAKAUER, ALEXANDER KLEIN and ERICH MENDELSOHN had already produced early Modern Movement buildings of some distinction that suited the demands of rapid development. Equally appropriate was the sparse Bauhaus modernism of the early Dessau years brought by ARIEH SHARON and Munio Weinraub and from elsewhere in Europe by such figures as Dov KARMI and Ze'ev Rechter (*see* RECHTER, (1)), all of whom set up practice in Tel Aviv in the 1930s. All were at the peak of their powers and had already built housing in Tel Aviv and Haifa that was comparable with the European *Siedlungen* of the same period.

After independence (1948) Arieh Sharon was appointed Director and Chief Architect of the National Planning Agency, and by 1953 he had prepared a national development plan to cope with the fast-growing population. He opted for a dispersed settlement pattern, and *c.* 20 new towns were designated. Simple solutions were increasingly based on large-unit precast concrete techniques. Distinguished examples included Dov Karmi's Bar Shira and Lautman apartment buildings (1952–6) in Tel Aviv and the Mt Carmel and Kiryat Eliahu housing developments (1953–6) at Haifa by AL MANSFELD (with Munio Weinraub); many developments had, however, fallen into disrepair by the 1970s. Before the end of the 1950s construction had begun to catch up with housing demand, and institutional and public buildings grew in number. Examples include the F. R. Mann Auditorium (1957), Tel Aviv, by Rechter-Zarhy-Rechter (with Dov Karmi and Ram Karmi), reminiscent of the Royal Festival Hall, London; and the Soroka Health Centre and regional hospital (1959–62), Beersheba, by Arieh Sharon and Benjamin Idelson, a trend-setting structural rationalist building with sophisticated shading devices.

As financial constraints became less stringent in the 1960s, the provision of universities, hotels and commercial buildings also gathered momentum, and a more positive architecture began to emerge. Work in an increasingly contextual version of the International Style included the El Al headquarters (1962–3) by Karmi-Melzer-Karmi, which boasts a gently curving, almost Mendelsohnian façade with cylindrical end-features, and Sharon and Idelson's Brutalist Sick Fund Administrative Centre (1965), both Tel Aviv. More significantly, however, over the next two decades a recognizable Israeli architectural character evolved. It emerged from the combination of

1. Map of Israel; those sites with separate entries in this dictionary are distinguished by CROSS-REFERENCE TYPE

unitary elements (originally devised to expedite the provision of housing) in close stacking arrangements but also refers to the traditional urban aggregations of the Levant and takes full advantage of the flat roof as additional living space.

A movement towards more geometrical, even crystalline, forms followed and was often associated morphologically with the control of solar radiation. These developments can be seen in such works as the Municipal Building (1959–63) at Bat Yam by Alfred Neumann, Zvi Hecker (*b* 1931) and Eldar Sharon (*b* 1933), which is built up from close-stacked octahedra, or in the Danciger Teaching Laboratory (1960–64; see fig. 2) of the Technion, Haifa, by Neumann and Hecker; in both environmental control is achieved by means of spatial arrangements as opposed to shading devices such as *brises-soleil*. The Israel Museum (1960–65), Jerusalem, by Al Mansfeld (with Dora Gat), planned for expansion and elevated to a series of linked but discrete white cubes of various sizes, contrasts with the somewhat later, more conventional Tel Aviv Museum (1971) by Dan Eitan and Itzhak Yashar; the serrated edge of the great double curve of Yacov Rechter's Mivtachim Resort Hotel (1968), astride the ridge at Zikhron Ya'aqov, is one of the best examples of the integration of units in a single linear composition (*see* RECHTER, (2)). A number of foreign architects were commissioned in the 1960s: Philip Johnson designed the nuclear reactor building (1961) at Rehovot, a simple courtyard block, from which a monumental polygonal reactor tower with battered walls rises; Oscar Niemeyer designed buildings for the University of Haifa (1964;

partly completed); the unique ogee-domed Shrine of the Book at the Gottesman Centre for Rare Manuscripts, Hebrew University of Jerusalem (1959–65), is by Frederick Kiesler and Armand Bartos.

University development flourished, for example at Beersheba in the Negev and on two campuses in Jerusalem, as did hospital building. The Arieh Sharon practice completed seven hospitals and the Tel Aviv University Medical School between 1966 and 1976. Housing in many new and expanding provincial neighbourhoods is typified by the Sharons' neighbourhood development at Beersheba (1967–9; with Shmuel Schwartz) or the more lyrical designs of the Hassidic settlement (1976) at Hazor by DAVID REZNIK. After 1967 new peri-urban satellite neighbourhoods were built around Jerusalem. At Gilo, with a planning team led by AVRAHAM YASKY, a number of architects including Yacov Rechter, Ram KARMI and Saloh Hershmann produced new and often exciting contextual solutions throughout the 1970s. At Ramot, another Jerusalem satellite, housing development by Zvi Hecker between 1972 and 1985 enabled him to evolve a unique and carefully scaled angular style, modulated to give environmental comfort and a sense of enclosure.

The most important works in Israel by MOSHE SAFDIE also date from the second half of the 1970s and reflect changing Post-modernist attitudes to context. His designs (1974) for a square adjacent to the Western Wall of the Second Temple, Jerusalem, won acclaim, as did his proposal (1972) for the Mamillah Business District, Jerusalem, between the old and new cities. Most notable in the development of the structural and spatial innovation

2. Alfred Neumann and Zvi Hecker: Danciger Teaching Laboratory, the Technion, Haifa, 1960–64

associated with Safdie's work from this period is the Yeshivat Porat Joseph Rabbinical College (1971–80), Jerusalem. Although uncompromising in its expression of structure, the Yeshivat faithfully reflects the characteristics of its immediate context in the old city, and a similar attitude informs Safdie's work on the Hebrew Union College (completed 1986), Jerusalem. More significantly perhaps, similar changes can be seen in work by others from the same period, such as David Reznik's Jerusalem Centre for Near Eastern Studies (completed 1989), and in that of younger architects. Further large-scale immigration into Israel in the late 20th century led to more housing developments (with some of the errors of the 1950s being repeated). On a more positive note, however, efforts were increased to restore buildings of historical significance.

BIBLIOGRAPHY
G. Canaan: *Rebuilding the Land of Israel* (New York, 1954)
E. Spiegel: *New Towns in Israel* (Stuttgart, 1966)
Y. Golani and D. G. von Schwarze, eds: *Israel Builds, 1970: Interdisciplinary Planning* (Jerusalem, 1970)
A. Harlap: *Israel Builds* (Jerusalem, 1973)
——: *New Israeli Architecture* (New Brunswick, 1982)
'Contemporary Israeli Architecture', *Process: Archit.*, 44 (Feb 1984), pp. 5–159
'Jerusalem: A Report', *Baumeister*, lxxxii/3 (March 1984) [issue ded. to archit. of Jerusalem]
White City: International Style Architecture in Israel: A Portrait of an Era (exh. cat. by M. Levin, Tel Aviv, Mus. A.; New York, Jew. Mus.; 1984–5)
Build Ye Cities (exh. cat., ed. G. Duvshani and H. Frank; Tel Aviv, Inst. Architects & Town Planners, 1985)
M. Safdie: *Jerusalem: The Future of the Past* (Boston, 1989)
Archit. Israel, 9 (March 1991) [issue on the archit. dev. of Tel Aviv]
MICHAEL TURNER

III. Painting, graphic arts and sculpture.

The fine art produced in Israel after its official foundation grew out of trends that can be traced back to 1906, when the Bezalel School of Arts and Crafts was founded in Jerusalem (*see* BEZALEL; *see also* §X below). Although fuelled by a strongly Zionist impulse, such fine art as was produced was firmly rooted in the European traditions espoused by its first teachers: naturalism in the case of Samuel Hirszenberg (1865–1908) and BORIS SCHATZ; and Art Nouveau in the case of Ephraim Lilien (1874–1925). This often problematic dual allegiance, to the creation of distinctive indigenous art forms and also to a wider Western culture, became one of the enduring features of Israeli art. By the 1920s a new generation of artists had emerged. Such painters as Nachum Gutman (1898–1980) and REUVEN RUBIN attempted to convey a primitivistic vision of a Mediterranean Utopia, in which the Arab peasant assumed the exemplary role of heroic worker close to the land (e.g. Gutman's *Resting at Noon*, 1926; Tel Aviv, Mus. A.). These artists' determination to celebrate the promise of the present was reflected in a shifting of artistic life from the ancient, multi-cultural city of Jerusalem to the new Jewish metropolis of Tel Aviv. The Arab massacre of Jews in Hebron in 1929 and the struggle against the British Mandate, combined with the rise of European Fascism in the 1930s, led many Jews in Palestine to identify once more with diaspora Jewry. Strong links were forged with the Jewish artists of the Ecole de Paris, and a tendency to mystical expressionism prevailed, as in

3. Yosseff Zaritsky: *Yehiam*, oil on canvas, 2.08×2.28 m, 1951 (Tel Aviv, Museum of Art)

Synagogue in Safed (1939; Jerusalem, Israel Mus.) by Yitzhak Frenkel (1899–1981). Expressionist tendencies were strengthened by the arrival of German-Jewish artist refugees, such as JACOB STEINHARDT, who joined the Jerusalem circle of ANNA TICHO and LEOPOLD KRAKAUER, artists of similar origin who had emigrated earlier.

From the late 1930s events in Europe prompted many Jewish artists in Palestine to seek an identity unburdened by the traumas of recent history; some found this in a celebration of ancient Canaanite culture (e.g. ITZHAK DANZIGER). Only a few artists, including Marcel Janco, Igael Tumarkin and MORDECAI ARDON, themselves European émigrés, were to confront the subject of the Holocaust in their work (e.g. Ardon's *Missa dura*, 1958–9; London, Tate; *see also* JEWISH ART, §VII). Even the War of Independence (1948) featured only rarely in the art of this period.

In the early 1950s such left-wing artists as Naftali Bezem (*b* 1924), Moshe Gat (*b* 1935) and Avraham Ofek (1935–89) worked briefly in a socially critical, realist mode. *Kibbutz* artists, such as Yochanan Simon (1905–76), also adopted a realist style but tended to idealize and monumentalize the *kibbutz* way of life (e.g. Simon's *In the Shower*, 1952; Tel Aviv, Mus. A.). Most influential in the long term was the group known as NEW HORIZONS, founded in 1948 around YOSSEF ZARITSKY, in which a lyrical abstraction, inspired by the local light and colours but fuelled by a belief in the need for a universal language, soon became the dominant tendency in painting (e.g. Zaritsky's *Yehiam*, 1951; Tel Aviv, Mus. A.; see fig. 3). In sculpture, particularly memorial sculpture, a symbolic abstraction dominated for much of the second half of the 20th century (e.g. the environmental work *Negev Monument* (1963–8) at Beersheba by DANI KARAVAN).

Most of the young artists prominent in the 1960s, such as RAFFI LAVIE and Uri Lifshitz (*b* 1936), sought to reintroduce a raw figuration, often incorporating the printed or painted word into their mixed-media compositions (e.g. Lavie's *Composition*, 1968; Tel Aviv, Mus. A.). In the late 1960s and 1970s many artists, including Joshua Neustein (*b* 1940) and PINCHAS COHEN GAN, adopted a conceptual approach, working in the areas of mixed media, land art and performance art, and often incorporating political statements, as in Neustein's *Jerusalem River Project* (1970). Although in the 1980s there was a widespread return to traditional media, political events—the Arab–Israeli War of 1973, the elections of 1977, the invasion of Lebanon in 1982 and from 1987 the Palestinian Intifada—prompted more Israeli artists than ever before to question or attack the status quo (e.g. *Isaac! Isaac!* by Moshe Gershuni, 1982; Tel Aviv, Mus. A.).

BIBLIOGRAPHY

R. Shechori: *Art in Israel* (Tel Aviv, 1974)
B. Tammuz, D. Le Vité and G. Ofrat: *Sipura shel omanut Israel* [The story of art in Israel] (Tel Aviv, 1980)
Artists of Israel, 1920–1980 (exh. cat. by S. Tumarkin Goodman and others, New York, Jew. Mus., 1981)
A. Barzel: *Art in Israel* (Milan, 1987)
In the Shadow of Conflict: Israeli Art, 1980–1989 (exh. cat. by S. Tumarkin Goodman and others, New York, Jew. Mus., 1989)

MONICA BOHM-DUCHEN

IV. Ceramics.

Based on no Jewish tradition, Israeli ceramics have developed under the combined influence of regional traditions, archaeological finds and modern European trends. In the 1920s, the terracotta tiles from the BEZALEL craft workshops that were used to decorate some houses in Tel Aviv, and utensils of unglazed Arab pottery, summed up the production of ceramics in Palestine. In the 1930s, several women artists from Germany emigrated to Palestine. In 1932 Hava Samuel (1904–89) opened the first ceramics studio in Jerusalem. She was joined a year later by Paula Ahronson (*b* 1908), a Bauhaus graduate, and in 1934 they established in Rishon le Zion a workshop that remained active until 1979. Because of her immense influence, Hedwig Grossmann (*b* 1902), who arrived in 1933, must receive the credit for laying the foundation of ceramics in Israel. Unlike Samuel, whose work was characterized by ornamental glazes and Oriental folklorism, Grossmann laid stress on essential form and the use of local clays and earth colours, while rejecting external elements, such as glazes. Hanna Zuntz-Harag (*b* 1915), who arrived in 1940, was inspired by ancient Mediterranean pottery and, without renouncing glazes, developed simple, classic forms. In Haifa, where she worked, the ceramics of Elsbeth Cohen (1921–92) and Nehemia Azaz (*b* 1923) encouraged improvement in the designs of industrial pottery; it was, in fact, the growth of the pottery industry that brought about the establishment in 1958 of a ceramics department at Bezalel. However, under its head, Gedula Ogen (*b* 1929), who was a pupil of Grossmann, the department gave priority to ceramics as art. Her influence was felt in the animal sculpture that was in vogue in the 1960s, as well as in ceramic murals. The use of clay as a sculptural material had further support in the work of David Morris (*b* 1936) and, in particular, that of the sculptor and designer Siona Shimshi (*b* 1939).

Ceramic murals, often designed by painters, for public institutions, banks etc, flourished in Israel during the 1950s and 1960s. Aharon Kahana (1905–67), a founder-member of the abstract art movement New Horizons (for further discussion *see* §III above), was also a ceramicist; in the workshop he established in Ramat Gan he created, in a symbolic and archaic abstract style, decorated vessels and, later, murals made of tiles, painted, glazed or in relief. Other artists, among them Jean David (*b* 1908) and Marcel Janco, produced murals at the community ceramics studio of Ein Hod. In spite of little recognition by art institutions, many contemporary Israeli ceramicists, such as Lidia Zavadsky (*b* 1937), Magdalena Hefetz (*b* 1944), Nora Kochavi (*b* 1934), Naomi Bitter (*b* 1936), Maud Friedland (*b* 1928) and Meira Unna (*b* 1947), have chosen to treat ceramics as a fine rather than a decorative art. In the 1990s ceramicists gained the support of the ceramic industry in the Negev, resulting in co-operative projects (artists working with industrial materials) and exhibitions.

For bibliography *see* §VI below.

V. Metalwork.

For many years Israeli jewellery was identified with Yemenite jewellery, because Yemenite Jewish craftsmen had dominated the field from the opening of the Bezalel filigree department in 1908; it produced a variety of items, including, as well as jewellery, cups, saucers and Jewish ritual objects. From 1911 to 1914 there was in Ben-Shemen a Yemenite silversmiths' colony, also established by the founder of Bezalel, BORIS SCHATZ. The Bezalel silver was not, in fact, purely Yemenite in its designs; the ornament was characterized by flatness and symmetry, and some of the methods of making vessels were not Yemenite. Subsequent waves of immigration from San'a brought other skilled Yemenite workers, who continued Israeli craftsmanship in this genre. Bezalel also promoted high-quality work in solid silver and copper. In 1912, damascened work won an exclusive contract with Liberty, London. Bezalel metalwork is typically the combination of several techniques in one piece, as in the *Holy Ark* (1918–25; Chicago, IL, Maurice Spertus Mus. Jud.) and *Elijah's Chair* (see fig. 4). Long after the first Bezalel had closed in 1929, Yemenite silversmiths continued to work in this manner, often stamping their products with Bezalel's name.

Modern design for tableware and Jewish ritual objects was introduced by Yehuda Wolpert (*b* 1900) and David Gumbel (1909–92), immigrants from Germany, who directed the New Bezalel's metalwork department for some 20 years. While rejecting earlier romantic Orientalism and imitation of the past, they conformed to cultural tradition in the basic forms of the ritual objects, as well as in using Hebrew letters as a major ornament, a tendency that was continued by their graduates, including Menachem Berman (*b* 1929), Zelig Segal (*b* 1933) and Arie Ofir (*b* 1939). Taking another direction, Bianka Eshel-Gershuni (*b* 1932) challenged conventional jewellery-making by her unorthodox combinations of materials, such as gold with pieces of plastic, glass, feathers, little dolls or other ready-mades. In the 1970s she extended her scope to include body decorations and also sculpture. During the same period

4. *Elijah's Chair*, walnut, wool, silk, velvet, cameo, enamel, silver filigree, with brass and ivory reliefs and shell and leather inlay, 1.90×0.91×0.91 m, from the Bezalel workshop, 1918–25 (Jerusalem, Bezalel National Art Museum)

the tendency at Bezalel was to encourage goldsmiths and silversmiths, such as Deganit Schocken (*b* 1947), Vered Kaminsky (*b* 1953) and Esther Knobel (*b* 1949), to produce work that was a means of personal expression rather than decoration, while broadening the range of materials and sources of inspiration. The same latitude was extended to the makers of ritual objects.

For bibliography *see* §VI below.

VI. Textiles.

Among Jews, embroidery has traditionally been a women's craft. In 19th-century Jerusalem women often decorated the Sabbath tablecloths with depictions of the Holy Places, with the Wailing Wall at the centre. Weaving, spinning and lacework were taught in Jerusalem from the 1860s, and Boris Schatz's successful experience in Bulgaria of reviving the folk-rug industry gave a sound start to rug-making at Bezalel. Despite an initial lack of materials and skills, Bezalel's Persian knotted rugs in both wool and silk

soon became remarkably successful. In 1910 Queen Wilhelmina of the Netherlands (*reg* 1890–1948) purchased the *Song of Songs* rug (copy, 1920s; Jerusalem, Israel Mus.).

Julia Keiner (1900–92), who arrived from Germany in 1936 and opened a workshop in Jerusalem, wove textiles in modern designs; in 1952 she was commissioned to weave curtains for the United Nations Headquarters in New York. The weaving department at the New Bezalel, which Keiner founded in 1941 and headed until it closed in 1965, trained students in weaving wool, cotton and linen fabrics, in simple abstract patterns and natural monochrome colours, for clothing and furnishing.

At Maskit, the government craft enterprise founded by Ruth Dayan (*b* 1917) in 1954 and closed in October 1994, the main concern in the area of textiles was with adapting traditional techniques brought by Jews from Libya, southern Arabia, Azerbaijan and Bulgaria: by altering an object's function or design, or by switching to synthetic dyes, work could be produced on a larger scale. Adaptation of Yemenite and Bethlehem embroidery to modern clothing was a typical attempt by Maskit to create Israeli fashion. An outstanding success in this direction was the desert coat, inspired by the Bedouin abaya, which Finny Lietersdorf (1906–86) designed. Maskit also commissioned designs by modern Israeli artists, such as Siona Shimshi, for carpets and printed fabrics, as well as selling individual pieces of textile work. The establishment of the Shenkar College of Textiles and Fashion at the end of the 1960s marked the turning-point of textile design towards industrial production, while the conservation of ethnic fabrics was left to the museums. In the late 20th century the decline in traditional handmade textiles prompted some younger artists to explore the possibilities offered by FIBRE ART.

BIBLIOGRAPHY
R. Dayan and W. Feinberg: *Crafts of Israel* (New York, 1974)
Bezalel Academy, Jerusalem: Gold- und Silberschmiedeabteilung/Jewellery and Silversmithing Department (exh. cat., ed. F. Falk; Pforzheim, Schmuckmus.; Hanau, Dt. Goldschmiedehaus; London, Electrum Gal.; 1978)
Arts and Crafts in Eretz-Israel in the 19th Century (exh. cat., ed. Y. Fischer; Jerusalem, Israel Mus., 1979) [in Heb.]
Artisans d'Israël de la Fondation Alix de Rothschild, Jérusalem (exh. cat., Paris, Bib. Forney, 1990)
The Beginnings of Israeli Ceramics, 1932–1962 (exh. cat. by G. Ofrat, Jerusalem, Artists' House, 1991); also *Ariel*, 90 (1992), pp. 75–94
A. Mishory: 'Ceramics from Israel', *Ceramics Israel 92* (exh. cat., Ramat Gan, Beit Aharon Kahana; Geva, Mus. Angewandte Kst; 1992), pp. 6–9
N. Warshavsky and M. Klausner: 'Israeli Textile Art', *Ariel*, xcii (1993), pp. 67–74
Ceramics Biennale Beer-Sheva, 1993 (exh. cat. by H. Finkelstein, Beer-Sheva, Ben-Gurion University of the Negev, 1993)

For further bibliography *see* BEZALEL.

VII. Patronage.

Public patronage has always been the principal source of support for Israeli artistic activity, although the national resources made available have sometimes appeared narrow in comparison to the breadth of creative talent. From the 1920s, during the British Mandate, the Histadrut (Federation of Labour) initiated and supported various activities, including opening some studios for teaching art, organizing travelling exhibitions and lectures and supporting artists individually. After the establishment of the State, the Ministry of Education and Culture took charge of state patronage through the National Council of Culture and Art, founded in 1959 as the Ministry's advisory body, which in the 1990s continued to finance the participation of Israel in international exhibitions, to bestow grants and awards and to support the publication of art books and magazines.

The Jerusalem Foundation, established in 1966 by Teddy Kollek (*b* 1911; Mayor of Jerusalem 1965–93) with American and Israeli associates, has independent branches in seven other countries and dedicates *c.* 30% of its finances to arts and culture; it notably organized the installation of *c.* 100 sculptures by foreign and Israeli artists at sites around the city and has also founded and subsidized artists' studios as well as supporting the Jerusalem Print Workshop and some museums. Likewise, the Yehoshua Rabinowitz Tel Aviv Foundation for the Arts, founded in 1970 by Yehoshua Rabinowitz (Mayor of Tel Aviv 1969–74), awards grants, supports arts-related publications and has also commissioned 15 environmental sculptures by such artists as Dani Karavan and Itzhak Danziger.

Much support for Israeli art has come from foreign organizations and foundations; the budgets for acquisitions and special projects in Israeli museums have been highly dependent on international donations from such organizations as American Friends of the Israel Museum (Jerusalem) and British Friends of the Art Museums of Israel. An important contribution is made by the America-Israel Cultural Foundation (formerly the Norman Fund), a Jewish charitable organization founded in the USA in 1938, through its scholarship programme for students and young artists and through financial contributions to art institutions.

Private patronage has remained rare, perhaps in part because Israel provides no tax relief for donations to the arts. Several firms and individuals do, however, support artists and institutions: Ayala Zacks Abramov (*b* 1912), for example, donated works from her collections to museums as well as purchasing Israeli art for the Israel Museum and financing its pavilion for Israeli art (which was named after her). In addition she and her husband, Sam Zacks (1908–70), founded the Hazor Museum for Antiquities at Kibbutz Ayyelet Hashahar and an exhibition wing, the Sam and Ayala Zacks Hall, in the Tel Aviv Museum of Art.

BIBLIOGRAPHY
M. Levin and T. Goldschmidt: *Ha'Ir ke-muze'on: Omanut ve'adrikhalut modernit bi-Yerushalayim/The City as a Museum: Modern Art and Architecture in Jerusalem* (Jerusalem, 1980) [bilingual text]
'Steeped in Culture: The Jerusalem Foundation: Projects in the Arts', *Jerusalem Rep.* (13 Aug 1992) [suppl.]

VIII. Collecting and dealing.

The first collection to arrive in the country came from Russia in 1919 with Jacob Fereman and comprised *c.* 200 paintings by contemporary, if second-rate artists; it had some influence on local modernist trends. A large collection of Impressionist and German Expressionist art came to Jerusalem in 1928 with the merchant, publisher and patron of artists and writers Salman Schocken, who also commissioned several buildings from the architect Eric Mendelsohn in Germany and in Jerusalem. Valuable collections of modern and Jewish art and books came with Jewish German immigrants from 1933. The most notable is the collection of the textile manufacturer Erich Goeritz, of which 500 works (including examples by German artists and a unique group of Alexander Archipenko's early works) were lent to the Tel Aviv Museum (now the Tel Aviv Museum of Art) in 1933 and in 1956 donated by the Goeritz family. The high-quality Judaica collection of Joseph Stieglitz, begun by his father in Kraków (and which survived World War II partly in a suitcase buried in the ground), continued to develop in Tel Aviv, where Stieglitz was an international-scale dealer and expert in Jewish art and Judaica. His private collection was transferred to the Israel Museum, Jerusalem.

Notable among the young collections in Israel after 1948 was that of the artist Jacob Pins, who started to collect Japanese and Chinese art in Jerusalem in 1945 on a small scale. Over the years the collection grew and came to be a valuable source for research into prints and paintings. From the mid-1940s Ayala Zacks Abramov and Sam Zacks began to assemble a major collection of international Post-Impressionist and other modern paintings, drawings and sculpture, as well as Israeli art and Canadian modern art; a large proportion of the collections was donated to museums and institutions in Canada and Israel. One of the biggest and most important collections of Israeli art was begun in 1975 by Joseph Hackmey and the Israel Phoenix Assurance Company; eventually numbering *c.* 2000 works, the collection represents Israeli art from the 1920s onwards, although from the early 1990s the company also acquired European and American contemporary art. Collections of antiquities include the archaeological collection of Reuben Hecht, displayed in the museum at the University of Haifa, and a fine selection of antique jewels, maps and books, collected by the Mayor of Jerusalem and founder of the Israel Museum, Teddy Kollek (*b* 1911).

Art dealing was notably practised by two industrialists and collectors, who, after the closure of their factories, dedicated their efforts to art: Sam Dubiner, who opened the first professional commercial art gallery in Israel in Tel Aviv in 1961, exhibiting Israeli abstract artists; and Ephraim Ilin, who set up and directed the international investment company MODARCO (1971–6), which bought, commissioned or exhibited works by, among others, Willem De Kooning, Max Ernst and Arman. Although by the 1990s the art market in Israel was still limited, it was gradually developing. Auctions, mostly of Israeli art, were first held in 1977 by the Gordon Gallery, Tel Aviv, and in 1985 by Sotheby's (in their case mostly of Judaica). Among the incentives to the market is the fact that in Israel there is no capital gains tax and no inheritance tax (since 1972), and the law of protecting national heritage applies only to archaeology and (since 1972) Hebrew and Jewish books and manuscripts dating from before the 16th century. On the other hand imported art, like other goods, is subject to value-added tax, and taxes designed to protect Israeli products are payable on imported silver, textiles, ceramics, glass and other goods.

BIBLIOGRAPHY
A Tribute to Sam Zacks: Selected Paintings, Drawings and Sculptures from the Sam and Ayala Zacks Collection (exh. cat., Jerusalem, Israel Mus.; Tel Aviv, Mus. A.; 1976)

The Pins Collection: Chinese and Japanese Paintings and Prints (exh. cat., Jerusalem, Israel Mus., 1980)

IX. Museums.

In 1906 BORIS SCHATZ founded the Bezalel Museum adjacent to the Bezalel School of Arts and Crafts as a source of inspiration for students attempting to create a national art. The museum acquired works by Jewish artists, Judaica, Jewish ethnographical material, archaeological finds and natural history. The second director, Mordechai Narkiss (1897–1957), changed its emphasis to a general art museum with growing collections of European painting, prints and drawings, and Near-Eastern works of art. The Israel Museum, Jerusalem, founded in 1965, is Israel's largest and most important museum; only 15% of its budget comes from the State, however, and it is supported extensively by donations from Europe and the USA. In 1965 it incorporated the Bezalel National Art Museum, with departments of Israeli and European art, Asian art, ethnic art from Africa, the Americas and Pacific Islands, prints and drawings, photography and design; the Judaica and ethnography division contains, with *c.* 10,000 items, the world's most complete and diverse Judaica collection, including two complete 18th-century synagogues. Other divisions of the Israel Museum are the Billy Rose Sculpture Garden (designed in 1960–65 by Isamu Noguchi), the Shrine of the Book (which includes the Dead Sea Scrolls), the Samuel Bronfman Biblical and Archaeological Museum, and the Youth Wing. The Tel Aviv Museum of Art was established in 1932 by Meir Dizengoff (1861–1936), the city's first mayor, who donated his own house for this purpose. The museum's main exhibition hall was the venue for the proclamation of the State of Israel in 1948. In 1971 the Museum was rehoused, although temporary exhibitions have continued to be held in the Helena Rubinstein Pavilion for Contemporary Art since 1959. The collection (mainly of Israeli and other modern art) notably includes works by Alexander Archipenko from the Erich Goeritz Collection, lent in 1933 by Goeritz (1889–1955) and donated in 1956.

The first rural museum in Israel, the Ein Harod Museum of Art, was established in 1937 by the painter Chaim Atar (1902–53) at Kibbutz Ein Harod, and it contains a collection of Israeli art with special emphasis on artists associated with the *kibbutz* movement, as well as Jewish folk art and Judaica. From 1986 the museum organized the Israeli Photographic Biennale. Among museums dedicated to non-Western cultures, the L. A. Mayer Memorial Institute for Islamic Art (museum opened 1974, in memory of Leon Arie Mayer (1895–1959)) was inspired and financed by Vera Bryce Salomons (1888–1969) to celebrate the cultural heritage and artistic achievements of Israel's Muslim neighbours, particularly Iran; it also contains the Sir Salomons Collection of antique clocks and watches. Some Israeli museums are based on private collections, such as the Tikotin Museum of Japanese Art (founded 1959) in Haifa; the Wilfrid Israel House of Oriental Art (founded 1951) in Kibbutz Ha-Zore'a, containing Chinese, Indian and especially Cambodian art as well as Near Eastern ancient art and local archaeology; and the Bible Lands Museum, Jerusalem (opened 1992), with the collection of antiquities, most notably 1400 seals, of Elie

Borowski (*b* 1913), a dealer and specialist in Mesopotamian seals. Of the few museums that are dedicated to individual artists, notable examples are the Ticho House, Jerusalem, donated by ANNA TICHO, which exhibits her works and the Hanukkah lamp collection of her husband, Albert Abraham Ticho (1883–1960); the Rubin House, Tel Aviv, with its collection of paintings by REUVEN RUBIN; the Mané-Katz Museum, Haifa (*see* MANÉ-KATZ); and the Janco Dada Museum in Ein Hod, founded by Marcel Janco, which exhibits his works and holds exhibitions related to the Dada movement.

BIBLIOGRAPHY
L. Y. Rahmani: *The Museums of Israel* (London, 1976)
Annu. Rev.: Tel Aviv Mus., 2–3 (1984) [issue ded. to the history of the mus.]
'The Israel Museum at Twenty', *Ariel*, 60 (1985) [special issue]
Treasures of the Israel Museum, Jerusalem (Jerusalem, 1985)
N. Rosovsky and J. Ungerlei der-Mayerson: *The Museums of Israel* (New York, 1989)
Y. Inbar and E. Schiller, eds: *Muze'onim be-Yisra'el* [Museums in Israel] (Jerusalem, 1990)

X. Art education.

In 1906 the Bezalel School of Arts and Crafts was founded as part of the Zionist vision to serve practical and economic purposes and spiritual needs (*see* BEZALEL). Although the workshops established as part of the school were successful and exported high-quality *objets d'art* to Europe and the USA, the fine-art teaching was too conservative; many students left to study abroad. In 1925, however, Yitzhak Frenkel (1899–1981) returned from Paris and opened a studio that offered an alternative in the spirit of the Ecole de Paris. Conflict between modern and conservative tendencies characterized the dissent in 1945 of a teacher and several students from the studio for painting and sculpture directed by Aharon Avni, leading to the foundation of the Streichman and Stematsky studio, which despite its poor physical conditions ran a lively space for such artist students as Lea Nikel and Dani Karavan.

In 1930 the Bezalel was closed; it reopened in 1935 as the Bezalel Academy of Arts and Design, with greater emphasis being placed on the graphic arts and design and on Bauhaus-inspired teaching methods. The Bezalel gradually re-established its central position in Israeli artistic life after opening a department of fine arts (1967) and acquiring the status of an academic institution (1975); in 1990 its various departments were brought together at the Hebrew University campus on Mt Scopus. From the 1950s to the 1970s YEHEZKEL STREICHMAN and AVIGDOR STEMATSKY of the New Horizons group taught at the Avni Art Institute (established 1952) in Tel Aviv, which became a stronghold of lyrical abstraction. During the 1950s and 1960s it was the only establishment of its kind in Israel.

The Art Teachers Training College in Tel Aviv was founded in 1946 by the pedagogue Eliahu Beiles as an evening school, and in 1964 it became affiliated with the Ministry of Education. After 1966, when day-time courses became established under the directorship of Ran Shechori, the College began to develop into a major art school as well as a teacher-training institution. In 1972 it moved to Herzliya, then to Ramat Hasharon in 1977, and in 1987 it was affiliated to Beit Berl College as a means of gaining academic recognition. Elsewhere, fine art is taught at the University of Haifa, and a remarkable design department developed during the 1980s at the Center for Technological Education in Holon; architecture has been taught since 1925 at the Technion (Israel Institute of Technology) on Mt Carmel, near Haifa, which itself was built by ALEXANDER BAERWALD, the Technion's first professor of architecture.

BIBLIOGRAPHY
N. Shiloh-Cohen, ed.: *Bezalel, 1906–1929* (Jerusalem, 1983)
G. Ofrat: *New Bezalel, 1935–1955* (Jerusalem, 1987)

DALIA MANOR

XI. Art libraries and photographic collections.

Although art libraries in Israel were established prior to statehood in 1948, significant development began only in the mid-1960s. Among the most notable museum libraries is that of the Israel Museum in Jerusalem, established in 1969, which contains 100,000 volumes, collections of 220 periodicals and auction catalogues relating to the history of art, archaeology, Judaica, photography, crafts and design, numismatics, costumes and textiles, ancient and primitive cultures, Asian and Far Eastern cultures and museology. The library of the Israel Antiquities Authority, Jerusalem, established in 1935, houses 60,000 books and periodicals, mainly relating to the archaeology, history and civilizations of ancient Israel and the Ancient Near East. In addition to the library (est. 1965) at the L. A. Mayer Memorial Institute for Islamic Art, a substantial photographic collection includes 20,000 slides of Islamic art, architecture and archaeology, and 35,000 photographs of art objects. Two other notable museum libraries are the Tel Aviv Museum of Art library, established in 1938, with 45,000 volumes and 145 periodicals mainly devoted to contemporary art, architecture and design, in addition to catalogues of Israeli art since the 1920s; and the Haifa Museum of Art library, established in 1977, which has 22,000 volumes and 47 periodicals relating to archaeology, ancient Israel, the Middle East, the history of art, Jewish and Israeli art and museology.

There exists in addition a number of university libraries devoted to art, notably the Hebrew University's History of Art Department library (established 1964), Mt Scopus, Jerusalem, which specializes in Western, Oriental and African art and the history of architecture; it also houses a collection of 100,000 slides and several thousand photographs. The library (established 1970) of the Bezalel Academy of Arts and Design, Jerusalem, houses 30,000 books, catalogues and periodicals on art, architecture, graphic arts, photography, jewellery, ceramics and industrial design, together with 60,000 slides; and the library of the Faculty of Architecture at the Technion (Israel Institute of Technology), Haifa, has a large collection of books relating to all aspects of architecture. One of the most extensive photographic collections is that held by the Media Department of the University of Haifa Library, established in 1969, which has, aside from books and periodicals, 130,000 slides, 2000 architectural photographs and 360 video recordings relating to Western, Israeli, Islamic and Far Eastern art as well as the archaeology of the ancient world and the Near East.

LIA KOFFLER

Israelite. Name given to the dominant element in the population of Palestine in the 1st millennium BC. The Israelites are first referred to *c.* 1210 BC on a stele of the Egyptian pharaoh Merneptah. It is generally believed that they were semi-nomadic people who gradually migrated into Palestine from the east late in the 13th century BC, eventually dominating the local Canaanites, but a few scholars argue that Israel resulted from an internal revolt by oppressed peasants. The archaeological record is difficult to reconcile with the biblical account of a military invasion entailing the destruction of Canaanite cities such as Jericho, but it does demonstrate a major cultural change in Palestine *c.* 1200–1000 BC. Numerous farming villages arose in the hill country, and in the early Iron Age the elaborate products of Late Bronze Age Canaan gave way to a simpler material culture, less influenced by Aegean, Egyptian and Syrian fashions, with a gradual change from bronze to iron tools. While hazards of discovery may be responsible, the absence of temple buildings in Iron Age Palestine contrasts notably with their presence in the Bronze Age, and there is no evidence that Late Bronze Age (i.e. Canaanite) cult sites continued in use. Open-air hilltop shrines ('high places') may have existed, for example on Mt Ebal.

David (*reg* first half of the 10th century BC) successfully opposed the Philistines, who were settled along the coast, and established his capital in Jerusalem (*see* JERUSALEM, §I, 1) where his successor Solomon built a temple. Political stability brought wealth and encouraged major building projects. When Solomon died *c.* 930 BC, the kingdom divided into Judah, with its capital in Jerusalem, and Israel in the north, with its capital in SAMARIA. Shoshenq I (Shishak) of Egypt ravaged the land *c.* 925 BC (I Kings 14:25–6) and thereafter internal conflicts, and wars or alliances with other states, led to Israel's absorption by the Assyrian empire in 720 BC and the conquest of Judah by Babylon in 586 BC.

The splendours of Solomon's Jerusalem and its temple are known only from the Bible. Foreign craftsmen, such as masons from Byblos and a bronze-founder from Tyre (I Kings 5:18; 7:13–40), supplied skills the Israelites lacked. The temple shrine was 10×10×10 m; the main hall was the same width, but twice as long and higher, with an entrance porch. Walls of squared stone were panelled inside with imported cedar-wood, carved with plants and palms and entirely plated with gold. The sacred box, the Ark, stood in the shrine, guarded by gold-covered winged figures (the cherubim). Equipment of gold and bronze included elaborate wheeled stands cast in bronze, for moving basins of water. Two great bronze pillars (Jachin and Boaz) flanked the doorway. In Solomon's richly decorated palace stood a throne of carved ivory, plated with gold and flanked by lions. Commentators often consider the account in I Kings 6–7 unhistorical and exaggerated, the fantasy of later generations, but investigation of Ancient Near Eastern temples and contemporary records proves otherwise. The carved patterns described in the Bible conform to the known repertory of the times and the winged cherubim echo other guardian figures, while Solomon's throne is comparable to those of Egyptian and Phoenician kings.

Excavations have uncovered fortifications at Gezer, HAZOR and MEGIDDO, which are all of a similar kind and have been attributed to the reign of Solomon. Casemate city walls were pierced by gateways with projecting rectangular towers, behind which were three pairs of guardrooms. Casemate walls with less elaborate gates surrounded other towns. Houses built against the walls incorporated the casemates as rooms and so formed a concentric street. In many towns elaborate shafts and tunnels were dug within the walls to reach the water-table or springs (e.g. at Megiddo). 'Hezekiah's tunnel' in Jerusalem (late 8th century BC), an impressive feat of engineering 533 m long, was pierced by two gangs working from either end, twisting in their course, yet meeting.

At Hazor and Megiddo royal and administrative buildings of the 10th and 9th centuries BC had walls of fine ashlar masonry and attached or free-standing pillars with proto-Aeolic capitals. This style continued in the 8th-century BC palace at Samaria. In the 7th-century BC palace at Ramat Rahel, south of Jerusalem, small stone balusters girdled with palmettes and topped by capitals appear to have supported a window bar, as shown in contemporary ivory-carvings. Hints of architectural refinement appear in rock-cut tombs around Jerusalem. Panelling on internal walls and Egyptian cavetto-cornice mouldings on the façades presumably reproduce the house styles current among the rich. Private houses consisted of four or five rectangular rooms opening off three sides of a small courtyard, with pillars and mud-brick construction on stone foundations.

Israelite and Judaean crafts were those of the small town and countryside; the wealthy imported more artistic objects or the men to make them. Phoenician craftsmen imitating Egyptian designs carved ivory overlays for wooden furniture, while Syrians followed their local styles; examples of each were found in Samaria (see Amos 6:4 and see ANCIENT NEAR EAST §II, 3). Levantine gem-engravers and metalworkers took motifs from Egypt and Mesopotamia, and Israelite and Judaean artisans imitated some of these, notably in seal designs. An outstanding example is the seal of Shema, servant of Jeroboam II of Israel (c. 775 BC), displaying a fine roaring lion (cast in Jerusalem, Rockefeller Mus.). Glazed ware and glass are rare and were imported from Egypt and Phoenicia. Local pottery is plain, often burnished, well fired, serviceable and shapely. Sherds from Ramat Rahel bear a well-painted figure of a seated man. A jar found at Kuntillet Ajrud in the Negev bears crude painted figures in red and, more expertly, gazelles flanking a tree, with a lion below.

Biblical texts warned the Israelites against foreign influences and condemned them for succumbing to them. These entered society at every level, from Queen Jezebel's Baal priests (I Kings 18) and the luxury goods the rich enjoyed, to the fortune-tellers and charms ordinary folk employed. Religious laws against idolatry may account for the absence of sculptures, although the Bible reports those laws were often broken. The paucity of surviving material may be attributed to the continual occupation of sites and the destruction of earlier remains. Tribute to, and looting and destruction by, foreign rulers must also be a factor; Jehu, King of Israel, is depicted on the 'Black Obelisk'

(841 BC; London, BM) paying tribute to the Assyrian king, Shalmaneser III (reg 858–824 BC).

BIBLIOGRAPHY

J. W. Crowfoot and G. M. Crowfoot: *Early Ivories from Samaria* (1938), ii of *Samaria-Sebaste* (London, 1938–57)
R. B. K. Amiran: *Ancient Pottery of the Holy Land* (New Brunswick, 1970)
S. M. Paul and W. G. Dever: *Biblical Archaeology* (Jerusalem, 1973)
K. M. Kenyon: *The Bible and Recent Archaeology* (London, 1978, rev. 1987) [1987 ed. much rev. by P. R. S. Moorey]
A. Kempinski and R. Reich, eds: *The Architecture of Ancient Israel* (Jerusalem, 1992)

A. R. MILLARD

Israëls [Israels]. Dutch family of painters and printmakers.

(1) Jozef Israëls (*b* Groningen, 27 Jan 1824; *d* Scheveningen, 12 Aug 1911). He was, during his lifetime, the most internationally celebrated Dutch painter of the 19th century and a leader of the HAGUE SCHOOL. He was particularly noted for his scenes of life among the Dutch fishing and peasant communities.

1. LIFE AND WORK. From 1835 to 1842 he trained at the Academie Minerva in Groningen; his first teachers were Johan Joeke Gabriel van Wicheren (1808–97) and Cornelis Bernudes Buys (1808–72). In 1842 he continued his training in the studio of Jan Adam Kruseman in Amsterdam and took classes at the Koninklijke Academie, making his début in 1844 in Amsterdam. From September 1845 until May 1847 he was in Paris, where he worked in the studio of the history painter François-Edouard Picot and took classes at the École des Beaux-Arts under James Pradier, Horace Vernet and Paul Delaroche. After returning to the Netherlands he entered the competition for the Prix de Rome in painting at the Koninklijke Academie in Amsterdam. Between November 1847 and 1850 Israëls was again enrolled there and was recognized as one of several promising history painters in the circle of Jan Willem Pieneman, the Academie's principal director. It was at this time that he painted his first ambitious works, the biblical *Aaron and his Sons* (1848; untraced) and the more literary *Daydreaming* ('*Ophelia*') (1850; Dordrecht, Dordrechts Mus.), which established his reputation.

In the autumn of 1850 Israëls went to Düsseldorf; he returned a few months later via Oosterbeek, later to become a Dutch centre for painting *en plein air*, where the landscape painter Johannes Warnardus Bilders (1811–90) was staying. He settled temporarily in Amsterdam but returned in 1853 to Paris, from where he visited Barbizon. Although the sketches he made there show peasant interiors, the bulk of his work was hardly affected by the Barbizon school. He preferred to take his subjects either from Romantic poetry, inspired by the example of Ary Scheffer, or from Dutch national history, following the history painter Louis Gallait. In addition he continued painting small, sentimental genre paintings and portraits.

The strength of Israëls's initial ambition to become a history painter can be gauged in particular from *William of Orange in Council with the Regent Margaret of Parma* (1855; Amsterdam, Hist. Mus.), which he exhibited at the Exposition Universelle held in Paris in 1855. The painting had a mixed reception from critics, who seemed to prefer larger and more tragic scenes featuring ordinary people living in isolated communities. The generally unfavourable climate for history painting in the Netherlands at that time may also account for Israëls's decision to paint two scenes in 1856 featuring fishermen. It was especially with his large figure painting *Passing Mother's Grave*, also known as *The Way past the Graveyard* (1856; Amsterdam, Stedel. Mus.; see fig.), that Israëls introduced into Dutch art a powerful variant of French Realism. The success of this work encouraged him to specialize increasingly in paintings of fishermen. He portrayed both the grimmer side of the fisherman's life and his carefree open-air existence but, surprisingly, took little interest in the details of fishermen's working lives until the late 1880s. With the possible exception of the motifs of the card player and the distribution of bread, he also avoided the depiction of social conditions. Frequent subjects treated throughout his life include women awaiting the return of the fishermen (*After the Storm*, 1858; Amsterdam, Stedel. Mus.), the death of fishermen (*Fishermen Carrying a Drowned Man*, 1861; London, N.G.), fishermen's daughters at work (*Ida, the Fisherman's Daughter at the Door* or *Girl Knitting*, 1858; Antwerp, Kon. Mus. S. Kst.) and fishermen's children playing on the beach (*Children of the Sea* or *Little Boat*, 1863; Amsterdam, Stedel. Mus.).

In the 1860s Israëls began to paint more interior scenes, emphasizing such themes as motherhood (*Expectant Mother*, c. 1863; ex-Nunez priv. col., Breukelen), domestic harmony (*Happy Family*, c. 1870; Glasgow, A.G. & Mus.) and loving children (*Getting Better* or *Grandmother's Treasure*, 1862; New York, Met.). Other well-known subjects include orphans (*Katwijk Orphanage*, 1866; smaller replica,

Moscow, Pushkin Mus. F.A.), kitchen scenes (*Birthday Party* or *Woman Making Cakes*, c. 1872; ex-M. Newman Gal., London, 1973; see *Connoisseur* (April 1973), p. 57) and old women (*Sleepers*, c. 1868; Aberdeen, A.G.).

In 1871 Israëls moved from Amsterdam to The Hague, where several major figures of the Hague school were already living. It was in these surroundings that his interest in etching was aroused. Also from this period are his first major watercolours, in which he explored themes already adopted in his oil paintings. He had been using this technique for some time and from 1861 exhibited watercolours at the recently formed Société Belge des Aquarellistes. From 1871 Israëls also exhibited his watercolours in England and Scotland, where they were particularly popular. He made etchings for Dutch as well as foreign art dealers and for etching societies. Most important was his connection with the Paris firm Arnold & Tripp, which published *The Smoker* and *Shell Fisher* in 1882.

In the 1870s Israëls began to broaden his repertory to include peasant scenes. Early works in this genre, such as the *Shepherd's Prayer* (1863; Toledo, OH, Mus. A.) and *Cottage Madonna* (c. 1867; Detroit, MI, Inst. A.), suggest the influence of Millet, who became a major source of inspiration for Israëls. His peasant subjects, also frequently repeated, include coming back from work (*Return from the Fields*, c. 1878; sold New York, Sotheby's, 28 Oct 1982), having a meal (*Lunch in a Peasant Cottage in Karlshaven*, 1885; Dordrecht, Dordrechts Mus., which is a more elaborate version of the successful *Cobbler's Family at Supper* or *Frugal Meal*, 1876; Glasgow, A.G. & Mus.), the shepherd with his flock (*The Shepherd*, c. 1885; The Hague, Gemeentemus.) and the mother and child (*Maternal Bliss*, c. 1890; Amsterdam, Rijksmus.). Around 1880 Israëls became increasingly concerned to depict old age (*Growing Older*, 1878; The Hague, Gemeentemus.) and dying (*Alone in the World* or *Nothing Left*, c. 1880; The Hague, Rijksmus. Mesdag).

In 1881 Israëls met Max Liebermann; this was the beginning of a lasting friendship and reciprocal influence. In the early 1880s the emphasis of his work shifted towards depictions of labourers at work, often carrying heavy loads (*Fishermen's Wives from Zandvoort*, c. 1890; ex-Bedarida priv. col., Livorno). Towards the end of his life he was increasingly drawn to the Jewish environment as a source of inspiration (*Jewish Law Scribe*, 1902; Otterlo, Kröller-Müller) and also returned to biblical subjects (*Saul and David*, 1899; Amsterdam, Stedel. Mus.). This tendency must be viewed against the background of Israëls's strong identification with Rembrandt.

Throughout his life Israëls painted portraits; from the 1860s his sitters were primarily prominent persons (e.g. the *Liberal Statesman J. R. Thorbecke*, 1872; Leiden, Rijksuniv.). His portraits of fellow artists, such as *Willem Roelofs* (1892; The Hague, Gemeentemus.), also achieved fame. His *Self-portrait* (1908; Amsterdam, Rijksmus.) is a particularly revealing work. It shows the artist standing in front of his *Saul and David*. The subject had obsessed Israëls since his youth because of the contrast between melancholy (Saul) and idealism (David).

In broad terms Israëls's style can be said to have developed from colour towards tonal painting. His early history paintings show a smooth handling of the brush, a

Jozef Israëls: *Passing Mother's Grave* (or *The Way past the Graveyard*), oil on canvas, 2.44×1.78 m, 1856 (Amsterdam, Stedelijk Museum)

bright palette, strongly marked outlines and sharp contrasts between light and dark. In 1856 he began using broader brushstrokes and thicker layers of paint, his approach to form becoming less defined and his palette gradually darker. Not until the late 1870s was there any distinct change, with a grey tonality replacing his previously warm colour scheme and effective use of chiaroscuro and broad streaks replacing the subtly intermingled brushstrokes. Although he abandoned anecdotal detail, the titles remain as a reminder of the narrative character of his work. During his final period, from c. 1890, he used even broader brushstrokes, while brightening his palette again slightly.

Israëls's working methods have not yet been properly studied. On his journeys he recorded ideas for paintings in a sketchbook, later trying out several in watercolour. He stayed in fishing villages such as Zandvoort, Katwijk and Scheveningen and studied peasant life in Laren, Dongen and the country surrounding Delden. He also borrowed motifs from the work of such artists as his son (2) Isaac Israëls, Millet, Max Liebermann and other contemporaries or from the 17th-century Dutch genre painters. Israëls was not a *plein-air* painter. He usually placed his models in a fisherman's interior that he had reconstructed in his studio in the garden of his house in The Hague. He once remarked about his method: 'I choose a model which more or less corresponds with the type I have in mind, and then I paint from this model, *adding to it* what I have in my head.'

2. REPUTATION AND INFLUENCE. Israëls was a well-known artist in his own lifetime, not only within the Hague school circles but also abroad, particularly in Britain, Germany, North America and Italy. The distribution of reproductions caused his work to become popular at an early stage. His reputation was further enhanced by his participation in important international exhibitions: *Fishermen Carrying a Drowned Man* (1861; London, N.G.) was a triumphant success at both the Paris Salon of 1861 and the London International Exhibition of 1862. He was also fortunate in his contacts with art dealers, collectors and critics, for whose sake he would often travel. His work was appreciated in particular for its simplicity of subject-matter and the sensitivity with which it was rendered. Only the more radical critics thought it sentimental. The large number of exhibitions devoted to Israëls between 1885 and 1924 is an indication of the intense interest in his paintings. He received numerous medals and appointments. In The Hague he was Chairman of the painters' society, the Pulchri Studio, as well as the Hollandse Teeken-Maatschappij (Dutch Drawing Society); he was an honorary member of the Munich Secession, corresponding member of the Secession in Berlin and maintained close ties with the Venice Biennale.

Israëls became widely known for establishing Scheveningen fishing scenes as a popular genre. Among his followers in this were Adolphe Artz, Philip Lodewijk, Jacob Frederik Sadée (1837–1904) and Bernard Blommers. Israëls has also been considered the forerunner of the Laren school, which was led by Albert Neuhuys. In Britain he influenced the work of Frank Holl as well as the Newlyn school, the Glasgow Boys and painters at the Edinburgh School of Art, while in Germany he was a major source

of inspiration for Hans von Bartels. The early Dutch paintings of van Gogh also owed much to the subject-matter and handling of Israëls.

WRITINGS

Spanje, een reisverhaal [Spain, the record of a journey] (The Hague, 1899)

BIBLIOGRAPHY

C. Vosmaer: 'Jozef Israëls', *Onze hedendaagsche schilders* [Our painters of today] (The Hague, 1881)

J. Veth: 'Jozef Israëls', *Mannen van beteekenis in onze dagen* [Men of significance in our times], i (Haarlem, 1889), pp. 173–98

F. Netscher and P. Zilcken: *Jozef Israëls: L'Homme et l'artiste* (Amsterdam, 1890/R 1903) [incl. cat. of etchings to 1890]

P. Zilcken: 'Jozef Israëls, naar aanleiding van zijn zeventig-jarig jubileum' [Jozef Israëls, on the occasion of his 70th birthday], *De Gids*, lviii/1 (1894), pp. 369–87

M. Liebermann: 'Jozef Israëls', *Z. Bild. Kst*, xii (1901), pp. 145–56; also in *Die Phantasie in Malerei* (Frankfurt am Main, 1978); Eng. trans. as 'Jozef Israëls, the Man and his Work', *Pall Mall Gaz.* (Sept 1901), pp. 25–36

J. Veth: 'Modern Dutch Art: The Work of Jozef Israëls', *The Studio*, xxvi (1902), pp. 239–51

——: *Jozef Israëls en zijn kunst* (Arnhem and Nijmegen, 1904; Ger. trans., Amsterdam and Leipzig, 1906)

H. J. Hubert: *De etsen van Jozef Israëls: Een catalogus* [The etchings of Jozef Israels: a catalogue] (Amsterdam, 1909; Eng. trans., 1910)

J. Veth: 'Eenzelfde compositie bij Jozef Israëls en bij Millet' [A composition found in the work of both Jozef Israëls and Millet], *De Amsterdammer* (31 Jan 1909); rev. in *Onze Kst*, xi/2 (1912), pp. 41–8; Fr. trans. in *A. Flam. & Holl.*, xvii (1912), pp. 53–60

[J.] Tersteeg: *Een halve eeuw met Jozef Israëls* [Half a century with Jozef Israëls] (The Hague, 1910; Eng. trans., 1910)

M. Eisler: 'J. F. Millet en J. Israëls', *Onze Kst*, x/2 (1911), pp. 117–28

——: *Jozef Israëls* (London, 1924)

H. E. van Gelder: *Jozef Israels* (Amsterdam, [1947])

J. Knoef: 'Israëls-studiën, I: Een compositieprincipe', *Oud-Holland*, lxii (1947), pp. 79–86

Herdenkingstentoonstelling Jozef Israëls, 1824–1911 [Memorial exhibition Jozef Israëls, 1824–1911] (exh. cat., intro. J. de Gruyter; Groningen, Groninger Mus.; Arnhem, Gemeentemus.; 1961–2) [incl. bibliog.]

A. Boime: 'A Source for Van Gogh's Potato-eaters', *Gaz. B.-A.*, n. s. 5, lxvii (1966), pp. 249–53

J. de Gruyter: 'Jozef Israëls', *De Haagse School*, i (Rotterdam, 1968), pp. 46–59

The Hague School: Dutch Masters of the 19th Century (exh. cat., ed. R. de Leeuw, J. Silleris and C. Dumas; Paris, Grand Pal.; London, R.A.; The Hague, Gemeentemus.; 1983), pp. 187–99 [incl. bibliog.]

D. Dekkers: 'Jozef Israëls en Millet', *De school van Barbizon: Franse meesters van de 19de eeuw* (exh. cat., ed. J. Sillevis and H. Kraan; Ghent, Mus. S. Kst.; The Hague, Gemeentemus.; Paris, Fond. Custodia, Inst. Néer.; 1985–6), pp. 105–11; Eng. trans. (The Hague, 1985)

——: 'De kinderen der zee: De samenwerking tussen Jozef Israëls en Nicolaas Beets' [Children of the sea: the collaboration between Jozef Israëls and Nicolaas Beets], *Jong Holland*, ii/1 (1986), pp. 36–52

——: 'Jozef Israëls en de Koninklijke Akademie van Beeldende Kunsten te Amsterdam: Van kwekeling tot gevestigd schilder' [Jozef Israëls and the Royal Academy of Fine Arts in Amsterdam: from pupil to established painter], *Oud-Holland*, ci/1 (1987), pp. 65–86

J. Sillevis: 'Lettres de Jozef Israëls à Arnold et Tripp, marchands de tableaux à Paris (1881–92)', *Archv A. Fr.*, n. s., xxix (1988), pp. 141–62

D. Dekkers: *Een visserstragedie groot geschilderd: Jozef Israëls' 'Langs moeders graf'* [A fisherman's tragedy painted on a grand scale: Joseph Israëls's *Passing Mother's Grave*] (Zwolle, 1989)

The Age of van Gogh: Dutch Painting, 1880–1895 (exh. cat., Glasgow, Burrell Col.; Amsterdam, Rijksmus. van Gogh; 1990–91)

DIEUWERTJE DEKKERS

(2) Isaac (Lazarus) Israels (*b* Amsterdam, 3 Feb 1865; *d* The Hague, 7 Oct 1934). Son of (1) Jozef Israëls. He was largely self-taught, showing precocious talent and attending the Academie in The Hague in 1878–80. His first paintings date from 1880–84 and include a self-portrait, portraits of women and military subjects such as *Bugle Practice* (1881; The Hague, Rijksmus. Mesdag). They were composed in the studio in a precise style, soft grey and brown tones predominating, showing the influence of the Hague school. In 1887 Israels moved to Amsterdam, where he was at the centre of the Tachtigers (Eighties Movement) of writers and painters. Among his friends were George Hendrik Breitner, Lodewijk van Dyssel, Frans Erens, Max Liebermann, Jan Pieter Veth and Jan Voerman. In Amsterdam, after a brief and abortive period at the Rijksacademie, he sought a more fluent technique with which to record contemporary life. His drawings and watercolours are predominantly of cafés, cabarets, dance halls and the street life of Amsterdam. In 1889 he visited Paris, where he met Stéphane Mallarmé, Berthe Morisot, Odilon Redon and Emile Zola. In 1894 he painted *Three Servant Girls* (priv. col.), the first of his *plein-air* pictures. From then on he applied transparent colours (mainly pink, blues, green and light brown) to capture the fleeting effects of light in oil, watercolour and pastel. His oils were painted in flat broad strokes. For the rest of his life he employed his very personal Impressionist style, which emphasized the interplay of light, colour, line and movement. His favourite subjects were beach, street and park scenes (e.g. *Dressmaker in the Jardin des Tuileries*, Dordrecht, Dordrechts Mus.), seamstresses in fashion houses, cabarets and circuses, fairs, ballet schools and the theatre. He also painted portraits, nudes and occasionally still-lifes.

Between 1903 and 1914 Israels had a studio in Paris but played little part in the Parisian artistic world. In 1913–14 he was in London, and from 1915 to 1934 he was mainly in The Hague, except for travels abroad, including South-east Asia (1922). He also produced etchings (1912–13) and lithographs (1933).

BIBLIOGRAPHY
A. Wagner: *Isaac Israels* (Rotterdam, 1967, rev. Venlo, 1985) [with Eng. summary]
——: *Isaac Israels*, A. & Archit. Netherlands (Amsterdam, 1969)
ANNA WAGNER

Israyelyan, Rafayel (Sarqis) (*b* Tiflis [now Tbilisi], 17 Sept 1908; *d* Erevan, 8 Sept 1973). Armenian architect of Georgian birth. He studied, from 1928 to 1930, in the architectural faculty of the Academy of Arts, Tiflis, and then in the architectural faculty of the Institute of Communal Construction, Leningrad (now St Petersburg), from 1930 to 1932, and at the Academy of Arts, Leningrad, from 1932 to 1934. From 1936 he worked in Erevan, where he designed massive constructions of natural stone combining neo-classicism with Armenian architectural traditions, of which he was a more consistent interpreter than Alek'sandr T'amanyan. He built an intricate complex of wine cellars (1937) for the Ararat Trust, Erevan, its concise volumes blending organically with the rocky landscape. These are constantly undergoing alteration and renovation. Connected to the complex is a stone aqueduct over the River Hrazdan. During and after World War II, continuing the Armenian custom of commemorating the dead at springs, he built monuments in numerous towns and villages. He also revived the ancient Armenian tradition of the *khatchk'ar* (*see* ARMENIA, §IV, 1(ii)), a stele with relief decoration. Larger designs include the monument to *Victory in Erevan* (1950–67), on the Kanaker Plateau, and the monument to the *Battle of Sardarapat* (1968), near Hoktemberyan, where a tall, three-bay belfry

provides the focal point. The Museum of the Ethnography of Armenia (1968–78), Hoktemberyan, in which Armenian traditions are apparent in the massive outer stone casing and in the complex forms of the reinforced-concrete roofs, achieves its effect in the contrast of the monolithic, blank-walled exterior and the airy lightness of the interior. He also designed the Armenian church of St Vardan (1970s), New York, and a number of residential buildings, in which the unique character of his work, uniting characteristics of the 20th-century professional architect and of a traditional folk craftsman, is also realized.

WRITINGS
'Ob osvoyenii naslediya' [Concerning the mastery of one's heritage], *Tvorcheskiye problemy sovetskoy arkhitektury* [Creative problems in Soviet architecture], ed. E. Levinson and B. Muzaviev (Moscow, 1956), pp. 59–84
Hodvacner, usumnasirut 'yunner, aknarkner [Articles, studies and reviews] (Erevan, 1982)

BIBLIOGRAPHY
L. Babayan: 'Rafayel Israyelyan', *Sovetakan Arvest*, 11 (1958); *Garun*, 1 (1971)
Rafayel Israyelyan v vospominaniyakh sovremmenikov [Rafayel Israyelyan as recalled by his contemporaries] (Yerevan, 1981) [in Armen.]
A. M. Babayan and Yu. S. Yaralov: *Rafayel Israyelyan* (Moscow, 1986)
A. V. IKONNIKOV

Issakovitch, Serge (Ivan). *See* CHERMAYEFF, SERGE.

Issei Suda. *See* SUDA, ISSEI.

Isselburg [Eisselburg; Iselburg; Yselburg], **Peter** (*b* Cologne, *c.* 1580 or ?1568; *d* Bamberg or Nuremberg, 1630 or later). German draughtsman, engraver and printer. He is thought to have been a student of Crispijn van de Passe I or another Netherlandish artist. His work is known from 1606, when he was in Cologne, primarily producing frontispieces and prints for Cologne painters; by 1610 he was resident in Nuremberg. His work subsequently encompassed a broader spectrum of subjects, including religious works of modest significance but also portraits of scholars, generals and secular and clerical princes, for which he sketched many of the engraved models. His city panoramas are of historical interest and are distinguished by great technical proficiency. He also left a large number of sheets with emblems, costumes and scenes from history. In 1622 he was seriously warned by Nuremberg city council for engraving lampoons. He moved to Bamberg in 1623, where he became a printer (1625), then to Coburg *c.* 1626 and back to Nuremberg in 1630. He was regarded as one of the most important German artists in his day and from 1620 was the teacher of Joachim von Sandrart.

BIBLIOGRAPHY
ADB; Hollstein: *Ger.*; *NDB*; Thieme–Becker
J. von Sandrart: *Teutsche Academie* (1675–9); ed. A. R. Peltzer (1925), pp. 21, 242, 381, 410
E. Firmenich-Richartz and H. Keussen, eds: *Kölnische Künstler in alter und neuer Zeit, Johann Jacob Merlos neu bearbeitete und erweiterte Nachrichten von dem Leben und den Werken kölnischer Künstler* (Düsseldorf, 1895), pp. 453–73 [cat.]
K. Pilz: 'Nürnberg und die Niederlande', *Mitt. Ver. Gesch. Stadt Nürnberg*, xliii (1952), pp. 1–153 (107–8, 124)
Barock in Nürnberg, 1600–1750: Aus Anlass der Dreihundertjahrfeier der Akademie der Bildenden Künste (exh. cat., Nuremberg, Ger. Nmus., 1962), A 31–2, pp 42–3; B4, 5, 7–9, pp. 98–100
K. Sitzmann: *Künstler und Kunsthandwerker in Ostfranken* (2nd edn, Kulmbach, 1983), pp. 272f
WERNER WILHELM SCHNABEL

Isshō. *See* MARUYAMA ŌKYO.

Issiakhem, M'hamed [Isyākhim, M'hammad] (*b* Djennad, nr Azzefoun, 1928; *d* Algiers, 1 Dec 1985). Algerian painter. Wounded by a home-made bomb in 1943, his left arm was amputated and he was hospitalized for two years. From 1947 to 1951 he studied first at the Société des Beaux-Arts and then at the Ecole des Beaux-Arts in Algiers, while simultaneously training in miniature painting with Omar Racim. In 1953 he continued his studies at the Ecole Nationale Supérieure des Beaux-Arts in Paris, where he worked in the painting atelier of Raymond Legueult (1898–1978), graduating in 1958. While in Paris, Issiakhem witnessed the development of Abstract Expressionism and other artistic styles, which he quickly adopted. A pioneer of modern Algerian art, he was one of the founders of the Algerian National Union of Plastic Arts in 1963 and held exhibitions in Algeria and abroad. Attracted by left-wing ideas, he travelled to Vietnam in 1972 and Moscow in 1978. In his work, male figures are surrounded by forms, signs and blotches in sombre colours, while his female figures express drama and silent suffering (e.g. *Homage to Katia*; 1984; oil on canvas; Paris, Inst. Monde Arab.).

BIBLIOGRAPHY
W. Ali: *A Survey of Modern Painting in the Islamic World and the Development of the Contemporary Calligraphic School* (diss., U. London, SOAS, 1993)
W. ALI

Issyk. Burial site 50 km east of Almaty in Kazakhstan. The 3-km long site comprises 45 earthen mounds in an embankment ranging in width from 30 to 90 m and in height from 4 to 15 m. Some mounds show traces of looting, and one mound (diam. 60 m, h. 6 m) excavated by Kemal K. Akishev in 1969–70 had a crater in its surface, through which looters had gained access to the central burial site, now completely destroyed. However, another chamber entered from the side underneath the same embankment, 15 m to the south of the central grave, was undisturbed, and, judging from the wealth of objects found there, was the burial chamber of a tribal leader. Comparable with the European Scythian burial sites, it is the first and only burial complex of such a high-ranking person to have been excavated in Central Asia. The burial (mid-1st millennium BC) was established by Saka tribes, and both the costume and burial rites were similar to those used at TILLYA TEPE in northern Afghanistan in the 1st century AD.

The burial chamber (3.3×1.9 m) was constructed from treated pine beams (250–300 mm thick) from the Tian Shan Mountains, and the floor was covered with boards. The dead person lay at the northern end of the chamber on his back, with his head facing west. Vessels and other items were placed at the south and west ends of the chamber, and gold-leaf objects to decorate the clothing, headgear and footgear lay on and underneath the skeleton. Weapons, objects for personal hygiene, including a circular gilt bronze mirror with handles at the sides and two concentric circles on the back, and other objects were found beside the dead person. Metal plates and plaques of different sizes and shapes were found next to the skull over an area 650×300 mm. Parts of the headgear decoration found lying undisturbed 650 mm from the skull include a diadem attached to the base of the headgear; metal plates and plaques, six in the shape of a lion's jaws, others decorated with angry snow leopards standing on their back legs, a mountain goat, birds, trees, horses or mountain peaks; a miniature gold figurine (16×19 mm) of a mountain ram (argali), set on a convex rectangular stand by which it was attached to the upper part of the headgear; and two symmetrical metal plates with appliqué work (100×175 mm) depicting the protomes of a winged horse with the horns of a mountain goat, the side pieces of the headgear flanking the ram on the forehead. The deceased's gold jewellery comprised an earring, a pendant and two rings. Metal plaques with a tiger's head *en face* were sewn on to the fabric of the tribal leader's clothing between 59 horizontal and 59 vertical slats; they included 2411 small triangles, 30 small rectangles, 488 rectangles, 162 squares, 30 circles, 108 crescents and 113 rhomboids. The belt was made of massive rectangular plates on to which were affixed smaller plates in the shape of a reclining deer or a deer's head. An iron dagger, its upper side shaped like the head of two facing griffins and its handle and sheath decorated with gold plates depicting an elk and horse, and a sword, its upper side and cross encrusted with small gold plaques and gold thread twisted around the handle, were hung from the belt. Only 31 vessels were found. They included two silver bowls—a large one, the outside engraved with 32 rings and the inside decorated with two concentric circles, and a small one, the outside decorated with 26 signs resembling Aramaic letters but still undeciphered; a bronze bowl; two dishes, one large (675×375 mm) and one small (460×290 mm), made from a single piece of birch; ten ceramic ewers and six basins. Other finds include silver forks with the upper part of the handle in the shape of a bird's neck and head with a sharp beak.

BIBLIOGRAPHY
K. K. Akishev: *Kurgan Issyk: Iskusstvo sakov Kazakhstana* [Issyk Mound: the art of the Saka in Kazakhstan] (Moscow, 1978) [incl. Eng. summary]
YE. V. ZEYMAL'

Istanbul [Turk. İstanbul; anc. Byzantium, Gr. Byzantion; formerly Constantinople, Gr. Konstantinoupolis, Arab. and Ott. Quṣṭantiniya, Turk. Konstantiniye]. Largest city in the Republic of Turkey, occupying the most south-easterly peninsula of Europe and separated from its suburbs in Asia by the Bosphorus. The European part of Istanbul is bisected by a long salt-water inlet, the Golden Horn, on the south bank of which is the oldest section of the city and on the north bank the port of Galata. At the apex of the peninsula the waters of the Golden Horn and Bosporus (Bosphorus) meet and flow into the Sea of Marmara. From the 7th century BC until AD 330 the Greek settlement and Roman city on this site were known as Byzantion. As Constantinople, it was one of the great cities and eventually the capital of the Eastern Roman (subsequently Byzantine) empire from 330 to 1453, except for the years of Latin occupation (1204–61). As Istanbul, it was the capital of the Ottoman empire from 1453 to

1923, although the city continued to be called Constantinople in Western and some official Ottoman sources until the 20th century.

I. History and urban development. II. Art life and organization. III. Buildings.

I. History and urban development.

Whatever the prehistoric antecedents of Istanbul, the continuous historical development of the site began with the foundation of a Greek colony from Megara in the mid-7th century BC. Despite its strategic location, however, Byzantion did not become a leading cultural or political centre within the ancient Greek world. Not until AD 330, when Constantine the Great founded a new capital on the site, did the city acquire a role that profoundly influenced the history of Europe and Asia Minor for the next 1000 years. Although some of the most famous buildings from the Byzantine period survive in Istanbul, many more have perished without trace. Since only a fraction of the city has been excavated, the evidence for them comes mainly from the ancient writers, inscriptions and medieval and later views of the city and its structures. Fires, earthquakes, the ravages of war and neglect have all taken their toll.

Under Ottoman rule, Istanbul initially flourished. Great mosque complexes, markets and the splendid residences of the sultans and their courtiers mingled with the monuments of a bygone empire. Fires and earthquakes are also recorded for this period, but since the early 19th century the most dramatic change in Istanbul's urban development has been its gradual transformation into a Western-style city. Although in 1923 it was replaced by Ankara as the capital of the Turkish Republic, it has nevertheless had to contend with a rapidly expanding population and the pressing need to house growing numbers of Anatolians who come in search of work.

1. Before AD 532. 2. AD 532–1204. 3. 1205–1453. 4. 1454–1838. 5. 1839–1923. 6. After 1923.

1. BEFORE AD 532.

(i) Ancient Byzantion. (ii) The city of Constantine. (iii) From the Theodosian expansion to AD 532.

(i) Ancient Byzantion. The Megaran colony of Byzantion occupied the hilly eastern end of a peninsula defined on the south by the Sea of Marmara (anc. Propontis) and on the north by the Golden Horn; to the west the site was connected to the continent of Europe by a neck of land that was then more of an isthmus than an evenly tapering triangle. Byzantion enjoyed a commanding position at a point where a natural land route from Europe to Asia crossed the sea passage from the Black Sea to the Mediterranean. The sea, besides providing natural defences and rich fishing grounds, gave access to a wide range of imported products. The hinterland was rich in grain and timber, and good-quality building stone was close at hand in the marble quarries of the island of Prokonnesos in the Sea of Marmara. For all these advantages, Byzantion was not naturally well supplied with water or defensible on the landward side. Although a key strategic point in the wars for control of the region, the city was not able to fulfil its unique amphibious potential until it became part of the Roman Empire. Under the pax Romana, Byzantion was the eastern terminus of the two main Roman roads across the Balkans: the *via militaris* from the Middle Danube, and the Via Egnatia from the lower Adriatic and Thessaloniki. In common with all the Greek cities of the Balkan and Aegean area, Byzantion adopted the basic elements of Roman civic architecture: the arch, the vault, the dome and the basilica, and the construction of walls with brick facing and concrete and rubble core. The emperor Hadrian (*reg* AD 117–38) provided the city with an aqueduct, part of which still stands, and Septimius Severus, having destroyed the city after the revolt of 193–6, rebuilt it in a form that reinforced its Roman features and thus foreshadowed the city of Constantine (see fig. 1).

The nucleus of Byzantion consisted of an acropolis occupying the hill at the eastern tip of the peninsula (for the later development of this region *see* §III, 13(i) below), and a commercial–residential quarter spreading inland from the natural harbours just inside the Golden Horn. The acropolis housed the city's temples, which were dedicated to Aphrodite, Artemis, the Sun and Poseidon, and had a theatre (1i) on its eastern slope. To the west, the settlement developed around two main squares: the agora, later known as the Strategion (1ii), and the Tetrastoon, so named after its four porticos (but subsequently known as the Augustaion; 1iii). A transverse avenue, later known to Byzantines as the Mese, or central street, formed the eastern extremity of the Via Egnatia and connected the Tetrastoon with the main city gate. It was this southwestern quarter of the city that achieved its greatest development under Septimius Severus, who is said to have built the Baths of Zeuxippos (1iv), the Hippodrome (1v) for chariot racing and porticos lining the Mese. He also rebuilt the theatre and to the north of this added an arena, the Kynegion (1vi), for wild-beast shows.

(ii) The city of Constantine. In AD 324 Constantine began to transform Byzantion into a great imperial city bearing his name. The initial transformation was conditioned by the geographical constraints of the site, the prior existence of the ancient settlement and the Via Egnatia, and the Roman imperial ideology of the Tetrarchy (293–312). Within the walls Constantine built on the legacy of Septimius Severus, and outside expansion followed the axis of the Via Egnatia. The site of the Hippodrome determined the site of the Great Palace (1vii; *see* §III, 12 below), for in Rome and in the other cities where emperors had resided the palace closely adjoined the circus, thus allowing the emperor direct access to the box from which he watched the games.

Constantine's foundation, formally inaugurated on 11 May 330, was defined by a new set of land walls more than tripling the area of the city, which now consisted of an old and a new town. The newer part of the old town, comprising the Hippodrome, the Baths of Zeuxippos, the Tetrastoon and the porticos lining the Mese, was rebuilt on a grand scale, with the addition of various new structures grouped around the Tetrastoon: the Great Palace, a senate house (1viii), the imperial stoa known as the Basilica (1ix) and the domed, four-arched Milion (1x), which marked the end of the Via Egnatia. The main

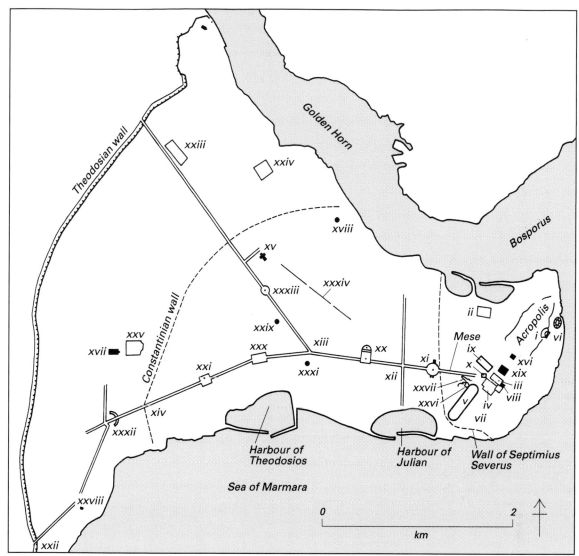

1. Plan of Constantinople showing major monuments, before AD 532: (i) Theatre; (ii) Strategion; (iii) Tetrastoon/Augustaion; (iv) Baths of Zeuxippos; (v) Hippodrome; (vi) Kynegion; (vii) Great (Sacred) Palace; (viii) Senate House; (ix) Basilica; (x) Milion; (xi) Forum of Constantine; (xii) Tetrapylon; (xiii) Capitol; (xiv) Golden Gate of Constantine/Gate of Satournios; (xv) Constantine's mausoleum/Church of the Holy Apostles; (xvi) Hagia Eirene; (xvii) St Mokios; (xviii) St Akakios; (xix) Hagia Sophia; (xx) Forum of Theodosios/Forum Tauri; (xxi) Forum of Arkadios; (xxii) Golden Gate; (xxiii) Cistern of Aetios; (xxiv) Cistern of Aspar; (xxv) Cistern of Mokios; (xxvi) Palace of Antiochos; (xxvii) Palace of Lausos; (xxviii) St John Stoudios; (xxix) St Polyeuktos; (xxx) Forum Bovis; (xxxi) Rotunda; (xxxii) Baths of Helenianai; (xxxiii) Column of Marcian; (xxxiv) Aqueduct of Valens

landmarks of the new town were a series of monumental structures along the continuation of the Mese: the circular Forum of Constantine (1xi), with its senate house and red porphyry column bearing the Emperor's statue; the Tetrapylon (1xii), where the Mese intersected with a transverse avenue connecting the Sea of Marmara and the Golden Horn; the group of statuary known as the Philadelphion near the Capitol (1xiii), at the point where the Mese forked; the ceremonial Golden Gate (also known as the Gate of Satournios; 1xiv), through which the southern branch of the Mese left the new city wall; and the Church of the Holy Apostles, Constantine's mausoleum (1xv); see

also §III, 9(i) below), just inside this wall near the northern branch of the avenue.

This programme was clearly designed to create a megalopolis on a par with Rome, Antioch and Alexandria. Its pretensions were emphasized by the importation of works of art looted from all over the Greek world. Yet Constantinople did not as yet represent a new departure in ancient urban planning. It was the last, albeit the greatest, in the series of Tetrarchic 'Romes from Rome', and like its predecessors, namely Trier, Milan, Thessaloniki and Nicomedia (now Ismit, Turkey), it replicated those features of Rome that served the administrative and ceremonial needs of an itinerant military court. It was not intended to replace Rome, or to displace the economic and cultural centre of Byzantion. Constantine, despite his Christianity, did not close the pagan temples on the acropolis. The cathedral church of Hagia Eirene (1xvi; *see* §III, 5 below) merely added to the row of cult centres in the old town, and the martyr churches of St Mokios (destr.; 1xvii) and St Akakios (destr. early 5th century, later rebuilt; 1xviii) were very much on the edge of the new town. None of these buildings constituted a new civic focus.

The urban space marked out by Constantine developed slowly under his immediate successors, who improved the water supply, harbour capacity and bathing facilities. The Christian character of the city became gradually more emphatic with the building of two major churches, Hagia Sophia (1xix; see §III, 1(i) below) and the new Holy Apostles, by Constantius II (*reg* 337–61), and the foundation of the first monasteries and welfare institutions. It was not, however, until after the disaster of 378 when Emperor Valens was killed in battle against the Goths that Roman emperors seriously invested in the future of Constantinople as an imperial and Christian capital.

(iii) From the Theodosian expansion to AD *532.* Although as mobile as any of his predecessors, Theodosios I was more at home in Constantinople than elsewhere, and his son Arkadios (*reg* 395–408) and grandson Theodosios II (*reg* 408–50) resided there permanently. Under this dynasty the pace of urban expansion quickened dramatically. New public monuments (*see* LATE ANTIQUITY, fig. 1) and a new public bath were erected in the old town, and at least two new fora (i.e. Forum of Theodosios or Forum Tauri and Forum of Arkadios; see fig. 1xx and xxi), dominated by triumphal columns, were laid out along the Mese. The urban infrastructure was enlarged by the creation of a new harbour, and by the construction of massive new fortifications both on the land and along the sea shore. The new land walls, which were entered by an even grander Golden Gate (1xxii), doubled the area of the Constantinian city. Their purpose seems to have been to protect the vast open-air reservoirs (often called cisterns; 1xxiii, xxiv and xxv) sunk on the high ground to the west of the Constantinian wall, which was left standing. The main expansion of the built-up area occurred within this wall, primarily on land reclaimed from the sea. The cells of this urban growth were units known as *oikoi* ('houses'), denoting both palatial mansions (e.g. Palace of Antiochos, 1xxv; and Palace of Lausos, 1xxvii) and tenement blocks. Churches, monasteries and welfare establishments also proliferated, partly under imperial patronage, but mainly on the initiative of wealthy individuals such as Stoudius, founder of St John Stoudios (lxxviii; *see* §III, 6 below).

By the mid-5th century Constantinople was coming of age as not only the New Rome but also a New Jerusalem, with a population estimated at between 300,000 and 600,000. From this point its appearance was regularly disfigured by two symptoms of overcrowding: devastating fires and popular violence associated with the Hippodrome games. Contemporary legislation gives the impression that the neat, rectangular ancient city was developing into a ramshackle medieval maze. The continued construction

of churches, many of them converted from private mansions, was also beginning to transform the aesthetic character of the city, especially since it was accompanied by the collection of Christian relics in preference to Greek statues and Egyptian obelisks. Yet such churches as St Polyeuktos (524–7; destr.; see fig. 1xxix), erected by ANICIA JULIANA, were clearly imposing public monuments, whose ample porticoed courtyards harmonized well with the monumental urban environment. The construction of fora and public baths slowed down but did not cease, and popular charioteers as well as emperors were honoured by public statues. Above all, the emperors of this period and their subordinates had both the material resources and the cultural incentive to build in the style and on the scale of their predecessors.

BIBLIOGRAPHY

EARLY SOURCES
Chronicon Paschale (7th century AD); Eng. trans., ed. M. Whitby and M. Whitby as *Chronicon Paschale: 284–628 AD* (Liverpool, 1989)

GENERAL
A. van Millingen: *Byzantine Constantinople: The Walls of the City and Adjoining Historical Sites* (London, 1899)
R. Janin: *Constantinople byzantine* (Paris, 1950, 2/1964)
T. F. Mathews: *The Early Churches of Constantinople: Architecture and Liturgy* (University Park, PA, and London, 1971)
C. Mango: *The Art of the Byzantine Empire, 312–1453: Sources and Documents* (Englewood Cliffs, 1972/R Toronto, Buffalo and London, 1986)
G. Dagron: *Naissance d'une capitale: Constantinople et ses institutions de 330 à 451* (Paris, 1974)
C. Mango: *Architettura byzantina* (Milan, 1974; Eng. trans., New York, 1976/R London, 1986)
A. Cameron: *Circus Factions* (Oxford, 1976)
T. F. Mathews: *The Byzantine Churches of Istanbul: A Photographic Survey* (University Park, PA, and London, 1976)
W. Müller-Wiener: *Bildlexicon zur Topographie Istanbuls: Byzantion-Konstantinupolis-Istanbul bis zum Beginn des 17. Jahrhunderts* (Tübingen, 1977)
A. Berger: *Das Bad in der byzantinischen Zeit* (Munich, 1982)
C. Mango: *Le Développement urbain de Constantinople (IVe–VIIe siècles)* (Paris, 1985, 2/1990)
——: 'The Development of Constantinople as an Urban Centre', *The 17th Byzantine Congress, Major Papers: Washington, 1985*; repr. C. Mango: *Studies on Constantinople* (Aldershot, Hants, and Brookfield, VT, 1993), pp. 117–36
T. S. Miller: *The Birth of the Hospital in the Byzantine Empire* (Baltimore, 1985)
A. Berger: *Untersuchungen zu den Patria Konstantinupoleos* (Bonn, 1988)
J. Durliat: *De la ville antique à la ville byzantine: Le Problème des subsistances* (Paris and Rome, 1990)
C. Mango: *Studies on Constantinople* (Aldershot, Hants, and Brookfield, VT, 1993)

2. AD 532–1204.

(i) From the Nika Riot (AD 532) to the early 7th century. (ii) Mid-7th century–1204.

*(i) From the Nika Riot (*AD *532) to the early 7th century.* The reign of Justinian I was undoubtedly a turning-point in the urban development of Constantinople. In 532 the Nika Riot left tens of thousands dead and the civic centre of the old town burnt to the ground. Ten years later the city was struck by an epidemic of bubonic plague, which killed half the population and recurred at regular intervals for the next two centuries. At the time of these disasters Justinian was a fanatical Christian autocrat much less concerned to preserve traditional civic culture than to ensure 'that everything might have a new look and be associated with his name' (Prokopios, *The Secret History*

XI.2). Although he rebuilt everything that had been destroyed in the fire of 532, he gave pride of place to the church of Hagia Sophia (see fig. 2(a) and §III, 1(ii) below), which rose from the ashes in a new form and on a vast, elevated scale, dominating the skyline like no other building. Hagia Sophia was the grandest of many churches that Justinian built or rebuilt. The emphasis on church-building was maintained by his successors JUSTIN II, Tiberios (reg 578–82) and Maurice (reg 582–602), so much so that a separate section of the imperial patrimony was earmarked for the financing of new churches. Under these 6th-century emperors, the city's religious establishments achieved the form in which they were to serve the populace for the next three centuries. Significant for the future, too, was the amount of investment in palace-building. Justinian

rebuilt and redecorated the Chalke ('Bronze Gate'; 2b), the main entrance to the Great Palace (2c; see §III, 12 below) and Justin II constructed the Chrysotriklinos ('Golden Throne Room'). This domed, apsidal structure, which seems to have resembled S Vitale in Ravenna (see RAVENNA, §2(vii)), was in a sense the secular equivalent of Hagia Sophia, and served as the hub of palace ceremonial until the 12th century.

The 6th century thus quickened the pace of transition from the open space of the ancient city, with its public squares, porticos, baths and entertainments, to the closed spaces of medieval Constantinople, where elaborate rituals were acted out behind high walls and artistic energies were channelled into the two-dimensional decoration of the interior surfaces of churches and palaces. Yet the degree

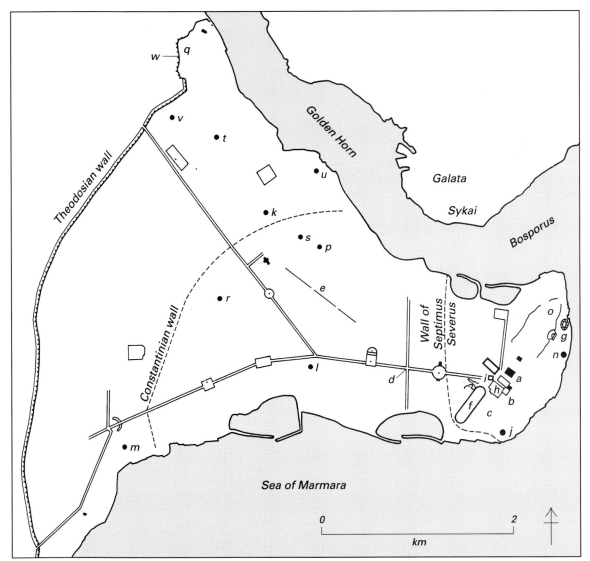

2. Plan of Constantinople showing major monuments, AD 532–1204: (a) Hagia Sophia; (b) Chalke ('Bronze Gate'); (c) Great Palace; (d) Tetrapylon; (e) Aqueduct of Valens; (f) Hippodrome; (g) Kynegion; (h) Augustaion; (i) Milion; (j) Nea Ekklesia ('New Church'); (k) Petrion; (l) Myrelaion; (m) St Mary Peribleptos; (n) St George of the Mangana; (o) Orphanage; (p) monastery of Christ Pantokrator; (q) Blachernai Palace; (r) monastery of Constantine Lips; (s) monastery of Christ Pantepoptes; (t) St Mary Pammakaristos; (u) Christ Evergetis; (v) Christ the Saviour in Chora; (w) early 7th-century wall

of transition at this stage should not be overstated. Justinian built a theatre in the city suburb of Sykai across the Golden Horn, and it should not be overlooked that Prokopios, in his account of the emperor's church and palace buildings (*Buildings* I.i.20–78; x.10–20), treats them as features of the general urban and suburban landscape, closely related to the sea shore, which the emperor improved, at great expense, with embankments and breakwaters. The 6th-century emperors continued the tradition of having themselves represented in public statues, and their successor Phokas (*reg* 602–10) placed his on a triumphal column near the Tetrapylon (2d). Seen in this light, the crises of 532 and 542 seem less decisive for the decline of the ancient city than the disruption of the food and water supplies in the reign of Heraklios (*reg* 610–41). The Persian conquest of Egypt (619) forced Heraklios to end the state distribution of bread to the city populace, and the invading Avars destroyed the Aqueduct of Valens (2e) in 626; it was not repaired until 768.

(ii) Mid-7th century–1204. The frustration of attempts by Heraklios and Constans II (*reg* 641–68) to transfer the seat of imperial government to the West, and the failure of massive attacks by the Avars (626) and Arabs (674–8 and 717–18), enabled Constantinople to survive as the political and ecclesiastical capital of a much-reduced empire. The walls, the main churches and philanthropic foundations, the Hippodrome (2f) and the Great Palace were kept in basic repair. Yet apart from some additions to the palace by Justinian II (*reg* 685–95; 705–11) there was no new building, and the occupied space within the walls contracted sharply, reflecting a considerable fall in population. The old public baths were abandoned for smaller establishments attached to religious institutions. The Kynegion (2g) became a place of execution, burials were allowed inside Constantine's wall, and several major squares became markets for livestock, slaves and hay. Public life centred on the Hippodrome and the Augustaion (2h), where changes in official ideology were publicized in pictures on the Chalke and the Milion (2i). The iconoclastic controversy (726–843) led to redecoration, but no rebuilding, of churches. The statues and secular monuments of late antiquity were contemplated with a mixture of superstitious dread and fanciful speculation about the city's early history.

From the reign of Constantine V (741–75) Constantinople, along with the rest of the Aegean area, experienced a slow demographic and economic revival which continued until 1204 and was reflected in the steady redevelopment of the city's built-up area. This redevelopment was characterized by investment in the magnate *oikos* ('house') at the expense of the civic environment as a monumental whole. Whether its nucleus was a secular (i.e. imperial or aristocratic) household or a religious (i.e. monastic or clerical) community, the *oikos* was a self-contained, inward-looking social, economic and architectural unit. Although the emperors of the 9th and 10th centuries restored the old public churches and certain civic monuments, in accordance with their ideology of imperial renewal, the new buildings which they constructed were mostly in or attached to the Great Palace. Initially the emperors lagged behind other private individuals in the foundation of

monasteries, preferring to expend most of their religious patronage on costly palatine-collegiate churches, such as the Nea Ekklesia ('New Church'; *c.* 880; destr. 15th century; 2j) of Basil I and the Christ Chalkites (next to the Chalke) of John I (*reg* 969–76). Basil I and Romanos I (*reg* 920–44), however, both founded monastic houses, the Petrion (*c.* 867–86; 2k, approx. location) and the Myrelaion (Turk. Bodrum Camii; 920; 2l), which adumbrated the series of great imperial 'abbeys' that constituted the most spectacular additions to the city in the 11th and 12th centuries. These foundations were characterized by their close personal association with the founder and his family, who were often buried in the monastery church, by the variety of functions—philanthropic, educational and medical, as well as monastic—that they combined, by their status as 'crown' trusts, and by their extensive property holdings throughout the Aegean area. The proliferation of imperial *oikoi* received an added boost with the accession of Alexios I Komnenos (*reg* 1081–1118), who altered the constitution to give his extended family an enormous share of imperial wealth and privilege, which allowed them to build splendid palaces and to found and endow monasteries on a comparable scale. The new imperial foundations of the 11th and 12th centuries were nearly all located in the more thinly populated parts of the city. St Mary Peribleptos (2m) of Romanos III Argyros (*reg* 1028–34) was in the south-west corner; and Michael IV (*reg* 1034–41) founded his monastery of SS Cosmas and Damian outside the walls, on the Golden Horn. The two largest foundations, St George of the Mangana (1048–54; destr.; 2n), founded by Constantine IX (see MACEDONIAN DYNASTY, (4)) and the Orphanage of St Paul (destr.; 2o, approx. location), an old establishment (possibly 6th century) that Alexios I refounded on a grander scale, were both in the relatively undeveloped acropolis area at the eastern end of the old city. John II built the monastery of Christ Pantokrator (2p; see §III, 2 below) on a hill between the aqueduct and the Golden Horn. It was the last in a chain of monasteries founded, refounded or sponsored by the Komnenian dynasty in the fairly empty space between the Blachernai quarter and the city centre (see below). This development was due in part to the tendency of Alexios I and his successors to reside at the Blachernai Palace (2q), which they extended, without, however, neglecting the Great Palace; the last major additions to this complex were made by Manuel I (*reg* 1143–80).

Church buildings still survive from the monastery founded by Constantine Lips in 907 (Turk. Fenarı Isa Cami; 2r), the Myrelaion, and a number of Komnenian foundations: Christ Pantepoptes (Turk. Eski Imaret Camii; before 1087; 2s; see EARLY CHRISTIAN AND BYZANTINE ART, fig. 23), St Mary Pammakaristos (2t; see III, 7 below), Christ Evergetis (possibly Turk. Gül Camii; *c.* 1100; 2u), Christ the Saviour in Chora (2v; see §III, 3 below), and the Pantokrator. Excavation has also revealed the impressive ground-plan of the Mangana monastery church. It is more difficult to visualize the appearance of the other structures of which the great Constantinopolitan *oikoi* were composed; the insignificant surviving fragments of the Great Palace and of the Orphanage of St Paul are little to go on. The one certain fact about all the buildings of this period is that they made extensive reuse of older buildings, which served as substructures and, above all, as quarries of choice marble spolia for jambs, lintels, paving and mural revetment. The growth and proliferation of large, consumer magnate houses necessarily involved an increase in the artisan and trading population of the city, which by the 11th century was sufficiently sizeable and organized to exert pressure at times of political crisis. The revival of commerce throughout the Mediterranean world also meant that Constantinople, as a centre of consumption, luxury manufacture and international exchange, attracted increasing numbers of foreign merchants. By the 12th century the citizens of the Italian maritime republics of Venice, Pisa and Genoa were emerging as the most prominent and successful groups. In return for naval help they received valuable trading concessions, including the right to occupy permanent trading quarters along the south coast of the Golden Horn. The Jews, meanwhile, had been moved from this area to the north of the inlet, where the stench from their tanneries was less likely to affect the city's central residential and business area.

In the 12th century and early 13th Constantinople impressed foreign visitors as a city of extraordinary size, splendour, and contrasts of wealth and poverty. Geoffroy de Villehardouin, the chronicler of the Fourth Crusade, estimated its population at 400,000 in 1204, and described the first impression that it made on the crusaders in the following words: '. . . all those who had never seen Constantinople before gazed very intently at the city, having never imagined there could be so fine a place in all the world. They noted the high walls and lofty towers encircling it (see fig. 3), and its rich palaces and tall churches, of which there were so many that no one would have believed it to be true if he had not seen it with his own eyes, and viewed the length and breadth of that city which reigns supreme over all others' (pp. 58–9). The diversion of the main body of the Fourth Crusade to Constantinople, however, dealt the city a blow from which it never recovered. In August 1203 a clash between some crusaders and some Muslim merchants led to the worst fire in living memory, which devastated the main commercial and residential district from shore to shore. The crusader assault in April 1204 was followed by looting and slaughter on a scale that appalled Villehardouin (pp. 94–5) and other Latin chroniclers of the event.

BIBLIOGRAPHY

EARLY SOURCES

Prokopios: *Buildings* (*c*. AD 553–5); ed. H. B. Dewing and G. Downey, Loeb Class. Lib. (London and New York, 1940/*R* 1971), pp. 3–97
——: *The Secret History*; trans. by G. A. Williams, Penguin Classics (Harmondsworth, 1966/*R* 1981), p. 94
Parastaseis syntomoi chronikai [Brief historical descriptions] (741–75); Eng. trans., ed. Averil Cameron and J. Herrin as *Constantinople in the Early Eighth Century: The Parastaseis syntomoi chronikai* (Leiden, 1984)
Geoffroy de Villehardouin: *La Conquête de Constantinople* (early 13th century); Eng. trans., ed. M. R. B. Shaw as Joinville and Villehardouin: *Chronicles of the Crusades* (London, 1963), pp. 29–160

GENERAL

D. Jacoby: 'La Population de Constantinople à l'époque byzantine: Un Problème de démographie urbaine', *Byzantion*, xxxi (1961), pp. 81–109
C. Mango: 'Antique Statuary and the Byzantine Beholder', *Dumbarton Oaks Pap.*, xvii (1963), pp. 53–75
D. Jacoby: 'Les Quartiers juifs de Constantinople à l'époque byzantine', *Byzantion*, xxxvii (1967), pp. 167–227

3. View of Constantinople and city walls; manuscript miniature (detail), folio size, 225×170 mm, 12th century (Rome, Vatican, Biblioteca Apostolica Vaticana, MS. gr. 1851, fol. 2*r*)

C. Mango: 'Les Monuments de l'architecture du XIe siècle et leur significance historique et sociale', *Trav. & Mém.*, vi (1976), pp. 351–65
G. Dagron: 'Le Christianisme dans la ville byzantine', *Dumbarton Oaks Pap.*, xxxi (1977), pp. 3–25
P. Magdalino: 'Manuel Komnenos and the Great Palace', *Byz. & Mod. Gr. Stud.*, iv (1978), pp. 101–14
B. Aran: 'The Church of Saint Theodora and the Monastery of Christ Evergetes', *Jb. Österreich. Byz.*, xxviii (1979), pp. 211–28
C. L. Striker: *The Myrelaion (Bodrum Camii)* (Princeton, 1982)
G. Dagron: *Constantinople imaginaire* (Paris, 1984)
P. Magdalino: 'The Byzantine Aristocratic *oikos*', *The Byzantine Aristocracy, IX–XII Centuries*, ed. M. Angold, Brit. Archaeol. Rep., Int. Ser., cci (Oxford, 1984), pp. 92–111
——: 'Church, Bath and Diakonia in Medieval Constantinople', *Church and People in Byzantium*, ed. R. Morris (Birmingham, 1990), pp. 165–88
J. Herrin: 'Byzance: Le Palais et la ville', *Byzantion*, lxi (1991), pp. 215–30

3. 1205–1453. The conquerors established an insolvent Latin empire of Constantinople that compounded the damage to the plundered city by melting down ancient bronze statues for coin and stripping the lead from palace roofs. The Venetians used their privileged share in the occupying regime to help themselves to works of art for their own city. The bronze horses (Venice, Mus. S Marco; formerly on the façade of S Marco but now replaced by copies) and the porphyry group of the *Tetrarchs* (*c*. AD 300; *see* ROME, ANCIENT, §IV, 2(ix) and fig. 82), which is set into the south-west corner of the façade of S Marco, are the best-known examples.

When the Greeks retook Constantinople in 1261, their emperor Michael VIII Palaiologos (*reg* 1258–82) did his best to repair the main imperial and ecclesiastical buildings and encouraged aristocratic families to restore their ancestral palaces and the religious houses with which they had connections. The surviving Byzantine churches of Istanbul reflect the vitality of this effort. Christ the Saviour in Chora, St Mary Pammakaristos, Constantine Lips (Turk. Fenarı Isa Camii; *see* CHURCH, fig. 12) and the Kalenderhane and Kilise mosques (for which the Byzantine names are unknown) were restored, redecorated or added to in the 13th and 14th centuries. There were even some new monastic foundations.

4. Map of Constantinople; from Cristoforo Buondelmonti: *Liber insularum archipelagi*, 1422 (London, British Library, MS. Cotton Vespasian A XIII)

Michael VIII, who was hailed as the New Constantine and commissioned a monumental bronze sculpture depicting him at the feet of the Archangel Michael, clearly hoped to restore the imperial capital to its former glory; but the territorial base of the restored empire was smaller than it had been before 1204 and contracted steadily after 1282, while defence commitments grew ever more burdensome, and power and wealth within the empire became increasingly devolved. Such provincial centres as Thessaloniki and Mystras flourished independent of the capital, and such government ministers as Theodore Metochites (1270–1332) built themselves magnificent palaces and monastery churches at a time when Andronikos II (*reg* 1282–1328) lacked the money to make basic repairs to public buildings. Chariot racing at the Hippodrome, which had continued until 1204, was not revived, and the Great Palace was almost completely abandoned.

Constantinople was one of the first European cities to be struck by the Black Death in 1347. After 1354 its European hinterland, already ravaged by decades of invasion and civil war, fell to the Ottoman Turks, who had occupied the Asiatic hinterland since the beginning of the century. The Byzantine aristocracy partially compensated for the loss of their agricultural estates by going into trade, but there they had to operate in the shadow of the privileged Italian merchants who were exempt from customs dues. The Genoese had attracted most local trade to their own fortified enclave of Pera (Galata) across the Golden Horn (whence the Jews had returned to the old city, this time to a quarter on the southern shore), while the Venetians had gained a virtual monopoly of the city's retail trade. Fifteenth-century travellers and the schematic plans of Constantinople that illustrate the manuscripts of Cristoforo Buondelmonti's *Liber insularum archipelagi* (see fig. 4) tell the same story: the New Rome that fell to the Turks on 29 May 1453 was largely a ghost town.

BIBLIOGRAPHY

EARLY SOURCES
Cristoforo Buondelmonti: *Liber insularum archipelagi* (1422); ed. G. Gerola: 'Le vedute di Constantinopolu di Cristoforo Buondelmonti', *Studi bizantini e neoellenici*, iii (1931), pp. 247–79

GENERAL
N. Oikonomides: *Hommes d'affaires grecs et latins à Constantinople (XIIIe–XVe siècles)* (Montreal, 1979)
G. Majeska: *Russian Travelers to Constantinople in the Fourteenth and Fifteenth Centuries* (Washington, DC, 1984)

For further bibliography *see* §§1 and 2 above.

PAUL MAGDALINO

4. 1454–1838. Ottoman rule brought new populations and new economic life to Istanbul, as the harbour once again became an important centre of trade and the resident European communities arranged new terms with the conqueror Mehmed II (*reg* 1444–81 with interruption) for commercial concessions. The Sultan made serious efforts to repopulate his new capital, and his giant mosque complex with its social-service and educational buildings (*see* §III, 9(ii) below) formed the core of a renewed quarter of the city; smaller complexes erected by his chief ministers served similar functions elsewhere. Mehmed ordered the construction of a fortress near the Byzantine Golden Gate (see fig. 1xiv above). Known as Yediküle, the fortress of the seven towers, it had a star-shaped plan anticipating similar designs in Italy (*see* MILITARY ARCHITECTURE AND FORTIFICATION, §IV, 3). Mehmed built his first palace (Turk. Eski Saray: 'old palace') in the centre of the city near the Forum Tauri (see fig. 1xx above), but soon selected the tip of the peninsula for a second and larger palace. Later known as Topkapı Palace, it remained the residence of the Ottoman sultans and their administrative centre until the 19th century (*see* §III, 13(ii)–(iv) below). Mehmed had declared the buildings of the city under his protection at the time of the siege, and much was preserved and adapted to new uses, including Hagia Sophia, which became the premier mosque of the Ottoman capital (*see* §III, 1(iii) below). Mehmed's two large new market halls became the centre of the Grand Bazaar (*see* §III, 14 below), and other significant topographical features of the Byzantine city, including the Mese, the Hippodrome and the terraced area where the Topkapı Palace now stands, were preserved or converted to new uses.

The new city, like the old, was divided into four major sections. On the European peninsula to the south of the Golden Horn, a river estuary serving as the harbour, stood the walled city proper, often known as Stambul. On the north side of the harbour, also in Europe, were the old Latin trading quarters. Across the Bosporus in Asia were the ancient suburbs of Üsküdar and Kadıköy, and along both shores of the Bosporus were a series of suburban villages. The entire metropolis was popularly called İstanbul, a name derived from the Greek *eis stin poli* ('to the city'), and in the Ottoman literary tradition even İslambol (Ott. Turk.: 'full of Islam'), but officially it remained Quṣṭantiniyya, the 'city of Constantine'. The repopulation of the city included not only transplanted Muslim populations, but non-Muslims as well; large Greek and Armenian minorities remained or emigrated from provincial centres, and under Bayezid II (*reg* 1481–1512), Jewish refugees from Spain founded a Ladino-speaking Sephardic community. The transformation of the Byzantine capital to a predominantly but not completely Muslim city was incremental, and the minority communities remained both large and influential until the end of the Ottoman empire.

The three successors of Mehmed II and their chief ministers built great imperial mosque complexes (*see* KÜLLIYE) to serve various quarters of the city; of these the Süleymaniye Mosque (see fig. 5; *see also* §III, 10 below) is the largest and most important. Enormous engineering effort was also invested in improving the water supply by repairing the Byzantine infrastructure and adding new dams, reservoirs and aqueducts; the repairs and additions made by the 16th-century architect Sinan (*see* SINAN (ii)) to the great Kırkçeşme aqueduct system are arguably his most significant contribution to the city with which he is so closely identified. The new organization of the city was both ethnic and geographic. Under the Ottoman *millet* system, customary and family law of the minority religious and ethnic groups were handled by their own courts, and such minorities tended to congregate in their own quarters of the city. The city was also divided into Ottoman administrative districts that dealt with local affairs of each quarter. Local water needs were met by endowed fountains (*see* ISLAMIC ART, §II, 7(i)(b) and fig. 66) of various types, given generally by private philanthropy, and educational and philanthropic institutions both Muslim and non-Muslim were under religious control within the quarters and communities. Fire-fighting was the duty of the military corps of janissaries until the 19th century.

Historical population estimates for the city tell the story of its growth after the conquest. In 1477, after extensive efforts at repopulation were well under way, the population is estimated to have been *c.* 65,000, three-fifths of whom were Muslim; by the beginning of the reign of Murad III (*reg* 1574–95) it had grown to half a million, with the proportion of Muslims slightly smaller. Two categories of civil disaster—fires and earthquakes—define the history of Istanbul to a major extent. Seven major earthquakes, the most severe in 1766, altered the architectural character of the Ottoman city by damaging or destroying major monuments. Some 30 major fires have been recorded; because of the traditional wooden architecture, narrow streets and high winds, together with deficiencies in fire-fighting organization and apparatus, vast areas were often destroyed. In the aftermath there were often significant shifts in the ethnic composition of neighbourhoods.

The building of the city was thus a continuous process. Although it is customary to dwell on the great architectural accomplishments of the 15th to 17th centuries, the repairs necessitated by disasters in later times and the Islamic practice of endowing public-service institutions and buildings (*see* ISLAM, §III) meant that even after the political and economic contraction of the Ottoman empire, the city was continually being renewed by the building of local mosques, fountains, schools and the like. The foreign trading quarters, formerly known as Galata and Pera, were

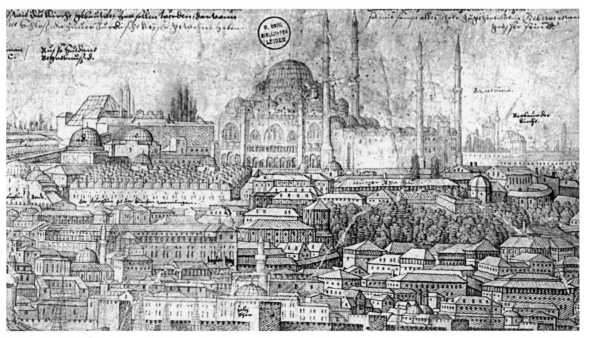

5. *View of the Süleymaniye Mosque* (detail) from the *Prospect of Constantinople* by Melchior Lorch, pen and brown ink, *c.* 12 m, *c.* 1559 (Leiden, Bibliotheek der Rijksuniversiteit Leiden, Cod. 1758)

divided into four administrative districts after the conquest; they became progressively more Europeanized after 1700. The expansion of the city outside the walls of the peninsula itself increased during the 18th century, especially with the construction of seaside residences of sultans, their families and court notables along the shores of the Bosporus and the upper end of the Golden Horn.

BIBLIOGRAPHY
Enc. Islam/2
E. Mamboury: *Istanbul touristique* (Istanbul, 1951)
A. Erzen: 'Über die Gründung und den Namen der Stadt Istanbul', *Akten des XI internationalen Byzantinistenkongress: Munich, 1958*, pp. 144–9
R. Mantran: *Istanbul dans la seconde moitié du XVIIe siècle* (Paris, 1962)
R. Lewis: *Everyday Life in Ottoman Turkey* (London and New York, 1971)
                              WALTER B. DENNY

5. 1839–1923. The transformation of Istanbul into a Western-style capital began in 1839 when Sultan Abdülmecid (*reg* 1839–61) signed the Tanzimat Charter, which heralded the reorganization of Turkish society on European lines. Commercial treaties with European countries opened the Ottoman empire to foreign capital. In the 19th century the relationship between the two sides of the Golden Horn altered as the north was developed at the expense of the south. The population of the city and its suburbs doubled from 391,000 in 1844 to 851,527 in 1886, after which it stabilized.

The physical boundaries of Istanbul expanded dramatically. Settlements on the north side of the Golden Horn developed in three main directions: from Taksim to Şişli, from Tophane to Dolmabahçe along the shoreline and from Dolmabahçe towards Teşvikiye and Nişantaşı on the hills above Beşiktaş. Karaköy developed into a business centre, the Bosporus shoreline from Karaköy to Tophane and Kabataş became a commercial waterfront, and Pera (Turk. Beyoğlu) became a Western-style centre. The transfer of power from the Istanbul peninsula to the north side of the Golden Horn was marked by the construction of imperial palaces between Dolmabahçe and Beşiktaş, while military barracks were built on the hills of Taksim and Maçka. Communication across the Golden Horn improved markedly: a bridge (1836; replaced 1872) connected Unkapanı on the south bank with Azapkapı on the north, while the Galata Bridge (1845; replaced 1863, 1878 and 1912) connected Eminönü with Karaköy.

The growth of the city to the north of the Golden Horn was encouraged in 1848, when a new settlement was created in Pangaltı by imperial order. By 1855 measures were being taken to organize the urban administration of the city, and the Commission for the Order of the City was established to initiate reform. Its aims included the straightening, widening, paving, lighting and cleaning of streets, and the construction of an infrastructure for water and sewage. The Sixth District, which included Pera, Galata and Tophane, became an experimental area for reform under the Sixth District Administration. The presence of a large European population in Galata probably determined this choice of district, and foreigners were encouraged to become involved in its administration. By 1858 Karaköy Square had been opened, and from 1863 to 1865 the walls of Galata were demolished and roads constructed on their trace. The Galata Tower, a Genoese foundation (1348), was converted to a fire observation

post. After a fire in 1870 destroyed more than 3000 buildings in Pera, new construction in brick or stone became obligatory. In 1869 a park was created in Taksim, followed shortly by another in Tepebaşı.

The new banks, offices, theatres, department stores, hotels and apartment blocks were constructed in four main styles: Neo-classical (the most prevalent), Gothic Revival, Islamic Revival and Art Nouveau (*see* ISLAMIC ART, §II, 7(i)(b)). The new European embassies constructed in Pera in classical styles competed with one another in monumentality, and many other buildings there adhered to the styles imposed by the embassies. The City of Pera Building (1876), which was constructed in the Second Empire style, had stores and shops on the ground floor and apartments on three upper floors. It became a landmark and a model for later apartment buildings, which lined the main arteries of Pera, Taksim and Pangaltı by 1900. The Franciscan church of St Anthony of Padua (1725; rebuilt 1913) in Pera is a large Gothic Revival building in red brick. The Land Registry Building (1908) in Sultanahmed and the Central Post Office Building (1909) in Sirkeci were both designed by VEDAT in a Neo-classical style. The Fourth Vakıf Han (1912–26) by KEMALETTIN is an immense seven-storey office block with a cut-stone façade in an Islamic revivalist style.

Areas destroyed by fire were the first to have new principles of urban planning put into practice. A fire in Aksaray in 1856, which destroyed over 650 buildings, led to the implementation of a regular urban pattern with wide streets. A large fire in Hocapaşa in 1865 also led to urban regularization, including the clearing of areas around historic monuments. The decision to move the imperial residence from Topkapı Palace was partly responsible for the slowed development on the peninsula, for after the construction on the western waterfront of the Bosporus of the grandiose palace at Dolmabahçe (1853–5; see fig. 6) by the architect Garabed Balyan (*see* BALYAN, (2)), the area around it was developed. To the north along the Bosporus waterfront Çırağan Palace was constructed for Abdülaziz (*reg* 1861–76). At Yıldız a palace complex was built for Abdülhamid II (*reg* 1876–1909); its several pavilions include the Sale Kiosk, Malta Kiosk and Çadir Kiosk.

Suburban development was encouraged by the growth of public transport services. The state ferryboat service, introduced in the 1850s, offered housing credit at locations along the shore of the Bosporus. A tramway system was also developed in the city, and the Tünel, an underground funicular linking Galata and Pera, opened in 1875. The railway line linking Istanbul with Sofia (Bulgaria) opened in 1874, and the line to Vienna was completed by 1888. Sirkeci station (1890) was designed by A. Jachmund in an eclectic Oriental style as the terminus of the Orient Express. On the Asian shore the railway line from Haydarpaşa to Izmit dated from 1873. A new era of transport began when the automobile arrived in Istanbul in the early 20th century.

With the growth of new urban professions, terraced housing for those of moderate income was introduced in Istanbul from the late 19th century. These houses were designed for low-level bureaucrats, minor merchants, craftsmen and artisans. With the exception of the ambitious Akaretler project in Beşiktaş, terraced houses were

6. Istanbul, view of Dolmabahçe Palace from the east, 1853–5

built in modest neighbourhoods and had regular layouts with simple façades.

As in other European cities, several grand schemes for the urban development of Istanbul were commissioned. They included Helmuth von Moltke's plan (1839) to create five major arteries in the peninsula, F. Arnodin's project (1900) for a ring-road with bridges encircling the city, and Joseph Antoine Bouvard's plans (early 20th century) for key areas of development. Such schemes, which were ambitious as well as dependent on European technology (*see* §II, 3 below), indicate the extent to which a European conception of the city had taken hold. When the Young Turks came to power in 1908, they introduced a new and more efficient municipal organization and carried out an extensive building programme while continuing to look to Europe as a source of inspiration.

BIBLIOGRAPHY
S. H. Eldem: *Boğaziçi Anıları: Reminiscences of the Bosporus* (Istanbul, 1979)
——: *Istanbul Anıları: Reminiscences of Istanbul* (Istanbul, 1979)
R. Holod and A. Evin, eds: *Modern Turkish Architecture* (Philadelphia, 1984)
Z. Çelik: *The Remaking of Istanbul: Portrait of an Ottoman City in the Nineteenth Century* (Seattle and London, 1987)

6. AFTER 1923. By the time the Turkish Republic was proclaimed on 29 October 1923, Istanbul had been replaced as capital by Ankara. This change in the city's status, together with the abolition of the Ottoman sultanate (*reg* 1281–1924), which had resided there, marked a total break with the past. Despite these changes, the urban development of Istanbul has proceeded apace and planning has remained a pressing issue.

From the outset of the republican era, the design of buildings in Turkey and notions of city planning were affected by the Modern Movement in architecture. In Istanbul, Sirri Arif's Bekir Bey House (1929) was the first Modernist building to be designed by a Turkish architect. In general, however, Istanbul did not initially offer as much scope for Modernist architecture as Ankara, and architects in the city such as SEDAD HAKKI ELDEM were inspired equally by Ottoman civic architecture, particularly the old residences of the Istanbul upper classes. European specialists continued to be invited to Turkey to aid urban planning. The first attempt under the republican government to control development by means of a master-plan was made in the 1930s, and the German and French planners Donat-Alfred Agache, Herman Elgötz, H. Lambert and MARTIN VON WAGNER acted as consultants. Their plans for urban growth, transportation, conservation and zoning, however, were not implemented. More important was the arrival in 1936 of the French architect and planner HENRI PROST, who drew up a plan for the city and remained there until 1951; parts of the plan he developed were still in application in the late 20th century. A second wave of urban planning occurred in the 1950s: among the European consultants were the German Hans Högg and the Italian Luigi Piccinato, but by this time a greater number of Turkish planners and architects had also become involved.

The rapid increase in population from the 1950s raised several new issues. Population growth went hand in hand with industrialization, urbanization, commercial development and land speculation, while migration from the countryside was creating squatter belts around the city. These changes were accompanied by the arrival of new architectural styles and construction techniques. The Istanbul Hilton Hotel (1952), by SKIDMORE, OWINGS & MERRILL with Eldem as the Turkish collaborator, became the precursor of high-rise hotels in Turkey, while the Hukukçular Apartments (1960–61) by Haluk Baysal and Melih Birsel is a prominent example of the new high-rise residential development for the middle and upper-middle classes. By the 1970s a new trend in housing was the construction of multi-block apartment complexes.

An important role in development after World War II was played by the Emlâk Kredi Bank, which provided long-term low-interest credit and became involved in housing construction. One of its first projects was the Levent district (begun 1947), followed by the Kosuyolu district (begun 1951). These projects consisted of single- and two-storey detached or terraced houses for middle-income families. By the late 1950s the Bank had broadened its activities and was constructing multistorey apartments: the first of this type was the Fourth Levent Development (1956–60), in which public amenities such as cinemas and sports facilities were included. The most comprehensive project was the Ataköy complex, a new city for 50,000 people, begun in 1957. Consisting mainly of multistorey apartments, it combined the use of reinforced concrete for high-rise blocks and masonry for low-level buildings.

Istanbul was transformed by the construction of the first suspension bridge across the Bosporus (1973), connecting the European and Asiatic quarters of the city with a network of new expressways and allowing huge numbers of emigrants from Anatolia to move into an integrated complex of outlying suburbs from Kumburgaz in the west to Izmit in the east and Sarıyer in the north. The needs of this new population have severely taxed the old infrastructure, and in times of political stability controversial but highly energetic governors have overseen dramatic new projects, including the conversion of the banks of the Golden Horn into a park, the building of gigantic sewerage projects, a new underground railway and conversion of such streets as the Grand Rue de Pera (Turk. İstiklâl Caddesi) into pedestrian shopping malls. Amid these efforts there has been some significant success at historical and scenic preservation, aided by enlightened tax laws. The destruction of many old houses and streets, particularly in the 1960s and 1970s, has given quite modest houses of the early 20th century a considerable value, and there is a growing awareness of the importance of conservation. There have also been significant failures, most notably the lack of preservation of any substantial part of the open spaces on the Bosporus, whose beauties have lessened significantly, and the sometimes almost unchecked and unregulated proliferation of shanty towns housing newcomers from Anatolia.

BIBLIOGRAPHY

N. Duranay, E. Gürsel and S. Ural: 'Cumhuriyetten bu yana Istanbul planlamasi' [Planning of Istanbul since the republic], *Mimarlık*, vii (1972), pp. 65–109
J. Cramer: 'Changes to the Urban Structure of Istanbul in the Past 100 Years', *A. & Archaeol. Res. Pap.*, xiv (1978), pp. 38–45

II. Art life and organization.

1. Before 1453. 2. 1453–1838. 3. After 1838.

1. BEFORE 1453. Much less is known about the careers, working methods and organization of Byzantine artists and artisans than is provided by Roman inscriptions, laws

and monuments for the period before the foundation of Constantinople (324–30). Even though the city, as a principal focus of imperial munificence, was filled in the course of the 4th century with sculpture from throughout the empire, it must have had its own masons, carpenters, plasterers and mosaicists. If, as is often supposed, the number of craftsmen working in precious metals and ivory, carving honorific statues and illuminating books, remained small until the 5th century, the capital would still have needed potters, weavers and glassmakers. About these, however, far less is known than of the artisans of Alexandria, Antioch and the cities of Asia Minor in the same period. The presence, scanty or otherwise, of these and other craftsmen in Constantinople is attested in an edict of 337, exempting them from public service in order that they might improve their skills and train their children (*Codex Theodosianus* XIII.iv.2).

Reflecting the low social esteem of craftsmen, they are shown as peripheral figures in a miniature glorifying ANICIA JULIANA, the sponsor of Dioskurides' *De materia medica* (*c.* 512; Vienna, Österreich. Nbib., Cod. med. gr. 1, fol. 6v). The book was made in Constantinople and also contains an image of a portrait painter at an easel (fol. 5v), set perhaps in one of the studios (Lat. *pergulae*) or workshops (Gr. *ergasteria*) in public places mentioned in a law of 372 (*Codex Theodosianus* XIII.iv.4). No ample account of the city's crafts exists before the *Book of the Eparch* of the early 10th century. This ordinance prescribes the work-sites and materials in which craftsmen could operate. Obviously incomplete—the preserved text does not mention, for instance, potters or ivory-carvers—it specifies the activities of many types of silk-workers, bronze-casters, silversmiths and others, restricting their workshops to particular parts of the city; these shops generally were to be located in the craftsmen's houses. Before this period, some impression of the range of artistic industries is gained from a list of trades said by Theodore of Stoudios, in a letter of 801 to Empress EIRENE, to have benefited from her restoration of icon veneration; these included those of architect, metalworker, goldsmith, weaver, dyer and woodworker.

The *Book of the Eparch* treats as normal the provision of materials by clients to those who executed their commissions. Such craftsmen were organized in guilds (Gr. *somateia*) under the city prefect (Gr. *eparchos*). Artisans directly subject to imperial authority in the 10th century were armourers and moneyers; control was also exercised by the Palace over workers in silk and gold. As these commodities were of strategic importance in negotiations with foreigners, goldsmiths were required to work in shops along the Mese, the central street of the city (see fig. 1 above), rather than at home. Western European church treasuries and museums preserve silks inwoven with the names of the emperors Romanos and Christophoros (i.e. the Siegburg Silk; 921–31; Berlin, Schloss Köpenick) and Basil and Constantine (i.e. the Gunther Tapestry; 976–1028; Bamberg, Domschatzkam.; *see* EARLY CHRISTIAN AND BYZANTINE ART, §VII, 8). The production of less pretentious fabrics is seldom recorded in any detail. A rare glimpse of female workers, seemingly associated in a guild, spinning, carding and weaving cloth and, at least in part, responsible for a festival called Agathe, is however provided in a description by Michael Psellos (1018–*c.* 1081).

While luxurious crafts could originate in the Great Palace, as under Constantine VII (*see* MACEDONIAN DYNASTY, (3)), most were produced by independent craftsmen working at home and aided by, at most, an apprentice or two and members of their families. Large monasteries, such as St John Stoudios and the Hodegon (9th century; rest. 12th century; destr.), had resident scribes and even prepared their own parchment in standard sizes. Although ornament and illumination were sometimes painted by the scribe, as in the case of the Theodore Psalter, they were usually given to professional painters to execute. A team of eight painters was responsible for the 430 miniatures in the MENOLOGION OF BASIL II (*c.* 1000; Rome, Vatican, Bib. Apostolica, MS. Vat. gr. 1613), though such huge undertakings were probably abnormal. At least one member of this team, known as PANTOLEON, also painted icons. Painters may have engaged in summer in the seasonal occupation of church decoration; those responsible for the wall paintings (after 1321) in Christ the Saviour in Chora monastery (*see* §III, 3(ii) below and WALL PAINTING, colour pl. II, fig. 1) probably also made its mosaics.

As the industrial centre of the empire from Justinian's time onwards, Constantinople was the prime producer of the materials of art, as for example the mosaic tesserae sent to Córdoba in the 10th century. It was also a main source of artists. From the early 14th century records survive of named individuals travelling abroad, exporting to the provinces and beyond the styles, techniques and tastes of the capital.

BIBLIOGRAPHY

EARLY SOURCES
Codex Theodosianus (438); Eng. trans., ed. C. Pharr as *The Theodosian Code and Novels and the Sirmondian Constitutions* (Princeton, 1952/*R* 1970)
Theodore of Stoudios, letter to Empress Eirene (801); *PG*, xcix (Paris, 1860), pp. 929–34
To eparchikon biblion [Book of the Eparch] (early 10th century); ed. J. Koder as *Das Eparchenbuch Leons des Weisen*, Corpus fontium historiae byzantinae, xxxii (Vienna, 1991)

GENERAL
M. Psellos: 'On the Female Festival of Agathe', *Messaionike Bibliotheke*, ed. K. N. Sathas, v (Paris, 1876), pp. 527–31; *R* as *Bibliotheca Graeca medii aeri* (Hildesheim and New York, 1972)
E. Cruikshank Dodd: *Byzantine Silver Stamps* (Washington, DC, 1961)
L. Cracco Ruggini: 'Le associazioni professionali nel mondo romano-bizantino', *XVIII Settimane di studio del Centro italiano di studi sull'alto medioevo: Spoleto, 1970*, pp. 59–193
P. A. Yannopoulos: *La Société profane dans l'empire byzantin des VIIe, VIIIe et IXe siècles* (Leuven, 1975)
B. Malich: 'Handwerk und Handwerksvereinigungen im Byzanz im Übergang zum Feudalismus', *Jb. Wirtschgesch.*, iv (1977), pp. 173–81
N. Oikonomides: *Hommes d'affaires grecs et latins à Constantinople (XIIIe–XVe siècles)* (Montreal, 1979)
J.-P. Sodini: 'L'Artisanat urbain à l'époque paléochrétienne (IVe–VIIe s.)', *Ktema*, iv (1979), pp. 71–119
A. Christophilopoulou: 'Systima basilikon istourgon: Ena somateion kratikon yphantourgon tou Iaiona' [A system of imperial weavers: a guild of state textile manufacturers of the 10th century], *Byzantion: Aphieroma ston Andrea N. Strato* [Byzantion: tribute to Andreas N. Stratos], i, ed. N. A. Stratou (Athens, 1986), pp. 65–72
A. Cutler and J. Nesbitt: *L'arte bizantina e il suo pubblico*, 2 vols (Turin, 1986)
E. Kislinger: 'Gewerbe im späten Byzanz', *Handwerk und Sachenkultur in Spätmittelalter. Internationaler Kongress: Krems an der Donau, 1986*, pp. 103–26
P. Schreiner: 'Die Organisation byzantinischer Kaufleute und Handwerker', *Untersuchungen zu Handel und Verkehr der vor- und frühgeschichtlichen Zeit in Mittel- und Nordeuropa*, ed. H. Jarkuhn and E. Ebel (Göttingen, 1989), pp. 44–61

ANTHONY CUTLER

2. 1453–1838. The artistic economy of Istanbul after the Turkish conquest developed along traditional Islamic lines within the established economy of the conquered city. Artists and craftsmen in the capital participated in the artistic life of the city either as servants of the Ottoman court or as tradesmen working in traditional crafts under the aegis of guild corporations and involved in selling their products in the bazaar.

The imperial palace (*see* §III, 13(ii) and (iii) below) was not only the residence of the sultan and seat of his administration but also a centre of patronage and production for many of the royal necessities and *objets d'art*. These included garments, jewellery, arms and armour, furnishings, tents, manuscripts and coins. The imperial corps of architects prepared designs, procured materials and kept account books for buildings ordered by the sultan and his entourage. The Çinili ('Tiled') Kiosk (see fig. 7 and §III, 13(ii) below) in Topkapı Palace, for example, is one of the most beautiful secular monuments of Ottoman architecture to be commissioned by a sultan. The corps also approved and supervised all major architectural projects throughout the empire, ensuring that the metropolitan styles of the capital were followed in the provinces.

7. Istanbul, Topkapı Palace, Çinili ('Tiled') Kiosk, 1473

Similarly the palace set the taste for luxury arts throughout the empire, for patterns prepared in the imperial design studio were used to prepare designs for textiles, ceramics and other arts. Court documents suggest that the court followed a fixed price schedule, which was often outmoded by inflation. The court was sometimes at a disadvantage in demanding work from artisans, and the more lucrative prospect of selling works of ceramics, textiles or carpets in the bazaar for high prices kept artisans from fulfilling royal commissions on a timely basis. The court style, which appeared in the decorations of the great public monuments of the sultans, their families and ministers, dictated popular artistic taste and standards. Court fashion was conspicuously presented to the public in numerous parades, processions and other ceremonies that formed a part of the public court ritual and projection of royal power in the Ottoman capital.

The situation of the tradesmen in Istanbul, especially by the 16th century, is comparable to that of European guilds in such centres as Florence. Guild corporations were grouped according to various media—weavers, copper-vessel makers, potters and tile-makers—and were highly structured internally, with strict standards for technical quality and artistic uniformity. The guilds were also regulated by the government, through price and quality controls implemented by an official known as the *mühtesib*. Complaints against artisans were adjudicated in the courts. Each guild had its own patron saint and its own quasi-religious ceremonies, many derived from the practices of Sufi brotherhoods, since most guilds were associated with a Sufi religious order. The tight control exercised by the guild militated against dramatic artistic innovation, but it also ensured a high level of technical quality in such media as textiles and ceramics, where the correlation between elaborate technique and high artistry was vital. Periodic fairs and great public displays of artistic work by the guilds, such as those chronicled in the great manuscripts of the *Surnāma* ('Imperial book of festivals'; *see* ISLAMIC ART, §§III, 4(vi)(e); VI, 2(iii)(a) and fig. 191; and VI, 3(i) and fig. 195), also served to publicize the works of artisans to a broad and discerning public.

The embellishment of the middle-class residence with artistic production—carpets, textiles, ceramics, metalwork, wood-carving and marquetry, architectural painting, embroidery and calligraphy—was a well-established tradition in Ottoman Istanbul, and countless works of art bear witness to the patronage of a prosperous urban middle class of merchants and bureaucrats who, following the example of the imperial court itself, sought to surround themselves with objects of beauty. In this patronage the various non-Muslim minorities were as enthusiastic as their Muslim counterparts, attested by the large numbers of ceramics, wooden objects, metalware and embroideries with Hebrew, Armenian and Greek inscriptions.

While artists themselves were largely anonymous, and names of artists attached to works of art in general made little economic impact, in certain media, notably album painting and calligraphy, the existence of a vigorous collectors' market for the works of important artists did affect the market and the public perceptions both of artists and of their production. The names of certain famous artists, such as the 16th-century painter VELI CAN or the 17th-century calligrapher HAFIZ OSMAN, appear to have wrought a particular magic on the price structure in the market-place.

BIBLIOGRAPHY
R. Mantran: *Istanbul dans la seconde moitié du XVIIe siècle* (Paris, 1962)
——: *La Vie quotidienne à Constantinople au temps de Soliman le Magnifique et des successeurs (XVIe et XVIIe siècles)* (Paris, 1965)
R. Lewis: *Everyday Life in Ottoman Turkey* (London and New York, 1971)
A. W. Fisher and C. G. Fisher: 'A Note on the Location of the Royal Ottoman Ateliers', *Muqarnas*, iii (1985), pp. 118–20
G. Necipoğlu: 'From International Timurid to Ottoman: A Change of Taste in Sixteenth-Century Ceramic Tiles', *Muqarnas*, vii (1990), pp. 136–70

WALTER B. DENNY

3. AFTER 1838. The signing of the Tanzimat Charter in 1839 by Abdülmecid (*reg* 1839–61) signalled the reorganization of Ottoman society along European lines, and over the following decades measures with important cultural implications were introduced. Cultural life was revitalized as Istanbul was opened to artistic ideas from Europe: European architects and artists came in increasing numbers, and some of their Turkish counterparts travelled to Europe to complete their education. This cultural interaction in the artistic life of the city continued to gather momentum after the demise of the Ottoman empire and the founding of the Republic of Turkey in 1923.

European notions about art and art education began to take root in 1883 when the Imperial Academy of Fine Arts was founded by OSMAN HAMDI, who modelled it on such European institutions as the Ecole des Beaux-Arts in Paris. The Academy quickly became the focus of artistic life in Istanbul and remained the only centre for European-style art education in Turkey until 1932, when an art department was formed at the Gazi Teachers' College in Ankara. In 1926 the Academy merged with the Academy of Fine Arts for Women, which had opened in 1914. Despite a further expansion of art education since the mid-20th century, including the opening of the State School of Applied Arts (1957), the Academy has remained prominent in the artistic life of the city, and in 1962 it became a faculty of Mimar Sinan University.

When it opened, the Academy had three departments—architecture, painting and sculpture—each of which filled a vacuum created by the decline of traditional methods of art education. From the mid-19th century, court architects had been chosen increasingly from the Armenian community (e.g. members of the BALYAN family) or commissioned from Europe, as in the case of Gaspare Trajano Fossati (*see* FOSSATI, (2)). The new system of architectural education established at the Academy helped to rectify this situation. The other establishment where architects could train was the College of Civil Engineering (1884), but it emphasized engineering rather than architecture. Both the Academy and the College of Civil Engineering employed European architects on their staff, and European architects occupied other important posts in the city: the Italian architect RAIMONDO D'ARONCO, who introduced Art Nouveau to Istanbul, served as chief architect to the imperial court from 1896 to 1908 and ran a large practice in the city. By the early 20th century, Turkish architects such as KEMALETTIN and VEDAT, who taught at the College of Civil Engineering and the Academy respectively, began to promote themselves within the new educational framework. The Academy came to the forefront of developments in taste in Turkey and in 1934 hosted the first seminar on Turkish national architecture, organized by SEDAD HAKKI ELDEM. Meanwhile, Eldem's colleague, the architect EMIN ONAT, became an influential figure at the College of Civil Engineering (since 1946 a faculty of Istanbul Technical University). At the same time, such European architects as PAUL BONATZ, Clemens Holzmeister, Gustav Oelsner and Bruno Taut (see TAUT, (1)) continued to play an active role in the cultural life of the city.

Painting was also affected by changes in patronage at the imperial court and was revitalized by the growth of new institutions and practices (see ISLAMIC ART, §VIII, 11(ii)). Painting in a European manner was first encouraged in Istanbul at the Imperial Artillery School (Mühendishane-i Berri-i Hümayun) and the Military Academy (Mekteb-i Fünunu Harbiye), which included drawing lessons in their curricula from 1793 and 1835 respectively. Similar drawing lessons were also introduced in high schools. By the late 19th century such Turkish painters as ALI AHMED, SÜLEYMAN SEYYIT and Osman Hamdi had studied in Europe and returned to Istanbul with European ideas. In the 20th century an increasing number of Turkish painters and sculptors have been educated in Europe, and European artists have continued to be invited to Istanbul. In 1937 the French painter Leopold Lévy was appointed head of the department of painting at the Academy, and the German sculptor RUDOLF BELLING became head of the sculpture department in 1936. The Republican government promoted European-style painting and sculpture far more than traditional Turkish art forms such as calligraphy, which was particularly threatened by the official decision in 1928 to replace Arabic script with the Latin alphabet (see ISLAMIC ART, §III, 2(v)).

Photography was introduced to Istanbul in the early 1840s, and several commercial studios were soon established, including those of Kargopoulo (1850) and Pascal Sébah (1857). The Abdullah brothers, who also opened a studio, had an exhibit at the Exposition Universelle in Paris in 1867 entitled 'Views of Istanbul and Historical Arms of Turkey'. As commercial photography developed, such military bodies as the War Ministry, the Navy Ministry, the Army Commands and the Palace Corps of Engineers took advantage of the new medium. Among the amateur photographers active in the city was the Ottoman sultan Abdülhamid II (reg 1876–1909), who ordered a photography studio for Yıldız Palace.

The idea of collecting and preserving antiquities developed in Istanbul in the mid-19th century. An imperial decree issued in 1869 urged the construction of a museum based on European examples. The museum movement got under way in 1876 when the Çinili ('Tiled') Kiosk (see fig. 7 above) at Topkapı Palace was converted into an archaeological museum and Philipp Anton Dethier (d 1881) was appointed director. After his death, Dethier was replaced by Osman Hamdi, who in 1883 attempted to influence Abdülhamid to issue an order against the traffic in antiquities, as Europeans were increasingly exporting their archaeological finds. Hamdi also began to

organize archaeological excavations. When the Çinili Kiosk became short of space, a new building designed in a Neo-classical style by the French architect Antoine Vallaury was constructed opposite. Opened to the public in 1891, it was enlarged several times (1899–1903, 1908). By this time the archaeological collection included Greek, Roman, Byzantine, Assyrian, Egyptian, Phoenician, Hittite and Islamic items, as well as antique coins, natural history specimens and a library. HALIL EDHEM ELDEM directed the museum after the death of his older brother Osman Hamdi in 1910, and in 1917 Eldem formed a committee for the conservation of historic monuments and sites in the Ottoman empire. Istanbul was the starting-point for the committee, and a commission of engineers and architects began to prepare an inventory of the city's monuments. Meanwhile, in 1914, the Museum of Turkish and Islamic Art was opened at the Süleymaniye Mosque complex.

When the capital was moved to Ankara, Istanbul ceased to be the centre of government patronage, but the monuments and art collections in the city became more accessible, and it retained a vigorous cultural life because of its location. In 1924 it was decided to repair buildings at Topkapı Palace and admit the public. In addition to the Archaeological Museum, the Museum of the Ancient Orient and the Museum of Turkish Ceramics in the Çinili Kiosk, Topkapı Palace houses collections of Islamic art, Chinese and Japanese porcelain and European items. Hagia Sophia was opened as a museum in 1935, and the fine Byzantine mosaics and wall paintings in Christ the Saviour in Chora (see §III, 3(ii) below) were restored between 1948 and 1958. The modern movement in Turkish art was encouraged in 1937 when the Museum of Painting and Sculpture was founded in Dolmabahçe Palace for the display of 19th- and 20th-century Turkish paintings and sculptures. The Vakıflar Carpet Museum was opened in 1979, and the Vakıflar Kilim and Flat-Woven Rug Museum in 1982. The Research Centre of Islamic History, Art and Culture (IRCICA) was founded in 1979.

For further discussion of museums in Istanbul see TURKEY.

BIBLIOGRAPHY
R. O. Arık: L'Histoire et l'organisation des musées turcs (Istanbul, 1953)
M. Önder: The Museums of Turkey and Examples of the Masterpieces in the Museums (Ankara, 1977)
M. Cezar: Sanatta batı'ya açılış ve Osman Hamdi [Western trends in art and Osman Hamdi] (Istanbul, 1979)
Z. Çelik: The Remaking of Istanbul: Portrait of an Ottoman City in the Nineteenth Century (Seattle and London, 1987)
E. Ihsanoğlu, ed.: Istanbul: A Glimpse into the Past (Istanbul, 1987)

III. Buildings.

1. Hagia Sophia. 2. Christ Pantokrator Monastery. 3. Christ the Saviour in Chora. 4. Church of the Kyriotissa. 5. Hagia Eirene. 6. St John Stoudios. 7. St Mary Pammakaristos. 8. SS Sergios and Bakchos. 9. Fatih Mosque. 10. Süleymaniye Mosque. 11. Sultan Ahmed I Mosque. 12. Great Palace. 13. Topkapı Palace. 14. Grand Bazaar.

1. HAGIA SOPHIA. Byzantine church near the apex of the city's peninsula (see fig. 2a above). From the date of its dedication in 360 until 1453, it served as the cathedral of Constantinople except between 1204 and 1261, when it was the cathedral of the Latin empire. The building was a mosque from 23 May 1453 until 1934, when it was

8. Istanbul, Hagia Sophia, interior from west end of nave, AD 537–62

secularized; it was opened as a museum on 1 February 1935.

(i) Before AD 532. (ii) AD 532–1453. (iii) After 1453.

(i) Before AD 532. Soon after the foundation of Constantinople in 330, a cathedral and episcopal complex of buildings was planned for the central and prominent site on the acropolis of ancient Byzantion (*see* §I, 1(ii) above), adjacent to the area on which the Great Palace (*see* §12 below) was being developed. Hagia Eirene ('Holy Peace'; *see* §5 below) was finished first and acted as the cathedral until Hagia Sophia ('Holy Wisdom') was dedicated under Constantius in 360. Thereafter they acted together as the principal churches of the empire and the seat of the Patriarch of Constantinople, as well as the site of major imperial public ceremonial. Despite the specific dedication of the churches to Holy Wisdom and to Holy Peace, they should probably be understood as dedicated to Christ, evoked by two of his attributes.

This first church of Hagia Sophia was a spacious colonnaded basilica, with galleries and a wooden roof, preceded by an atrium; it was damaged by fire in 404 and rededicated in 415 (the architectural sculpture of this phase is visible at ground-level outside the west narthex). The architectural importance of the first church is difficult to assess, as it lies largely beneath the present building. It represents a large congregational basilica of the kind that was built all over the empire of Constantine after 313 and belongs to a period when the subsequent power and importance of Constantinople as a capital could hardly have been anticipated. Nevertheless, the sources indicate that it was richly supplied with liturgical vessels and fittings in gold and silver. The western portico leading to the atrium was excavated in 1935 and the free-standing treasury in 1979. The architectural sculpture of this grand

portico belongs to the early 5th-century renovation and closely resembles the grand and impressive forms of the Golden Gate of Constantinople from the same period. The most recent reconstruction of the first Hagia Sophia suggests it was 52 m wide with a central nave and four aisles, and stretched about 100 m from the west of the atrium to the east wall of the church.

(ii) AD 532–1453. The church underwent numerous phases of building and decoration during this period.

(a) Architecture. (b) Decoration.

(a) Architecture. The first Hagia Sophia was largely destroyed by fire in the Nika riots of 15 January 532; the present vast central-planned domed cathedral, which replaced it and overlaid it, was built and decorated by 24 December 537 under the patronage of Justinian I (*reg* 527–65). The dome collapsed on 7 May 558 while work was in progress to repair serious earthquake damage inflicted on 14 December 557 but was reconstructed with a higher profile by 562. The church has remained in this definitive 6th-century form ever since, though it has been subject to structural repairs and alterations over the centuries (see fig. 8). Most obviously in the Byzantine period the entrance at the south-west vestibule was developed in the late 6th century, and extra buttresses were added around the structure. Other major repair work followed the earthquake of 989, when the Armenian architect Trdat (*fl* 989–1000) rebuilt the main western arch and a portion of the dome (for further structural alterations *see* §(iii) below).

The construction of the new Hagia Sophia in 532–7 produced a major work of world architecture and demonstrates the structural creativity of its period (*see* LIGHTING, fig. 1). The achievement was well recognized in a description by the contemporary court writer Prokopios. His text (*Buildings*), commissioned by Justinian I as a celebration of his universal patronage, highlights the church as the greatest building of the reign, even flatteringly attributing more of the architectural expertise to the emperor than to the two documented architects, ANTHEMIOS OF TRALLES and Isidore of Miletus. Their ability to raise a high dome over such an open space may have depended on a knowledge of the mathematical and geometrical theories of Heron of Alexandria (*fl* AD 62); if so, it may be possible to trace a continuity in architectural knowledge with the great buildings of imperial Rome, this time translated into the needs of the Christian religion. The interior space is both vast and highly complex in its organization: the broad nave is vaulted with an interlocking system of dome, semi-domes and apsed areas, and the aisles and galleries above are subdivided into various compartments. Architectural composition on this scale is complicated and takes the viewer some time to appreciate, just as it led in time to all sorts of structural problems, due to insufficient foundations, subsidence, earthquake damage and instabilities in the design. The architects probably gave less attention to the functional needs of the church, although they supplied the necessary sanctuary fittings, divisions in the floor and galleries for the catechumens. New uses were gradually found for these large spaces; the south gallery, for example, became the private areas of the emperor and patriarch, but it is less clear what cult functions were ever carried out in the north gallery.

The cathedral was well supplied with access ramps to the galleries, and numerous doors into the two narthexes and church. The octagonal Little Baptistery (c. 562) still survives to the south-west and would have stood next to the Patriarchal Palace (late 6th century; destr.). A vast clergy served the cathedral, and from the 11th century the liturgy was celebrated daily. It received great numbers of visitors and pilgrims, who could venerate the many Christian relics collected over the centuries and displayed all around the building.

In addition to its structural daring, Hagia Sophia is distinctive for a change in the character of the architectural sculpture. As in the slightly earlier Constantinopolitan churches of SS Sergios and Bakchos (see §8 below) and St Polyeuktos (524–7; destr.) commissioned by ANICIA JULIANA, there is a dissolution of the orders of Late Antique architecture into a fluid and more ornamental form of capital and cornice decoration (see EARLY CHRISTIAN AND BYZANTINE ART, §IV, 2). The design of the capitals is based on spiky acanthus forms, and they enclose monograms of the names of Justinian or (more rarely) his consort Theodora (c. 500–548). The spandrels of the gallery are revetted in *opus sectile* with vegetal and bird forms in white marble set against a background of dark marble. Overall the impression of the architectural carving and ornament is of contrasting dark and light forms. While some of the columns may have been recycled from earlier buildings, much of the marble was quarried from the nearby Marmara islands, and Hagia Sophia represents one of the last major buildings to use specially commissioned Proconnesian marble from these famous ancient quarries, which apparently ceased functioning in the 6th century; Proconnesian marble used in Constantinopolitan buildings after the 6th century was normally reused from earlier buildings. Many of the slabs of wall revetment were quarried and cut 'back-to-back' and set up in the church to create evocative and symmetrical patterns (it was a common conceit to 'see' figurative images in the abstract veining of the marble).

(b) Decoration. Under Justinian's patronage the original interior decoration of Hagia Sophia consisted of the abstract designs of the marble revetment on the vertical walls combined with swathes of mosaic 'carpet' decoration spread over the vast surfaces of the curving vaults. These mosaics included large areas of repetitive vegetal ornament and crosses of various forms and sizes (see ACANTHUS, fig. 2). This sort of symbolic Christian decoration must have evoked on earth the heavenly paradise of Christ. Even in the 10th century, when some figurative elements had been added to the mosaic decoration, the emissaries of VLADIMIR, Prince of Kiev, were highly sensitive to the created atmosphere in Hagia Sophia and reported (*The Russian Primary Chronicle*) of the divine liturgy in the church: 'We knew not whether we were in heaven or earth. For on earth there is no such splendour or such beauty, and we are at a loss how to describe it. We only know that God dwells there among men, and their service is fairer than the ceremonies of other nations. For we cannot forget that beauty.'

Throughout the Middle Ages the power of the aura created in Hagia Sophia cannot be understated, and the decoration functioned as much to impress the visitor as to enhance the services of worship and glorification of God, which were celebrated during both the day and night. At least up to 1204 and the subsequent plundering of possessions by the Crusaders, the decoration and treasures of Hagia Sophia became progressively denser and richer. Accounts of Russian pilgrims from the 12th century onwards, for example, speak of its amazing collection of famous relics and miracle-working icons. Even in the church under Justinian, figurative decoration was not entirely lacking; Paulos Silentarios's verse EKPHRASIS recited early in 563 in front of the Emperor describes the silver images on the sanctuary screen of the restored church as showing Christ, the Virgin and other saints (Mango, 1986, pp. 80–91). There must also have been painted portable icons in the church.

Figurative mosaics were added to the non-figurative decoration of the vaults at various stages. Although the evidence for their history mostly comes from archaeological exploration of the vaults since the 1930s, during the mid-19th century restoration of the mosque by Gaspare and Giuseppe Fossati (see FOSSATI, (2) and §(iii) below) a number of other mosaics were uncovered, which have since perished; their drawings and records are an invaluable adjunct to the study of Hagia Sophia (Mango, 1962). Up to the 1990s, the priority in the study of the mosaics, as of the architecture, has been thorough and accurate recording of the surviving materials.

During the reign of Justin II (*reg* 565–78), a new patriarchal palace (565–77) was added to the south-west corner of the church; one of its ceremonial rooms, the small *sekreton*, to which access could be gained from the west gallery of the church, had a mosaic vault decoration, which included busts of Christ and other saints. This figurative decoration was cut out and destroyed during the iconoclastic controversy (726–843) by Patriarch Niketas in 768/9. This decoration, which was not strictly in the public part of the church, is the only figurative mosaic set that is known to have been added to the church between the 6th century and the 9th.

The failure of the iconoclasts to eradicate figurative imagery from Byzantine Christianity led to a massive celebratory redecoration in Hagia Sophia in the 9th century, enthusiastically supported by 'Orthodox' emperors and patriarchs. Progressively from 867 the church received vast mosaic icons, and the interior must have been cluttered for some considerable time with enormous wooden scaffoldings to enable the artists to reach the dome, semi-domes, apse and the tympana above the nave. The first of these post-iconoclastic mosaics were those of the *Virgin and Child* in the couch of the main apse and *Archangel Michael* (largely destr.) and *Archangel Gabriel* in the arches in front of the apse. The inauguration of these mosaics was celebrated in a sermon delivered on 29 March 867 by Patriarch Photios (*reg* 858–67; 877–86) in the presence of the emperors Michael III and Basil I. This text represents a rare example of a Byzantine *ekphrasis* that describes an extant work of art (Mango, 1986, pp. 187–90); analysis of such a text helps to reveal how a Byzantine viewer treated religious art and how art functioned within

9. Istanbul, south gallery of Hagia Sophia, mosaic of *Virgin and Child with Emperor John II, Empress Eirene and their Son Alexios, c.* 1118–22

the culture, but as description it reveals a world of difference between modern and medieval perceptions.

The programme of decoration of the second half of the 9th century encompassed a scheme with the representation of Christ in the central dome; prophets and other saints in the tympana below, including a series of Church fathers and historical figures connected with Hagia Sophia itself, such as Patriarch Ignatios (*reg* 847–58; 867–77); the *Virgin and Child* in the apse; and some Gospel scenes, including the *Descent of the Holy Ghost*, in the galleries. At the same time another room in the Patriarchal Palace, the large *sekreton*, was decorated with a cycle of saints. The predominance of single figures in the post-iconoclastic decorative scheme of the church may have been the consequence of the type of architectural spaces available as much as any theological conception of the 'proper' character of church decoration.

The architecture of the church was a problem for the mosaic planners; the size and height of the available spaces were not ideal, and such figures as the *Virgin and Child* in the apse seem to modern observers on the floor of the church far too small for the position. What must be true is that the conspicuous decoration of Orthodox saints all over the church from the 9th century onwards was a firm and permanent reminder of the commitment of the Byzantine Church to the use of figurative icons in response to the failure of Iconoclasm in 843. Hereafter the visual distinctiveness of Orthodoxy was to be affirmed by the inclusion of images all over the church.

In later centuries a number of further panels were added. The most controversial in terms of meaning and date is the panel over the central door from the narthex into the nave in which an emperor kneels in front of Christ (*see* CHRISTIANITY, fig. 1). In style the mosaic seems

to belong to the late 9th century or the early 10th, and the emperor is most often identified as Leo VI (*see* MACEDONIAN DYNASTY, (2)).

The meaning of the panel may however be explained in much more general terms as a representation of the timeless power of the Byzantine emperor. The panel over the door from the south-west vestibule into the narthex may belong to the same period; it represents the *Virgin and Child* flanked by *Justinian I* and *Constantine I* and is more clearly a political statement about the status of these great emperors of Byzantine history and the heavenly protection offered to Constantinople and Hagia Sophia.

Several panels are preserved in the south gallery of the church, the private area for the emperor and his court and for the patriarch. Two adjacent panels on the east wall represent imperial donations to the church. The earlier of the two shows *Empress Zoe* (*reg* 1028–50) and *Constantine X* (*see* MACEDONIAN DYNASTY, (4)) offering respectively a legal document and a purse of money to Christ (*see* EARLY CHRISTIAN AND BYZANTINE ART, fig. 41). Close examination of this panel reveals that the extant mosaic is an alteration of a previous image and has three new heads and rewritten inscriptions. The earlier panel showed Empress Zoe with one of her two previous husbands, probably Romanos III Argyros (*reg* 1028–34), and their donation to Hagia Sophia. To the right of this panel is a 12th-century imperial donation (see fig. 9) representing John II (*reg* 1118–43) and his wife Eirene (*d* 1134), together with their son Alexios (co-emperor 1122). Their donation is offered to the Virgin and Child. The two panels present an ideal comparison of the methods and meanings of Byzantine art in two related images that are a century apart in date.

A third extant mosaic in this imperial enclosure is a monumental *Deësis*, which probably dates to 1261 (*see* EARLY CHRISTIAN AND BYZANTINE ART, fig. 45 and MOSAIC, colour pl. III, fig. 2) and marks the return of Hagia Sophia to the Orthodox rite after 57 years of Roman Catholic use. Features of this devotional panel are the softness of the impression given by the tones of the mosaic and the closeness of its style to central Italian painting of the late 13th century and the early 14th, particularly to that of Duccio (*see* ITALY, §III, 2).

The latest extant mosaics are the figures of the *Virgin, Emperor John V* (*reg* 1341–91) and *St John the Baptist* on the great eastern arch, with a *Hetoimasia* at the centre of the arch. They were probably set up in 1354–5, or soon after, following a collapse of the arch in 1346 due to earthquake damage. To the same restoration belonged a reset of the *Christ Pantokrator* (destr.) in the main dome and the seraphim (*in situ*) on the eastern pendentives.

BIBLIOGRAPHY

EARLY SOURCES
Prokopios: *Peri ktismaton/De aedificiis* (*c.* 553–5); Eng. trans., ed. H. B. Dewing and G. Downey as *Buildings* (1940/*R* 1971), vii of *Procopius*, Loeb Class. Lib. (London and New York, 1914–40)
Povest' vremmennykh (early 10th century); Eng. trans., ed. S. H. Cross and O. P. Sherbowitz-Wetzor as *The Russian Primary Chronicle* (Cambridge, MA, 1953), p. 111

GENERAL
C. Mango: *Materials for the Study of the Mosaics of St. Sophia at Istanbul* (Washington, DC, 1962) [analytical study of the dossier of available drawings, mostly 19th century, of the known decoration]
R. L. Van Nice: *St Sophia in Istanbul: An Architectural Survey*, 2 vols (Washington, DC, 1965–86)
T. F. Mathews: *The Early Churches of Constantinople: Architecture and Liturgy* (University Park, PA, 1971)
C. Mango: *The Art of the Byzantine Empire, 312–1453: Sources and Documents* (Englewood Cliffs, NJ, 1972/*R* Toronto, Buffalo and London, 1986)
T. F. Mathews: *The Byzantine Churches of Istanbul* (University Park, PA, 1976) [phot. record]
G. Majeska: *Russian Travelers to Constantinople in the Fourteenth and Fifteenth Centuries* (Washington, DC, 1984)
R. J. Mainstone: *Hagia Sophia: Architecture, Structure and Liturgy of Justinian's Great Church* (London, 1988)
R. Cormack: *The Byzantine Eye* (London, 1989) [documents mosaics]

ROBIN CORMACK

(iii) After 1453. After the conquest of Istanbul, Mehmed II rode in triumph through the city to Hagia Sophia and had the church converted into a congregational mosque. Several alterations were necessary: a wooden minaret was raised on the southern stair-turret of the west façade, and inside, a marble mihrab and minbar, orientated towards the qibla, the direction of Mecca, were introduced along with other furnishings and relics. Mehmed also had a brick minaret added to the south-east and the buttresses and retaining walls repaired. From the time of the conquest Hagia Sophia remained a source of inspiration to Ottoman architects for the design of imperial domed mosques in Istanbul and elsewhere (*see* ISLAMIC ART, §II, 7(i)(b)).

Between 1572 and 1574 Selim II (*reg* 1566–74) issued firmans ordering the structural consolidation of the building by strengthening the buttresses and building a minaret to replace the wooden structure of Mehmed II. Two identical minarets at the north and west corners were completed under Murad III (*reg* 1574–95). The chief court architect Sinan was also responsible for constructing the

mausoleum of Selim II in the south garden. The mausoleum was followed by another for Murad III by Davud Ağa and a third (1608) for Mehmed III (*reg* 1595–1603) by Ahmed Dalgıç. During the reign of Ahmed I (*reg* 1603–17) other major renovations were undertaken, including the plastering and whitewashing of the interior and exterior, so that most of the figural mosaics were obscured. The baptistery nearby was converted into a mausoleum for Mustafa I (*reg* 1617–18) by removing the font and raising the floor. In 1739 Mahmud I (*reg* 1730–54) built a library in the south aisle of the nave. The library, which housed some 5000 manuscripts, comprised several domed rooms revetted with Iznik tiles and enclosed with metal grilles, and the revenues from the Cağaloğlu Baths (1741) in Istanbul paid for its upkeep.

Between 1847 and 1849 Abdülmecid (*reg* 1839–61) commissioned a thorough restoration of Hagia Sophia. This second major structural repair under the Ottomans was carried out by Gaspare Trajano Fossati (*see* FOSSATI, (2)), assisted by his brother Giuseppe Fossati (1822–91). They consolidated the dome and vaults, heightened the brick minaret on the south-east to conform to the other three and repaired the leaning columns. During the course of their work the figural mosaics were cleaned of whitewash and plaster, but they were subsequently covered over for protection against further damage. Fossati also constructed the sultan's loge at the east end of the north aisle. The eight large calligraphic plaques (diam. 8 m) that hang from the piers at gallery level were also introduced. Bearing the names of God, Muhammad, the first four Caliphs, Hasan and Husayn in gold letters on a green ground, they are the work of Mustafa Izzat, who also renewed the Koranic inscription in the dome.

Hagia Sophia remained in use as the Ayasofya Mosque until the 20th century. Under the Republican government, the building lost its imperial status, and it was opened as a museum on 1 February 1935. Several years earlier the Byzantine Institute of America had begun to uncover and restore the mosaics, many of which had disappeared since the Fossati brothers examined them. This work was completed in 1964.

BIBLIOGRAPHY

G. Fossati: *Ayasofia, Constantinople as Recently Restored by Order of H. M. the Sultan Abdul Medjid* (London, 1852)
W. Emerson and R. L. Van Nice: 'Hagia Sophia and the First Minaret Erected after the Conquest of Istanbul', *Amer. J. Archaeol.*, liv (1950), pp. 28–40
M. Ahunbay and Z. Ahunbay: 'Structural Influence of Hagia Sophia on Ottoman Mosque Architecture', *Hagia Sophia: From the Age of Justinian to the Present*, ed. R. Mark and A. Çakmak (Cambridge, 1992), pp. 179–94
G. Necipoğlu: 'The Life of an Imperial Monument: Hagia Sophia after Byzantium', *Hagia Sophia: From the Age of Justinian to the Present*, ed. R. Mark and A. Çakmak (Cambridge, 1992), pp. 195–225

2. CHRIST PANTOKRATOR MONASTERY. Middle Byzantine monastery church on the Fourth Hill, overlooking the Golden Horn (see fig. 2p above). It was built as the funerary church of the Komnenian dynasty in the early 12th century. It was sacked by the Venetians in 1204, but towards the end of Latin rule it was used as their headquarters. Under the Palaiologan emperors the monastery was restored and resumed its role as one of the most important religious centres in Constantinople. After the Ottoman conquest, it was converted to a mosque (Turk. Zeyrek Camii).

(i) Architecture. The complex consists of two churches with a mausoleum chapel between them. They originally formed the centre of a large monastery that included a hospital, leprosarium and hospice for aged men. The monastery's *typikon*, or constitution, dated October 1136, prescribes the administration of the monastery and its dependencies. The detailed liturgical instructions have allowed scholars to identify the parts of the extant building and reconstruct its decoration, while soundings by Megaw during restoration work in the 1950s clarified the construction sequence. The south church, dedicated to Christ, was possibly begun by Empress Eirene between 1118 and 1124 and used by 80 monks. The north church of the Virgin Eleousa ('merciful') was erected shortly after 1124 by John II and intended for public worship. Both are large domed cross-in-square churches with upper galleries. John II also built the intervening two-domed mausoleum chapel (before 1136) dedicated to the Archangel Michael. Doors were cut to connect all parts of the complex, allowing commemorative processions to pass throughout, and an exonarthex was added to the south church.

The complex is one of a group of Middle Byzantine monastery churches with subsidiary chapels or parekklesia built for the burial of aristocratic founders, such as the north church of the monastery of Constantine Lips (Turk. Fenarı Isa Camii; 907) in Istanbul. The Pantokrator's great prestige is reflected by the fact that four emperors were buried here: John II, Manuel I (*reg* 1143–80), Manuel II (*reg* 1391–1425) and John VIII (*reg* 1425–48); the imperial tombs were removed when it was converted into a mosque.

(ii) Decoration. The Pantokrator's importance is reflected in its decoration, some of which survives. Stephen of Novgorod reported (*c.* 1350) seeing the exterior of the church and its gateways glitter with mosaics (Khitrowo, 1889). The present exterior is bare brick, but not undecorated. The masonry has been over-restored on the north and west sides, but the undulating east façade with its seven apses displays delicate ornamental brick patterns, tall blind niches and the recessed brick technique characteristic of Constantinople in the 12th century.

Most of the preserved interior decoration is in the south church; a magnificent *opus sectile* floor (rest. 1950s; see fig. 10) forms a continuous carpet over the sanctuary and nave. The pattern consists of squares and roundels outlined by interlaced borders, and corner panels containing figural scenes incised in white marble: the *Labours of Samson* in the east end, *The Zodiac* and *The Seasons* by the west portals, and hunting, marine and foliate motifs throughout. It resembles the badly damaged Middle Byzantine floor in St John Stoudios (*see* §6 below). Much of the marble wall revetment is preserved in the apse but the mosaic decoration that once covered the vaults above the second cornice has gone. The four red granite columns seen by Gyllius in the mid-16th century were replaced by Turkish Baroque columns, although several smaller colonettes remain in window openings, their formerly polychrome capitals displaying carved foliate crosses.

Fragments of the church's furnishings were discovered during restoration work, including pieces of the ciborium, the synthronon, a font, icon frames and several carved marble slabs from the sanctuary screens, some of which were spolia from the 6th-century church of St Polyeuktos. Small finds include rock crystal and cloisonné enamel. The most intriguing finds are fragments of coloured and painted glass with lead kames, which Megaw assigned to the 12th century on technical and stylistic grounds. They come from windows with life-size figures of standing saints and display some affinity to early French and Rhenish painted glass windows. Similar glass fragments have been found at other Middle Byzantine Constantinopolitan churches, including Christ the Saviour in Chora (early 12th century; *see* §3 below).

10. Istanbul, Christ Pantokrator Monastery, south church (1118–24), detail from the *opus sectile* floor in the nave, 12th century, restored 1950s

The north church of the Virgin Eleousa is less well preserved, its columns replaced by masonry piers and its marble revetment gone. The only mosaic visible in the Pantokrator complex is a gold foliate interlace pattern on a red ground in the soffit of a north window. The marble cornices are boldly carved with a vine and pomegranate interlace enclosing bird and animal motifs. No decoration remains in the central mausoleum chapel of St Michael or in the narthexes, which once contained the various imperial tombs (mostly destr.), including the black sarcophagus of Manuel I by the entrance to the south church and near the Stone of Unction, a relic he brought to Constantinople; their original position may be indicated by irregularities in the *opus sectile*. A verde-antico sarcophagus (Istanbul, Hagia Sophia Mus.) removed from the square outside the church in 1960 may have been that of Empress Eirene.

Icons and images mentioned in the liturgical details of the *Typikon* fall into three categories: individual sanctuary icons, narrative scenes on the walls and vaults, and images of *Christ Pantokrator* and the *Virgin Eleousa* over the doors. They were elaborately coloured and figured prominently in the commemorative processions. The scant evidence suggests a cycle of the Twelve Feasts in the south church, a Passion cycle in the central chapel with *St Michael* in one dome, and individual images in the narthexes. Throughout the complex, the choice and placement of images, like the liturgical specifications, clearly reflected the monastery's funereal and commemorative functions.

BIBLIOGRAPHY

P. Gyllius [Gilles]: *De topographia Constantinopoleos et de illius antiquitatibus* (Lyon, 1561; Eng. trans., London, 1729, rev. 2/1988), iv/2, p. 195ff
B. de Khitrowo: *Itinéraires russes en Orient* (Geneva, 1889)
A. Hergès: 'Le Monastère du Pantocrator à Constantinople', *Echos Orient*, ii (1898), pp. 70–88
G. Moravcsik: *Szent László Leánya es a Bizanci Pantokrator-Monostor/Die Tochter Ladislaus des Heiligen und das Pantocrator-Kloster in Konstantinopel* (Budapest and Constantinople, 1923) [dual text]
P. Schweinfurth: 'Der Mosaikfussboden der Komnenischen Pantokratorkirche in Istanbul', *Jb. Dt. Archäol. Inst.*, lxix (1954), cols 253–60
P. Underwood: 'Notes on the Work of the Byzantine Institute in Istanbul: 1954', *Dumbarton Oaks Pap.*, ix–x (1955–6), pp. 291–300
A. Megaw: 'Notes on Recent Work of the Byzantine Institute: Zeyrek Camii', *Dumbarton Oaks Pap.*, xvii (1963), pp. 335–64
J. Lafond: 'Les Vitraux historiés du moyen-âge découverts récemment à Constantinople', *Cah. Archéol.*, xviii (1968), pp. 231–8
C. Mango: 'Notes on Byzantine Monuments: Tomb of Manuel I Comnenus', *Dumbarton Oaks Pap.*, xxiii–xxiv (1969–70), pp. 372–5
P. Gautier: 'Le Typikon du Pantocrator', *Rev. Etud. Byz.*, xxxii (1974), pp. 1–145
W. Müller-Wiener and J. Cramer, eds: 'Istanbul-Zeyrek: Studien zur Erhaltung eines traditionellen Wohngebietes', *Mitt. Dt. Orient-Inst.*, xvii (1982), pp. 174–6

LAWRENCE E. BUTLER

3. CHRIST THE SAVIOUR IN CHORA. Byzantine church located just inside the Adrianople Gate (now Edirne Kapısı; see fig. 2v above) and one of the finest examples of Late Byzantine art. It served as the katholikon of the Chora Monastery; none of the conventual buildings survives. The church was rebuilt in its present form c. 1316–21 and decorated with wall paintings and mosaics commissioned by Theodore Metochites (1270–1332). The building was converted to a mosque about 1510 (Turk. Kariye Camii); it was restored under the direction of Paul Underwood between 1948 and 1958 and is now preserved as a museum.

(i) Architecture. The building's structural history is complex and scholars remain uncertain as to its origin, for although the foundations may date from the 6th and 9th centuries, the rising walls of the nave are no earlier than the late 11th century. In the early 12th century the sebastokrator Isaak Komnenos was probably responsible for rebuilding the nave on a cruciform plan with shallow cross-arms and a dome (diam. c. 7.4 m; for a plan of the church *see* PAREKKLESION). The present wide central apse with its deep barrel vault and two domed apsidal chambers on either side also belong to this period of construction. In design the church recalls much earlier structures, such as the church of the Dormitian (?early 8th century) at Nicaea (*see* IZNIK, §1) and Hagia Sophia in Thessaloniki (*see* THESSALONIKI, §III, 5(i)). By the early 14th century, however, the church was in a poor state of repair. Metochites was apparently appointed founder (*ktitor*) by the emperor, and he was responsible for reconstructing the nave dome and adding the ancillary chambers that envelop the building on three sides. To the north lies a two-storey annexe, which may have served as skeuophylakeion, library or diakonikon. To the west he erected two narthexes, the inner of which is not centred with regard to the nave and has domes of different sizes over its end bays. The outer narthex lies across the entire width of the church in six unequal compartments and was originally an open portico. A belfry (destr.) was positioned over the south-west corner. Along the building's south side is a substantial parekklesion, included to serve as a funeral chapel, with one domed and one vaulted bay. A Gothic-style flying buttress was added to the east to brace the apse. Metochites also built himself a palace near by, which has not survived.

The building exhibits a studied asymmetry. The construction of the walls is of high quality, with broad alternating bands of brick and stone. The exterior façades are further enlivened by blind and open arcades, with stepped responds and half-columns. The apses feature two tiers of recessed niches, and a variety of brick decoration appears throughout the building. The vaulting is of brick, with pumpkin domes and ribbed domes raised on windowed drums. An unusual form of sail vault is used in the narthexes. The roof-line is undulating, and the domes are scalloped on the exterior.

(ii) Mosaics and wall paintings. The mosaics and wall paintings of the Chora are among the key works of Late Byzantine art and the most complete to survive in Istanbul. The nave and narthexes were completed by 1321 and decorated in mosaic, while the parekklesion and lesser areas were painted. The dual dedication of the church to Christ and the Virgin is evident from the two mosaic panels in the lunette over the door to the inner narthex and, opposite, over the main entrance door: the former shows a bust of *Christ Pantokrator* with an inscription referring to him as 'the dwelling-place [Gr. *chora*] of the living'; the second depicts the *Virgin* between two angels and an inscription referring to her as 'the container [Gr. *chora*] of the uncontainable'. The same inscriptions appear in the framed mosaic icons of Christ and the Virgin that flank the iconostasis in the nave. The only other surviving

11. Istanbul, Christ the Saviour in Chora, mosaics in the inner narthex, looking south, after 1321

decoration in this part of the church is the *Dormition of the Virgin* over the west entrance.

The two fluted domes over the north and south bays of the inner narthex contain medallions of the *Virgin* and *Christ Pantokrator*, respectively, surrounded by figures from the genealogy of Christ. The domical vaults, lunettes and soffits of the north and two central bays show the *Life of the Virgin*, based on the apocryphal gospel of St James, beginning with the *Rejection of Joachim's Offering* and concluding with the *Annunciation* (see fig. 11). This programme continues in the lunettes of the outer narthex with the *Infancy of Christ*, which includes an extended section devoted to the *Journey of the Magi* and the *Massacre of the Innocents*. The soffits are decorated with medallion and full-length portraits of martyr saints; there were originally 50, of which 37 survive in whole or in part. The domical vaults show the *Ministry and Miracles of Christ*, concluding with scenes of healing in the lunettes and pendentives of the south bay of the inner narthex. The latter's east wall also includes the monumental *Deësis* mosaic showing Christ and the Virgin with the figures of two earlier donors at their feet, who are identified by inscription as Isaak Komnenos and 'the Lady of the Mongols, Melane the nun'. This was either Maria, half-sister of Andronikos II Palaiologos (*reg* 1282–1328), known as Despoina of the Mongols, or another Maria, an illegitimate daughter of Andronikos II, who married a Mongol khan. A dedicatory panel in the lunette over the door to the nave depicts Metochites offering a model of his church to the enthroned Christ.

The complex painted programme in the parekklesion was probably created by the artist of the mosaics. The emphasis on salvation and resurrection in the paintings above the cornice reflects the chapel's funerary function. Old Testament prefigurations of the Virgin are represented in the west bay, and a medallion of the *Virgin* occupies the centre of the dome, surrounded by angels, with four hymnographers in the pendentives. The east bay shows scenes from the Apocalypse, with a representation of the *Last Judgement* occupying the whole domical vault. On the north and south sides of the apse are *Christ Raising the Widow's Son* and *Christ Raising the Daughter of Jairus* respectively. The programme terminates with the *Anastasis* in the conch of the apse, showing Christ resurrecting both Adam and Eve (*see* WALL PAINTING, colour pl. II, fig. 1). Below the cornice there is a procession of standing military and ecclesiastical saints interrupted by four arcosolium tombs, which originally contained sarcophagi; fragments of their painted and mosaic decoration survive. Decorated tombs were also added to the narthexes. The latest one probably dates to the early 15th century and has paintings of the donors and an enthroned Virgin in a style that is apparently influenced by concurrent developments in Italian art.

Stylistically the main body of the Chora's decoration progresses from the nave to the narthexes and then to the parekklesion. The mosaics flanking the iconostasis are relatively conservative, and it has even been suggested that these date from the 12th century. The remainder is more experimental; Demus described its style as 'overripe'. The interests and budget of the patron seem to have provided the conditions for the rapid development of the style, allowing for lavish experimentation. Occasionally, however, this resulted in unsatisfactory solutions to problems of composition and detail. The many different types of figures, portrayed in a variety of unusual poses, are often set against a uniting landscape, architectural or decorative background. Compositions are often stretched or squeezed to fit the vaulting forms, and a sense of unrest dominates the narrative scenes. A mannerist aesthetic is revealed, in which the refinement of the parts becomes more important than the overall unity. The style of painting

is similar to that of the slightly earlier wall paintings in the churches of St Mary Pammakaristos (1310; *see* §7 below) and the Holy Apostles (1312–15; *see* THESSALONIKI, §III, 7(ii)) and may be detected through the remainder of the Byzantine period, as at Profitis Elias at Thessaloniki (*c.* 1360; *see* THESSALONIKI, §III, 7).

(iii) *Other decoration.* The walls of the nave and inner narthex preserve the best examples of Late Byzantine revetments; most of the revetment in the outer narthex was stripped in Ottoman times. The most common material is Proconnesian marble, arranged in mirrored panels and framed with verde- and rosso-antico. Large fields of other coloured stones are also used in the nave; all the material is apparently spolia. Champlevé relief appears in the spandrels of the apse windows, and an upper border of inlay links the 14th-century nave revetment to the 12th-century cornice. In the inner narthex the revetment patterns do not reflect the building's structural divisions, thus complementing the studied mannerism of the art and architecture.

Although much of the varied architectural sculpture is spolia, it was carefully selected and integrated into the building, such as the 6th-century 'false door' panels that line the secondary entrance to the nave. All the figural carving has been defaced. A foliated, arched frame with heavily undercut decoration is positioned above the nave icon of the Virgin, and decorated framing arches were added above two of the parekklesion tombs in the 14th century. A set of four reused capitals decorated with angels (perhaps 11th century) appear in the outer narthex.

The original flooring of the nave and inner narthex survives, with large repeating panels of Proconnesian marble, also framed in verde- and rosso-antico. All the surfaces that were not in themselves decorative were decorated. The cornices and much of the sculpture were painted, either following the carved patterns or creating *rinceau* designs on flat surfaces. The tie-beams, now lost, were similarly carved and painted. The carved or painted monograms of the founder appear in several places.

BIBLIOGRAPHY

O. Demus: 'Die Entstehung des Paläologenstils in der Malerei', *Bericht zum XI. Internationalen Byzantinisten-Kongress: Munich, 1958*, iv/2, pp. 1–63

D. Oates: 'A Summary Report on the Excavations of the Byzantine Institute in the Kariye Camii, 1957 and 1958', *Dumbarton Oaks Pap.*, xiv (1960), pp. 223–31

P. A. Underwood: *The Kariye Djami*, 3 vols (New York, 1966)

P. A. Underwood, ed.: *The Kariye Djami: Studies in the Art of the Kariye Djami and its Intellectual Background* (Princeton, 1975) [ess. drawn from the symp. on the mosaics and frescoes of the Kariye Djami: Washington, DC, 1960]

Ø. Hjort: 'The Sculpture of the Kariye Camii', *Dumbarton Oaks Pap.*, xxxiii (1979), pp. 201–89

R. G. Ousterhout: *The Architecture of the Kariye Camii* (Washington, DC, 1987)

ROBERT OUSTERHOUT

4. CHURCH OF THE KYRIOTISSA. Byzantine church on the Third Hill, *c.* 250 m east of the Aqueduct of Valens (AD 375; see fig.1xxxiv above). The church's dedication is based on the inscription 'Mother of God of Kyriotissa' accompanying two icons of the Virgin that were discovered during excavations to the north of the church by L. Striker and Y. Kuban from 1966; these excavations also helped to date the core of the building to the 12th century.

The present cross-domed church appears to rise from an almost square ground-plan with towering, barrel-vaulted transepts and a central dome on a 16-sided drum. The structure incorporates the walls of several earlier buildings: to the north are several round structures belonging to baths of the late 4th century or the early 5th, which were superseded as early as the 6th century by an apsidal building. The present apse and bema may belong to the diakonikon erected to the south of this c. 700. The two absidioles on the diakonikon's east side were built c. 700 and in the late 12th century, when the existing nave and narthexes were constructed. During the Latin occupation of Constantinople (1204–61) the northernmost absidiole was decorated with a painting of the *Life of St Francis* (probably c. 1250; see below). Under the Palaiologan emperors (1261–1453) slight alterations were made to the church furnishings. In the late 15th century the church was converted into a Dervish monastery (Turk. Kalendarhane Camii); the vestries on either side of the nave and the upper floors of the inner and outer narthexes were also demolished.

The earliest surviving decoration is a mosaic showing the *Presentation in the Temple* (c. AD 705–7) on the south wall of the prothesis, which may have belonged to the apsed building of c. 700. A mosaic of the *Archangel Michael* was found in the passage leading from the bema to the diakonikon, to the south of the apse. Its late Komnenian characteristics suggest that it is contemporary with the church's construction in the late 12th century. A well-preserved wall painting of the *Mother of God of Kyriotissa* dates from soon after and occupies a round-arched niche in a passage leading from the bema to the diakonikon that was subsequently walled up. Above the doorway leading to the inner narthex is another representation of the *Mother of God of Kyriotissa* that has all the stylistic features of the Palaiologan period.

The most surprising find was the wall painting of the *Life of St Francis* in the northernmost absidiole of the diakonikon. In style the paintings are close to the illumination in the Arsénal Bible (Paris, Bib. Arsenal, MS. 5211), which was probably produced between 1250 and 1254. The Kyriotissa paintings are therefore among the earliest known cycles of St Francis, and the first cycle of wall paintings. They also indicate that the church was used by the Franciscan Order during the Latin occupation of Constantinople. During the Palaiologan period the absidiole with the cycle of *St Francis* was walled over, and new paintings of the *Melismos* (the breaking of bread in the Eucharist), the *Dormition* and standing saints were applied to the walls of the diakonikon. Alterations and repairs to the marble inlay in the nave and to part of the *opus sectile* floor in the apse, most of which date from the late 12th century, can also be attributed to the Palaiologan period.

RBK

BIBLIOGRAPHY

E. Freshfield: 'Notes on the Church Now Called the Mosque of the Kalenders at Constantinople', *Archaeologia*, lv (1897), pp. 431–8
N. Bunov: 'Zur Erforschung der byzantinischen Baudenkmäler von Konstantinopel', *Byz. Z.*, xxxii (1932), pp. 49–62
J. Kollwitz: 'Zur frühmittelalterlichen Baukunst Konstantinopels', *Röm. Qschr.*, xlii (1934), pp. 233–50
C. L. Striker and Y. D. Kuban: 'Work at Kalenderhane Camii in Istanbul', *Dumbarton Oaks Pap.*, xxi (1967), pp. 267–71; xxii (1968), pp. 185–93; xxv (1971), pp. 251–8 [preliminary excav. rep.]
T. F. Mathews: *The Byzantine Churches of Istanbul: A Photographic Survey* (London, 1976), pp. 171–85
W. Müller-Wiener: *Bildlexikon zur Topographie Istanbuls* (Tübingen, 1977), pp. 153–8
A. Berger: 'Untersuchungen zur Patria Konstantinupoleos', *Poikilia Byz.*, viii (1988), pp. 477–82

LIOBA THEIS

5. HAGIA EIRENE. Byzantine church in the southern region of the city (see fig. 1xvi above), to the north of Hagia Sophia. According to several ancient sources it occupies the site of a church that predated the reign of Constantine I, but which he then rebuilt on a larger scale and dedicated to Eirene ('peace'). This second church was destroyed by the Nika riots fire of 532 and rebuilt by Justinian I. Damage caused by the earthquake of 740 resulted in the reconstruction of most of the church's superstructure. Surviving portions of Justinian's church include the atrium and some lower sections of the external walls. The present church is a three-aisled basilica (58×30 m) with a central dome (diam. c. 16 m) with windows, a domical vault without windows over the west bay of the nave, and barrel-vaulted galleries along the south, north and west sides. The present arcading with four columns dates from the 8th century, while the Justinianic atrium was probably similar in arrangement to that of St John at Ephesos with five columns (*see* EPHESOS, §I, 3).

The colonnades flanking the nave are composed of reused column shafts and Ionic impost capitals from the Justinianic period. The narthex was originally lined with marble revetment. Only remnants survive of the vault mosaics with tendrils and geometric ornament. The fragmented apse mosaic of a cross outlined in black on a three-stepped pedestal against a gold ground probably dates to the reign of the iconoclastic emperor Constantine V (*reg* 741–75). Two inscriptions extend across the entrance arch of the apse on the transition to the conch. The upper one begins with a quotation from Amos 9:6 and ends with a passage from Psalm 33:21. In the inscription beneath this is an extract from Psalm 65:5–6 that also appears in the apse of Hagia Sophia in Thessaloniki (*see* THESSALONIKI, §III, 5(ii)). All the inscriptions allude to the House of the Lord.

In the Middle Ages various repairs to the building were carried out. After the Turkish conquest, the church was used as an arsenal until it was fitted out as a museum in the 19th century.

BIBLIOGRAPHY

W. S. George: *The Church of Saint Eirene at Constantinople* (Oxford, 1913)
T. F. Mathews: *The Early Churches of Constantinople* (London, 1971)
——: *The Byzantine Churches of Istanbul* (London, 1976)
W. Müller-Wiener: *Bildlexikon zur Topographie Istanbuls* (Tübingen, 1977)
U. Peschlow: *Die Irenenkirche in Istanbul* (Tübingen, 1977)

6. ST JOHN STOUDIOS. Oldest surviving church (c. 450) in Istanbul. It was founded together with a monastery by the Roman patrician Stoudios on a plot to the south-west of the Constantinian city wall (see fig. 1xxviii above). All that remains is the ruined basilican church (30 ×26 m), which was preceded by an atrium and a two-storey narthex. The walls are built of alternating layers of stone and brick. A gallery originally surrounded the three-aisled interior, while the eastern apse, with its three-sided external shell, was occupied by a synthronon. In front of the apse was a cruciform crypt (arms c. 2 m

long), which was probably used to store relics. Windows in the aisles, galleries and clerestory provided generous lighting.

Of the rich interior decoration, the portal of the narthex's central bay survives complete with four Corinthian columns supporting a richly sculpted architrave, frieze and cornice, while in the nave, of the two rows of seven columns separating it from the side aisles, six columns on the north side still stand; they are of verde-antico surmounted by fine-toothed acanthus capitals and an entablature. The walls were covered with multicoloured revetment, and sculpted fragments indicate the existence of an ambo. Under Theodore of Stoudios, a leader against the iconoclastic decrees of Leo V (*reg* 813–20), the church was decorated with a series of saints' portraits. Sources also confirm that mosaics of *Christ*, the *Virgin*, cherubim and seraphim (before 900; destr.) covered the apse. The *opus sectile* floor, with its figural designs, dates from 1057–1180. In the 8th and 9th centuries the monastery became renowned for its scriptorium and remained an important pilgrimage centre throughout the Middle Ages.

Around 1500 the church was converted into a mosque (Turk. Imrahor Camii) by Ilyas Bey, Master of the Horse (Ott. Turk. *Imrahor*) under Sultan Bayezid II (*reg* 1481–1512). Damage of varying degrees by earthquakes and fires, most recently in 1920, had already led to the building's abandonment in 1894.

See also EARLY CHRISTIAN AND BYZANTINE ART, fig. 10.

BIBLIOGRAPHY
W. Müller-Wiener: *Bildlexikon zur Topographie Istanbuls* (Tübingen, 1977)
U. Peschlow: 'Die Johanneskirche des Studios in Istanbul', *Jb. Österreich. Byz.*, xxxii/4 (1982), pp. 429–35
M. Restle: 'Art. Konstantinopel', *Reallexikon zur byzantinischen Kunst*, ed. M. Restle and K. Wessel, xxvii (1989), pp. 378–84

FRANZ RICKERT

7. ST MARY PAMMAKARISTOS. The Pammakaristos monastery, overlooking the Golden Horn (see fig. 2t above), was founded by John Komnenos and his wife Anna Doukaina, probably during the second half of the 12th century. The Greek Orthodox Patriarchate was

12. Istanbul, St Mary Pammakaristos, parekklesion, dome mosaic of *Christ Pantokrator with Twelve Prophets, c.* 1310

transferred to the monastery in 1456, following the conquest of the city by the Ottoman Turks. In 1573 the building was converted to a mosque by Murad III (*reg* 1574–95), who called it Fethiye ('Victory') Mosque (Turk. Fethiye Camii) to commemorate his conquest of Georgia and Azerbaijan.

The original church was of the ambulatory type, with triple arcades in the north, west and south sides dividing the central domed area from the ambulatory, which was designed to hold the tombs of the founding family. The eastern side ended in three apses. Numerous ancillary chambers were added around the core during the following centuries, although the chronology has not been resolved. The narthex was built either during the original construction or in the late 13th century, when the monastery came under the patronage of the *protostrator* (military commander) Michael Doukas Glavas Tarchaneiotes. A portico was added along the north side, perhaps in 1294, terminating in a domed chapel.

About 1310 a parekklesion (*see* BRICK, fig. 7) was added to the south flank by the *protostrator's* widow, Maria, as a funeral chapel for her husband. It was built of brick and stone in the form of a miniature cross-in-square church with a twin-domed gallery above its narthex, and it is one of the finest examples of Late Byzantine architecture in the capital. The façades are lavishly decorated with arcades, niches, brick patterning and inscriptions. The domes are scalloped on the exterior and ribbed or fluted on the interior. Marble revetment, of which some fragments have survived, covered the interior walls, topped by a champlevé relief frieze. A dedicatory verse, written by Manuel Philes (*c.* 1275–*c.* 1345), was painted on the interior cornice and sculpted on the exterior cornice. An outer narthex was later added and perhaps vaulted in the 15th century. A belfry (destr.) was positioned above the western entrance. The main apse was removed when the church was converted into a mosque. The church was restored in the 1960s, and the parekklesion, now separated from the rest of the building, functions as a museum.

Fragments of wall painting dating from the 1290s are preserved in the south portico. These include the *Closed Door* and *Aaron and his Sons before an Altar*, set into a niche; the *Virgin Praying in her House*; and a fragment of a scene with *St Peter*. Large areas of the early 14th-century mosaic decoration of the parekklesion survive (*see* MOSAIC). The tiny naos dome contains a medallion of *Christ Pantokrator* ('all powerful') surrounded by 12 prophets (see fig. 12). A *Deësis* appears in the main apse, with an enthroned *Christ Yperagathos* ('the most benevolent') in the conch and the *Virgin* and *St John the Baptist* in the lunettes to either side. The subject is iconographically unusual and reflects the dedication of the chapel to Christ the Logos. Four archangels appear in the bema vault. Of the episodes from the Feast Cycle, only the *Baptism* and a fragment of the *Ascension* have survived. The small size of the chapel means that few areas of the upper walls or vaults are large enough for narrative scenes, and instead these are decorated with images of saints. The *pastophoria* are dark, small and practically inaccessible; its mosaics of saints are of poor quality and partly painted. The mosaics are stylistically uneven, both in quality and choice of models. The restrained classicism may be compared with the almost coeval decoration of Hagioi Apostoloi in Thessaloniki (*see* THESSALONIKI, §III, 7(ii)) and contrasted with the polished mannerism of the slightly later mosaics of Christ the Saviour in Chora (*see* §3(ii) above).

BIBLIOGRAPHY
H. Hallensleben: 'Die Baugeschichte der ehemaligen Pammakaristoskirche, der heutigen Fethiye camii zu Istanbul', *Istanbul. Mitt.*, xiii–xiv (1963–4), pp. 128–93
C. Mango and E. Hawkins: 'Report on Field Work in Istanbul and Cyprus, 1962–63', *Dumbarton Oaks Pap.*, xviii (1964), pp. 319–33
H. Belting, D. Mouriki and C. Mango: *The Mosaics and Frescoes of the Pammakaristos (Fethiye Camii) in Istanbul* (Washington, DC, 1976)
W. Müller-Wiener: *Bildlexikon zur Topographie Istanbuls* (Tübingen, 1977), pp. 132–5

ROBERT OUSTERHOUT

8. SS SERGIOS AND BAKCHOS. This former church, now a mosque (Turk. Küçük Ayasofya Camii), is the only surviving part of an extensive palace complex, which also included the adjoining basilica of SS Peter and Paul (erected 518–19; destr.) and the Palace of Hormisdas situated in the southern part of central Istanbul between the Hippodrome and the sea walls along the Marmara coast. A long inscription set into the architrave and monograms carved on the capitals identify the founders as Justinian I (*reg* 527–65) and his consort, Theodora (*c.* 500–548). The building was started after 527 and completed by 536. Together with the palace and SS Peter and Paul, it seems to have served as a Monophysite monastery, which was forcibly dissolved on the death of Theodora (548). In 580 fire destroyed most of the complex except for SS Sergios and Bakchos. The function of this building is disputed: the suggestion that it served as a palace church should probably be rejected in view of its date of construction and dedication.

The building consists of a central, domed octagon set within an irregular square shell, both of two storeys. The octagon opens eastwards into a forechoir and polygonal apse, while to the west it is preceded by a narthex and open colonnaded hall. The interior of the square shell is converted into an octagon by semicircular niches placed in the corners; these are echoed by exedrae on the diagonal axes of the central octagon. Eight piers support the dome, with two columns between each pair of piers, except on the eastern side, where the arch rises to full height. The articulation of the arcades corresponds to that of the outer shell: the two levels of columns are separated by a strongly moulded entablature, broken at the east bay. The 16-sided dome (diam. *c.* 15 m), composed of alternating flat and concave segments, rises directly above the upper storey of the octagon.

The church shared a narthex and atrium with the earlier basilica of SS Peter and Paul and may originally have communicated with it through three round arches (now blocked) to the south. The fact that SS Sergios and Bakchos was squeezed in between the basilica and palace may partly account for various irregularities of construction, including the misalignment of the central octagon and outer square. A more likely explanation, however, is that, while the complex design of the church was the work of an accomplished architect, its execution was left to a less capable master mason.

Centralized buildings enclosing a core with exedrae survive at S Vitale in Ravenna (*see* RAVENNA, §2(vii)), built at about the same time, and in Syria in the churches of SS Sergios, Bakchos and Leontios (512/13), Bosra, and St George (515), Izra'. Prokopios mentioned two similar churches in Constantinople: St John in the Hebdomon (built in 560 to replace an earlier church) and St Michael in Anaplus. The principle of a polygonal central structure within an outer shell was therefore well known when Justinian began the construction of Hagia Sophia (*see* §1(ii) above), and the hypothesis, frequently expressed, that SS Sergios and Bakchos served as a model for that more complicated building is questionable.

Of the church's interior decoration only the architectural sculpture survives. The high quality of the workmanship and careful choice of materials suggest that originally the walls and dome were decorated with marble revetment and mosaic respectively. The columns, of red Synnada marble in the semicircular niches and green Thessalian marble in the rectangular niches, are crowned by capitals of Proconnesian marble: folded capitals on the ground floor and Ionic imposts on the upper level. Both types are deeply undercut with fine acanthus decoration, which is also found on the triple architrave of the horizontal entablature. The architectural sculpture, similar to that from St Polyeuktos (524–7; destr.; see fig. 1xxix above and ANICIA JULIANA), is both an elaboration of that in St John Stoudios and a precursor of Hagia Sophia.

BIBLIOGRAPHY

R. Kautzsch: *Kapitellstudien: Beiträge zu einer Geschichte des spätantiken Kapitells im Osten vom vierten bis ins siebente Jahrhundert* (Berlin, 1936)

P. Underwood: 'Some Principles of Measure in the Architecture of the Period of Justinian', *Cah. Archéol.*, iii (1948), pp. 64–74

R. Janin: *Les Eglises et les monastères*, I/iii of *La Géographie ecclésiastique de l'empire byzantin* (Paris, 1953)

F. W. Deichmann: *Studien zur Architektur Konstantinopels im 5. und 6. Jahrhundert* (Baden-Baden, 1956), pp. 72–6, 103–7

P. Sanpaolesi: 'La Chiesa dei SS. Sergio e Bacco a Costantinopoli', *Riv. Ist. N. Archeol. & Stor. A.*, n. s., x (1961), pp. 116–80

O. Feld: 'Beobachtungen in der Küçük Ayasofya (Kirche der hl. Sergios und Bacchos) zu Istanbul', *Istanbul. Mitt.*, xviii (1968), pp. 264–9

T. F. Mathews: *The Early Churches of Constantinople: Architecture and Liturgy* (London, 1971), pp. 42–51

C. Mango: 'The Church of Saints Sergius and Bacchus at Constantinople and the Alleged Tradition of Octagonal Palatine Churches', *Jb. Österreich. Byz.*, xxi (1972), pp. 189–93

R. Krautheimer: 'Again Saints Sergius and Bacchus at Constantinople', *Jb. Österreich. Byz.*, xxiii (1974), pp. 251–3

C. Mango: *Architettura bizantina* (Milan, 1974; Eng. trans., New York, 1976), pp. 101–7

——: 'The Church of Sts Sergius and Bacchus Once Again', *Byz. Z.*, lxviii (1975), pp. 385–92

W. Müller-Wiener: *Bildlexikon zur Topographie Istanbuls* (Tübingen, 1977), pp. 177–83

C. Strube: *Polyeuktoskirche und Hagia Sophia: Umbildung und Auflösung antiker Formen, Entstehung des Kämpferkapitells* (Munich, 1984)

LIOBA THEIS

9. FATIH MOSQUE. This mosque forms part of a large complex (partially destr.) begun in 1461 by Mehmed II (*reg* 1444–81 with interruption). It occupies the site of the early 4th-century Church of the Holy Apostles (Gr. Apostoleion; see fig. 1xv above), which was built just inside the Constantinian walls on the highest hill of the city.

(i) Church of the Holy Apostles. One of the most famous and influential churches of the Byzantine empire, its foundation has usually been attributed to CONSTANTINE THE GREAT (*reg* 285–337). It survived as a ruin, until it was dismantled by Mehmed II (*see* §(ii) below). Consequently the physical remains of the church are no longer accessible, and modern understanding of the building rests on documentary evidence.

Two definite architectural campaigns and at least two interior redecorations are recorded, but many details remain conjectural. The final result of the first campaign was a church following the Greek-cross plan, but the initial form of the building is still subject to argument. Mango (1985, p. 27; 1990) has suggested that the church, which was intended to serve as Constantine's mausoleum, was originally a round building similar to the mausoleum of Galerius (Hagios Georgios) at Thessaloniki (*see* THESSALONIKI, §III, 2(i)) and that the cruciform church was built adjacent to it by his son Constantius II, who is known to have obtained its first relics in 356 and 357.

The church served as a burial place for Byzantine rulers until 1042. According to Prokopios (*Buildings* I.iv.9–10) it required repair in the 6th century, and JUSTINIAN I initiated a major restoration (536–50) that apparently replaced the old building with a new church. The latter was still cruciform and had five domes—one above each arm, and a taller one in the centre; it was decorated with mosaics between 565 and 578. Whether the church sustained damage during the iconoclastic controversy (726–843) is not known, but Basil I (*reg* 867–86; *see* MACEDONIAN DYNASTY, (1)) repaired it. The ekphrasis of the church, written between 931 and 944 by Constantinus Rhodius (Mango, 1972), suggests that Basil retained the plan and elevation of the 6th-century church but redecorated the interior: Constantinus's discussion of the mosaics does not survive in full but preserves descriptions of the *Christ* in the central dome, the *Virgin*, the *Apostles* and New Testament scenes that accord better with 9th- than with 6th-century iconography. While the church seems essentially to have retained its 9th-century programme of decoration, this evidently required minor alterations and repairs, for a second (also incomplete) ekphrasis, written between 1198 and 1203 by Nikolaos Mesarites (*d c.* 1220; Mango, 1972), differs from Constantinus's in some respects: Mesarites describes the mosaic of *Christ* in the dome but never mentions the *Virgin* and *Apostles*; nor does his list of New Testament scenes coincide fully with those listed by Constantinus.

The sanctity and importance of the church, assured by the relics and tombs it housed and attested by numerous chroniclers and liturgical commemorations, ensured the spread of the Greek-cross plan around the Mediterranean. Its most famous 'copy' is S Marco in Venice (*see* VENICE, §IV, 1(i)), while its mosaics seem to have inspired artists throughout the Byzantine empire during the 9th and 10th centuries.

BIBLIOGRAPHY

G. Downey: 'Nikolaos Mesarites' Description of the Church of the Holy Apostles at Constantinople', *Trans. Amer. Philos. Assoc.*, xlvii (1957), pp. 857–924

P. Grierson: 'Tombs and Obits of the Byzantine Emperors (337–1042)', *Dumbarton Oaks Pap.*, xvi (1962), pp. 1–65

R. Krautheimer: 'Zu Konstantins Apostelkirche in Konstantinopel', *Mullus: Festschrift Theodor Klauser* (Münster Westfalen, 1964), pp. 224–9; Eng. trans. in *Studies in Early Christian, Medieval and Renaissance Art* (London, 1969), pp. 27–34

——: 'A Note on Constantine's Church of the Holy Apostles in Constantinople', *Studies in Early Christian, Medieval and Renaissance Art* (London, 1969), pp. 197–201

C. Mango: *The Art of the Byzantine Empire, 312–1453: Sources and Documents* (Englewood Cliffs, NJ, 1972/*R* Toronto, Buffalo and London, 1986), pp. 199–201, 232–3

A. W. Epstein: 'The Rebuilding and Redecoration of the Holy Apostles in Constantinople: A Reconsideration', *Gr., Roman & Byz. Stud.*, xxiii (1982), pp. 79–92

C. Mango: *Le Développement urbain de Constantinople (IVe–VIIe siècles)* (Paris, 1985)

——: 'Constantine's Mausoleum and the Translation of Relics', *Byz. Z.*, lxxxiii (1990), no. 1, pp. 51–61; no. 2, p. 434

LESLIE BRUBAKER

(ii) Mehmed II's foundation. In 1470 Mehmed II had the ruined Church of the Holy Apostles (*see* §(i) above) dismantled, replacing it with a great mosque complex. The mosque became known as the Fatih ('Conqueror') Mosque, after the patron's sobriquet. Largely destroyed by the earthquake of 1766, the huge place of worship was the centrepiece of a vast complex of buildings (*see* KÜLLIYE), including eight major theological colleges, a hospital, an inn, a caravanserai and the tomb of the founder. The architect is known as Atık ('Old') Sinan to distinguish him from the famous 16th-century architect of the same name.

Surviving elements of the original mosque, archaeological evidence and early depictions show that it consisted of a huge dome (diam. *c.* 26 m) on a cubic base, extended to the south or qibla side by a semi-dome and on either side by three small domes. Smaller versions of the same plan may be seen in the mosques of Rum Mehmed Pasha (1471) in Üsküdar and Atık Ali Pasha (1497) in Istanbul. The first Fatih Mosque represents an incremental development in Ottoman mosque architecture, incorporating the innovations of the Üç Şerefeli ('Three Balcony'; 1437–47) Mosque at EDIRNE and presaging the mosque of Bayazid II (1505; *see* ISLAMIC ART, §II, 7(i)(b)) in Istanbul. The court and the details of the garden walls surviving from the first Fatih Mosque show the impact of the early Ottoman style of Bursa and Edirne in such features as the hipped arch and the main door, a virtual copy of the portal of the Üç Şerefeli. The ceramic tiles decorating the court are examples of Miletus ware from Iznik.

As a symbolic assertion of Ottoman dominance and a solution to the problems posed by repopulation and Islamization of a conquered city, the first Fatih Mosque served its patron well. The dome's immense size, however, probably contributed to the structural instability that led to its collapse and the destruction of most of the south part of the building in 1766. The mosque was subsequently rebuilt on the old foundations under the chief architect Mehmed Tahir. The massy and somewhat squat original form was not to contemporary Ottoman taste, and since the Baroque style then in vogue was evidently deemed equally inappropriate for the Fatih Mosque, the reconstruction was based on the classical scheme with four semi-domes pioneered by Sinan (*see* SINAN (ii)) at the Şehzade Mosque (1543–8) and used in both of the great 17th-century Ottoman royal mosques of Istanbul, that of Ahmed I (*see* §11 below) and the Yeni Valide. The dimensions of the original building were respected and significant parts of it preserved, including the forecourt, main doorway and wall around the back garden. Details, however, were executed in the Baroque style, as was the interior stencilling. The mosque has undergone periodic restoration and is a major centre for Islamic revivalism in Istanbul.

BIBLIOGRAPHY

Fatih Mehmed II Vakıfiyeleri [Endowments of the Fatih Mosque], Vakıflar Umum Müdürlüğü (Ankara, 1938)

A. Kuran: *The Mosque in Early Ottoman Architecture* (Chicago and London, 1968)

G. Goodwin: *A History of Ottoman Architecture* (Baltimore and London, 1971)

E. H. Ayverdi: *Osmanlı mimârisinde Fâtih devri* [Ottoman architecture in the period of the Conqueror], 2 vols (Istanbul, 1973–4)

10. SÜLEYMANIYE MOSQUE. This large mosque and its surrounding complex were commissioned by Süleyman II (*reg* 1520–66; see fig. 5 above) and planned and constructed between 1550 and 1557 by the court architect Sinan (*see* SINAN (ii)). Widely recognized as one of the premier monuments of Ottoman architecture, it was built above the Golden Horn on a hilltop site, part of which had been occupied by the Eski Saray ('Old Palace'). Owing to the survival of the account-books kept during construction and their exemplary publication, the Süleymaniye is the best documented as well as the largest of the great imperial foundations of the classical Ottoman period (*see* ISLAMIC ART, §II, 7(i)(b) and fig. 63). The entire complex (250×350 m) includes the mosque, four theological colleges, a school for the study of Prophetic traditions, a hospital, an alms-kitchen, an inn, a bath, primary school, a public fountain, several public toilets and the tombs of the founder and his wife, as well as a residence for the grounds-keeper (for illustration *see* KÜLLIYE).

The Süleymaniye is remarkable for its great size (the diameter of the dome is 26.2 m; the height of its crown is 53 m), its prodigious strength (the soffits of the four major arches are more than 4 m deep) and its ingenious system of geometric proportions. Apparently the plan of the building was drawn full-scale on the site, while construction was controlled by multiplication from a large wooden model, which was still extant in 1582 when it was carried on parade by the builders' guild. Analysis of the construction accounts demonstrates the Ottoman skill at handling the logistics of such a vast project, as well as the multiethnic nature of the building force. Some elements of the building, such as the great columns of the interior, are Classical or Byzantine spolia; the architectural inscriptions were designed by the great calligrapher AHMAD KARAHISARI; and the tile decorations represent the first major use in an Ottoman building project of polychrome underglaze-painted tiles from Iznik. The coloured glass windows of the qibla wall, executed by Master Ibrahim, curiously nicknamed 'the drunkard', are important examples of Ottoman stained glass (*see* ISLAMIC ART, §II, 9(v)). The building was also decorated with carved wooden doors and shutters, hundreds of square metres of carpets, and painted calligraphy and ornament. Contemporary Ottoman historical accounts and panegyrics refer metaphorically to the mosque and the Sultan's tomb in the garden behind it as paradise brought to earth; in plan and form the tomb deliberately invokes the Dome of the Rock (*see* JERUSALEM, §II, 1(iii)), which Süleyman had restored *c.* 1550.

The Süleymaniye is not an ornate building, contrary to historical descriptions stressing its lavish decoration. The

Iznik tiles on the interior and exterior are almost lost in the vast space, the coloured glass windows and inscriptions must be seen at close range to be deciphered, and the inscriptions and *muqarnas* elaborately carved in stone are confined to a few areas. The Süleymaniye reflects the piety and personal austerity of its creator in its many textual and symbolic references to orthodox Islamic tradition and in its reliance on the colour and texture of two simple materials, ivory-white stone for building and dark-grey lead for roofing, for its extraordinary effects. In some ways the structure is the ultimate Ottoman response to Justinian I's church of Hagia Sophia (*see* §1(ii) above). The basic elements of the plan of the great church were acknowledged, but whereas the church is intuitive, the mosque is rational; whereas the interior of the church is vague and mysterious, that of the mosque is clearly delimited; and whereas the church was veneered with marble, mosaic and stone, the mosque has austere and simple surfaces of stone and lead. The impression of vastness given by the Süleymaniye is one of artifice as much as size. The ring of small flying buttresses surrounding the dome, for example, makes the dome look much larger as well as strengthening it, and the arrangements of mass in the smaller domes, stepped and domed buttresses and minarets have been articulated so that the building presents a powerful and coherent image from every angle, while the screens of arches on its exterior lighten its massiveness and give it human scale. Although Sinan considered his greatest work the Selimiye Mosque (1575) in EDIRNE, in the eyes of many critics the Süleymaniye is his pre-eminent work and certainly the greatest imperial mosque of the Ottoman capital.

BIBLIOGRAPHY
Ö. L. Barkan: *Süleymaniye camii ve imareti inşaati (1550–1557)* [The construction of the Süleymaniye mosque and its adjoining buildings (1550–1557)], 2 vols (Ankara, 1972–9)
J. M. Rogers: 'The State and the Arts in Ottoman Turkey: The Stones of Süleymaniye', *Int. J. Mid. E. Stud.*, xiv (1982), pp. 71–96
G. Necipoğlu-Kafadar: 'The Süleymaniye Complex in Istanbul: An Interpretation', *Muqarnas*, iii (1985), pp. 92–117

11. SULTAN AHMED I MOSQUE. When Ahmed I (*reg* 1603–17) ascended the throne, no imperial mosque had been built in the city for 44 years. The Sultan selected MEHMED AĞA as chief architect and picked a site of immense symbolic significance. Whereas imperial mosque-complexes had been situated on imposing hilltop sites and provided infrastructure for the growing population in resettled quarters of the city, Ahmed's mosque (also known as the Blue Mosque) was placed in the heart of the city on a site containing the ruins of the Byzantine Great Palace (*see* §12 below) and facing the Hippodrome to the west. It confronted at a distance of some 200 m to the north the most venerated and important mosque in the capital, the converted church of Hagia Sophia (*see* §1 above).

With its six minarets and its semi-domes cascading on four axes, the mosque represents the ultimate evolution of the imperial Ottoman mosque after two centuries of linear development (*see* ISLAMIC ART, §II, 7(i)(b)). Taking as a point of departure Sinan's plan of the Şehzade Mosque (1543–8), with its four semi-domes, Mehmed Ağa created a structure with many references to the work of his predecessor. The main columnar supports recall those of

the Selimiye Mosque (1575) in Edirne; of the six minarets, four are at the corners of the mosque and two at the west end of the forecourt. By creating a forecourt of unprecedented size, the architect was able to avoid the awkward corner adjustments in the court and the sense of crowding that characterize some earlier courts. Although critics have long faulted the mosque for infelicities in architectural transitions, decoration and structural details, the siting, size, number of minarets, light-flooded interior and spacious forecourt make it the most popular and well-known of Ottoman mosques.

Problems during its construction, many of them financial, evidently included an inability to commission adequate ceramic decoration for the interior, and Iznik tiles from other monuments not protected by endowment were recycled. Most of the interior tiling made for the building, apart from that of the rear gallery walls, is of markedly inferior quality, although the overwhelming impression of colour has given rise to its nickname, the Blue Mosque. The exterior arcading of the mosque and courtyard walls, the massing of semi-domes and the four tall and two shorter minarets provide an indelible architectural impression, which marks growing Ottoman architectural self-confidence *vis-à-vis* Hagia Sophia and contrasts strikingly with the Byzantine church.

BIBLIOGRAPHY
Ca'fer Efendi (*d* 1623): *Risāle-i Mi'māriyye: An Early Seventeenth-century Ottoman Treatise on Architecture*, ed. and trans. H. Crane (Leiden, 1987)
G. Goodwin: *A History of Ottoman Architecture* (Baltimore and London, 1971), pp. 342–9

WALTER B. DENNY

12. GREAT PALACE. This was the principal residence of Byzantine emperors from Constantine the Great (*reg* 306–37) to Alexios I (*reg* 1081–1118) and the symbolic nerve centre of the empire. Also known as the Sacred Palace, it was the Byzantine equivalent of the Palatine in Rome (*see* ROME, §V, 3). The Great Palace was a large complex of buildings and gardens situated on a terraced, roughly trapezoidal site, measuring *c.* 600×500 m (see fig. 13), and overlooking the Sea of Marmara to the southeast (see fig. 1vii above). The complex was enclosed by the Hippodrome (see fig. 13a) to the west, by the Regia (a ceremonial extension of the Mese; 13b), the Augustaion (13c), and the Senate to the north (13d), and by the sea walls to the south and east. Modern understanding of the Great Palace depends heavily on the literary sources (e.g. the *Book of Ceremonies* by Constantine VII; *Theophanes continuatus*) and, to a lesser degree, on the meagre archaeological evidence. Of the few archaeologically explored components of the palace complex, the largest is an apsed hall (13e) preceded by a large peristyle court (13f) with splendid floor mosaics (first half of 6th century; Istanbul, Mosaic Mus.; *see* EARLY CHRISTIAN AND BYZANTINE ART, fig. 34), which feature hunting and pastoral scenes combined with figures from mythology. The isolated nature of these finds and the ambiguity of the written sources preclude any comprehensive architectural reconstructions of the palace despite repeated attempts since the 19th century.

In its scale and general character the Great Palace must have resembled a city, with numerous buildings, private harbours, avenues, open spaces, terraces, ramps and stairs,

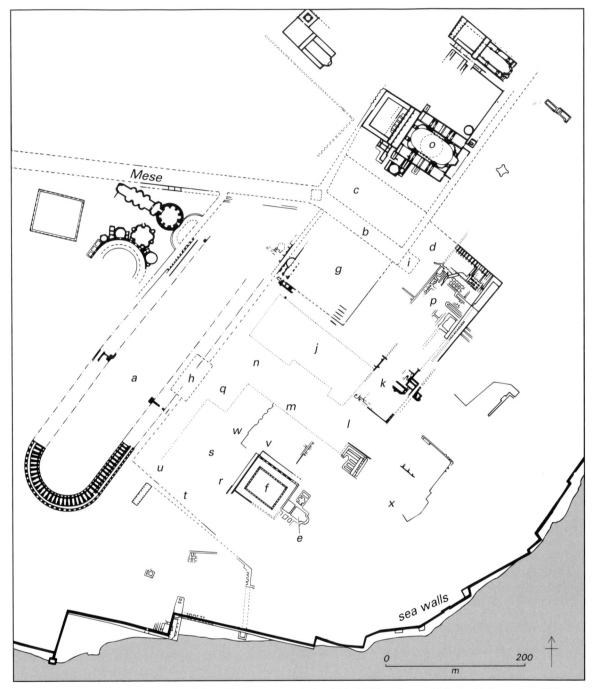

13. Istanbul, hypothetical plan of the Great Palace, 4th century AD to the late 15th: (a) Hippodrome; (b) Regia; (c) Augustaion; (d) Senate; (e) excavated apsed hall; (f) excavated peristyle court; (g) Baths of Zeuxippos; (h) Kathisma; (i) Chalke ('Bronze Gate'); (j) Delphax ('Tribunal'); (k) Triklinos of the Kandidates; (l) Consistorium; (m) Augusteus; (n) Triklinos of the 19 Couches; (o) Hagia Sophia; (p) Magnaura; (q) Daphne; (r) Chrysotriklinos; (s) Lausiakos; (t) Justinianos; (u) Skyla; (v) Trikonchos ('Hall of the Three Couches'); (w) Sigma; (x) Tzykanisterion

gardens, fountains and other amenities, built and rebuilt over nearly eight centuries. Rebuilding of palace components at new locations, but retaining their old names, along with the changing functions and names of preserved buildings, are among the factors contributing to the confusion in the current state of knowledge about the Great Palace. Notwithstanding these problems, it is possible to identify the main stages in its development.

The initial phase, under the auspices of Constantine the Great, produced the core of the palace complex, which, by all accounts, must have resembled several other imperial palaces built during the Tetrarchy (293–312) as at Antioch and Thessaloniki. Constantine's palace was an overtly urban complex, approached by the Regia. Adjacent to the Regia stood the large Baths of Zeuxippos (13g), a public bath also related to the palace compound. The entire western flank of the Great Palace bordered the Hippodrome, while the so-called Kathisma (13h)—a component of the palace with the imperial box for viewing the Hippodrome races, and rooms for other ceremonial functions—provided a palpable link between the Great Palace and the city itself. The ceremonial gate of the inner palace was known as the Chalke ('Bronze Gate'; 13i). It led into the Delphax ('Tribunal'; 13j), a large courtyard with access to the vast ceremonial halls: the Triklinos of the Kandidates (13k), the Consistorium (13l), the Augusteus (13m) and the Triklinos of the 19 Couches (formal dining hall; 13n). A raised passage (probably built by Justinian I) also connected the Chalke to the south-east corner of Hagia Sophia (13o). Other parts of the palace included the Magnaura (a three-aisled basilican reception hall; 13p) and the Daphne (the private residential wing; 13q).

The second major phase in the development of the Great Palace occurred in the 6th century, during the reigns of JUSTINIAN I and JUSTIN II. Justinian's building programme was spurred in large measure by the damage caused by the Nika riots (532), and it involved the rebuilding of structures along the north flank of the palace complex, including the Magnaura and the Chalke. The latter's ceiling was decorated with mosaics showing Justinian's victories over the Vandals in North Africa (533–4) and the Goths in Italy and in part of Spain (535–55); in the centre of the ceiling was a portrait of the imperial couple surrounded by senators.

Justin II is credited with the construction of the Chrysotriklinos (after 565; 13r), the octagonal domed throne-room, the resplendent decoration of which was finished by Tiberios I (reg 578–82). The Chrysotriklinos became in effect the new ceremonial nucleus of the palace, modifying the original Constantinian layout. It was intended to dazzle foreign dignitaries, as it did in the case of LIUDPRAND, who left a written account of his visit (c. 950).

The Great Palace was expanded again by Justinian II (reg 685–95; 705–11), who built the Lausiakos (13s) and the Justinianos (13t), two halls in the vicinity of the Chrysotriklinos. He is also credited with the construction of a wall enclosing the palace, and of another gate, the Skyla (13u), on the south side. This development marks the end of an 'open' relationship between the palace and the city, characteristic of Late Antique imperial palaces in general (see EARLY CHRISTIAN AND BYZANTINE ART, §II, 3(ii)(a)). This change was brought about, in all likelihood, by the growing urban tensions and violence. During the iconoclastic controversy (726–843) the Chalke acquired a particular significance in the arguments for and against the worship of images. On the building's façade was an icon of *Christ Chalkites* ('of the Chalke') shown standing on a footstool; in 726 or 730 Leo III Isaurikos (reg 717–41) removed the icon and replaced it with a cross as the first overt act of imperial iconoclasm. The image of Christ was restored c. 787 by Empress EIRENE, only to be removed once again by Leo V (reg 813–20) in 813 and replaced by

a cross at the start of the second period of iconoclasm. After the final victory of Orthodoxy in 843, Empress THEODORA commissioned a mosaic icon of Christ to be set up again.

By that time the iconoclastic emperor THEOPHILOS (reg 829–42) had already begun the next major phase in the development of the Great Palace, which continued under Michael II (reg 842–67), Basil I and Leo VI (see MACEDONIAN DYNASTY, (1) and (2) respectively). Theophilos was responsible for the strengthening of the sea walls and for a new two-storey ceremonial complex centred on the Trikonchos ('Hall of the Three Couches'; 13v), preceded by the Sigma court (13w) and surrounded by other pavilions. In its general character, this complex owed as much to the Late Antique palatine tradition as it probably did to the palaces of the Umayyads (see ISLAMIC ART, §II, 3(iii)), with whom Theophilos is known to have maintained close cultural contacts. Michael III is noted for several building restorations (particularly of the Chrysotriklinos) and adaptations, but his most celebrated addition to the Great Palace was the church of the Virgin of Pharos ('Lighthouse'), renowned for the relics it contained and for its splendour, if not for its size. By far the best-known church to be added to the Great Palace was the five-domed Nea Ekklesia ('New Church'; 881; destr.) under the auspices of Basil I. This emperor was responsible for one of the most extensive building programmes to the Great Palace, which must have substantially altered its appearance. Among his additions were two halls, known as the Kainourgion ('New Hall') and the Pentakoubiklon (a room divided into five bays), and a large court for polo games, known as the Tzykanisterion (13x). Leo VI is credited with the construction of a sumptuously decorated bathhouse.

In the following centuries the amount of construction within the Great Palace diminished. During the reign of Nikephoros II Phokas (reg 963–9) another line of fortification walls was erected, apparently enclosing the shrunken core of the Great Palace. The final decline of the Great Palace began under Alexios I Komnenos (reg 1081–1118), who moved the imperial residence to the new palace of Blachernai. Despite this shift, the Great Palace retained its ceremonial role for some time to come. Even some new construction occurred, as under Manuel I (reg 1143–80), who built two halls: the Manouelites and the Mouchroutas. The latter, known to have been the work of a Persian builder, had a painted and gilded stalactite ceiling akin to such ceilings in Islamic architecture.

During the Latin occupation of Constantinople (1204–61) the Great Palace was used, but was also despoiled of its major treasures. The Palaiologan emperors (1261–1453) never attempted to restore the abandoned, slowly decaying complex. Its final demise came in 1489–90, when a large quantity of gunpowder stored in one of the old buildings exploded, obliterating most of the surviving remnants.

BIBLIOGRAPHY

EARLY SOURCES

Constantine VII Porphyrogenitos: *Book of Ceremonies* (c. 959); Fr. trans., ed. A. Vogt as *Le Livre des cérémonies*, 2 vols (Paris, 1935)

Theophanes continuatus (c. 949–50), ed. I. Bekker (Bonn, 1838)

Liudprand, Bishop of Cremona: *Antapodosis* (c. 950); ed. F. A. Wright as *Works of Liuprand of Cremona* (London, 1930)

GENERAL

J. Labarte: *Le Palais impérial de Constantinople et ses abords* (Paris, 1861)

G. A. Paspates: *The Great Palace of Constantinople* (London, 1893)

J. Ebersolt: *Le Grand Palais de Constantinople et 'Le Livre des cérémonies'* (Paris, 1910)

J. B. Bury: 'The Great Palace', *Byz. Z.*, xxi (1912), pp. 210–25

E. Mamboury and T. Wiegand: *Die Kaiserpaläste von Konstantinopel* (Berlin, 1934)

G. Brett and others: *The Great Palace of the Byzantine Emperors* (Oxford, 1947)

S. Miranda: *Etude de topographie du Palais Sacré de Byzance* (Mexico City, 1956, rev. 1976)

D. Talbot Rice, ed.: *The Great Palace of the Byzantine Emperors: Second Report* (Edinburgh, 1958)

C. Mango: *The Brazen House: A Study of the Vestibule of the Imperial Palace of Constantinople* (Copenhagen, 1959)

R. Guilland: *Etudes de topographie de Constantinople byzantine*, Berliner Byzantinische Arbeiten, xxxvii (Berlin and Amsterdam, 1969)

W. Müller-Wiener: *Bildlexikon zur Topographie Istanbuls* (Tübingen, 1977), pp. 229–37

P. Magdalino: 'Manuel Komnenos and the Great Palace', *Byz. & Mod. Gr. Stud.*, iv (1978), pp. 101–14

——: 'The Bath of Leo the Wise and the "Macedonian Renaissance" Revisited: Topography, Iconography, Ceremonial, Ideology', *Dumbarton Oaks Pap.*, xlii (1988), pp. 97–118

J. Trilling: 'The Soul of the Empire: Style and Meaning in the Mosaic Pavement of the Byzantine Imperial Palace in Constantinople', *Dumbarton Oaks Pap.*, xliii (1989), pp. 27–72

J. Herrin: 'Byzance: Le Palais et la ville', *Byzantion*, 61 (1991), pp. 213–60

SLOBODAN ĆURČIĆ

13. TOPKAPI PALACE. Primary residence of the Ottoman sultans (*reg* 1281–1924) from the mid-15th century until the construction of Dolmabahçe Palace (1853) on the Bosporus. This vast conglomeration of buildings (now a museum) stands on a magnificent promontory on the tip of the peninsula overlooking the Bosporus and the inner harbour on the east and the Golden Horn on the north (see fig. 14). It is isolated from the city on the landward sides by walls on the south and west. Originally known as the New Palace, only in the 19th century did it come to be known as Topkapı ('Cannon-gate') Palace, after a shore pavilion (destr. 1862–3) built near a gate of that name. The layout of the palace, established by Mehmed II (*see* §(ii) below), is based on the First Court (see fig. 14i), an outer precinct or park, and an inner precinct of three courts (14ii, iii and iv) that constitute the palace proper.

BIBLIOGRAPHY

Topkapı Sarayı Müzesi rehberi [Guide to the Topkapı Palace Museum] (Istanbul, 1933)

F. David: *The Palace of Topkapı in Istanbul* (New York, 1970)

G. Goodwin: *A History of Ottoman Architecture* (Baltimore and London, 1971)

K. Çiğ, S. Batur and C. Köseoğlu: *The Topkapı Saray Museum: Architecture: The Harem and Other Buildings*, trans. and ed. J. M. Rogers (Boston, 1988)   □

(i) Before 1453. (ii) 1453–1622. (iii) 1623–1853. (iv) After 1853.

(i) Before 1453. The hill on which Topkapı Palace stands was the acropolis of ancient Byzantion (*see* §I, 1(i) above); it was surrounded with walls and graced with secular and religious structures, some of which have been excavated among the present buildings. The Temple of Poseidon, known to have been situated within the precincts of the palace, was transformed into the church of St Menas (before 10th century; destr.), and it has been suggested that the present Arcade of the Chamber of the Holy Mantle (Hırket-i Saadet; 14v) were built on the site. Under

Byzantine rule the steep slopes of the hill were terraced and cisterns built, of which 39 have been identified within the palace grounds. These cisterns were supplied from an ancient ashlar-lined well (Dolap Ocağı; 14vi), 5 m in diameter and 30 m deep. It later became the main water source for the palace, and it was repaired by Sinan during the reign of Süleyman (*reg* 1520–66).

The Mangana arsenal stood on the lower slopes of the eastern side of the hill, and its name was later applied to the whole district. Constantine IX (*reg* 1042–55) built the monastery and palace of Mangana; the latter was reportedly a large complex with five storeys, the last remains of which were razed by Isaak II Angelos (*reg* 1185–95). According to the sources this district contained numerous churches, among which were the Mangana monastery church of St George, Christ the Philanthropist Church, St Demetrios, St Lazaros and St Barbara. None of these buildings has been identified with the remains of various religious structures found on the site. One, discovered during excavations in 1937 in front of the old Inner Treasury Building (14vii) in the Second Court, is known as the Basilica of Topkapı Palace (5th century). A small baptistery with a trefoil plan was discovered in the basement of Room 2 of the Treasury Apartments (14viii), and an octagonal baptistery was cut by the wall surrounding the pool and the Fourth Court. Objects from the Roman and Byzantine periods found on the site include sarcophagi, baptismal fonts and parapet slabs, and fragments of architectural elements and sculpture, many of which were reused under the Ottomans. Sarcophagi and fonts were often used as the drinking basins of fountains or water tanks. The font in the Treasury Apartments was reportedly used as a safe for cash.

BIBLIOGRAPHY

K. Bittel: 'Grabung im Hof des Topkapı Sarayı', *Jb. Dt. Archäol. Inst.*, liv (1939), pp. 179–82

R. Demangel and E. Mamboury: *Le Quartier des Manganes et la première région de Constantinople* (Paris, 1939)

A. Ongan: '1937 yılında Türk Tarih Kurumu tarafından yapılan Topkapı Sarayı hafriyatı' [The excavations in Topkapı Palace conducted by the Turkish Historical Society in 1937], *Belleten*, iv (1940), pp. 318–55

H. Tezcan: *Sur-u Sultani içinin Bizans devri arkeologisi* [The archaeology of the Byzantine period within the imperial walls] (diss., U. Istanbul, 1983)

HÜLYA TEZCAN

(ii) 1453–1622. Within a few years of the conquest of Constantinople, Mehmed II constructed a palace in the centre of his capital as well as several large fortresses in or near the city. His selection of the magnificent site—easily defensible, highly visible and close to the symbolic centre of the ancient city—was a logical choice for the major imperial residence and administrative centre of the growing empire. Construction of the walls surrounding the palace was begun *c.* 1460 and completed in 1478. There are several gateways in the outer wall, but the major ceremonial route was a linear series of three great portals leading into the First, Second and Third Courts, with the audience throne-room beyond the third portal.

Remains from Mehmed's period include the encircling walls, the main portal for the entire complex (Emperor's Gate; Bab-ı Humayun), that of the palace proper (Middle Gate or Gate of Salutation; Bab es-Selam; 14ix), and a series of gardens and pavilions or kiosks, built first in the

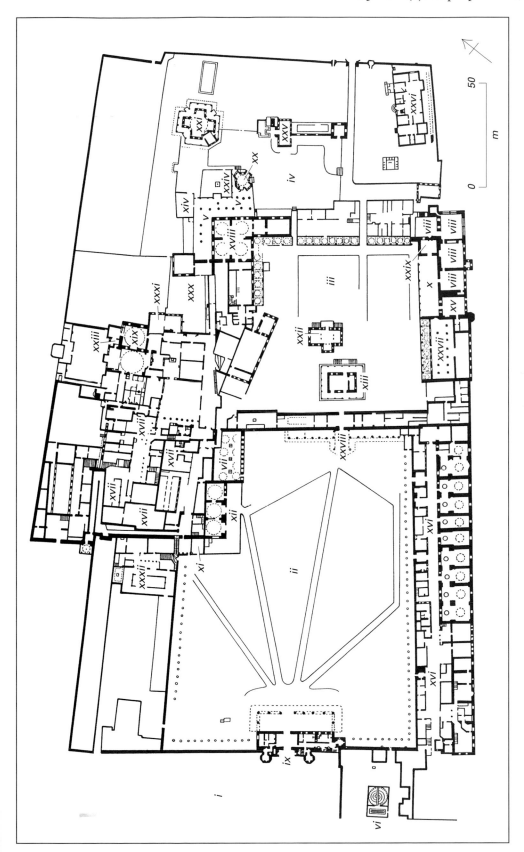

14. Istanbul, plan of Topkapı Palace, mid-15th century to the 20th: (i) First Court; (ii) Second Court; (iii) Third Court; (iv) Fourth Court; (v) Arcade of the Chamber of the Holy Mantle (Hırket-i Saadet); (vi) ancient well (Dolcap Ocağı); (vii) Inner Treasury; (viii) Treasury Apartments (Conqueror's Kiosk); (ix) Middle Gate or Gate of Salutation; (x) Arcade of the Conqueror's Kiosk (Fatih Köşkü); (xi) Tower of Justice; (xii) Council Hall (Divan) ; (xiii) Throne-room; (xiv) Circumcision Room (Sünnet Odası); (xv) baths of Selim II; (xvi) kitchens; (xvii) Harem; (xviii) Pavilion of the Holy Mantle (Privy Chamber); (xix) Bedroom of Murad III; (xx) Revan Kiosk; (xxi) Baghdad Kiosk; (xxii) Library of Ahmed III; (xxiii) Dining-room of Ahmed III; (xxiv) pool and fountain in Fourth Court; (xxv) Kiosk of Mustafa Pasha; (xxvi) Kiosk of Abdülmecid; (xxvii) Dormitory of the Expeditionary Force (Seferli Koğuş); (xxviii) Gate of the White Eunuchs (Akağalar; Gate of Felicity); (xxix) Treasury of the Ambassadors; (xxx) Courtyard of the Favourites; (xxxi) Apartments of the Heir Apparent (Cifre); (xxxii) Apartments of the Halberdiers with Tresses (Zülüflü Baltacıs)

palace proper and then in the park. Of these pavilions, the Çinili ('Tiled') Kiosk (see fig. 7 above) in the park, with its splendid decoration and complex axial arrangement of rooms, follows a 15th-century Timurid-style plan probably considered somewhat exotic in Istanbul at the time (*see* PALACE, §III). Inside the palace proper, the most important building to survive is the Arcade of the Conqueror's Kiosk (Fatih Köşkü; 14x), built in a corner of the Third Court at the top of the promontory on a cliff overlooking the conjunction of the Bosporus and the Sea of Marmara; the magnificent view from its covered porch and its great visibility from the water leave little doubt why the site was selected. The Tower of Justice (14xi), the highest structure in the complex, recalls in its original form a similar tower erected during Mehmed's reign in the palace at Edirne. The basic layout of the park and three interior courts established under Mehmed dictated the pattern of subsequent development.

The next major additions took place under Süleyman (*reg* 1520–66), when certain ceremonial parts of the palace were rebuilt on a larger scale, and the palace infrastructure was enlarged to support the burgeoning administrative bureaucracy of the empire. Major additions, evidently completed under the supervision of the Grand Vizier IBRAHIM PASHA, included the building of the Council Hall (Divan; 14xii) and the neighbouring Inner Treasury in the Second Court and the Throne-room (14xiii) in the Third Court. Although these structures have been greatly altered in subsequent rebuildings, their decorative tiles have been preserved in other parts of the palace, most notably on the walls of the Circumcision Room (Sünnet Odası; *c.* 1555–65; 14xiv) in the Fourth Court. The massive gilded iron doors in the Middle Gate were placed there *c.* 1525.

Under Selim II (*reg* 1566–74) the great Ottoman architect Sinan built his first important additions to the palace. New baths for the Sultan were erected and decorated with Iznik polychrome tiles of the highest quality (14xv). In 1574, after the kitchens in the Second Court were destroyed by fire, Sinan began the gigantic kitchens that still constitute the largest single structure in the palace (14xvi). Other additions made to the Harem (14xvii) were substantially altered, and much of the tile decoration was recycled by Ahmed I (*reg* 1603–17) for his great mosque (*see* §11 above). In the reign of Murad III (1574–95) the palace attained its present form with the construction (date uncertain) by Sinan of the Privy Chamber (now known as the Chamber of the Sacred Mantle; 14xviii), previously remodelled between 1512 and 1520 under Selim I, in the Fourth Court; vast additions to the Harem were also made, including the complex known as the Bedroom of Murad III (14xix), several seashore kiosks in the park and more housing for the palace staff. Murad's architectural patronage was heavily concentrated in the palace, for he was the first sultan since the conquest to forego building an imperial mosque in the capital. In particular, his architectural patronage involved massive purchases of ceramic tiles from Iznik. Contemporary documents sent from the palace to the administrative judge of Iznik complained that potters were producing more lucrative tablewares for sale in the bazaar rather than tiles for the palace. Murad's additions were altered by the stripping of

their tiles and by the intrusion of European taste in the 18th century.

During the reigns of Mehmed III (*reg* 1595–1603) and Ahmed I (*reg* 1603–17) little was added to Topkapı Palace. Ahmed's preoccupation with the building of his mosque even meant that the palace was stripped of tiles from structures damaged in the fire of 1574 for reuse in the mosque.

(iii) 1623–1853. The first major additions to the palace in the 17th century occurred during the reign of the bellicose Murad IV (*reg* 1623–40), who built in the Fourth Court the lovely Revan and Baghdad kiosks (14xx and 14xxi respectively) to commemorate his victories at Erevan (1635–6) and Baghdad (1638–9; *see* ISLAMIC ART, fig. 65). Based on the classical type of four-iwan plan, they have projecting eaves, domed central spaces and interiors with recessed cupboards and woodwork inlaid with mother-of-pearl. They typify Islamic and Ottoman palace structures. Their decoration in blue-and-white tiles deliberately patterned after those of a century earlier are self-conscious attempts to duplicate the glories of an earlier age.

The nearby Circumcision Room (Sünnet Odası), built in 1648 by Ibrahim (*reg* 1640–48), is an altogether simpler structure than Murad's two kiosks, but it is largely decorated on the exterior with tiles that once graced ceremonial buildings of Süleyman (*see* §(ii) above). Although it is not certain when these recycled tiles were added to the Circumcision Room, it is highly probable that these prototypes for the decoration of Murad's kiosks were moved to their present location *c.* 1648 as part of the same reverence and nostalgia for the art of the age of Süleyman. Ibrahim also erected the terrace that links the Circumcision Room with Murad's kiosks and the arcaded roof around the Chamber of the Holy Mantle.

Another fire in 1665 resulted in the wholesale redecoration of the Harem, although little of its plan and structure was changed. Once again the reverence for the 16th century is manifested in a tenacious adherence to polychrome underglaze-painted tiles in the Iznik mode, despite the poor quality. Although the redecoration is notable for its extreme dreariness, it does include direct imitations of the mass-produced tiles of the reign of Murad III.

Topkapı Palace continued to serve as the formal seat of government and primary imperial residence in Istanbul after 1687, but the palace gradually lost its predominance as the Ottoman sultans spent more time in their new suburban palaces on the Bosporus and at the Sweet Waters of Europe. Major additions during the reign of Ahmed III (1703–30) include the lovely Neo-classical library (14xxii) in the Third Court, built on the foundations of an earlier kiosk; the spectacular Dining-room in the Harem, painted with floral designs (14xxiii); and the pool and fountain in the Fourth Court (1729; 14xxiv; *see* ISLAMIC ART, fig. 66). These additions were held in significant esteem at the time, and the library and the pool were accurately and prominently depicted in the famous copy of the *Surnāma* ('imperial book of festivals') made for Ahmed III by the painter LEVNI.

Under Mahmud I (*reg* 1730–54) and Osman III (*reg* 1754–7) the Harem was redecorated in the Ottoman Baroque style, an Italianate rather than French-inspired mode of decoration that adds a jarring note when juxtaposed with the decoration of the Ottoman classical age. In 1752 Mahmud I rebuilt the Kiosk of Mustafa Pasha (14xxv) in the Fourth Court: the interior contains a Rococo ceiling, but this unusually spare and open building, with its large windows derived from the wooden residences along the Bosporus, injects a refreshing and forward-looking architectural note. The last significant royal addition to the palace was the Kiosk of Abdülmecid (c. 1840; 14xxvi) constructed by Sarkis Balyan (see BALYAN, (4)) on a built-up terrace beyond the Conqueror's Kiosk, with the same sweeping view of the Bosporus and the Sea of Marmara. This building, in the eclectic Europeanized style popularized by the Balyan family in the 19th century, is simply another typical seaside palace; its location within the Topkapı complex was due primarily to the magnificent view rather than to old imperial associations.

BIBLIOGRAPHY
E. H. Ayverdi: *Osmanlı mimârîsinde Fâtih devri* [Ottoman architecture in the period of the Conqueror], 2 vols (Istanbul, 1973–4)
S. Eldem and S. Akozan: *Topkapı Sarayı: Bir mimari araştırma* [Topkapı Palace: an architectural investigation] (Istanbul, 1982)
G. Necipoğlu: *Architecture, Ceremonial and Power: The Topkapı Palace in the Fifteenth and Sixteenth Centuries* (Cambridge, MA, and London, 1992)

WALTER B. DENNY

(iv) After 1853. Although Abdülmecid (*reg* 1839–61) moved his official residence to Dolmabahçe Palace (1853–5; see fig. 6 above), the sultans' ties with Topkapı Palace were not completely broken. The palace continued to be the residence of court officials and site of the treasury, ceremonies on the sultan's accession and handing over of the treasury were performed there, funerals for sultans began there, and the yearly visit to the Chamber of the Holy Mantle on 15 Ramadan continued to take place. The Kiosk of Abdülmecid was opened on occasion to accommodate foreign guests. The Sultan gave special permission for foreign ambassadors resident in Istanbul and their associates to visit the palace. They were able to tour two rooms in the Treasury and the Dormitory of the Expeditionary Force (Seferli Koğuş; now the Textile Department; 14xxvii), where a collection of 360 ceramic objects was exhibited. According to Georgina Max Müller, who toured the palace with such a group, they had to pay a substantial fee.

Topkapı Palace underwent various changes and repairs to suit the needs of its residents. The imperial historiographer Abdurrahman Şeref (1853–1925) was the first to receive special permission to spend a long time in the palace, where he established the condition of the buildings and recorded their inscriptions. Major repairs that changed the appearance of the Third Court were begun under Abdülhamid II (*reg* 1876–1909) and completed under Mehmed V Reşad (*reg* 1909–18) by VEDAT. A report in 1915 stated that the repairs had been poorly done and recorded mistakes. The demolition of the Music-room (Meşkhane) built by Selim III (*reg* 1789–1807) at the entrance to the Gate of the White Eunuchs (Akağalar; 14xxviii) was strongly criticized.

The palace was officially opened as a museum on 3 April 1924. The first campaign of restoration (1940–44) restored the kitchens and adjacent cooks' quarters, as well as the privy stables and Treasury Apartments. The Treasury

of the Ambassadors (14xxix), built in front of the Treasury Apartments under Mahmud I (*reg* 1730–54), was removed. The second restoration campaign (1959–62), directed by the architect Selma Emlar (1920–93), delineated the Harem water-supply and exposed the pool under the Courtyard of the Favourites (14xxx) in the Harem Apartments, known from its depiction in manuscript illustrations. The larder beside the kitchen was repaired, the dairy restored and the archives transformed into the textile depot. Under the architect Mualla Egüpoğlu Anhegger (*b* 1919), the restoration of the Harem continued. The most striking part was the removal of the decorated wooden partitions and penthouse from the Apartments of the Heir Apparent (Cifte; 14xxxi). The dome, which had been covered with a flat ceiling, was revealed when the ceiling was dismantled. İlban Öz (1931–92) restored the apartments of the Favourites and of Abdülhamid in the Harem and of the Halberdiers with Tresses (Zülüflü Baltacıs; 14xxxii). An exhibition hall was constructed (1978–80) on the rampart opposite the kitchens.

BIBLIOGRAPHY
G. M. Müller: *Letters from Constantinople* (London, 1897)
Abdurrahman Şeref: 'Topkapı Saray-ı Hümayunu' [The Imperial Palace of Topkapı], *Tarih-i Osmanî Encümeni Mecmuası* [Journal of the Ottoman Historical Society], v (1910), pp. 266–99; vi (1911), pp. 329–64; vii (1911), pp. 393–421; viii (1911), pp. 457–83; ix (1911), pp. 521–7; x (1911), pp. 585–94; xi (1911), pp. 649–57; xii (1912), pp. 713–30
T. Öz: 'Topkapı Sarayı Müzesi onarımları' [Restoration work at Topkapı Palace Museum], *Güzel Sanatlar*, vi (1949), pp. 6–74
S. Emler: 'Topkapı Sarayı restorasyon çalışmaları' [Restoration work on Topkapı Palace], *Türk Sanatı Tarihi Araştırma İncelemeleri*, i (1963), pp. 212–27
S. Eldem and S. Akozan: *Topkapı Sarayı: Bir mimari araştırma* [Topkapı Palace: an architectural investigation] (Istanbul, 1982) [rep. of the Permanent Commission on the Preservation of Ancient Monuments, 15 Oct 1915, pubd on pp. 100–102]
İ. Öz: 'Topkapı Sarayı Müzesi onarımları' [The restoration work on Topkapı Palace Museum], *Sanat*, vii (April 1982), pp. 65–77
M. E. Anhegger: *Topkapı Sarıında padişah evi (Harem)* [The sultan's house in Topkapı Palace (the Harem)] (Istanbul, 1986)

HÜLYA TEZCAN

14. GRAND BAZAAR. A first market hall (Turk. *bedesten*) was built *c.* 1460 on a site in the traditional commercial centre of Constantinople, near the major Byzantine fora and the Mese, the major east–west artery later known as Divan Yolu. A second market hall, known as Sandal Bedesten ('Market of Chairs'), was built near by also under Mehmed II (not under Süleyman as often supposed). Surrounding these market halls, a network of covered streets was built up over the centuries, with a wide variety of vaulting and dome systems adapted to the irregular plan and terrain. The major east–west street of Kalpakçılar is the most impressive space, while the triple-arcaded spaces on three sides of the Great Bedesten form one of the most distinctive and attractive aspects of the complex. The bazaar has suffered from major fires, the latest in 1954, resulting in substantial rebuilding and restoration. By the mid-20th century it comprised thousands of metres of covered ways connecting the two market halls with over a dozen caravanserais (see CARAVANSERAI) for manufacture, trade and accommodation. The covered streets of the Grand Bazaar (Turk. Kapalı Çarşı) are accessible through many peripheral gates that can be locked at night for security; this centre is surrounded by many other open bazaar streets and caravanserais, constituting the commercial core of Istanbul.

The average size of shops in the bazaar is very small, ranging from 10 to 18 sq. m. The majority are endowed property (*see* ISLAM, §III), their rents supporting mosques, schools and other religious, educational or charitable institutions. Shops have traditionally been organized by quarters within the bazaar. The several thousand shops in the Grand Bazaar originally catered for all the commercial and economic needs of the population; increasingly, however, merchants have moved towards business of interest to tourists, such as antiques, carpets, other traditional handicrafts and specialized clothing such as leather and embroidery items.

BIBLIOGRAPHY
E. H. Ayverdi: *Osmanlı mimârîsinde Fâtih devrî* [Ottoman architecture in the period of the Conqueror], iv (Istanbul, 1974)
Ç. Gülersoy: *Kapalı çarşının romanı* [The story of the covered bazaar] (Istanbul, 1979)

WALTER B. DENNY

Isthmia. Site in the northern Peloponnese, Greece, now in the village of Kyras Vrisi, near the east end of the Isthmus of Corinth. It flourished as the Sanctuary of Poseidon for 12 centuries. Evidence for sacrifices begins in the 11th century BC and continues, with a hiatus of two centuries following the sack of Corinth in 146 BC, to the mid-3rd century AD. Complete levelling of the site came *c.* AD 405 with the removal of building material for construction of the Hexamilion wall and fortress. Three large deposits of Archaic offerings and other objects produced the major part of the artefectural record. The Temple of Poseidon was discovered by Oscar Broneer in 1952, and in excavations from 1952 to 1967 he uncovered the central temenos, a shrine to the hero Melikertes-Palaimon, two stadia, a theatre and a Hellenistic settlement. Excavations by Paul Clement between 1967 and 1976 cleared the Roman bath, the Hexamilion fortress and fortification wall. Most finds from the sanctuary are in the Archaeological Collection at the site.

The sanctuary is located on a rocky plateau adjacent to the Corinth–Isthmus road. Offerings, in the form of bronze pins and terracotta boots, date from the 9th century BC; among later offerings were terracotta bulls, helmets, tripods and richly decorated pottery. The first Temple of Poseidon (begun *c.* 690–*c.* 650 BC) was built after the Corinthians had completed a similar temple at Corinth. Its peristyle (7×18 columns) was probably of wood, and the cella walls were embellished with a painted frieze. Within the porch stood a great marble basin (*perirrhanterion*) supported by four female figures standing on lions (mid-7th century BC; Isthmia, Archaeol. Col.; see fig.). Each woman holds the leash of a beast in one hand and its tail in the other, and painted designs originally enlivened the grey marble figures. Dedications made at the sanctuary throughout the 7th, 6th and early 5th centuries BC include arms and armour, tripods, cauldrons, chariots and horse-trappings, jewellery, bronze and terracotta vessels and figurines. The latter represent bulls, horses with riders, centaurs, athletes, a satyr and a maenad and Poseidon himself. Jumping weights (*halteres*) were dedicated by athletes. A miniature gold bull, fragments of life-size bronze statues, a Poros limestone kouros and over 130

Isthmia, *perirrhanterion*, marble, h. excluding base 1.26 m, from the Temple of Poseidon, mid-7th century BC (Isthmia, Archaeological Collection)

silver coins represent a richer class of offerings. Outside the temple stood over 75 Corinthian terracotta *perirrhanteria*. After the burning of the Archaic temple (*c.* 470–450 BC), a Classical successor was built on the same site. It was made of local Poros limestone with a peristyle of 6 by 13 columns surmounted by a marble sima. A single row of internal columns was an archaistic feature. Severely damaged by fire *c.* 390 BC, it was soon rebuilt and survived, with Roman repairs, until the 4th century AD. Sculptural fragments have been recovered from an early Antonine cult group of *Poseidon and Amphitrite* on a base decorated with reliefs of the *Kalydonian Boar Hunt* and the *Slaughter of the Niobids* (mid-2nd century AD; Isthmia, Archaeol. Col.)

The first stadium at Isthmia was built shortly after pan-Hellenic games were instituted in 582/580 BC. It is the earliest Greek stadium of which substantial traces remain. In the Classical period (*c.* 480–*c.* 323 BC) a unique starting device had 16 gates controlled by cords set into a triangular pavement. In the late 4th century BC a new stadium was constructed in a natural hollow south-east of the temple. The theatre was built *c.* 50 m north-east of the temple to accommodate musical and oratorical contests. The three-sided auditorium and rectilinear *orchestra* cut into a gently sloping hillside represent an early form of theatre design that probably belongs to the 5th century BC. The *skene* (stage building) included a narrow *proskenion* (porch). The theatre was rebuilt twice in the 4th century BC and remodelled in Roman times, though it retained a high, shallow stage and deep *orchestra*.

The myth of Melikertes-Palaimon is associated wth the Isthmian Games by the 5th century BC, but his cult place has not been identified. The hero was given a new shrine *c.* AD 50. At its greatest extent the Roman Palaimonion contained a sacrificial pit and a circular monopteral temple with a passage beneath. Statues of *Sisyphus* and the prophet *Blastos* (2nd century AD) adorned the cult area, together with images of officials and a group, of which only fragments remain, representing *Pan with Three Muses* (Isthmia, Archaeol. Col.). Extensive Roman baths (2nd century AD) to the north of the sanctuary apparently overlie a Greek bathing establishment with a large pool. The central room contains a black and white mosaic of Italian type depicting sea creatures and geometric designs.

BIBLIOGRAPHY

O. Broneer: *Temple of Poseidon* (1973), i of *Isthmia* (Princeton, NJ, 1971–)

——: *Topography and Architecture* (1973), ii of *Isthmia* (Princeton, NJ, 1971–)

E. R. Gebhard: *The Theater at Isthmia* (Chicago, 1973)

M. C. Sturgeon: *Sculpture I, 1952–1967* (1987), iv of *Isthmia* (Princeton, NJ, 1971–)

E. Gebhard and F. Hemans: 'University of Chicago Excavations at Isthmia, 1989', *Hesperia*, lxi (1992), pp. 1–77

T. Gregory: *The Hexamilion and Fortress* (1993), v of *Isthmia* (Princeton, NJ, 1971–)

I. Ranbitschek: *Metal Objects, exclusive of Arms and Armour*, vii of *Isthmia* (Princeton, NJ, 1971–) [in preparation]

ELIZABETH R. GEBHARD

Istoria [historia]. Term first used in the 15th century to refer to the complex new narrative and allegorical subjects that were then enlarging the repertory of painters. While remaining in use, its meaning became less clearly defined and more generalized in the 16th century. It appeared prominently for the first time in Books II and III of Leon Battista Alberti's pioneering treatise on painting, *De pictura* (written 1435), where the author referred to *historia* as the most ambitious and most difficult category of works a painter can attempt.

Alberti explained that they derive from the finest texts of Christianity and antiquity and involve numerous figures. Educated friends of the artist may supply him with an *inventione*; his visualization of the words is an *istoria*. He further explained that the *istoria* is for the painter what the colossal statue was in antiquity for the sculptor, except that the painter's project requires greater intelligence (*ingenium*): variety, decorum and dignity are requisite. The painting must be eloquent and hold the attention of both the senses and the mind of the spectator. Alberti gave such examples as Timanthes' lost painting of the *Sacrifice of Iphigenia*; Apelles' lost *Calumny*; ancient representations of the *Three Graces*; a well-known, but unidentified *istoria* in Rome showing the *Bearing of the Dead Meleager*, possibly the one formerly housed at the Palazzo Sciarra, Rome, and now lost (Bober, Rubinstein and Woodford, 1987, p. 147); and Giotto's *Navicella* (destr.) in St Peter's, Rome. Apelles' lost *Calumny* was re-created later in the century by Botticelli (Florence, Uffizi) and Mantegna (drawing; London, BM); the *Three Graces* was re-created by Botticelli (*Primavera*; Florence, Uffizi) and Raphael (Chantilly, Mus. Condé); and the *Meleager* was transformed into a relief *all'antica* of the *Pietà* by Luca Signorelli (see fig.).

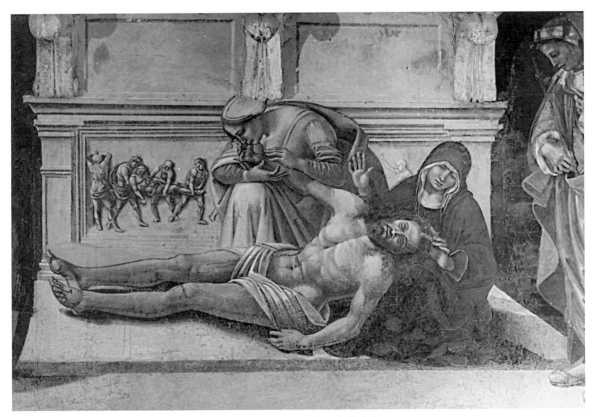

Luca Signorelli: *Pietà* (1499–1504), detail of fresco, chapel of S Brizio, Orvieto Cathedral

The complexity of the endeavour is such that Alberti suggested the use of preparatory drawings. He recommended nine or ten figures, ranging in age and attitude. The nude should be shown only with modesty, and any ugliness in live models ameliorated. Movement should be used to convey emotion; expression to engage the viewer's attention. One figure in particular should address the viewer. Although figures are the essence of the *istoria*, Alberti allowed for the inclusion of animals, landscape and buildings. He thus expected the artist to be broadly knowledgeable. The concept of *istoria* provided Alberti with his highest level of generality for analysing pictures. Proposing that the spectator should 'enter' not only the space of a picture but also the experience depicted, he understood an *istoria* to be more than simply narrative subject-matter, rather it represented an instant of an idealized but essentially true reality, a reality that accorded with nature and with art. Exacting in both its naturalism and its DECORUM, an *istoria* could achieve both likeness and beauty and create a context in which beauty asserts its proper prevalence over mere conspicuousness. In an *istoria*, the senses serve the mind rather than distracting it.

The discussion that preceded Lorenzo Ghiberti's creation of the doors of the Baptistery, Florence (*Gates of Paradise*, ?1426–52; *see* GHIBERTI, (1) and figs 4–6) included some precedent for Alberti's concept of *istoria*, though the subject of the debate was the programme to be given to the artist rather than specifically what he would create (Krautheimer and Krautheimer-Hess, 1956, doc. 52). Leonardo Bruni and Niccolò Niccoli both used the word, Bruni specifying that the '*historie*' should be '*illustri*' (clear) and '*significanti*' (meaningful). He stressed variety as part of the first quality. In his mid-15th-century *commentarii*; Ghiberti used the word of his compositions on both sets of doors (*I commentarii*; ed. J. von Schlosser, Berlin, 1912).

Leonardo not only composed *istorie* but also mused on the challenge in his notebooks. Like Alberti, he cautioned against crowding yet recommended variety. He also emphasized the expressive function of movement while stipulating that decorum be observed. Leonardo's recommendations on how to represent a battle or a night scene, a storm or a deluge, follow on from Alberti's suggestions for *istorie*, though they rely less on the authority of literature and more on actual observation. Nor was this sort of theorizing restricted to Florence. Jacopo de' Barbari of Venice in a letter of 1500–1501 (Serrolini, 1944) closely associated poetical invention in painting and the need for copiousness in an *istoria*; Dürer wrote to Willibald Pirckheimer in 1506 that he had seen no *historien* of interest in Venice. Mantegna and then Raphael perfected the type, emphasizing the dramatic interaction of figures without disrupting the compositional wholeness of the group.

After Alberti the word *istoria* continued to be an important part of the vocabulary for thinking about art, although it did not always have the prestigious connotation he gave it. It might designate little more than the difference between a narrative subject and an iconic one, as when Vasari referred to the Martelli *David* (Washington, DC, N.G.A.) of Donatello as an *istoria*. He elsewhere refers to the *istoria* as a type that might involve between four and twenty figures, the crucial requirement being their mutual integration. This is the standard 16th-century definition: an *istoria* is a painting or relief sculpture in the grand manner, copious, unified and likely to be didactic. Giovanni Battista Armenini acknowledged (1587) that in his day *istorie* were usually relegated to ornamental friezes and recommended a choice of subject appropriate to the patron and to the function of the room. For a patron who has accomplished no great deed, the deeds of renowned Romans could be substituted.

Though often *istorie* had been compared with *favole* or *poesie* (*see* POESIA), during the Counter-Reformation the contrast was emphasized. Galileo Galilei called Torquato Tasso's poetry a collection of *favolette*, like sketches by Baccio Bandinelli or Parmigianino, whereas Ariosto provided *storie integre*. A corresponding phenomenon is the reversal of the connotations of *istorie* and *inventione*: whereas for Alberti the latter made the former possible, later writers often think of the *istoria* as provoking the *inventione*. The *istoria*, in this newer formulation, must be faithful to what actually occurred. Giovanni Andrea Gilio da Fabriano cites Gregory the Great on pictures as the books of the illiterate (Barocchi, 1961): the painter's role is one of a humble translator, whose business is accuracy rather than inventiveness and displays of genius. Michelangelo's *Last Judgement* (1541; Rome, Vatican, Sistine Chapel; *see* ROME, fig. 3), with its Dantesque flavour, is at issue, as is Raphael's *Fire in the Borgo* (Rome, Vatican, Stanze di Raffaello; *see* RAPHAEL, fig. 4) with its visual reference to Troy. For Giovanni Paolo Lomazzo, however, such caution applied only to sacred stories and those in dignified places: he also allowed for *istorie* that are neither grand nor serious, nor differentiated from fictions. Both Paolo Pino and Raffaello Borghini theorized about the devising of *istorie* that did not depend on texts—as, earlier, had Leonardo, not to mention Apelles. Borghini cited Michelangelo as such an artist, for example, in his cartoons for the *Battle of Cascina* (destr.).

The early concept of *istoria* referred to but few existing works. By the 16th century the word was applied to a plethora of works, including Lucas van Leyden's prints. Rather than suggesting extraordinary ambitiousness, it stipulated only a many-figured scene presented with optimal vividness. No longer did the concept preside over the triumvirate of invention, colouring and design: *istoria* had become a means rather than an end. For Alberti, to construct an *istoria* was to claim *ingenium*; for Lodovico Dolce, in his *Dialogo della pittura* (1557), the *istoria* is no more than the artist's material, to which must be added some ingenious composition and design if there is to be praiseworthy invention.

BIBLIOGRAPHY
L. B. Alberti: *De pictura* (Basle, 1540); trans. and ed. C. Grayson as part of *On Painting and on Sculpture* (London, 1972)
L. Dolce: *Dialogo della pittura* (Venice, 1557); trans. and ed. M. W. Roskill as *Dolce's 'Aretino' and Venetian Art Theory of the Cinquecento* (New York, 1968)
R. Borghini: *Il Riposo* (Florence, 1584); ed. M. Rosci (Milan, 1967), p. 61
G. Lomazzo: *Trattato dell' arte della pittura, scoltura et architettura* (Milan, 1584); ed. R. Ciardi in *Scritti sulle arti* (Florence, 1974)
G. B. Armenini: *De' veri precetti della pittura* (Ravenna, 1587; Eng. trans., New York, 1977), bk III, chaps x, xiv
G. Galilei: *Considerazioni al Tasso* (Rome, 1793); x of *Opere*, ed. A. Favaro, A. Garbasso and G. Abetti, 20 vols (Florence, 1968)
L. Serrolini: *Jacopo de' Barbari* (Padua, 1944), pp. 105–7

R. Krautheimer and T. Krautheimer-Hess: *Lorenzo Ghiberti* (Princeton, 1956, rev. 3/1982) [doc. 52: Bruni's letter]

P. Barocchi: *Trattati d'arte del cinquecento fra Manierismo e Controriforma* (Bari, 1961) [incl. Gilio da Fabriano's *Dialogo* . . . (1564)]

M. Baxandall: *Giotto and the Orators* (Oxford, 1971), pp. 130–34

C. Hope: 'Artists, Patrons and Advisers in the Italian Renaissance', *Patronage in the Renaissance*, ed. G. Lytle and S. Orgel (Princeton, NJ, 1981), pp. 293–343

H. Mühlmann: *Ästhetische Theorie der Renaissance: Leon Battista Alberti* (Bonn, 1981), pp. 161–72

P. P. Bober, R. Rubinstein and S. Woodford: *Renaissance Artists and Antique Sculpture: A Handbook of Sources* (London, 1987)

D. Rosand: '*Ekphrasis* and the Renaissance of Painting: Observations on Alberti's Third Book', *Florilegium Columbianum: Essays in Honor of Paul Oskar Kristeller* (New York, 1987), pp. 147–65

PATRICIA EMISON

Isturitz. Cave site in south-west France in the Pyrenees. It is one of the outstanding European sites of the Upper Palaeolithic period (*c.* 40,000–*c.* 10,000 BP; *see also* PREHISTORIC EUROPE, §II): in addition to a long stratigraphic sequence indicating Mousterian, Aurignacian, Gravettian, Solutrean and Magdalenian occupations, it has yielded examples of wall art and numerous pieces of portable art, now in the Musée des Antiquités Nationales, Saint-Germain-en-Laye. Excavations in the two huge halls—the 'Salle d'Isturitz' and the 'Salle Saint-Martin'—were conducted from 1912 to 1922 by Emmanuel Passemard and from 1928 to 1958 by René and Suzanne de Saint-Périer. Their work produced evidence of a rich Upper Palaeolithic stone tool industry and many bone and antler tools of the same date, indicating an intensively and frequently occupied base camp.

All of the Upper Palaeolithic levels also produced examples of portable art, and some of the tools are decorated: these include two Upper Magdalenian projectile heads, one engraved with a horse and the other with a frieze of horses' heads, and a pierced baton with a low-relief carving of an ibex. A large series of antler rods with convex–concave cross-sections ('*baguettes demi-rondes*') is richly decorated with low-relief chevrons, angles and spirals (*see* PREHISTORIC EUROPE, fig. 13); some were also carved with figural designs, including a horse's head with barbed signs and two engraved bison heads. Engraved bone discs and *contours découpés* (flat bones cut to form the silhouette of the subject) are typical of Middle Magdalenian cultures. Most of the *contours découpés* are small, with drilled holes, but there are larger examples, including one of a horse and one of a bison, both nearly 100 mm long. Another bison carved from a large flat bone measures 220 mm long; its two halves were found 100 m apart. Among examples of portable art are 137 figurines and numerous low reliefs of fine local sandstone or marl. Most of the figurines were broken according to a standardized pattern, suggesting intentional action. Some have been attributed to the Aurignacian (*c.* 40,000–*c.* 25,000 BP), Gravettian (*c.* 30,000–*c.* 10,000 BP) and Solutrean (*c.* 20,000–*c.* 18,000 BP) cultures, but most belong to the Magdalenian (*c.* 18,000–*c.* 10,000 BP). Horses and bison are the most frequently represented species, but bears also occur; mammoths, ibex and fish are rare. These pieces vary in size, but some must have been quite long. Engravings on bone, depicting bison and occasionally birds, are common. One fragmentary piece (l. 105 mm) portrays two naked women with raised arms; two bison are engraved on the reverse. Both the bison and one of the women are marked with barbed signs, and the women wear bracelets, anklets and necklaces. Another rare subject is a man engraved alongside horses' heads on a flat stone, while a horse's head carved from amber represents an exceptional find.

BIBLIOGRAPHY

R. de Saint-Périer: 'La Grotte d'Isturitz I: Le Magdalénien de la Salle Saint-Martin', *Archives de l'Institut de Paléontologie Humaine* (Paris, 1930)

R. de Saint-Périer and S. de Saint-Périer: 'La Grotte d'Isturitz II: Le Magdalénien de la Grande Salle', *Archives de l'Institut de Paléontologie Humaine* (Paris, 1936)

E. Passemard: 'La Caverne d'Isturitz en Pays Basque', *Préhistoire*, ix (1944), pp. 1–45

R. de Saint-Périer and S. de Saint-Périer: 'La Grotte d'Isturitz III: Les Solutréens, les Aurignaciens et les Moustériens', *Archives de l'Institut de Paléontologie Humaine* (Paris, 1952)

L. Mons: 'Les Statuettes animalières en grès de la grotte d'Isturitz (Pyrénées Atlantiques): Observations et hypothèses de fragmentation volontaire', *L'Anthropologie*, xc (1986), pp. 701–12

——: 'Les Figurations de bisons dans l'art mobilier de la grotte d'Isturitz (Pyr.-Atlantiques)', *Ant. N.*, xviii–xix (1986–7), pp. 91–9

H. Delporte: *L'Image des animaux dans l'art préhistorique* (Paris, 1990)

JOACHIM HAHN

István Kassai. *See* STEFAN.

Isyakhim, M'hammad. *See* ISSIAKHEM, M'HAMED.

Italia, Angelo (*b* Licata, 8 May 1628; *d* Palermo, 5 May 1700). Italian architect. Described as an 'architectus et sculptor', he joined the Jesuit novitiate in Palermo in November 1671. He then worked as an architect for the Jesuits at Sciacca and Marsala (*c.* 1674) and the Jesuit colleges at Termini Imercse (*c.* 1679) and Mazara del Vallo (*c.* 1682). His church of S Francesco Saverio (1684–1709), Palermo, has four hexagonal chapels inserted between the arms of a Greek cross. The plan probably reflects the church designs of Guarino Guarini (ii), which Italia must have seen when he was in Messina in 1672. The chapels, with Doric columns in the style of Jacopo Vignola, rise through two storeys and open on to the central space through an arcade. The triglyphs of the frieze bulge forward under the projecting curve of the cornice and become consoles, as if supporting a balcony. The upper parts of the campanile's exterior recall the bell-towers of the Chiesa Madre (begun 1665), Palma de Montechiaro, which is also attributed to Italia.

S Gerolamo, the church of the Jesuit college at Polizzi Generosa (1681–5), is similar to S Francesco, but its chapels and unpierced drum are octagonal, while the articulation of its interior by pilasters makes the design more coherent but less inventive. Italia's interest in polychromy, which is apparent at S Francesco, was developed at the Cappella del Crocifisso (from 1688), Monreale Cathedral. His characteristic use of grotesques, scrolls and foliage is best seen in the cupola (*c.* 1679) of the Carmine, Palermo, which is decorated with brightly coloured tiles and has Michelangelesque caryatids on the exterior of the drum. He also designed plans for the new towns of Avolà, Noto and Lentini after the 1693 earthquake. His hexagonal plan for Avolà adopted the ideals of symmetry and hierarchical organization while providing open spaces and straight, broad streets to minimize damage in a future earthquake.

BIBLIOGRAPHY

V. Palazzotto: *Angelo Italia e S Francesco Saverio* (Palermo, n.d.)
T. Viscuso: *Aspetti dell'architettura barocca in Sicilia: Guarino Guarini e Angelo Italia* (Palermo, n.d.)
A. Blunt: *Sicilian Baroque* (London, 1968)
M. L. Stella: 'L'architetto Angelo Italia', *Palladio*, n. s., xviii (1968), pp. 155–76

HELEN HILLS

Italianates, Dutch. *See* DUTCH ITALIANATES.

Italica [Sp. Itálica; now Santiponce]. City 6 km northwest of Seville, founded in 206 BC by Scipio Africanus (236–184/3 BC). It was always a small, agricultural community, its earliest settlement occupying two hills: Cerro de San Antonio to the west, originally the industrial quarter, and Cerro de los Palacios to the east, the residential area. Remains, perhaps of two temples, one a capitolium, have been found on Los Palacios (before 27 BC). Some fragments of Ibero-Roman sculpture are probably also of Republican date (Seville, Mus. Arqueol. Prov.), while a terracotta acroterion representing the *Mistress of the Beasts* (*c.* 100 BC; Seville, Condesa de Lebrija priv. col., see García

1. Map of Italy; those areas with separate entries in this dictionary are distinguished by CROSS-REFERENCE TYPE

y Bellido, p. 9, fig. 11) may have decorated one of the city's early temples.

Augustus may have raised the city to the status of a *municipium*, and Trajan (AD 53) and Hadrian (AD 76) were both born there; Hadrian made the city a full *colonia*. During the 2nd century AD a residential quarter on an orthogonal plan, with two houses per block, spread out to the north. An elaborate bath complex was built on Los Palacios, and the theatre was bedded into its slopes; outside the walls was an amphitheatre even larger than those at Arles and Nîmes. A massive temple complex, perhaps dedicated to Trajan, was built at this time in the new city. The houses were luxurious peristyle buildings decorated with mosaic pavements. Most were single-storey, and a few had shops attached. The mosaic style relates to that practised in Italy, but the device of combining polychrome and black-and-white technique is typically Iberian. Subjects include birds, mythological narratives, portraits of divinities and one Nilotic scene showing a battle between pygmies and cranes (*in situ* and Seville, Mus. Arqueol. Prov.). Notable sculptures from Italica (1st and 2nd centuries AD; Seville, Mus. Arqueol. Prov.) include heroic nude statues of *Trajan* and *Hadrian* and a torso of *Diana* (second version, New York, Hisp. Soc. America, D201) from the baths of Los Palacios; nude images of *Hermes* and *Venus* from the theatre; and portraits of *Augustus, Livia, Nero* and *Marcus Aurelius* and a fine head of *Alexander the Great*, from elsewhere in the city.

Although not an important city, Italica probably suffered in the general upheaval in southern Iberia caused by the 2nd- and 3rd-century AD invasions of North African tribesmen. It must also have suffered in the 3rd century AD from the turmoil that culminated in the Germanic invasions; the northern suburb was largely abandoned at this date.

BIBLIOGRAPHY

A. García y Bellido: *Colonia Aelia Augusta Italica* (Madrid, 1960, 2/1979)
M. Bendala Galán: 'Excavaciones en el Cerro de los Palacios', *Itálica (Santiponce, Sevilla)*, Excavaciones Arqueológicas en España, cxxi (Madrid, 1982), pp. 29–75
J. M. Luzón Nogué: *La Itálica de Adriano* (Seville, 1982)
P. Léon: *Traianeum de Itálica* (Seville, 1988)

WILLIAM E. MIERSE

Italus, Franciscus. *See* FRANCISCUS ITALUS.

Italy [Repubblica Italiana]. South European country. Mainland Italy occupies a peninsula (1200 km from north to south) bordered by the Tyrrhenian Sea to the west, the Ionian Sea to the south and the Adriatic Sea to the east (see fig. 1). The principal offshore islands of Italy are SICILY and SARDINIA. To the north the Alps form the mountainous border with France, Switzerland, Austria and Slovenia. The Apennines are a limestone range running right down the peninsula into Sicily. Active volcanoes include Mt Vesuvius near Naples and Mt Etna in Sicily. The many and varied regions of Italy (pop. *c.* 57 million) include Piedmont and Lombardy in the north, which occupy the plain of the River Po and are home to TURIN and MILAN respectively; the Venetias to the east, including VENICE; Emilia Romagna to the north-east of the Apennines, with the major towns of BOLOGNA and RAVENNA; Liguria, a coastal region to the west of the Apennines that includes GENOA (see fig. 2); fertile Tuscany, with its great artistic centres of FLORENCE and SIENA; Umbria, the heartland of the Etruscan civilization in central Italy; Latium, the cradle of the Roman civilization, with ROME, Italy's capital, at its centre (see fig. 3); and Campania, which runs along the Bay of NAPLES (see fig. 4). The climate is continental in northern Italy, harsh in the mountainous regions but temperate and Mediterranean in most of the country. Agriculture (including wine production), engineering, motor manufacturing and tourism are major industries. Italy has been the home of several cultures of the greatest importance for Western art, from the ETRUSCAN civilization to the mighty Roman Empire (*see* ROME, ANCIENT) to the artistic flowering of the RENAISSANCE. This survey covers the art of the country in the historical periods (for earlier periods *see* PREHISTORIC EUROPE and VILLANOVAN).

I. Introduction. II. Architecture. III. Painting. IV. Sculpture. V. Interior decoration. VI. Furniture. VII. Ceramics. VIII. Glass. IX. Metalwork. X. Objects of vertu. XI. Textiles. XII. Patronage. XIII. Collecting and dealing. XIV. Museums. XV. Art libraries and photographic collections. XVI. Art education. XVII. Historiography.

DETAILED TABLE OF CONTENTS

I. Introduction   619

II. Architecture   622
   1. Ancient, 8th century BC–c. AD 313   622
   2. Early Christian and medieval, c. AD 313–c. 1400   623
     (i) Early Christian and Lombard, 4th–10th centuries   623
     (ii) Romanesque, 11th–13th centuries   624
     (iii) Gothic, 13th–14th centuries   627
   3. Renaissance and Mannerism, c. 1400–c. 1600   628
     (i) Early Renaissance, c. 1400–c. 1500   628
       (a) Tuscany   628
       (b) Lombardy   630
       (c) The Marches and the Veneto   630
       (d) Rome   631
     (ii) High Renaissance, c. 1500–c. 1520   632
     (iii) Late Renaissance and Mannerism, c. 1520–c. 1600   634
       (a) Florence   634
       (b) Rome   634
       (c) The Veneto   635
   4. Baroque and Rococo, c. 1600–c. 1750   636
     (i) Introduction   636
     (ii) Rome   637
     (iii) Southern Italy   639
     (iv) Northern Italy   641
   5. Neo-classicism to early Modernism, c. 1750–c. 1900   642
     (i) Rome and southern Italy   644
     (ii) Northern Italy   646
   6. After c. 1900   648
     (i) *Stile Liberty* and the Futurist legacy, c. 1900–c. 1920   648
     (ii) *Novecentismo, Razionalismo* and the establishment styles, c. 1920–c. 1946   648
     (iii) Neo-Realism and Neo-Liberty to *La Tendenza*, c. 1946–c. 1970   649
     (iv) Post-modernism, after c. 1970   651

III. Painting   652
   1. Ancient, 8th century BC to late Roman   652
   2. Early Christian and medieval, before c. 1400   653
     (i) Early Christian, c. AD 200–c. 600   653
     (ii) Early medieval, c. AD 600–c. 1100   654
     (iii) Late medieval, c. 1100–c. 1400   654
   3. Early Renaissance, c. 1400–c. 1500   657
     (i) Introduction   658
       (a) Humanism, the Antique and illusionism   658
       (b) Format   658
       (c) Technique   658
       (d) Subject-matter and patronage   659
       (e) Status of the artist   660
     (ii) Regional survey   661
       (a) Florence   661
       (b) Other centres   662
   4. High Renaissance and Mannerism, c. 1500–c. 1600   663
     (i) Florence   663
     (ii) Rome   664
     (iii) Venice   665
     (iv) Other schools and artists   667
   5. Baroque and Rococo, c. 1600–c. 1750   668
     (i) Bologna and Emilia Romagna   669
     (ii) Rome   670
       (a) Early Baroque, c. 1590–c. 1620   670
       (b) High Baroque, c. 1620–c. 1650   670
       (c) Late Baroque and Rococo, c. 1650–c. 1750   672
     (iii) Naples   672
     (iv) Florence and Tuscany   672
     (v) Lombardy and northern Italy   674
     (vi) Genoa   674
     (vii) Venice and the Veneto   675
   6. Neo-classicism to early modernism, c. 1750–c. 1900   676
   7. After c. 1900   679
     (i) c. 1900–1945   679
     (ii) From 1946   681

IV. Sculpture   683
   1. Ancient, 8th century BC–c. AD 313   683
   2. Early Christian and medieval, c. AD 313–c. 1400   685
     (i) Introduction   685
     (ii) Early Christian, 4th–6th centuries AD   686
     (iii) Lombard, Romanesque and Gothic, 6th–14th centuries   686
   3. Renaissance and Mannerism, c. 1400–c. 1600   688
     (i) Early Renaissance, c. 1400–c. 1480   689
       (a) Florence   689
         – Introduction   689
         – Types of sculpture   689
         – 'Sweet style'   690
         – 'Dramatic style'   691
       (b) Rome   691
       (c) Lucca, Siena and Bologna   691
       (d) Venice and the Veneto   692
         – Late Gothic   692
         – Early Renaissance   692
     (ii) High Renaissance, c. 1480–c. 1530   693
       (a) Venice   693
       (b) Florence   694
       (c) Michelangelo in Florence and Rome   694
       (d) Impact in Europe   695
     (iii) Mannerism, c. 1530–c. 1600   695
       (a) Florence   695
       (b) Rome   696
       (c) Venice   697
       (d) Milan   697

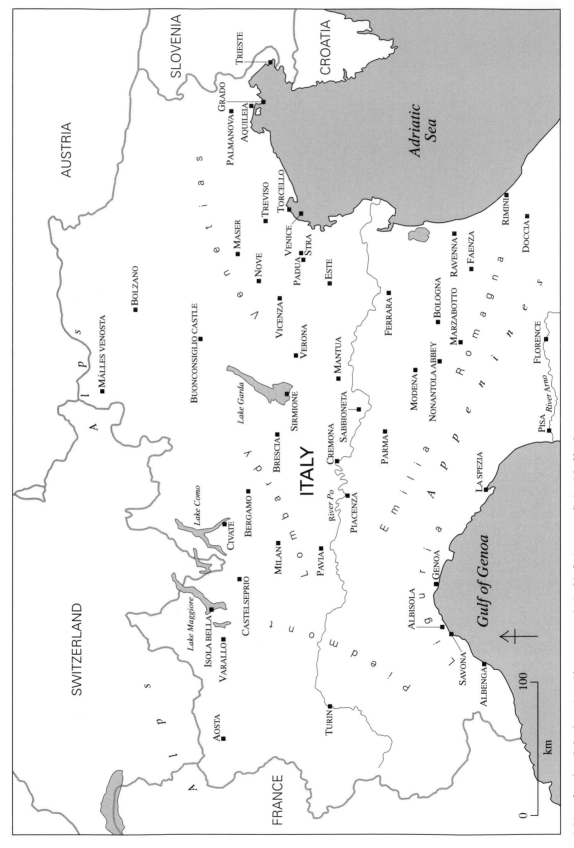

2. Map of northern Italy; those sites with separate entries in this dictionary are distinguished by CROSS-REFERENCE TYPE

4. Baroque, *c.* 1600–*c.* 1750   697
  (i) Rome   697
  (ii) Bologna and Emilia   699
  (iii) Florence and Tuscany   699
  (iv) Milan and Lombardy   700
  (v) Genoa and Liguria   701
  (vi) Turin and Piedmont   702
  (vii) Venice and the Veneto   702
  (viii) Kingdom of Naples   703
5. Neo-classicism to early modernism, *c.* 1750–*c.* 1900   704
6. After *c.* 1900   707

V. Interior decoration   709
1. Before 1450   709
2. 1450–1599   711
3. 1600–1699   712
4. 1700–*c.* 1750   716
5. *c.* 1750–*c.* 1800   717
6. *c.* 1800–1900   719
7. After 1900   721

VI. Furniture   721
1. Before *c.* 1450   721
2. *c.* 1450–1599   723
3. 1600–1799   726
4. 1800–1900   729
5. After 1900   731

VII. Ceramics   732
1. Maiolica   732
  (i) Before 1500   732
  (ii) 1500 and after   733
2. Porcelain   736
  (i) Before 1720   736
  (ii) 1720–75   737
  (iii) After 1775   739

VIII. Glass   740

IX. Metalwork   741
1. Gold and silver   741
2. Base metals   743

X. Objects of vertu   744
1. Hardstones   744
  (i) Rock crystal   744
  (ii) Other   746
2. Tortoiseshell   748
3. Wax modelling   749
4. Coral   750
5. Niello and enamel   750
6. Jewellery   750

XI. Textiles   752
1. Silk   752
2. Lace   754
3. Tapestry   755
  (i) Before 1500   755
  (ii) 1500–1624   757
  (iii) 1625–1800   757
  (iv) After 1800   758
4. Embroidery   758

XII. Patronage   760
1. Roman, before *c.* AD 313   760
2. Early Christian to early medieval, *c.* AD 313–*c.* 1200   761
  (i) Papal court   761
  (ii) Monastic orders and secular rulers   762

3. Medieval, *c.* 1200–*c.*1400   762
4. Renaissance, *c.* 1400–*c.* 1600   762
5. Baroque, Rococo and Neo-classicism, *c.* 1600–*c.* 1861   762
6. Nation state, from 1861   763

XIII. Collecting and dealing   765
1. Middle Ages–17th century   765
2. 18th–20th centuries   768

XIV. Museums   770
1. Renaissance collections   770
2. The Renaissance and Baroque gallery   771
3. The age of Neo-classicism   771
4. The Napoleonic age and the Restoration   772
5. The early nation state   774
6. After World War I   775

XV. Art libraries and photographic collections   776

XVI. Art education   777
1. Apprenticeships   777
2. Academies   778
3. Education of women artists   780

XVII. Historiography   780
1. 14th–16th centuries   780
2. 17th–20th centuries   781

I. Introduction.

In the late 8th century BC Greek colonists settled in South Italy and Sicily, and at the same time the Etruscan civilization developed in central Italy. Rome itself was ruled by Etruscan kings in the 6th century BC. Under the Roman Republic (509–27 BC), Etruscan power declined, and Italy began to be unified under Roman rule. The power of Rome and Italy extended under the Empire (31 BC–AD 476), although the importance of Roman provinces abroad gradually exceeded that of Italy itself, until in AD 330 Constantinople (now Istanbul) became the new capital of the Empire. Successive waves of invasions, first by Germanic barbarian tribes in the 4th and 5th centuries and then by the Lombards (568–774; *see also* LOMBARD ART), combined with the growing power of the papacy centred on Rome, all contributed to the severing of political ties with the Byzantine Empire in the East. For a short period in the 9th century northern Italy was part of the Frankish empire (*see also* CAROLINGIAN ART), and in 962 the German king Otto I was crowned Holy Roman Emperor at Rome (*see also* OTTONIAN ART). The medieval period was characterized by the struggle for supremacy between the papacy and the Empire, though theoretically they were the spiritual and temporal arms of the same entity. Many northern Italian cities became powerful and independent city states, though divided in their allegiance to the emperors or the popes. Southern Italy followed a different course: Arab influence was strong from the 9th century, but from the mid-11th century the Normans established control there, with Roger II becoming King of Sicily in 1130. Charles of Anjou ruled as King of Naples and Sicily from 1266, and in the 15th century the so-called Kingdom of the Two Sicilies became a Spanish possession.

3. Map of central Italy; those areas with separate entries in this dictionary are distinguished by Cross-reference type

The 14th century was a period of weakening papal and imperial authority in Italy (for a time the papacy was situated at Avignon in France), but one also of great cultural and intellectual revival—the beginnings of the Renaissance. The communal governments of the city states fell to powerful families, such as the Medici in Florence, who made their cities magnificent centres of the arts. Frequent wars between the city states led to a long period of foreign domination from 1494, first under Charles VIII of France, then under the Spanish in the 16th and 17th centuries (the Habsburg Charles V was both Holy Roman Emperor and King of Spain) and the Austrian empire in the 18th century.

Italy was invaded by Napoleon I Bonaparte in 1796, but after the restoration of peace in Europe in 1815 a popular Italian unification movement, the Risorgimento, worked to rid Italy of its foreign powers, in particular the harsh rule of Austria. By 1860, with the help of France, England and Sardinia, independence was secured for most of northern Italy. Giuseppe Garibaldi's conquest of Sicily and southern Italy led to a unified Kingdom of Italy in 1861, Venetia being added in 1866 and Rome in 1870.

A rise of nationalism after World War I—in which Italy joined the Allies, although it gained little and suffered much—combined with social and political crisis proved to be fertile conditions for the rise of the Fascists. Their leader, Benito Mussolini, assumed dictatorial powers from the mid-1920s. Italy allied with Nazi Germany in World War II; after their defeat, a republic was formed in 1946

4. Map of southern Italy; those sites with separate entries in this dictionary are distinguished by CROSS-REFERENCE TYPE

and achieved rapid economic growth and industrialization. Italy joined the European Economic Community (now the European Union) in 1958, becoming one of its leading member states. In the 1990s a revised electoral system and popular dissatisfaction with political corruption and instability led to a rejection of the Christian Democrat- and Socialist-dominated coalitions of the post-war years.

BIBLIOGRAPHY

D. Mack Smith: *Italy: A Modern History* (Bari, 1959, rev. London, 2/1969)

H. Hearder and D. P. Waley, eds: *A Short History of Italy* (Cambridge, 1963)

G. Procacci: *Histoire d'Italie* (Paris, 1968); trans. by A. Paul as *A History of the Italian People* (London, 1970)

J. J. Norwich: *The Italian World: History, Art and Genius of a People* (London, 1983)

II. Architecture.

1. Ancient, 8th century BC–*c*. AD 313. 2. Early Christian and medieval, *c*. AD 313–*c*. 1400. 3. Renaissance and Mannerism, *c*. 1400–*c*. 1600. 4. Baroque and Rococo, *c*. 1600–*c*. 1750. 5. Neo-classicism to early Modernism, *c*. 1750–*c*. 1900. 6. After *c*. 1900.

1. ANCIENT, 8TH CENTURY BC–*c*. AD 313. The Greeks who colonized South Italy and Sicily from the 8th century BC brought with them the technology and aesthetics of temple building (*see* GREECE, ANCIENT, §II, 1(i)(a)). Their stone-cut, post and lintel, columnar architecture was based on rules of form and proportion, the Doric and Ionic orders and optical refinements such as curvature and entasis, as seen in the best-preserved Classical temple in Italy, the 5th-century BC Doric second Temple of Hera at PAESTUM. Colonial temples deviated from those of the Greek mainland in their frontal orientation and longer proportions, as in the 6th-century BC Temple of Apollo at Syracuse, and in the unorthodox use of the orders, as in the 6th-century BC Temple of Athena at Paestum, which also had no pediment; both of these may reflect a relaxed attitude on the part of colonial builders towards the theoretical preoccupations of mainland architects. Their taste for massive forms can be seen in the unfinished late 5th-century BC temple at SEGESTA (see fig. 5), or in one of the largest of all Doric temples, Temple G at SELINUS (begun late 6th century BC).

From the 7th to the 2nd century BC the Etruscans of central Italy developed a stone-built architecture that fused their own traditions with their admiration for Greek forms (*see* ETRUSCAN, §II). Like the Greeks in South Italy, the Etruscans settled in cities, some of which were organized into *insulae* (house-blocks) dominated by an *arx* (sacred citadel) and laid out on a grid plan with a *cardo* and a *decumanus* (major north–south and east–west streets respectively). It is difficult to say whether this plan was a Greek or Etruscan invention; it became the configuration that was emulated in later Roman colonies. City walls were built of stone, and by the 3rd century BC a few of these included arched gateways, later imitated by the Romans in their city walls. The Etruscans had distinctive burial practices. Underground tomb chambers were hewn out of the rock and decorated with wall paintings or stucco reliefs to emulate domestic architecture. The tomb plans may have been based on Etruscan house plans (rooms grouped around a central hall, as at the 2nd-century BC Tomb of the Volumnii, Perugia), an arrangement similar to the Roman atrium house (*see* ROME, ANCIENT, §II, 1(i)(c)), many examples of which were buried in ash at Pompeii. After the 6th century BC Etruscan temples resembled Greek temples, but with some variations: they were pseudo-peripteral, stood on high podia, had frontal emphasis with deep columnar porches, were divided into three cellae and utilized more wood and terracotta ornamentation. This configuration served as the basis for one of the first monumental buildings in Rome, the Temple of Jupiter on the Capitoline Hill, built by the last Etruscan king before he was expelled in 509 BC (*see* ROME, ANCIENT, §II, 2(i)(a)).

5. Ancient Greek temple at Segesta, late 5th century BC, unfinished

During the Republic and early Empire the city of Rome developed from an Etruscan city state to the largest urbanized metropolis of the ancient world (*see* ROME, §II, 1). Villages on the seven hills were joined by major streets leading to the Forum Romanum; architects experimented with arches and concrete in larger public buildings that served a growing population. As the political and spiritual centre of a vast empire until the early 4th century AD, Rome became the architectural model for its network of urbanized cities, municipalities and colonial satellites in Italy and in the more distant Roman provinces. By the late 1st century BC a revolutionary new phase in the history of architecture was ushered in by the marble quarried at Luna in Italy, by the influx of coloured marbles from across the Empire (*see* STONE, colour pl. VIII, fig. 2), by the development of concrete mixed with pozzolana and faced with tufa, travertine and brick, and by experimentation with the arch, vault and dome (*see* ROME, ANCIENT, §II, 1(ii)). According to Suetonius (*Augustus* XXVIII.iii), Augustus 'so beautified [Rome] that he could justly boast that he had found it built of brick and left it in marble'.

The process of Romanization and the formation of Roman town culture motivated the development of new types of buildings and the technologies to build them. Supported by a system of state and aristocratic patronage, professional architects such as Severus and Celer, Rabirius and Apollodoros of Damascus were commissioned to oversee massive public and private building projects and encouraged to experiment with new architectural forms, materials and technologies. The significance of these projects is reflected in the preface to Vitruvius' *On Architecture* (I.ii), in which the architect reminds the Emperor Augustus, to whom the book is dedicated, that the greatness of Rome's power is embodied in the distinguished authority of its public buildings. The architectural signs of Rome's sphere of influence were distinctive and numerous: fora, municipal basilicas, temples, monumental arches, arched city gateways, city walls and fortifications, monumental tombs, baths, amphitheatres, theatres, circuses, aqueducts, cisterns, granaries, markets, shops, *insulae*, atrium houses, villas and palaces. At POMPEII, HERCULANEUM and OSTIA one can still see these marks of a properly Romanized town.

While early Roman buildings were modelled on Greek and Etruscan temples, by the late 2nd century BC the Greek column and architrave, once a structural necessity, became a decorative adjunct of the Roman arcade, as seen in the Sanctuary of Fortuna Primigenia at PRAENESTE, the first large-scale authentically Roman terraced architectural complex in which curvilinear forms shaped by concrete make an early appearance. No longer content with the technological limitations of the Greek post-and-lintel systems, Roman builders experimented with an arched and vaulted concrete technology that shaped and moulded exterior and interior spaces with fluid curves. Hemicycles, apses, barrel vaults, groin-vaulted ceilings and monumental domes lit by oculi at their apexes, such as that of Hadrian's Pantheon (*see* ROME, §V, 8), became the hallmark of Roman architecture. To meet the growing demands of a sophisticated Imperial clientele, an expanding population and a vast administrative bureaucracy, Roman architects and engineers of the 1st century AD to the early 4th used concrete vaulted technology for increasingly complex, experimental, large-scale private and public projects, such as the Domus Aurea, Nero's grandiose domed palace in Rome (*see* ROME, §V, 5), the Colosseum, the largest amphitheatre in Rome (*see* ROME, §V, 6), the curvilinear terraced and annular vaulted Markets of Trajan (*see* ROME, ANCIENT, §II, 2(i)(e)), the multistorey apartment complexes (*insulae*) at Ostia, Hadrian's extensive villa complex at Tivoli (*see* TIVOLI, §2(i)), the colossal Baths of Caracalla (*see* ROME, §V, 10) and the Basilica of Maxentius (*see* ROME, §V, 11), the largest built in Rome. These remarkable architectural achievements expressed Rome's political programmes and intentions in monumental forms that represented a new age of architecture. Their structural principles and shapes soon appeared in every important city and town in Italy and in the provinces, displaying the image of Rome and her claims, and having an indelible impact on all Western art and architecture.

BIBLIOGRAPHY

Vitruvius: *On Architecture*

D. S. Robertson: *A Handbook of Greek and Roman Architecture* (Cambridge, 1929, rev. 2/1943); repr. as *Greek and Roman Architecture* (London, 1969; rev. Cambridge, 1971)

M. E. Blake: *Ancient Roman Construction in Italy from the Prehistoric Period to Augustus* (Washington, DC, 1947)

——: *Roman Construction in Italy from Tiberius through the Flavians* (Washington, DC, 1959)

A. Böethius: *The Golden House of Nero: Some Aspects of Roman Architecture* (Ann Arbor, 1960)

F. E. Brown: *Roman Architecture* (New York, 1961)

E. Nash: *Pictorial Dictionary of Ancient Rome*, 2 vols (London and New York, 1961–2, 2/1968)

W. L. MacDonald: *The Architecture of the Roman Empire*, 2 vols (New Haven, 1965–86, i rev. 2/1982)

P. MacKendrick: *The Mute Stones Speak: The Story of Archaeology in Italy* (New York, 1966)

L. Banti: *The Etruscan Cities and their Culture* (London, 1973)

J. B. Ward-Perkins: *Cities of Ancient Greece and Italy: Planning in Classical Antiquity* (London, 1974)

A. Böethius: *Etruscan and Early Roman Architecture*, Pelican Hist. A. (Harmondsworth, 1978)

J. B. Ward-Perkins: *Roman Imperial Architecture*, Pelican Hist. A. (Harmondsworth, 1981)

F. B. Sear: *Roman Architecture* (London and Ithaca, 1982)

J. Rykwert: *The Idea of a Town: The Anthropology of Urban Form in Rome, Italy, and the Ancient World* (2nd edn, Cambridge, 1988)

T. W. Potter: *Roman Italy* (2nd edn, Berkeley, CA, 1990)

J. R. Clarke: *The Houses of Roman Italy, 100 BC–AD 250: Ritual, Space, and Decoration* (Berkeley, CA, 1991)

SUSAN SILBERBERG-PEIRCE

2. EARLY CHRISTIAN AND MEDIEVAL, *c.* AD 313–*c.* 1400.

(i) Early Christian and Lombard, 4th–10th centuries. (ii) Romanesque, 11th–13th centuries. (iii) Gothic, 13th–14th centuries.

(i) Early Christian and Lombard, 4th–10th centuries. In AD 313, with the Edict of Milan, the Emperor Constantine authorized Christian worship and founded a number of churches in Rome, the designs of which became the inspiration for many others in the Middle Ages. The Basilica Constantiana (now S Giovanni in Laterano; begun *c.* 313; altered), the first, is regarded as the mother of churches, but St Peter's (*c.* 320–29/30; rebuilt) on the Vatican Hill became pre-eminent owing to its possession of this Apostle's tomb (*see* ROME, §II, 2). Both churches faced west, and the interior of each was divided into five aisles by columns; those flanking the central vessel carried an entablature, while the columns dividing the inner aisles

6. S Maria in Cosmedin, Rome, interior, 6th century AD, enlarged 8th century, restored 12th century

from the outer supported arcades (*see* ROME, figs 33 and 47). The cemetery churches outside the walls that were founded during or just after Constantine's reign (notably S Sebastiano, *c.* 313–37 (*see* EARLY CHRISTIAN AND BYZANTINE ART, fig. 13); SS Pietro e Marcellino, before 324–6; S Lorenzo, *c.* 330; and S Agnese, 337–50; all rebuilt) had an eastern apse surrounded by an ambulatory, a design that resembled the imperial circuses. Other early buildings include Santa Croce in Gerusalemme, built within the Sessorian palace, the octagonal baptistery at the Lateran (*c.* 315; altered; *see* ROME, §V, 15(iii)) and the circular mausoleum of S Costanza (next to S Agnese; *see* ROME, §V, 18), the best preserved of all Constantinian churches, with its two concentric arcades carried by 24 paired columns.

Roman churches of the following period, now substantially altered, include S Paolo fuori le Mura (begun 385; rebuilt after 1823), with a plan close to that of St Peter's, but with an arcaded rather than a trabeated nave colonnade; S Pudenziana (*c.* 390), converted from a *domus ecclesiae*; S Maria Maggiore, built by Pope Sixtus III, with Ionic columns supporting an entablature (*see* ROME, §V, 20); S Sabina (422–32), with a round-headed nave arcade and large windows in the clerestory and apse; the circular church of S Stefano Rotondo (468–83; *see* ROME, §V, 22), with an Ionic colonnade; and the later phases of S Lorenzo

(579–90) and S Agnese fuori le Mura (625–38), both with galleries.

Elsewhere in Italy, the Early Christian period is represented in Milan by S Lorenzo (founded 370s; altered; *see* MILAN, fig. 17), a double-shell, quatrefoil structure with four square towers; in Umbria by the graceful little temple at Clitunno and by S Salvatore, Spoleto, both buildings showing traces of Roman Imperial architecture, the latter with paired, fluted Corinthian columns at the corners of the sanctuary; and in Campania by Paulinus's basilica at CIMITILE-NOLA, with a trilobe apse, and by S Gennaro extra moenia and S Giorgio Maggiore, Naples (both *c.* 400; part destr.), both with arched openings in the apse wall.

The architecture of RAVENNA and the surrounding area during the 5th and 6th centuries should be considered separately. The earliest intact structure is the mausoleum of Galla Placidia (*c.* 425–50), a small cruciform building built of brick, the exterior wall lightened by a series of blind arcades and pilasters. Of slightly later date are the Orthodox and Arian baptisteries, both octagonal, with projecting niches in alternate sides. The austere, two-storey mausoleum of Theodoric (*c.* 526), also with a centralized plan, partly resembles Imperial Roman mausolea, but certain decorative elements show the intervention of foreign craftsmen (*see* RAVENNA, §2(iii) and fig. 3). The building that best represents Byzantine architecture in Ravenna is Justinian's church of S Vitale (begun 530; ded. 547), the design of which is related to Hagia Sophia and SS Sergios and Bakchos in Constantinople (now Istanbul). It has an octagonal plan with two tiers of arcaded exedrae between the piers supporting the dome and a long narthex with apsidal terminations set obliquely to the axis of the building. The basilicas of S Giovanni Evangelista (424–34), S Apollinare Nuovo and S Apollinare in Classe (see RAVENNA, figs 5 and 4 respectively) have broad, spacious and well-lit interiors, punctuated by the calm rhythms of the columnar arcades, and polygonal apses. Later churches related to them in the north Adriatic include the cathedrals of AQUILEIA, Torcello (see TOR-CELLO, §1) and Grado, Pomposa Abbey (8th–9th century) and S Pietro in Sylvis, Bagnacavallo. Also at Ravenna, the 8th-century 'Palace of Theodoric' has a corbelled loggia that seems to anticipate Romanesque solutions.

The most important structures built under the Lombards (mid-6th century to 8th) are the baptistery at Lomello; S Maria in Valle, Cividale; S Salvatore, Brescia; and S Sofia, BENEVENTO. The Carolingian and Ottonian periods are represented in northern Italy by the rebuilt apse of S Ambrogio, Milan; by S PIETRO AL MONTE, CIVATE; and by buildings at Biella (baptistery), Galliano (S Vincenzo and the quadrilobed baptistery) and Rome (e.g. S Cecilia in Trastevere and S Maria in Cosmedin; see fig. 6).

See also EARLY CHRISTIAN AND BYZANTINE ART, §II, 2(i)(a).

(ii) Romanesque, 11th–13th centuries. Despite the development of Romanesque architecture in the 11th and 12th centuries (see ROMANESQUE, §II), traditional forms persisted in Italy, even in the late Middle Ages, and their survival led to marked regional differences. In Lombardy, where specialized masons were most numerous, S Ambrogio, Milan, was rebuilt with a rib-vaulted nave of four (now three) double bays with galleries and a simple gabled façade overlooking an atrium (see MILAN, fig. 14). S Abbondio (ded. 1095; see ROMANESQUE, fig. 8), Como, has double aisles flanking the nave, a long, groin-vaulted choir and eastern apse, with the subsidiary apses at the ends of the aisles enclosed in the thickness of the walls. At S Fedele, Como, an aisled, trilobe east end is grafted on to a basilican nave. S Michele, Pavia, seems to be directly derived from S Ambrogio, with the addition of long, barrel-vaulted transepts and a gabled screen façade divided into three by shafting on dosserets and articulated by dwarf galleries beneath the roofline (see PAVIA, §2(ii)(a) and fig. 3).

A development of these Lombard solutions can be seen in Emilia in the design of Modena Cathedral, begun in 1099 (see MODENA, §1(i) and fig. 1). The façade, articulated by robust buttresses and embellished with a two-storey porch and triple-arched gallery (which continues around the perimeter of the building), has bold chiaroscuro contrasts. Almost all the Po Valley churches built in the 12th and 13th centuries took their inspiration from Modena, but they still retained Lombard characteristics. The cathedrals of Parma, Piacenza and Cremona (for illustration *see* CREMONA), for example, have two-storey porches, but their plain façades crowned with dwarf arcading belong to the traditions of Lombardy. The external features of

Ferrara Cathedral (ded. 1135; completed 13th century; see fig. 7), however, are more obviously derived from Modena.

Churches in Piedmont and Liguria show a blend of French and Lombard styles; notable buildings are the Sacra of San Michele (1130s–1160s), perched on a hilltop, and S Andrea, Vercelli, with arcading under the eaves and Gothic elements. In the Veneto, the eclectic church of S Zeno Maggiore (*c.* 1135), Verona, has a basilican interior with large diaphragm arches, an alternating main arcade and a wooden roof with a trefoil cross-section in the form of an inverted keel. Buildings along the Adriatic coast such as S Fosca (see TORCELLO, §2) and Murano Cathedral have some Byzantine features, but the domed church of S Marco, Venice, rebuilt from 1063, is unique (see VENICE, fig. 14): its plan may follow that of Justinian's church of the Holy Apostles (destr.) in Constantinople. The churches of the Adriatic littoral further south, in the Marches, mostly combine Lombard and Byzantine elements. The 12th-century baptistery at Ascoli Piceno resembles that of Lomello, while S Vittore, Chiusi, and S Claudio, Chienti, have inscribed cross plans with a central dome supported by columns. The two traditions are combined at Santa Maria di Portonovo (*c.* 1100; see ROMANESQUE, fig. 7) and Ancona Cathedral (ded. 1128), the finest Romanesque monument in the region.

Buildings in Tuscany were conservative and followed Early Christian models. An important feature of Florentine Romanesque is exemplified by the ancient Baptistery, the reconsecration of which in 1059 implies a thorough remodelling if not a total reconstruction: the striking use of coloured marble inlays to form lively geometrical patterns (see FLORENCE, fig. 13) is seen also at S Miniato al Monte, with an interior articulated by the rhythmic alternating system of columnar and quadrilobed piers, the latter rising to diaphragm arches (see FLORENCE, fig. 21). The first examples of Pisan Romanesque, S Piero in Grado (early 10th century; see PISA, §III, 2) and Pisa Cathedral (from 1063; see PISA, §III, 1(i) and figs 3, 4 and 5 and ROMANESQUE, fig. 6), also show strong Early Christian roots, but at the cathedral these are revived with almost triumphalistic overtones through a suggestive combination of structural and decorative elements: the nave with double aisles and the large, aisled transepts, the numerous columns, the oval crossing dome and the rich arcading of the exterior, enlivened by coloured marble inlay (lozenge motifs etc). Buildings inspired by Pisa Cathedral include S Paolo a Ripa d'Arno, Pisa; S Michele in Foro, Lucca, and the cathedral of S Martino, Lucca (see LUCCA, §3, and fig. 2); S Giovanni Fuorcivitas, Pistoia, and S Maria della Pieve, Arezzo, in Tuscany; and Cagliari Cathedral and S Gavino, Porto Torres, in Sardinia.

The churches of Umbria and northern Lazio show some clearly indigenous features as well as northern Romanesque and Lombard influences. In Umbria, screen façades are broken horizontally by cornices and sometimes enriched with geometrical designs and at least one rose window (e.g. Assisi Cathedral, S Pietro and the cathedral at Spoleto). Narni Cathedral has a depressed main arcade; S Silvestro, Bevagna, has quadrant barrel vaults over the aisles, ultimately of Burgundian origin; and, in Lazio, S Pietro, Tuscania, shows archaic features in its main arcade. In Rome, the churches of the 11th to the 13th centuries,

7. Ferrara Cathedral, from the south-west, dedicated 1135

often built over earlier structures, adhere closely to Early Christian basilican traditions; they include SS Quattro Coronati (1116), S Clemente (ded. ?1118/19; *see* ROME, §V, 17; for illustration *see* SCHOLA CANTORUM) and S Maria in Trastevere (rebuilt from 1141; *see* ROME, §V, 21(ii) and fig. 59). The Roman marble-working families created distinctive interior church furnishings and also cloisters, notably those of S Paolo fuori le Mura (*c.* 1193–1228) and S Giovanni in Laterano (1220–32; *see* COSMATI and STONE, colour pl. XII). Also characteristic of this period are the numerous brick bell-towers, rectangular in plan, the storeys marked by windows of one, two or three arches.

In southern Italy a few fundamental types underlie the regional styles. Abbot Desiderius's church at Montecassino (1066; destr. 1349; *see* MONTECASSINO, fig. 1), with three aisles, a slightly projecting transept and three aligned apses, is reflected in many buildings in southern Lazio (e.g. S Maria della Libera, Aquino), the Abruzzo (S Liberatore alla Maiella) and Campania (the cathedrals of Salerno, Amalfi, Ravello, Sessa Aurunca and Caserta Vecchia). The aisles continue directly into the apses at Sant'Angelo in Formis, also built by Desiderius (after 1072), and the church was the model for numerous buildings scattered over a wide area in Campania (e.g. San Pietro ad Montes Abbey, S Maria di Foroclaudio and the first phase of Carinola Cathedral) and the Abruzzo (S Pietro ad Oratorio, nr Capestrano, San Clemente al Vomano).

In Apulia, under Norman rule from the mid-11th century, the picture is more complex. The most outstanding structure, S Nicola (begun in 1087; remodelled after 1156; *see* BARI (ii), §2(i)), is distinguished by the straight eastern wall that screens the projection of the three apses, as well as by the galleries, the niches along the flanks of the nave and the sculptured portals (*see* BARI (ii), fig. 2) and windows with their protruding animals. These elements were adopted at the cathedrals of Bari, Bitonto (begun 1175) and Trani (from 1098), although in the last the screening eastern wall was never executed. Different solutions, sometimes inspired by both Montecassino and S Nicola, Bari, and often including elements of Byzantine architecture, appear in other Apulian buildings. Some churches have timber cupolas (e.g. S Benedetto, Conversano; Ognissanti, nr Valenzano); others have framed lozenge motifs like the Pisan churches (e.g. Tróia Cathedral).

In Campania, Apulia and Basilicata, a small group of churches with a semicircular ambulatory and radiating chapels shows French influence: Aversa Cathedral, Santa Trinità (begun 1135), Venosa, and Acerenza Cathedral (12th–13th century). In Calabria, one group, which includes the Cattolica, Stilo, is related to Byzantine traditions; the other includes churches with a staggered apse plan of Cluniac derivation, the earliest of which may be Santa Trinità (begun 1063; ruined), Mileto, with another example at Gerace Cathedral.

Architecture in Norman Sicily shows the influence of earlier Byzantine and Islamic traditions as well as southern Italian features. In Palermo, Byzantine influence is demonstrated at S Maria dell'Ammiraglio (begun *c.* 1143), with its inscribed, cross-in-square plan and central dome (*see* PALERMO, fig. 4), while the sharply defined forms and surfaces and small, stilted cupolas along the lengths of S Cataldo and S Giovanni degli Eremiti (c. 1142–8) were inspired by Arab buildings. In the Cappella Palatina (1131–40), the Latin, basilican plan is transformed by rich Byzantine mosaic decoration and by the painted Islamic *muqarnas* ceiling (see ISLAMIC ART, fig. 35). Cefalù Cathedral (founded 1131; see CEFALÙ, fig. 1), on the other hand, shows French Romanesque influence, and many of its features are reflected in Monreale Cathedral, the most eloquent symbol of the synthesis of the various cultural traditions that converge in Sicily (see MONREALE, fig. 1).

Among the most characteristic secular buildings from this period are the numerous tower houses of central Italy, notably those in Rome, Pisa, San Gimignano and Bologna (the Asinelli and Garisenda towers). In Sicily the palaces of the Norman period (the Zisa and Cuba palaces in Palermo) reflect Arab taste also in the luxuriant vegetation of their surrounding gardens.

(iii) Gothic, 13th–14th centuries. The appearance of Gothic in Italy was associated either with the spread of a religious order or with political events (see also GOTHIC, §II, 1). The first clearly Gothic structures were introduced by the Cistercians (see CISTERCIAN ORDER, §III, 1), who brought teams of monks skilled in building from France and a church type characterized by rational organization and austere detail. Cruciform plans with rectangular choirs flanked by smaller, rectangular chapels and barrel or rib vaults with emphatic transverse arches and façades with rose windows are all common features of early Cistercian churches at S Paolo alle Tre Fontane (founded by St Bernard in 1138–40), Rome, Fossanova (ded. 1208; see CISTERCIAN ORDER, fig. 1) and Casamari (ded. 1217) in Lazio, and San Galgano (begun by 1224; ruined), near Siena. Of the many Cistercian buildings in northern Italy, Chiaravalle Abbey (ded. 1220) near Milan, built in brick, is notable for its combination of French Gothic and Romanesque traditions.

More independent of northern European models, but in many ways linked with the Cistercian type, is the architecture of the mendicant orders (see FRANCISCAN ORDER, §III and DOMINICAN ORDER, §III). S Francesco, Assisi, begun in 1228, two years after St Francis's death, comprises two churches, one on top of the other: the lower, Romanesque in flavour, resembles a vast crypt, while the graceful, light-filled upper church is articulated by clustered pilasters and spanned by pointed rib vaults (see ASSISI, §II, 1). Other major Franciscan churches are Santa Croce (begun c. 1294; see FLORENCE, fig. 18), with a plan attributed to ARNOLFO DI CAMBIO, and the domed basilica of Il Santo (see PADUA, fig. 3). Among the most notable Dominican churches are S Maria Novella (begun c. 1275; see FLORENCE, fig. 20) and S Maria sopra Minerva, one of the very few Gothic buildings in Rome.

The first Gothic cathedrals were built in the second half of the 13th century in central Italy, by lay architects, on the initiative of individual cities. The architects who worked on Florence Cathedral, with its basilican nave and domed, centralized east end, included Arnolfo di Cambio and Francesco Talenti, while Giotto designed the lower section of the campanile (see FLORENCE, §IV, 1). Among the most important expressions of the new taste were

Orvieto Cathedral (begun 1290; see ORVIETO, figs 2 and 3), which has the most refined façade of Italian Gothic, and Siena Cathedral, with a west front that resembles that of Orvieto (see SIENA, fig. 6). Most other Italian buildings are more Romanesque than Gothic in appearance (e.g. Genoa Cathedral and S Petronio, Bologna), and only Milan Cathedral demonstrates a true taste for northern European Gothic (see MILAN, figs 12 and 13). Begun c. 1285–6 under Giangaleazzo Visconti, Duke of Milan, the project involved French and German architects as well as Italians. German influence was responsible for the strong Late Gothic character of the earliest parts, but the work continued until the 19th century, when the design of the façade was finally established.

A mature Gothic style can be seen in the great public buildings of this period, especially those of north-central Italy, for example the Palazzo del Comune, Piacenza, the Doges' Palace in Venice (see VENICE, fig. 23), the Palazzo Pubblico, Siena (see SIENA, fig. 9), the Palazzo Vecchio, Florence (see FLORENCE, §IV, 8), the Palazzo dei Consoli, GUBBIO, and the Palazzo dei Priori, Perugia. In southern Italy, the castles associated with Frederick II include CASTEL DEL MONTE, notable for its compositional rigour.

BIBLIOGRAPHY

GENERAL
C. Boito: *Architettura del medio evo in Italia* (Milan, 1880)
O. Mothes: *Die Baukunst des Mittelalters in Italien* (Jena, 1883)
C. Enlart: *Origines françaises de l'architecture gothique en Italie* (Paris, 1894)
A. Venturi: *Storia* (1901–40), i–iii
C. Enlart: *L'Art roman en Italie: L'Architecture et la décoration* (Paris, 1924)
C. Ricci: *L'architettura romanica in Italia* (Stockholm, 1925)
P. Toesca: *Il medioevo* (Turin, 1927)
G. C. Argan: *L'architettura italiana del duecento e trecento* (Florence, 1937, rev. Bari, 1978)
H. Thuemmler: 'Die Baukunst des 11. Jahrunderts in Italien', *Röm. Jb. Kstgesch.*, iii (1939), pp. 141–226
P. Toesca: *Il trecento* (Turin, 1951)
G. Chierici: *Il palazzo italiano dal secolo XI al secolo XIX*, i (Milan, 1952)
R. Wagner Rieger: *Die italienische Baukunst zu Beginn der Gotik*, 2 vols (Graz, 1956–7)
——: 'Zur Typologie italienischer Bettelordenskirchen', *Röm. Jb. Kstgesch.*, ii (1957–8), pp. 266–98
H. Decker: *Italia romanica: Die hohe Kunst der romanischen Epoche in Italien* (Vienna and Munich, 1958)
L. Fraccaro de Longhi: *L'architettura delle chiese cistercensi italiane* (Milan, 1958)
J. W. Franklin: *The Cathedrals of Italy* (London, 1958)
H. Decker: *Gotik in Italien* (Vienna and Munich, 1964)
J. White: *Art and Architecture in Italy, 1250–1400*, Pelican Hist. A. (Harmondsworth, 1966)
H. E. Kubach: *Architettura romanica* (Milan, 1972)
L. Grodecki: *Architettura gotica* (Milan, 1976)
E. Bririo, ed.: *Repertorio delle cattedrali gotiche*, ii (Milan, 1986)
G. Brucher: *Die sakrale Baukunst Italiens im 11. und 12. Jahrhundert* (Cologne, 1987)

NORTHERN ITALY
G. Merzario: *I maestri comacini*, i (Milan, 1893)
G. T. Rivoira: *Le origini dell'architettura lombarda e delle sue principali derivazioni nei paesi d'oltr'Alpe* (Milan, 1908)
A. Kingsley Porter: *Lombard Architecture*, 3 vols (New Haven, 1917)
R. Krautheimer: 'Lombardische Hallenkirchen', *Jb. Kstwiss.*, v (1928), pp. 176–91
P. Verzone: *L'architettura romanica del Vercellese* (Vercelli, 1934)
——: *L'architettura religiosa dell'alto medio evo nell'Italia settentrionale* (Milan, 1942)
E. Arslan: 'L'architettura dal 568 al mille', *Storia di Milano*, ii (Milan, 1954), pp. 499–608
——: 'L'architettura romanica milanese', *Storia di Milano*, iii (Milan, 1954), pp. 395–521

C. Ceschi: *Architettura romanica genovese* (Milan, 1954)

M. Magni: *Architettura romanica comasca* (Milan, 1960)

A. M. Romanini: *L'architettura gotica in Lombardia*, 2 vols (Milan, 1964)

P. Salvini: *Il duomo di Modena e il romanico nel modenese* (Modena, 1966)

A. C. Quintavalle: *Romanico padano: Civiltà d'Occidente* (Florence, 1969)

F. W. Deichmann: *Ravenna: Hauptstadt des spätantiken Abendlandes*, 2 vols (Wiesbaden, 1969–76)

E. Arslan: *Venezia gotica: L'architettura civile gotica veneziana* (Milan, 1970)

H. Dellwing: *Studien zur Baukunst der Bettelorden im Veneto: Die Gotik der monumentalen Gewölbebasiliken* (Munich, 1970)

A. C. Quintavalle: *La cattedrale di Parma e il romanico europeo* (Parma, 1974)

S. Chierici: *La Lombardia*, Italia Romanica, i (Milan, 1978)

S. Chierici and D. Citi: *Il Piemonte, la Val d'Aosta, la Liguria* (Milan, 1979)

S. Stocchi: *L'Emilia-Romagna* (Milan, 1984)

CENTRAL ITALY

M. Salmi: *L'architettura romanica in Toscana* (Milan and Rome, 1926)

I. C. Gavini: *Storia dell'architettura in Abruzzo*, 2 vols (Rome, 1927–8)

W. Paatz: *Werden und Wesen der Trecento Architektur in Toskana* (Burg, 1937)

U. Tarchi: *L'arte nell'Umbria e nella Sabina*, ii–iv (Milan, 1937–40)

R. Krautheimer and others: *Corpus basilicarum christianarum Romae*, 5 vols (Vatican City, 1937–80)

W. Kroenig: 'Hallenkirchen in Mittelitalien', *Röm. Jb. Kstgesch.*, ii (1938), pp. 1–141

R. Bonelli: *Il duomo di Orvieto e l'architettura italiana del duecento e trecento* (Città di Castello, 1952)

M. Moretti: *Architettura medievale in Abruzzo (dal VI al XVI secolo)* (Rome, 1969)

A. Trombetta: *Arte medievale nel Molise* (Campobasso, 1971)

J. Raspi Serra: *La Tuscia romana* (Milan, 1972)

R. Pardi: *Monumenti medievali umbri* (Perugia, 1975)

P. Sanpaolesi: *Il duomo di Pisa e l'architettura romanica toscana delle origini* (Pisa, 1975)

D. Negri: *Chiese romaniche in Toscana* (Pistoia, 1978)

A. Prandi and others: *L'Umbria* (Milan, 1979)

R. Krautheimer: *Rome, Profile of a City, 312–1308* (Princeton, 1981)

R. Bonelli, ed.: *Francesco d'Assisi: Chiese e conventi* (Milan, 1982)

I. Moretti and R. Stopani: *La Toscana* (Milan, 1982)

P. Rossi: *Civita Castellana e le chiese medievali del suo territorio* (Rome, 1986)

SOUTHERN ITALY

H. W. Schulz: *Denkmäler der Kunst des Mittelalters in Unteritalien*, i–iv (Dresden, 1860)

E. Bertaux: *L'Art dans l'Italie méridionale de la fin de l'empire romain à la conquête de Charles d'Anjou*, i–ii (Paris, 1903); rev. A. Prandi (Rome, 1978)

G. Agnello: *L'architettura sveva in Sicilia* (Rome, 1935)

S. Bottari: *Chiese basiliane della Sicilia e della Calabria* (Messina, 1939)

H. M. Schwarz: 'Die Baukunst Kalabriens und Siziliens im Zeitalter der Normannen', *Röm. Jb. Kstgesch.*, vi (1942–44), pp. 1–112

S. Bottari: *Monumenti svevi di Sicilia* (Milan, 1950)

R. Delogu: *L'architettura del medioevo in Sardegna* (Rome, 1953)

G. di Stefano: *Monumenti della Sicilia normanna* (Palermo, 1955, rev. Palermo, 1979)

A. Petrucci: *Cattedrali di Puglia* (Rome, 1960)

W. Kroenig: *Il duomo di Monreale e l'architettura normanna in Sicilia* (Palermo, 1966)

A. Venditti: *Architettura bizantina nell'Italia meridionale*, 2 vols (Naples, 1967)

C. Bozzoni: *Calabria normanna: Ricerche sull'architettura dei secoli undecimo e dodicesimo* (Rome, 1974)

P. Belli d'Elia: *Alle sorgenti del romanico: Puglia XI secolo* (Bari, 1975)

R. Pardi: *Monumenti medievali umbri* (Perugia, 1975)

G. Carbonara: *Iussu Desiderii: Montecassino e l'architettura campano-abruzzese nell'undicesimo secolo* (Rome, 1979)

C. A. Willemsen: *I castelli di Federico II nell'Italia meridionale* (Naples, 1979)

M. D'Onofrio and V. Pace: *La Campania* (Milan, 1981)

P. Belli d'Elia: *La Puglia* (Milan, 1986)

G. Cassata and others: *La Sicilia* (Milan, 1986)

C. Garzya Romano: *La Basilicata, la Calabria* (Milan, 1988)

MARIO D'ONOFRIO

3. RENAISSANCE AND MANNERISM, *c.* 1400–*c.* 1600.

(i) Early Renaissance, *c.* 1400–*c.* 1500. (ii) High Renaissance, *c.* 1500–*c.* 1520. (iii) Late Renaissance and Mannerism, *c.* 1520–*c.* 1600.

(i) Early Renaissance, c. *1400*–c. *1500.* The stylistic changes in Italian architecture in the 15th century involved the abandonment of the Gothic usages of the previous centuries in favour of a return to the architectural vocabulary and proportional system of Roman antiquity, interpreted in a way that met the social and religious requirements of a new epoch: the RENAISSANCE.

(a) Tuscany. (b) Lombardy. (c) The Marches and the Veneto. (d) Rome.

(a) Tuscany. Italian Renaissance architecture originated in Florence *c.* 1420, in the work of FILIPPO BRUNELLESCHI, alongside similar developments in painting and sculpture. Besides the adoption of the Classical system of proportions, consistently applied to plans and elevations, Brunelleschi's most influential innovations were the round-headed arch on columns and the employment of the Classical orders, Corinthian being his own preference. He reintroduced the hemispherical dome combined with pendentives, previously unknown in central Italy but employed in Byzantine architecture. Brunelleschi's use of grey *pietra serena* elements with white stucco walls became the characteristic colour scheme of Florentine Renaissance interiors. He employed these features in all his own works, beginning with the loggia of the Ospedale degli Innocenti (from 1419; *see* FLORENCE, fig. 1), in the longitudinal churches of S Lorenzo, with the Old Sacristy (1419–29), and Santo Spirito (from 1436; *see* RENAISSANCE, fig. 1), as well as the Pazzi Chapel (begun *c.* 1430), Santa Croce (*see* BRUNELLESCHI, FILIPPO, figs 5 and 6). They provided the model for the rest of the century in Florence: clear, uncluttered lines, systematic proportions and use of *all'antica* vocabulary.

Although Brunelleschi employed individual Classical motifs, he did not 'revive' Classical architecture: his most frequent sources were such Tuscan Romanesque buildings as the Florentine Baptistery (*see* FLORENCE, fig. 13). The Classical revival was effected by the other major innovator of the century, LEON BATTISTA ALBERTI, who applied his theoretical knowledge of ancient Roman architecture to his own projects, adapting Classical vocabulary for contemporary building types. Between them Brunelleschi and Alberti created the early Renaissance style in architecture, which spread throughout Italy during the century. Brunelleschi's influence was due principally to his achievement in erecting the dome of Florence Cathedral, designed in 1418 (*see* FLORENCE, fig. 12). His resolution of the problem of roofing over the largest space since antiquity, for which he not only devised the double-shell dome but also a system for its erection without centering, was Brunelleschi's most important technical invention (*see* BRUNELLESCHI, FILIPPO, fig. 1). Forced to build it with a Gothic curve, since there was no possibility of external buttressing, Brunelleschi exploited this for the visual effect of red brick cells with white stone ribs.

In Brunelleschi's last works, Santo Spirito and the barely started S Maria degli Angeli (1434; abandoned on his death), the planarity of his earlier works was replaced by a greater plasticity of forms, with the use of engaged columns instead of pilasters, and semicircular chapels. The major innovation at S Maria degli Angeli was the employment of a circular plan, influenced by the Temple of Minerva Medica, Rome. The centrally planned church became a significant development of the Renaissance, evolving throughout the 15th century and reaching maturity in the 16th. Alberti described the circle as the perfect shape in Nature and its derivations—rectangular and polygonal—as ideal for the 'temple' or church (*De re aedificatoria* IV). Alberti himself employed the Greek-cross plan, at S Sebastiano (from 1460; *see* §(b) below), Mantua, possibly derived from such Early Christian tombs as that of Galla Placidia, Ravenna. The basilican type was, however, most frequently employed for liturgical reasons.

Florentine palace design was transformed (*see* FLORENCE, §I, 3; *see also* PALAZZO), producing buildings with a symmetrical structure, the façades divided into rectangular bays, three storeys high, each storey differentiated slightly—the *piano nobile* being the most splendid—crowned with a Classical cornice. The central, rectangular, arcaded courtyard became an essential feature. MICHELOZZO DI BARTOLOMEO designed the earliest, the Palazzo Medici (1444–60; now Palazzo Medici-Riccardi; for illustration *see* PALAZZO). Its façade is graduated from rusticated, rock-faced blocks on the ground floor, via a sharply channelled but smooth-faced treatment on the *piano nobile* to completely smooth ashlar on the top floor. The upper two storeys have regularly disposed, round-headed, biforate windows with a central colonette. The basic plan was followed by all other palace builders in Florence and was exported elsewhere, for example Urbino and Ferrara. Florentine influence is also apparent in Giuliano da Maiano's Palazzo Cuomo (begun 1466; *see* MAIANO, (1)) in Naples. Giuliano was the greatest exponent of Florentine taste in Naples. In Florence variations were confined to exteriors, which could be rusticated (e.g. Palazzo Gondi, 1490s; Palazzo Strozzi, begun 1489; see fig. 8) or covered with *intonaco* (e.g. Palazzo Pazzi-Quaratesi, 1460s), perhaps with *sgraffito* decoration.

Only Alberti's Palazzo Rucellai (begun *c.* 1453; *see* ALBERTI, LEON BATTISTA, fig. 2) differed significantly. Its façade has three orders of pilasters, each with its own entablature, applied decoratively, not structurally. In accordance with Alberti's theoretical beliefs, the windows, although round-headed, have a lintel below the arch, supported by the central colonette. It was not emulated in Florence, and its successors are found outside Florence, at Pienza and Rome (*see* §(d) below). In the 15th century such palaces were for residence only. Rooms ran in a single file around the courtyard and usually had no specific purpose, except for the room used by the head of the household. A contemporary description of the Palazzo Medici records a splendidly decorated interior with wooden panelling articulated by *all'antica* pilasters and gilding, contrasting with the sober exterior. Only the chapel, frescoed (1459–61) by Benozzo Gozzoli, remains to give some indication of its original appearance.

Models were produced for the major projects (*see* ARCHITECTURAL MODEL), and they were usually of wood (e.g. Giuliano da Sangallo's for the Palazzo Strozzi; now in Florence, Pal. Strozzi; *see* SANGALLO, (1)). However,

8. Benedetto da Maiano, Giuliano da Sangallo and Cronaca: Palazzo Strozzi, Florence, begun 1489

Brunelleschi's model for the dome of Florence Cathedral used full-sized bricks. Most building workers were members of the Arte di Maestri del Legname e delle Pietra (Woodworkers' and Stonemasons' Guild) except for carpenters and metalworkers who had separate guilds.

As well as being a working architect, Alberti also wrote treatises on numerous subjects, including the first architectural treatise since antiquity, *De re aedificatoria* (Florence, 1485), modelled on Vitruvius and his own studies of Roman ruins. These studies set a pattern for later generations of architects (*see* TREATISE, §I). He first employed the temple front for the upper storey of the façade (*c.* 1458–70) of S Maria Novella (*see* FLORENCE, fig. 20), partially erected in the 14th century. Alberti designed the upper storey to harmonize with the lower by retaining the coloured marbles and applied a tetrastyle façade, with triangular pediment carried on pilasters, to the upper storey, the width only of the nave. He employed large volutes to link together the wide lower storey and narrow upper storey, a final resolution to the problem.

Alberti's ideas were also influential in the planning of PIENZA, the birthplace of Pius II, which was a rare example of 15th-century urban planning (*see* URBAN PLANNING, §II). Built between 1459 and 1464, the principal religious and government buildings are organized symmetrically around the trapezoid-shaped piazza, and some 40 buildings were either erected or refurbished. The cathedral is the main focus, opposite the Palazzo Comunale, with the Palazzo Piccolomini and the Episcopal Palace on either side. The architect Bernardo Rossellino (*see* ROSSELLINO,

(1), §2) based the pilastered façade of the Palazzo Piccolomini on that of the Palazzo Rucellai. It follows the Florentine palace plan, set around a central courtyard. The most novel feature is the three-storey loggias at the rear overlooking the valley towards Monte Amiata, bringing together an urban domestic building and open countryside, for the aesthetic pleasure of the view. Pius was much concerned with the comfort of the interior, ordering that rooms be high, with polished brick floors and fireplaces. Cisterns to collect water for distribution throughout the palace were installed on the roof. The internal layout of Pienza Cathedral was also dictated by Pius, who wished to emulate the hall churches he had admired in Austria. The façade, however, is *all'antica*, having a triumphal arch motif.

(b) Lombardy. Alberti's influence was above all outside Florence. His friendship with such important patrons as Pope Nicholas V, Lionello d'Este, Marchese of Ferrara (*see* ESTE (i), (3)), and Federigo da Montefeltro, Count (later Duke) of Urbino (*see* MONTEFELTRO, (1)), influenced their architectural projects. Throughout the 15th century the Renaissance style was gradually disseminated, especially in the princely states where rulers were anxious to show themselves as cultured patrons. The new style was usually adapted piecemeal into the regional style. Alberti's most influential designs were in Mantua, for the churches of S Sebastiano (begun 1460) and S Andrea (begun 1472), built under the patronage of the 2nd Marchese, Ludovico II Gonzaga (*see* ALBERTI, LEON BATTISTA, figs 4–8). In addition to the innovation of the Greek-cross plan for S Sebastiano, Alberti's design for the basilican church of S Andrea, begun only in the year of his death, was also innovative and influential. This church is aisleless with side chapels that are alternately large, with a high arched entrance, and small, with a rectangular entrance. The walls support the first large-scale barrel vault of the Renaissance, derived from the Roman baths and the Basilica of Maxentius, again demonstrating Alberti's skill in adapting antique forms to a modern building type. Subordinate spaces are organic continuations of the main space. The façade combines the Classical temple front, of triangular pediment on giant pilasters, and the triumphal arch.

Although the Gothic cathedrals of Milan and Pavia were still under construction, Duke Francesco Sforza of Milan (*see* SFORZA, (1)), who had received a humanist education and was allied with Florence, was anxious to introduce the new style into his capital. To that end he brought FILARETE to work for him. Filarete's major project was the Ospedale Maggiore (begun 1465; continued and altered by Giovanni Antonio Amadeo), the original appearance of which is recorded only in Filarete's treatise, the *Trattato di architettura* (1461–4), which describes the ideal city of Sforzinda, and was dedicated to the Duke. Filarete's advocacy of the centrally planned form proved important in the development of architectural theory in Milan. Michelozzo had been employed by the Medici in Milan to design a palace to serve as the headquarters of their bank, again known only from a Filarete drawing. His design for the Portinari Chapel (before 1468) of S Eustorgio reveals his sensitivity to the

Milanese love of decoration, which he combined with Florentine emphasis of the wall plane. This chapel was one of the most important examples of the introduction of Florentine ideas into Milan.

However, it was only the arrival (*c.* 1480) of Donato Bramante that brought Milanese architecture up to date. Duke Ludovico Sforza immediately employed Bramante, initially at S Maria presso S Satiro (1482–6) and in rebuilding the choir (1492; *see* MILAN, fig. 3) of the newly completed S Maria delle Grazie. Amadeo and Dolcebuono are also documented there. Bramante used his painter's knowledge of *trompe l'oeil* to design the false choir at S Maria presso S Satiro. It is only 500 mm deep but gives the illusion of an imposing barrel-vaulted structure, three bays deep (*see* BRAMANTE, DONATO, fig. 1). In S Maria delle Grazie (*see* BRAMANTE, DONATO, §I, 2(ii)(b) and fig. 2), Bramante was charged with turning the eastern end into a Sforza mausoleum. He created a centrally planned addition to the nave, with a square crossing crowned by a hemispherical dome, extending the choir itself and terminating the choir and transepts with apses. The overall concept is one of grandeur, enhanced by Bramante's manipulation of light, which floods the choir, separating it from the dark Gothic nave, producing a dramatic climax.

With Leonardo da Vinci, who was in Milan *c.* 1482–99 (*see* LEONARDO DA VINCI, §I, 2), Bramante explored the possibilities of central planning, which was to be of importance in his plans for St Peter's and which influenced his immediate followers. In the cloisters (1497) of S Ambrogio, Milan, Bramante employed three Classical orders for the first time, applying a different one to each of the three cloisters, which anticipates his works in Rome.

(c) The Marches and the Veneto. In Urbino, Federigo da Montefeltro appointed Luciano Laurana, Ingegniere et Capo di Tutti li Maestri (1468), to rebuild and extend his medieval palace, continuing the work of Maso di Bartolomeo (*see* URBINO, §4). The palace links together two separate buildings in an irregular plan and has two main façades. Federigo's wish to employ a Florentine architect indicates a knowledge of and desire to copy the Florentine palace. The principal façade, of three storeys, is symmetrically organized, with three regular doorways and evenly spaced windows on the *piano nobile*. The Palazzo Ducale at Urbino became the model for a ruler's palace. It incorporates public and private rooms, and the public reception rooms are reached by the monumental staircase from the courtyard (begun *c.* 1466; for illustration *see* LAURANA, LUCIANO), where the encircling inscription would remind visitors of Federigo's achievements. The courtyard, of the Palazzo Medici type, is here treated with greater sophistication, employing piers at the corners, giving an impression of greater support. The private rooms are located behind a second façade, a three-tiered loggia flanked by towers, overlooking the valley beyond, as at the Palazzo Piccolomini in Pienza.

The Renaissance style became fashionable in Venice in the 1480s, with the arrival of Pietro Lombardo (*see* LOMBARDO, (1)) and Mauro Codussi from Lombardy. Neither Michelozzo, who designed a library, nor Filarete, employed by the Duke of Milan to erect a palace there, had made any impact on the city's architecture. The

9. Antonio Gambello and Mauro Codussi: façade of S Zaccaria, Venice, 1458–90

Arsenal Gateway (*c*. 1451) was based on the Arch of the Sergii (*c*. 29–28 BC) at Pola (now Pula, Croatia) but had no immediate descendants. Codussi's S Michele in Isola (1469–77; *see* CODUSSI, MAURO, fig. 1) is the clearest expression of the new style, which is also seen in the Renaissance forms and unified design of the façade of S Zaccaria (see fig. 9). The Byzantine architecture of S Marco continued to dominate church architecture. This is most apparent in the prevalence of the centrally planned church with multiple domes, of which Codussi's S Maria Formosa (begun 1492) and S Giovanni Crisostomo (begun 1497) are examples. Although these both have Greek-cross plans they do have a principal orientation. Codussi employed the Brunelleschian scheme of column or pilaster plus arch and his own system of proportions.

Florence provided the model for changes to Venetian palaces, adapted to the requirements of the canal city. Irregular façades overlooking the canals were made symmetrical around the ground-floor entrance hall. Windows were confined to the front and rear façades, and in order to maximize light the *salone* on the *piano nobile* extended the full depth of the building, above the entrance, with large, round-headed windows grouped together in the centre, usually in threes as in the Palazzo Loredan (now Palazzo Vendramin-Calergi; begun *c*. 1502; *see* CODUSSI, MAURO, fig. 2). Codussi here employed a Classical order of engaged columns with entablature, radically different from the Gothic features of the earlier part of the century. Unlike Florentine palaces, those in Venice were occupied

by several households and might also be used as business premises.

(d) Rome. The state of Rome had greatly deteriorated during the Avignon residence of the popes (1309–73). On their return to Rome, successive popes found their funds deployed entirely on restoring the principal churches. NICHOLAS V, with Alberti and Rossellino as his architectural advisers, had ambitious plans for urban renewal but these were only effected in the 1480s by Sixtus IV (*see* ROME, §II, 3). Nicholas's principal contribution was the restoration of the ancient walls and the rebuilding of the choir of Old St Peter's (destr.; *see* ROME, §V, 14(i)(a)). The latter, designed by Rossellino, was the first work of Renaissance architecture in Rome, together with the Benediction Loggia (destr.) erected in front of the basilica by Pius II. The loggia employed a system of piers articulated by engaged columns on pedestals, adapted from the Colosseum. The proximity of the ancient sites was of major importance to the development of Roman Renaissance architecture. Although predominantly designed by such Tuscans as JACOPO DA PIETRASANTA, the architect of S Agostino (1479–83), a new monumentality distinguished Roman church interiors. Rather than a column and arch system, the arcade is borne by piers, with engaged columns, carrying groin vaulting, as in S Maria del Popolo (1472–7). By contrast, façades, which were of travertine stone, were planar, employing pilasters as decoration.

Few 15th-century Roman palaces survive. The Palazzo di S Giorgio (*c*. 1485–*c*. 1511; now Palazzo della Cancelleria; *see* ROME, §V, 23(i)), built for Cardinal Raffaele Riario, conforms to the Florentine palace type, with a central courtyard after the Urbino model (see fig. 10) while the façade is inspired by the Palazzo Rucellai. The travertine revetment of the main façade (completed by 1495) has applied pilaster orders. The round-headed windows set in rectangular frames derive from the Porta dei Borsari

10. Palazzo della Cancelleria, Rome, courtyard, *c*. 1485–*c*. 1511

11. Palazzo Venezia, Rome, courtyard, c. 1455–71

(1st century; *see* VERONA, fig. 1). The large palace incorporated shops for rent into its ground-floor, an antique device, which was used here for the first time in the Renaissance. The more common Roman palace type, with a stuccoed façade and stone cross-mullioned windows, prevailed to the end of the century, exemplified by the Palazzo S Marco (now Palazzo Venezia) built by Cardinal Pietro Barbo from 1455, adjoining his titular church. It employs individual features based on antique prototypes, including the coffered, barrel-vaulted entrance hall and the two-storey arcades of the incomplete courtyard (see fig. 11) with rectangular piers and engaged columns, Tuscan below—on high pedestals, supporting an entablature that breaks forwards over them—and Corinthian above; features that later became popular (*see* ORDERS, ARCHITECTURAL, §I, 2(iii)(a)).

By the end of the 15th century architects had become more informed about the ancient ruins, and a visit to Rome to study them was essential. Giuliano da Sangallo's numerous drawings of antiquities reveal the depth of such studies, and this knowledge was applied in the treatment of architectural forms, although ancient Roman techniques were revived only in the early 16th century.

(ii) High Renaissance, c. 1500–c. 1520. In the early 16th century a new style emerged, and Rome replaced Florence as the centre where major innovations occurred; their influence would be dominant for centuries. The papacy, now firmly re-established and with many building and decorative schemes in mind to restore Rome to its ancient splendour, drew artists from all over Italy. Bramante, who arrived *c.* 1500, was responsible for the development of the new architectural style.

Bramante studied the ancient remains at first hand, and such studies inform his architecture, from his first major Roman commission, the cloister (1500–04) of S Maria della Pace, for Cardinal Oliviero Carafa (*see* CARAFA, (1)). This developed further his concern, evinced in the S Ambrogio cloisters, with applying the orders in combination, here in a single structure. The arcade is carried on Doric piers with Ionic pilasters carrying the entablature; above, Composite piers alternate with Corinthian columns to support the upper entablature. Bramante was commissioned *c.* 1502 to erect a church on the supposed site of St Peter's martyrdom, at S Pietro in Montorio, the Tempietto (*see* BRAMANTE, DONATO, fig. 4). The first wholly circular building of the Renaissance, the Tempietto was highly influential; Bramante's contemporaries acknowledged his achievement in the use of the Classical vocabulary, and the Tempietto was illustrated by SEBASTIANO SERLIO in his treatise (Book III) among the examples of Classical works. It is this correct use of antique motifs that categorizes High Renaissance architecture. But even as Bramante achieved this synthesis of the Classical vocabulary, the need to adapt and invent imposed by the requirements of Christian architecture points towards the failure of those rules.

Despite its novelty, it was not the Tempietto but the project to rebuild St Peter's that was the most influential in Rome. This was initiated by Julius II (*see* ROVERE, DELLA (i), (2)), whose policies continued those of Sixtus IV, through the construction of new thoroughfares and the aggrandizement of Rome's appearance through new buildings (*see* ROME, §II, 3). The foundation stone of St Peter's was laid in 1506 (*see* ROME, §V, 14(ii)(a)). Bramante designed a centralized plan, a cross inscribed in a square, the central dome borne on four massive crossing piers, articulated by a giant order, with subsidiary chapels around the crossing and corner towers. The crossing piers and barrel vaulting of one arm were erected but, despite the appointment of numerous successors after Bramante's death, including Raphael and Giuliano da Sangallo, little progress was made before the appointment in 1546 of Michelangelo (*see* MICHELANGELO, §I, 4) as Architetto della Fabbrica. He revived Bramante's Greek-cross plan, greatly strengthening and enlarging the crossing piers and simplifying the organization of the interior. He completed the coffered barrel vaults around the crossing, but the liturgical requirement of a nave led to changes to his plans after his death. Both interior and exterior are articulated by a giant Corinthian order, carrying an entablature that encircles and binds together the whole. Michelangelo left a wooden model (1558–61) for a double-shell, hemispherical dome, subsequently altered to a pointed profile by GIACOMO DELLA PORTA in the 1580s.

The interest in centrally planned churches led to the erection of a number of them in the early 16th century, often on the outskirts of provincial towns, for example

Cola da Caprarola's S Maria della Consolazione (from 1508; see fig. 12), Todi, and Antonio da Sangallo (i)'s Madonna di S Biagio (begun 1518; for illustration *see* SANGALLO, (2)), Montepulciano, both of which were developed from the Greek cross. The former has a square plan with huge apses projecting from each side, emphasizing its space-moulding appearance; the latter a Greek cross with barrel-vaulted arms and corner towers.

Roman palaces assumed an increased monumentality, giving the city a more impressive aspect, beginning with Bramante's Palazzo Caprini (House of Raphael; *c.* 1510; destr.; *see* BRAMANTE, DONATO, fig. 6). The two-storey façade was divided horizontally into a commercial lower storey, with shops inserted into arched openings, the wall surfaces heavily rusticated, and a *piano nobile* with an engaged Doric order. The substitution of coupled half-columns for pilasters to articulate the wall gives a greater plasticity to the surfaces. Its influence was widespread, and it became the model for aristocratic palaces in Rome, Venice, Verona, Genoa and Bologna.

Contemporaneously, however, Antonio da Sangallo (ii) (*see* SANGALLO, (4)) established a more sober palace style with stuccoed façades, and stone used only for quoins and aedicular windows, as in his Palazzo Farnese (begun 1514; completed by Michelangelo after 1545; *see* ROME, §V, 25 and PALACE, fig. 1). Michelangelo designed the more sculpturesque appearance of the upper storey of the courtyard, employing overlapping pilasters to create a constant advance and recession. Ground-floor shops were abandoned, as being inappropriate for the owner's status.

12. Cola da Caprarola: S Maria della Consolazione, Todi, begun 1508; perhaps designed by Bramante

A new architectural type that was developed in the 16th century was the villa suburbana, usually located just outside the city wall, where cardinals and nobles retired for a day's leisure (*see* VILLA, §II). The earliest was a villa (1508–11; now the Villa Farnesina) in Rome, designed by BALDASSARE PERUZZI for Agostino Chigi (i) (*see* CHIGI, (1)). It was relatively simple, a U-shape with open loggia in the central bay, frescoed by Raphael and his workshop with mythological scenes, the façade having applied pilasters enlivened by grisaille decoration (destr.). Raphael's design for the Villa Madama (from 1518; with Antonio da Sangallo (i)) for Cardinal Giulio de' Medici (later Pope Clement VII; *see* MEDICI, DE', (9)), on the side of Monte Mario, deliberately drew on Classical texts describing ancient villas, following Vitruvius on the disposal of rooms. He exploited the hillside site to include hidden grottoes and a nymphaeum, and a Roman theatre was planned at the top of the slope. The garden loggia (*see* RAPHAEL, fig. 9), with a domed central bay opening from the circular courtyard, was decorated by Giulio Romano with frescoes and stuccowork based on those recently discovered in the Domus Aurea of Nero. Such features were exploited throughout the century, as in the Villa Giulia (from 1552) for Pope Julius II in Rome, by JACOPO VIGNOLA, Vasari and Bartolomeo Ammanati, and Vignola's Villa Farnese (from 1552) at Caprarola (*see* CAPRAROLA, VILLA FARNESE), a combination of palace and villa. Gardens (*see* GARDEN, §VIII, (4)(i)) were a vital feature of the villa suburbana, with hidden areas, unexpected fountains and nymphaea, which the improved hydraulic technology permitted, as in the later garden of fountains (1567–8) at the Villa d'Este, Tivoli (*see* TIVOLI, §3) by PIRRO LIGORIO.

Roman developments of the early 16th century were disseminated through Italy by the followers of Bramante and Raphael, especially after the Sack of Rome (1527), which led to the dispersal of artists from the city. Giulio Romano became court artist at Mantua, where he designed the Mannerist Palazzo del Te, the villa suburbana on the outskirts of the city, each façade of the single-storey building and its courtyard being different (*see* GIULIO ROMANO). The classical vocabulary has been treated with wit and imagination, structural members apparently collapsing and entablatures crumbling (*see* ORDERS, ARCHITECTURAL, fig. 6). The villa's garden loggia depends heavily on that of the Villa Madama.

In the later 16th century Andrea Palladio developed a new, highly influential villa style. The country villa was well known from antiquity, and both Vitruvius' and Pliny the younger's descriptions were examined for ideas in the Renaissance. The Medici in 15th-century Florence had made retreat to the country villa fashionable, but only at the end of the century was the fortified appearance of the earlier villas abandoned for the more refined appearance of the villa (1485–94) at Poggio a Caiano (*see* POGGIO A CAIANO, VILLA MEDICI) by Giuliano da Sangallo, where a temple front was applied for the first time in such a context. Palladio's villas were on extensive properties, frequently working farms, and his designs brought the farm buildings into the fabric of the building, although treated in such a way that their working function is entirely hidden. Palladio set out all his designs in Book II of his treatise *I quattro libri* (1570). The buildings were symmetrically organized around a central axis, their proportions related to musical harmonies. The façade invariably incorporated an adaptation of the Classical temple portico, as in his most influential villas, the Villa Barbaro (completed by 1558; *see* MASER, VILLA BARBARO, with illustration) and the Villa Rotonda, or Villa Capra (begun *c.* 1565/6; *see* PALLADIO, ANDREA, fig. 6 and VICENZA, §2).

(iii) Late Renaissance and Mannerism, c. *1520–*c. *1600.* The increased plasticity and restless advance and recession of planes became more marked throughout the century. Bramante's influence continued after his death (1514), but by Raphael's death in 1520 the newly established rules were already breaking down, leading to the Mannerist style in which the Classical vocabulary is employed in non-canonical ways (*see* MANNERISM). The practitioners were fully versed in the 'correct' usage but deliberately flouted the rules. Thus in the Palazzo Branconio dell'Aquila (1519; destr.), Rome, by RAPHAEL the half-columns of the ground-floor appeared to support the upper storeys, but had only a niche above them, and the order on the *piano nobile* is confined to the aediculae around the windows. Above the windows an attic storey had an exuberant stucco decoration. The curved façade of the Palazzo Massimo alle Colonne (1532–5), by Baldassare Peruzzi, also employs an order only on the ground-floor, in the loggia that supports the solid superstructure of rusticated wall.

(a) Florence. Florentine architecture of the 1520s and 1530s was heavily influenced by the work of Michelangelo, who developed his own Mannerist style, also based on a thorough grounding in Classical forms. In the New Sacristy (1519–34), S Lorenzo (*see* FLORENCE, §IV, 5), he retained the cube and dome of Brunelleschi's Old Sacristy, with stucco walls and *pietra serena* elements, but transformed it into a tightly compressed organization of architectural and sculptural forms. He raised the height of the chapel by inserting an attic, with blind, pedimented windows between cube and dome, and inserted wholly innovative wedge-shaped windows into the lunettes above. Tabernacles are squeezed above the doors in the side bays, as though there were insufficient space for them. The broken bases of their pediments became a much more elaborated feature during the century.

In the vestibule to the Biblioteca Laurenziana (begun *c.* 1524; *see* MICHELANGELO, §I, 4), the library attached to the church of S Lorenzo, Michelangelo's inventions were taken further. Because the entrance to the vestibule is at a lower level than that into the library, he treated the lower part of the wall as a basement, dividing it into alternating bays of wall surface and paired volutes. In the Laurenziana Michelangelo's apparently wayward treatment of Classical forms was to an extent necessitated because it was constructed above already extant buildings. However, his solutions were adopted as innovative features by such followers as Giorgio Vasari (*see* VASARI, (1)) in his designs for the Palazzo degli Uffizi (1559–74; *see* FLORENCE, §IV, 10) and BARTOLOMEO AMMANATI, who enlarged and modernized (1560–77) the Palazzo Pitti (*see* FLORENCE, §IV, 9(i)) and executed the staircase in the Laurenziana

vestibule. The influence of S Lorenzo is also apparent in GALEAZZO ALESSI's work at S Maria presso S Celso, Milan, from 1565.

(b) Rome. One of the major architectural projects in Rome was the rebuilding of the Capitoline Hill (after 1546), the heart of secular Roman government, which was then a ruin. Michelangelo clothed the 15th-century Palazzo dei Conservatori with a new façade, balanced by an identical, new building facing it, the Palazzo Nuovo, creating a wedge-shaped piazza (as at Pienza), approached by the ramped stairway up the hill (*see* MICHELANGELO, fig. 11). The Palazzo del Senatore at the head was also given a new façade, with a monumental staircase providing an entrance at *piano nobile* level. Michelangelo employed a giant Corinthian order of pilasters to unify the three structures. In the centre of the oval piazza that he laid out, Michelangelo placed the ancient statue of *Marcus Aurelius*, mounted on an oval pedestal, which he himself had designed. Other architects involved in the scheme were GUIDETTO GUIDETTI and GIACOMO DELLA PORTA. Michelangelo's most striking Mannerist work in Rome, however, was the Porta Pia (1561–4; see fig. 13); its carefully worked out design incorporates a mixture of eccentric elements, broken pediments, displaced sections of the orders, overlapping planes and fantastic ornamental details.

Church building in Rome had suffered a hiatus following the 1527 sack and 1530 flood, which devastated the city. From the mid-century, however, in a mood of penitence, many churches were rebuilt and new orders were founded, requiring new churches. Most important were the Jesuits, for whom Il Gesù was built by JACOPO VIGNOLA (*see* ROME, §V, 16), and the Oratorians, who built S Maria in

13. Michelangelo: Porta Pia, Rome, 1561–4

Vallicella (from 1575), to the designs of Martino Longhi (i). Il Gesù (1568–73), financed by Cardinal Alessandro Farnese, is a descendant of S Andrea, Mantua, having no aisles, but side chapels in the massive walls, which support the barrel vault of the nave. The nave is unusually wide, to enable the maximum numbers of people to see and hear the priest, of paramount importance for Counter-Reformation masses. The transepts are wide but shallow, barely protruding beyond the line of the exterior wall. The dome is supported by a very high drum, enhancing its visibility from the surrounding cramped streets. Il Gesù became one of the 16th century's most influential buildings, for as the Jesuits travelled the world they modelled churches on it everywhere. Vignola also revived the centrally planned church in later 16th-century Rome, at S Andrea (1561) in Via Flaminia and S Anna dei Palafrenieri, both small in scale but introducing the oval plan, which was influential for the development of the Baroque, in that it appeared to reconcile centrality with directionality.

Church façades became more monumental, projecting a powerful image of the Church Triumphant. Typically they were symmetrically balanced around a massive portal, building up from quieter outer bays, with paired pilasters at the corners, to paired pilasters and engaged columns framing the massive central portal where the entablature projects forwards and is intersected by a monumental pediment. Above, the bays culminate in a central tabernacle. Side bays contain niches, so that little of the wall surface remains and a constant movement backwards and forwards is maintained without rest. Volutes link upper and lower elements, now with an increased monumentality and plasticity. This begins with Giacomo della Porta's design for the Gesù façade (completed 1577), reaching fruition only at the end of the century with that of S Susanna (1597–1603) by CARLO MADERNO, which looks forward to the Baroque, in the way that Mannerist tension and ambiguity are resolved by the substitution of steadily cumulative plasticity directed towards the centre.

(c) The Veneto. A more formal Roman Renaissance style was transmitted to Venice by Jacopo Sansovino who fled there in 1527, as did SEBASTIANO SERLIO. In 1529 Sansovino was appointed *proto* to the procurators of S Marco, with responsibility for the architecture of the Piazza di S Marco. Here he designed the Libreria Marciana (1537; now the Biblioteca Nazionale Marciana; *see* VENICE, §IV, 7(i)) in the Roman Renaissance style, the Zecca (public mint; 1535–7) and the three-bay loggetta (c. 1537–42; *see* SANSOVINO, JACOPO, fig. 3) at the foot of the campanile. The two-storey arcades of the library façade, with a Doric order of engaged columns, point to the ancient Theatre of Marcellus, Rome, as source, but the balconies of each storey and the swags of the upper cornice are typically Venetian. The whole of the piazza was given a similar treatment, turning it into a spectacular atrium for the basilica. As with the Capitoline Hill, the regularization of façades of buildings with disparate functions gives a unified appearance to an important urban space.

The Zecca, needing to appear strong and impregnable, has a rusticated façade, although the rustication is treated in a more playful manner than formerly and covers even the Doric half-columns of the *piano nobile* in the form of

banding (a feature found also at the Palazzo del Tè, Mantua). The probable source was the Porta Maggiore, Rome, which was characteristic of the Mannerist phase of later Imperial architecture. Sansovino also adapted the Classical vocabulary for his palace façades, combining monumentality and correct use of the orders with the requirements of the Venetian palace for large windows and canal entrance, as in the Palazzo Corner della Cà Grande (begun 1545), ultimately derived from Bramante's Palazzo Caprini, Rome.

In his design for the monastic church of S Francesco della Vigna (from 1534), however, Sansovino relied more on the architecture of his native Tuscany, deriving its aisleless, barrel-vaulted interior, with side chapels, from S Salvatore al Monte (1490–1504) by CRONACA. The façade (1562–c. 1570; *see* fig. 14) was built by Palladio, who succeeded Sansovino in 1570 as municipal architect. It continues the tradition of adapting the Classical temple façade, into which he introduced the novel feature of a thermal window. In his own church interiors for S Giorgio Maggiore (from 1566; *see* PALLADIO, ANDREA, §I, 1(iii)) and Il Redentore (begun 1576; *see* PALLADIO, ANDREA, fig. 7), both in Venice, Palladio depended on Bramante's moulded architecture and the Roman example. Nevertheless, Palladio believed, like Michelangelo, that just as Christianity was superior to pagan religions, so Christian churches should surpass ancient temples.

The sack of Rome also caused MICHELE SANMICHELI to return to his native Verona, where he introduced the Roman style, both antique and contemporary. The Venetian government put him in charge of its fortifications (*see* VERONA, §1), but his best-known works are the pilgrimage church of the Madonna di Campagna (1559), San Michele Extra, near Verona, and the city gates of Verona, although he also designed palaces. The Madonna di Campagna derives in part from Bramante's Tempietto, having a domed rotunda surrounded externally by a Doric colonnade, but projecting above it into a high drum supporting a Pantheon-type dome, with hemispherical interior and saucer-shaped exterior. It also follows Antonio da Sangallo (ii)'s S Maria di Monte d'Oro (begun 1523), near Montefiascone. The influence of Bramante is also apparent in Sanmicheli's palace designs, including the Palazzo Pompei (previously Lavezola; ?1530s) based on the Palazzo Caprini. Sanmicheli's city gates, the Porta Nuova (1535–40; *see* CITY GATE, fig. 3) and Porta Palio (c. 1547), both incorporate a triumphal arch motif into a rusticated surface.

Outside Rome, the major innovations of the later 16th century were those of Palladio. While his urban palaces derive largely from the Roman High Renaissance style, he nevertheless introduced novel features: in the loggias of Palazzo Chiericati (from 1550), Vicenza, for example, the façade unexpectedly consists of a central bay with a ground-floor loggia and solid *piano nobile* and two-tiered loggias on either side (*see* PALLADIO, ANDREA, fig. 2). It presents the appearance, therefore, less of a private residence than of a public square based on the Roman forum. Of the later 16th-century architects, Palladio had the greatest influence.

14. Andrea Palladio: façade of S Francesco della Vigna, Venice, 1562–*c.* 1570

BIBLIOGRAPHY

Portoghesi
A. Venturi: *Storia* (1901–40)
J. Durm: *Die Baukunst der Renaissance* (Leipzig, 1914)
J. Baum: *Baukunst und dekorative Plastik der Frührenaissance* (Stuttgart, 1920)
D. Frey: *Architettura della rinascenza* (Rome, 1924)
W. J. Anderson and A. Stratton: *The Architecture of the Renaissance in Italy* (London, 1927)
G. Giovannoni: *Saggi sull'architettura del rinascimento* (Milan, 1935)
J. S. Ackermann: 'Architectural Practice in the Italian Renaissance', *J. Soc. Archit. Historians*, xiii/3 (1954), pp. 3–11
W. Lotz: 'Architecture in the Later Sixteenth Century', *Coll. A. J.*, xvii/2 (1958), pp. 129–39
R. Bonelli: *Da Bramante a Michelangelo: Profilo dell'architettura del cinquecento* (Venice, 1960)
L. Heydenreich: 'Il bugnato rustico nel quattro- e nel cinquecento', *Boll. Cent. Int. Stud. Archit. Andrea Palladio*, ii (1960), pp. 40–41
B. Lowry: *Renaissance Architecture* (London, 1962)
M. Tafuri: *L'architettura del manierismo nel cinquecento europeo* (Bari, 1966)
E. Battisti: 'Storia del concetto di manierismo in architettura', *Boll. Cent. Int. Stud. Archit. Andrea Palladio*, ix (1967), pp. 204–10
W. Hager: 'Strutture spaziali del manierismo nell'architettura italiana', *Boll. Cent. Int. Stud. Archit. Andrea Palladio*, ix (1967), pp. 257–71
L. Benevolo: *Storia dell'architettura del rinascimento* (Bari, 1968)
P. Murray: *The Architecture of the Italian Renaissance* (London, 1969; rev. 3/1986/R 1988)
M. Tafuri: *L'architettura dell'umanesimo* (Bari, 1969)
H. Burns: 'Quattrocento Architecture and the Antique: Some Problems', *Classical Influences on European Culture, 500–1500*, ed. R. R. Bolgar (London, 1971), pp. 269–87
L. Heydenreich and W. Lotz: *Architecture in Italy, 1400–1600*, Pelican Hist. A. (Harmondsworth, 1974)

R. Pane: *Il rinascimento nell'Italia meridionale*, i (Milan, 1975)
G. Hersey: *Pythagorean Palaces: Magic and Architecture in the Italian Renaissance* (Ithaca, 1976)
L. Benevolo: *The Architecture of the Renaissance* (London, 1978)
A. Bruschi and others: *Scritti rinascimentali di architettura* (Milan, 1978)
W. Lotz: *Studies in Italian Renaissance Architecture* (Cambridge, MA, 1981)
A. Buck and B. Guthmueller, eds: *La città italiana del rinascimento fra utopia e realtà* (Venice, 1983)
K. Bering: *Baupropaganda und Bildprogrammatik der Fruehrenaissance in Florenz, Rom und Pienza* (Frankfurt am Main, 1984)
R. DeFusco: *L'architettura del quattrocento* (Turin, 1984)
J. Onians: *Bearers of Meaning* (New Jersey, 1988)

LYNDA STEPHENS

4. BAROQUE AND ROCOCO, *c.* 1600–*c.* 1750.

(i) Introduction. (ii) Rome. (iii) Southern Italy. (iv) Northern Italy.

(i) Introduction. Italian architecture of the 17th century and the early 18th was grounded in Renaissance principles of design but developed from this rich tradition the distinctive and highly expressive style known as the BAROQUE, and in later stages as the ROCOCO. From the Renaissance, Baroque architects inherited a basic repertory of building types: churches, city palaces and, less frequently, suburban villas. Structural innovations were modest, but compositionally the most progressive buildings tended to be complex and their embellishment exuberant. Curved wall planes, projecting columns, rhythmic bay arrangements, controlled illumination, extensive sculptural

accents and a special sensitivity to site and location are just some of the features found in the more adventurous buildings of the time.

Italian Baroque architecture was above all rhetorical, and the most grandiloquent buildings of the period had a religious function. Churches constructed in the aftermath of the Counter-Reformation usually sought to overpower audiences with a spectacle that, in the words of Bernini, 'would reach out to Catholics in order to reaffirm their faith, to heretics to reunite them with the church and to agnostics to enlighten them with the true faith'. If Renaissance architecture was to be contemplated on an intellectual level, Baroque architecture was to be experienced with the emotions and the senses.

Only rarely were truly innovative buildings constructed for secular patrons. Just as private portraiture seldom possessed the expressive power of religious narrative in contemporary Italian painting and sculpture, so secular architecture usually deferred to sacred construction. The principal palaces built in Rome during the period were for papal families, but even the grandest of these tended to be more conservative than the ecclesiastical commissions awarded by the same pontiffs. The essentially urban nature of Italian cultural life resulted in an even more modest number of distinctive country villas (*see* VILLA, §II). Flamboyant solutions were not sought by every Italian architect of the Baroque age, however, and a strong undercurrent of conservatism ran through the period. Even Bernini, so demonstrative a sculptor, designed buildings of such taciturn character and Vitruvian correctness that they might be mistaken for designs of the High Renaissance. Francesco Borromini and Guarino Guarini were less constrained by tradition, but their work attracted almost no followers among their contemporaries.

During this period Italy had yet to become a unified political state. The peninsula shared a language and a religion but otherwise consisted of a shifting medley of republics, duchies, principalities, foreign domains and the territorially limited papal states. The papacy maintained spiritual hegemony over all of Catholic Europe, but as its temporal power and, consequently, its cultural influence was circumscribed, regional traditions remained pronounced. Climatic differences between north and south and the varying traits of local building materials further contributed to the diversity of architectural practice.

In the early 17th century, architects were still trained through apprenticeships or by rising through the ranks of the building trades, and a few crossed over from successful careers as painters or sculptors. By the end of the century, however, the Accademia di S Luca in Rome had begun to offer courses and competitions that drew aspiring architects from all over Italy and from abroad (*see* ROME, §VI). It did not take long for the academy's offerings to become academic, promoting a vision of architecture that favoured classicizing correctness over Baroque fantasia, and polished urbanity over the charm of regional inflection. Several of those who received their training at the academy in the early 18th century were later destined to play leading roles in the genesis of NEO-CLASSICISM, which developed in the mid-18th century partly as a reaction against the Rococo. But the Accademia di S Luca did not absorb all the architectural talent in this period. Many architects

throughout Italy, particularly in the provinces, fashioned from the vocabulary of the Baroque the elegant and playful style known as the Rococo. Despite their chronological differences or stylistic preferences, few of the architects active in the period were as concerned with theory and critical debate as were members of the profession in previous or subsequent eras. This was an age when creative practice took precedence over abstract formulation.

(ii) Rome. The period began with the decision of Pope Paul V (*see* BORGHESE, (1)) to complete the still unfinished basilica of St Peter's (consecrated 1626; *see* ROME, §V, 14(ii)(a)). Carlo Maderno was commissioned in 1608 to add a nave and thereby transform the basilica into a more conventional longitudinal space. This concept was conventional because it followed the example of a number of Roman Counter-Reformation churches, beginning with Il Gesù, the mother church of the Jesuit Order (*see* ROME, §V, 16). Il Gesù was begun in 1568, and the intervening years of the 16th century were not known for creative imagination. Maderno is credited with revitalizing the moribund practices that he inherited through a few modest innovations, most notably by giving greater emphasis to the centre of more vigorously articulated façades and by substituting engaged columns for the flat pilasters favoured by his predecessors. He did so first on the façade of S Susanna (1597–1603; *see* MADERNO, CARLO, fig. 1) and again on the front of St Peter's, where he skilfully blended his frontispiece with the existing side walls by Michelangelo.

Theologians of the late 16th century, including Carlo Borromeo, had argued that major churches should customarily be built in the form of a Latin cross. For decades after the Counter-Reformation this was done, but by the second third of the 17th century such prescriptions were increasingly overlooked and a remarkable group of small, cleverly planned centralized churches came into being. The most ingenious of these were the work of Bernini, Borromini and Pietro da Cortona. Borromini's S Carlo alle Quattro Fontane (or S Carlino; begun 1634; *see* BORROMINI, FRANCESCO, figs 1, 2 and 3) was the least bound by tradition of any kind. Its lozenge-shaped plan has undulating interior walls articulated with robust three-quarter columns, while its pendentives and cupola are densely overlaid with figural and geometric relief. The façade (designed later in the architect's career) brims with the movement of counter-curving wall planes and the variation of structural and ornamental motifs. Cortona's church of SS Luca e Martina (completed 1670s; *see* CORTONA, PIETRO DA, fig. 5) was also started in 1634. Its plan is a more conventional Greek cross, but the forceful expression of the orders and the widespread use of sculptural relief departs noticeably from the interior treatment of Renaissance prototypes (see fig. 15). As in Borromini's S Carlo, the colour scheme is monochromatic, but the upper parts of the walls are more brightly illuminated than the lower. Proportionally, churches of this period were also relatively taller than those of previous centuries.

Bernini built the church of S Andrea al Quirinale (begun 1658; *see* BERNINI, (2), §I, 3(ii)) for the Jesuits, just down the street from S Carlo alle Quattro Fontane. It has an oval ground-plan which, owing to the shallowness of the

15. Pietro da Cortona: interior of SS Luca e Martina, Rome, completed 1670s

site, is set transversely to the ritual axis. The principal articulation is with pilasters, and the oval dome rests directly on the lower elevation with no transitional pendentives (as at S Carlo or SS Luca e Martina) to disturb the fluidity of the upward movement. However, the relative simplification of architectural form in Bernini's church is balanced by his lavish use of colour and materials. Rich marbles, prominent sculpture, a focal painting on the altar and gilded vaulting create a sumptuously pictorial effect.

The façades of Roman Baroque churches loudly proclaim the special blessings to be found within. The fronts of centralized churches are the most varied, and they usually reflect the character of the interior. Early in the period, when longitudinal churches were more common or when new façades were given to existing buildings, one type was particularly popular. Derived from Il Gesù, it has two storeys with a wide lower storey surmounted by a narrow upper one topped by a pediment. As architects reverted to this scheme throughout the first half of the 17th century, they expressed the component elements with increasing boldness. Orders project more vigorously from the wall, pediments are multiplied and encased one within the other, and free-standing and relief sculpture abounds. The expressive effect achieved in such High Baroque façades as SS Vincenzo e Anastasio (*see* LONGHI (ii), (3), fig. 1) and S Maria in Campitelli (for illustration *see* RAINALDI, (2)) is similar to that of the *scaenae frons* of ancient Roman theatres. The affinity of architectural styles in the two periods has often been remarked upon.

Church façades also play a prominent role in the urban planning of Baroque Rome. When Innocent X (*see* PAMPHILI, (1)) resystemized the Piazza Navona (*see* ROME,

§II, 3), he commissioned a large family palace, the Palazzo Pamphili (1645–50; *see* RAINALDI, (1)), from Girolamo Rainaldi, and the Four Rivers Fountain (1648–51; *see* BERNINI, (2), §I, 1(iii)) from Bernini. However, in adding the family church of the Pamphili, S Agnese in Agone (1652–3; see fig. 16 and RAINALDI, (2)), he gave the piazza its dominant aspect. The centralized interior of this church does not overwhelm, but the exterior is as magnificent as any in Rome. Designed sequentially by four architects—Girolamo and Carlo Rainaldi, Borromini and finally Bernini—the gently undulating façade is crowned by a splendid dome and two bold towers. This stately composition is, in effect, a High Baroque revision of St Peter's, but its presence in the Piazza Navona transcends religious necessity or papal self-promotion to become a centrepiece in the civic pageantry of Baroque Rome. Similar attitudes lay behind Alexander VII's commission in 1661 of a pair of identical churches, S Maria dei Miracoli and S Maria in Montesanto (completed 1670s), in the Piazza del Popolo to serve as propylaea to the city for visitors entering Rome from its principal northern gate. They were designed by Carlo Rainaldi, aided by Bernini and Carlo Fontana (*see* FONTANA (v), (1)). The functional need for these churches may have been open to question, but the Classical porticos play a clear semiotic role in providing a stately introduction to the architectural marvels of Rome.

Secular architecture of 17th-century Rome was rarely so grandiloquent. The boldest solutions tended to involve iconographic rather than expressive innovations. Departing from convention, Maderno designed the Palazzo Barberini (1622–4), the family residence of Urban VIII, as

16. Girolamo Rainaldi, Carlo Rainaldi, Francesco Borromini and Gianlorenzo Bernini: exterior of S Agnese in Agone, Rome, 1652–3

an expanded version of a Renaissance villa *suburbana* (*see* §3(ii) above) with winged pavilions, while Bernini adopted the giant orders from Michelangelo's Palazzo del Senatore for the façade of Alexander VII's Palazzo Chigi (begun 1664; now the Palazzo Chigi-Odescalchi; *see* ORDERS, ARCHITECTURAL, fig. 8). More typical was Innocent X's Palazzo Pamphili in the Piazza Navona. As prototypes for later construction, only the Palazzo Chigi was to have any significant influence.

In the later 17th century there was a marked decline in new building works. Overbuilding in previous decades combined with an economic downturn and the distraction of Turkish expansion to the east of Italy limited all but the smallest undertakings. A revival of building activity did not occur until the second quarter of the 18th century. At that time, two distinctively different styles became discernible. The first, known as the Rococo, was generically related to the fanciful work of Borromini. However, where Borromini explored the dynamic potential of interior space and the sculptural value of exterior elevations, Rococo architects such as FILIPPO RAGUZZINI or DOMENICO GREGORINI preferred simpler, more graceful plans and delicately worked surface embellishments. In Raguzzini's Piazza di S Ignazio (1727–35; see fig. 17), a cluster of modestly scaled apartment blocks with gently curving façades, acute and obtuse corner angles, and elegant stucco garnishings about doors and windows provide a refined response to the cumbersome Gesù-inspired façade of the

adjacent Baroque church of S Ignazio. The delicacy of Raguzzini's style, like that of other Rococo architects, was largely dependent on the creative use of stucco, an inexpensive and malleable material that had not been used with such freedom since antiquity.

The grandest undertaking of the Roman Rococo was the Spanish Steps (or Scalinata della Trinità dei Monti; 1723–6; *see* ROME, fig. 9), constructed on the designs of FRANCESCO DE' SANCTIS. Set into the steep hillside between the Piazza di Spagna and the church of the Trinità dei Monti, the staircase consists of an alternating sequence of single and double ramps linked by spacious landings that provide a scenic and unhurried passage in either direction. As in the Piazza di S Ignazio, the Spanish Steps follow no rules and make no theoretical statements. Rococo architects and their patrons rarely sought to impress or influence a wider audience.

A second approach to architecture at this time followed from more rational principles. Known as Academic Classicism or Late Baroque Classicism, its adherents were on the whole sympathetic to the aims of the Accademia di S Luca, which was involved in appointing the juries that chose the winners of the major architectural competitions held in the city. The most important competition, which took place in 1732, was for the façade of S Giovanni in Laterano (*see* ROME, §V, 15(ii)). Alessandro Galilei's winning entry set the norm for large public commissions in Rome for years to come (*see* GALILEI, ALESSANDRO, fig. 2). Compact but stately, the façade employs a limited vocabulary of giant pilasters and half-columns arranged in parallel planes. Sculpture is confined to the roofline, and there are few ornamental frills. Decorum and propriety replace the charm and whimsy that were hallmarks of the Rococo. The spare formalism of the Lateran façade was not restricted to sacred structures. Some Roman palaces and villas of the second third of the century likewise tended towards a reductive classicism. The front of the Palazzo Poli, the architectural backdrop for the Trevi Fountain (for illustration *see* SALVI, NICOLA), exemplifies the style in a public secular building. The centrepiece of Nicola Salvi's façade (begun 1732) is a massive re-creation of the Arch of Constantine (*see* ROME, fig. 30), an ancient monument that was undergoing restoration just as work commenced on the Trevi. The tripartite composition of the façade looks back to Bernini's Palazzo Chigi, but the antiquarian flavour of the triumphal arch is prophetic of the more literal historicism of Neo-classicism.

(iii) Southern Italy. The lands to the south of Rome remained for the most part under Spanish domination in the 17th and 18th centuries. Isolated politically and culturally from the rest of Italy, and with considerable wealth concentrated in the hands of a few landowners and the Church, the architecture of Naples, Apulia and Sicily was regionally distinctive and frequently fashioned from costly materials. Southern Baroque was also a relatively late style with the most remarkable buildings constructed in the later 17th century and the 18th.

In Naples, the period begins with the work of COSIMO FANZAGO, who endowed the city with an array of palaces, churches, chapels and public monuments (*see* NAPLES, §I, 4). Many of his commissions are memorable less for the

17. Filippo Raguzzini: Piazza di S Ignazio, Rome, 1727–35; isometric view

originality of their ground-plans and façades than for the richness of their interior embellishment. At the Certosa di S Martino, where he worked from 1623, Fanzago restricted himself to white and grey marbles for the fancifully detailed exterior of the main cloister (1623–43), but the interior of the church has floors and walls covered with the colourful marbles and intarsia that so appealed to Neapolitan tastes (*see* NAPLES, §IV, 3). Later architects in Naples were structurally more daring and preferred lighter decorative effects, frequently executed in stucco. The churches of Domenico Antonio Vaccaro typify the fullest flowering of the Neapolitan Baroque, locally called the *barochetto*. The centralized Concezione a Montecalvario (1718–24) is open and airy, its whitewashed skeletal structure embellished with stucco in a confectionary manner (*see* VACCARO, (2)).

Palace design in Naples was greatly influenced by the work of FERDINANDO SANFELICE. Neapolitan palaces were taller than elsewhere, and Sanfelice turned this to his advantage, making the staircase a focal point. Of his many stairways that open on to a courtyard, that in his own palace (now nos 2–6, Via della Sanità) is the most breathtaking. Five bays wide and four storeys tall, the double flights and landings are extensively perforated with openings that afford scenographic views of the courtyard and garden.

Further south in Apulia, and especially in Lecce, one finds a provincial variant of the Baroque that is as idiosyncratic as any in Italy. From the late 16th century to the mid-18th, Apulian architecture brimmed with exuberance. It is characterized by three features in particular: an unorthodox handling of the Classical orders, the continued use of such old-fashioned forms as the Gothic pointed arch, and the unrestrained use of sculptural relief. In common with all of the fervently Catholic south, sacred architecture was most prominent. Church interiors on the whole are modest and structurally conservative, but façades in Lecce are extravagant. The exterior of the church of the Rosary (1691–1728) by Giuseppe Zimbalo (1620–1710) is fairly typical. The two-storey façade is articulated in parallel planes, but virtually every inch of flat surface is carved in intricate relief. Spiral-fluted columns and panelled pilasters compete with sculpted figures for public attention. The overall expressive effect recalls CHURRI-GUERESQUE architecture in Spain while lesser details seem to be of Islamic origin.

The Piazza del Duomo in Lecce is one of the loveliest public spaces in Italy. Largely constructed in the 17th and 18th centuries, it contains the cathedral, episcopal palace and a seminary, but no commercial buildings. The square itself is a cul-de-sac without thoroughfares of any kind. Part of its charm derives from the warm golden colour of the local stone. Easily carved when first quarried, it hardens with time, lending itself to the extensive and unusual sculptural embellishment for which the region is renowned.

In Sicily, Baroque architecture came into its own only in the 18th century (*see* SICILY, §4). The most ingenious buildings in and around Palermo were villas built for the nobility in the suburban towns of Piana dei Colli and Bagheria. All are now in lamentable states of decay, but they were once among the most fabulous country houses in Europe. Walled off from the surrounding landscape,

their plans favoured curved but relatively spare exterior façades with the main façade usually providing a backdrop for double flights of extremely complicated stairways. The Villa Palagonia in Bagheria, begun by Tommaso Napoli (1655–1725) in 1705, has, since the time of Goethe, been celebrated for its strange assortment of sculptured monstrosities as well as for its highly imaginative architecture. After the great earthquake of 1693, much of the south-eastern part of Sicily was rebuilt in the Baroque style. Syracuse, Catania, Ragusa, Modica and Noto were the main centres of new construction. Syracuse Cathedral was also rebuilt (1728–54); its façade by Andrea Palma (1664–1730; see fig. 18) typifies Sicily's stylistic independence from architectural currents then in fashion elsewhere in Italy. With its bold array of projecting columns, craggy broken pediments and abundant sculpture, the façade has little in common with the Rococo or Late Baroque classicism. In Modica and Ragusa, ROSARIO GAGLIARDI went even further in providing the cathedrals with gently curving, three-storey façades, which loom above great flights of steps. It is characteristic of Sicilian architecture that ornament does not compete with the Classical orders for expressive primacy.

The small town of NOTO is the gem of the Sicilian Baroque. Built from scratch after the earthquake, it remains one of Italy's most thoroughly Baroque towns. The master plan, attributed to ANGELO ITALIA but thought to be based on Vincenzo Scamozzi's 1615 design for an ideal city (*see* SCAMOZZI, (2) and MILITARY ARCHITECTURE AND FORTIFICATION, fig. 24), resulted in an integrated gridlike layout of streets, squares and major buildings. As city architect, Gagliardi was the principal designer involved in the rebuilding, but he was assisted by his nephew VINCENZO SINATRA. The appeal of their works was

18. Andrea Palma: façade of Syracuse Cathedral, 1728–54

enhanced by the local building material, a pale yellow stone.

(iv) Northern Italy. North Italian architecture of the 17th and 18th centuries was even more diversified than that of the south. This was due in part to the myriad political affiliations that divided the city states north of Rome, and partly to the greater strength of Renaissance traditions in such cities as Florence and Venice. Florence remained a virtual anachronism as even such accomplished architects as MATTEO NIGETTI (e.g. Cappella dei Principi, 1604–48, in S Lorenzo; *see* FLORENCE, §IV, 5) and Gherardo Silvani (*see* SILVANI, (1)) were content to design tame, Mannerist variations on the work of BERNARDO BUONTALENTI, with whom they had both collaborated. In Venice the influence of Andrea Palladio was even more powerful, but one Venetian architect, BALDASSARE LONGHENA, did rise to prominence. His church of S Maria della Salute (begun 1631; *see* VENICE, §IV, 5) has been called the first major Baroque church in Italy. Conspicuously located at the head of the Grand Canal, it follows in many respects Palladio's nearby churches of S Giorgio Maggiore (from 1566) and Il Redentore (begun 1576; *see* PALLADIO, ANDREA, fig. 7), but in the more permissive atmosphere of the 17th century Longhena employed a compact, centralized plan where Palladio could not. In the interior (see fig. 19), Longhena's dependence on Palladio is apparent in his scenographic linkage of independent spatial units—rotunda, ambulatory and choir—that moves the eye episodically through the building. Decoratively, he followed Palladio's example by using engaged columns on high pedestals, which contrast colouristically with white

walls. But Longhena's church transcends all models: its tall proportions are majestic, and its voluminous dome with bold scroll buttresses and sculptural embellishments is one of the most splendid in all of Italy.

Later Venetian architects including DOMENICO EGIDIO ROSSI, who was influential in mediating Italian styles to northern Europe, Andrea Tirali (1657–1737) and Giovanni Antonio Scalfarotto (*c.* 1690–1764) rejected Longhena's picturesque style in favour of an even more literal Palladian classicism. Reflecting the conservatism of a city the political and cultural fortunes of which had become increasingly insecure, the solemn historicism of their work was deeply prophetic of Neo-classicism. Tirali's façade for S Nicolò da Tolentino (1706–14) and Scalfarotto's SS Simeone e Giuda (1718–38), although derived from Palladio, are the direct precursors of such classicizing structures as the Ste Geneviève by JACQUES-GERMAIN SOUFFLOT in Paris (begun 1755; altered from 1791; now the Panthéon).

Architecture in Bologna and Milan played a significant role in the formation of the early Baroque style. In church interiors particularly, such architects as Lorenzo Binago (1554–1629), FRANCESCO MARIA RICCHINI and GIOVANNI AMBROGIO MAZENTA strove towards more coherent if, still by local tradition, compartmentalized ground-plans, while they vigorously deployed free-standing or engaged columns in place of the flat pilasters favoured in the later Renaissance. Ricchini's S Giuseppe (1607–16) in Milan and Mazenta's S Salvatore (completed 1623) in Bologna were models for subsequent developments in Rome. The wider influence of the region is also reflected by the fact that many of the architects who became important in Rome—including Domenico Fontana, Carlo Maderno and Francesco Borromini—were themselves of Lombard origin.

Later, in the 18th century, Milan had in Marco Bianchi one of the more refined advocates of the Rococo style. His church of S Francesco da Paola (1723–35) is constructed on a violin-shaped plan and embellished externally and internally with elegant stuccowork that recalls the RÉGENCE STYLE in France. Bianchi's Bolognese contemporary CARLO FRANCESCO DOTTI took a different approach. In his mountain-top sanctuary of the Madonna di S Luca (1723–57) and the Arco del Meloncello (1718–32), which are linked by a lengthy arcade, Dotti created imaginative structures with boldly sweeping curves, open loggias and complex interplays between variously scaled orders. His feeling for mass and the sculptural values of architectural framework owes more to 17th- than 18th-century practice. The plan of the sanctuary interior is based on Pietro da Cortona's SS Luca e Martina in Rome (*see* §(ii) above), and there are few concessions to current tastes for the Rococo or Academic Classicism. The closest parallel is with Sicilian architecture of the 18th century where similarly bold but outdated architectural forms were also commonplace. The term 'Ultra-Baroque' has sometimes been used to describe the character of such innovative provincial developments.

By far the most progressive advances in earlier north Italian architecture occurred in Piedmont, especially in the capital city of Turin (*see* TURIN, §I, 1). GUARINO GUARINI stands out among all other 17th-century architects. He

19. Baldassare Longhena: interior of S Maria della Salute, Venice, begun 1631

20. Guarino Guarini: dome of the chapel of the Holy Shroud (S Sindone), Turin Cathedral, 1668–82

began designing churches for the Theatine Order while teaching in their seminaries in Modena, Messina and Paris. In 1666 he moved to Turin and began work on the church of S Lorenzo (begun 1634; Guarini's scheme begun 1668) and the chapel of the Holy Shroud (Santa Sindone; Guarini's work begun 1668) in the cathedral. In both cases Guarini inherited commissions started by others, but he transformed both structures so radically as to defy every architectural convention. His inspiration may have been Borromini, whom he probably met during an eight-year stay in Rome (1639–47), but Guarini also explored earlier and wider periods of architectural history than previous Italian architects. While the specific prototypes for the extraordinary cross-ribbed vaults that crown S Lorenzo and the chapel of the Holy Shroud (see fig. 20) have never been identified, it is generally agreed that they were derived from 10th-century Hispano-Moorish vaults. In a posthumously published treatise, *Architettura civile* (1737), Guarini claimed that 'vaults are the principal parts of buildings', and his analysis of medieval construction went beyond Hispano-Moorish practices to include even those of the Late Gothic period. His willingness to explore and assimilate non-Classical sources of inspiration is as evident in his churches as in the treatise.

Guarini also designed a remarkable private palace in Turin. The Palazzo Carignano (begun 1679; *see* GUARINI, GUARINO, fig. 4) was commissioned by the Prince of Carignan, Emanuel-Philibert, a cousin of Victor-Amadeus II, Duke of Savoy. Located in the city centre, the palace is large and imposing. Its 15-bay façade is broken into alternating straight, concave, convex, concave and straight sections. The vertical organization is even more complex, with two superimposed orders of irregularly spaced pilasters framing seven windows in each bay. The façade, furthermore, is executed in brick, which gives it a texture and colouristic richness. The window surrounds of the *piano nobile* are of special interest. Alluding to the recent victory of the owner—who was Commander General of the Regiment of Carignano—over the Iroquois tribe in Quebec, Canada, they suggest stylized representations of North American Indian peoples. This anthropomorphic transformation of architectonic motifs looks back to Borromini, but unlike the Rococo architects who shared Borromini's taste for surface embellishment, Guarini followed his example in designing dynamic spatial configurations as well.

Piedmontese architecture of the 18th century followed the same stylistic dichotomy between Rococo and Academic Classicism that occurred in Rome. The two principal personalities were the Sicilian Filippo Juvarra and Bernardo Antonio Vittone. Juvarra's monastery church of La Superga (1717–31; *see* JUVARRA, FILIPPO, fig. 1), which stands high on a mountain overlooking Turin, is a domed rotunda with projecting Classical portico and twin bell towers. The formal pedigree is unabashedly Roman: the dome derives from St Peter's, the portico from the churches in the Piazza del Popolo and the towers from S Agnese in the Piazza Navona. The overall impression is one of Classical poise and authority, but despite its eclectic sources inside and out, the church possesses an organic vitality that

distinguishes it from the more historically detached, doctrinaire designs of the Neo-classical architects of the next generation.

In 1718 Juvarra started to rebuild the Palazzo Madama (completed 1721; see fig. 21) in Turin for the French-born mother of Victor-Amadeus II. An addition to a medieval fortress in the centre of the city, this sober structure bears a striking resemblance to the garden façade (1669–85) of Louis XIV's palace at Versailles (*see* VERSAILLES, §1). By the 18th century Versailles had become as important a model for European state architecture as were the Roman churches for sacred architecture. Juvarra's façade of the Palazzo Madama makes few concessions to local tradition and, although not without embellishment, it avoids any suggestion of the curved planes and complex rhythms seen at Guarini's nearby Palazzo Carignano.

Vittone trained in Rome and in 1733 returned to Piedmont, where he is believed to have briefly entered Juvarra's studio before going on to edit Guarini's *Architettura civile* for publication. Vittone's own designs reconcile stylistic features found in the work of both Guarini and Juvarra. Vittone was primarily a church architect, and he constructed some three dozen churches in and around Turin. S Chiara in Bra (1742–8) is typical in having a centralized quatrefoil plan, the lower façade of which is based on Juvarra's church of the Carmine in Turin, while the vaulting (*see* VITTONE, BERNARDO ANTONIO, fig. 2) is dependent on Guarini. From such different sources, Vittone fashioned an interior that is uncompromisingly Rococo in the lightness of its structure and the delicacy of its pastel-toned decoration. He continued to practise this style even as Neo-classicism gathered momentum everywhere around him. It is he, more than any other Italian architect, who symbolizes the last flourish of the Italian Baroque.

BIBLIOGRAPHY

R. Wittkower: *Art and Architecture in Italy, 1600–1750*, Pelican Hist. A. (Harmondsworth, 1958, rev. 1991)
E. Bassi: *Architettura del sei e settecento a Venezia* (Naples, 1962)
L. Grassi: *Province del barocco e del rococo: Proposta di un lessico biobibliografico di architetti in Lombardia* (Milan, 1966)
R. Pommer: *Eighteenth-century Architecture in Piedmont* (New York, 1967)
A. Blunt: *Sicilian Baroque* (New York, 1968)
P. Portoghesi: *Roma barocca* (Cambridge, 1970)
M. Calvesi and M. Manieri-Elia: *Architettura barocca a Lecce e in terra di Puglia* (Rome, 1971)
A. Blunt: *Neapolitan Baroque and Rococo Architecture* (London, 1975)
C. Elling: *Rome: The Biography of her Architecture from Bernini to Thorwaldsen* (Boulder, CO, 1975)
A. M. Matteucci and others: *Architettura, scenografia, pittura di paesaggio: L'arte del settecento emiliano* (Bologna, 1980)
R. Krautheimer: *The Rome of Alexander VII* (Princeton, 1985)
T. Magnuson: *Rome in the Age of Bernini*, 2 vols (Stockholm, 1986)
J. Varriano: *Italian Baroque and Rococo Architecture* (New York and Oxford, 1986)
E. Debenedetti, ed.: *L'architettura da Clemente XI a Benedetto XIV: Pluralità di tendenze*, Studi sul settecento romano, v (Rome, 1989)
P. Waddy: *Seventeenth-century Roman Palaces: Use and the Art of the Plan* (New York, 1990)

JOHN VARRIANO

5. NEO-CLASSICISM TO EARLY MODERNISM, *c.* 1750–*c.* 1900. In the mid-18th century the Rococo style declined in Italy, to be supplanted by a NEO-CLASSICISM of French derivation, which had already made its appearance in the work of Filippo Juvarra (*see* §4(iv) above). In

21. Filippo Juvarra: façade of the Palazzo Madama, Turin, 1718–21

the 19th century Italian architecture moved towards Eclecticism, and as Modernism approached it embraced the *Stile Liberty*, an Italian form of Art Nouveau.

(i) Rome and southern Italy. (ii) Northern Italy.

(i) Rome and southern Italy. Italian Neo-classicism first developed in Rome, around the middle of the 18th century, in the tempietti, pavilions, propylaea and imitation ruins designed by CARLO MARCHIONNI for the Villa Albani (*see* ROME, §V, 27) and by ANTONIO ASPRUCCI and Cristoph Unterberger (*see* UNTERBERGER, (3)) for the Villa Borghese. An important architect of this period was LUIGI VANVITELLI, who had trained in Rome in the circle of Domenico Fontana and Nicola Salvi and produced his first work there, S Maria degli Angeli (1748–65). The church had been started in 1562 by Michelangelo on the ruins of the Baths of Diocletian, and Vanvitelli completed it in a Neo-classical style, reducing Michelangelo's nave to a transept and grafting on a new nave perpendicular to it, thus creating a much greater effect of space. In 18th-century Roman architecture the most prominent figure was Giuseppe Valadier, a builder and urban planner of Neo-classical taste, whose name is linked in particular with the creation of the Piazza del Popolo, for which he drew up designs from 1793 and which was finally completed in 1824. The piazza, which is the starting point for the Corso and Via del Babuino, had been laid out in the 1660s by Carlo Rainaldi. Valadier gave it an ellipsoidal form, centred around the existing Egyptian obelisk. What makes it unique and beautiful in its singular setting is the link with the gardens on the Pincian Hill, which descend to it in terraces, loggias and ornamental waterworks. Valadier also executed several façades of Roman churches, including S Pantaleo (begun 1806; for illustration *see* VALADIER, (1)) and S

Andrea delle Fratte (1826); he also rebuilt Urbino Cathedral (1789–1801) and a few palaces in Macerata and Rimini, in which classicist rigour was softened with elements derived from Palladio and Vignola.

In the following period Eclecticism triumphed in Rome, perhaps more than elsewhere. Classical forms were combined with Renaissance, Mannerist and Baroque elements, especially after 1871 when Rome became the capital of Italy and many public buildings, banks and ministries were built. Gaetano Koch (*see* KOCH, (2)) designed the Piazza delle Terme (now Piazza della Repubblica; 1886–90; see fig. 22) in the form of a great exedra with porticos, on the perimeter of the one that in antiquity enclosed the colossal Baths of Diocletian. He used stylistic features of the late 16th century in a neo-Baroque spatial design. This combined harmoniously with the curved lines of the two Palazzi dell'Esedra set on steps, the proportions of the levels and even the decorative cornices, which show a French influence in the manner of Charles Garnier. In the centre of the exedra is the great Fountain of the Naiads, a masterpiece of the *Stile Liberty* and at the same time the last, vigorous revival of the monumental fountains of papal Rome. Koch is also noted for a few Roman palazzi, although not so much for the Banca Nazionale (now the Banca d'Italia; completed 1892) on Via Nazionale, with its oppressive and solemn borrowings from Antonio da Sangallo (ii), as for the Palazzo Margherita (1886–90; now the American Embassy), a work of rare elegance in its overall composition. Koch's Palazzo Pacelli (from 1880) in Corso Vittorio Emanuele, in its faithful 16th-century style, shows a balanced respect for the surrounding historical environment.

Other important architects active in Rome included Pio Piacentini (*see* PIACENTINI, (1)), who designed the Renaissance Revival Palazzo delle Esposizioni (1882) in Via

22. Gaetano Koch: Piazza delle Terme (now Piazza della Repubblica), Rome, 1886–90

Nazionale, and GUGLIELMO CALDERINI, who designed the huge Palazzo di Giustizia (begun 1888; opened 1910) after winning the competition in 1887. As ideal models he had in mind Mannerist architecture, the stage sets of the Bibbiena family and Piranesi's *Carceri*. From these sources he drew inspiration for the palazzo, an immense square structure with a strong chiaroscuro look, the design of which is cluttered with a profusion of ornaments, columns, statues, reliefs, festoons, plaques and medallions applied to every part. However, the greatest, vain celebration of Italy's patriotic history and Rome as the new capital of the realm was the immense monument to *Victor-Emanuel II*, King of Italy (1885–1911), designed by GIUSEPPE SACCONI. His plan triumphed over 293 entries submitted by the major architects and sculptors, including Giovanni Battista Basile and Raimondo D'Aronco. The effect of the monument is discordant and pretentious: a slightly curved gallery of 16 columns rises above the huge pile, adorned with sculptural groups and allegorical reliefs, and it mars the piazza, obstructing it with terraces and flights of steps.

One of the most important projects in southern Italy in the mid-18th century was the Palazzo Reale at Caserta, near Naples, which was designed in 1751 by Vanvitelli for Charles III of Naples (*see* BOURBON, §II(4)) and started the following year. Around the palace the King meant to build a whole city for his court and the administration of the kingdom, which was to replace Naples as Versailles had replaced Paris. The project was never realized because of changed political conditions, although it was already nearly complete on paper, and the palace remained isolated and uncompleted. Its façades, with well-proportioned orders one above the other and a limited use of curved lines, clearly reflect the Neo-classical manner, while the great octagonal, central entrance hall and the majestic staircases are essentially Baroque in proportion and scenographic effect. Some of the most beautiful rooms were later designed in the French Empire style: the Sala di Astrea and the Sala di Marte, designed in 1807 by Antonio De Simone for Joseph Bonaparte (*reg* 1806–8), and the gold and white Sala del Trono richly decorated by Gaetano Genovese (1795–1860) in 1839. Even the palace park illustrated the change in style. Instead of the layout on terraces typical of the Italian tradition, it offers long, broad perspectives in the French taste of André Le Nôtre—while at the same time wisely continuing to use water, dynamically rather than statically as in France, with a great cascade plunging down the hill through basins and pools (for further discussion *see* CASERTA, PALAZZO REALE).

In Naples Vanvitelli also built the Foro Carolino (now the Piazza Dante; from 1758) and the church of SS Annunziata (rebuilt from 1760) with an aisleless nave and side chapels. Adapting his design to the particular conditions of the land, Vanvitelli created an ingenious and complex effect that brings to mind the manner of Juvarra. Work on this church was interrupted by his death and it was finished in 1782 by his son Carlo Vanvitelli (1734–1821). In Naples the most coherent Neo-classical monument was Pietro Bianchi's church of S Francesco di Paola (from 1808), commissioned by King Ferdinand I for his return to the throne. This construction combines elements taken from the Pantheon in Rome (circular plan, portico, hemispherical dome) with others derived from Piazza S Pietro, also in Rome (the columns that form the two wings at the sides of the portico). In Palermo Neo-classicism still survived towards the end of the 19th century, when the rest of Italy had returned to 'national' styles. The Teatro Massimo, with its cold portico in Greek style, was begun in 1875 by Giovanni Battista Basile and was finished by his son Ernesto Basile (*see* BASILE, (2)) in 1897. Ernesto developed a Sicilian version of Art Nouveau, making Palermo a centre of *Stile Liberty.*

(ii) Northern Italy. In Venice, after the brilliant affirmation of Baldassare Longhena, there was a stronger tendency to react against the Baroque, clearing away decorations, widening and chopping structures up in a manner often reminiscent of Vincenzo Scamozzi. This tendency emerged with great precision and clarity in the architecture of Giorgio Massari. His works included the Jesuit church of S Maria del Rosario (or del Gesuati; 1725–36), the façade of which is both Baroque and Palladian, and the Palazzo Grassi (1748). The greatest interpreter of Neo-classicism in Venice at the end of the 18th century was Giovanni Antonio Selva, who had worked in England. Selva, a former pupil of Tommaso Temanza, built the Teatro della Fenice (1789; destr. 1996; for illustration *see* SELVA, GIOVANNI ANTONIO), which was rather conventional in appearance but structurally extremely functional. Giacomo Quarenghi was also linked with Venetian Neo-classicism; he internally reconstructed the church of S Scolastica (1771–7) in Subiaco.

In the 17th century Florence had resisted the influence of the Baroque. Classicizing forms, however, favoured by the local tradition, continued to find a favourable climate in the second half of the century, especially in the work of Zanobi del Rosso (1724–98), who designed the central part and the right wing of the church of S Filippo Neri (or Chiesa Nuova), at S Firenze, the façade of which (the left wing) had been remodelled from *c.* 1715 by Ferdinando Ruggieri. The whole of the vast prospect is limpid and cold; nor do the cornice motifs and broken arches, clearly inspired by Bernardo Buontalenti, succeed in giving it warmth (for further discussion *see* RUGGIERI, (2)). Florentine Neo-classical forms, however, were less cold than elsewhere. The most important personality was that of GASPARO MARIA PAOLETTI, who created the Neo-classical Meridiana annex to the Palazzo Pitti, the Leopoldine baths (from 1772) at Montecatini Terme and the extension (1776) of the Villa del Poggio Imperiale. Here he elegantly renovated the salons on the first floor, built two large courts at the sides of the entrance court and erected the south façade without projecting wings. Other architects engaged at the villa were PASQUALE POCCIANTI, who

designed and started the main entrance (north) façade *c.* 1804, and GIUSEPPE CACIALLI, who executed it *c.* 1807.

In the second half of the 19th century building activity in Florence was intense, especially when the city was capital of Italy (1865–70). Unfortunately, part of the old medieval centre was later demolished and rebuilt, creating the unwieldy Piazza Vittorio Emanuele (1893–5). In the same period the Gothic Revival façades of Santa Croce (Niccola Matas; 1857–63) and the cathedral (Emilio De Fabris; completed 1887) were produced. Florence had, however, the good fortune to receive from GIUSEPPE POGGI a development plan, which took account of all the main problems, from water supply to the natural expansion of the city's life beyond Michelangelo's walls. Poggi worked on this from 1864 to 1877, and he obtained a rational solution for traffic with a circuit of wide avenues replacing the old fortifications, culminating with the Viale dei Colli (1865–7), including Piazzale Michelangelo and the powerful ramps and stairs of S Niccolò, which connected the city with its southern hills, facilitating access to such important monuments as the churches of S Miniato and S Salvatore (for further discussion *see* FLORENCE, §I, 6).

Milan was the only city where Neo-classicism achieved consistent and unitary effects, which can be seen through three distinct phases. The first, characterized by a sense of measure and equilibrium still tinged with 16th-century Mannerism, coincided with the government of Maria Theresa and Joseph II (*reg* 1780–90). The second, inspired by rules of rigorous imitation of Athenian and Roman monuments, corresponds to the brief period of Napoleonic rule in Italy (1796–1814). The third, harking back to Renaissance forms, coincided with the restoration of Austrian rule in 1814.

The chief interpreter of the first phase was Giuseppe Piermarini, a follower of Vanvitelli with whom he worked at Caserta. Called to Milan in 1769 by Archduke Ferdinand Habsburg, he began rebuilding the Palazzo Ducale (later Palazzo Reale), taking inspiration from the solemn severity of the Caserta façade (1769–89). Piermarini, who was later appointed Archducal Architect, worked in Milan for about 30 years, and his designs were distinguished by their simplicity and clarity. After the Palazzo Ducale, his most important works were the Villa Regio-Ducale (1776–80) at Monza, the Palazzo Belgioioso (1772–82) with its broad façade and a single order, the middle section of which is enlivened by pilasters and columns, and his best-known work, the Teatro alla Scala (1776–8). The heavy, projecting, three-arched portico of the theatre darkens and constricts the central section of its façade, where the elements derived from Palladio and Scamozzi reflect a chiaroscuro conception that was really alien to the sensibility of the architect (for illustration *see* PIERMARINI, GIUSEPPE). But the interior of the Scala, thanks to Piermarini's studies of his Italian and French forerunners, blends the grandiosity of Vanvitelli's style with the extreme neatness and elegance of Neo-classical ornamentation. It is a model of theatres built by Italians in Italy and abroad. Leopoldo Pollack and SIMONE CANTONI were followers of Piermarini and continued his style. The Viennese Pollack collaborated with Piermarini at the Villa Regio-Ducale from 1776 to 1778 and subsequently created the Villa Belgioioso (1790–96; now Villa Reale; for illustration *see* POLLACK, (1)), Monza, whose best feature is the garden façade, a design that is both controlled and magnificent, with fluted Ionic columns articulated at the ends by two short, pedimented wings. After renovating (1778–83) the façade and salon of the Palazzo Ducale in Genoa, Cantone moved to Milan, where his most important works included the Palazzo Pertusati (1789–91; destr.). He also built the Villa Olmo (1780–94) at Como, one of the most beautiful and coherent Neo-classical works in Lombardy (see fig. 23).

The second phase of Milanese Neo-classicism is typified by Luigi Cagnola, who succeeded Piermarini as state architect. This phase was the coldest and most rhetorical. Piermarini's forms—clear, measured and simplified in structure and decoration—gave place to a Neo-classicism inspired 'aux Grecques et aux Romains', or in other words by the 'Empire style'. Cagnola's best-known work is the Arco della Pace (or del Sempione; from 1807; *see* MILAN, fig. 6), which combines elements of the Arch of Constantine (the three vaults) with elements from the Arch of Titus (the reliefs inside the central vault). With the return of the Austrians, the arch, begun in homage to Napoleon, was dedicated to peace; similarly, another important work by this architect, the so-called Atrium of Porta Marengo (1801–14) at Porta Ticinese, was originally built in memory of the Battle of Marengo (1800). Cagnola also built the fine bell-tower (1824–9) of the parish church of Urgnano, one of the most sensitive interpretations of ancient architecture, and his own Villa di Inverigo (1813–33) at Como (for illustration *see* CAGNOLA, LUIGI). To GIOVANNI ANTONIO ANTOLINI, another eminent architect of the period, Napoleon assigned in 1801 the difficult task of formulating a new urban plan for Milan. The city was to have centred around the Castello Sforzesca, with a huge piazza—the Foro Bonaparte—cleared by the destruction of the bastions erected under Spanish rule. The project was logical and on the whole functional; it would have made Milan one of the most modern capitals of Europe. Because of political events, however, it was never carried out (for further discussion *see* MILAN, §I, 4). Other architects working in the city were LUIGI CANONICA, who designed the Park of Monza (1805) with a boulevard linking it to Milan, and Giuseppe Zanoia (1752–1817) and

CARLO AMATI, both appointed by Napoleon to design the façade (1806–13) of Milan Cathedral, the prime expression of Italian interest in Gothic art. Amati was also responsible for the church of S Carlo al Corso (1838–47), a typically Neo-classical structure clearly inspired by the Pantheon in Rome.

In the third phase, that of the Restoration, Milanese architecture moved away from archaeological solemnity and took its inspiration instead from the lively intellectualism of the 16th century. There were no outstanding figures among the architects, who were by then looking towards the Eclecticism of the second half of the 19th century. However, one major figure was Giuseppe Mengoni, designer of the new Piazza del Duomo (1861)—which he enlarged to the point of dwarfing the Gothic cathedral—and the Galleria Vittorio Emanuele (begun 1863; for illustration *see* MENGONI, GIUSEPPE), a great structure on a Greek-cross plan with a two-ordered triumphal arch and a grandiose iron and glass dome rising above a wide central octagon: one of those powerful, colossal structures that were the pride of the newly united Italy. The façade (1886–92) of the Palazzo Marino in Piazza della Scala was created by LUCA BELTRAMI, who had studied and worked in Paris with Charles Garnier and who also restored the Castello Sforzesca (from 1893) following the contemporary principle of returning monuments to their original appearance. He gave the 16th-century palazzo a look influenced by Piermarini, in harmony with the prevalent character of the city; he garnished it, however, with projections and decorative features in a style that suggested early Art Nouveau influences, as did RAIMONDO D'ARONCO's original neo-Greek competition-winning proposal for a new façade to an existing pavilion in the Parco del Valentino, Turin, in which the Prima Esposizione Italiana di Architettura (1890; executed in simplified form; destr.) was to be housed. Thus the origins of the *Stile Liberty* may be glimpsed.

In Genoa the local 17th-century tradition, characterized by sumptuous scenographic effects, was continued by Gregorio Petondi, who placed an atrium with a vast twin-flight staircase in the Palazzo Balbi in Via Cairoli. The Teatro Carlo Felice (1826–7; damaged 1944; largely

23. Simone Cantoni: Villa Olmo, Como, 1780–94

destr. 1976; rebuilt 1989–90) presents a typically Neo-classical character; its façade is characterized by a monumental Doric portico. It was the work of CARLO FRANCESCO BARABINO, to whom Genoa also owes the layout of the city centre. In Padua Giuseppe Jappelli created the influential Caffè Pedrocchi (begun 1826; for illustration *see* JAPPELLI, GIUSEPPE), in which Neo-classical and Greek Revival style forms were adapted to the particular function of a public resort. In Turin the most important architect of the later 19th century was Alessandro Antonelli, who built the Mole Antonelliana (from 1863); this was originally intended to serve as a synagogue, but it was bought by the city council in 1877 and became a monument to Victor-Emanuel II. It has a square plan, decorated on the outside with a gallery; on this rises a cupola in the form of a four-sided pyramid, terminating in a tall spire (for illustration *see* ANTONELLI, ALESSANDRO). The cupola is formed of robust interwoven iron beams, which allow the greatest possible reduction in the thickness of the walls.

BIBLIOGRAPHY

A. Melani: *Architettura italiana* (Milan, 1884)
G. Damerini: *Un architetto veneziano dell'ottocento: Giuseppe Iappelli* (Venice, 1934)
S. Caronia-Roberti: *Ernesto Basile e cinquant'anni di architettura in Sicilia* (Palermo, 1935)
M. Lizzani: *Il Vittoriano* (Rome, 1937)
N. Tarchiani: *L'architettura italiana dell'ottocento* (Florence, 1937)
M. Kirchmayr: *L'architettura italiana: Dalle origini ai giorni nostri* (Turin, 1946)
F. Peggiori: *Milano, 1800–1943* (Milan, 1947)
V. Golzio: *Il seicento e il settecento* (Turin, 1950)
E. Kauffmann: *Architecture in the Age of Reason: Baroque and Post-Baroque in England, Italy and France* (Cambridge, MA, 1955)
C. Maltese: *Storia dell'arte italiana, 1785–1943* (Turin, 1956)
H. R. Hitchcock: *Architecture: Nineteenth and Twentieth Centuries*, Pelican Hist. A. (Harmondsworth, 1958)
M. Pittaluga: *Dall'arte del cinquecento all'arte contemporanea* (1959), iii of *L'arte italiana* (Florence, 1958–9)
M. S. Briggs: *Architecture in Italy* (London and New York, 1961)
A. Venditti: *Architettura neoclassica a Napoli* (Naples, 1961)
F. Borsi: *L'architettura dell'unità d'Italia* (Florence, 1966)
C. L. V. Meeks: *Italian Architecture, 1759–1914* (New Haven, 1966)
T. West: *A History of Architecture in Italy* (London, 1968)
F. Bellonzi: *Architettura, pittura, scultura dal Neoclassicismo al Liberty* (Rome, 1978)
R. De Fusco: *L'architettura dell'ottocento: Storia dell'arte in Italia* (Turin, 1980)
R. Bossaglia: 'L'architettura dell'ottocento: Recente bibliografia italiana', *Stud. Stor. A.*, iv (1981–2)
E. Bairati and D. Riva: *Il Liberty in Italia* (Bari, 1985)
J. L. Varriano: *Italian Baroque and Rococo Architecture* (New York, 1986)
R. A. Etlin: *Modernism in Italian Architecture, 1890–1940* (Cambridge, MA, 1991)
L. Benevolo: *Roma dal 1870 al 1990* (Bari, 1992)

PETER BOUTOURLINE YOUNG

6. AFTER *c.* 1900.

(i) *Stile Liberty* and the Futurist legacy, *c.* 1900–*c.* 1920. (ii) *Novecentismo, Razionalismo* and the establishment styles, *c.* 1920–*c.* 1946. (iii) Neo-Realism and Neo-Liberty to *La Tendenza, c.* 1946–*c.* 1970. (iv) Post-modernism, after *c.* 1970.

(i) Stile Liberty *and the Futurist legacy,* c. *1900–*c. *1920.* The Prima Esposizione Internazionale d'Arte Decorativa Moderna (Turin, 1902) brought to Italy the best international examples of ART NOUVEAU, including work by Victor Horta, Joseph Maria Olbrich, Charles Rennie Mackintosh and Tiffany. Although there had been a few examples of Art Nouveau (It. *Stile Liberty* or *Stile floreale*) influence before 1902, it was the spectacular exhibition

buildings themselves (destr.) by Raimondo D'Aronco and Annibale Rigotti that pointed the way to a coherent style. There followed a period before World War I in which attempts were made at stylistic renewal, some of them related to Art Nouveau, others more characteristic of *fin-de-siècle* Eclecticism. The former ranged from the Casa Ferrario (1902–4) of ERNESTO PIROVANO, on the Via Spadari, Milan, and the structural originality of the work of Gino Coppede (1866–1927), to the sculptural *Stile Liberty* of the Hotel Tre Croci (1912), Varese, of GIUSEPPE SOMMARUGA, or the florid Palazzo Beri-Meregalli (1911–14), Milan, by Giulio Ulisse Arata (1881–1962). Eclectic buildings ranged through the neo-Baroque pavilions of the Premio Cinquantenario dell'Unità d'Italia (1911), Rome, by Marcello Piacentini (with CESARE BAZZANI; *see* PIACENTINI, (2)), to Bazzani's own Palazzo delle Belle Arti (opened in 1911; now Galleria Nazionale d'Arte Moderna), Rome, and the Biblioteca Nazionale (from 1907), Florence, completed after World War I, and the grandiose Stazione Centrale (1912–31), Milan, by ULISSE STACCHINI (*see* MILAN, fig. 7).

FUTURISM, inspired by the rapid, if late, industrialization and growth of the northern cities after the Risorgimento, had its primary impact on architecture and attitudes to urban planning when a series of evocative perspective drawings by ANTONIO SANT'ELIA (the *Città Nuova* series) and MARIO CHIATTONE were shown in an exhibition of Nuove Tendenze, in Milan, May 1914. They portrayed thrusting skyscrapers and rapid transport systems, utopian but credible, and the polemic that accompanied them denounced all compromise with historicism. Although the movement continued spasmodically into the 1920s (Virgilio Marchi (1895–1960), FORTUNATO DEPERO, ENRICO PRAMPOLINI), it left no built monuments that carry its name. Nevertheless, Sant'Elia had 'imagined a future so radically different from the past that it irrevocably altered the terms of the debate concerning modern architecture in Italy' (Doordan, p. 17) and, more importantly, 'made Futurism a turning point in the development of Modern theories of design' (P. R. Banham: *Theory and Design in the First Machine Age* (London, 1960), p. 99; *see* MODERN MOVEMENT).

By contrast with what Etlin termed the 'cultural firecrackers' of Futurism, however, contemporary development in Rome (*see* ROME, §II, 4) and elsewhere by members of the Associazione Artistica fra i Cultori di Architettura, led by GUSTAVO GIOVANNONI and Piacentini, was studied and deliberate. Under the influence of CAMILLO SITTE and CHARLES BULS the concept of *ambientismo* (contextual integration of new buildings) was espoused and a policy of *diradamento* ('thinning out') adopted at historically sensitive city sites. Schemes included Giovannoni's proposals for the Caprera (1907–11) and Via Coronari (1913) areas in Rome. Developing a principle proposed by Camillo Boito in the 1880s, an urban vernacular style was advocated as a background for historic monuments, and it was used for numerous apartments and houses in and around Rome in the 1920s.

(ii) Novecentismo, Razionalismo *and the establishment styles,* c. *1920–*c. *1946.* NOVECENTISMO (*see also* NOVECENTO ITALIANO) in architecture, which aimed to imbue

functional forms with Italian overtones by using Classical elements to embellish them, was first associated with young architects returned from World War I, including GIOVANNI MUZIO, Emilio Lancia (1890–1973), GIO PONTI and Mino Fiocchi (1893–1983). Muzio's Ca' Brutta (1919–22), Milan, was the most significant early example, and, although initially ridiculed, it was rapidly assimilated into the urban fabric as an acceptable combination of modern forms with a unique and recognizable Italian character. Works of this kind were built throughout the 1920s by, for example, Piero Portaluppi (1888–1976; e.g. mixed urban development, Corso Venezia and Via Salvini, 1926), Aldo Adreani (*b* 1887; e.g. Palazzo Fidia, 1926–8) and Lancia and Ponti (Casa Borletti, 1927–8), all Milan.

Meanwhile, GRUPPO 7 was formed (Milan, 1926) and *Razionalismo* came into being with a manifesto that declared its alignment with the European *nouveau esprit* (*see* RATIONALISM (ii)). Early projects were exhibited at the 3rd Biennale in Monza (1927), and at the first Esposizione dell'Architettura Razionale (Rome, 1928), arranged by ADALBERTO LIBERA and Gaetano Minucci (1896–1980). Contributing to the latter were LUCIANO BALDESSARI and ALBERTO SARTORIS, founder-members of the Congrès Internationaux d'Architecture Moderne (CIAM) and originators of the unsuccessful Movimento dell'Architettura Razionale (MAR), who also exhibited at the Esposizione per la Decenniale della Vittoria (Turin, 1928), organized by Gruppo Sei, as did GIUSEPPE PAGANO, Ettore Sottsass (1892–1953) and EDOARDO PERSICO. By the second half of the 1920s, however, such

Novecento architects as GIUSEPPE DE FINETTI (e.g. Casa della Meridiana, Milan, 1924–5) and Pino Pizzigoni (1901–67; e.g. Villa Pizzigoni, Bergamo, 1925–7), who were influenced by Adolf Loos, and others who had worked in northern Europe were already beginning to converge with *Razionalismo*. Radical early Rationalist buildings included the Novocomum apartment building (1928–9), Como, by GIUSEPPE TERRAGNI, the seven-storey Gualino office buildings (completed 1929), Turin, by Pagano and Gino Levi-Montalcini (1902–74) and the Casa Elettrica (1930; destr.) at the 4th Biennale, Monza, by FIGINI AND POLLINI with Gruppo 7.

The Movimento Italiano dell'Architettura Razionale (MIAR) was formed by members of Gruppo 7 in 1930, and the second exhibition of members' work (Rome, 1931) resulted in confrontation with the architectural establishment (Bazzani, Giovannoni and Piacentini). MIAR was disbanded, but compromise followed and Rationalist influence continued to grow—theoretically and polemically through the pages of *Casabella* and *Quadrante* (from May 1933), through the publicity from the Milan Triennale, as well as through a widening range of executed projects. The works of those members of MIAR active in Rome stood astride the events of 1931: Giuseppe Capponi (1893–1936; e.g. Casa Nebbiosi, 1929–30) and Pietro Aschieri (1859–1952; e.g. Casa Lavoro per i Ciechi di Guerra, 1931), who combined a Baroque interest in form with plain surfaces; and the near Purist Palestra per la Scherma (1934–6) of LUIGI MORETTI. Rapprochement

24. Giuseppe Terragni: Casa del Fascio (now Casa del Popolo), Como, 1933–6

with authority had been signalled by Libera's spectacular Modernist façade for the Mostra della Rivoluzione Fascista (Rome, 1932) and he, as well as MARIO RIDOLFI and GIUSEPPE SAMONÀ, all completed major Post Office buildings (1933–5). Elsewhere, overtly Rationalist designs for important buildings included the S Maria Novella Railway Station (1933–5) of GIOVANNI MICHELUCCI at Florence; Sabaudia (1933–4), the second of Mussolini's five new agricultural towns, by Luigi Piccinato (1899–1983); and buildings resulting from Adriano Olivetti's long-running patronage which began in 1934 in the Val d'Aosta (*see* BBPR ARCHITECTURAL STUDIO). Most of the major works of *Razionalismo* date from *c.* 1936: the highly influential Sala delle Medaglie d'Oro at the Mostra dell'Aeronautica Italiano (Milan, 1934), symbolizing the *aggiornamento* wing of the movement; the Salone d'Onore at the 6th Triennale, Milan (1936), characterizing the dilemma between Rationalist purity and Classical spatial values, both by Persico and MARCELLO NIZZOLI; and the work of the Como group: FRANCO ALBINI, Cesare Cattaneo (1912–43), PIETRO LINGERI and Terragni, whose apartment buildings (1933–5) in Milan and Casa del Fascio (1933–6; now Casa del Popolo; see fig. 24), Como, represented the culmination of the movement between the wars.

Little of the Neo-classical origins of *Novecentismo* remained in such buildings as Muzio's dormitories (1934) for the Università Cattolica del Sacro Cuore, or Ponti's Casa Marmont apartment building (1933–4; with Antonio Fornaroli and Eugenio Soncini), both in Milan. Furthermore, when Piacentini was commissioned in 1932 to build the Città Universitaria in Rome (completed 1935), he invited several Rationalists to join him as collaborators. Aschieri, Michelucci, Capponi and Pagano, as well as Ponti, all produced campus buildings within Piacentini's guidelines. Important buildings of the later 1930s included the rigorously rectilinear Dispensario Antitubercolare (1936), Alessandria, by IGNAZIO GARDELLA, and Ponti's Montecatini building (1936), Milan, although there were already signs of growing concern for traditional values, seen for example in the restoration (1936–7) by CARLO SCARPA of Ca' Foscari, Venice. The regulatory plan (1937) for the site of the 1942 Esposizione Universale di Roma (EUR; originally known as E 42; cancelled because of World War II), which was, for Mussolini, to be the nucleus of the Third Rome, was prepared by a group including Piacentini, Pagano and Piccinato. Although Rationalist buildings were included (e.g. BBPR's Post Office, 1940; destr.), the official monumentalism eventually proved unacceptable to the Rationalists: *Casabella* was closed by government order in 1943, and dissenting architects went underground.

(iii) Neo-Realism and Neo-Liberty to La Tendenza, *c. 1946–c. 1970.* The contrast of BBPR's celebrated memorial grid (Milan, 1946) with the solemn Monument to the Fallen Italians (1949) at Mauthausen, by MARIO LABÓ, both raised to war victims, symbolized the continuing dilemma between Rationalist innovation and respect for tradition. Populist post-war ideology promoted practical attitudes to reconstruction, and, in the spirit of Ridolfi's *Manuale*, first-generation Rationalists produced a decade

or so of Neo-Realist housing. For example in Rome, Ridolfi and LUDOVICO QUARONI directed a young team including CARLO AYMONINO and Mario Fiorentino (1918–82) (e.g. INA-Casa housing project, Via Tiburtino, 1949–54); in Milan, Gardella, Albini and BBPR built the Cesate low-rise housing and the five-storey Mangiagalli workers' housing development (both 1950–51); in Naples, there was Libera's unashamedly structural twelve-storey apartment block of 1954; and in Genoa, the vast concrete Forte di Quezzi complex (1955–7) by Carlo Daneri (1900–72). The policy of encouraging regional dispersal of industry was typified by the Olivetti factory at Pozzuoli (1954), Naples, by Luigi Cosenza (1905–84).

Bruno Zevi (*b* 1918) founded the Associazione per l'Architettura Organica (1945) and for a number of years through its magazine *Metron* created a dialectic with postwar *Razionalismo*. Its influence on artefacts was limited but was seen briefly in the early 1950s, for example in the work of Scarpa and Samonà, who was professor at the Instituto Universitaria di Architettura, Venice. Concern for urban values had once again become apparent in the work of such architects as Michelucci (e.g. Borsa Merci, Pistoia, 1947–50) and Albini (e.g. INA offices, Parma, 1950). In Venice, Samonà elevated urban planning to a new level of importance through both his writings and a team of distinguished teachers, which during the 1960s included Aymonino, VITTORIO GREGOTTI and ALDO ROSSI.

In their sensitive designs for historic interiors Albini and Scarpa were in the vanguard of the continuing 'confrontation with history' when, in 1957, ERNESTO NATHAN ROGERS published in *Casabella* the historically orientated, early work of Roberto Gabetti (*b* 1925) and Aimaro Isola (*b* 1928). In 1958 BBPR's celebrated Torre Velasca (see fig. 25), Milan, created international crosscurrents of criticism from which the label NEO-LIBERTY arose. Similar influences were apparent in other contemporary buildings such as the Democratic Party headquarters (EUR; 1958) by Saverio Muratori (1910–73), and more importantly in the Casa Baldi (1959), Via Flaminia, near Rome, by PAOLO PORTOGHESI. Neo-Liberty represented a uniquely Italian reaction to the anonymity of INTERNATIONAL STYLE formalism—as, for example, in Ponti's Pirelli Building (1956–8; for illustration *see* PONTI, GIO), Milan, to the growing use of industrialized techniques in the work of such architects as ANGELO MANGIAROTTI and GINO VALLE, and to the large-scale structural virtuosity of PIER LUIGI NERVI and RICCARDO MORANDI. There were substantial undercurrents of postCIAM Brutalism in such buildings as the Instituto Marchiondi (1959), Milan, by Vittoriano Viganò (*b* 1919), but rarely so competently handled as in the social housing of GIANCARLO DE CARLO (Baveno and Novara, 1951; Matera, 1945–57) and his uniquely contextual solutions for the Free University of Urbino (1958–64). Neo-Expressionism, characterized by Michelucci's church of S Giovanni Battista (1964), Campi Bisenzio, near Florence, also appeared in this period. Rossi and Giorgio Grassi (*b* 1935) met the burgeoning pluralism of the 1960s head-on with a fresh response to the dilemma posed by Modernism in

25. BBPR Architectural Studio: Torre Velasca, Milan, 1958

the context of the city in their influential books, *L'archi-tettura della città* (1966) and *La construzione logica dell'architettura* (1967) respectively.

(iv) Post-modernism, after c. 1970. Iconoclastic radical groups such as SUPERSTUDIO (1966–78) in Florence and such architects as ETTORE SOTTSASS jr were active in the early 1970s and ran against the avant-garde Rationalist formalism of the Venetian school. An example of the latter, Aymonino's red and grey ten-storey Gallaratese housing development (1967–72), Monte Amiata, Milan, was closely juxtaposed with a white four-storey block by Rossi (1967–73) in a sparse reductionist aesthetic—the genotype of Tendenza Neo-Rationalism (*see* TENDENZA; *see also* RATIONALISM (ii)). Rossi's school (1972) at Fagnano Olona and the competition-winning San Cataldo Cemetery (1971–6; 1980–82 with Gianni Braghieri), Mo-dena, seemed to confirm the uncompromising graphic autonomy of the movement, as did the work of Grassi (e.g. Students' residences, Chieti, from 1976; with Antonio Monestiroli, *b* 1940) and others associated with the Venice school, for instance Valeriano Pastor (*b* 1927) and Luciano Semirani (*b* 1933), both active in Trieste, or Ugo Polesello

(*b* 1930), working in Rome. Meanwhile, pluralist pragmatic attitudes ranged widely from the High Tech rebuilding of the architectural school at the Politecnico di Milano (1970–79) by Viganò, through the International Style formalism of MARCO ZANUSO (e.g. IBM headquarters, Milan, 1972–5; IBM factory, Rome, 1979–83) or the vigorous surface interest in the work of Adolfo Natalini (*b* 1941), a founder-member of Superstudio, in Como and Bologna.

Historicist reminiscence also persisted throughout the 1970s in the work of such architects as Guido Canella (*b* 1932), Gabetti and Isola and others: Portoghesi pur-posely integrated historical elements with Modernist de-sign and technology and is regarded as a pioneer of international POST-MODERNISM. He was responsible for the first exhibition of Post-modern architecture at the 1980 Venice Biennale, for which a number of architects built façades to illustrate the double-coded nuances of Post-modern design. His almost Surrealist bank headquar-ters (1984) at Campobasso gives new meaning to the term 'broken pediment'. Post-modern influence can be seen, for example, in Valle's later work (e.g. housing on La Giudecca, Venice, 1986), and that of younger architects such as Francesco Venezia (*b* 1944) in the mid-1980s in Naples and Sicily and Paolo Zermani (*b* 1958) in Varano (Florence). In spite of the aesthetic shift towards what Braghieri termed 'mannerism. . .and a tireless determina-tion to keep on inventing', Rossi's later work retained its international influence. From the simplicity of low-rise housing (Bergamo, 1977; Mantua, 1979) to the monu-mental pylons of the Centro Torri shopping centre (de-signed 1985; built 1988), Parma, or the serene Pertini memorial (1990) in Milan, its invention is self-evident, as is its national influence in the work of the next generation: Antonio Monestiroli (*b* 1940) in Milan and Udine, Franco Stella (*b* 1944) in Thiene, Bruno Minardi (*b* 1946) in Ravenna; and Emilio Puglielli (*b* 1947) in Como and Brescia.

BIBLIOGRAPHY
G. Veronesi: *Difficoltà politiche dell'architettura in Italia, 1920–1940* (Milan, 1953)
G. E. Kidder Smith: *Italy Builds* (London, 1955)
B. Zevi: *Storia dell'architettura moderna* (Turin, 1955, rev. 2/1975)
A. Galardi: *Neue italienische Architektur* (Stuttgart, 1967)
G. Fanelli: *Architettura moderna in Italia, 1900–1940* (Florence, 1968)
V. Gregotti: *New Directions in Italian Architecture* (London and New York, 1968)
C. Cresti: *Appunti storici e critici sull'architettura italiana dall 1900 ad oggi* (Florence, 1971)
L. Patetta, ed.: *L'architettura in Italia, 1919–1943: Le polemiche* (Milan, 1972)
L. Patetta and S. Danesi: *Il razionalismo e l'architettura in Italia durante il fascismo* (Venice, 1976)
C. Conforti, G. De Giorgi and A. Muntoni: *Il dibattito architettonico in Italia, 1945–1975* (Rome, 1977)
M. Nicoletti: *L'architettura Liberty in Italia* (Bari, 1978)
C. De Seta: *Architetti italiani nel novecento* (Bari, 1982)
M. Estermann-Juchler: *Faschistische Staatbaukunst: Zur ideologischen Funktion der öffentlichen Architektur im faschistischen Italien* (Cologne, 1982)
V. Fraticelli: *Roma, 1914-1929: La città e gli architetti tra la guerra e il fascismo* (Rome, 1982)
M. Tafuri: *Storia dell'architettura italiana, 1944–85* (Turin, 1982); Eng. trans. by J. Levine (Cambridge, MA, and London, 1989)
C. De Seta: *La cultura architettonica in Italia tra le due guerre* (Bari, 1983)
E. Mantero and M. Novati: *Il razionalismo italiano* (Bologna, 1984)
A. Belluzzi and C. Conforti: *Architettura italiana, 1944–84* (Bari, 1985)
F. Dal Co and S. Polano, eds: 'Italian Architecture, 1945–1985', *A + U* (March 1988), pp. 1–208 [extra edition]

D. P. Doordan: *Building Modern Italy: Italian Architecture, 1914–1936* (New York, 1988)

G. Ciucci, ed.: *L'architettura italiana oggi* (Bari, 1989)

A. Burg: *Novecento milanese: I novocentisti e il rinnovamento dell'architettura a Milano fra il 1920 e il 1940* (Milan, 1991)

F. Dal Co and S. Polano, eds: '20th Century Architecture and Urbanism: Milano', *A + U* (Dec 1991), pp. 4–280 [extra edition]

R. A. Etlin: *Modernism in Italian Architecture, 1890–1940* (Cambridge, MA, and London, 1991)

JOHN MUSGROVE

III. Painting.

1. Ancient, 8th century BC to late Roman. 2. Early Christian and medieval, before *c.* 1400. 3. Early Renaissance, *c.* 1400–*c.* 1500. 4. High Renaissance and Mannerism, *c.* 1500–*c.* 1600. 5. Baroque and Rococo, *c.* 1600–*c.* 1750. 6. Neo-classicism to early modernism, *c.* 1750–*c.* 1900. 7. After *c.* 1900.

1. ANCIENT, 8TH CENTURY BC TO LATE ROMAN. The history of ancient painting in Italy is intimately connected with that of ancient Greece and the Greek world. Without the works of genuine Greek decorative and monumental painting that have been found in Italy the history of Greek art itself would be woefully incomplete. From the 8th century BC to the end of the Roman Empire, Italy served Greek artists as customer, employer and imitator. Hence the evolutionary periods of Greek art, Archaic, Classical and Hellenistic, are aptly applied to the history of Etruscan, South Italian or Italiote and Roman painting. At the same time there is evident in Italian painting (and in the other arts) a certain opposition to the dominant high style of Greek or Hellenicizing artists. This opposition has been described as 'primitive', 'popular' or 'bi-polar' and has been linked with other anti-Classical phenomena observable in Etruscan and Roman culture. Some scholars have attempted to define an indigenous Italian art or national style based on isolated, local traditions in Italic, Etruscan and Western Greek cultures, traditions that further coalesced during the political unification of Italy under the later Roman Republic. Accordingly the Roman preference for particulars over generalities—which would account for the Roman preference for history over philosophy, for example—gave rise to paintings of specific historical events as well as realistic portraiture, genres not represented in the Classical art of Greece. These genres or alternative tendencies within established genres might, therefore, be deemed characteristic of an Italian national style that co-existed with Greek art of a more idealizing style.

Monumental painting first appeared in Etruria in the form of wall paintings in tombs towards the end of the Orientalizing period (*c.* 600 BC; *see also* ETRUSCAN, §V). Painted chamber tombs of this period in Cerveteri and Veii incorporate motifs and figural style from Greek Orientalizing art, just as Villanovan vase painting was similarly influenced by Greek styles. The sequence of painted tombs from Tarquinia began *c.* 550 BC and established a type that lasted until *c.* 450 BC. The discovery of painted tombs near ELMALI in Anatolia has demonstrated

26. Wall painting of the Pumpu family in procession (detail; *c.* 200–*c.* 150 BC), Tomb of the Typhon, Tarquinia

clear iconographical and stylistic connections between East Greek painting and the tomb painting of Etruria, including Tarquinia. It is reasonable to assume, however, that the greater part of Greek influence on Etruscan tomb painting was transmitted by means of smaller, decorative objects.

Greek painting in the Early Classical style (c. 480–c. 450 BC) appeared first in Italy in the Tomb of the Diver discovered at PAESTUM in 1968. In addition to outline, reminiscent of Attic Red-figure vase painting (see GREECE, ANCIENT, §V, 6(i)), the painter employed modelling in flesh tones in order to create an illusion of depth. Attic influence on Etruscan painting can be detected in the first half of the 5th century BC, as in the profiles of the figures in the Tomb of the Chariots and the Tomb of the Triclinium at Tarquinia. Again, it is likely that contemporary Attic Red-figure vase painting served as a medium of transmission. While Etruscan vase painters also imitated contemporary Attic styles, a stylistic evolution in Etruscan vase painting comparable with that found in the Attic tradition cannot be demonstrated. This contrasts with South Italian Red figure vase painting, which does show a coherent evolution, despite (and perhaps because of) the likelihood of artistic interchange with peninsular Greek artists of the 4th century BC, so that South Italian painting is clearly enough established by c. 340 BC to suggest the possibility of Italian influence on the rest of the Greek world, including Macedonia, at this time.

South Italian influence has also been noted in one of the most important monuments of the Hellenistic period in Etruria, the paintings of the François Tomb at Vulci (c. 350–c. 300 BC; Rome, Villa Albani). In part Greek mythology with emphasis on the underworld, in part representing actual events and persons in Etruscan history, the programmatic iconography of the tomb parallels the two traditions in deliberate comparison. Etruscan tomb paintings of the 2nd century BC show even more interest in historical portraiture in an eschatological setting. The Tomb of the Typhon at Tarquinia (see fig. 26) shows members of the Pumpu family marshalled by psychopomps of the underworld, a scene without parallel in Greek art, said by Pallottino to anticipate the reliefs of the Ara Pacis in Rome.

Though historiographical in nature, the Italic element introduced in the François Tomb paintings was disruptive to the history of style in ways that primitivism, generally said to stand outside of history, may be considered opposed to the Classical stylistic sequence. The later formal achievements of Greek painting such as the single vanishing point, atmospheric perspective, broken colour and the like appear in subsequent Italian painting as scattered instances without much of an art historical context. The wall paintings from Pompeii, Herculaneum and Stabiae (see POMPEII, §IV and HERCULANEUM, §IV) show spectacular formal achievements that could only be the results of a brilliant evolutionary process in easel painting, but the same paintings offer no explanation of their origins within the context of house decoration.

The evidence from the cities buried by Vesuvius in AD 79 indicates that painters active in Italy during the first centuries BC and AD copied masterpieces of Greek easel painting for the purpose of decorating public and private buildings in fresco and mosaic. This body of painting, known also as Romano-Campanian painting, does present evidence of stylistic evolution and the emergence of new genres apart from the Greek achievements in style that it copies. Regarding entire walls and the decorative ensembles of entire rooms, Mau distinguished a sequence of four styles of Pompeian painting ranging from the tactile First Style, which imitated polychrome ashlar masonry, to the optical Fourth Style, which imitated back-lighted prospects of architectural fantasy. Paintings of the Second to the Fourth Styles abound in vignettes, among which may be classed sacro-idyllic landscapes, a genre first encountered within the Third Pompeian Style and which, consequently, may be considered as an Italian innovation. In the 2nd and 3rd centuries AD the compositions of wall paintings (most examples from Ostia) became simpler and the subject-matter less varied (see also ROME, ANCIENT, §V, 2). Analysis of the Late Roman figures in polychrome mosaic from the Imperial baths in Rome and of similar mosaics from the villa at Piazza Armerina in Sicily (c. 310–c. 325 AD) suggests that the artistic context of late Imperial graphic arts included Africa and Asia as well as Greece and Italy.

BIBLIOGRAPHY

EWA: 'Italo–Roman Folk Art'

A. Mau: *Pompeji in Leben und Kunst* (Leipzig, 1900, 2/1908); Eng. trans. by F. W. Kelsey (New York, 1899)

Monumenti della pittura antica scoperti in Italia (Rome, 1937–)

M. Pallottino: *Etruscologia* (Milan, 1942, rev. 7/1984)

A. Rumpf: *Malerei und Zeichnung*, Handbuch der Archäologie (Munich, 1953)

W. Dorigo: *Pittura tardoromana* (Rome, 1970); Eng. trans. by J. Cleugh and J. Warrington as *Late Roman Painting: A Study of Pictorial Records, 30 BC–AD 500* (London, 1971)

B. M. Felletti Maj: *La tradizione italica nell'arte romana* (Rome, 1977)

O. J. Brendel: *Etruscan Art*, Pelican Hist. A. (Harmondsworth, 1978)

See also WALL PAINTING, colour pl. I, fig. 2.

EUGENE DWYER

2. EARLY CHRISTIAN AND MEDIEVAL, BEFORE c. 1400. Owing to the loss of many of the wall paintings of this period, this section also includes mosaics.

(i) Early Christian, c. AD 200–c.600. (ii) Early Medieval, c. AD 600–c.1100. (iii) Late Medieval, c. 1100–c.1400.

(i) *Early Christian,* c. AD *200*–c. *600.* The first Christian painting in Italy was created for Roman patrons who were distinguished from their pagan counterparts principally by their adherence to the proscribed new faith. Its earliest context was private and funerary, and its treatment of Christian themes often cryptographic (see CATACOMB, §3). With Constantine's Edict of Toleration of 313, Christian painting attracted official patronage and appeared within a new, public context. Simultaneously, its repertory of subjects expanded and was guided increasingly by dogmatic interpretation. From the late 4th century onwards, the patronage of Christian painting became largely the prerogative of the Church.

The stylistic evolution of Early Christian painting mirrored that of Late Roman art. During the 3rd century this entailed a dynamic interplay between refined, residual classicism and a typical Late Antique predisposition towards abstraction and expressionism (*see* EARLY CHRISTIAN AND BYZANTINE ART, §III, 2). The two subcurrents prevail respectively in the representations of the *Good Shepherd* and the *Woman of Samaria* in the catacomb of Calixtus (*c.* 220) in Rome. In the *Orans with Shepherds* in the catacombs of the Cimitero Maggiore (*c.* 270), Rome, and elsewhere in the late 3rd century, the tendencies converge fluidly.

During the reigns of Diocletian and Constantine the style of such works as the wall painting of *Christ among the Apostles* in the catacomb of the Giordani (early 4th century), Rome, assumed a severe, monumental linearity related to that of official art of the Tetrarchy. The new style also appeared in the mosaic of *Christ Enthroned* in S Lorenzo (?*c.* 380), Milan, and at other monuments created under Constantius II (*reg* 337–61) and subsequently, but was characteristically tempered by a fresh classicizing impulse. The mosaic of the *Good Shepherd* in the mausoleum of Galla Placidia (*c.* 425–50; *see* RAVENNA, §2(ii)) and the apse mosaic of S Pudenziana (*c.* 427), Rome, demonstrate the persistence of the latter tendency in the early 5th century. As illustrated by the mosaics on the triumphal arch of S Maria Maggiore (*c.* 432; *see* ROME, §V, 20) and those in the dome of the Arian baptistery in Ravenna (*c.* 480; *see* RAVENNA, fig. 1), classicism and naturalism gradually gave way during the 5th century to an emphasis on symbolic content, hieratic arrangement and schematized form.

The last flowering of Early Christian painting in Italy occurred during the reign of Justinian I. The greatest achievement of this period, illustrated superbly by the apse mosaic of *Christ Enthroned between St Vitalis and Bishop Ecclesius* at S Vitale, Ravenna (*c.* 547; *see* RAVENNA, §2(vii)), and the apse mosaic of SS Cosma e Damiano (*c.* 525), Rome, resided in the success with which artists from Italy and Constantinople reconciled the conflicting stylistic tendencies of the 5th century. The Lombard conquest of Justinian's domains in Italy during the late 6th century coincided, in such monuments as the apse mosaic of S Apollinare in Classe (*c.* 549; *see* RAVENNA, fig. 4), with a dissolution of this classicizing style and a revival of late 5th-century abstraction and hieraticism. The same development is apparent in the earliest, Italian example of Christian manuscript illumination to survive, the illuminations of the ST AUGUSTINE GOSPELS (?6th century; Cambridge, Corpus Christi Coll., MS. 286).

(ii) Early medieval, c. AD *600–c. 1100.* Early medieval Italian painting was almost exclusively the creation of the Church and of such monastic communities as the Basilian and Benedictine establishments in southern Italy. Its characteristic forms were monumental wall decoration and manuscript illumination. Although the successive interventions in Italy of the Lombards and the Carolingian, Ottonian and Byzantine empires created political instability, they precipitated cultural contacts that ensured the continued development and vitality of Italian painting throughout this period.

In Rome, the austere linearity of the apse decoration of S Stefano Rotondo (642–9) and S Agnese fuori le mura (*c.* 630) perpetuated the style of late 6th-century painting.

The naturalism of frescoes to the right of the apse at S Maria Antiqua (*c.* 650–707; *see* ROME, §V, 19) illustrate a concurrent revival of Hellenizing classicism. Although similarly indebted to Early Christian tradition, the apse mosaic of S Venanzio (640–42) shows clear awareness of contemporary developments in Byzantine painting. A remarkable sensitivity for Classical form, and an apparent debt to Byzantium, are also evident in northern Italy, in the wall paintings of S Maria foris portas at CASTELSEPRIO (*c.* 700). From the 8th century onwards, Byzantine models were widely emulated, as in the wall paintings of S Sofia, BENEVENTO (*c.* 758–60), and S Vincenzo, near Volterra (*c.* 826–43) and in panel paintings such as the icon of *Maria Regina* (*c.* 705–7; Rome, S Maria in Trastevere; *see* TEMPERA, colour pl. I, fig. 2). Although modified occasionally by Carolingian and Early Christian elements, south Italian manuscripts, such as the 10th-century Exultet Roll (Rome, Vatican, Bib Apostolica, MS. Vat. lat. 9820), also followed Byzantine examples. Similarly, the Psalter (London, BL, Add. MS. 40731) and other manuscripts produced at Montecassino (*see* MONTECASSINO, §2(i)) under Abbot DESIDERIUS (*reg* 1058–86) combined the Franco-Saxon features of early 11th-century Cassinese illumination with a vigorously calligraphic interpretation of Byzantine style. Tempered by a Western approach to narrative and content, the latter trait also distinguishes the fresco decoration of SANT'ANGELO IN FORMIS (*c.* 1072–1100) and other wall paintings executed by Byzantine-trained artists under the auspices of Montecassino.

The impress of Byzantine tradition was less pronounced in Roman painting between 800 and 1100. In the mosaics of S Prassede and S Marco (827–44), the apse frescoes of S Sebastiano al Palatino (*c.* 980) and elsewhere, a widespread revival of Early Christian compositional schemes and subjects is instead apparent (*see* ICON, colour pl. I). By comparison, the sporadic productions of the 11th century were restricted largely to manuscripts, such as the *Remigus* from S Cecilia (Oxford, Bodleian Lib., Add. MS. D. 104), in which the principal source of inspiration was Ottonian miniatures (*see* OTTONIAN ART, §IV). In Lombardy, however, an important cycle of wall paintings survives at S Vincenzo, Galliano (*c.* 1007; *see* OTTONIAN ART, §IV, 1).

(iii) Late medieval, c. 1100–c. 1400. As in northern Europe, between 1100 and 1400 the revival of Greek and Roman letters was accompanied in Italy by a resurgence of intellectual activity. Along with continuing contacts with the Byzantine Empire and northern Europe, these developments had a decisive influence on the evolution of late medieval Italian painting. Throughout Italy, civic and private patronage began to rival that of the Church (although in Rome painting remained dependent on the beneficence of the papacy and curia), while artists enjoyed greater recognition and standing, changes that accelerated during the early Renaissance (*see* §3 below).

Roman painting of the 12th century was invigorated by a wave of Byzantine influence originating at Montecassino. In the apse mosaics of S Clemente (begun *c.* 1120; *see* ROME, fig. 55) and S Francesca Romana (*c.* 1150) and the fresco decoration of S Giovanni a Porta Latina (*c.* 1180), a comprehensive revival of Early Christian style and motifs is apparent as well. The spirit of revival and Byzantine influence also figured prominently in such 12th-century Umbro-Roman manuscripts as the Pantheon Bible (Rome, Vatican, Bib. Apostolica, MS. Vat. lat. 12958, fol. 4*v*; see fig. 27). The existence of active schools of painting in Tuscany during the 12th century is demonstrated by the survival of a few painted crucifixes from Pisa, Florence and Siena (see CRUCIFIX, §2) and by the productions of scriptoria in Florence and Lucca. The style of these works represents a distinguishable Romanesque idiom, in which Byzantine and north European influences predominate. In the frescoes of S PIETRO AL MONTE, CIVATE, as elsewhere in Lombard painting of the 12th century, a comparable balance was achieved between Byzantine and northern traditions.

A more purely Byzantine school of painting emerged under Norman patronage in Sicily during the 12th century, although local, Romanesque and Islamic elements are also apparent. Nevertheless, the evolution from the early Komnenian classicism of the mosaics of the east end of the Cappella Palatina in Palermo (c. 1140–43; see PALERMO, fig. 3) to the late Komnenian 'Baroque' of those of Monreale Cathedral (c. 1183; see MONREALE CATHEDRAL, §3) is one that echoed closely the development of

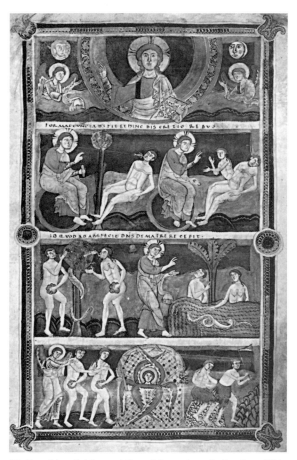

27. *Expulsion of Adam and Eve*, miniature from the Pantheon Bible, second quarter of the 12th century (Rome, Vatican, Biblioteca Apostolica, MS. Vat. lat. 12958, fol. 4*v*)

12th-century Byzantine painting in general. The earliest phase of that evolution is also represented in the Veneto, in the *Last Judgement* mosaic of Torcello Cathedral (see TORCELLO, §1) and the apse mosaics of S Marco (see VENICE, §IV, 1(iii)). In those mosaics executed in the nave of S Marco during the second half of the 1100s, however, the evidence of local craftsmanship and Romanesque tendencies is more pronounced.

Byzantine influence in Italian painting culminated in the 13th century. In the mosaics of S Marco, Venice, an early phase showing Byzantine features was followed, in the atrium mosaics of the second third of the 13th century, by a concerted revival of Early Christian motifs and techniques. The style of the mosaics executed from c. 1275 onwards in the western part of the nave, however, shows increasing influence of early Palaiologan painting. In northern Italy, frescoes in the baptistery at Parma (c. 1265) provide an accomplished but more provincial reflection of 13th-century Byzantine style. That style was also adopted in Umbria, in the frescoes of S Bevignate, near Perugia (c. 1277). Palaiologan miniatures served as the model for late 13th-century Bolognese illumination. By 1300, however, in such works as a Psalter in Paris (Bib. N., MS. lat. 18), the Byzantine element was superseded by French Gothic influences.

A similar pattern can be observed in 13th-century Tuscan and Roman painting. The BERLINGHIERI in Lucca and GIUNTA PISANO and COPPO DI MARCOVALDO in Florence followed the example of 12th-century Byzantine painting. Early Palaiologan influences were subsequently modified by that of French Gothic art in the work of the Florentine painter CIMABUE and the Sienese masters GUIDO DA SIENA and DUCCIO (see also CONSERVATION AND RESTORATION, colour pls IX and X). Byzantine and, later, Gothic influences also characterized painting in late 13th-century Rome.

In addition, the Roman masters of this period, such as PIETRO CAVALLINI, JACOPO TORRITI and FILIPPO RUSUTI, found important inspiration in antique and Early Christian art. At the end of the 13th century, Gothic and antique elements were combined with Franciscan-inspired humanism in a new, naturalistic style illustrated by the St Francis cycle in the Upper Church of S Francesco, Assisi (c. 1295; for illustration see MASTERS, ANONYMOUS, AND MONOGRAMMISTS, §I: MASTER OF THE ST FRANCIS LEGEND), and other works related to the early manner of the Florentine GIOTTO.

Painting in Florence during the 14th century was dominated by Giotto, whose frescoes of c. 1305 in the Arena Chapel, Padua (see PADUA, fig. 4 and PERSPECTIVE, colour pl. VIII, fig. 1), are distinguished by their unprecedented naturalism, psychological realism and monumentality. Among Giotto's numerous followers, MASO DI BANCO, Taddeo Gaddi (see GADDI (i), (2)) and BERNARDO DADDI continued his mastery of the human form and pictorial space. Towards the mid-14th century, the formal hieraticism and sombre religious tenor of 13th-century painting were reasserted, a tendency that came to the fore in the work of ANDREA DA FIRENZE (i), Andrea di Cione and his brother Nando di Cione (see CIONE, (1) and (2); see also PIGMENT, colour pl. XII, fig. 4). In the second half of the 14th century Agnolo Gaddi (see GADDI (i), (4)), GIUSTO DE' MENABUOI and others revived the naturalism

28. *Annunciation, Entry into Jerusalem, Judas and the Thirty Pieces of Silver, Last Supper* (early 1350s), fresco, Collegiata, San Gimignano

of Giotto's art with a heightened interest in anecdotal detail and developed with impressive sophistication his achievements in empirical perspective.

In Siena, the Gothic-inflected Byzantine manner of Duccio gave way in the works of SIMONE MARTINI (*see also* WALL PAINTING, colour pl. II, fig. 2) and the brothers Pietro and Ambrogio LORENZETTI to a more fully Gothic style influenced by Giotto. Throughout, the Sienese school retained its predisposition towards vibrant colour and surface detail and achieved significant innovations in the representation of pictorial space. As in Florence, a retrospective movement gained impetus in the middle decades of the 14th century, as exemplified by the severe visions in the New Testament frescoes in the Collegiata at San Gimignano (see fig. 28), which are often attributed to the putative BARNA. A renewed interest in the naturalism of early 14th-century Sienese painting, comparable to a similar trend in Florence, subsequently characterized the style of TADDEO DI BARTOLO and other Sienese masters active *c.* 1400.

Painting in Campania flourished briefly in the early 14th century, under the influence of Pietro Cavallini (active in S Maria Donnaregina, Naples, after 1310) and Giotto, but was typically conservative in its adherence to 13th-century figure types and compositional schemes. A more progressive spirit is evident in northern Italy: in Rimini, Giotto's example provided the impetus for the local school of fresco painting; in the scriptoria of Bologna, the Palaiologan and Gothic influences of the late 13th century were supplanted by that of Giotto's frescoes in Padua; and in Venice, the works of PAOLO VENEZIANO and LORENZO VENEZIANO reflect both the endurance of the indigenous Byzantine tradition and the impress of late 13th-century Roman painting. The revival of interest in the painting of Giotto in the late 14th century was paralleled in northern Italy in the frescoes in Verona and Padua by ALTICHIERO and JACOPO AVANZI. These artists' efforts in furthering Giotto's innovations in empirical perspective benefited also from the achievements of the early 14th-century Sienese masters and anticipated the innovations in perspective made in Florence in the early 15th century by Brunelleschi and Alberti.

BIBLIOGRAPHY

GENERAL

M. Salmi: *Italian Miniatures* (New York, 1957)
C. Ihm: *Die Programme der christlichen Apsismalerei vom IV. Jahrhundert bis zur Mitte des VIII. Jahrhunderts* (Wiesbaden, 1960)
G. Matthiae: *Pittura romana del medioevo*, 2 vols (Rome, 1965, rev. 2/1988)
——: *Mosaici medioevali delle chiese di Roma*, 2 vols (Rome, 1967)
W. F. Oakeshott: *The Mosaics of Rome* (New York, 1967)
E. Kitzinger: *The Art of Byzantium and the Medieval West: Selected Studies* (Bloomington and London, 1976)

EARLY CHRISTIAN

J. Wilpert: *Die römischen Mosaiken und Malereien der kirchlichen Bauten vom IV. bis XIII. Jahrhundert*, 4 vols (Freiburg, 1917)
G. Agnello: *La pittura paleocristiana in Sicilia* (Vatican City, 1952)
S. Bettini: *Pittura delle origini cristiane* (Novara, 1952)
H. P. L'Orange: *Mosaikk fra antikk til Middelalder* (Oslo, 1958)
K. Weitzmann: *Ancient Book Illumination* (Cambridge, MA, 1959)
P. L. Zovatto: *Mosaici paleocristiani delle Venezie* (Udine, 1963)
P. Du Bourguet: *Early Christian Painting*, Contact History of Art (London, 1965)
W. Dorigo: *Pittura tardoromana* (Milan, 1966)
A. Grabar: *The Beginnings of Christian Art, 200–395* (London, 1967)
——: *The Golden Age of Justinian* (New York, 1967)

——: *Christian Iconography: A Study of its Origins* (Princeton, 1968, rev. 2/1980)
G. Bovini: *Mosaici paleocristiani di Roma (secoli III–VI)* (Bologna, 1971)
——: *Ravenna Mosaics* (New York, 1978)
E. Kitzinger: *Byzantine Art in the Making* (Cambridge, MA, 1980)
C. Marabini: *I mosaici di Ravenna*, Documenti d'Arte (Novara, 1981)

EARLY MEDIEVAL

M. Avery: *The Exultet Rolls of South Italy*, 2 vols (Princeton, 1936)
J. Wettstein: *Sant'Angelo in Formis et la peinture médiévale en Campanie* (Geneva, 1960)
F. Bologna: *Early Italian Painting: Romanesque and Early Medieval* (Princeton, 1964)
H. Belting: *Studien zur beneventanischen Malerei* (Wiesbaden, 1968)
W. F. Volbach and others: *Europe of the Invasions* (New York, 1969)
O. Demus: *Romanesque Mural Painting* (New York, 1970)
W. F. Volbach and others: *Carolingian Art* (London, 1970)
C. R. Dodwell: *Painting in Europe, 800 to 1200*, Pelican Hist. A. (Harmondsworth, 1971)
L. Grodecki and others: *Le Siècle de l'an mil* (Paris, 1973)
G. Matthiae: *Pittori committenti fruitori nell'Italia altomedioevale* (Rome, 1977)

LATE MEDIEVAL

E. Bertaux: *L'Art dans l'Italie méridionale* (Paris, 1904)
O. Demus: *The Mosaics of Norman Sicily* (London, 1949/R New York, 1988)
E. B. Garrison: *Italian Romanesque Panel Painting: An Illustrated Index* (Florence, 1949, rev. 2/New York, 1976)
M. Meiss: *Painting in Florence and Siena after the Black Death* (Princeton, 1951, rev. 4/1978)
E. B. Garrison: *Studies in the History of Medieval Italian Painting*, 4 vols (Florence, 1953–62)
E. Carli: *Pittura medievale pisana* (Milan, 1958)
E. Borsook: *The Mural Painters of Tuscany from Cimabue to Andrea del Sarto* (London, 1960, rev. 2/1980)
W. F. Friedländer: *Florentine Gothic Painters from Giotto to Masaccio* (London, 1975)
B. Cole: *Giotto and Florentine Painting, 1280–1375* (New York, 1976)
A. Smart: *The Dawn of Italian Painting, c. 1250–1400* (Ithaca, NY, 1978)
G. Palumbo and others: *Giotto e i giotteschi in Assisi* (Assisi, 1979)
B. Cole: *Sienese Painting: From its Origins to the 15th Century* (New York, 1980)
E. Carli: *Sienese Painting* (New York, 1983)
J. H. Stubblebine, ed.: *Dugento Painting: An Annotated Bibliography*, Reference Publications in Art History (Boston, 1983)
O. Demus: *The Mosaics of S Marco in Venice*, 4 vols (Chicago, 1984)
L. Bellosi: *La pecora di Giotto* (Turin, 1985)
J. Poeschke: *Die Kirche S. Francesco in Assisi und ihre Wandmalereien* (Munich, 1985)
J. H. Stubblebine, ed.: *Assisi and the Rise of Vernacular Art* (New York, 1985)
P. Hills: *The Light of Early Italian Painting* (New Haven, 1987)

MARK R. PETERSEN

3. EARLY RENAISSANCE, *c.* 1400–*c.* 1500. Scholars have traditionally divided 15th-century painting in the Italian city states into three stylistic categories based primarily on developments in Florence, the most vigorous and influential centre of production. The earliest, the International Gothic style, which was prevalent throughout Europe, flourished in the first decades of the century in Florence; it was displaced by the style of the early Renaissance that emerged in the 1420s. In the last two decades of the century, Leonardo da Vinci developed a simplified, classicizing art that laid the foundations for the High Renaissance style, which flourished in Rome under the patronage of Pope Julius II in the early 16th century. Developments in painting were linked to the revival of interest in antiquity and to a related interest in naturalism and illusionism. Humanist attitudes about the dignity of the individual and faith in the human potential for achievement, as explicated, for example, in Giovanni Pico della Mirandola's *Oration on the Dignity of Man* (Florence,

1496), and the humanist emphasis on historical consciousness help to explain the increasing importance of new genres such as portraiture, self-portraiture, mythology and Classical history. (All artists and patrons mentioned in this section have their own articles in this dictionary, unless their dates of birth and death are given.)

(i) Introduction. (ii) Regional survey.

(i) Introduction.

(a) Humanism, the Antique and illusionism. (b) Format. (c) Technique. (d) Subject-matter and patronage. (e) Status of the artist.

(a) Humanism, the Antique and illusionism. The humanist union of Christianity with ancient literary and philosophical traditions was centred in Florence, where it was important for the development of attitudes about painting and art in general (*see also* HUMANISM, §1). Leading Florentine humanists included Poggio Bracciolini, Coluccio Salutati (1331–1406), Leonardo Bruni and Niccolò Niccoli. Cosimo de' Medici charged Bracciolini and others with the task of retrieving Classical manuscripts from monasteries throughout Europe, where they had remained in obscurity since the Middle Ages. A manuscript copying business, organized by the humanist bookseller Vespasiano da Bisticci, guaranteed that an increasing number of Classical texts were available. Neo-Platonism flourished around Lorenzo de' Medici, and the ideas of his humanist protégés, especially Marsilio Ficino, Angelo Poliziano and Pico della Mirandola, were given visual expression in the art of Sandro Botticelli and others.

Renaissance architects and sculptors drew inspiration from surviving works of antique architecture and sculpture, but there were few painted models. Painters, however, could and did study works of antique sculpture and also new works of sculpture, inspired by antique models, by such artists as Donatello and Nanni di Banco, as well as surviving monuments of ancient architecture and the new Renaissance architecture of Brunelleschi. Despite the lack of actual models, pictorial illusionism, a major factor in ancient painting, was encouraged by a passage from Pliny (*Natural History* XXXV.xxxvi.65) that described an ancient painting contest in which Zeuxis created a painting of grapes that was so realistic that birds flew up to the fruit. Zeuxis lost the contest, however, when he requested that a draped curtain that was actually a painted one be removed from a work by his rival Parrhasios. The most exacting examples of illusionistic painting demonstrate sharp outlining of forms, a unified light source, careful and vigorous modelling and space created with repoussoirs and scientific and atmospheric perspective. That truth to nature was often used as the yardstick by which to judge paintings is confirmed by literary sources, including writings by Leonardo and Girolamo Savonarola.

Scientific perspective was perhaps the most important single device used by 15th-century painters to create an illusion of space. It allowed the development of measurable illusionistic space and also controlled the relative diminution of figures and objects within that space; in addition, it encouraged the study of complex forms represented in foreshortening. Scientific perspective was developed by Brunelleschi, probably in 1413, out of his interest in recording ancient architectural remains, but a series of

simple rules made it available to all artists (*see* PERSPECTIVE, §II, 2(i)). The system was codified and examined in some detail by Leon Battista Alberti in his treatise *De pictura* (1435).

In the 15th century there was an increased interest in writing about art and important developments in art theory, especially in the writings of Alberti. His *De pictura* was highly influential and provided a theoretical basis for painting; his ideas became the basis for the development of 16th-century Italian art theory (*see* ALBERTI, LEON BATTISTA, §II, 1). Several artists studied figural proportion: Piero della Francesca wrote a treatise on the subject, *De prospectiva pingendi* (*see* PIERO DELLA FRANCESCA, §III), and Leonardo planned a similar work (*see* LEONARDO DA VINCI, §III).

(b) Format. A large altarpiece produced at the beginning of the century was usually a polyptych, a complex grouping of many panels, including narrative predellas and saints in pinnacles, within an exuberant, elaborately carved Late Gothic frame, the gold background and repeated forms of the frame giving unity to the whole (*see* COLOUR, colour pl. II, fig. 1). By the end of the century the typical altarpiece consisted of a *pala* (panel) set within classicizing pilasters and an entablature and enclosing a single illusionistic narrative or religious grouping. Private devotional works changed from small triptychs with folding wings to rectangular or round-arched panels within classicizing frames. During the second half of the century, terracotta relief sculpture such as that produced by the della Robbia workshop came to rival and even replace the traditional painted devotional panels in the home. In the course of the 15th century popular new painting types included the polygonal or round *desco da parto* (birth salver) painted on both sides and cassone chests with narrative scenes and figures painted on the front and sides, as well as inside. Late in the century the TONDO became a popular format for domestic religious images. The decorative borders for fresco paintings and large fresco cycles were gradually simplified and usually featured Classical Corinthian pilasters and entablatures.

Any assessment of 15th-century Italian painting is tentative because a high percentage of works are lost. Some documented categories, such as the *pitture infamanti* of executed criminals that were painted on the outside of public buildings, do not survive in a single example.

(c) Technique. The attention to precise detail and the subtle luminosity that were made possible by the new oil technique developed in the early 15th century by Netherlandish artists gradually transformed Italian painting in the second half of the century. Jan van Eyck and his works were well known in Italy. Alfonso I of Aragon, King of Naples and Sicily, owned at least three of his paintings, as well as works by Rogier van der Weyden and other Netherlandish artists. The collection of Isabella d'Este, Marchesa of Mantua, included a painting by van Eyck as did the Medici collection in Florence. Rogier van der Weyden worked for the Este family at Ferrara between 1449 and 1451. He is said to have been in Rome in 1450 and he also may have visited Florence. Antonello da

Messina's understanding of Netherlandish technique surpassed that of any of his Italian contemporaries. His sojourn in Venice (1475–6) transformed the development of Venetian painting. Justus of Ghent and the Spaniard Pedro Berruguete both worked in a Netherlandish style between 1473 and 1482 for Federigo da Montefeltro, Duke of Urbino (*see* URBINO, fig. 1). Hugo van der Goes's *Portinari Altarpiece* (*c.* 1473–8; Florence, Uffizi), commissioned by the Florentine banker Tommaso Portinari in Bruges for the family chapel in S Egidio, Florence, had a pronounced impact on Florentine artists when it arrived in the city in 1483. Certain of Leonardo's early works show an awareness of Netherlandish oil technique. His technique of colour modelling, which unifies the painting by developing a tonal structure that moves towards a darker tonality, rather than towards white as in tempera painting, is based on Netherlandish practice.

(d) Subject-matter and patronage. The vast majority of the paintings created were still religious in subject. The 14th-century interest in painted narrative cycles that filled chapels, confraternities and other appropriate settings continued into the new century. Important religious cycles were painted by Masaccio and Masolino (Florence, S Maria del Carmine; Rome, S Clemente, destr.), Masolino (1435; Castiglione Olona, Baptistery), Fra Filippo Lippi (1452–66; Prato Cathedral), Fra Angelico (1438–44, Florence, S Marco; 1448–9, Rome, Vatican, chapel of Nicholas V), Benozzo Gozzoli (1459, Florence, Pal. Medici–Riccardi; 1465, San Gimignano, S Agostino), Piero della Francesca (1452–7; Arezzo, S Francesco), Andrea del Castagno (1447; Florence, S Apollonia, Cenacolo), Alesso Baldovinetti (Florence, Santa Trìnita; destr.), Mantegna (1454–7; Padua, Eremitani, Ovetari Chapel; mostly destr. 1944), Ghirlandaio (1483–6, Florence, Santa Trìnita; 1485–90, Florence, S Maria Novella), Melozzo da Forlì (1477–80; Rome, SS Apostoli, frags in Rome, Vatican, Pin. Vaticana) and Filippino Lippi (1487–1502; Florence, S Maria Novella, Strozzi Chapel; Rome, S Maria sopra Minerva) and in the Sistine Chapel in the Vatican (1481–3). Paintings were also incorporated into complex decorative schemes with architecture and sculpture, as at the chapel of the Cardinal of Portugal (Florence, S Miniato), which has paintings by Antonio and Piero Pollaiuolo and Baldovinetti (*see* FLORENCE, §IV, 7).

In the Republics civic commissions from the state increased. In Venice, the Doge's Palace was decorated with frescoes by Gentile da Fabriano, Pisanello, Gentile Bellini, Alvise Vivarini and Carpaccio, all destroyed by fire in 1574 and 1577 (*see* VENICE, §IV, 6(ii)). The various *scuole* commissioned cycles from Carpaccio (1490s, Scuola di Sant'Orsola; 1494, Scuola Grande di S Giovanni Evangelista) and Gentile Bellini (1496; Scuola Grande di S Giovanni Evangelista; *see* VENICE, fig. 26). Other public decorations include the Pellegrinaio in the Ospedale di S Maria della Scala, Siena, the frescoed monuments to famous condottieri in Florence Cathedral by Uccello (1436; *see* UCCELLO, PAOLO, fig. 1) and Castagno (1456; *see* ANDREA DEL CASTAGNO, fig. 4) and the frescoes (1481–5) by Ghirlandaio in the Sala dei Gigli in the Palazzo della Signoria (later Palazzo Vecchio), Florence. Decorative cycles commissioned by rulers of city states elsewhere

include Mantegna's frescoes (1465–74) in the Camera degli Sposi in the Palazzo Ducale, Mantua, and his *Triumphs of Caesar* series (1487–94; London, Hampton Court, Royal Col.), the frescoes of *The Months* (completed 1470) at the Palazzo Schifanoia, Ferrara, by Francesco del Cossa and Ercole de' Roberti (*see* FERRARA, §4(ii)), works by Justus of Ghent and Pedro Berruguete for the *studioli* of Federigo da Montefeltro at Urbino and Gubbio and works by Perugino and Mantegna for the *studiolo* of Isabella d'Este

29. Neroccio de' Landi and the Griselda Master: *Claudia Quinta*, panel, 1.05×0.46 m, *c.* 1495 (Washington, DC, National Gallery of Art)

30. Domenico Ghirlandaio: *St Francis Restoring a Child to Life*, fresco from the *Life of St Francis* cycle (1479–85) in the Sassetti Chapel, Santa Trinita, Florence

in Mantua. The frescoes in the Borgia Apartments in the Vatican (1492–5) were commissioned by Pope Alexander VI from Bernardino Pinturicchio (*see* ROME, §V, 14(iii)(b)). Many secular works are lost, including several documented cycles in palaces in Ferrara.

There was an increasing interest in the use of narrative sequences for palazzo and villa decoration. The rapidly increasing wealth of the banking and mercantile class, especially in Florence, meant that businessmen could afford to decorate their town houses with works of art. While most of these paintings were religious in nature, some began to feature mythological or historical subjects. Uccello's three large paintings of the *Rout of San Romano* (1430s and mid-1450s; Florence, Uffizi; London, N.G. (*see* UCCELLO, PAOLO, fig. 3); Paris, Louvre) feature a very recent historical event (1432) and decorated a bed-room wall in the Medici town house on Via Larga, Florence (now Palazzo Medici–Riccardi). Themes from Classical history and mythology were first commonly represented on cassone panels (*see* CASSONE, §1) and *spalliere*, long rectangular panels, or series of panels, set into wainscoting that furnished the town houses of the Florentine merchant classes and that had been produced in the workshops of such artists as Apollonio di Giovanni, Pesellino and Scheggia (*see* SPALLIERA). Popular themes included lives of *Famous Men and Women*, Petrarch's *Triumphs* and subjects from Classical history and Ovid. Large-scale paintings of mythological subjects were at first rare. Among the earliest documented examples are Antonio and Piero Pollaiuolo's three large canvases depicting the *Labours of Hercules* (untraced; painted *c.* 1460 for the Medici town house in Florence). Two of the compositions survive (Florence, Uffizi), replicated on small-scale panels. Large-scale mythological and Classical works appeared by the 1470s and 1480s, for example Botticelli's *Primavera* and the *Birth of Venus* (*see* BOTTICELLI, SANDRO, figs 2 and 3) and Mantegna's *Triumphs of Caesar*. A special interest in ancient themes is evident in the works of Piero

di Cosimo at the end of the century. Some artists, for example Botticelli, tried to re-create the *Calumny*, an allegorical painting by the Greek painter Apelles described in a famous EKPHRASIS by the Greek author Lucian. Nudes and paintings of mythological themes were proba-bly among the works of art that were burnt by the followers of Savonarola in the 1490s. Secular decorations include Andrea del Castagno's series of *Famous Men and Women* (1449–51; ex-Villa Carducci, Legnaia; Florence, S Apol-lonia, Cenacolo) and the cycle of eight *Famous Men and Women* by various Sienese artists that includes Neroccio de' Landi's and the Griselda Master's *Claudia Quinta* (*c.* 1495; Washington, DC, N.G.A.; see fig. 29).

Portraiture of men and women of the mercantile and banking class began in Florence with profile representa-tions modelled on those depicted on ancient coins and medals, but during the second half of the century the three-quarter view became common. The inclusion of donors the same size as Christ, the Virgin and saints is found in works by Masaccio and Gentile da Fabriano in the 1420s. By the end of the century Ghirlandaio's frescoes (see fig. 30; see also fig.103 below) and Gentile Bellini's and Vittore Carpaccio's paintings for the Venetian *scuole* (*see* CARPACCIO, (1), figs 2 and 4) are crowded with portraits of citizens gathered at the margins of religious narratives against a backdrop of Florentine or Venetian architecture.

See also §XII, 4 below.

(e) Status of the artist. During the 15th century artists gradually began to sign their works or to include a self-portrait in the painting (e.g. Benozzo Gozzoli, Botticelli and Gentile Bellini) as a sign of their accomplishment. Some artists achieved individual fâme, as indicated in humanist and other writings, and the status of the artist as an intellectual was promoted by Alberti's treatises. The perceived importance of perspective and geometry for

artists, not to mention the usefulness of some Classical knowledge, helped to elevate painting above the mechanical arts to a new status as a liberal art. Communities and rulers were proud of artists who achieved an international reputation and who received commissions from other city states. Such artists often travelled widely, and their works were sent as gifts from one ruler to another. Those rulers of the various city states who had had a humanist education, such as Federigo II Montefeltro, Duke of Urbino; Gianfrancesco Gonzaga, 1st Marchese of Mantua, and his son Ludovico, 2nd Marchese of Mantua; Lionello d'Este, Marchese of Ferrara; Sigismondo Pandolfo Malatesta and Isabella d'Este, Marchesa of Mantua, began to retain artists at their courts as *stipendiati* and used works of art both to enhance their prestige and to promote their roles as enlightened rulers. The acceptance of artists at noble courts eventually helped to establish the basis for the respect accorded to Leonardo, Michelangelo, Raphael and Titian in the 16th century. The rise in social status enjoyed by the foremost Renaissance artists was supported by reports of the esteem accorded to artists in antiquity, as evidenced by passages in Pliny. Painters were commonly active in other areas of intellectual and cultural life, such as architecture, writing and science, as is seen in the careers of Leonardo, Michelangelo, Bramante and Francesco di Giorgio Martini.

At the same time, however, documents such as Neri di Bicci's *Ricordanze* give a clear indication of the many mundane tasks carried out in a typical 15th-century workshop: painting trade signs, banners, coats-of-arms, furniture, frames and cheap gessoed *Virgins*, designing tournament costumes and temporary decorations for festivals and gilding horse-trappings. Many aspects of the painter's life had changed little since the Middle Ages. The training of apprentices, for example, was still carried on in the workshop and could take as long as 13 years. Painters and apprentices were still subject to GUILD membership and rules, except in Florence, where membership of the Arte de' Medici e Speziali was not required and foreign artists could practise without fear of recrimination. Family dynasties, a result of the workshop tradition, were encouraged by guild rules and were common. In Florence, in the second half of the 15th century the two most successful workshops were those of Domenico Ghirlandaio and Andrea del Verrocchio, both of whom operated on a large scale. Verrocchio's workshop, in addition to turning out large quantities of paintings, engaged in sculptural and engineering projects. It employed a large workforce, from *garzoni* (shop-boys) to apprentices and assistants of varying skill.

(ii) Regional survey. There were other centres of production than Florence—Bologna, Ferrara, Mantua, Milan, Naples, Padua, Rome, Siena, Venice and Verona—but interaction with Florentine painters or their work, especially in the period *c.* 1440–70, was common. Many of these centres were dominated by a single artist or a small group of artists practising a unified style, usually under the inspiration of Florentine precedents. Later in the century other centres rose in importance and in turn exported their styles. Perugino and Raphael carried Umbrian trends to Florence, the Paduan style was carried to the Marches by Carlo

Crivelli, and the Venetian style had an impact throughout the Veneto and was even practised in Constantinople by Gentile Bellini.

(a) Florence. The International Gothic style in Italy (*see* GOTHIC, §IV, 5(xi)) is characterized by marginal realism, especially in the rendering of animals and plants, tall, elegant figures, extravagant decorative drapery patterns and 'doll's house' architecture. Florentine painters who worked in this style include Lorenzo Monaco, Masolino, the Master of 1419, Gentile da Fabriano (whose *Adoration of the Magi* (1423; Florence, Uffizi; *see* GENTILE DA FABRIANO, fig. 3) illustrates the style at its most characteristic) and the young Paolo Uccello.

Masaccio's new Renaissance style, which emerged in Florence in the 1420s, combined the weight and mass of Giotto's figures with a more subtle understanding of figural construction derived from a study of the Antique and the Classically inspired contemporary sculpture of Donatello and Nanni di Banco. In reaction to the prevailing International Gothic style, his works are, as the humanist Cristoforo Landino wrote, 'pure and without ornamentation'. Masaccio's serious, noble figures were placed in classicizing architectural settings within a coherent illusory space made possible by the new developments of scientific and atmospheric perspective. Masaccio's naturalistic style influenced the second generation of Florentine painters, Fra Angelico, Fra Filippo Lippi and Paolo Uccello, and had an impact on virtually all later Renaissance painting. Later artists added their own emphases. Domenico Veneziano specialized in subtlety of lighting, as for example in the *Annunciation* (*c.* 1445; Cambridge, Fitzwilliam; *see* fig. 31), part of the predella from the *St Lucy* Altarpiece (Florence, Uffizi). Andrea del Castagno concentrated on achieving sculpturesque effects, and Antonio and Piero Pollaiuolo powerful movement. Several artists began to take a more scientific approach to art. Antonio Pollaiuolo was followed in his interest in anatomy by Leonardo and Michelangelo. A new interest in mythological and allegorical themes, surely based on humanist interests, is evident in works from the second half of the century. Botticelli's *Primavera* and the *Birth of Venus*, two of the earliest large-scale paintings of mythological subjects since antiquity, exhibit a complex iconography that relates to Neo-Platonic debates of the period.

When Pope Sixtus IV wanted to fresco the Sistine Chapel in the Vatican Palace, between 1481 and 1483 (*see* ROME, §V, 14(iii)(b)), he called to Rome the Florentines Domenico Ghirlandaio, Botticelli and Cosimo Rosselli; the last was assisted by Piero di Cosimo. The other painters commissioned by Sixtus—Luca Signorelli, Perugino and Bernardino Pinturicchio (*see* ROME, fig. 44)—had all been influenced by Florentine innovations. The Florentine style had already been carried to Rome by Masaccio, and Uccello had worked in Venice (1425–*c.* 1430) and Padua (1445–6). Filippo Lippi, Fra Angelico, Andrea del Castagno, Antonio del Pollaiuolo and Leonardo were among the numerous artists who carried Florentine innovations to many parts of Italy. The Florentine sculptor Donatello lived in Padua from 1443 to 1453, and his works were greatly influential there as well as in Venice, Siena, Naples

31. Domenico Veneziano: *Annunciation*, panel, 273×540 mm, from the predella of the *St Lucy* Altarpiece, *c.* 1445 (Cambridge, Fitzwilliam Museum)

and Rome. Ghiberti's and Donatello's work on the font in the Siena Baptistery also influenced painters. Among the artists who came to Florence to study and/or work in the 15th century were Piero della Francesca and Perugino and Raphael from Umbria, and Domenico Veneziano and Jacopo Bellini from Venice. In the 1490s the preaching of Savonarola turned patrons and artists away from the humanist interests of preceding decades and led to the destruction of many secular works of art.

(b) *Other centres.* Painting in Siena in the 15th century is generally deemed conservative in comparison to that of Florence. Sienese patrons continued to admire the work of the 14th century, and religious attitudes in Siena suggest the impact of a central cultural figure in 15th-century Sienese life, St Bernardino of Siena (1380–1444, *can* 1450). Domenico di Bartolo, il Vecchietta and the other painters who worked on the fresco cycle (1441–4) depicting the activity of the hospital in the Pellegrinaio (hostel for pilgrims) at the Ospedale di S Maria della Scala, Siena (*see* SIENA, §III, 2 and fig. 8), adapted many Florentine elements. At the same time Sassetta, Giovanni di Paolo and others continued the venerable Sienese tradition of Duccio and Simone Martini, of delicate figures against a gold ground, and restricted their interest in Florentine innovations to spatial effects in the landscapes and architectural settings of their narrative scenes. Sienese patrons kept alive the demand for gold-backed *Virgins* and altarpieces such as those produced by Sano di Pietro until late in the century. The tense, linear and dramatic style of the Florentines Castagno and Antonio Pollaiuolo influenced the works of il Vecchietta and Matteo di Giovanni. Other Sienese artists influenced by Florence were Neroccio de' Landi and Francesco di Giorgio Martini. An unusual opportunity was given to 15th-century Sienese painters when they were asked to create compositions to be executed in stone for the pavement of their Cathedral.

Although somewhat worn and restored, pavement compositions by Pinturicchio, Matteo di Giovanni, Neroccio de' Landi and others survive. (*See also* SIENA, §II.)

In Padua, the interest in archaeology and in antique decorative motifs found in the works of Andrea Mantegna was probably inspired by the Classical interests of his teacher Francesco Squarcione. Donatello's presence in Padua also had an important impact on the development of Mantegna's style. Mantegna later took the Paduan style to Mantua and Ferrara. Carlo Crivelli carried it to the Marches, and it was promoted in Venice by the Bellini family. (*See also* PADUA, §2.)

In Venice, the International Gothic style as interpreted by Jacobello del Fiore, Paolo Veneziano and Antonio Vivarini gradually gave way to Florentine interests in space and scientific perspective, as may be seen in the dramatic vistas in the sketchbooks of Jacopo Bellini. In the works of his son Giovanni Bellini, the influence of the linear and sculpturesque style of Mantegna was at first paramount, but, apparently captivated by Antonello da Messina's use of the Netherlandish oil technique, Bellini gradually created a successful fusion of colour, light and atmosphere that laid the foundation for the developments of Giorgione and Titian in the 16th century. His brother Gentile Bellini and Vittore Carpaccio excelled at recording the full panoply of Venetian life, culture and customs in their works. (*See also* VENICE, §II, 2 and 3.)

Working in centres in Umbria and the Marches, Piero della Francesco created his own serene vision of Renaissance clarity based on Florentine models. In Naples, Niccolò Colantonio shows the influence of Flemish and French models. At Perugia, the most important artists were Giovanni Santi (the father of Raphael) and Perugino. In Bologna, Francesco Francia, a goldsmith, only began to paint in the 1490s. Rome had no native school worthy of papal patronage. In Milan, Bramante worked in the style of Mantegna before turning to architecture, and Leonardo exerted a great influence on the local tradition during his residency at the Sforza court (*c.* 1482–99). Other painters active in Lombardy included Vincenzo Foppa and il Bergognone. The major painters in Ferrara were Cosimo Tura, Francesco del Cossa and Ercole de' Roberti; those in Modena were Agnolo and Bartolommeo degli Erri.

BIBLIOGRAPHY

P. Burke: *Culture and Society in Renaissance Italy, 1420–1540* (London, 1972); rev. as *The Italian Renaissance: Culture and Society in Italy* (Princeton, 1986)

S. Y. Edgerton jr: *The Renaissance Rediscovery of Linear Perspective* (New York, 1975)

J. R. Hale: *Italian Renaissance Painting from Masaccio to Titian* (New York, 1977)

C. E. Gilbert: *Italian Art, 1400–1500: Sources and Documents* (Englewood Cliffs, 1980)

M. Wackernagel: *The World of the Florentine Renaissance Artist* (Princeton, 1981)

B. Cole: *The Renaissance Artist at Work* (New York, 1983)

——: *Sienese Painting in the Age of the Renaissance* (Bloomington, 1985)

B. Schultz: *Art and Anatomy in Renaissance Italy* (Ann Arbor, 1985)

M. Baxandall: *Painting and Experience in Fifteenth-century Italy* (Oxford, 1988)

M. A. Lavin: *The Place of Narrative: Mural Decoration in Italian Churches, 431–1600* (Chicago, 1990)

J. Shearman: *Only Connect: Art and the Spectator in the Italian Renaissance* (Princeton, 1992)

Maestri e botteghe: Pittura a Firenze alla fine del quattrocento (Florence, 1992)

C. F. Lewine: *The Sistine Chapel Walls and the Roman Liturgy* (University Park, PA, 1994)

A. B. Barriault: *Spalliera Paintings of Renaissance Italy* (University Park, PA, 1994)

E. Boorsook and F. S. Gioffredi, eds: *Italian Altarpieces 1250–1550: Function and Design* (Oxford, 1994)

Painting and Illumination in Early Renaissance Florence, 1300–1450 (exh. cat., New York, Met., 1995)

DAVID G. WILKINS

4. HIGH RENAISSANCE AND MANNERISM, *c.* 1500–*c.* 1600. In the first two decades of the 16th century the dominant artistic style was that of the High Renaissance. By 1520 the balance of artistic intentions was shifting, and style was developing in a number of ways that would collectively come to be known as MANNERISM. Awareness of antique philosophy and literature, art and architecture was seminal to the development of subject-matter and artistic style in this period. Painters, once equated with craftsmen, won equal status with practitioners of the traditional liberal arts. Heightened artistic consciousness intensified stylistic interaction between painting and sculpture and provoked debate as to the comparative values of each, the PARAGONE. Cross-currents of artistic practice were accelerated by the travels of artists and patrons and by the dissemination of drawings and prints.

(i) Florence. (ii) Rome. (iii) Venice. (iv) Other schools and artists.

(i) Florence. Artistic patronage was affected by political upheaval. Leonardo da Vinci and MICHELANGELO were in Florence periodically during the first decade, and both were central to the realization of High Renaissance art. Leonardo evolved idealized and monumental figures and harmonious compositions built on interdependent forms. He exploited the new oil medium to create subtle modulation of tone, soft *sfumato* effect (*see* CHIAROSCURO) and

atmospheric perspective (*see* PERSPECTIVE, §III), achieving a unified mood of figures and setting. The transformation from the bright naturalism of 15th-century altarpieces is exemplified by Leonardo's *Virgin of the Rocks* (*c.* 1490–1508; London, N.G.; *see* LEONARDO DA VINCI, fig. 2). Michelangelo's art was influenced by the philosophy of NEO-PLATONISM. His Doni *Tondo* (1503–4; Florence, Uffizi) is another example of traditional iconography reconsidered, combining male nudes derived from antique art with Christian imagery.

The art of Leonardo and Michelangelo was based on drawing (*see* DRAWING, colour pl. I, fig. 1), which remained significant for quick notation and for drawing from life and from antique exemplars. It was the basis of the central Italian concept of *disegno*, intellectualized, structural form and composition (*see* DISEGNO E COLORE). Drawing in metalpoint was superseded by pen and ink, black chalk and red chalk. In the High Renaissance painters made increasing use of the CARTOON, which was particularly important for the accurate transfer of design in fresco, the traditional medium for Florentine decorative art. In 1504 Leonardo and Michelangelo were commissioned to paint two battle scenes in the new council hall, the Sala del Gran Concilio, of the Palazzo della Signoria. Neither work was completed, but Leonardo's complex composition and Michelangelo's cartoon of the male nude in vigorous action (both recorded in copies) would be highly influential.

Raphael was in Florence on and off between 1504 and 1508 and responded to stylistic developments there. By late 1508, when Leonardo, Michelangelo and Raphael had left Florence, FRA BARTOLOMMEO and ANDREA DEL SARTO were the leading painters there. Del Sarto, who had assimilated the underlying Classical values of Leonardo and Michelangelo, also evolved an effective chiaroscuro and borrowed from the engravings of Albrecht Dürer, which were becoming available in Italy. The demand for portraiture was growing, and Leonardo's lessons—of breadth of form, turning figure and psychological presence in the half-length portrait—were fully assimilated in the second decade. Del Sarto's *Portrait of a Man* (*c.* 1517; London, N.G.) projects physical and mental alertness as the figure turns in space to engage with the viewer.

By *c.* 1515–18 Pontormo and ROSSO FIORENTINO had transformed del Sarto's classical art into a disturbing and irrational form of Mannerism. Pontormo united decentralized composition, irrational depiction of space, attenuated figures and exaggerated poses. He adopted irregular line from Dürer's prints and evolved a palette of light, bright colours, for example in the *Lamentation* (*c.* 1528; Florence, S Felicità; *see* PONTORMO, fig. 2). Rosso distorted figures into cyphers of emotional condition, and in Rome (1523–7) he adopted extremes of CONTRAPPOSTO and foreshortening.

Hopes for a renewal of the Republic ended with the accession of Cosimo I de' Medici as Duke of Florence in 1537 (*see* MEDICI, DE', (14)). Court patronage then dominated second-generation Mannerism. Agnolo Bronzino's paintings were sophisticated artifices in frozen elegance with a formal beauty of line and surface. His nudes displayed sexuality but pretended none, as in the allegory *Venus, Cupid, Folly and Time* (*c.* 1544–5; London,

32. Raphael: *School of Athens* (*c.* 1510–12), fresco, Stanza della Segnatura, Vatican, Rome

N.G.; *see* BRONZINO, fig. 2). His masklike portraits contrasted with the sensitive nervosity of Pontormo's. A great programme of decoration was instigated by Cosimo's personal appropriation of the Palazzo della Signoria (1540). Bronzino and Francesco Salviati made significant contributions, in which subject and content were subservient to formal aesthetics (*see* SALVIATI, FRANCESCO, fig. 2). The decorations designed by Giorgio Vasari (*see* VASARI, (1)) used stylized formulae to tedious effect, with obscure intellectual conceits. In this late form of Mannerism, known as High Maniera, Vasari's was the pervading influence. He subcontracted some of the decorative work, as in the *studiolo* (designed 1570; *see* STUDIOLO, fig. 2) for Cosimo's son Francesco (*see* MEDICI, DE', (16)), as well as altarpieces for S Maria Novella and Santa Croce. During the last three decades a tired version of Maniera artifice was continued by painters including Alessandro Allori (*see* ALLORI, (1)), GIROLAMO MACCHIETTI and MIRABELLO CAVALORI. Others more successfully sought a way out of Maniera conventions. SANTI DI TITO, for example, achieved a return to conventional form and clarity of composition and content, as in his *Vision of St Thomas Aquinas* (1593; Florence, S Marco). By this time, Vasari had done much to formalize the status of painters and painting with the publication of his artists' lives, the *Vite* (1550; revised 1568). His initiatives resulted in the founding of the first artists' academy, the Accademia del Disegno (1563).

(ii) Rome. Pope Julius II (*see* ROVERE, DELLA (i), (2)) transformed Rome into the artistic centre of central Italy. He compelled Michelangelo to fresco the ceiling of the Sistine Chapel (1508–12; *see* ROME, fig.42) and by 1509 had commissioned Raphael to fresco the Stanza della Segnatura (both Rome, Vatican). Michelangelo's art was rooted in the expressive possibilities of the human form, and in the Sistine ceiling his idealized male nudes and figures were developed with monumental force or in extreme torsion. His influence was extended through SEBASTIANO DEL PIOMBO, in Rome from 1511, for whom he supplied figure studies for such important commissions as the *Raising of Lazarus* (1517–19; London, N.G.).

Raphael's work in the Vatican set the standard of intellectual and executive ability required of the High Renaissance artist. He accommodated the decorative and propaganda intentions of his patrons, combining Christian and pagan iconography, realism, idealism and grace. He first projected a fully realized response to the monumental ruins of ancient Rome in the *School of Athens* (*c.* 1510–12; Rome, Vatican, Stanza della Segnatura; see fig. 32). He went on to create a chiaroscuro of expressive and dramatic force, and to stretch the classical style to its limits. Raphael's altarpieces and portraits epitomize High Renaissance achievement: the visionary *Sistine Madonna* (*c.* 1513–14; Dresden, Gemäldegal. Alte Meister); the *Transfiguration* (1517–20; Rome, Pin. Vaticana; *see* RAPHAEL, fig. 6), which includes two narrative subjects; the innovative three-quarter length, seated and turned *Pope Julius II* (c. 1512; London, N.G.); the courtly dignity of *Baldassare Castiglione* (c. 1514–15; Paris, Louvre; *see* RAPHAEL, fig. 8). His collaboration with the engraver MARCANTONIO RAIMONDI extended the artistic and commercial potential of engraving. Raphael employed a large workshop to execute his designs for various commissions from c. 1515, expanding the vocabulary of decorative art from antique examples.

After Raphael's death in 1520, his former assistants led Rome in the development of a new post-classical style, Mannerism. Giulio Romano, for example, used rhythmic tensions, heavily sculptural form, selfconscious poses and exaggerated perspective recession, as in the *Holy Family with SS James, John the Baptist and Mark* (?c. 1522; Rome, S Maria dell'Anima; *see* GIULIO ROMANO, fig. 2). He also made purely erotic drawings, which were engraved by Marcantonio. Rome continued to attract painters, including PARMIGIANINO in 1523, who assimilated the artifice of Mannerist aesthetics, as seen in the *Virgin and Child with SS John the Baptist and Jerome* (1527; London, N.G.).

In 1527 many artists fled after Rome was sacked by imperial troops. Their dispersal affected art elsewhere in Italy, and also in France. The material and psychological devastation of the sack affected the arts for several years. In 1534 Michelangelo returned from Florence. Pope Paul III (*see* FARNESE, (1)) ordered him to paint the altar wall of the Sistine Chapel with the *Last Judgement* (1536–41; Rome, Vatican; *see* ROME, fig. 43). The many nudes offended the increasing pietism of the Counter-Reformation, and after Michelangelo's death (1564) drapery was added to them. From c. 1530 Michelangelo extended the function of drawing, producing 'presentation drawings' as independent works. Made as gifts for friends, they introduced an art of personal, intellectual and spiritual communion between artist and recipient (*see* MICHELANGELO, fig. 9 and PRESENTATION DRAWING).

In the second half of the century stylistic trends became more complex. The cult of Michelangelo, the power and energy of human form manifest in his later works, affected such painters as DANIELE DA VOLTERRA and Francesco Salviati. Their work was, however, essentially developed High Maniera in its stylized artifice. Salviati's complex decorative schemes in the Salon dei Fasti Farnesi, Palazzo Farnese, Rome (c. 1549–63; *see* SALVIATI, FRANCESCO, fig. 4), exemplify this. With the sobering influence of the Counter-Reformation, the younger generation sought a classical temper to counter Maniera extremes. GIROLAMO MUZIANO, for example, revived a more natural form and logic of composition. His counter-Maniera style was taken to an extreme in Scipione Pulzone's pietistic art, as in his *Holy Family* (c. 1590; Rome, Gal. Borghese; for illustration *see* PULZONE, SCIPIONE). Parallel with this, some artists continued a Mannerist aesthetic, such as Federico Zuccaro, in the 1580s in Rome (*see* ZUCCARO, (2)). All these tendencies of the late century relied directly on various 16th-century precedents. MICHELANGELO MERISI DA CARAVAGGIO, who was in Rome by c. 1590, and Annibale Carracci, by 1595, introduced fresh concepts of realism and classicism, which provided new impetus for the next century.

(iii) Venice. Art in Venice was open to various influences: developments in central Italy, antiquity and her own Byzantine heritage. Dürer's visit in 1505–6 heightened awareness of northern realism and nature. Jacopo Sansovino (*see* SANSOVINO, (1)), PIETRO ARETINO and SEBASTIANO SERLIO, who arrived in 1527, significantly affected Venetian art. Despite the decline of the Venetian Empire, artistic patronage flourished. Experimenting with oil techniques, painters developed a distinctive style, *colorismo*, reliant on the optical experience of light, colour and surface impression.

In the first decade Giorgione introduced innovative subjects that accorded with the interests of humanists and literati, such as *The Tempest* (c. 1504; Venice, Accad.) and the nude *Sleeping Venus*, completed by Titian (c. 1509–10; Dresden, Gemäldegal. Alte Meister; for both *see* GIORGIONE, figs 3 and 5). He simplified preparatory underdrawing, initiating the Venetian freedom to extemporize during the painting process. His idealized, atmospheric and contemplative style was emulated by many painters. Giovanni Bellini (*see* BELLINI (3)), Giorgione, Titian and others contributed to the transformation of altarpieces and devotional works. Titian first fully realized a new scale, vision and drama in the *Assumption of the Virgin* (1516–18; Venice, S Maria Gloriosa dei Frari; *see* ALTARPIECE, fig. 4). He went on to explore asymmetrical composition and the dramatic interaction of man and nature.

The State used decorative art in the Doge's Palace to glorify the past. Decoration of *scuole* buildings proved an exceptional opportunity for the development of narrative and serial painting (*see* VENICE, §V). This is traceable through the achievements of the BELLINI family and Vittore Carpaccio (*see* CARPACCIO, (1)) in the 15th century to Titian and Jacopo Tintoretto (*see* TINTORETTO, (1)). Oil on canvas, rather than fresco, was the rule. By the mid-16th century the scope of portraiture in Italy had been radically extended to include half, three-quarter, full-length and seated figures, and single, double and group portraits. After Giorgione, Titian dominated Venetian portraiture. From the 1530s he developed a sensitive balance of lively realism and idealism, of individual and status, for princely patrons on the mainland. Such patronage opened other opportunities to him, including mythological subjects such as the *Bacchanal of the Andrians* (c. 1523–5; Madrid, Prado; *see* TITIAN, fig. 5) for Alfonso I d'Este, Duke of Ferrara. In the 'fancy portrait', a Venetian development of the first two decades, the model was depicted as a character or type (*see* PORTRAITURE, §I). Titian's *Venus of Urbino* (1538; Florence, Uffizi) was an extension of this type, accommodating voyeurism in the viewer. Francesco Salviati visited Venice in 1539–41, introducing his rhetorical, Mannerist style and elongated figures. BONIFAZIO DE' PITATI, PARIS BORDONE, PORDENONE and ANDREA SCHIAVONE also all worked in Venice.

The publications of PAOLO PINO and LUDOVICO DOLCE discussed the relative merits of Venetian *colorismo* and central Italian *disegno*. Dolce focused on Titian as Venice's most famous practitioner. Titian continued to enjoy important patronage outside Venice, especially for portraits, such as the propagandist *Charles V at Mühlberg* (1548; Madrid, Prado). Through the 1550s and 1560s he executed a series of paintings for Philip II of Spain (*see* HABSBURG, §II(2)), based on Ovid's *Metamorphoses*. In *Diana and Actaeon* (1559; Duke of Sutherland, on loan to Edinburgh, N.G.; see fig. 33) his free brushwork, colour, tone and shifting verticals increase the tension of glance and gesture.

In Venice, the combination of stylistic awareness and ambitious patronage produced innovative decorative schemes for Church and State. Illusionistic ceiling painting was adopted, using canvases inserted into geometrically compartmentalized wooden ceilings rather than fresco. Titian initiated a 45% angle of perspective for greater legibility from the ground, for example in *Cain and Abel* (1542–4; Venice, S Maria della Salute). By 1555 Paolo Veronese was resident in Venice and had begun work in S Sebastiano. Continuing into the 1570s, he decorated the whole church, a unified programme that was novel in Venetian churches. Consciousness of style led Jacopo Tintoretto from an early synthesis of forms derived from Michelangelo and Titian's use of colour to atmospheric evocation. He used Mannerist devices, such as repoussoir forms (in the very foreground) and the placement of significant figures in the middle-ground. His vitality and epic scale transformed the decoration of churches and *scuole*, climaxing in his extensive programme for the Scuola Grande di S Rocco, 1565–87 (*see* VENICE, §V, 4 and fig. 28). With the *Marriage at Cana* (1561; Venice, S Maria della Salute) he initiated a new genre for Venice, the great feast scene. This was developed variously by himself and Veronese. Veronese's rich colour and elegance of architectural settings affected a secular splendour, but with subtly controlled composition and content (*see* VERONESE, PAOLO, fig. 4). By the 1570s Titian and Veronese were assimilating Tintoretto's tonal force and dematerialized form, yet all retained artistic individuality. They responded to different commissions with versatility. The State's continuing employment of leading painters in the Doge's Palace culminated in the redecoration of the Sala del Maggior Consiglio, after a fire in 1577 (*see* VENICE, §IV, 6(ii)). Veronese's ceiling with the *Apotheosis of Venice*

33. Titian: *Diana and Actaeon*, oil on canvas, 1.88×2.03 m, 1559 (Duke of Sutherland, on loan to Edinburgh, National Gallery of Scotland)

(*c.* 1583) and Tintoretto's epic *Paradise* (1588–92) epitomize the decorative and ideological harmony of Venetian painting. By the end of the century, however, Venetian painting had lost the vigour of innovation.

In the Veneto, Jacopo Bassano created a novel rustic style, as in *Adoration of the Shepherds* (1568; Bassano del Grappa, Mus. Civ.; *see* BASSANO, (2), fig. 3). This type became popular through Europe. Development of the working country villa offered new decorative scope. At the Villa Barbaro, Maser, Veronese showed sensitivity to Andrea Palladio's architecture in his inventive frescoed allegories, landscapes and illusionistic caprices (*c.* 1561; *see* ILLUSIONISM, colour pl. IV). BATTISTA ZELOTTI established a career in villa decoration.

(iv) Other schools and artists. Court patronage dominated Mantua and Ferrara. ANDREA MANTEGNA was painter to the Gonzaga in Mantua until his death in 1506. In 1524 Giulio Romano arrived as court artist to Federico II Gonzaga, 5th Marquese and later 1st Duke of Mantua (*see* GONZAGA, (9)). Giulio revitalized Mantuan art. His brutal, lascivious and humorous decoration of the Palazzo del Tè (*c.* 1532–4) exploited the building's informal function, and his forceful illusionism and exaggeration of form had a wide impact. Federico Gonzaga also patronized Titian, who assimilated something of Giulio's style. In Ferrara Alfonso I d'Este (*see* ESTE (i), (8)) pressed for artistic contributions to his court from leading painters of Venice and central Italy, although Dosso Dossi effectively updated the local fanciful and courtly style by introducing the styles of Venetian art and Raphael (*see* DOSSI, (1)). The fantastic landscapes of NICOLÒ DELL'ABATE, a Modenese painter, owed much to the Ferrarese school, which declined after Alfonso's rule.

LORENZO LOTTO worked for provincial patrons in the Marches during several extended periods, as well as in Venice, Rome, Bergamo and Treviso. Aware of the mainstreams of painting, he developed a singular, intense style, as seen in the *Visitation* (*c.* 1535; Jesi, Pin. Civ.). Venetian influence spread through northern Italy to Brescia and Bergamo. Here, men of the increasingly important professional classes supported a burgeoning portrait business. In this, MORETTO da Brescia and his pupil Giovanni Battista Moroni overlaid Brescian naturalism with stylistic elements from Giorgione and Titian. By the late 1520s Moretto had adopted the northern, full-length, independent portrait. Moroni's greater realism is seen in *The Tailor* (*Portrait of a Man*, *c.* 1570; London, N.G.; *see* MORONI, GIOVANNI BATTISTA, fig. 2), which exceptionally represents a working artisan.

In Parma, Correggio used a broad knowledge of Italian art to evolve a style of energized illusionism and intense emotion that anticipated the Baroque, culminating in the *Assumption of the Virgin* (*c.* 1526–30; Parma Cathedral; *see* CORREGGIO, fig. 4). In his oil paintings he combined a soft *sfumato* derived from Leonardo with delicate colouring. In 1530 Parmigianino returned from Rome, bringing the exaggerated aesthetics of Roman Mannerism, for example in his *Virgin and Child with SS John the Baptist and Jerome* (*Vision of St Jerome*, 1527; London, N.G.; see fig. 34). In Bologna, Lodovico, Annibale and Agostino CARRACCI founded the first effective teaching academy

34. Parmigianino: *Virgin and Child with SS John the Baptist and Jerome* (*Vision of St Jerome*), oil on panel, 3.43×1.49 m, 1527 (London, National Gallery)

for artists shortly after 1582. They rejected the obscuring artifices of Mannerism and emphasized drawing from life as the basis for visual and ideological clarity. Their reappraisal of the classical tradition formed the basis for much of 17th-century art.

The expressive value of Sienese art was already modified by 15th-century Florentine rationalism. DOMENICO BECCAFUMI was outstanding as the Sienese painter who met contemporary developments on his own terms. He was in Rome in 1510–12 and knew the work of Raphael and Michelangelo. Returning to Siena in 1513, he increasingly heightened the emotional tenor of his work with effects of shot-colour or surprising hues (*see* CANGIANTI) reminding one of the force of colour in Michelangelo's Sistine Chapel ceiling.

In Italy a few women painters were materially successful. Foremost was Sofonisba Anguissola (*see* ANGUISSOLA, (1)) of Cremona. A noblewoman, she was taught painting as a dilettante skill but exceptionally achieved international fame. Lavinia Fontana of Bologna and FEDE GALIZIA of Milan were, like Marietta Tintoretto (*see* TINTORETTO, (2)), daughters of painters. Portraits of women were deemed suitable subjects: Fontana made her name with portraits of Bolognese noblewomen. *Woman with a Lapdog* (late 1590s; Baltimore, MD, Walters A.G.) exemplifies the suggestion of activity and presents character in her elegant images. Sofonisba's portraits included such innovative works as *Lucia, Minerva and Europa Anguissola Playing Chess* (1555; Poznań, N. Mus.). Social decorum prohibited women from studying the life-model and thus hindered their participation in the prestigious area of large, narrative painting. Nonetheless, Fontana produced religious and mythological subjects for private and public commissions (for illustration *see* FONTANA (ii), (2)). Galizia broadened her range by exploring the new genre of still-life. Recognition of the talents of a few women owed something to Renaissance emulation of similarly limited antique precedent. Professional women painters were seen as acting atypically, however, in what was deemed to be properly the male preserve of an intellectual and creative art.

EWA

BIBLIOGRAPHY

P. Pino: *Dialogo di pittura* (Venice, 1548); ed. E. Camesasca (Milan, 1954)
G. Vasari: *Vite* (1550, rev. 2/1568); ed. G. Milanesi (1878–85)
L. Dolce: *Dialogo della pittura intitolato l'Aretino* (Venice, 1557), ed. and Eng. trans. by M. Roskill (Princeton, 1968)
J. A. Crowe and G. B. Cavalcaselle: *A History of Painting in North Italy*, 2 vols (London, 1871); rev. 2, ed. T. Borenius, 2 vols (New York, 1912/R 1972)
J. Burkhardt: *Das Altarbild* (1893–4); Eng. trans. as *The Altarpiece in Renaissance Italy*, ed. P. Humphrey (Oxford, 1988)
B. Berenson: *The Drawings of the Florentine Painters*, 2 vols (London, 1903, rev. 2, 3 vols, Chicago, 1938/R 1970)
H. Tietze and E. Tietze Conrat: *The Drawings of the Venetian Painters of the 15th and 16th Centuries*, 2 vols (New York, 1944/R 1970)
B. Berenson: *Venetian School* (1957)
W. Friedlaender: *Mannerism and Anti-Mannerism in Italian Painting* (New York, 1957, rev. 2/1964, intro. D. Posner, R 1990)
P. Barocchi, ed.: *Trattati d'arte del cinquecento*, 3 vols (Bari, 1960–62)
S. J. Freedberg: *Painting of the High Renaissance in Rome and Florence*, 2 vols (Cambridge, MA, 1961/R New York, 1972, rev. 2/1985)
L. Crosato: *Gli affreschi nelle ville venete del cinquecento* (Treviso, 1962)
A. R. Turner: *The Vision of Landscape in Renaissance Italy* (Princeton, 1966, rev. 2/1974)
J. Shearman: *Mannerism*, Style & Civil. (Harmondsworth, 1967/R 1990)
B. Berenson: *Central and North Italian Schools* (1968)
J. Schulz: *Venetian Painted Ceilings of the Renaissance* (Berkeley, 1968)
F. Hartt: *History of Italian Renaissance Art: Painting, Sculpture, Architecture* (London, 1970, rev. New York and London, 4/1994)
P. Zampetti: *A Dictionary of Venetian Painters*, ii (Leigh-on-Sea, 1970)
S. J. Freedberg: *Painting in Italy, 1500–1600*, Pelican Hist. A. (Harmondsworth, 1971, rev. New Haven and London, 3/1993)
J. Wilde: *Venetian Art from Bellini to Titian*, Oxford Stud. Hist. A. & Archit. (Oxford, 1974/R 1989)
Women Artists, 1550–1950 (exh. cat. by A. Sutherland Harris and L. Nochlin, Los Angeles, CA, Co. Mus. A.; Austin, U. TX, A. Mus.; Pittsburgh, PA, Carnegie Mus. A.; New York, Brooklyn Mus.; 1976–7)

D. Rosand: *Painting in Cinquecento Venice: Titian, Veronese, Tintoretto* (New Haven and London, 1982)
The Genius of Venice, 1500–1600 (exh. cat., ed. J. Martineau and C. Hope; London, RA, 1983)
N. Huse and W. Wolters: *Venedig: Die Kunst der Renaissance: Architektur, Skulptur, Malerei, 1460–1590* (Munich, 1986); Eng. trans. by E. Japhcott (Chicago and London, 1990)
G. Briganti, ed.: *La pittura in Italia: Il cinquecento*, 2 vols (Milan, 1987)
N. Heller: *Women Artists: An Illustrated History* (New York, 1987)
B. Kempers: *Kunst, macht en mecenaat* (Netherlands, 1987); Eng. trans. by B. Jackson as *Painting, Power and Patronage: The Rise of the Professional Artist in the Italian Renaissance* (Harmondsworth, 1992/R 1994)

JESSICA HARNESS

5. BAROQUE AND ROCOCO, *c.* 1600–*c.* 1750. This century and a half encompassed Italian painting's final rejection of Mannerism, the absorption and consolidation of Counter-Reformation influences, the growth and development of the BAROQUE style and its eventual evolution into the so-called *Barocchetto* and ROCOCO styles. At the end of the period early Neo-classical ideas gained ground in Rome, fuelled not only by the archaeological discoveries of the early 18th century but also by the unbroken academic tradition dating back to the Carracci academy in the last years of the 16th century. The range of native Italian painters was immense, but the presence of important foreign artists played a significant role in the development of Italian painting; notable among these were Adam Elsheimer, Rubens, Claude and Poussin. Van Dyck's presence in Genoa and Palermo left its distinctive

35. Giovanni Benedetto Castiglione: *Genius of Castiglione*, etching, 365×243 mm, 1648 (London, British Museum)

mark on local artists. Early in the period Rome rapidly attained artistic pre-eminence through the pioneering work of Caravaggio and Annibale Carracci: by the end of the period Giambattista Tiepolo was the leading painter of the intensely reactivated Venetian school, by then enjoying the greatest international reputation. With respect to draughtsmanship, the principal centres of quality in this period remained Bologna, Florence and Rome. Chalk, for either rapid and expressive studies or for meticulous preparatory ones, was still the preferred medium for most major painters, with detailed studies often executed in pen, with heightening or washes. There was considerable activity in the art of etching, with Stefano della Bella and Giovanni Benedetto Castiglione—both of whom were influenced by Rembrandt—being notable virtuosi in the 17th century (see fig. 35). The leading etchers in 18th-century Italy were Giandomenico Tiepolo and Giovanni Battista Piranesi.

(i) Bologna and Emilia Romagna. (ii) Rome. (iii) Naples. (iv) Florence and Tuscany. (v) Lombardy and northern Italy. (vi) Genoa. (vii) Venice and the Veneto.

(i) Bologna and Emilia Romagna. Notwithstanding the rapid changes in Italian painting after 1600, an understanding of its principal tendencies originated mainly in Bologna from c. 1580, where the reforming style of the CARRACCI family, led by the immensely talented Annibale, with his brother Agostino and their cousin Lodovico, was fundamental in the evolution of many of the forms and general concepts of 17th-century Italian painting style. It is important to appreciate that these influential innovations occurred, in fact, two decades before the century opened. It is also important to understand that however significant the innovations of their near-contemporary Caravaggio, in Italy at least it was the Renaissance tradition as continued through the Carracci's clearly defined principles that prevailed until the Romantic period.

Although some of the features of the Carracci's painting derived from flourishing local Emilian traditions (e.g. the interest in genre in BARTOLOMEO PASSAROTTI) and from the influence of genre paintings by northern painters, such as Pieter Aertsen and Joachim Bueckelaer, which had attracted the interest of collectors in northern Italy, their individual interpretations became strikingly and increasingly novel. In addition to the example set by their own painting, their foundation in Bologna of the Accademia degli Incamminati ('of the Progressives') was vital in spreading their doctrine of sound draughtsmanship and the study of the best High Renaissance masters (including Titian, Veronese, Raphael and Michelangelo). The Carracci re-established the preparatory role of the drawn study in painting, using live models and general observation from nature, features that were permitted less emphasis by Mannerist artists. Caricature formed another enduring aspect of Annibale's drawings and became increasingly popular in Italy. Lodovico was a gifted teacher and remained in Bologna when Annibale moved definitively to Rome in 1595 to paint the great transitional work of the 16th/17th century, the vault fresco of the Galleria Farnese (see fig. 36).

From direct study in the Carracci academy came the leading Bolognese painters of the next generation, notably DOMENICHINO, GUERCINO and GUIDO RENI, painters with a classical ideal also indebted to Raphael. The influence of the Carracci academy continued throughout 17th-century Emilian art and, despite the evolution of the Roman Baroque, much painting in Rome too. The altarpiece as evolved in Bologna by Annibale and Lodovico was to remain the basis for such painting throughout the Baroque era: Annibale's moving *Pietà with SS Francis and Clare* of 1585 (Parma, G.N.) has been called the first Baroque altarpiece.

36. Annibale Carracci: *Loves of the Gods* (1597–1600), vault fresco, Galleria Farnese, Palazzo Farnese, Rome

Bolognese artists also made significant contributions to decorative fresco painting in the 17th century and the early 18th, and a flourishing school of specialists in *quadratura* (feigned architectural perspective) included Enrico Giovanni Haffner (*see* HAFFNER, (1)), GIROLAMO CURTI and DOMENICO MARIA CANUTI. The classicizing style of the Carracci was kept alive in the frescoes of MARCANTONIO FRANCESCHINI, the most sought-after decorator of his age, and of AURELIANO MILANI. Underlying these achievements lay the clear, firm drawing established by Annibale, which culminated in the superb draughtsmanship of Ubaldo and Gaetano Gandolfi (*see* GANDOLFI, (2)).

A notable Bolognese artist at the end of this period was Giuseppe Maria Crespi (*see* CRESPI (ii), (1)), whose genre, portraiture, religious and mythological works in his uniquely painterly manner set him apart from all his contemporaries.

(ii) Rome.

(a) Early Baroque, c. 1590–c. 1620. Understanding of the principal painting styles in early Baroque Rome must inevitably be based on the study of Annibale Carracci's frescoes in the Galleria Farnese, and especially the vault (1597–1600), which he decorated with scenes from Classical mythology celebrating the *Loves of the Gods* in a style combining his previous sources with a new empathy with the Antique. The studies he made for them in red chalk constitute a high point in Italian graphic art. The completed vault has a grandeur, vivacity and brilliant colour that was accepted by informed contemporaries as having equalled the Roman High Renaissance and wholly replaced the Mannerist style. Annibale's wealth of imagery, imaginative invention and immediacy attracted both painters and sculptors, ranging from Poussin and Bernini to the creators of the full Roman Baroque such as GIOVANNI LANFRANCO and PIETRO DA CORTONA.

The leading painter in Rome during Annibale's ascendancy was the CAVALIERE D'ARPINO, whose late Mannerist preciosity is one of the best gauges of official taste at the time, superseded only in advanced circles by an appreciation of Annibale. However, the arrival in Rome of the young Lombard MICHELANGELO MERISI DA CARAVAGGIO (*c.* 1592) launched an alternative convention, initially in limited circles. Few found themselves able to accept fully the styles of both Annibale and Caravaggio.

Ostensibly, Caravaggio's style relied on stark realism of detail, texture and incident (increasing during his brief and peripatetic career) accentuated by dramatic lighting. His early sources in northern Italian painting showed a preference for artists concerned with subtle light effects such as Giovanni Girolamo Savoldo and Giorgione, and his beginnings were influenced by the Lombard Counter-Reformation demands for directness of imagery. Like his Bolognese peers, however, Caravaggio was fully acquainted with the classic Roman exemplars in painting, quoted them and achieved comparable grandeur in such pictures as the *Entombment* (Rome, Pin. Vaticana).

Unlike Annibale's case, it was only while he was actually present in Rome that Caravaggio's influence prevailed strongly on Roman art. After he had fled Rome on committing a murder in 1606, although his Italian and foreign followers (he had no pupils as such) perpetuated

variants of his style, it was the classicism of the Bolognese that increasingly gained ground and, although transformed by later painters, enjoyed the longest-lasting influence. However, Caravaggio's followers in Rome included some of the most gifted painters of the rising generation: ORAZIO BORGIANNI, the Pisan Orazio Gentileschi (*see* GENTILESCHI, (1)), the Venetian CARLO SARACENI and the Mantuan BARTOLOMEO MANFREDI.

Few Italian painters resisted Caravaggio's dramatic chiaroscuro: even Reni, who sought a pure classicism, briefly succumbed. Of the few public commissions left by Caravaggio in Rome, the most important were those in the Contarelli Chapel (S Luigi dei Francesi) and the Cerasi Chapel (S Maria del Popolo). Unlike the work of the Carracci (notably in their religious painting), these paintings contain none of the salient features of the Baroque, such as cloud-borne figures, elaborate illusionism or the sort of religiosity that derived from Correggio. Outside Rome, Caravaggio's influence was felt most in Naples and least in the Veneto.

(b) High Baroque, c. 1620–c. 1650. The rise to prominence of the most inventive artistic mind of the Baroque age, the sculptor–painter–architect Gianlorenzo Bernini (*see* BERNINI, (2)), under the patronage of Cardinal Scipione Borghese (*see* BORGHESE, (2)) in the middle of the second decade was crucial for all of the visual arts and for the politics of art in Rome. In the 1620s the true Roman Baroque style emerged, in large part with the direct financial and inspirational aid of the new pope, the Tuscan Urban VIII (*see* BARBERINI, (1)). The direct connection between a pope's regional origins and the chauvinistic patronage of artists is fundamental in this period.

Bernini's novel dynamism in sculpture, which was indebted to his rapid and evocative pen-and-ink studies, was paralleled almost contemporaneously in painting by the innovations of Giovanni Lanfranco and Pietro da Cortona. Lanfranco had collaborated with Annibale, but in contrast to Domenichino, whose frescoes of scenes from the *Life of St Cecilia* (1613–14; Rome, S Luigi dei Francesi) epitomize neo-Raphaelesque classical poise, he quickly evolved a new, intensely dramatic manner using flickering light and shade such as another Emilian, Guercino, was later to intensify. Its culmination is his huge multifigural dome fresco of the *Assumption of the Virgin* (1625–7; Rome, S Andrea della Valle; *see* LANFRANCO, GIOVANNI, fig. 3). Being from Parma, Lanfranco had studied Correggio's dome frescoes, and in this dome he revitalized their illusionism. The viewpoint, unlike that of the great Venetian 16th-century ceilings, is of figures seen *di sotto in sù*, receding upwards in real depth, not merely on the surface of an uptilted easel painting. This was of crucial importance for all subsequent Baroque illusionism.

The Tuscan Pietro da Cortona had arrived in Rome in 1612 or 1613. He introduced further elements to the developing Baroque style during the 1620s, notably a fresh approach to the Antique, a sense of impressive scale, a robust style of draughtsmanship and an irresistible vigour of composition, gesture, drapery and colour. Cortona's large-scale figures are unprecedentedly energetic, particularly in his ceiling frescoes, for example his masterpiece,

37. Salvator Rosa: *Finding of Moses*, oil on canvas, 1.13×2.02 m, c. 1660 (Detroit, MI, Institute of Arts)

the decoration of the ceiling of the Gran Salone in the Palazzo Barberini (1633–9). Here the theme is *Divine Providence* as personified in the activity of Urban VIII: such unabashed flattery in a thin guise of allegory and symbolism was common in the iconography of Barberini Rome. Cortona later applied his dynamic use of spatial effects and Venetian colour in his frescoes for S Maria in Vallicella (1647–60) and the gallery ceiling of the Palazzo Pamphili.

It is possible to say that the Roman High Baroque style in large painted decorations derived from a combination of the ideas found in Lanfranco's dome and Cortona's ceiling, each in itself an assimilation of many previous visual inventions. Their scale alone established new expectations for such decorative schemes and continued to be emulated throughout Italy until the Neo-classical period. After the Barberini ceiling, the most important Roman examples include Giovanni Battista Gaulli's *Triumph of the Name of Jesus* (1678–9; Rome, Pal. Gesú; *see* GAULLI, GIOVANNI BATTISTA, fig. 1) and the *Glory of St Ignatius Loyola* (1688–94; Rome, S Ignazio) by ANDREA POZZO: the former uses the device of figures flying free in space, the latter is the major example of *quadratura*. Although comparable secular decorations were fewer, even in Rome, the style reached a high point in the ceiling fresco of the *Battle of Lepanto* (1675–8) by GIOVANNI COLI and FILIPPO GHERARDI on the gallery vault in the Palazzo Colonna: one of the most successful examples of the unity achieved in grand Roman Baroque interiors with fresco, coloured marbles, bronzes, large mirrors and extensive gilding (*see also* §V, 3 below).

The taste for such unparalleled grandiloquence was firmly established in Rome by 1630 but represented only one side of Roman taste, associated primarily with propaganda—papal, ecclesiastic or aristocratic. Another, more subtle facet was the taste for a less extrovert painting style, based not on dazzling optical effects obtained with the newly perfected spatial illusionism but on restrained and usually small-scale works for private contemplation. A compromise attempted by Andrea Sacchi sought a path midway between the two by combining grandiloquence with carefully defined individual gesture and expression: the result was expressed on its largest scale in his *Allegory of Divine Wisdom* (1629–31; Rome, Pal. Barberini; *see* SACCHI, ANDREA, fig. 1).

By its very nature, this less aggressive style appealed to a highly cultivated middle-class exemplified by the antiquarian and connoisseur Cassiano dal Pozzo. Two French painters who moved permanently to Rome, CLAUDE LORRAIN and NICOLAS POUSSIN, produced a Franco-Italian classical art of immense significance. Painting on a smaller scale than most of their Roman contemporaries, they evolved opposing but not irreconcilable interpretations of the classical ideal in landscape, mythology, history and religious themes. Their landscape innovations were built on an already firmly established Roman taste for evocative if fantastic landscape, introduced there by the Fleming Paul Bril and the Frankfurt painter Adam Elsheimer, and given convincing classical atmosphere by Annibale and Domenichino. Claude's effects rely on romantic groupings of natural landscape form and highly atmospheric light, while Poussin's landscape relies on the juxtaposition of meticulously arranged form revealed by lighting of great clarity. In contrast, SALVATOR ROSA created a Baroque landscape of wild and rocky terrain (see fig. 37). Both Claude and Poussin were brilliant draughtsmen, and their landscape drawings of the Roman Campagna are particularly memorable. However, Poussin was primarily a history painter, whose geometric compositions depend on their cerebral conception of the relationship between highly controlled form and specific human gesture, with colour playing a less important part as his career advanced. His learned and philosophical subjects provided inspiration for etchings by Salvator Rosa, PIETRO TESTA and Giovanni Benedetto Castiglione (*see* CASTIGLIONE, (1)). Poussin's classical art found an eloquent advocate in GIOVANNI PIETRO BELLORI, whose writings championed classical painting based on pre-established ideals and were fundamental in the formation of subsequent academic theory.

(c) Late Baroque and Rococo, c. 1650–c. 1750. The most significant single figure in Roman painting from the mid-century until his death in 1713 was Sacchi's gifted pupil CARLO MARATTI, ablest practitioner of late Baroque classicism. This is characterized by forms and compositions of great dignity and clarity, which contrast with the increasing fussiness of much later Baroque composition and retain allegiance to many of Raphael's principles. Maratti was, moreover, an exceptionally gifted draughtsman. His art appealed to the existing academic strand and even looked forward to Neo-classicism. Maratti's pupils dominated Roman painting after his death. Prominent among them were BENEDETTO LUTI, GIUSEPPE BARTOLOMEO CHIARI, AGOSTINO MASUCCI and FRANCESCO

MANCINI. The half-French MARCO BENEFIAL was also important in maintaining simplified late Baroque traditions, but arguably the leading talent in the city was the Neapolitan SEBASTIANO CONCA. Until the emergence in the mid-century of the Neo-classical painters Pompeo Batoni and the German Anton Raphael Mengs, a Romanized near-Rococo was practised by the Neapolitan FRANCESCO TREVISANI, resident in Rome from 1678.

The painting of Roman *vedute* and caprice views of monuments, many produced for the Grand Tour market, and records of major civic events (e.g. *Preparations in Piazza Navona...* (1729; *see* PANINI, GIOVANNI PAOLO, fig. 2) was dominated by the Piacenza-born Giovanni Paolo Panini, while GASPAR VAN WITTEL painted sensitive views of the city. After 1740 the many large etchings made by GIOVANNI BATTISTA PIRANESI created a European vision of the city for posterity in which the grandeur of the Baroque was united with the fantasy of the dawning Romantic age.

(iii) Naples. The Spanish presence in Naples imposed an alien religious and social mould. Neapolitan painting in the early 17th century was dominated by Caravaggio's brief sojourn there (1606–7), which jolted local painting out of a provincial Mannerist torpor. The continuing influence of his art was, however, greatly diminished by the classicism of Domenichino (in Naples in the 1630s) and the Roman Baroque of Lanfranco, who arrived in Naples in 1633; in turn a new vivacity was introduced by the Calabrese painter MATTIA PRETI, who arrived from

38. Francesco Solimena: *Dido Receiving Aeneas and Cupid Disguised as Ascanius*, oil on canvas, 2.07×3.10 m, *c.* 1720 (London, National Gallery)

Rome soon after the plague of 1656, which had claimed the lives of many artists in Naples. Caravaggio's style nonetheless found its most fervent Italian adherent in Naples, in the talented GIOVANNI BATTISTA CARACCIOLO. The ambiguous position of the Spanish painter–etcher JUSEPE DE RIBERA, who arrived in Naples in 1616, sets him apart from the Caravaggisti. Although a tenebrist painter at the outset, Ribera's individuality is always striking: the export of his painting to Spain (Velázquez visited him while in Italy) exerted incalculable influence there. Although he was capable of violent imagery, his compassionate *Crippled Child* (1642; Paris, Louvre) probably reflects his real perceptions of art's purpose.

In the 1620s and 1630s Neapolitan painting was predominantly naturalistic, and the art of such painters as Francesco Fracanzano (*see* FRACANZANO, (2)) and the MASTER OF THE ANNUNCIATION TO THE SHEPHERDS (*see* MASTERS, ANONYMOUS, AND MONOGRAMMISTS, §I) records a proletarian world with deep compassion. The minor genres flourished; ANIELLO FALCONE and Salvator Rosa developed a new kind of naturalistic battle scene; still-life, influenced by Caravaggio, attained a new and virtuoso character. In the 1640s aggressive naturalism yielded to a new refinement and painterly richness influenced both by the Bolognese tradition and by a renewed interest in Venetian art; the large workshop of the classicizing MASSIMO STANZIONE produced many altarpieces and frescoes, and Ribera's later compositions are in the fullest classical tradition.

The later 17th century in Naples is dominated by LUCA GIORDANO, whose renowned technical facility resulted in an immense output throughout Italy and Spain, where he spent ten years from 1692. Giordano's beginnings in the Ribera manner soon evolved into his personal style, where looser composition, pale colour and bravura paint handling are all increasingly in evidence. Many of his paintings prefigure the early proto-Rococo of Sebastiano Ricci (*see* RICCI (i), (1)), and his airy ceiling decorations were of fundamental importance in the Rococo's concept of space.

Neapolitan painting in the 18th century was dominated by Francesco Solimena (*see* SOLIMENA, (2) and fig. 38), whose style was derived from Giordano and Preti, among others. Solimena resisted the soft-outline forms favoured by Giordano, preferring carefully composed, sometimes ponderous and solidly outlined figures. He filled the international role previously Maratti's, and, as in Maratti's case, his pupils (including FRANCESCO DE MURA and CORRADO GIAQUINTO) benefited from his powerful position.

(iv) Florence and Tuscany. With the decline of the Medici in the 17th century, there were no native painters who might compare with the great 16th-century artists of Tuscany. Florence continued its dominance, with spasmodic activity in provincial centres such as Siena and Lucca. Among the major painters from elsewhere whose Florentine sojourn exerted profound influence were Salvator Rosa and Luca Giordano. The court portraitist was also an outsider, the Fleming GIUSTO SUTTERMANS, capable of striking Baroque likenesses. The one major Tuscan painter of the period, Pietro da Cortona, settled in Rome but painted two significant fresco masterpieces in

39. Francesco Cairo: *Herodias with the Head of St John the Baptist*, oil on canvas, 1.14×0.94 m, 1633–5 (Turin, Galleria Sabauda)

the Palazzo Pitti: the Sala della Stufa (1637) and, with the assistance of CIRO FERRI, the ceilings of the grand-ducal apartments, the so-called Planetary Rooms (1641–7). (For an illustration of the Sala di Giove *see* CORTONA, PIETRO DA, fig. 2.) The latter introduced the full Roman Baroque style to Florence. Their lavish stucco framework proved of immense consequence for subsequent European interiors, and the style was imported to Paris by Cortona's pupil GIOVANNI FRANCESCO ROMANELLI.

Florence too had produced 'reforming' painters in the later 16th century, notably SANTI DI TITO, JACOPO DA EMPOLI, LODOVICO CIGOLI and Cristofano Allori. The last may be viewed as bringing a tentative Baroque feeling to his work, while confirming many of the elements subsequently so characteristic of Florentine 17th-century painting—the three-quarter-length single-figure composition with a morbid or erotic psychology in the guise of biblical themes (as in Allori's *Judith with the Head of Holofernes*; *c.* 1615; Florence, Pitti; *see* ALLORI, CRISTOFANO, fig. 2). In Allori's wake a host of lesser figures, which included artists of considerable local importance, divided their production mainly between the religious and secular narrative painting always favoured in Florence, including altarpieces, although to a lesser extent than elsewhere in Italy. These include GIOVANNI BILIVERT, MATTEO ROSSELLI, JACOPO VIGNOLA, FRANCESCO FURINI, Cesare Dandini (*see* DANDINI, (1)), LORENZO LIPPI, CECCO BRAVO and GIOVANNI MARTINELLI.

Two painters with fundamentally opposed ideals transcended local limitations. CARLO DOLCI attained international fame in his lifetime for his flawless oil technique and brilliant colour based on 15th-century Flemish examples, applied to intensely religious imagery and superb portraiture: Dolci also subscribed to a deliberate revival of earlier painting styles, which enjoyed some vogue in Florence, partly as a direct result of Medici collecting. BALDASSARRE FRANCESCHINI became Florence's leading fresco decorator in his own version of Cortona's Florentine fresco style, achieving grandeur in his vast cupola fresco in the SS Annunziata but also able to paint with a strong dash of sharp Tuscan humour.

While the court and nobility avidly collected the work of local artists, it longed for the grandeur purveyed by the great outsiders: after Cortona, Luca Giordano was the most influential visitor to Florence, leaving one of the finest ceilings of the age, in the Palazzo Medici–Riccardi (1682–5), together with the superb *Glory of St Andrea Corsini* (1682) in the cupola of the Corsini Chapel, S Maria del Carmine. It was Giordano's visit that, possibly even more than Cortona's, alerted local painters to the need for a less insular approach, and the generation active in the last 20 years of the century owed him a huge debt: the series of ceiling frescoes in the Palazzo Corsini (1695) by ANTON DOMENICO GABBIANI and others is perhaps the most significant attempt in Florence by local artists to rival such schemes. Gabbiani was the most important exponent of contemporary Roman style to work in Tuscany.

The presence in Florence in 1706–7 of the Venetian Sebastiano Ricci coincided with the transition from the late Baroque to what in Italy is termed the *Barocchetto*, a style neither still fully Baroque nor yet Rococo. Ricci's delightful frescoes in the Marucelli (1706–7) and Pitti (?1707–8) palaces, along with other work in Florence, demonstrate the style's inclination, with a lightening of

palette and treatment of the human figure and very loose composition, towards the more evanescent aspects of the Rococo. In Ricci's wake came such Florentines as Vincenzo Meucci (1694–1766), GIOVANNI DOMENICO FERRETTI, ANTONIO FRANCHI and GIOVANNI CAMILLO SAGRESTANI. The Pisan GIOVANNI BATTISTA RANIERI DEL PACE dissolved Sagrestani's forms even further. In the first half of the 18th century there was much less interest in *veduta* painting in Florence than in Venice or Rome, although Gaspar van Wittel and GIUSEPPE ZOCCHI produced evocative views of the city and its environs.

(*v*) *Lombardy and northern Italy.* Lombardy experienced one of the most intense periods of Counter-Reformation change in the arts under the aegis of the Cardinal-Archbishop of Milan, Federico Borromeo (*see* BORROMEO, (2)). Counter-Reformation influence continued to prevail there much later than elsewhere in Italy; indeed, many influences are perceptible in Lombard painting.

Giulio Cesare Procaccini (*see* PROCACCINI, (4)) was the major painter, and his mixtures of vibrant colour and sprightly form show the various influences on local painting, including that of BARTHOLOMÄUS SPRANGER, and on Venetian art. Cerano (*see* CERANO, fig. 2) and MORAZZONE also form a transition from late Mannerism to the early Baroque. The more bizarre (and possibly more interesting) aspects of Lombard painting are seen in the tortured images of TANZIO DA VARALLO and FRANCESCO CAIRO (see fig. 39), whose half-length, swooning figures are closer to contemporary Florentine painting. Although Genoese, Alessandro Magnasco (*see* MAGNASCO, (2)) spent most of his career in Milan, creating macabre images of unusual subjects with virtuoso paintwork and flickering light. Giambattista Tiepolo's superb frescoes of 1740 in the Palazzo Clerici (see fig. 40) are the last works of international importance in the Milan of the period (*see* TIEPOLO, (1)).

The provincial Lombard centres made significant contributions to the minor genres. Cremona, where Vincenzo Campi (*see* CAMPI, (3)) painted comic genre scenes with exuberant still-lifes (*see* GENRE, fig. 1), is generally accepted as the cradle of still-life painting. In sharp contrast the still-lifes of the Bergamese EVARISTO BASCHENIS, such as his *Still-life with Musical Instruments and a Statuette* (Bergamo, Gal. Accad. Carrara; see fig. 41) introduce a new spatial sophistication and elegance.

(*vi*) *Genoa.* In the 17th century Genoa was a wealthy city. Its rich trading families were distinguished patrons and collectors and encouraged the rise of a native school of painting. In the early years many styles were current; Tuscan Mannerism was represented by such artists as VENTURA SALIMBENI and Aurelio Lomi (1556–1622); the more progressive Lombard school by Giulio Cesare Procaccini, who visited the city in 1618. Flemish pictures were popular with collectors, and there existed a colony of Flemish painters, including FRANS SNYDERS and Cornelis de Wael (*see* WAEL, DE, (2)); the visits of Rubens (1607 and 1620) and van Dyck (1623–4) were immensely influential, and these artists introduced a warmth of colour, of glowing reds and golds, and a new type of courtly portrait, which was developed by GIOVANNI BERNARDO CARBONE.

40. Giambattista Tiepolo: *Chariot of the Sun* (1740), ceiling fresco, Palazzo Clerici, Milan

41. Evaristo Baschenis: *Still-life with Musical Instruments and a Statuette*, oil on canvas, 886×1147 mm, *c.* 1660 (Bergamo, Galleria dell'Accademia Carrara)

In the 1620s native Genoese painters broke with Mannerism and created a lively naturalism. Rustic genre, influenced by Flemish painting, flourished in the art of SINIBALDO SCORZA, BERNARDO STROZZI and Giovanni Benedetto Castiglione, who specialized in journeys of the patriarchs, crowded with animals and still-life details (*see* CASTIGLIONE, (1), fig. 1). The religious pictures of Strozzi and GIOACCHINO ASSERETO are warmly naturalistic and distinguished by a freedom of handling and brilliant colour indebted to Rubens and van Dyck. The middle years of the century were dominated by DOMENICO FIASELLA, who had worked in Rome and brought to Genoa an awareness both of Caravaggism and of Roman classicism.

A revival of fresco, stimulated by the Carlone brothers (*see* CARLONE (i), (1) and (2)) and Fiasella, took place in the 1620s; it was developed in the 1670s and 1680s by Domenico Piola (*see* PIOLA, (1)) and Gregorio de' Ferrari (*see* FERRARI, DE', (1)), who together decorated many of the grandest palaces and churches. Their festive art is indebted to the Roman grandeur of Pietro da Cortona, and yet softened by a lyrical, poetic quality inspired by Correggio.

(vii) Venice and the Veneto. Although the Venetian 17th century does not lack distinction, its production must take second place to the period of its Rococo genius between 1700 and 1750. Talent in painting was not concentrated exclusively in Venice, and other centres, such as Padua and Vicenza, produced significant artists: Venice's rich painting heritage drew painters from elsewhere, much as the lure of the Antique drew them to Rome. Although the deaths of Veronese (1588) and Tintoretto (1594) brought an epoch to a close, the impact of the 16th-century painters continued to dominate the following century. This continuation (particularly of Titian's ideas, in whose studio he studied) is seen in the work of Palma Giovane (*see* PALMA, (3)), but it was the Paduan painter Alessandro Varotari, called PADOVANINO, who broke with such traditions to create a more up-to-date style: he was the most inspired teacher of his period, and his impact on the next generation was considerable. His best pupils included GIROLAMO FORABOSCO, PIETRO DELLA VECCHIA, GIULIO CARPIONI and PIETRO LIBERI. Each of these found notable inspiration in Titian.

The impact of outsiders on Venetian painting at this time was considerable, notwithstanding the brevity of some of their visits. Bernardo Strozzi's vibrant manner influenced by van Dyck captivated Venetian painters, who were then turning to smaller works, which contrast with the huge scale of much 16th-century Venetian painting. The Roman DOMENICO FETTI and the German JOHANN

LISS were also important. Liss left one altarpiece there, the *Inspiration of St Jerome* (*c.* 1627; Venice, S Nicolò da Tolentino), the bravura approach of which had considerable local impact. This was combined with the effect of the altarpieces of Francesco Ruschi (*c.* 1610–61), who introduced the latest Roman ideas between 1643 and 1656.

Subsequently, the presence in Venice of Pietro da Cortona and Luca Giordano was highly influential. Both painted altarpieces there in the 1660s and 1670s, and Giordano's pale palette and physical types were to have a direct bearing on the evolution towards the Rococo. It was, however, Sebastiano Ricci who finally bridged the gap, returning to settle in Venice in the early years of the new century after travelling widely. His style, neo-Veronese rather than full Rococo, was inspirational. One of his many pupils, GIOVANNI ANTONIO PELLEGRINI, like his teacher travelled to England, as well as to Düsseldorf and Paris. Their experience of the European scene, and also that of JACOPO AMIGONI who followed them, set the international tone of much 18th-century Venetian painting. Pellegrini and Amigoni both became fully fledged Rococo painters, while Giovanni Battista Piazzetta (*see* PIAZZETTA, (2)) remained the one Venetian painter of history and religious themes who resisted the new style's increasingly dazzling colour and dissolution of form, preferring a dignified, measured style.

The genius of Giambattista Tiepolo dominated Venice in this period. Tiepolo moved rapidly from an early Piazzetta-influenced style to the light manner ushered in by his frescoes in the patriarchal palace (now the Archbishop's Palace) at Udine of the later 1720s. By the 1730s he had evolved his uniquely loose aerial compositions, best seen in his frescoes, and was mainly active in Venice during the following decade. His frescoes in the Palazzo Labia, Venice, date from *c.* 1744; their combination of Veronese-inspired pageant and detail with technical brilliance, wit and illusion constitute one of the high points of the Rococo. His constant travels took him to Germany, where in 1750–53 he created the astonishing frescoes in the Kaisersaal of the Residenz at Würzburg (*see* TIEPOLO, (1), fig. 3), and to Madrid.

It seems natural that *vedute* and capriccios constituted some of Venice's most important output in this period, principally in the hands of LUCA CARLEVARIS, CANALETTO and Francesco Guardi (*see* GUARDI, (2)). Like that of Tiepolo, Canaletto's career took off in the 1720s, and he worked for an international clientele dominated by the English, painting increasingly meticulous views of Venice and, from the 1740s, the Veneto and even Rome. His English visit of 1746–55 further secured his reputation there, and his nephew BERNARDO BELLOTTO—regarded by some as the more original artist—carried his uncle's style to Dresden and Warsaw.

Pietro Longhi (*see* LONGHI (iii), (1)) exemplifies Venice's genre painting in the Rococo, with a prolific output of small scenes of everyday life in fashionable Venice, and occasional delightful surprises such as the *Rhinoceros* (Venice, Ca' Rezzonico). Portraiture enjoyed much less vogue than might have been expected, its two opposing facets represented by the official style of SEBASTIANO BOMBELLI and the intimate pastel portraits of ROSALBA

CARRIERA (*see* PASTEL, colour pl. IV), which gained her a European reputation.

BIBLIOGRAPHY

GENERAL

D. Mahon: *Studies in Seicento Art and Theory* (London, 1947)

R. Wittkower: *Art and Architecture in Italy, 1600–1750*, Pelican Hist. A. (Harmondsworth, 1958, rev. 3/1973)

F. Haskell: *Patrons and Painters* (London, 1962, rev. 2, New Haven and London, 1980)

E. Waterhouse: *Italian Baroque Painting* (London, 1962, rev. 2/1969)

L'ideale classico del seicento in Italia e la pittura di paesaggio (exh. cat., Bologna, Pal. Archiginnasio, 1962)

A. Moir: *The Italian Followers of Caravaggio* (Cambridge, MA, 1967)

J. Brown and R. Enggass: *Sources and Documents in the History of Art: Italy and Spain, 1600–1750* (Englewood Cliffs, 1970)

Pintura italiana del siglo XVII (exh. cat., ed. E. P. Sánchez; Madrid, Prado, 1970)

Caravaggio and his Followers (exh. cat. by R. E. Spear, Cleveland, OH, Mus. A., 1971; rev. 2, New York, 1975)

J. R. Martin: *Baroque* (New York, 1977)

J. Urrea Fernández: *La pintura italiana del siglo XVIII en España* (Valladolid, 1977)

C. McCorquodale: *The Baroque Painters of Italy* (Oxford, 1979)

Italian Still-life Painting from Three Centuries (exh. cat., ed. J. T. Spike; New York, N. Acad. Des., 1983)

The Age of Caravaggio (exh. cat., New York, Met.; Naples, Capodimonte; 1985)

A. Brejon de Lavergnée and N. Volle: *Musées de France: Répertoire des peintures italiennes du XVIIe siècle* (Paris, 1988)

M. Gregori and E. Schleier, eds: *La pittura in Italia: Il seicento*, 2 vols (Milan, 1988, rev. 1989)

Seicento: Le Siècle de Caravage dans les collections françaises (exh. cat. by A. Brejon de Lavergnée and N. Volle, Paris, Grand Pal.; Milan Pal. Reale; 1988–9)

G. Briganti, ed.: *La pittura in Italia: Il settecento*, 2 vols (Milan, 1989, rev. 1990)

CITY AND REGIONAL SURVEYS

H. Voss: *Die Malerei des Barock in Rom* (Berlin, 1924)

M. Levey: *Painting in XVIII Century Venice* (London, 1959)

R. Pallucchini: *La pittura veneziana del settecento* (Venice and Rome, 1960)

C. Dufour and others: *Dal seicento al primo novecento* (1970, rev. 1981), ii of *La pittura a Genova e in Liguria* (Genoa, 1970–71)

R. Causa: *La pittura del seicento a Napoli: Dal naturalismo al barocco* (Naples, 1972)

Il seicento lombardo: Catalogo dei dipinti e delle sculture (exh. cat., ed. M. Valsecchi; Milan, Pal. Reale, 1973)

The Twilight of the Medici: Late Baroque Art in Florence, 1670–1743 (exh. cat., ed. S. F. Rossen; Detroit, MI, Inst. A.; Florence, Pitti; 1974)

E. Waterhouse: *Roman Baroque Painting* (Oxford, 1976)

N. Spinosa, ed.: *Le arti figurative a Napoli nel settecento* (Naples, 1979)

L'arte del settecento emiliano: La pittura, l'Accademia Clementina (exh. cat., Bologna, Pal. Archiginnasio, 1979)

Painting in Florence, 1600–1700 (exh. cat. by C. McCorquodale, London, RA, 1979)

R. Pallucchini: *La pittura veneziana del seicento*, 2 vols (Milan, 1981)

Painting in Naples, 1606–1705: From Caravaggio to Giordano (exh. cat., ed. C. Whitfield and J. Martineau; London, RA, 1982)

S. Rudolph: *La pittura del '700 a Roma* (Rome, 1983)

Civiltà del 600 a Napoli (exh. cat., ed. S. Cassani; Naples, Capodimonte, 1984–5)

N. Spinosa: *La pittura napoletana del settecento*, 2 vols (Naples, 1986–7)

The Age of Correggio and the Carracci: Emilian Painting in the Sixteenth and Seventeenth Centuries (exh. cat. by G. Briganti and others, Washington, DC, N.G.A.; New York, Met.; Bologna, Pin. N.; 1986–7)

Baroque napolitain: La Peinture à Naples au 17 siècle (exh. cat. by N. Spinosa, B. de Giovanni and A. Roy, Strasbourg, Mus. B.-A. and Musées Château Rohan, 1994)

CHARLES MCCORQUODALE

6. NEO-CLASSICISM TO EARLY MODERNISM, *c.* 1750–*c.* 1900. During the second half of the 18th century, Italian painting remained pre-eminent. Italian artists travelled all over Europe at the invitation of the

courts. Venice, despite its unchecked political and economic decline, produced the greatest talents: *vedute* continued to be painted by Canaletto, Bernardo Bellotto and Francesco Guardi, while the tradition of monumental Venetian painting was represented by Giambattista and Giandomenico Tiepolo. In Rome, Pompeo Batoni's portraiture developed a new informality, apparent in such works as *Princess Cecilia Mahony Giustiniani* (1785; Edinburgh, N.G.). However, the most important development was that of NEO-CLASSICISM, which superseded the Rococo and the pastoral style associated with the literary Society of Arcadia. Neo-classicism began in Rome in 1755 with the theories of the German critic Winckelmann, followed by those of Anton Raphael Mengs (*see* MENGS, (2)), whose paintings included the frescoes of *Parnassus* (1760–61), commissioned by Cardinal Alessandro Albani for his villa (now Villa Torlonia) on the Via Salaria in Rome. Neo-classicism drew on the ideas of the Enlightenment, which considered the Greek art of Pericles' time as the highest aesthetic expressions of humanity. The new style was also stimulated by the archaeological interests of Giovanni Battista Piranesi and by the discovery of the Roman cities of Herculaneum (1738) and Pompeii (1748). Its development was heavily influenced by the sculptor Antonio Canova, who was based in Rome from 1780, and by David, who spent periods of time in Rome in the 1770s and 1780s. Neo-classicism was well established by the Napoleonic period in the early 19th century. Italian painters who practised in the style included ANDREA APPIANI, who worked mainly in Milan (e.g. *Apotheosis of the Emperor Napoleon*, completed 1808; formerly Milan, Pal. Reale; now Tremezzo, Villa Carlotta), and Vincenzo Camuccini (*see* CAMUCCINI, (2)), a Roman follower of David (e.g. *Death of Caesar*; see fig. 42). FELICE GIANI left important frescoes in the Palazzo Milzetti (1804–5)

and Palazzo Laderchi (1794–6), both in Faenza, and the new style was taught by the Tuscans LUIGI SABATELLI and PIETRO BENVENUTI, professors respectively at the Accademia di Belle Arti di Brera, Milan, and at the Accademia di Belle Arti in Florence. Plaster casts of ancient works and engravings of paintings (of which the greatest master was Raphael Morghen (*see* MORGHEN, (1)) and his school made a fundamental contribution to the academic studies.

After the fall of Napoleon the flow of commissions ceased, and the ideological and political commitment of painters declined. Artists turned to the more domestic aspects of painting (expressed by the Biedermeier taste of the Restoration period), to schools and trends opposed to the Neo-classical conception of 'ideal beauty' or 'truth', and to the recovery of national traditions. In Rome, still the centre of international culture, there flourished the school of JEAN-AUGUSTE-DOMINIQUE INGRES, who headed the Académie de France in Rome from 1830 to 1841. The NAZARENES, a group of mystically inclined German painters led by Friedrich Overbeck, found their models in the religious art of the early Italian Renaissance. Their example was followed by the members of the movement called PURISMO, including Tommaso Minardi and Luigi Mussini, working in parallel with writers of the period, who sought the origins of the Italian language in the 14th century. However, the most important new figurative culture was that of Romanticism, which in Italy at once took the form of 'historical Romanticism'. It flourished in the two Italian cities that had the liveliest intellectual life: Milan, with FRANCESCO HAYEZ, and Florence, with GIUSEPPE BEZZUOLI. Both men looked to Italian history for examples of national pride: for example, Hayez's *Sicilian Vespers* and Bezzuoli's *Entry of Charles VIII into Florence* (1829; Florence, Pitti). Another Romantic painter was the Neapolitan DOMENICO MORELLI.

42. Vincenzo Camuccini: *Death of Caesar*, oil on canvas, 4.0×7.0 m, 1793–9 (Naples, Museo e Gallerie Nazionali di Capodimonte)

In such works as *The Iconoclasts* (1855; Naples, Capodimonte) his declared aim was realism, while the content alluded to contemporary victims of persecution in Italy. After 1848, with the struggle for national independence, many painters became more openly political. Instead of historical events, artists began to portray episodes from contemporary life.

Landscape painting also began to show more attention to the real environment and the effects of light and colour, as VERISMO spread, in particular in Naples and Tuscany. In this field the most important group at first was the Neapolitan SCUOLA DI POSILLIPO, represented by Giacinto Gigante, Anton Sminck Pitloo and Filippo Palizzi. These artists reacted against Neo-classicism by returning to the 18th-century *veduta* genre favoured by such foreign artists as J. C. Dahl, Turner and Corot, for whom Naples was a favourite destination. The new trends in landscape painting were expressed in Tuscany by the Scuola di Staggia, so called because such artists as Serafino De Tivoli (1826–92), like their French colleagues of the Barbizon school, went to paint *en plein-air* at Staggia, near Siena. They formed part of the nucleus of the MACCHIAIOLI, formed in Florence between 1853 and 1860. This group's approach had many sources: the habit of painting from life; an analytical and positivist attitude to history, landscape and everyday life; contact with artists familiar with French Realism (e.g. Francesco Saverio Altamura (1826–97), Morelli and GIOVANNI COSTA), who gathered in Florence from all over Italy; and the influence of such photographers as the Alinari brothers. The Macchiaioli included Giovanni Fattori, Telemaco Signorini, Raffaello Sernesi (1838–66), Vito D'Ancona (1825–84), Vincenzo Cabianca (1827–1902), Silvestro Lega, Giuseppe Abbati (1836–68), Odoardo Borranni (1834–1905), Cristiano Banti (1824–1904) and the critic Diego Martelli. All of them were antagonistic to the teaching of the Accademia di Belle Arti in Florence; they also all took part in the struggle for the unification of Italy. In their small paintings they ignored drawing and chiaroscuro, creating their images entirely through the juxtaposition of spots of colour. Their main subjects were episodes from the war of unification of 1859 (e.g. Fattori's *Italian Camp during the Battle of Magenta,* 1859–61; Florence, Pitti), seascapes of Castiglioncello near Livorno, scenes of domestic and daily life and the countryside just outside the town. In Florence the Macchiaioli's style continued until the 20th century, practised by such artists as Egisto Ferroni (1835–1912), who were talented, although the critics often considered them provincial. Exchanges between Tuscan and Neapolitan painting, aiming at greater realism, continued to be frequent. The Macchiaiolo Adriano Cecioni, a painter, sculptor and theoretician, stayed from 1863 to 1867 in Naples, where he joined the SCUOLA DI RESINA, together with Federico Rossano (1835–1912), Marco De Gregorio (1829–76) and GIUSEPPE DE NITTIS.

In Piedmont, from 1861 to 1873 there was a landscape school devoted to realistic painting: the SCUOLA DI RIVARA, centred around Carlo Pittara (1836–90) and Alfredo D'Andrade, which took its inspiration from the work of Antonio Fontanesi, a painter with a wider European experience. Elements of true realism can be found in the work of the Abruzzese FRANCESCO PAOLO MICHETTI, the Neapolitan ANTONIO MANCINI and the Venetian GIACOMO FAVRETTO. These artists imitated the painting and folkloric themes of the Spanish Mariano Fortuny y Marsal, who worked in Rome and whose work became very popular after his death in 1874. A real interest in social themes appears in the paintings of GIOACCHINO TOMA (e.g. *Sacrament of the Orphan Girl,* 1877; Rome, G.N.A. Mod.; see fig. 43) and TEOFILO PATINI (e.g. *Spade and Milk,* 1883; Rome, Min. Agric.), who was especially dedicated to themes of labour. After 1870, however, the questioning of Risorgimento ideals coincided with the crisis of realism and the distrust of positivist research, which led to the reappearance of sentiment in works of art. In Lombardy this trend was represented by GLI SCAPIGLIATI, writers, musicians and artists, who included Domenico Induno, Gerolamo Induno, Tranquillo Cremona (e.g. *Ivy,* 1878; Turin, Gal. Civ. A. Mod.) and Daniele Ranzoni. They rebelled against bourgeois social conventions and academic hierarchies and lived like the bohemians of Paris. The painters took their inspiration from Giovanni Carnevali's everyday themes and quick, dense and cursive brushstrokes, and from Federico Faruffini (e.g. *Woman Smoking,* 1864–5; Milan, Civ. Mus. A. Contemp.), a solitary painter and traveller who died young in 1869.

Another factor in the crisis of Italian painting was the permanent exodus to Paris of many artists (e.g. Giuseppe De Nittis, Giovanni Boldini and Federico Zandomeneghi) who are counted among the French Impressionists. Near the turn of the century Symbolism took hold in Italy in reaction to *Verismo,* as a result of the critical revival of the English Pre-Raphaelites and the evocative visionary classicism of ARNOLD BÖCKLIN, who lived for a long time first in Rome and then in Florence. An important native artist was GIOVANNI COSTA, who saw in the Renaissance, especially the Italian Cinquecento, the basis for a revival of Italian painting—free of the official art of bourgeois realism, the crudity of *Verismo* and the foreign influence of Impressionism. In 1886 he founded the movement In Arte Libertas, which took hold so well that it in turn became the model for the new official art (e.g. mural cycles for public buildings by ADOLFO DE CAROLIS and GIULIO ARISTIDE SARTORIO). At the same time the renewal brought by French Neo-Impressionism to European painting received an important contribution from the Italian Divisionists, offshoots of Gli Scapigliati, whose influence continued into the new century. The most celebrated was GIOVANNI SEGANTINI, but important work was also produced by GAETANO PREVIATI, VITTORE GRUBICY, the Ligurian Rubaldo Merello (1875–1922) and PLINIO NOMELLINI, as well as GIUSEPPE PELLIZZA DA VOLPEDO and ANGELO MORBELLI, who were particularly interested in social themes.

BIBLIOGRAPHY

C. Maltese: *Storia dell'arte in Italia, 1785–1943* (Turin, 1960)
P. Barocchi: *L'ottocento: Dal bello ideale al preraffaellismo,* Testimonianze e polemiche figurative in Italia (Messina and Florence, 1972)
——: *Dal divisionismo al novecento,* Testimonianze e polemiche figurative in Italia (Messina and Florence, 1974), pp. 5–139
G. Previtali and F. Zeri, eds: *Storia dell'arte italiana,* pt 1, vol. ii (Turin, 1979), pp. 417–84; pt 2, vol. ii (Turin, 1982), pp. 793–1079; pt 2, vol. iii (Turin, 1982), pp. 5–172
A. Del Guercio: *La pittura dell'ottocento* (Turin, 1982)

43. Gioacchino Toma: *Sacrament of the Orphan Girl*, oil on canvas, 1.31×0.82 m, 1877 (Rome, Galleria Nazionale d'Arte Moderna)

N. Broude: *The Macchiaioli: Italian Painters of the Nineteenth Century* (New Haven, 1987)

Soldati e pittori nel Risorgimento italiano (exh. cat., ed. M. Corgnati; Turin, Circ. Ufficiale, 1987)

Il secondo '800 italiano: Le poetiche del vero (exh. cat. by R. Barilli and others, Milan, Pal. Reale, 1988)

E. Castelnuovo, ed.: *La pittura in Italia: L'ottocento* (Milan, 1992)

LIA BERNINI

7. AFTER *c.* 1900.

(i) *c.* 1900–1945. (ii) From 1946.

(i) c. 1900–1945. Around 1900 Italy still suffered from the fragility of recent unification. Industry had flourished in the northern cities, but this had exacerbated historic divisions by fuelling political radicalism, as well as massive emigration from the rural south. In the arts, strong local currents also persisted, from the southern Italian version of VERISMO to the *plein-air* tradition of the Tuscan Macchiaioli, pursued by OSCAR GHIGLIA and others. Official commissions, exemplified by the murals of GIULIO ARISTIDE SARTORIO for the Parliamentary Chamber of Deputies in Rome (1908), drew on the 'Italian tradition', while a flamboyant *Stile Liberty* (Art Nouveau) was popularized by the Prima Esposizione Internazionale d'Arte Decorativa in Turin (1902) and influenced such schemes as the murals by GALILEO CHINI for the Biennale building in Venice (1909). By contrast, the small politicized avant-garde was associated with the technique of Divisionism, as practised by GIOVANNI SEGANTINI, GAETANO PREVIATI and GIUSEPPE PELLIZZA DA VOLPEDO (e.g. *Fourth Estate*, 1901; Milan, Civ. Mus. A. Contemp.); combined with Symbolism, this was passed on by Duilio Cambellotti (1876–1960), GIACOMO BALLA and others to the younger generation.

As the only regular international exhibition in Italy, the Venice Biennale made the city a magnet for younger painters. These included AMEDEO MODIGLIANI and UMBERTO BOCCIONI, as well as GINO ROSSI and PIO SEMEGHINI, who exhibited with Nino Barbantini's Ca' Pesaro association (1908–20). These artists sought a cultural renewal, inspired by the philosophy of Benedetto Croce, Henri Bergson and Friedrich Nietzsche, and encouraged by the writings of Gabriele D'Annunzio, who romanticized the 'superman' as an attainable state of being. Such avant-garde theorists as Giovanni Prezzolini and GIOVANNI PAPINI (the editors of the Florentine periodicals *Leonardo* and *La Voce*) believed that this renewal necessitated the repudiation of the past, a view proclaimed most effectively in Filippo Tommaso Marinetti's 'Manifeste de fondation du Futurisme' (20 Feb 1909), published in Paris in *Le Figaro*.

Based in Milan, FUTURISM proposed a contemporary culture characterized by the 'simultaneity' of experience suitable to urban existence. Marinetti's strident language and deliberate provocations were widely admired and attracted the painters Boccioni, Luigi Russolo and Carlo Carrà. The radical aspirations of such works as Carrà's *Funeral of the Anarchist Galli* (1910–11; New York, MOMA; for illustration *see* CARRÀ, CARLO) continued to be expressed through Divisionism; however, after visiting Paris in 1911, the Futurists adopted a Cubist vocabulary of broken planes, transforming it into a means to dynamic expression (e.g. Boccioni's *Dynamism of a Human Body*, 1913–14; Milan, Civ. Mus. A. Contemp.). The Milanese painters were originally joined by Balla (in Rome), Gino Severini (in Paris) and Ardengo Soffici (in Florence), but the movement influenced a whole generation. Early participants included Leonardo Dudreville (1885–1975), Achille Funi and Ugo Giannattasio (1888–1960), as well as Fortunato Depero and Enrico Prampolini, who worked towards abstraction. The movement supported Italy's intervention in World War I (May 1915), but, despite the addition of Primo Conti, Ottone Rosai, Achille Lega (1899–1934) and others, such casualties as Boccioni curtailed its most energetic phase.

A significant number of painters remained independent of Futurism, concentrating on social and Symbolist themes. In Italy these included Romolo Romani (1885–1916) and AROLDO BONZAGNI, while Anselmo Bucci (1887–1955), UBALDO OPPI, LORENZO VIANI and Modigliani all worked in Paris. Only ALBERTO MAGNELLI, a visitor there in 1914, responded to Cubism by moving towards abstraction (e.g. *Composition No. 0522;* see fig. 44). Giorgio de Chirico's PITTURA METAFISICA also emerged in Paris. His empty cities, juxtapositions of unexpected objects (e.g. *Song of Love*, 1914; New York, MOMA) and faceless mannequins evoked a disconcerting quality antithetical to Futurism. During a wartime collaboration in Ferrara, this style inspired Carrà to produce work of a formal simplicity comparable to that of Italian 14th-century art. Championed by Mario Broglio's Roman

44. Alberto Magnelli: *Composition No. 0522*, 1915 (Paris, Pompidou, Musée National d'Art Moderne)

periodical *Valori plastici* (1918–21), Pittura Metafisica proved influential in the uncertain post-war climate. For many (such as Soffici, GIORGIO MORANDI and the sculptor Arturo Martini), it balanced the necessary destructiveness of Futurism with a constructive phase and established a new form for the Italian tradition.

Post-war disaffection over limited territorial gains and economic crises spilled over into street battles between Communists and Fascists, and in October 1922 the latter group's opportunist 'March on Rome' swept Benito Mussolini to power. The ambiguities of his programme allowed those who feared Bolshevism to ignore Fascist atrocities, while the avant-garde perceived him as a man of their own radical aspirations. The regime's early political difficulties ensured relatively little interference as various artistic groups vied for approval. Marinetti promoted Futurist artists, in particular after 1928 such AEROPITTURA artists as Gerardo Dottori and Tullio Crali (*b* 1910), as appropriately revolutionary. However, Mussolini publicly favoured the ideas of MARIO SIRONI and the critic Margherita Sarfatti, who founded the NOVECENTO ITALIANO movement in Milan in 1922, with Bucci, Funi, Oppi and others. Like 'call to order' trends abroad, their combination of realism and modern form evoked classical values, while such works as Sironi's *Solitude* (*c*. 1925; Rome, G.N.A. Mod.) conveyed a more searching melancholy. The group's *Prima Mostra del Novecento Italiano* in 1926 (Milan, Pal. Permanente) included such independent contributors as Carrà, Morandi, FELICE CARENA, VIRGILIO GUIDI and FERRUCCIO FERRAZZI, with the figure studies of FELICE CASORATI and ANTONIO DONGHI representing a remarkable form of Magic Realism. Many artists moved to France in the 1920s, either for financial reasons or in response to the murder of the Socialist deputy Giacomo Mattioti (June 1924) and the proclamation of the dictatorship (Jan 1925). However, few rejected Fascism unequivocally, and such periodicals as the bilingual *900* (1926–9), directed by Massimo Bontempelli (1878–1960), maintained cultural exchanges. This ambiguity was embodied in the Italiani di Parigi, a grouping of Severini, de Chirico, ALBERTO SAVINIO, FILIPPO DE PISIS, Renato Paresce (1886–1937) and MASSIMO CAMPIGLI, which was specifically organized by MARIO TOZZI for the *Novecento* show of 1926, and for further exhibitions in 1928 and 1930.

By 1930 political intervention was more marked. A system of official exhibitions was headed by the Milan Triennale and the Rome Quadriennale (from 1931). From 1928 it also became illegal to practise without belonging to the Confederazione dei Professionisti e degli Artisti, which in turn required Fascist Party membership. Although Mussolini's personality cult and allusions to Roman imperialism were widespread, the single official style demanded by the radical minister Roberto Farinacci was not implemented. Indeed, within the political constraints, debate continued. Soffici saw the rural *strapaese* tendency (associated with Rosai, and with Mino Maccari's radical Fascist periodical *Il Selvaggio*, 1928–42) as exemplary of social constants. By contrast, the loose grouping known as the SCUOLA ROMANA, which included Fausto Pirandello, Corrado Cagli, Guglielmo Janni (1892–1958) and Alberto Ziveri (*b* 1908), developed an expressionistic style. This reached a critical extreme in the related Scuola di Via

Cavour of Mario Mafai, Antonietta Raphael and Scipione, whose work suggested the underlying social malaise (e.g. Scipione's *Men Who Turn around*, 1930; Rome, G.N.A. Mod.; see fig. 45). Furthermore, non-figural work re-emerged, both with the activities of Prampolini and Magnelli in Paris and with the biomorphism of the Turinese Futurists around FILLIA. In 1935 the book *Kn* by Carlo Belli (*b* 1903) championed the geometric abstraction shown at the Milanese Galleria Il Milione; participants included MAURO REGGIANI, ATANASIO SOLDATI and OSVALDO LICINI and the group in Como of MARIO RADICE, MANLIO RHO and Carla Badiali (*b* 1907). Their views on purity and equilibrium, echoing the *Razionalismo* architects Giuseppe Terragni and Alberto Sartoris, were politically acceptable as an assertion of order.

Sironi remained crucial in reconciling Fascism with modernism. In 1933 he, Carrà, Funi and Campigli signed the *Manifesto della pittura murale* and, together with de Chirico and Severini, executed murals for the Milan Triennale. Subsequent schemes included the murals created by Funi in a Renaissance style at the Palazzo Comunale in Ferrara. The propagandizing subjects of many of the contemporary murals belied the country's isolation following the invasion of Ethiopia (1935–6) and participation in the Spanish Civil War (1936–8). Although some artists formed broad alliances around such periodicals as *Quadrante* (1933–6) and *Valori primordiali* (1938), in general attitudes were hardening. In 1939 Farinacci's Premio Cremona was instituted for works with specified Fascist themes; this was immediately counter-balanced by the

Premio Bergamo, established by the liberal Minister of National Education, Giuseppe Bottai. More insidious were the infamous anti-semitic Racial Laws of 1938, against which artists protested in Marinetti's manifesto *L'evoluzione dell'arte italiana*. The periodical CORRENTE (1938–40) became the forum for young discontented artists, with the critical realism of Renato Guttuso, Aligi Sassu, Renato Birolli and the sculptor Giacomo Manzù reflecting clandestine Communist sympathies. As the climate of suppression intensified with the outbreak of World War II and the Sicilian landings of 1943, the *Corrente* artists emerged as dominant forces in an art of resistance (e.g. Guttuso's *Crucifixion*, 1940–41; Rome, G.N.A. Mod.; for illustration *see* GUTTUSO, RENATO).

(ii) From 1946. On 11 June 1946 the declaration of the Republic broke with the past and ushered in an era of coalition governments dominated by the Catholic Christian Democrats. Artists tended towards the powerful Socialist and Communist parties, as the experience of the Resistance had established an equation between their activity and class struggle. A decade of shifting alliances ensued in which they attempted to balance these commitments. Debate centred on the validity of realism, which, although associated with Fascism, was officially favoured by the Communist Party. As Guttuso's influential work became more literal, this question divided the 'post-Cubist' FRONTE NUOVO DELLE ARTI (1946–8), which included Guttuso and his former *Corrente* associates Birolli, Ennio Morlotti, Emilio Vedova, Giulio Turcato, Giuseppe Santomaso and Antonio Corpora. The majority of this group turned towards abstraction; in 1947 Turcato joined the Roman FORMA group, founded by Pietro Consagra, Piero Dorazio, Mino Guerrini (*b* 1927), Achille Perilli (*b* 1927), Carla Accardi and others. A distinction between their synthetic work (inspired by abstract Futurism) and a greater purity of form led to the formation of the MOVIMENTO ARTE CONCRETA by Soldati, Bruno Munari, Gianni Monnet (1912–58) and Gillo Dorfles (*b* 1910) and Fontana's associated SPAZIALISMO (with such adherents as Roberto Crippa and Gianni Dova). Pure apolitical creativity was simultaneously asserted by the stylistically disparate Gruppo Origine founded in Rome by ALBERTO BURRI, Mario Ballocco, GIUSEPPE CAPOGROSSI, the sculptor Ettore Colla and the writer Emilio Villa. By 1952 a painterly *Art informel* was favoured by the former Fronte artists who, together with Afro, made up the GRUPPO DEGLI OTTO PITTORI ITALIANI. The appeal of *Art informel* and Abstract Expressionism was reinforced by examples (notably by Wols and Jackson Pollock) visible in Venice at the Biennale and the Peggy Guggenheim Collection, and by the presence in Rome of Roberto Matta and Cy Twombly (from 1957).

With the dominance of abstraction, Fontana and Burri emerged as leading figures, both nationally and internationally. They revised the spatial, gestural and material qualities of art in works that blurred the distinctions between painting and sculpture. These developments suggested tendencies explored by succeeding generations, especially the optical, mathematical and spatial structures of such groups of conceptual artists as GRUPPO N and GRUPPO T, active in the 1960s. In the late 1950s and early

45. Scipione: *Men Who Turn around*, oil on panel, 998×795 mm, 1930 (Rome, Galleria Nazionale d'Arte Moderna)

1960s PIERO MANZONI established his radical reputation with works questioning preconceived notions of art and mocking the value placed on dexterity. In this he was closely involved with French Nouveau Réalisme and such figures as Yves Klein. Manzoni's white *Achromes* (see fig. 46), together with related work by his associate ENRICO CASTELLANI and the paintings and sculpture of FRANCESCO LO SAVIO, established their art as a new point of departure for younger artists. The contemporary re-assessment of the post-war boom elicited other responses, which opposed 'high' art with the imagery of popular culture. These ranged from the use of the detritus of consumer society, in the abstract *décollages* (made of stripped billboards) by MIMMO ROTELLA and Enrico Baj's ARTE NUCLEARE, to the Pop images of VALERIO ADAMI and Mario Schifano (*b* 1934), and to paintings of details from everyday objects by DOMENICO GNOLI (ii), and works on mirrors by MICHELANGELO PISTOLETTO.

Political instability marked the decade between the university strikes of 1968 and the assassination of the former prime minister Aldo Moro in 1978; anti-authoritarianism metamorphosed into violence and terrorism from left and right. For many artists, social injustice and the Cold War made abstraction increasingly untenable;

this was particularly true of those brought together by the critic Germano Celant in exhibitions in 1967 and 1968 under the name ARTE POVERA. Although much of their work was sculptural, these artists made extensive use of photography: for example Giulio Paolini's *Young Man Looking at Lorenzo Lotto* (1967; artist's priv. col.; see 1989 RA exh. cat., no. 201) consists of a screenprinted photograph of a portrait by a Renaissance artist, which explores the relationship between artist, subject and modern spectator. The production of paintings by such figures as Jannis Kounellis earlier in the decade was superseded by joint events (e.g. the *Azione Povere*, 1968; Amalfi, Arsenale) and by three-dimensional pieces. The various forms of Arte Povera were united by a rigorous intellectualism, for which gesture and the nature of communication, man's relation to his culture (particularly explored by Luciano Fabro and Paolini) and material environment were recurring themes. These concerns, which dominated the decade, also attracted such artists as GINO DE DOMENICIS, CLAUDIO PARMIGGIANI, LUIGI ONTANI and VETTOR PISANI.

By 1979 younger artists, especially NICOLA DE MARIA, ENZO CUCCHI, SANDRO CHIA, FRANCESCO CLEMENTE and MIMMO PALADINO, reacted to the increasingly distant

46. Piero Manzoni: *Achrome*, kaolin on canvas, 1.30×1.63 m, 1958 (Turin, Galleria Civica d'Arte Moderna)

quality of much Arte Povera by turning to lush figural oil painting. The critic Achille Bonito Olica (*b* 1939) dubbed them the Transavanguardia to convey their 'cultural nomadism' and eclectic style, which became associated with Neo-Expressionist painters in the USA and Germany (e.g. Georg Baselitz). The works of Clemente and Paladino embraced influences exerted within increasingly multicultural societies, but their interests also reflected contemporary research into Pittura Metafisica and inter-war Italian culture. In the mid-1980s a neo-classical response to this process of reassessment emerged in the referential *Arte Colta* of SALVO, Roberto Barni (*b* 1939), Carlo Maria Mariani (*b* 1931), Alberto Abate (*b* 1946), Stefano Di Stasio (*b* 1948) and others. In common with the preceding generations, the radicalism of Arte Povera and the mythologizing of the Transavanguardia and *Arte Colta* attempted to address the legacy of Italy's cultural past. In establishing an intellectualism and stylistic pluralism that served subsequent artists such as Bruno Ceccobelli (*b* 1952), they succeeded in securing a particular identity for their own era.

BIBLIOGRAPHY

PERIODICALS
La Voce (1909–10/*R* Rome and Milan, 1969)
Valori Plast. (1918–21/*R* Rome and Milan, 1969)
900 Cah. Italie & Europe (1926–9)
Il Selvaggio (1928–42)
Quadrante (1933–6)
Valori Prim. (1938)
Corrente (1938–40)

GENERAL
C. Belli: *Kn* (Milan, 1935, rev. 1972)
U. Apollonio: *Pittura italiana moderna* (Venice, 1950)
A. Pica: *Storia della Triennale, 1918–1957* (Milan, 1957)
M. Drudi Gambillo and T. Fiori, eds: *Archivi del futurismo*, 2 vols (Rome, 1958–62)
D. Frigessi, ed.: *La cultura italiana del 900 attraverso le riviste*, 5 vols (Turin, 1960)
L'informale in Italia, fino al 1957 (exh. cat. by D. Durbé and M. Calvesi, Livorno, Pal. Com., 1963)
G. Perocco: *Artisti del primo novecento italiano* (Milan, 1965); rev. as *Le origini di arte moderna a Venezia, 1908–1920* (Treviso, 1972)
R. De Grada: *Pittura e scultura degli anni '60* (Milan, 1967)
F. Bellonzi and T. Fiori, eds: *Archivi del divisionismo*, 2 vols (Rome, 1968)
Vitalità del negativo nell'arte italiana, 1960–70 (exh. cat., ed. A. Bonito Oliva; Rome, Pal. Espos., 1970–71)
E. Crispolti: *L'informale: Storia e poetica*, 5 vols (Assisi and Rome, 1971)
P. Fossati: *L'immagine sospesa: Pittura e scultura astratte in Italia, 1934–1940* (Turin, 1971)
P. Barocchi, ed.: *Testimonianze e polemiche figurative in Italia dal divisionismo al novecento* (Messina and Florence, 1974)
F. Tempesti: *Arte dell'Italia fascista* (Milan, 1976)
R. Barilli: *L'arte in Italia nel secondo dopoguerra* (Bologna, 1979)
La metafisica: Gli anni venti (exh. cat., ed. R. Barilli and F. Solmi; Bologna, Gal. Com. A. Mod., 1980)
Identité italienne: L'Art en Italie depuis 1959 (exh. cat. by G. Celant, Paris, Pompidou, 1981)
Linee della ricerca artistica in Italia, 1960–1980 (exh. cat. by M. Calvesi, Rome, Pal. Espos., 1981)
A. Bonito Oliva: *La transavanguardia internazionale/Trans Avant Garde International* (Milan, 1982) [in It. and Eng.]
F. Carioli: *Magico primario: L'arte degli anni ottanta* (Milan, 1982)
Italian Art Now: An American Perspective (exh. cat., ed. D. Waldman; New York, Guggenheim, 1982)
Arte italiana, 1960–1982 (exh. cat. by C. Tisdall and others, London, ICA and Hayward Gal., 1982–3)
I. Mussa: *La pittura colta* (Rome, 1983)
L'informale in Italia (exh. cat., ed. R. Barilli and F. Solmi; Bologna, Gal. Com. A. Mod., 1983)
L'ultima avanguardia (exh. cat. by L. Vergine, Milan, Pal. Reale, 1983–4)
M. Calvesi: *Le due avanguardie: Dal futurismo alla pop art* (Bari, 1984)
Der Traum des Orpheus: Mythologie in der italienischen Gegenwartskunst, 1964–1984 (exh. cat., ed. H. Friedel; Munich, Lenbachhaus, 1984)
C. Cerritelli: *Il corpo della pittura: Critici e nuovi pittori in Italia, 1972–1976* (Turin, 1985)
Futurism and Futurisms (exh. cat., ed. P. Hulten; Venice, Pal. Grassi, 1986)
Italian Art, 1900–1945 (exh. cat., ed. P. Hulten and G. Celant; Venice, Pal. Grassi, 1989)
Italian Art in the 20th Century: Painting and Sculpture, 1900–1988 (exh. cat., ed. E. Braun; London, RA, 1989)
P. Barocchi, ed.: *Storia moderna dell'arte in Italia: Manifesti, polemiche, documenti: Dal novecento ai dibattiti sulla figura e sul monumentale (1925–1945)* (Turin, 1990)

MATTHEW GALE

IV. Sculpture.

1. Ancient, 8th century BC–c. AD 313. 2. Early Christian and medieval, c. AD 313–c. 1400. 3. Renaissance and Mannerism, c. 1400–c. 1600. 4. Baroque, c. 1600–c. 1750. 5. Neo-classicism to early modernism, c. 1750–c. 1900. 6. After c. 1900.

1. ANCIENT, 8TH CENTURY BC–c. AD 313. From the Archaic to the Hellenistic period, and especially in the 3rd and 2nd centuries BC, Greek art expanded all over the Mediterranean region. In that time a basically homogeneous artistic culture developed in Italy, extending from Apulia, which initially had contacts with Attic civilization and later with that of Epiros and Macedonia, to Campania and Etruria. The Etruscan civilization, which developed in the area bounded by the Arno and the Tiber (now Tuscany and part of Umbria and Lazio) between the 8th century BC and 40 BC, produced the liveliest and most autonomous art to emerge in the western regions under the inevitable influence of the Greek world. The so-called 'Archaic age' of Etruscan sculpture (*see* ETRUSCAN, §III) is divided into an 'Orientalizing period' (*c.* 700–*c.* 600 BC), characterized by ornamental geometric elements derived from the version of the Greek Geometric style that was common in the Greek colonies of South Italy, and a period of Ionic and Attic influence (*c.* 600–*c.* 400 BC) when Etruscan art was dominated by Greek culture. Only one great artist of this period is documented by ancient sources (Pliny: *Natural History* XXXV.157; Plutarch: *Poplio* xiii). This was Vulca, the master of the school of Veii to whom the large clay statues of *Apollo*, *Herakles* and *Hermes* (*c.* 515–*c.* 490 BC; Rome, Villa Giulia), found during excavation of the Portonaccio Temple in Veii, can be attributed (for illustration *see* VEII). Etruscan sculpture of between 560 and 460 BC, while clearly inspired by Greek models, exhibits a distinctive taste and remarkable technical qualities, especially in the handling of bronze (e.g. the *Chimaera* of Arezzo; Florence, Mus. Archeol.; see fig. 47 and ETRUSCAN, §III, 2). This was followed by a 'middle period' (*c.* 400–*c.* 225 BC), during which the Romans conquered and Etruria lost its sea power and its economic and cultural contacts with the Greek world, and by a 'Hellenistic age' (*c.* 225–*c.* 40 BC) when the styles and iconographic schemes of Hellenistic sculpture were repeated.

Latium and Rome, unlike the other Italic centres, did not produce their own characteristic art until the later Hellenistic period. In Latium, in the late 7th century BC and the early 6th, there were workshops where Latin-speaking craftsmen produced objects in typically Etruscan styles. The bronze *She-wolf* (Rome, Mus. Conserv.; *see* ROME, ANCIENT, fig. 60) that became the symbol of Rome,

47. *Chimaera* of Arezzo, bronze, h. 760 mm, Etruscan, ? between 560 and 460 BC (Florence, Museo Archeologico di Firenze)

datable to the middle of the 5th century BC, can be identified stylistically as the product of a workshop that might have been Etruscan or of South Italy. At that date there did not yet exist a Roman civilization with its own formal artistic modes.

The period from the beginning of the Social War (91–88 BC) to the victory of Octavian (later Augustus) over Mark Antony at Actium (31 BC) was decisive for the formation of a truly Roman artistic culture. Roman art was eclectic at its birth because of the art works of different dates and styles that increasingly flowed into Rome after the wars of conquest. Eclecticism characterizes the so-called Altar of Domitius Ahenobarbus (*c.* 100–70 BC; Munich, Glyp.; Paris, Louvre), probably the most ancient official Roman monument with low reliefs. Popular or plebeian art, a provincial current of Hellenism, played a secondary role in the formation and later development of Roman art. The most notable phenomenon of this period was the realistic Republican portrait, which exalted the old Roman peasant race of patrician origin.

The Augustan age (27 BC–AD 14) was marked by technical and formal perfection at the expense of sculptural richness. A typical work is the Ara Pacis (*see* ROME, §V, 4 and fig. 22) consecrated in 13 BC, in which a generally Italic-Roman conception is overlaid with heterogeneous

figural and ornamental elements. Few stylistic changes occurred during the Julian-Claudian dynasty. Only in the age of Claudius did the aristocratic and impersonal style soften a little and take on some warmth and colour. In the Flavian period (AD 69–96) there was a return to typically Hellenistic artistic tendencies, namely spatial and atmospheric illusion. In the Arch of Titus (*c.* 81) the typical Roman historical relief was already fully defined. The art of antiquity reached a climax in the storiated column (ded. 113) erected by Trajan for his forum (*see* ROME, §V, 7 and fig. 25). Its 200 m of reliefs in 23 circuits narrate the four campaigns of the two Dacian campaigns (AD 101–2 and 105–6). The scenes of official rites are represented with a sense of lively participation; the military scenes are full of movement and a new energy; the impetus of the army is described with remarkable clarity; the battle scenes express compassion for the defeated and understanding of the nobility of their desperate struggle against an invader superior in weapons and organization (*see also* ROME, ANCIENT, fig. 76). A significant development of Trajan's last years was the production of marble sarcophagi decorated on three sides with mythological reliefs.

If the art of Trajan's reign was the expression of a new condition of Roman society, that of Hadrian's age (AD 117–38) was influenced by the Emperor, himself an artist, and shows a consciously nostalgic love of Classical Greece. The most frequently copied Greek sculpture was the statue of *Antinous* (e.g. *see* ROME, ANCIENT, fig. 78). In historical sculpture the power and richness characteristic of Trajan's time were lost, but there remained a solid, pictorial plasticity full of movement. In the time of the early Antonines (Antoninus Pius, *reg* AD 138–61; Marcus Aurelius, *reg* 161–80) different perceptions, combined with the classicism inherited from Hadrian's time, led to new spatial relations, and between AD 180 and 190 a new, more expressive element emerged. Forms became less rigorous, partly because of the search for chromatic and spatial effects. The Column of Antoninus Pius (after AD 161; destr.; *see* ROME, ANCIENT, §IV, 1(iv)(b) and fig. 71), with reliefs describing the campaign of MARCUS AURELIUS against the Sarmatians and the Germans, was modelled on Trajan's Column, although it had fewer circuits (21) and was taller (41.95 m). This resulted in larger, less crowded figures in higher relief, increasing the column's effectiveness as propaganda although interfering with its architectural outline. The Emperor is often presented frontally, the sign of a break with Hellenistic naturalistic tradition and of the adoption of ideological or mythological elements. The equestrian statue of *Marcus Aurelius* also dates from this time (*see* ROME, ANCIENT, fig. 61).

The sculpture of the Severan period (AD 193–235) is stylistically dependent on that of the time of Marcus Aurelius and Commodus (*reg* AD 180–93). The language of the plebeian current appears on the Arch of the Argentarii (AD 203). The style of the triple arch, erected in the Forum Romanum on the return of Septimius Severus from the wars against the Parthians, is related to that of the Column of Antoninus Pius and set a precedent for the rest of the century (*see* ROME, ANCIENT, fig. 34). Portraiture also flourished in the 3rd century, and a series of monumental sarcophagi (e.g. the Ludovisi battle sarcophagus; Rome, Mus. N. Romano) was produced. Hellenistic form was progressively abandoned, and the expressive or irrational element became permanently established. The Arch of Constantine (ded. AD 315; *see* ROME, §V, 12 and fig. 30), erected by the Senate beside the Colosseum, is a monument of fundamental importance for understanding the art of this period. It is largely composed of reclaimed sculptures from the age of Trajan, Hadrian and Marcus Aurelius. The new elements are the two tondi on the narrow sides and the narrow frieze, crowded with figures, that narrates the main events of the war against Maxentius (*reg* AD 306–12) in the popular artistic idiom of the middle classes. The arch expresses a new ideology of Imperial sanctity, derived from the eastern empire. The simplifications and aulic character of Constantinian art were developed further from the mid-4th century AD to the mid-6th. The last expressions of ancient artistic civilization were not suffocated by the barbarian invaders. Although they did not understand it, they respected the ancient form, which, though emptied of its content, was to survive for those two centuries. It was finally extinguished, as a consequence of internal developments, only under the Byzantine emperors.

BIBLIOGRAPHY

Die antiken Sarkophagreliefs (Berlin, 1890–1975)
A. Riegl: *Die spätrömische Kunstindustrie nach den Funden in Oesterreich-Ungarn* (Vienna, 1901, 2/1927)
E. Strong: *La scultura romana da Augusto a Costantino* (Florence, 1923–6)
——: *Mostra augustea della romanità: Catalogo* (Rome, 4/1938)
M. Pallottino: *Arte figurativa ed ornamentale* (Rome, 1940), iii of *Civiltà romana* (Rome, 1937–40)
O. Vessberg: *Studien zur Kunstgeschichte der römischen Republik* (Lund, 1941)
P. E. Arias: *La scultura romana* (Messina, 1943)
R. Bianchi Bandinelli: *Storicità dell'arte classica* (Florence, 1943)
G. Becatti: *La colonna coclide istoriata: Problemi storici, iconografici, stilistici* (Rome, 1960)
R. Bianchi Bandinelli: 'Sulla formazione del ritratto romano', *Archeologia e cultura*, ed. R. Ricciardi (Milan and Naples, 1961), pp. 172–88
J. M. C. Toynbee: *The Art of the Romans* (London, 1963)
R. Bianchi Bandinelli: *Roma: L'arte romana nel centro del potere* (Milan, 1969)
R. Brilliant: *Roman Art from the Republic to Constantine* (London, 1974)
P. Zanker: *Klassicistische Statuen: Studien zur Veränderung des Kunstgeschmacks in der römischen Kaiserzeit* (Mainz, 1974)
R. Bianchi Bandinelli and M. Torelli: *Etruria—Roma* (Turin, 1976)
B. M. Felletti Maj: *La tradizione italica nell'arte romana* (Rome, 1977)
E. Simon: *Ara Pacis Augustae* (Tübingen, 1977)
G. Gualandi: 'L'apporto italico alla formazione della civiltà romana', *Popoli e civiltà dell'Italia antica*, vii, ed. M. Pallottino (Rome, 1978), pp. 287ff
O. J. Brendel: *Prolegomena to the Study of Roman Art* (Yale, 1980)
M. Torelli: *Typology and Structure of Roman Historical Reliefs* (Ann Arbor, 1982)

LUCA LEONCINI

2. EARLY CHRISTIAN AND MEDIEVAL, *c.* AD 313–*c.* 1400.

(i) Introduction. (ii) Early Chrsitian, 4th–6th centuries AD. (iii) Lombard, Romanesque and Gothic, 6th–14th centuries.

(i) Introduction. Italian sculpture underwent a variety of changes in the millennium after the adoption of Christianity in the 4th century AD as the official religion of the Empire. The legalization and eventual predominance of Christianity led to the adaptation of pagan imagery, necessitating the formulation of new means of artistic expression (*see* EARLY CHRISTIAN AND BYZANTINE ART, §I, 2(i)). In the early centuries of Christianity works were usually anonymous; much later (in the 12th and 13th centuries) signatures became more common and made statements in praise of the artists' abilities (e.g. Nicola Pisano at Pisa describing himself as the greatest living sculptor). Workshops were highly organized, with a successful sculptor training and employing several assistants who would learn by imitating the skills of the master. As a result, changes took place only slowly. The controls and restrictions placed on artists by the guilds contributed to this relative lack of innovation. Patronage was important, often determining both the stylistic and iconographic approach adopted. While most patronage was religious, secular patronage did exist, particularly for sarcophagi and small ivory panels.

Medieval Italian art was subject to many foreign influences because of Italy's central position geographically, politically and culturally. Pisa, Genoa and Venice all played important roles in the Crusades and established trading colonies in Eastern cities, facilitating the free passage of artistic styles and motifs between cultures. The arrival of the Normans in the south and the Lombards in the north introduced new influences that blended with native characteristics to create a number of distinctive Italian styles. Northern influences were balanced with the Classical tradition which survived in various forms throughout the period; this can be seen in the sarcophagus fragment embedded in the wall of Calvi Cathedral, where Lombard decoration and a flattened figural style were used to depict tritons and nereids holding up a portrait medallion, and it is particularly noticeable in the much later work of Nicola Pisano, Lorenzo Maitani and Andrea Pisano.

(ii) Early Christian, 4th–6th centuries AD. Monumental sculpture largely died out in the centuries following the foundation of Constantinople, although there are isolated examples, such as the 5th-century AD bronze Colossus of Barletta (*see* EARLY CHRISTIAN AND BYZANTINE ART, §IV, 1), an attempt to emulate the Augustan Imperial tradition. A much more important art form was the sarcophagus, which marks most clearly the change from Classical to Christian art. Initially Christian sculptors borrowed pagan motifs, but they gradually developed Christian equivalents. On the sarcophagus of Junius Bassus (*c.* AD 359; Rome, Grotte Vaticane; *see* SARCOPHAGUS, fig. 3), Classical architectural motifs were combined with figures that, while modelled almost in the round and clothed in Classical draperies, anticipate the more compressed figures of the following centuries. The dominant theme is Christian salvation. Borrowings from antiquity are apparent in, for example, the pagan god (on whom Christ tramples to signify the triumph of Christianity), which is based on a figure from Trajan's Column. Many important sarcophagi have survived in Ravenna, although the dating of most is contentious and it is uncertain whether they were made in a Byzantine workshop or in Ravenna itself. Iconography is again dominated by themes of salvation, although depictions of the Virgin may reflect the decision of the Council of Ephesos (AD 431) to confirm the Virgin's title 'Theotokos' (Mother of God). She appears as a subject in her own right on the early 5th-century AD sarcophagus of Isaccius (Ravenna, S Francesco) and the Pignatta sarcophagus or 'sarcophagus of Elisha' (Ravenna, Edicola Braccioforte), among others. The sense of movement and plasticity of the figures in these high-quality works demonstrate the survival in some areas of the Late Antique style. This co-existed with a more hieratic style exemplified in a sarcophagus showing *Christ with the Twelve Apostles* (Ravenna, S Apollinare in Classe), the figures of which are more compressed and two-dimensional, although inhabiting a space delineated by Classical architectural motifs.

Sculpture was important in the decoration of ecclesiastical buildings, both as an integral part of the fabric (Calvi) and for liturgical objects (*see* EARLY CHRISTIAN AND BYZANTINE ART, §IV, 2(i)). Many Early Christian basilicas, such as S Sabina, Rome, and S Ambrogio, Milan, had sets of doors decorated with narrative cycles (*see* DOOR, §II, 1). At S Sabina the cypress-wood doors (AD 422–32) were carved with Old and New Testament subjects, including one of the earliest depictions of the *Crucifixion*, almost certainly part of an exegetical programme. Liturgical furnishings included fonts, such as the huge porphyry example (*c.* AD 432) in the Lateran Baptistery, Rome, as well as pulpits, thrones and choir screens. The ambos of Bishop Agnellus (*reg* AD 556–69) and Bishop Marinianus (*reg* AD 597–606) in Ravenna Cathedral are decorated with animals within square panels. The remnants of the 6th-century AD marble choir screen commissioned by Mercurius in S Clemente, Rome, include the cross and a wreath

48. *Three Marys at the Tomb* and the *Ascension*, ivory plaque, 187×114 mm, early 5th century AD (Munich, Bayerisches Nationalmuseum)

combined with the patron's monogram and a closely woven basketwork design related to the elaborately carved capitals in S Vitale, Ravenna. (For an example of a 10th-century liturgical object *see* SITULA.)

Ivory plaques were important in the Early Christian period, being easily portable, and have survived in relatively large numbers (*see* EARLY CHRISTIAN AND BYZANTINE ART, §VII, 5). Their precious nature suggests important patrons, reflecting the spread of Christianity among the wealthy classes. A small, early 5th-century AD plaque (Munich, Bayer. Nmus.; see fig. 48) depicts the *Three Marys at the Tomb* and the *Ascension* in a Late Antique style and setting; the artist has created a sense of depth and has shown Christ as a clean-shaven Roman figure. This naturalism disappeared before the end of the 5th century AD, to be replaced by a more static hieratic quality, as demonstrated by the diptych of Boethius (AD 487; Brescia, Mus. Civ. Crist.) and the related five-part diptych showing scenes from the *Life of Christ* (Milan, Tesoro Duomo). Similar consular diptychs were produced in Constantinople into the 6th century AD.

(iii) Lombard, Romanesque and Gothic, 6th–14th centuries. The invasion of Italy in the 6th century AD by the Lombards brought wide-ranging and long-lasting changes.

In general, Lombard carving was highly decorative and non-representational, although notable figural works were produced. The Ratchis Altar (c. AD 737; Cividale del Friuli, Mus. Crist. & Tesoro Duomo) is simple in concept and demonstrates northern European or barbarian influences in the stylized depiction of figures (see also LOMBARD ART). The marked frontality with a lack of depth and perspective, giving the figures the appearance of being suspended in space, is far removed from the Classical tradition. The Sigwald Altar Frontal (c. AD 762–77) in Cividale del Friuli Cathedral is a more complex work, combining Eastern animal motifs with a cross with Celtic ornament, the *Tree of Life* and *The Evangelists* in roundels. The imitation of the northern champlevé metalwork style was probably inspired by a metal altar frontal.

The Lombards were masters in the use of stucco, which was used widely in Italian churches for decorative purposes until the revival of carving in hardstone in the Romanesque period. The combination of stucco with marble, fresco, mosaic and relief-carving in the 8th-century church of S Maria in Valle ('Tempietto'), Cividale, represents the finest extant example of Lombard art in northern Italy. The date of the stuccos remains disputed, suggestions ranging from the 8th to the 11th century.

During the Romanesque period the Classical tradition underwent a revival that is most apparent in the work of Lombard and Emilian artists (see ROMANESQUE, §III,

1(vi)). Lombard techniques that survived the destruction of the Lombard kingdom by the Franks (AD 774) became integral to the Italian Romanesque style. It is more organic and purer in form than that of Provence and the Languedoc, suggesting a closer and more continuous contact with the Classical tradition. The period was dominated by WILIGELMO and Benedetto Antelami. On the south façade (c. 1099–1110) of Modena Cathedral Wiligelmo's use of the pagan motif of genii with reversed torches, to which he gave a Christian symbolism, highlights his knowledge and understanding of the Classical tradition (see MODENA, §1(ii)). Wiligelmo was concerned with the manipulation of forms and masses in space. His follower NICHOLAUS carved the important reliefs (after c. 1120) on the façade of S Zeno Maggiore, Verona (see VERONA, fig. 4).

Lombard Romanesque sculpture reached its acme in the work of BENEDETTO ANTELAMI. His graceful figures in the marble *Deposition* (1178; Parma Cathedral; see PARMA, fig. 2) are naturalistic, although unemotional, and come closest to contemporary French work. On the Baptistery at Parma (see BAPTISTERY, fig. 3) Antelami used the cube and cylinder for the structure of his monumental, volumetric figures. They define their own space within the overall decorative programme and set the standard for later sculptors. The drapery style suggests the inspiration of a Late Antique model.

The Early Christian and Byzantine tradition of decorated doors was revived in the Romanesque period, at S

49. Nicola Pisano: *Adoration of the Magi* (1260), marble panel from his pulpit, 0.85×1.13 m, Baptistery, Pisa

Zeno (12th century), Verona, where bronze plaques were attached to a wooden base to create a set of monumental doors, and for the bronze doors of the Porta di S Ranieri, Pisa Cathedral (c. 1180), by BONANUS OF PISA. Andrea Pisano (see PISANO (ii), (1)) took Bonanus's doors as his model for the first set of bronze doors (c. 1329–36) for the Baptistery in Florence (see FLORENCE, §IV, 1(ii)(c) and fig. 14). The pulpit and throne remained predominant among church furniture throughout the Romanesque period and beyond. The 12th-century Gropina pulpit (Gropina, Pieve di S Pietro) indicates the continuing power of barbarian influences, while the vitality of the monolithic marble throne (c. 1197) in Bari Cathedral (see BARI (ii), §2(iii) and fig. 3) anticipates the masterpieces of the 14th century.

In the 13th and 14th centuries sculptural production was prolific, and numerous intermingling cross-currents laid the foundations for the Renaissance. There was tremendous regional variation and no continuous development. Nicola Pisano's outstanding pulpit (1260) carved for the Baptistery at Pisa exhibits a strong Classical style (see PISANO (i), (1) and fig. 1). One of its most startling figures is that of *Fortitude*, often described as the first monumental nude since antiquity. The *Adoration of the Magi* (see fig. 49), which consists of classicizing figures with foreshortened horses, points forward to the Renaissance. On his pulpit (1265–8) for Siena Cathedral (see PISANO (i), (1), fig. 2), Nicola was assisted by his son Giovanni and by ARNOLFO DI CAMBIO. The Pisani were more successful than any other artists in combining Classical motifs with the Gothic influences that were entering Italy from the north. Giovanni's prophets (c. 1287–97) for the façade of Siena Cathedral exhibit a closeness to German Gothic, while in his pulpit (1302–10) for Pisa Cathedral (see PISANO (i), (2) and PULPIT, fig. 1) a knowledge of contemporary French work is apparent. His free-standing *Virgin and Child between Two Angels* (1305–6) for the altar of the Arena Chapel, Padua, reflects the monumentality of Giotto's painted figures and the mannerism of contemporary French ivory-carvers and demonstrates the eclecticism that was to be such a powerful force in the 14th century.

Two important art forms in the 13th and 14th centuries were the EQUESTRIAN MONUMENT and the sculptural tomb. In the equestrian figures of *Can Grande I della Scala* (d 1329) and *Mastino II della Scala* (d 1277) in S Maria Antica, Verona (see VERONA, fig. 5), classicizing elements were combined with the depiction of contemporary armour. Another northern Italian example is the statue of *Bernabò Visconti* (1363; Milan, Castello Sforzesco) by Bonino da Campione. Tomb monuments also tended to glorify local rulers, as in the case of the tomb of *Azzo Visconti* (c. 1339; Milan, S Gottardo in Corte) by the workshop of Giovanni di Balduccio, which shows subject cities paying homage to Milan (see VISCONTI (i), (1)).

At the beginning of the 14th century LORENZO MAITANI executed a series of relief-carvings on the exterior of Orvieto Cathedral (c. 1310; see ORVIETO, fig. 3). Stylistically the work is an admixture of the Classical and Gothic, contributing to Italian sculpture an expressionism that would be influential later. It thus proved to be one of

many direct links in Italian art between the Classical past and the Renaissance via medieval sculpture.

BIBLIOGRAPHY

EWA: 'Late Antique and Early Christian Art: Sculpture'
A. Venturi: *L'arte romanica* (1904), iii of *Storia dell'arte italiana*, ed. A. Venturi (Milan, 1901–40)
P. Toesca: *Il medioevo* (1927), i of *Storia dell'arte italiana*, ed. A. Venturi (Milan, 1901–40)
M. Salmi: *La scultura romanica in Toscana* (Florence, 1928)
A. Haseloff: *La scultura pre-romanica in Italia* (Bologna, 1930; Eng. trans., Florence and Paris, 1930)
C. R. Morey: *Early Christian Art: An Outline of the Evolution of the Style and Iconography in Sculpture and Painting from Antiquity to the Eighth Century* (Princeton, 1942, rev. 1953)
R. Jullian: *L'Eveil de la sculpture italienne: La Sculpture romane dans l'Italie du nord* (Paris, 1945)
G. H. Crichton: *Romanesque Sculpture in Italy* (London, 1954)
H. Swarzenski: *Monuments of Romanesque Art* (Chicago, 1954, rev. 1967)
H. Decker: *Romanesque Art in Italy* (New York, 1959)
P. Verzone: *From Theoderic to Charlemagne: A History of the Dark Ages in the West*, A. World (Baden-Baden, 1967)
R. Krautheimer: *Studies in Early Christian, Medieval and Renaissance Art* (New York, 1969)
J. Beckwith: *Early Christian Art*, Pelican Hist. A. (Harmondsworth, 1970)
G. Henderson: *Early Medieval*, Style & Civiliz. (Harmondsworth, 1972)
P. Lasko: *Ars Sacra, 800–1200*, Pelican Hist. A. (Harmondsworth, 1972)
M. Schapiro: *Late Antique, Early Christian and Medieval Art* (New York, 1979)
M. F. Hearn: *Romanesque Sculpture: The Revival of Monumental Stone Sculpture in the Eleventh and Twelfth Centuries* (Ithaca, NY, 1981)
M. Stokstad: *Medieval Art* (New York, 1986)
J. Snyder: *Medieval Art: Painting–Sculpture–Architecture, 4th–14th Century* (Englewood Cliffs, 1989)

MICHAEL A. KISSANE

3. RENAISSANCE AND MANNERISM, *c*. 1400–*c*. 1600. The 15th and 16th centuries in Italy constituted one of the most vibrant epochs in the history of world sculpture. It is best divided into three periods, on broad, stylistic criteria: early Renaissance (*c*. 1400–*c*. 1480), High Renaissance (*c*. 1480–*c*. 1530) and Mannerism (*c*. 1530–*c*. 1600). These dates are approximate, as Italy was not then unified and progress varied between city states. Further divisions must be made to take account of the diverse approaches to sculpture in the city states, both in materials and in themes. Florentine sculptors rarely relinquished the stylistic initiative and quickly appropriated and adapted innovations that emerged elsewhere, for example Mannerism, from Rome. Rome did not play a leading role, owing to schisms in the Church, and to the Reformation, which checked papal expenditure. Certain popes did lavish money on sculpture, but each tended to employ favourites from his native city, and there seems not to have been sufficient continuity in patronage to support a major, homogeneous school of sculpture. Venice flourished during the whole period, and the doges appreciated sculpture as a means of symbolizing her achievements. Visiting artists from Tuscany (e.g. Donatello and Jacopo Sansovino) stimulated her out of her innate conservatism and spurred her cautious adoption of successive styles. Other city states came to prominence for limited periods: Milan, Siena, Bologna, Urbino, Ferrara, Padua, Mantua, Genoa, Naples and Sicily all boasted local schools of sculpture, which on occasion gave birth to master sculptors or masterpieces. These bursts of activity resulted in an efflorescence of sculpture all over Italy, with particular local flavours but of a consistently high quality, both in creative imagination and in terms of technique. Many of the best-known names in the history of art are those of

Italian sculptors from these two centuries, such as Lorenzo Ghiberti, Donatello, Andrea Verrocchio, Michelangelo, Benvenuto Cellini, Giambologna, Tullio Lombardo and Jacopo Sansovino.

(i) Early Renaissance, *c.* 1400–*c.* 1480. (ii) High Renaissance, *c.* 1480–*c.* 1530. (iii) Mannerism, *c.* 1530–*c.* 1600.

(i) Early Renaissance, c. 1400–c. 1480.

(a) Florence. (b) Rome. (c) Lucca, Siena and Bologna. (d) Venice and the Veneto.

(a) Florence. It was in Florence that a renewed interest in ancient culture, including remains of architecture and monumental sculpture, first emerged, towards the end of the 14th century. This resulted in a new Classically derived style, which appeared first in sculpture. Florence is the only city in which the full development of sculpture may be followed, from the Gothic legacy of the Middle Ages to the sublime productions of the High Renaissance, and thence to the poetic, almost abstracted, grace and wit of Mannerism.

Introduction. The period of Italian art known as the RENAISSANCE is usually regarded as beginning in 1401, the date of a competition to design a new pair of monumental bronze doors for the Baptistery at Florence. Before this date art was predominantly Gothic and medieval in character; afterwards it was predominantly influenced by the revival of interest in the ancient civilization of the Greeks and Romans. The Baptistery, the Campanile and the Cathedral (*see* FLORENCE, §IV, 1) became the epicentre of sculptural activity in the city in the Renaissance, a showpiece of the latest development in narrative reliefs and in statues devoted to religious subjects. The other centre of sculptural activity in the first quarter of the 15th century was the guildhall, Orsanmichele (*see* FLORENCE, §IV, 2). Each major guild had to furnish one of the external niches with a statue of its patron saint. The guilds felt themselves in direct rivalry, and there was a startling explosion of technical and stylistic innovation, as the greatest sculptors of the day vied to produce the most 'modern' statue.

Private patronage of sculpture existed as well as corporate, but it was confined to works for churches. Sacred locations permitted only a limited range of opportunities and subjects, however, and a major feature of the Renaissance is the gradual broadening of the scope of private patronage to encompass entirely new types of sculpture, inspired by ancient models, notably plaquettes and bronze statuettes of Classical subjects. Owing to the private and personal nature of such commissions, the full range of pagan, mythological and occasionally even erotic subjects could be addressed. Consequently it is in these minor fields of sculpture that the broadest exploration of antiquity occurs, and hence the 'real' Renaissance. After *c.* 1425 the pre-eminence of Florence as a centre of sculpture was due to the MEDICI family, who came to own probably the greatest collection of antiquities and perceptively employed a sequence of the finest sculptors: Donatello, Bertoldo di Giovanni, Verrocchio and Antonio del Pollaiuolo.

Types of sculpture. The pioneering role of sculptors in the early Renaissance was applied in four main types of sculpture: the narrative relief, the statue, the tomb and the portrait. The narrative relief became the first vehicle for the emergence of the Renaissance style, through direct references to ancient Roman sculptural prototypes, notably sarcophagi, as well as a renewed emphasis on realism and drama. The competition for the Baptistery doors in 1401 was won by Ghiberti, whose reliefs of scenes from the *Life of Christ* (*in situ*; *see* GHIBERTI, (1), fig. 1), while retaining Gothic elements, show the adoption and integration of antique motifs (Krautheimer). In a second set of doors for the Baptistery, showing scenes from the Old Testament (1452; *in situ*; *see* GHIBERTI, (1), fig. 4), he used larger panels, which enabled him to vie with paintings, in the inclusion of landscapes or architectural settings, just as DONATELLO was beginning to do in the same decade.

Ghiberti avoided the excesses of violence or drama that inspired some of Donatello's greatest relief sculpture. Trained by Ghiberti, Donatello soon evolved a personal style, influenced by ancient Roman models. This he expressed in a low-relief technique (*rilievo schiacciato*) that he invented between *c.* 1415 and 1425. He drew on the surface of the marble with a pointed chisel, indicating depth pictorially, by perspective rather than by physically excavating the marble. His contemporaries, MICHELOZZO DI BARTOLOMEO, NANNI DI BANCO and Luca della Robbia (*see* ROBBIA, DELLA, (1)), all preferred the ancient Roman convention of high relief, which is easier to control in the carving.

At the beginning of the 15th century, as in the Middle Ages, almost all statues were made for architectural settings, usually niches in churches. As the Renaissance evolved, the statue began to be liberated from such constraints, to be set at the centre of a courtyard, for example, or over a fountain basin. By the turn of the century, statues on grandiose pedestals began to be used to dominate squares and to articulate urban plans. Ultimately, in the 16th century, this formal approach was challenged by the Mannerist idea of scattering statues in gardens, to be encountered unexpectedly. The principal destinations for statues in the first third of the 15th century in Florence were the cathedral complex and the guildhall. For the cathedral façade and Campanile a number of marble statues were carved by the earliest representatives of Renaissance figure sculpture, Nanni di Banco, Donatello and NANNI DI BARTOLO. Donatello created a series of horrifyingly emaciated *Prophets*, derived from ancient Roman portraits. To Orsanmichele, Ghiberti contributed three saints cast in bronze (*see* GHIBERTI, (1) fig. 2), and Nanni di Banco made a particularly impressive group of four saints resembling Roman senators (for illustration see NANNI DI BANCO). The undoubted masterpiece in terms of expressiveness is Donatello's knight in armour, *St George* (*c.* 1414; *see* FLORENCE, fig. 17). Orsanmichele remained a focus of sculptural endeavour for many years; last to arrive was a splendid *St Luke* in bronze by GIAMBOLOGNA (1602). It was in the essentially private context of Medicean patronage that the emancipation of statuary from ecclesiastical constraints began. In the middle of the century Cosimo de' Medici commissioned from Donatello a statue in bronze of *David* (Florence, Bargello;

see STATUE, fig. 1), the first life-size statue of a male nude in the Renaissance, reviving an antique type. The *David* was first recorded in the courtyard of Cosimo's new palace, which was finished in the 1450s. For the garden of the palace, Donatello's *Judith and Holofernes* (*c.* 1465; Florence, Piazza della Signoria; see fig. 50) was the first functioning fountain statue of the Renaissance, and the first group of two integrated figures designed to be seen from all round.

Tombs in the Middle Ages were, to a greater or lesser extent, free-standing, architectural affairs. Donatello and Michelozzo translated the grand wall-tomb from the Gothic into a Renaissance idiom in the monument to the

50. Donatello: *Judith and Holofernes* (*c.* 1465), bronze, h. 2.36m, Piazza della Signoria, Florence

anti-Pope *John XXIII* (*c.* 1424–7; Florence, Baptistery), in which standard elements were framed in Classical architectural forms. Variations of this 'humanist tomb' (Pope-Hennessy, 1958) were made for most of the 15th century, for example the tombs of the chancellors of Florence (see below), and spread throughout Italy. Copies and variants of ancient Roman sarcophagi were also used (*see* SARCOPHAGUS, §III, 3). Slabs for setting in the floor were converted into the Renaissance idiom, and Donatello introduced a convincing image of the deceased in the tomb slab of *Bishop Pecci* (*c.* 1428; Siena Cathedral).

Possibly the greatest innovation in the repertory of the sculptor during the Renaissance was the revival of the portrait bust. Traditionally, this was held to have occurred only in the 1450s, for example Mino da Fiesole's *Piero de' Medici* (1453; Florence, Bargello; *see* BUST, fig. 2) and Antonio Rossellino's *Giovanni Chellini* (1456; London, V&A). Ghiberti had applied a self-portrait to his doors for the Baptistery (*c.* 1420), however, and Donatello's painted terracotta likeness of *Niccolò da Uzzano* (Florence, Bargello) suggests that he too was involved in the deliberate revival of the portrait in bust form *c.* 1430 (*see also* POLYCHROMY, colour pl. V, fig. 1). By mid-century, still more ambitious portrait statues were made, notably another Roman type, the equestrian monument: Donatello's *Gattamelata* (1447–53; Padua, Piazza Santo; *see* DONATELLO, fig. 4) and Verrocchio's *Bartolomeo Colleoni* (*c.* 1479–92; Venice, Campo SS Giovanni e Paolo; *see* VERROCCHIO, ANDREA DEL, fig. 4), both masterpieces of bronze founding. The concept of the portrait medal, making portraits in multiples, was evident from ancient coinage. The greatest exponents of the medal were Pisanello and MATTEO DE' PASTI, who portrayed many Renaissance rulers and intellectuals (*see* PISANELLO, fig. 2 and ALBERTI, LEON BATTISTA, fig. 1). Original casts were made in gold and/or silver (for illustration *see* GIAN CRISTOFORO ROMANO), and secondary ones in bronze. Analogous portraits were also carved in hardstones or cameos but were rarely reproduced in quantity, for technical reasons.

'Sweet style'. Ghiberti was a proponent of a moderate and appealing style of sculpture, ennobling humanity and Christianity in an idealized vision amalgamated from Gothic art and Roman remains. Nanni di Banco and Michelozzo also tended to adhere to this norm, but Donatello largely abandoned it from the 1420s. From *c.* 1430 this 'Sweet style' was reinforced by Luca della Robbia, whose *Cantoria* for Florence Cathedral (*see* ROBBIA, DELLA, (1), fig. 1) is one of its greatest manifestations. Luca then adapted ceramic glazing techniques to terracotta sculpture and produced a long series of works, including charming images of the Virgin and Child, portrait roundels and coats of arms. The second generation of Renaissance sculptors who came to maturity *c.* 1445–55, while Donatello was absent in Padua, absorbed the calm mood and delicacy of detail in Ghiberti's and Luca's mature work: Bernardo and Antonio ROSSELLINO, DESIDERIO DA SETTIGNANO and MINO DA FIESOLE. Bernardo developed several of the structual types invented by Donatello and Michelozzo, for instance the sacramental tabernacle and notably the 'humanist tomb', such as those for *Leonardo Bruni* (*d* 1444) and *Carlo Marsuppini* (*d* 1453) in Santa

Croce. Antonio's splendid tomb for *Cardinal James of Portugal* (d 1459) in S Miniato al Monte is part of a complete funerary chapel, including works by Luca, Antonio Pollaiuolo (see POLLAIUOLO, (1)) and ALESSO BALDOVINETTI that is the apogee of the 'Sweet Style' and one of the greatest artistic complexes in the world. Mino also carved tombs, including *Count Ugo of Tuscany* (Florence, Badia Fiorentina), and later introduced the style to Rome.

Mino's portrait busts of *Piero I de' Medici* and *Giovanni de' Medici* (both Florence, Bargello) are forceful images, although they lack the finesse of such busts as Antonio's *Giovanni Chellini* (1456; London, V&A). Delicate busts of women and of children were made by Antonio, Desiderio (e.g. Florence, Bargello) and Verrocchio (see fig. 51). Outside Florence, only the nine female busts by FRANCESCO LAURANA are significant: they show a degree of abstraction that appeals particularly to 20th-century viewers. Each of the Florentine sculptors discussed above executed reliefs of the Virgin and Child. Only Desiderio dared to try *rilievo schiacciato* (very shallow relief), and with great success (e.g. Turin, Gal. Sabauda; Philadelphia, PA, Mus. A.). Their designs were copied throughout central Italy.

'Dramatic style'. Donatello's major contribution to the history of art was the single-handed creation of a vigorous, and at times horrendous, alternative style in which to convey the darker aspects of the Old and New Testaments. His intensity of feeling and the speed and spontaneity of

51. Andrea del Verrocchio: *Woman Holding Flowers*, marble, h. 610 mm, 1475–80 (Florence, Museo Nazionale del Bargello)

his work are conveyed by a deliberate lack of finish. The urgency of Donatello's carving can be seen in the low relief of the *Ascension* (1420s; London, V&A; see DONATELLO, fig. 3), in which sketchy outlines and masses blocked out with the claw chisel are everywhere apparent. His stucco roundels of the Old Sacristy (1430s; Florence, S Lorenzo) are yet more spontaneous. The carved wood statue of *St John the Baptist* (1438; Venice, S Maria Gloriosa dei Frari) exceeds even his *Prophets* for the Campanile in its 'expressionism'. Younger sculptors continued Donatello's style for a generation or more: BERTOLDO DI GIOVANNI, Verrocchio and Pollaiuolo. Pollaiuolo's intensely felt, and aggressively linear and angular, style is perhaps the direct successor of the late style of Donatello: his observation of anatomy inspired Leonardo da Vinci and Michelangelo to dissect corpses in order to convey inner feelings visually. The intensity of Donatello's style was emulated in Rome by FILARETE, in Siena by VECCHIETTA and in Padua by BARTOLOMEO BELLANO and SEVERO DA RAVENNA. All of his immediate successors applied Donatello's style to the one type of ancient sculpture that he scarcely explored, the independent bronze statuette (see STATUETTE, §II).

(b) Rome. The development of sculpture in Rome was sporadic, as explained above. Around 1430 Donatello created two works there in fully Renaissance style, a tomb-slab for Giovanni Crivelli (Rome, S Maria in Aracoeli) and a sacramental tabernacle for St Peter's, which included a masterly low-relief scene of the *Entombment*. A major commission for a pair of bronze doors for St Peter's, intended to rival Ghiberti's Baptistery doors, was awarded to Filarete, who was not able to depict human figures convincingly and nobly. His other significant work of this period was one of the earliest datable bronze statuettes, a reduction of the ancient Roman equestrian *Marcus Aurelius* (Dresden, Skulpsamml.). Bronze masterpieces in Rome include il Vecchietta's striking effigy of *Bishop Girolamo Foscari* (d 1463) in S Maria del Popolo and Pollaiuolo's tombs in St Peter's for *Sixtus IV* (1493) and *Innocent VIII* (1498). The local school of the mid-15th century in Rome was composed exclusively of marble sculptors. First and foremost was ISAIA DA PISA, who was obviously indebted to ancient Roman sculpture for his rendering of anatomy and drapery (e.g. *Virgin and Child with SS Peter and Paul*, 1460s; Rome, Vatican, Grotte Vaticane). His tomb for *Cardinal Chiaves* in S Giovanni in Laterano was influential in Rome. Direct Tuscan influence on Roman marble carving came from Mino da Fiesole, who worked there frequently between 1454 and ?1480. From the far north of Italy, Andrea Bregno (see BREGNO, (2)) was active in Rome 1465–1501, furnishing sculpture to the Vatican and important churches, notably the *Riario* and *Della Rovere* monuments in SS Apostoli.

(c) Lucca, Siena and Bologna. These cities together constituted the focus of activity of the third great sculptor of the early Renaissance, Jacopo della Quercia. His first surviving commission (1403) was an important one, a marble group of the *Virgin and Child* for Ferrara Cathedral, in which the solid forms and classical faces betoken a potentially Renaissance mentality. The effigy of *Ilaria del*

Carretto (*d* 1405; Lucca Cathedral; *see* JACOPO DELLA QUERCIA, fig. 2) rests on a deliberately classicizing tomb chest, with putti supporting swags, derived from Roman sarcophagi; they were some of the earliest of a type of figure that became characteristic of the Renaissance period in Italy. Jacopo's fountain (Fonte Gaia) in the Siena *campo*, completed in 1419, includes a pair of free-standing, virtually nude, female statues with putti. In the relief of the *Expulsion from Paradise* on the end panel, the arrangement of his characteristic robust nudes shows little concern with illusionistic perspective and architectural settings. This is also evident in the gilt-bronze relief of the *Annunication to Zacharias* (1428–30) for the font in the Siena Baptistery, which has panels by Ghiberti and Donatello. Jacopo's last great commission (1425) was for ten reliefs for the main portal of S Petronio, Bologna. In those narrating the *Creation and Fall of Man* (see fig. 52) he set dramatically posed figures against a virtually abstract background, which he did not attempt to penetrate, as did Donatello. The figures in the reliefs of the *Early Life of Christ* are so large, with such exaggerated *contrapposto* that they seem about to burst the containing frame.

Siena remained a major sculptural centre in the Renaissance, owing not only to Jacopo but also to the contributions of Ghiberti and Donatello to the font, as well as to

Donatello's work there 1457–9, including the bronze statue of *St John the Baptist*. Il Vecchietta, inspired by Donatello, created a relief of the *Resurrection* (1472; New York, Frick) and a tautly muscled *Risen Christ* (1476; S Maria della Scala; *see* VECCHIETTA, fig. 2). He in turn trained FRANCESCO DI GIORGIO MARTINI, who practised all three fine arts; in sculpture, his most significant creations are in bronze, narrative scenes with the dramatic intensity of Donatello, a *Lamentation* (1476; Venice, S Maria del Carmine) and a *Flagellation* (1476–82; Perugia, G.N. Umbria). His over life-size *Angels* (1497) for the high altar of Siena Cathedral are masterpieces of lively modelling and great charm, continuing the style of Donatello into the period of the High Renaissance.

(d) Venice and the Veneto. Venice, which was established long after the Roman Empire had fallen, and isolated from mainland Italy, had links by sea with the Near and Far East. The prolonged influence of Byzantine art there, in the Veneto-Byzantine style, delayed the adoption of the Gothic style and subsequently that of the Renaissance (only c. 1450).

Late Gothic. The interest of Venetian sculptors in antiquity and its revival in Tuscany was strengthened with the arrival in 1416 from Florence of two stone-carvers, Niccolò di Piero Lamberti and his son Piero di Niccolò. Niccolò carved statues for the upper storey of the façade of S Marco (for illustration *see* LAMBERTI, (1)), and he (or another Florentine, Nanni di Bartolo) executed a prominent group of the *Judgement of Solomon* on the Doge's Palace, an effective scene but without the urgency of, for example, Donatello. The native school of sculpture was led by Giovanni BUON (i) and his son Bartolomeo. In 1422 both were working on a new Gothic palace, the Ca' d'Oro: Bartolomeo's splendid well-head for its courtyard (1427–8), with a figure of *Charity* copied from Ghiberti, is one of the finest examples of a class of sculpture that was virtually unique to Venice. For the Scuola Grande della Misericordia they carved a magnificent ogival lunette showing the *Madonna of Mercy* (London, V&A). Like the well-head, its figures are in deep relief and carved very broadly, giving a slightly 'abstract' feeling. The style is related to that of Jacopo della Quercia, who was in the Venetian area in this period. In 1438 the Buon sculptors were commissioned to carve the main gateway to the Doge's Palace, the Porta della Carta, including a statue of *Justice* (positioned 1441; for illustration, *see* BUON (i), (1)). Bartolomeo contributed an excellent bust of *Doge Francesco Foscari* (1423–57; part destr. 1797; Venice, Mus. Opera Pal.) and went on to work on the internal triumphant arch for the same entrance, the Arco Foscari, which spans the transition from Gothic to Renaissance style.

Early Renaissance. The arrival of Donatello in Padua in 1443 represented a major stylistic turning point in northeastern Italy. His dramatic style had been known in Venice for five years previously, since the delivery of his wooden figure of *St John the Baptist* (S Maria Gloriosa dei Frari). In Padua, the full majesty of his Renaissance style was revealed in such works as the equestrian monument to *Gattamelata* (*see* DONATELLO, fig. 4), a life-size bronze *Crucifix* and the statues of the *Virgin and Child* and *Saints*

52. Jacopo della Quercia: *Creation of Eve* (top) and *Temptation* (bottom), stone relief panels, (*c.* 1430–35), main portal of S Petronio, Bologna

for the high altar of S Antonio and the relief panels of the *Miracles of St Anthony* (S Antonio), with a brilliant use of perspective. His large workshop in Padua was a training ground in Tuscan Renaissance style and thought. Some stone-carving was done there, but the main thrust was modelling sculptures in wax for casting into bronze. The tradition of sculpture in bronze remained strong in Padua and Venice: it was reinforced by the arrival of another Florentine, Verrocchio, to make his rival equestrian monument of *Bartolomeo Colleoni*, in Venice itself (*see* VERROCCHIO, ANDREA DEL, fig. 4). The tradition of Donatello in Padua was continued by Giovanni d'Antonio Minello de' Bardi (*see* MINELLO, (1)), who modelled statues in terracotta, and in bronzeworking by Donatello's favourite pupil, Bartolomeo Bellano. Bellano's idiosyncratic style can be seen in his masterpiece, a series of bronze reliefs (1484–90; for illustration *see* BELLANO, BARTOLOMEO) for the choir-screen in S Antonio, combining the panoramic landscapes of Ghiberti with the tougher figure style of Donatello. His other major work, the monument to *Pietro Roccabonella* (*d* 1491; Padua, S Francesco), includes a powerful portrait of the humanist professor sitting at his desk reading.

In Venice itself, the Renaissance was first discernible in the work of Antonio Rizzo, notably in the monumental wall-tomb for *Doge Niccolò Tron* (*c.* 1476–80; S Maria Gloriosa dei Frari; for illustration *see* RIZZO, ANTONIO). A rival tomb for *Doge Pietro Mocenigo* (SS Giovanni e Paolo) by Pietro Lombardo (*see* LOMBARDO, (1)) was completed in 1481. Rizzo's life-size statue of the Doge is impressive, but Lombardo's figures are livelier and more authentically Classical. Rizzo remained the leading sculptor in Venice, nevertheless, and his masterpieces, nude figures of *Adam* and *Eve* on the Arco Foscari, are among the most memorable and influential statues of the 15th century in Venice. The proportions of the *Eve* are still basically Gothic; the full-bodied Renaissance type was realized in marble later by the sons of Pietro Lombardo, Tullio and Antonio.

(ii) High Renaissance, c. 1480–c. 1530. The beginning of the High Renaissance may be defined as the point at which artists had mastered the complete illusion of reality, through the use of perspective, light and shade, and anatomical knowledge. Sculptors could execute with ease even colossal figures in marble or bronze and render narratives convincingly in relief. They had reached the goal for which their predecessors had striven in the early 15th century, to equal Greco-Roman art in both realism and harmony. By 1470–80, however, most of the figural work still looked somewhat artificial: the figures were realistic but expressed only a limited range of emotions. In the High Renaissance, artists began to extend the range of expression they had inherited from antique art. The work of the great trio Leonardo, Michelangelo and Raphael is imbued with a feeling of spiritual presence and emotional reality and shows a completely free range of imagination in utilizing the vocabulary of Classical architecture.

(a) Venice. Tullio Lombardo produced the most perfectly cogitated tomb in 15th-century Venice, for Doge *Andrea Vendramin* (SS Giovanni e Paolo; *see* LOMBARDO,

(2), fig. 1), first mentioned in 1493. His introduction of a unifying architectural structure resembling a Roman triumphal arch heralded the arrival of the High Renaissance. This is also reflected in the tomb sculpture: the figure of *Adam* (New York, Met.) is the most purely Classical of all High Renaissance nudes. The fuller body type in his relief of *Bacchus and Ariadne* (*c.* 1510; Vienna, Ksthist. Mus.) shows Tullio's understanding of Classical sculpture. One of the masterpieces attributed to Antonio Lombardo is a marble bas-relief showing *Venus Anadyomene* (*c.* 1511; London, V&A; see fig. 53), perhaps produced for Alfonso I d'Este. The mastery of the Classical nude and its expressive possibilities puts the work on a par with contemporary painted nudes by Giorgione and Titian. Antonio worked on a monumental scale with equal success in the bronze altar and tomb of *Cardinal Giovanni Battista Zen* for S Marco. The life-size group in bronze of the *Virgin and Child* from the altar is the most truly Classical of the whole Italian Renaissance, surpassing all but the greatest Greco-Roman sculptures in intensity of emotion.

The sack of Rome in 1527 by the Germanic troops of Charles V had far-reaching repercussions even in the world of art. The many artists attracted to Rome by the Medici popes, Leo X and Clement VII, were forced to flee. The Florentine Jacopo Sansovino went to Venice: his masterpiece there is the Loggetta in the Piazza S Marco (*see* SANSOVINO, JACOPO, fig. 3), a perfectly integrated

53. Antonio Lombardo (attrib.): *Venus Anadyomene*, marble, 406×251 mm, *c.* 1511 (London, Victoria and Albert Museum)

complex of architecture and sculpture. It includes life-size bronze figures in the round, which show his characteristic fluent contrapposto and relaxed grace. Bronze was a new medium for Jacopo, previously famed as a marble-carver, and subsequently his best sculpture was modelled, such as the bronze reliefs (*c.* 1540) for the pulpits in the choir of S Marco and a fine door for the Sacristy.

(b) Florence. Verrocchio, who probably trained with Desiderio da Settignano, developed a mature style in opposition to that of Donatello: two of his major works, the *David* (Florence, Bargello) and the equestrian statue of *Bartolomeo Colleoni* (*see* VERROCCHIO, ANDREA DEL, figs 3–4), patently are intended as comments on Donatello's treatments of the same themes. Much of his best work was for the Medici, including tombs in the Old Sacristy at S Lorenzo. His basic contributions to the development of sculpture form a prelude to the style of the High Renaissance. In the *Cupid with a Dolphin* (Florence, Pal. Vecchio), made for the Medici villa at Careggi, he gave to a free-standing figure a sense of movement by the spiral twist of the body, legs and arms, counter-pointed by the wriggling dolphin. His novel and sophisticated composition was not fully utilized until the late 16th century, however, by Giambologna. Verrocchio's other advance was of more immediate relevance to the High Renaissance. In his ambitious group *Christ and St Thomas* on Orsanmichele (*c.* 1466–83; *see* VERROCCHIO, ANDREA DEL, fig. 1), he managed to suggest a psychological link between the two figures, conveying the sympathy of Christ for the weakness of human nature, as exemplified in the doubt felt by St Thomas. Verrocchio is remembered chiefly as the master of Leonardo, who probably joined his workshop *c.* 1466, in time to see most of the big sculptural commissions executed. This had a profound effect on Leonardo's career, although his most important sculptural project, an equestrian monument begun in 1489 for Ludovico Sforza, was never fully realized (*see* LEONARDO DA VINCI, §II, 3). Numerous preparatory drawings survive (e.g. Windsor Castle, Berks, Royal Lib.; *see* LEONARDO DA VINCI, fig. 7), and his studies of horses may be reflected in a number of small groups of *Fighting Horsemen* (e.g. Florence, Pal. Vecchio), modelled in terracotta by his associate Giovanni Francesco Rustici. Rustici's grandiose group in bronze of *St John the Baptist Preaching* (1506–11; Florence, Baptistery; for illustration *see* RUSTICI, GIOVANNI FRANCESCO) shows an acute observation of physiognomy, and hence of human character, derived from Leonardo.

The other major sculptors in Florence were Andrea Sansovino and his pupil Jacopo Sansovino. Andrea's art was the archetype of High Renaissance sculpture: suavely composed figures and compositions within superb, Classical architectural settings (e.g. the Corbinelli Altar; Florence, S Spirito). In the *Della Rovere* tombs (Rome, S Maria del Popolo), he aggrandized the 15th-century 'humanist tomb' by adapting the Classical triumphal arch as a frame. Andrea's life-size group of the *Virgin and Child with St Anne* (1512; Rome, S Agostino) and the *Madonna del parto* by Jacopo (1518–21; Rome, S Agostino; *see* SANSOVINO, JACOPO, fig. 2) are classic examples of High Renaissance compositional principles applied to sculpture.

Jacopo Sansovino was interested in the relationship between sculpture and painting and made models for painters including Pietro Perugino and Andrea del Sarto. His earliest masterpiece, a statue of *St James* (Florence Cathedral), is an elegant figure with brilliantly carved drapery, a strong contrast to the intensity of Michelangelo's unfinished work for the same series, the *St Matthew* (Florence, Accad.). A statue of *Bacchus* also emulated a figure by Michelangelo (both Florence, Bargello) but is lighter and more graceful. (For Jacopo's later work in Venice *see* §(a) above.)

(c) Michelangelo in Florence and Rome. Just as Donatello influenced the figural arts in Italy for the first half of the 15th century, Michelangelo dominated the painting, sculpture and architecture of the 16th century: his supremacy was challenged only in painting, by Raphael. Although he

54. Michelangelo: *David*, marble, h. 4.34 m (incl. base), 1501–4 (Florence, Galleria dell'Accademia)

studied sculpture only with an expert in bronze, Bertoldo di Giovanni, Michelangelo concentrated on carving marble, largely self-taught. The success of his early statues, such as the *David* (Florence, Accad.; see fig. 54), brought him to the notice of Pope Julius II, who commissioned him to design a huge tomb for St Peter's. This project occasioned some of Michelangelo's best statues: the *Moses* (Rome, S Pietro in Vincoli) and the series of *Slaves* (Florence, Accad.; Paris, Louvre; *see* MICHELANGELO, fig. 3). Under Julius's successor, the Medici pope Leo X, Michelangelo was forced to work on architectural projects for the family's parish church of S Lorenzo, Florence, including the New Sacristy (*see* MICHELANGELO, fig. 5), a memorial chapel. The figures representing the four times of day mourning the deceased Medici reclining on the sarcophagi are wonderful examples of his power of evoking an emotional response using anatomy in totally naked figures. Michelangelo endowed the art of sculpture with unprecedented prestige, expressed at the time ('*terribilità*') in terms of extreme admiration: 'divine', 'terrifying'. His work became known throughout Europe; it was so far advanced that it had little immediate effect, however. Interpretation came from a younger generation, although none approached the emotional intensity of Michelangelo; arguably, no one ever has.

(d) Impact in Europe. Italian sculptors were invited to England to embellish the great new buildings of the Tudor monarchs and their courtiers; it is often forgotten that the masterwork of Italian High Renaissance bronze casting is in London, Pietro Torrigiani's tomb of *Henry VII and Elizabeth of York* in Westminster Abbey (1512–18; *see* TORRIGIANI, PIETRO, fig. 1). Other Italian sculptors, including Giovanni de Maiano II, were employed by Cardinal Thomas Wolsey at Hampton Court. By the late 1520s an appreciation of at least the ornamental repertory of Renaissance sculpture was common to England, France and Germany. The French conquest of Milan had brought the Lombard Renaissance style and the works of Leonardo to the attention of the court. This resulted in a new style of château, culminating in the decoration of the palace of Fontainebleau by the Italians Rosso Fiorentino and Francesco Primaticcio, and the recruitment of Leonardo, and later of Benvenuto Cellini, to serve Francis I. Gothic elements made way for Classical ones; portal figures were replaced by caryatids (e.g. Cellini's *Satyrs* for the Porte Dorée at Fontainebleau); and correct Classical mouldings and the new grotesque ornaments were introduced, as well as roundels with busts. Renaissance sculpture spread thence to the Netherlands on tombs, fireplaces and roodlofts (in Notre-Dame, Bruges, there is a *Madonna* by Michelangelo himself) and to Germany, especially in bronze-casting at the traditional centres of craftsmanship in metal, Augsburg, Nuremberg and later Munich. Fountains, portraits and such small-scale sculpture as plaquettes and medals were favourites in the lands of the Holy Roman Empire under Maximilian I and Charles V.

In the Iberian Peninsula, during the 1490s, an extended visit to Portugal by Andrea Sansovino began a swing away from the Gothic style, later reinforced by Torrigiani's terracotta sculptures for Seville (1522; Mus. B.A.). It was further encouraged by influences from the dominions of Spain in Naples and the Netherlands. Michelangelo's work was admired from afar, and a celebrated Mannerist painter and sculptor, Alonso Berruguete (*see* BERRUGUETE, (2)), brought back the new style from his training in Italy. Its impact was reinforced later in the century by the great bronze statues, magnificent life-size portraits of the Habsburg dynasty and religious figures (Madrid, Prado; Escorial) produced for the Escorial by Leone LEONI and his son Pompeo.

(iii) Mannerism, c. 1530–c. 1600. In Italy, meanwhile, sculpture evolved beyond the classicizing stability and harmony of the High Renaissance in directions predicted by some of Michelangelo's works of the 1520s, towards Mannerism.

(a) Florence. Emancipated from architecture, sculpture appeared in squares, fountains and gardens, while miniature pieces were sought for the newly fashionable collector's cabinets. Distortions of anatomy and exaggerations of pose and gesture are characteristic of Mannerism but, in sculpture, limits are imposed by the weight and mass of the material. The simple grace of High Renaissance figure style dissolved into a purely sensuous treatment of pose and surface, frequently giving a feeling of sexual ambiguity, as in the *River God* (Paris, Louvre) by PIERINO DA VINCI and *Honour and Falsehood* (Florence, Bargello) by Vincenzio Danti (*see* DANTI, (1)). Technique was emphasized at the expense of emotional expression. Only in relief, where the figures are attached to a solid background, could the sculptor give rein to his imagination with anything like the freedom of the Mannerist painter. BACCIO BANDINELLI, Cellini and Pierino abandoned the narrative legibility of the High Renaissance for an emphasis on the play of forms on the surface and the sinuous contours of individual figures, as in the relief on the base of Cellini's *Perseus* (Florence, Loggia Lanzi; *see* CELLINI, BENVENUTO, fig. 3).

Michelangelo's groups of *Victory* (e.g. Florence, Pal. Vecchio), showing one figure treading down another, inspired numerous variations of this theme by younger sculptors including Baccio Bandinelli, BARTOLOMEO AMMANATI, Cellini and Danti. Other themes adumbrated by Michelangelo in the New Sacristy tombs were also explored, notably the recumbent 'river-god' pose and the figure in contrapposto, in, for example, Ammanati's Fountain of Neptune (Florence, Piazza della Signoria) and Danti's group of *Cosimo I and Virtues* (Florence, Uffizi). In the mid-16th century Giambologna took up several of the ideas in Michelangelo's lapsed commissions, in *Samson Slaying a Philistine* (1560; London, V&A; see fig. 55) and *Florence Triumphant over Pisa* (Florence, Bargello). In 1582 he achieved the highest ideal, according to Michelangelo, a group of three figures, the *Rape of a Sabine* (Florence, Loggia Lanzi; *see* GIAMBOLOGNA, fig. 2). He was also able to emulate the designs of Michelangelo and Leonardo for equestrian monuments with that to *Cosimo I* (Florence, Piazza della Signoria; *see* GIAMBOLOGNA, fig. 5), and produced several excellent public fountains, including the Neptune (Bologna, Piazza Nettuno; *see* FOUNTAIN, fig. 3), as well as numerous bronze statuettes.

A new range of sculpture also came into being at this time to articulate the formal garden, to ornament the

55. Giambologna: *Samson Slaying a Philistine*, marble, h. 2.09 m, 1560 (London, Victoria and Albert Museum)

fountain and to inhabit the newly fashionable artificial grotto. In 1537, Cosimo I employed Niccolò Tribolo to create a garden for his villa of Il Castello: this included a sequence of fountains; the bronze colossus Apennine, seemingly rising from a pond, by Ammanati; the Fountain of the Labyrinth, by Pierino da Vinci and Giambologna; and the Fountain of Hercules, crowned by Ammanati's bronze *Hercules Strangling Antaeus.* A grotto housed life-size coloured marble animals by Cosimo Fancelli (*in situ*), with bronze birds by Giambologna (Florence, Bargello;

see GIAMBOLOGNA, fig. 4). A larger grotto was built near the Palazzo Pitti, and in 1583 Michelangelo's four unfinished marble statues of *Slaves* (Florence, Accad.) were installed there, in a setting supervised by BERNARDO BUONTALENTI, with *Paris and Helen* by VINCENZO DE' ROSSI and a lovely, humorous Fountain of Venus by Giambologna. Towards the end of the century, at the ducal villa of Pratolino, Buontalenti installed still more complex grottoes, with moving elements powered hydraulically. Several major fountains were created behind the Palazzo Pitti in the Boboli Gardens, including Neptune by Stoldo Lorenzi (*see* LORENZI, (2)) and Ocean by Giambologna. These are examples of the 'cylix type', with one or more circular basins mounted on a central, ornamental stem, usually crowned with a statue. Sculptors created bold figures with strong contours, to be seen against the sky, and surrounded them with sea-creatures drawn from Classical mythology.

Another, novel, type of statue was engendered by these grottoes and gardens: genre figures of countryfolk, including vintners carrying grapes, harvesters with scythes and fowlers and huntsmen. Attuned to idyllic poetry, such images appeared as well in bronze statuettes by Giambologna and his followers. A more pyramidal fountain type, without raised basins, also originated in Florence in the middle of the 16th century. The Fountain of Neptune, in the Piazza della Signoria, has a central marble colossus by Ammanati, surrounded by bronze statues of marine deities and satyrs, produced by members of his team. This enormous project provided a training ground for younger sculptors, creating variations on such themes from antiquity, subsequently treated by Michelangelo, as the river-god and the fettered slave. Another Fountain of Neptune (1560s; Bologna, Piazza Nettuno; *see* FOUNTAIN, fig. 3) was the early masterpiece of Giambologna, who supplied all the figures in bronze, from a handsome, muscular Neptune to Sirens sensuously expressing water from their breasts. The Bolognese fountain is generally accounted superior aesthetically, and it launched Giambologna's international career. Perhaps his most bizarre fountain is a colossal stone structure of the Appenines, shown as a crouching, hoary old giant, squeezing water out of a dragon's mouth into a pool below (1570–80; Pratolino, Villa Medici; *see* MANNERISM, fig. 1).

(*b*) *Rome.* The concentration on grandiose tombs continued: most important were Bandinelli's wall-monuments to *Clement VII* and *Leo X* (S Maria sopra Minerva) and the erection of Michelangelo's tomb for *Julius II* in its final, abbreviated form (S Pietro in Vincoli) *c.* 1544, with the great seated figure of *Moses.* Guglielmo della Porta (*see* PORTA, DELLA, (3)) created the next significant tomb, for the Farnese pope *Paul III* (erected 1577; St Peter's) with an effective bronze portrait statue seated above carved recumbent female figures. The emphasis in sculpture remained almost entirely on marble statues for tombs and on portraits, until the last third of the 16th century when papal families began to require garden statuary and amusing fountains for new villas (e.g. Villa Orsini, Bomarzo). The most famous fountain was in Piazza Mattei, the Fountain of the Tortoises (1585) by TADDEO LANDINI: four bronze nude youths holding tortoises notionally supporting a basin. This was among the earliest secular public sculptures in Rome.

(c) Venice. Jacopo Sansovino's follower Alessandro Vittoria added to the grace of his master something of the robustness of Michelangelo. In sculpture Vittoria met the challenge of such contemporary painters as Titian and Jacopo Tintoretto, notably in dramatic figures (e.g. *St Jerome*; Venice, SS Giovanni e Paolo) and brilliantly characterized portrait busts (e.g. *Niccolò da Ponte*; Venice, Semin. Patriarcale; *see* VITTORIA, ALESSANDRO, fig. 3). Characteristically of Venice, much of his sculpture was to decorate public buildings, such as the coved stucco ceiling of the Scala d'Oro in the Doge's Palace, or the caryatids flanking the portal of Sansovino's library at S Marco. He also produced excellent bronze statuettes (e.g. *St Sebastian*; New York, Met.). The other prominent sculptor active at the end of the century, whose style was not dissimilar, was GIROLAMO CAMPAGNA from Verona. He carved dramatic narratives in marble, including a relief of *St Anthony* (1577; Padua, S Antonio) and an *Altar of the Deposition* (Venice, S Giuliano). In bronze, his masterpiece is the magnificent pyramidal altar group of the Trinity and the Four Evangelists supporting a huge globe bearing God the Father (1592–3; Venice, S Giorgio Maggiore). Around Campagna and Vittoria competent, if less imaginative, sculptors formed a veritable 'school': Tiziano Minio and DANESE CATTANEO, immediate followers of Sansovino; and then FRANCESCO SEGALA and TIZIANO ASPETTI from Padua and NICOLÒ ROCCATAGLIATA from Genoa.

(d) Milan. One of the greatest Italian sculptors of the Mannerist period, and one of the most influential, because he served Charles V both in the Netherlands and in Spain, was Leone Leoni from Milan. He made his name around 1550 with a spectacular series of life-size portrait statues in bronze, including one of *Gian Giacomo de' Medici*, which stands in a fine wall-monument designed by Michelangelo, in Milan Cathedral. He also produced impressive portraits of rulers allegorically trampling personifications of evil: *Ferrante Gonzaga* (Guastalla, Piazza Roma) and *Charles V* (Madrid, Prado). The latter has an intriguing feature, typical of the Mannerist mentality: the figure is nude but is normally clad in a removable suit of armour; in effect, two statues for the price of one.

BIBLIOGRAPHY

R. Krautheimer: *Lorenzo Ghiberti* (Princeton, 1956, rev. 2/1973)
J. Pope-Hennessy: *Italian Renaissance Sculpture* (London, 1958, rev. New York, 3/1985)
J. Montagu: *Bronzes* (London, 1963)
J. Pope-Hennessy: *Italian High Renaissance and Baroque Sculpture* (London, 1963, rev. 3/New York, 1985)
E. Borsook: *Companion Guide to Florence* (London, 1966, rev. 1988)
A. Radcliffe: *European Bronze Statuettes* (London, 1966)
C. Seymour jr: *Sculpture in Italy, 1400–1500*, Pelican Hist. A. (Harmondsworth, 1966)
J. Pope-Hennessy: *Essays on Italian Sculpture* (London, 1968)
C. Avery: *Florentine Renaissance Sculpture* (London, 1970/*R* 1982)
J. Pope-Hennessy: *The Study and Criticism of Italian Sculpture* (Princeton, 1980)
R. Olsen: *Italian Renaissance Sculpture* (London, 1992)
J. Poeschke: *Donatello and his World: Italian Renaissance Sculpture* (London and New York, 1993)

CHARLES AVERY

4. BAROQUE, *c.* 1600–*c.* 1750. Although the 17th and 18th centuries were a period of political and economic decay for Italy, the arts flourished. Italian artists produced a major new style, the BAROQUE, which lasted (though continuously evolving) for almost the whole period.

(i) Rome. (ii) Bologna and Emilia. (iii) Florence and Tuscany. (iv) Milan and Lombardy. (v) Genoa and Liguria. (vi) Turin and Piedmont. (vii) Venice and the Veneto. (viii) Kingdom of Naples.

(i) Rome. In 17th-century Rome the patronage of the popes and of the great religious orders, who wished to celebrate the glory of the papal city and of the Church Triumphant, offered spectacular opportunities to sculptors. Major commissions were for religious statuary, papal tombs and decorative sculptural cycles in Roman churches; private patrons required funerary monuments, the enrichment of chapels, portrait busts and mythological sculpture. The Baroque art of Gianlorenzo Bernini dominated, and, after the deaths of the more classical artists François Du Quesnoy (*see* DU QUESNOY, (2)) and ALESSANDRO ALGARDI, his vast studio reigned unchallenged for most of the 17th century. In the 18th century, commissions were smaller and the art less exuberant, reflecting both a decline in the economy of the Papal States and a new mood of pessimism brought about by the declining influence of the popes in international affairs. The grandeur and energy of the Baroque yielded to the restraint and tenderness of the Italian *Barocchetto*. In this period, due to the establishment in 1666 of the Académie de France in Rome, many of the important commissions were executed by French artists who were working in the city. In the early years of the 18th century Pierre Legros (ii) was the finest sculptor in Rome, and indeed in all Italy, and with him the medium of the relief sculpture attained a new importance.

The first important 17th-century sculptor in Rome was FRANCESCO MOCHI, a revolutionary figure who has now begun to receive due recognition. Born near Florence, he spent most of his career in Rome, but his work is widely scattered. The two life-size marble statues for his *Annunciation* group in Orvieto (1608; Orvieto, Mus. Opera Duomo) reveal a fully developed High Baroque style at a time when Bernini was still a child. The cloud-borne figure of Gabriel, still in full flight, sweeps downward, his garments billowing out widely (see fig. 56). Instead of the timidly devout Virgin portrayed by hundreds of artists, Mochi created a figure of heroic intensity, her body straining under extreme torsion, the sharp slashing lines of her tunic serving to exacerbate the sense of inner agitation. By 1611 Mochi had moved to Rome but at the end of the decade he was called to Piacenza to execute two great bronze equestrian statues of *Ranuccio Farnese* and his father *Alessandro Farnese* (Piacenza, Piazza Cavalli). In the orchestration of Baroque rhythms in these two statues, Mochi surpassed anything ever seen in sculpture before. While treating both horse and rider with considerable realism, he gave full rein to his fantasy with the wind-blown draperies and manes. These he exaggerated to create effects not unlike great cascades of water breaking over the figures. His best-known work is the colossal marble *St Veronica* (1635–40) in St Peter's in Rome, in which the saint is shown crying out as she rushes forward against the wind, holding in both hands the cloth with the

56. Francesco Mochi: *Angel Gabriel*, part of the *Annunciation* group, marble, 1608 (Orvieto, Museo Opera del Duomo)

miraculous imprint of the face of Christ. The movement of the figure, part of which is fully revealed through the clinging, silk-thin tunic, is set against the turbulence of garment folds that take on an illogical but wonderful life of their own. In the lower section of the figure they whip across the body in sharp knife-thin diagonals, at the waist they extend impossibly far out in the air, while around Veronica's right elbow they seem to churn in a rotary movement like some strange marine engine.

While Mochi was a great innovator, the presiding genius of the 17th century was Gianlorenzo Bernini (*see* BERNINI, (2)), who, during the latter part of his life, was the most famous artist in all of Europe. Almost everything he did demonstrates astonishing technical skill. In his group of *Aeneas, Anchises and Ascanius* (1618–19; Rome, Gal. Borghese), for example, made early in his career, he used the same marble to evoke the contrasting effects of the soft pudgy body of a young child, the hard musculature of a man in his prime and the sagging flesh of old age. His *David* (1623; Rome, Gal. Borghese) is a marvellous depiction of muscles under stress, the boy wound like a

tight spring about to be released, the lips sucked in, the nostrils dilated and the toes tense. This highly dynamic composition implies space outside itself, for unless the viewer visualizes the unseen Goliath, David's action has no meaning; and even though Bernini chose to show a split-second in time, his statue also implies past and future. One of Bernini's most original creations is the Baroque fountain. In these, as never before, water plays an integral part in the whole composition: it bursts up into the air and falls across sinuous sculpture that seems itself to be moving. Sound also plays an important role, as the water drips, splashes and gurgles away. Light, too, is often a major element in Bernini's compositions. In the Cornaro Chapel (1645–52; Rome, S Maria della Vittoria) it comes from a hidden window but becomes the divine inspiration that fills the tempestuous floating figure of *St Teresa* with ecstasy (*see* BAROQUE, fig. 1). In his *Longinus* (1629–38; Rome, St Peter's) the light streaming down from the dome of the basilica serves to crystallize the moment of the saint's miraculous conversion. Bernini's religious art is a celebration of the Catholic Counter-Reformation, of the Church Triumphant. The supreme expression of this can be seen in the Cathedra Petri (1657–66; *see* BERNINI, (2), fig. 2), a vast monument of marble, bronze, gold, gilt stucco and glass, which rises up in the sanctuary of St Peter's as high as a six- or seven-storey office building. It celebrates one of the church's most sacred relics: the small wood and ivory throne that is said to have been used by St Peter. This wooden chair is itself encased in a gigantic gilt-bronze throne, which serves as its reliquary. The heavy bronze throne seems to float, touched but not sustained by colossal statues of the Fathers of the Church, and bathed in the light of the Holy Ghost, which propels outward a vast multitude of gilded angels. A relief panel makes it clear that what is being celebrated is Christ's transfer of his earthly authority to St Peter and through Peter, as the first bishop of Rome, to the popes of the Roman Church. This was the dogma that the Protestants attacked the most, and thus the one that the Church most upheld.

At the same time that Bernini was developing his dynamic, expressionistic, High Baroque style, other sculptors in Rome were working in a different, quieter manner, which has been variously characterized as the Classical or Decorative Baroque. This trend is best exemplified by the works of the Flemish sculptor François Du Quesnoy and the Bolognese Alessandro Algardi, both of whom were active in Rome. The deep resonance and quiet dignity of Du Quesnoy's style finds full expression in his colossal *St Andrew* (1629–40; Rome, St Peter's). With all the small detail suppressed, a generalization of the real remains. Across the slowly turning figure the garment folds flow in long prominent shallow arcs, each seeming to echo the next, but always with variations. Much of Algardi's work is also in this manner, but it embraces a wider range of styles. It includes severe and unflattering realistic portraiture in a style known as Roman Verism, as for example in the bust of *Olimpia Maidalchini* (*c.* 1646–7; Rome, Pal. Doria-Pamphili) or the bronze effigy of *Innocent X* (1645–50; Rome, Pal. Conserv.); but it also includes an emphasis on purely decorative effects, as in the use of short, light, rippling curves of the garment folds that play across the body of the statue of *St Mary Magdalene* (shortly before 1629; Rome, S Silvestro al Quirinale).

In the mid- and late 17th century Bernini's dominance was almost complete, and he and his studio carried out the major sculptural cycles in Rome, among them the redecoration of the nave of St Peter's in the late 1640s and of S Maria del Popolo (1655–7). Among the more notable of Bernini's many followers are GIULIANO FINELLI, MELCHIORRE CAFFA, ERCOLE FERRATA, DOMENICO GUIDI, Giuseppe Mazzuoli (*see* MAZZUOLI, (1)) and ANTONIO RAGGI. Their work may best be appreciated in the altars in S Agnese in Rome, where the *Stoning of St Emerenziana* (begun 1660) is by Ercole Ferrata and the *Death of St Cecilia* by Antonio Raggi. Raggi, who developed an intense, mystical style, was the most original of these artists. A new era opened with the lavish and opulent altar of St Ignatius (1697–9) in the left transept of Il Gesù, on which many sculptors worked, none of whom was a Bernini follower, and several of whom were French, among them Pierre Legros (ii).

Baroque classicism was out of vogue during the years of Bernini's dominance, but it resurfaced at the beginning of the 18th century in a more enriched form. The best of the many Late Baroque sculptors who worked in this manner was CAMILLO RUSCONI. He made four of the twelve colossal marble statues of apostles, by seven sculptors, in S Giovanni in Laterano, which together constitute the largest contemporary sculptural project (1703–18), and which are almost all in the Classical Baroque style. Two were made by Legros (*see* LEGROS, (2)), the most original late 17th- and early 18th-century sculptor in Rome. His sculpture, which often contains distant echoes of late French Gothic, resembles nothing in the Italian tradition. In his *St Francis Xavier* (*c.* 1702; S Apollinare) all sense of the underlying body is lost beneath a marvellous play of two totally different sets of counterpointed rhythms. Below, the movements of the garment folds are larger and stronger, but they are interrupted by small, unexpected twists. Above, the rhythms are brief, trilling, the folds lightly shadowed, in a way that seems to bring every centimetre of the surface into a delicate rippling movement. His enormous marble relief of the *Apotheosis of the Blessed Aloysius Gonzaga* (1698–9; Rome, S Ignazio; for illustration *see* LEGROS, (2)) reveals his mastery of this medium. In the early 1730s the major sculptural decoration was that of the Corsini Chapel in S Giovanni in Laterano, where ten sculptors were employed. FILIPPO DELLA VALLE, Giuseppe Rusconi, AGOSTINO CORNACCHINI and GIUSEPPE LIRONI contributed marble statues of the *Cardinal Virtues*, which, lacking both the drama of the Baroque and the severity of Neo-classicism, represent the tender grace of the *Barocchetto*. Cornacchini was a Florentine and is remembered in Rome (if at all) for his huge *Charlemagne* (1720–25) for the narthex of St Peter's, although his smaller works in marble, such as the *Adoration of the Shepherds* (before 1720; Pistoia, Bib. Fabroniana), done in the light manner of the Roman *Barocchetto*, are more successful.

(ii) Bologna and Emilia. In the 17th century and the early 18th Bologna was an important artistic centre. It was the birthplace of the pre-eminent sculptor Alessandro Algardi,

who trained in drawing at the Carracci academy but then left the city early in his career. In Bologna sculptors were less important than the painters in part because, with the wealth concentrated in Rome, there was not enough regular financial support elsewhere in the Papal States for the costlier art of sculpture. During this period there was only one sculptor in Emilia of considerable importance: GIUSEPPE MAZZA. That his sculpture is almost entirely in stucco, rather than in marble or bronze, reflects the political and economic weakness of Bologna. Many of his sculptures, such as those that decorate the high altar of S Cristina in Bologna, are strongly influenced by the Emilian painter Giovanni Lanfranco. From Lanfranco he derived the poses of his reclining figures as well as the way in which their garment folds are made up of stiff, broad-based triangles. Occasionally, as in his *Madonna of Sorrows* in the church of the Madonna di Galliera in Bologna, he borrowed aspects of Bernini's late style to create effects of great intensity.

A new chapter in the history of Bolognese sculpture began with the work of ANGELO GABRIELLO PIÒ, who was trained by Camillo Rusconi in Rome. His *St Michael Overcoming a Demon* (Imola, S Agostino) is derived from the famous painting of the same subject by the Bolognese painter Guido Reni. In Piò's hands, however, the theme is radically revised in the manner of the French Rococo. The warrior saint, surrounded by gracefully billowing garments, is transformed into a slender, delicate dancer who does a rapid two-step across the body of his fallen foe. Piò's statue of *Prudence* (Bologna, Pal. Gozzadini) is still more elegant and elongated but equally Rococo. The life-size stucco figure is posed so as to form an upward-rising spiral whose circular movement is reinforced by the spiralling of the garment folds.

(iii) Florence and Tuscany. In Florence, where the ducal court was one of the grandest and most extravagant in Europe, the art of sculpture was held in the highest esteem. A great tradition of Florentine sculptors had worked in bronze, and this remained important in the 17th century, in monumental sculpture, in relief sculpture and, above all, in the small bronze statuette. Yet 17th-century sculptors also worked in marble and produced sculptural decoration for churches and palaces, and many portrait busts. Cosimo III de' Medici's patronage was particularly important to the development of Florentine Baroque sculpture (*see* MEDICI, DE', (27)); in 1673 he opened an academy in Rome and sent many Florentine sculptors there to study under CIRO FERRI and Ercole Ferrata, thus ensuring the creation of a court art that blends the elegance of a Tuscan tradition of bronze casting with something of the vigour of the Roman Baroque. Much 17th-century Florentine sculpture has a strong pictorial quality, perhaps due to the important role of Ciro Ferri.

In the first part of the 17th century Florentine sculpture was dominated by Pietro Tacca (*see* TACCA, (1)), a student of Giambologna, who held the enviable position of chief sculptor at the Medici court. The virtuosity and technical skill of the Florentine tradition is demonstrated by his fountain in the Piazza della SS Annunziata (see fig. 57), where two intertwined tritons atop a huge shell are composed entirely of monster and human features so aptly

57. Pietro Tacca: bronze fountain (cast by 1633), placed in 1640 in the Piazza della SS Annunziata, Florence

blended that it is difficult to tell where the one blends into the other. Tacca's equestrian monument of *Philip IV* (1634–40; Madrid, Plaza de Oriente; for illustration *see* TACCA, (1)) is the first full-scale statue of a rider on a rearing horse. The concept, dreamt of a century earlier by Leonardo, was realized by Tacca only with the advice of Galileo Galilei, who held the chair of mathematics at the nearby University of Pisa. It is an intensely Baroque composition, combining strong movement and split-second action.

Tacca's death in 1640 left a void in Florentine sculpture, which lasted until the rise of GIOVANNI BATTISTA FOGGINI. Foggini was one of the first to study (from 1673) at the Accademia Fiorentina in Rome, where he absorbed the dynamic Late Baroque of Ferrata and Ferri. In 1676 he returned to Florence and was immediately employed by the Medici court, serving as chief sculptor from 1678 and chief architect from 1694. His office required him to supervise large-scale sculptural projects, which were executed chiefly by assistants, and his three marble high reliefs (1675–91) in the Corsini Chapel in S Maria del Carmine introduced the Roman Baroque to Florence. Foggini preferred, however, in part because of an accident that left him crippled, to work on a small scale. His is a courtly art in which decorative effects and technical virtuosity replace intensity of expression. Two small bronzes, an *Apollo and Marsyas* (see fig. 58) and a *Mercury and Prometheus* (1716; both London, V&A), which were made as a pair, are, despite their grim subjects, the essence of charm and grace. Around their captive figures the lithe captors dance

as if in a ballet, their scarves fluttering around their slender bodies. Above the *Marsyas* group the rhythms are amplified by a typically 18th-century tree, with thinned-out foliage, angular branches and emphatic asymmetry.

The career of MASSIMILIANO SOLDANI, who was the last of the great Florentine bronzeworkers, runs parallel to that of Foggini in both training and patronage, but his work shows less refinement and more vigour. Among his masterpieces is a pair of bronze ewers (London, V&A). On each vase is a score of figures, some in high relief, others almost free-standing. Against a seemingly molten ground they surge and fall back, lunge and twist, crowding against one another, until the whole surface seems to be churning. Likewise, with Soldani's small bronze of *Venus Pulling Feathers from Cupid's Wings* (Ottawa, N.G.), it is the dynamics of the composition—everything sucked into one single diagonal downward sweep—that leaves the viewer momentarily breathless; but it is also recognized as a kind of game, with the action far beyond anything that could be justified by the subject.

After the death of Cosimo III, Florence declined as an art centre, and Florentine sculptors, among them Agostino Cornacchini, a pupil of Foggini, moved to Rome.

(iv) Milan and Lombardy. In the 17th century Milan was still dominated by the spirit of Carlo Borromeo (see BORROMEO, (1)), Cardinal and saint, who was the driving

58. Giovanni Battista Foggini: *Apollo and Marsyas*, bronze, h. 609 mm, 1716 (London, Victoria and Albert Museum)

force behind the major religious reforms of the late 16th century. His importance is symbolized by the statue of him, set high on a hill in Arona, that rises up 23 m, the height of an eight-storey building. Designed by the painter Cerano, it was built in 1694 by Siro Zanelli (*d* 1724) and BERNARDO FALCONE.

In contrast to Florence there was little demand for sculpture in bronze. What work there is in marble is chiefly in the form of narrative reliefs, either for Milan Cathedral or for the Certosa di Pavia. Much of this work is dull and uninspired, the result in part of the practice of requiring sculptors to follow designs that painters had made for them. Of the 17th-century examples the best are by Dionigi Bussola (*see* BUSSOLA, (1)), whose *Massacre of the Innocents* (Milan Cathedral) has about it an air of High Baroque excitement that most of the other reliefs lack. In the 18th century commissions in marble were more frequent. With the age of the Rococo came a new sense of grace, as with the *Guardian Angel*, a statuary group by Elia Vincenzo Buzzi (*see* BUZZI, (1)), or the *Allegory of Faith* by Antonio Calegari (1699–1777), in SS Cosma and Damiano in Brescia. More interesting, however, are the works done in stucco where, perhaps because the cost was very much less, the artists were given more freedom. A degree of expressive intensity far higher than in any of the marble sculptures can be seen, for example, in the *Deposition* in Piacenza or the *St John the Evangelist* in the oratory of S Ilario in Parma, both by Domenico Reti (*fl* 1663–1709).

Yet the most striking sculptures of this period are the great *tableaux vivants*: groups of life-size polychromed figures usually intended to reproduce a scene from the Bible as if it were happening before our very eyes. This type of sculpture is not to be seen in Milan, where it was thought of as naive and primitive, but in smaller Lombard towns. There it expresses a tradition that goes back to the morality plays of the late Middle Ages. Usually of terracotta, these *tableaux* are closely related to the polychromatic wood sculpture of south Germany and recall the close ties that long existed between Lombards and Germans. Among the many dramatic examples of this art form, one is Bussola's huge *Crucifixion* (1660–70) in the chapel of the Crucifixion of the Sacromonte in Varese. As if on a stage, but with the players frozen in time, as many as 50 figures in contemporary dress—knights in armour on charging horses, half-naked executioners, mourning women in differing states of grief—all surround a towering cross from which Christ gazes towards the scene of a heavenly host painted on a backdrop.

(v) Genoa and Liguria. In the 17th century sculpture in Genoa was predominantly religious, and the altars and chapels of many new churches received lavish sculptural decoration in polychrome marble. There was also a tradition of wood-carving, an artisan's craft that had long been practised throughout northern Italy. In the second half of the century two important sculptors, Filippo Parodi (*see* PARODI, (1)) and PIERRE PUGET, both of whom were aware of the new and exciting developments of the Roman Baroque, initiated a Genoese school of sculptors. In the 18th century public commissions for sculptural projects dropped sharply, due to Genoa's declining economy, although decorative mythological sculptures for gardens and sumptuous palace interiors were made. Throughout the period sculptors enjoyed a particularly close relationship with painters, and the influence of the lyrical grace of Correggio, and of the free and painterly rhythms of the Casa Piola and of Gregorio de' Ferrari, is often apparent.

Filippo Parodi was first trained in wood-carving; to learn to sculpt in marble he went to Rome where he spent six years (*c*. 1655–61) in Bernini's studio. His first major commission after his return was for four life-size marble figures: *Narcissus*, *Hyacinth*, *Flora* and *Clizia*, in the Palazzo Reale in Genoa, which are taken from themes in Ovid's *Metamorphoses*. The lightly clad male and female figures, which are all in gentle movement, show the mastery of anatomy and the skill in differentiating textures that Parodi learnt in Bernini's studio. Of Bernini's dramatic High Baroque manner, however, he took nothing: what he aimed at is grace. This is especially evident in his *Virgin and Child* (1675–8) in S Carlo in Genoa. The Virgin is a proud young aristocrat with Classical features. With one impossibly slender hand she holds a rambunctious Infant whose body swings outward in a broad arc. In the other, with a gesture that seems to acknowledge an adoring throng, she holds a scapular. An entirely different aspect of Parodi's art is represented by his painted wooden figures. His *Dead Christ* (1680–81; Genoa, S Luca), lying prone on the earth, is in concept intensely Spanish. In creating the slender elongated figure Parodi showed no interest in anatomical accuracy. His emphasis is entirely on the sense of physical suffering: the frail, battered body, the gaping wounds dripping with blood. In treating the theme in this manner, so different from the way it was handled in Italy during the Renaissance, Parodi was reflecting the views of the famous Spanish saint, Ignatius of Loyola, who taught the faithful to attempt to perceive biblical events in sensate, physical terms.

Puget worked in Genoa from 1661 to 1667 and again briefly in 1670 and 1680. But even in this short time his art shows a much wider range than Parodi's. His *Martyrdom of St Sebastian* in S Maria Assunta in Carignano, Genoa, while not entirely convincing anatomically, is a *tour de force* in the handling of textures, as well as in the exquisite refinement of the small-scale details, such as the decorative reliefs on the arms and armour. The art of Puget and Parodi may be compared in the sculptures of the *Immaculate Conception* they both made for churches in Genoa. Puget's was done in 1670 for the oratory of S Filippo Neri, Parodi's in 1699 for the church of S Luca. Puget's statue is a French Gothic Virgin translated into the terminology of the Baroque. The cloud-borne figure sways gracefully with the body forming an elongated 'S'. Across the centre of the torso the drapery billows out asymmetrically, far to the left. There is no clear indication of the body beneath the drapery or where the feet are placed. Instead the emphasis is on the rhythms of the drapery folds: the soft short lines of the light tunic, the hard sharp creases of the heavier cloak. In his version, Parodi copied but misunderstood the swaying body with the asymmetrical cloak. His Madonna, which is thoroughly Italian, rests her weight on one leg with the other slightly bent and clearly articulated through the drapery. From the knees up the body remains rigid but tilts to the left. This makes sense anatomically, but the pose is awkward and the figure seems unstable.

Garment folds are elaborate but all of a piece. There is almost no difference between the tunic and the cloak. In comparison with Parodi, Puget's stone cutting is sharper and more precise.

In the 18th century Domenico Parodi (ii), Filippo's son (*see* PARODI, (2)), continued the tradition of his father in marble but stylistically he is closer to Puget. His female *Allegory of Gentleness* (Genoa, S Filippo Neri) has the elongated proportions preferred by the new age and the serpentine pose that the Rococo took over from the Gothic, but lacks technical skill. The garments are clumsily carved, and the flowers the figure wears in her hair have thick crude rubbery petals. Bernardo and Francesco Maria SCHIAFFINO, both of whom were associated with the Casa Piola, created a more graceful, pictorial style; both produced mythological sculptures for aristocratic interiors, such as Francesco Maria's *Rape of Proserpina* (Genoa, Pal. Reale). FRANCESCO QUEIROLO, Bernardo's pupil, endowed with a superb technical mastery reminiscent of Puget, left Genoa to seek work in Rome and Naples (*see* §(viii) below).

(vi) Turin and Piedmont. In this period Piedmont became a highly military state in response to recurrent invasions from France and Spain. The most notable assemblage of Baroque sculpture in Piedmont is in the basilica of the Superga outside Turin, a church built to commemorate the victory of the Piedmontese army over Louis XIV in 1706. The marble relief (h. 5 m) over the high altar, by the Roman sculptor BERNARDINO CAMETTI, reflects this military orientation. It depicts, in a swirl of Baroque movement, the Blessed Amadeus of Savoy interceding with the Virgin and the Piedmontese forces, with resultant victory over the French. In the rotunda of the Superga are two more large marble reliefs, an *Annunciation* by Cametti and a *Birth of the Virgin* by Agostino Cornacchini.

Of the native sculptors, most were artisans who worked outside the court, in small provincial centres where they were called on to create the *tableaux vivants* that were popular in this period throughout northern Italy. These scenes, almost always set in churches, are something like the Neapolitan crèche, but with life-size figures of terracotta or wood, realistically painted in Renaissance or contemporary costume and arranged on the stage, very much as in the theatre. Two notable examples, which are thought to date from the late 17th century, are the *Massacre of the Innocents* and the *Road to Calvary* in the Sacromonte at Varallo. The most important Piedmontese sculptor is FRANÇOIS LADATTE, who was born in Turin but had exceptionally strong ties with France. As a youth he visited Paris in the entourage of the Prince of Carignan and then studied in Rome at the Académie de France. From 1734 to 1744 he was once more in Paris, where he executed several works for the Crown, including the large bronze relief of the *Martyrdom of St Philip* (1738) in the chapel at Versailles (*in situ*). Back in Turin in 1744, he provided the court with splendid small-scale examples of the French Rococo in its purest form, exquisitely refined half-length female nudes set among spiralling plant forms, shell motifs and flowers, or, in the manner of François Boucher, playful putti doing adult tasks. One of his most celebrated works is a clock (1775; Turin, Pal. Reale), set into a bronze cascade of draperies, banners, cannons, armour and the like, together with allegorical figures that represent *Military Glory Made Known by Time and Truth*.

(vii) Venice and the Veneto. In Venice sculpture, lacking the rich colours for which Venetian art is famous, had always been secondary to painting. Sculptors did, however, receive commissions to work in areas for which paintings were unsuitable, and much 17th- and early 18th-century sculpture was created for the formal gardens of the country houses that rich Venetian merchants owned to the north of the city. It is a commentary on the status of Venetian sculpture during this period that the best-known sculptor in Venice, JOSSE DE CORTE, came from far-off Flanders, and the best-known piece of sculpture by a Venetian, the *Modesty* (*c.* 1750; Naples, Cappella Sansevero) by ANTONIO CORRADINI, was commissioned in far-off Naples (see §(viii) and fig. 59 below). De Corte was trained in Antwerp but spent the last 20 years of his life in Venice, where all his principal works can be found. His monument to *Giorgio Morosini* in S Clemente all'Isola is characteristically Flemish both in the mass of small-scale detail that fills its empty spaces and in the Atlas terms that are bent far over, under the weight of the entablature that they carry. His *Winter,* now in the Palazzo Rezzonico but obviously made as a garden-piece, is in a different vein. The chubby Rubens-like infant is shown walking into a winter wind that blows open his fur coat and makes him hang on to his fur hat. Still different again is the high altar of S Maria della Salute, which de Corte probably executed after the designs of the architect Baldassare Longhena. This elaborate sculptural project, made up of many marble figures, is surmounted by a statuary group that represents Venice beseeching the Virgin to cause the plague to cease. On the left is the kneeling figure of *Venice,* her wind-blown cape twisted and deeply convoluted so as to produce a staccato linear rhythm accompanied by rapidly alternating patches of dark shadow and bright light. The rhythms are picked up again on the right, but in a more agitated form, in the figure of the *Plague* whom a torch-wielding cherub drives into flight.

In the latter part of the 17th century the leading sculptor was Orazio Marinali (*see* MARINALI, (1)), who worked in the Venetian mainland. For the basilica of Monte Bérico, near Vicenza, where he was occupied for many years, he created an extraordinary assemblage of statues in marble, stucco and bronze. Of these the most impressive is the figure of *Jonah* who is shown waving wildly and crying out, just after he has issued from the mouth of the whale. Admirable, too, are the marble angels on the façade: massive figures with robust limbs overlaid in part by thin, crinkly ribbon-like tunics. But his most original works are his genre pieces, such as the boy in the garden of the Villa Deliziosa outside Vicenza, who is shown in contemporary dress but in a deliberately gauche pose, twisting around with one leg and one arm up, as if suddenly overcome with embarrassment.

The outstanding figure of the first part of the 18th century is Antonio Corradini, who was born in Este in Veneto and served for a time as chief sculptor of the Venetian Republic, but who also spent long periods abroad, in Vienna, Dresden, Rome and Naples. His early work in Venice, such as his *Virginity* (1721; S Maria del Carmine), shows strong French influence, probably traceable to Pierre Puget as transmitted by Filippo Parodi, but this style he soon abandoned. From 1736 to 1740 he was in Dresden, where he executed some 15 statuary groups on mythological subjects, such as *Apollo Flaying Marsyas* and *Zephyrus and Flora* (both London, V&A), for the gardens of the Elector of Saxony. All these groups are in movement, but the figures are so simplified and their emotions so restrained that they constitute, stylistically, an anticipation of Neo-classicism. Later, in Rome (1740–44) he established a new type of statue: the veiled figure unveiled, with his *Tuccia* (Rome, Pal. Barberini), made for Cardinal Neri Corsini.

Antonio Bonazza (*see* BONAZZA, (2)) made many amusing garden statues with which he populated the park at the Villa Widman near Vicenza. Except for some allegories appropriate to a park (the *Four Seasons*, the *Four Winds*), the statues are all genre pieces, many of them representing the bourgeoisie who played such a prominent role in 18th-century Venetian society, but there are some from every station: they include a soldier in a hussar's uniform with a tall beaver hat, a gypsy fortune-teller in a costume with lots of lace, a woman spinning, a man who sings and plays a lute, a black woman who is pregnant and many more. Together they reflect at least some aspects of the 18th century: its light-heartedness, its dallying and above all its strong element of secularism.

(viii) Kingdom of Naples. In the early years of the 17th century many Tuscan sculptors worked in Naples, among them MICHELANGELO NACCHERINO and Pietro Bernini (*see* BERNINI, (1)). Yet the century was dominated by the Lombard COSIMO FANZAGO, who created a Neapolitan variant of the Baroque; he was concerned to unite sculpture and architecture and created highly original decorative sculptures, enriched by the glowing colours of polychrome marble. A more classical Baroque is to be seen in the works of such figures as GIULIANO FINELLI and Lorenzo Vaccaro (*see* VACCARO, (1)). The sculptors active in 18th-century Naples were all minor, but in Sicily Giacomo Serpotta (*see* SERPOTTA, (3)) created stucco decorations that seem to anticipate the French Rococo. Throughout the period the popular tradition of the Christian crib persisted, and many artists contributed lively realistic figures in polychrome sculpture.

Pietro Bernini, father of Gianlorenzo Bernini, introduced Florentine Mannerist sculpture to Naples. His most important Neapolitan work is the marble *Virgin and Child with the Infant St John the Baptist* (Naples, Mus. N. S Martino), which was completed by Fanzago. The interlocked figures turn in a rising spiral, a Mannerist device known as the 'figura serpentina', which was popularized in Florence by Giambologna. But Fanzago must have been responsible for the hard, sharp, angular garment folds, which create a staccato rhythm, counterpointing the spiralling movement of the figures.

Fanzago was not only the most important sculptor in 17th-century Naples but also the most important architect. At the entrance loggia of the main cloister (Chiostro Grande) of the Certosa di S Martino, where the architecture and the sculpture (1623–43) are both his, the marble

saints look down as if leaning out of windows, the turbulent convolutions of their drapery amplified by the massing of crowded undulating architectural motifs (*see* FANZAGO, COSIMO, fig. 1). The stone balustrades that Fanzago designed for the Certosa lie halfway between architecture and sculpture. Carved draperies and foliage overlay the architectural forms, and on top of the principal balusters there are gaping stone skulls, a motif especially prominent in Spain and Spanish Naples. His finest figure is his *Jeremiah* (1637–46) in the Gesù Nuovo, Naples. The aged prophet with his worn face and staring eyes calls to mind similar figures by Michelangelo in the Sistine Chapel. Like them the *Jeremiah* is in strong torsion, the upper half of the body twisting one way, the lower the other, and both overlaid with the dynamism of the deeply shadowed garment folds.

The grandest sculptural project of the middle years of the century was the decoration (1749–66) of the Cappella Sansevero (S Maria della Pietà dei Sangro), commissioned by Raimondo del Sangro, Prince of Sansevero. Corradini contributed portrait busts and allegorical figures, among them his celebrated *Modesty* (see fig. 59), a veiled figure with a garland of roses on the Caetani tomb. The most striking feature of Francesco Queirolo's *Allegory of Deception Unmasked* (1752–9) is the utterly convincing, partially free-standing rope net from which a mature male figure struggles to free himself: a virtuoso display of technical mastery. The gruesome *Dead Christ* (1753), covered with

59. Antonio Corradini: *Modesty*, allegorical figure from the Caetani tomb, (*c.* 1750), Cappella Sansevero, Naples

a transparent veil, by GIUSEPPE SANMARTINO, is in direct imitation of the work of Corradini.

By far the finest sculptor in the Kingdom of Naples during the 18th century was Giacomo Serpotta, who spent his entire career in Palermo, capital of Sicily. His work is entirely in stucco, marble statuary normally being too costly for a provincial centre. But Serpotta, unlike other sculptors, coated the fresh wet stucco figures with a thin layer of marble dust to give them a hard bright-white, porcelain-like surface. This formula was lost at the time of his death and has never been rediscovered. His best works are the decorations he made for oratories: simple rectangular halls that had both a social and a religious function and were dependent for their character on such decorations. In the oratory of S Cita, Palermo, as in other oratories in which Serpotta worked, his stuccos (see fig. 60) cover almost every part of the surface, from eye level to the top of the walls, a space of about 5 m. They occupy the whole of the front and back walls, and along the sides they crowd around the windows and fill the spaces in between. This *horror vacui*, which is quite foreign to the mainstream of the Italian tradition, comes from Spain. We see it in such distinctly Spanish architectural styles as Plateresque, where sculpture and ornament cover most of the façade, but it originated with the Moors, once rulers of much of Spain and all of Sicily. In contrast to other stuccoists, who loaded their sculpture with gilt, Serpotta's

surfaces are bright white with only small touches of gold, a colour scheme that anticipates the Rococo. His figures, too, seem far closer to the French Rococo than to the Roman Baroque or *Barocchetto*. Most of the life-size allegories are tall, slender female figures arranged in graceful swaying poses. Much attention is paid to the decorative effect of the costume and little to the body beneath. Around each of the principal figures are placed six or eight cherubs, who soar or plunge through the air, playing together or with bits of drapery, bunches of flowers or bowls of fruit. There are also framed stucco reliefs with biblical scenes and a large central panel that illustrates the victory of the Christians over the infidel Turks at Lepanto, but these are less effective, and the mood of the sculpture as a whole is light and secular. Along with the female allegories, many of whom seem too gay and pretty for what they represent, there are goat-footed satyrs bearing swags. Other figures are pure genre: a bare-footed old peasant woman, for example, and a young boy with his clothes in picturesque disarray.

BIBLIOGRAPHY

S. Vigezzi: *La scultura lombarda nell'età barocca* (Milan, 1930)
P. Fogaccia: *Cosimo Fanzago* (Bergamo, 1945)
G. Nicodemi: 'La scultura lombarda dal 1630 al 1706', *Stor. Milano*, xi (1958), pp. 517–46
R. Wittkower: *Art and Architecture in Italy, 1600–1750* (London, 1958, rev. Harmondsworth, 1980)
A. Romanini: 'La scultura milanese nel XVIII secolo', *Stor. Milano*, xii (1959), pp. 755–90
K. Lankheit: *Florentinische Barockplastik* (Munich, 1962)
P. Rotondi Briasco: *Filippo Parodi* (Genoa, 1962)
M. Bernardi: *Il barocco piemontese* (Turin, 1964)
A. Ballo: *Torino barocco* (Rome, 1965)
H. Hibbard: *Bernini* (London, 1965)
C. Semenzato: *La scultura veneta del seicento e del settecento* (Venice, 1966)
G. Carendente: *Giacomo Serpotta* (Turin, 1967)
A. Griseri: *Le metamorfosi del barocco* (Turin, 1967)
O. Ferrari: 'Le arti figurative', *Stor. Napoli*, vi/2 (1970), pp. 1233–345
E. Howard: *Genoa: History and Art in an Old Seaport* (Genoa, 1971)
E. Riccomini: *Ordine e vaghezza* (Bologna, 1972)
R. Causa: *L'arte nella certosa di S Martino a Napoli* (Naples, 1973)
L. Mallè: *Le arte figurative in Piemonte* (Turin, 1973)
The Twilight of the Medici: Late Baroque Art in Florence, 1640–1743 (exh. cat., ed. S. Rossen; Detroit, MI, Inst. A.; Florence, Pitti; 1974)
A. Blunt: *Neapolitan Baroque and Rococo Architecture* (London, 1975)
R. Enggass: *Early Eighteenth-century Sculpture in Rome* (University Park, PA, 1976)
Kunst des Barock in der Toskana: Studien zur Kunst unter den letzen Medici, Florence, Ksthist. Inst. (Munich, 1976)
E. Riccomini: *Vaghezza e furore* (Bologna, 1978)
F. Strazzullo: *La Real Cappella del tesoro de S Gennaro* (Naples, 1978)
L'arte del settecento in Emilia Romagna (exh. cat., ed. E. Riccomini; Bologna, Mus. Civ. and elsewhere, 1979)
R. Enggass: 'Settecento Sculpture in St Peter's: An Encyclopedia of Styles', *Apollo*, cxiii (1981), pp. 74–81
A. Nava Cellini: *La scultura del seicento* (Turin, 1982)
——: *La scultura del settecento* (Turin, 1982)
D. Garstang: *Giacomo Serpotta* (London, 1984)
J. Montagu: *Alessandro Algardi* (London, 1986)

ROBERT ENGGASS

5. NEO-CLASSICISM TO EARLY MODERNISM, *c.* 1750–*c.* 1900. In the second half of the 18th century many sculptors were still heavily influenced by the French Rococo. This can be seen in the work of ANGELO GABRIELLO PIÒ in Bologna, Elia Vincenzo Buzzi (*see* BUZZI, (1)) in Milan and FRANÇOIS LADATTE in Turin. In Rome important Late Baroque work was produced by such figures as PIETRO BRACCI, who provided the central

60. Giacomo Serpotta: *Strength* (detail), stucco, allegorical figure from his decoration (1688–1718) of the oratory of S Cita, Palermo, Sicily

group (completed 1762) in the Trevi Fountain. However, this style was superseded by the development of NEO-CLASSICISM, in particular during the last 20 years of the 18th century. The new style was inspired by a great interest in antique statuary: many splendid ancient works were catalogued and displayed in the new Museo Pio-Clementino in the Vatican, founded under Popes Clement XIV and Pius VI, and formally opened in 1780 (*see* §XIV). This museum was visited by ANTONIO CANOVA, who came to Rome from Venice for the first time in 1779 and settled there permanently from December 1780. In parallel with David's *Oath of the Horatii* (exh. Paris Salon 1785; Paris, Louvre), which marked the affirmation of the Neo-classical style in painting in Rome, Canova began his monument to *Clement XIV* (1783–7; Rome, SS Apostoli). This was new in conception compared to the works of contemporary sculptors, who were still tied to the style of Bernini. Its composition was simple, elegant and solemn, with the figures and architectural structure in an antique style. Canova then turned to ancient themes (e.g. *Cupid and Psyche Playing with a Butterfly*; see fig. 61), as well as Napoleonic portraits and such tombs as that of *Vittorio Alfieri* (1804–6; Florence, Santa Croce): the figure of *Italy* in this work was a model for the celebratory monuments of the Risorgimento. Along with his research on ancient art and his search for ideal beauty, Canova sought beauty in nature and in life studies. This was not the case with his Danish contemporary BERTEL THORVALDSEN, who lived nearly all his life in Rome. Thorvaldsen held scrupulously to the models of Greek sculpture, not only Classical but also Archaic, which he studied mainly through Roman copies. Canova found the correctness of his own approach confirmed in 1815, when he saw the vitality of the marbles of the Parthenon (London, BM). Canova's followers included Adamo Tadolini (*see* TADOLINI, (1)) from Bologna.

The Neo-classical sculptors in Rome also included GIUSEPPE CERACCHI and the Tuscan PIETRO TENERANI, a pupil of Thorvaldsen, who produced the *Abandoned Psyche* (1817; Florence, Pitti). In Florence there were Francesco Carradori (1747–1825) and Stefano Ricci (1765–1837), both professors at the Accademia di Belle Arti; in Liguria, Giuseppe Gaggini (1791–1867); and in Milan, Innocenzo Fraccaroli (1805–82) and later Abbondio Sangiorgio (1798–1879), Giovanni Putti (1771–1847), POMPEO MARCHESI, Benedetto Cacciatori (1794–1871) and GIOVANNI BATTISTA COMOLLI, all of whom worked on the important Arco della Pace (1807–59). This was commissioned by Napoleon I Bonaparte from the architect Luigi Cagnola and the sculptor Camillo Pacetti (*see* PACETTI, (2)), who was in charge of iconography and co-ordination of works. In the Veneto Luigi Zandomeneghi (1778–1850) produced such work as the *St Mary* and *St John* in S Maria in Pieve, Castelfranco Veneto. Southern Italian sculptors included Gennaro Calì (1799–1877) and Antonio Calì (1789–1866) in Naples and Leonardo Pennino (1765–1850) in Sicily.

While Romanticism appeared in Italian painting as early as the 1820s, sculpture remained largely tied to the forms of ideal beauty and antique subjects until the 1840s, although new developments were anticipated by the Tuscan Lorenzo Bartolini, who in his youth in Paris had

61. Antonio Canova: *Cupid and Psyche Playing with a Butterfly*, marble, 1796–1800 (Paris, Musée du Louvre)

known Ingres and Les Primitifs. He created the statue of the *Grape Presser* (1818; untraced; version of 1844, Brescia, Pin. Civ. Tosio-Martinengo), inspired not by the Classical Bacchus but by a 15th-century figure in the Camposanto of Pisa. However, this was not considered a revolutionary work because, although it was original, it fitted well into the ideology of PURISMO. Many Tuscan sculptors, for example Emilio Santarelli (1801–86), ULISSE CAMBI and Odoardo Fantacchiotti (1811–77), followed Bartolini's example by turning to the art of the Renaissance. In 1836, with the *Trust in God* (Milan, Mus. Poldi Pezzoli; *see* BARTOLINI, LORENZO, fig. 2), he succeeded admirably in expressing high moral sentiments in the nude, naturalistic figure of a young girl. Bartolini's continuing debt to the

62. Lorenzo Bartolini: funerary monument (1837–44) to *Countess Sophia Zamoyska*, marble, 0.80×1.94×0.84 m, Santa Croce, Florence

Renaissance is apparent in the funerary monument to *Countess Sophia Zamoyska* (see fig. 62). The influence of 15th-century sculpture, especially that of Donatello, led him to focus no longer on ideal beauty but on the imitation of nature, albeit in terms of an 'artistic' imitation that always respected the decorum of the subject and allowed the artist to correct any defects in the model. Bartolini's example found a response in the contemporary aesthetic and literary debates conducted in such works as Gjunio Carbone's *Intorno la imitazione artistica della natura* (Florence, 1842). He was joined in his search for natural beauty by the Tuscan sculptors Luigi Pampaloni (1791–1847), Emilio Demi (1797–1863), Pasquale Romanelli (1812–87), Pio Fedi (1816–92) and especially Giovanni Dupré (e.g. the *Dying Abel*, several versions, e.g. 1842; Paris, Louvre; see DUPRÉ, GIOVANNI, fig. 1). This movement had fundamental importance for the affirmation of naturalism, especially by VINCENZO VELA (e.g. *Spartacus*, original plaster, 1847; Ligornetto, Mus. Vela).

The first truly Romantic sculptor was Carlo Marochetti (1805–67), a pupil of Antoine-Jean Gros in Paris, along with Delacroix and Géricault. Marochetti worked in Turin for King Charles-Albert of Savoy (e.g. the monument to *Emanuel-Philibert of Savoy*, 1838; Turin, Piazza S Carlo) and gained great international fame, living for long periods in Paris and London. In Milan, along with Vela, there were Alessandro Puttinati (1801–72), whose work included *Paolo and Francesca* (1844; Milan, Gal. A. Mod.), Giovanni Strazza (1818–75), PIETRO MAGNI, Giosuè Argenti (1819–1901), Antonio Tantardini (1829–79) and ALFONSO BALZICO. Genoese sculptors in this period included Santo Varni (1807–85), who after some years of study in Florence taught for many years at the Accademia Ligustica di Belle

Arti in Genoa. The loftiest and most emotional Romantic sculpture is to be found in cemeteries. Among the best preserved examples of monumental complexes are the cemetery of Staglieno in Genoa and the English Cemetery in Florence. The cemetery of the cloisters of Santa Croce in Florence (now removed) was a major source of attraction for cultured tourists: only a few monuments remain, including the touching monument to the singer *Virginia de Blasis* (1839) by Pampaloni.

The first signs of Realism appeared in Italian sculpture in 1860, mainly through the work of Vela (then in Turin), ODOARDO TABACCHI and his pupils DAVIDE CALANDRA, PIETRO CANONICA, LEONARDO BISTOLFI, Giacomo Ginotti (1837–97) and ADRIANO CECIONI. However, academic sculpture was still yielding works of great value, for example Dupré's *Pietà* (1862–8; Siena, Cimitero Misericordia), which won a prize at the Exposition Universelle in Paris in 1867. At the end of the following decade the exclusive focus on reality was questioned in sculpture as in painting. This crisis was expressed through a disaggregation of forms whereby the solid composition of sculpture, and the 'bourgeois realism' still practised in the academies, were replaced by the creation of indistinct impressionistic shapes. This tendency was represented by Giuseppe Grandi (e.g. the monument to the *Cinque Giornate*, 1881–95; Milan, Piazza Cinque Giornate) and MEDARDO ROSSO (e.g. *The Concierge*; see fig. 63), as well as by Ernesto Bazzaro (1859–1937), PAOLO TROUBETZKOY and Eugenio Pellini (1864–1934). These artists belonged to GLI SCAPIGLIATI in Milan, who were violently

63. Medardo Rosso: *The Concierge*, wax, 385×340×180 mm, before 1884 (Rome, Galleria Nazionale d'Arte Moderna)

opposed to the Accademia di Belle Arti. They preferred to work in bronze or wax, which allowed them to create surfaces that were extremely lively and sensitive to light. Grandi and Rosso, in particular, were brilliant impressionistic sculptors.

Realist sculptors continued to produce interesting works, especially in Naples with the art of VINCENZO GEMITO, even after the Esposizione Italiana in Naples of 1877, when the sculptors Raffaele Belliazzi (1835–1917) and Raffaello Pagliaccetti (1839–1900) emerged. However, Italian sculpture in the second half of the 19th century, after the unification of Italy, mostly comprised the monuments to illustrious men and events of the Risorgimento, which increasingly populated the city squares. Among the most important artists in this genre were Francesco Barzaghi (1839–92) and Enrico Butti (1847–1932) in Milan, AUGUSTO RIVALTA in Florence, ETTORE XIMENES in Naples, and Emilio Gallori (1846–1924), Ercole Rosa (1846–93) and ETTORE FERRARI in Rome. In that city the celebration of the Italian Risorgimento was epitomized in the monument to *Victor-Emanuel II* (1883–1911) in the Piazza Venezia (*see also* §6 below).

BIBLIOGRAPHY
G. Carbone: *Intorno la imitazione artistica della natura* (Florence, 1842)
P. Emiliani Giudici: 'Classe XXIV: Scultura', *Esposizione italiana tenuta in Firenze nel 1861: Relazioni dei giurati*, iii (Florence, 1865), pp. 301–14
G. Dupré: 'Scultura: Classe III: Relazione', *Relazioni dei giurati italiani sulla Esposizione universale del 1867*, ii/2 (Florence, 1869), pp. 155–71
F. Sapori: *Scultura italiana moderna* (Rome, 1949)
C. Maltese: *Storia dell'arte in Italia, 1785–1943* (Turin, 1960)
M. Rheims: *La Sculpture au XIXe siècle* (Paris, 1972)
G. Previtali and F. Zeri, eds: *Storia dell'arte italiana*, pt 2, vol. ii (Turin, 1982), pp. 559–660, 793–1079
C. Del Bravo: 'Arte della restaurazione', *Le risposte dell'arte* (Florence, 1985), pp. 259–69
A. Panzetta: *Dizionario degli scultori italiani dell'ottocento* (Turin, 1989), rev. as *Dizionario degli scultori italiani dell'ottocento e del primo novecento* (Turin, 1994)
V. Vicario: *Gli scultori italiani dal neoclassicismo al Liberty* (Lodi, 1990, rev. 1994)
M. De Micheli: *La scultura dell'ottocento* (Turin, 1992)

LIA BERNINI

6. AFTER *c.* 1900. At the end of the 19th century much sculpture was commissioned to honour the heroes of the Risorgimento. In the squares of many cities colossal groups of statues were erected by the local administrations, and in the Piazza Venezia in Rome the monument to *Victor-Emanuel II* was completed in 1911. MEDARDO ROSSO took a critical view of such academic celebratory sculpture, preferring to depict everyday subjects in a tactile, impressionistic style. Until 1906 he continued the highly innovative work that he had been producing since the 1880s, in which the play of light broke up the sculptural forms. After his last sculpture, the wax *Ecce puer* (1906; Venice, Ca' Pesaro), which shows the influence of Symbolism, Rosso devoted himself to publicizing his work through such media as magazines and public displays of his technique with bronze. His formal innovations were highly influential on FUTURISM. In the *Manifesto dei pittori futuristi* (Milan) of 1910 Rosso's name already appeared among those of the small group of innovators who helped Italian art to emerge from provincialism. Rosso's importance was also stressed by UMBERTO BOCCIONI in *La scultura futurista* (Florence) of April 1912. Boccioni also added,

however, 'unfortunately the impressionistic approach has limited Medardo Rosso's experiments to a sort of high or low relief, which means that the figure is still conceived as a world unto itself, in a basically episodic way.'

Boccioni's own sculptural studies aimed to overcome the shortcomings that he perceived in Rosso's work, while taking his ideas as a point of departure. In particular, Boccioni concentrated on creating a sense of movement by representing the 'lines of force' of the figure or object in space. Closed lines were abolished, and the structure of the work was based on the abstract reconstruction of planes and volumes, as in the *Unique Forms of Continuity in Space* (1913; London, Tate; *see* FUTURISM, fig. 2). Like various contemporaries, including Picasso and Alexander Archipenko, Boccioni used mixed media. These included mechanically movable planes of wood or metal, as well as other materials designed to emphasize the work's dynamism. This practice was the outcome of many intuitions by the Futurist group. Around 1915 these innovations became more playful and festive; with the manifesto *Ricostruzione futurista dell'universo* (Milan, 1915), GIACOMO BALLA and FORTUNATO DEPERO invented ironic proposals for multi-media 'plastic complexes', involving experimentation with different noises, smells and colours. These ideas became the point of departure for the creations of ENRICO PRAMPOLINI and Depero and were exploited by the Futurists in theatrical performances.

Despite the continuing innovations of Futurist sculpture, one of the consequences of World War I, in which Boccioni died, was a re-affirmation of more conservative, classical values. As early as the end of the first decade of

64. Arturo Martini: *100-metre Runner* ('Il centometrista') bronze, 420×390×390 mm, 1935 (Venice, Galleria Internazionale d'Arte Moderna di Ca' Pesaro)

the century, ARTURO MARTINI had passed from his early expressionistic style, in which he used dynamic cut planes, to a more meditated and classical style, combining elements of modernism with a knowledge of ancient statuary (see fig. 64). In his mature work after World War I, Martini developed this style still further, with considerable success, gaining commissions for monumental sculpture throughout the Fascist period. In general during the 1920s Italian sculpture was characterized by a crude archaicism and a classicism with mythical themes. MARINO MARINI was among many artists who adopted a style influenced by Etruscan art. In the physiognomies of his figures, however, he achieved an expressive formal abstraction that became progressively more pronounced. Among the sculptors most closely associated with the Novecento Italiano movement was ADOLFO WILDT, who chose such officially favoured themes as patriotism, religion and the family. While such sculptors, drawing on Italian traditions, were identified with the values of the Fascist state, the second wave of Futurism, known as 'second Futurism', which produced such sculptors as Mino Rosso (1904–63), also claimed to represent Fascist ideals. This demonstrates the

relative pluralism of art in the Fascist period, in comparison with the situations in Nazi Germany and Soviet Russia.

In the 1930s, however, stronger attempts were made to dictate to artists the subject-matter of their work. On the one hand the traditional values of domesticity and rural life were promoted, while the strength of the authoritarian system was expressed through such monumental projects as the gigantic white marble statues that adorned the grandiose projects conceived by Benito Mussolini—the Stadio Mussolini and the EUR complex in Rome. MARIO SIRONI, the leading Italian exponent of mural painting, also produced public sculpture, for example the bas-reliefs of the *Italian People* (Milan, Pal. Giornali). During this period a cultural opposition to Fascism took shape, represented by the experiments of the abstractionists and the expressive figural language of the Scuola Romana, in particular the sculpture of ANTONIETTA RAPHAEL. The abstract work of FAUSTO MELOTTI was characterized by a geometric rigour combined with a musical rhythmic quality, while the early sculpture of LUCIO FONTANA included both figural and abstract work (e.g. *Abstract Sculpture*, 1934; Turin, Gal. Civ. A. Mod.).

65. Mario Merz: *Giap's Igloo*, iron, plastic, dirt and neon lights, 1.2×2.0×2.0 m, 1968 (Paris, Pompidou, Musée National d'Art Moderne)

The immediate period after World War II was characterized by a debate between the exponents of figural work, often with a specific social significance, and those who supported the intellectual experiments of abstract art. The anguish of the period was expressed by such works as Marini's *Horsemen*, the polychromed terracotta figures of Agenore Fabbri (*b* 1911) and by the tragic religious reliefs of GIACOMO MANZÙ (e.g. *Door of Death*, 1964; Rome, St Peter's; *see* DOOR, fig. 6). Other artists also returned to traditional idioms, including PERICLE FAZZINI, Francesco Messina (1900–95), who used Renaissance models, and EMILIO GRECO, whose works displayed a classical elegance. The abstractionists included PIETRO CONSAGRA, a member of the group FORMA, which claimed in its manifesto to express Marxism through visual abstraction. Abstract sculptures were also produced by ETTORE COLLA, who put together colossal assemblages of jetsam from the modern mechanized civilization, and EMILIO VEDOVA, whose work expressed the contemporary current of *Art informel*. The dynamic qualities of light in space were explored by FRANCESCO LO SAVIO (e.g. the *Metals*, executed 1961), whose work has also been seen as anticipating Minimalism and conceptual art. Probably the most important avant-garde sculptors of the immediate post-war era were Lucio Fontana and PIERO MANZONI. Fontana, the founder of SPAZIALISMO, produced such works as the *Spatial Environments*, in which he created patterns of neon lights in a room, in order to transform the visitor's experience of the space around him. Manzoni's work questioned the traditional conceptions of art with his 'living sculptures' and 'pneumatic sculptures', which the purchaser was supposed to inflate himself.

In the second half of the 1960s sculptors sought to express the instability of this politically troubled era with a new directness, such as PINO PASCALI in his *Self-propelled Cannon* (1965; Turin, Franz Paludetto priv. col.; see 1989 exh. cat., no. 188). Pascali, who died in 1967, was associated with the early development of ARTE POVERA, a term first used in 1967. Much of Arte Povera was sculptural, and explored issues connected with the wider development of conceptual art. The work often drew ironically on the Classical heritage or used unorthodox combinations of materials, as in the *Igloos* (e.g. *Giap's Igloo*; see fig. 65) by MARIO MERZ. JANNIS KOUNELLIS juxtaposed seemingly unrelated images in order to create complicated installations, which expressed his sense of the fragmentation and alienation of modern society. While the artists associated with Arte Povera continued to be active in the 1980s, this decade was also marked by the use of Neo-classical elements in the work of certain mythological artists, including Luigi Ontari. Non-figural art was also produced, including primitivist pieces by Mimmo Paladino (e.g. the artistic movement *Transavanguardia* and Nunzio (*b* 1954).

BIBLIOGRAPHY
A. Soffici: *Medardo Rosso* (Florence, 1929)
G. Castelfranco and M. Valsecchi: *Pittura e scultura italiana dal 1910 al 1930* (Rome, 1956)
G. Giampiero: *Spazialismo: Origini e sviluppi di una tendenza artistica* (Milan, 1956)
M. De Micheli: *Scultura italiana del dopoguerra* (Milan, 1958)
P. Bucarelli: *Scultori italiani contemporanei* (Milan, 1967)
R. De Grada: *Pittura e scultura degli anni '60* (Milan, 1967)
Recent Italian Painting and Sculpture (exh. cat. by G. Ballo and K. McShine, New York, Jew. Mus., 1968)
G. Celant: *Arte povera* (Milan, 1969)
U. Apollonio, ed.: *Futurismo* (Milan, 1970); Eng. trans. as *Futurist Manifestos* (London, 1973)
M. De Micheli: *La scultura del novecento* (Turin, 1981)
Anni trenta: Arte e cultura in Italia (exh. cat. by R. Barilli and others, Milan, Com. Milano, 1982)
Il segno della pittura e della scultura (exh. cat., Milan, Pal. Permanente, 1983)
M. Pratesi: 'Scultura italiana verso gli anni trenta e contemporanea rivalutazione dell'arte etrusca', *Boll. A.*, 3rd ser., xxviii (Nov–Dec 1984), pp. 91–106
M. Fagiolo dell'Arco: *Scuola romana: Pittura e scultura a Roma dal 1919 al 1943* (Rome, 1986)
Futurismo e futurismi (exh. cat., ed. P. Hulten; Venice, Pal. Grassi, 1986)
Italian Art in the 20th Century: Painting and Sculpture, 1900–1988 (exh. cat., ed. E. Braun; London, RA, 1989)

□

V. Interior decoration.

1. Before 1450. 2. 1450–1599. 3. 1600–1699. 4. 1700–*c*. 1750. 5. *c*. 1750–*c*. 1800. 6. *c*. 1800–1900. 7. After 1900.

1. BEFORE 1450. From the fall of the Roman Empire in AD 476 throughout the entire Romanesque period it is impossible to reconstruct with any accuracy the production of furniture and its arrangement in interiors due to the relative scarcity of either surviving examples or iconographical representations (*see* ROME, ANCIENT, §§X, 3, V and VI). During this period craftsmen's work—especially that in ivory, cloth and metals, with which seats were made—retained elements from the antique period. Elaborate hinges and locks were applied to simple and functional wooden furniture, which, with the exception of such fixed furniture as the throne and the bed, was moved, together with all the other objects that decorated castles, each time the court changed residence.

In contrast to the nomadic life of the nobles, who loved to surround themselves with precious furnishings, the middle-class town dwellers lived in simple tower houses, where each floor had a large room flanked by smaller spaces for the servants and storage. In medieval tower houses the hall had both a social function as a place where meetings were held and, more often, a domestic one, as a sitting-room for the family, which spent most of the day there. Tapestries were hung throughout the interior to provide protection from draughts and to brighten the walls with colour; benches and box seats were placed against the wall, while at meal-times tables were drawn up. Life in the castle also focused on the main hall, to which women had access. Next to it was the master bedroom, where bodyguards and servants often spent the night curled up at the foot of the bed. Sometimes noble residences had two halls: one for festivities and another for more ordinary meetings. According to the courtly romances, the knights' common room corresponded to the lady's bedroom on the floor immediately above; other rooms could be made by using tapestries or other hangings as partitions.

Given that the rooms were basically of two main types (the hall and the bedroom) and that there was a scarcity of furniture, the depiction of interiors in paintings varies little. In the *Birth of the Virgin* (1342; Siena, Mus. Opera

Duomo) by Pietro Lorenzetti, the room is furnished with a bed, encircled by a curtain, and a large chest, while thick hangings are the only furnishing for the room in the depiction (end of the 13th century/beginning of the 14th) by an anonymous Sienese artist in the Stanza della Torre of the Palazzo del Popolo of San Gimignano. During the Middle Ages the practice of decorating castle rooms with frescoes became more common. Beginning in the 13th century, first in France then in Italy, with the return of the Crusaders, who had been in contact with the sophisticated Middle Eastern civilization, the residences of noblemen became less austere. Palaces were no longer thought of merely as refuges to be used in times of war, but also as the ideal place to spend part of the year. The interiors, made more comfortable with the creation of huge fire-places, were decorated with painted or sculpted ornaments bearing foliage motifs, geometric interlace or coats of arms, which, in the Late Gothic period, were flanked by large compositions depicting chivalrous or courtly scenes.

Some interiors still retain the original paintings. In Piedmont, the Sala Baronale of the Castello della Manta with its frescoes (*c.* 1420) by Giacomo Jaquerio depicting the *Nine Worthies and the Fountain of Youth* is an important example of late medieval Gothic wall decoration (see fig. 66). The figures are depicted outdoors, in a flowery meadow, separated by fruit trees from which hang their shields and emblems, a device taken directly from French tapestries. In Lombardy, the Sala di Giustizia of the Rocca d'Angera (1320s), with its cross-vaults decorated with geometric designs and walls depicting the wartime exploits of Archbishop Ottone Visconti, contains one of the major fresco cycles of medieval secular art found in the region. Similarly, the mid-15th-century paintings in the Borromeo family palace in Milan are significant examples of a taste for luxury and self-promotion. The halls, rooms, corridors, passages and porticos of the court of the Gonzaga in Mantua were copiously decorated with ornate coats of arms and stories of chivalry. This decoration alternated with, and was sometimes even covered by, French tapestries, as recorded in the inventories of the early 15th century; the inventory compiled in 1407, after the death of Francesco I Gonzaga, for example, lists a large quantity of bed hangings, curtains, benches and bench coverings made in Italy and France. According to Vasari, ALTICHIERO painted many works for the della Scala family including, in the Sala del Podestà of their palace in Verona, a depiction of the *Jewish Wars* and various well-known personalities (all destr.). Primary sources also mention various frescoed halls, rich 'with gold and paintings', which Altichiero painted in the Palazzo Carrara, Padua (1370–79; fragment *in situ*), and the cycles based on the Arthurian legend in such castles in the Veneto as Castel Roncolo

66. Fresco decoration (*c.* 1420) by Giacomo Jaquerio in the Sala Baronale, Castello della Manta, Piedmont

and Castel Rodengo, and in the famous Saleta Lanzeloti in the Palazzo Ducale in Mantua.

Hunting scenes and episodes of court life were the subject of frescoes in country residences (*delizie*) of the Este family in Ferrara, for example the Castello di Belfiore where, at the end of the 14th century, Alberto d'Este had some rooms decorated with court scenes and pictures of young girls with animals on leashes. This last theme was also used by artists working for Giangaleazzo Visconti, 1st Duke of Milan, *c.* 1380 in the Castello di Pavia, which additionally had a 'room of mirrors' (*da li speghi*) where the ceiling was covered with tiny pieces of coloured glass, painted in gold with subjects taken from contemporary miniatures. In central Italy notable rooms of the late 14th century include the hall of the Collegio della Mercanzia in Perugia (*c.* 1390), where the walls and ceiling are lined with wood carved in the shape of small panels.

The decoration of noble residences in the medieval period was not limited to frescoed walls but also extended to other surfaces. The floors, mostly laid in brick in herringbone patterns, were sometimes decorated with marble mosaics or with ceramic tiles in geometric patterns. The vaulted ceilings were frescoed, while those with wooden beams were decorated with carvings, paintings, stucco or painted panels in harmony with the decoration of the walls. As further protection from the cold and damp the walls were lined with 2-m high panels called *spalliere*, which also served as headboards for beds, cots or as benches. During the 14th century *spalliere* were generally very simple and only rarely highlighted with gold; during the 15th century they were embellished with elaborate moulding and intarsia. Further decoration of the *spalliere* included the insertion of painted panels in the frame. According to the inventory of goods drawn up in 1431 for the Palazzo di Parte Guelfa in Florence, for example, the *spalliere* that surrounded the main hall were decorated with paintings.

In 14th- and 15th-century dwellings mobile tapestries were used, which could be hung or taken down when needed. Some—the rugs and bench and other covers placed over different types of furniture—were generally quite small and were prevalent. Other larger tapestries, such as the bed hangings, wall hangings and those used to cover wholly or in part the walls of the rooms, halls, *spalliere* and large doors, were less common. A real show of tapestries was restricted to such special occasions as public holidays or weddings. In the 15th century only the large noble families possessed an entire series of tapestries capable of completely covering the walls of their rooms; others had to content themselves with a few pieces, which they would hang on the more visible walls. This type of interior decoration, where more money was spent on tapestries than on furniture, continued throughout the century in the apartments of the noble families.

2. 1450–1599. Numerous dwellings dating from the second half of the 15th century and the 16th still exist in Italy. However, only their decoration is authentic as the furniture, when found, is the result of reconstructions by antiquarians. The lack of original furniture is partly compensated for by the information on interiors gathered from primary sources and contemporary paintings. The latter, while mainly depicting such domestic interiors as rooms or studies, constitute an irreplaceable source for understanding not only the taste of the period but also the function and arrangement of furniture in Renaissance dwellings. For example, the two bedrooms painted by Vittore Carpaccio at the end of the 15th century in the background of the *Dream of St Ursula* (Venice, Accad.) and of the *Birth of the Virgin* (Bergamo, Gal. Accad. Carrara) show respectively the differences between the furnishings in a sophisticated noble residence and the more practical, but no less refined, decoration of a middle-class dwelling. In the first painting the regal solemnity of the room is emphasized by the vast space, dominated by a monumental bed, and such decorative details as the relief work on the architraves over the doors, the sculptures placed on top of the bed and the small painted altarpiece hung to the right of it. The modest workmanship of the few pieces of furniture indicates their temporary arrangement in the room. In the *Birth of the Virgin* an entirely different type of room is depicted. It has much lower ceilings and is more functional, arranged to meet the needs of daily life. The bed is designed as an alcove so as to leave the rest of the room to serve as a sitting-room, and the wooden panel that partially lines the wall in front of the spectator has a shelf to hold several domestic objects. Domenico Ghirlandaio's fresco of the *Birth of the Virgin* (1485–90; Florence, S Maria Novella; *see* SPALLIERA, fig. 1) records the sumptuous late 15th- and 16th-century Florentine interiors that included paintings, glazed terracotta reliefs and multicoloured tapestries as well as elaborate wood panelling. The Borgherini family, when designing a luxurious nuptial suite (1511–15) in the Palazzo Borgherini, Florence, for Pierfrancesco Borgherini, employed Pontormo, Francesco Granacci, Bacchiacca and Andrea del Sarto to decorate panels with scenes from the *Story of Joseph* and had all the wooden furniture executed by Baccio d'Agnolo, the architect who had built the family palace and decorated it with doors and sculpted fireplaces (*in situ*) and inlaid furniture.

By the end of the 15th century the palaces of the nobility, which became steadily larger with vast courtyards often leading to gardens, were made more comfortable through the creation of numerous rooms designed for the needs of daily life or for functions, as can still be seen in the Palazzo Ducale in Urbino (*see* URBINO, §4). Alberti, in *De re aedificatoria*, stated that in royal palaces the apartments for the husband must be separate from those of the wife, just as the servants' quarters were to be set in another part of the palace. Next to the large ceremonial halls, the walls of which were covered with frescoes or tapestries, were the rooms and *studioli* (*see* STUDIOLO) designed to hold the family collections of art, books and precious objects. The walls of such rooms were lined with wooden cabinets, which were either inlaid or painted by the court painter, as in the respective studies of Borso d'Este (built *c.* 1448–65) in the Castello di Belfiore, near Ferrara, and of Piero de' Medici (destr.) in the Palazzo Medici, Florence, which was also decorated with glazed terracotta reliefs by Luca della Robbia. There are further examples in the *studioli* (which can still be visited) of Federigo II da Montefeltro, Duke of Urbino (1473–6), in the Palazzo Ducale, Urbino, of Isabella d'Este (1491–8)

67. Stucco decoration (1537–40) by Giovanni da Udine, Palazzo Grimani, Venice

(c. 1548), the Palazzo Cataldi (1558) and the Villa Pallavicino delle Peschiere (c. 1560). In Venice, Giovanni da Udine decorated the rooms of the Palazzo Grimani (1537–40) with frescoes and with stuccos incorporating festoon motifs, niches and busts in a classical Roman style (see fig. 67). This manner was also used—with variations—in the interiors of the palaces and villas designed by Jacopo Sansovino and Andrea Palladio.

Other decorative innovations introduced in the 16th century were painted maiolica floors (e.g. Cappella dell'Annunziata, S Sebastiano, Venice, 1510), the inclusion of ground-floor open galleries and porticos in the overall decorative scheme, and the increasingly majestic proportions of the staircase, which prepared the way for the dramatic interior decoration of the 17th century.

BIBLIOGRAPHY

G. Mariacher: *Ambienti italiani del trecento e quattrocento* (Milan, 1963)
M. Praz: *La filosofia dell'arredamento* (Milan, 1964)
A. González-Palacios, ed.: *Antiquariato: Enciclopedia delle arti decorative* (Milan, 1981)
A. Schiapparelli: *La casa fiorentina e i suoi arredi nei secoli XIV e XV* (Florence, 1983)
L. Collobi Ragghianti: *Ambienti del rinascimento* (Novara, 1986)
P. Thornton: *The Italian Renaissance Interior, 1400–1600* (London, 1991)

ENRICO COLLE

in Mantua and of Francesco I de' Medici, Grand Duke of Tuscany (1570–78), in the Palazzo Vecchio in Florence.

Up to the end of the 15th century the coffered ceilings, generally divided into squares, were decorated in relief. In the 16th century they were also decorated with paintings and elaborate inlay. The transition from simple painted motifs to inlay occurred gradually; first, such decorative elements as rosettes, acanthus leaves and moulded rods were inserted between the tablets of the coffers, followed by more complicated and creative solutions, where the area created by the crossing beams assumed various geometric forms decorated with elegant inlay that often formed frames for paintings. Fine examples are the coffered ceilings (1520–40) executed from the drawings of Baldassarre Peruzzi in both the Palazzo della Cancelleria and the Palazzo Massimo alle Colonne in Rome, and the later ceilings in the Palazzo Vecchio by Marco, Domenico and Giuliano Del Tasso (1478) in Florence, the Palazzo Ducale by Antonio and Paulo Mola (1506–8) and the Palazzo del Te from drawings by Giulio Romano (1525–34) in Mantua, and the Doge's Palace by Cristoforo Sorte (1581) and the Scuola Grande di S Rocco in Venice.

Stucco was one of the techniques used in the decoration of 16th-century interiors, which, like grotesque decoration, spread throughout Italy following the revival of classical models by Raphael and his school. Many rooms preserved intact in Roman palaces show the influence of the sophisticated and scenographic classical decorations of the Villa Madama (c. 1515–25; see STUCCO AND PLASTERWORK, §III, 10(i)(a)), as do the rooms of the Palazzo del Te, Mantua, where Giulio Romano created (1525–30) not only the wall and vault decorations, but also the floor mosaics based on designs fashionable in ancient Rome. In Genoa the Roman school influenced the decoration of the interiors of the Palazzo Doria (c. 1530), the Villa Cambiaso

3. 1600–1699. The 17th century was a period of decadence and decline in Italy. By the second half of the 16th century the Counter-Reformation stifled any attempt at intellectual activity, and the division of the Italian peninsula into a large number of small states in reality placed it under the supremacy of Spain. Spain dragged Italy into its own economic crisis, aggravating the burden of taxes, and the lifestyle of the bourgeois classes, who had been at the forefront of the Renaissance, became no longer fashionable. Instead, an exaggerated formalism and a pompous concept of nobility was the example followed by all and embodied by the few surviving courts, principally that of the pope, in Rome. Here, in the third decade of the 17th century, religious tensions subsided and the triumphant Church put aside its mourning dress; the opulent joy of life was joined with faith in the explosion of the Baroque. This was developed by Gianlorenzo Bernini (see BERNINI, (2)), PIETRO DA CORTONA and FRANCESCO BORROMINI under the pontificates of Gregory XV, Urban VIII, Innocent X and Alexander VII. The Baroque in all its artistic representations, above all in interior decoration, was a highly communicative, rhetorical and persuasive style involving theatrical illusion.

In the Baroque period there was a complete integration of all the constituent elements of interior decoration. The figure of the architect–decorator, responsible for both the architectural shell and its decoration, was born when the three founders of the style planned (or modified) churches and their decoration. The paradigm of the Baroque interior can be found in two works by Bernini in St Peter's, the baldacchino (1623–34) and the Cathedra Petri (1657–66; see BERNINI, (2), fig. 2); these two objects for ceremonial use were enlarged to giant proportions and surrounded by the most suggestive scenic devices (rays of light, rejoicing angels) to make the spectator feel 'dwarfed' and overwhelmed. Another essential characteristic of the Baroque was the use of ephemeral decoration to embellish exteriors (streets, squares) and interiors (churches, palaces), completely changing their shape and proportions on the occasion of specific ceremonies or anniversaries, for example to welcome a royal person, for a funeral or for the feast of a patron saint. The Baroque infiltrated other regions of Italy, producing unequal results ranging from the composed and sober style fashionable in Genoa—where the simplicity of the exteriors contrasts with the sumptuous interior decoration whose scenography is achieved through moulded and painted ceilings in stucco—to the rational structures of Guarino Guarini in Piedmont, a tendency towards grand decoration in Emilia, and a late Renaissance emphasis fashionable in Lombardy. In Tuscany the tradition of the 16th century lingered, but the influence of Rome is first evident in the Palazzo Capponi and the Palazzo Corsini. It culminated in the rooms decorated by Cortona in the Palazzo Pitti (see fig. 68), and these began the fashion for gilded stucco, subsequently to be widely imitated. The Baroque was late in reaching Venice; the bare walls and ceilings with gilded coffering or decorated with sumptuously framed canvases and frescoes surrounded by stucco decoration are no different from those of the previous century.

Ceremonies influenced the layout of rooms, their decorative themes and even the shape of the furniture. The division between reception rooms, private apartments and service areas—already outlined in the 16th century—became more apparent. Grand staircases, galleries and

rooms for special occasions were no novelty, but they increased so much in size and were decorated with such pomp that the principal rooms were reserved only for ceremonies for economic reasons (to light and heat such vast rooms involved considerable cost). The day-to-day life of the owners was carried on in a series of more private rooms, also characterized by a concept of scenographic layout, with grandiose suites of rooms in sequence, culminating in the bedroom. The doors were aligned (towards the windows, to take maximum advantage of the wall space) so as to allow a view of the whole but also to create a rational circulation. The apartments of husband and wife were generally separate, but in most cases their bedrooms were either adjacent or shared.

The owners of the house lived on the *piano nobile*, or first floor, which also housed the reception rooms. On the upper floors, progressively higher up as their importance decreased, were located the rooms of the other members of the family. Service rooms were at the top, with the sole exception of the kitchens, which, because of incoming supplies and the hydraulic system, were generally situated on the ground floor. Also here, and normally facing on to the central courtyard, were to be found the stables and carriage houses. On the other hand, shops and warehouses, either for the family's own activity or rented out, tended to disappear from the most important façades. The bathrooms, which were becoming more widely used (although many people, even those better off, were still

68. Frescoes and white and gilded stucco decoration (1643–4) by Pietro da Cortona, in the Sala di Marte, Palazzo Pitti, Florence

using basins and close-stools in their bedrooms), were mostly located within the thickness of a wall, generally adjacent to the principal bedrooms.

The staircase leading to the *piano nobile* was wide, its flights embellished with columns and statues in niches. Two rooms typical of the *piano nobile* of a Baroque house were the salon and the gallery. The salon was centralized on the façade and was used for balls and receptions. The gallery usually faced on to the interior square courtyard and had large windows that allowed the spectator to admire the works of art displayed there. The loggia was a kind of open gallery on one side of the house. It also served to accommodate the family collections, but during summer evenings it was possible to dine there. The most opulent houses also possessed other reception rooms, decorated with subtle cross-references so that, for example, the Salon of Peace complemented the Salon of War, the room dedicated to the Arts formed a pendant to that of the Sciences, and so on.

The most common heating system was the open fireplace, whose form and location against the wall had already been established during the Renaissance. The richest chimney-pieces were in marble, but there are also fine examples in stone with the family coat of arms carved in the centre. Braziers were much appreciated for their mobility; pottery stoves were particularly popular in the north. Rooms were lighted by lamps made of wood, silver or rock crystal, with the addition of crystal towards the end of the 17th century. Murano lamps, made of coloured glass in various shades, were a typical product of Venice. Torches were widely used, their supports sculpted in such human forms as telamons and Moors in painted and gilded wood. Candelabra were placed on tables and sconces fixed to the walls.

Painted decoration played a primary role in Baroque interiors; it appeared on walls, but it was principally on ceilings that it was most fully developed. The gallery of the Palazzo Farnese in Rome painted by Annibale Carracci (*see* CARRACCI, (3)) and Agostino Carracci (*see* CARRACCI, (2)) in 1597–1601 is the model of Baroque ceiling decoration, the high point of which is represented by the fresco painted in 1632–9 by Cortona in the salon of the Palazzo Barberini in Rome (*see* ROME, fig. 61). This masterpiece represents the *Triumph of Divine Providence*: the personified Virtues are interwoven with the heraldic symbols of the family in an exultation of the divinities. Much of the architectural setting, loaded with sculpted figures, was created through pictorial illusion in a fusion of painting, sculpture and architecture that here reached the climax of its achievement.

Quadraturismo (the genre of painted architecture with illusionistic effects) had been created in the 16th century and, in the second half of the century, had become a speciality of the Bolognese school. It spread from Emilia to Rome around 1600, with the Alberti and the Carracci. In the 17th century, this type of painting was greatly in vogue for special reception rooms, where the illusion was often highlighted by stucco elements alternating with the painting. Among the most important *quadraturisti* were: GIROLAMO CURTI, called Dentone, active in Bologna; Agostino Mitelli and ANGELO MICHELE COLONNA (see fig. 69), who were responsible for the illusionistic paintings

(1639–41) in the Palazzo Pitti, Florence; ANDREA POZZO, the major exponent of *quadraturismo* in Rome; and GIOVANNI COLI and FILIPPO GHERARDI from Lucca, who painted (1675–8) the frescoes of the gallery of the Palazzo Colonna in Rome, already begun ten years previously by Johann Paul Schor.

The materials and techniques employed for floors were the same as those of the previous century: parquet, marble (in slabs or inlaid), stone and ceramic tiles, with a particular preference in Tuscany and Rome for terracotta, which, in Rome, was alternated with enamelled tiles set in frames of marble or stone. The decorative elements adapted themselves to the curved lines and polychrome complexity of the Baroque, and a certain degree of attention was paid to the harmony between ceilings, floors and walls. From the middle of the 17th century, the custom of covering floors with carpets spread throughout Europe. Even Italy appears to have followed this fashion, although there were no distinguished carpet manufacturers in the peninsula.

Walls were covered with engraved and gilded leather, textiles and tapestries, the most important 17th-century tapestries being those of the Medici in Florence and the Barberini in Rome. Wood panelling was also used in northern areas. However, by far the most common was painted wall decoration, with figurative designs, geometric friezes and, above all, imitations of such precious materials as framed paintings, tapestries, curtains and marble incrustations. Mirrors, on an increasingly vast scale, had gilded or silvered frames and were painted with floral motifs at the joints. Wallpaper was used only sporadically, mainly in Venice, in imitation of such textiles as damask and velvet. Against these wall coverings were displayed a large quantity of paintings, often hung in multiple rows as well as above the doors, a location reserved for landscapes and still-lifes. Some reception rooms of great importance (for example, in the Vatican palaces) followed the fashion, generally applied to chapels of the nobility, of walls and floors inlaid with pieces of excavated marble.

With the exception of the prestigious reception table, all the furniture was lined up against the walls and was moved towards the centre of the room only when required to be used. However, the first impression on entering a Baroque interior was that offered by the ever-present gilding (on frames, *gineffe*, from which curtain pelmets were suspended, furniture and lamps), which contributed to a visual unification equal to that of the textile coverings. Textiles were employed in the creation of many pieces of furniture: chiefly beds, but also chairs, sofas and stools, which were rendered more comfortable than in the 16th century through the use of padding. Other furniture, especially tables, was concealed under rugs and fabric coverings. Beds and chairs were upholstered *en suite* with the wall coverings and window hangings, a fashion that started at the beginning of the 17th century. Each city had its own textile production, but some were famous for particular weaving techniques: thus Florence and Genoa exported brocaded and cut velvets, and Florence also produced the highly valued *teletta*, interwoven with threads of precious metals. Venice was famous for silk lampas, Bologna for voiles, and Naples supplied embroidered covers for a bedroom, complete with bed and chairs, for Louis XIV of France.

69. *Quadratura* decoration (1646–7) by Agostino Mitelli and Angelo Michele Colonna, in the Great Hall of the Palazzo d'Este, Sassuolo, Modena

BIBLIOGRAPHY

T. Pignatti: *Ambienti italiani del seicento e settecento* (Turin, 1964)

P. Thornton: *Authentic Decor: The Domestic Interior, 1620–1920* (London, 1984)

R. De Fusco: *Storia dell'arredamento* (Turin, 1985)

4. 1700–*c*. 1750. In the 18th century there was a cultural revolution in cosmopolitan Europe, in the course of which aesthetic pleasure, eroticism and the search for intimacy came to replace spirituality, ethical and heroic ideals and the sense of dignity. As a result of the restraining influence of the Church, Italy was only partially affected by this phenomenon. For this reason the style associated with this changed vision of the world—the Rococo—did not achieve the same success in Italy and appeared only in an attenuated form. The Baroque style had permeated Italian culture so deeply that it hampered the new style coming from France; therefore the term *Barocchetto* is used when referring to the style in vogue in Italy in the first half of the 18th century. In this style Baroque forms were simplified, lightened and reduced in dimension. Movement was created through graceful curves, and decorative motifs were adopted from the vocabulary of the Louis XV style, yet were always controlled by the principles of symmetry. The spirit of Italian Rococo, or *Barocchetto*, found greater scope for development in interior decoration than in architecture. The rooms were linear in structure, with a preference for the curved line, and colours were pale and luminous partly as a result of large windows, glass doors and mirrors. The search for comfort led to a reduction in the size of the rooms: for example, the grand salon and gallery, although retained in building design, were flanked by the boudoir and the small salon, decorated with exotic taste and considered much more fashionable.

A taste for the exotic was an important element of the Rococo, and in Italy it fed primarily on tales brought back by Jesuit missionaries; these produced such extraordinary images as the scenes of Native North American life (*in situ* painted on the silk wall panels of a small salon in the Palazzo Barberini in Rome. Materials became extremely costly and techniques very complicated. The complex outlines of the furniture were veneered with refined inlays of rare woods and, for the first time on a widespread basis, experiments were carried out into new possibilities for lacquers, crystal and wallpapers. Porcelain, produced at Doccia from 1737 and at Capodimonte from 1743, spread with incredible speed and was used both for objects and architectural decoration.

Rococo ceilings were often painted, as in the Baroque period, but illusionistic decoration was abandoned (except in Bologna) or toned down by the use of pale or subdued colours (as in Venice). Gilded stucco was widely used, and there were frequent, rather audacious decorative experiments, such as the ceiling of painted mirrors framed with gilded wood (*in situ*), designed by Benedetto Alfieri in 1739, that decorated the queen's *camera da toletta* in the Palazzo Reale, Turin. Stucco and painting were also employed on the walls, though the latter was usually conceived as decorative rather than high art. Tapestries became smaller. Mirrors extended from consoles and mantelpieces up to the ceiling and sometimes even took

over entire rooms. Textiles were also widely used for wall decoration, but the fabrics decorated by traditional techniques (velvets, damasks, brocades) were complemented by printed and painted textiles. Wallpapers became popular, especially from the 1730s, and the first manufacturer in Italy was probably the Remondini printworks at Bassano. The same materials as in the previous centuries were used for floors, with an increase in the popularity of inlaid parquet and a growing use of carpets. Furniture began to be placed slightly away from the edges of the room. The Roman *Barocchetto* interiors closest to the style of Louis XV, all dating from the 1750s, were the Salone d'Oro in Palazzo Chigi and the Villa Chigi in Via Nomentano, which combined rocaille outlines with Roman solemnity. Neo-classicism, which began at the same time as these decorative projects, was more suited to the city and impeded any further development of the *Barocchetto*.

With the rise to the throne of Charles III (*reg* 1734–59), Naples became the capital of a kingdom and a cosmopolitan city. Luxurious palaces and regal villas were constructed after the model of the palace of Versailles, while also being comfortable (*see also* §5 below). In Palermo the architectural projects of this period (Palazzo Bonagia, Villa la Favorita) retain a Baroque richness. However, brilliant stucco artists were active in Sicily, chief of whom was Giacomo Serpotta (*see* SERPOTTA, (3)) who created figural decoration full of 18th-century grace. The greater part of his work was carried out in churches (see fig. 60 above), but a few mid-century palaces still retain their stucco decoration (Palazzo Villafranca, Palazzo Gangi). In Turin, Victor-Amadeus II of Savoy called on FILIPPO JUVARRA to create such interiors as those in the Palazzina di Caccia at Stupinigi (1729–34), notably the grand *salone* in the central oval pavilion. Juvarra employed the carpenters Luigi Prinotto (*fl* 1722–33) and Pietro Piffetti (*c*. 1700–77), who produced furniture and elaborately inlaid wood panelling and parquet floors with an unusual Rococo syntax, an example of the profound French influence on the House of Savoy and Piedmontese society.

The *Barocchetto* in Genoa is characterized by luminous stuccowork and decorative frescoes on ceilings, corresponding to the delicate lacquering of the furniture. Bologna was the scene of much building; the palaces are grandiose, with frescoed decoration in a scenographic *quadratura* style. The Rococo reached Parma with Louise-Elisabeth, daughter of Louis XV, who went there to marry Duke Philip of Bourbon in 1739 and transferred to the city the tastes of the French court, as well as various pieces of French furniture that served as models for local decorators. In Florence, the extinction of the Medici family in 1737 and the consequent abandonment of their palace led to a lack of stimulus for interior decoration and the repetition of the stucco and gilt designs of Pietro da Cortona up to the advent of Neo-classicism. Characteristic of Lombardy are the villas built at Brianza and on the Lakes, with their refined, comfortable rooms decorated with stucco of a stylized elegance. In the Palazzo Clerici (1740) in Milan the Rococo is evident in the Venetian frescoes of Giambattista Tiepolo.

BIBLIOGRAPHY

A. González-Palacios, ed.: *Antiquariato: Enciclopedia delle arti decorative* (Milan, 1981) [with further bibliog.]

A. González-Palacios: *Il tempio del gusto: Le arti decorative in Italia fra classicismi e barocco: Roma e il regno delle Due Sicilie*, 2 vols (Milan, 1984)

P. Thornton: *Authentic Decor: The Domestic Interior, 1620–1920* (London, 1984)

R. De Fusco: *Storia dell'arredamento* (Turin, 1985)

A. González-Palacios: *Il tempio del gusto: Le arti decorative in Italia fra classicismi e barocco: La Toscana e l'Italia settentrionale*, 2 vols (Milan, 1986)

DANIELA DI CASTRO MOSCATI

5. *c.* 1750–*c.* 1800. After the mid-18th century there was a significant change in Italian domestic interiors as they began to be influenced by the Neo-classical ideas expressed in the *Encyclopédie* (Paris, 1751–65) by Denis Diderot and Jean le Rond d'Alembert. The distinction between public reception rooms and smaller private quarters was accentuated by furnishings specifically designed to meet the function of each room. In contrast to the exoticism often seen in the Rococo style, by 1760 themes based on the Antique had begun to appear in interiors. *Le antichità di Ercolano esposte* (8 vols, Naples, 1757–92), describing the finds at Herculaneum, provided a large repertory of ideas and motifs for scholars, collectors, patrons and Grand Tourists. Palmettes, beading, ribbons, cameos, classicizing profile portraits, trophies, lion heads, pelts and feet, dancing figures and grotesques appeared in painted decoration, furniture and objects in the interior. Popular colours were red, green, blue and white.

Among the most successful examples of the taste for the Antique was the Roman villa of Cardinal Alessandro Albani (*see* ROME, §V, 27), which Winckelmann admired as 'the most stupendous work ever imagined in our time'.

Built between 1755 and *c.* 1762 to a plan by Carlo Marchionni, it incorporated columns of porphyry, granite and oriental alabaster. In the garden were columns, sculptures, temples and curtains of trees, all carefully laid out to produce a studied, 'natural', rhythm. An early exponent of Neo-classicism was Anton Raphael Mengs, who painted the frescoes of *Parnassus* in the ballroom of the Villa Albani in 1760–61. Another notable example of Roman Neo-classicism is the Salone d'Oro (1765–7; see fig. 70) in the Palazzo Chigi. In Rome the taste for the Antique in interior decoration could also be seen in GIOVANNI BATTISTA PIRANESI's engravings and Neo-classical painting, but there was also room for such spirited fantasies as the cell of Padre Le Sueur in Santa Trinità dei Monti, frescoed *c.* 1766 by CHARLES-LOUIS CLÉRISSEAU. This was created as a ruined temple, complete with sarcophagi and furnishings. Reflecting the continuing appeal of the Rococo, however, a porcelain room of painted and relief chinoiserie tiles and figures, made at the Capodimonte Porcelain Factory, was created for the Palazzo Reale in Portici between 1757 and 1759 (now Naples, Pal. Reale; see fig. 71). The Palazzo Reale, Caserta (*see* CASERTA, PALAZZO REALE, and §6 below), contained Neo-classical frescoes painted in the late 1770s and the 1780s.

In the Veneto, the desire of the aristocracy and the bourgeoisie for 'villa life' was reflected in the interiors with allegorical frescoes that drew parallels between ancient history and the history of the commissioning families. Divans were placed along the walls in the open reception rooms, and the rooms held works of lacquer. Examples

70. Salone d'Oro (1765–7), Palazzo Chigi, Rome

71. Salottino di Porcellana, Palazzo Reale, Portici, designed by Giovanni Natali; tiles and figures made at the Capodimonte Porcelain Factory, 1757–9 (Naples, Palazzo Reale)

can be seen in the Villa Marcello, Levada (nr Padua), with frescoes (*c.* 1755) by Giovanni Battista Crosato and in the Villa Zenobio, Santa Bona Nuova (nr Treviso), with scenographic frescoes by Francesco Fontebasso and other *quadratura* painters. In the Villa Valmarana, Vicenza, frescoes (1757) by Giambattista Tiepolo (*see* TIEPOLO, (1)) and Girolamo Mengozzi-Colonna (*c.* 1688–1766) portray mythological scenes from the *Aeneid*, the *Iliad*, Ariosto's *Orlando furioso* and Tasso's *Gerusalemme liberata*. In the Gothic pavilion there are frescoes by Giandomenico Tiepolo, and rooms with pastoral scenes, and still others in the Chinese style. The vast central salon in the Villa Pisani (now Villa Nazionale Già Pisani), Stra, contains allegorical frescoes (1760) by Giambattista Tiepolo, while landscape decoration (1771) dominates in the Villa Giustiniani, Noventa Padovana, with views of Italianate gardens, picturesque villages and chinoiseries. The Villa Emo Capodilista, Montecchia (Padua), contains a prestigious *trompe l'oeil* (1770): this type of decoration, using false perspective, and with furniture in the Louis XVI style, was then in the fashion.

In Piedmont, many villas were enriched after 1760, during the reign of King Charles-Emanuel III of Sardinia, with interesting interiors containing Chinese-style wallpapers, porcelains from Vinovo and furniture in pastiglia. The repertory of motifs was simplified, as can be seen in the work of the architect BENEDETTO INNOCENTE ALFIERI, influenced as he was by French and Viennese examples. This can be seen in the stupendous rooms of the Palazzo Isnardi di Caraglio, Turin; the rooms were fitted with mirrors and gilt *boiseries* in 1770. Alfieri's Teatro Regio was illustrated in the *Encyclopédie*. The interior of the Palazzo dell'Accademia delle Scienze in Turin (1787), however, remains decidedly in the Louis XVI style, with *trompe l'oeil* architectural details painted by Giovannino Galliari. After 1750 an extreme Rococo style became popular in the aristocratic and bourgeois villas of Lombardy, in decorations executed by *quadratura* artists. Frescoes were painted by the scenographers Bernardino Galliari and Fabrizio Galliari in the ballrooms of Villa Crivelli, Castellazzo di Bollate (Milan), and in Villa Bettoni, Bugliaco, Lake Garda, where the furnishings were extraordinarily functional and elegant.

The Neo-classical style was supported in Milan by the Habsburg monarchy with the appointment of GIUSEPPE PIERMARINI as Imperial Royal Architect in 1769 and the establishment in 1770 of the Accademia di Belle Arti (transferred to Brera in 1773). Piermarini's work, in the most refined Neo-classical style, can be seen in the Palazzo Belgioioso (1772–82), the restoration of the Palazzo Ducale, and in the Villa di Monza (1776–80), with the *Story of Psyche* (1789) by ANDREA APPIANI. Of particular interest for interior decoration is the work of Giocondo Albertolli (*see* ALBERTOLLI, (1)). González-Palacios (1986) has shown that drawings by Albertolli, Appiani and Giuseppe Levati (1738–1828) were used by Giuseppe Maggiolini for his renowned furniture. Another high point of Neo-classicism was achieved by Leopoldo Pollack (*see* POLLACK, (1)) in the Villa Belgioioso (1790; now Villa Reale). The great reforms of the Enlightenment had contributed to the increase in the construction of villas on lakes, in Brianza and the Brescian highlands. Their interiors showed

a great mastery of stuccowork and furniture; for example in the Villa Olmo, Como, the Villa Carlotta, Tremezzo, with later reliefs by Bertel Thorvaldsen, the Villa Lechi, Montirone (Brescia), the Villa Ghirlanda Silva, Cinisello Balsamo, with its Neo-classical salon, and the Villa Melzi, Bellagio, by Albertolli. The Neo-classical style was an important phase and is well represented in the work of the Brescian architect Giacomo Quarenghi, who went (1779) to the court of Catherine the Great of Russia.

The renowned elegance of the work of GIUSEPPE MARIA BONZANIGO and other furniture-makers and carvers, including Francesco Bolgié (active 1769–1825), can be seen in the apartments of the dukes of Aosta on the second floor of the Palazzo Reale, Turin, executed (1775) under the direction of the architects Giuseppe Battista Piacenza (1735–1818) and Carlo Randoni (active 1786–1831). The low-relief decorations remain in the Louis XVI style: vases with mythological panels, friezes, garlands, torches, tripods and trophies were incorporated in fireplaces, mirrors, doors and over-door panels. The unity of the arts reached a high point in the work of the 1780s in the Palazzo Stupinigi. Bonzanigo worked on the interiors, together with Michele Antonio Rapous (active 1765–1792), who painted the floral still-lifes, and Vittorio Amedeo Cignaroli (1730–*c.* 1800), who created the Arcadian landscapes. Other examples of this style can be found in the Castello di Moncalieri, with preparatory drawings (Turin, Bib. Reale) by Leonardo Marini (active 1760–1806) for the furnishings. The 18th-century Enlightenment found a singular expression in the Castello di Masino, Ivrea, with its scenographic frescoes in the Salone degli Dei and especially those in the Galleria dei Poeti (1780).

6. *c.* 1800–1900. During the rule of Napoleon Bonaparte (1804–14) the dominant taste was for interiors and furnishings in the severe Empire style, encouraged and promoted by various members of the BONAPARTE family. The Palazzo Reale, Caserta, was decorated with figural low reliefs in the Neo-classical style, with marble floors, pilasters and ornate friezes, as can be seen in the Sala di Marte (1807–15; see fig. 72). The Neo-classical style was also apparent in the villas of the Veneto: monochrome mythological decoration was executed by Giambattista Canal (1745–1825), in the *Dancers and Hours* (1800) at the Villa Caselli, Cortello (nr Udine), and in the Villa Pisani (now Villa Nazionale Già Pisani), Stra, with antique subjects in the style of Canova. The decoration (1790–1824) of the Quartiere d'Inverno in the Palazzo Pitti, Florence, includes (1739–1811) frescoes by Giuseppe Maria Terreni in the Sala della Musica (1795) and, after 1859, the *Stories of Orpheus, Mercury and Allegories* in the Stanza del Pranzo. Other rooms, such as the Salone da Ballo, the Salotto Giallo, the Salotto Rosso and the bedroom were lavishly decorated in the Neo-classical style in the mid-19th century. In these interiors are found paintings and furniture from the Esposizione Nazionale held in Florence in 1861, and monumental mirrors. These are combined with Neo-classical furnishings, for example chests-of-drawers (1821) by Giuseppe Colzi, consoles (1825) by Giovanni Socchi (*fl* 1807–25) and upholstered furniture typical of the 1870s.

72. Sala di Marte (1807–15), Palazzo Reale, Caserta

After the fall of Napoleon, the Restoration brought a move towards historicist styles. Romanticism exalted nationalist styles and promoted aspects of picturesque and medieval architecture. The interiors of the Castello di Govone were replaced, and the ballroom frescoed by Luigi Vacca (1778–1854) and Fabrizio Sevesi (1773–1837). Similar new work was carried out in the Castello di Aglié, where the Galleria di Ponente was decorated in the TROUBADOUR STYLE. Another, more striking development can be seen in the royal interiors of Charles-Albert, King of Sardinia (reg 1831–49). The grandiose Castello di Racconigi was renovated, with the Margherie and the Serre decorated in the neo-Gothic style, and with neo-Etruscan salons and studies. The Neo-classical style was preferred for the Palazzo Reale, Turin, as a style celebrating sovereignty that could compete with the earlier Baroque magnificence of the reception rooms. The interiors were planned by PELAGIO PALAGI, who designed the Sala del Consiglio (1836), the Sala del Trono and the Sala da Ballo (1842), a masterpiece with mirrors, great chandeliers, 20 white marble Corinthian columns, with, on the ceiling, *Olympus*, and on the walls *Dancers* painted by Carlo Bellosio (1801–49) and Francesco Gonin. The Caffè Pedrocchi (1826–42; for illustration *see* JAPPELLI), Padua, by GIUSEPPE JAPPELLI reveals the eclecticism current at the time, and an addition to the café, the Pedrocchino (1837–9), is decorated in an exuberant Gothic Revival style. The Baroque style of decoration continued in Genoa until the early 19th century, supported by the Accademia Ligustica. A change in style dates from the 1840s, when

the Salone da Ballo in the Palazzo Reale was transformed. Here, the plan by Michele Canzio (1787–1868) had called for an inlaid pavement designed by Palagi, comparable to those he created for the Palazzo Reale, Turin. There are important wall and ceiling stuccos by Santo Varni (1807–85) and Giuseppe Ghezzi, the *Dancing Nymphs* undoubtedly inspired by Flaxman. In the Sala delle Udienze the great bronze and crystal chandeliers and the prestigious furnishings by Enrico Peters (active 1817–52) add weight to the celebrated Neo-classical programme.

From 1830 to 1850 the Louis-Philippe style favoured the demands of comfort, combined with a show of elegance. Antique objects were used as part of the decorative scheme, but replicas, ranging from Gothic through Renaissance, Baroque and the exotic, were not disdained. The international exhibitions offered many ideas, for objects and for new materials, until the advent of Eclecticism, when interiors were designed to create a theatrical effect, with different fabrics, curtains, articles of silver, enamel and coloured glass adopted by the bourgeoisie as status symbols. Important examples remain in the royal residences, at Castello della Mandria, Turin, from the reign of Victor-Emanuel II. Here, the neo-Baroque Sala da Pranzo, with aspects of the neo-Rococo and Louis-Philippe style, reveals exchanges with Paris and London, and especially a certain warmth that linked the aristocracy with the industrial bourgeoisie. This was reflected in the Castello di Sammezzano, Florence, conceived as a Moorish palace. In Genoa Gino Coppedé (1886–1927) worked on

MacKenzie Castle (1890), and in Milan CAMILLO BOITO was a noted influence.

7. AFTER 1900. The ideas of William Morris were important in Italy, and skilled craftsmanship was responsible for the eclectic richness of the early 20th century, which found new interpretations in the *Stile Liberty* (Art Nouveau), with its alternation of striking elements and simplification. An important example of Eclecticism can be seen in the interiors of the Palazzo Orfei, Venice (now Museo Fortuny), home of Mariano Fortuny y Madrazo (*see* FORTUNY, (2)). The *Stile Liberty* decades are represented by the Sala dei Pavoni (1901), Palazzo Castiglioni, Milan, by GIUSEPPE SOMMARUGA. The Prima Esposizione Internazionale d'Arte Decorativa Moderna, held in Turin in 1902, played an important role through the contribution of the architect Raimondo D'Aronco. Also significant was the work of PIETRO FENOGLIO, represented by the Casa Fenoglio (1902) on the corner of the Corso Francia and the Via Principe d'Acaja, Turin, and of Carlo Bugatti (*see* BUGATTI, (1)) who created a drawing-room (the 'Snail Room') based on large wheels as a tribute to industrial civilization. In Naples, Vincenzo Jerace (1862–1947) worked on the palazzo of the Prince of Sirignano, while in Sicily Ernesto Basile (*see* BASILE, (2)), a leading promoter of *Stile Liberty*, designed furnishings often produced by Vittorio Ducrot (1867–1942). Among other designers of the early 20th century, EUGENIO QUARTI encouraged a simplified floral style.

Futurism brought a sharp break with all previous traditions. Its high point came with the designs of ANTONIO SANT'ELIA, who saw the house as a 'visionary machine in which to live'. After 1920 the Art Deco style took a stance against the styles of the old bourgeoisie and was epitomized by the work of GABRIELE D'ANNUNZIO, which ranged between the eclectic and the bizarre, and is displayed in his home, Vittoriale degli Italiani in Gardone Riviera. Rationalism was championed in Italy by the Movimento Italiano per l'Architettura Razionale (MIAR), presented at an exhibition in Rome in 1928, and by the work of the designer GIO PONTI, founder of the magazine *Domus*. Ponti designed models for the Richard Doccia porcelain factory and furnishings for ships and homes. Furnishings continued to be designed by architects. GIUSEPPE TERRAGNI and PIETRO LINGERI experimented in Milan with modern shop design in the gallery–bookshop of Milione, working with an idea of a deep shop window for a more direct relationship with the public. In Turin, CARLO MOLLINO produced Surrealist furniture (see fig.73), of which some pieces (1965–73) remain in the Teatro Regio. In the late 20th century, in parallel with designs for museums by such architects as FRANCO ALBINI and CARLO SCARPA, the design of interiors showed an interest in the use of antique sculpture with contemporary graphic art.

BIBLIOGRAPHY

G. Chierici: *La Reggia di Caserta* (Rome, 1930)
M. Praz: *La filosofia dell'arredamento* (Milan, 1964)
L. Mallè: *Stupinigi: Un capolavoro del settecento europeo tra barocchetto e classicismo* (Turin, 1968)
C. Briganti: *Curioso itinerario delle collezioni ducali parmensi* (Milan, 1969)
G. Cuppini and A. M. Matteucci: *Ville del Bolognese* (Bologna, 1969)
Pelagio Palagi: Artista e collezionista (Bologna, 1976)
F. D'Arcais: *Gli affreschi nelle ville venete* (Milan, 1978)
Civiltà del settecento a Napoli, 1734–1799 (Naples, 1979–1980)
A. O. Cavina: 'Il settecento e l'antico', *Storia dell'arte italiana: Dal cinquecento all'ottocento*, ii (Turin, 1982), pp. 599–655
G. L. Hersey: 'Carlo di Borbone a Napoli e Caserta', *Storia dell'arte italiana: Momenti di architettura*, xii (Turin, 1983), pp. 215–70
A. González-Palacios: *Il tempio del gusto: Le arti decorative in Italia fra classicismi e barocco. Roma e il regno delle Due Sicilie*, 2 vols (Milan, 1984)
——: *Il tempio del gusto: Le arti decorative in Italia fra classicismi e barocco. La Toscana e l'Italia settentrionale*, 2 vols (Milan, 1986)
Porcellane e argenti del Palazzo Reale di Torino (Milan, 1986)
S. Pinto: 'Dalla rivoluzione alla restaurazione', *Arte di corte a Torino: Da Carlo Emanuele III a Carlo Felice* (Turin, 1987), pp. 101–28
C. Bertolotta: *Giuseppe Maria Bonzanigo: Intaglio minuto e grande decorazione* (Turin, 1989)
G. Briganti: *La pittura in Italia: Il settecento* (Milan, 1990)
C. Robbero, M. G. Vinardi and V. Defabiani: *Ville Sabaude* (Milan, 1990)
'Ambienti', *Grande enciclopedia dell'antiquariato* (Milan, 1991)
E. Colle: *Palazzo Pitti: Il Quartiere d'Inverno* (Milan, 1991)
A. González-Palacios: *Fasto romano: Dipinti, sculture e arredi dai palazzi di Roma* (Rome, 1991)
L. Lodi: *La Galleria di Palazzo Reale a Genova* (Genoa, 1991)

ANGELA GRISERI

VI. Furniture.

1. Before *c*. 1450. 2. *c*. 1450–1599. 3. 1600–1799. 4. 1800–1900. 5. After 1900.

1. BEFORE *c*. 1450. Information on medieval Italian furniture is limited and incomplete. With the exception of the bed and throne, which were considered fixed pieces and could therefore assume more elaborate shapes, furniture was distinctly functional. The fact that noble families frequently moved between various castles together with the threat of looting gave rise to the custom of transporting furniture from one residence to another. Tables, chairs and stools therefore had to be easily folded or dismantled, and the strong chests, which held household goods,

73. Furniture designed by Carlo Mollino in the Casa Miller (1938), Via Talucchi, Turin

74. Cassone, walnut and low-relief stucco, 1.42×0.55×0.58 m, from Florence, early 14th century (London, Victoria and Albert Museum)

precluded any bulky or impractical furnishings. Chairs were often made of iron, instead of wood, both in order to withstand the frequent moves and because medieval craftsmen perpetuated classical traditions, as can be seen in an example (Pavia, Castello Visconteo) produced in damascened metal in the 7th or 8th century. Romanesque furniture and, later, Gothic furniture was decorated with such motifs taken from contemporary architecture as arches, columns and rosettes. Pieces were constructed of planks joined with nails; later the corners were strengthened by strapping with metal, which was often worked with elaborate geometric designs. In 1322 the invention of the saw mill and the introduction of the dovetail joint revolutionized furniture production in Italy. As a result of these technical developments furniture became more solid and better suited for carving and intarsia work. In contemporary paintings beds are increasingly depicted with headboards and curtains, and box seats, tables and chairs are elaborately embellished. The bedroom shown in the miniature of the *Birth of St John the Baptist* (1416; Turin, Mus. Civ. A. Ant.) by Jan van Eyck, taken from the *Heures de Milan*, portrays several pieces of furniture, including a Gothic cabinet in the middle of the room, a cassone and two triangular stools built of turned members following the Romanesque practice, which remained in fashion throughout most of the 15th century. From the 14th century Italian craftsmen who worked and traded in wood—carvers and inlayers, coffermakers and coopers, sawyers and lumber tradesmen—organized themselves into a guild, which defended the rights of its members and discouraged unfair competition.

The CASSONE, also known depending on its use and the region as an *arca, cofano* or *forziere* when reinforced with hinges and locks, remained the most important piece of furniture in noble residences until the type disappeared in the 17th century. Vasari related that every Florentine palace had a cassone decorated on three sides with scenes representing hunting, jousting, romances or mythology

(see fig. 74), while the interior was lined with expensive cloth. The form of these chests was perfectly suited for accommodating panels decorated with intarsia inlays, paintings or reliefs in gilded pastiglia, for which Italian craftsmen exhibited particular technical and inventive skill.

In the 15th century tables were still produced in traditional medieval forms. Movable frames or trestles supported broad and simply decorated timber tops, which were draped with valuable textiles. Chairs, on the other hand, while deriving their X-form from the folding chairs already in use in ancient times, acquired different shapes. The Dantesca chair, for example, had four legs with crossed scissor hinges connected by four bars, while the Savonarola chair, a more elaborate version of this, took its name from a similar seat found in the cell of Girolamo Savonarola in the convent of S Marco in Florence. The design of the bed also changed in accordance with the new concept of interior decoration that took root during the Renaissance: the bedstead took on a monumental form and size, while wooden bed alcoves, enclosed by doors, were still used in the 15th century, an important example being the one (Urbino, Pal. Ducale) owned by Federigo II, Duke of Urbino (*see also* BED, §1 and fig. 1).

One of the major woodworking centres in Italy was Piedmont, where as early as 1300 choir-stalls were decorated with Gothic carving, for example those made for S Maria Maggiore, Susa (now in S Giusto Cathedral) and those of Novalesa (now in the parish church of Bardonecchia). Carving became increasingly elaborate during the 15th century due to the presence of foreign craftsmen. Decorative motifs were taken from the iconography of miniatures and displayed a taste for naturalism: plants and fantastic animals were depicted on the choir-stalls of Ivrea Cathedral (now reduced to chair backs; Turin, Mus. Civ. A. Ant.). The carving was often intricate, as in the choir of Aosta Cathedral executed in 1457 by the master carvers Jean Vion di Sauroens and Jean de Chetro.

Few pieces from the Gothic period survive in the Veneto. Perhaps the best examples are the sacristy armoire (*in situ*) from the Arena Chapel in Padua or, near Friuli, the stalls (*in situ*) from the Lombard temple of Cividale commissioned by the Abbess Margherita della Torre between 1371 and 1384. During the 15th century the practice of decorating furniture with intarsia became common in the Veneto, the main craftsmen being the Canozi family from Rovigo. The choir of S Giustina in Padua contains a group of inlaid furniture (1467–77) with representations in linear perspective made by Francesco da Parma and Domenico da Piacenza (*fl c.* 1480), testifying to the spread of Emilian culture in the Veneto area. As for domestic furniture, there are several cassoni decorated with pastiglia and partly painted in the Museo di Castelvecchio, Verona, and the Ca' d'Oro, Venice. Small cult objects were also widely dispersed, such as the portable altarpieces and picture frames produced in great number by the workshop of the EMBRIACHI family in Venice.

In the 14th century furniture in Tuscany, as in the rest of Italy, was still simple and functional in design, while in the 15th century it was embellished with an elaborate array of ornaments covering the traditionally solid form. In Siena the technique of intarsia, already well known in the 14th century, was used on both religious and secular furniture. Pastiglia was also widely used in Siena, particularly in decorating cassoni. Even in Florence the cassoni and dressers, with their solid architectural forms, were decorated with pastiglia, intarsia and tempera.

Umbria, influenced by the Tuscan style in furniture and intarsia, produced very high-quality furniture, mainly the work of masters from neighbouring regions. The choir (1331–40) of Orvieto Cathedral was executed by Giovanni Ammannati (*fl* 1305–40) and other Sienese craftsmen, while the Florentine Manno di Benincasa (1373–1455) was responsible for the choir (1435) of S Domenico in Città de Castello. The Tuscan Late Gothic style had some influence on domestic furniture, as can be seen in a cassone decorated with pastiglia (Gubbio, Pal. Com.) or a bench ornamented with intarsia (Bettona, Pin. & Mus. Civ.). Other examples of the great technical skill attained by central Italian craftsmen are the wood furnishings of Orvieto Cathedral (e.g. pulpit; Orvieto, Mus. Opera Duomo; see fig. 75) and of Ascoli Piceno Cathedral.

In southern Italy the art of woodworking did not reach its height in Naples until the first half of the 15th century. Masters from Arezzo and Verona, with the collaboration of local workers, executed the most exacting inlaid work, while masters from Brescia, Rome and the Veneto assisted Neapolitan workers in wood-carving, creating complex decorative forms. Flemish and Neapolitan artists collaborated on furniture inlaid with bone and ivory, which became a particularly widespread form of decoration during the second half of the 15th century.

2. *c.* 1450–1599. During the Renaissance, furniture-making, like other areas of fine and applied arts, increasingly took antique models as its source of inspiration. Furniture was decorated with motifs from contemporary architecture, pilasters, cornices and frames, next to which were placed such classical ornaments as vases, volutes, putti and leaf-work. Sometimes the decoration was inlaid

75. Pulpit, carved and inlaid wood, from Orvieto Cathedral, 14th century (Orvieto, Museo Opera del Duomo)

and portrayed objects, people or architecture arranged in strict perspective, as in the *studiolo* (1476; *see* STUDIOLO, fig. 1) of Federigo II da Montefeltro in the Palazzo Ducale in Urbino, where the inlaid panels with *trompe l'oeil* designs alternate with classicizing pilasters and entablatures. Later in the 15th century furniture became increasingly elaborate in decoration: from this time onwards grotesque masks, frond volutes, bean motifs, figures from mythology and geometric designs decorated the wooden surfaces of most domestic furniture. Mythological or allegorical scenes, executed in plaster, carving or painting, were depicted on cassoni (see fig. 76), while legs sculpted in the form of leaves and ending in lions' paws, of classical origin, were specifically adopted for tables. As the 16th century progressed decorative effects became increasingly sumptuous and robust, sometimes surpassing the form of the furniture itself (see fig. 77). The armchair made its appearance in this period, taking its place beside the traditional Savonarola and Dantesca chairs. The dresser gained considerable grandeur in form, and large beds, deprived of the chests that encircled them previously, were decorated with carved and gilded columns, while tables generally had lyre, balustrade or anthropomorphic legs with rails featuring carved grotesque masks and coats of arms.

76. Cassone, engraved and carved walnut, mid-16th century (San Marino, CA, Huntington Library and Art Gallery)

Florentine furniture acquired a distinctly majestic air along with an increasing precision in execution. Woodcarving assumed a major role in furniture decoration. Both BACCIO D'AGNOLO and Vasari (creator of the *studiolo* of Francesco I, Grand Duke of Tuscany, in the Palazzo Vecchio; *see* STUDIOLO, fig. 2) provided drawings for furniture and interior decoration. After the technique had been mastered in Milan and elsewhere, during the second half of the 16th century Florentine table-tops were inlaid with hardstones (*see* HARDSTONES, colour pl. I, fig. 1), a technique that was soon adopted for cabinets and cupboards (*see* §X, 2 below and FLORENCE, §III, 2(i)). Benedetto da Maiano and his brother Giuliano da Maiano (*see* MAIANO, DA, (1) and (2)), for example, executed the inlaid cabinets in the sacristy of Florence Cathedral and the door and ceiling (1476–81) of the Sala dell'Udienza of the Palazzo della Signoria (now Palazzo Vecchio). In 1588 Ferdinando I, Grand Duke of Tuscany, established the Galleria dei Lavori, enlarging and reorganizing the group of craftsmen assembled by Francesco I, and this specialized in the production of pietre dure. (It was later, in 1860, named the Opificio delle Pietre Dure.) The first artist in charge of the factory was Bernardo Buontalenti, but it became especially important in the 17th century (*see* §3 below). The del Tasso family, which began working towards the end of the 15th century in Benedetto's workshop, and took it over after his death, produced a number of significant works. The head of the family, Chimenti or Clemente *il vecchio* (1430–1516), produced furniture for Florentine churches together with his sons Leonardo (1466–?1500) and Zanobi (1469–1511). One of Chimenti's two brothers, Domenico *il vecchio* (1440–1508), executed some wood panels in 1475 for the Palazzo della Signoria. From 1488 he was active in Perugia, where, between 1490 and 1493, he carved the tribune, chair back and bench in the Sala dell'Udienza of the Collegio del Cambio. This work contained a variety of decorative motifs that would inspire wood-workers in Tuscany and Umbria for the next 50 years. Among the numerous family descendants, GIOVAN BATTISTA DI MARCO DEL TASSO carved the timber ceiling (*c.* 1550) of the Biblioteca Medicea-Laurenziana, Florence, after the designs of Michelangelo and decorated a number of rooms in the Palazzo Vecchio, displaying skill and decorative virtuosity in a technique that had elements of both engraving and carving.

In Siena, throughout the 15th century and part of the 16th, furniture and particularly cassoni were decorated with either pastiglia or paintings of secular subjects. The search for superficial, delicate effects and dense carving, as well as the free translation of grotesque motifs, is typical of Sienese art. In particular they characterize the work of Antonio Barilli (1453–?1529), who carved the choir of the S Giovanni Chapel in Siena Cathedral, which was then transferred to the Chiesa dell'Assunta in San Quirico d'Orcia, and the doors of the Vatican loggia in Rome. The quality of carving in Siena was very high throughout the 16th century, as can be seen in various pieces of furniture where the decoration is expressed as an ordered architectonic scheme.

Renaissance decorative motifs spread to Umbrian craftsmen through the collaboration between an inlayer from the Marches, Mariotto de Pesaro, and the Tuscan carvers Giusto da Incisa and Giovanni da Fiesole (*fl* 1472). The best examples of the new style in Umbria can be seen in the study (*c.* 1480) of the Palazzo Ducale in Gubbio and in the intarsia work of Giuliano da Maiano and Domenico del Tasso *il vecchio*, which influenced ANTONIO BENCIV-ENNI. In 1508 Bencivenni executed the intarsia work in the Sala dell'Udienza of the Collegio del Cambio in Perugia, which was imitated in numerous Umbrian cassoni. Also based on Tuscan models are the cabinets (1494) of Perugia Cathedral, the lectern (1492–7) of S Domenico in Gubbio and the later works of the inlayers Giovan Battista Bastone (*fl* 1505–30) from Perugia and Antonio Senaca, active during the first part of the 16th century.

Craftsmen from northern Italy helped to spread a type of intarsia similar to that of the Lendinara family, as

77. Chair, walnut, 1054×533 mm, from Venice, 16th century (London, Victoria and Albert Museum)

inlaid wardrobes (*c.* 1545–54) of the sacristy of Spoleto Cathedral, the doors of which are also decorated with painted figures by Francesco Nardini (*fl* 1550–60).

Domestic furniture known to be by Umbrian craftsmen is rare. Generally it has a clear architectonic form and is richly carved. An election ballot-box (Gubbio, Pal. Com.) shows Tuscan influence, as do stools and various cassoni, including a dowry chest (Perugia, G.N. Umbria) that is supported by sphinxes and decorated with satyrs, leaf volutes and other motifs, as well as with intarsia that displays more energy than Tuscan examples. Tuscan models were adopted for dressers, which were decorated with intricate carvings and grotesque masks on the doors. Venetian influence is also present in some cassoni and chairs with twisted bands of curls in the backs.

In Piedmont, at the end of the 15th century, the most common decorative motif on dressers, wardrobes, cassoni and doors was the 'pergamena' motif, copied from French furniture, which sometimes also included geometric braids, roses, stars and hearts. The carvings were often combined with plaques of wrought iron, and the hinges became decorative elements as they did in Emilia and some transalpine regions. Examples include the cassone (1468) with the Savoy and Piosassco coats of arms, the cassone with the coat of arms of the Challant family and the doors from the Valle d'Aosta (all Turin, Mus. Civ. A. Ant.).

In Liguria a flourishing aristocracy commissioned numerous pieces of furniture: the earliest extant domestic furniture dates to the mid-16th century. In 1514, however, Anselmo Fornari (active 1470–1521) from Castelnuovo Scrivia is known to have worked on the choir of S Lorenzo in Genoa. In the early 16th century domestic furniture arrived from Spain and Flanders, which influenced the style of Genoese furniture. Domenico da Vernio completed several cassoni in this period, and Perino del Vaga designed some dowry chests for Andrea Doria. Inlaid furniture was produced by Andrea de' Rocchi and Elia de' Rocchi (1500–22), who also carved the tarsia of Savona Cathedral. The Calvi family built elaborate organ cases, and the Garibaldi constructed frames for altarpieces, while the work of Filippo Santacroce (*d* 1609), the greatest Genoese carver of the 16th century, showed signs of Roman and Tuscan influence as can be seen in the choir of S Ambrogio. Around 1560 the first *bambocci* style chests-of-drawers appeared, characterized by a wealth of high-relief decoration composed of putti, caryatids and heads, which were also used to disguise the handles.

In Lombardy the art of wood intarsia reached its height at the end of the 15th century. The craftsmen who worked during the second half of the century include Lorenzo di Odrisio and Giacomo del Maino (*fl* 1469–1502), who worked in the Carthusian monastery in Pavia, and Baldino di Surso (*fl* 1477), who worked in S Michele in Pavia and in Piedmont. In Pavia, Giovanni Pietro Donati (active 1484–1516) and Giovanni Ambrogio Donati (*fl* 1484–97) executed (1484) the choir of S Francesco, where animals and plants are depicted in a highly stylized manner. In Cremona, Giovanni Maria Platina (*c.* 1455–1500) executed a monumental wardrobe (1477; Cremona, Mus. Civ. Ala Ponzone) for the sacristy and the choir of the cathedral (1482–9). Two of the most famous Italian inlayers were born in Bergamo and Brescia: Brother Damiano (*c.* 1480–

exemplified in the work of Andrea Campano from Modena who executed (1530–34) the choir of S Lorenzo in Spello with inlaid figures of saints and town views. The Bergamesque intarsia of S Maria Maggiore, Florence, drawn by Lorenzo Lotto, is clearly echoed in the choir doors (completed 1536) of S Pietro in Perugia by Damiano da Bergamo (*c.* 1490–1549). The choir-stalls (1526–35) of this latter church represent the most ambitious work of the 16th century, executed by various masters from Tuscany, Lombardy and other regions, led by Bernardino Antonibi from Perugia. They have very refined carving using grotesque motifs, which were taken up in the intarsia work by Battista Bolognese (*fl* 1535–7) and others. During this period the Umbrian masters achieved an independent style, and their carving exhibits an eye for detail and a skill that sometimes surpasses their Florentine counterparts. Carving and inserted paintings were often combined, a local characteristic that was already under way at the end of the 15th century. One example of this is the carved and

1542) and RAFFAELLO DA BRESCIA, who helped revive the technique of intarsia and promote its popularity. Cassoni, the only Lombardian furniture known from the end of the 15th century, were sometimes decorated with geometric inlay, but more often with pastiglia or paintings. However, during the 16th century, they were increasingly decorated with carvings of plant motifs and with ever-smaller pieces of inlay. The most famous carvers at this time were the Taurini family, originally from France, who worked in Lombardy from the mid-16th century until well into the 17th century. In Valtellina, carving was influenced by Bergamo, where a particular type of chest-of-drawers was developed with four drawers with boxwood and maple inlaid panels; this differed from the Mantuan model, which was made in softwood with three drawers. Some of the greatest Renaissance carvers were trained in Piacenza, Emilia, such as Domenico da Piacenza (*fl* 1467–88), creator of the choir (1467–77) of S Giustina in Padua, decorated with intarsia in perspective; Matteo Grattoni (*fl* 1550–1601), who carved the choir of S Maria di Campagna, near Piacenza; and Pasquale Testa (?1524–1587), who is recorded as working for Ottavio Farnese, 2nd Duke of Parma and Piacenza.

If in the Veneto during the 15th century there was a preference for carving furniture with such Gothic motifs as roses, and double- and lozenge-shaped openings, in the 16th century, thanks to the newly established cultural ties with Florence, Rome and the Low Countries, the local decorative repertory gained a wealth of new additions. Sixteenth-century Venetian furniture is actually very similar to Tuscan furniture, from which it derives its balanced architectonic design and classical decorative motifs. Jacopo Sansovino played a crucial role in this respect; his work spread the use of such decorative motifs as festoons, female heads framed with veils, and tablets with volutes, which were very popular and adopted even in cabinet-making. Apart from painted furniture by such well-known artists as Bonifazio de' Pitati and Andrea Schiavone, various types of furniture were decorated with intarsia, including the wardrobes and the choir (1494–9) of S Maria in Organo in Verona by Fra GIOVANNI DA VERONA, which constitute the finest examples of this craft in the Veneto area. Another notable piece of ecclesiastical furniture is the reliquary chest of Padua Cathedral, which an anonymous local craftsman carved with grotesque motifs. As for secular furniture, the cassone played an important part, even though wardrobes, chests-of-drawers and tables were beginning to acquire greater significance. During the first half of the 16th century the cassone was linked to the 15th-century types decorated with pastiglia or inlaid in the *certosina* style, but towards the middle of the century more elaborate forms with intricate carving and wooden panels depicting jousts or courtly scenes in pyrography appeared.

BIBLIOGRAPHY

F. Schottmuller: *Wohnungskultur und Möbel der italienischen Renaissance* (Stuttgart, 1921)
M. Tinti: *Il mobilio fiorentino* (Milan and Rome, 1929)
V. Pagliuzzi: 'Mobili del medioevo: Il cassone la cassapanca, il seggiolone dal secolo XII al secolo XV', *A. Illus.*, i (1968), pp. 38–42
C. Alberici: *Il mobile lombardo* (Milan, 1969)
A. González-Palacios: *Il mobile nei secoli*, i (Milan, 1969)
T. Miotti: *Il mobile friulano* (Milan, 1970)
M. Trionfi Honorati: *Il mobile marchigiano* (Milan, 1971)
L. Bandera: *Il mobile emiliano* (Milan, 1972)
G. Cantelli: *Il mobile umbro* (Milan, 1973)
C. Alberici: *Il mobile veneto* (Milan, 1980)
G. Manni: *Mille mobili emiliani* (Modena, 1980)
A. González-Palacios, ed.: *Antiquariato: Enciclopedia delle arti decorative* (Milan, 1981)
M. Boroli and S. Broggi: *Il mobile del rinascimento: Italia* (Novara, 1985)

ENRICO COLLE

3. 1600–1799. During the 17th and 18th centuries Italy existed as a collection of states, each with a separate identity—some independent, some subjected to other states and some ruled by foreign monarchies. Each one had its own court and its own nobility, members of which sought to demonstrate their status in the appearance of their residences. Rivalry between them stimulated the demand for furniture.

The furniture-makers belonged to organizations that, although they no longer had any political influence, retained their religious and charitable functions, and they maintained standards by admitting as members only those who had served an apprenticeship and passed tests of proficiency. They might also initiate such protectionist measures as the higher taxes and limited rights for foreign artisans imposed in Genoa or the expulsion of foreign workers from Venice during the mid-18th century. Within these organizations the craftsmen had different names in the various dialects: cabinetmakers (*ebanisti*) were called *rimesseri* in Venice, while joiners (*falegnami*) were known as *minusieri* in Turin, *marangoni da noghera* in Venice and *bancalari* in Genoa.

The development of furniture types followed a fairly similar pattern throughout Italy, although techniques and forms of decoration varied from one region to another. Tables in the 17th century were monumental, and the most elaborate ones had supports of gilded bronze and tops of marble, hardstone or scagliola; console tables had figurative supports, usually of carved and gilded wood. In the early 18th century the supports took on more fluent lines and were enriched with lacquer and inlay, while in the latter decades of the century the revival of antique styles encouraged the use of marble bases.

In the 17th century in Italy there was a development of the cabinet inlaid with precious metals and hardstones. The largest and most expensive mirrors were produced in Venice, although by the early 18th century most cities produced their own. The glasses were set in splendid frames, which sometimes received imaginative treatment, as in the case of the flowers painted by MARIO DEI FIORI in Rome to conceal the joins between the plates of glass. Clocks in the 17th century were generally incorporated into other pieces of furniture, such as cabinets. During the second half of the 17th century the three Campani brothers, Dietro Tommaso, Matteo and Giuseppe, were active in Rome. The clocks made by them were famous for their movements, known as *silenziosi*, *notturni* or *della morte*, in which an internal light enabled the dial to be read during the night. The dials were decorated by well-known artists, such as Carlo Maratti. In the 18th century many of the clocks had long cases or were set into sculptural groups or a Neo-classical temple of a size that permitted them to be used as mantel clocks.

In Rome (*see* ROME, §IV, 3) the emergence of the Baroque style during the 17th century can be attributed in part to the popes who were generous patrons of the arts—Clement VIII, Paul V, Urban VIII, Innocent X and Alexander VII. The decoration of the Vatican palaces, as well as the villas and other properties that belonged to the cardinals and their families, created a tradition of ostentatious splendour. The masters who worked for them adopted the Baroque style not only for ambitious projects but for the design of furniture as well. In the early years of the 17th century the austerity imposed by the Counter-Reformation is to be found in the severe and architectural style of the sacristy cupboards in the Jesuit churches of Il Gesù and S Ignazio; by the third decade of the century Gianlorenzo Bernini, the creator of the great baldacchino in St Peter's (1623–34), had designed and inspired a number of pieces of furniture that reject all sense of geometry and in which the carving, often gilded, dominates to the extent that they may be regarded as sculptures. Among Bernini's many followers was Johann Paul Schor (*see* SCHOR, (2)), who had great inventive talent; others imitated the master's bizarre forms, rendering them heavier. ALESSANDRO ALGARDI made designs for furniture that were as sumptuous as those of Bernini but tempered with a greater degree of classicism. The Baroque lasted for a long time in Rome, gradually becoming more ponderous to the point where it approached the grotesque around the turn of the century. It then became lighter in the 18th century, acquiring the graceful lines and decorative detail characteristic of the *Barocchetto*, the Italian version of the Rococo.

In 1769 GIOVANNI BATTISTA PIRANESI, in his folio *Diverse maniere d'adornare i cammini* (see fig. 78), codified his extremely sumptuous version of Neo-classicism. Piranesi's designs were to be influential throughout Europe; in Rome, under Pope Pius VI, they attained great grace and refinement in the work of Luigi Valadier and Giuseppe Valadier (*see* VALADIER, (1)), who were responsible for some of the furnishings in the Vatican, and in that of ANTONIO ASPRUCCI, who redecorated the interior of the Villa Borghese.

The principal technique employed in Rome was carving, while inlay was almost exclusively the work of such craftsmen from the north as Giacomo Herman (1615–85). Bronze was widely used, especially for the supports of tables and for the borders of marble tops, and gilding was much in evidence. Painted finishes, at which Mario dei Fiori excelled, were more common than lacquering. For table-tops marble was extensively used, especially the coloured marbles that were still to be found among the ancient ruins.

In Florence the grand ducal factory, the Galleria dei Lavori (*see* §2 above), established in 1588, was very important in the 17th century. Within the Galleria a hardstone workshop was set up in 1604 (*see* FLORENCE, §III, 2(i)). Characteristic of the work produced by the Galleria were ebony cabinets embellished with pietra dura decoration in naturalistic designs and gilt bronze. Chests, stools and other types of furniture were made in the same manner. Some of the pieces were presented by the Medici as gifts to foreign rulers and their ambassadors, and some have remained in the possession of their descendants. The

78. Giovanni Battista Piranesi: design from his *Diverse maniere d'adornare i cammini* (Rome, 1769), pl. 63

Galleria dei Lavori was the inspiration for the Gobelins factory, founded by the French king Louis XIV, where the Florentine DOMENICO CUCCI—renowned for his cabinets decorated with pietre dure—worked from 1644, having taken with him to France the secrets of his trade.

Another form of decoration associated with Florence in the 17th century is carving (typically of volutes and masks), superimposed on a structure that is strongly architectural in character. With the extinction of the ruling Medici dynasty in 1737 Florence gave up its role as innovator in the field of furniture. Lucca established a reputation in the 18th century for the production of lacquered and gilded pieces, influenced by French Louis XV and Louis XVI furniture. These styles co-existed with a fashion for open splat-back chairs based on English models.

Lombard furniture in the 17th and 18th centuries, despite the fact that the state was a Spanish dependency from 1535 until 1703, had affinities with other Italian and French models. Intarsia, popular in the previous period, was enriched with figurative motifs and by the use of bone and ivory, and characteristic pieces are cabinets inlaid with ivory, tortoiseshell and hardstones. Associated with furniture production in Bergamo and Brescia at the end of the 17th century is a chest ornamented with strips of walnut veneer and raised black borders. At Rovetta, near

Bergamo, the Fantoni workshop had been active since 1450 and with ANDREA FANTONI reached its height with the creation of furniture decorated with carving and inlaid with fantastic figures.

In 1706 Lombardy came under Austrian rule, and the resulting increase in wealth encouraged a demand for furniture, especially pieces in the Piedmontese, Venetian, Genoese and, above all, French manner. Neo-classicism reached Milan in the 1770s, when Giuseppe Piermarini was commissioned to remodel the Palazzo Ducale (now Palazzo Reale). GIUSEPPE MAGGIOLINI was among those who collaborated on this project, and he became known for the technical perfection of his work and the fine quality of the materials he employed in his inlaid furniture—especially his chests, commodes and game-tables (e.g. commode, 1790; Milan, Mus. Civ. Milano). Designs in the most fashionable taste—Neo-classical chinoiserie—were prepared for his inlay work by such artists as Andrea Appiani and Giuseppe Levati (1738–1828).

Piedmont prospered under the Savoy dynasty, and from the end of the 17th century many splendid pieces of furniture in the Rococo style were commissioned for the court in Turin and the nobility. Luigi Prinotto (fl 1712–76) is famed for his desks and stools (e.g. Turin, Pal. Reale) in the French manner inlaid with ivory decoration showing scenes of domestic and popular life and representations of historic events. The same technique was employed with unprecedented richness by Pietro Piffetti (1700–77), whose furniture is inlaid with wood, mother-of-pearl, ivory and tortoiseshell in complicated designs that resemble embroidery (e.g. cabinet, 1740–50, London, V&A; see fig. 79). The tradition of carving, relegated to the provinces during the 17th century, was reintroduced in an elegant Neo-classical form by GIUSEPPE MARIA BONZANIGO.

In Genoa at the turn of the 17th century furniture design was influenced by the work of the painters and draughtsmen Domenico Piola and Gregorio de' Ferrari. In the 18th century the city was distinguished for the production of fine veneered furniture. Typical of Genoa is decoration comprising floral designs within frames executed in lacquer in pastel colours, thinly applied so that it allows the wood to show through.

Venetian luxury furniture made in the early 17th century remained Mannerist in character, with projecting cornices and cartouches and heads in high relief. The style of carving changed towards the mid-century with the arrival of the Baroque, exemplified in the fantastic figures created by Francesco Pianta the younger (c. 1632–92). Also worthy of note is the carver Giacomo Piazzetta (see PIAZZETTA, (1)), some of whose decorative work for the Scuola di S Maria della Carità is in the Cappella del Rosario of SS Giovanni e Paolo. The outstanding craftsman at the turn of the century was Andrea Brustolon. For Pietro Venier he carved in boxwood and ebony a set of 40 pieces of furniture (Venice, Ca' Rezzonico; for illustration see BRUSTOLON, ANDREA), in which the Baroque idiom is coloured by exoticism in the figures of Moors, which function as supports, while cherubs and divinities are depicted among branches and rocks.

During the 18th century Venice was a favourite destination for tourists; even so, the city was economically in

79. Cabinet by Pietro Piffetti, mother-of-pearl veneered base and gilded bronze fittings, 1422×685×572 mm, 1740–50 (London, Victoria and Albert Museum)

decline. The *marangoni* proved themselves inventive in creating sophisticated-looking furniture with inexpensive materials, including lacquer, which here was often a painted gesso surface that had been varnished. The still cheaper imitation known as *lacca povera* was produced by decorating the piece with transfers, which were then varnished. Venetian inlayers made use of inexpensive wood, including walnut, and gilt-bronze mounts were imitated in carved and gilded wood. The bulbous forms of the furniture retained their popularity long into the 18th century, and Neo-classicism was slow to establish itself in Venice.

In Emilia 17th-century furniture-makers continued to work to the heavy designs of the previous century, in which decoration was limited to geometric carving and applied metalwork. Some lighter pieces were banded with walnut. In 1739 Louise-Elisabeth, daughter of Louis XV, married Philip of Bourbon, Duke of Parma, bringing Parisian taste with her to Parma.

In Modena Francesco I d'Este, Duke of Modena, began in 1634 the building of the Palazzo Ducale. He admired the Baroque and asked Bernini to send some of his pupils to work at the court in Modena. The technique of scagliola spread rapidly from Carpi to Modena and towards the end of the century to the rest of Emilia. During the 18th century lacquering, gilding and painting were all practised, as well as veneering. Neo-classicism was represented here by the adoption of Maggiolini's style.

Naples in the 17th century produced ebony cabinets with inlay and ornamentation in bronze, ivory and tortoise-shell; other pieces were painted or lacquered. Characteristically Neapolitan are small desks decorated with panels of painted glass and carriages and sedan chairs embellished with gilt-wood carvings and valuable textiles. In 1734 Naples became independent under Charles VII (later Charles III of Spain). He built a number of residences, at Portici, Capodimonte, Caserta and elsewhere. During his reign factories were established for work in pietre dure and crystal and for the manufacture of porcelain. This high level of specialization led to the development of such forms of decoration as *piquet*—tortoiseshell veneer inlaid with threads of gold and silver and with mother-of-pearl. The rediscovery of Pompeii and Herculaneum, and the production of the nine illustrated folios of *Antichità di Ercolano esposte* (1757–96), inspired in Naples from the 1770s an archaeological approach to the design of furniture.

BIBLIOGRAPHY

G. Morazzoni: *Il mobile genovese* (Milan, 1949)
C. Alberici: *Il mobile lombardo* (Milan, 1969)
C. Lizzani: *Il mobile romano* (Milan, 1970)
A. Putaturo Murano: *Il mobile napoletano del settecento* (Naples, 1977)
C. Alberici: *Il mobile veneto* (Milan, 1980)
A. González-Palacios: *Il tempio del gusto: Le arti decorative in Italia fra classicismi e barocco: Roma e il regno delle due Sicilie*, 2 vols (Milan, 1984)
R. Antonetto: *Minusieri ed ebanisti del Piemonte: Storia e immagini del mobile piemontese, 1636–1844* (Turin, 1985)
A. González-Palacios: *Il tempio del gusto: Le arti decorative in Italia fra classicismi e barocco: La Toscana e l'Italia settentrionale*, 2 vols (Milan, 1986)
G. Manni: *Mobili in Emilia: Con una indagine sulla civiltà dell'arredo alla corte degli Estensi* (Modena, 1986)

DANIELA DI CASTRO MOSCATI

4. 1800–1900. The Neo-classical style that had characterized the decoration and furnishings of Italian palaces at the end of the 18th century moved towards the contemporary French Directoire and Empire styles at the beginning of the 19th century. In Milan the workshop of GIUSEPPE MAGGIOLINI continued its activity under the patronage of the Viceroy, Prince Eugène de Beauharnais. This workshop did not, however, conform to the Empire style favoured by the Napoleonic court and was gradually overtaken by cabinetmakers and wood-carvers more attuned to the new demands. Marquetry furniture produced by Maggiolini and other northern Italian craftsmen continued to be produced in large numbers, although it was superseded by ornament in gilt bronze, for which the foundry of the brothers Francesco and Luigi Manfredini was renowned (e.g. three-legged table in gilt bronze, lapis lazuli and gilt silver, 1813; London, V&A). Carved furniture, painted white and gilt, remained fashionable in Milan, differing only in the motifs used, military trophies, Egyptian motifs and allegorical Greek and Roman themes

becoming typical (e.g. console table in wood carved with ram's head and medallion motifs, early 19th century; Milan, Castello Sforzesco). Much furniture of this kind was designed by the architect Luigi Canonica, an apprentice and follower of Piermarini, and the architect most favoured by the Napoleonic administration. Canonica's work (e.g. salon suite, Milan, Pal. Reale, depositi) shows a clear stylistic link to that of Percier and Fontaine in France.

In Venice and the Veneto, furniture that had previously been lacquered, or veneered in burr walnut, was now usually painted in polychrome, with gilt detail (e.g. salon suite in wood painted wtih Classical figures on a black ground, 1830s; Venice, Fond. Querini-Stampalia). Chests, night-tables, sideboards and small tables, often of mahogany veneer, were inlaid with such light-coloured woods as rose-wood, elm or cherry that imitated gilt-bronze mounts. There was little figurative marquetry work produced, as Venice, unlike other Italian centres, lacked the native tradition. Giuseppe Borsato (1770–1849), an important designer, produced decorations and furnishings for the royal palaces and those of the Venetian aristocracy for more than 40 years. These designs were published in 1831 in the renowned *Opera ornamentale*. Antonio Basoli (1774–1843) had worked in Bologna since the last years of the 18th century. His furniture designs reflect the influence of Neo-classicism, with additional elements of the exotic, Picturesque and Egyptian. He was one of the first to revive the Gothic style, although this had already been taken up by Bolognese stage designers, who had been quick to adopt neo-Gothic and neo-Egyptian motifs. Basoli also published an important collection of engravings, which showed not only decorations for rooms, stage sets and historical paintings, but also furniture and utensils.

Florence and Tuscany were the most active centres for the development of the Empire style. A major factor in this was Napoleon's sister, Elisa, Grand Duchess of Tuscany, who carried out a large programme of refurbishment of palaces in Lucca and Florence. She not only imported furniture from France, but also invited the French cabinetmaker Jean Baptiste Youf (1762–1838) to Lucca, where he settled in 1805. Youf made numerous pieces in the Empire style for the refurbishment of the Palazzo Pitti and other former residences of the Medici family. Youf's name often appears in the catalogues of exhibitions in Lucca, where between 1808 and 1812 he showed beds, tables, desks and dressing-tables in mahogany mounted with gilt bronze by the Valadier family. Pietro Massagli, Francesco Beccari, Giuseppe Beccari and Anastasio Barsanti were Italian craftsmen who worked with Youf in Lucca. Giuseppe Benvenuti, Giuseppe Colzi and Giovanni Socci (*fl* 1807–*c.* 1839) were active in Florence. Socci produced a mechanical writing-desk (1807; Florence, Pitti) that opened to reveal the chair, a type that was copied many times. Jacopo Ciacchi made two nighttables and a series of drum-shaped stools for Grand Duchess Elisa and, with Colzi, the furniture for Queen Mary Louise's bathroom in the Quartiere dei Volterrano in the Palazzo Pitti (e.g. commode; Florence, Pitti). Paolo Sani produced many of the console tables and chairs that can still be seen in the Palazzo Pitti, and the bronzeworker Pietro Corsini supplied most of the gilt-bronze mounts on the chests, mirrors and secrétaires commissioned by Grand

Duchess Elisa and later by Ferdinand III of Tuscany (*reg* 1790–1801; 1814–24).

In Siena the Empire style was skilfully interpreted in the furnishings of Agostino Fantastici (1782–1845), but Rome continued to produce furniture that remained stylistically linked to the 18th century. In the Kingdom of the Two Sicilies the royal palaces of Naples and Caserta and the Villa di Pórtici were refurnished in the Empire style under the Napoleonic regime. The work of the leading Parisian furniture-maker, Georges Jacob, had a strong influence, not only through a number of his pieces sent from France, but also through the craftsmen who came from France with Joachim Murat, King of Naples (*reg* 1808–15). Many of the pieces showing French influence can still be seen in the Palazzo Reale, Caserta, and the Palazzo Reale, Naples; they show the taste for rich decoration in bronze or gilt wood. This Neapolitan taste continued after the Napoleonic period, as seen in the work of the architect Antonio Niccolini, who had worked in Naples from 1807, and who produced a less rigidly academic and more eclectic Neo-classical language, as in, for example, the console tables, settees and chairs in the king's private apartment in the Palazzo Reale, Caserta. In these pieces the typical Empire frame is embellished with carved volutes of acanthus leaves, which look forward to the bold decoration of the neo-Baroque style.

In Italy, as in the rest of Europe, the Neo-classical style continued to be favoured by the restored monarchies. In Naples, Florence, Siena and Milan, until *c.* 1830, carved furniture, of mahogany or other woods, continued to be decorated with gilt-bronze mounts in the form of lion-heads, eagles and similar ornament derived from Percier and Fontaine. In Lombardy and Piedmont, Neo-classical motifs can be seen in the marquetry work of the Cremonese cabinetmaker and wood-carver Giovanni Mafezzoli (1776–1818), a pupil of Maggiolini, and in the marquetry pictures representing views of famous monuments, prisons and architectural perspectives produced by Ignazio Revelli (1756–1836) and his brother Luigi Revelli (1756–1856). Pelagio Palagi produced for Charles-Albert, King of Sardinia, the extraordinary furnishings of the Palazzo Reale in Turin and the Castello di Racconigi. Palagi employed several Piedmontese craftsmen to execute his furniture designs, among the most important of whom was the cabinetmaker and wood-carver Gabriele Cappello, known as Moncalvo, who made (1835–9) the furniture of the Gabinetto Etrusco in the Castello di Racconigi and the exquisite neo-Grecian pieces that furnished Charles-Albert's Medagliere in the Palazzo Reale, Turin.

In Liguria the workshop of the Descalzi brothers was distinguished for the production of the chiavari chair (Turin, Castello d'Agliè). This light and functional form was very popular throughout the 19th century. In the Veneto the furniture made by the architect Giuseppe Jappelli is worthy of note. The influence of the Biedermeier style and the English Regency and Sheraton styles was reflected in the work of Piero Moschini, who was active in Cremona during the first half of the 19th century. In Florence, the native 17th-century marquetry technique was revived by the brothers Luigi and Angiolo Falcini, in whose workshop Giovan Battista Gatti (1816–89), who worked in Faenza, was trained. In Rome, Florence and

Livorno, Federico Lancetti produced marquetry in mother-of-pearl, metals and coloured woods (e.g. table, Florence, Pitti); this art was passed to his apprentice Alessandro Monteneri of Perugia.

The introduction of mechanical production of furniture coincided with the rise of the Biedermeier style, which did not encourage the development of individual production of furniture. The opening of craft schools and the Accademia di Belle Arti in Florence, promoted by Pierre-Léopold of Lorraine to encourage local industry, had favoured such young cabinetmakers as the Sienese Angiolo Barbetti (1805–73) and Antonio Manetti (1805–87). During the post-Napoleonic period, these craftsmen developed a style based on traditional Renaissance ornament. This was seen as a nationalist style, in opposition to the French neo-Baroque. With the unification of Italy (1861) architects, designers and furniture-makers joined in the search for a national style. In Florence a reinterpretation of Renaissance elements, developed in a more monumental and exuberant manner, was proposed by Luigi Frullini (1839–1911; see fig. 80), Egisto Gaiani (1832–90), Francesco Marini (1822–99), Ferdinando Romanelli (1839–1911) and Rinaldo Barbetti (1830–1904). In northern Italy, particularly in Milan, Ferdinando Pogliani (1832–99) produced furniture with ivory and pietra dura inlays on an

80. Cupboard by Luigi Frullini, carved walnut, 2.48×1.37×0.58 m, *c.* 1878 (Paris, Musée d'Orsay)

ebony ground, thus reviving an art for which Milan had been famous in the 16th century. Such workshops as those of Giuseppe Speluzzi, Pietro Zaneletti, Carlo Zen and Carlo Bugatti (*see* BUGATTI, (1)) were more eclectic, searching for new decorative ideas and materials. Their furniture, with its Moorish character and its revolutionary vocabulary of motifs and materials, marked a watershed between Eclecticism and modernism.

During the last quarter of the century Besarel (1829–1902), active in Venice, and Salvatre Pagano and Luigi Mastrodonato, working in Naples, produced furniture showing a revived interest in Baroque carving, with complicated allegories giving way to the functional role. At the end of the century Italian furniture, as seen in the international exhibitions, was produced mainly for a bourgeois clientele.

BIBLIOGRAPHY

A. Basoli: *Compartimenti di camere per uso degli amatori e studenti delle belle arti* (Bologna, 1827)
——: *Raccolta di diversi ornamenti per uso degli amatori e studiosi delle belle arti del disegno* (Bologna, 1838)
G. Morazzoni: *Il mobile neoclassico italiano* (Milan, 1955)
C. Alberici: *Il mobile lombardo* (Milan, 1969)
A. González-Palacios: *Il mobile nei secoli*, 3 vols (Milan, 1969)
C. Garzya: *Interni neoclassici a Napoli* (Naples, 1978)
D. Worsdale: 'Later Neo-classical Florentine Furniture at Palazzo Pitti', *Furn. Hist.* (1978), pp. 49–57
C. Alberici: *Il mobile veneto* (Milan, 1980)
G. Cirillo and G. Godi: *Il mobile a Parma fra barocco e romanticismo* (Parma, 1983)
E. Cozzi: *Il mobile dell'ottocento* (Novara, 1984)
R. Antonetto: *Minusieri ed ebanisti del Piemonte* (Chieri, 1985)
A. González-Palacios: *Il tempio del gusto: La Toscana e l'Italia settentrionale* (Milan, 1986)
E. Colle: 'La culla del principe di Napoli e alcune note sull'intaglio napoletano dell'800', *Ant. Viva*, i (1987), pp. 46–53
——: 'Ebanisti e mobilieri toscani dell'ottocento', *L'artigianato del legno* (exh. cat., Prato, Mus. Com., 1988)
——: 'Monumenti domestici all'Esposizione fiorentina del 1861', *Artista* (1990), pp. 110–19
C. Paolini, A. Ponte and O. Selvafolta: *Il bello 'ritrovato'* (Novara, 1990)

5. AFTER 1900. The Art Nouveau style was slower to find acceptance in Italy than in other European countries, although it had no lack of supporters. Italy was, however, still divided by wide cultural, regional and economic differences, which tended to inhibit the spread of the new ideas. New designs appeared in Turin at the Prima Esposizione Internazionale d'Arte Decorativa Moderna of 1902, where the latest work in the Art Nouveau style could be seen emerging from the Martinotti furniture factory (active from 1831 in Turin) and the Aemilia Ars group (active 1898–1903). Work by the Milanese cabinet-makers Carlo Bugatti and Eugenio Quarti and the Palermo architect Ernesto Basile was also on show.

The new furniture made use of Art Nouveau decorative motifs, which appeared in carved work and in veneering and marquetry using such materials as bone, mother-of-pearl, tortoiseshell, tin, lead, parchment or brass. The furniture of Carlo Bugatti (*see* BUGATTI, (1)) was transformed with great freedom and inventiveness into bizarrely coloured interpretations of the Moorish style. After Bugatti moved to Paris *c.* 1904, the most prestigious furniture-maker in Milan was undoubtedly EUGENIO QUARTI. His use of precious materials and quality finishing justified his title as the 'goldsmith of furniture-makers' (e.g. piece with

mirror and shelves, 1900; see O. Selvafolta, *Il mobile del Novecento Liberty*, p. 70).

At the turn of the century a resurgence took place in the decorative and industrial arts in Palermo, steered chiefly by the architect Ernesto Basile (*see* BASILE, (2)) and the furniture-maker Golia Ducrot (1867–1943). Their furnishings were designed to harmonize with the interiors for which they were produced. To meet the demands of their wealthy international clients, Basile and Ducrot produced richly carved and inlaid furniture, but their work for more bourgeois clients, for example the oak study displayed at the Esposizione in Turin in 1902, was distinguished by the simplicity of line that enabled mass-production. Other producers adopted Art Nouveau forms, including the Aemilia Ars cooperative in Bologna and the factories of Carlo Zen (1851–1918) in Milan, Vittorio Valabrega in Turin (factory active *c.* 1900), Alberto Issel in Genoa, and Cutler and Girard in Florence.

Although work by the Futurists Giacomo Balla (e.g. cupboard for dining-room, 1918; priv. col.; see 1986 exh. cat., p. 323), Fortunato Depero and Enrico Prampolini remains an isolated phenomenon in comparison to industrial production, their experiments influenced later generations of architects and designers engaged in the planning of Rationalist interiors. For them each piece of furniture was seen as a 'plastic complex' that interacts with the surrounding space and the people who inhabit it, and thus assumes dynamic forms corresponding to human functions. After World War I a nationalist current that stressed the ethical content inherent in the Italian folk tradition was represented by the architect Marcello Piacentini. With Gustavo Giovannoni he exhibited three rooms containing traditional craftsmanship at the Mostra d'Arte Italiana in Rome in 1921, showing work by craftsmen from Emilia, Abruzzi, Sardinia, Siena and Amalfi. Duilio Cambellotti (1876–1960), on the other hand, sought to use his own classical training in conjunction with the archaic culture of the Roman Campagna, and produced wooden curule chairs, benches and chests in bold, classical form with folk decoration (e.g. lectern (1929) and armchair (*c.* 1920); Milan, priv. col.; see 1980 exh. cat., p. 202).

In northern Italy the first to adopt the Art Deco style as practised in France were the Atelier Borsani (active post-World War I–1950s) in Varedo and the Monti workshop in Milan. In Trieste the Stuard establishment of Gustavo Pulitzer Finali (1887–1967) and Ceas was more influenced by Germany. A simplified classical trend, running concurrently with Art Deco, was represented by GIOVANNI MUZIO and GIO PONTI, for example. A liberal use was made of pilasters, capitals, columns and tympani in both furniture and interiors, producing unprecedented compositional clarity and rigorous symmetry. This classicism emerged strongly at the Monza Biennale of 1927, together with furniture in the Novecento style with its highly simplified, massive shapes relieved by the contrast of light and dark woods (see fig. 81) and by the decorative use of burr walnut, thuya and rose-wood veneers. At the Monza Biennale of 1930, tubular metal furniture appeared; many factories were subsequently established to produce this type of furniture, which had a widespread use. At the end of the 1930s new ideas emerged, for example the basket chair and thinner, splayed legs, while curved lines

81. Chest-of-drawers by Gio Ponti, *c.* 1930 (private collection)

reappeared, often accompanied by rich inlay work. Later furniture designers include members of the CASTIGLIONI family, CARLO MOLLINO and ETTORE SOTTSASS.

BIBLIOGRAPHY

R. Bossaglia: *Il mobile Liberty* (Novara, 1971)
F. Bologna: *Dalle arti minori all'industrial design: Storia di un' ideologia* (Bari, 1972)
R. Bossaglia: *Il Deco italiano: Fisionomia dello stile 1925 in Italia* (Milan, 1975)
M. C. Tonelli: *Eugenio e Mario Quarti: Dall'ebanisteria Liberty all' arredamento moderno* (Milan, 1980)
La metafisica, gli anni venti (exh. cat., ed. R. Barilli and F. Solmi; Bologna, 1980)
Mobili italiani anni trenta (exh. cat., ed. D. Riva and C. Tonelli; Milan, Pal. Reale; 1982)
I. De Guttry, M. P. Maino and M. Quesada: *Le arti minori d'autore in Italia dal 1900 al 1930* (Rome and Bari, 1985)
A. M. Rutta: *Arredi futuristi* (Palermo, 1985)
O. Selvafolta: *Il mobile del novecento Art Deco* (Novara, 1985)
——: *Il mobile del novecento Liberty* (Novara, 1985)
Futurismo e futuristi (exh. cat., Venice, 1986)
M. C. Tonelli Michail: *Il design in Italia, 1925–1943* (Rome and Bari, 1987)

ENRICO COLLE

VII. Ceramics.

1. Maiolica. 2. Porcelain.

1. MAIOLICA.

(i) Before 1500. (ii) 1500 and after.

(i) Before 1500. The oldest Italian maiolicas considered to be of artistic value date from the end of the 14th century (for earlier periods *see* ROME, ANCIENT, §X, 8 and EARLY CHRISTIAN AND BYZANTINE ART, §VII, 1). During excavations of the Forum Romanum, Rome's civic centre, examples of ceramics were found that can be dated to between the 9th and 12th century and have relief decoration and silica-alkaline glazes. The 13th-century maiolicas

were derived from these prototypes, and their style is described as 'archaic'. Recent studies have proved that the centres of production were not only in central Italy—Florence, Siena, Grosseto, Faenza, Rimini, Orvieto, Assisi, Todi, Rome and Valentano—but also in some northern areas, for example in the Veneto, as well as in southern Italy and the Italian islands.

The products from all these areas have a rather thin, off-white glaze and are generally decorated with manganese-brown designs and a copper-green ground; cobalt-blue and iron-yellow were also sometimes used. The decorative themes, which were derived from medieval iconography, consist of stylized animals, monsters taken from the Roman Bestiaries, coats of arms, Gothic calligraphy and floral, vegetal and geometric motifs (e.g. bowl, end of the 14th century; London, V&A). Human figures were only rarely represented. The forms included small bowls, large two-handled dishes, urns, pitchers and albarelli (e.g. of *c.* 1380–1420; London, BM). Maiolicas decorated with *sgraffito* designs were also produced during this first 'archaic' phase. The technique, long considered to be a speciality of Ferrara, was also adopted, although to a lesser extent, by the potters of Venice (*see* VENICE, §III, 2), Bologna (*see* BOLOGNA, §III), Padua and Calabria.

During the early 14th century there was a gradual evolution of the 'Archaic' style towards a more sophisticated form of decoration known as the 'Severe' style. The first phase is known as the 'green' family (1425–50). Compared with the earlier maiolicas these display a marked improvement in both glaze and decoration. The manganese-brown contours are better defined and more precise and prevented the colours from running. The ornamental elements were influenced by imported Hispano-Moresque wares, and the representations of people and animals were set against a ground of dotted elements or tiny flowers. The most highly valued maiolicas of this period are attributed to Florence and are characterized by their vitality and by the well-painted, rounded figures. A second, more or less contemporary group, is known as the 'relief-blue' family (1430–60) and includes large albarelli decorated with thickly applied blue and purple oak leaves, coats of arms, fantastic animals and, more rarely, human figures or representations of animals (see fig. 82). These maiolicas, which were for the most part produced in Tuscany, were also copied in such other Italian centres of production as Faenza. The 'Italo-Moresque' family (1450–80), known as such because of the less intense monochrome blue or polychrome decorations, were even more decisively Florentine and were strongly inspired by Islamic lustrewares (e.g. jug, c. 1460–80; Oxford, Ashmolean). Generally the use of turquoise or a yellow-green was intended to imitate

82. Maiolica albarello of the 'relief-blue' family, h. 328 mm, probably from Florence, 1448–51 (London, British Museum)

a metallic surface. This type of Italian maiolica is less highly valued than the preceding type because the decoration is less incisive and the motifs somewhat monotonous.

During the second half of the 14th century FAENZA became the most important centre of ceramic production, developing a distinctive figurative repertory. The town was under the protection of the Manfredi family (1334–1501). Here, and later in Tuscany and other areas in central Italy, new styles were developed during the second phase of the 'Severe' style. The 'Gothic-floral' and 'peacock-feather eye' families (1460–95) were developed at the same time. Their decorative elements were inspired by both Islamic and Greco-Roman art. The chromatic range became increasingly rich and more imaginative; blue remained predominant, while the manganese-brown became more red and was accompanied by lively touches of yellow and a brilliant green. The 'peacock-feather eye' decoration was apparently in homage to Cassandra Pavona, the beautiful mistress of Galeazzo Manfredi, Lord of Faenza (d 1480). An important work from this period is the tile pavement in the Vaselli Chapel in S Petronio in Bologna (see TILE, fig. 12). Executed by Pietro Andrea (fl 1487–1526) from Faenza in 1487, it is decorated with such motifs as 'Persian palmettes', a kind of stylized flower resembling a pine cone, the 'peacock-feather eye' and half-bust portraits. Judging from the few extant examples, other tile pavements in a similar style were also common in Neapolitan churches.

In addition to these decorative motifs blue tendrils and arabesques painted on a white ground were introduced at the end of the 15th century. This form of decoration, known as *alla porcellana*, proved to be highly successful due to the popularity of the expensive blue-and-white Chinese porcelain that began to be imported into Europe at this time. One characteristic of the work produced towards the end of the 15th century was the frequent use of minute motifs in concentric frames on the reverse of plates and dishes. The popularity of *sgraffito* wares continued, and the style of decoration was influenced by the development of more naturalistic scenes.

(ii) 1500 and after. Although albarelli, pitchers and plates decorated with profiles of knights or maidens accompanied by an amorous phrase, an aphorism or a name were made from the late 15th century, the most outstanding examples dated from the early 16th (see fig. 83). Such objects were exchanged as engagement gifts. Some well-known albarelli with portraits of nobles painted in polychrome were produced in Naples for the court of Aragón. The last phase of the 'Severe' style, which dates from the early 16th century until the first decades of the 17th, is characterized by grotesque decoration. GROTESQUE designs were inspired by the discovery c. 1480 of the motifs on the walls of Nero's Domus Aurea (mostly destr. AD 104) in Rome.

The 16th century has appropriately been defined as the golden age of Italian maiolica. During the first two decades Faenza was still the principal centre of production; later important centres included CASTEL DURANTE GIOVANNI and Urbino (see URBINO, §3), where such potters as NICOLA DA URBINO, FRANCESCO XANTO AVELLI and FRANCESCO DURANTINO established workshops. Before

83. Maiolica dish with yellow-brown lustre, inscribed NEMO SUA SORTE CHONTENTUS ('No-one is happy with his own destiny'), diam. 415 mm, from Deruta, *c.* 1500–30 (London, British Museum)

84. Maiolica dish painted with the *Presentation of Psyche to the Gods by Eros*, diam. 481 mm, from Urbino, *c.* 1530 (London, Wallace Collection)

the 'Beautiful' style was established *c.* 1515, a transitional phase is evident, which is characterized by fantastic decoration in gaudy colours. Wares from Faenza were used as the model and the decoration reworked in a variety of ways in workshops in such centres as Siena, Gubbio, Padua, Venice and at the CAFAGGIOLO CERAMIC FACTORY.

The first *istoriato* (narrative) phase proved to be very popular during the second and third decades of the 16th century. The leading centre in this first phase continued to be Faenza due to the fame of Pietro 'Pirotto' Paterni (*see* PIROTTI), who ran a workshop known as the Casa Pirota (Pirotta). The work of the Pirotti family was so frequently imitated that it is often difficult to identify. *Istoriato* wares were often decorated with historical or mythological themes and were called 'New' style wares. Prints provided the potters with images of contemporary paintings and sculpture; in particular Raphael's work was frequently reproduced on maiolica from Urbino (e.g. dish depicting the *Presentation of Psyche to the Gods by Eros*, based on Raphael's fresco in the Villa Farnesina, see fig. 84).

During the early 16th century technical experiments were carried out, and one of the results was the successful production in DERUTA of lustrewares, until then only imported from Spain. In Gubbio (*see* GUBBIO, §2), another centre for the production of lustrewares, GIORGIO ANDREOLI became a specialist, and potters from neighbouring regions sent their works to him to be given this iridescent gold or red finish. Lustrewares are classified in the phase known as the second *istoriato* or the 'Beautiful' style. One of the typical shapes of this period is the conical vase in the form of a pine-cone. Around the 1520s potters in Faenza introduced the *berrettino* (grey-blue) ground, which was decorated with motifs in contrasting colours (e.g. plate, 1525; London, BM). A variation on this technique was a deep-blue ground decorated with light-blue or gold decoration. In Venice work of this kind was known as *smaltino*.

Maiolica sculpture was developed in the workshop of the DELLA ROBBIA family, who practised their art from the 15th century until the end of the 16th. Their work, decorated with vivid colours, consisted largely of low-relief votive icons depicting the Madonna and Child, or basins with holy scenes for use in convents. Girolamo della Robbia also produced such vessels as vases decorated with low-relief garlands of flowers and fruit; his reputation won him the respect of the French king Francis I who commissioned him to decorate the loggia (1527; destr. 1792) of the Château de Madrid in the Bois de Bologne, Paris.

Italian maiolica was also popular abroad; potters in Lyons, for example, were very influenced by the *istoriato* style, which they copied. In Spain the style of 16th-century maiolica was imported by a potter from Pisa called Francisco Niculoso (*d* 1529), who was responsible for such outstanding tile pictures framed with friezes and grotesques as those in the Oratory Chapel in the Alcázar, Seville.

Next to the grotesques, another very successful ornamental style was that called *a quartieri*. This involved dividing the ground of an object into areas of different colours filled with various motifs; the central medallion was often filled with a portrait (e.g. dish, *c.* 1520–25; London, Wallace). This decoration was extensively used by the potters of central Italy and later in Sicily. In Montelupo, at this time, wares were richly decorated for courtiers or for the pontifical court, as indicated by the presence of coats of arms superimposed on the figures.

During the second half of the 16th century Urbino became an increasingly important centre of production largely due to the success of the FONTANA and PATANAZZI families. They were particularly well known for their wares of the third *istoriato* phase, which is distinguished by abundant decorations with historical or mythological scenes framed by friezes or grotesques in a palette dominated by yellow and orange; it is also known as the 'Raphaelesque' style (*see* CERAMICS, colour pl. I, fig. 1). This style was often applied to such highly intricate forms as centrepieces, lobed dishes, cisterns and inkstands with such relief decoration as handles in the shape of griffins. Maestro Domenico (active 1562–8), a Venetian potter, produced an original version of the *istoriato* style, during the second half of the 16th century, which he created using a highly coloured palette; his work includes plates and pitchers decorated with medallions enclosing profiles, with borders of flowers and fruit in blue, yellow, green and orange (e.g. large plate, 1568; Faenza, Mus. Int. Cer.). For over a century these works were imitated by many workshops in Venice and Sicily.

In reaction to the strong figurative nature of the third *istoriato* phase, a more restrained style of decoration came into fashion during the second half of the 16th century, first in Faenza (*see* MEZZARISA, FRANCESCO DI ANTONIO) and subsequently in other workshops in central Italy. Known as the *compendiario* style, it attempted to emphasize the items' form, and the potters took inspiration from contemporary silverwares. A decoration of blue and yellow was applied to the ground of thick, white enamel. The best-known examples, called *bianchi di Faenza*, were usually sketchily decorated with coats of arms and floral motifs (*see* CALAMELLI, VIRGILIOTTO). This style lasted throughout the first half of the 17th century, when workshops in Naples and the Abruzzo produced inferior-quality imitations. A direct derivation of the popular style of *compendiario* is evident in the maiolica ceiling tiles in the church of S Donato in CASTELLI, Abruzzo, which were produced by local craftsmen between 1615 and 1617. In Apulia, particularly in the town of Laterza, large, ceremonial plates known as *piatti da pompa* were produced during the later 17th century. Inspired by the originals from Faenza, they were decorated in a more pictorial style, which was quite different from the *compendiario* style.

In the rest of Italy maiolica production underwent a different evolution during the 16th century and into the 17th with distinct regional styles that became increasingly influenced by the emergent Baroque style. Wares from the Middle East were still influential, as is seen in the choice of the Paduan workshops to produce *candiana* maiolica decorated with stylized, polychrome flowers inspired by Iznik and Persian designs (*see* PADUA, §3). In such other areas in the Veneto as Bassano and Angarano, the workshops produced the so-called *latesini* wares with milky-white grounds, emulating the *lattimo* glass of the contemporary Muranese glassblowers. These works are often highly decorative, painted with mythological or allegorical scenes set in arcadian landscapes.

Another highly original type of maiolica is the *arlecchini* ware produced in MONTELUPO; these large, brightly painted plates depict burlesque figures, soldiers or figures inspired by the characters from the *commedia dell'arte* (see

85. Maiolica plate with *arlecchini* decoration, diam. 243 mm, from Montelupo, *c.* 1600–60 (London, British Museum)

fig. 85). In Liguria the East-Asian influence was still evident in the blue-and-white maiolicas decorated with chinoiseries produced in such centres as ALBISOLA, SAVONA and Genoa (*see* GENOA, §3(ii)). The early wares display a calligraphic style, which was to be gradually replaced by a more figurative Baroque style. Seventeenth-century Ligurian ceramics achieved considerable commercial success and were exported to various parts of Europe; Nevers in France was influenced by these exported wares.

Ceramics produced in Lodi are distinguished by their high technical quality, the elegance of their composition and the excellence of their thick decoration, which was largely borrowed from Delftwares. Such workshops in Castelli as those of the Grue and Gentile families produced shields, vases and plates decorated with rural scenes, or with biblical or mythological subjects executed in a palette dominated by warm tones of brown, green and yellow. Towards the end of the 17th century, the more courtly products of the Castellian workshops—where the most important potter was Carlo Antonio Grue (1655–1723), father of FRANCESCO ANTONIO XAVERIO GRUE—were enriched with gold. The use of gold is indicative of an attempt to emulate imported Chinese and Japanese porcelain.

Production in Naples during the second half of the 17th century and the early 18th was influenced by both the mastery of the craftsmen from Abruzzo and Ligurian production. This resulted in the establishment of a school of pottery dedicated to the decoration of floors and walls with tiles that were more popular among contemporary architects than marble decoration. Among the better known and more complex examples are the tiled floor (1761) of the church of S Michele Arcangelo in Anacapri by Leonardo Chiaiese (active 1750–*c.* 1761), which depicts the expulsion from Paradise, and the intricate decoration of the tiled cloister (1740–42) of the convent of S Chiara in Naples, carried out by Donato Massa and his sons, Gennero (*fl*1742–50) and Giuseppe (1719–74). In Sicily, there was considerable activity in workshops throughout the island in such centres as Caltagirone, Sciacca, Burgio and Palermo. During the 17th and 18th centuries they produced vividly painted albarelli and vases in the form of an owl. In Apulia at the end of the 17th century the potter Angelo Antonio d'Alessandro (1642–1717) produced blue-and-white plates painted with beautiful and satirical scenes.

In most of the workshops in northern Italy the Rococo style and chinoiserie decoration dominated the production of the early 18th century. The works of GIACOMO BOSELLI in Savona seem to have been produced in virtual competition with contemporary porcelain. In order to obtain a wider chromatic range he frequently used enamels. Such floral motifs of East-Asian inspiration as the potato flower or carnation are found on wares produced by the Ferniani family in Faenza after 1724 until the end of the century. In Lombardy and Piedmont equally elegant maiolicas were produced, which are similar to those manufactured by the French faience factories in Marseille and Rouen. Printed materials were widely used as a source of inspiration and themes taken from the *commedia dell'arte* were favoured: for example figures painted in the style of Jacques Callot are often found on maiolica produced by Felice Clerici (1745–88) in Milan (*see* MILAN, §III, 2).

During the 18th century forms were largely based on those of silverware and porcelain: ceramics from Bassano, however, were often highly elaborate and were derived from naturalistic forms. The work produced in such smaller centres as Ariano Irpino and Cerreto Sannita in Campania were particularly imaginative; flasks or vases in the form of the female figure and spire-shaped centrepieces, inspired by marble prototypes in the Neapolitan piazzas, were manufactured. At the end of the 18th century, a cautious move towards the Neo-classical style is evident in, for example, the tableware painted in the workshops of the Callegari and Casali families in Pesaro (*see* PESARO, §2).

During the 19th century there was a deterioration in the quality of maiolica produced throughout Italy, due in part to the rise of cream-coloured earthenware and other materials for decorative objects. With the advent of Neo-classicism maiolica lost public favour, and marble and its derivatives were preferred for pavements. Such families as the Giustiniani (*see* GIUSTINIANI (ii)) from Naples continued production in the first half of the 19th century. During the second half of the 19th century Renaissance wares were widely copied in most of the major Italian centres of ceramic production. At the end of the century notable experiments were produced by the painter Filippo Palizzi (1818–99) in Naples, the Museo Artistico Industriele and Fedeli Cappellitti (1847–1920) in Repino, Abbruzzo.

BIBLIOGRAPHY

L. Mallé: *Maioliche italiane dalle origini al settecento* (Milan, n.d.)
G. Ballardini: *Corpus della maiolica italiana* (Rome, 1933–8)
——: *La maiolica italiana (dalle origini alla fine del cinquecento)* (Florence, 1938/R Faenza, 1975)
B. Rackham: *Catalogue of Italian Maiolica* (London, 1940, rev. 1977)
——: *Italian Maiolica* (London, 1952)
G. Liverani: *La maiolica italiana fino alla comparsa della porcellana europea* (Milan, 1958)
V. Brosio: *Porcellane e maioliche dell'ottocento* (Milan, 1964, rev. 1980)
J. Scott-Taggart: *Italian Maiolica* (London, 1972)
G. Conti: *L'arte della maiolica in Italia* (Milan, 1973)
G. Batini: *L'amico della ceramica* (Florence, 1974)
B. Rackham: *Capolavori della maiolica italiana* (Faenza, 1976)
G. C. Bojani, C. Ravanelli Guidotti and A. Fanfani: *La donazione Galeazzo Cora: Ceramiche dal medioevo al XIX secolo* (Milan, 1985)
Ceramic Art of the Italian Renaissance (exh. cat. by T. Wilson, London, BM, 1987)
L. Arbace: *Il conoscitore di maioliche italiane del rinascimento* (Milan, 1992)
LUCIANA ARBACE

2. PORCELAIN.

(i) Before 1720. (ii) 1720–75. (iii) After 1775.

(i) Before 1720. Italy was the first European country to manufacture porcelain; experiments were sponsored by Alfonso II, Duke of Ferrara, conducted between 1561 and 1571 and carried out by the brothers Camillo de Gatti da Urbino (*d* 1567) and Battista de Gatti da Urbino (*d* by 1578). Production, if any, has not been identified. The earliest manufacture for which there is an identifiable corpus of work is the so-called Medici porcelain (soft paste), produced in Florence between *c.* 1575 and *c.* 1587 under the patronage of Francesco I, Grand Duke of Tuscany (*see* FLORENCE, §III, 1). Production included deep dishes, ewers and pilgrim flasks (see fig. 86) decorated in underglaze blue. Systematic manufacture was apparently discontinued after Francesco's death (1587), although in 1620 the potter Niccolo Sistì described himself as having been summoned by Francesco's successor, Ferdinando I, to manufacture porcelain in Florence and later in Pisa.

86. Soft-paste porcelain pilgrim flask, h. 264 mm, made at the factory of the Medici in Florence, *c.* 1575–87 (Malibu, CA, J. Paul Getty Museum)

Sisti's work has not been identified, but tokens bearing the Medici arms recorded in 1613 may be attributed to the factory. Two soft-paste porcelain bowls dated 1627 and 1638 (London, V&A) are evidence of 17th-century porcelain manufacture in Italy. They differ in style: one is painted with floral and foliate ornament inspired by Ottoman pottery, while the other is decorated with European birds and trees. The paste, execution and inscriptions on both, however, suggest the same origin, possibly from a pottery in Padua.

(ii) 1720–75. There is no evidence of further porcelain manufacture in Italy until 1720 when a factory was established in Venice by Francesco Vezzi (1651–1740) and his son Giovanni Vezzi (*b* 1687) (*see* VEZZI PORCELAIN FACTORY).

In 1737 Marchese Carlo Ginori (1702–57), the ceramics technician Giorgio delle Torri (*fl* 1737–43) and the painter Karl Wendelin Anreiter von Zirnfeld (1702–57) founded a factory for the production of hard-paste porcelain in Doccia. Useful wares were decorated with relief, pierced and other decoration (see fig. 87), and figures and groups were also produced (for further discussion *see* DOCCIA).

During the 18th century several small porcelain factories were established in Piedmont. The earliest was established in Turin in 1737 by Giorgio Giacinto Rossetti (*d* 1779). In 1742 his staff included Jakob Helchis (*fl* 1730–49), a painter associated with the factory of Claudius Innocentius du Paquier (*fl* 1718–51) in Vienna, and Anton Wagner. Rossetti's factory apparently closed when Helchis returned to Vienna in 1746. Two classical-style hard-paste porcelain busts (Turin, Pal. Madama), one marked with Rossetti's initials, have been identified with the factory.

In the Palazzo Reale di Capodimonte, near Naples, Charles VII, King of Naples (later Charles III, King of Spain), founded the CAPODIMONTE PORCELAIN FACTORY in 1743. The chief modeller was GIUSEPPE GRICCI (see fig. 88). In 1759 the factory was transferred to the Buen Retiro in Madrid. It was succeeded in 1771 by the Royal Porcelain Factory, founded in Pórtici by Ferdinand I, King of Naples and the Two Sicilies, and moved to Naples in 1772 (see NAPLES, §III, 3). Tablewares and figures in both the Rococo and Neo-classical styles were made until the factory closed in 1806.

In the mid-1750s three rival factories were established in and around Venice. The first was that of Nathaniel Friedrich Hewelke and Maria Hewelke (both *fl* 1751–63), who had been porcelain merchants in Dresden until they were displaced by the Prussian occupation of Dresden during the Seven Years War (1756–63). In 1758 they received a 20-year privilege to manufacture porcelain 'in the manner of Saxony' in Udine and in 1761 they moved to Venice. There the ceramic technician Geminiano Cozzi (1728–97) became their partner until 1763, after which the Hewelkes probably returned to Saxony. The few extant examples of their wares are of a greyish, hard paste. Such useful wares as tea- and coffee-sets included pots with distinctively modelled knobbed spouts and handles, painted with enamelled flowers or figures in simple settings. An unidentified modeller produced rather stiff, naive figures and groups; more ambitious and accomplished,

87. Hard-paste porcelain platter, w. 318 mm, painted by Karl Wendelin Anreiter von Zirnfeld after Jacopo Ligozzi, made at the factory of Doccia, *c.* 1740 (New York, Metropolitan Museum of Art)

however, was a relief portrait (London, BM) signed by Fortunato Tolerazzi and dated 1763.

In 1761 Captain Filippo Cuccomos obtained a 40-year monopoly for porcelain manufacture in Rome. The monopoly was transferred in 1781 to Lanfranco Bosio, who bought his equipment from Cuccomos; Bosio left Rome in 1783, while Cuccomos apparently remained in business until 1784. Known production from the Cuccomos period consists of glazed and gilded hard-paste figures of saints, all dated 1769 (two examples, Gazzada, Mus. Villa Cagnola).

88. Soft-paste porcelain figure group of the *Rabbit-catchers* by Giuseppe Gricci, h. 164 mm, made at the Capodimonte Porcelain Factory, 1755–9 (New York, Metropolitan Museum of Art)

89. Hard-paste porcelain teapot, h. 182 mm, made at the Nove Factory, c. 1775 (London, Victoria and Albert Museum)

In 1762 Pasquale Antonibon (d ?1773) succeeded in producing a hard-paste porcelain at NOVE, near Bassano, after 12 years of experiments that had begun in 1750 in collaboration with the painter Johann Sigismund Fische (fl c. 1750–58) from Dresden. Fischer soon left to work at the Capodimonte Porcelain Factory, where he was recorded in 1754. Between 1760 and 1765 the French sculptor Jean-Pierre Varion (d 1780/1), a modeller from the factory of Vincennes, also worked at the Nove Factory. Manufacture at Nove was suspended between 1763 and 1765 when Antonibon fell ill, and some of his employees went to the COZZI PORCELAIN FACTORY in Venice (est. 1764). In 1765 production was resumed, and Nove remained in operation until Antonibon retired in 1773, when production was again suspended until 1781. During this lull in production, permission to manufacture porcelain at Angarano, near Bassano, was granted in 1778 to Baldassare Marinoni, who presumably employed workers from Nove; a figure group from this factory dated 1779 was recorded in 1876. Angarano is not mentioned after 1781 when much of the equipment was sold to Giovanni Maria Baccin (1744–1815), proprietor of Antonibon's maiolica factory in Nove. In 1781 Antonibon's porcelain factory was leased to Francesco Parolin, and in 1802 to Giovanni Baroni until 1825. It was finally closed in 1835.

The Cozzi Factory, which had received its privilege from the Venetian Senate in 1764, continued without interruption until 1812. It was the first commercial Italian factory and was conceived to compete with the increased importation of Chinese Export porcelain. According to a report of 1767 Cozzi employed forty-five workmen and had four kilns. In 1784 his staff of sixty-seven included seven turners, seven painters, two sculptors and five kiln workers, and his markets extended into the Near East.

The manufacture of Cozzi and Nove is very similar: both factories used the same clay from Vicenza, which resulted in the production of a greyish, hard-paste body. The glaze appeared somewhat shiny particularly on figures, while the earlier palettes were almost identical, the colours dark and often muddy, and some of the subjects depicted were the same. Given the exchange of workmen between the two factories these similarities were inevitable. Among Cozzi's painters were members of the Ortolani, Baccin and Fabris families, all of whom had also worked at Nove. A dish (1765; priv. col.) signed LO may be attributable to Ludovico Ortolani (b 1732) although he was evidently at Nove the same year. Cozzi's repertory was large and diverse. A production index of 1783, lists 66 types of painted decoration, 37 models of useful wares and 86 sculpture models, as well as numerous forms of vases, ornamental pieces and galanterie. These were enamelled with conventional mid-18th-century subjects: armorials (sometimes with pastoral scenes), chinoiseries, architectural landscapes, trellises covered with large flowers and clusters of fruit and flowers. Some of these were used at Nove with little variation (see fig. 89). Only at Cozzi was there extensive imitation of East Asian Export porcelain. Early Nove and Cozzi models of useful wares show how little they were influenced by the Saxon factory of Meissen; at both factories the sculptural vigour and playfulness of the work is more akin to contemporary maiolica production. Towards the end of the 18th century both factories yielded to French influence, imitating both the form and decoration of porcelain from the factory of Sèvres. The chief painter at Nove when Parolin was in charge of production was Giovanni Marcon, whose style can be identified in an écuelle and stand (c. 1785; Bassano del Grappa, Mus. Civ.) and a vase hollandais (c. 1790; London, V&A), both of which are signed and painted with groups of lively figures in landscapes. The useful wares of both factories were usually marked.

Figures from Cozzi illustrate the styles of several modellers although none are known by name; the source of their subject-matter is also unknown. One characteristic arrangement was a group of figures—children with rather heavy heads or dwarfs—circling a tree, fountain or other focal element often situated on a scrolled, Rococo base. Other modellers are identifiable in single figures of masqueraders, gentry or peasants, as well as in white-glazed groups of Classical and allegorical subjects, and in the figures of children known as enfants Boucher (after works by François Boucher) that were popularized by the factory of Sèvres. Nove is notable for its technically complex, multi-figural groups made under both Parolin and Baroni, such as the large-scale group (h. 578 mm) of Jupiter Defeating the Titans (London, V&A). These have been attributed to Domenico Bosello (1755–1821), the factory's chief modeller, whose career began at Cozzi. His only signed work is a portrait bust of Cristiano Antonio Sambugari (1789; Venice, Ca' Rezzonico), a priest from Nove. At the end of the 18th century both factories produced similar, polychrome genre figures and groups.

In 1765 Francesco Lodovico Birago (1719–90), Conte di Vische, organized a company in Vische, which made a hard-paste porcelain developed by him from a local clay. Its useful wares are simple, although somewhat inexpertly fired, and include forms based on Meissen versions of East-Asian models. Sculptures of *enfants Boucher*, copied from Vincennes models, were, however, technically more controlled and proficient. Although the factory received royal protection in 1766, economic and technical difficulties forced the stock to be sold in 1768.

(iii) After 1775. In 1776 Giovanni Vittorio Brodel (*fl* 1765–78), who had been a major shareholder in the Vische enterprise, in partnership with Pierre-Antoine Hannong (1739–94), obtained a patent from Victor-Amadeus III of Savoy for the manufacture of porcelain at Vinovo, near Turin. Brodel withdrew in 1778, and Hannong left the country in 1780, when the factory was briefly closed. It was reopened later the same year under the management of Vittorio Amedeo Gioanetti (1729–1815), a Torinese doctor and chemist. Between 1796 and 1815 production at Vinovo was reduced; when Gioanetti died he was succeeded by Giovanni Lomello, the factory's chief modeller. The factory finally closed in 1820. The undulating, Rococo tureens and the freely asymmetrical flower painting reflected Hannong's training in his father's faience factory in Strasbourg. After 1781 forms and decoration were based chiefly on models from Sèvres, Mennecy and the new commercial factories in Paris. Sculptural work at Vinovo varied considerably in skill and sophistication. The first chief modeller was Carlo Tamietti (*d* 1796), whose signature appears on two groups; the *Allegory of Savoy* and the *Miracle of St Hubert* (1778; both Turin, Pal. Madama). They are graceful compositions in the manner of early Neo-classical biscuit groups made at Sèvres. Both white-glazed and polychrome *enfants Boucher* were also produced. Some of the models are similar to those produced at Vische and were presumably introduced by Brodel. Hannong's influence can be seen in a brightly coloured figure of *Minerva* (*c.* 1768–80; Turin, Mus. Civ. A. Ant.) in the manner of Johann Wilhelm Lanz (*fl* 1748–61), who had been a modeller at Strasbourg between 1748 and 1754, and in simply modelled figures of country youths after the modeller Paul-Louis Cyfflé (1724–1806) from Lunéville. After 1796 Classical figures and religious subjects in biscuit porcelain predominated.

In 1778 the French sculptor Jean-Pierre Varion left Nove, entered into a partnership with Girolamo Franchini (1727–1808) and established a porcelain factory in Este. Production is thought to have started only after Varion's death. Franchini continued in business until at least 1825, and Varion's widow, Fiorina Fabris, went into partnership with Antonio Costa. A cream-tinted, hard-paste porcelain was produced, and the repertory was exclusively of allegorical and mythological figures. Well-rounded, graceful figures have been attributed to Varion, although, since they are datable to the 1780s, this is debatable. A single figure of an actor has been attributed to Franchini (Stazzi, 1964).

A signed and dated figure of a saint (1782; Genoa, Pal. Rosso) in biscuit porcelain is evidence of manufacture in Savona by GIACOMO BOSELLI in 1782. Contemporary records mention figural dessert-services made between 1787 and 1794. Boselli was joined in 1798 by Giuseppe Rubatto (1752–1825), an association confirmed by two vigorously modelled, soft-paste figures of a peasant couple

(ex-Goldblatt col.; see Lane, *Connoisseur* 1955, p. 164, figs 6, 7) in polychrome signed with both names. From 1808 Rubatto continued the manufacture until his death.

A second factory in Rome was founded in 1785 by the engraver Giovanni Trevisan, known as Volpato (1732–1803), and his son Giuseppe Volpato (*d* 1805). The Volpato factory reproduced Classical figures in biscuit for both the table and ornamental use. A Volpato catalogue, circulated in 1795, listed models similar in subject to those described in a catalogue issued in Rome by the bronze-founders Giovanni Zoffoli (*c.* 1745–1805) and Francesco Righetti. A direct connection between the two enterprises, however, has not been proved. Volpato's figures were usually placed on low plinths and often incised with his name. From 1805 Giuseppe's son Angelo Volpato (*d* 1831) managed the factory with his brothers. In 1831 the family withdrew from the business, which in 1857 was sold to Giuseppe Trocchi.

Porcelain manufacture at Vicenza began in 1788 under Conte Carlo Vicentini dal Giglio and was carried on to at least 1810 by Baldassar Sebellin. Hard-paste porcelain was produced at the factory, and there are a few extant examples of tablewares marked with a fleur-de-lis and sometimes an incised double v.

At Treviso hard-paste porcelain was manufactured by the brothers Andrea and Giuseppe Fontebasso by 1799 (e.g. bowl, London, BM). The majority of recorded examples are cups and saucers sketchily painted with figures in contemporary civilian and military dress. Items were marked with the name Treviso and sometimes include the initials of the proprietors; production ended *c.* 1835.

In 1827 a factory was established in Turin by a partnership headed by Frédéric Dortu (1787–after 1846). Two years later it was restyled Dortu Richard et Cie. After several changes of partnership it closed in 1864. Recorded pieces are of hard paste and include sculptural decorative models in a neo-Rococo style. In 1834 the San Cristoforo Factory was founded in Milan by Luigi Tinelli. It was sold to Giulio Richard in 1841 and was still in operation in 1881. During the Tinelli period production was chiefly of ornamental wares based on English and French models (examples, Laveno, Civ. Rac. Terraglia). Under Richard's ownership, the factory produced industrial as well as luxury porcelain. In 1896 Richard acquired the Doccia Factory.

BIBLIOGRAPHY

W. R. Drake: *Notes on Venetian Ceramics* (London, 1868)

A. Lane: 'Porcelain Figures of Este', *Faenza*, xxxix (1953), pp. 162–5

——: *Italian Porcelain* (London, 1954)

——: 'Giacomo Boselli: An Italian Potter of Savona', *Connoisseur*, cxxxvi (1955), pp. 161–4

G. Morazzoni and S. Levy: *Le porcellane italiane*, 2 vols (Milan, 1960)

F. Martinengo: 'Vinovo Porcelain', *Connoisseur*, cxlviii (1961), pp. 185–9

F. Stazzi: *Italian Porcelain* (New York, 1964)

H. Honour: 'Statuettes after the Antique: Volpato's Roman Porcelain Factory', *Apollo*, lxxxv (1967), pp. 371–3

V. Brosio: *Porcellane e maiolica dell'ottocento a Torino e Milano* (Milan, 1972)

——: *Rossetti, Vische, Vinovo: Porcellane e maioliche torinesi del settecento* (Milan, 1973)

E. Biavati: 'Giambattista Antonibon e compagno Francesco Parolin q.ᵃᵐ Alberto di Bassano: Porcellane delle Nove, 1781–1802', *Faenza*, lxi (1975), pp. 26–9

A. Mottola Molfino: *L'arte della porcellana in Italia*, 2 vols (Busto Arsizio, 1976–7)

P. Portoghesi and A. Pansera: *Gio Ponti alla manifattura di Doccia* (Brera, 1982)

F. Stazzi: *Le porcellane veneziane di Geminiano e Vincenzo Cozzi* (Venice, ?1982)

A. Caròla-Perrotti: *Le porcellane napoletane dell'ottocento, 1801–1860* (Naples, 1990)

C. Hess: ' "Primo esperimento in grande": A Pair of Vases from the Factory of Geminiano Cozzi', *Getty Mus. J.*, xviii (1990), pp. 141–56

V. P. Salabelle: *Porcellana di Capodimonte: La Real Fabbrica di Carlo di Borbone, 1743–1759* (Naples, 1993)

CLARE LE CORBEILLER

VIII. Glass.

The history of glass manufacture in Italy from the Middle Ages (for earlier periods *see* ROME, ANCIENT, §VIII, 2(ii) and EARLY CHRISTIAN AND BYZANTINE ART, §VII, 4) is almost entirely identified with the history of glass produced in Venice (*see* VENICE, §III, 3). In fact, it would be more accurate to refer to Murano, a city on a small island in the Venetian lagoon. Venetian glassmakers worked in Murano from 1291, when they were transferred there by a decree of the Magistrature of the Venetian Republic for fear of the fires caused by the furnaces in the city itself. Historical research has not yet ascertained what factors may have led to the rise of glassmaking in Venice and the Venetian lagoon. Documents show that glass was made there before AD 1000, and a few ancient documents suggest that the great artistic production of Venetian glass must have continued uninterrupted from Late Roman times (*see* GLASS, colour pl. VIII, fig. 3). Indeed the Venetians adopted and developed decorative styles, typological models and techniques from the Roman traditions.

The great success of the Murano glass industry led not only to the progressive widening of its commercial horizon, but also stimulated the formation and development of other, smaller glassmaking centres in Italy. These were founded by glassmakers who, despite the strict regulations, emigrated from Murano and influenced the development of techniques, tastes and the types of article produced. A major historiographical problem arises from the fact that the technology of glassmaking does not facilitate clear and certain distinctions between products manufactured in different geographical centres. The question is further complicated by the considerable stylistic uniformity of glass due to the predominance of Venetian taste, and the fact that Murano glass articles are not reliably attributable to any particular maker, although the early documents contain plenty of names. All these problems oblige the historian of Italian glassware to concentrate mainly on Venetian production, while verifying those contacts that existed between Venice and other, minor centres of production elsewhere in the peninsula.

Glassmaking seems to have been practised in the small Ligurian town of Altare, near Savona, since the 11th century. At first utilitarian objects were produced, but during the Renaissance pieces became more artistic, undoubtedly due to the contribution of craftsmen from Murano who had initiated the local craftsmen into the secrets of the art. While the activity in Altare is documented by early sources, it has not been possible to identify with certainty any piece produced there, as the typological and aesthetic characteristics were indistinguishable from those of Venetian glass. As they gained experience the Ligurian craftsmen refined their taste and techniques and contributed to the development of technical processes, especially for mirrors. They played an important role in creating the market for glass *à la façon de Venise* throughout Europe as they migrated in great numbers to Provence, Normandy and Belgium. The glassmakers of Altare were organized in a guild, the Università dell'Arte Vitrea, which adopted a statute in 1495 and worked to facilitate contacts and exchanges and establish new glassmaking centres in other countries.

Other glass factories existed in such cities in the Veneto region as Padua, Verona, Vicenza and Treviso. These were of minor importance, and at the end of the 16th century their slight activity completely ceased. However, in Tuscany the development of glass manufacture was more substantial; in Florence it began in the 16th century, and in the 17th century production spread to Prato, Pisa, Pistoia, Lucca, Arezzo and Empoli. Initially the interest of the Tuscan glassmakers was in the production of utilitarian wares, especially everyday tableware. In Florence there were a great number of glassmakers who specialized in the manufacture of drinking glasses. Also well known were the Tuscan *fiasche* (flasks) covered with straw jackets, which were used for transporting wines and other drinks. The government of Cosimo I, Grand Duke of Tuscany, gave the first stimulus to the production of artistic glass by inviting such noted Venetian craftsmen as Bartolo d'Alvise, who arrived in Florence in 1569. Such masters of other disciplines as the painter Jacopo Ligozzi and the engraver Stefano della Bella were commissioned to provide designs for glass. There was also a large and widespread production of Venetian-style glassware, which was so similar to Murano glass that it is hard to distinguish it. Another area in which Tuscan glassmaking had considerable fame—though only from the 17th century—was the production of pharmaceutical wares, medical instruments and different items for scientific uses: the research carried out in Tuscany by physicians, alchemists and scientists, including Galileo Galilei, favoured the specialized production of phials, alembics, lenses and various small vessels. A collection of this glassware from the Accademia del Cimento is preserved in the Museo di Storia della Scienza in Florence.

The importance of Tuscan glassmaking at the end of the 16th century and the beginning of the 17th is also documented in the publication *L'arte vetraria* (Florence, 1612) by Abbot Antonio Neri (1576–1614). Drawing on his own vast experience, the author gave a clear and exhaustive account of the systems, methods and typologies of glass manufacture. The production of glassware in Tuscany continued almost until the end of the 18th century, but under the last Medici rulers it progressively declined.

BIBLIOGRAPHY

G. Mariacher: *L'arte del vetro* (Verona, 1954)

G. Taddei: *L'arte del vetro in Firenze* (Florence, 1954)

G. Mariacher: *Il vetro soffiato* (Milan, 1960)

——: *Il vetro soffiato: Da Roma antica a Venezia* (Milan, 1960)

——: *Il vetro europeo dal XV al XX secolo* (Novara, 1964)

M. Causa: *L'arte del vetro dal rinascimento ai nostri giorni* (Milan, 1966)

G. Mariacher: *Specchiere italiane e cornici da specchio dal XV al XIX secolo* (Milan, 1969)

C. Bertelli: 'Vetri e altre cose della Napoli angioina' *Paragone*, xxiii/263 (1972), pp. 89–106

PAOLA D'ALCONZO

IX. Metalwork.

For pre-medieval metalwork *see* ROME, ANCIENT, §IX and EARLY CHRISTIAN AND BYZANTINE ART, §VII, 7.

1. Gold and silver. 2. Base metals.

1. GOLD AND SILVER. One of the earliest centres of goldsmiths' work in Italy was Venice: a statute of the Venetian guild of goldsmiths is dated 1233. The 'opus veneticum' of the 13th century, delicate filigree work influenced by that of East Asia, remained popular until the Renaissance. Siena was the most important centre during the 14th century, and the statutes of its guild of goldsmiths date from 1361, though they refer to other earlier organizations. The work produced there was influenced largely by the Gothic style and characterized by the use of translucent enamels, the chief exponent of which was GUCCIO DI MANNAIA (*see* GOTHIC, fig. 90). The combination of gold and enamel continued in the work of UGOLINO DI VIERI, while FRANCESCO D'ANTONIO was an important goldsmith of the second half of the 15th century. In Venice the powerful traditions of Byzantine art can be seen in the gold altarpiece in S Marco in which Byzantine enamels of the 10th–12th centuries are framed in a base (1345) in the International Gothic style by Giampaolo Boninsegna (*see also* ICON, colour pl. I). The Gothic style remained predominant in Venice until the mid-15th century, as can be seen in the gilded silver candlesticks (1462–71; Venice, Tesoro S Marco) made for the Doge Cristoforo Moro. Venice also produced much silver and gold tableware and cutlery during the 15th and 16th centuries.

The Renaissance vocabulary of forms was developed most strongly in Florence. Although goldsmiths in Florence had been obliged to stamp their work from as early as 1322, they had no official guild of their own during the Renaissance, but belonged to the Arte dei Mercanti di Por S Maria. The many goldsmiths' workshops in Florence provided training for some of the greatest names of the Renaissance. Filippo Brunelleschi became a master goldsmith in 1404, and Lorenzo Ghiberti (*see* GHIBERTI, (1)) served his apprenticeship with the goldsmith Bartolo di Michele, in turn training DONATELLO and Luca della Robbia. The silver altar of *St John the Baptist* (Florence, Mus. Opera Duomo) for the Baptistery contains four relief panels dating from the 15th century, among them the panel by ANDREA DEL VERROCCHIO of the *Beheading of St John the Baptist* (1477–80) on the right side of the

90. Silver panel of the *Beheading of St John the Baptist* by Andrea del Verrocchio, 360×380 mm, from the altar of *St John the Baptist*, 1477–80 (Florence, Museo dell'Opera del Duomo)

91. Gilded silver candlesticks by Giovan Battista Boucheron, h. 285 mm each, 1783 (London, Victoria and Albert Museum)

antependium (see fig. 90). The statue of *St John* in the central niche of the altar is the work of MICHELOZZO DI BARTOLOMEO, who was probably also trained by Ghiberti. The production of goldsmiths' work in Florence was boosted by the patronage of the Medici family in the 15th and 16th centuries. The technical expertise and formal refinement of Florentine work in this period can be seen in the golden artefacts in the Museo degli Argenti in the Palazzo Pitti, especially in the precious mountings of the Medici vases. One of the most important works from Genoa in the 15th century is the *Ark of St John the Baptist* (1433; Genoa Cathedral) by Teramo Danieli and Simone Caldara. Also held in the cathedral is the 16th-century *Cask of the Corpus Domini*, made through a collaboration between local and Nordic craftsmen. Prolific quantities of goldsmiths' work were produced in Sicily from the 14th century, mainly by Catalan and Tuscan craftsmen based in Palermo, Catania and Messina. The Catalan influence remained dominant in the 15th century, but by the 16th century, Renaissance forms had spread, though still linked to Spanish models, as in the work of Paoli Gili in Palermo. In the second half of the 16th century the measured, classical forms described in the treatises of Juan de Arje were disseminated by Nabilio Gagini.

Although statutes had existed in Rome from as early as 1358, in 1509 a new guild was formed, the Università degli Orefici Argentieri e Gioiellieri dell'Alma Città di Roma. Laws defined the standards for precious metals, and hallmarks of both the goldsmith and the assayer became obligatory. BENVENUTO CELLINI, the most renowned goldsmith in the 16th century, worked primarily in Rome and Florence between 1513 and 1540, and he recorded in his *Vita* (written *c.* 1558–67) the presence of many goldsmiths' workshops on the Via del Pellegrino. Among the most noteworthy of the goldsmiths working for the papal

court during the 16th century were VALERIO BELLI and CARADOSSO. In 1580 ANTONIO GENTILI produced two candlesticks (Rome, St Peter's) for Cardinal Alessandro Farnese. In Mantua GIULIO ROMANO designed silver tableware for Federico Gonzaga, designs illustrated in the *Libro de disegni per far vasella di argento et oro*. Cutlery in precious metals was produced in Milan, for example the 'Trivulzio' knives (Milan, Castello Sforzesco), with handles in nielloed silver, and cutlery (Milan, Mus. Poldi Pezzoli), the handles of which are decorated in relief. Milan was the centre for production of hardstone objects of vertu mounted in precious metals, gemstones and hardstones. Naples boasts a long tradition of goldsmiths' work, with roots in antiquity, but was heavily influenced by French and, later, Florentine styles. In 1437 Alfonso I of Aragón conferred on the Neapolitan goldsmiths the privilege of marking silverwork. A statute was granted for the Corporazione degli Orefici, confirmed in 1505.

One of the masterpieces of 17th-century Florentine work is the relief panel executed in gold, enamel and diamonds (Florence, Pitti) depicting Cosimo II, Grand Duke of Tuscany, kneeling in prayer. This formed part of an altar frontal (1617–24) commissioned by Cosimo from the grand ducal workshop for S Carlo Borromeo in Milan, the rest of which was lost, probably in the 18th century. While the Mannerist style, encouraged by the Counter-Reformation, spread throughout Italy, the High Baroque style was especially prevalent in Rome. Carlo Spagna (*fl* 1680), a member of an important family of goldsmiths, created a triangular base for Cardinal Farnese's Gentili candlesticks, and Giovanni Giardini produced in 1689 the crown, sceptre and funerary mask of Queen Christina of Sweden. Giardini is remembered for his treatise *Promptuarium artis argentariae*, a collection of drawings for silversmiths. In Naples the abundance of silver from the New World brought enormous wealth and, subsequently, extravagant use of the metal. An increase in the cult of relics led to a heightened demand for devotional objects, such as silver reliquaries and silver altar frontals, a typical example of the latter being that (1692–5; Naples, S Gennaro, Tesoro) by GIAN DOMENICO VINACCIA. Similar developments took place in Sicily, where one of the most prolific workshops was that of the Juvarra family. The founder of the family, Pietro Juvarra, was renowned for a gold chalice (Trapani, Mus. Reg.) covered with dense embossed decoration. His descendant Filippo Juvarra worked as a silversmith between 1693 and 1701 with his father and brothers and produced, among other important work, the gilded silver chalice (1695) in Messina Cathedral.

In the 18th century both the princely courts and Italian goldsmiths came under the influence of current French styles. JUSTE-AURÈLE MEISSONNIER was born in Turin and trained there with his father, a sculptor and silversmith. The goldsmith to the court of Savoy in Turin from 1737 was Andrea BOUCHERON, a pupil in Paris of Thomas Germain. Boucheron's son, Giovan Battista Boucheron, was appointed a royal goldsmith in 1763 and in 1776 became the director of the goldsmiths' workshop to Victor-Amadeus III. Giovan Battista Boucheron's classically inspired gilded silver candlesticks (1783; London, V&A; see fig. 91) exemplify the high-quality work produced during this period. At the end of the 18th century the Rococo style and the decorative vocabulary of chinoiserie took root in Turin and also in Genoa. The Rococo was, further, taken up in Venice in the 18th century, though much of the goldwork of the period was melted down in 1797 during the war with France. In Rome Giuseppe Gagliardi (1721–49) produced two monumental candelabra as part of the magnificent ensemble (1742–52) commissioned by John V of Portugal for the chapel of S João Batista in S Roque, Lisbon (candelabra *in situ*). Carlo Guarnieri, from the well-known Roman family of silversmiths, produced four gilded silver reliquaries (1745–74; Lisbon, Mus. S Roque). Though porcelain was more favoured in Naples in the 18th century, precious metals continued to be used for tableware and furniture. Of the religious work, the gold chalice (1761; Naples, S Gennaro, Tesoro) by the court jeweller Michele Lofrano is one of the few pieces to survive. In the second half of the 18th century there was a transition in Rome from flowing, dynamic lines to the restraint of the Neo-classical vocabulary. The VALADIER family, Luigi Valadier in particular, were instrumental in disseminating this style throughout Italy. The Valadier workshop continued operating under the control of successive generations of the family until the mid-19th century.

BIBLIOGRAPHY

C. G. Bulgari: *Argentari, gemmari e orafi d'Italia* (Rome, 1958–74)
S. Fornari: *Gli argenti romani* (Rome, 1968)
E. Catello and C. Catello: *Argenti napoletani dal XVI al XIX secolo* (Naples, 1973)
M. Accascina: *I marchi delle argenterie e oreficerie siciliane* (Trapani, 1976)
R. Bossaglia and M. Cinotti: *Tesoro e Museo del Duomo* (Milan, 1978)

2. BASE METALS. Copper, used in the manufacture of arms, utensils and church and domestic furnishings, is found in its natural state in numerous deposits in various parts of Italy, for example in the Campigliese and in Val di Cecine, and especially on the islands of Elba and Sardinia. These last two sources had considerable importance for the development of such ancient civilizations as the Etruscan and the Nuragic and were heavily exploited in Roman times. Bronze was also used for many church furnishings. Candelabra, lamps, censers and stational and processional crosses were made of bronze, sometimes gilded to imitate gold. Bronzeworkers practised their art in the same workshops as goldsmiths. Bronze was also widely used for architectural decoration from the 11th century (for a detailed survey of the many cast-bronze doors produced in Italy during the medieval and Renaissance periods, *see* DOOR, §II, 1(ii) and 2). Through its close relationship with the Byzantine Empire, where bronze-casting was widely practised, Venice enjoyed the services of excellent bronze founders; Venetian artisans cast Andrea Pisano's doors for the Baptistery, Florence, and the tabernacle railings of Orsanmichele, Florence.

During the 13th and 14th centuries Siena was a leading centre in the production of wrought iron; the Sienese 'magistri clavari', mentioned in contemporary documents for their ability to forge keys and locks, laid new foundations for the craft of ironworking. They sought to decorate such domestic items of basic form as oil lamps, andirons, coffers, lanterns and harness rings. They continued to excel in monumental works, for example the railings by Jacopo di Lello for Orvieto Cathedral, the railings of the Cappella del Sacro Cintolo, Prato Cathedral, and those of the Palazzo della Signoria, Siena. A guild of *fabbri* (smiths) was founded in Florence in the second half of the 13th century. The Republic ordered lanterns, standard-holders and torch-holders from the guild, to be placed outside the most important palazzi. A number of prominent families installed wrought-iron architectural pieces, notably the Strozzi in the 15th century, who had their *ferri* produced by Niccolò Caparra, described by Vasari as a 'master who in the working of iron had no equals'.

Bronze was widely used in the Renaissance for decorative arts, as it could be splendidly finished by chiselling and gilding, or by burnishing it to provide a glossy, dark surface. It was used for such architectural fittings as handles, door-knockers, torch-holders, flagpoles and harness rings. In domestic interiors it was used for sconces, writing equipment, fireplace furniture, lamps and furniture mounts. Small bronze statues of an essentially decorative nature were extremely popular and were often displayed in 16th-century *studioli*. These could be made more refined and elaborate by the use of dark lacquers or gilding (*see* BRONZE, §II). Such small-scale decorative works of art continued to be produced throughout the 16th century. Medals (*see* MEDAL, §II, 1 and 2), usually of bronze, were struck for commemorative purposes or as a form of portraiture. Plaquettes (*see* PLAQUETTE, §3(i)), commonly made of bronze, developed in Italy in the mid-15th century and remained important until the mid-16th century. Debate continues as to their original function. There were also lead castings of 16th-century medals and plaquettes: the material was cheaper and more malleable than bronze, but many of these lead items probably served as models for goldsmiths and bronzeworkers. Objects for domestic use during the Renaissance were also produced in copper, often gilded, using the same forms as those of precious metals.

In Italy, unlike Flanders and Germany, the only noteworthy brass works of art were produced in Venice during the 16th century. At first the ornament and techniques (engraving or inlay) were reproduced from pieces imported from the East, such as plates, cups, candle holders and incense burners (*see* VENETO-SARACENIC). During the course of the 16th century, however, the decorations reflected the classicizing influence of the Renaissance (see fig. 92). Venice was also a centre for the production of articles in pewter during the 16th century. Employed at first only to copy pieces originally made in precious metal, the use of pewter gradually spread throughout northern Italy. In Venice the activity of pewterers was greatly increased by the immigrant Flemish workers who settled there. Gradually the pewterers distanced themselves from silversmiths, although they continued to copy their models and use the same moulds. The expansion of the pewter trade was favoured by the Venetian sumptuary laws. From the 17th century onwards, Italian pewter began to decline.

The Counter-Reformation provided for an incredible wealth of Baroque church furnishings in copper, bronze and brass. For example, Bernini designed the gilt-bronze crucifix and candelabra (1657–61) for St Peter's, Rome. In Naples too, base metals formed part of broad decorative programmes. Bronze was used, for example, in the gates (1629) of the Cappella del Tesoro, S Gennaro, executed

92. Brass dish by Horatio Fortezza, diam. 450 mm, made in Venice, 1562 (London, Victoria and Albert Museum)

under the direction of COSIMO FANZAGO, and gilt copper was adopted for statues and bases for reliquary busts and ciboria, often in combination with ebony and lapis lazuli for greater visual impact. Bronze continued to be employed for railings and furniture decorations in the French style and for sconces used in week-day masses.

Wrought iron followed the Baroque and Rococo styles adopted in stuccowork, polychrome marbles, bronze and gilt wood. Until the second half of the 17th century Italy followed the lead of the Lucca workshops, which had played a leading role since the Renaissance. Later, the French influence became more prominent, using typical motifs of interlacing and streamers in railings and gates. Venice made an important contribution to the art of decorative ironwork with such examples of refined Rococo lightness as the gates of the Palazzo Pisani, but the most significant Italian ironworker in the 18th century was Giovan Battista Malagoli of Modena, who executed the most important commissions in that city. In southern Italy and in Sicily there was a continuation of a Spanish-influenced style based on naturalistic vegetal motifs (e.g. chandeliers, andirons and bedheads; Palermo, Pal. Cinese).

The production of bronze vases, lamps, clocks, desk fittings and table centrepieces in the Neo-classical style was influenced by the wealth of drawings and engravings by such artists as Giovani Battista Piranesi. During the 19th century, however, there was a marked decline in quality of Italian metalwork; many bronze pieces reproduced Renaissance objects with a confused stylistic eclecticism. Wrought iron was gradually replaced by rigidly geometric cast iron, to which were applied decorative motifs, cast from mechanical moulds, in slavish imitation of earlier styles. Copper also underwent a progressive decline with the spread of various galvanic processes by

which cheap reproductions of gold objects could be made. Experiments were also under way with various new alloys that provided cheap imitations of silver or bronze, and industrial methods made it possible to produce an enormous number of copies. The art of metalworking was revitalized with the advent of the *Stile Liberty* (Art Nouveau). Small objects for domestic use were produced in bronze or copper, and trays, statuettes, inkwells and ashtrays were produced with less costly metals such as brass, pewter and cast iron.

In the 20th century other metals, such as aluminium or brass, plated with nickel or chrome, lent themselves better to the many new possibilities opened up by industrial design. Iron, however, which was always linked with the modernist myth of the machine, found a vast number of applications in compositions using wires, plates, collages with gears, tubes, bars etc. This field of ironwork had a rich development, down to the late 20th-century experiments with non-representational and Neo-Dadaist art. A revival of wrought-iron work at the beginning of the 20th century was inspired by several master craftsmen: the works displayed at the Esposizione Internazionale d'Arte Decorativa in Monza in 1923, by ALESSANDRO MAZZUCOTELLI, Umberto Bellotto and others, marked the rebirth of an art that had always been alive in the Italian tradition and established the prestige of Italian wrought iron at an international level.

ANGELA CATELLO

X. Objects of vertu.

1. Hardstones. 2. Tortoiseshell. 3. Wax modelling. 4. Coral. 5. Niello and enamel. 6. Jewellery.

1. HARDSTONES.

(i) Rock crystal. (ii) Other.

(i) Rock crystal. In Italy rock crystal was extracted in large quantities near the Saint Gotthard Pass. In the Middle Ages, Venice was one of the most important centres for the working of rock crystal. After the sack of Constantinople in 1204, many antique pieces were brought to Venice from East Asia, including some vases that are still in the Tesoro di S Marco. This undoubtedly stimulated the spread of the art of carving hardstones. There must also have been some production in other Italian centres, for in the 13th century Abbot Suger of Saint-Denis Abbey in France obtained vases of sardonyx and rock crystal from Roger II of Sicily. The northern European tradition of work in rock crystal had a direct influence on Venetian production. The guild of workers in rock crystal is documented in Venice from 1284. It was regulated by a statute with rigorous obligations and rights; for example, it was forbidden to make false rock crystal of white glass. The craft was strongly encouraged, and each workshop had the right to train two apprentices, while artisans who decided to practise their craft in another city were subject to a fine. The main production was of beads; one section made large beads, another rosaries (in which case the artisans were called *paternostrai*), and yet another made small beads, sometimes called *margherite*, whose makers were called masters of the *arte sottile* or *margheritai*. Objects in rock crystal were commissioned mainly by the Church and the Italian courts and usually took the form of crosses,

caskets, reliquaries, pyxes or altar decorations, as, for example, the important altar (1290; Berne) of Andrew III of Hungary (*reg* 1290–1301), decorated with engraved rock crystal panels, panels of cabochon pietre dure and astylar crosses, in which can be seen miniature paintings on parchment. The work of the Venetian rock crystal carvers can also be found in Tuscany; a cross in Santa Croce, Florence, is signed and dated MCCC MAGISTER BERTUCIUS AURIFEX VENETUS ME FECIT.

Examples of rock crystal and pietre dure vases begin to appear in the inventories of the treasuries of the major Italian churches from the second half of the 13th century. During the Renaissance rock crystal carving reached its fullest development. The high level of quality attained by the Venetian craftsmen during this period can be seen in the work of such artisans as Valerio Belli of Vicenza, a medalmaker and gem engraver. He produced important pieces decorated with engraved crystal plaques, such as two gilded silver candelabra with rock crystal, lapis lazuli and other gems (1510–15; London, V&A). Belli was working *c.* 1515 in Rome, where he produced an enamelled gilded silver plate inset with small rock crystal plaques for Leo X, whose enamelled coat of arms appears on the bottom (Munich, Residenz). Belli's most celebrated work is undoubtedly the casket (1530–32; Florence, Pitti) made for Clement VII; the gilded silver has enamelled decorations and 24 small crystal plaques engraved with scenes of the *Passion* (see fig. 93). It was sent as a gift in 1533 to Francis I of France on the occasion of the marriage of his son, the future Henry II, to Catherine de' Medici. The casket returned to Florence with Christine of Lorraine, who married Ferdinando I de' Medici in 1589.

Another renowned engraver and medalmaker was GIOVANNI BERNARDI from Castelbolognese. He worked for Alfonso I d'Este in Ferrara after 1520, and from 1529 in Rome. He, too, produced an important casket (Naples, Capodimonte), begun in 1548 in collaboration with the goldsmith Manno di Bastiano Sbarri. The casket was commissioned by Alessandro Farnese, for whom Bernardi had made small rock crystal plaques carved with classical subjects based on engravings by Perino del Vaga. Bernardi engraved a scene of *Noah's Ark* on a rock crystal plate (Florence, Pitti) taken from further drawings by del Vaga.

During the 16th century rock crystal carving became one of the most important crafts in Milan (*see* MILAN, §III, 1). Among the most notable workshops in Milan were those run by the MISERONI (*see* HARDSTONES, colour pl. II, fig. 1) and SARACCHI families. Specialist workshops sprang up all over Europe, and many Italian masters were commissioned to work in the major courts. In the grand ducal workshop, the Galleria dei Lavori, in Florence, rock crystal carving was first practised by Milanese craftsmen (*see* FLORENCE, §III, 2(i)).

In the 17th century the art of rock crystal carving gradually declined. However, the use of the stone was still frequent in the production of liturgical objects. In Milan, as in Tuscany, during the first half of the century crosses and candelabra were assembled from turned or spiral-engraved elements, as, for example, Matteo Nigetti's altar cross resting on a block of natural rock crystal (completed 1632; Florence, SS Annunziata). In Naples painted rock crystal was frequently found in mosaic panels for altar frontals during the 17th century.

93. Rock crystal plaques and enamel decorations on a gilded silver casket by Valerio Belli, 267×150×145 mm, 1530–32 (Florence, Palazzo Pitti, Museo degli Argenti)

BIBLIOGRAPHY

E. Kris: *Meister und Meisterwerke der Steinschneidekunst in der italienischen Renaissance* (Vienna, 1929/*R* 1979)
W. Holzhausen: 'Bergkristallarbeiten des Mittelalters', *Z. Bild. Kst*, 64 (1930–31), pp. 199–205, 216–21
H. R. Hahnloser: 'Scola et artes cristellariorum de veneciis, 1284–1319: "Opus venetum ad filum"', *Venezia e l'Europa. Atti del XVIII Congresso internazionale di storia dell'arte: Venice, 1956*
H. R. Hahnloser, ed.: *Il tesoro di S Marco* (Rome and Florence, 1971)
H. R. Hahnloser: 'Opere di tagliatori veneziani di cristallo di rocca e di pietre dure del medioevo in Toscana', *Civiltà delle arti minori in Toscana. Atti del I convegno: Arezzo, 1971*
Palazzo Vecchio: Committenza e collezionismo medicei (exh. cat., Florence, Pal. Vecchio, 1980)
C. Strocchi: 'Cristalli di rocca: Una rivisitazione', *MCM*, 3 (1986), pp. 31–5

(ii) Other. The technique of carving pietre dure and polychrome marbles developed in a few cities during the Middle Ages. In Venice carvers of rock crystal (*see* §(i) above) also worked in jasper, serpentine, porphyry and various kinds of marble. In Rome the ancient art of mosaic had never died out. At the court of Frederick II of Sicily (*reg* 1295–1337) glyptic art was practised by specialized craftsmen who may have emigrated after the sack of Constantinople in 1204; one cameo traceable to Frederick II's court is the onyx cameo carved with a scene of animals entering the Ark. Medieval cameos usually depicted biblical and allegorical subjects.

The 15th-century humanist interest in the Classical past and the subsequent collecting of works of art from antiquity meant that antique pietre dure vases and cameos were used as models for Renaissance sculptors and gem-engravers. The interest in antiquity was so prevalent that there was a wide production of cameos imitating antique

94. White onyx cameo portrait of *Cosimo I de' Medici, Eleonora of Toledo and their Children* by Giovanni Antonio de Rossi, h. 188 mm, *c.* 1557–62 (Florence, Palazzo Pitti, Museo degli Argenti)

prototypes. There were, however, also subjects based on contemporary history or portraiture, for example the renowned large onyx cameo portrait of *Cosimo I de' Medici, Eleonora of Toledo and their Children* (*c.* 1557–62; Florence, Pitti; see fig. 94), made by the Milanese GIOVANNI ANTONIO DE ROSSI, who was active in Venice, Florence and Rome. Giuliano di Scipione Amici and Gaspare dei Tazoli were employed by the papal court in Rome, and Domenico Compagni, known as Domenico dei Cammei, worked for Ludovico Sforza, Duke of Milan. In Florence, Piero di Neri dei Rezzuti and Giovanni delle Opere, nicknamed 'delle Corniole' (*c.* 1470–1516), are documented as working for Lorenzo the Magnificent. A collaborator of Giovanni delle Corniole was PIER MARIA SERBALDI DA PESCIA, who carved the first Renaissance sculpture in porphyry, the *Venus with Cupid* (Florence, Pitti). Domenico di Polo, who served his apprenticeship in their workshop, carved a seal in stone plasma with the engraved image of *Hercules*, symbol of the Florentine Republic, for Cosimo I de' Medici, and a series of five cameos in pietre dure with the portrait of *Alessandro de' Medici* (Florence, Pitti).

During the 16th century, especially in Milan, craftsmen moved away from classical themes to religious subjects or portraits. Mythological images were still carved on vases or plaques for use in furniture and showed a marked taste for richly detailed landscape backgrounds. The great technical virtuosity of the Milanese craftsmen working in pietre dure around the middle of the 16th century can be seen in several vases, especially those in rock crystal (*see* §(i) above), and in furniture. Morigia mentioned, for example, that the workshop of Gasparo Miseroni produced for Emperor Rudolf II an inlay of jasper, lapis lazuli and crystals for an ebony table (untraced), designed by Giuseppe Arcimboldo and executed by Giuseppe Guzzi. An example of Milanese furniture of this type is the spinet signed and dated 1577 by the Milanese Annibale de' Rossi (London, V&A), which is adorned with cabochon stones set into panels of carved ivory with a keyboard of ivory and lapis lazuli. In Rome from the mid-16th century, table-tops were made in pietre dure and differently coloured marbles, often set in geometric patterns, usually with a large central panel framed by smaller bands (*see* HARD-STONES, colour pl. I, fig. 1). Combinations of inlays of different design can be seen in the fronts of cabinets made in Rome, such as the sumptuous cabinet at Stourhead House, Wilts. Pietre dure was used to embellish furniture and clocks and remained fashionable throughout the 17th century.

From the mid-16th century the art of pietre dure was widespread in all the major Italian cities. Florence, which had imported the techniques of mosaic, sculpture and gem-engraving, became the most important centre for this art (*see* FLORENCE, §III, 2(i)). Francesco Ferrucci del Tadda carved porphyry sculpture for Cosimo I de' Medici, whose interest in hardstones passed to his sons Francesco I and Ferdinando I. Milanese craftsmen were brought in to work on carved pietre dure vases with gold mounts, as in the lapis lazuli vase designed by Bernardo Buontalenti for Francesco I with mounts by Jacques Bylivert (see fig. 95), and on inlaid cabinets and tables. In 1588 the grand ducal workshop, the Galleria dei Lavori, was formally established.

95. Lapis lazuli vase designed by Bernardo Buontalenti with enamelled gold mounts by Jacques Bijlivert, h. 405 mm, 1583 (Florence, Palazzo Pitti, Museo degli Argenti)

The use of pietre dure for furniture decoration is also documented in Venice, although it is hard to identify the production of that city. There was a renowned cabinet (untraced) that belonged to Cardinal Grimani. Built in Venice in the second half of the 16th century, it was decorated with inlay and columns of polychrome marble and pietre dure and had 72 antique cameos set into the front. The art of pietre dure inlay was spread throughout the Veneto region by Tuscan craftsmen, especially the Florentine family of Corbarelli. Pietro Paolo Corbarelli (1589–1649) is documented as working in Padua from 1639, where he created polychrome marble and pietre dure decoration for the main altar of S Giustina and inlays (1648) for the altar of SS Sacramento. His son, Benedetto Corbarelli, worked mainly in Vicenza, where he lived from 1671. He and other members of the family, including Antonio Corbarelli, produced the decorations of the altar of S Corona. In 1681 the Duke of Modena called on Benedetto to direct a pietre dure workshop with two of his sons. In 1676 Antonio and his brother Francesco Corbarelli built the altar of the Cappella della Croce in the Basilica del Santo in Padua. Francesco, with his sons, set up a flourishing workshop in Brescia after 1683, and the work of his sons is documented in that city until the first

half of the 18th century. The activity of the Corbarelli family was mainly based on church commissions, especially the decoration of altars and ciboria. The ornamental repertory used by these craftsmen in their mosaic panels included naturalistic floral motifs, birds and insects, arabesques, religious figural scenes, urban perspectives and still-lifes with musical instruments. A craftsman active in Venice in the mid-17th century was Giovanni Ferro, whose signature and the date 1656 appear on the altar frontal inlaid in polychrome marble and pietre dure with a rich decoration of plant motifs in S Stefano.

Archival documentation attests that in Naples too, at the end of the 16th century and in the course of the 17th, specialized craftsmen from Florence and Carrara were working in polychrome marbles and pietre dure. Known works are linked with church commissions, especially altar frontals and altar decorations, where the use of polychrome marbles and such stones as lapis lazuli and painted rock crystal predominated. The inlays created in 1605–7 by the Carrara craftsmen Mario Marasi and Costantino Marasi in S Maria Nova use such ornamental motifs as volutes, candelabra and plants. Other Tuscan artisans active in the second and third decades of the 17th century were Francesco Balsimelli and Jacopo Lazzari (see LAZZARI, (1)). Plant motifs predominated in their work, revealing a close adherence to the Florentine Mannerist style; these, however, were not rendered with the naturalistic three-dimensional effect found in Tuscan work, but in a more abstract fashion. In the 17th century pietre dure was still being used as ornament in Milan, as in the cabinet (Milan, Ambrosiana) that belonged to the collector Manfredo Settala, the front of which is inlaid with cabochon and other cuts of hardstones and some Florentine mosaics of naturalistic subjects. Seventeenth-century Lombard production included complex altar frontals with sumptuous pietre dure inlays, examples of which can be seen in Milan, in S Antonio Abate (1654) and S Maria della Passione.

COSIMO FANZAGO, the greatest exponent of Neapolitan Baroque inlay work, produced an ornamental language that was completely different from Tuscan models and characterized by an abundance of plant motifs that were often coordinated with the decoration of the embroidered altar frontals. In 1738, on the initiative of Charles III, King of Spain, a pietre dure workshop was set up in S Carlo alle Mortelle. This workshop, which continued until 1861, was modelled on that in Florence and was run by a master craftsman from the grand ducal workshop, Francesco Ghinghi, a pupil of Giovanni Battista Foggini. From 1780 it was directed by Gaspare Donnini, and later by Giovanni Mugnai until 1805. The Neapolitan court workshop continued to produce work similar to the Florentine traditions of table-tops or inlaid panels with a prevalence of ornamental plant motifs set against a background of basanite. In the 19th century they also made cameos, tobacco-cases and jewellery. A parure with lapis lazuli medallions inlaid with shells, which formerly belonged to Caroline Murat (Los Angeles, CA, Co. Mus. A.), has been connected by A. González-Palacios with Naples manufacture; however, work of this type was also produced in Florence. In the mid-19th century Florence still held a privileged role in the production of pietre dure inlay. In 1860 the grand ducal workshop was turned into a State enterprise, the

Opificio delle Pietre Dure, which retained a vast Italian and foreign clientele. The traditional naturalistic motifs remained important and were adapted to contemporary taste at the turn of the century with *Stile Liberty* (Art Nouveau) floral motifs.

BIBLIOGRAPHY

Morigia: *La nobiltà di Milano* (Milan, 1595)

R. Ruotolo: 'La decorazione in tarsia e commessa a Napoli nel periodo tardomanierista', *Ant. Viva*, xiii/1 (1974), pp. 55–6

Palazzo Vecchio: Committenza e collezionismo medicei (exh. cat., Florence, Pal. Vecchio, 1980)

A. González-Palacios: 'Mosaici e pietre dure', *Quad. Antiqua.* (1982)

A. González-Palacios and S. Roettgen: *The Art of Mosaics: Selections from the Gilbert Collection* (Los Angeles, 1982)

M. I. Catalano: 'Marmi policromi e pietre dure', *Il seicento a Napoli* (exh. cat., Naples, Villa Pignatelli, 1984), pp. 386–7

Splendori di pietre dure (exh. cat., Florence, Pitti, 1988)

A. M. Massinelli: 'Lo studiolo "nobilissimo" del patriarca Giovanni Grimani', *Riv. Archaeol.*, vii (1990), pp. 41–50

A. M. Giusti: *Pietre Dure: Hardstone in Furniture and Decoration* (London, 1992)

ANNA MARIA MASSINELLI

2. TORTOISESHELL. Tortoiseshell has been used in Italy for the manufacture of a wide variety of objects since ancient times, as is shown by some of the objects found in the excavations of Pompeii. It is not possible, however, to study the production of tortoiseshell objects during the Middle Ages and the Renaissance, as none from this period survives. In Italy, as in the rest of western Europe, the golden age of tortoiseshell was undoubtedly the 17th and 18th centuries, when it was used for the decoration of furniture, musical instruments, clocks and even weapons, as well as for such smaller articles as boxes, desk- or toilet-sets, frames, tobacco-cases, trays and jugs.

Craftsmen working in tortoiseshell have been documented from the 17th century, particularly in Naples, where their products were in demand until the end of the 18th century. Inventories and other documents also include records of tortoiseshell furniture and objects in Sicily and in the Castello Valentino in Turin. The fact that the few tortoiseshell objects mentioned in documents are sometimes traceable to northern Italy, for example Venice, suggests that the art of tortoiseshell work was more widespread than is indicated by the provenance of extant objects. Precious tortoiseshell articles were often commissioned by ruling families, for example the Bourbons in Naples, as diplomatic gifts. This may explain why more works of probable Neapolitan origin are located in museums throughout Europe than are found in Naples.

The characteristics of 17th- and 18th-century Italian furniture inlaid in tortoiseshell are rather different from those of the French furniture-maker André-Charles Boulle and his numerous followers, French and otherwise. Boulle gave his name to a particular type of inlay work, which he probably invented, that incorporates tortoiseshell and gilt bronze. It has been suggested, however, that the development of the technique should be attributed to Italian craftsmen brought to France by Marie de' Medici, and that Boulle merely perfected it. In Italy the use of gilt bronze, which Boulle sometimes combined with pewter or copper, was much more sparing, and the materials most often used with tortoiseshell were ebony, sometimes ivory and, especially in the 18th century, mother-of-pearl. Seventeenth-century documents record cabinets in ebony and tortoiseshell (of which a number are extant) in patrician homes, especially in Naples; they were also often found in Sicily, where they were known as *alla napoletana*. In both areas writing-desks and small tables were also made in ebony and tortoiseshell, sometimes with touches of ivory; in some cases this material was simulated with paint. Two 17th-century works are particularly notable: a large clock (Naples, S Paolo Maggiore) veneered in tortoiseshell and pear-wood—the design of which was inspired by Baroque architecture and ornamentation—signed and dated 1678 by Lorenzo Snaiter, a furniture-maker working in Naples but perhaps of German origin; and a tabernacle from the second half of the 17th century (Naples, Certosa di S Martino), in ebony and tortoiseshell with copper, bronze and gilt-brass decoration, inspired by the style of the Lombard sculptor Cosimo Fanzago.

An 18th-century Neapolitan tortoiseshell-worker called Laurentini—about whom almost nothing is known—is traditionally credited with the invention of the technique of *piqué*: tortoiseshell inlaid with gold and silver and sometimes mother-of-pearl and ivory. It was used to make small, exquisite, delicate objects, for example boxes, candlesticks, combs, cases for various articles, frames, inkwells and trays, and is splendidly exemplified by two desk-sets of tortoiseshell inlaid with gold (London, Wallace; Bari, priv. col.), signed by Gennaro Sarao (*fl* second half of the 18th century). Such products were much in tune with the taste of the period and are recorded in inventories, for example those of the apartments of the Bourbons of Naples, as late as the second half of the 19th century. It is not always possible to attribute extant works in this technique to documented craftsmen, as the articles are often unsigned, although some signed works by Gennaro Savino, Nicola Starace and Nicola De Turris, as well as Sarao, are extant. Sometimes, however, the supposed signature of the tortoiseshell-worker is actually that of the silversmith, as in some works signed by De Turris, who was undoubtedly a goldsmith.

Outstanding examples of 18th-century furniture include a tortoiseshell, ebony and gilt-bronze prie-dieu (priv. col.; see 1979–80 exh. cat.); a beautiful table-top (Florence, Pitti) in tortoiseshell, ebony and mother-of-pearl, richly decorated with chinoiserie motifs; and various other tortoiseshell-veneered pieces of furniture in the Museo Correale di Terranova at Sorrento. Of the surviving musical instruments, perhaps the most beautiful example is a mandolin (Stuttgart, Württemberg Landesmus.), splendidly inlaid with tortoiseshell, mother-of-pearl, ivory and gold, signed and dated 1780 by the Neapolitans Antonio Vinaccia and Gioacchino Imparato. Other magnificent instruments with tortoiseshell decoration produced in Naples at the end of the 18th century and the beginning of the 19th are in the Kunsthistorisches Museum, Vienna.

In the 19th century the use of tortoiseshell was less widespread, though it continued to be used for such small articles as combs, fans, spectacle-frames and boxes. It became usual to substitute such cheaper, inferior materials as horn, suitably coloured, that simulated tortoiseshell. Towards the end of the 19th century, celluloid came into use and largely replaced tortoiseshell.

BIBLIOGRAPHY
H. C. Dent: *Piqué: A Beautiful Minor Art* (London, 1923)
F. Strazzullo: *Le manifatture d'arte di Carlo di Borbone* (Naples, 1979), pp. 267–8
A. González-Palacios: 'Le arti decorative e l'arredamento alla corte di Napoli, 1734–1805', *Civiltà del settecento a Napoli*, ii (exh. cat., Naples; Florence; 1979–80)
——: 'Mobili', *Civiltà del settecento a Napoli*, ii (exh. cat., Naples; Florence; 1979–80)
J. Fleming: 'Tartaruga', *Dizionario delle arti minori e decorative* (Milan, 1980)
——: 'Tartaruga', *Antiquariato: Enciclopedia delle arti decorative*, ed. A. González-Palacios (Milan, 1981)
A. González-Palacios: 'Pane, amore e tartaruga', *Bolaffi A.*, iv (1981), p. 43
R. Ruotolo: 'Mobili', *Civiltà del seicento a Napoli*, ii (exh. cat., Naples, 1984)

3. WAX MODELLING. From the Middle Ages ephemeral wax devotional objects, particularly ex-votos, were used in Italian churches. Vasari noted that most such effigies were rather crude, and that high-quality pieces were produced only by such artists as Andrea del Verrocchio. According to Vasari, he produced three wax statues in collaboration with one Orsino Ceraiuolo that were offered ex-voto for Lorenzo the Magnificent's escape from the plot in which his brother Giuliano de' Medici was killed. Vasari also stated that by the mid-15th century realistic representation of the human figure and illusionistic rendering of details in wax modelling were already established. The church of SS Annunziata in Florence was well known for its abundance of wax votive statues in the second half of the 16th century, although such works must certainly have been widespread throughout Italy until the 17th century, after which they became rarer and eventually disappeared.

Wax was used during the Renaissance for the production of models for sculptures or medals. From the first half of the 16th century three-dimensional works in wax were also used as models for paintings. In 1510, for example, the sculptor Jacopo Sansovino made a wax sculpture (London, V&A) of the *Deposition* for the painter Perugino. Despite its original purpose, this was the first wax creation judged by contemporaries to have intrinsic artistic value and was purchased as such by a member of the Gaddi family.

In the first half of the 16th century there was also a vogue for small portraits in white wax, for example those produced by Alfonso Lombardi of Ferrara. According to Vasari, these included portraits of such illustrious contemporaries as *Emperor Charles V*, *Pope Clement VII* and *Ludovico Ariosto*, although none has been preserved. In the second half of the 16th century naturalistic colouring was applied to similar portraits, made usually in the form of medals, the characteristic features of which, including the use of a profile view and the realistic approach, are similar to those in gold and silver. The most important portraitists in wax were, in fact, goldsmiths, for example PASTORINO PASTORINI of Siena and Antonio Abondio (*see* ABONDIO, (1)) of Trent. These small wax portraits were essentially for private use; in 16th-century Italy they were often displayed alongside precious gems, as was the custom with miniatures in northern Europe. Later, as the genre became more popular, they were hung on walls. Towards the end of the 16th century the production of statuettes in coloured wax became widespread in Italy. There was also a fashion for various kinds of relief sculpture in wax that can be classified into three types: those in white or coloured wax on a base of dark stone; those with figures and background both in coloured wax; and *tableaux*, which are wide, deep plaques with fully rounded wax figures.

Few of the works produced in the 16th and 17th centuries have been preserved, and surviving examples can rarely be attributed to known wax modellers. However, a few pieces by the most celebrated artist, GAETANO ZUMBO, have survived. He was active in Naples, Florence and Genoa and was noted for his morbid interest in the decomposition of human bodies, rendered in wax with an analytical realism perhaps inspired by Spanish works. Two of his important works are the *Corruption of Bodies* and *The Plague* (both *c.* 1690; Florence, Bargello), executed for Cosimo III, Grand Duke of Tuscany.

Other outstanding wax modellers and works of high quality also appeared at the end of the 17th century and the beginning of the 18th. In Bologna the most notable was Angelo Gabriello Piò and in Naples Giovan Francesco Pieri (1698–1773). The styles and formal approaches of these artists are different from those of Zumbo. The work of Piò is moderated by a more benevolent observation of the human figure; this is expressed in fully rounded figures (often portrait busts), realistically coloured and often even completed with genuine teeth and hair. Pieri worked in a similar style to that of the painters Giuseppe Bonito and Gaspare Traversi. He produced lively genre scenes, as well as portrait medallions of illustrious figures in the Bourbon court and small wax copies of pictures from the Farnese collection that belonged to Charles, King of Naples (later Charles III, King of Spain).

In the 18th century the patronage of wax modellers spread from the court and upper aristocracy to the lower nobility and the bourgeoisie: this was the last great flowering of the art, which ranged from the polychrome portraits in the late Baroque style to sober Neo-classical pieces, usually monochrome, and small, pretty, genre scenes. In the early 19th century the popularity of wax models declined, and wax modellers were relegated to a secondary role, that of reproducing anatomical models. After some illustrious but isolated 16th-century precedents, including work by Michelangelo and Lodovico Cigoli, and a more widespread practice in the 17th and 18th centuries, this specialized use of wax reached its maximum development in the 19th century, due especially to the work of the Florentine Clemente Susini (1754–1814). Although his works, which constitute the greater part of the collection of anatomical wax models in the Museo Zoologico 'La Specola' in Florence, were expressly intended for scientific use, a strong aesthetic interest is evident.

BIBLIOGRAPHY
G. Masi: 'Appunti d'archivio: La ceroplastica a Firenze nel XV–XVI secolo e la famiglia Benintendi', *Riv. A.*, ix (1916), pp. 124–42
A. Emiliani: 'Ritratti in cera del settecento bolognese', *A. Figurativa*, ii (1960), pp. 28–35
M. Bucci: *Anatomia come arte* (Florence, 1969)
D. Lightbown: 'Le cere artistiche del cinquecento', *A. Illus.*, iii (1970), pp. 30–39, 46–55
E. J. Pyke: *A Biographical Dictionary of Wax Modellers* (London, 1973)

A. González-Palacios: 'Giovan Francesco Pieri', *Antol. B.A.*, ii (1977), pp. 139–47
Congresso internazionale sulla ceroplastica nella scienza e nell'arte. Atti del I congresso: Firenze, 1977
A. González-Palacios: 'Arti decorative e arredamento', *Civiltà del settecento a Napoli*, ii (exh. cat., Naples; Florence; 1979–80)
Ritrattini in cera d'epoca neoclassica (exh. cat., Florence, 1981)

PAOLA D'ALCONZO

4. CORAL. In ancient Rome coral was considered a precious material; apart from its decorative uses in jewellery, for example in necklaces, seals, cameos and rings, it was thought to afford powerful protection against the evil eye. During the Middle Ages coral was used mainly in jewellery and for the decoration of goldsmiths' work and textiles. In the 14th and 15th centuries it was often left in its natural form, as in the candelabra in the Scuola Grande di S Rocco, Venice, whose arms, mounted on a silver base, consist solely of coral branches. In Naples the art of coral-carving was strongly promoted by the Aragón dynasty, which in the 15th century commissioned a large number of works that revealed a strong Spanish influence. The renowned Sicilian coral-carving developed between the 15th and 16th centuries, TRAPANI and Messina being the two major centres. In Trapani the work was almost all done by Jews, and when they were expelled from the island for political reasons in 1492 there was a serious crisis in the production of coral-carving. Throughout the 16th century and until the 18th century Trapani was the most important centre of coral-working. Other Italian cities, for example Amalfi, Florence and Naples, followed the Sicilian lead. Genoa, where, unlike Trapani, craftsmen did not specialize in a particular technique, was also renowned in the 16th century. Coral worked in Genoa was frequently exported, especially to India, Spain and Armenia. In Trapani during the 17th and 18th centuries copper or silver objects, for example trays, epergnes, chalices, reliquaries and monstrances, were decorated with small pieces of coral to create floral motifs or relief figures, often a depiction of the Virgin in glory surrounded by putti or of the Crucifixion. Some 17th-century examples are preserved in the Museo Nazionale di S Martino in Naples. During the 18th century coral was used throughout Italy to ornament ecclesiastical objects; these reflect the persistence of the Baroque style. There are a few examples of coral statuary of that period; a small crib in the Museo Nazionale di S Martino in Naples is similar in style to another in the Museo Pépoli in Trapani. The use of coral to decorate goldsmiths' work remained popular in the 19th century. In the 20th century jewellery made of coral ranging in colour from pale pink to strong red continues to be produced in great quantities, especially in the area around Naples. In Torre del Greco there is a flourishing industry producing coral objects based on historical models and in such new forms as pipes and umbrella handles.

BIBLIOGRAPHY
P. Leone de Castris: 'Corallo', *Antiquariato: Enciclopedia delle arti decorative*, ed. A. González-Palacios, xvi (Milan, 1981), pp. 400–02
B. Liverino: *Il corallo: Esperienze e ricordi di un corallaio* (Bologna, 1983)

5. NIELLO AND ENAMEL. Although a few medieval Italian works in niello are extant, the greatest development of this art took place during the Renaissance. Tuscany was the main area of production of niello, not only for such religious objects as paxes, reliquaries and antependiums but also for such secular pieces as side-arms, caskets, bookbindings and buckles. Along with Antonio del Pollaiuolo, Filippo Brunelleschi, Matteo di Giovanni and Bardinelli—who all often used niello—the Florentine masters of the art included MASO FINIGUERRA, who made the splendid niello pax with a depiction of the *Coronation of the Virgin* in the centre (*c.* 1452; Florence, Bargello). In Bologna, another important centre for niello work, a well-known master of the art was Francesco Francia, who produced gilded silver frames for paxes, often with a Pietà in niello. Other artists of the late 15th century and the early 16th who used niello included the sculptor and medallist Caradosso, who worked in Milan and Rome; Giovanni di Turino in Siena; Giacomo della Porta in Modena; and Peregrino da Cesena, as well as Benvenuto Cellini, Marcantonio Raimondi and Nicoletto da Modena. After the first half of the 16th century niello disappeared from the work of Italian goldsmiths; it was later used mainly for bookbindings throughout Europe.

Some of the most important pieces of Italian enamel were produced in the Byzantine period. In the 10th and 11th centuries cloisonné and champlevé enamels were used in increasingly varied ways, especially to decorate such liturgical objects as crosses, breviaries, reliquaries, paxes and thuribles. Among the most important works of this type is the reliquary of the True Cross (Rome, Vatican, Mus. Sacro), commissioned by Pope Paschal I. The Pala d'Oro (late 11th century; Venice, S Marco; *see* VENICE, §IV, 1(v)) may be considered the finest example of enamelwork in the Byzantine period. In this large altarpiece the technique of champlevé and cloisonné enamel are well combined, with enamelled figures of saints framed in a brilliant setting of precious stones mounted in gold. During the 14th century the technique of *basse taille* came into use in Italy, completely supplanting cloisonné and champlevé. Towards the mid-15th century enamel began to be used on copperplates, perhaps following a Flemish tradition; an important example is a pax in the form of a tabernacle (Milan, Mus. Poldi Pezzoli). In the 17th and 18th centuries the use of enamel was relegated to a secondary role, supplementing goldsmiths' work as decoration for jewellery, clocks, snuff-boxes or chivalric insignia.

BIBLIOGRAPHY
A. Lipinsky: *Oro, argento, gemme e smalti: Tecnologie delle arti dalle origini alla fine del medioevo* (Florence, 1975)
P. Leone de Castris: 'Niello', *Antiquariato: Enciclopedia delle arti decorative*, ed. A. González-Palacios, xli (Milan, 1981), p. 1018

FERNANDA CAPOBIANCO

6. JEWELLERY. The use of jewellery increased in Italy in the 13th century, when the necklines of dresses were adorned with jewelled borders in the antique Byzantine fashion. Rings are rarely found in inventories of the period. The symbolic value of stones was very important: sapphire was associated with virtue in Heaven and celestial beatitude on Earth, and emeralds stood for wealth. Coral was a popular ornament (*see* §4 above), and sales at huge prices are registered in notarial archives, especially in Genoa. The detailed sumptuary laws, which differed in the various Italian states, are useful guides for reconstructing the

different ways in which jewellery was used, but it is difficult to establish to what extent these laws were obeyed.

In the 14th century a typical form of jewellery was the paternoster, a rosary without a cross worn around the neck or the waist. Valentina Visconti (1366–1408) had one with enamel and pearls, while 14th-century Venetian documents mention numerous paternosters in crystal, amber, coral and silver. Ornaments of gold, pearls and precious stones were sewn to clothing; rings were usually made with a single gem mounted in a smooth setting of great value. In Florence a sumptuary law of 1355 prohibited the wearing of more than two rings, each of which could have only one gem; in Naples, however, rings of more elaborate design were made, and gem-engraving was practised.

In the Renaissance gem mountings were more refined, and the quality of the goldsmith's work was almost more important than the value of the stones. In Florence at the time of Lorenzo the Magnificent there were no less than 44 goldsmiths, and the art of gem-engraving was revived, notably by Giovanni delle Corniole. The Florentine idea of elegance favoured the whiteness of pearls, which were wound in long strings around the hair of Tuscan noblewomen. Another common form was the *vezzi*, short necklaces, often of coral or pearls; *vezzi* of black pearls can be seen in Antonio del Pollaiuolo's *Portrait of a Lady* (Milan, Mus. Poldi Pezzoli).

Vittoria Camponeschi Carafa, the mother of Pope Paul IV, had in her dowry a necklace of alternating silver and coral beads. The massive buckles favoured in the 14th century were converted into pendants and worn around the neck, suspended from ribbons or pearl necklaces. These often consisted of a circular section with a central gem, from which three pearls hung (see, for example, Domenico Ghirlandaio's portrait of *Giovanna Tornabuoni*; Lugano, Col. Thyssen-Bornemisza). Up to four or five rings were worn on each hand. In northern Italy earrings were rare, but in the south they were more common. Neapolitan inventories list some in the form of the sun, and in the fresco of *The Triumph of Death* at Palermo (Gal. Reg. Sicilia) the ladies wear beautiful earrings shaped like leaves.

The use of jewels to decorate dresses was elaborate. In 1468 Bona of Savoy, the bride of Galeazzo Maria Sforza, Duke of Milan, had a gown embroidered with pearls and rubies of the fabulous value of 50,000 ducats, while the dowry of Anna Maria Sforza, the wife of Alfonso I d'Este, Duke of Ferrara and Modena, contained 22,000 jewelled pins for clothing. Men wore great golden chains, medallions and brooches on their hats, and rings with gems and engraved stones. More than extravagant luxury, great collections of jewels were meant to display flourishing economic stability for political ends: Ludovico Sforza, Duke of Milan, showed his gem collections to foreign ambassadors and princes.

In the 16th century, at the height of Renaissance elegance, precious golden hair-nets embroidered with gems appeared. On their foreheads noblewomen would wear a splendid single gem or pearl, held by a light veil or slender chain. Rich trimmings adorned their gowns, and long jewelled fillets emphasized the cut of the garment. Necklaces became very rich, hanging in long cascades with alternating parts of finely chiselled gold, gems or enamel. In the 16th century, especially in Florence, splendid jewels, trinkets, buckles and pendants were finely chiselled and enamelled with images of animals and mythological figures, among other things; although no known pieces are attributed to him, Benvenuto Cellini described his work in this style in his books. Rings were worn less often in Italy than in northern Europe, and they were usually sober in form; engraved stones were increasingly favoured for rings, medallions and brooches. During the 16th century the vogue for earrings spread to the north of Italy; peculiar to Venice were earrings composed of a small ring to which a little fabric ribbon was tied. In Naples the combination of blue and white was frequently used, for example aquamarines and diamonds or pearls and blue enamel; this was probably derived from the Hispano-Moresque tradition.

In the course of the 17th century the importance of the worked mounting diminished; the value of the gems took precedence even if the mountings were of gold and enamel. Stones were still cut in rectangles or triangles, and in the second half of the century the rose style of diamond-cutting began to be used. In Piedmontese inventories from the end of the 17th century there are a few mentions of the brilliant cut; this style also appeared elsewhere in northern Italy at this time, whereas in Rome and the south it was found only in the early decades of the 18th century. Parures, comprising a necklace, bracelets, earrings and breastpins, came into use at this time and featured flowers, all mounted with the same type of precious stones. Flower jewels, worn as breastpins or in the hair, were elaborate floral shapes encrusted with large stones that stood out strikingly in mountings of a more open design. The longer necklaces of the Renaissance were shortened, and the Spanish style of a short jewelled or pearl necklace worn tightly around the neck became widely fashionable. These sometimes featured imposing cascades of pearls in numerous strings. Jewelled crosses worn around the neck or pinned to the breast were popular all over Italy, especially in Rome. Men's jewellery was limited to rings, jewelled honorific badges and dozens of precious buttons.

In Italy, unlike France, during the 17th and 18th centuries there were very few collections of engravings to show the work of famous jewellers. Many architects and painters took delight in designing jewellery, but there are very few jewellers for whom a significant number of designs or more than a few biographical facts are known. In the course of the 18th century gold mountings almost disappeared in favour of silver settings. Faceted or brilliant-cut stones were no longer embedded in their settings but were brought into greater relief. In the second half of the century the open setting was introduced. The brilliant diamond became very fashionable, although the use of coloured stones was never abandoned as it was in France. Items of jewellery were always grouped in parures; diamonds, emeralds, rubies, sapphires and pearls were now considered by far the most valuable and were often the only jewels to be inventoried. In Rome, a conservative city indifferent to French fashions, the brilliant cut became widespread only around the middle of the century. The largest jewellery-making centre to cut diamonds in this way was Venice, which for some centuries had been at the centre of the gem trade. The workshop of the Fondaco

96. Bracelet by Fortunato Pio Castellani, 12 links decorated with white and gold mosaic spelling NON RELINQVES ('you will not give up') and (reverse) NON RELINQVAM ('I will not give up'), l. *c.* 160 mm, *c.* 1860s (private collection)

dei Tedeschi was especially well known; Francesco III d'Este, Duke of Modena (*d* 1780), went there personally *c.* 1750 to supervise the recutting of the ducal diamonds in the brilliant style.

At the beginning of the 18th century ladies wore large braided frogs and combs on their bodices and jewelled flowers in their hair. These flowers were often *en tremblant*; in the course of the century light aigrettes and simple solitaire gems fixed to the hair also appeared. The richness of Venetian gems was notable: in 1771 Polisena Mocenigo owned 3552 diamonds weighing 1989 carats, and the splendour of the Labia family jewels dazzled visitors.

Peculiar to Rome at this time was the use of engraved cameos and gems; from various inventories, including those of the Colonna and Pamphili families, it is known that *c.* 1750 these were mounted in whole sets, long before that fashion became widespread in Europe. The very rich gems of the Roman patricians, of which many had originally belonged to the papacy, continued to be set in classically simple mountings. *Esclavage* necklaces of pearls or precious stones and large jewelled butterflies were particularly elegant.

At the end of the 18th century the influence of Neo-classical taste spread to jewellery. Sprays of diamonds for the hair and clothing were made in the form of ears of corn; earrings were made in Egyptian style or in the form of circles, stars or suns. The Napoleonic invasions brought ruin to many families in the Italian states, and as a result their jewellery was often sold, requisitioned, removed from the mountings or melted down. Those who still had economic means, or who shared the imperial fortunes, adapted themselves to the French styles; others continued to ignore the Empire style and went on using 18th-century forms of jewellery until the 1850s. Typical pieces of the Napoleonic era were corals, cameos and engraved lava; in Florence, jewellery with hardstone inlays; in Rome, engraved gems and cameos and miniature mosaics (*see also* JEWELLERY, fig. 7). Among the most celebrated engravers were BENEDETTO PISTRUCCI, GIUSEPPE GIROMETTI, Luigi PICHLER and NICOLA MORELLI, all working in Rome.

In Rome *c.* 1820 Fortunato Pio Castellani (*see* CASTEL-LANI, (1)) began his production of archaeologically inspired jewellery (see fig. 96). His trade, famous all over Europe, concentrated mainly on conventional types of jewellery, and he launched the elegant French floral style in Rome. His son Augusto Castellani (*see* CASTELLANI, (3)) consolidated the business by capitalizing on the revival of classical, Byzantine, Carolingian and medieval themes. Aside from the work of the Castellani, in the 19th century French taste predominated throughout Italy, although local influences never disappeared completely.

BIBLIOGRAPHY

A. Castellani: *Della oreficeria italiana* (Rome, 1872)
A. Bertoletti: *Le arti minori alla corte di Mantova nei secoli XV–XVI–XVII* (Milan, 1889)
P. Lanza di Scalea: *Donne e gioielli in Sicilia nel medioevo e nel rinascimento* (Palermo, 1892)
F. Malaguzzi Valeri: *La corte di Ludovico il Moro*, 3 vols (Milan, 1917)
M. Accascina: *L'oreficeria italiana* (Florence, 1934)
R. Berliner: *Italian Drawings for Jewellery* (New York, 1940)
C. G. Bulgari: *Argentieri, gemmari ed orafi d'Italia*, 4 vols (Rome, 1958)
G. Tescione: *Il corallo nella storia e nell'arte* (Naples, 1965)
G. Gregorietti: *Il gioiello nei secoli* (Milan, 1969)
L'oreficeria della Firenze del '400 (exh. cat., Florence, Ist. Stor. A., 1977)
D. Petochi: *I mosaici minuti romani nei secoli XVIII e XIX* (Rome, 1981)
G. C. Munn: *Les Bijoutiers Castellani et Giuliano: Retour à l'antique au XIXe siècle* (Paris, 1983; Eng. trans., London, 1984)
S. Aluffi-Pentini: *I gioielli delle famiglie romane dal barocco al romanticismo* (diss., U. Rome, 1987)
Ori ed argenti di Sicilia (exh. cat., Trapani, Mus. Reg., 1989)

STEFANO ALUFFI-PENTINI

XI. Textiles.

1. Silk. 2. Lace. 3. Tapestry. 4. Embroidery.

1. SILK. Silk-weaving was introduced into Sicily by the Fatimid Arabs, who controlled the island until its conquest by the Normans in AD 1071. The silks attributed to Sicily, for example those used in the coronation mantle of the Holy Roman Emperors (1133–4; Vienna, Schatzkam.; *see* ISLAMIC ART, fig. 183) made for Roger II and a 12th-century fragment (Hannover, Kestner-Mus.) inscribed 'made in a workshop of the realm', show a mix of Islamic and Byzantine influences. By 1300, however, silk-weaving was more strongly established in the northern city states. They had long been involved in the silk trade, and from the 8th century to the 12th there had been a special relationship between Venice and the Byzantine Empire, with Venice providing naval support against the Empire's enemies in return for lucrative trading rights. The sacking of Constantinople (1204) and the decline of the Empire encouraged the introduction of sericulture to Italy and the establishment of silk-weaving in Venice, Genoa, Lucca, Florence and later Milan and other cities. As early as 1265 Venetian statutes refer to the weaving of a variety of pure and mixed silks. The patterns encompassed plant, animal and heraldic motifs and even large-scale pictorial panels, such as the antependium (Regensburg Cathedral) with the figure of Bishop Heinrich von Rotteneck (*reg* 1277–93). The Vatican inventory of 1295 includes one silk from Genoa and many from Venice and Lucca with patterns of birds in roundels, their heads and claws brocaded with gold thread. Such silks continued to be purchased by the English court into the 1320s.

Italian silks were dramatically affected, however, by the opening-up of trade with East Asia following the establishment of the Mughal empire in the 13th century. In the

14th century dragons and phoenixes replaced the rather stylized birds and animals, while asymmetrical patterns, full of movement and often with a marked diagonal bias, replaced the rows of roundels. Different weaves were also adopted including lampas, five-shaft satin (used for both plain fabrics and damask) and velvet (*see* TEXTILE, §III, 1(i)). Plain velvet had been woven in the late 13th century, but first stripes and then small floral patterns were introduced; by 1376 three-colour velvets in two heights of pile were being woven in Lucca (*see* LUCCA, §2). Although plain silks continued to make up the bulk of Italian production, it was for these richly patterned goods that Italy was renowned.

The fanciful designs of the 14th century continued into the 15th, but, as foliage became a more dominant feature, they were replaced by formally arranged compartments containing pineapples or similar fruits and, later in the century, by large, asymmetrical undulating stems bearing fleshy leaves enclosing or terminating in large fruits. Lampas was largely replaced by damask and velvet, which in the mid-15th century was often woven in monochrome with voided patterns delicately outlined on the plain silk grounds. Polychrome and pile-on-pile velvets were also produced and, later in the 15th century, the silk grounds were increasingly replaced with gold cloth on which details of the pattern were defined with thin lines of velvet, while more substantial areas of pile were ornamented with loops of gold. Brocading was also used. Such expensive fabrics were made to order, as in the case of the vestments (1499–1502; Stonyhurst, Lancs) woven in Florence for Henry VII of England.

Some large-scale velvets and other silks in a 15th-century style continued to be woven throughout the 16th century, but new designs were introduced based on curvilinear lattices and sinuous arabesques entwined by or enclosing plants and animals. These large-scale patterns were woven in *cisolé* (cut and uncut pile) velvet (see fig. 97), brocatelle, damask and brocaded satin, fabrics which were also used for the small-scale patterns woven for use in dress from the mid-16th century. These designs were composed of small motifs—sprigs, broken branches, 'S'-shapes, birds and animals—sometimes enclosed in diapers but often simply arranged in straight or staggered rows. Towards the end of the 16th century and into the 17th rows of left-right curving sprigs were particularly popular.

During the 17th century the distinction between dress and furnishing silks became more evident, with the designs of the latter becoming increasingly large scale, and, although influenced by the development of the Baroque, continuing to hark back to 16th- and even 15th-century patterns. Dress silks developed differently; floral sprigs became a dominant feature, growing in size and becoming more delicate and naturalistic, often linked or enclosed by curvilinear stems. With the growth of the Baroque style in the mid-17th century, the stems became more vigorously curved, creating a feeling of movement, and the flowers became increasingly exotic. The sprigs were sometimes scattered across the surface, set within loosely defined compartments, confined within wide and narrow stripes or brocaded across them.

The design and production of dress silks was dramatically affected, however, by the reform and expansion of

97. *Cisolé* velvet, polychrome silks on a gold ground, probably made in Genoa, 1600–50 (Stockholm, St Jakob's Church); from an altar frontal of 1651

the French silk industry after 1664, and by the end of the century France was beginning to dominate the market. Although this had a drastic effect on the Italian silk industry, it did not destroy it. Patterned dress silks, usually in the French style, were woven throughout the 18th century, as were fine plain silks such as the organzine produced at Como, while Italy remained pre-eminent for the weaving of grand furnishing damasks and velvets, notably in Genoa (*see* GENOA, §3(i)), but also in Venice (famous for its brocatelles), Milan, Florence and Naples.

Although damaged by the Napoleonic Wars (1803–15), its concentration on fine, plain silks meant that the Italian industry was not as badly hit as France and England by the move away from elaborate dress silks in the late 18th century and the early 19th. Plain silks and patterned fabrics for ecclesiastical use (*see* VESTMENTS, ECCLESIASTICAL, §2) and furnishings remained central to the industry during the 19th century and, although less heavily industrialized than other countries, Italy was well represented at all the international exhibitions. In the first half of the 20th century such internationally important firms as those of Abegg and Ratti (Como) flourished, and, despite a difficult period after World War II, the Italian silk industry, often working on a small scale but drawing on traditional skills and concentrating on good design, continued to be of international importance.

BIBLIOGRAPHY

F. Podreider: *Storia dei tessuti d'arte in Italia* (Bergamo, 1928)

T. Broggi: *Storia del serificio comasco: La tecnica, i: Dalla origine alla fine del settecento* (Como, 1958)

P. Thornton: *Baroque and Rococo Silks* (London, 1964)

D. King: 'Some Unrecognised Venetian Woven Fabrics', *V&A Mus. Yb.* (1969)

D. Devoti: *L'arte del tessuto in Europa* (Milan, 1974)

R. B. Fanelli: *Il Museo del tessuto a Prato: La donazione Bertini* (Florence, 1975)

Tessuti italiani del rinascimento: Collezioni Franchetti, Carrand (exh. cat., Florence, Bargello, 1981)

Tessuti serici italiani, 1450–1530 (exh. cat., Milan, Castello Sforzesco, 1983)

La collezione Gandini del Museo Civico: I tessuti del XVIII e XIX secolo, Modena, Istituto per i Beni Artistici Culturali e Naturali della Regione Emilia-Romagna (Bologna, 1985)

L. Monnas: 'Developments in Figured Velvet Weaving in Italy during the 14th Century', *Bull. Liason Cent. Int. Etud. Textiles Anc.*, lxiii–lxiv (1986), pp. 63–100

M. King and D. King: *European Textiles in the Keir Collection, 400 BC to 1800 AD* (London, 1990)

SANTINA M. LEVEY

2. LACE. Cutwork and silk and metal-thread bobbin laces began to be made in Italy *c.* 1550. Venice soon emerged as a leading centre, and cutwork, in addition to fine embroidery, was made in the convent workrooms there. Italian cutwork, heavier than the Flemish equivalent, soon developed flowing patterns or more naive figurative ones. Cutwork and *reticella* with figurative and geometrical patterns continued to be made in parts of the eastern Mediterranean formerly ruled by Venice until the 20th century. An important series of pattern books for needle lace of all types, including *lacis*, was published in Venice from the 1540s. Bobbin lace was also made there, while other important centres were Genoa and Milan. In the

first half of the 17th century Genoa produced linen, silk and metal-thread laces in a solid technique, often incorporating wheat-ear motifs. Milan, also noted originally for silk and metal lace, developed a part lace in which bobbin-made tapes were formed into designs imitating the soft patterns of Flemish lace, like contemporary Venetian tape lace.

The growing expertise of the Venetian needle lacemakers enabled them soon after the mid-17th century to develop a system of specialization whereby large and sumptuous items could be made in a magnificent high-relief lace in rich Baroque patterns (*see* VENICE, §III, 4(ii)). This supreme luxury product proved hugely popular throughout Europe during the second half of the 17th century, and the later adaptation to lighter, frothier designs ensured that Venice remained the leading centre of production until *c.* 1700 (see fig. 98). A similarly bold Baroque bobbin lace is attributed to Milan, while the same kind of designs appeared on Italian silk and metal-thread lace. Milanese linen lace spread throughout Lombardy, to central Italy and even across the border to Austria and beyond. Variants of it continued to be produced, mainly for ecclesiastic use, until the 20th century.

Changes in fashion caused the Venetian lace industry to collapse early in the 18th century, although needle lace continued to be made for ecclesiastic purposes. The Genoese industry had already begun to decline in the late 17th century, and production eventually moved out to towns along the Ligurian coast. By the mid-18th century only small, cheap laces were produced in Milan, but in the second half of the century the fashion for light silk and linen bobbin laces restored some prosperity to the industries there and in Liguria and Lombardy. They were also successfully introduced into Venice, while a needle lace

98. Flounce of heavy raised linen needle lace (detail), 572×5030 mm, Venice, second half of the 17th century (Chicago, IL, Art Institute of Chicago)

with a cloudy square mesh, usually called 'Burano', was also made there at the end of the 18th century. These and the heavier peasant laces kept lacemaking alive in Italy until the art was revived in the late 19th century.

In 1872 a school of lace was established on the island of Burano, near Venice. The first needle laces made there reproduced 18th- and early 19th-century designs and techniques, and reproductions, especially of 17th-century Venetian lace, continued to form a large part of the output, as did the remodelling of antique lace. The school also developed a distinctive style of its own, which helped it survive until the late 20th century. Many other Italian lace schools adopted the policy of making reproduction laces, particularly late 16th- and early 17th-century bobbin laces, while the Società Aemilia Ars in Bologna (est. 1898) concentrated on cutwork and *reticella* and copies of the designs in the 16th-century pattern book by Archangelo Passerotti (1590–1627), although needle lace in the Art Nouveau style was also made. The reproduction and novelty laces produced by these schools and by more strictly commercial ventures, such as the bobbin-lace industry established at Pellestrina by the Venetian businessman Michelangelo Jesurum (*d* 1909), were highly successful at the beginning of the 20th century. In 1903 the Industrie Femminile Italiane was founded as a means of bringing all these products together on a national basis. An astonishing variety of work was shown at its inaugural exhibition in Genoa in the same year. A new venture, which started in 1908 and remained in being until 1968, was the bobbin-lace firm established by Mario Zennaro (1881–1962) at Rapallo, which again relied largely on reproduction lace, but also produced some work of strikingly modern design. This was, however, exceptional and by 1914 the industry in general was once again in decline, and few of the lace schools managed to survive the 1920s. In Cantù the school founded in 1883 was able to continue, as it produced lace in a purely contemporary idiom during the 1920s and 1930s after artists' designs. There was a further revival there in the 1950s, but the emphasis was still on traditional, two-dimensional lace.

BIBLIOGRAPHY

G. Romanelli Marone: *Lavori artistici femminili: Trine a fuselli in Italia* (Milan, 1902)

M. Jesurum: *Esemplari di merletti moderni: Raccolti da Michelangelo Jesurum* (Venice and Rome, 1910)

E. Ricci: *Old Italian Lace*, 2 vols (London and Philadelphia, 1913)

A. Mottola Molfino and T. Binaghi Olivari: *I pizzi: Moda e simbolo* (Venice, 1977)

L. Bellodi Casanova and others: *La Scuola dei Merletti di Burano* (exh. cat., Burano, Consorzio Merletti, 1981)

Cinque secoli di merletti europei: I capolavori (exh. cat., ed. D. Davanzo Poli; Burano, Consorzio Merletti, 1984)

G. Mariacher and others: *Il merletto di Pellestrina* (Pellestrina, 1986)

E. Parma Armani, ed.: *Il Museo del Pizzo al Tombolo di Rapallo: La manifattura Mario Zennaro, 1908–1968* (Genoa, 1990)

PATRICIA WARDLE

3. TAPESTRY.

(i) Before 1500. (ii) 1500–1624. (iii) 1625–1800. (iv) After 1800.

(i) Before 1500. The use of woven tapestry in Italy seems to have survived from antiquity into modern times almost without hiatus. During the early Middle Ages, however, probably only the very wealthiest sectors of society could afford these luxury weavings. Monumental woven representations, as well as sets of unrivalled dimensions, were used in St Peter's and other major basilicas in Rome. Tapestries were probably also employed to a lesser extent at the courts of kings and powerful overlords, although documentation is scarce and other textile hangings must have predominated. There are no records of where these tapestries were woven, but since the technique was known all over the Roman Empire, many may have been created locally.

The modern Italian term for woven tapestry, *arazzo*, derives from the phrase 'cloth' or 'hanging of Arras' (It. *panno di Arrazzo*, evolving to *panno de razo* and other variants), which is found in the Middle Ages in so many European languages. It indicates that by the late 14th century in Italy, as elsewhere, when tapestries had become a more usual and even necessary luxury accoutrement, the production centre from which the finest examples were obtained was Arras in France. Tapestries acquired in the 15th century from the north, through such middlemen as the Medici Bank of Florence, were either bought ready-made from weaver-merchants' stocks or were specially ordered according to the purchaser's requirements. A drawing or cartoon by an Italian artist was provided in some cases; such major artists as Leonardo da Vinci and Botticelli painted cartoons to be sent north for weaving. In Italy, as in northern Europe, tapestries were displayed for pomp, and sets were regularly loaned among allies, to achieve greater splendour for weddings and other grand occasions, or to decorate the chambers of a visiting notable.

By the early decades of the 15th century the increasing quantities of tapestries collected required major maintenance. Apparently, some collections justified the hiring of full-time, specialized foreign artisans, as opposed to locally trained upholsterers. Documents for this phenomenon at the courts of Mantua (from 1420) and Ferrara (from 1436) indicate that most of these workers had been trained in Flanders or France as master or journeyman weavers. They also acted as intermediaries for the purchase of tapestries from their homelands and set up looms of their own to weave smaller, but in many cases possibly choicer, pieces for their patrons. Court weavers are also documented at the papal court in Rome (from 1451/2–6), in Modena (1457, 1488), Correggio (1460–1506), Milan (by 1456), Urbino (*c.* 1470) and Naples (*c.* 1498). Numerous tapestries by them are recorded, although at this time the masters were never numerous enough, nor was the weaving sufficiently economical to affect the rate of importation from northern Europe. Only two pieces (*c.* 1475–6; Lugano, Col. Thyssen–Bornemisza and Cleveland, OH, Mus. A.), woven in Ferrara, which had the greatest number of court weavers in the 15th century, can still be identified.

Such masters filled a need for direct contacts: they not only facilitated relations during recurrent political turmoil in northern tapestry-producing areas, but, perhaps more importantly, they could obviate or unite with the services of traditional tapestry-ordering channels to assure more satisfactory results. By weaving certain commissions on site, they afforded their patrons more personalized and closer artistic and economic control. Thus, at about the same time as their appearance as full-time, court employees in Italy, northern masters also began roaming the peninsula as itinerant weaver-merchant-restorers. They catered to lesser noblemen, wealthy merchants and city governments, with a selection of wares for sale or to order. Alternatively, they offered the possibility of setting up looms temporarily, to execute a major project. Such commissions allowed a master weaver to test whether an area might support a permanent workshop, as suggested by extant contracts, which record the training of such local apprentices, for example the contract of Reinaut Woutersz. (pseud. Rinaldo Boteram; Rinaldo di Gualtieri; *fl* 1438–81) from Brussels in Siena. With the permission of Niccolo III d'Este, Marquese de Ferrara, for whom he may already have worked, Woutersz. went to Siena in 1438 and stayed until 1442, working on both public and private commissions. He was followed in 1443 by Giachetto di Benedetto da Razzo (*fl* 1441–57), whom the city of Siena contracted to teach for up to ten years and to weave three large tapestries (*Good Government*, *Peace* and *War*; all untraced), after Simone Martini's frescoes in the Palazzo Pubblico, Siena. Other temporary workshops are recorded in Florence (1455–7 and 1476–80), Bologna (*c.* 1460), Todi (1460), Perugia (1463–7), Ferrara (1464), Genoa (1496)

and elsewhere. Apparently only in Venice (by 1421) and Milan, however, did independent weaver-merchants find it profitable to settle on a long-term basis.

Woutersz. is among the best documented of these ambulatory masters. After his stay in Siena, he worked for the courts of Ferrara (1444–8), Mantua (1449–57) and Modena (1457). He finally set up an independent shop in Venice (*see* VENICE, §III, 4(i)), after which he seems to have concentrated on importing tapestries from Brussels, actively maintaining his court contacts in Ferrara and Mantua until at least 1481. Another peripatetic master was Livinus Gilii de Burgis (*fl* 1444–after 1473), who was recorded at various times at the Ferrara court (1444, 1463 and *c.* 1473), Florence (1455–7) and Milan (from 1463).

The themes of Italian tapestries at this time were much the same as Flemish ones: religious, mythological, historical, heraldic and allegorical. It seems, however, that fewer tapestries with such representations as millefleurs, *verdures*, landscapes or genre pieces were woven in Italy, probably because northern centres were so specialized in their design and mass-produced them so economically; mass-production would never, in fact, be a major factor in Italian tapestry weaving. Unlike in the north, where

99. Tapestry of the *Three Marys at the Tomb and Noli me tangere* from the *Passion* cycle, *c.* 2.02×11.30 m, designed and woven in ?Venice, *c.* 1420–30 (Venice, Museo di San Marco)

weavers relied on the use of cartoons for multiple sets, designs for Italian patrons were generally conceived to be woven only once, although some popular ones were later repeated. Another difference in Italian cartoons was that they were apparently almost always fully coloured—early northern tapestry cartoons were rarely coloured at all—whether they were to be woven locally or in the north. A third major difference between Italian and northern tapestries is the treatment of borders: northern tapestries had no borders until approximately the 1490s, whereas the *Passion* cycle (*c.* 1420–30; Venice, Mus. S Marco; see fig. 99) for the cathedral of S Marco, Venice (the earliest preserved tapestries from Italian designs) already had framing borders like those in contemporary Italian painted wall decoration.

(ii) 1500–1624. Few Italian courts that had employed tapestry weavers in the 15th century continued to do so into the 16th. Ferrara and Mantua, from which documented tapestries have survived, and Correggio are exceptions. In the early 16th century a group of independent weavers was hired by Gian Giacomo Trivulzio, Marchese di Vigevano, near Milan, to produce *The Months* series (Milan, Castello Sforzesco). Apparently only in Milan and Venice were independent weavers continuously active from the 15th century through the first decades of the 16th.

Sixteenth-century production at the marriage-related courts of Ferrara and Mantua was limited, however, until 1536, when the brothers Giovanni Karcher (*fl* 1517–62) and NICOLAS KARCHER in Ferrara (*see* FERRARA, §3) brought in a group of Brussels weavers, including JAN ROST, as reinforcements. Soon, production in Ferrara was so vigorous that Nicolas Karcher could set up his own workshop in Mantua in 1539 (*see* MANTUA, §3). In 1545, both Nicolas Karcher and Rost moved to Florence, to found independent workshops with subventions from Cosimo I, Grand Duke of Tuscany (*see* FLORENCE, §III, 3). In 1554 Nicolas Karcher returned to Mantua, where he had maintained a small workshop, while his and Rost's students were organized by the Duke into a court workshop, the Arazzeria Medicea (est. 1554). Weaving died out in Mantua in the 1560s and in Ferrara in the early 1570s, but the Arazzeria Medicea continued for almost 200 years producing tapestries for both the Medici and private patrons.

During the 16th century Italian workshops wove cycles of large tapestries and thus made some limited inroads into local importation from the north. Unlike most large Flemish cycles, the majority of Italian ones were carefully sized to fit specific areas. An interesting illustration of the dynamics of tapestry commissioning in Italy, in a set woven for a predetermined space, is the *Marian and Eucharistic* cycle (1562–1633) for Como Cathedral, which, because of the church's finances, took over 70 years to complete. Various cartoon painters were employed on the project including Giuseppe Arcimboldo, Sebastiano II Filippi, Alessandro Allori and Giovan Battista Recchi (*c.* 1590/1600–*c.* 1650); because of changing politics, economics and logistics, the weaving was executed in Brussels, Ferrara and Florence.

100. Tapestry of the *Meeting of Dante and Virgil*, 5.27×4.70 m, designed by Francesco Salviati and woven in the workshop of Jan Rost, Florence, *c.* 1541–9 (Minneapolis, MN, Minneapolis Institute of Arts)

Sixteenth-century Italian painters continued the practice of making coloured cartoons, best illustrated by Raphael and his school's cartoons for Pope Leo X's set of the *Acts of the Apostles* (cartoons, London, V&A; tapestries, Rome, Pin. Vaticana). In fact, these and other Raphael school cartoons for papal court tapestries sent to Brussels for weaving from *c.* 1515 to 1523 inspired Bernard van Orley (i) to revolutionize Flemish cartoons by adding colours and introducing High Renaissance spatiality and monumentality. The more varied colours and compositions of Italian tapestries may result not only from the Italian cartoons, but also from the Flemish weavers' reluctance to use dyes traditionally considered unstable or inferior and the painters' and weavers' inability to break completely with their long tradition of perspectiveless tapestry design.

Throughout the 16th century Italian tapestry borders continued to be more innovative than Flemish ones. They sometimes imitated Flemish fruit and flower garland models but more often display a great range of other types of motifs, from imitations of carved or geometric frescoed frames (see fig. 100) to tied-back curtains. Many were carefully coordinated with the central theme of the tapestry. From the 1540s, a recognizable local style of compartmentalized tapestry border evolved in Florence, which was especially favoured by Francesco Salviati, Johannes Stradanus and Alessandro Allori. This style later influenced Rubens's tapestry borders, which in turn revolutionized Flemish border design in the 1620s.

(iii) 1625–1800. Tapestry production was limited in Italy in the 17th century. The Arazzeria Medicea in Florence

continued at a progressively slower rate of production, serving mainly the Medici court and select private clients. In 1627 Cardinal Francesco Barberini (*see* BARBERINI, (2)) gathered French and Flemish weavers into a small personal factory in Rome, which produced work for the Barberini and their friends until 1683 (*see* ROME, §IV, 1).

During the 18th century there was a more ambitious revival of Italian tapestry weaving. Because tapestries were gradually fading from fashion in northern European decoration, the maintenance of the Gobelins in Paris, as well as the philanthropic patronage by the French kings of the Beauvais workshops for royal gifts, became increasingly a display of wealth and power. Italian princes, who emulated the French, began, therefore, to consider court tapestry workshops to be an attribute of majesty.

In 1710 Pope Clement XI invited French weavers to found a papal workshop at the orphanage of S Michele a Ripa in Rome. The workshop was active for 200 years. Between 1731 and 1737 Charles-Emanuel III, King of Sardinia and 17th Duke of Savoy, founded his own court workshop in Turin (*see* TURIN, §III), headed by Vittorio Demignot (*fl* 1710; *d* 1742), who had previously worked in Florence and Rome. This workshop functioned until *c*.1802, when the Savoys were exiled under Emperor Napoleon I. After the death of Gian Gaston, the last Medici Grand Duke, came the first signs of the demise of the Arazzeria Medicea, which was closed temporarily, and then, after producing a few works under the Lorraine heirs, was officially disbanded in 1744. In 1737 Charles VII, King of Naples (later Charles III, King of Spain), took advantage of the temporary suspension of the Arazzeria Medicea to convince a group of weavers to move from Florence to Naples (*see* NAPLES, §III, 1). The Naples workshop was active until 1798, after which Charles's heir, Ferdinand IV, King of Naples (*reg* 1759–1806), fled to Sicily for fear of the French invasion. There were also some independent tapestry workshops in Milan and Venice in this period.

In the 17th and 18th centuries Italian tapestry design was rarely in the artistic forefront as it had been before. Other artistic luxuries were becoming more fashionable in Italy, and the cult of painting had begun, so leading artists were asked to paint tapestry cartoons less frequently. Italian tapestry cartoons still differed from northern ones in demanding more naturalistic colours of the weavers and in being conceived as 'one-off' productions. General layouts, however, followed northern ones in style: borders widened in the 17th century, and became narrower or were excluded in the 18th. The practice of relating the borders thematically to the central compositions of a series continued mainly in Florence.

One unique genre of this period—copying oil paintings—appears to have been largely an Italian speciality. Although tapestry copies of paintings had for a long time appeared sporadically, PIETRO FEVÈRE in Florence was the first great exponent, supported by the Medici. This genre reached its apogee in Rome at the S Michele tapestry works, where a high percentage of cartoons were carefully copied from paintings in the Vatican collections. It was also practised in Naples, Turin and elsewhere in Italy.

(iv) After 1800. The S Michele workshop in Rome was the only court workshop to survive the Napoleonic era intact. In Turin the brief revival of weaving between 1823 and 1832 was an anomaly. The S Michele workshop became a training centre for most Italian tapestry weavers after this time, but by the early 20th century it had become more concerned with restoring the papal tapestries than with weaving, and from 1910 it was officially only a restoration, and later a conservation workshop.

At the end of the 19th century new tapestry workshops began to appear in Italy: first that of Erulo Eroli (1854–1916) in Rome, then that of Count Federigo Niccola Marcelli (*fl* early 20th century) in Florence and finally those of Ugo Scassa in Asti and Wanda Casaril (*b* 1933) in Venice. At the end of the 20th century all except the Florentine workshop were still active, although the workshop in Rome was mainly involved with restoration. The 20th-century phenomenon of the artist–tapestry-weaver was less strong in Italy than in other western countries. Eroli's workshop in Rome was the most noted example; weaving in Venice took this direction from the 1950s. After World War II a number of painters made cartoons for tapestries or had their paintings transposed into tapestry. Felice Casorati, Corrado Cagli and Antonio Corpora, for example, received an important commission in 1960 for cartoons for tapestries for the Italian luxury liner *Leonardo da Vinci*, to be woven at Asti, where many of Cagli's paintings were also made into weavings.

EWA: 'Arazzo'

BIBLIOGRAPHY

L. F. E. Müntz: *Histoire de la tapisserie en Italie, en Allemagne*, i of *Histoire générale de la tapisserie* (Paris, 1878–84)

J. Del Badia: 'Sulla parola "arazzo"', *Archv. Stor. It.*, xxv (1900), pp. 87–90

A. Schiaparelli: *La casa fiorentina e i suoi arredi nei secoli XIV e XV* (Florence, 1908/*R* with vol. of tables, ed. M. Sframeli and L. Pagnotta, 1983), i, pp. 194–290

M. Viale Ferrero: *Arazzi italiani* (Milan, 1961)

D. Heinz: 'Die italienische Tapisseriekunst bis zum Ende des 16. Jahrhunderts', *Europäische Wandteppiche*, i (Brunswick, 1963), pp. 257–76

M. Viale Ferrero: *Arazzi italiani del cinquecento* (Milan, 1963)

O. Ferrari: *Arazzi italiani del seicento e settecento* (Milan, 1968)

J. Shearman: *Raphael's Cartoons in the Collection of Her Majesty the Queen and the Tapestries for the Sistine Chapel* (London, 1972)

M. Stucky-Schürer: *Die Passionsteppiche von San Marco in Venedig* (Berne, 1972)

M. Siniscalco Spinosa: 'Italia', *Gli arazzi*, ed. A. González-Palacios (Milan, 1981), pp. 4–27

M. Viale Ferrero: 'Arazzo e pittura', *Stor. Archv. It.*, iii/4, pp. 117–58

Arazzi del cinquecento a Como (exh. cat., ed. N. Forti Grazzini; Como Cathedral, 1986)

B. Davidson: 'The *Furti di Giove* Tapestries Designed by Perino del Vaga for Andrea Doria', *A. Bull.*, lxx/3 (1988), pp. 424–50

P. Boccardo: *Andrea Doria e le arti* (Rome and Milan, 1989)

C. Adelson: *The Tapestry Patronage of Cosimo I de' Medici, 1545–1553*, 4 vols (diss., U. New York, 1990)

V. Baradel: 'Materie tessili e forme d'arazzo nell'arte contemporanea: Un'ipotesi di lettura', *Civici musei veneziani d'arte e di storia, centro studi di storia del tessuto e del costume*, ii (1990), pp. 45–55

R. Bonito Fanelli: 'L'arte dell'arazzo da William Morris alla Bauhaus', *Civici musei veneziani d'arte e di storia, centro studi di storia del tessuto e del costume*, ii (1990), pp. 35–44

B. Davidson: 'The *Navigatione d'Enea* Tapestries Designed by Perino del Vaga for Andrea Doria', *A. Bull.*, lxxii/1 (1990), pp. 35–50

N. Fortigrazzini: *Il patrimonio artistico del Quirinale. Gli arazzi* (Rome and Milan, 1994), i, pp. 15–168

CANDACE J. ADELSON

4. EMBROIDERY. The Italian embroidery industry was linked to that of woven silk (*see* §1 above) and, although

not as important, enjoyed a comparable international reputation. One of the earliest references to both crafts relates to the TIRAZ workshop in Palermo, Sicily, where the magnificent coronation mantle of the Holy Roman Emperors (1133–4; Vienna, Schatzkam.; *see* ISLAMIC ART, fig. 183) was made for the Norman king of Sicily, Roger II. The ground of red figured samite is worked with couched gold thread and some silk. Seed pearls decorate the border and outline the stylized palm tree and lions attacking camels, and the mantle is further decorated with cloisonné enamel plaques and precious stones. The continuing influence of the Near East can be seen in the design of roundels containing birds and animals that decorates the red silk and gold-embroidered chasuble in Anagni Cathedral, near Rome, which was a gift from Pope Boniface VIII (*reg* 1294–1303), while Venetian embroideries, such as the gold-embroidered antependium (*c.* 1330; London, V&A) designed by Paolo Veneziano (*fl c.* 1310–60s), show a strong Byzantine influence.

The embroiderers worked within close-knit communities of craftsmen in the city states, and in Florence, for example, they formed a section within the silk guild. Embroidered vestments of *opus florentinum, opus venitum* and *opus romanum* are listed in the Vatican inventory of 1295, and another of Boniface VIII's gifts to Anagni Cathedral is an antependium (*in situ*) made in Rome *c.* 1300. Worked with couched gold thread and coloured silks in split stitch, it is embroidered with figures set within two tiers of arcades. Florentine embroiderers used the same techniques, but their works show the influence of such local artists as Bernardo Daddi, to whose workshop are attributed the designs for two mid-14th-century antependia: one depicts the Coronation of the Virgin, scenes from the life of the Virgin and saints in arcades and is signed IACOBO CAMBI, 1336 (Florence, Bargello), and the other is embroidered with a central Crucifixion scene and is signed GERI LAPI RACNAMATORE ME FECIT IN FLORENTIA (?*c.* 1336; Manresa, Catalonia, church of S María). The links between embroidery and painting were emphasized technically by working the couched gold thread of the grounds over cords to form raised foliate patterns echoing those of the panel paintings.

Individual workshops compiled books of designs for use in several media, and artists of the calibre of Andrea del Sarto and Sandro Botticelli provided patterns specifically for embroidery. In 1469 Antonio del Pollaiuolo (*see* POLLAIUOLO, (1)) was commissioned to design the decorative panels depicting scenes from the *Life of St John the Baptist* for a set of vestments (*c.* 1469–80; Florence, Mus. Opera Duomo; see fig. 101) for the Baptistery in Florence. They were worked by 11 embroiderers, including Coppino di Giovanni di Bramante from Mechelen, possibly one of the Flemish embroiderers who introduced the *or nué* technique to Italy; this features extensively in the Baptistery panels, which also illustrate a skilled use of perspective.

With the exception of such rare pieces as the quilted cover (*c.* 1400; London, V&A, and Florence, Bargello) illustrating the *Story of Tristan*, little early secular embroidery survives, although it does appear in records and in paintings from the 15th century onwards. By that time pattern design was emerging as a distinct discipline, the impact of which was increased by the invention of the

101. Embroidered panel with *or nué* and split stitch, *Carrying of St John*, from the *Life of St John the Baptist*, designed by Antonio del Pollaiuolo for the Florence Baptistery vestments, *c.* 1469–80 (Florence, Museo dell'Opera del Duomo)

printing press and the publication, in the 16th century, of a series of embroidery pattern books, such as *Gli universali di tutte e bei dissegni, raccami e moderno lavori* (Venice, 1532) by Zoppino, illustrating all aspects of Late Gothic and Renaissance taste. Examples of the patterns survive mainly as borders on linen furnishings and items of dress; they are worked with monochrome silk in outline stitches or left voided in a ground covered with cross stitch. Alternatively, they were embroidered with white linen thread and elaborated with raised details and openwork. Grounds of linen *lacis* and of linen or silk burato were also used, the latter commonly decorated with all-over patterns in bright floss silks. The use of more complex designs worked in polychrome silks and metal threads is recorded in paintings and archives and survives in such rare pieces as the mid-16th-century cover of fine linen decorated with the *Loves of Jupiter and Neptune*, based on Ovid's *Metamorphoses* (Frankfurt am Main, Mus. Ksthandwk; Vienna, Österreich. Mus. Angewandte Kst).

By the early 17th century small-scale floral designs were being worked with silk and metal thread on silk grounds for both secular and ecclesiastical use. The flowers became increasingly large as the Baroque style developed, with naturalistic and exotic blooms combined in dramatic profusion. Delicate needle-painting techniques and moulded raised work were used for the finest pieces, but many large-scale items, such as pilaster hangings, were worked in appliqué. The bold technique, developed in the 16th century, of using two contrasting fabrics to make inlaid appliqué with designs based on furnishing silks, remained popular, but, by the later 17th century and into the first quarter of the 18th, smaller-scale appliqué was combined with more elaborate surface decoration.

Coarse-woven linen was employed as a ground for table-carpets, cushions and such furnishings as bed and wall hangings from the medieval period onwards. Unlike the canvaswork of northern Europe, it was usually embroidered with silk in such patterned stitches as chequer and Florentine (flame) stitch (e.g. of the 17th–18th centuries; London, V&A). Large pictorial hangings worked on linen canvas in a needle-painting technique were also produced in Italy; some were based on engraved copies of paintings, such as a late 17th-century set derived from works by Tintoretto, Poussin and Sébastien Bourdon (London, Hampton Court, Royal Col.; Buckingham Pal., Royal Col.), while others copied woven tapestries, but many had original designs and were valued in their own right. Naples is thought to have been one of the main centres of production.

The fact that different centres favoured different techniques can be seen in the ecclesiastical embroideries that continued to be of major importance. Many survive in church treasuries in Italy and other countries; Genoese work, for example, is represented by the magnificent collection of vestments (1686–91) in S Salvatore, Jerusalem, which was embroidered with polychrome silk and metal thread on red damask grounds, while Rome, which specialized in goldwork, produced six complete sets of gold-embroidered vestments and antependia for the chapel of St John the Baptist in the church of S Roque, Lisbon, when it was moved from Rome in 1747.

Although the production of large-scale wall hangings and heavy furnishings declined during the 18th century, lighter furnishings in the Rococo style, small pictures and much delicate floral embroidery for male and female dress were produced throughout Italy. In addition to surviving garments, there are samples and coloured patterns from the industries of Venice and Milan (examples in Venice, Correr; Milan, Castello Sforzesco).

Due to the patronage of the Roman Catholic Church, embroidery standards remained high during the 19th century, although the designs were mostly derivative versions of Rococo and even Baroque styles. Some traditional linen-based techniques were kept alive within rural communities, and these were drawn on when, at the end of the 19th century, there was a revival of all forms of craft. In 1903 the various workshops scattered throughout the country were coordinated by the cooperative organization Industrie Femminili Italiane. Standards were high, and some linen embroideries, including the so-called Assisi embroideries, have been confused with the 16th- and early 17th-century pieces on which they are based. Although the Industrie Femminili was beginning to fail commercially before World War I, Italy remained a centre for whitework and fine silk embroidery well into the 20th century.

BIBLIOGRAPHY

E. Ricci: *Ricami italiani* (Florence, 1925)
B. Kurth: 'Florentine Trecento-Stickerein', *Pantheon*, viii (1931), pp. 455–62
G. Morazzoni: *Ricami genovesi* (Milan, 1954)
A. Santangelo: *Tessuti d'arte italiani dal XII al XVIII secolo* (Milan, 1959; Eng. trans., London, 1964)
A. S. Cavallo: 'A Newly Discovered Trecento Orphrey from Florence', *Burl. Mag.*, cii (1960), pp. 505–14
L. Mortari: *Il tesoro della cattedrale di Anagni* (Rome, 1963)
M. Schuette and S. Müller-Christensen: *Das Stickereiwerk* (Tübingen, 1963; Fr. trans., Paris, 1963; Eng. trans., London, 1964)
R. Grönwoldt: 'Some Groups of Renaissance Orphreys of Venetian Origin', *Burl. Mag.*, cvii (1965), pp. 321–40
D. King: 'A Venetian Embroidered Altar Frontal', *V&A Mus. Bull.*, i/4 (1965), pp. 14–25
D. van Fossen: 'A Fourteenth-century Embroidered Florentine Antependium', *A. Bull.*, l (1968), pp. 141–52
A. Garzelli: *I ricami nella attività artistica di Pollaiuolo, Botticelli, Bartolo di Giovanni* (Florence, 1973)
P. Johnstone: 'Italy', *Needlework: An Illustrated History*, ed. H. Bridgeman and E. Drury (London, 1978), pp. 109–45
Ricamata pittura. Quadri ad argo dal XVII al XX secolo (exh. cat. by M. Amari, M. Rizzini and M. D. Lunghi, Milan, Pal. Permanente, 1991)
E. Parma: *Ricami e maioliche genovesi del seicento a Gerusalemme* (Genoa, 1992)

SANTINA M. LEVEY

XII. Patronage.

An exceptionally rich tradition of patronage developed in Italy. Until the rise of art collecting in the Renaissance, patronage broadly determined the history of architecture and the visual arts. Individual patrons, groups and institutions sought to display their worldly power or religious belief by commissioning works of art, the subjects and, sometimes, style of which they themselves dictated; each era set its stamp on art, and patrons freely commissioned changes to existing buildings. Only in the 19th century, with the development of a national art policy, were conscious efforts made to conserve and revive the great traditions of art and patronage. The history of patronage is not only a matter of the quantities of commissions issued by one group or another for this or that kind of art, but also of changes in the nature of relationships within which artists worked, and of attitudes to this.

1. Roman, before *c.* AD 313. 2. Early Christian to early medieval, *c.* AD 313–*c.* 1200. 3. Medieval, *c.* 1200–*c.* 1400. 4. Renaissance, *c.* 1400–*c.* 1600. 5. Baroque, Rococo and Neo-classicism, *c.* 1600–*c.* 1861. 6. Nation state, from 1861.

1. ROMAN, BEFORE *c.* AD 313. Emperors continued to build on the traditions of the Late Republic (*see also* ROME, ANCIENT, §I, 3). War booty and tax revenues made patronage in Rome possible, both for renovations and for new projects. Imperial commissions surpassed the scale and extent of previous art production, and the Emperor Augustus was the first to use art and architecture on a grand scale as a public expression of authority. His most celebrated commission was the Ara Pacis (ded. 9 BC) in the Campus Martius next to his mausoleum (*see* ROME, §V, 4). Emperors took responsibility for altars, temples, libraries, fora, theatres and stadia as well as aqueducts, ports, roads and town walls, as an aspect of public government. They also commissioned works of a more private nature, from funerary monuments and baths to palaces and villas. Even in Imperial times there were moves for and against personal show: Claudius and Vespasian led the criticism of Nero's lavish display of wealth in the Domus Aurea (*see* ROME, §V, 5). Symbols of honour in the form of triumphal arches and columns were not usually ordered by the emperor himself but by the Senate and people, or by successors and heirs. Imperial patronage thus embraced the emperor's own public and

private commissions and those of people who through choice or necessity were concerned with them. Together these various parties prescribed the face of the Empire in Italy and far beyond. There were periods of cultural expansion during the reigns of Domitian, Trajan and Hadrian. Trajan's Column (completed in AD 113; *see* ROME, §V, 7) in the forum named after him was the model for that of Marcus Aurelius (completed shortly before 193; *see* ROME, ANCIENT, §IV, 2(vii)) with contemporary reliefs representing a military victory. Thereafter the regions outside Italy became more important culturally: emperors were not of Italian origin and they put their resources into building projects elsewhere.

2. EARLY CHRISTIAN TO EARLY MEDIEVAL, *c.* AD 313–*c.* 1200. As the Empire was converted to Christianity, emperors built Christian churches. Between 312 and 315 a triumphal arch was built for Constantine (*see* ROME, §V, 12) near the Colosseum, in the style of and with sculpture from older monuments. After his victory over Maxentius (himself the patron of a basilica (*see* ROME, §V, 11), villa and circus), Constantine decided to give official recognition to the religion that was now nearly 300 years old and commissioned the construction and decoration of the Basilica Constantiniana (now S Giovanni in Laterano; *see* ROME, §V, 15(ii)) and St Peter's (*see* ROME, §V, 14(i)(a)). Furthermore he founded a new capital for the Roman Empire named after him: Constantinople (now Istanbul). Both interventions had major consequences for Italian patronage. Beyond Rome centres competed with the capital for power and wealth. Ravenna became the most important town in Italy. Theodoric, King of the Goths (*reg* 489–526), built a mausoleum there and built and decorated S Apollinare Nuovo (*see* RAVENNA, §2). The direct continuation of imperial patronage then became situated in Ravenna as the imperial seat of Byzantine Italy. Around 547 Justinian I, his wife Theodora, bishops, warriors and courtiers were commemorated in mosaic in S Vitale (*see* RAVENNA, §2(vii)). Archbishops

were active patrons too: their achievements included S Apollinare in Classe (completed 549; *see* RAVENNA, §2(v)).

(i) Papal court. In Rome itself, authority and patronage were wielded by the pope, and bishops and their entourages built, decorated, rebuilt and redecorated churches. The patriarchal basilica of S Maria Maggiore (*see* ROME, §V, 20) was founded by Sixtus III (*reg* 432–40), while the centrally planned S Stefano Rotondo (*see* ROME, §V, 22) was completed by Pope Simplicius (*reg* 468–83). Foundations for church building and decoration in Rome were also made by senators (SS Giovanni e Paolo; *c.* 410), clergy (S Sabina; 420–30) or a devout widow (S Vitale; early 5th century). In 609 the conversion of the city to Christianity was crowned by the completion of the Pantheon as the church of S Maria ad Martyres. As well as architecture, commissions were issued for mosaics (particularly apsidal), marbles (altars, thrones and screens around the choir and altar), reliquaries, antependia and icons in precious metals, expensive textiles and sometimes wall paintings. Images were carried in procession or elevated on rood beams in the centre of the church. Through these works of art the Christian service acquired an imposing context and focused attention on the Old and New Testaments and the lives and miracles of the saints. Those who commissioned the works were also pleased to be commemorated, often by name and sometimes by a portrait.

In the Carolingian period the decorations of the palace of LEO III near the Lateran included a mosaic of him kneeling before St Peter, with the Emperor Charlemagne, whom he had crowned in Old St Peter's on Christmas night 800, on the other side. New churches were built, expressly showing the popes as patrons. Paschal I (*reg* 817–24) was very active: his portrait frequently appears in mosaics, for example in the apse of S Prassede, Rome (see fig. 102). The large churches acquired new furnishings, as in the donations to St Peter's by Leo IV (*reg* 847–55).

S Clemente, S Maria in Cosmedin, SS Quattro Coronati and S Maria in Trastevere followed in the 12th century.

102. *Christ, Apostles, Saints and Pope Paschal I*, apse mosaic, early 9th century AD, S Prassede, Rome

Commissions in and around Rome for embellishing churches did not lead to new building types and decorative styles but did promote a new kind of marble-working, carried out in the 12th and 13th centuries by specialists from Latium, traditionally referred to as the COSMATI.

Funerary monuments formed an important aspect of papal patronage; the popes were portrayed lying on sarcophagi, praying in front of Mary or sometimes enthroned and giving the blessing. Cardinals, especially in the 13th century, similarly became patrons of funerary sculpture, mosaics and wall paintings. The expansion of patronage was carried on by the wealthy families of the popes and cardinals (e.g. the Orsini, COLONNA, Savelli and STEFANESCHI), both in Rome and far beyond. Papal patronage possessed a remarkable continuity despite periods of stagnation, such as the Migration Period, and sometimes during schisms. But whenever spiritual and worldly authority was challenged, art was used to reassert that authority. Calixtus II (*reg* 1119–24) had new rooms in the Lateran Palace decorated with wall paintings that emphasized the legitimacy of his papacy by showing antipopes trampled underfoot by the rightful *pontifex maximus*.

(ii) Monastic orders and secular rulers. Both rulers and popes gave support to the monastic orders, which encouraged particular types of patronage. From the 8th to the 12th centuries the Benedictine Order was culturally pre-eminent, and Abbot Desiderius (1058–87) instigated the rebuilding of the Benedictine abbey at Montecassino in the style of Early Christian churches in Rome. Desiderius also supported Byzantine artists and promoted the production of manuscripts (*see* MONTECASSINO, §§2(i) and (ii)). The Cistercians, who maintained vital contacts with the popes and French abbeys, modelled the abbey of Fossanova (begun 1163), their first new church in Italy, on French precedents. Their taste was more restrained than that of the Benedictines, who were criticized for ostentation. The complex was completed by Innocent III, who wished to strengthen the papacy by maintaining the balance of power with the monastic orders (*see* CISTERCIAN ORDER, §III, 1–2).

The popes also sought military support from secular rulers and financial support from the feudal families. Holy Roman Emperors gave occasional gifts to St Peter's but were primarily concerned with centres outside Italy. The Norman kings of Sicily built churches, castles and palaces as lasting proof of their status as the most powerful ruling house in Italy; the monasteries and the cathedrals of Cefalù (*see* CEFALÙ, §1) and Monreale (*see* MONREALE CATHEDRAL) and the palace chapel in Palermo (*see* PALERMO, §II, 2(ii)), profusely decorated with marble and mosaics, bear witness to their lavish patronage.

3. MEDIEVAL, *c.* 1200–*c.* 1400. Franciscans, Dominicans, Servites and Carmelites, mendicant orders that expanded rapidly in the 13th century, profited from the period's economic expansion. These orders looked less to the feudal élite and more to the city states, merchant families and secular princes. With the realignment of economic and political power, the centres of art changed; new cities set the tone, some older centres underwent a

renaissance and others ceased to play a part. At first the mendicant orders built small and simply decorated churches; their large churches acquired their lavish decorations later. The decoration of the church of S Francesco at Assisi, where St Francis was buried, became an important model for later patronage. Here, between 1260 and 1320 pilgrims' offerings, donations from popes and gifts from cardinals provided altars, seating and grandiose frescoes that draw a parallel between the life of St Francis and that of Christ. In the early years of the 14th century frescoes of the life of Francis and of such saints as Clare of Assisi and Anthony of Padua were painted in many Franciscan churches throughout Italy. Decorations were mainly financed through contributions from merchants and bankers who wished to be buried in a church, in imitation of popes, cardinals and clergy.

Monastic churches were generally provided with panel paintings. Large panels with Mary seated in majesty, known as Maestà, were usually commissioned by lay confraternities. Altarpieces were dedicated to the saints of the order, and polyptychs for the high altars could be commissioned by a lay brother, *conversus* (a monk converted later in life) or merchant family. After 1320 families as well as lay confraternities usually preferred to have their own chapels decorated with frescoes and altarpieces.

There was a steady rise in patronage all over Italy in this period. In Frederick II (*see* HOHENSTAUFEN, (2)) south Italy had an imperial master who shifted attention from Sicily to the area around Naples. Under his successors from the House of Anjou, Naples—unlike Amalfi and Salerno, ports that had flourished earlier—came into its own as a centre for patronage, with new, lavishly decorated castles and churches of the mendicant orders. In Pisa and Arezzo the bishops played a leading role, but elsewhere the initiative for building and decorating cathedrals lay with the chapter, guilds or rulers. The rise of the city states, which supported monastic churches, baptisteries and cathedrals and took direct responsibility for the town hall, encouraged a new and vigorous civic patronage.

An outstanding example of this is Siena, where the *comune* itself took charge. The *comune* commissioned the town's most famous painters to create, for Siena Cathedral, a series of altarpieces (dispersed) celebrating the city's patron saints. Through this commission these artists established themselves as a flourishing professional group and crowned their careers in Florence, and at the courts of Avignon and Naples. The decorations of the Palazzo Pubblico in Siena symbolized the authority of the city state and the rightfulness of its rule. The Republic's victory over the feudal lords was depicted by Simone Martini (*c.* 1330) in the assembly hall for the general council, known as the Sala del Mappamondo. The condottiere, Guidoriccio di Niccolo da Foligno, the general in the service of the *comune*, rides on a caparisoned horse towards the beleaguered city of Montemassi. Opposite this fresco Simone painted a *Maestà* (1315–16; Siena, Pal. Pub.; *see* SIENA, fig. 10 and WALL PAINTING, colour pl. II, fig. 2) encircled by the city's four patron saints, based on Duccio's *Maestà* (Siena, Mus. Opera Duomo), which was, at that time, the high altar of Siena Cathedral. In the Nine's meeting chamber in the room beyond, known as the Sala della Pace, Ambrogio Lorenzetti frescoed the *Allegory of Good* and *Bad Government* (1338–9; Siena, Pal. Pub.; *see* SIENA, fig. 12 and LORENZETTI, (2), fig. 2). On the east and west wall respectively he showed peace in the country and town and war; on the north wall he painted the dignitaries of the city state, under the authority of the Nine, arrayed in all their finery before a podium bearing personifications of good government and the virtues associated with it.

4. RENAISSANCE, *c.* 1400–*c.* 1600. The rich artistic developments of 15th-century Florence were encouraged above all by merchant families and, although noblemen and clergy continued to play a part, private commissions gradually became pre-eminent. Above all, the MEDICI issued commissions for churches and chapels and encouraged the innovations of Filippo Brunelleschi, Michelozzo Michelozzi, Leon Battista Alberti and Donatello. Merchant families displayed their wealth and power in the decoration of chapels, where they had themselves, their children, parents, relatives and name saints depicted. Around 1478 Francesco Sassetti commissioned Domenico Ghirlandaio to decorate a chapel in Santa Trinita; within the cycle of the *Life of St Francis* (see fig. 30 above) Ghirlandaio included Sassetti, his family and Lorenzo de' Medici, his employer at the Medici bank (see fig. 103). Sassetti's most important business partner, Giovanni Tornabuoni, had the same painter execute an altarpiece and frescoes in the Cappella Maggiore in S Maria Novella.

In the 15th century even the rulers of such small towns as Foligno and Rimini began to enrich their courts with works of art, while a great era of courtly patronage opened in Ferrara, Mantua and Urbino. Rulers commissioned

103. Domenico Ghirlandaio: *St Francis, Francesco Sassetti and Lorenzo de' Medici*, detail from a fresco of the *Life of St Francis* cycle (1479–85) in the Sassetti Chapel, Santa Trinita, Florence

paintings of saints, historical events, personifications of the arts, portraits of famous men and of themselves, their families and courtiers. Their court painters, among whom were Piero della Francesca, Mantegna and Raphael, thus gained social status, as of course did Leonardo da Vinci, Michelangelo and Titian, who were also in demand by a republican and international clientele. Vasari, successful court painter and architect to Cosimo I de' Medici, proudly described in his *Vite* the increasing artistic and social opportunities afforded to his profession, which he linked directly to the patronage of rulers, clergy and merchants.

In the 16th century, as the pontiff became increasingly influential as statesman and military commander in a European context, the papal court became the pre-eminent centre of culture, and Julius II (*see* ROVERE, DELLA(i), (2)), who is among the most celebrated of Italian patrons, and Leo X (*see* MEDICI, DE', (7)) issued a multitude of commissions for frescoes, portraits (*see* POLYCHROMY, colour pl. V, fig. 1), altarpieces, tombs and buildings. Michelangelo decorated the Sistine Chapel, and in the Vatican Stanze Raphael created a series of monumental narrative frescoes, of unprecedented formal and iconographical complexity, which gave visual expression to the history and authority of the Papal State; many lesser patrons were to see the possibilities of this new kind of history painting. In Florence, Cosimo I de' Medici (*reg* 1537–74) initiated a new aristocratic patronage; Giorgio Vasari's decoration of the Palazzo Vecchio extolled Medici traditions of patronage; commissions for tapestries, portraits and pictures displayed Cosimo's new princely splendour. Venice lacked a court, and the chief patrons were the State, religious communities and churches, and the lay confraternities, or *scuole*; the most magnificent commissions were those for the decoration of the Doge's Palace.

5. BAROQUE, ROCOCO AND NEO-CLASSICISM, *c.* 1600–*c.* 1861. In 17th-century Rome the popes remained the main art patrons, and the magnificence of their patronage expressed the renewed confidence of the Roman Catholic Church after the austere years of the Counter-Reformation; Urban VIII (*see* BARBERINI, (1)) and Alexander VII (*see* CHIGI, (3)) were the most influential patrons of their era. Popes and cardinals patronized the great churches, foremost among them St Peter's, which was transformed by the sculptures of Gianlorenzo Bernini, and by his monumental Piazza, and S Giovanni in Laterano, which was renovated by Francesco Borromini. Once again popes took responsibility for churches and the palaces connected to them, and for the laying out of streets, squares and fountains. In this period, in contrast to the conservatism of the 12th-century popes, papal patronage promoted the introduction of new building types and new styles of sculpture and painting, which led to the development of the Baroque. The patronage of the new religious orders, the Jesuits, Theatines and Oratorians, often rivalled the splendour of the popes. The Jesuits were outstandingly successful patrons (*see* JESUIT ORDER, §3) and took over responsibility for Il Gesù, S Ignazio and S Andrea al Quirinale (1658–70), the prestigious novitiate church designed by Bernini. The Oratorian church, the Chiesa Nuova, was frescoed by Pietro da Cortona.

The great papal families, the Medici, FARNESE, Barberini, BORGHESE, PAMPHILI, Chigi and Ottoboni (*see* OTTOBONI, PIETRO), became both patrons and collectors. They enriched their new palazzi (see fig. 104) and villas both with collections of antique sculpture and coins and with contemporary frescoes celebrating their family history and authority; they created magnificent picture galleries, displaying both Old Master and contemporary works. Patronage and collecting by families who enhanced their fortunes in Rome extended to their family seats in Siena, Florence and Parma.

Collecting had begun to develop in the 14th century (*see also* §XIII, 1 below). In the 17th century artists increasingly began to work for a circle of collectors and sometimes for dealers and for the art market. Consequently connections with patrons became less direct and written or verbal requirements concerning subjects less stringent. A new type of painting, small framed easel pictures on canvas or panel, dominated the market. Such distinguished private patrons as Cassiano dal Pozzo (*see* POZZO, (1)) were inspired by their intellectual and historical interests to become both collectors of antique sculpture and patrons of modern artists; Cassiano was a member of the Congregazioni degli Virtuosi and himself a draughtsman. In the

18th century papal patronage was less lavish, although both Clement XI (*see* ALBANI, (1)) and Clement XII (*see* CORSINI, (2)) played a distinguished role, and cardinals and princes continued to issue commissions. Clement XI commissioned the 12 marble statues of the Apostles that line the nave of S Giovanni in Laterano, while the church's façade and the Trevi Fountain were both instigated by Clement XII. In both Rome and Venice many Italian artists gained support from foreign patrons who were making the Grand Tour, and the courts of both Naples and Turin became significant centres of patronage, fostering the development of a Rococo style. Under Victor-Amadeus II of Savoy FILIPPO JUVARRA transformed the city of Turin.

6. NATION STATE, FROM 1861. Italy became an independent nation state in 1861. At first patronage was nationalistic, and various élite groups and organizations united and participated in collective commissions, thus pushing the private patron into the background. Italian patrons commissioned Italian artists to execute Italian subjects: in all large towns statues of the founders of the nation were erected. Garibaldi appeared standing in the provincial towns and mounted on a horse in the main centres. Favourite subjects for monuments were celebrated artists from the past as well as political leaders. Statues celebrating Italy's heroes together comprised a national canon: Leonardo da Vinci in Milan, Titian in Venice, Raphael in Urbino, and Giotto, Michelangelo and others in Florence. These 'great Italians' were also portrayed, or their names inscribed, on the façades of the newly built national museums. Thus they became an essential part of the national identity.

A feeling for tradition, local patriotism and national consciousness inspired the commission awarded to a group of Sienese painters for the decoration of the Sala del Risorgimento in the Palazzo Pubblico between 1870 and 1890. These decorations deliberately echo the symbolism and imagery of the 14th-century narrative frescoes. In place of the castles south of Siena, the provinces of Italy were depicted, Garibaldi replaced Guidoriccio and King Victor-Emanuel II took the place of the Nine Lords. Essentially an allegory of Italy, this commission, as did many others, arose through a private initiative, and its Sienese patrons intended to suggest the renaissance and continuing vitality of Sienese artistic traditions.

After the erection of national monuments in Turin and Florence, each briefly the capital, Rome definitively became Roma Capitale. This changed the nature and appearance of the city. Ministries were housed in monumental buildings, the decorations often connected to their area of policy. The artists have not won a place in the history books, nor have the history painters of Siena or the creators of monumental sculptures. The largest commission was for the national monument in honour of King Victor-Emanuel II at the foot of the Capitol and near the entrance to the excavated Imperial Fora. The competition held for this (1881 and 1882) was eventually won by GIUSEPPE SACCONI, and 30 years later, in 1911, after much discussion and controversy, the promised consecration took place. The ruler is mounted on a horse among sculptures, frescoes and mosaics that combine

104. Palazzo Barberini, Rome, by Carlo Maderno and others, begun 1624; engraved frontispiece to *Aedes Barberinae* by Guido Abbatini (Cambridge, University Library)

images of his qualities (Sacrifice, Harmony, Wisdom), the towns of Italy, the arts and the heroic days of the Risorgimento in a style that refers directly to the Imperial Fora (*see* ROME, fig. 10).

Public buildings—county halls, post offices and railway stations—of the Fascist regime (1922–44) were monumental and expensive. Their design was often taken from Imperial forms, but extensive figurative–symbolic subjects were frequently lacking. In the new EUR (Esposizione Universale di Roma) district in south Rome, Fascism was glorified through archaeology, film and photography, as well as in sculptural programmes. In the new station halls in Venice and Florence, photographs showed the traveller the sites, emphasizing famous tourist attractions.

The post-war Republic rejected the revivalist approach inspired by political and artistic interests. The famous cultural past, a source of collective inspiration and pride, also became a hindrance to artistic innovation. Few commissions were given to contemporary artists, and an arts policy was slow to emerge. Modern art is sustained by an international market: successful Italian artists sell much of their work to foreign collectors, and Italian collectors buy foreign art, though some daring dealers and museum curators have promoted the work of modern artists (*see* ROME, §IV, 6).

Thanks to more than 20 centuries of virtually unbroken patronage, Italy possesses the richest patrimony of any country. Official government policies for patronage have not been formulated because central, regional and municipal authorities possess more than enough monuments and museums. Palaces, town halls and even church buildings serve as public buildings and as museums. This inheritance attracts tourists from all over the world, but it also creates problems of cataloguing, conservation, restoration and presentation. The Church, too, plays little part in patronage nowadays. After 1950 the number of figurative–symbolic representations in churches declined, and ecclesiastical patronage no longer encouraged artistic innovation. New patrons have arisen, notably industrial sponsors, although their commissions have not been of the traditional kind. Leading industrial and commercial firms have given their support to architecture (e.g. Fiat commissioned Pier Luigi Nervi to build their factory in Turin (1955)) and, particularly, to design, for which Italy has established a high reputation. Cooperation between local and national government and private corporate sponsors has been a feature in the restoration of cultural monuments and the publication of expensive art books. Art publishing has joined museums and monuments to display the history of patronage in Italy.

BIBLIOGRAPHY
G. Vasari: *Vite* (1550, rev. 2/1568); ed. G. Milanesi (1878–85)
F. Haskell: *Patrons and Painters: A Study in the Relations between Italian Art and Society in the Age of the Baroque* (London, 1963)
P. Hirschfeld: *Mäzene: Die Rolle des Auftraggebers in der Kunst* (Munich, 1968)
M. Baxandall: *Painting and Experience in 15th-century Italy* (Oxford, 1974)
P. Burke: *Tradition and Innovation in Renaissance Italy: A Sociological Approach* (London, 1974)
R. Krautheimer: *Rome: Profile of a City, 312–1308* (Princeton, 1980)
G. F. Little and S. Orgel, eds: *Patronage in the Renaissance* (Princeton, 1981)
Della casa al museo: Capolavori da fondazioni artistiche italiane (exh. cat., Milan, Mus. Poldi-Pezzoli, 1981–2)
E. L. Goldberg: *Patterns in Late Medici Art Patronage* (Princeton, 1983)
T. Rodiek: *Das Monumento nazionale Vittorio Emanuele II. in Rom* (Frankfurt am Main, 1983)
R. Krautheimer: *The Rome of Alexander VII, 1655–67* (Princeton, 1985)
M. Warnke: *Hofkünstler: Zur Vorgeschichte des modernen Künstlers* (Keulen, 1985)
A. Quint: *Cardinal Federico Borromeo as a Patron and a Critic of the Arts and his Musaeum of 1625* (New York, 1986)
P. Zanker: *Augustus und die Macht der Bilder* (Munich, 1987); trans. as *The Power of Images in the Age of Augustus* (Ann Arbor, 1988)
H. Belting and D. Blume, eds: *Malerei und Stadtkultur in der Dantezeit: Die Argumentation der Bilder* (Munich, 1989)
I. Herklotz: 'Die Beratungsräume Calixtus II im Lateranpalast: Kunst und Propaganda am Ende des Investiturstreit', *Z. Kstgesch.*, lii (1989), pp. 145–214
C. Riebesell: *Die Sammlung des Kardinal Alessandro Farnese: Ein 'studio' für Künstler und Gelehrte* (Weinheim, 1989)
E. Borsook: *Messages in Mosaic: The Royal Programme of Norman Sicily, 1130–1187* (Oxford, 1990)
B. Kempers: *Painting, Power and Patronage: The Rise of the Professional Artist in Renaissance Italy* (London, 1992)
Roma tardo-antica e medievale, Studi & Testi, 355 (Vatican City, 1993)

B. KEMPERS

XIII. Collecting and dealing.

In ancient Rome, Greek works of art, acquired as spoils from all over the Hellenic world, were displayed in galleries and temples (*see* ROME, ANCIENT, §IV, 2(i)). Collecting in the modern sense began in earnest in Italy in the 14th century, when the necessary conditions developed: the existence of an art market with dealers, the practice of connoisseurship or the ability to distinguish authenticity and quality, and the availability of works of art. As Italy was acknowledged to have produced the greatest artists in the Western world, Italians tended to collect Italian works of art, as did collectors in the rest of Europe. Flemish paintings of the 15th century were the only foreign works regularly to enter Italian collections in the Renaissance. The Este of Ferrara and the Medici of Florence acquired Flemish pictures from their agents in the Netherlands, for by the 15th century the commercialization of artistic production was well under way. Only relatively few pictures were actually commissioned in northern Europe; Netherlandish works of art were sent to Italy in the normal course of international trade. Legislation relating to art was introduced earlier in Italy than anywhere else in Europe. This was to impose restrictions on the export of works of art and preserve the artistic patrimony of the Italian cities, especially in the Papal States. Italy was not a united country until 1861, and some of this legislation was just as much intended to control exports from Papal Rome to other Italian states as to control foreign collectors.

1. Middle Ages–17th century. 2. 18th–20th centuries.

1. MIDDLE AGES–17TH CENTURY. In the Middle Ages Church and State dominated art patronage and collecting. Commissions from individuals were rare. The earliest collectors' rooms of paintings were in bishops' palaces and church sacristies, for example the treasury of S Marco, Venice, which still has precious Byzantine goldsmith work, reliquaries and icons, mostly acquired as booty during the Crusades. The conquest of Constantinople produced an especially rich hoard. Objects in church treasuries were collected for the costliness of their materials and their religious associations rather than as works

of art in their own right. By the 15th century private patronage from individuals became increasingly common, and special objects were commissioned such as the devotional pictures of the *Virgin* or the *quadri da sposi*, for example the nuptial bed commissioned by Pierfrancesco Borgherini (see below), as well as allegorical pictures which resulted from a special relationship between artist and patron. These new classes of objects, as distinct from more monumental painting and sculpture for public places, created the materials for collecting.

The impetus for collecting, according to Burckhardt, developed in Renaissance Italy through the power of private patronage, which brought into being a whole new kind of easily portable object that could be bought and sold, an art that was made not only for secular and ecclesiastical princes but for the enjoyment of middle-class and patrician householders. With portable and saleable art came dealers. Indeed, it was a furniture painting by Pontormo and others on the Borgherini marriage bed that provoked the first international dealer in the history of painting, GIOVANBATTISTA DELLA PALLA, to act unscrupulously to obtain it for Francis I of France, although, as Vasari related in Pontormo's *Vita*, Borgherini's patriotic wife prevented the acquisition. (Of all the works known to have reached Francis I, only one survives: Niccolò Tribolo's *Nature*; see fig. 105.) Collecting ancient sculpture, as distinct from contemporary painting, existed in the early 15th century on a significant scale, although we have no detailed knowledge of it, but by the early 16th century there were specialized dealers such as Baldassare del Milanese in Rome, through whom Michelangelo sold his forged *Sleeping Cupid*. Similarly, as Held and Bury have shown, there were also specialist dealers in drawings and prints by that date, especially in the Netherlands. Collecting was accompanied by the beginnings of art history, most notably Vasari's *Vite*, in which he gave the first systematic account of the development of contemporary art, providing in anecdotal and methodical form a reassuring explanation of the importance of Italian art for collectors. His own collection of drawings stimulated a new fashion in collecting and in turn altered the form and function of drawing itself, for once drawings became collectors' items artists produced finished drawings as works of art in their own right.

By the end of the 16th century dealing in painting had so increased and international collecting had developed on such a large scale that the Grand Duke Ferdinando I de' Medici issued a decree in 1601 forbidding the exportation from Florence of works of art by 18 listed masters. The original list was drawn up by a committee of 12 artists from the Accademia del Disegno. Starting with Michelangelo and Raphael, it went on to Andrea del Sarto, Domenico Beccafumi, Rosso Fiorentino, Leonardo, Franciabiagio, Perino del Vaga, Pontormo, Titian, Francesco Salviati, Bronzino, Daniele da Volterra, Fra Bartolommeo, Sebastiano del Piombo, Filippino Lippi, Correggio and Parmigianino. With the exception of Filippino Lippi, those artists whose works were most sought after were masters of the High Renaissance, which indicates that the collecting of painting in the 16th century involved contemporary artists' works rather than those by Old Masters from the

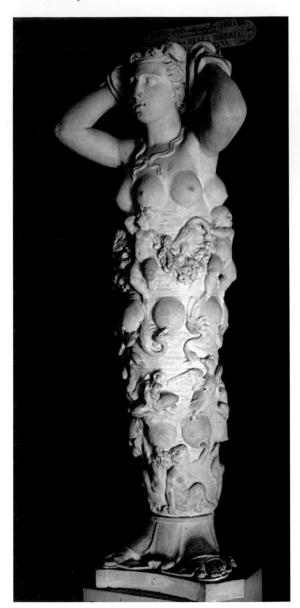

105. Niccolò Tribolo: *Nature*, marble, *c.* 1528 (Paris, Musée du Louvre)

14th or the 15th century, although Flemish and Netherlandish paintings from the earlier period were sometimes bought.

It was usual to buy pictures from painters' workshops but on occasion they were on sale at church doors and at fairs, such as the one represented by David Vinckboons in his painting of *Market Stalls* (see fig. 106), which shows pictures and other objects for sale in the market place. It is quite possible that even earlier, in the 15th century, the Antwerp fairs were significant markets for the sale of pictures that were often bound for Italy, but without documentary evidence this must remain a speculation. By the 18th century art exhibitions were reasonably frequent occurrences in Venice but, again, such events had probably

106. David Vinckboons: *Market Stalls*, oil on panel, 115×141 mm, 1608 (Brunswick, Herzog Anton-Ulrich Museum)

long been customary, even in the 16th century, for example in the Piazza S Marco on Ascension Day or in the Campo S Rocco on the saint's feast day, commemorated in Canaletto's picture of the *Feast Day of St Roch* (c. 1735; London, N.G.). In Venice, too, there came the first reasonably systematic account of patrician private collections: the *Notizia d'opere del disegno*, written between 1521 and 1543 by the Venetian patrician MARCANTONIO MICHIEL. The author was a connoisseur of a new kind, who had travelled extensively, and who recorded the most notable works of art in the Veneto in the houses of aristocrats, writers and politicians, such as Pietro Bembo, the Cornaro family and the Grimani. In the 17th century these collections of Venetian painting were to enrich major European collections such as that of the governor of the Southern Netherlands, the Archduke Leopold Wilhelm, in Brussels, whose gallery later formed the basis of the Kunsthistorisches Museum, Vienna. The various painted and engraved inventories of the Archduke's collection by David Teniers II (*see* TENIERS, (2)) contain copies of numerous Venetian works of art described by Michiel. Although Michiel's notes are always said, quite rightly, to demonstrate the wealth of Venetian collections, he was in fact extremely selective in what he chose to describe. In one instance, that of the collection of GABRIELE VENDRAMIN, remembered as the first owner of Giorgione's *The Tempest*, several later inventories record the richly varied

content of his collection and reveal how much richer the collection was than Michiel's notes would suggest.

In the 17th century Venice produced writings by artist–critics who also acted as *marchands amateurs*: CARLO RIDOLFI in *Le meraviglie* (1648) and MARCO BOSCHINI in the *Carta del navegar pittoresco* (1660) produced elaborate guides as to what was for sale in private collections; these guides were used by foreign collectors, who wanted not only to admire Venetian art but also to acquire it. To own paintings, probably through inheritance, and to buy pictures as a collector were two very different activities, one requiring little money for conservation, the other a great deal of finance, for the prices of Renaissance paintings were quite considerable by the 17th century. This was especially the case in Venice, which was a centre that attracted international collectors such as Thomas Howard, 14th Earl of Arundel, Leopoldo de' Medici and even Velázquez, who bought important Venetian paintings for the Spanish royal collections.

It became fashionable in the 17th century to acquire collections *en bloc*, as in the purchase (1627) by Charles I of England of the Gonzaga collection from Mantua. This trend continued into the 18th century, despite legislation to restrict it (*see* §2 below), as is shown by the spectacular acquisition by Frederick Augustus II, Elector of Saxony (1696–1763), of the collection of Francesco d'Este, Duke of Modena, in 1745, which created one of the greatest galleries of Italian art outside Italy.

The earliest protective legislation against the export of works of art had, in fact, occurred in Renaissance Rome, where the pontifical government recognized the spiritual and political values of their artistic patrimony. From the 15th century there had been ever-increasing signs of a growing preoccupation with the conservation and protection of ancient, medieval and modern works in a city that was continually developing. This can be traced, for instance, in Petrarch's letters concerning the preservation of Rome, in the Bull against the demolition of ancient buildings promulgated by Pius II (1462), in the Bull against the removal of works of art from churches by Sixtus IV (1474), as well as from the brief that Leo X assigned Raphael (1516). Later decrees made by Paul III (1534), Pius IV (1562) and Gregory XIII (1574) reveal a preoccupation with how to prevent national treasures from being appropriated. These attempts to safeguard the heritage of Rome preceded the firm legislation of 1624, when Cardinal Pietro Aldobrandini made it an offence to export works of art from the Pontifical States without a licence, and the even more rigorous edict of Cardinal Sforza in 1646, which made it clear that disciplinary measures would be taken against anyone who attempted to plunder or steal any beautiful work of art from Rome.

2. 18TH–20TH CENTURIES. Implicit in the papal decrees of 1686, 1701 and 1704 concerning the control of works of art, especially antiquities, was the gradual recognition of the unique position of esteem that Rome enjoyed with foreign nations. Three decades later, in 1733, similar edicts encouraged foreigners to settle in the city and to create the ever-growing number of foreign institutions that were founded to study the artistic and cultural heritage of the city in order to appropriate what was best for their own national concerns. Museums, such as the Museo Capitolino and the Museo Pio-Clementino (Vatican), were instituted and financed privately by individual popes in the 18th century as a means of preserving threatened objects, such as the Sacchetti collection, acquired by Benedict XIV. Once in a permanent and public home, treasures could not be sold abroad.

One of the most intelligent reforms to control the movement of works of art was the institution of a meticulous inventory of the works by famous artists held in religious buildings. The first such inventory was that made by Anton Maria Zanetti (ii) of works in the churches, confraternities and monasteries of Venice and the surrounding islands in 1733. Zanetti was nominated Ispettore alle Pubbliche Pitture and was himself responsible for the inventory, which resulted in the first systematic catalogue of Venetian painting and sculpture. A catalogue of works from some periods of Venetian painting, such as the 15th century, which had been much neglected by local historiographers, resulted in a radical re-evaluation of Venetian painting. The restoration of the works of art listed in this new catalogue was controlled by a board of experts in Venice, and in 1778 the Venetian Senate published a decree inspired by PIETRO EDWARDS for a laboratory to specialize in restoration. These decrees created a kind of dispersed gallery over the entire territory of the Venetian Republic and were imitated elsewhere.

The realization of the didactic and financial value of the artistic patrimony of Rome was to reach its apogee with Pius VII (reg 1800–23), the indefatigable enemy of Napoleon I Bonaparte, who had the imagination to appoint Canova as his Inspector General of Fine Arts. He also realized the significance both of the new archaeological history written by Winckelmann (1764) and of the history of Italian painting by the abbot Luigi Lanzi (1795–6) for the designation of what was important in Italian art and how this designation should affect the way it was displayed in newly created museums. Roman legislation culminated in several famous edicts during his pontificate, the most famous of which was promulgated by Cardinal Giuseppe Doria-Pamphili in 1802 in reaction to the Napoleonic confiscations. No antiquities whatsoever, even architectural details from buildings or fragments of stone, were to be exported from the Papal States; similarly no picture by an Old Master could be exported, with no exceptions made for foreigners who were resident in Rome or for ecclesiastics, even cardinals. All private collectors had to declare the contents of their collections, which were to be inspected annually.

Despite the long tradition of legislation against exporting works of art Rome suffered more than any other Italian city during the Napoleonic upheavals, as the French insisted that works of art should be included among the spoils, and works of art in princely collections could be legitimately sequestered. Some treasures, however, such as the collections of Classical sculpture in the Borghese Gallery, were sold legitimately by Prince Camillo Borghese (1755–1832) to his brother-in-law Napoleon.

At the beginning of the 19th century Napoleon had created a sort of national gallery of western Europe, the Musée Napoléon in Paris, containing objects looted from various subject countries, but principally from Italy, during his extensive campaigns there. The museum was briefly accessible to a European public after the Peace of Amiens. It provided the model for the development of national galleries elsewhere, the aim of which, unlike the newly developing public museums in Italy, was not to preserve the heritage of their own countries but to acquire the best Old Master paintings from Italy and elsewhere. As a result of the Napoleonic suppression of religious institutions in Italy between 1806 and 1812 private and public collections in Italy were greatly enriched, and the opportunities for foreign collectors increased. In the earliest years of its existence the National Gallery of London acquired pictures by benefaction, but in 1855, with the appointment of the first director, Sir Charles Eastlake (see EASTLAKE, (1)), the situation changed dramatically. He introduced a systematic acquisitions policy, primarily based on acquiring Renaissance paintings from Italy. To assist Eastlake the gallery employed a travelling agent, a German dealer who had previously been based in Paris, OTTO MÜNDLER, who kept a travel diary recording every remarkable Italian work of art that might be offered for sale to the gallery. Many of their most successful acquisitions were made in northern Italy, then under Austro-Hungarian domination, where the exportation of works of art was less rigorously controlled than in the Papal States. The most important dealer of the period was Giuseppe Baslini (1817–87) in Milan, who sold many masterpieces to the new national galleries in Berlin and London, as well as to the Milanese collector GIAN GIACAMO POLDI PEZZOLI.

The activities of these newly formed national galleries, as well as private collectors such as AUSTEN HENRY LAYARD, caused grave concern to patriotic Italians such as Giovanni Morelli and Giovanni Battista Cavalcaselle, who were intent on preserving the artistic heritage of a newly united Italy. However, one of the strange ironies of unification was the ensuing negative policies towards art, for only those works that symbolized the unity of the nation were considered worth preserving. From 1861 to 1902 there were frequent attempts to formulate legislation to control the movement of works of art, and there were constant tensions between the interests of the new state and the rights of private individuals, and the contrasting politics of regionalism versus centralization. In 1861, shortly after Francesco de' Sanctis had become Minister of Public Instruction in Italy, he commissioned Morelli and Cavalcaselle to catalogue all the important works of art in Umbria and the Marches. This catalogue was conceived both as a coercive instrument by which the administration could control the movement of works of art and also as the basis for determining the content of a projected regional museum in Urbino, one intended to be a prototype for regional museums elsewhere in Italy. Although the catalogue was completed, there was considerable local resistance to the museum. In other parts of Italy, over the next decades, great efforts were made to catalogue every object scientifically, *musei civici e comunali* gradually developed, and the risk of losing masterpieces was increasingly avoided. From 1875, with the introduction of entrance tickets, museums were gradually emancipated from the administration of academies of art, but this never resulted, as was intended, in funds for acquisitions to rival those of museums abroad. Despite all the legislation in the 19th century, a number of important pictures from famous Roman collections were sold abroad, notably and most scandalously from the collections of the Sciarra, Connestabile, Albani and Chigi families.

Italian art, which had determined European taste for so long, ceased to be of universal importance by the 20th century, when collecting in this immensely expensive area was dominated by American millionaires, many of whom, such as Benjamin Altman in New York, Isabella Stewart Gardner in Boston and John G. Johnson in Philadelphia, were advised by Bernard Berenson, then living in Florence, and the international firm of dealers with whom Berenson liaised, the Duveen brothers. Although American collectors entered the field relatively late, many great Italian masterpieces were bought by them after 1915, such as Raphael's *Small Cowper Madonna* and Giovanni Bellini's *Feast of the Gods* (both Washington, DC, N.G.A.). Nowadays the export of Italian Renaissance paintings from Italy is rigorously controlled, for Italian museums are the basis of another great modern industry: tourism. American collections such as the J. Paul Getty Museum make their best acquisitions in Italian Old Master paintings from the sales of great aristocratic English collections, originally created in the 19th century in the post-Napoleonic period.

See also §§XII above and XIV below, and PAUL VI.

BIBLIOGRAPHY

M. Michiel: *Notizia d'opere di disegno nella prima metà del secolo XVI, esistenti in Padova, Cremona, Milano, Pavia, Bergamo, Crema e Venezia* (MS., 1521–43); ed. J. Morelli (Bassano, 1800, rev. Bologna, 1884)

C. A. Levi: *Le collezioni veneziane d'arte e d'antichità dal secolo XIV ai nostri giorni* (Venice, 1800)

J. Burckhardt: 'Die Sammler', *Beitr. Kstgesch.* (Basle, 1898), pp. 297–510

R. Lanciani: *Storia degli scavi di Roma e notizie intorno le collezioni romane di antichità* (Rome, 1902)

A. Luzio: *La galleria dei Gonzaga venduta all'Inghilterra nel 1627–28* (Rome, 1912)

E. Jacobs: 'Das Museo Vendramin und die Sammlung Reynst', *Repert. Kstwiss.*, xlvi (1925), pp. 15–39

F. Lugt: 'Italiaansche kunstwerken in Nederlandsche verzamelingen van vroeger tijden', *Oud Holland*, liii (1936), pp. 97–135

E. K. Waterhouse: 'Paintings from Venice for Seventeenth-century England', *It. Stud.*, vii (1952), pp. 1–23

F. Lugt: *Les Marques de collections de dessins et d'estampes* (The Hague, 1956)

F. Haskell and M. Levey: 'Art Exhibitions in 18th Century Venice', *A. Ven.*, xii (1958), pp. 179–84

C. Pietrangeli: *Scavi e scoperte di antichità sotto il pontificato di Pio VI* (Rome, 1958)

J. Held: 'The Early Appreciation of Drawing', *Latin American Art and the Baroque Period in Europe: Studies in Western Art III: Acts of the 20th International Congress of Art: The History of Art: New York, 1961*, pp. 79ff

F. Haskell: *Patrons and Painters: Art and Society in Baroque Italy* (London, 1963, rev. New York and London, 1980)

K. Garas: 'Giorgione et giorgionisme au XVIIe siècle', *Bull. Mus. Hong. B.-A.*, xxv (1964), pp. 51–80

C. Gould: *Trophy of Conquest: The Musée Napoléon and the Creation of the Louvre* (London, 1965)

S. Savini-Branca: *Il collezionismo veneziano del '600* (Padua, 1965)

L. Berti: *Il principe dello studiolo* (Florence, 1967)

F. Haskell: 'Some Collectors of Venetian Art at the End of the Eighteenth Century', *Studies in Renaissance and Baroque Art Presented to Anthony Blunt on his 60th Birthday* (London, 1967), pp. 173–8

F. Boyer: *Le Monde des arts en Italie et de la France de la Révolution et de l'Empire* (Turin, 1970)

F. Hermann: *The English as Collectors: A Documentary Chrestomathy* (London, 1972)

A. Emiliani: *Il dibattito sulla tutela e la salvaguardia del patrimonio artistico e culturale italiano dal 1860 al 1923* (Bologna, 1973)

J. Fleming: 'Art Dealing in the Risorgimento', *Burl. Mag.*, cxv (1973), pp. 4–16; cxxi (1979), pp. 492–508, 568–80

A. Emiliani: *Una politica dei beni culturali* (Turin, 1974)

L. Campbell: 'The Art Market in the Southern Netherlands in the Fifteenth Century', *Burl. Mag.*, cxviii (1976), pp. 188–98

F. Haskell: *Rediscoveries in Art: Some Aspects of Taste, Fashion and Collecting in England and France* (Ithaca, NY, 1976)

A. Emiliani: *Leggi, bandi e provvedimenti per la tutela dei beni artistici e culturali negli antichi stati italiani, 1571–1860* (Bologna, 1978)

D. Robertson: *Sir Charles Eastlake and the Victorian Art World* (Princeton, 1978)

J. Anderson: 'A Further Inventory of Gabriel Vendramin's Collection', *Burl. Mag.*, cxxi (1979), pp. 639–48

P. Barocchi: 'Storiografia e collezionismo dal Vasari al Lanzi', *Storia dell'arte italiana*, ii (Turin, 1979), pp. 28–35

F. Haskell: 'La dispersione e la conservazione del patrimonio artistico', *Storia dell'arte italiana*, x (Turin, 1981), pp. 5–35

F. Haskell and N. Penny: *Taste and the Antique* (New Haven and New York, 1981)

J. Alsop: *The Rare Art Traditions: The History of Art Collecting and its Linked Phenomena wherever these Have Appeared* (London, 1982)

M. Bury: 'The Taste for Prints in Italy to c. 1600', *Prt Q.*, ii (1985), pp. 12–26

C. Dowd, ed.: 'The Travel Diaries of Otto Mündler', intro. J. Anderson, *Walpole Soc.*, li (1985)

O. Impey and A. MacGregor: *The Origins of Museums: The Cabinet of Curiosities in Sixteenth- and Seventeenth-century Europe* (Oxford, 1985)

J. Anderson: 'Il collezionismo e la pittura del cinquecento', *La pittura in Italia: Il cinquecento*, ed. G. Briganti (Milan, 1987, rev. 1988), i, pp. 559–68

J. Anderson: 'Collezioni e collezionisti della pittura veneziana del quattrocento: Storia, sfortuna e fortuna', *La pittura veneta del quattrocento*, ed. M. Lucco (Milan, 1989)

K. Pomian: *Collezionisti, amatori e curiosi: Parigi–Venezia, XVI–XVIII secolo* (Milan, 1989)
J. Hist. Coll. (1989–)

JAYNIE ANDERSON

XIV. Museums.

1. Renaissance collections. 2. The Renaissance and Baroque gallery. 3. The age of Neo-classicism. 4. The Napoleonic age and the Restoration. 5. The early nation state. 6. After World War I.

1. RENAISSANCE COLLECTIONS. In the Middle Ages the Church fulfilled the role of public art museum. Church treasuries, secure and apart, displayed to the faithful devotional objects: reliquaries, liturgical vessels, crosses and missals. Those of Monza Cathedral and of S Marco in Venice have survived almost intact. The STUDIOLO, a small chamber, secluded and secretive, resembling part monastic cell, part treasury, devoted to study and to the placement of rare objects, developed from these displays. This development took place primarily in Italy at the end of the 14th century, and by the mid-15th many Renaissance courts had *studioli*, often decorated with intarsia panels (recommended by Alberti) or with series of famous men or Roman emperors. The objects included natural curiosities, objects from archaeological excavations, small pictures, miniatures and finished drawings. A 1492 inventory of the Medici palace reveals the peculiar character of the objects in the *studiolo* of Lorenzo the Magnificent; it included ancient vessels of pietre dure, gold liturgical objects, small mosaics, engraved stones, statuettes, coins and medals. There were only a few paintings: small panels attributed to Jan van Eyck, Giotto and Andrea Mantegna.

Isabella d'Este (*see* ESTE (i), (6)), a ruthless collector of rare things, created a new kind of display in the Appartamento della Grotta in the Corte Vecchia of the Palazzo Ducale at Mantua (1522), which united picture gallery and cabinet (*see* CABINET (i)). Here, through an enclosed garden with Classical statues, one entered the GROTTO, with intarsia-decorated cabinets, vases and small antique sculptures; beyond the grotto lay the *studiolo*, with a splendid series of paintings by Mantegna, Lorenzo Costa and Perugino.

HUMANISM encouraged the collection of ancient art and Rome was the centre of such collections. Maarten van Heemskerck filled a sketchbook with drawings of displays of statues in Roman courtyards and gardens (1532–6; Berlin, Kupferstichkab.; see fig. 107). The arrangement of the display was sometimes casual, the statues picturesquely exhibited in a fragmentary state; or they might be restored and arranged decoratively, as in the courtyard of the Palazzo della Valle, belonging to Cardinal Andrea della Valle (1463–1534), where the display, designed by the sculptor Lorenzo Lotti, was admired by Giorgio Vasari. In Florence, too, the larger antique statues were placed in the garden or courtyard of the Medici palace and in a Medici garden at Piazza S Marco (*see* FLORENCE, §V, 2).

Under Julius II the most important Classical statues in Rome were brought to the Vatican. Here, to display them, Donato Bramante designed a statue court, the Cortile Belvedere (*c*. 1508), fragrant with orange trees and the play of fountains, adjoining the Villa Belvedere of Innocent VIII. The statues were displayed in decorated niches and antique masks set into the walls. The *Laokoon* was brought there immediately after its discovery in 1506; in 1509 there followed the *Apollo Belvedere* (both *in situ*) and in 1512 the *Cleopatra* (also known as the *Sleeping Ariadne*; Rome, Mus. Pio-Clementino). These great works of art became the property of the pope, partly as a symbol of prestige but also to guarantee their preservation and accessibility. Venetian collectors displayed a similar pride in preserving their heritage, and in 1523 Cardinal Domenico Grimani left his collection of antiquities to the city. These were later displayed, with his nephew Giovanni Grimani's 200 antique marble works, in Sansovino's Libreria Marciana and the Statuario Pubblico was established in 1596 as the first public archaeological museum. The collection constituted the nucleus of the present Museo Archeologico.

In the late 16th century museums and cabinets aimed at universality. Encyclopedic collections attempted to satisfy man's interest in his place in the universe; they included both *naturalia* (metals, minerals etc) and *artificialia* (works of art ingeniously wrought from such natural objects). The arrangement of princely and aristocratic scientific collections tended to follow an abstract and schematic scheme; in Francesco de' Medici's *studiolo* (1570–71; Florence, Pal. Vecchio) objects were stored in cupboards decorated by paintings that symbolized their qualities. The collections of private individuals were often linked to scholarly interests; for example, those of Ulisse Aldrovandi (*see* ALDROVANDI, (1)) in Bologna, Ferrante Imperato (1550–1625) in Naples and Francesco Calzolari (1522–1609) in Verona aided their scientific research into the natural world; Aldrovandi used artists to illustrate his collection and in turn his collection was studied by artists. Such museums also included material intended to supply visual information about history and geography. The collection of PAOLO GIOVIO in Como (described in his *Musaei Joviani descriptio* (1546)) was the most famous of many collections of portraits of famous men (parts survive; Como, Civ. Mus. Archeol.). His museum was copied

107. Maarten van Heemskerck: *Display of Roman Sculpture in the Loggia of the Villa Madama, Rome*, pen and brown ink, 179×214 mm, *c*. 1535 (Berlin, Kupferstichkabinett)

by Cristofano dell'Altissimo (*d* 1605) for Cosimo I de' Medici between 1552 and 1556, and this collection remains intact (Florence, Uffizi). The portraits were displayed in the Sala del Mappamondo (completed 1583) in the Palazzo Vecchio, where the cabinets of walnut were decorated with maps painted by Ignazio Danti and Stefano Buonsignori (1565–81).

In the 17th century magnificent private museums continued to be formed in north Italy, such as that of MANFREDO SETTALA in Milan (part in Milan, Ambrosiana). Here the illustration of the natural world was accompanied by craft activities, most notably a workshop producing ingenious lathe-turned items. The court gallery, too, might be linked to highly specialized artisans' workshops in which forms and techniques were elaborated. In Milan Cardinal Federico Borromeo regarded his museum as the complement to the art school, the Accademia del Disegno, and the library, the Biblioteca Ambrosiana, that he also founded. Included in his collection were paintings intended as models of excellence for contemporary artists, for example works by Titian, Bernardino Luini and other followers of Leonardo. Caravaggio's *Basket of Fruit* was the only Italian naturalist painting to accompany many landscapes and still-lifes by Jan Breughel. Borromeo described his collection in his *Musaeum* (1625) and many other 17th-century collectors issued printed catalogues. In Rome such museums were rarer in this period, although Cardinal Flavio Chigi (*see* CHIGI, (4)) and Athanasius Kircher formed great encyclopedic collections. Kircher's was displayed in the Jesuit Collegio Romano. In Florence Leopoldo de' Medici (*see* MEDICI, DE', (25)) broke with the encyclopedic approach to collecting and brought a new methodological seriousness to collections of both art and science.

2. THE RENAISSANCE AND BAROQUE GALLERY. Towards the end of the 16th century buildings began to be erected for the display of collections of Classical sculpture; sometimes these were centrally planned, but more frequently they were long galleries. In Florence Francesco I de' Medici commissioned Bernardo Buontalenti to transform the second floor of Vasari's Uffizi Palace, built as an administrative centre (*uffizi*: 'offices'), into an art gallery with large windows for lighting. The Uffizi (*see* FLORENCE, fig. 3) could be visited and constituted the first purpose-built art gallery. Under Ferdinando I the ancient statues were arranged along the corridor leading across the Ponte Vecchio to the Palazzo Pitti: one of the first instances of the protection of major works under cover, distinguishing them from less valuable sculpture destined for gardens or façades.

The Uffizi retained the universality of 16th-century collections. It incorporated goldsmiths' and engravers' workshops, a room displaying scientific instruments and an armoury that included antique and modern weapons and miscellaneous exotic and curious objects. The *artificalia* most highly valued for their materials or their art were collected in Buontalenti's Tribuna (designed *c.* 1580), an octagonal room lit from above and glowing with mother-of-pearl, scarlet lacquer and *pietra serena*. The inventory of 1589 describes a cabinet at the centre, inlaid with pietre dure and containing small precious objects.

The greater part of the collection was displayed on shelves running along the walls, alternating antique sculptures and modern bronzes with items of virtuoso craftsmanship and small paintings (some originals, others small copies of famous works on copper). Above hung a series of the most famous High Renaissance pictures (*see* DISPLAY OF ART, fig. 3). The Tribuna became celebrated throughout Europe and established a pattern for much later museum design.

Galleries, decorated with iconographically elaborate fresco cycles and intended to display antique sculptures, were built throughout Italy. In the Palazzo Ducale at Mantua, the Galleria della Mostra, designed by Antonio Maria Viani (finished 1612), also displayed paintings, set in a regular sequence of rectangular spaces in decorated walls, and cupboards full of objects in precious materials. At Sabbioneta, Vespasiano Gonzaga built a statue gallery (1583–90) almost 91 m long. Federico Zuccaro designed a gallery for Charles-Emanuel I of Savoy in Turin (1606–7; destr.). The most splendid sculpture galleries were built in Rome, at the Villa Medici (*c.* 1580), the Palazzo Sacchetti, the Palazzo Rucellai and the Palazzo Farnese.

In the 17th century, when the wealth of the papal nephews led to the creation of opulent collections of art, the gallery was a symbol of prestige, bearing witness to the taste and magnificence of its collector and owner. These collections were semi-public, open to connoisseurs, artists and travellers. Most easily accessible were the sumptuous villas and gardens built on the edges of Rome, such as the Villa Borghese and the Villa Ludovisi, where the statues were displayed both indoors and out, the latter in enchanting gardens.

Paintings were also collected, and the fashion for covering the walls of fine residences with them is mentioned as a novelty by the wealthy collector Vincenzo Giustiniani around 1610. In the 17th-century picture collection, or *quadreria*, paintings were arranged symmetrically, over the entire wall surface, in decorated spaces and with carved or gilded frames. The most valued paintings were placed in the best light. The pictures in these collections rarely dated from earlier than the 16th century, but they were varied in style and included landscapes and genre pictures. The first gallery built to hang modern paintings rather than to display ancient sculptures was the Galleria Colonna, built by Antonio del Grande and Girolamo Fontana II in the Palazzo Colonna (begun 1654; opened 1703), Rome, which still retains its 17th-century appearance (*see* DISPLAY OF ART, fig. 1).

3. THE AGE OF NEO-CLASSICISM. In the Enlightenment the museum was no longer intended as a show of wealth and taste, displayed in a princely residence. Instead it presented a rich cultural heritage, in a museum the architectural style of which reflected the aesthetic ideals of the exhibits. The good sovereign, aware of its propaganda value, would aim to establish a gallery in the capital, where his subjects could enjoy their artistic patrimony.

In 1734 Pope Clement XII sent the Albani collection of ancient statues to the Museo Capitolino, thus founding a new and highly influential public art museum. Yet its decoration remained traditional, and it was with the Villa

Albani, an opulent villa–museum, built for Cardinal Alessandro Albani by Carlo Marchionni, that a new style of museum building was created (see fig. 108). Here, under the supervision of Johann Joachim Winckelmann, who was the keeper of the collections, the sculptures were arranged by subject-matter; Anton Raphael Mengs's ceiling painting *Parnassus* championed the ideals of Classical art. There followed the Museo Pio-Clementino, built in the Vatican (1770–93; see fig. 109) for PIUS VI by Michelangelo Simonetti and Giuseppe Camporese. Here the architectural style was more consistently Neo-classical, with the Rotunda, where statues of the pagan gods were displayed, based on the Pantheon (*see* MUSEUM, fig. 4). Other rooms were designed to reflect the style of ancient Roman baths and palaces. The organization of the new museum with its thematic arrangement of the sculptures was indebted to Giovanni Battista Visconti and his son Ennio Quirino Visconti (1751–1818), who also prepared its catalogue. It became one of the most celebrated museums in the world, enormously influential on later museum architecture.

The will (1743) of the Palatine Electress Anna Maria Luisa, the last of the Medici, left the Medici collections to the city of Florence, with the new Habsburg–Lorraine grand dukes as trustees of her bequest. The subsequent reorganization of the Uffizi under grand dukes Leopoldo (1747–92) and Ferdinand III (1769–1824), advised by Giuseppe Bencivenni and Luigi Lanzi, was a triumph of the systematic approach that characterized the Enlightenment. The gallery was dedicated to ancient art and to the fine arts; the scientific instruments and natural curiosities were removed to a specialized physics museum. The *Niobid* group was brought from Rome in 1779 and displayed in a Neo-classical room (1780) designed by Gasparo Maria Paoletti. The paintings were arranged by schools, and exchanges with the Belvedere Gallery, Vienna, filled gaps in the collection. This was how Albrecht Dürer's *Adoration of the Magi* came to the Uffizi. The gallery was intended to illustrate art history rather than to be a temple of taste, and new emphasis was given to early Italian painting.

4. THE NAPOLEONIC AGE AND THE RESTORATION. Under Napoleonic rule the French requisitioned the most celebrated masterpieces for the Louvre in Paris. Other paintings, belonging to religious foundations that had been suppressed, came to form the great collections of the Brera in Milan (which included works from all over the

108. Loggia of the Villa Albani (1755–62), Rome, by Carlo Marchionni

109. Gallery of Busts, Museo Pio-Clementino (1770–93), Vatican, Rome, by Michelangelo Simonetti and Giuseppe Camporese; engraving by Vincenzo Feoli after Francesco Miccinelli

Marches), the Galleria dell'Accademia in Venice and the Pinacoteca in Bologna (1803). These museums, under the influence of French educational theories, became closely associated with academies of art, a study of their collections forming part of the curriculum for students of sculpture and painting. Established artists, too, were encouraged to use the collections for study. The paintings, generally altarpieces, were hung in large rooms and lit by lamps high above, as in 18th-century French museums. They were set in gold frames in an effort to impose unity. The early Italian paintings of each school were arranged chronologically, though often grouped rather indiscriminately.

The difficulties of organizing the new picture galleries were considerable; works were often stored for decades before being exhibited. The museum directors could sell or exchange them for other paintings, or for materials for didactic use, such as prints and plaster models. The Brera Academy, which started with almost exclusively religious paintings, exchanged some for portraits and examples of other genres. In one such exchange Carlo Crivelli's *Annunciation* (1486) was sent to the National Gallery in London. After the unification of Italy these galleries came under the direct control of the State but many works remained in storage for long afterwards, encouraging the practice, especially in Milan and Venice, of sending out

works to be hung in alternative locations, such as churches, where control of them often became impossible. In the course of the 19th century many paintings from the reserve collections in Venice were sent to the gallery of the Vienna Academy, where they were held until 1923. While the new galleries had first choice of the works belonging to suppressed monasteries and lay religious bodies, the largest number of paintings was acquired by art lovers or speculators to form great new private collections. The source of their contents gave these collections a very different character from that of the earlier picture gallery. A good example of this was the collection donated in 1797 by Conte GIACOMO CARRARA to the Academy he founded in Bergamo.

In 1815 the Treaty of Vienna called for the return of art works requested by their countries of origin and to a large extent this was accomplished. The Italian authorities renounced their claim to some works in order to guarantee the return of others considered more important. For example, the representatives of the Grand Duchy of Tuscany relinquished their claim to all their early Italian paintings in return for the guaranteed restitution of pietre dure tables that had been distributed among the various Napoleonic residences.

The Restoration did not mark any change in policy with regard to favouring museums as a suitable location for works of art that had once hung in churches or palaces. The works returned to the Papal States were placed in a new gallery in the Vatican Palace, organized as a study collection for artists. In Rome the desire to re-establish pre-Napoleonic cultural policy and celebrate those years when Rome had been the greatest centre of Neo-classical culture led to the building of the splendid Vatican museums in that style: the Museo Chiaramonti (1807–10), the Museo Gregoriano Egizio and Museo Gregoriano Etrusco (1837–9) and, one of the best examples of museum architecture of the Neo-classical age, the Braccio Nuovo (1817–22; for illustration see STERN, (2)). A flourishing programme of museum development also existed in Turin under Carlo Felici and Carlo Alberto of Savoy. The Museo Egizio, which became the most important in Italy, was established in 1824; in 1829 the Moggi di Morano collection was acquired (since 1839 housed in the Accademia Albertina). The most important museum of them all, the Pinacoteca Sabauda, was opened to the public in 1832. It contained paintings from the royal collections (with both Italian and Flemish masterpieces) and benefited from a vigorous acquisition policy (1839–65) whereby the collection gained a nucleus of Florentine works.

5. THE EARLY NATION STATE. On the eve of the unification of Italy the nation still lacked museums dedicated to sculpture and the decorative arts, especially of the Middle Ages and the Renaissance. In 1865 a new museum was established in Florence to remedy that omission: the Museo Nazionale in the Palazzo del Podestà, the Bargello. The intention was to form a collection similar to that of the Hôtel de Cluny in Paris or the Victoria and Albert Museum in London. The maiolica works, bronzes and arms from the Uffizi Gallery were transferred to the new institution. With the Uffizi's statues by Donatello and Michelangelo and the 16th-century marbles from the Salone del Cinquecento in the Palazzo Vecchio, the Bargello became the first great museum of Renaissance sculpture in Italy. The sector of decorative arts gained impetus only when the splendid collection of medieval art, mainly collected in France, was donated in 1888 by Jean and Louis Carrand.

Other developments in Florence included the removal of Michelangelo's *David* from outdoors into the shelter of the Accademia di Belle Arti (1873), where a splendid dais was built for it, designed by Emilio de Fabris. Finally, in 1891 the bas-reliefs made by Donatello and Luca della Robbia for the singing galleries of Florence Cathedral were placed in the Museo dell'Opera del Duomo, where they formed the nucleus of the collection of works belonging to the cathedral. This type of museum was founded in several other cities (Orvieto, c. 1850; Siena, 1870; Atri, 1912; Perugia, 1923; Milan, 1953; Pisa, 1979).

In 1861 as part of the renewed suppression of ecclesiastical bodies by the Kingdom of Italy, civic administrations gained control over works of art. In many cases they were simply sold off while in others they were left in their original locations (where eventually the question of their ownership gave rise to complex legal problems), but often, as in many small cities of central Italy, the opportunity was taken to set up or improve collections, most of which focused on medieval and Renaissance works.

In the second half of the 19th century there was a sharp increase in archaeological collections. Important new ones were founded, such as the Museo Archeologico in Florence (1881), which included the city's old collections but was mainly intended as a centre for materials from the Etruscan tombs, especially those excavated by Luigi Adriano Milani (1854–1914). In 1889 the archaeological museum of the Villa Giulia in Rome was founded to display materials from the excavations of southern Etruria and the Museo Nazionale Romano opened in the cloisters adjoining the Baths of Diocletian to receive the objects that were coming to light every day in the course of building works in the new capital. There the State established a collection worthy to stand beside the great municipal and papal collections of the Capitoline and the Vatican respectively. Some new museums resulted from the donation of private archaeological collections, such as the Museo Barracco, founded in Rome in 1902, and the Museo Provinciale of Lecce, where the Greek and Apulian vases donated by Duke Sigismondo Castromediano in 1868 formed the start of the collection. Other archaeological museums were enlarged: under Ernesto Schiaparelli (1856–1928), who became its director in 1894, the Museo Egizio in Turin was augmented with the fruits of important excavations in Egypt. The Museo Nazionale in Naples was enriched by excavations conducted by Giuseppe Fiorelli (1823–96), especially in the urban area of Pompeii.

In the second half of the 19th century the Italian museum scene was affected by the development of new types of private collections. In some of these paintings and sculpture were displayed in furnished rooms, often in the corresponding historical style; in others the works were presented in a more rigorously museological setting. Many of these collections came to constitute new museums, either independent or run by the State or local authorities. They included the Museo Poldi Pezzoli in Milan (1881, later increased by purchases of exquisite taste made by Giuseppe Bertini), the Museo Filangieri in Naples (1888), the Museo Borgogna in Vercelli (1907), the Museo Stibbert, Florence (1909), with its extraordinary collection of European and Japanese arms and armour, and the Galleria Franchetti at the Ca' d'Oro in Venice (1927).

The last years of the 19th century were a very positive period for the management of Italy's artistic patrimony. The Ministero della Pubblica Istruzione, after the heroic years of GIOVANNI BATTISTA CAVALCASELLE, included such figures as Adolfo Venturi (see VENTURI, (1)) and Giulio Cantalamessa. Even men of lesser fame such as CORRADO RICCI revealed a gift for organization and an attentiveness to public expectations that made him a great museum organizer. The collections were enriched by purchases, and works that had been loaned out were recalled. This was done, for example, when the Pinacoteca di Brera was being reorganized in 1903 by Corrado Ricci in consultation with the restorer Luigi Cavenaghi.

In 1902 the State acquired the Borghese collection, which was put on display in the 17th-century palace in the Borghese Gardens in Rome together with the paintings and sculpture from the family's city residence. Less successful was the Florentine initiative taken in 1919 of transferring the chief masterpieces of the Accademia gallery to the Uffizi, which robbed the Accademia of its character as a centre for works of the Florentine school and left it with a relatively second-rate collection.

6. AFTER WORLD WAR I. The years following World War I were less momentous. The establishment during the 1920s of a new museum in the Palazzo Venezia, the old seat of the Austro-Hungarian embassy, had a nationalistic flavour, though its collection of medieval and Renaissance art has helped remedy the paucity of collections of sculpture and decorative arts. In 1929 the Museo di Storia della Scienza was established in Florence, with objects related to Galileo's experiments and with instruments that have artistic as well as scientific interest. New excavations led to the establishment of the Museo di Spina in Ferrara (1935). In 1937, another archaeological venture, the Mostra Augustea della Romanità, was inaugurated with all the rhetorical fanfare typical of the period. This was a great assemblage of models and casts illustrating Roman civilization, an experiment in the creation of a didactic collection which now constitutes the Museo della Civiltà Romana at the EUR (Esposizione Universale di Roma). Most organizational efforts of the period seem to have been focused on the great international exhibitions of Italian art (London, 1930; Paris, 1935); in this the guiding spirit was Ugo Ojetti.

When World War II swept through Italy, many of the museums were evacuated, and often their buildings were damaged. For a time the nation's artistic heritage was brought to the public through temporary exhibitions; then came a major reorganization in which museums were redesigned according to 'modern' criteria. The works that were considered to be most aesthetically important were often singled out and displayed against an uncluttered background so that they could be appreciated as individual works of art. The educational role of museums and the history of their different collections were regarded as of secondary importance; indeed, some highly significant works were relegated to unsuitable storerooms. This approach obviously took little account of the complexity and richness of a museum's function, but nonetheless the high quality of many of these settings is indisputable. Particularly noteworthy is the architecture of CARLO SCARPA, who produced excellent designs that worked both in formal architectural terms and as settings for works of art. The Palazzo Abatellis in Palermo (1953–4), the Canova gallery of plaster casts in Possagno (1955–7), the Museo Correr in Venice (1960) and the Museo Civico di Castelvecchio in Verona (1964) were all designed by him.

The museum architecture of Franco Albini, for example in the Museo del Tesoro of San Lorenzo (1952–6) and the reorganization of the Palazzo Rosso in Genoa (1952–61), shows concern for the creation of a well-defined environment. A different setting, with strong expressive values, can be seen in the design for the Castello Sforzesco in Milan, created by the BBPR group (1956) just after the acquisition of Michelangelo's Rondanini *Pietà*. The new wing built to rehouse the Lateran museums (Mus. Gregoriano Profano; Mus. Missionari Etnol.; Mus. Pio-Crist.) in the Vatican, by Lucio Passarelli and his firm (1965–70), focused on the relationship between the museum's interior and its setting among the walls and gardens of the Vatican Palace.

The important role of museums, not only as great aesthetic experiences but also as repositories of artistic culture, was explicitly recognized around the end of the 1960s. This was not so much a matter of museum design as a recognition of their role in helping protect cultural heritage. Particularly significant were Giovanni Romano's views on the exhibition dedicated to the artistic patrimony of the Valle di Susa (see 1977 exh. cat.) and the research on the Umbrian area (1977–8) led by Bruno Toscano. A new area of concern arose involving the preservation of vestments and ceremonial objects that went out of use with the liturgical reform. This large patrimony, often of relatively recent date, includes such materials as textiles that present special problems of conservation. The State authorities have improved their record-keeping in an attempt to avoid the dispersal of these articles but the most effective move has been to house them in diocesan or parochial museums, often newly established for the purpose. Another recent element in the Italian scene has been the appearance of museums devoted to peasant culture. These are almost always run by local bodies but are not always organized with the rigour and intelligence that characterize their model, the Museo della Civiltà Contadina in San Marino di Bentivoglio (Bologna), founded in 1973.

In Italy collections of contemporary art have not received the attention granted to them in other countries. The 19th-century academic collection did not generally distinguish the collection of contemporary works from the older paintings. Almost all recent works were produced by the professors and pupils of the academy where the picture gallery was located. The Galleria d'Arte Moderna in Rome was founded in 1883 for the promotion and documentation of living Italian artists. In the period before World War II public and private collectors tended to disregard the great avant-garde movements (especially the French ones), their attention being primarily focused on the excellent work being produced by Italian painters between World Wars I and II. A selection of high-quality works indicating the Italian taste of the early decades of the century can be seen in the Galleria Ricci-Oddi, Piacenza, in a building especially constructed to house the collection in 1933. The large collections left to the Brera and to the city of Milan consist of Italian paintings, as does the collection that Alberto della Ragione donated to the city of Florence in 1970, which has an emphasis on post-war art. The only collection to provide a wider view of developments in 20th-century art is the Peggy Guggenheim Collection in Venice.

Since 1960 there has been more contact between the Italian art scene and developments elsewhere. A few Italian artists, such as Alberto Burri and Lucio Fontana, have been recognized as leading European artists, and Italian experiments and movements have entered the international arena. Collections of avant-garde works now feature the most important Italian artists alongside their foreign colleagues. New museums are being founded, often featuring great private collections (e.g. the Panza di Biumo collection in Varese, the movable works of which are destined for the Los Angeles Museum of Contemporary Art, and the Gori collection at Celle di Pistoia). These museums are also centres for documentation and open experimentation. The most important of them at present is the Museo d'Arte Contemporanea at the Castello Rivoli, near Turin, which was inaugurated in 1985.

BIBLIOGRAPHY

GENERAL

O. Campori: *Raccolta di cataloghi ed inventari inediti* (Modena, 1870)
Documenti inediti per servire alla storia dei musei d'Italia, i–iv, Ministerio della Pubblica Istruzione (Florence and Rome, 1878–80)
Le gallerie nazionali italiane, i–v, Ministerio della Pubblica Istruzione (Rome, 1894–1902)
Boll. A. (1907–)
Guida d'Italia, i–xvi, Touring Club of Milan (Milan, 1914–29 and subsequent editions)
Le arti, i–iii (Florence, 1938–41)
L. Moscona: 'Repertorio di musei e gallerie in Italia', *Civiltà nell'arte* (Bologna, 1960), pp. 379–416
Museologia (1972–)
I musei: I musei schede, Touring Club of Milan (Milan, 1980)

PERIODS AND STYLES OF COLLECTING

Enc. A. Ant.: 'Collezioni archeologiche'
W. Liebenwein: *Studiolo* (Berlin, 1977)
W. Prinz: *Die Entstehung der Galerie in Frankreich und Italien* (Berlin, 1977)
F. Haskell and N. Penny: *Taste and the Antique: The Lure of Classical Sculpture, 1500–1900* (New Haven and London, 1981)
P. Barocchi and G. Ragionieri, eds: *Gli Uffizi quattro secoli di una galleria: Atti del convegno: Firenze, 1982* (Florence, 1983)
A. Lugli: *Naturalia et mirabilia* (Milan, 1983)
C. Franzoni: 'Rimembranze d'infinite cose: Le collezioni rinascimentali di antichità', *Memoria dell'antico nell'arte italiana*, i (Turin, 1984), pp. 301–60
O. Impey and A. Macgregor, eds: *The Origin of Museums* (Oxford, 1985)

INDIVIDUAL COLLECTIONS

L. Lanzi: 'La Real Galleria di Firenze accresciuta e riordinata', *Nuovo G. Lett. Italia*, xlvii (1782/R Florence, 1982)
A. Venturi: *La R. Galleria Estense di Modena* (Modena, 1882)
M. Ruggiero: *Storia degli scavi di Ercolano* (Naples, 1885)
A. Baudi di Vesme: *Catalogo della Regia Pinacoteca di Torino* (Turin, 1899, 2/1909)
C. A. Levi: *Le collezioni veneziane d'arte e d'antichità dal secolo XVI ai nostri giorni* (Venice, 1900)
F. Malaguzzi Valeri: *Catalogo della Pinacoteca di Brera* (Milan, 1908)
A. de Rinaldis: *Museo Nazionale di Napoli: Guida*, i–ii (Naples, 1911)
S. Moschini Marconi: *Gallerie dell'Accademie di Venezia*, i–iii (Rome, 1955–70)
A. Emiliani, ed.: *La Pinacoteca Nazionale di Bologna* (Bologna, 1967)
A. Falchetti, ed.: *La Pinacoteca Ambrosiana* (Vicenza, 1969)
Palazzo Vecchio: Committenza e collezionismo medicei (exh. cat., Florence, Pal. Vecchio, 1980)
C. Pietrangeli: *I Musei Vaticani: Cinque secoli di storia* (Rome, 1985)
Omaggio a Donatello, 1386–1986: Donatello e la storia del museo (exh. cat., Florence, Bargello, 1985–6)
R. Grandi, ed.: *Il Museo civico d'arte industriale Davia Bargellini* (Bologna, 1987)
'Una città e il suo museo', *Boll. Mus. Civ. Ven.*, xxx/1–4 (1988)

SIGNIFICANT ISSUES AND FIGURES

In memoria di Corrado Ricci (Rome, 1935)
F. Haskell: *Rediscoveries in Art* (New York, 1967)
S. Cantacuzino: *Carlo Scarpa architetto poeta* (exh. cat., London, RIBA, 1974)
A. Emiliani: *Dal museo al territorio* (Bologna, 1974)
Valle di Susa: Arte e storia dall'XI al XVIII secolo (exh. cat., Turin, Gal. Civ. A. Mod., 1977)
L'Umbria: Manuali per il territorio, 2 vols (Rome, 1977–8)
Franco Albini: Architettura per un museo (Rome, 1980)
F. Haskell: 'La dispersione e la conservazione del patrimonio artistico', *Stor. A. It.*, x (1981), pp. 5–35
R. Longhi: *Critica d'arte e buongoverno, 1938–1969*, Opera Completa, xiii (Florence, 1985)
K. Pomian: *Collectionneurs, amateurs et curieux, Paris, Venise: XVIe–XVIIIe siècle* (Paris, 1987; It. trans., Milan, 1989)

ALESSANDRO CONTI

XV. Art libraries and photographic collections.

Although the term 'art library' became current in Italy only in the 20th century, the country has always had such libraries, many of which belong to the Ministry of Culture. Such libraries contain reading rooms especially devoted to the study of art. These older-established libraries exist in regional capitals (e.g. Milan, Bib. N. Braidense; Florence, Bib. Marucelliana) as well as in provincial centres (Parma, Bib. Palatina; Modena, Bib. Estense). In some of these libraries the artistic documentation originally pertained to specialized collections of drawings, manuscript illuminations or engravings; they generally include repertories and bibliographies and monographs on the artists and collections involved, with reference to the local areas. In addition to these sections of large libraries, Italy has various independent collections specializing in art, both public and private.

The Biblioteca dell'Istituto Nazionale d'Archeologia e Storia dell'Arte, based in the Palazzo Venezia in Rome, is considered to be the national art library. Founded in 1922, it is richly endowed, due partly to the donations of many art historians. Its most famous resources include the Roman topographic materials of the Lanciani collection, as well as a fund of drawings including the Valadier collection and a sketchbook of Salvator Rosa. The Biblioteca Luigi Poletti in MODENA, which belongs to the city, is dedicated exclusively to art history. It was founded in the 19th century by the architect LUIGI POLETTI, who donated his library and drawing collection to the city. The Castello Sforzesco in Milan houses the Biblioteca d'Arte as well as the library of the Achille Bertarelli collection of prints (also city-owned; Civica Raccolta delle Stampe Achille Bertarelli), which is one of the most important of its kind in Italy.

Many art history libraries are connected with the university teaching of this subject and they are found in the most important Italian faculties. The universities also maintain such architectural libraries as those of the Turin Politecnico and the Istituto Universitario di Architettura in Venice and the library of the Facoltà di arte e filosofia at Bologna University. Other art schools—specialist high schools, art institutes and academies—in many cities have links with libraries. Perhaps the best known of these is the library of the Accademia di Belle Arti di Brera in Milan, established at the beginning of the 19th century (*see* MILAN, §II, 4). The archaeological libraries administered by the Italian State are also often linked with universities. However, these specialized libraries are often for use only by members of the archaeological authorities. The same is frequently the case with the libraries of public bodies in charge of art and architecture.

Museum libraries are more numerous, for the wealth of Italian artistic heritage has favoured the creation of many institutions linked with both the great municipal collections and those of the nation. Examples include the libraries of civic museums in Venice, Padua, Verona, Reggio Emilia, Bolzano, Trieste, Piacenza and Bologna. More specialized museums also have documentary collections—for example the library of the Museo Internazionale delle Ceramiche in Faenza, the collection of documents in Vinci on Leonardo, the library of the Museo Nazionale delle Arti e delle Tradizioni Popolari in Rome, and that of the Museo Nazionale Preistorico ed Etnografico Pigorini, Rome. Another field served by specialized libraries is that of restoration; one example is the library of the pietre dure workshop (Opificio delle Pietre Dure) in Florence; another is the ADOLFO VENTURI library of the Istituto Centrale per il Restauro in Rome. There are also specialist libraries for contemporary art (e.g. Genoa, Mus. Villa Croce; Prato, Cent. A. Contemp. Luigi Pecci). In Venice the Archivio Storico dell'Arti Contemporaneae della Biennale possesses a vast library linked with the Biennale exhibitions in the fields of art, theatre and cinema.

Foreign art libraries have a number of important branches in Italy. The Bibliotheca Hertziana in Rome and the Kunsthistorisches Institut in Florence, both German, are very large and rich in documentation. Florence is also the home of the Berenson collection (specializing in the Renaissance), while the Ecole Française and many foreign academies have libraries in Rome. Many of the institutions already mentioned also hold print collections, especially those attached to the Ministry of Culture (e.g. Florence, Bib. N. Cent.). Some were originally based on 18th-century endowments (e.g. Florence, Bib. Marucelliana). Others, including the Bertarelli print collection in Milan, have been founded through private donations in the 20th century. The richest collections of engravings are those in museums (e.g. Florence, Uffizi). In Rome the Istituto Nazionale per la Grafica holds not only prints but also many original plates in the Calcografia Nazionale.

Museums also keep photograph collections, which are used as research tools. The various administrative bodies that oversee the Italian artistic, archaeological and architectural heritage also possess important photographic documents for use by those working in these fields. For the same purpose there are also regional centres for such autonomous regions as Friuli and Sicily. The specialized foreign institutes mentioned above also have collections of photographs dedicated to art history. At a national level the two most important photograph collections are that of the Istituto Centrale per il Catalogo e la Documentazione created by the National Photograph Office, which contains photographs of the whole artistic patrimony of Italy, and that of the Istituto Nazionale per la Grafica. The latter, which dates from the mid-19th century, contains images commissioned from various photographers to document the institute's rich collection.

There are also many specialized photograph collections, including the Istituto di Fotografia Alpina Vittorio Sella, Biella, in Piedmont and the huge collection of the Touring Club Italiano of Milan, with over 7000 photographs and slides dedicated to tourism. These centres are run mainly by private organizations such as publishing houses (e.g. Electa in Milan; Scala in Florence). The collections of historical photographs in the Civico Archivio Fotografico, Castello Sforzesco, in Milan and the Becchetti photograph library in Rome were both originally based on donations from collectors. However, the most important collection in the field of photographic history is the one in the ALINARI Museum in Florence, which contains not only the Alinari photograph collection but also, among others, those of GIACOMO BROGI and JAMES ANDERSON.

BIBLIOGRAPHY

C. Alberici: *Incontro con la Civica Raccolta delle Stampe Achille Bertarelli: Milano, Castello Sforzesco* (Milan, 1970, rev. 2/1980)
A. Cicinelli and S. Vasco Rocca, eds: *Repertorio delle fotografie del Gabinetto Fotografico Nazionale: Dipinti dei musei e gallerie di Roma* (Rome, 1978)
L. Gandolfi: *La biblioteca d'arte*, 2 vols (Milan, 1980)
Disegni e incisione della raccolta Marucelli (exh. cat., Florence, Bib. Marucelliana, 1984)
J. Viaux, ed.: *IFLA Directory of Art Libraries* (New York, 1985)
C. Bianchi and M. G. Maraviglia, eds: *Biblioteche d'arte e fondi di interesse artistico in territorio fiorentino* (Rome, 1988) [bilingual text]
C. Rotondi: 'La Biblioteca Marucelliana di Firenze', *Labyrinthos*, vii–viii (1988–9), pp. 167–275
A. Emiliani: *Il politecnico delle arti: Un libro bianco per la Pinacoteca Nazionale e l'Accademia di Belle Arti di Bologna* (Bologna, 1989)
ROSSELLA TODROS

XVI. Art education.

1. Apprenticeships. 2. Academies. 3. Education of women artists.

1. APPRENTICESHIPS. In the Roman period many architects and sculptors must have practised in small family businesses and thus learnt their trade there as well (*see* ROME, ANCIENT, §§II, 1(iv) and IV, 1(v)). Later training seems to have become more organized: the emperors Severus Alexander (*reg* 222–35) and Aurelian (*reg* 270–75) tried to promote architectural studies by making grants to teachers. Throughout the Middle Ages as well as the early Renaissance, workshop practice was the only common form of artistic instruction in Italy. The earliest known institutions to propagate this kind of training and to become not only centres of learning in general, but also the main sources for art patronage in particular, were religious. In the 11th century the Benedictine monastery at Montecassino (*see* MONTECASSINO, §2) became an establishment for the instruction of future Roman craftsmen after having been decorated by artists from Constantinople (now Istanbul). Other religious orders followed the Benedictines' example (*see* BENEDICTINE ORDER, §1). Many of them continued to maintain scriptoria for the writing and illumination of manuscripts, for example the Carmelite Order at S Maria del Carmine and the Dominican monastery of S Marco, both in Florence (*see* DOMINICAN ORDER, §III). These served as art schools for those clerical painters who became active in the early and mid-15th century.

The identity of the architect in medieval times was ambiguous, and expertise in any of the visual arts was accepted as a qualification to design and supervise the erection of important buildings, as was the case with Giotto; nor were the trades of sculptor, mason and architect rigidly distinguished from each other. Training at first was from father to son, or from an older member of a family to a younger one, in circumstances of some secrecy, which is one of the reasons why so few technical drawings have survived from this period. Formal apprenticeships emerged in the 13th century in the context of the craft guild system.

Workshop or bound apprenticeship also became a fully regulated system for lay artists. Dictated by the commercial guilds, it was promoted indiscriminately among all would-be craftsmen (*see* GUILD). The pupil, usually aged 13, was taken into the house of a recognized master for a training period lasting three to seven years. Paid a small annuity, the apprentice would, in Cennino Cennini's words: 'agree to stay with him, with love of obedience, submitting to serve him in order to attain perfection in the art'. Grinding and mixing colours, in addition to preparing panel and wall surfaces, for example, formed the basic foundation of the apprentice's training. These mechanical labours were followed by drawing exercises, which included copies of the master's study sheets and then of his paintings. Imitation remained the most important component of artistic training until the 19th century. The young Michelangelo, for example, who was active when a new concept of art education was beginning to emerge, copied Giotto's images at Santa Croce, Florence. Also, as a young man, Giorgio Vasari (see VASARI, (1)), one of the founders of a new system of artistic education in the late 16th century, copied the works of established painters in Urbino.

In late 16th-century Florence the apprentice was encouraged to continue his study in Rome. As a journeyman he could become his master's assistant, and after three or four years he was allowed to submit a test piece to be evaluated, not only by his master, but also by the guild representatives. He would then be able to work as a master craftsman and to acquire a permit to establish his own workshop (see FLORENCE, §II, 1). Apprenticeship remained such a popular system of artistic instruction in Italy that it continued to flourish even after the introduction of art academies. Thus in 17th-century Genoa no painter was permitted to exercise his or her craft without having learnt the rudiments of painting in a local workshop for seven years.

During the Renaissance, the nature of an architect's education depended substantially on his class origins. The sons of gentlemen studied literature and science; those who made the transition to architecture from the building trades had very little general education. Vasari nowhere referred to schools of architecture where formal training was given. Where he mentioned such matters in his biographies of architects he generally said that his subject was articled to a practising architect. As in the Middle Ages, architecture was often practised in conjunction with another profession, and both Filippo Brunelleschi and Baldassare Peruzzi learnt the first elements of design in a goldsmith's workshop. A frequent component of the architect's training was the study of the Antique, generally by way of measuring the remains of ancient Roman buildings and their details, a taste for which was often evinced by practitioners of other trades such as sculpture or joinery. For the first Renaissance students the very fabric of the ruins was a school of architecture, to be examined for hints as to how bricks were laid and stone blocks cramped together.

2. ACADEMIES. There were few successsful attempts in the late 15th century to develop a new concept of artistic instruction that promoted knowledge more than skill. Those that did succeed took the form of private teaching establishments, which were not subject to guild regulations and in which promising artists were no longer considered mere artisans. One of the first, in the late 1480s, was the academy that Lorenzo the Magnificent instituted in his garden at the Piazza S Marco (see FLORENCE, §V, 2). The collection of antique and modern statuary that the garden had housed was reorganized to

form a centre of practice for such promising young sculptors as Michelangelo. Such an establishment was new in Florence but not entirely unknown elsewhere in Italy. Basing artistic training on the study of ancient as well as contemporary reliefs, drawings and icons had been the guiding principle of the innovative *studium* that FRANCESCO SQUARCIONE had established in Padua in the 1440s. However, the Medicean centre differed from its Paduan precursor in that it did not advocate the traditional method of education through tutelage. Unlike Squarcione, BERTOLDO DI GIOVANNI, who supervised Lorenzo's collection of artworks, does not seem to have acted as master–teacher to the apprentice–pupils.

Leonardo da Vinci is said to have founded an academy at the castle of Ludovico Sforza in Milan during the 1490s, but its existence has not been proved. It was known as an intellectual circle rather than an institution where art was taught, and this Accademia Leonardi Vinci may have taken the form of debates, which Leonardo either initiated or attended. It may have produced, at least in part, the treatise on painting that Leonardo prepared from 1489 to 1518, which had a far-reaching impact on the development of an academic art education.

Besides the Medicean garden, the only documented private establishments for artistic training to embody new ideas were those of BACCIO BANDINELLI in Rome and Florence during the 1530s and 1540s respectively. The first, referred to as the Accademia di Bacchio Brandin, operated in the Belvedere court at the Vatican under the patronage of Pope Clement VII. In an engraving by Agostino dei Musi from 1531, it is shown as a centre where both experienced and inexperienced artists examined, copied and perhaps discussed statuettes of male and female nudes. Thus the emphasis of the academy appears to have been on learning through theoretical study as well as imitation. In engravings by ENEA VICO *c*. 20 years after Musi's, Bandinelli's second studio, called the Accademia, is shown to have grown in size and changed somewhat in essence. Bandinelli's Florentine school included not only various statuettes but also different sections of human skeletons, which would have been used for anatomy demonstrations. In addition, it appears to have encouraged aspiring artists—whom Vico shows divided into diverse groups and immersed in diverse activities rather than in copying one given cast—to draw from their imagination (see fig. 110).

One of the principal purposes of the Accademia del Disegno, founded in Florence as the Accademia e Compagnia del Disegno in 1563, was to create an official institution for the teaching of painting, sculpture and architecture (see also FLORENCE, §V, 1). In this sense, the Accademia e Compagnia del Disegno was to resemble the Accademia Fiorentina (founded 1542), which had also been founded under the patronage of Cosimo I de' Medici to promote the study of the arts and letters. Cosimo demonstrated his regard for the Accademia del Disegno as a worthwhile institution for artistic training by sending his son Giovanni de' Medici to study there. He later became a painter and architect. The academy formulated an educational programme, which was only partially implemented. Three senior members were to be elected annually by its officers to serve as teachers, either at the

110. Enea Vico: *Baccio Bandinelli's Academy, Florence*, engraving, 306×525 mm, *c.* 1551 (London, British Museum)

academy meeting place or in their own workshops. The other members were obliged, under financial penalty, to help promising artists. For teaching, the academy built up a studio collection of artworks: preparatory drawings, cartoons, sculptural models and architectural designs, in addition to examples of ancient sculpture. Anatomy classes, conducted at the hospital of S Maria Nuova, were also required. The programme also promoted the use of lectures in mathematics and perspective, to be presented at the academy meeting-place. The academy's programme did not replace workshop practice, however, and attempts in the late 16th century to introduce life-drawing classes and various courses on theory failed: the academy remained a fundamentally administrative organization. Nevertheless, it produced an academic curriculum that helped to change the concepts and some of the methods of traditional artistic practice. It was succeeded by the Accademia di Belle Arti in 1784.

Even more than the Accademia del Disegno in Florence, the Accademia di S Luca in Rome, founded on 14 November 1593 under the patronage of Pope Sixtus V, regarded the promotion of art education as its primary concern (*see* ROME, §VI). The programme included tuition for aspiring artists and theoretical study for all members. Formal classes were given in architecture in the same way as they were in painting and sculpture. Twelve visiting teachers were appointed annually, each to be on duty for one month and train beginners to draw from life and from artworks. Daily lectures on such topics as the nature of *disegno*, the pre-eminence of painting, composition and motion were also scheduled. Such academies as those in

Florence and Rome emerged in different Italian cities throughout the 17th century. An important example was the Accademia di S Luca, Milan, founded in 1620 and housed in the Biblioteca Ambrosiana under the auspices of Archbishop FEDERICO BORROMEO. Indeed, with its picture collection, its casts of antique statues, a paid model and a series of lectures, it was an educational establishment intended to train 24 students without fees.

Among the various didactic studios flourishing in Italy in the wake of the formation of the Florentine Accademia del Disegno, the most prestigious was the Carracci Academy in Bologna, founded in 1582 by Lodovico, Agostino and Annibale Carracci (*see* CARRACCI, (3)). It was known first as the Accademia delli Desiderosi and later as the Accademia delli Incamminati. In common with most of its counterparts, it began as an informal centre for life-drawing classes and grew into an establishment where artistic study focused on what was becoming a permanent collection of copies of famous statues, casts of ornamental details and a human skeleton. Indeed, it originated as a place where artists could practise life studies by sharing models' fees, and it evolved into a circle inspired by the academic tradition, where lectures or discussions became common on such theoretical and practical issues as anatomy, perspective and architecture. The academy included architecture in its programme of studies, with formal courses in drawing, perspective, mathematics and mechanics. It closed in 1620 following the death of Ludovico Carracci (*see* ACADEMY).

In the late 19th century, after the unification of Italy, technical education was reorganized on a systematic basis, and architects were taught along with engineers in *scuole d'applicazione*, though the Higher Technical Institute of Milan had a separate three-year course. Architectural students would also often attend the classes there of the school of *capomaestri* or master builders. The establishment of the Legge Gentile by the Fascist regime produced for the first time a uniform organization of national art education in Italy. Basic artistic instruction was undertaken by various art schools, specialized high schools and institutions, whereas advanced study was offered by a few select institutions for the industrial arts, architectural schools and academies for the fine arts, all propagating workshop practice. As well as the different architectural faculties, for example the ones at the universities of Rome and Palermo, the curricula of which have been constantly modernized since the late 1960s, most of the successful institutions for artistic training in Italy are those incorporating, or focusing on, the study of industrial design. Notable examples of these include the Istituto Europeo di Design, Milan, the Politecnico, Turin, and the Istituto Statale d'Arte, Monza. Apart from the universities, some schools (e.g. Domus Academy where courses last only ten months) serve as finishing schools for more advanced would-be architects and designers.

3. EDUCATION OF WOMEN ARTISTS. The few women artists known to have been active during the late Middle Ages (e.g. the miniaturists Allegra and Donella) had learnt their art in convents, where the education of daughters of wealthy families often included copying and decorating manuscripts. Most, if not all, of those who succeeded as artists throughout the early Renaissance had been trained in a similar fashion, for example Maria Ormani and Francesca da Firenze, who were both nuns. In the late Renaissance, female artists were either daughters of male artists, such as Lavinia Fontana (*see* FONTANA (ii), (2)), who had been able to learn the rudiments of her art at home, or members of noble families such as Sofonisba Anguissola (*see* ANGUISSOLA, (1)), who had gained what was then an exceptional education for a woman. The same trend continued during the Baroque when ELISABETTA SIRANI and Artemisia Gentileschi (*see* GENTILESCHI, (2)), among others, studied painting from their respective fathers. Gentileschi was the first woman to join the Florentine Accademia del Disegno (1616).

Aspiring female artists had no recourse to the kind of artistic instruction available to their male counterparts. In the late 14th century, the Painters' Guild in Perugia ignored their existence altogether, as did the University of Painters in Rome 100 years later. In the early 17th century, the Accademia di S Luca in Rome forbade women to attend meetings even though it admitted some of them as members. It was only in Bologna, where women outnumbered men, that the training of women illuminators, painters, sculptors and printers continued to be relatively common. Furthermore, the city prided itself on a famous university, which not only welcomed women but also produced renowned women scholars. The first private centre for artistic practice to be supervised exclusively by a woman was the studio of ROSALBA CARRIERA in Venice, in the 18th century. Carriera became the most successful female painter of her generation; she had started her professional training at home, under the guidance of her father, who was a lacemaker. Carriera went on to teach her two sisters, Giovanna and Angela, as well as two other women, Margherita Terzi and Angioletta Sartori (*d* 1760).

BIBLIOGRAPHY
C. Cennini: *Il libro dell'arte* (MS.; *c.* 1390); trans. and notes by D. V. Thomson jr (1933)
N. Pevsner: *Academies of Art Past and Present* (London, 1940, rev. New York, 1973)
D. Mahon: 'Art Theory in the Newly-founded Accademia di San Luca, with Special Reference to "Academic" Criticism of Caravaggio', *Studies in Seicento Art and Theory* (London, 1947/*R* Westport, CT, 1971), pp. 155–91
S. Macdonald: *The History and Philosophy of Art Education* (London, 1970), pp. 21–5
M. A. Jack: 'The Accademia del Disegno in Late Renaissance Florence', *16th C. J.*, vii/2 (1976), pp. 3–20
T. Maldonado: 'Arte, educazione, scienza: Verso una nuova creatività progettivale', *Casabella*, xlii (1978), pp. 10–16
C. Dempsey: 'Some Observations on the Education of Artists in Florence and Bologna During the Later Sixteenth Century', *A. Bull.*, lxii (1980), pp. 552–69
M. Wackernagel: *The World of the Florentine Renaissance Artist* (Princeton, 1981), pp. 328–37
B. Cole: *The Renaissance Artist at Work* (New York, 1983), pp. 30–34
A. M. Fundaro and others: 'La didattica', *L'Architettura*, xxix (1983), pp. 901–15
A. Hughes: '"An Academy for Doing", 1: The Accademia del Disegno, the Guilds and the Principate in Sixteenth-century Florence', *Oxford A. J.*, ix/1 (1986), pp. 3–10
W. Chadwick: *Women, Art and Society* (New York, 1990)

YAEL EVEN

XVII. Historiography.

1. 14th–16th centuries. 2. 17th–20th centuries.

1. 14TH–16TH CENTURIES. In Italy literature on art that combines a notion of history with a sense for the artist's individuality emerged during the Renaissance. The humanist view that history is made up of the stories of individuals led to the revival of the Classical tradition of famous men (*viri illustres*). Dante's, Petrarch's and Boccaccio's praise of Giotto and Simone Martini introduced the concept of artistic fame, which prepared the ground for the genre of the artist's biography. The first in a long line of writers of artists' lives was FILIPPO VILLANI. The chronicle of his native Florence (1381–8) included biographies of such painters as Cimabue, Giotto and Taddeo Gaddi. In the writings of the Florentine sculptor LORENZO GHIBERTI, art was for the first time treated in the context of historical development. Ghiberti focused on questions of style and quality, with only a distant interest in anecdotal reports on artists' lives. In his three *Commentarii* (*c.* 1447–55) he discussed art from antiquity to his own time, including in Book 2 the first autobiographical account of an artist. In the course of the 15th century Villani's inclusion of accounts on artists in conventional history was widely imitated. CRISTOFORO LANDINO, best known for his translation of Pliny, added a survey of artists and a list of Florentine cultural milestones to his commentaries on Dante (Florence, 1481) and Horace (Florence, 1482). Catalogues of artists were often appended to municipal or national histories, such as *De laudibus patavii* (*c.* 1440) by Michele Savonarola (*c.* 1385–1464), *Speculum lapidum* (Venice, 1502) by CAMILLO LEONARDI and *De illustratione urbis Florentiae* (1512) by UGOLINO VERINO. Bartolomeo Facio's *De viris illustribus*, written in 1456 at the court of

Alfonso I of Naples, was the first Italian book to include information on artists outside Italy, commending the work of the Netherlandish painters Jan van Eyck and Rogier van der Weyden (*see* FACIO, BARTOLOMEO). Similarly, Giovanni Santi's *La vita e le geste di Federico di Montefeltro duca d'Urbino*, written between 1484 and 1487, included a section on painting (*Disputa della pictura*) with comments on contemporary Italian as well as northern artists (*see* SANTI, GIOVANNI). The first work devoted to a single artist, the *Vita di Filippo Brunelleschi* (Florence, ?1480s), has been attributed to ANTONIO MANETTI. The influential writings of the humanist and architect Leon Battista Alberti, as well as the notebooks of Leonardo da Vinci, mark the peak of a tendency in 15th-century Italy to focus on art theoretical issues and matters linked to the natural sciences at the expense of historical thinking, which was taken for granted.

By far the most important figure for the historiography of the 16th century, and in some respects the founder of art history, was Giorgio Vasari, but his work was to some extent foreshadowed by that of ANTONIO BILLI, the ANONIMO MAGLIABECHIANO (*fl c.* 1537–57) and GIOVANNI BATTISTA GELLI. Billi's *Libro* (1516–35), a collection of notes on artists, became Vasari's most important source for the early period. The author known as the Anonimo Magliabechiano drafted a concise history of painting, similar to Vasari's first edition of the *Vite*, but he abandoned the project when the latter appeared in 1550. The same happened to a similar project of Venetian origin, the so-called *Anonimo Morelliano*, written by MARC-ANTONIO MICHIEL, which also remained unfinished as a result of the publication of Vasari's *Vite*. In an incomplete manuscript, Giovanni Battista Gelli left 20 short biographies of artists, typically Florentine in their point of view. A summary was published in the introduction to his two lectures on Petrarch's sonnets in praise of Simone Martini (Florence, 1549). Closer to Vasari was the historical approach of PAOLO GIOVIO, who sought to accompany the portrait gallery in his villa at Lake Como with a text on the lives of famous men that would have included artists, but which remained incomplete. All these writings, however, are overshadowed by the achievement of the learned artist GIORGIO VASARI, whose *Vite*, dedicated to Cosimo I de' Medici, were published in two editions (1550, 1568) and long remained the canonical model for later writers. Carefully making use of earlier texts, Vasari gave the genre of artists' biographies a new overall structure by organizing the lives from Cimabue to Michelangelo according to the Classical model of the three stages of human life. This division of the work into infancy, youth and maturity expressed his identification of the progress of art with a development in the imitation of nature. In the 1550 edition he continued the tradition of including biographies only of deceased artists, with the exception of Michelangelo, who for him represented the summit of perfection. The edition of 1568 introduced engraved portraits of artists and, more importantly, an additional fourth section in which Vasari described his own time. His writing was influenced by Florentine patriotism, which so stirred his imagination that truth sometimes suffered. His attempt to link the events of an artist's life with his work resulted in biographies rich in colourful anecdotes. There is no author

of artists' lives immediately following Vasari, with the exception of RAFFAELE BORGHINI, whose third and fourth books of *Il riposo . . .* (Florence, 1584) included lives of artists that are valuable for the later period not covered by Vasari. The rising status of the artist inspired individual biographies, among them Ascanio Condivi's life of Michelangelo (Rome, 1553) and autobiographies by Benvenuto Cellini, Baccio Bandinelli, Raffaello da Montelupo and Giovanni Paolo Lomazzo. Another form of art literature gained importance during the 16th century: the GUIDE-BOOK, linking topography with historiography. Noteworthy are Francesco Sansovino's *Venetia città nobilissima et singolare descritta* (Venice, 1581; *see* SANSOVINO, (2)) and Francesco Bocchi's guide to the *Bellezze di Firenze* (Florence, 1591; *see* BOCCHI, FRANCESCO).

2. 17TH–20TH CENTURIES. In the 17th century art literature was increasingly dominated by connoisseurs rather than artists. In Rome, GIOVANNI BAGLIONE, GIOVANNI BATTISTA PASSERI and LIONE PASCOLI followed the tradition of Vasari and continued to chronicle artists' lives. In his versatile work, GIULIO MANCINI updated Vasari with biographies on Caravaggio and the Carracci. He compiled a catalogue of painters and paintings in which he introduced connoisseurship as a tool for the assessment of authenticity and developed new views on the value of the individual style of artists, schools and periods. The most important successor to Vasari was GIOVANNI PIETRO BELLORI. The biographies in his *Vite de' pittori, scultori, et architetti moderni* (Rome, 1672) represent his personal selection of worthy artists and are thus a testimony to his classicist taste. Bellori replaced Vasari's ideal of perfection, Michelangelo, with Raphael, Annibale Carracci and his friend Carlo Maratti. In his preference of Greek to Roman art he anticipated Johann Joachim Winckelmann. FILIPPO BALDINUCCI, in his *Notizie de' professori del disegno da Cimabue in qua* (Florence, 1681–1728), intended to update Vasari's *Vite*. It simplified their threefold historical structure into a straightforward chronology. Baldinucci was also the author of the *Vita del Cavaliere Giovanni Lorenzo Bernini* (Florence, 1682) and published the first dictionary on the terminology of art (*Vocabolario toscano dell'arte del disegno*; Florence, 1681) as well as being the first to write on the technique of etching (Florence, 1686). His firm belief in the artistic primacy of his native Florence was strongly contested. CARLO CESARE MALVASIA asserted the superiority of Bologna in his *Felsina pittrice* (Bologna, 1678), while the painters CARLO RIDOLFI and MARCO BOSCHINI promoted Venetian art in their writings. Ridolfi's *Le meraviglie dell'arte . . .* (Venice, 1648) is a collection of biographies of Venetian artists; Boschini's *La carta del navegar pitoresco* (Venice, 1660) and his guidebook *Le ricche miniere della pittura veneziana* (Venice, 1674) eulogize Venetian art and the supremacy of colour.

In the 18th century art literature developed further in the direction of modern scholarship. A new awareness of methodology was accompanied by scholarly interest in the publication of documentary materials, and writings of the past. GIOVANNI GAETANO BOTTARI published a valuable collection of letters by artists (Rome, 1757–68), which was revised (1822–5) by Stefano Ticozzi and continued (1844) by Michelangelo Gualandi. Pietro Zani compiled an extensive encyclopedia that combined a dictionary of artists with a reference book on graphic art. At the same time, regional historiography was prolific. Every province, almost every town, produced its own 'Vasari' who composed a collection of local artists' lives; such compilations exist, for example, in Bologna, Ferrara, Venice, Padua, Verona, Treviso, Bergamo, Cremona, Genoa, Naples and Messina. The most innovative figure of the century was perhaps LUIGI LANZI. His *Storia pittorica della Italia* (Bassano, 1795–6) introduced a new structure into the traditional collection of artists' lives. Instead of the artist's biography, it was his art, more specifically his style, that determined his place within the book. The artist's personality was not treated separately, however, but considered together with his stylistic development. Lanzi also acted as adviser in the reorganization of the Galleria degli Uffizi from 1775 to 1782, during which paintings were arranged according to schools in order to reflect their place in art history.

At the beginning of the 19th century, but methodologically rooted in the 18th, Conte LEOPOLDO CICOGNARA published a history of Italian sculpture from the Middle Ages up to his own time, the *Storia della scultura . . .* (Venice, 1813–18), in which he explicitly continued the tradition of Winckelmann and Séroux d'Agincourt. Nineteenth-century scholarship prepared the ground on which modern art history is based. GAETANO MILANESI dedicated his research to the study of sources, documents and archives; among his publications is the famous and still definitive edition of Vasari's *Vite* (Florence, 1878–85). Much Italian art history was, however, dominated by the connoisseurs. GIOVANNI BATTISTA CAVALCASELLE, in collaboration with J. A. Crowe, published monumental histories on Flemish painting (1856), on Italian and north Italian painting (1864–6, 1871) and monographs on Titian (1877) and Raphael (1882–5). With the force of his visual memory, and the help of countless drawings of paintings taken during the team's extensive travels throughout Europe, Cavalcaselle was able to penetrate the field of style and attribution before the ready availability of photography. Another influential connoisseur was GIOVANNI MORELLI, who published under the pseudonym of Ivan Lermolieff. With the aid of photographs, Morelli developed an empirical method to establish the authorship and authenticity of works of art by examining such details as hands, ears or the fall of drapery.

In the 20th century the strong Italian tradition of the connoisseur was continued by ADOLFO VENTURI and CORRADO RICCI. Venturi's *Storia dell'arte italiana*, in 11 books divided into 25 volumes (1901–40), was the most extensive work ever dedicated to the art of one country. In 1902 BENEDETTO CROCE published his *Estetica . . .* in which, besides introducing the concept of works of art as the product of intuition, he laid new emphasis on the individual personality of the artist and proclaimed a synthesis of art history and aesthetic criticism. Croce influenced many Italian art historians, among them LIONELLO VENTURI, who in 1936 published his *History of Art Criticism*, and ROBERTO LONGHI, who became one of the most influential art historians of 20th-century Italy. Longhi's eloquent research, which continued the tradition of the connoisseur, included publications on Masaccio,

Piero della Francesca and Caravaggio; and in 1950 he founded the periodical *Paragone*. The development in the approach to art history that took place in the course of the century can be grasped from the ambitious *Storia dell'arte italiana*, published in 13 volumes by Einaudi (1979–83; ed. Giovanni Previtali and Federico Zeri). In opposition to the traditional historical chronology, to linear models of historic evolution and to the systematic approach, the *Storia dell'arte* drew an image of Italian art history that focused on topical problems. The monographic study of first-rate masters was replaced by research on secondary masters, and the emphasis shifted to the investigation of the artistic periphery. Attention was given to such topics as gardens, stamps, festive decoration or photography, and coverage extended to contemporary art. This publication, compiled as a series of essays by scholars of diverse—even divergent—views, aimed at a new and critical view on Italian art and provided an excellent documentation of the imaginative versatility of modern Italian scholarship.

See also TREATISE; ART HISTORY; CONNOISSEURSHIP.

BIBLIOGRAPHY

E. Panofsky: *Idea: Ein Beitrag zur Begriffsgeschichte der älteren Kunsttheorie* (Leipzig, 1924); Eng. trans. as *Idea: A Concept in Art Theory* (New York, 1968)
J. von Schlosser: *Die Kunstliteratur* (Vienna, 1924); updated Fr. trans. as *La Littérature artistique*, ed. P. di Paolo Stathopoulos (Paris, 1984)
——: 'Über die ältere Kunsthistoriographie der Italiener', *Mitt. Österreich. Inst. Geschforsch.*, xliii (1929), pp. 46–76
A. Blunt: *Artistic Theory in Italy, 1450–1600* (London, 1935)
L. Venturi: *Storia della critica d'arte* (Florence, 1948)
E. H. Gombrich: 'Kunstliteratur', *Atlantisbuch der Kunst: Eine Enzyklopädie der bildenden Künste* (Zurich, 1952), pp. 665–79; Eng. trans. as 'The Literature on Art', repr. in *A. Doc.*, xi/1 (1992), pp. 3–8
E. Gilmore Holt, ed.: *A Documentary History of Art*, 2 vols (Princeton, 1958)
L. Grassi: *Teorici e storia della critica d'arte*, 3 vols (Rome, 1970–79)
G. Bazin: *Histoire de l'histoire de l'art de Vasari à nos jours* (Paris, 1986)
U. Kultermann: *Geschichte der Kunstgeschichte: Der Weg einer Wissenschaft* (Munich, 1990)

STELLA VON BOCH

Itchō. *See* HANABUSA ITCHŌ.

Ithaka. Greek island in the Ionian Sea. According to Homeric tradition Ithaka was the home of Odysseus, but some scholars have disputed that the island bearing this name is the Homeric island, claiming that neighbouring Kephallinia or Leukas fits Homer's description better. Heinrich Schliemann conducted his first excavation here in 1868. Between 1930 and 1938 a series of excavations conducted by the British School at Athens attempted to prove that the traditional identification was correct. Although they discovered traces of settlement dating to the Early Bronze Age (*c.* 3600/3000–*c.* 2050 BC) and Late Helladic (*c.* 1600–*c.* 1050 BC) periods on the plateau of Pelikata in the north of the island, they found no palace for Odysseus. A cave on the beach near by at Polis had been used for a series of votive offerings from the Mycenaean (Late Helladic) era until the Roman period. Among the most remarkable finds were fragments of at least 12 cast bronze tripod stands (Stavros, Archaeol. Mus.), perhaps offered in the cave in the 8th century BC. A tourist in 75 BC, an unguent seller from Rome, recorded his visit with a graffito on a broken pot. Another sanctuary was explored on the saddle of Aetos between the two halves of the island. The first offerings here date from the 10th century BC and continue to the 6th century BC. Corinthian Geometric and Orientalizing pottery (Vathy, Archaeol. Mus.) is common and reflects the important position of Ithaka on the route to the new colonies in southern Italy. The same trade route brought Baltic amber as a frequent offering.

BIBLIOGRAPHY

Annu. Brit. Sch. Athens, xxxiii- (1932–3) [excavation reports]
J. N. Coldstream: *Geometric Greece* (London, 1977), pp. 182–4

K. A. WARDLE

Itinerants. *See* WANDERERS.

Itō, Chūta (*b* Yonezawa, Dewa Province [now Yamagata Prefect.], 1868; *d* 1954). Japanese architectural historian and architect. He graduated from the School of Engineering at Tokyo Imperial University in 1892 and then undertook graduate studies in architectural history. He participated in research on the oldest building in Japan, the temple of Hōryūji at Nara, and carried out a survey of the principal buildings that recorded details of the temple's proportions, construction and decoration. In 1898 he published the *Hōryūji kenchikuron* ('Discourse on the architecture of Hōryūji'), his first lengthy thesis. In 1897 he began to teach at the School of Engineering at the university; in 1901 he received his doctorate and in 1905 he became a full professor in the department where he continued teaching until his retirement in 1928.

In his research Itō was more interested in comparing the civilizations of the East and West, and the influences on them, rather than merely accumulating archaeological information. As he explained in his first thesis, for example, the architecture of Hōryūji was derived from the Gandhara style in India, having been transmitted to the Korean peninsula and then to Japan. At this time, *c.* 1905, Itō began to compile a systematic description of historical Japanese architecture, beginning with Shinto and Buddhist buildings and later expanding the study to include monuments from all periods. Although he concentrated on Japan, he also included Japanese works built in other countries, especially in China, Korea and India, three countries of particular interest to him. He also researched the indigenous architecture of China, India and Turkey, introducing it to Japan, and he attempted to systematize Asian architecture. He became a member of Japan's Society for the Preservation of Ancient Shrines and Temples in 1896 and thereafter worked continuously for the protection of ancient buildings.

Itō was also active as an architect, designing buildings that convey a unique Asian aesthetic. Important examples of his work include the Dragon Gate (1914; destr.), Tokyo; Okura Shūkokan Museum (1927), Tokyo; Memorial Hall for the Earthquake of 1923 (1930), Tokyo; and the Main Hall of the Temple of Tsukiji Honganji (1934), Tokyo. He was a member of the Japan Academy and in 1943 he was awarded the Cultural Medal of Japan.

WRITINGS

Hōryūji kenchikuron [Discourse on the architecture of Hōryūji] (Tokyo, 1898)
Itō Chūta kenchiku bunken [Chūta Itō's architectural documents], 6 vols (Tokyo, 1936–7)

Shina kenchiku sōshoku [Chinese architectural ornament], 4 vols (Tokyo, 1941–2)

BIBLIOGRAPHY

N. Kawazoe: *Contemporary Japanese Architecture* (Tokyo, 1968)
E. Tempel: *New Japanese Architecture* (New York, 1969)

EIZO INAGAKI

Itō, Toyō (*b* Seoul, Korea, 1 June 1941). Japanese architect. He graduated from the University of Tokyo in 1965 and then worked for the Metabolist architect Kiyonori Kikutake until 1969. In 1971 he opened his own office, URBOT, which was renamed Toyō Itō, Architect & Associates in 1979. An influential though far from prolific architect, Itō believed that architecture had become encumbered with irrelevant symbolism. He sought to erase conventional meaning from his works through minimalist tactics, inspired by early modernist movements such as Purism and the straightforward use of easily available industrial materials. He developed an aesthetic of lightweight, permeable membranes composed of fabrics, perforated aluminium panels and expanded metal sheets, which he believed was most suited to an increasingly mobile and informal urban lifestyle.

Although Itō made no explicit historical references, there are a number of parallels between his work and the traditional residential architecture of Japan. Like Itsuko Hasegawa and Yuzuru Tominaga, he was for a time influenced by Kazuo Shinohara, whose point of departure was traditional Japanese architecture. Itō's House in Nakano (1976) in Tokyo, for instance, reflects characteristics of the *shoin* (study) residences of the feudal period (Kamakura, Muromachi and Momoyama periods, 1185–1600; *see* JAPAN, §III, 4 (ii)(a)) in the way its space 'bends': its U-shaped plan prevents the interior from being seen in its entirety from any single point; the courtyard is not the centre of activity but merely a void; and the interior, in white, seems to be dematerialized. Itō's PMT Building (1978) in Nagoya, a three-storey structure housing offices and a showroom, also expresses dematerialization; it features two-dimensional geometrical elements that he called 'morphemes', assembled without any apparent unifying order or compositional centre and thus creating fragmented spaces.

Itō claimed that the reality of the urban environment resided in its surfaces. The 'superficial' character of his work was intended to underscore the absence of any deeper significance to the city beyond that which is immediately apparent. Silver Hut (1984), his own house, and Nomad (1986), a small restaurant, both in Tokyo, take the concept of dematerialization a step further. Silver Hut (see fig.), situated next to the House in Nakano, is a cluster of rooms arranged around a courtyard; the whole is roofed by seven vaults built of lozenge-shaped steel elements joined by high-tension bolts, resting on concrete columns. The floor is paved in Japanese tiles. Through the vaults and the tiling Itō expressed the mixture of high technology and tradition that characterized the contemporary Japanese city. At the same time, Silver Hut affords only a minimal sense of enclosure and the occupants live very close to nature; lightweight, movable screens articulate space, and a retractable cover over the courtyard

Toyō Itō: Silver Hut, Tokyo, 1984

provides protection against inclement weather. Itō compared modern urban dwellers to nomads and asserted that all they needed was a shelter that was slightly more permanent and solid than a yurt. In this sense Silver Hut may indeed be a house for today, yet the view that a house need not last more than a generation at best—with its implication that life is but a transitory experience—is rooted through Buddhism in Japanese history. In its fragility, transparency and relationship to nature, Silver Hut can be seen as a modern interpretation of the traditional house. It is one of the most important Japanese houses built in the 1970s and 1980s.

BIBLIOGRAPHY

A New Wave of Japanese Architecture (exh. cat., ed. K. Frampton; New York, Inst. Archit. & Urb. Stud., 1978)

H. Yatsuka: 'Architecture in the Urban Desert: A Critical Introduction to Japanese Architecture after Modernism', *Oppositions*, 23 (Winter 1981), pp. 1–35

Space Des., cclxiv (1986) [whole issue]

HIROSHI WATANABE

Itō Jakuchū [Shunkyō; Tobeian] (*b* Kyoto, 1716; *d* Kyoto, 1800). Japanese painter and printmaker.

1. EARLY DEVELOPMENT, BEFORE 1756. Jakuchū was born into a family of well-to-do merchants who owned a wholesale greengrocery business in the Nishiki district of Kyoto. As the eldest son, he was expected to succeed his father but contemporary accounts reveal that painting was the young Jakuchū's only real interest, and that his reclusive temperament made him ill-suited for business. The early death of Jakuchū's father, however, forced him to assume the headship of the family and business at the age of 23.

Jakuchū probably began his formal artistic training during his twenties, perhaps with Ōoka Shunboku (1680–

1763) or an unidentified painter of the academic KANŌ school. Jakuchū was also influenced by Chinese court painting (*see* CHINA, §V, 4(i)(c) and (d)), many examples of which could be seen in Kyoto's Zen monasteries, and by the decorative style associated with Ogata Kōrin (*see* OGATA, (1)). None of Jakuchū's early works is known to have survived. In his thirties Jakuchū became interested in Zen Buddhism and took the vows of a lay monk, which he kept until his death, choosing never to marry. It was around the same period that he began to sign his works Jakuchū, the name by which he is best known. This artist's name (*gō*) may have been conferred on him by his new friend and benefactor Daiten Kenjō (1719–1801), the abbot of Shōkokuji in Kyoto, where Jakuchū was able to study Chinese painting. The hanging scroll *Phoenix and Sun* (Boston, MA, Mus. F.A.) is thought to be one of the few extant paintings from this period of Jakuchū's life.

2. MATURE WORKS, 1756–1800. In 1756 Jakuchū was able to pass on his business responsibilities to a younger brother. The family's wealth freed him from economic worries and he was able to devote the rest of his life to painting. He was active and well respected in Kyoto's artistic circles throughout the second half of the 18th century. He lived and worked at his studio, Shin'enkan, until it was destroyed by fire in 1788, and thereafter at Sekihōji, a temple where he continued to paint in retirement until his death in 1800.

Jakuchū produced many of the highly individualistic works for which he is best known during his forties and fifties. Most important among these is the set of 30 scrolls painted in colours on silk, entitled *Dōshku saie* ('Colourful realm of living beings'; *c*. 1757–70; see fig.), which he initially presented to Shōkokuji in 1765. Jakuchū meant the series to show the multiplicity and intrinsic worth of

Itō Jakuchū: *Rooster, Sunflowers and Morning Glories*, hanging scroll, colours on silk, 1425×795 mm, 1759 (Tokyo, Imperial Household Collection); from the series *Dōshoku saie* ('Colourful realm of living beings')

all forms of life, although his choice of subjects was arbitrary. Eight of the 30 scrolls depict chickens, his favourite subject.

Jakuchū characteristically combines the bright colours and decorative patterns of *Yamatoe* (Japanese-style painting) with a keen observation of natural forms, executed in meticulous detail. The result of this synthesis was a hypernaturalism preceding that of MARUYAMA ŌKYO and exceeding it in intensity and energy.

Jakuchū specialized in *kachō* ('bird-and-flower') subjects, not only the more common themes, such as flowering plums and geese in autumn, but also less frequently depicted ones, such as vegetables, marine life and exotic and barnyard fowl. He is particularly known for his paintings of chickens, which he observed first-hand, along with the other more unusual birds that he kept on the grounds of his residence. He admired them for their vigour and striking plumage, and also possibly because the rooster

was traditionally associated with the nobility of the gentleman of superior virtue. A late example of his *kachō* painting is *Cacti and Fowl* (1790), a set of six sliding screens painted with bright colours on gold paper, in the Saifukuji, Osaka Prefecture.

Another dimension of his art is evident in forcefully brushed monochromatic works, for example the set of hanging scrolls *Sixteen Rakan* (Boston, MA, Mus. F.A.), the sliding screens *Roosters and Hens* (1790; Kyoto, N. Mus.) and the hanging scroll *Vegetable Parinirvana* (*c.* 1780; Kyoto, N. Mus.). In this treatment of the traditional theme of the death of the historical Buddha, a large white *daikon* (radish) takes the place of the reclining figure of Shakyamuni (Jap. Shaka) and is mourned by over 50 kinds of fruits and vegetables. Whimsical though the iconography may seem, it is also quite in keeping with Jakuchū's family business, and he may have painted it as a memorial following the death of his mother or brother.

Jakuchū experimented with other forms and media, producing works that are not easily categorized. These include the six-panel folding screen *White Elephant and Phoenix* (Tokyo, N. Mus.), which consists of a grid of thousands of small squares, each containing an even smaller coloured geometric design. The resulting mosaic-like pattern was a distinctive innovation but was not widely imitated. He also experimented with woodblock-printing techniques: he hand-stencilled colours on block-printed designs set against black backgrounds, as in a series of six *kachō* subjects (1771; Tokyo, Hiraki Ukiyoe Found.), and used an intaglio process called *taku hanga* ('rubbing print'), seen in the printed handscroll *Impromptu Pleasures Afloat* (1767; Boston, MA, Mus. F.A.). Such works serve only to emphasize the idiosyncratic nature of Jakuchū's contribution to the arts of the Edo period (1600–1868). Among those 18th-century artists who broke away from the established traditions of the Kanō school, Jakuchū stands out as one of the most original.

BIBLIOGRAPHY
Jakuchū tokubetsu tenkan zuroku [Catalogue of the special exhibition of Jakuchū] (exh. cat. by T. Kobayashi, Tokyo, 1971)
N. Tsuji: 'Jakuchū-hitsu *Dōshoku saie* tsuite' [On the 'Colourful realm of living beings' series of paintings by Jakuchū], *Museum* [Tokyo], 245 (1971), pp. 20–25
N. Tsuji: *Jakuchū* (Tokyo, 1974)
T. Tokuriki and others: *Jakuchū no taku hanga* [The rubbing prints of Jakuchū] (Tokyo, 1981)
Y. Sato: 'Itō Jakuchū', *Nihon no Bijutsu*, 256 (1987) [whole issue]
The Paintings of Jakuchū (exh. cat. by M. L. Hickman and Y. Sato, New York, Asia House Gals, 1989)

JOAN H. O'MARA

Itsukushima Shrine [Jap. Itsukushima jinja]. Japanese Shinto shrine in Miyajima, Saeki Province, Hiroshima Prefecture. It is 15 km south-west of Hiroshima on the island of Itsukushima, one island among many in the Seto Inland Sea. The island has traditionally been included among the three most beautiful sites in Japan. The name Itsukushima (Majestic Island) denotes a place where *kami* (Shinto deities) are worshipped, and in ancient times the entire island was acknowledged as a sacred site. The shrine is dedicated to the worship of the goddess Ichikishima hime no mikoto, who ensures safety at sea, and her two sisters, as well as to the five male 'cousin' deities who are collectively called *Marōdo no kami* ('guest gods'). At the shrine, there are two *honden* ('main sanctuaries'); Honsha ('head' or 'main shrine') for the worship of the three goddesses; and the Marōdo Jinja ('guest shrine') for the worship of the male guest deities. Many of the buildings of the Itsukushima Shrine, which are constructed of wood, are located on the sandy beach of Itsukushima cove. During high tide the sea-water flows under the floor of the buildings, making the shrine appear to float on water. Itsukushima is the only shrine in Japan sited in such a manner. Conceptually and architecturally, its closest parallels are in Amida Halls such as the Phoenix Hall (Hōōdō) at Byōdōin.

1. HISTORY. It is recorded that Itsukushima was established at the end of the 6th century AD. In 811 it was recognized by the Heian-period (794–1185) government as one of the powerful shrines, and in the mid-12th century it was revered by the most influential man of the time, the Prime Minister Taira no Kiyomori (1118–81). The Taira family were generous patrons of Itsukushima: in about 1168 Kiyomori aided a large-scale rebuilding of the shrine. According to contemporary records, this included such additions as 37 buildings and four *torii* (post-and-lintel gates). Kiyomori and his family also presented 33 illustrated scrolls of the Lotus Sutra (*Hokkekyō* or *Myōhō renge kyō*; Skt *Saddharmapuṇḍarīkasūtra*) to the shrine (12th century; Itsukushima Shrine col.; *see* JAPAN, §VI, 3(iii)).

The style and arrangement of the buildings of the shrine today are much as they were on their completion in the 12th century, and they reveal the influence of *shinden zukuri* ('sleeping hall construction'), an aristocratic style of residential architecture (*see* JAPAN, §III, 3(iii)). In 1207 and again in 1223 the buildings were destroyed by fire and underwent a reconstruction that lasted until 1241. In 1569

conflicts led to bloodshed in the shrine interior, and as the sanctity of the shrine had been defiled, the *honden* was rebuilt in 1571 by the powerful regional lord Mōri Terumoto (1553–1625).

2. ARCHITECTURE. The two main sanctuaries of the shrine were built on the beach and are connected to the land by a long *kairō* (roofed, semi-enclosed corridor), which winds intricately around the building and leads to the front of the *honden*. A *haiden* ('worship hall' or 'oratory hall') and *haraidono* ('purification rites hall') stand in front of the *honden*, as does a wooden *hirabutai* ('terrace'; 553 sq. m), in the centre of which is a *takabutai* (stage where court dances and musical performances (*bugaku*) are held). Midway along the *kairō* and at one end of the *hirabutai* are a few affiliated shrines. A *nō* stage (*see* JAPAN, §XIII, 1(i)) was also built on the beach and is visible from the corridor. Most of the shrine buildings that relate to Shinto were built on the beach. The Buddhist buildings associated with the shrine were erected on the land surrounding the inlet. Buddhist buildings such as the *gojū no tō* (five-storey pagoda), *tahōtō* (two-storey pagoda, of which the ground floor is square and surrounded by a *mokoshi* (lean-to pent roof) and the first floor is cylindrical) and the *daikyōdō* ('scripture recital hall') still stand, although in about 1868 many of the Buddhist buildings were destroyed as a result of anti-Buddhist sentiment on the part of the Meiji government (1868–1912).

It is understood from old records that the *honden* of the main shrine was of the same size and shape as that built in 1168. Even the design details were faithfully reproduced in a 12th-century style. The *honden* (w. 23.7m, depth 11.5 m) is the largest of its kind in Japan. Nine wooden columns are placed along the façade and five along the sides. The roof is in the gable-roof construction format (*kirizuma zukuri*), a form that was developed in ancient Shinto *honden*. The gable roofs are in the Double Nagare or flowing construction (*ryōnagare zukuri*) and thatched with Japanese cypress-bark shingles (*hiwadabuki*), a material seen only on structures built for the aristocracy. The gables and the use of cypress bark create a soft, elegantly curved roof line. The floor of the *honden* was placed relatively low, compared with the other shrines in Japan, so that at high tide the sea skims the floor. Splendid examples of *kumimono* (a bracket complex adapted from Buddhist architecture) are to be seen on the tops of the columns. The use of *kumimono* represents an advance in architectural style; ancient shrines did not have *kumimono*.

The important structural members, such as the columns, the *kōryō* ('rainbow beam'; a single beam running transversally) and the *kumimono*, are painted in bright vermilion. The windows and doors are painted green and the wall panels white. At the interior of the *honden* is an inner sanctuary surrounded by outer sanctuaries. The floor of the inner sanctuary is raised and has six *gyokuden* (small inner shrines), where the three goddesses are worshipped. This type of interior organization is unusual in Shinto shrine sanctuary buildings.

The *haiden* was reconstructed in 1241 (29.6×11.8 m) and is the largest and oldest among extant Japanese shrine *haiden*. Eleven columns run along the front and four on

Itsukushima Shrine, Miyajima, Hiroshima Prefecture; *torii*, re-erected 1875

the sides. The thatched roof is in the hip-and-gable construction (*irimoya zukuri*). The interior, with *kōryō* and *kaerumata* ('frog-leg struts'), is evidence of the beauty and power of such traditional structures. The *honden* is connected to the *haiden* by a short passageway.

The *haraidono* projects from the front of the *haiden*, and together these buildings form a T-shaped plan; even the roofs are joined. The *haraidono* was also rebuilt in 1241 (10.4×16.1 m). Four columns run along the front and seven along the sides. The spaces between the columns are open, with no doors or wall panels. Beautifully shaped *kaerumata* decorate the areas between the *kumimono*. A hip-and-gable roof faces the front of the building, with the eaves raised at the centre. The arrangement of the roof and the design details are exemplars of a refined architectural style that has survived from the 12th century.

The Marōdo Shrine was built about 30 m away from the main shrine, and the two are at right angles. The shrine comprises a *honden*, *haiden* and *haraidono*. This shrine was also rebuilt in 1241 and is a smaller version of the main shrine. The *kairō* connecting the main and Marōdo shrines to the land was gradually reconstructed between the last half of the 16th century and the early 17th. It is 4 m wide and 274 m long with several right angle turns. The passageway affords a view of the tranquil surroundings and the beautiful buildings. The *nō* stage, which abuts the passageway, was erected in 1568. The present stage, which was reconstructed in 1680, is a typical example of a *nō* stage, with a gabled roof facing the front.

The buildings of the main shrine were built facing the sea, and a *torii* (post-and-lintel gate) is located approximately 160 m from the front of the shrine (see fig.). It was re-erected in 1875 and stands 17 m high, with a 24 m roofing beam. Two columns support the roof elements, and four short wooden columns reinforce the structure against collapse. The lovely shape of the vermilion *torii* has become a symbol of Itsukushima.

The Buddhist five-storey pagoda and the *daikyōdō* are in alignment. The pagoda is a Chinese-style (*karayō*) structure built in 1407; the strong curvature of the pointed ends of the roof is a distinctive feature of the building. The *daikyōdō* (40×21 m) was built by the warlord TOYOTOMI HIDEYOSHI in 1587. Its tiled roof is hipped and gabled, and the ends of the roof tiles were wrapped in gold foil; however, such elements as the ceiling and doors were not built until after the building had been completed. The size and splendour of the building is indicative of Hideyoshi's status. Initially the *daikyōdō* was a Buddhist building, but it is now recognized as a shrine consecrated to the worship of Hideyoshi. The two-storey pagoda is located on the hillside opposite these two buildings. It was built in 1523 and features a skilful arrangement of square ground floor and cylindrical first floor, along with some regional design details.

BIBLIOGRAPHY

N. Asano, ed.: *Hihō*, x of *Itsukushima* [The treasure of Itsukushima] (Tokyo, 1967)

T. Fukuyama: *Nihon kenchikushi kenkyū* [Research on the history of Japanese architecture] (Tokyo, 1968)

E. Inagaki: *Nihon kenchikushi kiso shiryō shūsei* [Collection of the basic materials in Japanese architectural history], ii (Tokyo, 1971), pp. 60–68, 125–40

M. Miura: 'The Main Shrines of the Itsukushima Jinja, Hiroshima Prefecture', *Kenchiku Shigaku*, iv (1985), pp. 46–68

MASAYUKI MIURA

Itsunen Shōyū [Yiran Xingrong; Li; Rōun'an] (*b* Hangzhou, Zhejiang Province, China, 1601; *d* Nagasaki, 1668). Naturalized Japanese painter and Buddhist monk. Itsunen first came to Nagasaki from China, as a trader in Chinese medicines, in 1642. In 1644 he entered Kōfukuji, becoming its third abbot in 1645. Itsunen sought to increase the presence of the Chinese Chan (Jap. Zen) community in Japan, and, after repeated invitations, he persuaded the 33rd abbot of Wanfusi at Huangbo (Fujian Prov.), INGEN RYŪKI, to emigrate to Japan in 1654. Ingen eventually founded Manpukuji in Uji in 1663, which became the headquarters for the new Japanese sect of Ōbaku Zen. Itsunen was a gifted painter of Buddhist figural subjects working in styles related to those popular among late Ming period (1368–1644) Buddhist monks in Fujian Province. He is known to have copied works by Chen Xian (*fl* 1634–54) brought to Japan by Ingen. These include a painting of *Kannon* (Kyoto, N. Mus.). He also saw earlier Chinese and Japanese Buddhist paintings in Japanese temple collections. His artistic style may have been further influenced by his acquaintance with members of the KANŌ SCHOOL of painting. Some of his paintings exhibit typical Kanō-style brushwork: outlines which have highly exaggerated flourishes at the beginning and ending points of each stroke. In general, his style is distinguished by its elegant, sinuous outlines surrounding areas of light colour and ink-wash, which combine to create a sense of heightened naturalism. To the Japanese, these techniques imparted an unprecedented lifelike quality to the subject, and they were thus highly admired.

Itsunen brushed the most important paintings in all the early Japanese Ōbaku temples, frequently presenting them to Ingen. He specialized in formal portraits (*gazō*) of Chan (Zen) patriarchs and other subjects favoured in Ōbaku circles: *Shaka*, *Fugen*, *Monju*, *Hotei*, *Rakan* (Skt *Arhat*), *Nehanzu* (Death of the Buddha), *Kanzan* and *Jittoku* and *Byakue Kannon* (White-robed; Skt Avalokiteshvara). Many are inscribed by Ingen or MOKUAN SHŌTŌ. Among his best-known paintings is a triptych of *Shaka, Monju and Fugen* (1660; inscribed by Ingen in 1665; Uji, Manpukuji). Itsunen had many Japanese pupils in Nagasaki. Through them, his style proliferated in Japan, and he is now considered one of the founders of the Nagasaki school of painting. His most talented pupils were Nagasaki artists Watanabe Shūseki (1639–1707) and Kawamura Jakushi (1638–1707).

See also JAPAN, §VI, 4(vi)(c).

BIBLIOGRAPHY

J. Koga: *Nagasaki gashi iden* [Collected commentaries on the history of painting in Nagasaki] (Nagasaki, 1983)

R. Nishigori: 'Kokura Fukushūji shōzō Itsunen hitsu ressōzu no keifu' [The lineage of Itsunen's paintings of Zen patriarchs at Fukushuji of Kokura], *Bukkyō Geijutsu* (1986), no. 166, pp. 65–78

M. Ōtsuki, S. Katō and Y. Hayashi, eds: *Ōbaku bunka jinmei jiten* [Biographical dictionary of Ōbaku cultural figures] (Kyoto, 1988)

Ingen zenshi to Ōbakusō no Kaiga ten [Exhibition of Priest Ingen and Ōbaku sect painting] (exh. cat., Kobe, City Mus., 1991)

PATRICIA J. GRAHAM

Ittagi [Iṭṭagi]. Temple site in northern Karnataka, India, that flourished *c.* AD 650–1200. Its two monuments of interest are a ceremonial gateway (Skt *torana*), important because it bears an inscription from the time of the Chalukyas of Badami (*reg c.* 542–757; *see* CHALUKYA, §1), and the Mahadeva Temple, one of the finest surviving structures from the time of the Chalukyas of Kalyana (*reg* 973–1189; *see* CHALUKYA, §2).

Located on a terrace to the west of a large tank, the Mahadeva Temple is surrounded by the ruins of many subsidiary shrines. Built in 1112 by the general Mahadeva, who served in the army of Vikramaditya VI (*reg c.* 1076–1126), it was originally named Mahadeveshvara in his honour and is dedicated to Shiva as Mahadeva. Facing east, it consists of a pillared hall connected by a porch to a second hall (known locally as a *navaranga*) from which a vestibule leads to the sanctum. The pillared hall has extended eaves and domed ceilings supported by 54 columns in a variety of compounded types characteristic of medieval Karnataka. The porch connecting it with the *navaranga* contains an image of the bull Nandi, Shiva's vehicle.

The *navaranga* and sanctum are integrated by an architectural and decorative programme in the southern (Skt *drāviḍa*) manner as developed under Kalyana Chalukya patronage. The walls are articulated in a series of pilastered bays that carry ornate niches, compound piers and pillars supporting aediculae (*pañjara*). Constructed of a fine-grained chloritic schist, the surfaces are carved with a profusion of detail, rendered with striking precision and refinement. Small-scale sculpture decorates the base mouldings, pillar bases and lower walls. Quarter guardians and images of deities and worshippers fill the elaborately worked lantern ceilings, one of which carries the remains of a fine dancing Shiva.

The temple superstructure rises three storeys (*bhūmi*) above the cornice. The dense reticulation of the building elements shows a mixing of southern forms and northern organizational principles that is typical of later architecture in Karnataka. The original crowning element of the temple has been replaced. On the east side of the superstructure is a vaulted antefix (*śukanāsikā*) indicating the presence of the vestibule below.

See also INDIAN SUBCONTINENT, §§III, 5(i)(g) and 6(i)(f), and IV, 7(vi)(c).

BIBLIOGRAPHY
H. Cousens: *Chālukyan Architecture of the Kanarese Districts*, Archaeol. Surv. India, New Imp. Ser., xlii (Calcutta, 1926)
M. S. Nagaraja Rao: 'Sculptures and Paintings of the Badami Chalukyas', *The Chalukyas of Badami*, ed. M. S. Nagaraja Rao (Bangalore, 1978), pp. 304–13 [discusses the *torana*]
S. Huntington and J. Huntington: *The Art of Ancient India: Buddhist, Hindu, Jain* (New York, 1985), pp. 543–5
S. Rajasekhara: *Karnataka Architecture* (Dharwad, 1985)

GARY MICHAEL TARTAKOV

Itten, Johannes (*b* Südern-Linden, 11 Nov 1888; *d* Zurich, 25 May 1967). Swiss painter, textile designer, teacher, writer and theorist. He trained first as a primary school teacher in Berne (1904–6), where he became familiar with progressive educational and psychoanalytical ideas. He was, however, interested in art and music, and in 1909 he decided to become a painter. He enrolled at the Ecole des Beaux-Arts in Geneva but was so disappointed that he returned to teacher training in Berne. He read widely and developed an interest in religion and mystic philosophy. After qualifying he returned to Geneva and greatly enjoyed the course on the geometric elements of art run by the Swiss painter Eugène Gilliard (1861–1921). After travelling in Europe, in 1913 Itten went to Stuttgart to study at the academy of Adolf Hölzel, a pioneer of abstraction who was also convinced of the importance of automatism in art. Greatly impressed, Itten absorbed his teaching on colour and contrast and his analyses of Old Masters paintings. Encouraged by Hölzel, he made abstract collages incorporating torn paper and cloth.

Itten avidly read the journal *Der Blaue Reiter* and in 1915 painted his first important pictures, fusing his interpretations of Cubism and Expressionism into paintings such as the *Good Samaritan* (artist's estate, see Rotzler, p. 109). Others such as the *Bach Singer* (1916; Stuttgart, Gal. Stadt; see fig.) were strictly geometric in emphasis and used bold, contrasting colours rather than a muted Cubist palette. The *Bach Singer* relates to his interest in analogies between art and music. In the same year he painted his first abstract compositions, including *Horizontal-Vertical*

Johannes Itten: *Bach Singer*, oil on canvas, 1.55×0.95 m, 1916 (Stuttgart, Galerie der Stadt)

(Berne, V. Loeb priv. col., see Rotzler, p. 118) and *The Meeting* (Zurich, Ksthaus). He taught privately and in 1916 had his first one-man exhibition at the Sturm-Galerie in Berlin and moved to Vienna; there he established his own art school, where he developed a highly unconventional method of art education, which drew on the insights of progressive educationalists such as Friedrich Wilhelm August Fröbel (1782–1852), Johann Heinrich Pestalozzi (1746–1827), Maria Montessori (1870–1952) and Franz Cizek. These included the idea of the child's creativity and of learning through play. Despite his relative uncouthness he was soon absorbed into sophisticated Viennese society. Through Alma Mahler he was introduced to the musical circle of Alban Berg, Arnold Schönberg and others, which fuelled his interest in analogies of form and colour. In March 1919 Adolf Loos arranged an exhibition of his work, which comprised increasingly fragmented and dynamic compositions, for example the *Holy One* (1917; Amsterdam, Stedel. Mus.).

In October 1919 Itten was appointed to the Bauhaus at Weimar on the recommendation of Alma Mahler, Walter Gropius's wife at the time. He swiftly gained control of the carpentry, metal, carving, stained-glass and mural workshops. He also devised and taught the *Vorkurs*, an obligatory six-month preliminary course, which aimed to liberate students from preconceptions and develop their latent creative powers. The materials exercises sought to heighten students' sensitivity to their different qualities through paired contrasts such as rough-smooth, coarse-fine. Many different techniques were used, from highly naturalistic pencil drawing to two- and three-dimensional collages of waste material. In Itten's analyses of Old Masters the emphasis was not on formal composition but on the painting's underlying structure. When drawing from the nude the students were encouraged to capture what they considered to be the characteristic expression of each pose, often in rhythmic gestures.

Itten's charismatic personality came to dominate and then divide the school. A key issue was his allegiance to Mazdaznan, a life-system based on the ancient wisdom of Zoroaster and one of many cults that flourished during the Weimar Republic. He initially embraced it in 1909 to cure his dietary difficulties, but he soon became completely committed and incorporated it in his teaching. He introduced Mazdaznan breathing exercises for simultaneous relaxation and concentration on *Vorkurs* exercises and drew heavily on its conception of polarity. A devoted group of converts alienated the other students with their shaven heads, prayer, fasting and conviction of the insubstantiality of this world. Even the Bauhaus kitchen yielded to the Mazdaznan diet, and by summer 1921 the school was seriously divided.

Irreconcilable differences in approach had arisen between Itten and Gropius: whereas Itten wished to preserve the school as a contemplative enclave, Gropius had come to believe that the school must look outwards and establish contact with industry. In 1922 Itten withdrew from his teaching responsibilities, moving to the Mazdaznan community at Herrliberg in 1923, where he set up a weaving workshop with Gunta Stölzl (1897–1983). Some of the designs he produced here reflected his earlier abstract painting, for example a red woollen carpet of 1925 (artist's

estate, see Rotzler, p. 147). From this point on his work as a teacher and administrator took precedence over his production as an artist. In 1926 he left to set up his own school for painting, graphic art, photography and architecture in Berlin. In 1932 he also took on the direction of the Flächenkunstschule in Krefeld, where he educated designers for the textile industry; the school closed in 1938. In 1937 his work, deemed to be 'degenerate' by the Nazis, was represented in the *Entartete Kunst* exhibition (*see* ENTARTETE KUNST), held in Munich at the Archeologisches Institut. Itten emigrated to the Netherlands, where he taught briefly before returning to Switzerland to become director of the Kunstgewerbeschule and Museum in Zurich (1938–54). He joined the Swiss Werkbund and became closely involved with the textile industry, taking the post of director of the Textilfachschule in Zurich (1943–60). He was also involved in museum work, including the foundation of the Museum Rietberg in Zurich, of which he was director from 1952 to 1955.

In 1955 he began to paint intensively again; he frequently worked with decorative patterns based on natural forms and the idea of natural cycles, for example *Autumnal Structures* (chalk and pastel, 1963; artist's estate, see Rotzler, no. 828). He also returned to some of the abstract motifs of earlier works, such as the chequerboard composition, seen in *Composition (Easter Morning)* (1967; Locarno, Civ. Mus.).

WRITINGS

Kunst der Farbe (Ravensburg, 1961; Eng. trans., 1961, R 1970)
Gestaltungs- und Formenlehre. Mein Vorkurs am Bauhaus und später (Ravensburg, 1963, 2/1965; Eng. trans., 1964)

BIBLIOGRAPHY

H. M. Wingler: *Das Bauhaus* (Bramsche and Cologne, 1962, rev. 1975; Eng. trans., 1969, rev. 1976)
E. Roters: *Die Maler am Bauhaus* (Berlin, 1965; Eng. trans., 1969)
M. Franciscono: *Walter Gropius and the Creation of the Bauhaus in Weimar* (Urbana, 1971)
W. Rotzler, ed.: *Johannes Itten: Werke und Schriften* (Zurich, 1982)
R. Wick: *Bauhauspädagogik* (Cologne, 1982)

ANNA ROWLAND

Iturrino, Francisco (*b* Santander, 9 Sept 1864; *d* Cagnes-sur-Mer, nr Nice, 20 June 1924). Spanish painter. As a young man he moved with his family to Bilbao. He travelled to Belgium in 1883 to study engineering but ended up studying life drawing in Brussels in 1890. On his return to Spain he travelled through Andalucia, Salamanca and other parts of the country, choosing local models whom he painted as an exercise in the exploration of colour. In 1895 he travelled to Paris, to which he returned on numerous occasions; his most fruitful period there was from 1901 to 1908. In Paris he met Picasso, exhibiting with him at the Galerie Vollard in 1901. He also befriended Matisse and travelled with him to Seville (1909) and Tangiers (1911). He exhibited at the Salon d'Automne in Paris in 1903 and 1911 and took part in the Arte Moderno exhibitions in Bilbao (1900, 1905 and 1910), returning to Spain during World War I.

In typical paintings such as *Malaga Garden* (1913) and the undated *Nudes in a Landscape* and *Girls with Flowers* (all Madrid, Mus. A. Contemp.) he contrasted vigorous lines and forms with light colours. Giving particular importance to draughtsmanship and the play of light, he produced landscapes characterized by great expressive strength.

See also PINTURA DE LA LUZ.

BIBLIOGRAPHY
E. Lafuente Ferrari and J. de la Puente: *Francisco Iturrino* (Madrid, 1976)

PILAR BENITO

Itzatlán. *See* ETZATLÁN.

Iunet. *See* DENDARA.

Ivaldi [Ivaldy], **Humberto** (*b* Panama City, 24 Dec 1909; *d* Panama City, 10 March 1947). Panamanian painter. He studied under Roberto Lewis and in 1930 won a scholarship to the Academia de San Fernando in Madrid, where he spent five years. On his return to Panama, Ivaldi taught at the Escuela Nacional de Pintura, later becoming its Director, a post he held until his death. His academic background was apparent in the careful and detailed rendering of his traditional still-lifes and many portraits, for example *Mitzi Arias de Saint Malo* (*c.* 1947; Panama City, Guillermo Saint Malo priv. col., see E. Wolfschoon: *Las manifestaciones artísticas en Panamá*, Panama City, 1983, p. 444). His particular contribution within a Post-Impressionist idiom was most evident in genre paintings and in landscapes, such as *Wind on the Hill* (1945; Panama City, Jorge Angelini priv. col., see Wolfschoon, p. 443), which were often characterized by dynamic diagonal compositions, free brushwork and great sensitivity to the atmospheric quality of colours.

BIBLIOGRAPHY
H. Calamari: 'Breves apuntaciones sobre la obra de Humberto Ivaldi', *Supl. Lit. Panamá América* (23 March 1947), centrefold
R. Miró: 'Lewis, Amador, Ivaldi', *Rev. Lotería*, 219 (1974), pp. 72–80

MONICA E. KUPFER

Ivan. *See* IWAN.

Ivan III [Ivan the Great], Grand Duke of Muscovy (*b* Moscow, 22 Jan 1440; *reg* 1462–1505; *d* Moscow, 27 Oct 1505). Russian prince and patron. At the beginning of Ivan's reign, Moscow was pre-eminent among the Russian principalities, but there was no single Russian state. Ivan annexed the other principalities by dynastic marriage (Ryazan', 1464), purchase (Rostov, 1474) or force of arms (Novgorod, 1478 and Tver', 1485), leaving him the direct sovereign of almost all Russia. He also made considerable territorial gains at the expense of Lithuania, and he presided over the final emancipation of Russia from Tatar hegemony in 1480.

In 1472 he married Sophia (Zoë) Palaiologa, niece of Constantine XI (*reg* 1448–53), who had grown up in Rome, and who brought a number of Greeks and Italians to Moscow in her retinue. This seems to have encouraged Ivan to employ Italian architects and engineers in his reconstruction of the citadel (kremlin) of his capital. The construction of the cathedral of the Dormition (Uspensky) had originally been entrusted to Russian builders but after the partially erected building collapsed in the earthquake of 1474, Ivan brought Aristotele Fioravanti of Bologna to Moscow as its architect. Although Fioravanti incorporated elements from both Venice and Novgorod in his church (1475–9), his primary model was the cathedral of the Dormition (1158–60; rebuilt 1185–9) in the former grand-princely seat of Vladimir. A similar combination of the architect's native traditions with those of Vladimir is seen in the cathedral of the Annunciation (Blagoveshchensky; 1484–9) and the church of the Deposition (Rizpolozhensky; 1484–6) built by architects from Pskov, the westernmost of the Russian territories and virtually the only one to retain formal independence by the time of Ivan's death. The last of Ivan's great projects, the cathedral of the Archangel Michael (Arkhangel'sky; 1505–8) by Aleviz (Alevisio) Novy, again shows Venetian influence.

The aim of this building programme was the aggrandizement of Moscow as the symbol of the new autocratic status of its prince. This was not achieved without detriment to regional traditions, notably at Novgorod, but it did result in the establishment of Moscow as the country's unrivalled cultural centre.

BIBLIOGRAPHY
J. L. I. Fennell: *Ivan the Great of Moscow* (London, 1961)

RALPH M. CLEMINSON

Ivan, Johannes (*fl* 1449; *d* Alunda, Uppland, 1465). Painter, active in Sweden. He worked in the province of Uppland, and he may have been one of the many German artists and craftsmen to settle in Sweden during the Middle Ages. His earliest known works are the wall paintings in Östra Ryd church, near Stockholm, the first and probably the largest portion of which he signed in 1449 (a presumed addition was made in 1459). Shortly afterwards he executed the paintings in the churches of Lena and Vendel, Uppland, the latter in 1451–2 according to the signed inscription. An inscription (destr.) recorded that he died during the course of painting the chancel of Alunda church and was buried there. The paintings were completed by three artists of the so-called TIERP SCHOOL; the similarity of his style to that of the Tierp school painters suggests that at least some of them were trained by him.

Only the paintings in Vendel church still illustrate Johannes Ivan's style; the rest are badly damaged or completely destroyed. All his murals were painted *a secco*. The five-bay interior of the church is entirely covered with his paintings. The walls are divided into several registers, with mainly figural representations, while the vaults are predominantly decorated with vines and leaves, a typical feature of the Tierp school. The figures are slender and linear in character, and Johannes Ivan was one of the first Swedish artists to adopt an angular, broken drapery style. His paintings are colourful, and the use of light blue is especially notable. The distinctive choice of motifs, some of which recur in his work, suggest that he may have designed the programme himself or at least strongly influenced it. A unique *Crucifixion* with the followers of Christ at the base of the cross, one of whom carries a cross on his back, and a marked interest in the Immaculate Conception of the Virgin in the story of her birth (Vendel church) perhaps indicate Franciscan influence. It cannot be ascertained whether Johannes Ivan was a Franciscan, but his patrons in Östra Ryd, Johan Kristiernsson Vasa and his wife, Birgitta Gustafsdotter Sture, had shown their interest in the Order by building a family burial chapel in the Franciscan church in Stockholm.

BIBLIOGRAPHY
H. Cornell and S. Wallin: *Kirchenmalereien von Johannes Iwan* (Stockholm, 1957)
A. Nilsén: *Program och funktion i senmedeltida kalkmåleri: Kyrkmålningar i Mälarlandskapen och Finland, 1400–1534* [Programme and function in late medieval wall painting: church paintings in the Mälar provinces and Finland, 1400-1534] (Stockholm, 1986)
Å. Nisbeth: *Bildernas predikan* [The pictorial sermon] (Stockholm, 1986)
A. Nilsén: 'Marie obefläckade avlelse i kult och konst' [The Immaculate Conception in Swedish medieval cult and art], *Ksthist. Tidskr.*, lvi/1 (1987), pp. 6–15

ANNA NILSÉN

Ivanov, Aleksandr (Andreyevich) (*b* St Petersburg, 28 July 1806; *d* St Petersburg, 15 July 1858). Russian painter. He was the foremost religious painter in 19th-century Russia. While maintaining the traditions of his academic mentors, including his father Andrey Ivanov (*c.* 1772–1848), a history painter of some merit, and Aleksey Yegorov (1776–1851), Ivanov also investigated new formal resolutions that have been compared to those of Cézanne and Mikhail Vrubel'. Ivanov trained at the Academy of Arts, St Petersburg, from 1817 to 1828, first as an external student and subsequently full-time, receiving a gold medal for his *Joseph Interpreting the Dreams of his Fellow Prisoners, a Wine Merchant and a Caterer* (St Petersburg, Rus. Mus.). In 1830 he received a scholarship from the Society for the Encouragement of the Arts to study abroad, and from 1830 to 1857 he lived in Italy, at that time full of Russian artists studying under the auspices of the St Petersburg Academy of Arts or the Society for the Encouragement of the Arts, two august institutions that looked askance at innovative tendencies and urged their *pensionnaires* to uphold the classical tradition.

Ivanov arrived in Rome with a sound academic training and a deep respect for Raphael, Leonardo and Poussin. Although he spent most of his creative life in Rome, he travelled extensively both within Italy and in other European countries, drawing for inspiration on a wide variety of classical art from Giotto to Titian. He was part of the large international colony in Rome, where he was close to his fellow countryman Orest Kiprensky, and where he was sympathetic to the spiritual quest of the Nazarenes. However, Ivanov was an eccentric who held himself aloof from most activities of the Russian contingent in Rome, and his religious fervour, expressed in his many Biblical interpretations, was not compatible with the brilliant salon of Princess Zinaida Volkonskaya, for many years the social and intellectual centre for Russians in Rome, or the vainglorious caprices of Rome's other great Russian painter Karl Bryullov. On the other hand, Ivanov found a sympathetic friend in the writer Nikolay Gogol', whose portrait he painted in 1841 (St Petersburg, Rus. Mus.). Ivanov also seems to have found a common language with another expatriate, the political radical Alexander Herzen, whom he met in Rome and London in 1847 and 1856.

In spite of his many years abroad, Ivanov remained profoundly Russian and, like many of his generation, especially Gogol', he tended to imbue art with a messianic, apocalyptic purpose. Along with the democratic thinkers Vissarion Belinsky and Herzen, Ivanov wished to reform mankind and considered art a principal weapon in the

Aleksandr Ivanov: *Christ Appearing to the People*, oil on canvas, 5.4×7.5 m, 1837–57 (Moscow, Tret'yakov Gallery)

struggle for social transformation. While leading a monastic way of life, Ivanov retained a fanatical belief in Russia, implying that her destiny was that of a Third Rome, and he elaborated his ideas in his philosophical tract of 1847, *Mysli pri chtenii Biblii* ('Thoughts occurring to me as I read the Bible'), which affirmed that the Slavic peoples will bring about a Golden Age when 'mankind will live in complete peace, when wars will cease, and eternal peace will be established . . . All branches of the human intellect, requiring profound peace and tranquility, will attain their full development, particularly historical painting.'

Ivanov dedicated most of his time and effort to religious painting, specifically to the preparation and completion of his magnum opus *Christ Appearing to the People* (1837–57; Moscow, Tret'yakov Gal.; see fig.). Although some of Ivanov's Academy and early Italian paintings had treated religious and mythological scenes, for example *Apollo, Hyacinthus and Chiparis Making Music and Singing* (1831–4; Moscow, Tret'yakov Gal.) and *Christ Appearing to Mary Magdalene* (1834–5; St Petersburg, Rus. Mus.), it was his discovery and diligent study of particular artistic phenomena in Italy—a felicitous combination of circumstances—that encouraged him to consider the subject of the appearance of the Messiah. For example, Ivanov was much impressed with the Raphael frescoes at the Vatican, and he discovered Titian in Venice, Giotto in Padua and Giotto and Masaccio in Florence—confrontations that prompted him to use a large format for his masterpiece (5.4×7.5 m) and to think in terms almost of a mural rather than of an easel painting. Moreover, the year he arrived in Rome, Ivanov made the acquaintance of Friedrich Overbeck, the leader of the Nazarenes, and throughout the 1830s and 1840s the two men often met to discuss the relationship of painting to religious rebirth. Like Overbeck, Peter Cornelius and other members of the group, Ivanov looked back to the early Renaissance, particularly to Fra Angelico, in his aspiration to bring about an evangelical revival. At first Ivanov was convinced that his *Christ Appearing to the People* would herald a spiritual reawakening, but as time went by, and as the preparatory sketches increased from 228 in 1839 to 400 in the early 1850s, Ivanov's enthusiasm waned. When the completed work was finished in 1857 and exhibited at the Academy in St Petersburg the following year, it did not receive strong acclaim and was criticized for its lifelessness. Even so, the painting is important as a document of its time: the synthetic derivation of the composition (from Raphael, Poussin etc.), the inclusion of a likeness of Gogol' and a self-portrait in the crowd, the careful ethnographical researches that Ivanov conducted to ensure historical accuracy and especially the many fine landscape and figure studies—these are ramifications that help us to understand the new tastes and orientations of mid-19th-century Russian painting.

While Ivanov continued with his masterpiece, he also tested other themes and methods. In the 1840s he became interested in painting directly from nature and produced nudes *en plein air* of young boys that he befriended in Rome and Naples, for example *Naked Boy* (c. 1850; St Petersburg, Rus. Mus.). At the same time he investigated the rhythmical principles he found in the frescoes of Giotto and Piero della Francesca, something that led him to his cycle of audacious and innovative watercolours known as the *Biblical Sketches*. The themes that Ivanov chose, such as the *Angel Striking Zacharias Dumb* (1850s) and *Christ Walking on the Water* (1850s; both Moscow, Tret'yakov Gal.), were actually his interpretations of David Strauss's *Das Leben Jesu* (Tübingen, 1835–6), a copy of which he owned (contrary to the Papal ban). The melodic, transparent qualities of these watercolours, which some critics have compared to William Blake's illustrations to Dante, distinguish them immediately from the more sober, more reportorial style of the earlier work and bring to mind the *fin-de-siècle* painting of Viktor Borisov-Musatov and Mikhail Vrubel'. In the light of the experimental nature of these works it is not surprising that artists and critics of the avant-garde period at the turn of the century (such as Nikolay Punin) should have drawn attention to them, referring to their musical, abstract qualities.

BIBLIOGRAPHY

M. Alpatov: *Aleksandr Andreyevich Ivanov*, 2 vols (Moscow, 1956)
G. Zagyanskaya: *Peyzazhi Aleksandra Ivanova* [The landscapes of Aleksandr Ivanov] (Moscow, 1976)
M. Allenov: *Aleksandr Andreyevich Ivanov* (Moscow, 1980)
M. Alpatov: *Aleksandr Andreyevich Ivanov* (Leningrad, 1983)
V. Barooshian: *The Art of Liberation: Alexander A. Ivanov* (Boston, 1987)

JOHN E. BOWLT

Ivanov, Ivan. *See* SHADR, IVAN.

Ivanov, Sergey (Vasil'yevich) (*b* Ruza, nr Moscow, 16 June 1864; *d* Svistukha, nr Moscow, 16 Aug 1910). Russian painter and graphic artist. He studied at the Moscow School of Painting, Sculpture and Architecture (1878–82 and 1884–5) under Illarion Pryanishnikov and others. He was a member of the Wanderers from 1899 and of the Union of Russian Artists, of which he was one of the founders. Ivanov became dissatisfied with the traditional Wanderers-style realism of the late 19th century and early 20th and with the painting of genre scenes—'nice little scenes', as he called them—and he aspired to a strongly dramatic expressive art, in which 'the heartbeat of the human soul' could be felt. His series of pictures of migrants, capturing the tragedies of peasant life (e.g. *On the Road: Death of a Migrant*, 1889; Moscow, Tret'yakov Gal.), is marked by an austere verism.

Ivanov was an innovator in history painting, introducing strong foreshortening effects, framing the composition and seeking to give it the maximum emotional impact. Among his masterpieces of this period are *Foreigners Arriving in 17th-century Moscow* (1901; Moscow, Tret'yakov Gal.; see fig.), in which the emptiness of the snow-covered slope in the centre, separating a distant carriage with foreigners alighting in the background from a Muscovite couple in the foreground, seems to symbolize the gulf between two different civilizations, and *Muscovites on Campaign in the 16th Century* (1903; Moscow, Tret'yakov Gal.), in which the compositional device of ranks of soldiers advancing across the snow almost straight towards the observer lends the battle scene a particular force.

Taken as a whole, Ivanov's oeuvre, with its powerfully dramatic use of spatial rhythms and its muted, psychologically eloquent colours, shows the evolution from 19th-century Critical Realism towards Art Nouveau. Distinctive

Sergey Ivanov: *Foreigners Arriving in 17th-century Moscow*, oil on canvas, 1.52×2.32 m, 1901 (Moscow, Tret'yakov Gallery)

proto-Expressionist elements, which give him a kinship with such German contemporaries as Käthe Kollwitz, are particularly strong in a number of Ivanov's pictures devoted to the First Russian Revolution of 1905–7, such as *Execution by Firing Squad* (1905; Moscow, Cent. Mus. Revolution), in which the solitary figure of the shot man, crumpled face downwards in the midst of a suddenly emptied square, acts as a concentrated shock device of a cinematic type. Ivanov also worked actively as a draughtsman, producing, for example, sketches of settlers by various techniques between 1885 and 1888. He was also a successful lithographer and etcher, using the same historical and socio-dramatic themes as in his proto-Expressionist paintings.

BIBLIOGRAPHY
I. N. Granovsky: *S. V. Ivanov* (Moscow, 1962)
P. Suzdalev: *S. V. Ivanov* (Moscow, 1975)

M. N. SOKOLOV

Ivanov-Alliluyev, Sergey (Kuz'mich) (*b* St Petersburg, 1891; *d* Moscow, 1979). Russian photographer. He took up photography at the age of 12, developing an early interest in colour photography. He won his first award in 1913 at a colour photography exhibition in Nizhny Novgorod and became a professional photographer in 1921. In 1924 he was invited to join the Leningrad Cinephoto Factory as a photographer and in 1931 he became a film cameraman. During this period he created lyrical winter landscapes in soft focus, a feature typical of his photography as a whole, including *In Winter Dress* (1924) and *Forester's Hut* (1923), as well as works clearly reminiscent in their mood of romantic films, such as *Expectation*

(1924) and his summer landscape by a pond, *Here Nightingales Sing until Dawn* (1926). In 1933–45 he worked as a stills photographer at the Moscow Mosfil'm studio, where he collaborated with such film directors as Lev Kuleshov, Vsevolod Pudovkin, Sergey Eisenstein and Mikhail Romm. Ivanov-Alliluyev took part in all the major photographic shows and international exhibitions of the 1920s and 1930s. Along with Nikolay Andreyev, Yury Yeryomin, Vasily Ulitin and Nikolay Svishchov-Paola, among others, he represented the classical wing of Soviet photography. In the post-war years he produced portrait and architectural photographs for the TASS Photochronicle and led the creative seminar for the Photochronicle's press photographers' section.

BIBLIOGRAPHY
G. Shudakov: *Pioneers of Soviet Photography* (London and New York, 1983)
Sergei Ivanov-Alliluyev: Izbranniye fotografii [Selected photographs] (Moscow, 1986)
S. Morozov: *Tvorcheskaya fotografiya* [Creative photography] (Moscow, 1986)
D. Elliott, ed.: *Photography in Russia: 1840–1940* (Berlin, 1992)

A. N. LAVRENTIEV

Ivanovo. Village in Bulgaria about 20 km south of Rousse, near to which along the banks of the River Roussenski Lom a large number of churches and monks' cells were carved into the rock: the earliest information concerning them dates to the reign of Tsar Ivan Assen II (*reg* 1218–41). Traces of wall painting survive in five of the churches.

The earliest frescoes are those in the single-cell, apsed church of the Gospodev Dol; the flat, decorative style in which the full-length figures of saints and scenes from the *Passion* are depicted suggests a 13th-century date. Of greater interest are the paintings in the rock-cut monument known as Crkvata (Bulg.: 'the church'). This comprises a nave and a narthex, with the remains of a rock-cut chapel to the north. Its wall paintings, only about a third of which survive, were commissioned by Tsar Ivan Alexander (*reg* 1331–71), whose portrait decorates the north wall of the narthex. Scenes from the *Life of St John the Baptist* decorate the narthex ceiling, but the best-preserved paintings are those depicting the *Passion* cycle on the nave ceiling. They include *Christ Washing the Feet of the Disciples*, the *Last Supper*, *Peter's Denial and Repentance*, the *Trial before Annas and Caiaphas*, the *Mocking of Christ*, the *Christ Carrying the Cross* (shown in two episodes, which is rare), the *Elevation of the Cross*, the *Crucifixion*, the *Deposition* and the *Death of Judas*. Fragments from the cycle of the *Twelve Great Feasts* survive on the walls of the nave, while the rock-cut chapel has a number of scenes from the *Life of St Gerasimos*, now in poor condition. The paintings are characterized by their elongated figures, vigorous line and pastel colours. The other churches containing fragments of frescoes are the Zatrupanata Crkva (Bulg.: 'buried church'; 13th–14th centuries), the Moskov Dol (14th century) and the Saborenata Crkva (Bulg.: 'ruined church').

BIBLIOGRAPHY

A. Grabar: *La Peinture religieuse en Bulgarie* (Paris, 1928)
A. Vasiliev: *Ivanovskite stenopisi* [The wall painting at Ivanovo] (Sofia, 1953)

TANIA VELMANS

Ivanov-Shits, Illarion (Aleksandrovich) (*b* Voronezh, 28 March 1865; *d* Moscow, 1937). Russian architect. He graduated from the Institute of Civil Engineers, St Petersburg, and then went to Moscow, where he worked as a district architect. His subsequent career, during which he established a reputation as a designer almost exclusively of public service buildings, designing few private houses and no churches, can be divided into three phases. Characteristic of his early work in Moscow during the 1890s are the Belkin and Martyanov houses executed in flamboyant Renaissance and Baroque variants of historicism, and the brick-built Mazyrin municipal children's home on B. Tsaritsynskaya Street. From 1900 Ivanov-Shits was a member of the Technical Construction Council attached to the Moscow City Authority, where most of his buildings were necessitated by the social conditions of the large city or created to meet the needs of the poor. Works produced during this period include the House of the People (1903) in Vvedensky Square, the first such project in Moscow, and the tea-room theatre, Lefortovo district, and other buildings with auditoria. During the 1900s, with Lev Kekushev, V. F. Valkot (1874–1943) and Fyoder Shekhtel', Ivanov-Shits became a pioneer in Moscow of the classicizing northern version of Art Nouveau (Rus. *modern*). Notable examples of his work in this style include the Hirsh Theatre and Restaurant (1898–1902; destr.) on the corner of Povarskaya Street and Merzlyakovsky Lane; the Merchants' Club (1905–9) on M. Dmitrovka Street, with its foyer and two theatres with magnificent interiors; and the State Savings Bank (1913–14) on Rakhmanovsky

Lane, built in several stages, with a parade ground in front of the main façade and a massive banking hall with a glass roof. The Shanyavsky People's University Building (1910–13), Miusskaya Square, Moscow, is a strictly symmetrical composition, its main façade consisting of three projecting bays and a central, decorated loggia with a colonnade. By far his largest undertaking in this style, although restrained in its formal execution, is the Soldatenkova (now Botkinskaya) City Hospital complex (1908–12) in north-west Moscow.

From *c*. 1910 the third phase of Ivanov-Shits's career began, as his designs became increasingly Neo-classical in spirit, for example the Cas'yanov and Orlov houses (1910s) in Nikolopeskovsky Lane, near the Arbat, Moscow, and the unrealized projects for the Museum of the Patriotic War of 1812 (1912) and the Institute of Physical Methods for Treating Ex-Servicemen (1916). Similar in style are the Moscow City Bank (1925), the Weisbrot Hospital (1926) and the surgical block (1929) of the Helm'hol'z Hospital, all in Moscow. He also experimented briefly with Constructivism during the 1920s, for example in the sanatorium block in Barvikh, near Moscow, but in the 1930s he returned exclusively to the Neo-classical style, for example in the conversion (1932–4) of the Andreyevsky and Aleksandrovsky halls in the Great Kremlin Palace (1838–49; by Konstantin Ton) into the Assembly Hall of the Supreme Soviet of the USSR. His official appointments included architect (1918–21) to Narkomfin (People's Commissariat for Finance), consultant (1918–21) to the VTSSPS (All-Union Central Council of Professional Trade Unions) and to Lechsanupra (Department of Health and Sanitation), and architect to Lechsanupra (1933–7).

BIBLIOGRAPHY

V. G. Baranovsky: *Yubileyny spravochnik svedeniy o deyatel'nosti byvshikh vospitannikov Instituta Grazhdanskikh Inzhenerov: Stroitel'nogo Uchilishcha, 1842–1892* [Anniversary directory of information on the work of past students of the Institute of Civil Engineering: School of Construction] (St Petersburg, 1893)
Ye. Bagina: 'Illarion Ivanov-Shits, 1865–1937', *Stroitel'stvo & Arkhit. Moskvy*, iv (1986), pp. 24–6

YE. I. KIRICHENKO

Iványi Grünwald, Béla (*b* Somogysom, 7 May 1867; *d* Budapest, 24 Sept 1940). Hungarian painter. He studied painting at the Academy of Fine Arts in Budapest (1882–6), then in Munich (1886–7) and finally (1887–90) at the Académie Julian in Paris. He remained in Paris until 1892, taking part in exhibitions from 1889. Characteristic of his early pictures is the *Sword of God* (1890; Budapest, N.G.), a proto-Symbolist treatment of rural genre showing the influence of Jules Bastien-Lepage. After his return to Munich, Iványi Grünwald painted a large-scale genre painting entitled *Nihilists Drawing Lots* (1893; Budapest, N.G.), a work as notable for its dramatic use of chiaroscuro as for its deeply felt subject-matter. In response to a state commission for the 1896 Millennium Exhibition in Budapest he produced an enormous academic history painting, *King Béla IV's Return following the Invasion Suffered at the Hands of the Tartars* (Budapest, N.G.). A determining influence on Iványi Grünwald's development was his association in Munich with Simon Hollósy at the latter's anti-academic painting school. In 1896 Iványi Grünwald moved with the rest of Hollósy's circle to NAGYBÁNYA

COLONY (now Baia Mare, Romania), in order to concentrate on *plein-air* landscape painting. Iványi Grünwald's Nagybánya period, lasting from 1896 to 1907, was undoubtedly the most accomplished phase of his career. His painting by this time had distanced itself from the influence of Bastien-Lepage to concentrate on the changing effects of atmosphere. He emphasized, for example, the mood produced by light at various times of the day and night, as in *Evening by the Cattle Pen* (1896; Budapest, N.G.), and used extremely bright colours, not entirely typical of the Nagybánya school as a whole, as with the brilliant greens of *In the Valley* (1901; Budapest, N.G.). His subjects were taken from his immediate surroundings and the human figure is shown as an integral part of the landscape. Iványi Grünwald also taught in Hollósy's Nagybánya school until he took up an award in 1905 that enabled him to spend a year in Rome. In 1906 he held an exhibition of his works in the Ernst Museum, Budapest, and this event effectively heralded the end of his Nagybánya period.

Iványi Grünwald continued to work in Nagybánya for a few more years, but a change in his painting was brought about by the influence of younger Hungarian painters returning from Paris and working in the style of the Fauves. More direct inspiration was provided by the exhibition of modern French painting held in Budapest in 1907. Iványi Grünwald's paintings became more decorative, his outlines bolder, and his compositions based on flat shapes, as in *Landscape of Upper Bánya with the River Gutin* (1906–8; priv. col., see Telepy, 1985, no. 98). Decorative principles already dominated in the large panel of 1909 for the Révai Villa in Budapest, *Spring* (destr.; see Telepy, 1976, p. 18). At the Budapest National Salon in 1909 Iványi Grünwald won great acclaim for his paintings in the new style and he successfully solicited support from the mayor of the small town of Kecskemét to set up an artists' colony there (*see* KECSKEMÉT COLONY) in 1911. Iványi Grünwald's major work in this period was *Kecskemét Traders among Snow Mounds* (1912; Kecskemét, Katona Mus.), of which he painted a number of versions. In style these scenes were reminiscent of Gauguin's Brittany paintings, with boldly outlined planes of deep colour. After 1919 Iványi Grünwald moved to Budapest. He subsequently worked both there and at Lake Balaton on a series of landscapes that, for the most part, were vigorously painted and impressionistic in effect, for example *Oxen on the Shore of Lake Balaton* (1920; Budapest, N.G.).

BIBLIOGRAPHY
B. Lázár: *Iványi Grünwald Béla* (Budapest, 1921)
Iványi Grünwald Béla (exh. cat., ed. K. Telepy; Kecskemét, Katona Mus., 1967)
K. Telepy: *Iványi Grünwald* (Budapest, 1971)
——: *Iványi Grünwald Béla* (Budapest, 1985) [cat. rais.]

MARIA SZOBOR-BERNÁTH

Iveagh, 1st Earl of. *See* GUINNESS, EDWARD.

Iveković, Oton (*b* Klanjec, nr Zagreb, 17 April 1869; *d* Klanjec, 4 July 1939). Croatian painter and teacher. He studied painting in Zagreb under Ferdo Quiquerez and from 1886 he attended the Akademie der Bildenden Künste, Vienna, where he studied with Christian Griepenkerl (1839–1916) and August Eisenmenger (1830–1907). In 1892 he studied at the Akademie der Bildenden Künste, Munich, under Wilhelm von Lindenschmidt (1829–95) and also took master classes with Ferdinand Keller (1842–1922) at the Staatliche Akademie der Bildenden Künste, Karlsruhe. From 1895 he taught at the School of Arts and Crafts (now School for Applied Art and Design) in Zagreb and from 1908 to 1927 at the Art School (later Academy of Fine Arts) in the same city. At the end of the 19th century and the beginning of the 20th he was the most important history painter working in Croatia and the most prolific. Attracted by Vlaho Bukovac's Divisionist technique and his use of light, he adopted a palette of *plein-air* colours and skilfully incorporated them into his historical genre paintings. Some of his best-known works are *Nikola Zrinski Before the Charge from Siget* (1890; Zagreb, Hist. Mus. Croatia), the *Coronation of King Tomislav* (1905; Zagreb, Gal. Mod. A.), the *Arrival of the Croats* (1905), the *Croats Choosing Koloman for their King in 1102* (1906; both Zagreb, Golden Hall) and the *Battle of Stubica* (1919; Zagreb, Hist. Mus. Croatia).

BIBLIOGRAPHY
L. Babić: *Umjetnost kod Hrvata u XIX. stoljeću* [Croatian art in the 19th century] (Zagreb, 1934), pp. 113–16
S. Pintarić: 'Pejzaži Otona Ivekovića' [The landscapes of Oton Iveković], *Anali*, 5 (1985), pp. 49–56
M. Schneider: 'Historijsko slikarstvo Otona Ivekovića' [The historical painting of Oton Iveković], *Anali*, 5 (1985), pp. 37–47

ZDENKO RUS

Iverni [Yverni], **Jacques** (*fl* Avignon, 1410; *d* between 12 Dec 1435 and 22 March 1438). French painter. In 1411–12 he painted banners with the arms of Avignon, and in 1413 he was paid by Pierre d'Acigné, seneschal of Provence, for an altarpiece of 'Our Lord' for St Sauveur, Aix-en-Provence. For Cavaillon Cathedral, in 1422, he was commissioned to execute four stained-glass windows. In 1427 Iverni executed pennants for the municipal ship that sailed the Rhône, and also processional banners. A panel with a gold ground and the signature *Jacobus Iverini* depicting François de Nyons, Abbot of Ste Geneviève, Paris, kneeling before St Agricol and flanked by his arms, was recorded in St Agricol, Avignon, in the 18th century. None of these works is known to survive.

Iverni's only extant and secure work is a triptych of the *Virgin and Child Enthroned between SS Stephen and Lucy* (*c.* 1420; 1.61×1.91 m; Turin, Gal. Sabauda) inscribed *Yacobus Iverni de* [Av] *inione pinxsit*; it was once, apparently, followed by a date. In the predella, on either side of *Christ, the Man of Sorrows Flanked by SS Peter and Paul*, are the arms of the marchesi of Ceva from Ferrazzi in Piedmont, a family in contact with Avignon, where the altarpiece was presumably ordered. The work, with its bright hues, gold punch marks, miniature-like quality and dependence on Sienese models, conforms to the late International Gothic style of Avignon. An *Annunciation with St Stephen and Donors* (Dublin, N.G.), held to originate from a church in Avignon, is probably another work by Iverni, judging from its closely related style. Iverni, apparently a well-established painter, may have participated in the decoration of Notre-Dame-des-Doms, Avignon: the fresco there of the *Baptism* (*c.* 1423) may be his contribution.

BIBLIOGRAPHY
L. Venturi: 'Courrier d'Italie', *Ren. A.*, ii (1919), pp. 230–31
L. Labande: *Les Primitifs français: Peintres et peintres verriers de la Provence occidentale*, i (Marseille, 1932)
C. Sterling: *Les Peintres du Moyen Age* (Paris, 1942)
M. Roques: *Les Peintures murales du sud-est de la France: XIIIe au XVIe siècle* (Paris, 1961)
E. Kane: 'Jacques Yverni of Avignon', *Burl. Mag.*, cxxix (1987), pp. 491–8

PATRICK M. DE WINTER

Ives, Chauncey B(radley) (*b* Hamden, CT, 14 Dec 1810; *d* Rome, 2 Aug 1894). American sculptor, active in Italy. He trained as a wood-carver in New Haven, CT, and he may also have studied with the sculptor Hezekiah Augur. In 1838 Ives launched his career as a portraitist. Among the works that contributed to his rising reputation during the next two years were portraits of the professor *Benjamin Silliman* (plaster, *c.* 1840; New York, NY Hist. Soc.) and the architect *Ithiel Town* (marble, *c.* 1840; New Haven, CT, Yale U. A.G.).

Due to illness, Ives sought the milder climate of Italy; he lived in Florence from 1844 to 1851, when he settled permanently in Rome. In the third quarter of the 19th century, he rivalled Hiram Powers as the foremost American sculptor in Italy. Although he continued to produce portraits, Ives developed his reputation as a sculptor of idealized marble figures. He excelled at representations of childhood; for example his *Sans souci* (1863; Washington, DC, Corcoran Gal. A.) was particularly popular, and his workmen generated 22 copies of the dishevelled young girl who abandons her book for a daydream. The work reveals Ives's skill at combining 19th-century naturalism with traditional Neo-classicism; to contemporary audiences the anecdotal quality of the figure epitomized his artistic strength.

Ives catered to the vogue for Old Testament themes with his *Rebecca at the Well* (1854; New York, Met.). His classical subjects also met with extraordinary success. Defying American strictures against nudity, he modelled a *Pandora* in 1851. Using a contrived arrangement of drapery as a concession to modesty, Ives focused on Pandora's hesitant contemplation of the forbidden box. When Ives remodelled his celebrated creation in 1863 (New York, Brooklyn Mus.), the revised version was hailed as his masterpiece. *Undine Receiving her Soul* (1855; New Haven, CT, Yale U. A.G.), an almost life-size standing female figure, thinly veiled in flowing drapery, further reveals his skill at representing flesh in marble.

BIBLIOGRAPHY
L. Taft: *The History of American Sculpture* (New York, 1903, rev. 1930), pp. 112–13
W. Craven: *Sculpture in America* (Newark, 1968, rev. 1984), pp. 284–8
W. Gerdts: 'Chauncey Bradley Ives, American Sculptor', *Antiques*, xciv (1968), pp. 714–18
American Figurative Sculpture in the Museum of Fine Arts, Boston (Boston, 1986), pp. 44–7

JANET A. HEADLEY

Ivory. Material, technically known as dentine, from which the teeth of elephants and other mammals are mainly composed. It is similar in appearance to BONE and is chemically indistinguishable from it. When freshly cut it is creamy white in colour and displays a variety of grain patterns in transverse or longitudinal section depending on the type of animal from which it was derived.

1. Types. 2. Techniques. 3. History and uses. 4. Conservation.

1. TYPES. True ivory comes from the incisor teeth, or tusks, found in the upper jaw of the African and Asiatic elephant. Those of the African are normally larger and of better quality than the Asian; they average 23 kg in weight and measure up to 2 m in length and 0.18 m in diameter. Tusks weighing 70 kg, measuring 3 m in length, were not uncommon in the past: the largest known pair is reputed to have weighed 208 kg and measured 8 m in length. The tusks are conically hollow for about one third of their length from the proximal end. A distinguishing feature of elephant ivory is the appearance on the end grain or transverse section of the lines of Owen and the lines of Retsius, which give an engine-turned effect.

Mammoth ivory is virtually indistinguishable from elephant once worked, but it tends to age to a distinctly yellowish-cream colour and to have a more opaque surface finish. Considerable finds have been made on the Siberian tundra, and large quantities have been exported to Europe and East Asia. Mammoth ivory has sometimes been mineralized and stained during burial by mineral deposits. The Alaskan deposits produce a form known as odontolite, which can be a bright turquoise blue, but the more common, Siberian ivory is a mottled nutty brown.

Hippopotamus ivory is derived from six teeth set in the animal's lower jaw. Four are comparatively small and of limited utility, providing solid material no more than 100 mm long and 40 mm in diameter. The canines can reach a considerable size, but they are sharply curved and covered with a hard enamel layer that is difficult to remove even with modern techniques. The ivory is harder and whiter than elephant. It will take a higher polish and does not tend to yellow with age. The objects made from it are comparatively small and may reflect the triangular section of the unworked tooth.

Walrus ivory, also known as morse ivory, is derived from the highly modified canines carried by the male animal. They have an average length of 600 mm but a diameter of only 60 mm, although much larger examples have been reported. The tusks are hollow for 60–70% of their length and possess a thick core of highly crystalline secondary dentine, which can form up to 75% of their volume. Artefacts manufactured from walrus ivory are readily identified by their generally small cross-section and by the presence of secondary dentine.

Pig or boar's tusk ivory is derived from the modified canines of the wild pig (*Sus scrofa*). The tusks are very heavily curved, sometimes forming complete circles up to 100 mm in diameter, but they rarely exceed 20 mm in thickness. A tough enamel layer covers all but the extreme tip of the tusk. Objects manufactured from boar's tusk will always be of small diameter and usually triangular in section. The ivory is very dense, so no grain is visible even under moderate magnification.

Whales provide two further sources of ivory. The Arctic whale or narwhal has a highly modified left canine, which forms one spiral, conical tusk up to 2.5 m long. The right canine is similar in form, but only *c.* 30 mm long and both tusks are hollow for most of their length. The sperm-whale carries approximately 45 teeth in its lower jaw, each up to 200 mm long and 80 mm in diameter. About 50% of the tooth is hollow, but the tips provide much useful material. (*See also* SCRIMSHAW.)

In addition to bone, there are a number of substitutes for ivory. The helmeted hornbill has a large excrescence on top of its beak, known as the casque, which is composed of a material as dense as elephant ivory. It is rarely more than 60 mm long, 40 mm high and 20 mm wide, and it ranges in colour from a deep creamy white to pale orange. Vegetable ivory is actually the kernel of the nut of certain species of palm tree, principally *Phytelephas macrocarpa*. It is smooth and white when fresh but darker when dry. Synthetic ivory was first produced in 1865 by John Hyatt of New York. His composition was based on highly flammable nitrocellulose mixed with ivory-coloured pigments. Similar substances were manufactured under the trade names of Cellonite, Pyralin and Xylonite. In the 1920s and 1930s Ivorine and Ivorite were manufactured: these were essentially similar to the earlier products, but contained a plasticizer that made them less brittle and more versatile. Celluloid was particularly successful at imitating ivory grain. Since the 1960s epoxy and polyester resins have been used to make reasonable facsimiles of ivory. (*See also* PLASTIC, §1.)

For the identification of ivory *see* TECHNICAL EXAMINATION, §VIII, 8.

2. TECHNIQUES. Ivory can be sawn, drilled, filed and worked with scrapers. It can be fixed with and made into screws, and glued to itself or to other supports, for example wood. It is a very dense material and therefore capable of accepting both fine carved or engraved detail and a high degree of surface finish. It has reasonable bending properties and can be worked down to a very thin cross-section without breaking. Thin sections can be permanently curved by steam heating.

Much ivory carving is done in the round and conforms to the general shape and dimensions of the tusk or portion of tusk from which it was carved. The most obvious examples of this type of carving are oliphants (*see* OLIPHANT) or horns and the Chinese figurines representing the Eight Immortals of Daoism, which are heavily carved but still follow the shape of the tusk, even to the extent of incorporating its curvature into the design. The proximal end of the tusk, which is hollow and generally circular in section, is used in the manufacture of bangles, armlets and circular boxes. This obviates the need to create a hollow section.

The techniques employed by the modern carver (excluding the use of power tools) are largely the same as those used in antiquity since the development of metal tools. Coping and fret saws are relatively recent additions to the carver's kit, but the other tools, for example saws, chisels, gouges, gravers, files, drills and abrasives, differ from those of the ancient Egyptians only in the material of manufacture and the number of types available. For carvings in which the shape or size departs from that of the tusk, the ivory is first prepared by sawing out a block or slab that will accommodate the required design. Preliminary shaping is achieved by sawing away any large

unwanted areas. Detailed shaping follows, using chisels, gouges, knives and files. The chisels and gouges are rarely, if ever, struck with a mallet or hammer: hand pressure is used instead to produce a paring cut. Deep undercuts, as found in drapery, are produced by drilling and carving. Pierced work is produced by drilling a small through hole to allow access for the blade of a frame saw, a coping saw for coarse work or a piercing saw for fine work. Shallow patterning and precise detail is worked with simple points or engraver's tools, known as burins and gravers.

Turned work is produced on machines as simple as the bow lathe or as sophisticated as the ornamental turning lathe. The hand tools employed in turning can be the same as those used by the wood turner, especially when working between centres on spindle work. However, the density of ivory lends it to the use of the scraper. Seven main patterns are used, the straight, the round, the half round, the point, the bead and the left and right side. In addition, a wide range of special-profile scrapers is used to produce fixed patterns. In face-plate turning only the scrapers are used, as in ornamental work.

Veneers and inlay pieces are usually made by sawing the tusk longitudinally, but transverse sections of elephant ivory have been used to display the engine-turned effect seen on the end grain. Machine-made rotary-cut veneers have been made since the mid-19th century.

Ivory can be bleached and polished to enhance its natural translucency, or gilded, painted and stained with oils and dyes. Many ivories have lost their original polychromy, so their present appearance may be misleading.

3. HISTORY AND USES. Throughout history ivory has been used in many different cultures for a wide range of religious, secular and utilitarian objects, for jewellery, for inlay and marquetry, and even, when burnt, as a pigment (*see* PIGMENT, §II). Its popularity has been due to its attractive colour, its smooth, translucent appearance and the ease with which it can be carved and coloured. Also, for many cultures the exotic origin of ivory has made it a prestigious material with symbolic and magical associations. For art historians ivory is of special interest because it has been widely traded, it cannot be melted down and it survives when many other materials disintegrate. It is therefore an important indicator of stylistic evolution.

The earliest known ivories date from the Upper Palaeolithic era, when decorated jewellery and stylized representations of human and animal figures (see fig. 1) were made in mammoth ivory by people of the Gravettian culture (22,000–18,000 BC) living between south-west France and Siberia (*see* PREHISTORIC EUROPE, §II, 3(i)). Later, in the Ancient Near East, ivory was a valuable trade commodity, its status so great that it was frequently included in tribute and royal gifts (*see* ANCIENT NEAR EAST, §II, 3). It was used for both practical and luxury goods, some of the earliest examples being found in Egypt, where cosmetic items, jewellery and game-pieces were produced from Neolithic times to the end of the Dynastic period (*c.* 4500–30 BC; *see* EGYPT, ANCIENT, §XVII, 9). Ivory objects from the tomb of Tutankhamun (*reg c.* 1332–*c.* 1323 BC) indicate that almost every ivory-working technique was then known and used. As in other Near Eastern cultures, the material was gilded and coloured, carved in relief or in the round,

1. Ivory, tip of a mammoth's tusk carved with 'swimming' reindeer (possibly a handle for a dagger or spear-thrower), 30×207 mm, Upper Palaeolithic period (London, British Museum); found at Montastruc, near Toulouse, France, 1866

or applied to furniture and boxes in the form of veneer or inlay. Further to the east, ivory was used by the Indus civilization (*c.* 2550–2000 BC): pieces found at Harappa include fragments of inlay and such utilitarian items as combs.

Over the centuries ivory naturally became most widely used in the regions in which it was readily available, notably the Indian subcontinent, Africa and the Arctic regions of north-west America (*see* NATIVE NORTH AMERICAN ART, §§III, 1 and XV, 3) and Siberia (*see* TOBOL'SK). These

traditions developed independently of one another and are covered in detail in this dictionary under the relevant countries, civilizations and geographical regions. Although ivory was less widespread in Europe, its use was significant in the expression of certain artistic styles, especially during the Early Christian and Byzantine era and in the Middle Ages. Its history, which is also discussed in detail in the relevant style and country articles, forms a continuous tradition and is therefore summarized below.

(i) Ancient and Classical. In the 1st and 2nd millennium BC the distribution of ivory products throughout the Near East and Mediterranean area was largely due to the Phoenicians (*see* PHOENICIAN). The trade declined in the 8th century BC, but by then ivory had become established in neighbouring cultures for use in furniture and a variety of small objects, including toilette articles, seals and gamepieces (*see* CYCLADIC, §VIII; CYPRUS, §II, 5 (iii); HELLADIC, §VI; and MINOAN, §VI). In ancient Greece enormous chryselephantine statues were made in the 5th century, in which ivory, representing flesh, and gold foil were applied to a wooden base (*see* GREECE, ANCIENT, §§IV, 1(iii)(g) and X, 6(ii)); none survives.

In the Italian peninsula ivory was used by the Etruscans (*see* ETRUSCAN, §VII, 3), but the craft declined in the 3rd century. It was revived by the Romans in the 2nd century when the Carthaginian wars brought them into contact with the Hellenistic cultures of southern Italy and Sicily (*see* ROME, ANCIENT, §X, 4). Cheap imports from East Africa enabled the Romans to use ivory lavishly, even on buildings. It was still widely used for both secular and religious objects in the Early Christian era, but by the Byzantine period it was largely reserved for sacred images and liturgical objects (*see* EARLY CHRISTIAN AND BYZANTINE ART, §VII, 5). Many of these continued the formats originally used by the Romans: the CONSULAR DIPTYCH, for example, was adapted for book covers and a variety of devotional objects, while the pyx, a small round box readily made from a hollow tusk, was used for the sacramental bread.

(ii) Medieval. In northern Europe there was a native tradition based on marine ivory (*see* ANGLO-SAXON ART, §VI), but Byzantine ivories, acquired as gifts, booty or trade items, were highly prized, and from the 9th century a great revival of ivory-carving took place in which the Byzantine products were copied and even reused (*see* BOOKBINDING, colour pl. IV, fig. 2, CAROLINGIAN ART, §VI and OTTONIAN ART, §VI). Ivory was reintroduced to

2. Walrus ivory chess rook carved in the form of two standing lions, h. 102 mm, 11th century (London, British Museum); found at Bildeston, Suffolk, 1881

southern Europe by the Muslims in the 10th century. They produced very fine work in the royal workshops in Spain and later were probably responsible for many of the ivories produced in Italy and Sicily in the 11th, 12th and 13th centuries (*see* ISLAMIC ART, §VIII, 7). By the Romanesque period schools of ivory-carving had become established in Germany, Italy, England (see fig. 2), Spain and France (*see* ROMANESQUE, §VIII).

Ivory-carving in Europe peaked in the 13th and 14th centuries (*see* GOTHIC, §VII), when elephant ivory was widely available for use in a great range of liturgical and secular objects: tabernacles, reliquaries, statuettes, diptychs, triptychs, caskets and altarpieces; combs, lanterns, writing-tablets, knife-handles, buttons, belts and mirrorcases. The craft, which was now based in urban workshops rather than monasteries, became highly organized, and the products, in particular the Virgin and Child statuettes made in Paris in the 13th century, are among the most innovative, graceful and expressive art forms of the period.

(iii) 1600 and after. The craft declined during the religious and political upheavals of the Renaissance but flourished again in the 17th century and the early 18th, when supplies were plentiful, and ivory was used to advantage in new sculptural and decorative forms. In Germany and the Low Countries it was popular for low-relief plaques, small, virtuoso figure groups and illusionistic compositions in which it was combined with wood and precious metals. It was also increasingly used for such costly decorative and utilitarian objects as cutlery handles, tankards, table salts, powder flasks, perfume-bottle holders and fans. Ivory turning with a lathe became a favourite aristocratic hobby, so a number of elaborate turned objects were produced. On a more practical level, ivory was found to be ideal for anatomical models, scientific instruments, portrait medals and as a support for miniatures (*see* MINIATURE, §II).

Later, specialized machines were developed that further reduced the price and increased the variety of ivory objects. Apart from the ornamental turning lathe, which underwent continual development, notable innovations include H. Pape's veneer-cutting machine of 1826, Benjamin Steadman and Fenner Bush's rotary veneer cutter of the 1840s and machines for duplicating and reproducing carvings (see fig. 3) built by James Watt in 1800 and by Benjamin Cheverton (1794–1876) and John Hawkins in 1828. By the end of the 19th century ivory was used decoratively in jewellery and furniture inlay, as well as for a multitude of utilitarian and craft purposes, from shirt buttons to model ships. In the 20th century it was soon superseded by synthetic ivory, although true ivory was highly popular in the Art Deco period and has occasionally been used by sculptors. From the 1950s the availability of the material was severely curtailed by attempts to protect the African elephant. One of the few remaining legitimate sources is the deposits of mammoth tusk in Siberia, which is still used by the Yakut people to carve chess sets, decorated boxes and figurines for the export and tourist market.

For further information on European ivory *see* entries under individual countries; *see also* CASKET; CHESS SET; COMB, LITURGICAL; and SITULA.

3. Elephant ivory bust of *Antinous Vertumnus* (a favourite slave of the Emperor Hadrian), h. 125 mm, possibly 19th century (London, British Museum)

4. CONSERVATION. Ivory is a mixture of organic and inorganic material, the former being ossein, the latter hydroxyapatite, which is calcium phosphate in association with carbonate and fluoride. It is hygroscopic and anisotropic, so prone to splitting and warping on exposure to moisture and/or heat. The ossein is decomposed by hydrolysis on prolonged exposure to water, and the hydroxypatite is readily attacked by acids.

Ivory derived from an archaeological context is always degraded to some extent, which makes it porous, chalky and brittle. In this condition it is particularly prone to impact damage and delamination and will often require consolidation. Ivory excavated from a wet context requires very careful drying. Incorrect or badly controlled drying can result in warping and partial delamination or even the complete disintegration of the object. In this condition an ivory is very fragile, and the slightest pressure can cause cross-grain breaks. Material recovered from salty contexts will contain absorbed soluble salts, which have a tendency to crystallize out in the inter-lamellar spaces. This can cause serious delamination, or even the total loss of the outer surface of an ivory. The condition can be remedied by carefully controlled and timed washing in distilled water, followed by dehydration with organic solvents.

Degraded ivory can be cleaned with a non-ionic detergent in distilled water, provided that the exposure to water is kept to a minimum. Concretions on the surface of an object can often be removed by careful picking with a needle, or, where they are particularly firmly fixed, by treatment with dilute acids. Undegraded ivory can warp and split with the grain if exposed to adverse environments; objects or parts of objects that have been worked to a thin section are especially prone to this form of damage. If the ivory is both degraded and warped, it is not usually possible to correct the warping, but splits can often be closed by exposing the object to relative humidities in excess of 60%. If the humidity is then very gradually reduced to ambient, the cracks tend to stay closed. A common form of damage is cross-grain breakage caused by impact. These breaks are usually clean and present a good surface area, so they are easily repaired with a spirit-soluble adhesive. Difficulties arise if the break occurs across a small section or at a steep angle; it may then be necessary to reinforce the break area by dowelling or splinting. Where this is impractical, the only recourse is to stronger adhesives, usually the epoxy resins. Cyanoacrylates should never be used.

Ivory objects should be stored and displayed out of direct sunlight and away from sources of heat. The relative humidity of the display or storage area should be maintained at 50–55%, at 19°C. Where this is not possible, a stable environment that is neither too moist nor too dry is desirable.

BIBLIOGRAPHY

R. Owen: *Odontography: Or a Treatise on the Comparative Anatomy of Teeth* (London, 1840)
T. K. Penniman: *Pictures of Ivory and Other Animal Teeth, Bone, and Antler*, Occasional Papers on Technology, v (Oxford, 1952)
H. Hodges: *Artifacts* (London, 1964)
C. I. A. Ritchie: *Ivory Carving* (London, 1969)
N. S. Baer and L. J. Majewski: 'Ivory and Related Materials', *A. & Archaeol. Tech. Abstr.*, viii/2 (1970), pp. 229–72
R. Silverberg: *Mammoths, Mastodons and Man* (London, 1970)
H. J. Plenderleith and A. E. A. Werner: *The Conservation of Antiquities and Works of Art* (Oxford, 1971)
V. Arwas: *Art Deco Sculpture: Chryselephantine Statuettes of the Twenties* (New York, 1975)
H. Osborne, ed.: *The Oxford Companion to the Decorative Arts* (Oxford, 1975)
Tardy [H. Lengellé]: *Les Ivoires: Evolution décorative du 1er siècle à nos jours*, 2 vols (Paris, 1977)
D. Gaborit-Chopin: *Ivoires du moyen âge* (Fribourg, 1978)
R. D. Barnett: *Ancient Ivories of the Middle East and Adjacent Areas*, Quedem, xiv (Jerusalem, 1982)
B. Burack: *Ivory and its Uses* (Rutland, VT, 1984)
A. Cutler: *The Craft of Ivory: Sources, Techniques and Uses in the Mediterranean World, AD 200–1400* (Washington, DC, 1985)
A. MacGregor: *Bone, Antler, Ivory and Horn: The Technology of Skeletal Materials Since the Roman Period* (Beckenham, 1985)
[M. Vickers and others]: *Ivory: A History and Collector's Guide* (London, 1987)
O. Krzyszkowska: 'Ivory and Related Materials', *Bull. Inst. Class. Stud. U. London Suppl. Pap.*, lix (1990)
F. Minney: 'The Conservation and Reconstruction of a Late Bronze Age Ivory Inlaid Box from Palestine', *The Conservator*, xv (1991), pp. 3–7
Elephant: The Animal and its Ivory in African Art (exh. cat., ed. D. H. Ross; Los Angeles, UCLA, Fowler Mus. Cult. Hist.; New York, Met.; 1993–4)
A. Caubet and F. Poplin: 'Les Objets de matière dure animale: Etude du matériau', *Ras Shamra-Ougarit*, cxi

FRANK MINNEY

Ivory, Thomas (*b* ?Cork, *c.* 1732; *d* Dublin, Dec 1786). Irish architect. He was, with Thomas Cooley, the most prominent architect in Dublin in the 1770s. His importance possibly derived less from his buildings than from his post as master of the Dublin Society's School of Architectural Drawing, where from the early 1760s to his death he instructed many craftsmen and designers in architectural drawing and the rudiments of classical composition.

Ivory's most important buildings are Kilcarty (*c.* 1770–80), Co. Meath, and the Bluecoat School (King's Hospital; begun 1773) and Newcomen's Bank (*c.* 1781), both in Dublin. His partly executed designs for the Bluecoat School in the British Library are among the most beautiful Irish architectural drawings of the 18th century. They reveal Ivory's conservative, even old-fashioned approach, for here, as late as 1773, he proposed a Palladian composition enlivened with Baroque flourishes.

Never reluctant to repeat his designs, Ivory used the same basic layout in the Bluecoat drawings and at Kilcarty, a sophisticated and subtle farmhouse that he selfconsciously refused to turn into a villa. The Bluecoat elevations reappear in flawless Neo-classical guise in Newcomen's Bank, described by Maurice Craig as 'the only building in Dublin which looks as though it might have been designed by one of the Adams'. Ivory was no innovator but a sensitive exponent of conservative taste. In the 1770s he was upstaged by Thomas Cooley and eclipsed after 1781 by James Gandon. Henry Aaron Baker was his pupil.

BIBLIOGRAPHY

M. Craig: *Dublin, 1660–1860* (London, 1952/*R* Dublin, 1980)
E. McParland: *Thomas Ivory, Architect* (Ballycotton, 1973)
——: 'Thomas Ivory', *Bull. Irish Georg. Soc.*, xvii/1–2 (1974), pp. 15–18

EDWARD McPARLAND

Ivory Coast. *See* CÔTE D'IVOIRE.

Ivry, Pierre Contant d'. *See* CONTANT D'IVRY, PIERRE.

Iwan [aiwan, eyvan, ivan, liwan; Pers. *ayvān*, Arab. *īwān*]. Vaulted hall with walls on three sides and completely open on the fourth. In classical Persian and Arabic texts the term usually refers to a palace building or some formal part of a palace, such as a platform, balcony or portico; only among modern archaeologists and art historians is the word applied solely to this type of vaulted hall. The basic form of the iwan can be traced back to Mesopotamia and Iran during the time of the Parthians (*see* PARTHIAN) and Sasanians (*c.* 250 BC–AD 651), but its full architectural potential was realized by Islamic builders from Egypt to India, who made it a distinctive feature of their secular and religious monuments.

The origin and early development of the iwan are the subject of debate, and no convincing solution to these problems will be possible until more archaeological data is available from Iran and Central Asia, where the iwan became such an important architectural feature. Some large halls at Dura Europos in Mesopotamia, which have been tentatively dated to the 2nd century BC, have been cited as the earliest examples of the form (Downey), but these qualify only if the definition is extended to include a unit whose opening to the outside is significantly narrower than the full width of the room. The first unquestionable iwans occur in private houses that were excavated at

BIBLIOGRAPHY
Imperial Japan: The Art of the Meiji Era (1868–1912) (exh. cat. by F. Baekeland, Ithaca, NY, Cornell U., Johnson Mus. A., 1980)
K. Korezawa, ed.: 'Edo jidai no sho' [Calligraphy of the Edo period], *Nihon no Bijutsu*, 184 (1981) [whole issue]
S. Komatsu: *Karayō* [Chinese-style calligraphy], Nihon no sho [Japanese calligraphy], xii (Tokyo, 1983)

CECIL H. UYEHARA

Iximché. Site of Pre-Columbian Cakchiquel MAYA fortress capital in the Guatemalan highlands near Lake Atitlán. It flourished during the Post-Classic period (*c.* AD 900–1521) and was captured by the Spanish in 1524. Iximché was visited by John Lloyd Stephens and Frederick Catherwood in 1840 but was otherwise ignored until 1887, when Alfred Maudslay surveyed it and made a plan. Ceramics were studied by Robert Wauchope in the 1940s; excavation and restoration were done by G. F. Guillemín in the 1950s and 1970s, and a small museum (Iximché Archaeol. Mus.) was established in Tecpán near by.

In the Late Post-Classic period (*c.* AD 1200–1521) the Guatemalan highlands were in turmoil as numerous noble families sought to enhance their power. Civic centres were fortified and located or relocated on mountaintops. Architectural embellishment became more restricted and regressed from the grand to the utilitarian, as did sculpture and ceramics. Copper, silver and gold objects were imported from central Mesoamerica. Lineage and inherited rights for civic leaders, priests, craftsmen, merchants and farmers became extremely structured. The Cakchiquel rebelled against the Quiché Maya of Utatlán *c.* AD 1486 to establish a city state of their own at Iximché. Two ruling lineages maintained a treaty of friendship with the Aztecs but paid tribute to Motecuhzuma II. Although the present ruins are of the Post-Classic city, there is also evidence of Toltec influence from *c.* AD 800.

Iximché was protected by deep ravines on three sides and by dry moats, and the city centre comprised four large courtyards and two smaller ones. Natural features were levelled into terracing to accommodate the plazas and platforms. To serve the two lineages there were duplicate sets of palaces ballcourts, temples and other structures. The residential area extended far beyond the ravines. Although architecturally undistinguished and producing no outstanding works of art, Iximché is typical of Late Post-Classic Highland Maya fortress sites. Its structures and platforms show strong Central Highland influence, hastily constructed with little regard for traditional Maya styles of the Early Post-Classic period (*c.* AD 900–*c.* 1200). Emphasizing the *tablero* (*see* TALUD-TABLERO), buildings and platforms feature steep profiles reminiscent of Classic period construction at MONTE ALBÁN. Buildings, plaza walls and platforms of Court A and Court C were made with stone and mortar, plastered and painted and renewed on the death of each ruler. Thus Court A has three superimpositions of temples and other buildings. Court B and Court D were also compounds for élite citizens. Temple 2 in Court A has badly deteriorated wall paintings depicting subjects in a style similar to Mixtec codices (*see* MESOAMERICA, PRE-COLUMBIAN, §V). Several other structures also have traces of wall paintings. Sculpture was rare, but there were small objects of jade and obsidian and

offerings of obsidian knives and decapitated heads, emphasizing the importance of war and sacrifice. One such offertory contained 48 human skulls. Stephens reported two badly worn sculptures in 1840, now lost, and one sculpted boulder similar to those at KAMINALJUYÚ was later found.

Most burials were beneath buildings. One grave contained the body of an élite person wearing a gold crown, gold beads and a carved bone bracelet, stylistically reminiscent of the ornaments from Tomb 7 at Monte Albán. Also accompanying the burial were copper, jade, turquoise and carved shell objects and the skeletons of three, presumably sacrificed, individuals (Guatemala City, Mus. N. Arqueol. & Etnol.). This is the largest cache of gold ever found in the Maya area except for that from the Sacred Cenote at CHICHÉN ITZÁ. Temple 2 and other structures also contained large numbers of ceramic incense burners, cinnamon-coloured cups and white-on-red vessels, all typical of the Late Post-Classic Maya highlands and confirming highland Guatemala's position as an intermediary between Mesoamerica and Central American cultures.

For discussion of individual art forms in a wider context *see* PRE-COLUMBIAN MESOAMERICA.

BIBLIOGRAPHY
G. F. Guillemín: 'The Ancient Cakchiquel Capital of Iximché', *Expedition*, ix/2 (1967), pp. 22–35
M. P. Weaver: *The Aztecs, Maya and their Predecessors: Archaeology of Mesoamerica* (New York, 1972, rev. 2/1981)
C. B. Hunter: *A Guide to Ancient Maya Ruins* (Norman, 1974, rev. 2/1986), pp. 208–14
G. F. Guillemín: 'Urbanism and Hierarchy at Iximché', *Social Process in Maya Prehistory: Studies in Memory of Sir Eric Thompson*, ed. N. Hammond (London, 1977), pp. 227–64
J. Kelly: *The Complete Visitor's Guide to Mesoamerican Ruins* (Norman, 1982), pp. 403–5

DAVID M. JONES

Ixnard [Dixnard], Pierre-Michel [Michel, Pierre] d' (*b* Nîmes, 22 Nov 1723; *d* Strasbourg, 20 Aug 1795). French architect, active in Germany. He was originally called Pierre Michel and was the son of Jean Michel, a joiner in Nîmes. He followed his father's trade and in 1743 entered the guild of joiners in Nîmes. In 1751 he married Thérèse Isnard and set up in the village of Cadenet, south-west of Avignon, as a joiner; from 1754 he also called himself an architect. In 1755 he left Cadenet; he appears to have been working on an architectural project in 1758 in Paris. In the autumn of 1763 he travelled to Stuttgart to work as assistant to the stage designer Giovanni Niccolò Servandoni; he helped with drawings and the making of scenery for the celebrations of the birthday of Charles Eugene, Duke of Württemberg, the following February.

From March 1764 Pierre Michel assumed the striking aristocratic-sounding surname of d'Ixnard (the 'x' being, apparently, silent). He had become aware that his lack of formal education and his previous, rather lowly occupation attracted little attention in southern Germany. He passed himself off as a university-trained architect; he used the most recently published Neo-classical engravings by François de Neufforge and Jean-Charles Delafosse as patterns and was also familiar with the working practices of the French building trade. The beautifully finished drawings that he always had prepared by architectural draughtsmen made a particular impression in Germany. Moreover, thanks to his practical experience of the building trade, he could assess craftsmen's work and was himself industrious and adaptable. D'Ixnard thus embarked on a career as an architect in southern Germany—something he could never have done in France.

From May 1764 d'Ixnard was employed by Prince Joseph Wilhelm of Hohenzollern-Hechingen (1717–98): he remodelled some interiors (destr.) in the Schloss von Hechingen, south of Stuttgart, and designed a scheme, which was not carried out, for the reconstruction of the east wing of the castle. From 1765 he made modifications to Graf Königsegg-Aulendorf's hunting-lodge in the Königsegg forest in Swabia; the most striking feature is the staircase, from which large free-standing pairs of columns give on to the interior of the building. D'Ixnard constructed a similar staircase at the Palais Sickingen in Freiburg im Breisgau (from 1769), the interior of which was destroyed in 1944, and designed numerous interiors (from 1773) for the castle of the Teutonic Order in Ellingen, Franconia. Such minor commissions were sufficient to qualify d'Ixnard to be put in charge of the rebuilding of the Benedictine monastery and the abbey church of St Blasius in St Blasien, Waldshut (see fig.). The church is the first Neo-classical building in southern Germany; d'Ixnard's plans (Strasbourg, Archvs Mun.) show a rotunda, freely based on the Roman Pantheon. An indirectly lit dome, like that of the Dôme des Invalides in Paris, is supported by free-standing columns, while the extended choir is similarly enclosed by free-standing columns, perhaps inspired by the chapel at the château of Versailles. The façade consists of a portico flanked by two square towers. Building began in 1772, but despite modifications to the ambitious design of the dome, carried out for d'Ixnard in Paris, he had overreached himself, and in 1774 his contract was cancelled. Nicolas de Pigage from Mannheim was called on to complete the structure; nevertheless, the concept of the existing building is d'Ixnard's. The austere juxtaposition of simple volumes and the severity and sobriety of all the forms make this remote building an impressive example of Neo-classicism in southern Germany.

From 1773 d'Ixnard designed the abbey church at Buchau in Swabia, where six years earlier he had constructed residential wings for the canonesses. This is lighter and more delicate in concept. The narrow, rectangular interior is brightly illuminated on all sides with rectangular openings to the galleries at the sides and the chancel in the front. Against this clear architecture the numerous decorative motifs, which were again derived from designs by Neufforge and Delafosse, are a distinct contrast. D'Ixnard's biggest commission was the construction of a new palace (from 1777) in Koblenz, Germany, for the Electors of Trier. He planned a U-shaped layout, with a square *corps de logis* and contrasting side pavilions. A giant order of columns and pilasters and a domed roof over the central building strengthen the imposing effect. However, once again d'Ixnard's ambitions exceeded his abilities.

Pierre-Michel d'Ixnard: interior of the abbey church of St Blasius, St Blasien, begun 1772

Although the foundations were begun in 1778, he had not yet completed his plans. A supervisory committee that included the Trier court architect Johannes Seiz, a pupil of Balthasar Neumann, criticized d'Ixnard's scheme. In June 1779 he therefore sent all his drawings for assessment to the Académie Royale d'Architecture in Paris. Its findings in part endorsed the criticisms and also objected to the lack of 'purity' and 'nobility of style' in d'Ixnard's designs. In the autumn of 1779 the architect Antoine-François Peyre drew up the new and much reduced scheme from which the palace was constructed.

At the end of 1779 d'Ixnard was discharged from Koblenz and settled in Strasbourg. There he erected several civic buildings, among them Zum Spiegel (1782–5), the guildhall of the merchants' guild. He also designed the church (1780–83) in Hechingen, where he had begun his career; the library of the Collège Royal (1785–7) in Colmar; and the parish church (1790–91) in Epfig. During this late phase of his career d'Ixnard compiled two collections of his drawings for buildings: one consists of 102 drawings (Stuttgart, Württemberg. Landesmus.); the other, of 34 engraved plates, was published as *Recueil d'architecture* (Strasbourg, 1791).

D'Ixnard's buildings are not a transfer of French architecture to Germany. The gravity and severity of the individual elements of his buildings and their combinations would not have been possible in France in the 1760s and 1770s. The similarities are more to the *goût grec* prevalent in French decorative art and to the publications of Neufforge and Delafosse. However, working in small, remote German principalities, d'Ixnard was able to erect a number of buildings that are impressive by virtue of their plastic strength and the impact of their contrasting forms.

BIBLIOGRAPHY

L. Schmieder: *Das Benediktinerkloster St. Blasien: Eine baugeschichtliche Studie* (Augsburg, 1929)

L.-L. Vossnack: *Pierre Michel d'Ixnard, 1723–1795* (Remscheid, 1938)

H. A. Klaiber: 'Der Stuttgarter Architektur-Sammelband von Pierre Michel Dixnard', *Jb. Staatl. Kstsamml. Baden-Württemberg*, vi (1969), pp. 161–8

H. Heidegger and H. Ott, eds: *St. Blasien: Festschrift aus Anlass des 200 jährigen Bestehens der Kloster- und Pfarrkirche* (Munich and Zurich, 1983), pp. 195–291

E. Franz: *Pierre Michel d'Ixnard, 1723–1795: Leben und Werk* (Weissenhorn, 1985)

W. Schöller: 'Pierre-Michel d'Ixnard, Antoine-François Peyre und der Bau des Koblenzer Residenz-schlosses. Neue Forschungen', *Wallraf-Richartz-Jb.*, liii (1992), pp. 155-75

ERICH FRANZ

Ixtlán del Río. Site in Narayit state, Mexico. The term is also used for an associated regional style of pottery and figurines. The site has an architectural complex that dates largely from the Early Post-Classic period (*c.* AD 900–*c.* 1200), while the Narayit style is an earlier phenomenon, spanning the Middle and Late Pre-Classic periods (*c.* 1000 BC–*c.* AD 250). Quantities of chemical turquoise found at Ixtlán del Río and in its vicinity indicate that the region played an important role in long-distance trade. The site is now a national park.

The Pre-Classic period ceramics, and group and architectural figurines, are found over a wide area of Nayarit and adjacent sections of the state of Jalisco, but the main production centre may have been in the vicinity of Ixtlán del Río. The figurines are truly ethnographic documents, nearly always polychrome and almost 'baroque' in the amount of detail used. This attention to detail provides a wealth of information on costume, ornamentation, personal artefacts, economic activities and architecture. Some are clearly portraits, and again great attention is paid to such details as facial expressions and hand gestures. Warriors and group activity scenes are the best-known types. The group scenes often have architectural settings, ranging from individual houses on platforms to entire villages. One spectacular group scene in a modified Ixtlán style represents a ball-game in progress (Mexico City, Museo Diego Rivera de Anahuacalli); other scenes include festivals, processions, dances and combat.

Although the Early Post-Classic architectural complex has never been fully described, an account of the site was published by Edward Gifford in 1950. The central section is composed of about 15 large mounds and 12 smaller ones. The major mounds, which have been excavated and restored, are arranged into groups forming rectangular or square courts, each enclosing a patio surrounded by banquettes. The rectangular platforms have aprons facing the patios, and narrow, rectangular rooms with entries defined by columns are set towards the back of each. There was also a circular structure constructed from a rubble core with a fine stone veneer built over an earlier structure of the same format. It is connected to one of the rectangular platforms by a paved walkway, which may have been the floor of a ballcourt. At least three stairways led to the summit. Examples of architectural sculpture recovered from the monument are displayed in Tepic (Mus. Reg. Antropol. & Hist.). Prototypes of such circular platforms are found in the Teuchitlán–Tequila region of Jalisco, where they are associated with remains of the Classic period (*c.* AD 250–*c.* 900). They are thought to have been dedicated to Quetzalcóatl, especially in his manifestation as the wind god Ehecatl. Orientation to the four cardinal points is considered a major characteristic of the symbolism both of Ehecatl and of these structures. Other circular platforms of the Ixtlán style are found at Huitzilapa in Jalisco and Huajimíc in Nayarit.

BIBLIOGRAPHY

E. Gifford: 'Surface Archaeology of Ixtlan del Rio, Nayarit', *U. CA Pubns Amer. Archaeol. & Ethnol.*, xliii/2 (1950), pp. 183–302

I. Marquina: *Architectura prehispánica* (Mexico City, 1950, 2/1964/*R* 1981)

H. von Winning and O. Hammer: *Anecdotal Sculpture of Ancient West Mexico* (Los Angeles, 1972)

H. von Winning: *The Shaft Tomb Figures of West Mexico*, Southwest Museum Papers, xxiv (Los Angeles, 1974)

PHIL C. WEIGAND

Ixtolinque, Pedro Patiño. *See* PATIÑO IXTOLINQUE, PEDRO.

İyem, Nuri (*b* Istanbul, 10 March 1915). Turkish painter. He studied at the Fine Arts Academy in Istanbul where he was taught by the painters Ibrahim Çallı, Nazmi Ziya Güran and Hikmet Onat (1886–1977), and later by Léopold Lévy (1882–1966), becoming the first graduate of higher studies at the Academy in 1944. In 1941 he formed the New Group (Yeniler Grubu) to promote new ideas in painting and organized the first exhibition of this group under the title *Harbour Painters* (Liman Resim Sergisi). This exhibition led to a conflict with the doctrines of the Academy. İyem searched for a style relevant to life in Turkey in his figurative paintings, and he was inspired by social realism, although from *c.* 1955 he showed an interest in abstraction. He defended non-figurative art in his writings until 1965, after which he returned to the manner of his earlier figurative works, depicting the simple life of villagers. His work has been included in exhibitions in Europe, the USA and South America, and in Turkey at the Maya Gallery, Istanbul (1953); the Akdenız Art Gallery, Ankara (1978); the Baraz Gallery, Istanbul (1978); the Kile Art Gallery, Bebek (1985); and at Tüyap, Istanbul (1986).

BIBLIOGRAPHY
S. Tansuğ: *Çağdaş Türk sanatı* [Contemporary Turkish art] (Istanbul, 1986), pp. 227–8, 246, 251, *passim*
International Istanbul Contemporary Art Exhibitions (exh. cat., Istanbul, Hagia Eirene; Istanbul, Hagia Sophia Mus.,; Istanbul, Mil. Mus.; Istanbul, Mimar Sinan U., Mus. Ptg & Sculp.; 1987) [Turk. and Eng. texts]
G. Renda and others: *A History of Turkish Painting* (Geneva, Seattle and London, 1988), pp. 256, 282, 336, *passim*

☐

Iza, Washington (*b* Quito, 1947). Ecuadorean painter and engraver. He studied at the fine arts faculty of the Universidad Central de Quito. Together with José Unda (*b* 1948), Ramiro Jácome and Nelson Román (*b* 1945) he was a member of the group Los Cuatro Mosqueteros, which set up its own 'anti-Salon' in Guayaquil (1968) in opposition to the official Salon. In the early 1970s he exhibited work in a geometric style influenced by Op art, but he later revolutionized Ecuadorean art through the coarse realism and critical attitude of his more figurative work. His ironic aesthetic of ugliness dwelt principally on the human figure; although he was at first preoccupied with solitude and helplessness, in his later work he moved towards a magical neo-figurative style, as in *The Bath* (1982; Horacio Soler priv. col.). As a result of his involvement with the research group Piru, Iza was influenced by Pre-Columbian art in his choice of colours and motifs, and this led to a period of fantastic realism, sustained by superb draughtsmanship. The influence of José Luis Cuevas was also important for Iza, above all in his response to his environment in a country where ugliness was inextricably linked to modernization.

BIBLIOGRAPHY
H. Rodríguez Castelo: 'Iza', *Rev. Diners*, 24 (1984), pp. 42–5

CECILIA SUÁREZ

Izaguirre, Leandro (*b* Mexico City, 1867; *d* Mexico City, 1941). Mexican painter. He entered the Academia de San Carlos in Mexico City in 1884. After studying with Santiago Rebull and José Salomé Pina, he soon devoted himself to the painting of historical subjects favoured by liberal critics in an attempt to create a Mexican school of painting, as in *Columbus at Rábida* and the *Founding of Tenochtitlán* (both Mexico City, Mus. Pal. B.A.). The highest recognition he received was for a painting of greater breadth and aspiration, for which he was awarded a medal when it was exhibited in Philadelphia in 1893: the *Torture of Cuauhtémoc* (1892; Mexico City, Mus. Pal. B.A.) in which, with

a sort of academic realism, the dignity of the last Aztec emperor is portrayed in a sordid setting, contrasted with the suffering of the king of Tlacopan and the cold indifference of the conquistadors. He was a professor at the Academia, had work commissioned in Europe (1904–6) and worked as an illustrator for the magazine *Mundo ilustrado*.

BIBLIOGRAPHY
J. Fernández: *Arte moderno y contemporáneo de México* (Mexico City, 1952)
B. Espejo: *Historia de la pintura mexicana*, iii (Mexico City, 1989)

JORGE ALBERTO MANRIQUE

Izapa. Site of Pre-Columbian Highland Maya culture in Chiapas, Mexico. It is notable for its Late Pre-Classic period (*c.* 300 BC–*c.* AD 250) sculpture. The term Izapan is also more broadly applied to an important regional art style (see below). The visible ruins of Izapa cover *c.* 2 sq. km on the west margin of the River Izapa, in the southernmost district of Chiapas on the Mexico–Guatemala border, 32 km from the Pacific Ocean. The ruins were first reported to the Mexican Instituto Nacional de Antropología e Historia in 1935 and 1936 by José Coffin, and details about the area and some of the sculptures began to be published soon after (e.g. Culebro, 1939; Stirling, 1943; Orellana Tapia, 1952). Phillip Drucker of the Smithsonian Institution made a provisional map and excavated 12 trenches at Izapa as part of his Pacific Coast survey, and a deep deposit of Late Pre-Classic refuse was found at the site by Gareth Lowe in 1956. Archaeologists working under the auspices of the Brigham Young University New World Archaeological Foundation began intensive work at the site in 1961 and documented more than 50 carved monuments (Lowe, Lee jr and Martínez Espinosa, 1982).

The monuments were set up within numerous courtyards formed by ceremonial pyramidal platforms of earth faced with river cobbles. Their formal and iconographic features relate them to similar but distinctive features in the earlier OLMEC art of the Early Pre-Classic (*c.* 2000–*c.* 1000 BC) and Middle Pre-Classic (*c.* 1000–*c.* 300 BC) periods and to Classic-period (*c.* AD 250–*c.* 900) Maya art (*see also* MESOAMERICA, PRE-COLUMBIAN, §II, 2(i) and MAYA, §2). The stylistic term Izapan is used to describe the stone monuments of Izapa, ABAJ TAKALIK, KAMINALJUYÚ and other sites in the Chiapas–Guatemala highlands and the Pacific slope, even though the many variations of the style are not all found at Izapa. The sculptures at Izapa itself represent only the earliest phase (*c.* 300–*c.*50 BC) of a long sculptural tradition in this area. Tatiana Proskouriakoff was the first to suggest that the style was related to both Olmec and Maya art and probably transitional between the two. She also saw resemblances to the art of MONTE ALBÁN. George Kubler, Gareth Lowe and S. W. Miles observed connections between Izapa and Kaminaljuyú, and Michael Coe postulated connections between Olmec, Izapan and Maya cultures. Miles correlated the Izapan style monuments with the chronological framework of Highland ceramic phases, and detailed iconographic and formal analyses of the sculptures at Izapa itself have been done by Miles, Jacinto Quirarte and Garth Norman.

Mythic events dominate the thematic content of the art of Izapa: deities, supernatural beings and their human impersonators and worshippers are the primary themes in stelae, potbellied figures, tenoned silhouette carvings and effigy mushroom stones. The artists relied alternately on figuration and abstraction, sometimes using both approaches in the same image. Figurative solutions range from a stylized representation of a compound creature, such as the hovering winged figure of Stele 25, to realistic portrayals of animals, such as the crocodile with foliage growing from its tail on the same stele. Abstract elements are used to represent similar or matching compound creatures above and below the narrative scenes in most Izapa stelae. The arrangement of figures within primarily vertical formats in Izapan-style art follows a similar unpredictable alternation between symmetry and asymmetry. While some themes may be presented in bilateral fashion, most are presented asymmetrically. Small human and large divine and supernatural figures do not balance each other in established patterns. Each theme appears to dictate the manner of its presentation, with motifs moving freely between terrestrial and celestial bands into and out of narrative scenes. There is no clear distinction between narrative scenes and their borders. While some of the compound creatures may frame the scenes, they do not necessarily perform a secondary function either visually or thematically.

Although Izapan style images at first appear complex, neither the repertory of elements, motifs and themes nor their representation, is extensive. The predominantly curvilinear aspects of Izapan-style art give it a dynamic appearance (see fig.), but the figures and objects are precisely defined according to established pictorial conventions. The contours of all elements and motifs define both shape and volume. Inner fillets are rarely used to enhance the surfaces of the relief sculptures. Most early pieces seem to be primarily a series of positive and negative spaces in tension with one another. The area around and behind each object is given sufficient importance to ensure that the figures (the positive areas) do not become the central issue, and that negative areas are never simply background.

There are few formal similarities between the sculptures of the Olmec, Maya and Izapa areas. The relationship with Olmec art lies in the placement of the Izapan monuments within architectural contexts, and that with Maya art in the use of flat altar-like stones placed in front of some of the stelae. The few known Olmec stelae (such as Stele 2 and Stele 3 at LA VENTA, Tabasco) demonstrate a different approach to the representation of figures in space, with little physical and visual differentiation between figure and ground. The Olmec sculptor consistently placed all figures within the frontal plane, whereas the Izapa sculptor created different relief surfaces. The sophisticated use of overlapping, diminution of size and the placement of figures to establish a legible spatial framework, as in Izapa Stele 21, is lacking in both Olmec and Maya pieces. In Maya art the arrangement and placement of figures, as well as their poses and postures, are straightforward and predictable. With few exceptions, Maya images are symmetrically arranged. In contrast, the lateral displacement of images and glyphs, and the subtleties between positive and negative areas are more sophisticated than in Izapan art.

Izapa, Stele 5, showing a tree with human and supernatural beings framed by sky and water symbols, andesite, max. 1.58×1.60 m, c. 300 BC–c. AD 250

The compound creatures represented on Izapan stelae are formed from various combinations of bird, crocodile, jaguar and serpent features. A scroll-eyed bodiless head, part jaguar, part serpent, may represent a water deity. The use of the open jaw of a feline–serpent creature as a frame for the narrative programmes of Izapan stelae is related to Altar 4, Altar 5 and others at Olmec La Venta. The abstract configuration of the Izapa examples, however, is unique and reflects Izapan sculptors' propensity to abbreviate the rather complicated beings into a series of elements and signs. The long-lipped saurian heads are probably ancestral to similar heads found in Maya art. The relationship of these heads with downward-flying figures produced an abbreviated earth–sky symbol—the diagonal and crossed bands—used extensively in Maya hieroglyphs. Long-lipped heads with U-shaped elements and diagonal bands are the prototype for the later terrestrial 'dragon' heads found throughout Mesoamerica. The top- and base-line designs (composed of U-shapes, double opposed diagonal bands, J-forms, crenellated diagonal bands, scrolled collars, bodies of water and others at the bottom) represent the sky and earth as places where humans and deities act. A constantly changing environment is acknowledged by the variety of such designs, particularly of the earth design, in which variable aspects are demonstrated by the numerous stylized representations of the markings on compound reptilian and saurian bodies: sometimes the surface is a body of water with fishes swimming in it, as in Izapa Stele 1; at other times its fertile aspects are represented by terrestrial 'dragon' heads and crocodiles, as in Izapa Stele 2 and Stele 25. The double opposed diagonals and U-shaped elements found in the 'sky' bands of many Izapan stelae were later incorporated into costume details and glyphic notations in the Maya and Zapotec areas.

BIBLIOGRAPHY

C. A. Culebro: *Chiapas prehistórica: Su arqueología* (Huixtla, Chiapas, 1939)

I. Marquina: *Atlas arqueológico de la Republica Mexicana* (Mexico City, 1939)

M. W. Stirling: 'Some Monuments of Southern Mexico', *Bureau Amer. Ethnol. Bull.*, cxxxviii (1943) [whole issue]

P. Drucker: *Preliminary Notes on an Archaeological Survey of the Chiapas Coast* (New Orleans, 1948)

T. Proskouriakoff: *A Study of Maya Sculpture*, Carnegie Institution Publication, dxciii (Washington, DC, 1950)

R. Orellana Tapia: 'Zona arqueológica de Izapa', *Tlatoani*, i (1952), pp. 17–25

G. Lowe: *Archaeological Exploration of the Upper Grijalva River, Chiapas, Mexico*, Papers of the New World Archaeological Foundation, ii (Orinda, 1959)

G. Kubler: *The Art and Architecture of Ancient America*, Pelican Hist. A. (Harmondsworth, 1962, rev. 3/1984)

M. D. Coe: 'The Olmec Style and its Distribution', *Hb. Mid. Amer. Ind.*, iii (1965), pp. 739–75

G. Lowe: 'Desarollo y función del incensario en Izapa', *Estud. Cult. Maya*, ii (1965), pp. 185–96

S. W. Miles: 'Sculpture of the Guatemala–Chiapas Highlands and Pacific Slopes, and Associated Hieroglyphs', *Hb. Mid. Amer. Ind.*, ii (1965), pp. 237–75

M. D. Coe: *America's First Civilization* (New York, 1968)

G. Norman: *Izapa Sculpture*, 2 vols, Papers of the New World Archaeological Foundation, xxx (Provo, 1973–6)

J. Quirarte: *Izapan-style Art: A Study of its Form and Meaning*, Studies in Pre-Columbian Art and Archaeology, x (Washington, DC, 1973)

——: 'Early Art Styles of Mesoamerica and Early Classic Maya Art', *The Origins of Maya Civilization*, ed. R. E. W. Adams (Albuquerque, 1977), pp. 249–83

——: 'Tricephalic Units in Olmec, Izapan-style and Maya Art', *The Olmec and their Neighbors: Essays in Memory of Matthew W. Stirling* (Washington, DC, 1981)

G. Lowe, T. A. Lee jr and E. Martínez Espinosa: *Izapa: An Introduction to the Ruins and Monuments*, Papers of the New World Archaeological Foundation, xxxi (Provo, 1982)

JACINTO QUIRARTE

Izdebsky, Vladimir (Alekseyevich) (*b* Odessa, 1882; *d* New York, 1965). Ukrainian sculptor and impresario. After studying at the Art School in Odessa from 1897 to 1904, he lived in Germany (until 1909) where he was associated with Vladimir Bekhteyev (1878–1971), Vasily Kandinsky, Gabriele Münter and Alexei Jawlenski and was a founder-member of the Neue Künstlervereinigung München in 1909. Through his friends Izdebsky became especially interested in the latest Western trends in art, which he discussed in an essay for the Kiev journal *Iskusstvo i pechatnoye delo* ('Art and printing', 1910, nos 2–3). In 1908 he contributed sculptures to the 19th exhibition of the Association of South Russian Artists in Odessa.

One result of Izdebsky's exposure to the new movements in Munich was his decision to organize the grandiose *Internatsionnal'naya vystavka kartin, skulptury, gravyury i risunkov* ('International exhibition of paintings, sculpture, engraving and drawings'; often called the Izdebsky Salon), shown in 1909 in Odessa and subsequently in Kiev and St Petersburg. This was the largest exhibition of its kind in Russia (over 650 works) and included the work of many French, German and Italian artists, such as Giacomo Balla, Georges Braque, Maurice Denis, Albert Gleizes, Marie Laurencin, Henri Le Fauconnier, Henri Matisse, Jean Metzinger, Henri Rousseau and Paul Signac, as well as young Russian artists such as David Burlyuk and Vladimir Burlyuk, Alexandra Exter, Vasily Kandinsky, Mikhail Larionov, Il'ya Mashkov and Mikhail Matyushin. In January 1911 Izdebsky opened a second, more modest Salon,

consisting almost exclusively of contemporary Russian art. Naturally, Izdebsky used both opportunities to display his own sculpture (plaster and clay portraits and allegorical subjects much indebted to Rodin), but he never received wide acclaim either as an impresario or as an artist. Shortly after his second Salon Izdebsky emigrated to France, where he lived until moving to New York in 1930. During the 1930s to 1950s he continued to sculpt and also to write poetry.

BIBLIOGRAPHY

Katalog Internatsional'noy vystavki kartin, skulptury, gravyury i risunkov 1909–1910 [Catalogue of the international exhibition of paintings, sculpture, engraving and drawings, 1909–1910] (exh. cat., intro. V. Izdebsky; Odessa, 1909)

Salon 2: Mezhdunarodnaya khudozhestvennaya vystavka [Salon 2: international art exhibition] (exh. cat., intro. V. Izdebsky; Odessa, 1910)

D. Gordon: *Modern Art Exhibitions, 1900–1916*, ii (Munich, 1974)

JOHN E. BOWLT

Izis [Bidermanas, Izis (Isracl; Israëlis)] (*b* Marijampole, Lithuania, 17 Jan 1911; *d* Paris, 16 May 1980). French photographer of Lithuanian birth. He was apprenticed to a portrait photographer at the age of 13, learning techniques of soft focus and retouching against which he later rebelled as untruthful. He emigrated to Paris in 1930 and in 1934 opened a studio where he produced portraits. During World War II he was a member of the Resistance, photographing his comrades and working as a photo researcher. After the war he became a French citizen (1946) and worked as a freelance photographer before joining the staff of *Paris-Match* in 1949. He remained with the magazine for 20 years, specializing in photographs of painters, poets and writers. He also photographed Paris and the life within it, and throughout his life he retained a strong fascination for the city. On leaving *Paris-Match* in 1969 he worked as a freelance photographer until his death.

Izis was dismissive of methods and devices, such as light meters and flash-guns, that he thought would distract from his subject. He was not prolific; often he would wait a considerable time to capture the right image. A large proportion of his work appeared in a series of books during the 1950s and 1960s, most of them taking their inspiration from Paris. These include *Paris des rêves* (Paris, 1950), with a foreword by Jean Cocteau and texts by Blaise Cendrars, Paul Eluard, André Breton, Henry Miller and others, and *Paris des poètes* (Paris, 1967), with texts by Louis Aragon, Jacques Prévert, Eugène Ionesco and other writers. There were also books centred on places other than Paris, such as *Israël* (Paris, 1956), with a foreword by André Malraux and frontispiece and cover by Marc Chagall, and *Charmes de Londres* (Paris, 1952) with a text by Prévert.

PHOTOGRAPHIC PUBLICATIONS

Grand Bal du printemps, text by J. Prévert (Paris, 1951)
Paradis terrestre, text by Colette (Paris, 1953)
Le Cirque d'Izis, text by J. Prévert (Paris, 1965)
Le Monde de Chagall, text by R. McMullen (Paris, 1969)

BIBLIOGRAPHY

Contemp. Phots
Other Eyes (exh. cat. by P. Turner, London, Hayward Gal., 1976)
International Center of Photography: Encyclopedia of Photography (New York, 1984)

Izmir. *See* SMYRNA.

Iznik [formerly Nicaea; Nikaia]. Turkish town in the eastern bay of Lake Iznik (anc. Ascania), with important Byzantine and early Ottoman remains. The earliest settlements on the site date to the 1st millennium BC. In 316 BC Antigonos Monophthalmos, a general of Alexander the Great, expanded the existing town and called it Antigonia. It was conquered by Lysimachos in 301 BC and renamed Nicaea after his wife. In 281 BC it came under the rulers of Bithynia, gaining importance before falling to Roman domination in 72 BC. In the 3rd and 4th centuries AD it thrived as the site of an imperial treasury and a major military base on the strategic road linking the eastern provinces of the Roman Empire to Italy and the Rhine frontier. Byzantine rule lasted until 1081 when the city was captured by Sulayman and a group of Seljuk Turks and established as capital of the first Turkish state in Asia Minor. In 1097 it was reconquered for the Byzantine empire by the forces of the First Crusade. Between 1204 and 1261 it served as the residence of the Byzantine government in exile and the seat of the patriarch. It remained part of the reconstituted Byzantine empire until 1331, when it was taken by the Ottoman sultan Orhan (*reg* 1324–60). In 1402 it was sacked by the Tatar Mongols, but it was eventually returned to Ottoman rule, enjoying a period of renewed prosperity in the 16th and 17th centuries. After this period it fell into decline, until by the 20th century it had become a small village. Many of its ancient buildings were destroyed in 1922, when the Greeks were expelled by the Turks. Surviving monuments have suffered further damage as a result of Iznik's economic development since the 1960s.

1. BEFORE 1331. The city built by Lysimachos had a square plan (700 m sq.) with a grid pattern of streets. This was retained when Hadrian lavishly rebuilt Nicaea after its destruction by earthquake in AD 120. Although a few traces have survived of the street plan and monumental public buildings, the major monument of the Roman period is the well-preserved city walls. Begun by Hadrian, they were completed *c.* 268–9 and kept in continuous repair up to the 14th century. Repairs and substantial rebuildings in the 8th, 9th, 13th and 14th centuries altered their appearance, but they remained essentially on their 3rd-century plan, 5 km in length, enclosing a rectangular site. Nicaea was an important ecclesiastical centre and in 325 was chosen by Constantine the Great as the site of the First Ecumenical Council, which condemned Arianism and issued the Nicene Creed. From 378 the city was the seat of the metropolitan of Bithynia. At the same time, however, it apparently suffered some decline following earthquakes in 363 and 368 and the growth of Constantinople.

In the 6th century Justinian I restored several buildings, including a palace, and built a number of churches and monasteries. During the 7th and 8th centuries Nicaea suffered with other cities the effects of the empire's economic collapse and Arab invasion, but its walls guaranteed it a major military role. In 787 the Seventh Ecumenical Council was summoned to the city by Eirene and brought to an end the first period of the iconoclastic controversy (726–87). Two important churches have survived as ruins in the city. Hagia Sophia, which was probably

the cathedral and the site of the Council of 787, lies in the centre of Nicaea. It is an aisled basilica with piers, largely rebuilt following the devastating earthquake of 1065 but on the foundations of an earlier church, probably of the 5th or 6th century. Traces of fine marble decoration and fragments of possibly 13th-century wall painting have been preserved.

The second was the monastery church of Hyakinthos, known in modern times as the church of the Dormition. It was destroyed in 1922, and only the lower portions of the walls, part of its *opus sectile* pavement and fragments of its marble decoration remain. However, it was recorded and photographed before World War I. Probably built in the early 8th century (although a date in the late 6th century or 7th cannot be ruled out), it was a very rare example of Byzantine architecture from this period. The church had three apses and a narthex, and a cruciform nave surmounted by a dome resting on four massive piers

Iznik, church of the Dormition, mosaic depicting *Virgin and Child*, mid-9th century AD (destr. 1922)

and separated from the aisles by arcades. It contained an important series of mosaics. In the apse was a *Virgin and Child* standing on a pedestal with three rays descending from the hand of God (see fig.). In the sanctuary vault were four angels, two on either side of the Virgin, dressed in imperial court costume and each bearing a labarum and an orb. These mosaics were mid-9th century copies of those erected before *c*. 730, which had been removed during the iconoclastic period and replaced by non-figural images, including a cross in the apse. The narthex (rebuilt after 1065) was also partly decorated with mosaics. In the lunette above the door leading into the nave was a half-length figure of the *Virgin Orans*; in the summit of the vault of the central bay was an eight-armed cross within a circle, surrounded by four medallions containing the busts of *Christ, St John the Baptist, Joachim* and *Anna*. In the four pendentives of the vault were the *Evangelists* seated at their desks. Above the door leading into the south aisle was a standing *Virgin and Child* flanked by an emperor and an imperial official; the latter was presumably the monastery's patron and rebuilder after 1065, the eunuch Nikephoros. Two mosaic panels on the nave piers, one showing *Christ Antiphonitis* ('the guarantor'), the other the *Virgin Eleousa* ('merciful'), are likely to have been contemporary with the narthex mosaics. Traces of three other 13th-century churches have also been discovered, one of which may have been the church of Hagios Tryphon, known to have been built by Theodoros II Laskaris (*reg* 1254–8; *see* EARLY CHRISTIAN AND BYZANTINE ART, §II, 2(iv)(b)).

BIBLIOGRAPHY

T. Schmit: *Die Koimesis-Kirche von Nikaia* (Berlin, 1927) [important pls]
A. M. Schneider: *Die römischen und byzantinischen Denkmäler von Iznik-Nicaea*, Istanbuler Forschungen, xvi (Berlin, 1943)
C. Mango: 'The Date of the Narthex Mosaics of the Church of the Dormition at Nicaea', *Dumbarton Oaks Pap.*, xiii (1959), pp. 242–52
P. A. Underwood: 'The Evidence of Restorations in the Sanctuary Mosaics of the Church of the Dormition at Nicaea', *Dumbarton Oaks Pap.*, xiii (1959), pp. 235–42
U. Peschlow: 'Neue Beobachtungen zur Architektur und Ausstattung der Koimesiskirche in Iznik', *Istanbul. Mitt.*, xii (1972), pp. 145–87
C. Foss and D. Winfield: *Byzantine Fortifications: An Introduction* (Pretoria, 1986), pp. 79–120
C. Barber: 'The Koimesis Church, Nicaea', *Jb. Österreich. Byz.*, xli (1991), pp. 43–60

MARK WHITTOW

2. 1331 AND AFTER. Taken by the Ottoman sultan Orkhan in 1331, the town became an important centre of early Ottoman architecture and tile and ceramic production. Orkhan converted Hagia Sophia into a mosque and built an adjacent madrasa (1331–4; destr.), the first in the Ottoman empire. The mosque had a five-bay porch in front of two rectangular units and an axial iwan opening on to a domed central hall (*see* ISLAMIC ART, §II, 6(ii)(b)). It is the earliest example of a T-plan mosque, suitable both for prayer and as a convent for itinerant dervishes. The Mosque of Haci Ozbek contains the oldest Ottoman building inscription, dating from 1333. A three-bay porch (destr.) on the west side originally led to the square prayer-hall covered by a dome (inter. diam. 7.9 m) supported on Turkish triangles. In 1334 Orhan founded a small mosque-bath–kitchen complex outside the city walls, 400 m beyond the southern Yenisehir Gate.

The same types of building were constructed in the second half of the 14th century. The Green Mosque (Turk. Yeşil Cami; 1378–92) was built by the architect Haci bin Musa on the orders of the grand vizier Hayreddin Pasha, a member of the Candarli family of statesmen. A three-bay porch leads through a three-bay vestibule to a square prayer-hall covered by a dome (diam. 11 m). The exterior walls are of cut stone; the interior has a marble dado and a richly carved marble mihrab, the earliest of its kind. The brick minaret (rest.) decorated with green- and other-coloured tiles has given the mosque its name. Near by stands the imaret (kitchen) of Nilüfer Hatun (1388), built by Murad I (*reg* 1360–89) in honour of his mother. It repeats the type of plan used in the Mosque of Orkhan for a secular use. The walls are constructed of alternating courses of stone and brick, and tiled domes of different sizes cover the individual units. It has been converted into the Archaeological Museum.

Madrasas, tombs and baths also survive from the early Ottoman period. The madrasa of Süleyman Pasha, son of Orkhan, is the oldest surviving Ottoman madrasa; it already displays the classical form of a closed, domed classroom and domed rooms for students grouped in a U-shape around an arcaded courtyard. Notable tombs include the Kirgizlar Türbe with a conical roof; the Türbe of Sari Saltuk, an open baldacchino on four columns; and the Candarli Türbe (1387) with two domed square halls of unequal size. The Hamams of Murad I and of Haci Hamza are double baths; that of Ismail Bey is smaller but has fine stucco decoration.

Iznik had long produced simple pottery wares, such as the blue-and-black-painted earthenware known as Miletus ware, but some time in the late 15th century potters began to produce blue-and-white ceramics of a technical standard unmatched in the Islamic world since the frit-wares produced at Kashan in the early 13th century (*see* ISLAMIC ART, §V, 3(iv)). Numerous kiln sites have been discovered in the city and its environs. Iznik vessels and tiles (*see* ISLAMIC ART, §V, 4(iii), 5(ii) and figs 177–9, and TILE, colour pl. IX, fig. 1) have a dense fritted body, white slip and transparent glaze. The decorative palette soon evolved to include turquoise, black, grey-green, pale purple and a characteristic tomato red. Motifs were first inspired by Chinese prototypes but soon displayed a distinct repertory of flowers, serrated leaves and stems typical of the Ottoman court style. The finest pieces (*see* CERAMICS, colour pl. IV, fig. 1) were produced in the mid-16th century. Quality declined until the 18th century, when Kütahya replaced Iznik as the main centre of ceramic production.

BIBLIOGRAPHY
Enc. Islam/2
K. Otto-Dorn: *Das islamische Iznik* (Berlin, 1941)
A. Lane: *Later Islamic Pottery* (London, 1957), pp. 40–60
——: 'The Ottoman Pottery of Isnik', *A. Orient.*, ii (1957), pp. 254–81
A. Kuran: *The Mosque in Early Ottoman Architecture* (Chicago, 1968), pp. 17, 21, 34–5, 61–3 and 78–9
O. Aslanapa: 'Pottery and Kilns from the Iznik Excavations', *Forschungen zur Kunst Asiens in Memoriam Kurt Erdmann* (Istanbul, 1969), pp. 140–46
G. Goodwin: *A History of Ottoman Architecture* (London and Baltimore, 1971), pp. 38–9, 44, 71–2
O. Aslanapa: 'Iznik çini fırınları 1985 çalışmaları' [The 1985 season at the Iznik tile kilns], *VIII. kazı sonuçları toplantısı* [Eighth conference on excavation results], ii (Ankara, 1986), pp. 315–34

N. Atasoy and J. Raby: *İznik: The Pottery of Ottoman Turkey* (Istanbul and London, 1989)

ÇİĞDEM KAFESÇİOĞLU

Izquierdo, Francisco Hurtado. *See* HURTADO IZ-QUIERDO, FRANCISCO.

Izquierdo, María (*b* San Juan de los Lagos, Jalisco, 30 Oct ?1906; *d* Mexico City, 3 Dec 1955). Mexican painter and printmaker. She moved to Mexico City to study at the Academia de San Carlos and soon afterwards briefly shared a studio with Rufino Tamayo, who influenced her artistic development and taught her how to use gouache and watercolour. She exhibited in New York in 1929 and later made woodcuts with the Liga de Escritores y Artistas Revolucionarios, an association founded in 1934.

In her paintings Izquierdo embraced popular traditions both in her masterly use of colour and in her tendency towards a naive or primitive style. Her work has a provincial flavour, reflected in her favourite subjects: still-lifes, cupboards, altars, fruit, horses, portraits and the circus, for which she felt a special attraction.

BIBLIOGRAPHY
H. García Rivas: *Pintores mexicanos* (Mexico City, 1965), pp. 220–21
M. Helm: *Modern Mexican Painters* (New York, 1974), pp. 117, 140, 142–6, 148
O. Debroise: *Figuras en el trópico: Plástica mexicana, 1920–1940* (Barcelona, 1984), pp. 153–66

LEONOR MORALES

Izsó, Miklós (*b* Disznóshorvát [now Izsófalva], 9 Sept 1831; *d* Budapest, 29 May 1877). Hungarian sculptor. He fought in the Hungarian revolt against Austrian rule (1848–9) and was forced into hiding. In 1851 he went to Rimaszombat (now Rimavská Sobota, Slovakia), where he became a stone-carver in Antal Jakovctz's workshop, and was acquainted with István Ferenczy, the first significant 19th-century Hungarian sculptor. Between 1853 and 1856 Izsó studied sculpture under Ferenczy and developed his skills at the local art school. In 1856 he moved to Pest (now part of Budapest), where he continued to work as a stone-carver. In the following year he went to Vienna, working in Hans Gasser's workshop and later with Anton Dominik Fernkorn and Johann Meixner (1819–72). He carved in marble the designs of portraits executed by others, for example Ferenczy's portrait of *Ferenc Kazinczy* (Szeghalom, Kazinczy Mem. Mus.) and Gasser's of *Count István Széchenyi* (Nagycenk, Széchenyi Mem. Mus.). In November 1859 he registered at the Akademie der Bildenden Künste, Munich, under the patronage of young Hungarians living in Vienna. He studied there for one and a half years and then returned permanently to Hungary.

Izsó's greatest objective was to protect the Hungarians' national identity, immortalizing their way of life and other characteristics. His work in Munich already showed signs of this, for example *Piping Shepherd* (gypsum, 1860; Sárospatak, Mus. Reformed Ch.) and the very successful *Melancholy Shepherd* (marble, 1861–2; Budapest, N.G.). He continuously produced small-scale genre figures (e.g. *Harvesting Woman*, terracotta, *c.* 1863) and genre scenes (e.g. *Gypsy Laokoon*, terracotta, 1869; both Budapest, N.G.). His *Dancing Peasant* series of fourteen terracotta and one gypsum sculptures (1870–75; all Budapest, N.G.) constituted a rebirth of sculpture after a period characterized by anti-art tendencies. These small-scale figures combine a sense of national identity with forms derived from Hellenistic art. National dress was represented not only for its ethnographic interest but also to emphasize body forms and movement. Izsó also executed *c.* 25 busts of important Hungarian historical, artistic and literary personalities, including a few of his famous contemporaries (e.g. *János Arany*, marble, 1862; Budapest, N.G.). The gypsum bust of the doctor and natural scientist *Balogh Pál Almási* (1864; Budapest, N.G.) is a characteristically forceful example.

An important aspect of Izsó's work was his public sculpture, for example the full-length statue of the linguist *Miklós Révay* (1863–5) for the Hungarian Academy of Sciences (Roosevelt Square, Budapest). On this building he also executed the national coat of arms in the centre of the façade. Although Izsó designed four other public sculptures (portraying Count István Széchenyi, Vitéz Mihály Csokonai, András Dugonics and Sándor Petőfi), only that of Csokonai was realized during his lifetime. This important bronze statue (1867–71; Debrecen, Calvin Square) depicts the great poet of the Hungarian Enlightenment in national dress, a lute in his left hand, with luxuriant vines around his feet; it is notably different from the gypsum maquette (1867; Debrecen, Presbyterian Coll. Eccles Mus.), which captures the poet's fiery spirit. The sculpture of Dugonics (1876) planned for Szeged and that of Petőfi (1882) for Budapest were completed after Izsó's death by his follower Adolf Huszár (1842–85) in both smaller and larger versions.

BIBLIOGRAPHY
T. Szana: *Izsó Miklós élete és munkái* [Miklós Izsó's life and work] (Budapest, 1897)
——: 'Miklós Izsó', *Művészettörténeti Értesítő*, 1–2 (1933), pp. 13–31
A. Weiss: *Izsó Miklós élete és művészete* [Miklós Izsó's life and art] (Budapest, 1939)
G. Soós: *Izsó Miklós levelei* [Miklós Izsó's letters] (Budapest, 1958)
——: *Izsó*, Művészet Kiskönyrtára [Little art library] (Budapest, 1966)
L. Fülep: *Magyar művészet* [Hungarian art] (Budapest, 1971), pp. 63–76, 169–93

S. KONTHA

Izue, Yutaka [Hiroshi; Kan] (*b* Kyoto, 29 Aug 1931). Japanese architect. He graduated from the Civil Engineering Department of Ritsumeikan University, Kyoto, in 1957 and worked for two years at the Engineering Bureau of Kyoto University. From 1959 to 1976 he was a designer for Takenaka Komuten Co. Ltd, one of the largest construction companies in Japan, where he became vice-president. During this period he received training and learnt the essence of traditional Japanese aesthetics from Hiroyuki Iwamoto, Director of the design department and winner of the competition for the National Theatre in Tokyo.

In 1976 Izue established his own office in Osaka and started his career designing houses such as the Benigara Colour House (1977), Marugame, a traditional-style house in a rural setting, with red ochre-coloured walls. In the 1980s he became interested in *sukiya zukuri* ('tea house construction'; *see* JAPAN, §XIV, 2), an eclectic style of traditional Japanese residential architecture in which different materials and styles are combined according to the architect's personal idea of spiritual beauty. The freedom and individuality of modern *sukiya*, developed by Isoya

Yoshida, allowed the architect to incorporate modern materials in traditional design. Izue, who appreciated the beauty to be found in the transparency and reflections of ice, used industrial materials such as aluminium, stainless steel and glass in an austere manner to make a sharp contrast with the surrounding environment. Examples of this work include the Shinsaibashi Tower (1980), Osaka, the Okakei building (1983), Tokyo, and many other housing and hotel projects such as the Hotel Liberty (1985), Osaka, a modernist building with curved walls clad in silvery aluminium.

WRITINGS
'Shadow and Form', *Japan Architect*, 176 (1971), pp. 98–9
BIBLIOGRAPHY
'A Benigara Color House', *Japan Architect*, 248 (1977), pp. 9–22
'Hotel Liberty', *Japan Architect*, 351 (1986), pp. 46–9

TOSHIAKI NAGAYA

Izumo Grand Shrine [Jap.: Izumo Taisha; Kizuki ōyashiro]. Japanese Shinto shrine in Taisha, Hikawa-gun, Shimane Prefecture. Located about 300 km west of Kyoto in a small town on the Sea of Japan, Izumo Grand Shrine is one of Japan's most important Shinto shrines, dedicated, like ISE SHRINE, to the worship of the ancestral *kami* (deity) of the imperial house.

1. HISTORY. Izumo Grand Shrine was founded in ancient times. According to a myth in the *Kojiki* ('Record of ancient matters'; AD 712), when the ancestors of the imperial house descended from heaven and demanded that Ōkuninushi no mikoto (or Ōnamuchi no mikoto), the *kami* who was worshipped at the shrine, should give the country to them, he asked for a splendid palace like the imperial palace as his reward. This is said to be the origin of the *honden* ('main sanctuary') of the shrine. The *Kojiki* also notes that the Izumo region where the Grand Shrine is located was an important area in legends concerning the rise of the imperial house. In AD 765 numerous *shinpu* (fiefs of a shrine) were given by the court, and when priests succeeded to the position of *daiguji* (chief priest of the shrine) it was customary to read a *kan'yogoto* (Shinto prayer) to celebrate the reign of the emperor at court. This is thought to have occurred for the first time in 716. The ceremony took place at this shrine only, because of its particularly high standing.

The *honden* of the shrine has always been known for its size. In a ballad dating from 970 the large wooden structures of the period were mentioned: Izumo Grand Shrine was the largest; the Daibutsuden (Great Buddha Hall) of Tōdaiji in Nara was second largest; and the buildings of the Kyoto imperial court were third. It is recorded that the *honden* collapsed in 1031, 1061, 1109, 1141, 1172 and 1235, perhaps, as legends suggest, because the buildings were too large, but the cause has not been established with certainty. After the 13th century, with the breakdown of the economic system, which supported shrines, the *honden* at Izumo, like those at other shrines, was reduced in size. Legend states that its original height was 96 m; afterwards it was 48 m, then 24 m, until it was reduced to 13.5 m at the end of the 14th century. In 1486 the *honden* was destroyed by fire, and in 1519 the daimyo of this region, Amago, had it rebuilt. He also added Buddhist structures—a three-storey pagoda and Buddhist halls (*Butsudō*)—on the shrine grounds. In 1609 Toyotomi Hideyori (1593–1615), the son of warlord TOYOTOMI HIDEYOSHI, rebuilt the *honden* to a height of 20 m. In 1667, the region's *daimyo*, Matsudaira, obtained the backing of the Edo shogunate in order to restore the *honden*, and it was again rebuilt to a height of 24 m. At the same time, the Buddhist buildings on the shrine grounds were dismantled as the practice of combining Buddhist and Shinto buildings was no longer favoured. The present *honden* (see fig.) dates from the reconstruction of 1744, but some buildings still stand that were reconstructed in 1667. However, the *haiden* ('worship' or 'oratory hall'), which is located in front of the *honden*, was rebuilt in 1953 after its destruction by fire. It is not in a traditional architectural style.

2. ARCHITECTURE AND LAYOUT. A number of wooden buildings stand on a long, narrow area of flat land at Izumo. Near the northern end of this area is the south-facing *honden*, which is enclosed by an interior fence with a two-storey gate on the south side. Smaller *honden* have been built outside the fence, aligned to the east and west. These buildings are devoted to the worship of the two wives of Ōkuninushi no mikoto, and another small sanctuary on the eastern side to the worship of the two goddesses who saved Ōkuninushi. They are surrounded on the east, north and west by an exterior fence; to the south is a *kairō* (roofed, semi-enclosed corridor). The façade of the *honden* has a single-storey gate, outside which to the south is the *haiden*. At each end of the *kairō* stands a long, narrow building, the Jūku sha, which is the lodging for the *kami* of Japan when they gather at the shrine for one month every year. Running from the south side of the *haiden* is a long *sandō* (approach to the shrine) where a *torii* (post-and-lintel gate) has been erected. The environs of the shrine have grown thick with vegetation.

(i) The style of the honden. The present-day *honden* is a square wooden structure (each side 10.9 m). It is one of the largest among Japanese *honden* and is famous as an example of an ancient architectural style called *taisha*

Izumo Grand Shrine, side view of the *honden* ('main sanctuary'), rebuilt 1744

zukuri ('Grand Shrine construction') which has apparently been transmitted unaltered from ancient times.

The arrangement of the nine columns on the building's exterior, in which the vertical and horizontal latticework is omitted every third column, creates a simple, pure form. The wooden floor is raised, and on both sides and at the back thick wooden boards have been inserted between the columns to create a wall. Double hanging doors (*tobira*) have been hung on the right side of the façade, while on the left a *shitomi* (latticed section), open at top and bottom, acts as a window. Inside, at the back on the right, is a *shinza* ('seat of the *kami*') which contains a small sanctuary built for *kami* worship. On the front section of the *shinza* wooden boards form a wall between the columns, and as a result the *shinza* is not directly visible from the *tobira*. The *shinza* faces west, so that worshippers pray to the *kami* from the side rather than from the front of the building. This type of arrangement is seen only in *taisha zukuri* buildings and does not exist in other modes of construction. The column that stands in the centre of the *honden* is a special type called *shinno mihashira* ('a sacred-centre column'). With a diameter of 1.09 m it is bigger than the other columns in the *honden*; the diameter of those on both sides is 0.73 m and those on the façade and rear 0.87 m.

Running round the four sides of the *honden* is a *mawari'en* (verandah) with a width of 2.7 m on three sides and 3.6 m along the façade. There is a covered staircase with 15 steps leading up to the *mawari'en* on the right side of the façade; the front of the building is therefore asymmetrical. A railing is attached to both the *mawari'en* and the steps. The columns are not capped with the complex wooden bracketing system (*kumimono*) that is used in Japanese shrines and temples built after the introduction of Buddhist architecture: this feature was not present in *taisha zukuri*.

The roof of the building is in *kirizuma zukuri* ('gabled-roof construction'); the façade gable is a special characteristic. This type of roof construction is rare among Japanese shrine *honden*. The roof is laid with *hiwadabuki* (Japanese cypress-bark shingles); the ends of the roof elements reach a thickness of 0.91 m, and the entire area measures 584 sq. m. The central column on the façade and the rear has been placed slightly further out than the columns on either side and the tops of the columns are of a form called *munamochi bashira* (column supporting ridge-tree). Buildings constructed in *taisha zukuri*, and Ise Shrine, which is built in *shinmei zukuri*, are the only buildings that have *munamochi bashira*. The line of the roof is gently curved; however, it is thought that in ancient times the roof-line was straight. On the top of the roof ridge near each end are 7.9 m-long *chigi* (forked roof finials) and between them are *katsuogi* (ridge billets). The roof over the steps leading to the *honden* is also gabled; this protects the area from rain.

The exterior of the building is unpainted; the ceiling of the interior is decorated in brilliant colours with an abstract cloud design. The *honden* has generally been left in the ancient style, except that originally the columns would have been placed in holes dug into the ground whereas the columns of the present building rest on stone bases.

(ii) Affiliated buildings. Most of the other buildings associated with the shrine were built during the reconstructions of 1667 and 1744. The two-storey gate, which is located at the front of the *honden*, is called a *rōmon* and is characteristic of both shrines and temples. It is roofed in *irimoya zukuri* ('hip-and-gable construction') and is surrounded by a *mawari'en*. There are four columns on the front (which is 8.5 m wide) and three on the sides (4.8 m deep). Only shrine priests are permitted inside this gate. Flanking the *honden* on each side are three sanctuaries erected to the four female *kami*. The structures are a variation on *taisha zukuri*, having steps in the centre rather than on the right side. The buildings are 3.64 m sq. The single-storey gate (8.7×5.0 m) in front of the *rōmon* has a gabled roof. Common worshippers pray from the outside of this gate. Located to the east and west there are two narrow *honden*, unique in style to Izumo shrine, called the Jūku sha ('nineteen shrines') because each *honden* has a row of 19 adjoining small rooms (each with a façade of 1.8 m and sides of 1.9 m). On the front of each *honden* are double doors. For one month every year, when the *kami* in Japan are said to gather at Izumo, these buildings serve as their lodgings.

The *taisha zukuri honden* style is seen only in the Izumo area (that is, in the eastern half of Shimane Prefecture). The oldest extant *taisha zukuri honden* is at the Kamosu Jinja (Kamosu Shrine, Oba, Matsue), which was rebuilt in 1583 and is an important early example of the ancient style. The façade of this *honden* is 5.15 m long and the sides 5.76 m. The *munamochi bashira* extends further out from the surrounding columns than at Izumo. Other examples of shrines in this style are the Manai Jinja (Manai Shrine, 1662, Yamashiro, Matsue) and the Sada Jinja (Sada Shrine, 1807, Kashima, Yatsuka Province, Shimane Prefecture).

See also SHINTO and JAPAN, §III, 3(i).

BIBLIOGRAPHY

S. Horiguchi: 'The Ancient Form of Izumo Shrine', *Japan Architect* (March 1961), pp. 8–13

Y. Watanabe: *Ise to Izumo* [Ise Shrine and Izumo Shrine], iii of *Nihon no bijutsu* [Arts of Japan] (Tokyo, 1964); Eng. trans. by R. Ricketts as *Shinto Art: Ise and Izumo Shrines*, Heibonsha Surv. Jap. A., iii (New York and Tokyo, 1974)

T. Fukuyama: *Nihon kenchikushi kenkyū* [Research on the history of Japanese architecture] (Tokyo, 1968)

E. Inagaki: *Jinja to reibyō* [Shinto shrines and mausolea], xvi of *Genshoku Nihon no bijutsu* [Arts of Japan, illustrated] (Tokyo, 1968)

M. Hayashino: *Jinja no kenchiku* [Shrine architecture] (Kyoto, 1974)

T. Fukuyama: 'Jinja kenchiku no kenkyū' [Research on shrine architecture], *Fukuyama Toshio chosakushū* [Writings of Toshio Fukuyama], ed. K. Yasuda (Tokyo, 1984)

MASAYUKI MIURA

İzzet Efendi. *See* MUSTAFA İZZET.

J

Jabach [Jabaque], **Everard** [Eberhardt; Evrard] (*b* Cologne, 10 July 1618; *d* Paris, 6 March 1695). French banker, financier, patron and collector of German birth. He formed two of the most important and prestigious collections of paintings and drawings assembled by a private citizen in the 17th century. Housed in his Paris mansion in the Rue Neuve-Saint-Merry, his first collection included over 100 paintings and almost 6000 drawings. It subsequently formed the basis of the collections of Louis XIV (*see* BOURBON, §I(9)), after having been ceded to the King in 1662 and 1671. After this Jabach formed a second collection, less magnificent than the first, but still of great quality.

1. EARLY LIFE AND FIRST COLLECTION, TO 1660. Jabach was born into a powerful family based in Cologne that had made its fortune from the middle of the 15th century in banking and the fur trade. He was initiated by his father at an early age into the worlds of finance and of art collecting. On the latter's death in 1636, Everard was left an immense fortune as well as numerous works of art that included an altarpiece by Albrecht Dürer (elements dispersed between Cologne, Wallraf-Richartz-Mus.; Frankfurt am Main, Städel Kstinst.; and Munich, Alte Pin.). In memory of his father, Jabach commissioned an altarpiece from Rubens for St Peter's in Cologne, his own parish church. This work, the *Crucifixion of St Peter*, was still in the workshop of Rubens at the artist's death in 1640, but was purchased from his heirs by Jabach in the following year and placed in the church.

At this period Jabach devoted himself to business and travel. A visit to London around 1636–7, where he admired the prestigious collections of Charles I and Thomas Howard, 2nd Earl of Arundel, seems to have confirmed his vocation as a collector. About 1638 Jabach moved to Paris, where he gained the confidence and respect of Cardinal Mazarin, whose banker he became. Anthony van Dyck executed his portrait (St Petersburg, Hermitage) in 1641.

Jabach soon acquired a reputation as a determined and large-scale collector, whose immense fortune allowed him to make spectacular acquisitions. He was also recognized internationally as an expert and was instrumental in Mazarin's acquisition of Titian's *Venus of the Pardo* and Correggio's *Jupiter and Antiope* (both Paris, Louvre). His own collection expanded rapidly, especially when that of Charles I (*see* STUART, House of, (6)) was sold at auction in the two years following his execution in 1649. The bulk of these works had originated from the collection of the Dukes of Mantua (*see* GONZAGA, (17)), and Jabach was one of the biggest buyers. Jabach was also active when parts of Lord Arundel's collection were sold in 1653, buying the famous drawings from the *Libro de' disegni* that had once belonged to Giorgio Vasari. In 1658 Jabach bought a house close to the corner of the Rue Neuve-Saint-Merry and the Rue Saint-Martin, where he was able to display his sumptuous collection. The Hôtel Jabach was subsequently enlarged by Pierre Bullet in 1669 (destr.; for illustration see Marot, n.d.).

2. SALES TO LOUIS XIV, 1662 AND 1671. From 1661 Jabach was negotiating with Cardinal Mazarin and then his Surintendant des Finances Nicolas Fouquet to sell part of his collection to the Crown. It was not, however, until 1662 that he sold capital works to Louis XIV for 330,000 livres. The items sold included 'pictures, busts and bronzes'. Among the paintings were some of the masterpieces of Italian art now in the Musée du Louvre: Leonardo da Vinci's *St John the Baptist*; Giulio Romano's *Nativity* and *Triumph of Titus and Vespasian*; the *Concert champêtre* attributed to Giorgione; Titian's *Young Woman at her Toilet, Allegory of Alfonso of Avalos, Supper at Emmaus* and *Entombment*; Guido Reni's four paintings of the *Labours of Hercules*; Caravaggio's *Death of the Virgin*; and Correggio's *Allegory of Virtue*.

Around 1666 Jabach had many of the Old Master drawings in his collection engraved by Michel Corneille (i), Jean-Baptiste Corneille, Jacques Rousseau and others. His business affairs continued to flourish until 1670, when under the stringent controls of Jean-Baptiste Colbert's administration his financial situation began to deteriorate to the point where he was obliged to negotiate the sale of the rest of his collection to the King on particularly unfavourable conditions. He was forced by Colbert to give up to the Crown marble and bronze sculptures, furnishings, silverware and gems on which Jabach himself had put a value of 581,025 livres, and in March 1671 he sold to the King 101 paintings and 5542 drawings for the sum of 220,000 livres (for details of the sale see Reiset, 1879, and de Grouchy). Among the paintings were Veronese's *Susanna and the Elders* and *Esther before Ahasuerus*; Domenichino's *St Cecilia*; Claude's *Straits of Suza Taken by Louis XIII*; and Hans Holbein (ii)'s portrait of *Erasmus* (all Paris, Louvre). But above all Jabach's inestimable collection of drawings, the most famous of its time, went to enrich the royal collections. Italian drawings of the High Renaissance predominated, among them outstanding works by Raphael and Michelangelo, but there were also over 300 mounted Flemish and German ones, including sheets by Dürer, as well as a quantity by modern masters. Jabach had divided them by school and compiled an inventory (Paris, Bib. N., MS. FR. 869). The best drawings, about half the number, were on mounts with a gilt band and Jabach's collector's mark on the reverse of the mount. The residue of unmounted sheets was stamped on the verso of the drawings. Today Jabach's drawings, most of which had come from such illustrious cabinets as those of Vasari, the Dukes of Mantua, Charles I and Desneux de La Noue, are among the most highly prized in the Louvre's collection.

3. LATER LIFE AND SECOND COLLECTION, AFTER 1671. The crisis over, prosperity returned to Jabach's affairs. In 1671 he was appointed Director of the Compagnie des Indes and also of the Aubusson manufactory. He began to build a second collection around the large portrait by Charles Le Brun of *Jabach with his Family* (1660; Berlin, ex-Kaiser-Friedrich Mus.), which he had kept back from the 1671 sale. At his death there were 687 paintings, less outstanding than the earlier collection and including copies of his previously owned works, as well as paintings by Rubens, Bruegel, Rembrandt, Frans Snyders, Sébastien Bourdon, Holbein, Jacopo Bassano, Lorenzo Lotto, Parmigianino and the Cavaliere d'Arpino. He also assembled over 4000 drawings. Details of the collection were recorded in an inventory (Paris, Archvs Louvres) compiled in the year following Jabach's death. This includes descriptions of subjects, media, dimensions, and even estimates of value, thus indicating the state of the art market at the end of the 17th century. The collection was gradually dispersed by Jabach's children. A number of drawings were acquired by the Venetian connoisseur Anton Maria Zanetti (i) and others by Pierre-Jean Mariette. The largest part went to Pierre Crozat (*see* CROZAT, (1)).

UNPUBLISHED SOURCES

Paris, Archvs Louvres, *Mémoire estat inventaire et réglement de droitz dans la famille de feu Sr Evrard Jabach, et de dame Anne Marie de Groot sa veuve du 17 juillet 1696, reconnu par devant nottaire le dernier octobre aud. an*

BIBLIOGRAPHY

J. Marot: *Recueil des plans, profils et élévations des plusiers palais, chasteaux, églises, sépultures, grotes et hostels bâtis dans Paris* (Paris, n.d./R 1970) [7 pls]

——: *Recueil de 283 estampes, gravées à l'eau-forte par les plus habiles peintres du tems, d'après les desseins des grands maistres, que possédait autrefois M. Jabach et qui depuis sont passés au Cabinet du Roi* (Paris, 1754)

F. Reiset: 'Préface', *Notice des dessins, cartons, pastels, miniatures et émaux exposés dans les salles du 1er étage au Musée impérial du Louvre* (Paris, 1866)

E. Bonnaffé: *Les Collectionneurs de l'ancienne France: Notes d'un amateur* (Paris, 1873), pp. 52, 62, 74, 104–6

L. Clément de Ris: *Les Amateurs d'autrefois* (Paris, 1877), pp. 125–52

F. Reiset: [Lettres et papiers relatifs à la vente 1671] (Paris, 1879)

E. Bonnaffé: *Dictionnaire des amateurs français au XVIIe siècle* (Paris, 1884), pp. 142–5, 330–31

Vicomte de Grouchy: 'Everhard Jabach, collectionneur parisien (1695)', *Mém. Soc. Hist. Paris & Ile-de-France*, xxi (1894), pp. 1–76

F. Lugt: *Marques* (1921), no. 2959

A. Hulftegger: 'Notes sur la formation des collections de peintures de Louis XIV', *Bull. Soc. Hist. A. Fr.* (1954), pp. 124–34

F. Lugt: *Marques*, suppl. (1956), no. 2959

J. Thuillier: 'Les Tableaux et les dessins d'Evrard Jabach', *L'Oeil*, 81 (1961), pp. 32–41, 83

Collections de Louis XIV, dessins, albums, manuscrits (exh. cat., preface R. Bacou; Paris, Mus. Orangerie, 1977)

C. Monbeig-Goguel: 'Le *Libro de' disegni* de Giorgio Vasari dans la première collection Jabach', *Collections de Louis XIV, dessins, albums, manuscrits* (exh. cat., Paris, Mus. Orangerie, 1977), pp. 45–7

F. Viatte: 'Les Dessins italiens dans la collection Jabach', *Collections de Louis XIV, dessins, albums, manuscrits* (exh. cat., Paris, Mus. Orangerie, 1977), pp. 42–5

R. Bacou: 'Everard Jabach: Dessins de la seconde collection', *Rev. A.* [Paris], 40–41 (1978), pp. 141–50

C. Monbeig-Goguel and F. Viatte: *La Collection Jabach: Dessins acquis en 1671 pour la collection royale*, i of *Répertoire systématique des fonds*, Paris, Louvre, Cab. Dessins cat. (1978) [typescript]

A. Schnapper: 'Jabach, Mazarin, Fouquet, Louis XIV', *Bull. Soc. Hist. A. Fr.* (1982), pp. 85–6

C. Monbeig-Goguel: 'Taste and Trade: The Retouched Drawings in the Everard Jabach Collection at the Louvre', *Burl. Mag.*, cxxx (1988), pp. 821–35

ALEXANDRA SKLIAR-PIGUET

Jabbadar, 'Aliquli. *See* 'ALIQULI JABBADAR.

Jaca. Spanish city situated in the Aragon valley in the north of Huesca province.

1. HISTORY AND URBAN DEVELOPMENT. Jaca was an Iberian *castrum*, and there is archaeological evidence for its urban development during the Roman period. At the time of the Arab invasion it became the centre of Christian resistance in the central Pyrenees, an area that became the County, then the Kingdom, of Aragon. In addition to its excellent strategic position Jaca was also an important staging post in the network of communications revitalized by the pilgrimage to Santiago de Compostela and by the growth of commerce in Europe in the 11th and 12th centuries. This encouraged its rapid urban development, sanctioned by the privileges granted by King Sancho Ramírez (*reg* 1063–94) in 1076 and the installation there of the bishopric of Aragon. The reconquest of Huesca (1096) and of Saragossa (1118) deprived Jaca of its political significance, but its importance as a commercial and frontier centre has continued.

The three nuclei that shaped the city constituted in 1076 are still visible. On the east of the historic centre is the ancient citadel, converted into a royal residence and defined by a semi-elliptical street outlining the old walled enclosure. The adjoining monastery of S Pedro el Viejo, perhaps founded after the reconquest of the city in 920, defines the second, ecclesiastical nucleus to the north, where the Romanesque cathedral now stands. The commercial area developed to the south, around the parish church of Santiago, and spread to the cathedral; in between this area and the walls lay the Jewish quarter. An influx of inhabitants, mostly from beyond the Pyrenees, who were attracted by the franchises granted by Sancho Ramírez, led to the demolition of the city walls as early as the beginning of the 12th century. Outside the walls to the north-east, along the road to the Samport pass, the district of Burnao (Burgo Novo) grew up.

BIBLIOGRAPHY

J. M. Lacarra: 'Desarrollo urbano de Jaca en la edad media', *Estud. Edad Med. Corona Aragón*, iv (1951), pp. 139–55

A. Ubieto Arteta: 'El románico de la catedral jaquesa y su cronología', *Príncipe Viana*, xxv (1964), pp. 187–200

L. H. Nelson: 'The Foundation of Jaca (1076): Urban Growth in Early Aragon', *Speculum*, liii (1978), pp. 688–708

2. CATHEDRAL. The construction of the cathedral cannot have been begun before 1076, when Jaca was established as an episcopal see and capital of the Kingdom of Aragon. A donation *ad laborem*, made by King Sancho Ramírez before his death in 1094, indicates the period of the earliest sculpture. The conquest of Huesca and the transfer of the capital of the kingdom and diocese there in 1098 suggests that there was a slowing down and possibly a temporary interruption of the work. In about 1105 a chapel was being built adjoining the east end and integral to the cloisters; it was consecrated before 1130. The relative modesty of the church (for plan *see* ROMANESQUE, fig. 12), with its alternating piers and columns originally supporting a wooden roof, contrasts with the ambitious sculptural programme, begun by a master from Frómista. The repertory of motifs and the stylistic echoes of the Husillos sarcophagus from Frómista (Madrid, Mus. Arqueol. N.) is enriched at Jaca by other antique sources, among which can be recognized sarcophagi of the *imago clipeata*, marine and Dionysiac *thiasos* types. The two sculptured portals are among the earliest of Hispano-Languedocian Romanesque. The west portal bears a penitential programme, with the *Story of Daniel* and themes derived from bestiaries surmounted by a chi-rho signifying the Trinity, a common motif on both sides of the Pyrenees. On the south portal tympanum is an original composition inspired by the margins of Gospel canon tables, which also served as a model for portals at Oloron and Morlaas. Of the splendid capitals, that representing the *Sacrifice of Isaac* (*see* ROMANESQUE, fig. 29) stands out for its vigour and pathos, as well as for the fine treatment of the nude. The presence in Jaca of sculptors from the circle of Bernardus Gelduinus in Toulouse led to a synthesis of Toulouse and local styles, shown in the superb capitals leading from the cloister. The carvings on these, like the capitals of the columns in the church, were completed by an inferior artist, the Master of the Sarcophagus of Doña Sancha, and his workshop, active *c.* 1110–40.

BIBLIOGRAPHY

G. Gaillard: *Les Débuts de la sculpture romane espagnole: León, Jaca, Compostelle* (Paris, 1938), pp. 87–119
S. Moralejo: 'Une Sculpture du style de Bernard Gilduin à Jaca', *Bull. Mnmtl*, cxxxi (1973), pp. 7–16
——: 'Sobre la formación del estilo escultórico de Frómista y Jaca', *Actas del XXIII congreso internacional de historia del arte: Granada, 1973*, i, pp. 427–33
D. L. Simon: 'Daniel and Habakkuk in Aragon', *J. Brit. Archaeol. Assoc.*, n. s. 2, xxxviii (1975), pp. 50–54
Homenaje a don José María Lacarra de Miguel en su jubilación del profesorado, i (Saragossa, 1977), pp. 173–207 [articles by M. Durliat, S. Moralejo]
J. M. Caamaño Martínez: 'En torno al tímpano de Jaca', *Goya*, 142 (1978), pp. 200–07
M. Durliat: 'Les Origines de la sculpture romane à Jaca', *Acad. Inscr. & B.-Lett.: C. R. Séances* (Oct 1978), pp. 363–99
Cah. Saint-Michel Cuxa, x (1979), pp. 79–129 [articles by S. Moralejo, D. L. Simon, S. C. Simon]
S. H. Caldwell: 'The Easter Context of Jaca Cathedral's West Tympanum', *A. Hist.*, iii (1980), pp. 25–40
Cah. Saint-Michel Cuxa, xi (1980), pp. 239–67 [articles by D. L. Simon, S. C. Simon]
S. Moralejo: 'Un reflejo de la escultura de Jaca, en una moneda de Sancho Ramírez (†1094)', *Scritti di storia dell'arte in onore di Roberto Salvini* (Florence, 1984), pp. 29–35

S. MORALEJO

Jachmann, Christine (*b* Lüneburg, 18 Nov 1946). German architect. She studied architecture and urban planning at the Technische Universität, Berlin, and established an architectural practice in Berlin and Cologne in 1972. She specialized in social housing and was greatly concerned with the problem of humanizing such dwellings, especially within the context of large, crowded cities such as Berlin. Her Wohnanlage am Park (1978–80), a complex of 234 flats, shops and a restaurant in Wilmersdorf, Berlin, is built around a courtyard and backs on to a spacious park, yet each flat has a balcony and with it the possibility of a terrace-garden. The building itself exhibits a spare, almost minimalist geometry. A more fully synthesized relationship between architectural form and nature is seen in the Glashaus (1983) in Grunewald, a building with six flats, the design of which is integral with its rectangular site. In plan the building (a right-angled triangle) interconnects with the open space of a courtyard, occupying about one-quarter of the site. Balconies again provide additional space for greenery. The plans of the individual flats echo this interest in interlocking geometric forms, the two flats on each roughly triangular floor being separated by a bisecting diagonal. Variants on this dividing principle generate inventively shaped and flowing spaces within the flats themselves, which are mirror images of one another. Jachmann also designed a block of 120 model flats for the Internationale Bauaustellung (IBA; 1988–90; unexecuted), Berlin.

BIBLIOGRAPHY

Die Mehrfamilienvilla als Bautyp: Vier neue Häuser im Grunewald (Berlin, 1983)
C. Lorenz: *Women in Architecture: A Contemporary Perspective* (New York, 1990), pp. 62–3

WALTER SMITH

Jäckel, Matěj Václav [Mathias Wenzel] (*b* Wittichenau, 1655; *d* Prague, after 16 Jan 1738). Bohemian sculptor. He probably trained in southern Germany or Austria, where he was able to familiarize himself with the Roman Baroque style, particularly with Gianlorenzo Bernini's oeuvre. Before 1684 he settled in Prague, where he ran a large and productive workshop, executing wood and sandstone sculpture in a rather stiff Baroque idiom. His statues decorated the façades and interiors of numerous churches in Prague and its provinces. His earliest known works were for the Carmelite church of St Joseph in the Lesser Quarter of Prague: stone statues on the façade and three carved wooden altars with ornaments and statues (1695–9) inside the church. Although these figures lack dynamism of pose, their surfaces are enlivened by a rich treatment of the drapery folds. In 1696 Jäckel supplied five stone statues for the façade of the Pauline convent on the Old Town Square, Prague; the statues of angels at the side are Berniniesque in character. After 1699 he made a group of stone statues of Jesuit saints for the portico of St Ignatius and also supplied some wooden statues of Apostles for the niches of the church's interior; to the same period belong his statues on the façade of St James in the Lesser Quarter of Prague, and perhaps some of the altars there. All these works emphasize the fact that Jäckel's art is based on a wood-carving technique: the statues' bodies are slightly elongated, their gestures are somewhat overemphatic, the faces idealized; but the hands are realistically executed. The drapery changes from being smooth and static, with thin folds, to a dramatic display of swinging hems, which sometimes assume the shape of conch-like fans.

Jäckel's oeuvre achieved its peak in the first decade of the 18th century. About 1701–2 he supplied the church of St Francis, Prague, with two side altars decorated with foliage, putti and flying angels. Before 1710 he executed the high altar, with a representation above it of the *Trinity*, in a Glory lit from a window in the manner of Bernini's Glory above the Cathedra Petri in Rome—the first time that such a device had been used in Prague. The flanking statues of St Helena and St Augustine are lofty and noble. In 1705 Jäckel added the wooden statues of *St Joseph, St Mary Magdalene, St John the Baptist* and *St John of Nepomuk* to those already in the church, the work of Jeremias Süssner (*d* 1690). Jäckel's reputation rests chiefly on three sculptural groups for the Charles Bridge. The first is the somewhat old-fashioned *St Anne with the Virgin and Child* (1707). For the sculptural group of the *Virgin and Child with SS Dominic and Thomas Aquinas* (1708), Jäckel chose a traditional triangular composition, which gives an impression of having been translated from a print into plastic shape. The group of the *Virgin and Child with St Bernard* (1709) corresponds to the later phase of Jäckel's style; the kneeling figure of *St Bernard*, in a dialogue with the central statue of the *Virgin*, is only partly balanced on the other side by a group representing the *Instruments of the Passion*, and thus a dynamically open composition succeeds a closed one.

In 1705–13 Jäckel worked on a massive column of *St John of Nepomuk*, placed close to the Cistercian monastery in Sedlec; on a statue of the *Virgin* for the convent there; and on a statue representing the *Immaculate Conception* for the façade of the church. It was becoming obvious that his work was losing ground to the two masters of the succeeding generation, Matyáš Bernard Braun and Jan Brokof; already in 1712 Jäckel's stone statues for the façade of the Břevnov monastery church of St Margaret appeared disproportionately small-scale against Christoph Dientzenhofer's monumental architecture, while the eight statues of Benedictine saints (1718) that he made for the church's interior seem outdated in comparison with Petr Brandl's dynamic paintings. Jäckel's high altar gives the impression of a Late Renaissance aedicula, rather than a monumental altar. In his angels (1722–4) on the attic gable of the Knights of the Cross Church, Prague, he attempted to come to terms with the prevailing dynamic Berniniesque style of Braun.

In the following years Jäckel's physical strength diminished, and so members of his workshop, particularly Ignác Weis (*d* 1756), possibly his son-in-law, came to have an increasing share in his works. This is probably true of the statues made in 1724 for the Premonstratensian church in Chotěšov, and particularly so of a big group of stone statues (after 1726) made for the garden façade of the Jesuit church of St Bartholomew, Prague. Only in Jäckel's last known work, a double altar (1728–31) in St Vitus's Church, Dobřany, did he return to the expressive realism of his early works.

BIBLIOGRAPHY

Thieme–Becker

P. Toman: *Nový slovník československých výtvarných umělců* [New dictionary of Czechoslovak artists], i (Prague, 1947), p. 408
O. J. Blažíček: *Sochařství baroku v Čechách* [Baroque sculpture in Bohemia] (Prague, 1958), pp. 99–103
V. Vančura: 'Příspěvek k pražskému dílu M. V. Jäckela' [M. V. Jäckel's work in Prague], *Umění*, xxxv (1987), pp. 356–63

IVO KOŘÁN

Jack of Diamonds [Rus. Bubnovy Valet]. Group of Russian avant-garde painters active in Moscow from 1910 to 1917. It was founded by Mikhail Larionov, Natal'ya Goncharova, Aristarkh Lentulov, Pyotr Konchalovsky, Robert Fal'k, Il'ya Mashkov and Aleksandr Kuprin, young artists who found membership of existing art societies no longer compatible with their experimental styles of painting. Regular participants included Alexandra Exter, David Burlyuk and Vladimir Burlyuk. The name 'Jack of Diamonds', chosen by Larionov, suggested not only the roguish behaviour of the avant-garde but also their love of popular graphic art forms such as old printed playing cards.

The group's first exhibition took place in Moscow in 1910, and, following the example of the exhibitions sponsored by the magazine GOLDEN FLEECE, they invited contributions from foreign artists such as Albert Gleizes, Albert Le Fauconnier and members of the 'Neue Künstlervereinigung München', including Kandinsky, Gabriele Münter and Alexei Jawlenski. In this first exhibition the influence of the LUBOK (popular Russian print) was especially evident in the work of Larionov and Goncharova. Crude in style and content, Larionov's *Soldiers* (1910; Los Angeles, CA, Co. Mus. A.), with obscenities scribbled across the canvas, caused a scandal at the exhibition. Other leaders of the group were inspired more by Fauvism and contemporary German art. Mashkov's *Portrait of Vinogradova* (1909; Moscow, Tret'yakov Gal.), with its bold arabesques, daring colouring and simplified portraiture, recalls Henri Matisse, and Konchalovsky's magnificently ugly *Portrait of Antaro* (?1910; untraced) bears the stamp of Kees van Dongen.

During 1911 Larionov and Goncharova organized their own group called the DONKEY'S TAIL and seceded from the Jack of Diamonds group on ideological grounds. Their complaints about the group's reliance on Western models instead of on indigenous Russian sources were shared by seven other artists, including Kazimir Malevich, who also resigned from the group. Twice as many young artists who wished to be associated with the group filled the gap, however, and Lentulov, Konchalovsky, Mashkov, Fal'k and Kuprin became the leaders.

In their second, third and fourth exhibitions of 1912–14 (all in Moscow; the exhibition of 1913 was a smaller version of one that opened in St Petersburg), the Jack of Diamonds group invited a wide range of French and German artists to participate. They included not only Fauves such as Matisse, Derain, Kees van Dongen and Vlaminck but also Cubists: Robert Delaunay, Gleizes, Le Fauconnier, Léger, Braque and Picasso. Works by artists of Die Brücke and Der Blaue Reiter, such as Ernst Kirchner, Erich Heckel, Franz Macke, Franz Marc and Kandinsky, were also shown. Moreover the Jack of Diamonds almanac of 1913 included translations of Le

Fauconnier's 'La Sensibilité moderne et le tableau' and Apollinaire's essay 'Fernand Léger'. Such painters had a profound effect upon the Jack of Diamonds group, who began to synthesize these trends in their art from 1912 to 1914. Konchalovsky, Fal'k and Kuprin now concentrated more on still-lifes than portraits and painted brightly coloured works in which the subjects were faceted and rearranged in a mildly Cubist way. The work of new participants, such as Nadezhda Udal'tsova and Lyubov' Popova, who had both worked in Paris under Le Fauconnier and Jean Metzinger, was much more radical and in a thoroughly Cubist vein.

Jack of Diamonds failed to exhibit as a group in 1915, preferring to contribute works individually to *Vystavka zhivopisi: 1915 god* ('Exhibition of painting: The year 1915'), a large avant-garde exhibition in Moscow. Their penultimate exhibition was held during 1916, but without the participation of either Konchalovsky or Mashkov. Instead the exhibition was dominated by artists from Petrograd (St Petersburg): Natan Al'tman, Jean Pougny and Ol'ga Rozanova, who showed several works described as 'Non-objective compositions'. The exhibition also included nearly 70 Suprematist paintings by the prodigal Malevich and his friend Ivan Klyun. Jack of Diamonds dissolved following their final exhibition in Moscow in 1917.

WRITINGS

Bubnovy Valet [Jack of Diamonds] (Moscow, 1913)

BIBLIOGRAPHY

Bubnovy Valet (exh. cats, Moscow, 1910–14, 1916–17; St Petersburg, 1913) [illus. album of works shown at the first exh.]

A. Grishchenko: 'O gruppe khudozhnikov "Bubnovy Valet"' [About the 'Jack of Diamonds' group of artists], *Apollon*, vi (1913), pp. 31–8

Vystavka proizvedeniy khudozhnikov gruppy 'Bubnovy Valet' [Exhibition of works by the 'Jack of Diamonds' group of artists] (exh. cat., ed. V. Midler; Moscow, 1927)

G. Pospelov: 'O "valetakh" bubnovykh i "valetakh" chervonnykh' [On the 'Jacks' of Diamonds and the 'Jacks' of Hearts], *Panorama Isk. '77* [Panorama of Arts '77] (1978), pp. 127–42

G. Pospelov: *Karo-Bube: Aus der Geschichte der Moskauer Malerei zu Beginn des 20. Jahrhunderts* (Dresden, 1984)

Sieben Moskauer Künstler/Seven Moscow Artists, 1910–1930 (exh. cat., Cologne, Gal. Gmurzynska, 1984)

ANTHONY PARTON

Jacks, Robert (*b* Melbourne, 1943). Australian painter. He originally trained as a sculptor at the Royal Melbourne Institute of Technology (1959–65), holding his first one-man exhibition in 1966. Two years later he participated in the Field Exhibition that opened the new National Gallery of Victoria in Melbourne with a survey of recent developments in Australian painting. Although he achieved considerable early success within Australia, he left in 1968 to visit Canada and later New York and Texas. In New York he was influenced by some members of the ART & LANGUAGE group of conceptual artists, and began to move away from painting to minimal, serial and post-minimal drawings and constructions. He exhibited a group of these in the Cultural Center, New York, in 1970. In 1974 he returned to Australia to become artist-in-residence at the University of Melbourne. At this stage he was concentrating almost exclusively on drawing, partly under the influence of Sol LeWitt. From these drawings Jacks worked his way back into painting. The lyricism of his earlier manner was gone and a more severe architectonic

feeling for abstract forms took its place. After teaching briefly at the Sydney College of the Arts in the late 1970s he returned to settle in Melbourne, where he re-established himself as one of the leading painters of his generation.

PATRICK MCCAUGHEY

Jackson, A(lexander) Y(oung) (*b* Montreal, 3 Oct 1882; *d* Kleinburg, Ont., 5 April 1974). Canadian painter. He worked as a commercial artist in Montreal (1895–1906) and Chicago (1906–7) and attended evening classes at the Art Institute of Chicago in 1906. Determined to become a painter, he went to Paris in 1907 and studied at the Académie Julian under Jean-Paul Laurens. He returned to Montreal in 1909 but in 1913 moved to Toronto, where he became associated with other painters who later banded together as the GROUP OF SEVEN, notably J. E. H. MacDonald, Arthur Lismer and Fred Varley. One of the first large paintings in which he established the terms of his approach to the open Canadian landscape, *Terre Sauvage* (1913; Ottawa, N.G.; for illustration *see* GROUP OF SEVEN), was painted in the studio of a future member of the group, Lawren S. Harris. He shared a studio with Tom Thomson from January 1914 and in October 1914 went with him, Lismer and Varley to paint in Algonquin Provincial Park, developing with them an intense dedication to the painting of the northern landscape.

In 1915 Jackson enlisted in the Canadian Army and saw active service in France. Wounded in June 1916 he spent several months of convalescence in England and then returned to reserve battalion duties. In July 1917 he met Lord Beaverbrook, who arranged his appointment to the War Art programme of the Canadian War Records. He worked in the war zone in France in the autumn of 1917 and again in the spring of 1918 before returning to London, where he produced oil paintings such as *Springtime in Picardy* (1918; Toronto, A.G. Ont.) based on sketches he had made in France. He returned to Canada in September 1918 and was discharged from the Army in April 1919. Later that year, together with Lawren S. Harris, MacDonald and Franz Johnston (1888–1949), he went on a box-car trip to paint in the Algoma district of northern Ontario, and in February 1920 he travelled alone to paint in the Georgian Bay region. The paintings produced by Jackson as a result of these trips, such as *First Snow, Algoma* (1919–20; Kleinburg, Ont., McMichael Can. A. Col.) and *October Morning, Algoma* (1920; U. Toronto, Hart House), demonstrate the evolution of his mature style in the treatment of the sweeping vistas as a pattern of schematic shapes in vivid colours.

Jackson was one of the most active and vocal members of the Group of Seven, formed in 1920, becoming an insistent advocate of the nationalist purpose of their representation of the Canadian landscape. He travelled widely, painting not only in Ontario but also in Quebec (e.g. *Early Spring, Quebec*, 1923; Ottawa, N.G.), in western Canada and (in 1927 and 1930) in northern Canada and the Arctic, as in *Beothic at Bache Post, Ellesmere Island* (*c.* 1928; Ottawa, N.G.); he was accompanied on his first visit to the Arctic by a friend Frederick G. Banting (1891–1941), the co-discoverer of insulin and an enthusiastic amateur painter.

In the later decades of his life Jackson epitomized in the public's eyes the essential character of the Group of Seven's advocacy of a national school of painting in landscapes such as *Country Road, Alberta* (*c.* 1954; Toronto, A.G. Ont.). He was an influential and commanding figure in Canadian art for many years, with a particularly public presence after moving in 1968 to a flat in the McMichael Canadian Art Collection in Kleinburg, Ontario, north of Toronto, where an important group of his paintings was placed on permanent display.

WRITINGS
A Painter's Country: The Autobiography of A. Y. Jackson (Toronto and Vancouver, 1958)

BIBLIOGRAPHY
A. H. Robson: *A. Y. Jackson* (Toronto, 1938)
A. Y. Jackson: Thirty Years of Painting (exh. cat., intro. A. Lismer; Montreal, Dominion Gal., 1946)
A. Y. Jackson: Paintings, 1902–1953 (exh. cat., ed. S. J. Key; Toronto, A.G. Ont., 1953)
N. J. Groves: *A. Y.'s Canada* (Toronto and Vancouver, 1968)
O. J. Firestone: *The Other A. Y. Jackson* (Toronto, 1979)
For further bibliography see GROUP OF SEVEN.

DAVID BURNETT

Jackson, Daryl (*b* Clunes, Victoria, 7 Feb 1937). Australian architect. He studied architecture at the Royal Melbourne Institute of Technology (1954–6) and at the University of Melbourne (1957–8). Between 1960 and 1964 he worked for Chamberlin, Powell & Bon in England and Paul Rudolph and Skidmore, Owings & Merrill in the USA. In 1965 he returned to Melbourne and worked in the practice he had set up with Evan Walker (*b* 11 Oct 1935) in 1963. Jackson's work, predominantly in the public realm, is informed by a commitment to architecture as a democratic social art. Early buildings designed by the firm were informally planned around meandering pedestrian routes incorporating 45° splays derived from the work of Rudolph and Louis Kahn. A Brutalist vocabulary of off-form concrete, unpainted blockwork and metal glazing systems was used, notably in the Harold Holt Pool (1967; with Kevin Borland), Melbourne, and the Canberra School of Music (1972–6). In the late 1970s the firm produced work of a less assertive character, highly sensitive to human activity and context, using white-painted brick and concrete; examples include the State Bank Residential College, Baxter (1977), Victoria, the McLachlan Federal Government Offices (1978), Canberra, and extensions (1978) to the Canberra School of Art. After Walker left the practice in 1979, Jackson's work became more eclectic and complex, incorporating Post-modern devices such as deconstructivist diagonal shifts in plan and free-standing screens to create layered façades. Several works of the 1980s employ steel structures with lightweight cladding panels, often in coloured horizontal bands, as in the National Sports Centre Swimming Pool (1982), Canberra. He later turned increasingly to classically based compositions, particularly in urban projects such as the office tower (1992) at 120 Collins Street, Melbourne. He was awarded the Gold Medal of the Royal Australian Institute of Architects in 1987.

WRITINGS
Daryl Jackson: Architecture, Drawings and Photographs (South Melbourne, 1984)

BIBLIOGRAPHY
J. Taylor: *Australian Architecture since 1960* (Sydney, 1986, rev. 2/1990)
M. Roehrs, ed.: 'Daryl Jackson: RAIA Gold Medal 1987', *Archit. Austra-lia*, lxxvi/7 (1987), pp. 51–82

RORY SPENCE

Jackson, Gilbert (*fl* 1621–40). English painter. He was made free of the Painter-Stainers Company in London in December 1640, but he had probably been active before that date in the provinces as well as in London. He was patronized by country families and by members of the learned professions. He does not appear to have worked for the court. His style changed little within the period in which he is known to have been working. His earliest works, such as the portrait of *Edward Somerset, 4th Earl of Worcester* (1621; Lord Dormer priv. col.), were influenced by George Geldorp or Paul van Somer, but he was only superficially influenced by van Dyck. His portraits are provincial, if not archaic, in style, rough and unpolished in quality. The sense of character is lively and sympathetic, and the attention to detail and colour (which is often very pretty) may reflect the influence of Marcus Gheeraerts (ii). The compositions, however, though often decorative, are flat and linear. Jackson's sitters seldom appear to stand convincingly in space, though the space itself, whether an interior or a landscape, is often interestingly delineated. His manner is close to that of Edward Bower and is most clearly illustrated in full-length portraits, such as *William Hickman* (1634; Raveningham, Norfolk, Sir Nicholas Bacon priv. col.), *Portrait of a Boy* (Mapledurham, Oxon, Mr John Eyston priv. col.) and *Lord Bellasys* (1636; London, N.P.G.; *see* ENGLAND, fig. 17). His signature, written in a distinctive spiky script, is sometimes shortened to the form *Gil. Jack.*

BIBLIOGRAPHY
M. Whinney and O. Millar: *English Art, 1625–1714*, Oxford Hist. Eng. A. (Oxford, 1957), pp. 78–9
The Treasure Houses of Britain (exh. cat., ed. G. Jackson-Stops; Washington, DC, N.G.A., 1985), p. 128

OLIVER MILLAR

Jackson, John (*b* Lastingham, Yorks, 31 May 1778; *d* London, 1 June 1831). English painter. He was first apprenticed to his father, a tailor, who disapproved of his artistic inclinations. The support of the local magnate Henry Phipps, 1st Earl of Mulgrave (1755–1831), and then of the great Regency patron Sir George Beaumont, Bart, however, meant that he was able to go to the Royal Academy Schools in London in 1804, where he became a friend of B. R. Haydon and David Wilkie. He was elected ARA in 1815 and RA in 1817. He went to the Netherlands in 1816 and to Rome via Switzerland in 1819 with Sir Francis Chantrey. He was a prolific and successful portrait painter somewhat influenced by Thomas Lawrence and Henry Raeburn, producing strong, incisive, highly individualized likenesses, such as that of *Sir John Soane* (1828; London, N.P.G.). It may be that this last quality was unacceptable to the most fashionable English sitters, for he never displaced Lawrence as the leading portrait painter of the day, despite his attractive handling and colour. His directness of approach may be a reflection of his adherence to Methodism, and one of his first portraits was a posthumous depiction of John Wesley (untraced).

BIBLIOGRAPHY

Redgrave
H. C. Morgan: *The Life and Works of John Jackson* (diss., U. London, 1956)
H. Honour: 'John Jackson', *Connoisseur Yb.* (1957), p. 91

ROBIN SIMON

Jackson, John Baptist [Jean-Baptiste] (*b c*. 1701; *d c*. 1780). English wood-engraver and wallpaper manufacturer. He trained as a wood-engraver, first in London with Edward Kirkall (1695–1750) and then *c*. 1726 in Paris under Jean-Michel Papillon. He parted from Papillon on bad terms and went on to Rome, and then Venice, specializing in the chiaroscuro technique. His six *Heroic Landscapes* (1745; *see* WOODCUT, fig. 5) after gouaches by Marco Ricci were printed in 7–10 colours. He returned to London in 1746 and founded a wallpaper manufacturing company in Battersea. There he applied the chiaroscuro technique to produce wallpaper panels printed with oil-based colours, imitating the appearance of the print rooms of the day with their framed engravings and landscapes in roundels surrounded by Baroque frames (e.g. London, V&A). He also engraved imitation stucco arrangements of ornamental foliage in the Italian style, as well as statues and trophies. He published a vigorous defence of his claims for recognition as an inventor of the technique of printing and engraving in chiaroscuro in a treatise of 1754. The sweeping scale of his work gave new life to the art of wallpaper manufacture, and the Italian influences that he succeeded in assimilating into an original and expressive style contrasted sharply with the then predominating vogue for Chinese papers. Various documents and an album attributed to Jackson's workshop are preserved in the Victoria and Albert Museum, London.

See also PRINTS, §III, 6.

WRITINGS

An Essay on the Invention of Engraving and Printing in Chiaro Oscuro, as Practised by Albert Dürer, Hugo di Carpi, etc., and the Application of it to the Making of Paper Hangings of Taste, Duration and Elegance, by Mr Jackson of Battersea (London, 1754)

BIBLIOGRAPHY

J. Kainen: *John Baptist Jackson: Eighteenth-century Master of the Colour Woodcut* (Washington, DC, 1962)

BERNARD JACQUÉ

Jackson, John Richardson (*b* Portsmouth, 17 Dec 1819; *d* Southsea, 10 May 1877). English engraver. In 1836 he became the pupil of Robert Graves, from whom he learnt the craft of line-engraving. His reputation was established subsequently, however, as a mezzotint engraver. One of his most prominent achievements in this technique was the large plate after Edwin Landseer's *Otter and Salmon* (exh. RA 1842; Sir J. Fitzherbert priv. col.), declared for publication by Francis Graham Moon in July 1847. Jackson also reproduced many portraits by such painters as Joshua Reynolds, Thomas Lawrence and George Richmond. He exhibited 27 works at the Royal Academy between 1854 and 1876.

BIBLIOGRAPHY

DNB
R. K. Engen: *Dictionary of Victorian Engravers* (Cambridge, 1979)

ANTHONY DYSON

Jackson [née Kellogg], **Martha** (*b* Buffalo, NY, 1907; *d* Los Angeles, CA, 4 July 1969). American dealer and collector. She came from a wealthy family and studied art and art history in New York and Baltimore. She began collecting modern art in Baltimore in the 1940s. In 1953 she opened a gallery in New York. At this time her private collection favoured 20th-century American painting, particularly the Abstract Expressionists. In later years it reflected the artists she exhibited.

While she showed Willem de Kooning's second series of *Woman* paintings in 1955 and work by Adolph Gottlieb in 1957, as a dealer Jackson was best known for her championship of younger artists. These included such Americans working in Paris as Sam Francis, Clare Frankenstein and Paul Jenkins and second-generation Abstract Expressionists such as Alfred Leslie (*b* 1927), Michael Goldberg (*b* 1924), Grace Hartigan and Joan Mitchell. She gave Morris Louis one of his few New York shows within his lifetime. She was also instrumental in introducing many post-war European artists to New York in the 1950s, including Karel Appel, Alberto Burri, Lucio Fontana, Barbara Hepworth, Germaine Richier, William Scott (*b* 1913) and Antoni Tàpies. In 1960 she was one of the earliest presenters of junk art and gave John Chamberlain his first major show. In 1965 she held the first show of *Optical Painting* or Op art.

BIBLIOGRAPHY

Private Collection of Martha Jackson (exh. cat., Baltimore, U. MD, Mus. A., 1973)
Martha Jackson Memorial Collection (exh. cat. by H. Rand, Washington, DC, N. Mus. Amer. A., 1984)
A. D. Robson: *The Market for Modern Art in New York in the 1940s and 1950s* (diss., U. London, 1988), pp. 187–201

A. DEIRDRE ROBSON

Jackson, Sir **Thomas Graham** (*b* Hampstead, London, 21 Dec 1835; *d* Wimbledon, London, 7 Nov 1924). English architect and writer. Jackson, the son of a solicitor, was educated at Brighton College and Wadham College, Oxford, of which he became a Fellow in 1865. He served his articles (1858–61) in the office of George Gilbert Scott the elder and then set up practice in London in 1861. His early work—including St Peter's Church (1872–4), Hornblotton, Somerset —attracted little attention, although his book *Modern Gothic Architecture* (1873) was widely praised: in it Jackson advocated the use of an eclectic English Renaissance style, which he himself used with few exceptions throughout his career.

In 1876 he made his name by winning the competition for the new Examination Schools, Oxford, and went on to work for no fewer than 11 colleges there. He also carried out restoration or other work on practically every university building and designed the new High Schools for Boys and Girls (1879–81). His best buildings are in Oxford, foremost among them being Hertford College, which he virtually rebuilt from 1884 onwards, and the new quadrangle for Brasenose (1880–1911). Elsewhere, he did much work at public schools, most extensively for Radley College (1891–1922), Oxon, and Brighton College (1882–1922), and most notably at Giggleswick, N. Yorks, where he built a half-Gothic, half-Byzantine chapel (1897–1901). He built a number of new churches, of which St John the Evangelist (1887–90), Northington, Hants, is the most impressive, and private houses, the best known being 2 Kensington Court, London, for which he also designed a piano (1883–5). In London he built for the Drapers' and Grocers' Companies and for the Middle Temple, and in Cambridge he designed the block of university buildings in Downing Street (1899–1918).

Jackson had a considerable public reputation; he was elected ARA in 1892 and RA in 1896 and was Master of the Art Workers' Guild, 1896, but although he continued to enter all the principal public competitions he met with no further success. This failure led to much adverse criticism. He was well known as an 'artist–architect' and was a leading opponent of the proposed registration of architects, editing (with Richard Norman Shaw) *Architecture: A Profession or an Art* (1892). He was strongly in favour of closer links between architecture and allied arts; his buildings were usually adorned with sculpture, wood-carving and other decoration, and he also designed table glass (for James Powell & Sons), organ cases, bookplates, book covers and a barge (for Oriel College, Oxford, 1892). The range of his talents was wide; he could design simple functional buildings as well as elaborate expensive ones, and his own brand of eclecticism involved considerable versatility in the understanding and combining of a number of styles.

The work for which he became most famous was the major restoration of Winchester Cathedral (1905–12), which involved massive underpinning by means of bags of concrete placed by a diver beneath the waterlogged foundations; it was for this that he was created Baronet in 1913, the first hereditary title to be granted to a British architect. Jackson had been awarded the Royal Gold Medal in 1910, but towards the end of his career, although he continued to be highly respected, he was increasingly regarded as reactionary, for his new buildings lay outside the mainstream of architectural development.

Jackson was a scholarly and sensitive man, whose special study of the architecture of Dalmatia is still a standard work, and this interest led to the commission to build a campanile (1889) for Zadar Cathedral. The last years of his life were taken up with writing, mostly on architectural history, and work unfinished at the time of his death was completed by his son, Basil Hippisley Jackson.

WRITINGS

Modern Gothic Architecture (London, 1873)
Dalmatia, the Quarnero and Istria, 3 vols (Oxford, 1887)
ed. with R. N. Shaw: *Architecture: A Profession or an Art* (London, 1892)
Wadham College, Oxford (Oxford, 1893)
The Church of St Mary the Virgin, Oxford (Oxford, 1897)
Reason in Architecture (London, 1906) [lectures delivered at the Royal Academy]
Byzantine and Romanesque Architecture, 2 vols (Cambridge, 1913, rev. New York, 2/1975)
Gothic Architecture in France, England and Italy, 2 vols (Cambridge, 1915, rev. New York, 2/1975)
The Renaissance of Roman Architecture in Italy, England and France, 3 vols (Cambridge, 1921–3, rev. New York, 2/1975)
Architecture (London, 1925, rev. Freeport, NY, 2/1972)

BIBLIOGRAPHY

B. H. Jackson, ed.: *Recollections of Thomas Graham Jackson* (Oxford, 1950)
J. M. Crook: 'T. G. Jackson and the Cult of Eclecticism', *In Search of Modern Architecture*, ed. H. Searing (London, 1982), pp. 102–20
Sir Thomas Graham Jackson, Bart., R.A. 1835–1924: An Exhibition of his Oxford Buildings (exh. cat., ed. J. Bettley; Oxford U., Delegates Exam. Sch., 1983)

JAMES BETTLEY

Jackson, William Henry (*b* Keesville, NY, 4 April 1843; *d* New York, 30 June 1942). American photographer. Jackson began his career as a colourist and retoucher in photographic studios in New York and Vermont. After enlisting in the infantry and working as a sketcher of camp life, he began to travel. He reached Omaha, NE, in 1867 and set up a photographic studio with his brother Edward Jackson. He began to make expeditions along the Union Pacific Railroad, photographing the Pawnee, Omaha and Winnebago people, and points of interest in and around Omaha. He gained a contract with the E. & H. T. Anthony Company to supply them with 10,000 views of American scenery. In 1870 the government surveyor Ferdinand V. Hayden visited Jackson's studio and invited him to join his US Geological and Geographical Survey of the Territories. Jackson worked with Hayden every year until 1878, using wet collodion negatives to photograph the Oregon trail (1870; *see* NATIVE NORTH AMERICAN ART, fig. 12), Yellowstone (1871), the Teton Mountains (1872), the Rocky Mountains (1873), the Southwest (1877) and the Northern territories (1878). The painter Thomas Moran accompanied several of the expeditions, advising Jackson on the composition of his images and using Jackson's photographs to compose his own paintings. Moran appears as the lone figure (a device Jackson often used to heighten the romantic grandeur of the scenery) in the photograph *Hot Springs on the Gardiner River, Upper Basin* (1871; Rochester, NY, Int. Mus. Phot.).

Jackson made a great reputation with the landscapes he produced on these trips. In 1872 sets of *Yellowstone's Scenic Wonders* containing nine images were bound and given to members of the US Congress, where they proved influential in the decision to create the national park. In 1873 Jackson photographed the *Mountain of the Holy Cross in the Rockies* (Rochester, NY, Int. Mus. Phot.) with its unusual marking and made his first panoramic views; he sold many images of the mountain, some to popular magazines. The US government published two books of his photographs that year, *Photographs of Yellowstone National Park* and *Views in Montana and Wyoming Territories*. In 1874 more photographs were published: *The U.S. Geological Survey Rocky Mountains Natural Surroundings* included Jackson's pictures of the 'lost cities' of Mesa Verde, McElmo Canyon and Hovenweep. In 1875 he added the 20×24 inch mammoth plate camera to his equipment. The resulting images, the largest ever produced in the field, were made much of in the press. He exhibited several of his photographs as painted transparencies in the Centennial Exposition in Philadelphia in 1876 and gained much attention.

In 1879 Jackson discontinued his work for the government and set up the Jackson Photographic Co. in Denver, CO. Railway companies hired him to photograph their routes to stimulate travel; using collodion dry plate materials he produced promotional images for the Denver and Rio Grande Railroad Company, the Colorado Central and the Pacific Railroad. Over a period of about 15 years Jackson made *c.* 30,000 images. During the summers he travelled extensively throughout the USA, Canada and Latin America. In 1893 he exhibited at the Columbia Exposition, Chicago, and was the fair's official photographer. To commemorate the event he produced a special album of 100 views that sold for £1000. In 1894 he published *Wonder Places . . . The Most Perfect Pictures of Magnificent Scenes in the Rocky Mountains . . . Masterworks of the World's Greatest Photographic Artist*. That same year he accompanied the World Transportation Commission on a worldwide study tour of public transportation systems; the magazine *Harper's Weekly* commissioned his pictures of the trip. When the tour ended, Jackson became head cameraman and part owner of the Photochrom Company of Detroit and worked there until the company collapsed in 1924. Although retired, he helped to execute a series of painted murals of the Hayden geological surveys for the Department of the Interior in 1936 and worked for the National Park Service painting scenes from memory in 1937. His autobiography *Time Exposure* was published in 1940.

WRITINGS

Time Exposure: An Autobiography (New York, 1940/R Albuquerque, 1986)

BIBLIOGRAPHY

C. S. Jackson: *Picture Maker of the Old West, William Henry Jackson* (New York, 1947)
H. Driggs: *The Old West Speaks: Water-color Paintings by William Henry Jackson* (New York, 1956)
L. R. Hafen and A. W. Hafen, eds: *The Diaries of William Henry Jackson, Frontier Photographer* (Glendale, CA, 1959)
H. M. Miller: *Lens on the West: The Story of William Henry Jackson* (Garden City, NY, 1966)
William H. Jackson (exh. cat., ed. B. Newhall and D. E. Edkins; Fort Worth, TX, Amon Carter Mus., 1974) [essay by W. L. Broecker]
P. B. Hales: *William Henry Jackson and the Transformation of the American Landscape* (Philadelphia, 1988)

SHERYL CONKELTON

Jacob (i). German family of architects. A master mason named Jacob is mentioned in 1302 and 1307 at Xanten Cathedral, North Rhine-Westphalia. It is possible, but not very likely, that he began its construction in 1263; the building follows St Yved, Braisne (France), in plan and elevation, but Cologne Cathedral in its details. A son or nephew, also called Jacob (*d* Xanten, 1374), is first mentioned at Xanten in 1302. It is recorded that he made a wooden model (destr.) of a tracery window, and that his assistants worked to wooden templates. He worked in Prussia from 1360 to 1361 but returned to Xanten.

Thieme–Becker   BIBLIOGRAPHY

ARNOLD WOLFF

Jacob (ii). French family of furniture-makers. Georges Jacob I (*b* Cheny, 6 July 1739; *d* Paris, 5 July 1814) arrived in Paris in 1755 and became a Maître Ebéniste on 4 September 1765. His first business was in the Rue de Cléry, Paris, from 1767 and the Rue Meslée from 1775. At the start of his career he produced curvilinear models often decorated with carved flowers and foliage (e.g. 1777; Paris, Louvre), characteristic of chairs at the end of the reign of Louis XV. His reputation rests on the production of numerous, sometimes innovative varieties of high-quality seats in the Louis XVI and Empire styles, for which his work was seminal. He was probably the first to use the common Louis XVI form of tapering, fluted legs headed by a rosette within a square (e.g. of 1780–90; Paris, Mus. Nissim de Camondo), and he introduced console-shaped legs that terminated in a volute below the seat rail (e.g. *fauteuil de toilette*, 1770; Paris, Louvre) and promoted the use of baluster-shaped arm supports (e.g. *fauteuil à la reine*; Paris, Mus. A. Déc.), also using them on the later Empire-style seats. He was one of the first, following the English, to use mahogany for seats. His production, which included beds (*see* BED, fig. 2), console tables and screens, and later cabinet work, strongly featured carved decoration, ranging from the standard Louis XVI motifs of twisted ribbons, foliate *rinceaux*, stylized acanthus leaves, guilloche, beading and fluting to the Turkish-style suite of furniture (Paris, Louvre) supplied in 1777 to Charles, Comte d'Artois (later King Charles X), and carved by Jean-Baptiste Rode (1735–99), which prefigured the Empire style (*see* BOURBON, §I(14)). Much of the carving and gilding was executed by the Jacob workshops, but on certain occasions outside craftsmen were used.

In 1789 Jacob supplied Jacques-Louis David with a suite of mahogany furniture (untraced) for which David had provided drawings inspired by Roman antiquity. Intended as props for his studio, they appear in a number of David's paintings, such as the *Lictors Bringing Brutus the Bodies of his Sons* (1789; Paris, Louvre; *see* NEO-CLASSICISM, fig. 1). Jacob's friendship with David caused him to be relatively untroubled by the Revolution, despite his having worked prolifically for the Garde-Meuble de la Couronne from 1773, and his business became one of the chief suppliers to the Revolutionary government and later to the Emperor Napoleon I (*see* COMPIÈGNE).

Georges Jacob I retired in 1796, making his business over to his sons Georges Jacob II (*b* Paris, 1768; *d* Paris, 23 Oct 1803) and François-Honoré-Georges Jacob (1770–1841), who stamped their work JACOB FRÈRES RUE MES-LÉE. When Georges Jacob II died, Georges Jacob I became his son's partner, and thereafter the business was styled Jacob-Desmalter et Cie and the work stamped with JACOB D. R. MESLÉE for 'Jacob-Desmalter, Rue Meslée'. The business was one of the most important of the period, and by 1808 it employed 332 workmen and produced mostly restrained, predominantly mahogany, furniture in the Empire style. Although the business had severe financial difficulties and went bankrupt in 1813, François-Honoré-Georges continued until his son Alphonse-George Jacob (1799–1870) succeeded him in 1825. Alphonse-George Jacob sold the business in 1847 to Joseph-Pierre-François Jeanselme (*d* 1860).

BIBLIOGRAPHY

H. Lefuel: *Georges Jacob, ébéniste du XVIIIe siècle* (Paris, 1923)
S. Grandjean: *Empire Furniture, 1800–1825* (London, 1965)
D. Ledoux-Lebard: *Les Ébénistes du XIXe siècle 1795–1889, leurs oeuvres et leurs marques* (Paris, 1984)
P. Kjellberg: *Le Mobilier français du XVIIIe siècle* (Paris, 1989)

ELEANOR JOHN

Jacob, Max (*b* Quimper, 12 July 1876; *d* Drancy, 5 March 1944). French draughtsman, painter and writer. On leaving school he went to Paris, where he led a bohemian existence in Montmartre, writing reviews of exhibitions for the *Gazette des Beaux-Arts* and painting stage scenery in oils. He produced pastels and gouaches (e.g. *Portrait of Guillaume Apollinaire*, *c.* 1910; Orléans, Mus. B.-A.) that show him to be a recorder of avant-garde cultural life in Paris. He was closely involved in Cubist and modernist circles there, painting under the influence of Picasso. His literary output began with tales for children, and his first books of poems, illustrated by Picasso and published by Daniel-Henry Kahnweiler, marked an important stage in the history of fine books (*Oeuvres burlesques et mystiques du Frère Matorel, mort au couvent de Barcelone*, Paris, 1912; *Le Siège de Jérusalem*, Paris, 1914). He also produced prose poems (e.g. *Cornet à dés*, Paris, 1917), lyrical verse, novels and short stories, which all bear witness to the sharp and ironic eye he cast on society. They echo, albeit ironically, his spiritual path, which was distinguished by two visions, in 1909 and 1915. Jacob was a convert to Catholicism, and from 1921 he lived in retreat at Saint-Benoît-sur-Loire, devoting himself to a devout life, interrupted by brief trips abroad.

In 1927 Jacob returned to Paris, where he led a dissolute existence, which disgusted him but which nurtured his poetry. Returning to Saint-Benoît to meditate in the shades of the monastery, he lived on his paintings and drawings. Jacob had first illustrated his own writings in 1920 and this culminated in 40 drawings for the poetry collection *Visions des souffrances et de la mort de Jésus, fils de Dieu* (Paris, 1928). Throughout the 1920s and 1930s he exhibited deliberately naive religious and genre scenes (e.g. *Feast-day at Quimper*, 1925; Quimper, Mus. B.-A.). He gained a contract with the Galerie Petit, Paris, in 1927–31, and his sparse linear drawings played an increasing role in his activities in the 1930s. Arrested by the Germans because of his Jewish origins, he died in the camp at Drancy.

WRITINGS
ed. J. de Palacio: *Max Jacob*, Les Revues des lettres modernes, 474/478 (Paris, 1973–81)

BIBLIOGRAPHY
Y. Belaval: *La Rencontre avec Max Jacob* (Paris, 1946)
R. G. Cadou: *Esthétique de Max Jacob* (Paris, 1956)
Europe (April–May, 1958) [special issue]
R. Plantier: *L'Univers poétique de Max Jacob* (1963)
Hommage à Max Jacob, 1876–1944 (exh. cat., Paris, Mus. Montparnasse, 1976–7)
M. Pleynet: *Max Jacob: Dessins* (Paris, 1978)
P. Andreu: *Vie et mort de Max Jacob* (Paris, 1982)
Max Jacob, l'archange foudroyé (exh. cat., Orléans, Mus. B.-A., 1994)
Max Jacob et Picasso (exh. cat., Quimper, Mus. B.-A.; Paris, Mus. Picasso; 1994)

HENRI BÉHAR

Jacob, Pierre. *See* TAL-COAT, PIERRE.

Jacob, Sir **Samuel Swinton** (*b* 14 Jan 1841; *d* Weybridge, 4 Dec 1917). English engineer, architect and writer, active in India. He was educated at Cheam and then at the East India Company Military College at Addiscombe where he was one of the last batch of graduates. He entered the Bombay Artillery in 1858, qualifying five years later as a surveyor and engineer. After initial service in the Public Works Department, and a brief spell with the Aden Field Force in 1865–6, he was appointed Chief Engineer to Jaipur state where he spent his entire working life.

An extremely prolific engineer and architect, he was responsible for a large number of important irrigation schemes but was also a pioneer and one of the most accomplished exponents of eclectic 'Indo-Saracenic' architecture. His *Jeypore Portfolio of Architectural Details* (1890), published for the Maharajah, is a vast, scholarly compendium of architectural details of north Indian buildings that became a recognized pattern book and standard reference work. His principal works include the Anglican church (1870–75), Mayo Hospital and the Albert Hall and Museum (now the Government Central Museum of Jaipur, 1876–87), Jaipur, where he also made extensive alterations to the palace complex; Gorton Castle, Simla; the Victoria Memorial Hall, Peshawar; Mayo College (1875), Ajmer; St John's College, Agra; the State Bank at Madras; Lallgarh Palace (1895), Bikaner; and Daly College (*c.* 1905), Indore; and numerous civic and college buildings at Lucknow. On his return to England in 1911, he was brought in briefly to advise on Indian materials and detailing during the preparation of the plans for the new Indian capital at New Delhi until ill-health forced his retirement.

See also INDIAN SUBCONTINENT, §III, 8(i).

BIBLIOGRAPHY
Obituary, *The Times* (7 Dec 1917); *RIBA J.*, n.s. 3, xxv (1918), p. 72
E. W. Sandes: *The Military Engineer in India* (Chatham, 1933–5)
T. R. Metcalf: 'A Tradition Created: Indo-Saracenic Architecture under the Raj', *Hist. Today*, xxxii (1982), pp. 40–45
P. Davies: *Splendours of the Raj: British Architecture in India, 1660–1947* (London, 1985)
T. R. Metcalf: *An Imperial Vision: Indian Architecture and Britain's Raj* (London and Boston, 1989)

PHILIP DAVIES

Jacobean style. Term loosely used to describe British art and architecture produced during the reign (1603–25) of James I of England (James VI of Scotland). Portraiture dominated both miniature and easel painting in this period, during which the decorative and jewel-like manner of the Elizabethan era was carried to an extreme. John de Critz, Robert Peake, William Larkin and other court artists were much in demand for their iconic depictions of sitters, in which clothes, jewellery and heraldic insignia are minutely detailed. In the work of Daniel Mijtens I and Paul van Somer, there emerges a greater interest in the physical setting; this can be seen, for example, in Mijtens's use of a gallery and distant garden for the background to his pendant portraits of *Thomas Howard, 2nd Earl of Arundel* and *Alathea, Countess of Arundel* (both 1618; Arundel Castle, W. Sussex) and in van Somer's *Queen Anne at Oatlands* (1618; Windsor Castle, Berks, Royal Col.), whose background includes Inigo Jones's fashionable Serlian gate for Oatlands Palace, Surrey (destr.).

Jacobean architecture is most readily associated with the large brick-built prodigy houses of the English ruling class; they include Audley End (*c.* 1603–16), Essex, Hatfield House (1607–12), Herts, and Blickling Hall (designed 1616–17), Norfolk. Extravagantly massed and silhouetted, early 17th-century country houses were frequently enlivened with arcades or loggias and ogee-capped towers; such features as balustrades and porches were often carved with Mannerist decorative motifs by Flemish or Flemish-trained masons, or by English masons working from pattern books. The Jacobean style thus contrasts strongly with the purer Renaissance classicism of Inigo Jones's Palladian buildings, commissioned by the court towards the end of James's reign. The so-called Jacobethan Revival houses of the Victorian period were modelled on the forms and detailing of Elizabethan as well as Jacobean architecture, for example Bear Wood (1865–74), Berks, by

Robert Kerr, or Hewell Grange (1884–91), Hereford & Worcs, by G. F. Bodley and Thomas Garner.

BIBLIOGRAPHY

J. Summerson: *Architecture in Britain, 1530–1830*, Pelican Hist. A. (Harmondsworth, 1953, rev. 7/1983)
E. K. Waterhouse: *Painting in Britain, 1530–1790*, Pelican Hist. A. (Harmondsworth, 1953, rev. 4/1978)
E. Mercer: *English Art, 1553–1625*, Oxford Hist. Eng. A. (Oxford, 1962)
M. Whinney: *Sculpture in Britain, 1530–1830*, Pelican Hist. A. (Harmondsworth, 1964, rev. 2/1988 by J. Physick)

ALICE T. FRIEDMAN

Jacobello d'Antonio [Jacopo di Antonello; ?Pino da Messina] (*b* ?Messina, ?*c.* 1456; *d* ?*c.* 1488 or after 1508). Italian painter, son of ANTONELLO DA MESSINA. He is first documented in his father's will of February 1479, in which he is named as the chief beneficiary. Documents between then and 1482 indicate that he assumed responsibility for the workshop and for completing work left unfinished by his father; in early 1480 he took his cousin Antonio de Saliba into the *bottega* as an apprentice. The documentary silence after the early 1480s has led to the suggestions that he may have 'emigrated' to Venice, which he probably first visited with his father in 1475–6, or, more likely, that he died young, before 1490.

A *Virgin and Child* (1480; Bergamo, Gal. Accad. Carrara) is Jacobello's only surviving signed and dated work; its *cartellino* bears a tribute to his deceased father. The painting may originally have been commissioned from Antonello, although the execution is entirely by Jacobello (Previtali). The poses are derived from his father's work: the Virgin from the *St Gregory* altarpiece (1473; Messina, Mus. Reg.) and the Child from the S Cassiano Altarpiece (1475; fragments, Vienna, Ksthist. Mus.). Analogies can also be drawn with the slight harshness and calligraphic touch of the Benson–Mackay *Virgin and Child* (Washington, DC, N.G.A.), considered a father–son collaboration, but both works are poorly preserved. Jacobello's collaboration in several of Antonello's other late works, including his *Pietà* (Madrid, Prado), has also been proposed: this would explain not only the enamel-like surface (unlike the more delicate finish of his father's work) but also the slightly obvious appeal to religious emotionalism (which his father tended to handle with greater subtlety).

The attribution of an imposing *Virgin and Child* (Syracuse, Archbishop's Pal.), with its strong reminiscences of Antonello's S Cassiano Altarpiece in composition and spatial organization, has received some support. However, its indebtedness to the more rigorous stylistic characteristics of the turn of the century creates problems if the case for Jacobello's early demise is sustained.

BIBLIOGRAPHY

G. di Marzo: *Di Antonello e dei suoi congiunti* (Palermo, 1903/R 1983), pp. 23–85 and documents [app.]
Antonello e la pittura del '400 in Sicilia (exh. cat., ed. G. Vigni and G. Caradente; Messina, Pal. Comm., 1953), pp. 79–80
S. Bottari: *La pittura del '400 in Sicilia* (Messina and Florence, 1954), pp. 58–62, 87–8
M. G. Paolini: 'Antonello e la sua scuola', *Stor. Sicilia*, v (1979), pp. 50–51
G. Previtali: 'Da Antonello da Messina a Jacopo di Antonello, 2: Il Cristo deposto del Museo del Prado', *Prospettiva*, xxi (1981), pp. 45–57

Antonello da Messina (exh. cat., ed. A. Marabottini and F. Sricchia Santoro; Messina, Mus. Reg., 1981), pp. 212–16
F. Sricchia Santoro: *Antonello e l'Europa* (Milan, 1986), pp. 137–42

JOANNE WRIGHT

Jacobello del Fiore (*fl* Venice, 1400; *d* 1439). Italian painter. Together with Niccolò di Pietro and Zanino di Pietro, he was one of the most important Venetian painters of the first third of the 15th century. His work marks the transition from a local, retardataire style based on the example of Paolo Veneziano and his school to a fully developed Late Gothic style of remarkable decorative complexity. However, to a greater degree than his two contemporaries, Jacobello's work remained tied to Venetian precedent, and it has been undervalued. He was the most refined Venetian painter of his generation and a narrator of exceptional skill who influenced such artists as Michele Giambono and, to a lesser degree, Antonio Vivarini.

1. EARLY LIFE AND WORKS. Jacobello was active as a painter in Venice as early as 1400, but his earliest documented works were all destined for places on the Adriatic coast. In 1401 he was in Pesaro, where he painted an altarpiece for the church of S Cassiano. This was followed in 1407 by the triptych with the *Madonna of Mercy* in the centre for Montegranaro, outside Pesaro; its inscription reads *in venezia* and it must have been sent from Venice to the church for which it was commissioned. A third picture for Pesaro, an altarpiece of 1409, has also been documented. Of these three works, only the second can be identified with certainty, though it is possible that the altarpiece of 1409 is identical with a polyptych from S Francesco, Pesaro (Pesaro, Mus. Civ.). Conservative—almost retardataire—in design, with stiff, schematic figures, the two surviving altarpieces evolved from a purely local Venetian training and show no awareness of the international or courtly style introduced into Venice by Michelino da Besozzo and Gentile da Fabriano. It is small wonder that Jacobello's audience was drawn not from the university environment of Padua or the Lombard-oriented culture of Verona, but from provincial centres along the Adriatic and from the signory of Venice.

On 11 January 1412 Jacobello's annual stipend from the signory, the considerable sum of 100 ducats, was reduced to 50 because of the war Venice was conducting in Dalmatia. Jacobello was probably among the artists who, between 1409 and 1415, decorated the Sala del Maggior Consiglio in the Doge's Palace in Venice. This was the most important Venetian commission of the first half of the 15th century, responsible for putting Venetian artists in direct contact with the most advanced painters of the mainland. Gentile da Fabriano and Pisanello are both known to have painted a scene, and Michelino da Besozzo, whom circumstantial evidence indicates was in Venice at least between 1410 and 1414, probably participated as well. It was, in any event, after 1410 that Jacobello's work underwent a transformation. For the Doge's Palace in 1415 he painted a heraldic *Lion of St Mark* (*in situ*): Michelino's influence is apparent in its softly modelled forms, in the decorative sweep of its wings and in the abstract pattern created by its tail. It was perhaps at the same time that Jacobello painted the *Madonna of Mercy* (Venice, Accademia; the inscription and date, 1436, are false), in which both the heavy-limbed child and the broad areas of raised pastiglia decoration are derived from Michelino and used to a marvellously decorative effect.

2. THE 'TRIPTYCH OF JUSTICE'. Jacobello's next dated work, the great *Triptych of Justice* painted for the Magistrato del Proprio in the Doge's Palace (1421; Venice, Accad.; see fig. 1), marks the beginning of an indigenous Venetian Late Gothic style. In 1648 Ridolfi recorded that the painting was installed above an *armaio* (cupboard) and inscribed: *1421. 23. Novembrio. Jacobellus de Flore Pinxt*; the present, abbreviated name and date on the centre panel obviously derive from the original inscription. The Magistrato del Proprio was a civil and criminal court, and the commission celebrated both functions. In the centre panel, seated on the hindquarters of two lions (a reference to Solomon's throne), is a crowned figure personifying both Justice and Venice. In one hand she holds the scales with which the evidence is weighed, and in the other a sword, the means of punishment. Her breastplate is emblazoned with a sun in relief. A figure identical save for the substitution of a scroll for the scales was carved, possibly in 1422, on a roundel of the Doge's Palace facing the Piazzetta, and it is identified by an inscription as *Venecia*. Crowning the Porta della Carta is a similar figure, executed some two decades later by Bartolomeo Buon (i), identified as *Justicia*. The scroll behind Jacobello's figure is inscribed with a Latin distich: 'I will carry out the admonition of the angels and the holy word: gentle with the pious, harsh with the evil, and haughty with the proud'. To the left, St Michael uses the sword to slay an extravagantly oriental dragon, while the scroll he holds urges Venetia–Justitia to reward or punish according to merit and to 'commend the purged souls to the scales of benignity'. To the right Gabriel, his movement encumbered by a welter of drapery, raises his right hand while with his left hand he unfurls a scroll identifying himself as the messenger of the virgin birth and of peace among men

and urging Venetia–Justitia (now equated with the Virgin) to lead men through the darkness. The pose of each figure is echoed by the pattern made by the individual scrolls. As with Michelino, the shape of the picture field, delimited by the frame (which is in large part original), played a determining role in the composition of each panel. Gilded pastiglia is used with an abandon that is almost without parallel. Jacobello's *Justice* triptych established the pattern of Venetian painting for more than a decade. Giambono's *St Michael* (Florence, I Tatti) pays homage to it and so also does Michele di Matteo's altarpiece of the *Virgin with Saints* (Venice, Accad.).

3. THE 'LIFE OF ST LUCY' AND FINAL YEARS. Jacobello's masterpiece is the series of scenes illustrating the *Life of St Lucy* (Fermo, Pin. Com.). These were commissioned for a coastal town on the Adriatic, and, although it has been argued that they were painted in Fermo, they may well have been painted in Venice and then dispatched to the church of S Lucia, where they are first mentioned in an inventory of 1728. Originally they must have been arranged in two superimposed tiers on either side of a central panel or sculpted image of the saint, similar to the altarpiece painted in Paolo Veneziano's workshop in the mid-14th century for the abbey church of S Lucia in Jurandor, near Baska (Trieste, Mus. Civ. Stor. & A.). This type of altarpiece derives from Romanesque dossals, and it continued to be employed into the third quarter of the 15th century, when Bartolomeo Vivarini painted the altarpiece of the *Virgin* (now in a false frame; New York, Met.).

With only one exception, Jacobello illustrated the same events from St Lucy's life as had Paolo Veneziano. In the first scene St Lucy visits the tomb of St Agatha, who appears to her in a dream; in the second, she distributes her possessions to the poor; in the third she refuses to sacrifice to idols; in the fourth oxen are unable to drag her to a brothel; in the fifth an unsuccessful attempt is made to burn her at the stake; in the sixth she is stabbed in the throat; in the seventh she receives Holy Communion

1. Jacobello del Fiore: *Triptych of Justice*, oil and gilt on panel, 1.97×4.82 m, 1421 (Venice, Galleria dell'Accademia)

before dying; and in the eighth she is buried. Jacobello employed a good deal more architecture and landscape than had Paolo to describe the setting of each scene, but he nonetheless remained faithful to his predecessor's conception of narrative. Although Jacobello's flowering meadows and curving rocky hills must derive from scenes similar to those of Gentile da Fabriano's polyptych of the *Coronation of the Virgin* (Milan, Brera), Jacobello has in no sense tried to emulate the naturalism that distinguishes Gentile's scenes. His buildings have the toy-like fragility of Paolo Veneziano's cover for the Pala d'Oro (Venice, Mus. S Marco), and, for example in *St Lucy Distributing her Possessions* (see fig. 2), there is a total inconsistency between the upper and lower storeys. The figures move almost as if they were dancing, only occasionally seeming to set their feet on the ground. 'Jacobello held to the Greek [Byzantine] style', wrote Vasari, and in a sense he was correct, although his verdict perhaps obscures two facts. The first is that Jacobello's work was of primary importance to the subsequent generation of artists, like Giambono. The second is that Jacobello's approximation to the narrative style of Paolo Veneziano occurs in his mature, not in his youthful, work and is at least partially a reaction to contact with those three great non-Venetians: Michelino, Gentile and Pisanello. This has not always been grasped, and the *St Lucy* series has been dated relatively early in Jacobello's career. However, if the scenes are compared to the indisputably early *Adoration of the Magi*

triptych (Stockholm, Nmus) or the small scene of *Tobias with the Angel* (Tulsa, OK, Philbrook A. Cent.), where the forms are stiffer, the figures more schematic and the decorative sense less evolved, an early dating proves untenable. In this sense, Jacobello's development runs parallel to that of Zanino and Niccolò di Pietro, though his frame of reference was exclusively local.

Jacobello died in 1439, but there is no securely documented work after 1421 and almost two decades of activity are therefore a matter of speculation. He had an adopted son, Ercole del Fiore, who in 1461 stated that he was a painter, and it may be that Ercole acted as an assistant in Jacobello's shop and is the author of such weak pictures as the *Coronation of the Virgin from Ceneda* (Venice, Accad.) or other related works that have been associated with Jacobello. The most important of these is an altarpiece painted for S Pietro, Fermo (Denver, CO, A. Mus.), which Zeri argued is an early work, but which is certainly later than the *St Lucy* series and not necessarily by Jacobello.

BIBLIOGRAPHY

I. Chiappini di Sorio: 'Per una datazione tarda della Madonna Correr di Jacobello del Fiore', *Boll. Mus. Civ. Ven.*, 4 (1968), pp. 11–25

F. Zeri: 'Jacobello del Fiore: La pala di S Pietro a Fermo', *Diari Lavoro*, i (1971), pp. 36–40

I. Chiappini di Sorio: 'Note e appunti su Jacobello del Fiore', *Not. Pal. Albani*, ii (1973), pp. 23–8

S. Sinding-Larsen: *Christ in the Council Hall: Studies in the Religious Iconography of the Venetian Republic*, Acta Archaeol. & A. Hist. Pertinentia, v (1974), pp. 56, 67, 167–75

K. Christiansen: *Gentile da Fabriano* (Ithaca, NY, 1982), pp. 70–71, n. 15

'K. Christiansen: 'La pittura a Venezia e in Veneto nel primo quattrocento', *La pittura in Italia: Il quattrocento*, i (Milan, 1987), pp. 124–8

M. Lucco: Venetia 1400–1430', *La pittura nel Veneto: Il quattrocento*, i (Milan, 1989), pp. 13–34

KEITH CHRISTIANSEN

Jacobello di Bonomo (*fl* 1370–90). Italian painter. In 1375 he signed a panel of *St Ursula* (ex-S Michele, Vicenza). In 1384 he contracted to take on two pupils, and in 1385 he signed a polyptych of the *Virgin and Child with Saints* (Santarcangelo di Romagna, Municipio), which is the basis for all attributions. If polyptychs of *St Augustine and Other Saints* (Arquà Petrarca, Santa Trinità) and the *Madonna of Humility and Saints* (Lecce, Mus. Prov. Sigismondo Castromediano) are, as Pallucchini argues, early works of Jacobello's, they indicate a development under the influence of Lorenzo Veneziano. The Santarcangelo polyptych, however, shows a marked departure in style and may suggest a knowledge of other Italian traditions. Lorenzo's daintiness is replaced by the solidity typified by the figure of St Catherine. Draperies are less exuberant, the underlying forms more insistent, with a greater interest in sculptural mass than in linear pattern. The recession of the Virgin's throne is more ambitious and accurate than that of thrones drawn by Lorenzo's followers, Catarino or Stefano di Sant'Agnese. Furthermore, Jacobello's figures are bulkier and his faces less elongated. His facial modelling is less refined, more graphic than painterly, and his characters appear less abstracted than Stefano's. Jacobello's style at its most impressively ponderous is seen in some of the saints from a polyptych of the *Virgin and Child with Saints* in Prague Cathedral.

BIBLIOGRAPHY

P. Paoletti: 'Un' ancona di Jacobello di Bonomo', *Rass. A.*, iii (1903), pp. 65–6

2. Jacobello del Fiore: *St Lucy Distributing her Possessions*, 700×520 mm, panel from the *Life of St Lucy* altarpiece, tempera and gilt on panel, *c.* 1410 (Fermo, Pinacoteca Comunale)

R. Longhi: *Viatico per cinque secoli di pittura veneziana* (Florence, 1946)

S. Marconi: 'Restauro di dipinti di Lorenzo Veneziano', *Boll. A.*, xxxiv (1949), pp. 156–61

F. Bologna: 'Contributi allo studio della pittura veneziana', *A. Ven.*, v (1951), pp. 21–31; vi (1952), pp. 7–18

P. Toesca: *Storia dell'arte italiana*, ii: *Il trecento* (Turin, 1951)

B. Berenson: *Venetian School*, i (1957), p. 94

L. Puppi: 'Contributi a Jacobello di Bonomo', *A. Ven.*, xvi (1962), pp. 19–30

R. Pallucchini: *La pittura veneziana del trecento* (Venice, 1964), pp. 200–07 [full set of pls]

JOHN RICHARDS

Jacobi [Jacobi Reiss], **Lotte** [Johanna Alexandra] (*b* Thorn, W. Prussia [now Torun, Poland], 17 Aug 1896; *d* Concord, NH, 9 May 1990). American photographer of German birth. From 1925 to 1927 she studied photography and film at the Bavarian State Academy of Photography, Munich. She took over her father's photographic studio in Berlin in 1927 and became noted for celebrity portraits. Because of Nazism she left Berlin to establish a studio in New York (1935). She avoided a specific style, often presenting subjects casually, for example the portrait of *Albert Einstein* (1938; see Wise, p. 100) wearing a leather jacket. Another aspect of her professional work was published as *Theatre and Dance Photographs* (Woodstock, VT, 1982). She used the term 'photogenics' to describe the abstract black-and-white images that she produced by moving torches and candles over light-sensitive paper. In 1955 she moved to Deering, NH, and opened a studio.

BIBLIOGRAPHY

K. Wise, ed.: *Lotte Jacobi*, intro. J. A. Fasanelli (Danbury, NH, 1978)

M. K. Mitchell, ed.: *Recollections: 10 Women of Photography* (New York, 1979)

JOHN FULLER

Jacobs, Henri (François Eugène) (*b* Brussels, 3 Dec 1864; *d* Brussels, 29 Nov 1935). Belgian architect. He began his career in 1892 by winning a competition for the construction of small workers' houses in Laeken, Brussels. In 1899, also as a result of a competition, he became architect to Le Foyer Schaerbeekois, the organization providing low-cost housing in Schaerbeek, Brussels. Between 1900 and 1910 he built seven groups of low-cost housing for the organization, mainly designed as houses divided into flats. The composition of their façades was sober and rational, incorporating an Art Nouveau stylistic vocabulary similar to that of Paul Hankar: contrasting materials, visible lintels and small iron columns, the use of colour, particularly yellow and red brick, and *sgraffito* decoration.

Jacobs was one of the few Art Nouveau architects specializing in the public sector. In 1907 the construction of a school complex in Rue Josaphat in Schaerbeek earned him an unchallenged reputation in this field. The school was considered at the time to be truly palatial: as well as normal school buildings, it also included a gymnasium, swimming-pool and industrial school, all set out around vast playgrounds according to a clearly articulated layout. The interior spaces and façades, which were influenced by both Victor Horta and Paul Hankar, henceforth constituted a model for school buildings in Belgium. Between 1904 and 1922 Jacobs built at least another ten schools in Brussels; he also built private houses, the most interesting

of which was his own house (1903), often decorated with *sgraffito* designs that owe much to Privat-Livemont. He was awarded several prizes in local competitions.

BIBLIOGRAPHY

F. Borsi, R.-L. Delevoy and H. Wieser-Benedetti: *Bruxelles 1900: Capitale de l'Art Nouveau* (Rome, 1972)

J. H. Baudon and others: *Brussels, 1890–1978: Guide d'architecture* (Brussels, 1978), pl. 72–3

MARIE DEMANET

Jacobsen, Arne (Emil) (*b* Copenhagen, 11 Feb 1902; *d* Copenhagen, 24 March 1971). Danish architect and designer. He studied at the Arkitektskole of the Kunstakademi in Copenhagen (Dip. Arch., 1928). He began his career with elegant single-family houses influenced by Danish country house architecture of *c.* 1800. However, as a result of a series of prominent commissions, he soon became known outside architectural circles as an advocate of ultra-modern architecture, although he was disinclined to support 'trends' in architecture or issue manifestos. In 1929, in collaboration with Flemming Lassen (1902–84), he designed the cylindrical 'House of the Future' for the *Bygge- og Bolig Udstillingen i Forum* (Building and home exhibition in the Forum) in Copenhagen, and over the next few years he left his mark on Copenhagen's newly laid-out riviera at Klampenborg with such projects as the beach development at Bellevue (1932), the housing complex Bellavista (1934), Bellevue Summer Theatre (1937) and the service station at Skovshoved harbour (1938). In these projects Jacobsen drew upon the central European early modernist white Cubist style, also revealing his well-developed feeling for architectonic form and for the characteristics of the site. Stelling's House (1937–8), Gammel Torv 6, Copenhagen, despite its modest and restrained modernism, aroused violent protest, although it was later regarded as a model example of successful new building in historical surroundings.

In 1937, with Erik Møller, Jacobsen won the competition for the town hall in Århus (executed 1939–42). Again protests followed, partly because public opinion expected a tower for such a building: they designed a convincing structure in the form of an open ferro-concrete skeleton around a solid core. In 1939, with Lassen, he won the competition for the town hall in Søllerød, near Copenhagen (executed 1940–42). Both town halls were built at a time when Jacobsen acknowledged great admiration for Gunnar Asplund's works, particularly his later projects. Asplund's influence is most evident in the town halls' meticulous and luxurious detailing, whose complexity is a far cry from the ideals of Functionalism. However, their elegant plans with parallel transposed office wings have more affinity with Vilhelm Lauritzen's project for Radio House (1934) in Copenhagen, a type of design to which Jacobsen turned with variations in his plan for the Elektrizitätswerke office blocks (1963) in Hamburg.

As well as these large projects Jacobsen designed numerous single-family houses and smaller developments, generally in brick with tiled roofs in the compact form Kay Fisker had evolved as part of the Danish Functionalist tradition. The fish-smoking house (1943) at Odden harbour is of modest format but characteristic. From 1943 to

1945 Jacobsen lived as a refugee in Stockholm. In collaboration with his wife, Jonna Jacobsen (*b* 1908), a textile printer, he designed textiles and wallpapers based on his watercolour studies of Danish flora, which became immensely popular. The terraced house development Søholm (1950), near Bellavista in Klampenborg, secured Jacobsen's international reputation. The small development was planned to take full advantage of the opposition of the view and the direction of the sunlight; it caused a stir in the early post-war years when quality was often sacrificed to quantity, and architectural integrity was rare. An equally sensitive treatment of familiar elements is evident in Hårby School (1951), the exhibition building at Glostrup (1952) and Munkegård School (1952–6), Gentofte.

During this period Jacobsen was obviously inspired by the industrial image in the International Style, as expressed for example in works by Skidmore, Owings & Merrill and by Eero Saarinen. This is reflected in three curtain-wall structures, which are simplified almost to the point of abstraction: the office block for Jespersen and Sons (1953), Copenhagen; Rødovre Town Hall (1955); and the SAS Royal Hotel (1958–60). Similarly, the Carl Christensen Factory at Ålborg (1957; see fig.) exemplifies Jacobsen's success in good proportioning and simplicity in a design. In the SAS Royal Hotel Jacobsen designed all the furnishing and fittings too. By 1960 Jacobsen's application of the International Style relaxed in favour of a freer and more individual approach, with emphasis on sculptural and structural aspects. This was expressed in an increasing number of international commissions such as the courtyard houses (1957) at Hansaviertel, Berlin; St Catherine's College (1964), Oxford; the town centre (1964; completed 1976), Castrop-Rauxell, Germany; Christianeum College (1965–71), Hamburg; the town hall of Mainz (1968; executed 1970–73); and the Danish Embassy (1971; executed 1972–6) in London. Jacobsen's last big Danish project was the National Bank in Copenhagen, which won the competition of 1961 (first stage executed 1965–71). Jacobsen died unexpectedly halfway through the work. His practice was continued by his close colleagues Hans Dissing (*b* 1926) and Otto Weitling (*b* 1930), who completed the works under construction. On their own initiative they created distinctive buildings abroad including the National Bank (1984), Baghdad, and the Staatliches Kunstmuseum (1986), Düsseldorf.

Although Jacobsen introduced several new international trends to Denmark, he did so without programmatic intentions: his architecture was not polemical. On the contrary, with an intuitive understanding of contemporary movements he aimed consistently for an architecture of elegance and comfort, which in his younger days made him too 'fashionable' for pure Functionalists, while those shackled by tradition could not accept his originality. His sources of inspiration are often clear (for example, Lever House was the model for the SAS Royal Hotel), yet Jacobsen was no mere imitator. His uncompromising mastery of the overall form and the variety of treatment of detail, space and surroundings meant that he often surpassed the original concept. As an architect of international standing his work inevitably acquired an air of exclusivity, but he never made distinctions over the differing prestige values of his commissions, taking on even quite modest projects, as in the industrial plans for Novo (1934–69), Toms Factories (1960–62) and many

Arne Jacobsen: Carl Christensen Factory, Ålborg, 1957

smaller housing developments. Although he designed furniture and a wide range of items for particular houses, the objects were later released for mass production. In particular, his unpretentious chair, the Ant (*myren*), made of moulded wood, became internationally famous, as did the sculpturally shaped Swan (*svanen*) and Egg (*aegget*) chairs, originally designed for the SAS Royal Hotel. His work in landscape gardening also had the same effortlessly sure touch. He laid out both the park-like surroundings of Toms Factories and the intimate courtyard gardens of Munkegård School and often enhanced the public areas in his buildings with a very sensitive use of plants. In addition, he was an outstanding draughtsman and water-colourist. In 1956 he was appointed Professor Extraordinary at the Arkitektskole of the Kunstakademi in Copenhagen, but his association with the school was chiefly a formal one.

BIBLIOGRAPHY

Between 1957 and 1978 most of Jacobsen's buildings were illustrated in *Arkitektur DK*.

J. Pedersen: *Arkitekten Arne Jacobsen* [Arne Jacobsen the architect] (Copenhagen, 1954)
T. Faber: *Arne Jacobsen* (Stuttgart, 1964)
J. Kastholm: *Arne Jacobsen* (Copenhagen, 1968)
B. Funk and W. Jung: *Das Mainzer Rathaus* (Mainz, 1974)
Arne Jacobsen, Danish Ministry of Foreign Affairs (Copenhagen, 1976)
R. P. Hackney: *The Life and Work of Arne Jacobsen: The Complete Design Approach to Architecture*, 4 vols (PhD thesis, U. Manchester, 1979)
L. Rubino: *Arne Jacobsen* (Rome, 1980)
D. Sharp: *Sources of Modern Architecture* (London, 1981), p. 62 [biog. and select bibliog.]
E. Møller and K. Vindum: *Århus Rådhus* [Århus town hall] (Copenhagen, 1991)

JØRGEN SESTOFT

Jacobsen, Carl (Christian Hillmann) (*b* Copenhagen, 2 March 1842; *d* Copenhagen, 11 Jan 1914). Danish brewer and collector. In 1879 he founded the Ny Carlsberg Bryggeri and later became the director of both the Gammel Carlsberg and Ny Carlsberg breweries. With money from his inheritance and with revenues from the brewery, he established such trust funds for art as the Albertinalegat in 1879 and the Museumslegat in 1883. In 1878 he had begun to assemble his own large art collection, acquiring such works as Eugène Delaplanche's marble figure of a woman, *Music* (1878; Copenhagen, Ny Carlsberg Glyp.). In 1882, encouraged by the sculptor Rasmus Secher Malthe (1829–93), Jacobsen obtained a major collection of plaster models by Hermann Wilhelm Bissen. In the same year he established the Ny Carlsberg Glyptotek and opened it to the public in his home in Valby, Copenhagen. In 1888 his collection of contemporary sculpture was also donated to the public. For the next ten years he continued to make large purchases of French and antique sculpture and, through his association with the German archaeologist Wolfgang Helbig, acquired several Roman portrait busts. These also formed part of his collection at Valby. In 1897 Jacobsen's collection was installed in Copenhagen in a new building of Venetian Renaissance design by Hack Kampmann and Jens Vilhelm Dahlerup (1836–1907). The corner rooms with the lantern-towers are, however, by Jacobsen. In order to ensure the growth of the collection, the Ny Carlsberg Bryggeri was handed over in 1902 to the Ny Carlsbergfondet, the aims of which were to support

painting, architecture, ornamental gardening and art scholarship. The favourable conditions under which he collected, and the large sums of money he made available for that purpose, resulted in the acquisition of many significant works of art for Denmark. His awareness of contemporary trends in sculpture was important for Danish artists seeking to establish a direct relationship with French sculptors. His son Helge Jacobsen (1882–1946) was also a collector.

WRITINGS
Ny Carlsberg Glyptoteks tilblivelse [The making of the Ny Carlsberg Glyptotek] (Copenhagen, 1906)

DBL
BIBLIOGRAPHY
J. Steenstrup: *Carl Jacobsens liv og gerning* [Carl Jacobsen's life and work] (Copenhagen, 1922)
T. Holck Colding: 'J. C. Jacobsen og Carl Jacobsen som maecener' [J. C. Jacobsen and Carl Jacobsen as patrons of the arts], *Meddel. Ny Carlsberg* (1976) [with Fr. summary]

GRETHE KUSK

Jacobsen, Egill (*b* Copenhagen, 16 Dec 1910). Danish painter. He studied at the Kongelige Danske Kunstakademi in Copenhagen from 1932 to 1933. Early influences upon him included the Danish painters Harald Giersing, Jens Søndergaard and Edvard Weie. However, he quickly discovered an individual, highly painterly form of expression using intense colours. After his début at the Kunstnernes Efterårsudstilling (Artists' autumn exhibition) in Copenhagen in 1932, he went to Paris, where the work of Pablo Picasso and Henri Matisse had a great impact on him. At the same time he sought inspiration in the folk art of Africa and in this he found a subject that ran through all his work: the mask. He was enchanted by its simple, archetypal form and in 1936 he exhibited mask pictures for the first time. The figurative and the colouristic aspects of his work culminated in *Orange Object* (1940; Copenhagen, Stat. Mus. Kst), which revealed the mask picture as simultaneously grotesque and Constructivist in character.

Jacobsen worked primarily in oils, and he moved from the fabulous and enigmatic to a much simpler form of expression. *Hay Man* (1943; Copenhagen, E. Johansson priv. col., see Hovdenakk, p. 173), for example, displays both a clear geometric construction and a powerful use of colour. A markedly expressionist use of colour resulted from his close connection with the COBRA group, especially with Asger Jorn and Ejler Bille. As one of the most outstanding Danish abstract artists, Jacobsen was one of the first members of Cobra in 1948, taking part in the group's exhibition *La Fin et les moyens* at the Petite Galerie du Séminaire des Arts in Brussels in 1949. For Jacobsen, as for the other Cobra members, colour was a guiding principle as well as the actual means of expression. In Jacobsen's work such celebratory and strong colours as green, yellow, red and blue are particularly apparent, as, for example, in the *Olive Eater* (1951; Århus, Kreditforen. Danmark). With many important decorative projects (e.g. a mural for Hvidovre Rådhus, 1936–8) and exhibitions to his credit, Jacobsen maintained a consistently high artistic level, recognized for his life-enhancing and harmonious pictorial universe. He continued to use the same motifs of masks and mask-like forms.

BIBLIOGRAPHY
C. Dotremont: *Egill Jacobsen* (Copenhagen, 1963)
P. Hovdenakk: *Egill Jacobsen: Malerier/Paintings 1928–1965* (Copenhagen, 1980) [Eng. and Dan. text; contains cat. rais.]

MICHAEL FLINTHOLM

Jacobsen, Holger (*b* Odense, 30 Oct 1876; *d* Copenhagen, 27 March 1960). Danish architect. He studied at the Arkitektskole of the Kunstakademi in Copenhagen (1898–1905). After he left he won the competition of 1905 for Bispebjerg Crematorium (executed 1905–7, extended 1919 and 1927). In 1907 he built the new church at Tåstrup. Jacobsen adopted a personal historicism dominated by mannered classicistic motifs that accorded with such contemporary trends as Art Nouveau and neo-classicism. He was among the first to rediscover C. F. Hansen's architecture and shared the art historian Vilhelm Wanscher's enthusiasm for Michelangelo and the grand Italian style. In 1914 he rebuilt the Circus building in Copenhagen. After Hack Kampmann's death, working with Aage Rafn he took over the detailed planning and building of the Police Headquarters (1920–24), which, like the crematorium and the Circus building, was based on the Pantheon in Rome.

From 1919 until his death Jacobsen designed plans for a number of extensions to the Royal Theatre and built the adjoining New Stage (1929–31), one of his greatest achievements. The latter incorporates variations of motifs from the Police Headquarters in the mussel-shell acoustic ceiling in the auditorium and the pointed star in the coffered ceiling of the foyer. Some of the best artists of the time carried out the decorations in cohesive baroque style. His own house (1926) at Rosbæksvej 6, Copenhagen, is a paraphrase of the Villa Pia in the Vatican.

BIBLIOGRAPHY
'Kirke ved Taæstrup', *Arkitekten DK*, x/31 (1908), pp. 365–70
'Krematoriet paa Bispebjaerg', *Arkitekten DK*, xix/19 (1917), pp. 149–55
'Cirkusbygningen', *Arkitekten DK*, xxi (1919), pp. 325–8
'Holger Jacobsens sommerhus ved Gilleleje', *Arkitekten DK*, xxix (1927)
K. Millech: Obituary, *Arkitekten DK*, lxii (1960), p. 179
Nordisk klassicism/Nordic Classicism, 1910–1930 (exh. cat., ed. S. Paavilainen; Helsinki, Mus. Fin. Archit., 1982)

LISBET BALSLEV JØRGENSEN

Jacobsen, Robert (*b* Copenhagen, 4 June 1912). Danish sculptor. He supported himself from 1926 by a variety of jobs. In 1930, self-taught, he began to make sculptures in wood. His early works were influenced by an exhibition of German Expressionism that he saw in Copenhagen in 1932; his pieces included roughly carved, primitive, doll-like figures, which were partly painted. In the early 1940s he turned to carving in stone and *c.* 1944–5 made some figures in granite of imps and goblins inspired by Viking art, for example *Granite Sculpture* (1944–5; Randers, Kstmus.). He was actively involved at this period in the movement that later led to the formation of Cobra and was a friend of Asger Jorn and Richard Mortensen.

In 1947 Jacobsen went to Paris, where Mortensen introduced him to Hans Arp, Jean Deyrolle, Jean Dewasne, Auguste Herbin, Alberto Magnelli, Serge Poliakoff and Victor Vasarely, and he started to make abstract sculptures such as *Graphics in Iron* (1950; Paris, Pompidou) in welded iron in a very pure Constructivist style, with clean-cut

shapes and a spatial arrangement of forms, while also producing some grotesque figures in scrap metal. His abstract works subsequently tended to become more complex in form and larger in scale and included a number of pieces coloured black, blue or red. He returned to Denmark in 1969 and settled at Tagelund, near Egtved. His later works include *Positive/Negative Sculpture* (iron and brass, 1981) in Meinertz, Denmark, a combination of linear forms and spirals.

BIBLIOGRAPHY
J. Dewasne: *Le Sculpteur: Robert Jacobsen, sculpteur danois* (Copenhagen, 1951)
Der Bildhauer Robert Jacobsen und seine Welt (exh. cat., Kiel, Christian Albrechts-U., Ksthalle, 1975)
Robert Jacobsen/Parcours (exh. cat., Toulon, Mus. Toulon; Rennes, Mus. B.-A. & Archéol.; Paris, Mus. Rodin; 1984)
Robert Jacobsen: Raum und Zeichen Werke des Bildhauers Robert Jacobsen (exh. cat., Mannheim, Städt. Ksthalle; Marl, Skulpmus.; 1987)

RONALD ALLEY

Jacobsthal, Paul Ferdinand (*b* 23 Feb 1880; *d* 27 Oct 1957). German prehistorian and Classical scholar. He was educated at the universities of Berlin, Göttingen and Bonn, where he gained his doctorate. He was a lecturer at Göttingen University from 1908 to 1912 and Professor of Classical Archaeology at Marburg University from 1912 to 1935. He left Nazi Germany for England, becoming a lecturer at Christ Church, Oxford, from 1937 to 1947, then a Student of Christ Church and University Reader in Celtic Archaeology until his retirement in 1950. He was an Honorary Fellow of the Society of Antiquaries and a Corresponding Fellow of the British Academy. Jacobsthal's examination of the floral decoration of Greek vases, chiefly the designs under the handles, marked a new era in the study of ancient ornament, and his work on reliefs from Melos was seen as a model of its kind. His background in Classical archaeology gave a new dimension to his increasing interest in the relationship between the Classical world of Greece and Italy and the Celtic world of central and northern Europe, fields which had hitherto been studied entirely separately. The combination of the better chronological framework of Classical art and Jacobsthal's interest in the careful analysis of the forms in Celtic art, as well as his knowledge of Oriental material, resulted in the publication of *Early Celtic Art* (1944). This was the first scholarly treatise on the Early La Tène style of European Iron Age art (*see also* CELTIC ART and PREHISTORIC EUROPE, §VI) and Jacobsthal's best-known work. He died before finishing the sequel, a volume on later Celtic art, which was to concentrate particularly on the British Isles. His influence on subsequent studies of Celtic art has been overwhelming, and the style terms he coined, as well as his chronology, remain widely used throughout Europe.

WRITINGS
Der Blitz in der orientalischen und griechischen Kunst (1906)
Göttinger Vasen (1912)
with A. Langsdorf: *Die Bronzeschnabelkannen* (1927)
Ornamente griechischer Vasen (1927)
Die melischen Reliefs (1931)
Early Celtic Art (Oxford, 1944)
Greek Pins in their European and Asiatic Setting (Oxford and New York, 1956)

SARA CHAMPION

Jacobsz., Dirck [Dirk] (*b c.* 1497; *d* Amsterdam; *bur* 27 June 1567). North Netherlandish painter, son of JACOB CORNELISZ. VAN OOSTSANEN. His birthdate is estimated from van Mander's claim that he died at the age of almost 70. His birthplace is unknown, but by about the age of three he was living in Amsterdam, where his father purchased a house in 1500. Dirck himself is documented in the city from 1546 until his burial. About 1550 he married Marritgen Gerritsdr., by whom he had two children, Maria Dircksdr. and Jacob Dircksz. War, also a painter. Dirck was trained by his father, probably around 1512, when Jan van Scorel was an apprentice. The two young artists may have remained friends, for in later years elements of Jan's mature, more Mannerist style can be seen in Dirck's paintings. Not only were Dirck's father and his brother, the little-known painter Cornelis Jacobsz. (*d* 1526–33), artists, his uncle Cornelis Buys I (*fl c.* 1490–1524), usually identified as the MASTER OF ALKMAAR (*see* MASTERS, ANONYMOUS, AND MONOGRAMMISTS, §I), and his cousin Cornelis Buys II (*c.* 1500–45/6) also practised the craft. They all signed their pieces with a shared housemark flanked by their respective initials. But whereas Dirck's kinsmen painted a variety of subjects, he concentrated on portraiture, thus becoming one of the first Dutch artists to specialize.

Dirck's identified oeuvre is very small. His earliest and most important work is *The Crossbowmen* (1529; Amsterdam, Rijksmus.), the first militia portrait in Dutch art. Along with Jan van Scorel's *Twelve Members of the Haarlem Brotherhood of Jerusalem Pilgrims* (*c.* 1528; Haarlem, Frans Halsmus.), this work marked the start of independent group portraiture in the northern Netherlands. Dirck avoided Jan's linear arrangement and united his two rows of men through gesture or touch. Yet, like van Scorel, he conceived of this and subsequent militia pieces as a series of single likenesses, with each figure interacting independently with the viewer. Dirck Jacobsz.'s portraits resemble those of his father in their delicate linear sensibility and their focus on individualized physiognomy, but his subjects' large gesturing hands are distinctive. Van Mander related that a certain Jacob Rauvert was so taken with a 'speaking' hand in a portrait by Dirck that he offered a large sum if the artist would cut it from the picture. The expressive language of gesture was exploited by other north Netherlandish artists of this generation, for example, Joos van Cleve, Jan Cornelisz. Vermeyen and Jan van Scorel.

A more flowing and less detailed style is found in Dirck's later group paintings, such as his militia companies from 1561 (St Petersburg, Hermitage) and 1565 (Amsterdam, Rijksmus.). The coarser surfaces and increased chiaroscuro effects create less rigid poses and more spontaneous expressions, and he increasingly personalized the scenes by giving his sitters props to hold. His ability to capture a likeness led to his being asked to paint the donor portraits on the wings of polyptychs by other artists. The triptych with the *Virgin and Child* (1530; Stuttgart, Staatsgal.) and the altarpiece of the *Rest on the Flight into Egypt* (Utrecht, Catharijneconvent) have shutters and landscapes by Dirck and religious figures painted by Jacob Cornelisz. and Pieter Coecke respectively. The painted donors are not involved in the religious scene but instead

Dirck Jacobsz.: *Pompeius Occo*, oil on panel, 660×540 mm, *c.* 1534 (Amsterdam, Rijksmuseum)

gaze out at the viewer with a slightly bored and worldly air. The three panels of the composition are united only by the landscape background. The technique, with its atmospheric mists, vaguely Roman ruins and loose brushstrokes, reveals the influence of Jan van Scorel.

Dirck often introduced genre elements, such as an hourglass or a skull, into his single portraits to blend genre and likeness into a *vanitas* or *memento mori* (see fig.). But his true gift lay in organizing crowds so as to give equal emphasis to each figure, whether only two, as in the portrait of *Jacob Cornelisz. Painting his Wife* (Toledo, OH, Mus. A.), or twelve, as in *The Crossbowmen* (1563; Amsterdam, Rijksmus.). Such democracy was often achieved at the cost of a unified composition. Yet in his painted portraits Dirck Jacobsz. excelled as a good draughtsman, whose controlled mastery of bone structure helped him to capture his sitter's character.

BIBLIOGRAPHY

K. van Mander: *Schilder-boeck* ([1603]–1604), fol. 207*v*

G. J. Hoogewerff: 'Een portret van Dirk Jacobsz.', *Oud-Holland*, xxxii (1914), pp. 81–8

M. J. Friedländer: *Die altniederländische Malerei* (Berlin, 1924–37), xiii (1936), pp. 133–40; Eng. trans. as *Early Netherlandish Painting* (Leiden, 1967–76), xiii (1975)

B. Haak: 'Het portret van *Pompejus Occo* door Dirck Jacobsz.', *Bull. Rijksmus.*, vi (1958), p. 27

Kunst voor de beeldenstorm: Noordnederlandse kunst, 1525–1580, 2 vols (exh. cat. by J. P. Filedt Kok, W. Halsema-Kubes and W. T. Kloek, Amsterdam, Rijksmus., 1986), ii, pp. 197–8

JANE L. CARROLL

Jacobsz., Hugo [Huge; Huygh] (*b* ?Koudekerck, nr Leiden, *c.* 1460; *d* Leiden, ?1534–8). North Netherlandish painter and draughtsman. Although there is archival information about the life of Hugo Jacobsz., father of LUCAS VAN LEYDEN, nothing can be said with certainty about his artistic activity; van Mander called him an 'outstanding painter in his time'. According to the archives of the Hieronymusdal monastery near Leiden, then an important artistic centre, between 1475 and 1481 he was an assistant to the painter Brother Tyman. By 1485 he was established as an independent artist in Leiden and in 1488 he is recorded as living in Gouda. He returned to Leiden before October 1494. Attempts (Dülberg, Gibson) to identify him with the south Netherlandish Master of the Turin Crucifixion, so-called after a triptych in the Museo Civico d'Arte Antica, Turin, have failed to find much support. More convincing is the identification with the MASTER OF THE ST JOHN ALTARPIECE (*see* MASTERS, ANONYMOUS, AND MONOGRAMMISTS, §I), named after the three panels of an altarpiece in the St Janskerk, Gouda. These panels of *c.* 1512 show certain parallels with the early prints of Lucas van Leyden in the treatment of figures and landscape, but they do not seem to have exerted any influence on the style and painting technique of Lucas van Leyden who, according to van Mander, was apprenticed to his father Hugo Jacobsz.

BIBLIOGRAPHY

Thieme–Becker
K. van Mander: *Schilder-boeck* ([1603]–1604), fol. 211*v*

F. Dülberg: 'Die Persönlichkeit des Lucas van Leyden', *Oud-Holland*, xiv (1899), pp. 65–83
W. S. Gibson: 'Lucas van Leyden and his Two Teachers', *Simiolus*, iv (1969–70), pp. 90–99
J. D. Bangs: *Cornelis Engebrechtsz.'s Leiden* (Assen, 1979), pp. 92–6
K. G. Boon: 'The Life and Work of Hugo Jacobsz. before 1500', *Essays in Northern European Art Presented to Egbert Haverkamp-Begemann on his Sixtieth Birthday* (Doornspijk, 1983), pp. 43–8

For further bibliography *see* MASTERS, ANONYMOUS, AND MONOGRAMMISTS, §I: MASTER OF THE ST JOHN ALTARPIECE.

J. P. FILEDT KOK

Jacobsz., Juriaen [Jurriaen] (*b* Hamburg, *bapt* 19 Dec 1624; *d* Leeuwarden, 1685). German painter. He is thought to have been apprenticed in Hamburg and to have continued his training (*c.* 1642–51) in Antwerp under Frans Snyders, who clearly influenced his work. A visit to Amsterdam is evident from some portraits (1649; Hamburg, Ksthalle) which show the influence of Ferdinand Bol; he was documented there between 1658 and 1665/6. Subsequently Jacobsz. became court painter to William Frederick of Orange in Leeuwarden, though he occasionally travelled to Hamburg. He painted predominantly animals and hunting scenes, and still-lifes in the style of Frans Snyders. Examples of these genres are a *Piece of Veal Attacked by a Dog* (1651; Hamburg, Ksthalle) and *Wild Boar Hunt* (1659; St Petersburg, Hermitage). The

Lambert Jacobsz.: *Old Prophet Meeting the Man of God*, oil on canvas, 825×1110 mm, 1629 (Amsterdam, Rijksmuseum, on loan to Amsterdam, Rembrandthuis)

style of his portraits initially resembled that of van Dyck, later that of Ferdinand Bol.

BIBLIOGRAPHY

J. A. Renckens: 'Jurriaen Jacobsz. als Amsterdams Portrettist', *Oud-Holland*, lxvi (1951), pp. 184–6

H. Lungagnini: *Der Hamburger Maler Juriaen Jacobsz., 1624–1685: Leben und Werk* (diss., U. Hamburg, 1970)

KARIN KLEINEWEFERS

Jacobsz., Lambert (*b* Amsterdam, *c.* 1598; *d* Leeuwarden, 24 June 1636). Dutch painter. He was the son of a well-to-do Mennonite cloth merchant in Amsterdam. He served his apprenticeship there among the artists now called the Pre-Rembrandtists. After his marriage in 1620, commemorated by the poet Joost van den Vondel (1587–1639), he settled in Leeuwarden, his wife's native city, where he became a preacher in the Mennonite community and worked primarily as a painter. He was also active as an art dealer, as is known from his estate inventory, which records transactions in Amsterdam with the Mennonite art dealer and patron of Rembrandt, Hendrick van Uylenburgh. Two of Jacobsz.'s pupils were Govaert Flinck and Jacob Backer. His son, the painter ABRAHAM VAN DEN TEMPEL probably also studied with him before becoming Backer's pupil *c.* 1642–6.

Jacobsz.'s work can be divided into two stylistic groups. His small-figured works on biblical themes, set in Italianate landscapes with antique ruins, poultry, livestock and other animals, are similar in manner and subject to the work of the Pre-Rembrandtists. The Italianate elements have led art historians to postulate a trip to Italy, though in the marriage poem Vondel actually asserted the contrary, and no traces of such a visit are known. The Italianate aspects could be the result of his contact, as a dealer, with works in this style. The *Old Prophet Meeting the Man of God* (1629; see fig.) is one example of a small-figured work; it depicts a subject that was painted by, among others, the Pre-Rembrandtist Claes Moeyaert.

The second group of paintings, Jacobsz.'s pictures of single figures, which are shown half- or three-quarter length and almost life-size at a table or against a solid background, can best be compared with the work of the Utrecht Caravaggisti. There are fewer works in this group, and these are mostly in private collections. Striking examples include the *Apostle Paul* (1629) and a series of *Four Church Fathers* (all Leeuwarden, Fries Mus.). The model for the *Apostle Paul* may have been Lubbert Gerritsz., the painter's maternal grandfather and a prominent figure in Amsterdam Mennonite circles (van der Meij-Tolsma, 1989). Jacobsz.'s activities as a Mennonite preacher brought him into conflict with the authorities, but despite this his patrons undoubtedly came from several different religious groups. Except for a couple of drawings, no other works on paper survive.

BIBLIOGRAPHY

H. L. Straat: 'Lambert Jacobsz.: Schilder', *Vrije Fries*, xxviii (1928), pp. 53–76

H. F. Wijnman: 'Nieuwe gegevens omtrent den schilder Lambert Jacobsz.' [New data on the painter Lambert Jacobsz.], *Oud-Holland*, xlvii (1930), pp. 145–7; li (1934), pp. 241–55

M. Halbertsma: 'Lambert Jacobsz., een Amsterdammer in Leeuwarden', *Vrije Fries*, lii (1972), pp. 15–25

M. van der Meij-Tolsma: 'Lambert Jacobsz. (*ca.* 1598–1636): Een Amsterdams historieschilder in Leeuwarden', *17de Eeuw*, iv/2 (1988), pp. 29–55

——: 'Lambert Jacobsz. (*ca.* 1598–1636): Kunstschilder en doopsgezind leraar te Leeuwarden' [Lambert Jacobsz.: painter and Mennonite teacher in Leeuwarden], *Doopsgezinde Bijdr.*, xv (1989), pp. 79–96

MARIJKE VAN DER MEIJ-TOLSMA

Jacob (Jansz.) van Haarlem. *See under* MASTERS, ANONYMOUS, AND MONOGRAMMISTS, §I: MASTER OF THE BRUNSWICK DIPTYCH.

Jacob [Jacques] van Lathem. *See under* LIEVEN VAN LATHEM.

Jacob (Claesz.) van Utrecht [Traiectensis, Jacobus] (*b* ?Utrecht, *c.* 1480; *d* ?Lübeck, after 1530). North Netherlandish painter, active in the southern Netherlands and Germany. Presumably after initial training as a painter in Utrecht, he moved to Antwerp, where he became a master in the Guild of St Luke in 1506. The Antwerp archives mention as his pupils Jasper de Vos in 1511 and Heynken Francx in 1512. Dating from the following year is the earliest work attributed to him, a triptych with the *Descent from the Cross* (1513; Berlin, Gemäldegal.). Surprisingly, it shows little evidence of the influence of the great Antwerp masters. Instead, the presence of many over-populated subsidiary scenes alongside the main events suggests a knowledge of Westphalian painting. The artist was also inspired by prints of Albrecht Dürer's graphic work.

Jacob certainly had first-hand knowledge of developments in German art. Around 1515, for the abbey of Gross-St Martin in Cologne, he painted two altarpiece wings with scenes from the *Life of St Bernard of Clairvaux*, the *Birth of Christ* and the *Adoration of the Magi* (Cologne, Wallraf-Richartz-Mus.; Berchtesgaden, Schlossmus.). He probably stayed in Cologne for some time. From this work it is clear that Jacob van Utrecht was also familiar with paintings by the Flemish Primitives, as in it he quoted passages from Jan van Eyck's portrait of *Baudoin de Lannoy* (Berlin, Gemäldegal.) and his portrait of Joris van der Paele in the *Virgin and Child with Canon van de Paele* (Bruges, Groeningemus.).

From 1519 until 1530 Jacob van Utrecht lived in Lübeck, initially with the patrician Bruskow family. He is mentioned in a document of 1523 as Master Jakob of Utrecht. He was also a member of the Leonhard Brotherhood, a society of Lübeck merchants, which implies that he was not only active as a painter but also as an art dealer. The majority of his surviving oeuvre consists of portraits of Lübeck patricians. Seven are signed, but another fourteen can be attributed to him on stylistic grounds: the figures are half-length, with drooping shoulders, pictured in three-quarter view with part of the face in shadow. There is no light in the eyes, and the eyelids are heavy, giving the face a frozen and somewhat drowsy expression. The rather heavy hands hold a flower, ring, rosary or book. There is usually a table or stone ledge in front of the sitter, and on it a number of objects, placed as if in a still-life, perhaps intended to allude to some specific aspect of the sitter. Hair and beards are painted in short parallel lines, and furs are also treated in a distinctive way. Backgrounds are mainly dark and closed off, and in many cases the sitter's coat of arms appears in one of the upper corners,

Jacob van Utrecht: *Virgin and Child*, oil on panel, 760×610 mm, 1520 (Lübeck, St Annen-Kloster); central panel from a triptych

as, for example, in the *Portrait of a Man* (Stockholm, Nmus.), which depicts a member of the Shute family of Lübeck. Exceptions to this formula included the *Portrait of a Man with a White Beard* (1523; ex-Kaiser-Friedrich-Mus., Berlin; destr. 1945), which had a background landscape with water and mountains. These paintings show parallels with the work of Joos van Cleve and Bartholomäus Bruyn the elder.

Jacob van Utrecht also received religious commissions in Lübeck. One of the most important is the *Virgin and Child with Donors* (1520; Lübeck, St Annen-Mus.; see fig.), a triptych for the councillor Hinrich Kerckring, who is portrayed on the left wing. His wife Katharina is on the right wing. These donor portraits show the same characteristics as his individual portraits. Only from the 1520s, while Jacob van Utrecht was working in Lübeck, did the influence of Antwerp artists (mainly Joos van Cleve but also the Master of 1518 and the Master of Frankfurt) become more apparent in his work.

BIBLIOGRAPHY

L. Baldass: 'Jacob van Utrecht', *Z. Bild. Kst*, xxxi (1920), pp. 241–7
M. J. Friedländer: 'Anmerkung über Jacob van Utrecht', *Z. Bild. Kst*, xxxi (1920), p. 284
W. Neumann: 'Ein Flügelaltar von Jacobus van Utrecht', *Oud-Holland*, xl (1922), pp. 19–23
M. J. Friedländer: 'Neues über Jacob van Utrecht', *Oud-Holland*, lviii (1941), pp. 6–17
J. J. De Mesquita: 'Nog meer werk van Jacob van Utrecht', *Oud-Holland*, lviii (1941), pp. 59–75, 135–47
Bilder im Blickpunkt: Jacob van Utrecht und der Altar von 1513 (exh. cat. by R. Grosshaus, W. Berlin, Gemäldegal., 1982)

ELS VERMANDERE

Jacob von Schweinfurt. *See* HAYLMANN, JACOB.

Jacomart [Baco, Jaime] (*b* Valencia, *c.* 1411; *d* Valencia, 1461). Spanish painter. He enjoyed the patronage of King Alfonso V of Aragon (*reg* 1416–58) and of his son John II (*reg* 1458–79). In 1440 he was summoned to Italy by Alfonso, who was laying siege to Naples; he abandoned the work he had in progress and left Valencia late in 1442. He became court painter in 1444 and returned to Valencia in 1446 but left again in 1447 to accompany Alfonso to Tivoli on a military campaign against the Florentines. He is mentioned in Valencia again from 1451 until his death.

Numerous documents attest that Jacomart was held in high esteem as a painter, but most of his surviving works were made in collaboration with Pere Rexach and Juan Rexach. There are references to several altarpieces (all untraced) painted, before his departure for Italy, for Valencia Cathedral (1441) and for the parish church in Burjasot and for S María la Mayor, Morella. None of his Italian works, including the altarpiece painted for S Maria della Pace (1444), Naples, and the decoration of 20 standards for the royal infantry (1447), survives.

Jacomart's style has always been hard to define since there are no surviving works painted by himself alone. For example the *SS Lawrence and Peter* retable (Catí, parish church), which Jacomart was commissioned to paint in 1460, seems to have been carried out to a large extent by his assistants, in view of the lack of skill in both technique and design. Its restoration will make a more accurate judgement possible. Furthermore, the *St Anne* retable, painted for the funerary chapel of the Borgias at Játiva and attributed to Jacomart, must now be attributed to Pere Rexach, following the discovery of a document establishing the commissioning of the work to that artist in 1452.

BIBLIOGRAPHY

Documents concerning Jacomart have been published in *Archv A. Valenc.*, xvi (1930), pp. 5–34; *An. Cent. Cult. Valenc.*, xlviii (1963), p. 73; xlix (1964), pp. 92–7; *Archv A. Valenc.*, xxxvi (1965), p. 28; xxxviii (1966), pp. 19–30; xliii (1972), pp. 50–51
E. Tormo: *Jacomart y el arte hispano-flamenco cuatrocentista* (Madrid, 1913)
C. R. Post: *A History of Spanish Painting* (Cambridge, MA, 1935–60), vi, pp. 14–127; vii, pp. 875–9; x, pp. 357–9
V. Aguilera Cerni: 'Jacomart', *Archv A. Valenc.*, xxxii (1961), pp. 80–95
L. de Saralegui: 'De pintura valenciana medieval: En torno al binomio Jacomart-Rexach', *Archv A. Valenc.*, xxxiii (1962), pp. 5–12
A. J. Pitarch: 'Jacomart—Rexach', *La pintura gótica en la corona de Aragón* (exh. cat., Saragossa, Mus. Camón Aznar, 1980), p. 120
C. Soler d'Hyver: 'Jacomart—Rexach', *Valencia: Su pintura en el siglo XV* (exh. cat., Valencia, Banco de Santander, 1982)
X. Company: *La pintura valenciana de Jacomart a Pau de Sant Leocadi: El corrent hispanoflamenc i els inicis del Renaixement* (Barcelona, (1987)

CLAUDIE RESSORT

Jácome, Ramiro (*b* Quito, 10 Sept 1948). Ecuadorean painter, draughtsman and printmaker. He was self-taught. Working in the neo-figurative style that revitalized Ecuadorean art in the 1970s, he was a member with José Unda (*b* 1948), Washington Iza and Nelson Román (*b* 1945) of the Los Cuatro Mosqueteros group, which was opposed to the art promoted by the official Salon. The members of the group formed their own 'anti-Salon' in Guayaquil in 1968. Jácome's incisive and ironic drawing style fed on ugliness, the grotesque and the horrific. He experimented with colour, space and line, as well as with abstraction, incorporating indigenous chromatics and magical elements. His desire to demythologize the history of America led him to paint the series *El camino de El Dorado* to illustrate a compilation of poetic texts published in 1979. This was followed in 1991 by the series *500 Years* on the theme of the discovery of America and another on *Famous and Anonymous Characters of Quito*. He also criticized urban life, as in *Megapopolis* (1990; artist's col.). He used various materials, including acrylic, oil and ink on canvas and wood, and also worked with engraving and screen-printing. Jácome's work was widely exhibited, and he took part in the Venice Biennale (1990); he was also awarded numerous prizes, including first prize at the Salón Nacional Mariano Aguilera in Quito (1980).

WRITINGS
El camino de El Dorado (Quito, 1979)

BIBLIOGRAPHY
J. Icaza: *Huasipungo* [illus. by Jácome] (Quito, n.d.)
Algo sobre Jácome (exh. cat., Quito, Mus. Camilo Egas Banco Cent., 1983)
H. Rodríguez Castelo: 'Ramiro Jácome', *Rev. Diners*, 18 (1983), pp. 36–40

CECILIA SUÁREZ

Jacometti, Pietro Paolo (*b* Recanati, 1580; *d* Recanati, 1655). Italian sculptor, painter, architect and bronze caster. He is known primarily for his bronzes, which combine an adherence to traditional standards of 15th-century Lombardy and a move towards the more dramatic qualities of the Baroque. With his brother, Tarquino Jacometti (1570–1638), he was instructed in drawing and sculpting by his uncle, Antonio Calcagni, but the influence of his lifelong teacher Cristoforo Roncalli was always uppermost in his works. The brothers became business partners, collaborating in casting bronze low reliefs, fountains and baptismal fonts, but Pietro Paolo also produced individual items.

The Jacometti brothers collaborated in such bronze works as the fountain (1619–20) in the Piazza della Madonna, Loreto; the Galli fountain, Loreto; the fountain (1619) in the Piazza del Popolo, Faenza; and on fonts in Recanati Cathedral (1622) and S Giovanni Battista, Osimo (1622–8). Pietro Paolo also produced the bronze portrait of *Vincenzo Cataldi* (Ascoli Piceno, S Francesco) and bronze reliefs of the *Bacchanal* (Recanati, Pal. Leopardi) and *Virgin and Child* (1627; Ancona, Gesù). His bronze relief of the *Transfer of the Holy House* (1634; Recanati, Pal. Com., façade) shows the influence of Roncalli's fresco of the *Coronation of the Virgin* (destr.; fragments remain) in the cupola of S Casa, Loreto.

BIBLIOGRAPHY
Bénézit; Thieme–Becker
F. Baldinucci: *Notizie* (1681–1728); ed. F. Ranalli, v (1846), pp. 324–5, 598–9
G. Pauri: *I Lombardi-Solari e la scuola recanatese di scultura: Sec. XVI–XVII* (Milan, 1915), pp. 85–104
L. Marchetti and C. Bevilacqua: *Italian Basilicas and Cathedrals* (Novara, 1950), pp. 55–6
J. D. Sisson: *Storia dell'arte italiana* (Neudeln, 1975), pp. 749–57
F. Grimaldi and K. Sordi: *Pittori a Loreto: Committenze tra '500 e '600* (Ancona, 1988), pp. 102, 243

JOANNE A. RUBINO

Jacometto Veneziano (*fl* Venice, 1472–97). Italian painter and illuminator. Knowledge of the artistic activity of Jacometto is based almost exclusively on the notebooks of Marcantonio Michiel, who recorded a number of his works in the patrician houses of Venice and Padua in the first half of the 16th century. In Pietro Bembo's house Michiel saw a small picture with scenes from the life of a saint, and portraits of Bembo as a child of eleven and of his brother Carlo as a newborn baby in 1472; in the house of Francesco Zio Michiel saw four miniatures by Jacometto in a Book of Hours; in the house of Zuanantonio Venier he saw a small picture with animals painted in chiaroscuro; in the house of Antonio Pasqualino he saw a number of drawings; in the house of Gabriele Vendramin he saw a portrait painted (or ?drawn) in chiaroscuro, and a small book of vellum with pen drawings of animals and candelabra; and finally, in the house of Michele Contarini in 1543 the author saw 'a little portrait of Messer Alvise Contarini . . . , who died some years ago; and on the same panel there is a portrait of a nun of San Secondo. On the cover of these portraits there is a small (?)deer in a landscape; and their leather case is decorated with foliage stamped with gold. This most perfect work is by the hand of Jacometto.' It is clear from the testimony of Michiel that Jacometto practised chiefly as a manuscript illuminator and as a painter of small-scale panels, most of which were portraits. It is also clear that his work was much in demand among patrician collectors, and that, unlike most art of the generation before Giorgione, it was much admired by Michiel himself. The high reputation the artist enjoyed among his contemporaries is confirmed by the humanist Michele da Placiola, who in a letter of September 1497 praised the young Giulio Campagnola by saying that his miniatures 'are not inferior to those of the late Jacometto, who was the best in the world'.

Unfortunately, none of the works recorded by Michiel has survived, with the probable exception only of the portrait of *Alvise Contarini*, together with its companion-piece and their painted covers, which most modern scholars identify with a pair of miniature portraits of a man and woman on panel in the Lehman collection (New York, Met.). The identification is confirmed by the extraordinary delicacy of their handling, and also by their stylistic relationship with Flemish painting and with the art of Antonello da Messina. Michiel had said, in fact, of Antonello's *St Jerome* (London, N.G.) (which he considered to be by Jan van Eyck or Memling), that he thought the face had been painted, and the whole figure repainted, by Jacometto. On the basis of the Lehman portraits, a number of other portraits have been attributed to the artist. Some of these attributions are controversial, because of the difficulty of comparing the style of works painted on a different scale; but among the most convincing are three male portraits (London, N.G., nos 2509, 3121; New York, Met., no. 49.7.3). Evidence that Jacometto did on occasion work on a larger scale is provided by a Venetian inventory of 1564, which lists a 'large portrait' by him. Similarly, a number of manuscript illuminations and incunabula have also been attributed to the artist by analogy with the Lehman portraits; these attributions, too, remain controversial.

BIBLIOGRAPHY
Thieme–Becker
M. A. Michiel: *Notizia d'opere di disegno* (MS. before 1552); ed. G. Frizzoni (Bologna, 1884); ed. T. Frimmel as *Der Anonimo Morelliano* (Vienna, 1888), pp. 20, 22, 82, 94, 98, 108, 112, 114
T. Frimmel: 'Bemerkungen zu Jacometto Veneziano', *Stud. & Skiz. Gemäldeknd.*, ii (1915–16), pp. 16ff
G. Gronau: 'Zu Jacometto Veneziano', *Stud. & Skiz. Gemäldeknd.*, ii (1915–16), pp. 48ff

Italian Illuminated Manuscripts from 1400 to 1550 (exh. cat. by O. Pächt, Oxford, Bodleian Lib., 1948)

M. Davies: *The Earlier Italian Schools*, London, N.G. cat. (London, 1951, 2/1961/R 1986), pp. 257–60

F. Heinemann: *Giovanni Bellini e i Belliniani*, 2 vols (Venice, 1962)

J. Pope-Hennessy: *The Portrait in the Renaissance* (Princeton, 1966)

G. Mariani Canova: *La miniatura veneta del rinascimento* (Venice, 1969)

O. Pächt and J. J. G. Alexander: *Illuminated Manuscripts in the Bodleian Library*, Oxford: *Italian School* (Oxford, 1970)

B. Fredericksen and F. Zeri: *Census of Pre-nineteenth-century Italian Paintings in North American Public Collections* (Cambridge, MA, 1972), p. 100

F. Zeri: *Italian Paintings: Venetian School*, New York, Met. cat. (New York, 1973), pp. 34–6

L. Armstrong: *Renaissance Miniature Painters and Classical Imagery: The Master of the Putti and his Venetian Workshop* (London, 1981)

J. Pope-Hennessy: *Italian Paintings* (1987), i of *The Robert Lehman Collection* (Princeton, 1987), pp. 240–43

PETER HUMFREY

Jacopino da Reggio (*fl* 1265–*c.* 1300). Italian illuminator. He is recorded in many documents relating to the copying of books, and he signed the decoration of a copy of Gratian's *Decretals* (Rome, Vatican, Bib. Apostolica, MS. Vat. lat. 1375) to which several illuminators contributed. If this signature is accepted as belonging not to a stationer who had the manuscript illustrated, but to the principal illuminator who organized the work and was himself responsible for the most important decoration, then Jacopino can be identified as the most important Bolognese master working in the Byzantine style at the end of the 13th century, and the illuminator of the Bible of Clement VII (Paris, Bib. N., MS. lat. 18). Compared with the equally Byzantine-influenced but more lively narrative style of the Girona Master who illuminated the Bible of Charles V (Girona, Bib. Capitolare), Jacopino evolved an extremely courtly style in which Byzantine elements are combined with decorative features derived from Limoges enamels and others that suggest knowledge of the Isaac Master at Assisi. His illustrations tend to be included as small pictures, rather than being in a freer relationship with the rubrics and script. The stylistic tendencies of his collaborators suggest that the Paris Bible, another in London (BL, Add. MS. 18720), the Book of Psalms in Bible D.II.3 (Turin, Bib. N. U.) and probably Aristotle's *Opera* (Paris, Bib. N., MS. lat. 6297) all precede Jacopino's work on the *Decretals* (MS. Vat. lat. 1375). Other work by his collaborators on this manuscript can be dated after 1300. Another manuscript of the *Decretals* in the Vatican (Rome, Vatican, Bib. Apostolica, MS. Pal. lat. 629) and a Psalter (Paris, Bib. N., MS. fond. Smith-Lesouëf 21) are possibly even later works.

BIBLIOGRAPHY

R. Longhi: 'Postilla all'apertura sugli umbri', *Paragone*, xvii/195 (1966), pp. 3–8

——: *Opere complete*, vii (Florence, 1974), pp. 158–62

A. Conti: *La miniatura bolognese: Scuole e botteghe* (Bologna, 1981), pp. 44–54

F. Avril and M.-T. Gousset: *Manuscrits enluminés d'origine italienne*, ii, Paris, Bib. N. cat. (Paris, 1984), nos 123–5

ALESSANDRO CONTI

Jacopino di Francesco Bavosi. *See* MASTERS, ANONYMOUS, AND MONOGRAMMISTS, §I: PSEUDO-JACOPINO.

Jacopo, Mariano del Buono di. *See* MARIANO DEL BUONO DI JACOPO.

Jacopo Biondi da Bologna, Cristoforo di. *See* CRISTOFORO DI JACOPO BIONDI DA BOLOGNA.

Jacopo (di Paride Parisati) da Montagnana (*b* Montagnana, ?1440–50; *d* Padua, between 20 April and 14 Aug 1499). Italian painter. He began his career in Padua, where between 1458 and 1461 he was trained by the little-known Bolognese artist Francesco Brazalieri (1410–after 1484). According to Vasari and Ridolfi he was a pupil of Giovanni Bellini; although no formal relationship is documented, it is clear that Jacopo was strongly influenced by the Venetian painter. The dominant influence on his art, however, was Andrea Mantegna, whose altarpiece for S Zeno, Verona, was painted in Padua in 1457–9. Jacopo is recorded in 1469 as a member of the painters' guild of Padua. His principal surviving and securely attributed works are nearly all frescoes in Padua, Belluno and Monteorte. A wider range of his activities is suggested by the papal vestments (Padua, Santo) that he designed for Sixtus IV in 1472.

Most of Jacopo's major projects have been badly damaged or completely destroyed. Of works executed in the Santo, Padua, nothing remains of the frescoes of 1469–77 for the Gattamelata Chapel and only one scene, the *Mystic Marriage of St Catherine*, survives from the frescoes of 1487–8 for the Chiostro del Noviziato. Only fragments remain of a remarkable fresco cycle (1489–90) of scenes from Roman history in the Palazzo dei Nobili, Belluno, which was destroyed in 1838 along with his frescoes on its façade. The interior frescoes, with their celebration of Classical civic virtues, were recorded in engravings by Melchiorre Toller (1800–46) and in drawings by Ippolito Caffi (1809–66).

Of Jacopo's surviving work, the frescoes of scenes from the *Lives of SS Stephen and Paul* and the *Life of Christ* in S Stefano, Belluno, date from 1485–6. In Padua he was commissioned by Bishop Pietro Barozzi (*d* 1507) to decorate his private chapel at the Palazzo Vescovile, where in 1494 he produced figures of the *Evangelists* and *Church Fathers* on the ceiling and *Christ among the Apostles* on the walls, and in 1495 an altarpiece whose central *Annunciation*, depicted in an extensive architectural setting in sharp perspective, is flanked by panels of the *Archangels Michael and Raphael with Tobias*. The Santuario di Monte Ortone, Monteortone, contains his most important extant work, a cycle of 1494–7 incorporating scenes from *Genesis* and the *Life of the Virgin* as well as representations of *Prophets* and *Church Fathers*. The prominent architectural elements rendered in perspective make clear his continuing debt to Mantegna. The two panels of the *Annunciation* (Venice, Accad.), which were originally organ shutters for Monte Ortone, probably date from the same years as the fresco cycle. The cleaned panels reveal Jacopo's ability and sensitivity as a colourist but, in comparison with Mantegna or the leading contemporary painters of Venice, his work has something of an awkward and provincial quality.

BIBLIOGRAPHY

G. Vasari: *Vite* (1550, rev. 2/1568); ed. G. Milanesi (1878–85), iii, p. 170

C. Ridolfi: *Meraviglie* (1648); ed. D. von Hadeln (1914–25), i, pp. 78, 91

A. Moschetti: 'Di Jacopo da Montagnana e delle opere sue', *Boll. Mus. Civ. Padova*, n. s. i, 3 (1925), pp. 149–58; n. s. iv, 3–4 (1928), pp. 165–219; n. s. vi, 1–4 (1930), pp. 122–88; n. s. x–xi (1934–9), pp. 31–90; also as book (Padua, 1940)

C. Furlan: 'Jacopo da Montagnana', *Dopo Mantegna: Arte a Padova e nel territorio nei secoli xv e xvi* (exh. cat., ed. F. Feltrin; Padua, Pal. Ragione, 1976), pp. 35–9

M. Lucco: *Catalogo del Museo Civico di Belluno*, 2 vols (Vicenza, 1983), i, pp. 5–7; ii, pp. 182–3

——: 'La pittura del secondo quattrocento nel Veneto occidentale', *La pittura in Italia: Il quattrocento*, ed. F. Zeri (Milan, 1987), i, pp. 147–83; ii, p. 656

JOHN G. BERNASCONI

Jacopo da Pontormo. *See* PONTORMO, JACOPO DA.

Jacopo d'Avanzi. *See* AVANZI, JACOPO.

Jacopo da Voragine [Jacobus de Voragine; Varagine] (*b* Varazze, nr Genoa, *c.* 1230; *d* Genoa, 13–14 July 1298; *fd* 13 July). Italian archbishop and writer. Born into a poor and undistinguished family, he joined the Dominican Order in 1244. As Provincial of Lombardy (1267–77; 1281–6) he travelled extensively in Italy, and in 1292 he was appointed Archbishop of Genoa. Recognized for his piety, gentleness and works of charity, Jacopo acquired a reputation for holiness. His cult spread throughout north-west Italy, and he was beatified in 1816.

Jacopo da Voragine wrote a number of works, including sermons and the *Chronica civitatis Januensis*, an important source for the history of Genoa, but he is best known for the *Legenda aurea*, or *Golden Legend*. Written in Latin and composed sometime between 1255 and 1266, it was originally titled *Legenda sanctorum*; the honorific 'aurea' was added *c.* 1300. This hagiographical encyclopedia contains 182 chapters of varying length, arranged according to the liturgical calendar. A derivative work, it was compiled from earlier, largely unknown sources. It is, however, an outstanding example of a literary genre that was particularly popular in the late Middle Ages. In recounting the lives of the saints, hagiographers aimed to inspire devotion and virtuous conduct. To this end, the historical facts were altered and emphasis was placed on miraculous or extraordinary events; in addition, borrowed or fictional material was frequently introduced in order to embellish otherwise prosaic accounts. Both the Dominicans and the Franciscans drew on these *vitae* as the basis for their sermons, urging the faithful to emulate the examples of the saints in their daily lives.

The text of the *Golden Legend* does show a limited reliance on two abridged legendaries that enjoyed a wide circulation during the 13th century: the *Abbreviatio in gestis et miraculis sanctorum* attributed to Jean de Mailly and the *Epilogus in gesta sanctorum* by Bartholomew of Trent. Nevertheless, certain traits distinguish the *Golden Legend* from all other works of its genre: the curious etymologies of the saints' names that preface many of the chapters and the authoritarian, decidedly puritanical bias of the text. The latter and the lack of historicity met with harsh criticism from theologians and scholars in the 16th century, but its advocates, who included the Jesuit John van Bolland (1596–1665), emphasized the scholarly merits and piety of its author and argued that its enormous success during the 14th and 15th centuries proved conclusively that the book met the needs of its medieval audience.

That the *Golden Legend* outstripped all its predecessors and contemporary rivals in popularity is evident from the number of extant manuscripts and incunabula (e.g. New York, Pierpont Morgan Lib., MS. 672). Among 14th-century editions, the *Légende dorée*, a French translation by Jean de Vignay, is the most precise; it served as the basis for the 14th-century anonymous prose translation in English, the *Gilte Legende*, as well as for William Caxton's *Golden Legend* of *c.* 1483. Adaptations of Jacopo da Voragine's text, the *Leben der Heiligen* and the *Prosapassionals*, proliferated in German and Dutch editions in the 15th century, and many of the later volumes contained woodcut illustrations. By the end of the 15th century, a substantial number of saints had been added to the original roster, undoubtedly in response to local and regional demand.

From the late 13th century, the *Golden Legend* inspired the iconography of numerous works of art, although artists frequently drew on more than one text in developing their narrative cycles (these included the Bible, the Apocryphal Gospels, the *Meditations on the Life of Christ* as well as the *Golden Legend*). Important Italian narrative cycles, such as Cimabue's frescoes in the upper church of S Francesco, Assisi (*c.* 1277–80), and those of Giotto in the Arena Chapel at Padua (*c.* 1303–6), are indebted to the *Golden Legend*, as are the five scenes by Maso di Banco depicting the *Legend of St Silvester and the Emperor Constantine* in the Bardi di Vernio Chapel in Santa Croce, Florence (*c.* 1330s–40s). Equally faithful to the text is the iconography of the *Raising of the Son of Theophilus* and *St Peter in Cathedra* in the Brancacci Chapel of S Maria del Carmine, Florence, begun by Masaccio (1427) and continued by Filippino Lippi (*c.* 1485). It was also the source for the *Legend of the True Cross* as represented in the fresco cycle by Piero della Francesca in S Francesco, Arezzo (*c.* 1453–4). One of the earliest works to be derived from the *Golden Legend* in northern Europe is the series of scenes from the *Life of St Eustace* in a stained-glass window in the north aisle of the nave of Chartres Cathedral (*c.* 1300). A detail from the cycle portrays the saint's conversion: while hunting, the Roman general Placidas encounters a stag

Life of St Eustace (detail), stained-glass window, Chartres Cathedral, *c.* 1300; iconography inspired by Jacopo da Voragine's *Golden Legend*

with a crucifix between its antlers and kneels before it in adoration (see fig.). Similar cycles or individual representations of St Eustace can be found in contemporary monuments in France, Austria and Sicily as well as in manuscripts. A scene from his *Life* appears in the Belles Heures of Jean, Duc de Berry (New York, Cloisters, MS. 54.1.1, fol. 164*v*), illuminated by the de Limbourg brothers *c.* 1408–9. The manuscript is notable for the fact that below most of the picture cycles are four lines of prefatory text in Latin derived from the etymologies in the *Golden Legend*.

The widespread popularity of the *Golden Legend* during the late Middle Ages was followed by a marked decline in the Renaissance. Emile Mâle deserves much of the credit for the resurgence of interest in the book during the 20th century. It is now recognized as both an essential literary source for the iconography of late medieval and Renaissance art and a valuable document for religious and cultural historians, providing a remarkable insight into popular piety in the late Middle Ages.

WRITINGS

Legenda aurea: Vulgo historia lombardica dicta [MS.; 1255–66]; ed. T. Graesse (Dresden, 1846, rev. 3/Bratislava, 1890/*R* 1965); Eng. trans. and adaptation by G. Ryan and H. Ripperger, 2 vols (London, 1941/*R* 1969); Eng. trans. by W. G. Ryan, 2 vols (Princeton, 1993)

BIBLIOGRAPHY

E. Mâle: *L'Art religieux du XIIIe siècle en France: Etude sur l'iconographie du moyen âge et sur ses sources d'inspiration* (Paris, 1898; Eng. trans. of 3rd edn by D. Nussey as *The Gothic Image: Religious Art in France of the Thirteenth Century* (New York and London, 1958)

H. Delehaye: *Les Légendes hagiographiques* (Besançon, 1903, Brussels, 3/1927); Eng. trans. as *The Legend of the Saints* (Notre Dame, IN, 1961)

F. Wilhelm: *Deutsche Legenden und Legendäre* (Leipzig, 1907), pp. 74–93

G. Monleone: *Studio introduttivo* (1941); i of *Jacopo da Varagine e la sua Cronaca di Genova*, 3 vols (Rome, 1941)

M. Jeremy: 'Caxton's *Golden Legend* and Voragine's *Legenda aurea*', *Speculum*, xxi (1946), pp. 212–21

R. E. Seybolt: 'Fifteenth-century Editions of the *Legenda aurea*', *Speculum*, xxi (1946), pp. 327–38

——: 'The *Legenda aurea*, Bible, and *Historia scholastica*', *Speculum*, xxi (1946), pp. 339–42

L. Réau: *Iconographie des saints*, 3 vols (1958–9); iii of *Iconographie de l'art chrétien* (Paris, 1955–9), pp. 468–71

G. Schiller: *Ikonographie der christlichen Kunst* (Gütersloh, 1966, rev. 1969; Eng. trans., London and Greenwich, 1971)

E. H. Beatson and others: *The Belles Heures of Jean, Duke of Berry* (New York, 1974)

K. Kunze: 'Jacopo de Voragine', *Die deutsche Literatur des Mittelalters: Verfasserlexikon*, ed. W. Stammler, iii (Berlin, 1981), pp. 448–66

Legenda aurea: Sept siècles de diffusion. Actes du colloque international sur la Legenda aurea: Texte latin et branches vernaculaires: Montreal, 1983

B. Dunn-Lardeau and D. Coq: 'Fifteenth and Sixteenth-century Editions of the Légende dorée', *Bib. Humanisme & Ren.*, xlvii/1 (1985), pp. 87–101

S. L. Reames: *The Legenda aurea: A Re-examination of its Paradoxical History* (Madison, 1985)

JOAN ISOBEL FRIEDMAN

Jacopo de' Barbari. *See* BARBARI, JACOPO DE'

Jacopo del Casentino (*fl c.* 1315–?1349). Italian painter. He was the subject of a biography by Vasari, who incorrectly identified him as a member of the Landini family still active at the end of the 14th century, and as a fellow Aretine from Pratovecchio. This source, combined with the dearth of documentary evidence, is to blame for much of the confusion surrounding Jacopo. The only clue to his origins is his name, 'de Casentino', given in his one

signed work, the Cagnola Triptych (Florence, Uffizi), and as he is called in the two contemporary notices that mention him; the evidence of his surviving work, however, indicates a Florentine training in the milieu of the St Cecilia Master, and a career confined to the first half of the 14th century. The chronology of his works is uncertain, and only two of his panels are dated: a *Presentation in the Temple* (Kansas City, MO, Nelson–Atkins Mus. A.) that bears a plausible date of 1330 on its reconstructed frame, and a fragmentary *Virgin and Child* (Crespino sul Lamone, S Maria) dated 1342.

Jacopo's artistic lineage is clearly evident in the decoration of the Velluti chapel of *c.* 1322 in Santa Croce, Florence. Its murals, stained glass and the dispersed altarpiece of *St Michael* (Florence, Acton priv. col.) indicate something of his ambitions and prominence. Like other members of the so-called 'Miniaturist Tendency' (Offner and Steinweg), with whom he is associated and has been confused, his most engaging work is found in small-scale narrative scenes, but, unlike these artists, he also painted many larger panels, and he is no longer associated with any examples of manuscript illumination. In such panels as *St Menas Surrounded by Eight Scenes from his Life* (Florence, S Miniato al Monte; see fig.), the values of his training are combined with the influence of Giotto. Probably painted in the mid-1320s, the small, flanking scenes are illustrative in character, but the central figure of the standing saint has a solidity and volume derived from Giotto. The latter's influence is also evident in the large *Maestà* altarpiece (Florence, Pal. A. Lana, S Maria della Tromba) that is already ascribed to Jacopo in such pre-Vasarian sources as the *Libro di Antonio Billi* (*c.* 1516–30; Florence, Bib. N. Cent.), in a series of narrative works that are among his most successful, for example an *Annunciation* (Milan, Mus. Poldi Pezzoli), and in a finely crafted *Virgin Enthroned* (Ann Arbor, U. MI Mus. A., 1960/2.123) that reflects the example of Giotto's Ognissanti *Virgin and Child* (Florence, Uffizi). Jacopo's sources were eclectic, and such works as the polyptych on the high altar of Santa Croce in Florence by Ugolino di Nerio offered a ready formula, evident in a divided polyptych of the *Virgin and Child* (Brussels, Mus. A. Anc., 794) and *Four Saints* (Houston, TX, Menil Col. 60-01). Similarly, Bernardo Daddi exercised, as he did for other painters during the 1320s and 1330s, a powerful lead, seen in a *Virgin and Child* panel (Pozzolatico, S Stefano).

Jacopo's economic success and the respect of his peers is reflected in his election in 1339 as the first *consigliere* of the newly founded painters' guild, the Compagnia di S Luca. Moreover, in a will of 1347, he is cited as the testator's choice of painter for a commission for S Maria Novella, which may never have been undertaken. During the 1340s, however, his output appears to have diminished. The iconic character of a late work, the panel of *St Bartholomew* (Florence, Uffizi), painted after 1339 for the pier of the Arte dei Pizzicagnoli in Orsanmichele, although a reflection of Jacopo's lingering connection with the St Cecilia Master, seems to prefigure the direction of Florentine painting after the middle of the century. His death probably came not in 1358, as has long been supposed on the unreliable evidence of the *Annali Camaldulensis* infused the Late Gothic art of Nicola Pisano (i) with a new appreciation of antiquity, paving the way for such later artists as Antonio Federighi and Francesco di Giorgio in Siena, Niccolò dell'Arca in Bologna and, most notably, Michelangelo. He worked for a wide spectrum of patrons—the papal states, noble and mercantile families and the cities of Siena and Florence—and was the only Sienese artist of his century to achieve a truly national reputation.

1. Life and work. 2. Working methods and workshop. 3. Critical reputation.

1. LIFE AND WORK.

(i) Early style: works in Lucca and Ferrara, to 1408. (ii) The Fonte Gaia, Siena (1408–19), the Trenta Chapel, Lucca (1412–22), and related works. (iii) The late years, 1425–38: reliefs for S Petronio, Bologna, and other works.

(i) Early style: works in Lucca and Ferrara, to 1408. Jacopo was the son of Piero d'Angelo (*fl* 1370–1410), a minor goldsmith and sculptor, and had a brother, Priamo (1438–67), who was a painter. His birthdate is uncertain; Vasari describes in his *Lives* (1568) an equestrian statue (untraced), carved when Jacopo was 19, for the funeral of the condottiere Giovanni d'Azzo Ubaldini (*d* 1390). This would suggest a birthdate of 1370–71, but Vasari later asserts that Jacopo died in 1438 at the age of 64, indicating a birthdate of 1374. This has been extended to 1375 (Seymour) or even 1380 (Beck); Jacopo remains, at all events, a contemporary of his Florentine rivals and collaborators Brunelleschi, Ghiberti and Donatello. He presumably received his first training from his father, the only known works by whom are three gilded angels (untraced), carved for the main altar of Siena Cathedral and a stiff, somewhat retardataire polychromed wooden *Annunciation* (Benabbio, nr Lucca, S Maria). A modest role for Jacopo in the carving of the Benabbio group has often been suggested. Piero was documented in Lucca from 1391 to 1394, where one of his patrons was the city's ruler, Paolo Guinigi (*d* 1432), later to become a patron of Jacopo. The latter may have accompanied his father from Siena to Lucca, commencing what became a frequent practice of travelling between these cities. Lucca had a long and rich sculptural tradition and an apprenticeship with a Lucchese master should not be ruled out, though it was from the works of Pisano and Arnolfo di Cambio in Siena Cathedral that Jacopo learnt his true craft. In Pisa, which he doubtless visited, he must have studied the rich repository of antiquities located in the Camposanto; his earliest extant pieces reveal a thorough assimilation of both Roman techniques and motifs. However, no convincing hypothesis concerning his early work has been advanced. A depiction of the *Man of Sorrows* (now inserted into the Altar of the Sacrament) and a relief from the tomb monument of *St Aniello* (both Lucca Cathedral) have been suggested as examples of Jacopo's youthful work in Lucca, but neither is entirely convincing. Seymour postulated an alternative Bolognese journey and apprenticeship, and did not rule out a trip to France.

The need to establish a significant early body of works for Jacopo is particularly critical considering the importance of the artist's first firmly fixed activity: an invitation, in 1400–01, to participate in the prestigious competition for the bronze doors of the Baptistery in Florence. The impressive list of competitors included Ghiberti (the

Jacopo del Casentino: *St Menas Surrounded by Eight Scenes from his Life*, tempera on panel, 1.85×1.06 m, mid-1320s (Florence, S Miniato al Monte)

(1761), but in 1349, the date appended to his name in the rolls of his guild.

BIBLIOGRAPHY
G. Vasari: *Vite* (1550, rev. 2/1568); ed. G. Milanesi (1878–85), i, pp. 669–675
H. Horne: 'A Commentary upon Vasari's Life of Jacopo dal Casentino', *Riv. A.*, vi (1909), pp. 95–113
R. Offner and K. Steinweg: *Corpus* (1930–79), III/ii (1930), pt ii, pp. 87–186, 260–64; III/vii (1957), pp. v–vi, 93–142; rev. M. Boskovits, III/ii (1987), pp. 22–4, 381–551, 588–95
M. Boskovits: *Corpus* (1984), pp. 56–60, 296–316
A. Ladis: 'The Velluti Chapel in Santa Croce, Florence', *Apollo*, cxx (1984), pp. 238–45

ANDREW LADIS

Jacopo della Pila. *See under* MINO DEL REAME.

Jacopo della Quercia [della Fonte; della Guercia; di Pietro d'Angelo] (*b* Siena, ?1374; *d* Siena, 20 Oct 1438). Italian sculptor. He was the most significant non-Florentine sculptor of the 15th century: a transitional figure in the development of Italian Renaissance sculpture, who eventual winner), Brunelleschi, Niccolò di Pietro Lamberti, Simone da Colle, Niccolò d'Arezzo and Francesco di Valdambrino. Jacopo's trial piece no longer exists, but Vasari's contention that it was well-designed but lacked a knowledge of true perspective is prophetic of the artist's later relief style. Vasari further claimed that while in Florence Jacopo also designed the crowning relief of the Porta della Mandorla (Florence Cathedral), an assertion surprisingly still repeated by some modern scholars (Brunetti).

Jacopo travelled next to Ferrara, where his first extant documented sculpture can be found. In 1403 he was contracted to carve the marble statue of the *Virgin and Child* (see fig. 1) for the Silvestri Chapel in the cathedral (Ferrara, Mus. Duomo; the date of 1408 on the back of the monument is not original). The Virgin, a full, thickset figure, sober and unadorned, is seated on a modest throne

1. Jacopo della Quercia: *Virgin and Child*, marble, 1403 (Ferrara, Museo del Duomo)

and stylistically follows the tradition of Arnolfo di Cambio. The severely frontal figure stares vacantly ahead, and the rigid lines of the statue are only partially relieved by the gentle flow of her mantle and veil. A statuette of *St Maurelius* (Ferrara, Mus. Duomo) is the only other work associated, however tentatively, with this Ferrarese period.

By 1406 Jacopo was again in Lucca, where he began work on the tomb of *Ilaria del Carretto* (1405–7/8; Lucca Cathedral; see fig. 2), the young and beautiful second wife of Paolo Guinigi; she died in childbirth on 8 December 1405. This work represents a landmark in Renaissance funerary design, though what survives is not the complete monument, which was dismantled in 1430 when Guinigi was expelled from Lucca. The original design probably included a canopy to crown the sarcophagus bearing the recumbent effigy. Compared to the massive, simplified forms of Jacopo's earlier work in Ferrara, the figure of Ilaria is a masterpiece of delicacy, intricacy and finesse. Her head gently resting on a pair of puffy, tasselled pillows, Ilaria lies in eternal repose, her hands softly folded across her chest. In a side view, beautifully swelling curves rise in a sweep from the faithful dog curled at her feet to the high wide collar of the Gothic dress that frames her lovely face. The most unusual feature of the tomb, however, is the frieze of nude putti carrying heavy swags of leaves and fruits that decorates the sides of the sarcophagus. Though putti were a familiar motif on Classical funerary monuments, this is the first use of them on a large scale in the Renaissance. Their robust, fleshly forms stand out in marked contrast to the delicate, fine-boned effigy of Ilaria. Bacci was the first to note the marked distinction in style between the aggressive putti on the south side and the more reticent figures on the north side of the tomb. The latter are the work of Francesco di Valdambrino, a frequent early collaborator who is documented in Lucca during the period of the tomb's construction.

(ii) The Fonte Gaia, Siena (1408–19), the Trenta Chapel, Lucca (1412–22), and related works. In December 1408 Jacopo, having returned to Siena, signed a contract to build a new fountain in the Piazza del Campo, the central space of the city: the prestigious commission indicates that he was recognized as Siena's leading sculptor. The Fonte Gaia (Siena, Pal. Pub.; the version in the Piazza del Campo is a copy) took its name ('fountain of joy') from the festivity that greeted the arrival of water when it was first brought to this hilltop site in the mid-14th century. The Fonte Gaia was dedicated to the Virgin, traditional protectress of the city, and its iconography was intended to harmonize with and expand on the themes of good government found in the 14th-century frescoes in the Palazzo Pubblico opposite. The contract was modified in January 1409 to specify a greater number of figures and an increased payment. A brown ink drawing on vellum, preserved in two sections (New York, Met.; London, V&A) details the new plan. The fountain was to include reliefs of the *Virgin and Child* (this central section is missing from the drawing) surrounded by the four *Cardinal Virtues*, *Faith*, the *Angel Gabriel* and the *Virgin Annunciate*. Two free-standing statues, the *Rhea Silvia* and the *Acca Larentia*, the real and adopted mothers of the twins Romulus and Remus, legendary founders of Siena,

2. Jacopo della Quercia: tomb of *Ilaria del Carretto*, marble, h. 880 mm, 1405–7/8 (Lucca Cathedral)

were to be placed at the corners. The scheme was altered yet again in 1415. The fountain as it is now consists of a large rectangular basin, with multiple spouts, surrounded by low walls on three sides, the remaining portion open to allow for direct access to the piazza. The interior of the walls is decorated with shallow niches containing large-scale figures in high relief of the *Virgin and Child*, flanked by *Angels* and by the *Theological and Cardinal Virtues* and *Wisdom*, plus scenes of the *Creation of Adam* and the *Expulsion from the Garden* and at the corners, as originally planned, the *Rhea Silvia* and the *Acca Larentia*.

Progress was extremely slow. Jacopo began to carve the figures in 1414, but did not finish until 1419. The unusually porous material used for the fountain has deteriorated, making it hard to determine the style and chronology of specific parts. But the sections generally agreed to be later—the free-standing figures and the Genesis scenes, Jacopo's first attempt at narrative sculpture—reveal his growing confidence. The former are among the earliest free-standing nude female figures of the Renaissance. (Bacci attributes the *Rhea Silvia* to Francesco di Valdam-brino, on purely stylistic grounds.) The relief of the *Creation* depicts a powerfully muscular but generalized figure of Adam, who strains upwards towards a downward-inclining God the Father. The figures are tightly compressed in the foreground plane with little attention to depth or indication of landscape setting. Janson (1962) has suggested certain parallels between the pose of Adam and the Early Christian ivory of *Adam in the Garden* (AD 400; Florence, Bargello). Andrea Pisano's reliefs for the Campanile (Florence) also provide stylistic and icon-ographic precedents, yet no direct borrowing can be recognized as Jacopo assimilated and internalized all his

sources. The *Expulsion* (see fig. 3) is both better preserved and more dramatic. The figures of Adam, Eve and the Avenging Angel, all shown parallel to the relief plane, appear too large to have passed through Jacopo's gates of Paradise. The Angel must use physical force to expel the sinners. The striding pose of Adam can be related to an antique source—a Meleager-type sarcophagus (e.g. Pisa, Camposanto, no. 64)—yet it is modified by an awareness of Nicola Pisano's figure style.

The reason for Jacopo's dilatoriness in completing the fountain was that he accepted commissions elsewhere. One of these was for a carved marble statue of an *Apostle* (1411–13; though del Bravo suggests *c.* 1420) for Lucca Cathedral, originally placed high on the north flank of the exterior as part of a series of twelve figures. Intended to be seen from below at a distance, both the upper torso and the head are enlarged. This vigorous, youthful figure has been likened to Giovanni Pisano's *Prophets* (Siena, Mus. Duomo) for the façade of Siena Cathedral or even to Donatello's *St George* (Florence, Bargello). The main alternative to work on the Fonte Gaia came, however, from Lorenzo Trenta, a wealthy merchant from Lucca, who contracted Jacopo to design his family chapel in S Frediano, Lucca. Work on the Trenta Chapel (1412–22) continued concurrently with the Fonte Gaia over the next decade, being interrupted in December 1413 when Jacopo and his assistant Giovanni di Francesco da Imola (*d* before 13 Jan 1425) were denounced, in a letter sent to the city's ruler Paolo Guinigi, for theft, rape and sodomy. Jacopo somehow escaped punishment altogether, but his assistant was imprisoned for three years. Perhaps these circumstances explain why Jacopo was suddenly available to begin work on the Fonte Gaia in Siena in 1414. He

3. Jacopo della Quercia: *Expulsion from the Garden*, marble, relief sculpture from the Fonte Gaia, formerly in the Piazza del Campo, Siena, 1414–19 (Siena, Palazzo Pubblico)

returned to Lucca in March 1416, but only after he had been supplied with a letter of safe conduct.

Jacopo's first work in the Trenta Chapel consisted of an intricately carved marble altar dedicated to the patron saints of the chapel: Richard, Jerome and Ursula. This is basically a conservative *sacra conversazione* with the *Virgin and Child* enthroned against a cloth of honour in a shallow central niche. To the viewer's left and right, standing in self-contained niches framed by pilasters, are *SS Ursula and Lawrence* and *SS Jerome and Richard*. All the niches are surmounted by steeply pitched gables. Half-length figures of the *Prophets* are located on pinnacles above the saints; some sort of decorative element once also rose above the niche containing the *Virgin and Child*. Likewise missing are the Gothic finials planned to complete the elaborate frame. At the base is an elaborate historiated predella with scenes from the *Lives of the Saints* enframing a central *Lamentation*. The saints of the Trenta altar bear a striking resemblance to the *Virgin* and the *Virtues* from the Fonte Gaia, having the same small oval heads with pointed chins and thick necks. The remoteness of expression harks back to the Ferrara *Madonna*, but now the figures are wrapped in heavy draperies with elaborate convoluted folds. While some parts of the work are Giovanni da Imola's, most scholars assign to Jacopo the major share of the execution. The inscription at the base has the date of 1422, which may apply to the completion of the predella. The predella scenes, especially the bold *Martyrdom of St Lawrence*, are clearly more complex and more dependent on dramatic tension. Conceivably they could belong to this later date.

Jacopo also designed for the chapel the tomb effigies (1416) of *Lorenzo Trenta* (d 1439) and his wife, *Isabetta Onesti* (d 1426). The tomb slabs, set into the pavement in front of the altar, have suffered considerable wear. Compared to the high relief of the Ilaria monument, the Trenta tombs offered only a moderate degree of projection. Lorenzo Trenta is shown recumbent with his head, swathed in a voluminous turban, resting on a huge pillow. His body is slightly inclined towards his wife. The effigy of Isabetta complements that of her husband, although she appears to be more active, her drapery more agitated and linear. This effigy has been attributed (Seymour, 1973) to Giovanni da Imola, but both are inscribed 1416, a year when he was still in prison.

Already busy in both Siena and Lucca, with the Fonte Gaia still relatively untouched and the Trenta Chapel awaiting completion, Jacopo took on yet another project. In 1416 Lorenzo Ghiberti advised the authorities on the creation of a new font in the Siena Baptistery. Ghiberti designed the hexagonal marble basin with panels for six bronze narrative reliefs, which he planned to be separated by bronze statuettes of the *Virtues* set in shallow niches. Ghiberti executed two of the reliefs, including the most prominent, the *Baptism of Christ*, but it soon became apparent that Sienese participation was politically advisable, and Jacopo was brought into the project. On 16 April 1417 Jacopo was awarded two reliefs, to be completed within a year: the *Annunciation to Zacharias* and the *Banquet of Herod* (the latter later given to Donatello), with the remaining scenes assigned to Turino di Sano and his son, Giovanni Turini. But lacking experience in working with bronze, Jacopo procrastinated. In autumn 1419 a new contract had to be drawn up; the following year the authorities threatened to begin legal action against Jacopo, who counter-sued. The dispute was finally settled in August 1425, but the Sienese had to wait until July 1430 for the final delivery.

Exactly what preoccupied Jacopo between 1419, when the last payments for the Fonte Gaia were recorded, and 1425, the onset of the S Petronio commission, is hard to identify. No major new projects were begun, and he appears to have been in Siena for most of the time. In 1420 he was elected prior for the Terzo di Martino along with his colleague, Domenico di Niccolò de' Cori. In 1421 he received a commission to carve an *Annunciation* for the Collegiata in San Gimignano (*in situ*). The two life-size, polychromed wooden statues represent his sole documented effort in this medium, so popular in Siena where marble was often difficult to obtain. The grouping of the figures is deliberately conservative in style, recalling the International Gothic idiom of the Ilaria effigy. Jacopo's stylistic range can be seen in his ability to be innovative on the one hand, and respectful of past traditions on the other. The latter characteristic is particularly visible in the delicate swaying stance of the long-limbed, high-waisted, lithesome *Virgin*, who places her arm protectively across her chest. The figure of *Gabriel* is less conventional yet he complements the *Virgin* completely in terms of posture and glance. The delicate polychromy and the gilding serve to enhance both the youth and the ethereal quality of the two figures. The general sophistication of this group suggests that Jacopo was no novice at working in wood, which has led scholars to attribute a number of other wood sculptures to him. The most widely accepted attributions are: a *Virgin with Saints* from S Martino (*c.* 1423–5; Siena, Mus. Duomo); a *Virgin and Child* (*c.* 1430; Paris, Louvre) and a *St John the Baptist* (*c.* 1430; Siena, S Giovanni).

(iii) The late years, 1425–38: reliefs for S Petronio, Bologna, and other works. The last years of Jacopo's life were perhaps his most active and productive. He seems to have divided his time equally between Siena and Bologna, finishing one much delayed project while beginning another. The Siena Baptistery authorities, surprisingly in view of earlier delays, commissioned him in 1427 to design the upper portion of the baptismal font. This consists of a hexagonal marble tabernacle set on a thick, fluted base that rises from a pillar in the centre of the basin. Five of the six faces of the tabernacle contain marble prophets, clothed in voluminous draperies and situated before scallop-shaped niches defined by pilasters. Only one of these prophets, the *King David*, facing the entranceway, has been specifically identified, although all are highly individualized. The remaining face consists of a small *sportello*, or door, behind which the baptismal oil would have been kept, ornamented with a gilt bronze relief of the *Virgin and Child* by Giovanni Turini. The tabernacle is capped by a heavy cornice, above which rises a dome with six small pediments. Originally six gilt music-making putti, by Donatello and Turini, were placed at the corners (four *in situ*). On top of the dome are two diminishing pillars that serve as the base for the marble statue of *John the Baptist*, attributed to Jacopo in most recent literature. The major work on the tabernacle was finished by 1430, although the font itself was not completed for four years.

Jacopo received final payment in August 1430 for his relief of the *Annunciation to Zacharias* on the lower part of the font. This is adjacent to Donatello's *Banquet of Herod* and tries to re-create that work's illusion of space. In earlier reliefs, Jacopo had allowed the figures, set against essentially flat architectural backgrounds, to dominate. In the *Annunciation*, however, he set his figures within a complicated temple consisting of three bays connected by massive arches. This arcade-like arrangement deliberately resembled Donatello's banquet hall but lacked his manipulation of perspective to provide a coherent space. Jacopo even tried to rival Donatello's manner of modelling forms, which varied from figures seen almost entirely in the round to those in low relief in the background. The stance of the figures, particularly that of Zacharias, is difficult to comprehend, indicating the sculptor's fundamental indifference to anatomy.

Jacopo's reliefs in Istrian stone for the Porta Magna of S Petronio in Bologna (see fig. 4) are much more successful. These sculptures, his preoccupation during the last thirteen years of his life, are recognized as his masterworks. On 28 March 1425 he was commissioned to design a complicated portal for the west façade of this late medieval church, located in the very heart of the papal states, and produced a design for a round-arched entranceway framed by historiated pilasters with Old Testament reliefs, eighteen busts of prophets, five New Testament reliefs in the architrave above the door, decorative colonnettes and a lunette above the door containing free-standing statues of

the *Virgin and Child*, *St Petronius* and the patron, Cardinal *Lodovico Alemanno*, papal legate to Bologna. Beck (1970) has established that the *Virgin and Child*, the prophet busts, the lintel reliefs and the colonnettes were all carved first, during the period 1426–September 1428, while the Old Testament scenes and *St Petronius* were added in 1429/30. The original plan was modified in 1428: Jacopo's idea had been for a kneeling figure of the papal legate being presented to the Virgin Mary by Pope Martin V, but the legate had to be replaced by a figure of St Ambrose when the Bolognese rebelled and evicted Cardinal Alemanno.

The adjacent statue of *St Petronius* is a powerful figure, the expressive quality of his face heightened by the nervous chisel strokes of his short, cropped beard. As befits the city's patron saint, he holds a model of Bologna, complete with its huge towers, in his right hand. (The third free-standing figure, *St Ambrose*, was carved in 1510 by Domenico Aimo.)

As a group, the Old Testament panels are carved in lower relief than those in the lintel and are higher rather than wider, thus allowing the heroic nude figure to dominate the relief field. Although relatively small in size, Jacopo's figures give the impression of monumentality. In the *Creation of Adam*, the figural arrangement is the exact reverse of the scene from the Fonte Gaia. Jacopo has even retained the unusual triangular halo of God the Father. The arrangement of the figures, however, seems less tightly compressed. The body of Adam is also more idealized than the earlier work, but is still in Jacopo's typical style—thick-necked, heavy-limbed and with an exaggerated musculature that gives little hint of the skeletal structure underneath. The convoluted, tubular drapery folds of God's robes are typical of the artist's late manner. The *Temptation* is one of the most innovative scenes iconographically as it shows Adam and Eve at equal fault for the Fall. Adam glares angrily at Eve, who has her eyes closed. The two figures are shown on either side of the Tree of Knowledge, whose large central form bisects the relief plane.

The *Expulsion* also takes its basic format from the Fonte Gaia, except that, instead of obediently striding forward, Adam now turns his head and raises his arms in defiance, and a mountain closes off the space to the right, further reducing any sense of depth. Here, as in the *Annunciation to Zacharias*, Jacopo again avoided the Florentine science of perspective.

With so many sculptures to carve for the Portal, Jacopo was frequently absent from Siena. In 1434 the Sienese, however, finally lured him back with the promise of a new project: he was commissioned to design a small loggia on one of the major thoroughfares that runs parallel to the Piazza del Campo. The Loggia di San Paolo, or della Mercanzia, was only partially complete at his death. Attributed to Jacopo are the elaborate capitals of the lower storey, as well as the design for the six niches on the massive piers. These were intended to house statues, which Jacopo was also to have supplied. However, they were not carved until the late 1450s and early 1460s and then by Antonio Federighi and il Vecchietta.

In addition to the new commission, further honours were awarded to Siena's leading artist. In 1435 he was

4. Jacopo della Quercia: Porta Magna, S Petronio, Bologna, 1425–30

knighted, was again selected Priore to the city council and also named Operaio of the cathedral, a powerful and influential appointment that put him in charge of a large workshop. During these final years he became involved with the decoration of a chapel belonging to Cardinal Antonio Casini in Siena Cathedral. A fragmentary relief (Siena, Mus. Duomo) depicting the kneeling cardinal being presented to the Virgin and Child by his patron saint,

Anthony Abbot, is associated with him. While the conception may indeed be Jacopo's, the work depended upon assistants for much of the actual execution. The Vari-Bentivoglio monument (Bologna, S Giacomo Maggiore) and the tomb of *Antonio Budrio* (S Michele in Bosco) are also attributed to Jacopo with considerable workshop participation.

Jacopo was buried in the church of S Agostino in Siena. Soon after his death his executor, Priamo della Quercia, was confronted by the cathedral authorities over his brother's unsanctioned use of assistants from the cathedral workshop for his own purposes and his misappropriation of money and materials. Priamo was obliged to make a substantial repayment.

2. WORKING METHODS AND WORKSHOP. Jacopo della Quercia was unusually versatile, being able to create diverse works in three different media: marble, bronze and wood. He was, however, primarily a carver, with marble his preferred medium. He appears to have been particular about the condition of his marble blocks, making several documented trips to the Carrara quarries, near Lucca, early in his career, and later to Milan, Verona, and Venice in connection with the acquisition of stone for the Porta Magna. Interestingly, he often developed a different style for his works carved in wood. Although there are fewer attributable works in this medium, they are of equal quality to some of his best sculptures in marble. He appears to have done only the carving; the polychroming or gilding was assigned to other masters. These painters were skilled artisans in their own right. The San Gimignano statue of the *Virgin* is inscribed on the base M. CCCC. XXVI MARTINUS BARTHOLOMEI PINXIT, while the *Gabriel* is inscribed with Jacopo's name. Here the painter, Martino di Bartolomeo (*d* 1434/5), seems to claim equality with the sculptor. Jacopo's highly active bottega probably produced various wooden sculptures associated with his name, among them the *St Leonard* (*c.* 1411; Massa, S Maria degli Ulivi), the *Annunciation* (*c.* 1410; Berlin, Gemäldegal.) and a *Virgin Annunciate* (*c.* 1410; Siena, S Raimondo al Refugio). Related to the wooden sculptures are a series of half-length terracotta and stucco *Madonnas* (e.g. Florence, Fond. Romano and Mus. Bardini; Washington, DC, N.G.A.), which are usually assigned to his bottega, but must ultimately be traceable back to a lost prototype by Jacopo.

Jacopo is known to have worked in bronze as early as 1401–2 in Florence when competing for the Baptistery doors. Thirty years later he seems to have met with only slightly greater success when his *Annunciation to Zacharias* was finally completed. His reluctance to work in this medium is further demonstrated by his insistence on retaining for himself only the marble portions of the Baptistery Tabernacle while delegating the bronze areas to associates.

Since many of his projects involved multiple pieces, Jacopo often had to rely on drawings to clarify his complicated schemes to his patrons. For the Fonte Gaia he himself provided the drawing illustrating the first (1408) plan, now subdivided into two fragments (New York, Met.; London, V&A). As Vasari noted, the drawing is extremely detailed, more befitting the hand of a painter of

miniatures than a sculptor. The second contract for the Fonte Gaia, dated 22 January 1419, specified, again, a full-scale drawing to be displayed on the wall of the Palazzo Pubblico, overlooking the proposed site of the fountain. The contract for the Porta Magna, dated 28 March 1425, mentioned a pen-and-ink drawing by Quercia ('fatto di suo mano'), since lost and known only through a 16th-century copy by Peruzzi (Bologna, S Petronio, Sacristy). The painter Sassetta, at Jacopo's own request, received payment for a full-scale drawing of the Siena Baptistery font in December 1427.

The demands placed on the artist by his patrons and his practice of accepting multiple commissions led Jacopo, in his later years, to rely more and more on his bottega to handle the overload and to cope during his prolonged absences. He had two workshops: one in Siena, the other in Bologna, both manned by an extremely capable and trusted group of associates who were later mentioned in his will. In Bologna the workshop was headed by Cino di Bartolo (*d* 1474), while in Siena Pietro di Tommaso del Minella (1391–1458) was most often in charge, particularly in connection with the construction of the Loggia di San Paolo. Among other artists listed at various times in Jacopo's employ, we find the names of Castorlo di Nanni (*fl* 1440s), Paolo and Tonio di Baccio and the young Antonio Federighi. None, with the exception of Federighi, produced important work independently. Despite all the assistance he received from colleagues and shophands, Quercia was rarely able to meet a promised deadline. He was in fact a poor manager, both of materials and of time, and in his last years was accused of misusing funds, materials and even *garzoni* from the cathedral workshop.

3. CRITICAL REPUTATION. Jacopo della Quercia was held in high regard by his own colleagues, contemporaries and rivals. Ghiberti discussed him in his *Commentarii* in connection with the Florentine competition. Antonio Filarete, in his *Trattato di architettura*, proclaimed him one of the finest sculptors in Italy, as did Giovanni Santi in his comments on the arts presented *c.* 1492 to Federico da Montefeltro, Duke of Urbino. Michelangelo held him in high esteem and based his own Genesis scenes (Rome, Vatican, Sistine Chapel ceiling) on Jacopo's reliefs for the Porta Magna. Giorgio Vasari devoted a section of his *Lives* to Jacopo and expanded it in the second edition (1568). With support of this kind his reputation remained high, especially in Italy. Outside Italy the tomb of *Ilaria del Carretto* was his most celebrated work. John Ruskin, who saw the tomb in 1845, was deeply moved by it and wrote that it had inspired his 'true study of Italian, and all other art'.

In the 20th century interest in Jacopo della Quercia was considerably heightened after the exhibition of Sienese art held in London in 1904 by the Burlington Fine Arts Guild, and since that time major monographs have been published by Supino (1926), Bacci (1929), Seymour (1973) and Beck (1991). An exhibition held in Siena in honour of the sexcentenary of his birth (1974) presented not only Jacopo's career but also his relationship to his sources, contemporaries and followers.

BIBLIOGRAPHY

EARLY SOURCES

G. Vasari: *Vite* (1550, rev. 2/1568); ed. G. Milanesi (1878–85), ii, pp.109–30

G. Milanesi: *Documenti per la storia dell'arte senese*, 3 vols (Siena, 1854–6)

S. Borghesi and L. Banchi: *Nuovi documenti per la storia dell'arte senese* (Siena, 1898)

L. Ghiberti: *I commentarii*, Book 2, in *Lorenzo Ghibertis Denkwürdigkeiten*, ed. J. Schlusser (Berlin, 1912), pp. 35–51

A. Filarete: *Treatise on Architecture*, ed. J. R. Spencer (New Haven, 1965)

G. Santi: *La vita e la gesta di Federico di Montefeltro duca d'Urbino*, ed. L. Michelini Tocci, Studi e Testi, 305–6 (Vatican City, 1985)

GENERAL

Thieme–Becker

E. T. Cook and A. Wedderburn, eds: *The Works of John Ruskin* (London, 1903–12), xi, p. 239; xxviii, p. 146; xxxiv, pp. 171–2

C. Ricci: *Il Palazzo Pubblico di Siena e la mostra d'arte senese* (Bergamo, 1904)

Antica arte senese (exh. cat., Siena, Pal. Pub., 1904)

P. Schubring: *Die Plastik Sienas im Quattrocento* (Berlin, 1907)

C. Raggianti: 'Scultura lignea senese e non senese', *Crit. A.*, xviii (1950), pp. 480–96

J. Pope-Hennessy: *Italian Gothic Sculpture*, iii of *An Introduction to Italian Sculpture* (London, 1955, rev. 1972/*R* New York, 1985)

H. W. Janson: *History of Art* (New York, 1962), p. 311

Scultura dipinta: Maestri di legname e pittori a Siena (exh. cat., Siena, Pin. N., 1987)

MONOGRAPHS

C. Cornelius: *Jacopo della Quercia: Eine kunsthistorische Studie* (Halle, 1896)

I. B. Supino: *Jacopo della Quercia* (Bologna, 1926)

P. Bacci: *Jacopo della Quercia: Nuovi documenti e commenti* (Siena, 1929)

Catalogo della mostra di scultura d'arte senese del XV secolo nel quinto centenario della morte di Jacopo della Quercia (1438–1938) (exh. cat., Siena, Pal. Pub., 1938)

L. Biagi: *Jacopo della Quercia* (Florence, 1946)

A. Bertini: *L'opera di Jacopo della Quercia* (Milan, 1962)

O. Morisani: *Tutta la scultura di Jacopo della Quercia* (Milan, 1962)

C. Seymour jr: *Jacopo della Quercia Sculptor* (New Haven and London, 1973) [with critical bibliog.]

Jacopo della Quercia nell'arte del suo tempo (exh. cat., ed. G. Chelazzi Dini; Siena, Pal. Pub.; Grosseto, Mus. Archeol.; 1974)

J. Beck: *Jacopo della Quercia* (New York, 1991)

SPECIALIST STUDIES

V. Davia: *Le sculture delle porte della basilica di San Petronio* (Bologna, 1834)

C. F. Carpellini: *Di Giacomo della Guercia e della sua fonte nella piazza del Campo* (Siena, 1860, 2/1869)

A. Michel: '*La Madone et l'Enfant*: Statue en bois peint et doré attribuée à Jacopo della Quercia', *Mnmts Piot*, 3 (1896), pp. 261–9

I. B. Supino: *Le sculture delle porte di San Petronio in Bologna* (Florence, 1914)

E. Lazareschi: 'La dimora a Lucca di Jacopo della Guercia e di Giovanni da Imola', *Bull. Sen. Stor. Patria*, xxxii (1925), pp. 63–97

E. Caratti and R. Longhi: 'Un'osservazione circa il monumento d'Ilaria', *Vita artistica*, i (1926), pp. 94–6

P. Bacci: 'Le statue dell'Annunciazione intagliata nel 1421 da Jacopo della Quercia', *La Balzana*, i (1927), pp. 149–75

G. Brunetti: 'Jacopo della Quercia and the Porta della Mandorla', *A. Q.* [Detroit], xv (1952), pp. 119–31

R. Krautheimer: 'A Drawing for the Fonte Gaia in Siena', *Bull. Met.*, x (1952), pp. 265–74

N. Rondelli: 'Jacopo della Quercia a Ferrara, 1403–1408', *Bull. Sen. Stor. Patria*, n. s. 2, lxxi/23 (1964), pp. 131–42

A. C. Hanson: *Jacopo della Quercia's Fonte Gaia in Siena* (London, 1965)

C. Ragghianti: 'Novità per Jacopo della Quercia', *Crit. A.*, xii (1965), pp. 35–47

A. M. Matteucci: *La Porta Magna di San Petronio in Bologna* (Bologna, 1966)

H. Klotz: 'Jacopo della Quercias Zyklus der "Vier Temperamente" am Dom zu Lucca', *Jb. Berlin. Mus.*, ix (1967), pp. 81–99

J. T. Paoletti: *The Baptistery Font at Siena* (diss., New Haven, CT, Yale U., 1967)

A. Kosegarten: 'Das Grabrelief des San Aniello Abbate im Dom von Lucca: Studien zu den früheren Werken des Jacopo della Quercia', *Mitt. Ksthist. Inst. Florenz*, xiii/3–4 (1968), pp. 223–72

C. Seymour jr: '"Fatto di suo mano": Another Look at the Fonte Gaia Fragments in London and New York', *Festschrift Ulrich Middeldorf*, ed. A. Rosengarten and P. Tigler (Berlin, 1968), pp. 93–105

J. H. Beck: *Jacopo della Quercia e il portale di San Petronio: Ricerche storiche, documentarie e iconografiche* (Bologna, 1970)

C. del Bravo: *Scultura senese del quattrocento* (Florence, 1970)

M. Paoli: 'Jacopo della Quercia e Lorenzo Trenta: Nuove osservazioni e ipotesi per la cappella in San Frediano di Lucca', *Ant. Viva*, xix/3 (1980), pp. 27–36

A. Emiliani and others: *Jacopo della Quercia e la facciata di San Petronio a Bologna: Contributi allo studio della decorazione e notizie sul restauro* (Bologna, 1981)

C. Gnudi: 'Per una revisione critica della documentazione riguardante la "Porta Magna" di San Petronio', *Jacopo della Quercia e la facciata di San Petronio a Bologna*, ed. R. Manaresi (Bologna, 1981), pp. 13–118

J. Beck and A. Amendola: *Ilaria del Carretto di Jacopo della Quercia* (Milan, 1988)

J. Beck: *Jacopo della Quercia*, 2 vols (New York, 1991)

ELINOR M. RICHTER

Jacopo del Meglio. *See* COPPI, GIACOMO.

Jacopo del Sellaio [Jacopo di Arcangelo di Jacopo] (*b* Florence, *c.* 1441; *d* Florence, 1493). Italian painter. He is first mentioned in his father's *catasto* (land registry declaration) of 1446 as a child of five. By 1460 he had joined the Compagnia di S Luca in Florence, and in October 1473 he appears in their records sharing a studio with Filippo di Giuliano (*fl* 1473–91). His first documented commission, of 10 December 1477, was for two panels with an *Angel Annunciate* and a *Virgin Annunciate* for S

Jacopo del Sellaio: *Angel Annunciate* and *Virgin Annunciate*, oil on panel, 1.47×0.36 mm, 1477 (Florence, S Lucia dei Magnoli)

Lucia dei Magnoli in Florence (*in situ*; see fig.). For the same church he was asked to clean and restore a painting of *St Lucy* (*in situ*) usually attributed to Pietro Lorenzetti. Sellaio's paintings show a brittle, linear technique and a light, pastel palette, clearly indebted to Botticelli. Vasari describes both Sellaio and Botticelli as fellow pupils of Fra Filippo Lippi.

Vasari names three paintings by Sellaio in Florence: two in S Frediano and one in S Maria del Carmine. The latter work is undocumented and perished in the fire of 1771. However, Sellaio certainly had some association with the Carmine, since on 1 January 1484 he was elected *capitano* for the Compagnia di S Maria delle Laudi, which owned a chapel in the Carmine and whose secretary was Neri di Bicci. Eighteenth-century descriptions of S Frediano list a *Pietà* and a *Crucifixion*, which critics have associated with the two paintings by Sellaio seen there by Vasari. On 8 February 1483 Sellaio was commissioned to paint a *Pietà* for the chapel of the Compagnia di S Frediano (nicknamed La Brucciata) in the church of the same name. Payments for the altarpiece continued until 1489, and it was not finished when Jacopo died, for in 1506 his son Arcangelo del Sellaio (1478–1531), who had inherited his father's studio, was asked to complete the work within one year. In 1517 there was a dispute over the cost, and Giuliano Bugiardini and Ridolfo Ghirlandaio were called in to arbitrate. Mackowsky (1899) convincingly identified this work with a *Pietà with Saints* (ex Kaiser-Friedrich Museum, Berlin, inv. no. 1055; destr.) in which the figure of St Fredianus is derived from the same saint in Lippi's Barbadori altarpiece (Paris, Louvre). Sellaio's other work for S Frediano, a huge *Crucifixion with the Virgin, St John and Six Saints*, survives in the 17th-century church of that name. It probably pre-dated the lost *Pietà*.

The two *Annunciation* panels, the *Crucifixion* in S Frediano and the destroyed *Pietà* formed the basis for a large number of attributions to Sellaio (Berenson). The impact of Filippo Lippi on his style is difficult to assess, Botticelli's influence being more apparent in early works, such as the *Annunciation* panels. Sellaio's linear style is both more rigid and more flaccid than that of his contemporary, and his narrative scenes, often set in beautifully rendered landscapes, more anecdotal. In religious works, such as the *Penitent St Jerome* (*c.* 1485; Stockholm, N. Mus.) and the *Trinity with Saints and Donors* (*c.* 1480–85; Tokyo, N. Mus. W.A.), the principal subject is surrounded by a number of miniature scenes, unrelated to the main figures but presumably included as an aid to Christian devotion.

Sellaio's delicate colour sense and feeling for narrative are put to more effective use in such secular scenes as those he painted for cassoni and other items of domestic furniture, as in the pair of panels illustrating the story of Cupid and Psyche (one panel, Cambridge, Fitzwilliam). Sellaio also illustrated the *Trionfi* of Petrarch in four beautiful panels (Fiesole, Mus. Bandini).

The dating of Sellaio's works presents various problems, but throughout the 1470s and 1480s he appears to have been frequently dependent on Botticelli as a source of inspiration. The face of the Christ Child in a *Virgin and Child* (Florence, Gal. Corsini), for example, is copied from

that in Botticelli's Bardi altarpiece (1484–5; Berlin, Gemäldegal.), and the style of the two masters came so close at this time that one work, the *Virgin of the Sea* (*c.* 1485–90; Florence, Accad.), continues to be attributed to Botticelli, or even Filippino Lippi, although Berenson rightly ascribed it to Sellaio. The professional relationship between the two painters still requires further study, as indeed does the entire career of Sellaio himself.

BIBLIOGRAPHY

G. Vasari: *Vite* (1550, rev. 2/1568); ed. G. Milanesi (1878–85), ii, pp. 627, 642–3

H. Mackowsky: 'Jacopo del Sellaio', *Jb. K. Preuss. Kstsamml.*, xx (1899), pp. 192–202, 271–84 [cat. of works]

O. H. Giglioli: 'L'antica Cappella Nenti nella Chiesa di Santa Lucia dei Magnoli a Firenze e le sue pitture', *Riv. A.*, iv (1906), pp. 184–8

H. P. Horne: 'Jacopo del Sellaio', *Burl. Mag.*, xiii (1908), pp. 210–13

G. Bacci: 'La Compagnia di S Maria delle Laudi e di S Agnese nel Carmine di Firenze', *Riv. Stor. Carmelitano*, iii (1931–2), p. 118

L. H. Heydenreich: 'Ein In-Memoriam-Bild des Jacopo del Sellaio', *Schönes Heim*, l/1 (1952), pp. 252–3

B. Berenson: *Florentine School*, i (1963), pp. 195–9

C. L. Baskins: 'Jacopo del Sellaio's *Pietà* in San Frediano', *Burl. Mag.*, cxxxi (1989), pp. 474–8

ELIOT W. ROWLANDS

Jacopo di Antonio (*d* Florence, 13 Dec 1454). Italian painter. He was a pupil of Andrea del Castagno (Vasari). His only surviving work is a series of cherubs (docmented 1451) painted to frame Giotto's Badia polyptych (Florence, Uffizi). Of secondary importance (and consequently perhaps not entirely by his hand), this work has some charm and was admired by Jacopo's contemporaries. The putti are stylistically close to paintings grouped under the name of the MASTER OF PRATOVECCHIO (*see* MASTERS, ANONYMOUS, AND MONOGRAMMISTS, §I) and particularly to fragments of a fresco from the church of Ognissanti, of identical date. Jacopo di Antonio was the cousin of Giovanni di Francesco, and it is possible that he, rather than Giovanni, may have painted a triptych commissioned by the nuns of the Convento del Paradiso, Pian di Ripoli, near Florence. This triptych may perhaps be identified with the *Virgin and Child with SS Bridget and Michael*, known as the Poggibonsi altarpiece (Malibu, CA, Getty Mus.) painted *c.* 1450. If so, Jacopo may perhaps be identified with the Master of Pratovecchio; further evidence suggests that he worked for the same localities as this artist.

BIBLIOGRAPHY

G. Vasari: *Vite* (1550; rev. 2/1568); ed. G. Milanesi (1878–85), ii, p. 682

U. Procacci: 'Di Jacopo di Antonio e delle 'compagnie' di pittori nel corso degli Adimari nel XV secolo', *Riv. A.*, xxxv (1960), pp. 3–70

F. Hartt and G. Corti: 'New Documents Concerning Donatello, Luca and Andrea della Robbia, Desiderio, Mino, Uccello, Pollaiuolo, Filippo Lippi, Baldovinetti and Others', *A. Bull.*, xliv (1962), p. 162

U. Procacci: 'La tavola di Giotto dell'altare maggiore della chiesa della Badia fiorentina', *Scritti di storia dell'arte in onore di Mario Salmi*, ii (Rome, 1962), pp. 9–45

A. Padoa Rizzo: 'Ristudiando i documenti: Proposte per il "Maestro di Pratovecchio" e la sua tavola eponima', *Studi di storia dell'arte sul medio evo e il rinascimento nel centenario della nascita di Mario Salmi*, ii (Florence, 1992), pp. 579–99

ANNA PADOA RIZZO

Jacopo di Cione. *See* CIONE, (4).

Jacopo di Mino del Pellicciaio. *See* GIACOMO DI MINO DEL PELLICCIAIO.

Jacopo di Paolo (*fl* 1371–1426). Italian illuminator and painter. He was the nephew of the Bolognese illuminator Niccolò di Giacomo. He illuminated two statutes of the *Arte della seta* (Bologna, Archv Stato, Cod. min. 56, before 1413; Cod. min. 59, 1424), but he was principally a painter, taught undoubtedly by Niccolò's friend Simone dei Crocefissi, in whose house Jacopo witnessed a loan in 1371. He was enrolled in both the painters' and goldsmiths' guilds and held many public offices in Bologna. In 1393 he designed sculpture for the façade of S Petronio (founded 1390), and in 1402 he was commissioned to supply a new model for the building.

Some 25 works by Jacopo survive. His most important early panel, the *Annunciation* (Bologna, Pal. Com.), was painted for the Camera degli Atti *c.* 1385–90. Its composition and two-bay interior derive from the celebrated *Annunciation* fresco by a follower of Bernardo Daddi in SS Annunziata, Florence; its fresh pinks, blues and yellows reflect such Florentine artists as Giovanni del Biondo. The youthful, curiously flattened faces with emphatic features are typically Bolognese, but the strikingly angular drapery is Jacopo's own. The *Journey of the Magi*, which forms the predella of the carved altarpiece of the Cappella Bolognini (*c.* 1415; Bologna, S Petronio), is notable for its genre detail. Jacopo's major late work is the polyptych of the *Coronation of the Virgin* (1420; Bologna, S Giacomo). Here the figures are taller, faces leaner and more dramatic, and the central Christ and the Virgin with high domed foreheads seem French-inspired. The subtle colours range from lavender and rose to vermilion, and the drawing is sharper. Jacopo's influence lasted for 50 years in Bologna; his sons Orazio (*fl* 1410; *d* 1449) and Paolo (*fl* 1410–18) and son-in-law Michele di Matteo were all painters.

BIBLIOGRAPHY

F. Filippini and G. Zucchini: *Miniatori e pittori a Bologna: Documenti dei secoli XIII e XIV* (Florence, 1947), pp. 135–46, 212

F. Arcangeli: *Pittura bolognese del '300* (Bologna, 1978), pp. 240–55 [with notes by A. Conti]

R. Gibbs: 'Two Families of Painters at Bologna in the Later Fourteenth Century', *Burl. Mag.*, cxxi (1979), pp. 560–68

C. Volpe: 'La pittura gotica: Da Lippo di Dalmasio a Giovanni da Modena', *La basilica di S Petronio in Bologna* (Bologna, 1983), pp. 213–94

R. D'Amico and R. Grandi, eds: *Il tramonto del medioevo a Bologna: Il cantiere di San Petronio* (Bologna, 1987)

ROBERT GIBBS

Jacopo d'Ognabene, Andrea di. *See* ANDREA DI JACOPO D'OGNABENE.

Jacopo Filippo d'Argenta [Jacopo Filippo de' Medici] (*b* Argenta, Emilia, *c.* 1438; *d* ?Ferrara, *c.* 1501). Italian illuminator. In 1456 he was a *garzone* not yet of age in the workshop of the illuminator Taddeo Crivelli, then working on Borso d'Este's Bible (Modena, Bib. Estense MS. V. G.12, lat. 422–3). In 1469 Jacopo was in Bologna. From 1477 until 1501 he produced most of the decoration in fourteen Antiphonals and two Graduals for Ferrara Cathedral (Mus. Duomo; two excised leaves in Cleveland, OH, Mus. A.). While in Ferrara in the early 1490s Jacopo also painted most of the decoration of eight Antiphonals and five Graduals for the Convent of S Francesco, Brescia (Brescia, Pin. Civ. Tosio-Martinengo). The frontispiece for a copy of Pliny's *Natural History* (Turin, Bib. N.U.), a miniature of the *Virgin and Child* in a Book of Hours (Basle, Kstmus.) and single miniatures (New York, Met.; Washington, DC, N.G.A.; ex-Wildenstein Col., Paris) have also been attributed to Jacopo.

With his main collaborator, Fra Evangelista da Reggio, Jacopo developed a highly successful page layout with sumptuous borders that included medallions derived from those in the Bible of Borso d'Este but with ornamental frames made of larger, crisper elements. He also designed robust decorative initials that frame figures set against rocky, visionary landscapes. Jacopo's style is characterized by rigid and incisively drawn forms and the juxtaposition of sharp, contrasting tonalities. He was overwhelmingly influenced by Cosimo Tura's works of *c.* 1470, which he freely adapted in his miniatures.

BIBLIOGRAPHY

E. Calabi: 'I corali miniati del convento di S Francesco a Brescia', *Crit. A.*, xiii (1938), pp. 57–67, pls 36–43

B. G. Vigi: 'Jacopo Filippo d'Argenta, il maggior miniatore dei corali della cattedrale di Ferrara', *La Bibliofilia*, lxxxv (1983), pp. 201–22

PATRICK M. DE WINTER

Jacoulet, Paul (*b* Paris, 23 Jan 1902; *d* Tokyo, March 1960). French draughtsman, printmaker and painter. Shortly after his birth his father accepted a teaching post in Japan, and the family moved there in 1906. A delicate only child, Jacoulet integrated with difficulty in the energetic military academy at Yokohama. Yet he became an accomplished linguist and musician and pursued his interest in nature with drawings of insects, butterflies and seashells. During World War I he worked as an interpreter at the French embassy in Tokyo but in his spare time explored the world of *nō* drama and *bunraku* puppetry. The popular and derivative *ukiyoe* style of his first prints was soon abandoned, as Jacoulet found his individual path in designs of exotic and romantic subjects, influenced by his admiration, on visits to Paris, of the work of Gauguin, Matisse and Egon Schiele. Voyages through the islands of Saipan and Truk in 1929 inspired his first attempt at a series of related prints, *Seven Women of the South Seas* (woodcuts; published 1934), also known as the *Rainbow* (or *Baren*) series, and for a later, much celebrated, series *In the Official Box* (woodcuts; 1942), sometimes referred to as the 'Manchurian Princesses'. These series were carved, respectively, by Kazuo Yamagishi (*b* 1883) and Kentaro Maeda (*b* 1891), who also worked on other projects with Jacoulet. In 1946 *Time* magazine reported an exhibition of Jacoulet's work (Tokyo, Fifth Air Force, Inf. & Educ. Sect.; Tokyo, Armed Forces Educ. Cent.) the 'hit of the Tokyo art season'. Jacoulet revised his methods to design directly on the key-block, rather than executing the meticulous paintings usually supplied to printers for guidance. By 1954 he was devoting all his time to printmaking. In his last decade, despite his declining health, the artist immersed himself in numerous projects, including a proposal for 120 prints of the disappearing peoples of the Asian and Pacific world, which he hoped would secure his international reputation. Overseeing the production of fresh works, often designed in triplicate, exhausted him, and he died of diabetic shock. Of his life's work of *c.* 30,000 woodcuts and several hundred watercolours, 166 prints remain, variable in quality but including some singular achievements.

BIBLIOGRAPHY

F. Wells: *Paul Jacoulet, Woodblock Artist* (Tokyo, 1957)
O. Statler: *The Prints of Paul Jacoulet* (East Dennis, MA, 1975)
R. Miles: *The Prints of Paul Jacoulet, 1934–1960* (London, 1982)

Jacovleff, Alexandre. See YAKOVLEV, ALEKSANDR.

Jacqmain, André (*b* Brussels, 15 Jan 1921). Belgian architect. He studied under Henri Lacoste (*b* 1885) at the Académie Royale des Beaux-Arts, Brussels (graduated 1944), where he learnt an independent style and a mid-20th-century eclecticism. His very first works, for example the house and studio (1955; in collaboration with Victor Mulpas), Brussels, of the sculptor Olivier Strebelle (*b* 1927) demonstrate his detachment from the functionalist sectarianism of the 1950s. A forerunner of Postmodernism, he distinguished himself by a very sophisticated treatment of volumes and forms, in which the rigour of execution and architectural intent often approach mannerism. Later works include the Urvater house (1960) and the headquarters (1963–7) of the Glaverbel company, both in Brussels; various university buildings (1962–72) at Liège and Louvain-la-Neuve; the Belgian Pavilion at Expo '70 (1970), Osaka; and numerous blocks of offices and flats in Brussels and Antwerp.

BIBLIOGRAPHY

G. Bekaert and F. Strauven: *La Construction en Belgique, 1945–1970* (Brussels, 1971), pp. 323–7
'A. Jacqmain et l'Atelier de Genval, en collaboration avec P. Loze', *Entretiens sur l'architecture* (Brussels, 1988)

C. MIEROP

Jacquand, Claudius [Claude] (*b* Lyon, 11 Dec 1803; *d* Paris, 2 April 1878). French painter, designer and printmaker. In 1821 he entered the atelier of Fleury Richard in the Ecole des Beaux-Arts, Lyon. He exhibited for the first time at the Lyon Salon of 1822, in 1824 receiving a first-class medal at the Paris Salon for a *Prison Courtyard* (untraced). He lived in Lyon until his mother's death in 1836, when he settled in Paris. During the 1830s his pictures sold well: Louis-Philippe bought seven paintings for Versailles, and commissioned cartoons of the *Death of the Duc d'Orléans* (1847) for the stained-glass windows of the Chapelle St Ferdinand at Dreux. Although the fall of Louis-Philippe in 1848 deprived Jacquand of official commissions, financial mismanagement of the family polish factory obliged him to earn his living from painting. Between 1852 and 1855 he lived in Boulogne-sur-Mer where he decorated the Salle d'honneur in the Hôtel de Ville. He also obtained the commission for several paintings (1852–4) for Notre-Dame, Roubaix. Government commissions gradually returned: he was asked to decorate the chapel of the Virgin in St Philippe du Roule, Paris (1858–60), and the chapel of St Bernard, St Bernard de la Chapelle, Paris (1867). Jacquand also painted the archivolt of the chapel of the Virgin, St Martin d'Ainay, Lyon (1863).

For his easel paintings Jacquand chose subjects that he knew would appeal to the emotions of his public, for example *Sick Savoyard Child* (1822; untraced) and *Young*

Girl Being Cared for by Nuns in Hospital (1824; priv. col.). He was not a history painter, rather a painter of historical anecdote, and he sometimes chose fanciful settings and anachronistic costumes, but he had a gift for selecting the right moment to represent. He was an eclectic reader and adroitly visualized precise literary descriptions as in his *Death of Adelaide de Comminges* (1831; priv. col.) after Froissard and the *Fifth of March at Perpignan* (1837; priv. col.) after Alfred de Vigny. He also made lithographs for Lyon magazines. Jacquand's concentration on meticulous detail was the fruit of his training in Lyon and his study of 17th-century Dutch painting.

BIBLIOGRAPHY

D. Richard: 'Claudius Jacquand "cet habile artiste"', *Bull. Mus. Ingres*, xiv (1980), pp. 23–9

MADELEINE ROCHER-JAUNEAU

Jacquard, Antoine (*b* ?Poitiers; *fl* 1612; *bur* ?11 July 1652). French designer and engraver. He executed *c.* 92 prints using a technique of short, sharp, clear lines, similar to those of Théodore de Bry and Etienne Delaune. Between 1612 and 1640 he worked for print-sellers in Poitiers and for the Jesuits, for whom he made the *Allegory on the Canonization of SS Ignatius and Francis Xavier* (1622; Weigert, no. 26). In addition to religious subjects and illustrations, Jacquard engraved series of lively and imaginative ornamental prints, mostly on black ground, including locks, watchcases and dials (e.g. W 60–65), as well as handles and hilts for swords (e.g. W 48–53) decorated with mythological and human figures. He also produced allegories, such as the *Five Senses* (1624; W 27–32), and some portraits, for example *André de Nesmond* (1617; W 24) and what may well be a self-portrait in the *Artist's Shop Sign*, which depicts a warrior and two armourers. His series of *Divers portraits et figures faites sur les moeurs des habitants du Nouveau Monde* (W 35–47) has friezes showing the sports and games of the American Indians.

BIBLIOGRAPHY

H. Clouzot: *Antoine Jacquard et les graveurs poitevins du XVIIème siècle* (Paris, 1906)
R.-A. Weigert: *Inventaire du fonds français: Graveurs du dix-septième siècle*, Paris, Bib. N., Cab. Est. cat., v (Paris, 1968), pp. 442–8 [w]

VÉRONIQUE MEYER

Jacquard [Jacard; Jacart; Jacquart; Jakard; Jaquard; Jaquart], **Joseph-Marie** [Charles Marie; J. C.; Joseph Charles] (*b* Lyon, 7 July 1752; *d* Oullins, 7 Aug 1834). French silk-weaver and inventor. The son of a master weaver, he too became a weaver, having tried various other jobs. In the late 1790s, after fighting in the French Revolution, he turned his attention to improving the loom used for weaving patterned silks. This effort resulted in a drawloom for which he was accorded a patent on 23 January 1801 and awarded a bronze medal at the Second Public Exposition of the Products of French Industry in the autumn of the same year. He introduced the punch-card-controlled loom mechanism that bears his name in 1804 but never patented it (in this regard, it is often confused with the drawloom). The Jacquard mechanism, being the first practical application of punch-cards to the automatic control of a manufacturing process, had significance beyond the textile industry. It offered a solution to certain problems faced by 19th-century inventors of computing machines and can be considered a distant ancestor of 20th-century computers.

Work began on the punch-card device in late 1803 or early 1804, when Jacquard went to Paris to demonstrate a fishnetting machine that he had designed. While in Paris he found, then studied, the long-abandoned automatic loom mechanism for weaving patterned fabrics developed by Jacques Vaucanson (1709–82). Thinking that Vaucanson's loom might provide ideas for his own research, he made a model of it, which he brought back to Lyon. By December 1804 he had developed his own mechanism by combining Vaucanson's cylinder (c. 1748) with ideas from two earlier loom mechanisms: Basile Bouchon's band of punched paper (c. 1739) and Jean Philippe Falcon's (c. 1705–65) laced-together punch-cards (1741). Jacquard's device, set on top of a standard treadle loom, for the first time enabled a lone weaver to produce silks with woven patterns of almost unlimited complexity, a task that had previously required a weaver and one or more helpers.

The first documentary evidence of the invention appears in the minutes of Lyon's Chamber of Commerce meeting of 6 December 1804; the minutes of the following meeting, held on 13 December 1804, include an enthusiastic report submitted by three members of the Chamber who had observed Jacquard's loom in action. Initial problems with mechanical aspects of the device were solved gradually. By 1819 the attachment was in common use in the French silk industry, and during the rest of the 19th century it spread throughout the world. It could still be found in the late 20th century, but by then most looms were equipped with less cumbersome, more efficient computer-assisted pattern-control mechanisms.

See also TEXTILES, §II, (1)(ii)(b).

BIBLIOGRAPHY

G. Piobert: 'Machines à tisser les étoffes façonnées à basses et à hautes lisses', *Rapports du jury mixte international: Exposition Universelle, 1855* (Paris, 1856), pp. 380–83
P. Eymard: 'Historique de métier Jacquard', *An. Sci. Phys. & Nat. Agric. & Indust.*, vii (1863), pp. 34–56
C. Ballot: *L'Introduction du machinisme dans l'industrie française* (Paris and Lille, 1923), pp. 334–82

RITA J. ADROSKO

Jacque, Charles(-Emile) (*b* Paris, 23 May 1813; *d* Paris, 7 May 1894). French painter, printmaker and illustrator. In 1830 he worked briefly for an engraver who specialized in cartography, and in that year he produced his first etching, a copy of a head after Rembrandt. From 1831 to 1836 Jacque served in the infantry, seeing action in the siege of Antwerp in 1832. During military service he found time to sketch scenes of army life and is reputed to have submitted two works to the Salon of 1833 in Paris. In 1836 he went to London where he found employment as an illustrator. He was back in France in 1838 and visited his parents in Burgundy, where he became enamoured of the countryside.

Jacque's graphic works in the early 1840s include caricatures published in *Le Charivari* in 1843 and a number of vignettes and illustrations that appeared in the publications of the firm Curmer. More significant, however, are his etchings; this medium was beginning to undergo a revival in popularity at the time (*see* ETCHING, §V), to a large extent through Jacque's efforts. Working in

etching and drypoint, he produced numerous small prints of rustic life, beggars, farm animals, cottages and landscapes. An auction of the works of Georges Michel in 1841 profoundly influenced Jacque, who began to emulate the older master, painting landscapes with windmills at Montmartre and later on the Clignancourt plains (e.g. *Herd of Swine*; priv. col., see Miquel, p. 547).

By 1843 Jacque was closely associated with the Realist movement. Although he had previously exhibited only prints at the Salon, in 1846 the State commissioned a painting showing a herd of cattle milling about a pond at twilight, *Herd of Cattle at the Drinking Hole* (Angers, Mus. B.-A.). Meanwhile, he had befriended Jean-François Millet (ii), and in the spring of 1849 the two artists, seeking to avoid an outbreak of cholera in the capital, moved their families to adjoining properties in Barbizon. Thereafter Jacque divided his time between Barbizon, by then an established artists' colony (*see* BARBIZON SCHOOL), Montrouge, where he maintained another studio, and Paris. He increasingly concentrated on painting, treating his rustic subjects, barnyard scenes and images of grazing livestock with an unerring though more descriptive realism than that of Millet. The works of this period are often small and painted on panel, such as the barn scene, *The Sheepfold* (1857; New York, Met.), and *Poultry* (Amsterdam, Hist. Mus.), one of many similar compositions in which fowl with brightly coloured plumage are shown against sunlit masonry walls. In the 1850s and 1860s Jacque continued to produce prints, often working in a larger format as in the etchings *The Sheepfold* (1859), *The Storm* (1865–6) and *Edge of the Forest: Evening* (1866).

In addition to his artistic endeavours, Jacque pursued numerous speculative ventures: he raised poultry and in 1858 published *Le Poulailler: Monographie des poules indigènes et exotiques*; he cultivated asparagus; and he invested in real estate. In the course of these activities Jacque alienated his fellow artists in Barbizon and still failed to attain financial security. In the 1870s he became involved with a factory at Le Croisic that produced Renaissance- and Gothic-style furniture, utilizing fragments of original pieces. Although he did not regularly participate in the Salon after 1870, he continued to paint, relying on various dealers for sales. He treated the same subjects, working in thicker impasto and relying increasingly on his palette knife. Many of his later works, including *Forest Pastures near Bas Bréan* (Montreal, Mus. F.A.), are marked by a sombre note bordering on pathos. Jacque's position improved in his last years: he received a gold medal at the Exposition Universelle in 1889 and, outliving his Barbizon colleagues, he benefited from the Anglo-American vogue for landscape in the late 19th century. Working in Jacque's immediate circle were a brother, Léon Jacque (*b* 1828), and two sons, Emile Jacque (1848–1912) and Frédéric Jacque (*b* 1859).

BIBLIOGRAPHY

J. M. J. Guiffrey: *L'Oeuvre de Charles Jacque: Catalogue de ses eaux-fortes et pointes sèches* (Paris, 1866)
H. Béraldi: *Les Graveurs du XIXe siècle* (Paris, 1885–92), viii, pp. 162–92
F. C. Emanuel: 'The Etchings of Charles Jacque', *The Studio*, xxxiv (1905), pp. 216–22
P. Miquel: *Le Paysage français au XIXe siècle, 1824–1874*, iii (Maurs-la-Jolie, 1975), pp. 532–63

Millet and his Barbizon Contemporaries (exh. cat. by G. Weisberg, Tokyo, Keio Umeda Gal., 1985), pp. 160–64

Jacquemart, Jules(-Ferdinand) (*b* Paris, 3 Sept 1837; *d* Paris, 26 Sept 1880). French etcher, illustrator and water-colourist. He received his early training from his father, Albert Jacquemart (1808–75), an amateur artist, botanical illustrator, collector and author. From the outset he distinguished himself with illustrations of various *objets d'art*. His earliest recorded work is an etching of 1859 showing a selection of Japanese and Chinese artefacts, and with Philippe Burty, Henri Fantin-Latour and Félix Brac-quemond, among others, he formed a society to study and promote Japanese culture (*see* JAPONISME). Also in 1859 he entered into an association with the *Gazette des beaux-arts* that lasted for most of his career. To this periodical he contributed plates illustrating the extraordinary range of objects owned by such notable collectors as Charles, Duc de Morny, Victor, Duc de Luynes, and members of the Rothschild family, as well as those found in the Louvre. In these etchings he proved remarkably adept at rendering reflections and varying textures and colours.

In the process of engraving plates for the *Histoire artistique, industrielle et commerciale de la porcelaine* (Paris, 1862), written by his father and E. Le Blant, Jacquemart prepared watercolour studies on vellum (e.g. *Sèvres Vase*, 1862; Baltimore, MD, Walters A.G.). In addition, he produced illustrations for other publications treating 16th-century bookbindings (1864), the ceramics of Valenci-ennes (1868), treasures of the French crown (1868), the history of ceramics (1873) and American medals (1880). He published etchings reproducing paintings by Old Masters and contemporary artists, the most extensive work in this category being *Etchings of Pictures in the Metropolitan Museum, New York* (London, 1874). Although he established his reputation as an etcher of works of art, Jacquemart was also an able watercolourist, special-izing in landscapes, and in 1879 was a founder-member of the Société des Aquarellistes Français.

See also CHINA, §VII, 3(vii).

BIBLIOGRAPHY
L. Gonse: *L'Oeuvre de Jules Jacquemart* (Paris, 1876)
H. Beraldi: *Les Graveurs du XIXe siècle* (Paris, 1885–92), viii, pp. 192–213
Japonisme: Japanese Influence on French Art, 1854–1910 (exh. cat. by G. P. Weisberg and others, Cleveland, Mus. A., 1975)

WILLIAM R. JOHNSTON

Jacquemart-André. French collection formed by Edouard(-François) André (*b* Paris, 13 Dec 1833; *d* Paris, 16 July 1894) and his wife Nélie(-Barbe-Hyacinthe) Jac-quemart (*b* Paris, 25 July 1841; *d* Paris, 14 May 1912). Edouard André was the son of the banker and politician César-Ernest André. After service in the French army he, too, became a banker. In 1864 he was elected *député*, remaining in the Assemblée Nationale until 1876. He began collecting at the Duc de Morny's sale in 1865; in the same year he bought paintings by Fragonard (e.g. *Old Man Wearing a Cap*, c. 1769; Paris, Mus. Jacquemart-André) and Rembrandt. His wife, Nélie Jacquemart, had been a pupil of Léon Cogniet and became one of the most successful of society portrait painters. She exhibited at the Salon from 1863, showing portraits between 1868 and

1878; they included those of *Adolphe Thiers*, President of the French Republic (1872 Salon), and *Baron Robert de Montesquiou* (1878 Salon; both untraced). During the 1860s she also completed religious paintings for the church at Suresnes, Hauts-de-Seine (1863) and for two churches in Paris: St Jacques-du-Haut-Pas (e.g. *St Eugène*, 1867; *in situ*) and Notre Dame de Clignancourt (e.g. the *Presentation of Christ* and the *Nativity*, both 1869; *in situ*). She met Edouard André in 1868 and painted his portrait (Paris, Mus. Jacquemart-André) in 1872. They were married in 1881 and lived in the splendid *hôtel particulier* that André had commissioned from the architect Henri-Joseph-Au-bert Parent (1819–95) at 158 Boulevard Haussmann and which was constructed between 1870 and 1875. The house became the centre of glittering social success and home for dazzling collections. Shortly after their marriage, the couple sold their collection of modern paintings and thereafter concentrated on acquiring Italian Old Master paintings, sculpture and works of art and some 18th-century French paintings. Among many great master-pieces, they bought Mantegna's *Ecce homo* (*c.* 1500; Paris, Mus. Jacquemart-André) in 1891. Their collection of objects of *haute curiosité* is comparable in importance to those of Debruge-Dumenil and Charles Stein (1840–99), if on a less lavish scale. They made regular trips to Italy, on the last of which, in 1893, they bought the great series of frescoes (*c.* 1749–50; Paris, Mus. Jacquemart-André) by Giambattista Tiepolo commemorating the journey of Henry III, King of France, to Venice. In 1902 Mme Jacquemart bought the Abbaye de Chaalis, Val d'Oise, from Prince Murat and spent huge sums restoring it to its former splendour. Following the example of Henri d'Or-léans, Duc d'Aumale, she bequeathed her houses and collections and 5,000,000 francs for their maintenance to the Institut de France. The hôtel in the Boulevard Hauss-man now houses the Musée Jacquemart-André.

BIBLIOGRAPHY
DBF
G. Lafenestre: 'La Peinture au Musée Jacquemart-André', *Gaz. B.-A.*, n. s. 3, x (1913), pp. 437–64; xi (1914), pp. 32–50, 101–16
A. Michel: 'La Sculpture au Musée Jacquemart-André', *Gaz. B.-A.*, n. s. 3, x (1913), pp. 465–78; xi (1914), pp. 51–8
L. Deshairs: 'La Tapisserie et le mobilier au Musée Jacquemart-André', *Gaz. B.-A.*, n. s. 3, xi (1914), pp. 117–35
G. Lafenestre: 'Le Musée Jacquemart-André', *Rev. Deux Mondes* (1914), pp. 767–95   □

Jacquemart de Hesdin [Esdin; Esdun; Hodin; Odin; Oudain] (*b* ?Hesdin, Artois; *fl* 1384; *d* after 1413). South Netherlandish illuminator, active in France. He was one of the Netherlandish artists who moved to France to work for the French royal family from the middle of the 14th century. By studying the work of Jean Pucelle and Italian painters he not only evolved his techniques of modelling and rendering of space but also modified the realism characteristic of Netherlandish painting to develop his own more refined style. On 28 November 1384 Jacque-mart was paid for the first time by the administration of Jean, Duc de Berry (*see* VALOIS, (3)). The payment concerned expenses that he and his wife had incurred in Bourges; he was also reimbursed for his clothing for the following winter months. Thereafter he was paid a regular salary by the Duc. In 1398, while he was working in the castle of Poitiers, he, his assistant Godefroy and his brother-in-law Jean Petit were accused of having stolen colours and patterns from Jean de Hollande, another painter in the service of the Duc de Berry. Jacquemart stayed temporarily in Bourges the following year. He may have been in contact with John I of Aragon in 1409.

None of the recorded payments provides information on Jacquemart's work, but inventories of the Duc de Berry's manuscripts show that he collaborated on two Books of Hours. The inventory of 1402 describes a Très Belles Heures, 'enluminées et ystoriées de la main de Jaquemart de Odin', identified as the Book of Hours in Brussels (Brussels, Bib. Royale Albert 1er, MSS. 11060–61), in which he illuminated the Hours of the Virgin and of the Passion. The inventory of 1413 includes the Grandes Heures (before 1409; Paris, Bib. N., MS. lat. 919), stipulating that the large miniatures are by 'Jaquemart de Hodin et autres ouvriers de Monseigneur'. The 17 or so full-page miniatures were cut out, and only one survives, the *Road to Calvary* (Paris, Louvre; see fig.), which reveals the influence of Sienese art, particularly of Simone Martini, and Jacquemart's own realistic, narrative approach. Painting in other manuscripts has been attributed to Jacquemart on the basis of these works. The illumination of a manuscript known as the Petites Heures (Paris, Bib. N., MS. lat. 18014) was probably begun *c.* 1375–80 by Jean le Noir; presumably after his death, Jacquemart and others continued the work between 1384 and 1390. Jacquemart

was responsible for the illumination of the Hours of the Virgin. In addition to the influence of Jean Pucelle, Jacquemart's work reflects a considerable interest in Italian painting, which led to his confident representation of space. His awareness of a more naturalistic rendering of reality was sharpened by contact with the work of Jan Boudolf of Bruges, who had been painter to King Charles V, and of André Beauneveu, with whom he collaborated on the Psalter of the Duc de Berry (*c.* 1386; Paris, Bib. N., MS. fr. 13091). Jacquemart painted only two miniatures for the Psalter, one (fol. 106*r*) based on the *Fool* in Pucelle's Breviary of Jeanne d'Evreux (Chantilly, Mus. Condé, MS. 51, fol. 35*v*). He also collaborated *c.* 1385–94 on the Bible of Pope Clement VII (Rome, Vatican, Bib. Apostolica, MSS. lat. 50–51).

In the payment of 1384 Jacquemart was described as a painter rather than as an illuminator. Since his work on the Duc de Berry's manuscripts was not extensive, it is possible that, like Beauneveu, he worked only occasionally as an illuminator and painted in other media for the Duc. The designs for the stained-glass windows (*c.* 1400–05; destr.) of the Sainte-Chapelle, Bourges, may perhaps be attributed to him. A sketchbook consisting of silverpoint drawings on six sized boxwood panels and compiled from *c.* 1380 to shortly after 1400 (New York, Pierpont Morgan Lib., MS. 346) has been associated with Jacquemart.

BIBLIOGRAPHY

Thieme-Becker

E. Panofsky: *Early Netherlandish Painting*, i (Cambridge, MA, 1953), pp. 42–50
O. Pächt: 'A Forgotten Manuscript from the Library of the Duke of Berry', *Burl. Mag.*, xcviii (1956), pp. 146–53
——: 'Un Tableau de Jacquemart de Hesdin?', *Rev. des A.*, vi (1956), pp. 149–60
K. Morand: *Jean Pucelle* (Oxford, 1962), pp. 26–30
G. Troescher: *Burgundische Malerei* (Berlin, 1966), pp. 222–6
M. Meiss: *French Painting in the Time of Jean de Berry: The Late Fourteenth Century and the Patronage of the Duke*, i (London, 1967), pp. 135–93, 267–85, 321–3, 331–7, 342–3
M. Thomas: *Les Grandes Heures de Jean, Duc de Berry* (Paris, 1971)
A. Châtelet: 'Un Artiste à la cour de Charles VI: A propos d'un carnet d'esquisses du XIVe siècle conservé à la Pierpont Morgan Library', *L'Oeil*, ccxvi/216 (1972), pp. 16–23, 62
Les Fastes du Gothique: Le Siècle de Charles V (exh. cat., ed. G. Pélegrin; Paris, Grand Pal., 1981), pp. 341–7, 430–31
C. Sterling: *La Peinture médiévale à Paris, 1300–1500*, i (Paris, 1987), pp. 124, 230, 408, 411, 414, 426

M. SMEYERS

Jacquemart de Hesdin: *Road to Calvary*, 379×283 mm (Paris, Musée du Louvre); detached miniature from the Grandes Heures of Jean, Duc de Berry, before 1409 (Paris, Bibliothèque Nationale, MS. lat. 919)

Jacquemin [de Lenoncourt], Gérard (*fl* 1460; *d* Toul, 1491). French architect and sculptor. Claims that he was born at Commercy in 1371 are unproven. Owing to the faulty reading of his lost epitaph in the Cordeliers' church at Toul by Dom Calmet, his Christian name has been wrongly given as Rogier and the date of his death as 1460. From 1460 Jacquemin was engaged by the cathedral chapter of Toul as 'masson'; in a document of 1474 he is described as 'maître'. His most important work was for the façade of Toul Cathedral (now St Etienne), designed by Tristan de Hattonchatel (*fl* 1460). The original plans for the project have disappeared, so it is impossible to evaluate Jacquemin's contribution to the creation of this magnificent Flamboyant façade, on which he worked until his death.

As a sculptor Jacquemin worked in the service of René II, Duke of Lorraine. In 1480 the latter commissioned an

Annunciation (untraced) for the oratory of his palace, and in 1481 an altarpiece for his chapel in St Georges, Nancy. In 1485 Jacquemin sculpted the equestrian statue of *René II* for the façade of Toul Cathedral. The statue was smashed in 1793 during the Revolution, although traces can be seen above the north portal. He received 200 gold crowns for this work, which was completed in 1489, and he was called 'mason, sculptor and master of works for the portal of the cathedral church of Toul'.

BIBLIOGRAPHY

Dom Calmet: *Bibliothèque lorraine ou histoire des hommes illustres* (Nancy, 1751), pp. 536–7
E. Martin: *Le Chapitre de Toul aux XIVe et XVe siècles* (Nancy, 1896)
L. Maxe-Werly: *Notes et documents pour servir à l'histoire de l'art et des artistes dans le Barrois* (Paris, 1896)
G. Save: 'Gérard Jacquemin et le portail de Toul', *Bull. Soc. A. E.* (1899), pp. 1–14
A. Villes: *La Cathédrale de Toul* (Metz, 1983), pp. 56–8

MARIE-CLAIRE BURNAND

Jacques (i). French family of sculptors.

(1) Pierre Jacques (*b* Reims, *c.* 1516–20 or *c.* 1545; *d* Reims, 1596). Between 1573 and 1577 he was in Rome, according to the dates inscribed on several pages of the sketchbook (Paris, Bib. N.) that is almost his sole authenticated work. It contains 96 folios of drawings after antique statues, bas-reliefs and architectural details. The drawings, which are mostly in brown ink and black chalk but occasionally in red chalk or sepia, show the sculptor's interest in multiple views of a single statue, such as the bent-up knee of a crouching *Knife-grinder*; some are of flayed figures and skeletons. In dated drawings, methods of shading reveal three main stages in Jacques's graphic development: the earliest are marked by hesitant hatching, followed by carefully contoured parallel lines or zigzagging, and finally by sure, swift outline sketches. He drew most often in the della Valle, del Bufalo, and Cesi collections and copied many details from the reliefs on Trajan's Column and on the Roman arches, as well as sculpture on the Campidoglio. Among other collections, he visited those of the Farnese family and of the Savelli family, where he studied the *Labours of Hercules* sarcophagus (Rome, Mus. Torlonia). He also drew contemporary works, among them Michelangelo's *Risen Christ*. His sketchbook of drawings made on the site (one of the few such to be preserved) is an essential source for the study of antique statues and reliefs in Roman collections in the latter half of the 16th century.

A 17th-century inscription by the owner of the sketchbook mentions sculptural projects by Pierre Jacques in the churches and parishes of Reims: the wood Crucifix of the church of St Pierre-le-Vieil (now at St Jacques) and the high altar for the same church, destroyed in the French Revolution. Fragments of a *Nativity* altarpiece (Reims, Mus. St-Rémi) can reasonably be attributed to Jacques (see Jadart, Reinach), and so perhaps can an altarpiece of the *Apostles* (1541) in Reims Cathedral (Jadart). Other pieces of sculpture in Reims have traditionally been attributed to him: the tomb (1565; untraced) of *Marie de Guise*, formerly in St Pierre-les-Dames, and the statue of *St Andrew* (1586) in St André. Jacques's mausoleum of *Bishop Jérôme Bourgeois* (after 1583, according to the epitaph), formerly in St Pierre-aux-Monts, Châlons-sur-Marne, is known from a drawing by Roger de Gaignières (Paris, Bib. N.). The imposing effigy (now in Châlons Cathedral), carved in bas-relief, from the surviving lower part is comparable in quality to works by Germain Pilon. In August 1583 Pierre Jacques signed a contract for the construction of the high altar (untraced) of St Pierre-le-Vieil. He is last described as a 'master image-maker' in a document of February 1595.

(2) Nicolas Jacques (*b* Reims, *c.* 1578; *d* Reims, 1649). Son of (1) Pierre Jacques. He probably trained with his father. Few of his works survive, but his documented commissions include a massive stone statue of *Louis XIII*, made on the occasion of his coronation in Reims (1610), a wood tabernacle (1626; untraced) for the church of the Carmelite monastery, Reims, and an altar front (1628; untraced) ordered by the equerry Nicolas Thiret for the abbey of Notre-Dame-du-Trésor, Normandy. In Reims he sculpted an equestrian statue of *Louis XIII* (1634) on the pediment of the Hôtel de Ville; six stone statues of the *Apostles* (1636; *in situ* on the pillars of the choir) for St Maurice; a major stone altar (1637; untraced) in the Augustinian monastery; and the engraved marble epitaph in the Carmelite church of *Gérard Siga* (1644), a cathedral chaplain. A terracotta statuette (signed and dated 1647; priv. col., see de Traverse and Ronot, p. 30, illus. 3) of the *Comte de Toulouse*, one of the six secular peers of France, proves that Jacques was requested to provide models for the figural decoration of the silver reliquary of St Rémi, commissioned in 1648 from the Reims goldsmith Antoine Lespicier. (It was destroyed with the tomb in 1793.) In 1648 Jacques undertook various sculptural commissions at St Rémi: the rood screen, porticos (probably including the south portico) and choir enclosures. His son François Jacques (*b* Reims, *c.* 1628; *d* Reims, 20 July 1664), together with the master mason Henri Gentillastre, undertook in 1659 the construction of the north portico of the choir of St Rémi; he created a decorative ensemble of marble and jasper that is still *in situ*. He fell to his death while erecting a figure on the portal of the Carmelite chapel.

BIBLIOGRAPHY

Thieme–Becker

H. Jadart: 'Les Jacques: Sculpteurs rémois des XVIe, XVIIe et XVIIIe siècles', *Réun. Soc. B.-A. Dépt.*, xiv (1890), pp. 568–96
S. Reinach: *L'Album de Pierre Jacques, sculpteur de Reims: Dessiné à Rome de 1572–1577* (Paris, 1902) [facs. repr. with intro.]
P. G. Hübner: *Le statue di Roma: I. Quellen und Sammlungen*, Röm. Forsch. Bib. Hertz., II (Leipzig, 1912), pp. 66–7
L. Pressouyre: 'Sculptures funéraires du XVIe siècle à Châlons-sur-Marne', *Gaz. B.-A.*, n. s. 5, lix (1962), pp. 143–52
P. M. de Traverse and H. Ronot: 'Une Maquette originale de Jacques pour la châsse de Saint Remi à Reims', *Bull. Soc. Hist. A. Fr.* (1974), pp. 27–33

PHILIPPE ROUILLARD, RUTH OLITSKY RUBINSTEIN

Jacques (ii). *See* BACKER, JACOB DE.

Jacques, Charles. *See* STERLING, CHARLES.

Jacques d'Amboise, Bishop of Clermont-Ferrand. *See under* AMBOISE, D'.

Jacques d'Armagnac, Duc de Nemours (*b c.* 1433; *d* Paris, 4 Aug 1477). French patron. The son of Bernard d'Armagnac, Comte de Pardiac, and Eleanor of Bourbon la Marche, he became Duc de Nemours in 1461. He was in favour with Louis XI until 1465, when he defected to the League of the Public Weal led by Charles the Bold, Duke of Burgundy, intent on maintaining the independence of the feudal states from the Crown. An army led by Peter II, Duke of Bourbon, forced Jacques to capitulate; he was subsequently beheaded. He is remembered as a discriminating bibliophile as well as for his political machinations. Jacques employed several copyists, among them Guillaume Olery, who was also a painter. Evrard d'Espinques (a German) and Master Guillaume Alixandre (*fl* 1476-7) of Paris were his resident illuminators. Around 1465 JEAN FOUQUET painted for him 12 large illuminations in the *Antiquités judaïques* (Paris, Bib. N., MSS fr. 247 and nouv. acq. fr. 21013). In 1473 the Duke had the illuminator decorate a larger version of the same work (Paris, Bib. N., MS. 9186). Jacques d'Armagnac was apparently Maître François's most faithful patron, commissioning from him a manuscript of the *Mirroir historiale* of Vincent de Beauvais (Chantilly, Mus. Condé, MS. 1196), copied by Gilles Gracien and bearing a date of 1460. About 1465, Jacques commissioned from Maître François the decoration of 'le Mignon' or *Compendium historiale* (Geneva, Bib. Pub. & U., MS. fr. 79). About 1476 Maître François, in collaboration with the illuminator Jacques de Besançon, produced for the Duke the illustrations of Nicole Oresme's translation of Petrarch's *De remediis utrisque fortunae* (Vienna, Österreich. Nbib., Codex 2559). The painting by Maître François of a copy of the *Cité de Dieu* for Jacques d'Armagnac (The Hague, Rijkmus. Meermanno–Westreenianum, MS. LO AII) came to an abrupt halt on account of the patron's incarceration and death. Jacques d'Armagnac inherited prestigious volumes commissioned by his grandfathers Jacques of Bourbon and Jean, Duc de Berry. In 1476 his properties were confiscated; the books, bearing his ex-libris, were appropriated by Peter II (*see* BOURBON, §I(3)), Tanneguy du Chastel (*c.* 1425-77), Vicomte de La Bellière, and Jean du Mas, Seigneur de l'Isle. Over 70 manuscripts from the collection have been identified in the Bibliothèque Nationale, Paris; others are in the Bibliothèque de l'Arsenal and the Bibliothèque Mazarine, Paris, and in Brussels (Bib. Royale Albert 1er), Chantilly (Mus. Condé), Dresden (Sächs. Landesbib.), London (BL) and Vienna (Österreich. Nbib.).

BIBLIOGRAPHY

L. Delisle: *Le Cabinet des manuscrits de la Bibliothèque impériale* [vol. I]; ...*de la Bibliothèque nationale* [vols II-3], 3 vols (Paris, 1868-81)
A. Thomas: 'Jacques d'Armagnac bibliophile', *J. Sav.* (1906), pp. 633-44
P. Durrieu: *Les Antiquités judaïques et le peintre Jean Fouquet* (Paris, 1908)
E. P. Spencer: 'Dom Louis de Busco's "Psalter" ', *Gatherings in Honor of Dorothy E. Miner*, ed. U. McCracken (Baltimore, 1974), pp. 227-40
C. Sterling: *La Peinture médiévale à Paris 1300-1500*, ii (Paris, 1990)

Jacques de Baerze (*fl* before 1384-after 1399). South Netherlandish sculptor. He was commissioned by Louis II de Mâle, Count of Flanders and Duke of Brabant, to produce two carved altarpieces (untraced): one for the chapel of the castle of Dendermonde, another for the hospice of the Cistercian abbey of Bijloke, outside Ghent. Philip the Bold, Duke of Burgundy, and from 1384 also ruler of Flanders through his marriage to Margaret of

Flanders (1350-1405), having admired these works, commissioned two similar altarpieces from the sculptor in 1390 for the charterhouse of Champmol, which he had founded in 1385 outside Dijon. In August 1391 the two altarpieces were transported to Burgundy from Dendermonde. Documents suggest that these were to be completed in Dijon, but instead, for unexplained reasons, they were returned to Flanders one year later, where the overall supervision of their completion, as well as painting and gilding, was entrusted to Philip's principal Netherlandish painter, MELCHIOR BROEDERLAM. In August 1399 the two finished altarpieces were brought back to Champmol and were favourably judged by a committee that included the sculptor Claus Sluter, the painter Jean Malouel, the goldsmith Hennequin de Haacht and Guillaume, nephew of the former court painter Jean de Beaumetz. By the end of November 1399 the larger triptych was installed on an altar endowed by Jean, Duc de Berry, and the second in the chapter house.

The two triptychs are mostly intact (Dijon, Mus. B.-A.). In the central field of the larger one (1.67×5.02 m; *see* GOTHIC, fig. 51) is the *Crucifixion* flanked by the *Adoration of the Magi* and the *Entombment* (the original *Christ* is in Chicago, IL, A. Inst.). The interior of each wing has five standing saints, and on the exterior are painted scenes of the *Infancy of Christ* by Broederlam. In the second triptych of saints and martyrs (1.59×5.02 m) the central element is also tripartite: the *Martyrdoms of SS Catherine and Barbara* in the centre is flanked by the *Martyrdom of St John the Baptist* and by the *Temptation of St Anthony* (on whose feast day Philip was born). Again, in the interior of each wing are five standing saints; the painted exteriors are lost. The predominant effect of these works is achieved by the busy carved scheme of reticulated gilt tracery, gables, canopies and crockets over compact groupings of delicately coloured doll-like figures. This type of stage-like construction, the forerunner of Brabantine altarpieces, was hitherto limited in France to goldsmiths' work and ivory panels. One standing figure in the Crucifixion altarpiece, *St George*, is especially lively and may have been modelled after a large statue carved by Sluter for the Champmol ducal oratory, which de Baerze had probably seen when in Dijon in 1391. The care and personalized character of the commissions are exemplified by the tooled lower borders bearing the arms and monograms of the Duke and Duchess. Jacques de Baerze also produced for the same patron an unspecified number of other 'tables entaillées', which in late 1395 or early 1396 he brought from Dendermonde to Paris, where Philip usually resided. These additional commissions and Broederlam's own busy production probably account for the excessive delay in completing the two altarpieces for Champmol.

BIBLIOGRAPHY

C. Monget: *La Chartreuse de Dijon d'après les documents des Archives de Dijon*, i (Montreuil-sur-Mer, 1898)
D. Roggen: 'De twee retabels van De Baerze te Dijon', *Gent. Bijdr. Kstgesch.*, i (1934), pp. 91-107
P. de Winter: *The Patronage of Philippe le Hardi, Duke of Burgundy, 1364-1404* (diss., New York U., Inst. F.A., 1976)

PATRICK M. DE WINTER

Jacques de Besançon (i). *See under* FRANÇOIS, MAÎTRE.

Jacques de Besançon (ii). *See* MASTERS, ANONYMOUS, AND MONOGRAMMISTS, §I: MASTER OF JACQUES DE BESANÇON.

Jacques & Hay. Canadian furniture-manufacturing partnership formed in 1835 by John Jacques (*b* ?Cumbria, 9 Nov 1804; *d* Toronto, 14 Feb 1886) and Robert Hay (*b* Tibbermore, Tayside, 18 May 1808; *d* Toronto, 24 July 1890). Both trained cabinetmakers, they worked mostly in the Victorian styles popularized by John Claudius Loudon, A. J. Downey and Charles Locke Eastlake. Although few pieces are labelled, their products are identifiable as high-quality 19th-century Ontario furniture. Established at Toronto and New Lowell, Ontario, this partnership was among the first to use steam-powered machinery and mass-production methods. Parts were cut, shaped and partially decorated by machine, then assembled and finished by hand. Solid black walnut, stained a medium brown, was the principal wood used, and decorative detail was supplied in burl veneer or inlays of bird's-eye maple or fruitwood. By 1865 Jacques & Hay had become the largest furniture manufacturer in Canada; they supplied many public institutions, such as Osgoode Hall, Toronto, and University College (part of the University of Toronto), and private homes such as Spadina, in Toronto. Following the retirement of Jacques in 1870 and of Hay in 1885, the company was reorganized and renamed under Charles Rogers (*b* ?Glasgow, 1816; *d* Toronto, 8 July 1891), its chief carver and designer.

DCB

BIBLIOGRAPHY

P. Dunning: 'The Jacques & Hay Style?', *Can. Colr*, ix/6 (1974), pp. 14–17

R. Cathcart: *Jacques & Hay: 19th Century Toronto Furniture Makers* (Erin, Ont., 1986)

JOHN A. FLEMING

Jacquet. French family of sculptors. They probably came from Grenoble and were active in Paris and the surrounding region from the 16th century to the end of the 17th. Antoine Jacquet, also known as Antoine de Grenoble (*b* ?Grenoble, *c*. 1500–05; *d* Avon, Seine-et-Marne, before June 1572), was a sculptor, mason and architect. He worked at the château of Fontainebleau from 1538, executing stucco decoration, providing architectural models and casting bronze. Among his other works was ornamental sculpture executed under the direction of Francesco Primaticcio for the tomb of *Henry II* in Saint-Denis Abbey. His son (1) Mathieu Jacquet, a contemporary of Germain Pilon and sculptor of the famous *Belle cheminée* at the château of Fontainebleau, was the most eminent member of the family.

Three of Mathieu's sons were also sculptors: Germain Jacquet (*b* Paris, 26 April 1574; *d* Paris; *bur* 8 March 1635) was the godson of Germain Pilon and inherited his father's royal appointments as Garde des Antiques du Roi (1610) and Sculpteur Ordinaire du Roi (1611). He modelled the wax head of *Henry IV* for the effigy used at his funeral (1610; destr.) and, like his father, was principally active as a tomb sculptor, though none of his works in this genre is known to survive. He is also known to have collaborated with Barthélemy Tremblay and with his brothers Nicolas Jacquet (*b* Paris, *c*. 1581; *d* before 1622) and Pierre Jacquet

(*b* Paris; *bapt* 8 April 1582; *d* before 1638). It is possible that a small bronze group of *Neptune with Three Sea Horses* (Amsterdam, Rijksmus.) is the work on this subject that Germain and Pierre are recorded as having made together in 1621.

Germain's son Alexandre Jacquet (*b* Paris; *bapt* 26 May 1614; *d* Paris, 28 May 1686) inherited his father's title of Garde des Antiques du Roi (1637) and, after beginning his career in Paris, went in 1649 to Rome, where he worked in Alessandro Algardi's studio. He contributed a rectangular stucco high-relief panel of *Judas Betraying Christ* to the redecoration of S Giovanni in Laterano (1649; *in situ*). After his return to Paris he contributed stone trophies (destr.) to the restoration of the Porte Saint-Antoine and quantities of decorative stone sculpture (1664 and 1665; destr.) to the Tuileries and Louvre palaces and also (1671–85; *in situ*) to the château of Versailles. It is not clear whether a reference to a Mathieu, Jean and Jacques Jacquet, who were responsible for the richly carved pendentive boss (stone, 1542) in the apsidal chapel at St Gervais, Paris, relates to the same family.

(1) Mathieu Jacquet (*b* Avon, Seine-et-Marne, *c*. 1545; *d* Paris, after March 1611). He was trained in the stylistic tradition of the FONTAINEBLEAU SCHOOL, coming also under the influence of Germain Pilon. Jacquet moved to Paris around 1570, and his early work continued in the decorative Mannerist tradition of his father and the other artists and craftsmen who had worked on the decoration of the château of Fontainebleau. From 1583 he worked frequently for the powerful Neufville de Villeroy family on funerary monuments and on their various houses. His career in royal service began in 1590, when he was put in charge of the abandoned works for the Valois Chapel at Saint-Denis Abbey, but was disrupted by the political disturbances of the early years of Henry IV's reign. Jacquet held the title of Sculpteur Ordinaire du Roi from 1595 and was Garde des Antiques du Roi from 1608 to 1610.

One of the specialities of Jacquet's workshop was the production of monumental chimney-pieces, such as those (all destr.) for the château of Ollainville, Essonne (1572), the château of Conflans, Seine (1600), and the château of Liancourt, Oise (1610). A particularly fine two-tier chimney-piece (4.62×2.55 m, white and coloured marbles; Paris, Louvre) from the Château de Villeroy at Mennecy, Essonne, has been plausibly attributed to Jacquet. The lower tier consists of an architrave supported by two herms, while the elaborate upper tier has two graceful female personifications of Victory about to crown a male portrait bust in an oval niche, garlanded with fruit and flowers.

The principal achievement of Jacquet's career in royal service was also a chimney-piece, the so-called *Belle cheminée*, commissioned by Henry IV in 1597 (completed in 1600; 7×6 m, white and coloured marbles and bronze; dismantled 1725, fragments Fontainebleau, Château, and Paris, Louvre) for the Grande Salle on the first floor of the east wing of the Cour des Fontaines at the château of Fontainebleau. Universally admired by contemporaries, its appearance is recorded in a drawing of 1676 by François d'Orbay (Paris, Archvs N.). Its principal feature was a relief of *Henry IV on Horseback* (marble; Fontainebleau,

Mathieu Jacquet: *Nicolas III de Neufville de Villeroy* and *Madeleine de l'Aubespine*, marble, 1599–1602 (Magny-en-Vexin, Val d'Oise, St Martin); the figure (right) of *Nicolas IV de Neufville de Villeroy* is not by Mathieu Jacquet

Château) in the upper tier, flanked by allegorical statues of *Peace* and *Clemency* (both marble; Fontainebleau, Château). The frieze above the hearth consisted of reliefs representing, in the centre, *Henry IV at the Battle of Ivry* (probably designed by Antoine Caron) and, on either side, winged Victories with palm branches and the insignia of the orders of chivalry, and buxom winged putti clasping flags, crowns and the royal cipher (marble; Paris, Louvre). The influence of Germain Pilon is clear in the figure types and the treatment of hair and draperies, but the finesse, knowledge of anatomy and seriousness of Pilon's sculpture are missing, replaced instead by an exuberant, but slightly rigid, application of Mannerist style.

Among Jacquet's decorative works for private patrons was the portal of the château of Mery-sur-Oise, Val-d'Oise (stone and coloured marbles, 1580; destr.), and the sculptural decoration in the chapel of the Château de Villeroy at Mennecy (1588; destr.). He also produced a large number of garden fountains, including two for the Villeroy family for their châteaux at Conflans and Mennecy, of which none is known to survive.

In the field of funerary sculpture Jacquet created a body of work that, while lacking the magisterial authority of Pilon's, is nevertheless distinguished by comparison with the craftsman-like pieces of contemporary sculpture workshops. He produced all types of monuments, ranging from incised tomb slabs and simple wall tablets to elaborate combinations of architecture and sculpture, such as the alabaster, limestone and coloured marble monument to *Jean Baudouin* (1584; Péronne, Somme, St Jean-Baptiste) with its tympanum relief of the deceased kneeling before the crucified Christ; and the black marble and white marble cenotaph of *Madeleine d'Alesso* in the chapel of the château of Ussé, Indre-et-Loire, which has two graceful angels carrying torches flanking the inscription. Lost monuments include those in stone and marble to *Jean de l'Aubespine* (1596), formerly in Orléans Cathedral; to

Henriette de Clèves (1601), formerly in Nevers Cathedral; and to *Antoine Guyot* (1603), formerly in St Gervais, Paris. One of Jacquet's more important monuments was that to the poet *Philippe Desportes* (1607) formerly in Bon-Port Abbey near Pont-de-l'Arche, Eure. It consisted of a circular, bronze high-relief portrait medallion (Paris, Louvre) set into the pedestal of a black marble Doric column surmounted by a gilt-bronze cross (destr. but recorded in a drawing by François-Roger de Gaignières; Paris, Bib. N., Cab. Est.). The three-quarter profile portrait of the poet is modelled with great delicacy and has a melancholy irony of expression. A similar sense of life is to be found in some of Jacquet's other funerary portraits, of which the busts of *Jean d'Alesso* (bronze, originally painted *au naturel*, 1581; Paris, Louvre) and *Pomponne de Bellièvre* (marble, 1608; Versailles, Château) are extant examples. The bust of *Jean d'Alesso*, from the Minim convent at Passy near Paris, and the bust of *Pomponne de Bellièvre*, from St Germain-l'Auxerrois, Paris, originally formed part of similar wall monuments in the form of pedimented classical tabernacles, flanked by allegorical figures of *Justice* and *Peace* (Paris, Ecole B.-A.) in relief, with an oval niche in the centre for the portrait.

In his large-scale tombs with praying effigies Jacquet was clearly influenced by the volumetric simplicity of such works by Pilon as the monument to *Cardinal René de Birague* (Paris, Louvre). Many of Jacquet's monuments of this kind are destroyed and the statues lost. However, the marble figures of *Nicolas III de Neufville de Villeroy* and his daughter-in-law *Madeleine de l'Aubespine* survive (see fig.), and the disposition of the figures in profile within the elaborate architectural framework of the monument (destr.) is known from a drawing by Gaignières (Paris, Bib. N., Cab. Est.). The statues display an enormous technical virtuosity, combining powerfully modelled faces with melancholy expressions, a minute description of details of costume and a simplicity and strength of contour. A similar combination of qualities can be found in the recumbent marble effigy of Neufville's other daughter-in-law *Marguerite de Mandelot* (Laon, Mus. Archéol. Mun.), originally part of her tomb in the church of the Cordeliers at Pontoise. In addition to such tomb effigies and funerary portraits, two images of *Henry IV*, a bronze head (Paris, Louvre) and a marble bust (Fontainebleau, Château) have been plausibly attributed to Jacquet, in view of their stylistic affinities with the bust of *Jean d'Alesso* and the medallion of *Philippe Desportes*. He is known to have worked with Nicolas Guillain, and Thomas Boudin was his pupil.

BIBLIOGRAPHY

Lami [for all family members]; Souchal [for Alexandre Jacquet]
E. J. Ciprut: *Mathieu Jacquet, sculpteur d'Henri IV* (Paris, 1967) [with bibliog. of earlier lit.]
A. Le Blant: 'Sculpteurs du temps d'Henri IV d'après les documents du Minutier central à Paris', *Actes du 96e congrès national des sociétés savantes: Toulouse, 1971*, i, pp. 399–413
——: 'Autour de Mathieu Jacquet dit Grenoble (fin 16e-début 17e siècle)', *Actes du 97e congrès national des sociétés savantes: Nantes, 1972*, pp. 377–89
M. Beaulieu: *Renaissance française (1978)*, ii of *Description raisonnée des sculptures du Musée du Louvre* (Paris, 1950–), pp. 106–12 [for Mathieu Jacquet]

GENEVIÈVE BRESC-BAUTIER

Jacquet, Alain (*b* Neuilly sur-Seine, nr Paris, 22 Feb 1939). French painter, sculptor and printmaker. He briefly studied architecture in 1960 at the Ecole des Beaux-Arts in Paris but was self-taught as a painter. Sympathetic to Nouveau Réalisme but wishing to counter the lyricism of *Art informel* in the context of painting, he adopted a cool representational style, often using clichéd imagery. Such works brought him within the orbit of Pop art. Among his first paintings exhibited at the *2e Biennale de Paris* (Paris, Mus. A. Mod. Ville Paris, 1961) next to an installation by Martial Raysse were visual puns on several vividly coloured compositions entitled *Jeu de Jacquet* (1961; see 1978 exh. cat.), a pun on his name and the game of backgammon, on which he based their formats. In 1962 he instituted a series of paintings entitled *Camouflages*, in which he superimposed a vulgar symbol on to a reproduction of a work of art: a Shell petrol pump on Botticelli's Venus (*Camouflage, Shell*, 1963; D. Varenne priv. col., see Livingstone, p. 144), a false circulation panel on Leda (Camouflage, Leda, 1963; Boulois priv. col.), coloured blobs over Michelangelo's Christ.

In 1965 Jacquet helped initiate MEC ART, extolling the photo-mechanical reproduction of imagery in silkscreened paintings in theoretically endless variations. He pursued the process to an extreme by exaggerating the scale and by deliberate misregistrations of the photoscreen, particularly in his series *Déjeuner sur l'herbe* (1964–5; e.g. Paris, Fonds N. A. Contemp.), in which he photographically reinterpreted Manet's painting (1863; Paris, Mus. d'Orsay) in modern dress and undress, using as his models the French critic Pierre Restany and other friends. He produced dozens of variations of this single image, the largest of them on the side of a building (see 1978 exh. cat.), so as to call into question traditional concepts concerning originality and the uniqueness of the work of art. In other parodies of works by earlier artists he modified the images further still by modernizing dress, accessories and hairstyles, as in *La Source* (1965; see Livingstone, p. 145), after Ingres's painting of the same name (1856; Paris, Louvre).

From 1969 Jacquet spent more of his time in New York than in Paris, continuing in his paintings and in sculptures posing as real objects such as floorboards and burlap sacks to rely on modern reproductive processes as a way of generating his imagery. By such means he furthered his investigation of the relationship between artifice and reality. In the 1970s he initiated a sustained series of paintings in which he represented planet Earth as seen in photographs taken from outer space.

BIBLIOGRAPHY

Alain Jacquet: Donut Flight 6078 (exh. cat. by S. Pagé and P. Restany, Paris, Mus. A. Mod. Ville Paris, 1978)

P. Restany: *Alain Jacquet: Le Déjeuner sur l'herbe, 1964–1989, 25e anniversaire* (Paris, 1989)

M. Livingstone: *Pop Art: A Continuing History* (London and New York, 1990), pp. 143–6, 158, 256, 259

D. Smith: *Alain Jacquet* (Paris, 1990)

ELISABETH LEBOVICI

Jade. Descriptive term rather than the name of a specific material that in the West refers to two silicate minerals, nephrite and jadeite, which are notable for their hardness, toughness and attractive appearance when worked into a variety of objects. Green is the colour usually associated with jade but many other colours are known (see colour pl. IV). The Chinese term *yu* refers not only to jade but also to softer stones such as serpentine, steatite, pyrophyllite, muscovite, olivine and sillimanite; all these minerals have been identified among early Chinese 'jades' (*see* CHINA, §XIII, 11). Other minerals exist that resemble jade to a certain degree such as idocrase, grossular, amazonite and chrysoprase. Also, nephrite and jadeite are not simple minerals: other minerals are often included within their structure.

1. Types and properties. 2. Techniques. 3. History, sources and uses.

1. TYPES AND PROPERTIES. Nephrite is a calcium magnesium silicate from the amphibole group of minerals. It is a compact variety of the mineral series tremolite–actinolite in which the fibrous hair-like crystals are tightly felted and matted together; this dense structure accounts for its extreme toughness and hardness. Nephrite has a hardness of 6.5 on the Mohs hardness scale. (The scale ranges from 1 to 10, diamond at 10 being the hardest.) The specific gravity of nephrite is 2.90–3.09, so it is three times denser than water. Its mean refractive index is 1.62. Polished nephrite has an oily or waxy lustre. The colour of nephrite ranges widely from white, yellow and various shades of green, to brown, grey and black. The Chinese called white or pale-coloured nephrite 'mutton fat jade' (*yang zhi yu*). The nephrite of ancient Chinese jades (*c.* 7000–256 BC) is often variegated rather than being one colour throughout. The green of nephrite can be due to traces of iron, but white jade sometimes has a high iron content. The green colour can also be attributed to chromium and nickel, and a red–brown colour can be due to the presence of titanium.

Jadeite is a sodium aluminium silicate mineral from the pyroxene group. It is rarer than nephrite. The individual blocklike crystals of jadeite are interlocked in a complex way to give a granular appearance which is especially noticeable at broken edges. The crystals are not fibrous and matted as in nephrite, and therefore jadeite is less tough. It is somewhat harder than nephrite, being 7 on the Mohs scale, and also denser, with a specific gravity of

1. Nephrite cup, greenish-white with chalky-white areas of soft altered nephrite, h. 96 mm, from China, 5th–4th centuries BC (Washington, DC, Freer Gallery of Art)

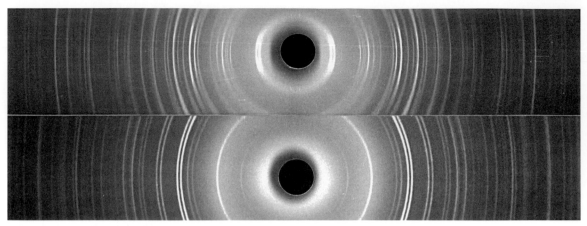

2. X-ray diffraction patterns of nephrite (above) and jadeite (below)

3.30–3.36. Its mean refractive index is 1.66. Polished jadeite has a vitreous appearance. The typical colour of jadeite is a bright emerald green, but it can also be black, white, red, pink, orange, purple or blue. The emerald green colour in Burmese jade is thought to be due to chromium, and chromium has been identified in green Mesoamerican jades. Central American jadeite generally has less variety in colour than the Burmese material, ranging from shades of green, including one that is almost blue, to grey and white. Diopside–jadeite, in various shades of green, and albitic jadeite, which is white or pale grey mottled with green, are two varieties found exclusively in Central America. Chloromelanite is a dark green to black variety of jadeite found in Mesoamerica and New Guinea and, in the forms of tools, in European Neolithic sites. Ureyite, a deep green sodium chromium silicate analogous to jadeite, is found in Burma, and in Mexico and South Africa with jadeite.

Chinese nephrite tomb jade, dating from the Neolithic period through the Zhou period (from c. 6500 BC to c. 1100–256 BC), has sometimes undergone alteration during burial; it is known as 'calcified' or 'calcined' jade or described as having 'jade patina' (see fig. 1). The light-coloured, sometimes patchy, altered areas retain the shape or design of the original except when decomposition has progressed so far as to cause loss of the surface. The alteration is evidently caused by exposure to ammoniacal conditions during burial, probably due to the decomposition of bodies in the tombs. These altered areas are still nephrite but are softer than normal jade.

In another type of alteration the nephrite develops a curious opaque, chalky, ivory-like appearance. This is called 'chicken-bone white' (ji gu bai) jade by the Chinese and is also sometimes termed 'burnt' jade. Nephrite assumes this appearance when heated to 1025° C, whereupon it alters to diopside, a different calcium magnesium silicate. Areas with this appearance on Chinese nephrite jades have been identified as diopside and some late Neolithic Chinese nephrite jades are known to have been deliberately exposed to fire. Jadeite when heated behaves quite differently: it turns glassy and small pieces may even melt out of shape.

Various tests can be used to identify jade. Determination of hardness can suggest that the mineral is jadeite or nephrite and not some softer mineral, but it will not differentiate between the two jades. Neither mineral can be scratched by a metal tool such as a penknife, though misleading results may arise from testing soft areas of surface alteration. Also, there are minerals that are as hard as jade and might be mistaken for it: bowenite, for example, a pale green variety of serpentine, has a hardness of 6 and looks very much like jade. Determination of specific gravity or refractive index may indicate if the mineral is jadeite or nephrite, or neither, but it will not provide certain identification.

X-ray powder diffraction is the most definitive identification method and requires only a tiny sample the size of a few grains of salt scraped from the object. Identification of the unknown sample depends on the fact that every crystalline material gives a reproducible and individual pattern, recorded either as lines on photographic film (see fig. 2) or as peaks in a graph. This method can differentiate nephrite from jadeite and both varieties of jade from other minerals.

2. TECHNIQUES. The hardness of jade has always presented a challenge to those who mine and work it. Quarrying of nephrite jade from the mines in Sino-Central Asia was described as early as 1133 in a Chinese lapidarium, Yun lin shi pu, by Du Wan. Fires were built next to the jade to heat it and water was then thrown against the rock face, causing it to crack because of the rapid temperature change. Wooden wedges were used to drive the pieces apart. This treatment damaged the material, so the best jade came from pebbles and boulders found in streams. The brown rind often found on these boulders is sometimes incorporated into the design of carved jades (see colour pl. IV). In Burma jadeite was mined by methods similar to those used in Sino-Central Asia, using heat and wedges to extract the extensive occurrences from mines dug into the hillsides; also, boulders and loose blocks of jade were found in the river valleys.

The breaking and chipping techniques used to carve other stones are not effective on jade because of its toughness. Even though Chinese jades are often described as carved, the working of jade from ancient times to the present day has always been achieved by abrasion with a harder material. In early times without metal tools this was a slow and laborious process, and even with modern abrasives jade cannot be worked rapidly. The first abrasive used in China, and probably the only one available for several millennia, was quartz, a commonly occurring mineral with a hardness of 7, harder than jade. Early artisans could have used quartz sand, crushed sandstone or crushed loess, the main constituent of which is fine quartz particles. Crushed almandine garnets (hardness 7.5), the "red sand" of Chinese jade workers in the 1930s, were probably used beginning in the Song period. A new abrasive that appeared in the 12th century may have been emery, a naturally occurring black mineral mixture containing corundum (hardness 9), the "black sand" of the 1930s workers.

The abrasive is applied with various tools. At an early date only bamboo or bone drills were used. The earliest reference to rotary cutting and grinding tools (see fig. 3) was made c. 1500 by a Chinese author, in *Taicang zhou zhi* (Topography of Taicang), in Jiangsu Province, but there is some evidence of the use of rotary tools on earlier objects, a significant development in the technique of jadeworking. Metal tools, probably first copper and then iron, were another significant advance, introduced in the late Zhou period (c. 1050–256 BC). The use of rotary tools was probably essential for the working of hollow jade vessels. An early reference to 'toad fat' used for working jade probably referred to a grease containing abrasive

3. Chinese jade worker, Shanghai; from a photograph by James Marshall Plummer, c. 1935

material. Jade-bead workers in Idzumo province, Japan, still use oil with the abrasive, but Chinese workers suspend the abrasive in water. Jadeworking methods in the 20th century give some clues as to earlier procedures, the chief difference being that harder abrasives such as carborundum, a synthetic product (hardness 9.5), and diamond (hardness 10) are now available. It has been suggested that diamond abrasive, the hardest material, was available to the early Chinese, but no definite evidence for this exists.

Since jade was so expensive and difficult to work, the pieces were often created with a minimum of change to the contours of the stone and any discarded pieces were reused. Forms were designed to coincide with the natural colour variations in the mineral (see colour pl. I).

The jadeworking techniques of the Maori were described by Captain James Cook, the discoverer of New Zealand, in 1769. Their methods had probably been unchanged for centuries. They had no metal and made use of slate, flint and laminae of sandstone for abrading and cutting. Holes were made with rotary drills of wood, bamboo or hollow bone, used with wet sand. (In North America, in the Fraser River area of British Columbia, workers used thin flat slabs of sandstone as saws.)

Information on jadeworking techniques in Mesoamerica comes from a text (1558–9) by the Spanish missionary Bernardino de Sahagún, describing the art of the lapidary as practised by the Aztecs at the time of the Spanish Conquest in the 16th century. These techniques must have been derived from, and been essentially the same as, those used in earlier indigenous cultures. The material was shaped and rubbed down with some hard stone and then ground and polished, using wood or bamboo with suitable abrasives, probably garnet, pyrite, haematite and quartz, which are as hard as jade or even slightly harder. Evidence of working techniques can also be inferred from the objects themselves. Objects from Guatemala show evidence of pecking, grinding, rasping, sawing, drilling, reaming, polishing, incising, graving and string sawing. Sawing may have been done with copper tools, otherwise with hard wood or bamboo, used with abrasives. Drilling may have been done with jade-tipped rods; cylindrical, pointed jade objects that may be drill points have been found. Crushed jade was also used as an abrasive.

See also MESOAMERICA, PRE-COLUMBIAN, §VIII.

3. HISTORY, SOURCES AND USES. The names of the jade minerals have a complex history. No reference to jade occurs in Western mineralogical or pharmacological literature before the discovery of the Americas in the 16th century. When Marco Polo (1254–1324) described jadeworking in Sino-Central Asia in the late 13th century, he described the stone there as jasper and chalcedony. The Spaniards found a green stone, called *chalchihuitl* by the Aztecs, being used for decorative carving by the natives of Mesoamerica. They attributed curative properties, especially for the kidneys, to this stone and hence named it *piedra de ijada* ('stone of the loins'). From the French *pierre l'ejade* came *le jade*, and thus jade. When carved stone objects from East Asia began to reach Europe in the mid-17th century, the name jade was transferred to them, though by that time Mesoamerican jade was rare and

nearly forgotten. Nephrite as a mineral name first appeared at the end of the 18th century; it derived from the Latin *lapis nephriticus*, another version of the Spanish name. Finally, in 1863 the French mineralogist Alexis Damour established the existence of two distinct jade minerals of different chemical composition, the one from Sino-Central Asia for which he retained the name nephrite, and the one from Central America and Burma for which he coined the name jadeite. The Chinese use the word *yu* to describe any stone used for carving, not just nephrite and jadeite. The name *feicui*, the Chinese word for kingfisher, originally applied to a fine green nephrite from Sino-Central Asia; it was revived in the 19th century to apply to emerald green Burmese jadeite.

(i) Asia. (ii) The Pacific. (iii) The Americas. (iv) Europe and Africa.

(i) Asia. Although China is a jade-carving centre where ritual and ceremonial pieces have been produced from at least the 7th millennium BC to the present day (*see* CHINA, §VIII), no sources of jade are known in China proper. Tao Hongjing, a 5th-century medical writer, quoted in the Ming pharmacopoeia *Bengao gangmu*, mentioned sources of jade in Shaanxi and Henan provinces and the *Shanhai jing* ('Classic of mountains and seas'), a geographical and mythical description dating partly to the Warring States period, gives 200 references to supposed jade sources in China, but no sources there have yet been affirmed. Apparently the confusion arose from the broad application of the term *yu*. Current studies by Chinese scholars may eventually be able to specify origins of raw nephrite in China proper. From early times until the 19th century the only source of nephrite for the Chinese was Sino-Central Asia, now the Chinese province of Xinjiang. Jade is found there near Yarkand and Kashgar and in river valleys of the western Kunlun mountain range that divides Tibet from the Taklamakan Desert. North of Khotan, an oasis on a loop of the ancient silk route across Central Asia, two of these rivers come together, the Karakash (the Turkic *kara*: *ka:ş* means black jade) and the Yurungkash (*ürüñ ka:ş* means white jade). The jade trade in Khotan was witnessed by Marco Polo in 1272, and mention is made of jade mines in those valleys by a Manchu writer, Qishiyi, in *Xiyou wenjian lu* ('Observations from the "Western Regions"', 1777). In the early 1870s European travellers described seeing pale green jade in veins over 3 m thick in the workings there. Nephrite was also known in the Mansi area north of the east Tian shan range.

From the late 14th century to the late 15th the jade-producing areas of Sino-Central Asia were controlled by the Timurids. They established a two-way trading relationship with the Ming dynasty emperors in China, and the earliest extant Islamic jades are attributed to them (see colour pl. III, fig. 1). Their descendants, the Mughals, introduced jadeworking to India in the 16th century, and at the end of the century the Mughal emperor Akbar (*reg* 1556–1605) gave a certain trader the rights to prospect the banks of the rivers near Kashgar. Sino-Central Asia continued to be the source worked by the Mughals (see colour pl. III, fig. 2). The Ottoman Turks, too, used jade, producing lavishly decorated nephrite objects (see fig. 4) from the 16th century, and their source must also have

4. Nephrite tankard, pale green inlaid with jewels and gold, h. 135 mm, from Turkey, Ottoman empire, second half of the 16th century (Istanbul, Topkapı Palace Museum)

been Sino-Central Asia. (*See also* INDIAN SUBCONTINENT, §VII, 11 and ISLAMIC ART, §VIII, 8.)

The only other known source of nephrite in continental Asia is central Siberia in the area of Lake Baikal. In 1850 the French engineer J. P. Alibert observed water-worn nephrite boulders weighing up to two tonnes in the rivers. Nephrite was also found along the Onot River south of Irkutsk. Siberian jade is green with minute flecks of black chromite scattered through it: the Chinese call it 'spinach' jade (*bocai yu*). It was used in prehistoric times in this area for axes, ornaments and trade pieces and appears to have been exported to China in the Neolithic period, though written evidence of this trade exists only from the 19th century. In the 19th century jade was used by Russian jewellers and lapidaries. Peter Carl Fabergé used Siberian jade for the bases of his decorated eggs and for the leaves of artificial flowers. The Russians also used the material for monumental purposes; the sarcophagus of Alexander III (*reg* 1881–94) was made of Siberian nephrite.

The finest jadeite in the world comes from northern Burma, near the villages of Tawmaw and Hpakan, in the Kachin Mountains near Mogaung, and in the valley of the Uru River. At one time it was thought that the Chinese discovered it there in the 13th century, but it is now known that extensive trade between the two countries started only in the late 18th century, during the reign of the emperor Qianlong (*reg* 1736–96; for example of jade of this period see colour pl. II, fig. 2). Burma became an important source of jade for the Chinese and spectacular objects were produced. The Chinese sometimes refer to Burmese jade as Yunnan jade because it entered China through Yunnan Province, just north of the jade-producing area of Burma.

In addition to the nephrite of Sino-Central Asia and Siberia and the jadeite of Burma, confirmed jade mineral deposits in continental Asia include nephrite in Korea and jadeite in the polar Ural Mountains of Russia and in the east Sayan Mountains of Siberia. Jadeite occurs in several locations in Japan, but only the jadeite found in the Niigata Prefecture in central Japan seems to have been exploited as a raw material. Jadeite *magatama*, comma-shaped beads, have been found in large numbers in grave sites in Japan (2nd–3rd century AD) and Korea (4th–6th century AD). Since 1961 nephrite has been mined on the island of Taiwan, but this source was not exploited in earlier times.

(ii) The Pacific. There are several occurrences of jade in the South Pacific area, and jade tools have been widely reported throughout Oceania. Nephrite, most commonly dark or grass green, occurs in New Zealand where it is called greenstone; it was used by the Maoris, who probably arrived in New Zealand in the mid–14th century, for tools, weapons and ornaments. Nephrite is found in New South Wales, Australia and, in small quantities, in New Caledonia. Jadeite is known in the Celebes and in New Guinea, where unworked loose nephrite and nephrite celts as well as chloromelanite have also been found. (*See also* MAORI.)

(iii) The Americas. Radiocarbon dating has shown that jadeite was worked by the indigenous races of Central America and Mexico as early as 1500 BC: the Olmecs, the Maya and, finally, the Aztecs used it for ornaments, amulets and badges of rank (see fig. 5 and colour pl. II, fig. 1). The first carved jades were brought to Europe by Spanish navigators, but jadeworking in Mesoamerica ceased soon after the Spanish Conquest. Local cultures were destroyed and all knowledge and appreciation of the material disappeared. The source of the jadeite used in Mesoamerican jades was uncertain until the finding of jadeite in Guatemala in 1952, followed by subsequent finds of jadeite throughout the area. Until then, Burma had been suggested as the source of the raw materials, although this was unlikely because the appearance of Central American jade differs from the Burmese material and diopside–jadeite, which does not occur in Burma, was common among Maya and Aztec carved objects. (*See also* SOUTH AMERICA, PRE-COLUMBIAN, §II, 6(i), and MESOAMERICA, PRE-COLUMBIAN, §VIII and fig.33.)

In South America nephrite is known at a single locality at Babytinga, Bahia, Brazil, and nephrite celts are known among the aborigines of the Amazon River basin. Jade artefacts, not definitely identified, are reported from Peru, Colombia and Chile.

In North America nephrite occurs in Alaska and British Columbia. Jade was worked by the Inuit of Alaska, where enormous nephrite deposits are found along the Kobuk River in the area of Jade Mountain. In British Columbia large deposits are located along the Fraser River, where artefacts worked by the Native Americans dating to 1500 BC have been found. (*See also* NATIVE NORTH AMERICAN ART, §III, 1–3.) Nephrite and jadeite occur in the western United States, but no artefacts have been reported. The nephrite of Wyoming, first discovered in 1936, is the best North American material and compares well with nephrite

5. Jadeite miniature mask, 70×55 mm, Teotihuacán culture, Mexico, Classic period, AD 200–900 (Washington, DC, Dumbarton Oaks Research Library and Collections)

from Sino-Central Asia and Siberia. Both minerals occur in California and a few isolated deposits have been reported elsewhere. In the late 19th century Chinese gold-miners and railroad workers exported tonnes of nephrite to China from California and British Columbia. It is possible that some Chinese carved jades of the period may have been made from this material.

(iv) Europe and Africa. In Europe jade was used by Neolithic lake dwellers for axes and celts of nephrite, jadeite and chloromelanite. Nephrite was first located in Europe in 1885, near Jordansmuhl in Silesia, Poland. Until then, it was thought that the material for European Neolithic jades was imported from Asia. Both minerals are now known to occur in Poland, Italy, Germany and Switzerland, and prehistoric jade ceremonial weapons have been found in Spain, Portugal, Germany and Great Britain.

In Africa a single nephrite deposit is known in Zimbabwe and nephrite is also reported in Egypt in the Eastern Desert; the use of nephrite and jadeite for artefacts in Ancient Egypt is unconfirmed.

See also CENTRAL ASIA, §I, 8(v).

BIBLIOGRAPHY
B. de Sahagún: *Historia general de las cosas de Nueva España* (1558–9; trans. A. Anderson and C. Dibble, Santa Fe, 1955)
W. F. Foshag: 'Mineralogical Studies on Guatemalan Jade', *Smithsonian Inst. Misc. Col.*, cxxxv/5 (1957) [monograph]

J. Needham: *Mathematics and the Science of the Heavens and the Earth* (Cambridge 1959), iii of *Science and Civilization in China*, Section 25: Mineralogy; pp. 663–9: Jade and Abrasives

E. H. West: 'Jade: Its Character and Occurrence', *Expedition*, v/2 (1963), pp. 3–11

W. A. Deer, R. A. Howie and J. Zussman: *An Introduction to the Rock-forming Minerals* (London, 1966)

S. H. Hansford: *Chinese Carved Jades* (London, 1968)

A. M. Gaines and J. L. Handy: 'Mineralogical Alteration of Chinese Tomb Jades', *Nature*, ccliii (1975), pp. 433–4

A. R. Woolley: 'Jade Axes and Other Artefacts', *The Petrology of Archaeological Artefacts*, ed. D. R. C. Kempe and A. P. Harvey (Oxford, 1983), pp. 256–76

Xia Nai: *Jade and Silk of Han China*, trans. & ed. Chu-tsing Li (Kansas City, 1983)

R. L. Bishop, E. V. Sayre and L. Van Zelst: 'Characterization of Mesoamerican Jade', *Application of Science in Examination of Works of Art* (Boston, 1985), pp. 151–6

Jeffrey Yu-teh Kao: *The Archaeology of Ancient Chinese Jades: A Case Study from the Late Shang Period Site of Yinxu* (diss., Cambridge, MA, microfilm, Ann Arbor, 1985)

P. E. Desautels: *The Jade Kingdom* (New York, 1986)

T. W. Lentz and G. D. Lowry: *Timur and the Princely Vision: Persian Art and Culture in the Fifteenth Century* (Washington, DC, 1989)

Wen Guang and Jing Zhichun: 'Chinese Neolithic Jade: A Preliminary Geoarchaeological Study', *Geoarchaeology*, vii/3 (1992), pp. 251–75

ELISABETH WEST FITZHUGH

Jadot (de Ville-Issey), Jean-Nicolas (*b* Lunéville, 22 Jan 1710; *d* Ville-Issey, 1 June 1761). French architect, active in central Europe and Italy. Jadot came from a family of court architects in Lorraine. He trained on a variety of Germain Boffrand's schemes for Leopold, Duc de Lorraine (1679–1729), and may have spent periods of study in Paris and Rome. In 1732 he was appointed Architecte Ordinaire to Leopold's son François III (later Emperor Francis I) and accompanied his master, then Grand Duke, to Florence and, when he became Emperor, to Vienna. In 1740 Jadot was ennobled as Baron de Ville-Issey (Lorraine) and in 1753 he was appointed Intendant des Bâtiments Royaux under the Emperor's brother Charles Alexander, Governor of the Austrian Netherlands. Jadot's first known work is the Temple to Hymen and Peace in Lunéville, a firework structure built on the occasion of the marriage in 1736 between François and Maria-Theresa of Austria. In 1737 he moved to Florence, where, for the entry of the ruling couple, he erected a triumphal arch (1738–9) at the Porta San Gallo. From 1745 Jadot was resident in Vienna, where he built (1750) the menagerie at Schönbrunn Castle: the animals' cages are set in the segments of a circle, at the centre of which is a pavilion based on a design by François Blondel. He also designed the University (1753; now the Academy of Sciences) in a style dependent on French models.

Numerous plans survive for unrealized works, reconstructions and other schemes (Vienna, Albertina, and U. Paris, Bib. Doucet). These include the façade of St Jacques, Lunéville; plans for the Bagni di Pisa (lost, but known to have been splendid) and the Palazzo Pitti in Florence; a large-scale extension project for the Vienna Hofburg, and the Ambassador's staircase there; the Burgtheater in the Michaelerplatz; and three palaces for Prince Charles Alexander. Designs survive for imperial fortresses and castles at Buda in Hungary (executed) and Bratislava and Holič in Slovakia, the villa of Mariemont in Belgium (executed, but burnt down in 1794) and the modernization of the ducal sepulchral chapel at the Palais Ducal in Nancy.

Jadot was a sensitive, if unadaptable, architect, and he obviously had difficulties realizing his plans. His life and work were entirely devoted to the service of the ruling dynasty of Lorraine. He brought a French style, imbued with individual Italian decorative elements, to Vienna, and in the service of the court he repeatedly returned to the inspiration of Versailles (e.g. façade of the Universität in Vienna; Schönbrunn Menagerie; Ambassador's staircase, Hofburg). This, as well as his studies for palace façades with colonnades (in part for the Vienna Hofburg), for which his main inspiration was the eastern façade of the Louvre and the earlier triumphal arch in Florence (inspired by the Arch of Constantine), characterize his work as early Neo-classical.

BIBLIOGRAPHY

Macmillan Enc. Architects

J. Schmidt: *Die alte Universität in Wien und ihr Erbauer Jean Nicolas Jadot* (Vienna and Leipzig, 1929)

L. Hautecoeur: *Architecture classique* (1943–57)

J. Garms: 'Jadot und Italien—Zwischen Lothringen und Wien'; *Röm. Hist. Mitt.*, xxxi (1989), pp. 319–38

JÖRG GARMS

Jaeckel, Willy (*b* Breslau [now Wrocław, Poland], 10 Feb 1888; *d* Berlin, 30 Jan 1944). German painter and printmaker. He studied painting at the art academies in Breslau (1906) and Dresden (1908). In 1911 he returned to Breslau and worked as a decorative painter. His first exhibition at the Galerie Fritz Gurlitt in Berlin in 1913 was a success. His important portfolios of prints also brought him recognition: *Memento Mori* (1914–15) was suppressed for its anti-war sentiments; *Biblische Motive* (Berlin, 1916) and *Das Buch Hiob* (Berlin, 1917) were followed by numerous illustrations to Dante, Goethe, Whitman and others. His work was clearly Expressionistic at this time. Drafted during World War I, he was given leave of absence to paint four large murals (destr.; see 1975 exh. cat., pls 4–7) for the TET factory in Hanover. In 1919 he was elected a member of the Preussische Akademie der Künste.

The experience of the war made him move to a small southern German village to study religious, theosophical and philosophical concepts (1919–24). At this time he began his large (over 200 items) graphic portfolio *Menschgott—Mensch—Gottmensch* (Berlin, 1921). On his return to Berlin he was appointed professor at the Staatliche Kunsthochschule in Berlin (1925) and was awarded the Rome Prize in 1928. Around 1923 he moved towards a brooding realism, concentrating on still-lifes, portraits and moody female nudes. In 1933 he was dismissed by the Nazis but reinstated due to the students' protest. His work was included in the infamous exhibition of *Entartete Kunst* in 1937. In 1943 his studio was destroyed by bombs. He himself died in a bombing raid.

BIBLIOGRAPHY

G. Biermann: 'Jaeckels Monumentalgemälde für die TET-Fabrik in Hannover', *Almanach auf das Jahr 1920*, ed. F. Gurlitt (Berlin, 1920)

E. Cohn-Wiener: *Willy Jaeckel* (Leipzig, 1920)

A. Maerkisch: *Willy Jaeckel: Das graphische Werk* (Dresden, 1963)

Willy Jaeckel (exh. cat., Regensburg, Ostdt. Gal., 1975)

D. Klein: *Der Expressionist Willy Jaeckel* (Cologne, 1990)

PETER W. GUENTHER

Jægerspris [formerly Abrahamstrup]. Castle and garden in north Zealand, Denmark, *c.* 50 km north-west of Copenhagen. The small castle, on a spur between Isefjord and Roskilde fjord, is partly medieval but dates mostly from the 16th and 18th centuries, the east wing having been built in 1730–32 by Johan Conrad Ernst (1666–1750). It is now a museum containing the furniture and collections of King Frederick VII (*reg* 1848–63) and his third wife, Countess Danner, who occupied it between 1854 and 1863. North and east of the castle is the memorial grove. In 1776 the heir presumptive to the Danish throne, Prince Frederick (1753–1805), excavated a Bronze Age tumulus, which he dedicated to his mother, the Dowager Queen Juliana Maria (1729–96). This was a time when there was an upsurge of interest in national history and origins, and the project was conceived of turning these ancient remains into a political monument to Denmark's past. Johannes Wiedewelt was commissioned to transform the mound into a Roman-inspired monument—circular, terraced, fenced in and planted with trees, among which were set seven memorial columns bearing the names of Danish kings since the time of the sagas.

Owing to the mental instability of King Christian VII (*reg* 1766–1808), the regime was led by his unpopular stepmother, the Dowager Queen, whose prime minister, Ove Høegh Guldberg (1731–1808), saw the memorial grove as a means of emphasizing national unity and diverting attention from the regime's unpopularity. He commissioned Wiedewelt to produce 56 columns commemorating famous Danes, Norwegians and Holsteiners (Denmark then included Norway and Schleswig-Holstein). The sculptor sought a national, non-Roman style to express the spirit of the North, reflected in his use of simple, geometric forms. The columns (1779–89) were positioned throughout the grove, as if at random, undoubtedly after the model of Lord Chief Justice Mansfield's garden (later Kenwood, Hampstead London) before its remodelling by Humphry Repton *c.* 1797. Although not a landscape garden, the memorial grove was the first romantic garden in Denmark.

BIBLIOGRAPHY
T. H. Colding: *Jægerspris-Slottets bygningshistorie og dets samlinger* [Jægerspris Castle's building history and collections] (Copenhagen, 1965)
H. Lund: *Mindelunden ved Jægerspris* [The memorial grove at Jægerspris] (Copenhagen, 1975)
HAKON LUND

Jaén [anc. Aurinx]. Spanish city located due north of Granada and east of Córdoba, in the centre of the autonomous region of Andalusia, with a population of *c.* 100,000. Originally a Roman settlement named Aurinx, the city was subsequently occupied by the Moors until 1246. Among the remaining evidence of that period are the 11th-century Moorish baths beneath the convent of S Teresa. Overlooking the city from the west is the Castillo de S Catalina, rebuilt after the Christian Reconquest on Moorish foundations. Other buildings of interest include the Gothic church of S Ildefonso, the façade of which was designed by VENTURA RODRÍGUEZ and whose *retablo mayor* was produced by Pedro Roldán (*see* ROLDÁN, (1)) and José Roldán.

Jaén Cathedral, sacristy, by Andrés de Vandelvira, from 1555

Of principal interest, however, is the cathedral of La Asunción, consecrated in 1660. The first cathedral building, as in other cities following the Reconquest, was a converted mosque. In the late 14th century Bishop Nicolás de Biedma carried out extensive alterations to this. Rebuilding began *c.* 1500, beginning at the east end, under the master mason Pedro López to a plan by Enrique Egas (*see* EGAS, (3)). Work proceeded until doubts were expressed as to the building's safety. Committees of masons were called in to advise in 1523 and 1525, and the second of these recommended that most of the work should be demolished. One section of the early work remains visible: the lower part of the east wall, with a band of fine Hispano-Flemish ornament. In 1534 ANDRÉS DE VANDELVIRA produced a new plan, which was largely executed, although it took over a century to complete. Vandelvira directed operations until his death in 1579, building the chapter house and sacristy (from 1555; see fig.) at the south-east corner and the chapels flanking the chancel to the south, with the south transept front. It seems that funds ran out, as work then stopped for over 50 years.

In 1634 the remaining parts of the unsatisfactory earlier building were demolished, and the east end and crossing were erected (1634–54) under Juan de Aranda. Pedro de Portillo continued work on the crossing, building the central dome. In 1667 Eufrasio López de Rojas was appointed; by his death in 1684, he had built most of the nave and west front (the latter to his own design); the façade was decorated with statues and reliefs by Pedro Roldán. The western towers were completed in 1688 by Blas Antonio Delgado, Miguel Quesada and José Gallego. Under Gallego work on the vaults and roof over the nave continued until the 1720s. Gallego also built the choir (occupying the two easternmost bays of the nave, as is common in Spanish cathedrals), with its magnificent flanking walls in the ornate, curvilinear Churrigueresque style. The stalls themselves, however, date partly from the 16th century and partly from the 17th.

The plan and form of the cathedral are mostly Vandelvira's and developed Diego de Siloe's design for Granada Cathedral (begun 1528). Despite the long building period, the cathedral at Jaén is generally homogeneous in style, following Vandelvira's Mannerist classical formula. The major exception is the west front, by López de Rojas, in a more strongly Baroque idiom with a giant order of Corinthian semi-columns raised on high pedestals. Vandelvira planned the interior as a form of hall church, with the aisles as tall as the nave, divided by Corinthian columns on tall pedestals. The transepts project very slightly, and there are lower chapels flanking each bay. The two interiors completed by Vandelvira are highly dramatic: the sacristy has paired columns supporting arches against the walls, with a great barrel vault over. Finally the *sagrario* (sacrarium) in the north-east corner is an important example of Neo-classical style. Designed by Ventura Rodríguez in 1761, it has an oval ground-plan, with paired Corinthian columns supporting a dome with hexagonal coffering, rather French in spirit. Begun in 1764, it was completed in 1801 by Rodríguez's nephew Manuel Martín Rodríguez.

BIBLIOGRAPHY

G. Alamos: *La iglesia catedral de Jaén* (Jaén, 1971)
P. Galera Andreu: *Arquitectura y arquitectos en Jaén a fines del siglo XVI* (Jaén, 1982)

STEPHEN BRINDLE

Ja'far [Ja'far ibn 'Alī al-Tabrīzī al-Baysunghurī] (*b* Tabriz; *fl* 1412–31). Persian calligrapher. According to the Safavid chronicler Dūst Muḥammad, Ja'far was trained in the classic six scripts by Shams al-Din Qattabi, whose line of tutelage went back to the 14th-century master 'ABDALLAH SAYRAFI. Ja'far was trained in *nasta'līq* by 'Abdallah, supposedly the son of MIR 'ALI TABRIZI, the inventor of the script. Ja'far served at the court of the Timurid ruler Shahrukh (*reg* 1405–47) in Herat and supervised the scriptorium of Prince Baysunghur (*see* TIMURID, §II (7)). Signed and dated works by Ja'far range from a manuscript (Tehran, Majlis Lib.) of the *Dīvān* (collected poetry) of Hasan Dihlavi, copied in 1412–13, to a Miscellany (Dublin, Chester Beatty Lib., MS. 122), copied in 1431–32. He was the calligrapher of the celebrated manuscript (Tehran, Gulistan Pal. Lib., MS. 4752) of the *Shāhnāma* ('Book of kings') made for Baysunghur in 1429–30, and internal evidence suggests that a unique example of an early Timurid report (Pers. *'arẓadāsht*) from an unnamed supervisor of an artistic establishment to an unnamed patron is a report from Ja'far to Baysunghur *c.* 1429. Ja'far's mastery of the classic scripts, particularly *thuluth*, *naskh* and *muḥaqqaq* (*see* ISLAMIC ART, §III, 2(iii)), is evident in the specimens of his calligraphy preserved in several albums (e.g. Istanbul, Topkapı Pal. Lib., H. 2153, fols 27*r*, 58*r*, 160*v*). His *nasta'līq* is typical of early examples of the script in which the individual graphic units are placed at a 30° angle to the horizontal writing line, but his script did not reach the fluidity shown by SULTAN 'ALI MASHHADI nor the elegance achieved by the next generation of *nasta'līq* calligraphers trained by Ja'far in Herat, such as

Shaykh Mahmud Zarin–qalam (*fl* 1442–66) and Azhar (*fl* 1421–72). Ja'far was also the teacher of 'Abdallah Tabbakh (*fl* 1429–61), who continued the line of tutelage in Herat.

WRITINGS

Report (*c.* 1429; Istanbul, Topkapı Pal. Lib., H. 2153, fol. 98*r*); Eng. trans., ed. W. M. Thackston in *A Century of Princes: Sources on Timurid History and Art* (Cambridge, MA, 1989), pp. 323–7

BIBLIOGRAPHY

Dūst Muḥammad: Preface to the Bahram Mirza Album (MS.; 1544); Eng. trans., ed. W. M. Thackston in *A Century of Princes: Sources on Timurid History and Art* (Cambridge, MA, 1989), pp. 335–50
Muṣṭafā 'Alī: *Manāqib-i hunarvarān* [Virtues of artists] (1587); ed. I. M. Kemal (Istanbul, 1926), pp. 28–32
Qāżī Aḥmad ibn Mīr Munshī: *Gulistān-i hunar* [Rose-garden of art] (*c.* 1606); Eng. trans. by V. Minorsky as *Calligraphers and Painters* (Washington, DC, 1959), pp. 64, 100
M. Bayani: *Aḥvāl va āthār-i khūshnivīsān* [Biographies and works of calligraphers], 2nd edn in 4 vols (Tehran, Iran. Solar 1363/1984–5), i, pp. 114–23

WHEELER M. THACKSTON

Jaffna [Sinh. Yapane; Tamil Yalpanam; anc. Nagadipa]. Peninsula and city in the dry zone in the extreme north of Sri Lanka. The peninsula—*c.* 137 km long, *c.* 13–40 km wide and with an area of 2580 sq. km—is nearly separated from the rest of the island by the Jaffna lagoon (also known as Elephant Pass lagoon). Ruins of Buddhist monasteries mainly built prior to the 10th century are extant at Kantharodei, Tellippalai, Mallakam, Chunnakam, Puttur, Sambiliturai, Vallipuram, Kankesanturai, Nilavarei, Anakottei, Puloli, Uduvil and Keeramalai. Quantities of such finds as bases of stupas (Sinh. *dāgaba*s) with diameters ranging from 2.45 m to 7 m, granite and white limestone images of the Buddha and bodhisattvas, images of gods and goddesses, sculptured slabs and other objects were recovered from these sites (Jaffna, Archaeol. Mus.).

From the 13th century AD to the early 17th the peninsula was the location of the independent Tamil kingdom. The site of its last capital was at Nallur, now in the suburbs of the city of Jaffna; little remains of the royal palace, but the Kandaswamy Temple (rebuilt 1807) is still the focus of a major annual festival. There are also well-preserved Hindu temples (*kovi*ls) at Mavatupuram and Nagamma, as well as important temples at Vallipuram and Nainativu. Images of Hindu deities (Jaffna, Archaeol. Mus.) have been found at Kantharodei, Nallur and Kayts.

Jaffna was ruled successively by the Portuguese, Dutch and British from the late 16th century until the mid-20th century. There are ruined Portuguese churches at Myladdi and Chankanai (1641) and also remains of colonial-period churches at Achchaveli and Vadukkodai; the latter, established by the Portuguese, was later modified by the Dutch. The well-preserved fort (1680) within the city of Jaffna is star-shaped in plan and stands as a monument to Dutch military architecture (*see also* MILITARY ARCHITECTURE AND FORTIFICATION, §III, 2(v)(b) and fig. 18). Its ramparts (h. 6 m) and battlements are surrounded by a moat and by later outworks (1792), with a total area of 55 acres. The fort contains offices, prisons, the so-called King's House (once the residence of the Dutch and British commanders) and the church known as the Groote Kerk (1706). There are other small forts in the Jaffna peninsula: one near the Elephant Pass lagoon and two on the island of Kayts. Other structures of note are a gate made of palmyra wood (2.44×1.52 m; Jaffna, Archaeol. Mus.) and two large bell-towers at Point Pedro, Sri Lanka's most northerly point.

See also SRI LANKA, §III, 4.

BIBLIOGRAPHY
C. Rasanayagam: *Mudaliyar: Ancient Jaffna, Being a Research into the History of Jaffna from Very Early Times to the Portuguese Period* (Madras, 1926)
S. Natesan: 'The Northern Kingdom', *History of Ceylon*, i, pt 2 (Colombo, 1960), pp. 691–702
C. W. Nicholas: 'Historical Topography of Ancient and Medieval Ceylon', *J. Ceylon Branch Royal Asiat. Soc.*, n. s. vi (1963) [special issue]
K. Indrapala: *Dravidian Settlements in Ceylon and the Beginnings of the Jaffna Kingdom* (diss., U. London, 1966)
M. D. Raghavan: *Tamil Culture in Ceylon: A General Introduction* (Colombo, 1971)
S. Pathmanathan: *The Kingdom of Jaffna* (Colombo, 1978)
E. T. Kannangara: *Jaffna and the Sinhalese Heritage* (Colombo, 1984)
W. A. Nelson: *The Dutch Forts of Sri Lanka* (Edinburgh, 1984)

H. T. BASNAYAKE

Jagamara, Michael Nelson. *See* NELSON TJAKAMARRA, MICHAEL.

Jagan (*fl c.* 1580–90). Indian miniature painter. He was named 11th of the 17 painters listed in the *Āyīn-i Akbarī*, a contemporary account of the administration of the Mughal emperor Akbar (*reg* 1556–1605) as it was *c.* 1590. His three folios in the *Dārābnāma* ('Story of Darab'; *c.* 1580–85; London, BL, Or. 4615, fols 31*r*, 115*v* and 122*r*) have a dramatic impact, but the compositions are more suited to the narrative line and large format of the *Hamzanāma* ('Tales of Hamza'; *c.* 1567–82; alternatively dated *c.* 1562–77) on which he must have worked. However, his illustrations as sole artist in the *Razmnāma* ('Book of wars'; 1582–6; Jaipur, Maharaja Sawai Man Singh II Mus., MS. AG. 1683–1850; fols 47–8, 72 and 106) are well-balanced and follow the Persian conventions he learnt while working on designs for the *Timūrnāma* ('History of Timur'; 1584; Bankipur, Patna, Khuda Bakhsh Lib.; fols 26*v*, 59*v*, 115*v*, 131*v* and 138*v*). No attributions survive in subsequent manuscripts, but Jagan's inclusion in the *Āyīn-i Akbarī* suggests he was still alive in 1590 since, unlike Daswanth (included in the list as a master although he had died in 1584), his oeuvre was limited. Jagan may perhaps be identified as Jaganath, designer of one folio in the 1584 *Timūrnāma*, who contributed to historical and literary manuscripts in the 1590s.

BIBLIOGRAPHY
E. S. Smart: *Paintings from the Babur-nama* (diss., U. London, SOAS, 1977)
The Imperial Image: Paintings for the Mughal Court (exh. cat. by M. C. Beach, Washington, DC, Freer, 1981)

PHILIPPA VAUGHAN

Jagat. Temple site in south-west Rajasthan, India, associated with goddess worship. Sculptures from the site (6th century AD; Udaipur, City Pal. Mus.) are mainly of mother goddesses (Skt *mātṛkā*). Jagat's most important extant monument is the Ambika (Durga) temple, datable by a pilgrim's inscription to *c.* AD 960–61. Additional temple inscriptions of 1059 and 1187, recording various donations, indicate that Jagat was an active religious centre until the late 12th century.

The Ambika temple, resting on a moulded base, consists of a sanctum with a multi-spired superstructure. The temple's dedication is to Durga as Slayer of the Buffalo Demon, and her image is placed in the inner sanctum and in the central niches of the sanctum's exterior (*see* INDIAN SUBCONTINENT, fig. 188). The sanctum is fronted by a cruciform hall with stone lattice windows and an elaborate tiered roof. A porch with a balustrade and heavy awning gives entry into the hall. Goddesses appear on the exterior of the vestibule, on the lintel of the sanctum's doorframe and on the doorframe of a detached hall in front of the temple. Also, there are five goddess icons on the base mouldings below the central sections of the temple walls.

The sanctum's images include Brahmi, Vaishnavi and Maheshvari, three of the seven mother goddesses (*sapta mātṛkā*) and vital consorts (*śakti*) of Brahma, Vishnu and Shiva. The presence of goddesses clustered around the central figure of Durga suggests the temple is dedicated to Durga as the supreme deity, the others being her differentiated aspects. This echoes the imagery of the *Devī Māhātmya* (a section of the *Mārkaṇḍeya Purāṇa*), where the goddesses are created by Durga to help her slay the demons Śumbha and Niśumbha.

BIBLIOGRAPHY
R. C. Agrawala: 'Some Unpublished Sculptures from Southwestern Rajasthan', *Lalit Kalā*, vi (1959), pp. 63–71
V. S. Agrawala, trans.: *Devī Māhātmya* (Varanasi, 1963)
R. C. Agrawala: 'Khajuraho of Rajasthan: The Temple of Ambika at Jagat', *A. Asiat.*, x (1964), pp. 43–65
——: 'Inscriptions from Jagat, Rajasthan', *J. Orient. Inst., Maharajah Sayajirao U. Baroda*, xiv (1964–5), pp. 75–8
Krishna Deva: *Temples of North India* (New Delhi, 1969)
M. A. Dhaky: 'The Genesis and Development of the Maru-Gurjara Temple Architecture', *Studies in Indian Temple Architecture*, ed. P. Chandra (New Delhi, 1975), pp. 114–65

WALTER SMITH

Jagger, (Charles) Sargeant (*b* Kilnhurst, nr Sheffield, 17 Dec 1885; *d* London, 16 Nov 1934). British sculptor. He was a highly regarded student at the Royal College of Art, London (1908–11), whose early sculpture showed a fanciful treatment of classical and literary themes. In 1914 he gave up the Prix de Rome to enlist in the army. He began work on *No Man's Land* (1919–20; London, Tate) while still convalescing from war wounds. This low relief presents a stark vision of trench warfare. Corpses stranded on barbed wire are ranged across a ravaged landscape, while the solitary live figure of the look-out in the foreground, a surrogate for the spectator, uses them for cover. Jagger attempted to maintain such realism in commissioned war memorials, most successfully in the Royal Artillery memorial (1921–5; London, Hyde Park Corner; *see* MONUMENT, PUBLIC, fig. 4). His obsessive concern for detail, shared by the regimental committee who commissioned the work, reached its zenith in the stone replica of a howitzer, which surmounts his vivid representation of war as hard and dangerous labour. Although he remained in demand as a sculptor of monuments, it is for his war memorials that he is chiefly remembered. He received a Military Cross in World War I and was made an ARA in 1926.

WRITINGS
Modelling and Sculpture in the Making (London, 1933)
'The Sculptor's Point of View', *The Studio*, cvi (Nov 1933), pp. 251–4

BIBLIOGRAPHY
N. Penny: 'English Sculpture and the First World War', *Oxford A. J.*, iv/2 (1981), pp. 36–42 (40–42)
Charles Sargeant Jagger: War and Peace Sculpture (exh. cat., ed. Ann Compton; London, Imp. War Mus., 1985)

JOHN GLAVES-SMITH

Jagiellon, House of. Eastern European dynasty of rulers, patrons and collectors. In 1386 Jogaila, Grand Duke of Lithuania (*d* 1434), claimed the throne of Poland through marriage to Jadwiga (*reg* 1384–99), daughter of Louis I, King of Hungary and Poland, and became Vladislav II Jagiellon of Poland. He was succeeded by his sons, Vladislav III (*reg* 1434–44) and Kasimir IV (*reg* 1447–92). Kasimir's sons (1) Vladislav II, elected King of Bohemia (1471) and of Hungary (1490), and (2) Sigismund I, King of Poland and Grand Duke of Lithuania (*reg* 1506–48), were both notable patrons of Renaissance artists. The patronage of (3) Louis II, King of Bohemia and Hungary (*reg* 1516–26), son of Vladislav II, was limited by the political instability of his kingdoms and his lack of financial resources. As Louis II's sister, Anne, was married to the future Ferdinand I, Holy Roman Emperor, the latter claimed Bohemia and Hungary after Louis was killed at the Battle of Mohács in 1526, although the claim was disputed. (4) Sigismund II Augustus, King of Poland and Grand Duke of Lithuania (*reg* 1548–72), son of Sigismund I and the last ruler of the Jagiellon dynasty, formed an important collection of books, paintings, textiles and metalwork. On his death in 1572 the throne of Poland passed to Henry of Valois, later Henry III, King of France, but in 1587 Sigismund III, a member of the Swedish House of Vasa, was elected king.

BIBLIOGRAPHY
J. Białostocki: *The Art of the Renaissance in Eastern Europe: Hungary, Bohemia, Poland* (Oxford, 1976)
Polen im Zeitalter der Jagiellonen, 1386–1572 (exh. cat., Schallaburg, Schloss, 1986)

□

(1) Vladislav [Władisław] **II,** King of Bohemia and Hungary (*b* 1 March 1456; *reg* Bohemia 1471–1516, Hungary 1490–1516; *d* 13 March 1516). He was the son of Kasimierz IV Jagiellon, King of Poland (*reg* 1447–92), and was elected King of Bohemia after the death of George Podiebrad (*reg* 1457–71). On the death of Matthias Corvinus in 1490 he was also elected King of Hungary, where he subsequently mainly resided. During his reign in Hungary the royal authority declined owing to political and social unrest and the increasing threat of a Turkish invasion. In Prague he initially lived in the Royal Residence of the Old Town near the Powder Tower, which was built in his honour from 1475 by Matthias Rajsek. Building in the castle began in 1477. In the Vladislav Hall (completed 1502; *see* RIED, BENEDIKT, fig. 2) Benedikt Ried applied many architectural details derived from the work patronized by Matthias Corvinus at Buda. The altarpiece for the chapel of Křivoklát Castle (*in situ*) was made by court artists before 1490, and the wall paintings of the Wenceslas Chapel (before 1509) in Prague Cathedral are by the painter of the altar in Litoměřice. In Hungary Vladislav continued the projects of Matthias Corvinus, as can be seen in fragments of Renaissance-style carvings (Budapest, Hist. Mus.) from both Buda and a villa at Nyék, near

Buda. Vladislav is depicted on his dual royal seal (after 1490), on illuminated letters patent of nobility, for example those of John Pethő of Gerse (1507; Budapest, Hung. N. Archvs), and on coins. The votive picture (Budapest, Mus. F. A.) showing him with his children and St Laszlo before the Virgin was painted by Bernhard Strigel in 1511–12.

BIBLIOGRAPHY
J. Homolka and others: *Pozdné gotické umění v Čechách, 1471–1526* [Late Gothic art in Bohemia, 1471–1526] (Prague, 1978) [Eng., Ger. and Rus. summaries]
Matthias Corvinus und die Renaissance in Ungarn, 1458–1541 (exh. cat., ed. G. Stangler and others; Schallaburg, Schloss, 1982)

ERNŐ MAROSÍ

(2) Sigismund I [Sigismund the Old], King of Poland and Grand Duke of Lithuania (*b* 1 Jan 1467; *reg* 1506–48; *d* Kraków, 1 April 1548). Brother of (1) Vladislav II. One of his mentors was the Italian humanist Filippo Buonaccorsi (1437–96). Between 1498 and 1501 he stayed at the court of his brother Vladislav II in Buda, where he became acquainted with early Italian Renaissance art and architecture commissioned or collected by King Matthias Corvinus. In 1502 Sigismund invited FRANCISCUS ITALUS to Kraków from Hungary and commissioned him to execute the arcaded tomb (1502–5) of his brother *John I Albert* in Wawel Cathedral, the first example of the Tuscan Renaissance style in Poland. In 1507 Sigismund initiated the rebuilding of the north wing of Wawel Castle in the Renaissance style. Until 1516 the works were directed by Franciscus Italus and then continued by Bartolomeo Berrecci. At the same time the interiors of the castle were refurbished. The spacious courtyard surrounded by arcaded loggias, carved coffers, tapestries and murals of battle scenes and historical, mythological and astrological subjects made Wawel Castle one of the most outstanding residences in central Europe (*see* KRAKÓW, §IV, 2 and fig. 4).

Sigismund's most remarkable foundation, however, was his domed burial chapel, known as the Sigismund Chapel (1517–33; *see* KRAKÓW, fig. 5), built in Wawel Cathedral to the designs of Berrecci, who also directed the 30 artists involved, mostly Tuscans. Although Sigismund allowed Berrecci to inscribe his name in the chapel, appreciating the perfection of his work, he did not appoint him court artist, limiting his protection to the period stipulated in the contract. The King's fondness for Italian art was shared by his wife, the Italian princess Bona Sforza (1494–1557), who appears with Sigismund and their son and daughter on four signed medals (1532; Modena, Gal. & Mus. Estense) by Giovanni Maria Mosca Padovano.

Although most of the architectural and sculptural commissions went to Italian artists, on the advice of the bankers Jan Boner (*d* 1523) and Seweryn Boner (1486–1549) some works came from the imperial court of Nuremberg, Breslau (now Wrocław) and Brussels. The bronze tomb slab (1510) of the King's brother *Cardinal Frederick* (1468–1503) in Wawel Cathedral and the gates (1530–32) of the Sigismund Chapel were both made by the Vischer foundry. The silver altar (1531–8; *in situ*) for the same chapel was executed by artists from Nuremberg, including Pankraz Labenwolf, Peter Flötner, Melchior Baier, Hans Dürer and Georg Pencz, who made use of

PLATE I   Jade

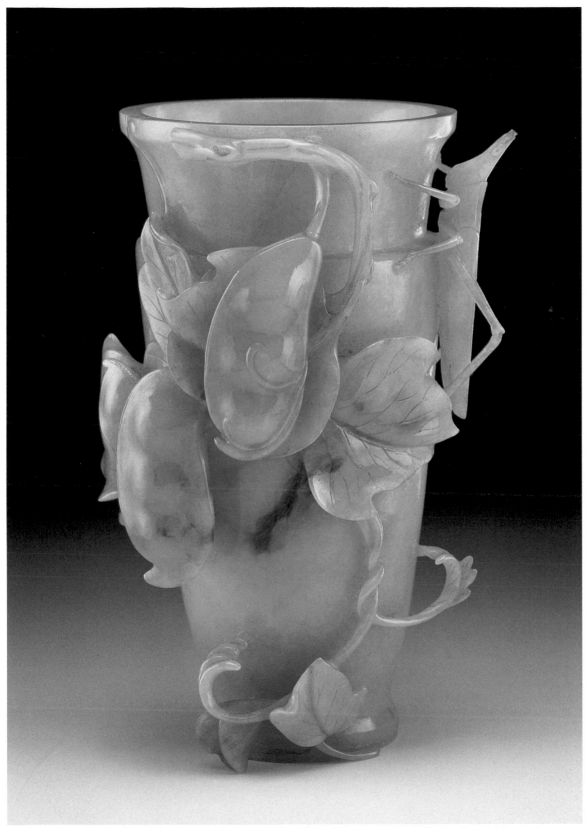

Jadeite vase, carved with a design of grasshoppers, h. 200 mm, from China, 19th century (Taipei, Ritz Jewellery and Arts Co.)

1. Jade burial mask of Pacal (*reg* AD 615–84), from the Temple of the Inscription, Palenque, Mexico, Classic Maya period (ex-National Museum of Anthropology, Mexico City)

2. Nephrite lanterns, h. 435 mm, from the palace of Emperor Qianlong (*reg* 1736–96), Beijing, China (Taipei, Ritz Jewellery and Arts Co.)

PLATE III   Jade

1. Nephrite cup with dragon-shaped handle, h. 64 mm, probably from China, 14th century, inscribed early 15th with the name Ulughbeg (London, British Museum)

2. Nephrite wine vessel, inlaid with enamelled gold plant motifs, h. 104 mm, diam. 116 mm, from India, Mughal, 18th century (London, Victoria and Albert Museum)

Jade snuff bottles, Chinese, 18th–19th centuries: (*clockwise from top*) pebble jade, carved in the shape of a fish between the fronds of a lotus plant, h. 80 mm, 1720–80 (the green glass stopper is not the original); flawless nephrite, tourmaline stopper, gilt silver collar, h. 55 mm, 1720–1830; Trojan Embellished Jade, nephrite, carved with bamboo shoot design, coral stopper possibly original, h. 58 mm, perhaps from the Imperial Palace workshops, Beijing, 1750–1830; Meng Haoran Suzhou Jade, nephrite, carved with Meng Haoran riding a donkey, coral stopper, vinyl collar, h. 70 mm, from Suzhou, 1740–1850; Master of the Rocks Noble Occupations Pebble, nephrite, carved with a mountainous landscape, jadeite stopper, h. 63 mm, 1740–1860; (*centre*) Dwyer Lilac Jadeite, jadeite body and stopper, gilt bronze collar, h. 54 mm, 1770–1880 (all Mary and George Bloch private collection)

woodcuts by Albrecht Dürer. Other artists from Nuremberg included the bell-founder Jan Beham (fl 1517–33), who cast the largest bell in Poland, known as 'Sigismund', for Wawel Cathedral in 1520. Sebastian Tauerbach (d 1552) from Wrocław sculpted 194 heads, of which 30 survive in situ, that adorn the coffered ceiling (1531–5) in the Deputies' Hall of Wawel Castle. Among Polish artists of note at Sigismund's court were Stanisław Samostrzelnik (c. 1480–1541), who produced the Renaissance miniatures for the prayer books of the King and Queen (1524, London, BL, and 1527, Oxford, Bodleian Lib., respectively).

Not all of Sigismund's commissions reflected Renaissance influence, for the richly decorated portals (completed 1529) of Wawel Castle, by Benedikt, and the monstrance that the King presented to the Paulite Order in Jasna Góra, Częstochowa (1542; in situ), are both Late Gothic. Sigismund also collected tapestries, enlarging his already rich collection in 1533 with a commission for 66 from Antwerp. His patronage at Wawel Castle initiated what became known as the 'Wawel Renaissance' in Polish art, and his example was followed by other members of his court, including Chancellor Krzysztof Szydłowiecki (1467–1532), Bishop Piotr Tomicki (1464–1535) and the poet and humanist Andrzej Krzycki (1482–1537), who served as Sigismund's secretary and artistic adviser.

BIBLIOGRAPHY
A. Bochnak: 'Mecenat Zygmunta Starego w zakresie rzemiosła artystycznego' [Sigismund the Old's patronage of decorative arts], Studia do dziejów Wawelu, ii (Kraków, 1960), pp. 131–301 [Fr. summary]
L. Kalinowski: 'Treści artystyczne i ideowe Kaplicy Zygmuntowskiej' [The artistic programme and philosophical content of the Sigismund Chapel], Studia do dziejów Wawelu, ii (Kraków, 1960), pp. 1–129 [Fr. summary]
S. Mossakowski: 'Renesansowy pałac na Wawelu a polska myśl polityczna i filozoficzna epoki' [The Renaissance palace on Wawel Hill and contemporary Polish political and philosophical thought], Renesans: Sztuka i ideologia [Renaissance: art and ideology] (Warsaw, 1976), pp. 349–80
Polen im Zeitalter der Jagiellonen, 1386–1572 (exh. cat.; Schallaburg, Schloss, 1986)

JERZY KOWALCZYK

(3) Louis II, King of Bohemia and Hungary (b Buda, 1 July 1506; reg 1516–26; d Mohács, 29 Aug 1526). Son of (1) Vladislav II. Court art dwindled in his reign, due largely to the political discord and financial difficulties in the kingdom and the menace of a Turkish invasion. The King was portrayed in his childhood by Bernhard Strigel (Vienna, Ksthist. Mus.) and in a votive icon (1511–12; Budapest, Mus. F.A.) but later mainly on coins and medals, for example the commemorative coin (1508; Budapest, N. Mus.) and medal for his coronation (1508; Prague, N. Mus.), a coin and medal (1525; Kremnica) depicting him with his wife, Mary of Hungary, by Bernhard Behaim and medals (1526; Budapest, N. Mus.) struck at his death by Hieronymus Magdeburger (fl 1508–18), Christoph Fuessl and Hans Daucher. Louis II is also depicted in the law book of the town of Znojmo (1523; Znojmo, Distr. Archvs, Cod. 286/A), and in copies of portraits by Hans Krell (fl 1522–c. 1586) of Brussels, who was in his service from 1522 to 1526, and of a posthumous portrait (1533) by Bernard van Orley, commissioned by Mary of Hungary. After Louis II's death at the Battle of Mohács, Mary became regent of the Netherlands from 1531, where she

maintained a court famous for its art (see HABSBURG, §I (7)).

BIBLIOGRAPHY
I. Schlégl: 'Ikonographie König Ludwigs II. von Ungarn', Miscellanea Jozef Duverger, i (Ghent, 1968), p. 163
Matthias Corvinus und die Renaissance in Ungarn, 1458–1541 (exh. cat., ed. G. Stangler and others; Schallaburg, Schloss, 1982), p. 500

ERNŐ MAROSÍ

(4) Sigismund II Augustus, King of Poland and Grand Duke of Lithuania (b Kraków, 1 Aug 1520; reg 1548–72; d Knyszyn, 7 July 1572). Son of (2) Sigismund I. He was the last ruler of the Jagiellon dynasty. His teacher was the Italian humanist Johannes Silvius Amatus Siculus. Sigismund II governed the duchy of Lithuania from 1544 and assumed control of Poland after his father's death. He was an enthusiastic bibliophile and collected books from the mid-1540s. His library, which numbered some 4000 beautifully bound volumes with impressed bookplates and the inscription MONUMENTUM SIGISMUNDI AUGUSTI, included many treatises on the theory of art and architecture, both civil and military. His interest in architecture was renowned, but few of his foundations have survived, particularly those in his main residence, VILNIUS (for example the Lower Castle), while others, including the castle at Warsaw and Vilnius Cathedral, have been redesigned; only the hunting castle at Niepołomice has survived unaltered.

The most eminent artists joined Sigismund's court and received regular salaries and even titles, such as the knighthood conferred on Giovanni Jacopo Caraglio; on this occasion Sigismund probably commissioned Paris Bordone to execute his allegorical portrait (Kraków, N. A. Cols). His love of craftsmanship resulted in a very rich collection of goldsmiths' and jewellers' works, textiles, arms, armour, harnesses and cannons. In 1555 the King summoned Kunz Lochner the younger (1510–67) from Nuremberg to execute sumptuous armour for a horse and rider (Stockholm, Livrustkam.).

An important part of the King's collection comprised textiles imported from the Near East and the Netherlands; he also engaged Armenian embroiderers. On the occasion of his marriage to Catherine of Habsburg (1533–72) in 1553 the interior of Wawel Castle, Kraków, was adorned with 132 carpets recently brought from Turkey and the collection of tapestries inherited from his parents or imported from Brussels from 1549. The tapestries numbered about 350 in 1573; only 141 of these remain in Poland (e.g. in Wawel Castle) and depict biblical themes, verdure with animals, grotesques with the Polish and Lithuanian coat of arms and the King's initials. They were designed by Michiel Coxcie and artists from the circle of Pieter Coecke van Aelst, Cornelis Floris and Cornelis Bos and executed by the workshops of Willem I (fl 1534–48) and Jan de Kempeneer (fl 1541–54), Pieter van Aelst the younger, Jan van Tiegen (fl 1562–70), Catherine Leyniers and Frans Ghieteel.

At Vilnius Castle Sigismund maintained a picture gallery with imported paintings, including works by Titian and Veronese. He also possessed a series of miniature portraits of the Jagiellon family (Kraków, N. Mus.) by the workshop of Lucas Cranach (ii). Many of the King's medals were executed in Poland by such foreign artists as Domenico

Veneziano (*fl* 1548), Steven van Herwijck and Giovanni Maria Mosca Padovano, who also designed and made Sigismund's tomb in the Sigismund Chapel. The influence of the court was more marked in the duchy of Lithuania than in the kingdom of Poland since the King spent more time in Vilnius than in Kraków.

BIBLIOGRAPHY
J. Szablowski, ed.: *The Flemish Tapestries at Wawel Castle in Cracow: Treasure of King Sigismund Augustus Jagiello* (Antwerp, 1972)
S. Cynarski: *Zygmunt August* (Wrocław, 1988)
                                                    JERZY KOWALCZYK

Jahangir. *See under* MUGHAL.

Jahn, Helmut (*b* Nuremberg, 4 Jan 1940). American architect of German birth. A graduate of the Technische Hochschule in Munich (1965), he pursued architectural studies at the Illinois Institute of Technology (IIT), Chicago, where he studied with Myron Goldsmith and Fazlur Khan (1929–82). Having joined the respected Chicago architectural firm of C. F. Murphy in 1967, he became Principal of the renamed office Murphy/Jahn (1981), then President (1982) and Chief Executive officer (1983). Jahn's reputation is due to the great number, prominence and memorable character of his buildings. Using broad references from architectural history and appealing to a public visual memory nurtured on cartoons and Hollywood movies, he made use of a wide range of sources from the recent and distant past for his architectural compositions. Many of his works—eclectic pastiches that unite familiar and exotic elements—overwhelm the surrounding context and baffle the visitor with colour, megalomaniac scale, and effective use of sophisticated American construction techniques. New materials and structural ideas are used by Jahn with a consummate virtuosity that endows his buildings with the dramatic expression, movement and restrained energy previously reserved for the harnessed power of applied modern science (rockets, nuclear stations). Simultaneously with the scene designers of contemporary science-fiction films, he realized the fantastic architecture projected in the 1920s and 1930s for a 'brave new world'. This quality and its immediate visual appeal are most evident in the skyscrapers of the 1980s such as the Xerox Centre (1980), Chicago, the addition to the Board of Trade (1982), Chicago, and his 701 Fourth Avenue South office building (1984), Minneapolis.

Jahn also built commissions outside the city centre. His suburban office and commercial structures, such as those in Naperville and Evanston, near Chicago, have transformed their areas, endowing them with a new urban character. In the United Airlines Terminal in O'Hare Airport (1987), Chicago, Jahn used visual effects of light and colour to alleviate the boredom and uniformity of an artificial environment while efficiently processing large numbers of travellers. In contrast, at the State of Illinois Center (1985), Chicago, he combined the successful architectural vocabulary of the Hyatt Hotels (conceived in the early 1970s by John Portman) with ironic Postmodernism and a coral-pink and powder-blue colour scheme, endowing public space with an aimless leisure and whimsy unsuited to the gravity of a governmental

institution. His projects of the late 1980s to 1990s include Hyatt Hotels in Amsterdam, Frankfurt am Main and Munich, and numerous skyscrapers, in Houston, Los Angeles, Philadelphia and New York (Park Avenue, Lexington Avenue, the Television City project, Times Square). In New York the potentially harmful effect of their excessive height was ignored in favour of their capricious conception as anchors for dirigible airships.

Jahn taught at Harvard University, Cambridge, MA (Elliot Noyes Visiting Professor of Architecture, 1981), and Yale University, New Haven, CT (Davenport Visiting Professor of Architectural Design, 1983), and received an honorary doctoral degree from St Mary's College, South Bend, IN (1980). He received numerous awards, including those from the American Institute of Architects, *Progressive Architecture* and other institutions concerned with building. His work was exhibited in Chicago, New York, San Francisco, Toronto, Milan, Venice, Paris, Frankfurt, Buenos Aires and Tokyo.

See also CHICAGO, fig. 2.

BIBLIOGRAPHY
C. Jencks: *Late-Modern Architecture* (New York, 1980)
P. Goldberger: *The Skyscraper* (New York, 1981)
The Architecture of Helmut Jahn: An Introductory Bibliography (Monticello, IL, 1983)
P. Portoghesi: *Postmodern: The Architecture of the Post-industrial Society* (New York, 1984)
J. A. Joedicke, ed.: *Helmut Jahn: Design einer neuen Architektur* (Stuttgart and Zurich, 1986) [parallel Eng. and Fr. trans.]
H. Klotz: *Vision der Moderne* (Frankfurt, 1986)
N. Miller: *Helmut Jahn* (New York, 1986)
                                                    MARTHA POLLAK

Jaimes Sánchez, Humberto (*b* San Cristóbal, 25 June 1930). Venezuelan painter and printmaker. He studied at the Escuela de Artes Plásticas y Aplicadas de Caracas (1947–50) and was a member of the Taller Libre de Arte in 1949. Jaimes Sánchez lived in Europe from 1954 to 1957, studying architecture at the Ecole des Beaux-Arts, Paris (1955–6). His painting initially drew its inspiration from American archaeology, but in 1956 he executed his first lyrical abstract works. Later he executed his so-called 'psychological paintings'; the exploration of colour and material characterized all his work. He was a member of the Informalistas group between 1960 and 1962. In 1961 he began printmaking, joining the group of engravers El Taller in 1962. In the same year he won the Premio Nacional de Pintura at the Venezuelan Salón Oficial for *Fragments of Earth* (1961; Caracas, Gal. A. N.). He was also a member of Presencia 70 (1970–71).

BIBLIOGRAPHY
R. Delgado: *Humberto Jaimes Sánchez* (Caracas, 1969)
A. Boulton: *Historia de la pintura en Venezuela: Epoca contemporánea*, iii (Caracas, 1972)
Humberto Jaimes Sánchez: Tierras psicológicas—Exposición antológica (exh. cat. by J. Calzadilla, Caracas, Gal. A. N., 1980)
                                    MARÍA ANTONIA GONZÁLEZ-ARNAL

Jainism. Religion established in India and founded there in its present form by Mahavira during the 6th century BC.

1. HISTORY AND DEVELOPMENT. Like Buddhism, Jainism arose out of the breakdown of the Vedic world-view that occurred during the period immediately preceding the 6th century BC (*see* INDIAN SUBCONTINENT, §I, 7(ii)). However, although Buddhism and Jainism appeared around the same time, their development followed very different courses. While Buddhism became an active missionary religion, spreading throughout Asia but meanwhile losing its foothold in India, Jainism continued as a living religion on the subcontinent, though it was less successful as a missionary movement (until recently its activities were confined to India). The Jainas made remarkable cultural contributions, especially in the fields of philosophy, literature and art (*see* INDIAN SUBCONTINENT, §II, 3). Apart from engaging in stupa-building, they also built cave temples such as that at Hathigumpha in Orissa (2nd century BC). Jaina places of pilgrimage are adorned with a sumptuousness of which the marble temples of Rajasthan at Mt Abu (*see* MT ABU, §2) are exquisite examples (*see also* INDIAN SUBCONTINENT, fig. 10), and Jaina illustrated manuscripts constitute a distinctive art form (*see* INDIAN SUBCONTINENT, §V, 3(ii)(a)). In 1981 the Jainas constituted 0.48% of the Indian population, representing an influential and prosperous minority.

The Jaina tradition considers Mahavira, the founder of modern Jainism (see fig.), as the last in a line of 24 masters known as *tīrthaṅkaras*, or 'ford-builders' (across the ocean of suffering; *see* INDIAN SUBCONTINENT, fig. 11). Modern scholars also tend to regard Parshvanatha, the 23rd *tīrthaṅkara*, as a historical figure. Mahavira was born at Vaishali in Bihar to a *kṣatriya* (warrior class) family; his father Siddhartha was the chief of the Jnatr clan and his mother Trishala also came from a royal family. It is likely that they were followers of Parshvanatha. The child was named Varddhamana; Mahavira ('great hero') and Jina ('victor') were later titles accorded to him after his attainment of omniscience. According to some sources, Mahavira remained single but others maintain that he married and fathered a daughter who also married. All agree, however, that at the age of 30, after the death of his parents, he renounced the world and became a religious mendicant practising extreme austerities, in the course of which he also discarded clothing. After 12 years he achieved omniscience (*kevalajñāna*) while seated in meditation under a tree. Following 30 years of successful public ministry he died, aged 72, at Pava (near Patna) in 468 BC according to current scholarly opinion, and in 527 or 526 BC according to the Jaina tradition.

During the course of his itinerant career Mahavira reformed the order of Parshvanatha, insisting on the observance of nudity. This issue led directly to an extremely important event in the early history of Jainism, when adherents of the faith divided into two main branches over the question of this practice: the Digambara ('sky-clad') sect who regarded nudity as essential for salvation, and the Shvetambara ('white-clad') faction, who considered it dispensable. The Digambaras assign this event to the 4th century BC, and the Shvetambaras to the 1st century AD. The fact that the main centre of the Shvetambara sect is now in Gujarat, while the Digambara sect centres around Mysore, is due to historical factors. The differences between the two sects extend beyond the role of nudity in religious life to such questions as whether the Jina, though omniscient, otherwise leads a normal existence, whether women can attain liberation and whether offerings may be received inside the house. The understanding of the Jaina canon, which is written in the 'half-Magadhi' (*ardha-māgadhī*) dialect of Prakrit, differs according to the sect. The Digambaras believe that the original canon, consisting of the Twelve Limbs (*aṅga*s), was irretrievably lost in the chain of circumstances leading to the schism and only accord canonical status to two texts: the *Ṣaṭkhaṇḍāgama* and the *Kaṣāyaprābhṛta*, compilations that preserve sections of the lost material. The Shvetambaras, accepting the loss, reconstructed the canon and gave it formal authority at a council held at Valabhi, now in Gujarat, in the 5th century AD. It consists of 45 texts: the Eleven *Aṅga*s; the Twelve *Upāṅga*s ('secondary texts'); the Ten *Prakīrṇaka*s ('miscellaneous texts'); the Six *Cheda sūtra*s ('discrete texts'); the Four *Mūla sūtra*s ('root texts'); the *Nandī sūtra* ('benediction') and the *Anuyogadvāra* ('door of inquiry').

Jaina manuscript painting on paper showing Mahavira distributing alms, western India, 1490 (London, Victoria and Albert Museum)

2. DOCTRINE. The teachings of Jainism rest on the fundamental dualism between matter and spirit. According to Jainism the soul, in its natural state of pristine purity, is free from all sorrow; it would naturally rise to the abode of the released souls (*siddhaśilā*) at the top of the universe were it not tainted by *karma* ('action'). In Jainism *karma* is regarded as a very subtle form of matter contaminating the soul in the same way that a beam of light may be interpenetrated by dust. The size of the soul is neither atomic nor all-pervasive, as in Hindu systems, but is co-extensive with the body and approximates its size even in the state of release. Jainism thus differs from Buddhism in admitting a soul, from Hinduism regarding its dimension and from both faiths in attributing to *karma* a material quality and also in attributing souls to all objects, animate or inanimate.

The Jaina system can be summarized as comprising the doctrines of the 'five spatials' (*astikāya*s), the 'six substances' (*dravya*s), the 'seven principles' (*tattva*s) and the 'nine categories' (*padārtha*s). The term *astikāya*, literally 'that which possesses a body', is used to describe the category of spatial relationships, i.e. the property of simultaneously being in association with several spatial points. The five spatials are spirit (*jīva*), matter (*pudgala*), motion (*dharma*), rest (*adharma*) and space (*ākāśa*); time (*kāla*) is added to complete the 'six substances'. Spirit, or *jīva*, the first of the spatials and substances, is also interpreted as 'embodied being', a comprehensive concept including all micrological, botanical and zoological life forms. Living beings are classified according to the number of senses they possess. For instance, worms possess only touch and taste but bees have smell and sight as well; human beings represent the highest members of the class, as they possess all five senses and mind. *Jīva*s are destined for four states of existence—divine, human, infernal or sub-human—in accordance with their *karma*. The living *jīva*s, by themselves all soul, are trapped in a second, non-living, substance (*ajīva*); the remaining five substances—matter, motion, rest, space and time—are therefore all classified as non-living.

If the five spatials and six substances encapsulate the cosmology of Jainism, the seven principles comprise its soteriology. In addition to the living and non-living (*jīva* and *ajīva*), these principles are inflow (*āsrava*), bondage (*bandha*), stoppage (*saṁvara*), outflow (*nirjarā*) and liberation (*mokṣa*). Briefly, contact between the living and the non-living leads to the inflow of *karma* from the non-living into the living, causing karmic bondage. Through proper spiritual practice such ingress can be stopped, and the *karma* that is already present in the system can be removed or made to flow out. Once the embodied being has thus been purged of all traces of *karma*, liberation can be attained in a single lifetime, after passing through 14 stages of spiritual advancement.

If this scheme is further extended to include the concepts of good and bad *karma* (*punya* and *pāpa*) then the seven principles become the nine categories, which offer a summary of Jaina philosophy. It might be added that the process of the expulsion of *karma* from the system requires the exercise of 'proper faith, knowledge and conduct', known as the 'three jewels' (*triratna*) and the observance of the 'five great vows' (*mahāvrata*s) of non-violence (*ahiṁsā*), truth (*satya*), continence (*brahma*), non-stealing (*asteya*) and non-possession (*aparigraha*) undertaken by Jaina monks and nuns; less rigorous vows (*aṇuvrata*s) apply to householders. The vows are interpreted more strictly in Jainism than in the Hindu system, with non-violence sometimes being carried to extreme limits. Frequent fasting constitutes an important element of ascetic practices, and the ideal mode of dying—fasting to death (known as the rite of *sallekhanā*)—is open to both the religious and to householders. The Jainas have also developed a sophisticated system of philosophy, as exemplified by their concept of epistemological relativism (*anekāntavāda*), which in effect states that several contradictory statements about a referent may all be true from different standpoints, a doctrine that not only encourages a comprehensive approach to philosophical issues but also promotes religious tolerance. As a philosophical system, Jainism may be seen as standing midway between Hinduism—which emphasizes the permanent aspect of reality at the expense of virtually denying ontological status to its changeable aspect—and Buddhism (which reverses the emphasis) in according equal status to permanence and change as constituents of reality.

BIBLIOGRAPHY
H. Jacobi: 'Jainism', *Encyclopedia of Religion and Ethics*, vii, ed. J. Hastings (Edinburgh, 1919), pp. 465–74
H. von Glasenapp: *Der Jainismus* (Berlin, 1925/*R* Hildesheim, 1964)
W. Schubring: *Die Lehre der Jainas, nach den alten Quellen dargestellt* (Berlin, 1935; Eng. trans. by W. Beurlen, Delhi, 1962)
A. Chakravarti: 'Jainism: Its Philosophy and Ethics', *The Cultural Heritage of India*, i, ed. H. Bhattacharyya (Calcutta, 1937; rev. 1958), pp. 414–33
H. Jain: 'Jainism: Its History, Principles, and Precepts', *The Cultural Heritage of India*, i, ed. H. Bhattacharyya (Calcutta, 1937; rev. 1958), pp. 400–413
S. Sangvi: 'Some Fundamental Principles of Jainism', *The Cultural Heritage of India*, i, ed. H. Bhattacharyya (Calcutta, 1937; rev. 1958), pp. 434–41
C. L. Jain: *Jain Bibliography* (Calcutta, 1945)
L. Alsdorf: *Les Etudes Jaina: Etat présent et tâches futures* (Paris, 1965)
N. N. Bhattacharyya: *Jaina Philosophy: Historical Outline* (New Delhi, 1976)
P. S. Jaini: *The Jaina Path of Purification* (Berkeley, 1979)
C. Caillat: 'Jainism', *The Encyclopedia of Religion*, vii, ed. M. Eliade (New York, 1987), pp. 507–14

ARVIND SHARMA

Jaintiapur. *See under* SYLHET.

Jaipur [Sawāi Jaipur; Jai Nagar]. Capital city of the Indian state of Rajasthan. It was founded in 1727 by Maharaja Sawai Jai Singh (*reg* 1700–43) as a new capital to succeed AMER. Jai Singh's main adviser in building the city was his courtier Vidyadhar Chakravarty. The city was designed on a grid pattern consisting of rectangular blocks (Hindi *cokri*) enclosed within a strong crenellated wall. Its most remarkable feature is the planned distribution of space (*see* INDIAN SUBCONTINENT, fig. 129). At the heart of the city is the sprawling palace complex (popularly known as 'City Palace') with its adjacent astronomical observatory, reflecting Jai Singh's interest in the study of the stars and planets (*see* OBSERVATORY, fig. 1). Temples, shops, large family houses (*hāvelī*s) and gardens are neatly arranged along wide roads and lanes intersecting at right angles. The shops lining the principal roads were designed to be of uniform size with similar façades.

The most important structures dating from the reign of Jai Singh are the Chandra Mahal in the City Palace complex, the observatory, the temple dedicated to Govindadeva (an aspect of Krishna) within the palace complex and a number of large *havelis*. Sawai Ishvari Singh (*reg* 1743–50) built the beautifully carved white marble cenotaph of Jai Singh at the royal cremation site at Gaitore and the imposing tower known as Swarga Shuli or Isar Lat in the heart of the city. His brother Sawai Madho Singh I (*reg* 1750–68) built the Madho Nivas in the City Palace complex, the Jal Mahal palace on an island in Man Sagar Lake, Madho Vilas outside the northern gate of the city and the unique landscape garden in the south-east corner of the city known as Sisodiya Rani ka Bagh. Sawai Pratap Singh (*reg* 1778–1803), a great devotee of Krishna, built temples to this deity as well as the monument known as the Hawa Mahal ('Palace of the Wind'). This building consists of a façade with small rooms, halls, passages and open court-yards behind it, and it may have been intended as a place from which women of the court could view processions and celebrations.

A new spate of building activity was undertaken in the mid-19th century. During the reign of Sawai Ram Singh II (*reg* 1835–80) SAMUEL SWINTON JACOB was appointed the State Engineer-in-Chief. His finest building is the Albert Hall, which houses the Central Museum. Other buildings from the period of Ram Singh II and his successor Sawai Madho Singh II (*reg* 1880–1922) are the Mubarak Mahal in the City Palace complex, the town hall, Mayo Hospital (also designed by Jacob) and the Rambagh Palace (now a hotel). It was probably during the reign of Ram Singh II that buildings in Jaipur were coloured a uniform earthy pink (obtained by mixing finely ground terracotta in the wash) giving rise to the epithet, the 'Pink City'. Modernization continued during and after the reign of the last Maharaja, Sawai Man Singh II (*reg* 1922–49). Buildings in an international modern style have been constructed mainly outside the old city walls. Traditional crafts still practised in the city include gem-cutting, enamelling, jewellery-making and the production of hand-loom block-printed textiles. Among the city's outstanding museums are the Maharaja Sawai Man Singh II Museum, housed in parts of the City Palace, and the Government Central Museum.

BIBLIOGRAPHY
J. Tod: *Annals and Antiquities of Rajast'han* (London, 1829–32; ed. W. Crooke, Oxford, 1920)
H. L. Showers: *Notes on Jaipur* (Jaipur, 1916)
Dasarath Sharma, ed.: *Rajasthan through the Ages*, i (Bikaner, 1966)
K. C. Jain: *Ancient Cities and Towns of Rajasthan* (Delhi, 1972)
A. K. Roy: *History of Jaipur City* (New Delhi, 1978)
J. N. Sarkar: *A History of Jaipur* (rev. and ed. by R. Singh, New Delhi, 1984)
G. H. R. Tillotson: *The Rajput Palaces: The Development of an Architectural Style, 1450–1750* (London, 1987)

ASOK KUMAR DAS

Jaisalmer. City in the Thar Desert of western Rajasthan, India. Founded in AD 1156 by Maharawal Jaisal (*reg* second half of 12th century), it prospered owing to its strategic position on caravan routes linking India with Sind and west Asia. Wealthy Jaina merchants added to the city's affluence. They imported large numbers of manuscripts and paintings, the earliest dating to *c.* 1200, which are now

stored in the Shri Jinabhadra Suri Gyan Grantha Bhandar, a library located in the Shri Sambhavanathji Temple (1431). Other Jaina temples also date to the 15th century. Buildings such as the Jina Chandraprabha Temple (1453) demonstrate a revival of the Maru–Gurjara style that flourished in Rajasthan and Gujarat in the 11th and 12th centuries. Of several Brahmanical temples, the most important are the Surya (1437), Lakshmi Narayana (1437) and Ratnesh-vara Mahadeva (1441). The first two were built by Maharawal Bairi Singh (*reg* 1436–48), the third by his wife, Ratna Kanwar.

The massive fort was built on a triangular hill known as Trikuta (h. *c.* 80 m). Although this was no doubt an ancient site, the surviving portions date principally from the 16th century. Between 1577 and 1623 three elegantly carved gateways were built, seven circular bastions were added to the defensive walls and a second enclosure wall was constructed. More bastions were added between 1633 and 1647, bringing the total to 99. Additional gateways date from 1722–55. The settlements outside the fort were encircled with a boundary wall by Maharawal Mulraj II (*reg* 1762–1820). A group of royal palaces was built inside the fort between 1722 and 1820, among them the Rang Mahal of Mulraj II, where several wall paintings survive. The multi-storey mansions (*havelis*) built by nobles and merchants are distinctive for their sumptuousness. The celebrated Patua *havelis* (*c.* 1810) have wall surfaces punctuated by projecting enclosures and balconies, all enmeshed in delicately carved screens (*see* INDIAN SUBCONTINENT, fig. 116). A school of mural painting survives from *c.* 1820, the date of the Rang Mahal murals, as do miniatures from *c.* 1860. The style is strongly indebted to the schools of Jodhpur and Jaipur (*see* INDIAN SUBCONTINENT, §V, 4(iii)(e)).

Jaisalmer declined in the late 19th century, when, with the development of railways and the port of Bombay, the land route lost its importance. As a craft centre, modern Jaisalmer is known for its block-printed and tie-dyed handloom textiles, embroideries and objects carved from the fine-grained local sandstone.

See also INDIAN SUBCONTINENT, §III, 7(ii)(b).

BIBLIOGRAPHY
S. Toy: *The Strongholds of India* (London, 1957)
M. A. Dhaky: 'Renaissance and the Late Māru–Gurjara Temple Architecture', *J. Ind. Soc. Orient. A.*, n. s. i (1965–6), pp. 4–22
N. K. Sharma: *Jaisalmer: The Golden City* (Jaisalmer, 1978)
R. A. Agrawala: *History, Art and Architecture of Jaisalmer* (Delhi, 1979)
R. Rewal: 'An Indian Portfolio: Jaisalmer', *Mimar: Archit. Dev.*, xx (April–June, 1986), pp. 69–78
G. H. R. Tillotson: *The Rajput Palaces: The Development of an Architectural Style, 1450–1750* (London, 1987)
S. Nand: *Art and Architecture of Jaisalmer* (Jodhpur, 1990)

WALTER SMITH

Jakab, Dezső. *See under* KOMOR & JAKAB.

Ják Abbey. Benedictine abbey church in the county of Vas, south-western Hungary. The abbey, dedicated to St George, was founded by Martinus Magnus of the Ják family *c.* 1220 and built mostly in the 1230s. There are contemporary wall paintings in the central chancel, showing St George, and on the ground floor (south bay) of the west gallery, where they presumably show the founder with his family, and his burial scene. In 1256, after the Mongol invasion (1241–2), the church was reconsecrated in the presence of Bishop Omode of Györ (Ger. Raab).

Ják Abbey Church is one of the best preserved and most highly developed examples of a Hungarian type of church, whose basic construction (a three-aisled, transept-less basilica with three eastern apses and a west front with twin towers) evolved in the 12th century. It was derived partly from Lombardy (the ground-plan) and partly from Normandy (the two-tower façade) and reached its apogee in the 13th century. A characteristic feature of these buildings is the connection of the two storeys of the west gallery with the corresponding rooms in the towers. At Ják one notable feature of the ground-plan is the vaulted rectangular bay in front of the semicircular central apse; another is the richly decorated west portal, which gives unusual emphasis to the west front. In the interior the linkage of the west gallery and the towers is shown to full effect. The external articulation of the north wall is evidence of an earlier plan *ad quadratum*, but this was changed to *ad triangulum*, which reduced the five bays originally planned for the nave to four. Compound piers support pointed arches. The heavy, ribbed north aisle vault dates from the reconsecration.

The decoration of the east and west fronts, the most important parts of the exterior, is partly figurative and partly composed of geometric motifs derived from Normandy. The massive west portal (see fig.) is the formal and iconographical focus of the building: slightly projecting, it completely fills the space between the two towers, its deep jambs articulated by six pairs of columns. The inner archivolts are round, the outer ones pointed, and the whole surface is covered with Norman geometric motifs, together with Late Romanesque and Early Gothic plant and animal ornament originating from the Upper Rhine and southern Germany. The tympanum has the usual Christ in Majesty with two angels, and the composition culminates in the group of Apostles arranged in a triangle, standing in trefoil niches with the figure of Christ at the top. The sculptures are related to the corresponding figures on the Fürstenportal of Bamberg Cathedral. The masters trained in Normandy were also active elsewhere in Hungary in this period, but it was only at Ják that they appear to have been given such a leading role.

The sculptured decoration at Ják not only shows contemporary central European connections but also represents a strand of local artistic development, which reached its highest level in this work. Ják was evidently the centre of a local architectural type and style with related buildings (cathedrals, dynastic monasteries etc); masons' marks give evidence of this. The local influence of the Ják style is reflected in several village churches across the Danube and even in the quatrefoil-planned parish church (the chapel of St James) in Ják itself. The tympanum of the south entrance to the abbey church, which was used by the monks, contains an *Agnus Dei* flanked by a pair of dragons, which also served as a model for local parish churches. The west door was undoubtedly used by the patrons, and the west end of the church gives strong emphasis to them. The upper storey of the west gallery has a finely made tripartite niche seat for the patrons facing the chancel. Presumably there was also an altar

Ják Abbey, west front, founded *c.* 1220

there. The iconographic programme of the wall paintings in the ground floor and the exceptional emphasis given to the west portal strongly suggest that in monastic churches closely associated with their patrons the west gallery had a liturgical function to do with their representation. Of the medieval furnishings, one wooden Virgin survives, on the altar in the north aisle.

During the Turkish period (1526–1686), the church was given a defensive wall, of which the gate-house survives, bearing the arms of the builder, Abbot Ferenc Folnai, and the date 1663. The first detailed description of the church is found in the *Visitatio canonica* of 1697. The Baroque decoration dates from the 18th century. The surviving parts of this were moved to the chapel of St James during the last restoration. The ruins of the medieval abbey disappeared in the 18th century. After a few minor repairs in the 18th and 19th centuries, a thorough restoration was carried out between 1896 and 1904 by László Gyalus under the direction of Frigyes Schulek. Although this preserved the structure and most of the details, considerable parts of the walls, the south row of piers and the spire were rebuilt. The nave and south aisle were vaulted for the first time, but many damaged features were replaced with exact copies. The original fragments are in Szombathely Museum, Vas.

BIBLIOGRAPHY

T. Gerevich: *Magyarország romankori emlékei* [The Romanesque monuments of Hungary] (Budapest, 1938), pp. 109–15, 186–92, 221–3

J. Csemegi: *A jáki apátsági templom* [The abbey church in Ják] (Vasi Szemle, 1939), pp. 12–37

T. Bogyay: *A jáki apátsági templom és Szent Jakab kápolna* [The abbey church and chapel of St James in Ják] (Szombathely, 1943)

——: *Normannische Invasion, Wiener Bauhütte, ungarische Romanik*, Forsch. Kstgesch. & Christ. Archäol. (Baden-Baden, 1954)

I. Hoefelmayer-Straube: *Ják und die normannische Ornamentik in Ungarn* (Freising, 1954)

D. Dercsényi: 'Zur siebenhundertjährigen Feier der Kirche von Ják', *Acta Hist. A. Acad. Sci. Hung.*, vii (1957), pp. 173–202

G. Entz: 'Westemporen in der ungarischen Romanik', *Acta Hist. A. Acad. Sci. Hung.*, ix (1959), pp. 1–19

D. Dercsényi: *Romanesque Architecture in Hungary* (Budapest, 1972)

G. Entz: 'Die Wandmalereien der Westempore in Ják', *Kunstgeschichte und Denkmalpflege, Walter Frodl zum 65 Geburtstag gewidmet* (Vienna, 1975), pp. 172–81

D. Dercsényi: *Die Kirche in Ják* (Budapest, 1979)

G. Entz: 'Zur Frage der Westemporen in der mittelalterlichen Kirchen-architektur Ungarns', *Architektur des Mittelalters: Funktion und Gestalt*, ed. F. Möbius and E. Schubert (Weimar, 1983), pp. 240–45

GÉZA ENTZ

Jakamarra, Michael Nelson. *See* NELSON TJAKAMARRA, MICHAEL.

Jakard. *See* JACQUARD, JOSEPH-MARIE.

Jakarta [formerly Batavia; Djakarta; Jayakarta; Sunda Kelapa]. Port city on the north coast of West Java at the estuary of the Cwilung River, capital of the Republic of Indonesia. The oldest part of the city stands on the site of Sunda Kelapa, which from at least the 12th century was an important emporium for the export of merchandise produced in the hinterland of West Java. In 1527 the Muslim Sundanese prince Fatahillah founded a Muslim principality based on Sunda Kelapa, which he renamed Jayakarta ('City of Victory') and which during the next 100 years became an important international trading centre, frequented by Portuguese, Dutch and Asian merchants. In 1617 the Dutch East India Company (VOC) was given permission to establish a trading post at Jayakarta, and only two years later a Dutch force under Jan Pieterszoon Coen captured the city, renaming it Batavia and making it the headquarters of the VOC in Asia.

The site was ideally placed for trading purposes on the Bay of Jakarta, commanding the Sunda Straits between Sumatra and Java. The Dutch first built a fortress (Kasteel) on the east bank of the Ciwilung River near the estuary, surrounded by a wall and moats. By the end of the 17th century the Dutch settlement had already outgrown the fortress area and had begun to spread to the higher land to the south, and it was here on the west bank of the Ciwilung River that a new city grew up in the area known as Kota. The Batavia of the 17th and 18th centuries was built in direct imitation of such Dutch cities as Amsterdam. Little attempt was made to adapt the plan of the city or the design of individual buildings to the exigencies of the hot and humid climate. Long straight streets were constructed, interspersed with waterways, and the earliest houses were narrow and tall, with a small inner courtyard, a steep staircase leading to the upper floors, small windows, high roofs and gables.

In 1799 the VOC was abolished, and in 1806 the Dutch colonies in the East Indies passed under the control of the kingdom of the Netherlands, then ruled by Louis Bonaparte. He appointed Marshal Herman Willem Daendels to govern Java on his behalf. Daendels, who was in Batavia from 1808 to 1811, pulled down the old walls of the city and used the stones to create a new centre in the suburb of Weltevreden. However, the Kota area remained the commercial centre of Batavia until a new harbour was constructed (1866–77) at Tanjung Priok, 14 km to the east; at the end of the 20th century, many whitewashed, two-storey warehouses with tiled roofs were still standing in this part of the city. The most important surviving building in the quarter is the former town hall (Stadhuis), now the Jakarta City Museum, on the south side of Taman Fatahillah. Designed by W. J. van der Welde in 1707–10, it is a two-storey brick building modelled on the contemporary town hall in Amsterdam, with an elegant octagonal cupola and a triple-arched portico surmounted by a pediment. In 1974 it was restored and converted into a museum illustrating the history of the VOC in Batavia. To the left of the City Museum is the Wayang Museum, built in 1912 on the site of a Dutch 17th-century church and cemetery and housing a fine collection of Indonesian and other puppets. Near Kota Railway Station is the Portuguese Church, now known as the Gereja Zion, designed by E. Ewout Verhagen and built between 1693 and 1695 for the Mardijkers, Christian (Dutch Reformed) descendants of the Portuguese-speaking Indian slaves brought by the Portuguese to Batavia during the 17th century. The oldest church in Jakarta, it was restored in 1920 and again in 1978. It contains fine carved ebony panelling, pews, pulpit and organ loft, and four copper chandeliers.

During the early 19th century Batavia became centred round two squares in Weltevreden: the Waterlooplein (now Lapangan Banteng) and, to the east of the Waterlooplein, the Koningsplein (now Medan Merdeka). The most important buildings in Lapangan Banteng are the former governor's palace (now the Department of Finance), built between 1809 and 1828 in a restrained Neo-classical style, and the Roman Catholic cathedral, built in 1901 in a somewhat ponderous neo-Gothic style, with two latticed metal spires. The square is dominated by a statue of a man breaking his chains, erected in 1963 to commemorate the withdrawal of the Dutch from Irian Jaya and its accession to the Indonesian republic. In the centre of Medan Merdeka is the National Monument (Monas) erected under President Sukarno, an obelisk 132 m high, made of Italian marble and surmounted by a gilded bronze flame symbolizing independence. At the base of the obelisk is a Museum of National History. On the north side of Medan Merdeka is the Istana Negara (National Palace), built in the late 18th century as a country house by a rich Dutch merchant named J. A. van Braam. It is a single-storey building in classical style. Immediately behind this is the Istana Merdeka (Freedom Palace), originally known as the Koningsplein Palace and built in 1873–9 for the Dutch governor. Although almost 100 years later than the Istana Negara, it is very similar in style, comprising a single storey with a colonnaded front. Both palaces are now only used for state occasions. On the west side of the square is the National Museum, built between 1862 and 1868 as the headquarters of the Batavian Society for Arts and Science, also in classical style with a colonnaded portico. In front of the museum is a statue of a bronze elephant on a high pedestal presented by the Thai king Chulalongkorn (Rama V) on his visit to Batavia in 1871.

Just off the north-east corner of Medan Merdeka is the Istiqlal Mosque, opened by President Sukarno in 1978 and reputed to be the largest mosque in South-east Asia. It is built almost entirely of marble, and the roof over its vast praying area is supported by 12 massive pillars. On the east side of Taman Merdeka is one of Jakarta's finest churches, the Gereja Emmanuel (formerly Willemskerk), a circular building in classical style built by J. H. Horst between 1834 and 1839. It contains an organ constructed in the Netherlands in 1843. Many of the 19th- and early 20th-century European houses in the vicinity of Taman Merdeka and along the Molenvliet Canal (now Jalan Hayam Wuruk) and Jalan Gajah Mada are still standing. They are mostly single-storey with red-tiled roofs, deep verandahs and marble or red-tiled floors. At the back there is usually a courtyard, round which are the servants' quarters, kitchens and stables, and often containing a well.

In the early 20th century further suburbs were built, notably in the areas now called Menteng to the south of Medan Merdeka and Kemayoran to the south-east. After World War II and the independence of Indonesia in 1945, the name of the city was changed to Jakarta, and the suburb Kebayoran was developed still further to the south as a residential quarter. During the 1960s and 1970s many high-rise office blocks, banks, embassies and luxury hotels in a nondescript international style were built on either side of Jalan Thamrin, a street running due south from the south-west corner of Medan Merdeka.

BIBLIOGRAPHY

F. de Haan: *Oud Batavia*, 2 vols (Batavia, 1922)
P. D. Milone: *Queen City of the East: The Metamorphosis of a Colonial Capital* (diss., Berkeley, U. CA, 1966)
L. Blusse: 'Batavia, 1619–1740: The Rise and Fall of a Chinese Colonial Town', *J. SE Asian Stud.*, xii/1 (1981), pp. 159–78
A. Heuken: *Historical Sights of Jakarta* (Jakarta, 1982/*R* Singapore, 1989)
J. Taylor: *The Social World of Batavia: European and Eurasian in Dutch Asia* (Madison, WI, 1983)
S. Abeyasekere: *Jakarta: A History* (Singapore, 1987)
M. Jayapal: *Old Jakarta* (Kuala Lumpur, 1993)

JOHN VILLIERS

Jakob von Landshut (*b* Landshut, *c.* 1450; *d* Strasbourg, 6 Aug 1509). German architect. His father may have been Ulrich Iserecker, architect to the city of Landshut about the middle of the 15th century, whose son Jakob was residing outside the district in 1469. Jakob's mark appears on the church of Herrnsheim, near Worms, built *c.*1470–90. He may have participated in other buildings of Bavarian inspiration in the same region, such as the church of Bechtolsheim and the Lady chapel of Worms Cathedral. In 1492 Jakob arrived in Strasbourg, where in 1495 he became Master of the Works. From 1494 to 1505 he built the St Laurent porch on the north transept façade. In 1496 he built a bell-tower (destr. 1533) on the cathedral podium. In 1506 he restored the parapet of the St Catherine Chapel. He was trained by one of the successors of Hans von Burghausen and, with knowledge of the architecture of his native city, he also appears to have been influenced by the Swabian style of Matthäus Böblinger. The vault of the St Laurent porch, and even more its façade, with its canopy composed of angular re-entrants and its decorative richness, constitutes one of the most elaborate masterpieces of Late Gothic in the southern Empire. A more timid first plan for this façade survives in the Musée de l'Oeuvre Notre-Dame.

BIBLIOGRAPHY

D. Harster: 'L'Architecture du portail Saint-Laurent de la cathédrale', *Bull. Cathédrale Strasbourg*, xiv (1980), pp. 21–39
B. Schock-Werner: *Das Strassburger Münster im 15. Jahrhundert* (Cologne, 1983), pp. 200–13, 361–7

ROGER LEHNI

Jakopič, Rihard (*b* Ljubljana, 12 April 1869; *d* Ljubljana, 21 April 1943). Slovenian painter. In 1887–9 he studied at the Akademie der Bildenden Künste in Vienna under Franz Rumpler (1848–1922), in 1890 in Munich under Karl Raupp (1837–1918), and from 1903 to 1904 in Prague under Vojtěch Hynais. He was the principal organizer of artistic and cultural life in Slovenia in his time. In 1909 an exhibition hall, the Jakopič Pavilion, Ljubljana, was erected on his initiative; he was also the founder of a private school of painting in Ljubljana and the originator of contemporary Slovenian art, together with his colleagues Ivan Grohar and Matej Sternen (1870–1949). At first he practised a similar style to that of Anton Ažbé, under whom he had studied in Munich, but after seeing Monet's paintings he turned enthusiastically to Impressionism. He painted series of pictures in which he tried to capture the atmosphere of the Slovenian landscape in the Impressionist manner. During 1903–5 he made informal experimental sketches whose dispersed composition and heavy impasto were like abstract colour studies, for example the *Sunny Hillside* (1903; Ljubljana, N. G.). From then until 1917 he mostly depicted brightly coloured interiors with vivid contrasts of cold and warm colours suggestive of the Fauvists, although in atmosphere and texture more akin to *Intimisme*.

After World War I Jakopič often painted distorted figures with firm gestural strokes, his colours consisting of shades of red and blue juxtaposed in vivid contrast. A typical example is the *Blind Man* (1926; Ljubljana, Gal. Mod. A.), which conveys a more universal, symbolic vision of mankind.

BIBLIOGRAPHY

A. Podbevšek: *Jakopič* (Ljubljana, 1941)
Rihard Jakopič (exh. cat., text Z. Kržišnik; Ljubljana, Gal. Mod. A., 1970)
Z. Kržišnik: *Rihard Jakopič* (Ljubljana, 1971)

JURE MIKUŽ

Jakubonis, Gediminas (*b* Kupiškis, 8 Mar 1927). Lithuanian sculptor. He studied at the State Institute of Applied and Decorative Art in Kaunas, first under Viktoras Polis, then Juozas Mikėnas (1901–64). His graduation work was a decorative relief, *Training Horses* (1952), for the Vilnius Hippodrome. He continued to explore the possibilities of decorative sculpture in his relief *Lithuanian Dancer* (1958) for the façade of the club of the cement factory in Naueyi Akmyane. His war memorial in the village of Purcipius (1961) became his best known work, largely because of the significance given such monuments during the years of Soviet power. The main figure, *Grieving Mother*, is of gabbro and is close in style to Kārlis Zāle's ensemble at the Brothers' Cemetery (1924–38) in Riga, while its painfully expressive form resembles the work of Ivan Meštrović and Anton Starkopf. The use of female attire characteristic of the local area and the method of working with the material recall folk sculpture and gave rise to many imitations. In the following years Jakubonis received political commissions from Russia, including a monument to *Lenin* on Il'ich Square in Moscow (bronze and granite, 1967). The monument to *Adam Mickiewicz* (granite, 1979–82) by the church of St Anne in Vilnius was designed to fit the context of the surrounding city and unites the detailed forms of Lithuanian sculpture of the 1930s, as seen in the work of Vincentas Grybas (1890–1941) and Juozas Mikėnas, with other 20th-century sculptural tendencies. Jakubonis also produced medals in the tradition of Petras Rimša.

BIBLIOGRAPHY
S. Budrys: *Gediminas Jakubonis* (Vilnius, 1963)

SERGEY KUZNETSOV

Jakuchū. *See* ITŌ JAKUCHŪ.

Jal, Auguste (*b* Lyon, 1795; *d* Vernon, 1873). French art critic and journalist. His career began in 1818 with a pamphlet, *Mes visites au Musée Royal du Luxembourg* (Paris, 1818), in which he divided the history of painting in France into three ages: the golden age of Poussin and Claude, the period of decadence of Boucher and Carle Vanloo, and the era of revival of Joseph-Marie Vien and David. His most significant contributions to art criticism were his works on the Paris Salons, written between 1819 and 1833, particularly those of 1824 and 1827, which provide useful insight into the debate between classicism and Romanticism that emerged in French painting during the 1820s.

Jal perceived decadence in the Neo-classical paintings at the Salon of 1824, which he criticized for over-emphasis on precise rendering and excessive use of academic form. He defined Romanticism as a school of painting disdaining style and correctness, and he accused Delacroix of careless drawing, strident colour and a lack of decorum in the *Massacres at Chios* (exh. Salon 1824; Paris, Louvre), although he admired the force, energy and vivacity of the painting. Jal proclaimed France to be in an artistic crisis and imagined David returning to head the Romantic school, to which he would bring his good taste in drawing and imaginative ideas to serve as a corrective. He allied himself with Stendhal and, anticipating the criticism of Charles Baudelaire, called for a renunciation of outmoded Neo-classical themes along with the painting of modern history in France.

Jal began his work on the Salon of 1827 with a harsh critique of the politics of the Académie Royale and the injustices of the jury system. He recognized that the Salon functioned as a powerful political arena and stated that Romanticism in painting echoed the cannon shots of 1789. He recommended the suppression of the jury system and official expositions, urging public freedom of expression. He condemned the Neo-classical artists exhibiting at the Salon for their lack of inspiration and originality. He labelled the Romantics schismatics, and accused them of espousing ugliness as their ideal. He advocated the portrayal of the human figure modelled on the most pleasing natural forms and drawn in a correct yet imaginative style. Jal recognized Delacroix as the leading painter of the Romantic school and praised his powers as a colourist, although he criticized his inchoate treatment of form. He continued his evaluation of Delacroix's work in his discussion of the Salon of 1831 and discovered in *Liberty Leading the People* (1830; Paris, Louvre) a new poetry and an energetic expression of bold thought. He found the figures in the painting uniformly ugly, but argued that the strangeness of style should be viewed as part of Delacroix's special character. Jal thus moved to an acceptance of Delacroix on his own terms rather than through the filter of a critic's preconceived notions of appropriate form and style.

Jal demonstrated that he had broadened his aesthetic base beyond the classic–Romantic antithesis in 1833. In this discussion he openly endorsed the Romantic school of painting and emphasized significant individuality in artistic expression as the key to appreciation. He predicted the decline of history painting at the Salon and signalled the ascension of landscape as the new tendency of modern art.

WRITINGS
Mes visites au Musée Royal du Luxembourg ou coup d'oeil critique de la galerie des peintres vivans (Paris, 1818)
L'Ombre de Diderot et le bossu du Marais: Dialogue critique sur le Salon de 1819 (Paris, 1819)
L'Artiste et le philosophe: Entretiens critiques sur le Salon de 1824 (Paris, 1824)
Esquisses, croquis, pochades, ou tout ce qu'on voudra sur le Salon de 1827 (Paris, 1828)
Le Peuple au sacre: Critiques, observations, causeries faites devant le tableau de M. Le Baron Gerard, premier peintre du Roi (Paris, 1829)
Salon de 1831: Ebauches critiques (Paris, 1831)
Salon de 1833: Les Causeries du Louvre (Paris, 1833)
Souvenirs d'un homme de lettres (Paris, 1877/R Geneva, 1973)

BIBLIOGRAPHY
C. M. Puppin: *The Art Criticism of Auguste Jal: The Formation of a Romantic* (MA thesis, Bryn Mawr Coll., 1977)

THERESE DOLAN

Jalabert, Charles(-François) (*b* Nîmes, 1 Jan 1819; *d* Paris, 8 March 1901). French painter. Against the wishes of his father, a jeweller, he enrolled in the Ecole de Dessin of Nîmes, directed by Alexandre Colin (1798–1875). A promising pupil, he received the first prize in drawing in 1835 and in painting in 1836 and 1837. A year later he moved to Paris to work briefly for one of his father's associates who urged him to study at the Ecole des Beaux-Arts, where he entered the atelier of Paul Delaroche. He competed three times for the Prix de Rome, faring best with his first attempt in 1841, when he obtained a second prize. However, he submitted his entry of 1843, *Oedipus and Antigone* (Marseille, Mus. B.-A.), to the initial exhibition of the Amis des Arts in Nîmes, winning a gold medal.

Jalabert followed Delaroche to Italy, where he stayed at his own expense until 1846. In Rome in 1844 he began work on *Virgil, Horace and Varius in the House of Maecenas* (Nîmes, Mus. B.-A.), which he intended as the counterpart to the large history paintings sent home by Prix de Rome winners. Embodying all the characteristics of academic history painting, this idealized view of Virgil reading the *Georgics* to his patron launched the artist's career in France: it received a third-class medal at the Salon of 1847 and was purchased by the State.

With Delaroche's sponsorship, Jalabert was introduced to wealthy and influential patrons, including Achille Fould (1800–67) and Emile Pereire. He became associated with the dealer Adolphe Goupil, who popularized his stock through the distribution of prints. Goupil found a ready market for Jalabert's small figure paintings recalling his Italian sojourn, such as the *Peasant Girl* (untraced, see 1981 exh. cat., p. 43), a genre so successfully exploited by Léopold Robert and Ernest Hébert, for his Renaissance subjects, including *Romeo and Juliet* (untraced, see 1981 exh. cat., p. 52) and *Raphael's Studio* (untraced, see 1981 exh. cat., p. 53), and for his religious works. The avoidance of heroic themes from antiquity and the preference for anecdotal, often sentimental subjects from the more recent past were characteristic of Delaroche and his pupils.

Jalabert's official recognition included a commission in 1850 from the Sèvres Manufactory for paintings of the *Four Evangelists* (Sèvres, Mus. N. Cér.), which served as designs for the enamelled plaques presented to Prince Albert at the Great Exhibition of 1851 in London. At the Salon of 1853 Empress Eugénie purchased for her chapel in the Tuileries the *Annunciation* (destr.), originally commissioned by the State for Alès Cathedral. Jalabert won a first-class medal at the Salon of 1853 for *Orpheus* (Baltimore, MD, Walters A.G.); this painting, showing nymphs in a forest glade listening enraptured to the Thracian poet, was praised for the lyrical treatment of the subject and for the delicate nuances and harmonies of its execution. Following his exhibition of several paintings, including *Christ in the Garden of Olives* (Douai, Mus. Mun.), at the Exposition Universelle of 1855, Jalabert was awarded the Légion d'honneur. After a trip to Italy in 1857 with his pupil Adolphe Jourdan (1825–89) and Albert Goupil, his dealer's son, Jalabert embarked on two projects that proved ideally suited to his temperament: the ceiling decoration, *Night Unfurling her Veils*, for a bedroom in Pereire's hôtel on the Rue du Faubourg St-Honoré (now the British Embassy) and another, *Homage to Aurora*, for the boudoir of Constant Say's hôtel on the Place Vendôme (now the Morgan Bank).

From the mid-1860s Jalabert devoted his time to portraiture. In 1864 a commission from Charles Asseline, the former secretary to Louis-Philippe, for portraits of *Louis-Philippe Albert d'Orléans, Comte de Paris* and *Isabelle, Comtesse de Paris* (1865; untraced, see 1981 exh. cat., p. 64), who were residing in exile in Twickenham, England, linked the artist with the house of Orléans. The following year, while in England, he painted portraits of the Comte's younger brother, *Robert d'Orléans, Duc de Chartres*, and *Françoise, Duchesse de Chartres* (1865; untraced). On a third trip in 1866 he received commissions for a series of portraits from Henri d'Orléans, Duc d'Aumale for various members of his family. These works, together with a posthumous portrait of *Marie-Amélie*, ordered by the Duc d'Aumale in 1880, are in the Musée Condé, Chantilly. Jalabert remained active until his death, dividing his time between Nîmes and Bougival.

BIBLIOGRAPHY
T. Gautier: *Les Beaux-arts en Europe*, ii (Paris, 1855), pp. 8–9
C. Blanc: *Les Artistes de mon temps* (Paris, 1876), p. 474
E. Reinaud: *Charles Jalabert: L'Homme, l'artiste d'après sa correspondance* (Paris, 1903)
Charles-François Jalabert, 1819–1901 (exh. cat. by A. Jourdan, Nîmes, Mus. B.-A., 1981)

WILLIAM R. JOHNSTON

Jalayirid [Jalā'irid]. Islamic dynasty that ruled in Iraq and Azerbaijan from 1336 to 1432. A Mongol family that established itself in Baghdad after the Ilkhanid sultanate began to collapse, the Jalayirids vied with the Muzaffarid and Qaraqoyunlu dynasties, as well as with the Golden Horde and the Timurid dynasty. The Jalayirids lost Azerbaijan to the Qaraqoyunlu after the Timurid invasion, and in 1412 the Qaraqoyunlu took Baghdad. The last Jalayirids were vassals of the Timurids. The architecture of the early Jalayirids (*see* ISLAMIC ART, §II, 6(i)(a)) apparently continued earlier local styles, with superb geometric brick and stucco decoration and fine inscriptions. The major building to survive in Baghdad is the funerary complex (1356–9) built by Mirjan, the amir who governed the city for the Jalayirids. It includes a madrasa and a caravanserai, the Khan al-Mirjan (or Khan al-Urtma), with a glum interior nevertheless well lit by windows under transverse barrel vaults. Several metal wares can be identified with Jalayirid patronage on the basis of inscriptions, but the art form most closely associated with the dynasty, particularly with Ahmad (*see* (1) below), is manuscript illustration (*see* ISLAMIC ART, §III, 4(v)(c)). In this transitional period Chinese and Near Eastern pictorial elements were fused into a coherent whole, new formulae for the depiction of space were developed, and the emotionalism of the early 14th century gave way to the lyricism that was characteristic of later Persian painting.

BIBLIOGRAPHY
Y. A. Godard: 'Bassin de cuivre au nom de Shaikh Uwais', *Athār-é Irān*, i (1936), pp. 371–3
D. Duda: 'Die Buchmalerei der Galā'iriden', *Der Islam*, xlviii (1971), pp. 28–76; li (1972), pp. 153–220
B. Gray: *The Arts of the Book in Central Asia, 14th–16th Centuries* (London and Paris, 1979), pp. 93–120
B. W. Robinson: 'A Survey of Persian Painting (1350–1896)', *Art et société dans le monde iranien*, ed. C. Adle (Paris, 1982), pp. 13–89
S. S. Blair: 'Artists and Patronage in Late Fourteenth-century Iran in the Light of Two Catalogues of Islamic Metalwork', *Bull. SOAS*, xlviii (1985), pp. 53–9
J. S. Cowen: *Kalila wa Dimna: An Animal Allegory of the Mongol Court: The Istanbul University Album* (New York, 1989)

(1) Ahmad Jalayir [Aḥmad Jalā'ir ibn Shaykh Uways] (*b* c. 1364; *reg* 1382–1410; *d* Tabriz, 1410). Iraqi sultan, poet and patron. According to the 16th-century chronicler DUST MUHAMMAD, Ahmad succeeded his father as the leading patron in Baghdad, employing 'ABD AL-HAYY and then JUNAYD as chief painters. Twice forced into exile by Timur (1393–4 and 1401–4), Ahmad ruled western Iran three times and three manuscripts survive from each reign. During the first, he commissioned a copy of Nizami's *Khamsa* ('Five poems'; Baghdad, 1386–8; London, BL, Or. MS.13299); a 'cosmology' completed on 10 March 1388 (Paris, Bib. N., MS. supp. pers.332) often misidentified as a Persian translation of al-Qazvini's '*Ajā'ib al-makhluqāt* ('Wonders of creation'); and a copy of *Kalila and Dimna*, completed on 10 August 1392 (Paris, Bib. N., MS. supp. pers.913). Upon returning to Baghdad in 1394, Ahmad resumed his book patronage. The most impressive work is a copy of Khwaju Kirmani's *Dīvān* ('Collected poems'), copied by 'Ali ibn Ilyas al-Tabrizi al-Bavarji ('the Taster') at Baghdad in February–March 1396. The manuscript (London, BL, Add. MS.18113) now contains nine paintings including one (fol. 45*v*) signed by Junayd; an additional page was detached and mounted in the album that Dust Muhammad compiled for the Safavid prince Bahram Mirza (1544; Istanbul, Topkapı Pal. Lib., H 2154, fol. 20*v*). Two astrological manuscripts also date from this period: the *Kitāb al-Bulhān* done at Irbil in 1399 (Oxford, Bodleian Lib., Or. MS. 133) and a contemporary text used for casting horoscopes (dispersed: Ham House, Surrey, NT, Keir priv. col., III.29–68, and U. Sarajevo, Inst. Orient. Res.). During Ahmad's last reign, he ordered two copies of his own poems. One (Baghdad, 1406–7; Istanbul, Mus. Turk. & Islam. A., 2046) contains only fine illumination, but the other (Washington, DC, Freer, 32.30–37) made at Tabriz has eight pages of marginal painting in grisaille. On stylistic grounds, an incomplete copy of Nizami's *Khusraw and Shirin* copied by Mir 'Ali ibn Hasan al-Sultani at Tabriz (Washington, DC, Freer, 31.29–37) can also be attributed to the period.

BIBLIOGRAPHY

Dūst Muḥammad: Preface to the Bahram Mirza Album (1544); Eng. trans., ed. W. M. Thackston in *A Century of Princes: Sources on Timurid History and Art* (Cambridge, MA, 1989), pp. 335–50

D. E. Klimburg-Salter: 'A Sufi Theme in Persian Painting: The Diwan of Sultan Ahmad Gala'ir in the Freer Gallery of Art, Washington, D.C.', *Kst Orients*, xi (1977), pp. 43–84

V. A. Prentice: 'A Detached Miniature from the *Masnavis* of Khwaju Kermani', *Orient. A.*, xxvii (1981), pp. 60–66

S. Carboni: 'Two Fragments of a Jalayirid Astrological Treatise in the Keir Collection and in the Oriental Institute in Sarajevo', *Islam. A.*, ii (1987), pp. 149–86

BASIL GRAY

Jalea, Ion (*b* Casimcea, 19 May 1887; *d* Bucharest, 7 Nov 1983). Romanian sculptor. He studied sculpture in Bucharest at the School of Arts and Crafts (1903–7) under Ştefan Ionescu-Valbudea (1856–1918), Vladimir Hegel (1839–1918) and Anibal Spoldy, and then at the Fine Arts School (1907–11) under Dimitrie Paciurea. In 1915 he studied under Henri Bouchard at the Académie Julian in Paris and also attended Rodin's studio at Meudon. Between 1919 and 1922, despite the loss of a hand during World War I, he continued his studies at the Académie de la Grande Chaumière, Paris, becoming a great admirer of the monumental style of Emile-Antoine Bourdelle. He exhibited at the Salon d'Automne, Paris, in 1920 and 1921. Jalea introduced mythological subjects such as Prometheus, Hercules, Minerva and Pegasus into Romanian sculpture, and he also drew on Romanian folklore for his subject-matter, with such bronzes as the *Stone-breaker* and *Briar* (both h. 380 mm, 1913–14; Constanţa, Mus. A.), as well as the *Resting Archer* (h. 1.2 m, 1926; Bucharest, N. Mus. A.), which had a Herculean anatomy, architecturally structured and reminiscent of Bourdelle's figures, although in this case the physiognomy had the robustness of an indigenous type. In the 1920s he also produced a series of small statuary groups in clay, plaster and bronze, featuring rustic subjects such as *Ploughman* (bronze, h. 90 mm, 1924–8; Constanţa, Mus. A.) and *People with Sacks* (bronze, h. 220 mm, 1924–8; Constanţa, Mus. A.). Instead of giving an idyllic view of the peasant's existence, these cultivated an almost aggressive realism to convey the hardships faced

by agricultural labourers. Among his best-known public works are the monuments to the French soldiers who died in Romania (marble, h. 2.8 m, 1920; Bucharest, Cişmigiu Gdn) and to the Romanian soldiers taken captive (stele with relief, h. *c.* 2.5 m, 1923; Dieuze, France). With Cornel Medrea he made the circular relief at the mausoleum of Maraşeşti (1938); he also sculpted the *Spiru Haret* statue (marble, h. 3.2 m, 1935; Bucharest, University Square) and more recently the equestrian bronzes of *Mircea the Old* (h. 4.6 m, 1973; Tulcea) and *Decebal* (h. 4.2 m, 1976; Deva). Jalea was a founder-member of Arta Română in 1918, of the Salon of Romanian Artist Sculptors, of the Criterion group and of the Arta association.

BIBLIOGRAPHY

P. Comarnescu: *Ion Jalea* (Bucharest, 1962)

G. Oprescu: *Sculptura românească* [Romanian sculpture] (Bucharest, 2/1965), pp. 115–21, 147–9

A. Arghir: 'Structuri georgice in opera lui Ion Jalea' [Georgic structures in Ion Jalea's works], *Tomis*, iv (1972)

IOANA VLASIU

Jaley, Jean-Louis-Nicolas (*b* Paris, 27 Jan 1802; *d* Neuilly, 30 May 1866). French sculptor. He was a pupil of his father, Louis Jaley (1763–1838), a medal engraver, and of Pierre Cartellier. In 1820 he entered the Ecole des Beaux-Arts, Paris, winning the Prix de Rome in 1827 with the relief *Mucius Scaevola before Porsenna* (Paris, Ecole N. Sup. B.-A.). His stay in Rome profoundly affected his style, which was influenced by the sculpture of antiquity and the paintings of Raphael. After his return to Paris, *c.* 1834, he contributed sculpture to all the major state building projects of the July Monarchy (1830–48) and the Second Empire (1851–70), including statues of *Jean-Sylvain Bailly* and *Victor Riqueti, Marquis de Mirabeau* (both marble, 1833) for the Chambre des Députés, Paris, of *St Ferdinand* (stone, 1837–9) for the church of La Madeleine, Paris, and those representing *London* and *Vienna* (both stone, 1862) for the Gare du Nord, Paris (all *in situ*). Jaley also achieved contemporary renown for the elegant, Raphaelesque female nudes that he exhibited regularly at the Salon, with titles such as *Prayer* (marble, exh. Salon 1831; Paris, Louvre) and *Modesty* (marble, exh. Salon 1834; Paris, Min. Finances).

BIBLIOGRAPHY

Lami

A. Le Normand: *La Tradition classique et l'esprit romantique* (Rome, 1981), pp. 218, 222

ISABELLE LEMAISTRE

Jallier, Noël (*fl* 1546–50). French painter. In 1550 he was paid for 14 large history paintings in the château of Oiron, Deux-Sèvres. These have been identified with the series painted *a secco* in the gallery in the north wing of the château, rediscovered in 1974. Painted in 1546–9 for Claude Gouffier, Grand Ecuyer of France, and dedicated to Francis I, they illustrate episodes from the *History of Troy* as described in Virgil's *Aeneid*. The ensemble was clearly inspired by the decorations of the Galerie François I at the château of Fontainebleau (*see* FONTAINEBLEAU, §1), but while the figure style is indebted to that of Rosso Fiorentino and Francesco Primaticcio, the composition and elaborate illusionistic painted framing reveal knowledge of contemporary Roman decorative cycles by such artists as Perino del Vaga and Daniele da Volterra. This led Blunt to suggest that Jallier may have visited Rome in the course of executing the paintings. No other works by Jallier are known, but the Oiron paintings are among the most impressive surviving decorations of their period in France and the first examples of large-scale decorations painted by a French artist before 1550.

BIBLIOGRAPHY

M. Dumolin: *Le Château d'Oiron* (Paris, 1931)
A. Blunt: *Art and Architecture in France, 1500–1700*, Pelican Hist. A. (Harmondsworth, 1953, rev. 5/1982)
J. Guillaume: 'Oiron: Fontainebleau poitevin', *Mnmts Hist.*, ci (1979), pp. 76–93

PHILIPPE ROUILLARD

Jamaer, Pierre-Victor (*b* Brussels, 1825; *d* Brussels, 10 April 1902). Belgian architect. He was trained by Joseph Jonas Dumont and spent much of his career working on the restoration or reconstruction of a large number of medieval and Renaissance monuments in Brussels as a member of the city's architectural staff; he became its Chief Architect in 1864. Most of his original designs were of Gothic Revival or Flemish Renaissance Revival character, reflecting his archaeological interests. His own house (1874–9) at 62 Avenue de Stalingrad, Brussels, was the most remarkable of these designs. The exposed timber structure of its gabled façade recalled the destroyed wooden houses of 15th- and 16th-century Brussels. Jamaer's major work involved the restoration of several buildings in the Grand'Place, Brussels, which began with his participation in the restoration (1850s) of the 15th-century Gothic Hôtel de Ville and the complete rebuilding (1873–85) in Gothic Revival style of the 16th-century Maison du Roi. In 1883 he began to restore the lavish Baroque façades of the square's distinctive guildhouses, including no. 7, la Maison du Renard (1883–4), no. 11, la Maison de la Rose, and no. 12, la Maison du Mont-Thabor,

(1885–7) and no. 5, la Maison de la Louve (1890–92), among others. This last project, substantially financed by the city of Brussels, was promoted by burgomaster Charles Buls, the well-known antiquarian and urban-planning theorist. Jamaer also did restoration work on the Eglise de la Chapelle, Place de la Chapelle, Brussels (1851–60 and 1866–98), and designed numerous houses and municipal buildings in the Belgian capital, such as the Ecole Communale, Rue Haute (1882–6), and the monumental entrance to the municipal cemetery at Evere, near Brussels (1878–9).

BIBLIOGRAPHY

G. Anciaux: 'Nécrologie: P. V. Jamaer, architecte', *L'Emulation*, xxvii (1902), cols 33–5

ALFRED WILLIS

Jamaica. Caribbean island, the third largest among the Greater Antilles. It lies 144 km south of Cuba and covers an area of 11,425 sq. km (see fig. 1). It is a lush island traversed by a mountain range, and it includes an area of unusual limestone formations, the Cockpit Country. The population is *c.* 2.4 million.

I. Introduction. II. Cultures. III. Architecture. IV. Painting, graphic arts and sculpture. V. Interior decoration and furniture. VI. Ceramics. VII. Metalwork. VIII. Patronage. IX. Collecting and dealing. X. Museums. XI. Art education.

I. Introduction.

When Columbus arrived in Jamaica in 1494 it was inhabited by Arawak-speaking Taino Amerindians. Juan de Esquivel conquered the island in 1509, and by 1513 the first Africans were brought to be personal servants to the Spanish. Within decades the indigenous population had died out through war and European disease. They were replaced by West Africans bought by the Portuguese to

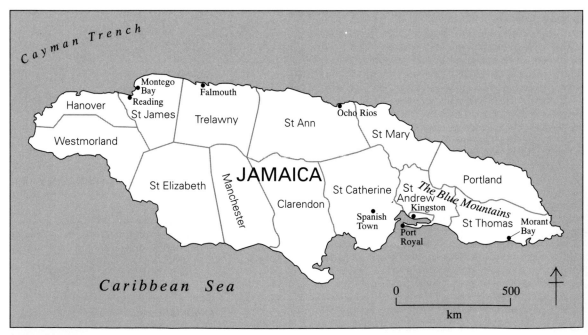

1. Map of Jamaica

work as slaves on sugar plantations. In 1655 an English expeditionary force landed and captured Spanish Town, which had been the capital since 1635. The Spanish released the slaves to hinder English occupation and abandoned the island after about five years. Many of the slaves fled into the interior Cockpit Country, where they and their descendants became known as Maroons and waged war against the new colonists until 1739 when a peace treaty was negotiated, which granted 1500 acres and certain rights to the Maroons. Port Royal, near Kingston, a base for the buccaneer Henry Morgan, was destroyed in an earthquake in 1692. There was a further wave of slave importation from the late 17th century. Many Kikong- and Yoruba-speaking peoples arrived, particularly in the 1770s. The slaves were emancipated in 1838, when most of them left the plantations to settle in the mountains. From 1840 to 1865, 8000 West Africans arrived to work as waged labourers on the plantations. Kingston became the capital in 1870. In 1958 Jamaica joined the Federation of the West Indies but withdrew in 1961 and gained independence within the Commonwealth in 1962. There was a high rate of emigration from the mid-20th century, but at the end of the 20th century the natural annual increase in population was *c.* 1.5%. Approximately 90% of the population is of West African descent; the remainder includes people of Chinese, East Indian and European origin. Maroon settlements still exist at St Mary, Portland and St Elizabeth. Sugar is still the main export crop, although in 1990 bauxite and alumina accounted for two-thirds of merchandise exports, while bananas, coffee, cocoa, citrus, tobacco, spices and illegal ganja (marijuana) are also grown. Jamaica's official second foreign exchange earner is tourism.

BIBLIOGRAPHY
C. V. Black: *History of Jamaica* (London, 1958, 2/1983)
Jamaica J., i– (1967–)
F. E. Hurwitz and S. J. Hurwitz: *Jamaica: A Historical Portrait* (New York, 1971)
M. Binney, J. Harris and K. Martin: *Jamaica's Heritage* (Kingston, 1991)
JANET HENSHALL MOMSEN

II. Cultures.

1. Amerindian. 2. Afro-Caribbean.

1. AMERINDIAN. The language and culture of Jamaica's first inhabitants, the Taino Amerindians, were similar to those of the indigenous peoples of Hispaniola, Puerto Rico and eastern Cuba (*see also* CARIBBEAN ISLANDS, §II, 1). Archaeological remains include rather crude pottery decorated with red or black paint and geometric designs incised on the borders of the vessels. These correspond to what archaeologists of the Antilles consider sub-Taino styles of pottery. This evidence suggests that the first inhabitants of the islands arrived towards the 12th century, possibly from Hispaniola. Ethno-historical references to their culture are scant, since chroniclers of the Spanish Conquest focused on Hispaniola. In a letter to the Catholic kings, discovered in the late 20th century, Columbus described aspects of the aboriginal art while informing of the arrival of a large canoe with a Jamaican *cacique* (Sp.: Indian chief), his family and servants. He drew attention to the fine and elaborate ornaments and paraphernalia of the individuals: the canoe was decorated with painted

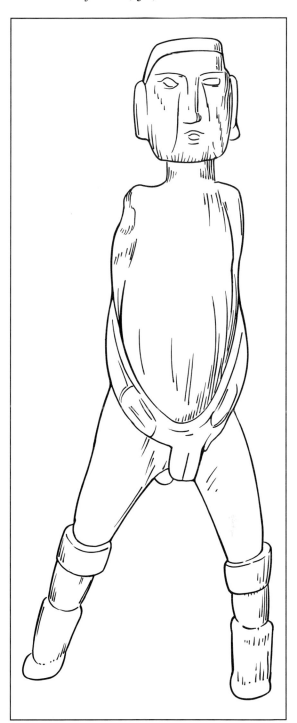

2. Amerindian idol, Guaiacum-wood, h. 1.03 m, AD 1000–1500, from Carpenters Mountains, Parish of Vere, Jamaica, found 1797 (London, British Museum)

designs; the men wore colourful red-and-white feather head ornaments; one had a banner-like woven-cotton cloth; another carried a wooden trumpet carved with bird motifs; over his chest the *cacique* bore a large stone-bead necklace with a gold ornament in the form of an 'iris flower' and 'on his head a garland of small white stone beads with a few hanging over his forehead, while from his ears hung two large gold tablets with strings of marble beads and even though naked, he wore a belt of small stone beads'.

The best examples of the Amerindian art of Jamaica are three idols (1000–1500; London, BM) carved from Guaiacum-wood, discovered in 1797 in a cave in Carpenters Mountains, Parish of Vere. The bird-headed idol (h. 880 mm) has conch-shell incrustation for teeth in its beak-like mouth. Its tubular body has extended upper appendages that simulate arms or perhaps wings. The legs have carved bands under the knees, like the cotton ones commonly used by the Tainos. The second (see fig. 2), an anthropomorphic, armless idol (h. 1.03 m), has legs stretched wide apart. Its gaping mouth reveals conch-shell teeth. This idol has representations of the cotton leggings and also the round ear-plugs used by the Tainos. The third idol (h. 390 mm), representing the upper torso of a human figure, carries on its head a round dish or canopy, which was used to deposit the hallucinogenic *cohoba* powder or snuff, used by the Taino shamans in their rituals (*see* SOUTH AMERICA, PRE-COLUMBIAN, §I, 3(ii)). Under the eyes, vertical grooves, which possibly contained shell incrustations, may represent tears. In 1983 Lee reported the discovery in St Ann of a gold-leaf disc (16×21 mm; now in Kingston, Inst. Jamaica), probably used as an ornament. The use of stone by Amerindians in Jamaica was limited to celts, mortars and rather simple corporal ornaments. Other examples of the Amerindian art of Jamaica include pictographs. These were discovered at Mountain River Cave in St Catherine. They are painted with a black pigment, possibly a type of bituminous material (Watson). The 148 identifiable pictographs are mostly of animals, such as iguanas, turtles, birds and frogs. Some anthropomorphic figures as well as some abstract pictographs were also uncovered. There is also evidence of a few petroglyphs. Ethno-historical sources reveal that Jamaican Amerindians played *batey*, the ceremonial ball-game of the Tainos, using a rubber ball. By the late 20th century, however, no special monolith-lined court, such as those of Puerto Rico and Hispaniola, had been found.

BIBLIOGRAPHY

T. A. Joyce: *Central American and West Indian Archaeology* (London, 1916)
S. Loven: *Origins of the Tainan Culture of the West Indies* (Göteborg, 1935)
J. W. Lee: 'A Pre-Columbian Gold Artifact from Jamaica', *Proceedings of the 10th Congress for the Study of Pre-Columbian Cultures of the Lesser Antilles: Montreal, 1985*, pp. 343–5
K. Watson: 'Amerindian Cave Art in Jamaica', *Jamaica J.*, xxi/1 (1988)
I. Rouse: *The Tainos: Rise and Fall of the People who Greeted Columbus* (New Haven, 1992)

RICARDO E. ALEGRÍA, MELA PONS-ALEGRÍA

2. AFRO-CARIBBEAN. The Africans imported as servants, and then as slaves, came from many peoples of West Africa, the majority being Asante from the Gold Coast and Yoruba and Ibo of southern Nigeria. Smaller numbers of Kongo and Mandingo were also prominent, particularly among the later Free Africans. Despite the island's slave laws and Christianity, which together exerted control over a people already stripped of virtually all possessions, many slaves secretly and surreptitiously continued to practise their traditions, particularly in music,

dance, beliefs, language and other customs. The Maroons (from the Spanish *cimarron*, 'wild and untamed'), for example, who had formed from bands of escaped slaves, communicated by means of talking drums and their *abeng*, a cow-horn bugle used also as a musical instrument and for ceremonial occasions. Their secret language contained many Akan words. African culture can still be observed within the modern Maroon, Kumina and Nago communities in Jamaica. Following independence the rise of nationalism led to a re-examination and renewed appreciation of Afro-Jamaican cultural expression. The African Caribbean Institute at the Institute of Jamaica in Kingston was established in 1972 as the principal cultural agency for the study and dissemination of research on Africa and its heritage in the Caribbean.

Although Christianity is the dominant religion on the island, a number of African religious beliefs and cults have been practised. Obeah, for example, was brought to the Caribbean by the Asante and flourished for over 300 years. In 1772 the historian Edward Long wrote disparagingly of the practice: 'Some of these execrable wretches in Jamaica introduced what they called the "myal dance" and established a kind of society into which they initiated all they could. The lure hung out was that every Negro initiated into the myal society would be invulnerable to the white man; and, although they might appear to be slain, the obeahman could, at his pleasure, restore the body to life.' In response to the threat to the planters' authority, the government's suppression of the cult in an effort to control the black population ensured its entrenched secrecy within Jamaican society. It is therefore difficult to estimate the extent to which it has been practised, although it became less popular over time. Practitioners, both men and women, may be associated with one of two forms of Obeah, or a combination of both. Some Obeahmen or -women have balm yards (herb gardens) and use local roots, herbs and other natural substances, such as earth, blood, bones, feathers and ashes, in established forms clearly related to African antecedents. Others are associated with religious cults, claiming to be able to control spirits to do their bidding. Obeah can, however, be worked for any number of reasons.

Kumina (or Cumina) is regarded as the most African of the Jamaican religious cults and is believed either to have been brought with the Free Africans between the 1840s and 1860s or to have received new stimulation from their arrival. Many of the Free Africans settled in St Thomas, where the cult has remained strongest. Kumina groups were also formed in Portland, St Catherine, Kingston and other areas. Extensive research has revealed a Bantu, and more specifically a Kongo, ancestry for this cult. Kumina ritual is largely conducted in Kikongo, the language of the Kongo peoples, and the name Kumina itself is a Kikongo word meaning to act or move rhythmically. Kumina people also refer to themselves by the Bantu term Bongo. The ceremonies of Kumina, a cult of ancestor worship, are performed for such specific reasons as births, deaths, weddings, wakes, entombments and thanksgiving. Kumina comprises both rites of incorporation and rites of passage. Singing, dancing and drumming are the three key elements of Kumina ceremonies. The goat-skin-covered hollow drums, played only by men, include the large *kimbanda* or *kbandu* and the smaller *kyas* or *cass*. Their importance lies in their hypnotic rhythms, through which control is exercised over certain spirits. Both men and women may become leaders following a long apprenticeship. They then hold the pre-eminent position within the group, since they control such spirits as the sky gods, earthbound gods and ancestral zombies.

Myalism, another Jamaican possession–healing cult, was probably first associated with Obeah, in that its potions and trances were employed to counteract the influences of the latter. Myal men are also bush-healers, using herbs for healing and protection; they also became associated with 'shadow catching', capturing and controlling 'duppies' (ghosts of dead people). The traditional dance of *gombay* is considered a Myal dance. Myalism reached its zenith between Emancipation and the 'Great Revival', an orgy of religious conversion in 1860–61. Thereafter, Myalism appears to have disappeared, and many of its elements were absorbed into Revivalism, another spirit cult, which gained great impetus at this time, developing from a synthesis of African religious beliefs and Christianity. This cult is celebrated in several forms, the two major ones being Revival Zion (or Zion) and Pocomania (now more commonly known as Puk Kumina). The state of possession or 'getting into the spirit', a notable feature of services, is induced through a ritual that includes music and songs borrowed from orthodox religion, but uniquely performed accompanied by drumming, dancing, clapping, groaning and the chanting of prayers. One of the best-known contemporary leaders is Revival Shepherd Mallica 'Kapo' Reynolds, whose fame derives primarily from his reputation as an acclaimed Intuitive artist (*see* §IV below). Early Revivalist meetings were held in consecrated areas called the 'seal ground' or 'mission ground', part of the leader's yard, where a temporary booth was erected. In the late 20th century some bands (or groups) began to construct more permanent churches. Revivalism has been important in preserving traditional Jamaican folk culture and has inspired the development of various Jamaican art forms.

The origins of Rastafarianism remain obscure, but it came to national attention in the 1930s. The inspiration of Marcus Garvey's Universal Negro Improvement Association and his teachings on the pre-eminence of black culture, the need for self-improvement and self-reliance of Africans aroused a black consciousness and pride. Rastafarianism emerged from this movement, against the backdrop of organized labour and political groups. Its principal icon and eventual Messiah was Haile Selassie (1891–1975), who became Emperor of Abyssinia (now Ethiopia) in 1930. The identifying symbol of the lion, with the red, green and gold Ethiopian flag flying, is another reference to Selassie's title as the Lion of Judah. The movement's two fundamental doctrines are that Haile Selassie was the black reincarnation of Christ and that repatriation to Africa assured the redemption of black people in their spiritual home. Thus Rastafarianism came to reflect the national search for a cultural identity that absorbed Jamaica at this time and beyond independence. Rastafarians differentiate themselves from 'Babylon' (or mainstream society) in such aspects of everyday life as speech, dress, behaviour and diet. While an adherent must retain his beard (a symbol of his pact with Jah or Jehovah)

and his Bible as his source of knowledge and wisdom, a more extremist group called 'locksmen' popularized long, uncombed hair or dreadlocks in emulation of the lion's mane, which has now become an identifiable trademark of all cult members. The use of marijuana or 'ganja' as a biblical herb is associated with the cult's meditative nature, through which wisdom and communication with God can be achieved. Rastafarianism's close identification with the performing and visual arts has given the cult visibility at an international level, especially in popular music. The paintings of Albert Artwell (*b* 1942) are defined by his personal revelation of Rastafari, and other artists have begun to employ the trappings and idioms of Rastafarianism to create a new iconography.

A fusion of European, African and Creole cultures can be seen in Jonkonnu (or John Canoe), a traditional feature of Jamaican Christmas celebrations involving bands of costumed masqueraders roaming the streets of towns and villages (*see also* CARNIVAL). The practice appears to have started early in Jamaican history, among the slave population, and was widely popularized by the late 18th century. It was initially suppressed by the government, who feared that such gatherings might encourage rebellion and covert communication via drums and conch-shells among the blacks. The masquerade includes music, dance, pantomime and drama. The word Jonkonnu itself may be linked to the Ewe terms *dzono* or *dzonko*, and *kunu* or *nu*, meaning deadly sorcerer or sorcerer man respectively. This reinforces hypotheses that Jonkonnu originated from West

3. Isaac Mendes Belisario: *Koo Koo or Actor-boy*, character from the Jonkonnu masquerade, lithograph, 399×495 mm, 1837 (St Michael, Barbados Museum)

African secret societies such as the Poro and Egungun, especially since all the players are masked men. The earliest forms and characters of the masquerade were closely associated with secrecy and magic, and such early characters as Cow Head, Horse Head, Jack in the Green and Pitchy Patchy bear a strong resemblance to West African parallels. The 19th-century artist Isaac Mendes Belisario (?1795–1849) documented Jonkonnu characters in a print series in the 1830s (see fig. 3).

Among the crafts brought to Jamaica from Africa is basketry. Local materials are used, including bamboo, wiss or withe, thatch palm, sisal or jippa jappa. Some forms of basket betray the African origin. The Jamaican bankra, for example, a rectangular travelling basket with handles and a cover, is clearly derived from the bonkara of Ghana, which has a similar function of transportation of goods and food to market. Jamaica's traditional coarse earthenware, such as *yabbahs* and monkey jars (see fig. 7 below), have distinctive African features (*see* §VI below). Archaeological research at Morant Bay in St Thomas has provided evidence of the technological skills of the early Maroons, who produced ironwork for domestic use and weapons. African sources have been identified in the motifs used in the grillwork and fretwork designs that decorated older buildings, for example patterns of the *adinkra* cloths of the Asante of Ghana (Bryan; *see* §IV below).

During the 1850s the Rev. James Phillippo recorded the continuity of a wood-carving tradition, noting, 'Fifteen or twenty years ago in a Negro burying ground, at no great distance from the author's residence in Spanish Town, there was scarcely a grave that did not exhibit from two to four rudely carved images.' Such funerary statuary may reflect a continuity with the burial traditions of the Akan peoples of West Africa. The Jamaican traditional walking-stick is still subconsciously associated with the symbol of an Obeahman's power. More recently the artists David Miller and his son (of the same name) reinterpreted West African imagery and form: David Miller jr, for example, has re-examined the African physiognomy in his wooden sculpture.

BIBLIOGRAPHY

J. H. Bell: *Obeah: Witchcraft in the West Indies* (1889/*R* 1970)
O. Senior: *A–Z of Jamaican Heritage* (1983, 2/1988)
R. F. Thompson: *Flash of the Spirit: African and Afro-American Art and Philosophy* (New York, 1983)
V. Poupeye-Rammelaere: 'The Rainbow Valley: The Life and Work of Brother Everald Brown', *Jamaica J.*, xxi/2 (1988), pp. 2–14
C. Goucher: 'John Reeder's Foundry: A Study of 18th Century African-Caribbean Technology', *Jamaica J.*, xxiii/1 (1989), pp. 39–43
D. Armstrong: 'Recovering an Early 18th-Century Afro-Jamaican Community: Archaeology of the Slave Village at Seville, Jamaica', *Proceedings of the 13th International Congress for Caribbean Archaeology: Curaçao, 1990*, pp. 344–62
V. Poupeye-Rammelaere: 'The Iconography of Marcus Garvey: Part 2', *Jamaica J.*, xxiv/2 (1992), pp. 24–33

III. *Architecture.*

The first Spanish colonists settled at Sevilla La Nueva (now New Seville; mostly destr.). The earliest Spanish domestic buildings were simple timber-framed, palm-thatched, square or oblong huts based on Amerindian designs (reconstruction of Amerindian hut in St Catherine, Arawak Ind. Mus.). Manufacture of local clay bricks and roof tiles is recorded as early as 1527. The island's first governor, Juan de Esquivel, erected a two-storey fortified dwelling of cut stone, with external walls over 1.20 m thick, on 2.40 m-wide foundations. The settlement was soon abandoned in favour of Villa de la Vega (now Spanish Town), which comprised 400 to 500 buildings laid out on the characteristic Spanish grid plan with a central square. In the 17th century houses were generally small with high timber walls raised on a masonry base and roofed with locally manufactured clay tiles. Little survives from over 150 years of Spanish colonization.

When the English captured Jamaica in 1655 Spanish Town was mostly destroyed, and the building materials were reused. During visits in 1687 the physician and botanist HANS SLOANE, who later wrote the comprehensive, two-volume *Natural History of Jamaica* (1707 and 1725), described Jamaican houses as being bungalows of timber and plaster with shuttered windows and inner courtyards in the Spanish mode. More important buildings were constructed in masonry, for example the cathedral of St James (begun 1655) on the site of an early 16th-century Franciscan chapel. The development of sugar cultivation gave rise to the construction of houses such as Drax Hall (1690), facing the sea on the St Ann coast, a broad-roofed masonry and timber-boarded house. Several of the plantation houses were fortified against raids, such as that by the French in 1694. Stokes Hall (c. 1710), St Thomas, and Colbeck Castle (c. 1748), St Catherine (both ruined), are examples: they have massive corner towers and loopholes for cross-fire defence.

Port Royal had developed to serve the sugar trade during the 17th century and boasted masonry buildings up to four storeys high before it was destroyed by an earthquake in 1692. Kingston was founded in 1693. Houses there were built lower and wider, with verandahs, arcades and sash windows in the emerging Jamaican Georgian style. Surviving examples in this style include the town houses at Falmouth and the government buildings at Spanish Town. In Spanish Town elaborate public buildings were built around the main square. These included the House of Assembly (1762) on the east side, with a ground-floor arcade and deep colonnaded verandah facing the square, and on the west King's House (1762), a splendid H-shaped building in the Georgian style, built under the direction of Henry Craskell (*fl*1760s), the government engineer; after a fire (1925) it was restored around the remaining façade. Both buildings are in brick with stone dressings. Nineteenth-century plantation houses include Rose Hall (rest. 1969), St James; Marlborough, Manchester; and Bellevue, St Andrew (all c. 1770–80). Built in ashlar masonry, with regularly spaced sash windows with and without jalousies, they show increasingly Neo-classical features, such as the tetrastyle portico at Marlborough.

Falmouth, a port founded on the north coast at the end of the 18th century, remains the most complete Jamaican colonial urban environment. Most of the buildings were constructed in the early 19th century. While some brick houses with their small entrance porches exhibit the influence of the Queen Anne style, Barrett House (1799), with its colonnaded verandah on the street front supporting an enclosed, boarded upper storey, is more typically Caribbean Georgian style. Other notable buildings in

4. Courthouse, Falmouth, 1815, restored 1926

Falmouth include the school (1815; formerly the barracks), the elegant classical Courthouse (see fig. 4) and the Caribbean Georgian church (1795).

When plantation society declined following Emancipation few new mansions were built. The basic characteristics of Jamaican architecture remained unchanged, however, until well into the 19th century. Devon House (1881), Kingston, successfully adapted the English Neo-classical style with a pilastered façade complemented by a colonnaded verandah. Vernacular architecture developed along similar lines to the chattel house found elsewhere in the Caribbean. Many of these small timber houses are concentrated in the Falmouth area. They retain the Georgian sense of proportion in a symmetrical façade with a central door and a window on either side. Front porches are often trimmed with white-painted 'gingerbread' fretwork, echoed by railings and white-painted roof crests. The side windows are often protected by 'coolers' or awnings.

Little construction took place during the first decades of the 20th century following the degeneration of the sugar industry, which was compounded by the worldwide depression. It was only during the post-World War II period with the beginning of the tourist industry that architectural activity again increased. Many of the new buildings constructed from the 1950s were holiday homes, such as Ocean View, Reading, which incorporated the ruins of an old stone warehouse with jalousied windows to create a simple bungalow, and Casa del Sol, Reading, a low-lying villa, with jalousied windows and doors opening

on to a wide, covered terrace. In the 1980s local artists and architects were involved in a lively debate concerning their collaboration to enhance the Jamaican lifestyle: the architect Patrick Stranigar's designs for the Jamaican Conference Centre (1985), Kingston, involved experimentation with traditional materials to produce such elements as acoustic baskets, wicker ceiling tiles and macramé sound baffles as part of his search for a Jamaican architectural iconography.

BIBLIOGRAPHY

T. A. L. Concannon: 'Houses of Jamaica', *Jamaica J.*, i/1 (1967), pp. 35–9

Buildings in Jamaica, Jamaica Information Service (Kingston, 1970)

V. Radcliffe: *The Caribbean Heritage* (New York, 1976)

D. Buisseret: *Historic Architecture of the Caribbean* (London, 1980)

P. Grosner: *Caribbean Georgian: The Great and Small Houses of the West Indies* (Washington, DC, 1982)

S. Slezin and others: *Caribbean Style* (London and New York, 1985)

P. Stranigar: 'Art in Architecture', *A. Jamaica*, iv/2 (1985), pp. 24–35

M. Holden: 'Acoustics: Handcrafted in Jamaica—Jamaica Conference Centre', *Archit. Rec.*, clxxiv/12 (1986), pp. 134–7

ALISSANDRA CUMMINS

IV. Painting, graphic arts and sculpture.

Little remains on the island of the material culture of Jamaica's Amerindian population (*see* §II, 1 above), while the Spaniards themselves left little of artistic merit. The most important remains are the New Seville Carvings (Kingston, N.G.; see fig. 6 below), a group of architectural friezes and ornaments carved by European craftsmen in local limestone and probably intended to adorn the

Governor's residence in the former capital of Sevilla La Nueva (now New Seville). In contrast, the English colonizers left a rich heritage of 18th- and 19th-century art. Of particular interest is the monument in Portland stone (1784–6) to *Admiral Rodney* by the English sculptor John Bacon the elder in the main square in Spanish Town. The nearby cathedral and other churches on the island boast some fine examples of Neo-classical funerary sculpture by Bacon, John Flaxman and others. The important paintings of the period were produced by itinerant artists, such as the Englishman George Robertson (1748–88), who drew and painted in Jamaica and on his return to England published six aquatints of Jamaican landscapes. James Hakewill (1778–1843) produced a collection of 21 aquatint views published in 1825, while Joseph Bartholomew Kidd (*d* 1889) published 50 hand-coloured lithographs, including *Views of Jamaica*. Of particular interest is Isaac Mendes Belisario (?1795–1849), who settled in Jamaica in 1835; he produced portraits of prominent citizens, some fine landscapes and several topical lithographs chronicling important national events (see also fig. 3 above). During the 19th century several American painters arrived in Jamaica, notably Ralph Albert Blakelock, Frederick Edwin Church and Martin Johnson Heade, all of whom painted fine Jamaican landscapes.

A truly Jamaican art, however, did not begin to develop until the early 20th century. What is commonly called the Jamaican Art Movement is usually considered to have begun in 1922, the year that the young EDNA MANLEY, who was born and had studied in England, arrived in Jamaica, where her mother had been born. Manley immediately identified with Jamaica and in the 1920s and 1930s produced an impressive body of heroic carvings, notably a series that monumentalized Jamaican womanhood. Beginning with the carving *Negro Aroused* (1935; see fig. 5), her work was given a political edge as she became intimately involved with the developing nationalist political movement spearheaded by her husband, Norman Manley. Other artists emerged during the late 1930s, notably ALBERT HUIE and ALVIN MARRIOTT, who were either directly inspired by Manley's work or encouraged by her active efforts to forge a truly Jamaican art.

A watershed year in Jamaica's political development, 1938 was also important to the development of Jamaican art: the first All Island Exhibition of Art and Craft was staged, with great success. By 1940 the Institute of Jamaica in Kingston (est. 1876), prompted by the fervour of this burgeoning art movement, established classes. Manley was one of the prime movers behind this initiative and was among the early tutors. Through these classes, several new artists came to the fore, including RALPH CAMPBELL, DAVID POTTINGER and Henry Daley (1918–50). Although instructed in essentially European naturalistic and Post-Impressionist styles, these artists were inculcated with the nationalist ethos and the need for the development of an indigenous iconography. By 1950 the classes were institutionalized into the Jamaica School of Art and Craft. Several important artists also developed outside the Manley orbit and the institute. They included GLORIA ESCOFFERY, CARL ABRAHAMS, RONALD MOODY, NAMBA ROY and the first of Jamaica's Intuitive painters, JOHN DUNKLEY, a unique visionary.

5. Edna Manley: *Negro Aroused*, mahogany, h. 635 mm, 1935 (Kingston, National Gallery)

The 1960s and 1970s were periods of both entrenchment of traditional values and of marked experimentation. While BARRINGTON WATSON developed a figurative style rooted in 19th-century academicism, KARL PARBOOSINGH and EUGENE HYDE drew on more recent styles, in particular a figurative expressionism and Abstract Expressionism. This latter 'American import' (as it was viewed, suspiciously, by some) also found favour with Milton Harley (*b* 1936) and KOFI KAYIGA. Other 20th-century movements were also belatedly established at this time. Surrealism, for example, found a ready breeding-ground in the work of painter COLIN GARLAND and of sculptor Winston Patrick (*b* 1946), whose biomorphic forms later gave way to illusionistic abstractions in wood. Hope Brooks, another abstractionist, developed a highly personal style, which relies on subtle textural effects within limited All-over painted canvases. DAVID BOXER also utilized marked textural effects but to different ends. Espousing what were termed New Imagist ideas, born of an investigation of such European figurative artists as Francis Bacon and Dubuffet, Boxer created icons of a doomed post-nuclear civilization. After the outstanding example of Dunkley, several Intuitive artists of undeniable talent surfaced, principally the true *naïfs* Gaston Tabois (*b* 1931) and SIDNEY MCLAREN, and three highly inventive artists steeped in local folklore and traditions, whose works at times moved into mysterious mystical realms: KAPO

(Mallica Reynolds), EVERALD BROWN and Albert Artwell (*b* 1942).

In the late 1970s MILTON GEORGE, a fine colourist inspired by Matisse and Parboosingh, emerged as a major painter; during the 1980s his work took on a marked satirical edge as more weighty subjects entered his repertory. Also during the 1980s a wave of younger artists came to prominence, many of them graduates of the Jamaica School of Art. Especially notable was a loosely defined Neo-expressionist group who drew heavily on the New Imagist trends of Boxer and the more recent developments of Milton George. The finest of these include Robert Cookhorne (*b* 1960). A more abstract approach combined with textural interests also characterized the work of many young female graduates of the Jamaica School of Art, for example Margaret Chen, who returned to Jamaica after spending nearly a decade studying in Canada. Several important Intuitive artists also came to attention in the 1980s, notably William Joseph (*b* 1919), with his elemental 'Neo-African' carvings, and Leonard Daley (*b c.* 1930), whose paintings are filled with wildly expressionistic grotesques.

BIBLIOGRAPHY
The Intuitive Eye (exh. cat., intro. D. Boxer; Kingston, N.G., 1979)
P. Beshoff: 'Namba Roy: Maroon Artist and Writer', *Jamaica J.*, xvi/3 (1983), pp. 34–8
Jamaican Art, 1922–1982 (exh. cat., by D. Boxer, Washington, DC, Smithsonian Inst.; Kingston, N.G.; 1983)
P. Bryan: 'Towards an African Aesthetic in Jamaican Intuitive Art', *A. Jamaica*, iii/3–4 (1985), pp. 2–11
P. Archer Straw and K. Robinson: *Jamaican Art* (Kingston, 1990)
D. Boxer: *Edna Manley: Sculptor* (Kingston, 1990)

DAVID BOXER

V. Interior decoration and furniture.

In Jamaica, as elsewhere in the Caribbean, the simple huts built by the first Spanish colonists in the early 16th century had little decoration and few furnishings. The inner walls of these timber buildings were plastered with mud, the floor covered with lime concrete. Little remains of the basic furnishings constructed to traditional Spanish designs. The Spaniards were, however, quick to adapt the woven cotton hammocks of the Amerindians to their own use. The New Seville Carvings (see fig. 6), doorjambs associated with the Governor's Mansion in Sevilla la Nueva (now New Seville), are redolent of an Italianate or Spanish Renaissance grotesque style, with confronting foliate scrolls and local bird motifs. These carvings remain the only known examples of such decoration of the period, as interior decoration was clearly limited in less exalted households.

The migration of planters from the Lesser Antilles, and particularly Barbados, during the second half of the 17th century almost certainly influenced early interior decoration and furniture design in Jamaica. Jamaican inventories for these early plantation houses (the 'Great Houses') suggest generally smaller buildings than those in Barbados during the same period. The interior rooms probably included a large hall, one or more parlours, a dining-room, several service rooms and the master's chamber on the ground floor. The remaining chambers, rarely more than three in number, were situated upstairs, while the kitchen was generally in a separate building behind the house.

6. New Seville Carvings, doorjamb, limestone, h. 1.37 m, *c.* 1530 (Kingston, National Gallery)

Dunn suggested that the best rooms in the house might have been wainscoted, painted or covered with hangings. As with English houses of the same period, the hall remained the centre of activity. Accounts for Bybrook Plantation include the purchase of some dozen cane chairs for the Great House. By the end of the 17th century, however, absentee landlords began to return to London. Thus, the impetus for creative design in furnishing and decorating the Great Houses became more or less stagnant, despite the accumulated wealth of the plantocracy.

Inventories dating from 1674 to 1701 record the presence of skilled and semi-skilled workers in Port Royal, including cabinetmakers, glaziers, carpenters and joiners. The wealthiest sugar planters also built town houses in Port Royal, often larger and more elaborately furnished than the plantation houses. John Taylor recorded (1688) that 'the merchants and Gentry live here to the hight [sic] of splendor in full ease and plenty'. An inventory for the six-room house of the Port Royal shoemaker John Waller listed three beds, a hammock, ten chairs, four stools, four tables, one desk, four chests, two carpets used to cover the tables, two pictures and two mirrors. Inventories of more wealthy households include cabinets inlaid with ivory and tortoiseshell, floral satin chairs, two harpsi-chords, looking-glasses, oil paintings and framed maps. The hall was often furnished with 50 to 60 chairs and several tables. Few surviving houses, however, predate the 19th century, and none has completely original furnishings to indicate how the interiors were arranged.

While evidence exists of a thriving local furniture industry, the record books of Waring & Gillow Ltd of England record an increasing export trade to the Caribbean during the 18th century, and by 1770 the Jamaican trade exceeded that of any other island. The large range of mahogany items in demand between 1745 and 1785 included billiard and backgammon tables, Pembroke tables, Windsor chairs, pier tables, bed pillars carved in the 'Gothic stile', wardrobes and close stool chairs. Two cases of paper hangings listed such patterns as 'Border No. 1: Black and white on stone; Border No. 17: Sprig on straw, Bengall and sprig on blue, and stripe green on crimson'. In most cases, however, the furniture was sent specula-tively, with only a few pieces sent in response to a specific order. By the end of the 18th century the growing number of absentee landlords and the decline in the sugar industry resulted in the virtual disappearance of this prosperous trade with Jamaica.

The interior of the Great House at Good Hope (c. 1755) possesses some fine Neo-classical woodwork. Bryan Castle (c. 1750) is noted for its interior staircase, fine woodwork and classical doorframes executed in stucco. Old King's House (1762; destr. 1925), Spanish Town, impressed observers with its classical proportions and huge reception hall (h. 9.75 m). It was lavishly decorated with a gallery to the west, and archaeological evidence has revealed frag-ments of painted wall plaster decorated with a black-and-white geometric stencil design consisting of a trellis motif and a lineal dot design. Edward Long, describing the ballroom in 1774, stated that:

> the great saloon . . . is well proportioned; being seventy-three by thirty feet and the height about thirty-two: from the ceiling, which is coved, hung two brass gilt lustres. A screen of seven large Doric pillars, divides the room from an upper and lower gallery of communication, which range the whole length on the West side, and the upper is secured with an elegant entrelas of figured iron work. The East [side] . . . is finished with Doric pilasters; upon each of which are brass girandoles double-gilt.

During the 19th century the pre-eminence of the merchant class led to the development of elegant house-holds and country seats. In 1825 James Hakewill described the interior of Rose-Hall (c. 1770), St James, noting that on the left of the entrance hall:

> is the eating-room, and on the right the drawing room, behind which are other apartments for domestic use. The right wing, fitted up with great elegance, and enriched with painting and gilding, was the private apartment . . . and the left wing is occupied as servants' apartments and offices. The principal staircase, into the body of the house, is a specimen of joinery in mahogany and other costly woods seldom excelled, and leads to a suite of chambers in the upper storey.

The naturalist Philip Gosse's description (1844–5) of Phoenix Park offers a vivid account of a typical building:

> Jamaican houses are commonly built on one principle. . . .the furnished part of the house is all on the same level. . . .a visitor [enters through] the front door, [into] a spacious hall, of the form of a cross, extending the whole length and breadth of the house. This large hall is the characteristic of all Jamaican houses, it forms the principal sitting room. . . .the two square areas formed by one side of the cross are filled by bedrooms; but with these exceptions the whole of the sides and ends of the hall are either occupied by windows, or open, and furnished with jalousies. . . .this large and cool apartment is furnished with a cross, ottomans, tables, chairs etc, not differing from ours; but there is no fireplace, nor any carpet. Instead of the latter the floor is made of the most beautiful of the native woods, in the selection of which much taste is often displayed, as also in arrangement, so that the various colours of the wood may harmonize or contrast well with each other. Mahogany, green-heart, breadnut and blood-heart are among the trees whose timber is employed for floors.

Devon House, Kingston, built by George Stiebel in 1881, was refurbished in the 1960s in the style of a late 19th-century Great House. The furnishings are of both European and Caribbean manufacture. The ballroom has round low-relief cherub decorations in the plasterwork ceiling, and a rare Meissen porcelain chandelier hangs in one of the bedrooms. In the dining-room, two ornately carved sideboards and two cellarettes are typical of 19th-century mahogany West Indian pieces. The dining table and chairs are 20th-century reproductions of Chippendale geometric pattern pieces originally owned by a Jamaican family. Government House, Kingston, was described by James Froude in 1888 as having:

> long airy darkened galleries, and into these the sitting rooms open, which are of course still darker with a subdued green light. . . .the floors are black, smooth, and polished, with loose mats for carpets. All the arrangements are made to shut out heat and light. The galleries have sofas to lounge on.

During the early 1870s T. N. Aguilar established Agui-lar's Furnishing Warehouse in Kingston, importing heavy horse-hair Victorian furniture from the United Kingdom and offering a cabinetmaking service that had developed by the 1930s into one of the most successful furnishing businesses in Jamaica. Similar concerns, such as Fenton's Cabinet Establishment (est. 1919) and the Jamaica Furni-ture Co. Ltd, (est. 1928) also flourished during the 1930s, employing local craftsmen to produce furniture in cedar, pine and mahogany. This furniture was much influenced by the severe simplicity of contemporary British Art Deco design. Master craftsmen such as Thomas Theophilus Jackson (1888–1983), originally apprenticed to the Scottish firm of Kearn Brothers, continued to command a faithful following until well into the 1960s. His Neo-Victorian, intricately carved mahogany furniture was extremely pop-ular. John Dunkley, as well as producing highly individual paintings and carvings, also decorated furniture in brilliant enamel colours with representations of flowers, leaves and fruit. The first interior design business in Jamaica was also established in the 1930s, when Cayman Islander Burnett

Webster (1909–92) began to design contemporary furniture and interiors. Much influenced by European Art Deco, his designs show close affinities with the work of sculptor Edna Manley and artist Koren Der Harootian (b 1909), with whom he exhibited during this period. Webster's Decorator's Store (1933–9), which received attention abroad, carried his line of finely crafted furniture designs, often carved and detailed by the young sculptor Alvin Marriott. From the mid-20th century the furnishing of Jamaican interiors has generally been the result of the successful marketing of items of European and American manufacture, although a small minority continue to support the efforts of Jamaican artists and fine craftsmen. The establishment of Things Jamaican in the early 1980s by a government agency formed to stimulate the development of craftsmanship remains a popular source for reproductions of Jamaican antiques. The Life of Jamaica Building (1983), Kingston, has contributed to the prestige of Jamaican design. The interior, designed by Hester Rousseau, employs natural local materials and Jamaican craftsmanship. The sisal wall hanging with copper accents, the abstract mahogany wall sculpture, and the mahogany and brass boardroom door were all created by the Jamaican sculptor Winston Patrick (b 1946).

BIBLIOGRAPHY

B. Edwards: *History, Civil and Commercial, of the British Colonies in the West Indies*, 2 vols (London, 1793)

P. H. Gosse: *A Naturalist's Sojourn in Jamaica* (London, 1851)

C. S. Cotter: 'Discovery of the Spanish Carvings', *Jam. Hist. Rev.*, iii (1948), pp. 227–33

W. A. Roberts: *Old King's House, Spanish Town* (Kingston, 1959)

K. E. Ingram: 'The West Indian Trade of an English Furniture Firm in the 18th Century', *Jam. Hist. Rev.*, iii/3 (1962), pp. 22–37

J. Richards: 'The Chandeliers from Old King's House, Spanish Town', *Jamaica J.*, i/1 (1967)

R. S. Dunn: *Sugar and Slaves: The Rise of the Planter Class in the English West Indies, 1624–1713* (Chapel Hill, 1972)

The Formative Years: Art in Jamaica, 1922–1940 (exh. cat. by D. Boxer, Kingston, N.G., 1978)

Devon House: Guide to the Collection (Kingston, 1984)

N. James: 'T. T. Jackson: A Tribute to One of Jamaica's Master Craftsmen', *A. Jamaica*, iii/1–2 (1984)

S. Dello Strologo: 'Devon House: The House of Dreams', *Jamaica J.*, xvii/2 (1984), pp. 33–40

'Corporate Collection', *A. Jamaica*, iv/1–2 (1985)

VI. Ceramics.

Excavations in the late 20th century at the Old King's House, Spanish Town, revealed a large collection of ceramics, including 16th- and 17th-century Spanish maiolica, Delftware, ceramics from the Wedgwood factory in England, as well as quantities of Chinese porcelain. Excavations in the 17th-century town of Port Royal also uncovered numerous sherds of large water-jars. These jars may possibly have been manufactured locally and have salt-glazed interiors, unglazed exteriors with white-painted rims, and with striped and ladder designs on the body and handles of some wares. Excavations at Spanish Town also revealed evidence of a ceramic folk tradition dating primarily from the 18th century, when the majority of African slaves arrived in the island. These vessels were clearly influenced by West African ceramic traditions, primarily Akan in origin. The number of handmade pots found in dated sites are convincing evidence of the evolution of an indigenous ceramic tradition, which blended European and possibly Arawak influences with African features and forms to produce an identifiable Afro-Jamaican ware by the second half of the 18th century.

Mathewson suggested that two distinct types of earthenware were produced concurrently for both the European and African communities. The vessels for the European market were flat-bottomed, often lead glazed, with strap handles. Pots of African derivation were more often hemispherical with a round base, and unglazed tureens, carafes, saucers and cooking-pots were among the wares produced. Simple, decorative designs were sometimes incised on the surface of these vessels, and one earthenware bowl exhibits pseudomorphs of rivets imitating contemporary European metal cooking-pots. Of more interest, however, are the isolated geometric motifs, which may represent a type of maker's mark, evidence, perhaps, of even greater specialization than has so far been documented. The Afro-Jamaican ceramic tradition continued throughout the 19th century and remains well established in the 20th. Most Jamaican kitchens still contain a monkey jar (see fig. 7) and a *yabbah*. Ma Lou [pseud. of Louisa Jones] (1916–92) was the best-known modern producer of traditional hand-coiled pottery; her cooking-pots, coal stoves and *yabbahs* are highly regarded as a fine craft in Jamaica.

During the 1920s Cecil Baugh (b 1908) worked in the traditional hand-coiled technique. In 1936, in association with Wilfred Lord, he formed the Cornwall Clay Works in Montego Bay, which operated until 1941. He continued to experiment with new glazes, forms and designs during

7. Earthenware monkey jar by Cecil Baugh, h. 355 mm, 1984 (Kingston, National Gallery)

the 1940s. In 1948 Baugh received a British Council scholarship for his first formal training with Bernard Leach at St Ives in Cornwall, England. Following his return to Jamaica in 1950, he became Ceramics Tutor at the newly formed Jamaica School of Art and Craft in Kingston, a position he held for 24 years. Recognized as the pioneer of modern ceramics on the island, Baugh was the recipient of many national awards. His work was a major influence on most of the major contemporary ceramicists, including Gene Pearson (*b* 1946), Jean Taylor-Bushay (*b* 1948), Norma Rodney Harrack (*b* 1947), Donald Johnson (*b* 1948) and Bella Johnson, the Clonmell Potters, Philip Bryan and David Dunn (*b* 1954). Walford Campbell is a young artist who has gained prominence in the last decades of the 20th century. With Marguerite Stanigar and Margaret McGluie, who have opted for a Post-Modernist approach, they represent an exciting new direction in Jamaican ceramics.

BIBLIOGRAPHY
R. D. Mathewson: 'Jamaican Ceramics', *Jamaica J.*, vi/2 (1972), pp. 54–6
P. Cumper: 'Cecil Baugh, Master Potter', *Jamaica J.*, ix/2–3 (1975), pp. 18–27
N. Harrack: 'Ceramics in Jamaica: An Overview', *A. Jamaica*, iii/1–2 (1984), pp. 8–11
C. Baugh and L. Tanna: *Baugh: Jamaica's Master Potter* (Jamaica, 1986)
Jamaica J., xxiv/1 (1991), pp. 23–31
V. Poupeye-Rammelaere: *Personal Communication* (Jamaica, 1992)

VII. Metalwork.

There is little evidence of sources of precious and base metals in Jamaica. Black asserted, however, that

> at the time of the discovery the Indians in the Greater Antilles were found to possess some gold in the form of ornaments. Most of this appears to have been produced in Haiti and Puerto Rico, finding its way to the other islands in the course of trade. Jamaica had very little gold and such as there was the Indians collected by a simple method [from the river].

The earliest Spanish settlers adopted similar methods in their mining operations on the banks of the Rio Minho, near the Longville Estate at Clarendon. Within a few years of their arrival the Spaniards had also assiduously collected by exchange much Arawak gold and many ornaments.

Metals necessary for the consolidation of settlement were imported into the island from the 16th century, to be worked by the skilled craftsmen who settled for that purpose. After the English took control of the island in 1655, Jamaica provided a strategic base from which to launch attacks on the Spanish Empire. Much of the wealth of the island was acquired as a result of buccaneering activities that were eventually based at Port Royal. Henry Morgan's raids on Porto Bello, Panama, in 1667, and Panama City in 1671 were two such exercises. The latter raid on the royal houses, the Governor's Palace, the Law Courts and the Treasury, filled with gold and silver from Peru, netted the buccaneers over 750,000 pieces of eight and brought extraordinary wealth into Jamaica. It found a ready market among the thriving community at Port Royal. Over the next few decades the city rapidly developed as the trading centre and chief market of the island. Francis Hanson offered a contemporary description of the city at its zenith in 1682:

> Port Royal, being as it were the Store or Treasury of the West Indies, is always like a continual Mart or Fair where all sorts of choice Merchandizes are daily imported, not only to furnish the island, but vast quantities are thence again transported to supply the Spaniards, Indians, and other nations, who in exchange return us bars and cakes of Gold, wedges and pigs of Silver, Pistoles, Pieces of Eight and several other Coyns of both Mettles, with store of wrought Plate, Jewels, rich Pearl Necklaces, and of Pearl unsorted or undrill'd several Bushels; besides which, we are furnished with the purest and most fine sorts of Dust Gold from Guiney. . .some of which our Goldsmiths there work up, who being yet few grow very wealthy, for almost every House hath a rich Cupboard of Plate, which they carelessly expose.

Excavations of the sunken Port Royal site have also revealed the existence of quantities of pewter artefacts (Kingston, N.G.), evidence of the skilled pewterers who supplied the burgeoning population. Jamaican inventories of the 17th and 18th centuries confirm the extensive use of pewter plates, flatware, candlesticks and bowls in the majority of households. By the late 17th century a number of large firms were engaged in the importation of silverware and bullion.

Another art form that emerged during the late 17th century was that of etched and inlaid tortoiseshell cases and boxes for wigs and combs. Examples in the Cunda collection (Kingston, N.G.) are richly decorated with floral designs reminiscent of English crewel-work of the period. Reputedly inspired by the patronage of Lady Lynch, the Governor's wife, this work seems to have been produced mainly at Port Royal. At least two distinct styles have been identified, using such motifs as local trees and Amerindian and armorial designs, which can be seen in finely engraved silver mounts. Only one craftsman, Paul Bennett, has been positively identified, being the only maker of combs listed among the Port Royal craftsmen in 1763.

Despite conditions or war and serious internal problems in the early 18th century, the beginning of prosperity in Jamaica and the rise in power and wealth of the Creole proprietors occurred during this period. Also at this time Kingston developed, as did the lavish lifestyle of the privileged, supported by the development of the sugar industry. Wealthy planters, for example Samuel Long and the Governor, Sir Thomas Lynch, lived ostentatiously. Lynch's silver service consisted of some 42 dishes and plates, 44 spoons and forks, and an assortment of candlesticks, basins, condiment pots and beakers, and was valued at £361.

In 1760 the young English coppersmith John Reeder arrived in Jamaica in the company of a local property owner, who encouaged him to start his own foundry operations. By 1772 Reeder had prospered sufficiently to acquire land in St Thomas-in-the-East for the purpose of erecting mills 'with a waterwork for the smelting and other manufactures of iron and other metals'. Various descriptions confirm that the foundry worked both iron and non-ferrous metals, including copper, brass and lead, producing items that ranged from iron boilers and rollers to lead bullets, brass howitzers, mortars and petards, and providing the general outfitting for British warships and other vessels. Skilled foundry-workers included English craftsmen as well as African–Jamaicans. Reeder surmised that

'Africans were perfect in every branch of the iron manufacture so far as it relates to casting and turning...and in wrought iron'. It success was short-lived, however, as by 1782 the Governor-General ordered that the foundry be dismantled in the face of a threatened invasion of the island. By this period a hallmark representing a crocodile's head had been established for Jamaica. A cruet with three vase-shaped castors (*c.* 1750; Kingston, Devon House) by Charles Allan bears this mark. While it is clear that, stylistically, metalworkers followed trends established in England, there is some evidence to suggest that silversmiths in Jamaica adopted local motifs in their work. J. Ewan (*fl* early 1800s) is known to have used a breadfruit motif on flatware of that period.

During the first decades of the 20th century some large firms, for example L. A. Henriques and Swiss Stores, continued to employ qualified craftsmen to produce small items and jewellery, but the majority of their stock was imported from Europe. During the 1930s C. A. Scott, a lumber and hardware merchant, established an ironworks at Montego Bay that produced domestic and industrial iron, brass and other metals. The emphasis, however, remained largely on imports. The establishment of the Jamaica School of Art in 1950, however, did much to foster a renewal of interest in local design. Along with tutoring and designing at the jewellery workshop at the Polio Rehabilitation Center, the Edinburgh-trained silversmith Pat Byer acted by 1968 as external examiner for jewellery at the School of Art. For two periods in the 1970s she was also tutor in jewellery at the school. Through these activities, and with the establishment of her studio in the early 1960s, Byer played a significant part in the development of metalworking in the island. In 1984 her presentation piece to Queen Elizabeth II (see fig. 8) re-established Jamaica's hallmark of a crocodile. The Jamaica School of Art, now the Edna Manley School for the Visual Arts, continues to play an influential role under the leadership of the master goldsmith Garth Sanguinetti, who was trained by the Gorman company in the USA. Some of the school's more recent and active graduates include Ralf Bender, Hugh Bromfield, Paul Henriques, Philip Cadien, Georgia Brown and Jasmine Girvon.

BIBLIOGRAPHY
C. V. Black: *History of Jamaica* (London, 1958, 2/1983)
I. Baxter: *The Arts of an Island* (Metuchen, 1970)
R. F. Marx: *Report on Silver and Pewter Recovered from the Sunken City of Port Royal, Jamaica* (Kingston, 1971)
R. S. Dunn: *Sugar and Slaves: The Rise of the Planter Class in the English West Indies, 1624–1713* (Chapel Hill, 1972)
C. Goucher: 'John Reeder's Foundry: A Study of 18th-century African–Caribbean Technology', *Jamaica J.*, xxiii/1 (1989), pp. 39–43

ALISSANDRA CUMMINS

VIII. Patronage.

In the 18th and 19th centuries rich landowners sought the service of artists to paint portraits and to document the picturesque 'views' on their plantations. In the 1770s, for example, the English artists George Robertson (1748–88) and Phillip Wickstead (*fl* 1763–86) were brought to the island in the employ of the wealthy English landowner William Beckford. The colonial government also commissioned British sculptors to execute monuments, such as John Bacon the elder's monument to *Admiral Rodney*

8. Pat Byer: *Jamaica Box*, sterling silver studded with jadeite, agate, carnelian and amethyst, 355×317 mm, 1983 (British Royal Collection)

(1784–6), commemorating his victory in the Battle of the Saints, and Edward Hodges Baily's monument to *Sir Charles Metcalf*, Governor of Jamaica from 1839 to 1842. In the 20th century the Church was an important patron of contemporary artists, beginning with Edna Manley's *Crucifix* (1950) for All Saints Anglican Church in Kingston. Several works by Manley, Alvin Marriott, Osmond Watson, Karl Parboosingh and Christopher Gonzalez, among others, may be found in churches, principally in Kingston.

Direct state patronage increased dramatically following independence (1962) and the consequent desire adequately to portray the new heroes of Jamaica and to commemorate their deeds. The most important works include the statues of *Sir Alexander Bustamante* (1972) and of *Norman Manley* (1971) in the Parade Square, Kingston, the *Garvey* statue in St Anns Bay, the *Bob Marley* statue (1985) in Kingston and the *Don Quarrie* statue at the National Stadium, all by Alvin Marriott; the *Sam Sharpe* monument by Kay Sullivan (*b* 1944) in Montego Bay; the *Paul Bogle* statue (1965) in Morant Bay by Manley; and the panels on the tomb of *Norman Manley* (1975) at the National Heroes Park, Kingston, by Christopher Gonzalez. By the late 20th century patronage was private, corporate and institutional.

IX. Collecting and dealing.

Until 1974, when the National Gallery was established, public collecting of Jamaican art was restricted to the activities of the Institute of Jamaica in Kingston. In 1974 the Institute's collection of 20th-century works was transferred to the National Gallery, while 18th- and 19th-century works were transferred to the National Library. The National Gallery's collection has since grown dramatically; by the mid-1990s it housed over one thousand works. Apart from its principal collection of Jamaican art, it has a small international collection, which includes mainly 20th-century Caribbean, British and American works. With the acquisition of Edna Manley's *Land* in 1948, the University of the West Indies in Kingston began a programme of collecting, which has proved, however, to be erratic, as have the collecting habits of many of the corporations that boast collections.

The principal private collector of the 1960s and 1970s was A. D. Scott, who acquired hundreds of works that virtually define the backbone of mainstream art of the period. In 1990 Scott donated 40 key works to the National Gallery. During the 1980s there was a marked increase in the number of private collectors, including Wallace Campbell. Through both local and international purchases, Campbell amassed not only a major Jamaican collection, but also an important Caribbean group, principally of Haitian and Cuban paintings.

Privately owned galleries are responsible for most sales of artwork in Jamaica. In general they exhibit a cross-section of artists of various styles and reputation with little specialization. Harmony Hall in Ocho Rios, however, demonstrated an allegiance to the Intuitives, while Frame Centre Gallery in Kingston has tended to concentrate on essentially modernist artists, for example Kofi Kayiga and Milton George.

DAVID BOXER

X. Museums.

The National Gallery of Jamaica in Kingston was founded in 1974 as a division of the Institute of Jamaica. Some 380 modern Jamaican works were then transferred from the Institute, including Edna Manley's *Negro Aroused* (1935; see fig. 5 above), the first modern Jamaican work to be acquired by the Institute (1937). In 1979 the National Gallery curated the landmark exhibition *Intuitive Eye*, bringing together the works of such Jamaican artists working outside the mainstream as Everald Brown and Kapo. Since 1974 the size of the permanent collection has more than tripled. The Gallery's policy is to spend its small acquisitions budget only on Jamaican art. Acquisitions are supplemented by loans and donations from artists, collectors, public institutions and corporations. About a quarter of the collection is on permanent display in an installation that focuses on the development of modern Jamaican art. This includes such specialized galleries as the Larry Wirth Collection of work by Kapo, and the A. D. Scott Collection of modern Jamaican art. There is also a display of pre-20th-century Jamaican art and a small international collection. New galleries that are planned are the Edna Manley Memorial Gallery, a ceramics gallery and a photography gallery. The gallery presents an average of four to five exhibitions each year and offers educational services. Originally located in Devon House, Kingston, the National Gallery moved in 1982 to the Roy West Building, a modern building that is rented by the government. Plans exist for a Cultural Centre in New Kingston, which will include a permanent National Gallery building. In St Catherine, the Arawak Indian Museum includes a reconstruction of a typical pre-conquest Caribbean dwelling.

BIBLIOGRAPHY
'The National Gallery of Jamaica', *Jamaica J.*, xvi/4 (1983), pp. 29–36

XI. Art education.

In the 1940s art classes were held at the Junior Centre of the Institute of Jamaica. In 1950 the Jamaica School of Art was founded, largely through the efforts of artist Edna Manley and Institute of Jamaica officials Philip Sherlock and Robert Verity. The school has fostered both the fine arts and design. Originally small and rather informal, it has grown into a fully accredited tertiary-level institution, with a total student population of *c.* 500. The majority are Jamaican, but the school also attracts foreign students, mainly from the English-speaking Caribbean. In 1976 the School became a part of the Cultural Training Centre campus, located in the New Kingston area, together with the schools of dance, drama and music. In 1987 the School was renamed the Edna Manley School for the Visual Arts.

BIBLIOGRAPHY
Forty Years: Edna Manley School for the Visual Arts, 2 vols (exh. cat. by V. Poupeye-Rammelaere, Kingston, N.G. and Edna Manley Sch. Visual A., 1990)

VEERLE POUPEYE

Jamal al-Din ibn 'Abdallah al-Mawsuli Yaqut al-Musta'simi. *See* YAQUT AL-MUSTA'SIMI.

Jamalgarhi [Jamālgarhī]. Buddhist monastery on a small hill 13 km from Mardan, north-east of Peshawar, Pakistan, which flourished from *c.* AD 100 to *c.* 400. The site was discovered by Alexander Cunningham in 1848. In 1852, two British officers, Stokes and Lumsden, searched unsuccessfully for relics in the main stupa and collected sculptures (destroyed in the Crystal Palace fire, London, 1866). Major excavations were undertaken by the Punjab government in 1873 and by the Archaeological Survey of India in the 1920s. The finds are now divided between museums in Pakistan, India and England (Pakistan: Peshawar Mus., Lahore Mus.; India: Chandigarh, Govt Mus. & A.G.; Calcutta, Ind. Mus.; Patna Mus.; Bombay, Prince of Wales Mus.; Lucknow, State Mus.; England: London, BM and V&A).

Only the circular base of the main stupa survives, encircled by a ring of 15 chapels. Stairs lead to a lower rectangular courtyard containing votive stupas and shrines and descend again to a second courtyard. These areas produced the majority of schist sculptures from the site. Stucco figures were also found on the main stupa and chapel façades. The principal buildings include a series of halls but no monastery. Instead, separate terraced units, each comprising several houses, shrines and a stupa, extend across the steep escarpment of the site. Diaper masonry is used throughout, except for a few earlier rubble walls, and the so-called Conference Hall, which is built in a transitional style between diaper and semi-ashlar masonry. The most important inscription from Jamalgarhi is a stone slab dated in the year 359 of an unspecified era. KUSHANA coins have also been found, the earliest from Kanishka I with issues of Vasudeva I and his successors predominating. The latest coins found are silver issues of Kidara.

See also INDIAN SUBCONTINENT, §IV, 5(i).

UNPUBLISHED SOURCES
New Delhi, Cent. Archaeol. Lib. [attached to Govt Body Archaeol. Surv. of India] and London, BL, Orient. & India Office Lib. [Phot. cols of the Archaeol. Surv. India, Frontier Circ. The photographs are listed in

Frontier Circ. annu. rep. London, BL, Orient. & India Office Lib. holdings: (1902–4), serial nos 44–7; (1907–8), nos 172–6; (1908–9), nos 394–5, 398–9; (1911–12), nos 1005–6; (1920–22), nos 1814–28, 1849–1961]

BIBLIOGRAPHY

E. C. Bayley: 'Notes on Some Sculptures Found in the District of Peshawar', *J. Asiat. Soc. Bengal*, xxi (1852), pp. 606–21

A. Cunningham: *Archaeol. Surv. India Rep., 1872–3*, v (Simla, 1875), pp. 46–53

H. Hargreaves: 'Excavations at Jamālgarhī', *Archaeol. Surv. India, Frontier Circ.* (1920–21), pp. 2–7, 20–28 and *Archaeol. Surv. India Annu. Rep.* (1921–2), pp. 54–62

——: 'Conservation and Clearance at Jamālgarhī', *Archaeol. Surv. India Annu. Rep.* (1922–3), pp. 19–22; (1923–4), pp. 16, 19–22

E. Errington: *The Western Discovery of the Art of Gandhāra, and the Finds of Jamālgarhī* (diss., U. London, SOAS, 1987)

E. ERRINGTON

Jambukola. *See* DAMBULLA.

James I [James VI], King of England and Scotland. *See* STUART, House of, (2).

James, C(harles) H(olloway) (*b* Gloucester, ?1893; *d* London, 8 Feb 1953). English architect and writer. He received his formative architectural training as assistant to Edwin Lutyens and later Barry Parker and Raymond Unwin. His subsequent career epitomized the continuation of the Neo-classical tradition in English architecture during the 1920s and 1930s, particularly in housing. Immediately after World War I he became involved in domestic architecture, much of it for municipal clients. He designed several housing schemes in the early 1920s, including Dellcot Close (1922), Welwyn Garden City, and Swanpool Garden Suburb (1919), Lincoln. Swanpool was characteristic of the Neo-Georgian influence of the City Beautiful movement that the Liverpool School of Town Planning had exerted on the government housing programmes of the inter-war period. The houses were designed as simple brick boxes relieved by tall chimneys and bell cast roofs, laid out around cul-de-sacs and avenues radiating from a central square. James prepared urban plans for Norwich and Leamington Spa, and he lectured widely on the subject as well as being the author of a number of influential publications. He also made a contribution to public building with his Norwich City Hall (1932–8; with S. Rowland Pierce (1896–1966); see ENGLAND, fig. 12), a modern interpretation of the classical theme that drew obvious parallels with the city hall (1911–23) in Stockholm.

His designs for Slough Town Hall (1934–6; partly executed) and Hertford County Hall (1939) also show a Scandinavian influence. The house he designed for himself, Hornbeams (1939), Hampstead, London, received much attention for its restrained but elegant Neo-Georgian exterior and interior planning.

WRITINGS

with F. R. Yerbury: *Small Houses for the Community* (London, 1924)
Modern English Houses and Interiors (London, 1925)

BIBLIOGRAPHY

R. Philips: 'An Architect's Own House: Hornbeams, Hampstead', *Country Life*, lxxxvi (5 Aug 1939), pp. 124–5

Obituary: *Archit. J.*, cxvii (1953), p. 214; *RIBA J.*, lx (1953), p. 206

James, Charlie [Jameson, Charles; Yakuglas] (*b* Port Townsend, WA, *c.* 1870; *d* Alert Bay, BC, 1938). Native American Kwakiutl wood-carver. He was the son of Kugwisi'la'ogwa, a Kwakiutl woman from Fort Rupert, BC, and a white American sawmill owner from Port Townsend. When his mother died in 1877, he was adopted by her tribe and inherited the right to work as a wood-carver, receiving training from a kinsman. As a child, James's left hand was injured in a shotgun accident, and he probably began carving because he was unable to participate in other activities. He was one of the first Kwakiutl wood-carvers to establish a reputation outside his own society, and he is best known for the hundreds of small totem poles he carved for sale to non-natives in the last 20–30 years of his life. James also produced traditional objects, including totem poles and masks, for use in potlatches and other Kwakiutl social events. The mask of *Sisiutl*, the dangerous 'double-headed serpent' (before 1914; Victoria, BC, Prov. Mus.; see fig.), for example, was used in the Tlásulá ('weasel dance'), one of the two principal ceremonial complexes in Kwakiutl society. James was instrumental in establishing what might be termed the Fort Rupert substyle of Southern Kwakiutl art, introducing new forms and the use of colour (*see* NATIVE NORTH AMERICAN ART, §III, 2). This substyle, distinct from the more flamboyant style of such wood-carvers of the Blunden Harbour–Smith Inlet area as Charles George, jr and the Seaweed family (*see* SEAWEED, WILLIE), was further developed and elaborated by his stepson MUNGO MARTIN (Naka'pankam). James's stepdaughter Ellen Newman Neal (Kakasolas, 1916–66) also learnt carving from him.

Charlie James: mask of *Sisiutl*, the double-headed serpent, painted wood, before 1914 (Victoria, BC, Provincial Museum)

BIBLIOGRAPHY

The Legacy: Continuing Traditions of Canadian Northwest Coast Indian Art (exh. cat. by P. L. Macnair, A. L. Hoover and K. Neary, Victoria, BC, Prov. Mus., 1980)

P. Nuytten: *The Totem Carvers: Charlie James, Ellen Neal, Mungo Martin* (Vancouver, BC, 1982)

MARTINE REID

James, Edward (Frank Willis) (*b* Chichester, Sussex, 16 Aug 1907; *d* Xilitla, Mexico, 2 Dec 1984). English patron and collector. He inherited his fortune from his mother and spent it on the arts. He remodelled and redecorated Monkton House (West Dean Estate, Chichester), built for his parents by Sir Edwin Lutyens, with a collection that included the sofa designed by Salvador Dalí, *Mae West's Lips*, and *The Metamorphosis of Narcissus*; Magritte's *La Reproduction interdit* (a portrait of James); Leonora Carrington's *Cock Crow*; Delvaux's *Prostitutes*; Bérard's *On the Beach*; Pavel Tchelitchew's *Edith Sitwell*; and many other works by Eugene Berman, Ernst, Tanguy, and other artists of the Surrealist and Neo-Romantic circle. To occupy his wife, the dancer Tilly Losch, he commissioned *Les Ballets 1933*, produced in Paris and London; *Die Sieben Todsünden* by Bertolt Brecht and Kurt Weill; *Les Songes* by Darius Milhaud, and others, with décors by Bérard, Dalí and Tchelitchew.

After an acrimonious divorce, James led a peripatetic life in North America, finally settling at Xilitla in the Mexican jungle, where he designed and built a series of fantastic towers. He paid for the preservation of Watts Towers in Los Angeles, a ceramic fantasy built by Simon Rodia between 1921 and 1954. James endowed West Dean Park as a crafts college and intended to establish an arts foundation, but in 1986 his trustees sold his collection (at Christie's & Co., London) amidst great controversy. James wrote a number of books, including a novel, *The Gardener Who Saw God* (London, 1932), with illustrations by Tchelitchew, and two books of poems, *The Next Volume* (London, 1932), illustrated by Rex Whistler, and *The Bones of My Hand* (Oxford, 1935).

BIBLIOGRAPHY

P. Purser: *Where Is He Now?* (London, 1978)

G. Melly: *Swans Reflecting Elephants* (London, 1982)

C. Aslet and G. Stamp: *Monkton: A Vanishing Surrealist Dream* (London, 1986)

PHILIP CORE

James, Henry (*b* New York, 15 April 1843; *d* London, 28 Feb 1916). American writer, naturalized British in 1915. Taken to Europe as a child, he visited its museums and on his return to America briefly studied painting under William Morris Hunt. His early fiction shows the effect of further visits to Europe in 1869–70 and 1872–4. During the 1870s he wrote art criticism and short stories for various American periodicals; 30 of his articles on art (1868–97) are reprinted in J. L. Sweeney's *The Painter's Eye* (London, 1956). He was among the first to appreciate Burne-Jones and wrote with authority on all the traditional schools of European painting but was dismissive of Impressionism, until his *American Scene* (1907), in which he praises Impressionist works he had seen in Farmington, MA (priv. col.). In 1876 he took up permanent residence in London and after 1885 paid annual visits to the American painters Frank Millet (1846–1912), Edwin Austin Abbey and Sargent in Broadway, Worcs. James wrote about Sargent's work in *Picture and Text* (New York, 1893), which also includes an essay on Daumier. The theme of his novel *The Tragic Muse* (1890), written during this period, is the seriousness of the painter's vocation. He was commissioned to write *William Wetmore Story and his Friends* (Boston, 1903), although he did not like Story's sculpture. Works of art continue to appear in the late fiction as metaphors. In *The Golden Bowl* (1905) a pagoda, Holman Hunt's *Scapegoat* (Port Sunlight, Lady Lever A.G.) and a crystal bowl are central to the plot; the pagoda, a symbol of mystery, stands for the adultery that Maggie Verver senses but has no proof of until the flawed bowl, a symbol of her marriage and an object revealing her husband's adultery, is broken. James anticipated Proust in his appreciation of Vermeer in *The Outcry* (1909). Sargent painted James's portrait on the occasion of the latter's birthday in 1913 (London, N.P.G.).

BIBLIOGRAPHY

V. H. Winner: *Henry James and the Visual Arts* (Charlottesville, 1970)

A. R. Tintner: *The Museum World of Henry James* (Ann Arbor, 1986)

——: *Henry James and the List of the Eyes: Thirteen Artists in his Fiction* (Baton Rouge, 1993)

ADELINE TINTNER

James, Isaac (*fl* 1600; *d* after 1624–5). English sculptor of Dutch descent. The James family is said to have come from the town of Haastrecht, near Gouda, and to have established a branch in England during the reign of Henry VIII (1509–47). Isaac was a tomb sculptor resident in the parish of St Martin-in-the-Fields, Westminster, from 1600 until 1624/5. He is first recorded in partnership with Bartholemew Atye (*d c.* 1617), a sculptor of the City of London with whom he made the monuments to *Sir Edward and Lady Denny* (1600–01; Waltham Abbey, Essex) and *Sir Richard Kingsmill* (1601–2; Highclere, Hants, St Michael's). Both are typical of their time and country with their stiffly posed, expressionless effigies and coarsely carved ornament. His sole authorship of the dignified memorial to *Henry, Lord Norris* and his family (*c.* 1611; London, Westminster Abbey) is known from a legal battle with the man who undertook to paint and gild it. Norris and his wife are shown recumbent, with their sons kneeling life-size on either side of them, beneath an eight-poster canopy with an upper stage adorned by military reliefs and surmounted by a figure of Fame. This upper stage is probably derived from a temporary triumphal arch erected by the Italian merchants of London for the ceremonial passage of James I through the City in 1604.

Isaac James's other major work was the monument to *Sir Thomas Walmesley* (1613–14; Blackburn, Lancs., St Mary's), which was destroyed during the Civil War. The sculptor's pupil Nicholas Stone the elder gave him what was probably just a minor part to play when he made him his 'partner . . . in cortisay' in the memorial to *Henry Howard, Earl of Northampton* (1615–16; Dover, Kent, formerly St Mary in Castro; largely destr.).

BIBLIOGRAPHY

M. Whinney: *Sculpture in Britain, 1530–1830*, Pelican Hist. A. (Harmondsworth, 1964, rev. by J. Physick, 1988), pp. 55–6

ADAM WHITE

James, John (*b* ?1673; *d* Greenwich, 15 May 1746). English architect, surveyor and writer. He was educated by his father in Basingstoke, Hants, before being apprenticed to the king's Master Carpenter, Matthew Banckes. From Banckes he received his training as carpenter and surveyor and must have worked at Hampton Court Palace and Chelsea Hospital, London, and on private houses. James's association with Banckes (and his marriage to Banckes's niece, Hannah, in 1697) laid the foundations of his style and his circle of contacts with other surveyors and craftsmen.

James earned his reputation as one of the most experienced and dependable surveyors of his time, undertaking a variety of work—carpentry, measurement, supervision, inspection and advice, designing and any combination of these. His earliest recorded employment was at the Royal Hospital for Seamen, Greenwich, in 1699, as assistant clerk of works. He designed little, but his association there with Nicholas Hawksmoor was an important influence on his early work, and the buildings at Greenwich were a lasting source of inspiration. He worked there until his death, eventually succeeding to Hawksmoor's post. He was also surveyor to St Paul's from 1723 and Westminster Abbey from 1725 and was consulted about the restoration of other cathedrals.

In 1716 he became surveyor to the Commissioners for the 1711 Act for Building Fifty New Churches in London, through whom he received many of his ecclesiastical commissions. Of eight churches attributable to him, the most impressive is St George's (1721–5), Hanover Square, London. It is faced in stone and features his interpretation of the hexastyle temple front. A more modest church is St Mary's (1714–15), Twickenham, near London, in finely laid brick, with giant Doric pilasters in stone supporting pediments on each side. He favoured simple shapes and rectangular plans, following Christopher Wren and Inigo Jones.

James designed large and small country houses for a wide circle of patrons drawn from his contacts in Hampshire and London. Although Banckes was grounded in Restoration architecture, James was at his most impressionable during the brief development of the Baroque in England. His earliest known country house, at Herriard (1703–6, destr. 1965), Hants, reflected this dual influence.

In 1711 James was one of the first to set out in writing (Oxford, Bodleian, MS. Rawl.B376, fols 8–9) ideas on plainness and restraint, perhaps inspired by French architectural treatises and exemplified by Inigo Jones. These ideas emerged transformed a few years later as the basis for a Palladian revival.

However, James evolved a plain style of simplified Baroque, which is seen in his own house, Warbrook (1724), at Eversley, Hants. Conservative in temperament, he moved only slowly to accommodate some elements of Palladian design, as illustrated in a later house, Standlynch (now Trafalgar House; 1731–4), near Downton, Wilts. Wricklemarsh (1723–4, destr. 1787), Blackheath, Kent (now London), was exceptional in his work, being wholly in the style of Jones. James, who was adept at producing what his patrons required, built Wricklemarsh for a wealthy businessman who probably wanted to be as fashionable as possible.

He translated three books: Andrea Pozzo's *Rules and Examples of Perspective Proper for Painters and Architects* (1693; trans. 1707), Claude Perrault's *A Treatise of the Five Orders of Columns in Architecture* (1683; trans. 1708 and 1722) and Antoine-Joseph Dezallier d'Argenville's *The Theory and Practice of Gardening* (1709, 1722; trans. 1712 and 1728). Although this last translation has led to James's name being associated with garden design, the only known documented instance of such work was at Swallowfield, Berks, where he designed a bathhouse and supervised canal building (1718–26).

BIBLIOGRAPHY
Colvin
K. Downes: *English Baroque Architecture* (London, 1966)
J. Brushe: 'Wricklemarsh and the Collections of Sir Gregory Page', *Apollo*, cxxii (1985), pp. 364–71
S. R. Jeffery: 'John James and George London at Herriard: Architectural Drawings in the Jervoise of Herriard Collection', *Archit. Hist.*, xxviii (1985), pp. 40–70
——: 'An Architect for Standlynch', *Country Life*, clxxix (13 Feb 1986), pp. 404–6
——: *English Baroque Architecture: The Work of John James* (diss., U. London, 1986)
J. Brushe: 'Some Designs by John James', *The Georgian Group Journal* (1994), pp. 4–10
SALLY JEFFERY

James, M(ontague) R(hodes) (*b* Goodnestone, Kent, 1 Aug 1862; *d* Eton, Berks, 12 June 1936). English scholar and art historian. He was educated at Eton College and King's College, Cambridge, and was Director of the Fitzwilliam Museum (1893–1908), Provost of King's College (1905–17), Vice-Chancellor of Cambridge University (1913–15) and Provost of Eton College (1918–36). His prodigiously extensive work was in three main areas: the study of apocryphal biblical writings, cataloguing of medieval manuscripts and the study of iconography in all forms of art. In the field of apocryphal writings his work was mainly on those of the New Testament, on which he published the standard collection of texts in English translation, *The Apocryphal New Testament* (Cambridge, 1924). His cataloguing of the medieval manuscript collections of Eton College Library (Berks), the Fitzwilliam Museum and colleges of Cambridge, Westminster Abbey and Lambeth Palace, London, John Rylands University Library of Manchester, and the University of Aberdeen Library has given him a lasting reputation. His strong interest in iconography ensured that in his catalogues that aspect of the manuscripts was always accurately described. He published studies of the iconography of Apocalypses, Bestiaries, the Saints' Lives, the narrative cycles of the Old and New Testaments and of apocryphal texts. He was mainly interested in English material, and he published many facsimiles of English illuminated manuscripts with exhaustive commentaries. Although his catalogues, by modern standards, have some limitations, the body of his published work laid the foundations for all subsequent study of English manuscript painting and medieval iconography.

WRITINGS
The Sculptures in the Lady Chapel at Ely (London, 1895)
A Descriptive Catalogue of the Manuscripts in the Library of Corpus Christi College, Cambridge (Cambridge, 1911)
The Treatise of Walter de Milemete (London, 1913)
The Bestiary (Cambridge, U. Lib., MS. Ii.4.46) (Oxford, 1928) [facs.]
The Apocalypse in Art (London, 1931)

The Canterbury Psalter (London, 1935) [facs.]
'Pictor in carmine', *Archaeologia*, xciv (1951), pp. 141–66

BIBLIOGRAPHY
R. W. Pfaff: *Montague Rhodes James* (London, 1980) [with full bibliog.]

NIGEL J. MORGAN

James of St George (*fl* 1261; *d* 1309). Savoyard mason and military engineer. He was employed by Edward I to design castles in Wales and Scotland and was one of the most significant figures in the history of 13th-century military architecture. His long career has been ingeniously reconstructed by A. J. Taylor from the household rolls of the counts of Savoy and the English royal building accounts.

1. Life. 2. Works. 3. Influence.

1. LIFE. James of St George was first heard of in 1265 assisting his father in the building of Yverdon Castle in Savoy from 1261 to *c.* 1271. From 1271 to 1275 he worked at a number of other Savoyard castles including Chambéry, Chillon and Voiron. The most important commission before his departure for England in 1276, and the one from which he derived his name, was the castle of St Georges-d'Espéranche for Philip I, Count of Savoy.

He is recorded in the English royal building accounts in 1278 directing the work at the castles of Flint and Rhuddlan in north Wales, the earliest of a chain of fortresses that Edward I built as part of three military campaigns mounted in response to the Welsh uprisings of 1276, 1282 and 1294. Throughout this period and until his death Master James was in overall charge of the building works. Claims by earlier scholars that he was simply an administrative official were effectively dismissed by Taylor in 1950, and it now seems certain that his was the creative mind behind all Edward's Welsh castles. The documentary record of his English career is incomplete, but he was involved in the works at Ruthin and Denbigh in October 1282, and in the accounts prepared for 1283–6 for the castles of Caernarfon (*see* CAERNARFON CASTLE), Conwy, Criccieth and Harlech in Gwynedd he is described as 'Master of the King's Works in Wales'. In 1284 he was receiving a high level of pay unprecedented in the Royal Works. In 1284–5 he is documented building the royal apartments at Conwy Castle, and he was in Gascony with Edward I between 1286 and 1289. On his return to England he was further rewarded for his outstanding service by his appointment as constable of Harlech Castle for the period 1290–93. The revolt of the Welsh prince Madoc in 1294 led to renewed work on Caernarfon Castle and town walls directed by James's deputy, WALTER OF HEREFORD, as well as the construction of a new fortress at Beaumaris. Only for Beaumaris do the accounts actually describe James of St George as master of the work. Two years later Edward turned his attention to war in Scotland, and in 1302 Master James was with him receiving instructions for the strengthening of Linlithgow Castle, Lothian. He was also present at the siege of Stirling Castle in 1304. By 20 May 1309 he was dead.

2. WORKS. Master James's work in Savoy has been altered by later hands, but the remains of the castle of St Georges-d'Espéranche show it to have been a symmetrical rectangle, the corners of which were marked by tall, octagonal towers. His other Savoyard castles had the more usual round towers, and the use of the multangular shape at St Georges probably symbolizes its special role as the palace (*palacium*) and favoured residence of Count Philip. In choosing this form, he and Master James were perhaps following the example of Frederick II, whose favourite Castel del Monte (1240) in southern Italy was distinguished from the other Hohenstaufen castles there by its centralized polygonal plan. The counts of Savoy were the vassals of the English king, and their mountainous domain was not unlike the upland country of Wales and Scotland, over which Edward I was to reassert his power in the coming years. Edward's employment of James of St George accords well with the long-established tendency of the English court to look to France for architectural inspiration. That so much authority in architectural matters should be given to a foreigner is partly a reflection of the significant Savoyard presence in Edward's administration and partly a recognition that the conquest of Wales and Scotland could only be secured with the aid of a master mason familiar with the most advanced military technology and accustomed to warfare in mountainous regions.

Flint and Rhuddlan (1277–*c.* 1282), built to secure supply lines from Chester along the north Welsh coast, are among the most perfect castle plans of their time. Flint is a quadrangle reinforced by three round towers and a massive cylindrical donjon, set in a moated quadrant, which was intended to guard the main gate and provide a strongly defended place of ultimate retreat. In Edward's castles it initiates the principle of concentrating accommodation and defensive strength at the gates, and it is similar to earlier French fortifications, notably the Tour de Constance (*c.* 1249) at Aigues-Mortes and the donjon of Coucy Castle (1225–42). Rhuddlan (see fig. 1a), the earliest of Master James's concentric castles, is entirely different: its rhomboid inner bailey is entered by twin-towered gatehouses at the oblique angles while the dry moat, revetted in stone, is commanded by the lower, outer curtain wall. With the building of Harlech (see figs 1b and 2) the concentric idea was applied to an irregular square on a prominent site at the edge of a rocky sea-cliff. The inner bailey is a square clasped by round angle towers, while its landward curtain wall straddles a large, powerful keep-gatehouse containing some of the principal apartments. Quadrangular castles of precisely this type had already been built in France (e.g. Dourdon, Essone, *c.* 1220) and the twin-towered gatehouse is a typically French feature also found at Péronne, Somme, and Angers in the mid-13th century.

The use of concentric defences, however, seems to have originated in the Middle East, the principle deriving from earlier Byzantine fortifications such as the 5th-century walls of Constantinople; some of Master James's applications of this and other devices are close enough to the antique models to suggest direct imitation rather than intervention of derivative medieval models. This is especially true of Caernarfon Castle (*see* CAERNARFON CASTLE, fig. 1), where Taylor has argued that the Theodosian defences of Constantinople were copied with remarkable accuracy.

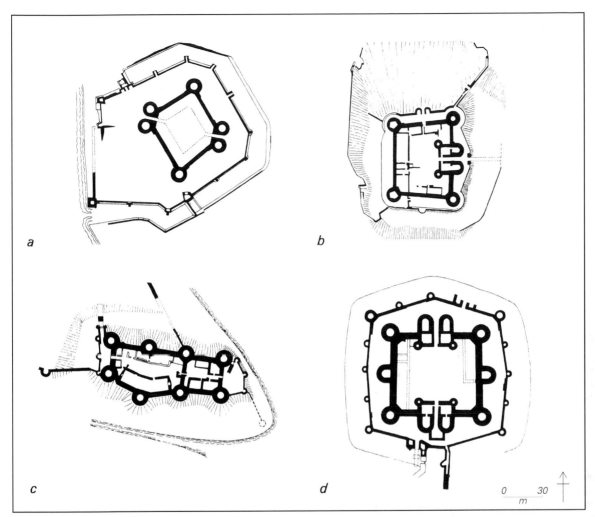

1. James of St George: plans of castles: (a) Rhuddlan, 1277–*c*. 1282; (b) Harlech, 1283–95; (c) Conwy, 1283–9; (d) Beaumaris, 1295–1300 (outer curtain wall, 1309–30)

Master James's special genius for exploiting topography is seen at Conwy (see fig. 1c above). Here he displaced a Cistercian abbey, the precincts of which occupied a defensible rock spur projecting into the Conwy estuary, and built a formidable rectangular castle of two adjacent baileys punctuated by eight round towers, two at the western and eastern extremities protecting gates leading into a pair of barbicans. This represents a partial but effective application of the concentric principle to a constricted site. The castle forms the strongest point in an impressive circuit of town walls built to protect the English burgesses whom Edward was settling in a series of planned towns, after the model of southern French *bastides* such as Aigues-Mortes and Carcassonne. The town and castle of Caernarfon (1283–1327) were laid out in a similar fashion, and the treatment of the town walls is close to those of Conwy. In the castle, however, the polygonal towers and walls are striped in broad bands of light and dark masonry marking it out from the rest of the Edwardian group; speculation that these features, bearing on its political function and symbolic meaning, implied the hand of someone other than Master James, has been effectively countered (Taylor, 1953). While it now seems safe to credit Master James with the general layout of the castle, it cannot be proved that he supervised the first phase of construction (1283–92) before the appointment of Walter of Hereford as master of the work for the second phase in 1295; indeed, masonry details of the castle suggest that Hereford might have been executant architect of the early work as well.

Beaumaris, Gwynedd, built after the uprising of 1294 to consolidate the English conquest of Anglesey, has a flat, clear site that allowed the building of a beautifully symmetrical, concentric fortress in which the inner ward, defended by a pair of large gatehouses and six towers, rises above a more lightly built outer curtain wall (see fig. 1d above). The castle was never completed, but the inner curtain was the main work of the period 1295–1300. The distinctive octagonal outer curtain with its cycle of 16 towers was carried out between 1309 and 1330, after Master James's death but to his designs (*see* MILITARY ARCHITECTURE AND FORTIFICATION, fig. 10).

2. James of St George: Harlech Castle, 1283–95, view from the south

The handsome, austere castle chapels at Conwy and Beaumaris are both strongly influenced by the Rayonnant style. The only more ambitious religious building with which James of St George is known to have been involved is the new Cistercian abbey of Maenan, Gwynedd, established by Edward to replace the convent at Conwy in 1283. He dealt with the conveyance of the land but the subsequent demolition of the buildings has removed any evidence that might support or refute his responsibility for their design.

3. INFLUENCE. Master James's work was undoubtedly an important factor in the development of castle design throughout the British Isles around 1300. His documented works in Scotland have not survived but the gatehouse of Kildrummy Castle (after 1303), Grampian, is similar to that at Harlech, and it could be influenced by James's work. Within the Royal Works, Chirk (?after 1308) in north Wales has a plan similar to the inner ward at Beaumaris; the inner bailey of the King's castle at Beeston (after 1300), Cheshire, uses its topographical advantages in exactly the same way as Harlech and has a similar gatehouse, while the royal castle of Roscommon in central Ireland, rebuilt from 1278 to 1284, is an obvious relative of Harlech and Flint. The gatehouses of Edward I's alterations to the castles of Chester (1292–3; destr.) and Corfe (1280–85), Dorset, were of the twin-towered type, which Master James established as a standard element of his work; the feature recurs in the smaller royal castles of St Briavel's (1292–3), Glos, and Rockingham (c. 1280–90), Northants. Similar Edwardian gatehouses can be found in several castles outside the sphere of the Royal Works, for example Tonbridge (c. 1300), Kent; Powis (early 14th century), Powys, NT; and Dunstanburgh (1315), Northumb. The appearance in early 14th-century England of a type of fortified residence similar in certain respects to St Georges-d'Espéranche is also noteworthy and can

perhaps only be explained in terms of Master James's influence. The early examples are poorly preserved but the remains of the country palace of Edward's Chancellor, Bishop Walter Langton, at Eccleshall (1310–c. 1320), Staffs, are substantial enough to demonstrate the kinship, and the well-preserved Maxstoke Castle (1345), Warwicks, gives a good idea of how St Georges-d'Espéranche must once have looked.

Not all innovations in English late 13th-century fortification should be attributed to Master James. He cannot, for example, be credited with the introduction of the principle of concentric defence at Caerffili (c. 1268–71), Mid Glam. Master James appears not to have played a very significant role in transmitting the more decorative details of French Gothic to England, though it is conceivable that the square-headed and segmentally arched windows of Conwy and Harlech encouraged the use of these devices in Decorated church architecture (e.g. the chancels of Skipwith, N. Yorks, and Byfield, Northants).

BIBLIOGRAPHY

Harvey

A. J. Taylor: 'Master James of St George', *Eng. Hist. Rev.*, cclvii (1950), pp. 433–57

——: 'The Castle of St Georges d'Espéranche', *Antiqua. J.*, xxxiii (1953), pp. 33–47

H. M. Colvin, ed.: *The History of the King's Works*, 2 vols (London, 1963)

A. J. Taylor: 'Castle-building in Thirteenth Century Wales and Savoy', *Proceedings of the British Academy*, lxiii (1977), pp. 265-92

J. M. MADDISON

Jameson [née Murphy], **Anna Brownell** (*b* Dublin, 17 May 1794; *d* London, 17 March 1860). English writer of Irish birth. Her father, Denis Murphy (*d* 1842), was a miniature painter. The family moved to England in 1798; Jameson, substantially self-educated, worked as a governess between 1810 and 1825. Her first book, *Diary of an Ennuyée* (London, 1826), was based on a tour of Italy that she made as a governess, and it discusses both Classical sculpture and Renaissance painting. In 1825 she married

Robert Jameson, a barrister, but a series of colonial appointments, in the West Indies and then in Canada, combined with their basic incompatibility to keep them apart. In 1832 *Characteristics of Women*, two volumes of essays on Shakespeare's heroines, won her critical esteem, which was reinforced by the publication of *Visits and Sketches* in 1834. In this book, written after a trip to Germany during which she became acquainted with August Wilhelm Schlegel and Ottilie von Goethe, she introduced British readers to developments in contemporary art and the new German methods of organizing museum collections chronologically. It also deals with the professional identity of women artists, past and present. By now, her parents and unmarried sisters entirely depended on her for support.

Mrs Jameson began to specialize in art around 1840, and with her pioneering series for the *Penny Magazine*, subsequently republished as *Memoirs of the Early Italian Painters* (1845), she brought art history within the province of popular education. Her two guidebooks, *A Handbook to the Public Galleries of Art in and near London* (1842) and *Companion to the Most Celebrated Private Galleries of Art in London* (1844), set new standards of accuracy and sophistication. However, her most distinctive contribution lay in her historical approach to Christian symbolism in art. Conversant with German art history as represented by Carl Friedrich von Rumohr and the early works of Karl Schnaase, as well as with current French and Italian theories on art, she was fully aware that the art of the past was the product of cultural values very different from those of the present. Her four-part work, *The Poetry of Sacred and Legendary Art* (1848–64), was the first extended study of Christian iconography in English, which presupposed less that images were created to instruct the illiterate than that they were informed by popular 'legends' that interacted with doctrine. Her insight into mythopoeic modes and the distinction between latent and overt meanings in Christian legends and the art they inspired was similarly significant. This framework was underwritten by a wide knowledge of art, sureness of judgement and a graceful literary style, which helped to make her books both popular and widely influential.

WRITINGS

Diary of an Ennuyée (London, 1826)
Characteristics of Women, 2 vols (London, 1832)
Visits and Sketches at Home and Abroad, 4 vols (London, 1834)
A Handbook to the Public Galleries of Art in and near London (London, 1842)
Companion to the Most Celebrated Private Galleries of Art in London (London, 1844)
Memoirs of the Early Italian Painters, 2 vols (London, 1845)
The Poetry of Sacred and Legendary Art (London, 1848–64), in four parts: *The Poetry of Sacred and Legendary Art* (1848); *Legends of the Monastic Orders* (1850); *Legend of the Madonna* (1852); *The History of Our Lord as Exemplified in Works of Art*, 2 vols (completed by Lady Elizabeth Eastlake; 1864, rev. 2/1865)
G. H. Needler, ed.: *Letters of Anna Jameson to Ottilie von Goethe* (London, 1939)

BIBLIOGRAPHY

DNB
G. MacPherson: *Memoirs of the Life of Anna Jameson* (London, 1878)
C. Thomas: *Love and Work Enough: The Life of Anna Jameson* (Toronto, 1967)
——: 'Anna Jameson: Art Historian and Critic', *Woman's A. J.* (Spring/Summer 1980), pp. 20–22
A. M. Holcomb: 'Anna Jameson (1794–1860): Sacred Art and Social Vision', *Women as Interpreters of the Visual Arts, 1820–1979*, ed. C. R. Sherman and A. M. Holcomb (Westport, CT, and London, 1981)
——: 'Anna Jameson: The First Professional English Art Historian', *A. Hist.*, vi (1983), pp. 171–87
——: 'Anna Jameson on Women Artists', *Woman's A. J.*, viii (1987–8), pp. 15–24

ADELE M. ERNSTROM

Jamesone, George (*b* Aberdeen, ?1589–90; *d* Aberdeen, ?Nov 1644). Scottish painter. He was the first native portrait painter of real ability; his certain extant works are exclusively busts and half-lengths. His father, Andrew Jamesone, a successful and wealthy mason, enjoyed social and political connections with the Scottish nobility that were to serve his son well. Jamesone was apprenticed to the painter John Anderson in 1612 at the age of 22; this period of training seems to have ended by 1617, although Jamesone's earliest known work, a portrait of *Sir Paul Menzies of Kinmundy* (U. Aberdeen), dates from 1620. In 1624 he married the relatively wealthy Isabel Tosche and during the 1620s went on to produce numerous portraits of distinguished sitters. These include the attributed full-lengths of *John Leslie, 6th Earl of Rothes* (1625) and *Anne Erskine, Countess of Rothes, with her Two Children* (1626; both sold London, Christie's, 22 June 1973, lots 16–17; for illustration of lot 16 see Thomson, fig. 23), as well as *Mary Erskine, Countess Marischal* (1626; Edinburgh, N.P.G.; *see* SCOTLAND, fig. 8) and *Arthur Johnston* (*c.* 1629; U. Aberdeen). About this time Jamesone began to establish connections in Edinburgh, opening a studio there in 1633, although he never gave up his Aberdeen practice. When Charles I arrived in the capital for his coronation in 1633, Jamesone was involved in making triumphal decorations for the event, supplying a set of roughly worked and brightly coloured portraits of the king's ancestors (ex-Newbattle Abbey Coll., Lothian; sold Edinburgh, Dowell's, 2 July 1971). By 1634 he was acquainted with Sir Colin Campbell, 8th Laird of Glenorchy, who became an important patron, with the artist perhaps also advising on Campbell's art acquisitions. One notable series of pictures he made for Campbell is the *Ladies of Glenorchy* (e.g. Invereil House, Lothian; remainder dispersed at sale, Invereil House, 3 March 1969), a set of eight head-and-shoulders portraits, each in a feigned oval surround, of the wives of former Glenorchy lairds: these were intended as companion pieces to the genealogical set of Campbell's male predecessors that had been painted at his Taymouth home in 1633 by an unknown German artist.

In 1636 Jamesone took on John Michael Wright as his apprentice for five years. During this period he produced some of his own best works, including portraits of three brothers, *Sir David Carnegie, 1st Earl of Southesk*, *Sir John Carnegie, 1st Earl of Northesk* and *Sir Alexander Carnegie of Balnamoon* (all 1637; Kinnaird Castle, Tayside), as well as portraits of *Sir George Stirling of Keir* (1637) and his wife *Margaret Napier* (*c.* 1637; both Dunblane, Tayside, A. Stirling of Keir priv. col.). He also made a number of half-length self-portraits, in one of which (*c.* 1637; Aberdeen A.G.) he holds a miniature portrait and in another (*c.* 1637–40; ex-Cullen House, Grampian) depicts himself in his studio, one wall of which is hung with pictures that include a sea-piece and a large mythological picture, although no examples of work by Jamesone in either of these genres is known. Despite his success and substantial income, the growing political dispute between Charles I and the Church of Scotland was to make life increasingly difficult for Jamesone. The King's attempts to impose episcopacy on the Church led to Presbyterians organizing a national Covenant in opposition; the Bishops' Wars that followed were a prelude to the English civil wars of the 1640s. Aberdeen, caught in the crossfire, was for a time occupied in 1638. Jamesone was identified as an anti-Covenanter and spent the latter half of 1640 incarcerated in Edinburgh's Tolbooth. After his release he continued to take commissions, although his last portraits, for example *William Kerr, 3rd Earl of Lothian* (Yester House, Lothian) and that of his wife *Anne Kerr, Countess of Lothian* (Monteviot House, Borders), both painted in 1644, show a serious decline in quality. In September of that year many citizens of Aberdeen were killed when the city was sacked by anti-Covenanter forces, an event that may have contributed to Jamesone's own death shortly after.

BIBLIOGRAPHY

H. Walpole: *Anecdotes of Painting in England* (1762–71); ed. R. N. Wornum (1876), i, pp. 346–50
A. Cunningham: *The Lives of the Most Eminent British Painters, Sculptors and Architects*, v (London, 1832), pp. 1–33
J. Bullock: *George Jamesone: The Scottish Vandyck* (Edinburgh, 1855)
M. W. Brockwell: *George Jamesone and Some Primitive Scottish Painters* (London, 1939)
D. Thomson: *The Life and Art of George Jamesone* (Oxford, 1974)

DAVID CAST

Jamete, Esteban [Jamet, Etienne] (*b* Orléans, *c.* 1515; *d* Cuenca, Aug 1565). French sculptor and architect, active in Spain. He was the son of master mason Jamet Loxin and came to Salamanca in 1535. His work combines the Italian influence seen in French sculpture of the early 16th century with heraldic motifs of the Isabelline style, and these often merge harmoniously in a manner characteristic of Plateresque. He enriched the traditional biblical iconography with symbolic figures, myths and allegories and structured his compositions with a free use of architectural elements.

According to his statement to the Tribunal of the Inquisition in Cuenca on 26 April 1557, Jamete worked initially as a sculptor in Medina del Campo and then for the imperial secretary, Francisco de los Cobos, in Valladolid, where he was also active in the monastery of S Francisco. He executed works in Burgos Cathedral in collaboration with Felipe Vigarny, and in Toledo Cathedral (*c.* 1536) with Alonso de Covarrubias on the interior decoration of the mid-15th-century Puerta de los Leones, on the Renaissance chapel of S Juan (begun 1537; now Treasury) and on the choir-stalls (upper tier completed 1543). In Madrid he worked on the funerary monument of the *Bishop of Calahorra* (1539–40; Madrid, Mus. Arqueol. N.), and in Ubeda, Jaén, with Andrés de Vandelvira on the decoration of the Sacra Capilla, for Francisco de los Cobos (from 1540). In Seville in 1544–5 he worked in the monastery of Las Cuevas and for the municipality. From 1545 he lived in Cuenca, where he was active on sculptural and architectural commissions in the cathedral

and principal churches of the diocese. On 15 May 1558 he was sentenced to three years' imprisonment for violent behaviour and heresy, and, although released after a year, he spent the rest of his life under surveillance.

BIBLIOGRAPHY

J. Domínguez Bordona, ed.: *Proceso inquisitorial contra el escultor Esteban Jamete* (Madrid, 1933)
F. Chueca Goitia: *Arquitectura del siglo XVI*, A. Hisp., xi (Madrid, 1953)
——: *Andrés de Vandelvira, Arquitecto* (Jaén, 1971), pp. 117–25
M. L. Rokiski Lazaro: *Arquitectura del siglo XVI en Cuenca* (Cuenca, 1985)

CRISTIANO TESSARI

Jami, Domenico de. *See* AIMO, DOMENICO.

Jamnitzer. German family of gold- and silversmiths, sculptors, designers and draughtsmen. Hans Jamnitzer I (*d* Nuremberg, between 19 Dec 1548 and 13 March 1549), a goldsmith of Vienna, settled his family in Nuremberg, where his descendants worked successfully for at least three generations. The most notable member of the family was his son (1) Wenzel Jamnitzer I. In 1534 Wenzel married Anna Braunreuchin (*d* 1575), who bore him four daughters and seven sons, of whom three, Hans Jamnitzer II (1539–1603), Abraham Jamnitzer (1555–91/1600) and Wenzel Jamnitzer II (1548–72), also learnt the goldsmith's craft and worked in their father's establishment, together with his brother Albrecht Jamnitzer (*d* 1555). Only his grandson, (2) Christoph Jamnitzer, was his equal in artistic feeling and invention.

BIBLIOGRAPHY

M. Frankenburger: 'Beiträge zu Geschichte Wenzel Jamnitzers und seiner Familie', *Stud. Dt. Kstgesch.*, xxx (1901)
M. Rosenberg: *Jamnitzer: Alle erhaltenen Goldschmiedearbeiten, verlorene Werke, Handzeichnungen* (Frankfurt, 1920)
——: *Der Goldschmiede Merkzeichen*, iii (Frankfurt am Main, 1925), pp. 53–68, nos 3832–40
E. Kris and O. von Falke: 'Beiträge zu den Werken Christoph und Hans Jamnitzers', *Jb. Preuss. Kstsamml.*, xlvii (1926)
K. Pechstein: 'Jamnitzer-Studien', *Jb. Berlin. Mus.*, viii (1966)
G. Kuhr: 'Stammtafel des Familie Jamnitzer', *Mitt. Ver. Gesch. Stadt Nürnberg*, lxi (1974), pp. 122–128
K. Pechstein: 'Beiträge zu Jamnitzerforschung', *Anz. Ger. Nmus.* (1984), pp. 71–6
Wenzel Jamnitzer und die Nürnberger Goldschmiedekunst, 1500–1700 (exh. cat., Nuremberg, Ger. Nmus., 1985)
Schätze deutscher Goldschmiedekunst von 1500 bis 1920 aus dem Germanischen Nationalmuseum (exh. cat., ed. K. Pechstein and others; Nuremberg, Ger. Nmus., 1992)

(1) Wenzel Jamnitzer I (*b* ?Vienna, 1507–8; *d* Nuremberg, 19 Dec 1585). He is first recorded as a master goldsmith and a burgher of Nuremberg, and nothing is known of his apprenticeship. In 1543 he took up the post of engraver in the city mint and later held important honorary offices in Nuremberg, becoming a member of the Great Council in 1556 and the Small Council in 1573. His mark is the head of a lion *en face*, with the letter W beneath.

Few of Jamnitzer's early works are known, but they include the so-called *Ernestinischer Willkomm* (*c.* 1541; Coburg, Veste Coburg), composed of four superimposed vessels of differing sizes, which was commissioned by John-Frederick the Magnanimous, Elector of Saxony (1532–47). Jamnitzer's early works are characterized by ornamentation in the style of Peter Floetner, the arabesque motif playing an important part, constantly varied and combined with other ornamental forms, as is shown in the drawings in Jamnitzer's Berlin sketchbook (1545–6; Berlin, Kstbib. & Mus.). The sketchbook reveals Jamnitzer's capabilities as a graphic artist, and demonstrates that the style of Floetner's human figures, as well as that of his ornament, exercised a lasting influence on him; this is particularly evident in a charcoal drawing of a female figure personifying *Geometry* (1537; untraced) and signed WI.

In 1544 Jamnitzer was commissioned by the Holy Roman Emperor Charles V to make a ceremonial sword and sheath (coloured and signed drawing, Weimar, Schlossmus.), which were executed but lost in Spain at the beginning of the 17th century. The combination of arabesque ornament with figural decoration, including grotesques, masks and above all animal forms, anticipates the use of fully evolved classical ornament, for example friezes and caryatids, and plant and animal forms, cast from life, on his masterpiece, the *Mother Earth* centrepiece (1549; Amsterdam, Rijksmus.; see fig. 1). The stem is in the form of a caryatid, and the bowl is decorated with the most sumptuous ornament of cornucopia, masks, fabulous beasts, and figurative and natural forms. This work places him alongside the potter Bernard Palissy, the French representative of the *style rustique*. Jamnitzer, however, did not regard the courtly and the rural as in opposition but, in the tradition of Dürer, sought to unite natural forms with classical ornament. The centrepiece was commissioned by the city council of Nuremberg as a gift for Charles V or his son, later Philip II, King of Spain, but, contrary to expectations, neither returned to Nuremberg after 1549, and therefore the large cartouche in the Renaissance style on the underside of the foot, which must have been designed to contain a dedicatory inscription, remains blank.

Jamnitzer executed work for three other Habsburg emperors—Ferdinand I, Maximilian II and Rudolf II. For Maximilian II he made a silver saddle-bow (plaster cast, Basle, Hist. Mus.), a display casket (1570; Madrid, Mus. Monasterio Descalzas Reales) and the 'Emperor's Cup' (1570; Berlin, Tiergarten, Kstgewmus.). The last two may have been gifts presented to Maximilian by the city of Nuremberg on the occasion of his first visit in 1570. The ceremonial cup is in the most sumptuous late Renaissance style; the ornamentation of the lid includes a figure of *Maximilian II* with imperial insignia, crown, sword and sceptre, and four princes stand at his feet—Johann Jakob Khuen von Belasy, Archbishop of Salzburg (*reg* 1560–86), Veit von Würzburg, Bishop of Bamberg (*reg* 1566–77), Friedrich von Wirsberg, Bishop of Würzburg (*reg* 1558–72), and Albert V, Duke of Bavaria (*reg* 1550–79). This cup inaugurated a completely new type of commemorative piece, which re-emerged in the 19th century and was widely popular throughout Germany. The display casket was another of Jamnitzer's innovations. The introduction of architectonic forms for chests and display caskets such as that of 1570 are already evident in designs in his Berlin sketchbook.

Jamnitzer's earliest caskets were almost completely covered with silver foil, revealing the outlines of the wooden carcase, but his style later changed considerably: the decoration and carcase, the latter mostly of ebony,

1. Wenzel Jamnitzer I: *Mother Earth* centrepiece, silver gilt, h. 1 m, 1549 (Amsterdam, Rijksmuseum)

providing very striking colour contrast to the silver panels, were harmonized in a more balanced relationship, despite the use of over-elaborate decoration, and the figurative programme was widely extended, individual figures being placed within framed panels (e.g. casket, formerly Berlin; silver panels, now London, V&A). The casket made for Maximilian II, now used as a reliquary, bears Jamnitzer's full signature and the inscription *1570 Noric aurifaber Venclaus Gamnitzer, ista aeterni fecit ductus amore boni.* Preliminary designs, drawings and models of the casket are extant, including the lead casts on the Amerbach Kabinet (Basle, Hist. Mus.) and a model of *Fortitude* (*potentia*), one of the Virtues (Berlin, Tiergarten, Kstgewmus.). With his display caskets Jamnitzer introduced a tradition that was imitated and extended in Augsburg in the 17th century in large, ebony cabinets with applied decoration.

Another of Jamnitzer's important works was the ornamental Fountain of Prague commissioned by Maximilian II in 1568 and delivered to Rudolf II in 1578. This silver and gilt-bronze fountain (h. *c.* 3 m), surmounted by the imperial crown, was originally intended for the Neubau, the newly built part of Vienna, but was melted down in 1748. Only the four gilt-bronze figures (Vienna, Ksthist. Mus.) of *Flora*, *Ceres*, *Bacchus* and *Vulcan*, representing the Seasons, which supported the fountain, survive, although there is also a description by a student from Altdorf dating from the first half of the 17th century (Nuremberg, Ger. Nmus.). The form and decoration of the fountain represented an allegory of imperial power and the House of Habsburg, and it was similar to another executed in a different art form for Maximilian II, whose apotheosis is depicted in an engraving (1565–70; preliminary drawing, Vienna, Albertina) by Jost Amman.

In addition to the Habsburg emperors, Jamnitzer was also commissioned by the dukes of Bavaria, archdukes of Austria and the electors of Saxony. The figure of *Philosophy* on a writing-cabinet (1562; Dresden, Grünes Gewölbe), commissioned by Augustus I, Elector of Saxony, is reminiscent of the figure of *Tellus* on the famous salt of Francis I (1540–43; Vienna, Ksthist. Mus.) by Cellini; the Classical simplicity of the substructure is reminiscent of Etruscan sarcophagi. The lid of a writing-case (*c.* 1570; Vienna, Ksthist. Mus.; see fig. 2), made for Archduke Ferdinand

II of the Tyrol (1529–95) is divided into ten square compartments containing such tiny creatures, cast from life, as a snail, lizards, beetles, a shell, a frog and a mouse, while the sides are also covered with lifelike casts of small creatures, grasses and flowers. An unmarked table clock (1560; Munich, Residenz), probably commissioned from Jamnitzer by a duke of Bavaria, is profusely ornamented with lizards, tortoises and herbs etc, cast from life; a design for the piece is also extant (Berlin, Kupferstichkab.). Jamnitzer was always as fascinated by the possibilities of combining gold with other materials as by the combined use of different techniques of goldwork. This is evident in his cylindrical goblet (*c.* 1550; Nuremberg, Ger. Nmus.) for the Pfinzing family, with its conical-shaped, painted Venetian glass tapering at the bottom; a jasper bowl (1560–70; Munich, Residenz) with silver-gilt mounts; and in his ornamental ewer (*c.* 1570; Munich, Residenz; *see* SHELL, colour pl. I, fig. 1), the body of which consists of a trochus shell.

Jamnitzer is known to have executed work for Nuremberg patrician families; in the Imhoff family archives an account book, belonging to Andreas Imhoff, records deliveries of jewellery, cutlery, tableware and mugs by Jamnitzer to the family. A double drinking cup (dated 1564) for the Tucher family consists of two almost identical embossed goblets of neo-Gothic form; this was originally a wedding gift and bears the arms of the families of Tucher and Pfinzing on the inner side of each foot on round enamel medallions. Jamnitzer supplied silver-gilt mounts for some enamelled copper jugs dated 1562.

2. Wenzel Jamnitzer I: writing-case, silver, 60×227×102 mm, *c.* 1570 (Vienna, Kunsthistorisches Museum)

Jamnitzer made constant efforts to extend the creative possibilities of his workshop, for example by lavish decoration of a silver display casket, the juxtaposition of 'artificial writing-desks' containing a variety of mathematical and other specialized instruments, or the invention of new machines and devices, such as that for stamping ornamental borders. He also advocated the 'Columbine' cup as one of the standard admission masterpieces set by the goldsmiths' guild. As with his goldsmith's work, he exercised a decisive stylistic influence on the increasingly important craft of ornamental engraving, although few examples by him are known.

Jamnitzer's designs were engraved mostly by Virgil Solis (*see* SOLIS, (1)), Jost Amman and Matthias Zündt. Drawing played a significant role throughout Jamnitzer's career, and he was influenced by ornament from the Netherlands; in this connection his acquaintance with Erasmus Hornick of Antwerp, who lived for a period in Nuremberg, was especially fruitful. In his later years Jamnitzer devoted himself especially to the invention and manufacture of scientific and technical instruments, devising, for example, a standard calibrated gauge for metals. *Perspective* (1568; preliminary drawings, Berlin, Kupferstichkab. and Wolfenbüttel, Herzog August Bib.), dedicated to Maximilian II, documents this interest.

The importance that scientific and technical problems held for Jamnitzer may be seen from the fact that he was painted (1562–3; Geneva, Mus. A. & Hist.) by Nicolas Neufchâtel, holding in his left hand the calibrated metalgauge that he had developed. A portrait of Jamnitzer engraved by Amman shows him engaged in the projection of a geometrical body on to the two-dimensional plane of a page. The Nuremberg goldsmith Jakob Hofmann (1512–64) struck a commemorative coin with Jamnitzer's likeness in his own lifetime (dated 1563; see 1985 exh. cat., no. 629), and there are further portrait medallions (see 1985 exh. cat.) by Jamnitzer's son-in-law Valentin Maler (1540–1603), who probably also executed the bronze epitaph portrait (Nuremberg, Ger. Nmus.).

Jamnitzer's reputation as the foremost German goldsmith for many years rested entirely on the *Mother Earth* centrepiece, which remained in Nuremberg until 1880; by the 1920s, however, many scholars emphasized his wideranging oeuvre. His work received an impressive and comprehensive appreciation in the exhibition held at the Germanisches Nationalmuseum, Nuremberg, in 1985 commemorating the 400th anniversary of his death.

ADB; *NDB*

BIBLIOGRAPHY

M. Engelmann: 'Mathematische Instrumente Wenzel Jamnitzers', *Mitt. Sächs. Kstsamml.*, v (1914)

E. Kris: 'Der Stil "Rustique": Die Verwendung des Naturabgusses bei Wenzel Jamnitzer und Bernard Palissy', *Jb. Ksthist. Samml. Wien*, n. s., i (1926), pp. 137–208

P. Kupf: *Jamnitzer an den von ihm konstruierten Perspektivapparat sitzend, von J. Amman: mehrere Medaillen von H. Bolsterer und V. Maler*, cf. G. Habich: *Die deutschen Schaumünzen des XVI. Jahrhunderts* (1931)

E. W. Braun: 'Verschollene Zimmerbrunnen Wenzel Jamnitzers', *Jber. Ger. Nmus.-Nürnberg*, xcvi (1951), p. 29–36

E. Zinner: *Deutsche und niederländische Astronomische Instrumente des 11.–18. Jahrhunderts* (Munich, 1956), pp. 394–6

S. A. Bendini: 'The Perspective Machine of Wenzel Jamnitzer', *Technol. & Cult.*, ix (1968), pp. 197–202

K. Pechstein: 'Zeichnungen von Wenzel Jamnitzer', *Anz. Ger. Nmus.* (1970), pp. 81–95

I. Franke: 'Wenzel Jamnitzers Zeichnungen zur Perspectiva', *Münchn. Jb. Bild. Kst*, n. s. 2, xxiii (1972), pp. 165–86

E. Mulzer: 'Das Jamnitzerhaus und der Goldschmied Wenzel Jamnitzer', *Mitt. Ver. Gesch. Stadt Nürnberg*, lxi (1974), pp. 48–89

K. Pechstein: 'Der Merkelsche Tafelaufsatz von Wenzel Jamnitzer', *Mitt. Ver. Gesch. Stadt Nürnberg*, lxi (1974) pp. 90–121

SILVIA GLASER, KLAUS PECHSTEIN

(2) Christoph Jamnitzer (*b* Nuremberg, 12 May 1563; *d* Nuremberg, 1618). Grandson of (1) Wenzel Jamnitzer I. He did not qualify as a master goldsmith until he was 29, having perhaps served his apprenticeship in the workshop of Hans Petzolt. There are records of his journey to Prague in 1609, and it is thought that he spent some time in Italy. While he mastered the Italian repertory of form, he preferred to use an idiom that was part neo-Gothic and part bizarrely exaggerated, both trends being popular in Nuremberg *c.* 1600 and after. Research has revealed that Christoph was a particularly fine draughtsman; *c.* 80 drawings can now be definitely ascribed to him, including pictures from family albums and designs for book illustrations, sculptural work, fountains, plaques and items made by goldsmiths. His best-known work is the *Neuw Grottessken Buch* (Nuremberg, 1610), a pattern-book of grotesque ornaments including mythological scenes, the Four Elements and the Four Seasons, enriched with many subtle cultural and contemporary allusions.

About 20 of the items he made as a goldsmith have been preserved, of which the 'Dragon' ewer (*c.* 1618; Dresden, Grünes Gewölbe; bowl lost), the 'Elephant' table-fountain (*c.* 1610; Berlin, Tiergarten, Kstgewmus.), and the 'Trionfi' ewer and basin (1603; Vienna, Ksthist. Mus.), are among the most splendid. Both artistically and iconographically the last is exceptionally significant as regards the court of Rudolf II, who commissioned the set, in Prague: the scenes on both the ewer and basin, which

Christoph Jamnitzer: 'Milo of Croton' cup, silver gilt, h. 220 mm, 1616 (Nuremberg, Germanisches Nationalmuseum)

are based on Petrarch's *Trionfi*, show a combination of the Habsburg concept of empire, the virtues of the ruler, the prophecies of Daniel and a neo-Platonic concept of love and eternity. His reputation as a sculptor is primarily related to his designs for the six recumbent figures on the doorways of the Rathaus at Nuremberg (1617) and to small-scale sculpture, which is usually incorporated into his silver- and goldsmithing (see fig.). A portrait of *Christoph Jamnitzer* (1597; Nuremberg, Ger. Nmus.) by Lorenz Strauch shows him with a small statuette of *Bacchus* as a wax *bozzetto*. He is portrayed not as a craftsman but as a free artist, a sculptor. This estimate is repeated in his own drawing depicting *Minerva Presenting Man with the Liberal Arts* (London, V&A).

Jamnitzer was a master of pictorial inventiveness: his individual figures were generally taken directly from international printed graphic conventions, or slightly adapted. Moreover, he embossed, engraved and chased his own work; his chasing was particularly outstanding. With his strong tendency to add on to his compositions, his strange elongated, scalloped ornamentation and an unnaturalistic, Mannerist approach to creating figures he showed himself to be one of the last great artists of the international late Mannerist movement *c.* 1600.

BIBLIOGRAPHY

K. Pechstein, 'Der Nürnberger Goldschmied und Zeichner Christoph Jamnitzer (1563–1618)', *Fränk. Lebensbild.*, x (1982), pp. 179–92

GÜNTER IRMSCHER

Jan II (Kazimierz), King of Poland. *See* VASA, (4).

Jan III, King of Poland. *See* JOHN SOBIESKI.

Janák, Pavel (*b* Prague, 12 March 1882; *d* Prague, 1 Aug 1956). Czech architect, designer, theorist and teacher. He graduated in architecture from the Czech Technical University, Prague, where he studied under Josef Schulz and Josef Zítek, and from 1906 to 1907 he was a student of Otto Wagner at the Akademie der Bildenden Künste, Vienna. In 1908 he worked in Jan Kotěra's studio in Prague. His early work was influenced by the modernism of Wagner and Kotěra, but he perceived a danger of uniformity in a purely rationalist approach to architecture. In 1911, together with Josef Chochol, Josef Gočár, Vlastislav Hofman (1884–1964), Emil Filla, Václav Špála, Antonín Procházka, Otto Gutfreund and others, he founded the Group of Fine Artists, which sought a more artistic approach to architecture, and in 1912 he and Gočár founded the Prague Art Workshops for the design of arts, crafts and furniture. Within the Group of Fine Artists, Janák developed the principles of CZECH CUBISM, and in such essays as 'Hranol a pyramida' (1911), and 'Obnova průčelí' (1912–13), he elaborated the theory for architectural Cubism. This attempted to dematerialize a building's mass by the three-dimensional surface sculpturing of the façade with abstract, prismatic forms. The principal building by Janák to embody these ideas was a house (1913) in Pelhřimov, where he created a distinctive reconstruction of an existing Baroque building with Cubist details. More numerous examples of the Cubist influence in his work are found in the applied arts and furniture design, particularly chairs (*see* CZECH REPUBLIC, fig. 23).

After World War I the prismatic surface forms of Cubism were replaced by curved and spherical elements to produce Rondocubism, which incorporated elements of Czech vernacular art and was briefly seen as a national style. Dating from this period are the two main achievements of Janák's work: the crematorium (1921) in Pardubice and the building of the Riunione Adriatica di Sicurta (1922–4), Prague. Janák also took part in the interior design of the Czechoslovak pavilion at the Exposition Internationale des Arts Décoratifs et Industriels Modernes (1925) in Paris. Janák then spent a short period building brick family houses in Prague, when he adopted a Functionalist approach; however, with the exception of the Juliš Hotel (1927–30), Prague, he never achieved the purity of expression associated with that style. His chief field remained housing in all its aspects, from the overall architectural concept to interiors and the detail of functional fittings and equipment. From 1921 Janák taught at the Academy of Applied Arts in Prague, and from 1924 to 1942 he was President of the Union of Czech Crafts (Werkbund). He was the principal organizer of the Werkbund exhibition (1932) at Baba in Prague, which was devoted to Functionalist housing, undertaking the overall planning of the site and designing one of the houses.

Throughout his career Janák was involved with the restoration of architectural monuments, and after the mid-1920s he worked on the reconstruction and completion of the Černín Palace in Prague. In 1936 he succeeded Jože Plečnik as Chief Architect of Hradčany Castle, Prague, where his main achievements included the reconstruction of the Riding School and Ballgame Hall (1950). Janák believed that architects should treat monuments with as much care as if they were visiting a private home, and through his work in this field he became a founder of the modern discipline of architectural conservation and restoration in Czechoslovakia.

WRITINGS

'Hranol a pyramida' [The prism and the pyramid], *Umělecký Měsíčník* (1911–12), pp. 162–70
'Obnova průčelí' [The restoration of the façade], *Umělecký Měsíčník* (1912–13), pp. 85–95
'Architektura: Hmota či duch' [Architecture: matter or spirit], *Styl*, 10 (1925), pp. 170–74
Vybrané stati [Selected essays], *Acta Umělecko-Průmyslové Muz.*, xix (1985)

BIBLIOGRAPHY

M. Benešová: *Pavel Janák* (Prague, 1959)
I. Margolius: *Cubism in Architecture and the Applied Arts: Bohemia and France, 1910–1914* (London, 1979)
M. Benešová: 'Sto let od narození Pavla Janáka' [Centenary of the birth of Pavel Janák], *Archit. ČSR*, xli (1982), pp. 122–4
Pavel Janák 1882–1956: Architektur und Kunstgewerbe (exh. cat., ed. V. Šlapeta and O. Herbenová; Prague; Vienna; 1984)
Z. Lukeš, V. Šlapeta and A. Adlerová: 'Pavel Janák', *Tschechische Kunst 1878–1914: Auf dem Weg in die Moderne* (exh. cat., Darmstadt, Inst. Mathildenhöhe, 1984–5), pp. 92–5
R. Sedláková and M. Lamarová: 'Pavel Janák', *Tschechische Kunst der 20er und 30er Jahre: Avantgarde und Tradition* (exh. cat., Darmstadt, Inst. Mathildenhöhe, 1988–9), pp. 157–63
Český kubismus [Czech cubism] (exh. cat., ed. J. Švestka and T. Vlček; Düsseldorf, Kstver.; Prague, N.G.; 1991–2)
The Art of the Avant-Garde in Czechoslovakia 1918–1938 (exh. cat., ed. J. Anděl; Valencia, IVAM, 1993)
Prague 1891–1941: Architecture and Design (exh. cat., Edinburgh, City A. Centre, 1994)

RADOMÍRA SEDLÁKOVÁ

Janáky, István (*b* Hódmezővásárhely, 26 Dec 1901; *d* Budapest, 13 Jan 1966). Hungarian architect. He graduated in 1929 from the Hungarian Palatine Joseph Technical University, Budapest, and then worked in Móric Pogány's office until 1936, when he established his own practice. His most significant work of this period is the Palatinus Lido (1937) on Margaret Island, Budapest, which is notable for its subtle arrangement of masses and its graceful façade with loggia, which helps it to blend in with its environment. After 1948 Janáky worked with other leading architects in a state design office, where he prepared several designs in a classicizing spirit, which he had to revise for ideological reasons in the early 1950s. In 1950–53 he took part in the renovation of the Royal Palace (1891–1905; by Alajos Hauszmann), Budapest, during which the original neo-Baroque buildings were simplified by classicizing forms. By the 1960s he was able to build functionalist public buildings without formal, politically inspired constrictions. A notable example is the Golden Sands Hotel (1957–62) in Kecskemét, which reflects his recurrent interest in hotel design. The simply planned, five-storey building with loggia perfectly complements the atmosphere of its setting, and the high quality of the interior decoration is characteristic of his buildings. He was also involved until his death in the construction of the Technical University of Heavy Industry in Miskolc.

BIBLIOGRAPHY

P. Kisdi: 'Megemlékezés Janáky Istvánról' [In remembrance of István Janáky], *Magyar Építőművészet*, xv/3 (1966), pp. 50–57

M. Major: 'Emlékezés egy építészre' [In remembrance of an architect], *Kortárs*, x (1966), pp. 751–8

A. Ferkai: 'Janáky István', *Opeion*, i/1 (1982), pp. 11–17 [with list of works]

FERENC VADAS

Janco [Iancu], Marcel (*b* Bucharest, 1895; *d* Ein Hod, 1984). Romanian painter, printmaker, architect and writer. He was a pupil of the painter Iosif Iser and from 1915 studied architecture in Zurich. With Tristan Tzara, Hans Arp, Richard Huelsenbeck and Hugo Ball, Janco participated in the Dada performances of the Cabaret Voltaire (*see* DADA, §1). Janco made props and posters for the Dada group and illustrated with engravings the books of Tristan Tzara; he broke with Dada in 1922. In 1918 he became involved with the NEUE LEBEN group in Basle. After returning to Romania in 1920 he took part in all the major avant-garde exhibitions, showed at the Maison d'Art in Bucharest (1922) and was a member of the group Contimporanul (1924), which published an eponymous review and organized the first international avant-garde exhibition in December 1924. Janco was prolific as an artist, drawing, painting, engraving, designing buildings (e.g. Wexler House, 1931, Bucharest, with his brother, Jules Janco) and also writing manifestos and articles. As well as abstract graphic compositions, in which he explored the possibilities of a universal formal language, Janco produced works of traditional genres. In his portraits in Indian ink he took up the formal aspects of Expressionism. His paintings also display such elements. Although some abstract reliefs of *c.* 1918–20 show an inclination towards geometric abstraction, Janco never fully came to terms with it. In 1940 he emigrated, settling in Tel Aviv. The move marked a renewal in his art, away from abstraction to vigorous interpretations of the colourful local life. He also became involved in progressive art education. In 1948

he founded the New Horizons group, and in 1953 he set up the artists' colony of Ein Hod in the ancient Arab village of Carmel. In 1967 he was awarded the Grand Prix National d'Israel.

BIBLIOGRAPHY

M.-L. Mendelson: *Marcel Janco* (Tel Aviv, 1962)

R. Bogdan: 'Miscarea artistica de avantgarda din Romania si implicatiile ei pe plan mondial' [The avant-garde artistic movement in Romania and its global implications], *Pagini de arta moderna romaneasca* [Pages of Romanian modern art] (Bucharest, 1974)

V. M. Enache: *Marcel Iancu in Romania* (diss., Bucharest, Nicolae Grigorescu Acad. A., 1976)

H. Seiwert: *Marcel Janco* (Frankfurt am Main, 1993)

IOANA VLASIU

Jandial. *See under* TAXILA.

Janeček, Ota (*b* Pardubičky, nr Pardubice, 15 Aug 1919). Czech painter, sculptor and illustrator. In 1938–9 he studied at the Czech Technical University in Prague and in 1941–2 at the School of Applied Art in Prague. His first exhibition in the capital was in 1942, at the Elán Gallery. In 1943 he became a member of the Mánes Union of Artists and in 1945 of the Hollar Society of Czech Artists. In the 1940s he produced a number of paintings of female figures in which he strove to recapture the style of Modigliani, endeavouring to link it with the German Renaissance tradition. After 1943 his interest in Cubism led him to re-evaluate the Cubist conception of nature, as seen in his paintings of grass, birds, butterfly wings, etc. (e.g. *Grasses*, *White Cabbage Butterfly*, both 1948; both Prague, N.G., Trade Fair Pal.). In the late 1940s he returned for a while to a realistic approach to art, working at drawing and illustration as well as painting. In *Paradise* (1949; Prague, N.G. Czech. Eur. Graph. A.), for instance, he was evidently inspired by folk art. By the late 1950s his work began to show the influence of Paul Klee and of Seurat's pointillism, which inspired him to create new vibrant colour effects, as in *Suburban Garden* (1957; untraced). These effects became a permanent feature of his work. In this period he concentrated mainly on drawing, particularly female nudes and portraits. His interest in capturing natural elements led him to non-figurative brushwork, paraphrasing the richness of natural forms, as in the cycles *Organisms* (1960–61; some works, Prague, N.G., Trade Fair Pal.) and *Forms* (1961–3; Prague, N.G., Trade Fair Pal.) as well as sculptures, e.g. *Form* (1962–3; Litoměřice, Gal. F.A.) and *Sculpture* (1962–6; Brussels, Banque de Paris et des Pays-Bas). By the early 1970s he had arrived at a stylistic synthesis of his previous themes and artistic ideas, which continued to reflect his personal lyricism.

BIBLIOGRAPHY

P. Hartmann: *Soupis grafického díla Oty Janečka* [The graphic work of Ota Janeček] (Prague, 1961)

Ota Janeček, 1959–1961 (exh. cat. by P. Hartmann, Prague, Špála Gal.; London, Grosvenor Gal.; 1962)

Ota Janeček, 1941–1970 (exh. cat. by P. Hartmann, Pardubice, E. Boh. Gal., 1970)

P. Hartmann: *Ota Janeček* (Prague, 1973)

Ota Janeček (exh. cat. by J. Kotalík, L. Hlaváček and Z. Vaníček, Cardiff, N. Mus., 1984)

L. Hlaváček: *Ota Janeček* (Prague, 1989)

HANA LARVOVÁ

Janet. *See* CLOUET.

Janet-Lange [Janet, Ange-Louis] (*b* Paris, 26 Nov 1815; *d* Paris, 25 Nov 1872). French painter, illustrator and lithographer. On 5 October 1833 he entered the Ecole des Beaux-Arts in Paris, where he was a pupil of Horace Vernet, Ingres and Alexandre Marie Colin (1798–1875), but was most influenced by Vernet. He made his début at the Salon of 1836 with two paintings, a *Stud Farm* and *Post Stable* and continued to exhibit there until 1870. His subjects consist mostly of hunting scenes and episodes from contemporary French history. Among the latter are works depicting the Crimean War of 1853–6, (e.g. *Episode from the Battle of Koughil, Crimea*, exh. Salon 1859; Epinal, Mus. Dépt. Vosges & Mus. Int. Imagerie), Napoleon III's campaigns in Italy in 1859 (e.g. *Napoleon III at Solferino, 24 June 1859*, exh. Salon 1861; Versailles, Château, on dep. Rennes, Cercle Mil.) and the Mexican expedition of 1861 (e.g. the *Battle of Altesco in Mexico*, exh. Salon 1864). He also painted religious subjects, for example *Agony in the Garden* (exh. Salon 1839; Castelnaudary, Mus. Archéol. Lavragais).

In 1846 Marshal Nicolas-Jean Soult (1769–1851) commissioned Janet-Lange to make a series of drawings of military uniforms, and these now form part of the archives of the French Ministry of War. He also produced a great number of drawings and lithographs, distinguished by their precision, for the magazine *L'Illustration* and for such other illustrated periodicals as the *Journal amusant* and the *Journal pour rire*. He contributed illustrations of oriental figures to the *Tour du monde* (1862–73), a periodical that was hailed by the critic Léon Lagrange in 1864 as the most lively illustrated publication produced by Hachette. Janet-Lange's illustrations for it were engraved on wood. In addition he illustrated such books as Augustin Thierry's *Histoire de la conquête de l'Angleterre* (1866). He also made a number of Bonapartist lithographs (e.g. *Louis-Napoleon Bonaparte Elected by 7,500,000 Votes*, 1852) chronicling and celebrating the policies and campaigns of Louis-Napoleon Bonaparte (later Napoleon III). Around 1847 he contributed a few cartoons for the publication *Code civil illustré* (1847).

BIBLIOGRAPHY
Bellier de La Chavignerie-Auvray; Bénézit; Thieme–Becker
L. Lagrange: 'Les Illustrations du *Tour du monde*', *Gaz. B.-A.*, xvi (1864), pp. 179–83
H. Beraldi: *Les Graveurs du XIXe siècle*, viii (Paris, 1889), pp. 221–2
Inventaire du fonds français après 1800, Paris, Bib. N., Dépt. Est. cat., xi (Paris, 1960), pp. 247–55

ATHENA S. E. LEOUSSI

Jänggl [Janckl], **Franz** (*b* Sankt Margarethen im Gurktal, Carinthia, 1650; *d* Vienna, 15 Feb 1734). Austrian master builder and mason. He was awarded his master's certificate in Vienna in 1683. Jänggl's building business was soon one of the largest of its kind and was often called upon for important building projects. In 1702 he was paid for drawings for the church at MELK ABBEY, which must have been in connection with the first rebuilding project. His participation in the building work at the Peterskirche (begun 1702 by Gabriele Montani and continued by Johann Lukas von Hildebrandt) and the Maria Treu (1716–31), both in Vienna, was probably as a builder, although the original description of him as 'opcris inventor' led people to suppose that he was the architect, an idea refuted by the artistic disparity, however, between these churches and the buildings known to be by him. It is certain that Jänggl designed, with some incorporation of existing material, country churches at Trauttmannsdorf, Neudorf bei Staatz and Biedermannsdorf, each of which aims for a crossing with shallow transepts. This basic plan can also be seen at the Mariahilferkirche in Vienna, for which Jänggl produced plans in 1711 (these may be the plans preserved in the Barnabite provincial archives in Milan, which possibly show an early planning stage). Jänggl is also associated with the former church of St Florian (1709) in Matzleinsdorf, Vienna. The main body is an elongated octagonal shape with conches on the diagonal but not the cross axes. The Trinitarierkirche (begun 1717) in Pressburg (now Bratislava) was also by Jänggl; the central area is a longitudinal oval with niches on the cross axis and smaller niches on the diagonal ones. He was also responsible for building work at the abbey church of Göttweig from 1719, but here no significant independent design role can be ascribed to him. Among the secular buildings for which Jänggl may have been responsible is the Palais Bartolotti-Partenfeld (1720) in Vienna, formerly believed to have been the work of Johann Lukas von Hildebrandt. The overall similarity to Hildebrandt's style can be explained by the fact that Jänggl was often employed to carry out the former's designs. By 1730 Franz Anton Pilgram, Jänggl's cousin and adopted son, was largely responsible for the work of the building firm, which he took over in name after 1734.

BIBLIOGRAPHY
B. Grimschitz: 'Johann Lucas von Hildebrandts Kirchenbauten', *Wien. Jb. Kstgesch.*, vi (1929), pp. 216–56
W. Posch: 'Quellen und Daten zur Geschichte der Mariahilferkirche', *Wien. Geschbl.*, x (1955), pp. 8–13
B. Grimschitz: *Johann Lucas von Hildebrandt* (Vienna and Munich, 1959)
E. Spiesberger: 'Ein Beitrag zur Lebensgeschichte des Bau- und Maurermeisters Franz Jänggl', *Das Josefstädter Heimat-Museum*, 49–50 (Vienna, 1968)
P. Voit: *Franz Anton Pilgram* (Budapest, 1982)
M. A. Jelonek: *Franz Jänggl: Ein unbekannter Wiener Barockmeister*, Diss. Kstgesch., 19 (Cologne and Vienna, 1984)

W. GEORG RIZZI

Janin, Jules(-Gabriel) (*b* Saint-Etienne, Loire, 16 Feb 1804; *d* Passy, Seine, 20 June 1874), French writer. In 1836 he took over from Geoffroy and Hoffmann as drama critic on the *Journal des débats*. He rejected the dogmatic approach of his predecessors, and his readers quickly came to appreciate his lively and elegant style and his sometimes paradoxical opinions. Through his articles in the *Journal des débats*, some of which are collected in *Histoire de la littérature dramatique* (1853–8), he exercised a near absolute sovereignty over literary and theatrical circles. He wrote many novels as well as countless prefaces, introductions and essays, and contributions to a great number of literary reviews and newspapers. In the field of art he wrote for *L'Artiste*, which established itself as the official mouthpiece of Romantic art from 1831 onwards. Other works on art include *Fontainebleau, Versailles, Paris* (1837), *Versailles et son musée historique* (1837), *Galeries historiques de Versailles: Histoire de France* (1838–41), *Voyage en Italie* (1839) as well as *La Normandie historique, pittoresque et monumentale* (1844). It is in these lesser-known works and also in his approach to literary criticism that the guiding principles behind Janin's writings on art become apparent.

In his *Voyage en Italie* Janin displayed a somewhat effusive admiration for the monuments of cities that he visited, such as Genoa, Turin, Lucca and Pisa. Most notably this lyrical discovery of Italian art (essentially Renaissance art) found expression in his Florentine memoirs in the same volume, in particular in the detailed description of his visit to the Galleria degli Uffizi. This descriptive and oratorical approach is also found in *Versailles et son musée historique*. After describing the château of Versailles, which, between 1789 and 1830, was 'deserted and devastated', he praised—somewhat exuberantly—the role of Louis-Philippe, King of France, who, in the space of a few years, was able to make this palace once more 'the seat of French glory and majesty', endowing it with a fine museum of French history, a 'highly intelligent and original' conception. Janin was not, in fact, really an art critic: though a talented and lyrical commentator on famous examples of French architecture, he is chiefly remembered as a drama critic.

WRITINGS
Fontainebleau, Versailles, Paris (Paris, 1837)
Versailles et son musée historique (Paris, 1837)
Galeries historiques de Versailles: Histoire de France, 4 vols (1838–41)
Voyage en Italie (Paris, 1839)
La Normandie historique, pittoresque et monumentale (Paris, 1844)
Histoire de la littérature dramatique, 6 vols (Paris, 1853–8)
Regular contributions to *J. Débats* (1836–) and *L'Artiste*

BIBLIOGRAPHY
A. Piedagnel: *Jules Janin* (Paris, 1874, 2/1877)

PAUL GERBOD

Janinet, Jean-François (*b* Paris, 1752; *d* Paris, 1 Nov 1814). French printmaker. He was probably apprenticed to his father François Janinet, a gem-engraver from Burgundy. Between *c.* 1770 and *c.* 1772 he worked in the studio of LOUIS-MARIN BONNET, who had a considerable reputation as an engraver in the crayon manner and pastel manner. Their collaboration continued later with the production of coloured mounts with gilt decorations. Although Janinet began by executing engravings in the crayon manner, his reputation was based on his perfection of the process of colour printing with a series of plates and the subtle use of special mattoirs and thin layers of ink imitating the tonal effects of brush-and-ink washes, watercolours or gouaches (*see* GOUACHE MANNER, §2). In 1772 he published a small oval-print from several plates, *The Meeting* (*Inventaire de fonds français*, no. 2), after Clément-Pierre Marillier, with an inscription that asserted 'Cette Planché gravé à l'imitation du lavie en couleur par F. Janinet/le seul qui ait trouvé cette manière'. He was essentially a reproductive artist, and he left a copious oeuvre. His prints were rarely dated, but they can be classified according to his successive Paris addresses after 1780 (before then he frequently moved house). Between 1781 and 1787 he lived in the Place Maubert and between 1787 and 1792 in the Rue Hautefeuille. His later works were mainly published by the partnership of Esnauts and Rapilly. He seems to have found success and wealth early on. His career continued throughout the political upheavals of the French Revolution and changes in public taste. He tackled a wide variety of subjects: drawing books in

the crayon manner such as *Principes de dessin d'après nature* (1773); genre scenes—which won him most renown—such as the *Pleasant Disarray* (1779; after Baudouin), the *Friendly Peasant Girl* (after Saint-Quentin), and his most popular works, after Lafrensen, *The Comparison* (1786), the *Difficult Confession* (1787) and *The Indiscretion* (1788). He also worked on mythological scenes such as the *Toilet of Venus* (1784; after François Boucher); small-scale portraits such as those of the milliner *Rose Bertin* and of *Queen Marie-Antoinette* (both 1787); portraits of actresses on stage, for example *Madame Dugazon in the Role of Nina* and *Mlle Contat* as Suzanne in Beaumarchais's *Le Mariage de Figaro* (see fig.). In a similar vein was the set of 176 plates illustrating Le Vacher de Charnois's *Costumes et annales des grands théâtres de Paris* (1786–9), which Janinet took charge of and for which he made most of the engravings. During the Revolution Janinet was obliged to reproduce the austere allegories of Jean-Guillaume Moitte: *La Liberté* and *L'Egalité*, but he also produced a historical series from his own drawings, consisting of 52 plates in the wash manner: *Principaux événements depuis l'ouverture des Etats généraux*.

In addition to a number of fine Roman landscapes engraved after watercolours by Hubert Robert, Janinet also executed two series of views of Paris, in colour, after the drawings of the architect Jean-Nicolas-Louis Durand,

Jean-François Janinet: *Mlle Contat as Suzanne in 'Le Mariage de Figaro'*, wash manner print, 175×120 mm, 1785 (Paris, Bibliothèque Nationale)

which record the appearance of many buildings now destroyed: *Vues des plus beaux édifices publics et particuliers de la ville de Paris* (*c*. 1787) as well as 63 new views in a circular format (1792). In 1810, in collaboration with his pupil J.-B. Chapuy, he engraved 83 plates in the wash manner for the *Vues des plus beaux édifices publics et particuliers de la ville de Paris et des châteaux royaux*. Janinet claimed to be a 'physicist', and this pretension led to an abortive ascent in a balloon on 11 July 1784, which engendered much mockery and many caricatures. Besides Chapuy, his pupils included Antoine Carrée and Charles-Melchior Descourtis; the latter became his equal in the reproduction of watercolours and was the author of the prints *Village Fair* and the *Village Wedding*. Janinet had a daughter, Sophie, who exhibited a number of prints in the wash manner, under her married name of Giacomelli, at the Salons between 1799 and 1804.

BIBLIOGRAPHY
Portalis–Beraldi
M. Hébert and Y. Sjöberg, eds: *Inventaire du fonds français: Graveurs de XVIIIe siècle*, Paris, Bib. N., Dépt. Est. cat., xii (Paris, 1973), pp. 1–94
Regency to Empire: French Printmaking, 1715–1814 (exh. cat. by V. Carlson and J. Ittmann, Baltimore, MD, Mus. A.; Minneapolis, MN, Inst. A., 1984), p. 258
Graveurs français de la seconde moitié du XVIIIe siècle (exh. cat., Paris, Louvre, 1985)

MADELEINE BARBIN

Janini, Joaquim Pla. *See* PLA JANINI, JOAQUIM.

Janis, Sidney (*b* Buffalo, NY, 8 July 1896; *d* New York, 23 Nov 1989). American dealer, collector and writer. He first worked as a professional ballroom dancer, aeronautical mechanic and businessman. During business trips to New York he began visiting museums and art galleries in the 57th Street area. He moved to New York in 1924, married Harriet Grossman (1898–1963) in 1925 and in 1926 founded the M'Lord Shirt Company. He began collecting art in 1926, acquiring one of the finest collections of the Ecole de Paris in the USA. On successive trips to Europe, he met Fernand Léger, Pablo Picasso, Piet Mondrian, Constantin Brancusi, Marcel Duchamp and other major European artists. After acquiring *The Dream* by Henri Rousseau (New York, MOMA) he became interested in American naive painters, including Grandma Moses and Morris Hirshfield, on whom he published a study in 1942.

Having dissolved his business in 1939 to devote himself full-time to writing and lecturing on art, in 1949 Janis opened the Sidney Janis Gallery with an exhibition of work by Léger, followed by shows devoted to other European modernists such as Robert Delaunay, Hans Arp and Vasily Kandinsky, and to movements such as Dada (1953), Futurism (1954) and Analytical Cubism (1956). In the 1950s he became the dealer for major Abstract Expressionist painters, including Jackson Pollock, Willem de Kooning, Mark Rothko, Franz Kline and Robert Motherwell, although with his *New Realists* exhibition in 1962 he was also the first to document the arrival of Pop art as a recognized art movement. He continued to hold museum-quality shows of European artists such as Arp and Alberto Giacometti while also representing Pop artists such as George Segal and Tom Wesselmann and younger American artists who emerged in the 1980s. In 1967 he announced the gift of the Sidney and Harriet Janis collection containing more than 100 20th-century works, including Picasso's *Painter and Model* (1928) and Umberto Boccioni's *Dynamism of a Soccer Player* (1913), to the Museum of Modern Art, New York.

WRITINGS
They Taught Themselves: American Primitive Painters of the 20th Century (New York, 1942)
Abstract & Surrealist Art in America (New York, 1944)

BIBLIOGRAPHY
A. H. Barr and W. Rubin: *Three Generations of Twentieth-century Art: The Sidney and Harriet Janis Collection of the Museum of Modern Art* (New York, 1972)
L. de Coppet and A. Jones, eds: *The Art Dealers* (New York, 1984) pp. 32–41

RUTH BASS

Jan Joest von Kalkar. *See* JOEST, JAN.

Jank, Angelo (*b* Munich, 30 Oct 1868; *d* Munich, 9 Oct 1940). German painter, illustrator, teacher and poster designer. The son of the painter Christian Jank (1833–88), he attended Simon Hollósy's private art school in Munich before studying (1891–6) at the Akademie der Bildenden Künste, also in Munich, under Ludwig von Löfftz (1845–1910) and Paul Höcker (1854–1910). From 1896 he exhibited at the Munich Secession, and he became a member of DIE SCHOLLE, founded in 1899. A regular contributor to the journal *Jugend* and at the forefront of modernism, he made his mark as a humorous illustrator, portraying allegories and scenes from military life. Jank also designed posters (e.g. *Underworld*, 1896; Berlin, Mus. Dt. Gesch.). He taught at the Damenakademie (1899–1907). Having come to prominence as a portrayer of events from German history with three monumental paintings for Berlin's Reichstag building (destr.) in 1905, he collaborated with Adolf Münzer (1870–1952) and Walter Püttner (1872–1953) on frescoes (1906) in the Schwurgerichtssaal of the Neuer Justizpalast in Munich. Between 1907 and 1937 he was a professor at the Munich Akademie. In such works as *Soldiers Bearing the Coffin of Fritz von Uhde* (1911; Munich, Neue Pin.) Jank created an intense atmosphere. He used an impressionist style with flat brushstrokes in depictions of hunts and horse races to capture the powerful movements of horse and rider, for example *Jockey Racing Over Hurdles* (1909; Wuppertal, von der Heydt-Mus.).

BIBLIOGRAPHY
Thieme–Becker
R. Braungart: 'Angelo Jank', *Dt. Kst & Dek.*, xxix (1911–12), pp. 30–44
H. Ludwig and others, eds: *Münchener Maler im 19. Jahrhundert*, ii (Munich, 1982), pp. 242-5

A. ZIFFER

Jankowski, Stanislaw. *See under* STĘPINSKI, ZYGMUNT.

Janlet, (Charles-)Emile (*b* Brussels, 1 Jan 1839; *d* Brussels, 14 Sept 1918). Belgian architect. He was the son of the architect Félix Janlet (1808–68) and received his professional training at the Académie Royale des Beaux-Arts, Brussels, and in the studios of his father and of Henri Beyaert. Collaborating occasionally with his brother, Gustave Janlet, he rapidly gained prominence as one of the leading architects of Brussels and a conspicuous proponent of the Flemish Renaissance Revival that was coming into fashion in the early 1870s. Indeed Janlet's Ecole Communale no. 13 (1876–9), Place Anneessens, Brussels, marked the maturity of that style in Belgium. Similar to the exterior of this school was Janlet's contemporary and widely acclaimed Belgian façade (destr.) in the Rue des Nations at the Paris Exposition Universelle (1878). Both buildings had scroll gables and exhibited a distinctive red, white and black structural polychromy of native Belgian materials, so that sympathetic critics could justifiably regard them as prototypes, both formally and materially, of a 'national' style of Belgian building. Janlet designed a number of other Flemish Renaissance Revival buildings and then moved towards the creation of a more sober, rational architecture with his designs for the Mechelen railway station (1888; destr.; see P. Pastiels: 'Les Gares d'antan' [Brussels], *Direction commerciale de la Société nationale des chemins de fer belges, 1978*, p. 66) and the Musée des Sciences Naturelles (1898–1903; now Institut des Sciences Naturelles) in the Parc Léopold, Brussels. These buildings, which featured little historicist ornamentation, used large areas of glass between skeletal structural elements of iron and masonry respectively. Janlet was a member of the Commission Royale des Monuments et des Sites, and he exercised considerable influence over the replanning and rebuilding, in revived vernacular historical styles, of many Belgian cities devastated during World War I, notably Leuven.

BIBLIOGRAPHY
C. Lagasse de Locht: 'Nécrologie', *Bull. Comm. Royales A. & Archéol.*, lvii (1918), pp. 123–9
J. Brunfaut: 'Notice sur Emile Janlet', *Annu. Acad. Royale Sci., Lett. & B.A. Belgique*, xcvii (1931), pp. 207–14
P. Uyttenhove and J. Celis: *De wederopbouw van Leuven na 1914* [The rebuilding of Leuven after 1914] (Leuven, 1991)

ALFRED WILLIS

Janmot, (Anne-François-)Louis (*b* Lyon, 21 May 1814; *d* Lyon, 1 June 1892). French painter and poet. He belonged to the Lyon school of painting, characterized by idealistic and mystical tendencies similar to those of the Nazarenes and the Pre-Raphaelites. His Christian beliefs, which are very apparent in his art, were strongly influenced by neo-Catholic apologists. From 1831 Janmot studied at the Ecole des Beaux-Arts in Lyon. In 1833 he went to Paris, where he became a student of Victor Orsel at the Ecole des Beaux-Arts. He also attended Ingres's studios in Paris and Rome. His technique was deeply indebted to Ingres, but emotionally and intellectually he was more closely allied with Delacroix, whose enthusiasm for the literature of Dante and Shakespeare he shared. Janmot's style combined the precision of Ingres with the meditative devotion of Orsel. His predilection for heraldic compositions, based on symmetry and repetition, his use of profile and flattened form and his luminous colour were all influenced by a love of such early Italian painters as Giotto and Fra Angelico. Janmot's style has much in common with that of fellow Lyonnais and pupil of Ingres, Hippolyte Flandrin.

The majority of Janmot's paintings were commissions for churches. The *Resurrection of the Son of the Widow of Nain* (1840; Puget-Ville Church, Var) is indebted to Ingres's *Martyrdom of St Symphorien* (1884; Autun Cathedral). His *Agony in the Garden* (1840; Col. Ouillins)

demonstrates his doctrinaire pro-Catholic beliefs, with such scenes as Savonarola and the Polish defence of the national religion in the background. Other religious works include *St Francis Xavier* (1843; Lyon, St Paul) and an *Assumption of the Virgin* (1844) for the Mulatière Church, Lyon. Janmot also executed murals, sometimes in fresco, as for example at St Polycarpe (1856; destr.), Lyon; St François de Sales (1859), Lyon; and St Etienne du Mont (1866), Paris. His fresco (1878–9) in the chapel of the Franciscains-de-Terre-Sainte, Lyon, was his last state commission.

Janmot's most ambitious work was a series of 18 allegorical paintings, 16 drawings (Lyon, Mus. B.-A.) and poetic verses called *La Poème de l'âme* on which he worked for over 40 years. The series traces the spiritual and physical history of a soul. Recurrent themes include maternal affection and divine and terrestrial love. *La Poème de l'âme* contains autobiographical references and allusions to such contemporary political events as the Revolution of 1848. It attracted the attention of Paul Chenavard, Delacroix and Baudelaire at the Paris Exposition Universelle of 1855, but it was not well received by the public. Janmot's personal and poetic approach to his subject-matter as well as his pictorial imagination make him an important link between Romanticism and Symbolism. His work was admired by Pierre Puvis de Chavannes, Maurice Denis and Odilon Redon.

WRITINGS
La Poème de l'âme (Paris, 1881, rev. Lyon, 1978)
Opinion d'un artiste sur l'art (Paris, 1887)
BIBLIOGRAPHY
E. Hardouin-Fugier: *Louis Janmot, 1814–1892* (Lyon, 1981) [with comprehensive bibliog.]

NADIA TSCHERNY

Janneck, Franz Christoph (*b* Graz, 10 Oct 1703; *d* Vienna, 13 Jan 1761). Austrian painter. He was a pupil of Matthias Vanguš (*fl* 1716) in Graz before he came to Vienna, where he was first mentioned in documents of the 1730s. His younger brother, Mathias Jakob, studied at the Viennese academy in 1728–30 and in 1733. About 1735 Janneck travelled in Austria and southern Germany; in Frankfurt am Main he met Karl Aigen (1684–1762), Christian Hilfgott Brand and Josef Orient (1677–1747). In 1740 the Viennese academy, joining the 'Frey-Compagnie' (a voluntary military company) in 1741. With Paul Troger, and later with Michelangelo Unterberger, he held the office of assessor at the academy between 1752 and 1758.

Like his friend Johann Georg Platzer, Janneck painted cabinet pictures illustrating conversation scenes and religious, secular and mythological themes, for example *Nymphs* (*c.* 1730; Vienna, Niederösterreich. Landesmus.). Janneck's colours, however, are more restrained than Platzer's; his pictures are more tranquil and are not as detailed. The figures are often dressed in 17th-century costumes and are modelled on the work of French and Netherlandish painters, such as Watteau, Frans van Mieris, Willem van Mieris, Caspar Netscher and Adriaen van der Werff. Janneck also painted portraits of fellow artists, landscapes in the Flemish manner (similar to those of Josef Orient), for example *Landscape with Mountains and a River* (1729; Graz, Steiermärk. Landesmus.), and religious scenes.

BIBLIOGRAPHY

W. Hilger: '"Kammermaler" des österreichischen Spätbarock', *Joseph Haydn und seine Zeit* (Eisenstadt, 1972), p. 157
Österreichische Barockmaler aus der Nationalgalerie in Prag (exh. cat. by P. Preiss, Vienna, Belvedere, 1977), pp. 70–73
E. Baum: *Katalog des Österreichischen Barockmuseums im Unteren Belvedere in Wien*, i (Vienna, 1980), pp. 252–9

ELISABETH HERRMANN-FICHTENAU

Jan of Opava [Johann von Troppau] (*fl* 1368). Bohemian scribe, illuminator and priest. A canon of Brno and priest in Lanškroun, he both wrote and illuminated the Evangeliary now called after him (Vienna, Österreich. Nbib., Cod. 1182). According to an inscription on fol. 190*v* the book was completed in 1368. Armorial evidence suggests that it was made for Duke Albert III of Austria (*reg* 1358–95), a son-in-law of the Emperor Charles IV (*reg* 1346–78). It was probably a gift from Jan of Středa, the Imperial Chancellor; letters from him to the prior of the Augustinian monastery in Brno during the 1370s mention *Johannes scriptor noster*. The Evangeliary is the last of a group of manuscripts produced by the most outstanding illuminators of Charles's reign. Jan of Středa was among the patrons of this workshop, and one of the artists who worked on the Evangeliary also illuminated a Missal (Prague Cathedral, St Vitus's Treasury, Cim. 6) for the Chancellor after he became Bishop of Olomouc in 1364. Although several hands can be identified in the illumination of the Evangeliary, Jan of Opava must be credited with the overall design. Each Gospel is preceded by a page illustrating 12 scenes from the life of the Evangelist, and an elaborate full-page initial. The subtle colouring and soft modelling of the figures are close to contemporary wall painting, particularly that in the chapel of the Holy Cross in Karlštejn Castle (*see* KARLŠTEJN CASTLE, §2).

BIBLIOGRAPHY

E. Trenkler: *Das Evangeliar des Johannes von Troppau* (Klagenfurt and Vienna, 1948)
G. Schmidt: 'Johann von Troppau und die vorromanische Buchmalerei', *Festschrift K. H. Usener* (Marburg, 1967), pp. 275–92

AMANDA SIMPSON

Jan of Středa [John of Neumarkt] (*b c.* 1310; *d* 23 Dec 1380). Bohemian notary, cleric, collector and patron. He began his career as a notary (and later prothonotary) in the service of John of Luxembourg, King of Bohemia, and from 1353 to 1374 was Emperor Charles IV's chancellor. He became (successively) Bishop of Naumburg, Litomyšl and Olomouc. As an outstanding diplomat and organizer he was one of the Emperor's leading advisers on a variety of subjects, including art. His humanist leanings were developed by his contact with Francesco Petrarch and Cola di Rienzi. About 1353 Jan was portrayed as the donor of Italianate paintings in the sacristy of the Augustinian church of St Thomas (*c.* 1285; altered) in the Malá Strana district in Prague. Before leaving for Italy he endowed the church with part of his library, which included works by Seneca, Livy, Valerius Maximus, Dante, Petrarch and others. He attracted some outstanding illuminators to the imperial scriptorium, where seven magnificent codices were illustrated, including his famous *Liber viaticus* (before 1364; Prague, N. Mus. Lib., MS. XIII.A.12). It was decorated by an illuminator intimately acquainted with Italian painting, especially Sienese. The *bas-de-page* biblical scenes may have been imitated from the work of the Parisian Master of the Boqueteaux. Of the other manuscripts in the so-called '*Viaticus* group' the miniature of the *Resurrection* (Prague, St Vitus Cathedral Lib., Cod. J. XXVI, fol. 59*v*) is the closest in style. Two more freely painted full-page miniatures in the *Laus Mariae* of Konrad von Heimburg (Prague, N. Mus. Lib., Cod. XVI.D.13, of which one is fol. 34*v*) are probably somewhat later (*c.* 1360). The softer appearance of the forms is also characteristic both of the prayerbook of Archbishop Arnošt of Pardubice (Prague, N. Mus.) and the Missal of Jan of Středa (after 1364; Prague, St Vitus Cathedral Lib., Cim. 6).

BIBLIOGRAPHY

M. Dvořák: 'Die Illuminatoren des Johann von Neumarkt', *Jb. Kstsamml. Allhöch. Ksrhaus.*, xxii (1901), pp. 35–126
K. Chytil: *Památky českého umění iluminátorského: I. Knihovna Národního Musea* [Examples of Bohemian illumination: I. National Museum Library] (Prague, 1915)
J. Krofta: *Mistr brevíře Jana ze Středy* [The master of the breviary of Jan of Středa] (Prague, 1940)
G. Schmidt: 'Malerei bis 1450', *Gotik in Böhmen*, ed. K. M. Swoboda (Munich, 1969), pp. 179–84
J. Krása: 'Knižní malba' [Book illumination], *České umění gotické* [Bohemian Gothic art] (exh. cat., ed. J. Pešina; Academica Praha; Prague, 1970), pp. 244–58, 264–73
——: 'Knižní malba' [Book illumination], i/2 of *Dějiny českého výtvarného umění* [History of Czech fine art] (Prague, 1984–), pp. 405–39

KAREL STEJSKAL

Janoušek, František (*b* Jesenný, nr Semily, 6 May 1890; *d* Prague, 23 Jan 1943). Czech painter. He studied at the Academy of Fine Arts in Prague from 1917 to 1922. In 1921 he became a pupil of Vojtěch Hynais. He was a member of the Mánes Union of Artists (SVU Mánes). Overall, his figure compositions, still-lifes and landscapes display Neo-classicist and lyrical, Cubist tendencies. In 1929 he adopted a more Surrealist style, with imaginative, illusionistic paintings of ill-defined symbolic objects with organic and anthropomorphic associations. In 1932 he took part in the first group exhibition of Surrealism in Czechoslovakia, arranged by SVU Mánes in Prague under the title *Poesie 1932*. After 1935 his work culminated in raw, expressive visions of an imagined biological and psychic universe with destructive and apocalyptic elements anticipating the catastrophe of world war. From 1939 to 1942, when he was not permitted to exhibit his work in public, he taught at the SVU Mánes School.

BIBLIOGRAPHY

František Janoušek (exh. cat., Prague, Mánes Exh. Hall, 1947)
František Janoušek: Obrazy z let 1932–1942 [František Janoušek: pictures 1932–1942] (exh. cat., Prague, Rlwy Workers Cent. Cult. Office, 1990)
J. Chalupecký: *František Janoušek* (Prague, 1991)

HANA MYSLIVEČKOVÁ

Illustration Acknowledgements

We are grateful to those listed below for permission to reproduce copyright illustrative material and to those contributors who supplied photographs or helped us to obtain them. The word 'Photo:' precedes the names of large commercial or archival sources who have provided us with photographs, as well as the names of individual photographers (where known). It has generally not been used before the names of owners of works of art, such as museums and civic bodies. Every effort has been made to contact copyright holders and to credit them appropriately; we apologize to anyone who may have been omitted from the acknowledgements or cited incorrectly. Any error brought to our attention will be corrected in subsequent editions. Where illustrations have been taken from books, publication details are provided in the acknowledgements below.

Line drawings, maps, plans, chronological tables and family trees commissioned by the *Dictionary of Art* are not included in the list below. All of the maps in the dictionary were produced by Oxford Illustrators Ltd, who were also responsible for some of the line drawings. Most of the line drawings and plans, however, were drawn by the following artists: Diane Fortenberry, Lorraine Hodghton, Chris Miners, Amanda Patton, Mike Pringle, Jo Richards, Miranda Schofield, John Tiernan, John Wilson and Philip Winton. The chronological tables and family trees were prepared initially by Kate Boatfield and finalized by John Johnson.

Iraq Magnum Photos/Photo: Steve McCurron

Ireland *2* Irish Architectural Archive, Dublin/Photo: Chandler Collection, Dublin; *3*, *15* Irish Architectural Archive, Dublin; *4*, *13* Photo: Hugh Doran; *5* Irish Architectural Archive, Dublin/Photo: William Garner; *6* Photo: Aer Rianta, Dublin; *7* Board of Trinity College, Dublin; *8–12* National Gallery of Ireland, Dublin; *14* Photo: Irish Tourist Board; *16* National Trust Photo Library, London/Photo: Patrick Prendergast; *17–19* Photo: Desmond Fitzgerald, Knight of Glin; *20–21*, *24* National Museum of Ireland, Dublin; *22* Douglas Bennett; *23* National Museum of Women in the Arts, Washington, DC

Ireland, Northern *1–3* Trustees of the Ulster Museum, Belfast

Irian Jaya *1*, *3* Rijksmuseum voor Volkenkunde, Leiden; *2* Royal Tropical Institute (K.I.T.), Tropenmuseum, Amsterdam/Photo: L. Lange

Iron and steel *1* Architectural Association, London/Photo: Paul Oliver; *2* Photo: Institution of Civil Engineers Archive, London; *3* Photo: Anthony Kersting, London; *4* Photo: Overseas Agenzia Fotografica, Milan; *5* Photo: © Julius Shulman, Hon. AIA, Los Angeles, CA; *6* Museum of Modern Art, New York (Gift of the Artist)/© DACS, 1996; *7* Musée National d'Art Moderne, Paris; *8* Howard and Jean Lipman, Cannondale, CT/Photo: Rudolph Buckhardt; *9* Board of Trustees of the Victoria and Albert Museum, London; *10* Trustees of the British Museum, London

Isabey: (1) Jean-Baptiste Isabey Musées d'Angers

Isabey: (2) Eugène Isabey Photo: © RMN, Paris

Isenbrandt, Adriaen Photo: © ACL, Brussels

Isenmann, Caspar Musée d'Unterlinden, Colmar

Isfahan *2* Photo: Ancient Art and Architecture Collection, London; *3–4* Photo: Bernard O'Kane

Islam *1–3* Photo: Robert Harding Picture Library, London

Islamabad Photo: Douglas Dickens, London

Islamic art *1*, *78*, *160*, *240* Freer Gallery of Art, Smithsonian Institution, Washington, DC; *5* Millet Library, Istanbul; *6–7*, *14*, *93*, *101*, *118*, *124–5*, *132–4*, *191*, *195*, *238* Topkapı Palace Museum, Istanbul; *8*, *153*, *185*, *235* Photo: © RMN, Paris; *9* Harvard University Art Museums, Cambridge, MA; *10* Princeton University Libraries, Princeton, NJ; *11* British Library, London (MS. 22412, fol. 1v–2r); *12* Cleveland Museum of Art, Cleveland, OH (Purchase from the J.H. Wade Fund); *13* Photo: Archivi Alinari, Florence; *15*, *27*, *40*, *44*, *49*, *79* Photo: Bernard O'Kane; *17*, *24*, *35*, *56*, *58* Photo: Anthony Kersting, London; *18*, *81* Photo: Ancient Art and Architecture Collection, London; *19* British Library, London (no. L.R.403.b.5); *21* Photo: Aerofilms of Borehamwood; *23*, *31*, *223* Photo: Sheila S. Blair; *25* Yale University Press Picture Library, London/Photo: Roger Wood; *28*, *32–33*, *43* Photo: J. Powell, Rome; *30* Photo: A.D.H. Bivar; *34*, *54*, *74* Photo: Jonathan M. Bloom; *37* Ashmolean Museum, Oxford (Creswell Archive; MAE1, pl. 82c; neg. C.1010), *38* Ashmolean Museum, Oxford (Creswell Archive; MAE1, pl. 116a; neg. C.3411); *39* Photo: J. Schmidt; *41* Photo: Yasser Tabbaa; *42* Photo: Rahmi Hüseyin Ünal; *45–46* Deutsches Archäologisches Institut, Madrid/Photo: Peter Witte; *47* Photo: Geraldine Smith-Parr Banerji; *48* On loan/Photo: Overseas Agenzia Fotografica, Milan, *51* Photo: Yolande Crowe; *52* Photo: Islamic Architecture Archive, Edinburgh; *53* Photo: Howard Crane; *57* British Library, London (no. 746.e.67); *59*, *73* Photo: Robert Harding Picture Library, London; *60*, *217* Photo: Ampliaciones y Reproducciones MAS, Barcelona; *61*, *72* Photo: Sheila S. Blair and Jonathan M. Bloom; *62* Ashmolean Museum, Oxford (Creswell Archive; neg. C.6723); *63* Photo: Dr Donna Kurtz; *64* Photo: Overseas Agenzia Fotografica, Milan/Photo: Lucy Johnson; *65–6* Photo: Lucy Johnson; *67*, *71* Photo: Warwick Ball; *69*, *77* Photo: Eugenio Galdieri; *70* Photo: Scorpion Publications, Buckhurst Hill, Essex; *75* Photo: Marianne Barrucand; *76* Photo: British Architectural Library, RIBA, London; *80* Photo: Walter B. Denny; *82* Photo: Overseas Agenzia Fotografica, Milan; *83* Ashmolean Museum, Oxford (Creswell Archive; MAE1, pl. 30b; neg. C.137); *86* British Library, London (no. T39887); *87* Prof. Sevgi Aktüre, Metu, Department of Architecture, Ankara; *90* Photo: John Warren; *94–8*, *128*, *131*, *137* Trustees of the Chester Beatty Library, Dublin; *99* Freer Gallery of Art, Smithsonian Institution, Washington, DC (no. 31.37b); *102*, *111*, *196* Bibliothèque Nationale de France, Paris; *103* British Library, London (Or. MS. 2265, fol. 2v); *104* British Library, London (Or. MS. 2265, fol. 195r); *105* Freer Gallery of Art, Smithsonian Institution, Washington, DC (no. 30.75r); *106* Biblioteca Apostolica Vaticana, Rome; *107* British Library, London (Or. MS. 2265, fol. 15); *108* Collection of Prince Sadruddin Aga Khan; *109*, *172*, *207*, *251* Keir Collection, Richmond; *110* Bildarchiv, Österreichische Nationalbibliothek, Vienna; *112* Photo: Patrimonio Nacional Archivo Fotografico, Madrid; *113* Central Library, Istanbul University; *114* Library, Edinburgh University; *115* Arthur M. Sackler Gallery, Smithsonian Institution, Washington, DC; *116* National Library of Russia, St Petersburg; *117* Musée d'Art et d'Histoire, Geneva; *119* British Library, London (Add. MS. 18113, fol. 31); *120* British Library, London (MS. 27261, fol. 38); *121*, *143* Gulistan Palace Library and Museum, Tehran; *122*, *249* L.A. Mayer Memorial, Institute for Islamic Art, Jerusalem; *123* Metropolitan Museum of Art, New York (Fletcher Fund, 1963; no. 63.210.28); *126* Metropolitan Museum of Art, New York (Promised gift of Mr and Mrs Stuart Cary Welch, Jr; Partially owned by the Metropolitan Museum of Art, New York, and Arthur M. Sackler Museum, Harvard University, Cambridge, MA; no. 1988.430); *127* Freer Gallery of Art, Smithsonian Institution, Washington, DC (no. 46.12.132); *129* British Library, London (Or. MS. 2265, fol. 213); *130* Royal Collection, Windsor Castle/© Her Majesty Queen Elizabeth II; *135* Los Angeles County Museum of Art, Los Angeles, CA (Nasli M. Heeramaneck Collection; Gift of Joan Palevsky); *138*, *154*, *220* Museum of Turkish and Islamic Art, Istanbul; *139* Syndics of Cambridge University Library; *140* Hermitage Museum, St Petersburg; *141* Museo Arqueológico Provincial, Córdoba; *142* Photo: VAAP, Moscow; *144*